lonely planet

Japan

Sapporo & Hokkaidō
p561

Northern Honshū (Tōhoku)
p492

The Japan Alps & Central Honshū
p206

Mt Fuji & Around Tokyo
p153

Kyoto
p288

Tokyo
p70

Hiroshima & Western Honshū
p426

Kansai
p349

Shikoku
p630

Kyūshū
p673

Okinawa & the Southwest Islands
p749

THIS EDITION WRITTEN AND RESEARCHED BY

Chris Rowthorn,
Ray Bartlett, Andrew Bender, Laura Crawford, Craig McLachlan,
Rebecca Milner, Simon Richmond, Phillip Tang, Benedict Walker,
Wendy Yanagihara

PLAN YOUR TRIP

IAN TROWER/GETTY IMAGES ©

SUMIYOSHI TAISHA, OSAKA, P359

ON THE ROAD

Contents

ON THE ROAD

MARTIN ROUSSEAU/GETTY IMAGES ©

MARUYAMA KŌEN, KYOTO, P303

Contents

PETER ADAMS/GETTY IMAGES ©

Welcome to Japan

Japan is a world apart – a cultural Galápagos where a unique civilisation blossomed, and today thrives in delicious contrasts of traditional and modern. Its spirit is strong, warm and welcoming.

Culture

Standing at the far-eastern end of the Silk Road and drawing influences from the entire continent, Japan has spent millennia taking in and refining the cultural bounties of Asia to produce something distinctly Japanese. From the splendour of a Kyoto geisha dance to the spare beauty of a Zen rock garden, Japan has the power to enthral even the most jaded traveller. Traditional culture is only half the story: an evolving contemporary-art scene, dynamic design and a voracious appetite for pop-culture trends all help shape the fascinating old-meets-new cultural landscape.

Accessible Exoticism

Travellers to Japan have always found themselves entranced by a culture that is by turns beautiful, unfathomable and downright odd. Staying in a ryokan (traditional Japanese inn) is utterly different from staying in a hotel. Sitting in a robe on tatami (woven floor matting) eating raw fish and mountain vegetables is probably not how you dine back home. Getting naked with strangers to soak in an onsen (hot spring) might seem strange at first, but try it and you'll find it's relaxing. And with helpful locals, spotless facilities and excellent public transport, you can experience this exoticism with ease.

Food

Savouring the delights of Japanese cuisine on its home turf is half the reason to come to Japan, and you can easily build an itinerary around trying regional specialties and dining in sublime restaurants. Eat just one meal in a top-flight Tokyo sushi restaurant – or gulp down fresh noodles at a station counter – and you'll see why. The Japanese attention to detail, genius for presentation and insistence on the finest ingredients results in food that can change your idea of what is possible in the culinary arena.

Outdoors

The wonders of Japan's natural world are a well-kept secret. The hiking in the Japan Alps and Hokkaidō is world class, and with an extensive hut system you can do multiday hikes with nothing more than a knapsack on your back. Down south, the coral reefs of Okinawa will have you wondering if you've somehow been transported to Thailand. And you never have to travel far in Japan to get out into nature: in major hubs like Kyoto, just a short trip from the city will get you into forested mountains.

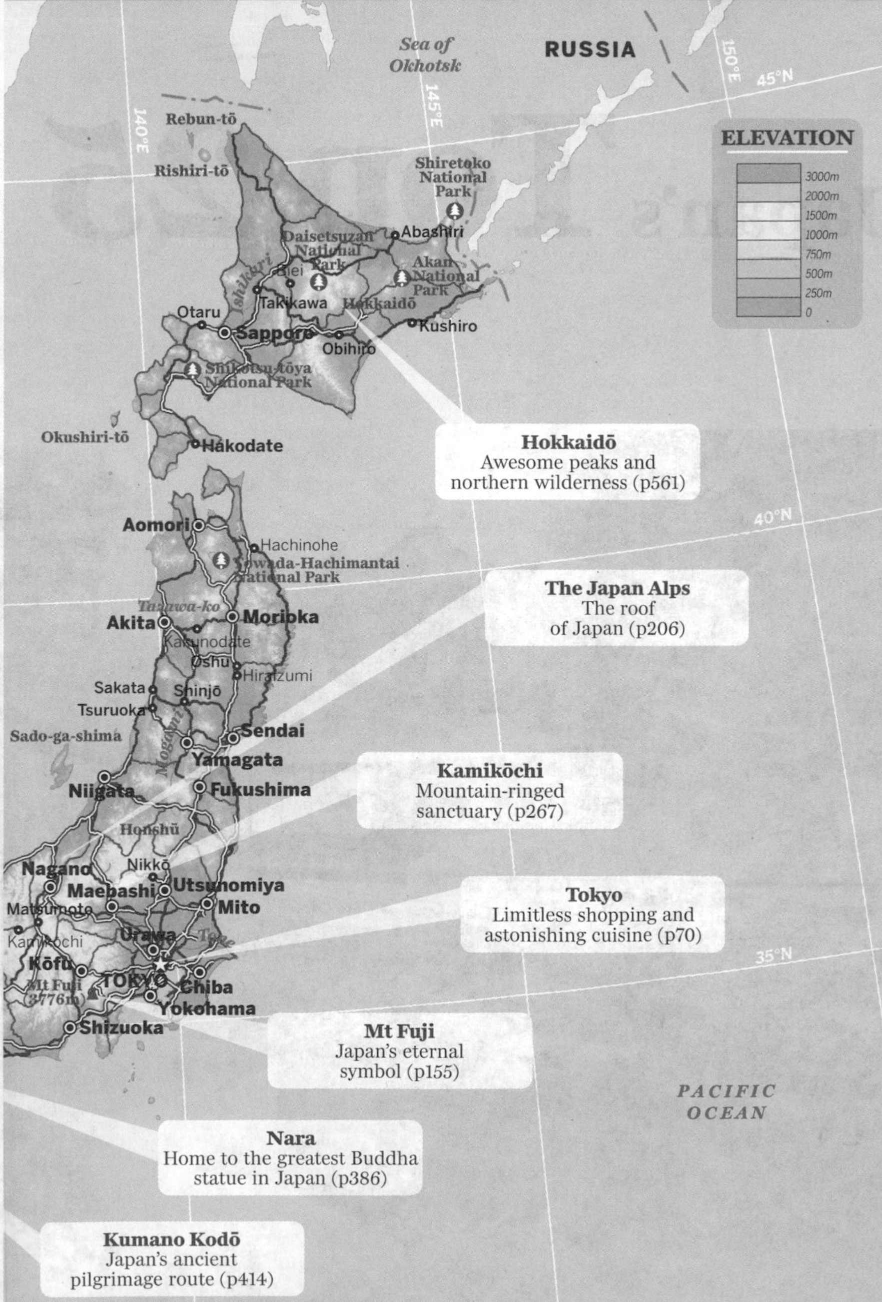

0 500 km
0 250 miles
Sea of Okhotsk
RUSSIA
145°E
150°E
140°E
45°N
40°N
35°N
Rebun-tō
Rishiri-tō
ELEVATION
3000m
2000m
1500m
1000m
750m
500m
250m
0
Shiretoko National Park
Daisetsuzan National Park
Abashiri
Biei
Akan National Park
Takikawa
Hokkaidō
Otaru
Sapporo
Kushiro
Obihiro
Shikotsu-tōya National Park
Okushiri-tō
Hakodate
Hokkaidō
Awesome peaks and northern wilderness (p561)
Aomori
Hachinohe
Towada-Hachimantai National Park
The Japan Alps
The roof of Japan (p206)
Tazawa-ko
Akita
Morioka
Kakunodate
Ōshu
Hiraizumi
Sakata
Shinjō
Tsuruoka
Sendai
Sado-ga-shima
Yamagata
Kamikōchi
Mountain-ringed sanctuary (p267)
Niigata
Fukushima
Honshū
Nikkō
Nagano
Maebashi
Utsunomiya
Tokyo
Limitless shopping and astonishing cuisine (p70)
Matsumoto
Mito
Urawa
Kamikōchi
Kōfu
TOKYO
Chiba
Mt Fuji (3776m)
Yokohama
Shizuoka
Mt Fuji
Japan's eternal symbol (p155)
PACIFIC OCEAN
Nara
Home to the greatest Buddha statue in Japan (p386)
Kumano Kodō
Japan's ancient pilgrimage route (p414)
Ogasawara Archipelago (500km)

Japan's Top 25

1

Kyoto Temples & Gardens

1 With more than 1000 temples to choose from, you're spoiled for choice in Kyoto. Spend your time finding one that suits your taste. If you like things gaudy and grand, you'll love the splendour of Kinkaku-ji. If you prefer *wabi-sabi* to rococo, you'll find the tranquillity of Hōnen-in or Shōren-in more to your liking. And don't forget that temples are where you'll find the best gardens: some of them are at Ginkaku-ji, Ryōan-ji and Tōfuku-ji.

Below left: Ginkaku-ji (p308)

Onsen

2 There's nothing like lowering yourself into the tub at a classic Japanese onsen (natural hot spring bath; p63). You can feel the muscles in your back relax and the 'ahhh' that you emit is just a simple way of saying 'Damn, I'm glad I came to Japan!' If you're lucky, the tub is outside and there's a nice stream running nearby. The Japanese have turned the simple act of bathing into a folk religion and the country is dotted with temples and shrines to this most relaxing of faiths.

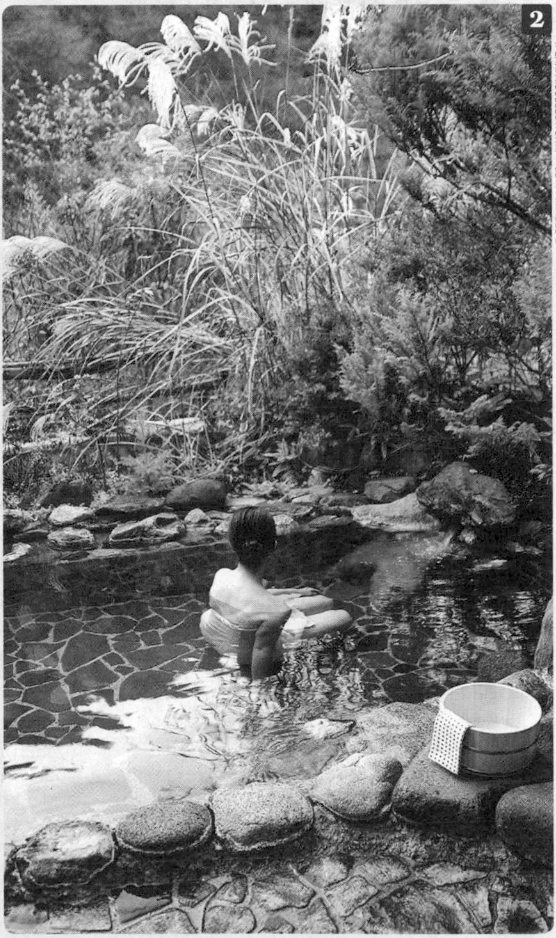

2

3

SHYMAN / GETTY IMAGES ©

4

LOTTIE DAVIES / GETTY IMAGES ©

Japanese Cuisine

3 Japan is a foodie paradise and the cuisine (p816) is incredibly varied, running the gamut from simple *soba* (buckwheat noodles) to multicourse *kaiseki* (haute cuisine) banquets. In a city such as Tokyo or Kyoto, you could eat a different Japanese speciality every night for a month without repeating your meal. There's no doubt that a food tour of Japan will be memorable, but there's one problem: once you try the real thing in Japan, the restaurants back home will pale in comparison. The only solution is another trip to Japan!

Cherry-Blossom Viewing (Hanami)

4 If you think of the Japanese as sober, serious people, join them under a cherry tree laden with blossoms in the springtime. It's as if the cherries release a narcotic that removes inhibitions. They'll drench you in sake and beer, stuff you with snacks, pull out portable karaoke systems and perhaps even dance. Japan is a happy place when the cherry blossoms are out. Two of the best places to experience *hanami* are Tokyo's Ueno-kōen and Kyoto's Maruyama-kōen. Above: Yoyogi-kōen (p89)

ISU / GETTY IMAGES ©

KEVIN FRATES / GETTY IMAGES ©

Staying in a Ryokan

5 Eat in your bedroom. Spend the day lounging about in a robe. Soak in a bath while looking at a garden. Don't lift a finger except to bring food to your mouth. Sound relaxing? Then we highly recommend a night in a good ryokan (traditional Japanese inn). The Japanese had the whole spa thing figured out long before they ever heard the word 'spa'. From first-class to the most humble, every ryokan (p843) will give you a taste of how the Japanese used to live.

Castles

6 Japan's castles (p31) have about as much in common with their European counterparts as kimonos have with Western dinner dresses. Their graceful contours belie the grim military realities behind their construction. Towering above the plains, they seem designed more to please the eye than to protect their lords. If you have an interest in samurai, shoguns and military history, you'll love Japan's castles. In original or re-built form, they are found across the country – the recently renovated Himeji-jō is a must-see. Above: Himeji-jō (p381)

HIROSHI HIGUCHI / GETTY IMAGES ©

Shopping in Tokyo

7 If it's available to humanity, you can buy it in Japan. Whether it's ¥10,000 (US$100) melons or curios from ¥100 shops (where everything goes for about US$1), you'll be amazed at the sheer variety of the goods on offer in Tokyo. Head to the boutiques of Ginza to see the glitterati do their shopping, or join the mere mortals in Shibuya and Shinjuku. And no trip to Tokyo would be complete without a visit to Tsukiji Market, the largest fish market in the world.

Above: Shibuya crossing (p87)

Arashiyama's Bamboo Grove

8 Western Kyoto is home to one of the most magical places in all of Japan: the famed bamboo grove in Arashiyama. The visual effect of the seemingly infinite stalks of bamboo is quite different from any forest we've ever encountered – there's a palpable presence to the place that is impossible to capture in pictures, but don't let that stop you from trying. If you've seen *Crouching Tiger, Hidden Dragon*, you'll have some idea of what this place is about.

Mt Fuji

9 Even from a distance Mt Fuji (p155) will take your breath away. Close up, the perfectly symmetrical cone of Japan's highest peak is nothing short of awesome. Dawn from the summit? Pure magic. Fuji-san is Japan's most revered and timeless attraction. Hundreds of thousands of people climb it every year, continuing a centuries-old tradition of pilgrimages up this sacred volcano. Those who'd rather search for picture-perfect views from the less daunting peaks nearby can follow in the steps of Japan's most famous painters and poets.

8

LIGHTPOEM / GETTY IMAGES ©

9

TAKAO NISHIDA / GETTY IMAGES ©

10
MEGUMI TANAKA / GETTY IMAGES ©

11
DAN HERRICK / GETTY IMAGES ©

12
MALCOLM P CHAPMAN / GETTY IMAGES ©

Hiking in the Japan Alps

10 Close your eyes and picture Japan. If all you see are geisha, Zen gardens, bullet trains and hypermodern cities, you might be in for a real surprise when you get into the Japan Alps (p206). Hike right into the heart of the high peaks here and you'll be in awe of so much mountain splendour. You can go hut-to-hut among the peaks for a week with nothing on your back but a solid day pack.

Daibutsu (Great Buddha) of Nara

11 Here's the drill: go to the temple of Tōdai-ji (p389) in Nara and stop for a moment outside the main hall. Then, without looking up, step into the hall. Calm your thoughts. Now raise your eyes to behold the Great Buddha. This is probably the closest you can come to enlightenment without years of meditation. There are few sights in Japan that have as much impact as this cosmic Buddha – you can almost feel the energy radiating from its bulk.

Hiroshima

12 Seeing the city's leafy boulevards, it's hard to picture Hiroshima (p427) as the devastated victim of an atomic bomb. It's not until you walk through the Peace Memorial Museum that the terrible reality becomes clear. But outside the quiet of Peace Memorial Park, energetic and forward-thinking Hiroshima rolls on. A visit here is a heartbreaking, important history lesson, but the modern city and its people – not to mention the food – ensure that's not the only memory you'll take when you leave. Above right: Peace Memorial Park (p427)

y
uring
e event

Oku-no-in at Kōya-s

14 Riding the funicular up to sacred Buddhist monastic of Kōya-san, you almost feel like you ascending to another world. The place permeated with a kind of august spiritual grandeur, and nowhere is this feeling stronger than in the vast Oku-no-in cemetery. Trails weave their way among towering cryptomeria trees and by the time you arrive at the main hall, the sudden appearance of a Buddha seems like the most natural thing in the world.

DENNIS FLAHERTY / GETTY IMAGES ©

DAMIEN DOUXCHAMPS / GETTY IMAGES ©

16

KOICHI KAMOSHIDA / GETTY IMAGES ©

Naoshima & Inland Sea Contemporary Art

15 The island-turned-art enclave of Naoshima (p460) is studded with standout modern art galleries and installations, drawing more visitors to the Inland Sea each year. Cycle around the sites, drop into an offbeat cafe, and soak in a mural-lined public bathhouse. Nearby islands, such as Teshima with its curved concrete art museum and 'heartbeat archive', are emerging as arty highlights as well. A couple of days on the islands is a great way to check out groundbreaking art against a beautiful natural backdrop. Top left: *Pumpkin* by Yayoi Kusama

Skiing

16 Travellers are finally becoming savvy about one of Japan's greatest secrets: skiing and snowboarding (p48). From the Japan Alps in Central Honshū to the Siberian-blasted Hokkaidō highlands, there are powder-covered runs to suit everyone. Well-priced equipment rental shops will have you up on the slopes in no time at all, while onsen are waiting to receive you for a unique après-ski experience. Indeed, there is nothing quite like a hot bath and a cold sake after an adrenaline-fuelled day of black diamonds. Left: Sapporo Teine (p570)

Kabuki

17 For otherworldly bizarreness, few theatrical spectacles come close to kabuki (stylised Japanese theatre). It doesn't really matter if you don't understand the words, as the colour and action of kabuki make it one of the most entertaining, if flummoxing, ways to lose yourself in Japan. While your kids might feel differently, we're pretty sure that you'll find kabuki to be one of those experiences that resonates long after leaving these islands. Catch a show at Tokyo's refurbished Kabuki-za or Kyoto's Minami-za theatre.

Walking Ancient Pilgrimage Routes

18 Japan is criss-crossed with ancient pilgrimage routes, many of which are still traversed by pilgrims. In the wilds of southern Kansai, the Kumano Kodō (p414) links three Shintō shrines with a network of mountainous trails, punctuated by welcoming rest stops and inns. It's the closest you'll come to Nepal-style 'teahouse' trekking in Japan. Nearby, on Shikoku, the 88 Temple Route is Japan's most famous Buddhist pilgrimage – tackle it on foot, by bicycle or on a bus tour. Below: Kumano Kodō

Yakushima

19 A quick ferry ride from the Kyūshū port town of Kagoshima, the island of Yakushima (p752) is a world of jagged mountains and primeval moss-strewn forests. This Unesco World Heritage island is a hiker's paradise, where you can spend the day exploring the peaks and then soak your bones in seaside onsen, some of which are at the water's edge and can only be entered when the tide is right. For non-hikers, there are sandy beaches and snorkelling to enjoy.

19

Tsumago–Magome Hike

20 A beautifully preserved post town in southern Nagano Prefecture, Tsumago is home to traditional wooden inns that once hosted travelling samurai lords. From Tsumago, follow the old Nakasendō post road (p225) up through sleepy alpine hamlets, old-growth cedar forests and waterfalls to the mountain pass Magome-tōge. Here you can rest at a teahouse before continuing to Magome, where fantastic mountain views are a backdrop to old inns and shops. The 7.8km hike winds through a world of farmhouses, waterwheels and rice paddies that time seems to have passed by.

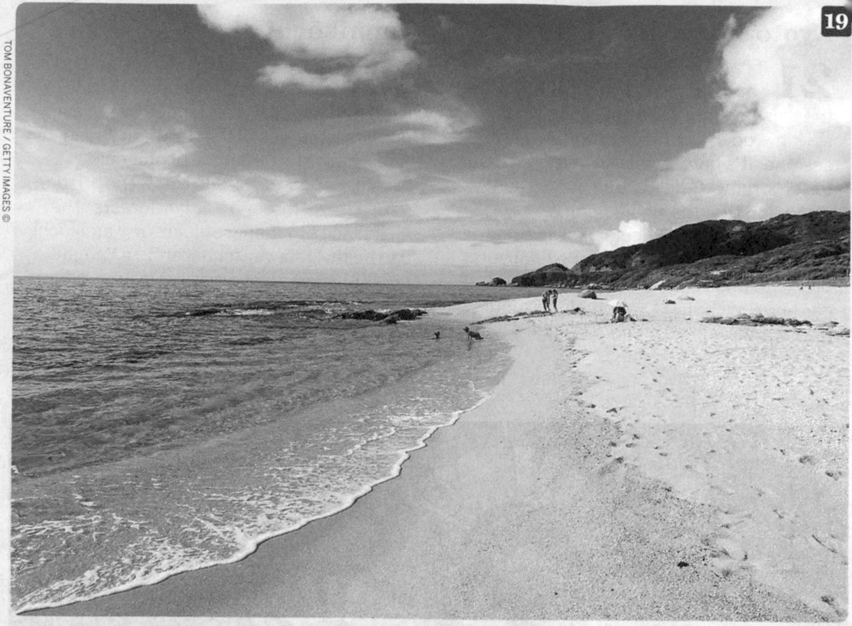

Left: Tsumago (p226)

Kyoto's Geisha Dances

21 It can't be stressed enough: if you find yourself in Kyoto (p288) when the geisha dances are on – usually in the spring – do everything in your power to see one. It's hard to think of a more colourful, charming and diverting stage event. You'll find that the whole thing takes on the appearance of a particularly vivid dream. When the curtain falls after the final burst of colour and song, the geisha might continue to dance in your mind for hours afterwards.

Kamikōchi

22 One of the most stunning natural vistas in Japan, Kamikōchi (p267) is a highland valley surrounded by the eye-popping summits of the Northern Japan Alps. Trails start from the photogenic bridge, Kappa-bashi, and follow the pristine Azusa-gawa through tranquil forests. The birthplace of Japanese alpinism, Kamikōchi can be the gateway for ascending Yariga-take (3180m) or for a one-hour stroll along the river to reach hot springs. In winter, you can trek in and have the valley to yourself for a snowshoe jaunt.

21

22

MARTIN ROUSSEAU / GETTY IMAGES ©

MASAMI GOTO / GETTY IMAGES ©

Tokyo's Modern Architecture

23 Japan may be known for its traditional temples, but Tokyo's cityscape is a veritable open-air museum of contemporary structures. The capital has come a long way from copying the Eiffel Tower – these days you'll find dozens of inspired and original works by a pantheon of the world's greatest designers. Fill up on such architectural eye-candy as the chic boutiques in Omote-sandō, the quirky postmodern projects on Odaiba, or even the new army of office towers in Marunouchi. Above: Tokyo International Forum (p78)

Festivals

24 You might imagine the people of Japan as buttoned-down conformists. If so, check out a really rollicking *matsuri* (festival) while you're here. The fact is, these people know how to really let loose. From giant festivals such as Kyoto's Gion Matsuri to local ones held in tiny hamlets, a festival may well be the highpoint of your trip. And don't be surprised if you're asked to participate. Top right: Gion Matsuri (p321)

Wild Hokkaidō

25 The last region of Japan to be 'pacified' by the central government, Hokkaidō (p561) remains the wildest part of the country. The scale here is totally different from any other part of Japan: the sky is bigger, the distances are greater and the natural landscape less tamed (this is the last redoubt of the brown bear in Japan). If you like your nature wild and woolly, take time to make a trip up to Japan's northernmost island.

Need to Know

For more information, see Survival Guide (p855)

Currency

Yen (¥)

Language

Japanese

Visas

Visas are issued on arrival for most nationalities for stays of up to 90 days.

Money

Post offices and some convenience stores have international ATMs. Most hotels and department stores, but only some restaurants and ryokan, accept credit cards.

Mobile Phones

Only 3G phones work in Japan. Data SIMs are available. Mobile phone rental is common and easy.

Time

Japan Standard Time (GMT/UTC plus nine hours)

When to Go

High Season (Apr & May, Aug)

- Flights are pricey around the Golden Week (early May), O-Bon (mid-August) and New Year.
- Honshū cities are busy in the cherry blossom (late March to early April) and autumn foliage (November) seasons.

Shoulder (Jun & Jul, Sep–Dec)

- June and July is rainy season in most of Japan (except Hokkaidō) – it doesn't rain every day but it can be pretty humid.
- Autumn (September to mid-December) is usually cool and clear.

Low Season (Jan–Mar)

- Winter is cool or cold in most of Honshū, but it's fine for travel.
- Be ready for snow in the mountains.
- Many businesses close over the New Year period (end December and early January).

Useful Websites

Lonely Planet (www.lonelyplanet.com/japan) Destination information, hotel bookings, traveller forum and more.

HyperDia (www.hyperdia.com) Comprehensive train schedules and fares.

Japan National Tourism Organization (www.jnto.go.jp) Official tourist site.

Japan Meteorological Agency Tropical Cyclone Page (www.jma.go.jp/en/typh) Up-to-date weather satellite images (good for checking on typhoons).

Japan Ministry of Foreign Affairs (www.mofa.go.jp) Links to embassies and consulates.

Important Numbers

Drop the 0 in the area code when dialling from abroad.

Ambulance & fire	☎119
Police	☎110
Country code	☎81
International access code	☎001
International operator	☎0051
Local directory	☎104

Exchange Rates

Australia	A$1	¥87
Canada	C$1	¥86
Europe	€1	¥117
New Zealand	NZ$1	¥65
UK	£1	¥134
US	US$1	¥83

For current exchange rates, see www.xe.com

Daily Costs

Budget: Less than ¥8000

- Dorm bed: ¥2800
- Set meal at casual restaurant: ¥800
- Train and bus tickets: ¥1500
- One temple or museum entry: ¥500

Midrange: ¥8000–¥20,000

- Double room at a business hotel: ¥12,000
- Dinner at an *izakaya* (Japanese-style pub): ¥4000
- Train and bus tickets: ¥1500
- Temple and museum entries: ¥1000

Top End: More than ¥20,000

- Double room in a top hotel: ¥23,000
- Meal at a good sushi restaurant: from ¥10,000
- Train tickets or taxi ride: ¥4500
- Temple and museum entries: ¥1000

Opening Hours

Banks 9am to 3pm weekdays

Bars 6pm to midnight or later, closed one day a week

Department stores 10am to 7pm, closed one or two days a month

Museums 9am or 10am to 5pm, closed Monday

Offices 9am to 5pm or 6pm weekdays

Post offices Local: 9am to 5pm weekdays; Central: 9am to 7pm weekdays, 9am to 3pm Saturday

Restaurants 11am to 2pm and 6pm to 11pm, closed one day a week

Smaller shops 9am to 5pm, may be closed Sunday

Arriving in Japan

Narita Airport Express train or highway bus to central Tokyo costs around ¥3000 (one to two hours). Both run frequently from 6am to 10.30pm. Taxis to the city cost about ¥30,000.

Haneda Airport Train or bus to central Tokyo costs ¥400 to ¥1200 (30 to 45 minutes). Both run frequently from 5.30am to midnight. Taxis, your only option for before-dawn arrivals, cost between ¥4000 and ¥10,000.

Kansai International Airport (KIX) Express trains run regularly to Kyoto (from ¥2850, 75 minutes) and Osaka (¥1430, 35 minutes). Buses cost ¥1050 to ¥1550 to central Osaka (50 minutes), ¥2550 to Kyoto (90 minutes). Trains and buses stop running close to midnight. A shared taxi service to Kyoto costs ¥3600; a standard taxi to Osaka from ¥14,500.

Getting Around

Japan has a brilliant public-transport system. For online timetables and fares see HyperDia (www.hyperdia.com).

Train Japan's rail system is fast, efficient and reliable and you can get just about anywhere by train. Consider purchasing a Japan Rail Pass.

Ferry You can make long inter-island hops by ferry for low prices and see a different side of Japan.

Bus If a part of Japan is not served by train or ferry, it's almost certainly served by good local or long-distance buses.

Car Rental cars are widely available, roads are great, driving is safe, and a car will give you plenty of freedom. Especially recommended in Hokkaidō and Okinawa. Drive on the left.

For much more on **getting around**, see p868

First Time Japan

For more information, see Survival Guide (p855)

Checklist

- ➡ Purchase a Japan Rail Pass (p875)
- ➡ Get an international licence if you plan to rent a car in Japan
- ➡ Make sure your passport is valid for at least six months past your arrival date
- ➡ Inform your debit- or credit-card company that you will be travelling abroad
- ➡ Get travel insurance

What to Pack

- ➡ Slip-on shoes, as you'll be taking off your shoes a lot
- ➡ Prescription medicines, which can be time-consuming to purchase
- ➡ Toiletries and personal-hygiene items: almost everything is available in Japan, but you might have a hard time finding preferred brands
- ➡ As little as possible – you can buy most things you'll need

Top Tips for Your Trip

- ➡ Get a Japan Rail Pass. These allow you to make unlimited use of the extensive, fast and efficient Japan Rail system.
- ➡ Stay at least one night in a ryokan (traditional Japanese inn) and visit at least one onsen (hot spring bath).
- ➡ Learn a couple of basic Japanese phrases. The locals will love you for trying.

What to Wear

Japan experiences four distinct seasons, each of which has changeable weather. For the hot, humid months (late May to early September) go with light, breathable clothes. For the cold months (early December to March), a fleece and shell/windbreaker is a good idea. For everything in between, be flexible: bring a light fleece, cardigan or jacket that you can put on or take off as needed.

As for dress code, most adult males don't wear shorts in Japan (unless they're exercising or hiking), but foreign males can do so without problems. For upscale restaurants and bars, you don't need anything nicer than 'smart casual' clothing.

Sleeping

Reservations are an absolute necessity in the high seasons (from late March to mid-May, in mid-August and during the New Year period), particularly in places like Kyoto and Nara. It's also a good idea to book ahead in other seasons as the Japanese are not used to 'walk in' guests.

- ➡ **Hotels** Choose from international luxury brands, efficient business hotels, cramped capsule hotels and slightly scandalous 'love hotels'.
- ➡ **Ryokan** A stay in a traditional inn is highly recommended.
- ➡ **Hostels and guesthouses** Inexpensive lodgings, many catering specifically to foreign travellers, are plentiful in tourist destinations.

Money

Many Japanese ATMs don't accept foreign-issued cards, but ATMs in Japanese post offices and 7-Eleven convenience stores do. Likewise, credit cards are not universally accepted in Japan, though can be used at most hotels, department stores, upscale restaurants, JR ticket offices and even some taxis. Still, you should never assume that you can use your credit card – always carry sufficient cash as a backup.

Bargaining

Bargaining is not really done in Japan. The only place where haggling is practised is at flea markets, such as the ones held twice a month in Kyoto.

Tipping

Tipping is not expected in Japan and the Japanese never do it. Leaving money on the table in a restaurant will usually result in the waiter chasing you down the street to give it back. However, if you feel like you've received excellent service from a guide or your personal maid at a ryokan, then place some money in an envelope and hand it to the person (handing cash over without an envelope is considered crass in these situations).

Phrases to Learn Before You Go

Is there a Western-/Japanese-style room?
洋室/和室はありますか?
yō·shi·tsu/wa·shi·tsu wa a·ri·mas ka

Some lodgings have only Japanese-style rooms, or a mix of Western and Japanese – ask if you have a preference.

Please bring a (spoon/knife/fork).
(スプーン/ナイフ/フォーク)をください。
(spūn/nai·fu/fō·ku) o ku·da·sai

If you haven't quite mastered the art of eating with chopsticks, don't be afraid to ask for cutlery at a restaurant.

How do I get to ...?
…へはどう行けばいいですか?
... e wa dō i·ke·ba ī des ka

Finding a place from its address can be difficult in Japan. Addresses usually give an area (not a street) and numbers aren't always consecutive. Practise asking for directions.

I'd like a nonsmoking seat, please.
禁煙席をお願いします。
kin·en·se·ki o o·ne·gai shi·mas

There are smoking seats in many restaurants and on bullet trains so be sure to specify if you want to be smoke-free.

What's the local speciality?
地元料理は何がありますか?
ji·mo·to·ryō·ri wa na·ni ga a·ri·mas ka

Throughout Japan most areas have a speciality dish and locals usually love to talk food.

Etiquette

No one expects you to know all the rules. Do what would be polite in your own country, and you won't go too far wrong.

➡ **Greetings** Japanese tend to bow rather than shake hands, but you aren't expected to strictly follow this custom. If a Japanese person bows to you, simply incline your head a little in return. Wait for the opposite party to offer their hand for a handshake.

➡ **Giving and receiving** Use two hands when giving or receiving a name/business card (business cards are enormously important in Japan). Ditto for presents or important documents. And when giving money, try to put it into an envelope.

➡ **Shoes** Take off your shoes when stepping onto tatami mats, into a private home or into the hall of a temple. Step out of the shoes onto the mats. The point is to keep the inside free from outside dirt.

➡ **Religious sites** Temples are religious places, so don't enter the grounds or main halls dressed like you're out for a day at the beach, and speak quietly while in the main halls. Shrines tend to be a little more casual, but flip-flops and cut-off shorts aren't going to impress anyone.

➡ **Flexibility** Not all restaurants are willing to alter dishes to suit dietary preferences or requirements, and not every ryokan has slippers or futons big enough for some foreign guests.

What's New

New Bullet Train Line (Hokuriku Shinkansen Line)

The Hokuriku *shinkansen* (bullet train) cuts travel time between Tokyo and Kanazawa to just over two hours. This new line makes it extremely easy and comfortable to do the Tokyo–Kyoto Kanazawa loop, one of the top one-week Japan travel itineraries.

Cheap Yen

The Japanese yen has plunged recently against most currencies, making Japan (at least areas outside of Tokyo) seem positively cheap in comparison to some destinations.

Haneda Airport Expansion

Tokyo's 'second' airport, Haneda International Airport, is now serving an increasing number of international flights. This is a huge boon to travellers, since Haneda is significantly closer to central Tokyo than Narita Airport.

Discount Narita Express (N'EX) Tickets

Tourists can purchase return Narita Express tickets for ¥4000, which is more than 30% off the standard return fare. Check online for the latest as deals are prone to change. (p150)

Better Wi-fi Coverage

While most hotels in Japan used to offer only in-room LAN cable internet access, wi-fi is becoming the new norm. Free wi-fi is also becoming increasingly available in restaurants, cafes, bars, airports and even some train stations. Some major cities even offer wi-fi on the street.

More Japan Rail passes

Japan Rail has released a raft of new pass options for tourists, including a three-day Kantō area (Tokyo and surrounds) pass covering Narita, Nikkō and Fuji-san; a four-day pass for travel in Hiroshima and Western Honshū; a four-day Hokuriku travel pass; and a five-day pass for travel in Kansai and to Hiroshima. (p875)

Tsukiji Market Moving

Tsukiji's famous fish market is on course to move to a new home on Tokyo Bay in late 2016. Only a short time remains to see this classic Tokyo sight in its present form. (p79)

New Tax Exemptions

Until recently, only certain non-consumable items such as electronics were tax-exempt for tourists, but now many consumable items such as food, cosmetics, beverages and medicine also qualify for tax-exempt status when making purchases over ¥5000. Look for signs indicating special tax-exempt stores.

Okada Museum of Art

Showcasing the dazzling Japanese, Chinese and Korean art treasures of industrialist Okada Kazuo, this mammoth museum is a great addition to Hakone's showcases of world-class art. (p175)

For more recommendations and reviews, see lonelyplanet.com/japan

Why I Love Japan

By Chris Rowthorn, Author

I've spent most of my adult life in Japan and now it feels like home to me. I love the food: it's incredibly varied and nourishing and there seems to be no end to the culinary discoveries you can make. I love the combination of a hike in the mountains followed by a long soak in an onsen. But, most of all, I love the meticulous and careful nature of the Japanese people, reflected in every aspect of Japanese life, from trains that run right on time to sublime works of art. Put it all together and you come away with a country that still intrigues me even after two decades of living there.

For more about our authors, see page 904

Above: Tsukiji Outer Market (p80), Tokyo

Japan

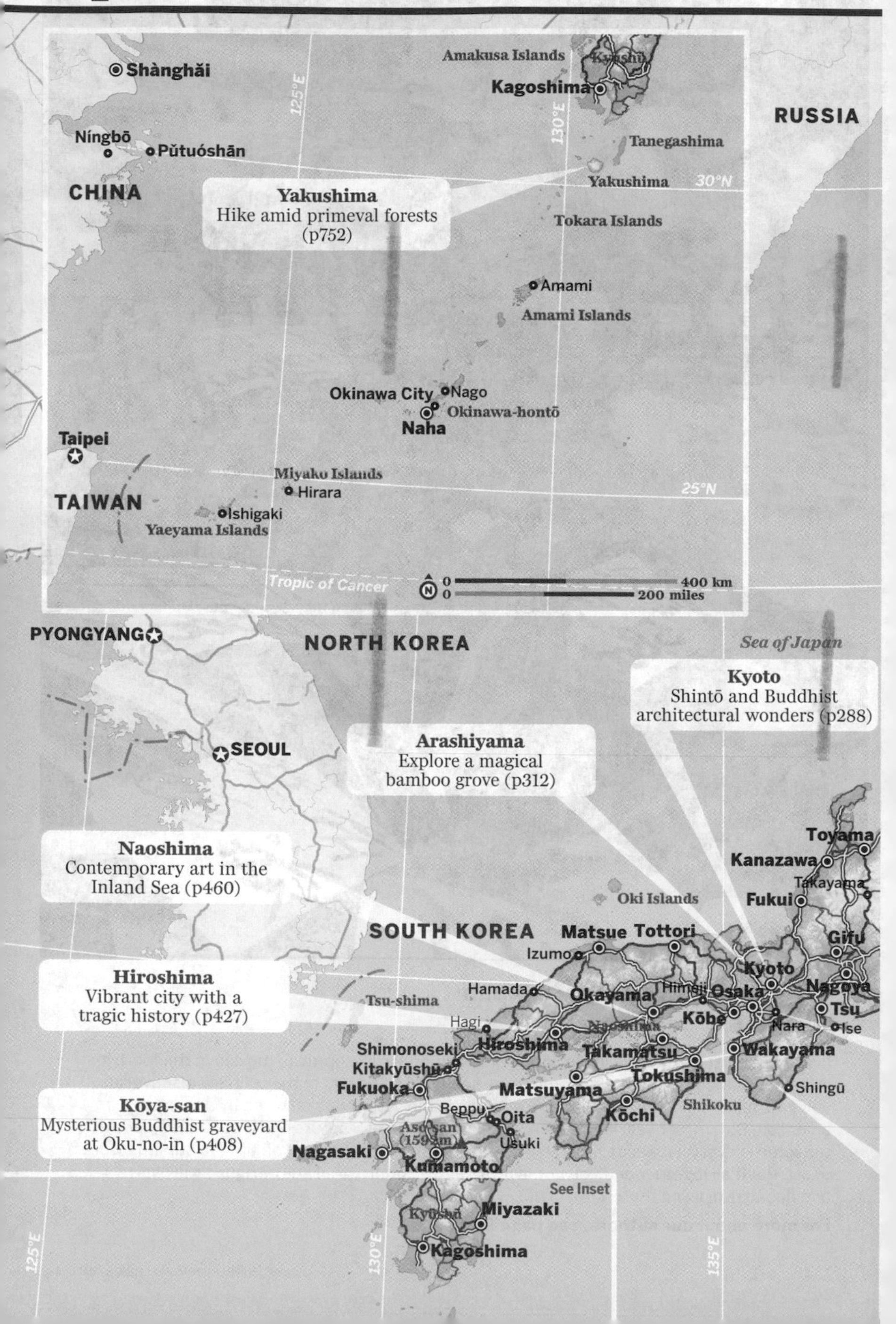

Yakushima
Hike amid primeval forests
(p752)

Kyoto
Shintō and Buddhist
architectural wonders (p288)

Arashiyama
Explore a magical
bamboo grove (p312)

Naoshima
Contemporary art in the
Inland Sea (p460)

Hiroshima
Vibrant city with a
tragic history (p427)

Kōya-san
Mysterious Buddhist graveyard
at Oku-no-in (p408)

Shànghǎi
Amakusa Islands
Kyūshū
Kagoshima
125°E
130°E
RUSSIA
Níngbō
Pǔtuóshān
Tanegashima
CHINA
Yakushima
30°N
Tokara Islands
Amami
Amami Islands
Okinawa City
Nago
Okinawa-hontō
Naha
Taipei
Miyako Islands
Hirara
25°N
TAIWAN
Ishigaki
Yaeyama Islands
Tropic of Cancer
0 — 400 km
0 — 200 miles
PYONGYANG
NORTH KOREA
Sea of Japan
SEOUL
Toyama
Kanazawa
Takayama
Fukui
Oki Islands
SOUTH KOREA
Matsue
Tottori
Gifu
Izumo
Kyoto
Hamada
Okayama
Himeji
Osaka
Nagoya
Tsu-shima
Kōbe
Tsu
Hagi
Naoshima
Nara
Ise
Shimonoseki
Hiroshima
Takamatsu
Wakayama
Kitakyūshū
Tokushima
Fukuoka
Matsuyama
Shingū
Beppu
Kōchi
Shikoku
Oita
Aso-san
(1592m)
Usuki
Nagasaki
Kumamoto
See Inset
Kyūshū
Miyazaki
Kagoshima
125°E
130°E
135°E

If You Like...

Temples, Shrines & Gardens

You'll find the Japan of your imagination – immaculately raked gardens, quiet Buddhist temples and mysterious Shintō shrines – all across the archipelago, even in the ultramodern capital of Tokyo.

Kyoto Start with must-see places such as Ginkaku-ji (p308), Kinkaku-ji (p310) and Fushimi Inari-Taisha (p314) and then find your own personal favourite among the nearly endless offerings.

Nara Stand in awe before the Great Buddha (Daibutsu) at Tōdai-ji (p389) and then let it all sink in at the superb garden at Isui-en (p387).

Kanazawa Some call this small city a 'mini-Kyoto', but Kanazawa isn't a 'mini' anything – it's big on temples and has one of the best gardens in Japan: Kenroku-en (p242).

Tokyo That's right: amid all that concrete you'll find centuries-old Sensō-ji (p107) and the grand Meiji-jingū (p89).

Culinary Adventure

Who doesn't come to Japan to eat? And we don't just mean 'extreme eating'; we mean some of the Japanese food you might have tried back home, only much better versions.

Tokyo With more Michelin stars than any city on earth, this is the place for the best Japanese food in the country, as well as some of the best French and Italian food you'll find anywhere. (p122)

Tsukiji Simply pointing out that the Tsukiji Fish Market is the biggest in the world doesn't begin to convey the size, variety and excitement of the place. (p79)

Kyoto If you want to sample *kaiseki* (haute cuisine) in traditional surroundings, dine with a geisha, or sample the offerings in Japanese sweet shops, this is the place to go. (p331)

Osaka The culinary rallying cry for Osakans is 'eat 'til you drop!'. The food is plebeian and plentiful. Grab a pair of chopsticks and join the fray. (p363)

Okinawa Okinawan cuisine is as close as Japan comes to China, and the impressive array of pork and noodle dishes is a must-try for any self-respecting gourmand. (p763)

Kōya-san This mountain-top monastic complex has literally and figuratively elevated Buddhist vegetarian fare to new heights. (p412)

Onsen (Hot Springs)

Kinosaki Japan's classic onsen town is everything an onsen town ought to be: quaint, friendly and packed with homey ryokan. (p422)

Kayōtei If your finances run to a night or two here, you will surely be glad you made the trip to this sublime onsen. (p250)

Hongū Trek for a few days along Japan's ancient pilgrimage route, the Kumano Kodō, then soak your sore muscles in the three great onsen near the village of Hongū. (p417)

Takaragawa Onsen This is the place to try the classic onsen experience: sitting in a hot bath looking at the snowy banks of a rushing river. (p286)

Urami-ga-taki Onsen They don't make onsen with more scenic and soothing locations than this one on the island of Hachijō-jima. (p189)

Shopping

Forget sumo and judo – Japan's national sport is shopping. Whether your taste runs to expensive boutiques or ¥100 shops, if you're a shopper you have to come to Japan.

Tokyo Japan's capital has the widest selection of stores on the planet, selling everything from gadgets to Gucci bags. (p140)

Kyoto The old capital has a brilliant selection of traditional goods (think ceramics, antiques, scrolls, tea-ceremony articles and kimonos), as well as plenty of trendy boutiques, well-stocked department stores and the two best flea markets in the country. (p342)

Osaka The Osakans come in for quite a ribbing from their fellow Japanese: they're famed for driving a hard bargain and shopping with abandon. (p370)

Kanazawa Some of the finest lacquerware and woodworking in Japan is produced and sold in this charming Sea of Japan city. (p249)

Tsuboya Pottery Street Way down in the city of Naha, on the main island of Okinawa, you'll find one of Japan's most vibrant ceramics centres. (p766)

Modern Architecture

Tokyo Tokyo is an architect's playground: check out the Tokyo Metropolitan Government Offices (p92), the Tokyo Sky Tree (p108), the International Forum building (p78) and hundreds more.

Naoshima This island-cum-art-museum is graced with several Andō Tadao creations and lots of other fantastic buildings. (p460)

JOHN SONES SINGING BOWL MEDIA / GETTY IMAGES ©

IPPEI NAOI / GETTY IMAGES ©

Top: Shoppers in Akihabara (p145)

Bottom: Tokashiki-jima (p775), Kerama Islands

Kanazawa While it's more famous for its temples and gardens, Kanazawa gets a lot of visits from architecture buffs who come to see the 21st Century Museum of Contemporary Art. (p243)

Osaka Don't miss Osaka's own Arc de Triomphe, the Umeda Sky Building, and then head over to marvel at the Abeno Harukas building; at 300m, it's the highest building in the city. (p351)

Festivals

Perhaps you imagine the Japanese to be a serious and staid people. If so, check out one of the country's wilder *matsuri* (festivals) to see them bust loose, and join the fun!

Gion Matsuri The main event here (a parade of floats) is pretty tame, but the evenings leading up to this great Kyoto summer festival get pretty wild. Put on a *yukata* (robe) and stroll through town, stopping for beer and snacks as you go. (p321)

Hanami Strictly speaking, the Japanese cherry-blossom-viewing parties *(hanami)* that take place up and down the archipelago in March and April aren't *matsuri*, but they sure feel like festivals.

Hatsu-mōde Again, the first shrine visit of the year *(hatsu-mōde)* is not a *matsuri* in the strict sense, but if you find yourself at a popular Shintō shrine on New Year's Eve or New Year's Day, you'll see why we've included it here.

Kishiwada Danjiri Matsuri In one of the wilder events in Japan, the locals haul floats through the streets, sometimes at surprising speeds. Join the fun, but stand well back when those things go by. (p361)

Pop Culture

Whether it be *cosplay* (costume play), manga (Japanese comics) or 'maid cafes', Japan is one huge pop-culture playground. Check out where it all begins: Tokyo.

Akihabara Better known as 'Akiba', Tokyo's main electronics district is alive with the pulse of *otaku* (geek) trends. (p97)

Shibuya Shibuya is the shopping mecca at the centre of Tokyo's youth universe. Keep your eyes peeled and you'll see several trends coming into being as you walk down the street. (p86)

Ghibli Museum If you know the name Miyazaki Hayao (the king of Japanese anime), or if your kids do, you'll want to make a half-day trip out of Tokyo to see his museum. (p93)

Beaches

Few people associate Japan with beaches, but the country has some real stunners, many in the southwest islands of Okinawa.

Sakibaru Kaigan This lovely stretch of white sand and clear water on Amami-Ōshima is a winner by any definition. (p760)

Kerama Islands It's impossible to pick a favourite beach on these three charming islands – the fun is in exploring each one and finding your own white-sand paradise. (p774)

Hoshisuna-no-hama While the beach here is nothing to sneeze at, it's the drop-off at the edge of the coral reef that really gets our motor running. (p786)

Shirara-hama This blinding-white stretch of sand in Kansai's Wakayama Prefecture is backed by one of the worst tourist circuses in the country, but swim a few hundred metres offshore and it's all a distant memory. (p414)

Castles

For anyone with an interest in Japan's feudal era (think samurai, shoguns and *daimyō*), a visit to a Japanese castle is sure to get the imagination working.

Himeji-jō The queen of all Japanese castles, the 'White Egret Castle' is a must-see for all Japanese castle fans. (p381)

Hikone-jō Within easy day-trip distance of Kyoto, Hikone-jō is a beautiful castle that makes up for its lack of size with a fine view and graceful lines. (p385)

Osaka-jō It's not original and it's not subtle, but it sure looks good from a distance or when the cherries in the surrounding park are in bloom. (p354)

Matsuyama-jō Dominating the city of Matsuyama on the island of Shikoku, this is easily one of Japan's finest original castles. (p659)

Shuri-jō Way down in Okinawa, this rebuilt castle is a completely different kettle of fish from its mainland cousins – the Chinese influence is clear. (p769)

Month by Month

TOP EVENTS

Gion Matsuri, July

Cherry-Blossom Viewing, April

Takayama Matsuri, April

Yuki Matsuri, February

Tenjin Matsuri, July

January

Japan comes to life after the lull of the New Year holiday. Winter grips the country in the mountains and in the north, but travel is still possible in most places.

Shōgatsu (New Year)

New Year (31 December to 3 January) is one of the most important celebrations in Japan and includes plenty of eating and drinking. The central ritual, *hatsu-mōde,* involves the first visit to the local shrine to pray for health, happiness and prosperity during the coming year. Keep in mind that a lot of businesses and attractions shut down during this period and transport can be busy as people head back to their hometowns.

Seijin-no-hi (Coming-of-Age Day)

On the second Monday in January, ceremonies are held for boys and girls who have reached the age of 20. A good place to see the action is at large shrines, where you'll find crowds of girls in kimonos and boys in suits or kimonos.

Skiing

Although many ski areas open in December, the ski season really gets rolling in January.

February

It's still cold in February in most of Japan (with the exception of Okinawa). Skiing is in full swing and this is a good time to soak in onsen (hot springs).

Setsubun Matsuri

On 2, 3 or 4 February, to celebrate the end of winter and drive out evil spirits, the Japanese engage in throwing roasted beans while chanting *'oni wa soto, fuku wa uchi'* (meaning 'out with the demons, in with good luck'). Check local shrines for events.

Yuki Matsuri

Drawing over two million annual visitors, Sapporo's famous snow festival really warms up winter in Hokkaidō in early February. Teams from around the world compete to create the most impressive ice and snow sculptures. After touring the sculptures, head to one of the city's friendly pubs and eateries to warm up with sake and great local food. (p571)

March

By March it's starting to warm up on the main islands of Japan. Plums start the annual procession of blossoms across the archipelago. This is a pleasant time to travel in Honshū, Kyūshū and Shikoku.

Plum-Blossom Viewing

Not as famous as the cherries, but quite lovely in their own right, Japan's plum trees bloom from late February into early March. Strolling among the plum orchards at places like Kyoto's Kitano Tenman-gū is a fine way to spend an early spring day in Japan.

AnimeJapan

Formerly known as the Tokyo International Anime Fair, this is the world's largest anime (Japanese animation) fair. Held on 21 and 22 March at the Tokyo Big Sight event hall, this is a must-see event for fans of Japanese pop culture (www.anime-japan.jp).

April

Spring is in full swing by April. The cherry blossoms usually peak early in April in most of Honshū. Japan is beautiful at this time, but places like Kyoto can be crowded.

Cherry-Blossom Viewing

When the cherry blossoms burst into bloom, the Japanese hold rollicking *hanami* (blossom viewing) parties. It's hard to time viewing the blossoms: to hit them at their peak in Tokyo or Kyoto, you have to be in the country from around 25 March to 5 April.

Takayama Matsuri

The first part of this festival (p232), the Sannō Matsuri, is held on 14 and 15 April. The festival floats here are truly spectacular. Book well in advance if you want to spend the night or come back in October for the second part, the Hachiman Matsuri. (p232)

May

May is one of the best months to visit Japan. It's warm and sunny in most of the country. Book accommodation well in advance during the April/May Golden Week holidays.

Golden Week

Most Japanese are on holiday from 29 April to 5 May, when a series of national holidays coincide. This is one of the busiest times for domestic travel, so be prepared for crowded transport and accommodation.

Sanja Matsuri

The grandest of all Tokyo festivals is held on the third weekend in May. It features hundreds of *mikoshi* (portable shrines) paraded through Asakusa, starting from Asakusa-jinja.

June

June is generally a lovely time to travel in Japan – it's warm, but not sweltering. Keep in mind that the rainy season generally starts in Kyūshū and Honshū sometime in June. It doesn't rain every day, but it can be humid.

Japan Alps Hiking Season

Most of the snow has melted off the high peaks of the Japan Alps by June and hikers flock to the trails. Check conditions before going, however, as big powder years can mean snow lingering on trails late into summer.

July

The rainy season ends in Honshū sometime in July and, once it does, the heat cranks up and it can be very hot and humid. Head to Hokkaidō or the Japan Alps to escape the heat.

Mt Fuji Climbing Season

Mt Fuji (p155) officially opens to climbing on 1 July, and the months of July and August are ideal for climbing the peak. (p155)

Gion Matsuri

Held on 17 and 24 July, this is the mother of all Japanese festivals. Dozens of huge floats are pulled through the streets of Kyoto by teams of chanting citizens. On the three evenings preceding the first parade, people stroll through Shijō-dōri's street stalls dressed in beautiful *yukata* (light cotton kimonos).

Tenjin Matsuri

Held on 24 and 25 July, this is your chance to see the city of Osaka let its hair down. Try to make the second day of the festival, when huge crowds carry *mikoshi* (portable shrines) through the city.

August

August is hot and humid across most of Japan. Once again, Hokkaidō and the Japan Alps can provide some relief. Several of the year's best festivals and events happen in August.

Summer Fireworks Festivals

Cities and towns across Japan hold spectacular summer fireworks festivals in late July and early August. Some of the nation's top events include the Sumida-gawa Fireworks Festival (Tokyo, late July), Uji-gawa Fireworks Festival (near Kyoto, early August), Lake Biwa Fireworks Festival (near Kyoto, early August) and the Naniwa Yodogawa Fireworks Festival (Osaka, early August).

Aomori Nebuta Matsuri

Held for several days in early August, this is one of Japan's more colourful festivals. On the final day of the festival, enormous parade floats are pulled through Aomori by teams of chanting dancers. (p531)

Matsumoto Bonbon

Matsumoto's biggest event takes place on the first Saturday in August, when hordes of people perform the 'bonbon' dance through the city streets.

Peace Memorial Ceremony

On 6 August, a memorial service is held in Hiroshima for victims of the WWII atomic bombing of the city. Thousands of paper lanterns are floated down the river. (p433)

Awa-odori Matsuri

The city of Tokushima, on the southern island of Shikoku, comes alive from 12 to 15 August for the nation's largest and most famous *bon* dance (p636). These dances are performed to welcome the souls of the departed back to this world (and this is usually considered a good excuse to consume vast quantities of sake). Teams of dancers take to the streets to perform, and the best troupes are awarded prizes. (p636)

O-Bon (Festival of the Dead)

This Buddhist observance, which honours the spirits of the dead, occurs in mid-August (it is one of the high-season travel periods). This is a time when ancestors return to earth to visit their descendants. Lanterns are lit and floated on rivers, lakes or the sea to help guide them on their journey. See also Daimon-ji Gozan Okuribi.

Daimon-ji Gozan Okuribi

Huge fires in the shape of Chinese characters and other symbols are set alight in Kyoto during this festival, which forms part of O-Bon. It's one of Japan's most impressive spectacles. (p321)

Earth Celebration

The island of Sado-ga-shima, off the coast of Northern Honshū, is the scene of this internationally famous festival of dance, art and music. The festival is held in the third week of August. (p502)

September

Sometime in early to mid-September, the heat breaks and temperatures become very pleasant on the main islands. Skies are generally clear at this time, making it a great time to travel.

Kishiwada Danjiri Matsuri

Huge *danjiri* (festival floats) are pulled through the narrow streets in the south of Osaka during this lively festival on 14 and 15 September. Much alcohol is consumed and occasionally the *danjiri* go off course and crash into houses. (p361)

October

October is one of the best months to visit Japan: the weather can be cool or warm and it's usually sunny. The autumn foliage peaks in the Japan Alps at this time.

Matsue Suitōro

Held on Saturdays, Sundays and holidays throughout October in the Western Honshu city of Matsue, this festival of light and water takes place at Matsue-jō, the city's scenic castle, which is incredibly atmospheric after dark. Try to catch the lively battles of rival drumming groups.

Asama Onsen Taimatsu Matsuri

In early October, Asama Onsen holds this spectacular fire festival. Groups of men, women and children parade burning bales of hay through narrow streets to an enormous bonfire at Misha-jinja.

Kurama-no-hi Matsuri

On 22 October, huge flaming torches are carried through the streets of the

BRENT WINEBRENNER / GETTY IMAGES ©

SOT / GETTY IMAGES ©

Top: Takayama Matsuri (p33)

Bottom: Shichi-go-san

tiny hamlet of Kurama in the mountains north of Kyoto. This is one of Japan's more primeval festivals.

November

November is also beautiful for travel in most of Japan. Skies are reliably clear and temperatures are pleasantly cool. Snow starts to fall in the mountains and foliage peaks in places like Kyoto and Nara. Expect crowds.

Shichi-Go-San (7-5-3 Festival)

This is a festival in honour of girls aged three and seven and boys aged five. On 15 November, children are dressed in their finest clothes and taken to shrines or temples, where prayers are offered for good fortune.

December

December is cool to cold across most of Japan. The Japanese are busy preparing for the New Year. Most things shut down from 29 or 30 December, making travel difficult (but transport runs and accommodation is open).

FRANK DEIM/ GETTY IMAGES ©

Plan Your Trip
Itineraries

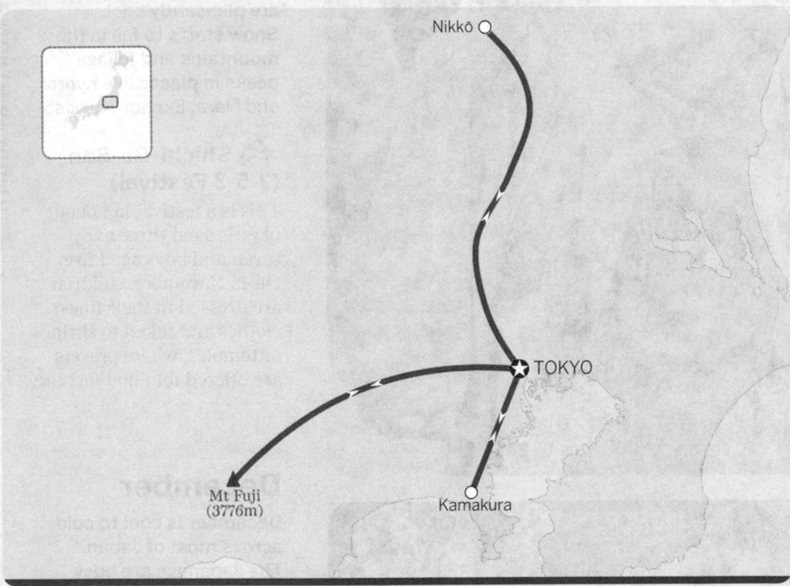

Tokyo, Mt Fuji & Around

With air connections to most of the world, as well as some of the world's best restaurants, shops and nightlife, Tokyo makes a great introduction to Japan. And you don't have to travel far outside the city to see some of Japan's great natural and traditional wonders.

To make the most of your stay in **Tokyo**, try to base yourself in an area that's interesting and also well served by transport connections, such as Shinjuku, Shibuya, Ginza, Roppongi or Marunouchi (Tokyo Station area). In any of these places, you can walk to a huge variety of restaurants and shops, and train/subway stations are always nearby. Of course, it's also perfectly possible to stay in slightly less convenient but cheaper areas like Asakusa or Ueno.

On your first morning in town, visit Tsukiji Market – if you're jetlagged and up early anyway, make the best of it with a market tour. After the obligatory sushi breakfast, head up to Asakusa to visit the temple of Sensō-ji, then over to nearby Ueno for the Tokyo National Museum. The next day, take the loop line to Harajuku and walk to Meiji-jingū, the city's finest

Tokyo Tower (p83)

Shintō shrine, then take a stroll down chic Omote-sandō. From there, head to Shibuya to soak up some of modern Tokyo. Make sure you spend an evening wandering east Shinjuku, where you'll get the full experience of Tokyo's neon madness. Other urban areas to check out include Ginza for high-end shopping, Akihabara for electronics and geek culture, and Roppongi for international nightlife.

Break up your time in Tokyo with day trips to nearby attractions. The temples and shrines at **Nikkō** are among the most spectacular in Japan. For a taste of old Japan, a day poking among the Zen temples at **Kamakura** is a brilliant way to escape the crowds of the capital. Finally, it would be a shame to come all the way to Japan and not see **Mt Fuji**. You can get to the base of the mountain and back in a day from Tokyo, but climbing it will involve spending the night on the mountain. Either way, we recommend checking the weather first – the mountain is covered by clouds much of the year, so try to wait for a break in the weather to make the trip.

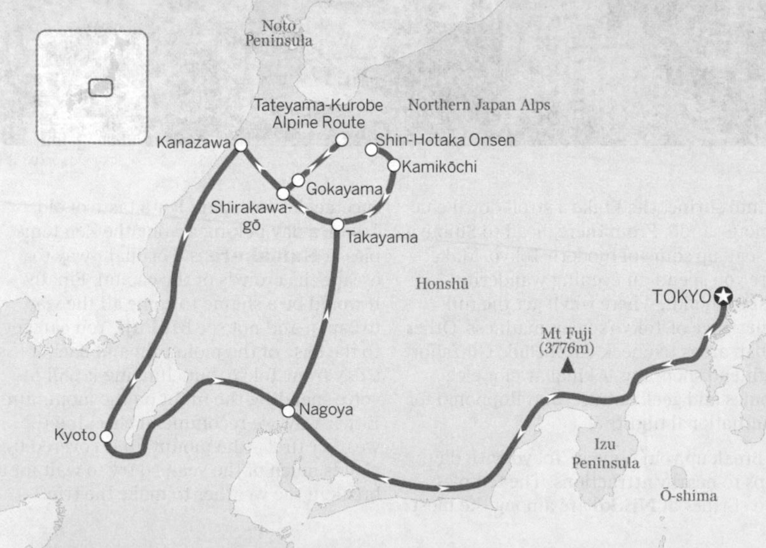
Noto Peninsula
Tateyama-Kurobe Alpine Route
Northern Japan Alps
Kanazawa
Shin-Hotaka Onsen
Kamikōchi
Gokayama
Shirakawa-gō
Takayama
Honshū
TOKYO
Mt Fuji (3776m)
Nagoya
Kyoto
Izu Peninsula
Ō-shima

WAN RU CHEN / GETTY IMAGES ©

DAJ / GETTY IMAGES ©

Top: Shirakawa-gō (p236)
Bottom: Kenroku-en (p242), Kanazawa

Tokyo, the Japan Alps & Kyoto

The Tokyo–Japan Alps–Kyoto route is the classic Japan itinerary and the best way to get a quick taste of the country. You'll experience three faces of Japan: the modern wonders of Tokyo, the traditional culture of Kyoto and the natural beauty of the Japan Alps.

While you can do this itinerary in any season, keep in mind that the Japan Alps can be snow covered any time from early November to late March – this rules out hiking unless you're an experienced winter mountaineer – but you can visit the attractive cities of Takayama and Kanazawa any time of year.

Let's assume that you'll fly into **Tokyo**, where you can spend a few days experiencing the best that the capital has to offer. Don't worry about skipping some of the city's traditional sights, because you'll be heading to Kyoto, and you'll get your fill of shrines and temples there.

From Tokyo, take the *shinkansen* (bullet train) to **Nagoya** then an express to **Takayama**. Spend a day here checking out the restored Sanmachi-suji, then head into the Japan Alps via **Kamikōchi** or nearby **Shin-Hotaka Onsen**. Return to Takayama and rent a car so you can visit the thatched-roof villages of **Shirakawa-gō** and **Gokayama**. From there, if you feel like some more alpine scenery, drive northeast and head back into the Japan Alps via the **Tateyama-Kurobe Alpine Route** (the drive is open from late spring to early autumn). Next, travel to **Kanazawa** (some rental agencies will allow you to drop the car in Kanazawa, otherwise, you can also go from Takayama to Kanazawa by bus with a stop in Shirakawa-gō en route). In Kanazawa, check out the famous garden of Kenroku-en, the 21st Century Museum of Contemporary Art and the Nagamachi district.

From Kanazawa, there are several daily express trains that will get you to **Kyoto** in a little over two hours. In Kyoto, take some time to visit the sights (including 17 Unesco World Heritage Sites, and literally hundreds of temples and shrines), then jump on the *shinkansen* and get yourself back to Tokyo in time for your flight home.

2 WEEKS Kansai & Points West

While many people fly into Tokyo and base themselves there, Kansai, which is home to the ancient capital of Kyoto, is an equally appealing place to stay, especially if you're a fan of traditional culture. And with a Japan Rail Pass, you can easily head west to see Hiroshima, Miyajima and Naoshima.

Served by Kansai International Airport, which has connections to many parts of the world, **Kyoto** is the obvious place to stay: it's roughly in the middle of Kansai and it's got a wide range of accommodation, not to mention the nation's finest temples, gardens and shrines. Spend a day exploring the Higashiyama area (both southern and northern), followed by another day strolling the bamboo groves of Arashiyama. Then, hop on a train for a day trip to **Nara** to see the sights of Nara-kōen including Tōdai-ji, with its enormous Buddha figure.

If you want to see a modern Japanese metropolis in high gear, **Osaka** is only about 30 minutes by train from Kyoto. You can easily explore the city, grab some dinner and a drink and make it back to Kyoto before the trains stop running.

For those with a spiritual bent, a trip to the mountain-top Buddhist retreat of **Kōya-san** is highly recommended. Spend the night in one of the temple lodgings there before returning to Kyoto. More adventurous travellers will also want to check out Japan's ancient pilgrimage route, the **Kumano Kodō** in southern Kansai.

Kyoto also makes a good base for exploring some of the important sights in Western Honshū and the Inland Sea. **Hiroshima** can be visited as a day trip from Kyoto if you use the *shinkansen* and get an early start. However, it's more relaxing to spend the night in nearby **Miyajima**, home of the iconic 'floating' torii (Shintō shrine gate) of Itsukushima-jinja. Art lovers might also consider stopping for a night or two at **Naoshima**, the island-turned-art museum in the Inland Sea.

Finally, if all this toing and froing makes you tired, finish off your Kansai adventure with an overnight trip up to **Kinosaki**, where you can soak away your cares in some of Japan's best hot springs.

KEREN SU / GETTY IMAGES ©

DAN HERRICK / GETTY IMAGES ©

Top: Kangen-sai, a Shintō ritual at Itsukushima-jinja (p438), Miyajima
Bottom: Woman in geisha costume, Gion (p303), Kyoto

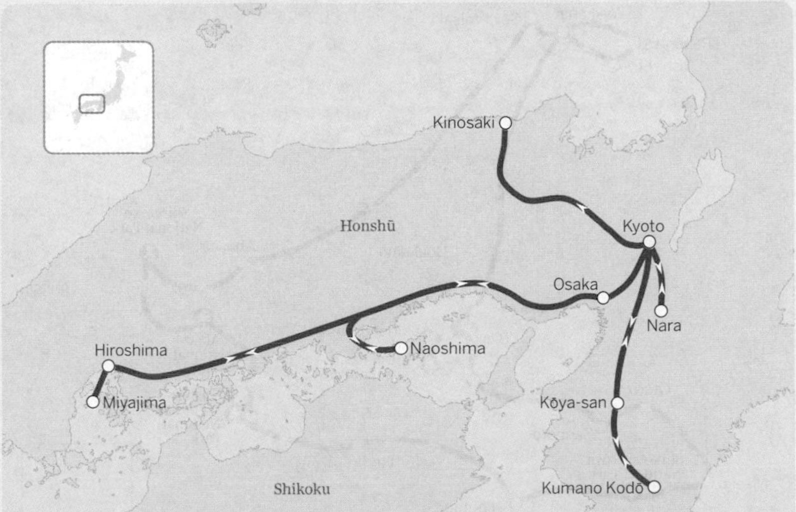

Kinosaki
Honshū
Kyoto
Osaka
Nara
Hiroshima
Naoshima
Miyajima
Kōya-san
Kumano Kodō
Shikoku

本
倉
庫
港
運
会
社
小
樽

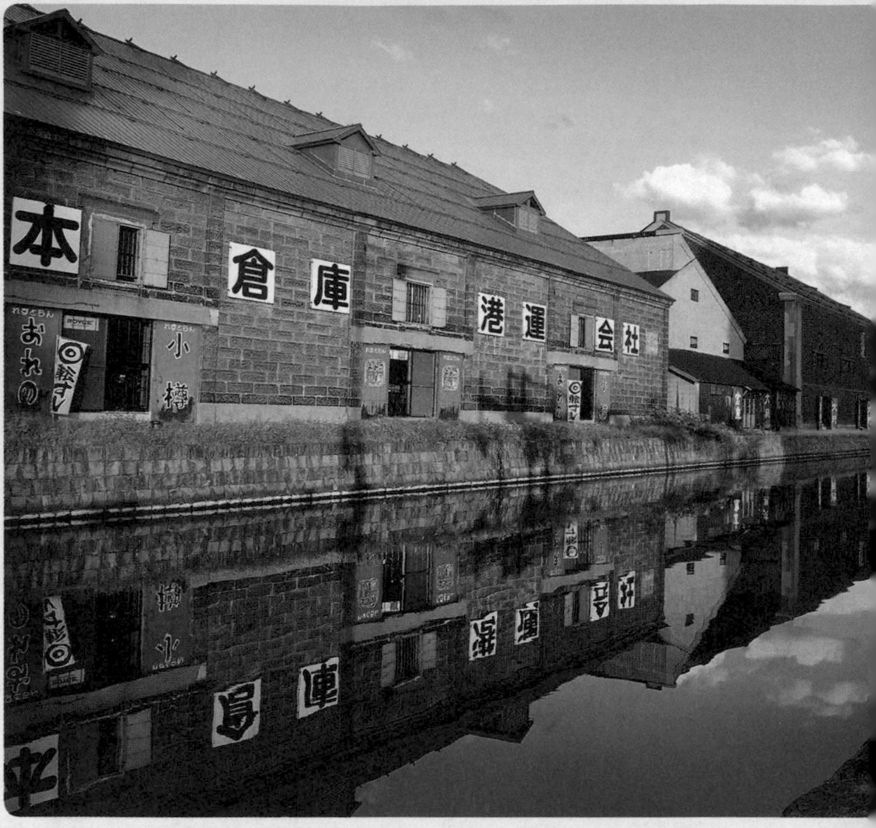

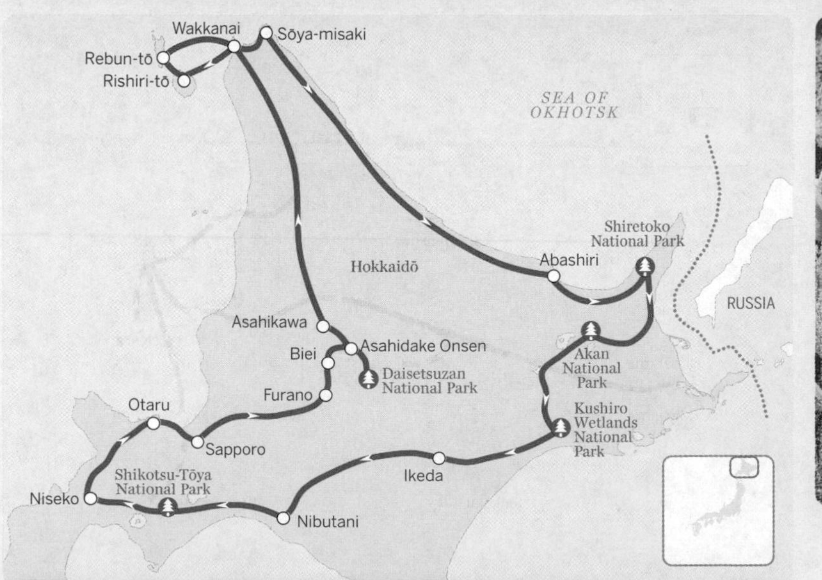

Wakkanai
Sōya-misaki
Rebun-tō
Rishiri-tō
SEA OF
OKHOTSK
Shiretoko
National Park
Abashiri
Hokkaidō
RUSSIA
Asahikawa
Asahidake Onsen
Biei
Daisetsuzan
National Park
Furano
Akan
National
Park
Kushiro
Wetlands
National
Park
Otaru
Sapporo
Shikotsu-Tōya
National Park
Niseko
Ikeda
Nibutani

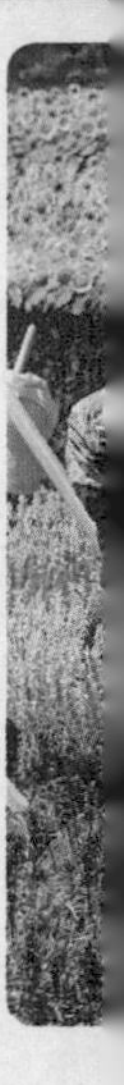

The Wilds of Hokkaidō

Step off the Tokyo–Kyoto tourist trail and head to Hokkaidō, Japan's northernmost major island. It's like a different Japan, with 20% of the country's land area, but only 5% of its population. There are magnificent national parks, mountains, lakes and onsen – plus the Ainu, Hokkaidō's indigenous people. We recommend a road trip...

Cheap tickets on budget airlines make flying to Hokkaidō a great option. Fly into the island's gateway, New Chitose Airport, pick up a rental car with an English-speaking navigation system (surprisingly good value!) and hit the road. Hokkaidō is doable by train, but there aren't a lot of lines and if you're into the outdoors, it's difficult to get where you want to be by train.

Head to **Sapporo** for your first few days, to settle in. The prefectural capital, with 1.9 million people, is Japan's fifth largest city and full of action, including the legendary Snow Festival in February. When it's time to hit the road, set your sights on the lavender fields and gourmet attractions of **Furano** and **Biei**. If you like the mountains, head up to **Asahidake Onsen** and hike in **Daisetsuzan National Park**.

After a stop in **Asahikawa** to taste Otokoyama sake, head up to **Wakkanai**, where Russian-language street signs may surprise you. **Rishiri-tō** and **Rebun-tō** are a must for outdoorsy types. Head out there by ferry, either with or without your car. Back on the mainland, round **Sōya-misaki**, Japan's northernmost point, and drive down the desolate Okhotsk sea coast to **Abashiri** for a blue beer at Abashiri Beer.

After hiking and soaking in onsen at World Heritage–listed **Shiretoko National Park**, head southwest to **Akan National Park** and its hiking, Ainu and onsen hotspots. Check out the red-crested cranes at **Kushiro Wetlands National Park**, then drive to the wine and gourmet area around **Ikeda**.

For more Ainu experiences, drop into **Nibutani** before doing the rounds of **Shikotsu-Tōya National Park**, including the caldera lakes of Shikotsu-ko and Tōya-ko, and a soak in Noboribetsu Onsen. After some action at **Niseko** (skiing, hiking or biking, depending on the season), head to romantic **Otaru** for some seafood before driving back to cosmopolitan Sapporo.

BY ALAN TSAI / GETTY IMAGES ©

KEREN SU / GETTY IMAGES ©

Top: Otaru (p583)
Bottom: Flower farm, Furano (p597)

Kyūshū & Shikoku

Relatively few tourists make the journey southwest to the islands of Kyūshū and Shikoku, which is a shame, as these two islands are home to some of the country's most beautiful scenery, welcoming people and delicious food. Southern Kyūshū is also a particularly good option for escaping the bitter cold of winter.

While there are some international flights to Fukuoka in Kyūshū, it's likely that you'll approach this area from Kansai or Tokyo. Take a *shinkansen* to the city of Okayama in Western Honshū. Here, catch a special *Nampū* express train across the Inland Sea down into the mountainous heart of Shikoku and spend a night or two in one of the thatched-roof cottages in **Iya Valley** (note that it's also possible to drive here, which will give you more freedom to explore the area). From the valley, you can head south to do some surfing at **Ohkihama** or west to climb **Ishizuchi-san**. Finally, take a dip in the wonderful Dōgo Onsen in the castle town of **Matsuyama**.

From Matsuyama you can recross the Inland Sea and join the Sanyō Shinkansen line that will take you southwest to the island of **Kyūshū** (consider a stop at Hiroshima en route). Your first stop in Kyūshū should be **Fukuoka**, Kyūshū's largest city, which is crammed with spirited dining and nightlife in the lanes of Tenjin and Daimyō. From here, you can head southeast to the hot spring resort of **Beppu** or southwest to **Nagasaki**. While Nagasaki is best known to Westerners for its tragic history, most visitors are surprised to find a vibrant city with great food and lots of opportunities to learn about Japan's early contacts with the West.

From either Beppu or Nagasaki, head south, possibly stopping en route at the semiactive volcano of **Aso-san**, then make your way to **Kagoshima**, a city with a laid-back, almost tropical, vibe. Sengan-en garden and Sakurajima volcano are must-sees, before going south for a sand bath in the seaside town of **Ibusuki**.

Finally, if you have time and enjoy hiking, take a ferry from Kagoshima to the island of **Yakushima** for some walks and onsen before making your way north and homeward.

Top: Umi Jigoku (p741), Beppu
Bottom: Hakata *rāmen* (noodles in soup), Fukuoka (p676)

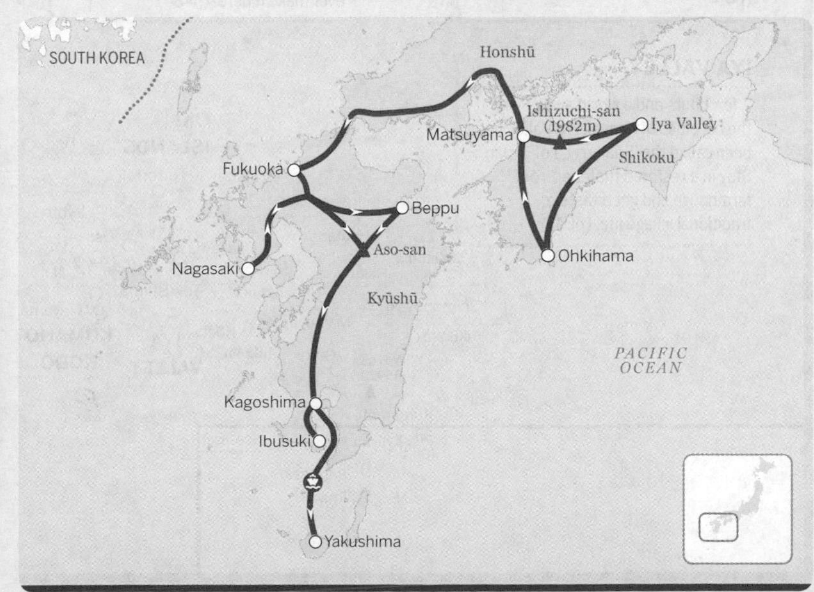
SOUTH KOREA
Honshū
Ishizuchi-san
(1982m)
Matsuyama
Iya Valley
Shikoku
Fukuoka
Beppu
Aso-san
Nagasaki
Ohkihama
Kyūshū
PACIFIC
OCEAN
Kagoshima
Ibusuki
Yakushima

Off the Beaten Track: Japan

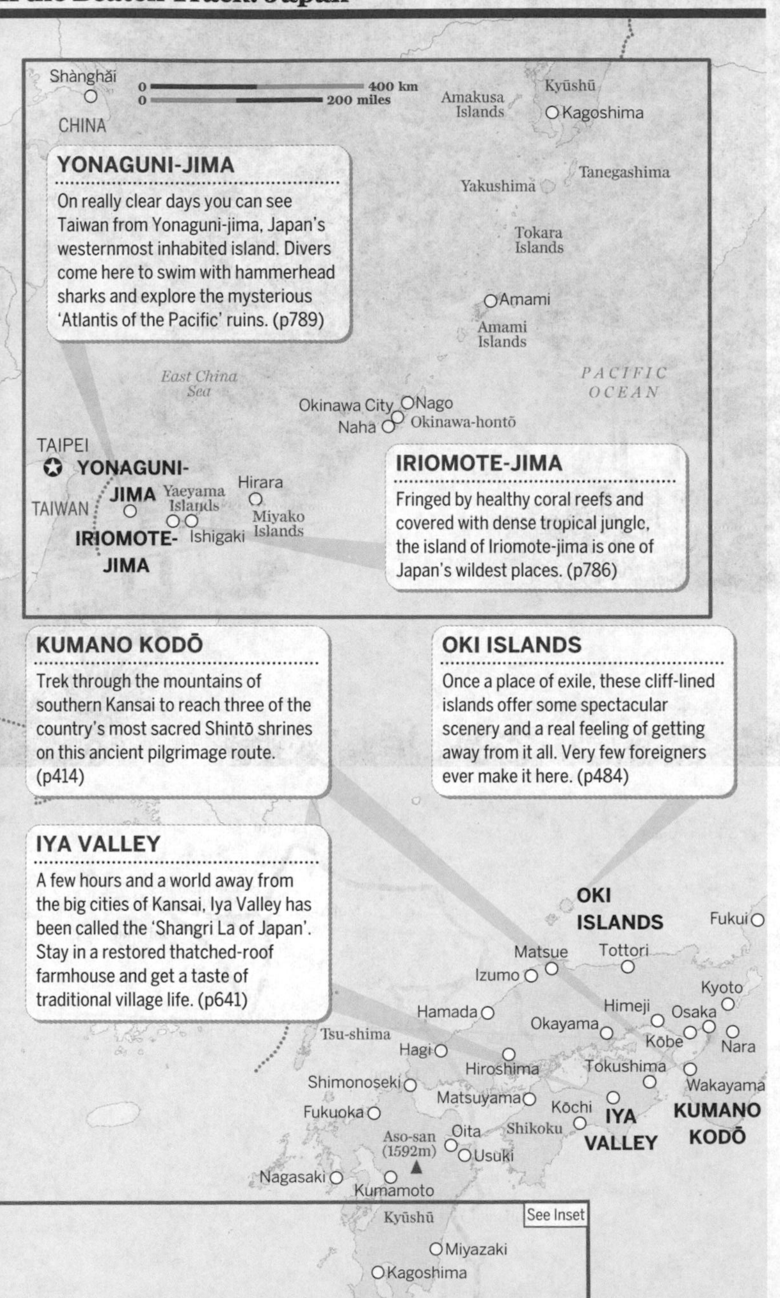

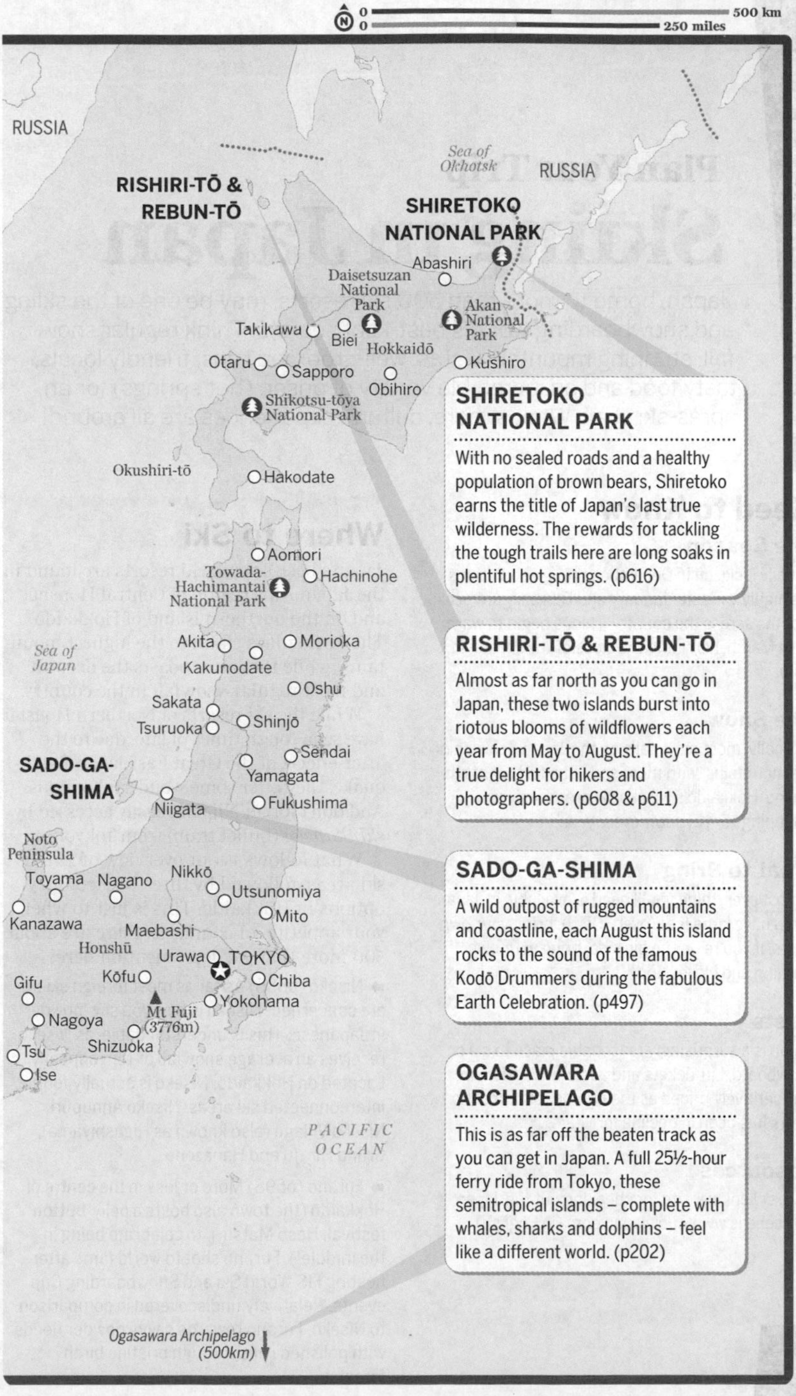

0 — 500 km
0 — 250 miles

RUSSIA
RISHIRI-TŌ & REBUN-TŌ
Sea of Okhotsk
RUSSIA
SHIRETOKO NATIONAL PARK
Abashiri
Daisetsuzan National Park
Akan National Park
Takikawa
Biei
Hokkaidō
Otaru
Sapporo
Kushiro
Obihiro
Shikotsu-tōya National Park
Okushiri-tō
Hakodate
Aomori
Towada-Hachimantai National Park
Hachinohe
Sea of Japan
Akita
Morioka
Kakunodate
Oshu
Sakata
Tsuruoka
Shinjō
Sendai
SADO-GA-SHIMA
Yamagata
Niigata
Fukushima
Noto Peninsula
Toyama
Nagano
Nikkō
Utsunomiya
Kanazawa
Mito
Maebashi
Honshū
Urawa
TOKYO
Kōfu
Chiba
Gifu
Mt Fuji (3776m)
Yokohama
Nagoya
Shizuoka
Tsu
Ise
PACIFIC OCEAN
Ogasawara Archipelago (500km)

SHIRETOKO NATIONAL PARK

With no sealed roads and a healthy population of brown bears, Shiretoko earns the title of Japan's last true wilderness. The rewards for tackling the tough trails here are long soaks in plentiful hot springs. (p616)

RISHIRI-TŌ & REBUN-TŌ

Almost as far north as you can go in Japan, these two islands burst into riotous blooms of wildflowers each year from May to August. They're a true delight for hikers and photographers. (p608 & p611)

SADO-GA-SHIMA

A wild outpost of rugged mountains and coastline, each August this island rocks to the sound of the famous Kodō Drummers during the fabulous Earth Celebration. (p497)

OGASAWARA ARCHIPELAGO

This is as far off the beaten track as you can get in Japan. A full 25½-hour ferry ride from Tokyo, these semitropical islands – complete with whales, sharks and dolphins – feel like a different world. (p202)

Plan Your Trip
Skiing in Japan

Japan, home to more than 500 ski resorts, may be one of the skiing and snowboarding world's best-kept secrets. Think regular snowfall, stunning mountain vistas, well-groomed runs, friendly locals, tasty food and an incredible variety of onsen (hot springs) for an après-ski soak. What's more, cultural experiences are all around!

Need to Know

The Season

Usually kicks off in December, though conditions are highly variable. January and February are peak months across the country. Things begin to warm up in March, heralding the close of the season in April.

The Snow

Basically, more snow falls on the Japan Sea side of the mountains, with more snow the further north you go. Hokkaidō's Niseko ski area receives a whopping 15m of snow every year!

What to Bring

Almost everything you'll need is available in Japan. If you have large feet (over 30cm), bring your own boots. If you're on the big side, bring your own clothing and gloves, too.

Costs

Japan is a surprisingly reasonable place to ski or snowboard. Lift tickets and accommodation are competitively priced as the number of domestic skiers has been in decline for years.

Resources

An excellent website for checking out the Japan ski scene is www.snowjapan.com (in English).

Where to Ski

Japan's best-known ski resorts are found in the Japan Alps region of Central Honshū, and on the northern island of Hokkaidō. The former lays claim to the highest mountains, while the latter boasts the deepest and most regular snowfall in the country.

While the ski resorts of Northern Honshū have seen tough times of late, due to the after-effects of the Great East Japan Earthquake, they offer some wonderful options. And don't forget Niigata, easily accessed by *shinkansen* (bullet train) from Tokyo.

What follows is our overview of 12 top ski areas, followed by three backcountry options in Hokkaidō. This is just to whet your appetite, of course, as there are about 500 more that we don't mention here!

➡ Niseko (p586) As far as most foreign skiers are concerned, Niseko is how you say 'powder' in Japanese. This is understandable, as Niseko receives an average snowfall of 15m annually. Located on Hokkaidō, Niseko is actually four interconnected ski areas: Niseko Annupuri, Niseko Village (also known as Higashiyama), Grand Hirafu and Hanazono.

➡ Furano (p598) More or less in the centre of Hokkaidō (the town also hosts a belly-button festival, Heso Matsuri, to celebrate being in the middle!), Furano shot to world fame after hosting FIS World Ski and Snowboarding Cup events. Relatively undiscovered in comparison to Niseko, Furano rewards savvy powder fiends with polished runs through pristine birch forests.

➡ Sapporo Teine (p570) So close to Sapporo, Hokkaidō's capital, that buses run from downtown hotels. You can swish down slopes used in the 1972 Sapporo Winter Olympics by day and enjoy the raucous restaurants, bars and clubs of Susukino by night.

➡ Hakuba (p269) The quintessential Japan Alps ski resort, Hakuba offers eye-popping views in addition to excellent and varied skiing in seven resorts. Hakuba hosted Winter Olympic events in 1998 and is led by the legendary Happō-One Ski Resort (pronounced 'hah-poh-oh-nay').

➡ Shiga Kōgen (p280) Also in the Japan Alps, Shiga Kōgen is one of the largest ski resorts in the world, with an incredible 21 different areas, all interconnected by trails and lifts and accessible with one lift ticket. With such a variety of terrain on offer, there is something for everyone here.

➡ Nozawa Onsen (p278) This quaint little Swiss-style village is tucked high up in the Japan Alps. It offers a good variety of runs, including some challenging mogul courses. Snowboarders will enjoy the terrain park and half-pipe, and there's even a cross-country skiing course that traverses the peaks.

➡ Echigo-Yuzawa Onsen (p504) Talk about easy to get to! Echigo-Yuzawa Onsen has its own *shinkansen* station on the Jōetsu line to Niigata and you can literally go skiing as a day-trip from Tokyo (77 minutes one way by the fastest service!). GALA Yuzawa is the resort to head to here.

➡ Naeba (p505) Home to Dragondola, reportedly the longest gondola in the world (5.5km), Naeba has two massive ski areas, centred around the Prince Hotel Naeba, that cater to your every whim and fancy.

➡ Myōkō Kōgen (p506) Much less developed than the other resorts listed here, Myōkō Kōgen is directly north of Nagano city and close to the Sea of Japan. Head here for an off-the-beaten-path ski holiday in the powder-rich Myōkō mountain range.

Skiier in Nagano Prefecture (p271)

➡ Zaō Onsen Ski Resort (p515) Arguably the top ski slopes in Northern Honshū, Zaō has a huge selection of beginner and intermediate runs, broad winding courses and, of course, excellent après-ski onsen options.

➡ Tazawako Ski Park (p527) Akita Prefecture's largest winter sports destination, Tazawako Ski Park's slopes wind down Akita Komaga-take and overlook the shores of Tazawa-ko. Expect fewer foreigners but a friendly welcome.

➡ Daisen (p490) This is our wildcard! Offering the best skiing in western Japan, this stand-alone exposed volcano (1729m) is only 10km from the Sea of Japan in Tottori Prefecture and catches heavy snowfall in winter. Daisen White Resort is where it's at.

DID YOU KNOW?

➡ The first Winter Olympics held outside Europe or North America was at Sapporo in 1972.

➡ Snowboarding first debuted as an Olympic sport at the 1998 Nagano Winter Olympics.

Backcountry Options

Some excellent options for backcountry skiing exist in Japan, though this is a relatively new sphere of adventure tourism and most Japanese skiers stick to the mainstream.

➡ Asahidake (p600) An extreme experience on a smoking volcano in Daisetsuzan National Park. Hokkaidō's highest mountain, Asahidake offers

Skiing in Japan

HOKKAIDŌ

There's lots of snow up here in the northerly latitudes, along with ski resorts such as Niseko, Furano and Sapporo Teine. There are also some great backcountry ski opportunities. (p561)

NORTHERN HONSHŪ

Great snowfall and off-the-beaten-path ski resorts for foreigners, such as Zaō Onsen Ski Resort and Tazawako Ski Park. (p492)

NIIGATA

Head here for excellent snow and accessibility, and resorts such as Echigo-Yuzawa Onsen, Naeba and Myōkō Kōgen. (p495)

JAPAN ALPS

Featuring Japan's highest mountains, there are ski resorts everywhere, including Hakuba, Shiga Kōgen and Nozawa Onsen. (p206)

DAISEN

For the best skiing in western Japan, head to this stand-alone volcano (1729m) near the Sea of Japan coast. (p490)

THE JAPANESE WAY OF SKIING

Snow is snow, skis are skis – right? How different can it be to ski in Japan? Not very much, but keep the following in mind:

➡ Lift-line management can be surprisingly poor in Japan.

➡ Not all resorts use the green/blue/black coding system for difficulty.

➡ The majority of Japanese skiers start skiing at 9am, have lunch exactly at noon, and get off the hill by 3pm. If you work on a slightly different schedule, you will avoid a lot of the crowds.

➡ Off-piste and out-of-bounds skiing is often high quality but also illegal at most ski areas, resulting in the confiscation of your lift pass if you're caught by the ski patrol. Cut the ropes at your own risk.

one ropeway (500 vertical metres), dry powder and scenic views, but is not for beginners.

➡ Kurodake (p604) At Sōunkyō Onsen on the northeastern side of Daisetsuzan National Park in Hokkaidō, Kurodake has one ropeway and lift and is becoming popular with those who like vertical and challenging terrain.

➡ Rishiri-tō (p609) Extreme skiing is possible on Rishiri-zan, a classic volcanic cone on its own remote island off the coast of northern Hokkaidō. No lifts and plenty of walking. You'll need a guide from Rishiri Nature Guide Service.

Costs

Many people unfamiliar with skiing in Japan often assume that it will cost an arm and a leg to ski here. But, even after factoring in the international air ticket, it might actually be cheaper to ski for a week in Japan than in your home country. Are we mad? Well, let's check the numbers.

➡ **Lift tickets and equipment rental** A full-day lift ticket at most ski areas in Japan costs between ¥4000 and ¥5500. This is significantly less than a full day at large resorts in North America or Europe. Full equipment rental is typically no more than ¥5000 per day (both ski and snowboard sets are available). The Japanese tend to be connoisseurs of quality, which means that you need not worry about getting stuck with shabby and/or outdated gear.

➡ **Accommodation** You can find plenty of upmarket accommodation in the ¥6500 to ¥10,000 range at major ski areas in Japan, and this price will often include one or two meals. This is often less than half of what you'd expect to pay for similar accommodation in North America or Europe. The budget traveller will find a variety of backpacker-type hostels near most resorts, and families will be glad to know that young children (under six years of age) can usually stay for free or at a significant discount.

➡ **Food** On-slope meals top out at around ¥1000, cheaper than what you'd pay in North America or Europe. The restaurant selection anywhere you go is also varied, including the likes of *rāmen* (egg noodles), udon (wheat noodles), *karē-raisu* (curry rice) and *gyūdon* (sliced beef on rice), as well as more familiar fast-food options including sandwiches, pizza, burgers and kebabs.

➡ **Transport** Airport-to-resort transport in Japan costs no more than in other countries, and is usually faster and more efficient (and, unlike in North America, you don't need to rent a car).

Can You Say 'Ski' in Japanese?

That's right: it's 'ski' (all right, it's pronounced more like 'sukee'), but the point is that communication won't be much of a problem on your Japan ski trip.

Tackling the language barrier has never been easier: most of the better-known resorts employ a number of English-speaking foreigners. They work the lifts and in the cafeterias, and often find employment in the hotels or guesthouses that are most popular with foreign guests.

All major signs and maps are translated into English, and provided you have some experience at large resorts back home, you'll find the layout and organisation of Japanese resorts to be pretty intuitive.

The information counters at the base of the mountains always have helpful and polite staff available to answer questions.

Plan Your Trip
Travel with Children

Japan is a great place to travel with kids. The usual concerns that parents have about safety and hygiene are simply not an issue in ultrasafe and spotless Japan. Instead, your biggest challenge will probably be keeping your kids entertained. In this chapter, we'll show you how.

Best Regions for Children

Tokyo

Tokyo Disney Resort and the youth meccas of Shibuya and Harajuku are only the beginning of Tokyo's child-friendly attractions.

Kansai

Nara offers a giant park filled with friendly deer and eye-popping sights like the Great Buddha; there's even a restaurant where the kids can eat lunch while operating a giant train set.

Okinawa & the Southwest Islands

The sand is white, the water warm and the coral gorgeous. If the weather's bad for snorkelling, take the kids to one of the world's best aquariums.

Kyoto

Cycling the backstreets, wandering the shopping arcades, picnicking by the river and hiking in the hills will please the kids. And Kiyomizu-dera is as close to child-friendly as temples come.

Sapporo & Hokkaidō

If your kids ski or snowboard, they'll love the powder snow up in Hokkaidō.

Japan for Children

You'll find that the Japanese love kids and will fawn over the young ones, declaring them to be *kawaii* (cute).

Entertainment

You'll find Japan is a very easy place to travel and keep the kids entertained. Most towns have playgrounds and parks for younger children, and older children will enjoy the game centres, amusement parks, shopping and movies (usually screened in English). Of course, some kids will love exploring the shrines, temples and museums; alternatively, head outdoors for hiking, skiing and snorkelling.

Food

Food can be an issue if your child is a picky or unadventurous eater – even adults can find some Japanese cuisine challenging.

➡ If you're going to a *kaiseki* (haute cuisine) place, have your lodgings call ahead to ask for some kid-friendly dishes. Ditto if you'll be dining at your ryokan (traditional Japanese inn).

➡ If necessary, have your lodgings write your child's dietary restrictions or allergies for you in Japanese.

➡ You'll find a lot of so-called 'family restaurants' in Japan, which usually serve

Western food (pizza, fried chicken, fries) or offer special kids' meals (sometimes called *o-ko-sama ranchii*). *Shokudō* (all-round eateries) also tend to serve something that children will eat.

➡ If your child simply will not eat Japanese food, don't worry: the big cities are chock-a-block with international restaurants, and fast-food joints can be found even in smaller towns. In rural areas, where only Japanese food may be available, you can stock up beforehand on food your child likes at a supermarket.

Facilities

➡ There are nappy-changing facilities in some public places, such as department stores and larger train stations.

➡ Cots are available in most hotels (but not usually in ryokan) and can be booked in advance.

➡ High chairs are available in lots of restaurants (though in many restaurants everyone simply sits on the floor).

➡ There are child-care agencies in larger cities, although outside Tokyo few have English-speaking staff.

Infants

➡ Nappies (diapers) are readily available. A picture on the package usually indicates if they are for boys or girls. Bottles, wipes and medications are available at large pharmacies.

➡ Breastfeeding is generally not done in public. That said, in a quiet part of a park or a playground, with something like a shawl to cover the child, it is usually fine. Some department stores, hospitals and public attractions have rooms where mothers can breastfeed.

PLANNING

Very little special planning is necessary for travellers with children heading to Japan, but consider bringing any medicines that your child takes regularly. You might also bring a few favourite books (English-language children's books can be found in large cities, but prices are high and the selection is limited). The only other thing you might want to pack is small plastic forks and spoons (not all restaurants have these on hand).

➡ Most supermarkets stock a good selection of baby food, but you may need to ask a clerk to help you read the contents.

Getting Around

➡ Most trains and buses have *yūsen zaseki* (priority seating for those who are elderly, disabled, pregnant or with young children).

➡ Child seats in taxis are generally not available, but most car-rental agencies will provide one if you ask in advance.

➡ Most cities are fairly accessible to those with strollers, and train stations and many large buildings have elevators (lifts). However, many attractions, such as temples and shrines, do not have ramps. An issue, particularly in Kyoto, is the relative lack of pavements away from the main streets (luckily, the Japanese tend to be safe drivers!).

Children's Highlights

Let's face it: even the most precocious kid will eventually get tired of temples, gardens and shrines. Here are a few hints to keep the little ones entertained in Japan.

Amusement parks Japan is famous for its amusement parks, including Tokyo Disney Resort (p111) and Universal Studios Japan (p361).

Trains Children will love Japan's trains, whether they're riding the *shinkansen* (bullet train) or just watching them from the platform. And if you go to Kyoto, don't miss the Umekōji Steam Locomotive Museum (p293).

Museums Japan has plenty of kid-friendly museums, including Kyoto's International Manga Museum (p295) and Tokyo's Ghibli Museum (p93), a must for any fan of Miyazaki Hayao's animated films.

Shōtengai At the downtown *shōtengai* (market streets) – with ¥100 shops and game centres – there's plenty to keep kids occupied. And, because they're usually covered, they're great on rainy days. Tokyo, Kyoto and Osaka are particularly rich in *shōtengai*.

Skiing & snowboarding If you're in Japan in the winter, the kids will love spending a day on the slopes. Try Shiga Kōgen (p280) in Nagano or Niseko United (p586) in Hokkaidō.

Beaches While Okinawa has the best beaches in Japan, you'll find decent strips of sand along the shores of most of Japan's major islands.

Nabe (hot pot)

Eat & Drink Like a Local

Japanese food is one of the world's most diverse, refined and delicious cuisines. If you're like most visitors to Japan, enjoying the genuine article on its home turf is a big reason for visiting the country. More than likely, you will have some of the most memorable meals of your life while exploring Japan.

BRIAN FARRELL / GETTY IMAGES ©

The Year in Food

Few cultures are as seasonally aware as the Japanese. Indeed, the ancient Japanese calendar divided the year into 24 separate seasonal periods. This appreciation of the seasons finds its greatest expression in the country's food culture.

Spring (Mar–May)

The new growth of spring finds its way onto tables in the form of *takenoko* (bamboo shoots), *sansai* (mountain vegetables) and *wagashi* (Japanese sweets) with plum- and cherry-blossom motifs.

Summer (Jun–Aug)

The Japanese fight the heat of summer by eating cooling dishes like *reimen* (cold *rāmen*) and cold *zaru soba* (noodles served on a plate). *Unagi* (eel) is also eaten, as it's thought to strengthen the body against the summer heat. After meals, juicy peaches, pears and watermelon are served for dessert.

Autumn (Sep–Nov)

Chestnut dishes and persimmons are popular, as are *wagashi* with maple-leaf motifs.

Winter (Dec–Feb)

The Japanese warm up in winter by eating *nabe* (hot pot) dishes and drinking *amazake* (warm, fermented rice milk). This is also the season for *fugu* (pufferfish) and oysters.

Food Experiences

Meals of a Lifetime

➡ **Kitcho Arashiyama** (p338) A meal at this Kyoto *kaiseki* (Japanese haute cuisine) restaurant can approach a religious experience.

➡ **Kyūbey** (p123) For over-the-top sushi in approachable surroundings, you can't go wrong at this Tokyo sushi-lover's paradise.

➡ **Dōtombori** (p357) Join the locals in their favourite pastime – *kuidaore* (eating until you drop) – at the cheap, hearty restaurants and food stalls in Osaka's Dōtombori arcade.

➡ **Gyōshintei** (p168) This Nikkō restaurant serves vegetarian food raised to the level of haute cuisine overlooking a beautiful garden.

➡ **Yabure-Kabure** (p476) In Western Honshū's Shimonoseki, this buzzing spot offers one of Japan's most lauded (and notorious) dishes – *fugu* (pufferfish) – prepared in numerous delicious ways.

➡ **Azumaya Honten** (p542) Try this all-you-can eat noodle joint in Morioka (Northern Honshū) for a famous local speciality: *wanko soba*, a noodle dish usually consumed in vast quantities. The average customer puts away 50 or so bowls.

➡ **Hirome Ichiba** (p651) This bustling market in the Shikoku city of Kōchi is a great place to sample regional delicacies and rub shoulders with the locals in the communal dining area.

➡ **Tsukiji Market** (p79) Explore the world's biggest fish market to whet your appetite and then sit down to a breakfast of the world's freshest sushi.

Cheap Treats

➡ **Tachi-kui restaurants** The name means 'stand and eat', and if you don't mind eating on your feet, you can get good noodle and rice dishes at places like this for around ¥200.

➡ **Convenience stores** Japanese convenience stores stock an astonishing variety of food, drinks and snacks, including ready-made *bentō* (boxed meals) and *onigiri* (rice-ball snacks).

➡ **Depachika** These department-store food floors usually stock a wide variety of ready-made food. An hour or so before closing, they'll often mark things down by as much as 50%.

➡ **Bakeries** Ubiquitous in Japan, bakeries usually stock a wide variety of sandwiches and pastries.

Dare to Try

➡ **Fugu** This is the 'deadly' pufferfish that gave Homer Simpson so much trouble. It's a speciality of Western Honshū, best consumed in winter.

➡ **Nattō** These partially fermented soybeans with the scent of ammonia are the litmus test by which Japanese judge a foreigner's sense of culinary adventure (don't be surprised if someone asks you: 'Can you eat *nattō*?').

➡ **Uni** With the flavour of a distilled tidal pool and the appearance of a small orange brain, *uni* (sea urchin) is usually described on English-language sushi menus as 'challenging'.

➡ **Namako** Even most Japanese are put off by sea cucumber. If you can eat this and actually enjoy it, our hats are off to you.

➡ **Shirako** This is the sperm-filled reproductive gland of a male fish. No further comment.

Local Specialities

You'll find that every island and region of Japan has its own *meibutsu* (speciality).

Tokyo

➡ **Sushi** Get it fresh from Tsukiji Fish Market or at one of the high-end sushi restaurants across the city.

➡ **Nouveau rāmen** Of course you can get every type of regional Japanese *rāmen* in Tokyo, but you can also sample some new twists on these familiar noodles.

Mt Fuji & Around Tokyo

➡ **Hōtō noodles** A speciality of the Fuji area is *hōtō* (hand-cut noodles), served as part of hearty mountain stews containing thick miso, pumpkin, sweet potato and other vegetables.

➡ **Yuba** A popular traditional dish in the Nikkō area is *yuba* (the skin that forms when making tofu), which is cut into strips and used in everything from udon (thick white wheat noodle) dishes, to sashimi, to *age yuba manju* (fried bean buns).

The Japan Alps & Central Honshū

➡ **Kishimen** A hearty, flat type of udon noodle that is wildly popular in Nagoya.

➡ **Miso-katsu** A type of *tonkatsu* (deep-fried pork cutlet) served with a miso-flavoured sauce.

➡ **Soba** Nagoya prides itself on producing some of Japan's finest *soba* (buckwheat noodles).

➡ **Sashimi and sushi** Kanazawa and the Noto Peninsula are famous for impossibly fresh seafood.

Kyoto

➡ **Kaiseki** Kyoto is the best place to sample Japan's traditional haute cuisine.

➡ **Sweets** You can find *wagashi* (Japanese sweets) from Okinawa to Hokkaidō, but Kyoto has the largest selection and an incredible variety of long-established sweet shops.

DANITA DELIMONT / GETTY IMAGES ©

Woman eating oysters

➡ **Tofu** Known for its pure underground water and high-quality beans, Kyoto tofu is revered as some of the best in the country.

Kansai

➡ **Okonomiyaki** For hearty *okonomiyaki* (savoury pancakes), Osaka's Dōtombori is the place to go.

➡ **Rāmen** It's hardly surprising that down-to-earth Osaka is the best place in Japan to get acquainted with *rāmen*.

➡ **Street food** No city in Japan has a better selection of street food than Osaka, including several *tako-yaki* (grilled octopus dumpling) stands that attract huge crowds from dawn to dusk.

Hiroshima & Western Honshū

➡ **Hiroshima-yaki** You can't visit Hiroshima without sampling the city's distinctive style of *okonomiyaki*, which features noodles as a key ingredient.

Sashimi

➡ **Oysters** In winter, oyster lovers from across Japan seek out the bivalves harvested from the Inland Sea near Hiroshima.

Northern Honshū (Tōhoku)

➡ **Gyūtan** Beef tongue grilled over charcoal might not sound that appealing, but when served with a squeeze of lemon, it's fantastic.

➡ **Kiritanpo** Kneaded rice grilled on bamboo spits may sound a bit odd, but it's pretty tasty, especially when served with a soy-based broth and vegetable hot pot.

➡ **Jaja-men** These flat noodles are Morioka's most famous noodle dish – usually served all-you-can-eat.

➡ **Tanrei karakuchi sake** A distinctive style of crisp, dry sake produced in Niigata Prefecture, an area famous for its pure water and excellent rice.

Sapporo & Hokkaidō

➡ **Craft beer** Sapporo is in the middle of a huge craft-beer boom and local brews are attracting worldwide attention.

➡ **Crab cuisine** Hokkaidō is famous for its king crab and nothing tastes better than freshly caught crab boiled and served with a bit of melted butter and lemon.

➡ **Jingisukan** The Japanese pronunciation of Ghenghis Khan, this all-you-can-eat lamb dish is usually washed down with endless mugs of draft beer.

➡ **Sapporo rāmen** A hearty *rāmen* dish based on a miso-flavoured soup.

Shikoku

➡ **Sanuki udon** This speciality of Shikoku's Kagawa Prefecture is famous for its smooth texture and distinctive taste. It usually comes in very small serves and customers often compete to see how many bowls they can eat.

Kyūshū

➡ **Hakata rāmen** *Rāmen* served in a soup with an intensely flavourful pork broth.

➡ **Yaki-curry** Curry rice topped with cheese and grilled – sort of like curry au gratin.

➡ **Chikin nanban** Sweet fried chicken served with tartar sauce.

SHAYNE HILL XTREME VISUALS / GETTY IMAGES ©

Snake inside a bottle of *awamori*

➡ **Chirin-chirin** A Nagasaki speciality of sweet citrus-flavoured shaved ice served from pushcarts.

➡ **Shippoku-ryori** A type of *kaiseki* cuisine with Portuguese and Chinese influences – a speciality of Nagasaki.

Okinawa & the Southwest Islands

➡ **Gōyā champurū** A stir-fry containing bitter melon (an Okinawan vegetable).

➡ **Sōki-soba** Bowls of hot noodles served with thick slices of tender marinated pork.

➡ **Mimigā** Sliced pig's ears marinated in vinegar.

➡ **Awamori** Okinawan firewater brewed from rice, occasionally 'flavoured' by the addition of a poisonous snake in the bottle.

How to Eat & Drink

When to Eat

➡ **Breakfast** The traditional Japanese breakfast consists of rice, miso soup and a few side dishes such as a small cooked fish and *nattō*. These days, unless they're staying at a ryokan, modern Japanese tend to eat thick slices of supermarket bread and perhaps a boiled egg, washed down with tea or coffee.

➡ **Lunch** Eaten at midday, this is usually a rice-based meal with various side dishes such as cooked meat or fish. Noodles (*soba,* udon or *rāmen*) are also popular.

➡ **Dinner** Usually eaten between 6pm and 8pm, dinner is often a rice-based meal supplemented with cooked meat or fish, although noodles are also sometimes consumed. If a person eats out, especially in a big city, they'll likely eat foreign fare as often as Japanese.

Where to Eat

It's said that Japan has the highest number of restaurants per capita of any country on earth. One reason for this is that few Japanese entertain guests at home; it's much more common to eat out. Most Japanese restaurants specialise in one dish or type of cuisine.

In addition to Japanese restaurants of every stripe, you'll find a wide range of foreign restaurants in Japanese cities, with French, Italian, Chinese and Thai being the most popular.

Menu Decoder

For a full explanation of the restaurants and dishes you'll encounter in Japan, see Japanese Cuisine (p816).

➡ **Setto** (セット) A set menu/course

➡ **Morning setto** (モーニングセット) A breakfast set (usually an egg, toast and coffee)

➡ **Teishoku** (定食) Another term for set menu/course

➡ **Tabe-hōdai** (食べ放題) All-you-can-eat

➡ **Viking** (バイキング) Another term for all-you-can-eat

➡ **Nomi-hōdai** (飲み放題) All-you-can-drink

➡ **Ippin ryōri** (一品料理) À la carte

➡ **Nomimono** (飲み物) Drinks

Plan Your Trip
Japan on a Budget

Japan has a reputation as being a particularly expensive place to travel. In reality, Japan is among the least expensive countries in the developed world, especially with the recent drop in the yen. Of course, you can still burn through a lot of cash if you're not careful, so read on for some tips on how to really stretch those yen.

It's Cheaper Than You Think

Everyone has heard the tale of the guy who blundered into a bar in Japan, had two drinks and got stuck with a bill for US$1000. Urban legends like this date back to the heady days of the Bubble Era in the 1980s. Sure, you can still drop money like that on a few drinks in exclusive establishments in Tokyo (if you can get past the guy at the door), but you're more likely to be spending ¥700 (US$6) per beer in Japan.

The fact is, Japan's image as one of the world's most expensive countries is just that: image. Anyone who has been to Japan recently knows that it can be cheaper to travel in Japan than in parts of Western Europe, the US, Australia or even the big coastal cities of China. Still, there's no denying that Japan is not Thailand. In order to best accommodate your budget, we've put together the following list of money-saving tips.

Accommodation

➡ **Cheap business hotels** In many cases, cheap business hotels, which are proliferating across Japan, can be cheaper than youth hostels, especially if you're travelling as a couple. There are several good budget chains that offer double or twin rooms for about ¥6500 (US$55). One of the best-value chains is Toyoko Inn, which offers free internet, breakfast (and sometimes

Top Free Sights

Tokyo

For Tokyo's most impressive Shintō shrine and a soothing green space, head to Meiji-jingū (p89). And for one of the best views over Tokyo – all the way to Fuji-san on clear days – head to the observatories in the Tokyo Metropolitan Government Offices (p92).

Kyoto

Kyoto's imperial properties – Kyoto Imperial Palace (p295), Sentō Gosho (p297), Katsura Rikyū (p316) and Shūgaku-in Rikyū Imperial Villa (p309) – all have gorgeous gardens and are free to visit. The Imperial Palace Park (p297), in particular, is perfect for a picnic, a stroll or a lazy afternoon nap. Kyoto also boasts Fushimi Inari-Taisha (p314), one of the most impressive sights in the country (and completely free!).

Nara

The green expanse of Nara-kōen (p387) is filled with temples, museums and a herd of semi-wild deer.

Ise

The Gekū, or Outer Shrine, of Ise-jingū (p419) is one of the most spiritually powerful spots in all of Japan.

dinner), free phone calls in Japan and a host of other perks.

➡ **Capsule hotels** A night in a capsule hotel will set you back around ¥3000 (US$25) per person. Best of all, hip new capsule hotels have opened recently that cater to travellers (including women) rather than drunk salarymen.

➡ **Guesthouses** You'll find good, cheap guesthouses in many of Japan's cities, where a night's accommodation costs about ¥3500 (US$30) per person.

Transport

➡ **Japan Rail Pass** (p875) Like the famous Eurail Pass, this is one of the world's great travel bargains, and is the best way to see a lot of Japan without going broke. It allows unlimited travel on Japan's brilliant nationwide rail system, including the lightning-fast *shinkansen* (bullet train).

➡ **Seishun Jūhachi Kippu** (p877) For ¥11,850, you get five one-day tickets good for travel on any regular Japan Railways train. You can literally travel from one end of the country to the other for around US$100. However, these can only be purchased and used during certain periods.

➡ **Local travel passes** Always check for special transport passes in the areas you explore. Deals are being introduced all the time, so it never hurts to enquire at the tourist information office when you arrive.

➡ **Car hire** (p871) Consider renting a car to explore places not well served by public transport, or in places where public transport is expensive. Highway tolls can really add up, but you always have the option of staying on local roads.

➡ **Bus** (p871) Several budget highway bus services have opened in Japan in recent years. These can drastically reduce your intercity travel costs on certain routes (usually between major cities like Kyoto and Tokyo).

Eating

➡ **Shokudō** You can get a good, filling meal in these all-round Japanese eateries for about ¥700 (US$6), the tea is free and there's no tipping. Try that in New York.

➡ **Bentō** The ubiquitous Japanese box lunch, or *bentō,* costs around ¥500 and is both filling and nutritious.

➡ **Use Your Noodle** You can get a steaming bowl of tasty *rāmen* (egg noodles) for as little as ¥500, and ordering is a breeze – you just have to say *'rāmen'* and you're away. *Soba* (buckwheat noodles) and udon (thick white wheat noodles) are even cheaper – as low as ¥350 per bowl.

Shopping

➡ **Hyaku-en shops** *Hyaku-en* means ¥100, and, like the name implies, everything in these shops costs only ¥100, or just a bit less than US$1. You'll be amazed at what you can find in these places – some even sell food.

➡ **Flea markets** A good, new kimono costs an average of ¥200,000 (US$1700), but you can pick up a fine, used kimono at a flea market for ¥1000 (US$9). Whether you're shopping for yourself or for presents for the folks back home, you'll find some incredible bargains at Japan's flea markets.

Attractions

➡ **Shrines and temples** The vast majority of Shintō shrines in Japan cost nothing to enter. Likewise, the grounds of many temples can be toured for free (often, you only have to pay to enter the halls or a walled garden).

➡ **Museums and galleries** A surprising number of museums and galleries in Japan are free, while others are free a few days each month. The local tourist information office can usually supply a list of free places.

➡ **Parks and gardens** Most parks and many gardens in Japan are free to enter.

➡ **Sentō** Japan's public baths usually cost around ¥400 and are the ultimate 'only in Japan' experience. Ask at your lodgings to see if there is a good one nearby.

➡ **Strolling** It costs nothing to walk around the city or village where you are staying, and this can be one of the most rewarding, relaxing and fascinating parts of your trip.

Plan Your Trip

Hiking in Japan

Blessed with a geography that is more than two-thirds mountain terrain, Japan offers outdoors enthusiasts the most diverse climate in all of Asia. From the rugged shores and wind-weathered peaks of Hokkaidō in the north, to the tropical island jungles of Okinawa in the south, this country has it all.

Where to Hike

Mt Fuji & Around Tokyo

Mt Fuji Japan's highest and best-known mountain (p155), at 3776m. A gruelling climb that more than 300,000 make each summer, many hiking overnight to be at the peak at sunrise.

Takao-san A popular day hike (p170) less than an hour west of Shinjuku. Can be walked year-round, has a high point of 599m and is good for families.

Oku-Tama Region One of Tokyo's top hiking getaway spots (p171), with mountains, waterfalls, woodlands and walking trails. Head to Mitake-san for the day.

Kamakura The 3km Daibutsu hiking course (p198) winds its way past ancient temples and shrines to the giant Buddha statue at Hase.

The Japan Alps & Central Honshū

Home to the North, Central and South Alps, central Honshū is a hiking hot spot for Japan.

North Alps Excellent high-mountain trails. From Kamikōchi (p268), climb Yariga-take (3180m) and Oku-Hotaka-dake (3190m). From Murodō on the Tateyama-Kurobe Alpine Route (p260), climb Tateyama (3015m) and Tsurugi-dake (2999m). From Hakuba (p270), take the gondola and chairlifts to climb Karamatsu-dake (2695m).

Hakusan A sacred peak in Hakusan National Park, (p256) the 'white mountain' is criss-crossed with great hiking trails.

Need to Know

The Land

Japan is on the Pacific 'Rim of Fire' and is one of the most geologically active areas in the world. Think high mountains, volcanoes, earthquakes and hot springs. Fuji-san is 3776m and 21 peaks top 3000m.

The Season

Lower latitude and lower altitude hikes can be walked year-round. With heavy winter snowfalls, higher peaks such as the North, Central and South Alps, and those in Hokkaidō have a July-to-October season. The official season for climbing Mt Fuji is 1 July to mid-September.

What to Bring

Almost everything you'll need is available in Japan. If you have large feet, bring your own hiking boots. If you're on the big side, bring your own clothing.

Multiday hikes

Mountain hut rates can include meals and bedding, so week-long hikes can be done with minimal gear. There are plenty of camping areas, but you'll need to carry everything.

Resources

For details on 69 great hikes, grab Lonely Planet's *Hiking in Japan*. For more on hikes throughout Japan, check out www.hikinginjapan.com.

Nakasendō Walk the 8km hike (p225) from Magome to Tsumago in the attractive Kiso Valley.

Kyoto

Kyoto may be known for its culture, but it is also surrounded by mountains.

Fushimi Inari-Taisha A 4km pathway up Inari-yama in southeast Kyoto is lined with thousands of red *torii* (shrine gates) and hundreds of stone foxes (p314).

Kurama & Kibune Only 30 minutes north of Kyoto, two tranquil valleys are linked by a trail over the ridge between them. A peaceful escape from the city. (p318)

Daimonji-yama There is no finer walk in the city than the 30-minute climb to the viewpoint above Ginkaku-ji in Northern Higashiyama. (p315)

Kansai

There is great hiking in the Kansai region.

Kumano Kodō Walk on ancient pilgrimage routes in the wilds of the Kii Peninsula (p414). Or go the whole way and walk the 500km 33 Sacred Temples of Kannon Pilgrimage.

Hikes from Tenri The Rokku Gaaden hike from Ashiya, just east of Kōbe, and the Yamanobe-no-michi both ramble through the Nara countryside – consider these couple of day hikes within easy reach of Osaka or Kyoto.

Hiroshima & Western Honshū

Daisen A five-hour return climb of this 1729m stand-alone volcano affords excellent views of the San-in region (p490).

Sandan Gorge An 11km ravine about 50km northwest of Hiroshima, Sandan-kyō (p435) gives access to waterfalls, forests and fresh air.

Miyajima There's good walking to be had on this well-known island not far from Hiroshima. Climb the high point of Misen (530m; p439).

Northern Honshū (Tōhoku)

Dewa Sanzan The collective name for three sacred peaks – Haguro-san, Gas-san and Yudono-san – which represent birth, death and rebirth respectively. The climb up Gas-san (1984m) is a good challenge (p517).

Bandai-san There are great tracks to climb this 1819m peak (p510) in Fukushima Prefecture.

Hakkōda-san Wildflower-filled marshes, a ridge trail and peaks in Aomori Prefecture (p538).

Sapporo & Hokkaidō

There's so much hiking on hand that you could spend weeks in the northern wilds.

Daisetsuzan National Park Pick your walks in this massive park (p601) in the centre of Hokkaidō, with day trips to a week-long challenge the length of the park.

Shiretoko National Park This World Heritage Site (p616) offers day walks to a three-dayer, plenty of hot springs and *higuma* (brown bears).

Akan National Park Brilliant day-trip options including Me-Akan-dake (1499m; p624) and O-Akan-dake (1371m; p624).

Rishiri-zan A standalone volcano (1721m; p608) on its own island off the northern coast of Hokkaidō.

Shikoku

Ishizuchi-san At 1982m, the highest peak (p665) in western Japan. Great day and overnight hikes in Ehime Prefecture.

Tsurugi-san Shikoku's second-highest peak (1955m; p644) provides both easy walks and multiday hiking opportunities.

88 Temple Pilgrimage The 1200th birthday of Kōbō Daishi's legendary 1400km 88-temple pilgrimage (p641) around Shikoku was in 2015.

Kyūshū

Aso-san Good hiking at the world's largest volcanic caldera (p714), 128km in circumference! Walk around the crater rim to the high peaks.

Kirishima-Yaku National Park Excellent options including climbing Karakuni-dake (1700m), Kirishima's highest peak (p727).

Kaimon-dake This beautifully symmetrical 924m cone (p730) on the Satsuma Peninsula is a brilliant day walk.

Okinawa & the Southwest Islands

Yakushima Lots of hiking options on this World Heritage–listed island (p753). Climb Miyanoura-dake (1935m) or hike on myriad tracks that criss-cross the island.

Iriomote-jima A Japanese jungle hike (p786) on one of Okinawa Prefecture's westernmost islands.

Plan Your Trip
Visiting an Onsen

With thousands of onsen (hot springs) scattered across the archipelago, the Japanese have been taking the plunge for centuries. The blissful relaxation that follows a good long soak can turn a sceptic into a convert, and is likely to make you an onsen fanatic.

Onsen Basics

Some locals will tell you that the only distinctively Japanese aspect of their culture – that is, the only thing that didn't ultimately originate in mainland Asia – is the bath. There are accounts of onsen bathing in Japan's earliest historical records, and over the millennia the Japanese have turned the simple act of bathing in an onsen into something like a religion.

Onsen water comes naturally heated from a hot spring and often contains a number of different minerals. Onsen are reputed to makes one's skin *sube-sube* (smooth), while the chemical composition of particular waters are also believed to help cure such ailments as high blood pressure, poor circulation and even infertility.

The minerals in some onsen can discolour jewellery, particularly silver. But don't worry too much if you forget to take off your wedding ring before jumping in the tub – after a few hours, the discolouration usually fades.

Japan's other form of public bathhouse – *sentō* – can also be found throughout the country. What sets an onsen apart from a *sentō* is the nature of the water: *sentō* water comes from the tap and is mechanically heated.

Need to Know

Onsen Lingo

男湯 (otoko-yu) male bath; most commonly used term

女湯 (onna-yu) female bath; most commonly used term

男性の湯 (dansei-no-yu) male bath

女性の湯 (josei-no-yu) female bath

家族の湯 (kazoku-no-yu) family bath

露天風呂 (rotemburo) outdoor bath

外湯 (soto-yu) public bath

内湯 (uchi-yu) private bath

Costs

Some of Japan's finest onsen are free. Just show up with a towel and your birthday suit, splash a little water on yourself and plunge in. If there is an entry charge it will rarely be more than ¥1000 (US$9).

Online Resources

Sento Guide (www.sentoguide.info) Best English-language resource about bathhouses across Japan.

Onsen Soaker (www.onsensoaker.blogspot.com) Blogger who's dipped in over 1500 baths.

Onsen Types & Locations

While onsen can be stand-alone baths, more commonly you'll find many clustered together in a particular location, such as Hakone, Beppu and Noboribetsu. If you want to bathe in the great outdoors, look for the terms *rotemburo* or *notemburo*.

Facilities can be publicly run or attached to a traditional Japanese inn, either *minshuku* or ryokan, many of which admit day visitors. For the ultimate onsen experience book an overnight stay at a ryokan with its own private hot-spring bath. That way you can take your time in the tub, relax in your room (which may also have a private onsen bath) and eat sumptuous food.

Onsen Etiquette

Known as *hadaka no tsukiai* (naked friendship), communal bathing is seen in Japan as a great social leveller. Bathing isn't just a pastime, it's a ritual – one so embedded in Japanese culture that everyone knows exactly what to do. This can be intimidating to the novice, but the main thing you need to know to avoid causing alarm is to wash yourself before getting into the bath. It's also a good idea to memorise the characters for men (男) and women (女), which will be marked on the *noren* (curtain) hanging in front of the respective baths.

Konyoku (mixed bathing) was the norm in Japan until the Meiji Restoration, when the country sought to align itself with more 'civilised' Western ideas and outlawed the practice. It's rare to encounter *konyoku* in Japan's urban centres, but in the countryside and on smaller islands (where baths may be no more than a pool in a riverbed blocked off with stones or a tidal basin beside crashing waves) the practice is more common.

Upon entering an onsen or *sentō*, the first thing you'll encounter is a row of lockers for your shoes. After you pay your admission and head to the correct changing room, you'll find either more lockers or baskets for your clothes. Take everything off here, entering the bathing room with only the small towel that will either be provided for free or a small charge.

That little towel performs a variety of functions: you can use it to wash (but make sure to give it a good rinse afterwards) or to cover yourself as you walk around. It is not supposed to touch the water though, so leave it on the side of the bath or – as the locals do – folded on top of your head.

Before you step into the bath, park yourself on a stool in front of one of the taps and give yourself a thorough wash. Make sure you rinse off all the suds. When you're done, it's polite to rinse off the stool for the next person. At more humble bathhouses you might have little more than a ladle to work with; in that case, crouch low and use it to scoop out water from the bath to pour over your body – taking care not to

TATTOO WARNING

Be warned that if you have any tattoos, you may not be allowed to enter a public onsen or *sentō*. The reason for this is that *yakuza* (Japanese mafia) almost always sport tattoos. Banning people with tattoos is an indirect way of banning gangsters. Unfortunately, to avoid the appearance of unfairness (and because Japan is a country where rules are rigorously adhered to), the no-tattoo rule often applies to locals and foreign visitors alike.

If your tattoo is small enough, cover it up with Band-Aids and you'll have no problem. Otherwise, ask the staff at the front desk if you can go in despite your tattoos. The phrase to use is, *'Irezumi wa daijōbu desu ka'* (Are tattoos okay?). A few public facilities have started to allow visitors with tattoos to enter, but be prepared for some patrons to complain.

Another option is to enquire whether a public spa has private baths you can book – some do. Similarly, some onsen ryokan also have private baths.

ONSEN IN PRINT

➡ *The Japanese Spa: A Guide to Japan's Finest Ryokan and Onsen* (Akihiko Seki & Elizabeth Heilman Brooke; 2005) Lush coffee-table book.

➡ *A Guide to Japanese Hot Springs* (Anne Hotta with Yoko Ishiguro; 1986) Some classic gems.

➡ *Japan's Hidden Onsen* (Robert Neff; 1995) Contains some fantastic finds.

➡ *Japanese Spa Resorts* (Jinling Qu; 2012) Gorgeous, glossy offering.

splash water into the tub – and scrub a bit with the towel.

In the baths, keep splashing to a minimum and your head above the water. Before heading back to the changing room, wipe yourself down with the towel to avoid dripping on the floor.

Best Onsen Experiences

With so many onsen bubbling up across Japan, it's perfectly feasible to organise your travel itinerary around visiting some of the best. Following are some of our absolute favourites:

Tokyo Located on the artificial island of Odaiba in Tokyo Bay, Ōedo Onsen Monogatari (p110) is a super-onsen modelled on an Edo-period town. There is a huge variety of tubs, including outdoor tubs, as well as restaurants, relaxation rooms and shops.

Around Tokyo Hakone (p172) is excellent for its proximity to Tokyo and fab mix of public onsen and luxurious onsen ryokan. The wooden onsen bath at Rendai-ji's Kanaya Ryokan (p185) on the Izu Peninsula is massive, atmospheric and offers mixed bathing.

The Japan Alps & Central Honshū The top two for this area are Shirahone Onsen (p263) and Kaga Onsen (p250), although running a close third is the amazing and remote Nakabusa Onsen (p269).

Kyoto Only 30 minutes north of Kyoto, Kurama Onsen (p320) is a great place to soak away city stresses or relax after a hike in the surrounding hills.

Kansai Kinosaki (p422) is the quintessential onsen town, with seven public baths and dozens of onsen ryokan. Relax in your accommodation taking the waters as it pleases you, and when you get tired of your ryokan's bath, hit the streets in a *yukata* (light cotton kimono) and *geta* (wooden sandals) and visit the public baths.

Western Honshū & the Inland Sea Contemporary art and Japanese bathing culture collide memorably in Naoshima Bath – I Heart Yū (p461), the only *sentō* in the country with a life-sized model of an elephant in the bathroom. On the Japan Sea coast Yunotsu (p488) offers preserved wooden buildings and a pair of atmospheric public baths.

Northern Honshū In Aoni Onsen stay at the oil-lamp-lit Rampu-no-yado (p539). At Nyūtō Onsen, slip into the milky, mineral rich waters of Tsuru-no-yu (p529), which has been in business for four centuries.

Hokkaidō Well off the beaten track, the forest-surrounded *konyoku* (mixed bathing) Fukiage Roten-no-yu (p605) in central Hokkaido is as natural as they come – plus it's free.

Shikoku Legend has it that Dōgo Onsen (p662) in Matsuyama was discovered in 'the age of the gods'. Since the castle-style building's construction in 1894, the onsen has been featured in several literary classics, most famously in Natsume Sōseki's *Botchan*.

Kyūshū Beppu (p739) draws the onsen-tourist crowds, but for something different head to Ibusuki (p729), famous for sand baths where onsen steam rises through the sand in which bathers are buried up to their necks.

Okinawa & the Southwest Islands Yakushima's Hirauchi Kaichū Onsen (p754) is for the brave, as it's an outdoor, seaside pool with little privacy unless you happen to get it to yourself. However, it's only ¥100 and you can't beat the setting.

Regions at a Glance

Tokyo

Food
Culture
Shopping

Sushi & More

Not only does Tokyo have more restaurants than any other city in the world, it has more great ones. Whether it's sushi right from the source at Tsukiji Fish Market or a late-night bowl of *rāmen,* you will eat well – very well – here.

Past, Present & Future

Tokyo is famous for its pop culture – its eccentric street fashion, lurid anime and *kawaii* (cute) characters. But there is so much more: dig deeper in the city's excellent museums, and look to the future on those giant video screens.

Shop, Shop, Shop

Didn't think you were getting out of here empty-handed, did you? Tokyo is a shopper's paradise, offering everything from traditional crafts to the latest lifestyle gadgets.

p70

Mt Fuji & Around Tokyo

Ryokan
Outdoors
Culture

Ryokan & Onsen

Some of Japan's most beloved ryokan and onsen are just a few hours from Tokyo. Each area offers its own regional flavour – rugged onsen towns to the north, lakeside resorts to the west, and laid-back coastal villages to the south.

Outdoor Activities

Outdoor options include hiking among cedar groves or up volcanoes, white-water rafting, snow skiing, surfing and swimming with dolphins.

Shrines & Temples

The cultural legacies of different historical eras come to life in the vibrant shrines and temples of Nikkō and the more austere ones of medieval Kamakura.

p153

The Japan Alps & Central Honshū

Onsen
Villages
Skiing

Ultimate Onsen

The mountainous heart of Japan bubbles over with exquisite hot springs and fantastic inns to enjoy them. Gaze up at snowy peaks while steam rises from your body.

Thatched Roofs

Travel to the remote village of Shirakawa-gō (or, even remoter, Ainokura) and fall asleep to the sound of chirping frogs in a centuries-old thatched-roof farmhouse.

Powder Peaks

Ski some of Asia's best slopes, commanding breathtaking views of the northern Japan Alps. Après-ski soaking in hot springs is mandatory.

p206

Kyoto

Temples
Culture
Food

Shintō & Buddhist Masterpieces

With over 1000 Buddhist temples and more than 400 Shintō shrines, Kyoto is *the* place to savour Japanese religious architecture and garden design. Find a quiet temple to call your own for the morning or join the throngs at a popular shrine.

Japan's Cultural Storehouse

Whether it's geisha, tea ceremonies, painting, theatre performances or textiles, Kyoto is Japan's cultural capital.

Cuisine: Refined & Otherwise

If you're after *kaiseki* (haute cuisine) in sublime surroundings, go to Kyoto. But if a steaming bowl of *rāmen* is more your speed, you'll find endless choices here, too.

p288

Kansai

Food
Nature
Onsen

Gourmet Playground

Kyoto is the place to experience *kaiseki*, Japan's impossibly refined haute cuisine, while nearby Osaka is known for heaping portions of delicious down-home food.

Rugged Mountains & Pilgrimage Routes

Southern Kansai (Wakayama and southern Nara) is a world of mountains, winding rivers and Shintō shrines. Pilgrims have been communing with the gods here for thousands of years.

Seaside & Riverside Onsen

From the quaint town of Kinosaki in the north to the riverside Hongū in the south, Kansai has plenty of hot springs to relax in after a day of soaking up the culture.

p349

Hiroshima & Western Honshū

Islands
Food
History

Island Adventures

An art-filled weekend, a mountain hike, a beachside frolic or an escape to slow-paced solitude – you can take your pick on one of Western Honshū's countless islands.

Seafood Heaven

Seafood is king along the salty coasts of Western Honshū, and every seaside town has its speciality. Don't miss the chance to risk your life for a plate of pufferfish in *fugu*-mad Shimonoseki.

History

Visit revered Izumo Taisha, a shrine as old as Japan's recorded history, or explore a 17th-century silver mine. Or learn about more recent history in the city of Hiroshima.

p426

Northern Honshū (Tōhoku)

Outdoors
Onsen
Culture

Parks & Peaks

Northern Honshū is blessed with some spectacular mountains. Temperate summers lure hikers, while snowy winters attract powder fiends and snow bunnies.

Rustic Escapes

That image you have of milky-white waters and stars overhead or the steamy wooden bathhouse all by its lonesome in the mountains – that's Tōhoku.

Festivals & Ancient Rites

Nobody in Japan does festivals like they do up here. Ancient customs and beliefs live on in Tōhoku, preserved by centuries of isolation. Sample food prepared the way it has been for generations, or follow in the footsteps of mountain ascetics.

p492

Sapporo & Hokkaidō

Outdoors
Food
Onsen

Pristine Wilderness

Hokkaidō is where all your preconceived notions of Japan will be shattered: walks in the park span days on end; ocean voyages navigate precarious ice floes; and skiers carve snow drifts reaching several metres in depth.

Unique Cuisine

Flash-frozen salmon sashimi, soup curries, massive crabs and Sapporo lager are just some of Hokkaidō's much-revered culinary specialities.

Hidden Onsen

Soak in hidden steaming hot pools surrounded by thick forest and towering mountains.

p561

Shikoku

Nature
Temples
Surfing

Japan's Shangri La Valley

A short drive from the mainland madness, Iya Valley has dramatic gorges, ancient vine bridges and a hint of sustainable living. Raft or hike along the pristine Yoshino-gawa.

Good Buddha

The 88-temple pilgrimage is a rite of passage for many Japanese who, dressed in white and armed with a walking stick, lower the pulse, raise the gaze and seek to honour the great Buddhist saint, Kōbō Daishi.

Surfing Shikoku

There's good surfing from the fishing villages of Tokushima Prefecture to the wild bluffs at Ashizuri-misaki. And the consistent crowd-free swells at Ohkinohama Beach should be legendary.

p630

Kyūshū

History
Nature
Onsen

Storied Gateway

Christian rebellions led to over two centuries of seclusion, during which Nagasaki's Dejima Island was Japan's window to the world. Visit the city to learn about this fascinating chapter of Japanese history.

Mountains of Fire

The active volcanoes Aso-san and Sakurajima are the most famous of Kyūshū's mountains, with fantastic hiking in between. The ever-present chance of eruption gives residents a unique *joie de vivre*.

In Hot Water – and Hot Sand

Soak away riverside in intimate Kurokawa Onsen or in one of Beppu's onsen, or get buried in a sand bath in Ibusuki. Even Kyūshū's biggest city, Fukuoka, has natural onsen.

p673

Okinawa & the Southwest Islands

Beaches
Hiking
Food

Sun-Soaked

Splash out on the gorgeous golden beaches of the Kerama Islands, where you can whale-watch in winter and have the sand all to yourself.

Super Cedars

Climb into the green, pulsing heart of Yakushima, where ancient cedar trees grow really, really big. Looking more like a *Star Wars* set than earth, this is the closest we've come to an otherworldly experience.

Island Cuisine

Tuck into a plateful of *gōyā champurū,* Okinawa's signature stir-fry with bitter melon. Add some *awamori,* the local firewater, and you'll be ready to grab the *sanshin* (banjo) and party.

p749

On the Road

Tokyo

03 / POP 13.39 MILLION

Includes ➡

Best Places to Eat

- Kyūbey (p123)
- Shinsuke (p129)
- Nagi (p127)
- Tonki (p125)
- Yanmo (p127)

Best Places to Stay

- Sawanoya Ryokan (p121)
- Shibuya Granbell Hotel (p119)
- Nui (p121)
- Claska (p118)
- Hotel S (p117)

Why Go?

Tokyo (東京) is a city forever reaching into the future, resulting in sci-fi streetscapes of crackling neon and soaring towers. It is constantly reinventing itself – most recently as a culinary and pop-culture mecca (and a must-visit for anyone interested in either). Yet it is also a city steeped in history, and you can find traces of the shogun's capital on the kabuki stage or under the cherry blossoms in Ueno Park.

There are excellent museums here, along with everything else you could ask of Japan – grand temples, atmospheric shrines, fascinating contemporary architecture, elegant gardens and, yes, even hot springs. Tokyo, however, is also a place where sightseeing can take a backseat. To get to know the city is to enjoy it as the locals do: by splurging on sushi in Ginza, scouting new looks in Harajuku or just wandering the lanes of one of the city's more atmospheric quarters, such as Yanaka or Kagurazaka. And don't forget the varied and often outrageous nightlife – more proof of Tokyo's indefatigable spirit.

When to Go

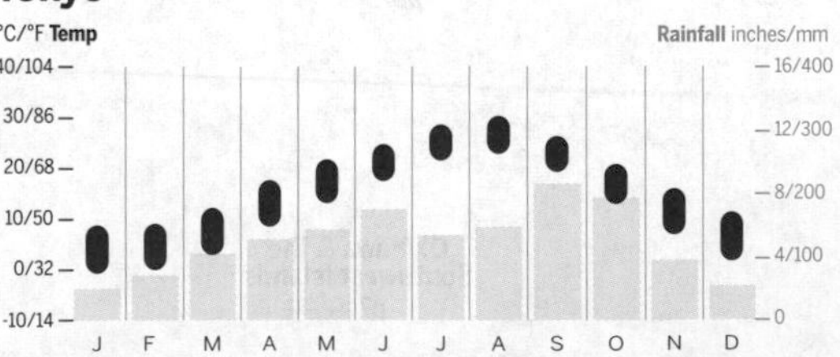

Mar & Apr Cherry-blossom viewing is in full swing – bring a *bentō* and spread the picnic blanket.

May–Sep Hot and humid, but lively summer festivals more than make up for it.

Oct–Dec Crisp, cool and sunny days. Falling gingko leaves turn Tokyo's streets to gold in December.

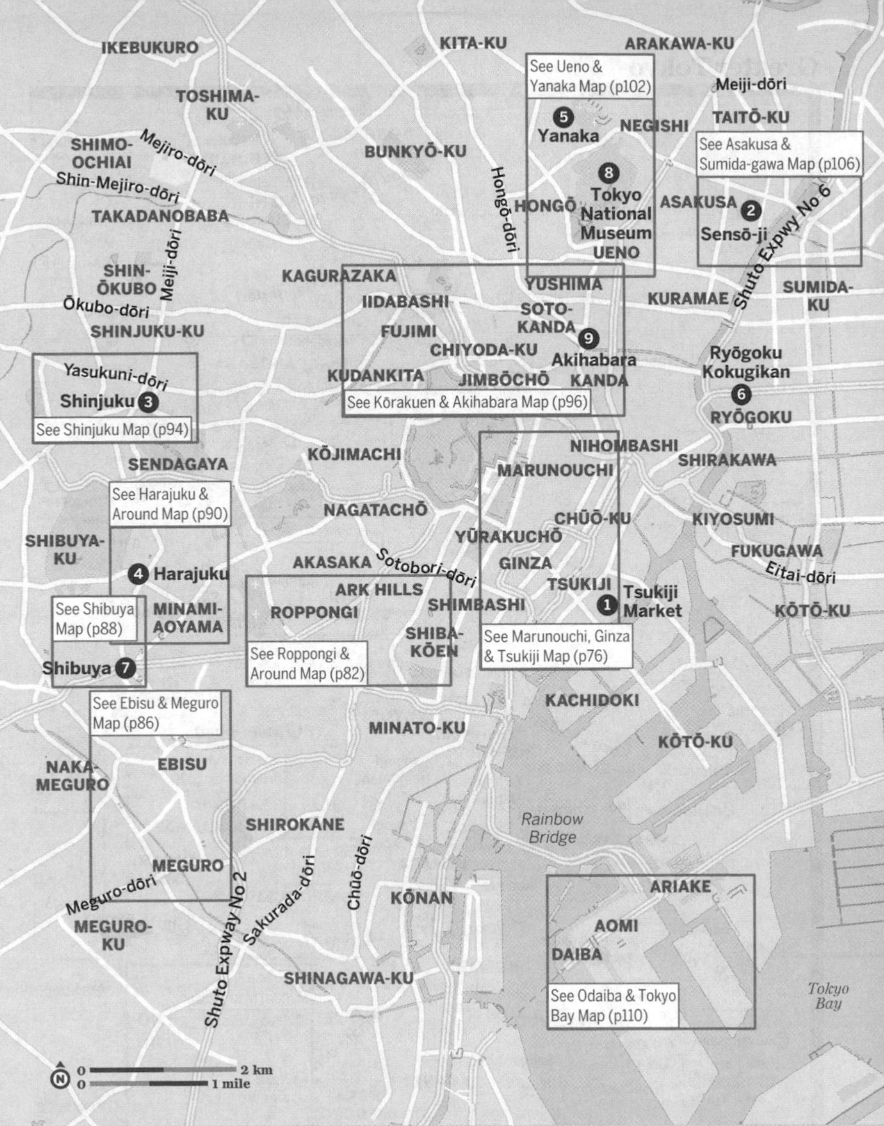

Tokyo Highlights

1 Gawking at the colourful sea creatures on sale at **Tsukiji Market** (p79).

2 Soaking up the atmosphere at Asakusa's centuries-old temple, **Sensō-ji** (p107).

3 Raising a glass in the colourful nightlife district of **Shinjuku** (p134).

4 Joining the city's eccentric fashion tribes as they shop in **Harajuku** (p143).

5 Losing yourself in the vestiges of the old city in **Yanaka** (p98).

6 Catching the salt-slinging, belly-slapping ritual of sumo at **Ryōgoku Kokugikan** (p139).

7 Getting swept up in the crowds and neon lights of **Shibuya** (p86).

8 Seeing the world's largest collection of Japanese art at the **Tokyo National Museum** (p99).

9 Venturing into the belly of the pop culture beast that is **Akihabara** (p97).

Greater Tokyo

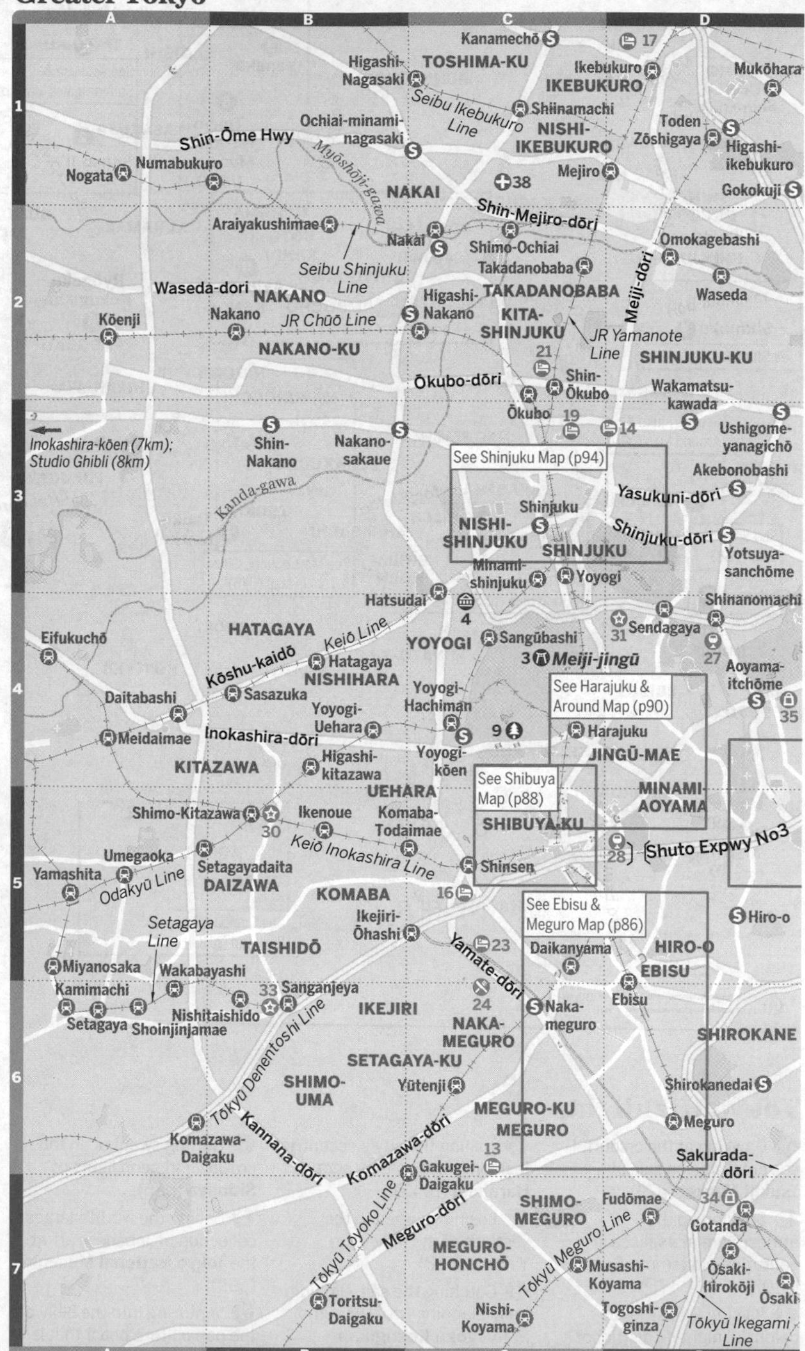

0 2 km
0 1 mile
Sugamo
Arakawa Streetcar Line
Sengoku
Shin-Ōtsuka
BUNKYŌ-KU
NISHI-NIPPORI
Nishi Nippori
ARAKAWA-KU
Nippori
Sendagi
YANAKA
NEZU
Uguisudani
Minamisenju
Minowa
Kokusai-dōri
TAITŌ-KU
Iriya
Sumida River
Sumida-gawa
Myōgadani
Todai-mae
UENO
Nezu
Ueno
Keisei Ueno
HONGŌ
See Asakusa & Sumida-gawa Map (p106)
ASAKUSA
OSHIAGE
Inarichō
Asakusa
Tokyo Sky Tree Station
KOISHIKAWA
Edogawabashi
Kasuga
See Ueno & Yanaka Map (p102)
Shin-okachimachi
KAGURAZAKA
Kōrakuen
Suidōbashi
JR Chūō Line
Iidabashi
Suehirochō
AKIHABARA
Ochanomizu
Akihabara
KURAMAE
Kuramae
Asakusabashi
SUMIDA-KU
KUDANKITA
Kudanshita
Jimbōchō
Kanda
Bakuroyokoyama
Ryōgoku
Edo-Tokyo Museum
Keiyō-dōri
CHIYODA-KU
Higashi-nihombashi
Shuto Expwy No 7
RYŌGOKU
Narita (60km)
See Kōrakuen & Akihabara Map (p96)
Hamachō
Kikukawa
Morishita
Kōjimachi
Hanzōmon
CHŪŌ-KU
Ningyōchō
SHIRAKAWA
Yotsuya
Imperial Palace
MARUNOUCHI
Kiyosumi-shirakawa
Tokyo
KYŌBASHI
Kayabachō
Kokkai-gijidōmae
Sakuradamon
Akasaka-mitsuke
Yūrakuchō
KIYOSUMI
KIBA
Hatchōbori
KŌTŌ-KU
Akasaka
Tameike-sannō
Kasumigaseki
Ginza
Monzen-nakachō
FUKAGAWA
Toranomon
GINZA
ROPPONGI
Etchujima
Eitai-dōri
Kiba
Shimbashi
Tsukiji
Roppongi
Tsukijishijō
Tsukishima
SHIBA-KŌEN
Shiodome
TSUKIJI
Keiyō Line
See Roppongi & Around Map (p82)
See Marunouchi, Ginza & Tsukiji Map (p76)
Daimon
Hamamatsuchō
Azabu-jūban
Akabanebashi
KACHIDOKI
Toyosu
Shibakōen
Takeshiba Pier
KŌTŌ-KU
Hinode
Shin-Toyosu
Tokyo Disney Resort (6km)
Mita
Shijo-mae
Tatsumi
Tamachi
Shirokane Takanawa
Shibaura Futō
Site of Tsukiji Fish Market (from late 2016)
Ariake Tennis-no-mori
Bayshore Line Expwy
Shinonome
Sengakuji
Chūō-dōri
Ariake Tennis-no-mori
Kokusai Tenjijō
Ariake
See Odaiba & Tokyo Bay Map (p110)
ARIAKE
Takanawadai
Odaiba Kaihin-kōen
Kokusai-tenjijō Seimon
Shinagawa
Daiba
Tokyo Teleport
Tennōzu-Isle
Kita-Shinagawa
AOMI
Aomi
Fune-no-Kagakukan
Tokyo Bay
SHINAGAWA-KU
Shin-Banba
Telecom Center
Haneda (10km)
TOKYO

Greater Tokyo

Top Sights
1 Edo-Tokyo Museum ... H3
2 Imperial Palace ... F4
3 Meiji-jingū ... C4

Sights
4 Japanese Sword Museum ... C4
5 Museum of Contemporary Art, Tokyo (MOT) ... H4
6 Rikugi-en ... E1
7 Sengaku-ji ... E6
8 Sumo Museum ... G3
9 Yoyogi-kōen ... C4

Activities, Courses & Tours
10 Arashio Stable ... G3
11 Hato Bus Tours ... F5
Ryōgoku Kokugikan ... (see 8)

Sleeping
12 Andon Ryokan ... G1
13 Claska ... C6
14 E Hotel Higashi-Shinjuku ... D3
15 Hōmeikan ... F2
16 Hotel Fukudaya ... C5
17 Kimi Ryokan ... D1
18 K's House Tokyo ... G2
19 Ladies 510 ... C3
20 Nui ... G2
21 Sekitei ... C2
22 Toco ... G1
23 Weekly Dormy Inn Meguro Aobadai ... C5

Eating
24 Higashi-Yama ... C6
Tomoegata ... (see 8)
25 TY Harbor Brewery ... E7

Drinking & Nightlife
26 Fukurou-no-mise ... G5
27 Mori-no Beer Garden ... D4
28 Oath ... D5
29 Popeye ... G3

Entertainment
30 Honda Theatre ... B5
31 National Nō Theatre ... D4
32 National Theatre ... E4
33 Setagaya Public Theatre ... B6

Shopping
34 Good Day Books ... D7
35 Japan Traditional Crafts Aoyama Square ... D4
36 Tolman Collection ... F5

Information
37 Australian Embassy ... E5
38 Seibo International Catholic Hospital ... C1
39 Tokyo Regional Immigration Bureau ... F7

History

For most of its history, Tokyo was called Edo (literally 'Gate of the River') due to its location at the mouth of the Sumida-gawa. It was a remote fishing village until the warrior poet Ōta Dōkan put up a castle here in the 15th century. Then, in 1603, warlord Tokugawa Ieyasu decided to make Edo Castle the centre of his new shogunate (military government). From that point, Edo quickly transformed into a bustling city and, by the late 18th century, it had become the most populous city in the world.

In 1868, after civil war and the resignation of the last Tokugawa shogun, authority reverted to the emperor – an act known as the Meiji Restoration. The capital was officially moved from Kyoto to Edo, which was then renamed Tokyo, meaning Eastern Capital.

Following the Meiji Restoration, Japan ended its 250 years of self-prescribed isolation and began to welcome foreign influence with open arms, particularly in the capital. Western fashions and ideas were adopted as Tokyo eagerly sought to take its place among the pantheon of the world's great cities.

In 1923 the Great Kantō Earthquake and ensuing fires levelled much of the city. It was once again torn to shreds during the devastating Allied air raids in the final years of WWII.

Emerging from the rubble after the US occupation, Tokyo quickly propelled itself towards modernity in the 1950s and '60s. A soaring economic crescendo followed, culminating in the giddy heights of the 1980s 'bubble economy'.

The humbling 'burst' in the '90s led to a recession that still continues today. Yet Tokyo remains the beating heart of its island nation, never ceasing to reinvent itself while holding significant global influence over pop culture, design and technology.

Sights & Activities

Tokyo is endless in size and scope and can feel more like a collection of cities than one cohesive whole. In Edo times, the city was divided into Yamanote ('uptown' or 'high city') and Shitamachi ('downtown' or 'low city'). On the elevated plain west of the castle (now the Imperial Palace), Yamanote was where the feudal elite built their estates. In the east, along the banks of the Sumida-gawa, Shitamachi was home to the working classes, merchants and artisans.

Even today, remnants of this distinction exist: the east side of the city is still a tangle of alleys and tightly packed quarters. Neighbourhoods such as Asakusa and Ueno retain a down-to-earth vibe, more traditional architecture and an artisan tradition – the closest approximation to old Edo that remains.

Yamanote developed into the moneyed commercial and business districts of today. Further west, newer neighbourhoods such as Shinjuku and Shibuya developed after the Great Kantō Earthquake and WWII – this is the hypermodern Tokyo of riotous neon and giant video screens.

Of course it's not really that simple. You'll discover incongruous pockets of juxtaposed old and new – a tiny shrine lodged among skyscrapers, a glowing spire rising from a jumble of low-slung buildings – that are oh-so-Tokyo.

Marunouchi (Tokyo Station area) 丸の内（東京駅）

The Imperial Palace marks the centre of the city. Though the palace itself is closed to the public, a large proportion of the grounds are now parks open to all, including Kitanomaru-kōen, which has a handful of museums.

To the east of the palace you'll find the bustling business district of Marunouchi. In the past decade, several glossy towers have replaced the tired, almost Soviet-style structures that once characterised Marunouchi. Naka-dōri, which runs parallel to the palace between Hibiya and Ōtemachi stations, is a pretty, tree-lined avenue with upscale boutiques and patio cafes. Once famous for being deserted at nights and on weekends, Marunouchi is now an increasingly popular place to hang out.

★Imperial Palace PALACE

(皇居; Kōkyo; Map p72; 03-3213-1111; http://sankan.kunaicho.go.jp/english/index.html; 1 Chiyoda, Chiyoda-ku; S Chiyoda line to Ōtemachi, exits C13b & C10) FREE The Imperial Palace grounds occupy the site of the original Edo-jō, the Tokugawa shogunate's castle when they ruled the land. As it's the home of Japan's emperor and some of the imperial family, the palace is off limits. You can take a free tour of some of the surrounding grounds. If you're not on the tour, two bridges – the iron Nijū-bashi and the stone Megane-bashi – comprise a famous landmark that can be viewed from the southwest corner of Imperial Palace Plaza.

Behind the bridges rises the Edo-era Fushimi-yagura watchtower.

For tours (lasting around one hour, 15 minutes) you must book ahead through the Imperial Household Agency's website or by phoning. Reservations are taken between a month and four days in advance – you'd be wise to apply as early as possible. Tours run twice daily from Monday to Friday (10am and 1.30pm), but not on public holidays nor afternoons from late July through to the end of August.

In its heyday this was the largest fortress in the world, though little remains of it today apart from the moat and stone walls. The present palace, completed in 1968, replaced the one built in 1888, which was largely destroyed during WWII.

The main park of the verdant palace grounds is the Imperial Palace East Garden, which is open to the public without reservations. You must take a token upon arrival and return it at the end of your visit.

➡ Imperial Palace East Garden

(東御苑; Kōkyo Higashi-gyoen; Map p76; http://sankan.kunaicho.go.jp; 1 Chiyoda, Chiyoda-ku; 9am-4pm Nov-Feb, to 4.30pm Mar–mid-Apr, Sep & Oct, to 5pm mid-Apr–Aug, closed Mon & Fri year-round; S Chiyoda line to Ōtemachi, exit C13b or C10) FREE Crafted from part of the original castle compound, these lovely free gardens allow you to get close-up views of the massive stones used to build the castle walls, and even climb the ruins of one of the keeps, off the upper lawn. The number of visitors at any one time is limited, so it never feels crowded. Most people enter through Ōtemon, the closest gate to Tokyo Station, and once the principal entrance to Edo Castle.

Kitanomaru-kōen (Kitanomaru Park) PARK

(北の丸公園; Map p96; www.env.go.jp/garden/kokyogaien/english/index.html; S Hanzōmon line to Kudanshita, exit 2, or Takebashi line, exit 1a) This large park north of the Imperial Palace grounds is home to noteworthy museums as well as the **Nippon Budōkan** (日本武道館; Map p96; 3216-5100; http://nipponbudokan.web.fc2.com; 2-3 Kitanomaru-kōen, Chiyoda-ku; S Hanzōmon line to Kudanshita, exit 2) concert hall. The gate at the park's northern end, **Tayasu-mon**, dates from 1636, making it

Marunouchi, Ginza & Tsukiji

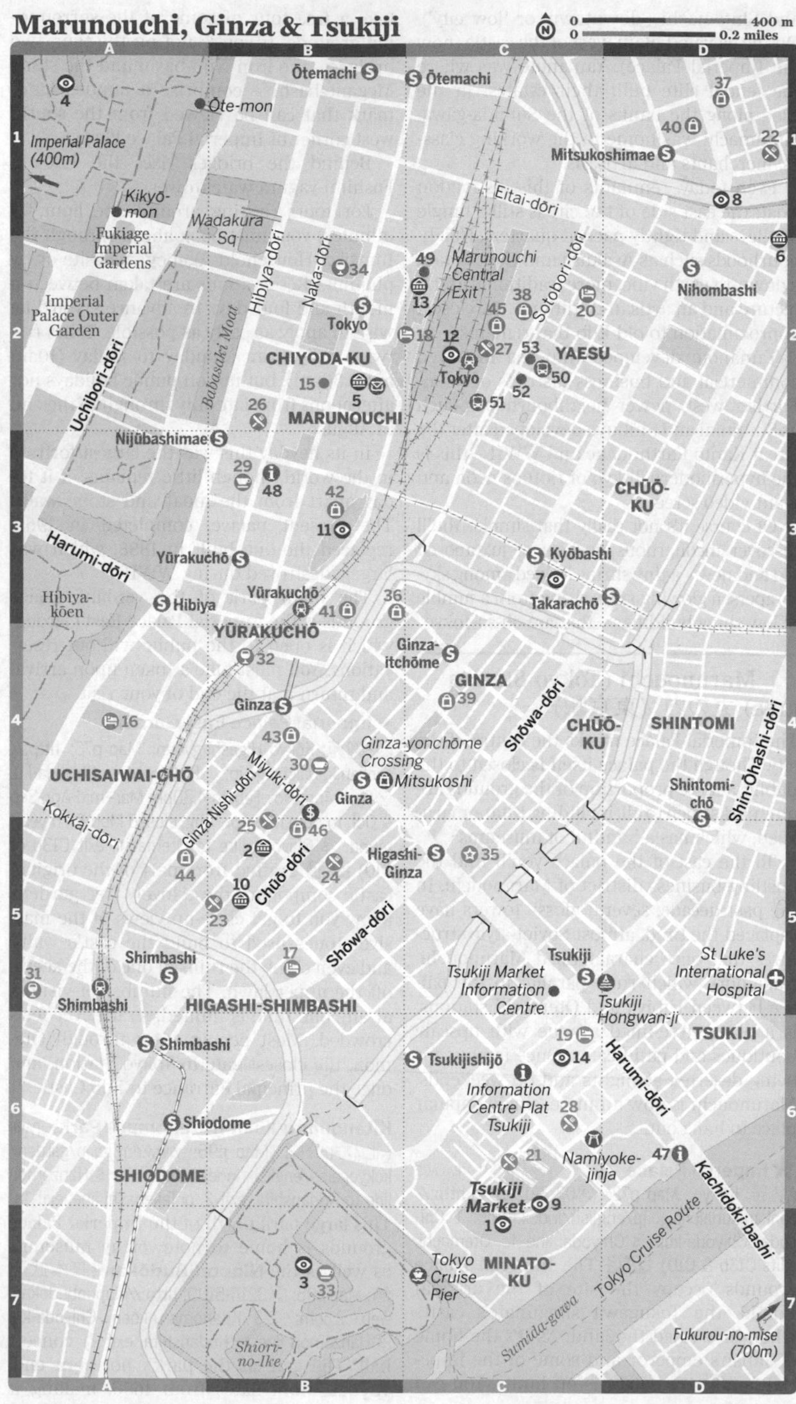

Marunouchi, Ginza & Tsukiji

Top Sights
1 Tsukiji Market C7

Sights
2 Ginza Graphic Gallery B5
3 Hama-rikyū Onshi-teien B7
4 Imperial Palace East Garden A1
5 Intermediatheque B2
6 Kite Museum D2
7 National Film Centre C3
8 Nihombashi (Nihonbashi) D1
9 Seafood Intermediate Wholesalers' Area C6
10 Shiseido Gallery B5
11 Tokyo International Forum B3
12 Tokyo Station C2
13 Tokyo Station Gallery C2
14 Tsukiji Outer Market C6

Activities, Courses & Tours
15 SkyBus B2

Sleeping
16 Imperial Hotel A4
17 Mitsui Garden Hotel Ginza Premier B5
18 Tokyo Station Hotel C2
19 Tōkyū Stay Higashi-Ginza C6
20 Yaesu Terminal Hotel C2

Eating
21 Daiwa Sushi C6
22 Hōnen Manpuku D1
23 Kyūbey B5
24 Maru B5
Meal MUJI Yūrakuchō .... (see 41)
25 Ore-no-dashi B5
26 Rose Bakery Marunouchi B2
27 Tokyo Rāmen Street C2
28 Trattoria Tsukiji Paradiso! C6

Drinking & Nightlife
29 Cafe Salvador B3
30 Cha Ginza B4
31 Kagaya A5
32 Manpuku Shokudō B4
33 Nakajima no Ochaya B7
34 So Tired B2

Entertainment
35 Kabuki-za C5

Shopping
36 Akomeya B3
37 Coredo Muromachi D1
38 Daimaru C2
Dover Street Market Ginza .... (see 46)
39 Itōya C4
40 Mitsukoshi D1
41 Muji B3
42 Ōedo Antique Market B3
43 Sony Building B4
44 Takumi A5
45 Tokyo Character Street C2
46 Uniqlo B5

Information
47 Fish Information Center D6
48 JNTO Tourist Information Center B3
49 JR East Travel Service Center C2

Transport
50 Access Narita C2
51 JR Highway Bus Terminal C2
52 Nippon Rent-a-Car C2
53 Toyota Rent-a-Car C2

the oldest remaining gate to the Edo Castle compound. The area surrounding it along the moat explodes with cherry blossoms (and flower photographers) in spring.

➡ National Museum of Modern Art (MOMAT)
(国立近代美術館; Kokuritsu Kindai Bijutsukan; Map p96; ☎03-5777-8600; www.momat.go.jp/english; 3-1 Kitanomaru-kōen, Chiyoda-ku; adult/student ¥420/130, extra for special exhibitions; ⏲10am-5pm Tue-Thu, Sat & Sun, to 8pm Fri; Ⓢ Tōzai line to Takebashi, exit 1b) This collection of over 9000 works is one of the country's best. All pieces date from the Meiji period onwards and impart a sense of a more modern Japan through portraits, photography and contemporary sculptures and video works. There's a wonderful view from the museum towards the Imperial Palace East Garden.

➡ Crafts Gallery
(東京国立近代美術館 工芸館; Map p96; www.momat.go.jp/english; 1 Kitanomaru-kōen, Chiyoda-ku; adult/child ¥210/70, 1st Sun of month free; ⏲10am-5pm Tue-Sun; Ⓢ Tōzai line to Takebashi, exit 1b) Housed in a vintage red-brick building this annexe of MOMAT stages excellent changing exhibitions of *mingei* (folk crafts): ceramics, lacquerware, bamboo, textiles, dolls and much more. Artists range from living national treasures to contemporary artisans. The building was once the headquarters of the imperial guards, and was rebuilt after its destruction in WWII.

Tokyo Station LANDMARK
(東京駅; Map p76; www.tokyostationcity.com/en; 1-9 Marunouchi, Chiyoda-ku; 🅡 JR lines to Tokyo Station) Following a major renovation and expansion completed in time for

its centenary in 2014, Tokyo Station is in grand form. Kingo Tatsuno's elegant brick building on the Marunouchi side has been expertly restored to include domes faithful to the original design, decorated inside with relief sculptures. Tokyo Station Hotel (p117) occupies the south end of the building; to the north is **Tokyo Station Gallery** (Map p76; www.ejrcf.or.jp/gallery; Tokyo Station, 1-9-1 Marunouchi, Chiyoda-ku; differs for each exhibition; 10am-6pm Tue-Thu, Sat & Sun, to 8pm Fri; JR lines to Tokyo, Marunouchi north exit), which hosts interesting exhibitions and the useful JR East Travel Service Center (p148).

Tokyo Station City, the name for the general nontransport complex, includes, on the eastern Yaesu side, **Daimaru** (Map p76; 03-3212-8011; www.daimaru.co.jp/tokyo; 1-9-1 Marunouchi, Chiyoda-ku; 10am-9pm, restaurants 11am-11pm; JR lines to Tokyo Station, Yaesu exit) department store, and a vast and bewildering network of underground shopping and dining arcades. Here you can pick up a *bentō* (boxed lunch) – perfect for long train rides – and souvenirs from across Japan.

Intermediatheque MUSEUM

(Map p76; 03-5777-8600; www.intermediatheque.jp; 2nd & 3rd fl, JP Tower, 2-7-2 Marunouchi, Chiyoda-ku; 11am-6pm Tue, Wed, Sat & Sun, to 8pm Thu & Fri; JR Yamanote line to Tokyo, Marunouchi exit) FREE Dedicated to interdisciplinary experimentation, Intermediatheque cherry picks from the vast collection of the University of Tokyo (Tōdai) to craft a fascinating and wholly contemporary museum experience. Go from viewing the best ornithological taxidermy collection in Japan to a giant pop-art print or the beautifully encased skeleton of a dinosaur. A handsome Tōdai lecture hall is reconstituted as a forum for events including the playing of 1920s jazz recordings on a gramophone or old movie screenings.

Tokyo International Forum ARCHITECTURE

(東京国際フォーラム; Map p76; 03-5221-9000; www.t-i-forum.co.jp; 3-5-1 Marunouchi, Chiyoda-ku; JR Yamanote line to Yūrakuchō, central exit) FREE This architectural marvel designed by Rafael Viñoly houses a convention and arts centre, with seven auditoriums and a spacious courtyard in which concerts and events are held. The eastern wing looks like a glass ship plying the urban waters; take the lift to the 7th floor and look down on the tiny people below.

Visit for the twice-monthly Ōedo Antique Market (p141) and the daily food trucks serving bargain meals and drinks to local office workers.

National Film Centre ARTS CENTRE

(東京国立近代美術館フィルムセンター; Map p76; www.momat.go.jp/english/nfc/index.html; 3-7-6 Kyōbashi, Chūō-ku; screenings adult/student ¥500/300, gallery ¥200/70; gallery 11am-6.30pm Tue-Sat, check website for screening

TOKYO IN...

Two Days

Start the day with a pilgrimage to Meiji-jingū (p89) in **Harajuku**, followed by a stroll through the pop-culture bazaar Takeshita-dōri (p89). Check out the stunning contemporary architecture along Omote-sandō (p90) before heading to **Shibuya** to see Shibuya Crossing (p87). After dark, hit **Shinjuku** for noodles at Nagi (p127) and a drink in one of the bohemian watering holes of Golden Gai.

The following day, get an early start at Tsukiji Market (p79), followed by a sushi breakfast at one of the market stalls. Visit the landscape garden Hama-rikyū Onshi-teien (p80) then continue up to **Ginza**, home to department stores and art galleries. Catch an act of kabuki at Kabuki-za (p138).

Four Days

On day three, visit the old side of town for some sightseeing in **Asakusa** and **Ueno**, finishing with an afternoon amble through the atmospheric Yanaka neighbourhood and dinner at Shinsuke (p129).

Make the fourth morning a relaxing one and get your onsen on at Ōedo Onsen Monogatari (p110). Spend the afternoon exploring one of Tokyo's more off-beat neighbourhoods, such as bohemian **Shimo-Kitazawa** or anime-mad **Akihabara**. In the evening, head to **Roppongi**. The excellent Mori Art Museum (p81) stays open until 10pm, after which you can head out into the wilds of the neighbourhood's infamous nightlife.

times; S Ginza line to Kyōbashi, exit 1) Here you'll find an archive of Japanese and foreign films, as well as books, periodicals, posters and other materials. There are daily screenings of classic films at bargain prices but few have English subtitles. There are English captions, however, on the worthwhile 7th-floor gallery, which charts the history and evolution of Japanese cinema as well as hosting special movie-themed exhibitions.

Nihombashi (Nihonbashi) BRIDGE
(日本橋; Map p76; www.nihonbashi-tokyo.jp; S Ginza line to Mitsukoshimae, exits B5 & B6) Guarded by bronze lions and dragons this handsome 1911-vintage granite bridge over Nihombashi-gawa is sadly obscured by the overhead expressway. It's notable as the point from which all distances were measured during the Edo period and as the beginning of the great trunk roads (the Tōkaidō, the Nikkō Kaidō etc) that took *daimyō* (feudal lords) between Edo and their home provinces.

Kite Museum MUSEUM
(凧の博物館; Map p76; 03-3271-2465; www.tako.gr.jp/eng/museums_e/tokyo_e.html; 5th fl, 1-12-10 Nihombashi, Chūō-ku; adult/child ¥200/100; 11am-5pm Mon-Sat; S Ginza line to Nihombashi, exit C5) There are 300 or so kites in this small but fascinating museum, located above the restaurant Taimeiken, including brilliantly painted ones based on folk characters, woodblock prints or samurai armour. None are particularly old (they're made of paper, after all), but they're amazing to admire nonetheless. Ask for an English booklet at reception.

Ginza & Tsukiji 銀座・築地

Ginza is Tokyo's answer to New York's Fifth Ave or London's Oxford St. In the 1870s the area was the first neighbourhood in Tokyo to modernise, welcoming Western-style brick buildings, the city's first department stores, gas lamps and other harbingers of globalisation.

Today, other shopping districts rival it in opulence, vitality and popularity, but Ginza retains a distinct snob value. It's therefore a superb place to window-shop and people-watch. Ginza is also Tokyo's original gallery district, and there are still many in the neighbourhood.

The heart of Ginza is the yon-chōme crossing, where Chūō-dōri and Harumi-dōri intersect. Cars are banned from Chūō-dōri on weekend afternoons, creating what locals call 'pedestrian heaven'.

A short walk to the southeast is a luxury commercial centre of a different sort: Tsukiji Market.

MUSEUM DISCOUNTS

Valid for two months, the **Grutt Pass** (www.rekibun.or.jp/grutto; pass ¥2000) has coupons for discounted – and sometimes free – admission to over 70 museums in greater Tokyo, including the biggies (Tokyo National Museum, Edo-Tokyo Museum, Mori Art Museum etc). Purchase the pass at any of the affiliated museums.

★ **Tsukiji Market** MARKET
(東京都中央卸売市場 Tokyo Metropolitan Central Wholesale Produce Market; Map p76; 03-3261-8326; www.tsukiji-market.or.jp; 5-2-1 Tsukiji, Chūō-ku; 5am-1pm; closed Sun, most Wed & all public holidays; S Hibiya line to Tsukiji, exit 1) FREE Fruit, vegetables, flowers and meat are also sold here, but it's seafood – around 2000 tonnes of it traded daily – that Tsukiji is most famous for. The frenetic **inner market** (*jōnai-shijō*) – officially known as the Seafood Intermediate Wholesalers' Area – is slated to move to Toyosu by late 2016; the equally fascinating **outer market** (*jōgai-shijō*) comprising hundreds of food stalls and restaurants, will stay put.

Before setting off here check the market's online calendar to make sure it's open, and for instructions on attending the **tuna auctions**, which start around 5am.

➡ **Seafood Intermediate Wholesalers' Area**
(水産仲卸業者売場; Map p76; 9-11am) This area of the Tsukiji market, which opens to the public from 9am, is where you can see all manner of sea creatures lain out in styrofoam crates. It's a photographer's paradise, but you need to exercise caution to avoid getting in the way. Handcarts and forklifts perform a perfect high-speed choreography – not accounting for the odd tourist.

Don't come in large groups, with small children or in nice shoes. By 11am the crowds have dwindled and the sprinkler trucks plough through to prep the empty market for tomorrow's sale.

VISITING THE TUNA AUCTION

Tsukiji's famous tuna auction is without a doubt one of Tokyo's highlights, but it's only for the hardy. Up to 120 visitors a day are allowed to watch from a gallery between 5.25am and 6.15am. You must be at the **Fish Information Center** (おさかな普及センター; Osakana Fukyū Senta; Map p76; Kachidoki Gate, 6-20-5 Tsukiji, Chūō-ku), by the market's Kachidoki-mon, at 5am to register as a visitor.

It's first-come, first-served, so to ensure you make the cut, it's a good idea to arrive by 4am. Public transport doesn't start up early enough to get you there on time, so you'll have to take a taxi or hang out nearby all night.

The market has banned visitors to the tuna auction in the past, so please be on your best behaviour so as not to give the authorities any reason to do so again. Note that the auction is often closed to visitors during part of December and January due to the holiday rush.

The whole show will pack up in November 2016, when the market is scheduled to move to a new location in Toyosu, an island of reclaimed land in Tokyo Bay; it's not clear yet whether visitors will be allowed in to the auction in the new market.

➡ Tsukiji Outer Market
(場外市場; Jōgai Shijō; Map p76; ⏲5am-2pm; Ⓢ Hibiya line to Tsukiji, exit 1) Here, rows of vendors hawk related goods, such as dried fish and seaweed, rubber boots and crockery. It's far more pedestrian friendly than the inner market, too. There's also the market's Shintō shrine, Namiyoke-jinja, whose deity protects seafarers.

Hama-rikyū Onshi-teien GARDENS
(浜離宮恩賜庭園; Detached Palace Garden; Map p76; www.tokyo-park.or.jp/park/format/index028.html; 1-1 Hama-rikyū-teien, Chūō-ku; adult/child ¥300/free; ⏲9am-5pm; Ⓢ Ōedo line to Shiodome, exit A1) This beautiful garden, one of Tokyo's finest, is all that remains of a shōgunal palace that once extended into the area now occupied by Tsukiji Market. The main features are a large duck pond with an island that's home to a charming tea pavilion, **Nakajima no Ochaya** (中島の御茶屋; Map p76; www.tokyo-park.or.jp/park/format/restaurant028.html; tea set ¥500; ⏲9am-4.30pm), as well as some wonderfully manicured trees (black pine, Japanese apricot, hydrangeas etc), some of which are hundreds of years old.

Ginza Graphic Gallery GALLERY
(ギンザ・グラフィック・ギャラリー; Map p76; ☎03-3571-5206; www.dnp.co.jp/gallery/ggg; 7-7-2 Ginza, Chūō-ku; ⏲11am-7pm Tue-Fri, to 6pm Sat; Ⓢ Ginza line to Ginza, exit A2) FREE Monthly changing exhibits of graphic arts from mostly Japanese artists but with the occasional Western artist. Focuses on advertising and poster art. The annual Tokyo Art Directors Conference exhibition takes place here in July.

Shiseido Gallery GALLERY
(資生堂ギャラリー; Map p76; ☎03-3572-3901; www.shiseido.co.jp/e/gallery/html; Basement fl, 8-8-3 Ginza, Chūō-ku; ⏲11am-7pm Tue-Sat, to 6pm Sun; Ⓢ Ginza line to Shimbashi, exit 1 or 3) FREE The cosmetics company Shiseido runs its experimental art space out of the basement of its Shiseido Parlour complex of cafes and restaurants. An ever-changing selection, particularly of installation pieces, lends itself well to the gallery's high ceiling.

Roppongi & Around 六本木

Once primarily known for its debauched nightlife, Roppongi has reinvented itself over the last decade and now has an air of sophistication (at least during the day).

The transformation started with the opening in 2003 of Roppongi Hills, an enormous, labyrinthine complex that took developer Mori Minoru no fewer than 17 years to plan and construct. He envisioned improving the quality of urban life by centralising home, work and leisure into a utopian microcity.

A grand vision realised? It's a matter of opinion, but similar structures, such as Tokyo Midtown (2005), which now anchors the other side of Roppongi, followed. The latest is Toranomon Hills (2014), another development from Mori Building.

Also part of Roppongi's reinvention was the opening of three major art museums – Mori Art Museum, Suntory Museum of Art and the National Art Center Tokyo – which make up what is known as 'Art Triangle Roppongi'. There are other gallery spaces fitted in between.

Roppongi Hills LANDMARK
(六本木ヒルズ; Map p82; www.roppongihills.com/en; 6-chōme Roppongi, Minato-ku; ⌚11am-11pm; Ⓢ Hibiya line to Roppongi, exit 1) It's over a decade old, but Roppongi Hills remains the gold standard for real-estate developments in Tokyo. The centrepiece of the office, shopping, dining and entertainment complex is the 54-storey Mori Tower, home to the Mori Art Museum and Tokyo City View observatory. Scattered around it is public art such as Louise Bourgeois' giant, spiny **Maman spider sculpture** and the benches-cum-sculptures along Keyakizaka-dōri, as well as the re-created Edo-style **Mohri Garden**.

★ **Mori Art Museum** MUSEUM
(森美術館; Map p82; www.mori.art.museum; 52nd fl, Mori Tower, Roppongi Hills, 6-10-1 Roppongi, Minato-ku; adult/student/child ¥1500/1000/500; ⌚10am-10pm Wed-Mon, to 5pm Tue, Sky Deck 10am-10pm; Ⓢ Hibiya line to Roppongi, exit 1) Atop Mori Tower this gigantic gallery space sports high ceilings, broad views and thematic programs that continue to live up to all the hype associated with Roppongi Hills. Contemporary exhibits are beautifully presented and include superstars of the art world from both Japan and abroad.

Admission to the musem is shared with **Tokyo City View** (東京シティビュー; Map p82; ☎03-6406-6652; www.roppongihills.com/tcv/en; 52nd fl, Mori Tower, Roppongi Hills, 6-10-1 Roppongi, Minato-ku; incl with admission to Mori Art Museum, observatory only adult/student/child ¥1500/1000/500; ⌚10am-11pm Mon-Thu & Sun, to 1am Fri & Sat; Ⓢ Hibiya line to Roppongi, exit 1), which wraps itself around the 52nd floor. From this 250m-high vantage point you can see 360-degree views of the seemingly never-ending city. Weather permitting you can also pop out to the rooftop Sky Deck (additional ¥500; 11am to 8pm) for alfresco views.

Tokyo Midtown LANDMARK
(東京ミッドタウン; Map p82; www.tokyo-midtown.com/en; 9-7 Akasaka, Minato-ku; ⌚11am-11pm; Ⓢ Ōedo line to Roppongi, exit 8) With a similar design and urban-planning blueprint to the one that made Roppongi Hills so successful, this sleek complex brims with sophisticated bars, restaurants, shops, art galleries, a hotel and leafy public spaces. Escalators ascend alongside human-made waterfalls of rock and glass, bridges in the air are lined with backlit *washi* (Japanese handmade paper) and planters full of soaring bamboo draw your eyes through skylights to the lofty heights of the towers above.

Behind the complex is **Hinokichō-kōen**. Formerly a private garden attached to an Edo-period villa, Hinokichō was reopened as a public park. The adjacent **Midtown Garden** is a cherry-tree-lined grassy space that makes a perfect spot for a picnic.

Suntory Museum of Art MUSEUM
(サントリー美術館; Map p82; ☎03-3479-8600; www.suntory.com/sma; 4th fl, Tokyo Midtown, 9-7-4 Akasaka, Minato-ku; admission varies, free for children & junior-high-school students; ⌚10am-6pm Sun-Thu, to 8pm Fri & Sat; Ⓢ Ōedo line to Roppongi, exit 8) Since its original 1961 opening, the Suntory Museum of Art has subscribed to an underlying philosophy of lifestyle art. Rotating exhibitions focus on the beauty of useful things: Japanese ceramics, lacquerware, glass, dyeing, weaving and such. Its current Midtown digs, designed by architect Kuma Kengō, are both understated and breathtaking.

21_21 Design Sight MUSEUM
(21_21デザインサイト; Map p82; ☎03-3475-2121; www.2121designsight.jp; Tokyo Midtown, 9-7-6 Akasaka, Minato-ku; adult/child ¥1000/free; ⌚11am-8pm Wed-Mon; Ⓢ Ōedo line to Roppongi, exit 8) An exhibition and discussion space dedicated to all forms of design, the 21_21 Design Sight acts as a beacon for local art enthusiasts, whether they be designers themselves or simply onlookers. The striking concrete and glass building, bursting out of the ground at sharp angles, was designed by Pritzker Prize–winning architect Andō Tadao.

Tokyo Midtown Design Hub GALLERY
(Map p82; ☎03-6743-3776; www.designhub.jp; 5th fl, Midtown Tower, 9-7-1 Akasaka, Minato-ku; Ⓢ Ōedo line to Roppongi, exit 8) FREE Tokyo Midtown prides itself on being at the cutting edge of contemporary Japanese design. This gallery, tucked away on the 5th floor of Midtown Tower, hosts interesting exhibitions around this theme. Some exhibitions tackle social issues, while others facilitate dialogue between disciplines.

National Art Center Tokyo MUSEUM
(国立新美術館; Map p82; ☎03-5777-8600; www.nact.jp; 7-22-1 Roppongi, Minato-ku; admission varies by exhibition; ⌚10am-6pm Wed, Thu & Sat-Mon, to 8pm Fri; Ⓢ Chiyoda line to Nogizaka, exit 6) Designed by Kurokawa Kishō, this architectural beauty has no permanent collection, but boasts Japan's largest exhibition space

Roppongi & Around

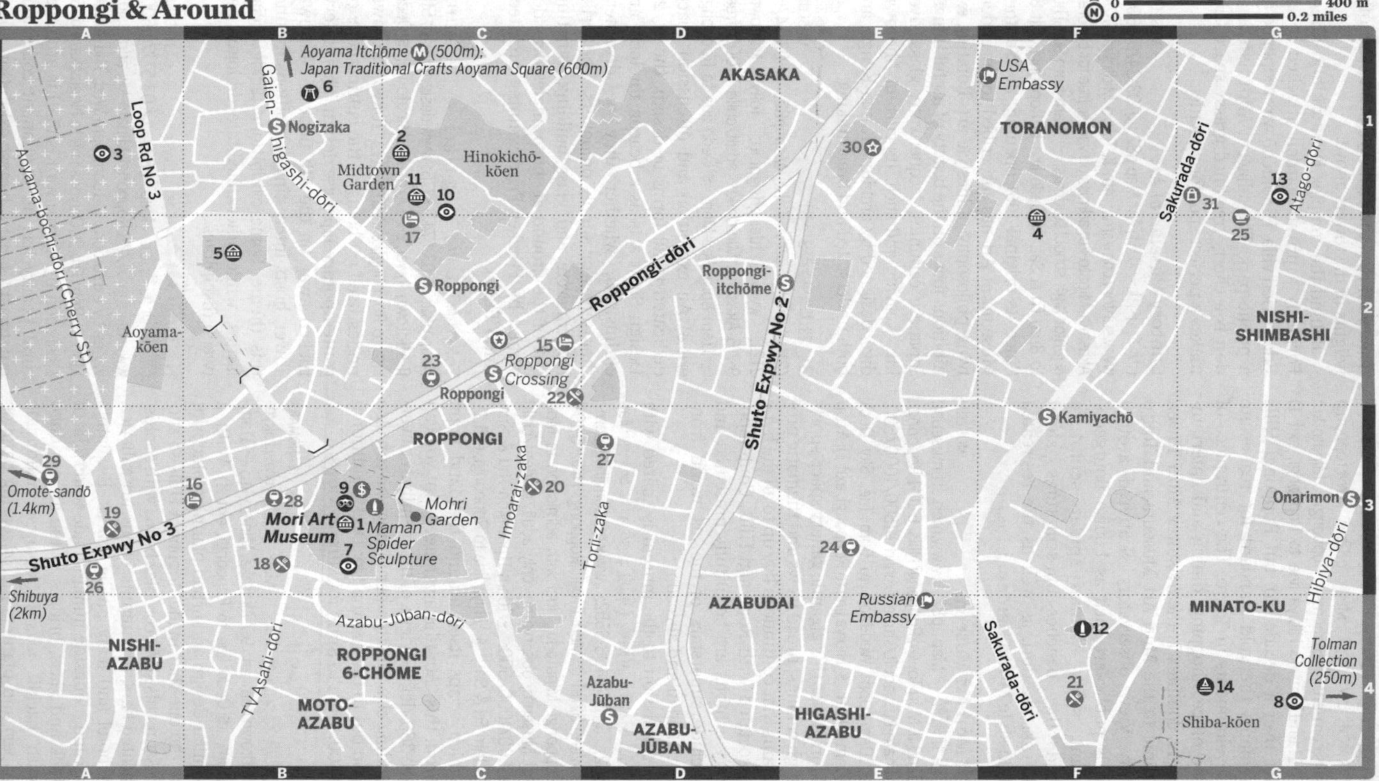

Roppongi & Around

for visiting shows, which have included Renoir, Modigliani and the Japan Media Arts Festival. Apart from exhibitions, a visit here is recommended to admire the building's awesome undulating glass facade, its cafes atop giant inverted cones and the great gift shop Souvenir From Tokyo (p142).

Nogi-jinja SHINTO SHRINE

(乃木神社; Map p82; www.nogijinja.or.jp; 8-11-27 Akasaka, Minato-ku; 9am-5pm; S Chiyoda line to Nogizaka, exit 1) This shrine honours General Nogi Maresuke, a famed commander in the Russo-Japanese War. Hours after Emperor Meiji's funerary procession in 1912, Nogi and his faithful wife committed ritual suicide, following their master into death. An **antiques flea market** is held on the shrine grounds on the fourth Sunday of each month (9am to 4pm).

Aoyama Rei-en CEMETERY

(青山霊園; Map p82; 2-32-2 Minami-Aoyama, Minato-ku; S Chiyoda line to Nogizaka, exit 5 or Ginza line to Gaienmae, exit 1B) The cherry-tree-lined paths of Japan's first public cemetery are used by locals as shortcuts through the neighbourhood and as a place for picnics during *hanami* (cherry-blossom viewing) season. Accessible either from Roppongi or Aoyama it's a peaceful place for a stroll and the elaborate stone-carved tombs are rather impressive.

Tokyo Tower TOWER

(東京タワー; Map p82; www.tokyotower.co.jp/english; 4-2-8 Shiba-kōen, Minato-ku; adult/child main deck ¥900/400, plus special deck ¥1600/800; observation deck 9am-10pm; S Ōedo line to Akabanebashi, Akabanebashi exit) Something of a shameless tourist trap, this 1958-vintage tower remains a beloved symbol of the city's post-WWII rebirth. At 333m it's 13m taller than the Eiffel Tower, which was the inspiration for its design. It's also painted bright orange and white in order to comply with international aviation safety regulations.

The main observation deck is at 145m (there's another 'special' deck at 250m). There are loftier views at the more expensive Tokyo Sky Tree.

Zōjō-ji BUDDHIST TEMPLE

(増上寺; Map p82; 03-3432-1431; www.zojoji.or.jp/en/index.html; 4-7-35 Shiba-kōen, Minato-ku; dawn-dusk; S Ōedo line to Daimon, exit A3) FREE One of the most important temples of the Jōdō (Pure Land) sect of Buddhism, Zōjō-ji dates from 1393 and was the funerary temple of the Tokugawa regime. It's an impressive sight, particularly the main gate, **Sangedatsumon** (解脱門; Map p82), constructed in 1605, with its three sections designed to symbolise the three stages one must pass through to achieve nirvana. The **Daibonsho** (Big Bell; 1673) is a 15-tonne

LOCAL KNOWLEDGE

CHERRY-BLOSSOM VIEWING

When it comes to cherry-blossom viewing, parks such as Ueno-kōen (p99), Yoyogi-kōen (p89), Inokashira-kōen (p93) and Shinjuku-gyoen (p93) are obvious choices. Here are two spots known only by locals that blissfully fly under the radar in spring:

Meguro-gawa: Naka-Meguro's canal is lined with *sakura* (cherry trees) that form an awesome pale pink canopy. Local restaurants set up food stalls and, rather than staking out a seat, visitors stroll under the blossoms, hot wine in hand.

Aoyama Rei-en (p83): This sprawling cemetery, with many famous inhabitants, comes alive with cherry blossoms that blanket the tombs and statues. It's a pretty, if unusual, *hanami* spot. Why should the living have all the fun?

whopper considered one of the great three bells of the Edo period.

Musée Tomo MUSEUM
(智美術館; Map p82; 03-5733-5131; www.musee-tomo.or.jp; 4-1-35 Toranomon, Minato-ku; adult/student ¥1000/500; 11am-6pm Tue-Sun; S Hibiya line to Kamiyachō, exit 4B) One of Tokyo's most elegant and tasteful museums is named after Kikuchi Tomo, whose collection of contemporary Japanese ceramics wowed them in Washington and London before finally being exhibited at home. Exhibitions change every few months but can be relied on to be atmospheric and beautiful.

Toranomon Hills LANDMARK
(Map p82; http://toranomonhills.com; 1-23 Toranomon, Minato-ku; ; S Ginza line to Toranomon, exit 1) Opened in June 2014, the 52-storey, 247m Toranomon Hills complex, topped by the Andaz Hotel, is Mori Buildings' latest modification of Tokyo's cityscape. Apart from the hotel, there are pleasant places to eat and drink and a small public garden.

The complex sits at the head of the new tree-lined boulevard Shin-Tora-dōri (also referred to as General MacArthur Rd), a section of Circular Route 2, a major highway construction project that will link Ariake on Odaiba through to Yotsuya and Kanda in time for the 2020 Olympics.

Ebisu & Meguro 恵比寿・目黒

Named for the prominent beer manufacturer that once provided a lifeline for most of the neighbourhood's residents, Ebisu has morphed into a hip neighbourhood with a generous smattering of excellent restaurants and bars.

A short zip along the 'Skywalk' from Ebisu Station takes you to **Yebisu Garden Place** (恵比寿ガーデンプレイス; Map p86; www.gardenplace.jp; 4-20 Ebisu, Shibuya-ku; JR Yamanote line to Ebisu, east exit), another one of Tokyo's 'microcities' with a string of shops and restaurants, office buildings and two museums. The large central plaza regularly hosts events and markets on weekends.

One stop south of Ebisu is Meguro, another mid-sized node on the JR Yamanote line. Meguro is off the tourist trail, but has a handful of worthwhile sights. It's also known as Tokyo's interior-design district, as dozens of interior shops line its main drag, Meguro-dōri.

Beyond Ebisu and Meguro are some of Tokyo's more attractive residential neighbourhoods, including **Daikanyama** and **Naka-Meguro**. Daikanyama is an upscale residential enclave with sidewalk cafes, fashionable boutiques and an unhurried pace. Neighboring Naka-Meguro is Daikanyama's bohemian little sister, home to secondhand shops and secret lounge bars.

Tokyo Metropolitan Museum of Photography MUSEUM
(東京都写真美術館; Map p86; 03-3280-0099; www.syabi.com; 1-13-3 Mita, Meguro-ku; admission ¥600-1650; 10am-6pm Tue, Wed, Sat & Sun, to 8pm Thu & Fri; JR Yamanote line to Ebisu, east exit) Tokyo's principal photography museum is closed through August 2016 for renovations. In addition to drawing on its extensive collection, the museum also hosts travelling shows (usually several exhibitions happen simultaneously; ticket prices depend on how many you see). The museum is at the far end of Yebisu Garden Place, on the right side if you're coming from Ebisu Station.

Beer Museum Yebisu MUSEUM
(エビスビール記念館; Map p86; 03-5423-7255; www.sapporoholdings.jp/english/guide/yebisu; 4-20-1 Ebisu, Shibuya-ku; 11am-7pm Tue-Sun; JR Yamanote line to Ebisu, east exit) FREE Photos, vintage bottles and posters document the rise of Yebisu, and beer in general, in

Japan at this small museum located where the actual Yebisu brewery stood until 1988. At the 'tasting salon' you can sample four kinds of Yebisu beer (¥400 each). It's behind the Mitsukoshi department store at Yebisu Garden Place.

Yamatane Museum of Art MUSEUM
(山種美術館; Map p86; ☎03-5777-8600; www.yamatane-museum.or.jp; 3-12-36 Hiroo, Shibuya-ku; adult/student/child ¥1000/800/free, special exhibits extra; ⏰10am-5pm Tue-Sun; 🚆JR Yamanote line to Ebisu, west exit) When Western ideas entered Japan following the Meiji Restoration (1868), many artists set out to master oil and canvas. Others poured new energy into *nihonga* – Japanese-style painting, usually done with mineral pigments on silk or paper – and the masters are represented here. From the collection of 1800 works, a small number are displayed in thematic exhibitions.

Meguro-gawa RIVER
(目黒川; Map p86; Ⓢ Hibiya line to Naka-Meguro) Lined with cherry trees and a walking path, the Meguro-gawa (not so much a river as a canal) is what gives the neighbourhood Naka-Meguro its unlikely village vibe. On either side you'll find all manner of quirky boutiques, plus cafes overlooking the water.

Tokyo Metropolitan Teien Art Museum MUSEUM
(東京都庭園美術館; Map p86; www.teien-art-museum.ne.jp; 5-21-9 Shirokanedai, Minato-ku; admission varies; ⏰10am-6pm, closed 2nd & 4th Wed each month; 🚆JR Yamanote line to Meguro, east exit) Although the Teien museum hosts regular art exhibitions – usually of decorative arts – its appeal lies principally in the building itself: it's an art-deco structure, a former princely estate built in 1933, designed by French architect Henri Rapin. The museum reopened in late 2014 after a lengthy renovation and now includes a modern annexe designed by artist Sugimoto Hiroshi.

Institute for Nature Study PARK
(自然教育園; Shizen Kyōiku-en; Map p86; ☎03-3441-7176; www.ins.kahaku.go.jp; 5-21-5 Shirokane-dai, Meguro-ku; adult/child ¥310/free; ⏰9am-4.30pm Tue-Sun Sep-Apr, to 5pm Tue-Sun May-Aug, last entry 4pm; 🚆JR Yamanote line to Meguro, east exit) What would Tokyo look like left to its own natural devices? Since 1949 this park, affiliated with the Tokyo National Museum, has let the local flora go wild. There are wonderful walks through its forests, marshes and ponds. No more than 300 people are allowed in at a time, which makes for an even more peaceful setting.

Meguro Parasitological Museum MUSEUM
(目黒寄生虫館; Map p86; ☎03-3716-1264; http://kiseichu.org; 4-1-1 Shimo-Meguro, Meguro-ku; ⏰10am-5pm Tue-Sun; 🚌2 or 7 from Meguro Station to Ōtori-jinja-mae, 🚆JR Yamanote line to Meguro, west exit) FREE Here's one for fans of the grotesque: this small museum was established in 1953 by a local doctor concerned by the increasing number of parasites he was encountering due to unsanitary postwar conditions. The grisly centrepiece is an 8.8m-long tapeworm found in the body of a 40-year-old Yokohama man.

The museum is about a 1km walk from Meguro Station; the entrance is on the ground floor of a small apartment building, just uphill from the Ōtori-jinja-mae bus stop.

Sengaku-ji BUDDHIST TEMPLE
(泉岳寺; Map p72; www.sengakuji.or.jp; 2-11-1 Takanawa, Minato-ku; ⏰7am-6pm Apr-Sep, to 5pm Oct-Mar; Ⓢ Asakusa line to Sengaku-ji, exit A2) The story of the 47 *rōnin* (masterless samurai) who avenged their master, Lord Asano – put to death after being tricked into pulling a sword on a rival – is legend in Japan. They were condemned to commit seppuku (ritual disembowelment) and their remains were

WORTH A TRIP

SHIMO-KITAZAWA

If hippies – not bureaucrats – ran Tokyo, the city would look a lot more like Shimo-Kitazawa (下北沢). This neighbourhood of narrow streets has been a favourite haunt of generations of students, musicians and artists. There's an active underground music and theatre scene, plus loads of quirky boutiques, secondhand shops, cafes and bars. The neighbourhood's main drag, the Minami-guchi shōtengai (market street), in front of the train station's south exit, is a good place to start exploring. For maps and more information, see www.shimokitazawahills.com.

Both the Odakyū line (from Shinjuku, seven minutes; ¥154) and the Keiō Inokashira line (from Shibuya, three minutes; ¥124) stop at Shimo-Kitazawa.

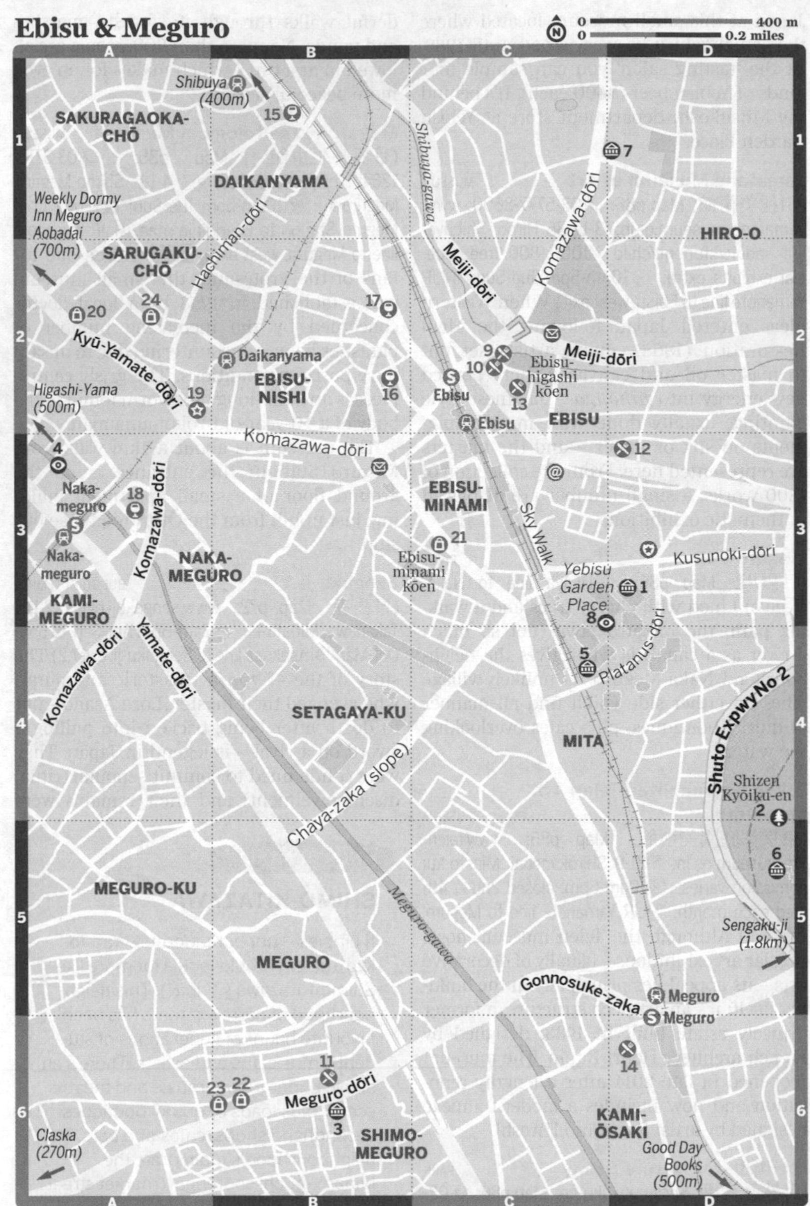

buried at this temple. It's a sombre place, with fresh incense rising from the tombs, placed there by visitors moved by the samurais' loyalty.

Shibuya & Around 渋谷

Shibuya is the centre of the city's teen culture, and its brightly dressed, bleached-hair denizens aren't shy about living loud. If a local friend asks to meet you at Shibuya, you'll

Ebisu & Meguro

Sights
1 Beer Museum Yebisu D3
2 Institute for Nature Study D4
3 Meguro Parasitological Museum B6
4 Meguro-gawa A3
5 Tokyo Metropolitan Museum of Photography C4
6 Tokyo Metropolitan Teien Art Museum D5
7 Yamatane Museum of Art D1
8 Yebisu Garden Place C3

Eating
9 Afuri C2
10 Ebisu-yokochō C2
11 Ganko Dako B6
12 Ippo D3
13 Ouca C2
14 Tonki D6

Drinking & Nightlife
15 Air B1
16 Buri B2
17 Enjoy House B2
18 Nakame Takkyū Lounge A3

Entertainment
19 Unit A2

Shopping
20 Daikanyama T-Site A2
21 Kapital C3
22 Meguro Interior Shops Community (MISC) B6
23 Meister B6
24 Okura A2

probably gather at **Hachikō** (ハチ公) plaza in front of the station. The always-buzzing Shibuya Crossing leads from the station to the pedestrian street Center-gai, Shibuya's main artery.

On the east side of the station, the 34-floor Shibuya Hikarie building, which opened in 2012, is full of upmarket shops and restaurants that threaten to attract grown-up sophisticates to Shibuya.

★ Shibuya Crossing — STREET

(渋谷スクランブル交差点; Shibuya Scramble; Map p88; JR Yamanote line to Shibuya, Hachikō exit) Rumoured to be the world's busiest, this intersection in front of Shibuya Station is famously known as 'The Scramble'. It's an awesome spectacle of giant video screens and neon, guaranteed to give you a 'Wow – I'm in Tokyo!' feeling. People come from all directions at once – sometimes over a thousand with every light change – yet still manage to dodge each other with a practiced, nonchalant agility.

Hachikō Statue — STATUE

(ハチ公像; Map p88; Hachikō Plaza; JR Yamanote line to Shibuya, Hachikō exit) Come meet Tokyo's most famous pooch, Hachikō. This Akita dog came to Shibuya Station everyday to meet his master, a professor, returning from work. The professor died in 1925, but Hachikō kept coming to the station until his own death 10 years later. The story became legend and a small statue was erected in the dog's memory in front of Shibuya Station.

Myth of Tomorrow — PUBLIC ART

(明日の神話; Asu no Shinwa; Map p88; JR Yamanote line to Shibuya, Hachikō exit) Okamoto Tarō's mural, *Myth of Tomorrow* (1967), was commissioned by a Mexican luxury hotel but went missing two years later. It finally turned up in 2003 and, in 2008, the haunting 30m-long work, which depicts the atomic bomb exploding over Hiroshima, was installed inside Shibuya Station. It's on the 2nd floor, on the way to the Inokashira line.

Shibuya Center-gai — STREET

(渋谷センター街; Shibuya Sentā-gai; Map p88; JR Yamanote line to Shibuya, Hachikō exit) Shibuya's main drag is closed to cars and chock-a-block with fast-food joints and high-street fashion shops. At night, lit bright as day, with a dozen competing soundtracks (coming from who knows where), wares spilling onto the streets, shady touts and strutting teens, it feels like a block party – or Tokyo's version of a classic Asian night market.

Dōgenzaka — NEIGHBOURHOOD

(道玄坂; Love Hotel Hill; Map p88; JR Yamanote line to Shibuya, Hachikō exit) Dōgenzaka, named for a 13th-century highway robber, is a maze of narrow streets. Home to one of Tokyo's largest clusters of love hotels (hotels for amorous encounters), it's also known as Love Hotel Hill. It's more than a little seedy, but some of the older hotels have fantastical (if not a bit chipped and crumbling) facades.

Spain-zaka — STREET

(スペイン坂; Map p88; JR Yamanote line to Shibuya, Hachikō exit) Shibuya's most atmospheric little alley is typical Tokyo bricolage with a Mediterranean flavour; a mismatch of architecture styles, cutesy clothing stores and a melting pot of restaurants all along a narrow, winding brick lane.

Shibuya

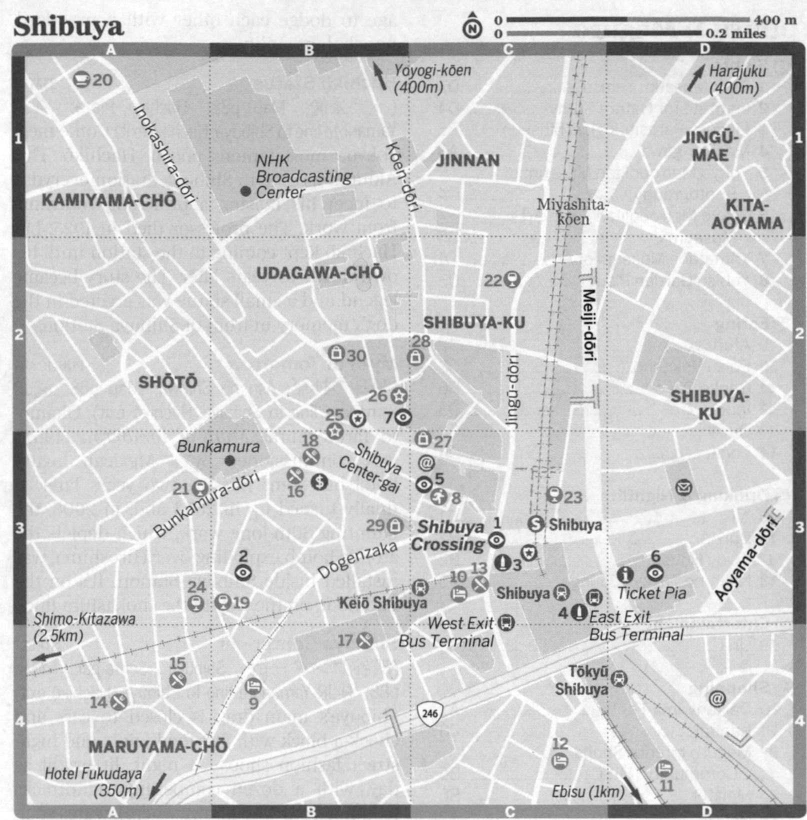

Shibuya Hikarie BUILDING

(渋谷ヒカリエ; Map p88; ☎03-5468-5892; www.hikarie.jp; 2-21-1 Shibuya, Shibuya-ku; JR Yamanote line to Shibuya, east exit) This glistening 34-storey tower, which opened in 2012, is just the first step in what promises to be a massive redesign of Shibuya. Sandwiched between the shops on the lower floors and the offices on the upper floors are a couple of worthwhile cultural sights on the 8th floor.

➡ **d47 Museum**

(Map p88; www.hikarie8.com/d47museum; 8th fl, Hikarie bldg, 2-21-1 Shibuya, Shibuya-ku; 11am-8pm; JR Yamanote line to Shibuya, east exit) FREE Lifestyle brand D&D Department combs the country for the platonic ideals of the utterly ordinary: the perfect broom, bottle opener or salt shaker (to name a few examples). See rotating exhibitions of its latest finds from all 47 prefectures at this one-room museum. The excellent d47 Design Travel shop is next door.

➡ **Tomio Koyama Gallery**

(小山登美夫ギャラリー; Map p88; www.tomiokoyamagallery.com; 8th fl, Hikarie bldg, 2-21-1 Shibuya, Shibuya-ku; 11am-8pm; JR Yamanote line to Shibuya, east exit) FREE This is a branch of one of Tokyo's more influential contemporary art galleries, which shows both Japanese and international artists.

Purikura no Mecca ARCADE

(プリクラのメッカ; Map p88; 1-23-10 Jinnan, Shibuya-ku; purikura ¥400; 10am-9pm; JR Yamanote line to Shibuya, Hachikō exit) It's easy to see why teens get sucked into the cult of *purikura* ('print club', aka photo booths): the digitally enhanced photos automatically airbrush away blemishes and add doe eyes and long lashes for good measure (so you come out looking like an anime version of yourself). After primping and posing, decorate the images on screen with touch pens.

Shibuya

Harajuku 原宿

Harajuku is Tokyo's catwalk, where the city's fashionistas come to shop and show off. But not everything here is about frippery and frivolity: there's also Tokyo's signature Shintō shrine, Meiji-jingū, plus excellent art museums.

Fans of contemporary architecture will want to check out Omote-sandō – the boulevard lined with boutiques designed by Japan's award-winning architects.

★Meiji-jingū SHINTO SHRINE

(明治神宮; Map p72; www.meijijingu.or.jp; 1-1 Yoyogi Kamizono-chō, Shibuya-ku; dawn-dusk; JR Yamanote line to Harajuku, Omote-sandō exit) FREE Tokyo's grandest Shintō shrine is dedicated to the Emperor Meiji and Empress Shōken. Constructed in 1920, the shrine was destroyed in WWII air raids and rebuilt in 1958; however, unlike so many of Japan's postwar reconstructions, Meiji-jingū has an authentic feel. The towering 12m wooden *torii* gate that marks the entrance was created from a 1500-year-old Taiwanese cyprus.

➡ Meiji-jingū Gyoen

(明治神宮御苑; Inner Garden; Map p90; admission ¥500; 9am-4.30pm, to 4pm Nov-Feb; JR Yamanote line to Harajuku, Omote-sandō exit) On the grounds of Meiji-jingū is the strolling garden, Meiji-jingū Gyoen. It was once a feudal estate; after it came under imperial control, the Meiji Emperor himself designed the garden as a gift to the Empress Shōken. There are peaceful walks, a good dose of privacy on weekdays, and spectacular irises in June.

Yoyogi-kōen PARK

(代々木公園; Map p72; JR Yamanote line to Harajuku, Omote-sandō exit) If it's a sunny and warm weekend afternoon you can count on there being a crowd lazing around the large grassy expanse that is Yoyogi-kōen. You can also usually find revellers and noisemakers of all stripes, from hula-hoopers to African drum circles to a group of retro greasers dancing around a boom box. It's an excellent place for a picnic and probably the only place in the city where you can reasonably toss a frisbee without fear of hitting someone.

Takeshita-dōri STREET

(竹下通り; Map p90; JR Yamanote line to Harajuku, Takeshita exit) This is Tokyo's famous teen-fashion bazaar, where trendy duds sit alongside the trappings of various fashion subcultures (colourful tutus for the *decora;* Victorian dresses for the Gothic Lolitas). Be

Harajuku & Around

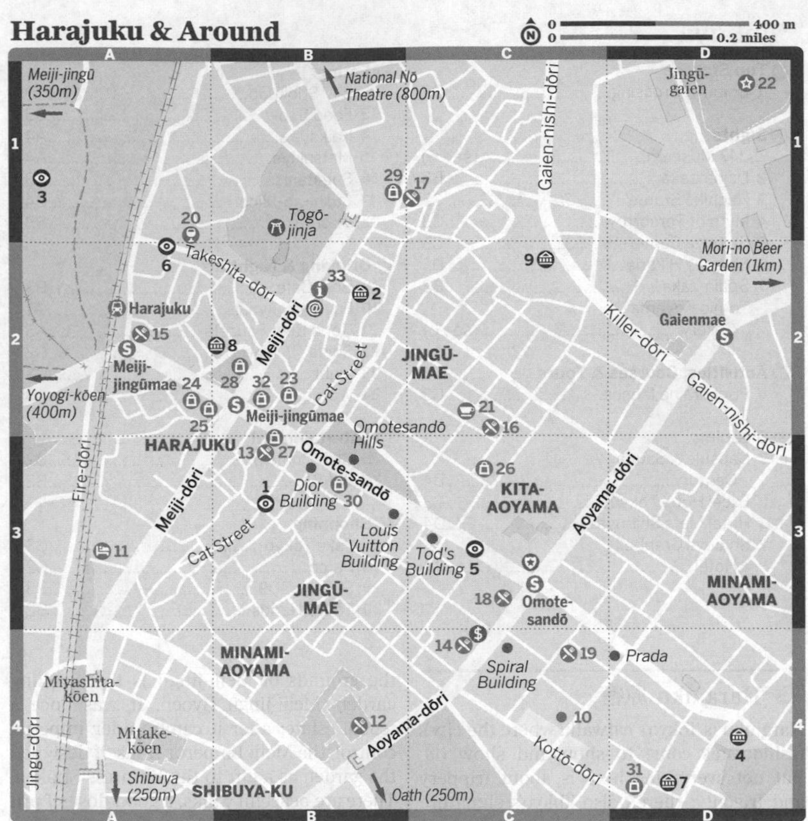

warned: this pedestrian alley is a pilgrimage site for teens from all over Japan, which means it can get packed.

Omote-sandō STREET

(表参道; Map p90; Ⓢ Ginza line to Omote-sandō, exits A3 & B4, 🚉 JR Yamanote line to Harajuku, Omote-sandō exit) This regal boulevard was originally designed as the official approach to Meiji-jingū. Now it's a fashionable strip lined with high-end boutiques. Those designer shops come in designer buildings, which means Omote-sandō is also one of the best places in the city to see contemporary architecture.

Ukiyo-e Ōta Memorial Museum of Art MUSEUM

(浮世絵太田記念美術館; Map p90; ☎03-3403-0880; www.ukiyoe-ota-muse.jp; 1-10-10 Jingūmae, Shibuya-ku; adult ¥700-1000, child free; ⏱10.30am-5.30pm Tue-Sun, closed 27th to end of month; 🚉 JR Yamanote line to Harajuku, Omote-sandō exit) This small, peaceful museum houses the excellent *ukiyo-e* (woodblock prints) collection of Ōta Seizo, the former head of the Toho Life Insurance Company. Seasonal, thematic exhibitions are easily digested in an hour and usually include a few works by masters such as Hokusai and Hiroshige.

The shop in the basement sells beautifully printed *tenugui* (traditional hand-dyed thin cotton towels).

Cat Street STREET

(キャットストリート; Map p90; 🚉 JR Yamanote line to Harajuku, Omote-sandō exit) Had enough of crowded Harajuku? Exit, stage right, for Cat Street, a windy road lined with a mish-mash of boutiques and more room to move. The retail architecture is also quite a spectacle, as this is where smaller brands strike their monuments to consumerism if they can't afford to do so on the main drag.

Harajuku & Around

Design Festa GALLERY

(デザインフェスタ; Map p90; ☎03-3479-1442; www.designfestagallery.com; 3-20-2 Jingūmae, Shibuya-ku; ⏰11am-7pm; 🚉JR Yamanote line to Harajuku, Takeshita exit) FREE Design Festa has been a leader in Tokyo's DIY art scene for over a decade. The madhouse building itself is worth a visit; it's always evolving. Inside there are a dozen small galleries rented by the day. Design Festa also sponsors a twice-yearly exhibition, actually Asia's largest art fair, at Tokyo Big Sight.

Watari Museum of Contemporary Art MUSEUM

(ワタリウム美術館; Watari-Um; Map p90; ☎03-3402-3001; www.watarium.co.jp; 3-7-6 Jingūmae, Shibuya-ku; adult/student ¥1000/800; ⏰11am-7pm Tue & Thu-Sun, to 9pm Wed; Ⓢ Ginza line to Gaienmae, exit 3) This progressive and often provocative museum was built in 1990 to a design by Swiss architect Mario Botta. Exhibits range from retrospectives of works by established art-world figures (such as Yayoi Kusama and Nam June Paik) to graffiti and landscape artists – with some exhibitions spilling onto the surrounding streets.

There's an excellent art bookstore, **On Sundays** (⏰11am-8pm), in the basement.

Nezu Museum MUSEUM

(根津美術館; Map p90; ☎03-3400-2536; www.nezu-muse.or.jp; 6-5-1 Minami-Aoyama, Minato-ku; adult/student/child ¥1000/800/free, special exhibitions ¥200 extra; ⏰10am-5pm Tue-Sun; Ⓢ Ginza line to Omote-sandō, exit A5) Nezu Museum offers a striking blend of old and new: a renowned collection of Japanese, Chinese and Korean antiquities in a gallery space designed by contemporary architect Kuma Kengo. Select items from the extensive collection are displayed in seasonal exhibitions.

Taro Okamoto Memorial Museum MUSEUM

(岡本太郎記念館; Map p90; http://taro-okamoto.or.jp; 6-1-19 Minami-Aoyama, Minato-ku; adult/child ¥620/310; ⏰10am-6pm Wed-Mon; Ⓢ Ginza line to Omote-sandō, exit A5) A painter and sculptor, Okamoto Tarō was Japan's most recognised artist from the post-WWII period, a rare avant-garde figure with mass

LOCAL KNOWLEDGE

HARAJUKU FESTIVALS

During the warmer months, festivals take place most weekends at the plaza across from Yoyogi-kōen (p89).

appeal. His works are both playful and sinister, life-affirming and chaotic. This small museum, which includes a sculpture garden, is inside the artist's former home.

Shinjuku & West Tokyo 新宿

Here in Shinjuku, much of what makes Tokyo tick is crammed into one busy district: upscale department stores, anachronistic shanty bars, buttoned-up government offices, swarming crowds, streetside video screens, hostess clubs, hidden shrines and soaring skyscrapers.

At the heart of Shinjuku is the sprawling train station, which acts as a nexus for over three million commuters each day, making it the busiest in the world. The west side of the station, called **Nishi-Shinjuku**, is a perfectly planned expanse of gridded streets and soaring corporate towers. Tokyo's municipal government moved here in 1991 from Yūrakuchō; the newest landmark is the elliptical, webbed **Mode Gakuen Cocoon Tower** (Map p94; 1-7-3 Nishi-shinjuku, Shinjuku-ku; JR Yamanote line to Shinjuku, west exit).

The east side of Shinjuku is one of Tokyo's largest – and liveliest – entertainment districts. It's also home to the city's biggest red-light district, Kabukichō.

The JR Chūō line heads west of Shinjuku to some of Tokyo's original commuter towns, characterised by classic 1960s shopping arcades and an ambivalent, if not dismissive, attitude towards the development seen elsewhere in the city. Here you'll find the charming suburb of Kichijōji, oft-voted the best place to live in Tokyo, and the Ghibli Museum just beyond.

WORTH A TRIP

RIKUGI-EN

Tokyo's most beautiful garden, **Rikugi-en** (六義園; Map p72; 6-16-3 Hon-Komagome, Bunkyō-ku; adult/child ¥300/free; 9am-5pm; JR Yamanote line to Komagome, south exit) was designed to reflect the aesthetic of traditional Waka poetry. Built by a feudal lord in 1702, it has walkways that pass over hills and stone bridges, and by trickling streams and scenes inspired by famous poems. There's a teahouse where you can drink *matcha* (powdered green tea; ¥500) alfresco while overlooking the garden's central pond.

★Tokyo Metropolitan Government Offices — BUILDING

(東京都庁; Tokyo Tochō; Map p94; www.metro.tokyo.jp/ENGLISH/TMG/observat.htm; 2-8-1 Nishi-Shinjuku, Shinjuku-ku; observatories 9.30am-11pm; S Ōedo line to Tochōmae, exit A4) FREE Tokyo's seat of power, designed by Tange Kenzō, looms large and looks somewhat like a pixelated cathedral. Take an elevator from the ground floor of Building 1 to one of the twin 202m-high observatories for panoramic views over the never-ending cityscape (the views are virtually the same from either tower). On a clear day, look west for a glimpse of Mt Fuji.

Shinjuku I-Land — PUBLIC ART

(新宿アイランド; Map p94; 6-5-1 Nishi-Shinjuku, Shinjuku-ku; S Marunouchi line to Nishi-Shinjuku) An otherwise ordinary office complex, Shinjuku I-Land (1995) is home to more than a dozen public artworks, including one of Robert Indiana's *Love* sculptures and two *Tokyo Brushstroke* sculptures by Roy Liechtenstein. The courtyard, with stonework by Giulio Paolini and a dozen restaurants, makes for an attractive lunch or coffee stop.

Japanese Sword Museum — MUSEUM

(刀剣博物館; Map p72; www.touken.or.jp; 4-25-10 Yoyogi, Shibuya-ku; adult/student/child ¥600/300/free; 9am-4.30pm Tue-Sun; Keiō New line to Hatsudai, east exit) In 1948, after American forces returned the *katana* (Japanese swords) they'd confiscated during the postwar occupation, the national Ministry of Education established a society, and this museum, to preserve the feudal art of Japanese sword-making. There are dozens of swords on display here, with English explanations throughout.

The museum's location, in a residential neighbourhood, is not obvious. Head down Kōshū-kaidō to the Park Hyatt and make a left, then take the second right under the highway, followed by another quick right and left in succession. There's a map on the website.

Kabukichō — NEIGHBOURHOOD

(歌舞伎町; Map p94; JR Yamanote line to Shinjuku, east exit) Tokyo's most notorious red-light district, which covers several blocks north of Yasukuni-dōri, was famously named for a kabuki theatre that was never built. Instead you'll find an urban theatre of a different sort playing out in the neighbourhood's soaplands (bathhouses just shy of anti-prostitution laws), peep shows, cabarets, love hotels and fetish bars. It's generally safe to walk through, though men and women both may attract unwanted attention – best not to go alone.

Hanazono-jinja SHINTO SHRINE

(花園神社; Map p94; 5-17 Shinjuku, Shinjuku-ku; 24hr; Marunouchi line to Shinjuku-sanchōme, exits B10 & E2) During the day merchants from nearby Kabukichō come to this Shintō shrine to pray for the solvency of their business ventures. At night, despite signs asking revellers to refrain, drinking and merrymaking carries over from the nearby bars onto the stairs here.

Shinjuku-gyoen PARK

(新宿御苑; Map p94; 3350-0151; www.env.go.jp/garden/shinjukugyoen; 11 Naito-chō, Shinjuku-ku; adult/child ¥200/50; 9am-4.30pm Tue-Sun; Marunouchi line to Shinjuku-gyoenmae, exit 1) Though Shinjuku-gyoen was designed as an imperial retreat (completed 1906), it's now definitively a park for everyone. The wide lawns make it a favourite for urbanites in need of a quick escape from the hurly-burly of city life. Don't miss the recently renovated greenhouse, with its giant lily pads and perfectly formed orchids, and the cherry blossoms in spring.

Harmonica-yokochō MARKET

(ハーモニカ横丁; http://hamoyoko.com; 1-2 Kichijōji-Honchō, Musashino-shi; JR Chūō line to Kichijōji, north exit) With low ceilings and red paper *chōchin* (lanterns), this old covered market has a definite vintage feel. Some of the vendors – the fish mongers, for example – are equally old-school, but there are some trendy boutiques and bars here too. There's a morning market every third Sunday (7am to 10am). Look for the entrance across the street from Kichijōji Station's north exit.

Inokashira-kōen PARK

(井の頭公園; www.kensetsu.metro.tokyo.jp/seibuk/inokashira/index.html; 1-18-31 Gotenyama, Musashino-shi; JR Chūō line to Kichijōji, Kōen exit) One of Tokyo's best parks, Inokashira-kōen has a big pond in the middle with rowboats and swan-shaped pedal boats for rent. There's also an island with an ancient shrine to the sea goddess Benzaiten. Walk straight from the Kōen exit of Kichijōji Station, cross at the light and veer right at Marui ('0101') department store; the park is at the end of the lane. Along the way, you'll pass shops selling takeaway items such as *yakitori* (grilled chicken skewers) and hot dogs.

★Ghibli Museum MUSEUM

(ジブリ美術館; www.ghibli-museum.jp; 1-1-83 Shimo-Renjaku, Mitaka-shi; adult ¥1000, child ¥100-700; 10am-6pm Wed-Mon; JR Chūō line to Mitaka, south exit) Master animator Miyazaki Hayao, whose Studio Ghibli produced *Princess Mononoke* and *Spirited Away*, designed this museum. Fans will enjoy the original sketches; kids, even if they're not familiar with the movies, will fall in love with the fairy-tale atmosphere (and the big cat bus). Don't miss the original 20-minute animated short playing on the 1st floor.

Tickets must be purchased in advance, and you must choose the exact time and date you plan to visit. Purchase tickets online through a travel agent before you arrive in Japan or from a kiosk at any Lawson convenience store in Tokyo (the trickier option, as it will require some Japanese-language ability to navigate the ticket machine). Both options are explained in detail on the website, where you will also find a useful map.

Getting to Ghibli (which is pronounced 'jiburi') is all part of the adventure. A minibus (round trip/one way ¥320/210) leaves for the museum approximately every 20 minutes from Mitaka Station (bus stop no 9). Alternatively, you can walk there by following the canal and turning right when you reach Inokashira-kōen (which will take about 15 minutes). The museum is on the western edge of Inokashira-kōen, so you can also walk there through the park from Kichijōji Station in about 30 minutes.

Kōrakuen & Around 後楽園

Kōrakuen and its surrounds formed part of the Edo-era Yamanote district of villas belonging to the governing elite. A short walk away is the neighbourhood of Kagurazaka, an atmospheric former geisha district.

Koishikawa Kōrakuen GARDENS

(小石川後楽園; Map p96; 1-6-6 Kōraku, Bunkyō-ku; adult/child ¥300/free; 9am-5pm; JR Sōbu line to Iidabashi, exit C3) Established in the mid-17th century as the property of the Tokugawa clan, this formal strolling garden incorporates elements of Chinese and Japanese landscaping. It's among Tokyo's most attractive gardens, although nowadays the *shakkei* (borrowed scenery) also includes

Shinjuku

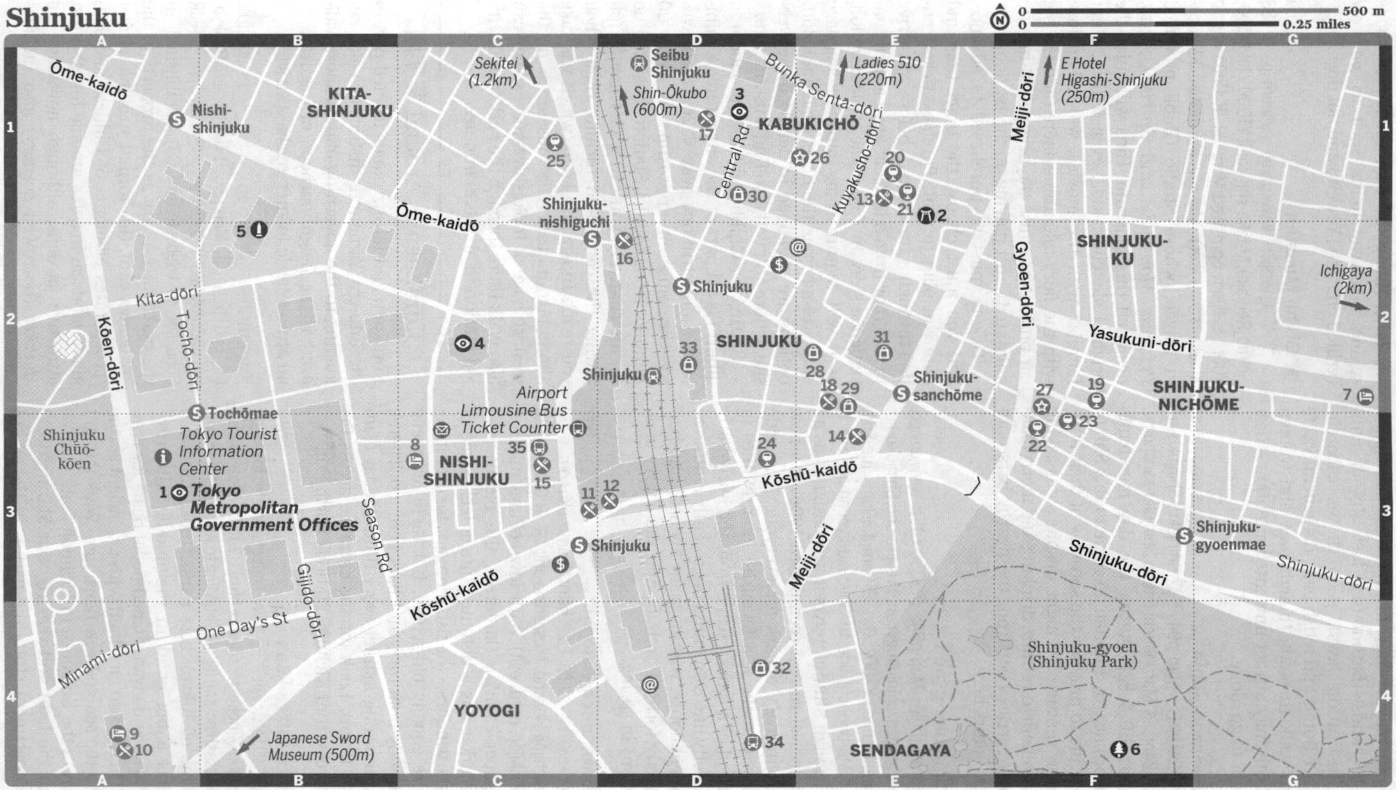

0 500 m
0 0.25 miles
Ōme-kaidō
Nishi-shinjuku
KITA-SHINJUKU
Sekitei (1.2km)
Seibu Shinjuku
Shin-Ōkubo (600m)
3
KABUKICHŌ
Bunka Sentā-dōri
Ladies 510 (220m)
E Hotel Higashi-Shinjuku (250m)
Meiji-dōri
17
25
26
20
Central Rd
Kuyakusho-dōri
30
13
21
2
Ōme-kaidō
Shinjuku-nishiguchi
5
16
SHINJUKU-KU
Gyoen-dōri
Ichigaya (2km)
Shinjuku
Kita-dōri
Kōen-dōri
Tochō-dōri
4
33
SHINJUKU
28
31
Yasukuni-dōri
Shinjuku
Airport Limousine Bus Ticket Counter
18
29
Shinjuku-sanchōme
27
19
SHINJUKU-NICHŌME
7
Tochōmae
Tokyo Tourist Information Center
Shinjuku Chūō-kōen
8
NISHI-SHINJUKU
35
15
14
24
23
22
Kōshū-kaidō
1 Tokyo Metropolitan Government Offices
11
12
Season Rd
Shinjuku
Meiji-dōri
Shinjuku-gyoenmae
Shinjuku-dōri
Gijido-dōri
Kōshū-kaidō
One Day's St
Minami-dōri
Shinjuku-gyoen (Shinjuku Park)
32
YOYOGI
9
10
Japanese Sword Museum (500m)
34
SENDAGAYA
6
A B C D E F G
1 2 3 4

Shinjuku

Top Sights
1 Tokyo Metropolitan Government Offices A3

Sights
2 Hanazono-jinja E1
3 Kabukichō D1
4 Mode Gakuen Cocoon Tower C2
5 Shinjuku I-Land B2
6 Shinjuku-gyoen F4

Sleeping
7 Citadines G2
8 Kadoya Hotel C3
9 Park Hyatt Tokyo A4

Eating
10 Kozue A4
11 Lumine C3
12 Mylord D3
13 Nagi E1
14 Nakajima E3
15 Numazukō C3
16 Omoide-yokochō D2
17 Shinjuku Asia-yokochō D1
18 Tsunahachi E2

Drinking & Nightlife
19 Advocates Café F2
20 Albatross G E1
21 Araku E1
22 Arty Farty F3
23 Bar Goldfinger F3
New York Bar .... (see 9)
24 Samurai D3
25 Zoetrope C1

Entertainment
26 Robot Restaurant E1
27 Shinjuku Pit Inn F2

Shopping
28 Bicqlo E2
29 Disk Union E2
30 Don Quijote D1
31 Isetan E2
32 Kinokuniya D4
33 RanKing RanQueen D2

Transport
34 JR Highway Bus Terminal D4
35 Shinjuku Highway Bus Terminal C3

the other-worldly Tokyo Dome. Don't miss the **Engetsu-kyō** (Full-Moon Bridge), which dates from the early Edo period; the name will make sense when you see it.

Tokyo Dome City Attractions AMUSEMENT PARK
(東京ドームシティアトラクションズ; Map p96; ☎03-3817-6001; www.tokyo-dome.co.jp/e; 1-3-61 Kōraku, Bunkyō-ku; attractions ¥420-1030; ⏰10am-9pm; 🚉JR Chūō line to Suidōbashi, west exit) The top attraction at this amusement park next to Tokyo Dome is the 'Thunder Dolphin' (¥1030), a roller coaster that cuts a heart-in-your-throat course in and around the tightly packed buildings of downtown. There are plenty of low-key, child-friendly rides as well. You can buy tickets for individual rides or a day pass (adult/child ¥3900/2100; after 5pm adult ¥2900).

Baseball Hall of Fame & Museum MUSEUM
(野球体育博物館; Map p96; www.baseball-museum.or.jp; 1-3-61 Kōraku, Bunkyō-ku; adult/child ¥600/200; ⏰10am-6pm Tue-Sun Mar-Sep, to 5pm Oct-Feb; 🚉JR Chūō line to Suidōbashi, west exit) How did baseball come to be a Japanese obsession? This museum chronicles baseball's rise from a hobby imported by an American teacher in 1872 to the Japanese team winning the bronze medal at the 2004 Olympics. Be sure to pick up the comprehensive English-language pamphlet. The entrance to the museum is adjacent to Gate 21 of Tokyo Dome.

Yasukuni-jinja SHINTO SHRINE
(靖国神社; Map p96; ☎03-3261-8326; www.yasukuni.or.jp; 3-1-1 Kudan-kita, Chiyoda-ku; ⏰6am-5pm; Ⓢ Hanzōmon line to Kudanshita, exit 1) Literally 'For the Peace of the Country Shrine', Yasukuni is the memorial shrine to Japan's war dead, around 2.5 million souls. Completed in 1869, it has unusual *torii* gates made of steel and bronze. It is also incredibly controversial: in 1979 14 class-A war criminals, including WWII general Hideki Tōjō, were enshrined here.

For politicians, a visit to Yasukuni, particularly on 15 August, the anniversary of Japan's defeat in WWII, is considered a political statement. It's a move that pleases hawkish constituents but also one that draws a strong rebuke from Japan's Asian neighbours, who suffered greatly in Japan's wars of expansion during the 20th century.

Yūshū-kan MUSEUM
(遊就館; Map p96; ☎03-3261-8326; www.yasukuni.or.jp; 3-1-1 Kudankita, Chiyoda-ku; adult/student ¥800/500; ⏰9am-4pm; Ⓢ Hanzōmon line to Kudanshita, exit 1) Most history museums in

Kōrakuen & Akihabara

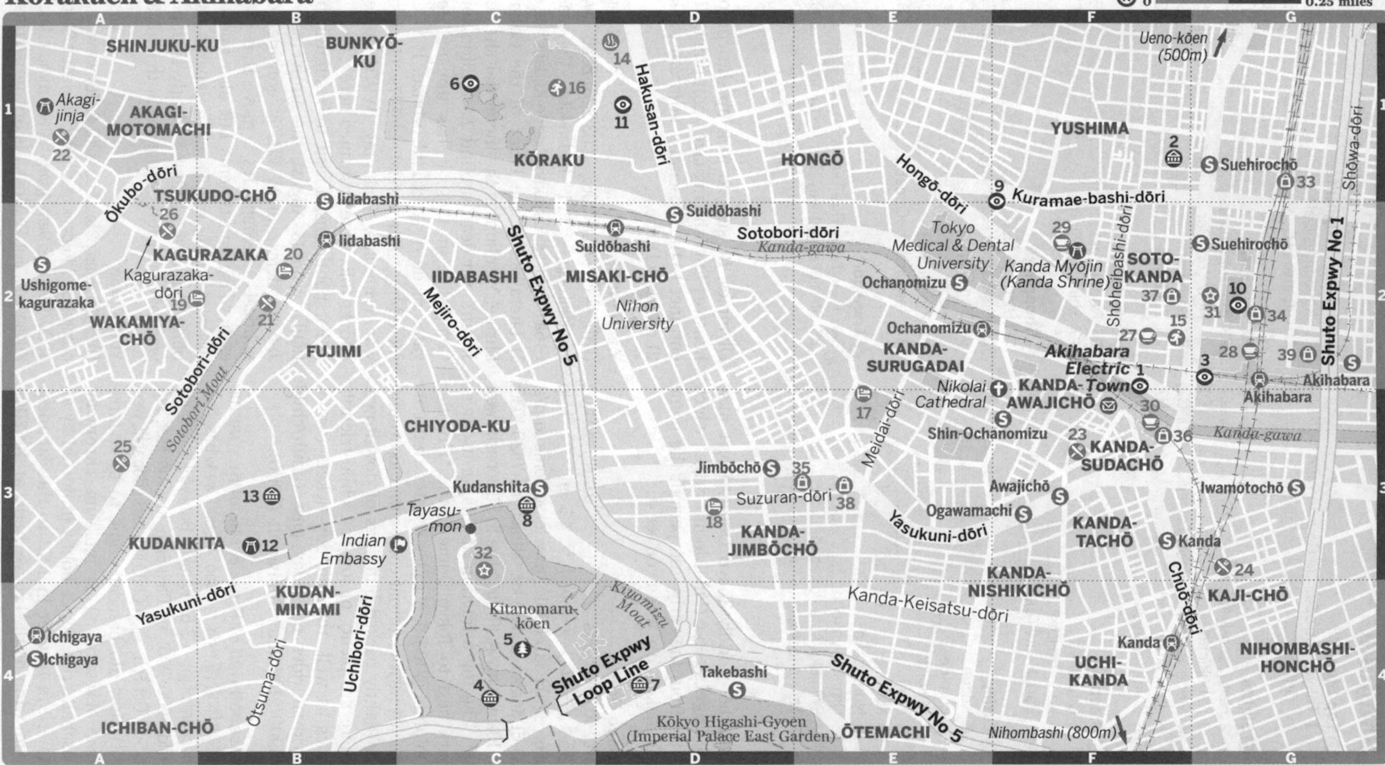

Kōrakuen & Akihabara

Top Sights
1 Akihabara Electric Town F2

Sights
2 3331 Arts Chiyoda F1
3 Akihabara Radio Center G2
Baseball Hall of Fame & Museum .... (see 16)
4 Crafts Gallery C4
5 Kitanomaru-kōen (Kitanomaru Park) C4
6 Koishikawa Kōrakuen C1
7 National Museum of Modern Art (MOMAT) D4
8 National Shōwa Memorial Museum C3
9 Origami Kaikan F1
10 Tokyo Anime Center Akiba Info G2
11 Tokyo Dome City Attractions D1
12 Yasukuni-jinja B3
13 Yūshū-kan B3

Activities, Courses & Tours
14 Spa LaQua D1
15 Super Potato Retro-kan F2
16 Tokyo Dome C1

Sleeping
17 Hilltop Hotel E3
18 Sakura Hotel Jimbōchō D3
19 The Agnes Hotel A2
20 Tokyo Central Youth Hostel B2

Eating
21 Canal Cafe B2
22 Kado A1
23 Kanda Yabu Soba F3
24 Kikanbō G3
Komaki Shokudō .... (see 34)
25 Kururi A3
26 Le Bretagne A2

Drinking & Nightlife
27 @Home Cafe F2
28 AKB48 Cafe G2
29 Imasa F2
30 N3331 .... F3

Entertainment
31 AKB48 Theatre G2
32 Nippon Budōkan C3

Shopping
33 2k540 Aki-Oka Artisan G1
34 Chabara G2
35 Jimbōchō Bookstores E3
36 mAAch ecute F3
37 Mandarake Complex F2
38 Ohya Shobō E3
39 Yodobashi Akiba G2

Japan skirt the issue of war or focus on the burden of the common people. Not so here: Yūshū-kan begins with Japan's samurai tradition and ends with its defeat in WWII. It is also unapologetic and has been known to boil the blood of some visitors with its particular view of history.

National Shōwa Memorial Museum MUSEUM
(昭和館; Shōwa-kan; Map p96; ☎03-3222-2577; www.showakan.go.jp; 1-6-1 Kudan-minami, Chiyoda-ku; adult/student/child ¥300/150/80; ⊙10am-5.30pm; 🚇Hanzōmon line to Kudanshita, exit 4) This museum of WWII-era Tokyo gives a sense of everyday life for the common people: how they ate, slept, dressed, studied, prepared for war and endured martial law, famine and loss of loved ones. An English audio guide (free) fills in a lot.

Spa LaQua ONSEN
(スパ ラクーア; Map p96; www.laqua.jp; 5th-9th fl, Tokyo Dome City, 1-3-61 Kōraku, Bunkyō-ku; admission weekday/weekend ¥2634/2958; ⊙11am-9am; Ⓢ Marunouchi line to Kōrakuen, exit 2) One of Tokyo's few true onsen, this chic spa complex relies on natural hot-spring water from 1700m below ground. There are indoor and outdoor baths, saunas and a bunch of add-on options, such as *akasuri* (Korean-style whole-body exfoliation). It's a fascinating introduction to Japanese health and beauty rituals.

Akihabara & Around 秋葉原

'Akiba' is the centre of Tokyo's *otaku* (geek) subculture. But you don't have to obsess about manga (Japanese comics) or anime (Japanese animation) to enjoy this quirky neighbourhood. It's equal parts sensory overload and cultural mind-bender. Surrounding districts that had been declining are on the upswing, thanks to some interesting cultural and commercial developments that have popped up in formerly abandoned buildings.

★ Akihabara Electric Town NEIGHBOURHOOD
(秋葉原電気街; Akihabara Denki-Gai; Map p96; 🚇JR Yamanote line to Akihabara, Electric Town exit) Post WWII, Akihabara Station became synonymous with a black market for radio parts and other electronics. After the 1960s

and '70s when the district was *the* place to hunt for bargains on new and used electronics, Akihabara saw its top shopping mantle increasingly usurped by discount stores elsewhere in the city. It has long since bounced back by reinventing itself as the centre of the *otaku* (geek) universe, catching J-pop culture fans in its gravitational pull.

Now you are as likely to find intricately designed plastic models of anime characters, self-penned pornographic comics and *cosplay* (costume play) outfits as you are electric circuits, fuses and wires in the place locals call Akiba. To make some sense of it all pick up an English map at **Tokyo Anime Center Akiba Info** (東京アニメセンター Akiba Info; Map p96; www.animecenter.jp; 2nd fl, Akihabara UDX Bldg, 4-14-1 Soto-Kanda, Chiyoda-ku; ⊙11am-7pm Tue-Sun; JR Yamanote line to Akihabara, Electric Town exit); the helpful staff here also speak English.

Akihabara Radio Center BUILDING
(秋葉原ラジオセンター; Map p96; 1-14-2 Soto-Kanda, Chiyoda-ku; ⊙hours vary; JR Yamanote line to Akihabara, Electric Town exit) Strictly for old-school electronics *otaku*, this two-storey warren of several dozen electronics stalls under the elevated railway is the original, still-beating heart of Akihabara. By old-school, we mean connectors, jacks, LEDs, switches, semiconductors and other components. It's worth a peek as a cultural study; the easiest access is the narrow entrances under the tracks on Chūō-dōri.

DON'T MISS

KAGURAZAKA

In the beginning of the 20th century, Kagurazaka (神楽坂) was a fashionable *hanamachi* – a pleasure quarter where geisha entertained. Though the geisha have disappeared, the neighbourhood retains the glamour and charm of decades past, with winding cobblestone streets and cosy cafes. To access the most enchanting backstreets, walk from Iidabashi Station up Kagurazaka Hill and turn right at the Royal Host restaurant. Don't miss **Hyogo-yokochō**, the neighbourhood's oldest lane and its most atmospheric – it's often used in television and movie shoots. With many excellent restaurants, Kagurazaka is also a foodie favourite; try Le Bretagne (p128) or Kado (p128).

3331 Arts Chiyoda GALLERY
(Map p96; 03-6803 2441; www.3331.jp/en; 6-11-14 Soto-Kanda, Chiyoda-ku; ⊙noon-7pm Wed-Mon; ; Ginza line to Suehirochō, exit 4) FREE Interesting galleries and creative studios now occupy this former high school which has morphed into a forward-thinking arts hub for Akiba. It's a fascinating place to explore. There's a good cafe and shop selling cute design items, as well as a play area for kids stocked with recycled toys and colourful giant dinosaurs made of old plastic toys.

Origami Kaikan CRAFTS
(おりがみ会館; Map p96; 03-3811-4025; www.origamikaikan.co.jp; 1-7-14 Yushima, Bunkyō-ku; ⊙shop 9am-6pm, gallery 10am-5.30pm Mon-Sat; JR Chūō or Sōbu lines to Ochanomizu, Hijiri-bashi exit) FREE This exhibition centre and workshop is dedicated to the quintessential Japanese art of origami, which you can learn to do yourself in classes here. There's a shop/gallery on the 1st floor, a gallery on the 2nd, and a workshop on 4th where you can watch the process of making, dyeing and decorating origami paper.

Super Potato Retro-kan ARCADE
(スーパーポテトレトロ館; Map p96; www.superpotato.com; 1-11-2 Soto-kanda, Chiyoda-ku; ⊙11am-8pm Mon-Fri, from 10am Sat & Sun; JR Yamanote line to Akihabara, Electric Town exit) Are you a gamer keen to sample retro computer games? On the 5th floor of this store specialising in used video games, there's a retro video arcade where you can get your hands on some old-fashioned consoles.

Ueno & Yanaka 上野・谷中

Ueno is the cultural heart of Tokyo and has been the city's top draw for centuries. At the centre of the neighbourhood is a sprawling park, Ueno-kōen, with the city's greatest concentration of museums, including the Tokyo National Museum.

Within walking distance is Yanaka, famous locally as the neighbourhood time forgot. Having survived, miraculously, the Great Kantō Earthquake and the allied fire-bombing of WWII (not to mention the slash-and-burn modernising of the postwar years), Yanaka has a high concentration of vintage wooden structures. But that's not all that makes the neighbourhood unique: it has more than a hundred temples, relocated from around Tokyo during an Edo-era episode of urban restructuring. Many artists

POP PHENOMENON: AKB48

Love them or hate them, these days there's no escaping AKB48, a super girl group with no fewer than 60 rotating members. Formed in 2005, AKB48 was meant to be an accessible idol group for Akiba's *otaku* (geeks). A decade later, AKB48 is now a full-on mainstream pop phenomenon with countless endorsements and record sales figures.

The group performs daily (in shifts) at its very own workhouse…er…theatre in the heart of Akihabara, **AKB48 Theatre** (Map p96; www.akb48.co.jp/english/overseas/index.html; 8th fl, Don Quijote, 4-3-3 Soto-Kanda, Chiyoda-ku; JR Yamanote line to Akihabara, Electric Town exit). Tickets for sell-out shows are awarded by lottery; overseas visitors can try their luck by sending an email to sfar@akb48.co.jp one month in advance of coming to Japan – see the weblink for further details.

While the AKB48 members have attracted a lot of male fans (and simultaneously picked up criticism for sexualising teens as young as 13), they've also got a lot of female fans their own age. Sister groups now exist in Jakarta and Shanghai.

If you're curious to see what the fuss is all about, you can pop into the **AKB48 Cafe** (Map p96; http://akb48cafeshops.com; 1-1 Kanda Hanagaoka-chō, Chiyoda-ku; 11am-11pm; JR Yamanote line to Akihabara, Electric Town exit). Here videos of the group play on loop and lookalike waitresses serve cutesy concoctions to slack-jawed fans.

also live and work in the area. Simply put, it's a fantastic place to wander.

★Tokyo National Museum MUSEUM
(東京国立博物館; Tokyo Kokuritsu Hakubutsukan; Map p102; 03-3822-1111; www.tnm.jp; 13-9 Ueno-kōen, Taitō-ku; adult/student/child & senior ¥620/¥410/free; 9.30am-5pm Tue-Thu year-round, to 8pm Fri, to 6pm Sat & Sun Mar-Dec; JR Yamanote line to Ueno, Ueno-kōen exit) If you visit only one museum in Tokyo, make it this one. The Tokyo National Museum holds the world's largest collection of Japanese art, including ancient pottery, Buddhist sculptures, samurai swords, colourful *ukiyo-e* (woodblock prints), gorgeous kimonos and much, much more. Visitors with only a couple of hours to spare should hone in on the Honkan (Main Gallery) and the enchanting Gallery of Hōryū-ji Treasures, which displays masks, scrolls and gilt Buddhas from Hōryū-ji (in Nara Prefecture, dating from 607).

With more time, you can explore the recently renovated, three-storied Tōyōkan (Gallery of Eastern Antiquities), with its collection of Buddhist sculpture from around Asia and delicate Chinese ceramics. The Heiseikan, accessed via a passage on the 1st floor of the Honkan, houses the Japanese Archaeological Gallery, full of pottery, talismans and articles of daily life from Japan's prehistoric periods. For a few weeks in spring and autumn, the garden, which includes several vintage teahouses, opens to the public.

The museum regularly hosts temporary exhibitions (which cost extra); these can be fantastic, but often lack the English signage found throughout the rest of the museum.

★Ueno-kōen PARK
(上野公園; Map p102; 5am-11pm; JR Yamanote line to Ueno, Ueno-kōen & Shinobazu exits) Sprawling Ueno-kōen has wooded pathways that wind past centuries-old temples and shrines – even a zoo. At the southern tip is a large pond, **Shinobazu-ike**, choked with lily pads. Stroll down the causeway to Benten-dō, a temple dedicated to Benzaiten (the water goddess). From here you can get a good look at the birds and botany that thrive in the park; you can also rent row boats (per hour ¥600). Navigating the park is easy, thanks to large maps in English.

Ueno Tōshō-gū SHINTO SHRINE
(上野東照宮; Map p102; www.uenotoshogu.com; 9-88 Ueno-kōen, Taitō-ku; admission ¥500; 9.30am-4.30pm; JR Yamanote line to Ueno, Shinobazu exit) Like its counterpart in Nikkō (p163), this shrine inside Ueno-kōen was built in honour of Tokugawa Ieyasu, the warlord who unified Japan. Resplendent in gold leaf and ornate details, it dates from 1651 (though it recently underwent a touch-up). You can get a pretty good look from outside the gate, if you want to skip the admission fee.

In January and February there is a spectacular peony garden (joint admission ¥1000).

Tokyo National Museum

HISTORIC HIGHLIGHTS

It would be a challenge to take in everything the sprawling Tokyo National Museum has to offer in a day. Fortunately, the Honkan (Main Gallery) is designed to give visitors a crash course in Japanese art history from the Jōmon era (13,000–300 BC) to the Edo era (AD 1603–1868). The works on display here are rotated regularly, to protect fragile ones and to create seasonal exhibitions – you're always guaranteed to see something new.

Buy your ticket from outside the main gate then head straight to the Honkan with its sloping tile roof. Stow your coat in a locker and take the central staircase up to the 2nd floor, where the exhibitions are arranged chronologically. Allow two hours for this tour of the highlights.

The first room on your right starts from the beginning with **ancient Japanese art ❶**. Be sure to pick up a copy of the brochure Highlights of Japanese Art at the entrance.

Continue to the **National Treasure Gallery ❷**. 'National Treasure' is the highest distinction awarded to a work of art in Japan. Keep an eye out for more National Treasures, labelled in red, on display in other rooms throughout the museum.

Moving on, stop to admire the **art of the Imperial court ❸**, the **samurai armour and swords ❹** and the **ukiyo-e and kimono ❺**.

Next, take the stairs down to the 1st floor, where each room is dedicated to a different craft, such as lacquerware or ceramics. Don't miss the excellent examples of **religious sculpture ❻** and **folk art ❼**.

Finish your visit with a look inside the enchanting **Gallery of Hōryū-ji Treasures ❽**.

REBECCA MILNER ©

Ukiyo-e & Kimono (Room 10)
Chic silken kimono and lushly coloured *ukiyo-e* (woodblock prints) are two icons of the Edo era (AD 1603–1868) *ukiyo* – the 'floating world', or world of fleeting beauty and pleasure.

Japanese Sculpture (Room 11)
Many of Japan's most famous sculptures, religious in nature, are locked away in temple reliquaries. This is a rare chance to see them up close.

MUSEUM GARDEN
Don't miss the garden if you visit during the few weeks it's open to the public in spring and autumn.

Heiseikan & Japanese Archaeology Gallery

Research & Information Centre

❽

Hyōkeikan

Kuro-mon

Main Gate

Gallery of Hōryū-ji Treasures
Surround yourself with miniature gilt Buddhas from Hōryū-ji, said to be one of Japan's oldest Buddhist temples, founded in 607. Don't miss the graceful Pitcher with Dragon Head, a National Treasure.

REBECCA MILNER ©

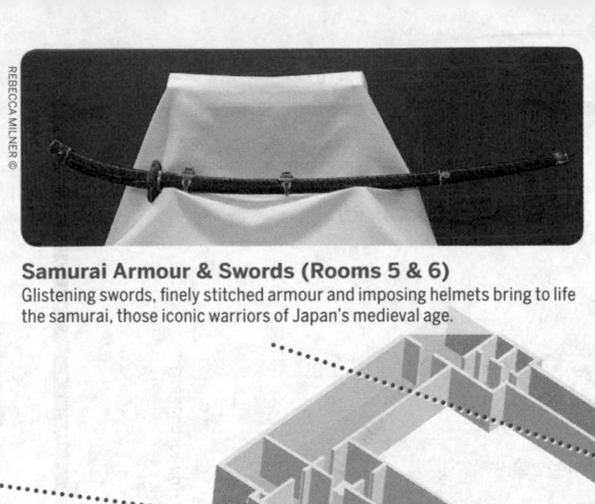

REBECCA MILNER ©

Samurai Armour & Swords (Rooms 5 & 6)

Glistening swords, finely stitched armour and imposing helmets bring to life the samurai, those iconic warriors of Japan's medieval age.

REBECCA MILNER ©

Art of the Imperial Court (Room 3-2)

Literature works, calligraphy and narrative picture scrolls are displayed alongside decorative art objects, which allude to the life of elegance led by courtesans a thousand years ago.

5 4 1 3 2 7 6

Honkan (Main Gallery) 2nd Floor

Honkan (Main Gallery) 1st Floor

Museum Garden & Teahouses

Honkan (Main Gallery)

Tōyōkan (Gallery of Eastern Antiquities)

National Treasure Gallery (Room 2)

A single, superlative work from the museum's collection of 87 National Treasures (perhaps a painted screen, or a gilded, hand-drawn sutra) is displayed in a serene, contemplative setting.

GIFT SHOP

The museum gift shop, on the 1st floor of the Honkan, has an excellent collection of Japanese art books in English.

Dawn of Japanese Art (Room 1)

The rise of the Imperial court and the introduction of Buddhism changed the Japanese aesthetic forever. These clay works from previous eras show what came before.

Folk Culture (Room 15)

See artefacts from Japan's historical minorities – the indigenous Ainu of Hokkaidō, the Kirishitan (persecuted Christians of the middle ages) and the former Ryūkyū Empire, now Okinawa.

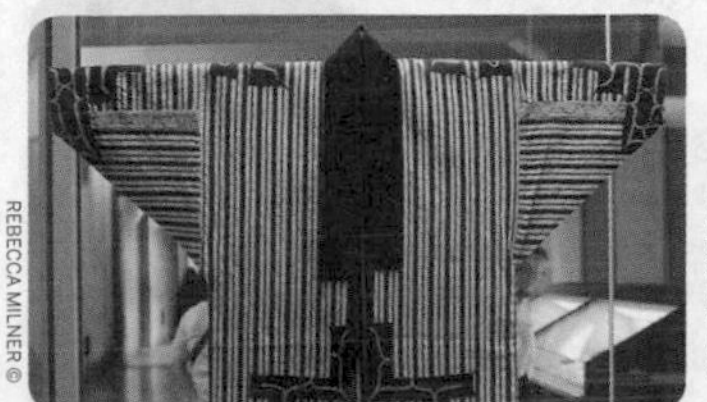

REBECCA MILNER ©

REBECCA MILNER ©

Ueno & Yanaka

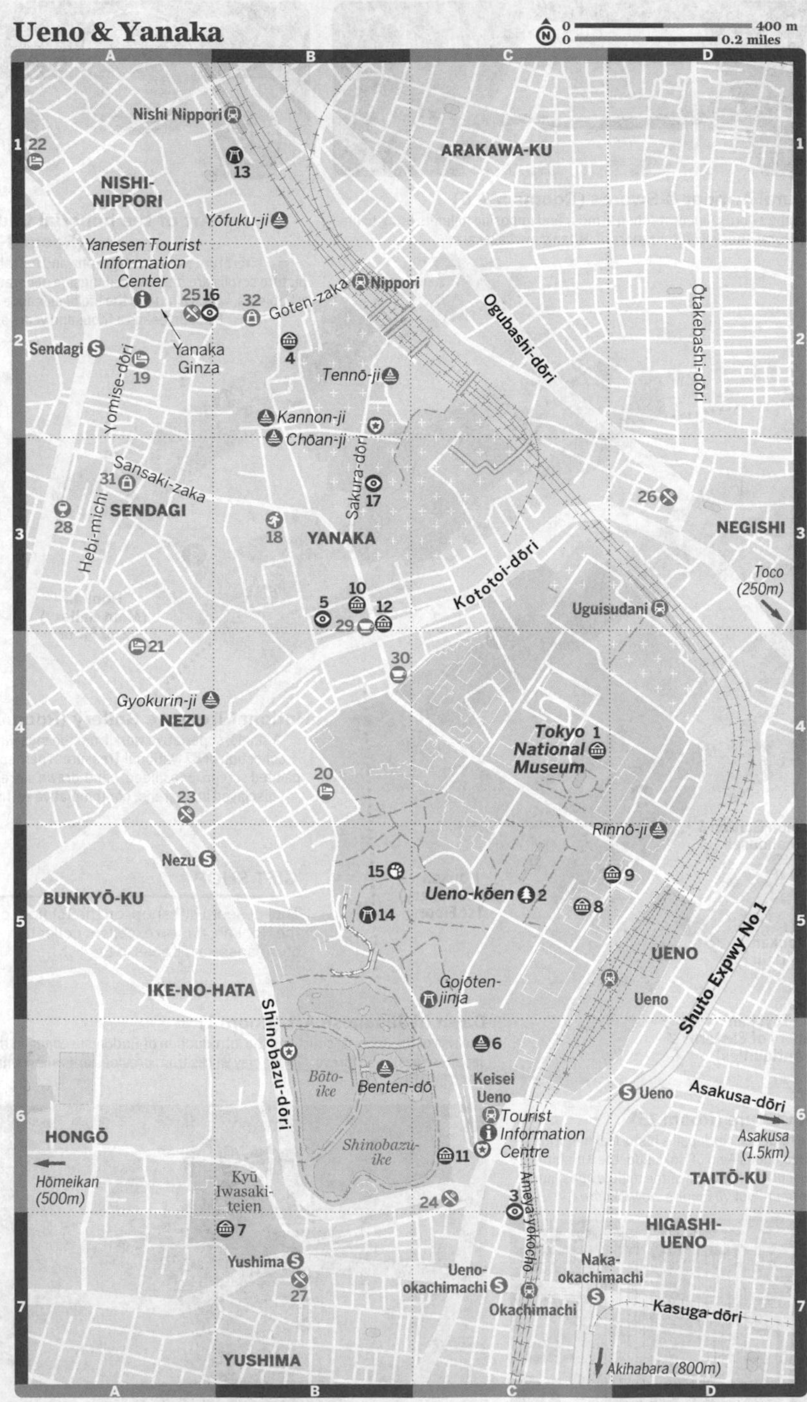
0 400 m
0 0.2 miles
Nishi Nippori
ARAKAWA-KU
NISHI-NIPPORI
Yōfuku-ji
Yanesen Tourist Information Center
Goten-zaka
Nippori
Ogubashi-dōri
Ōtakebashi-dōri
Sendagi
Yomise-dōri
Yanaka Ginza
Tennō-ji
Kannon-ji
Chōan-ji
Sakura-dōri
Sansaki-zaka
SENDAGI
Hebi-michi
YANAKA
NEGISHI
Kototoi-dōri
Toco (250m)
Uguisudani
Gyokurin-ji
NEZU
Tokyo National Museum
Rinnō-ji
Nezu
BUNKYŌ-KU
Ueno-kōen
UENO
Shuto Expwy No 1
IKE-NO-HATA
Gojōten-jinja
Ueno
Shinobazu-dōri
Bōto-ike
Benten-dō
Keisei Ueno
Tourist Information Centre
Asakusa-dōri
Asakusa (1.5km)
HONGŌ
Shinobazu-ike
TAITŌ-KU
Hōmeikan (500m)
Kyū Iwasaki-teien
Ameya-yokochō
HIGASHI-UENO
Yushima
Ueno-okachimachi
Naka-okachimachi
Okachimachi
Kasuga-dōri
YUSHIMA
Akihabara (800m)

Ueno & Yanaka

Kiyōmizu Kannon-dō BUDDHIST TEMPLE

(清水観音堂; Map p102; 1-29 Ueno-kōen, Taitō-ku; 9am-4pm; JR Yamanote line to Ueno, Shinobazu exit) Ueno-kōen's Kiyōmizu Kannon-dō is one of Tokyo's oldest structures: established in 1631 and in its present position since 1698, it has survived every disaster that's come its way. It's a miniature of the famous Kiyomizu-dera in Kyoto and is a pilgrimage site for women hoping to conceive.

Ueno Zoo ZOO

(上野動物園; Ueno Dōbutsu-en; Map p102; www.tokyo-zoo.net; 9-83 Ueno-kōen, Taitō-ku; adult/child ¥600/free; 9.30am-5pm Tue-Sun; JR Yamanote line to Ueno, Ueno-kōen exit) Japan's oldest zoo is home to animals from around the globe, but the biggest attractions are two giant pandas that arrived from China in 2011 – Rī Rī and Shin Shin. There's also a whole area devoted to lemurs, which makes sense given Tokyoites' love of all things cute.

National Science Museum MUSEUM

(国立科学博物館; Kokuritsu Kagaku Hakubutsukan; Map p102; www.kahaku.go.jp; 7-20 Ueno-kōen, Taitō-ku; adult/child ¥600/free; 9am-5pm Tue-Thu, Sat & Sun, to 8pm Fri; JR Yamanote line to Ueno, Ueno-kōen exit) The Japan Gallery here showcases the rich and varied wildlife of the Japanese archipelago, from the bears of Hokkaidō to the giant beetles of Okinawa. Elsewhere in the museum: a rocket launcher, a giant squid, an Edo-era mummy and a digital seismograph that charts earthquakes in real time. There's English signage throughout, plus an English-language audio guide (¥300).

National Museum of Western Art MUSEUM

(国立西洋美術館; Kokuritsu Seiyō Bijutsukan; Map p102; www.nmwa.go.jp; 7-7 Ueno-kōen, Taitō-ku; adult/student ¥420/130, 2nd & 4th Sat free; 9.30am-5.30pm Tue-Thu, Sat & Sun, to 8pm Fri; JR Yamanote line to Ueno, Ueno-kōen exit) The permanent collection here runs from medieval Madonna-and-child images to 20th-century abstract expressionism, but is strongest in French impressionism, including a whole gallery of Monet. The main building was designed by Le Corbusier in the late 1950s and is now on Unesco's World Heritage List.

Shitamachi Museum MUSEUM

(下町風俗資料館; Map p102; 03-3823-7451; www.taitocity.net/taito/shitamachi; 2-1 Ueno-kōen, Taitō-ku; adult/child ¥300/100; 9.30am-4.30pm Tue-Sun; JR Yamanote line to Ueno, Shinobazu exit) This museum re-creates life in the plebeian quarters of Tokyo during the Meiji and Taishō periods (1868–1926), before the city was twice destroyed by the Great Kantō Earthquake and WWII. There are old tenement houses and shops that you can enter.

Ameya-yokochō MARKET

(アメヤ横町; Map p102; 4 Ueno, Taitō-ku; JR Yamanote line to Ueno, Ueno-kōen exit) Step into

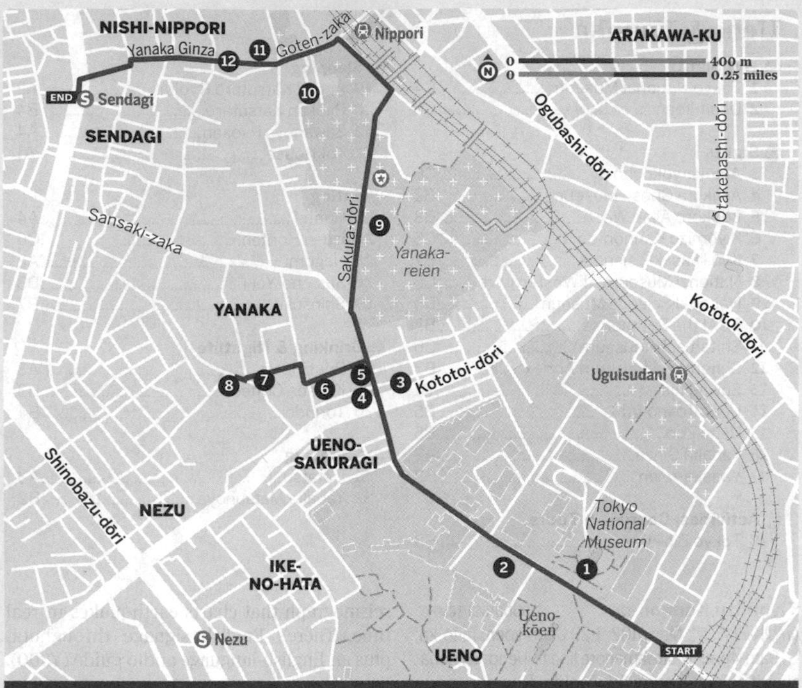

City Walk
Strolling Yanaka

START TOKYO NATIONAL MUSEUM
END SENDAGI STATION
LENGTH 3KM; TWO HOURS

If you have time, visit the ❶ **Tokyo National Museum** (p99) before you start exploring Yanaka, with its temples, galleries and old wooden buildings. If not, simply follow the road northwest out of ❷ **Ueno-kōen** (p99) until you hit Kototoi-dōri. At the corner is the ❸ **Shitamachi Museum Annex**, actually a preserved, century-old liquor store. Across the street is ❹ **Kayaba Coffee** (p136), if you need a pick-me-up.

From here, it's a short walk to ❺ **SCAI the Bathhouse**, a classic old public bathhouse turned contemporary art gallery. It's a worthwhile detour to continue down to the ❻ **studio** of painter Allan West, and to see the ancient, thick-trunked ❼ **Himalayan cedar tree** on the corner. In and around here, you will pass by many temples, including ❽ **Enju-ji**, where Nichikasama, the 'god of strong legs' is enshrined; it's popular with runners. Feel free to stop in at any of the temples; just be respectful and keep your voice low.

Now double back towards the entrance of ❾ **Yanaka-reien**, one of Tokyo's most atmospheric and prestigious cemeteries (also a favourite sunning spot of the neighborhood's many stray cats). When you exit the cemetery, continue with the train tracks on your right, climbing until you reach the bridge, which overlooks the tracks (a favourite destination for trainspotters).

Head left and look for the sign pointing towards the ❿ **Asakura Chōso Museum**, the home studio of an early 20th-century sculptor and now an attractive museum. Back on the main drag, continue down the ⓫ **Yūyake Dandan** – literally the 'Sunset Stairs' – to the classic mid-20th-century shopping street, ⓬ **Yanaka Ginza**. Pick up some snacks from the vendors here, then hunker down on a milk crate on the side of the road with the locals and wash it all down with a beer.

Walk west and you can pick up the subway at Sendagi Station.

this alley paralleling the JR Yamanote line tracks, and glitzy Tokyo feels like a distant memory. This open-air market got its start as a black market, post WWII, when American goods were sold here. Today, it's filled with vendors selling everything from fresh seafood and spices to jeans and sneakers.

Kyū Iwasaki-teien HISTORIC BUILDING
(旧岩崎邸庭園; Map p102; ☎3823-8340; http://teien.tokyo-park.or.jp/en/kyu-iwasaki/index.html; 1-3-45 Ike-no-hata, Taitō-ku; adult/child ¥400/free; ⏲9am-5pm; S Chiyoda line to Yushima, exit 1) This grand residence was once the villa of Hisaya Iwasaki, son of the founder of Mitsubishi, and is now a fascinating example of how the cultural elite of the early Meiji period tried to straddle east and west. Built in 1896, it has been open to the public since 2001.

Yanaka Ginza STREET
(谷中銀座; Map p102; 🚉JR Yamanote line to Nippori, north exit) Yanaka Ginza is pure, vintage mid-20th-century Tokyo, a pedestrian street lined with butcher shops, vegetable vendors and the like. Most Tokyo neighbourhoods once had stretches like these (until supermarkets took over). It's popular with Tokyoites from all over the city, who come to soak up the nostalgic atmosphere, plus the locals who shop here.

Asakura Chōso Museum MUSEUM
(朝倉彫塑館; Map p102; www.taitocity.net/taito/asakura; 7-16-10 Yanaka, Taitō-ku; adult/student ¥400/150; ⏲9.30am-4.30pm Tue-Thu, Sat & Sun; 🚉JR Yamanote line to Nippori, north exit) Sculptor Asakura Fumio (artist name Chōso; 1883–1964) designed this atmospheric house himself, which includes a central water garden, a studio with vaulted ceilings and a 'sunrise room'. It's now a museum with a number of the artist's signature realist works, mostly of people and cats, on display.

Yanaka-reien CEMETERY
(谷中霊園; Map p102; 7-5-24 Yanaka, Taitō-ku; 🚉JR Yamanote line to Nippori, west exit) One of Tokyo's largest graveyards, Yanaka-reien is the final resting place of more than 7000 souls, many of whom were quite well known in their day. It's also where you'll find the tomb of Yoshinobu Tokugawa (徳川慶喜の墓), the last shogun.

Edokoro Allan West ART STUDIO
(繪処アランウエスト; Map p102; ☎03-3827-1907; www.allanwest.jp; 1-6-17 Yanaka, Taitō-ku; ⏲1-5pm, from 3pm Sun, closed irregularly; S Chiyoda line to Nezu, exit 1) FREE A long-time Yanaka resident, Allan West paints gorgeous screens in the traditional Japanese style, making his paints from scratch just as local artists have done for centuries. Visitors are welcome to pop into his studio when he's there.

SCAI the Bathhouse GALLERY
(スカイザバスハウス; Map p102; ☎03-3821-1144; www.scaithebathhouse.com; 6-1-23 Yanaka, Taitō-ku; ⏲noon-6pm Tue-Sat; S Chiyoda line to Nezu, exit 1) FREE Once a 200-year-old bathhouse, now a cutting-edge gallery space, SCAI showcases Japanese and international artists in its austere vaulted space.

Shitamachi Museum Annex HISTORIC BUILDING
(下町風俗資料館; Map p102; 2-10-6 Uenosakuragi, Taitō-ku; ⏲9.30am-4.30pm Tue-Sun; S Chiyoda line to Nezu, exit 1) FREE This century-old liquor shop (which operated until 1986) has been returned to its original state, with old sake barrels, weights, measures and posters.

Asakusa & Sumida-gawa 浅草・隅田川

Welcome to Tokyo's east side, the area long known as Shitamachi (the 'low city'), where the city's merchants and artisans lived during the feudal period. Asakusa, with its ancient temple and crafts shops, retains a lot of that old Edo spirit.

The neighbourhoods across the Sumida-gawa look much like they have for decades, too, having experienced little of the development seen elsewhere in the city – save for Tokyo Sky Tree. Given its location, among low-lying residential buildings and unburied electrical wires, Tokyo's newest landmark looks as though it was dropped here by aliens.

Ryōgoku, also east of the Sumida-gawa, is home to the national sumo stadium Kokugikan (p139) – you'll often see chubby wrestlers around Ryōguku Station.

MEGURIN BUS

The **Megurin bus** (めぐりん; www.city.taito.lg.jp/index/kurashi/kotsu/megurin; ⏲single-ride/day pass ¥100/300) runs three useful routes around Ueno and Asakusa that connect many sights. Pick up a map at a tourist information centre or print one from the website.

Asakusa & Sumida-gawa

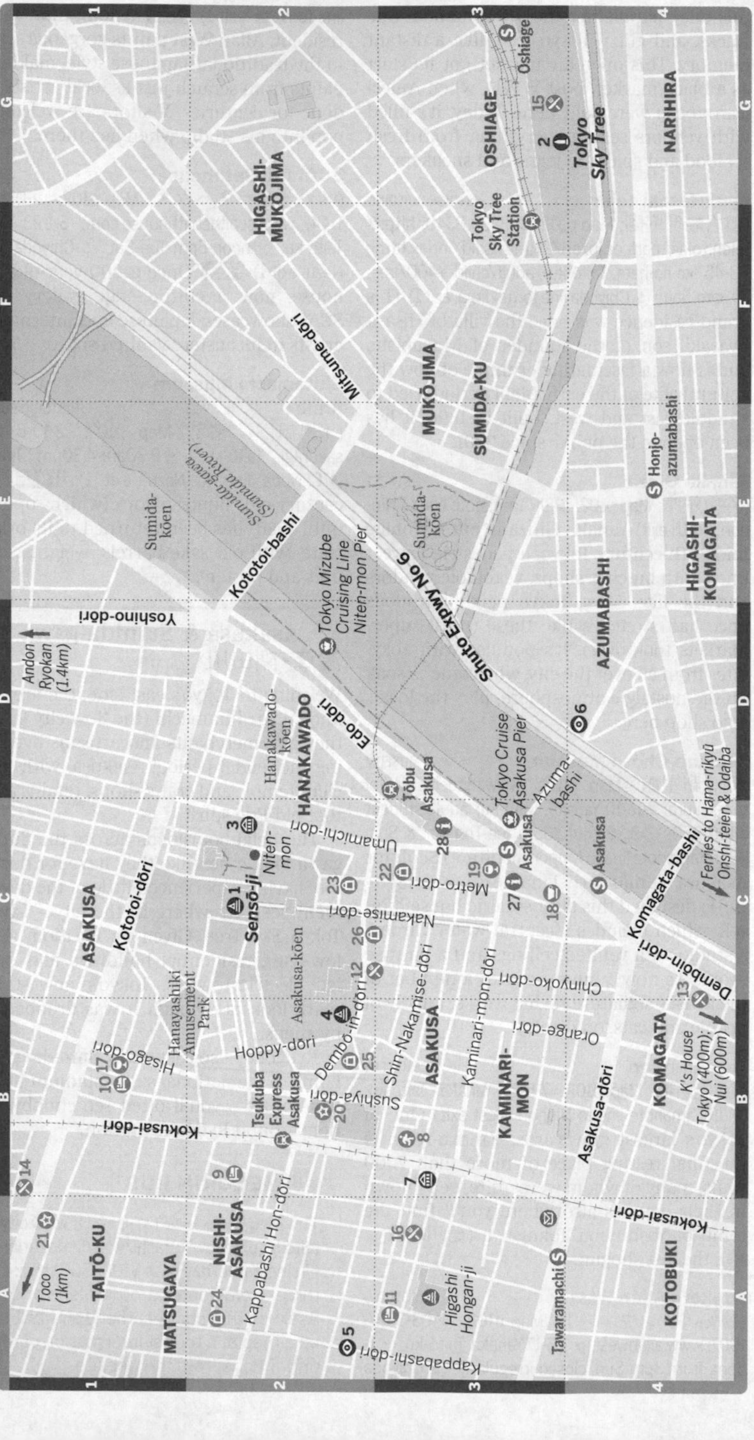

Asakusa & Sumida-gawa

Top Sights
1 Sensō-ji C2
2 Tokyo Sky Tree G3

Sights
3 Amuse Museum C2
4 Chingo-dō B2
5 Kappabashi-dōri A2
6 Super Dry Hall D4
7 Taiko Drum Museum B3

Activities, Courses & Tours
8 Jakotsu-yu B3
Mokuhankan .... (see 25)

Sleeping
9 Khaosan World B2
10 Sukeroku No Yado Sadachiyo B1
11 Tokyo Ryokan A3

Eating
12 Daikokuya C2
13 Komagata Dojō C4
14 Otafuku B1
15 Rokurinsha G3
16 Sometarō A3

Drinking & Nightlife
17 'Cuzn Homeground B1
18 Ef C3
19 Kamiya Bar C3

Entertainment
20 Asakusa Engei Hall B2
21 Oiwake A1

Shopping
22 Bengara C3
23 Fujiya C2
24 Ganso Shokuhin Sample-ya A2
Solamachi .... (see 15)
25 Tokyo Hotarudo B2
26 Yonoya Kushiho C2

Information
27 Asakusa Culture Tourist Information Center C3
28 Tōbu Sightseeing Service Center C3

★ Sensō-ji — BUDDHIST TEMPLE

(浅草寺; Map p106; ☎3842-0181; www.senso-ji.jp; 2-3-1 Asakusa, Taitō-ku; 24hr; S Ginza line to Asakusa, exit 1) FREE Tokyo's most visited temple enshrines a golden image of Kannon (the Buddhist Goddess of Mercy), which, according to legend, was miraculously pulled out of the nearby Sumida-gawa by two fishermen in AD 628. The image has remained on the spot ever since; the present structure dates from 1958. Entrance to the temple complex is via the fantastic, red **Kaminari-mon** (雷門; Thunder Gate).

Through the gate, protected by Fūjin (the god of wind) and Raijin (the god of thunder), is **Nakamise-dōri**, the temple precinct's shopping street. Here everything from tourist trinkets to genuine Edo-style crafts is sold. At the end of Nakamise-dōri is the temple itself, and to your left you'll spot the 55m **Five-Storey Pagoda** (五重塔). It's a 1973 reconstruction of a pagoda built by Tokugawa Iemitsu and is even more picturesque at night, all lit up.

It's a mystery as to whether or not the ancient image of Kannon actually exists, as it's not on public display. This doesn't stop a steady stream of worshippers from visiting. In front of the temple is a large incense cauldron: the smoke is said to bestow health and you'll see people rubbing it into their bodies through their clothes.

At the eastern edge of the temple complex is **Asakusa-jinja** (浅草神社), a shrine built in honour of the brothers who discovered the Kannon statue that inspired the construction of Sensō-ji. (Historically, Japan's two religions, Buddhism and Shintō were intertwined and it was not uncommon for temples to include shrines and vice versa). The current building, painted a deep shade of red, dates to 1649 and is a rare example of early Edo architecture. It's also the epicentre of one of Tokyo's most important festivals, May's Sanja Matsuri.

Super Dry Hall — ARCHITECTURE

(フラムドール; Flamme d'Or; Map p106; 1-23-1 Azuma-bashi, Sumida-ku; S Ginza line to Asakusa, exit 4) Designed by Philippe Starck and completed in 1989, the Asahi Beer headquarters, with its telltale golden plume, is a Tokyo landmark. The golden bit – which weighs more than 300 tonnes – is open to interpretation: Asahi likes to think it is the foam to the building's beer mug. Locals call it the 'golden turd'.

Amuse Museum — MUSEUM

(アミューズミュージアム; Map p106; www.amusemuseum.com; 2-34-3 Asakusa, Taitō-ku; adult/student ¥1080/864; 10am-6pm; S Ginza line to Asakusa) Here you'll find a fascinating collection of Japanese folk articles, mainly clothing, gathered by famed ethnologist

Tanaka Chūzaburō. On another floor there's a video tutorial (with English subtitles) on how to find secret meaning in *ukiyo-e* (woodblock prints). Don't miss the roof terrace, which looks over the Sensō-ji temple complex.

Chingo-dō BUDDHIST TEMPLE

(鎮護堂; Map p106; 2-3-1 Asakusa, Taitō-ku; ⏲6am-5pm; Ⓢ Ginza line to Asakusa, exit 1) This small, peaceful temple is actually part of Sensō-ji but has a separate entrance on Dembō-in-dōri. It pays tribute to the *tanuki* (racoon-like folkloric characters), who figure in Japanese myth as mystical shape-shifters and merry pranksters. They are also said to protect against fire and theft, which is why you'll often see *tanuki* figurines in front of restaurants.

Taiko Drum Museum MUSEUM

(太鼓館; Taiko-kan; Map p106; www.miyamoto-unosuke.co.jp/taikokan; 4th fl, 2-1-1 Nishi-Asakusa, Taitō-ku; adult/child ¥500/150; ⏲10am-5pm Wed-Sun; Ⓢ Ginza line to Tawaramachi, exit 3) There are hundreds of drums from around the world here, including several traditional Japanese *taiko*. The best part is that you can actually play most of them (those marked with a music note).

★Tokyo Sky Tree TOWER

(東京スカイツリー; Map p106; www.tokyo-skytree.jp; 1-1-2 Oshiage, Sumida-ku; admission 350m/450m observation decks ¥2060/3090; ⏲8am-10pm; Ⓢ Hanzōmon line to Oshiage, Sky Tree exit) Tokyo Sky Tree opened in May 2012 as the world's tallest 'free-standing tower' at 634m. Its silvery exterior of steel mesh morphs from a triangle at the base to a circle at 300m. There are two observation decks, at 350m and 450m. You can see more stuff during daylight hours – at peak visibility you can see up to 100km away, all the way to Mt Fuji – but it is at night that Tokyo appears truly beautiful.

The panorama from the lower observatory, the Tembō Deck, is spectacular. Don't miss the small section of glass floor panels, where you can see – dizzyingly – all the way to the ground. The upper observatory, the Tembō Galleria, beneath the digital broadcasting antennas, features a circular glass corridor for more vertiginous thrills. The elevator between the two has a glass front, so you can see yourself racing up the tower as the city grows smaller below.

The ticket counter is on the 4th floor. You'll see signs in English noting the wait and the current visibility. Try to avoid visiting on the weekend, when you might have to wait in line.

At the base is Tokyo Sky Tree Town, which includes the shopping centre Solamachi (p146).

DON'T MISS

PAPER FORTUNES

Getting an *omikuji* (paper fortune) is part of the fun of visiting a shrine or temple, and Sensō-ji (p107) has them in English (on the reverse). They're sold from what can best be described as a very analogue vending machine. Put a ¥100 coin in the slot, grab a silver canister and shake it. Extract a stick and note its number (in kanji), then find the matching drawer and withdraw a paper fortune, returning the stick to the canister. If you get a bad one – and some are harsh! – never fear. Just tie the paper on the nearby rack, ask the gods for better luck and try again.

★Edo-Tokyo Museum MUSEUM

(江戸東京博物館; Map p72; ☎03-3626-9974; www.edo-tokyo-museum.or.jp; 1-4-1 Yokoami, Sumida-ku; adult/child ¥600/free; ⏲9.30am-5.30pm Tue-Fri & Sun, to 7.30pm Sat; Ⓡ JR Sōbu line to Ryōgoku, west exit) This history museum does an excellent job laying out Tokyo's miraculous transformation from feudal city to modern capital, through city models, miniatures of real buildings, reproductions of old maps and *ukiyo-e* (woodblock prints). Don't miss the life-sized replica of the original Nihonbashi. There is English signage throughout and there's also a free audio guide available (¥1000 deposit).

Sumo Museum MUSEUM

(相撲博物館; Map p72; www.sumo.or.jp/sumo_museum; 1-3-28 Yokoami, Sumida-ku; ⏲10am-4.30pm Mon-Fri; Ⓡ JR Sōbu line to Ryōgoku, west exit) FREE On the ground floor of Ryōgoku Kokugikan Stadium, this small museum displays the pictures of all the past *yokozuna* (top-ranking sumo wrestlers), or for those who lived before the era of photography, *ukiyo-e*. During sumo tournaments, the museum is only open to ticket holders; otherwise it's free to enter.

TOKYO FOR CHILDREN

A popular destination for local families is **Odaiba**. Here, kids can meet ASIMO the humanoid robot at the National Museum of Emerging Science & Innovation (p109) and run loose at virtual-reality arcade Tokyo Joypolis (p111). Onsen themepark Ōedo Onsen Monogatari (p110) is also geared towards families.

With its zoo (p103) and National Science Museum (p103), **Ueno** is another good bet. The area's Tokyo National Museum (p99) has samurai swords, as does the Japanese Sword Museum (p92) in **Shinjuku**.

The magical Ghibli Museum (p93) honours Japan's own animation genius, Miyazaki Hayao *(Princess Mononoke, Spirited Away)* and is part of a larger park, Inokashira-kōen (p93). If your kids have caught the Japanese character bug, reward good behaviour with a trip to toy emporiums KiddyLand (p143) and Tokyo Character Street (p140).

Japanese kids are wild about trains – chances are yours will be, too. The southern terrace at Shinjuku Station overlooks the multiple tracks that feed the world's busiest train station. Another treat is a ride on the driverless Yurikamome Line that weaves in between skyscrapers. See **Tokyo Urban Baby** (www.tokyourbanbaby.com) for more suggestions about tackling Tokyo with small children.

Older kids and teens should also get a kick out of Tokyo's pop culture and neon streetscapes. **Shibuya** and **Harajuku** in particular are packed with the shops, restaurants and arcades that local teens love. Memorialise your trip with photos at Shibuya's Purikura no Mecca (p88), and don't forget to get in a round of karaoke.

Museum of Contemporary Art, Tokyo (MOT) MUSEUM

(東京都現代美術館; Map p72; www.mot-art-museum.jp; 4-1-1 Miyoshi, Kōtō-ku; adult/child ¥500/free; 10am-6pm Tue-Sun; S Ōedo line to Kiyosumi-Shirakawa, exit B2) For a primer in the major movements of post-WWII Japanese art, a visit to the permanent collection gallery here should do the trick. Temporary exhibitions, on changing subjects (including fashion, architecture and design) cost extra. The building's stone, steel and wood architecture by Yanagisawa Takahiko is a work of art in its own right. The museum is on the edge of Kiba-kōen, a well-signposted 10-minute walk from the subway station.

Odaiba & Tokyo Bay
お台場・東京湾

Odaiba is a collection of artificial islands in Tokyo Bay. Developed mostly in the '90s, it's a bubble-era vision of urban planning, where the buildings are large, the streets are wide and the waterfront is the main attraction. Love it or hate it, you'll definitely feel like you're in an alternate Tokyo.

With its giant malls and entertainment centres, Odaiba is popular with families and also as a teen date spot.

Travelling to Odaiba is most fun on the driverless Yurikamome train, which departs from Shimbashi Station and snakes through skyscrapers before crossing the Rainbow Bridge.

National Museum of Emerging Science & Innovation (Miraikan) MUSEUM

(未来館; Map p110; www.miraikan.jst.go.jp; 2-3-6 Aomi, Kōtō-ku; adult/child ¥620/210; 10am-5pm Wed-Mon; Yurikamome line to Telecom Centre) *Miraikan* means 'hall of the future', and the fascinating exhibits here present the science and technology that will shape the years to come. Lots of hands-on displays make this a great place for kids and curious adults. There are several demonstrations, too, including the humanoid robot ASIMO and the lifelike android Otonaroid. The Gaia dome theatre/planetarium has an English audio option and is popular; reserve your seats as soon as you arrive.

Odaiba Kaihin-kōen PARK

(お台場海浜公園; Odaiba Marine Park; Map p110; www.tptc.co.jp/en/park/tabid/846/Default.aspx; 1-4-1 Daiba, Minato-ku; 24hr; Yurikamome line to Odaiba Kaihin-kōen) One of the best views of Tokyo is from this park's promenades and elevated walkways – especially at night when old-fashioned *yakatabune* (low-slung wooden boats), decorated with lanterns, traverse the bay. Also here you'll find an 800m-long man-made **beach** and an 11m replica of the **Statue of Liberty** (Map p110) – a very popular photo op with the Rainbow Bridge in the background.

Odaiba & Tokyo Bay

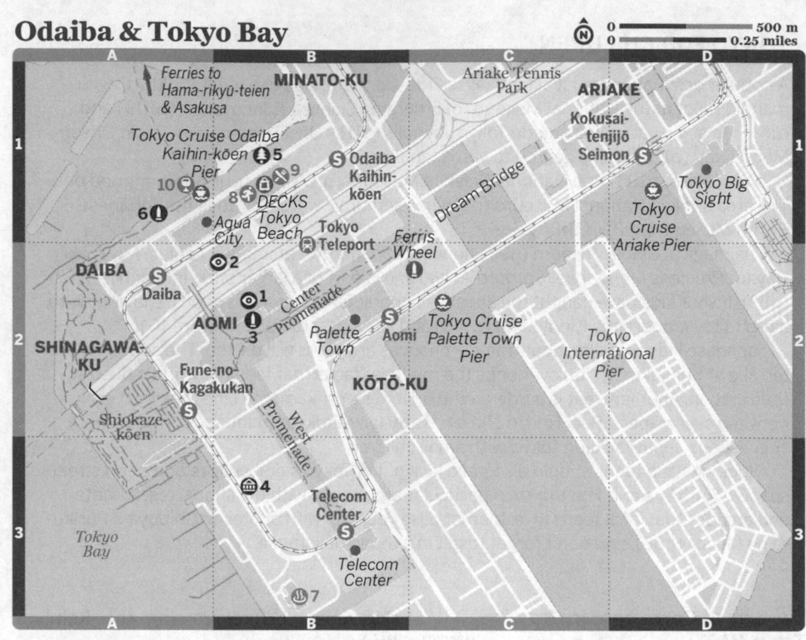

Odaiba & Tokyo Bay

Sights
1 Diver City Tokyo Plaza ... B2
2 Fuji TV ... B2
3 Gundam ... B2
4 National Museum of Emerging Science & Innovation (Miraikan) ... B3
5 Odaiba Kaihin-kōen ... B1
6 Statue of Liberty ... A1

Activities, Courses & Tours
7 Ōedo Onsen Monogatari ... B3
8 Tokyo Joypolis ... B1

Eating
Bills ... (see 9)
9 Odaiba Takoyaki Museum ... B1

Drinking & Nightlife
10 Jicoo the Floating Bar ... A1

Diver City Tokyo Plaza MALL
(Map p110; ☎03-6380-7800; www.divercity-tokyo.com; 1-1-10 Aomi, Kōtō-ku; Yurikamome line to Daiba) This Odaiba mall distinguishes itself more with its nonshopping attractions, including the mixed amusement and sports park **Round1 Stadium**, a rooftop **skate park** and **Gundam Front Tokyo** (http://gundamfront-tokyo.com/en), an exhibition based on the popular robot anime. An 18m-tall model of one of the **Gundam** (ガンダム; Map p110) robots stands in front of the mall and is a great photo op.

Fuji TV ARCHITECTURE
(フジテレビ; Map p110; ☎03-5500-8888; 2-4-8 Daiba, Minato-ku; observation deck adult/child ¥500/300; 10am-6pm Tue-Sun; Yurikamome line to Daiba) Designed by the late, great Tange Kenzō, the Fuji TV headquarters building is recognisable by the 90-degree angles of its scaffolding-like structure. It is topped by a 1200-tonne ball, which includes an observation deck. Pick up an English guide at the desk out front for information on a self-guided tour.

★**Ōedo Onsen Monogatari** ONSEN
(大江戸温泉物語; Map p110; www.ooedoonsen.jp; 2-6-3 Aomi, Kōtō-ku; adult/child from ¥1980/900, after 6pm from ¥1480/900; 11am-9am, last entry 7am; Yurikamome line to Telecom Centre, Rinkai line to Tokyo Teleport with free shuttle bus) Just to experience the truly Japanese phenomenon that is an amusement park centred on bathing is reason enough to visit. The baths, which include gender-divided indoor tubs and *rotemburo* (outdoor baths), are filled with real onsen (hot-spring) water,

pumped from 1400m below Tokyo Bay. The *iwashioyoku* (hot-stone bath) and *tsunaburo* (hot-sand bath) cost extra, as do massages, and require reservations. Visitors with tattoos will be denied admission.

Upon entering, visitors change their clothes for a choice of colourful *yukata* (light cotton kimonos) to wear while they stroll around the complex, which is a lantern-lit re-creation of an old Tokyo downtown area, with food stalls and games. There's also a communal outdoor footbath so mixed groups and families can hang out together.

It's not a bad place to crash overnight, but there's a surcharge of ¥2000 per person if you stay between 2am and 5am, plus ¥3980 if you book a sleeping cabin. This makes it as expensive as some business hotels.

Tokyo Joypolis AMUSEMENT PARK
(東京ジョイポリス; Map p110; http://tokyo-joypolis.com; 3rd-5th fl, Decks Tokyo Beach, 1-6-1 Daiba, Minato-ku; adult/child ¥800/300, all-rides passport ¥3900/2900, passport after 5pm ¥2900/1900; ⏲10am-10pm; Yurikamome line to Odaiba Kaihin-kōen) This indoor amusement park is stacked with virtual-reality attractions and adult thrill rides, such as the video-enhanced Halfpipe Canyon; there are rides for little ones, too. Separate admission and individual ride tickets (most ¥500) are available, but if you plan to go on more than a half-dozen attractions the unlimited 'passport' makes sense.

Tokyo Disney Resort AMUSEMENT PARK
(東京ディズニーリゾート; www.tokyodisneyresort.co.jp; 1-1 Maihama, Urayasu-shi; 1-day ticket for 1 park adult/child ¥6400/4200, after 6pm ¥3400; ⏲varies by season; JR Keiyō line to Maihama) At this very popular resort, you'll find not only Tokyo Disneyland, modelled after the California original, but also Tokyo DisneySea, a clever add-on that caters more to adults and Disney-run hotels. Tickets can be booked online and it's worth packing a *bentō* (boxed meal), as on-site restaurants are almost always overrun with diners.

Courses

A Taste of Culture COOKING
(www.tasteofculture.com) Established by noted Japanese culinary expert Elizabeth Andoh, these courses encompass everything from market tours to culinary classes, all imbued with deep cultural knowledge. Courses are seasonal and fill up fast. Half-day courses (including lunch) start at ¥7000 per person.

Buddha Bellies COOKING
(http://buddhabelliestokyo.jimdo.com) Professional sushi chef and sake sommelier Ayuko leads small classes in sushi, *bentō* and udon making. Prices start at ¥7000 per person for a 2½-hour course.

Ohara School of Ikebana IKEBANA
(小原流いけばな; Map p90; ☎03-5774-5097; www.ohararyu.or.jp; 5-7-17 Minami-Aoyama, Minato-ku; per class ¥4000; S Ginza line to Omote-sandō, exit B1) Every Thursday, from 10.30am to 12.30pm, this well-regarded ikebana school teaches introductory flower-arrangement classes in English. Sign up via email by 3pm the day before.

Mokuhankan PRINTMAKING
(木版館; Map p106; ☎070-5011-1418; http://mokuhankan.com/parties; 2nd fl, 1-41-8 Asakusa, Taitō-ku; per person ¥2000; ⏲10am-5.30pm; Tsukuba Express to Asakusa, exit 5) Try your hand at making *ukiyo-e* (woodblock prints) at this studio run by expat David Bull. Hour-long 'print parties' take place daily; you can sign up online. There's a shop here too, where you can see Bull and Jed Henry's humorous *Ukiyo-e Heroes* series – prints featuring video-game characters in traditional settings.

PUBLIC BATHHOUSES

Prior to Japan's post-WWII economic revolution, most private homes didn't have bathrooms. Instead people washed – and gossiped – at their neighbourhood *sentō* (public bathhouse). Though their numbers are dwindling, there are still about 1000 bathhouses in Tokyo; most neighbourhoods have at least one.

A welcoming place to experience this local culture is at **Jakotsu-yu** (蛇骨湯; Map p106; ☎03-3841-8645; www.jakotsuyu.co.jp; 1-11-11 Asakusa, Taitō-ku; admission ¥460; ⏲1pm-midnight Wed-Mon; S Ginza line to Tawaramachi, exit 3). It has English signage and no policy against tattoos. Unlike most *sentō*, the tubs here are filled with pure hot-spring water, naturally the colour of weak tea. Another treat is the lovely, lantern-lit, rock-framed *rotemburo* (outdoor bath). It's an extra ¥200 for the sauna; ¥140 for a small towel.

1

3

TODD FONG PHOTOGRAPHY / GETTY IMAGES ©

LARRY DALE GORDON / GETTY IMAGES ©

1. Takeshita-dōri (p89)
A neverending procession of shoppers fills this teen-fashion bazaar in trendy Harajuku.

2. Sumo (p846)
Young wrestlers train and live at sumo stables. To see a tournament in Tokyo, visit Ryōgoku Kokugikan (p139).

3. Tsukiji Market (p79)
After seeing all the action at this famous seafood market, breakfast on miso, rice and – of course – fresh fish.

LOTTIE DAVIES / GETTY IMAGES ©

1
TAKARADA
GAMERS
アキバ
を侵略
でゲソ
侵略！イカ娘
ブルーレイ&DVD①
12/24発売
ブルーレイには触手がついてくる？
カラオケパセラ × コラボ決定!!
カラオケパセラ電気街館
2010年11月中旬OPEN
カラオケパセラ昭和館
コンセプトルーム
続々増加中
楽しいパセラの忘年会
19店舗予約受付中
0120-759-835
0120-706-738
秋葉原
野村ビル
俺の妹がこんなに可愛いわけがない
BD&DVD第1巻
12.22発売!
完全生産限定版は本編DISC+特典CDの2枚組!
www.oreimo-anime.com
TOKYO MXほかにてTVアニメ好評放送中!
TY FREE
SCOUNT
IMPUESTOS
カド☆ゲマ
AKIHABARA
GAMERS
ANIBRO
SCOUNT
MOBILES
ラカラダ
美的免税商品
2nd Floor
Discount
computer

LAURIE NOBLE / GETTY IMAGES ©

SYLVAIN GRANDADAM / GETTY IMAGES ©

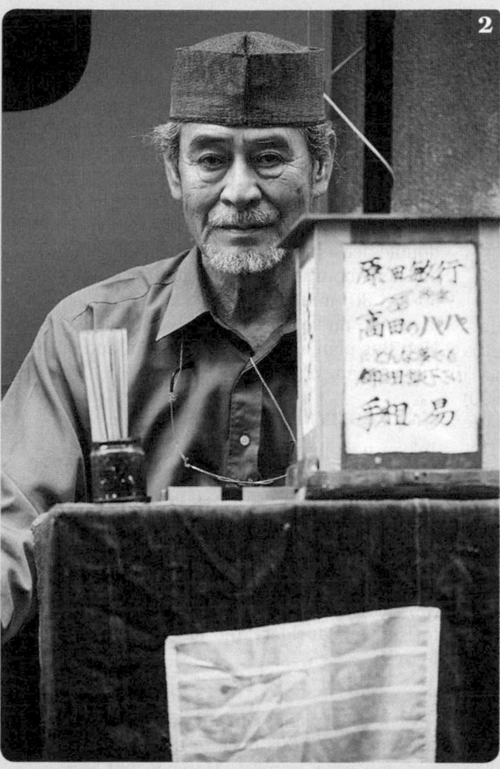

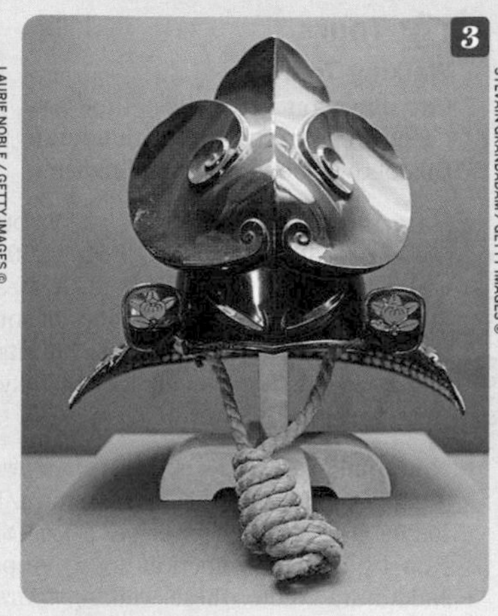

1. Akihabara (p97)
Shops specialising in electronics, manga and anime are a drawcard of this Tokyo neighbourhood.

2. Fortune teller, Tokyo
Traditional culture still thrives in Japan – even in one of its most futuristic cities.

3. Tokyo National Museum (p99)
Samurai helmets, Japanese art and detailed kimonos are on display at this showstopping museum.

4. Sensō-ji (p107)
Asakusa's atmospheric, centuries-old Buddhist temple is also Tokyo's most-visited.

MAREMAGNUM / GETTY IMAGES ©

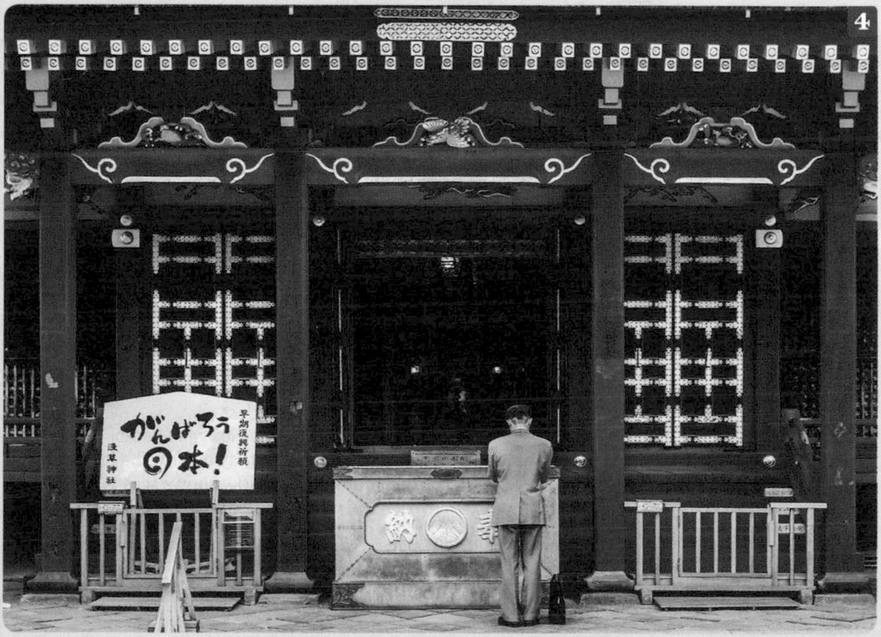

Tours

Walking Tours

Cut down on getting-lost time and get a deeper read on the city with a guide. All of the following offer tours in English.

Haunted Tokyo Tours GUIDED TOUR
(www.hauntedtokyotours.com; from ¥3000 per person) Fun and friendly English-speaking guides take amblers to the scenes of some of the city's most notorious ghost haunts and urban legends. You'll never look at Tokyo the same way again.

New Tsukiji Tour WALKING
(http://homepage3.nifty.com/tokyoworks/TsukijiTour/newtsukijitour.html; tour per person ¥7500) Run by ex-Tsukiji auction-house employee Nakamura Naoto, these walking tours (for one to six people) start at 3am and take you behind the scenes of the market.

Tokyo Metropolitan Government Tours GUIDED TOUR
(www.gotokyo.org/en/tourists/guideservice/guideservice/index.html) The Tokyo government tourism bureau can arrange free or fairly cheap walking tours in one of seven different languages with volunteer guides. There are several routes to choose from, each lasting about three hours.

Tokyo SGG Club GUIDED TOUR
(www2.ocn.ne.jp/~sgg) FREE Free guided tours of Asakusa (11am to 1.15pm Saturday and Sunday) and Ueno (10.30am to 1.30pm Wednesday and Friday) on a first-come, first-served basis.

Bus Tours

The following companies offer a variety of reliable bus tours with English-speaking guides.

Hato Bus Tours BUS TOUR
(Map p72; 3435-6081; www.hatobus.com; per person ¥1500-12,000; JR Yamanote line to Hamamatsuchō, south exit) Tokyo's most well-known bus-tour company offers hour-long, half-day and full-day bus tours of the city. Shorter tours cruise by the sights in an open-air double-decker bus; longer ones make stops. Tours leave from the Hato Bus Terminal in Hamamatsuchō.

Gray Line BUS TOUR
(3595-5948; www.jgl.co.jp/inbound/index.htm; per person ¥4000-9700) Offers half-day and full-day tours with stops, covering key downtown sights, as well as tours to Hakone. Pick-up service from major hotels is available, otherwise most tours leave from in front of the Dai-Ichi Hotel in Shimbashi (near Ginza).

SkyBus BUS TOUR
(Map p76; 3215-0008; www.skybus.jp; 2-5-2 Marunouchi, Chiyoda-ku; tours adult/child from ¥1600/700, Sky Hop Bus adult/child ¥2500/1200; ticket office 9am-6pm; JR Yamanote line to Tokyo, Marunouchi south exit) Open-top double-decker buses cruise through different neighbourhoods of the city (for roughly 50 to 80 minutes); most have English-language audio guidance aboard. The Sky Hop Bus plan allows you to hop on and off buses on any of the three routes.

Festivals & Events

Tokyo has hundreds of annual festivals, with the biggest ones happening during the warmer months. Here are some of the major ones; see **Go Tokyo** (www.gotokyo.org/en) for month-by-month listings.

Tokyo International Anime Fair FAIR
(www.tokyoanime.jp/en) Events and exhibitions for industry insiders and fans alike in late March.

Hanami CHERRY BLOSSOMS
(花見) Cherry-blossom-viewing obsession takes over as locals flock to the city's parks and cemeteries from late March to mid-April.

Design Festa ART
(www.designfesta.com) In mid-May a wide showcase of work from budding designers and artists is displayed at Tokyo Big Sight. A second showing takes place in November.

Sanja Matsuri PARADE
(三社祭) Tokyo's biggest festival takes place over the third weekend in May and features a parade of hundreds of *mikoshi* (portable shrines) through Asakusa.

Mitama Matsuri CULTURAL
(みたままつり) Yasukuni-jinja celebrates the summer festival of the dead with 30,000 paper lanterns in mid-July.

Sumida-gawa Fireworks FIREWORKS
(隅田川花火大会 Sumida-gawa Hanabi Taikai) Held on the last Saturday of July, the largest of the summer fireworks shows sees 20,000 pyrotechnic wonders explode over Asakusa.

Tokyo Designers Week DESIGN
(www.tdwa.com/en_index.html) In late October, the international design world convenes for

a week of exhibitions at Meiji-jingū Gyoen, plus satellite shows at shops and galleries.

Gishi-sai CULTURAL

(義士祭) On 14 December, a memorial service is held at Sengaku-ji to honour the 47 masterless samurai who famously avenged their master, and locals don their best medieval garb.

Emperor's Birthday CULTURAL

(www.kunaicho.go.jp) This day – 23 December – is one of only two days a year that the Imperial Palace is open to the public; the other is 2 January.

Sleeping

Tokyo is known for being an expensive place for accommodation; however, more and more attractive budget and midrange options are popping up every year. The best deals are on the east side of town in Ueno and Asakusa.

Wherever you decide to stay, advanced booking is highly recommended. You will almost always find cheaper hotel rates online (often from the hotel's own website).

Note that some budget and midrange options do not accept credit cards – come prepared with cash.

Marunouchi (Tokyo Station area) 丸の内（東京駅）

Yaesu Terminal Hotel BUSINESS HOTEL ¥¥

(八重洲ターミナルホテル; Map p76; 03-3281-3771; www.yth.jp; 1-5-14 Yaesu, Chūō-ku; s/d ¥11,500/16,500; @; JR lines to Tokyo, Yaesu north exit) This sleek little business hotel on cherry-tree-lined Sakura-dōri has contemporary lines and a minimalist look. Though room sizes are generally tiny, they're decently priced for this neighbourhood and showcase modern, sporting, contemporary art by radiographic artist Steven Meyers.

Tokyo Station Hotel LUXURY HOTEL ¥¥¥

(東京ステーションホテル; Map p76; 03-5220-1112; www.tokyostationhotel.jp; 1-9-1 Marunouchi, Chiyoda-ku; r from ¥41,000; @; JR lines to Tokyo, Marunouchi south exit) Representing a return to the classics, the Tokyo Station Hotel has brushed up handsomely as part of the heritage building's restoration. Rooms are spacious and decorated in an opulent European fashion, with tall ceilings, marble counters and dripping chandeliers. Some rooms have views of the Imperial Palace.

Ginza & Tsukiji 銀座・築地

★Mitsui Garden Hotel Ginza Premier HOTEL ¥¥

(三井ガーデンホテル銀座プレミア; Map p76; 03-3543-1131; www.gardenhotels.co.jp; 8-13-1 Ginza, Chūō-ku; r from ¥16,000; @; S Ginza line to Shimbashi, exit 1) If you book ahead and online, this upmarket business hotel is a steal. It is reasonably priced and has a great location, pleasantly decorated rooms, and a high-rise lobby with killer Shiodome and Tokyo Tower views.

Tōkyū Stay Higashi-Ginza BUSINESS HOTEL ¥¥

(東急ステイ東銀座; Map p76; 03-5551-0109; www.tokyustay.co.jp; 4-11-5 Tsukiji, Chūō-ku; s/d from ¥14,000/19,900; @; S Hibiya line to Tskuji, exits 1 & 2) With a giant red snapper painted on the side of the building you can't miss this place in Tsukiji's outer-market area. It's a combination of business hotel and longer-stay apartments with all the comfortable, compact rooms fitted with washing machines/dryers and kitchenettes.

Imperial Hotel LUXURY HOTEL ¥¥¥

(帝国ホテル; Map p76; 03-3504-1111; www.imperialhotel.co.jp; 1-1-1 Uchisaiwai-chō, Chiyoda-ku; s/d from ¥42,770/48,710; @; S Hibiya line to Hibiya, exit A13) The present building is the successor to Frank Lloyd Wright's 1923 masterpiece, and small tributes to the architect's style can be found in the lobby and elsewhere. The rooms are not the most stylish in Tokyo but are large, comfortable and generally have impressive views; the ones on the Imperial floor are the most up-to-date. Service here is virtually peerless.

Roppongi 六本木

★Hotel S BOUTIQUE HOTEL ¥¥

(ホテル S; Map p82; 03-5771-2469; http://hr-roppongi.jp; 1-11-6 Nishi-Azabu, Minato-ku; r from ¥18,200; @; S Hibiya line to Roppongi, exit 2) The eight styles of room at this boutique property capture the arty design spirit of Roppongi. Some of the more expensive duplex-type rooms have Japanese design elements such as tatami (in charcoal) and circular *hinoki* (wooden baths). The entry-level rooms are also a cut above the usual. There are serviced apartments here, too, if you're planning a longer stay.

B Roppongi BUSINESS HOTEL ¥¥

(ザ・ビー六本木; Map p82; 5412-0451; www.theb-hotels.com/the-b-roppongi/en/index.html;

3-9-8 Roppongi, Minato-ku; s/d incl breakfast from ¥13,600/14,100; ; Hibiya line to Roppongi, exit 5) The slick, white-brown rooms here range in size from 10 to 31 sq metres, albeit with small, prefab bathrooms. Atmosphere is business-casual and the location is perfect for Roppongi's nocturnal attractions. If it's full there are a couple of other B hotels nearby in Akasaka.

Ritz-Carlton Tokyo LUXURY HOTEL ¥¥¥
(ザ・リッツ・カールトン東京; Map p82; 03-3423-8000; www.ritzcarlton.com; Tokyo Midtown, 9-7-1 Akasaka, Minato-ku; s/ste from ¥73,500/126,500; ; Hibiya line to Roppongi, exit 8) The Ritz-Carlton's lobby – with giant paintings by Sam Francis and views clear to the Imperial Palace – is on the 45th floor, and capacious rooms go up from there. Concierges can do just about anything, and if you send your shoes for a complimentary shine they return in a lovely wooden box.

Ebisu & Meguro 恵比寿・目黒

★ **Claska** BOUTIQUE HOTEL ¥¥
(クラスカ; Map p72; 03-3719-8121; www.claska.com/en/hotel; 1-3-18 Chūō-chō, Meguro-ku; s/d from ¥13,200/20,900, weekly per night s ¥8200; ; No 1, 2 or 7 from Meguro Station to Shimizu, Tōkyū Tōyoko line to Gakugei Daigaku, east exit) The Claska is hands-down Tokyo's most stylish hotel, though you might not know it from the retro business-hotel facade. No two rooms are alike: some have tatami and floor cushions; others have spacious terraces and glass-walled bathrooms. Its 20 rooms fill up fast. The only drawback is the out-of-the-way location, about 2km west of Meguro Station.

Weekly Dormy Inn Meguro Aobadai BUSINESS HOTEL ¥¥
(ウィークリードーミーイン目黒青葉台; Map p72; 03-6894-5489; www.hotespa.net/weekly/meguro/en; 3-21-8 Aobadai, Meguro-ku; s/d from ¥7400/12,400; ; Hibiya line to Naka-Meguro) If you prefer to base yourself somewhere less hectic – but no less fun – try this business hotel in hip Naka-Meguro. Rooms include a hotplate and fridge. There are laundry machines and free bicycle rentals, too. Wi-fi is weak in some rooms, but fine in the lobby. Breakfast (rice balls) and even dinner (noodles) is included.

Shibuya & Harajuku 渋谷・原宿

Capsule & Sauna Century CAPSULE HOTEL ¥
(カプセル&サウナセンチュリー; Map p88; 03-3464-1777; www.century-grp.com; 1-19-14 Dōgenzaka, Shibuya-ku; capsules from ¥3990; ; JR Yamanote line to Shibuya, Hachikō exit) This men-only capsule hotel perched atop Dōgenzaka hill includes large shared bathrooms, massage chairs and coin-laundry machines; the 'deluxe' capsules are slightly bigger. It's a clean, well-run place, and major credit cards are accepted. It's also pretty popular, so it's a good idea to reserve a spot before you head out for the night.

WHERE TO STAY

Marunouchi Central, with convenient transport links; no budget options and quiet at night.

Ginza & Tsukiji Great shopping and dining; near the fish market; crowded, expensive area.

Roppongi Art museums and nightlife at your door; noisy all night.

Ebisu & Meguro Hip drinking and dining scene; removed from major sights.

Shibuya & Harajuku Buzzing streetscape, with good shopping, restaurants and transit links; very crowded and possible sensory overload.

Shinjuku Transport hub with plenty of dining and nightlife; crowded, with many cheaper options in the red-light district.

Kōrakuen & Akihabara Central with good transit links and budget options; drab district with little dining and nightlife.

Ueno & Yanaka Traditional ryokan, budget options and good airport access; most accommodation in quiet residential neighbourhoods.

Asakusa Backpacker central with old-city atmosphere and great hostels; long train rides to other parts of the city.

Dormy Inn Premium Shibuya Jingūmae BUSINESS HOTEL ¥¥
(ドーミーインプレミアム渋谷神宮前; Map p90; ☎03-5774-5489; www.hotespa.net/hotels/shibuya; 6-24-4 Jingūmae, Shibuya-ku; s/d from ¥11,490/15,990; JR Yamanote line to Harajuku, Omote-sandō exit) This flashy new property from the Dormy Inn chain of business hotels has typically small rooms with double beds (140cm) but a host of perks: free breakfast and noodles in the evening, laundry facilities, a communal bath and shuttle service to Shibuya Station (7am to noon).

Hotel Fukudaya RYOKAN ¥¥
(ホテル福田屋; Map p72; ☎03-3467-5833; www2.gol.com/users/ryokan-fukudaya/index.html; 4-5-9 Aobadai, Meguro-ku; s/d from ¥6600/11,500; Keiō line to Shinsen) Hotel Fukudaya offers futons in crisp, white linens on fresh tatami (woven reed mats); the western-style rooms are cheaper, but not as nice. Some rooms have private baths, but there is also a communal *o-furo* (Japanese-style bath). It's in a residential neighbourhood, a seven-minute walk from Shinsen Station or a 20-minute walk from Shibuya.

★ **Shibuya Granbell Hotel** BOUTIQUE HOTEL ¥¥¥
(渋谷グランベルホテル; Map p88; ☎03-5457-2681; www.granbellhotel.jp; 15-17 Sakuragaoka-chō, Shibuya-ku; s/d from ¥13,000/22,000; JR Yamanote line to Shibuya, south exit) Though priced about the same as a business hotel, the Granbell is far more stylish. Some rooms have glass-enclosed bathrooms, Simmons beds and pop-art curtains. The hotel is on the quieter side of Shibuya, towards Daikanyama; still, it's just a few minutes' walk to the station.

The Granbell is also available during the day for a 'rest' (from ¥10,500 for five hours), meaning it doubles as an upscale love hotel.

Hotel Mets Shibuya BUSINESS HOTEL ¥¥¥
(ホテルメッツ渋谷; Map p88; ☎03-3409-0011; www.hotelmets.jp/shibuya; 3-29-17 Shibuya, Shibuya-ku; s/d incl breakfast from ¥15,500/25,000; JR Yamanote line to Shibuya, new south exit) Super convenient and comfortable, the Hotel Mets is inside Shibuya Station's quiet south exit. For a business hotel it's fairly stylish and the double beds clock in at a roomy 160cm. Bonus: breakfast is included, either a buffet spread or toast and eggs at the in-house cafe. Reception is on the 4th floor.

Excel Hotel Tōkyū HOTEL ¥¥¥
(エクセルホテル東急; Map p88; ☎03-5457-0109; www.tokyuhotelsjapan.com/en/TE/TE_SHIBU/index.html; 1-12-2 Dōgenzaka, Shibuya-ku; s/d from ¥24,948/34,452; JR Yamanote line to Shibuya, Hachikō exit) This hotel is right on top of Shibuya Station, a location you'll be grateful for after a long day. Rooms are spacious though ordinary. Prices rise along with the floor numbers, but you can get a pretty good view with a simple upgrade for ¥2000 per night to a 'city view' room. The hotel is part of the Mark City complex.

Shinjuku 新宿

Ladies 510 CAPSULE HOTEL ¥
(レディース510; Map p72; ☎03-3200-1945; www.capsule510.jp/ladies510; 2-40-1 Kabukichō, Shinjuku-ku; capsule ¥4300; JR Yamanote line to Shinjuku, east exit) This is a clean, well-run capsule hotel just for women in Kabukichō. Park your stuff in the narrow locker on arrival and switch to the pyjamas provided; towels, hairbrushes and skin creams are also included. There's a shared bath, sauna, cafe and free iPad rentals. It's a small place and fills up early on weekends.

E Hotel Higashi-Shinjuku BUSINESS HOTEL ¥¥
(イーホテル東新宿; Map p72; www.shinjukuhotel.co.jp/eng; 2-3-15 Kabukichō, Shinjuku-ku; s/d from ¥9000/11,000; Ōedo line to Higashi-Shinjuku, exit A1) This traveller favourite has an excellent location – just in front of the Higashi-Shinjuku subway station – friendly staff and lots of city info. Rooms are typically small but have a clean, modern feel and comfortable double beds. Those on the main street might get some noise, but some have nice night views. There's a coffee shop on the ground floor.

Sekitei RYOKAN ¥¥
(石亭; Map p72; ☎03-3365-5931; http://license-kanren.com/sekitei?lang=en; 2-15-10 Hyakunin-chō, Shinjuku-ku; s/d ¥7800/11,400; JR Yamanote line to Shin-Ōkubo) A 15-minute walk north of Shinjuku, Sekitei is a quiet, personable inn with clean and comfortable tatami rooms. Try to book the one with the rock garden running through the centre. Staff speak some English. There's a small lounge and laundry room.

Citadines APARTMENT ¥¥
(シタディーン; Map p94; ☎03-5379-7208; www.citadines.com; 1-28-13 Shinjuku, Shinjuku-ku; r from ¥14,256; Marunouchi line to

Shinjuku-gyoenmae, exit 2) Bright and modern, Citadines has compact studios with queen-sized beds, kitchenettes and a sitting area. Rooms sleep up to three. It's a bit far from the Shinjuku action, though those staying for more than a few days will likely come to appreciate the relative quiet. There's a fitness room and laundrette. English is spoken.

Kadoya Hotel HOTEL ¥¥
(かどやホテル; Map p94; ☎03-3346-2561; www.kadoya-hotel.co.jp; 1-23-1 Nishi-Shinjuku, Shinjuku-ku; s/d from ¥9000/14,000; ; JR Yamanote line to Shinjuku, west exit) Kadoya has been welcoming foreign tourists for decades and is above all friendly and accommodating. The standard rooms show their age, but are clean and comfortable, and a steal for Nishi-Shinjuku. The newer 'comfort' rooms (from ¥19,500) have more space, Simmons beds, Japanese-style bathtubs and the best decor. There's also a coin laundry.

★ **Park Hyatt Tokyo** LUXURY HOTEL ¥¥¥
(パークハイアット東京; Map p94; ☎03-5322-1234; http://tokyo.park.hyatt.com; 3-7-1-2 Nishi-Shinjuku, Shinjuku-ku; d from ¥43,000; ; S Ōedo line to Tochōmae, exit A4) The Park Hyatt still looks as tasteful and elegant as it did when it opened 20 years ago. The hotel starts on the 41st floor of a Tange Kenzō-designed skyscraper in west Shinjuku, meaning even the entry-level rooms have otherworldly views. Perks for guests include complimentary mobile-phone rentals (you pay for outgoing calls only) and morning yoga classes.

MISSING THE MIDNIGHT TRAIN

Cinderellas who've stayed out partying past midnight and found that their last train has turned into a *kabocha* (pumpkin) needn't fret. If dancing the rest of the night away doesn't appeal, and an astronomically priced taxi ride doesn't compute, try a **manga kissa** instead. These 'comic-book coffee shops' have private cubicles for reading, watching DVDs, catching up on email and, more often than not, sleeping.

Overnight packages – as low as ¥1500 for up to eight hours – are a bargain. Check in at the reception desk, prepay for your stay and while away the wee hours; some even have shower stalls and will rent you a hair dryer and a blanket. **Gran Cyber Cafe Bagus** (www.bagus-99.com/internet_cafe) is one of the nicer chains, with convenient branches in Shinjuku, Shibuya and Roppongi.

Kōrakuen & Akihabara 後楽園・秋葉原

Kimi Ryokan RYOKAN ¥
(貴美旅館; Map p72; ☎03-3971-3766; www.kimi-ryokan.jp; 2-36-8 Ikebukuro, Toshima-ku; s/d from ¥4860/6590; ; JR Yamanote line to Ikebukuro, west exit) Easily one of the best budget ryokan in Tokyo, this convivial inn has tatami rooms of various sizes and a Japanese-style lounge area that's conducive to meeting other travellers. Clean showers and toilets are shared, and there's a lovely Japanese cypress bath. Book well in advance.

Tokyo Central Youth Hostel HOSTEL ¥
(東京セントラルユースホステル; Map p96; ☎03-3235-1107; www.jyh.gr.jp/tcyh; 18th fl, 1-1 Kagurakashi, Shinjuku-ku; dm ¥4050, with YHA discount ¥3450; ; JR Sōbu line to Iidabashi, west exit) Sitting right on top of Iidabashi Station, which handles five train lines, this clean, well-managed hostel has fantastic transport access. It also has luxury hotel-worthy night views. The drawbacks: a utilitarian atmosphere, wi-fi in the lobby only and an 11pm curfew. Sleeping is on basic wooden bunks in gender-segregated dorm rooms. There's a breakfast buffet (¥600) and laundry machines.

There's little signage out front, but it's in the big office building in front of Iidabashi Station; take the elevator to the 18th floor.

Sakura Hotel Jimbōchō HOSTEL ¥
(サクラホテル池袋; Map p96; ☎03-3261-3939; www.sakura-hotel.co.jp; 2-21-4 Kanda-Jimbōchō, Chiyoda-ku; dm/s/d from ¥3300/6300/8450; ; Marunouchi line to Jimbōchō, exit A6) A long-standing, great budget option with a sociable atmosphere. Staff are bilingual and helpful, and the rooms, though basic and tiny, are comfortable and clean. There's a 24-hour cafe, a laundry and internet access.

Hilltop Hotel HISTORIC HOTEL ¥¥
(山の上ホテル; Map p96; ☎03-3293-2311; www.yamanoue-hotel.co.jp; 1-1 Kanda-Surugadai, Chiyoda-ku; s/d from ¥20,396/21,584; ; JR Chūō or Sōbu lines to Ochanomizu, Ochanomizu exit) This art-deco gem from the 1930s exudes personality and charm, with antique wooden furniture and a wood-panelled lounge.

Mishima Yukio wrote his last few novels here. The older rooms in the main building come with antique writing desks and leather upholstered chairs.

The Agnes Hotel BOUTIQUE HOTEL ¥¥¥
(アグネスホテル; Map p96; ☎03-3267-5505; www.agneshotel.com/foreign/english.html; 2-20-1 Kagurazaka, Shinjuku-ku; s/d ¥22,000/27,000; ; JR Sōbu line to Iidabashi, west exit) Tucked away on a side street in atmospheric Kagurazaka, Agnes feels like a secluded retreat (even though it's only a few minutes' walk to the train station). The 56 rooms, big enough to move around in, are done up in soft colours and come with cushy armchairs.

Ueno & Yanaka 上野・谷中

★**Toco** HOSTEL ¥
(トコ; Map p72; ☎03-6458-1686; http://backpackersjapan.co.jp; 2-13-21 Shitaya, Taitō-ku; dm/r from ¥2700/6500; ; S Hibiya line to Iriya, exit 4) A group of friends renovated this old wooden building (which dates to 1920 and was once frequented by geisha) and turned it into one of Tokyo's most attractive hostels. Private tatami rooms and dorms with wooden bunks surround a small garden, and there's a funky bar-lounge out front.

★**Sawanoya Ryokan** RYOKAN ¥¥
(旅館澤の屋; Map p102; ☎03-3822-2251; www.sawanoya.com; 2-3-11 Yanaka, Taitō-ku; s/d from ¥5184/9720; ; S Chiyoda line to Nezu, exit 1) Sawanoya is a gem in quiet Yanaka, with very friendly staff and all the traditional hospitality you would expect of a ryokan. The shared cypress and earthenware baths are the perfect balm after a long day (some rooms have their own bath, too). The lobby overflows with information about travel options in Japan and bicycles are available for rent.

Hōmeikan RYOKAN ¥¥
(鳳明館; Map p72; ☎03-3811-1181; www.homeikan.com; 5-10-5 Hongō, Bunkyō-ku; s/d from ¥8100/14,040; ; S Ōedo line to Kasuga, exit A6) Atop a slope in a quiet residential neighbourhood, this beautifully crafted wooden ryokan is an old-world oasis in the middle of Tokyo. The main Honkan wing dates from the Meiji era and is registered as an important cultural property, though we prefer the Daimachi Bekkan, with its winding corridors and garden. Rates include breakfast.

Annex Katsutarō Ryokan RYOKAN ¥¥
(アネックス勝太郎旅館; Map p102; ☎03-3828-2500; www.katsutaro.com; 3-8-4 Yanaka, Taitō-ku; s/d from ¥6500/10,800; ; S Chiyoda line to Sendagi, exit 2) More like a modern hotel than a traditional ryokan, the family-run Annex Katsutarō has spotless, thoughtfully arranged tatami rooms with attached bathrooms. Though a bit of a walk from the sights in Ueno, it's ideal for exploring the old Yanaka district. Breakfast and bicycles are available for a small fee.

Ryokan Katsutarō RYOKAN ¥¥
(旅館勝太郎; Map p102; ☎03-3821-9808; www.katsutaro.com; 4-16-8 Ike-no-hata, Taitō-ku; s/d from ¥5500/9000; ; S Chiyoda line to Nezu, exit 2) The original Ryokan Katsutarō has a quiet and family-like atmosphere, with very affable managers. Though the building may be aged, the eight tatami rooms have been renovated without ruining the inn's character; some have en suite baths, others don't. Bicycle rental is available.

TokHouse RENTAL HOUSE ¥¥
(Map p102; ☎090-9674-4198; www.tokhouse.com; 3-52-9 Sendagi, Bunkyō-ku; s/d/q from ¥8000/10,000/13,000; ; JR Yamanote line to Nishi-Nippori, west exit) For the price of a room in a business hotel you can get your own apartment, with a fully equipped kitchen, in the heart of Yanaka. There's a two-night minimum and a ¥5000 to ¥6000 cleaning fee; ask about discounts for families with children. Richard, the American owner and a long-time Tokyo resident, has lots of tips for exploring the area.

Asakusa & Sumida-gawa 浅草・隅田川

★**Nui** HOSTEL ¥
(ヌイ; Map p72; ☎03-6240-9854; http://backpackersjapan.co.jp/nui_en; 2-14-13 Kuramae, Taitō-ku; dm/d from ¥2700/6800; ; S Ōedo line to Kuramae, exit A7) In a former warehouse, this hostel has raised the bar for stylish budget digs in Tokyo. High ceilings mean bunks you can comfortably sit up in and there is an enormous shared kitchen and workspace. Best of all is the ground-floor bar and lounge, with furniture made from salvaged timber; it's a popular local hang-out.

Khaosan World HOSTEL ¥
(Map p106; www.khaosan-tokyo.com/en/world/index.html; 3-15-1 Nishi-Asakusa, Taitō-ku; dm/d from ¥2200/8400, f ¥12,000; ;

LONG-TERM RENTALS

If you're planning to stick around for a couple weeks or more, a furnished apartment or a room in a share house (aka gaijin house) might be a better deal.

Sakura House (www.sakura-house.com) has dozens of share houses around the city and has long been a right of passage for expats getting started in Tokyo. Alternatively, **Kimi Information Center** (www.kimiwillbe.com) offers short- and long-stay, furnished and unfurnished apartments for the budget-minded, plus information on English-teaching jobs.

Tsukuba Express to Asakusa, exit A2) Hands down Tokyo's most oddball hostel, Khaosan World has taken over an ageing love hotel and left much of the design elements intact – things like mirrored ceilings and glittering brocade wallpaper (don't worry: it's clean). There's a wide variety of rooms to choose from, including ones with tatami floors and capsule-style bunks. There are cooking and laundry facilities, too.

Andon Ryokan RYOKAN ¥
(行燈旅館; Map p72; 03-3873-8611; www.andon.co.jp; 2-34-10 Nihonzutsumi, Taitō-ku; s/d from ¥6020/7140; @; S Hibiya line to Minowa, exit 3) About 2km north of Asakusa, the minimalist and modern Andon Ryokan is fabulously designed in form and function. It has tiny but immaculate tatami rooms and a spectacular upper-floor spa, which can be used privately. The owner collects antiques and will serve you breakfast on dishes worth more than your stay.

K's House Tokyo HOSTEL ¥
(ケイズハウス東京; Map p72; 03-5833-0555; http://kshouse.jp; 3-20-10 Kuramae, Taitō-ku; dm/s/d ¥2900/4500/7200; @; S Ōedo line to Kuramae, exit A6) This homey, modern hostel, with comfy sofas in the living room, cooking facilities and a roof terrace, is a backpacker fave. From exit A6, walk northwest along Asakusa-dōri and turn left at the first corner. K's House is the yellow building at the end of the block.

Tokyo Ryokan RYOKAN ¥
(東京旅館; Map p106; 090-8879-3599; www.tokyoryokan.com; 2-4-8 Nishi-Asakusa, Taitō-ku; r from ¥7000; ; S Ginza line to Tawaramachi, exit 3) This tidy inn has only three tatami rooms and no en suite bathrooms but tonnes of charm. There are touches of calligraphy, attractive woodwork and sliding screens. The owner, an avid traveller, speaks fluent English and is very knowledgeable about Asakusa.

Sukeroku No Yado Sadachiyo RYOKAN ¥¥
(助六の宿貞千代; Map p106; 03-3842-6431; www.sadachiyo.co.jp; 2-20-1 Asakusa, Taitō-ku; d with/without 2 meals from ¥33,600/19,600; @; S Ginza line to Asakusa, exit 1) This stunning ryokan virtually transports its guests to old Edo. Gorgeously maintained tatami rooms are spacious for two people, and all come with modern, Western-style bathrooms. Splurge on an exquisite meal here, and make time for the *o-furo* (traditional Japanese bath), one made of fragrant Japanese cypress and the other of black granite. Look for the rickshaw parked outside.

Eating

When it comes to Tokyo superlatives, the city's eating scene takes the cake. There are more restaurants in this pulsing megalopolis than in any other city in the world. And the quality is unparalleled, too – you're rarely more than 500m from a good, if not great, restaurant.

Best of all, you can eat well on any budget in pretty much every neighbourhood. Lunch is usually excellent value, with many pricier restaurants offering cheaper courses during the noontime hours. Reservations are necessary only at upmarket restaurants, though they're a good idea at midrange places (especially on Friday and Saturday evenings) if you have a party larger than two.

Older neighbourhoods such as Ueno and Asakusa are known for their traditional, sometimes century-old, restaurants. Cosmopolitan Roppongi has the most variety in terms of international cuisine. For sushi, Ginza and Tsukiji are tops; Ginza is also known for its upscale restaurants. Westside neighbourhoods such as Ebisu, Shibuya and Harajuku have more trendy joints. Of course there are numerous exceptions to all of this, too!

Marunouchi (Tokyo Station area) 丸の内（東京駅）

Rose Bakery Marunouchi BAKERY ¥
(ローズベーカリー　丸の内; Map p76; 03-3212-1715; http://rosebakery.jp; Meiji-Yasada Bldg, 2-1-1 Marunouchi, Chiyoda-ku; cakes & quiches from ¥410, lunch set ¥1350; 11am-7pm; ; S Chiyoda line to Nijūbashimae, exit 3) Tokyo has taken

to Paris' Rose Bakery style of dining. Branches of this delicious organic cafe have popped up here in the Comme des Garçons boutique as well as at the same fashion company's Dover Street Market in Ginza and Isetan in Shinjuku. Vegetarians are well served but it is also for those who fancy a full English fry-up for weekend brunch.

Tokyo Rāmen Street RĀMEN ¥

(東京ラーメンストリート; Map p76; www.tokyoeki-1bangai.co.jp/ramenstreet; B1 First Avenue Tokyo Station, 1-9-1 Marunouchi, Chiyoda-ku; rāmen from ¥800; ⏲7.30am-10.30pm; 🚆JR lines to Tokyo Station, Yaesu south exit) Eight hand-picked *rāmen-ya* operate minibranches in this basement arcade on the Yaesu side of Tokyo Station. All the major styles are covered – from *shōyu* (soy-sauce base) to *tsukemen* (cold noodles served on the side). Long lines form outside the most popular but they tend to move quickly.

Meal MUJI Yūrakuchō DELI ¥

(MealMUJI有楽町; Map p76; ☎03-5208-8241; www.muji.net/cafemeal/; 3-8-3 Marunouchi, Chiyoda-ku; meals from ¥780; ⏲10am-9pm; 🚭🖉; 🚆JR Yamanote line to Yūrakuchō, Kyōbashi exit) Those who subscribe to the Muji lifestyle will be delighted to know that the 'no name brand' experience goes beyond neutral-toned notebooks, containers and linens. Meal MUJI follows the 'simpler is better' mantra with fresh deli fare uncluttered by chemicals and unpronounceable ingredients.

★ **Hōnen Manpuku** JAPANESE ¥¥

(豊年萬福; Map p76; ☎03-3277-3330; www.hounenmanpuku.jp; 1-8-16 Nihombashi-Muromachi, Chūō-ku; mains ¥1280-1850; ⏲11.30am-2.30pm & 5-11pm Mon-Sat, 5-10pm Sun; 🗐; Ⓢ Ginza line to Mitsukoshimae, exit A1) Offering a riverside terrace in warmer months, Hōnen Manpuku's interior is dominated by giant *washi* (Japanese handmade paper) lanterns beneath which patrons tuck into bargain-priced beef or pork sukiyaki and other traditional dishes. Ingredients are sourced from gourmet retailers in Nihombashi. Lunchtime set menus are great value.

Ginza & Tsukiji 銀座・築地

Ore-no-dashi JAPANESE ¥

(俺のだし; Map p76; ☎03-3571-6762; www.oreno.co.jp/en/eaterycat/dashi; 7-6-6 Ginza; dishes from ¥380-1480; ⏲5pm-2am Mon-Fri, 4-11pm Sat & Sun; 🗐; Ⓢ Ginza line to Ginza, exit A2) The Ore-no chain – where you stand to eat gourmet dishes prepared by skilled chefs at bargain prices – has been a massive success in Ginza. This one specialises in *oden* – delicious morsels simmered in *dashi*-stock. There are seats here too and a good wine list.

Daiwa Sushi SUSHI ¥¥

(大和寿司; Map p76; ☎03-3547-6807; Bldg 6, 5-2-1 Tsukiji, Chūō-ku; sushi set ¥3500; ⏲5am-1.30pm Mon-Sat, closed occasional Wed; 🚭; Ⓢ Ōedo line to Tsukijishijomae, exit A1) Waits of over one hour are commonplace at Tsukiji's most famous sushi bar, after which you'll be expected to eat and run. But it's all worth it once your first piece of delectable sushi hits the counter. Unless you're comfortable ordering in Japanese, the standard set (seven *nigiri*, plus *maki* and miso soup) is a good bet; there's a picture menu.

Trattoria Tsukiji Paradiso! ITALIAN ¥¥

(Map p76; ☎03-3545-5550; www.tsukiji-paradiso.com; 6-27-3 Tsukiji, Chūō-ku; mains ¥1500-3600; ⏲11am-2pm & 6-10pm; Ⓢ Hibiya line to Tsukiji, exit 2) Paradise for food lovers, indeed. This charming, aqua-painted trattoria plays on its proximity to Tsukiji with seafood pasta dishes that will make you want to lick the plate clean. Its signature linguine is packed with shellfish in a scrumptious tomato, chilli and garlic sauce. Lunch (from ¥980) is a bargain; book for dinner.

★ **Kyūbey** SUSHI ¥¥¥

(久兵衛; Map p76; ☎03-3571-6523; www.kyubey.jp; 8-7-6 Ginza, Chūō-ku; sushi sets lunch ¥5000-8400, dinner from ¥10,500; ⏲11.30am-2pm & 5-10pm Mon-Sat; 🗐; Ⓢ Ginza line to Shimbashi, exit 3) Since 1936, Kyūbey's quality and presentation has won it a moneyed and celebrity clientele. Even so, this is a supremely foreigner-friendly and relaxed restaurant. Expect personal greetings in English by the owner Imada-san and his team of talented chefs who will make and serve your sushi, piece by piece.

Maru JAPANESE ¥¥¥

(銀座圓; Map p76; ☎03-5537-7420; www.maru-mayfont.jp/ginza; 2nd fl, Ichigo Ginza 612 Bldg, 6-12-15 Ginza, Chūō-ku; lunch/dinner from ¥1100/6000; ⏲11.30am-2pm & 5.30-9pm Mon-Sat; 🗐; Ⓢ Ginza line to Ginza, exit A3) Maru offers a modern take on *kaiseki* (Japanese haute cuisine) dining. The chefs are young and inventive and the appealing space is dominated by an open kitchen counter across which you can watch them work. Its good-value lunches offer a choice of mainly fish dishes.

Roppongi & Around 六本木

The basement of Tokyo Midtown (p81) has dozens of reasonably priced options, as well as takeaway counters – perfect for a picnic lunch in the garden out back.

Tsurutontan NOODLES ¥

(つるとんたん; Map p82; www.tsurutontan.co.jp; 3-14-12 Roppongi, Minato-ku; udon ¥680-1800; 11am-8am; ; S Hibiya line to Roppongi, exit 5) Huge bowls of udon (thick, wheat noodles) are the speciality here. Go for simple (topped with seaweed or pickled plum), exotic (udon carbonara) or filling (Tsuruton *zanmai*: topped with fried tofu, tempura and beef).

Chinese Cafe 8 CHINESE ¥

(中国茶房８; Map p82; 03-5414-5708; www.chinesecafe8.com; 2nd fl, 3-2-13 Nishi-Azabu, Minato-ku; dishes from ¥550; 24hr; ; S Hibiya line to Roppongi, exit 1) Cheap-and-cheerful Chinese known for its cheeky decor, Peking Duck served at any hour and abrupt service (in that order).

Tokyo Curry Lab CURRY ¥

(東京カレーラボ; Map p82; 2nd fl, Tokyo Tower, 4-2-8 Shiba-kōen, Minato-ku; meals ¥1000-1350; 11am-10pm; ; S Hibiya line to Kamiyachō, exit 1) Curry rice is like baked beans on toast – a comfort food beloved by nearly all Japanese. This neatly designed outlet, tucked under the soaring spires of Tokyo Tower has a sci-fi feel with personal TVs at each bar stool. The hilariously illustrated place mats (you'll see) make the perfect 'Tokyo is weird' souvenir.

Gonpachi IZAKAYA ¥

(権八; Map p82; 03-5771-0170; www.gonpachi.jp/nishiazabu; 1-13-11 Nishi-Azabu, Minato-ku; skewers ¥180-1500, lunch sets weekday/weekend from ¥800/2050; 11.30am-3.30am; ; S Hibiya line to Roppongi, exit 2) Over the past decade this cavernous old Edo-style space (which inspired a memorable set in Quentin Tarantino's *Kill Bill*) has cemented its rep as a Tokyo dining institution. *Kushiyaki* (charcoal-grilled skewers) are served here alongside noodles, tempura and sushi. Other, less-memorable branches are scattered around the city.

Jōmon IZAKAYA ¥¥

(ジョウモン; Map p82; 03-3405-2585; www.teyandei.com/jomon_rop; 5-9-17 Roppongi, Minato-ku; skewers ¥150-1600; 6pm-5am; ; S Hibiya line to Roppongi, exit 3) This wonderfully cosy kitchen has bar seating, rows of ornate *shochu* (liquor) jugs lining the wall and hundreds of freshly prepared skewers splayed in front of the patrons – don't miss the heavenly *zabuton* beef stick (¥400). It's almost directly across from the Family Mart – look for the name in Japanese on the door.

★Tofuya-Ukai KAISEKI ¥¥¥

(とうふ屋うかい; Map p82; 03-3436-1028; www.ukai.co.jp/english/shiba; 4-4-13 Shiba-kōen, Minato-ku; lunch/dinner set menu from ¥5500/8400; 11.30am-10pm, last order 8pm; ; S Toei Ōedo line to Akabanebashi, exit 8) One of Tokyo's most gracious restaurants is located in a former sake brewery (moved from northern Japan), with an exquisite traditional garden, in the shadow of Tokyo

TOKYO'S TOP DINING EXPERIENCES

➡ Making an early morning trip to Tsukiji Market, followed by a sushi breakfast in the market. Daiwa Sushi (p123) is among the most famous spots, but there are countless other options.

➡ Sipping sake at the wooden counter of a traditional *izakaya* (Japanese pub-eatery), such as Shinsuke (p129).

➡ Noshing on *yakitori* and knocking back beers with Tokyo's workday warriors under the train tracks in Yurakuchō. Try Manpuku Shokudō (p131).

➡ Splurging on an *omakase* (chef's tasting menu) meal at a top-class sushi restaurant, such as Kyūbey (p123).

➡ Crowding into one of Tokyo's hot new 'standing restaurants' that specialise in luxe food for less. Try Ore-no-dashi (p123).

➡ Dining Edo-style at one of the city's historic, centuries-old restaurants, such as Komagata Dojō (p131).

➡ Grabbing late-night noodles after a rousing round of karaoke. Try Tsurutontan or Afuri.

Tower. Seasonal preparations of tofu and accompanying dishes are served in the refined *kaiseki* (Japanese haute cuisine) style. Make reservations well in advance.

Ebisu & Meguro 恵比寿・目黒

★Tonki TONKATSU ¥

(とんき; Map p86; 1-2-1 Shimo-Meguro, Meguro-ku; meals ¥1900; ⏲4-10.45pm Wed-Mon, closed 3rd Mon of month; ; JR Yamanote line to Meguro, west exit) One of Tokyo's best *tonkatsu* (crumbed pork cutlet) restaurants, Tonki has a loyal following. The seats at the counter – where you can watch the perfectly choreographed chefs – are the most coveted. From the station, walk down Meguro-dōri, take a left at the first alley and look for a white sign and *noren* (doorway curtains) across the sliding doors.

Afuri RĀMEN ¥

(あふり; Map p86; 1-1-7 Ebisu, Shibuya-ku; noodles from ¥750; ⏲11am-5am; ; JR Yamanote line to Ebisu, east exit) Hardly your typical, surly *rāmen-ya,* Afuri has upbeat young cooks and a hip industrial interior. The unorthodox menu might draw eye-rolls from purists, but house specialities such as *yuzu-shio* (a light, salty broth flavoured with yuzu, a type of citrus) draw lines at lunchtime. Order from the vending machine.

Ganko Dako STREET FOOD ¥

(頑固蛸; Map p86; 3-11-6 Meguro, Meguro-ku; 6 for ¥500; ⏲11am-1am; JR Yamanote line to Meguro, west exit) This street stall dishes out steaming hot *tako-yaki* (grilled octopus dumplings). It's located, unfortunately, across from the Meguro Parasitological Museum; nonetheless, Ganko Dako draws them in – check out the celebrity signings on the wall.

Ouca ICE CREAM ¥

(櫻花; Map p86; www.ice-ouca.com; 1-6-6 Ebisu, Shibuya-ku; ice cream from ¥390; ⏲11am-11.30pm Mar-Oct, noon-11pm Nov-Feb; JR Yamanote line to Ebisu, east exit) Green tea isn't the only flavour Japan has contributed to the ice-cream playbook; other delicious innovations available at Ouca include *kuro-goma* (black sesame) and *beni imo* (purple sweet potato).

★Higashi-Yama JAPANESE ¥¥

(ヒガシヤマ; Map p72; ☎03-5720-1300; www.higashiyama-tokyo.jp; 1-21-25 Higashiyama, Meguro-ku; lunch/dinner courses from ¥2500/4500; ⏲11.30am-2pm Tue-Sat, 6pm-1am Mon-Sat; ; Ⓢ Hibiya line to Naka-Meguro) Higashi-Yama serves gorgeous modern Japanese cuisine paired with gorgeous crockery. The interior, a rustic take on minimalism, is stunning too. The restaurant is all but hidden, on a side street with little signage; see the website for a map. Tasting courses make ordering easy; the 'chef's recommendation' course (¥8200) is a worthwhile splurge. Best to book ahead.

Ippo IZAKAYA ¥¥

(一歩; Map p86; ☎03-3445-8418; 2nd fl, 1-22-10 Ebisu, Shibuya-ku; dishes ¥500-1500; ⏲6pm-3am; JR Yamanote line to Ebisu, east exit) This mellow little *izakaya* (Japanese pub-eatery) specialises in simple pleasures: fish and sake (there's an English sign out front that says just that). The friendly chefs speak some English and can help you decide what to have grilled, steamed, simmered or fried. The entrance is up the wooden stairs.

Ebisu-yokochō STREET FOOD ¥¥

(恵比寿横町; Map p86; www.ebisu-yokocho.com; 1-7-4 Ebisu, Shibuya-ku; dishes ¥500-1500; ⏲5pm-late; JR Yamanote line to Ebisu, east exit) Locals love this retro arcade chock-a-block with food stalls dishing up everything from grilled scallops to *yaki soba* (fried buckwheat noodles). Seating is on stools, while tables are fashioned from various items such as repurposed beer crates. It's a loud, lively (and smoky) place, especially on a Friday night.

Shibuya 渋谷

For more options, check out the restaurants on the 6th and 7th floors of Shibuya Hikarie (p88); the basement (level 3) food court has good takeaway options, too.

d47 Shokudō JAPANESE ¥

(d47食堂; Map p88; www.hikarie8.com/d47shokudo/about.shtml; 8th fl, Shibuya Hikarie, 2-21-1 Shibuya, Shibuya-ku; meals ¥1100-1680; ⏲11am-2.30pm & 6-11pm; ; JR Yamanote line to Shibuya, east exit) There are 47 prefectures in Japan and d47 serves a changing line-up of *teishoku* (set meals) that evoke the specialities of each, from the fermented tofu of Okinawa to the stuffed squid of Hokkaidō. A larger menu of small plates is available in the evening. Picture windows offer bird's-eye views over the trains coming and going at Shibuya Station.

Sagatani SOBA ¥

(嵯峨谷; Map p88; 2-25-7 Dōgenzaka, Shibuya-ku; noodles from ¥280; ⏲24hr; ; JR Yamanote line to Shibuya, Hachikō exit) Proving Tokyo is only expensive to those who don't know better, this all-night joint serves up bamboo steamers of delicious noodles for just ¥280 (and beer for ¥150). 'Splurge' on the ごまだれそば (*goma-dare soba;* buckwheat noodles with sesame dipping sauce) for ¥380. Look for the stone mill in the window and order from the vending machine.

Food Show SUPERMARKET ¥

(フードショー; Map p88; basement fl, 2-24-1 Shibuya, Shibuya-ku; 10am-9pm; ; JR Yamanote line to Shibuya, Hachikō exit) This takeaway paradise in the basement of Shibuya Station has steamers of dumplings, crisp *karaage* (Japanese-style fried chicken), heaps of salads and cakes almost too pretty to eat. Look for discount stickers on *bentō* (boxed meals) and sushi sets after 5pm. A green sign pointing downstairs marks the entrance at Hachikō Plaza.

Viron BAKERY ¥

(Map p88; 5458-1770; 33-8 Udagawa-chō, Shibuya-ku; sandwiches ¥600-1200; 9am-10pm; ; JR Yamanote line to Shibuya, Hachikō exit) A fantastic French bakery (it apparently imports the flour from the motherland), Viron serves takeaway sandwiches and quiches.

DON'T MISS

DEPARTMENT-STORE FOODHALLS

Depachika (デパ地下; department-store basements) house food halls with a staggering array of tempting edibles, both sweet and savoury. Everything is of the highest quality and gorgeously packaged for presentation as gifts.

Treat yourself to museum-quality cakes, flower-shaped *wagashi* (Japanese sweets) or a *bentō* that almost looks too good to eat. After 5pm the prices of some items, such as sushi sets, are slashed – a boon for those looking for a cheap, tasty dinner to go. This is also the place to pick up souvenirs such as green tea and rice crackers.

Two *depachika* to try are Isetan (p145) and **Mitsukoshi** (三越; Map p76; 03-3241-3311; www.mitsukoshi.co.jp; 1-4-1 Nihombashi-Muromachi, Chūō-ku; 10am-7pm; Ginza line to Mitsukoshi-mae, exit A2). Food Show also has department-store-like treats.

Kaikaya SEAFOOD ¥¥

(開花屋; Map p88; 03-3770-0878; www.kaikaya.com; 23-7 Maruyama-chō, Shibuya-ku; lunch from ¥780, dishes ¥680-2300; 11.30am-2pm & 5.30-11.30pm Mon-Fri, 5.30-11.30pm Sat & Sun; ; JR Yamanote line to Shibuya, Hachikō exit) Kaikaiya is one chef's attempt to bring the beach to Shibuya. Most everything on the menu is caught in nearby Sagami Bay and the super-fresh seafood is served both Japanese and Western-style. You must try *maguro no kama* (tuna collar). Kaikaya is a boisterous, popular place; reservations are recommended.

Sushi-no-Midori SUSHI ¥¥

(寿司の美登利; Map p88; www.sushinomidori.co.jp; 4th fl, Mark City, 1-12-3 Dōgenzaka, Shibuya-ku; meals ¥800-2800; 11am-10pm; ; JR Yamanote line to Shibuya, Hachikō exit) Locally famous for its generous, exceedingly reasonable sushi sets, Sushi-no-Midori almost always has a line. Take a number from the ticket machine (and, if the line is long, head out for a little shopping). It's least crowded around 3pm on weekdays.

★**Matsukiya** SUKIYAKI ¥¥¥

(松木家; Map p88; 03-3461-2651; 6-8 Maruyama-chō, Shibuya-ku; sukiyaki from ¥5250; 11.30am-1.30pm & 5-11pm Mon-Sat; ; JR Yamanote line to Shibuya, Hachikō exit) Matsukiya's chefs have been making *sukiyaki* (thinly sliced beef, simmered and then dipped in raw egg) since 1890 and they really, really know what they're doing. It's worth upgrading to the premium course (¥7350) for even meltier meat, cooked to perfection at your table. There's a white sign out front and the entrance is up some stairs. Reservations are recommended.

Harajuku 原宿

Sticky sweet crêpes are the official food of teeny-bopper Takeshita-dōri.

★**Harajuku Gyōza-rō** GYŌZA ¥

(原宿餃子楼; Map p90; 6-4-2 Jingūmae, Shibuya-ku; 6 gyōza ¥290; 11.30am-4.30am; ; JR Yamanote line to Harajuku, Omote-sandō exit) *Gyōza* (dumplings) are the only thing on the menu here, but you won't hear any complaints from the regulars who queue up to get their fix. Have them *sui* (boiled) or *yaki* (pan-fried), with or without *niniku* (garlic) or *nira* (chives) – they're all delicious. Expect to wait on weekends.

Maisen TONKATSU ¥

(まい泉; Map p90; http://mai-sen.com; 4-8-5 Jingūmae, Shibuya-ku; lunch/dinner from ¥995/1680; 11am-10pm; ; Ginza line to Omote-sandō, exit A2) You could order something else (like fried shrimp), but everyone else will be ordering the famous *tonkatsu* (breaded, deep-fried pork cutlets). There are different grades of pork on the menu, including prized *kurobuta* (black pig), but even the cheapest is melt-in-your-mouth divine. The restaurant is housed in an old public bathhouse. A takeaway window serves delicious *tonkatsu sando* (sandwich).

Kyūsyū Jangara RĀMEN ¥

(九州じゃんがら; Map p90; 1-13-21 Jingūmae, Shibuya-ku; rāmen ¥630-1130; 10.45am-midnight Mon-Fri, from 10am Sat & Sun; ; JR Yamanote line to Harajuku, Omote-sandō exit) Come to this popular shop to sample the elegantly thin noodles, silky *chāshū* (roast pork) and *karashi takana* (hot pickled greens) for which Kyūshū-style *rāmen* (noodles in broth) is famous. You can't go wrong with ordering *zembu-iri* (everything in).

Sakura-tei OKONOMIYAKI ¥

(さくら亭; Map p90; 03-3479-0039; www.sakuratei.co.jp; 3-20-1 Jingūmae, Shibuya-ku; okonomiyaki ¥950-1350; 11am-11pm; ; JR Yamanote line to Harajuku, Takeshita exit) Grill your own *okonomiyaki* (savoury pancakes) at this funky place inside the gallery Design Festa (p91). During lunch (11am to 3pm) you can get 90 minutes of all-you-can-eat, plus a drink, for just ¥1060.

Mominoki House ORGANIC ¥¥

(もみの木ハウス; Map p90; http://omotesando.mominokihouse.net; 2-18-5 Jingūmae, Shibuya-ku; lunch/dinner set from ¥800/3200; 11.30am-10pm; ; JR Yamanote line to Harajuku, Takeshita exit) Boho Tokyoites have been coming here for tasty macrobiotic fare since 1976. The casual, cosy dining room has seen some famous visitors too, such as Paul McCartney. Chef Yamada's menu is heavily vegetarian, but also includes free-range chicken and *Ezo shika* (Hokkaidō venison, ¥4800).

★ **Yanmo** SEAFOOD ¥¥¥

(やんも; Map p90; www.yanmo.co.jp/aoyama/index.html; basement fl, T Place bldg, 5-5-25 Minami-Aoyama, Minato-ku; lunch/dinner course from ¥1100/7560; 11.30am-2pm & 6-10.30pm Mon-Sat; ; Ginza line to Omote-sandō, exit A5) Fresh caught seafood from the nearby Izu Peninsula is the speciality at this upscale, yet unpretentious restaurant. If you're looking to splash out on a seafood dinner, this is a great place to do so. The reasonably priced courses include sashimi, steamed and grilled fish. Lunch is a bargain, but you might have to queue. Reservations are essential for dinner.

Shinjuku 新宿

Shinjuku has an overwhelming number of restaurants in all styles and budgets. If you want to narrow down your choices – or grab a quick bite without having to brave the crowds – head to one of the *resutoran-gai* (restaurant 'towns') found on the top floor of most department stores; both **Lumine** (ルミネ; Map p94; www.lumine.ne.jp/shinjuku; Shinjuku Station, Shinjuku-ku; 11am-11pm; JR Yamanote line to Shinjuku, south exit) and **Mylord** (ミロード; Map p94; www.shinjuku-mylord.com; Shinjuku Station, Shinjuku-ku; 11am-11pm; JR Yamanote line to Shinjuku, south exit), inside Shinjuku Station near the south exit, have reasonably priced options.

One stop north of Shinjuku on the Yamanote line, **Shin-Ōkubo** is Tokyo's Little Seoul, home to many authentic Korean restaurants.

★ **Nagi** RĀMEN ¥

(凪; Map p94; www.n-nagi.com; 2nd fl, Golden Gai G2, 1-1-10 Kabukichō, Shinjuku-ku; rāmen from ¥820; 24hr; ; JR Yamanote line to Shinjuku, east exit) The house speciality at this atmospheric noodle joint, up a treacherous stairway in Golden Gai, is *niboshi rāmen* (egg noodles in a broth flavoured with dried sardines). There is almost always a wait; first purchase your order from the vending machine inside, then claim your spot at the end of the line. Look for the sign with a red circle.

Nakajima KAISEKI ¥

(中嶋; Map p94; 03-3356-4534; www.shinjyuku-nakajima.com; basement fl, 3-32-5 Shinjuku, Shinjuku-ku; lunch/dinner from ¥800/8640; 11.30am-2pm & 5.30-10pm Mon-Sat; ; Marunouchi line to Shinjuku-sanchōme, exit A1) In the evening, this Michelin-starred restaurant serves exquisite *kaiseki* (Japanese haute cuisine) dinners. On weekdays, it also serves a set lunch of humble *iwashi* (sardines) for one-tenth the price; in the hands of Nakajima's chefs they're divine. The line for lunch starts to form shortly before the restaurant opens at 11.30am. Look for the white sign at the top of the stairs.

Omoide-yokochō YAKITORI ¥

(思い出横丁; Map p94; Nishi-Shinjuku 1-chōme, Shinjuku-ku; skewers from ¥100; noon-midnight, hours vary by shop; ; JR Yamanote line to Shinjuku, west exit) Since the postwar days, smoke has been billowing night and day from the *yakitori* stalls that line this alley by the train tracks, literally translated as 'Memory Lane' (and less politely known as Shonben-yokochō, or 'Piss Alley'). Several stalls have English menus.

Numazukō SUSHI ¥

(沼津港; Map p94; basement fl, My bldg, 1-10-1 Nishi-Shinjuku, Shinjuku-ku; plates ¥90-550; 11am-10.30pm; ; JR Yamanote line to Shinjuku, west exit) Shinjuku's best *kaiten-sushi* (conveyor-belt sushi) restaurant has a long, snaking counter and a huge menu; it's pricier than most but the quality is worth it. It's below the Shinjuku Higway Bus Terminal, two basement floors down. You can also get there via an underground passage from Shinjuku Station; look for the fish-shaped sign over the door.

Shinjuku Asia-yokochō ASIAN ¥

(新宿アジア横丁; Map p94; rooftop, 2nd Toa Hall bldg, 1-21-1 Kabukichō, Shinjuku-ku; dishes from ¥650; 5pm-5am; ; JR Yamanote line to Shinjuku, east exit) A rooftop night market that spans the Asian continent, Asia-yokochō has vendors dishing out everything from Korean *bibimbap* to Vietnamese *pho*. It's noisy, a bit chaotic and particularly fun in a group.

Tsunahachi TEMPURA ¥¥

(つな八; Map p94; 03-3352-1012; www.tunahachi.co.jp; 3-31-8 Shinjuku, Shinjuku-ku; lunch/dinner from ¥1296-2268; 11am-10.30pm; ; JR Yamanote line to Shinjuku, east exit) Tsunahachi has been expertly frying prawns and seasonal vegetables for nearly 90 years. The sets are served in courses so each dish comes piping hot. Sit at the counter for the added pleasure of watching the chefs at work. Indigo *noren* (curtains) mark the entrance.

Kozue JAPANESE ¥¥¥

(梢; Map p94; 03-5323-3460; http://tokyo.park.hyatt.jp/en/hotel/dining/Kozue.html; 40th fl, Park Hyatt, 3-7-1-2 Nishi-Shinjuku, Shinjuku-ku; lunch/dinner course from ¥2700/15,000; 11.30am-2.30pm & 5.30-9.30pm; ; Ōedo line to Tochōmae, exit A4) It's hard to beat Kozue's combination of exquisite, seasonal Japanese cuisine, artisan crockery and soaring views over Shinjuku from the floor-to-ceiling windows. Reservations are essential.

Kōrakuen & Around 後楽園

Tokyo Dome City has dozens of restaurants, mostly family-friendly chains.

Kururi RĀMEN ¥

(麺処くるり; Map p96; 3-2 Ichigaya-Tamachi, Shinjuku-ku; noodles ¥700-950; 11am-9pm; JR Sōbu line to Iidabashi, west exit) The line-up of *rāmen* fanatics outside this cramped, anonymous noodle shop proves its street cred among connoisseurs. The *miso-rāmen* (みそらぁめん) broth is swamp-thick, incredibly rich and absolutely delicious. There's no sign, but it's next to a liquor shop with a striped awning; buy a ticket inside from the machine.

Le Bretagne FRENCH ¥

(ル ブルターニュ; Map p96; 03-3235-3001; www.le-bretagne.com/e/top.html; 4-2 Kagurazaka, Shinjuku-ku; crêpes ¥750-1850; 11.30am-10.30pm Tue-Sat, to 10pm Sun; ; JR Sōbu line to Iidabashi, west exit) This French-owned cafe, hidden on a cobblestone lane in Kagurazaka, is credited with starting the Japanese rage for crêpes. Savoury buckwheat galettes are made with ham and cheese imported from France; the sweet ones – served with the likes of caramelised butter, apple compote and ice cream – are divine.

Kado TRADITIONAL JAPANESE ¥¥

(カド; Map p96; 03-3268-2410; http://kagurazaka-kado.com; 1-32 Akagi-Motomachi, Shinjuku-ku; lunch/dinner sets from ¥800/3150; 11.30am-2.30pm & 5-11pm; ; Tōzai line to Kagurazaka, exit 1) Set in an old wooden house, Kado specialises in *katei-ryōri* (home-cooking). Dinner is a set course of seasonal dishes (such as grilled quail or crab soup). At lunch there's no English menu, so your best bet is the カド定食 (*kado teishoku*), the daily house special. Bookings are required for dinner; the restaurant has a wooden facade and a white lantern out front.

Canal Cafe ITALIAN ¥¥

(カナルカフェ; Map p96; 03-3260-8068; www.canalcafe.jp; 1-9 Kagurazaka, Shinjuku-ku; lunch from ¥1600, dinner mains ¥1500-2800; 11.30am-11pm Tue-Sat, to 9.30pm Sun; ; JR Sōbu line to Iidabashi, west exit) Along the moat that forms the edge of Kitanomaru-kōen, this is one of Tokyo's best alfresco dining spots. The restaurant serves tasty wood-fired pizzas, seafood pastas and grilled meats, while over on the 'deck side' you can settle in with a sandwich, muffin or coffee.

Akihabara & Around 秋葉原

Kanda Yabu Soba SOBA ¥

(神田やぶそば; Map p96; ☎03-3251-0287; www.yabusoba.net; 2-10 Kanda-Awajichō, Chiyoda-ku; noodles ¥700-2000; ⊙11.30am-8.30pm; 📵; Ⓢ Marunouchi line to Awajichō, exit A3) This venerable buckwheat noodle shop has had a total rebuild following a fire in 2013. When you walk in, staff singing out the orders is one of the first signs that you've arrived in a singular, ageless place. Come here for classic handmade noodles and accompaniments such as shrimp tempura *(ten-seiro soba)* or slices of duck *(kamo-nanban soba)*.

Kikanbō RĀMEN ¥

(鬼金棒; Map p96; http://karashibi.com; 2-10-8 Kaji-chō, Chiyoda-ku; rāmen from ¥780; ⊙11am-9.30pm Mon-Sat, to 4pm Sun; 🚉 JR Yamanote line to Kanda, north exit) The *'karashibi'* (カラシビ) spicy *miso-rāmen* here has a cult following. Choose your level of *kara* (spice) and *shibi* (mouth-numbing sensation created by Japanese *sanshō* pepper). We recommend *futsu-futsu* (regular for both) for first-timers; *oni* (devil) level costs an extra ¥100. Look for the red curtains at the door and buy an order ticket from the vending machine.

Komaki Shokudō VEGAN ¥

(こまきしょくどう; Map p96; http://konnichiha.net/fushikian; Chabara, 8-2 Kanda Neribei-chō, Chiyoda-ku; set meals from ¥980; ⊙11am-7.30pm; 🚉 JR Yamanote line to Akihabara, Electric Town exit) A Kamakura cooking school specialising in *shōjin-ryōri* (Buddhist-style vegan cuisine) runs this cafe within the Chabara food market. The chefs' nonmeat meals and dishes are very tasty and they sell some of the ingredients they use. Round off your meal with excellent coffee from Yanaka Coffee opposite.

Ueno & Yanaka 上野・谷中

In and around the open-air market Ameya-yokochō (p103) there are numerous casual restaurants that open up onto the street. It's a fun place to dine in the evenings. Yanaka Ginza (p105) has snack vendors and takeaway counters.

★Shinsuke IZAKAYA ¥¥

(シンスケ; Map p102; ☎03-3832-0469; 3-31-5 Yushima, Bunkyō-ku; ⊙5-9.30pm Mon-Fri, to 9pm Sat; 🚭📵; Ⓢ Chiyoda line to Yushima, exit 3) In business since 1925, Shinsuke is pretty much the platonic ideal of an *izakaya*: long cedar counter, 'master' in *happi* (traditional short coat) and *hachimaki* (traditional headband), and smooth-as-silk *dai-ginjo* (premium grade sake). The only part that seems out of place is the friendly staff who go out of their way to explain the dishes in English.

This is the kind of place that should be intimidating for travellers, but isn't at all, and the food – modern updates of classics – is fantastic. Don't miss the *kitsune raclette* – deep-fried tofu stuffed with raclette cheese.

Hantei TRADITIONAL JAPANESE ¥¥

(はん亭; Map p102; ☎03-3828-1440; www.hantei.co.jp/nedu.html; 2-12-15 Nezu, Bunkyō-ku; lunch/dinner course from ¥3150/2835; ⊙noon-3pm & 5-10pm Tue-Sun; 📵; Ⓢ Chiyoda line to Nezu, exit 2) Housed in a beautifully maintained, century-old traditional wooden building, Hantei is a local landmark. Delectable skewers of seasonal *kushiage* (fried meat, fish and vegetables) are served with small, refreshing side dishes. Lunch courses include eight sticks and dinner courses start with six, after which you'll receive additional rounds (¥210 per skewer) until you say stop.

Sasa-no-Yuki TOFU ¥¥

(笹乃雪; Map p102; ☎03-3873-1145; 2-15-10 Negishi, Taitō-ku; dishes ¥400-700, lunch/dinner course from ¥2200/5000; ⊙11.30am-8pm Tue-Sun; ✎📵; 🚉 JR Yamanote line to Uguisudani, north exit) 🍃 Sasa-no-Yuki opened its doors in the Edo period, and continues to serve its signature

SELF-CATERING

The abundance of *konbini* (convenience stores) make self-catering a no-brainer in Tokyo. However, if you're craving good chocolate or crusty bread, check out these expat favourites:

Kinokuniya International Supermarket (紀ノ国屋 インターナショナル; Map p90; www.super-kinokuniya.jp/store/international; basement fl, AO bldg, 3-11-7 Kita-Aoyama, Minato-ku; ⊙9.30am-9pm; ✎; Ⓢ Ginza line to Omote-sandō, exit B2) Rather pricey, but stocked with fresh bread, flawless fruit, imported cheeses and chocolates galore.

Natural House (ナチュラルハウス; Map p90; www.naturalhouse.co.jp; 3-6-18 Kita-Aoyama, Minato-ku; ⊙10am-10pm; ✎; Ⓢ Ginza line to Omote-sandō, exit B4) 🍃 Good for organic produce, hearty brown bread and vegetarian *bentō*.

LOCAL KNOWLEDGE

THE WAY OF RĀMEN

Chef Ivan Orkin of **Ivan's Rāmen** (www.ivanramen.com; 3-24-7 Minami-Karasuyama, Setagaya-ku; ⌚11.30am-2pm & 6-11pm Mon, Tue, Thu & Fri, 11.30am-9.30pm Sat & Sun, closed Wed & 4th Tue; 🄴; 🅁Keio line to Rokakōen) filled us in on the art of noodle slurping and his favourite shops.

How to Eat It

Rāmen is like a brick-oven pizza – if you let it sit for a few minutes it becomes something different. So you need to start slurping right away, even if it burns a little. Keep slurping, make noise and don't chew.

Where to Eat It

Nagi (p127) is one of my favourites. The one in Golden Gai is a great place to go after drinking. I also like Kikanbō (p129) in Kanda. It's sort of new wave. It serves very serious, delicious spicy *miso-rāmen*.

dishes, with tofu made fresh every morning with water from the shop's own well. Some treats to expect: *ankake-dofu* (tofu in a thick, sweet sauce) and *goma-dofu* (sesame tofu). The best seats overlook a tiny garden with a koi pond.

Izu-ei Honten UNAGI ¥¥

(伊豆栄本店; Map p102; www.izuei.co.jp; 2-12-22 Ueno, Taitō-ku; set meals ¥2160-4860; ⌚11am-9.30pm; 🚭🄴; 🅁JR Yamanote line to Ueno, Hirokōji exit) Izu-ei's twin delights are its delicious *unagi* (eel) and its elegant, traditional atmosphere, with waitresses in kimonos and tatami seating (there are chairs, too).

Nagomi YAKITORI ¥¥

(和味; Map p102; ☎03-3821-5972; 3-11-11 Yanaka, Taitō-ku; skewers from ¥180; ⌚5pm-midnight; 🄴; 🅁JR Yamanote line to Nippori, north exit) On Yanaka Ginza, Nagomi deals in juicy skewers of *ji-dori* (free-range chicken). There are plenty of grilled veggie options, too. Wash it all down with a bowl of chicken soup *rāmen*. Look for the sake bottles in the window.

Asakusa & Sumida-gawa 浅草・隅田川

Don't miss the snack vendors on Nakamise-dōri, dishing out traditional treats such as *mochi* (sticky-rice cakes) stuffed with sweet bean paste.

Daikokuya TEMPURA ¥

(大黒家; Map p106; www.tempura.co.jp/english/index.html; 1-38-10 Asakusa, Taitō-ku; meals ¥1550-2100; ⌚11am-8.30pm Mon-Fri, to 9pm Sat; 🄴; 🅂Ginza line to Asakusa, exit 1) Near Nakamise-dōri, this is the place to get old-fashioned tempura fried in pure sesame oil, an Asakusa speciality. It's in a white building with a tile roof. If there's a queue (and there often is), try your luck at the annexe one block over.

Rokurinsha RĀMEN ¥

(六厘舎; Map p106; www.rokurinsha.com; 6th fl, Solamachi, 1-1-2 Oshiage, Sumida-ku; rāmen from ¥850; ⌚10.30am-11pm; 🚭🄴; 🅂Hanzōmon line to Oshiage, exit B3) Rokurinsha's speciality is *tsukemen* – *rāmen* noodles served on the side with a bowl of concentrated soup for dipping. The noodles here are thick and perfectly al dente and the soup is a rich *tonkotsu* (pork bone) base. It's an addictive combination that draws lines to this outpost in Tokyo Sky Tree Town.

Sometarō OKONOMIYAKI ¥

(染太郎; Map p106; 2-2-2 Nishi-Asakusa, Taitō-ku; mains ¥390-880; ⌚noon-10pm; 🄴; 🅂Ginza line to Tawaramachi, exit 3) Sometarō is a fun and funky place to try *okonomiyaki* (savoury Japanese-style pancakes filled with meat, seafood and vegetables that you cook yourself). This historic, vine-covered house is a friendly spot where the menu includes a how-to guide for even the most culinarily challenged.

Tomoegata NABE ¥

(巴潟; Map p72; www.tomoegata.com; 2-17-6 Ryōgoku, Sumida-ku; lunch/dinner from ¥860/3130; ⌚11.30am-2pm & 5-11pm; 🄴; 🅁JR Sōbu line to Ryōgoku, east exit) If you're keen to try *chanko-nabe* – the hearty, protein-rich stew that fattens up sumo wrestlers – Tomoegata is a great place to do it. The daily lunch special includes a reasonably sized individual serving of *chanko-nabe*. In the evening, groups can splash out on huge steaming pots filled with beef, scallops, mushrooms and tofu.

Komagata Dojō TRADITIONAL JAPANESE ¥

(駒形どぜう; Map p106; ☎03-3842-4001; 1-7-12 Komagata, Taitō-ku; mains from ¥1550; ⏰11am-9pm; 🚭📋; Ⓢ Ginza line to Asakusa, exits A2 & A4) Since 1801, Komagata Dojō has been simmering and stewing *dojō* (Japanese loach, which looks something like a miniature eel). *Dojō-nabe* (loach hotpot), served here on individual *hibachi* (charcoal stoves), was a common dish in the days of Edo, but few restaurants serve it today. The open seating around wide, wooden planks heightens the traditional flavour. There are lanterns out front.

★**Otafuku** TRADITIONAL JAPANESE ¥¥

(大多福; Map p106; ☎03-3871-2521; www.otafuku.ne.jp; 1-6-2 Senzoku, Taitō-ku; oden ¥110-550, course ¥5400; ⏰5-11pm Tue-Sat, to 10pm Sun; 📋; 🚉Tsukuba Express line to Asakusa, exit 1) Celebrating its centenary in 2015, Otafuku specialises in *oden,* classic Japanese stew. It's simmered at the counter and diners pick what they want from the pot, one or two items at a time. You can dine cheaply on radishes and kelp, or splash out on scallops and tuna – either way you get to soak up Otafuku's convivial, old-time atmosphere.

Look for a shack-like entrance and lantern on the northern side of Kototoi-dōri.

Odaiba & Tokyo Bay お台場・東京湾

All of Odaiba's giant malls have restaurant floors with family-friendly options.

Bills INTERNATIONAL ¥

(ビルズ; Map p110; www.bills-jp.net; 3rd fl Seaside Mall, DECKS Tokyo Beach, 1-6-1 Daiba, Minato-ku; mains from ¥1300; ⏰9am-10pm Mon-Fri, 8am-10pm Sat & Sun; 🚭📶📋👶; 🚉Yurikamome line to Odaiba Kaihin-kōen) Australian chef Bill Granger has had a big hit with his restaurant chain in Japan – unsurprising given how inviting and spacious a place this is. The menu includes his classics such as ricotta hotcakes, and lunch and dinner mains such as *wagyu* burgers. The terrace also has great bay views.

Odaiba Takoyaki Museum JAPANESE ¥

(お台場たこ焼きミュージアム; Map p110; 4th fl, Seaside Mall, DECKS Tokyo Beach, 1-6-1 Daiba, Minato-ku; takoyaki from ¥400; ⏰11am-9pm; 🚉Yurikamome line to Odaiba Kaihin-kōen) Seven stalls dish up variations on the classic fried batter and octopus balls *(tako-yaki)* usually served from street stalls at festivals and events.

TY Harbor Brewery AMERICAN ¥¥

(Map p72; ☎03-5479-4555; www.tyharborbrewing.co.jp; 2-1-3 Higashi-Shinagawa, Shinagawa-ku; lunch set ¥1200-1700, dinner mains from ¥1700; ⏰11.30am-2pm & 5.30-10pm; 🚭📋; Ⓢ Rinkai line to Tennōzu Isle, exit B) In a former warehouse on the waterfront, TY Harbor serves up excellent burgers, steaks and crab cakes with views of canals around Tennōzu Isle. It also brews its own beer on the premises. Call ahead to book a seat on the terrace.

Drinking & Nightlife

Tokyo's nightlife is undoubtably one of the city's highlights. Whatever stereotypes you may have accepted about Japanese people being quiet and reserved will fall to pieces after dark. Tokyo is a 'work hard, play hard' kind of place and you'll find people out any night of the week.

Shinjuku is the city's largest nightlife district. Roppongi is known as the place where *gaijin* (foreigners) congregate – it can feel a bit like entering the world of *Bladerunner* or *Star Wars,* where throngs of the galaxy's most unscrupulous citizens gather under the neon lights. Ginza and Marunouchi are loaded with places for local office workers to unwind. These include expense-account joints as well as ramshackle *izakaya.*

Nightclubs are mostly clustered in Shibuya and Roppongi. Most of the big clubs have discount flyers that can be printed or downloaded from their websites. Everyone needs to show photo ID at the door.

It's not all about the booze: Tokyo has some fantastic cafes, too, including some wacky themed ones.

Marunouchi (Tokyo Station area) 丸の内（東京駅）

Cafe Salvador CAFE

(Map p76; www.cafecompany.co.jp/brands/salvador/marunouchi; 3-2-3 Marunouchi, Chiyoda-ku; ⏰7am-11pm Mon-Fri, 10am-11pm Sat, 10am-8pm Sun; @📶; 🚉JR Yūrakuchō line to Yūrakuchō, Kokusai Forum exit) Comfy sofas, piles of glossy magazines, quirky art on the walls, free wi-fi and plenty of electricity outlets make this affordable counter-service cafe one of the most convivial along ritzy Naka-dōri. Plenty of caffeinated drinks are supplemented by salads, sandwiches and fresh bakes.

Manpuku Shokudō IZAKAYA

(まんぷく食堂; Map p76; ☎03-3211-6001; www.manpukushokudo.com; 2-4-1 Yūrakuchō,

Chiyoda-ku; cover charge ¥300; ⏲24hr; 🚆JR Yamanote line to Yūrakuchō, central exit) Down your beer or sake as trains rattle overhead on the tracks that span Harumi-dōri at Yūrakuchō. This convivial *izakaya,* plastered with old movie posters, is open round the clock and has bags of atmosphere.

So Tired BAR

(ソータイアード; Map p76; ☎03-5220-1358; www.heads-west.com/shop/so-tired.html; 7th fl, Shin-Marunouchi Bldg, 1-5-1 Marunouchi, Chiyoda-ku; ⏲11am-4am Mon-Sat, to 11pm Sun; 🚆JR lines to Tokyo, Marunouchi north exit) The best thing about this bar on the lively 7th floor of the Shin-Maru Building is that you can buy a drink at the counter and take it out to the terrace. The views aren't sky-high; instead, you feel curiously suspended among the office towers, hovering over Tokyo Station below.

Ginza & Tsukiji 銀座・築地

★Kagaya IZAKAYA

(加賀屋; Map p76; ☎03-3591-2347; www1.ocn.ne.jp/~kagayayy/index.html; B1 fl, Hanasada Bldg, 2-15-12 Shimbashi, Minato-ku; ⏲7pm-midnight Mon-Sat; 🚆JR Yamanote line to Shimbashi, Shimbashi exit) It is safe to say that there is no other bar owner in Tokyo who can match Mark Kagaya for brilliant lunacy. His side-splitting antics are this humble *izakaya*'s star attraction, although his mum's nourishing home-cooking also hits the spot. Bookings are essential.

Cha Ginza TEAHOUSE

(茶・銀座; Map p76; www.uogashi-meicha.co.jp/shop/ginza; 5-5-6 Ginza, Chūō-ku; tea set ¥600; ⏲11am-6pm, shop until 7pm Tue-Sun; Ⓢ Ginza line to Ginza, exit B3) At this slick contemporary tearoom, it costs ¥600 for either a cup of perfectly prepared *matcha* (green tea), and a small cake or two, or for a choice of *sencha* (premium green tea). Buy your token for tea at the shop on the ground floor which sells top-quality teas from various growing regions in Japan.

Fukurou-no-mise CAFE

(フクロウのみせ; Map p72; http://ameblo.jp/fukurounomise; 1-27-9 Tsukishima, Chuo-ku; entry incl a drink from ¥2000; ⏲2-6pm Wed & Thu, 2-9pm Fri, noon-9pm Sat, noon-6pm Sun; Ⓢ Ōedo line to Tsukishima, exit 10) Make like Harry Potter with many beautiful breeds at this originator of the bird-cafe concept. The owls are well looked after and nonchalant about having their photo taken on your shoulder. One-hour slots are reserved on a first-come, first-served basis; turn up early before the cafe opens to secure a place.

Roppongi & Around 六本木

★SuperDeluxe LOUNGE

(スーパー・デラックス; Map p82; ☎03-5412-0515; www.super-deluxe.com; B1 fl, 3-1-25 Nishi-Azabu, Minato-ku; admission varies; Ⓢ Hibiya line to Roppongi, exit 1b) This groovy basement performance space, also a cocktail lounge and club of sorts, stages everything from hula-hoop gatherings to literary evenings and creative presentations in the 20 x 20 PechaKucha (20 slides x 20 seconds) format. Check the website for event details. It's in an unmarked brown-brick building by a shoe-repair shop.

★Pink Cow BAR

(ピンクカウ; Map p82; www.thepinkcow.com; B1 fl, Roi Bldg, 5-5-1 Roppongi, Minato-ku; ⏲5pm-late Tue-Sun; Ⓢ Hibiya line to Roppongi, exit 3) With its animal-print decor, rotating display of local artwork and terrific all-you-can-eat buffet (¥2000) every Friday and Saturday, the Pink Cow is a funky, friendly place to hang out. Also hosts stitch-and-bitch evenings, writers' salons and indie-film screenings; it's a good bet if you're in the mood to mix with a creative crowd.

Agave BAR

(アガヴェ; Map p82; ☎03-3497-0229; www.agave.jp; B1 fl, 7-15-10 Roppongi, Minato-ku; ⏲6.30pm-2am Mon-Thu, to 4am Fri & Sat; Ⓢ Hibiya or Ōedo line to Roppongi, exit 2) Rawhide chairs, *cruzas de rosas* (crosses decorated with roses) and tequila shots for the willing make Agave a good place for a long night in search of the sacred

DON'T MISS

SUMMER BEER GARDENS

Summer beer gardens are a Tokyo tradition (typically running late May to early September). **Mori no Beer Garden** (森のビアガーデン; Map p72; www.rkfs.co.jp/brand/beer_garden_detail.html; 1-7-5 Kita-Aoyama, Minato-ku; men/women ¥4000/3800; ⏲5-10pm Mon-Fri, 3-10pm Sat & Sun; 🚆JR Sōbu line to Shinanomachi) hosts up to 1000 revellers for all-you-can-eat-and-drink spreads of beer and barbecue under a century-old tree.

worm. Luckily, this gem in the jungle that is Roppongi is more about savouring the subtleties of its 400-plus varieties of tequila than tossing back shots of Cuervo.

These LOUNGE
(テーゼ; Map p82; ☎03-5466-7331; www.these-jp.com; 2-15-12 Nishi-Azabu, Minato-ku; cover charge ¥500; ⏲7pm-4am, to 2am Sun; Ⓢ Hibiya line to Roppongi, exit 3) Pronouced *tay*-zay, this delightfully quirky, nook-ridden space calls itself a library lounge and overflows with armchairs, sofas, and books on the shelves and on the bar. Imbibe champagne, whiskies or seasonal-fruit cocktails. Bites include escargot garlic toast, which goes down nicely with a drink in the secret room on the 2nd floor. Look for the flaming torches outside.

Janome CAFE, BAR
(ジャノメ; Map p82; http://littletyo.com; 1-2-1 Atago, Minato-ku; ⏲8.30am-11pm Mon-Fri, noon-6pm Sat; 📶; Ⓢ Hibiya line to Kamiyachō, exit 3) Once a sushi shop and some vacant land, Janome is the base for the 'Little Tokyo' project, which combines a quirky cool cafe, bar, gallery and design shop with an events space. With free wi-fi it's a great hang-out in an area that, thanks to the adjacent Toranomon Hills development, is on the up and up.

Muse CLUB
(ミューズ; Map p82; ☎03-5467-1188; www.muse-web.com; B1 fl, 4-1-1 Nishi-Azabu, Minato-ku; admission women/men incl 2 drinks free/¥3000; ⏲9pm-late Mon-Fri, from 10pm Sat & Sun; Ⓢ Hibiya line to Roppongi, exit 3) This catacomb-like underground club with intimate booths, dance floors and billiards, has an excellent mix of locals and foreigners. There's something for everyone here, whether you want to dance up a storm or just feel like playing darts or table tennis.

Ebisu & Meguro 恵比寿・目黒

★Nakame Takkyū Lounge LOUNGE
(中目卓球ラウンジ; Map p86; 2nd fl, Lion House Naka-Meguro, 1-3-13 Kami-Meguro, Meguro-ku; cover before/after 10pm ¥500/800; ⏲7pm-2am Mon-Sat; Ⓢ Hibiya line to Naka-Meguro) *Takkyū* means table tennis and it's a serious sport in Japan. This hilarious bar looks like a university table-tennis clubhouse – right down to the tatty furniture and posters of star players on the wall. It's in an apartment building next to a parking garage (go all the way down the corridor past the bikes); ring the doorbell for entry.

Buri BAR
(ぶり; Map p86; ☎03-3496-7744; 1-14-1 Ebisu-nishi, Shibuya-ku; ⏲5pm-3am; 🚉 JR Yamanote line to Ebisu, west exit) Buri – the name means 'super' in Hiroshima dialect – is one of Ebisu's most popular *tachinomi-ya* (standing bars). On almost any night you can find a lively crowd packed in around the horseshoe-shaped counter. Generous quantities of sake (over 50 varieties; ¥750) are served semifrozen, like slushies, in colourful jars.

Air CLUB
(エアー; Map p86; www.air-tokyo.com; basement fl, Hikawa Bldg, 2-11 Sarugaku-chō, Shibuya-ku; cover from ¥2500; ⏲from 10pm Thu-Tue; 🚉 Tōkyū Tōyoko line to Daikanyama) DJs spin mostly house and techno here, and the sound system is top of the line. Expect a good night out on any Friday or Saturday night. Keep an eye out for Frames (フレイムス) – the entrance to the basement club is inside. Bring ID.

Enjoy House BAR
(Map p86; http://enjoyhouse.jugem.jp; 2nd fl, 2-9-9 Ebisu-nishi, Shibuya-ku; drinks from ¥600; ⏲noon-late; 🚉 JR Yamanote line to Ebisu, west exit) Decked out with velveteen booths, fairy lights and foliage, Enjoy House is a deeply funky place to spend the evening. DJs spin regularly, but there's still no cover charge. By day it's a burger shop. Look for the name painted in red letters in English on the 2nd-floor window.

Shibuya 渋谷

★Good Beer Faucets BAR
(グッドビアフォウセッツ; Map p88; http://shibuya.goodbeerfaucets.jp; 2nd fl, 1-29-1 Shōtō, Shibuya-ku; beer from ¥800; ⏲5pm-midnight Mon-Thu & Sat, to 3am Fri, 4-11pm Sun; 🚭📶; 🚉 JR Yamanote line to Shibuya, Hachikō exit) With 40 shiny taps, Good Beer Faucets has one of the city's best selections of Japanese craft brews and regularly draws a full house of locals and expats. The interior is chrome and concrete (and not at all grungy). Come for happy hour (5pm to 8pm Monday to Thursday, 4pm to 7pm Sunday) and get ¥200 off any beer.

Womb CLUB
(ウーム; Map p88; ☎03-5459-0039; www.womb.co.jp; 2-16 Maruyama-chō, Shibuya-ku; cover ¥2000-4000; ⏲11pm-late Fri & Sat, 4-10pm Sun; 🚉 JR Yamanote line to Shibuya, Hachikō exit) A longtime (in club years, at least) fixture on the Tokyo nightlife scene, Womb gets a lot of big-name

international DJs playing mostly house and techno. Frenetic lasers and strobes splash across the heaving crowds, which usually jam all four floors. Warning: can get sweaty.

Tight BAR
(タイト; Map p88; www.tight-tokyo.com; 2nd fl, 1-25-10 Shibuya, Shibuya-ku; drinks from ¥500; 6pm-2am Mon-Sat, to midnight Sun; JR Yamanote line to Shibuya, Hachikō exit) This teeny-tiny bar is wedged among the wooden shanties of Nonbei-yokochō, a narrow nightlife strip along the JR tracks. Like the name suggests, it's a tight fit, but the lack of seats doesn't keep regulars away: on a busy night, they line the stairs. Look for the big picture window.

Beat Cafe BAR
(Map p88; www.facebook.com/beatcafe; basement fl, 2-13-5 Dōgenzaka, Shibuya-ku; drinks from ¥500; 7pm-5am; JR Yamanote line to Shibuya, Hachikō exit) Join an eclectic mix of local and international regulars at this comfortably shabby bar among the nightclubs and love hotels of Dōgenzaka. It's a known hang-out for musicians and music fans; check the website for info on parties (and after parties). Look for Gateway Studio on the corner; the bar is in the basement.

Fuglen Tokyo CAFE
(Map p88; www.fuglen.com; 1-16-11 Tomigaya, Shibuya-ku; 8am-10pm Mon & Tue, to 1am Wed-Sun; ; S Chiyoda line to Yoyogi-kōen, exit 2) This Tokyo outpost of a long-running Oslo coffee shop serves Aeropress coffee by day and creative cocktails by night.

Harajuku 原宿

Two Rooms BAR
(トゥールームス; Map p90; 03-3498-0002; www.tworooms.jp; 5th fl, AO bldg, 3-11-7 Kita-Aoyama, Minato-ku; 11.30am-2am Mon-Sat, to 10pm Sun; S Ginza line to Omote-sandō, exit B2) Expect a crowd dressed like they don't care that wine by the glass starts at ¥1500. You can eat here too, but the real scene is at night by the bar. Call ahead (staff speak English) on Friday or Saturday night to reserve a table on the terrace, which has sweeping views towards the Shinjuku skyline.

Harajuku Taproom PUB
(原宿タップルーム; Map p90; http://bairdbeer.com/en/taproom; 2nd fl, 1-20-13 Jingūmae, Shibuya-ku; 5pm-midnight Mon-Fri, noon-midnight Sat & Sun; ; JR Yamanote line to Harajuku, Takeshita exit) Baird's Brewery is one of Japan's most successful and consistently good craft breweries. This is one of its two Tokyo outposts, where you can sample more than a dozen of its beers on tap; try the top-selling Rising Sun Pale Ale. Japanese pub-style food is served as well.

Omotesando Koffee CAFE
(Map p90; http://ooo-koffee.com; 4-15-3 Jingūmae, Shibuya-ku; espresso ¥250; 10am-7pm; S Ginza line to Omote-sandō, exit A2) Tokyo's most *oshare* (stylish) coffee stand is a minimalist cube set up inside a half-century-old traditional house. Be prepared to circle the block trying to find it, but know that an immaculate macchiato and a seat in the garden await you.

Oath BAR
(Map p72; http://bar-oath.com; 4-5-9 Shibuya, Shibuya-ku; 9pm-5am Mon-Thu, to 8am Fri & Sat, 5-11pm Sun; S Ginza line to Omote-sandō, exit B1) A tiny space along a somewhat forlorn strip of highway, Oath is a favourite after-hours destination for clubbers – helped no doubt by the ¥500 drinks and lack of cover charge. Underground DJs spin here sometimes, too.

Shinjuku 新宿

★Zoetrope BAR
(ゾートロープ; Map p94; http://homepage2.nifty.com/zoetrope; 3rd fl, 7-10-14 Nishi-Shinjuku, Shinjuku-ku; 7pm-4am Mon-Sat; JR Yamanote line to Shinjuku, west exit) A must-visit for whisky fans, Zoetrope has no less than 300 varieties of Japanese whisky (from ¥700) behind its small counter – including some no longer commercially available. The owner speaks some English and can help you pick from the daunting menu. He'll also let you choose the soundtrack to play alongside the silent films he screens on the wall.

New York Bar BAR
(ニューヨークバー; Map p94; 03-5323-3458; http://tokyo.park.hyatt.com; 52nd fl, Park Hyatt, 3-7-1-2 Nishi-Shinjuku, Shinjuku-ku; 5pm-midnight Sun-Wed, to 1am Thu-Sat; Ōedo line to Tochōmae, exit A4) You may not be lodging at the Park Hyatt, but you can still ascend to the 52nd floor to swoon over the sweeping nightscape from the floor-to-ceiling windows at this bar (of *Lost in Translation* fame). There's a cover charge of ¥2200 after 8pm (7pm Sunday) and live music nightly; cocktails start at ¥1800. Note: dress code enforced.

GAY & LESBIAN TOKYO

Tokyo's gay and lesbian enclave is **Shinjuku-nichōme** ('Ni-chōme'). There are hundreds of establishments crammed into a space of a few blocks, including bars, dance clubs, saunas and love hotels. Unfortunately, not all welcome foreigners; those listed below are all safe bets. **Utopia Asia** (www.utopia-asia.com) also has a good list of friendly places (including a small map of Ni-chōme). Outside of the neighbourhood, parties take place at larger venues; look for flyers around Ni-chōme.

Advocates Café (アドボケイツカフェ; Map p94; http://advocates-cafe.com; 2-18-1 Shinjuku, Shinjuku-ku; ⏲6pm-4am, to 1am Sun; Ⓢ Marunouchi line to Shinjuku-sanchōme, exit C8) Many a night out in Ni-chōme starts 'on the corner' at this tiny bar that spills out onto the street. Anyone and everyone is welcome.

Arty Farty (アーティファーティ; Map p94; www.arty-farty.net; 2nd fl, 2-11-7 Shinjuku, Shinjuku-ku; ⏲6pm-1am; Ⓢ Marunouchi line to Shinjuku-sanchōme, exit C8) A welcoming spot open to men and women, Arty Farty has been a gateway to the community for many a moon. There's a small dance floor here that gets packed on weekends.

Bar Goldfinger (Map p94; http://goldfingerparty.com/bar/top; 2-12-11 Shinjuku, Shinjuku-ku; ⏲from 6pm Thu-Mon, closing time varies; Ⓢ Marunouchi line to Shinjuku-sanchōme, exit C8) The most popular of the few ladies-only joints in Ni-chōme also hosts Tokyo's hottest lesbian party, Goldfinger.

Tokyo Rainbow Pride (www.tokyorainbowpride.com) takes place in late April. The **Tokyo International Lesbian & Gay Film Festival** (www.tokyo-lgff.org) usually hits screens in mid-July.

Samurai BAR
(サムライ; Map p94; http://jazz-samurai.seesaa.net; 5th fl, 3-35-5 Shinjuku, Shinjuku-ku; ⏲6pm-1am; 🚆JR Yamanote line to Shinjuku, southeast exit) Never mind the impeccable record collection, this eccentric jazz *kissa* (cafe where jazz records are played) is worth a visit just for the owner's impressive collection of 2500 *maneki-neko* (beckoning cats). Look for the sign next door to Disc Union and take the elevator. There's a ¥300 cover charge (¥500 after 9pm); drinks from ¥650.

Akihabara & Around 秋葉原

Imasa CAFE
(井政; Map p96; ☎03-3258-0059; www.kanda-imasa.co.jp; 2-16 Soto-Kanda, Chiyoda-ku; drinks ¥600; ⏲11am-4pm Mon-Fri; 🚆JR Chūō or Sōbu lines to Ochanomizu, Hijiribashi exit) It's not every day you get to sip coffee or tea in a cultural property. Imasa is the real deal, an old timber merchant's shophouse dating from 1927 but with Edo-era design and detail, and a few pieces of modern furniture. Very few houses like this exist in Tokyo or are open to the public.

@Home Cafe CAFE
(@ほぉ〜むカフェ; Map p96; www.cafe-athome.com; 4th-7th fl, 1-11-4 Soto-Kanda, Chiyoda-ku; drinks from ¥500; ⏲11.30am-10pm Mon-Fri, 10.30am-10pm Sat & Sun; 🚆JR Yamanote line to Akihabara, Electric Town exit) *Kawaii* (cute) waitresses, dressed as French maids, play children's games with customers at this quintessential 'maid cafe'. You'll be welcomed as *go-shujinsama* (master) the minute you enter. It's a little titillating, perhaps, but this is no sex joint – just (more or less) innocent fun for Akiba's *otaku*. Dishes, such as curried rice, are topped with smiley faces.

N3331 CAFE
(Map p96; ☎03-5295-2788; http://n3331.com; 2nd fl, mAAch ecute 1-25-4 Kanda-Sudachō, Chiyoda-ku; ⏲11am-10.30pm Mon-Sat, to 8.30pm Sun; 🚆JR Yamamote line to Akihabara, Electric Town exit) Climb the original white-tile-clad stairs to the former platform of Mansei-bashi Station to find this ultimate trainspotters' cafe. Through floor-to-ceiling windows, watch commuter trains stream by while you sip on coffee, craft beer or sake and enjoy snacks.

Ueno & Yanaka 上野・谷中

Torindō TEAHOUSE
(桃林堂; Map p102; 1-5-7 Ueno-Sakuragi, Taitō-ku; tea set ¥810; ⏲9am-5pm; Ⓢ Chiyoda line to Nezu, exit 1) Sample a cup of paint-thick *matcha* (powdered green tea) at this tiny teahouse

on the edge of Ueno-kōen. Tradition dictates that the bitter tea be paired with something sweet, so choose from the artful desserts in the glass counter, then pull up a stool at the communal table. It's a white building with persimmon-coloured door curtains.

Kayaba Coffee CAFE
(カヤバ珈琲; Map p102; http://kayaba-coffee.com; 6-1-29 Yanaka, Taitō-ku; drinks from ¥400; 8am-11pm Mon-Sat, to 6pm Sun; S Chiyoda line to Nezu, exit 1) This vintage 1930s coffee shop (the building is actually from the '20s) in Yanaka is a hang-out for local students and artists. Come early for the 'morning set' (coffee and a sandwich for ¥700). In the evenings, Kayaba morphs into a bar.

Bousingot BAR
(ブーザンゴ; Map p102; 03-3823-5501; www.bousingot.com; 2-33-2 Sendagi, Bunkyō-ku; drinks from ¥450; 6-11pm Wed-Mon; S Chiyoda line to Sendagi, exit 1) It's fitting that Yanaka, which refuses to trash the past, would have a bar that doubles as a used bookstore. Sure, the books are in Japanese but you can still enjoy the atmosphere with some resident book lovers.

Asakusa & Sumida-gawa 浅草・隅田川

★ **Popeye** PUB
(ポパイ; Map p72; www.40beersontap.com; 2-18-7 Ryōgoku, Sumida-ku; 5-11pm Mon-Sat; ; JR Sōbu line to Ryōgoku, west exit) Popeye boasts an astounding 70 beers on tap, including the world's largest selection of Japanese beers – from Echigo Weizen to Hitachino Nest Espresso Stout. The happy-hour deal (5pm to 8pm) offers select brews with free plates of pizza, sausages and other munchables. It's extremely popular and fills up fast; get here early to grab a seat.

Kamiya Bar BAR
(神谷バー; Map p106; 03-3841-5400; www.kamiya-bar.com; 1-1-1 Asakusa, Taitō-ku; 11.30am-10pm Wed-Mon; S Ginza line to Asakusa, exit 3) One of Tokyo's oldest Western-style bars, Kamiya opened in 1880 and is still hugely popular – though probably more so today for its enormous, cheap draft beer (¥1020 for a litre). Its real speciality, however, is Denki Bran, a herbal liquor that's been produced in-house for over a century. Order at the counter, then give your tickets to the server.

'Cuzn Homeground BAR
(Map p106; http://homeground.jpn.com; 2-17-9 Asakusa, Taitō-ku; beer ¥800; 11am-6am; ; S Ginza line to Tawaramachi, exit 3) Run by a wild gang of local hippies, 'Cuzn is the kind of bar where anything can happen: a barbecue, a jam session or all-night karaoke, for example.

Ef CAFE
(エフ; Map p106; 03-3841-0442; www.gallery-ef.com; 2-19-18 Kaminari-mon, Taitō-ku; coffee

GOLDEN GAI

This warren of tiny alleys and narrow, two-storey wooden buildings began as a black market following WWII. It later functioned as a licensed quarter, until prostitution was outlawed in 1958. Now those same buildings are filled with more than a hundred closet-sized bars. Each is as unique and eccentric as the 'master' or 'mama' who runs it. That Golden Gai – prime real estate – has so far resisted the kind of development seen elsewhere in Shinjuku is a credit to these stubbornly bohemian characters.

Bars here usually have a theme – from punk rock to photography – and draw customers with matching expertise and obsessions (many of whom work in the media and entertainment industries). Since regular customers are their bread and butter, many establishments are likely to give tourists a cool reception. Don't take it personally. Japanese visitors unaccompanied by a regular get the same treatment; this is Golden Gai's peculiar, invisible velvet rope. On the other hand, there are bars that expressly welcome tourists (with English signs posted on their doors). Note that most bars levy a cover charge (usually ¥500 to ¥1500).

The best way to experience Golden Gai is to stroll the lanes and pick a place that suits your mood. If you're stumped, **Albatross G** (アルバトロスG; Map p94; www.alba-s.com/index.html; 1-1-7 Kabukichō, Shinjuku-ku; cover charge ¥500, drinks from ¥500; 7pm-5am; JR Yamanote line to Shinjuku, east exit) and **Araku** (亜楽; Map p94; www.facebook.com/bar.araku; 2nd fl, G2-dōri, 1-1-9 Kabukichō, Shinjuku-ku; 8pm-5am Mon-Sat; JR Yamanote line to Shinjuku, east exit) are two good bets. Noodle shop Nagi (p127) is here, too.

¥550; ⏲11am-midnight Mon, Wed, Thu & Sat, to 2am Fri, to 10pm Sun; Ⓢ Ginza line to Asakusa, exit 2) Set in a 19th-century wooden warehouse that beat the 1923 earthquake and WWII, this wonderfully cosy space serves coffee, tea and, after 6pm, cocktails and beer. Be sure to check out the gallery in the back.

Odaiba & Tokyo Bay お台場・東京湾

★Jicoo the Floating Bar COCKTAIL BAR

(ジークザフローティングバー; Map p110; ☎0120-049-490; www.jicoofloatingbar.com; admission ¥2600; ⏲8-10.30pm Thu-Sat; 🚉Yurikamome line to Hinode or Odaiba Kaihin-kōen) For a few nights a week, the futuristic cruise-boat Himiko, designed by manga and anime artist Leiji Matsumoto, morphs into this floating bar. Board on the hour at Hinode pier and the half-hour at Odaiba Kaihin-kōen. The evening-long 'floating pass' usually includes some sort of live music. Space is limited; make a reservation online in advance.

Ageha CLUB

(アゲハ; www.ageha.com; 2-2-10 Shin-Kiba, Kōtō-ku; admission ¥2500-4000; ⏲11pm-5am Fri & Sat; 🚉Yūrakuchō line to Shin-Kiba, main exit) This gigantic waterside club, the largest in Tokyo, rivals any you'd find in LA or Ibiza. Top international and Japanese DJs appear here. Free buses run to the club from the east side of Shibuya Station on Roppongi-dōri; check the website for details and bring photo ID.

☆ Entertainment

Live Music

In Tokyo you can hear everything from classical to folk to electronica. A good number of 'live houses' – small venues where indie and up-and-coming bands perform – are clustered in Shibuya. **Tokyo Dross** (www.tokyodross.blogspot.jp) pulls together listings of the best upcoming shows.

★WWW LIVE MUSIC

(Map p88; www-shibuya.jp/index.html; 13-17 Udagawa-chō, Shibuya-ku; tickets ¥2000-5000; 🚉JR Yamanote line to Shibuya, Hachikō exit) Tokyo's newest, big-hitting music venue used to be an art-house cinema. It still has the tiered floor (though the seats are gone) so everyone can see the stage. The line-up varies from indie pop to punk to electronica, but this is one of those rare venues where you could turn up just about any night and hear something good.

Unit LIVE MUSIC

(ユニット; Map p86; ☎03-5459-8630; www.unit-tokyo.com; 1-34-17 Ebisu-nishi, Shibuya-ku; admission ¥2500-5000; 🚉Tōkyū Tōyoko line to Daikanyama) On weekends, this subterranean club has two shows: live music in the evening and a DJ-hosted event after hours. Acts range from Japanese indie bands to overseas artists making their Japanese debut. Unit is less grungy than other Tokyo live houses; it draws a stylish young crowd and, thanks to its high ceilings, it doesn't get too smoky.

Shinjuku Pit Inn JAZZ

(新宿ピットイン; Map p94; ☎03-3354-2024; www.pit-inn.com; basement fl, 2-12-4 Shinjuku, Shinjuku-ku; admission from ¥3000; ⏲matinee 2.30pm, evening show 7.30pm; Ⓢ Marunouchi line to Shinjuku-sanchōme, exit C5) This is not the kind of place you come to talk over the music. Aficionados have been coming here for more than 40 years to listen to Japan's best jazz performers. Weekday matinées feature new artists and cost only ¥1300.

Club Quattro LIVE MUSIC

(クラブクアトロ; Map p88; ☎03-3477-8750; www.club-quattro.com; 32-13-4 Udagawa-chō, Shibuya-ku; tickets ¥3000-4000; 🚭; 🚉JR Yamanote line to Shibuya, Hachikō exit) This small, intimate venue has the feel of a slick nightclub. Though there's no explicit musical focus, emphasis is on rock and roll and world music, generally of high quality. Expect a more grown-up, artsy crowd than the club's location – near Center-gai – might lead you to expect.

Oiwake TRADITIONAL MUSIC

(追分; Map p106; ☎03-3844-6283; www.oiwake.info; 3-28-11 Nishi-Asakusa, Taitō-ku; admission ¥2000 plus 1 food & 1 drink; ⏲5.30pm-midnight; 🚉Tsukuba Express to Asakusa, exit 1) Oiwake is one of Tokyo's few *minyō izakaya*, pubs where traditional folk music is performed. It's a homey place, where the waitstaff and the musicians – who play *tsugaru-jamisen* (a banjo-like instrument), hand drums and bamboo flute – are one and the same. Sets start at 7pm and 9pm; children are welcome for the early show. Seating is on tatami.

Suntory Hall CLASSICAL MUSIC

(Map p82; ☎03-3505-1001; www.suntory.com/culture-sports/suntoryhall; Ark Hills, 1-13-1 Akasaka, Minato-ku; Ⓢ Ginza line to Tameike-sannō, exit 13) This is one of the best venues to attend a classical music concert, with a busy schedule including accomplished musicians. Its

DON'T MISS

FILM FESTIVALS

Film fans will want to check out one of Tokyo's two film festivals, when works by Japanese directors are screened with English subtitles. The **Tokyo International Film Festival** (TIFF; www.tiff-jp.net/en/) takes place in October. The less-commercial **Tokyo Filmex** (http://filmex.net), held in November, focuses on the works of local and Asian directors.

2000-seat main hall has one of the largest organs in the world.

Theatre & Dance

Kabuki is Tokyo's signature form of performing arts. You can also catch other forms of traditional theatre, such as *nō* (stylised dance-drama) and bunraku (classic puppet theatre), throughout the year, though performances are irregular.

Contemporary theatre in Tokyo doesn't hold the same cultural sway that kabuki did in its heyday. Still, in pockets of the city, public and underground theatres play to full houses. To learn more about Tokyo's contemporary theatre scene, check out **Tokyo Stages** (www.tokyostages.wordpress.com).

The city's annual international theatre festival, **Festival/Tokyo** (www.festival-tokyo.jp/en/), takes place in November.

★Kabuki-za TRADITIONAL THEATRE

(歌舞伎座; Map p76; ☎03-3545-6800; www.kabuki-bito.jp/eng; 4-12-15 Ginza, Chūō-ku; tickets ¥4000-20,000, single-act tickets ¥800-2000; Hibiya line to Higashi-Ginza, exit 3) The flamboyant facade of this venerable theatre, recently completely reconstructed to incorporate a tower block, makes a strong impression. It is a good indication of the extravagant dramatic flourishes that are integral to the traditional performing art of kabuki. Check the website for performance details and to book tickets; you'll also find an explanation about cheaper one-act, day seats.

A full kabuki performance comprises three or four acts (usually from different plays) over an afternoon or an evening (typically 11am to 3.30pm or 4.30pm to 9pm), with long intervals between the acts. Be sure to rent a headset for blow-by-blow explanations in English, and pick up a *bentō* to snack on during the intervals.

If four-plus hours sounds too long, 90 sitting and 60 standing tickets are sold on the day for each single act. They are at the back of the auditorium but still provide good views. Some acts tend to be more popular than others, so ask ahead about which to catch and arrive at least 1½ hours before the start of the performance.

Setagaya Public Theatre PERFORMING ARTS

(世田谷パブリックシアター; Map p72; ☎03-5432-1526; www.setagaya-pt.jp; 4-1-1 Taishidō, Setagaya-ku; tickets ¥3500-7500; Tōkyū Den-en-toshi line to Sangenjaya, Carrot Tower exit) The best of Tokyo's public theatres, Setagaya Public Theatre puts on contemporary dramas as well as modern *nō* and sometimes *butoh* (an avant-garde form of dance). The smaller **Theatre Tram** shows more experimental works. Both are located inside the Carrot Tower building connected to Sangenjaya Station, a five-minute train ride from Shibuya.

National Nō Theatre TRADITIONAL THEATRE

(国立能楽堂; Kokuritsu Nō-gakudō; Map p72; ☎03-3423-1331; www.ntj.jac.go.jp/english; 4-18-1 Sendagaya, Shibuya-ku; tickets from ¥2600; JR Sōbu line to Sendagaya) The traditional music, poetry and dances that *nō* is famous for unfold here on an elegant cypress stage. Each seat has a small screen that can display an English translation of the dialogue. Shows take place only a few times a month.

Robot Restaurant CABARET

(ロボットレストラン; Map p94; ☎03-3200-5500; www.robot-restaurant.com; 1-7-1 Kabukichō, Shinjuku-ku; tickets ¥7000; shows at 4pm, 5.55pm, 7.50pm & 9.45pm; JR Yamanote line to Shinjuku, east exit) This Kabukichō spectacle is wacky Japan at its finest, with giant robots manned by bikini-clad women and enough neon to light all of Shinjuku. Reservations aren't necessary but they're highly recommended. If you've booked ahead, be sure to arrive at least 30 minutes before the show. Look for discount tickets in English-language free mags around town.

National Theatre TRADITIONAL THEATRE

(国立劇場; Kokuritsu Gekijō; Map p72; ☎03-3265-7411; www.ntj.jac.go.jp/english; 4-1 Hayabusa-chō, Chiyoda-ku; tickets from ¥1500; S Hanzōmon line to Hanzōmon, exit 1) This is the capital's premier venue for traditional performing arts with 1600-seat and 590-seat auditoriums. Performances include kabuki, *gagaku* (music of the imperial court) and bunraku. Earphones with English translation are available for hire (¥650 plus ¥1000 deposit). Check the website for performance schedules.

Asakusa Engei Hall COMEDY
(浅草演芸ホール; Map p106; ☎03-3841-6545; www.asakusaengei.com; 1-43-12 Asakusa, Taitō-ku; adult/student ¥2800/2300; ⊙shows 11.40am-4.30pm & 4.40-9pm; S Ginza line to Tawaramachi, exit 3) Asakusa was once full of theatres like this one, where traditional *rakugo* (comedic monologue) and other forms of comedy are performed along with juggling, magic shows and the like. It's all in Japanese, but the linguistic confusion is mitigated by lively facial expressions and props, which help translate comic takes on universal human experiences.

Honda Theatre THEATRE
(本多劇場; Map p72; www.honda-geki.com; 2-10-15 Kitazawa, Shibuya-ku; 🚂 Keiō Inokashira line to Shimo-Kitazawa, south exit) This is the original – and the biggest – of Shimo-Kitazawa's independent *shōgeki-jō* (small theatres). If you have a fair helping of Japanese ability, this is a good place to start digging into Tokyo's theatre scene.

Sport

Sumo is fascinating, highly ritualised and steeped in Shintō tradition. It's also the only traditional Japanese sport that still has enough clout to draw big crowds and dominate prime-time TV.

Tournaments take place in Tokyo at Ryōgoku Kokugikan in January, May and September. Other times of year you can drop in on an early morning practice session at one of the stables, where the wrestlers train and live, such as Arashio Stable.

Baseball is more of an obsession than a sport in Japan, and it's worth getting tickets to a game if only to see the fans go wild at each play and to witness the perfectly choreographed 7th-inning stretch. Within Tokyo, the Yomiuri Giants and Yakult Swallows are cross-town rivals.

Baseball season runs from April through October. Check the schedules on the stadium websites.

★ Ryōgoku Kokugikan SUMO
(両国国技館, Ryōgoku Sumo Stadium; Map p72; ☎3623-5111; www.sumo.or.jp; 1-3-28 Yokoami, Sumida-ku; admission ¥2200-14,800; 🚂 JR Sōbu line to Ryōgoku, west exit) If you're in town when a tournament is on – for 15 days each January, May and September – catch the big boys in action at Japan's largest sumo stadium. Doors open at 8am, but the action doesn't heat up until the senior wrestlers hit the ring around 2pm. Tickets can be bought online one month before the start of the tournament.

A limited number of general-admission tickets are sold only on the day of the match from the box office in front of the stadium. You'll have to line up very early (say 6am) on the last couple of days of the tournament to snag one.

If you get there in the morning when the stadium is still pretty empty, you can usually sneak down to the box seats. You can rent a radio (¥100 fee, plus ¥2000 deposit) to listen to commentary in English. Stop by

KARAOKE: WAY MORE FUN THAN IT SOUNDS

Of course no discussion of Tokyo nightlife would be complete without mentioning the national pastime that is karaoke (カラオケ). You'll find branches of major chains such as **Big Echo** (ビッグエコー) and **Karaoke-kan** (カラオケ館) around major train stations. Most offer a sizeable selection of songs in English.

Karaoke is charged per person per half-hour. It's often cheaper to go for a meal plan – though we make no promises about the food. Tack on a *nomihōdai* (飲み放題; all-you-can-drink) option and let your inner diva shine.

These favourites are a cut above the typical yodelling parlour:

Festa Iikura (フェスタ飯倉; Map p82; ☎5570-1500; www.festa-iikura.com; 3-5-7 Azabudai, Minato-ku; 3hr room & meal plan from ¥5000; ⊙5pm-5am Mon-Sat; S Hibiya line to Kamiyachō, exit 2) Serves the best karaoke food in town. Classy sushi dinner courses include three hours of karaoke, and there's a rack of costumes to play with free of charge.

Shidax Village (シダックスビレッジ; Map p88; ☎3461-9356; 1-12-13 Jinnan, Shibuya-ku; per 30min Mon-Thu ¥580, Fri-Sun ¥610; ⊙11am-5am Sun-Thu, to 6am Fri & Sat; 🚂 JR Yamanote line to Shibuya, Hachikō exit) Outshines all the other karaoke joints in Shibuya with comparatively spacious rooms.

the basement restaurant to sample *chanko-nabe* (the protein-rich stew eaten by the wrestlers) for just ¥250 a bowl.

★Tokyo Dome BASEBALL

(東京ドーム; Map p96; www.tokyo-dome.co.jp/e; 1-3 Kōraku, Bunkyō-ku; tickets ¥2200-6100; JR Chūō line to Suidōbashi, west exit) Tokyo Dome (aka 'Big Egg') is home to the Yomiuri Giants. Love 'em or hate 'em, they're the most consistently successful team in Japanese baseball. If you're looking to see the Giants in action, the baseball season runs from the end of March to the end of October. Tickets sell out in advance; get them early at www.giants.jp/en.

If you'd rather root for the underdog (whoever is playing the Giants), you can drown your sorrows in the beer served by the *uriko,* young women with kegs strapped to their backs, who work the aisles with tireless cheer.

Arashio Stable SUMO

(荒汐部屋; Arashio-beya; Map p72; 03-3666-7646; www.arashio.net/tour_e.html; 2-47-2 Hama-chō, Nihombashi, Chūō-ku; S Toei Shinjuku line to Hamachō, exit A2) FREE Catch morning sumo practice between 7.30am and 10am at this friendly stable. Call the day before to double-check that practice is on; more info on the English website.

Jingū Baseball Stadium BASEBALL

(神宮球場; Jingū Kyūjo; Map p90; 03-3404-8999; www.jingu-stadium.com; 3-1 Kasumigaoka-machi, Shinjuku-ku; tickets ¥1600-4600; S Ginza line to Gaienmae, exit 3) Jingū Baseball Stadium, built in 1926, is home to the Yakult Swallows, Tokyo's number-two team (but number one when it comes to fan loyalty). Pick up tickets from the booth in front of the stadium; same-day outfield tickets cost just ¥1600 (¥500 for children) and are usually available. Night games start at 6pm; weekend games start around 2pm.

> **GETTING TICKETS**
>
> Found a show or event that takes your fancy? **Ticket Pia** (チケットぴあ; 0570-02-9111; http://t.pia.jp; 10am-8pm) handles just about everything, including concerts and theatre performances major and minor. Tickets (when not sold out) can be purchased up to three days before the show. There are convenient branches on the 4th floor of Shibuya Hikarie (p88) and inside the Asakusa Tourist Information Center (p148).

Shopping

Ginza is Tokyo's original shopping district, full of department stores and boutiques. For younger shoppers, however, the fashion scene has shifted westward, to trendy neighbourhoods such as Shibuya and Harajuku.

Tokyo still has a strong artisan tradition and you can find craft stores in older neighbourhoods such as Ueno and Asakusa.

Major hubs such as Shibuya, Shinjuku, Ikebukuro and Ueno, which have department stores, electronic stores and popular chain stores, are all convenient shopping destinations. Akihabara has a particularly high concentration of electronics stores, and is the place to go for anime and manga.

More and more stores are offering duty-free shopping so make sure to have your passport on you.

Marunouchi (Tokyo Station area) 丸の内（東京駅）

Coredo Muromachi MALL

(コレド室町; Map p76; http://mi-mo.jp/pc/lng/eng/muromachi.html; 2-2-1 Nihonbashi-Muromachi, Chūō-ku; 11am-7pm most shops; S Ginza line to Mitsukoshimae, exit A4) Spread over three buildings, this stylish new development hits its stride at Coredo Muromachi 3. It houses several well-curated floors of top-class, Japanese-crafted goods including cosmetics, fashion, homewares, spectacles and speciality food.

Muji CLOTHING, HOMEWARES

(無印良品; Map p76; www.muji.com; 3-8-3 Marunouchi, Chiyoda-ku; 10am-9pm; JR Yamanote line to Yūrakuchō, Kyōbashi exit) The flagship store of the famously understated brand sells elegant, simple clothing, accessories and homewares. There are scores of other outlets across Tokyo, including a good one in Tokyo Midtown, but the Yūrakuchō store also has bicycle rental and a great cafeteria.

Tokyo Character Street TOYS

(東京キャラクターストリート; Map p76; www.tokyoeki-1bangai.co.jp; B1 First Avenue Tokyo Station, 1-9-1 Marunouchi, Chiyoda-ku; 10am-8.30pm; JR lines to Tokyo Station, Yaesu exit) From Doraemon to Domo-kun, Hello Kitty to Ultraman, Japan knows *kawaii* (cute) and how to merchandise it. In the basement on the Yaesu side of Tokyo Station, some 15 Japanese TV networks and toy manufacturers operate stalls selling official plush toys, sweets, accessories and the all-important miniature character to dangle from your mobile phone.

Ginza 銀座

★ Akomeya FOOD

(Map p76; 03-6758-0271; www.akomeya.jp; 2-2-6 Ginza, Chūō-ku; shop 11am-9pm; restaurant 11.30am-10pm; Yūrakuchō line to Ginza-itchome, exit 4) Rice is at the core of Japanese cuisine and drink. This stylish store sells not only many types of the grain but also products made from it (such as sake), a vast range of quality cooking ingredients and a choice collection of kitchen, home and bath items.

Takumi CRAFTS

(たくみ; Map p76; 03-3571-2017; www.ginza-takumi.co.jp; 8-4-2 Ginza, Chūō-ku; 11am-7pm Mon-Sat; Ginza line to Shimbashi, exit 5) You'll be hard pressed to find a more elegant selection of traditional folk crafts, including toys, textiles and ceramics from around Japan. Ever thoughtful, the shop also encloses information detailing the origin and background of the pieces if you make a purchase.

Dover Street Market Ginza FASHION

(DSM; Map p76; 03-6228-5080; http://ginza.doverstreetmarket.com; 6-9-5 Ginza, Chūō-ku; 11am-8pm Sun-Thu, to 9pm Fri & Sat; Ginza line to Ginza, exit A2) A department store as envisioned by Kawakubo Rei (of Comme des Garçons), DSM has seven floors of avant-garde brands, including several Japanese labels and everything in the Comme des Garçons line-up. The quirky art installations alone make it worth the visit.

Sony Building ELECTRONICS

(ソニービル; Map p76; 03-3573-2371; www.sonybuilding.jp; 5-3-1 Ginza, Chūō-ku; 11am-7pm; Ginza, Hibiya, Marunouchi line to Ginza, exit B9) Where Sony shows off and sells its latest digital and electronic gizmos. Kids will love the free Playstation games, while adults tend to lose an hour or so perusing all the latest audio and video accessories.

Uniqlo FASHION

(ユニクロ; Map p76; www.uniqlo.com; 5-7-7 Ginza, Chūō-ku; 11am-9pm; Ginza line to Ginza, exit A2) This now global brand has made its name by sticking to the basics and tweaking them with style. Offering inexpensive, quality clothing, this is the Tokyo flagship store with 11 floors and items you won't find elsewhere.

DON'T MISS

TOKYO'S BEST MARKETS

Flea markets, antiques fairs and farmers markets pop up regularly in Tokyo. In addition to these favourites, see www.frma.jp (in Japanese) for an up-to-date schedule of flea markets and www.japanfarmersmarkets.com for farmers markets.

Oedo Antique Market (大江戸骨董市; Map p76; 03-6407-6011; www.antique-market.jp; 3-5-1 Marunouchi, Chiyoda-ku; 9am-4pm 1st & 3rd Sun of month; JR Yamanote line to Yūrakuchō, Kokusai Forum exit) Quality vendors selling retro and antique Japanese goods set up twice a month.

Tsukiji Outer Market (p80) Daily morning market brimming with food and food-related items.

UNU Farmers Market (Map p90; www.farmersmarkets.jp; 10am-4pm Sat & Sun; Ginza line to Omote-sandō, exit B2) Weekend farmers market with colourful produce and food trucks; there's a small antiques market here on Saturdays, too.

Itōya ARTS & CRAFTS

(伊東屋; Map p76; www.ito-ya.co.jp; 2-7-15 Ginza, Chūō-ku; 10.30am-8pm Mon-Sat, to 7pm Sun; Ginza line to Ginza, exit A13) Nine floors of stationery-shop love await visual-art professionals and seekers of office accessories, with both everyday items and luxury such as fountain pens and Italian leather agendas. You'll also find *washi* (fine Japanese handmade paper), *tenugui* (beautifully hand-dyed thin cotton towels) and *furoshiki* (wrapping cloths).

Roppongi & Around 六本木

Japan Traditional Crafts Aoyama Square CRAFTS

(伝統工芸 青山スクエア; Map p72; http://kougeihin.jp/home.shtml; 8-1-22 Akasaka, Minato-ku; 11am-7pm, Mon-Sun except New Year's holidays; Ginza line to Aoyama-itchōme, exit 4) Supported by the Japanese Ministry of Economy, Trade and Industry, this is as much a showroom as a shop exhibiting a broad range of traditional crafts, including lacquerwork boxes, woodwork, cut glass, paper, textiles and earthy pottery. The emphasis is on high-end pieces, but you can find beautiful things in all price ranges here.

Tolman Collection ARTS & CRAFTS

(トールマンコレクション; Map p72; ☎03-3434-1300; www.tolmantokyo.com; 2-2-18 Shiba-Daimon, Minato-ku; ⊙11am-7pm Wed-Mon; Ⓢ Ōedo line to Daimon, exit A3) Based in a traditional wooden building, this reputable gallery represents nearly 50 leading Japanese artists of printing, lithography, etching, woodblock and more. Quality prints start at around ¥10,000 and rise steeply from there. From Daimon Station, walk west towards Zōjo-ji temple. Turn left at the shop Create. You'll soon see the gallery on your left.

Souvenir From Tokyo SOUVENIRS

(スーベニアフロムトーキョー; Map p82; www.souvenirfromtokyo.jp; basement fl, National Art Center Tokyo, 7-22-2 Roppongi, Minato-ku; ⊙10am-6pm Sat-Mon, Wed & Thu, to 8pm Fri; Ⓢ Chiyoda line to Nogizaka, exit 6) An expert selection of homegrown design bits and bobs that make for perfect, unique souvenirs: a mobile by Tempo, zig-zag tote from Mint Designs or a set of cheeky tea cups from Amabro, for example.

Japan Sword ANTIQUES

(日本刀剣; Map p82; ☎03-3434-4324; www.japansword.co.jp; 3-8-1 Toranomon, Minato-ku; ⊙9.30am-6pm Mon-Fri, to 5pm Sat; Ⓢ Ginza line to Toranomon, exit 2) If you're after a samurai sword or weaponry, this venerable place sells the genuine article – including antique sword guards and samurai helmets dating from the Edo period – as well as convincing replicas crafted by hand. Be sure to enquire about export and transport restrictions.

Ebisu & Meguro 恵比寿・目黒

★Okura FASHION, ACCESSORIES

(オクラ; Map p86; 20-11 Sarugaku-chō, Shibuya-ku; ⊙11.30am-8pm Mon-Fri, 11am-8.30pm Sat & Sun; Ⓡ Tōkyū Tōyoko line to Daikanyama) Almost everything in this enchanting shop is dyed a deep indigo blue – from sweatshirts to scarves. There are some beautiful, original items, though unfortunately most aren't cheap. The shop itself looks like a rural house, with worn, wooden floorboards and white-washed walls. Note: there's no sign out the front, but look for the traditional building.

Kapital FASHION

(キャピタル; Map p86; ☎03-5725-3923; http://kapital.jp; 2-20-2 Ebisu, Shibuya-ku; ⊙11am-8pm; Ⓡ JR Yamanote line to Ebisu, west exit) One of Japan's hottest brands, Kapital is a world away from Tokyo's pop image. The label is known for its premium denim, dyed a dozen times the traditional way, earthy knits and lushly patterned scarves.

Daikanyama T-Site BOOKS

(代官山T-SITE; Map p86; http://tsite.jp/daikanyama; 17-5 Sarugaku-chō, Shibuya-ku; ⊙7am-2am; Ⓡ Tōkyū Tōyoko line to Daikanyama) Locals love this stylish shrine to the printed word, which has a fantastic collection of books on travel, art, design and food (some are in English). The best part is that you can sit at the in-house Starbucks and read all afternoon – if you can get a seat, that is.

Good Day Books BOOKS

(グッド デイ ブックス; Map p72; www.gooddaybooks.com; 3rd fl, 2-4-2 Nishi-Gotanda, Shinagawa-ku; ⊙11am-8pm Mon-Sat, to 6pm Sun; Ⓡ JR Yamanote line to Gotanda, west exit) Tokyo's best source for secondhand English-language books has a good selection of titles on Japanese culture and language. From Gotanda Station, head right from the ticket gates, then right again, following the tracks until you see the Big Size Shoes store on the ground floor.

Shibuya 渋谷

★Tōkyū Hands VARIETY

(東急ハンズ; Map p88; http://shibuya.tokyu-hands.co.jp; 12-18 Udagawa-chō, Shibuya-ku; ⊙10am-8.30pm; Ⓡ JR Yamanote line to Shibuya, Hachikō exit) This DIY and *zakka* (miscellaneous goods) store has eight fascinating floors of everything you didn't know you needed. Like reflexology slippers, bee-venom face masks and cartoon-character-shaped rice-ball moulds. It's perfect for souvenir hunting.

Fake Tokyo FASHION

(Map p88; ☎03-5456-9892; www.faketokyo.com; 18-4 Udagawa-chō, Shibuya-ku; ⊙noon-10pm; Ⓡ JR Yamanote line to Shibuya, Hachikō exit) This is one of the best places in the city to discover hot new Japanese designers. It's actually two shops in one: downstairs is Candy, full of brash, unisex streetwear; upstairs is Sister, which specialises in more ladylike items, both new and vintage. Look for the 'Fake Tokyo' banners out front.

Shibuya 109 FASHION

(渋谷109; Ichimarukyū; Map p88; www.shibuya109.jp/en/top; 2-29-1 Dōgenzaka, Shibuya-ku; ⌚10am-9pm; 🚉JR Yamanote line to Shibuya, Hachikō exit) See all those dolled-up teens walking around Shibuya? This is where they shop. Nicknamed *marukyū*, this cylindrical tower houses dozens of small boutiques, each with their own carefully styled look. Even if you don't intend to buy anything, you can't understand Shibuya without making a stop here.

Parco DEPARTMENT STORE

(パルコ; Map p88; ☎03-3464-5111; www.parco-shibuya.com; 15-1 Udagawa-chō, Shibuya-ku; ⌚10am-9pm; 🚉JR Yamanote line to Shibuya, Hachikō exit) Not your typical fussy department store, Parco customers are more likely to be art-school students than ladies who lunch. Lots of Japanese fashion designers have shops here.

Harajuku 原宿

The web of alleys behind the mall Omote-sandō Hills is known as Ura-Hara (literally 'behind Harajuku'). This is where you'll find the small boutiques and vintage shops that keep the neighbourhood's indie spirit alive.

★Sou-Sou FASHION

(そうそう; Map p90; ☎03-3407-7877; http://sousounetshop.jp; 5-3-10 Minami-Aoyama, Minato-ku; ⌚11am-8pm; Ⓢ Ginza line to Omote-sandō, exit A5) Sou-Sou gives traditional Japanese clothing items – such as split-toed *tabi* socks and *haori* (coats with kimono-like sleeves) – a contemporary spin. It is best known for producing the steel-toed, rubber-soled *tabi* shoes worn by Japanese construction workers in fun, playful designs.

Laforet FASHION

(ラフォーレ; Map p90; www.laforet.ne.jp; 1-11-6 Jingūmae, Shibuya-ku; ⌚11am-8pm; 🚉JR Yamanote line to Harajuku, Omote-sandō exit) Laforet has been a beacon of cutting-edge Harajuku style for decades. Don't let the Topshop on the ground floor fool you; lots of quirky, cult favourite brands still cut their teeth here.

Musubi CRAFTS

(むす美; Map p90; http://kyoto-musubi.com; 2-31-8 Jingūmae, Shibuya-ku; ⌚11am-7pm Thu-Tue; 🚉JR Yamanote line to Harajuku, Takeshita exit) *Furoshiki* are versatile squares of cloth that can be folded and knotted to make shopping bags and gift wrap. This shop sells pretty ones in both traditional and contemporary patterns. There is usually an English-speaking clerk who can show you how to tie them, or pick up one of the English-language books sold here.

KiddyLand TOYS

(キデイランド; Map p90; www.kiddyland.co.jp/en/index.html; 6-1-9 Jingūmae, Shibuya-ku; ⌚10am-9pm; 🚉JR Yamanote line to Harajuku,

SPECIALITY SHOPPING DISTRICTS

Historically, Tokyo's *machi* (towns) were organised by trade. It's still possible to find streets devoted to selling just one kind of thing. Here are our favourites:

Kappabashi-dōri (合羽橋通り; Map p106; Ⓢ Ginza line to Tawaramachi, exit 3) The country's largest wholesale restaurant-supply and kitchenware district sells bamboo steamer baskets, lacquer trays, neon signs and *chōchin* (paper lanterns). It's also where restaurants get their freakishly realistic plastic food models. Get kits to make your own at **Ganso Shokuhin Sample-ya** (元祖食品サンプル屋; Map p106; www.ganso-sample.com; 3-7-6 Nishi-Asakusa, Taitō-ku; ⌚10am-5.30pm; Ⓢ Ginza line to Tawaramachi, exit 3).

Jimbōchō (Map p96; Ⓢ Hanzōmon line to Jimbōchō, exits A1, A6 or A7) This neighbourhood has over 170 new and secondhand booksellers. Don't miss **Ohya Shobō** (大屋書房; Map p96; ☎3291-0062; www.ohya-shobo.com; 1-1 Kanda-Jimbōchō, Chiyoda-ku; ⌚10am-6pm Mon-Sat; 🚉Hanzōmon line to Jimbōchō, exit A7), which carries *ukiyo-e* (woodblock prints), Edo-era manga and vintage maps.

Meguro Interior Shops Community (ミスク; Map p86; http://misc.co.jp/; Meguro-dōri; 🚉JR Yamanote Line to Meguro, west exit) Dozens of homewares shops are spread out over a 3km stretch of Meguro-dōri, which runs through wealthy residential neighbourhoods. **Meister** (マイスター; Map p86; www.meister-mag.co.jp; 4-11-4 Meguro, Meguro-ku; ⌚11am-8pm Thu-Tue; 🚌No 1, 2, 6 or 7 from Meguro Station to Moto-Keibajō-mae) and **Do**, inside the Claska (p118), are two favourites. Note that many stores close on Wednesday.

Omote-sandō exit) This multistorey toy emporium is packed to the rafters with character goods. It's not just for kids either; you'll spot plenty of adults on a nostalgia trip down the Hello Kitty aisle.

Tokyo's Tokyo SOUVENIRS
(トーキョーズトーキョー; Map p90; 5th fl, Tōkyū Plaza, 4-30-3 Jingūmae, Shibuya-ku; ⏲11am-9pm; 🚊JR Yamanote line to Harajuku, Omote-sandō exit) Tokyo's Tokyo is betting that you'd love to find something slightly wacky, pop-culture-inflected and 'only in Tokyo' to bring home with you. It's stocked with accessories from local fashion designers, surprisingly useful gadgets and other fun trinkets.

Gallery Kawano KIMONO
(ギャラリー川野; Map p90; www.gallery-kawano.com; 4-4-9 Jingūmae, Shibuya-ku; ⏲11am-6pm; 🚊Ginza line to Omote-sandō, exit A2) Gallery Kawano has a good selection of vintage kimonos in decent shape, priced reasonably (about ¥5000 to ¥15,000). The staff will help you try one on and pick out a matching *obi* (sash); they're less excited about helping customers who try things on but don't intend to buy.

6% Doki Doki FASHION, ACCESSORIES
(ロクパーセントドキドキ; Map p90; www.dokidoki6.com; 2nd fl, 4-28-16 Jingūmae, Shibuya-ku; ⏲noon-8pm; 🚊JR Yamanote line to Harajuku, Omote-sandō exit) Tucked away on an Ura-Hara backstreet, this bubblegum-pink store sells acid-bright accessories that are part raver, part schoolgirl (and 100% Harajuku).

Oriental Bazaar SOUVENIRS
(オリエンタルバザー; Map p90; www.orientalbazaar.co.jp; 5-9-13 Jingūmae, Shibuya-ku; ⏲10am-6pm Mon-Wed & Fri, to 7pm Sat & Sun; 🚊JR Yamanote line to Harajuku, Omote-sandō exit) Oriental Bazaar stocks a wide selection of souvenirs at very reasonable prices. Items to be found here include fans, pottery, *yukata* (light summer kimonos) and T-shirts, some made in Japan, but others not (read the labels).

Condomania SPECIALITY SHOP
(コンドマニア; Map p90; 6-30-1 Jingūmae, Shibuya-ku; ⏲11am-9.30pm; 🚊JR Yamanote line to Harajuku, Omote-sandō exit) This irreverent outpost must be Tokyo's cheekiest rendezvous point. Popular items include *omamori* (traditional good-luck charms) with condoms tucked inside.

Chicago Thrift Store VINTAGE
(シカゴ; Map p90; 6-31-21 Jingūmae, Shibuya-ku; ⏲10am-8pm; 🚊JR Yamanote line to Harajuku, Omote-sandō exit) Chicago is crammed with all sorts of vintage clothing, but best of all is the extensive collection of used kimonos and *yukata*, priced very low, in the back.

Shinjuku 新宿

★Don Quijote VARIETY
(ドン・キホーテ; Map p94; ☎03-5291-9211; www.donki.com; 1-16-5 Kabukichō, Shinjuku-ku; ⏲24hr; 🚊JR Yamanote line to Shinjuku, east exit) This fluorescent-lit bargain castle is filled to the brink with weird loot. Chaotic piles of knockoff electronics and designer goods

RETAIL ARCHITECTURE IN OMOTE-SANDŌ

The magnificent parade of sculpture-like stores along Omote-sandō (p90) also functions as a walk-through showroom for the who's who of contemporary (mostly) Japanese architects.

Tōkyū Plaza The entrance to this castle-like structure by up-and-coming architect Nakamura Hiroshi is a dizzying hall of mirrors; there's a roof garden on top.

Omotesandō Hills This low-slung concrete mall, designed by Andō Tadao, spirals around a sunken atrium.

Dior The filmy exterior, which seems to hang like a dress, is the work of Pritzker Prize–winner SANAA (Sejima Kazuyo and Nishizawa Ryūe).

Louis Vuitton Aoki Jun's design, which uses panels of tinted glass behind sheets of metal mesh, is meant to evoke a stack of trunks.

Tod's Itō Toyo designed the criss-crossing ribbons of concrete that take their inspiration from the zelkova trees below; what's more impressive is that they're also structural.

Prada This convex glass fishbowl is the work of Herzog & de Meuron, also Pritzker Prize winners.

sit alongside sex toys, fetish costumes and packaged foods. Though it's now a national chain, it started as a rare (at the time) 24-hour store for the city's night workers.

Isetan DEPARTMENT STORE
(伊勢丹; Map p94; www.isetan.co.jp; 3-14-1 Shinjuku, Shinjuku-ku; 10am-8pm; S Marunouchi line to Shinjuku-sanchōme, exits B3, B4 & B5) Most department stores play to conservative tastes, but this one doesn't. Women should head to the Re-Style section on the 2nd floor for an always changing line-up of up-and-coming Japanese designers. Men get a whole building of their own (connected by a passageway). Don't miss the basement food hall, featuring some of the country's top purveyors of sweet and savoury goodies.

RanKing RanQueen VARIETY
(ランキンランキン; Map p94; basement fl, Shinjuku Station, Shinjuku-ku; 10am-11pm; JR Yamanote line to Shinjuku, east exit) If it's trendy, it's here. This clever shop stocks only the top-selling products in any given category, from eyeliner and soft drinks to leg-slimming massage rollers. Look for it just outside the east-exit ticket gates of JR Shinjuku Station.

Disk Union MUSIC
(ディスクユニオン; Map p94; 3-31-4 Shinjuku, Shinjuku-ku; 11am-9pm; JR Yamanote line to Shinjuku, east exit) Scruffy Disk Union is known by local audiophiles as Tokyo's best used CD and vinyl store. Eight storeys carry a variety of musical styles; if you still can't find what you're looking for, there are several other branches in Shinjuku that stock more obscure genres (pick up a map here).

Bicqlo CLOTHING, ELECTRONICS
(ビックロ; Map p94; 3-29-1 Shinjuku, Shinjuku-ku; 10am-10pm; S Marunouchi line to Shinjuku-sanchōme, exit A5) This mash-up store brings two of Japan's favourite retailers – electronics outfitter Bic Camera and budget clothing chain Uniqlo – under one roof. So you can match your new camera to your new hoodie. It's bright white: you can't miss it.

Kinokuniya BOOKS
(紀伊國屋書店; Map p94; www.kinokuniya.co.jp; Takashimaya Times Sq, 5-24-2 Sendagaya, Shibuya-ku; 10am-8pm; JR Yamanote line to Shinjuku, south exit) The 6th floor has a broad selection of foreign-language books and magazines, including English-teaching texts.

Akihabara & Around 秋葉原

★Mandarake Complex MANGA, ANIME
(まんだらけコンプレックス; Map p96; www.mandarake.co.jp; 3-11-2 Soto-Kanda, Chiyoda-ku; noon-8pm; JR Yamanote line to Akihabara, Electric Town exit) When *otaku* dream of heaven, it probably looks a lot like this giant go-to store for manga and anime. Eight storeys are piled high with comic books and DVDs, action figures and cell art just for starters. The 5th floor, in all its pink splendour, is devoted to women's comics, while the 4th floor is for men.

★2k540 Aki-Oka Artisan CRAFTS
(アキオカアルチザン; Map p96; www.jrtk.jp/2k540; 5-9-23 Ueno, Taitō-ku; 11am-7pm Thu-Tue; Ginza line to Suehirochō, exit 2) This ace arcade under the JR tracks (its name refers to the distance from Tokyo Station) offers an eclectic range of stores selling Japanese-made goods – everything from pottery to cute aliens, a nod to Akihabara from a mall that is more akin to Kyoto than Electric Town. The best for colourful crafts is **Nippon Hyakkuten** (日本百貨店; http://nippon-dept.jp).

mAAch ecute MALL
(Map p96; www.maach-ecute.jp; 1-25-4 Kanda-Sudachō, Chiyoda-ku; 11am-9pm Mon-Sat, to 8pm Sun; Chūō or Sōbu lines to Akihabara, Electric Town exit) JR has another shopping and dining hit on its hands with this complex crafted from the old station and railway arches at Mansei-bashi. Crafts, homewares, fashions and food from across Japan are sold here; look out for **Tatazumai**, which stocks more than 50 types of craft beer, cider and sakes, and **Obscura Coffee Roasters**.

Chabara FOOD
(ちゃばら; Map p96; www.jrtk.jp/chabara; 8-2 Kanda Neribei-chō, Chiyoda-ku; 11am-8pm; JR Yamanote line to Akihabara, Electric Town exit) This under-the-train-tracks shopping mall focuses on artisan food and drinks from across Japan, including premium sake, soy sauce, sweets, teas and crackers – all great souvenirs and presents.

Yodobashi Akiba ELECTRONICS
(ヨドバシカメラAkiba; Map p96; www.yodobashi-akiba.com; 1-1 Kanda Hanaoka-chō, Chiyoda-ku; 9.30am-10pm; JR Yamanote line to Akihabara, Shōwa-tōriguchi exit) This is the monster branch of Shinjuku's Yodobashi Camera where many locals shop. It has eight floors

BEST SHOPS FOR...

Anime & Manga Mandarake Complex (p145)

Crafts Takumi (p141)

Fashion Laforet (p143)

Foodstuffs Akomeya (p141)

Kimonos Gallery Kawano (p144)

Souvenirs Tōkyū Hands (p142)

Vintage Tokyo Hotarudo

of electronics, cameras, toys, appliances, CDs and DVDs at an in-store branch of Tower Records, and even restaurants. Ask about export models and VAT-free purchases.

Ueno & Yanaka 上野・谷中

Isetatsu CRAFTS

(いせ辰; Map p102; ☎3823-1453; 2-18-9 Yanaka, Taitō-ku; ⏲10am-6pm; Ⓢ Chiyoda line to Sendagi, exit 1) Dating back to 1864, this venerable stationery shop specialises in *chiyogami:* gorgeous, colourful paper made using woodblocks.

Yanaka Matsunoya HOMEWARES

(谷中松野屋; Map p102; www.matsunoya.jp; 3-14-14 Nishi-Nippori, Arakawa-ku; ⏲11am-7pm Wed-Fri & Mon, from 10am Sat & Sun; Ⓡ JR Yamanote line to Nippori, west exit) On Yanaka Ginza, Matsunoya sells household goods – baskets, brooms and canvas totes, for example – simple in beauty and form, handmade by local artisans.

Asakusa & Sumida-gawa 浅草・隅田川

★ **Tokyo Hotarudo** VINTAGE

(東京蛍堂; Map p106; http://tokyohotarudo.com; 1-41-8 Asakusa, Taitō-ku; ⏲11am-8pm Wed-Sun; Ⓡ Tsukuba Express to Asakusa, exit 5) This curio shop is run by an eccentric young man who prefers to dress as if the 20th century hasn't come and gone already. If you think that sounds marvellous, then you'll want to check out his collection of vintage dresses and bags, antique lamps, watches and decorative *objet*. The entrance is tricky: look for a vertical black sign with a pointing finger.

Bengara CRAFTS

(べんがら; Map p106; www.bengara.com; 1-35-6 Asakusa, Taitō-ku; ⏲10am-6pm Mon-Fri, to 7pm Sat & Sun, closed 3rd Thu of month; Ⓢ Ginza line to Asakusa, exit 1) By now you're familiar with *noren,* the curtains that hang in front of shop doors. This store sells beautiful ones, made of linen and coloured with natural dyes (like indigo or persimmon) or decorated with ink-brush paintings. There are smaller items too, such as pouches and book covers, made of traditional textiles.

Yonoya Kushiho ACCESSORIES

(よのや櫛舗; Map p106; 1-37-10 Asakusa, Taitō-ku; ⏲10.30am-6pm Thu-Tue; Ⓢ Ginza line to Asakusa, exit 1) Even in a neighbourhood where old is not out of place, Yonoya Kushiho stands out: this little shop has been selling handmade boxwood combs since 1717. Yonoya also sells old-fashioned hair ornaments (worn with the elaborate up-dos of courtesans in the past) and modern trinkets.

Fujiya CRAFTS

(ふじ屋; Map p106; 2-2-15 Asakusa, Taitō-ku; ⏲10.30am-6.30pm Fri-Wed; Ⓢ Ginza line to Asakusa, exit 1) Fujiya specialises in *tenugui:* dyed cloths of thin cotton that can be used as tea towels, kerchiefs, gift wrap (the list goes on; they're surprisingly versatile). Here they come in traditional designs and there are also humorous modern ones.

Solamachi MALL

(ソラマチ; Map p106; 1-1-2 Oshiage, Sumida-ku; ⏲10am-9pm; Ⓢ Hanzōmon line to Oshiage, exit B3) It's not all cheesy Sky Tree swag here at this mall under the tower (though you can get 634m-long rolls of Sky Tree toilet paper). Shops on the 4th floor offer a better-than-usual selection of Japanese-y souvenirs, including pretty trinkets made from kimono fabric and quirky fashion items.

Orientation

Officially, central Tokyo is made up of 23 *ku* (wards). Unofficially, central Tokyo is whatever falls within the JR Yamanote line, the elevated rail loop that circles the city. Many of the stations on the Yamanote line are transit hubs and, as a result, are the most developed. A good many of the city's sights, accommodation, bars and restaurants lie in neighbourhoods on the loop, which include Marunouchi (Tokyo Station), Ebisu, Shibuya, Harajuku, Shinjuku, Akihabara and Ueno.

The Imperial Palace grounds form the city's incongruously verdant core. No roads pass through here, and no subways pass under, meaning that navigating the very centre of the city is necessarily a circuitous affair.

Tokyo is the antithesis of the neat grid, which can make it difficult to connect the dots without a map (smart phones are a lifesaver and fortunately Tokyo has more and more free wi-fi). Only major boulevards have names, though these sometimes change when the road bends or joins with another.

Central neighbourhoods with significant tourist spots usually have maps and street signs in English.

Information

DANGERS & ANNOYANCES

For a megalopolis with over 13 million people (and more than 37 million in Greater Tokyo), Tokyo is a surprisingly safe place. That said, you should exercise the same caution you would in your home country.

Touts for bars and clubs in Roppongi and Shinjuku's Kabukichō can be aggressive. Be wary of following them; while not common, spiked drinks followed by theft, extortion or, in extreme cases, assault, have occurred. Overcharging is the more likely outcome.

Women should note that *chikan* (gropers) do haunt crowded trains, though they usually prey on local women (who are presumed less likely to make a scene). During rush hour, many express trains heading to the suburbs have women-only cars (marked in pink).

EMERGENCY

Emergency Interpretation (emergency translation 03-5285-8185, medical info 03-5285-8181; www.himawari.metro.tokyo.jp/qq/qq13enmnlt.asp; medical info 9am-8pm, emergency translation 5-8pm Mon-Fri, 9am-8pm Sat & Sun) In English, Chinese, Korean, Thai and Spanish.

Police (警視庁; Keishichō; emergency 110, general 03-3501-0110; www.keishicho.metro.tokyo.jp) There are 24-hour staffed *kōban* (police boxes) near most major train stations.

INTERNET ACCESS

Most accommodation in Tokyo has, at the very least, complimentary wi-fi in the lobby. With the **Japan Connected** (www.ntt-bp.net/jcfw/en.html) app you can get online inside most city subway stations, 7-Eleven convenience stores, and in Roppongi Hills and other locations. If you need to get on a computer, here are some options:

FedEx Kinko's (フェデックスキンコーズ; ¥250 per 20min) Outposts all over central Tokyo (including branches in Shinjuku and Shibuya) have a few computer terminals each, as well as printing and photocopying services.

Terminal (Map p90; http://theterminal.jp/index.html; 3rd fl, 3-22-12 Jingūmae, Shibuya-ku; ¥325 per 30min; 24hr; JR Yamanote line to Harajuku, Takeshita exit) Tokyo's nicest internet cafe has big-screen Macs with Adobe software and good coffee.

LEFT LUGGAGE

Most train stations have coin lockers (priced ¥300 to ¥600 per day, depending on size), where you can store stuff for up to three days.

Both Narita and Haneda airports have left-luggage facilities, which average about ¥500 per day. Porter services can ship your bags ahead to your hotel for about ¥2000.

JR East Travel Service Center (p148) keeps bags for ¥500 per day and can transport your luggage anywhere within the city for ¥1500.

LOST & FOUND

Lost items are recovered at an astonishing rate – it is always worth trying. If you lose something on the street, check in with the nearest *kōban* (police box).

Major train stations have Lost & Found windows (marked in English); at smaller ones enquire at the station window. If that fails, have your accomodation call the hotline number for the appropriate train operator.

JR East Infoline (in English 050-2016-1603; 10am-6pm)

Toei Transportation Lost & Found (03-3816-5700; 9am-8pm)

Tokyo Metro Lost & Found (03-3834-5577; www.tokyometro.jp/en/support/lost/index.html; 9am-8pm)

MEDIA

Metropolis (www.metropolisjapan.com) is a free English-language magazine for the expat community, with reviews and event listings. It comes out twice a month and can be found at places popular with foreigners; the online version is updated more frequently.

MEDICAL SERVICES

The following hospitals have English-speaking doctors. For a comprehensive list of medical services with English-speaking staff, check out http://japan.usembassy.gov/e/acs/tacs-tokyo-doctors.html.

Seibo International Catholic Hospital (聖母病院; Map p72; 03-3951-1111; www.seibokai.or.jp; 2-5-1 Nakaochiai, Shinjuku-ku; JR Yamanote line to Mejiro, main exit)

St Luke's International Hospital (聖路加国際病院; Seiroka Kokusai Byōin; Map p76; 03-3541-5151; www.luke.or.jp; 9-1 Akashi-chō, Chūō-ku; S Hibiya line to Tsukiji, exits 3 & 4)

MONEY

Getting cash is easier in Tokyo than elsewhere in Japan, and even though most places take credit cards, it's still a good idea to have some cash as back up. Post offices and 7-Eleven convenience stores with international ATMs can be found in every neighbourhood. Major hubs including Shinjuku, Shibuya, Roppongi and Ginza also have 24-hour **Citibank** (シティバンク; www.citibank.co.jp/en) ATMs that accept cards from every country.

Mitsubishi UFJ bank operates **World Currency Shop** (www.tokyo-card.co.jp/wcs/wcs-shop-e.php) foreign exchange counters that will exchange a broad range of currencies, including Chinese yuan, Korean won and Taiwan, Hong Kong, Singapore and New Zealand dollars. They're located near major shopping centres.

POST

You're never more than a couple of hundred metres from a post office in central Tokyo. Post offices in major hubs keep later hours.

TELEPHONE

There are several mobile phone rental companies operating out of both airports. Some have cheaper base fees, while others have cheaper call rates; it's a good idea to shop around for a package that best suits your needs (data or calls).

Narita www.narita-airport.jp/en/guide/service/list/svc_19.html.

Haneda www.haneda-airport.jp/inter/en/premises/service/internet.html#mobilePhone

TOURIST INFORMATION

There are tourist information centres at both terminals at **Narita Airport** (1st fl, terminals 1 & 2; ⌚8am-10pm) and in the international terminal of **Haneda Airport** (2nd fl Arrival Lobby; ⌚5.30am-1am) with English-speaking staff who can help you get oriented. They cannot, however, make bookings.

Asakusa Culture Tourist Information Center (浅草文化観光センター; Map p106; ☎03-3842-5566; http://taitonavi.jp; 2-18-9 Kaminarimon, Taitō-ku; ⌚9am-8pm; Ⓢ Ginza line to Asakusa, exit 2) Run by Taitō-ku, this TIC has lots of info on Asakusa and Ueno, and a Pia ticket counter (for purchasing tickets to concerts and shows), near the entrance to Sensō-ji.

JNTO Tourist Information Center (Map p76; ☎03-3201-3331; www.jnto.go.jp; 1st fl, Shin-Tokyo Bldg, 3-3-1 Marunouchi, Chiyoda-ku; ⌚9am-5pm; 🚉 JR Yamanote line to Yūrakuchō, Tokyo International Forum exit) Run by the Japan National Tourism Organisation (JNTO), this TIC has information on Tokyo and beyond.

Moshi Moshi Information Space (もしもしインフォメーションスペース; Map p90; 3-235 Jingūmae, Shibuya-ku; 🚉 JR Yamanote line to Harajuku, Omote-sandō) Ship your shopping home, get your nails done and pick up loads of local info at this somewhat unorthodox tourist information centre run by a private organisation.

Tokyo Tourist Information Center (東京観光情報センター; Map p94; ☎03-5321-3077; www.gotokyo.org; 1st fl, Tokyo Metropolitan Government bldg 1, 2-8-1 Nishi-Shinjuku, Shinjuku-ku; ⌚9.30am-6.30pm; Ⓢ Ōedo line to Tochōmae, exit A4) Combine a trip to the observatories at the Tokyo Metropolitan Government Offices with a stop at the city's official TIC. There's another branch located right outside the ticket gates of the Keisei Ueno line (which services Narita Airport).

TRAVEL AGENCIES

JR East Travel Service Center (JR東日本訪日旅行センター; Map p76; www.jreast.co.jp/e/customer_support/service_center_tokyo.html; Tokyo Station, 1-9-1 Marunouchi, Chiyoda-ku; ⌚7.30am-8.30pm; 🚉 JR Yamanote line to Tokyo, Marunouchi north exit) Tourist information, luggage storage, money exchange, and bookings for ski and onsen getaways. There are branches in the two airports, too.

USEFUL WEBSITES

Go Tokyo (www.gotokyo.org/en) Tokyo metropolitan goverment tourism website, with attraction and festival information.

Metropolis (www.metropolisjapan.com) Comprehensive events listings, plus articles on what's going on in Tokyo.

Time Out Tokyo (www.timeout.jp/en/tokyo) Lots of reviews, plus a reliable weekend guide.

Tokyo Art Beat (www.tokyoartbeat.com) Bilingual art and design guide with a regularly updated list of exhibitions.

Tokyo Cheapo (www.tokyocheapo.com) Tips for how to get the most for your money.

Tokyo Fashion (www.tokyofashion.com) The lowdown on the latest trends and brands, as well as fashion-related events.

Tokyo Food Page (www.bento.com) Restaurant directory compiled by a *Japan Times* dining columnist; some information is outdated.

VISAS

Tokyo Regional Immigration Bureau (東京入国管理局; Tokyo Nyūkoku Kanrikyoku; Map p72; ☎03-5796-7111; www.immi-moj.go.jp/english/index.html; 5-5-30 Kōnan, Minato-ku; ⌚9am-noon & 1-4pm Mon-Fri; 🚌99 from Shinagawa Station, east exit to Tokyo Nyūkoku Kanrikyo-ku-mae, 🚉 Rinkai line to Tennōzu Isle) Handles all things visa-related for greater Tokyo.

SMOKING IN THE CITY

Tokyo has a different take on smoking than most Western cities: it is OK to smoke in most restaurants, bars and clubs, but not on city streets. Look for official smoking areas (easily spotted by oversized ashtray bins and clouds of smoke) around train stations.

RIVERBOAT CRUISE

Riverboats were once a primary means of transportation in Tokyo, and the Sumida-gawa was the main 'highway'. You can experience this centuries-old tradition (and happily combine sightseeing and transport) by hopping on one of the water buses run by **Tokyo Cruise** (水上バス; Suijō Bus; ☎0120-977-311; http://suijobus.co.jp).

Of the four routes, the Sumida-gawa line is the most popular; it runs from Asakusa to Hama-rikyū Onshi-teien (¥740, 35 minutes) and terminates at Hinode Pier on Tokyo Bay.

The Asakusa–Odaiba Direct Line connects Asakusa with Odaiba Kaihin-kōen (¥1560, 50 minutes), also via the Sumida-gawa. If you're planning to take this route, try to catch one of the two spaceship-like boats, *Himiko* or *Hotaluna*, designed by famous manga artist Matsumoto Leiji.

Tokyo Mizube Cruising Line (東京水辺ライン; ☎5608-8869; www.tokyo-park.or.jp/waterbus) runs similar ferries, leaving from Nitenmon Pier in Asakusa for Odaiba, stopping conveniently at Ryōgoku (¥310, 10 minutes).

ℹ Getting There & Away

AIR

Tokyo has two major airports: **Narita Airport** (NRT; 成田空港; ☎0476-34-8000; www.narita-airport.jp) and **Haneda Airport** (HND; 羽田空港; ☎international terminal 03-6428-0888; www.tokyo-airport-bldg.co.jp/en). Narita is 66km east of Tokyo, in neighbouring Chiba Prefecture. Haneda Airport is more convenient, within the city limits and near Tokyo Bay. Most international flights operate through Narita, while domestic travel is usually funnelled through Haneda. However, Haneda opened an international wing in October 2010 and is now handling an increasing number of international flights. Some flights into Haneda arrive in the middle of the night, when public transport isn't running – so you'll need to factor in the cost of a taxi.

Immigration and customs procedures are usually straightforward, but they can be time consuming. Non-Japanese visitors are finger-printed and photographed on arrival. Note that Japanese customs officials can be very scrupulous; backpackers arriving from anywhere even remotely exotic (the Philippines, Thailand etc) can expect at least some questions and perhaps a thorough search.

It is important to note that there are two distinct terminals at Narita, separated by a five-minute train ride. Be sure to check which terminal your flight departs from, and give yourself plenty of time to get out to Narita. Airport officials recommend leaving at least four hours before your flight.

BOAT

Ferries and high-speed jet foils depart for the Izu and Ogasawara Islands from **Takeshiba Pier** (竹芝桟橋; Takeshiba Sanbashi; Map p72; www.tptc.co.jp/en/tarminal/tabid/1502/Default.aspx; 1-16-3 Kaigan, Minato-ku; 🚉JR Yamanote line to Hamamatsuchō, north exit).

BUS

Long-distance buses are usually cheaper than trains and every once in a while actually more convenient. The most popular bus route is the one that travels to Mt Fuji from the **Shinjuku Highway Bus Terminal** (新宿高速バスターミナル; Map p94; ☎03-5376-2222; www.highway-bus.com/html/gp/foreign/en/access/index.html; 1-10-1 Nishi-Shinjuku, Shinjuku-ku; ⏰6am-11.30pm; 🚉JR Yamanote line to Shinjuku, west exit). Same-day tickets can be purchased on the ground floor of the terminal, where there is a timetable in English; advance-ticket sales are on the 2nd floor.

JR Highway Bus (JR 高速バス; ☎03-3844-1950; www.jrbuskanto.co.jp/bus_route_e/) runs night buses to major cities around Japan, including those in the Kansai and Tōhoku regions, from bus terminals in **Shinjuku** (Map p94; ⏰6.20am-midnight; 🚉JR Yamanote line to Shinjuku, south exit) and at **Tokyo Station** (Map p76; ⏰6am-12.30am; 🚉JR Yamanote Line to Tokyo, Yaesu south exit); prices are signficantly cheaper than *shinkansen* (bullet train) tickets, but journeys take twice as long.

TRAIN

The following information pertains to cross-country travel from Tokyo.

JR Lines

There are several *shinkansen* (bullet train) lines that connect Tokyo with the rest of Japan – they are the most convenient way to move around the country. Note that some make more stops than others; Japan Rail Pass holders can't ride the fastest trains, *nozomi* and *mizuho*, on the Tōkaidō line. All lines pass through Tokyo Station; the Jōetsu and Tōhoku lines also pass through Ueno Station. The Tōkaidō line stops at Shinagawa.

Jōetsu line Northbound for Niigata.

Nagano line Splinters off from the Jōetsu line, bound for Nagano; the Hokuriku line continues to Kanazawa.

Tōhoku line Runs northeast through Sendai all the way to Aomori, from where you can continue on to Hokkaidō. Branch lines head to Akita and Yamagata.

Tōkaidō line Zips through Central Honshū, stopping in Kyoto and Osaka, then changes its name to the Sanyō line before terminating in Kyūshū.

Private Lines

Tokyo's private train lines service the city's sprawling suburbia, but also connect the capital to several worthwhile day-trip destinations. All private lines depart from a major station along the JR Yamanote line, with the exception of the Tobu Nikkō line.

Keiō line Connects Shinjuku with the popular hiking spot, Takao-san.

Odakyū line Heads southwest from Shinjuku to Odawara, where you can transfer to trains for Hakone.

Tobu Nikkō line Connects Asakusa with Nikkō to the north.

Tōkyū Tōyoko line Runs south from Shibuya to Yokohama.

Getting Around

TO/FROM NARITA AIRPORT

With the exception of very early morning flights, public transport can usually meet all arrivals and departures.

Depending on where you're headed, it's generally cheaper and faster to travel into Tokyo by train than by limousine bus. However, rail users will probably need to change trains somewhere, and this can be frustrating on a jetlagged first visit.

Bus services provide a hassle-free direct route to many major hotels, and you don't have to be a hotel guest to use them; a short taxi ride (and there are always taxis waiting in front of big hotels) can take you the rest of the way.

We do not recommend taking a taxi from Narita – it'll set you back around ¥30,000. Figure on one to two hours to get to/from Narita.

Bus

Friendly Airport Limousine (☎ 03-3665-7220; www.limousinebus.co.jp/en; 1-way fare ¥3150) Operates scheduled, direct, all-reserved buses between Narita Airport and major hotels and train stations in Tokyo. The journey takes 1½ to two hours depending on traffic. At the time of research, discount round-trip 'Welcome to Tokyo Limousine Bus Return Voucher' tickets (¥4500) were available for foreign tourists; ask at the ticket counter at the airport.

Access Narita (アクセス成田; Map p76; ☎ 0120-600-366; www.accessnarita.jp) Discount buses connect Narita Airport to Tokyo Station and Ginza (¥1000, one to 1¼ hours). There's no ticket counter at the airport; just go directly to bus stop 31 at Terminal 1 or stops 2 or 19 at Terminal 2. You can reserve tickets online (a safer bet for trips to the airport), but unfortunately only in Japanese.

Train

Keisei Skyliner (京成スカイライナー; www.keisei.co.jp/keisei/tetudou/skyliner/us) The quickest service into Tokyo runs nonstop to Nippori (¥2470, 36 minutes) and Ueno (¥2470, 41 minutes) stations, where you can connect to the JR Yamanote line or the subway (Ueno Station only). Trains run twice an hour, 8am to 10pm. Foreign nationals can purchase advanced tickets online for slightly less (¥2200).

The Skyliner & Tokyo Subway Ticket, which combines a one-way ticket on the Skyliner and a one-, two- or three-day subway pass, is a good deal.

Keisei Main Line (京成本線) *Kaisoku kyūkō* (limited express; ¥1030, 71 minutes to Ueno) trains follow the same route as the Skyliner but make stops. This is a good budget option. Trains run every 20 minutes during peak hours.

Narita Express (N'EX; 成田エクスプレス; www.jreast.co.jp/e/nex) A swift and smooth option, especially if you're staying on the west side of the city, N'EX trains depart Narita approximately every half-hour between 7am and 10pm for Tokyo Station (¥3020, 53 minutes). They also run less frequently into Shinagawa (¥3110, 65 minutes), Shibuya (¥3110, 73 minutes), Shinjuku (¥3190, 80 minutes) and Ikebukuro (¥3190, 86 minutes).

Tourists can purchase return N'EX tickets for ¥4000 (valid for 14 days), a discount of more than 30% off the standard return fare. Check online or inquire at the JR East Travel Service centres at Narita Airport for the latest deals.

Long-haul JR passes are valid on N'EX trains, but you must obtain a seat reservation (no extra charge) from a JR ticket office.

TO/FROM HANEDA AIRPORT

From downtown Tokyo, it takes far less time to reach Haneda Airport than Narita. Taxis to the city centre cost around ¥6000; this will be your only option if your flight gets in before dawn.

Friendly Airport Limousine (www.limousinebus.co.jp/en) Coaches connect Haneda with major hubs such as Shibuya (¥1030), Shinjuku (¥1230), Roppongi (¥1130) and Ginza (¥930); fares double after midnight. Travel times vary wildly, taking anywhere from 30 to 90 minutes depending on traffic. The last bus of the day departs for Shibuya Station at 12.30am; service resumes at 5.45am.

Keikyū (☎ 03-5789-8686; www.haneda-tokyo-access.com/en) Airport *kyūkō* (limited-express) trains depart several times an hour (5.30am to midnight) for Shinagawa (¥410, 12 minutes) on the JR Yamanote line. From Shinagawa, some trains continue along the Asakusa subway line,

TRAIN TIPS

➡ Figure out the best route to your destination with the app **Navitime for Japan Travel** (www.navitime.co.jp/lp/transit/); you can download routes to be used offline, too.

➡ Avoid rush-hour (around 8am to 9.30am and 5pm to 8pm), when 'packed in like sardines' is an understatement.

➡ Note the time of your last train (they stop running around midnight). The last train of the night can also be especially crowded (often with swaying drunks).

➡ If you can't work out how much to pay, one easy trick is to buy a ticket at the cheapest fare (¥133 for JR; ¥165 for Tokyo Metro; ¥174 for Toei) and use one of the 'fare adjustment' machines, near the exit gates, to settle the difference at the end of your journey.

➡ When the platform is crowded, Tokyoites form neat lines on either side of where the doors will be when the train pulls up. Once you're on the train though, all's fair when it comes to grabbing a seat.

➡ It's considered bad form to eat or drink on the train (long-distance trains are an exception). Talking on the phone or having a loud conversation is also frowned upon.

➡ Most train stations have multiple exits – make sure you get the right one (which can save you a lot of time and confusion above ground). There are usually maps in the station that show which exits are closest to major area landmarks.

➡ Stand to the left on the escalators.

which serves Higashi-Ginza, Nihombashi and Asakusa stations.

Tokyo Monorail (東京モノレール; www.tokyo-monorail.co.jp/english) Leaving approximately every 10 minutes (5am to midnight) for Hamamatsuchō Station (¥490, 15 minutes), which is a stop on the JR Yamanote line.

BICYCLE

Tokyo may not have many bike lanes, but that doesn't stop a lot of locals from taking to the city on two wheels. Cycling is an excellent way to get around, and to see how the city fits together. Some guesthouses (especially around Ueno and Asakusa) have bikes to lend.

In addition to the following, check out **Rentabike** (www.rentabike.jp) for a list of other rental places around town.

Cogi Cogi (☎03-5459-7330; http://cogicogi.jp/index_en.asp; ¥1500 per day; ⏲10am-7pm) This bike-sharing system has ports around the city. There are instructions in English, but it's a little complicated to use and requires you to sign up in advance online.

Tokyo Bike Gallery (Map p102; www.tokyobike.com; 4-2-39 Yanaka, Taitō-ku; ¥1000 per day; ⏲11.30am-5.30pm Fri-Tue; 🅡JR Yamanote line to Nippori, west exit) This showroom for hipster bicycle manufacturer Tokyo Bike also rents seven-speed city bikes for the afternoon. Reserve one in advance by sending an email with your name, desired day and height.

BUS

Municipal buses criss-cross the city and cost ¥210 a ride; there are no transfer tickets. There's a change machine at the front of the bus, under the box where you deposit your fare.

Most buses have digital signage that switches between English and Japanese. That said, the subway is far more convenient and faster for most tourist destinations. One useful bus is the number 1 bus that leaves from platform 58 of the east exit bus terminal at Shibuya and stops at Roppongi.

CAR & MOTORCYCLE

Riding a bike through Tokyo can actually be faster than driving a car. With the city's chaotic traffic, exorbitant parking rates and network of one-way streets, we do not recommend renting a vehicle to get around.

If you're keen on renting a car to get out of the metropolis, consider taking a train away from central Tokyo (or at least to the edge) and renting a car from there.

Both **Nippon Rent-a-car** (Map p76; ☎English service desk 03-3485-7196; www.nipponrentacar.co.jp/english; ⏲9am-5pm Mon-Fri) and **Toyota Rent-a-car** (Map p76; ☎5954-8020, toll-free in Japan 0800-7000-815; https://rent.toyota.co.jp/en) have branches in and around Tokyo and are used to dealing with overseas travellers. Note that you will need an International Driving Permit.

TAXI

It rarely makes economic sense to take a taxi, unless you've got a group of four. The meter starts at a steep ¥730, which gives you 2km of travel. After that, the meter starts to clock an additional ¥90 for every 280m (and up to ¥90

TRAIN PASSES & DISCOUNT PACKAGES

Suica & Pasmo Cards

Getting prepaid train passes – the interchangeable Suica and Pasmo – is highly recommended, even for a short trip. With this card, fitted with an electromagnetic chip, you'll be able to breeze through the ticket gates of any train or subway station in the city without having to work out fares or transfer tickets. Fares for pass users are slightly less (a couple of yen per journey) than for paper-ticket holders.

Both Suica and Pasmo cards can be purchased from ticket-vending machines in most train and subway stations (Suica from JR line machines and Pasmo from subway and commuter line machines). A minimum charge of ¥1000 plus a ¥500 deposit (refundable if you turn your card into a train station window) is required. You can charge the cards, in increments of ¥1000, at the same vending machines.

To use it, simply wave it over the card reader; you will need to do this to enter and exit the station.

City Passes

The following are really only worth it if you plan to hit a number of neighbourhoods in one day. If you're coming through Narita, the **Skyliner & Tokyo Subway Ticket** (www.keisei.co.jp/keisei/tetudou/skyliner/us/value_ticket/subway.html; tickets ¥2800-3500) is a better deal.

Tokyo Metro One-Day Open Ticket (adult/child ¥710/360) Unlimited rides on Tokyo Metro subway lines only. Purchase at Tokyo Metro stations.

Common One-Day Ticket (adult/child ¥1000/500) Valid on all 13 lines operating underground in Tokyo. Purchase at Tokyo Metro or Toei stations.

Tokyo Combination Ticket (adult/child ¥1590/800) Unlimited same-day rides on Tokyo Metro, Toei and JR lines operating in Tokyo. Purchase at stations serviced by any of these lines.

for every two minutes you sit idly in traffic). Figure around ¥3000 for a ride from Roppongi to Ginza. It's best to have cash on you, as not all taxis take credit cards.

While it's possible to hail a cab from the street, your best bet is a taxi stand in front of a train station. Taxis with their indicator in red are free; green means taken.

Even in Tokyo, most cabbies don't speak English and have trouble finding all but the most well-known spots. Fortunately many have GPS systems, so have an address or a business card for your destination handy.

TRAIN & SUBWAY

Tokyo's train network includes JR lines, a subway system, and private commuter lines. It's so thorough, especially in the city centre, that you rarely have to walk more than 10 minutes from a station to your destination. Stations have English signage. Note that trains and subways run only from 5am to midnight.

Tickets are sold from vending machines near the automated ticket gates. Look for the newer touch-screen ones that have an English option. Fares are determined by how far you ride; there should be a fare chart above the ticket machines. You'll need a valid train ticket to exit the station.

JR Lines

Carving out the city's centre, the elevated **Yamanote line** does a 35km-long loop around the metropolis, taking in most of the important areas. Another useful JR route is the **Chūō line**, also above ground, which cuts across the city centre from Tokyo Station to Shinjuku and points further west. Tickets are transferable on all JR lines.

Private Lines

Private lines connect downtown Tokyo with the suburbs, but a few service popular destinations.

Keiō Inokashira line Travels from Shibuya to Kichijōji, stopping at Shimo-Kitazawa and Inokashira-kōen.

Tōkyū Tōyoko line Connects Shibuya with Daikanyama and Naka-Meguro.

Yurikamome line Driverless trains run from Shimbashi to the islands of Odaiba.

Subway Lines

There are a total of 13 colour-coded subway lines zigzagging through Tokyo. Four are operated by Toei; nine belong to Tokyo Metro. Transfers between lines within the same group are seamless; if you plan to switch between Toei trains and Tokyo Metro trains, you'll need to purchase a transfer ticket at the start of your journey.

Mt Fuji & Around Tokyo

Includes ➡

Best Onsen

- Jinata Onsen (p188)
- Urami-ga-taki Onsen (p189)
- Kanaya Ryokan (p185)
- Hakone Yuryō (p173)

Best Sacred Sites

- Tōshō-gū (p163)
- Fuji Sengen-jinja (p159)
- Daibutsu (p196)
- Narita-san Shinshōji (p202)

Why Go?

With ancient sanctuaries, hot springs, mountains and beaches, the region surrounding Tokyo is a natural foil for the dizzying capital. Really, you couldn't design it any better if you tried.

Authentic country ryokan, regional cuisines and cedar-lined trails are all within two hours of central Tokyo, as well as the symbol of Japan itself, alluring Mt Fuji. There's history here too, including a medieval capital and ports that were among the first to open to the West. These are, for better or for worse, well-visited places and you'll find transport and communication to be a comparative breeze.

Ferries and flights also provide relatively fast access to the Izu Islands, but if you're really looking to get away from it all then set your compass for the World Heritage–listed Ogasawara archipelago that trickles some 1000km south from Tokyo and where you can spot whales, swim with dolphins and snorkel alongside green turtles and a rainbow assortment of tropical fish.

When to Go

Kawaguchi-ko

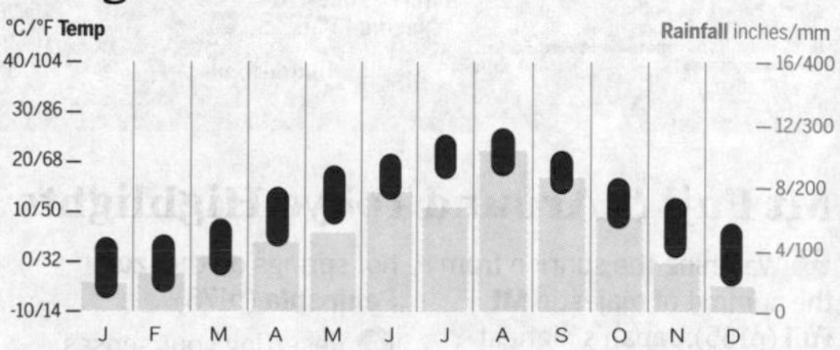

Apr & May Experience the flush of spring in the mountains north and west of Tokyo.

Jul & Aug The official season for Mt Fuji climbing or beach-hopping around the Izu Peninsula.

Sep–Nov Pleasant temperatures and fewer crowds, save when the autumn leaves blaze red.

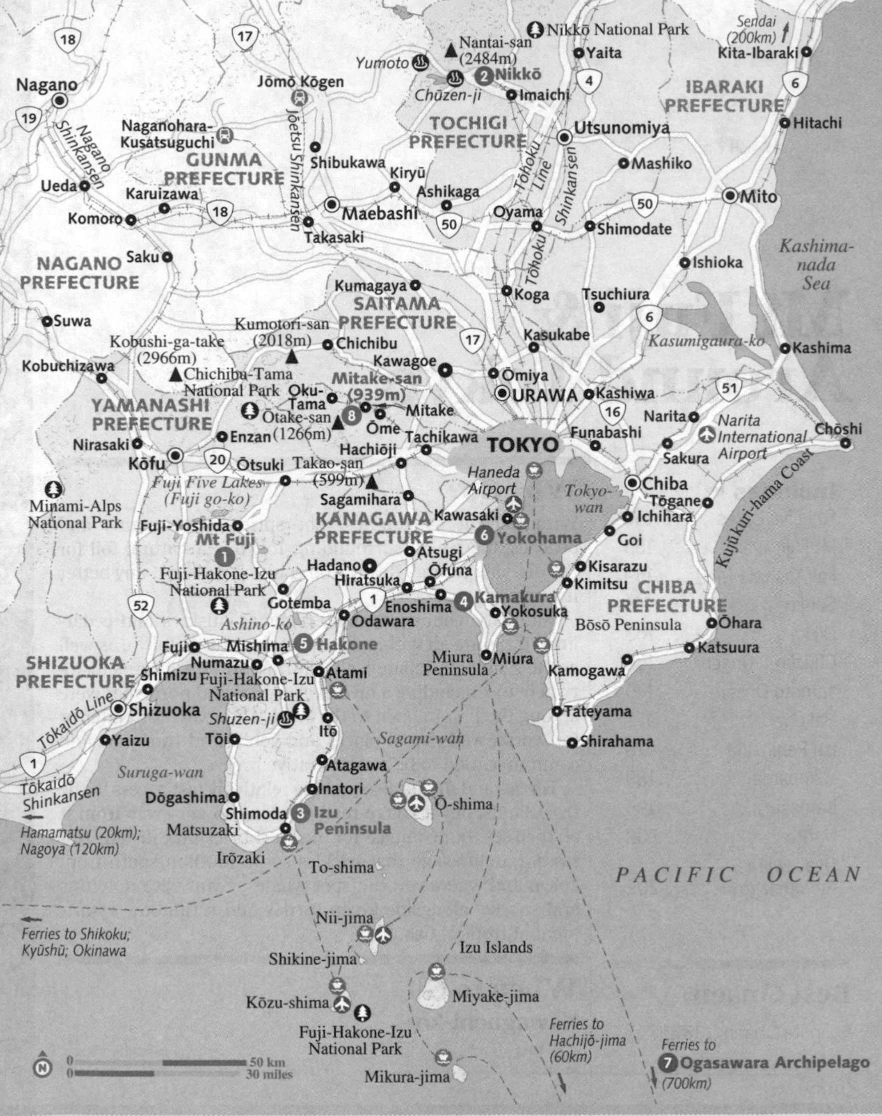

Mt Fuji & Around Tokyo Highlights

1. Watching the sunrise from the summit of majestic **Mt Fuji** (p155), Japan's highest mountain and national symbol.

2. Taking in the grandeur of old Edo at the dazzling shrines and temples of **Nikkō** (p163).

3. Flip-flopping between sandy beaches and seaside hot springs on the **Izu Peninsula** (p178).

4. Resetting your senses in the Zen temples of the medieval capital of **Kamakura** (p196).

5. Hopping between onsen, art museums and hiking trails around gorgeously scenic **Hakone** (p172).

6. Sampling craft beer and jazz tunes in cosmopolitan **Yokohama** (p189).

7. Getting back to nature on the pristine, subtropical **Ogasawara Archipelago** (p202).

8. Hiking, rafting or canyoning at **Mitake** (p171), the forested western edge of Tokyo.

FUJI FIVE LAKES 富士五湖

☎555

Japan's highest and most famous peak is this region's natural draw, but even if you don't intend climbing Fuji-san, it's still worth coming to enjoy the visual and natural delights around the volcano's northern foothills; the five lakes here act as natural reflecting pools for the mountain's perfect cone.

Yamanaka-ko is the easternmost lake, followed by Kawaguchi-ko, Sai-ko, Shōji-ko and Motosu-ko. Particularly during the autumn *kōyō* (foliage) season, the lakes make a good overnight trip out of Tokyo, for leisurely strolling, lake activities and for hiking in the nearby mountains.

Fuji-Yoshida and Kawaguchi-ko are the most accessible and developed areas, with the latter the most popular place to stay, with the best range of accommodation. Both make good bases if you plan on climbing Mt Fuji and don't intend on overnighting in a mountain hut.

Getting There & Away

The Fuji Five Lakes area is most easily reached from Tokyo by bus or train, with Fuji-Yoshida and Kawaguchi-ko being the principal gateways. It's also possible to bus in from Tokyo straight to the Kawaguchi-ko Fifth Station on the mountain during the official climbing season. If you want to combine travel to Mt Fuji and Hakone, consider the Fuji Hakone Pass (p173) from Tokyo.

Coming from Western Japan (Kyoto, Osaka), you can take an overnight bus to Kawaguchi-ko.

BUS

Frequent Keiō Dentetsu (p158) and Fujikyū Express (p159) buses (¥1750, one hour and 50 minutes) operate directly to Kawaguchi-ko Station, and Fujisan Station in Fuji-Yoshida, from the **Shinjuku Highway Bus Terminal** (☎03-5376-2222; http://highway-buses.jp; Yamanote line to Shinjuku, west exit).

Coming from Western Japan, the overnight bus departs from Osaka's Higashi-Umeda Subway Station (¥8700, 10.15pm) via Kyoto Station (¥8200, 11.18pm) to Kawaguchi-ko Station (arrives 8.32am).

TRAIN

JR Chūō line trains go from Shinjuku to Ōtsuki (*tokkyū* ¥2570, one hour; *futsū* ¥1320, 1½ hours), where you transfer to the Fuji Kyūkō line for Fujisan (the station for Fuji-Yoshida; ¥1020, 45 minutes) and Kawaguchi-ko (¥1140, 50 minutes).

Getting Around

From Fujisan Station it's an eight-minute bus ride (¥240) or five-minute train (¥220) to Kawaguchi-ko Station.

The **Retro-bus** (two-day passes adult/child ¥1200/600) has hop-on-hop-off service from Kawaguchi-ko Station to all of the sightseeing spots around the western lakes. One route follows Kawaguchi-ko's northern shore, and the other heads south and around Sai-ko and Aokigahara.

There is a **Toyota Rent-a-Car** (☎0555-72-1100, in English 0800-7000-815) a few minutes' walk from Kawaguchi-ko Station; head right from the station, turning right at the next intersection. **Sazanami** (⏲7am-5pm summer, 9am-5pm winter), on Kawaguchi-ko's southeast shore, rents regular bicycles (¥400/1500 per hour/day), electric pedal-assisted bicycles (¥600/2600 per hour/day) and rowboats (¥1000/2500 per hour/day).

Mt Fuji 富士山

Of all Japan's iconic images, Mt Fuji (3776m) is the real deal. Admiration for the mountain appears in Japan's earliest recorded literature, dating from the 8th century. Back then the now dormant volcano was prone to spewing smoke, making it all the more revered. In 2013, the year Fuji was granted World Heritage status, some 300,000 people climbed the country's highest peak.

The Japanese proverb 'He who climbs Mt Fuji once is a wise man, he who climbs it twice is a fool' remains as valid as ever. While reaching the top brings a great sense of achievement (particularly at sunrise), be aware it's a gruelling climb and one that's not known for its beautiful scenery or being at one with nature. During the climbing season routes are packed with trekkers, and its barren apocalyptic-looking landscape is worlds away from Fuji's beauty that's viewed from afar. At the summit, the crater has a circumference of 4km, but be prepared for it to be clouded over.

When to Go

The official climbing season is from 1 July to 31 August. It's a busy mountain during these two months. To avoid the worst of the crush, head up on a weekday or start earlier during the day to avoid the afternoon rush, and spend a night in a mountain hut.

Authorities strongly caution against climbing outside the regular season, when the weather is highly unpredictable and

Mt Fuji Area

first-aid stations on the mountain are closed. Despite this, many people do climb out of season, as it's the best time to avoid the crowds. During this time, climbers generally head off at dawn, and return early afternoon – however mountain huts on the Kawaguchi-ko Trail stay open through mid-September when weather conditions may still be good; a few open the last week of June, when snow still blankets the upper stations.

Outside of the climbing season, check weather conditions carefully before setting out (see www.snow-forecast.com/resorts/Mount-Fuji/6day/top), bring appropriate equipment, do not climb alone, and be prepared to retreat at any time. A guide will be invaluable.

Once snow or ice is on the mountain, Fuji becomes a very serious and dangerous undertaking and should only be attempted by those with winter mountaineering equipment and plenty of experience. It's highly advised that off-season climbers register with the local police department for safety reasons; fill out the form at the Kawaguchi-ko or Fuji-Yoshida Tourist Information Centers.

Trails

The mountain is divided into 10 'stations' from base (First Station) to summit (Tenth). From the base station is the original pilgrim trail, but these days most climbers start from the halfway point at one of the four Fifth Stations, all of which can be accessed via bus or car. The intersection of trails is not well marked and it's easy to get lost, particularly on the way down, ending up at the wrong exit point; this is a good reason to climb with experienced guides.

To time your arrival for dawn you can either start up in the afternoon, stay overnight in a mountain hut and continue early in the morning, or climb the whole way at night.

Mt Fuji Area

Top Sights
1 Itchiku Kubota Art Museum C1

Sights
2 Fuji Sengen-jinja B4
3 Fuji Viewing Platform B3
4 Fuji Visitor Center A4
5 Ide Sake Brewery A3
6 Kōyō-dai B1
7 Narusawa Hyōketsu & Fugaku Fuketsu B2
8 Sai-ko Iyashi-no-Sato Nenba B1
9 Togawa-ke Oshi-no-ie Restored Pilgrim's Inn B4

Activities, Courses & Tours
10 Benifuji-no-yu D2
11 Fuji-Q Highland A4
12 Kachi Kachi Yama Ropeway B3
13 Kōan Motosu A2
14 Panorama-dai A1

Sleeping
15 Camp Village Gnome B1
16 Fuji Lake Hotel A3
17 Fujisan Hotel C3
18 Fuji-Yoshida Youth Hostel B3
19 Higashi Fuji Lodge C3
20 Kawaguchi-ko Station Inn A3
Kōan Motosu Inn .... (see 13)
Kozantei Ubuya .... (see 29)
21 K's House Mt Fuji A3
22 Lake Motosu Campground A2
23 Maisan-chi B4
24 Mt Fuji Hostel Michael's B3
25 Murahamasō A1
26 PICA Yamanaka-ko Village D3
27 Solar Cafe & Farm B1
28 Sunnide Resort C1
Taishikan .... (see 17)
29 Tominoko Hotel C1

Eating
30 Akai A3
31 Hōtō Fudō A4
Matsuya Cafe .... (see 24)
Michael's American Pub .... (see 24)
32 Sakurada Udon B4
33 Sanrokuen A3

Drinking & Nightlife
Zero Station .... (see 21)

Information
34 Fuji-Yoshida Tourist Information Center B4
35 Kawaguchi-ko Tourist Information Center A3

Transport
36 Sazanami A3
37 Toyota Rent-a-Car A3

You do not want to arrive on the top too long before dawn, as it will be very cold and windy, even at the height of summer.

Traditional Route

Historically, Fuji pilgrims began at Sengen-jinja near present-day Fuji-Yoshida, paying their homage to the shrine gods before beginning their 19km ascent up the sacred mountain. Today, the **Yoshidaguchi Trail** offers climbers a chance to participate in this centuries-old tradition. Purists will tell you this is the only way to climb, saying that the lower reaches are the most beautiful, through lush forests along an isolated path.

It takes about five hours to reach the old Yoshidaguchi Fifth Station – you can cut this down by half by catching the climbing season bus from Fujisan Station to Umagaeshi (¥500).

The trail meets up with the one leaving from the new Kawaguchi-ko Fifth Station at the Sixth Station. Count on around 12 hours to complete the climb from Fuji's base to summit.

Fifth Station Routes

Around 90% of climbers opt for these more convenient, faster routes. The four routes are Kawaguchi-ko, also known as Yoshida (2305m); Subashiri (1980m); Fujinomiya (2380m); and Gotemba (1440m). Allow five to six hours to reach the top (though some climb it in half the time) and about three hours to descend, plus 1½ hours for circling the crater at the top.

The **Kawaguchi-ko Trail** is by far the most popular route. It's accessed from Kawaguchi-ko Fifth Station (aka Mt Fuji Fifth Station), and has the most modern facilities and is easiest to reach from Kawaguchi-ko town.

The less trodden, but more scenic forested **Subashiri Trail** is a good alternative. As it merges with the Kawaguchi-ko Trail at the Eighth Station, it's possible to combine the two by heading up via the Kawaguchi-ko path and descending via Subashiri by schussing down its loose volcanic sand. Though be aware you'll end up at Subashiri Fifth Station, so it might not be an option if you've parked your car at Kawaguchi-ko Fifth Station.

CLIMBING MT FUJI: KNOW BEFORE YOU GO

Make no mistake: Mt Fuji is a serious mountain, high enough for altitude sickness, and on the summit it can go from sunny and warm to wet, windy and cold remarkably quickly. Even if conditions are fine, you can count on it being close to freezing in the morning, even in summer. Also be aware that visibility can rapidly disappear with a blanket of mist rolling in suddenly.

At a minimum, bring clothing appropriate for cold and wet weather, including a hat and gloves. Also bring at least two litres of water (you can buy more on the mountain during the climbing season), as well as a map and snacks. If you're climbing at night, bring a torch (flashlight) or headlamp, and spare batteries. Also bring plenty of cash for buying snacks, other necessities and souvenirs from the mountain huts and to use their toilets (¥200).

Descending the mountain is much harder on the knees than ascending; hiking poles will help. To avoid altitude sickness, be sure to take it slowly and take regular breaks. If you're suffering severe symptoms, you'll need to make an immediate descent.

For summit weather conditions, see www.snow-forecast.com/resorts/Mount-Fuji/6day/top.

Other Fifth Stations are **Fujinomiya**, which is best for climbers coming from the west (Nagoya, Kyoto and beyond) and the seldom-used and neglected **Gotemba Trail**, a tough 7½ hour climb to the summit.

Sleeping

From the Fifth Stations and up, dozens of mountain huts offer hikers simple hot meals and a place to sleep. Conditions are spartan (a blanket on the floor sandwiched between other climbers), but reservations are recommended and are essential on weekends. It's also important to let huts know if you decide to cancel at the last minute and be prepared to pay to cover the cost of your no-show.

Taishikan (太子館; ☎0555-22-1947; http://www.mfi.or.jp/w3/home0/taisikan; per person with two meals from ¥8500) and **Fujisan Hotel** (富士山ホテル; ☎0555-22-0237; www.fujisanhotel.com; per person without/with 2 meals from ¥5950/8350) at the Eighth Station (Kawaguchi-ko Trail) usually have an English speaker on hand. Most huts allow you to rest inside as long as you order something. Camping on the mountain is not permitted, other than at the designated campsite near the Kawaguchi-ko Fifth Station.

The Subashiri Fifth Station has the atmospheric **Higashi Fuji Lodge** (☎0555-75-2113; r ¥5000), which is very convenient for the off-season trekkers, and cooks up steaming *soba* (buckwheat noodles) with local mushrooms and Fuji herbs.

Tours

All of the following can arrange private tours.

Fuji Mountain Guides WALKING TOUR
(☎048-999-5816; www.fujimountainguides.com; two-day tours per person from US$325) Aimed at foreign visitors, these excellent tours are run both in and out of season by highly experienced and very professional American bi-lingual guides.

Discover Japan Tours TOUR
(www.discover-japan-tours.com/en; 2-day tours per person ¥10,000) Reputable company offering guided tours from Tokyo for groups of two or more, and specialising in less-frequented routes.

Fujiyama Guides TOUR
(☎0555-23-7554; www.fujiyamaguides.com) As well as standard two-day ascents of Fuji, this company offers three-day pilgrim tours starting at Fuji Sengen-jinja. Prices for one/two people start from ¥149,000/78,000 for the three-day tours (per person), and ¥84,000/64,000 for the two-day tours.

Information

Mt Fuji Climbing Guide (www.mountfujiguide.com) and **Climbing Mt Fuji** (www17.plala.or.jp/climb_fujiyama/index.html) are good online resources, and the *Climbing Mt Fuji* brochure, available at the Fuji-Yoshida or Kawagiuchi-ko Tourist Information Centers, is also worth picking up.

Getting There & Around

For those wanting to start trekking as soon as they arrive from Tokyo, **Keiō Dentetsu Bus** (☎03-5376-2222; www.highwaybus.com) runs direct buses (¥2700, 2½ hours; reservations necessary) from the Shinjuku Highway Bus

Terminal to Kawaguchi-ko Fifth Station (it does not operate in winter).

Buses run from both Kawaguchi-ko Station and Fujisan Station to the starting point at Kawaguchi-ko Fifth Station (one way/return ¥1540/2100, 50 minutes) roughly mid-April to early December. In the trekking season, buses depart hourly from around 7am until 8pm (ideal for climbers intending to make an overnight ascent). Returning from Fifth Station, buses head back to town from 8am to 9pm.

In the off-season, the first bus inconveniently leaves Kawaguchi-ko and Fujisan Stations at 9.10am, and the last bus returns at 3.30pm, meaning most trekkers will need to get a taxi in the morning (around ¥12,000, plus ¥2100 in tolls) to have enough time before getting the bus back. The bus schedule is highly seasonal; call **Fujikyū Yamanashi bus** (☎0555-72-6877; http://transportation.fujikyu.co.jp) or your hotel for details.

In the low season you should be able to find other trekkers to share a taxi at K's House (p160). Car hire is another option (particularly good if you're in a group), costing around ¥6800 per day plus fuel and tolls.

To get to the Subashiri Fifth Station trail, you can catch a bus from Kawaguchi-ko to Gotemba (¥1470), from where regular buses head to the Subashiri access point; Gotemba can also be accessed directly from Tokyo either by bus or train.

Fuji-Yoshida 富士吉田

One of the main gateway towns for the Fuji Five Lakes area, this is the location of the original inns that pilgrims stayed at before ascending Fuji. Its central district, **Gekkō-ji**, feels like the little town that time forgot, with original mid-20th-century facades. Fujisan Station is in the centre of Fuji-Yoshida.

Sights & Activities

Fuji Sengen-jinja SHINTO SHRINE

(冨士浅間神社; ☎0555-22-0221; http://sengenjinja.jp/index.html; 5558 Kami-Yoshida, Fuji-Yoshida; ⏲grounds 24hr, staffed 9am-5pm) FREE A necessary preliminary to the Mt Fuji ascent was a visit to this deeply wooded, atmospheric temple, which has been located here since the 8th century. Notable points include a 1000-year-old cedar; its main gate, which is rebuilt every 60 years (slightly larger each time); and its two one-tonne *mikoshi* (portable shrines) used in the annual Yoshida no Himatsuri (Yoshida Fire Festival). From Fujisan Station it's a 20-minute uphill walk, or take a bus to Sengen-jinja-mae (¥150, five minutes).

Togawa-ke Oshi-no-ie Restored Pilgrim's Inn HISTORIC BUILDING

(御師旧外川家住宅; 3-14-8 Kami-Yoshida; adult/child ¥100/50; ⏲9.30am-4.30pm, closed Tue) Fuji-Yoshida's *oshi-no-ie* (pilgrims' inns) have served visitors to the mountain since the days when climbing Mt Fuji was a pilgrimage rather than a tourist event. Very few still function as inns but Togawa-ke Oshi-no-ie offers some insight into the fascinating Edo-era practice of Mt Fuji worship.

Fuji-Q Highland AMUSEMENT PARK

(www.fuji-q.com; 5-6-1 Shin-Nishihara; admission only adult/child ¥1400/800, day pass ¥5200/3800; ⏲9am-5pm Mon-Fri, to 8pm Sat & Sun) As well as a high-octane amusement park with spectacular roller coasters providing a memorable way to bag Fuji views, Fuji-Q's compound is home to Thomas Land, a theme park based on Thomas the Tank Engine, a resort hotel, onsen and shops. Fun for all the family, one stop west of Fujisan Station.

Festivals & Events

Yoshida no Himatsuri CULTURAL

This annual festival (26–27 August) is held to mark the end of the climbing season and to offer thanks for the safety of the year's climbers. The first day involves a *mikoshi* procession and the lighting of bonfires on Fuji-Yoshida's main street. On the second day, the focus is Sengen-jinja.

Sleeping & Eating

Maisan-chi GUESTHOUSE ¥

(☎0555-24-5328; http://maisanchi.jimdo.com; 4-6-46 Shimo-Yoshida; dm/s/d with shared bathroom and breakfast ¥2700/3700/5400; 📶) On a backstreet and doubling up as a charming cafe specialising in desserts, this old Japanese-style building offers simple, friendly tatami (tightly woven floor matting) rooms and a dorm with bunk beds.

Fuji-Yoshida Youth Hostel HOSTEL ¥

(☎0555-22-0533; www.jyh.or.jp; 3-6-51 Shimo-Yoshida; r per person from ¥2900; 📶) Popular old lodging with small, slightly dingy, tatami rooms, but some have mountain views. There are basic self-catering facilities and limited English is spoken. It's a 15-minute walk on the main road away from Fujisan Station; look for the sign on the left-hand side and turn down the small alley on the left just before it.

Mt Fuji Hostel Michael's HOSTEL ¥
(☎0555-72-9139; www.mfi.or.jp/mtfujihostel; 3-21-37 Shimo-Yoshida; dm from ¥2900;) Efficiently run, modern Western-style hostel above the expat and local favourite **Michael's American Pub** (マイケルズアメリカンパブ; 795-1 Shimo-Yoshida; meals ¥600-1200; ⊙11.30am-3.30pm Sun-Fri, 7pm-2am Fri-Wed;).

Sakurada Udon JAPANESE ¥
(桜井うどん; 5-1-33 Shimo-Yoshida; noodles ¥350; ⊙10am-2pm Mon-Sat) Fuji-Yoshida is famous for its *te-uchi udon* (chunky white flour noodles) with some 60 places serving them for lunch. Just off the main drag this is a good spot to sample the dish sitting cross-legged on tatami. Look for the blue *noren* (curtains) next to the Status Pub.

Matsuya Cafe CAFE ¥
(まつや茶房; 294-3 Shimo-Yoshida; sandwiches from ¥500; ⊙10am-7pm Tue-Sun;) Stop by for well-brewed coffee, grilled-cheese sandwiches and a chat with the savvy, English-speaking owner. It's in a wooden merchant's house from the 1930s on the main drag; look for an old hanging wooden sign.

Information

Fuji-Yoshida Tourist Information Center (☎0555-22-7000; ⊙9am-5pm) Next to Fujisan (Mt Fuji) train station, the clued-up staff can provide info on climbing, and brochures and maps of the area.

Kawaguchi-ko 河口湖

Even if you have no intention of climbing Mt Fuji, the sprawling town of Kawaguchi-ko, set around the lake of the same name, is a great spot to hang out and enjoy what the Fuji Five Lakes region has to offer, along with great mountain views. Also enquire at the tourist office about several public onsen in the area; staff may have discount coupons for the onsen.

Sights & Activities

★**Itchiku Kubota Art Museum** MUSEUM
(久保田一竹美術館; www.itchiku-museum.com; 2255 Kawaguchi; adult/child ¥1300/400; ⊙9.30am-5pm Apr-Nov, 10am-4pm Dec-Mar) In an attractive Gaudí-influenced building, this excellent museum exhibits the kimono art of Itchiku Kubota (1917–2003). A small number of lavishly dyed kimonos from his life's work of continuous landscapes are displayed at any one time, in a grand hall of cypress. You might see Mt Fuji in the wintertime or the cherry blossoms of spring spread across oversized kimonos. Take the bus to the Kubota Itchiku Bijyutsukan-mae stop.

Kachi Kachi Yama Ropeway ROPEWAY
(カチカチ山ロープウェイ; www.kachikachiyama-ropeway.com; 1163-1 Azagawa; one way/return adult ¥410/720, child ¥210/360; ⊙9am-5pm) On the lower eastern edge of the lake, this ropeway runs to the **Fuji Viewing Platform** (1104m). If you have time, there is a 3½-hour hike from here to **Mitsutōge-yama** (三つ峠山; 1785m); it's an old trail with excellent Fuji views. Ask at Kawaguchi-ko Tourist Information Center for a map.

Fuji Visitor Center VISITOR CENTRE
(富士ビジターセンター; ☎0555-72-0259; www.yamanashi-kankou.visitor/index.html; 6663-1 Funatsu; ⊙8.30am-5pm) FREE Get up to speed on Mt Fuji at this well-presented visitor centre. An English video (12 minutes) with blockbuster movie soundtrack is a little cheesy but gives a good summary of the mountain and its geological history. There's also an observation deck and restaurant.

Ide Sake Brewery BREWERY
(☎0555-72-0006; www.kainokaiun.jp; 8 Funatsu; tours ¥500; ⊙tours 9.30am & 3pm) Using the spring waters from Mt Fuji, this small-scale sake brewery has been producing Japan's favourite tipple for over 150 years, and its tours (around 40 minutes) provide a fascinating insight into the production process and include tasting of various sakes and a souvenir glass. Only a little English is spoken and reservations are essential.

Sleeping

★**K's House Mt Fuji** HOSTEL ¥
(☎0555-83-5556; http://kshouse.jp/fuji-e/index.html; 6713-108 Funatsu; dm from ¥2500, d with/without bathroom ¥7800/6800;) K's is expert at providing a welcoming atmosphere, spacious Japanese-style rooms and helpful English-speaking staff. There's a fully loaded kitchen, mountain bikes for hire, comfy common areas to meet fellow travellers/climbers and free pickup from Kawaguchi-ko Station. Its bar **Zero Station** (6713-108 Funatsu; ⊙6pm-midnight) is stumbling distance away. Rooms fill up fast during the climbing season.

Kawaguchi-ko Station Inn HOSTEL ¥
(☎0555-72-0015; www.st-inn.com; 3639-2 Funatsu; dm/s/d ¥2800/4320/8700;) Across from the station, this spotless hostel offers mixed dorms (some with Fuji views), laundry facilities, English-speaking staff and a top-floor bath looking out to Mt Fuji in the distance. There's an 11.30pm curfew.

Tominoko Hotel HOTEL ¥¥
(☎0555-72-5080; www.tominoko.net; 55 Asakawa; r per person with 2 meals from ¥8925; P@) Given its views of Fuji across the lake, this place is a steal. Rooms are modern, smart Western-style twins with plenty of space. Ask for one on an upper level to score a balcony. Also has a *rotemburo* (outdoor bath).

Fuji Lake Hotel HOTEL ¥¥
(☎0555-72-2209; www.fujilake.co.jp; 1 Funatsu; r per person with 2 meals from ¥15,552; @) On Kawaguchi-ko's south shore, this stylish 1935 vintage hotel offers either Mt Fuji or lake views from its Japanese-Western combo rooms. Some rooms have private *rotemburo*, otherwise there's a common onsen.

Sunnide Resort HOTEL ¥¥
(サニーデリゾート; ☎0555-76-6004; www.sunnide.com; 2549-1 Ōishi; r per person with two meals from ¥13,000, cottages from ¥16,000; @) Offering views of Mt Fuji from the far side of Kawaguchi-ko, friendly Sunnide has hotel rooms and cottages with a delicious outdoor bath. You can splash out in the stylish suites or go for the discounted 'backpacker' rates (¥4400, no views), if same-day rooms are available. Breakfast/dinner costs from ¥2000/1800.

Kozantei Ubuya RYOKAN ¥¥¥
(湖山亭うぶや; ☎0555-72-1145; www.ubuya.co.jp; 10 Asakawa; r per person with 2 meals from ¥20,100; @) Elegant and ultra stylish, Ubuya offers unobstructed panoramic views of Mt Fuji reflected in Kawaguchi-ko that are simply unbeatable. Splash out on the more expensive suites to enjoy the scene while soaking in an outdoor tub on your balcony decking. One for the honeymooners.

Eating

Akai IZAKAYA ¥
(赤井; mains from ¥430; ⊙6-11pm, closed Thu;) Great little *izakaya* (pub-eatery) serving sensational whole grilled fish and various *yaki-soba* (fried noodles). It's off Rte 137, behind the petrol station near the Ogino supermarket.

Hōtō Fudō NOODLES ¥¥
(ほうとう不動; ☎0555-72-8511; www.houtoufudou.jp; 707 Kawaguchi; hōtō ¥1080; ⊙11am-7pm) *Hōtō* are Kawaguchi-ko's local noodles, hand-cut and served in a thick miso stew with pumpkin, sweet potato and other vegetables. It's a hearty meal best sampled at this chain with five branches around town. This is the most architecturally interesting one, an igloo-like building in which you can also sample *basashi* – horsemeat sashimi (¥1080).

Sanrokuen TEPPANYAKI ¥¥
(山麓園; ☎0555-73-1000; 3370-1 Funatsu; set meals ¥2100-4200; ⊙11am-7.30pm Fri-Wed;) Here diners sit on the floor around traditional *irori* charcoal pits grilling their own meals – skewers of fish, meat, tofu and vegies. From Kawaguchi-ko Station, turn left, left again after the 7-Eleven and after 600m you'll see the thatched roof on the right.

Information

Kawaguchi-ko Tourist Information Center
(☎0555-72-6700; ⊙8.30am-5.30pm Sun-Fri, to 7pm Sat) Next to Kawaguchi-ko Station. Has English speakers as well as maps and brochures.

Sai-ko 紅葉台

Sai-ko (www.saiko-kankou.jp) is a quiet lake area good for hiking, fishing and boating. Mt Fuji is mostly obstructed but there are great views from the **Kōyō-dai** lookout, near the main road, and from the western end of the lake.

Sights

Narusawa Hyōketsu & Fugaku Fuketsu CAVE
(鳴沢氷穴, 富岳風穴; 8533 Narusawa-mura; one cave adult/child ¥280/130, both caves ¥500/250; ⊙9am-5pm) Not for the claustrophobic, it takes about 10 minutes to walk through the

TOKYO DAY-TRIP PLANNER

Many destinations make possible day trips from Tokyo:

One-way travel up to an hour Yokohama, Kamakura, Mt Takao, Oku-Tama Region, Narita, Omiya

One-way travel up to two hours Fuji Five Lakes, Hakone, Nikkō, Atami, Itō, Mito

Narusawa Hyōketsu (ice cave), formed by lava flows from an eruption of Mt Fuji in 864, to the end to see the ice pillars, which are at their peak in April. A 20-minute walk down the road is the similar Fugaku Fukestu (wind cave, also known as the lava cave), which was used to store silk worm cocoons in the past.

Sai-ko Iyashi-no-Sato Nenba CULTURAL CENTRE
(西湖いやしの里根場; 2710 Nenba; adult/child ¥350/150; 9am-5pm) Built in 2006 on the site of historic thatched-roof houses washed away in a typhoon 40 years earlier, these reconstructed frames offer an insight into a forgotten time. There are demonstrations of silk and paper crafts, as well as restaurants specialising in *soba* and *hōtō*. The Retro-bus stops right out front.

Sleeping & Eating

Camp Village Gnome CAMPGROUND ¥
(0555-82-2921; www.hamayouresort.com; 1030 Saiko; camping per person from ¥1000, tent rental ¥3000;) Ex-model and outdoors author Tokichi Kimura is the convivial English-speaking owner of this pleasant lakeside campsite opposite the Hamayou Resort. There are BBQ facilities, a simple cafe with wi-fi, and canoe rental (¥3000, three hours).

Solar Cafe & Farm GUESTHOUSE ¥
(0555-85-3329; https://www.facebook.com/pages/Earth-Embassys-Solar-Cafe-Organic-Farm/172381866148527?sk=info&tab=overview; 8529-74 Narusawa-mura; camping/treehouse/r from ¥2000/4000/4800; cafe 11am-3pm Mon, Tue & Fri, 11am-6pm Sat & Sun) It's possible to camp, stay in a treehouse (by a noisy main road) or in one of the two spacious tatami rooms to the rear of this woodsy, eco-friendly cafe where they serve food from their organic farm. There's a solar shower (in summer) but otherwise it's a 20-minute walk to Yurari Onsen for a hot bath. Working on the farm is also an option.

Shōji-ko 精進湖

Further west from Sai-ko, low-key, tiny Shōji-ko is said to be the prettiest of the Fuji lakes and offers Mt Fuji views, fishing and boating.

Murahamasō (村浜荘; 0555-87-2436; www.murahamasou.com; 807 Shōji; r per person with 2 meals ¥7500;) is a traditional lodging where some rooms have lake and mountain (not Mt Fuji) views and all have shared bathrooms. Some English is spoken.

Motosu-ko 本栖湖

For a preview of this lake, look at the ¥1000 bill, where Mt Fuji rises majestically from the north shore of Motosu-ko.

It's a popular spot for outdoor activities. The **Panorama-dai** (パノラマ台) hiking trail ends here in a spectacular, spot-on view of Mt Fuji. It's a one-hour hike from the trailhead, a 20-minute walk beyond the Motosu-Iriguchi bus stop (¥1230, 45 minutes from Kawaguchi-ko).

Kōan Motosu (0555-38-0117; www6.nns.ne.jp/~kouan) offers paddleboarding (¥1500/4000 per hour/day), kayaking (¥2000 per person, one hour) and even scuba diving in the lake!

Sleeping

Kōan Motosu Inn CAMPGROUND ¥
(0555-38-0117; www6.nns.ne.jp/~kouan; 2926 Nakanokura; camping per person ¥600, tent rental ¥1000, cabin sleeping 6 from ¥17,280) Kōan has two campgrounds on the lake, this one with Fuji views, jacuzzi, helpful English-speaking owner and attached restaurant and shop, as well as cabins, should you not wish to camp. It's a short walk downhill from the Tourist Information Center. Its second site occupies a more shaded forest area on the far west side of the lake.

Lake Motosu Campground CAMPGROUND ¥
(0555-87-2345; 18 Motosu; camping ¥3000, bungalow sleeping 4/6 ¥5250/6300) If you don't have a tent, this place also offers simple tatami-mat bungalows set in a wooded area on the lake, with campfires, shared bathroom blocks and a store selling snacks, beer and camping items. Futon rental is ¥620 per set and no English is spoken.

It's on the main road, about 300m on the left from the lake entrance.

Yamanaka-ko 山中湖村

The region's largest lake, Yamanaka-ko is popular with locals. The southern shore is overdeveloped and has a tourist-trap feel, but the northern side is more appealing with a sleepier vibe.

One of the reasons to visit is for the **Benifuji-no-yu** (山中湖温泉紅富士の湯; 0555-20-2700; www.benifuji.co.jp; adult/child ¥700/200, towel rental ¥210; 10am-8.30pm) onsen. Ignore the faded hotel facade; inside the views improve dramatically when Mt Fuji is clear in sight as you soak in the outdoor stone and *hinoki* (cypress) baths.

Sleeping & Eating

PICA Yamanaka-ko Village CABIN ¥¥
(PICA山中湖ヴィレッジ; ☎0555-62-4155; http://yamanakako.pica-village.jp; 506-296 Hirano; cottages sleeping 6 from ¥16,500;) On Yamanaka-ko's southern shore, this is a nicely designed complex of wooden cottages of varying sizes in a garden setting with attached restaurants, gift shop and a very popular hammock cafe. There are other PICA camps near Fuji-Yoshida and Sai-ko – see the website for details.

NORTH OF TOKYO

North of Tokyo, the Kantō plain gives way to a mountainous, forested landscape providing a fine backdrop for the spectacular shrines of Nikkō and the beautiful nearby lake Chūzenji-ko. The whole area is within the 400-sq-km Nikkō National Park, sprawling over Fukushima, Tochigi, Gunma and Niigata Prefectures, and offering some excellent hiking opportunities and remote onsen.

Nikkō 日光

☎0288 / POP 98,000

Ancient moss clinging to a stone wall; rows of perfectly aligned stone lanterns; vermilion gates; and towering cedars: this is only a pathway in Nikkō, a sanctuary that enshrines the glories of the Edo period (1600–1868). Scattered among hilly woodlands, Nikkō is one of Japan's major attractions. Its key World Heritage Site temples and shrines are an awesome display of wealth and power by the Tokugawa shogunate.

All this means that in high season (summer and autumn) and at weekends, Nikkō can be extremely crowded and the spirituality of the area can feel a little lost. Spending the night here allows for an early start before the crowds arrive. However, we highly recommend a couple of nights so you can explore the gorgeous natural scenery in the surrounding area, much of it national park, as well as Nikkō's other sights and activities, including an imperial palace and onsen.

History

In the middle of the 8th century the Buddhist priest Shōdō Shōnin (735–817) established a hermitage at Nikkō. For centuries the mountains served as a training ground for Buddhist monks, though the area fell gradually into obscurity. Nikkō's enduring fame was sealed, however, when it was chosen as the site for the mausoleum of Tokugawa Ieyasu, the warlord who established the shogunate that ruled Japan for over 250 years.

Ieyasu was laid to rest among Nikkō's towering cedars at a much less grand Tōshō-gū in 1617. Seventeen years later his grandson, Tokugawa Iemitsu, commenced work on the colossal shrine that can be seen today, using an army of some 15,000 artisans from across Japan, who took two years to complete the project.

Sights

★Tōshō-gū SHINTO SHRINE
(東照宮; www.toshogu.jp; 2301 Sannai; adult/child ¥1300/450; ⏲8am-4.30pm Apr-Oct, 8am-3.30pm Nov-Mar) A World Heritage Site, Tōshō-gū is a brilliantly decorative shrine in a beautiful natural setting. Among its notable features is the dazzling 'Sunset Gate' Yōmei-mon.

As the shrine gears up for its 400th anniversary, a major restoration program is underway. Until at least 2018, the Yōmei-mon and Shimojinko (one of the Three Sacred Storehouses) will be obscured by scaffolding. Don't be put off visiting, as Tōshō-gū remains an impressive sight. A new museum building is also set to open during 2015.

DON'T MISS

RAILWAY MUSEUM, OMIYA

The fascinating **Railway Museum** (鉄道博物館; www.railway-museum.jp/; 3-47 Onari-chō, Omiya-ku, Saitama-shi; adult/student/child ¥1000/500/200; ⏲10am-5.30pm Wed-Mon) in Omiya, 25km north of central Tokyo, charts the evolution from steam to modern-day technology of Japan's railways. It's packed with lovingly preserved rolling stock and is a must for rail enthusiasts who can climb aboard classic carriages and even get behind the controls of a *shinkansen* (bullet train).

The museum is linked to Omiya Station by the New Shuttle train (¥190, five minutes) and can easily be visited on the way to or from Nikkō.

Nikkō

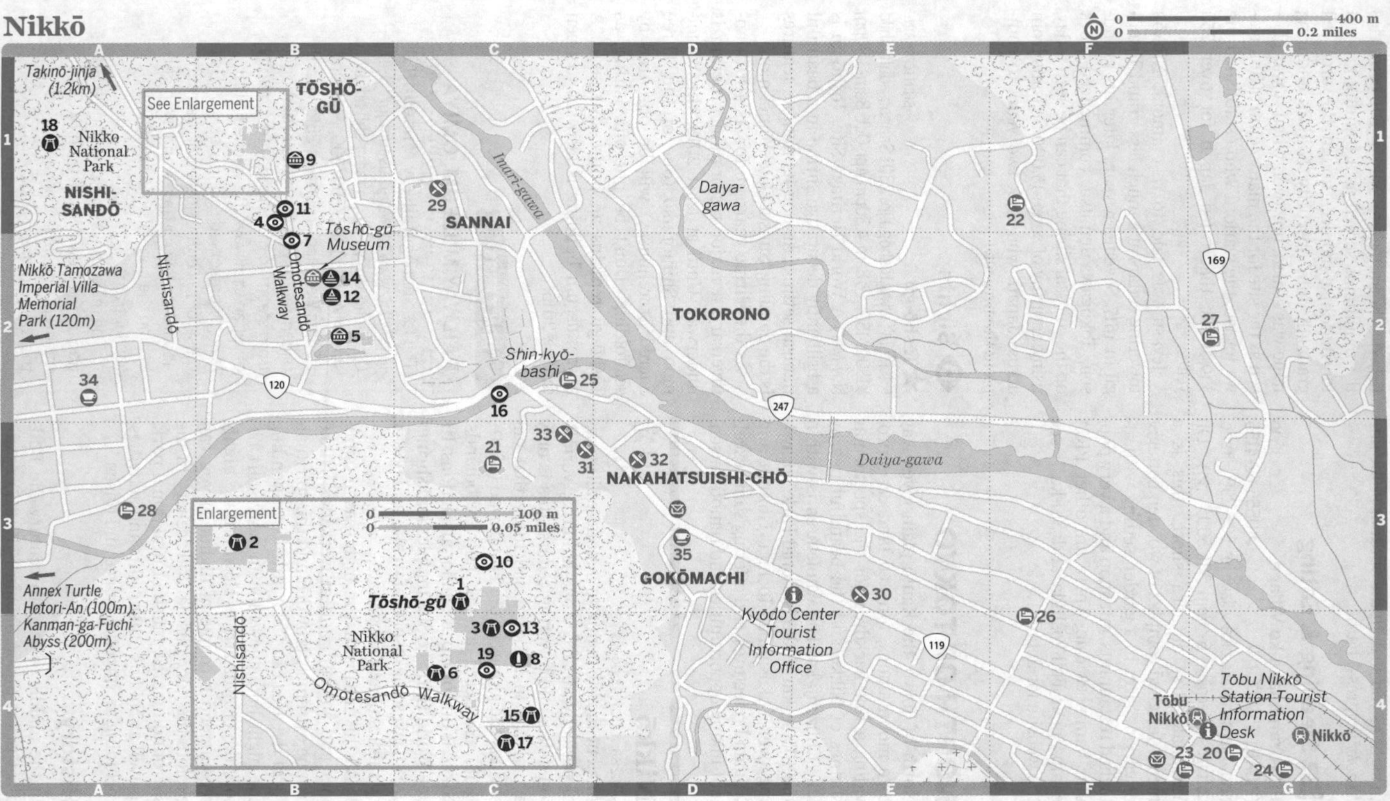
0 400 m
0 0.2 miles
A
B
C
D
E
F
G
1
2
3
4
Takinō-jinja (1.2km)
See Enlargement
TŌSHŌ-GŪ
18
Nikko National Park
9
NISHI-SANDŌ
11
4
7
Tōshō-gū Museum
Omotesandō Walkway
14
12
5
Nishisandō
Nikkō Tamozawa Imperial Villa Memorial Park (120m)
29
SANNAI
Inari-gawa
Daiya-gawa
TOKORONO
22
169
27
34
120
Shin-kyō-bashi
25
16
247
21
33
31
32
NAKAHATSUISHI-CHŌ
Daiya-gawa
28
Annex Turtle Hotori-An (100m); Kanman-ga-Fuchi Abyss (200m)
Enlargement
0 100 m
0 0.05 miles
2
10
1
Tōshō-gū
3
13
19
8
6
Nikko National Park
Omotesandō Walkway
15
17
35
GOKŌMACHI
Kyōdo Center Tourist Information Office
30
26
119
Tōbu Nikkō
Tōbu Nikkō Station Tourist Information Desk
Nikkō
23
20
24

Nikkō

Top Sights

1	Tōshō-gū	C3

Sights

2	Futarasan-jinja	B3
3	Gōhonsha	C4
4	Gōjūnotō	B1
5	Hōmotsu-den	B2
6	Honji-dō	C4
7	Ishi-dorii	B2
8	Nemuri-neko	C4
9	Nikkō Tōshō-gū Museum of Art	B1
10	Okumiya	C3
11	Omote-mon	B1
12	Rinnō-ji	B2
13	Sakashita-mon	C4
14	Sambutsu-dō	B2
15	Sanjinko	C4
16	Shin-kyō	C2
17	Shinkyūsha	C4
18	Taiyūin-byō	A1
19	Yōmei-mon	C4

Sleeping

20	Nikkō Guesthouse Sumica	G4
21	Nikkō Kanaya Hotel	C3
22	Nikkō Park Lodge	F1
23	Nikkō Park Lodge Guesthouse	F4
24	Nikkō Station Classic Hotel	G4
25	Nikkorisou Backpackers	C2
26	Nikkosan BackPackers Inn	F4
27	Rindō-no-Ie	G2
28	Turtle Inn Nikkō	A3

Eating

29	Gyōshintei	C1
30	Hi no Kuruma	E3
31	Hippari Dako	C3
32	Meguri	D3
33	Nagomi-chaya	C3

Drinking & Nightlife

34	Nikkō Coffee	A2
35	Yuzawaya	D3

The stone steps of **Omotesandō** lead past the towering stone *torii* (entrance gate) **Ishi-dorii** (石鳥居), and the **Gōjūnotō** (五重塔; Five Storey Pagoda), an 1819 reconstruction of the mid-17th-century original, to **Omote-mon** (表門), Tōshō-gū's main gateway, protected on either side by Deva kings.

In Tōshō-gū's initial courtyard are the **Sanjinko** (三神庫; Three Sacred Storehouses); on the upper storey of the Kamijinko (upper storehouse) are relief carvings of 'imaginary elephants' by an artist who had never seen the real thing. Nearby is the **Shinkyūsha** (神厩舎; Sacred Stable) adorned with relief carvings of monkeys. The allegorical 'hear no evil, see no evil, speak no evil' simians demonstrate three principles of Tendai Buddhism.

Further into Tōshō-gū's precincts, to the left of the drum tower, is **Honji-dō** (本地堂), a hall known for the painting on its ceiling of the Nakiryū (Crying Dragon). Monks demonstrate the hall's acoustic properties by clapping two sticks together. The dragon 'roars' (a bit of a stretch) when the sticks are clapped beneath its mouth, but not elsewhere.

Once the scaffolding comes off in 2018, the **Yōmei-mon** (陽明門; Sunset Gate) will be grander than ever, its gold leaf and intricate, coloured carvings and paintings of flowers, dancing girls, mythical beasts and Chinese sages all shiny and renewed. Worrying that the gate's perfection might arouse envy in the gods, those responsible for its construction had the final supporting pillar placed upside down as a deliberate error.

Gōhonsha (御本社), the main inner courtyard, includes the **Honden** (本殿; Main Hall) and **Haiden** (拝殿; Hall of Worship). Inside these halls are paintings of the 36 immortal poets of Kyoto, and a ceiling-painting pattern from the Momoyama period; note the 100 dragons, each different. *Fusuma* (sliding door) paintings depict a *kirin* (a mythical beast that's part giraffe and part dragon).

To the right of the Gōhonsha is **Sakashita-mon** (坂下門), into which is carved a tiny wooden sculpture of the **Nemuri-neko** (眠り猫; Sleeping Cat) that's famous for its life-like appearance (though admittedly the attraction is lost on some visitors). From here there's an uphill path through towering cedars to the appropriately solemn **Okumiya** (奥宮), Ieyasu's tomb.

Bypassed by nearly everyone at Tōshō-gū is the marvellous **Nikkō Tōshō-gū Museum of Art** (日光東照宮美術館; ☎0288-54-0560; http://www.toshogu.jp/shisetsu/bijutsu.html; 2301 Yamanouchi; adult/child ¥800/400; ⏲9am-4.30pm Apr-Oct, 9am-3.30pm Nov-Mar) in the old shrine offices, showcasing fine paintings on its doors, sliding screens, frames and decorative scrolls, some by masters including Yokoyama Taikan and Nakamura Gakuryo. Follow the path to the right of Omote-mon to find it.

Taiyūin-byō SHINTO SHRINE
(大猷院廟; adult/child ¥550/250; ⌚8am-4.30pm Apr-Oct, 8am-3.30pm Nov-Mar) Ieyasu's grandson Iemitsu (1604–51) is buried here and although it houses many of the same elements as Tōshō-gū (storehouses, drum tower, Chinese-style gates etc), the more intimate scale and setting in a cryptomeria forest make it very appealing.

Look for dozens of lanterns donated by *daimyō* (domain lords), and the gate Niō-mon, whose guardian deities have a hand up (to welcome those with pure hearts) and a hand down (to suppress those with impure hearts).

Inside the main hall, 140 dragons painted on the ceiling are said to carry prayers to the heavens; those holding pearls are on their way up, and those without are returning to gather more prayers.

Rinnō-ji BUDDHIST TEMPLE
(輪王寺; ☎0288-54-0531; http://rinnoji.or.jp; 2300 Yamanouchi; adult/child ¥400/200; ⌚8am-4.30pm Apr-Oct, 8am-3.30pm Nov-Mar) This Tendai-sect temple was founded 1200 years ago by Shōdō Shōnin. The exterior of the **Sambutsu-dō** (三仏堂; Three-Buddha Hall) is under wraps for restoration until 2020. Inside sit a trio of 8m gilded wooden Buddha statues: Amida Nyorai (a primal deity in the Mahayana Buddhist canon), flanked by Senjū (deity of mercy and compassion) and Batō (a horse-headed Kannon).

Rinnō-ji's **Hōmotsu-den** (宝物殿 Treasure Hall; admission ¥300) houses some 6000 treasures associated with the temple; the separate admission ticket includes entrance to the Shōyō-en strolling garden.

Futarasan-jinja SHINTO SHRINE
(二荒山神社; www.futarasan.jp; adult/child ¥200/100) Set among cypress trees, this very atmospheric shrine was also founded by Shōdō Shōnin; the current building dates from 1619, making it Nikkō's oldest. It's the protector shrine of Nikkō itself, dedicated to Nantai-san (2484m), the mountain's consort, Nyotai-san, and their mountainous progeny, Tarō. There are other branches of the shrine on Nantai-san and by Chūzenji-ko.

Nikkō Tamozawa Imperial Villa Memorial Park HISTORIC SITE
(日光田母沢御用邸記念公園; ☎0288-53-6767; www.park-tochigi.com/tamozawa; 8-27 Hon-chō; adult/child ¥510/260; ⌚9am-4pm Wed-Mon) About 1km west of Shin-kyō bridge, this splendidly restored imperial palace of more than 100 rooms showcases superb craftsmanship, with parts of the complex dating from the Edo, Meiji and Taishō eras. Apart from the construction skills involved, there are brilliantly detailed screen paintings and serene garden views framed from nearly every window.

Visit in autumn to see the gardens at their most spectacular.

Takinō-jinja SHINTO SHRINE
(滝尾神社) FREE About 1km north of Futarasan-jinja, close by the Shiraito Falls, is this serene, delightfully less crowded shrine that has a history stretching back to 820. The stone gate, called **Undameshi-no-torii**, dates back to Iemitsu's time. Before entering, it's customary to try your luck tossing three stones through the small hole near the top.

Maps available at the tourist offices show the route to the shrine, which also passes the tomb of Shōdō Shōnin.

Shin-kyō HISTORIC SITE
(神橋; crossing fee ¥300) This much-photographed red footbridge is located at the sacred spot where Shōdō Shōnin was said to have been carried across the Daiya River on the backs of two giant serpents. The bridge is a reconstruction of the 17th-century original.

Kanman-ga-Fuchi Abyss PARK
(憾満ガ淵) Escape the crowds along this wooded path lined with a collection of *jizō* statues (the small stone effigies of the Buddhist protector of travellers and children). After passing the Shin-kyō bridge, follow the Daiya River west for about 1km, crossing another bridge near Jyoko-ji temple en route.

It's said that if you try to count the statues there and again on the way back, you'll end up with a different number, hence the nickname 'Bake-jizō' (ghost *jizō*).

Tours

Tochigi Volunteer Interpreters & Guides Association TOUR
(NikkoTVIGA@hotmail.co.jp) Offers free guided tours between November and March, but not of the World Heritage area. Contact in advance.

Festivals & Events

Yayoi Matsuri CULTURAL
Procession of *mikoshi* held at Futarasan-jinja on 16 and 17 April.

Tōshō-gū Grand Festival CULTURAL

Nikkō's most important annual festival is held on 17 and 18 May and features horseback archery on the first day and a 1000-strong costumed re-enactment of the delivery of Ieyasu's remains to Nikkō on the second.

Tōshō-gū Autumn Festival CULTURAL

Autumnal repeat on 16 and 17 October of the May festival.

Sleeping

★ Nikkō Guesthouse Sumica GUESTHOUSE ¥

(日光ゲストハウス 巣み家; ☎090-1838-7873; www.nikko-guesthouse.com; 5-12 Aioi-chō; dm/r per person without bathroom from ¥3500/4000; 📶) Run by a lovely, clued-up couple, this tiny guesthouse is set in an artfully renovated wooden house steps from both train stations. Dorms are a bit cramped, but they're tidy, as are the private tatami-mat doubles; all with fan only and shared bathrooms. There's an 11pm curfew.

Nikkorisou Backpackers HOSTEL ¥

(☎080-9449-1545; http://nikkorisou.com/eng.html; 1107 Kamihatsu-ishi-machi; dm/s/d with shared bathroom from ¥2600/3600/6200; 📶) The closest hostel to the World Heritage site offers a riverside location, a relaxed, friendly vibe and a good-sized kitchen for self-catering. The rental bicycles at ¥500 a day are a good deal.

Nikkō Park Lodge GUESTHOUSE ¥

(日光パークロッジ; ☎0288-53-1201; www.nikkoparklodge.com; 2828-5 Tokorono; dm/d from ¥2990/7980; 🚭@📶) In the wooded hills north of town, this well-kept guesthouse has Western-style rooms, a spacious dorm, a homely lounge with log fire and English-speaking staff who are a great source of info. There's an afternoon pick-up service, otherwise it's around ¥700 by taxi from the station.

There's also a second **guesthouse** (☎0288-53-1201; www.nikkoparklodge.com; 11-6 Matsubara-chō; r from ¥12,000) across from Tōbu Station.

Nikkosan BackPackers Inn HOSTEL ¥

(☎080-3971 9670; takuuucommunity@gmail.com; 1-362-8 Inari-machi; dm/s with shared bathroom ¥3000/3500; 📶) This new minimalist-design hostel is located in an old wooden house on a quiet backstreet just five minutes' walk north of Tōbu Station.

Rindō-no-Ie MINSHUKU ¥

(りんどうの家; ☎0288-53-0131; www3.ocn.ne.jp/~garrr/Rindou.html; 1462 Tokorono; r per person without bathroom from ¥3500; 🚭@📶) Small but well-maintained tatami rooms, tasty meals and pick-up service. Breakfast/dinner is ¥700. It's across the river, about a 15-minute walk northwest of the train station; see the website for a map.

Annex Turtle Hotori-An INN ¥¥

(☎0288-53-3663; www.turtle-nikko.com; 8-28 Takumi-chō; s/tw ¥6500/12,600; 🚭@📶) More modern than the original Turtle Inn, with Japanese- and Western-style rooms plus river views from the onsen bath.

Turtle Inn Nikkō INN ¥¥

(タートル・イン・日光; ☎0288-53-3168; www.turtle-nikko.com; 2-16 Takumi-chō; s/tw without bathroom ¥4750/9200, with bathroom ¥5800/9900; 🚭📶) A long-time favourite with spacious rooms, both Japanese and Western style. Take a bus to Sōgō-kaikan-mae, backtrack about 50m, turn right along the river and walk for about five minutes; you'll see the turtle sign on the left.

Nikkō Kanaya Hotel HOTEL ¥¥¥

(日光金谷ホテル; ☎0288-54-0001; www.kanayahotel.co.jp; 1300 Kamihatsu-ishimachi; tw from ¥17,820; @📶) This grand lady from 1893 wears her history like a well-loved, if not slightly worn, dress. The newer wing has Japanese-style rooms with excellent vistas, spacious quarters and private bathrooms;

WORTH A TRIP

NIKKŌ INN

Nikkō Inn (☎0288-27-0008; www.nikko-inn.jp; 333 Koshiro; cottage from ¥13,000; 📶) Located just 30 minutes' train ride from Nikkō in pastoral Shimo-goshiro, Nikkō Inn offers six Japanese-style cottages, sleeping between two and seven people, and overlooking rice fields. Each wooden house has tatami rooms with rice-paper screens and traditional verandahs, plus modern kitchen and bathroom facilities.

On the doorstep is a village of 1000 people and the mountains of Nikkō. Shimo-goshiro is on the Tōbu line from Asakusa (¥1160, 2¼ hours), four stops before Nikkō (¥350). The cottages are a five-minute walk from the station.

the cheaper rooms in the main building are Western style and have an appealing old-fashioned ambience.

Wi-fi in the lobby only, where you'll find the bar is deliciously dark and amenable to drinking whisky. Rates rise steeply in high seasons.

Nikkō Station Classic Hotel HOTEL ¥¥¥
(☎0288-53-1000; www.nikko-stationhotel.jp; s/d from ¥11,000/20,000; ⊜@📶) Opposite the JR station, this smart midrange hotel has modern stylish decor, comfortable Western-style rooms, buffet breakfast (¥2000) and a communal bath filled with onsen water.

Eating & Drinking

A local speciality is *yuba* (the skin that forms when making tofu) cut into strips; better than it sounds, it's a staple of *shōjin ryōri* (Buddhist vegetarian cuisine). You'll see it all over town, in everything from noodles *(yuba soba)* to fried bean buns *(age yuba manju)*.

Hippari Dako YAKITORI ¥
(ひっぱり凧; 1011 Kamihatsu-ishimachi; meals ¥550-900; ⏲11am-8pm; 🖉📋) An institution for over a quarter of a century among foreign travellers, as layers of business cards tacked to the walls testify, this no-frills restaurant serves comfort-food meals, including curry *udon*, *yuba* sashimi and *yaki-udon* (fried noodles).

Hi no Kuruma OKONOMIYAKI ¥
(ひの車; 597-2 Gokō-machi; mains ¥500-1500; ⏲noon-3pm & 6-9pm Thu-Tue; 📋) A popular choice for cheap and easy grill-your-own meals. Look for the small parking lot and red-brown-green-and-white Japanese sign.

★**Meguri** VEGAN ¥¥
(909 Nakahatsuishi-machi; lunch ¥1400; ⏲11.30am-6pm Sat-Wed; 🖉📋) A young, dedicated couple dish up lovingly prepared tasty vegan Japanese meals in this former art shop with an amazing painting on its ceiling. Arrive as soon as they open if you want to secure lunch, as it's a popular place and once they've run out of food it's sweets and drinks only.

Nagomi-chaya JAPANESE ¥¥
(和み茶屋; ☎0288-54-3770; 1016 Kamihatsuishi; dishes/set-course meals from ¥450/1620; ⏲11.30am-4pm Thu-Tue) A faithful picture menu makes ordering simple at this sophisticated arts-and-crafts-style cafe near the top of Nikkō's main drag. The beautifully prepared *kaiseki*-style lunches are a great deal.

★**Gyōshintei** KAISEKI ¥¥¥
(尭心亭; ☎0288-53-3751; www.meiji-yakata.com/gyoushin; 2339-1 Sannai; set-courses lunch/dinner from ¥2138/4514; ⏲11am-7pm; 🖉📋) Splash out on deluxe spreads of vegetarian *shōjin-ryōri*, featuring local bean curd and vegetables served half a dozen delectable ways, or the *kaiseki* courses, which include fish. The elegant tatami dining room overlooks a carefully tended garden, which is part of the Meji-no-Yakata compound of chic restaurants close to the World Heritage sites.

★**Nikkō Coffee** CAFE
(日光珈琲; http://nikko-coffee.com; 3-13 Honchō; coffee ¥550, meals from ¥1000; ⏲10am-5pm Tue-Sun) A century-old rice shop has been sensitively reinvented as this retro-chic cafe with a garden, where expertly made hand-dripped coffee is served alongside cakes and snack meals, such as bacon, cheese and egg galette (buckwheat pancake) or pork curry.

Yuzawaya CAFE
(湯沢屋; www.yuzawaya.jp; 946 Kamihatsu-ishimachi; tea sets from ¥450; ⏲11am-4pm Mon-Fri, to 5pm Sat & Sun) In business since 1804, this teahouse specialises in *manjū* (buns filled

OFF THE BEATEN TRACK

KANIYU ONSEN

In the midst of the mountainous Okukino region of 'secret onsen' you'll find **Kaniyu Onsen** (加仁湯; ☎0288-96-0311; www.naf.co.jp/kaniyu; 871 Kawamata; r per person with 2 meals from ¥13,110; onsen day visitor ¥500; ⏲day visitors 9am-3pm), a rustic ryokan with milky sulphuric waters in its multiple outdoor baths, a few of which are mixed bathing. To get here from Nikkō, take the Tōbu line to Shimo-imachi, change to a Kinugawa Onsen–bound train, then board the bus to Meoto-buchi (¥1540; 1½ hours; four daily). From here, it's a gentle 1½-hour hour hike up a beautiful river valley past several waterfalls.

You'll need to leave Nikkō before 9am to make it to Kaniyu and back in a day, and that will only give you around one hour at the onsen. If you'd prefer to take it at a more leisurely pace, plan an overnight stay. Either way, before setting off check the latest transport details with one of Nikkō's tourist offices.

with sweet azuki-bean paste) and other traditional sweets; look for the green-and-white banners.

Information

Kyōdo Center Tourist Information Office (☎0288-54-2496; www.nikko-jp.org; 591 Gokomachi; ⊙9am-5pm) This is the main tourist information office with English speakers (guaranteed between 10am and 2pm) and maps for sightseeing and hiking. There are several computers available for internet use.

Nikkō Post Office (日光郵便局; ☎0288-54-0101; 896-1 Nakahatsuishi-machi) Three blocks northwest of the Kyōdo Center Tourist Information Office. There is another branch (Rte 119; ⊙8.45am-7pm Mon-Fri, 9am-5pm Sat & Sun) across the street from Tōbu Nikkō Station on Rte 119; both have international ATMs.

Tōbu Nikkō Station Tourist Information Desk (☎0288-54-0864; ⊙8.30am-5pm) At the Nikkō train station, there's a small information desk where you can pick up a town map and get help in English to find buses, restaurants and hotels.

Getting There & Around

Nikkō is best reached from Tokyo via the Tōbu Nikkō line from Asakusa Station. You can usually get last-minute seats on the hourly reserved *tokkyū* (limited-express) trains (¥2700, 1¾ hours). *Kaisoku* (rapid) trains (¥1360, 2½ hours, hourly from 6.20am to 5.30pm) require no reservation, but you may have to change at Shimo-imaichi. Be sure to ride in the last two cars to reach Nikkō (some cars may separate at an intermediate stop).

JR Pass holders can take the Tohoku *shinkansen* (bullet train) from Tokyo to Utsunomiya (¥4930, 54 minutes) and change there for an ordinary train to Nikkō (¥740, 45 minutes).

Both JR Nikkō Station (designed by Frank Lloyd Wright) and the nearby Tōbu Nikkō Station lie southeast of the shrine area within a block of Nikkō's main road (Rte 119, the old Nikkō-kaidō). From the station, follow this road uphill for 20 minutes to reach the shrine area, past restaurants, souvenir shops and the main tourist information centre, or take a bus to the Shin-kyō bus stop (¥200). Bus stops are announced in English. Buses leave from both JR and Tōbu Nikkō Station; buses bound for both Chūzen-ji Onsen and Yumoto Onsen stop at Shin-kyō and other stops around the World Heritage Sites.

TRAIN & BUS PASSES

Tōbu Railway (www.tobu.co.jp/foreign) Offers two passes covering rail transport from Asakusa to Nikkō (though not the *tokkyū* surcharge, from ¥1040) and unlimited hop-on-hop-off bus services around Nikkō. Purchase these passes at the **Tōbu Sightseeing Service Center** (Map p106; ☎0288-3841-2871; www.tobu.co.jp/foreign; ⊙7.45am-5pm) in Asakusa Station.

All Nikkō Pass (adult/child ¥4520/2280) Valid for four days and includes buses to Chūzen-ji Onsen and Yumoto Onsen.

Two-Day Nikkō Pass (adult/child ¥2670/1340) Valid for two days and includes buses to the World Heritage Sites.

TŌBU NIKKŌ BUS FREE PASS

If you've already got your rail ticket, two-day bus-only passes allow unlimited rides between Nikkō and Chūzen-ji Onsen (adult/child ¥2000/1000) or Yumoto Onsen (adult/child ¥3000/1500), including the World Heritage Site area. The **Sekai-isan-meguri** (World Heritage Bus Pass; adult/child ¥500/250) covers the area between the stations and the shrine precincts. Buy these at Tōbu Nikkō Station.

Chūzen-ji Onsen
中禅寺温泉

☎0288

This highland area 11.5km west of Nikkō offers some natural seclusion and striking views of Nantai-san from Chūzen-ji's lake, Chūzenji-ko. The lake itself is 161m deep and a fabulous shade of deep blue in good weather with the usual flotilla of sightseeing boats.

Sights

Kegon-no-taki WATERFALL
(華厳ノ滝 Kegon Falls; 2479-2 Chūgūshi; adult/child ¥550/330; ⊙7.30am-6pm May-Sep, 8am-5pm Oct-Apr) The big-ticket attraction of Chūzen-ji is this billowing, 97m-high waterfall. Take the elevator down to a platform to observe the full force of the plunging water or view up high on the viewing platform.

Futarasan-jinja SHRINE
(二荒山神社; 2484 Chūgūshi; ⊙8am-4.30pm) FREE This shrine complements the shrines at Tōshō-gū and is the starting point for pilgrimages up Nantai-san. It's about 1km west of the falls, along the lake's north shore.

Chūzen-ji Tachiki-kannon BUDDHIST TEMPLE
(中禅寺立木観音; 2578 Chūgūshi; adult/child ¥500/200; ⊙8am-4.30pm) This eponymous

temple, located on the lake's eastern shore, was founded in the 8th century and houses a 6m-tall Kannon statue from that time.

Italian Embassy Villa Memorial Park HOUSE, PARK
(イタリアン大使館別荘記念公園; 2482 Chūgūshi; ⌚9am-4.30pm Apr-Nov, closed Mon Apr, May, Nov) FREE The former summer residence of Italy's ambassadors (from 1928 to 1997) has a pleasant sun terrace with excellent views across Chūzen-ji lake. Walking here from the bus station takes around 25 minutes.

Sleeping & Eating

Chūzenji Pension INN ¥
(中禅寺ペンション; ☎0288-55-0888; www.chuzenji-pension.com; 2482 Chūgūshi; r per person from ¥5400;) A salmon-pink-painted hostelry set back from the lake's eastern shore with nine mostly Western-style rooms that feel a bit like grandma's house. It has onsen baths and, in the separate restaurant, a cosy fireplace. Bicycle rental (¥500 per hour) is also available.

Nikkō Lakeside Hotel HOTEL ¥¥¥
(日光レークサイドホテル; ☎0288-55-0321; www.tobuhotel.co.jp/nikkolake; 2482 Chūgūshi; s/d from ¥16,500/25,000;) Although dating to 1894, the rooms here are all blandly modern, but the classy dining room still carries an old-time resort feel and there's a smart cafe with outdoor decking overlooking manicured lawns. The wooden bathhouse with milky sulphuric water is also open to day trippers (¥1000, 12.30pm to 5pm).

KAI Nikko RYOKAN ¥¥¥
(界日光; ☎050-3786-0099; http://kai-nikko.jp/; 1661 Chūgūshi; r per person with two meals ¥30,000;) Hoshino Resorts took over this 20-year-old, 33-room mega-ryokan in 2014 and have given it some contemporary sparkle. Super spacious tatami rooms feature Western-style beds and killer lake views. There are enormous onsen baths and a nightly Nikko Geta folk-dance show. English is spoken and the food is delicious.

Getting There & Away

Buses run from Tōbu Nikkō Station to Chūzen-ji Onsen (¥1150, 45 minutes) or use the economical Tōbu Nikkō Bus Free Pass (p169), available at Tōbu Nikkō Station.

Yumoto Onsen 湯元温泉

Yumoto Onsen is a hot-springs village (quieter than nearby Chūzen-ji Onsen), accessed by bus (¥890, 30 minutes) or by a rewarding three-hour hike on the **Senjōgahara Shizen-kenkyu-rō** (戦場ヶ原自然研究路; Senjōgahara Plain Nature Trail).

For the latter option, take a Yumoto-bound bus and get off at **Ryūzu-no-taki** (竜頭ノ滝; ¥460, 20 minutes), a lovely waterfall overlooked by a teahouse, that marks the start of the trail. The hike follows the Yu-gawa across the picturesque marshland of **Senjōgahara** (mainly on wooden plank paths), alongside the 75m-high falls of **Yu-daki** (湯滝) to the lake **Yu-no-ko** (湯の湖), then around the lake to Yumoto Onsen.

Look for a row of stone lanterns near the final village bus stop that lead to the temple **Onsen-ji** (温泉時; adult/child ¥500/300; ⌚9am-4pm), which has a humble bathhouse (with extremely hot water) and a tatami lounge for resting weary muscles. Should you plan to stay overnight, a luxurious option is **Yu-no-Mori** (ゆの森; ☎0288-62-2800; www.okunikko-yunomori.com; 1662 Yumoto Onsen; r per person with 2 meals from ¥25,000;), with elegant rooms decorated in natural tones.

From Yumoto Onsen you can return to Nikkō by bus (¥1700, 1½ hours).

WEST & SOUTHWEST OF TOKYO

Nature conquers concrete at the western edge of Tokyo, where there's great hiking at Takao-san and in the Oku-Tama Region. Southwest are the classic hot-spring resorts of Hakone and the laid-back seaside onsen and beach towns of the Izu Peninsula.

Takao-san 高尾山

☎042

Gentle Takao-san (599m) is a highly popular day trip from Tokyo with year-round hiking. It's rather built up compared with other regional hikes, but can make for a perfect family outing if you avoid busy weekends and holidays.

One of Takao's chief attractions is the temple **Yaku-ō-in** (薬王院; ☎042-661-1115; www.takaosan.or.jp/english/about.html; 2177 Takaomachi, Hachioji-shi; ⌚24hr) FREE, best known for the **Hi-watari Matsuri** (Fire-Crossing Ceremony), which takes place on the second Sunday in March, near Takaosanguchi Station. Priests walk across hot coals with bare feet amid the ceremonial blowing of conch shells. Members of the public are also welcome to participate.

The most popular **hiking trail** (No 1) leads you past the temple; allow about 3¼ hours return for the 400m ascent. Alternatively, a cable car and a chairlift can take you part of the way up (adult/child one way ¥480/240, return ¥930/460). Keiō line offices have free trail maps in English, or check www.takaotozan.co.jp.

From Shinjuku Station, take the Keiō line (*jun-tokkyū;* ¥370, 47 minutes) to Takaosanguchi. The tourist village, trail entrances, cable car and chairlift are a few minutes away to the right. JR Pass holders can travel to Takao Station on the JR Chūō line (48 minutes) and transfer to the Keiō line to Takaosanguchi (¥120, two minutes).

Oku-Tama Region
奥多摩周辺

☎0428

Oku-Tama is Tokyo's best spot for easy hiking getaways and for river activities along the Tama-gawa. Among the many operators who run rafting and canyoning adventures from near Mitake's train station is Canyons (p286).

From **Takimoto** (滝本) in the valley you can either ride a **cable car** (www.mitaketozan.co.jp; one way/return ¥590/1110; ⊙7.30am-6.30pm), or hike up for around an hour via a beautiful ancient cedar-lined pilgrims' path to **Mitake-san** (御岳山; elevation 939m), a charming old-world mountain hamlet that seems light years from Tokyo's bustle. Another 30 minutes on foot from the terminus, up dozens of steps, is **Musashi Mitake-jinja** (武蔵御嶽神社; ☎0428-78-8500; www.musashimitakejinja.jp; 176 Mitake-san, Ome-shi; ⊙24hr) FREE, a Shintō shrine and pilgrimage site said to date back some 1200 years. The site commands stunning views of the surrounding mountains.

Pick up trail maps at the **Mitake Visitors Centre** (御岳ビジターセンター; ☎0428-78-9363; 38-5 Mitake-san; ⊙9am-4.30pm Tue-Sun), 250m beyond the cable-car station, near the start of the village, close to where you'll find the pilgrims' lodge **Baba-ke Oshi-Jutaku**, an amazing thatched roof building dating from 1866.

The five-hour round-trip **hike** from Musashi Mitake-jinja to the summit of **Ōtake-san** (大岳山; 1266m) is highly recommended. Although there's some climbing involved, it's a fairly easy hike and the views from the summit are excellent – Mt Fuji is visible on clear days.

If you're not spending the night on Mitake-san, note that the cable car operates from 7.30am to 6.30pm.

Sleeping & Eating

Komadori San-sō MINSHUKU ¥
(駒鳥山荘; ☎0428-78-8472; www.komadori.com; 155 Mitake-san, Ome-shi; r per person with shared bathroom from ¥5500, with two meals ¥10,000; @📶) Below Musashi Mitake-jinja, towards the back end of the village, this former pilgrims' inn brims with bric-a-brac and history – it's been in the same family for 17 generations. The rooms and the verandah have excellent views and the friendly English-speaking owners are a delight.

Meals are excellent and you can also arrange to take a dawn hike to stand under a waterfall, an ascetic practice known as *takigyo*.

Mitake Youth Hostel HOSTEL ¥
(御嶽ユースホステル; ☎78-8774; www.jyh.or.jp; 57 Mitake-san, Ome-shi; dm member/non-member ¥2880/3480; 🚭📶) Part of the comfortable ryokan Reiun-sō, this hostel has fine tatami rooms inside a handsome old building that used to be a pilgrims' lodge. It's midway between the top of the cable car and Musashi Mitake-jinja, about a minute beyond the visitors centre.

Momiji-ya NOODLES ¥
(紅葉屋; ☎0428-78-8475; 151 Mitake-san, Ome-shi; mains ¥750-1200; ⊙10am-4.30pm; 📖) Near the gate of Musashi Mitake-jinja, this cosy shop has mountain views out the back windows and *kamonanban soba* (noodles in hearty duck broth).

Getting There & Away

Take the JR Chūō line from Shinjuku Station, changing to the JR Ōme line at Tachikawa Station or Ōme Station depending on the service, and get off at Mitake (¥890, 90 minutes). Buses (¥280, 10 minutes) run from Mitake Station to Takimoto, for the cable car.

WORTH A TRIP

MITO

Capital of Ibaraki Prefecture and a one-time castle town, Mito (水戸) is best known for **Kairaku-en** (偕楽園; ☎029-244-5454; www.koen.pref.ibaraki.jp/park/kairakuen01.html; 1-3-3 Tokiwachō; ⏲6am-7pm mid-Feb–Sep, 7am-6pm Oct–mid-Feb) FREE, one of the three most celebrated landscape gardens in Japan.

Created in 1842 by the *daimyō* of the Mito *han* (domain), a member of the clan of the Tokugawa shogun, Kairaku-en' means 'the garden to enjoy with people', and it was one of the first gardens in the nation to open to the public. Covering 32 acres, the gardens are most popular for their 3000 *ume* (plum-blossom) trees; some 100 varieties bloom in late February or early March. A **plum-blossom festival** happens around this time. The three-storey pavilion **Kobun-tei** (好文亭; admission ¥190; ⏲9am-5pm), within the garden, is a 1950s reproduction of the *daimyō's* villa (the original was destroyed in WWII).

From Tokyo, JR Jōban line trains depart from Ueno Station for Mito (*tokkyū;* ¥3610, 70 minutes). During the plum-blossom festival, connect by local train to Kairaku-en Station (¥200, five minutes); otherwise take a bus to Kairaku-en bus stop (¥250, 15 minutes) or walk (about 30 minutes) from the station's south exit along the lake Senba-ko.

Hakone 箱根

☎0460 / POP 13,200

Offering serene onsen, world-class art museums, traditional inns and spectacular mountain scenery crowned by Mt Fuji, Hakone can make for a blissful escape from Tokyo. **Ashino-ko** (芦ノ湖) is the lake at the centre of it all, the setting for the iconic image of Mt Fuji with the *torii* gate of the Hakone-jinja rising from the water.

Naturally, it's popular, particularly on weekends and holidays when it can get very busy. If you follow the herd, it can also feel highly packaged. To beat the crowds, plan your trip during the week, go hiking and sample some of Hakone's off-beat gems.

Information

Try www.hakone.or.jp/en for online information.

Hakone-Yumoto Tourist Information Center (☎0460-85-8911; www.hakone.or.jp; ⏲9am-5.45pm) Make your first stop at the most clued-up of several tourist information centres scattered around Hakone. This is the best place for maps and information about hiking trails and all the attractions. Staffed by helpful English speakers, it's across the main road from the train station.

Getting There & Away

The Odakyū line (www.odakyu.jp) from Shinjuku Station goes directly into Hakone-Yumoto, the region's transit hub. Use either the convenient Romance Car (¥2080, 90 minutes) or *kyūkō* (regular-express) service (¥1190, two hours); the latter may require a transfer at Odawara.

JR Pass holders can take the Kodama *shinkansen* (¥3880, 50 minutes) or the JR Tōkaidō line (*futsū* ¥1790, one hour; *tokkyū* ¥2390, one hour) from Tokyo Station or the Shōnan-Shinjuku line from Shinjuku (¥1490, 80 minutes) to Odawara and change there for trains or buses for Hakone-Yumoto.

The narrow-gauge, switchback Hakone-Tōzan line runs from Odawara via Hakone-Yumoto to Gōra (¥670, one hour).

Getting Around

Part of Hakone's popularity comes from the chance to ride assorted *norimono* (modes of transport): switchback train (from Hakone-Yumoto to Gōra), cable car (funicular), ropeway (gondola), ship and bus. Check out www.odakyu.jp/english/course/hakone, which describes this circuit.

BOAT

From Tōgendai, sightseeing boats criss-cross Ashino-ko to Hakone-machi and Moto-Hakone (adult/child ¥1000/500, 30 minutes).

BUS

The Hakone-Tōzan and Izu Hakone bus companies service the Hakone area, linking most of the sights. Hakone-Tōzan buses, included in the Hakone Freepass, run between Hakone-machi and Odawara (¥1180, 55 minutes) and between Moto-Hakone and Hakone-Yumoto (¥960, 35 minutes).

CABLE CAR & ROPEWAY

Gōra is the terminus of the Hakone-Tōzan railway and the beginning of the cable car to Sōun-zan, from where you can catch the Hakone Ropeway line to Ōwakudani and Tōgendai.

LUGGAGE FORWARDING

At Hakone-Yumoto Station, deposit your luggage with **Hakone Baggage Service** (箱根キャリーサービス; 0460-86-4140; per piece from ¥800; 8.30am-7pm) by noon, and it will be delivered to your inn within Hakone from 3pm. Hakone Freepass holders get a discount of ¥100 per bag.

Hakone-Yumoto 箱根湯元温泉

This onsen resort town, spanning the Sukomo River, is the starting point for most visits to Hakone. Though heavily visited, it offers a high concentration of good onsen, the main attraction here.

Sights & Activities

Kei Hiraga Museum MUSEUM
(平賀敬美術館; www.hiraga-key-museum.com; 613 Yumoto; adult/child ¥600/300; 10am-5pm Fri-Tue) Dedicated to the sometimes sexually explicit, Pigalle-inspired paintings of Kei Hiraga (1936–2000), this museum is run by the late artist's wife in their old-style villa. Combine admiring the art with a soak in the villa's onsen for an extra fee of ¥500. Cross the Haya-kawa at Yumoto-bashi and take the first right; the museum is down a small lane.

★**Hakone Yuryō** ONSEN
(箱根湯寮; 0460-85-8411; www.hakoneyuryo.jp; 4 Tonosawa; adult/child ¥1400/700, private baths from ¥3900; 10am-8pm Mon-Fri, 10am-9pm Sat & Sun) A free shuttle bus will whisk you in three minutes from Hakone-Yumoto station to this idyllic onsen complex ensconced in the forest. The *rotemburo* are spacious, and leaf shaded. There are also private ones you can book in advance. No tattoos allowed.

It's about a five-minute walk from Tonosawa Station on the Hakone-Tōzan line.

Tenzan Tōji-kyō ONSEN
(天山湯治郷; www.tenzan.jp; 208 Yumoto-chaya; adult/child ¥1300/650; 9am-10pm) Soak in *rotemburo* of varying temperatures and designs (one is constructed to resemble a natural cave) at this large, popular bath 2km southwest of town. To get here, take the 'B' course shuttle bus from the bridge outside the Hakone-Yumoto Station (¥100). Tattoos are allowed.

Furasato ONSEN
(ふるさと; 0460-85-5559; www.hakone-furusato.com; 191 Yumoto-chaya; admission ¥850; 9am-6pm Mon-Fri, to 8pm Sat & Sun) This classy ryokan has atmospheric *rotemburo* and indoor onsen that are open to day trippers. A minibus runs here from Hakone-Yumoto station (¥100; 9am to 6.30pm)

Sleeping

Hakone-no-Mori Okada HOTEL ¥
(箱根の森おかだ; 0460-85-6711; www.hakonenomori-okada.jp; 191 Yumoto-chaya; r per person from ¥6100;) Offers pleasant Western- and Japanese-style rooms at reasonable room-only rates; two meals start from around ¥3000 per person extra. Guests have free access to **Yu-no-Sato** (湯の里; 0460-85-3955; www.yunosato-y.jp; 191 Yumoto-chaya; adult/child ¥1400/600; 11am-11pm) onsen.

Omiya Ryokan RYOKAN ¥¥
(0460-85-7345; www.o-miya.com; 116 Yumoto-chaya; r with breakfast from ¥9300, weekends with 2 meals ¥13,400;) Lower weekday prices make this simple ryokan an attractive proposition for its tatami rooms, some with mountain views. There's a small indoor onsen. To get here, take the 'B' course bus from Hakone-Yumoto Station.

★**Fukuzumirō** RYOKAN ¥¥¥
(福住楼; 0460-85-5301; www.fukuzumi-ro.com; 74 Tōnozawa; s/d per person incl 2 meals from ¥22,150/38,000;) This exquisite 125-year-old inn sports detailed woodwork, public

HAKONE TRAVEL PASSES

Odakyū's **Hakone Freepass**, available at Odakyū stations and Odakyū Travel branches, is an excellent deal, covering the return fare to Hakone and unlimited use of most modes of transport within the region, plus other discounts at museums and facilities in the area. It's available as a two-day pass (adult/child from Shinjuku ¥5140/1500, from Odawara if you're not planning on returning to Shinjuku ¥4000/1000) or a three-day pass (adult/child from Shinjuku ¥5640/1750, from Odawara ¥4500/1250). Freepass-holders need to pay an additional limited-express surcharge (¥890 each way) to ride the Romance Car.

If you plan to combine Hakone with Mt Fuji, also consider the **Fuji Hakone Pass** (adult/child ¥7400/3700), a three-day pass offering discount round-trip travel from Shinjuku as well as unlimited use of most transportation in the two areas.

Hakone Region

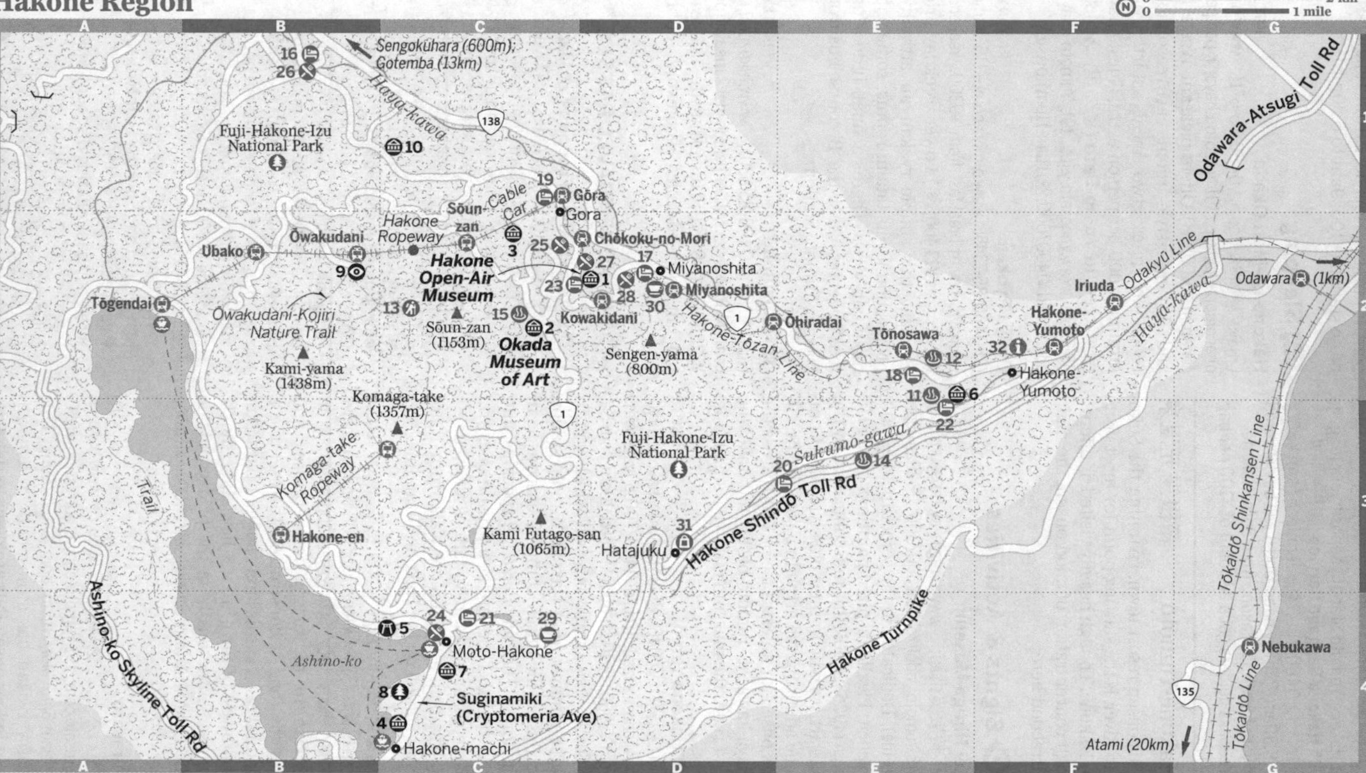

Hakone Region

Top Sights

1	Hakone Open-Air Museum	D2
2	Okada Museum of Art	C2

Sights

	Hakone Geomuseum	(see 9)
3	Hakone Museum of Art	C2
4	Hakone Sekisho	C4
5	Hakone-jinja	C4
6	Kei Hiraga Museum	E2
7	Narukawa Art Museum	C4
8	Onshi Hakone Kōen	C4
9	Ōwakudani	B2
10	Pola Museum of Art	C1

Activities, Courses & Tours

11	Furasato	E2
12	Hakone Yuryō	E2
13	Sōun-zan	C2
14	Tenzan Tōji-kyō	E3
15	Yunessun	C2
	Yu-No-Sato	(see 11)

Sleeping

16	Fuji Hakone Guest House	B1
17	Fujiya Hotel	D2
18	Fukuzumirō	E2
	Hakone Sengokuhara Youth Hostel	(see 16)
19	Hakone Tent	C1
	Hakone-no-Mori Okada	(see 11)
20	KAI Hakone	E3
21	Moto-Hakone Guesthouse	C4
22	Omiya Ryokan	E3
23	Yudokoro Chōraku	C2

Eating

24	Bakery & Table	C4
25	Gyōza Center	C2
26	Hanasai	B1
	Itoh Dining by Nobu	(see 3)
27	Kappeizushi	D2
28	Miyafuji	D2

Drinking & Nightlife

29	Amazake-chaya	C4
30	Naraya Cafe	D2

Shopping

31	Hatajuku Yosegi Kaikan	D3

Information

32	Hakone-Yumoto Tourist Information Center	F2

onsen baths and rooms with sun terraces with views of the Haya-kawa; the small, quiet room overlooking the garden was a favourite of author Kawabata Yasunori. It's about 10 minutes' walk down from Tōnozawa Station on the Hakone-Tōzan railway, or a short taxi ride from Hakone-Yumoto.

KAI Hakone RYOKAN ¥¥¥

(界箱根; ☎050-3786-0099; http://global.hoshinoresort.com/kai_hakone/; 230 Yumoto-chaya; s/d with 2 meals from ¥31,000/62,000; @ 📶) Less than a 10-minute bus ride from Hakone-Yumoto, this sleek resort is nestled amid soaring stands of bamboo, and overlooks the river. Spacious rooms mix traditional and contemporary styles. Highlights include infinity-style onsen pools, English-speaking staff and delicious *kaiseki* meals.

Miyanoshita & Kowakidani 宮ノ下・小涌谷

The first worthwhile stop on the Hakone-Tōzan railway towards Gōra, Miyanoshita has antique shops along the main road and a pleasant **hiking** trail skirting up 800m Sengen-yama (浅間山). The trailhead is just below Fujiya Hotel, marked by a shrine. Next stop along is Kowakidani, home to a giant onsen complex and the highly impressive collection of the Okada Museum of Art.

Sights & Activities

★ Okada Museum of Art MUSEUM

(岡田美術館; ☎0460-87-3931; www.okada-museum.com; 483-1 Kowakidani; adult/student ¥2800/1800; ⏰9am-4.30pm) Showcasing the dazzling Japanese, Chinese and Korean art treasures of industrialist Okada Kazuo, this mammoth museum should not be missed. You could spend hours marvelling at the beauty of so many pieces, including detailed screen paintings and exquisite pottery. The museum is opposite the Kowakien stop.

An outdoor footbath cafe-restaurant in a traditional wooden villa and lush hillside garden merging into the forest round out the experience.

Yunessun ONSEN

(箱根小涌園ユネッサン; www.yunessun.com; 1297 Ninotaira; Yunessun adult/child ¥2900/1600, Mori-no-Yu adult/child ¥1900/1200, both ¥4100/2100; ⏰9am-7pm Mar-Oct, 9am-6pm Nov-Feb) Best described as an onsen amusement park with a variety of baths and outdoor water slides, Yunessun is mixed bathing so bring a swimsuit; the connected

Mori-no-Yu complex (11am to 9pm) is traditional single-sex bathing. Take a bus from Hakone-machi, Gōra or Hakone-Yumoto to the Kowakien stop. There's also a variety of accommodation here.

Sleeping & Eating

Fujiya Hotel HOTEL ¥¥¥
(富士屋ホテル; 0460-82-2211; www.fujiyahotel.jp; 359 Miyanoshita; d from ¥21,670;) One of Japan's finest Western-heritage hotels, the beautifully detailed Fujiya opened in 1878 and played host to Charlie Chaplin back in the day (Room 45). Now sprawled across several wings, it remains dreamily elegant. It's worth a visit to soak up the retro atmosphere, stroll through the hillside gardens and greenhouse, and to have tea in the lounge.

Miyafuji SUSHI ¥¥
(鮨みやふじ; www.miyanoshita.com/miyafuji/index.html; 310 Miyanoshita; meals from ¥1680; 11.30am-3pm & 5.30-8pm Fri-Wed;) A short walk uphill from Fujiya Hotel this friendly sushi shop is known for its *aji-don* (brook trout over rice). Look for the English sign.

Naraya Cafe CAFE ¥¥
(ナラヤカフェ; 404-13 Miyanoshita; coffee from ¥350; 10.30am-6pm, closed Wed) Beside the station, this woodsy cafe and craft store is a pleasant pit stop for drinks and light meals. You can also soak your toes in the footbath on the terrace looking out over the mountains.

Chōkoku-no-mori & Gōra
彫刻の森・強羅

Chōkoku-no-mori is the stop for the Hakone Open-Air Museum, one of the area's top attractions. The Hakone-Tōzan line terminates at the next station Gōra, which is the starting point for the funicular and cable-car trip to Tōgendai on Ashino-ko.

Sights & Activities

★Hakone Open-Air Museum MUSEUM
(彫刻の森美術館; www.hakone-oam.or.jp; 1121 Ninotaira; adult/child ¥1600/800; 9am-4.30pm) On a rolling, leafy hillside setting, this safari for art lovers includes an impressive selection of 19th- and 20th-century Japanese and Western sculptures (including works by Henry Moore, Rodin and Miró) as well as an excellent Picasso Pavilion with more than 300 works ranging from paintings and glass art to tapestry.

Kids will love the giant crochet artwork/playground with its Jengalike exterior walls. End the day by soaking your feet in the outdoor footbath. Hakone Freepass holders get ¥200 off the admission price.

Hakone Museum of Art MUSEUM
(箱根美術館; www.moaart.or.jp; 1300 Gōra; adult/child ¥900/free; 9.30am-4.30pm, closed Thu) Sharing grounds with a lovely velvety moss garden and teahouse (¥700 *matcha* green tea and sweet), this museum has a collection of Japanese pottery dating from as far back as the Jōmon period (some 5000 years ago). The gardens are spectacular in autumn.

Sleeping & Eating

★Hakone Tent HOSTEL ¥
(050-5874-1900; http://hakonetent.com; 1320-257 Gōra; dm/s/d/tr with shared bathroom ¥3500/4000/9000/13,500;) Best hostel by far in Hakone, with an ace contemporary design blending punk and trad elements in a stylish makeover of a rundown ryokan to include a sleek, wooden lobby bar and lounge. Shin, Candy and their mates, the friendly young Japanese who run the place, got the place started through crowdfunding.

Yudokoro Chōraku RYOKAN ¥
(湯処長楽; 0460-82-2192; 525 Kowakudani; r per person from ¥5150) Simple, homely ryokan with lovely owners, spacious tatami rooms with kitchenettes and onsen bath, and outdoor barrel tubs (available for outside guests, ¥550). It's a 10-minute walk uphill from the Hakone Open-Air Museum, on the left.

Eating

Gyōza Center JAPANESE ¥
(餃子センター; 0460-82-3457; www.gyozacenter.com; 1300 Gōra; mains from ¥800; 11.30am-3pm & 5-8pm, closed Sat;) The humble *gyōza* (dumpling) stars at this cosy, long-running restaurant in a dozen different varieties. No vegetarian options though, unfortunately. It's between Gōra and Chōkoku-no-mori Stations on a corner, with an English sign.

Kappeizushi SUSHI ¥
(かっ平寿し; 0460-82-3278; 1143-49 Ninotaira; meals from ¥1000; 10am-8pm Wed-Mon;) A few doors downhill from the Hakone Open-Air Museum, this friendly sushi place also does tasty *chirashi-zushi* (rice topped with assorted sashimi). Look for the small sign in the window.

Itoh Dining by Nobu JAPANESE ¥¥¥
(☎0460-83-8209; http://www.itoh-dining.co.jp/; 1300-64 Gōra; lunch/dinner from ¥3000/7000; ⊙11.30am-3pm & 5-9pm) Savour some premium Japanese beef, cooked *teppanyaki*-style in front of you by the chef at this elegant restaurant, a branch of the celeb chef Nobu's dining empire. It's just uphill from Koenshimo station on the funicular, one stop from Gōra.

Sōun-zan & Sengokuhara 早雲山・仙石原

From Gōra, continue to near the 1153m-high summit of Sōun-zan by cable car (¥410, 10 minutes) then transfer to the **Hakone Ropeway**, a 30-minute, 4km gondola ride to Tōgendai (one way/return ¥1330/2340), stopping at Ōwakudani en route. In fine weather Mt Fuji looks fabulous from here.

Tōgendai can also be reached by road from Sengokuhara, a sizeable town with some good-value lodgings, places to eat and various niche interest museums, of which the Pola Museum of Art is by far the best.

Sights & Activities

Pola Museum of Art MUSEUM
(www.polamuseum.or.jp; 1285 Kozukayama; adult/child ¥1800/700; ⊙9am-4.30pm) Showcasing the top-drawer collection of the late Suzuki Tsuneshi, son of the founder of the Pola Group (cosmetics company), this quality museum is located in an equally impressive architecturally designed building. Artworks in the collection include those from such famous names as Van Gogh, Cézanne, Renoir, Matisse, Picasso and Rodin.

Ōwakudani VOLCANO
(大桶谷; www.kanagawa-park.or.jp/owakudani) FREE The 'Great Boiling Valley' was created 3000 years ago when Kami-yama erupted and collapsed, also forming Ashino-ko. Hydrogen sulfide steams from the ground here and the hot water is used to boil onsen *tamago*, eggs blackened in the sulphurous waters, which you can buy to eat (they're fine inside).

The **Ōwakudani-Tōgendai Nature Trail** is a one-hour hike you can do here but don't linger if the toxic gases are strong as they are dangerous.

Hakone Geomuseum MUSEUM
(☎0460-83-8140; www.hakone-geomuseum.jp; 1251 Sengokuhara; adult/child ¥300/200; ⊙9am-4.30pm) In a gift shop and restaurant complex opposite the ropeway station, this well-designed natural history exhibit is a fun way to learn about the volcanic forces that created Hakone. Good for kids and curious adults.

Sōun-zan HIKING
There are various hiking trails on this mountain including one to Kami-yama (1¾ hours) and another up to Ōwakudani (1¼ hours). The latter is sometimes closed due to the mountain's toxic gases. Check at the tourist information office.

Sleeping & Eating

Hakone Sengokuhara Youth Hostel HOSTEL ¥
(箱根仙石原ユースホステル; ☎0460-84-8966; www.theyh.com; dm members/nonmembers ¥3822/4470, r per person ¥5400) This hostel, adjacent to and also run by the Fuji Hakone Guest House, has Japanese-style shared and private rooms. Rates rise by ¥1000 to ¥2000 in high seasons. Use of the outdoor bath is ¥500 per person for 30 minutes.

Fuji Hakone Guest House GUESTHOUSE ¥¥
(富士箱根ゲストハウス; ☎0460-84-6577; www.fujihakone.com; 912 Sengokuhara; s/d from ¥6500/11,100) Run by a welcoming English-speaking family, this guesthouse has handsome tatami rooms, cosy indoor and outdoor onsen with divine volcanic waters, and a wealth of information on sights and hiking in the area. Take the T-course bus to Senkyōrō-mae from Odawara Station (stop 4; ¥1050, 50 minutes) or Tōgendai (¥380, 10 minutes). There's an English sign close by.

Hanasai JAPANESE ¥
(花菜; ☎0460-84-0666; 919 Sengokuhara; mains from ¥1000; ⊙11.30am-2.30pm & 5.30-9pm Wed-Mon) Slurp noodles and tuck into hearty traditional stews as you soak up the old Japanese atmosphere of this friendly family-run restaurant. It's a few minutes' walk from Fuji Hakone Guest House.

Hakone-machi & Moto-Hakone 箱根町・元箱根

The sightseeing boats across Ashino-ko deposit you at either of these two towns, both well touristed and with sights of historical interest.

Sights

Hakone Sekisho MUSEUM
(箱根関所, Hakone Checkpoint Museum; www.hakonesekisyo.jp; 1 Hakone-machi; adult/child

¥500/250; ⌚9am-4.30pm Mar-Nov, to 4pm Dec-Feb) You're free to walk through this 2007 reconstruction of the feudal-era checkpoint on the Old Tōkaidō Hwy, but if you want to enter any of the buildings you'll need to buy a ticket. One displays Darth Vader–like armour and grisly implements used on law-breakers. There's basic English explanations on only some displays.

Narukawa Art Museum MUSEUM
(成川美術館; ☎0460-83-6828; www.narukawamuseum.co.jp; 570 Moto-Hakone; adult/child ¥1200/800; ⌚9am-5pm) Art comes in two forms here – in the exquisite Japanese-style paintings, *nihonga*, on display, and in the stunning Mt Fuji views from the panorama lounge looking out across the lake. Don't miss the cool kaleidoscope displays.

Hakone-jinja SHINTO SHRINE
(箱根神社; ⌚9am-4pm) A pleasant stroll around Ashino-ko follows a cedar-lined path to this shrine set in a wooded grove, in Moto-Hakone. Its signature red *torii* (gate) rises from the lake; get your camera ready for that picture-postcard shot.

Onshi Hakone Kōen PARK
(恩賜箱根公園; 171 Moto-Hakone; ⌚9am-4.30pm) FREE On a small peninsula near the Hakone Sekisho is this scenic park. Don't miss the elegant hilltop Western-style building, once used by the imperial family, and now a lovely cafe; weather permitting it has Fuji views across the lake.

DON'T MISS

OLD HAKONE HIGHWAY

Up the hill from the lakeside Moto-Hakone bus stop is the entrance to the stone-paved Old Hakone Hwy (箱根旧街道), part of the Edo-era Tokkaidō Hwy that connected the shogun's capital with Kyoto. You can walk back to Hakone-Yumoto via the trail through the woods, which will take about 3½ hours.

About 30 minutes' walk from Moto-Hakone you'll also pass wonderful **Amazake-chaya** (甘酒茶屋; 395-1 Futoko-yama; drinks & snacks from ¥400; ⌚7am-5.30pm) and the small village of **Hatajuku** (畑宿), where you can visit the **Hatajuku Yosegi Kaikan** (畑宿寄木会館; ☎0460-85-8170; 103 Hakone-machi) to find out more about the craft of marquetry practiced in the area.

Sleeping & Eating

Moto-Hakone Guesthouse MINSHUKU ¥
(元箱根ゲストハウス; ☎0460-83-7880; www.fujihakone.com; 103 Moto-Hakone; dm/s/tw/tr without bathroom ¥3780/4860/9180/14,040;) Offering simple but pleasant Japanese-style rooms and common areas with laundry and kitchen facilities. Breakfast is ¥750. From Odawara Station, take the platform 3 bus to Hakone-machi or Moto-Hakone and get off at Ōshiba (¥1130, one hour); the guesthouse is a one-minute walk away.

Bakery & Table INTERNATIONAL ¥¥
(☎0460-85-1530; www.bthjapan.com; 9-1 Moto-Hakone; mains ¥1000-2500) There are options that appeal to everyone at this lakeside venue with a footbath terrace outside. The take-out bakery is on the ground floor, a cafe is one floor up and the restaurant serving fancy open sandwiches and crêpes is above that.

Izu Peninsula 伊豆半島

The Izu Peninsula (Izu-hantō), about 100km southwest of Tokyo in Shizuoka Prefecture, is where the famed *Kurofune* (Black Ships) of US Commodore Perry dropped anchor in 1854. Contemporary Izu has a cool surfer vibe, lush greenery, rugged coastlines and abundant onsen. Weekends and holidays see crowds descend on the east coast, particularly in summer. It's generally quieter on the rugged west coast, which has, weather permitting, Mt Fuji views over Suruga-wan.

Atami 熱海

☎0557 / POP 40,000

The onsen and seaside resort of Atami is both the gateway to Izu, and its largest town. Despite its dramatic hillside location, rampant development has robbed it of charm.

However, well worth a look before striking out for the rest of the peninsula is the hilltop **MOA Museum of Art** (MOA美術館; ☎0557-84-2511; www.moaart.or.jp; 26-2 Momoyama-chō; adult/student ¥1600/800; ⌚9.30am-4.30pm, closed Thu), which sports an excellent collection of Japanese and Chinese pottery and paintings, spanning more than 1000 years and including national treasures. It also has a serene tea garden set among Japanese maples and bubbling brooks. Almost stealing the show is MOA's grandiose entrance, with escalators leading up 200m past ceilings that glow in changing neon colours that make you feel like you're about to board a spaceship. Buses run here from platform 8 outside Atami Station (¥170, eight minutes). Otherwise you can get here via the **Yu-Yu bus** (tickets ¥700) if you plan to spend the day sightseeing.

Sun Beach is an attractive sight in the evening, with its sands illuminated by coloured floodlights.

If you plan to hang around, **Toyoko-Inn** (0557-86-1045; www.toyoko-inn.com; 12-4 Kasuga-chō; s/d incl breakfast from ¥5840/6980; @) has well-priced, comfortable rooms.

Atami Tourist Office (0557-81-5279; http://shizuokatourism.com/atami-city/; 9am-5.30pm Apr-Sep, 9am-5pm Oct-Mar), on the right as you exit Atami Station, has discount tickets to MOA (¥1400) as well as town maps.

Getting There & Away

JR trains run from Tokyo Station to Atami on the Tōkaidō line (Kodama *shinkansen* ¥3670, 50 minutes; Odoriko ¥3280, 1¼ hours; Acty *kaisoku* ¥1940, 1½ hours).

Tokai Kisen (03-5472-9999; www.tokaikisen.co.jp) runs hydrofoils from Atami port to the island of Ō-Shima (¥5790, 45 minutes). Prices are seasonal. To reach Atami port, take the bus from platform 7 at Atami station (¥230).

Itō & Around 伊東

0557

This commendably laid-back seaside town sports some wonderful ryokan and onsen that provide a perfect antidote to the hectic city pace.

Sights & Activities

Tōkaikan HISTORIC BUILDING

(東海館; 12-10 Higashi Matsubara-chō; adult/child ¥200/100; 9am-9pm, tearoom 10am-5pm) Next to K's House hostel, this inn, established in 1928, is now a national monument for its elegant woodwork. Each of its three storeys was designed by a different architect. Architecture buffs will love it and there's a convivial tearoom with river views on the ground floor. Pay ¥500 if you wish to take a dip in its onsen baths (big and small, alternating daily between male and female).

Ikeda Museum of 20th Century Art MUSEUM

(池田20世紀美術館; 0557-45-2211; www.nichireki.co.jp/ikeda; 614 Totari; adult/child ¥1000/500; 9am-5pm, closed Wed) Art lovers will not want to miss out on this treasure trove of big names, such as Dalí, Warhol, Picasso, Lichtenstein and Miró, all on show in an abstract silver cube-shaped building. Take the bus from platform 6 at Itō Station (¥680, 30 minutes).

Mt Ōmuro MOUNTAIN

(大室山; return chairlift ¥500; 9am-4pm) From Izu's seashore you can see this grassy dormant rice-bowl volcano peaking above the hills. Ride the four-minute chairlift to the 580m summit where you can take in coastal views of Mt Fuji. There's a 1km walk around the crater, bizarrely enough with an archery centre in the middle. Take the bus bound for Shaboten Kōen and Ōmuroyama from Itō Station (¥710, 40 minutes).

Nagisa Park PARK

At the southern end of Orange Beach, a short walk from K's House, this grassy park is studded with photogenic bronze sculptures by local artist Shigeoka Kenji.

Ryokufuen ONSEN

(緑風園; 0557-37-1885; www.ryokufuen.com; 3-1 Otonashi-chō; admission ¥1000; 1.30-10pm) Soak away in this tranquil *rotemburo* with its rocky waterfall under a canopy of trees. K's House guests receive a 50% discount with voucher. Follow the river inland from K's House and you'll reach it in less than 10 minutes; it's next to Otonashi-jinja.

Yokikan ONSEN

(0557-37-3101; www.yokikan.co.jp; 2-24 Suehiro-chō; admission ¥1000; 11am-3pm) Part of a hotel, this outdoor rooftop *rotemburo* has the novelty of only being accessible via a rickety in-house funicular. It's mixed bathing, with distant views over the town and the water.

Hotel Sun Hatoya ONSEN

(ホテルサンハトヤ; 0557-36-4126; www.sunhatoya.co.jp; 572-12 Oyukawa; adult/child ¥2000/1500; 8.30am-7pm) In a region famous for onsen, it's not surprising people are starting to get creative: this plush bathhouse boasts not only ocean views, but fish-tank-lined walls full of colourful fish, turtles and sharks.

Jōgasaki HIKING

(城ヶ崎) South of Itō is the striking Jōgasaki coast, with its windswept cliffs formed by lava. A moderately strenuous cliffside hike (about 6.5km), with volcanic rock and pine forests, winds south of the sci-fi–looking lighthouse to Izu-Kōgen Station. Add on

Izu Peninsula

Izu Peninsula

Sights
1 Gyokusenji B5
2 Shuzen-ji Treasure Museum B2

Sleeping
Ernest House .... (see 6)
3 Kanaya Ryokan B4
4 Seaside Dōgashima A3
5 Umibe-no-Kakureyu A3
6 Wabi Sabi B5

Eating
Cafe Mellow .... (see 6)
7 South Cafe B5

another 1.5km for the walk from Jōgasaki-kaigan Station to the coast.

Along the way you'll cross the 48m-long **Kadowaki-no-Umi** suspension bridge with waves crashing 23m below. From Itō Station, take the Jōgasaki-guchi bound bus (¥700, 40 minutes) to the lighthouse.

Sleeping

★ **K's House Itō Onsen** HOSTEL ¥
(ケイズハウス伊東温泉; ☎0557-35-9444; http://kshouse.jp/ito-e/index.html; 12-13 Higashi Matsubara-chō; dm from ¥2950, s/d per person from ¥3900/3400;) A 100-year-old

ryokan with a charming riverside setting full of carp and heron, K's House is the real reason to come to Itō. The Japanese-style dorms, private rooms and common areas are beautifully maintained and classically stylish. With a fully equipped kitchen, bicycle rental, helpful staff, and public and private onsen, this is an outstanding deal.

Yamaki Ryokan RYOKAN ¥¥

(山喜旅館; ☎0557-37-4123; www.ito-yamaki.co.jp; 4-7 Higashi Matsubara-chō; r per person from ¥5400;) A block east of the Tōkaikan is this charming wooden inn from the 1940s with an onsen bath and pleasant rooms, some with ocean views. Limited English. Ask for reservations at the Tourist Information Center.

Eating & Drinking

For a small seaside town, Itō is jam-packed with eateries and small bars. Fish, predictably, is a local speciality.

Kunihachi IZAKAYA ¥

(国八; 12-13 Higashimatsubara-chō; dishes ¥370-800; 5.30pm-midnight;) A cute *izakaya* cluttered with eclectic decor. The menu caters to all with cheap and tasy dishes such as jumbo *okonomiyaki* alongside more adventurous options like fried crocodile and horse or deer sashimi. It has a great vegetarian selection, too.

Hamazushi SUSHI ¥

(はま寿司; 546-40 Oyukawa; sushi Mon-Fri/Sat & Sun from ¥90/100; 11am-10.30pm;) In a town famous for fish, it says something about this *kaiten-sushi* (sushi train) place that people are prepared to queue for cheap and tasty morsels of seafood. Opposite the beach near Marine Town.

Fuji Ichi SUSHI ¥¥

(ふじいち; www.fujiichi.com/eng.html; 7-6 Shizumi-chō; sets from ¥1500; 10am-3pm Mon-Fri, to 3.30pm Sat & Sun) The coastal road is lined with restaurants and fishmongers – this is both. Run by a laid-back Japanese Kiwi, this casual upstairs eatery is noted for its grilled fish and squid (cooked DIY on hot plates), but you can't miss with the sashimi set (*sashimi teishoku*, ¥1100). Heading south, it's a block past the Aoki supermarket on the right.

Izu Kogen Brewery PUB FOOD ¥¥

(www.izubeer.com/; Marine Town, 571-19 Oyukawa; pizzas from ¥1000; 10am-9pm) Enjoy delicious thin-crust pizzas while sipping microbrewed beer and looking out to the sea. Then soak your toes in the foot onsen outside afterwards. Can life get any better?

Freaks BAR

(2-3 Matsukawa-chō; 8pm-1am) Intimate bar spinning soul and funk vinyl, on the main road towards the station from K's House.

Information

For online info, check out www.itospa.com.

Tourist Information Center (☎0557-37-6105; 9am-5pm) Across from Itō Station with helpful, English-speaking staff, loads of info on the Izu Peninsula and a detailed Itō map.

Getting There & Away

The JR limited-express Odoriko service runs from Tokyo Station to Itō (¥3610, one hour and 40 minutes). Itō is connected to Atami by the JR Itō line (¥320, 22 minutes).

From Itō, the Izukyūkō (aka Izukyū) line goes to Shimoda (¥1620, 1 hour), stopping at Jōgasaki-kaigan (¥580, 25 minutes). There are six buses daily to Shuzen-ji (¥1130, one hour).

Shimoda 下田

☎0558 / POP 24,000

Shimoda holds a pivotal place in Japan's history as the spot where the nation officially opened to the outside world after centuries of near isolation. The small port's laid-back vibe is also perfectly suited to an exploration of its surrounding beaches, which are some of the best in Izu.

Sights

★Perry Road STREET

It takes less than 10 minutes to walk the length of this quaint cobbled street shadowing a narrow canal to Ryōsen-ji. However, the appealing ambience of old houses under willow trees, now occupied by cafes, jazz bars, boutique shops and restaurants, will encourage you to linger.

Ryōsen-ji & Chōraku-ji BUDDHIST TEMPLE

FREE A 15-minute walk south of Shimoda Station is **Ryōsen-ji** (了仙寺), site of the treaty that opened Shimoda, signed by Commodore Perry and representatives of the Tokugawa shogunate. The temple's **Black Ship Art Gallery** (了仙寺宝物館; Hōmotsukan; 3-12-12 Shimoda; adult/child ¥500/150; 8.30am-5pm) displays artefacts relating to Perry, the Black Ships, and Japan as seen through foreign eyes and vice versa.

Shimoda

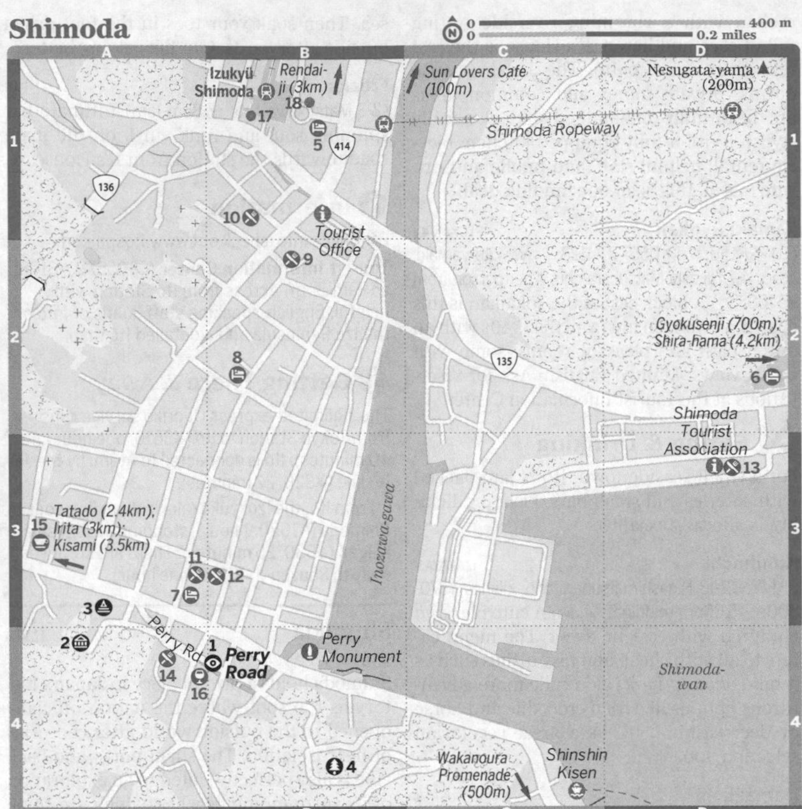

Behind and up the steps from Ryōsen-ji is **Chōraku-ji** (長楽寺), where a Russo-Japanese treaty was signed in 1854; look for the cemetery and *namako-kabe* (black-and-white lattice-patterned) walls.

Gyokusenji TEMPLE
(玉泉寺; www1.ocn.ne.jp/~gyokusen/; 31-6 Kakisaki; museum adult/child ¥400/200; 8am-5pm) Founded in 1590, this Zen temple is most famous as the first Western consulate in Japan, established in 1856. A small **museum** has artefacts of the life of American Townsend Harris, the first consul general. It's a 25-minute walk from Shimoda Station, or take bus 9 to Kakisaki-jinja-mae (¥170, five minutes).

Shimoda Kōen & Wakanoura Promenade Park PARK
(下田公園・和歌の浦遊歩道) If you keep walking east from Perry Rd, you'll reach the pleasant hillside park of Shimoda Kōen, which overlooks the bay. It's loveliest in June, when the hydrangeas are in bloom.

Tours

Shimoda International Club TOUR
(sicshimoda@yahoo.co.jp) Offers guided tours (¥200 per person) on weekends and holidays.

Sleeping

Yamane Ryokan RYOKAN ¥
(やまね旅館; 0558-22-0482; 1-19-15 Shimoda; r per person from ¥4500) You wouldn't guess this place has been running for over 60 years from its tidy, well-maintained Japanese-style rooms. The owner speaks little English but is very friendly and the central location is excellent. Facilities are shared; breakfast is available for ¥1000.

Ōizu Ryokan RYOKAN ¥
(大伊豆旅館; 0558-22-0123; 3-3-25 Shimoda; r per person ¥3500) Offering plain but comfy

Shimoda

Top Sights
1 Perry Road........B4

Sights
2 Black Ship Art Gallery........A4
3 Ryōsen-ji & Chōraku-ji........A3
4 Shimoda Kōen & Wakanoura Promenade Park........B4

Sleeping
5 Hotel Marseille........B1
6 Kurofune Hotel........D2
7 Ōizu Ryokan........A3
8 Yamane Ryokan........B2

Eating
9 Gorosaya........B2
10 Musashi........B1
11 Nami Nami........A3
12 Porto Caro........B3
13 Ra-Maru........D3
14 Shimoda Kappou Enn........A4

Drinking & Nightlife
15 Cubstar........A3
16 Soul Bar Tosaya........A4

Transport
17 Nippon Rent-a-Car........B1
18 Toyota Rent-a-Car........B1

Japanese-style rooms, with shared bathrooms that include a two-seater onsen. It's at the southern end of town, two blocks north of Perry Rd. Check-in is from 3pm and reservations are advised as it is sometimes closed during the week.

Hotel Marseille BUSINESS HOTEL ¥¥
(0558-23-8000; www.hotel-marseilles.jp; 1-1-5 Higashi Hongo; s/d from ¥8000/15,500;) The Marseille adds a little *je ne sais quoi* to the standard business-hotel offering with well-maintained, pleasant rooms and a tea lounge offering guests free coffee in the morning.

Kurofune Hotel HOTEL ¥¥¥
(黒船ホテル; 0558-22-1234; www.kurofune-hotel.com; 3-8 Kakizaki; r per person from ¥13,800;) This glitzy old-line hotel has bay views, seafood dinners, palm trees by the *rotemburo* and a heated swimming pool. Rooms are Japanese-style except for the suites, some of which have their own *rotemburo* (from ¥40,500 per person).

Eating & Drinking

Musashi NOODLES ¥
(むさし; 0558-22-0934; 1-13-1 Shimoda; mains ¥650-1000; 11am-4pm Wed-Mon) In business since 1916, serving hearty comfort food such as *kamo nabeyaki udon* (duck hotpot, ¥1000). There's a big badger out the front.

Ra-Maru CAFE ¥
(1-1 Sotogaoka; burgers from ¥1000; 10am-4.30pm;) Diner serving tasty Shimoda fish burgers with camembert, and shrimp burgers with a big dollop of fresh avocado, with a side of onion rings and cold beer. Just behind the harbour museum at the fishing port.

★Gorosaya JAPANESE ¥¥
(ごろさや; 0558-23-5638; 1-5-25 Shimoda; set menus ¥1700-3300; 11.30am-2pm & 5-9pm;) Elegant, understated ambience and fantastic seafood. The *Isōjiru* soup is made from over a dozen varieties of shellfish and looks like a tide pool in a bowl. The *sashimi-don* (rice bowl), not on the English menu, is also excellent. Look for the wooden fish decorating the entrance.

Shimoda Kappou Enn JAPANESE, ITALIAN ¥¥
(下田割烹えん; 0558-36-4255; http://shimoda-enn.jp/; Matthews Sq, 3-13-11 Shimoda; meals ¥1000-3200; 11.30am-2pm & 5-10pm Wed-Mon) The most stylish place to eat on Perry Rd, Kappou Enn serves fine-quality Japanese and fusion Italian dishes made from the best local seafood. A hearty seafood rice bowl is served at lunch and is also part of the great-value set-course menus in the evening. One of the chefs speaks English.

Porto Caro ITALIAN ¥¥
(ポルトカーロ; 0558-22-5514; 3-3-7 Shimoda; mains ¥950-1360; 6-8.30pm Thu-Tue;) This trattoria is run by Yokoyama Ikuyo, a friendly woman who wrote a book about Mishima Yukio (the famous writer, actor and film director) whom she met as a teenager – hence she has Mishima's favourite cake, the madeleine, on the menu. The Shimoda seafood pasta with a delicate wasabi sauce is excellent, as are the tasty simple pizzas.

Nami Nami IZAKAYA ¥¥
(開国厨房なみなみ; 0558-23-3302; 3-3-26 Shimoda; skewers/small plates from ¥150/550; 5pm-midnight) This friendly counter bar has a retro vibe and an inventive menu. Local fish *(honjitsu no sakana)* and assorted delicacies are served *yakitori*-style or

SURFIN' SHIMODA

The beaches around Shimoda are some of Japan's best surf spots. While it's an all-year-round surfing destination, waves are best between June and September. **Shira-hama** (白浜海岸) is the most popular and its small but constant break gets packed in summer. There's also a **reef break** at the front of the Shimoda Prince Hotel, a short walk uphill from Papa's Restaurant. **Shirahama Mariner** (☎0558-22-6002; www.mariner.co.jp; ⊙9am-9pm) and **Irie Surf & Cafe** (⊙9am-7pm Wed-Mon) both rent boards (¥3000) and offer lessons (per two hours ¥5000).

The beaches in **Kisami** (きさみ), just south of Shimoda, are among some of the best. **Ōhama** (大浜) has the largest stretch of sand and consistent waves, **Irita** (入田) is especially good when a southerly rolls in, and **Tatado** (多々戸) has arguably the most consistent waves on the peninsula. **Baguse Surf School** (☎0558-22-2558; http://baguse.jp; 58-8 Tatado; ⊙10am-4pm Apr-Nov) in Tatado offers lessons (from ¥5500, 1½ hours) and board rentals (from ¥3300). **Real** (☎0558-27-0771; www.real-surf.com; 1612-1 Kisami) also rents out boards (from ¥3000) and conducts lessons (¥9500 including all gear; 1½ hours) at Ōhama – its website has lots of English info on the surf scene.

breaded and fried. It's two doors up from Ōizu Ryokan, with a yellow sign.

Soul Bar Tosaya BAR
(土佐屋; http://tosaya.net; 3-14-30 Shimoda; snacks from ¥600; ⊙6pm-midnight) In the heart of Perry Rd, this unique place mashes up a traditional residence from the era of the Black Ships with a soul-music bar complete with disco ball. It also serves meals.

Cubstar CAFE
(☎0558-27-3225; www.cubstar.com; 4-7-22 Shimoda; coffee/mains ¥500/1000; ⊙11am-10pm Wed-Mon; 📶) Run by a cool couple who abandoned Tokyo for the slower life of Shimoda, this quirkily decorated cafe offers excellent coffee, light meals and alcoholic beverages. Look for it opposite the green-painted church.

ℹ Information

Check the online guide at www.shimoda-city.info.

Shimoda Tourist Association (☎0558-22-1531; 1-1 Sotogaoka; ⊙9am-5pm) Pick up the useful *Shimoda Guidebook* (¥840) and free walking map, and book accommodation. In the port area near the harbour museum. English is spoken. There's another office in the city centre, where no English is spoken but they can call the office here.

Sun Lovers Cafe (www.sunloverscafe.com; 1-21-9 Higashi-hongo; ⊙11am-5.30pm Tue-Sat) Free internet, book swapping, tourist info and light meals.

Tourist Office (観光案内所; ☎0558-22-1531; http://shimoda-city.info; 1-1 Sotogaoka; ⊙10am-5pm) Opposite the station; staff speak very little English.

ℹ Getting There & Away

Shimoda is as far as you can go by train on the Izu Peninsula. Limited-express Odoriko *tokkyū* trains run to Shimoda from Tokyo Station (¥6090, 2¾ hours) or Atami (¥3400, 80 minutes); regular Izukyūkō trains run from Atami (¥1890, 1½ hours) and Itō (¥1570, one hour). Try to catch Izukyū's Resort 21 train, with sideways-facing seats for full-on sea views.

Tōkai buses run to Dōgashima (¥1360, one hour) via Matsuzaki.

Shinshin Kisen (神新汽船株式会社; ☎03-3436-1146; http://shinshin-kisen.jp) ferries serve the Izu Islands Kōzu-shima, Shikine-jima and Nii-jima (adult/child ¥5040/2520, Thu-Tue).

Car rental is available at **Nippon Rent-a-Car** (☎0558-22-5711; www.nipponrentacar.co.jp; Shimoda eki-mae) and **Toyota Rent-a-Car** (トヨタレンタカー; ☎reservations in English 0800 7000 815; car rental from ¥6500 per day; ⊙8am-8pm) by the train station.

Shira-hama 白浜海岸

☎0558

Less than 10km north of Shimoda, Shirahama (meaning white-sand beach) is an attractive beach town that gets packed out with students in summer and on holiday weekends and is a popular spot with Kantō-area surfers.

Off the main road is the pleasant 2400-year-old **Shirahama-jinja** shrine, a nice spot to wander with a striking *torii* (gate) on the rocky edge of the beach.

🛏 Sleeping & Eating

Asanami HOSTEL ¥
(麻なみ; ☎090-4868-8078; http://asanami.main.jp; 1741-2 Shira-hama; dm/r with shared bathroom

from ¥1500/2000; 📶) As cheap as a bed gets, this surfer's flophouse is across the road from Shirahama-jinja and has an equally shacklike cafe-bar attached.

Pension Sakuraya PENSION ¥¥
(ペンション桜家; ☎0558-23-4470; www.izu-sakuraya.jp; 2584-20 Shira-hama; r per person with shared/private bathroom from ¥5400/5940; 📶) A 10-minute walk up a steep hill from the beach, this homely guesthouse has been welcoming visitors for over 27 years. All rooms have fridges, as well as sea or mountain views. The English-speaking owner is a good source of info.

Pension Shirahama Mariner PENSION ¥¥
(☎0558-22-6002; www.mariner.co.jp; 2752-16 Shira-hama; r per person ¥8000; 📶) Upstairs from Hana Cafe, rooms here are comfy with homely touches such as colourful bedspreads and rugs. There's a bit of traffic noise but with these spectacular ocean views, who cares?

Hana Cafe CAFE ¥
(2752-16 Shira-hama; pizzas from ¥980; ⌚9am-9pm; 📶) Across from the ocean, this sun-drenched beach cafe does cheap and cheerful meals, beer, cocktails and Hawaiian coffee.

Papa's Restaurant CAFE ¥¥
(☎0558-22-0225; pizzas from ¥1050; ⌚11am-3pm & 5-10pm, closed Tue) A cosy diner with vintage toy cars, gingham tablecloths and surfboards on the walls. Serves light fare such as shrimp tacos and pizza. It's a five-minute walk uphill from the beach, on the right.

ℹ Getting There & Away

Bus 9 runs from Shimoda to Shira-hama (¥320, 10 minutes).

Kisami きさみ

☎0558

Our pick of Izu's seaside getaways is laid-back Kisami, most famous for its long surf beach **Ōhama** (大浜), but also well placed for access to other nearby surf beaches **Irita** (入田) and **Tatado** (多々戸). There are several decent places to stay and, in season, plenty of eating and drinking options.

Sleeping & Eating

A great place to read up on dining options in the area is on Wabi Sabi guesthouse's blog: www.wabisabishimoda.com/activities.

★**Wabi Sabi** GUESTHOUSE ¥
(☎0558-22-4188; www.wabisabishimoda.com; 2735 Kisami; dm/r with shared bathroom from ¥3500/5000; 📶) An idyllic retreat enveloped by greenery but only five minutes' walk from Ōhama. The old Japanese house perfectly embodies the *wabi-sabi* rough beauty aesthetic and is expertly managed by Angela and Yasu, who also run nearby **Tabi Tabi** (☎0558-22-4188; www.tabitabiizu.com; r from ¥4500; 📶), another appealing guesthouse with tatami rooms and shared bathrooms.

Ernest House B&B ¥¥
(アーネストハウス; ☎0558-22-5880; www.ernest-house.com; 1893-1 Kisami; r per person from ¥5000; 🚭@📶) Two minutes' walk from Ōhama surf beach, this clapboard pension, named after Hemingway, has a quaint beach house vibe. The attached **Cafe Mellow** (☎0558-27-2327; 1893-1 Kisami; meals ¥300-950; ⌚11am-11pm, closed Tue; 📶) is a local hang-out offering outdoor decking with comfy chairs, and serving beach fare such as burgers, pizza and seafood BBQs (order a day ahead).

★**South Cafe** INTERNATIONAL ¥¥
(☎0558-25-5015; www.southcafe.net; 918-2 Kisami; mains ¥1000-1200) With the best combination of food, atmosphere and good-value prices in Kisami, this relaxed place is well worth dragging yourself away from the beach for. Excellent sandwiches, salads, pizzas and curries among other things (including must-have brownies). It's a five-minute walk inland from the Kisami bus stop, just past the convenience store Lawsons.

ℹ Getting There & Away

From Izukyū Shimoda Station take an Irōzaki-bound bus (platform 3 or 4; ¥270) to Kisami, from where Ōhama is a 15-minute walk.

Rendai-ji 蓮台寺

☎0558

The town of Rendai-ji is home to one of the best onsen baths on the peninsula. Built in 1929, the rambling wooden **Kanaya Ryokan** (金谷旅館; ☎0558-22-0325; http://homepage2.nifty.com/kanaya/; 114-2 Kouchi; r per person from ¥7500, with 2 meals from ¥15,000; onsen for outside guests ¥1000; 🅿📶) is fabulously traditional, although the cheapest rooms are relatively simple. There are no restaurants nearby, so go for the inn's meals or pack your own. The star attraction is the biggest all-wood *(hinoki)* bath in Japan (with mixed bathing), called the *sennin-furo* (1000-person bath, a vast exaggeration although you can swim in it). Women can cover up with a towel (BYO or buy one for ¥200). The women-only bath is nothing to sneeze at, and both sides have private outdoor baths as well.

Another ryokan allowing outside guests to use its onsen is **Rendai-ji-so** (蓮台寺荘; ☎0558-22-3501; www.rendaijiso.jp; 305 Rendai-ji; r with 2 meals from ¥13,000 per person; onsen for outside guests ¥1000; ⏲noon-7pm; 📶) which has several separate men's and women's baths on offer, a beautiful rockpool *rotemburo* and a *hinoki* outdoor bath under a wooden hut where you can soak to the sounds of whistling birds.

From Izukyū Shimoda Station take the Izukyū line to Rendai-ji Station (¥170, five minutes); note that the express doesn't stop here. For Kanaya, go straight across the river and main road to the T-junction and turn left; the onsen is 50m ahead on the right.

Matsuzaki 松崎

☎0558

Things are much quieter on the west coast of the Izu Peninsula. The sleepy port of Matsuzaki is known for its streetscapes and attractive setting on the Naka River: some 200 traditional houses with *namako-kabe* plasterwork and tile lattice walls are concentrated in the south of town, on the far side of the river. One you can see inside is **Nakasetei** (中瀬邸; ☎0558-43-0587; 1-315 Matsuzaki; admission ¥100; ⏲9am-5pm), an old kimono shop and residence, with a striking retro-design clock tower and a footbath.

Also worth a look is the **Izu Chōhachi Art Museum** (伊豆の長八美術館; 23 Matsuzaki; adult/child ¥500/free; ⏲9am-5pm) showcasing the detailed plasterwork art of native son Chōhachi Irie (1815–99); magnifying glasses are available so you can get a better look at the fine detail of his art.

Opposite the museum, **Sakura** (さくら; 22-3 Matsuzaki; mains/set meals from ¥800/1500; ⏲11.30am-7pm) is a simple canteen offering a good range of dishes from sashimi set meals to noodles. **Mingei Sabō** (民芸茶房; 495-7 Matsuzaki; sets ¥1050-3150; ⏲7.30am-8.30pm), near the port, has fresh local seafood.

Pick up an English map of the town at the **Tourist Association** (☎0558-42-0745; http://izumatsuzakinet.com; ⏲8.30am-5pm); it's 10 minutes' walk south of the bus station, across the Naka River. You can store your luggage at the bus station office for the day (¥100).

From Shimoda Station buses run to Matsuzaki (¥1270, one hour). Buses run to Shuzen-ji (¥2150, 1½ hours) via Dōgashima, complete with fantastic views over Suruga-wan to Mt Fuji.

Dōgashima 堂ヶ島

☎0558

Dramatic rock formations line the seashore around Dōgashima, a short bus ride from Matsuzaki. They are best seen from **cruises** (☎0558-52-0013; http://www.izudougasima-yuransen.com/en/index.html) lasting between 20 and 50 minutes (¥1200/2200), which depart from the jetty just below the **Tourist Information Center** (☎0558-52-1268; www.nishiizu-kankou.com; ⏲8.30am-5pm Mon-Fri, all week Jul & Aug) in front of the village bus stop.

The cliff-edge park here has excellent views too; don't miss the **Tensōdō** (天窓洞), a natural window in a cave's roof. A short walk away is **Sawada-kōen Rotemburo** (沢田公園; 2817-1 Sawada Nishina; adult/child ¥600/200; ⏲9am-6pm Wed-Mon, to 8pm Jul & Aug), an amazing spot on a cliff overlooking the ocean. It gets very busy at sunset. To get here, take a Dōgashima bus from Matsuzaki and get off at Sawada. From here it's about a 10-minute walk, on the hill overlooking the fisherman's harbour.

Seaside Dōgashima (シーサイド堂ヶ島; ☎0558-52-0117; http://sea-dou.izu-oyado.com/; 2121-3 Dōgashima; d from ¥10,500) has simple tatami rooms with ocean views and shared bathrooms. Much higher class is **Umibe No Kakureyu** (海辺のかくれ湯; ☎0558-52-1118; www.n-komatu.co.jp; 2941 Nishina; per person incl 2 meals from ¥50,000; @📶), where traditional design meets contemporary standards. A variety of baths are on offer, including a sensational *rotemburo* right on the beach with crashing waves. It's a five-minute walk from the Dōgashima bus stop.

Buses run to Dōgashima from Shimoda (¥1400, one hour), via Matsuzaki (¥270, eight minutes).

Shuzen-ji Onsen 修善寺温泉

☎0558

Inland Shuzen-ji Onsen is a quaint hot-spring village in a lush valley bisected by the rushing Katsura-gawa. The narrow lanes, bamboo forest path and criss-crossing red-lacquered pedestrian bridges are perfect for strolling. One of Japan's finest onsen ryokan is here as well.

There's a **Tourist Information Office** (☎0558-99-9501; www.shuzenji.info; ⏱9am-5pm) at Shuzen-ji Station, where you can pick up a sightseeing map in English. Shuzen-ji Onsen is less than a 10-minute bus ride from the station (¥220).

In the middle of the village is its namesake temple, **Shuzen-ji** (修善寺), said to have been founded over 1200 years ago by Kōbō Daishi, the priest credited with spreading Buddhism throughout much of Japan. You can wander the pleasant temple grounds for free but there's a fee if you wish to see inside the small **treasure museum** (修禅寺宝物殿; ☎0558-72-0053; http://shuzenji-temple.com; 964 Shuzen-ji; adult/child ¥300/200; ⏱8.30am-4.30pm), which contains ancient carved buddhas and other religious works of art.

Also worth a look is the **Ginza Shoko Kanazawa Museum** (銀座金澤翔子美術館; ☎0558-73-2900; www.shokokanazawa.net; 970 Shuzen-ji; adult/child ¥600/300; ⏱11am-3pm Fri-Wed). Kanazawa Shoko (www.k-shoko.org), who has Down syndrome, has been doing calligraphy since she was five years old. Her vividly expressive pieces are displayed in an annexe of the Arai Ryokan.

History and art aside, the real reason to visit Shuzen-ji is for its onsen. Inns around town offer day-use bathing. Try **Hako-yu** (筥湯; 925 Shuzen-ji; admission ¥350; ⏱noon-8.30pm), an elegant, contemporary facility identified by its 12m-high wooden tower.

Right on the river is a footbath called **Tokko-no-yu** (独鈷の湯, Iron-Club Waters; ⏱24hr) FREE, which legend says was created by Kōbō Daishi himself.

Sleeping & Eating

Goyōkan RYOKAN ¥¥

(五葉館; ☎0558-72-2066; www.goyokan.co.jp; 765-2 Shuzen-ji; r per person without bathroom from ¥10,410, with 2 meals ¥17,430; 📶) Stylish tatami rooms, some with river views, are offered at this small contemporary ryokan. There are no private facilities, but the shared (indoor) baths are made of stone and *hinoki* cypress. Some English is spoken.

★ **Arai Ryokan** RYOKAN ¥¥¥

(新井旅館; ☎0558-72-2007; www.arairyokan.net; 970 Shuzen-ji; r per person incl 2 meals from ¥21,750; 📶) Long beloved by Japanese artists and writers, this gem of an inn was founded in 1872 and has kept its traditional, wood-crafted heritage. The main bath hall, designed by artist Yasuda Yukihiko, is grand and the riverside rooms are magnificent in autumn, when the maples are ablaze. Take your pick between rooms looking onto the river or peaceful garden.

Zenfutei Nana ban NOODLES ¥¥

(禅風亭な〻番; 761-1-3 Shuzen-ji; meals ¥630-1890; ⏱10am-4pm Fri-Wed; 📋) This institution serves the local speciality *zendera soba* (¥1260) with a stalk of fresh wasabi root to grate yourself. Look for the white and black banners a few doors downhill from Goyōkan.

Getting There & Away

From Tokyo, take the Tōkaidō line to Mishima (Kodama *shinkansen* ¥4400, one hour) then transfer to the Izu-Hakone Tetsudō for Shuzen-ji (¥500, 35 minutes). Buses connect Shuzen-ji Station to Shuzen-ji Onsen (¥210, 10 minutes), Itō (¥1100, one hour), Shimoda (¥2140, 1½ hours) and Dōgashima (¥1970, 1½ hours).

Izu Islands 伊豆諸島

The peaks of a submerged volcanic chain extending 300km into the Pacific are what make up the Izu Islands (伊豆諸島; Izu-shotō). Soaking in an onsen while gazing at the ocean is the classic Izu Islands activity, as is hiking up the mostly dormant volcanoes and along the pristine beaches. Snorkeling, surfing and fishing are also popular. Island hopping is possible on daily ferries that run up and down the archipelago, but check schedules carefully (they change frequently).

Easily reached by ferries and flights, the islands feel worlds away from Tokyo and surrounds – even at the height of summer, when booking ahead for the limited accommodation on the islands is a must.

For more information, in Japanese, on the whole chain, which includes To-shima (利島), Kozu-shima (神津島), Miyake-jima (三宅島) and Mikura-jima (御蔵島), where it's possible to swim with dolphins, see www.tokyo-islands.com.

Getting There & Away

AIR

ANA (全日空グループ エアーニッポン; ☎0120-02-9222; www.ana.co.jp) has flights from Tokyo's Haneda Airport to Ō-shima (from ¥9590, 35 minutes) and Hachijō-jima (from ¥12,390, 55 minutes).

New Central Airservice (www.central-air.co.jp) flies between Chōfu Airport (on the Keiō line about 20 minutes from Shinjuku) and Ō-shima (¥11,800, 30 minutes) and Nii-jima (¥14,100, 40 minutes) as well as some of the other islands. Helicopters operated by **TAL** (http://tohoair-tal.jp) can also be used to hop between the islands.

BOAT

Tōkai Kisen (東海汽船; ☎03-5472-9999; www.tokaikisen.co.jp) operates hydrofoils and ferries from Tokyo's Takeshiba Pier, a 10-minute walk from the north exit of Hamamatsu-chō Station.

Hydrofoils service Ō-shima (¥9200, 1¾ hours), Nii-jima (¥11,800, 2½ hours), Shikine-jima (¥11,800, 2½ hours) and the other inner islands. The slower, cheaper overnight passenger ferry also stops at all of the islands from north to south, before making its way back to Tokyo. These islands are also serviced by ferries from the Izu Peninsula from Atami and Shimoda ports.

The passenger ferry *Salvia-maru* services Hachijō-jima (¥11,580, 11 hours) and the other outer islands.

Prices change seasonally or to reflect fuel prices.

Ō-SHIMA 大島

☎04992 / POP 8600

The largest of the Izu Islands, the closest to Tokyo and generally the most interesting to visit is Ō-shima. It has a rustic charm and is particulary known for its profusion of scarlet camellia flowers (best viewed in February and March) as well as its active volcano **Mihara-san**, which last erupted in 1990. A road runs to the 754m summit of the volcano from where you can walk another 45 mintues to peer into the still-steaming crater; **Ō-shima Tourist Association** (大島観光協会; ☎04992-2-2177; www.izu-oshima.or.jp; ⊙8.30am-5pm) can arrange a nature guide should you wish to trek the entire caldera.

Hire a car or scooter in the main port of **Motomachi** (元町) to reach Ō-shima's rocky southernmost point, **Toushiki-no-hana** (トウシキの鼻) with good swimming in sheltered pools below Tōshiki Camp-jō.

Walkable from the port is **Motomachi Hama-no-yu** (元町浜の湯; adult/child ¥400/240; ⊙1-7pm Sep-Jun, 11am-7pm Jul & Aug), an attractive outdoor onsen with great views of the ocean and Mt Fuji, too, if the weather is clear; it's mixed, so bring your bathing suit. Nearby you can also take a dip at the indoor onsen baths and swimming pool of **Gojinka Onsen** (御神火温泉; adult/child ¥1000/600; ⊙9am-9pm). Discount tickets for both facilities are available from the souvenir shops near the port where you'll also find the Ō-shima Tourist Association.

Sleeping

Tōshiki Camp-jō CAMPGROUND ¥
(トウシキキャンプ場; ☎04992-2-1446) Walkable from the Kaiyō kokusai kōkō-mae bus stop, this well-maintained stretch of grass has a nice location overlooking the sea, as well as showers and a communal cooking area. Book through the Oshima Town Office.

Island Izu Ō-shima CAPSULE HOTEL ¥
(アイランド伊豆大島; ☎04992-2-0665; http://hotelislandizuoshima.muse.weblife.me/; 2-3-12 Motomachi; capsule ¥4200;) New, top-quality capsule hotel with facilities for both men and women plus a friendly welcome. Just five minutes' walk uphill south of the port.

Akamon HOTEL ¥¥
(ホテル赤門; ☎¥2-1213; www.ooshima-akamon.com; 1-16-7 Motomachi; r per person from ¥13,000) The tatami rooms here are nicer than the bland exterior suggests, and there's an onsen bath. It's just up the road from Motomachi port.

NII-JIMA 新島

This island attracts surfers from all over Kantō who converge on **Habushi-ura** (羽伏浦), a blazing 6.5km stretch of white sand that runs over half Nii-jima's length. The waves and tide are very strong so take care.

Nii-jima's other main attraction is **Yunohama Onsen** (湯の浜温泉; ⊙24hr) FREE, a *rotemburo* with several tubs built into the rocks overlooking the Pacific.

You can camp at **Habushi-ura Camp-jo** (羽伏浦キャンプ場) with a stunning mountain backdrop and only 10 minutes' walk to the Habushi-ura beach. There are showers and plenty of barbecue pits.

Saro (サロー; ☎5-2703; www.saro-niijima.jp; 3-3-4 Honmura; r per person with 2 meals from ¥8500;) guesthouse offers simple but stylish rooms and a hip cafe; some English is spoken. The **Nii-jima Tourist Association** (新島観光協会; ☎5-0001; ⊙8am-4pm) is about 200m south of the pier.

SHIKINE-JIMA 式根島

About 6km south of Nii-jima, tiny Shikine-jima sports **Jinata Onsen** (地鉈温泉; ⊙24hr) FREE. It's one of the most dramatically located onsen we've seen: at the end of a narrow cleft in the rocky coastline. The waters, stained a rich orange from iron sulphide, are naturally 80°C; mixed with the cool ocean, they're just right. The tide affects the temperature, so bathing times change daily; check before making the steep descent.

Kamanoshita Camp-jo (釜の下キャンプ場; ⌚Sep-Nov & Mar-Jun) is near a fine beach and two free onsen. No showers here. The **Shikine-jima Tourist Association** (式根島観光協会; ☎7-0170; ⌚8am-5pm) is at the pier.

HACHIJŌ-JIMA 八丈島

About 290km south of Tokyo, Hachijō-jima has a culture all its own, with two dormant volcanos – 854m **Hachijō-Fuji** (八丈富士) and 700m **Mihara-yama** (三原山) – and plenty of palms, attracting visitors for its hiking, diving and onsen. The island is also famous in Japan for being riddled with luminous mushrooms. If you go in June, the forests light up at night with over seven different species.

Urami-ga-taki Onsen (裏見ケ滝温泉; ⌚10am-9pm) FREE is not to be missed. At the southern end of the island, a 30-minute drive from Sokodo Port, just below the road, it overlooks a waterfall – pure magic in the early evening.

Project WAVE (☎2-5407; www3.ocn.ne.jp/~p-wave/english.html) offers a variety of ecotourism options, including hiking, birdwatching, sea-kayaking and scuba diving. **Sokodo Camp-jō** (底土キャンプ場; ☎04996-2-1121; 4188 Mitsune) is an excellent camping ground with toilets, cold showers and cooking facilities.

Hachijōjima Tourism Association (八丈島観光協会; ☎2-1377; ⌚8.15am-5.15pm) is next to the town hall on the main road.

SOUTH OF TOKYO

Tokyo's cultural presence looms large in the Kantō area, but the area just to the south stands on its own. Yokohama, Japan's second-largest city, has a distinctly different urban spirit. Further south, the old capital and coastal town of Kamakura brims with temples, shrines and surprisingly hip restaurants.

Yokohama 横浜

☎045 / POP 3.7 MILLION

Even though it's just a 20 minute train ride south of central Tokyo, Yokohama has an appealing flavour and history all its own. Locals are likely to cite the uncrowded, walkable streets or neighbourhood atmosphere as the main draw, but for visitors it's the breezy bay front, creative arts scene, multiple microbreweries, jazz clubs and great international dining.

History

Up until the mid-19th century, Yokohama was an unassuming fishing village. Things started to change rapidly, however, in 1853 when the American fleet under Commodore Matthew Perry arrived off the coast to persuade Japan to open to foreign trade.

From 1858, when it was designated an international port, through to the early 20th century, Yokohama served as a gateway for foreign influence and ideas. Among the city's firsts-in-Japan: a daily newspaper, gas lamps and a train terminus (connected to Shimbashi in Tokyo).

The Great Kantō Earthquake of 1923 destroyed much of the city, but the rubble was used to reclaim more land, including Yamashita-kōen. The city was devastated yet again in WWII air raids; occupation forces were initially based here but later moved down the coast to Yokosuka. Despite all this, central Yokohama retains some rather fine early-20th-century buildings.

Sights & Activities

Minato Mirai 21 みなとみらい 21

Over the past three decades Yokohama's former shipping docks have been transformed into this planned city of tomorrow ('Minato Mirai' means 'port future'). There are plenty of pleasant recreation areas including the old **Akarenga Sōkō** (横浜赤レンガ倉庫; www.yokohama-akarenga.jp; 1-1-2 Shinkō, Naka-ku; ⌚11am-8pm; Ⓢ Bashamichi) red-brick warehouses transformed into a shopping, dining and events space, the waterfront **Zō-no-hana Park** and a series of breezy **promenades** connecting the area's main attractions.

★ **Hara Model Railway Museum** MUSEUM
(原鉄道模型博物館; www.hara-mrm.com; 2nd fl, Yokohama Mitsui Building, 1-1-2 Takashima, Nishi-ku; adult/child ¥1000/500; ⌚11am-5.30pm Wed-Mon; 🚉 Yokohama) The result of Hara Nobutaro's lifelong obsession with trains, this superb collection of model trains and other railway-associated memorabilia is every kid's and trainspotter's dream come true. Even

Yokohama

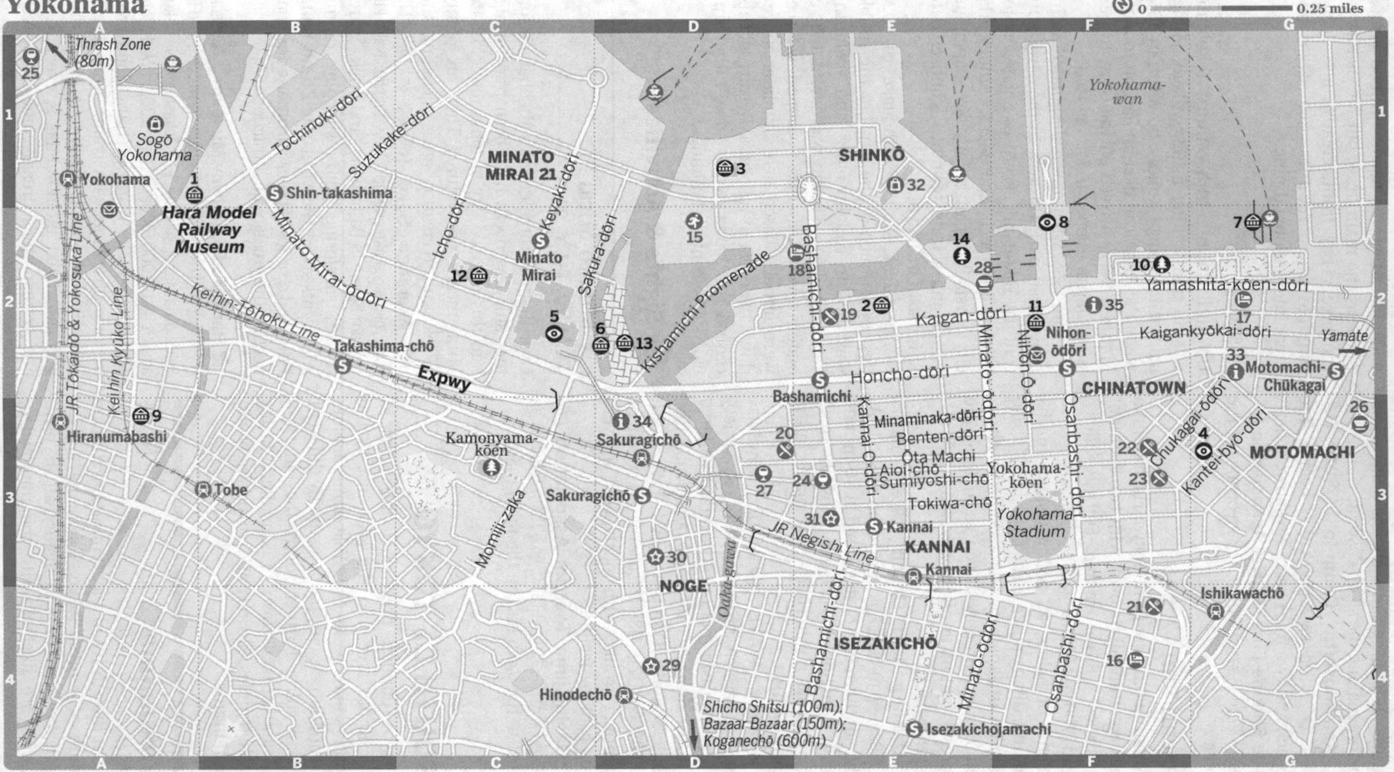
Thrash Zone (80m)
Sogō Yokohama
Yokohama
Hara Model Railway Museum
Shin-takashima
Tochinoki-dōri
Suzukake-dōri
MINATO MIRAI 21
Keyaki-dōri
Icho-dōri
Minato Mirai
Sakura-dōri
Minato Mirai-ōdōri
Keihin-Tōhoku Line
JR Tōkaidō & Yokosuka Line
Keihin Kyūko Line
Takashima-chō
Expwy
Hiranumabashi
Tobe
Kamonyama-kōen
Momiji-zaka
Sakuragichō
SHINKŌ
Kishamichi Promenade
Bashamichi-dōri
Bashamichi
Kaigan-dōri
Honcho-dōri
Kannai Ō-dōri
Minaminaka-dōri
Benten-dōri
Ōta Machi
Aioi-chō
Sumiyoshi-chō
Tokiwa-chō
Yokohama-kōen
Yokohama Stadium
Minato-ōdōri
Nihon Ō-dōri
Nihon-ōdōri
Osanbashi-dōri
Yokohama-wan
Yamashita-kōen-dōri
Kaigankyōkai-dōri
Yamate
Motomachi-Chūkagai
CHINATOWN
Chukagai-ōdōri
Kantei-byō-dōri
MOTOMACHI
Kannai
KANNAI
JR Negishi Line
NOGE
Ōoka-gawa
ISEZAKICHŌ
Ishikawachō
Hinodechō
Shicho Shitsu (100m); Bazaar Bazaar (150m); Koganechō (600m)
Isezakichojamachi
500 m
0.25 miles

Yokohama

Top Sights
1 Hara Model Railway Museum A1

Sights
2 BankART Studio NYK E2
3 Cup Noodles Museum D1
4 Kantei-byō G3
5 Landmark Tower C2
6 Nippon Maru Sailing Ship D2
7 NYK Hikawa Maru G2
8 Ōsanbashi International Passenger Terminal F2
9 Tattoo Museum A3
10 Yamashita-kōen F2
11 Yokohama Archives of History F2
12 Yokohama Museum of Art C2
13 Yokohama Port Museum D2
14 Zō-no-hana Park E2

Activities, Courses & Tours
15 Yokohama Cosmoworld D2

Sleeping
16 Hostel Zen F4
17 Hotel New Grand G2
18 Navios Yokohama E2

Eating
19 Araiya E2
Bills .... (see 32)
20 Charcoal Grill Green D3
21 Colombus Okonomiyaki F4
22 Manchinrō Honten F3
23 Masan-no-mise Ryūsen F3

Drinking & Nightlife
24 Bashamichi Taproom E3
25 Grassroots A1
26 Peace Flower Market G3
27 Yokohama Brewery D3
28 Zō-no-hana Terrace E2

Entertainment
Airegin .... (see 24)
29 Club Sensation D4
30 Downbeat Bar D3
31 Kamome E3

Shopping
32 Akarenga Sōkō E1

Information
33 Chinatown 80 Information Center G2
34 Sakuragichō Station Tourist Information D3
35 Yokohama Convention & Visitors Bureau F2

if you don't care much for trains, the sheer scale of the collection and beautiful detail of the exhibits is captivating. The highlight is the mammoth gauge one diorama of moving locomotives where you can act as train driver.

Landmark Tower TOWER
(ランドマークタワ; www.yokohama-landmark.jp; 2-2-1 Minato Mirai, Nishi-ku; adult/child ¥1000/500; ⏲10am-10pm; Ⓢ Minato Mirai) Standing an impressive 296m high (70 storeys) the Landmark Tower has one of the world's fastest lifts (45km/h). On clear days from the 69th floor Sky Garden observatory there are views to Tokyo and Mt Fuji, and you can get a glimpse into games taking place at Yokohama Stadium.

Yokohama Museum of Art GALLERY
(横浜美術館; www.yaf.or.jp/yma; 3-4-1 Minato Mirai, Nishi-ku; adult/child ¥500/free; ⏲10am-6pm, closed Thu; Ⓢ Minato Mirai) The focus of the Yokohama Triennale (next to be held in 2017), this museum hosts exhibitions that swing between safe-bet shows with European headliners to more daring contemporary Japanese artists. There are also permanent works including Picasso, Miró and Dalí in the catalogue.

Cup Noodles Museum MUSEUM
(www.cupnoodles-museum.jp; 2-3-4 Shinkō, Naka-ku; adult/child ¥500/free; ⏲10am-5pm Wed-Sun; Ⓢ Bashamichi) Dedicated to Momofuku Ando's instant *rāmen* invention, this slickly designed, interactive museum includes a cutesy animation theatre on the history of the Cup Noodle. The highlight is the chance to design your own Cup Noodles (¥300) by colouring your cup, selecting your ingredients and having it air sealed to take home to enjoy.

Yokohama Port Museum MUSEUM
(横浜みなと博物館; www.nippon-maru.or.jp; 2-1-1 Minato Mirai, Nishi-ku; museum & ship adult/child ¥600/300; ⏲10am-5pm Tue-Sun; 🚉 Sakuragichō) Explore the docked **Nippon Maru** (日本丸), a four-masted barque (built in 1930) that retains many original fittings. As you exit, the comprehensive, and somewhat dry, port museum takes you through the city's port history; kids will love the simulated ship ride.

Yokohama Cosmoworld AMUSEMENT PARK

(横浜コスモワールド; http://cosmoworld.jp; 2-8-1 Shinkō, Naka-ku; rides ¥100-800; ⏲11am-9pm Mon-Fri, 11am-10pm Sat & Sun; Ⓢ Minato Mirai) Perfect for the kiddies, this busy amusement park is home to one of the world's tallest Ferris wheels, the 112.5m Cosmo Clock 21.

Yamashita-kōen Area 山下公園周辺

This seaside, landscaped **park** (山下公園周辺; Ⓡ Motomachi-Chukagai) is perfect for strolling and ship watching.

BankART Studio NYK GALLERY

(www.bankart1929.com; 3-9 Kaigan-dōri, Naka-ku; admission varies; ⏲cafe 11.30am-11pm, gallery hours vary; Ⓢ Bashamichi) In a former warehouse, this multi-floor gallery is a fixture on the local arts scene. It hosts changing exhibitions from local and international artists, and you can sift through flyers for local events over drinks in the 1st-floor cafe before stocking up on art and design books in the excellent attached shop.

Ōsanbashi International Passenger Terminal BUILDING

(大さん橋国際客船ターミナル; 1-1-4 Kaigan-dōri, Naka-ku; ⏲24hr; Ⓢ Nihon-ōdōri) FREE Just to the west of Yamashita-kōen, this sleek, award-winning pier has an attractive **roof deck** where you can sit on the lawn or benches to take in the harbour views.

Yokohama Archives of History MUSEUM

(横浜開港資料館; www.kaikou.city.yokohama.jp/en/; 3 Nihon-ōdōri, Naka-ku; adult/child ¥200/100; ⏲9.30am-5pm, closed Mon; Ⓢ Nihon-ōdōri) Inside the former British consulate, displays in English chronicle the city's history with paintings, sketches, model ships and photographs, from the opening of Japan at the Yokohama port through to the mid-20th century.

NYK Hikawa Maru MUSEUM

(氷川丸; www.nyk.com/rekishi/e/index.htm; Yamashita-kōen, Naka-ku; adult/child ¥200/100; ⏲10am-4.30pm Tue-Sun; Ⓢ Motomachi-Chūkagai) Moored at the eastern end of Yamashita-kōen, this restored 1930s passenger ship has art-deco fixings and stories to tell. Inside, you can wander from the 1st-class cabins (one of the staterooms was used by Charlie Chaplin) to the engine room.

Chinatown, Motomachi and Yamate 中華街・元町・山手

Yokohama's frenetic Chinatown packs some 600 speciality shops and restaurants within a space of several blocks, marked by 10 elaborately painted gates. It's very touristy, but fun to visit for a meal or evening stroll. At its heart is the elaborately decorative temple **Kantei-byō** (関帝廟; 140 Yamashita-chō; ⏲9am-7pm; Ⓢ Motomachi-Chūkagai) FREE, dedicated to Kanwu, the god of business.

Across the nearby Nakamura River is Motomachi, a pleasant, upscale shopping and dining area overlooked by the bluff of Yamate, the old foreign quarter where you can find several preserved Western-style residences from the early 20th century. The most convenient subway for all these areas is Motomachi-Chūkagai.

Other Areas

Sankei-en GARDENS

(三渓園; www.sankeien.or.jp; 58-1 Honmoku-sannotani, Naka-ku; adult/child ¥500/200; ⏲9am-4.30pm) Opened to the public in 1906, this beautifully landscaped garden features walking paths among ponds, 17th-century buildings, several fine tea-ceremony houses and a 500-year-old, three-storey pagoda. The inner garden is a fine example of traditional Japanese garden landscaping. From Yokohama or Sakuragichō Station, take bus 8 to Honmoku Sankei-en-mae bus stop (10 minutes).

Tattoo Museum MUSEUM

(☎045-323-1073; www.ne.jp/asahi/tattoo/horiyoshi3; 1-11-7 Hiranuma , Nishi-ku; admission ¥1000; ⏲noon-6pm, closed 1st, 10th and 20th of the month; Ⓡ Tobe) Famous tattoo artist Horiyoshi III and his wife run this very personal museum that's a must for tattoo lovers as well as anyone interested in Japan's subculture. It's so packed you can hardly move with its display of needles and other tattoo paraphernalia. It's a short walk north of Tobe, one train stop south of Yokohama Station.

Shin-Yokohama Rāmen Museum MUSEUM

(新横浜ラーメン博物館; www.raumen.co.jp/ramen; 2-14-21 Shin-Yokohama, Kohoku-ku; adult/child ¥310/100, dishes around ¥900; ⏲11am-10pm Mon-Sat, 10.30am-10pm Sun; Ⓡ Shin-Yokohama) Nine *rāmen* restaurants from around Japan were handpicked to sell their wares in this inventive replica of a 1958 *shitamachi* (downtown district). It's a short walk from the Shin-Yokohama station – ask for directions at the information centre at the station.

Sleeping

Yokohama has plenty of midrange business hotel chains, such as Toyoko Inn (www.toyoko-inn.com/eng) with several central locations. Those on a budget should head to Kotobukichō and Matsukage-chō near Ishikawachō Station, where there's a high concentration of hostels. It's a neighbourhood known for the down and out, but it's perfectly safe, cheap and a five-minute walk to Chinatown.

Hostel Zen HOSTEL ¥
(☎045-342-9553; http://zen.ilee.jp/; 3-10-5 Matsukage-chō, Naka-ku; r incl breakfast from ¥3000; ; Ishikawachō) The best of the area's many cheapo hostels is Zen, which offers bright, clean Japanese-style rooms. Some are decent sized, others are squashy, and a few have been given makeovers by artists, so ask the helpful staff to let you check a few out first. There's a good breakfast spread and rooftop-decking area with funky furniture and umbrellas.

Hotel New Grand HOTEL ¥¥¥
(ホテルニューグランド; ☎045-681-1841; www.hotel-newgrand.co.jp; 10 Yamashita-chō, Naka-ku; s/d or tw from ¥14,256/33,264; @; S Motomachi-Chūkagai) Dating from 1927, the New Grand has a prime waterfront location and elegant old-world charm, particularly in its original lobby. It was once a favourite of visiting foreign dignitaries such as General McArthur and Charlie Chaplin. The bay-view rooms are the ones you want to go for.

Navios Yokohama HOTEL ¥¥¥
(ナビオス横浜; ☎045-633-6000; www.navios-yokohama.com; 2-1-1 Shinkō, Naka-ku; s/d from ¥8640/15,120; @; S Bashamichi) Rooms are spotless and central, with city or sea views. Rates increase on weekends.

Eating

Colombus Okonomiyaki OKONOMIYAKI ¥
(お好み焼きころんぶす; 1-3-7 Matsukage-chō, Naka-ku; mains ¥890-1120; 11.30am-10pm Mon-Thur, 11.30am-11pm Fri & Sat, 3-10pm Sun; ; Ishikawachō) Friendly staff grill up tasty *okonomiyaki* at your table from a choice of prawn, squid or veg at this smart eatery. It's a two-minute walk from the Ishikawachō Station. Turn right from the north exit, then take a left at the first traffic lights and Colombus is 50m on your right.

Bills INTERNATIONAL ¥¥
(ビルズ; www.bills-jp.net; Akarenga Sōkō Bldg 2, 1-1-2 Shinko, Naka-ku; mains ¥1000-2000; 9am-11pm Mon-Fri, 8am-11pm Sat & Sun; ; S Bashamichi) Australian celebrity chef Bill Granger's Yokohama outlet has been a huge hit with locals – expect to wait in line on weekends and holidays if you've not booked. Try his famous ricotta hotcakes or berry pancakes.

Charcoal Grill Green GASTROPUB ¥¥
(http://bashamichi.greenyokohama.com/; 6-79 Benten-dōri, Naka-ku; mains ¥1100-1400; 11.30am-2pm & 5pm-midnight Mon-Sat; ; S Bashamichi) The most central branch of this convivial charcoal grill and bar with three craft beers on tap to go with smoky steaks, BBQ pork and delicious prawn pizzas.

Masan-no-mise Ryūsen CHINESE ¥¥
(馬さんの店龍仙; www.ma-fam.com; 218-5 Yamashita-chō, Naka-ku; mains from ¥1050; 7am-3am; ; Ishikawachō) You can't miss friendly old Mr Ma sitting outside his small Shanghai-style eatery, as he has done for years. The walls are liberally wallpapered with photos of tasty-looking dishes. It has two other branches in Chinatown.

★ **Araiya** JAPANESE ¥¥¥
(荒井屋; ☎045-226-5003; www.araiya.co.jp; 4-23-1 Kaigan-dōri, Naka-ku; set meal lunch/dinner from ¥2300/3500; 11am-3pm & 5-10pm; ; S Bashamichi) Yokohama has it's own version of the beef hotpot dish *sukiyaki*, called *gyū-nabe*. This elegantly designed restaurant with waitresses in kimonos is the place to sample it.

Manchinrō Honten CHINESE ¥¥¥
(萬珍樓本店; ☎045-681-4004; www.manchinro.com; 153 Yamashita-chō, Naka-ku; lunch/dinner courses from ¥2800/6000; 11am-10pm; ; Motomachi-Chūkagai) This elegant Cantonese restaurant is one of Chinatown's oldest (1892) and most respected. It serves a great selection of dim sum from 11am to 4pm. Look for the English sign next to the tradtional gate.

Drinking & Nightlife

Beer lovers rejoice! Yokohama is packed with microbreweries and quality craft-beer bars. **Yokohama Oktoberfest** is held over two weeks at Akarenga Sōkō (p189) in

OFF THE BEATEN TRACK

KOGANECHŌ

Prostitution was once rife in **Koganechō** (黄金町), an atmospheric Yokohama district squeezed between the train tracks connecting Hinoechō and Koganechō stations and the Ōka River, roughly 2km southwest of Minato Mirai. But since the local authorities cleaned up the red light district in 2005, it has sprouted galleries, art studios, boutiques and fun cafes and bars such as **Shicho Shitsu** (http://shicho.org; Koganechō, Naka-ku; ⌚11am-7pm Sun-Fri, 11am-late Sat; 🚉Koganechō), which has a packed schedule of live gigs. There are residencies for artists whose murals and installations decorate the area and whose work is sold in **Bazaar Bazaar** (⌚11am-2pm & 3-7pm; 🚉Koganechō). The annual art festival **Koganechō Bazaar** (www.koganecho.net) amps up the creativity; check the website for other events throughout the year.

early October and features around 80 beers and much carousing in the spirit of the German festival. Also popular is the **Great Japan Beer Festival Yokohama** (www.beertaster.org/index-e.html), which is held in mid-September and features around 200 craft beers from across Japan.

Bashamichi Taproom PUB
(馬車道　タップルーム; www.bairdbeer.com; 5-63-1 Sumiyoshi-chō, Naka-ku; meals from ¥700; ⌚5pm-midnight Mon-Fri, noon-midnight Sat & Sun; Ⓢ Bashamichi) Set over three floors with a rooftop beer garden, this Baird Brewing Company pub offers some 14 beers on tap, 10 of which are from the brewery itself, ranging from pale ales to chocolate flavours. Try a sampler set for ¥1000 if you're struggling to decide. It also dishes up authentic American-style BBQ dishes.

Yokohama Brewery BREWERY
(www.yokohamabeer.com; 6-68-1 Sumiyoshi-chō, Naka-ku; ⌚11.30am-3pm & 6-11pm Mon-Fri, 11.30am-11pm Sat, 11.30am-9pm Sun; 🚉Sakuragichō) Sample five on-tap beers from the oldest craft brewery in Japan at this spacious restaurant-bar. A tasting set of all five is ¥1500. The food, using organic ingredients from farms in Kanagawa prefecture, is also very tasty.

Grassroots BAR
(http://stovesyokohama.com/grassroots; 2-13-3 Tsuruyachō, Kanagawa-ku; ⌚5pm-1am Mon-Fri, 4pm-1am Sat & Sun; 🚉Yokohama) Gigs, live art shows and DJ events are held in this psychedelically decorated basement space a short walk north of Yokohama Station. It also serves a good selection of international beers and tasty pub meals such as fish burgers and grilled tuna steaks with avocado mash.

Peace Flower Market CAFE
(http://peaceflowermarket.jp; 1-39-1 Motomachi, Naka-ku; ⌚9am-8pm Mon & Wed-Sat; Ⓢ Motomachi-Chūkagai) On the quieter road shadowing the main drag through Motomachi you'll find this convivial cafe and florist that also offers a variety of artsy-crafty classes. It's hard to resist the gourmet selection of baked goods, including muffins and scones in a variety of flavours.

Zō-no-hana Terrace CAFE
(象の鼻テラス; www.zounohana.com; 1 Kaigan-dōri, Naka-ku; ⌚10am-6pm; Ⓢ Nihon-ōdōri) A life-size sculpture of an elephant (*zō* in Japanese) and baby elephants, plus food and drink with elephant design themes, makes this bayside cafe a delightful place to go for a refreshing drink. There are often art shows and other events held here, too.

Thrash Zone BAR
(http://www.beerdrinkinginternational.com; 1F Tamura Bldg, 2-10-7 Tsuruyachō, Kanagawa-ku; ⌚6-11.30pm; 🚉Yokohama) Stacked Marshall amps and walls covered with punk posters set the scene at this small bar popular with local beer-and-music fans. Knock back frothies from a choice of 13 craft 'extreme' beers (full body and high alcohol) from Japan and American breweries to a soundtrack of heavy metal and punk tunes on the screen.

☆ Entertainment

Live music is prominent here, with Yokohama particularly noted for its love of jazz. The Kannai-Bashamichi area is considered the hub of jazz.

★Kamome LIVE MUSIC
(カモメ; www.yokohama-kamome.com; 6-76 Sumiyoshi-chō, Naka-ku; cover ¥2000-3500; ⌚7-10.30pm Mon-Fri, 6-10.30pm Sat & Sun; Ⓢ Bashamichi) The best place for serious live music, with a line-up that includes veteran and

up-and-coming talents playing jazz, funk, fusion and bossa nova. The interior is stark and sophisticated, the crowd stylish and multigenerational.

Club Sensation LIVE MUSIC

(http://sensation-jp.com; 3-80 Miyagawachō; cover from ¥3000; ⏲6pm-1am Tue-Sun; 🚇Hinodechō) Intimate British-themed rock cafe-bar, run by Japanese rockers, hosting local and international bands.

Airegin JAZZ

(www.yokohama-airegin.com; 5-60 Sumiyoshi-chō, Naka-ku; cover incl 1 drink ¥2500; ⏲7.30-11pm; 🚇Bashamichi) Up a flight of stairs is where you'll find this intimate, smoky and genuine jazz bar that's been swinging since '72. It's run by a passionate jazz-loving couple and top-notch performances bring in an appreciative and knowledgeable audience.

Downbeat Bar JAZZ

(ダウンビート; ☎045-241-6167; www.yokohama-downbeat.com; 2nd fl, Miyamoto Building, 1-43 Hanasaki-chō, Naka-ku; ⏲4-11.30pm Mon-Sat; 🚇Sakuragichō) *Jazz kissa*, which fall somewhere between cafes and bars, boast extensive jazz-record collections. This is one of the oldest (1956) in Yokohama, with more than 3000 albums and some serious speakers. Occasional live music means an occasional cover charge. Look for the 2nd-floor red awning.

ℹ Information

POST

Yokohama Port Post Office (5-3 Nihon-ōdori, Naka-ku; ⏲9am-7pm Mon-Fri, 9am-5pm Sat, 9am-12.30pm Sun) International ATM and parcel/post facilities.

TOURIST INFORMATION

See www.yokohamajapan.com and www.yokohamaseasider.com as well as the following tourist offices, all of which have an English speaker.

Chinatown 80 Information Center (横浜中華街インフォメーションセンター; ☎045-681-1252; ⏲10am-9pm) A few blocks from Motomachi-Chūgakai Station.

Sakuragichō Station Tourist Information (☎045-211-0111; ⏲9am-6pm) Maps, brochures and hotel bookings. Outside south exit of Sakuragichō Station.

Yokohama Convention & Visitors Bureau (☎045-221-2111; www.yokohamajapan.com; 1st fl, Sangyo-Boeki Center, 2 Yamashita-chō, Naka-ku; ⏲9am-5pm Mon-Fri) A 10-minute walk from Nihon-ōdori station. English spoken; very helpful with recommendations, maps and brochures. Excellent website.

Yokohama Station Tourist Information Center (☎045-441-7300; ⏲9am-7pm) Helpful staff in the east–west corridor at the station; English is spoken and they can book accommodation.

ℹ Getting There & Away

JR Tōkaidō, Yokosuka and Keihin Tōhoku lines run from Tokyo Station (¥470, 40 minutes) via Shinagawa (¥290, 18 minutes) to Yokohama Station. Some Keihin Tōhoku line trains continue along the Negishi line to Sakuragichō, Kannai and Ishikawachō. From Shinjuku, take the Shōnan-Shinjuku line (¥550, 35 minutes).

The Tōkyū Tōyoko line runs from Shibuya to Yokohama (¥270, 30 minutes), after which it becomes the Minato Mirai subway line to Minato Mirai (¥450, 34 minutes) and Motomachi-Chūkagai (¥480, 40 minutes).

The Tōkaidō *shinkansen* stops at Shin-Yokohama Station, northwest of town, connected to the city centre by the Yokohama line.

ℹ Getting Around

BOAT

Sea Bass ferries (www.yokohama-cruising.jp) connect Yokohama Station with Minato Mirai 21 (¥420, 10 minutes) and Yamashita-kōen (¥700, express/local 20/30 minutes) from approximately 10am to 7pm. From Yokohama Station, take the east exit and pass through Sogō department store to reach the dock.

BUS

Although trains are more convenient, Yokohama has an extensive bus network (adult/child ¥210/110 per ride). A special Akai-kutsu ('red shoe') bus loops every 20 minutes from 10am to around 7pm through the major tourist spots for ¥100 per ride.

SUBWAY & TRAIN

The Yokohama City blue line *(shiei chikatetsu)* connects Yokohama with Shin-Yokohama (¥240, 11 minutes), Sakuragichō (¥210, six minutes) and Kannai (¥210, five minutes). JR trains connect Yokohama with Shin-Yokohama (¥170, 15 minutes), Sakuragichō (¥140, three minutes) and Kannai (¥140, five minutes).

The **Minato Burari** day pass covers municipal subway and bus rides (including the Akai-kutsu bus, but not the Minato Mirai line) around Minato Mirai and Yamashita-kōen (adult/child ¥500/250); purchase it at any subway station.

Kamakura 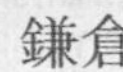

☎0467 / POP 173,500

The glory days of Japan's first feudal capital (from 1185 to 1333) coincided with the spread of populist Buddhism in Japan. This legacy is reflected in the area's proliferation of stunning temples. Kamakura also has a laid-back, earthy vibe complete with organic restaurants, summer beach shacks and surfers – which can be added to sunrise meditation and hillside hikes as reasons to visit. Only an hour from Tokyo, it tends to get packed on weekends and holidays, so plan accordingly.

History

In 1180 aspiring warlord Minamoto no Yoritomo set up his base at Kamakura, far away from the debilitating influences of Kyoto court life, close to other clans loyal to his family and, having the sea on one side and densely wooded hills on the others, easy to defend.

After victories over the old foes the Taira, Yoritomo was appointed shogun in 1192 and governed Japan from Kamakura. When he died without an heir, power passed to the Hōjō, the family of Yoritomo's wife. Ruling power remained in Kamakura until 1333, when, weakened by the cost of maintaining defences against threats of attack from Kublai Khan in China, the Hōjō clan was defeated by Emperor Go-Daigo. Kyoto once again became the capital.

By the Edo period, Kamakura was practically a village again. With the opening of a rail line at the turn of the last century, the seaside town was reborn as a summer resort. Summer homes of wealthy Tokyoites still line the Shōnan coast.

Sights & Activities

★Kenchō-ji — BUDDHIST TEMPLE

(建長寺; www.kenchoji.com; 8 Yamanouchi; adult/child ¥300/100; 8.30am-4.30pm) Established in 1253, Japan's oldest Zen monastery is still active today. The central Butsuden (Buddha Hall) was brought piece by piece from Tokyo in 1647. Its Jizō Bosatsu statue, unusual for a Zen temple, reflects the valley's ancient function as an execution ground – Jizō consoles lost souls. Other highlights include a bell cast in 1253 and the juniper grove, believed to have sprouted from seeds brought from China by Kenchō-ji's founder some seven centuries ago.

The temple once comprised seven buildings and 49 subtemples, most of which were destroyed in the fires of the 14th and 15th centuries. However, the 17th and 18th centuries saw its restoration, and you can still get a sense of its original splendour.

Engaku-ji — BUDDHIST TEMPLE

(円覚寺; www.engakuji.or.jp; 409 Yamanouchi; adult/child ¥300/100; 8am-4.30pm Mar-Nov, to 4pm Dec-Feb) One of Kamakura's five major Rinzai Zen temples, Engaku-ji was founded in 1282 as a place where Zen monks might pray for soldiers who lost their lives defending Japan against Kublai Khan. All of the temple structures have been rebuilt over the centuries; the Shariden, a Song-style reliquary, is the oldest, last rebuilt in the 16th century. At the top of the long flight of stairs is the Engaku-ji bell, the largest bell in Kamakura, cast in 1301.

Tsurugaoka Hachiman-gū — SHINTO SHRINE

(鶴岡八幡宮; http://hachimangu.or.jp; 2-1-31 Yukinoshita; 9am-4pm) FREE Kamakura's most important shrine is, naturally, dedicated to Hachiman, the god of war. Minamoto Yoritomo himself ordered its construction in 1191 and designed the pine-flanked central promenade that leads to the coast. The sprawling grounds are ripe with historical symbolism: the Gempei Pond, bisected by bridges, is said to depict the rift between the Minamoto (Genji) and Taira (Heike) clans.

Behind the pond is the **Kamakura National Treasure Museum** (鎌倉国宝館; ☎0467-22-0753; 2-1-1 Yukinoshita, Kamakura Kokuhōkan; adult/child ¥200/100; 9am-4.30pm Tue-Sun), housing remarkable Buddhist sculptures from the 12th to 16th centuries.

Daibutsu — MONUMENT

(大仏; www.kotoku-in.jp; Kōtoku-in, 4-2-28 Hase; adult/child ¥200/150; 8am-5.30pm Apr-Sep, to 5pm Oct & Nov) Kamakura's most iconic sight, an 11.4m bronze statue of Amida Buddha (*amitābha* in Sanskrit), is in Kōtoku-in, a Jōdo sect temple. Completed in 1252, it's said to have been inspired by Yoritomo's visit to Nara (where Japan's biggest Daibutsu holds court) after the Minamoto clan's victory over the Taira clan. Once housed in a huge hall, today the statue sits in the open, the hall having been washed away by a tsunami in 1495.

For an extra ¥20, you can duck inside to see how the sculptors pieced the 850-tonne statue together.

Kamakura

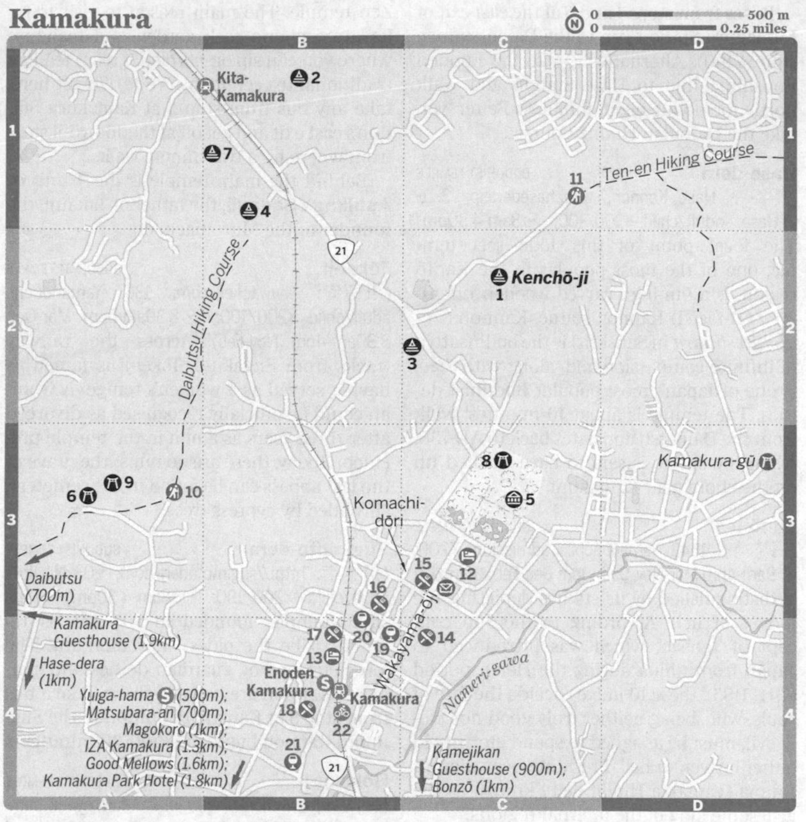

Kamakura

Top Sights
1 Kenchō-ji C2

Sights
2 Engaku-ji B1
3 Ennō-ji C2
4 Jōchi-ji B1
5 Kamakura National Treasure Museum C3
6 Sasuke-inari-jinja A3
7 Tōkei-ji B1
8 Tsurugaoka Hachiman-gū C3
9 Zeniarai-benten A3

Activities, Courses & Tours
10 Daibutsu Hiking Course A3
Engaku-ji .... (see 2)
Kenchō-ji .... (see 1)
11 Ten-en Hiking Course C1

Sleeping
12 Hotel Ajisai C3
13 Hotel New Kamakura B4

Eating
14 Bowls Donburi Café C4
15 Imoyoshi C3
16 Kamakura Ichibanya B3
17 Sông Bé Cafe B4
18 Wander Kitchen B4

Drinking & Nightlife
19 Bar Ram B4
20 Milk Hall B4
21 Univibe B4

Transport
22 Kamakura Rent-a-Cycle B4

Buses from stops 1 and 6 at the east exit of Kamakura Station run to the Daibutsu-mae stop (¥190). Alternatively, take the Enoden Enoshima line to Hase Station and walk north for about eight minutes. Better yet, take the Daibutsu Hiking Course.

Hase-dera BUDDHIST TEMPLE
(長谷寺, Hase Kannon; www.hasedera.jp; 3-11-2 Hase; adult/child ¥300/100; ⏲8am-4.30pm) The focal point of this Jōdo sect temple, one of the most popular in the Kantō region, is a 9m-high carved wooden *jūichimen* (11-faced) Kannon statue. Kannon (*avalokiteshvara* in Sanskrit) is the bodhisattva of infinite compassion and, along with *Jizō*, is one of Japan's most popular Buddhist deities. The temple is about 10 minutes' walk from the Daibutsu and dates back to AD 736, when the statue is said to have washed up on the shore near Kamakura.

Ennō-ji BUDDHIST TEMPLE
(円応寺; 1543 Yamanouchi; admission ¥200; ⏲9am-4pm Mar-Nov, 9am-3pm Dec-Feb) Ennō-ji is distinguished by its statues depicting the judges of hell. According to the Juo concept of Taoism, which was introduced to Japan from China during the Heian period (794–1185), these 10 judges decide the fate of souls, who, being neither truly good nor truly evil, must be assigned to spend eternity in either heaven or hell. Presiding over them is Emma (Yama), a Hindu deity known as the gruesome king of the infernal regions.

Jōmyō-ji BUDDHIST TEMPLE
(浄妙寺; 3-8-31 Jomyoji; adult/child ¥100/50; ⏲9.30am-4.30pm) This Tokasan temple of the Rinzaishu Kenchō-ji sect was originally a tantric Buddhist temple and converted to a Zen temple. The main reason to visit is for its atmospheric rock garden and teahouse where you can sip on *matcha* (green) tea in a traditional tea ceremony (¥600). To get here, take any bus from stop 5 at Kamakura Station's east exit and get off at the Jōmyō-ji stop, from where it's a two-minute walk.

Behind the main temple is the **Tomb of Ashikaga Sadauji**, the father of Takauji, the founder of the Muromachi era.

GET ZEN

Too many temples and before you know it you're feeling anything but 'Zen'. *Zazen* (seated meditation) can help you discover what you're missing – after all, temples were originally designed for this purpose (and not sightseeing). Both **Engaku-ji** (⏲5.30-6.30am Apr-Oct, 6-7am Nov-Mar) FREE and **Kenchō-ji** (temple admission ¥300; ⏲5-6pm Fri & Sat, enter before 4.30pm) hold beginner-friendly, public *zazen* sessions. Instruction is in Japanese, but you can easily manage by watching everyone else; arrive at least 15 minutes early.

Tōkei-ji BUDDHIST TEMPLE
(東慶寺; www.tokeiji.com; 1367 Yamanouchi; adult/child ¥200/100; ⏲8.30am-5pm Mar-Oct, 8.30am-4pm Nov-Feb) Across the railway tracks from Engaku-ji, Tōkei-ji is famed as having served as a women's refuge. A woman could be officially recognised as divorced after three years as a nun in the temple precincts. Today, there are no nuns; the grave of the last abbess can be found in the cemetery, shrouded by cypress trees.

Sugimoto-dera BUDDHIST TEMPLE
(杉本寺; http://sugimotodera.com; 903 Nikaidō; adult/child ¥200/100; ⏲8am-4.30pm) This small temple, founded in AD 734, is reputed to be the oldest in Kamakura. The ferocious-looking guardian deities and statues of Kannon are its main draw. Take a bus from stop 5 at Kamakura Station to the Sugimoto Kannon bus stop (¥200, 10 minutes).

Hōkoku-ji BUDDHIST TEMPLE
(報国寺; www.houkokuji.or.jp; 2-7-4 Jōmyō-ji; bamboo garden ¥200; ⏲9am-4pm) Down the road from Sugimoto-dera, on the right-hand side, is this Rinzai Zen temple with quiet, landscaped gardens where you can relax under a red parasol with a cup of Japanese tea (¥500).

Zuisen-ji BUDDHIST TEMPLE
(瑞泉寺; www.kamakura-zuisenji.or.jp; 710 Nikaidō; adult/child ¥200/100; ⏲9am-4.30pm) The grounds of this secluded picturesque Zen temple make for a pleasant stroll and include gardens laid out by Musō Soseki, the temple's esteemed founder. To get here, take the bus from stop 4 at Kamakura Station and get off at Ōtōnomiya (¥200, 10 minutes); turn right where the bus turns left in front of Kamakura-gū, take the next left and keep following the road for 10 to 15 minutes.

Daibutsu Hiking Course HIKING
This 3km wooded trail connects Kita-Kamakura with the Daibutsu in Hase (allow about 1½ hours) and passes several small, quiet temples and shrines, including **Zeniarai-**

benten (銭洗弁天; 2-25-16 Sasuke; ⏲8am-4pm) FREE, one of Kamakura's most alluring Shintō shrines.

The path begins at the steps just up the lane from pretty **Jōchi-ji** (浄智寺; 1402 Yamanouchi; adult/child ¥200/100; ⏲9am-4.30pm), a few minutes from Tōkei-ji. Along the course you'll pass Zeniarai-benten, where a cavelike entrance leads to a clearing where visitors come to bathe their money in natural springs, with the hope of bringing financial success. From here, continue down the paved road, turn right at the first intersection, walk along a path lined with cryptomeria and ascend through a succession of *torii* to **Sasuke-inari-jinja** (佐助稲荷神社; 2-22-10 Sasuke; ⏲24hr) FREE before meeting up with the Daibutsu path once again. To hike in the opposite direction, follow the road beyond Daibutsu and the trail entrance is on the right, just before a tunnel.

Ten-en Hiking Course HIKING
(天園ハイキングコース) From Zuisen-ji you can access this trail, which winds through the hills for two hours before coming out at Kenchō-ji. From Kenchō-ji, walk around the Hojo (Main Hall) and up the steps to the trail.

Tours

Kamakura Welcome Guides TOUR
(www1.kamakuranet.ne.jp/kwga) Offers free half-day tours on Fridays with volunteer guides in English; five days' notice is required.

Festivals & Events

Kamakura Matsuri CULTURAL
A week of celebrations held from the second Sunday to the third Sunday in April. It includes a wide range of activities, most of which are centred on Tsurugaoka Hachiman-gū.

Bonbori Matsuri CULTURAL
From 6 or 7 to 9 August, hundreds of lanterns are hung around Tsurugaoka Hachiman-gū.

Reitai Matsuri CULTURAL
On 14 September from 11am to 1pm there's a procession of *mikoshi* (portable shrines); on 16 September from 1pm there's a display of horseback archery.

Sleeping

Kamakura Guesthouse GUESTHOUSE ¥
(鎌倉ゲストハウス; ☎0467-67-6078; www.kamakura-guesthouse.com; 273-3 Tokiwa; dm ¥3000; 🚭📶) While it's away from the action, the cheap Japanese dorms and common area with *irori* (fireplace) set in a traditional cypress home make this a nice place to hang out. Take the Enoden bus from stop 1 at the east gate of Kamakura Station to Kajiwaraguchi (¥240); it's a one-minute walk from there.

There are bicycles for rent (per day ¥500) and a communal kitchen. *Zazen* meditation tours to Engaku-ji are offered on weekdays.

IZA Kamakura HOSTEL ¥
(IZA 鎌倉; ☎0467-33-5118; http://izaiza.jp; 11-7 Sakanoshita; dm/d or tw ¥3500/8000; 🚭📶) This surfies hang-out hostel is steps from the beach and has a very studenty vibe, but is also handy for Hase's temples. There's a bar and bike rental (per day ¥1000).

★**Kamejikan Guesthouse** GUESTHOUSE ¥¥
(☎0467-25-1166; www.kamejikan.com; 3-17-21 Zaimokuza; dm/d from ¥3200/9000; 🚭@📶) A three-minute walk to the beach, this lovely guesthouse has nice touches such as paper lampshades and a small cafe and bar (open noon-5pm Saturday and Sunday). Choose from six-bed dorms or private doubles, all with common tiled bathrooms. Catch bus 12, 40 or 41 to Kuhonji from Kamakura Station.

English-speaking owner Masa is a good source of info and rents bodyboards and bicycles (per day ¥500).

Hotel New Kamakura HOTEL ¥¥
(ホテルニューカマクラ; ☎0467-22-2230; www.newkamakura.com; 13-2 Onarimachi; s/d from ¥4200/11,000; @) Charming, slightly shabby, ultraconvenient and a steal, this hotel built in 1924 has both Western- and Japanese-style rooms. There's red carpet and a vintage vibe, though the economy rooms are rather plain. Exit west from Kamakura Station, and take a sharp right down the alley.

Hotel Ajisai HOTEL ¥¥
(クラシカルホテルあじさい; ☎0467-22-3492; www.hotel-ajisai.com; 1-12-4 Yukinoshita; s/tw from ¥7500/15,000; 🚭@) A businesslike, affordable option with small, basic Western-style rooms conveniently located near Tsurugaoka Hachiman-gū. The 4th-floor rooms have shrine views.

Kamakura Park Hotel HOTEL ¥¥¥
(鎌倉パークホテル; ☎0467-25-5121; www.kamakuraparkhotel.co.jp; 33-6 Sakanoshita; s/tw from ¥19,000/26,000; 🚭@📶) A bit 1980s plush, the large Western-style rooms come with ocean views and marble baths. It's a 12-minute walk along the coast from Hase Station.

Eating

Vegetarians can eat well in Kamakura; pick up the free, bilingual *Vegetarian Culture Map* at the Tourist Information Center.

Bowls Donburi Café JAPANESE ¥

(鎌倉どんぶりカフェbowls; http://bowls-cafe.jp; 2-14-7 Komachi; meals ¥880-1680; 11am-3pm & 5-10pm;) The humble *donburi* (rice bowl) gets a hip, healthy remake at this modern bright cafe, with toppings such as roasted tuna, soy sauce and sesame oil. You get a discount if you discover the word *atari* at the bottom of the bowl. Also serves excellent coffee and has free wi-fi and computer terminals with internet.

Wander Kitchen INTERNATIONAL ¥

(0467-61-4751; http://wanderkitchen.net; 15 Onarimachi; sweets/lunch from ¥400/1000; noon-8pm;) It's worth searching out this charmingly decorated, retro-chic wooden house with a small garden out front for its cool vibe and tasty meals, cakes and drinks. It's tucked away just off the main street about five minutes' walk south of the west exit of Kamakura Station.

Sông Bé Cafe ASIAN FUSION ¥

(ソンベカフェ; www.song-be-cafe.com; 13-32 Onarimachi; dishes from ¥780; 11.30am-8.30pm, closed Wed;) This mellow day-to-evening joint serves up dishes such as *pad thai* (rice noodles) and green curry, with vegies sourced from the local farmers market, and Southeast Asian beers to match. The friendly owner also serves a good selection of teas and tasty *zenzai* (red bean) desserts.

Kamakura Ichibanya RICE CRACKERS ¥

(鎌倉壱番屋; 22-6156 Komachi-dōri; packages from ¥80; 9am-6.30pm) Specialises in *sembei* (rice crackers); watch staff grilling them in the window or buy some of the 50 packaged varieties, including curry, wasabi, garlic, *mentaiko* (spicy cod roe) or *uni* (sea urchin). Look for the baskets on the corner.

Imoyoshi ICE CREAM ¥

(いも吉館; www.imoyoshi.com; 1-9-21 Yukinoshita; scoop ¥320; 10am-6pm) Famous for soft-serve sweet-potato ice cream. Has several branches around town.

★ **Matsubara-an** NOODLES ¥¥

(松原庵; 0467-61-2299; http://matsubara-an.com/kamakura/shop.php; 4-10-3 Yuiga-hama; mains ¥860-1720; 11am-9pm;) Dinner reservations are recommended for this upscale *soba* restaurant in a lovely old house. Try the tempura *goma seiro soba* (al dente noodles served cold with sesame dipping sauce). Dine alfresco or indoors where you can watch noodles being handmade. From Yuiga-hama Station (Enoden line) head towards the beach and then take the first right. Look for the blue sign.

Bonzō SOBA ¥¥

(梵蔵; 0467-73-7315; http://bonzokamakura.com; 3-17-33 Zaimokuza; dishes ¥300-2000, set-course menu from ¥3500; 11.30am-3pm & 6-9pm, closed Thu;) Intimate, rustic Michelin-star restaurant that specialises in handmade *ju-wari* (100% soba), including *kamo seiro* (cold soba in hot broth) with wild duck imported from France. The homemade sesame tofu is incredibly creamy and not to be missed. Catch bus 12, 40 or 41 to Kuhon-ji.

Magokoro FUSION ¥¥

(麻心; 2nd fl, 2-8-11 Hase; meals ¥800-1300; 11am-3pm & 5-9pm, Tue-Sun;) Mixing ocean views with an organic hemp-based menu, Magokoro offers vegetarian hemp taco rice, macriobiotic cakes and even a hemp beer. From Hase Station it's a short walk to the beach and a left turn onto the coastal road.

Good Mellows CAFE ¥¥

(www.goodmellows.com; 27-39 Sakanoshita; burgers from ¥850; 9am-8.30pm Tue-Sun, 9am-3pm Mon;) Americana meets Japanese kitsch

ENOSHIMA

A short ride on the Enoden line from Enoden Kamakura will take you to beachside Enoshima where rocky Enoshima Island is the main attraction. Cross the bridge that begins on the beach and head up the narrow cobblestone lane (or the escalator if you prefer) to **Enoshima-jinja** (江島神社; 0466-22-4020; http://enoshimajinja.or.jp; 2-3-8 Enoshima; 9am-4pm), a shrine to the sea goddess Benzaiten. The island is a popular date spot, and cliffside restaurants offer sunset views along with local specialties like *sazae* (turban shell seafood). There's a park and some caves, too. During the summer, Enoshima's black-sand beach transforms into a sort of Shibuya-by-the-sea, as super-tan teens crowd the sand.

opposite the beach, with neatly stacked charcoal-grilled burgers of bacon, mozzarella and avocado washed down with a Dr Pepper or a cold beer. Once a month or so it stays open till 11.30pm on Saturday with DJs playing.

Drinking

Milk Hall CAFE, BAR

(ミルクホール; www.milkhall.co.jp; 2-3-8 Komachi; 11am-8pm Mon-Fri, 11am-9pm Sat & Sun) Also an antiques shop and daytime cafe, by evening Milk Hall morphs into a moody bar with a good whisky menu and live jazz on some nights. Head two blocks down Komachi-dōri, take a left and then another left down the first alley.

Univibe BAR

(0467-67-8458; www.univibe.jp; 7-13-2F Onaricho; 11am-5pm & 6pm-late;) Spacious upstairs bar kitted-out in retro vintage decor, with friendly bartenders, table football and a relaxed vibe. A five-minute walk from the Kamakura JR station.

Bar Ram BAR

(バー・ラム; 2-11-11 Komachi; drinks from ¥500; 5pm-late) A hole in the wall in the lanes off Komachi-dōri, this *tachinomiya* (drink-while-standing bar) has plenty of old Rolling Stones vinyls and friendly banter. Look for the English sign.

Information

For information about Kamakura, see www.city.kamakura.kanagawa.jp/english.

Kamakura Post Office (郵便局; 0467-22-1200; 1-10-3 Komachi; 9am-7pm Mon-Fri, 9am-3pm Sat) Has ATMs inside.

Tourist Information Center (鎌倉市観光協会観光総合案内所; 0467-22-3350; 9am-5pm) Just outside the east exit of Kamakura Station; the English-speaking staff are helpful and can book accommodation. Pick up a guide to Kamakura's temples (¥1700), as well as free brochures and maps for the area.

Getting There & Away

JR Yokosuka-line trains run to Kamakura from Tokyo (¥920, 56 minutes) and Shinagawa (¥720, 46 minutes), via Yokohama (¥340, 27 minutes). Alternatively, the Shōnan Shinjuku line runs from the west side of Tokyo (Shibuya, Shinjuku and Ikebukuro, all ¥920) in about one hour, though some trains require a transfer at Ōfuna, one stop before Kita-Kamakura. The last train from Kamakura back to Tokyo Station is 11.20pm and Shinjuku 9.16pm.

JR Kamakura-Enoshima Free Pass (adult/child ¥700/350) Valid for one day from Ōfuna or Fujisawa stations; unlimited use of JR trains around Kamakura, the Shōnan monorail between Ōfuna and Enoshima, and the Enoden Enoshima line.

Odakyū Enoshima/Kamakura Free Pass (from Shinjuku/Fujisawa ¥1470/610) Valid for one day; includes transport to Fujisawa Station (where it meets the Enoden Enoshima line), plus use of the Enoden.

Getting Around

You can walk to most temples and shrines from Kamakura or Kita-Kamakura Stations. Sites in the west, like the Daibutsu, can be reached via the Enoden line from Kamakura Station to Hase (¥200) or by bus from Kamakura Station stops 1 and 6.

Kamakura Rent-a-Cycle (レンタサイクル; per hr/day ¥800/1800; 8.30am-5pm) is outside the east exit of Kamakura Station, and right up the incline.

OFF THE BEATEN TRACK

GANKOYAMA

Amid lush, old-growth forests of Chiba's Bōsō-hanto (Bōsō Peninsula), **Gankoyama** (ガンコ山; 045-834-7640; www.gankoyama.com; Minami-boso; 2-day course from ¥8500) is a rustic hamlet of simple loghouses built on platforms amid the soaring cedars. You can sign up for day and overnight courses to practise yoga, and learn forest survival skills and how to make treehouses.

It's run by friendly, well-travelled, eco-friendly folk and you can get here by bus or train in less than two hours from Tokyo (see the website for details).

EAST OF TOKYO

The main attractions of Chiba Prefecture, east and southeast of Tokyo, are the ancient pilgrim town of Narita on the doorstep of the international airport, and decent surf beaches along the 66km **Kujūkuri-hama** (九十九里浜) coastline, on the Pacific side of the Bōsō Peninsula. For more details about the breaks here, see www.surfinginjapan.com.

Narita 成田

☎0476 / POP 127,000

The home of Japan's main international airport is a surprisingly pleasant place to visit with an esteemed temple, terrific places to eat and plenty of accommodation that is perfect if you have an early morning flight or would prefer to ease yourself into Japan after your arrival. The town's major festival is the **Narita Gion Matsuri**, held on the Friday to Sunday closest to 8 July.

Sights

Narita-san Shinshōji BUDDHIST TEMPLE
(成田山新勝寺; www.naritasan.or.jp; 1 Narita; 24hr) FREE The landscaped grounds of this venerable temple, founded in 940, are among the largest in Japan, and are laced with walking paths. The temple buildings are splendid, particularly the Niomon entrance gate and three-storeyed pagoda.

Omote-sandō STREET
Local ordinances have preserved the traditional architectural look of Narita's main shopping drag as it winds its way towards the Narita-san Shinshōji. Along its sinuous path you'll find souvenir, craft and medicinal shops, and restaurants.

Tourist Pavilion MUSEUM
(www.nrtk.jp; 383-1 Nakamachi; 9am-5pm, closed Mon) FREE Halfway down Omote-sandō, this museum has local-history exhibits, as well as some of the floats used in the Narita Gion Matsuri on display.

Sleeping

Numerous chains operate hotels near the airport and in Narita town.

Ninehours Narita Airport CAPSULE HOTEL ¥
(☎0476-33-5109; http://ninehours.co.jp/en/narita/; Narita International Airport Terminal 2, 1-1 Furugome; capsule ¥3900;) You can hardly get closer to the airport than this brilliant white, futuristic-styled capsule hotel, which is in the basement car park of terminal two.

Kirinoya Ryokan RYOKAN ¥¥
(桐之屋旅館; ☎0476-22-0724; www.naritakanko.jp/kirinoya; 58 Tamachi; s/d with shared bathroom from ¥3500/9000;) The English-speaking owner of this workaday ryokan, just a five-minute walk south of Narita-san temple, can trace his lineage back 50 generations, and his rambling old inn is filled with samurai armour and swords. Meals and station pick-up/drop off (until 7pm) are also available.

Eating & Drinking

Kawatoyo Honten JAPANESE ¥¥
(川豊本店; www.unagi-kawatoyo.com; 386 Nakamachi; meals from ¥2300; 10am-5pm Tue-Sun;) *Unagi* (eel) is a speciality of Narita and this place, opposite the Tourist Pavilion, is the place to sample it. You can watch the chefs carving up live eels right at the front table (not for the squeamish).

Edoko Sushi JAPANESE ¥¥
(江戸ッ子寿司; 536-10 Hanazakichō; set meals from ¥1200; 11.30am-2.30pm & 5-9.30pm) Next to the popular pub/club **Barge Inn** (ザ・ヴァージン; www.naritabarginn.com; 538 Hanizakichō; meals around ¥1500; 4pm-2am Mon-Fri, 11am-2am Sat & Sun), near the train station end of Omote-sandō, is this convivial joint where the sushi toppings are extra generous.

5.2.4 Garage Cafe CAFE
(www.5-2-4.net; 512 Kamichō; coffee from ¥410; 8am-7pm;) Cool cafe serving good coffee, homemade bakes, beer and light meals.

Information

Narita Tourist Information Center (☎0476-24-3198; 8.30am-5.15pm) Pick up a map at the Narita Tourist Information Center, just outside the eastern exit of JR Narita Station.

Getting There & Away

From Narita International Airport you can take the private Keisei line (¥260, 10 minutes) or JR (¥200/240 from Terminal 2/1, 10 minutes); Keisei-line trains are more frequent. From Tokyo, the easiest way to get to Narita is via the Keisei line from Keisei Ueno Station, taking the Cityliner (¥1250, 41 minutes), or the express (*tokkyū;* ¥840, 71 minutes). Note that most JR Narita Express trains do not stop at Narita.

OGASAWARA ARCHIPELAGO

About 1000km south of Ginza, but still within Tokyo Prefecture, the World Natural Heritage listed Ogasawara Archipelago (小笠原諸島; Ogasawara-shotō) is a nature-lover's paradise with pristine beaches surrounded by tropical waters and coral reefs. Snorkelling, whale-watching, swimming with dolphins and hiking are all on the bill.

Just as fascinating as its natural attractions is the human history. Mapped by the Japanese back in the 16th century, the islands' earliest inhabitants were a motley crew of Europeans and Pacific Islanders who set up provisioning stations for whaling ships working the Japan whaling grounds in 1830. Around 100 of the descendants of these settlers, known as *obeikei*, still live on the islands, accounting for the occasional Western family name and face. US Commodore Matthew Perry stopped here in 1853 en route to Japan proper when the archipelago was known as the Bonin Islands – it gained the name Ogasawara in 1875 when the Meiji government claimed the territory.

The gun emplacements at the ends of most of the islands' beaches were built by the Japanese during WWII, though the big battles were fought further south on Iwo-jima. After the war the islands were occupied by the US military until 1968 when they reverted back to Japan.

The only way to get here is by a 25½-hour ferry ride from Tokyo. The ferry docks at Chichi-jima (父島; Father Island), the main island of the 30-strong group. A smaller ferry connects Chichi-jima to Haha-jima (母島; Mother Island), the only other inhabited island.

Getting There & Away

Ogasawara Kaiun (小笠原海運; ☎03-3451-5171; www.ogasawarakaiun.co.jp/english/) runs the *Ogasawara-maru*, which sails at least once a week between Tokyo's Takeshiba Pier (10 minutes' walk from Hamamatsu-chō Station) and Chichi-jima (2nd class from ¥25,100 in July and August, from ¥22,570 September to June, 25½ hours); check the website for the exact departure schedule and current prices.

The *Hahajima-maru* sails five times a week between Chichi-jima and Haha-jima (¥3780, two hours). Other operators run day cruises from Chichi-jima to Haha-jima.

Chichi-jima 父島

☎04998 / POP 2068

Beautifully preserved, gorgeous Chichi-jima has plenty of accommodation, restaurants, even a bit of tame nightlife. But the real attractions are the excellent beaches, outdoor activities and access to the Ogasawara's amazing natural heritage.

OGASAWARA: KNOW BEFORE YOU GO

- There is an ATM accepting foreign cards at the post office in Chichi-jima, but not on Haha-jima. Neither island has a foreign-currency-exchange service and while a few places accept credit cards, you can't rely on it.
- For visits in July and August make sure you book accommodation well in advance. Note there's no camping on the islands.
- For more information, check out **Ogasawara Village Tourist Information** (www.ogasawaramura.com) and **The Bonin Base** (http://ludysbonin.com).

Sights & Activities

The two best beaches for snorkelling are on the north side of the island, a short walk over the hill from the village. **Miya-no-hama** (宮之浜) has decent coral and is sheltered, making it suitable for beginners. About 500m along the coast (more easily accessed from town) is **Tsuri-hama** (釣浜), a rocky beach that has better coral but is more exposed.

Good swimming beaches line the west side of the island, getting better the further south you go. The neighbouring coves of **Kopepe** (コペペ海岸) and **Kominato-kaigan** (小港海岸) are particularly attractive. From Kominato-kaigan, you can walk along a trail over the hill and along the coast to the beguiling white sand of **John Beach** (ジョンビーチ), but note that it's a two-hour walk in each direction and there is no drinking water – bring at least 3L per person. The path to nearby **Jinny Beach** is off-limits; the strong current makes it unsafe to swim to here, though sea kayaking is possible.

Many operators, including Stanley Minami, the English-speaking skipper of the **Pink Dolphin** (☎04998-2-2096; www.chichijimapinkdolphin.jp/english.html; half-/full-day tours ¥5000/10,000), a glass-bottom boat, offer dolphin-swimming and whale-watching, as well as trips to Minami-jima, an uninhabited island with a magical secret beach called **Ōgi-ike** (扇池).

Pelan Sea Kayak Club (☎04998-2-3386; www.pelan. jp) offers tours to some of the island's more enchanting spots (per half-/full

NATURAL OGASAWARA

Known as the Galapagos of Japan, the Ogasawaras are oceanic islands that have never been connected with other land masses, meaning the nature here includes many rare endemic species. Of note are the Japanese wood pigeon, 90% of the snails on the island, and the Bonin flying fox. Between April and August green turtles haul themselves ashore to lay their eggs on the islands' beaches. Botantists by day should look out for the white rhododendron boninense, while by night green pepe luminous mushrooms glow in the dark.

For most visitors though it's the chance to watch whales and dolphins that is the Ogasawara's big draw. From January to April humpback whales come within 500m of shore. At other times you can see sperm whales around 10km to 30km offshore – if you're very lucky, one may rise with the fabled giant squid *Architeuthis*, photographed for the first time ever in 2004, in its mouth.

day ¥5000/10,000). Fees include equipment rental and meals cooked Pelan-style, on a wood-burning camp stove. Catching and grilling your own fish is optional.

At Ōgiura Beach, **Rao Adventure Tours** (☎04998-2-2081; http://web.me.com/boninrao/RAO/English_Page.html) organises jungle tours (per half-day ¥5000) and surf lessons (per day ¥15,000).

Sleeping

★Pelan Village ECO-RESORT ¥
(☎04998-2-3386; www.pelan.jp; r per person with shared bathroom from ¥5000;) A Never-Never Land of cosy rough wooden cabins, walkways and ladders perched on a leafy mountainside, Pelan Village offers a sustainable eco-retreat ideal for self-caterers. It is not, however, for dilettantes – conventional soaps and detergents are banned because water run-off goes directly to the crops.

Banana Inn GUESTHOUSE ¥
(バナナ荘; ☎04998-2-2050; www.chichijimapinkdolphin.jp/banana.html; r with shared bathroom from ¥5500; @) Steps from the ferry pier, this humble inn has basic Japanese- and Western-style rooms but lots of hospitality. The owner, John Washington, an Ernest Hemingway-type who enjoys discussing local history, is usually in residence in March.

Ogasawara Youth Hostel HOSTEL ¥
(小笠原ユースホステル; ☎04998-2-2692; www.oyh.jp; dm members/nonmembers ¥3530/4130; @) Clean, well-run hostel about 400m southwest of the pier with small bunk-bed dorms; book early during summer.

Rockwells GUESTHOUSE ¥¥
(ロックウェルズ; ☎04998-2-3838; rockwells.co.jp/ogasawara; r per person with shared bathroom & 2 meals from ¥9200;) A young and friendly English-speaking family runs this simple accommodation and a bar right on Ōgiura Beach. The meals are delicious.

Tetsuya Healing Guest House GUESTHOUSE ¥¥
(てつ家; ☎04998-2-7725; www.tetuyabonin.com; r per person from ¥10,800; @) Offers thoughtfully designed rooms, open-air baths and multicourse meals that make innovative use of local ingredients. It's a five-minute walk from Kominato-kaigan beach.

Eating & Drinking

Cafe Hale JAPANESE ¥
(☎04998-2-2373; www.papasir.com; meals ¥1000; ⏲9am-8pm Fri-Tue;) Hale's deck, facing Chichi-jima's port, is a top spot to enjoy a delicious lunch of sashimi on a bowl of rice, or a slice of lemon cheesecake.

Also here is an upmarket **guesthouse** (s/d with breakfast ¥24,840/34,560) with three smartly furnished en-suite rooms.

Bonina INTERNATIONAL ¥
(☎04998-2-3027; mains from ¥1000; ⏲6pm-midnight) Friendly restaurant and bar serving simple fare of rice dishes, pizza and tacos. Also open for lunch when the Tokyo ferry is in town. It's in front of Futami Bay, steps from the port.

★USK Coffee CAFE
(☎04998-2-2338; Kita-fukurozawa; ⏲1-5pm Fri, 10am-5pm Sat & Sun) Out of an Airstream caravan on the road to the Kominato-kaigan, English-speaking Ku and Yusuke serve thirst-quenching caffeinated drinks, made from beans grown on their adjacent plot, along with homemade cookies and cakes. A top spot to relax and refresh.

Yankee Town BAR
(ヤンキータウン; ☎080-2567-7168, 04998-2-3042; ⏲8pm-2am Thu-Tue) Follow the main coastal road towards Okumura for around

10 minutes east of the main pier to find this convivial driftwood bar run by island-born Rance Ohara. A great place to chill with a beer or cocktail; there is occasionally live music also, making it the town's livliest bar.

Contact Rance about history tours of the island.

Information

Chichi-jima Tourism Association (父島観光協会; ☎ 04998-2-2587; ⏲ 8am-5pm) In the B-Ship building, about 250m west of the pier, near the post office. Ask for the helpful *Guide Map of Chichi-jima;* English spoken.

Ogasawara Visitor Center (小笠原ビジターセンター; ⏲ 8.30am-5pm) Right on the beach past the village office, it has displays in English about the local ecosystem and history.

Getting Around

Rental scooters (available from ¥2400 per day) are the best way to get around as buses are infrequent and you'll be able to explore more of the island. You can rent them from **Ogasawara Kanko** (☎ 04998-2-3311; ⏲ 8am-6pm) if you have an international driving licence.

Haha-jima 母島

☎ 04998 / POP 466

Around 50km south of Chichi-jima is the much-less-developed Haha-jima. Outside the summer season, you may find yourself staring out over cerulean waters or spotting rare birds all by your lonesome.

Sights & Activities

Before leaving the only village on the island, scoot over to the **green turtle sanctuary** on the south side of the harbour – around 135 turtles are hatched here a year and released back into the sea.

A road runs south from the village to the start of the **Minami-zaki Yūhodō** (南崎遊歩道), a hiking course that continues all the way to the **Minami-zaki** (南崎; literally 'southern point') – the route is jungly and at times slippy and muddy. Along the way you'll find **Hōraine-kaigan** (蓬莢根海岸), a narrow beach with a decent offshore coral garden, and **Wai Beach** (ワイビーチ), with a drop-off that sometimes attracts eagle rays. Minami-zaki itself has a rocky, coral-strewn beach with ripping views of smaller islands to the south. Though tempting, the waters beyond the cove can whisk swimmers away.

Above Minami-zaki you'll find **Kofuji** (小富士), an 86m-high peak with fantastic views in all directions. Back in town, a four-hour hike loops through rare indigenous flora to **Mt Chibusa** (乳房山; 463m), the highest peak on the island. There are good snorkelling spots at the far north of the island at **Kita Minato** (北港湊).

Dive shop **Club Noah** (クラブノア母島; ☎ 04998-3-2442; http://noah88.web.fc2.com; 1 dive ¥7980, gear rental ¥7500; ⏲ cafe 9am-5pm) also runs jungle hiking and marine-life ecotours (from ¥5200). It's in a white building next to the turtle sanctuary; inside there's a **cafe** serving light meals (from ¥500).

Sleeping & Eating

Anna Beach Haha-jima Youth Hostel HOSTEL ¥
(アンナビーチ母島ユースホステル; ☎ 04998-3-24-68; www.k4.dion.ne.jp/~annayh; dm members/nonmembers from ¥5780/6380; 🚭📶) A friendly family runs this tidy, cheery youth hostel in a bright-yellow Western-style house overlooking the fishing port.

Island Resort Nanpū HOTEL ¥¥
(民宿 ナンプー; ☎ 0120-188-887; www.hahajima-nanpu.com/english; tw with breakfast & dinner from ¥12,000; 🚭@📶) Cosy, well-run lodge with glossy wood-panelled rooms, friendly owners and good food at its restaurant **Austro** (11.30am to 2pm and 6pm to 11pm), also open to nonguests.

Information

Haha-jima Tourist Association (母島観光協会; ☎ 04998-3-2300; www.hahajima.com/en; ⏲ 8am-noon & 1-5pm) In the passenger waiting room at the pier and only open on ferry days.

Getting Around

Scooters (per day from ¥3000) are the best way to get around the island. They can be rented from most lodgings.

The Japan Alps & Central Honshū

Includes ➡

Best Vistas

- Kamikōchi (p267)
- Shin-Hotaka Ropeway (p265)
- Tateyama-Kurobe Alpine Route (p260)
- Utsukushi-ga-hara-kōgen (p258)
- Noto-kongō Coast (p252)

Best Rotemburo

- Nakabusa Onsen (p269)
- Yarimikan (p266)
- Ōshirakawa Rotemburo (p238)
- Shin-Hotaka-no-yu (p266)
- Lamp no Yado (p255)

Why Go?

Japan's heartland in both geography and outlook, Central Honshū (本州中部, 'Honshū Chūbu') stretches out between the sprawling leviathans of Greater Tokyo and Kansai. The awesome Japan Alps (日本アルプス) rise sharply near the border of Gifu and Nagano prefectures before rolling north to the dramatic Sea of Japan coast.

World-class skiing, hiking and onsen can be found in the region's photogenic alpine uplands. All but one of Japan's 30 highest peaks (Mt Fuji) are here. Kanazawa oozes culture: temples and tearooms that served lords and housed geisha are beautifully preserved. Takayama's riverside streetscapes satisfy admirers from Japan and abroad. Matsumoto's magnificent castle and alpine backdrop ensure its popularity.

Nagoya, a gateway city famed for technical know-how, is Japan's fourth largest city. Combining urban delights with transport connections to just about everywhere, Nagoya secures the region's worthy place as a priority on any itinerary.

When to Go

Nagoya

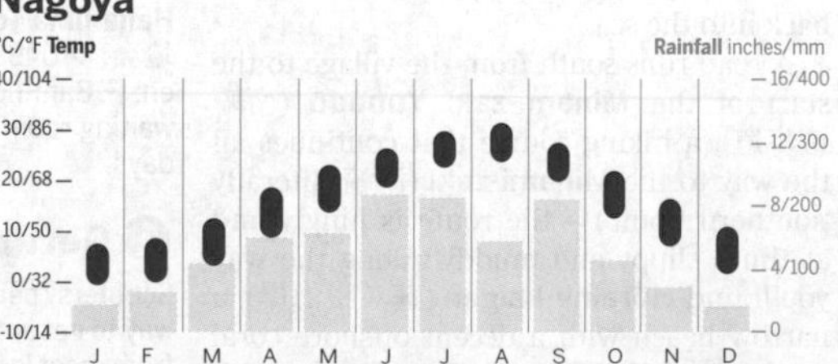

Jan–Mar Nagano's slopes satiate snow-starved skiers.

Sep–Nov Kamikōchi and Hida's many mountain onsen offer great spots for autumn's brilliant show.

Apr & May Come for cherry blossoms and the great Takayama Matsuri (festival).

The Japan Alps & Central Honshū Highlights

1. Walk the **Nakasendō** (p225) between Tsumago and Magome.
2. Sleep in a thatch-roofed house at World Heritage–listed **Ainokura** (p239).
3. Dissolve your troubles in the remote *rotemburo* of **Nakabusa Onsen** (p269).
4. Travel the spectacular high-altitude **Tateyama-Kurobe Alpine Route** (p260).
5. Hike against the picture-perfect alpine backdrop of **Kamikōchi** (p267).
6. Re-imagine a shogun's reign at Fukui's **Ichijōdani Asakura Clan Ruins** (p240).
7. Ski till you drop at Hakuba's **Olympic resorts** (p269).
8. Explore Zen at Kanazawa's **D.T. Suzuki Museum** (p242).
9. Seek the key to salvation in Nagano's **Zenkō-ji** (p272).
10. Go train-spotting in Nagoya's **JR SCMAGLEV & Railway Park** (p218).

Climate

Central Honshū's climate varies with its landscape. The best times to visit are generally April through May and late September to early November; temperatures are mild and clear skies prevail. Mid-April is the best time for *hanami* (cherry-blossom viewing) in the Alps. Expect heavy rains in the *tsuyu* (monsoon) season, typically a few weeks in June, then sticky summers capped with typhoons as late as October.

Road closures are commonplace in the Japan Alps when the snow sets in from November to March, although higher peaks might remain snowcapped as late as June. Hiking season runs from July to September, until autumn ushers in a brilliant display of *kōyō* (turning leaves), peaking in mid-October.

Getting There & Away

Chūbu Centrair International Airport (NGO), outside Nagoya, is an excellent gateway to the region with a variety of global connections. Komatsu (KMQ) and Toyama (TOY) airports to the north service domestic and a handful of intra-Asia routes. Nagoya is a major rail hub on the Tōkaidō Shinkansen (bullet train) line between Tokyo and Osaka. The Nagano Shinkansen connects Tokyo and Nagano. The long anticipated Hokuriku Shinkansen extension of the Nagano line commenced services from Nagano to Toyama and Kanazawa in March 2015.

Getting Around

Nagoya is Chūbu's transport terminus. Rail access is by the north–south JR Takayama and Chūō lines, with hubs in Takayama, Matsumoto and Nagano. The JR Hokuriku line follows the Sea of Japan coast, linking Fukui, Kanazawa and Toyama, with connections to Kyoto and Osaka.

Bus companies JR, Meitetsu, Nōhi and Alpico operate seasonal services from Nagoya, Takayama and Matsumoto to numerous destinations in Chūbu's mountainous middle.

Renting a car is well suited for trips to the Noto peninsula, and for those wanting to get up high and off the beaten track. Be prepared for slow, steep and windy roads that can be treacherous at times and are not for the faint-hearted; plan your explorations carefully. Google Maps has rudimentary routing capabilities in English and many rental cars include GPS navigation systems (some with English menus).

HIKING THE JAPAN ALPS

Central Honshū, a hiker's delight, is blessed with half of the nation's 100 famous mountains as well as many national parks. Enthusiastic hikers should pick up Lonely Planet's *Hiking in Japan*.

NAGOYA

052 / POP 2.26 MILLION

Home proud Nagoya, birthplace of Toyota and *pachinko* (a vertical pinball-style game), is a manufacturing powerhouse. Although Nagoya's GDP tops that of many small countries, this middle child has grown accustomed to life in the shadow of its bigger brothers, Tokyo and Kansai. In contrast to its industrial core, Nagoya has cosmopolitan aspects including some fantastic museums, significant temples and excellent shopping. Parks and green spaces in the inner wards prevail and are well maintained. Nagoyans take pride in the unpretentious nature of their friendly, accessible city.

Nagoya sits between Tokyo and Kyoto/Osaka on the Tōkaidō Shinkansen line. It's the gateway for journeys north into Chūbu's big mountain heart and a great base for day trips.

History

As the ancestral home of Japan's 'three heroes' – Oda Nobunaga (unifier of Japan), Toyotomi Hideyoshi (second unifier of Japan) and Tokugawa Ieyasu (founder of Japan's last shogunate) – Nagoya's influence is long-standing, although it did not become a unified city until 1889.

In 1609, Tokugawa ordered the construction of Nagoya-jō, which became an important outpost for 16 generations of the Tokugawa family (also called the Owari clan), whose dictatorial yet prosperous reign in a time known as the Edo period held sway until 1868 when the restoration of Emperor Meiji saw the ultimate demise of feudal samurai culture in Japan.

Nagoya grew into a centre for commerce, industry and transport; during WWII some 10,000 Mitsubishi Zero fighter planes were produced here. Manufacturing prominence led to massive Allied bombing – almost 4000 citizens were killed, over 450,000 were forced to leave their homes and roughly one quarter of the city was destroyed. From these ashes rose the Nagoya of today with its wide avenues, subways, skyscrapers and parks.

Sights

Don't confuse this museum with the Toyota Exhibition Hall (p218) and factory tours.

Nagoya Station Area

Midland Square LANDMARK

(ミッドランドスクエア; ☎052-527-8877; www.midland-square.com/english; 4-7-1 Meieki; ⊙shops 11am-8pm, restaurants 11am-11pm; 🚉Nagoya) Nagoya's tallest building (247m) houses Toyota's corporate HQ and showroom, boutique shopping on the lower floors and a beehive of offices in the middle. On levels 44 to 46 **Sky Promenade** (スカイプロメナード; ☎052-527-8877; www.midland-square.com/sky-promenade; 4-7-1 Meieki; adult/child ¥750/500; ⊙11am-9.30pm; 🚉Nagoya) features Japan's tallest open-air observation deck and a handful of high-altitude, high-priced eats. You can reach them via adventurously lit passageways.

Noritake Garden GARDENS

(ノリタケの森, Noritake no Mori; ☎052-561-7290; www.noritake.co.jp/eng/mori; 3-1-36 Noritake-shinmachi; ⊙10am-6pm Tue-Sun; Ⓢ Kamejima) FREE Pottery fans will enjoy a stroll around Noritake Garden, the 1904 factory grounds of one of Japan's best-known porcelain makers, featuring remnants of early kilns and the pleasant **Noritake Gallery** (☎052-562-9811; ⊙10am-6pm Tue-Sun), exhibiting paintings, sculptures and ceramic works. You can also glaze your own dish (from ¥1800) in the **Craft Centre & Museum** (☎052-561-7114; adult/child/senior ¥500/300/free; ⊙10am-5pm Tue-Sun), which demonstrates the production process. The 'Box Outlet Shop' has ironically unboxed wares at discounted prices. English signs throughout.

Toyota Commemorative Museum of Industry & Technology MUSEUM

(トヨタテクノミュージアム産業技術記念館, Toyota Techno-museum Zangyō Gijutsu Kinenkan; ☎052-551-6115; www.tcmit.org/english; 4-1-35 Noritake-shinmachi; ⊙9.30am-5pm Tue-Sat; 🚉Meitetsu Nagoya line to Sako) The world's largest car manufacturer had humble beginnings in the weaving industry. This interesting museum occupies the site of Toyota's original weaving plant. Rev-heads will find things textile heavy before warming to the 7900 sq metre automotive and robotics pavilion. Science-minded folk will enjoy countless hands-on exhibits. Displays are bilingual and there's an English-language audio tour available.

Nagoya Castle Area

Nagoya-jō CASTLE

(名古屋城; ☎052-231-1700; www.nagoyajo.city.nagoya.jp; 1-1 Honmaru; adult/child ¥500/free; ⊙9am-4.30pm; Ⓢ Shiyakusho, exit 7) The original structure, built between 1610 to 1614 by Tokugawa Ieyasu for his ninth son, was levelled in WWII. Today's castle is a concrete replica (with elevator) completed in 1959. Renovations are ongoing. On the roof, look for the 3m-long gilded *shachi-hoko* – legendary creatures possessing a tiger's head and carp's body. Inside, find treasures, an armour collection and the histories of the Oda, Toyotomi and Tokugawa families. The beautiful year-round garden, **Ninomaru-en** (二の丸園) has a number of pretty teahouses.

Painstaking reconstruction of the **Honmaru Palace** (1624–44) using traditional materials and methods commenced in 2009. The project is scheduled for completion in 2018.

Tokugawa Art Museum GALLERY

(徳川美術館; Tokugawa Bijutsukan; ☎052-935-6262; www.tokugawa-art-museum.jp/english; 1017 Tokugawa-chō; adult/child ¥1200/500; ⊙10am-5pm Tue-Sun; 🚌Me-guru stop 11) A must for anyone interested in Japanese culture and history, this museum has a collection of over 10,000 pieces that includes National Treasures and Important Cultural Properties once belonging to the shogun family. A priceless 12th-century scroll depicting *The Tale of Genji* is usually locked away, except during a short stint in late November; the rest of the year, visitors must remain content with a video.

Tokugawa-en GARDENS

(徳川園; ☎052-935-8988; www.tokugawaen.city.nagoya.jp/english; 1001 Tokugawa-chō; adult/senior ¥300/100; ⊙9.30am-5.30pm Tue-Sun; 🚌Me-guru stop 10) This delightful Japanese garden adjacent to the Tokugawa Art Museum was donated by the Tokugawa family to Nagoya city in 1931, but destroyed by bombing in 1945. From that time until a three-year restoration project was completed in 2004, the site was used as a park. Water is its key element – there's a lake, river, bridges and waterfall. Each spring 2000 peonies and irises burst into bloom, and maples ignite in the autumn.

Central Nagoya

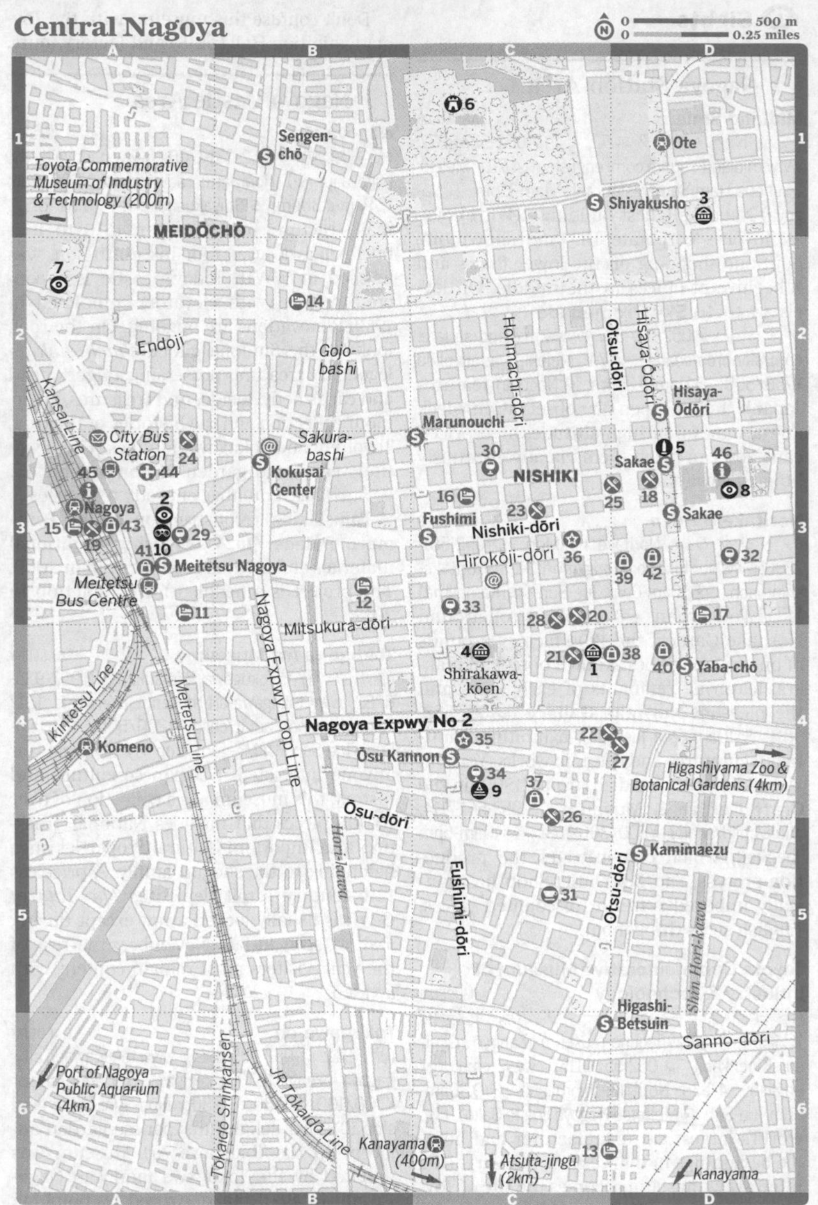

Nagoya City Archives HISTORIC BUILDING

(名古屋市政資料館, Nagoya Shisei Shiryō-kan; ☎052-953-0051; 1-3 Shirakabe, Higashi-ku; ⏲9am-5pm Tue-Sun; Ⓢ Shiyakusho, exit 3) FREE Built in 1922 this grand Taisho-era Court of Appeal now houses the city archives. While the archives themselves are difficult to navigate for non-Japanese speakers, the attractive neo-baroque building, with its fine stained-glass ornamentation, is worth a look.

Central Nagoya

Sights

1 International Design Centre Nagoya C4
2 Midland Square A3
3 Nagoya City Archives D1
4 Nagoya City Science Museum C4
5 Nagoya TV Tower D3
6 Nagoya-jō C1
Noritake Craft Centre and Museum .... (see 7)
Noritake Gallery .... (see 7)
7 Noritake Garden A2
8 Oasis 21 .... D3
9 Ōsu Kannon C4
10 Sky Promenade A3

Sleeping

11 Daiwa Roynet Nagoya Ekimae A3
12 Hilton Nagoya B3
13 Hostel Ann C6
14 Kyoya Ryokan B2
15 Nagoya Marriott Associa Hotel A3
16 Nishitetsu Inn Nagoya Nishiki C3
17 the b Nagoya D3

Eating

18 Chomoranmen D3
19 Din Tai Fung A3
20 Indus C3
21 Love Pacific Cafe C4
22 Misen C4
23 Sōhonke Ebisuya Honten C3
24 Tarafuku A3
25 Torigin Honten D3
26 Trattoria Cesari C4
27 Yabaton Honten D4
28 Yamamotoya Sōhonke C3

Drinking & Nightlife

29 7 Days Brew A3
30 Coat of Arms C3
31 GROK C5
32 Red Rock Bar & Grill D3
33 Shooters C3
34 Smash Head C4
The 59's Sports Bar & Diner .... (see 18)

Entertainment

35 Electric Lady Land C4
36 Nagoya Blue Note C3

Shopping

Kintetsu .... (see 41)
37 Komehyō C4
38 Loft Department Store D4
39 Maruei D3
40 Matsuzakaya D4
41 Meitetsu A3
42 Mitsukoshi D3
43 Takashimaya A3

Information

44 Tachino Clinic A3
45 Tourist Information Center (Nagoya Station) A3
46 Tourist Information Center (Sakae) D3

Fushimi & Sakae

The area between Fushimi and Sakae subway stations is ground zero for shopping and people-watching. **Hisaya-ōdōri-kōen** (Central Park) is usually bustling and Sakae's side streets fill with revellers well into the night.

Nagoya TV Tower TOWER

(名古屋テレビ塔; ☎052-971-8546; www.nagoya-tv-tower.co.jp; 3-6-15 Nishiki; adult/child/senior ¥700/300/600; ⏲10am-9pm; Ⓢ Sakae, exit 4b, 5a) Nagoya's much-loved TV tower, completed in 1954, was the first of its kind in Japan. The tower's central location makes its 100m-high **Sky Balcony** a great place to get the lie of the land. Better still, the sprawling beer garden and Korean barbecue at its base is unrivalled in town.

Oasis 21 LANDMARK

(オアシス２１; ☎052-962-1011; www.sakaepark.co.jp/en; 1-11-1 Higashi-sakura, Higashi-ku; Ⓢ Sakae, exit 4a) Oasis 21 is a bus terminal and transit hub with a difference. Its iconic 'galaxy platform' – an elliptical glass-and-steel structure filled with water for visual effect and cooling purposes – caused quite a stir when it was first built. Feel free to climb the stairs and walk around it while you're waiting for your next ride; it's most fun at night when it's adventurously lit.

Nagoya City Science Museum MUSEUM

(名古屋市科学館, Nagoya-shi Kagaku-kan; ☎052-201-4486; www.ncsm.city.nagoya.jp/en; 2-17-1 Sakae; adult/child ¥800/500; ⏲9.30am-5pm Tue-Sun; Ⓢ Fushimi, exit 5) This new hands-on museum claims the world's largest dome-screen planetarium with some seriously out-of-this-world projection technology. There's also a tornado lab and a deep-freeze lab complete with indoor aurora. Despite scheduled shows being kid-centric and in Japanese, the cutting-edge technology of this impressive, centrally located facility is worth experiencing.

International Design Centre Nagoya GALLERY

(国際デザインセンター, Kokusai Dezain Sentaa; 052-265-2105; www.idcn.jp/en; 3-7F, 3-18-1 Sakae; 11am-8pm Wed-Mon; S Yaba-chō, exit 5 or 6) FREE Housed in the swooping **Nadya Park** complex is this secular shrine to the deities of conceptualisation, form and function. Everything from art deco to postmodernism, Electrolux to Isamu Noguchi, Arne Jacobsen to the Mini Cooper, is represented in these significant galleries.

Once sated, design-heads should gravitate to the Loft Department Store (p216), also in Nadya Park, to burn some cash.

Further Afield

The area between Ōsu Kannon and Kamimaezu stations, crammed with retailers, eateries and street vendors, has a delightfully young and alternative vibe. Patient shoppers can be rewarded with funky vintage threads and offbeat souvenirs.

From Kamimaezu station, take exit 9 and walk north two blocks. Turn left onto Banshoji street (万松寺通), a covered shopping arcade that becomes Ōsu Kannon street and continues on to Ōsu Kannon temple. The streets either side are alive with activity. Further south, the busy yet compact Kanayama Station area is an alternative base to Meieki and Sakae.

Ōsu Kannon BUDDHIST TEMPLE

(大須観音; 052-231-6525; www.osu-kannon.jp; 2-21-47 Osu, Naka-ku; 24hr; S Ōsu Kannon, exit 2) FREE The much-visited Ōsu Kannon temple traces its roots back to 1333. The temple, devoted to the Buddha of Compassion was moved to its present location by Tokugawa Ieyasu in 1610, although the present buildings date from 1970. The library inside holds the oldest known handwritten copy of the *kojiki* – the ancient mythological history of Japan.

Atsuta-jingū SHINTO SHRINE

(熱田神宮; 052-671-4151; www.atsutajingu.or.jp; 1-1-1 Jingū; S Jingū-mae or Jingū-nishi, exit 2) Although the current buildings were completed in 1966, Atsuta-jingū has been a shrine for over 1900 years and is one of the most sacred Shintō shrines in Japan. Nestled among ancient cypress, it houses the sacred *kusanagi-no-tsurugi* (grass-cutting sword), one of the three regalia that, according to legend, were presented to the Imperial Family by the sun goddess Amaterasu-Ōmikami. There's a changing collection of over 4000 Tokugawa-era swords, masks and paintings on display in the **Treasure Hall** (宝物館; adult/child ¥300/150; 9am-4.30pm, closed last Wed & Thu of each month).

Nagoya/Boston Museum of Fine Arts MUSEUM

(名古屋ボストン美術館, Nagoya Boston Bijutsu-kan; 052-684-0101; www.nagoya-boston.or.jp/english; 1-1-1 Kanayama-chō; adult/senior/child ¥1300/900/free; 10am-7pm Tue-Fri, to 5pm Sat & Sun; Kanayama, south exit) This collaborative effort between Japanese backers and the Museum of Fine Arts Boston showcases an impressive collection of Japanese and international masterpieces.

Higashiyama Zoo & Botanical Gardens ZOO

(東山動植物園, Higashiyama Dōshokubutsu-en; 052-782-2111; www.higashiyama.city.nagoya.jp/14_english; 3-70 Higashiyama-motomachi, Chikusa-ku; adult/senior/child ¥500/100/free; 9am-5pm Tue-Sun; S Higashiyama-koen or Hoshigaoka) Some visitors might find the size of the enclosures at this otherwise well-kept zoo a little disheartening. A low admission price and the expansive, attractive, annexed Botanical Gardens earn this recommendation, especially for those travelling with kids. The zoo is a three-minute walk from Higashiyama-koen Station. If you're more interested in the gardens, use Hoshigaoka Station.

Port of Nagoya Public Aquarium AQUARIUM

(名古屋港水族館, Nagoya-ko Suizoku-kan; 052-654-7080; www.nagoyaaqua.jp; 1-3 Minatomachi, Minato-ku; combo ticket incl admission to all facilities ¥2400; 9.30am-5.30pm Tue-Sun; S Nagoya-ko) One of Nagoya's favourite attractions, this port-side aquarium boasts one of the largest outdoor tanks in the world, where resident dolphins frequently perform for crowds of up to 3000 spectators per show. We'll leave it up to you to decide how you feel about animals held and bred in captivity: this one claims its own conservation efforts. Be sure to check out the permanently moored **Fuji Icebreaker** ship, now an **Antarctic Museum**.

Festivals & Events

There are plenty of lively festivals and events to enjoy in a city of this size. A good, up-to-date resource can be found online at www.nagoya-info.jp/en/event.

Atsuta Matsuri CULTURAL
The largest and most auspicious celebration held at Atsuta-jingū on 5 June, with parades, martial arts displays and fireworks.

Nagoya Bashō SPORTS
(愛知県体育館, Aichi-ken Taiiku-kan; ☎052-971-2516; www.sumo.or.jp/eng; 1-1 Ninomaru; tickets from ¥3000) One of six annual sumo championship tournaments, Nagoya Bashō is held over two weeks in July at Aichi Prefectural Gymnasium. Arrive early in the afternoon to watch the lower-ranked wrestlers up close.

Minato Matsuri PARADE
Held around 'Ocean Day' (third Monday in July) is this street festival in Nagoya Port, with a parade, dancing, fireworks and a water-logging contest dating back to the Edo period.

World Cosplay Summit CULTURAL
(www.worldcosplaysummit.jp/en) If you're in Nagoya in July/August, be sure to see if your stay coincides with some of the events of this truly unique visual feast, when *cosplayers* (costume players) and anime fans from around the world come together to…well, play, in costume!

Nagoya Matsuri PARADE
Nagoya's big sha-bang takes place mid-October in Hisaya-ōdōri-kōen. Celebrating Nagoya's 'three heroes', the lively procession includes costumes, *karakuri ningyō* floats, folk dancing and decorated cars.

Sleeping

If you're passing through, stay near Nagoya or Kanayama stations for convenience. The area between Fushimi and Sakae will suit you better if you want to hit the town or shop 'til you drop. Ryokan do not have en-suite facilities. Be sure to take note of the station exits.

the b Nagoya HOTEL ¥
(ザ・ビー 名古屋; ☎052-241-1500; www.theb-hotels.com/en; 4-15-23 Sakae; s/d from ¥4800/6400; ; Ⓢ Sakae, exit 13) A smart, well-managed hotel with a brilliant location opposite Hisaya-ōdōri-kōen, between Sakae and Yaba-cho subway stations. Well-designed rooms are tiny but tasteful. Online special rates including breakfast offer excellent value.

Hostel Ann HOSTEL ¥
(Ann案; ☎052-253-7710; www.hostelann.com; 2-4-2 Kanayama; dm/s/d ¥2900/4000/7000; @; Ⓢ Kanayama, north exit) A short walk north of Kanayama station in a pleasant residential block, this former ryokan has been nicely remodelled to offer cheap digs for backpackers. From the station, walk north on Otsu-dōri, pass NTK hall (on your left) and turn right. Walk two short blocks and then turn left – the hostel is to the right.

Nishitetsu Inn Nagoya Nishiki HOTEL ¥¥
(西鉄イン名古屋錦; ☎052-209-5454; www.n-inn.jp/english/hotels/nagoya; 2-10-12 Nishiki; s/d ¥7,800/14,400; ; Ⓢ Fushimi, exit 1) You'll find this immaculate, stylish business hotel smack in the middle of it all: it's so central that you can crawl home if need be. Rooms are predictably compact yet functional and have a pleasant feel, with natural tones and accents. Cheaper rates can be found online.

Daiwa Roynet Nagoya Ekimae HOTEL ¥¥
(ダイワロイネットホテル名古屋駅前; ☎052-541-3955; www.daiwaroynet.jp/english/nagoyaekimae; 1-23-20 Meieki-minami; s/d from ¥7900/10,900; ; JR Nagoya, Sakura-dōri exit) If you're merely transiting in Nagoya and need cheap, clean (and yes, compact) digs near the station, look no further than this modern business hotel with refreshingly comfortable bedding. It's under 10 minutes' walk from the station.

★ **Hilton Nagoya** HOTEL ¥¥¥
(ヒルトン名古屋; ☎052-212-1111; www.hilton.com; 1-3-3 Sakae; s/d from ¥19,000/24,000; P@; Ⓢ Fushimi, exit 7) This characteristic Hilton benefits from an excellent location and features spacious, stylish rooms with Japanese accents, a selection of suites and an executive floor. There's also complimentary bicycle rental, a courtesy station shuttle service, two restaurants, three bars and a gym. Most rooms have good views.

Kyoya Ryokan RYOKAN ¥¥¥
(京屋旅館; ☎052-571-2588; http://kyoya.to; 2-11-4 Habashita, Nishi-ku; s/d incl 2 meals from ¥11,800/15,600; ; Ⓢ Kokusai Center) This popular ryokan centred around an attractive Japanese garden can get a little noisy when busy, but it has a lovely common bath and an even lovelier self-contained private suite. It's a little bit of a hike from the station, but the friendly owners are eager to help and speak some English.

Nagoya Marriott Associa Hotel HOTEL ¥¥¥
(名古屋マリオットアソシアホテル; ☎052-584-1111; www.associa.com/english/nma; 1-1-4 Meieki; s/d from ¥24,000/32,000; @; JR

Nagoya) Perched above JR Nagoya Station, it takes a while to get in/out and around the mammoth Marriott Associa, which tops everything in town. The 774 spacious rooms (all 35 sq m or larger) are located between the 20th and 49th floors, have huge windows with great views (some rooms have views from the tub) and luxurious, although somewhat dated appointments.

ANA Crowne Plaza Grand Court HOTEL ¥¥¥
(ANAクラウンプラザホテルグランコート名古屋; 052-683-4111; www.anacrowne-plaza-nagoya.jp/english; 1-1-1 Kanayama; s/d ¥20,000/28,000; P @; Kanayama, south exit) Conveniently located adjacent to Kanayama Station, this solid international hotel offers decent-sized, well-appointed rooms with a view. Significantly lower rates can usually be found through Crowne Plaza in your home country.

Eating

Nagoya may not be overburdened with tourist attractions, but it is a fantastic place to experience Japan's passion for food. The city is famous for bold local specialities that translate well to non-Japanese palates: *kishimen* are soft, flat, handmade wheat noodles; *miso-nikomi udon* are noodles in hearty miso broth; and *miso-katsu* is a fried breaded pork cutlet topped with miso sauce. *Kōchin* (free-range chicken), *hitsumabushi* (charcoal-grilled eel) and *tebasaki* (chicken wings) are other local specialities. For cheap international eats, head to the storefronts of the Ōsu Shopping Arcade, with street vendors hawking everything from kebabs to *karaage* (fried chicken), crêpes and pizza.

Sōhonke Ebisuya Honten NOODLES ¥
(総本家えびすや本店; 052-961-3412; 3-20-7 Sakae; dishes from ¥750, sets from ¥800; 11am-1am; S Sakae, exit 3) The massive noodle bowls at this, the head branch of one of Nagoya's best-known *kishimen* chains, are toasty, tasty and cheap. You can often see the noodles being made by the chef. There's a picture menu: try the *karē kishimen* (curry noodles, ¥900).

Love Pacific Cafe VEGAN ¥
(ラブ・パシフィックカフェ; 052-252-8429; 3-23-38 Sakae; items from ¥600; 11.30am-5pm Tue-Sun; ; S Yaba-chō, exit 4) Lovers of wholesome, delicious, healthy foods are in for a treat at this trendy, friendly, vegan cafe preparing lunch sets and cafe items that are free of dairy, egg and white sugars. The changing menu usually features a choice of two soups, the organic salad bar and a main: the tofu teriyaki burgers are delicious.

Indus INDIAN ¥
(インダス; 052-261-8819; 3-13-31 Sakae, Princess Garden Hotel 1F; lunch from ¥735, buffet ¥980; 11am-10pm; ; S Yaba-chō, exit 6, or Sakae, exit 7) A cheery, clean and colourful Indian institution where you can get serious with curry. The all-you-can-eat buffet is great value and includes your choice of three curries (including meat), an enormous naan bread, rice, salad, pappadams and a drink. There's a full à la carte menu and vegetarian options.

Chomoranmen NOODLES ¥
(ちょもらん麺; 052-963-5121; 3-15-10 Nishiki; items ¥630-1080; 11.30am-midnight; Sakae, exit 3) Opposite the Nagoya TV Tower, these cheap, chunky handmade *rāmen* bowls will fill you up. The walls are enshrined with photos of famous patrons. Someone should be happy to help you with the vending machine used to take orders if you get stuck.

★**Trattoria Cesari** ITALIAN ¥¥
(トラットリア　チェザリ; 052-238-0372; 3-36-44 Ōsu; pizza from ¥650, mains from ¥1150; 11am-3pm & 6-10pm; ; S Kamimaezu, exit 8) You may be surprised to find an Italian trattoria of this calibre and value smack bang in the heart of...Nagoya! Prepare to queue on weekends as folks line up for chef Makishima's famous Napoletana pizzas. There's an extensive à la carte menu of Italian favourites, masterfully prepared and presented in an atmosphere reminiscent of the homeland.

Yabaton Honten TONKATSU ¥¥
(矢場とん本店; 052-252-8810; www.english.yabaton.com; 3-6-18 Ōsu; dishes ¥1050-2400; 11am-9pm; ; S Yaba-chō, exit 4) This has been the place to try Nagoya's famed *miso-katsu* since 1947. Signature dishes are *waraji-tonkatsu* (schnitzel-style flattened, breaded pork) and *teppan-tonkatsu* (breaded pork cutlet with miso on a sizzling plate of cabbage). Walk under the expressway and look for the four-storey pig, across the street to your right. It's on the corner, next to McDonald's. Check the website for other locations.

Misen CHINESE ¥¥
(味仙; 052-238-7357; www.misen.ne.jp; 3-6-3 Ōsu; dishes ¥480-4800; 11.30am-2pm & 5pm-

1am Sun-Thu, to 2am Fri & Sat; ; S Yaba-chō, exit 4) Folks line up for opening at this big Chinese joint where the *Taiwan rāmen* (台湾ラーメン) induces rapture – it's a spicy concoction of ground meat, chilli, garlic and green onion, served over noodles in a hearty clear broth. Other faves include *gomoku yakisoba* (五目焼きそば; stir-fried noodles) and *kinoko-itame* (stir-fried mushrooms). There's a limited picture menu.

Din Tai Fung TAIWANESE ¥¥
(鼎泰豐; 052-533-6030; 1-1-4 Meieki, 12F Takashimaya Department Store; items from ¥432; 11am-10pm; JR Nagoya, Sakura-dōri exit) The Nagoya branch of this globally acclaimed Taiwanese chain, located in the Takashimaya department store at Nagoya station is likely to please with its literally 'mouth-watering' *xiao long bao* soup dumplings *(shōronbō)* and an extensive menu of dim-sum delights. Best for duos and groups of friends: the more the merrier.

Yamamotoya Sōhonke NOODLES ¥¥
(山本屋総本家; 052-241-5617; 3-12-19 Sakae; dishes ¥976-1842; 11am-3pm & 5-10pm; ; S Yaba-chō, exit 6) This is the place to go for soupy *miso-nikomi udon* – the chain has been doing it since 1925. The basic dish costs ¥976 and goes up from there. From Yaba-chō Station, take exit 6, turn left, cross Otsu-dōri and walk two blocks down Shirakawa-dōri. It's on your right and has a large white sign with black Japanese writing.

Tarafuku IZAKAYA ¥¥
(たら福; 052-566-5600; 3-17-26 Meieki; small plates ¥440-980; 5pm-1am Tue-Sun; ; Nagoya, Sakura-dōri exit) Atmosphere seeps from this ambitious *izakaya,* which transformed a decrepit building into an airy urban oasis. French-influenced dishes made with seasonal ingredients might include potato croquettes in a fried tofu crust, tomato and eggplant au gratin, or house-cured beef in wine sauce. There are wine and cocktail lists.

Torigin Honten JAPANESE ¥¥¥
(鳥銀本店; 052-973-3000; 3-14-22 Nishiki; kaiseki courses ¥3900-10,000; 5pm-midnight; ; S Sakae, exit 2) Come here for a unique *kōchin kaiseki* experience with immaculately presented servers and a wonderfully traditional atmosphere. Courses consist of *kōchin* chicken served in many forms, including *kushiyaki* (skewered), *kara-age* (deep-fried), *zōsui* (mild rice hotpot) and sashimi (what you think it is).

★ **Atsuta Hōraiken Honten** SEAFOOD ¥¥¥
(あつた蓬莱軒本店; 052-671-8686; 503 Gōdo-chō; sets from ¥2500; 11.30am-2pm & 4.30-8.30pm Thu-Tue; S Temma-chō, exit 4) The head branch of this *hitsumabushi* chain, in business since 1873, is revered for good reason. Patrons queue during the summer peak season for *hitsumabushi,* eel basted in a secret *tare* (sauce) served atop rice in a covered lacquered bowl (¥3600); add green onion, wasabi and *dashi* (fish broth) to your taste. Other *teishoku* (set menus) include tempura and steak.

Drinking & Nightlife

If you're looking to drink and make friends, Nagoya is the place to do so before heading north into Chūbu's sleepy interior. A large expat population means there are plenty of bars that are accessible and welcoming to foreign visitors, but not overrun by them.

GROK CAFE, BAR
(グロック; 052-332-2331; 1-6-13 Tachibana; 5pm-midnight Tue-Fri, noon-midnight Sat & Sun; S Kamimaezu, exit 7) We love this friendly, colourful and a little bit hippy two-storey cafe/bar. Whether you're with friends or flying solo, you're bound to feel comfortable. It's a little off the beaten track, but that's part of its charm. You can't miss it from the street.

Coat of Arms PUB
(コート・オブ・アームズ; 052-228-6155; www.coatofarms.jp/en; 2-6-12 Nishiki; 11.30am-midnight Tue-Sun; S Marunouchi, exit 5) This fresh and fun pub created by a bunch of booze-loving expats has an excellent outdoor patio (smoking permitted), two non-smoking interior floors, theme nights, weekly specials and a variety of unique craft beers and spirits to savour.

Smash Head PUB
(スマッシュヘッド; 052-201-2790; 2-21-90 Ōsu; noon-midnight Wed-Mon; S Ōsu Kannon, exit 2) Through the passageway to the left of the main Ōsu Kannon temple building, you'll find this teeny motorcycle and Vespa repair shop/pub (that's right). Guinness and Corona are the beers of choice, patrons are cool, and fish and chips costs ¥850.

The 59's Sports Bar & Diner BAR
(ザ フィフティーナインスポーツ バーアンドダイナー; 052-971-0566; 3-15-10 Nishiki; 5pm-late; @; S Sakae, exit 3) Cowboys and cowgirls greet you in this cruisy, colourful, fun and friendly basement bar. Staff will

make you feel welcome and may try to matchmake; with all-you-can-drink nights, they may succeed.

7 Days Brew PUB
(セブンデイズブリュー; ☎052-581-8844; 4-4-21 Meieki; ⏰5pm-1am Mon-Fri, from 11.30am Sat & Sun; 🚉JR Nagoya, Sakura-dōri exit) Tucked behind Midland Sq, this basement gem is a must for lovers of 'craft' beers and supporters of the microbrewery phenomenon. It's fresh, funky and the food rates too. Great atmosphere.

Red Rock Bar & Grill PUB
(レッドロックバーアンドグリル; ☎052-262-7893; www.theredrock.jp; 4-14-6 Sakae; ⏰5.30pm-1am Sun-Thu, 5.30pm-3am Fri & Sat; wi-fi; Ⓢ Sakae, exit 13) On a Sakae side street, Aussie-owned Red Rock attracts locals and expats alike. A fun menu includes such imports from Terra Australis as crocodile nuggets (that's right), lamb wraps and (we're told) the best meat pies north of Down Under. There's free wi-fi.

Shooters BAR
(シューターズ; ☎052-202-7077; www.shooters-nagoya.com; 2-9-26 Sakae; ⏰5pm-1am Mon-Thu, 11.30am-3am Fri-Sun; Ⓢ Fushimi, exit 5) Things can get rather raucous at Nagoya's largest American-themed sports bar: over a dozen big screens attract plenty of *gaijin* and their admirers. The bar menu includes mouth-watering burgers, hearty pasta and spicy Tex-Mex – some come just for the food.

Club Mago CLUB
(☎052-243-1818; www.club-mago.co.jp; 2-1-9 Shinsakae; cover charge varies; Ⓢ Shinsakae, exit 2) You'll love it or you'll hate it. This 'sexy' mega-club complex sometimes pulls international acts. Its throng of *gaijin* and Japanese punters often pulses with excitement.

☆ Entertainment

Nagoya's nightlife might not match Tokyo's or Osaka's in scale but it makes up for it in enthusiasm. Check venue homepages for listings.

Electric Lady Land LIVE MUSIC
(エレクトリックレディランド; ☎052-201-5004; www.ell.co.jp; 2-10-43 Ōsu; Ⓢ Ōsu Kannon, exit 2) An intimate live venue showcasing the underground music scene in a cool, post-industrial setting. Nationally known bands play the 1st-floor hall, while up-and-coming acts have the smaller 3rd.

Nagoya Blue Note LIVE MUSIC
(名古屋ブルーノート; ☎052-961-6311; www.nagoya-bluenote.com; B2F 3-22-20 Nishiki; Ⓢ Sakae, exit 8) If you're into jazz, big band or blues, you're likely to find your fancy at this long-standing Nagoyan institution.

Shopping

Nagoya's manufacturing roots make it a great place to shop. Both Meieki and Sakae boast gargantuan malls and department stores, good for clothing, crafts and foods. Big players are **Maruei** (丸栄; ☎052-264-1211; 3-3-1 Sakae; Ⓢ Sakae), **Mitsukoshi** (三越; ☎052-252-1111; 3-5-1 Sakae; Ⓢ Sakae, exit 16) and **Matsuzakaya** (松坂屋; ☎052-251-1111; www.matsuzakaya.co.jp/nagoya; 3-16-1 Sakae; Ⓢ Yaba-chō, exit 6) in Sakae; and **Takashimaya** (高島屋; ☎052-566-1101; 1-1-4 Meieki; 🚉JR Nagoya, Sakura-dōri side), **Meitetsu** (名鉄; ☎052-585-1111; 1-2-1 Meieki; 🚉Meitetsu Nagoya) and **Kintetsu** (近鉄; ☎052-582-3411; 1-2-2 Meieki; 🚉Kintetsu Nagoya) near Nagoya Station.

Regional crafts include *Arimatsu-narumi shibori* (elegant tie-dyeing), cloisonné ceramics and *seki* blades (swords, knives, scissors etc).

In Ōsu, along Akamon-dōri, Banshō-ji-dōri and Niomon-dōri, are hundreds of funky vintage boutiques and discount clothing retailers. Ōsu Kannon temple hosts a colourful antique market on the 18th and 28th of each month, while Higashi Betsuin temple has a flea market on the 12th of each month.

East of Ōsu, Otsu-dōri has a proliferation of manga shops.

Komehyō DEPARTMENT STORE
(コメ兵; ☎052-242-0088; www.en.komehyo.co.jp; 2-20-25 Ōsu; ⏰10.30am-7.30pm Thu-Tue; Ⓢ Ōsu Kannon, exit 2) Enjoy the genius of Komehyō, Japan's largest discounter of secondhand, well...everything. Housed over seven floors in the main building, clothes, jewellery and accessories are of excellent quality and are sold at reasonable prices. With patience, you can find some real bargains, especially at 'yen=g' on the 7th floor, where clothing is sold by weight.

Loft Department Store DEPARTMENT STORE
(ロフト; ☎052-219-3000; 3-18-1 Sakae, Nadya Park; ⏰10.30am-8pm; Ⓢ Yaba-chō, exit 5 or 6) The Nagoya branch of one of Japan's coolest department stores has a definite design bent. You can't miss the yellow and black livery.

Orientation

Running east of the station, Sakura-dōri, Nishiki-dōri and Hirokōji-dōri are the three main drags, intersected first by Fushimi-dōri then Otsu-dōri. The majority of the mainstream action is found within this grid. Just east of Otsu-dōri is the long and narrow Hisaya-ōdōri-kōen (aka Central Park), Nagoya's much loved Eiffel-esque TV Tower and the wacky Oasis 21 complex. Following Otsu-dōri north will get you to Nagoya-jō, while the vibrant Ōsu district, Atsuta-jingū shrine and bustling Kanayama station area, are to the south.

Nagoya's subway system has English signs and services all the hot spots – Fushimi and Sakae stations are your mainstays for shopping, accommodation and nightlife.

Information

INTERNET ACCESS

Nagoya International Centre (名古屋国際センター; ☎052-581-0100; www.nic-nagoya.or.jp/en; 1-47-1 Nagono; ⊙9am-7pm Tue-Sun; Ⓢ Kokusai Center) This not-for-profit organisation provides information, consultation and referral services in English. There's also an internet corner on the 3rd floor (¥100 per 15 minutes) and a library with over 30,000 items in various languages.

FedEx Kinko's Fushimi (フェデックスキンコーズ伏見店; ☎052-231-9211; 1F Kirin Hirokōji Bldg, 2-3-31 Sakae; ⊙24hr; Ⓢ Fushimi, exit 4) Rental PCs available for internet access as well as scanning and printing services.

INTERNET RESOURCES

There are a number of useful websites for up-to-date information on what's happening in Nagoya. The homepages of the Nagoya Convention and Visitors Bureau (www.nagoya-info.jp/en) and Nagoya International Centre (www.nic-nagoya.or.jp/en) are brimming with information. Also try www.nagoya-info.com for English-language listings.

MEDICAL SERVICES

Aichi Prefectural Emergency Medical Guide (愛知県救急医療ガイド; ☎052-263-1133, automated service 050-5810-5884; www.qq.pref.aichi.jp) Phone or follow the English link on this prefectural homepage for a list of medical institutions with English-speaking staff, including specialities and hours of operation.

Tachino Clinic (たちのクリニック; ☎052-541-9130; 3F Dai-Nagoya Bldg, 3-26-8 Meieki; ⊙9.30am-1pm & 2.30-6pm Mon-Wed & Fri, 9.30am-1pm Thu & Sat; 🚉JR Nagoya, Sakura-dōri exit) This medical clinic a short walk from Nagoya station has English-speaking staff.

MONEY & POST

Citibank has 24-hour Cirrus ATMs on the 1st floor of the Sakae Parkside Place building (Sakae subway station, exit 2) and in the arrival lobby at Central Japan International Airport. Most 7-Eleven convenience stores and Japan Post ATMs dispense cash from foreign cards.

JR Towers Post Office (タワーズ内郵便局; ☎052-586-5530; 1-1-4 Meieki; 🚉JR Nagoya) Within the JR station complex, on the Sakura-dōri side.

TOURIST INFORMATION

English-language street and subway maps are widely available at Tourist Information Centers (TICs) and hotels. The *Nagoya Pocket Guide* (www.nagoyapocketguide.com) is particularly handy, as are the *Nagoya Navi Map* and *Nagoya Shopping and Dining Guide*, which you can also download at www.nagoya-info.jp/en/brochures.

Nagoya has three helpful Tourist Information Center branches stacked with resources in English and Japanese and at least one English speaker on hand.

Tourist Information Center – Nagoya Station (名古屋駅観光案内所; ☎052-541-4301; 1-1-14 Meieki; ⊙9am-7pm; 🚉JR Nagoya)

Tourist Information Center – Kanayama (金山観光案内所; ☎052-323-0161; LOOP Kanayama 1F, 1-17-18 Kanayama; ⊙9am-7pm; 🚉Kanayama, north exit)

Tourist Information Center – Sakae (栄町観光案内所; ☎052-963-5252; Oasis 21 B1F, 1-11-1 Higashisakura; ⊙10am-8pm; Ⓢ Sakae)

Getting There & Away

AIR

On a manmade island in Ise-wan, 35km south of the city, **Central Japan International Airport** (NGO; ☎056-938-1195; www.centrair.jp/en) has become a tourist attraction for locals who come for the dozens of well-priced shopping and dining options, to plane-spot from the enormous observation deck, or to soak in the **Fū-no-yu** (風の湯; Central Japan International Airport, SkyTown 4F; adult/child with towel ¥1030/620; ⊙8am-10pm) hot-spring baths. For travellers, the airport is far friendlier and less frantic than its big brothers in Tokyo and Osaka. With excellent transport connections, it's a great arrival port into Japan from around 30 international destinations in Europe, North America and Asia. Domestic routes serve around 20 Japanese cities, though you'll find some are reached faster by train.

BOAT

Taiheiyo Ferry (☎052-582-8611; www.taiheiyo-ferry.co.jp/english) sails snazzy ships between Nagoya and Tomakomai (Hokkaidō, from ¥9500, 40 hours) via Sendai (from ¥6500, 21 hours 40 minutes) every other evening at 7pm, with daily services to Sendai. Take the Meikō subway line to Nagoya-kō Station and go to Nagoya Port.

BUS

JR and Meitetsu Highway buses operate services between Nagoya and Kyoto (¥2500, 2½ hours, hourly), Osaka (¥3000, three hours, hourly), Kobe (¥3300, 3½ hours), Kanazawa (¥4060, four hours, 10 daily), Nagano (¥4000, 4½ hours) and Tokyo (¥5000, six hours, 14 daily). Overnight buses run to Hiroshima (¥8500, nine hours).

New kid on the block, **Willer Express** (www.willerexpress.com) offers airline-style seating and online reservations in English at *heavily* discounted rates. Key routes from Nagoya include Tokyo (from ¥3200, six hours) and Fukuoka (from ¥6500, 11½ hours overnight).

Departure points vary by carrier and destination, although almost all highway buses depart from somewhere in Meieki (JR Nagoya Station). Some routes also depart from Oasis 21. JR Highway buses depart from the JR Highway Bus Terminal near the Shinkansen entrance (north side) of JR Nagoya Station. Meitetsu Highway buses depart from the Meitetsu Bus Centre. Willer Express buses depart from a variety of locations, depending on the route. Be sure to confirm your departure location with your carrier at the time of booking.

TRAIN

All lines lead to Meieki (JR Nagoya Station), a hybrid terminus of the JR and private Meitetsu and Kintetsu train lines, as well as subway and bus stations. Here you'll find a labyrinthine world of passageways, restaurants and retailers, and above, the soaring JR Central Towers and Midland Sq complexes. Be sure to leave plenty of time if making a rail transfer!

Nagoya is a major *shinkansen* hub, connecting with Tokyo (¥10,360, 1¾ hours), Shin-Osaka (¥5830, 50 minutes), Kyoto (¥5070, 35 minutes), Hiroshima (¥13,290, 2¼ hours) and Hakata/Fukuoka (¥17,500, 3¼ hours).

To get into the Japan Alps, take the JR Chūō line to Matsumoto (*Shinano tokkyū* ¥5510, two hours) or onwards to Nagano (¥7130, 2¾ hours). A separate line (JR Takayama line) serves Takayama (*Hida tokkyū*, ¥5510, 2¼ hours).

The private Meitetsu line has routes in and around Nagoya (Tokonome, Inuyama, Gifu) covered.

Getting Around

TO/FROM THE AIRPORT

Central Japan International Airport is easily accessed from Nagoya and Kanayama stations via the Meitetsu *Kūkō* (Airport) line (*tokkyū*, ¥1230, 28 minutes). A taxi from central Nagoya costs upwards of ¥13,000.

BUS

The gold **Me-guru bus** (名古屋観光ルートバスメーグル; www.nagoya-info.jp/en/routebus; day pass adult/child ¥500/250) follows a one-way loop near attractions in the Meieki, Sakae and castle areas. Ticket holders receive discounted admissions to many attractions. It runs hourly from 9.30am to 5pm Tuesday to Friday and twice hourly on weekends. No bus on Mondays.

SUBWAY

Nagoya has an excellent subway system with six lines, clearly signposted in English and Japanese. Fares cost ¥200 to ¥320 depending on distance. One-day passes (¥740, including city buses ¥850, available at ticket machines), include subway transport and discounted admission to many attractions. On Saturday and Sunday the *donichi eco-kippu* (Saturday and Sunday eco-ticket) gives the same benefits for ¥600 per day.

AROUND NAGOYA

In the suburbs of Nagoya, outlying Aichi-ken and the southern part of Gifu-ken, there are some interesting destination museums and towns reached easily by train.

Greater Nagoya

★ JR SCMAGLEV & Railway Park MUSEUM
(JR リニア・鉄道館, JR Rinia Tetsudō-kan; ☎050-3772-3910; http://museum.jr-central.co.jp/en; Kinjofuto 3-2-2; adult/child ¥1000/500; ⏲10am-5.30pm Wed-Mon; 🚉JR Aonami line to Kinjofuto) Trainspotters will be in heaven at this fantastic hands-on museum. Featuring actual *Maglev* (the world's fastest train – 581km/h), *shinkansen* and historical rolling stock and rail simulators, this massive museum offers a fascinating insight into Japanese post-war history through the development of a railroad like no other. The 'hangar' is 20 minutes from Nagoya on the Aonami line, found on the Taiko-dōri side of JR Nagoya station.

Toyota Exhibition Hall MUSEUM
(トヨタ会館, Toyota Kaikan; ☎museum 0565-29-3345, tours 0565-29-3355; www.toyota.co.jp/en/about_toyota/facility/toyota_kaikan; 1 Toyota-chō; ⏲9.30am-5pm Mon-Sat, tours 11am; 🚉Aichi Kanjō line to Mikawa Toyota) FREE See up to 20 shiny examples of the latest automotive technology hot off the production line and witness first hand how they're made here at Toyota's global HQ. Fascinating two-hour tours

TOKONAME POTTERY FOOTPATH

Clay beneath the ground has made the bayside community of Tokoname a ceramic-making hub for centuries – at one time 400 chimneys rose above its centre. The area still produces some ¥60 trillion in ceramics annually and makes an interesting excursion from Nagoya or nearby Central Japan International Airport.

The **Pottery Footpath** (やきもの散歩道, Yakimono Sanpō-michi) is a hilly 1.8km trail around the town's historic centre. Start by collecting a walking map from the Tourist Information Center inside Tokoname Station. Lining the well signposted path are kilns, cafes and galleries, with numbered plaques corresponding to the walking map indicating the stops along the way. A series of *maneki-neko* (ceramic 'lucky' cats) greets you as you head toward the beginning of the path. If you look up, you'll see **'Toko-nyan'**, the mother of all lucky cats, looming above: one for the Instagrammers.

Circa 1850 the restored **Takita Residence** (瀧田家, Takita-ke; ☎0569-36-2031; 4-75 Sakae-machi; admission ¥300; ⏲9am-4.30pm Tue-Sun), stop 8, was the home of a shipping magnate. Inside are replicas of *bishu-kaisen* (local trading ships) and displays of ceramics, lacquer and furniture. Continuing on, the pipe-and-jug-lined lane at **Dokan-zaka Hill** (stop 9) is particularly photogenic. Around the back of the **Climbing Kiln Square** (*Noborigahama-hiroba*, stop 13) you'll find 10 of the square chimneys that served the gigantic 1887 kiln. It's a five-minute detour from here to the **Inax Live Museum** (イナックスライブミュージアム; ☎0569-34-8282; www1.lixil.co.jp/ilm/english; 1-130 Okueichō; adult/child ¥600/200; ⏲10am-5pm, closed 3rd Wed of month), showpiece of one of Japan's largest ceramics manufacturers and housing some 150 elaborately decorated Meiji- and Taisho-era toilets (you read correctly) and Japan's only tile museum.

When you need a rest, atmospheric **Koyō-an** (古窯庵; ☎0569-35-8350; 4-87 Sakae-machi; dishes ¥480-1780; ⏲11.30am-5pm Tue-Sun; 🗐) serves homemade *soba* (buckwheat noodles) on beautiful local pottery, or why not dine near the giant cat, at cosy **Nakamura-ya** (うなぎの中村屋; ☎0569-35-0120; 2-53 Sakae-machi; sets ¥1350-3600; ⏲11.30am-2.30pm Thu-Tue), whose specialities are *una-don* (eel on rice) and Nagoya's famous *hitsumabushi*?

The private Meitetsu line connects Tokoname with Nagoya (*tokkyū* ¥660, 33 minutes) and Central Japan International Airport (¥310, five minutes). The Pottery Footpath begins a few hundred metres from the train station.

of Toyota Motor Corporation's main factory are conducted Monday through Saturday at 11am, but you need to book from two weeks to three months in advance. Allow two hours to get to Toyota city from central Nagoya; refer to the website for directions and reservations.

Arimatsu Tie-Dyeing Museum MUSEUM
(有松鳴海絞会館, Arimatsu Shibori Kaikan; ☎052-621-0111; www.shibori-kaikan.com; 3008 Arimatsu; adult/child ¥300/100; ⏲9.30am-5pm Thu-Tue; 🚉Meitetsu main line to Meitetsu Arimatsu) This museum upholds the 400-year-old tradition of *shibori* (tie-dyeing). Downstairs, you'll find historical artefacts, a gift shop and a video introducing this painstaking and beautiful craft. Upstairs, a number of women patiently demonstrate the art. If you fancy and have the time (up to three hours) you can try it yourself. It costs ¥1050 to ¥3150 depending on the item: reservations are required. Arimatsu is about 20 minutes from Nagoya on the Meitetsu main line, towards Toyohashi.

Inuyama 犬山

☎0568 / POP 74,650

Inuyama's Kiso-gawa (river), aka the 'Japanese Rhine', paints a pretty picture beneath its castle, a National Treasure. By day, the castle, quaint streets, manicured Uraku-en and 17th-century Jo-an Teahouse make for pleasant strolling, while at night the scene turns cinematic as fishermen perform the anicent art of *ukai* (p223) by firelight.

Just south of the castle are the picturesque Shinto shrines **Haritsuna Jinja** (針綱神社; ☎0568-61-0180; 65-1 Kitakoken) FREE and **Sankō-Inari Jinja** (三光稲荷神社; ☎0568-61-0702; 41-1 Kitakoken), the latter with interesting statues of *komainu* (protective dogs).

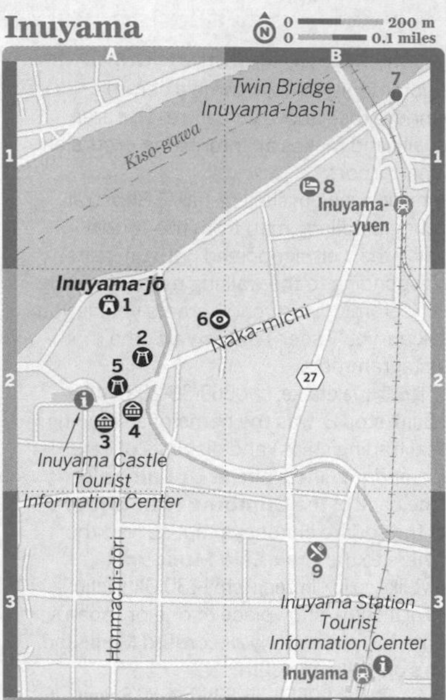

Inuyama

Top Sights

1 Inuyama-jō A2

Sights

2 Haritsuna Jinja A2
3 Inuyama Artifacts Museum/Castle & Town Museum A2
4 Karakuri Exhibition Room (Annex) A2
5 Sankō-Inari Jinja A2
6 Uraku-en & Chashitsu Jo-an A2

Activities, Courses & Tours

7 Kiso-gawa Cormorant Fishing B1

Sleeping

8 Rinkō-kan B1

Eating

9 Narita B3

Since 1635 townsfolk have celebrated the **Inuyama Matsuri** (festival) on the first weekend in April. A scaled-down version is held on the fourth Saturday in October. A government designated Intangible Cultural Asset, the festival features a parade of 13 three-tiered floats strewn with 365 lanterns. Atop each float elaborate *karakuri ningyō* (marionettes) perform to music.

Sights & Activities

★Inuyama-jō CASTLE

(犬山城; ☎0568-61-1711; 65-2 Kitakoken; adult/child ¥500/100; ⊙9am-4.30pm; 🚉Meitetsu Inuyama-yuen) A National Treasure, Japan's oldest standing castle is said to have originated as a fort in 1440. The current *donjon* (main keep), built atop a 40m rise beside the Kiso-gawa, dates from 1537 and has resisted war, earthquake and restoration, remaining the penultimate example of Momoyama-era architecture. Inside are steep, narrow staircases and military displays – the view from the top is worth the climb. The castle is 15 minutes' walk from Meitetsu Inuyama-yuen Station.

Inuyama Artifacts Museum/Castle & Town Museum MUSEUM

(犬山市文化史料館・城とまちミュージアム, Inuyama-shi Bunka Shiryō-kan/Shiro to Machi Myūjiamu; ☎0568-62-4802; 8 Kitakoken; admission ¥100, free with admission to Inuyama-jō; ⊙9am-4.30pm; 🚉Meitetsu Inuyama-yuen) This museum, located one block south of Haritsuna Jinja and Sankō-Inari Jinja was reopened in October 2012 after extensive renovations. It houses two of the Inuyama festival floats and various artefacts related to cormorant fishing, Inuyama-jō and the town's history.

Karakuri Exhibition Room (Annex) MUSEUM

(からくり展示館（別館, Karakuri Tenji-kan (Bekkan); ☎0568-61-3932; 69-2/69-3 Kitakoken; admission ¥100, free with admission to Inuyama-jō; ⊙9am-4.30pm; 🚉Meitetsu Inuyama-yuen) This small annexe exhibits Edo- and Meiji-era *karakuri ningyō* (marionettes). On Saturdays and Sundays at 10.30am and 2pm, you can see the wooden characters in action. On Fridays and Saturdays between 10am and 4pm, there are demonstrations of how the puppets are made by artisan Tamaya Shobei the 9th, who is the only living *karakuri ningyō* Master from an unbroken lineage.

Uraku-en & Chashitsu Jo-an GARDENS

(有楽苑・茶室如安; ☎0568-61-4608; 1 Gomonsaki; adult/child ¥1000/600; ⊙9am-5pm Mar-Nov, 9am-4pm Dec-Feb; 🚉Meitetsu Inuyama-yuen) Within the pretty garden of Uraku-en in the grounds of the Meitetsu Inuyama Hotel, you'll find 'Jo-an', one of the finest teahouses in Japan. Another of Inuyama's National Treasures, Jo-an was built in 1618 in Kyoto by Oda Urakusai, younger brother of Oda Nobunaga, and relocated here in 1972. You can enjoy tea on the grounds for an additional ¥500.

Kiso-gawa Cormorant Fishing BOAT TOUR
(木曽川鵜飼い, Kiso-gawa Ukai; ☎0568-61-2727; evening tours adult/child from ¥2600/1300) From 1 June to 15 October, the spectacle of this ancient practice takes place close to Inuyama-yūen Station, by the Twin Bridge Inuyama-bashi. Book your ticket on a **Kisogawa Kankō** spectator boat at the Tourist Information Center or near the cormorant-fishing pier. Up-close-and-personal tour boats depart nightly at 7pm from June to August, 30 minutes earlier in September and October. Daylight tours depart at 11.30am and include a lunchbox (adult/child ¥3800/2900). You can always watch from a distance on the riverbank for free.

Festivals & Events

In addition to **Inuyama Matsuri**, the city also hosts the summer **Nihon Rhine Matsuri** culminating in fireworks, every 10 August on the banks of the river.

Sleeping & Eating

If you can't find the kind of accommodation you're looking for, consider staying in nearby Gifu or Nagoya.

Inuyama International Youth Hostel HOSTEL ¥
(犬山国際ユースホステル; ☎0568-61-1111; www.inuyama-hostel.com/en; 161 Himuro; s/d from ¥3300/4400; @; 🚇Meitetsu Inuyama-yuen) This large hostel with a variety of room types and communal bathing is a little isolated, but reasonably priced. Meals must be reserved (breakfast/dinner ¥840/1580) and there are no facilities nearby. It's a 30-minute walk from Inuyama-yūen Station, or about ¥1350 in a taxi.

Rinkō-kan RYOKAN ¥¥
(臨江館; ☎0568-61-0977; www.rinkokan.jp; 8-1 Nishidaimon; r per person incl 2 meals from ¥10,800; @; 🚇Meitetsu Inuyama-yuen, west exit) Overlooking the river, this cheery 20-room ryokan has stone common baths including *rotemburo*. Some rooms have in-room bathrooms and a variety of packages are available, including good deals for single travellers.

Narita FRENCH ¥¥
(フレンチ創作料理なり多; ☎0568-65-2447; 395 Higashikoken; 5-course meal from ¥3200; ⏲11am-9pm; 🚇Meitetsu Inuyama, west exit) Fancy five-course French cusine in an Edo-period building with an attractive garden – lovely! From the station, turn right at the lights, walk two blocks to the next set of lights, then turn right. It's on your right.

Information

Inuyama has two Tourist Information Centers that dispense English-language materials and assist with accommodation and activities reservations. On the web, visit www.ml.inuyama.gr.jp/en.

Inuyama Station Tourist Information Center (犬山市観光案内所 (犬山駅; ☎0568-61-6000; ⏲9am-5pm)

Inuyama Castle Tourist Information Center (犬山市観光案内所 (犬山城; ☎0568-61-2825; 12 Kitakoken; ⏲9am-5pm)

Getting There & Around

Inuyama is connected with Nagoya (*tokkyū* ¥550, 25 minutes) and Gifu (¥450, 35 minutes) via the Meitetsu Inuyama line. The castle and *ukai* area are slightly closer to Inuyama-yūen Station than Inuyama Station.

Around Inuyama 犬山近辺

The region surrounding Inuyama has a few unusual and worthwhile attractions, as well as some decent farmland scenery. Check transport connections before you set out.

Sights

★Meiji-mura MUSEUM
(明治村; ☎0568-67-0314; www.meijimura.com/english; 1 Uchiyama; adult/senior/child ¥1700/1300/1000; ⏲9.30am-5pm Mar-Oct, to 4pm Nov-Feb, closed Mon Dec-Feb) Known for unifying Western and Japanese architectural elements, few Meiji-era buildings have survived due to war, earthquakes and development. In 1965 this open-air museum was created to preserve this unique style. Over 60 buildings from around Japan were painstakingly dismantled, transported and reassembled in this leafy lakeside location. Favourites include the entry facade of Frank Lloyd Wright's Tokyo Imperial Hotel, Kyoto's St Francis Xavier's Cathedral, and Sapporo's telephone exchange.

Buses to Meiji-mura (¥410, 20 minutes) depart every 20 to 30 minutes from Inuyama Station's east exit. If you're driving, parking is ¥800.

Ōagata-jinja SHINTO SHRINE
(大縣神社; ☎0568-67-1017; 3 Aza Miyayama; 🚇Meitetsu Komaki line to Gakuden) This ancient shrine set on a lovely hillside is dedicated

to the female Shintō deity Izanami and attracts women seeking marriage or fertility. See if you can find the large *hime-ishi* (姫石; princess stone) and other items resembling giant female genitals. The popular Hime-no-miya Matsuri takes place here on the Sunday before 15 March (or on 15 March if it's a Sunday). Locals pray for good harvests and prosperity by parading through the streets bearing a *mikoshi* (portable shrine) with more replica vaginas.

Ōagata-jinja is a 25-minute walk from Gakuden Station (¥220 from Inuyama, seven minutes). To reach the shrine, turn right at the exit and follow Route 177 east, all the way across the river and up the hill. Sadly, recent expansion of a nearby industrial landfill threatens the tranquillity of the shrine. Beware the many noisy, smelly dumptrucks sharing the narrow road to your destination.

Tagata-jinja SHINTO SHRINE

(田県神社; 152 Tagata-chō; Meitetsu Komaki line to Tagata-jinja-mae) Izanagi, the male counterpart of female deity Izanami, is commemorated at this shrine, with countless wooden and stone phalluses to celebrate. You can buy souvenirs from ¥500. The **Tagata Hōnen-sai Matsuri** takes place on 15 March at Tagata-jinja, when the highly photogenic, 2m-long, 60kg 'sacred object' is paraded excitedly around the neighbourhood. Arrive well before the procession starts at 2pm. Tagata-jinja is five minutes' walk west of Tagata-jinja-mae Station on the Meitetsu Komaki line (¥290 from Inuyama, nine minutes).

Gifu 岐阜

058 / POP 410,410

Historically Gifu has a strong association with Oda Nobunaga, *daimyō* (domain lord) of the castle and bestower of the city's name in 1567. It was later visited by famed haiku poet Matsuō Bashō, who witnessed *ukai* here in 1688; Charlie Chaplin did the same in his day.

Although contemporary Gifu shows little evidence of those historic times (due to a colossal earthquake in 1891 and the decimation of WWII), redevelopment has created a vibrant and accessible downtown core. Noteworthy attractions include the lovely Gifu Park and one of the three Great Buddhas of Japan. Add some pretty mountains, a wide river and excellent transportation links, and a stopover here becomes a viable alternative to big city Nagoya.

Sights

Visitors generally arrive into JR Gifu or Meitetsu Gifu stations, but sightseeing is centred about a 15-minute bus ride north of this area around Gifu-kōen, the Nagara River and the picturesque 'old-town' of Kawara-machi.

Shōhō-ji (Gifu Great Buddha) BUDDHIST TEMPLE

(正法寺; 058-264-2760; 8 Daibutsu-chō; adult/child ¥200/100; 9am-5pm; N80, N32-N86 to Gifu-kōen) The main attraction of this orange-and-white temple is the papier-mâché *daibutsu* (Great Buddha, circa 1832), one of the three Great Buddha statues of Japan. It's 13.7m tall and is said to have been fashioned over 38 years using a tonne of paper Sutras.

Gifu-kōen PARK

(岐阜公園; N80, N32-N86 to Gifu-kōen) At the foot of Mt Kinka-zan, this is one of the loveliest city parks in Japan, with plenty of water and trees set into the hillside.

Gifu-jō CASTLE

(岐阜城; 058-263-4853; 18 Tenshukaku; adult/child ¥200/100; 9.30am-4.30pm; N80, N32-N86 to Gifu-kōen) Perched atop Mt Kinka-zan with sweeping views over the cities of Gifu and Nagoya, this castle is a 1956 concrete replica of Oda Nobunaga's stronghold, destroyed in 1600, the ruins of which were finished off in WWII. There's an hour-long hiking trail from the park below.

Kinka-zan Ropeway ROPEWAY

(金華山ロープウエー; 058-262-6784; 257 Senjōjiki-shita; return adult/child ¥1080/620; 9am-5pm year-round, extended hours during holiday periods) Gifu's castle is most easily reached by this cable car within Gifu-kōen, whisking you 329m to the summit in under five minutes.

Nagara River Ukai Museum MUSEUM

(長良川うかいミュージアム, Nagara-gawa Ukai Myūjiamu; 058-210-1555; http://ukaimuseum.jp; 51-2 Choryo; adult/child ¥500/250; 9am-6.30pm Wed-Mon 1 May-15 Oct, 9am-4.30pm Wed-Mon 16 Oct-30 Apr; City loop or N-line bus to Ukai-ya) This museum is the only one of its kind and features exhibits on everything you could possibly want to know about cormorant fishing in Japan.

UKAI: THE ANICENT ART OF CORMORANT FISHING

The cities of Inuyama and Gifu remain some of the few places in the world where the ancient (and some say barbaric) practice of cormorant fishing continues as it has done for centuries. Estimates date the practice, which falls under the auspices of the Imperial Household Agency (the first and finest fish of the year are sent to the emperor) at over 1300 years. The masters (called *ushō*) are so skilled that their craft is passed on from father to son.

During the *ukai* season (from 1 June to 15 October), *ushō* set off after dusk in 13m traditional boats, with an iron basket containing a burning fire suspended by a pole at the front of the boat. Trained cormorants (large black, long-necked diving birds known for their voracious appetites), tethered by neck ropes to their masters, are released from the boats to dive for *ayu* (sweetfish). The ropes prevent the birds from swallowing the largest fish, which get lodged in their throats. Each bird will hold around six large fish until the master pulls it back into his boat and the fish are regurgitated. Although many shirk at this apparent cruelty, masters claim the birds are not harmed by their training.

While it's not for everyone, the spectacle of the fires reflected off the water and the opportunity to witness a unique and relatively unchanged traditional way of what was originally a means of feeding one's family, make watching *ukai* 'something different' if you're in the area.

Activities

Nagara-gawa Cormorant Fishing BOAT TOUR
(長良川鵜飼い, Nagara-gawa Ukai) The spectacle of *ukai* (cormorant fishing) and the glow of the lanterns drifting along the river east of the Nagara-bashi is a sight to behold. For a closer view, sightseeing boats depart nightly in season (1 June to 15 October) from the **Cormorant Fishing Viewing Boat Office** (鵜飼観覧船事務所; ☎058-262-0104; www.gifucvb.or.jp/en; 1-2 Minato-machi; adult/child ¥3400/1700; ⌚departures 6.15pm, 6.45pm & 7.15pm 1 June-15 Oct; 🚌N80, N32-N86, direction Takatomi, stop Nagara-bashi) below the bridge, which also takes reservations by phone (strongly advised). Food and drinks are not available on the boats.

Sleeping

The narrow streets a few blocks north of JR Gifu and west of Meitetsu Gifu stations, between Kinkabashi-dōri and Nagarabashi-dōri, are dotted with open eateries, *izakaya* and a welcoming nocturnal vibe. Many hotels are in this general vicinity.

Dormy Inn Gifu Ekimae HOTEL ¥¥
(ドーミーイン岐阜; ☎058-267-5489; www.hotespa.net/hotels/gifu; 6-31 Yoshino-machi; s/d from ¥7700/10,900; 🚉JR Gifu, north exit) Opened in September 2012, this new kid on the block is five minutes' stroll along the elevated walkway from JR Gifu Station. Light-filled rooms are functionally compact with fresh, inviting decor. There's an on-site onsen and the guest laundry has gas-powered dryers (so you can actually get a decent amount of clothes dried). Breakfast is available.

Daiwa Roynet Hotel Gifu HOTEL ¥¥
(ダイワロイネットホテル岐阜; ☎058-212-0055; www.daiwaroynet.jp/gifu; 8-5 Kanda-machi; s/d from ¥5800/7700; ⊖@; 🚉Meitetsu Gifu) Close to Meitetsu Gifu station, there's a splash of colour in the rooms of this pleasant business hotel, where everything is at your doorstep.

Eating & Drinking

Gyōza Gishuu DUMPLING ¥
(餃子専門店 岐州; ☎058-266-6227; 1-31 Sumidamachi; items from ¥200; ⌚5.30pm until sold out Wed-Mon) This humming hole-in-the-wall does soupy fried *gyōza* (¥400) and *ebi chahan* (shrimp fried rice, ¥700) and, of course, beer. Go straight from JR Gifu Station along the street between Kinkabashi-dōri and Nagarabashi-dōri. It's on the corner of the second block, to your right.

Shanthy INDIAN ¥¥
(☎058-262-7328; 2-13-2 Sumida-machi; lunch from ¥700, dinner set ¥1280; ⌚11.30am-2.30pm & 5.30-10.30pm; 📝) This spacious Indian restaurant is great value; dinner sets include salad, curry, naan or rice and a drink (including wine).

Senryū TEPPANYAKI ¥¥¥
(潜龍; ☎058-231-1151; 14 Nagara; set menus from ¥9936; ⌚11.30am-9.30pm) Since 1966 this

delightful restaurant has been preparing succulent Hida-beef in private tatami rooms in a traditional Japanese house. Set on the banks of the Nagara river in view of Gifu castle, and overlooking a manicured garden, the setting is delightful. If you're looking for an authentic teppanyaki experience (priced accordingly), you've found it. Some Japanese language ability is advantageous.

Bier Hall BAR
(ビアホール; ☎058-266-8868; 2-8 Tamamiya-chō; ⏲5.30pm-1am Mon-Sat) The friendly staff at this popular and spacious pub will make you feel welcome. Guinness is the beer of choice and simple meals are cheap and tasty. It's easily likeable.

Shopping

Gifu's craft tradition includes *wagasa* (oiled paper parasols/umbrellas) and elegantly painted *chōchin* (paper lanterns), though the number of real artisans is dwindling – souvenir shops sell mass-produced versions. The Tourist Information Center has a map of high-quality makers and retailers. Expect to pay ¥10,000 and over for the good stuff.

Sakaida Eikichi Honten HANDICRAFTS
(坂井田永吉本店; ☎058-271-6958; 27 Kanōnakahiroe-chō; ⏲9.30am-5.30pm Mon-Sat) This high-end *wagasa*-maker is a 10-minute walk from JR Gifu Station. Turn left from the south exit, and turn right at the second stoplight. It's on the next corner.

Ozeki Chōchin HANDICRAFTS
(オゼキ; ☎058-263-0111; www.ozeki-lantern.co.jp; 1-18 Oguma-chō; ⏲9am-5pm Mon-Fri; 🚌Ken-Sōgōchōsha-mae) Find beautiful paper lanterns here, by Higashi Betsuin temple.

Information

Tourist Information Center (☎058-262-4415; JR Gifu Station; ⏲9am-7pm Mar-Dec, 9am-6pm Jan & Feb) Within Gifu Station, friendly staff can direct you to maps, accommodation and bicycle rentals (¥100 per day).

Getting There & Around

Gifu is a blink from Nagoya on the JR Tōkaidō line (*tokkyū* ¥470, 20 minutes). Meitetsu trains take longer and are more expensive (¥550, 28 minutes) but also serve Inuyama (¥450, 35 minutes) and Central Japan International Airport (*tokkyū* ¥1340, 64 minutes).

JR Gifu and Meitetsu Gifu Stations are a few minutes' walk apart, joined by a covered elevated walkway.

Buses to sights (¥200) depart from stops 11 and 12 of the bus terminal by JR Gifu Station's Nagara exit, stopping at Meitetsu Gifu en route. There's also a city-loop bus from stop 10. Check before boarding as not all buses make all stops.

Gujō-Hachiman 郡上八幡

☎0575 / POP 42,872

Nestled in the mountains at the confluence of several rivers, Gujō-Hachiman is a picturesque town famed for its **Gujō Odori** folk dance festival. It's also where plastic food models were invented.

Following a tradition dating to the 1590s, townsfolk engage in frenzied dancing on 32 nights between mid-July and early September. Visitor participation is encouraged, especially during *tetsuya odori*, the four main days of the festival (13 to 16 August), when the dancing goes all night.

Otherwise, the town's sparkling rivers, narrow lanes and stone bridges maintain appeal. A famous spring, **Sōgi-sui**, near the centre of town, is something of a pilgrimage site, named for a Momoyama-era poet. People who rank such things place Sōgi-sui at the top of the list for clarity.

Sights & Activities

Gujō Hachiman-jō CASTLE
(郡上八幡城; ☎0575-65-5839; 659 Hachiman-chō; adult/child ¥310/150; ⏲9am-5pm) Twenty minutes hike from Jōka-machi Plaza bus terminal you'll find the pride of Gujō, a 1933 reconstruction of the previous fortress, originally constructed in 1559 but destroyed in the Meiji period. The handsome, hilltop castle contains various weaponry and has wonderful views across the valley. There is no access by public transportation.

Shokuhin Sample Kōbō WORKSHOP
(食品サンプル工房創作館; ☎0575-67-1870; www.samplekobo.com; 956 Hachiman-chō; ⏲9am-5pm Fri-Wed) FREE Realistic food models have been one of life's great mysteries, until now. In an old merchant house, this hands-on workshop lets you see how it's done and try creating them yourself (reservation required). Tempura (three pieces, ¥1000) and lettuce (free) make memorable souvenirs. It's about five minutes' walk from Jōka-machi Plaza, across the river.

Sleeping

Bizenya Ryokan RYOKAN ¥¥

(備前屋旅館; ☎0575-65-2068; http://gujyo-bizenya.jp; 264 Yanagi-machi; r per person from ¥5400; P) This quietly upscale ryokan near Shin-bashi faces a lovely garden. Some rooms have private facilities; plans with or without meals are available.

Nakashimaya Ryokan RYOKAN ¥¥

(中嶋屋旅館; ☎0575-65-2191; www.nakashimaya.net; 940 Shinmachi; r per person ¥5800; P) Nakashimaya Ryokan is a delightfully well-kept, compact and comfortable inn with shared facilities. It's between the station and the Tourist Association. There's an organic cafe next door.

Yoshida-ya Ryokan & City Hotel RYOKAN ¥¥

(旅館吉田屋; ☎0575-67-0001; www.yoshidayaryokan.com; 160 Tonomachi; Japanese-style r per person incl 2 meals from ¥15,000, Western s/d without meals ¥6500/12,000) By the bus terminal, this pleasant ryokan has been in business since 1880. It offers both traditional Japanese (shared bath and toilet) and spacious (though gaudy) Western-style rooms, and there's an on-site restaurant.

Information

Tourist Association (観光協会; ☎0575-67-0002; www.gujohachiman.com/kanko; 520-1 Shimadani; ⏲8.30am-5pm) By Shin-bashi, pick up a walking map in English or rent a bicycle (per hour ¥300, per day ¥1500). For guided tours in English, email Gujoinus in advance. Self-guided walking tours can be found online at www.gujohachiman.com/kanko/old_site/index_e.htm.

Getting There & Away

The most convenient access to Gujō-Hachiman is via bus from Gifu (¥1520, one hour). Be sure to get off at the Jōka-machi Plaza stop, which is not the end of the line. Nohi bus also operates services from Nagoya (¥1850, 1½ hours) and Takayama (¥1650, 1¼ hours) but these services only stop at the Gujō-Hachiman Highway Interchange on the outskirts of town.

The private Nagaragawa Tetsudō line serves Gujō-Hachiman from Mino-Ōta (¥1350, 80 minutes, hourly), with connections via the JR Takayama line to Nagoya (*tokkyū* ¥2320, 45 minutes; *futsū* via Gifu ¥1140, one hour) and Takayama (*tokkyū* ¥3770, 1¾ hours; *futsū* ¥1940, three hours), but the station is located inconveniently away from the sights.

KISO VALLEY NAKASENDŌ

☎0264

The Nakasendō (木曽谷中仙道) was one of the five highways of the Edo period connecting Edo (now Tokyo) with Kyoto. Much of the route is now followed by National Roads, however, in this thickly forested section of the Kiso Valley, there exist several sections of the twisty, craggy post road that have been carefully restored, the most impressive being the 7.8km stretch between Magome and Tsumago, two of the most attractive Nakasendō towns. Walking this route is one of Japan's most rewarding tourist experiences.

Magome 馬籠

In Gifu Prefecture, pretty Magome is the furthest south of the Kiso Valley post towns. Its buildings line a steep, cobblestone pedestrian road (unfriendly to wheelie suitcases) whose rustic shopfronts and mountain views will keep your finger on the shutter.

Sights & Activities

From Magome (elevation 600m), the 7.8km hike to Tsumago (elevation 420m) follows a steep, largely paved road until it reaches its peak at the top of Magome-tōge (pass) – elevation 801m. After the pass, the trail meanders by waterfalls, forest and farmland. The route is easiest in this direction and is clearly signposted in English; allow three to six hours to enjoy it.

If fitness or ability prevent you from appreciating this amazing walk, there is an easier way. The Magome-Tsumago bus (¥600, 30 minutes, two to three daily in each direction) also stops at Magome-tōge. If you alight and begin the walk here, it's a picturesque 5.2km downhill run through to Tsumago.

Both towns offer a handy baggage forwarding service from either Tourist Information Center to the other. Deposit your bags between 8.30am and 11.30am, for delivery by 1pm.

Tōson Kinenkan MUSEUM

(藤村記念館; ☎0264-69-2047; 4256-1 Magome; adult/child ¥550/100; ⏲9am-4pm) Magome was the birthplace of author Shimazaki Tōson (1872–1943). His work records the decline of two provincial Kiso families and this heavily Japanese museum is devoted to his life and times.

Sleeping & Eating

Minshuku Tajimaya MINSHUKU ¥¥
(民宿但馬屋; ☎0264-69-2048; www.kiso-tajimaya.com; 4266 Magome; s/d with 2 meals ¥9720/17,280;) This pleasant historical inn has compact rooms and friendly staff, although the location of the bathrooms can be inconvenient. The array of local specialities served in the common dining area is impressive, as are the *hinoki* (cypress baths).

Magome-Chaya MINSHUKU ¥¥
(馬籠茶屋; ☎0264-59-2038; http://en.magome chaya.com; 4296 Magome; r per person with 2 meals from ¥7980) This popular *minshuku* is almost halfway up the hill, near the water wheel. Room-only plans are available.

Information

Tourist Information Center (観光案内館; ☎0264-59-2336; ⊙9am-5pm) Located somewhat inconveniently halfway up the hill, to the right. A baggage forwarding service to Tsumago is available.

Getting There & Away

Nakatsugawa Station on the JR Chūō line serves Magome, though it is some distance from the town. Nakatsugawa is connected with Nagoya (*tokkyū* ¥2500, 55 minutes) and Matsumoto (*tokkyū* ¥3770, 1¼ hours).

Buses leave hourly from Nakatsugawa Station for Magome (¥540, 30 minutes). There's also an infrequent bus service between Magome and Tsumago (¥600, 25 minutes), via Magome-tōge.

Meitetsu operates highway buses that connect Tokyo's Shinjuku Station with Magome (¥4500, 4½ hours). Note that the stop is at the highway interchange; from here it's a 1.3km uphill walk, unless timed with the bus from Nakatsugawa.

Tsumago 妻籠

Tsumago feels like an open-air museum, about 15 minutes' walk from end to end. It was designated by the government as a protected area for the preservation of traditional buildings, where modern developments such as telephone poles aren't allowed to mar the scene. The dark-wood glory of its lattice-fronted buildings is particularly beautiful at dawn and dusk. Film and TV crews are often spotted here.

On 23 November, the **Fuzoku Emaki** parade is held along the Nakasendō in Tsumago, featuring townsfolk in Edo-period costume.

Sights & Activities

Waki-honjin (Okuya) & Local History Museum MUSEUM
(脇本陣（奥谷）・歴史資料館, Rekishi Shiryōkan; adult/child ¥600/300; ⊙9am-5pm) The former rest stop for the *daimyō's* retainers, this *waki-honjin* was reconstructed in 1877 by a former castle builder under special dispensation from Emperor Meiji. It contains a lovely moss garden and a special toilet built in case Meiji happened to show up (he never did). The adjacent Local History Museum houses elegant exhibitions about Kiso and the Nakasendō, with some English signage.

Tsumagojuku-honjin HISTORIC BUILDING
(妻籠宿本陣; adult/child ¥300/150; ⊙9am-5pm) It was in this building that the *daimyō* themselves would spend the night, although the building's architecture is more noteworthy than its exhibits. A combined ticket (adult/child ¥700/350) includes admission to Waki-honjin and the Local History Museum, opposite.

Kisoji Resort ONSEN
(木曽路館, Kisoji-kan; ☎0264-58-2046; 2278 Azuma; baths ¥700; ⊙9am-7pm) A few kilometres above Tsumago, you'll find this *rotemburo* with panoramic mountain vistas, a sprawling dining room and a souvenir shop.

Sleeping & Eating

Oyado Daikichi MINSHUKU ¥¥
(御宿大吉; ☎0264-57-2595; r per person with 2 meals from ¥8600;) Popular with foreign visitors, this traditional-looking inn benefits from modern construction and has a prime location on the top of the hill – all rooms have a lovely outlook. It's at the very edge of town.

★Fujioto RYOKAN ¥¥
(藤乙; ☎0264-57-3009; www.tsumago-fujioto.jp; r per person with 2 meals from ¥10,800;) The owner of this unpretentious, welcoming inn speaks some English, Italian and Spanish. It's a great place to have your first ryokan experience as most staff are able to communicate with travellers well, especially over the wonderful *kaiseki* dinner, served in the dining room. Corner upstairs rooms have lovely views. You can also stop by for lunch – try the Kiso Valley trout (¥1350).

Matsushiro-ya RYOKAN ¥¥
(松代屋旅館; ☎0264-57-3022; r per person with/without 2 meals ¥10,800/5400; ⊙Thu-Tue)

Showing signs of age, this is one of Tsumago's most historic lodgings (parts date from 1804). It has large tatami rooms and plenty of authentic charm.

Yoshimura-ya NOODLES ¥

(吉村屋; ☎0264-57-3265; dishes ¥700-1500; ⏰10am-5pm;) If you're hungry after a long walk, the handmade *soba* here will fill you up.

Information

Tourist Information Center (観光案内館; ☎0264-57-3123; www.tumago.jp/english; 2159-2 Azuma; ⏰8.30am-5pm) Tsumago's Tourist Information Center is in the centre of town, by the antique phone booth. Some English is spoken and there's English-language literature. Ask here for any directions.

Getting There & Away

Nagiso Station on the JR Chūō line serves Tsumago, though it is some distance from the town. A few *tokkyū* daily stop in Nagiso (from Nagoya ¥2840, one hour); otherwise change at Magome's Nakatsugawa Station (*futsū* ¥320, 20 minutes).

There's an infrequent bus service between Magome and Tsumago (¥600, 25 minutes), via Magome-tōge.

Buses run between Tsumago and Nagiso Station (¥270, 10 minutes, eight per day).

Kiso-Fukushima 木曽福島

North of Tsumago and Magome, Kiso-Fukushima is larger and considerably more developed than its southern neighbours, but its historical significance as an important checkpoint on the Nakasendō and its riverside position make it a pleasant lunch stop en route to (or from) Matsumoto.

Sights

From Kiso-Fukushima train station, turn right and head downhill towards the town centre and the Kiso-gawa. Sights are well signposted. Look for Ue-no-dan (上の段), the historic district of atmospheric houses, many of which now house retailers.

Fukushima Checkpoint Site MUSEUM

(福島関所跡, Fukushima Sekisho-ato; adult/child ¥300/150; ⏰8am-5pm Apr-Oct, 8.30am-4pm Nov-Mar) This is a reconstruction of one of the most significant checkpoints on the Edo-period trunk roads. From its perch above the river valley, it's easy to see the barrier's strategic importance. Displays inside show the implements used to maintain order, including weaponry and *tegata* (wooden travel passes), as well as the special treatment women travellers received.

Eating

★Kurumaya Honten NOODLES ¥

(くるまや本店; ☎0264-22-2200; 5367-2 Kiso-machi, Fukushima; mains ¥630-1575; ⏰10am-5pm Thu-Tue;) One of Japan's most renowned *soba* shops, the classic presentation here is cold *mori* (plain) or *zaru* (with strips of nori seaweed) with a sweetish dipping sauce. It's near the first bridge at the bottom of the hill; look for the gears above the doorway.

Bistro Matsushima-tei ITALIAN ¥¥

(ビストロ松島体; ☎0264-23-3625; 5250-1 Ue-no-dan; mains ¥1155-1900, lunch sets ¥1200-1800; ⏰lunch & dinner daily Jul-Oct, Thu-Tue Nov-Jun) In Ue-no-dan, Bistro Matsushima-tei serves a changing selection of handmade pizzas and pastas in an atmospheric setting befitting the building's history.

Information

Tourist Information Center (木曽町観光協会, Kiso-machi Kankō Kyōkai; ☎0264-22-4000; 2012-10 Kiso-machi, Fukushima; ⏰9am-4.45pm) Across from the train station, these friendly ladies have some English maps, but appreciate some Japanese-language ability.

Getting There & Away

Kiso-Fukushima is on the JR Chūō line (*Shinano tokkyū*), easily reached from Matsumoto (¥2150, 38 minutes), Nakatsugawa (¥2150, 34 minutes) and Nagoya (¥4100, 1½ hours).

Narai 奈良井

A lesser known but important example of a Nakasendō post town, Narai is a gem, tucked away in the folds of a narrow valley. Once called 'Narai of a thousand houses', it flourished during the Edo period when its proximity to the highest pass on the Nakasendō made it a popular resting place for travellers. Today, it's a conservation area with a preserved main street showcasing some wonderful examples of Edo-period architecture.

Narai is famed for *shikki* (lacquerware). Plenty of quality souvenir shops line the street, many with reasonable prices.

Sights

Nakamura House HISTORIC BUILDING
(中村邸; 0264-34-2655; adult/child ¥300/free; 9am-4pm) This wonderfully preserved former merchant's house and garden looks as if it has stood still while time passed by.

Sleeping & Eating

★ **Echigo-ya** RYOKAN ¥¥
(ゑちごや旅館; 0264-34-3011; www.naraijyuku-echigoya.jp; 493 Narai; r per person incl 2 meals from ¥15,660) In business for over 220 years, this charming family-run ryokan is one of a kind. With only two guestrooms, Echigo-ya provides a unique opportunity to experience the Japanese art of hospitality in its most undiluted form. Expect to feel like you've stepped back in time. Some Japanese-language ability will help make the most of the experience. Book well in advance. Cash only.

Oyado Iseya MINSHUKU ¥¥
(御宿伊勢屋; 0264-34-3051; www.oyado-iseya.jp; 388 Narai; r per person incl 2 meals from ¥9500) The streetfront of this former merchant house built in 1818 has been beautifully preserved. It's now a pleasant 10-room inn; guestrooms are in the main house and a newer building out back.

Matsunami SHOKUDO ¥
(松波; 0264-34-3750; 397-1 Narai; set menus from ¥850; 11.30am-8pm Wed-Mon) This delightful little eatery on a corner serves simple favourites such as special-sauce *tonkatsu-don* (deep-fried pork cutlet on rice).

Information

Tourist Information Center (奈良井宿観光協会; 0264-54-2001; www.naraijuku.com) Inside Narai station, it has some English-language leaflets and a map. Little English is spoken.

Getting There & Away

Only *futsū* (local) trains stop at Narai, which is on the JR Chūō line. It takes no more than an hour or three to see the sights, making it a neat day trip from Matsumoto (¥580, 50 minutes), but you could easily pass a peaceful evening here. From Nagoya, change trains at Nakatsugawa (¥1320, 1½ hours) or Kiso-Fukushima (¥410, 20 minutes).

HIDA REGION

Visitors flock to the utterly delightful, ancient, mountainous Hida Region (飛騨地域) for its *onsen ryokan* (traditional hot-spring inns), the World Heritage–listed villages of Ogimachi and Ainokura, and its centrepiece, Takayama, one of Japan's most likeable cities. Hida's signature architectural style is the thatch-roofed *gasshō-zukuri*, while its culinary fame rests in Hida-*gyū* (Hida beef), *hoba-miso* (sweet miso paste grilled at the table on a magnolia leaf) and *soba*.

Takayama 飛騨高山

0577 / POP 92,000

Takayama (officially known as Hida Takayama) boasts one of Japan's most atmospheric townscapes and best-loved festivals, and a

GASSHŌ-ZUKURI ARCHITECTURE

Hida winters are unforgiving. Inhabitants braved the elements long before the advent of propane heaters and 4WD vehicles. The most visible symbol of their adaptability is *gasshō-zukuri* architecture, as seen in the steeply slanted, straw-roofed homes that dot the regional landscape.

Sharply angled roofs prevent snow accumulation, a serious concern in an area where most mountain roads close from December to April. The name *gasshō* comes from the Japanese word for prayer, because the shape of the roofs was thought to resemble hands clasped together. *Gasshō* buildings often feature pillars crafted from stout cedars to lend extra support. The attic areas are ideal for silk cultivation. Larger *gasshō-zukuri* buildings were inhabited by wealthy families, with up to 30 people under one roof. Peasant families lived in huts so small that today they'd only be considered fit for tool sheds.

The art of *gasshō-zukuri* construction is dying out. Most remaining examples have been relocated to folk villages, including Hida-no-sato (p231), Ogimachi (p237), Suganuma (p238) and Ainokura (p239). Homes that are now neighbours may once have been separated by several days of travel on foot or sled. These cultural preservation efforts have made it possible to imagine a bygone life in the Hida hills.

visit here should be considered a high priority for anyone travelling in Central Honshū.

Its present layout dates from the late 17th century and incorporates a wealth of museums, galleries and temples for a city of its compact size. Meiji-era inns, hillside shrines and temples, and a pretty riverside setting beckon you. Excellent infrastructure and friendly, welcoming locals seal the deal. Give yourself two or three days to enjoy it all. Takayama is easily explored on foot and is the perfect start or end point for trips into the Hida region and the Northern Japan Alps.

Sights & Activities

Most sights are clearly signposted in English and are within walking distance of the station, which sits between the main streets of Kokubunji-dōri and Hirokōji-dōri. Both run east and cross the Miya-gawa where they become Yasugawa-dōri and Sanmachi-dōri, respectively. Once across the river you're in the middle of the infinitely photogenic Sanmachi-suji district, with its sake breweries, cafes, retailers and immaculately preserved *furui machinami* (古い町並み; old private houses).

Sanmachi-suji

This original district of three main streets of merchants (Ichino-machi, Nino-machi and Sanno-machi) has been immaculately preserved. Sake breweries are designated by spheres of cedar fronds hanging above their doors; some are open to the public in January and early February, but most sell their brews year round. You'll find artisans, antiques, clothiers and cafes. Day and night, photographic opportunities abound.

Takayama Shōwa-kan MUSEUM

(高山昭和館; ☎0577-33-7836; 6 Shimoichino-machi; adult/child ¥500/300; ⏲9am-5pm) This nostalgia bonanza from the Shōwa period (1926–1989) concentrates on the years between 1955 and 1965, a time of great optimism between Japan's postwar malaise and pre-Titan boom. Lose yourself among the delightful mishmash of endless objects, from movie posters to cars and everything in between, lovingly presented in a series of themed rooms.

Yoshijima Heritage House HISTORIC BUILDING

(吉島家, Yoshijima-ke; ☎0577-32-0038; 1-51 Ōjin-machi; adult/child ¥500/300; ⏲9am-5pm Mar-Nov, 9am-4.30pm Wed-Sun Dec-Feb) Design buffs shouldn't miss Yoshijima-ke, which is well covered in architectural publications. Its lack of ornamentation allows you to focus on the spare lines, soaring roof and skylight. Admission includes a cup of delicious shiitake tea, which you can also purchase for ¥600 per can.

Kusakabe Folk Crafts Museum MUSEUM

(日下部民藝館, Kusakabe Mingeikan; ☎0577-32-0072; 1-52 Ōjin-machi; adult/child ¥500/300; ⏲9am-4.30pm Mar-Nov, 9am-4pm Wed-Mon Dec-Feb) This building dating from the 1890s showcases the striking craftsmanship of traditional Takayama carpenters. Inside is a collection of folk art.

Takayama Museum of History & Art MUSEUM

(飛騨高山まちの博物館, Hida-Takayama Machi no Hakubutsukan; ☎0577-32-1205; 75 Kamiichino-machi; ⏲museum 9am-7pm, garden 7am-9pm) FREE Not to be confused with the Hida Takayama Museum of Art, this free museum is situated around pretty gardens and features 14 themed exhibition rooms relating to local history, culture, literature and the arts.

Hida Folk Archaeological Museum MUSEUM

(飛騨民族考古館, Hida Minzoku Kōko-kan; ☎0577-32-1980; 82 Kamisanno-machi; adult/child ¥500/200; ⏲7am-5pm Mar-Nov, 9.30am-4pm Dec-Feb) A former samurai house boasting interesting secret passageways and an old well in the courtyard.

Sakurayama Hachiman-gū Shrine & Around

Takayama Festival Floats Exhibition Hall MUSEUM

(高山屋台会館, Takayama Yatai-kaikan; 178 Sakura-machi; adult/child ¥820/410; ⏲8.30am-5pm Mar-Nov, 9am-4.30pm Dec-Feb) A rotating selection of four of the 23 multi-tiered *yatai* (floats) used in the Takayama Matsuri can be appreciated here. These spectacular creations, some dating from the 17th century, are prized for their flamboyant carvings, metalwork and lacquerwork. Some floats feature *karakuri ningyō* (marionettes) that perform amazing feats courtesy of eight accomplished puppeteers manipulating 36 strings.

The museum is on the grounds of the stately **Sakurayama Hachiman-gū** (桜山八幡宮; ☎0577-32-0240; www.hidahachimangu.jp/english; 178 Sakura-yama) FREE shrine, which presides over the festival and is dedicated to the protection of Takayama.

Takayama

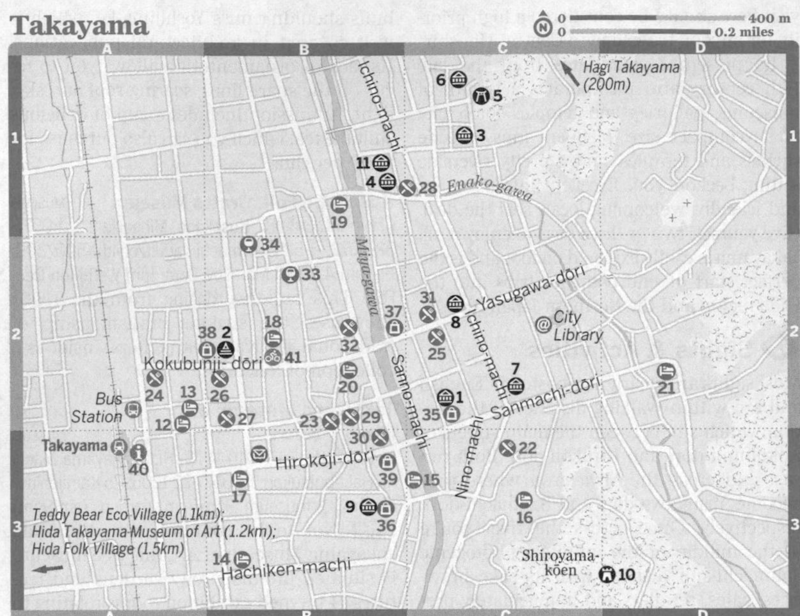

Karakuri Museum MUSEUM

((飛騨高山獅子会館)からくりミュージアム; ☎0577-32-0881; 53-1 Sakura-machi; adult/child ¥600/400; ⏲9am-4.30pm) On display are over 800 *shishi* (lion) masks, instruments and drums related to festival dances. The main draw is the twice-hourly puppet show where you can see the mechanical *karakuri ningyō* in action.

Teramachi, Shiroyama-kōen & Around

These lovely, hilly districts to the east are linked by a well-signposted walking path. Teramachi has over a dozen temples and shrines you can wander around before taking in the greenery of Shiroyama-kōen. Various trails lead through the park and up the mountainside to the ruins of the castle, **Takayama-jō** (高山城跡; Shiroyama-kōen).

Takayama-jinya HISTORIC BUILDING

(高山陣屋; ☎0577-32-0643; 1-5 Hachiken-machi; adult/child ¥430/free; ⏲8.45am-4.30pm Sep-Jul, to 6pm Aug) These sprawling grounds south of Sanmachi-suji house the only remaining prefectural office building of the Tokugawa shogunate, originally the administrative centre for the Kanamori clan. The present main building dates back to 1816 and was used as local government offices until 1969. There's also a rice granary, garden and a torture chamber with explanatory detail. Free guided tours in English are available (reservations advised).

Hida Kokubun-ji BUDDHIST TEMPLE

(飛騨国分寺; ☎0577-32-1395; 1-83 Sōwa-chō; treasure hall adult/child ¥300/250; ⏲9am-4pm) The original buildings of Takayama's oldest temple were constructed in the 8th century, but later destroyed by fire. The oldest of the present buildings dates from the 16th century. The temple's treasure hall houses some Important Cultural Properties, and the courtyard boasts a three-storey pagoda and an impressively gnarled gingko tree believed to be 1200 years old.

Around Takayama

Hida Takayama Museum of Art MUSEUM

(飛騨高山美術館, Hida Takayama Bijutsukan; ☎0577-35-3535; www.htm-museum.co.jp; 1-124-1 Kamiokamoto-chō; adult/child ¥1300/800; ⏲9am-5pm) Lovers of art-nouveau and art-deco glassware and furniture will appreciate this large private gallery, set back from town with a ritzy cafe, its own London Bus shuttle (ask at the Tourist Information Center) and a spectacular glass fountain by René Lalique.

Takayama

Sights
1 Hida Folk Archaeological Museum....... C2
2 Hida Kokubun-ji.......................................B2
3 Karakuri Museum C1
4 Kusakabe Folk Crafts Museum..............B1
5 Sakurayama Hachiman-gū......................C1
6 Takayama Festival Floats Exhibition Hall...C1
7 Takayama Museum of History & Art C2
8 Takayama Shōwa-kan............................ C2
9 Takayama-jinya.......................................B3
10 Takayama-jō...D3
11 Yoshijima Heritage House....................B1

Sleeping
12 Best Western Hotel A2
13 Guesthouse Tomaru................................ A2
14 Hida Takayama Temple Inn Zenkō-ji B3
15 Honjin Hiranoya C3
16 Hōshōkaku.. C3
17 K's House Takayama.............................. B3
18 Rickshaw Inn B2
Spa Hotel Alpina .... (see 17)
19 Sumiyoshi Ryokan.................................. B1
20 Tanabe Ryokan B2
21 Yamakyū.. D2

Eating
22 Center4 Hamburgers..............................C3
23 Chapala B2
24 Chitose..A2
25 Ebisu-Honten C2
26 Heianraku B2
27 Kotarō B2
28 Kyōya C1
29 Macrobiotique Okaa-san........................B2
30 Restaurant Le Midi B3
31 Takumi-ya..C2
32 Tenaga Ashinaga.....................................B2

Drinking & Nightlife
33 Desolation Row..B2
34 Red Hill Pub B2

Shopping
35 Itae Matsuoka C2
36 Jinya-mae Asa-ichi...................................B3
37 Miya-gawa Asa-ichi B2
38 Suzuki Chōkoku..B2
39 Washi no Yamazaki B3

Information
40 Tourist Information Center....................A3

Transport
41 Hara Cycle B2

Teddy Bear Eco Village GALLERY
(飛騨高山テディベアエコビレッジ; ☎0577-37-3525; www.teddyeco.jp/english; 3-829-4 Nishinoishiki-machi; adult/child ¥600/400; ⌚10am-4pm) You'll know if you're one of *those* people who *have* to see this collection of over 1000 little fluffy guys from around the world, some over 140 years old, housed in a building just a little bit older. The annexed cafe is a lovely spot to enjoy a healthy something in the outdoors. Ask for directions at the Tourist Information Center.

Hida Folk Village HISTORIC BUILDING
(飛騨の里, Hida-no-Sato; ☎0577-34-4711; www.hidanosato-tpo.jp/english12; 1-590 Kamiokamoto-chō; adult/child ¥700/200; ⌚8.30am-5pm) The sprawling, open-air Hida-no-Sato is a highly recommended half-day trip. It features dozens of traditional houses and buildings that were dismantled at their original sites throughout the region and rebuilt here. Well-presented displays offer the chance to envision rural life in previous centuries. During clear weather, there are good views of the Japan Alps. To get here, hire a bicycle or catch a bus from Takayama bus station (¥200, 10 minutes); be sure to check return bus times.

Sleeping

One of Takayama's delights is its variety of excellent accommodation across all styles, for all budgets. If visiting during festival times, book accommodation months in advance and expect to pay a 20% premium. The Ryokan Hotel Association (www.takayamaryokan.jp/english) can further assist with lodging enquiries.

★ **Rickshaw Inn** HOTEL ¥
(力車イン; ☎0577-32-2890; www.rickshawinn.com; 54 Suehiro-chō; s without bathroom from ¥4200, tw with/without bathroom from ¥11,900/10,200; ⊜@) Well positioned on the fringe of Takayama's entertainment district, this travellers' favourite is great value. There's a range of room types, a small kitchen, laundry facilities and a cosy lounge. Friendly English-speaking owners are founts of information about Takayama.

Guesthouse Tomaru GUESTHOUSE ¥
(飛騨高山ゲストハウスとまる; ☎0577-62-9260; www.hidatakayama-guesthouse.com; 6-5 Hanasato-machi; dm ¥2800, s & d ¥6500-7500, tr ¥9000; @🛜) Visitors love the friendly homestay vibe of this small, centrally

TAKAYAMA MATSURI

One of Japan's great festivals, the **Takayama Matsuri** takes place in two parts. On 14 and 15 April is the Sannō Matsuri, when a dozen *yatai*, decorated with carvings, dolls, colourful curtains and blinds, are paraded through the town. In the evening the floats are decked out with lanterns and the procession is accompanied by sacred music. Hachiman Matsuri, on 9 and 10 October, is a slightly smaller version. If you're planning to see these popular festivals, book accommodation months in advance.

located guesthouse. Pleasant rooms with homely touches are kept spotlessly clean. There's free wi-fi and a shared kitchen.

Hida Takayama Temple Inn Zenkō-ji HOSTEL ¥
(飛騨高山善光寺宿坊; ☎0577-32-8470; www.takayamahostelzenkoji.com; 4-3 Tenman-machi; dm ¥2500, s ¥3000; P ⊖ ☎) Good karma washes over this branch of Nagano's famous Zenkō-ji temple, where donations are accepted in return for accommodation. Private rooms are generously proportioned around a courtyard garden. Even the dorms have temple charm. There's a shared kitchen and no curfew for respectful guests.

K's House Takayama HOSTEL ¥
(☎0577-34-4410; www.kshouse.jp/takayama-e; 4-45-1 Tenman-machi; dm/s/d per person from ¥2900/4800/3600; ☎) This sparkly hostel has caused a stir on the Takayama hostel scene. All rooms, including dorms, have private bathroom, TV and wi-fi. There's a kitchen and common area, and bicycle rentals are available.

★Sumiyoshi Ryokan RYOKAN ¥¥
(寿美吉旅館; ☎0577-32-0228; www.sumiyoshi-ryokan.com; 4-21 Hon-machi; r per person with/without 2 meals from ¥11,000/7000; P @) The kind owners of this delightfully antiquey inn, set in a Meiji-era merchant's house, have been welcoming guests from abroad for years. Some rooms have river views through panes of antique glass, and the common baths are made of wood and slate tiles. One room has a private bath.

Yamakyū RYOKAN ¥¥
(山久; ☎0577-32-3756; www.takayama-yamakyu.com; 58 Tenshōji-machi; r with/without meals from ¥8100/5940; P @ ☎) Occupying a lovely hillside spot opposite Hokke-ji temple, Yamakyū is a 20-minute walk from the train station. Inside, antique-filled curio cabinets, clocks and lamps line the red-carpeted corridors. All 20 tatami rooms have a sink and toilet, and the common baths are of a high standard. Some English is spoken. This is an excellent choice for a ryokan experience without the expense.

Spa Hotel Alpina HOTEL ¥¥
(スパホテルアルピナ; ☎0577-33-0033; www.spa-hotel-alpina.com; 5-41 Nada-chō; s/tw from ¥7460/13,140; P ⊖ @) This glorified business hotel has a slightly clinical feel for a 'spa hotel', but offers comfortable beds, bright rooms and a fantastic rooftop onsen with views across the city. Discounted rates can be secured online.

Best Western Hotel HOTEL ¥¥
(ベストウェスタンホテル高山; ☎0577-37-2000; www.bestwestern.co.jp; 6-6 Hanasato-machi; s/d/tw from ¥6900/12,700/13,700; ⊖ ☎) Popular with overseas guests, this tourist hotel's refurbished rooms have a splash of colour. Good-value rates can be found online and sometimes include a breakfast buffet. It's a hop, skip and a jump from the station.

★Honjin Hiranoya RYOKAN ¥¥¥
(本陣平野屋; ☎0577-34-1234; www.honjinhiranoya.co.jp/english; 1-5 Hon-machi; r per person with 2 meals from ¥12,600; P) For something a little different, choose the contemporary elegance of the executive rooms in the more expensive Kachoan wing. Otherwise opt for a classical river-view room in the Bekkan (Annexe) wing. There's a free shuttle bus from the train station, or it's a 10-minute walk. Expect the highest service levels, English-speaking staff and exquisite cuisine. Highly recommended.

Hagi Takayama RYOKAN ¥¥¥
(萩高山; ☎0577-32-4100; www.takayama-kh.co.jp/english; 280 Hachiman-machi; r per person with 2 meals from ¥10,800; P) This elevated hotel on the immediate outskirts of downtown has wonderful views from all rooms and delightful communal bathing areas. Rooms in the main wing were refurbished most recently. Expect traditional service, fine local cuisine and a wonderful green location in the hills above Takayama, which makes

it ideal for those with a car; parking in the town below can be tricky.

Hōshōkaku RYOKAN ¥¥¥
(宝生閣; ☎0577-34-0700; www.hoshokaku.co.jp/english; 1-88 Baba-machi; r per person with 2 meals from ¥9720; P) Surrounded by the greenery of Shiroyama-kōen, this upscale hillside ryokan on the edge of town has wonderful outdoor rooftop hot springs with city views and sumptuous *kaiseki* cuisine. If arriving by train, it's easiest to grab a taxi out here.

Tanabe Ryokan RYOKAN ¥¥¥
(旅館田邊; ☎0577-32-0529; www.tanabe-ryokan.jp; 58 Aioi-chō; r per person with 2 meals from ¥12,960; @) This elegant, atmospheric inn has a premium, central location and friendly, welcoming staff who speak some English. All tatami rooms have an en-suite bath, although the lovely common baths with their beamed ceilings are worth enjoying. A sumptuous dinner of *kaiseki*-style Hida cuisine completes the experience.

Eating

Takayama's specialities include *soba, hoba-miso, sansei* (mountain vegetables) and Hida-*gyū* (Hida beef). Street foods include *mitarashi-dango* (skewers of grilled rice balls seasoned with soy sauce) and *shio-sembei* (salty rice crackers). Hida-*gyū* turns up on *kushiyaki* (skewers), in *korokke* (croquettes) and in *niku-man* (steamed buns). If you're on a budget, keep an eye out for the numerous bakeries around town where you can stock up on delicious, inexpensive fresh breads and sandwiches.

Heianraku CHINESE ¥
(平安楽; ☎0577-32-3078; 6-7-2 Tenman-machi; dishes from ¥700; ⏰11.30am-1.30pm & 5-10pm Wed-Mon;) Atmospheric, inexpensive, welcoming and delicious are all words that spring to mind when describing this wonderful second-generation eatery serving up Chinese delights in a traditional Japanese shopfront on Kokubunji-dōri. It's a few steps before Hida Kokubun-ji on the opposite side of the street. The *gyōza* and meatballs are spot on. English is spoken.

Chitose NOODLES ¥
(ちとせ; ☎0577-32-1056; 6-19 Hanasato-machi; noodles from ¥500; ⏰11am-3pm & 5-7.30pm Wed-Mon) Delicious, chunky *yaki-soba* (fried noodles) and *chūka-soba* noodle soups are the speciality at this cheap-as-chips local fave that will fill your belly and satisfy your wallet. Top your *yaki-soba* with a deliciously drippy fried egg to complete the experience. Highly recommended.

Chapala MEXICAN ¥
(チャパラ; ☎0577-34-9800; 1 Hanakawa-chō; mains ¥500-980; ⏰6-10.30pm Mon-Sat, closed 1st Mon of each month;) The enthusiastic, local owner of this friendly restaurant does a great job bringing the flavours of Mexico to a quiet Japanese street. The taste and dainty portions of tacos, quesadillas and guac' and chips won't match California or Guadalajara, but the place is adorable and patrons love it. Where else can you eat tacos with chopsticks while swilling Coronas and sake?

Ebisu-Honten NOODLES ¥
(恵比寿本店; ☎0577-32-0209; www.takayama-ebisu.jp/emenu; 46 Kamini-no-machi; noodle bowls from ¥880; ⏰10am-5pm Thu-Tue;) These folks have been making *teuchi* (handmade) *soba* since 1898. Try their cold *zaru soba* (¥880) to strip it bare and taste the flavour of the noodles. The *tororo nameko soba* (¥1220) is also very good: noodles in a hot soup with boiled mushroom and grated mountain potato. The building has an interesting red-glass sign with white characters and a little roof on it.

Tenaga Ashinaga SHOKUDO ¥
(てながあしなが; ☎0577-34-5855; 3-58-11 Hon-machi; small plates from ¥200, meals from ¥680; ⏰11am-9pm;) If you're looking for a tasty, uncomplicated meal, this large, well-positioned eatery near Kaji-bashi is a good choice. A diverse English and Japanese photo menu has most of your favourites, such as *udon, rāmen* and *donburi,* as well as meatier choices. The location attracts many foreign clientele whose smiling faces line the photo wall outside.

START YOUR DAY THE RIGHT WAY: MORNING MARKETS

Daily *asa-ichi* (morning markets) are a wonderful way to wake up and meet people. The **Jinya-mae Asa-ichi** (1-5 Hachiken-machi) is in front of Takayama-jinya; the larger **Miya-gawa Asa-ichi** (宮川朝市) runs along the east bank of the Miya-gawa, between Kaji-bashi and Yayoi-bashi. Stalls range from farm-fresh produce to local arts and crafts. Autumnal apples are out of this world!

Center4 Hamburgers BURGERS ¥¥

(0577-36-4527; www.tiger-center4.com; 94 Kamiichino-machi; burgers from ¥760; 11am-9.30pm;) Word has spread that this young Japanese couple are living their dream, welcoming visitors from around the world – so you might have to wait for a table to enjoy their delicious comfort food, prepared with love. On the menu: juicy home-style burgers (including vegie), club sandwiches, and chilli and clam chowder, served up in a funky dining room that feels like the extension of someone's home.

Top it off with a world beer, a decent red or a milkshake and you'll be too floaty to waste time feeling guilty about taking a break from *soba*.

Kotarō TONKATSU ¥¥

(小太郎; 0577-32-7353; 6-1 Tenman-machi; meals ¥1050-2100; 11.30am-2pm & 5-9pm Thu-Tue;) Expect satisfaction from this compact workman-like eatery whose chef has spent over 25 years mastering the art of *tonkatsu* and other fried goodies. Generous *teishoku* (from ¥1050) feature crispy, crunchy *katsu*, cooked to perfection, accompanied by perfectly balanced sides: fluffy rice, rich miso soup, fruit, salad and pickles. Try the cheese *katsu* (¥1350) for something different.

Kyōya SHOKUDO ¥¥

(京や; 0577-34-7660; 1-77 Ōjin-machi; mains ¥700-5000; 11am-10pm Wed-Mon;) This traditional eatery specialises in regional dishes such as *hoba-miso* and Hida-*gyū soba*. Seating is on tatami mats around long charcoal grills, under a cathedral ceiling supported by dark timbers. It's on a corner, by a bridge over the canal. Look for the sacks of rice over the door.

Takumi-ya BEEF ¥¥

(匠家; 0577-36-2989; 2 Shimo-ni-no-machi; mains downstairs ¥680-980, upstairs from ¥1500; 11am-3pm & 5-9pm Thu-Tue;) Hida-*gyū* on a burger budget. Adjacent to Takumi-ya's butcher shop is a casual restaurant specialising in *rāmen* in Hida-beef broth and Hida *gyū-don* (beef and onion over rice). The pricier upstairs restaurant serves *yakiniku* (Korean-style barbecue).

Macrobiotique Okaa-san VEGETARIAN ¥¥

(マクロビオティックお母さん; 0577-35-1057; www.okahsan.com/english; 46 Yuraku-chō; set meals ¥1000-2000; 8am-6pm Mon-Sat;) This friendly macrobiotic food store and cafe prepares meat-free macrobiotic meals that your body will love. Daily set meals start at ¥1000 and include rice, miso soup, pickles and two or more vegetarian delights.

Restaurant Le Midi FRENCH ¥¥¥

(0577-36-6386; www.le-midi.jp/english; 2-85 Hon-machi; appetisers ¥650-3400, Hida-gyū dishes ¥2400-7500; 11.30am-2pm & 6-9pm Fri-Wed;) One street back from the river, this upscale restaurant serves traditional French cuisine with a Japanese twist. Mouth-watering appetisers include Hida-beef carpaccio and onion gratin soup. Lunch set meals range from ¥1800 to ¥4800 and set-course dinners including hors d'oeuvres, mains, soup, salad and coffee start at ¥4800. For dessert, the local *sukune kabocha* (pumpkin) pudding is a must. If you're feeling French and fancy, you're unlikely to be disappointed.

Drinking & Nightlife

Once you've had a wonderful day in the sun, you might feel like carrying on into the night but, for the moment, your options are limited. Asahi-machi, north of Kokubun-ji-dōri and west of the Miya-gawa, is Takayama's sprawly bar district, but don't expect too much.

★Red Hill Pub PUB

(レッド・ヒル; 0577-33-8139; 2-4 Sowa-chō; 7pm-midnight;) You'll feel like you're walking into a friend's living room in this cosy, dimly lit basement bar. The hip and happy owner, Hisayo, deftly adjusts the vibe to suit the patrons present. It's sometimes soulful and smooth, sometimes rocking and raucous. If it's quiet and you're alone, you'll still have someone fascinating to talk to – Hisayo speaks excellent English. She also prepares tasty snacks and offers an excellent selection of brews and killer cocktails.

Desolation Row BAR

(デゾレーション ロウ; 090-8077-5966; 30 Asahi-machi; 8pm-late) If you're a fan of Bob Dylan, you'll likely connect with Ken, the friendly owner of this mellow bar with a real rustic charm. Ken speaks some English, but the language of music is universal. As is the language of whisky…and beer. Look for the galvanised iron front and the big blue door.

Shopping

Takayama is renowned for arts and crafts. Look for *ichi ittobori* (woodcarvings), *shunkei* lacquerware, and the rustic *yamada-*

yaki and decorative *shibukusa-yaki* styles of pottery. Between Sanmachi-dōri and Yasugawa-dōri, near the Takayama Museum of History and Art, are plenty of wonderful *kobutsu* (古物; antique) shops. With patience and smarts you can find some excellent deals – seeking them out is half the fun.

Takayama's most ubiquitous souvenirs are *saru-bobo* (monkey babies), little red dolls with pointy limbs and featureless faces, recalling the days when grandmothers fashioned dolls for children out of whatever materials were available.

Itae Matsuoka CRAFTS
(板画まつおか; ☎0577-32-3293; 92 Kamisanno-machi) The lovely Ms Matsuoka has no staff, so if she's not in, she's not in. But if you can find her little shop selling beautiful Japanese *hanga* (woodblock prints) you will be rewarded. Even when it's right before your very eyes, it can be hard to spot.

Washi no Yamazaki CRAFTS
(和紙の山崎; ☎0577-32-4132; 1-22 Hon-machi; ⏲9am-5pm) This wonderful family-run store sells *washi* (handmade Japanese paper).

Suzuki Chōkoku CRAFTS
(鈴木彫刻; ☎0577-32-1367; 1-2 Hatsuda-machi; ⏲9am-7pm Wed-Mon) Helmed by the one-time head of the local *ittobori* (woodcarving) association, here you'll find figurines from ¥750 to *how much?*

Information

Free wi-fi is available for visitors throughout the downtown area. Check in with the Tourist Information Center upon your arrival for the wi-fi password, which gets you access for one week.

Takayama Post Office (高山郵便局; ☎0577-32-0540; 5-95-1 Nada-machi), a few blocks east of the train station, has ATMs dispensing cash to foreign cards.

City Library (高山市図書館; ☎0577-32-3096; 2-115 Baba-machi; ⏲9.30am-9.30pm) Come for free internet access, or just to gawk at this wonderful historic building, which is east of Sanmachi-suji.

Tourist Information Center (飛騨高山観光案内所; ☎0577-32-5328; www.hida.jp/english; ⏲8.30am-5pm Nov-Mar, 8.30am-6.30pm Apr-Oct) Directly in front of JR Takayama Station, knowledgeable English-speaking staff dispense English and other language maps and a wealth of pamphlets on sights, accommodation, special events and regional transport. Staff are unable to assist with accommodation reservations.

Getting There & Away

From Tokyo or Kansai, the most efficient way to reach Takayama is via Nagoya on the JR Takayama line (*Hida tokkyū* ¥5510, 2½ hours); the mountainous train ride along the Hida-gawa is *gorge*-ous. Some trains continue on to Toyama (¥2840, 90 minutes), where you can connect to Kanazawa (¥2150, 40 minutes).

Nōhi Bus (濃飛バス; ☎0577-32-1688; www.nouhibus.co.jp/english) operates highway bus services between Takayama and Tokyo's Shinjuku Station (¥6690, 5½ hours, several daily, reservations required), Matsumoto (¥3190, 2½ hours) and Kanazawa (¥3390, 2¼ hours). Takayama's bus station is adjacent to the train station. Schedules vary seasonally and some routes don't run at all during winter, when many roads are closed.

Getting Around

Most sights in Takayama can be covered easily on foot. You can amble from the train station to Teramachi in about 20 minutes. Takayama is bicycle-friendly but rentals can be expensive. Try **Hara Cycle** (ハラサイクル; ☎0577-32-1657; 61 Suehiro-chō; 1st hr ¥300, additional hr ¥200, per day ¥1300; ⏲9am-8pm Wed-Mon). Some lodgings lend bikes for free.

Hida-Furukawa 飛騨古川

☎0577 / POP 25,446

Just 15 minutes by train from Takayama, Hida-Furukawa is a relaxing riverside town with a friendly, ageing population, eager to preserve their local history and culture. Photogenic streetscapes, peaceful temples and interesting museums are framed by the Hida mountains. Each April the town comes to life for the Hida-Furukawa Matsuri, also known as Hadaka Matsuri (Naked Festival).

Sights & Activities

★**Satoyama Experience** BICYCLE TOUR
(☎0577-73-5715; www.satoyama-experience.com; 8-8 Furukawa-chō nino-machi; half-day tours from ¥4700; ⏲9am-6pm Fri-Wed) The fantastic crew at Satoyama Experience are eager to introduce you to their beloved region, its culture and people. Small-group cycling tours include a friendly, English-speaking guide, mountain-bike rental and insurance. A variety of tours (including walking) cater to different levels of fitness, but all capture the spirit and scenery of Hida. The team can also connect you with some unique, traditional accommodation (for longer stays) in town and around – just ask. Highly recommended.

At the time of writing, Satoyama Experience was expanding its operations into Takayama. Enquire for details.

Seto-kawa & Shirakabe-dōzō HISTORIC SITE
(瀬戸川と白壁土蔵街) You'll find this lovely historic canal district five minutes' walk from JR Hida-Furukawa Station, boasting white-walled shops, storehouses, private homes and carp-filled waterways. Across the canal, Ichino-machi is sprinkled with woodworking shops, sake breweries (marked by spheres of cedar fronds above the entrance) and traditional storehouses.

Honkō-ji BUDDHIST TEMPLE
(本光寺; ☎0577-73-2938; 1-17 Furukawa-chō) Riverside Honkō-ji is Hida's largest wooden temple, showcasing the fine craftsmanship of Furukawa's carpenters. Originally established in 1532, the current buildings date from 1913 following a fire that destroyed 90% of the town.

Carpentry Museum MUSEUM
(匠文化館, Takumi Bunkakan; ☎0577-73-3321; 10-1 Ichino-machi; adult/child ¥300/100; ⏲9am-4.30pm Fri-Wed winter, 9am-5pm daily rest of year) Across from Hida-Furukawa Matsuri Kaikan, this museum dedicated to the history of Japanese carpentry and its unique methods is a must for woodworkers and design fans. In a hands-on room, you can try assembling blocks of wood cut into different joint patterns – not as easy as it sounds.

Festivals & Events

Furukawa Matsuri PARADE
(古川祭り) Furukawa Matsuri – informally known as Hadaka Matsuri (Naked Festival) – takes place every 19 and 20 April with parades of *yatai*. The highlight is an event known as Okoshi Daiko in which, on the night of the 19th, squads of boisterous young men dressed in *fundoshi* (loin cloths) and fuelled by sake, parade through town, competing to place small drums atop a stage bearing a giant drum. OK, it's not *naked* naked, but we didn't make up the name.

Kitsune Himatsuri PARADE
(きつね火祭り) During the 'Fox Fire Festival' on the fourth Saturday in September, locals dress up as foxes, parade through the town by lantern light and enact a wedding at Okura Inari-jinja. The ceremony, deemed to bring good fortune, climaxes with a bonfire.

Sleeping & Eating

Hida Tomoe Hotel HOTEL ¥¥
(飛騨ともえホテル; ☎0577-73-2056; www.tomoe-jp.com; 10-27 Kanamori-chō; r per person with/without meals from ¥10,290/5250; @) This attractive business hotel by the train station has Western- and Japanese-style rooms, most with bath and toilet, as well as a pretty common bath. Including meals means farm-fresh local *kaiseki* cuisine by the *irori* (fireplace).

Ichino-machi Cafe CAFE ¥
(壱之町珈琲店; ☎0577-73-7099; 1-12 Ichino-machi; ⏲11am-5pm Wed-Mon; wi-fi) Chiffon cake, melon bread and local Hida-beef curry are all items you might find on the menu in this handsome cafe within a restored traditional *machiya* (merchant house). Free wi-fi is a bonus.

Information

Hida-Furukawa train and bus stations adjoin each other east of the town centre. Sights are within 10 minutes' walk. There's a Tourist Information Center at the bus station with some English maps and leaflets, though little English is spoken.

Getting There & Around

Trains run frequently between Takayama and Hida-Furukawa, three stops north of Takayama (*futsū*, ¥240, 15 minutes). Central Furukawa is an easy stroll, or hire bikes at the **Miyagawa** (☎0577-73-2321; bicycle rental per hr ¥200) taxi office near the train station. Staff here can also store your luggage for ¥200 per day.

Shirakawa-gō & Gokayama 白川郷・五箇山

The remote, mountainous districts of Shirakawa-gō and Gokayama, between Takayama and Kanazawa, are best known for farmhouses in the thatched *gasshō-zukuri* style. They're rustic and lovely whether against the vibrant colours of spring, draped with the gentle mists of autumn, or peeking through a carpet of snow, and they hold a special place in the Japanese heart.

In the 12th century, the region's isolation is said to have attracted survivors from the Taira (Heike) clan, which was virtually wiped out by the Minamoto (Genji) clan in a brutal battle in 1185. During feudal times, Shirakawa-gō, like the rest of Hida, was under the direct control of the Kanamori clan, connected to the Tokugawa shogun, while

Gokayama was a centre for the production of gunpowder for the Kaga region, under the ruling Maeda clan.

Fast-forward to the 1960s when construction of the gigantic Miboro Dam over the Shōkawa river was to submerge entire villages. Many *gasshō* houses were relocated to their current sites. Although primarily preserved for tourism, these working villages still present a view of rural life found in few other parts of Japan.

Most of Shirakawa-gō's sights are in the heavily visited village of Ogimachi, linked by expressway to Takayama. The less-crowded, more isolated villages of Suganuma and Ainokura, in the Gokayama district of Toyama Prefecture, have the most ambience; other sights are spread over many kilometres along Rte 156. All three villages are Unesco World Heritage Sites.

Passionate debate continues around the impact tour buses have upon these unique communities, and how best to mitigate disruption to daily life. It's a case of not biting the hand that feeds you.

To avoid the crowds, steer clear of weekends, holidays, and cherry-blossom and autumn-foliage seasons. To best appreciate life here, stay overnight in a *gasshō-zukuri* inn. Accommodation is basic and advance reservations are recommended.

Getting There & Away

Nōhi Bus Company (www.nouhibus.co.jp/english) operates seven buses daily linking Shirakawa-gō with Takayama (one way ¥2470, return ¥4420, 50 minutes) and Kanazawa (one way ¥1850, return ¥3290, 1¼ hours). Some buses require a reservation. Weather delays and cancellations are possible between December and March.

Just before Ainokura, buses divert from Rte 156 for Rte 304 towards Kanazawa. From the Ainokura-guchi bus stop it's about 400m uphill to Ainokura before the descent into the village.

Kaetsuno Bus (www.kaetsunou.co.jp) operates at least four buses a day between Takaoka station on the JR Hokuriku line, Ainokura (¥1000, 90 minutes) and Ogimachi (¥1800, two hours), stopping at all major sights. If you want to get off at unofficial stops (eg Kuroba Onsen), tell the driver.

For self-drivers, there are exits for Shirakawa-gō (Ogimachi) and Gokayama (Ainokura) on the Tokai-Hokuriku expressway from Takayama. Alternatively, take the expressway to Shirakawa-gō (Ogimachi) then follow windy Rte 156 to the villages of Gokayama at your own pace. From Hakusan, the scenic toll road Hakusan Super-Rindō (cars ¥3240) ends near Ogimachi. In colder months, check conditions in advance with regional tourist offices before setting out on any National Roads.

Ogimachi 荻町

05769

The Shirakawa-gō region's central settlement has some 600 residents and the largest concentration of *gasshō-zukuri* buildings – over 110. It's also the most accessible. Pick up a free English-language map at the **Tourist Information Center** (観光案内所; 05769-6-1013; 2495-3 Ogimachi; 9am-5pm), by the main bus stop outside the Folk Village. Be sure to bring enough cash – ATMs are sparse and credit cards rarely accepted.

Sights & Activities

Shirakawa-gō's big festival is held on 14 and 15 October at **Shirakawa Hachiman-jinja** (other festivals continue until the 19th), and features groups of dancing locals taking part in the lion dance and *niwaka* (improvised buffoonery). The star is *doburoku,* a very potent unrefined sake.

Gasshō-zukuri Folk Village MUSEUM
(合掌造り民家園, Gasshō-zukuri Minka-en; 05769-6-1231; 2499 Ogimachi; adult/child ¥500/300; 8.40am-5pm Apr-Nov, 9am-6pm Fri-Wed Dec-Mar) Over two dozen *gasshō-zukuri* buildings have been relocated here, although the arrangement feels contrived. Several houses are used for demonstrating regional crafts such as woodwork, straw handicrafts and ceramics (in Japanese only; reservations required). Many items are for sale. You're free to wander the grounds for a picnic, but carry your rubbish out of town.

Shiroyama Tenbōdai VIEWPOINT
(Observation Point) This lookout on the site of a former castle provides a lovely overview of the valley. It's a 15-minute walk via the road behind the east side of town. You can climb the path (five minutes) from near the intersection of Rtes 156 and 360, or there's a shuttle bus (¥200 one way) from the Shirakawa-gō bus stop.

Wada-ke HISTORIC BUILDING
(和田家; 05769-6-1058; adult/child ¥300/150; 9am-5pm) Shirakawa-gō's largest *gasshō* house is a designated National Treasure. It once belonged to a wealthy silk-trading family and dates back to the mid-Edo period. Upstairs you'll find silk harvesting equipment and a valuable lacquerware collection.

Myōzen-ji Folk Museum MUSEUM
(明善寺郷土館; ☎05769-6-1009; adult/child ¥300/150; ⊙8.30am-5pm Apr-Nov, 9am-4pm Dec-Mar) Adjacent to Myōzen-ji, Ogimachi's small temple, Myōzen-ji Folk Museum displays the traditional paraphernalia of daily rural life.

Ōshirakawa Rotemburo ONSEN
(大白川露天風呂; ☎05769-6-1311; admission ¥300; ⊙8.30am-5pm mid-Jun–Oct, to 6pm Jul & Aug) This tiny, middle-of-nowhere onsen is 40km from Ogimachi, along a mountainous windy road with blind curves, impassable much of the year. There's no public transport, which is part of the charm, as are the views of Lake Shiramizu. Getting here from Ogimachi takes at least 90 minutes and requires determination and a car, or a taxi and lots of cash.

Sleeping & Eating

For online reservations at one of Ogimachi's many *gasshō* inns, try www.japaneseguest houses.com/db/shirakawago. Rates include two meals. Expect a nightly heating surcharge (¥400 and up) during cold weather.

★ **Magoemon** INN ¥¥¥
(孫右ェ門; ☎05769-6-1167; 360 Ogimachi; r per person with 2 meals from ¥10,260; Ⓟ) For an authentic and atmospheric retreat, this building is 300 years old and oozes history and charm. The friendly family owners speak no English and appreciate your efforts to communicate in Japanese. Meals are served around the handsome *irori*. Three of the six large rooms (shared facilities) face the river.

Kōemon INN ¥¥¥
(幸エ門; ☎05769-6-1446; 546 Ogimachi; r per person with 2 meals ¥8600; Ⓟ) In the centre of Ogimachi, Kōemon has five rooms with heated floors, dark-wood panelling and shared bathrooms. The fifth-generation owner speaks English well and his love of Shirakawa-gō is infectious.

Shimizu INN ¥¥¥
(民宿志みづ; ☎05769-6-1914; www.shimizuinn.com; 2613 Ogimachi; r per person with 2 meals ¥8800; Ⓟ) This homestyle inn at the southern end of town has a picturesque outlook. There are three small guestrooms and a common bath in a building that is over 200 years old.

Shirakawa-gō-no-yu ONSEN ¥¥¥
(白川郷の湯; ☎05769-6-0026; www.shirakawa gou-onsen.jp/english; 337 Ogimachi; r per person with 2 meals from ¥10,000) Day bathers (adult/child ¥700/300) in the town's only onsen can choose from a sauna, small *rotemburo* and large communal bath from 10am to 9.30pm. Overnight guests get to enjoy the facilities without the crowds.

Toyota Shirakawa-gō Eco-Institute HOTEL ¥¥¥
(トヨタ白川郷自然学校; ☎05769-6-1187; www.toyota.eco-inst.jp; 223 Magari; d per person from ¥12,200; Ⓟ) 🍃 Ten minutes' drive in the hills above Ogimachi brings you to this eco-lodge, which caters heavily to groups, but welcomes individual travellers. Countless activities are available and sumptuous French cuisine is served. Varying rates reflect the variety of room types.

Ochūdo CAFE ¥
(落人; ☎090-5458-0418; 792 Ogimachi; lunch ¥1000; ⊙10.30am-5pm; 📖) Set around a large *irori* hearth in a 350-year-old *gasshō* house, this delightful cafe serves curry rice, tea and coffee.

Irori SHOKUDO ¥
(いろり; ☎05769-6-1737; 374-1 Ogimachi; dishes from ¥432, set menu from ¥1296; ⊙lunch; 🖊📖) At the entrance to Ogimachi, this bustling eatery serves regional specialities such as *hoba-miso, yaki-dofu* (fried tofu) and *soba* or *udon teishoku*. You can eat at tables or around the *irori*.

Gokayama District 五箇山

☎0763

North along the Shōkawa river, in Toyama Prefecture, the Gokayama district is isolated and sparsely populated. Although there are a number of *gasshō-zukuri* buildings scattered along Rte 156, the villages of Suganuma and Ainokura have the best examples. To get here, drive north on Rte 156 from Shirakawa-gō. You'll reach Suganuma first, then Ainokura. The **Gokayama Tourist Information Center** (五箇山観光総合案内所; ☎0763-66-2468; 754 Kaminashi; ⊙9am-5pm) is in the village of Kaminashi.

SUGANUMA 菅沼

Down a steep hill off Rte 156, 15km north of Ogimachi, this pretty riverside collection of nine *gasshō-zukuri* houses is a World Heritage Site. It feels more like a residential museum than a working village, and there's no accommodation here.

Sights & Activities

Gokayama Minzoku-kan MUSEUM
(五箇山民族間; ☎0763-67-3652; 436 Suganuma; adult/child ¥300/150; ⊙9am-4.30pm) You can see items from traditional life and displays illustrating traditional gunpowder production, for which the area was famed, at this folklore museum in Suganuma.

Kuroba Onsen ONSEN
(くろば温泉; 1098 Kamitaira-hosojima; adult/child ¥600/300; ⊙10am-9pm Wed-Mon) About 1km north of Suganuma along Rte 156, Kuroba Onsen is a complex of indoor-outdoor baths with a lovely view. Its low-alkaline waters are good for fatigue and sore muscles.

KAMINASHI 上梨

Between Suganuma and Ainokura, in the hamlet of Kaminashi, you'll find **Murakami-ke** (村上家; ☎0763-66-2711; www.murakamike.jp; 742 Kaminashi; adult/child ¥300/150; ⊙8.30am-5pm Apr-Nov, 9am-4pm Dec-Mar), one of the oldest *gasshō* houses in the region (dating from 1578). Now a small museum, the proud owner delights in showing visitors around and might sing you some local folk songs. Close by, the main hall of **Hakusan-gū shrine** dates from 1502. It's an Important Cultural Property.

On 25 and 26 September, the **Kokiriko Matsuri** features costumed dancers performing with rattles that move like snakes. On day two, everyone joins in.

AINOKURA 相倉

Enchanting Ainokura, a World Heritage Site, is the most impressive of Gokayama's villages. The valley boasts over 20 *gasshō* buildings amid splendid mountain views. The village's remote location attracts less tour buses than Ogimachi, so it's much quieter. If you want to really step back in time and hear the sound of your thoughts, spend a night here – it's magical after the buses leave.

Sights

Ainokura Minzoku-kan MUSEUM
(相倉民族館; ☎0763-66-2732; admission ¥200; ⊙8.30am-5pm) Stroll through the village to this interesting folklore museum, with displays of local crafts and paper. It's divided into two buildings, the former Ozaki and Nakaya residences.

Gokayama Washi-no-Sato GALLERY
(五箇山和紙の里; ☎0763-66-2223; 215 Higashinakae; adult/child ¥200/150; ⊙8.30am-5pm) North of Ainokura on Rte 156 you'll find this roadside attraction, which explains the art of making *washi* (handmade paper) and gives you the chance to try it out (from ¥500, reservations required, limited English). You can also buy some in the gift shop.

Sleeping

Remote Ainokura is a great place for a *gasshō-zukuri* stay. Some Japanese ability will help you with reservations and getting by. Rates may be higher in winter due to a heating charge.

Ainokura Campground CAMPGROUND ¥
(相倉キャンプ場; ☎0763-66-2123; 611 Ainokura; per person ¥500; ⊙mid-Apr–late Oct) This lovely basic campground is about 1km from the village of Ainokura.

Yomoshiro MINSHUKU ¥¥¥
(民宿与茂四郎; ☎0763-66-2377; 395 Ainokura; per person with 2 meals ¥8800) Try this welcoming four-room inn, whose owner will demonstrate the *sasara,* a kind of noisemaker, upon request.

Goyomon MINSHUKU ¥¥¥
(民宿五ヨ門; ☎0763-66-2154; 438 Ainokura; per person with 2 meals ¥8000) This is a small, family-oriented homestay.

Chōyomon MINSHUKU ¥¥¥
(民宿長ヨ門; ☎0763-66-2755; 418 Ainokura; per person with 2 meals ¥8000) You can't get much more rustic than this 350-year-old place in the centre of Ainokura village.

FUKUI PREFECTURE

Northwest of Gifu Prefecture, little Fukui-ken (福井県) is off the beaten path for many travellers, but has a handful of special attractions including one of the world's most influential Zen centres, some pretty 'forgotten' towns and fascinating architectural ruins.

Fukui 福井

☎0776 / POP 268,000

Unfortunate Fukui city was decimated in the 1940s, first by war, then by earthquake. Most of the sights of interest are scattered around the compact prefecture, a short drive from town. Consider car rental and an overnight stay: country roads make for easy driving and the scenery is lovely.

Sights & Activities

Yokokan Garden GARDEN
(養浩館庭園; ☎0776-21-0489; 3-11 Hōei; admission ¥210; ⏲9am-4.30pm) This quaint garden in Fukui city, formerly a mansion of the Matsudaira clan, has a pretty teahouse where you can sit in silence and contemplate life, or feed the voraciously hungry *koi* (carp).

Daihonzan Eihei-ji BUDDHIST TEMPLE
(大本山永平寺; ☎0776-63-3640; http://global.sotozen-net.or.jp/eng/temples/foreigner/Eihei-ji.html; 5-15 Shihi, Eiheiji; adult/child ¥500/200; ⏲9am-5pm) In 1244 the great Zen master Dōgen (1200–53), founder of the Sōtō sect of Zen Buddhism, established Eihei-ji, the 'Temple of Eternal Peace', in a forest outside Fukui. Today it's one of Sōtō's two head temples, a palpably spiritual place amid mountains, mosses and ancient cedars. That said, day trippers visiting the complex of over 70 buildings might not find the constant throng of visitors and activities as peaceful as they might desire.

Aspirants affiliated with a Sōtō Zen organisation can attend Eihei-ji's four-day, three-night **sanzen religious experience program** (☎0776-63-3640; http://global.sotozen-net.or.jp/eng/temples/foreigner/Eihei-ji.html; 5-15 Shihi, Eiheiji; fee ¥12,100), which follows the monks' training schedule, complete with 3.50am prayers, cleaning, *zazen* and ritual meals in which not a grain of rice may be left behind. There are commonly some 150 priests and disciples in residence. Knowledge of Japanese isn't necessary, but it helps to be able to sit in the half-lotus position. Book at least a month in advance.

The compound is often closed for periods varying from a week to 10 days for religious observance. Sanrō temple stays cost ¥8000 per night and must be booked a month in advance.

To get to Eihei-ji from Fukui, take the Keifuku bus (¥720, 30 minutes, hourly); buses depart from the east exit of JR Fukui Station.

Tōjinbō LANDMARK
(東尋坊) Legend says these rock formations 25km northwest of Fukui came about when Tōjinbō, an evil priest, was cast off the cliff by angry villagers in 1182; the sea surged for 49 days thereafter, a demonstration of the priest's fury from beyond his watery grave. To see the rocks, visitors can take a boat trip (¥1300, 30 minutes) or ascend the gaudy tower (¥500).

To get to Tōjinbō from Fukui city, catch a train to Awara Onsen Station (*futsū* ¥320, 16 minutes) and then a bus (¥730, 40 minutes).

Fukui Dinosaur Museum MUSEUM
(福井県立恐竜博物館; ☎0779-88-0001; www.dinosaur.pref.fukui.jp/en; 51-11 Muroko-chō Terao, Katsuyama; adult/child ¥720/410; ⏲9am-5pm) Kids love the larger-than-life replicas and fossilised relics of the Jurrasic Park–styled Fukui Dinosaur Museum, one of the three largest museums of its kind in the world. There are plenty of English explanations and over 40 main exhibits (including interactive ones) concerned with natural history, prehistoric flora, fauna and the dinosaurs that once roamed Japan and other parts of the world. The closest train station is Katsuyama on the privately owned Echizen line, but your best bet is self-driving.

DON'T MISS

ICHIJŌDANI ASAKURA CLAN RUINS

The truly unique experience that is the **Ichijōdani Asakura Clan Ruins** (一乗谷朝倉氏遺跡, Ichijōdani Asakura-shi Iseki; ☎0776-41-2330; http://info.pref.fukui.lg.jp/bunka/asakura_museum/080_english/ruin.php; 4-10 Abaka; admission ¥210; ⏲9am-4.30pm) is just a short drive through pretty countryside from Fukui city. Designated a National Historic Site, this unexpected find boasts one of the largest town ruins in Japan. Perched in a narrow valley between modest mountains, it's easy to see why the Asakura clan would have built their small fortified city here: it's very beautiful. You're free to wander along the restored street of merchants, houses and stroll through the lush grasses, following the remnants of the buildings up the hillside. It's a wonderful spot to sit, picnic and contemplate.

Sleeping & Eating

Fukui Phoenix Hotel HOTEL ¥¥
(福井フェニックスホテル; ☎0776-21-1800; www.phoenix-hotel.jp/e; 2-4-18 Ote; s/d/tw from ¥6500/10,000/12,000; P 📶) A hop, skip and

a jump from JR Fukui Station, this refurbished hotel has tastefully decorated rooms, free wi-fi, a coin laundry and a variety of room types (including suites) for those wanting a little more room to spread out. Parking is available nearby for ¥1000.

Yūbuan NOODLES ¥¥
(遊歩庵; ☎0776-76-3519; 1-9-1 Chūō; ⊙11.30am-7pm) On the Reikishi-no-michi street outside the West Exit of Fukui Station, you'll find this delightful variance on the usual *soba* theme. The speciality is *oroshi soba sanmai* (¥1300), a double serve of thick flattened *soba* noodles with three flavours to dip in: *oroshi* (grated daikon), *tororo* (puréed mountain potato) and *wasabi*.

Information

Fukui Tourist Information Center (福井市観光案内所; ☎0776-20- 5348; 1-1-1 Chūō; ⊙8.30am-7pm) Enquire here, inside JR Fukui Station, for local maps and itineraries.

Getting There & Away

JR trains connect Fukui with Kanazawa (*tokkyū* ¥2500, 45 minutes; *futsū* ¥1320, 1½ hours), Tsuruga (*tokkyû* ¥2150, 35 minutes; *futsū* ¥970, 55 minutes), Kyoto (¥4420, 1½ hours) and Osaka (¥5510, two hours).

There are a bunch of car-rental options outside the East Exit of JR Fukui Station, including Toyota Rent-a-Car.

Echizen-Ōno 越前大野

☎0779 / POP 84,024

The delightful village of Echizen-Ōno was designed by Kanamori Nagachika in 1575 based on the layout of Kyoto at that time, earning it the nickname 'little Kyoto'. Today, the town is overlooked on most itineraries, but this little ageing village has a very special quality; even if the rest of the world seems to have forgotten it exists, the locals certainly haven't. Their town square has been lovingly maintained and updated. Even as their population grows increasingly older and their buildings start to decline, there's a palpable spirit of *ganbatte* (never give up) that shows in the immaculately clean, although sometimes almost empty, streets.

Ōno's **Teramachi** (temple row) features around 20 temples arranged side by side, some still operational, others closed down; most are still carefully cared for by their ageing owners and patrons. It's a truly stirring spot for a contemplative walk; an even better location for budding photographers.

Atop a hill overlooking the town, **Echizen Ōno-jō** (越前大野城; ☎0779-66-0234; 3-109 Shiromachi, Ono; admission ¥200; ⊙9am-4pm Apr-Nov), a little *yamashiro* (mountain castle) is a true delight, even if it is a replica and you have to climb all those stairs. Originally built in 1576, today's version went up in 1968 to exacting specifications. The views of the surrounding valleys and mountains are something special. In the right conditions, the castle appears as if it were above a sea of clouds.

Ringed by attractive mid-sized mountains and bathed in history, there's a whole lot more of Echizen-Ōno to uncover than listed here. Why not make friends with the locals at the **Tourist Information Center** (越前大野観光案内所; ☎0779-65-5521; www.ono-kankou-jp; 10-23 Motomachi; ⊙9am-4pm) and tell them we sent you?

SAIL AWAY?

Tsuruga, south of Fukui and north of Biwa-ko, is a thriving port and train junction. If you've still got a sense of adventure, **Shin Nihonkai Ferry Company** (☎0770-23-2222; www.snf.jp; 2nd class from ¥9300) has nine sailings a week to Tomakomai, Hokkaidō (19½ hours nonstop, 30½ hours with stops). Several of these stop en route at Niigata (¥5200, 12½ hours) and Akita (¥6500, 20 hours). Buses timed to ferry departures serve Tsuruga-kō port from JR Tsuruga Station (¥340, 20 minutes).

ISHIKAWA PREFECTURE

Ishikawa-ken (石川県), comprising the former Kaga and Noto fiefs, is rich in culture, history and natural beauty. In ancient times the prefecture was at the forefront of wealth and culture in Japan. Cut to March 2015 and Ishikawa steals the spotlight again with the opening of the Hokuriku Shinkansen, making the region easier to reach than ever before.

Kanazawa, the Kaga capital and power base of the feudal Maeda clan, boasts traditional architecture and one of Japan's most famous gardens. To the north, the Noto Peninsula has sweeping seascapes and quiet fishing villages. Hakusan National Park, near the southern tip of the prefecture, offers great hiking. You can find good overviews at www.hot-ishikawa.jp.

Kanazawa 金沢

076 / POP 462,360

Kanazawa's array of cultural attractions makes it the drawcard of the Hokuriku region. Best known for Kenroku-en, a castle garden dating from the 17th century, it also boasts beautifully preserved samurai and geisha districts, attractive temples, a wealth of museums and a wonderful market. We recommend a two- or three-day stay to take it all in.

History

During the 15th century Kanazawa was under the control of an autonomous Buddhist government, ousted in 1583 by Maeda Toshiie, head of the powerful Maeda clan. Kanazawa means 'golden marsh' – in its heyday the region was Japan's richest, producing about five million bushels of rice annually. This wealth allowed the Maeda to patronise culture and the arts. Kanazawa remains a national cultural hot spot.

An absence of military targets spared the city from destruction during WWII. Its myriad historical and cultural sites are wonderfully preserved and integrate neatly with the city's share of contemporary architecture.

Sights

Kanazawa is a sprawling city with two almost parallel rivers traversing its core. Most areas of interest are located a good distance from the impressive JR Kanazawa Station area, into which most visitors arrive. With the recent arrival of the Hokuriku Shinkansen speeding into town, this area is abuzz with activity. The terminus of the city's substantial bus network, which can at first seem a little confusing, is also here. Have patience: you'll orient yourself soon enough.

Heading south of the station along Hyakumangoku-dōri, you'll reach Kōrinbō (the shopping and business district) before arriving in Katamachi, by the banks of the Sai-gawa; this is the place to eat, drink and be merry. If you're staying near the station, note that buses stop early in the evening and taxis back from the action cost at least ¥1300.

Teramachi and Nishi-chaya-gai are just over the bridge from Katamachi, but the mainstay of sights are to its east. To their north, across the Asano-gawa, lies pretty Higashi-chaya-gai in the shadow of hilly Utatsuyama's many temples. Heading west will loop you back to the station, passing Ōmi-chō Market, a must see.

★D.T. Suzuki Museum — MUSEUM

(鈴木大拙館; 076-221-8011; www.kanazawa-museum.jp/daisetz/english; 3-4-20 Honda-machi; adult/senior/child ¥300/200/free; 9.30am-4.30pm Tue-Sun) This spiritual museum is a tribute to Daisetsu Teitaro Suzuki, one of the foremost Buddhist philosophers of our time. Published in Japanese and English, Suzuki is largely credited with introducing Zen to the west. This stunning concrete complex embodies the heart of Zen. Come to learn about the man and practise mindfulness by the water mirror garden.

★Kenroku-en — GARDENS

(兼六園; 076-234-3800; www.pref.ishikawa.jp/siro-niwa/kenrokuen/e/; 1-1 Marunouchi; adult/child ¥310/100; 7am-6pm Mar-15 Oct, 8am-4.30pm 16 Oct-Feb) Ranked as one of the top three gardens in Japan, this Edo-period garden draws its name (*kenroku* means 'combined six') from a renowned Sung-dynasty garden in China that dictated six attributes for perfection: seclusion, spaciousness, artificiality, antiquity, abundant water and broad views. Kenroku-en has them all. Arrive before the crowds to increase your chances of silent contemplation.

It is believed that the garden, originally belonging to an outer villa of Kanazawa-jō, was developed from the 1620s to the 1840s and was so named in 1822. It was first opened to the public in 1871.

Kanazawa Castle Park — LANDMARK

(金沢城公園, Kanazawa-jō Kōen; 076-34-3800; www.pref.ishikawa.jp/siro-niwa/kanazawajou/e/; 1-1 Marunouchi; buildings/grounds ¥310/free; grounds 5am-6pm Mar-15 Oct, 6am-4.30pm 16 Oct-Feb, castle 9am-4.30pm) Built in 1580, this massive structure was called the 'castle of 1000 tatami' and housed the Maeda clan for 14 generations until it was ultimately destroyed by fire in 1881. The elegant surviving gate **Ishikawa-mon** (built in 1788) provides a dramatic entry from Kenroku-en; holes in its turret were designed for hurling rocks at invaders. Two additional buildings, the **Hishi-yagura** (diamond-shaped turret) and **Gojikken-nagaya** (armoury), were reconstructed by traditional means in 2001. Restoration and archaeological work is ongoing.

Ōmi-chō Market MARKET

(近江町市場; 35 Ōmi-chō; ⌚9am-5pm) Between Kanazawa Station and Katamachi, you'll find this market, reminiscent of Tokyo's Tsukiji. A bustling warren of fishmongers, buyers and restaurants, it's a great place to watch everyday people in action or indulge in the freshest sashimi and local produce. The nearest bus stop is Musashi-ga-tsuji.

21st Century Museum of Contemporary Art GALLERY

(金沢21世紀美術館; ☎076-220-2800; www.kanazawa21.jp; 1-2-1 Hirosaka; ⌚10am-6pm Tue-Thu & Sun, 10am-8pm Fri & Sat) FREE A low-slung glass cylinder, 113m in diameter, forms the perimeter of this contemporary gallery, which celebrated its 10th birthday in 2014. Entry to the museum is free, but admission fees are charged for exhibitions by contemporary artists from Japan and abroad. Inside, galleries are arranged like boxes on a tray. Check the English-language website for event info and exhibition admission fees.

Kanazawa Phonograph Museum MUSEUM

(金沢蓄音器館; ☎076-232-3066; 2-11-21 Owari-chō; admission ¥300; ⌚10am-5pm) Audio buffs will dig this museum of old-time phonographs and SP records, with daily demonstrations at 11am, 2pm and 4pm.

Ishikawa Prefectural Museum of Traditional Products & Crafts MUSEUM

(石川県立伝統産業工芸館; ☎076-262-2020; www.ishikawa-densankan.jp/english/info; 2-1 Kenroku-machi; adult/child ¥260/100; ⌚9am-5pm, closed 3rd Thu of month Apr-Nov, closed Thu Dec-Mar) This small museum offers fine displays of over 20 regional crafts. Pick up the free English-language headphone guide.

Nagamachi District

Once inhabited by samurai, this attractive, well-preserved district (Nagamachi Buke-yashiki) framed by two canals features winding streets lined with tile-roofed mud walls.

Nagamachi Yūzen-kan MUSEUM

(長町友禅館; ☎076-264-2811; www.kagayuzen-club.co.jp/english; 2-6-16 Nagamachi; admission ¥350; ⌚9am-noon & 1-4.30pm Fri-Wed) In a non-traditional building at the edge of the Nagamachi district, the Nagamachi Yūzen-kan displays some splendid examples of *Kaga Yūzen* kimono dyeing and demonstrates the process. Enquire ahead about trying the silk-dyeing process yourself (¥4000).

Higashi-chaya-gai

Just north of Asano-gawa, Higashi-chaya-gai (Higashi Geisha District) is an enclave of narrow streets established early in the 19th century for geisha to entertain wealthy patrons. The slatted wooden facades of the geisha houses are romantically preserved.

Shima MUSEUM

(志摩; ☎076-252-5675; www.ochaya-shima.com/english; 1-13-21 Higashiyama; adult/child ¥400/300; ⌚9am-6pm) An Important Cultural Asset, this well-known, traditional-style former geisha house dates from 1820 and has an impressive collection of elaborate combs and *shamisen* picks.

Kaikarō MUSEUM

(懐華樓; ☎076-253-0591; www.kenrokuen.jp/en/kaikaro; 1-14-8 Higashiyama; admission ¥700; ⌚9am-5pm) In Higashi-chaya-gai, Kaikarō is an early-19th-century geisha house refinished with contemporary fittings and art including a red lacquered staircase.

Teramachi District

This hilly neighbourhood south of Sai-gawa, southwest of the centre, was established as a first line of defence and contains dozens of temples.

Myōryū-ji BUDDHIST TEMPLE

(妙立寺; ☎076-241-0888; 1-2-12 Nomachi; admission ¥800; ⌚9am-4.30pm Mar-Nov, 9am-4pm Dec-Feb, reservations required) In Teramachi, fascinating Myōryū-ji (aka Ninja-dera), completed in 1643, was designed to protect its Lord in case of attack. It contains hidden stairways, escape routes, secret chambers, concealed tunnels and trick doors. Contrary to popular belief, this ancient temple has nothing to do with ninja. Admission is by tour only (in Japanese with an English guidebook). You must phone for reservations (in English).

Festivals & Events

Kagatobi Dezomeshiki CULTURAL

In early January scantily clad firemen brave the cold, imbibe sake and demonstrate ancient fire-fighting skills on ladders.

Kanazawa

A
B
C
D
1
2
3
4
5
6
7
Moroe Ōdōri
Kanazawa Tourist Information Center
Shōwa Ōdōri
Kanazawa
23
13
36
37
22
14
Ishikawa Foundation for International Exchange
17
12
10
Hyakumangoku-dōri
15
Tamagawa-kōen
Ohori Ōdōri
Hyakumangoku-dōri
7
4
9
NAGAMACHI
Chūō-dōri
34
20
18
21
KŌRINBŌ
Kenroku-en
2
24
Hirosaka
3
26
29
31
28
KATAMACHI
Sai-gawa
30
Honda Ōdōri
Nishi-inter Ōdōri
TERAMACHI
Myōryū-ji (250m); Kutani Kosen Gama Kiln (750m)
1
D.T. Suzuki Museum

Asano-gawa Enyūkai MUSIC

Performances of traditional Japanese dance and music are held on the banks of the Asano-gawa during the second weekend of April.

Hyakumangoku Matsuri PARADE

In early June Kanazawa's main annual festival commemorates the first time the region's rice production hit one million *koku* (around 150,000 tonnes). There's a parade of townsfolk in 16th-century costumes, *takigi nō* (torch-lit performances of *nō* drama), *tōrō nagashi* (lanterns floated down the river at dusk) and a special *chanoyu* (tea ceremony). It's at Kenroku-en.

Sleeping

★Pongyi GUESTHOUSE ¥

(ポンギー; ☎076-225-7369; www.pongyi.com; 2-22 Rokumai-machi; dm ¥2700, s/d ¥4500/6000; @) Run by a friendly Japanese man who did a stint in Southeast Asia as a monk, Pongyi is a charmingly renovated old shop alongside a canal. Cosy dorms are located in an annexed vintage *kura* (mud-walled storehouse).

Tōyoko Inn Kanazawa Kenroku-en Kōrinbō HOTEL ¥

(東横イン金沢兼六園香林坊; ☎076-232-1045; www.toyoko-inn.com; 2-4-28 Korinbo; s/d from ¥4200/6700) About 15 minutes' walk from both Katamachi and JR Kanazawa Station you'll find this business hotel with clean, cheap and cheerful little rooms and a free shuttle to Kanazawa Station.

★Holiday Inn ANA Kanazawa Sky HOTEL ¥¥

(☎076-233-2233; www.holidayinn.com; 15-1 Musashi-machi; s/d from ¥6500/8800; wi-fi) Centrally located between JR Kanazawa Station and the sights, across the road from Ōmi-chō Market, this recently renovated hotel is an excellent midrange choice with comfortable bedding and great views. It's on top of the M'Za department store, whose basement-level food court is all too convenient.

Yōgetsu MINSHUKU ¥¥

(陽月; ☎076-252-0497; 1-13-22 Higashiyama; r per person with/without breakfast from ¥5000/4500) Located in the heart of the picturesque Higashi-chaya district, this beautifully renovated 200-year-old geisha teahouse has only three rooms and features a *goemon-buro* (cauldron-shaped bath). No English is spoken, there's no wi-fi and it's tucked away,

Kanazawa

Top Sights
- 1 D.T. Suzuki Museum ... D7
- 2 Kenroku-en ... D6

Sights
- 3 21st Century Museum of Contemporary Art ... D6
- Gojikken-nagaya ... (see 4)
- 4 Hishi-yagura ... D5
- 5 Ishikawa Prefectural Museum of Traditional Products & Crafts ... E6
- 6 Kaikarō ... F3
- 7 Kanazawa Castle Park ... D5
- 8 Kanazawa Phonograph Museum ... E3
- 9 Nagamachi Yūzen-kan ... A5
- 10 Ōmi-chō Market ... C3
- 11 Shima ... F3

Sleeping
- 12 Holiday Inn ANA Kanazawa Sky ... C3
- 13 Hotel Dormy Inn Kanazawa ... B1
- 14 Hotel Nikkō Kanazawa ... B2
- 15 Hotel Resol Trinity ... C4
- 16 Kanazawa Hakuchōrō Hotel ... E4
- 17 Pongyi ... A3
- 18 Tōyoko Inn Kanazawa Kenroku-en Kōrinbō ... C5
- 19 Yōgetsu ... F3

Eating
- 20 Aashirwad ... B5
- 21 Cottage ... B5
- 22 Daiba Kanazawa Ekimae ... B2
- 23 Forus Department Store ... B1
- 24 Janome-sushi Honten ... C6
- 25 Kanazawa Todoroki-tei ... E3
- 26 Osteria del Campagne ... B7
- Sentō ... (see 10)
- 27 Tamura ... E4

Drinking & Nightlife
- 28 Baby Rick ... B7
- 29 Cambio APT ... B7
- 30 Pilsen ... B7
- 31 Polé Polé ... B7

Entertainment
- 32 Ishikawa Prefectural Nō Theatre ... E7

Shopping
- 33 Ishikawa Craft Store ... E5
- 34 Murakami ... B5
- 35 Sakuda Gold Leaf Company ... F3

Transport
- 36 Hokutetsu Rent-a-Cycle ... A1
- 37 JR Kanazawa Station Rent-a-Cycle ... A2

but it's perfect if tranquillity, history and authenticity are what you're after.

Hotel Resol Trinity HOTEL ¥¥
(ホテルレソルトリニティ; ☎076-221-9629; www.resol-hotel.jp/resol/en/hotels/trinity-kanazawa; 1-18 Musashi-machi; s/d from ¥6300/8000; @) This lovely niche hotel is a breath of fresh air. Rooms have a splash of colour and have been designed to make you feel comfortable in a compact space. Its location is central to everything: you can walk to JR Kanazawa Station, Katamachi and Kenroku-en in about 15 minutes.

Hotel Dormy Inn Kanazawa HOTEL ¥¥
(ドーミーイン金沢; ☎076-263-9888; www.hotespa.net/hotels/kanazawa; 2-25 Horikawa-shinmachi; s/d from ¥5990/7990; @) Around the corner from JR Kanazawa Station, this popular, modern tourist hotel has well-designed, functional rooms, a calcium-rich onsen *rotemburo* on the top floor, and a coin laundry.

★ **Hotel Nikkō Kanazawa** HOTEL ¥¥¥
(ホテル日航金沢; ☎076-234-1111; www.hnkanazawa.jp; 2-15-1 Honmachi; r from ¥12,800;) Kanazawa's most luxurious hotel, near JR Kanazawa Station, has a wide range of room types from singles to lavish suites, and an impressive selection of on-site restaurants and bars. Most rooms have exceptional views. The hotel turned 20 in 2014, but all rooms have been recently refurbished. The 'Luxe Style' and 'Stylish' rooms are worth the extra coin.

Kanazawa Hakuchōrō Hotel HOTEL ¥¥¥
(金沢白鳥路ホテル; ☎076-222-1212; www.hakuchoro.com; 6-3 Marunouchi; s/tw from ¥13,000/19,000; P@) This interesting hotel adjacent to Kanazawa Castle Park and near Higashi-chaya-gai is quiet and removed from the action. Formal, Western-style rooms are showing their age, but their generous dimensions compensate. There's a lovely lobby, a restaurant and common onsen baths. Free parking.

Eating

Seafood is the staple of Kanazawa's *Kaga ryōri* (Kaga cuisine); even the most humble train-station *bentō* usually features some type of fish. *Oshi-zushi*, a thin layer of fish pressed atop vinegar rice, is said to be the precursor to modern sushi. Another favourite is *jibuni*, flour-coated duck or chicken stewed with shiitake and green vegetables.

The shiny, revitalised JR Kanazawa Station building is brimming with food outlets. Its neighbour, **Forus department store**, has great restaurants on the 6th floor. Ōmichō Market (p243) has fresh-from-the-boat eateries, but most of the evening action is in Katamachi.

★Sentō CHINESE ¥
(仙桃; ☎076-234-0669; 88 Aokusa-machi, 2F Ōmichō Ichiba; dishes from ¥600, set menus from ¥900; ⏲11am-3pm & 5-10.30pm Wed-Mon) Upstairs in Ōmi-chō Market, talented chefs from Hong Kong prepare authentic Szechuan- and Hong Kong–style dishes (including dim sum) from scratch. Healthy (yellow bean oil is used) and delicious lunch and dinner set menus are excellent value. The spicy, salted squid is exquisite, but we just had to come back for a second bowl of *tantanmen* (sesame and chilli *rāmen*). Sluuuurp!

Full of Beans CAFE ¥
(☎076-222-3315; www.fullofbeans.jp; 41-1 Satomi-chō; meals from ¥800; ⏲11.30am-3.30pm & 5-10pm Thu-Tue) A variety of Japanese and *yōshoku* (Western-style) meals are served in this stylish cafe in the quieter backstreets of Katamachi – the website homepage will give you a sense of the vibe. It's a good place to try the Kanazawa speciality, *hanton raisu* (¥900) – a bowl of rice topped with an omelette, fried seafood, ketchup and tartare sauce. YUM.

Aashirwad NEPALESE ¥
(アシルワード; ☎076-262-2170; 2-12-15 Kōrinbō; starters from ¥300, curries from ¥900; ⏲11am-10pm; 📋) Authentic and flavoursome Nepali and Indian cooking served in funky, atmospheric surroundings on a quaint Kōrinbō backstreet. The staff are friendly, and the ambience and quality of this recent appearance on the Kanazawa restaurant scene are impressive. An extensive menu has all your favourites, but you have to try the *momo* (Nepalese dumplings) for ¥650.

Daiba Kanazawa Ekimae IZAKAYA ¥
(台場金沢駅前店; ☎076-263-9191; 6-10 Konohana-machi, Kanazawa Miyako Hotel 1F; items from ¥420; ⏲11am-3pm & 5pm-midnight; 📋) This trendy spot in the Kanazawa Miyako Hotel building has a comprehensive Japanese menu and a limited English one with all the Western favourites and some local specialities. It's a great place for your first *izakaya* experience, with lots of small plates and beer. Highly recommended.

Cottage INTERNATIONAL ¥
(コテージ; ☎076-262-3277; 2-8-16 Seseragi-dōri, rear of Kōrinbō 109; dishes from ¥780; ⏲noon-2.30pm & 6-9.30pm Thu-Tue) This popular home-style restaurant run by a friendly Irish and Japanese husband-and-wife team has moved to a new location. The food and welcoming vibe are still top notch, while thin-crust pizza, flavourful pastas and hearty Irish stews feature on the eclectic, rotating menu.

Osteria del Campagne ITALIAN ¥¥
(オステリアデルカンパーニュ; ☎076-261-2156; 2-31-33 Katamachi; mains from ¥950, set menus from ¥3900; ⏲5pm-midnight Mon-Sat; 📋) This cosy, quietly fashionable Italian bistro serves lovely set-course menus, while à-la-carte offerings include house-made focaccia, salads, pastas, desserts and hors d'oeuvres you can eat with chopsticks! There's an English menu and friendly, professional staff.

Janome-sushi Honten SUSHI ¥¥
(蛇之目寿司本店; ☎076-231-0093; 1-1-12 Kōrinbō; set menu ¥1000-3400, Kaga ryōri sets from ¥4000; ⏲11am-2pm & 5-11pm Thu-Tue; 📋) Regarded for sashimi and Kaga cuisine since 1931, one of our Japanese friends says that when he eats here, he knows he's really in Kanazawa. You can't go wrong with the *saabisu ranchi* (lunch specials, from ¥1000).

Kanazawa Todoroki-tei BISTRO ¥¥
(金沢とどろき亭; ☎076-252-5755; 1-2-1 Higashiyama; plates from ¥1200; ⏲11.30am-2.30pm & 6-10pm) The art-deco, woody, candelit atmosphere of this Western-style bistro near Higashi-chaya-gai is a big selling point. The Taisho-era (1912–26) building with vaulted ceilings is a little rough around the edges, but that's part of its charm: it's not too snooty. Eight-course dinners are good value, starting at ¥3500 per person. Think romance.

Tamura IZAKAYA ¥¥
(田村; ☎076-222-0517; 2-18 Namiki-machi; courses from ¥2000; ⏲5-11.30pm Thu-Tue; 📋) Favoured by Japanese celebrities, this riverside joint is as affable as its owner (who speaks some English). If you're going to do it, you're best to let him run the show – courses start at ¥2000, with the deluxe *omakase* at ¥8800.

TRADITIONAL CRAFTS

During the Edo period Kanazawa's ruling Maeda family fuelled the growth of important crafts. Many are still practised today.

Kanazawa & Wajima Lacquerware

To create Kanazawa and Wajima lacquerware, decoration is applied to luminous black lacquerware through *maki-e* (painting) or gilding. Artists must take great care that dust does not settle on the final product.

Ōhi Pottery

The deliberately simple, almost primitive designs, rough surfaces, irregular shapes and monochromatic glazes of Ōhi pottery have been favoured by tea practitioners since the early Edo period. Since that time one family, with the professional name Chōzaemon, has been keeper of the Ōhi tradition.

Kutani Porcelain

Kutani porcelain is known for its elegant shapes, graceful designs and bright, bold colours. The style dates back to the early Edo period and shares design characteristics with Chinese porcelain and Japanese Imari ware. Typical motifs include birds, flowers, trees and landscapes.

Kaga Yūzen Silk Dyeing

The laborious, specialised method of *Kaga Yūzen* silk dyeing is characterised by strong colours and realistic depictions of nature, such as flower petals that have begun to brown around the edges. White lines between elements where ink has washed away are a characteristic of *Kaga Yūzen*.

Gold Leaf

It starts with a lump of pure gold the size of a ¥10 coin, which is rolled to the size of a tatami mat, as little as 0.0001mm thick. The gold leaf is cut into squares of 10.9cm – the size used for mounting on walls, murals or paintings – or then cut again for gilding on lacquerware or pottery. Kanazawa makes over 98% of Japan's gold leaf.

Drinking & Nightlife

Most of Kanazawa's bars are jam-packed into high-rises in Katamachi – many are barely disguised hostess bars. For a mellower evening, soak in the ambience of Higashi-chaya-gai.

Cambio APT BAR

(☎076-207-7524; 2-2-14 Katamachi, 2F SILK Bldg; ⊙7pm-midnight) Smack in the heart of Katamachi you'll find this shiny, new welcoming bar. The friendly young owner spent time in Canada and is happy to chat. There's a ¥400 seating charge.

Pilsen PUB

(ぴるぜん; ☎076-221-0688; http://pilsen.jp; 1-9-20 Katamachi; ⊙5pm-midnight Mon-Sat) This decent-sized German beer hall has been pulling pints and serving wurst, cheese and pasta since 1968 to an interesting mix of locals and foreigners.

Baby Rick BAR

(ベイビーリック; ☎076-263-5063; www.babyrick.com; 1-5-20 Katamachi; ⊙5pm-3am) Class and character in the heart of Katamachi. This basement bar has an extensive picture menu and a billiards table, and attracts a lively crowd. There's a ¥500 cover charge after 10pm.

Polé Polé BAR

(ポレポレ; ☎076-260-1138; 2-31-30 Katamachi) Kanazawa's grungy *gaijin*-friendly reggae/dive bar is littered with years of sawdust and peanut shells: not one for grandma. What's great about it are the friendly, open-minded staff and patrons who are happy to chat if you want or chill in the shadows if you don't.

Entertainment

Ishikawa Prefectural Nō Theatre THEATRE

(石川県立能楽堂; ☎076-264-2598; www.nohgaku.or.jp; 3-1 Dewa-machi; performance prices vary; ⊙9am-4.30pm Tue-Sun) *Nō* theatre is alive and well in Kanazawa. Weekly performances take place here during summer.

Shopping

The Hirosaka shopping street, between Kōrinbō 109 department store and Kenroku-en, has some upmarket craft shops on its south side. Other major department stores are towards JR Kanazawa Station (Forus, Meitetsu M'za) and on Hyakumangoku-dōri between Kōrinbō and Katamachi (Daiwa, Atrio Shopping Plaza). The fresh and funky Tatemachi Shopping Promenade is also here.

Ishikawa Craft Store CRAFTS
(石川県観光物産館, Ishikawa-ken Kankō-bussankan; ☎076-222-7788; 2-20 Kenroku-machi; ⏲10am-6pm) An overview of Kanazawa crafts, under one roof.

Murakami FOOD
(村上; ☎076-264-4223; 2-3-32 Nagamachi; ⏲8.30am-5pm) If a flowering tree made of candy excites you, head to Murakami. At this handsome *wagashi* (Japanese candy) shop you'll also find *fukusamochi* (red-bean paste and pounded rice in a crêpe) and *kakiho* (soybean flour rolled in black sesame seeds).

Sakuda Gold Leaf Company CRAFTS
(金銀箔工芸さくだ; ☎076-251-6777; www.goldleaf-sakuda.jp; 1-3-27 Higashiyama; ⏲9am-6pm) Here you can observe the *kinpaku* (gold leaf) process and pick up all sorts of gilded souvenirs including pottery, lacquerware and, er...golf balls. It also serves tea containing flecks of gold leaf, reputedly good for rheumatism. Even the toilet walls are lined with gold and platinum.

Information

There are post offices in Katamachi and in Kanazawa Station. Coin-operated laundries can be found in Higashi-chaya-gai and Katamachi. Online, check out www4.city.kanazawa.lg.jp for general city information.

Kanazawa Tourist Information Center (石川県金沢観光情報センター; ☎076-232-6200, KGGN 076-232-3933; http://kggn.sakura.ne.jp; 1 Hirooka-machi; ⏲9am-7pm) This excellent office inside Kanazawa Station has incredibly helpful staff and a plethora of well-made English-language maps, pamphlets and magazines including *Eye on Kanazawa.* The friendly folk from the Goodwill Guide Network (KGGN) are also here to assist with hotel recommendations and free guiding in English – two weeks' notice is requested.

Ishikawa Foundation for International Exchange (☎076-262-5931; www.ifie.or.jp; 1-5-3 Honmachi; ⏲9am-8pm Mon-Fri, to 5pm Sat & Sun) Offers information, a library, satellite-TV news and free internet access. It's on the 3rd floor of the Rifare building, a few minutes' walk southeast of JR Kanazawa Station.

Getting There & Away

AIR

Nearby **Komatsu Airport** (KMQ; www.komatsu airport.jp) has air connections with major Japanese cities, as well as Seoul, Shanghai and Taipei.

BUS

JR Highway Bus operates express buses from in front of JR Kanazawa Station's east exit to Tokyo's Shinjuku Station (¥8000, 7½ hours) and Kyoto (¥4100, 4¼ hours). Hokutetsu buses serve Nagoya (¥4100, four hours). Nōhi Bus Company services Takayama, via Shirakawa-go (¥3390, 2¼ hours).

TRAIN

The JR Hokuriku line links Kanazawa with Fukui (*tokkyū* ¥2500, 45 minutes; *futsū* ¥1320, 1½ hours), Kyoto (*tokkyū* ¥6380, 2¼ hours), Osaka (*tokkyū* ¥7130, 2¾ hours) and Toyama (*futsū* ¥980, one hour).

Fares and travel times for the brand-new, blink-of-an-eye journey between Kanazawa and Toyama on the long-anticipated Hokuriku Shinkansen can be found online at http://english.jr-central.co.jp/info/. The direct journey between Kanazawa and Tokyo (¥14,120) is now just 2½ hours.

For the latest scheduled services of the Thunderbird Limited Express service between Osaka/Kyoto and Kanazawa, check www.hyper dia.com.

Getting Around

JR Kanazawa Station is the hub for transit to/from and around Kanazawa.

Full-size bikes can be rented from **JR Kanazawa Station Rent-a-Cycle** (駅レンタサイクル; ☎076-261-1721; per hr/day ¥200/1200; ⏲8am-8.30pm) and **Hokutetsu Rent-a-Cycle** (北鉄レンタサイクル; ☎076-263-0919; per 4hr/day ¥630/1050; ⏲8am-5.30pm), in the offices of Nippon Rent-a-Car, both by the West exit.

There's also a pay-as-you-go bicycle rental system called 'Machi-nori'. The bikes are a bit dinky, but with a bit of planning, the system functions well. For the lowdown in English, go to www.machi-nori.jp/pdf/machinoriEnglishmap.pdf.

Buses depart from the circular terminus in front of the station's east exit. Any bus from station stop 7, 8 or 9 will take you to the city centre (¥200, day pass ¥900). The Kanazawa Loop Bus (single ride/day pass ¥200/500, every 15 minutes from 8.30am to 6pm) circles the major tourist attractions in 45 minutes. On Saturday, Sunday and holidays, the Machi-bus goes to Kōrinbō for ¥100.

Airport buses (¥1130, 45 minutes) depart from station stop 6. Some services are via Katamachi and Kōrinbō 109, but take one hour to reach the airport.

Numerous car-rental agencies are dotted around the station's west exit.

Kaga Onsen 加賀温泉

☎0761

This broad area consisting of three hot-spring villages – Katayamazu Onsen, Yamashiro Onsen and Yamanaka Onsen – is centred on Kaga Onsen and Daishōji Stations along the JR Hokuriku line and is famed for its *onsen ryokan*, lacquerware and porcelain. Of the three villages, Yamanaka Onsen is the most scenic.

Sights & Activities

Kutaniyaki Art Museum MUSEUM

(石川県九谷焼美術館; ☎0761-72-7466; www.kutani-mus.jp/en; 1-10-13 Daishōji Jikata-machi; adult/child ¥500/free; ⊙9am-5pm Tue-Sun) Stunning examples of bright and colourful local porcelain are on display here, an eight-minute walk from Daishōji Station.

Zenshō-ji BUDDHIST TEMPLE

(全昌寺; ☎0761-72-1164; 1 Daishōji Shinmei-chō; admission ¥500; ⊙9am-5pm) The Daishōji Station area is crammed with temples including Zenshō-ji, which houses more than 500 amusingly carved Buddhist arhat sculptures.

Yamanaka Onsen ONSEN

In lovely Yamanaka Onsen, the 17th-century haiku poet Bashō rhapsodised on the chrysanthemum fragrance of the local mineral springs. It's still an ideal spot for chilling at the **Kiku no Yu** (菊の湯; admission ¥420; ⊙6.45am-10.30pm) bathhouse, and for river walks by the Kokusenkei Gorge, spanned by the elegant **Korogi-bashi** (Cricket Bridge) and the whimsical, modern-art **Ayatori-hashi** (Cat's Cradle Bridge). Yamanaka Onsen is accessible by bus (¥410, 30 minutes) from Kaga Onsen Station.

Kosōyu ONSEN

(古総湯; admission ¥500, Sōyu combined ticket ¥700; ⊙6am-10pm) Close to Kaga Onsen Station, Yamashiro Onsen is a sleepy town centred on a magnificent wooden bathhouse that was recently rebuilt. Kosōyu has beautiful stained-glass windows and a rest area on the top floor; neighbouring Sōyu is a larger, more modern bathhouse.

Sleeping

The friendly folk at the **Yamanaka Onsen Tourism Association** (山中温泉観光協会; ☎0761-78-0330; www.yamanaka-spa.or.jp/english; 5-1 Yamanaka Onsen) and the **Yamashiro Onsen Tourist Association** (山代温泉観光協会; ☎0761-77-1144; www.yamashiro-spa.or.jp/foreign/en; 3-70 Hokubu; ⊙9am-5pm) can help with the difficult task of choosing from the many ryokan in this region: most are expensive, indulgent and delightful.

★**Beniya Mukayū** RYOKAN ¥¥¥

(べにや無何有; ☎0761-77-1340; www.mukayu.com; 55-1-3 Yamashiro Onsen; per person with 2 meals from ¥34,000; P @) The friendly staff at this award-winning ryokan are committed to upholding the Japanese art of hospitality. Gorgeously minimalist, there's a sense of Zen pervading every aspect of the guest experience, from the welcoming private tea ceremony, to the gentle morning yoga classes. Rooms are a beautiful fusion of old and new – most feature private outdoor cypress baths.

Mukayū's cuisine showcases only the best and freshest local seasonal ingredients, exquisitely prepared and presented. Spa treatments leave you gently breathless.

★**The Kayōtei** RYOKAN ¥¥¥

(かよう亭; ☎0761-78-1410; www.kayotei.jp; 1-20 Higashi-machi, Yamanaka Onsen; per person with 2 meals from ¥40,110; P @) This delightful, opulent ryokan along the scenic Kokusenkei Gorge has only 10 rooms, giving it an intimate feel. Some rooms have private outdoor baths, with views over the gorge and a beautiful hidden waterfall.

Kissho Yamanaka RYOKAN ¥¥¥

(吉祥やまなか; ☎0761-78-5656; www.kissho-yamanaka.com/english; 1-14-3 Higashi-machi, Yamanaka Onsen; r per person with 2 meals from ¥19,500) If you can afford the out-of-this-world pricing, go for the 'Miyabi' room with its private outdoor bath, 88 sq m of luxury space and to-die-for views of the valley. Otherwise most of the elegant Western- or Japanese-style rooms have great views and are comfortably appointed.

Getting There & Around

The JR Hokuriku line links Kaga Onsen with Kanazawa (*tokkyū* ¥1510, 25 minutes; *futsū* ¥760, 44 minutes) and Fukui (*tokkyū* ¥1330, 21 minutes; *futsū* ¥580, 33 minutes). **Willer Express** (from outside Japan 050-5805-0383; http://willerexpress.com) operates bus services from Tokyo to Kaga Onsen from ¥5000.

Ride the 'O-sanpo' shuttle bus (two-day pass ¥500) around Yamanaka Onsen, and enquire at the Tourist Association or your accommodation about the irregular tour bus to Daihonzan Eihei-ji (p240).

In Yamashiro Onsen 'Can bus' (two-day pass ¥1200) operates a similar service around the various sights and onsen in the area.

Noto Peninsula 能登半島

Rugged seascapes, rural life, seafood and a light diet of cultural sights make Noto Peninsula (Noto-hantō) a pleasant escape from Hokuriku's urban sprawl. The lacquer-making town of Wajima is the hub of the rugged north, known as Oku-Noto, and the best place to stay overnight. Famous products include *Wajima-nuri* lacquerware, *Suzu*-style pottery, locally harvested sea salt and *iwanori* seaweed.

Self driving from Kanazawa is easily the best way to see the peninsula. The 83km Noto Yūryo (能登有料; Noto Toll Rd) speeds you as far as Anamizu (toll ¥1180). Noto's mostly flat west coast appeals to cyclists, but cycling is not recommended on the Noto-kongō and east coasts because of steep, blind curves.

Getting There & Around

In the centre of Oku-Noto, Noto Satoyama Airport connects the peninsula with Tokyo (Haneda). Hokutetsu runs buses between Kanazawa and Wajima (¥2200, two hours, 10 daily) and, less frequently, Monzen (¥740, 35 minutes).

Most sights can be reached by road only: hiring a car from Kanazawa is recommended. Otherwise, for the west Noto coast, take the JR Nanao line from Kanazawa to Hakui (*tokkyū* ¥1410, 45 minutes; *futsū* ¥760, one hour) and connect to buses. For Oku-Noto, trains continue to Wakura Onsen, connecting to less frequent buses.

Lower Noto Peninsula 能登半島下

0767

The small town of **Hakui** (羽咋) is Noto's western transit hub, with frequent train connections to Kanazawa and less frequent bus connections along Noto's west coast. With about twice the population, the town of **Himi** (氷見) in neighbouring Toyama Prefecture, about 40 minutes' drive east, is also a pleasant starting point from which to tackle the peninsula.

Sights & Activities

★Myōjō-ji BUDDHIST TEMPLE

(妙成寺; 0767-27-1226; Yo-1 Takidani-machi; admission ¥500; 8am-5pm Apr-Oct, 8am-4.30pm Nov-Mar) Founded in 1294 by Nichizō, a disciple of Nichiren, the imposing Myōjō-ji remains an important temple for the sect. The grounds comprise 10 Important Cultural Properties, most notably the strikingly elegant five-storey pagoda. The Togi-bound bus from JR Hakui Station can drop you at Myōjō-ji-guchi bus stop (¥430, 18 minutes); from here, it's less than 10 minutes' walk.

Kita-ke HISTORIC BUILDING

(喜多家; 0767-28-2546; Ra 4-1 Kitakawashiri, Hodatsushimizu; adult/child ¥500/200; 8.30am-5pm Apr-Oct, to 4pm Nov-Mar) During the Edo period the Kita family administered over 200 villages from Kita-ke, the pivotal crossroads of the Kaga, Etchū and Noto fiefs. Inside this splendid, sprawling family home and museum are displays of weapons, ceramics, farming tools, fine and folk art, and documents. The garden has been called the Moss Temple of Noto.

It's about 1km from the Komedashi exit on the Noto Toll Rd. By train, take the JR Nanao line to Menden Station and walk for 20 minutes.

Chirihama Nagisa Driveway SCENIC DRIVE

(千里浜なぎさドライブウエイ) At times this 8km compacted strip of beach sand resembles Florida's Daytona Beach as buses, motorcycles and cars roar past the breakers and revellers barbecue in the sun.

Sleeping

Hotel Grantia Himi HOTEL ¥¥

(ホテルグランティア氷見; 0766-73-1771; 443-5 Kanō; s/d from ¥5500/9500; P) This smart, comfortable business hotel is a good resting point if you're driving to the Noto Peninsula from Toyama or Gokayama. It's in

Noto Peninsula

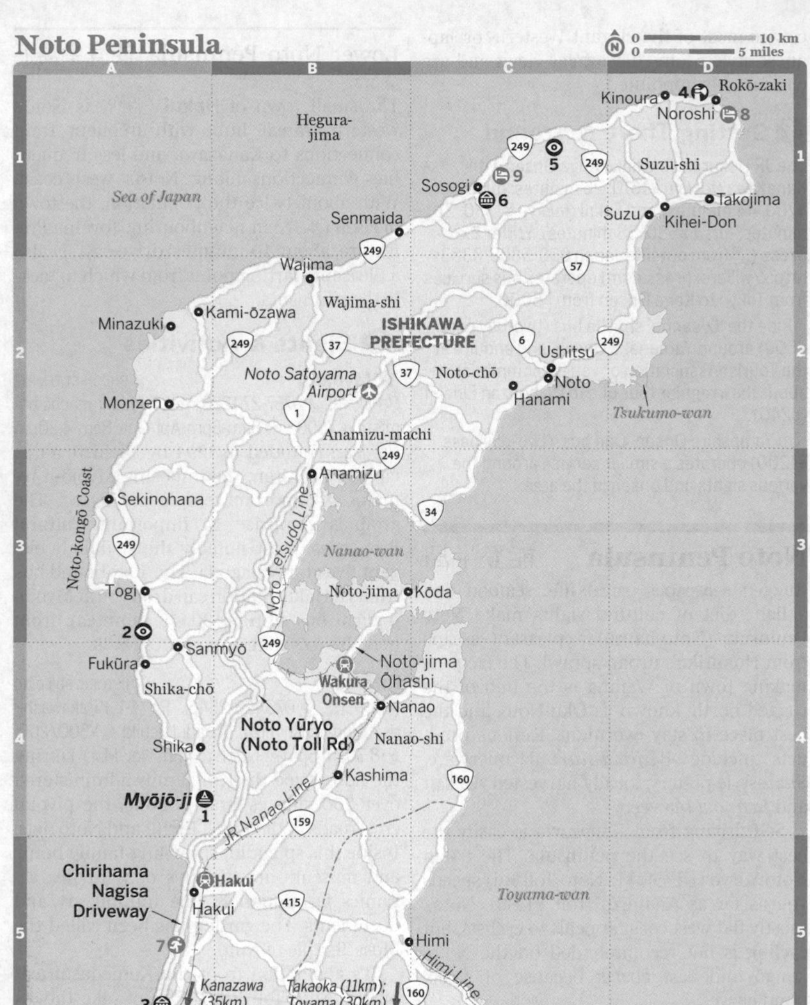

the car park of a shopping mall and there are plenty of shops and amenities nearby to keep you occupied.

Noto-kongō Coast 能登金剛

0768

This rocky, cliff-lined shoreline extends for about 16km between Fukūra and Sekinohana, and is adorned with dramatic rock formations. The manicured little town of **Monzen** is the area's transport hub with buses servicing Kanazawa (¥2250, 2½ hours), Hakui (¥1560, 1½ hours) and Wajima (¥790, 35 minutes).

Sights

Sōji-ji Soin BUDDHIST TEMPLE

(総持寺祖院; 0768-42-0005; 1-18 Monzen; adult/child ¥410/150; 8am-5pm) This beautiful temple in Monzen was established in 1321 as the head of the Sōtō school of Zen, but now functions as a branch temple. Temple buildings were damaged by the 2007 Noto earthquake and remain under fastidious reconstruction. Sōji-ji Soin welcomes visitors to experience one hour of *zazen* (seated meditation; ¥300, 9am to 3pm), serves *shōjin-ryōri* (Buddhist vegetarian cuisine; ¥2500 to ¥3500) and can accommo-

Noto Peninsula

Top Sights

Sights

Activities, Courses & Tours

Sleeping

date visitors (with two meals ¥6500; single women are prohibited). Reserve at least two days in advance.

Ganmon CAVE

(厳門) There's a lot of hype about this interesting though unexciting sea cave carved into the cliff by the force of the waves. Think souvenir shops and restaurants galore.

Wajima 輪島

0768 / POP 31,500

About 20km northeast of Monzen, this fishing port is the largest town in Oku-Noto and is historically famed for *Wajima-nuri* (lacquerware). Although significantly damaged in the 2007 Noto Earthquake (magnitude 6.9), the town centre has been lovingly rebuilt, making it a pleasant place to spend the night and wake to enjoy the lively morning market.

Sights & Activities

Asa-ichi MARKET

(朝市, Morning Market; 8am-noon, closed 10th & 25th of month) This entertaining morning market features a few hundred ageing fishwives hawking fresh-off-the-trawler seafood, lacquerware, pottery and souvenirs, with sass and humour that transcends language. Haggle politely if you dare.

Ishikawa Wajima Urushi Art Museum MUSEUM

(石川輪島漆芸美術館; 0768-22-9788; adult/student ¥600/300; 9am-4.30pm) This modern museum, about a 15-minute walk west of the former train station, has a large, rotating collection of lacquerware. Phone ahead, as it closes between exhibitions.

Kiriko Kaikan MUSEUM

(キリコ会館; 0768-22-7100; adult/child ¥600/350; 8am-5pm) Here you can view a selection of the impressive illuminated lacquered floats used in the Wajima Taisai festival, some up to 15m tall; take the bus to Tsukada bus stop (¥150, six minutes).

Festivals & Events

Gojinjō Daikō Nabune Matsuri MUSIC

This festival culminating on 31 July features wild drumming by performers wearing demon masks and seaweed head gear.

Wajima Taisai PARADE

Wajima's famous, towering, illuminated *kiriko* festival floats parade through the streets to much excitement in late August.

Sleeping & Eating

Wajima has dozens of *minshuku* known for seafood meals worth staying in for. There are nice restaurants by the harbour, though some close by early evening and English is uncommon.

Sodegahama Camping Ground CAMPGROUND ¥

(袖が浜キャンプ場; 0768-23-1146; campsites per person ¥1000) Take the local *noranke* bus (¥100) or Nishiho bus (direction Zōza 雑座) to Sodegahama, or hike for 20 minutes to reach this beachfront campground.

★ **Tanaka** RYOKAN ¥¥

(お宿たなか; 0768-22-5155; www.oyado-tanaka.jp; 22-38 Kawai-machi; r per person with 2 meals from ¥8790; P) This immaculate 10-room inn has beds on tatami, hot-spring baths (including a private-use *rotemburo*, extra charge), dark woodwork, paper lanterns and ambience aplenty. The *kaiseki* meals here feature local seafood and laquerware.

Route Inn Wajima HOTEL ¥¥

(ホテルルートイン輪島; 0768-22-7700; 1-2 Marine Town; s/d ¥6500/10,500; P) With decent-sized rooms and great views from the upper floors, this modern, harbourside tourist hotel has all you need if you're passing through, including free breakfast.

Madara-yakata SEAFOOD ¥

(まだら館; 0768-22-3453; 4-103 Kawai-machi; dishes from ¥800; 11am-7pm) This restaurant near the Asa-ichi serves local specialities including *zōsui* (rice hotpot), *yaki-zakana* (grilled fish) and seasonal seafood, surrounded by folk crafts.

WORTH A TRIP

TAKAOKA

Consider a day trip to the pleasant city of Takaoka (高岡), famed for the production of bronze temple bells and household products and home to a handful of interesting sights and one special temple.

A National Treasure, **Zuiryū-ji** (瑞龍寺; ☎0766-22-0179; www.zuiryuji.jp; 35 Sekihon-machi; adult/child ¥500/200; ⏰9am-4.30pm) is the temple of the second generation of the family of feudal Lord Maeda Toshinaga and is famed for its manicured lawns, steep roofs and all-round aesthetics. If you come just before 9am there's every chance you'll have the place to yourself, with the exception of the temple *deshi* (disciple) raking stones and opening *shōji* before the day's visitors arrive.

Intricate bronze casting is one of Takaoka's foremost traditional crafts. The **Risaburō Foundry** (鋳物工房利三郎; ☎0766-24-0852; 8-11 Kanaya-machi; admission free, casting ¥3000; ⏰10am-5pm) FREE has been producing traditional Takaoka bronzeware since the Meiji era and allows visitors a rare and fascinating glimpse into the casting process, as well as the opportunity to participate in the process themselves.

It was from the strength of this industry that construction of the **Takaoka Great Buddha** (高岡大仏; ☎0766-23-9156; 11-29 Ōte-machi; ⏰6am-6pm) FREE statue began in 1907. The statue was completed in 1933 but moved to its present location in 1981 after the ground supporting it began to give way from the weight of the bronze. It's now a symbol of the city and sometimes referred to as one of the three Great Buddhas of Japan.

Takaoka is served by local trains from Himi, at the base of the Noto Peninsula (¥320, 35 minutes) and Toyama (¥320, 20 minutes). The new Shin-Takaoka Station opened in March 2015, approximately 1km from the former Takaoka station, bringing the Hokuriku Shinkansen into town. For details on the new service, refer to www.hyperdia.com.

Once here it's easy to get around on bikes, which can be rented from April through November from the **Takaoka Station Tourist Information Center** (高岡駅観光案内所; ☎0766-20-1547; www.takaoka.or.jp/en; bike rental per day ¥200; ⏰9am-5pm).

Umi-tei Notokichi SEAFOOD ¥¥
(海亭のと吉; ☎0768-22-6636; 4-153 Kawai-machi; dishes ¥600-2500; ⏰11am-2pm & 5-8pm Thu-Tue) A popular local haunt for generations, you'll be hard pressed to better experience seafood elsewhere in Japan. Purists should keep it simple and go for the *sashimi moriawase* (sashimi of the day, ¥1500). It also does a mean version of *katsudon* (crumbed pork cutlet on rice, ¥1000).

Information

Tourist Information Center (輪島観光協会; ☎0768-22-1503; ⏰8am-7pm) Limited English is spoken by the friendly staff of this office at the former Wajima train station, now the bus station. They do have English-language maps and can help with accommodation bookings.

Suzu & Noto-chō 珠洲・能登町

☎0768

Travelling from Wajima towards the tip of the peninsula you'll pass the famous slivered *dandan-batake* (rice terraces) at **Senmaida** (千枚田) before arriving in the coastal village of **Sosogi** (曽々木). From Wajima, Ushitsu-bound buses stop in Sosogi (¥740, 40 minutes).

Close by you'll find the **mado-iwa** (窓岩; window rock) rock formation just offshore, and a number of hiking trails. In winter look for *nami-no-hana* (flowers of the waves), masses of foam that form when waves gnash Sosogi's rocky shore.

The road northeast from Sosogi village passes **sea-salt farms** (珠洲製塩) onward to the tiny village of Suzu and remote cape Rokkō, the peninsula's furthest point. Nearby, you can amble up to the **lighthouse** in the village of **Noroshi** (狼煙) and then head west along the cape. The road circles around the tip of the peninsula, heading south past less dramatic scenery, back to civilisation.

Sights

Senmaida Rice Terraces LANDMARK
(白米千枚田段々畑) Once a common sight in Japan, this ancient method of farming is disappearing – these 'thousand' terraced rice paddies snaking up the hillside are both fascinating and beautiful in all seasons.

Tokikuni Residences HISTORIC BUILDINGS

One of the few survivors of the Taira clan, Taira Tokitada was exiled to this region in 1185. His ancestors eventually divided and established separate family residences here, both now Important Cultural Properties. The first, **Tokikuni-ke** (時国家; ☎0768-32-0171; 13-4 Machino-machi, Minamitoki-kuni; adult/child ¥600/300; ⏲8.30am-5pm), was built in 1590 in the style of the Kamakura period and has a *meishō tei-en* (famous garden). A few minutes' walk away, **Kami-tokikuni-ke** (上時国家; ☎0768-32-0171; 13-4 Machino-machi, Minamitoki-kuni; adult/child ¥500/400; ⏲8.30am-5pm) has an impressive thatched roof and elegant interior. It was completed in the early 19th century.

Sleeping & Eating

Yokoiwaya MINSHUKU ¥¥

(横岩屋; ☎0768-32-0603; Ku-2 Machino-machi, Sosogi; r per person incl 2 meals from ¥8350; Ⓟ) Waterfront *minshuku* Yokoiwaya in Sosogi has welcomed guests for over 150 years (and it shows). It's known for seafood dinners. Look for the paper lantern, or request pick-up from Sosogi-guchi bus stop (曽々木口バス停).

★ **Lamp no Yado** RYOKAN ¥¥¥

(ランプの宿; ☎0768-86-8000; www.lampnoyado.co.jp; 10-11 Jike; r per person incl 2 meals from ¥18,000; Ⓟ) Remote Lamp no Yado is a place of its own: a 13-room wooden waterside village beneath a cliff. The building goes back four centuries, to when people would escape to its curative waters for weeks at a time. It's been an inn since the 1970s. Decadent rooms have private bathrooms, and some have their own *rotemburo*. The pool is almost superfluous. This is a romantic destination ryokan, but not for those on a budget or with a fear of tsunami.

TOYAMA PREFECTURE

Toyama Prefecture (富山県) is big in pharmaceuticals, zipper manufacturing and mountains. Visitors come for the latter, the Tateyama range to Toyama city's east and south.

Toyama 富山

☎076 / POP 421,950

The most likely reason you'll find yourself in Toyama is to journey on the Tateyama-Kurobe Alpine Route (p260) or the new Hokuriku Shinkansen, which commenced services in March 2015. Be sure to sample the plethora of seafood restaurants outside the station's south exit, which is also where the hotels are. Sights can be reached by tram, bus or rental bicycles.

In October 2014 Toyama's picturesque mountain-ringed bay was inducted into the Unesco-endorsed Most Beautiful Bays in the World Club, making it the second bay in Japan to be awarded this prestigious title, recognising both the natural beauty of the bay and its unique ecosystem. Toyama Bay's nutrient-dense waters are fed from nearby mountains and sustain a wide variety of marine life including the uncommon *hotaruika* (firefly squid) and *shiroebi* (white shrimp).

Sights

Kansui Park PARK

(環水公園; ☎076-444-6041; Minatoirifune-chō) This immaculately maintained park built on reclaimed land around Toyama's canal and lock system is a wonderful place for a stroll or a picnic. It's a popular spot with locals in the warmer months and has plenty of attractions such as birdwatching enclaves and lover's towers to keep you occupied.

Chōkei-ji BUDDHIST TEMPLE

(長慶寺; ⏲24hr) This hilltop temple has a wonderful outlook, but you'll come to see the 500-plus stone statues of *rakan* (Buddha's disciples) lined up in the forest.

Toyama Municipal Folkcraft Village MUSEUM

(富山市民俗民芸村; 1118-1 Anyōbō; adult/child ¥500/250; ⏲9am-5pm) Here you'll find folk art, ceramics, *sumi-e* (ink brush paintings) and more in a cluster of hillside buildings. Toyama's free Museum Bus (10 minutes, hourly from 10.30am to 4.30pm) can get you here, from in front of the Toyama Excel Hotel Tōkyū.

Iwase

North of the city centre is the bayside Iwase neighbourhood, the well-preserved main street of the former shipping business district. Now it's filled with shops and private homes, and even the banks look interesting. Take the Portram light-rail line from Toyama Station's north exit to the terminus, Iwase-hama (¥200, 25 minutes), make a sharp left to cross the canal via Iwase-bashi (岩瀬橋) and you'll see signs in English.

OFF THE BEATEN TRACK

HAKUSAN NATIONAL PARK 白山国立公園

Geared for serious hikers and naturalists, this stunning national park straddles four prefectures: Ishikawa, Fukui, Toyama and Gifu. Within are several peaks above 2500m, the tallest being Hakusan (2702m), a sacred mountain that has been worshipped since ancient times. In summer folks hike and scramble uphill for mountain sunrises. In winter skiing and onsen bathing take over. The alpine section of the park is criss-crossed with trails, offering treks of up to 25km. For well-equipped hikers, there's a 26km trek to Ogi-machi in the Shōkawa Valley.

Those looking to hike on and around the peaks are required to stay overnight in giant dorms at either **Tateyama Murodō Sansō** (館山室堂山荘; ☎076-463-1228; www.murodou.co.jp; dm with 2 meals ¥7700; ⊙May-Nov) or **Nanryū Sansō** (南竜; ☎076-259-2022; http://city-hakusan.com/hakusan/naryusanso; dm with 2 meals ¥7900, camp sites ¥300, 5-person cabins ¥12,400; ⊙1 Jul-15 Oct). Getting to either requires a hike of 3½ to five hours. When the lodges are full, each person gets about one tatami mat's worth of sleeping space. Camping is prohibited in the park except at Nanryū Sansō camping ground: advance reservations are strongly advised.

The closest access point is Bettōdeai. From here it's 6km to Murodō (about 4½ hours' walk) and 5km to Nanryū (3½ hours). The villages of **Ichirino**, **Chūgū Onsen**, **Shiramine** and **Ichinose** have *minshuku*, ryokan and camping. Rates per person start from around ¥300 for camp sites, or around ¥7800 for rooms in inns with two meals.

Visiting requires commitment. The main mode of transport is the **Hokutetsu Kankō** (☎076-237-5115) bus from Kanazawa Station to Bettōdeai (¥2100, two hours). From late June to mid-October, up to three buses operate daily. Return fares (¥10,800) include a coupon for a stay at Murodō Centre. If you're driving from the Shōkawa Valley, you can take the spectacular Hakusan Super-Rindō toll road (cars ¥3240).

Rather than back track, you can return via Higashi-Iwase Station on the Portram.

Sleeping & Eating

Comfort Hotel Toyama Eki-mae HOTEL ¥¥
(コンフォートホテル富山駅前; ☎076-433-6811; www.choice-hotels.jp; 1-3-2 Takara-machi; s/d with breakfast from ¥5800/8500; @ 📶) Across the street and to the right as you exit the train station, this business hotel has pleasant, well-maintained modern rooms and professional staff.

Toyama Excel Hotel Tōkyū HOTEL ¥¥¥
(富山エクセルホテル東急; ☎076-441-0109; www.tokyuhotelsjapan.com/en; 1-2-3 Shintomi-chō; s/d from ¥10,900/18,400; P @) Toyama's fanciest digs has 210 rooms in a variety of configurations and two restaurants. Rooms on higher floors have fantastic views.

Shiroebi-tei SEAFOOD ¥
(白えび亭; ☎076-432-7575; mains ¥730-2200; ⊙10am-8pm; 📋) Locals swear by this workman-like institution on the 3rd floor of Toyama Station. The staple is *shiroebi tendon* (white shrimp tempura over rice, ¥730). There's a picture menu.

Drinking & Nightlife

Pot Still PUB
(☎076-433-3347; www.pot-still.net/english; 2-3-27 Sakura-chō; ⊙7pm-late) This Irish pub has a weird name and an even weirder sign, but more importantly it has Guinness on tap, killer fish and chips (¥900), pool, darts and a foreigner-friendly environment.

Information

Tourist Information Center (観光案内所; ☎076-432-9751; http://foreign.info-toyama.com/en; ⊙8.30am-8pm) Inside Toyama Station this office stocks maps and pamphlets on Toyama and the Tateyama-Kurobe Alpine Route. Some English is spoken and bicycles can be rented for free.

Getting There & Away

Daily flights operate between Toyama and major Japanese cities, with less frequent flights to Seoul and Shanghai.

The JR Takayama line runs south to Takayama (*tokkyū* ¥2770, 90 minutes) and Nagoya (*tokkyū* ¥6930, four hours). JR's Hokuriku line runs west to Kanazawa (*tokkyū* ¥2100, 39 minutes; *futsū* ¥950, one hour) and Osaka (*tokkyū* ¥7980, 3¼ hours), and northeast to Niigata (¥6620, three hours).

The Hokuriku Shinkansen commenced services in March 2015 creating a high-speed link from Toyama to Kanazawa, Nagano and onwards to Tokyo. For fares and timetable information, see www.hyperdia.com.

Buses are available between Toyama, Takaoka and Gokayama; see http://foreign.info-toyama.com/en for details.

MATSUMOTO & AROUND

Boasting some of Japan's most dramatic scenery, the Northern Japan Alps (北日本アルプス) of Gifu, Toyama and Nagano Prefectures, accessed from Matsumoto, contain stunning peaks above 3000m, accessible even to amateur hikers. Also called the Hida Ranges, the most spectacular scenery is protected within the 174,323 hectare Chūbu-Sangaku National Park (中部山岳国立公園). Highlights include hiking the valleys and peaks of Kamikōchi, doing it easy on the Shin-Hotaka Ropeway and soaking up the splendour of Hida's many mountain *rotemburo*. The northern part of the park extends to the Tateyama-Kurobe Alpine Route (p260).

Meanwhile, ever-lovable Matsumoto makes the most of its wonderful geography, vibrant city centre and photogenic original castle.

Information

Numerous English-language maps and pamphlets are published by the Japan National Tourism Organization (JNTO) and local authorities. Most detailed hiking maps are in Japanese.

There are few banks in the area, though there is an ATM at Hirayu Onsen's post office, which keeps shorter hours than most. Be sure you have enough cash before setting out.

Getting There & Around

Matsumoto (Nagano Prefecture) and Takayama (Gifu Prefecture) are the gateway cities into the peaks, while the main transit hubs when you're up there are Hirayu Onsen and Kamikōchi. Buses make the journey from Takayama. From Matsumoto it's a bus, or a ride on the private Matsumoto Dentetsu train to Shin-Shimashima (don't you just love that name!) and then a bus. Either way, the journey is breathtaking.

Hiring a car is a good option if windy roads don't bother you and you're not overnighting in Kamikōchi – the road between Naka-no-yu and Kamikōchi is open only to buses and taxis. Otherwise, buses serve the mountainous villages; a variety of passes are available.

Matsumoto 松本

0263 / POP 243,000

Embraced by seven great peaks to the west (including Yariga-take, Hotaka-dake and Norikura-dake, each above 3000m) and three smaller sentinels to the east (including beautiful Utsukushi-ga-hara-kōgen), Matsumoto occupies a protected position in a fertile valley no more than 20km across at its widest. Views of the regal Alps are never far away and sunsets are breathtaking.

Formerly known as Fukashi, Nagano Prefecture's second-largest city has been here since the 8th century. In the 14th and 15th centuries it was the castle town of the Ogasawara clan and continued to prosper through the Edo period to the present.

Today, Matsumoto is one of Japan's finest cities – an attractive, cosmopolitan place loved by its residents. Admirers from around the world come to enjoy its superb castle, pretty streets, galleries, cafes and endearing vistas. With plenty of well-priced, quality accommodation and excellent access to, from and around the town, Matsumoto is the perfect base for exploring the Japan Alps and the Kiso and Azumino Valleys.

Sights & Activities

★Matsumoto-jō CASTLE

(松本城; 0263-32-9202; 4-1 Marunōchi; adult/child ¥610/310; 8.30am-5pm early Sep–mid-Jul, to 6pm mid-Jul–Aug) Must-see Matsumoto-jō is Japan's oldest wooden castle and one of four castles designated National Treasures – the others are Hikone, Himeji and Inuyama. The striking black and white three-turreted *donjon* was completed around 1595, earning the nickname Karasu-jō (Crow Castle). You can climb steep steps all the way to the top, with impressive views and historical displays on each level. Don't miss the recently restored *tsukimi yagura* (moon-viewing pavilion). The **Goodwill Guide Group** (0263-32-7140) offers free one-hour tours by reservation.

Admission includes entry to the Matsumoto City Museum.

Former Kaichi School MUSEUM

(旧開智学校, Kyū Kaichi Gakkō; 0263-32-5275; 2-4-12 Kaichi; admission ¥300; 8.30am-4.30pm daily Mar-Nov, Tue-Sun Dec-Feb) A few blocks north of the castle, the former Kaichi School is both an Important Cultural Property and the oldest elementary school in Japan, founded in 1873. It opened its doors as an education museum in 1965. The building itself is an excellent example of Meiji-era architecture.

Matsumoto City Museum of Art MUSEUM
(松本市美術館, Matsumoto-shi Bijutsukan; ☎0263-39-7400; 4-2-22 Chūō; adult/child ¥410/200; ⏲9am-5pm Tue-Sun) This sleek museum has a good collection of Japanese artists, many of whom hail from Matsumoto or whose works depict scenes of the surrounding countryside. Highlights include the striking avant-garde works of local-born, internationally renowned Kusama Yayoi.

Nakamachi

The charming former merchant district of Nakamachi (中町) by the Metoba-gawa, with its *namako-kabe kura* (lattice-walled storehouses) and Edo-period streetscapes, makes for a wonderful stroll. Many buildings have been preserved and transformed into cafes, galleries and craft shops specialising in wood, glass, fabric, ceramics and antiques.

Nawate-dōri STREET
(縄手道り) Nawate-dōri, a few blocks from the castle, is a popular place for a stroll. Vendors along this riverside walk sell antiques, souvenirs and delicious *taiyaki* (filled waffle in the shape of a carp) of varying flavours. Look for the big frog statue by the bridge.

Matsumoto Timepiece Museum MUSEUM
(松本市時計博物館, Matsumoto-shi Tokei Hakubutsukan; ☎0263-36-0969; 4-21-15 Chūō; adult/student ¥300/150; ⏲9am-5pm Tue-Sun) Home to Japan's largest pendulum clock (on the building's exterior) and over 300 other timepieces, including fascinating medieval Japanese creations, this museum shows Japan's love of *monozukuri,* the art of creating things.

Further Afield

Northeast of downtown, **Utsukushi-ga-hara Onsen** (Map p274; 美ヶ原温泉; not to be confused with Utsukushi-ga-hara-kōgen) is a pretty spa village, with a quaint main street and views across the valley. **Asama Onsen** (Map p274; 浅間温泉) has a history that's said to date back to the 10th century and include writers and poets, though it looks quite generic now. Both areas are easily reached by bus from Matsumoto's bus terminal.

Matsumoto

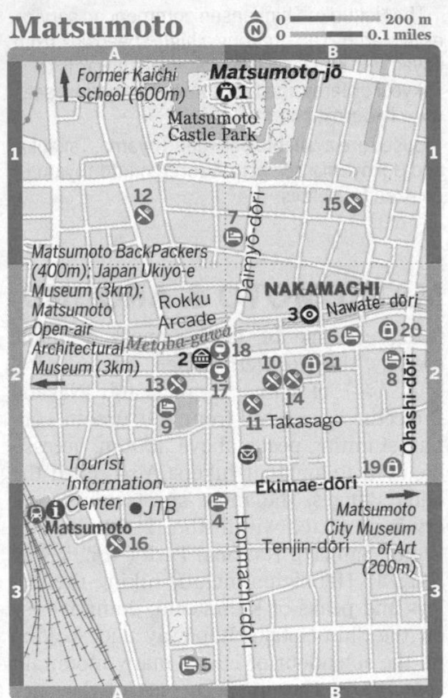

To the east of Matsumoto, the stunning alpine plateau of **Utsukushi-ga-hara-kōgen** (美ヶ原高原; 2000m) boasts over 200 varieties of flora that come alive in the summer. It's a great day trip from Matsumoto, reached via an ooh-and-ahh drive along twisty mountain roads called Azalea Line and Venus Line (open late April to early November). A car will give you the freedom to explore the beauty, but there's also a bus in season (¥1500 one way, 1½ hours).

Utsukushi-ga-hara Open Air Museum MUSEUM
(Map p274; 美ヶ原美術館, Utsukushi-ga-hara Bijutsukan; ☎0263-86-2331; http://utsukushi-oam.jp; adult/child/student ¥1000/700/800; ⏲9am-5pm late Apr-early Nov) Atop Utsukushi-ga-hara-kōgen plateau you'll find this seemingly random sculpture garden with some 350 pieces, mostly by Japanese sculptors. The surrounding countryside provides an inspiring backdrop. Nearby are pleasant walks and the opportunity to see cows in pasture (a constant source of fascination in Japan). Buses (¥1500, 1½ hours) run several times daily during the warmer months, although a rental car is a good option if windy roads don't faze you.

Matsumoto

Top Sights
1 Matsumoto-jō B1

Sights
2 Matsumoto Timepiece Museum A2
3 Nawate-dōri B2

Sleeping
4 Dormy Inn Matsumoto A3
5 Hotel Buena Vista A3
6 Marumo B2
7 Marunouchi Hotel B1
8 Nunoya B2
9 Richmond Hotel A2

Eating
10 Delhi B2
11 HU LA LA B2
12 Kane A1
13 Menshō Sakura A2
14 Nomugi B2
15 Shizuka B1
16 Tōfu Ryōri Marui A3

Drinking & Nightlife
17 Coat A2
18 Old Rock A2
Sorpresa .... (see 5)

Shopping
19 Belle Amie B2
20 Chikiri-ya B2
21 Nakamachi Kura-chic-kan B2

Transport
Matsumoto Bus Terminal .... (see 16)

Japan Ukiyo-e Museum MUSEUM
(日本浮世絵美術館; www.japan-ukiyoe-museum.com; 2206-1 Koshiba; adult/child ¥1200/600; ⏲10am-5pm Tue-Sun) Housing more than 100,000 wood-block prints, paintings, screens and old books, this renowned museum exhibits but a fraction of its collection. The museum is approximately 3km from JR Matsumoto Station, 15 minutes' walk from Ōniwa Station on the Matsumoto Dentetsu line (¥180, six minutes), or about ¥2000 by taxi.

Matsumoto Open-Air Architectural Museum MUSEUM
(松本市歴史の里, Matsumoto-shi Rekishi-no-sato; ☎0263-47-4515; 2196-1 Shimadachi; adult/child ¥400/300; ⏲9am-4.30pm Tue-Sun) Adjacent to the better known Japan Ukiyo-e Museum (p259), amid fields and rice paddies beneath the gaze of the Alps, stand these five examples of striking late Edo- and early Showa-era architecture for you to explore.

Festivals & Events

Locals love to celebrate – you're never far from a festival here.

Matsumoto-jō Sakura Matsuri CULTURAL
Three days after the cherry blossoms are declared in full bloom (early April), the castle and its *sakura* trees are illuminated spectacularly and entry to the inner compound is free.

Matsumoto-jō Taiko Matsuri MUSIC
The castle grounds and beyond ring out with the sound and energy of Taiko drumming during this awesome festival, held the balmy last weekend of July.

Matsumoto Bonbon PARADE
Matsumoto's biggest event takes place on the first Saturday in August, when over 25,000 people of all ages perform the 'bonbon' dance through the streets, well into the hot summer's night. Be prepared to be drawn into the action.

Takigi Nō Matsuri THEATRE
This atmospheric festival during August features *nō* performances by torchlight, outdoors on a stage in the park below the castle.

Saitō Kinen Matsuri MUSIC
About a dozen classical music concerts are held in memory of revered Japanese conductor and music educator Saitō Hideo (1902–72) from mid-August to mid-September. Ozawa Seiji, conductor emeritus of the Boston Symphony Orchestra, is the festival director.

Asama Onsen Taimatsu Matsuri PARADE
Around the start of October, Asama Onsen celebrates the spectacular and slightly manic fire festival, wherein groups of men, women and children, shouting 'wa-sshoi!', like a mantra, parade burning bales of hay through narrow streets to an enormous bonfire at Misha-jinja.

DON'T MISS

TATEYAMA-KUROBE ALPINE ROUTE

From mid-April to mid-November, the popular seasonal 90km Tateyama-Kurobe Alpine Route (立山黒部アルペンルート) connects Tateyama (Toyama Prefecture) with Shinano-ōmachi (Nagano Prefecture) via a sacred mountain, a deep gorge, a boiling-hot spring and glory-hallelujah mountain scenery. It's divided into nine sections, with different modes of transport including your own two feet. Reservations are *strongly* advised.

Travel is possible in either direction; as the route is often only travelled one way, we'd suggest using the route to travel between Kanazawa/Toyama and Matsumoto. Full details can be found online at www.alpen-route.com/english. There are hundreds of steps en route and plenty of walking. Be sure to forward your baggage to your destination hotel before you set off (details on the website).

The fare for the entire route is ¥10,850 one way or ¥18,260 return; tickets for individual sections are available. It takes at least six hours, one way. If you're starting in Toyama and are not heading to Matsumoto, you may find a return trip to Murodō (¥6710), the route's highest point (2450m), sufficient.

Start the journey before 9am at Dentetsu Toyama station on the chug-a-lug regional Toyama Chiho line bound for **Tateyama** (¥1200, one hour). The first stage of the route is the cable car up to **Bijodaira** (美女平; seven minutes).

Next is a bus journey up to **Murodō** (室堂; 50 minutes) via the spectacular alpine plateau of **Midagahara Kōgen**, where you can break the trip and do the 15-minute walk to see **Tateyama caldera** (立山カルデラ), the largest nonactive crater in Japan. The upper part of the plateau is often covered with deep snow well into spring; snowploughs keep the road clear by pushing vast walls of snow to each side of the road, forming a virtual tunnel of ice.

Ten minutes' walk from Murodō is **Mikuri-ga-ike** (みくりが池) pond, where you'll find Japan's highest *onsen ryokan* (www.mikuri.com/english). Twenty minutes further on is **Jigokudani Onsen** (Hell Valley Hot Springs) – no bathing here, the waters are boiling! To the east, you can make the steep two-hour hike to the peak of **O-yama** (雄山; 3003m) for an astounding panorama. Experienced and equipped long-distance hikers can continue south to Kamikōchi.

When you're ready, board the trolley bus that tunnels through Mt Tateyama for 3.7km to **Daikanbō** (10 minutes). From here, the Tateyama Ropeway whisks you 488m down to **Kurobe-daira** (seven minutes) with breathtaking views of the valley below. You're free to stop between sections at your own pace, or go with the flow of the crowds. The next step is the underground Kurobe cable car to **Kurobeko** (¥840, five minutes). You'll emerge to see the massive **Kurobe Dam**: it's a 15-minute walk across it to the impressive observation deck.

When you're ready to proceed, trolley buses (16 minutes) will whisk you through a 5.8km tunnel to the end of your journey at **Ogizawa**. From here there's one last bus to **Shinano-ōmachi Station** (40 minutes, elevation 712m) – you made it!

Continue on to Azumino, Matsumoto or beyond at your leisure.

Sleeping

Matsumoto is compact enough that you can stay anywhere downtown and get around easily. Most business hotels are by the train station, but there are some great traditional options in picturesque Nakamachi.

Matsumoto Backpackers HOSTEL ¥
(☎0263-31-5848; http://matsumotobp.com/en; Shiraita 1-1-6; dm per person ¥3000; 📶) By the river, just a few minutes' walk from JR Matsumoto Station, you'll find this clean, friendly addition to the Matsumoto traveller's scene. These are the cheapest, most central dorm beds in town.

★**Marunouchi Hotel** HOTEL ¥¥
(丸の内ホテル; ☎0263-35-4500; http://matsumoto-marunouchi.com/eng; 3-5-15 Ōte; s/d from ¥6600/9000; 📶) It's hard to fault this new hotel, occupying a prime spot near the castle. Right-priced rooms are refreshingly stylish and comfortable; deluxe rooms approach Western standard sizes at 27 sq m. Standard rooms are more compact, but cheaper. Suites are a nice option for those

wanting something special. Some rooms even have views of the castle.

★ Nunoya INN ¥¥
(ぬのや旅館; 0263-32-0545; www.mcci.or.jp/www/nunoya/en; 3-5-7 Chūō; r per person from ¥4500) Few inns have more heart than this simple, traditional charmer, meticulously kept by its friendly owner. The spotless inn has shiny dark-wood floors and atmospheric tatami rooms. No meals are served, but you're right in the heart of the best part of town. If you don't mind sharing a bathroom, the rate is a bargain for this much character.

Seifūsō RYOKAN ¥¥
(静風荘; 0263-46-0639; www.ryokanseifuso.jp/english; 634-5 Minami-asama; s/d from ¥3990/8280; P @) Free pick-up (arrange in advance) and free bicycles make up for the fact that this inn is closer to Asama Onsen than Matsumoto. It's run by a friendly family who love to welcome overseas guests. The Japanese-style rooms are clean and bright, have a nice outlook and shared baths. Once you're there, take bus 2 to get back into town.

Dormy Inn Matsumoto HOTEL ¥¥
(ドーミーイン松本; 0263-33-5489; www.hotespa.net/hotels/matsumoto; 2-2-1 Fukashi; s/d from ¥5790/8390; P @) This newer property has compact, well-designed rooms with pleasant, neutral decor. There's an onsen featuring a sunny *rotemburo* and the breakfast buffet is decent. Otherwise, there's everything travellers need, including a good location and a functional laundry. Deals can be found online (in Japanese).

Marumo RYOKAN ¥¥
(まるも; 0263-32-0115; www.avis.ne.jp/~marumo/index.html; 3-3-10 Chūō; r per person ¥5250;) Between Nakamachi and the river, this creaky wooden ryokan dates from 1868 and has lots of traditional charm, including a bamboo garden and coffee shop. Although the rooms aren't huge and don't have private facilities, it's quite popular, so book ahead.

Richmond Hotel HOTEL ¥¥
(リッチモンドホテル松本; 0263-37-5000; www.richmondhotel.jp/en/matsumoto; 1-10-7 Chūō; s/d from ¥6500/9500; @) A few minutes' walk from JR Matsumoto Station, this 204-room business hotel is in great shape and in a great location. The deluxe double rooms are large by Japanese standards, and reasonably priced. There's a Gusto family restaurant (with picture menu) downstairs.

Hotel Buena Vista HOTEL ¥¥¥
(ホテルブエナビスタ; 0263-37-0111; www.buena-vista.co.jp/english; 1-2-1 Honjō; s/tw from ¥9460/18,740; @) An oldie but a goodie – Matsumoto's sharpest Western hotel recently received a makeover in its public spaces and rooms, leaving it looking quite the part. The executive rooms and the suites are the way to go, if you're going to do it. Many rooms have exceptional views.

Sugimoto RYOKAN ¥¥¥
(旅館すぎもと; 0263-32-3379; http://ryokan-sugimoto.com; 451-7 Satoyamabe; r per person from ¥15,000; ; Utsukushi-ga-hara Onsen line, Town Sneaker North Course) A lack of English-speaking staff at this upscale ryokan in Utsukushi-ga-hara Onsen may be its only downfall for non-Japanese speakers. With some fascinating elements, such as the art collection, underground passageway and bar full of single malts, this is a unique property. Rooms range in size and decor, but all are ineffably stylish and the cuisine is, appropriately, top-notch.

Eating

For a quick coffee and cake, cafes line the banks of the Metoba-gawa and Nawate-dōri.

Delhi CURRY ¥
(デリー; 0263-35-2408; 2-4-13 Chūō; curries with rice ¥650-850; 11.30am-6pm Thu-Tue;) One of our favourites, this little 'ma and pa' outfit has been serving delicious curry rice (Japanese style) in an adorable former storehouse by the river since 1970. If you like *tonkatsu*, you must try the *katsu karē* (¥850). Cheap and cheerful.

Kane TAIWANESE ¥
(香根; 0263-36-1303; 2-8-5 Ōte; dishes ¥700-900; 5.30pm-2am;) This simple Taiwanese eatery near the castle serves amazing spicy soups, noodles and vegies, as well as the standard array of Chinese fare at very reasonable prices. There's a picture menu.

Menshō Sakura RĀMEN ¥
(麺匠佐蔵; 0263-34-1050; 1-20-26 Chūō; rāmen from ¥750; 11.30am-3pm & 5.30-10pm) Miso fans and rāmen fans should not go past this purveyor of fine noodles. *Miso rāmen* and black *Kuro-miso rāmen* are the specialities of the house: both rank highly. The *gyōza* are crunchy and the beer is cold. Ask the friendly staff for help with the vending machine if you get stuck.

KUROBE GORGE RAILWAY 'TOROKKO DENSHA'

For those wanting to do something a little different, consider this unique (if not a little bumpy) exploration into the heart of the Kurobe Valley in tiny train carriages originally used for the construction of the Kurobe Dam system. Running from Unazuki to Keyaki-daira, when the **Kurobe Gorge Railway** (黒部峡谷トロッコ電車; 0765-62-1011; www.kurotetu.co.jp/en; 11 Kurobe Kyokokuguchi, Kurobe; one way to Keyaki-daira ¥1710; 9am-5pm) is not careening through seemingly endless tunnels, the views of the surrounding forested mountains are breathtaking, especially in autumn, and the opportunity to explore some truly remote and astounding mountain *rotemburo* and inns is definitely rewarding.

The new Kurobe-Unazukionsen Station on the Hokuriku Shinkansen line has dramatically improved access and will no doubt increase visitor numbers. For detailed information on services transporting passengers between Kurobe-Unazukionsen Station and the Unazuki terminus of the Kurobe Gorge Railway, see the Kurobe Gorge Railway website.

Once you arrive at the railway you must purchase tickets for each leg of the journey separately. Due to high passenger demand, this is not a hop-on/hop-off service. The entire journey from Unazuki to Keyaki-daira takes about 80 minutes. It's suggested you take the full journey then decide which stops you'd like to get off at along the way. You'll need to purchase tickets to your next destination from each station.

The remote **Kuronagi-onsen** is a must-see: look out for bears along the path. Also recommended is the **Iwa-buro** cave bath, a short walk from Kanetsuri Station. The restaurant at Keyaki-daira can get very busy at times – bring sandwiches and snacks with you for the journey, as well as some warm clothing: even in summer it can get very chilly in the tunnels.

Be sure to sit on the right side of the train for the outbound journey from Unazuki, and the left side of the train coming back (from Keyaki-daira), or you'll miss the best photo ops and develop resentment towards your neighbouring passengers. Carriages are allocated, but seats aren't reserved and it's first-come, first-served.

HU LA LA HAWAIIAN ¥

(フ・ラ・ラ; 0263-50-7677; 2-5-13 Chūō; burgers from ¥690; 11.30am-10pm) This Hawaiian-themed restaurant flips the best burgers in Matsumoto, hands down. There's a bunch of other fun and tasty stuff on the menu as well; it's great for little kids and big kids alike or when you're drowning in a sea of *soba* and need the taste of home.

Tōfu Ryōri Marui TOFU ¥

(とうふ料理まるゐ; 0263-46-0635; 1-2-30 Fukashi, ESPA 7F; set menus from ¥880; 10am-9pm) On the 7th floor of the ESPA building opposite JR Matsumoto Station, you'll find this outpost of an Asama Onsen family business that has been making tofu for over 80 years. Lovers of the food's versatility will appreciate this delicious cuisine but don't make the assumption that all dishes are vegetarian. Look for the orange and white *noren* curtain. Try the *Agedashi teishoku* (fried silken tofu set menu, ¥940).

Nomugi NOODLES ¥¥

(野麦; 0263-36-3753; 2-9-11 Chūō; soba ¥1100; 11.30am-5pm Thu-Mon;) In Nakamachi, this is one of central Japan's finest *soba* shops. Its owner used to run a French restaurant in Tokyo before returning to his home town. Keeping things Zen, there are two dishes: *zaru-soba* and *kake-soba*. Oh, and beer.

Shizuka IZAKAYA ¥¥

(しづか; 0263-32-0547; 4-10-8 Ōte; plates from ¥480; noon-11pm Mon-Sat;) This wonderfully traditional *izakaya* serves favourites such as *oden* and *yakitori* as well as some more challenging specialities...

Drinking & Nightlife

Old Rock PUB

(オールドロック; 0263-38-0069; 2-30-20 Chūō; mains from ¥750; 11.30am-2.30pm & 6pm-midnight) In the perfect spot a block south of the river, across from Nakamachi, you'll find this popular pub with good lunch specials and, appropriately, a wide range of beers.

Coat BAR
(メインバーコート; ☎0263-34-7133; 2-3-24 Chūō; ⏲6pm-12.30am Mon-Sat) This sophisticated little whisky bar is run by a colourful character who'd love to pour you a single malt or one of his original cocktails.

Sorpresa BAR
(ソルプレーサ; ☎0263-37-0510; Hotel Buena Vista 14F, 1-2-1 Honjō; ⏲5.30pm-midnight) Come for the unbeatable views from this swanky top-floor bar at the Buena Vista Hotel. It's also a high-end French restaurant, if you fancy, but it's possible to come just to imbibe.

Shopping

Matsumoto is synonymous with *temari* (embroidered balls) and doll-making. Takasago street, one block south of Nakamachi, has several doll shops. **Parco Department Store** is unmissable in the city centre.

Belle Amie HANDICRAFTS
(ベラミ; ☎0263-33-1314; 3-7-23 Chūō; ⏲10am-6pm) *Temari* and dolls are found here. Doll styles include *tanabata* and *oshie-bina* (dressed in fine cloth).

Nakamachi Kura-chic-kan CRAFTS
(中町・蔵シック館; ☎0263-36-3053; 2-9-15 Chūō; ⏲9am-5pm) A pun on 'classic' in English, 'kura' in Japanese and 'chic' in French, Nakamachi Kura-chic-kan showcases locally produced arts and crafts.

Chikiri-ya GLASS
(ちきりや; ☎0263-33-2522; 3-4-18 Chūō; ⏲9am-5pm) Glass and pottery aficionados will find this wonderful boutique a must.

Information

Although small streets radiate somewhat confusingly from the train station, soon you're on a grid.

Online, visit http://welcome.city.matsumoto.nagano.jp.

Main Post Office (☎0263-35-0081; 2-3-5 Chūō)

JTB (☎0263-35-3311; 1-2-11 Fukashi) For train and bus reservations.

Tourist Information Center (松本市観光案内所; ☎0263-32-2814; 1-1-1 Fukashi; ⏲9.30am-5.45pm) This excellent Tourist Information Center inside JR Matsumoto Station has friendly English-speaking staff and a wide range of well-produced English-language materials on the area.

Getting There & Away

AIR

Shinshū Matsumoto airport has flights to Fukuoka, Osaka and Sapporo.

BUS

Alpico runs buses between Matsumoto and Shinjuku in Tokyo (¥3400, 3¼ hours, 24 daily), Osaka (¥5850, 5¾ hours, two daily; one longer overnight service) and Nagoya (from ¥3600, 3½ hours, 10 daily). Nohi Bus services Takayama (¥3900, 2½ hours, at least six daily). Reservations are advised. The Matsumoto Bus Terminal is in the basement of the ESPA building opposite JR Matsumoto Station.

CAR

Renting a car is a great way to explore the beauty outside town, but expect narrow, windy roads. There are several agencies around the train station. Rates generally start at around ¥6500 per day.

TRAIN

Matsumoto is connected with Tokyo's Shinjuku Station (*tokkyū* ¥6380, 2¾ hours, hourly), Nagoya (*tokkyū* ¥5510, two hours) and Nagano (Shinano *tokkyū* ¥2320, 50 minutes; Chūō *futsū* ¥1140, 1¼ hours). There are also infrequent direct services to Osaka (*tokkyū* ¥8850, 4½ hours).

Getting Around

Matsumoto-jō and the city centre are easily covered on foot and free bicycles are available for loan – enquire at the Tourist Information Center. Three 'town sneaker' loop bus routes operate between 9am and 5.30pm for ¥200 per ride (¥500 per day); the blue and orange routes cover the castle and Nakamachi.

An airport shuttle bus connects Shinshū Matsumoto airport with downtown (¥600, 25 minutes); a taxi costs around ¥5000.

Shirahone Onsen 白骨温泉

☎0263

Intimate, dramatic and straddling a deep gorge, this onsen resort town is one of Japan's most beautiful – it's heavenly during autumn and a wonderland in winter. *Onsen ryokan* with open-air baths surround the gorge. Meaning 'white bone', it is said that bathing in the silky, milky-blue hydrogen-sulphide waters of Shirahone for three day ensures you will go for three years without a cold.

OFF THE BEATEN TRACK

SLEEP ABOVE THE CLOUDS

If you're looking for something a little bit different, along the lines of isolation and indulgence, there are two very special places to rest your weary head in the mountains above Matsumoto. From April to November, consider a night at the singular **Ohgatou Hotel** (王ヶ頭ホテル; ☎0263-31-2751; www.ougatou.jp; Utsukushi-ga-hara-kōgen; d per person with 2 meals from ¥15,000) atop the beautiful Utsukushi-ga-hara-kōgen. Rooms are plush, comfy and reasonably priced for their standard. Oversized suites have decadent baths overlooking the plateau and the cloud line: you'll think you're on Cloud Nine as you wake.

For something a little pricier, fancier and more traditional, the exclusive **Tobira Onsen Myōjin-kan** (扉温泉明神館; ☎0263-31-2301; http://myojinkan.tobira-group.com; 8967 Iriyamabe; s/d per person with 2 meals from ¥32,500/26,000) has been nestled quietly in the mountains above Matsumoto (en route to Utsukushi-ga-hara-kōgen) since 1931. There's a variety of room types: many have private onsen baths, each enjoys wonderful vistas of the natural surrounds. The communal indoor and outdoor baths will leave you feeling like you're floating on air. For your investment, expect nothing less than exquisite French and *kaiseki* cuisine and the epitome of customer service.

Both rare gems are best enjoyed with cash in your wallet and the freedom of a rental car.

Activities

Kōkyō Notemburo ONSEN
(公共野天風呂; ☎0263-93-3251; admission ¥510; ⏰8.30am-5pm Apr-Nov) This riverside *rotemburo*, deep within the gorge at Shirahone Onsen, is separated by gender; the entrance is by the bus stop.

Sleeping & Eating

★**Awanoyu Ryokan** RYOKAN ¥¥¥
(泡の湯旅館; ☎0263-93-2101; www.awanoyu-ryokan.com; 4181 Shirahone Onsen; r per person incl 2 meals from ¥27,000; Ⓟ) Awanoyu Ryokan typifies mountain *onsen ryokan*. Uphill from Shirahone, it has been an inn since 1912 (the current building dates from 1940). Light-filled guest rooms have private facilities. There are also single-sex common baths and *konyoku* (mixed bathing): the waters are so milky that you can't see below the surface, so don't be shy. Reservations essential.

Tsuruya Ryokan RYOKAN ¥¥¥
(つるや旅館; ☎0263-93-2331; www.tsuruya-ryokan.jp; 4202-6 Shirahone Onsen; r per person with 2 meals from ¥10,650; Ⓟ) Lovely Tsuruya Ryokan has both contemporary and traditional touches and great indoor and outdoor baths. Each of its 28 rooms has lovely views of the gorge; rooms with private toilet and sink are available for an extra charge. Book in advance.

Information

Tourist Information Center (観光案内所; ☎0263-93-3251; www.shirahone.org; 4197-4 Azumino; ⏰9am-5pm) The Tourist Information Center maintains a list of inns that open their baths (admission from ¥600) to the public each day.

Hirayu Onsen 平湯温泉

☎0578

This onsen village is a hub for bus transport and the best base for day trips to Kamikōchi, neighbouring Shirahone and Fukuchi Onsens, and the Shin-Hotaka Ropeway. There is a pleasant, low-to-the-ground cluster of onsen lodgings, about half of which open for day-bathers. Even the bus station has a rooftop *rotemburo* (¥600).

Sleeping & Eating

Hirayu Camping Ground CAMPGROUND ¥
(平湯キャンプ場; ☎0578-89-2610; www.hirayu-camp.com; 768-36 Hirayu; camp site per adult/child ¥700/500, bungalow from ¥5800, parking from ¥1000; ⏰end Apr-Oct; Ⓟ) To reach the small Hirayu Camping Ground, turn right from the bus station – it's about 700m ahead, on the left.

Ryosō Tsuyukusa MINSHUKU ¥¥
(旅荘つゆくさ; ☎0578-89-2620; http://tuyukusa-hirayu.com; 621 Hirayu; s/d per person with 2 meals ¥9000/8000; Ⓟ) Ryosō Tsuyukusa is an eight-room mum-and-dad *minshuku* with decent tatami rooms and a cosy mountain-view *rotemburo* of hinoki cypress. Go downhill from the bus station and turn left at the first narrow street; it's on the left. Little English is spoken.

Hirayu-no-mori RESORT ¥¥

(ひらゆの森; ☎0578-89-3338; www.hirayunomori.co.jp/contents/english; 763-1 Hirayu; r per person with 2 meals from ¥7500, bath day use ¥500; P) Practically in its own forest uphill from the bus station, this sprawling *onsen ryokan* boasts 16 different *rotemburo* pools, plus indoor and private baths. After 9pm the baths are exclusively for overnight guests. Rooms are Japanese-style, and meals are hearty and local.

Okada Ryokan RYOKAN ¥¥

(岡田旅館; ☎0578-89-2336; www.okadaryokan.com; 505 Hirayu; r per person with 2 meals from ¥8800; P 📶) Although not much English is spoken, the kind staff at this hulking ryokan downhill from the bus station provide a warm welcome. Large but dated rooms have private facilities and the common baths and *rotemburo* are excellent. Unlike many ryokan in the area, single travellers can get rates here without meals – but beware the slim pickings for nearby restaurants.

Miyama Ouan RYOKAN ¥¥¥

(深山桜庵; ☎0578-89-2799; www.hotespa.net/hotels/miyamaouan; 229 Hirayu; r per person with 2 meals from ¥19,200) This recently built chain ryokan has traditional service, modern technology and intimate personal touches. The 72 rooms, in a variety of sizes and styles, are beautifully finished with cypress woods and chic design – all have private facilities. The private *kazoku-buro* (family-use) *rotemburo* is a little piece of heaven. Staff will even collect you from the bus station.

Information

Tourist Information Center (観光案内所; ☎0578-89-3030; 763-191 Hirayu; ⏲9.30am-5.30pm) The Tourist Information Center opposite the bus station has leaflets, maps and can book accommodation. Surprisingly, little English is spoken.

Fukuchi Onsen 福地温泉

☎0578

This tiny onsen town a short ride north of Hirayu Onsen follows a steep hill with beautiful views and a handful of outstanding baths. Otherwise, there's not even a village here. By bus from Hirayu Onsen, you can get off at Fukuchi-Onsen-Kami stop and walk downhill to check out the ryokan, then pick up the bus to return to Hirayu or travel onwards to Shirahone Onsen.

Activities

Mukashibanashi-no-sato (Isurugi-no-yu) ONSEN

(昔ばなしの里（石動の湯; ☎0578-89-2614; bath ¥500; ⏲8am-5pm, closed irregularly) This restaurant-cum-onsen is set back from the street in a traditional farmhouse with fine indoor and outdoor baths, free on the 26th of each month. Out the front is an unmissable vintage knick-knack shop adorned with Shōwa-era movie posters and advertisements. If you're travelling by bus, get off at Fukuchi-Onsen-Kami bus stop.

Sleeping & Eating

★**Yumoto Chōza** RYOKAN ¥¥¥

(湯元長座; ☎0578-89-2010; www.cyouza.com/english; 786 Fukuchi; r per person with 2 meals from ¥19,000; P) Opposite Fukuchi-Onsen-shimo bus stop, the entrance to Yumoto Chōza is reached by a rustic, covered walkway, as if to take you back in time. Think bold, dark woods and handsome traditional architecture. Half of the 32 rooms have en suites and *irori* and there are five indoor baths and two stunning *rotemburo* – day visitors can bathe between 2pm and 6pm for ¥750. Advance reservations essential.

Yamazato-no-iori Soene RYOKAN ¥¥¥

(山里のいおり　草円; ☎0578-89-1116; www.soene.com; 831 Fukuchi; r per person with 2 meals from ¥15,300; 📶) This rustic ryokan is over 100 years old and atmosphere abounds. Its indoor and outdoor baths are absolutely delightful, as are the views. Rooms are spacious and have an air of romance about them. Delicious *kaiseki* cuisine is served in the dining room. A little English is spoken and there's wi-fi in the lobby. Open year round, this is one for all seasons.

Shin-Hotaka Onsen 新穂高温泉

☎0578

This delightful sleepy hollow north of Fukuchi Onsen is famed for the Shin-Hotaka Ropeway, Japan's longest.

Activities

★**Shin-Hotaka Ropeway** ROPEWAY

(新穂高ロープウェイ; ☎0578-89-2252; www.okuhi.jp/Rop/english.pdf; Shin-Hotaka; one way/return ¥1600/2900; ⏲8.30am-4.30pm) From a starting elevation of 1308m, two cable cars whisk you to 2156m towards the peak of

Nishi Hotaka-dake (2909m). Views from the top are spectacular, both from observation decks and walking trails. In winter, snow can be shoulder deep. In season, properly equipped hikers with ample time can choose from a number of hikes beginning from the top cable-car station (Nishi Hotaka-guchi), including hiking over to Kamikōchi (three hours), which is much easier than going the other way.

Nakazaki Sansou Okuhida-no-yu ONSEN
(中崎山荘奥飛騨の湯; ☎0578-89-2021; 710 Okuhida Onsengo Kansaka; adult/child ¥800/400; ⏲8am-8pm) Over 50 years old but completely rebuilt in 2010, this facility commands a spectacular vista of the mountains. The milky waters of its large indoor baths and *rotemburo* do wonders for dry skin.

Shin-Hotaka-no-yu ONSEN
(新穂高の湯; ☎0578-89-2458; Okuhida Onsen-go Kansaka; ⏲8am-9pm May-Oct, closed Nov-Apr) FREE Exhibitionists will love this bare-bones *konyoku* (mixed bathing) *rotemburo* by the Kamata-gawa, visible from the bridge that passes over it. Entry is free (or by donation). Enter through segregated change rooms, and emerge into a single large pool. Be sure to mind your manners. When in Rome...

Sleeping & Eating

★ Yarimikan RYOKAN ¥¥¥
(槍見舘; ☎0578-89-2808; www.yarimikan.com; Okuhida Onsen-gun Kansaka; r per person with meals from ¥16,350; P) Yarimikan is a wonderfully traditional *onsen ryokan* on the Kamata-gawa, with two indoor baths, eight riverside *rotemburo* (some available for private use) and 15 rooms. Guests can bathe 24 hours a day (it's stunning by moonlight) and day visitors are accepted between 10am and 2pm for ¥500. Cuisine features local Hida beef and grilled freshwater fish.

It's just off Rte 475, a few kilometres before the Shin-Hotaka Ropeway.

Nonohana Sansō INN ¥¥¥
(野の花山荘; ☎0578-89-0030; www.nono87.jp; r per person with 2 meals from ¥13,000, day guests adult/child ¥800/500; ⏲day guests 10am-5pm; P) Along a road that ascends from Rte 475, Nonohana Sansō opened its doors in 2010. All tatami guestrooms are traditionally styled and have private facilities, although the lobby and lounge are refreshingly contemporary. There's an open kitchen preparing local specialities and the large *rotemburo* have a fantastic outlook – they're open to day visitors.

NORTHERN JAPAN ALPS SAMPLE BUS FARES & DURATIONS

Within the Alps, schedules change seasonally. Alpico's 'Alps-Wide Free Passport' (¥10,290) gives you four days unlimited rides between Matsumoto and Takayama, within the Chūbu-Sangaku National Park and including Shirakawa-gō.

Tourist information centres can direct you to the latest schedules and fares.

FROM	TO	FARE (¥; ONE WAY)	DURATION (MIN; ONE WAY)
Takayama	Hirayu Onsen	1570	55
	Kamikōchi	2720	80
	Shin-Hotaka	2160	90
Matsumoto	Shin-Shimashima	700 (train)	30
	Kamikōchi	2650	95
Shin-Shimashima	Naka-no-yu	1700	50
	Kamikōchi	1950	70
	Shirahone Onsen	1450	75
Kamikōchi	Naka-no-yu	770	15
	Hirayu Onsen	1160	25
	Shirahone Onsen	1350	35
Hirayu Onsen	Naka-no-yu	580	10
	Shin-Hotaka	920	30

Information

Oku-Hida Spa Tourist Information Center (奥飛騨温泉郷観光案内所; ☎0578-89-2614; ⊙10am-5pm) On Hwy 471 before the bridge, as the road turns into Hwy 475 towards the ropeway.

Kamikōchi 上高地

☎0260

In the late 19th century, foreigners 'discovered' this mountainous region and coined the term 'Japan Alps'. A British missionary, Reverend Walter Weston, toiled from peak to peak and sparked Japanese interest in mountaineering as a sport. He is now honoured with a festival on the first Sunday in June, the official opening of the hiking season. Kamikōchi has become a base for day trippers, hikers and climbers who come for snowcapped peaks, bubbling brooks, wild monkeys, wildflowers and ancient forests. That said, it wouldn't be Japan without the crowds: timing is everything.

Kamikōchi is closed from 15 November to 22 April, and in peak times (late July to late August, and during the foliage season in October) it can seem busier than Shinjuku Station. June to July is rainy season. It's perfectly feasible to visit as a day trip but you'll miss out on the pleasures of staying in the mountains and taking uncrowded early-morning or late-afternoon walks.

Visitors arrive at Kamikōchi's sprawling bus station. A 10-minute walk along the Azusa-gawa takes you to **Kappa-bashi**, a bridge named after a legendary water sprite. Hiking trails begin here.

Activities

Bokuden-no-yu ONSEN

(卜伝の湯; ☎0260-95-2407; admission ¥700; ⊙noon-5pm) Not for the claustrophobic, the area's most unusual onsen – a tiny cave bath dripping with minerals – is found near the Naka-no-yu bus stop, to the left of the bus-only tunnel into Kamikōchi. Pay at the small shop for the key to the little mountain hut housing the onsen. It's yours privately for up to 30 minutes.

Sleeping & Eating

Accommodation in Kamikōchi is expensive and advance reservations are essential. Some lodgings shut down power in the middle of the night (although emergency lighting stays on).

Dotted along the trails and around the mountains are dozens of spartan *yamagoya* (mountain huts), which provide two meals and a futon from around ¥8000 per person; some also serve simple lunches. Enquire before setting out to make sure there's one on your intended route.

The bus station has a very limited range of eateries and retailers: bring essential munchies and take your rubbish with you.

Tokusawa-en CAMPGROUND ¥

(徳澤園; ☎0260-95-2508; www.tokusawaen.com/english.html; per person incl 2 meals camp site/dm ¥500/10,000, d & tw ¥14,900; ⊙May-Oct) A marvellously secluded place in a wooded dell about 7km northeast of Kappa-bashi. It's both a camping ground and a lodge, and has Japanese-style rooms (shared facilities) and hearty meals served in a busy dining hall. Access is by walking only, and takes about two hours.

Forest Resort Konashi CAMPGROUND ¥

(森のリゾート小梨, Mori no rizōto Konashi; ☎0260-95-2321; www.nihonalpskankou.com; per person incl 2 meals camp site from ¥800, tw from ¥11,000; ⊙office 7am-7pm) About 200m past the Kamikōchi Visitor Centre, this camping ground can get crowded. Rental tents are available from ¥7000 (July and August) and there's a small shop and restaurant.

Kamikōchi Gosenjaku Hotel & Lodge HOTEL ¥¥

(上高地五千尺ホテル・ロッヂ; ☎hotel 0260-95-2111, lodge 0260-95-2221; www.gosenjaku.co.jp/english; 4468 Kamikōchi; per person incl 2 meals lodge skier's bed from ¥10,000, s/tw ¥24,000/12,000, hotel d from ¥17,500) By Kappa-bashi this compact lodge recently expanded to include a small hotel. The lodge has 34 Japanese-style rooms and some 'skier's beds'; basically curtained-off bunks. Rooms all have sink and toilet, but baths are shared. The hotel is more upscale with a combination of comfortable Western and Japanese rooms, some with balconies.

Kamikōchi Nishi-itoya Sansō INN ¥¥¥

(上高地西糸屋山荘; ☎0260-95-2206; www.nishiitoya.com; 4469-1 Kamikōchi; per person incl 2 meals dm from ¥8500, d from ¥9720; ⊗@📶) This friendly lodge, west of Kappa-bashi, has a cosy lounge and dates from the early 20th century. Rooms are a mix of Japanese and Western styles, all with toilet. The shared bath is a large onsen facing the Hotaka mountains.

★**Kamikochi Imperial Hotel** HOTEL ¥¥¥
(上高地帝国ホテル; 0260-95-2001; www.imperialhotel.co.jp/j/kamikochi; Azumino Kamikochi; s & tw from ¥29,400; @) Expect exceptional service and rustic, European Alps–styled rooms in this historic red-gabled lodge completed in 1933. Prices are elevated, but a wide range of stay plans are available and the hotel occasionally offers excellent packages including French haute cuisine. You may have to book a year in advance!

Kamonji-goya SHOKUDŌ ¥
(0260-95-2418; dishes from ¥700; 8.30am-4pm;) Kamikōchi's signature dish is *iwana* (river trout) grilled whole over an *irori*. This is *the* place to try it. The *iwana* set is ¥1500, or there's *oden* (fish-cake stew), *soba* and *kotsu-sake* (dried *iwana* in sake) served in a lovely ceramic bowl. It's just outside the entrance to Myōjin-ike.

Information

Kamikōchi is entirely closed from 15 November to 22 April. Serious hikers should consider insurance (保険; *hoken;* from ¥1000 per day), available at Kamikōchi bus station.

Kamikōchi Tourist Information Center (上高地インフォメーションセンター; 0260-95-2433; 8am-5pm) This invaluable resource at the bus station complex provides information on hiking and weather conditions and distributes the English-language *Kamikōchi Pocket Guide* with a map of the main walking tracks.

Kamikōchi Visitor Centre (上高地ビジターセンター; 0260-95-2606; 8am-5pm) Ten minutes' walk from Kamikōchi bus station along the main trail, this is the place for information on Kamikōchi's flora, fauna, geology and history. You can also book guided walks to destinations including Taishō-ike and Myōjin-ike (per person from ¥500). English-speaking nature guides (from ¥2000 per hour) and climbing guides (around ¥30,000 a day) may be available.

Getting Around

Private vehicles are prohibited between Naka-no-yu and Kamikōchi; access is only by bus or taxi as far as the Kamikōchi bus station. Those with private cars can use car parks en route to Naka-no-yu in the hamlet of Sawando for ¥500 per day; shuttle buses (¥1800 return) run a few times per hour.

Buses run via Naka-no-yu and Taishō-ike to the bus station. Hiking trails commence at

HIKING & CLIMBING IN KAMIKŌCHI

The Kamikōchi river valley offers mostly level, short-distance, signposted walks.

A recommended four-hour hike begins east of Kappa-bashi, heading past Myōjin-bashi (one hour). By Myōjin-bashi, the idyllic **Myōjin-ike** (pond) marks the innermost shrine of **Hotaka-jinja** (admission ¥300). From Myōjin-bashi, continue on to Tokusawa (another hour) before returning the same way.

West of Kappa-bashi, you can amble alongside the river to **Weston Relief** (monument to Walter Weston; 15 minutes) or to Taishō-ike (40 minutes).

Popular hiking destinations include the mountain hut at **Dakesawa** (2½ hours up) and fiery **Yakedake** (four hours up, starting about 20 minutes west of the Weston Relief, at Hotaka-bashi). From the peaks, it's possible to see all the way to Mt Fuji in clear weather.

Long-distance hikes vary in duration and have access to mountain huts; enquire at the Information Center for details. Japanese-language maps of the area show routes and average hiking times between huts, major peaks and landmarks. Favourite hikes and climbs (think human traffic jams during peak seasons) include **Yariga-take** (3180m) and **Hotaka-dake** (3190m). A stunning but steep hike connects Kamikōchi and Shin-Hotaka. From Kappa-bashi, the trail crosses the ridge below Nishi-Hotaka-dake (2909m) at Nishi-Hotaka Sansō (cottage; three hours) and continues to Nishi-Hotaka-guchi, the top station of the Shin-Hotaka Ropeway (p265). The hike takes nearly four hours in this direction but is far easier in reverse. Serious hikers should consider treks to pristine **Nakabusa Onsen** (three days) or **Murodō** (five days), the latter being the apex of the Tateyama-Kurobe Alpine Route (p260).

Hikers and climbers should be well prepared. Temperatures can plummet suddenly, sleeting rain or blinding fog set in rapidly and there is no refuge on the peaks during thunderstorms.

In winter, deserted Kamikōchi makes a beautiful **cross-country skiing** spot for the initiated: hike in from the entrance to the KamaTunnel on Rte 158.

Kappa-bashi, which is a short walk from the bus station.

Azumino 安曇野

☎0263

The city of Azumino was formed in 2005, when the towns of Toyoshina, Hotaka, Akashina and three smaller villages amalgamated. It's also the traditional name of the picturesque valley in which they're located. An easy day trip from Matsumoto, the area is home to Japan's largest wasabi farm and is a popular starting point for mountain hikes.

Sights & Activities

Dai-ō Wasabi-Nōjo FARM

(大王わさび農場; ☎0263-82-2118; 3640 Hotaka; ⊙9am-5pm) FREE Fancy some wasabi beer? This farm, a 15-minute bike ride from JR Hotaka Station is *de rigueur* for wasabi lovers. An English map guides you among wasabi plants (130 tons of wasabi are grown in flooded fields here annually) amid rolling hills, restaurants, shops and workspaces.

Rokuzan Bijutsukan GALLERY

(碌山美術館; ☎0263-82-2094; 5095-1 Hotaka; adult/child ¥700/150; ⊙9am-4pm daily May-Oct, Tue-Sun Nov-Apr) Ten minutes' walk from JR Hotaka Station, Rokuzan Bijutsukan showcases the work of Meiji-era sculptor Rokuzan Ogiwara (aka 'Rodin of the Orient') and his Japanese contemporaries in a delightful garden setting.

Jōnen-dake HIKING

(常念岳) From JR Hotaka Station it's 30 minutes by taxi (around ¥5000) to reach the Ichinosawa trailhead, from where experienced hikers can climb Jōnen-dake (2857m); the ascent takes about 5½ hours. There are many options for hikes extending over several days, but you must be properly prepared. Hiking maps are available at the Tourist Information Center, although the detailed ones are in Japanese.

Sleeping

Route Inn Azumino Toyoshina Eki-minami HOTEL ¥¥

(ホテルルートイン安曇野豊科駅南; ☎0263-73-0044; 4677-1 Toyoshina; s/d from ¥6850/11,900; wi-fi) This newer hotel is located adjacent to Toyoshina Station – perfect for explorations into the Azumino area. Rooms are compact and comfortable, and there's a communal bath, wi-fi and complimentary light breakfast buffet.

★ **Nakabusa Onsen** RYOKAN ¥¥¥

(中房温泉; ☎0263-77-1488; www.nakabusa.com; 7226 Nakabusa; r per person with 2 meals from ¥9654; ⊙Apr-Nov; P) With over a dozen indoor, outdoor and sand baths, this rambling resort at the end of a twisty mountain road to nowhere will delight anyone seeking a peaceful retreat. The older *honkan* wing has basic rooms, while the newer *bekkan* wing is more comfortable. In late autumn gawk at stunningly colourful foliage against the backdrop of snowcapped peaks. Enquire at the Tourist Information Center for the limited bus schedule (¥1700, one hour) from Azumino to Nakabusa Onsen or rent a car (and nerves of steel).

Ariake-so INN ¥¥¥

(有明荘; ☎0263-84-6511; r per person with 2 meals from ¥9800; ⊙Apr-late Nov; P) En route to Nakabusa Onsen, this seasonal forest lodge has basic dorm-style rooms and a nourishing onsen (day use ¥600).

Information

Tourist Information Center (観光案内所; ☎0263-82-9363; www.azumino-e-tabi.net/en; 5952-3 Hotaka; ⊙9am-5pm Apr-Nov, 10am-4pm Dec-Mar) This friendly, home-proud tourist office opposite JR Hotaka Station has helpful English-speaking staff and rents out bicycles – a great way to explore the area. They've done a great job on their English homepage.

Getting There & Away

Hotaka is the gateway city to the Azumino valley. JR Hotaka Station is 28 minutes (*futsū* ¥320) from Matsumoto on the JR Ōito line.

Hakuba 白馬

☎0261

At the base of one of the highest sections of the Northern Japan Alps, Hakuba is one of Japan's main skiing and hiking centres. In winter skiers from across Japan, and increasingly overseas, flock to Hakuba's seven ski resorts. In summer the region draws hikers attracted by easy access to the high peaks. There are many onsen in and around Hakuba-mura, the main village, and a long soak after a day of action is the perfect way to ease your muscles.

The region was struck by a powerful 6.7 magnitude earthquake on 21 November 2014, causing significant damage to Hakuba and neighbouring villages, though tourism was not greatly affected.

Activities

Happō-One Ski Resort SKIING
(Map p274; 八方尾根スキー所; ☎0261-72-3066; www.happo-one.jp/english; 1-day lift ticket ¥5000; ⏲Dec-Apr) Host of the downhill races at the 1998 Winter Olympics, Happō-One is one of Japan's best ski areas, with superb mountain views and beginner, intermediate and advanced runs catering to skiers and snowboarders. For the lowdown, check the excellent English-language homepage.

With a total of 23 lifts, half the terrain is rated intermediate, and there are more skiers than boarders. The resthouse at the top of the 'Adam' gondola, Usagidaira 109, is the ski area's centre point, with two chairlifts from there heading up to the highest elevation of 1830m.

From Hakuba Station, a five-minute bus ride (¥260) takes you into the middle of the lively little village of Hakuba-mura. In winter, shuttles make the rounds of the village, lodges and ski base.

Hakuba 47 Winter Sports Park & Hakuba Goryū Ski Resort SKIING
(Map p274; Hakuba47ウインタースポーツパーク・白馬五竜スキー場; www.hakuba47.co.jp; 1-day lift ticket ¥5000; ⏲Dec-Apr) The interlinked areas of Hakuba 47 Winter Sports Park and Hakuba Goryū Ski Resort form the second major ski resort in the Hakuba area. There's a good variety of terrain at both areas, with about an equal number of skiers and boarders. Like Happō-One, this area boasts fantastic mountain views.

A free shuttle bus from Hakuba-mura and Hakuba-eki provides the easiest access.

Hakuba Cortina Kokusai SKIING
(Map p274; 白馬コルチナ国際; www.hakubacortina.jp/ski; 1-day lift ticket ¥3600; ⏲Dec-Apr) At the northern end of the valley, Hakuba Cortina is popular with Japanese families who revel in the resort's facilities – a massive ski-in European-style structure with hotel, restaurants, ski rental and deluxe onsen – and those who want quieter slopes. Its seven lifts and 16 courses cater to all levels of skiers.

Mimizuku-no-yu ONSEN
(みみずくの湯; 5480 Ō-aza Hokujō; adult/child ¥500/250; ⏲10am-9.30pm, enter by 9pm) One of Hakuba's many onsen; many contend this has the best mountain views from the tub.

Evergreen Outdoor ADVENTURE SPORTS
(www.evergreen-hakuba.com) This gang of friendly, outdoorsy folk offer an array of adventures with English-speaking guides year-round from about ¥5000. On offer are canyoning and mountain biking, as well as snowshoeing and backcountry treks in the winter.

Hiking

In summer you can take the gondola and the two upper chairlifts, then hike along a trail for an hour or so to Happō-ike on a ridge below Karamatsu-dake (唐松岳; 2695m). From here, follow a trail another hour up to Maru-yama, continue for 1½ hours to the Karamatsu-dake San-sō (mountain hut) and then climb to the peak of Karamatsu-dake in about 30 minutes.

Sleeping & Eating

Snowbeds Backpackers HOSTEL ¥
(スノーベッズバックパッカーズ; ☎0261-72-5242; www.snowbedsjapan.com; dm per person from ¥3900; P@📶) This foreign-run backpackers has cheap but cramped bunk rooms and a nice communal area with a wood stove. It's close to the nightlife. Private rooms are also available.

Hakuba Panorama Hotel INN ¥¥
(白馬パノラマホテル; ☎0261-85-4031; www.hakuba-panorama.com; 3322-1 Hokujō; d per person incl breakfast from ¥7600; P📶) About 300m from one of the lifts at Happō-One, this Australian-run outfit has bilingual Japanese staff, an on-site travel agency and a variety of room types with en suite bathrooms. There's a guest laundry and a wonderful onsen.

★**Ridge Hotel & Apartments** HOTEL ¥¥¥
(☎0261-85-4301; www.theridgehakuba.com; 4608 Hakuba; d from ¥10,400, apt from ¥36,000; P@📶) Sophisticated, sexy and stylish, this stunning property has it all, year round: location, amenities, views. A variety of room types range from the sublime (Western-style rooms with Japanese elements) to the ridiculous (a gorgeous loft balcony suite in the shadow of the slopes). Obliging, attentive staff speak English well. Splurge if you can.

Hakuba Tokyu Hotel HOTEL ¥¥¥
(白馬東急ホテル; ☎0261-72-3001; www.tokyuhotelsjapan.com/en/; Happō-wadanomori; s/d incl breakfast from ¥19,200/27,200; P 📶) This elegant year-round hotel has large rooms with great views and a wonderful garden, popular for weddings. The Grand Spa boasts the highest alkaline content in the area, and there's both French and Japanese restaurants.

Hakuba Highland Hotel HOTEL ¥¥¥
(白馬ハイランドホテル; ☎0261-72-3450; www.hakuba-highland.net; 1582 Hokujō; d per person with 2 meals from ¥9680; P) This older hotel has sensational views over the Hakuba range and a great indoor-outdoor onsen, but it's away from the action. In winter there's a free shuttle bus to the main resorts, each about 20 minutes' drive away.

Bamboo Coffee Bar CAFE ¥
(☎0261-85-0901; www.bamboohakuba.com; ⏲8am-6pm; 📶) On the left as you exit JR Hakuba Station, this wonderful modern cafe serves delicious specialty coffees, sweet treats and panini sandwiches. The mellow tunes, friendly staff and free wi-fi (with purchases) make it a great place to log on and get your bearings.

Drinking & Entertainment

Tanuki's SPORTS BAR
(タヌキズ; ☎090-7202-9809; 6350-3 Hokujo; ⏲noon-late Thu-Tue) This neat little bar to your right as you exit JR Habuka Station serves juicy original burgers and your favourite fast foods in a welcoming environment with free pool, darts and foozball on the second floor.

Tracks Bar BAR
(☎0261-75-4366; tracksbar.info) Located between Kamishiro Station and Goryū, this is a favourite night spot for the younger, foreign crowd, with live music, pool tables, wood-burner stoves and sports on a huge screen.

The Pub PUB
(☎0261-72-4453; www.thepubhakuba.com; ⏲4.30pm-late; @📶) The only English pub in the village is found in a Swiss-style chalet on the grounds of the Momonoki hotel. By Japanese standards, it's huge and happening. There's a daily happy hour, free internet and wi-fi.

Hakuba Bike Bar BAR
(白馬バイクバー; www.bikebar-hakuba.com) This fun, disco-lit basement bar in Hakuba Goryū has a refreshingly hippie vibe – these guys think they're pretty cool, and by many standards, they are. It's about 10 minutes' walk from the Sky 4 Gondola and has billiards, early-evening film nights for families (Ninja juice is served) and karaoke.

Information

Hakuba Accomodation Information Centre (白馬宿泊情報センター, Hakuba Shukuhaku Jōhō Sentā; ☎0261-72-6900; www.hakuba1.com/english; ⏲7am-6pm) For information, maps and lodging assistance. Located to the right of Hakuba Station.

Hakuba Tourist Information Center (白馬村観光案内所; ☎0261-72-3232; www.vill.hakuba.nagano.jp/english; ⏲8.30am-5.30pm) Provides maps and leaflets relating to tourism in the area. In addition to all things winter, the website has detailed information on summer gondola operating schedules and fares. It's just outside Hakuba Station.

Getting There & Away

Hakuba is connected with Matsumoto by the JR Ōito line (*tokkyū* ¥2320, one hour; *futsū* ¥1140, 1½ hours). Continuing north, change trains at Minami Otari to meet the JR Hokuriku line at Itoigawa: it's a pretty journey on a little two-carriage train, taking an hour from Minami Otari to Itoigawa with connections to Niigata, Toyama and Kanazawa.

There is one direct service per day (Super Azusa #3) from Shinjuku to Hakuba, via Matsumoto (*tokkyū* ¥7780, four hours). It departs Shinjuku at 7.30am and returns from Hakuba at 2.38pm.

Alpico group operates buses from Nagano Station (¥1600, approximately 70 minutes) and Shinjuku Nishi-guchi in Tokyo (¥4850, 4½ hours), as well as a 'Ninja' bus service direct from Narita airport (from ¥9000). See www.alpico.co.jp/traffic/express/narita_hakuba/en for for details.

NAGANO & AROUND

Formerly known as Shinshū and often referred to as the 'Roof of Japan', Nagano Prefecture (長野県) is a wonderful place to visit for its regal mountains, rich cultural history, fine architecture and cuisine.

In addition to a hefty chunk of the Chūbu-Sangaku National Park, Nagano boasts several quasi-national parks that attract skiers, mountaineers and onsen aficionados.

Nagano, the prefectural capital and past host of the Olympic Games, is home to Zenkō-ji, a spectacular temple of national significance.

Nagano 長野

026 / POP 381,500

Mountain-ringed prefectural capital Nagano has been a place of pilgrimage since the Kamakura period, when it was a temple town centred on the magnificent Zenkō-ji, which still draws more than four million visitors per year.

Since hosting the Winter Olympics in 1988, the city has reverted to its friendly small-town self, while still retaining plenty of accommodation options and some nice restaurants.

Zenkō-ji occupies a prominent place to the north of this grid city. Chūō-dōri leads south from the temple, doing a quick dog-leg before hitting JR Nagano Station, 1.8km away; it is said that street-planners considered Zenkō-ji so auspicious that it should not be approached directly from the train. The Nagano bus terminal is to the west of the train station, but most buses also stop in front of JR Nagano Station, where the terminus of the private Nagano Dentetsu ('Nagaden') line is also located.

Sights

Zenkō-ji BUDDHIST TEMPLE

(善光寺; 026-234-3591; www.zenkoji.jp; 491 Motoyoshi-chō; 4.30am-4.30pm summer, 6am-4pm winter, varied hr rest of yr) FREE Founded in the 7th century, National Treasure Zenkō-ji is home to the revered statue Ikkō-Sanzon, said to be the first Buddhist image to arrive in Japan (AD 552). Not even 37 generations of emperors have seen the image, though millions of visitors flock here to view a copy every seven years during the Gokaichō Matsuri. Zenkō-ji's immense popularity stems partly from its liberal welcoming of pilgrims, regardless of gender, creed or religious belief. Its chief officiants are both a priest and a priestess. The current building dates from 1707.

Any bus from bus stop 1 in front of JR Nagano Station's Zenkō-ji exit will get you to the temple (¥100, about 10 minutes; alight at the Daimon bus stop).

Festivals & Events

Gokaichō Matsuri RELIGIOUS

Five million pilgrims come to Zenkō-ji every seven years from early April to mid-May

ZENKŌ-JI LEGENDS

Few Japanese temples inspire the fascination Zenkō-ji does, thanks in part to the legends related to it. The following are just a few:

The Key to Salvation Visitors may descend Okaidan (admission ¥500), a staircase to a twisting pitch-black tunnel beneath the altar. Not for the claustrophobic, the idea is that in the darkness, all are equal, seeking the same thing – a heavy metallic object said to be the key to salvation. Grope the right hand wall while avoiding your fellow aspirants. Can you find it?

Ikkō-Sanzon Three statues of the Amida Buddha were brought to Japan from Korea in the 6th century and remain the temple's raison d'être, wrapped like a mummy and kept in an ark behind the main altar. It's said that nobody has seen Ikkō-Sanzon for 1000 years, but in 1702, to quell rumours that the ark was empty, the shogunate ordered a priest to confirm its existence and take measurements. That priest remains the last confirmed person to have viewed it.

The Doves of San-mon Legend claims there are five white doves hidden in the plaque of the **San-mon** (山門（三門)) gate; the five short strokes in the characters for Zenkō-ji do look remarkably dove-like. See if you can spot them too. In the upper character (善, Zen) they're the two uppermost strokes; in the middle character (光, kō) they're the strokes on either side of the top; and in the 'ji' (寺) it's the short stroke on the bottom left.

Binzuru It is said that Binzuru, one of Buddha's disciples, a healer, had attained enlightenment, but was instructed to remain on earth in service. You'll find his statue just inside, worn down where visitors have touched it to help heal ailments of the corresponding parts of their own bodies.

Nagano

Sights
1 Niō-mon ... B1
2 San-mon ... B1
3 Zenkō-ji ... B1

Sleeping
4 1166 Backpackers ... A2
5 Chisun Grand Nagano ... B4
6 Hotel Metropolitan Nagano ... A4
7 Matsuya Ryokan ... B1
8 Shimizuya Ryokan ... B2

Eating
9 Asian Night Market ... B2
10 Fujiki-an ... B2
11 Gohonjin Fujiya ... B2
12 India the Spice ... A4
13 Marusei ... B1
14 Yayoi-za ... A2

Drinking & Nightlife
15 Groovy ... B3
Izakaya Hanbey ... (see 12)
16 Shinshū Nagaya Sakaba ... A4

Information
17 Nagano Tourist Information Center ... B4

to view a copy of Zenkō-ji's sacred Buddha image – the only time it can be seen. The festival will be held in 2015 and 2022.

Enka Taikai FIREWORKS
A fireworks festival with street food on 23 November.

Sleeping

Visitors have the opportunity to experience *shukubō* (temple lodging) at one of Zenkō-ji's subtemples. Contact Zenkō-ji to book at least one day in advance. Expect to pay ¥7000 to ¥10,000 per person with two meals.

1166 Backpackers HOSTEL ¥
(1166 バックパッカーズ; 026-217-2816; www.1166bp.com; 1048 Nishi-machi; dm/r ¥2600/5600; @) This intimate, woody hostel is set amid older buildings in the back streets near Zenkō-ji. Look for the beige building with a chalk signboard outside. No meals are served, but there's a kitchen and dining area for guests.

★ Shimizuya Ryokan RYOKAN ¥¥
(清水屋旅館; 026-232-2580; www.chuoukan-shimizuya.com; 49 Daimon-chō; r per person with breakfast from ¥6600; @) On Chūō-dōri, a few blocks south of Zenkō-ji, this ryokan has been in the family for 130 years. The rustic, dark-wood interior has plenty of interesting ups, downs, nooks and crannies. There are shared bathrooms and a laundry. Meal plans are available.

Matsuya Ryokan RYOKAN ¥¥
(松屋旅館; 026-232-2811; Zenkō-ji Kannai; r per person from ¥6300, with 2 meals from ¥10,500) Six generations of the Suzuki family have maintained this traditional inn just inside Zenkō-ji's Niō-mon (仁王門), next to the statue of Enmei Jizō. It's the closest lodging to the temple. Meals are seasonal *kaiseki*. Add ¥1000 per person for rooms with private facilities.

Hotel Metropolitan Nagano HOTEL ¥¥
(ホテルメトロポリタン長野; 026-291-7000; www.metro-n.co.jp; 1346 Minami-Ishido-chō; s from ¥9000, d & tw from ¥12,400; P @) Opposite the train station, the Metropolitan

Nagano Prefecture

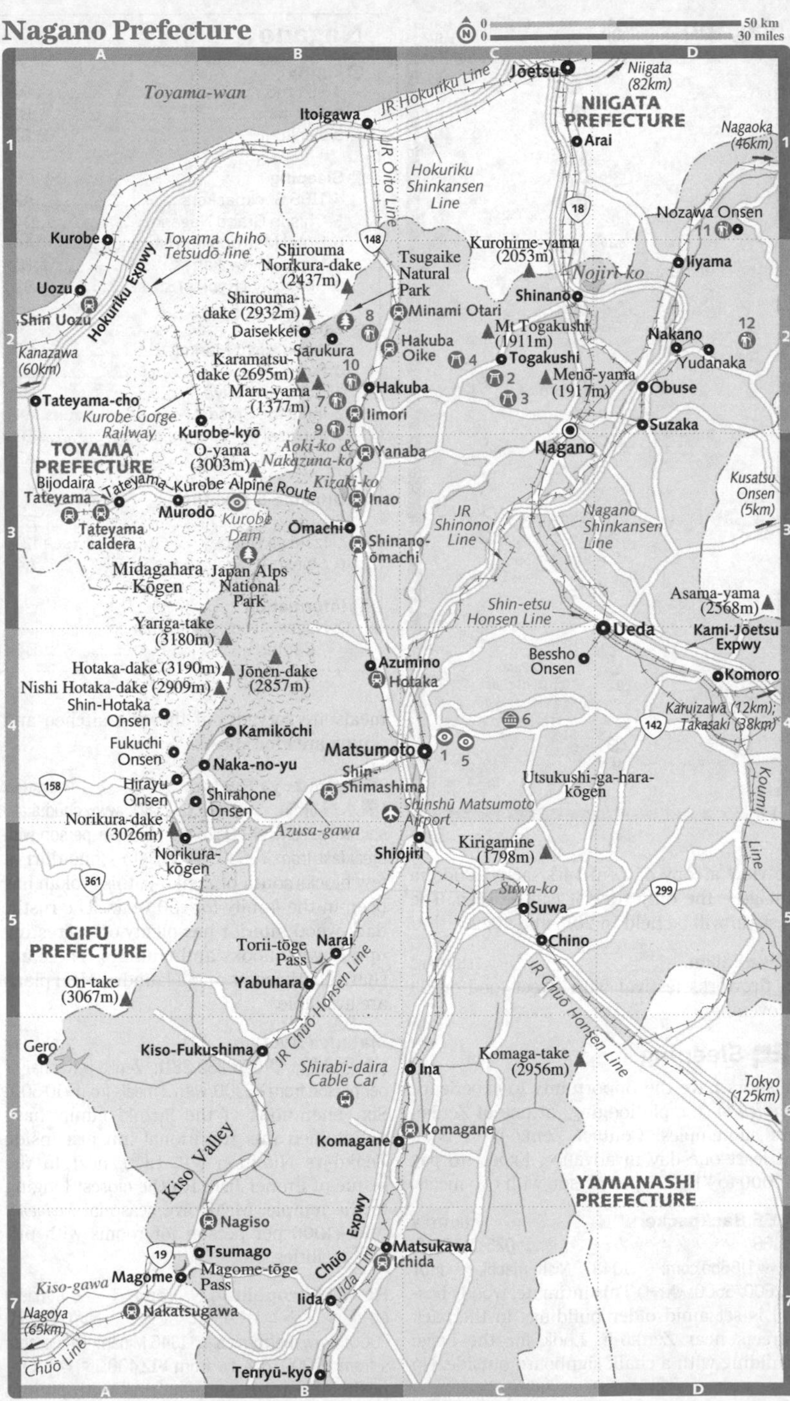

THE JAPAN ALPS & CENTRAL HONSHŪ

Nagano Prefecture

Sights

1 Asama Onsen C4
2 Togakushi-Chūsha C2
3 Togakushi-Hōkōsha C2
4 Togakushi-Okusha C2
5 Utsukushi-ga-hara Onsen C4
6 Utsukushi-ga-hara Open Air Museum C4

Activities, Courses & Tours

7 Hakuba 47 Winter Sports Park B2
8 Hakuba Cortina Kokusai B2
9 Hakuba Goryū Ski Resort B2
10 Happō-One Ski Resort B2
11 Nozawa Onsen Snow Resort D1
12 Shiga Kōgen D2

has elegant and spacious rooms by Japanese standards. There's a cafe, restaurant and top-floor lounge with sweeping views. Japan Rail Pass holders get a 20% discount.

Chisun Grand Nagano HOTEL ¥¥
(チサングランド長野; 026-264-6000; www.solarehotels.com; 2-17-1 Minami-Chitose; s/d from ¥6300/7500;) Formerly the Holiday Inn, this hotel was built for Olympic guests and features large, Western-style rooms, including impressive Junior Suites. Excellent rates can be found online.

Eating

India the Spice CAFE ¥
(インディア・ザ・すぱいす; 026-226-6136; 1418 Minami-ishido-chō; mains from ¥800; 11.30am-11pm Mon-Thu & Sun, to midnight Fri & Sat) This eccentric cafe is festooned with every kind of wall clock imaginable, and specialises in variations on the theme of curry; lunch set menus include *omu-karē* (rice wrapped in an omelette in keema curry sauce; ¥900). Going up Chūō-dōri, turn right at the 'Joy Style' London Bus, then take another right. There are vine leaves around the entrance.

Asian Night Market THAI ¥
(アジアンナイトマーケット; 026-214-5656; http://asian-night-market.net; 2-1 Higashi-go-chō; most dishes under ¥1000; noon-11pm;) This hippie joint is part boutique, selling clothes and knick-knacks from Southeast Asia, and part bar-restaurant with English-speaking staff serving sumptuous Thai food. There's also free wi-fi. You can view the menu online. The Chinese broccoli and obligatory pad thai are wonderful.

Marusei JAPANESE ¥
(丸清食堂; 026-232-5776; 486 Motoyoshi-chō; dishes ¥600-1800; 11am-6pm Thu-Tue) A stone's throw from Zenkō-ji on Nakamise-dōri, unassuming Marusei serves *soba* and *tonkatsu* among other dishes; the generous Marusei *bentō* (¥1350) lets you try both.

Yayoi-za JAPANESE ¥¥
(弥生座; 026-232-2311; 503 Daimon-chō; dishes ¥575-4600; lunch & dinner Wed-Mon, closed 2nd Wed each month;) This establishment has been serving *seiro-mushi* (ingredients steamed in a wood-and-bamboo box) for over 150 years. The standard is *monzen seiro-mushi* (local beef and vegetables). For dessert, try *kuri-an cream* (chestnut-paste mousse).

Fujiki-an NOODLES ¥¥
(藤木庵; 026-232-2531; 67 Daimon-chō; mains ¥850-1700; 11am-3pm Wed-Mon;) Fujiki-an has been making fresh *soba* in the north of Nagano Prefecture since 1827, but you wouldn't know it by the clean contemporary lines of this outlet. There's a picture menu. *Seiro-mori soba* (cold *soba* on a bamboo mat) lets the flavour shine; other favourites are tempura, *kinoko* (mushroom) and *nishin* (herring).

★ **Gohonjin Fujiya** FUSION ¥¥¥
(藤屋御本陣; 026-232-1241; 80 Daimon-chō; small plates from ¥700, courses ¥2500-7500; lunch Mon-Fri, dinner nightly;) Until recently this imposing 1923 building was Nagano's most venerable Hotel Fujiya, and had been since 1648. It has since been transformed into the city's most elegant Western restaurant and function centre. The spectacular dining room is called Wisteria and mixes Japanese and art-deco motifs.

Drinking & Nightlife

Shinshū Nagaya Sakaba IZAKAYA
(信州長屋酒場; 026-269-8866; http://marutomisuisan.jpn.com/nagaya-shinsyu; 1418-12 Minami-ishidō-chō; dishes from ¥390) Some English is spoken at this lively *izakaya* with a great menu, selection of sake and an ambience that is straight out of another era.

Izakaya Hanbey IZAKAYA
(居酒屋半兵エ; 026-269-8000; Takahashi Dai 2 Bldg 1F, 1418 Minami-ishidō-chō; items from ¥70; 5pm-late) The Nagano branch of this

THE SNOW MONKEYS OF YUDANAKA

One of Japan's most misrepresented tourist areas, Yudanaka is best known for the snow monkeys of the **Jigokudani Monkey Park** (地獄谷野猿公苑, Jigokudani Yaen-kōen; ☎0269-33-4379; www.jigokudani-yaenkoen.co.jp; 6845 Ōaza-heian; adult/child ¥500/250; ⊙8.30am-5pm Apr-Oct, 9am-4pm Nov-Mar), made famous by the 1992 film *Baraka*, in which wild monkeys appear to bathe in natural onsen pools. The park has been in operation since 1964 and is showing its age, but thousands flock here each year to see the over-photographed troupe of Japanese macaques, who are lured with food from their natural habitat into the man-made pools. They're at times a little savage as they run wildly around you on the concrete paths. The monkeys are a few hundred steps' climb from the car park, which is itself at the end of a 1.6km winding uphill road. The ruse is most convincing in winter when snow hides the industrial debris by the river, although the only way in is via a limited operation shuttle bus on that slippery, windy road.

If you're determined to make the trip, take the Nagano Dentetsu line from Nagano to the Yudanaka terminus (*tokkyū* ¥1260, 45 minutes) then take the bus for Kanbayashi Onsen Guchi and get off at Kanbayashi Onsen (¥230, 15 minutes, eight daily). Walk uphill along the road about 400m until you see the sign reading 'Monkey Park', then begin your rather gruelling uphill walk.

izakaya chain, plastered with Shōwa-era movie posters and advertisements, is particularly cool, as are the inexpensive all-you-can-drink courses. The amusing English menu features such delights as 'raw guts' and 'raw uterus' – both for ¥70: bargain. There's *gyōza, yakitori, okonomiyaki* (pancake) and *kushiage* (grilled skewers) too!

Groovy LIVE MUSIC
(グルービー; ☎026-227-0480; http://nagano groovy.web.fc2.com; 1398 Kitaishido-chō; cover ¥1000-3500; ⊙vary) A music spot popular with jazz lovers for its live shows; check the website for schedule info.

Information

The Nagano Visitor's Guide can be found online at www.nagano-cvb.or.jp/foreign/en.

Nagano Ekimae Post Office (長野駅前郵便局; ☎026-227-0983; 1355-5 Suehiro-chō; ⊙9am-6pm Mon-Sat) Full postal and ATM services.

Nagano Tourist Information Center (長野市観光情報センター; ☎026-226-5626; ⊙9am-6pm) Inside JR Nagano Station, this friendly outfit has good English-language colour maps and guides to Nagano and the surrounding areas.

Getting There & Away

Nagano's station buildings were revamped in preparation for the Hokuriku Shinkansen. For the latest pricing and journey times from this station, check www.hyperdia.com.

Nagano Shinkansen run twice hourly from Tokyo Station (Asama, ¥7680, 1¾ hours). The JR Shinonoi line connects Nagano with Matsumoto (*Shinano tokkyū* ¥2320, 50 minutes; *Chūō futsū* ¥1140, 1¼ hours) and Nagoya (*Shinano tokkyū* ¥6810, three hours).

If you're travelling on *futsū* (local) trains on the JR Chūō line between Nagano, Matsumoto and beyond, don't schedule an onward connection too tightly as trains are occasionally delayed by weather and wild pigs!

Togakushi 戸隠

☎026

Popular with hikers in spring, summer and autumn, and with skiers in the winter, this pretty forested region in the mountains northwest of Nagano city makes a lovely day trip or a peaceful overnight stay. Togakushi has been famed for *soba* for centuries.

Pick up English-language maps from the Nagano Tourist Information Center or download one at www.togakushi-21.jp.

Sights

Togakush-jinja SHINTO SHRINE
(戸隠神社; Map p274; ☎026-254-2001) Comprising three sub-shrines – **Togakushi-Hōkōsha** (宝光社), **Togakushi-Chūsha** (中社) and **Togakushi-Okusha** (奥社) – each a few kilometres apart, Togakushi Shrine honours the 1911m-high Mt Togakushi. Intimate Chūsha is the most easily accessible; one tree here is said to be 700 years old. From Okusha bus stop it's 2km (40 minutes) to Okusha, the innermost shrine, via a

magnificent 500m-long cedar-lined path (杉並木; *suginamiki*) planted in 1612.

From Okusha, avid alpinists can make the strenuous climb to the top of Mt Togakushi. In winter Okusha is inaccessible except for hearty snowshoers, and businesses are closed.

Togakushi Folk Museum & Ninja House MUSEUM
(戸隠民俗館・忍者からくり屋敷, Togakushi Minzoku-kan & Ninja Karakuri Yashiki; ☎026-254-2395; 3688-12 Togakushi; adult/child ¥500/350; ⏲9am-5pm mid-Apr–mid-Nov; 🚌Okusha) Above the Okusha bus stop you'll find this museum housing artefacts from a time when local *yamabushi* (mountain monks) practised what became known as *ninpo* (the art of stealth). The 'Ninja House' is the most fun, cleverly concocted with trick doors, hidden staircases and a room that slopes upwards.

Sleeping & Eating

Togakushi Campground CAMPGROUND ¥
(戸隠キャンプ場; ☎026-254-3581; www.togakusi.com/camp/; 3694 Togakushi; sites from ¥3000, bungalows from ¥5000, cabins from ¥9000, cottages from ¥18,000; ⏲end Apr-end Oct; 🚌Togakushi Kyanpu-jo) This beautiful, sprawling campground a few kilometres from Okusha has its own babbling brook, 350 camp sites, 30 bungalows, 33 cabins and six self-contained cottages. It's best in October when the leaves are turning and it's just about ready to close for the winter. Rental tents are available (¥4000). From Nagano, take the bus to 'Togakushi Kyanpu-jo' stop.

Yokokura Ryokan RYOKAN ¥
(横倉旅館; ☎026-254-2030; 3347 Chūsha; dm with/without 2 meals ¥5065/3045, r per person with meals from ¥7200; P) Yokokura Ryokan is in a thatched-roof building from the early Meiji era, about 150m from the steps up to Chūsha. It's both a hostel and a ryokan, with tatami-room dorms (gender separate) and private rooms. Room-only plans are available.

Okusha no Chaya CAFE ¥
(奥社の茶屋; ☎026-254-2222; 3506 Togakushi; mains from ¥820; ⏲10am-4.30pm late Apr-late Nov) By Okusha bus stop, Okusha no Chaya serves fresh *soba* and other staples behind a glass wall overlooking the forest; delicious soft-serve ice cream comes in seasonal flavours such as tomato, chestnut and wasabi.

Uzuraya Soba NOODLES ¥
(うずら家そば; ☎026-254-2219; 3229 Togakushi; dishes ¥400-1800; ⏲10.30am-4pm Thu-Tue; 🖉) This wonderful noodle shop claims that Togakushi is the home of *soba* and it may be right. It's directly across from the steps to Chūsha shrine. Tempura *soba* is king.

Getting There & Away

Buses depart Nagano hourly (from 7am to 7pm) and arrive at Chūsha-Miyamae bus stop by Chūsha shrine in about an hour (one way/return ¥1250/2250). To Okusha the one way/return fare is ¥1350/2400. The Togakushi Kōgen Free Kippu pass (¥2500) gives unlimited rides on buses to and around Togakushi for three days. Buy tickets inside the Alpico Bus office in front of Nagano Station's Zenkō-ji exit.

Obuse 小布施

☎026 / POP 11,070

This lovely little town northeast of Nagano occupies a big place in Japanese art history and has a handful of interesting museums. The famed *ukiyo-e* (woodblock print) artist Hokusai (1760–1849) worked here during his final years. Obuse is also famed for *kuri* (chestnuts), which you can sample steamed with rice or in ice cream and sweets.

The town is increasingly popular with local day trippers – avoid weekends and holidays.

Sights

Hokusai Museum GALLERY
(北斎館, Hokusai-kan; ☎026-247-5206; 485 Ōaza Obuse; adult/child ¥500/free; ⏲9am-5.30pm Apr-Sep, 9am-4.30pm Oct-Mar) Japan's most famous *ukiyo-e* (woodblock) artist, Hokusai, spent his final years in Obuse. Over 30 of his works are exhibited in this gallery, which recently reopened after extensive renovations. It's a 10-minute well-signposted walk from the Obuse train station.

Takai Kōzan Kinenkan MUSEUM
(高井鴻山記念館; ☎026-247-4049; 805-1 Ōaza Obuse; admission ¥300; ⏲9am-6pm Apr-Sep, 9am-5pm Oct-Mar) Takai Kōzan, Hokusai's friend and patron, was a businessman and an accomplished classical artist specialising in elegant Chinese-style landscapes. His life and work is commemorated in this small museum.

Japanese Lamp & Lighting Museum MUSEUM

(日本のあかり博物館, Nihon no Akari Hakubutsukan; 026-247-5669; 973 Obuse-machi; adult/child ¥510/free; 9am-4.30pm daily May, Aug, Oct & Nov, Thu-Tue rest of yr) Showcasing lighting through Japanese history, including oil lamps and lanterns, this neat museum will flip the switches of design aficionados.

Taikan Bonsai Gallery GALLERY

(盆栽美術館大観, Bonsai Bijutsukan Taikan; 026-247-3000; 10-20 Obuse-machi; adult/child Apr-Nov ¥500/300, Dec-Mar ¥300/free; 9am-5pm) Come here to appreciate the delicate art of bonsai, including some rare species. Admission includes entry to a small gallery of landscapes.

Sleeping & Eating

★**Masuichi Kyakuden** RYOKAN ¥¥¥

(桝一客殿; 026-247-1111; www.kyakuden.jp/english; 815 Obuse-machi; d per person with breakfast from ¥14,400) Delightful, original, stylish and enchanting: all describe this reasonably priced gem in the heart of Obuse. Twelve rooms – huge by Japanese standards – beautifully synergise old and new, and are constructed from antique *kura* storehouses around a chestnut garden. Disappear into the peace, tranquillity and refinement.

Chikufūdō DESSERTS

(竹風堂; 026-247-2569; 973 Obuse-machi; 8am-6pm) Sample chestnut confections at Chikufūdō, established in 1893. *Dorayakisan* (chestnut paste in pancake dumplings) are the standard.

Information

A la Obuse Guide Centre (ア・ラ・小布施ガイドセンター; 026-247-5050; 789-1 Ōaza Obuse; 9am-5pm) You can get maps and hire bikes (¥400 for half a day) here, en route to the museums from the Obuse train station. There's also a cafe, gift store and quaint guesthouse (single from ¥8400, twin from ¥12,600) if you decide to stick around.

Getting There & Away

Obuse is reached via the Nagano Dentetsu (Nagaden) line from Nagano (*tokkyū* ¥750, 26 minutes; *futsū* ¥650, 34 minutes).

Nozawa Onsen 野沢温泉

0269 / POP 3800

This wonderful working village tucked in a picturesque corner of the eastern Japan Alps is both a humming winter ski resort and a year-round onsen town – worth visiting any time of year. Settled as early as the 8th century, it's compact and quaint, though the maze of narrow streets will challenge even the best of drivers. Dotted around the village are free public onsen and a range of excellent accommodation. Outside the busy ski season, it's possible to briefly escape modernity and get a sense of life in an ancient mountain village.

Activities

Onsen water is still wisely used by many villagers for laundry, cooking and heating. There are 13 free onsen (open 6am to 11pm) dotted about the town, each with a history. Our favourite is **Ō-yu**, with its fine wooden building, followed by the scalding-hot **Shin-**

SHINSHŪ CUISINE

Nagano Prefecture is renowned for its food ranging from familiar to downright challenging. Local foods are usually preceded by the region's ancient name, '*Shinshū*' (信州).

ringo (りんご) Apples: we think these are the best in the world. Ubiquitous in autumn.

kuri (栗) Chestnuts, especially in Obuse.

teuchi soba (そば) Handmade buckwheat noodles, eaten either cold (*zaru-soba;* with wasabi and soy-based dipping sauce) or hot (*kake-soba;* in broth).

oyaki (おやき) Wheat buns filled with vegetables, baked or steamed.

wasabi (わさび) Japanese horseradish, grown in bogs particularly in Hotaka. Look out for wasabi cakes and ice cream.

basashi (馬刺し) Raw horse meat.

hachinoko (鉢の子) Bee larvae.

inago (稲子) Crickets.

yu, and the atmospheric old **Kuma-no-te-arai** (Bear's Bathroom). The waters here are hot and full of minerals – if you have silver jewellery, leave it in your room unless you don't mind it temporarily turning black.

Some baths are cordoned off because they are so hot that only hardened locals are permitted to enter them!

★Nozawa Onsen Snow Resort SNOW SPORTS
(Map p274; 野沢温泉スキー場; www.nozawaski.com/winter/en; 1-day lift ticket ¥4800; 8.30am-4.30pm Dec-Apr) Nozawa Onsen Snow Resort, one of Honshū's best, dominates the 'upper' village. The relatively compact resort with 21 lifts is easy to navigate and enjoy with a variety of terrain at all levels. The main base is around the Higake gondola station, where there are beginner and kid-friendly runs.

Snowboarders should try the Karasawa terrain park or the half-pipe at Uenotaira; advanced skiers will enjoy the steep and often mogulled Schneider Course. The lively village is great for after-ski action.

Festivals & Events

Dōsojin Matsuri CULTURAL
(道祖神祭り) Each year on 15 January crowds gather for the famous Dōsojin' Matsuri, a kind of cleansing ritual for men aged 25 and 42, the so-called 'unlucky ages' in Japan. The 42-year-olds' task is to defend a purpose-built two-storey shrine, which they sit upon as it is beseiged by fire at the hands of the 25-year-olds and onlookers.

Copious amounts of sake are imbibed by all, the defenders come down after a while, and the shrine is set ablaze with great enthusiasm. Seriously!

Sleeping

Lodge Nagano INN ¥
(ロッジながの; 050-5532-6026; www.lodgenagano.com; 6846-1 Toyosato; r per person incl breakfast from ¥4500, r in summer from ¥4000;) This popular foreign-run guesthouse attracts lots of Aussie skiers – there's Vegemite in the dining room. It's a friendly, fun place with bunk dorms and tatami rooms, some with private bath.

Address Nozawa APARTMENT ¥¥
(アドレス野沢; 0269-67-0360; www.addressnozawa.com; 9535 Nozawa Onsen; studios from ¥9000; @) This innovative, boutique property opened in 2011. Formerly a traditional inn, new owners sought to create a space that combined Japanese and European design elements and have done just that. Large Western-style rooms with tatami floors feature fresh colours, soft downy beds, bright bathrooms and a full kitchen stocked with breakfast provisions. There's an on-site onsen bath, kids' room, ski storage and plenty of high technology.

★Mura-no-hoteru Sumiyoshi-ya RYOKAN ¥¥¥
(村のホテル住吉屋; 0269-85-2005; http://sumiyosiya.com; 8713 Toyosato; r per person with 2 meals from ¥17,820; @) This wonderful ryokan, the oldest in town, has a wide range of inviting traditional room types, many with private bathrooms and great views. The communal onsen baths with stained-glass windows are dreamy. Limited English is spoken but the friendly staff are committed to excellence in service.

Kiriya Ryokan RYOKAN ¥¥¥
(桐屋旅館; 0269-85-2020; www.kiriya.jp; 8714-2 Nozawa Onsen; r per person with 2 meals from ¥13,500; P) This friendly ryokan has been in the family for generations. The owner's attentive service and excellent English ensure its abiding popularity with overseas guests. All rooms have private toilets. Some have their own baths in addition to the large communal onsen baths. There's a guest laundry and a wonderful garden.

Eating

Pasta di Pasta ITALIAN ¥
(パスタディパスタ; 0269-85-5055; www.pastadipasta.net; 8376-145 Toyosato; dishes ¥500-1200; lunch & dinner, hrs vary seasonally) Freshly cooked pasta, pizza and appetisers are the order of the day in this cosy upstairs eatery. The not-too-creamy *wafū sanshū no kinoko* pasta (three kinds of mushroom) is delicious.

Tōyō Râmen NOODLES ¥
(東洋ラーメン; 0269-85-3363; 9347 Toyosato; lunch & dinner) Chunky *rāmen* bowls and mouth-watering *tezukuri* (handmade) *gyōza* are dished out year round in this 30-seat Chinese eatery.

Drinking & Nightlife

Main Street Bar Foot BAR
(マインストリトバーフット; @) A casual place on the main street, with free internet (with drink purchase) and foozball.

Stay BAR
(ステイ; www.seisenso.com) Stay is a cosy basement bar that's open late and is run by a music-loving Japanese man who has lived abroad.

Information

Nozawa Onsen Visitor Centre (野沢温泉ビジターセンター; ☎0269-85-3155; www.nozawakanko.jp/english; 9780-4 Toyosato; ⌚8.30am-6pm) In the centre of the village. Has English-speaking staff who can assist with accommodation and tour bookings.

Getting There & Away

There are direct buses between JR Nagano Station's east exit and Nozawa Onsen (¥1500, 90 minutes, seven buses per day in winter, three buses per day in summer).

Alternatively, take a JR Iiyama-line train between Nagano and Togari Nozawa Onsen Station (¥760, one hour). Regular buses connect Togari Nozawa Onsen Station and Nozawa Onsen (¥310, 20 minutes, nine per day). The bus station/ticket office is about 200m from the main bus stop, which is directly in the middle of town. This can be a little confusing, but there are staff around to help get people where they need to be.

Shiga Kōgen 志賀高原

☎0269

The site of several events during the 1998 Nagano Olympics and the 2005 Special Olympics World Winter Games, Shiga Kōgen (Map p274) is Japan's largest ski resort and one of the largest in the world: there are 21 linked areas covering 80 runs.

Outside winter the mountain's lakes, ponds and overlooks make it an excellent destination for hikers. If you're not here to hike or ski, there's no compelling reason to visit.

Activities

Shiga Kōgen Ski Area SKIING
(志賀高原スキー場; ☎0269-34-2404; www.shigakogen.gr.jp; 1-day lift ticket ¥5000; ⌚8.30am-4.30pm Dec-Apr) This conglomeration of 21 ski areas is covered by one lift ticket, which gives access to all areas as well as the shuttle bus between various base lodges. Check out www.snowjapan.com for information on each of the individual areas.

There is a huge variety of terrain for all skill levels. In the Hasuike area, in front of the Shiga Kōgen ropeway station, the office has English speakers who can help you navigate the slopes and book accommodation. **Hasuike** ski area is central and is good for learners and families; **Nishitate-yama** has long courses and great views; **Yakebitai-yama** is one of the biggest areas with a huge variety of terrain and panoramic views.

Sleeping & Eating

★**Villa Ichinose** INN ¥¥
(ヴィラ・一の瀬; ☎0269-34-2704; www.villa101.biz/english; 7149 Hirao; r per person from ¥5000; P 📶) With a great location in front of the Ichinose bus stop, English-speaking staff and a friendly atmosphere, this inn is popular with overseas guests. Japanese-style rooms have toilet only and Western-style rooms have their own bathroom. There's wi-fi in the lobby and a 24-hour public bath on the 2nd floor.

Hotel Shirakabasō HOTEL ¥¥¥
(ホテル白樺荘; ☎0269-34-3311; www.shirakaba.co.jp/english; 7148 Hirao; r per person incl 2 meals from ¥12,500; P 📶) Close to the cable-car base station and the Sun Valley ski area is this pleasant little hotel with a variety of rooms and its own indoor and outdoor onsen baths.

Hotel Sunroute Shiga Kōgen HOTEL ¥¥¥
(ホテルサンルート志賀高原; ☎0269-34-2020; www.sunroute.jp/english; r per person incl 2 meals from ¥11,500; P) Popular with a Western crowd, this hotel is a three-minute walk from the Ichinose Diamond ski lift, with great access to other ski areas. The Western-style rooms have en-suite baths; some have mountain views. Staff communicate well in English.

Chalet Shiga INN ¥¥¥
(シャレー志賀; ☎0269-34-2235; www.shigakogen.jp/chalet/en; r per person with 2 meals from ¥10,200; P) Chalet Shiga is both convenient to the slopes and has a popular sports bar on site. Both Western- and Japanese-style rooms are available.

Getting There & Away

Nagaden runs direct buses between JR Nagano Station and Shiga Kōgen (¥1700, 70 minutes), with frequent departures in ski season. You can also take a train from Nagano to Yudanaka and continue to Shiga Kōgen by bus – take a Hase-ike-bound bus and get off at the last stop (¥780, approximately 40 minutes).

Bessho Onsen 別所温泉

0268

With some interesting temples and reputedly excellent waters, this mountain-ringed onsen town is worth passing through if you're nearby, but overall lacks something cohesive as a destination.

Historically, it's been referred to as 'Little Kamakura' for the fact that it served as an administrative centre during the Kamakura period (1185–1333). It was also mentioned in *The Pillow Book* by the Heian-era poetess Sei Shōnagon – no doubt it was infinitely more appealing then. That said, it does have some lovely elements, a National Treasure temple and a stunning example of traditional *onsen ryokan*.

Sights & Activities

There are three central onsen (admission ¥150), each open from 6am to 10pm: **Ō-yu** (大湯) has a small *rotemburo*; **Ishi-yu** (石湯) is famed for its stone bath; and **Daishi-yu** (大師湯), most frequented by the locals, is relatively cool.

Anraku-ji BUDDHIST TEMPLE

(安楽時; 0268-38-2062; adult/child ¥300/100; 8am-5pm Mar-Oct, 8am-4pm Nov-Feb) Of the Sōtō Zen sect, Anraku-ji is the oldest Zen temple in Nagano. Dating from AD 824–34, it's a National Treasure, renowned for its octagonal pagoda. The temple is a 10-minute walk from the Bessho Onsen train station.

Kitamuki Kannon BUDDHIST TEMPLE

(北向観音; 0268-38-2023; 24hr) FREE The grounds of this Tendai temple have some impressive ancient trees and sweeping valley views. Once an awe-inspiring vista, there's no longer anything particularly contemplative about the valley development below. The temple's name comes from the fact that this Kannon image faces north, a counterpart to the south-facing image at Zenkō-ji in Nagano. A 5km hike from here are the temples **Chūzen-ji** and **Zenzan-ji**, which do feel like a real escape.

Sleeping & Eating

★**Ryokan Hanaya** RYOKAN ¥¥¥

(旅館花屋; 0268-38-3131; http://hanaya.naganoken.jp; 169 Bessho Onsen; r per person with 2 meals from ¥11,880; P) Ryokan Hanaya is a step back in time to the Taishō era (1912–1925) – a traditional gem set amongst wonderful manicured Japanese gardens. Spacious tatami rooms open onto the scenery; 14 beautiful, though ageing, rooms each have unique motifs and history. All have their own toilets; some have onsen baths. Expect the most attentive level of service and cuisine (served in your room), though little English is spoken. The *rotemburo* in the garden are blissful.

Uematsu-ya INN ¥¥¥

(上松屋; 0268-38-2300; www.uematsuya.com/english; 1628 Bessho Onsen; r per person with 2 meals from ¥9500; P) Uematsu-ya is a well-kept, good-value inn occupying a nine-storey building atop a hill. Its Japanese- and Western-style rooms all have their own bathrooms. Deluxe rooms are larger, on higher floors and have a private terrace. There are also indoor onsen and lovely *rotemburo*. Some English is spoken.

Information

Bessho Onsen Ryokan Association (別所温泉旅館組合; 0268-38-3510; www.bessho-spa.jp; 1853-3 Bessho Onsen; 9am-5pm) Located at the train station, this small office provides tourist information and can assist with lodging reservations, though some Japanese ability will be handy.

Getting There & Away

Access is by train, via Ueda. From Nagano, take the JR *shinkansen* (Asama, ¥1410, 12 minutes) or the private Shinano Tetsudō line (¥750, 42 minutes). From Tokyo, take the JR *shinkansen* (Asama, ¥5980, 1½ hours). Once at Ueda, change to the private Ueda Dentetsu line to Bessho Onsen (¥570, 28 minutes).

Karuizawa 軽井沢

0267 / POP 19,020

Karuizawa is a picturesque resort town situated in a small, fertile valley beneath the shadow of Mt Asama, one of the most active volcanoes on Honshū. The volcano's last significant eruption was in 2009, from which ashfall was reported as far as Tokyo. Despite the distant potential for volcanic cataclysm, Karuizawa has long been a popular retreat from Tokyo's summer heat. In 1957 a young Emperor Akihito met his future bride, Empress Micihiko, on a tennis court here. Since then, the town has had a reputation as a place for romance. It's a popular spot for weddings.

With easy access from Tokyo and Nagano by *shinkansen,* a range of accommodation, restaurants and a shopping outlet that even anti-shoppers will find hard to resist, Karuizawa makes an excellent day trip or overnight destination. That said, occupancy is generally high and room rates are among the highest in Japan.

Hiring a car will help you enjoy all the area has to offer.

Sights & Activities

Old Karuizawa (旧軽井沢; Kyū Karuizawa), also known as 'Old Karuizawa Ginza', is an attractive main street lined with boutiques, galleries and cafes. Follow Karuizawa-hondōri north from the train station for about 1km, then turn right onto Kyū-karuizawa Main Street – you can't miss it.

Former Mikasa Hotel MUSEUM
(旧三笠ホテル; ☎0267-42-7072; 1339-342 Karuizawa; admission ¥400; ⏲9am-5pm) This property, one of the first Western hotels in Japan, welcomed guests from 1906 to 1970. An exceptional example of elaborate Meiji-era architecture, it's now a museum for you to explore.

Usui Pass Lookout LOOKOUT
(碓氷峠見晴台, Usui Tōge Miharadai) FREE On the border of Gunma and Nagano Prefectures, about 4km northeast of Old Karuizawa, you'll find this observation platform with stunning views of Mt Asama and surrounding mountains. There's no public transport – for directions, ask at the Karuizawa Tourist Association office.

Mt Asama Magma Stone Park PARK
(鬼押出し園, Onioshidashi-en; ☎0267-86-4141; www.princehotels.co.jp/amuse/onioshidashi; 1053 Kanbara, Tsumagoi-mura; adult/child ¥650/450; ⏲8am-4.30pm) In Gunma Prefecture, here's your chance to get up close and personal with Mt Asama – so close, you could almost touch it. Formed in 1783 by Asama's last violent eruption, this 'Hurled by Demons' Park has a surreal landscape of jagged, hardened magma juxtaposed with verdant green fields; volcanic soil is extremely fertile. Enquire at the Karuizawa Tourist Association office for bus fares and times.

'Umi' Museum of Contemporary Art GALLERY
(軽井沢現代美術館, Karuizawa Gendai-bijutsukan; ☎0267-31-5141; http://moca-karuizawa.jp; 2052-2 Nagakura; adult/senior/child ¥1000/800/500; ⏲10am-5pm Fri-Mon Apr-Jun & Oct-Nov, daily Jul-Sep) This light-filled gallery showcases an impressive collection of contemporary works by Japanese artists who have found fame abroad. It's in a lovely forested spot.

Sleeping

APA Hotel Karuizawa Ekimae HOTEL ¥¥
(APAホテル軽井沢駅前; ☎0267-42-0665; www.apahotel.com; 1178-1135 Karuizawa; s/d from ¥8500/14,500; P @) Only two minutes' walk from the north exit of JR Karuizawa Station, this neat business hotel is a great choice if you're here to shop and are looking for value and convenience.

Cottage Inn Log Cabin CABINS ¥¥
(☎0267-45-6007; www.log-cabin.co.jp/en; 3148-1 Naka-Karuizawa; per person s/tw/tr from ¥12,000/6000/5700; P) As the name suggests, these fully self-contained cabins have a rustic appeal in a forested setting, five minutes' walk from Naka-Karuizawa Station. It's a great option for travelling families.

Dormy Club Karuizawa HOTEL ¥¥¥
(ドーミー倶楽部軽井沢; ☎0267-44-3411; www.hotespa.net/hotels/karuizawa; 482 Senriga-taki-naka; s/d from ¥16,800/27,600; P @) This secluded 24-room tourist hotel between Karuizawa and Hoshino Onsen has friendly staff and stylish, well-designed rooms. *Shinkan* (new-wing) rooms have balconies and gorgeous light-filled bathrooms.

Ancient Hotel HOTEL ¥¥¥
(☎0267-42-3611; www.ancient-hotel.com/en/; 2126 Nagakura; d per person incl 2 meals from ¥30,000; P ᯤ) Sleek lines, muted tones and gentle accents allow this beautifully designed hotel to blend gracefully into its natural surroundings. It's a place of understated luxury, relaxation and tranquillity. This attention to detail and aesthetic sensibility flows through to the cuisine, which is presented so beautifully you'll have to eat very slowly indeed.

Hoshino-ya RYOKAN ¥¥¥
(星のや; ☎050-3786-0066; http://global.hoshinoresort.com/hoshinoya_karuizawa; Hoshino Karuizawa; r per person from ¥19,000; ᯤ) This stunning ecoresort in the onsen village of Hoshino, just outside Karuizawa, is anything but basic. Modern rooms and villas incorporate traditional design elements and are positioned around a pond in a beautiful forest setting. All have cypress tubs and are exquisitely furnished around the premise that less is more. Enjoy 24-hour room ser-

vice from the resort's three restaurants. You may have to share the decadent onsen pools with day visitors (¥1200).

Eating

Roast Chicken Kastanie DINER ¥

(カスターニエ; ☎0267-42-3081; 23-2 Karuizawa-higashi; dishes from ¥500; ⏰11am-2pm & 5-9pm Thu-Tue; 📖) For something a little uncommon in Japan, pop in to this original diner for succulent and tender roast chicken dinners, roast vegetables, sausage platters and all manner of Western treats, presented with Japanese attention to detail. Try the roast avocado with teriyaki sauce – yum!

Kawakami-an FUSION ¥¥

(川上案; ☎0267-42-0009; 6-10 Karuizawa; plates from ¥440; ⏰11am-10pm) This is a wonderful place to sample a wide variety of Japanese and Western dishes, including an excellent large serve of *tempura soba* or, for something different, avocado and camembert salad. Or just stop in for coffee and dessert.

Shopping

Karuizawa Prince Shopping Plaza MALL

(軽井沢・プリンスショッピングプラザ; ☎0267-42-5211; www.karuizawa-psp.jp; ⏰10am-7pm) Outside the south exit of JR Karuizawa Station, this gargantuan outlet shopping mall has most of the big names. There's a high likelihood of finding bargains and hard-to-find or only-in-Japan merchandise. Set among acres of grassland, with its own lake, plenty of dining options and great views to Mt Asama, it's easy to lose time here, even if you're not a big shopper. Shopaholics should allocate *plenty* of time.

Information

Karuizawa Tourist Association (軽井沢観光協会, Karuizawa Kankō Kyōkai; ☎0267-45-6050; www.karuizawa-kankokyokai.jp) Grab your English-language publications and maps at this office inside the JR Karuizawa Station building. Some English is spoken.

Getting There & Away

Karuizawa is a stop on the Nagano Shinkansen line, from Nagano (Asama, ¥3160, 33 minutes) or Tokyo (Asama, ¥5390, 70 minutes). There are twice-hourly services in both directions at most times.

Alternatively, the private *Shinano Tetsudō* line from Nagano operates local trains (¥1640, 1¼ hours) and there are five buses per day from Tokyo's Ikebukuro station (¥2600, three hours).

GUNMA PREFECTURE

Mineral baths seem to bubble out of the ground at every turn in the mountainous landscape of Gunma Prefecture (群馬県; Gunma-ken). Its most famous onsen town is Kusatsu, but there are many others that are far less commercial. All that water and mountains adds up to great outdoor activities ranging from skiing in winter to rafting and canyoning in spring and summer.

Takasaki

☎0273 / POP 371,300

Takasaki is a pretty city, famed for *daruma* dolls, pasta and a handful of great day trips. It's an excellent *norikaeru-machi*: place to change trains or stop over if you're travelling between Tōhoku and the Japan Alps. You'll find cheap eats and beds near the train station, which is the branching-out point for the Jōestu (to Niigata) and Hokuriku (to Nagano, Kanazawa and Toyama) Shinkansen lines.

Sights & Activities

★Tomioka Silk Mill HISTORIC BUILDING

(富岡製糸場; ☎0274-64-0005; www.tomioka-silk.jp/hp/en; 1-1 Tomioka, Tomioka; adult/child ¥500/250; ⏰9am-5pm) Listed as a World Heritage Site in 2014, Tomioka Silk Mill provides a wonderful look back into the history of silk production, with excellent English-language narration. Completed in 1872, the mill was once one of the largest producers of silk in the world. Today, its buildings are some of the only Meiji-era government factories preserved in excellent condition.

It's a fascinating day trip from Takasaki. To get here take the Joshin Dentetsu line from Takasaki to Joshu Tomioka station, then walk 10 minutes.

Usui Tōge Railway Village MUSEUM

(碓氷峠鉄道文化村, Usui Tōge Tetsudō Bunka Mura; ☎0273-80-4163; 407-16 Yokokawa; adult/child ¥500/free; ⏰9am-5pm) Kids, adults and trainspotters alike will love, love, love this rail-graveyard-cum-beloved-museum of the holy locomotive, with rolling stock, stations, carriages, simulators and years of Japanese rail history in a wonderful rural setting. Take the train from Takasaki to Yokokawa station (¥500, 30 minutes), the end of the Shinetsu main line.

Byakui Dai-kannon BUDDHIST STATUE
(白衣大観音; ☎0273-22-2269; http://takasakikannon.or.jp; 2710-1 Ishiharamachi; adult/child ¥300/100; ⏲9am-5pm) Built in 1936, this statue of Kannon (Goddess of Mercy) is one of the largest in Japan, standing at 41.8m tall and weighing over 6000 tonnes. You can walk inside the statue up to her shoulder for excellent views. To get here, take the *gururin* bus (¥200, 20 minutes) from JR Takasaki Station to Jigen-in temple.

Haruna Jinja SHINTO SHRINE
(榛名神社; ☎0273-74-9050; www.haruna.or.jp; 849 Harunasan-machi) FREE Believed to be the home of the God of Water, Fire and Agriculture, there has been a shrine of some form here, amongst forested mountains, for almost 1400 years. It is said a visit brings good fortune for love and money. A 700m path to the shirne takes you to a tree that some date as old as 1000 years. Take a bus from JR Takasaki Station (70 minutes) or drive.

Sleeping

APA Hotel Takasaki Ekimae HOTEL ¥¥
(アパホテル高崎駅前; ☎0273-326-3111; www.apahotel.com/hotel/shutoken/01_takasaki-ekimae/english; 232-8 Yashima-chō; s/d from ¥7500/12,000) A short walk from JR Takasaki Station, this business hotel has friendly staff, comfortable beds and oddly large TVs for its small rooms.

Hotel Metropolitan Takasaki HOTEL ¥¥
(ホテルメトロポリタン高崎; ☎0273-235-3311; http://takasaki.metropolitan.jp; 222 Yashima-chō; s/d from ¥7100/12,900) Adjoining JR Takasaki Station this hotel is Takasaki's most stylish and convenient with excellent views from higher floors, and well-appointed rooms.

Eating & Drinking

Harappa Honten PASTA
(はらっぱ本店; ☎0273-22-5445; JR Takasaki Station Bldg 5F, 222 Yashima-chō; pasta from ¥940; ⏲11am-3.30pm & 5-10pm) In the JR Takasaki Station building, you'll find this local pasta favourite serving every pasta dish conceivable, from the ones you've heard of to a bunch of Takasaki originals. The carbonara was particularly naughty but nice.

Red Lion Takasaki PUB
(☎0273-325-1405; 33-2 Tōri-machi; ⏲5pm-2am) A fun pub with a good selection of beers and great bar food, central to JR Takasaki Station.

Information

Takasaki Tourist Information Center (高崎観光案内所; ☎0273-27-2192; www.gtia.jp/kokusai/english; ⏲9am-8pm) Inside JR Takasaki Station, these friendly folks have a bunch of English-language publications and can advise you how to get to sights further afield.

Getting There & Away

Frequent *shinkansen* services race into Takasaki from Tokyo (¥4410, one hour) and onwards to Karuizawa (¥2600, 15 minutes), Nagano (¥4530, 45 minutes), Kanazawa and Toyama on the new Hokuriku extension. For up-to-date fares and travel times, check www.hyperdia.com.

You can also travel from here on the Jōestu line to Niigata (¥7470, 1¼ hours) to begin your explorations of the Tōhoku region.

Kusatsu Onsen

☎0279 / POP 3340

Consistently rated one of Japan's top onsen towns since the Edo period for its pungent, anti-bacterial, emerald-coloured waters, Kusatsu is also a great base for winter skiing, suitable for all levels; see www.kusatsu-kokusai.com/winter.

The downside is that Kusatsu gets busy during holiday periods and there's little in the way of contemporary style that you may find at other resorts, with several run-down accommodations resting on their laurels. The Yugama crater lake at Mt Shirane is currently off limits because of volcanic activity.

Sights & Activities

★ **Sai-no-kawara** ONSEN
(西の河靄天風呂; www.kusatsu.ne.jp/otaki/roten/; 521-2 Ōaza Kusatsu; adult/child ¥500/300; ⏲7am-8pm Apr-Nov, 9am-8pm Dec-Mar) In leafy Sai-no-kawara kōen is this incredibly tranquil 500-sq-metre *rotemburo* separated by a bamboo wall into men's and women's baths, that can easily fit 100 people. It's a 15-minute walk west from Yubatake spring or stop 15 on the Kusatsu Round Bus.

Yubatake SPRING
(湯畑, Hot-Water Field) Yubatake is the main attraction in the town centre and the source of hot-spring water in the area. Its milky blue sulphuric water flows like a waterfall at 4000L per minute and is topped with wooden tanks from which Kusatsu's ryokan fill their baths. The area is atmospherically lit up at night.

Ōtakinoyu ONSEN
(大滝乃湯; www.kusatsu.ne.jp/otaki/otaki; 596-13 Ōaza Kusatsu; adult/child ¥800/400; ⏲9am-9pm) Ōtakinoyu is known for its tubs at a variety of temperatures, some almost impossibly hot; try different ones for an experience known as *awase-yu* (mix-and-match waters). It's a five-minute walk downhill east of Yubatake.

Sleeping & Eating

Ijimaken Ryokan RYOKAN ¥¥
(飯島館; ☎0279-88-3457; r per person with shared bathroom & 2 meals/room only from ¥6690/4630;) Run by friendly owners, this is a good deal despite the mishmash of odd decor; stuffed animals, fake flowers and the like. Go for the upstairs rooms with balcony area and loads of natural light. It's a two-minute walk downhill from the bus terminal with no English sign.

Kusatsu Onsen Boun RYOKAN ¥¥¥
(草津温泉望雲; ☎0279-88-3251; www.hotelboun.com; 433-1 Kusatsu-machi; r per person from ¥14,000;) Beautiful Boun offers traditional decor with elegant touches, featuring tatami rooms and common areas brightened with ikebana artwork, mossy gardens, waterfalls and a bamboo decking atrium. There's a large onsen in a big wooden bathhouse and *rotemburo* with garden outlook. A three-minute walk from Yubatake.

Mikuniya NOODLES ¥
(三国家; 386 Ōaza Kusatsu; dishes from ¥650; ⏲11am-2pm) Fill up on tasty bowls of *sansai soba* (buckwheat noodles with mountain vegetables) at this popular place on the shopping street that runs behind Yubatake towards Sai-no-kawara. Look for the renovated wooden building with the black door curtains, or the line out the front.

Yumehana JAPANESE ¥
(夢花; http://kusatsu-yumehana.com; set menus from ¥980; ⏲10am-10pm) This popular lunch spot is diagonally opposite the bus station and serves filling *teishoku* (set meals) mainly based around tempura and *soba* or udon noodles. There's no English menu but a picture menu makes things easier. It closes on certain days depending on the season.

Entertainment

Yumomi LIVE PERFORMANCE
(Netsu-no-yu; adult/child ¥500/250; ⏲performances 9.30am-4.30pm Apr-Nov, 9.30-10.30am Dec-Mar) Although it's a touristy 30-minute show, this is a unique opportunity to see *yumomi,* in which local women stir the waters to cool them while singing folk songs. There's a chance to do it yourself at most shows (four or five daily from April to November) and the afternoon ones also include local dances. Netsu-no-yu is beside Yubatake.

Information

City Hall Tourist Section (☎0279-88-0001; ⏲8.30am-5.30pm Mon-Fri) Stop in at the City Hall Tourist Section, next to the bus station. Occasionally there's an English speaker on hand and there is a touch screen information terminal in English.

Kusatsu Onsen Ryokan Information Centre (草津温泉旅館案内センター; ☎0279-88-3722; ⏲9am-6pm) The Kusatsu Onsen Ryokan Information Centre, in the white building opposite the bus station, can help with accommodation bookings and has a recommended walking map. For more town info, see www.kusatsu-onsen.ne.jp/foreign/index.html.

Getting There & Away

JR Buses connect Kusatsu Onsen to Naganohara-Kusatsuguchi Station (¥690, 25 minutes, free for JR Pass holders). *Tokkyū* Kusatsu trains run from Ueno to Naganohara-Kusatsuguchi Station (¥4750, 2½ hours) three times a day. Alternatively, take the Jōetsu Shinkansen to Takasaki (¥5280, one hour) and transfer to the JR Agatsuma line (¥1140, 1½ hours).

JR Bus Kantō (☎03-3844-1950; www.jrbuskanto.co.jp) offers direct service to Kusatsu Onsen (¥3290, four hours) from Tokyo's Shinjuku Station's New South exit; reservations required.

Minakami & Takaragawa Onsen

☎0278 / POP 21,000

In the northern region of the Gunma Prefecture is the sprawling onsen town of Minakami. Surrounded by beautiful natural forests and mountains, and cut through by the gushing Tone-gawa (Tone River) it's a mecca for outdoor-adventure sports, hiking and skiing enthusiasts.

The area is also home to Takaragawa Onsen (about 30 minutes away by road), a riverside spa ranked among the nation's best.

Activities

★Takaragawa Onsen ONSEN

(宝川温泉; www.takaragawa.com; admission ¥1500; ⏲9am-5pm) This stunning outdoor onsen offers four large rock pools cascading beside Tone-gawa and shaded by a lush forest riddled with meandering paths, wooden huts, and folk and religious statues. All the pools, bar one for women only, are mixed but modesty towels are available (¥100). Buses run here hourly from Minakami Station (¥1150, 40 minutes).

You can also get off at Takaragawa Iriguchi (¥1050, 30 minutes), from where it's a short walk to the onsen.

The curious junk and gems you'll pass on your way to the baths are decades' worth of gifts from local villagers. Several bears in cages are the only downside here.

Hōshi Onsen Chōjūkan ONSEN

(法師温泉長寿館; www.houshi-onsen.jp; 650 Nagai; admission for day trippers ¥1000; ⏲10.30am-1.30pm Thu-Tue) The main bathhouse at this ryokan is a handsome wooden structure from 1896, with rows of individual bathing pools and a unique style of water bubbling up from below. It's mixed bathing, with an additional modern bathhouse just for women and *rotemburo*.

Tanigawa-dake Ropeway ROPEWAY

(谷川岳ロープウェイ; www.tanigawadake-rw.com; return ¥2060; ⏲8am-5pm) Tanigawa-dake Ropeway takes you via gondola to the peak of Tenjin-daira, from where hiking trips, ranging from a couple of hours to all day, are available from May to November. There's skiing and snowboarding in winter. From Minakami Station, take a 20-minute bus ride to Ropeway-Eki-mae bus stop (¥670, about hourly).

Ask at the Tourist Information Center about a discounted combined ropeway and return bus ticket.

Sleeping

Tenjin Lodge LODGE ¥¥

(天神・ロッジ; ☎0278-25-3540; www.tenjinlodge.com; 220-4 Yubiso; r per person from ¥5000; 📶) Ideally located at the foot of Tanigawa-dake, across from a lovely waterfall and nearby swimming holes, this lodge offers comfy, spacious Japanese- and Western-style rooms; ask for a riverside one. Welcoming hosts offer home-cooked meals (breakfast ¥800, dinner ¥1200) and plenty of local knowledge and adventure-sports options.

★Hōshi Onsen Chōjūkan RYOKAN ¥¥¥

(法師温泉長寿館; ☎0278-66-0005; www.houshi-onsen.jp; 650 Nagai; r per person incl 2 meals from ¥13,800; P) Perfectly rustic and supremely photogenic, this lodging is one of Japan's finest *onsen ryokan*, with a stunning 1896 wooden bathhouse. From Gokan Station (two stops before Minakami) take a bus to Sarugakyō (¥730, 40 minutes) then change to another infrequent bus for Hōshi

ADVENTURE SPORTS IN MINAKAMI

Minakami is Japan's year-round adventure-sports destination, with the exception of November when many of the operators take a break before the start of the winter season.

In the spring melt (between April and June) the Tone-gawa (利根川) is the source of Japan's best white-water activities. Tour operators with English guides include **Canyons** (☎0278-72-2811; www.canyons.jp; rafting half/full day from ¥8000/14,000), **I Love Outdoors** (☎0278-72-1337; www.iloveoutdoors.jp/en; 169-1 Shikanosawa; rafting & canyoning ¥8000, canoeing from ¥6500) and **H2O Guide Services** (☎0278-72 6117; http://h2o-guides.jp; rafting/canyoning tours from ¥8000). During summer, when water levels drop and it gets warmer, each outfitter offers canyoning trips. Both Canyons and I Love Outdoors can arrange packages in their own lodges.

A variety of mountain-biking tours are offered by **MTB Japan** (☎0278-72-1650; www.mtbjapan.com), while the team at Tenjin Lodge offers hiking in the warmer months and off-piste skiing, snowboarding and snowshoeing in the winter. If none of that is heart-thumping enough for you, take a plunge with **Bungy Japan** (☎0278-72 8133; www.bungyjapan.com; 143 Obinata; 1st jump from ¥7500; ⏲10am-4pm Mon-Fri, 9am-5pm Sat & Sun).

Serious climbers will also want to tackle Tanigawa-dake (1977m), Tenjin-dake and Ichino-kura. Tanigawa-dake is suited to experienced climbers only: it has claimed quadruple the number of deaths of Mt Everest. When hiking, exercise caution for bears (see p616).

Onsen (¥590, 15 minutes), or take a taxi (¥3000).

Ōsenkaku RYOKAN ¥¥¥

(汪泉閣; ☎0278-75-2611; www.takaragawa.com; 1899 Fujiwara; s/d with 2 meals & shared bathroom from ¥13,400/20,600;) They hardly come more traditional than this riverside inn split over three buildings, the oldest of which is the 1936 No 1 Annexe – so close to the rushing water it sounds as if you're in it! Slip off your choice of *yukata* (cotton robe) and you can be, as the ryokan has 24-hour use of adjacent Takaragawa Onsen.

The dinner banquet is good and includes bear-meat soup; if you'd prefer not to eat this, ask for no *kuma-jiru* (熊汁) when reserving.

Eating & Drinking

La Biere PIZZA ¥

(ラ・ビエール; ☎0278-72-2959; www.3-sui.com/labiere.html; pizzas from ¥800; 11am-2.30pm & 5-8.30pm Wed-Mon;) Simple and tasty wood-fired pizzas are served in this cute pizzeria with pot plants and umbrella-covered decking out the front. Takeaway is also available. In Minakami Village, a 15-minute walk from the train station.

I Love Outdoors Cafe CAFE ¥¥

(☎0278-72-1337; www.iloveoutdoors.jp/cafe; 169-1 Shikanosawa; mains from ¥1000; 9am-9pm;) It looks like a paint box has exploded in this cafe, a five-minute walk from Minakami Station. It serves burgers and pizza, as well as cold UK craft beers. There are plans for backpacker dorms next door – check the website for details.

Kadoya SOBA ¥¥

(そば処角弥; ☎0278-72-2477; www.kadoya-soba.com; 189-1 Yubiso; soba for 2 from ¥2700; 11am-2.30pm) Expect to queue at this popular 'local' specialising in *hegi soba* (*soba* flavoured with seaweed and served on a special plate, a *hegi*). The noodles are hand-rolled fresh every day and staff close up shop once they sell out. A five-minute walk from Alpine Cafe.

Alpine Cafe CAFE, BAR

(☎0278-72-2811; http://canyons.jp; 45 Yubiso; 4pm-late Thu-Sun Dec-Oct;) Run by the Canyons crew, this popular cafe-bar offers riverside barbecues in the summer, a pool table, plenty of beer, hamburgers and occasional live music. It's also where you'll be put up if you're on one of Canyons' adventure tour packages.

Information

Minakami Onsen Tourist Information Center (水上温泉旅館協同組合; ☎0278-72 2611; www.minakamionsen.com; 8.30am-4.30pm Jun-Oct, 9am-4.30pm Nov-May) Across from Minakami Station, this office has very helpful English-speaking staff, brochures and bus schedules. Also see www.enjoy-minakami.jp.

Getting There & Away

From Ueno, take the Joetsu Shinkansen (¥4200, 50 minutes) or JR Takasaki line (¥1940, two hours) to Takasaki and transfer to the Jōetsu line (¥970, one hour). You can also catch the Joetsu Shinkansen to Jōmō Kōgen from Tokyo/Ueno (¥5390/5180, 1¼ hours), from where buses run to Minakami (¥620, 25 minutes).

Kyoto

☎ 075 / POP 1.47 MILLION

Includes ➡

Best Places to Eat

- ➡ Omen (p337)
- ➡ Kyōgoku Kane-yo (p333)
- ➡ Roan Kikunoi (p334)
- ➡ Kitcho Arashiyama (p338)
- ➡ Yoshikawa (p334)

Best Places to Stay

- ➡ Tawaraya (p323)
- ➡ Capsule Ryokan Kyoto (p321)
- ➡ Hyatt Regency Kyoto (p329)
- ➡ Westin Miyako Kyoto (p330)
- ➡ Dormy Inn Premium Kyoto Ekimae (p322)

Why Go?

For much of its history, Kyoto (京都) *was* Japan. Even today, Kyoto is *the* place to go to see what Japan is all about. Here is where you'll find all those things you associate with the Land of the Rising Sun: ancient temples, colourful shrines and sublime gardens. Indeed, Kyoto is the storehouse of Japan's traditions, and it's even the place where the Japanese go to learn about their own culture.

With 17 Unesco World Heritage Sites, more than 1600 Buddhist temples and over 400 Shintō shrines, Kyoto is one of the world's most culturally rich cities. And traditional architecture is only half the story: there are also dazzling geisha dances, otherworldly kabuki (stylised Japanese theatre) performances, and an incredible range of shops and restaurants. All told, it's fair to say that Kyoto ranks with Paris, London and Rome as one of those cities that everyone should see at least once.

When to Go

Kyoto

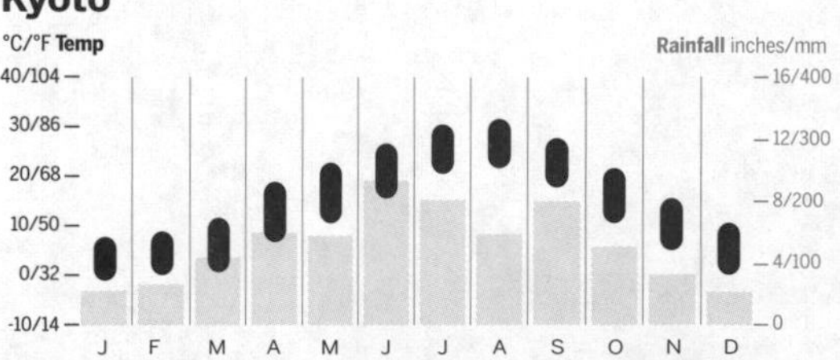

Late Mar–mid-Apr Kyoto in cherry-blossom season is one of the world's great sights.

May–Sep Summer is hot and humid and June is rainy, but summer evenings are magical.

Oct–early Dec Fall foliage makes the perfect backdrop for Kyoto's temples, shrines and gardens.

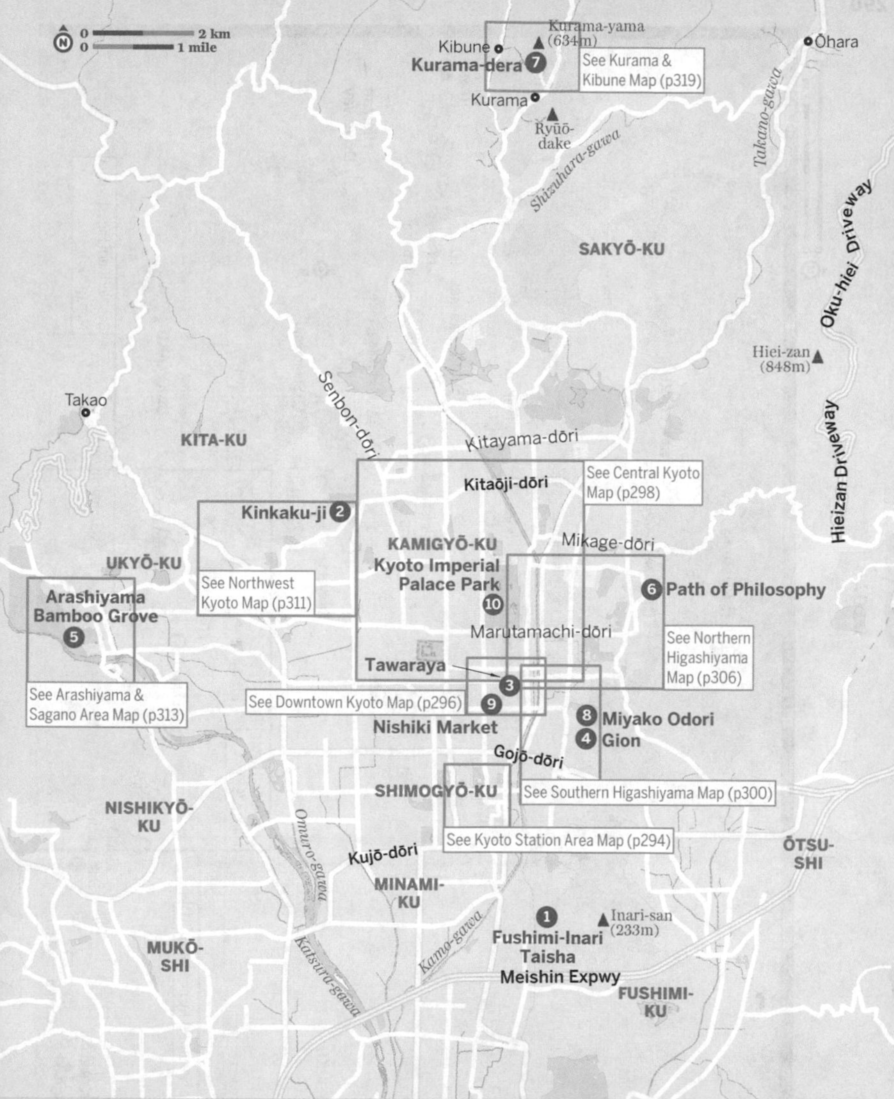

Kyoto Highlights

1 Wandering through arcades of vermilion shrine gates at **Fushimi-Inari Taisha** (p314).

2 Marvelling at the golden hall of **Kinkaku-ji** (p310) floating over its tranquil pond.

3 Spending a night in a traditional Kyoto ryokan, such as **Tawaraya** (p323).

4 Strolling through atmospheric **Gion** (p303).

5 Immersing in the green fantasy world of **Arashiyama Bamboo Grove** (p312).

6 Pondering the meaning of it all as you stroll along the **Path of Philosophy** (p305).

7 Climbing to the mountain temple of **Kurama-dera** (p318).

8 Being charmed by Geisha at **Miyako Odori** (p341).

9 Browsing **Nishiki Market** (p294) for Kyoto specialities.

10 Picnicking in the spacious grounds of **Kyoto Imperial Palace Park** (p297).

Greater Kyoto

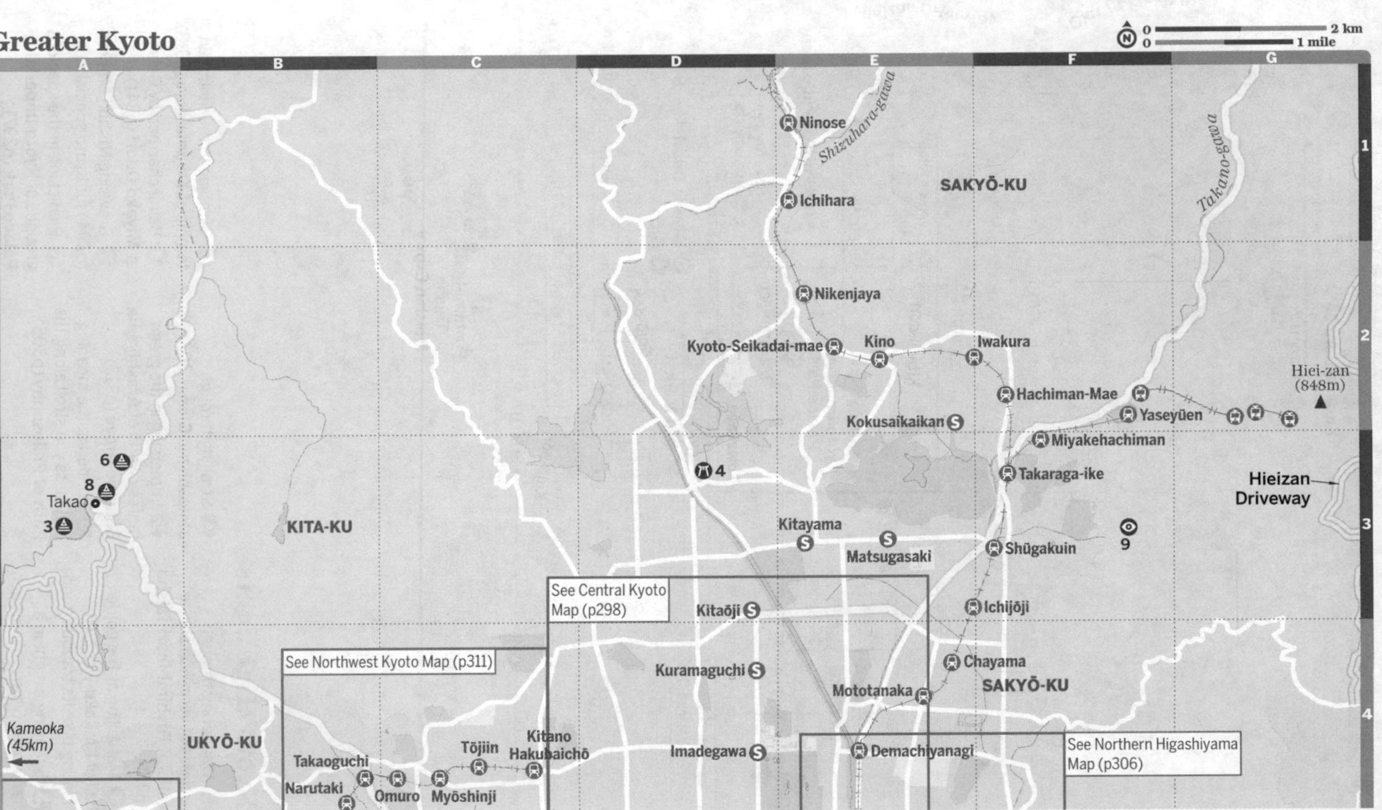

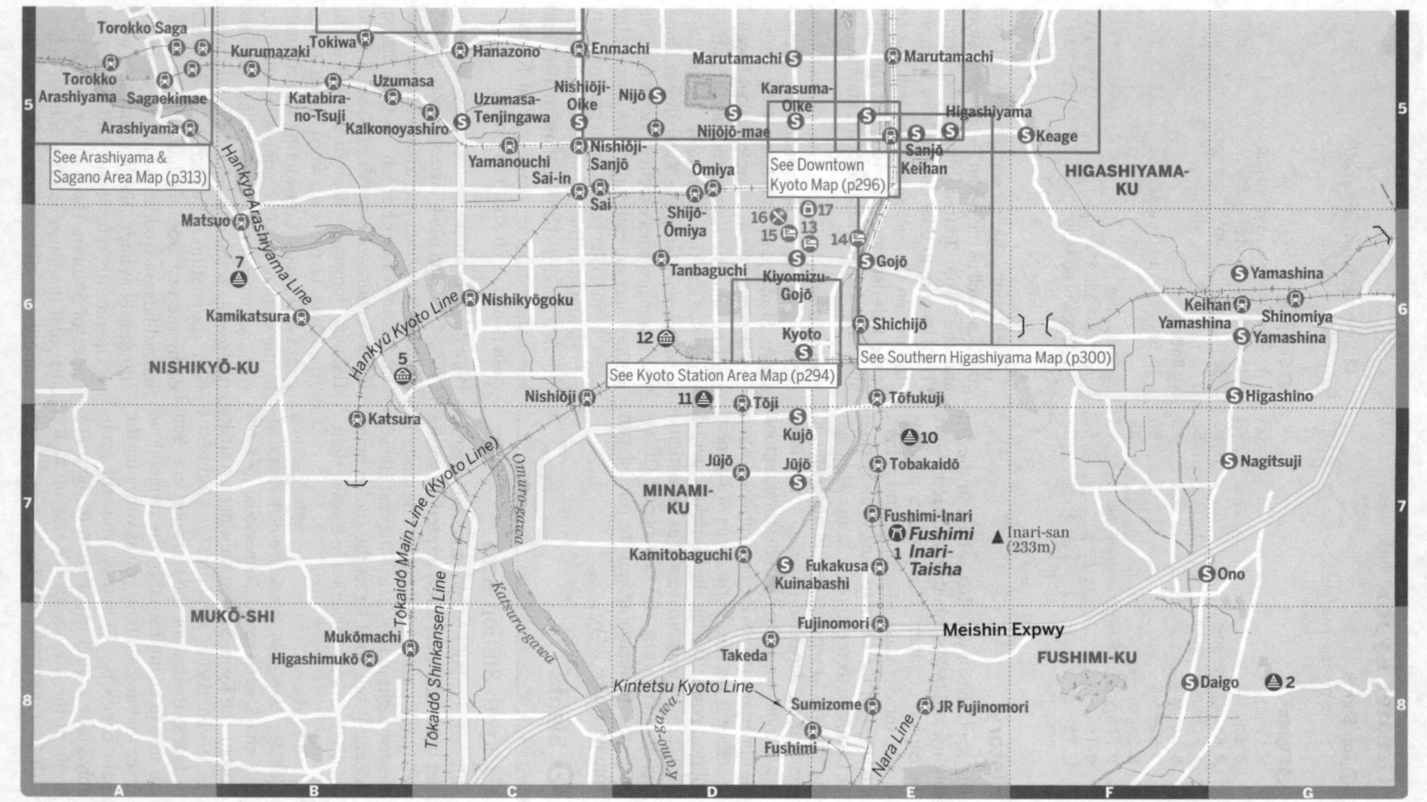

Torokko Saga
Torokko Arashiyama
Sagaekimae
Arashiyama
Kurumazaki
Tokiwa
Katabira-no-Tsuji
Uzumasa
Kaikonoyashiro
Uzumasa-Tenjingawa
Hanazono
Enmachi
Nishiōji-Oike
Nijō
Yamanouchi
Sai-in
Sai
Nishiōji-Sanjō
Marutamachi
Karasuma-Oike
Nijōjō-mae
Ōmiya
Shijō-Ōmiya
Marutamachi
Higashiyama
Sanjō
Keihan
Keage
HIGASHIYAMA-KU
See Arashiyama & Sagano Area Map (p313)
See Downtown Kyoto Map (p296)
Hankyū Arashiyama Line
Matsuo
7
Kamikatsura
Hankyū Kyoto Line
Nishikyōgoku
Tanbaguchi
12
Kiyomizu-Gojō
Gojō
Kyoto
Shichijō
16
17
15
13
14
See Kyoto Station Area Map (p294)
See Southern Higashiyama Map (p300)
NISHIKYŌ-KU
5
Katsura
Nishiōji
11
Tōji
Kujō
Tōfukuji
10
Jūjō
Jūjō
Tobakaidō
MINAMI-KU
Fushimi-Inari
Fushimi Inari-Taisha
1
Inari-san (233m)
Kamitobaguchi
Fukakusa
Kuinabashi
Yamashina
Keihan Yamashina
Shinomiya
Yamashina
Higashino
Nagitsuji
Ono
Omuro-gawa
Katsura-gawa
Tōkaidō Main Line (Kyoto Line)
Tōkaidō Shinkansen Line
MUKŌ-SHI
Mukōmachi
Higashimukō
Fujinomori
Meishin Expwy
Takeda
Kintetsu Kyoto Line
Sumizome
JR Fujinomori
Fushimi
Kamo-gawa
Nara Line
FUSHIMI-KU
Daigo
2
A
B
C
D
E
F
G
5
6
7
8

Greater Kyoto

Top Sights
1 Fushimi Inari-Taisha ... E7

Sights
2 Daigo-ji ... G8
3 Jingo-ji ... A3
4 Kamigamo-jinja ... D3
5 Katsura Rikyū ... B6
6 Kōzan-ji ... A3
7 Saihō-ji ... B6
8 Saimyō-ji ... A3
9 Shūgaku-in Rikyū Imperial Villa ... F3
10 Tōfuku-ji ... E7
11 Tō-ji ... D6
12 Umekōji Steam Locomotive Museum ... D6

Sleeping
13 Citadines Karasuma-Gojō Kyoto ... D6
14 Hotel Sunroute Kyoto ... E6
15 Tōyoko Inn Kyoto Gojō Karasuma ... D6

Eating
16 Shunsai Tempura Arima ... D6

Shopping
Kōbō-san Market ... (see 11)
17 Wagami no Mise ... D6

History

The Kyoto basin was first settled in the 7th century, and by 794 it had become Heian-kyō, the capital of Japan. Like Nara, a previous capital, the city was laid out in a grid pattern modelled on the Chinese Tang-dynasty capital, Chang'an (contemporary Xi'an). Although the city was to serve as capital of Japan and home to the Japanese imperial family from 794 to 1868 (when the Meiji Restoration took the imperial family to the new capital, Tokyo), the city was not always the focus of Japanese political power. During the Kamakura period (1185–1333), Kamakura served as the national capital, and during the Edo period (1600–1867), the Tokugawa shogunate ruled Japan from Edo (now Tokyo).

Sights

Kyoto Station Area

Although most of Kyoto's attractions are further north, there are a few attractions within walking distance of the station. The most impressive sight in this area is the vast Higashi Hongan-ji, but don't forget the station building itself – it's an attraction in its own right.

Kyoto Station NOTABLE BUILDING
(京都駅; Map p294; Karasuma-dōri, Higashishiokōji-chō, Shiokōji-sagaru, Shimogyō-ku; Kyoto Station) The Kyoto Station building is a striking steel-and-glass structure – a kind of futuristic cathedral for the transport age. You are sure to be impressed by the tremendous space that arches above you as you enter the main concourse. Moreover, you will probably enjoy a brief exploration of the many levels of the station, all the way up to the 15th-floor observation level.

The station building contains several food courts, as well as the Isetan Department Store and the Kyoto Tourist Information Center (TIC). Be sure to take the escalator from the 7th floor on the east side of the building up to the 11th-floor glass corridor that runs high above the main concourse of the station.

Kyoto Tower NOTABLE BUILDING
(京都タワー; Map p294; Karasuma-dōri, Shichijō-sagaru, Shimogyō-ku; admission ¥770; 9am-9pm, last entry 8.40pm; Kyoto Station) Located right outside the Karasuma (north) gate of Kyoto Station, this retro tower looks like a rocket perched atop the Kyoto Tower Hotel. The tower provides excellent views in all directions and you can really get a sense of the Kyoto *bonchi* (flat basin). It's a great place to get orientated to the city upon arrival. There are free mounted binoculars to use, and these allow ripping views over to Kiyomizu-dera and as far south as Osaka.

Higashi Hongan-ji BUDDHIST TEMPLE
(東本願寺; Map p294; Karasuma-dōri, Shichijō-agaru, Shimogyō-ku; 5.50am-5.30pm Mar-Oct, 6.20am-4.30pm Nov-Feb; Kyoto Station) FREE A short walk north of Kyoto Station, Higashi Hongan-ji (Eastern Temple of the True Vow) is the last word in all things grand and gaudy. Considering its proximity to the station, the free admission, the awesome structures and the dazzling interiors, this temple is the obvious spot to visit when near the station. The temple is dominated by the vast **Goei-dō** hall, said to be the second-largest wooden structure in Japan, standing 38m high, 76m long and 58m wide.

The recently refurbished hall contains an image of Shinran, the founder of the sect, although the image is often hidden behind sumptuous gilded doors. The adjoining

Amida-dō hall is presently under restoration. This restoration is expected to be completed in December 2015, but the hall is not slated to open until the spring of 2016.

There's a tremendous **coil of rope** made from human hair on display in the passageway. Following the destruction of the temple in the 1880s, a group of female temple devotees donated their locks to make the ropes that hauled the massive timbers used for reconstruction.

Higashi Hongan-ji was established in 1602 by Shogun Tokugawa Ieyasu in a 'divide and conquer' attempt to weaken the power of the enormously popular Jōdo Shin-shū (True Pure Land) school. The temple is now the headquarters of the Ōtani branch of Jōdo Shin-shū.

Nishi Hongan-ji BUDDHIST TEMPLE

(西本願寺; Map p294; Horikawa-dōri, Hanayachō-sagaru, Shimogyō-ku; 6am-5pm Nov-Feb, 5.30am-5.30pm Mar, Apr, Sep & Oct, to 6pm May-Aug; Kyoto Station) FREE A vast temple complex located about 15 minutes' walk northwest of Kyoto Station, Nishi Hongan-ji comprises five buildings that feature some of the finest examples of architecture and artistic achievement from the Azuchi-Momoyama period (1568–1600). The **Goei-dō** (main hall) is a marvellous sight. Another must-see building is the **Daisho-in** hall, which has sumptuous paintings, carvings and metal ornamentation. A small garden and two *nō* (stylised Japanese dance-drama) stages are connected with the hall. The dazzling **Kara-mon** has intricate ornamental carvings.

Tō-ji BUDDHIST TEMPLE

(東寺; Map p290; 1 Kujō-chō, Minami-ku; admission to grounds free, Kondō, Kōdō & Treasure Hall ¥500 each, pagoda, Kondō & Kōdō ¥800; 8.30am-5.30pm, to 4.30pm Sep-Mar; S Karasuma line to Kyoto, Kintetsu Kyoto line to Toji) One of the main sights south of Kyoto Station, Tō-ji is an appealing complex of halls and a fantastic pagoda that makes a fine backdrop for the monthly flea market held on the grounds. The temple was established in 794 by imperial decree to protect the city. In 823 the emperor handed it over to Kūkai (known posthumously as Kōbō Daishi), the founder of the Shingon school of Buddhism.

Umekōji Steam Locomotive Museum MUSEUM

(梅小路蒸気機関車館; Map p290; Kankiji-chō, Shimogyō-ku; adult/child ¥400/100, train ride ¥200/100; 10am-5pm, closed Mon, except 25 Mar-7 Apr & 21 Jul-7 Aug; Kyoto City bus 33, 205 or 208 from Kyoto Station to Umekō-ji Kōen-mae) A hit with steam-train buffs and kids, this excellent museum features 18 vintage steam locomotives (dating from 1914 to 1948) and related displays. It is in the former JR Nijō Station building, which was recently relocated here and thoughtfully reconstructed. You can take a 10-minute ride on one of the smoke-spewing choo-choos (departures at 11am, 1.30pm and 3.30pm).

KYOTO IN...

Two Days

On the morning of your first day, head to **Southern Higashiyama** and visit Kiyomizu-dera (p302), Chion-in (p303) and Maruyama-kōen (p303). If you've still got energy left for the afternoon, continue north after lunch to explore the **Northern Higashiyama** area. Start at Nanzen-ji (p305) and then follow the Path of Philosophy (p305) up to Hōnen-in (p308) and Ginkaku-ji (p308). On the following day, head west to **Arashiyama and Sagano** and explore Tenryū-ji (p312), the Arashiyama Bamboo Grove (p312), Ōkōchi Sansō (p312) and Giō-ji (p314).

Four Days

On your first few days in Kyoto, follow the two-day itinerary above, but consider visiting Southern Higashiyama and Northern Higashiyama on separate days so you can slow down and spend a little more time exploring, stopping into some of the smaller sites en route. After hitting these areas and the **Arashiyama and Sagano** area, take a break from temple-hopping and visit a museum such as the Kyoto National Museum (p301) or a downtown sight such as Nishiki Market (p294). If you like hiking, consider taking a half-day trip up to **Kurama** (p318). Finally, be sure to spend one evening of your stay exploring Gion (p303) and Ponto-chō (p295).

Kyoto Station Area

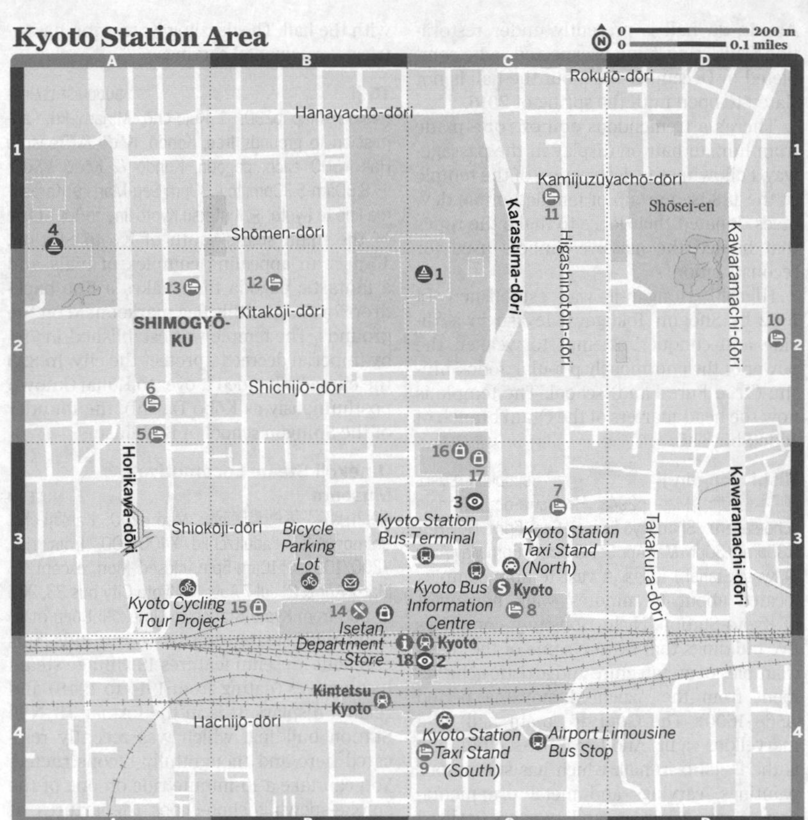

Downtown Kyoto

Downtown Kyoto looks much like any other Japanese city, but there are some excellent attractions to be found here; if you'd like a break from temples and shrines, then the area can be a welcome change. It's also good on a rainy day because of the number of covered arcades and indoor attractions.

Nishiki Market MARKET

(錦市場; Map p296; Nishikikōji-dōri, btwn Teramachi & Takakura, Nakagyō-ku; 9am-5pm; S Karasuma line to Shijō, Hankyū line to Karasuma or Kawaramachi) If you're interested in seeing all the really weird and wonderful foods that go into Kyoto cuisine, wander through Nishiki Market. It's in the centre of town, one block north of (and parallel to) Shijō-dōri, running west off Teramachi shopping arcade. This market is a great place to visit on a rainy day or if you need a break from temple-hopping. The variety of foods on display is staggering, and the frequent cries of *irasshaimase!* (welcome!) are heart-warming.

Museum of Kyoto MUSEUM

(京都文化博物館; Map p296; Takakura-dōri, Sanjō-agaru, Nakagyō-ku; admission ¥500, extra for special exhibitions; 10am-7.30pm, closed Mon; S Karasuma or Tōzai lines to Karasuma-Oike) This museum is worth visiting if a special exhibition is on (the regular exhibits are not particularly interesting and don't have much in the way of English explanations). On the 1st floor, the **Roji Tempō** is a reconstruction of a typical merchant area in Kyoto during the Edo period (this section can be entered free; some of the shops sell souvenirs and serve local dishes). Check the *Kyoto Visitor's Guide* website (www.kyotoguide.com) for upcoming special exhibitions.

Kyoto Station Area

Sights
1 Higashi Hongan-ji C2
2 Kyoto Station C4
3 Kyoto Tower C3
4 Nishi Hongan-ji A1

Sleeping
5 Budget Inn A2
6 Capsule Ryokan Kyoto A2
7 Dormy Inn Premium Kyoto Ekimae C3
8 Hotel Granvia Kyoto C3
9 Ibis Styles Kyoto Station C4
10 K's House Kyoto D2
11 Matsubaya Ryokan C1
12 Ryokan Shimizu B2
13 Tour Club A2

Eating
14 Cube B3
Eat Paradise .... (see 14)
Kyoto Rāmen Kōji .... (see 14)

Shopping
15 Bic Camera B3
16 Kōjitsu Sansō C3
17 Yodobashi Camera C3

Information
18 Kyoto Tourist Information Center B4

Kyoto International Manga Museum MUSEUM
(京都国際マンガミュージアム; Map p296; www.kyotomm.jp/english; Karasuma-dōri, Oike-agaru, Nakagyō-ku; adult/child ¥800/300; 10am-6pm, closed Wed; S Karasuma or Tōzai lines to Karasuma-Oike) This fine museum has a collection of some 300,000 manga (Japanese comic books). Located in an old elementary school building, the museum is the perfect introduction to the art of manga. While most of the manga and displays are in Japanese, the collection of translated works is growing. In addition to the galleries that show both the historical development of manga and original artwork done in manga style, there are beginners' workshops and portrait drawings on weekends.

Visitors with children will appreciate the children's library and the occasional performances of *kami-shibai* (humorous traditional Japanese sliding-picture shows), not to mention the Astroturf lawn where the kids can run free. The museum hosts six-month-long special exhibits yearly: check the website for details.

Ponto-chō NEIGHBOURHOOD
(先斗町; Map p296; Ponto-chō, Nakagyō-ku; S Tōzai line to Sanjo-Keihan or Kyoto-Shiyakusho-mae, Keihan line to Sanjo, Hankyū line to Kawaramachi) There are few streets in Asia that rival this narrow pedestrian-only walkway for atmosphere. Not much to look at by day, the street comes alive by night, with wonderful lanterns, traditional wooden exteriors, and elegant Kyotoites disappearing into the doorways of elite old restaurants and bars.

Central Kyoto

The area we refer to as Central Kyoto includes the Kyoto Imperial Palace Park, Nijō-jō, a couple of important shrines and the Nishijin weaving district. It's flat and easy to explore either by bicycle or on foot.

Kyoto Imperial Palace HISTORIC BUILDING
(京都御所, Kyoto Gosho; Map p298; Kyoto Gosho, Nakagyō-ku; S Karasuma line to Marutamachi or Imadegawa) The Kyoto Imperial Palace, known as the Gosho in Japanese, is a walled complex that sits in the middle of the Kyoto Imperial Palace Park. While no longer the official residence of the Japanese emperor, it's still a grand edifice.

The original imperial palace was built in 794 and was replaced numerous times after

VISITING THE IMPERIAL PALACE

Imperial Household Agency (宮内庁京都事務所; Map p298; 211-1215; 8.45am-noon & 1-5pm Mon-Fri; S Karasuma line to Imadegawa) Permission to visit the Gosho is granted by the Kunaichō, the Imperial Household Agency, which is inside the walled park surrounding the palace, a short walk from Imadegawa Station on the Karasuma line. You have to fill out an application form and show your passport. Children can visit if they are accompanied by adults over 20 years of age (but are forbidden entry to the other three imperial properties of Katsura Rikyū, Sentō Gosho and Shūgaku-in Rikyū).

Downtown Kyoto

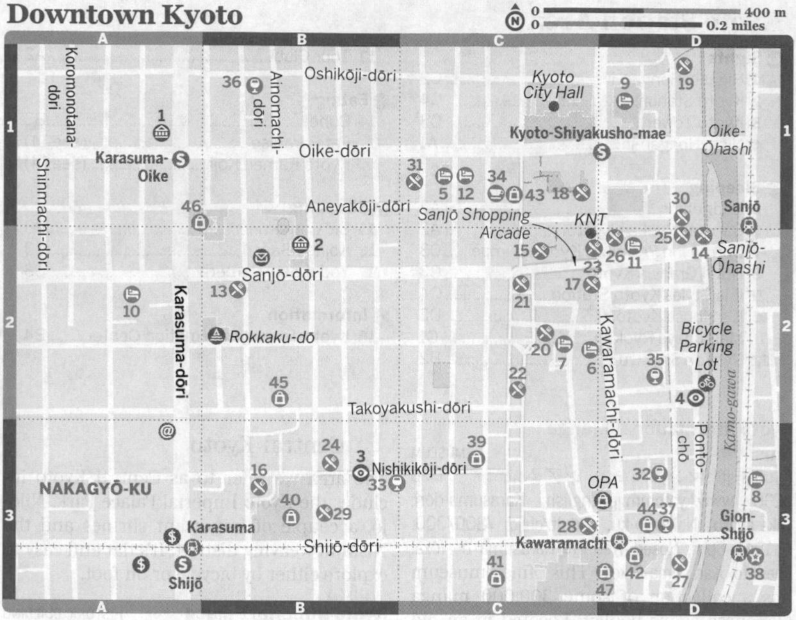

Downtown Kyoto

Sights
1 Kyoto International Manga Museum ... A1
2 Museum of Kyoto ... B2
3 Nishiki Market ... B3
4 Ponto-chō ... D2

Sleeping
5 Hiiragiya Ryokan ... C1
6 Hotel Unizo ... C2
7 Hotel Vista Premio Kyoto ... C2
8 JAM Hostel Kyoto Gion ... D3
9 Kyoto Hotel Ōkura ... D1
10 Mitsui Garden Hotel Kyoto Sanjō ... A2
11 Royal Park Hotel The Kyoto ... D2
12 Tawaraya ... C1
Yoshikawa ... (see 31)

Eating
13 Biotei ... B2
14 Ganko ... D2
15 Honke Tagoto ... C2
16 Ippūdō ... B3
17 Karafuneya Coffee Sanjō Honten ... C2
18 Kerala ... C1
19 Kiyamachi Sakuragawa ... D1
20 Kyōgoku Kane-yo ... C2
21 Mishima-tei ... C2
22 mumokuteki cafe ... C2
23 Musashi Sushi ... C2
24 Nishiki Warai ... B3
25 Ootoya ... D2
26 Rāmen Kairikiya ... D2
27 Roan Kikunoi ... D3
28 Tagoto Honten ... C3
29 Tsukiji Sushisei ... B3
30 Tsukimochiya Naomasa ... D1
31 Yoshikawa ... C1

Drinking & Nightlife
32 A Bar ... D3
33 Iketsuru Kajitsu ... B3
34 Park Café ... C1
35 Rocking Bar ING ... D2
36 Sake Bar Yoramu ... B1
Sama Sama ... (see 30)
37 World Peace Love ... D3

Entertainment
38 Minami-za ... D3

Shopping
39 Aritsugu ... C3
40 Daimaru ... B3
41 Fujii Daimaru Department Store ... C3
42 Kyoto Marui ... D3
43 Kyūkyo-dō ... C1
44 Nijūsan-ya ... D3
45 Rakushikan ... B2
46 Shin-Puh-Kan ... A1
47 Takashimaya ... D3

KYOTO TIPS

In Kyoto there are a few things to keep in mind to make your stay easier and perhaps a little safer:

- Look both ways when exiting a shop or hotel onto a sidewalk, especially if you have young ones in tow: Kyoto is a city of cyclists and there is almost always someone on a bicycle tearing in your direction.
- Bring a pair of slip-on shoes to save you from untying and tying your laces each time you visit a temple.
- Don't take a taxi in the main Higashiyama sightseeing district during cherry-blossom season – the streets will be so crowded that it will be faster to walk or cycle.
- Head for the hills to find the most beautiful sights. Yes, the centre has some great spots, but as a general rule, the closer you get to the mountains, the more attractive the city gets.

destruction by fire. The present building, on a different site and smaller than the original, was constructed in 1855. Enthronement of a new emperor and other state ceremonies are still held here.

The Gosho does not rate highly in comparison with other attractions in Kyoto and you must apply for permission to visit. However, the surrounding Kyoto Imperial Palace Park is open to the public from dawn to dusk and can be visited freely without any application procedure. It's Kyoto's premier green space.

Sentō Gosho Palace

(仙洞御所; Map p298; ☎211-1215; Kyoto Gyōen, Nakagyō-ku; Ⓢ Karasuma line to Marutamachi or Imadegawa) The Sentō Gosho is the second imperial property located within the Kyoto Imperial Palace Park (the other one is the Gosho, which is located about 100m northwest). The structures within this walled compound are not particularly grand, but the magnificent gardens, laid out in 1630 by renowned landscape designer Kobori Enshū, are excellent.

It was originally constructed in 1630 during the reign of Emperor Go-Mizunō as a residence for retired emperors. The palace was repeatedly destroyed by fire and reconstructed; it continued to serve its purpose until a final blaze in 1854, after which it was never rebuilt. Today only two structures, the **Seika-tei** and **Yūshin-tei** teahouses, remain.

Visitors must obtain advance permission from the Imperial Household Agency and be more than 20 years old. One-hour tours (in Japanese) start daily at 11am and 1.30pm. The route takes you past lovely ponds and pathways and, in many ways, a visit here is more enjoyable than a visit to the Gosho, especially if you are a fan of Japanese gardens.

Kyoto Imperial Palace Park

(京都御苑; Map p298; Kyoto gyōen, Nakagyō-ku; ⏲dawn to dusk; Ⓢ Karasuma line to Marutamachi or Imadegawa) FREE The Kyoto Imperial Palace (Kyoto Gosho) and Sentō Gosho are surrounded by the spacious Kyoto Imperial Palace Park, which is planted with a huge variety of flowering trees and open fields. It's perfect for picnics, strolls and just about any sport you can think of. Take some time to visit the pond at the park's southern end, which contains gorgeous carp. The park is most beautiful in the plum- and cherry-blossom seasons (late February and late March, respectively).

Nijō-jō CASTLE

(二条城; Map p298; 541 Nijōjō-chō, Nijō-dōri, Horikawa nishi-iru, Nakagyō-ku; admission ¥600; ⏲8.45am-5pm, closed Tue in Dec, Jan, Jul & Aug; Ⓢ Tōzai line to Nijō-jō-mae) The military might of Japan's great warlord generals, the Tokugawa shoguns, is amply demonstrated by the imposing stone walls and ramparts of their great castle, Nijō-jō, which dominates a large part of northwest Kyoto. Hidden behind these you will find a superb palace surrounded by beautiful gardens. As you might expect, a sight of this grandeur attracts a lot of crowds, so it's best to visit just after opening or shortly before closing.

This castle was built in 1603 as the official Kyoto residence of the first Tokugawa shogun, Ieyasu. The ostentatious style of its construction was intended as a demonstration of Ieyasu's prestige and also to signal the demise of the emperor's power. As a safeguard against treachery, Ieyasu had the interior fitted with 'nightingale' floors, as well as concealed chambers where bodyguards could keep watch.

Central Kyoto

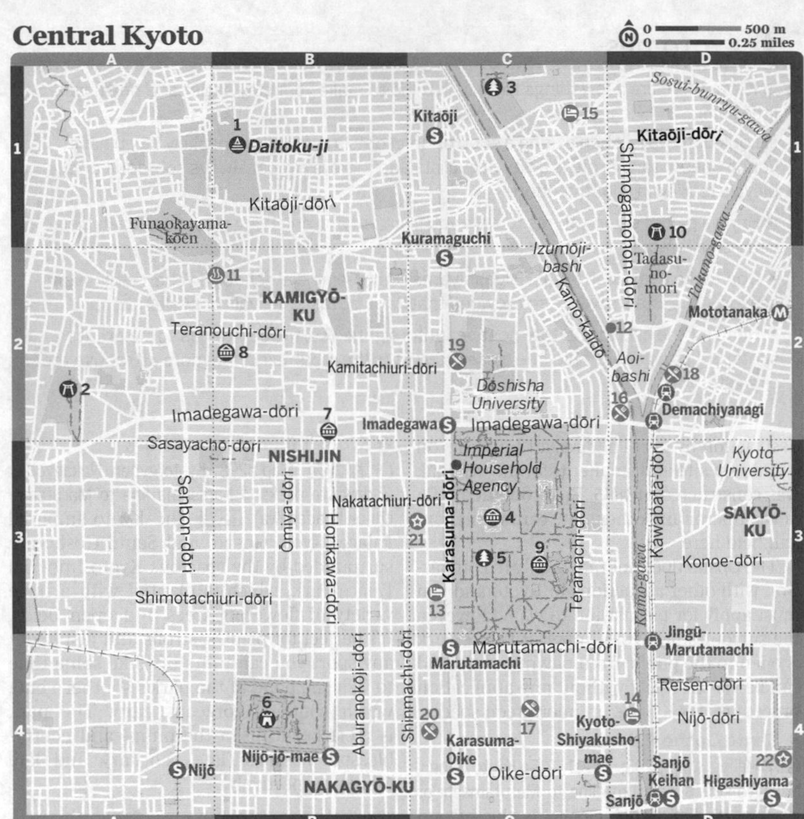

After passing through the grand **Karamon gate**, you enter **Ninomaru** palace, which is divided into five buildings with numerous chambers. The **Ōhiroma Yonno-Ma** (Fourth Chamber) has spectacular screen paintings. Don't miss the excellent **Ninomaru Palace Garden**, which was designed by the tea master and landscape architect Kobori Enshū.

★Daitoku-ji BUDDHIST TEMPLE

(大徳寺; Map p298; 53 Daitokuji-chō, Murasakino, Kita-ku; ⏲dawn-dusk; Ⓢ Karasuma line to Kitaōji) FREE Daitoku-ji is a separate world within Kyoto – a world of Zen temples, perfectly raked gardens and wandering lanes. It's one of the most rewarding destinations in this part of the city, particularly for those with an interest in Japanese gardens. The temple serves as the headquarters of the Rinzai Daitoku-ji school of Zen Buddhism. The highlights among the 24 subtemples include **Daisen-in**, **Kōtō-in**, **Ōbai-in**, **Ryōgen-in** and **Zuihō-in**.

Nishijin NEIGHBOURHOOD

(西陣; Nishijin, Kamigyō-ku; 🚌 Kyoto City bus 9 to Horikawa-Imadegawa) Nishijin is Kyoto's traditional textile centre, the source of all those dazzling kimono fabrics and *obi* (kimono sashes) that you see being paraded about town. The area is famous for Nishijin-ori (Nishijin weaving). There are quite a few *machiya* (traditional Japanese town houses) in this district, so it's a good place simply to wander.

Nishijin Textile Center MUSEUM

(西陣織会館; Map p298; ☎451-9231; Horikawa-dōri, Imadegawa-sagaru, Kamigyō-ku; ⏲9am-5pm; 🚌 Kyoto City bus 9 to Horikawa-Imadegawa) FREE In the heart of the Nishijin textile district, this is worth a peek before starting a walk around the area. There are also displays of completed fabrics and kimonos, as well as

Central Kyoto

Top Sights
1 Daitoku-ji......B1

Sights
2 Kitano Tenman-gū......A2
3 Kyoto Botanical Gardens......C1
4 Kyoto Imperial Palace......C3
5 Kyoto Imperial Palace Park......C3
6 Nijō-jō......B4
7 Nishijin Textile Center......B2
8 Orinasu-kan......B2
9 Sentō Gosho Palace......C3
10 Shimogamo-jinja......D1

Activities, Courses & Tours
11 Funaoka Onsen......B2
12 Haru Cooking Class......D2

Sleeping
13 Palace Side Hotel......C3
14 Ritz-Carlton Kyoto......D4
15 Ryokan Rakuchō......C1

Eating
16 Bon Bon Café......D2
17 Café Bibliotec Hello!......C4
18 Falafel Garden......D2
19 Papa Jon's......C2
20 Saryo Zen Cafe......C4

Entertainment
21 Club Ōkitsu Kyoto......C3
22 Kyoto Kanze Kaikan Nō Theatre......D4

Shopping
Tenjin-san Market......(see 2)

weaving demonstrations and occasional kimono fashion shows. Unfortunately, it's often overrun by large tour groups. It's on the southwest corner of the Horikawa-dōri and Imadegawa-dōri intersection.

Orinasu-kan MUSEUM
(織成館; Map p298; 693 Daikoku-chō, Kamigyō-ku; adult/child ¥500/350; 10am-4pm, closed Mon; Kyoto City bus 9 to Horikawa-Imadegawa) This atmospheric, and usually quiet, museum, housed in a Nishijin weaving factory, has impressive exhibits of Nishijin textiles. The **Susamei-sha** building across the street is also open to the public and worth a look.

Shimogamo-jinja SHINTO SHRINE
(下鴨神社; Map p298; 59 Izumigawa-chō, Shimogamo, Sakyō-ku; 6.30am-5pm; Kyoto City bus 205 to Shimogamo-jinja-mae, Keihan line to Demachiyanagi) FREE This shrine, dating from the 8th century, is a Unesco World Heritage Site. It is nestled in the fork of the Kamo-gawa and Takano-gawa rivers, and is approached along a shady path through the lovely Tadasu-no-mori. This wooded area is said to be a place where lies cannot be concealed and is considered a prime location to sort out disputes. The trees here are mostly broadleaf (a rarity in Kyoto) and they are gorgeous in the springtime.

Kyoto Botanical Gardens PARK
(京都府立植物園; Map p298; Shimogamohangi-chō, Sakyō-ku; gardens adult ¥200, child free-¥150, greenhouse adult ¥200, child free-¥150; 9am-5pm, greenhouse 10am-4pm, closed 28 Dec-4 Jan; S Karasuma line to Kitayama) The Kyoto Botanical Gardens occupy 240,000 sq metres and feature 12,000 plants, flowers and trees. It is pleasant to stroll through the rose, cherry and herb gardens or see the rows of camphor trees and the large tropical **greenhouse**. This is a good spot for a picnic. It's also a great spot for a *hanami* (cherry-blossom viewing) party, and the blossoms here tend to hold on a little longer than those elsewhere in the city.

Kamigamo-jinja SHINTO SHRINE
(上賀茂神社; Map p290; 339 Motoyama, Kamigamo, Kita-ku; 6am-5pm; Kyoto City bus 9 to Kamigamo-misonobashi) FREE Kamigamo-jinja is one of Japan's oldest shrines and predates the founding of Kyoto. Established in 679, it is dedicated to Raijin, the god of thunder, and is one of Kyoto's 17 Unesco World Heritage Sites. The present buildings (more than 40 in all), including the impressive **Haiden** hall, are exact reproductions of the originals, dating from the 17th to 19th centuries.

Southern Higashiyama

The Higashiyama (東山) district, which runs along the base of the Higashiyama mountains (Eastern Mountains), is the main sightseeing district in Kyoto, and it should be at the top of your Kyoto itinerary. It is thick with impressive sights: fine temples, shrines, gardens, museums, traditional neighbourhoods and parks.

Sanjūsangen-dō Temple BUDDHIST TEMPLE
(三十三間堂; Map p300; 657 Sanjūsangendōmawari-chō, Higashiyama-ku; admission ¥600; 8am-4.30pm Apr-Oct, 9am-3.30pm Nov-Mar; Kyoto

Southern Higashiyama

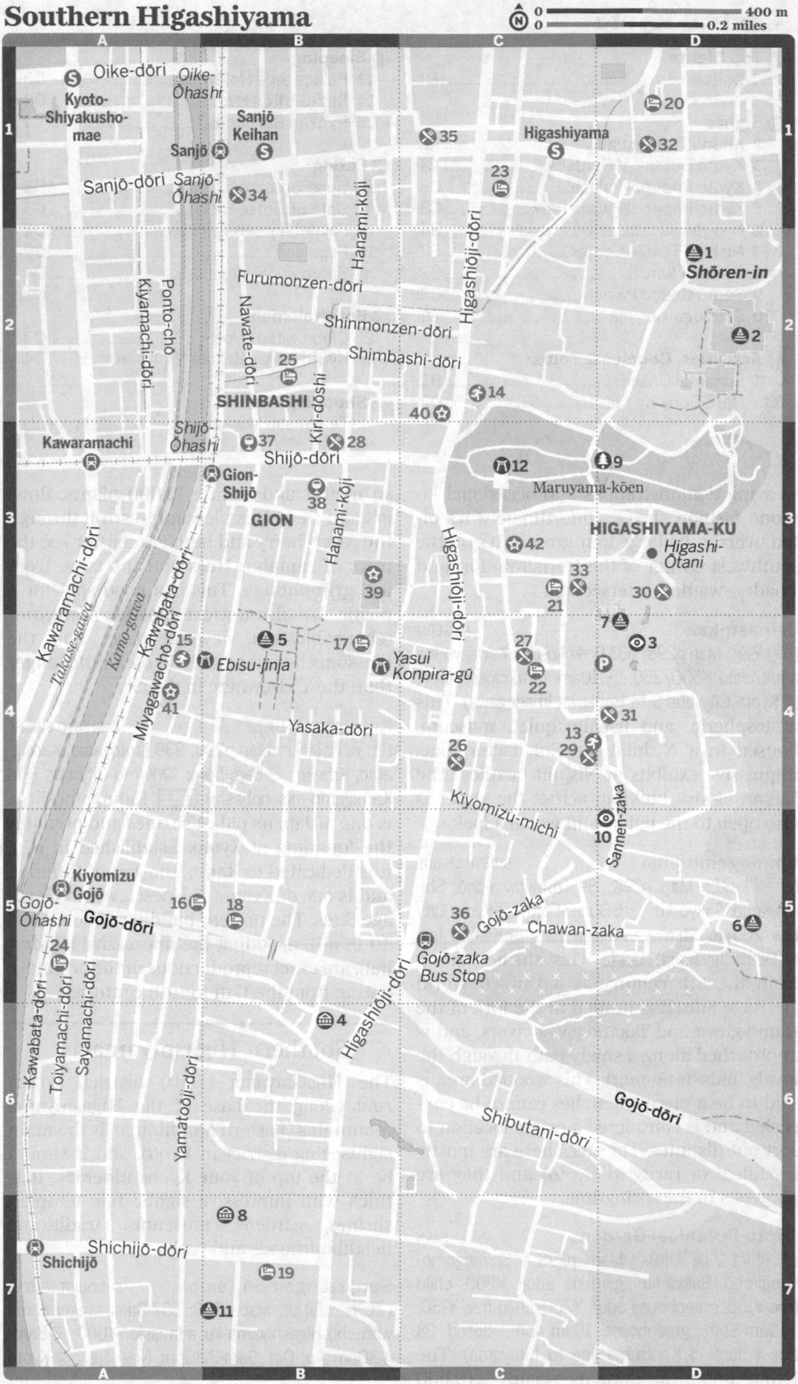

0 — 400 m
0 — 0.2 miles

A B C D
1 2 3 4 5 6 7

Oike-dōri
Oike-Ōhashi
Kyoto-Shiyakusho-mae
Sanjō Keihan
Sanjō
Sanjō-dōri
Sanjō-Ōhashi
34
35
Higashiyama
20
32
23
Hanami-kōji
Higashiōji-dōri
1
Shōren-in
Furumonzen-dōri
Ponto-chō
Kiyamachi-dōri
Nawate-dōri
Shinmonzen-dōri
2
Shimbashi-dōri
25
Kiri-dōshi
SHINBASHI
14
40
Kawaramachi
Shijō-Ōhashi
37
28
Shijō-dōri
12
9
Gion-Shijō
38
Maruyama-kōen
GION
Hanami-kōji
Kawaramachi-dōri
HIGASHIYAMA-KU
Higashi-Ōtani
42
Kawabata-dōri
33
39
21
30
Kamo-gawa
Miyagawachō-dōri
Takase-gawa
Higashiōji-dōri
7
15
5
17
27
3
Ebisu-jinja
Yasui Konpira-gū
22
41
Yasaka-dōri
31
13
26
29
Kiyomizu-michi
Sannen-zaka
10
Kiyomizu Gojō
Gojō-Ōhashi
Gojō-dōri
16
18
36
Gojō-zaka
Chawan-zaka
6
24
Gojō-zaka Bus Stop
Higashiōji-dōri
4
Kawabata-dōri
Toiyamachi-dōri
Sayamachi-dōri
Yamatoōji-dōri
Gojō-dōri
Shibutani-dōri
8
Shichijō
Shichijō-dōri
19
11

A B C D

Southern Higashiyama

Top Sights
1 Shōren-in D2

Sights
2 Chion-in D2
3 Gion D4
4 Kawai Kanjirō Memorial Hall B6
5 Kennin-ji B4
6 Kiyomizu-dera D5
7 Kōdai-ji D4
8 Kyoto National Museum B7
9 Maruyama-kōen D3
10 Ninen-zaka & Sannen-zaka D5
11 Sanjūsangen-dō Temple B7
12 Yasaka-jinja C3

Activities, Courses & Tours
13 Camellia Tea Experience C4
14 En C2
15 Maika A4

Sleeping
16 Gion Apartments A5
Gion Hatanaka .... (see 42)
17 Gion House B4
18 Gojō Guest House B5
19 Hyatt Regency Kyoto B7
20 Koto Inn D1
21 Motonago C3
22 Ryokan Uemura C4
23 Sakara Kyoto C1
24 Seikōrō A5
25 Shiraume Ryokan B2

Eating
26 Café 3032 .... C4
27 Hisago C4
28 Kagizen Yoshifusa B3
29 Kasagi-ya C4
30 Kikunoi D3
31 Omen Kodai-ji D4
32 Oshokujidokoro Asuka D1
33 Rakushō C3
34 Rāmen Santōka B1
35 Ryūmon C1
36 Sobadokoro Shibazaki C5

Drinking & Nightlife
37 Gael Irish Pub B3
38 Gion Finlandia Bar B3

Entertainment
39 Gion Corner B3
40 Gion Odori C2
41 Kyō Odori A4
42 Kyoto Cuisine & Maiko Evening C3
Miyako Odori .... (see 39)

City bus 206 or 208 to Sanjūsangen-dō-mae, Ⓢ Keihan line to Shichijō) This superb temple's name refers to the 33 *sanjūsan* (bays) between the pillars of this long, narrow building. The building houses 1001 wooden statues of Kannon (the Buddhist goddess of mercy); the chief image, the 1000-armed Senjū-Kannon, was carved by the celebrated sculptor Tankei in 1254. It is flanked by 500 smaller Kannon images, neatly lined in rows. The visual effect is stunning, making this a must-see in Southern Higashiyama and a good starting point for exploration of the area.

Kyoto National Museum MUSEUM

(京都国立博物館; Map p300; www.kyohaku.go.jp; 527 Chaya-machi, Higashiyama-ku; adult/student ¥500/250; ⌚9.30am-6pm, to 8pm Fri, closed Mon; 🚌Kyoto City bus 206 or 208 to Sanjūsangen-dō-mae, 🚆Keihan line to Shichijō) The Kyoto National Museum is Kyoto's premier art museum and plays host to the highest level exhibitions in the city. It was founded in 1895 as an imperial repository for art and treasures from local temples and shrines. In the original **main hall** there are 17 rooms with displays of over 1000 artworks, historical artefacts and handicrafts. The new **Heisei Chishinkan**, designed by Taniguchi Yoshio and opened in 2014, is a brilliant modern counterpoint to the original building.

While the permanent collection is worth a visit, the special exhibitions are the real highlights. Check the Tourist Information Center (TIC) or the Kyoto Visitor's Guide website to see what's on while you're in town.

Kawai Kanjirō Memorial Hall MUSEUM

(河井寛治郎記念館; Map p300; 569 Kanei-chō, Gojō-zaka, Higashiyama-ku; admission ¥900; ⌚10am-5pm, closed Mon & around 11-20 Aug & 24 Dec-7 Jan, dates vary each year; 🚌Kyoto City bus 206 or 207 to Umamachi) This small memorial hall is one of Kyoto's most commonly overlooked little gems. The hall was the home and workshop of one of Japan's most famous potters, Kawai Kanjirō (1890–1966). The 1937 house is built in rural style and contains examples of Kanjirō's work, his collection of folk art and ceramics, his workshop and a fascinating *nobori-gama* (stepped kiln). The museum is near the intersection of Gojō-dōri and Higashiōji-dōri.

Kiyomizu-dera BUDDHIST TEMPLE

(清水寺; Map p300; 1-294 Kiyomizu, Higashiyama-ku; admission ¥300; ⌚6am-6pm; 🚌Kyoto City bus 206 to Kiyōmizu-michi or Gojō-zaka, 🚆Keihan line to Kiyomizu-Gojō) A buzzing hive of activity perched on a hill overlooking the basin of Kyoto, Kiyomizu-dera is one of Kyoto's most popular and most enjoyable temples. It may not be the tranquil refuge that many associate with Buddhist temples, but it represents the popular expression of faith in Japan. For those with children in tow, this temple is sure to delight as there are plenty of things to do here.

This ancient temple was first built in 798, but the present buildings are reconstructions dating from 1633. As an affiliate of the Hossō school of Buddhism, which originated in Nara, it has successfully survived the many intrigues of local Kyoto schools of Buddhism through the centuries and is now one of the most famous landmarks of the city (which means it can get very crowded during spring and autumn).

The **Hondō** (Main Hall) has a huge verandah that is supported by pillars and juts out over the hillside. Just below this hall is the waterfall **Otowa-no-taki**, where visitors drink sacred waters believed to bestow health and longevity. Dotted around the precincts are other halls and shrines. At **Jishu-jinja**, the shrine up the steps above the main hall, visitors try to ensure success in love by closing their eyes and walking about 18m between a pair of stones – if you miss the stone, your desire for love won't be fulfilled! Note that you can ask someone to guide you, but if you do, you'll need someone's assistance to find your true love.

Before you enter the actual temple precincts, check out the **Tainai-meguri**, the entrance to which is just to the left (north) of the pagoda that is located in front of the main entrance to the temple (there is no English sign). We won't tell you too much about it as it will ruin the experience. Suffice to say that by entering the Tainai-meguri, you are symbolically entering the womb of a female bodhisattva. When you get to the rock in the darkness, spin it in either direction to make a wish.

The steep approach to the temple is known as **Chawan-zaka** (Teapot Lane) and is lined with shops selling Kyoto handicrafts, local snacks and souvenirs.

Check at the Tourist Information Center (TIC) for the scheduling of special night-time illuminations of the temple held in the spring and autumn.

KYOTO'S BEST TEMPLES & SHRINES

Nanzen-ji (p305) The one temple that has it all: expansive grounds, a fine *kare-sansui* (dry landscape) garden, intimate subtemples and soaring halls.

Shōren-in (p303) A rarely visited retreat on the main Southern Higashiyama tourist route with a superb garden.

Hōnen-in (p308) A pocket sanctuary hidden above the Path of Philosophy.

Daitoku-ji (p298) A walled-in world of Zen temples that will delight fans of Japanese gardens.

Kurama-dera (p318) A mountaintop temple in the hills north of Kyoto that really feels close to the gods.

Fushimi Inari-Taisha (p314) A mountain covered with hypnotic arcades of *torii* (Shinto shrine gates) – one of Japan's most distinctive sights.

Shimogamo-jinja (p299) A historic and lovely shrine approached by a soothing tree-lined arcade.

Ninen-zaka & Sannen-zaka NEIGHBOURHOOD

(二年坂・三年坂; Map p300; Higashiyama-ku; 🚌Kyoto City bus 206 to Kiyomizu-michi or Gojō-zaka, 🚆Keihan line to Kiyomizu-Gojō) Just downhill from and slightly to the north of Kiyomizu-dera is one of Kyoto's loveliest restored neighbourhoods, the Ninen-zaka–Sannen-zaka area. The name refers to the two main streets of the area: Ninen-zaka and Sannen-zaka, literally 'Two-Year Hill' and 'Three-Year Hill' (the years referring to the ancient imperial years when they were first laid out). These two charming streets are lined with old wooden houses, traditional shops and restaurants.

If you fancy a break, there are many teahouses and cafes along these lanes.

Kōdai-ji BUDDHIST TEMPLE

(高台寺; Map p300; 526 Shimokawara-chō, Kōdai-ji, Higashiyama-ku; admission ¥600; ⌚9am-5pm; 🚌Kyoto City bus 206 to Yasui, Ⓢ Tōzai line to Higashiyama) This exquisite temple was founded in 1605 by Kita-no-Mandokoro in memory of her late husband, Toyotomi Hideyoshi. The extensive grounds include gardens designed by the famed landscape architect Kobori Enshū, and teahouses designed by the renowned master of the tea ceremony, Sen no Rikyū.

The temple holds three annual special night-time illuminations, when the gardens are lit by multicoloured spotlights. The illuminations are held from mid-March to early May, 1 to 18 August and late October to early December.

Maruyama-kōen PARK

(円山公園; Map p300; Maruyama-chō, Higashiyama-ku; S Tōzai line to Higashiyama) Maruyama-kōen is a favourite of locals and visitors alike. This park is the place to come to escape the bustle of the city centre and amble around gardens, ponds, souvenir shops and restaurants. Peaceful paths meander through the trees and carp glide through the waters of a small pond in the park's centre.

Yasaka-jinja SHINTO SHRINE

(八坂神社; Map p300; 625 Gion-machi, Kita-gawa, Higashiyama-ku; 24hr; S Tōzai line to Higashiyama) FREE This colourful and spacious shrine is considered the guardian shrine of the Gion entertainment district. It's a bustling, colourful place that is well worth a visit while exploring Southern Higashiyama; it can easily be paired with Maruyama-kōen, the park just up the hill.

Chion-in BUDDHIST TEMPLE

(知恩院; Map p300; 400 Rinka-chō, Higashiyama-ku; admission inner buildings & garden ¥500, grounds free; 9am-4.30pm; S Tōzai line to Higashiyama) A collection of soaring buildings and spacious courtyards, Chion-in serves as the headquarters of the Jōdo sect, the largest sect of Buddhism in Japan. It's the most popular pilgrimage temple in Kyoto and it's always a hive of activity. For visitors with a taste for the grand, this temple is sure to satisfy.

Chion-in was established in 1234 on the site where Hōnen, one of the most famous figures in Japanese Buddhism, taught his brand of Buddhism (Jōdo, or Pure Land, Buddhism) and eventually fasted to death.

The oldest of the present buildings date to the 17th century. The two-storey **San-mon**, a Buddhist temple gate at the main entrance, is the largest temple gate in Japan and prepares you for the massive scale of the temple. The immense main hall contains an image of Hōnen. It's connected to another hall, the **Dai Hōjō**, by a 'nightingale' floor (that sings and squeaks at every move, making it difficult for intruders to move about quietly).

Up a flight of steps southeast of the main hall is the temple's **giant bell**, which was cast in 1633 and weighs 70 tonnes. It is the largest bell in Japan. The bell is rung by the temple's monks 108 times on New Year's Eve each year.

★ **Shōren-in** BUDDHIST TEMPLE

(青蓮院; Map p300; 69-1 Sanjōbō-chō, Awataguchi, Higashiyama-ku; admission ¥500; 9am-5pm; S Tōzai line to Higashiyama) This temple is hard to miss, with its giant camphor trees growing just outside the walls. Fortunately, most tourists march right on past, heading to the area's more famous temples. That is their loss, because this intimate little sanctuary contains a superb landscape garden, that you can enjoy while drinking a cup of green tea (ask at the reception office).

Gion NEIGHBOURHOOD

(祇園周辺; Map p300; Higashiyama-ku; S Tōzai line to Sanjō, R Keihan line to Gion-Shijō) Gion is the famous entertainment and geisha quarter on the eastern bank of the Kamo-gawa. While Gion's true origins were in teahouses catering to weary visitors to Yasaka-jinja (a neighbourhood shrine), by the mid-18th century the area was Kyoto's largest pleasure district. Despite the looming modern architecture, congested traffic and contemporary nightlife establishments that have compromised its historical beauty, there are still some places left in Gion for an enjoyable walk.

Hanami-kōji runs north–south and bisects **Shijō-dōri**. The southern section is lined with 17th-century traditional restaurants and teahouses, many of which are exclusive establishments for geisha entertainment. At the south end you reach **Gion Corner** and **Gion Kōbu Kaburen-jō Theatre** (祇園甲部歌舞練場).

If you walk from Shijō-dōri along the northern section of Hanami-kōji and take your third left, you will find yourself on **Shimbashi** (sometimes called Shirakawa Minami-dōri), which is one of Kyoto's most beautiful streets and, arguably, the most beautiful street in all of Asia, especially in the evening and during cherry-blossom season. A bit further north lie **Shinmonzen-dōri** and **Furumonzen-dōri**, running east–west. Wander in either direction along these streets, which are packed with old houses, art galleries and shops specialising in antiques – but don't expect flea-market prices.

City Walk Southern Higashiyama

START GOJŌ-ZAKA BUS STOP ON HIGASHIŌJI-DŌRI
END JINGŪ-MICHI BUS STOP ON SANJŌ-DŌRI
LENGTH 5KM; FOUR HOURS

Take bus 18, 100, 206 or 207 to the starting point, then walk up the Gojō-zaka slope. Head uphill until you reach the first fork in the road; bear right and continue up Chawan-zaka (Teapot Lane). At the top of the hill, you'll come to Kiyomizu-dera. Before you enter the temple, we recommend you pay ¥100 to descend into the 1 **Tainai-meguri**, the entrance to which is just left of the main temple entrance. Next, enter 2 **Kiyomizu-dera** (p302).

After touring Kiyomizu-dera, exit down Kiyomizu-michi. Continue down the hill until you reach a four-way intersection; take a right here down the stone-paved steps. This is Sannen-zaka, an atmospheric lane lined with traditional shops and cafes.

Halfway down Sannen-zaka, the road curves to the left. Follow it a short distance, then go right down a flight of steps into Ninen-zaka. Soon on your left you will find tiny 3 **Kasagi-ya** (p335), which has been serving tea and Japanese-style sweets for as long as anyone can remember. At the end of Ninen-zaka zigzag left (at the vending machines) then right (just past the parking lot), and continue north. Soon, on your left, you'll come to the entrance to 4 **Ishibei-kōji** – perhaps the most beautiful street in Kyoto. Take a detour to explore this lane, then retrace your steps and continue north, passing almost immediately the entrance to 5 **Kōdai-ji** (p302) on the right up a long flight of stairs.

After Kōdai-ji continue north to the T-junction; turn right and then take a quick left. You'll cross the wide pedestrian arcade that leads to Ōtani cemetery and then descend into 6 **Maruyama-kōen** (p303). In the centre of the park you'll see the giant Gion *shidare-zakura,* Kyoto's most famous cherry tree.

From the park, you can head west into the grounds of 7 **Yasaka-jinja** (p303). Then return to the park and head north to tour the grounds of the impressive 8 **Chion-in** (p303). From here it's a quick walk to 9 **Shōren-in** (p303). From Shōren-in walk down to Sanjō-dōri.

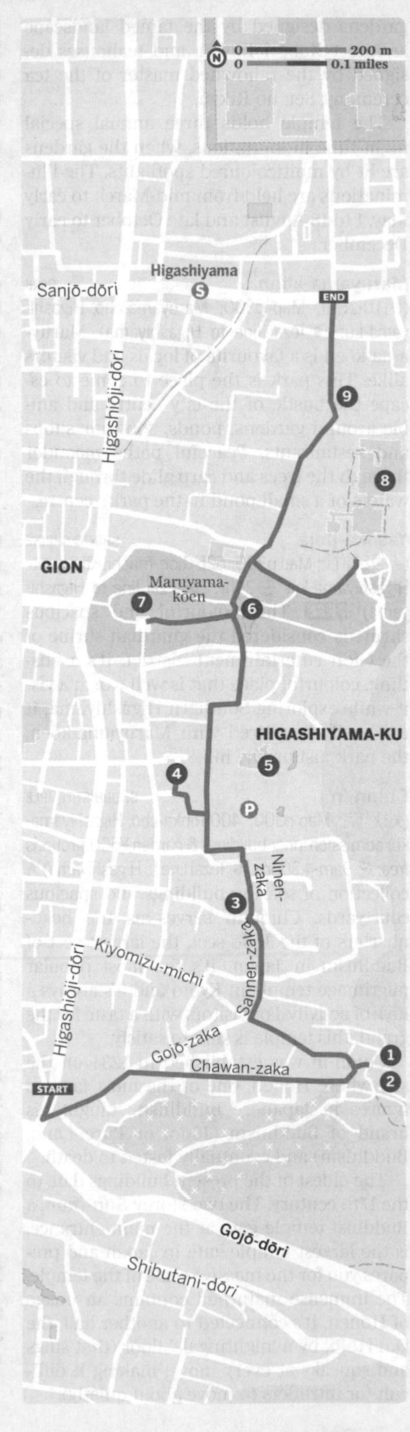

Kennin-ji BUDDHIST TEMPLE
(建仁寺; Map p300; 584 Komatsu-chō, Yamatoōji-dōri, Shijo-sagaru, Higashiyama-ku; admission ¥500; ⏲10am-4pm; Keihan line to Gion-Shijō) Founded in 1202 by the monk Eisai, Kennin-ji is the oldest Zen temple in Kyoto. It is an island of peace and calm on the border of the boisterous Gion nightlife district and it makes a fine counterpoint to the worldly pleasures of that area. The highlight at Kennin-ji is the fine and expansive *karesansui* (dry-landscape rock garden). The painting of the twin dragons on the roof of the **Hōdō** hall is also fantastic.

Northern Higashiyama

The northern Higashiyama area includes such first-rate attractions as Nanzen-ji, Ginkaku-ji, Hōnen-in and Shūgaku-in Rikyū. You can spend a wonderful day walking from Keage Station on the Tōzai subway line all the way north to Ginkaku-ji via the Tetsugaku-no-Michi (Path of Philosophy), stopping in the countless temples and shrines en route.

★**Nanzen-ji** BUDDHIST TEMPLE
(南禅寺; Map p306; 86 Fukuchi-chō, Nanzen-ji, Sakyō-ku; admission Hōjō garden ¥500, San-mon gate ¥400, grounds free; ⏲8.40am-5pm Mar-Nov, to 4.30pm Dec-Feb; Kyoto City bus 5 to Eikandō-michi, S Tōzai line to Keage) This is one of the most rewarding temples in Kyoto, with its expansive grounds and numerous subtemples. At its entrance stands the massive **San-mon**. Steps lead up to the 2nd storey, which has a fine view over the city. Beyond the gate is the main hall of the temple, above which you will find the **Hōjō**, where the Leaping Tiger Garden is a classic Zen garden well worth a look.

Nanzen-ji Oku-no-in BUDDHIST TEMPLE
(南禅寺奥の院; Map p306; Fukuchi-chō, Nanzen-ji, Sakyō-ku; ⏲dawn-dusk; Kyoto City bus 5 to Eikandō-michi, S Tōzai line to Keage) FREE Perhaps the best part of Nanzen-ji is overlooked by most visitors: Nanzen-ji Oku-no-in, a small shrine hidden in a forested hollow behind the main precinct. It's here that pilgrims pray while standing under the falls, sometimes in the dead of winter.

To get here, walk up to the red-brick aqueduct in front of Nanzen-in. Follow the road that runs parallel to the aqueduct up into the hills, and walk past (or through) Kōtoku-an, a small subtemple on your left. Continue up the steps into the woods until you reach a waterfall in a beautiful mountain glen.

Tenju-an BUDDHIST TEMPLE
(天授庵; Map p306; 86-8 Fukuchi-chō, Nanzen-ji, Sakyō-ku; admission ¥400; ⏲9am-5pm Mar-mid-Nov, to 4.30pm mid-Nov–Feb; Kyoto City bus 5 to Eikandō-michi, S Tōzai line to Keage) A subtemple of Nanzen-ji, Tenju-an is located on the south side of San-mon, the main gate of Nanzen-ji. Constructed in 1337, Tenju-an has a splendid garden and a great collection of carp in its pond.

Konchi-in BUDDHIST TEMPLE
(金地院; Map p306; 86-12 Fukuchi-chō, Nanzen-ji, Sakyō-ku; admission ¥400; ⏲8.30am-5pm Mar-Nov, to 4.30pm Dec-Feb; Kyoto City bus 5 to Eikandō-michi, S Tōzai line to Keage) Just southwest of the main precincts of Nanzen-ji, this fine subtemple has a wonderful garden designed by Kobori Enshū. If you want to find a good example of the *shakkei* (borrowed scenery) technique, look no further.

Eikan-dō BUDDHIST TEMPLE
(永観堂; Map p306; 48 Eikandō-chō, Sakyō-ku; admission ¥600; ⏲9am-5pm; Kyoto City bus 5 to Eikandō-michi, S Tōzai line to Keage) Perhaps Kyoto's most famous (and most crowded) autumn-foliage destination, Eikan-dō is a superb temple just a short walk south of the famous Path of Philosophy. Eikan-dō is made interesting by its varied architecture, its gardens and its works of art. It was founded as Zenrin-ji in 855 by the priest Shinshō, but the name was changed to Eikan-dō in the 11th century to honour the philanthropic priest Eikan.

In the **Amida-dō** hall at the southern end of the complex is a famous statue of Mikaeri Amida Buddha glancing backwards.

From Amida-dō, head north to the end of the curving covered **garyūrō** (walkway). Change into the sandals provided, then climb the steep steps up the mountainside to the **Tahō-tō** pagoda, from where there's a fine view across the city.

Path of Philosophy (Tetsugaku-no-Michi) NEIGHBOURHOOD
(哲学の道; Map p306; Sakyō-ku; Kyoto City bus 5 to Eikandō-michi or Ginkakuji-michi, S Tōzai line to Keage) The Tetsugaku-no-Michi is one of the most pleasant walks in all of Kyoto. Lined with a great variety of flowering plants, bushes and trees, it is a corridor of colour throughout most of the year. Follow

Northern Higashiyama

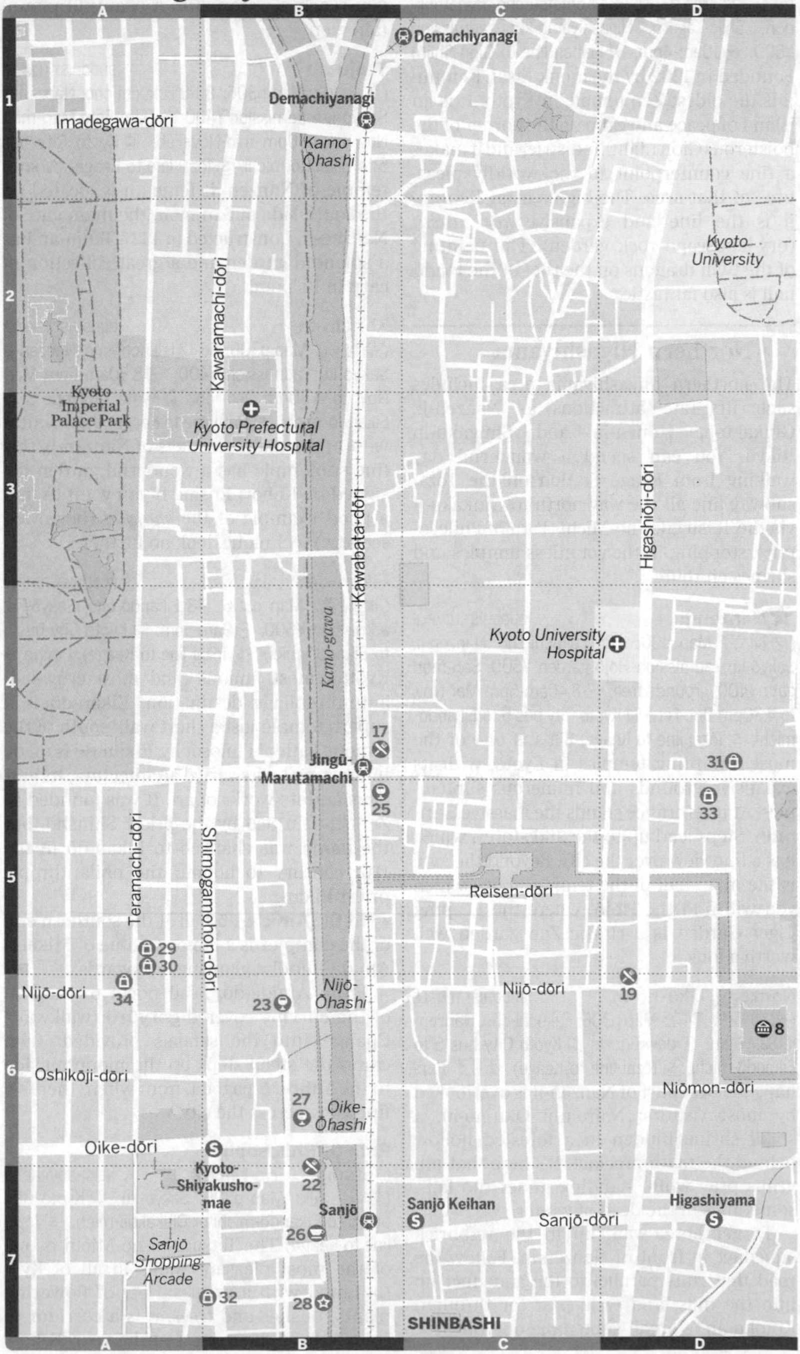

A B C D

1 2 3 4 5 6 7

Demachiyanagi
Demachiyanagi
Imadegawa-dōri
Kamo-Ōhashi
Kyoto University
Kawaramachi-dōri
Kyoto Imperial Palace Park
Kyoto Prefectural University Hospital
Higashiōji-dōri
Kawabata-dōri
Kamo-gawa
Kyoto University Hospital
17
Jingū-Marutamachi
31
25
33
Teramachi-dōri
Shimogamohon-dōri
Reisen-dōri
29
30
Nijō-dōri
34
Nijō-Ōhashi
23
Nijō-dōri
19
8
Oshikōji-dōri
27
Oike-Ōhashi
Niōmon-dōri
Oike-dōri
Kyoto-Shiyakusho-mae
22
Sanjō
Sanjō Keihan
Higashiyama
Sanjō-dōri
26
Sanjō Shopping Arcade
32
28
SHINBASHI

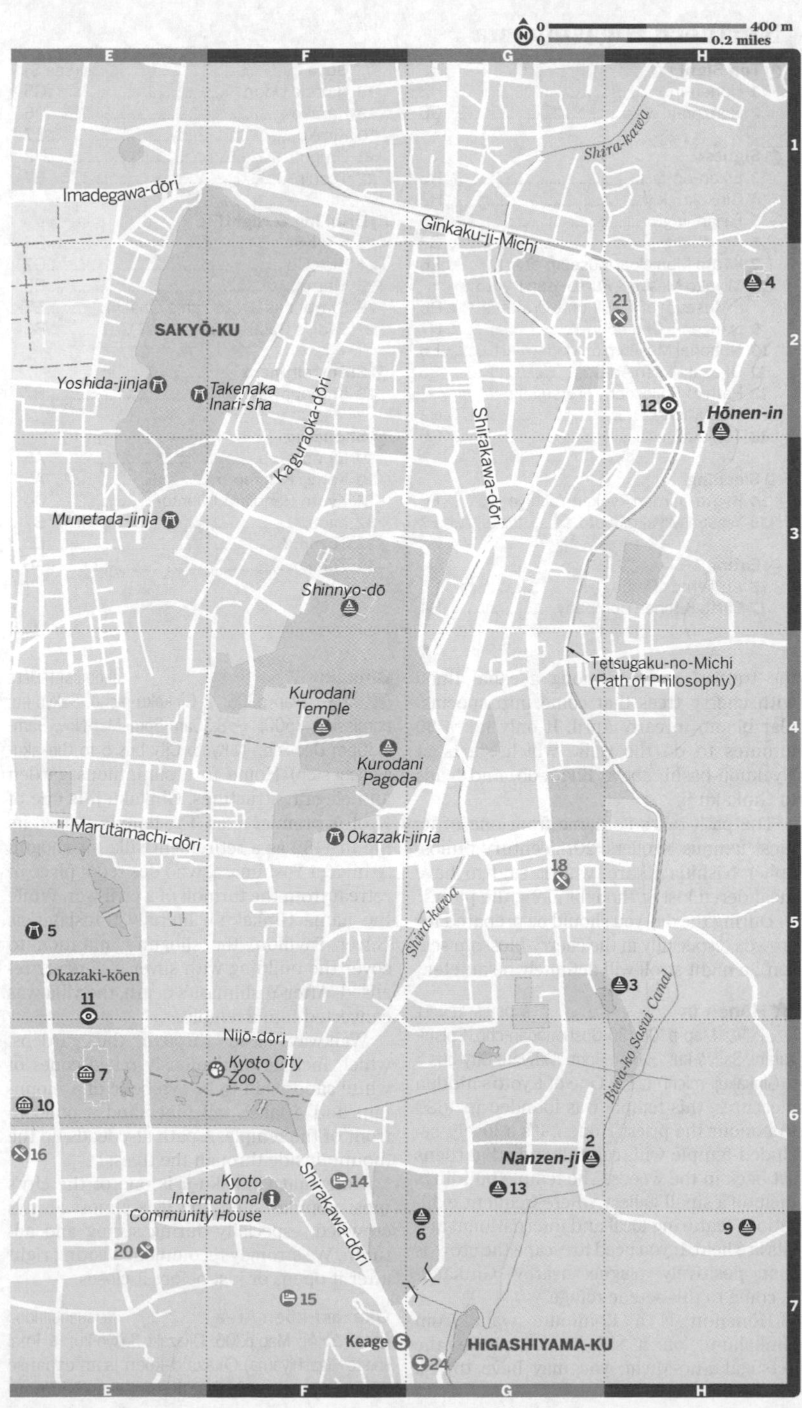
0 400 m
0 0.2 miles
E
F
G
H
1
2
3
4
5
6
7
Imadegawa-dōri
Ginkaku-ji-Michi
Shira-kawa
SAKYŌ-KU
Yoshida-jinja
Takenaka Inari-sha
Kaguraoka-dōri
Shirakawa-dōri
12
Hōnen-in
1
4
21
Munetada-jinja
Shinnyo-dō
Tetsugaku-no-Michi (Path of Philosophy)
Kurodani Temple
Kurodani Pagoda
Marutamachi-dōri
Okazaki-jinja
18
Shira-kawa
5
Okazaki-kōen
11
3
Biwa-ko Sosui Canal
Nijō-dōri
Kyoto City Zoo
7
10
16
2
Nanzen-ji
Kyoto International Community House
14
13
6
9
Shirakawa-dōri
20
15
Keage
HIGASHIYAMA-KU
24

Northern Higashiyama

Top Sights
1 Hōnen-in H2
2 Nanzen-ji G6

Sights
3 Eikan-dō H5
4 Ginkaku-ji H2
5 Heian-jingū E5
6 Konchi-in G7
7 Kyoto Municipal Museum of Art E6
8 Miyako Messe & Fureai-Kan Kyoto Museum of Traditional Crafts D6
9 Nanzen-ji Oku-no-in H7
10 National Museum of Modern Art E6
11 Okazaki-kōen Area E5
12 Path of Philosophy (Tetsugaku-no-Michi) H2
13 Tenju-an G6

Sleeping
14 Kyoto Garden Ryokan Yachiyo F6
15 Westin Miyako Kyoto F7

Eating
16 Au Temps Perdu E6
17 Earth Kitchen Company B4
Goya .... (see 8)
18 Hinode Udon G5
19 Karako D6
20 Kiraku E7
21 Omen H2
22 Tōsuirō B7

Drinking & Nightlife
23 Bar K6 .... B6
24 Kick Up G7
25 Metro B5
26 Starbucks Kyoto Sanjō-Ōhashi B7
27 Tadg's Gastro Pub B6

Entertainment
28 Kamogawa Odori B7

Shopping
29 Ippōdō Tea A5
30 Kamiji Kakimoto A5
31 Kyoto Handicraft Center D4
32 Mina B7
33 Tōzandō D5
34 Zōhiko A6

the traffic-free route along a canal lined with cherry trees that come into spectacular bloom in early April. It only takes 30 minutes to do the walk, which starts at Nyakuōji-bashi, above Eikan-dō, and leads to Ginkaku-ji.

The path takes its name from one of its most famous strollers, 20th-century philosopher Nishida Kitarō, who is said to have meandered lost in thought along the path.

During the day you should be prepared for crowds (especially in the cherry-blossom season); a night stroll will definitely be quieter.

★ Hōnen-in — BUDDHIST TEMPLE

(法然院; Map p306; 30 Goshonodan-chō, Shishigatani, Sakyō-ku; 6am-4pm; Kyoto City bus 5 to Ginkakuji-michi) FREE One of Kyoto's hidden pleasures, this temple was founded in 1680 to honour the priest Hōnen. It's a lovely, secluded temple with carefully raked gardens set back in the woods. The temple buildings include a small gallery where frequent exhibitions featuring local and international artists are held. If you need to escape the crowds that positively plague nearby Ginkaku-ji, come to this serene refuge.

Hōnen-in is a 12-minute walk from Ginkaku-ji, on a side street above the Tetsugaku-no-Michi; you may have to ask for directions.

Ginkaku-ji — BUDDHIST TEMPLE

(銀閣寺; Map p306; 2 Ginkaku-ji-chō, Sakyō-ku; admission ¥500; 8.30am-5pm Mar-Nov, 9am-4.30pm Dec-Feb; Kyoto City bus 5 to Ginkaku-ji-michi stop) Home to a sumptuous garden and elegant structures, Ginkaku-ji is one of Kyoto's premier sites. The temple started its life in 1482 as a retirement villa for shogun Ashikaga Yoshimasa, who desired a place to retreat from the turmoil of a civil war. While the name Ginkaku-ji literally translates as 'Silver Pavilion', the shogun's ambition to cover the building with silver was never realised. After Yoshimasa's death, the villa was converted into a temple.

Walkways lead through the gardens, which include meticulously raked cones of white sand (said to be symbolic of a mountain and a lake), tall pines and a pond in front of the temple. A path also leads up the mountainside through the trees.

Note that Ginkaku-ji is one of the city's most popular sites, and it is almost always crowded, especially during spring and autumn. We strongly recommend visiting right after it opens or just before it closes.

Okazaki-kōen Area — NEIGHBOURHOOD

(岡崎公園; Map p306; Okazaki, Sakyo-ku; S Tōzai line to Higashiyama) Okazaki-kōen is an expanse of parks and canals that lies between Niōmon-dōri and Heian-jingū. Two of Kyoto's significant museums can be found here, as well as two smaller museums. If you find yourself in Kyoto on a rainy day and need to do some indoor sightseeing, this area has enough to keep you sheltered for most of the day.

Kyoto Municipal Museum of Art MUSEUM
(京都市美術館; Map p306; 124 Enshōji-chō, Okazaki, Sakyō-ku; admission varies; 9am-5pm, closed Mon; S Tōzai line to Higashiyama) This fine museum holds several major exhibitions a year, as well as a variety of free shows. It's always worth stopping by to see if something is on while you are in town. The pond behind the museum is a great place for a picnic.

National Museum of Modern Art MUSEUM
(京都国立近代美術館; Map p306; www.momak.go.jp/english; Enshōji-chō, Okazaki, Sakyō-ku; admission ¥430; 9.30am-5pm, closed Mon; S Tōzai line to Higashiyama) This museum is renowned for its Japanese ceramics and paintings. There is an excellent permanent collection, which includes many pottery pieces by Kawai Kanjirō. The coffee shop here overlooks a picturesque canal.

Miyako Messe & Fureai-Kan Kyoto Museum of Traditional Crafts MUSEUM
(みやこめっせ・京都伝統産業ふれあい館; Map p306; 9-1 Seishōji-chō, Okazaki, Sakyō-ku; 9am-5pm, closed 18 & 19 Aug, 29 Dec-3 Jan; S Tōzai line to Higashiyama) FREE This multipurpose hall has excellent displays of Kyoto crafts. Exhibits include wood-block prints, lacquerware, bamboo goods and gold-leaf work. It's located in the basement of Miyako Messe (Kyoto International Exhibition Hall).

Heian-jingū SHINTO SHRINE
(平安神宮; Map p306; Nishitennō-chō, Okazaki, Sakyō-ku; admission garden ¥600; 6am-5pm Nov-Feb, 6am-6pm Mar-Oct; S Tōzai line to Higashiyama) One of Kyoto's more popular sights, this shrine was built in 1895 to commemorate the 1100th anniversary of the founding of Kyoto. The shrine buildings are colourful replicas, reduced to a two-thirds scale, of the Imperial Court Palace of the Heian period (794–1185). About 500m in front of the shrine is a massive steel **torii** (shrine gate). Although it appears to be entirely separate, this is actually considered the main entrance to the shrine itself.

The vast **garden** here, behind the shrine, is a fine place for a wander and particularly lovely during the cherry-blossom season. With its large pond and Chinese-inspired bridge, the garden is a tribute to the style that was popular in the Heian period. It is well known for its wisteria, irises and weeping cherry trees.

One of Kyoto's biggest festivals, the **Jidai Matsuri** is held here on 22 October. On 2 and 3 June, **Takigi nō** is also held here. Takigi nō is a picturesque form of *nō* (stylised dance-drama performed on a bare stage) performed in the light of blazing fires. Tickets cost ¥3000 if you pay in advance (ask at the Tourist Information Center for the location of ticket agencies) or you can pay ¥4000 at the entrance gate.

Shūgaku-in Rikyū Imperial Villa NOTABLE BUILDING
(修学院離宮; Map p290; 211-1215; Shūgaku-in, Yabusoe, Sakyō-ku; Kyoto City bus 5 from Kyoto Station to Shūgakuinrikyū-michi) FREE Lying at the foot of Hiei-zan, this superb imperial villa is one of the highlights of northeast Kyoto. It was designed as a lavish summer retreat for the imperial family. The gardens here, with their views down over the city of Kyoto, are worth the trouble it takes to visit.

Construction of the villa was begun in the 1650s by Emperor Go-Mizunō, following his abdication. Work was continued by his daughter Akeno-miya after his death in 1680.

The villa grounds are divided into three enormous garden areas on a hillside – lower, middle and upper. Each has superb tea-ceremony houses: the upper, **Kami-no-chaya**, and lower, **Shimo-no-chaya**, were completed in 1659, and the middle teahouse, **Naka-no-chaya**, was completed in 1682. The gardens' reputation rests on their ponds, pathways and impressive use of *shakkei* (borrowed scenery) in the form of the surrounding hills. The view from Kami-no-chaya is particularly impressive.

One-hour tours (in Japanese) start at 9am, 10am, 11am, 1.30pm and 3pm; try to arrive early. A basic leaflet in English is provided and more detailed literature is for sale in the tour waiting room.

You must make reservations through the Imperial Household Agency – usually several weeks in advance.

Hiei-zan & Enryaku-ji TEMPLE
(延暦寺; 4220 Honmachi, Sakamoto, Sakyō-ku; admission ¥700; 8.30am-4.30pm, 9am-4pm in winter; Kyoto bus to Enryakuji Bus Center,

Keihan bus to Enryakuji Bus Center) Located atop 848m-high Hiei-zan (the mountain that dominates the skyline in the northeast of the city), the Enryaku-ji temple complex is an entire world of temples and dark forests that feels a long way from the hustle and bustle of the city below. A visit to this temple is a good way to spend half a day hiking, poking around temples and enjoying the atmosphere of a key site in Japanese history.

Enryaku-ji was founded in 788 by Saichō, also known as Dengyō-daishi, the priest who established the Tenzai school. This school did not receive imperial recognition until 823, after Saichō's death; however, from the 8th century the temple grew in power. At its height, Enryaku-ji possessed some 3000 buildings and an army of thousands of *sōhei* (warrior monks). In 1571 Oda Nobunaga saw the temple's power as a threat to his aims to unify the nation and he destroyed most of the buildings, along with the monks inside. Today only three pagodas and 120 minor temples remain.

The complex is divided into three sections: **Tōtō**, **Saitō** and **Yokawa**. The Tōtō (eastern pagoda section) contains the **Kompon Chū-dō** (Primary Central Hall), which is the most important building in the complex. The flames on the three dharma lamps in front of the altar have been kept lit for more than 1200 years. The **Daikō-dō** (Great Lecture Hall) displays life-sized wooden statues of the founders of various Buddhist schools. This part of the temple is heavily geared to group access, with large expanses of asphalt for parking.

The Saitō (western pagoda section) contains the Shaka-dō, which dates from 1595 and houses a rare Buddha sculpture of the Shaka Nyorai (Historical Buddha). The Saitō, with its stone paths winding through forests of tall trees, temples shrouded in mist and the sound of distant gongs, is the most atmospheric part of the temple. Hold on to your ticket from the Tōtō section, as you may need to show it here.

The Yokawa is of minimal interest and a 4km bus ride away from the Saitō area. The Chū-dō here was originally built in 848. It was destroyed by fire several times and has undergone repeated reconstruction (most recently in 1971). If you plan to visit this area as well as Tōtō and Saitō, allow a full day for in-depth exploration.

Northwest Kyoto

Northwest Kyoto has many excellent sights spread over a large area. Highlights include Kinkaku-ji (the famed Golden Pavilion) and Ryōan-ji, with its mysterious stone garden. Note that three of the area's main sights – Kinkaku-ji, Ryōan-ji and Ninna-ji – can easily be linked together to form a great half-day tour out of the city centre.

Kitano Tenman-gū SHINTO SHRINE

(北野天満宮; Map p298; Bakuro-chō, Kamigyō-ku; 5am-6pm Apr-Sep, 5.30am-5.30pm Oct-Mar; Kyoto City bus 50 from Kyoto Station to Kitano-Tenmangū-mae) FREE The most atmospheric Shintō shrine in Northwest Kyoto, Kitano Tenman-gū is also the site of Tenjin-San Market, one of Kyoto's most popular flea markets. It's a pleasant spot for a lazy stroll and the shrine buildings themselves are beautiful. The present buildings were built in 1607 by Toyotomi Hideyori; the grounds contain an extensive grove of plum trees, which burst into bloom in early March.

Kinkaku-ji BUDDHIST TEMPLE

(金閣寺; Map p311; 1 Kinkakuji-chō, Kita-ku; admission ¥400; 9am-5pm; Kyoto City bus 205 from Kyoto Station to Kinkakuji-michi, Kyoto City bus 59 from Sanjo-Keihan to Kinkakuji-mae) Kyoto's famed 'Golden Pavilion', Kinkaku-ji is one of Japan's best-known sights. The main hall, covered in brilliant gold leaf, shining above its reflecting pond is truly spectacular. Needless to say, due to its beauty, the temple can be packed any day of the year. Thus, we recommend going early in the day or just before closing, ideally on a weekday.

The original building was built in 1397 as a retirement villa for shogun Ashikaga Yoshimitsu. His son converted it into a temple. In 1950 a young monk consummated his obsession with the temple by burning it to the ground. The monk's story was fictionalised in Mishima Yukio's *The Golden Pavilion*. In 1955 a full reconstruction was completed that followed the original design, but the gold-foil covering was extended to the lower floors.

Ryōan-ji BUDDHIST TEMPLE

(龍安寺; Map p311; 13 Goryōnoshitamachi, Ryōan-ji, Ukyō-ku; admission ¥500; 8am-5pm Mar-Nov, 8.30am-4.30pm Dec-Feb; Kyoto City bus 59 from Sanjō-Keihan to Ryoanji-mae) You've probably seen a picture of the rock garden here – it's one of the symbols of Kyoto and one of

KYOTO SIGHTS

Northwest Kyoto

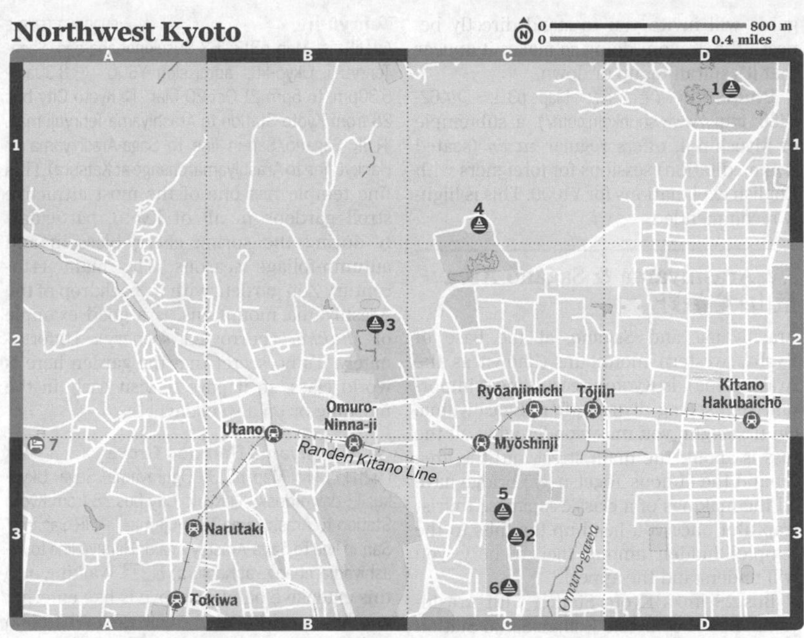

Northwest Kyoto

Japan's better-known sights. Ryōan-ji belongs to the Rinzai school and was founded in 1450. The garden, an oblong of sand with an austere collection of 15 carefully placed rocks, apparently adrift in a sea of sand, is enclosed by an earthen wall. The designer, who remains unknown to this day, provided no explanation.

Ninna-ji BUDDHIST TEMPLE

(仁和寺; Map p311; 33 Omuroōuchi, Ukyō-ku; admission to Kondō hall ¥500, Reihōkan ¥500, grounds free; 9am-5pm Mar-Nov, 9am-4.30pm Dec-Feb; Kyoto City bus 59 from Sanjo-Keihan to Omuro Ninna-ji, Kyoto City bus 26 from Kyoto Station to Omuro Ninna-ji) Few travellers make the journey all the way out to this sprawling temple complex, but most who do find it a pleasant spot. It's certainly a good counterpoint to the crowded and more famous temples nearby. If you're after something a bit off the beaten track in northwest Kyoto, this temple may fit the bill.

Myōshin-ji BUDDHIST TEMPLE

(妙心寺; Map p311; 1 Myoshin-ji-chō, Hanazono, Ukyō-ku; admission to main temple free, other areas of complex ¥500; 9.10-11.50am & 1-3.40pm; Kyoto City bus 10 from Sanjo-Keihan to Myōshin-ji Kita-mon-mae) Myōshin-ji is a separate world within Kyoto, a walled-off complex of temples and subtemples that invites lazy strolling. The subtemple of **Taizō-in** here contains one of the city's more interesting gardens. Myōshin-ji dates from 1342 and belongs to the Rinzai school. There are 47 subtemples, but only a few are open to the public.

From the north gate, follow the broad stone avenue flanked by rows of temples to the southern part of the complex. The eponymous **Myōshin-ji** temple here is roughly in the middle of the complex. Your entry fee entitles you to a tour of several of the buildings of the temple. The ceiling of the **Hattō** (Lecture Hall) here features Tanyū Kanō's unnerving painting *Unryūzu* (meaning 'Dragon glaring in eight directions'). Your guide will invite you to stand directly beneath the dragon; doing so makes it appear that it's spiralling up or down.

Shunkō-in (春光院; Map p311; ☎462-5488; http://www.shunkoin.com/), a subtemple of Myōshin-ji, offers regular *zazen* (seated Zen meditation) sessions for foreigners with English explanations for ¥1000. This is highly recommended.

Arashiyama & Sagano Area 嵐山・嵯峨野

Arashiyama and Sagano, at the base of Kyoto's western mountains (known as the Arashiyama), is Kyoto's second-most important sightseeing district after Higashiyama. On first sight, you may wonder what all the fuss is about; the main street and the area around the famous Tōgetsu-kyō bridge have all the makings of a classic Japanese tourist trap. But once you head up the hills to the temples hidden among the greenery, you will understand the appeal.

Bus 28 links Kyoto Station with Arashiyama. Bus 11 connects Keihan Sanjō Station with Arashiyama. The most convenient rail connection is the JR Sagano/San-in line from Kyoto Station or Nijō Station to Saga-Arashiyama Station (be careful to take only local trains, as the express trains do not stop at Saga-Arashiyama). You can also take the Hankyū line from downtown Kyoto to Arashiyama Station, but this involves changing trains at Katsura. A fast way to get there from the middle of Kyoto (both downtown and central) is to take the Tōzai subway line to the western-most stop (Uzumasa-Tenjin-gawa) and take a taxi from there to Arashiyama (the taxi ride will take about 15 minutes and cost around ¥1600).

Kameyama-kōen PARK

(亀山公園; Map p313; Sagaogurayama, Ukyō-ku; Kyoto City bus 28 from Kyoto Station to Arashiyama-Tenryuji-mae, JR Sagano/San-in line to Saga-Arashiyama or Hankyū line to Arashiyama, change at Katsura) Just upstream from Tōgetsu-kyō and behind Tenryū-ji, this park is a nice place to escape the crowds of Arashiyama. It's laced with trails, one of which leads to a lookout over Katsura-gawa and up into the Arashiyama mountains. It's especially attractive during cherry-blossom and autumn-foliage seasons. Keep an eye out for monkeys, which occasionally descend from the nearby hills to pick fruit.

Tenryū-ji BUDDHIST TEMPLE

(天龍寺; Map p313; 68 Susukinobaba-chō, Saga-Tenryū-ji, Ukyō-ku; admission ¥600; 8.30am-5.30pm, to 5pm 21 Oct-20 Mar; Kyoto City bus 28 from Kyoto Station to Arashiyama-Tenryuji-mae, JR Sagano/San-in line to Saga-Arashiyama or Hankyū line to Arashiyama, change at Katsura) This fine temple has one of the most attractive stroll gardens in all of Kyoto, particularly during the spring cherry-blossom and autumn-foliage seasons. The main 14th-century Zen garden, with its backdrop of the Arashiyama mountains, is a good example of *shakkei* (borrowed scenery). Unfortunately, it's no secret that the garden here is world class, so it pays to visit early in the morning or on a weekday.

★Arashiyama Bamboo Grove PARK

(嵐山竹林; Map p313; Ogurayama, Saga, Ukyō-ku; dawn-dusk; Kyoto City bus 28 from Kyoto Station to Arashiyama-Tenryuji-mae, JR Sagano/San-in line to Saga-Arashiyama or Hankyū line to Arashiyama, change at Katsura) FREE Walking into this extensive bamboo grove is like entering another world – the thick green bamboo stalks seem to continue endlessly in every direction and there's a strange quality to the light. You'll be unable to resist trying to take a few photos, but you might be disappointed with the results: photos just can't capture the magic of this place. The grove runs from just outside the north gate of Tenryū-ji to just below Ōkōchi Sansō villa.

★Ōkōchi Sansō HISTORIC BUILDING

(大河内山荘; Map p313; 8 Tabuchiyama-chō, Sagaogurayama, Ukyō-ku; admission ¥1000; 9am-5pm; Kyoto City bus 28 from Kyoto Station to Arashiyama-Tenryuji-mae, JR Sagano/San-in line to Saga-Arashiyama or Hankyū line to Arashiyama, change at Katsura) This is the lavish estate of Ōkōchi Denjirō, an actor famous for his samurai films. The sprawling stroll gardens may well be the most lovely in all of Kyoto, particularly when you consider the brilliant views eastwards across the city. The house and teahouse are also sublime. Be sure to follow all the trails around the gardens. Hold onto the tea ticket you were given upon entry to claim the tea and cake that comes with admission.

The following sights are all located north of Ōkōchi Sansō. Strolling from Ōkōchi Sansō all the way to Adashino Nembutsu-ji is a nice way to spend a few hours in Arashiyama and Sagano.

Arashiyama & Sagano Area

Arashiyama & Sagano Area

Top Sights

1 Arashiyama Bamboo Grove B3
2 Ōkōchi Sansō B3

Sights

3 Adashino Nenbutsu-ji A1
4 Arashiyama Monkey Park Iwatayama C4
5 Giō-ji A1
6 Jōjakkō-ji B2
7 Kameyama-kōen B3
8 Nison-in B2
9 Rakushisha B2
10 Tenryū-ji C3

Sleeping

11 Hoshinoya Kyoto B3

Eating

12 Arashiyama Yoshimura C3
13 Kitcho Arashiyama C3
14 Komichi B2
15 Shigetsu C3
16 Yoshida-ya C3

Jōjakkō-ji BUDDHIST TEMPLE

(常寂光寺; Map p313; 3 Ogura-chō, Sagaogurayama, Ukyō-ku; admission ¥400; ⏲9am-5pm; 🚌Kyoto City bus 28 from Kyoto Station to Arashiyama-Tenryuji-mae, 🚆JR Sagano/San-in line to Saga-Arashiyama or Hankyū line to Arashiyama, change at Katsura) This temple is perched on top of a mossy knoll and is famed for its brilliant maple trees, which turn a lovely crimson red in November, and its thatched-roof Niō-mon gate. The Hondō was constructed in the 16th century out of wood sourced from Fushimi-jō.

Rakushisha HISTORIC BUILDING

(落柿舎; Map p313; 20 Hinomyōjin-chō, Sagaogurayama, Ukyō-ku; admission ¥200; 9am-5pm Mar-Dec, 10am-4pm Jan & Feb, closed 31 Dec & 1 Jan; Kyoto City bus 28 from Kyoto Station to Arashiyama-Tenryuji-mae, JR Sagano/San-in line to Saga-Arashiyama or Hankyū line to Arashiyama, change at Katsura) This building was the hut of Mukai Kyorai, the best-known disciple of the illustrious haiku poet Bashō. Legend holds that Kyorai dubbed the house Rakushisha (literally 'House of the Fallen Persimmons') after he woke one morning following a fierce storm to find the persimmons he had planned to sell were all fallen from the trees in the garden and scattered on the ground.

Nison-in BUDDHIST TEMPLE

(二尊院; Map p313; 27 Monzenchōjin-chō, Saganison-in, Ukyō-ku; admission ¥500; 9am-4.30pm; Kyoto City bus 28 from Kyoto Station to Arashiyama-Tenryuji-mae, JR Sagano/San-in line to Saga-Arashiyama or Hankyū line to Arashiyama, change at Katsura) This is a popular spot with maple-watchers. Nison-in was originally built in the 9th century by Emperor Saga. It houses two important Kamakura-era Buddha statues side by side (Shaka on the right and Amida on the left). The temple features lacquered nightingale floors.

Giō-ji BUDDHIST TEMPLE

(祇王寺; Map p313; 32 Kozaka-chō, Sagatoriimoto, Ukyō-ku; admission ¥300; 9am-5pm, with seasonal variations; Kyoto City bus 28 from Kyoto Station to Arashiyama-Tenryuji-mae, JR Sagano/San-in line to Saga-Arashiyama or Hankyū line to Arashiyama, change at Katsura) This tiny temple near the north end of the main Arashiyama sightseeing route is one of Kyoto's hidden gems. Its main attraction is the lush moss garden outside the thatch-roofed hall of the temple.

Adashino Nenbutsu-ji BUDDHIST TEMPLE

(化野念仏寺; Map p313; 17 Adashino-chō, Sagatoriimoto, Ukyō-ku; admission ¥500; 9am-4.30pm, to 3.30pm Dec-Feb; Kyoto City bus 28 from Kyoto Station to Arashiyama-Tenryuji-mae, JR Sagano/San-in line to Saga-Arashiyama or Hankyū line to Arashiyama, change at Katsura) This rather unusual temple is where the abandoned bones of paupers without kin were gathered. More than 8000 stone images are crammed into the temple grounds, dedicated to the repose of their spirits. The abandoned souls are remembered with candles each year in the Sentō Kuyō ceremony held here on the evenings of 23 and 24 August. The temple is not a must-see attraction, but it's certainly interesting and the stone images make unusual photographs.

Arashiyama Monkey Park Iwatayama PARK

(嵐山モンキーパークいわたやま; Map p313; 8 Genrokuzan-chō, Arashiyama, Ukyō-ku; adult/child ¥550/250; 9am-5pm 15 Mar-Oct, to 4pm Nov-14 Mar; Kyoto City bus 28 from Kyoto Station to Arashiyama-Tenryuji-mae, JR Sagano/San-in line to Saga-Arashiyama or Hankyū line to Arashiyama, change at Katsura) Though it is common to spot wild monkeys in the nearby mountains, here you can encounter them at a close distance and enjoy watching the playful creatures frolic about. It makes for an excellent photo opportunity, not only of the monkeys but also of the panoramic view over Kyoto. Refreshingly, it is the animals who are free to roam while the humans who feed them are caged in a box!

You enter the park near the south side of Tōgetsu-kyō, through the orange *torii* (shrine gate) of Ichitani-jinja. Buy your tickets from the machine to the left of the shrine at the top of the steps. Just be warned: it's a steep climb up the hill to get to the monkeys. If it's a hot day, you're going to be drenched by the time you get to the spot where they gather.

Southeast Kyoto

Southeast Kyoto contains some of Kyoto's most impressive sights, including Tōfuku-ji, with its lovely garden, and Fushi-Inari-Taisha, with its hypnotically beautiful arcades of Shintō shrine gates.

Tōfuku-ji BUDDHIST TEMPLE

(東福寺; Map p290; 15-778 Honmahi, Higashiyama-ku; admission garden ¥400, Tsūtenkyō bridge ¥400, grounds free; 9am-4pm Apr-Oct, 8.30am-4pm Nov-early Dec, 9am-3.30pm early Dec-Mar; Keihan line to Tōfukuji, JR Nara line to Tōfukuji) Home to a spectacular garden, several superb structures and beautiful precincts, Tōfuku-ji is one of the finest temples in Kyoto. It's well worth a special visit and can easily be paired with a trip to Fushimi Inari-Taisha (the two are linked by the Keihan train line).

★**Fushimi-Inari Taisha** SHINTO SHRINE

(伏見稲荷大社; Map p290; 68 Yabunouchi-chō, Fukakusa, Fushimi-ku; dawn-dusk; JR Nara line to Inari, Keihan line to Fushimi-Inari) FREE With seemingly endless arcades of vermilion *torii* (shrine gates) spread across a thickly wooded mountain, this vast shrine complex is a world unto its own. It is, quite simply, one of the most impressive and memorable sights in all of Kyoto.

The entire complex, consisting of five shrines, sprawls across the wooded slopes of Inari-san. A pathway wanders 4km up the mountain and is lined with dozens of atmospheric sub-shrines.

Fushimi Inari was dedicated to the gods of rice and sake by the Hata family in the 8th century. As the role of agriculture diminished, deities were enrolled to ensure prosperity in business. Nowadays, the shrine is one of Japan's most popular, and is the head shrine for some 40,000 Inari shrines scattered the length and breadth of the country.

As you explore the shrine, you will come across hundreds of stone foxes. The fox is considered the messenger of Inari, the god of cereals, and the stone foxes, too, are often referred to as Inari. The key often seen in the fox's mouth is for the rice granary. On an incidental note, the Japanese traditionally see the fox as a sacred, somewhat mysterious figure capable of 'possessing' humans – the favoured point of entry is under the fingernails.

The walk around the upper precincts of the shrine is a pleasant day hike. It also makes for a very eerie stroll in the late afternoon and early evening, when the various graveyards and miniature shrines along the path take on a mysterious air. It's best to go with a friend at this time.

On 8 April there's a Sangyō-sai festival with offerings and dances to ensure prosperity for national industry. During the first few days in January, thousands of believers visit this shrine as their *hatsu-mōde* (first shrine visit of the New Year) to pray for good fortune.

Daigo-ji BUDDHIST TEMPLE

(醍醐寺; Map p290; 22 Higashiōji-chō, Daigo, Fushimi-ku; admission Sampō-in ¥600, Kondō Hall & Pagoda ¥600, grounds free; ⌚9am-5pm Mar-Nov, to 4pm Dec-Feb; S Tōzai line to Daigo) Daigo-ji is a sprawling temple complex located in the Daigo district of Kyoto, which lies on the east side of the Higashiyama mountains, accessible by the Tōzai subway line. Outside of the cherry-blossom season (early April), it's not a high-priority destination, but it makes a good half-day trip for those who like hiking and want a break from the more famous temples in the city centre.

Daigo-ji was founded in 874 by Shobo, who gave it the name Daigo (meaning 'the ultimate essence of milk'). This refers to the five periods of Buddha's teaching, which were compared to the five forms of milk prepared in India; the highest form is called *daigo* in Japanese.

The temple was expanded into a vast complex on two levels: **Shimo Daigo** (lower) and **Kami Daigo** (upper). Kami Daigo is atop **Daigo-yama**, behind the temple. During the 15th century those buildings on the lower level were destroyed, with the sole exception of the five-storey pagoda. Built in 951, this pagoda is treasured as the oldest of its kind in Japan and is the oldest existing building in Kyoto.

In the late 16th century, Hideyoshi took a fancy to Daigo-ji and ordered extensive rebuilding. It is now one of the Shingon school's main temples. To explore Daigo-ji thoroughly and at a leisurely pace, mixing some hiking with your temple-viewing, you will need at least half a day.

The subtemple **Sampō-in** is a fine example of the amazing opulence of that period. The Kanō paintings and the garden are special features.

From Sampō-in it's a steep and tiring 50-minute climb up to Kami Daigo. To get here, walk up the large avenue of cherry trees, through the Niō-mon gate, out the back gate of the lower temple, up a concrete incline and into the forest, past the pagoda.

KYOTO'S BEST HIKES

Daimonji-yama There is no finer walk in the city than the 30-minute climb to the viewpoint above Ginkaku-ji (p308) in Northern Higashiyama. The trail leaves from a parking lot just above and behind the temple. You might have to ask a local to point you in the right direction – ask for 'Daimonji-yama no haikingu kosu'.

Fushimi Inari-Taisha Paths lined with *torii* (Shintō shrine gates) criss-cross this mountain shrine in southeast Kyoto. The one-hour pilgrimage loop around the top of the mountain is highly recommended.

Kurama to Kibune The two-hour walk over the top of Kurama-yama from Kurama to Kibune via the mountain temple of Kurama-dera (p318) is one of the best easy half-day trips out of the city.

To get to Daigo-ji, take the Tōzai line subway east from central Kyoto to the Daigo stop, and walk east (towards the mountains) for about 10 minutes. Make sure that the train you board is bound for Rokujizō, as some head to Hama-Ōtsu instead. Admission to the grounds is free most of the year but during the cherry-blossom and autumn-foliage seasons it costs ¥600.

Uji 宇治

Uji is a small city to the south of Kyoto. Its main claims to fame are Byōdō-in and tea cultivation. Uji's stone bridge – the oldest of its kind in Japan – has been the scene of many bitter clashes in previous centuries.

Uji can be reached by rail in about 40 minutes from Kyoto on the Keihan Uji line or JR Nara line. When arriving in Uji by Keihan train, leave the station, cross the river via the first bridge on the right, and then turn left to find Byōdō-in. When coming by JR, the temple is about 10 minutes' walk east (towards the river) of Uji Station.

Byōdō-in BUDDHIST TEMPLE

(平等院; ☎0774-21-2861; 116 Uji-renge, Uji-shi; admission ¥600; 8.30am-5.15pm; JR Nara line or Keihan line to Uji) Byōdō-in is the star attraction in the Kyoto suburb of Uji. It's home to one of the loveliest Buddhist structures in Japan: the **Hōō-dō** hall, which is depicted on the back of the Japanese ¥10 coin. Perched overlooking a serene reflecting pond, this recently refurbished hall is a stunning sight. Paired with a stroll along the banks of the nearby Uji-gawa, this temple makes a good half-day trip out of Kyoto City.

This temple was converted from a Fujiwara villa into a Buddhist temple in 1052. The Hōō-dō (Phoenix Hall), the main hall of the temple, was built in 1053 and is the only original building remaining. The phoenix used to be a popular mythical bird in China and was revered by the Japanese as a protector of Buddha. The architecture of the building resembles the shape of the bird and there are two bronze phoenixes perched opposite each other on the roof.

The Hōō-dō was originally intended to represent Amida's heavenly palace in the Pure Land. This building is one of the few extant examples of Heian-period architecture, and its graceful lines make you wish that far more had survived the wars and fires that have plagued Kyoto's past. Inside the hall is the famous statue of Amida Buddha and 52 *bosatsu* (Bodhisattvas) dating from the 11th century and attributed to the priest-sculptor Jōchō.

Nearby, the **Hōmotsukan Treasure House** contains the original temple bell and door paintings and the original phoenix roof adornments. Allow about an hour to wander through the grounds.

Southwest Kyoto

Saihō-ji BUDDHIST TEMPLE

(西芳寺; Map p290; 56 Jingatani-chō, Matsuo, Nishikyō-ku; admission ¥3000; Kyoto City bus 28 from Kyoto Station to Matsuo-taisha-mae, Kyoto bus 63 from Sanjō-Keihan to Koke-dera) Saihō-ji, one of Kyoto's best-known gardens, is famed for its superb moss garden, hence the temple's nickname: Koke-dera (Moss Temple). The heart-shaped garden, laid out in 1339 by Musō Kokushi, surrounds a tranquil pond. In order to limit the number of visitors, you must apply to visit and then copy a sutra with ink and brush before exploring the garden.

While copying a sutra might seem daunting, it's actually fairly self-explanatory and if you're lost, just glance at what the Japanese visitors are doing. It's not necessary to finish the entire sutra, just do the best you can. Once in the garden, you are free to explore on your own and at your own pace.

To visit Saihō-ji you must make a reservation. Send a postcard at least one week before the date you wish to visit and include your name, number of visitors, address in Japan, occupation, age (you must be over 18) and desired date (choice of alternative dates preferred). The address: Saihō-ji, 56 Kamigaya-chō, Matsuo, Nishikyō-ku, Kyoto-shi 615-8286, JAPAN.

Enclose a stamped self-addressed postcard for a reply to your Japanese address. You might find it convenient to buy an Ōfuku-hagaki (send and return postcard set) at a Japanese post office.

Katsura Rikyū HISTORIC BUILDING

(桂離宮; Map p290; Katsura Detached Palace; Katsura Misono, Nishikyō-ku; Kyoto City bus 33 to Katsura Rikyū-mae, Hankyū line to Katsura) FREE Katsura Rikyū, one of Kyoto's imperial properties, is widely considered to be the pinnacle of Japanese traditional architecture and garden design. Set amid an otherwise drab neighbourhood, it is (literally) an island of incredible beauty. The villa was built in 1624 for the emperor's brother,

Prince Toshihito. Every conceivable detail of the villa – the teahouses, the large pond with islets and the surrounding garden – has been given meticulous attention.

Tours (in Japanese) start at 10am, 11am, 2pm and 3pm, and last 40 minutes. Try to be there 20 minutes before the start time. An explanatory video is shown in the waiting room and a leaflet is provided in English.

You must make reservations, usually several weeks in advance, through the Imperial Household Agency. There are those, however, who feel that the troublesome application process, the distance of the villa from downtown and the need to join a regimented tour detracts from the experience.

The villa is a 15-minute walk from Katsura Station, on the Hankyū line. A taxi from the station to the villa will cost around ¥700. Alternatively, Kyoto bus 33 stops at Katsura Rikyū-mae stop, which is a five-minute walk from the villa.

Ōhara (大原)

Since ancient times Ōhara, a quiet farming town about 10km north of Kyoto, has been regarded as a holy site by followers of the Jōdo school of Buddhism. The region provides a charming glimpse of rural Japan, along with the picturesque Sanzen-in, Jakkō-in and several other fine temples. It is most popular in autumn, when the maple leaves change colour and the mountain views are spectacular. During the peak foliage season of November, this area can get very crowded, especially on weekends.

Kyoto bus 17 or 18 from Kyoto Station will drop you to the Ōhara stop (¥600, one hour).

Sanzen-in BUDDHIST TEMPLE

(三千院; 540 Raikōin-chō, Ōhara, Sakyō-ku; admission ¥700; 9am-5pm Mar-Nov, to 4.30pm Dec-Feb; Kyoto bus 17 or 18 from Kyoto Station to Ōhara) Famed for its autumn foliage, hydrangea garden and stunning Buddha images, this temple is deservedly popular with foreign and domestic tourists alike. The temple's garden, **Yūsei-en**, is one of the most photographed sights in Japan, and rightly so.

Take some time to sit on the steps of the **Shin-den** hall and admire the beauty of the Yūsei-en. Then head off to see **Ōjō-gokuraku-in** (Temple of Rebirth in Paradise), the hall in which stands the impressive Amitabha trinity, a large Amida image flanked by attendants Kannon and Seishi (god of wisdom). After this, walk up to the garden at the back of the temple where, in late spring and summer, you can walk among hectares of blooming hydrangeas.

Sanzen-in was founded in 784 by the priest Saichō and belongs to the Tendai school. Saichō, considered one of the great patriarchs of Buddhism in Japan, also founded Enryaku-ji.

If you're keen for a short hike after leaving the temple, continue up the hill to see the rather oddly named **Soundless Waterfall** (Oto-nashi-no-taki; 音無の滝). Though in fact it sounds like any other waterfall, its resonance is believed to have inspired Shōmyō Buddhist chanting.

The approach to Sanzen-in is opposite the bus stop; there is no English sign but you can usually just follow the Japanese tourists. The temple is located about 600m up this walk on your left as you crest the hill.

Jakkō-in BUDDHIST TEMPLE

(寂光院; 676 Kusao-chō, Ōhara, Sakyō-ku; admission ¥600; 9am-5pm Mar-Nov, to 4.30pm Dec-Feb; Kyoto bus 17 or 18 from Kyoto Station to Ōhara) Jakkō-in sits on the opposite side of Ōhara from the famous Sanzen-in. It's reached by a very pleasant walk through a quaint 'old Japan' village. It's a relatively small temple and makes an interesting end point to a fine walk in the country.

The history of the temple is exceedingly tragic. The actual founding date of the temple is subject to some debate (it's thought to be somewhere between the 6th and 11th centuries), but it acquired fame as the temple that harboured Kenrei Mon-in, a lady of the Taira clan. In 1185 the Taira were soundly defeated in a sea battle against the Minamoto clan at Dan-no-ura. With the entire Taira clan slaughtered or drowned, Kenrei Mon-in threw herself into the waves with her son

KITAYAMA AREA

Starting on the north side of Kyoto city and stretching almost all the way to the Sea of Japan, the Kitayama (Northern Mountains) are a natural escape prized by Kyoto city dwellers. Attractions here include the village of Ōhara, with its pastoral beauty, the fine mountain temple at Kurama, the river dining platforms at Kibune, and the trio of mountain temples in Takao.

Antoku, the infant emperor. She was fished out – the only member of the clan to survive.

She was returned to Kyoto, where she became a nun and lived in a bare hut until it collapsed during an earthquake. Kenrei Mon-in was then accepted into Jakkō-in and stayed there, immersed in prayer and sorrowful memories, until her death 27 years later. Her tomb is located high on the hill behind the temple.

The main building of this temple burned down in May 2000 and the newly reconstructed main hall lacks some of the charm of the original. Nonetheless, it is a nice spot.

Jakkō-in is west of Ōhara. Walk out of the bus stop up the road to the traffic lights, then follow the small road to the left. You might have to ask directions on the way.

Kurama & Kibune 鞍馬・貴船

Only 30 minutes north of Kyoto on the Eiden Eizan main line, Kurama and Kibune are a pair of tranquil valleys long favoured by Kyotoites as places to escape the crowds and stresses of the city below. Kurama's main attractions are its mountain temple and its onsen (hot springs). Kibune, over the ridge, is a cluster of ryokan overlooking a mountain stream. It is best enjoyed in the summer, when the ryokan serve dinner on platforms built over the rushing waters of the Kibune-gawa, providing welcome relief from the summer heat.

The two valleys lend themselves to being explored together. In the winter you can start from Kibune, walk for an hour or so over the ridge, visit Kurama-dera and then soak in the onsen before heading back to Kyoto. In the summer the reverse is best; start from Kurama, walk up to the temple, then down the other side to Kibune to enjoy a meal suspended above the cool river.

If you happen to be in Kyoto on the night of 22 October, be sure not to miss the **Kurama-no-hi Matsuri** (Kurama Fire Festival), one of the most exciting festivals in the Kyoto area.

To get to Kurama and Kibune, take the Eiden Eizan line from Kyoto's Demachiyanagi Station. For Kibune, get off at the second-to-last stop, Kibune Guchi, take a right out of the station and walk about 20 minutes up the hill. For Kurama, go to the last stop, Kurama, and walk straight out of the station. Both destinations are ¥410 and take about 30 minutes to reach.

Kurama-dera BUDDHIST TEMPLE

(鞍馬寺; Map p319; 1074 Kurama Honmachi, Sakyō-ku; admission ¥200; ⌚9am-4.30pm; Eiden Eizan line from Demachiyanagi to Kurama) Located high on a thickly wooded mountain, Kurama-dera is one of the few temples in modern Japan that still manages to retain an air of real spirituality. This is a magical place that gains a lot of its power from its brilliant natural setting.

The temple also has a fascinating history. In 770 the monk Gantei left Nara's Tōshōdai-ji in search of a wilderness sanctuary in which to meditate. Wandering in the hills north of Kyoto, he came across a white horse that led him to the valley known today as Kurama. After seeing a vision of the deity Bishamon-ten, guardian of the northern quarter of the Buddhist heaven, Gantei established Kurama-dera just below the peak of Kurama-yama. Originally belonging to the Tendai school of Buddhism, Kurama has been independent since 1949, describing its own brand of Buddhism as Kurama-kyō.

The entrance to the temple is just up the hill from Kurama Station. A tram goes to the top for ¥100 or you can hike up in about 30 minutes (follow the main path past the tram station). The trail is worth taking (if it's not too hot), since it winds through a forest of towering old-growth cryptomeria trees, passing by **Yuki-jinja** (Map p319), a small Shintō shrine, on the way. Near the peak, there is a courtyard dominated by the **Honden** (Main Hall); behind this a trail leads off to the mountain's peak.

At the top, you can take a brief detour across the ridge to **Ōsugi-gongen** (Map p319), a quiet shrine in a grove of trees. Those who want to continue to Kibune can take the trail down the other side. It's a 1.2km, 30-minute hike from the Honden to the valley floor of Kibune. On the way down are two mountain shrines, **Sōjō-ga-dani Fudō-dō** (Map p319) and **Okuno-in Maō-den** (Map p319), which make pleasant rest stops.

Takao 高雄

Takao is a secluded mountain village tucked far away in the northwestern part of Kyoto. It is famed for autumn foliage and the temples of Jingo-ji, Saimyō-ji and Kōzan-ji.

There are two options for buses to Takao: an hourly JR bus that leaves from Kyoto Station, which takes about an hour to reach the Takao stop (get off at the Yamashiro-Takao stop); and Kyoto city bus 8 from Shijō-

Kurama & Kibune

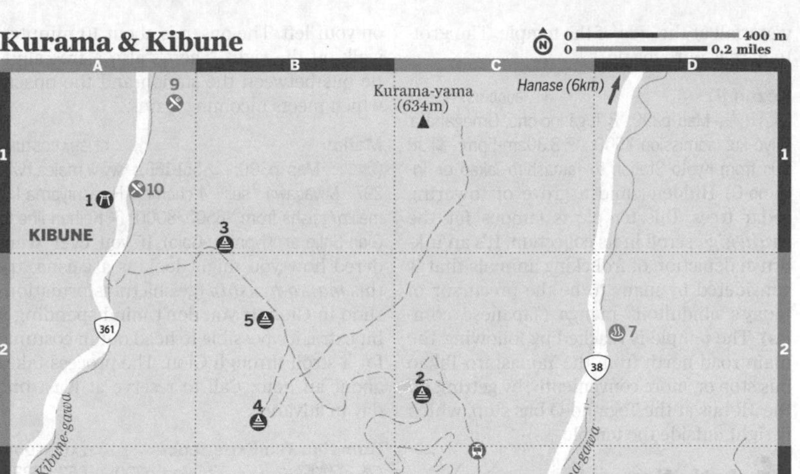

Kurama & Kibune

Sights

1 Kibune-jinja.......A1
2 Kurama-dera.......C2
3 Okuno-in Maō-den.......B1
4 Ōsugi-gongen.......B2
5 Sōjō-ga-dani Fudō-dō.......B2
6 Yuki-jinja.......C3

Activities, Courses & Tours

7 Kurama Onsen.......D2

Eating

8 Aburaya-Shokudō.......C3
9 Hirobun.......A1
10 Kibune Club.......A1
11 Yōshūji.......C3

Karasuma (get off at the Takao stop). To get to Jingo-ji from these bus stops, walk down to the river, then look for the steps on the other side.

Jingo-ji BUDDHIST TEMPLE
(神護寺; Map p290; 5 Takao-chō, Umegahata, Ukyō-ku; admission ¥500; 9am-4pm; JR Bus from Kyoto Station to Yamashiro-Takao) This mountaintop temple is one of our favourites in all of Kyoto. It sits at the top of a long flight of stairs that stretch from the Kiyotaki-gawa to the temple's main gate. The Kondō (Gold Hall) is the most impressive of the temple's structures, located roughly in the middle of the grounds at the top of another flight of stairs.

After visiting the Kondō, head in the opposite direction along a wooded path to an open area overlooking the valley. Here you'll see people tossing small discs over the railing into the chasm below. These are *kawarakenage,* light clay discs that people throw in order to rid themselves of their bad karma. Be careful, it's addictive and at ¥100 for two it can get expensive (you can buy the discs at a nearby stall). The trick is to flick the discs very gently, convex side up, like a frisbee. When you get it right, they sail all the way down the valley – taking all that bad karma with them (try not to think about the hikers down below).

To get to Jingo-ji, walk down to the river from the the Yamashiro-Takao bus stop and climb the steps on the other side.

Saimyō-ji BUDDHIST TEMPLE
(西明寺; Map p290; 2 Makino-chō, Umegahata, Ukyō-ku; admission ¥500; 9am-5pm; JR Bus from Kyoto Station to Yamashiro-Takao) About five minutes upstream from the base of the steps that lead to Jingo-ji, this fine little temple is one of our favourite spots in Kyoto. See if you can find your way round to the small

waterfall at the side of the temple. The grotto here is pure magic.

Kōzan-ji BUDDHIST TEMPLE

(高山寺; Map p290; 8 Toganoo-chō, Umegahata, Ukyō-ku; admission ¥600; 8.30am-5pm; JR Bus from Kyoto Station to Yamashiro-Takao or Toga-no-O) Hidden amid a grove of towering cedar trees, this temple is famous for the *chuju giga* scroll in its collection. It's an ink-brush depiction of frolicking animals that is considered by many to be the precursor of today's ubiquitous manga (Japanese comics). The temple is reached by following the main road north from the Yamashiro-Takao bus stop or, more conveniently, by getting off the JR bus at the Toga-no-O bus stop, which is right outside the temple.

Activities

Funaoka Onsen ONSEN

(船岡温泉; Map p298; 82-1 Minami-Funaoka-chō-Murasakino, Kita-ku; admission ¥410; 3pm-1am Mon-Sat, 8am-1am Sun & holidays; Kyoto City Bus 9 from Kyoto Station to Horikawa-Kuramaguchi) This old bath on Kuramaguchi-dōri is Kyoto's best. It boasts an outdoor bath, a sauna, a cypress-wood tub, an electric bath, a herbal bath and a few more for good measure. To get there, head west about 400m on Kuramaguchi-dōri from the Kuramaguchi-Horikawa intersection. It's on the left, not far past the Lawson convenience store. Look for the large rocks.

Be sure to check out the *ranma* (carved wooden panels) in the changing room. Carved during Japan's invasion of Manchuria, the panels offer insight into the prevailing mindset of that era. (Note the panels do contain some violent imagery, which may disturb some visitors.)

Kurama Onsen ONSEN

(鞍馬温泉; Map p319; 520 Kurama Honmachi, Sakyō-ku; admission outdoor bath only ¥1000, outdoor & indoor bath ¥2500; 10am-9pm; Eiden Eizan line from Demachiyanagi to Kurama) One of the few onsen within easy reach of Kyoto, Kurama Onsen is a great place to relax after a hike. The outdoor bath has fine views of Kurama-yama, while the indoor bath area includes some relaxation areas in addition to the tubs. For both baths, buy a ticket from the machine outside the door of the main building.

To get to Kurama Onsen, walk straight out of Kurama Station and continue up the main street, passing the entrance to Kurama-dera on your left. The onsen is about 10 minutes' walk on the right. There's also a free shuttle bus between the station and the onsen, which meets incoming trains.

Maika GEISHA COSTUME

(舞香; Map p300; 551-1661; www.maica.tv/e; 297 Miyagawa suji 4-chōme, Higashiyama-ku; maiko/geisha from ¥6500/8000; Keihan line to Gion-Shijo or Kiyomizu-Gojo) If you ever wondered how you might look as a geisha, try this *maiko-henshin* (geisha transformation) shop in Gion. If you don't mind spending a bit extra, it's possible to head out in costume for a stroll through Gion. The process takes about an hour. Call to reserve at least one day in advance.

Camellia Tea Experience TEA CEREMONY

(茶道体験カメリア; Map p300; 525-3238; www.tea-kyoto.com; 349 Masuya-chō, Higashiyama-ku; tea ceremony per person ¥2000; Kyoto City bus 206 to Yasui) Camellia is a superb place to try a simple Japanese tea ceremony. It's located in a beautiful old Japanese house just off Ninen-zaka, not far from Kiyomizu-dera. The host, Atsuko, speaks fluent English and explains the ceremony simply and clearly, while managing to perform an elegant ceremony without making guests nervous. The website has an excellent map and explanation.

En TEA CEREMONY

(えん; Map p300; 080-3782-2706; 272 Matsubara-chō, Higashiyama-ku; tea ceremony per person ¥2000; 3-6pm, closed Wed; Kyoto City bus 206 to Gion or Chionin-mae) This is a small teahouse near Gion where you can experience the Japanese tea ceremony with a minimum of fuss or expense. English explanations are provided and tea ceremonies are held at 3pm, 4pm, 5pm or 6pm (check the website for latest times, as these may change). Reservations are recommended in high season. It's a little tricky to find: it's down a little alley off Higashiōji-dōri – look for the sign just south of Tenkaippin Rāmen.

Courses

Uzuki COOKING COURSE

(www.kyotouzuki.com; 3hr class per person ¥4000) If you want to learn how to cook some of the delightful foods you've tried in Kyoto, we highly recommend Uzuki, a small cooking class conducted in a Japanese home for groups of two to four people. You will learn how to cook a variety of dishes and then sit down and enjoy the fruits of your labour. You can consult beforehand if you have particular dishes you'd like to cook. The fee includes all ingredients. Reserve via the website.

Haru Cooking Class COOKING COURSE

(料理教室はる; Map p298; http://www.kyoto-cooking-class.com/index.html; Shimogamo Miyazaki-chō 166-32, Sakyō-ku; per person from ¥5900; ⏲classes from 2pm daily, reservation required) Haru Cooking Class is a friendly one-man cooking school located in a private home a little bit north of Demachiyanagi. The school's teacher, Haru, speaks great English and can teach both vegetarian and non-vegetarian cooking. He also offers tours of Nishiki Market. Reserve by email.

Festivals & Events

There are hundreds of festivals happening in Kyoto throughout the year. Listings of these can be found in the free *Kansai Scene* weekly magazine or on www.kyotoguide.com. The following are some of the major and most spectacular festivals. These attract hordes of spectators from out of town, so you will need to book accommodation well in advance.

Setsubun Matsuri at Yoshida-jinja RELIGIOUS

This festival is held on the day of *setsubun* (2, 3 or 4 February; check with the TIC), which marks the last day of winter in the Japanese lunar calendar. In this festival, people climb up to Yoshida-jinja in the Northern Higashiyama area to watch a huge bonfire (in which old good-luck charms are burned). It's one of Kyoto's more dramatic festivals. The action starts at dusk.

Aoi Matsuri PARADE

The Hollyhock Festival dates back to the 6th century and commemorates the successful prayers of the people for the gods to stop calamitous weather. These days the procession involves imperial messengers carried in ox carts and a retinue of 600 people dressed in traditional costume. The procession leaves at around 10am on 15 May from the Kyoto Gosho and heads for Shimogamo-jinja.

Gion Matsuri PARADE

Kyoto's most important festival, Gion Matsuri reaches a climax on 17 July with a parade of over 30 floats and a smaller parade on 24 July. On the three evenings preceding the 17th, people gather on Shijō-dōri dressed in beautiful *yukata* (light summer kimonos) to look at the floats and carouse from one street stall to the next.

Daimon-ji Gozan Okuribi CULTURAL

This festival is celebrated on 16 August as a means of bidding farewell to the souls of ancestors. Enormous fires, in the form of Chinese characters or other shapes, are lit on five mountains. The largest fire is burned on Daimon-ji-yama, just above Ginkaku-ji, in Northern Higashiyama. The fires start at 8pm and the best perspective is from the banks of the Kamo-gawa.

Jidai Matsuri PARADE

The Festival of the Ages is of comparatively recent origin, only dating back to 1895. More than 2000 people, dressed in costumes ranging from the 8th century to the 19th century, parade from Kyoto Gosho to Heian-jingū on 22 October.

Kurama-no-hi Matsuri CULTURAL

In perhaps Kyoto's most dramatic festival, the Kurama Fire Festival, huge flaming torches are carried through the streets of Kurama by men in loincloths on 22 October (the same day as the Jidai Matsuri). Note that trains to and from Kurama will be completely packed with passengers on the evening of the festival (we suggest going early and returning late).

Sleeping

The most convenient areas in which to be based, in terms of easy access to shopping, dining and sightseeing attractions, are downtown Kyoto and the Higashiyama area. The Kyoto Station area is also a good location, with excellent access to transport and plenty of shops and restaurants. Transport information in the following listings is from Kyoto Station, unless otherwise noted.

Kyoto Station Area

★Capsule Ryokan Kyoto CAPSULE HOTEL ¥

(カプセル旅館京都; Map p294; ☎344-1510; www.capsule-ryokan-kyoto.com; 204 Tsuchihashi-chō, Shimogyō-ku; capsule ¥3500, tw per person from ¥3990; @ 📶; Ⓢ Karasuma line to Kyoto, 🚉 JR Tōkaidō main line to Kyoto) This unique new accommodation offers ryokan-style capsules (meaning tatami mats inside the capsules), as well as comfortable, cleverly designed private rooms. Each capsule also has its own TV and cable internet access point, while the private rooms have all the amenities you might need. Free internet, wifi and other amenities are available in the comfortable lounge.

It's near the southeast corner of the Horikawa–Shichijo intersection.

★Tour Club GUESTHOUSE ¥

(ツアークラブ; Map p294; ☎353-6968; www.kyotojp.com; 362 Momiji-chō, Higashinakasuji, Shōmen-sagaru, Shimogyō-ku; d/tw/tr per person ¥3490/3885/2960; ⊖@🛜; Ⓢ Karasuma line to Kyoto, Ⓡ JR Tōkaidō main line) This clean, well-maintained guesthouse remains a favourite of foreign visitors to Kyoto. Facilities include internet access, a small Zen garden, laundry, wi-fi, and free tea and coffee. Most private rooms have a private bathroom and toilet, and there is a spacious quad room for families. This is probably the best choice in this price bracket.

From Kyoto Station turn north off Shichijō-dōri two blocks before Horikawa (at the faux-Greco building) and keep an eye out for the English sign.

Budget Inn GUESTHOUSE ¥

(バジェットイン; Map p294; ☎344-1510; www.budgetinnjp.com; 295 Aburanokōji-chō, Aburanokōji, Shichijō-sagaru, Shimogyō-ku; tr/q/5-person r per person ¥3660/3245/2996; ⊖@🛜; Ⓢ Karasuma line to Kyoto, Ⓡ JR Tōkaidō main line) This well-run guesthouse is an excellent choice in this price bracket. It has eight Japanese-style private rooms, all of which are clean and well maintained. All rooms have private bathroom and toilet, and can accommodate up to five people, making it good for families. The staff is very helpful and friendly, and internet access, laundry and wi-fi are available.

Matsubaya Ryokan RYOKAN ¥

(松葉家旅館; Map p294; ☎351-3727; www.matsubayainn.com/; Kamijuzūyachō-dōri, Higashinotōin nishi-iru, Shimogyō-ku; r per person from ¥4400; @🛜; Ⓢ Karasuma line to Kyoto, Ⓡ JR Tōkaidō main line) A short walk from Kyoto Station, this newly renovated ryokan has clean, well-kept rooms and a management that is used to foreign guests. Some rooms on the 1st floor look out on small gardens. Western (¥500 to ¥900) or Japanese breakfast (¥1000) is available.

Ryokan Shimizu RYOKAN ¥

(京の宿しみず; Map p294; ☎371-5538; www.kyoto-shimizu.net; 644 Kagiya-chō, Shichijō-dōri, Wakamiya-agaru, Shimogyō-ku; r per person from ¥5250, Sat & nights before holidays plus ¥1080; ⊖@; Ⓢ Karasuma line to Kyoto, Ⓡ JR Tōkaidō main line) A short walk north of Kyoto Station's Karasuma central gate, this friendly ryokan has a loyal following of foreign guests, and for good reason: it's clean, well run and fun. Rooms are standard ryokan style with one difference: all have private bathrooms and toilets. Bicycle rental is available.

K's House Kyoto GUESTHOUSE ¥

(ケイズハウス京都; Map p294; ☎342-2444; http://kshouse.jp/kyoto-e/; 418 Naya-chō, Dotemachi-dōri, Shichijō-agaru, Shimogyō-ku; dm from ¥2400, s/d/tw per person from ¥3800/3100/3100; ⊖@🛜; Ⓢ Karasuma line to Kyoto, Ⓡ JR Tōkaidō main line) K's House is a large 'New Zealand–style' guesthouse with both private and dorm rooms. The rooms are simple but adequate and there are spacious common areas. The rooftop terrace, patio and attached bar-restaurant make this a very sociable spot and a good place to meet other travellers and share information.

★Ibis Styles Kyoto Station HOTEL ¥¥

(イビススタイルズ 京都ステーション; Map p294; ☎693-8444; www.ibis.com/gb/hotel-9418-ibis-styles-kyoto-station/index.shtml; 47 Higashikujō-Kamitonoda-chō, Minami-ku; r from ¥6500-10,000; Ⓢ Karasuma line to Kyoto, Ⓡ JR Tōkaidō main line) This great new business hotel just outside the south entrance to Kyoto Station offers excellent value. The rooms are small but packed with features you need. The staff are extremely efficient. All in all, this is a great option for the price.

★Dormy Inn Premium Kyoto Ekimae HOTEL ¥¥

(ドーミーインPREMIUM京都駅前; Map p294; ☎371-5489; www.hotespa.net/hotels/kyoto; Higashishiokōji-chō 558-8, Shimogyō-ku; tw/d from ¥12,500/11,890; @; Ⓢ Karasuma line to Kyoto, Ⓡ JR Tōkaidō main line to Kyoto) Located almost directly across the street from Kyoto Station, this efficient new hotel is a great choice. Rooms are clean and well maintained and the on-site spa bath is a nice plus.

★Hotel Granvia Kyoto HOTEL ¥¥¥

(ホテルグランヴィア京都; Map p294; ☎344-8888; www.granviakyoto.com; Karasuma-dōri, Shiokōji-sagaru, Shimogyō-ku; tw/d from ¥16,000/21,000; ⊖@≋; Ⓢ Karasuma line to Kyoto, Ⓡ JR Tōkaidō main line) Imagine being able to step out of bed and straight into the *shinkansen* (bullet train). This is almost possible when you stay at the Hotel Granvia, which is located directly above Kyoto Station. The rooms are clean, spacious and elegant, with deep bathtubs. This is a very professional operation with good on-site restaurants, some of which have views over the city.

Downtown Kyoto

★**Hotel Sunroute Kyoto** HOTEL ¥¥

(ホテルサンルート京都; Map p290; ☎371-3711; www.sunroute.jp/english/hotelinfo/kinki/kyoto/; 406 Nanba-chō, Kawaramachi-dōri, Matsubara-sagaru, Shimogyō-ku; r from ¥6300-10,000; @📶; 🚉Hankyū line to Kawaramachi) Located within easy walking distance of downtown, this brand-new hotel is a superb choice in this price bracket. As you'd expect, rooms aren't large, but they have everything you need. It's well run and comfortable with foreign travellers. In-room internet is LAN cable only, but there's free wi-fi in the 2nd-floor lobby.

Hotel Unizo HOTEL ¥¥

(ホテルユニゾ京都; Map p296; ☎241-3351; www.hotelunizo.com/eng/kyoto; Kawaramachi-dōri, Sanjō-sagaru, Nakagyō-ku; s/d/tw from ¥10,000/17,000/19,000; 🚭@📶; 🚌Kyoto City bus 5 to Kawaramachi-Sanjō, S Tōzai line to Kyoto-Shiyakusho-mae) They don't get more convenient than this business hotel: it's smack in the middle of Kyoto's nightlife, shopping and dining district – you can walk to hundreds of restaurants and shops within five minutes. It's a standard-issue business hotel, with tiny but adequate rooms and unit bathrooms. Nothing special, but it's clean, well run and used to foreign guests.

Royal Park Hotel The Kyoto HOTEL ¥¥

(ロイヤルパークホテル ザ 京都; Map p296; ☎241-1111; www.rph-the.co.jp/en/kyoto/; Sanjō-dōri, Kawaramachi higashi-iru, Nakagyō-ku; s/d from ¥10,000/12,500; 📶; S Tōzai line to Kyoto-Shiyakusho-mae, 🚉Keihan line to Sanjō) Located on Sanjō-dōri, a stone's throw from the river, this hotel commands a super-convenient location, with tons of shops and restaurants within easy walking distance. The hotel has a modern, chic feel, and rooms are slightly larger than at standard business hotels. The French bakery downstairs makes breakfast a breeze.

Hotel Vista Premio Kyoto HOTEL ¥¥

(ホテルビスタプレミオ京都; Map p296; ☎256-5888; www.hotel-vista.jp/kyoto-kawaramachi/index_e.html; Matsugae-chō 457, Kawaramachi-dōri, Rokkaku nishi-iru, Nakagyō-ku; s/tw from ¥6800/11,000; @📶; S Tōzai line to Kyoto-Shiyakusho-mae) Newly refurbished, and tucked into a lane between two of Kyoto's main downtown shopping streets, this is a really smart, clean hotel. There are some nice Japanese design touches in the rooms, which are compact but adequate. Overall, it's good value for the money and a super-convenient location.

Mitsui Garden Hotel Kyoto Sanjō HOTEL ¥¥

(三井ガーデンホテル 京都三条; Map p296; ☎256-3331; www.gardenhotels.co.jp/eng/sanjo; 80 Mikura-chō, Sanjō-dōri, Karasuma nishi-iru, Nakagyō-ku; s/d/tw from ¥6000/8700/9600; @; S Tōzai or Karasuma lines to Karasuma-Oike) Just west of the downtown dining and shopping district, this is a clean and efficient hotel that offers good value for the price and reasonably comfortable rooms.

★**Tawaraya** RYOKAN ¥¥¥

(俵屋; Map p296; ☎211-5566; 278 Nakahakusan-chō, Fuyachō, Oike-sagaru, Nakagyō-ku; r per person incl 2 meals ¥55,891-74,520; 🚭@; S Tōzai line to Kyoto-Shiyakusho-mae, exit 8) Tawaraya has been operating for more than three centuries and is one of the finest places to stay in the world. From the decorations to the service to the food, everything is simply the best available. It's a very intimate, warm and personal place that has many loyal guests.

★**Hiiragiya Ryokan** RYOKAN ¥¥¥

(柊屋; Map p296; ☎221-1136; www.hiiragiya.co.jp/en; Nakahakusan-chō, Fuyachō, Aneyakōji-agaru, Nakagyō-ku; r per person incl 2 meals ¥34,560-86,400; 🚭@; S Tōzai line to Kyoto-Shiyakusho-mae, exit 8) This elegant ryokan has long been favoured by celebrities from around the world. Facilities and services are excellent and the location is hard to beat. Ask for one of the newly redecorated rooms if you prefer a polished sheen; alternatively, request an older room if you fancy some 'Old Japan' *wabi-sabi* (imperfect beauty).

Kyoto Hotel Ōkura HOTEL ¥¥¥

(京都ホテルオークラ; Map p296; ☎211-5111; http://okura.kyotohotel.co.jp/english/; 537-4 Ichinofunairi-chō, Kawaramachi-dōri, Oike, Nakagyō-ku; s/d/tw from ¥13,600/23,000/18,400; 🚭@; S Tōzai line to Kyoto-Shiyakusho-mae, exit 3) This towering hotel in the centre of town commands an impressive view of the Higashiyama Mountains. Rooms are spacious and clean and many have great views, especially the excellent corner suites – we just wish we could open a window to enjoy the breeze.

You can access the Kyoto subway system directly from the hotel, which is convenient on rainy days or if you have luggage. You can often find great online rates for the Ōkura and it's one of the better value places in this price bracket.

TIM HUGHES / GETTY IMAGES ©

1. Kyoto Station (p292)
Kyoto Tower is reflected in the facade of this futuristic building.

2.Daigo-ji (p315)
This Buddhist temple was founded in AD 874. Its five-storey pagoda is the oldest of its kind in Japan.

3. Nishiki Market (p294)
Offering a staggering range of weird and wonderful ingredients, this is a must-see for foodies.

4. Traditional dress
Women in kimono stroll past women dressed as geisha in Kyoto.

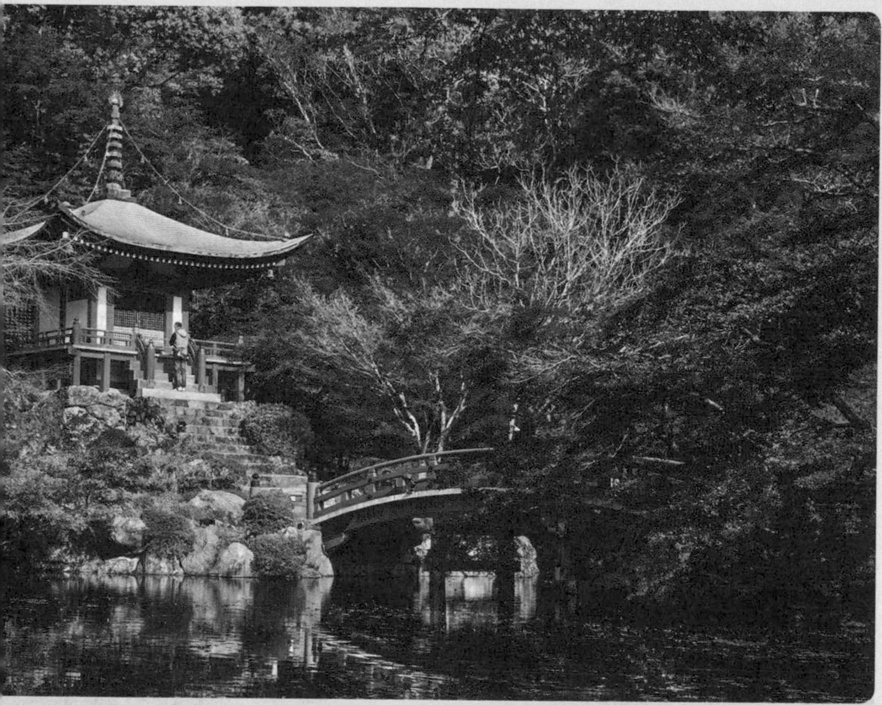

YU KODAMA / GETTY IMAGES ©

FUTURE LIGHT / GETTY IMAGES ©

WIBOWO RUSLI / GETTY IMAGES ©

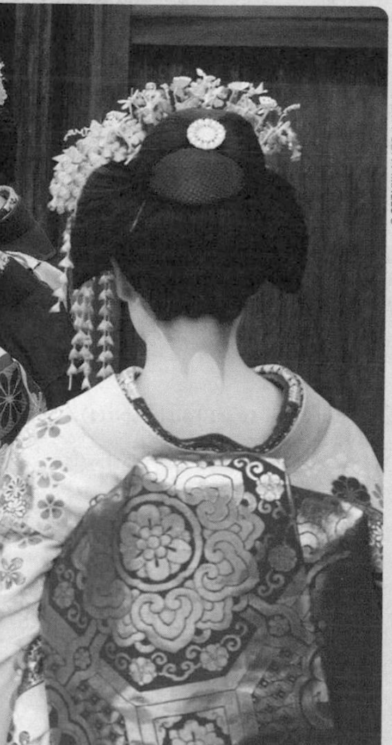

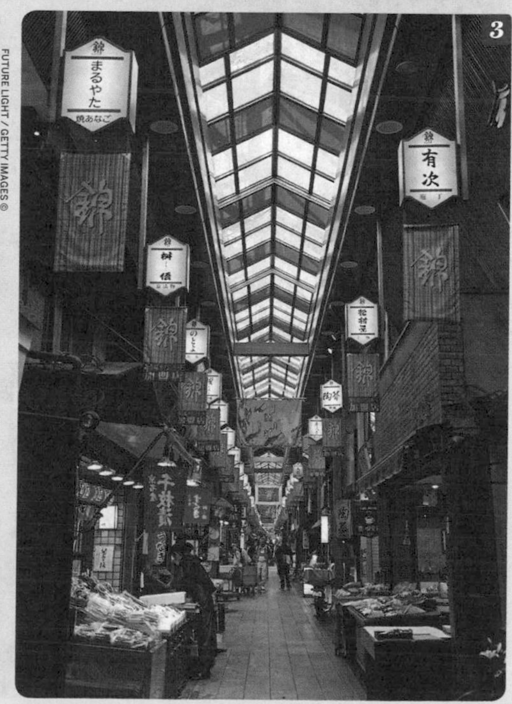

SANTI RODRIGUEZ / GETTY IMAGES ©

1. Fushimi-Inari Taisha (p314)
Arcades of vermilion *torii* (shrine gates) spread across this vast Shintō shrine complex, one of Kyoto's most memorable sights.

2. Kyoto Station (p292)
Not just a transport hub, Kyoto Station is an architectural marvel of glass and steel.

3. Kiyomizu-dera (p302)
Set on a hill overlooking Kyoto, this popular, crowded Buddhist temple offers a look at how faith is expressed in Japan today.

MICHAEL MARQUAND / GETTY IMAGES ©

Yoshikawa RYOKAN ¥¥¥
(吉川; Map p296; ☎221-5544; www.kyoto-yoshikawa.co.jp; 135 Matsushita-chō, Tominokōji, Oike-sagaru, Nakagyō-ku; r per person incl 2 meals from ¥32,400 (low season), ¥48,600 (high season); @; S Tōzai or Karasuma lines to Karasuma-Oike) Located in the heart of downtown, within easy walking distance of two subway stations and the entire dining and nightlife district, this superb traditional ryokan has beautiful rooms and a stunning garden. The ryokan is famous for its tempura and its meals are of a high standard. All rooms have private bathrooms and toilets.

Ritz-Carlton Kyoto HOTEL ¥¥¥
(ザ・リッツ・カールトン京都; Map p298; ☎746-5555; www.ritzcarlton.com/en/Properties/Kyoto; 543 Hokoden-chō, Nijō-Ōhashi-hotori, Nakagyō-ku; r ¥65,000-200,000; @ 📶 🏊; S Tōzai line to Kyoto-Shiyakusho-mae, 🚉 Keihan line to Sanjō or Jingū-Marutamachi) The new Ritz-Carlton is an oasis of luxury that commands perhaps the finest views of any hotel in the city – it's located on the banks for the Kamo-gawa and huge windows in the east-facing rooms take in the whole expanse of the Higashiyama mountains. The rooms are superbly designed and supremely comfortable, with plenty of Japanese touches.

Common areas are elegant and the on-site restaurants and bars are excellent. Finally, there are fine spa, gym and pool facilities.

Central Kyoto

Gojō Guest House GUESTHOUSE ¥
(五条ゲストハウス; Map p300; ☎525-2299; www.gojo-guest-house.com/; Gojōbashi higashi 3-396-2, Higashiyama-ku; dm ¥2600, s/tw ¥3500/6600; @; 🚉 Keihan line to Kiyomizu-Gojō) This is a fine guesthouse in an old wooden Japanese house, which makes the place feel more like a ryokan than your average guesthouse. It's a relaxed and friendly place at home with foreign guests. The staff speak good English and can help with travel advice. Best of all, it has *gaijin* (foreigner)-sized futons!

Palace Side Hotel HOTEL ¥¥
(ザ・パレスサイドホテル; Map p298; ☎415-8887; www.palacesidehotel.co.jp; Okakuen-chō, Karasuma-dōri, Shimotachiuri-agaru, Kamigyō-ku; s/tw/d from ¥6300/10,200/10,200; 🚭 @; S Karasuma line to Marutamachi) Overlooking the Kyoto Imperial Palace Park, this excellent-value hotel has a lot going for it, starting with friendly English-speaking staff, great service, washing machines, an on-site restaurant, well-maintained rooms and free internet terminals. The rooms are small but serviceable.

Ryokan Rakuchō RYOKAN ¥¥
(洛頂旅館; Map p298; ☎721-2174; 67 Higashi-hangi-chō, Shimogamo, Sakyō-ku; s/tw/tr ¥5300/9240/12,600; 🚭 @ 📶; 🚌 Kyoto City bus 205 to Furitsudaigaku-mae, S Karasuma line to Kitaōji) There is a lot to appreciate about this fine foreigner-friendly ryokan in the northern part of town: there is a nice little garden; it's entirely nonsmoking; and the rooms are clean and simple. Meals aren't served, but staff can provide you with a good map of local eateries. The downside is the somewhat out-of-the-way location.

Tōyoko Inn Kyoto Gojō Karasuma HOTEL ¥¥
(東横INN京都五条烏丸; Map p290; ☎344-1045; www.toyoko-inn.com/hotel/00040/; Gojō Karasuma-chō 393, Karasuma-dōri, Matsubara-sagaru, Shimogyō-ku; s/tw incl breakfast from ¥6804/10,044; @; S Karasuma line to Gojō) Those familiar with the Tōyoko Inn chain know that this hotel brand specialises in simple, clean, fully equipped but small rooms at the lowest price possible. There are all kinds of extras: free breakfast, free telephone calls inside Japan, and reduced rates on rental cars. Staff will even lend you a laptop if you need to check your email.

It's a little south of the city centre, but easily accessed by subway from Kyoto Station.

Citadines Karasuma-Gojō Kyoto HOTEL ¥¥¥
(シタディーン京都　烏丸五条; Map p290; ☎352-8900; www.citadines.jp/kyoto; Matsuya-chō 432, Gojō-dōri, Karasuma higashi-iru, Shimogyō-ku; tw/d from ¥28,600; @; S Karasuma line to Gojō) On Gojō-dōri, a bit south of the main downtown district, but within easy walking distance of the Karasuma subway line (as well as the Keihan line), this serviced apartment-hotel is a welcome addition to the Kyoto accommodation scene. The kitchens allow you to do your own cooking and other touches make you feel right at home.

Southern Higashiyama

JAM Hostel Kyoto Gion GUESTHOUSE ¥
(JAM ジャムホステル京都祇園; Map p296; ☎201-3374; www.jamhostel.com; 170 Tokiwa-chō, Higashiyama-ku; dm per person ¥2000-4000; 🚉 Keihan line to Gion Shijō) This new guesthouse boasts a convenient location on the

edge of Gion and a sake bar downstairs that is a convivial place for guests to mix with local regulars. There are a variety of simple but clean dorm rooms and shared bathing facilities.

Gion Apartments APARTMENT ¥¥
(ザギオンアパートメンツ; Map p300; www.thegionapartments.com/home; Yamatooji-dōri, Gōjo-agaru, Higashiyama-ku; apt per night from ¥12,000; ; Keihan line to Kiyomizu-Gojō) This is a collection of several well-maintained apartments on the south end of Gion. Each of the apartments has a kitchenette, laundry facilities and private shower/bath. The apartments are within walking distance of Gion, downtown Kyoto and the Southern Higashiyama tourist district.

Ryokan Uemura RYOKAN ¥¥
(旅館うえむら; Map p300; fax 561-0377; Ishibe-kōji, Shimogawara, Higashiyama-ku; r incl breakfast per person ¥10,000; ; Kyoto City bus 206 to Higashiyama-Yasui) This beautiful little ryokan is at ease with foreign guests. It's on a quaint, quiet cobblestone alley, just down the hill from some of Kyoto's most important sights. The owner prefers bookings by fax and asks that cancellations also be made by fax – with so few rooms, it can be costly when bookings are broken without notice.

Book well in advance, as there are only three rooms. There's a 10pm curfew.

★ **Hyatt Regency Kyoto** HOTEL ¥¥¥
(ハイアットリージェンシー京都; Map p300; 541-1234; www.kyoto.regency.hyatt.com/en/hotel/home.html; 644-2 Sanjūsangendō-mawari, Higashiyama-ku; r from ¥28,512; ; Keihan line to Shichijō) The Hyatt Regency is an excellent, stylish and foreigner-friendly hotel at the southern end of Kyoto's Southern Higashiyama sightseeing district. Many travellers consider this the best hotel in Kyoto. The staff are extremely efficient and helpful (there are even foreign staff members – a rarity in Japan). The on-site restaurants and bar are excellent.

The stylish rooms and bathrooms have lots of neat touches. The concierges are knowledgeable about the city and they'll even lend you a laptop to check your email if you don't have your own.

Shiraume Ryokan RYOKAN ¥¥¥
(白梅; Map p300; 561-1459; www.shiraume-kyoto.jp/index_en.html; Gion Shimbashi, Shirakawa hotori, Shijōnawate-agaru, higashi-iru, Higashiyama-ku; r per person incl 2 meals ¥23,760-37,800, per person incl breakfast only ¥16,200-27,000 ; @; Keihan line to Gion-Shijō) Looking out over the Shirakawa Canal in Shimbashi, a lovely street in Gion, this ryokan offers excellent location, atmosphere and service. The decor is traditional with a small inner garden and nice wooden bathtubs. This is a great spot to sample the Japanese ryokan experience.

Gion Hatanaka RYOKAN ¥¥¥
(祇園畑中; Map p300; 541-5315; www.thehatanaka.co.jp/english/; Yasaka-jinja Minami-mon mae, Higashiyama-ku; r per person incl 2 meals from ¥25,000; ; Kyoto City bus 206 to Higashiyama-Yasui) Gion Hatanaka is a fine ryokan right in the heart of the Southern Higashiyama sightseeing district (less than a minute's walk from Yasaka-jinja). Despite being fairly large, it manages to retain an intimate and private feeling. In addition to bathtubs in each room, there is a huge wooden communal bath. The rooms are clean, well designed and relaxing.

This ryokan offers regularly scheduled geisha entertainment that nonguests are welcome to join.

Seikōrō RYOKAN ¥¥¥
(晴鴨楼; Map p300; 561-0771; http://ryokan.asia/seikoro; 467 Nishi Tachibana-chō, 3 chō-me, Toiyamachi-dori, Gojō-sagaru, Higashiyama-ku; r per person incl 2 meals from ¥21,600; @; Keihan line to Kiyomizu-Gojō) The Seikōrō is a classic ryokan with a grandly decorated lobby. It's fairly spacious, with excellent, comfortable rooms, attentive service and a fairly convenient midtown location. Several rooms look over gardens and all have private bathrooms.

KYOTO'S BEST RYOKAN

Tawaraya (p323) A serene haven in the heart of the city, this ryokan is often rated the best in Japan.

Hiiragiya Ryokan (p323) With a beautiful new wing and a *wabi-sabi* old wing, Hiiragiya offers the classic ryokan experience.

Seikōrō An elegant ryokan near the river with rates within the range of mere mortals.

Shiraume Ryokan A boutique ryokan in the heart of Gion with a loyal following of discerning guests.

Motonago RYOKAN ¥¥¥

(旅館元奈古; Map p300; ☎561-2087; www.motonago.com/en/top.html; 511 Washio-chō, Kōdaiji-michi, Higashiyama-ku; r per person incl 2 meals from ¥18,367; ⊖@📶; 🚌Kyoto City bus 206 to Gion) This ryokan may have the best location of any in the city, and it hits all the right notes for one in this class: classic Japanese decor, friendly service, nice bathtubs and a few small Japanese gardens.

Gion House RENTAL HOUSE ¥¥¥

(ザ祇園ハウス; Map p300; ☎353-8282; www.thegionhouse.com; 563-12 Komatsu-chō, Higashiyama-ku; per night from ¥23,000; 📶; 🚌Kyoto City bus 206 to Higashiyama-Yasui, 🚇Keihan line to Gion-Shijō) This beautifully decorated traditional Japanese house stands right on the edge of Gion and would make the perfect getaway for those seeking something other than a run-of-the-mill hotel. It's spacious and comfortable, and there's everything you need to take care of yourselves for a few days in the old capital.

Sakara Kyoto INN ¥¥¥

(桜香楽; Map p300; http://sakarakyoto.com; 541-2 Furukawa-chō, Higashiyama-ku; r ¥11,000-25,000; @📶; S Tōzai line to Higashiyama) This modern Japanese-style inn is conveniently located in a covered pedestrian shopping arcade just south of Sanjō-dōri, about 50m from Higashiyama subway station. It's great for couples and families, and rooms can accommodate up to five people. Each room has bath/shower, kitchenette and laundry facilities. Reservation is by email only.

Northern Higashiyama

★Westin Miyako Kyoto HOTEL ¥¥¥

(ウェスティン都ホテル京都; Map p306; ☎771-7111; www.miyakohotels.ne.jp/westinkyoto; Keage, Sanjō-dōri, Higashiyama-ku; d/tw from ¥16,200, Japanese-style r from ¥18,360; ⊖@📶🏊; S Tōzai line to Keage, exit 2) This grande dame of Kyoto hotels overlooks the Higashiyama sightseeing district (meaning it's one of the best locations for sightseeing in Kyoto). Rooms are clean and well maintained, and staff are at home with foreign guests. Rooms on the north side have great views over the city to the Kitayama mountains.

There is a fitness centre, as well as a private garden and walking trail. The hotel even has its own ryokan section for those who want to try staying in a ryokan without giving up the convenience of a hotel.

Koto Inn RENTAL HOUSE ¥¥¥

(古都イン; Map p300; ☎751-2753; koto.inn@gmail.com; 373 Horiike-chō, Higashiyama-ku; per night from ¥15,000; ⊖@📶; S Tōzai line to Higashiyama) Conveniently located near the Higashiyama sightseeing district, this vacation rental is good for families, couples and groups who want a bit of privacy. It's got everything you need and is decorated with lovely Japanese antiques. While the building is traditionally Japanese, all the facilities are fully modernised.

Kyoto Garden Ryokan Yachiyo RYOKAN ¥¥¥

(旅館八千代; Map p306; ☎771-4148; www.ryokan-yachiyo.com; 34 Fukuchi-chō, Nanzen-ji, Sakyō-ku; r per person incl 2 meals ¥18,900-42,000; ⊖📶; S Tōzai line to Keage, exit 2) Located just down the street from Nanzen-ji, this large ryokan is at home with foreign guests. Rooms are spacious and clean, and some look out over private gardens. English-speaking staff are available.

Northwest Kyoto and Arashiyama & Sagano Area

Utano Youth Hostel HOSTEL ¥

(宇多野ユースホステル; Map p311; ☎462-2288; http://yh-kyoto.or.jp/utano/index.html; Nakayama-chō 29, Uzumasa, Ukyō-ku; dm/tw per person ¥3300/4000; 🚌Kyoto City bus 26 to Yūsu-Hosuteru-mae) The best hostel in Kyoto, Utano is friendly and well organised and makes a convenient base for the sights of northwest Kyoto (but keep in mind that it's a hike to reach any other part of town). If you want to skip the hostel food, turn left along the main road to find several coffee shops offering cheap *teishoku* (set-course meals). There is a 10pm curfew.

Shunkō-in TEMPLE LODGE ¥

(春光院; Map p311; ☎462-5488; rev.taka.kawakami@gmail.com; Myōshinji-chō 42, Hanazono, Ukyō-ku; per person ¥4000-5000; @; 🚇JR Sagano/San-in line to Hanazono) This is a *shukubō* (temple lodging) at a subtemple in Myōshin-ji. It's very comfortable and quiet and the main priest here speaks fluent English. For an extra ¥1000 you can try Zen meditation and go on a guided tour of the temple. Being in the temple at night is a very special experience.

Hoshinoya Kyoto RYOKAN ¥¥¥

(星のや京都; Map p313; ☎871-0001; http://kyoto.hoshinoya.com/en; Arashiyama Genrokuzan-chō 11-2, Nishikyō-ku; r per person incl meals from

¥70,296; Kyoto City bus 28 from Kyoto Station to Arashiyama-Tenryuji-mae, JR Sagano/San-in line to Saga-Arashiyama or Hankyū line to Arashiyama, change at Katsura) Sitting in a secluded area on the south bank of the Hozu-gawa in Arashiyama (upstream from the main sightseeing district), this modern take on the classic Japanese inn is quickly becoming a favourite of well-heeled visitors to Kyoto in search of privacy and a unique experience. Rooms feature incredible views of the river and the surrounding mountains.

The best part is the approach: you'll be chauffeured by a private boat from a dock near Togetsu-kyō bridge to the inn (note that on days following heavy rains, you'll have to go by car instead). This is easily one of the most unique places to stay in Kyoto.

Kansai Airport

Hotel Nikkō Kansai Airport HOTEL ¥¥
(ホテル日航関西空港; 072-455-1111; www.nikkokix.com; Senshū Kūkō Kita 1, Izumisano-shi, Osaka-fu; s/tw/d from ¥9500/11,000/14,500; ; JR Haruka Airport Express to Kansai Airport) The only hotel at the airport is the excellent Hotel Nikkō Kansai Airport, connected to the main terminal building by a pedestrian bridge (you can even bring your luggage trolleys right to your room). The rooms here are in good condition, spacious and comfortable enough for brief stays.

Eating

Kyoto is a great place to explore Japanese cuisine and you'll find good restaurants regardless of your budget. If you tire of Japanese food, there are also plenty of excellent international restaurants to choose from. You'll find the thickest concentration of eateries in downtown Kyoto, but also great choices in Southern Higashiyama/Gion and in and around Kyoto Station.

Because Kyoto gets a lot of foreign travellers, you'll find a surprising number of English menus and most places are quite comfortable with foreign guests.

Kyoto Station Area

The new Kyoto Station building is chock-a-block with restaurants, and if you find yourself anywhere near the station around mealtime, this is probably your best bet in terms of variety and price.

There are several food courts scattered about the station building. The best of these can be found on the 11th floor on the west side of the building: the **Cube** (ザ キューブ; Map p294; 371-2134; 11F Kyoto Station Bldg, Karasuma-dōri, Shiokōji-sagaru, Shimogyō-ku; 11am-10pm; Karasuma line to Kyoto, JR Tōkaidō main line to Kyoto) food court and Isetan department store's **Eat Paradise** (イートパラダイス; Map p294; 352-1111; 11F Kyoto Station Bldg, Karasuma-dōri, Shiokōji-sagaru, Shimogyō-ku; 11am-10pm; Kyoto Station) food court. In Eat Paradise, we like Tonkatsu Wako for *tonkatsu* (deep-fried pork cutlets), Tenichi for sublime tempura, and Wakuden for approachable *kaiseki* fare. To get to these food courts, take the west escalators from the main concourse all the way up to the 11th floor and look for Cube on your left and Eat Paradise straight in front of you.

Other options in the station include **Kyoto Rāmen Koji** (京都拉麺小路; Map p294; 361-4401; 10F Kyoto Station Bldg, Karasuma-dōri, Shiokōji-sagaru, Shimogyō-ku; rāmen ¥700-1000; 11am-10pm; Kyoto Station), a group of seven *rāmen* (noodles in broth) restaurants on the 10th floor. Buy tickets from the machines, which don't have English but have pictures on the buttons. In addition to *rāmen,* you can get green-tea ice cream and other Japanese desserts at Chasen, and *tako-yaki* (grilled octopus dumplings) at Miyako.

About five minutes' walk north of the station, Yodobashi Camera (p343) has a wide selection of restaurants on the 6th floor, and an international supermarket with lots of takeaway items on the B2 floor.

Downtown Kyoto

Downtown Kyoto has the best variety of approachable Japanese and international restaurants.

★**Ippūdō** RĀMEN ¥
(一風堂; Map p296; 213-8800; Higashinotō-in, Nishikikōji higashi-iru, Nakagyō-ku; rāmen ¥750-950; 11am-2am; ; Karasuma line to Shijō) There's a reason that there's usually a line outside this *rāmen* joint at lunchtime: the *rāmen* is awesome and the bite-sized *gyōza* (Chinese dumplings) are to die for. We recommend the *gyōza* set meal (¥750 or ¥850 depending on your choice of *rāmen*). It's on Nishiki-dōri, next to a post office and diagonally across from a Starbucks.

Saryo Zen Cafe CAFE ¥
(茶寮「然」カフェ; Map p298; Zenkashoin Kyoto Muromachi Store, 271-1 Takoyakushi-chō,

Muromachi-dōri, Nijō-sagaru, Nakagyō-ku; drinks from ¥1000; ⏲10am-7pm, closed 2nd & 4th Mon; 🗐; S Karasuma or Tōzai line to Karasuma-Oike) This brilliant modern tea room is a great place for a break – a break from sightseeing and a break from the international coffee chains that are taking over the city. You can enjoy a cup of *matcha* (powdered green tea) here served with a delicious Kyoto sweet, all in extremely comfortable surroundings.

Kerala INDIAN ¥

(ケララ; Map p296; ☎251-0141; 2nd fl, KUS Bldg, Kawaramachi-dōri, Sanjō-agaru, Nakagyō-ku; lunch/dinner from ¥850/2500; ⏲11.30am-2pm & 5-9pm; 🖉 🗐; S Tōzai line to Kyoto-Shiyakusho-mae) This narrow restaurant upstairs on Kawaramachi-dōri is Kyoto's best Indian restaurant. The ¥850 lunch set menu is an excellent deal, as is the vegetarian lunch, and the English menu is a bonus. Dinners run closer to ¥2500 per head and are of very high quality. Finish off the meal with the incredibly rich and creamy coconut ice cream.

Café Bibliotec Hello! CAFE ¥

(カフェビブリオテイックハロー！; Map p298; ☎231-8625; 650 Seimei-chō, Nijō-dōri, Yanaginobanba higashi-iru, Nakagyō-ku; meals from ¥1000, coffee ¥450; ⏲11.30am-midnight; 🗐; S Tōzai line to Kyoto-Shiyakusho-mae) As the name suggests, books line the walls of this cool cafe located in a converted *machiya* (traditional Japanese town house). You can get the usual range of coffee and tea drinks here, as well as light cafe lunches. It's popular with young ladies who work nearby and it's a great place to relax with a book or magazine. Look for the plants out the front.

Nishiki Warai OKONOMIYAKI ¥

(錦わらい; Map p296; ☎257-5966; 1st fl, Mizukōto Bldg, 597 Nishiuoya-chō, Nishikikōji-dōri, Takakura nishi-iru, Nakagyō-ku; okonomiyaki from ¥680; ⏲11.30am-midnight; 🗐; S Karasuma line to Shijō, R Hankyū line to Karasuma) This Nishiki-dōri restaurant is a great place to try *okonomiyaki* (Japanese pancakes) in casual surroundings. It can get a little smoky, but it's a fun spot to eat. It serves sets from as little as ¥680 at lunch. It's about 20m west of the west end of Nishiki Market; look for the English sign in the window.

Karafuneya Coffee Sanjō Honten CAFE ¥

(からふねや珈琲三条本店; Map p296; ☎254-8774; 39 Daikoku-chō, Kawaramachi-dōri, Sanjō-sagaru, Nakagyō-ku; meals from ¥900; ⏲9am-1am; 🗐; S Tōzai line to Kyoto-Shiyakusho-mae, R Keihan line to Sanjō) This casual coffee and dessert shop, downtown on Kawaramachi-dōri, is in the middle of Kyoto's main shopping district. It's a great spot for a pick-me-up during a day of retail therapy.

Japan is famous for its plastic food models, but this place takes them to a whole new level – it's like some futuristic dessert museum. We like the centrepiece of the display: the mother of all sundaes that goes for ¥10,000 to ¥18,000 and requires advance reservation to order. Lesser mortals can try the tasty *matcha* parfait for ¥780 or any of the cafe drinks and light meals on offer.

Biotei VEGETARIAN ¥

(びお亭; Map p296; ☎255-0086; 2nd fl, M&I Bldg, 28 Umetada-chō, Sanjō-dōri, Higashinotōin nishi-iru, Nakagyō-ku; lunch from ¥860; ⏲lunch & dinner, closed Sun, Mon, dinner Thu & lunch Sat; 🖉 🗐; S Tōzai or Karasuma lines to Karasuma-Oike) Located diagonally across from the Nakagyō post office, this is a favourite of Kyoto vegetarians and has an English menu. It serves daily sets of Japanese vegetarian food (the occasional bit of meat is offered as an option, but you'll be asked your preference). The seating is cramped but the food is very good and carefully made from quality ingredients.

Honke Tagoto NOODLES ¥

(本家田毎; Map p296; ☎221-3030; 12 Ishibashi-chō, Sanjō-dōri, Kawaramachi Nishi iru, Nakagyō-ku; noodle dishes from ¥840; ⏲11am-9pm; 🗐; S Tōzai Line to Kyoto Shiyakusho-mae) One of Kyoto's oldest *soba* restaurants makes a good break for those who have overdosed on *rāmen*. It's in the Sanjō covered arcade and you can see inside to the tables.

Rāmen Kairikiya RĀMEN ¥

(ラーメン魁力屋; Map p296; ☎251-0303; 1st fl, Hijikata Bldg, 435-2 Ebisu-chō, Kawaramachi-dōri, Sanjō-agaru, Nakagyō-ku; rāmen from ¥650; ⏲11am-3am; 🗐; S Tōzai line to Kyoto-Shiyakusho-mae) Not far from the Sanjō–Kawaramachi intersection, this popular *rāmen* specialist welcomes foreigners with an English menu and friendly staff. It's got several types of *rāmen* to choose from and tasty sets that include items like fried rice, fried chicken or *gyōza*, all for about ¥950.

Tsukimochiya Naomasa SWEETS ¥

(月餅家 直正; Map p296; ☎231-0175; 530 Kamiōsaka-chō, Kiyamachi-dōri, Sanjō-agaru, Nakagyō-ku; tsukimochi ¥150; ⏲9.30am-7pm, closed Thu; R Keihan line to Sanjō) This classic old sweet shop, about 50m north of Sanjō-dōri on Kiyamachi-dōri, is a great place to get acquainted with traditional Kyoto sweets. Just point at what looks good and staff will wrap it up nicely for you. There's no English sign; look for the traditional Kyoto exterior and the sweets in the window. It's closed on the third Wednesday of the month.

Ootoya SHOKUDŌ ¥

(大戸屋; Map p296; ☎255-4811; 2nd fl, Goshoame Bldg, Sanjō-dōri, Kawaramachi higashi-iru, Nakagyō-ku; meals from ¥480; ⏰11am-11pm; Ⓢ Tōzai line to Kyoto-Shiyakusho-mae, 🚉 Keihan line to Sanjō) Ootoya is a clean, modern Japanese restaurant that serves a range of standard Japanese dishes at bargain-basement prices. It's popular with Kyoto students and young office workers. The large picture menu makes ordering a breeze. Look for the English sign, then climb a flight of steps.

Musashi Sushi SUSHI ¥

(寿しのむさし; Map p296; ☎222-0634; Kawaramachi-dōri, Sanjō-agaru, Nakagyō-ku; all plates ¥140; ⏰11am-10pm; 📋; Ⓢ Tōzai line to Kyoto-Shiyakusho-mae, 🚉 Keihan line to Sanjō) If you've never tried a *kaiten-sushi* (conveyor-belt sushi restaurant), don't miss this place – all the dishes are a mere ¥140. It's not the best sushi in the world, but it's cheap, reliable and fun. Needless to say, it's easy to eat here: you just grab what you want off the conveyor belt.

Kyōgoku Kane-yo UNAGI ¥¥

(京極かねよ; Map p296; ☎221-0669; 456 Matsugaechō, Rokkaku, Shinkyōgoku higashi-iru, Nakagyō-ku; unagi over rice from ¥1200; ⏰11.30am-9pm; 📋; Ⓢ Tōzai line to Kyoto-Shiyakusho-mae) This is a good place to try *unagi* (eel), that most sublime of Japanese dishes. You can choose to either sit downstairs with a nice view of the waterfall, or upstairs on the tatami. The *kane-yo donburi* (eel over rice; ¥1200) set is excellent value. Look for the barrels of live eels outside and the wooden facade.

Tsukiji Sushisei SUSHI ¥¥

(築地寿司清; Map p296; ☎252-1537; 581 Obiya-chō, Takakura-dōri, Nishikikōji-sagaru, Nakagyō-ku; sushi sets ¥1296-3150; ⏰11.30am-3pm & 5-10pm Mon-Fri, 11.30am-10pm Sat, Sun & holidays; 📋; Ⓢ Karasuma line to Shijō) On the basement floor, next to Daimaru department store, this simple sushi restaurant serves excellent sushi. You can order a set or just point at what looks good. You can see inside the restaurant from street level, so it should be easy to spot.

Ganko SUSHI ¥¥

(がんこ; Map p296; ☎255-1128; 101 Nakajima-chō, Sanjō-dōri, Kawaramachi higashi-iru, Nakagyō-ku; lunch ¥1000-2500, dinner around ¥5000; ⏰11am-11pm; 📋; Ⓢ Tōzai line to Kyoto-Shiyakusho-mae or Sanjō Keihan, 🚉 Keihan line

KYOTO SPECIALITIES

Tofu Kyoto's famously good groundwater and preponderance of Buddhist monks (who were, at least historically, vegetarian) make Kyoto's tofu the most revered in Japan. You'll find it in restaurants across the city, but to see the full range of what can be done with it, try **Tōsuirō** (豆水楼; Map p306; ☎251-1600; Kiyamachi-dōri, Sanjō-agaru, Nakagyō-ku; lunch/dinner ¥2000/5000; ⏰11.30am-2pm & 5-9.30pm Mon-Sat, noon-8.30pm Sun; Ⓢ Tōzai line to Kyoto-Shiyakusho-mae).

Kyō-wagashi In a city where the cuisine carefully echoes the four seasons and the tea ceremony is practised with all the ardour of a religion, it's not surprising that sweets have achieved an incredible level of sophistication and variety. Try some seasonal favourites at places such as Kagizen Yoshifusa (p335), Saryo Zen Cafe (p331) or Tsukimochiya Naomasa.

Kyō-kaiseki *Kaiseki* is arguably the most refined cuisine in the world, and the Kyoto version, *kyō-kaiseki*, is the pinnacle of the art. Indeed, there's no finer place on earth to sample this superb fare than in Kyoto, as the entire city acts as part of the experience. Some of the city's great temples of *kaiseki* include Kikunoi (p336), Roan Kikunoi (p334) and Kitcho Arashiyama (p338).

Mitarashi dango Small dumplings of rice flour on skewers covered with a sweet sauce, these typical Kyoto snacks are the perfect way to power yourself through an afternoon of sightseeing. You'll see them on sale near popular temples and shrines and in Nishiki Market (p294).

to Sanjō) This giant four-storey dining hall is part of Kansai's biggest sushi chain. The ground floor is the sushi area (you can order non-sushi dishes here as well); it has a long sushi counter and plenty of tables (and room for a stroller if you have tots in tow). It's very popular with both tourists and locals.

mumokuteki cafe VEGETARIAN ¥¥

(ムモクテキカフェ; Map p296; www.mumokuteki.com/cafe/index_e.html; 2nd fl, Human Forum Bldg, 351 Iseya-chō, Gokomachi-dōri, Rokkaku-sagaru, Nakagyō-ku; meals from ¥1500; 11.30am-10pm; ; Hankyū line to Kawaramachi) This vegetarian cafe hidden above a shop in the Teramachi shopping arcade is a lifesaver for many Kyoto vegetarians. The food is tasty, varied and served in casual surroundings. Most of it is vegan, but non-vegan options are clearly marked on the menu. It's hidden up a flight of steps above a clothing shop called Spinns.

The steps up to the restaurant are located inside the shop.

Tagoto Honten KAISEKI ¥¥

(田ごと本店; Map p296; 221-1811; 34 Otabi-chō, Shijō-dōri, Kawaramachi nishi-iru, Nakagyō-ku; lunch/dinner from ¥1600/3400; lunch 11am-3pm, dinner 4.30-9pm; ; Keihan line to Shijō, Hankyū line to Kawaramachi) Across the street from Takashimaya department store, this longstanding Kyoto restaurant serves approachable *kaiseki* fare in a variety of rooms, both private and common. Its *kiku* set (¥2000) includes some sashimi, a bit of tempura and a variety of other nibblies. *Kaiseki* dinner courses start at ¥6480 and you must make reservations in advance.

★Roan Kikunoi KAISEKI ¥¥¥

(露庵菊乃井; Map p296; 361-5580; http://kikunoi.jp/english/store/roan/; 118 Saito-chō, Kiyamachi-dōri, Shijō-sagaru, Shimogyō-ku; lunch/dinner from ¥4000/10,000; 11.30am-1.30pm & 5-8.30pm; ; Hankyū line to Kawaramachi, Keihan line to Gion-Shijō) Roan Kikunoi is a fantastic place to experience the wonders of *kaiseki* cuisine. It's a clean, intimate space located right downtown. The chef takes an experimental and creative approach to *kaiseki* and the results are a wonder for the eyes and palate. It's highly recommended. Reserve through your hotel or ryokan concierge.

★Yoshikawa TEMPURA ¥¥¥

(吉川; Map p296; 221-5544; www.kyoto-yoshikawa.co.jp/; Tominokōji, Oike-sagaru, Nakagyō-ku; lunch ¥3000-25,000, dinner ¥6000-25,000; 11am-2pm & 5-8.30pm; ; S Tōzai line to Karasuma-Oike or Kyoto-Shiyakusho-mae) This is the place to go for delectable tempura. It offers table seating, but it's much more interesting to sit and eat around the small counter and observe the chefs at work. It's near Oike-dōri in a fine traditional Japanese-style building. Reservation required for tatami room; counter and table seating unavailable on Sunday.

Shunsai Tempura Arima TEMPURA ¥¥¥

(旬菜天ぷら 有馬; Map p290; 344-0111; 572 Sanno-chō, Muromachi-dōri, Takatsuji-agaru, Simogyō-ku; meals from ¥5000; 11.30am-2pm & 5.30-10.30pm, closed Thu; ; S Karasuma line to Shijō) Tempura is one of Japan's most divine dishes and this friendly downtown restaurant is a great place to try it. It's a tiny family-run joint that is at home with foreign guests. The English-language menus and set meals make ordering a breeze. It's on a corner with a small English sign.

Mishima-tei JAPANESE ¥¥¥

(三嶋亭; Map p296; 221-0003; 405 Sakurano-chō, Teramachi-dōri, Sanjō-sagaru, Nakagyō-ku; sukiyaki lunch/dinner from ¥9500/12,700; 11.30am-10pm, closed Wed; ; S Tōzai line to Kyoto-Shiyakusho-mae) This is an inexpensive place to sample sukiyaki. The quality of the meat here is very high, which is hardly surprising when you consider there is a butcher right downstairs. There is an English menu and a discount for foreign travellers! It's in the intersection of the Sanjō and Teramachi covered arcades.

Kiyamachi Sakuragawa KAISEKI ¥¥¥

(木屋町 櫻川; Map p296; 255-4477; Kiyamachi-dōri, Nijō-sagaru, Nakagyō-ku; lunch/dinner sets from ¥5000/10,000; 11.30am-2pm & 5-9pm, closed Sun; S Tōzai line to Kyoto-Shiyakusho-mae) This elegant restaurant on a scenic stretch of Kiyamachi-dōri is an excellent place to try *kaiseki*. The modest but fully satisfying food is beautifully presented and it's a joy to watch the chef in action. The warmth of the reception adds to the quality of the food. Reservations are recommended and smart casual is the way to go here.

Central Kyoto

★Papa Jon's CAFE ¥

(パパジョンズカフェ 本店; Map p298; 415-2655; 642-4 Shokokuji-chō, Karasuma-dōri, Kamidachiuri higashi-iru, Kamigyō-ku; lunch from ¥850; 10am-9pm, closed irregularly; ; S Karasuma line to Imadegawa) A three-minute walk from the north border of the Kyoto Imperial Palace Park, this clean, well-lit place serves brilliant New York cheesecake and great coffee drinks. Other menu items include pizza, homemade quiche, soup and tasty salads. Paintings by local artists are on display. It's a great lunch stop in Central Kyoto.

Bon Bon Café CAFE ¥

(ボンボンカフェ; Map p298; ☎213-8686; Kawaramachi, Imadegawa, Higashi-iru, Kita-gawa, Kamigyō-ku; coffee/sandwiches from ¥350/500; ⏲11am-11pm; 🚆Keihan line to Demachiyanagi) If you find yourself in need of a light meal or drink while you're in the Demachiyanagi area, this casual open-air cafe is an excellent choice. There is a variety of cakes and light meals on offer. It's on the west bank of the Kamo-gawa and outdoor seats here are very pleasant on warm evenings.

Southern Higashiyama

Kasagi-ya TEAHOUSE ¥

(かさぎ屋; Map p300; ☎561-9562; 349 Masuya chō, Kōdai-ji, Higashiyama-ku; tea & sweets from ¥600; ⏲11am-6pm, closed Tue; 📋; 🚌Kyoto City bus 206 to Higashiyama-Yasui) At Kasagi-ya, on Sannen-zaka near Kiyomizu-dera, you can enjoy a nice cup of *matcha* (powdered green tea) and a variety of sweets. This funky old wooden shop has atmosphere to boot and friendly staff – which makes it worth the wait if there's a queue. It's hard to spot – you may have to ask one of the local shop owners.

Rakushō CAFE ¥

(洛匠; Map p300; ☎561-6892; 516 Washio-chō, Kodaijikitamon-dōri, Shimogawara higashi-iru, Higashiyama-ku; tea from ¥500; ⏲9am-6pm, closed irregularly; 📋; 🚌Kyoto City bus 204 to Higashiyama-Yasui) This casual Japanese-style tea room on Nene-no-Michi in the heart of the Southern Higashiyama sightseeing district is well placed for a break while doing the main tourist route in this area. The real attraction is the small *koi* (Japanese carp) pond adjoining the tea room. The owner is a champion *koi* breeder and his fish are superb!

Café 3032 CAFE ¥

(カフェ サンゼロサンニ; Map p300; ☎531-8869; 102 Tatsumi-chō, Higashiōji-dōri, Matsubara-agaru, Higashiyama-ku; light meals from ¥600; ⏲8am-10pm, closed irregularly; 📋; 🚌Kyoto City bus 206 to Higashiyama-Yasui) This super-casual cafe on Higashiōji, just down the hill from the main Southern Higashiyama sightseeing district, is a great place for a light lunch or cuppa while exploring the area. There's an English menu and foreign visitors are welcomed. The fare includes sandwiches, curry, beer and coffee.

Kagizen Yoshifusa TEAHOUSE ¥

(鍵善良房; Map p300; ☎561-1818; www.kagizen.co.jp/en/; 264 Gion machi, Kita-gawa, Higashiyama-ku; kuzukiri ¥900; ⏲9.30am-6pm, closed Mon; 📋; 🚆Hankyū line to Kawaramachi, Keihan line to Gion-Shijō) This Gion institution is one of Kyoto's oldest and best-known *okashi-ya* (sweet shops). It sells a variety of traditional sweets and has a lovely tea room out the back where you can sample cold *kuzukiri* (transparent arrowroot noodles) served with a *kuro-mitsu* (sweet black sugar) dipping sauce, or just a nice cup of *matcha* and a sweet.

Rāmen Santōka RĀMEN ¥

(らーめん山頭火; Map p300; ☎532-1335; http://santouka.co.jp/en/; Yamatoōji-dōri, Sanjō-sagaru Higashi gawa, Higashiyama-ku; rāmen from ¥770; ⏲11am-2am Mon-Sat, 11am-midnight Sun & national holidays; 📋; Ⓢ Tōzai line to Sanjō-Keihan, 🚆Keihan line to Sanjō) The young chefs at this sleek restaurant dish out some seriously good Hokkaidō-style *rāmen* (noodles in a meat broth with meat and vegetables). You will be given a choice of three kinds of soup when you order: *shio* (salt), *shōyu* (soy sauce) or miso – we highly recommend you go for the miso soup.

Oshokujidokoro Asuka SHOKUDŌ ¥

(お食事処明日香; Map p300; ☎751-1941; 144 Nishi-machi, Sanjō-dōri, Jingū-michi nishi-iru, Higashiyama-ku; meals from ¥850; ⏲11am-11pm, closed Mon; 📋; Ⓢ Tōzai line to Higashiyama) With an English menu, and a staff of friendly Kyoto *mama-sans* who are at home with foreign customers, this is a great place for a cheap lunch or dinner while sightseeing in the Higashiyama area. The tempura *mori-awase* (assorted tempura set) is a big pile of tempura for only ¥1000. Look for the red lantern and pictures of the set meals.

Hisago NOODLES ¥

(ひさご; Map p300; ☎561-2109; 484 Shimokawara-chō, Higashiyama-ku; meals from ¥900; ⏲11.30am-7.30pm, closed Mon; 📋; 🚌Kyoto City bus 206 to Higashiyama-Yasui) If you need a quick meal while in the main Southern Higashiyama sightseeing district, this simple noodle and rice restaurant is a good bet. It's within easy walking distance of Kiyomizu-dera and Maruyama-kōen. *Oyako-donburi* (chicken and egg over rice; ¥980) is the speciality of the house.

There is no English sign; look for the traditional front and the small collection of food models on display. In the busy seasons, there's almost always a queue outside.

Omen Kodai-ji NOODLES ¥¥

(おめん 高台寺店; Map p300; ☎541-5007; 358 Masuya-chō, Kodaiji-dōri, Shimokawara higashi-iru, Higashiyama-ku; noodles from ¥1150, set menu ¥1800; ⏰11am-9pm, closed irregularly; 🚌Kyoto City bus 206 to Higashiyama-Yasui) This branch of Kyoto's famed Omen noodle chain is the best place to stop while exploring the Southern Higashiyama district. It's in a remodelled Japanese building with a light, airy feeling. The signature udon (thick white wheat noodles) are delicious and there are many other à la carte offerings.

Sobadokoro Shibazaki NOODLES ¥¥

(そば処柴崎; Map p300; ☎525-3600; 4-190-3 Kiyomizu, Higashiyama-ku; soba from ¥1026; ⏰11am-6pm, closed Tue except national holidays; 📖; 🚌Kyoto City bus 206 to Kiyomizu-michi, 🚆Keihan line to Kiyomizu-Gojō) For excellent *soba* noodles and well-presented tempura sets (among other things) in the Kiyomizu-dera area, try this comfortable and spacious restaurant. After your meal, head upstairs to check out the sublime collection of Japanese lacquerware. Look for the low stone wall and the *noren* curtains hanging in the entryway.

Ryūmon CHINESE ¥¥

(龍門; Map p300; ☎752-8181; Sanjō-dōri, Higashiōji nishi-iru, Higashiyama-ku; dinner set from ¥3000; ⏰5pm-5am; Ⓢ Tōzai line to Higashiyama or Sanjō-Keihan, 🚆Keihan line to Sanjō) This place may look like a total dive but the food is reliable and authentic, as the crowds of Kyoto's Chinese residents will attest. There's no English menu but there is a picture menu and some of the wait staff can speak English.

★Kikunoi KAISEKI ¥¥¥

(菊乃井; Map p300; ☎561-0015; http://kikunoi.jp/english/store/; 459 Shimokawara-chō, Yasakatoriimae-sagaru, Shimokawara-dōri, Higashiyama-ku; lunch/dinner from ¥4000/15,000; ⏰noon-1pm & 5-8pm; 🚭📖; 🚆Keihan line to Gion-Shijō) This is one of Kyoto's true culinary temples, serving some of the finest *kaiseki* (Japanese haute cuisine) in the city. Located in a hidden nook near Maruyama-kōen, this restaurant has everything necessary for the full over-the-top *kaiseki* experience, from setting, to service, to exquisitely executed cuisine, often with a creative twist. Reserve through your hotel or ryokan concierge.

Northern Higashiyama

★Goya OKINAWAN ¥

(ゴーヤ; Map p306; ☎752-1158; 114-6 Nishida-chō, Jōdo-ji, Sakyō-ku; meals from ¥700; ⏰noon-5pm & 6pm-midnight, closed Wed; 📖; 🚌Kyoto City bus 5 to Ginkakuji-michi) We love this Okinawan-style restaurant for its tasty food, stylish interior and comfortable upstairs seating. It's perfect for lunch while exploring northern Higashiyama and it's just a short walk from Ginkaku-ji. At lunch it serves simple dishes like taco rice (¥880) and *gōya champurū* (bitter melon stir-fry; ¥730), while dinners comprise a wide range of *izakaya* (Japanese pub) fare.

Kiraku OKONOMIYAKI ¥

(きらく三条本店; Map p306; ☎761-5780; 208 Nakanochō, Sanjō-Shirakawa, Higashiyama-ku; okonomiyaki from ¥1000; ⏰11.30am-2pm & 5pm-midnight, closed Mon; Ⓢ Tōzai line to Higashiyama or Keage) This approachable and friendly *okonomiyaki* restaurant on Sanjō, close to Nanzen-ji and other popular Northern Higashiyama sights, is an excellent place to stop for lunch while exploring the area or for dinner after a long day of sightseeing. In addition to the usual *okonomiyaki* favourites, you'll find dishes like *gyōza* (Chinese dumplings) and *yaki-soba* (fried noodles).

Karako RĀMEN ¥

(からこ; Map p306; ☎752-8234; 12-3 Tokusei-chō, Okazaki, Sakyō-ku; rāmen from ¥650; ⏰11.30am-2pm & 6pm-2am, to 1am Mon, closed Tue; 📖; 🚌Kyoto City bus 206 to Higashiyama-Nijō) Karako is our favourite *rāmen* (noodles in a meat broth with meat and vegetables) restaurant in Kyoto. While there's not much atmosphere, the *rāmen* is excellent – the soup is thick and rich and the *chāshū* (roast pork slices) melt in your mouth. We recommend that you ask for the *kotteri* (thick soup) *rāmen*. Look for the lantern outside.

Falafel Garden ISRAELI ¥

(ファラフェルガーデン; Map p298; ☎712-1856; http://www.falafelgarden.com/english/index.html; 15-2 Kamiyanagi-chō, Tanaka, Sakyō-ku; falafel from ¥410; ⏰11am-9.30pm; 🌿📖; 🚆Keihan line to Demachiyanagi) This funky place near

Demachiyanagi Station serves excellent falafel and a range of other dishes, as well as offering a set menu (from ¥1000). We like its open, relaxed feeling, but the main draw is those tasty falafels!

Hinode Udon NOODLES ¥
(日の出うどん; Map p306; ☎751-9251; 36 Kitanobō-chō, Nanzenji, Sakyō-ku; noodles from ¥450; ⏲11am-3.30pm, closed Sun, 1st & 3rd Mon, except for Apr & Nov; 📄; 🚌Kyoto City bus 5 to Eikandō-michi) Filling noodle and rice dishes are served at this pleasant shop with an English menu. Plain *udon* (thick white wheat noodles) are only ¥500, but we recommend you spring for the *nabeyaki udon* (pot-baked *udon* in broth) for ¥950. This is a good lunch spot when temple-hopping in the Northern Higashiyama area.

Earth Kitchen Company BENTŌ ¥
(あーすきっちんかんぱにー; Map p306; ☎771-1897; 9-7 Higashi Maruta-chō, Kawabata, Marutamachi, Sakyō-ku; lunch ¥735; ⏲10.30am-6.30pm Mon-Fri, closed Sat & Sun; 📄; 🚆Keihan line to Jingū-Marutamachi) Located on Marutamachi-dōri near the Kamo-gawa, this tiny spot seats just two people but does a bustling business serving tasty takeaway lunch *bentō* (boxed meals). If you fancy a picnic lunch for your temple-hopping and the ease of an English menu, this is the place.

★Omen NOODLES ¥¥
(おめん; Map p306; ☎771-8994; 74 Jōdo-ji Ishibashi-chō, Sakyō-ku; noodles from ¥1150; ⏲11am-9pm, closed Thu & 1 other day a month; 📄; 🚌Kyoto City bus 5 to Ginkakuji-michi) This elegant noodle shop is named after the thick white noodles that are served in broth with a selection of seven fresh vegetables. Just say *omen* and you'll be given your choice of hot or cold noodles, a bowl of soup to dip them in and a plate of vegetables (put these into the soup along with sesame seeds).

There's also an extensive à la carte menu. You can get a fine salad here, brilliant *tori sansho yaki* (chicken cooked with Japanese mountain spice), good tempura and occasionally a nice plate of sashimi. Best of all, there's an English menu. It's about five minutes' walk from Ginkaku-ji in a traditional Japanese house with a lantern outside. Highly recommended.

Au Temps Perdu FRENCH ¥¥
(オ・タン・ペルデュ; Map p306; ☎762-1299; 64 Enshōji-chō, Okazaki, Sakyō-ku; food/drink from ¥1300/500; ⏲closed Mon; 📄; Ⓢ Tōzai line to Higashiyama) Overlooking the Shirakawa Canal, just across the street from the National Museum of Modern Art, this tiny indoor/outdoor French-style cafe offers some of the best people-watching in Northern Higashiyama. It's easy to pull a baby stroller up to these outdoor tables.

DEPARTMENT-STORE DINING

Yes, we know: the idea of dining in a department store sounds as appetising as dining in a gas station. However, Japanese department stores, especially those in large cities such as Tokyo and Kyoto, are loaded with good dining options. And, unlike many street-level shops, they're usually fairly comfortable with foreign diners (if there's any communication trouble, they can always call down to the bilingual staff at the information counter).

On their basement floors, you'll find *depachika* (from the English word 'department' and the Japanese word *chika,* which means 'underground'). A good *depachika* is like an Aladdin's cave of gustatory delights that rivals the best gourmet shops in any Western city. Meanwhile, on their upper floors, you'll usually find a *resutoran-gai* ('restaurant city') that includes restaurants serving all the Japanese standards – sushi, noodles, *tonkatsu*, tempura – along with a few international restaurants, usually French, Italian and Chinese.

If you're feeling peckish in downtown Kyoto, here are some good department-store-dining options:

Takashimaya (p343) This elegant department store has an incredible food floor (on the B1 level) and the best department store *resutoran-gai* in the city (on the 7th floor).

Daimaru (p344) On the north side of Shijō, between Kawaramachi and Karasuma streets, Daimaru has a food floor that rivals the one at Takashimaya (note the awesome Japanese sweets section) and a solid *resutoran-gai* on the 8th floor.

Northwest Kyoto and Arashiyama & Sagano Area

Komichi CAFE ¥

(こみち; Map p313; ☎872-5313; 23 Ōjōin-chō, Nison-in Monzen, Saga, Ukyō-ku; matcha ¥650; ⏰10am-5pm, closed Wed; 🚌Kyoto City bus 28 from Kyoto Station to Arashiyama-Tenryuji-mae, 🚆JR Sagano/San-in line to Saga-Arashiyama or Hankyū line to Arashiyama, change at Katsura) This friendly little teahouse is perfectly located along the Arashiyama tourist trail. In addition to hot and cold tea and coffee, it serves *uji kintoki* (shaved ice with sweetened green tea) in summer and a variety of light noodle dishes year-round. The picture menu helps with ordering. The sign is green and black on a white background.

Yoshida-ya SHOKUDŌ ¥

(よしだや; Map p313; ☎861-0213; 20-24 Tsukurimichi-chō, Saga Tenryū-ji, Ukyō-ku; lunch from ¥650; ⏰10.30am-5pm, closed Wed; 🚌Kyoto City bus 28 from Kyoto Station to Arashiyama-Tenryuji-mae, 🚆JR Sagano/San-in line to Saga-Arashiyama or Hankyū line to Arashiyama, change at Katsura) This quaint and friendly little *teishoku-ya* (set-meal restaurant) is the perfect place to grab a simple lunch while in Arashiyama. All the standard *teishoku* favourites are on offer, including dishes such as *oyakodon* (egg and chicken over a bowl of rice; ¥900).

Arashiyama Yoshimura NOODLES ¥¥

(嵐山よしむら; Map p313; ☎863-5700; Togetsu-kyō kita, Saga-Tenryū-ji, Ukyō-ku; soba dishes from ¥1080, set meals from ¥1600; ⏰11am-5pm; 📖; 🚌Kyoto City bus 28 from Kyoto Station to Arashiyama-Tenryuji-mae, 🚆JR Sagano/San-in line to Saga-Arashiyama or Hankyū line to Arashiyama, change at Katsura) For a tasty bowl of *soba* noodles and a million-dollar view over the Arashiyama mountains and the Togetsu-kyō bridge, head to this extremely popular eatery just north of the famous bridge, overlooking the Katsura-gawa. There's an English menu but no English sign; look for the big glass windows and the stone wall.

Shigetsu VEGETARIAN, JAPANESE ¥¥

(篩月; Map p313; ☎882-9725; 68 Susukinobaba-chō, Saga-Tenryū-ji, Ukyō-ku; lunch sets incl temple admission ¥3500, ¥5500 & ¥7500; ⏰11am-2pm; 🌿; 🚌Kyoto City bus 28 from Kyoto Station to Arashiyama-Tenryuji-mae, 🚆JR Sagano/San-in line to Saga-Arashiyama or Hankyū line to Arashiyama, change at Katsura) To sample *shōjin-ryōri* (Buddhist vegetarian cuisine), try Shigetsu in the precincts of Tenryū-ji. This healthy fare has been sustaining monks for more than a thousand years in Japan, so it will probably get you through an afternoon of sightseeing, although carnivores may be left craving something. Shigetsu has beautiful garden views.

Kitcho Arashiyama KAISEKI ¥¥¥

(吉兆嵐山本店; Map p313; ☎881-1101; www.kitcho.com/kyoto/shoplist_en/arashiyama/; 58 Susukinobaba-chō, Saga-Tenryūji, Ukyō-ku; lunch/dinner from ¥36,750/42,000; ⏰11.30am-3pm & 5-9pm, closed Wed; 🚆JR Sagano/San-in line to Saga-Arashiyama) Considered one of the best *kaiseki* restaurants in Kyoto (and Japan, for that matter), Kitcho Arashiyama is the place to sample the full *kaiseki* experience. Meals are served in private rooms overlooking gardens. The food, service, explanations and atmosphere are all first rate. We suggest having a Japanese person call to reserve, or make a booking online via its website.

Ōhara

Seryō-Jaya SHOKUDŌ ¥¥

(芹生茶屋; ☎744-2301; 24 Shorinin-chō, Ōhara, Sakyō-ku; lunch sets from ¥1000; ⏰11am-5pm; 🚌Kyoto bus 17 or 18 from Kyoto Station to Ōhara) Just by the entry gate to Sanzen-in, Seryō-Jaya serves tasty *soba* noodles and other fare. There is outdoor seating in the warmer months. Look for the food models.

Kurama & Kibune

Visitors to Kibune from June to September should not miss the chance to cool down by dining at one of the picturesque restaurants beside the Kibune-gawa. Meals are served here on platforms (known as *kawa-doko*) suspended over the river, as cool water flows just underneath. Most of the restaurants offer some kind of lunch special for around ¥3000. For a full *kaiseki* dinner spread (¥5000 to ¥10,000), have a Japanese speaker call to reserve in advance. Be warned that restaurants in Kibune have been known to turn away solo diners.

Aburaya-Shokudō SHOKUDŌ ¥

(鞍馬　油屋食堂; Map p319; ☎741-2009; 252 Honmachi, Kurama, Sakyō-ku; udon & soba from ¥600; ⏰10.30am-4.30pm; 🚆Eiden Eizan line from Demachiyanagi to Kurama) Just down the steps from the main gate of Kurama-dera, this classic old-style *shokudō* (all-round restaurant) reminds us of what Japan was like before it got rich. The *sansai teishoku* (¥1750) is a delightful selection of vegetables, rice and *soba* topped with grated yam.

Kibune Club CAFE ¥

(貴船倶楽部; Map p319; ☎741-3039; 76 Kibune-chō, Kurama, Sakyō-ku; coffee from ¥500; 11am-6pm; ; Eiden Eizan line from Demachiyanagi to Kibune-guchi) The exposed wooden beams and open, airy feel of this rustic cafe make it a great spot to stop for a cuppa while exploring Kibune. In winter it sometimes cranks up the wood stove, which makes the place rather cosy. It's easy to spot.

★Yōshūji VEGETARIAN ¥¥

(雍州路; Map p319; ☎741-2848; 1074 Honmachi, Kurama, Sakyō-ku; meals from ¥1080; 10am-6pm, closed Tue; ; Eiden Eizan line from Demachiyanagi to Kurama) Yōshūji serves superb *shōjin-ryōri* in a delightful old Japanese farmhouse with an *irori* (open hearth). The house special, a sumptuous selection of vegetarian dishes served in red lacquered bowls, is called *kurama-yama shōjin zen* (¥2700). Or if you just feel like a quick bite, try the *uzu-soba* (*soba* topped with mountain vegetables; ¥1080).

You'll find it halfway up the steps leading to the main gate of Kurama-dera; look for the orange lanterns out the front.

Hirobun JAPANESE ¥¥

(ひろ文; Map p319; ☎741-2147; 87 Kibune-chō, Kurama, Sakyō-ku; noodles from ¥1000, kaiseki courses from ¥8600; 11am-9pm; Eiden Eizan line from Demachiyanagi to Kibune-guchi) This is a good place to sample riverside or 'above-river' dining in Kibune. There's a friendly crew of women here who run the show and the food is quite good. Note that it does not accept solo diners for *kaiseki* courses (but you can have noodles). Look for the black-and-white sign and the lantern. Reserve for dinner.

Drinking & Nightlife

Kyoto has a great variety of bars, clubs and *izakaya* (Japanese pub-eateries), all of which are good places to meet Japanese folks. And if you happen to be in Kyoto in the summer, many hotels and department stores operate rooftop beer gardens with all-you-can-eat-and-drink deals and good views of the city.

In addition to the places listed here, all the top-end hotels listed in the Sleeping section have at least one good bar on the premises. We particularly like Tōzan Bar at the Hyatt (p329).

★World Peace Love CLUB

(ワールドピースラブ; Map p296; ☎213-4119; http://world-kyoto.com/; Basement, Imagium Bldg, 97 Shin-chō, Nishikiyamachi, Shijō-agaru, Shimogyō-ku; admission ¥2500-3000, drinks from ¥500; 8pm-1am, closed irregularly but usually Mon, Tue & Thu; Hankyū line to Kawaramachi) World is Kyoto's largest club and it naturally hosts some of the biggest events. It has two floors, a dance floor and lockers where you can leave your stuff while you dance the night away. Events include everything from deep soul to reggae and techno to salsa.

Tadg's Gastro Pub PUB

(ダイグ ガストロ パブ; Map p306; ☎213-0214; http://tadgs.com; 1st fl, 498 Kamikoriki-chō, Nakagyō-ku; drinks from around ¥500; lunch & dinner until late, closed Wed; S Tōzai line to Kyoto-Shiyakusho-mae) Looking out on a particularly scenic stretch of Kiyamachi-dōri, Tadg's is a great place for a drink or two in the evening and you can choose from an extensive selection of craft beers, along with a variety of wines, sake and spirits. Seating is available, including an enclosed garden out the back for smokers.

Sama Sama BAR

(**サマサマ; Map p296; ☎241-4100; 532-16 Kamiōsaka-chō, Kiyamachi, Sanjō-agaru, Nakagyō-ku; drinks ¥600-700; 8pm-2am, closed Mon; S Tōzai line to Kyoto-Shiyakusho-mae) This place seems like a very comfortable cave somewhere near the Mediterranean. Scoot up to the counter or make yourself at home on the floor cushions and enjoy a wide variety of drinks, some of them from Indonesia (like the owner). It's down an alley just north of Sanjō; the alley has a sign for Sukiyaki Komai Tei.

Gion Finlandia Bar BAR

(ぎをん フィンランディアバー; Map p300; ☎541-3482; 570-123 Gion-machi minamigawa, Higashiyama-ku, (Hanamikōji, Shijō-sagaru hitosuji -me nishi-iru minamigawa); per drink about ¥900; 6pm-3am; Keihan Line to Gion-Shijō) This stylish Gion bar in an old geisha house is a great place for a civilised drink. The 1st floor is decorated with Finnish touches while the upstairs retains a Japanese feeling, with sunken floors and tatami mats. Admission is ¥500 and you can expect to pay around ¥3000 for a few drinks.

Sake Bar Yoramu BAR
(酒バー　よらむ; Map p296; ☎213-1512; www.sakebar-yoramu.com/index_eng.html; 35-1 Matsuya-chō, Nijō-dōri, Higashinotoin, higashi-iru, Nakagyō-ku; sake tasting sets from ¥1200; ⊙6pm-midnight, closed Sun-Tue; Ⓢ Karasuma or Tōzai lines to Karasuma-Oike) Named for Yoramu, the Israeli sake expert who runs Sake Bar Yoramu, this bar is highly recommended for anyone after an education in sake. It's small and can only accommodate a handful of people. By day, it's a *soba* restaurant.

Bar K6 BAR
(バーK６; Map p306; ☎255-5009; 2nd fl, Le Valls Bldg, Nijō-dōri, Kiyamachi higashi-iru, Nakagyō-ku; drinks from around ¥600; ⊙6pm-3am, to 5am Fri & Sat; Ⓢ Tōzai line to Kyoto-Shiyakusho-mae, 🚆 Keihan line to Jingu-Marutamachi) Overlooking one of the prettiest stretches of Kiyamachi-dōri, this upscale modern Japanese bar has a great selection of single malts and some of the best cocktails in town. There's even a local craft brew on offer. It's popular with well-heeled locals and travellers staying at some of the top-flight hotels nearby.

Gael Irish Pub BAR
(ザガエルアイリッシュパッブ; Map p300; ☎525-0680; 2nd fl, Ōtō Bldg, Nijūikken-chō, Shijō-dōri, Yamatoōji-agaru, Higashiyama-ku; drinks from ¥500; ⊙5pm-1am, later Thu-Sun; 🚆 Keihan line to Gion-Shijō) A cosy little Irish bar on the doorstep of Gion. It offers good food, excellent beer and friendly staff, as well as occasional live music. It's a great place to meet local expats and see what's going on in town. It's up a flight of steps.

Rocking Bar ING BAR
(ロック居酒屋ING; Map p296; ☎255-5087; www.kyotoingbar.com/; 2nd fl, Royal Bldg, 288 Minamikurayama-chō, Nishikiyamachi-dōri, Takoyakushi-agaru, Nakagyō-ku; drinks from ¥550; ⊙6pm-2am Sun-Thu, to 5am Fri & Sat; 🚆 Hankyū line to Kawaramachi) This *izakaya*-cum-bar on Kiyamachi is one of our favourite spots for a drink in Kyoto. It offers cheap bar snacks (¥350 to ¥750) and drinks, good music and friendly staff. It's in the Royal building; you'll know you're getting close when you see all the hostesses out trawling for customers on the streets nearby.

Kick Up BAR
(キックアップ; Map p306; ☎761-5604; Higashikomonoza-chō 331, Higashiyama-ku; drinks/food from ¥600/500; ⊙7pm-midnight, closed Wed; Ⓢ Tōzai line to Keage) Located just across the street from the Westin Miyako Kyoto, this wonderful bar attracts a regular crowd of Kyoto expats, local Japanese and guests from the Westin. It's subdued, relaxing and friendly.

Iketsuru Kajitsu JUICE BAR
(池鶴果実; Map p296; ☎221-3368; Nishikikōji-dōri, Yanaginobanba higashi-iru, Nakagyō-ku; juice ¥450; ⊙9am-6.30pm, closed Wed; Ⓢ Karasuma line to Shijō, 🚆 Hankyū line to Karasuma) We love this fruit-juice specialist in Nishiki Market. In addition to all the usual favourites, it sometimes has durian on hand and can whip up a very unusual durian juice. Look for the fruit on display – it's on the south side of the market, a little east of Yanaginobanba-dōri.

Park Café CAFE
(パークカフェ; Map p296; ☎211-8954; 1st fl, Gion Bldg, 340-1 Aneyakō-ji kado, Gokomachi-dōri, Nakagyō-ku; drinks from ¥450; ⊙noon-11pm; Ⓢ Tōzai line to Kyoto-Shiyakusho-mae) This cool little cafe always reminds us of a Melbourne coffee shop. It's on the edge of the Downtown Kyoto shopping district and is a convenient place to take a break. The comfy seats invite a nice long linger over a cuppa and the owner has an interesting music collection.

Starbucks Kyoto Sanjō-Ōhashi CAFE
(スターバックス京都三条大橋店; Map p306; ☎213-2326; 113 Nakajima-chō, Sanjō-dōri, Kawaramachi higashi-iru, Nakagyō-ku; coffee drinks from ¥300; ⊙8am-11pm; 🚭📶) This Starbucks branch makes a great meeting point when exploring downtown Kyoto. The free wi-fi is also super convenient (just make sure you register in advance online).

A Bar IZAKAYA
(居酒屋Ａ（あ）; Map p296; ☎213-2129; www.a-bar.net/; 2nd fl, Reiho Kaikan, 366 Kamiya-chō, Nishikiyamachi-dōri, Shijō-agaru, Nakagyō-ku; drinks from ¥350; ⊙6pm-1am; 🚆 Keihan line to Gion-Shijō, Hankyū line to Kawaramachi) This is a raucous student *izakaya* with a log-cabin interior located in the Kiyamachi area. There's a big menu to choose from and everything's cheap (dishes ¥160 to ¥680). The best part comes when staff add up the bill – you'll swear they've undercharged you by half!

Metro CLUB
(メトロ; Map p306; ☎752-4765; http://www.metro.ne.jp/; BF Ebisu Bldg, Kawabata-dōri, Marutamachi-sagaru, Sakyō-ku; admission ¥500-3000;

about 7pm-3am; Keihan line to Jingū-Marutamachi) Metro is part disco, part 'live house' (small concert hall) and it even hosts the occasional art exhibition. It attracts an eclectic mix of creative types and has a different theme nightly, so check ahead in *Kansai Scene* to see what's going on. Tourists are entitled to one free drink (bring your passport).

☆ Entertainment

Most of Kyoto's cultural entertainment is of an occasional nature, and you'll need to check with the TIC or *Kansai Scene* to find out whether anything interesting coincides with your visit.

Geisha Dances & Entertainment

In the spring and autumn, Kyoto's geisha (or, properly speaking, *geiko* and *maiko*) perform fantastic dances, usually on seasonal themes. For a small additional fee, you can participate in a brief tea ceremony before the show. We *highly* recommend seeing one of these dances if you are in town when they are being held. Ask at the tourist information centre or at your lodgings for help with ticket purchases. Tour companies can also help with tickets.

★Gion Odori DANCE

(祇園をどり; Map p300; 561-0224; Gion, Higashiyama-ku; admission/incl tea ¥3500/4000; shows 1.30pm & 4pm; Kyoto City bus 206 to Gion) This is a quaint and charming geisha dance put on by the geisha of the Gion Higashi geisha district. It's held from 1 to 10 November at the **Gion Kaikan Theatre** (祇園会館), near Yasaka-jinja.

★Miyako Odori DANCE

(都をどり; Map p300; 541-3391; www.miyako-odori.jp/english/; Gionkobu Kaburenjo, 570-2 Gionmachi-minamigawa, Higashiyama-ku; seat reserved/nonreserved/reserved incl tea ¥4200/2500/4800; shows 12.30pm, 2pm, 3.30pm & 4.50pm; Kyoto City bus 206 to Gion, Keihan line to Gion-Shijō) Presented by the Gion Kōbu geisha district, this is our favourite geisha dance in Kyoto. It's a real stunner and the colourful images will remain with you long after the curtain falls. It's held throughout April at the Gion Kōbu Kaburen-jō Theatre, on Hanami-kōji, just south of Shijō-dōri.

Kamogawa Odori DANCE

(鴨川をどり; Map p306; 221-2025; Ponto-chō, Sanjō-sagaru, Nakagyō-ku; normal/special seat/special seat incl tea ¥2000/4000/4500; shows 12.30pm, 2.20pm & 4.10pm; Tōzai line to Kyoto-Shiyakusho-mae) Geisha dances from 1 to 24 May at Ponto-chō Kaburen-jō Theatre in Ponto-chō.

Kitano Odori DANCE

(北野をどり; 461-0148; Imadegawa-dōri, Nishihonmatsu nishi iru, Kamigyō-ku; admission/with tea ¥4000/4500; shows 1.30pm & 4pm) At Kamishichiken Kaburen-jō Theatre (上七軒歌舞練場), east of Kitano-Tenman-gū; 15 to 25 April.

Kyō Odori DANCE

(京おどり; Map p300; 561-1151; Miyagawachlō Kaburenjo, 4-306 Miyagawasuji, Higashiyama-ku; seat reserved/nonreserved ¥4000/2000, incl tea plus ¥500; shows 12.30pm, 2.30pm & 4.30pm; Keihan line to Gion-Shijō) Put on by the Miyagawa-chō geisha district, this wonderful geisha dance is among the most picturesque performances of the Kyoto year. It's held from the first to the third Sunday in April at the **Miyagawa-chō Kaburen-jō Theatre** (宮川町歌舞練場), east of the Kamo-gawa between Shijō-dōri and Gojō-dōri.

Kyoto Cuisine & Maiko Evening DANCE

(ぎおん畑中; Map p300; 541-5315; www.kyoto-maiko.jp; Hatanaka Ryokan, 505 Minamigawa, Gion-machi, Yasaka-jinja Minamimon-mae, Higashiyama-ku; per person ¥18,000; 6-8pm Mon, Wed, Fri & Sat; Kyoto City bus 206 to Gion or Chionin-mae, Keihan line to Gion-Shijō) If you want to witness geisha perform and then actually speak with them, one of the best opportunities is at Gion Hatanaka (p329), a Gion ryokan that offers a regularly scheduled evening of elegant Kyoto *kaiseki* food and personal entertainment by real Kyoto *geiko* (fully fledged geisha) and *maiko* (apprentice geisha).

Traditional Culture, Theatre & Music

Musical performances featuring the koto (13-stringed instrument played flat on the floor), *shamisen* (three-stringed, banjo-like instrument) and *shakuhachi* (Japanese bamboo flute) are held in Kyoto on an irregular basis. Traditional performances of *bugaku* (court music and dance) are often held at Kyoto shrines during festival periods. Occasionally contemporary *butō* dance is also performed in Kyoto. Check with the tourist information centre to see if any performances are scheduled to be held while you are visiting the city.

★Minami-za THEATRE
(南座; Map p296; ☎561-0160; www.kabuki-bito.jp/eng/contents/theatre/kyoto_minamiza.html; Shijō-Ōhashi, Higashiyama-ku; performances ¥4000-27,000; Keihan line to Gion-Shijō) The oldest kabuki theatre in Japan is the Minami-za theatre in Gion. The major event of the year is the **Kaomise festival** (1 to 26 December), which features Japan's finest kabuki actors. Other performances take place on an irregular basis – check with the TIC. The most likely months for performances are May, June and September.

Kyoto Kanze Kaikan Nō Theatre THEATRE
(京都観世会館; Map p298; ☎771-6114; 44 Okazaki Enshoji-chō, Sakyō-ku; admission ¥3500-13,000; 9.30am-5pm, closed Mon; Tōzai line to Higashiyama) This is your best bet for performances of *nō*.

Club Ōkitsu Kyoto JAPANESE CULTURE
(京都桜橘倶楽部「桜橘庵」; Map p298; ☎411-8585; www.okitsu-kyoto.com; 524-1 Motosuchimikado-chō, Kamichōjamachi-dōri, Shinmachi higashi-iru, Kamigyō-ku; Karasuma line to Imadegawa) Ōkitsu provides an upmarket introduction to various aspects of Japanese culture including tea ceremony and the incense ceremony. The introduction is performed in an exquisite Japanese villa near the Kyoto Imperial Palace and participants get a real sense of the elegance and refinement of traditional Japanese culture.

It also offers kimono dressing upon request (note that kimono dressing is not offered alone: it must be part of a package including tea ceremony and/or incense ceremony).

Gion Corner THEATRE
(ギオンコーナー; Map p300; ☎561-1119; www.kyoto-gioncorner.com/global/en.html; Yasaka Kaikan, 570-2 Gionmachi Minamigawa, Higashiyama-ku; admission ¥3150; performances nightly 6pm & 7pm, Fri, Sat & Sun only 1 Dec-2nd week Mar; Keihan line to Gion-Shijō) Gion Corner presents shows that include a bit of tea ceremony, koto music, ikebana (the art of flower arranging), *gagaku* (court music), *kyōgen* (ancient comic plays), *kyōmai* (Kyoto-style dance) and *bunraku* (classical puppet theatre). It's geared to a tourist market and is fairly pricey for what you get.

Shopping

The heart of Kyoto's shopping district is around the intersection of Shijō-dōri and Kawaramachi-dōri. The blocks to the north and west of here are packed with stores selling both traditional and modern goods. Kyoto's largest department stores (Kyoto Marui, Takashimaya, Daimaru and Fujii Daimaru) can be found in this area.

Some of the best shopping can be had along Kyoto's three downtown shopping arcades: **Shinkyōgoku shopping arcade**, **Teramachi shopping arcade** and Nishiki Market (p294). Teramachi and Shinkyōgoku run parallel to each other in the heart of downtown. The former has a mix of tasteful and tacky shops; the latter specialises in tacky stuff for the hordes of schoolkids who visit Kyoto every year. Nishiki branches off Teramachi to the west, about 100m north of Shijō-dōri.

The place to look for antiques in Kyoto is Shinmonzen-dōri, in Gion. The street is lined with great old shops, many of them specialising in one thing or another (furniture, pottery, scrolls, prints etc). You can easily spend an afternoon strolling from shop to shop, but be warned: if something strikes your fancy you're going to have to break out the credit card – prices here are steep!

Teramachi-dōri, between Oike-dōri and Marutamachi-dōri, has a number of classic old Kyoto arts, crafts, antiques and tea shops. This is probably the best place for shopping if you're after 'old Kyoto' items.

★Aritsugu HOMEWARES
(有次; Map p296; ☎221-1091; 219 Kajiya-chō, Nishikikōji-dōri, Gokomachi nishi-iru, Nakagyō-ku; 9am-5.30pm; Hankyū line to Kawaramachi) While you're in the Nishiki Market, have a look at this store – it's where you can find some of the best kitchen knives in the world. It also carries a selection of excellent and unique Japanese kitchenware.

★Wagami no Mise HANDICRAFTS
(倭紙の店; Map p290; ☎341-1419; 1st fl, Kajinoha Bldg, 298 Ōgisakaya-chō, Higashinotōin-dōri, Bukkōji-agaru, Shimogyō-ku; 9.30am-5.30pm, to 4.30pm Sat, closed Sun; Karasuma line to Shijō) A short walk from the Shijō-Karasuma crossing, this place sells a fabulous variety of *washi* (Japanese handmade paper) for reasonable prices. It's one of our favourite shops in Kyoto for souvenirs.

★Zōhiko LACQUERWARE
(象彦; Map p306; ☎229-6625; www.zohiko.co.jp/english/; 719-1 Yohojimae-chō, Teramachi-dōri, Nijō-agaru, Nakagyō-ku; 10am-6pm; Tōzai line to Kyoto-Shiyakusho-mae) Zōhiko is the best

MARKETS

If you're in town when one of the following markets is on, by all means go! Markets are the best places to find antiques and bric-a-brac at reasonable prices, and are the only places in Japan where you can actually bargain for a better price.

➡ On the 21st of each month, **Kōbō-san Market** (弘法さん (東寺露天市); Map p290; ☎691-3325; 1 Kujō-chō, Tō-ji, Minami-ku; ⌚dawn to dusk, 21st of each month; 🚉Kintetsu line to Tōji) is held at Tō-ji to commemorate the death of Kōbō Daishi (Kūkai), who in 823 was appointed abbot of the temple.

➡ Another major market, **Tenjin-san Market** (天神さん(北野天満宮露天市); Map p298; ☎461-0005; Kitano Tenman-gū, Bakuro-chō, Kamigyō-ku; ⌚dawn to dusk, 25th of each month; 🚌Kyoto City bus 50 or 101 to Kitano Tenmangū-mae) is held on the 25th of each month at Kitano Tenman-gū, marking the day of the birth (and, coincidentally, the death) of the Heian-era statesman Sugawara Michizane (845–903).

place in Kyoto to buy one of Japan's most beguiling art/craft forms: lacquerware. If you aren't familiar with just how beautiful these products can be, you owe it to yourself to make the pilgrimage to Zōhiko. You'll find a great selection of cups, bowls, trays and various kinds of boxes.

If you want a gift or souvenir that really makes an impression, this is a great choice!

★Takashimaya DEPARTMENT STORE
(高島屋; Map p296; ☎221-8811; Shijō-Kawaramachi Kado, Shimogyō-ku; ⌚10am-8pm, restaurants to 9.30pm; 🚉Hankyū line to Kawaramachi) The grande dame of Kyoto department stores, Takashimaya is almost a tourist attraction in its own right, from the mind-boggling riches of the basement food floor to the wonderful selection of lacquerware and ceramics on the 6th floor. And don't miss the kimonos!

★Mina SHOPPING CENTRE
(ミーナ京都; Map p306; ☎222-8470; Kawaramachi-dōri, Shijō-agaru, Nakagyō-ku; ⌚restaurants 11am-midnight; 🚉Keihan line to Gion-Shijō, Hankyū line to Kawaramachi) One of Kyoto's trendiest shopping malls, Mina has branches of two of Japan's most interesting chains: Uniqlo, a budget clothing brand that has spread overseas, and Loft, a fashionable department store that stocks all manner of curio and gift items.

Kōjitsu Sansō OUTDOOR EQUIPMENT
(好日山荘; Map p294; ☎708-5178; 5th fl, Kyoto Yodobashi Camera, Karasuma-dōri, Shichijō-sagaru, Shimogyō-ku; ⌚9.30am-10pm; 🚉Kyoto Station) On the 5th floor of the Yodobashi Camera building, this is one of Kyoto's biggest outdoor goods shops. If you're heading up to the Japan Alps to do some hiking, you might want to stop here before getting on the train.

Bic Camera ELECTRONICS
(ビックカメラ; Map p294; ☎353-1111; 927 Higashi Shiokōji-chō, Shimogyō-ku; ⌚10am-9pm; 🚉Kyoto Station) This vast new shop is directly connected to Kyoto Station via the Nishinotō-in gate; otherwise, it's accessed by leaving the north (Karasuma) gate and walking west. You will be amazed by the sheer amount of goods this store has on display.

Yodobashi Camera ELECTRONICS
(ヨドバシカメラ; Map p294; ☎351-1010; 590-2 Higashi Shiokōji-chō, Shimogyō-ku; ⌚9.30am-10pm; 🚉Kyoto Station) This mammoth shop sells a range of electronics, camera and computer goods, and also has a restaurant floor, supermarket, bookshop, cafe and, well, the list goes on. It's a few minutes' walk north of Kyoto Station.

Kamiji Kakimoto HANDICRAFTS
(紙司柿本; Map p306; ☎211-3481; 54 Tokiwagi-chō, Teramachi-dōri, Nijō-agaru, Nakagyō-ku; ⌚9am-6pm; 🚉Keihan line to Jingū-Marutamachi) This is one of our favourite places to buy *washi* in Kyoto. It's got such unusual items as *washi* computer printer paper and *washi* wallpaper, along with great letter writing and wrapping paper.

Rakushikan HANDICRAFTS
(楽紙館; Map p296; ☎221-1070; Takoyakushi-dōri, Takakura nishi-iru, Nakagyō-ku; ⌚10.30am-6pm, closed Mon, first/last week of the year; Ⓢ Karasuma line to Shijō) This *washi* specialist is a true wonderland for artists, creative types and anyone who knows just how beautiful this handmade paper can be. There are three

floors to explore and occasional *washi*-making demonstrations.

Kyūkyo-dō HANDICRAFTS

(鳩居堂; Map p296; ☎231-0510; 520 Shimo-honnōjimae-chō, Teramachi-dōri, Aneyakōji-agaru, Nakagyō-ku; ⏰10am-6pm Mon-Sat, closed Sun & 1-3 Jan; Ⓢ Tōzai line to Kyoto-Shiyakusho-mae) This old shop in the Teramachi covered arcade sells a selection of incense, *shodō* (Japanese calligraphy) goods, tea-ceremony supplies and *washi*. Prices are on the high side but the quality is good. Overall, this is your best one-stop shop for distinctively Japanese souvenirs.

Kyoto Handicraft Center CRAFTS

(京都ハンディクラフトセンター; Map p306; ☎761-7000; http://www.kyotohandicraftcenter.com/; 21 Entomi-chō, Shōgoin, Sakyō-ku; ⏰10am-7pm; 🚌 Kyoto City bus 206 to Kumano-jinja-mae) The Kyoto Handicraft Center sells a good range of Japanese arts and crafts. You can find such things as wood-block prints, Japanese dolls, damascene crafts, pearls, clothing and books. English-speaking staff are on hand and currency exchange is available. It's within walking distance of the main Higashiyama sightseeing route.

Tōzandō SWORDS

(東山堂; Map p306; ☎762-1341; 24 Shōgoin Entomi-chō, Sakyō-ku; ⏰10am-7pm; 🚌 Kyoto City bus 206 to Kumano-jinja-mae) If you're a fan of Japanese swords and armour, you have to visit this wonderful shop on Marutamachi (diagonally opposite the Kyoto Handicraft Center). It has authentic swords, newly made Japanese armour, martial arts goods etc, and there's usually someone on hand who can speak English.

Ippōdō Tea TEA

(一保堂茶舗; Map p306; ☎211-3421; www.ippodo-tea.co.jp/en/; Teramachi-dōri, Nijō-agaru, Nakagyō-ku; ⏰9am-7pm Mon-Sat, to 6pm Sun & holidays; Ⓢ Tōzai line to Kyoto-Shiyakusho-mae) This old-style tea shop sells the best Japanese tea in Kyoto. Its *matcha* makes an excellent and lightweight souvenir. Try a 40g container of *wa-no-mukashi* (meaning 'old-time Japan') for ¥1600, which makes 25 cups of excellent green tea. Ippō-dō is north of the city hall, on Teramachi-dōri. It has an adjoining teahouse (open 11am to 5.30pm).

Nijūsan-ya ACCESSORIES

(二十三や; Map p296; ☎221-2371; Shijō-dōri, Kawaramachi higashi-iru, Shimogyō-ku; ⏰10am-8pm; 🚉 Hankyū line to Kawaramachi) Boxwood combs and hair clips are one of Kyoto's most famous traditional crafts, and they are still used in the elaborate hairstyles of the city's geisha and *maiko*. This tiny hole-in-the-wall shop has a fine selection for you to choose from (and if you don't like what's on view, you can ask if it has other choices in stock – it usually does).

Daimaru DEPARTMENT STORE

(大丸; Map p296; ☎211-8111; Tachiuri Nishi-machi 79, Shijō-dōri, Takakura nishi-iru, Shimogyō-ku; ⏰10am-8pm, restaurants 11am-9pm, closed 1 Jan; Ⓢ Karasuma line to Shijō, 🚉 Hankyū line to Karasuma) Daimaru has fantastic service, a brilliant selection of goods and a basement food floor that will make you want to move to Kyoto.

Fujii Daimaru Department Store DEPARTMENT STORE

(フジイダイマル; Map p296; ☎221-8181; Shijō-dōri, Teramachi nishi-iru; ⏰10.30am-8pm; Ⓢ Hankyū line to Kawaramachi) This smallish department store is very popular with local young ladies who flock here to peruse the interesting selection of up-to-the-minute fashions and jewellery. Older Kyotoites head to the basement food floor to snag great bargains on a wide selection of food, including great takeaway sushi and tropical fruit.

Kyoto Marui DEPARTMENT STORE

(丸井; Map p296; ☎257-0101; 68 Shin-chō, Shijō-dōri, Kawaramachi higashi-iru, Shimogyō-ku; ⏰10.30am-8.30pm, restaurants to 10pm; 🚉 Hankyū line to Kawaramachi) This new youth-oriented department store hails from Tokyo and brings some of that fashion sense with it. It's a good place to see what's hot with the local fashionistas.

Shin-Puh-Kan SHOPPING CENTRE

(新風館; Map p296; ☎213-6688; Karasuma-dōri, Aneyakōji-kudaru, Nakagyō-ku; ⏰shops 11am-8pm Sun-Thu, to 9pm Fri & Sat, restaurants 11am-11pm, closed irregularly; Ⓢ Karasuma line to Karasuma-Oike) This interesting shopping complex has a variety of boutiques and restaurants clustered around a huge open-air atrium. The offerings run to the cutting-edge and ephemeral, which attracts the young kids who congregate here. Occasional art and music performances are held in the atrium.

ℹ Orientation

Kyoto is laid out in a grid pattern and is extremely easy to navigate. Kyoto Station, the city's main station, is located at the southern end of the city, and the JR and Kintetsu lines operate from here. The real centre of Kyoto is located around Shijō-dōri, about 2km north of Kyoto Station via Karasuma-dōri. The commercial and nightlife centres are between Shijō-dōri to the south and Sanjō-dōri to the north, and between Kawaramachi-dōri to the east and Karasuma-dōri to the west.

Although some of Kyoto's major sights are in the city centre, Kyoto's best sightseeing is on the outskirts of the city, along the base of the eastern and western mountains (known as Higashiyama and Arashiyama, respectively). Sights on the east side are best reached by bus, bicycle or the Tōzai subway line. Sights on the west side are best reached by bus or train (or by bicycle if you're very keen). Outside the city itself, the mountain villages of Ōhara, Kurama and Takao make wonderful day trips and are easily accessible by public transport.

Information

INTERNET ACCESS

The city of Kyoto has recently launched a free wi-fi access program for foreign travellers, with hot spots across the city. You must email to get the access code. Go to http://kanko.city.kyoto.lg.jp/wifi/en/ to find a map of hot spots and to get started. Note that access is limited to three hours, but you can get another access code for additional hours.

Kinko's (キンコーズ; Map p296; ☎213-6802; 651-1 Tearaimizu-chō, Karasuma-dōri, Takoyakushi-sagaru, Nakagyō-ku; 1st 10min ¥270, then every 10min ¥216; ⏲24hr; Ⓢ Karasuma line to Shijō or Karasuma-Oike) This copy shop has several terminals where you can log on to the internet. It's expensive but conveniently located.

MEDICAL SERVICES

Kyoto University Hospital (京都大学医学部附属病院; Map p306; ☎751-3111; 54 Shōgoinkawahara-chō, Sakyō-ku; ⏲8.30am-11am; Ⓡ Keihan line to Jingū-Marutamachi) Best hospital in Kyoto. There is an information counter near the entrance that can point you in the right direction.

MONEY

Most of the major banks are near the Shijō-Karasuma intersection, two stops north of Kyoto Station on the Karasuma line subway.

International transactions (such as wire transfers) can be made at **Bank of Tokyo-Mitsubishi UFJ** (三菱東京ＵＦＪ銀行; Map p296; ☎211-4583; Ⓢ Karasuma line to Shijō), which is at the southeast corner of this intersection. Other international transactions can be made at **Citibank** (シティバンク; Map p296; ☎212-5387; ⏲office 9am-3pm Mon-Fri, ATM 24hr; Ⓢ Karasuma line to Shijō), just west of this intersection.

You can change travellers cheques at most post offices around town, including the Kyoto Central Post Office, next to Kyoto Station. Post offices also have ATMs that accept most foreign-issued cards. If your card doesn't work at postal ATMs, try the ATMs in 7-Eleven convenience stores. Failing that, try Citibank, which has a 24-hour ATM that accepts most foreign-issued cards.

POST

Kyoto Central Post Office (京都中央郵便局; Map p294; ☎365-2471; 843-12 Higashishiokōji-chō, Shimogyō-ku; ⏲9am-9pm Mon-Fri, to 7pm Sat & Sun, ATMs 12.05am-11.55pm Mon-Sat, to 9pm Sun & holidays; Ⓢ Karasuma line to Kyoto) Conveniently located next to Kyoto Station (take the Karasuma exit; the post office is on the northwestern side of the station). There's an after-hours service counter on the southern side of the post office, open 24 hours a day, 365 days a year. The ATMs here are open *almost* 24 hours a day.

TOURIST INFORMATION

Kyoto International Community House (京都国際交流開会, KICH; Map p306; ☎752-3010; 2-1 Torii-chō, Awataguchi, Sakyō-ku; ⏲9am-9pm, closed Mon; Ⓢ Tōzai line to Keage, exit 2) An essential stop for those planning a long-term stay in Kyoto, KICH can also be quite useful for short-term visitors. It has a library with maps, books, newspapers and magazines from around the world, and a board displaying messages regarding work, accommodation, rummage sales etc.

You can send and receive faxes, and use the internet (register at the information counter). You can also pick up a copy of its excellent *Guide to Kyoto* map and its *Easy Living in Kyoto* book (note that both of these are intended for residents). You can also chill out in the lobby and watch CNN news.

Kyoto Tourist Information Center (京都総合観光案内所; TIC; Map p294; ☎343-0548; 2F Kyoto Station Bldg, Shimogyō-ku; ⏲8.30am-7pm; Ⓢ Karasuma line to Kyoto) Located in the main concourse on the 2nd floor of the Kyoto Station building that runs between the *shinkansen* station and the front of the station (near Isetan department store), this is the main tourist information centre in Kyoto. English speakers are always on hand and, occasionally, speakers of other European and Asian languages are available.

It stocks useful maps of the city, as well as bus maps, and can answer most of your questions. Note that it's called 'Kyo Navi' in Japanese (in case you have to ask someone).

TRAVEL AGENCIES

KNT (近畿日本ツーリスト; Map p296; ☎255-0489; 437 Ebisu-chō, Kawaramachi-dōri,

Sanjo-agaru, Nakagyō-ku; ⏲10.30am-7pm Mon-Fri, to 6.30pm Sat & Sun)

USEFUL WEBSITES

Kansei Scene (www.kansaiscene.com) Free monthly magazine and website that covers upcoming events in Kansai (including Kyoto).

Kyoto Visitor's Guide (www.kyotoguide.com) Official source of up-to-date tourist and travel information.

Getting There & Away

Travel between Kyoto and other parts of Japan is a breeze. Kansai is served by the Tōkaidō and San-yō *shinkansen* (bullet train) lines, several JR main lines and a few private rail lines. It is also possible to travel to/from Kyoto and other parts of Honshū, Shikoku and Kyūshū by long-distance highway buses. Finally, Kyoto is served by two airports (Kansai International Airport and Osaka Itami Airport). Kyoto is also relatively close to Nagoya, in case you can only get a flight to Centrair airport.

AIR

Kyoto is served by Osaka Itami Airport (ITM), which principally handles domestic traffic, and Kansai International Airport (KIX), which principally handles international flights. There are frequent flights between Tokyo and Itami (around ¥25,000, 80 minutes), but unless you're very lucky with airport connections you'll probably find it as quick and more convenient to take the *shinkansen*. There are ample connections to/from both airports, though the trip to/from Kansai International Airport takes longer and costs more.

BUS

Overnight JR buses run between Tokyo Station (Nihonbashi-guchi/arrival, Yaesu-guchi/departure long-distance bus stop) and Kyoto Station Bus Terminal (京都駅前バスターミナル).

The trip takes about eight hours and there are usually departures nightly, at 10.10pm, 10.30pm, 11pm (daily from Tokyo to Kyoto) and 11pm (daily from Kyoto to Tokyo). The fare starts at ¥5400 one way. There is a similar service to/from Shinjuku Station's Shin-minami-guchi in Tokyo.

Other JR bus transport possibilities include Kanazawa (one way from ¥3800) and Hiroshima (one way from ¥4450).

TRAIN

Kyoto is on the Tōkaidō-San-yō *shinkansen* line, which runs between Tokyo and Kyūshū, with stops at places such as Nagoya, Osaka, Kōbe, Himeji and Hiroshima en route. The *shinkansen* operates to/from Kyoto Station (Kyoto's main train station). On the Tokyo end, it operates from Tokyo, Shinagawa and Shin-Yokohama stations.

From Kyoto, fares and times for Nozomi (the fastest type of *shinkansen*) include Tokyo (¥13,080, 2¾ hours), Nagoya (¥5070, 40 minutes), Shin-Osaka (¥1420, 13 minutes), Hiroshima (¥10,570, two hours) and Hakata (¥15,120, 2¾ hours).

Nara The private Kintetsu line (sometimes written in English as the Kinki Nippon railway) links Kyoto (Kintetsu Kyoto Station, south side of the main Kyoto Station building) and Nara (Kintetsu Nara Station). There are fast direct *tokkyū* (limited express; ¥1110, 33 minutes) and ordinary express trains (¥610, 40 minutes), which may require a change at Saidai-ji.

The JR Nara line also connects Kyoto Station with JR Nara Station (express ¥710, 41 minutes). This is a great option for Japan Rail Pass holders.

Osaka The fastest train other than the *shinkansen* between Kyoto Station and Osaka is the JR *shinkaisoku* (special rapid train), which takes 29 minutes (¥560). In Osaka, the train stops at both Shin-Osaka and Osaka Stations.

There is also the cheaper private Hankyū line, which runs between Hankyū Kawaramachi, Karasuma and Ōmiya Stations in Kyoto and Hankyū Umeda Station in Osaka (*tokkyū* or limited express Umeda-Kawaramachi ¥400, 40 minutes). These trains are usually more comfortable than the JR trains, and if you board at Kawaramachi or Umeda, you can usually get a seat.

Alternatively, you can take the Keihan main line between Demachiyanagi, Sanjō, Shijō or Shichijō Stations in Kyoto and Keihan Yodoyabashi Station in Osaka (*tokkyū* to/from Sanjō ¥410, 51 minutes). Yodoyabashi is on the Midō-suji subway line. Again, these are more comfortable than JR trains and you can usually get a seat if you board in Demachiyanagi or Yodoyabashi.

Tokyo The *shinkansen* line has the fastest and most frequent rail links. The journey can also be undertaken by a series of regular JR express trains, but keep in mind that it takes around eight hours and involves several changes along the way. The fare is ¥8210. Get the staff at the ticket counter to write down the exact details of each transfer for you when you buy your ticket.

Getting Around

TO/FROM THE AIRPORT

Osaka Itami Airport (ITM) 大阪伊丹空港

There are frequent limousine buses between Osaka Itami Airport and Kyoto Station (the Kyoto Station airport bus stop is opposite the south side of the station, in front of Avanti department store). Buses also run between the airport and various hotels around town, but on a less regular basis (check with your hotel). The journey should take around 55 minutes and the cost is ¥1280. Be sure to allow extra time in case of traffic.

At Itami, the stand for these buses is outside the arrivals hall; buy your tickets from the machines and ask one of the attendants which stand is for Kyoto (hint: you've got a better chance of getting a seat if you board at the South Terminal).

MK Taxi (p348) offers limousine van service to/from the airport for ¥2400. Call at least two days in advance to reserve, or ask at the information counter in the arrivals hall on arrival in Osaka.

Kansai International Airport (KIX) 関西国際空港

The fastest, most convenient way to travel between KIX and Kyoto is on the special Haruka airport express, which makes the trip in about 75 minutes. Most seats are reserved (¥3370), but there are usually two cars on each train with unreserved seats (¥2850). Open seats are almost always available, so you don't have to purchase tickets in advance. First and last departures from Kyoto to KIX are 5.46am and 8.15pm; first and last departures from KIX to Kyoto are 6.30am Monday to Friday, 6.40am Saturday, Sunday and holidays and 10.16pm. Note that the Haruka is one of the few trains in Japan that is frequently late (although not usually by more than a few minutes). We suggest leaving a little extra time when heading from Kyoto to the airport to catch a flight.

If you have time to spare, you can save some money by taking the *kankū kaisoku* (Kansai airport express) between the airport and Osaka Station and taking a regular *shinkaisoku* to/from Kyoto. The total journey by this method takes about 95 minutes with good connections and costs ¥1750, making it the cheapest option (note that you can save ¥130 by exiting and re-entering at Osaka Station).

It's also possible to travel by limousine bus between Kyoto and KIX (¥2550, about 90 minutes). In Kyoto, the bus departs from the same place as the Itami-bound bus.

A final option is the **MK Taxi Sky Gate Shuttle limousine van service** (☎778-5489; www.mk-taxi-japan.com), which will pick you up anywhere in Kyoto city and deliver you to KIX for ¥3600. Call at least two days in advance to reserve. The advantage of this method is that you are delivered from door to door and you don't have to lug your baggage through the train station. MK has a counter in the arrivals hall of KIX, and if there's room they'll put you on the next van to Kyoto. A similar service is offered by **Yasaka Taxi** (☎803-4800).

BICYCLE

Kyoto is a great city to explore on a bicycle; with the exception of outlying areas it's mostly flat and there is a bike path running the length of the Kamo-gawa.

Unfortunately, Kyoto must rank near the top in having the world's worst public facilities for bike parking, and the city regularly impounds bikes parked outside regulation bike-parking areas. If your bike does disappear, check for a poster in the vicinity (in both Japanese and English) indicating the time of seizure and the inconvenient place you'll have to go to pay a ¥2000 fine and retrieve your bike.

There are two bicycle-parking lots in town that are convenient for tourists: one in front of Kyoto Station and another off Kiyamachi-dōri, between Sanjō-dōri and Shijō-dōri. It costs ¥150 per day to park your bicycle here. Be sure to hang onto the ticket you pick up as you enter.

Kyoto Cycling Tour Project (京都サイクリングツアープロジェクト; KCTP; Map p294; ☎354-3636; www.kctp.net/en; 552-13 Higashi-Aburanokoji-chō, Aburanokōji-dōri, Shiokōji-sagaru, Shimogyō-ku; ⊙9am-7pm; Ⓢ Karasuma line to Kyoto, Ⓡ JR line to Kyoto) A great place to rent a bike. These folk rent bikes (¥1000 per day) that are perfect for getting around the city. KCTP also conducts a variety of excellent bicycle tours of Kyoto with English-speaking guides. These are a great way to see the city (check the website for details).

PUBLIC TRANSPORT

Bus

Kyoto has an extensive network of bus routes providing an efficient way of getting around at moderate cost. Many of the routes used by visitors have announcements in English. The core timetable for buses is between 7am and 9pm, though a few run earlier or later.

Maps & Information The main **Kyoto Bus Information Centre** (京都バス案内所; Map p294) is located in front of Kyoto Station. Here you can pick up bus maps, purchase bus tickets and passes (on all lines, including highway buses), and get additional information.

The TIC stocks the *Bus Navi: Kyoto City Bus Sightseeing Map*, which shows the city's main bus lines. But this map is not exhaustive. If you can read a little Japanese, pick up a copy of the regular (and more detailed) Japanese bus map available at major bus terminals throughout the city, including the main bus information centre.

Terminals & Stations Kyoto's main bus terminals are also train stations: Kyoto Station, Sanjō Station, Karasuma-Shijō Station and Kitaōji Station. The bus terminal at Kyoto Station is on the north side and has three main departure bays (departure points are indicated by the letter of the bay and number of the stop within that bay).

Bus stops usually have a map of destinations from that stop and a timetable for the buses serving that stop.

Riding Buses Three-digit numbers written against a red background denote loop lines: bus 204 runs around the northern part of the city and buses 205 and 206 circle the city via Kyoto Station. Buses with route numbers on a blue background take other routes.

When heading for locations outside the city centre, be careful which bus you board. Kyoto City buses are green, Kyoto buses are tan and Keihan buses are red and white.

Entry to the bus is usually through the back door and exit is via the front door. Inner-city buses charge a flat fare (¥230 for adults, ¥120 for children aged six to 12, free for those younger), which you drop into the clear plastic receptacle on top of the machine next to the driver on your way out. A separate machine gives change for ¥100 and ¥500 coins or ¥1000 notes.

On buses serving the outer areas, take a *seiri-ken* (numbered ticket) on boarding. When alighting, an electronic board above the driver displays the fare corresponding to your ticket number (drop the *seiri-ken* into the ticket box with your fare).

Subway

Kyoto has two efficient subway lines, which operate from around 5.30am to around 11.30pm. The minimum fare is ¥210 (children ¥110).

The quickest way to travel between the north and south of the city is the Karasuma subway line. The line has 15 stops and runs from Takeda in the far south, via Kyoto Station, to the Kyoto International Conference Hall (Kokusaikaikan Station) in the north.

The east–west Tōzai subway line crosses Kyoto from Uzumasa-Tenjingawa in the west, meeting the Karasuma line at Karasuma-Oike Station, and continuing east to Sanjō Keihan, Yamashina and Rokujizō, in the east and southeast.

TAXI

Kyoto taxi fares start at ¥640 for the first 2km. The exception is **MK Taxi** (☎778-4141; www.mktaxi-japan.com), where fares start at ¥600.

MK Taxi also provides tours of the city with English-speaking drivers. For a group of up to four, prices start at ¥22,300 for a three-hour tour.

Kansai

Includes ➡

Best Places to Eat

- ➡ Shoubentango-tei (p367)
- ➡ Café Absinthe (p365)
- ➡ Imai Honten (p367)
- ➡ Kōbe Plaisir (p379)
- ➡ Yokarō (p386)

Best Temples & Shrines

- ➡ Kasuga Taisha (p393)
- ➡ Ise-jingū (p418)
- ➡ Nachi Taisha (p416)
- ➡ Oku-no-in (p409)
- ➡ Tōdai-ji (p389)

Why Go?

If you had to choose only one region of Japan to explore, Kansai (関西) would be an easy choice. It's the heart of Japan; nowhere else in the country can you find so much of historical and cultural interest in such a compact area.

Osaka, the region's hub and Japan's third largest city, shows off Japanese urban life in all its mind-boggling intensity, while Kōbe retains some of the international feeling that dates back to its days as a foreign treaty port. Nara, Japan's first permanent capital, is thick with traditional sights, including Japan's largest Buddha at the awe-inspiring Tōdai-ji Temple. In Mie Prefecture, Ise Grand Shrine is one of the three most important sites in Shintō, while in Wakayama-ken there are great hiking and onsen (hot springs), a rugged coastline and the mountaintop Buddhist temple complex of Kōya-san, one of Japan's most intensely spiritual places.

Kyoto and Osaka are the main cities of Kansai and both make good bases for exploration.

When to Go

Osaka

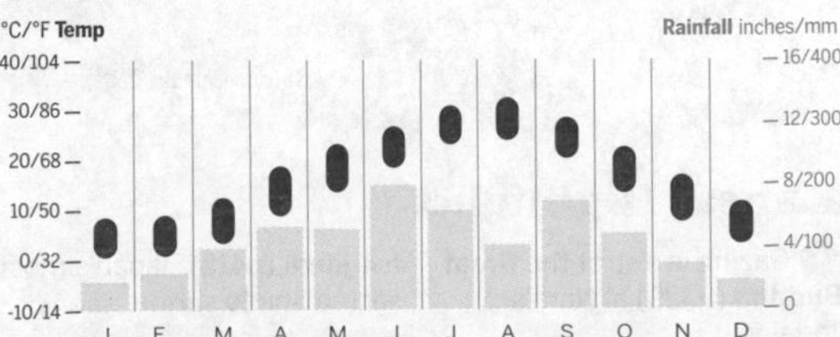

Late Mar–mid Apr The beauty of the cherry blossoms is over the top.

May–Sep July and August are hot and sticky, but summer is a great time to explore.

Oct–early Dec Kansai's sights are sublime against a backdrop of bright red maple leaves.

Kansai Highlights

1 Gazing in awe at the **Great Buddha** (p389) at Nara's Tōdai-ji.

2 Feasting your eyes on the colourful human parade of Osaka's **Dōtombori area** (p356).

3 Feeling the power radiating from the main hall of **Ise-jingū** (p418), Japan's most sacred Shintō shrine.

4 Wandering the mystical forest of Kōya-san's **Oku-no-in** (p409).

5 Soaking in the restorative waters of the three onsen at **Hongū** (p417).

6 Walking the ancient pilgrimage trails of Wakayama's **Kumano Kodō** (p414).

7 Donning a *yukata* (light cotton kimono) and strolling from onsen to onsen in the quaint town of **Kinosaki** (p422).

OSAKA

☎06 / POP 2.7 MILLION

Japan's third-largest city, ultra-urban, hard-working Osaka (大阪) is an unabashed antidote to the fashion-forward frenzy of Tokyo and the prim propriety of Kyoto. This longtime capital of commerce is filled with down-to-earth citizens speaking colourful *Kansai-ben* (Kansai dialect) and neon-clad streetscapes bursting with over-the-top 3D signage.

Most of all, Osaka is famous for good food. The phrase *kuidaore* ('eat 'til you drop') is heard so frequently here that it's practically the city motto. Delicacies from *okonomiyaki* (savoury pancakes) to conveyor-belt sushi were invented here and continue to thrive.

Even if Osaka isn't particularly attractive – at times it seems like an endless expanse of concrete boxes, *pachinko* (pinball) parlours and elevated highways – the city makes up for it with some architectural and cultural gems, pretty riversides, energetic shopping districts for the highbrow and the lowbrow and refreshingly open residents.

Sightseeing highlights include Osaka Castle, Osaka Aquarium Kaiyūkan, the *Blade Runner*–style nighttime scenery of the Dōtombori area, the gloriously gaudy retro storefronts of the Shin-Sekai neighborhood and the peaceful Open-Air Museum of Old Japanese Farmhouses.

But more than any specific sights, Osaka's real treasures are in the bustling street life in its arcades, markets and byways. And Osaka really comes into its own at night, when locals come out for tasty eats and good times.

History

Osaka has been a major port and mercantile centre from the beginning of Japan's recorded history. During its early days, Osaka (then called 'Naniwa', a name still heard today) was Japan's base for trade with Korea and China. In the late 16th century, Osaka rose to prominence when Toyotomi Hideyoshi, having unified all of Japan, chose Osaka as the site for his castle. Merchants set up around the castle and the city grew into a busy economic hub. This development was further encouraged by the Tokugawa shogunate, which adopted a hands-off approach to the city, allowing merchants to prosper unhindered by government interference.

As a primary manufacturing and munitions hub during WWII, Osaka was subject to numerous bombing raids during the last half-year of the war (March to August 1945), which killed upwards of 10,000 people and levelled much of the city centre.

In the modern period, Tokyo has usurped Osaka's position as Japan's economic hub, but Osaka remains a business powerhouse, ringed by factories churning out the latest in electronics and hi-tech.

Sights & Activities

Umeda & Osaka Station Area 梅田・大阪駅周辺

Also known as Kita (north), this neighbourhood is the city's centre of gravity by day, with office buildings, department stores, shopping complexes and hotels, plus the transit hubs of JR Osaka Station and multiple train and subway lines converging at Umeda Station. There are few great attractions, but Kita does have the eye-catching Umeda Sky Building and Grand Front shopping complex, department stores, lots of eateries and big-city bustle.

★Umeda Sky Building NOTABLE BUILDING
(梅田スカイビル; Map p352; www.kuchu-teien.com; 1-1-88 Ōyodonaka, Kita-ku; admission ¥700; ⏲observation decks 10am-10.30pm, last entry 10pm; 🚉JR line to Osaka) Opened in 1993 and named one of the world's top 20 buildings, the Sky Building resembles a 40-storey, space-age Arc de Triomphe. Twin towers are connected at the top by a 'floating garden' (really a garden-free observation deck) with breathtaking 360-degree city views day or night. Getting there is half the fun – an escalator in a see-through tube takes you up the last five storeys, between the towers (not for vertigo sufferers). Its architect, Hara Hiroshi, also designed Kyoto Station (p292).

The building is reached via an underground passage, a short walk north of Osaka and Umeda Stations.

Ohatsu Tenjin Shrine SHINTO SHRINE
(お初天神, Tsuyu no Tenjinja; Map p354; ☎06-6311-0895; www.tuyutenjin.com/en; 2-5-4 Sonezaki; ⏲6am-midnight; Ⓢ Midō-suji line to Umeda, 🚉JR line to Osaka) FREE Hiding in plain sight amid the skyscrapers of Umeda, this 1300-year-old shrine owes its fame to one of Japan's best-known tragic plays (based on true events) about star-crossed lovers

Osaka

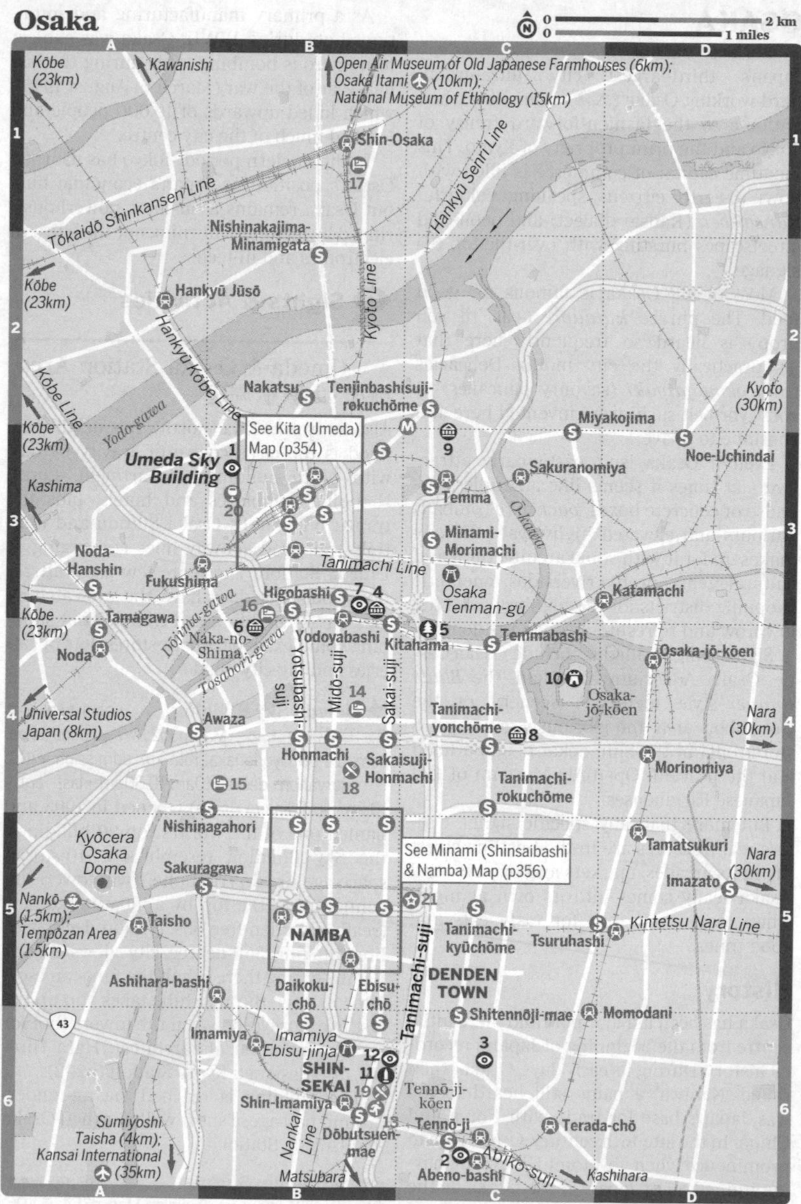

Ohatsu, a prostitute, and Tokubei, a merchant's apprentice. Rather than live apart, they committed double suicide here in 1703, to remain together forever in the afterlife. History aside, the shrine looks pretty modern and well-scrubbed, festooned throughout with mementos to the lovers, including *ema* (votive plaques) inscribed by visitors.

There's a flea market here on the first Friday of each month.

Osaka

Osaka Museum of Housing & Living MUSEUM
(大阪くらしの今昔館, Osaka Kurashi no Konjaku-kan; Map p352; http://konjyakukan.com; 8th fl, 6-4-20 Tenjinbashi; admission ¥600; ⌚10am-5pm, closed Tue, day after national holiday & 3rd Mon; Ⓢ Tanimachi line to Tenjinbashisuji-rokuchōme, exit 3) Two subway stops from Umeda, this museum contains a life-sized reproduction of an 1830s Osaka neighbourhood: shophouses, drug stores, an old-style *sentō* (public bath) and more. Enhancing the Edo Period mood, lighting shifts between day and night, shops sell traditional toys and unique souvenirs, and for ¥200 visitors can rent kimono for photo ops. Invest ¥100 in the English audio guide, since English signage is limited. The building is right behind as you exit the station.

Just outside is lively **Tenjinbashi-suji** shopping street, which, at 3km, claims to be Japan's longest shopping street. Pick up an English-language guide at the museum or along the route.

Naka-no-shima 中之島

South of Umeda, sandwiched between the rivers Dōjima-gawa and Tosabori-gawa, this island is an oasis of trees and riverside walkways. It's also home to **Osaka City Hall** (大阪市役所; Map p352), the neo-Renaissance **Osaka Central Public Hall** (大阪市中央公会堂; Map p352), and the park **Naka-no-shima-kōen** (中之島公園; Map p352) on the eastern end of the island, a good place for an afternoon stroll or picnic lunch.

If coming from Kyoto, the Keihan line runs direct to Yodoyabashi Station, or take JR trains to Osaka Station and walk (about 1km), or take the subway Midō-suji line to Yodoyabashi.

Museum of Oriental Ceramics MUSEUM
(大阪市立東洋陶磁美術館; Map p352; www.moco.or.jp; 1-1-26 Naka-no-shima; admission ¥500; ⌚9.30am-5pm, closed Mon; Ⓢ Midō-suji line to Yodoyabashi, exit 1) This museum has one of the world's finest collections of Chinese and Korean ceramics, with smaller galleries of Japanese ceramics and Chinese snuff bottles. At any one time, approximately 400 of the gorgeous pieces from the permanent collection are on display, and there are often special exhibits (with an extra charge). From the station, cross the river and go right, passing the Central Public Hall.

National Museum of Art, Osaka MUSEUM
(国立国際美術館; Map p352; www.nmao.go.jp; 4-2-55 Naka-no-shima; admission ¥430, special exhibits extra; ⌚10am-5pm, to 7pm Fri, closed Mon; Ⓢ Yotsubashi line to Higō-bashi) This impressive museum houses regularly changing exhibitions of modern (post-1945) Japanese and international art. Also arresting is its underground construction by architect Cesar Pelli; it's like a submarine with walls over 3m thick with light that filters down through skylights above the lobby. The entrance is marked by a large sculpture of steel tubes above ground, said to resemble a butterfly. It's towards the western end of Naka-no-shima.

Kita (Umeda)

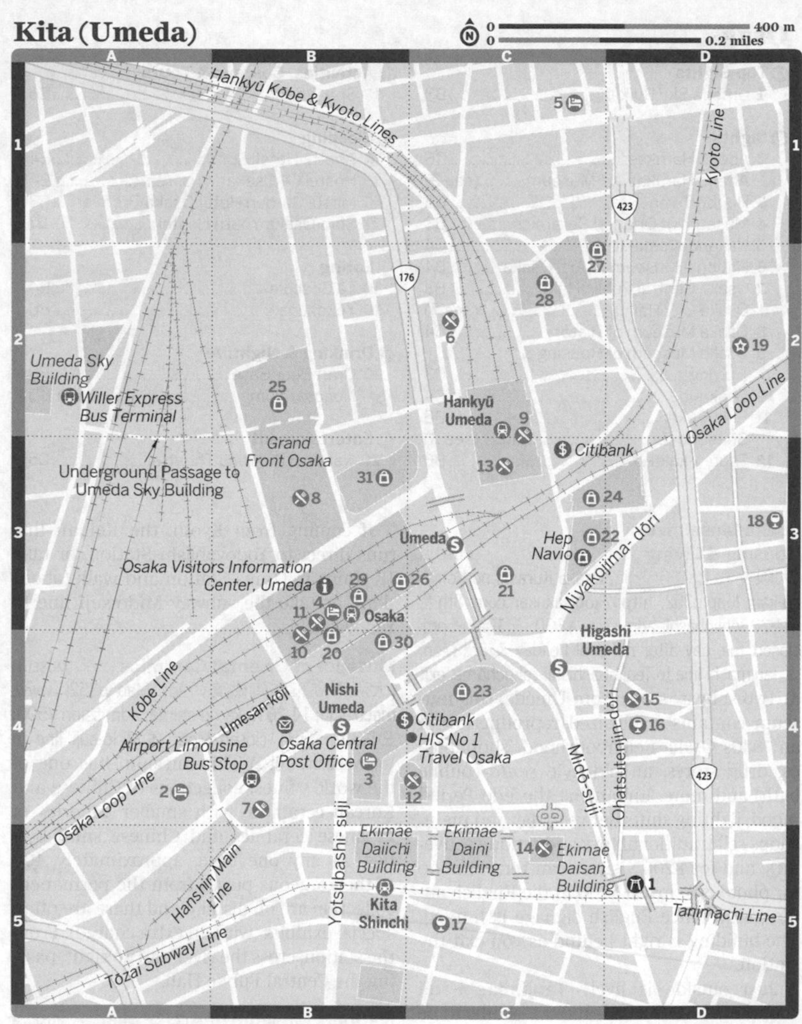

Central Osaka

Osaka-jō CASTLE

(大阪城, Osaka Castle; Map p352; www.osakacastle.net; 1-1 Osaka-jō; grounds/castle keep free/¥600, ¥900 combined with Osaka Museum of History; 9am-5pm, to 7pm Aug; S Chūō or Tanimachi line to Tanimachi 4-chōme, exit 9, JR Osaka Loop line to Osaka-jō-kōen) After unifying Japan in the late 16th century, General Toyotomi Hideyoshi (p801) built this castle (1583) as a display of power, using, it's said, the labour of 100,000 workers. Although the present structure is a 1931 concrete reconstruction (refurbished 1997), it's nonetheless quite a sight, looming dramatically over the surrounding park and moat. Inside is an excellent collection of art, armour, and day-to-day implements related to the castle, Hideyoshi and Osaka. An 8th-floor observation deck has 360-degree views.

Hideyoshi's original granite structure was said to be impregnable, yet it was destroyed in 1614 by the armies of Tokugawa Ieyasu (p803), rebuilt 15 years later, then razed again when another generation of the Tokugawa clan refused to cede it to the forces of the Meiji Restoration in 1868.

Kita (Umeda)

Sights

1 Ohatsu Tenjin Shrine............................ D5

Sleeping

2 Hearton Hotel Nishi-Umeda.................. A4
3 Hilton Osaka.. B4
4 Hotel Granvia Osaka............................. B3
5 Hotel Sunroute Umeda.......................... C1

Eating

6 Ganko Umeda Honten........................... C2
7 Gourmet Traveler................................. B4
8 Grand Front Osaka............................... B3
9 Hankyū Sanbangai................................ C2
Hilton Plaza....................................(see 3)
10 Kaiten Sushi Ganko............................ B4
11 Kani Chahan-no-Mise.......................... B3
12 Osaka Maru Building.......................... C4
Robatayaki Isaribi...........................(see 6)
13 Satoyama Dining................................ C3
Shinkiraku.....................................(see 3)
14 Umeda Hagakure................................ C5
15 Yukari... D4

Drinking & Nightlife

16 Blarney Stone......................................D4
17 Captain Kangaroo.................................C5
18 G Physique...D3
Windows on the World...................(see 3)

Entertainment

19 Osaka Nōgaku Hall..............................D2

Shopping

20 Daimaru Umeda....................................B4
21 Hankyū Department Store....................C3
22 Hankyū Men's.......................................C3
23 Hanshin Department Store...................C4
24 Hep Five...C3
25 Kōjitsu Sansō.......................................B2
26 Lucua...B3
27 Maruzen & Junkudō Umeda..................C2
28 NU Chayamachi....................................C2
29 Pokemon Centre...................................B3
30 Tokyu Hands..B4
31 Yodobashi Umeda Building..................B3

The castle and park are at their colourful best (and most crowded) in the cherry-blossom and autumn-foliage seasons.

Osaka Museum of History MUSEUM
(大阪歴史博物館, Osaka Rekishi Hakubutsukan; Map p352; www.mus-his.city.osaka.jp; 4-1-32 Ōtemae; admission ¥600, ¥900 combined with Osaka Castle; 9.30am-5pm, to 8pm Fri, closed Tue; S Tanimachi or Chūō line to Tanimachi-yonchōme, exit 9) Built above the ruins of Naniwa Palace (c 650), visible through the basement floor, this museum houses dramatically illuminated recreations of the old city and life-sized figures in the former palace court. There are also interesting early-20th-century displays, and great views of Osaka-jō. English explanations are sparse, so rent an English-language audio guide (¥200).

The museum is just southwest of the castle park, in a sail-shaped building adjoining the NHK Broadcast Center.

Shinsaibashi & Amerika-Mura 心斎橋・アメリカ村

Around Shinsaibashi subway station, the wide boulevard Midō-suji divides these two busy districts. East of Midō-suji, **Shinsaibashi** is one of Japan's great shopping zones, most notably in the eight-block long **Shinsaibashi-suji Shopping Arcade** (心斎橋筋商店街, Shinsaibashi Shōtengai; Map p356; www.shinsaibashi.or.jp/lang/en), large department stores like **Daimaru** (Map p356; www.daimaru.co.jp/shinsaibashi; 1-7-1 Shinsaibashi-suji; 10am-8pm, restaurant floors until 10pm; S Midō-suji line to Shinsaibashi, exit 4) and international couture boutiques on the main street. Shinsaibashi connects with Dōtombori in the south.

East of the arcade, the streets are crowded with hostess bars, clubs and pubs.

West of Midō-suji, **Amerika-Mura** (America Village, aka Ame-Mura) is a compact enclave of hip, youth-focused and offbeat shops, plus cafes, bars, tattoo and piercing parlours, hair salons and a few discreet love hotels. Ame-Mura owes its name to shops that sprang up after WWII, selling American goods such as Zippo lighters and T-shirts.

These days, the best reason to visit Ame-Mura is to check out the street life – hordes of Japanese teens sporting the latest fashion in clothing and hair – and to shop for secondhand clothes and music; look for English signage.

In the middle of Ame-Mura is **Triangle Park** (三角公園, Sankaku-kōen; Map p356; S Midō-suji line to Shinsaibashi, exit 7), an all-concrete 'park' with benches for sitting and watching the fashion parade. Just east is **Shinsaibashi Big Step** (心斎橋ビッグステップ; Map p356; www.big-step.co.jp/en; 1-6-14 Nishi-Shinsaibashi; shops 11am-8pm, restaurants 11am-10pm; S Midō-suji line to Shinsaibashi, exit 7), an eight-storey mall with dozens of

Minami (Shinsaibashi & Namba)

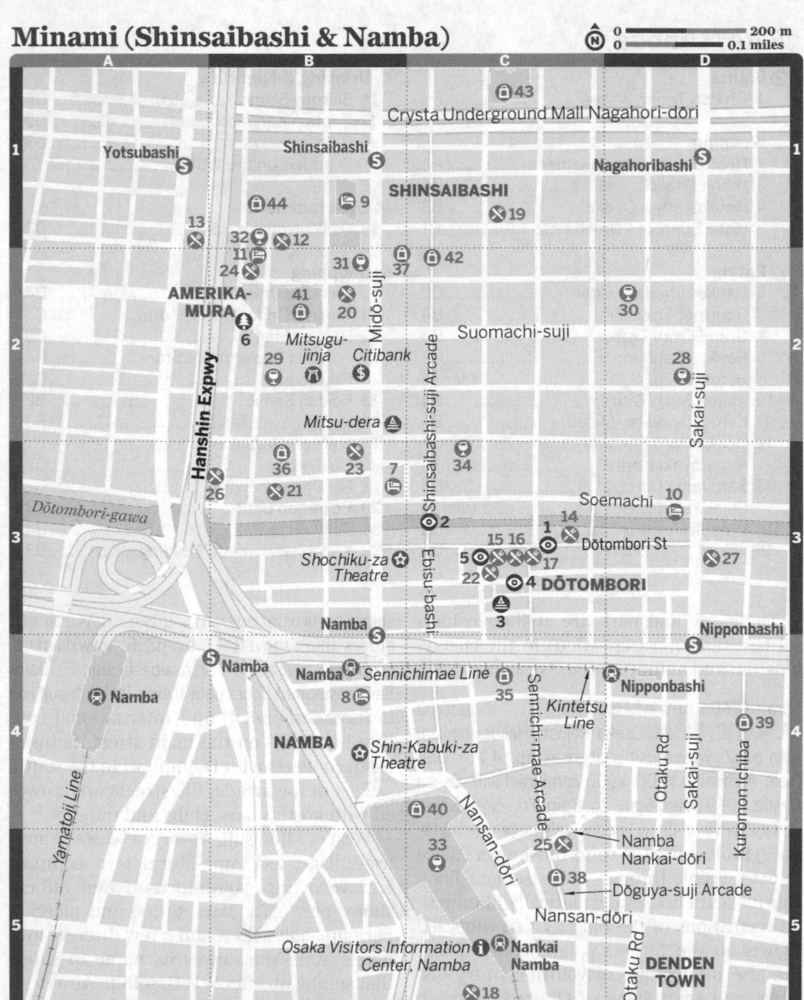

fashion and lifestyle shops and mid-priced restaurants; if that doesn't suit, try the old-fashioned game arcade **Silver Ball Planet** (3rd floor).

Around Ame-Mura, you'll notice **street lamps** like stick-figure people, some painted by artists. Other landmarks are the **Peace on Earth mural** (1983), painted by Osaka artist Seitaro Kuroda; and, of course, a mini **Statue of Liberty**.

For budget travelers, the southern end of Ame-Mura is the best place to eat and drink in Osaka in the evening, as it has many cheap *izakaya* (Japanese pub-eatery) and restaurants.

From Shinsaibashi station on the Midō-suji subway line, take exit 5 for Shinsaibashi Shopping Arcade. For Ame-Mura, take exit 7 and walk west past OPA. The Nagahori Tsurumi-ryokuchi line also stops at Shinsaibashi.

Dōtombori 道頓堀

Highly photogenic Dōtombori is the city's liveliest night spot and centre of the Minami (south) part of town. Its name comes from

Minami (Shinsaibashi & Namba)

the 400-year-old **Dōtombori-gawa canal**, now lined with pedestrian walkways and a riot of illuminated billboards glittering off its waters (the running man advertising Glico candy is a landmark). Best views are from the bridge **Ebisu-bashi** (戎橋; Map p356; S Midō-suji line to Namba) at night.

Just south and parallel to the canal is the pedestrianised **Dōtombori Street** (道頓堀; Map p356; S Midō-suji line to Namba), where dozens of restaurants and theatres vie for attention with the flashiest of signage: a giant 3D crab, puffer fish, dragon and more. There are plenty of tourists here.

South of Dōtombori Street is **Hōzen-ji** (法善寺; Map p356), a tiny temple hidden down a narrow paved alley off Sennichi-mae Arcade. The temple is built around a moss-covered **statue of Fudō-myōō**, the fearsome-looking Buddhist deity. People show their respects by splashing water over the statue, hence its bushy appearance. Parallel to this alley is atmospheric **Hōzen-ji Yokochō** (法善寺横丁; Hōzen-ji Alley; Map p356; S Midō-suji line to Namba), dotted with traditional restaurants and bars.

Further south, toward Nankai Namba Station, is a maze of arcades with more restaurants, *pachinko* (pinball) parlours, strip clubs and more.

The nearest stations to Dōtombori are Namba, on the Midō-suji line, or Nippon-bashi, on the Sakai-suji and Sennichimae lines.

Tennō-ji & Around 天王寺公園

Shin-Sekai NEIGHBOURHOOD
(新世界; Map p352; S Sakai-suji line to Ebisu-chō, exit 3 or Midō-suji line to Dōbutsuen-mae, exit 5)
A century ago, Shin-Sekai ('new world') was home to an amusement park that defined cutting edge. Now this entertainment district mixes down-on-its-heels with retro cool. It's centred on the crusty, trusty, 103m-high steel-frame tower **Tsūten-kaku** (通天閣; Map p352; admission ¥700; S Midō-suji or Sakai-suji lines to Dōbutsu-en-mae Station, exit 5, R JR or Nankai lines to Shin-Imamiya Station), which was built 1912 and rebuilt 1956 and is surrounded by ancient *pachinko* parlours, rundown theatres and a few homeless folks and suspicious-looking characters. Shin-Sekai still attracts plenty of visitors for nostalgia and cheap eateries behind over-the-top signage, especially for *kushikatsu*

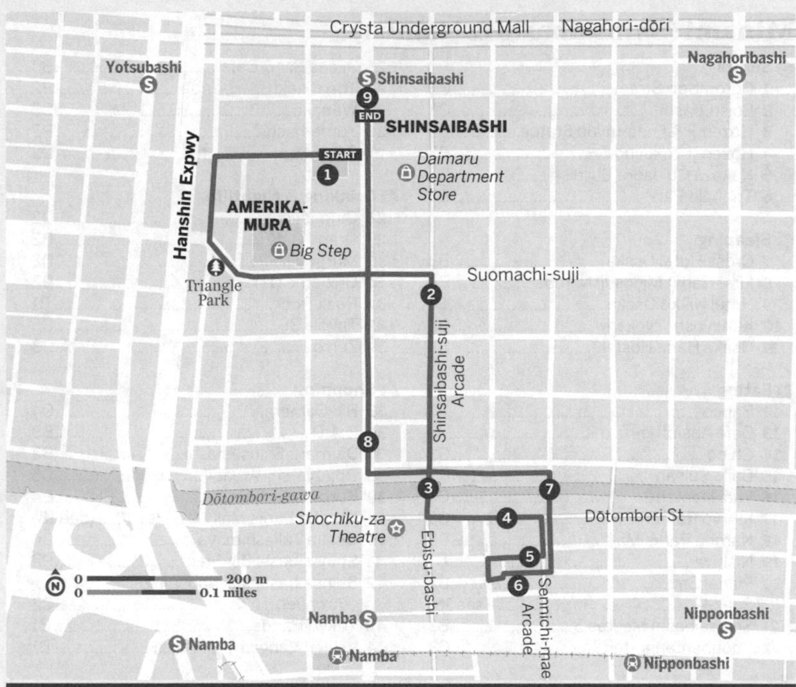

City Walk
Sights of Minami

START SHINSAIBASHI STATION
END SHINSAIBASHI STATION
LENGTH 2.2KM; 2½ HOURS

Try to time your walk so you're in Dōtombori after dark for the full neon-lit experience. Start with a wander around the colourful neighbourhood of **1 Amerika-Mura**. Then cross over Midō-suji and step into the throng in **2 Shinsaibashi-suji**, Shinsaibashi's famous *shōtengai* (market street).

After inching past shops, game parlours and eateries, with the high-pitched call of *irasshaimase!* (welcome!) coming at you from every angle, you'll be released out the end and onto **3 Ebisu-bashi**. This bridge is a popular place for photos down the canal Dōtombori-gawa, with the neon garishness of the buildings on both sides. Here also is the joyful Glico running man. Glance back to see the masses coming down the arcade.

At the end of the bridge, look right to glimpse the neo-Renaissance facade of Shochiku-za Theatre. Go left by the Kani Dōroku restaurant giant crab, another local landmark, into **4 Dōtombori Street** to walk past countless restaurants, *tako-yaki* (octopus dumplings) stands, spiky-haired touts and more big signs (big pufferfish, big dragon, big hand holding sushi, etc). Look out for Kuidaore Tarō, the 60-odd-year-old mechanical clown found drumming here when not on tour.

Before the big cow, take a right down Sennichi-mae arcade. Turn again at the cobblestoned alley with the wooden signboard for **5 Hōzen-ji Yokochō** (法善寺横丁), and you're suddenly in an older, quieter Osaka, charmingly lantern-lit in the evening. At the end, go left then through the temple gateway to tiny **6 Hōzen-ji**.

Continue past the temple back to Sennichi-mae arcade and the Dōtombori strip, then cross over **7 Tazaemon-bashi**. At the other side of the bridge, head down to the waterside walkway – a good spot to grab a plate of *tako-yaki*. Follow the walkway under Ebisu-bashi and up onto **8 Midō-suji**, where you can stroll the boulevard all the way north to **9 Shinsaibashi Station**.

(deep-fried meat and vegetables on skewers; see p365).

Abeno Harukas NOTABLE BUILDING

(あべのハルカス; Map p352; www.abenoharukas-300.jp/en; 1-1-43 Abeno-suji; observation deck ¥1500; ⏲observation deck 10am-10pm; Ⓢ Midō-suji or Tanimachi lines to Tennōji, JR lines to Tennōji, Kintetsu line to Abeno-bashi) FREE Japan's tallest building (300m, 60 storeys), this Cesar Pelli–designed tower opened in March 2014 and dominates Osaka's southern skyline, offering sweeping city views. It houses Japan's largest department store (Kintetsu, floors B2–14), other shops, a hotel, offices, restaurants (p366) and observation decks. Admission is free except for the top-level **Harukas 300 observation deck** and the **Abeno Harukas Art Museum** (あべのハルカス美術館; Map p352; ☎06-4399-9050; www.aham.jp; 16th fl, Abeno Harukas, 1-1-43 Abenosuji; varies by exhibition; ⏲10am-8pm Tue-Fri, 10am-6pm Sat & Sun), where temporary shows so far have encompassed everything from Renaissance painting to tantric Buddhist artifacts.

Although Abeno Harukas is Japan's tallest building, the tallest *structure* is Tokyo Sky Tree (p108), at 634m.

Shitennō-ji BUDDHIST TEMPLE

(四天王寺; Map p352; 1-11-18 Shitennō-ji; admission ¥300; ⏲8.30am-4.30pm Apr-Sep, to 4pm Oct-Mar; Ⓢ Tanimachi line to Shitennōji-mae, south exit) Founded in 593, Shitennō-ji is one of the oldest Buddhist temples in Japan, although only the big stone *torii* (Shintō shrine gate) is original, and is the oldest of its kind in the country (1294). Shitennō-ji is best visited for the lovely strolling garden, **Honbō Teien** (本坊庭園; Map p352; admission ¥300; ⏲10am-4pm; Ⓢ Tanimachi line to Shitennōji-mae, south exit), just northeast of the main precincts. Otherwise, the grounds are a somewhat desolate expanse of raked gravel, although there's a five-storey pagoda, which (unusually) you can climb up.

On the 21st and 22nd of each month there is a very good **flea market** outside the temple, with antiques and secondhand goods, including old kimono.

★**Sumiyoshi Taisha** SHINTO SHRINE

(住吉大社; 2-9-89 Sumiyoshi; ⏲dawn-dusk; Hankai line from Tennō-ji to Sumiyoshi-tori-mae, Nankai main line to Sumiyoshi-taisha) FREE Dedicated to Shintō deities of the sea and sea travel, this graceful shrine was founded in the early 3rd century and is considered the headquarters for all Sumiyoshi shrines in Japan. The buildings are faithful replicas of the ancient originals, with a couple that date back to 1810, and grounds are criss-crossed by a tree- and lantern-lined waterway spanned by a bright orange drum bridge. It's a rare Shintō shrine that predates the influence of Chinese Buddhist architectural styles.

Spa World BATHS

(スパワールド; Map p352; ☎06-6631-0001; www.spaworld.co.jp; 3-4-24 Ebisu-higashi; 3 hr/day pass Mon-Fri ¥2400/2700, Sat & Sun ¥2700/3000, midnight-5am additional ¥1300; ⏲10am-8.45am next day; Ⓢ Dōbutsu-en-mae Station, exit 5, JR or Nankai lines to Shin-Imamiya Station) 'Spa World' isn't a mere euphemism. Just south of Shin-Sekai, this gargantuan, seven-storey onsen (hot-spring) bathing complex contains dozens of options from saunas to salt baths, styled after a mini-UN's worth of nations including Japan, Finland, Canada, ancient Rome and, er, Atlantis. 'Asian' and 'European' bathing zones are separated by gender (bathe in the buff, towels provided) and switch monthly. Swimsuits (rental ¥600, or bring your own) or special outfits (provided) are worn in swimming pools, eateries and *ganbanyoku* (stone baths; additional ¥800 to ¥1000).

It's not cheap, but many visitors stay and splash for hours and hours and chow down at one of many casual eateries. Visitors with tattoos are not permitted.

Tempōzan 天保山

Trudging through the urban morass of Kita or Minami, you could easily forget that Osaka is actually a port city. Remind yourself with a trip to Tempōzan, a bayside development with attractions especially appealing for those with children. Take the Chūō subway line to Osakakō Station, come down the stairs of exit 1 and walk towards the big wheel.

Between the sights, Tempōzan Marketplace is a shopping centre best visited for **Naniwa Kuishinbo Yokochō** (なにわ食いしんぼ横丁; 1-1-10 Kaigan-dōri; ⏲11am-8pm; Ⓢ Chūō line to Osakakō Station, exit 1), a faux 1960s-nostalgic food court where stalls sell Osaka specialities.

★**Osaka Aquarium Kaiyūkan** AQUARIUM

(海遊館; www.kaiyukan.com; 1-1-10 Kaigan-dōri; adult/child ¥2300/1200; ⏲10am-8pm; Ⓢ Chuō line to Osakakō, exit 1) Kaiyūkan is easily one of

LOCAL KNOWLEDGE

OSAKA ICONS

New York has the Statue of Liberty and Brussels the Mannekin Pis, and Osaka is doubly blessed with two icons. You'll see them pretty much all over town.

Kuidaore Tarō A (frankly a little creepy looking) clown banging a drum. Instantly recognisable by his red-and-white striped outfit and round glasses, he represents the city's culture of *kuidaore* ('eat 'til you drop'). Find the most famous Kuidaore Tarō in the vestibule of the **Nakaza Cuidaore Building** (中座くいだおれビル; Map p356; 1-7-21 Dōtombori) in Dōtombori.

Billiken Ever-smiling (and also a bit creepy looking) Billiken sits, toes out, like a golden Kewpie doll on a pedestal reading 'The God of Things as they Ought to Be' in English. If the English slogan seems odd, it's explained by the fact that he was invented in the early 1900s as a good-luck charm by an art teacher in Kansas City, Missouri, USA. In Osaka, Billiken debuted in 1912, for the opening of the Tsūten-kaku (p357) tower. A Billiken figurine is said to bring good fortune to its purchaser, and better fortune if received as a gift.

the world's best aquariums. An 800m-plus walkway winds past displays of sea life from around the Pacific 'ring of fire': Antarctic penguins, coral-reef butterflyfish, unreasonably cute Arctic otters, Monterey Bay seals and unearthly jellyfish. Most impressive is the ginormous central tank, housing a whale shark, manta and thousands of other fish and rays. There are good English descriptions, but the audio guide (¥500) gives more detail. Expect lots of families and school groups.

Giant Ferris Wheel FERRIS WHEEL
(大観覧車, Daikanransha; 1-1-10 Kaigan-dōri; admission ¥800; ⏲10am-10pm; Ⓢ Chuō line to Osakakō, exit 1) Among the biggest in the world, this 112m-high Ferris wheel offers unbeatable views of Osaka Bay and the seemingly endless Osaka/Kōbe conurbation. Give it a whirl at night to enjoy the vast carpet of lights.

Other Areas

The Open-Air Museum of Japanese Farmhouses and the National Museum of Ethnology are both north of Osaka and accessible via the Midō-suji line, so it's feasible to see both in the same day if you set out early.

★Open-Air Museum of Old Japanese Farmhouses MUSEUM, PARK
(日本民家集落博物館, Nihon Minkashuraku Hakubutsukan; ☎06-6862-3137; www.occh.or.jp/minka; 1-2 Hattori Ryokuchi; admission ¥500; ⏲9.30am-5pm, closed Mon; Ⓡ Kita-Osaka Kyūko line to Ryokuchi-kōen, west exit) Set in leafy Ryokuchi-kōen, this fine open-air museum features a collection of traditional Japanese country houses, transported here and painstakingly reconstructed. Most striking is the giant *gasshō-zukuri* (steeply slanting thatch-roofed) farmhouse from Gifu Prefecture, and a thatched-wall farmhouse from Nagano, which looks to be wearing a shaggy coat. The whole place comes alive with fiery red maple leaves during November.

Take the Kita-Osaka Kyūko line (an extension north from the Midō-suji subway line; ¥90 surcharge) to Ryokuchi-kōen Station. From the west exit, go straight (past McDonald's), follow the road down to Hattori Ryokuchi Park (服部緑地公園), and walk through the park to the museum.

★National Museum of Ethnology MUSEUM
(国立民族学博物館; ☎06-6876-2151; www.minpaku.ac.jp; 10-1 Senri Expo Park; adult/child ¥420/110; ⏲10am-5pm, closed Wed; Ⓡ Midō-suji line to Senri-chūō, then Osaka Monorail to Banpaku-kinen-kōen) Located within the expansive Osaka World Expo Park (Banpaku-kōen), this fabulous museum brims with interesting and colourful objects for a whirlwind tour through many of the world's cultures. Exhibits range from Bollywood movie posters to Ainu textiles, Ghanaian barbershop signboards to Bhutanese mandalas and Japanese festival floats – even a Filipino jeepney. Note: there's limited English signage so it's best to get an audio guide.

From the station, cross the bridge to the park and follow the signs to the museum. From Kyoto, take the Hankyū line to Minami Ibaraki Station and change to the Osaka Monorail.

Universal Studios Japan THEME PARK
(ユニバーサルスタジオジャパン, Universal City; www.usj.co.jp/e; 1-day pass adult/child ¥7200/4980, 2-day pass ¥12,110/8420; hours vary seasonally; JR line to Universal City) Modelled after sister parks in the USA, 'USJ' bursts with Hollywood movie-related rides, shows, shops and restaurants. Top billing goes to the new, ¥45 billion (!) **Wizarding World of Harry Potter**, a painstakingly re-created Hogsmeade Village (shop for magic wands, Gryffindor capes and butterbeer) plus the 'Harry Potter and the Forbidden Journey' thrill ride through Hogwart's School. Wizarding World admission is by timed ticket. Other popular rides include **Spider-Man**.

Leaflet maps and signage are in English, though narrations and entertainment are in Japanese.

Long queues are common at the park's major venues (90 minutes is not unusual on the Harry Potter ride). To shorten waits, USJ offers a variety of fast passes that allow you to bypass queues, at an (often significant) extra charge; check the website.

To get here, take the JR Loop line to Nishi-kujō Station, then switch to a Universal Studios shuttle train (total trip ¥180, 15 minutes). There are also some direct trains from Osaka Station (same fare).

Momofuku Andō Instant Ramen Museum MUSEUM
(インスタントラーメン発明記念館; 072-752-3484; www.instantramen.museum.jp; 8-25 Masumi-cho, Ikeda; 9.30am-4pm, closed Tue; Hankyū line to Hankyū Ikeda Station) FREE From its humble invention in 1958 by Andō Momofuku, (1910–2007; later chair of Nissin Foods), instant rāmen has grown into a global business. Exhibits at this offbeat museum showcase its birthplace, instant noodles from around the world, and a 'tunnel' of Nissin products. For many visitors, the highlight is customising your own package of instant rāmen to take away and eat later (¥300), including decorating the cup.

Get the free English-language audio guide (¥2000 yen deposit). Expect long queues at weekends. It's about a 10-minute walk from the station.

Festivals & Events

Tōka Ebisu CULTURAL
From 9 to 11 January, huge crowds of more than a million people flock to the Imamiya Ebisu-jinja (今宮戎神社) to receive bamboo branches hung with auspicious tokens. The shrine is near Imamiya Ebisu Station on the Nankai line.

Sumo Spring Tournament SUMO
(Haru Bashō; www.sumo.or.jp; tickets ¥3500 to ¥10,000) The big fellas rumble into Osaka in March for this major tournament in the sumo calendar, held in the Prefectural Gymnasium (府立体育会館, Furitsu Taiiku-kan) in Namba.

★ **Tenjin Matsuri** CULTURAL
Held on 24 and 25 July, this is one of Japan's three biggest festivals. Try to make the second day, when processions of *mikoshi* (portable shrines) and people in traditional attire start at Osaka Temman-gū and end up in hundreds of boats on the O-kawa. As night falls, there is a huge fireworks display.

Kishiwada Danjiri Matsuri CULTURAL
Osaka's wildest festival, on 14 and 15 September, is a kind of running of the bulls except with *danjiri* (festival floats), many weighing over 3000kg. The *danjiri* are hauled through the streets by hundreds of people using ropes – take care and stand back. Most of the action takes place on the second day and the best place to see it is west of Kishiwada Station on the Nankai *honsen* line (main rail line, from Nankai Station).

Sleeping

Osaka has plenty of accommodation for all budgets – check websites for discounted rates. Stay in Minami for access to a larger selection of restaurants and shops, or in Kita for fast access to long-distance transport.

If exploring Osaka from a base in Kyoto, keep in mind that trains stop running before midnight (party-goers take note).

Umeda, Osaka Station & Naka-no-Shima Areas

Hearton Hotel Nishi-Umeda BUSINESS HOTEL ¥¥
(ハートンホテル西梅田; Map p354; 06-6342-1122; www.hearton.co.jp; 3-3-55 Umeda; s/tw/tr from ¥8100/11,400/15,000; S Yotsubashi line to Nishi-Umeda, JR lines to Osaka Station, west exit) At 18 storeys and 430 rooms, this large business hotel doesn't set any new style standards, but it boasts cheery staff, clean, comfy rooms, Japanese-Western breakfast buffet (¥1080 extra) and laundry machines, all a quick walk from JR Osaka Station and subway stops. Request a

south-facing room unless you're OK with train noise.

Hotel Sunroute Umeda BUSINESS HOTEL ¥¥
(ホテルサンルート梅田; Map p354; ☎06-6373-1111; www.sunroute.jp/english; 3-9-1 Toyosaki; s/d from ¥9720/14,040; ; Midō-suji line to Nakatsu) If you prefer to be away from the Osaka Station area, the Sunroute is a good business hotel about 15 minutes' walk north, and convenient for Hankyū Umeda Station. Rooms are small but fresh, with neutral colours, and some have good city views.

★**Mitsui Garden Hotel Osaka Premier** HOTEL ¥¥¥
(三井ガーデンホテル大阪プレミア; Map p352; ☎06-6444-1131; www.gardenhotels.co.jp/eng/osaka-premier; 3-4-15 Naka-no-shima; s/d/tw from ¥22,700/26,000/26,000; ; Yotsubashi line to Higobashi Station, exit 2) On Naka-no-shima, this handsome new hotel exudes contemporary cool, from its granite lobby and fabric wall coverings to the city's best river views (request an east-facing room). Rooms offer wooden floors, clean, spare lines, lots of power outlets and large bathrooms with separate WC and bathing areas, and there are guest laundry machines and attractive common baths.

Check the website for significant discounts (some via the MGH Members club, which has free registration). It's about a five-minute walk from the subway station, along the river, or a hotel shuttle bus serves JR Osaka Station.

Hotel Granvia Osaka HOTEL ¥¥¥
(ホテルグランヴィア大阪; Map p354; ☎06-6344-1235; www.granvia-osaka.jp; 3-1-1 Umeda; s/d/tw from ¥16,632/26,136/34,452; ; JR lines to Osaka Station) Above JR Osaka Station, this hotel has 700-plus rooms (on floors 21 to 27) that run the gamut from could-use-an-update to futuristic luxe (on the top level 'Granvia' floor). A glass roof over the tracks cuts out virtually all train noise. Request an outward-facing room for skyline views.

Hilton Osaka HOTEL ¥¥¥
(ヒルトン大阪; Map p354; ☎06-6347-7111; osaka.hilton.com; 1-8-8 Umeda; s from ¥21,622, d or tw from ¥25,780; ; JR line to Osaka) Across from JR Osaka Station's south exit, this large, excellent hotel is at home with foreign guests. Newly renovated rooms have wood finishes, *shoji* (paper screens) and *fusuma*-style (sliding door) windows, blackout panels and plenty of power outlets. Facilities include a well-equipped fitness centre with 15m pool and the 35th-floor Windows on the World bar (p368). There are seemingly infinite restaurant choices steps away.

Central Osaka, Shinsaibashi & Namba Areas

Osaka Hana Hostel HOSTEL ¥
(大阪花宿; Map p356; ☎06-6281-8786; http://osaka.hanahostel.com; 1-8-4 Nishi-Shinsaibashi; dm/tw/tr from ¥2800/7200/9600; ; Midō-suji line to Shinsaibashi, exit 7) This great budget option in the heart of Amerika-Mura has a variety of rooms for singles, families and groups. Besides the six-bed dorms, there are private, mostly Japanese-style rooms with and without (small) en suite, and studios with kitchenette and bigger en suite. There are two kitchen/lounge areas, clean, shared facilities, and a helpful team of well-travelled English-speaking staff.

First Cabin Midosuji Namba HOTEL ¥
(ファーストキャビン御堂筋難波; Map p356; ☎06-6631-8090; www.first-cabin.jp; 4th fl, Namba Midōsuji Bldg, 4-2-1 Namba; r per person ¥5900; ; Midō-suji line to Namba, exit 13) Imagine spending the night in a first-class suite of an Airbus A380 – inside an office building. Cabins, closed off by sliding screens, contain private TV, locker and power outlets. They're segregated by gender, as are large common baths and showers. It's a top location with friendly service, but noise can travel; pack earplugs (like on that plane).

A lounge serves simple, inexpensive meals for breakfast and dinner.

Kaneyoshi Ryokan RYOKAN ¥¥
(かねよし旅館; Map p356; ☎6211-6337; www.kaneyosi.jp; 3-12 Soemonchō; per person from ¥6480; ; Sennichimae line to Nipponbashi, exit 2 or Midō-suji line to Namba, exit 14) In business for nearly a century and right by Dōtombori – try for a room at the back, for river views – Kaneyoshi's current (1980s) building feels a bit dated, but there are eager-to-please staff, clean, comfy tatami (tightly woven floor matting) rooms with private bathrooms, and a simple common bath on the top (6th) floor. There are no non-smoking rooms (though rooms are well aired).

Note that although it's in the nightlife district, the doors close at midnight.

Arietta Hotel HOTEL ¥¥

(アリエッタホテル大阪; Map p352; ☎06-6267-2787; www.thehotel.co.jp/en/arietta_osaka; 3-2-6 Azuchi-machi; s/tw incl breakfast from ¥7776/10,800; ; Midō-suji line to Honmachi, exit 3) About 10 minutes' walk north of the Minami district, the Arietta has a warm, boutique-hotel feel, minimalist decor in good-sized rooms, with wood floors and tiled bathrooms, welcoming staff and a simple breakfast of breads, coffee and juice, all competitively priced. From the station, turn right at the first corner, and it's two-and-a-half blocks ahead on the right.

★ **Cross Hotel Osaka** HOTEL ¥¥¥

(クロスホテル大阪; Map p356; ☎06-6213-8281; www.crosshotel.com/osaka; 2-5-15 Shinsaibashisuji; s/d/tw from ¥16,170/24,255/27,720; ; Midō-suji line to Namba, exit 14) The Cross Hotel rocks a trendy, urban look with black, white and dark red motif, stylish restaurants, a cafe and a seasonal outdoor terrace for enjoying a generous breakfast buffet. Rooms are average size, but spacious Japanese-style bathrooms are a rare treat. Service is excellent and you'd have to sleep under Ebisu-bashi bridge for a more central location. Look for online specials.

Hotel Nikkō Osaka HOTEL ¥¥¥

(ホテル日航大阪; Map p356; ☎06-6244-1281; www.hno.co.jp; 1-3-3 Nishi-Shinsaibashi; s/d ¥30,000/36,000; ; Midō-suji line to Shinsaibashi, exit 8) Along tree-lined Midō-suji, this luxe choice has pampering service, a sleek, newly updated look, comfortable, spacious rooms with fine mattresses, great eastern or western views from upper floors, 10 (count 'em) restaurants and lounges and its own subway exit. Discounted rates are often available online.

Other Areas

★ **Hostel 64 Osaka** HOSTEL ¥

(Map p352; ☎6556-6586; www.hostel64.com; 3-11-20 Shinmachi; dm/s/d from ¥3500/6000/8100; ; Chuō line to Awaza, exit 2) This non-traditional hostel in a quiet neighbourhood northwest of Shinsaibashi is a little out of the way but worth the trip. There are Japanese- and Western-style private rooms, a small dorm with beds separated by screens, and a cosy lounge that doubles as a cafe-bar and simple breakfast room. Expect welcoming, knowledgeable staff and retro interiors befitting the 1960s building. Bathrooms are shared and there's no elevator. From the station, exit right, turn right at the third stoplight and make the first left.

Shin-Osaka Youth Hostel HOSTEL ¥

(新大阪ユースホステル; Map p352; ☎06-6370-5427; http://osaka-yha.or.jp/shin-osaka-eng; Koko Plaza, 1-13-13 Higashinakajima; dm/tw ¥3400/9200; ; JR line to Shin-Osaka, east exit) Five minutes southeast of Shin-Osaka Station, this efficiently run hostel sits on the top floors of a contemporary, 10-storey tower with great views across the city. Rooms and common areas are big, well equipped and spotless; private rooms are great value. There's a daytime lockout (you can still use the lounge), midnight curfew and breakfast for ¥500.

Eating

Umeda & Osaka Station Areas

Umeda Hagakure NOODLES ¥

(梅田はがくれ; Map p354; ☎06-6341-1409; B2 fl, Osaka Ekimae Daisan Bldg, 1-1 Umeda; noodles ¥600-1100; 11am-2.45pm & 5-7.45pm Mon-Fri, 11am-2.30pm Sat & Sun; JR line to Osaka) Two storeys underground and three decades old, this shop is cramped and workmanlike, but locals queue for udon noodles made before your eyes. Cold noodles are the speciality; try refreshing *namajoyu* (with ground *daikon* radish and *sudachi* lime; ¥600) or *tenzaru* (with tempura; ¥1100). Order from the picture menu, and get hand-gesture eating instructions from the owner.

Avoid weekdays between noon and 1pm, when the office-worker lunch crowd descends.

DON'T MISS

KUROMON MARKET

This landmark market in a covered arcade, **Kuromon Ichiba** (黒門市場, Kuromon Market; Map p356; www.kuromon.com; most shops 10am-5pm, closed Sun; Sennichimae or Sakai-suji line to Nippon-bashi, exit 10) is where the locals shop for fresh fish, meat, vegetables, pickles and more. In addition to fresh and prepared foods, some shops sell *bentō* and have lunch counters. It's one block east of Sakai-suji, about 10 minutes' walk from central Namba.

★Robatayaki Isaribi IZAKAYA, YAKITORI ¥¥
(炉ばた焼き漁火; Map p354; ☎06-6373-2969; www.rikimaru-group.com/shop/isaribi.html; 1-5-12 Shibata; dishes ¥324; ⊙5-11.15pm; 🄴; 🅡JR line to Osaka) Head downstairs to this spirited, friendly *izakaya* for standards such as skewered meats, seafood, vegies fresh off the grill and giant pieces of *tori no karaage* (fried chicken). The best seats are at half-round counters, where your chef will serve you using a very long paddle. Most dishes are ¥324.

It's on the street along the west side of Hankyū Umeda Station, to the left of the signage featuring a guy wearing a headband.

Yukari OKONOMIYAKI ¥¥
(ゆかり; Map p354; ☎06-6311-0214; www.yukarichan.co.jp; Ohatsutenjin-dōri; okonomiyaki ¥800-1460; ⊙11am-1am; 🅥🄴; 🅡JR line to Osaka) This popular restaurant in the Ohatsutenjin-dōri arcade serves up that great Osaka favourite, *okonomiyaki* (savoury pancakes), cooked on a griddle in front of you. There are lots to choose from the picture menu, including vegetarian options, but the *tokusen mikkusu yaki* (mixed *okonomiyaki* with fried pork, shrimp and squid; ¥1080) is a classic. Look for the red-and-white signage out the front.

Ganko Umeda Honten JAPANESE ¥¥
(がんこ梅田本店; Map p354; ☎06-6376-2001; www.gankofood.co.jp; 1-5-11 Shibata; meals ¥780-5000; ⊙11.30am-4am, to midnight Sun; 🄴; 🅡JR line to Osaka) At the main branch of this Osaka institution, a large dining hall serves a wide variety of set-course meals and sushi (à la carte or in sets), offering traditional, quality ingredients at a reasonable price. It's on the street along the west side of Hankyū Umeda Station. Look for the logo of the guy wearing a headband.

Satoyama Dining BUFFET ¥¥
(里山ダイニング; Map p354; 17th fl, Hankyū Terminal Bldg, 1-1-4 Shibata; lunch/dinner ¥1944/2700 for up to 90 minutes; ⊙11am-11.30pm; 🚭🅥👪; 🅡JR line to Osaka) Satoyama's all-you-can-eat 'Viking' (buffet) set-up lets you choose from mostly Japanese home-style dishes, while enjoying great views of the Hep Five Ferris wheel. Come after 8.30pm and you'll pay the lunch price for dinner. There are also discounts for kids. Enter the building across from Kinokuniya at Hankyu Umeda Station; take the elevator to the 17th floor.

Shinsaibashi & Amerika-Mura

Shinsaibashi restaurants offer a refreshing break from shopping or people watching, while Ame-Mura has some good cafes and some of Japan's cheapest *izakaya* and chain restaurants.

Banco CAFE ¥
(バンコ; Map p356; ☎080-6113-2504; http://banco.ciao.jp; 1-9-26 Nishi-Shinsaibashi; lunch ¥850; ⊙noon-2am; 🄴; 🅢Midō-suji line to Shinsaibashi, exit 7) In a handy Ame-Mura location, this intimate space has art-filled walls and streetside tables, friendly service, live jazz on some Sundays and, importantly, good coffee, panini and salumi – good for a relaxed lunchtime or evening pit stop. Alcohol is also served.

Planet 3rd CAFE ¥
(プラネットサード心斎橋店; Map p356; 1-5-24 Nishi-Shinsaibashi; mains lunch ¥702-961, dinner ¥790-1120; ⊙7am-midnight; 🚭@🄴; 🅢Midō-suji line to Shinsaibashi, exit 7) This large, comfortable hipster cafe in Ame-Mura serves good coffee, drinks and eclectic light meals: pastas, sandwiches, salads, soy-milk-based French toast, sausage and cabbage burrito, and tuna and avocado rice bowls. It's all amid modernist decor with big windows for people watching and a few iPads for guest use. Downside: it can be a bit smoky.

Yume-hachi IZAKAYA ¥
(ゆめ八; Map p356; ☎06-6212-7078; www.yume-hachi.jp; 1st fl, 2-16-9 Nishi-Shinsaibashi; dishes all ¥330; ⊙6pm-3am Sun-Thu, until 5am Fri & Sat; 🄴; 🅢Midō-suji line to Namba or Shinsaibashi) This spacious, funky 'freestyle' *izakaya* attracts a younger crowd for large serves of cheap yet decent food, cool design and good beats. In addition to standard *izakaya* fare are some unconventional choices such as camembert-potato *mochi* (dumplings), Jamaican-style jerk chicken and Indonesian *nasi goreng* (fried rice).

Tori Kizoku IZAKAYA, YAKITORI ¥
(鳥貴族; Map p356; ☎06-6251-7114; 2nd fl, 1-8-15 Nishi-Shinsaibashi; dishes & drinks ¥294; ⊙6pm-5am; 🄴; 🅢Midō-suji line to Shinsaibashi, exit 7) The name means 'chicken nobility', but prices at this popular Osaka-based *yakitori* chain are decidedly for regular folk. Look for the yellow-and-red sign and the number 280 (the price of all the generously portioned grilled skewers, plus tax), then climb the narrow stairs to the dining room with

LOCAL KNOWLEDGE

FIVE ESSENTIAL OSAKA FOODS

Okonomiyaki Thick, savoury pancakes filled with shredded cabbage and your choice of meat, seafood, vegetables and more (the name means 'cook as you like'). Often prepared on a *teppan* (steel plate) set into your table, the cooked pancake is brushed with a savoury Worcestershire-style sauce, decoratively striped with mayonnaise and topped with dried bonito flakes, which seem to dance in the rising steam. Slice off a wedge using tiny trowels called *kote*, and – warning – allow it to cool a bit before taking that first bite. Try it at Chibō (p367) in Dōtombori or Yukari in Umeda.

Tako-yaki The octopus dumpling counterpart to *okonomiyaki*: balls made of batter with a dollop of octopus (*tako* in Japanese) in the middle, served with picked ginger, topped with savoury sauce, powdered *aonori* (seaweed), mayonnaise and bonito flakes, and typically eaten with toothpicks. Any good street fair will have a booth selling them, or **Wanaka** (わなか; Map p356; ☎06-6631-0127; 11-19 Sennichi-mae ; tako-yaki from ¥450 per 8; ⏲10am-11pm Mon-Fri, from 8.30am Sat & Sun) is a classic *tako-yaki* stand just north of the Dōguya-suji arcade (p371).

Kushikatsu *Yakitori* is grilled meat, seafood and/or vegetables on a stick, and *kushikatsu* is the same ingredients crumbed, deep fried and served with a savoury dipping sauce (double-dipping is a serious no-no). Goes very well with beer. The Shin-Sekai neighbourhood is famed for *kushikatsu* restaurants in the lanes south of Tsūten-kaku tower, including Yokozuna (p367).

Kaiten-sushi Whether you call it conveyor-belt sushi, sushi-go-round or sushi train, sit at the counter and the plates of sushi come to you. This Osaka invention (in the 1950s) was long considered downmarket, but as Japan has gravitated toward cheap eats in the Great Recession, *kaiten-sushi* bars have been raising the quality. It'll never be a sushi master experience, but it's hard to beat for cheap and quick. Try it at Daiki Suisan (p367) or the Eki Marché branch of Ganko (p366).

Kappō-ryōri Osaka-style *kaiseki*, a sophisticated, multi-course meal of seasonal dishes served on refined crockery to match the high-quality cuisine. It can be frightfully expensive, but Shoubentango-tei (p367) does a reasonably priced version in soothing surrounds.

booths separated by untreated wood slats, and streaming J-pop hits.

Shinsaibashi Madras 5 CURRY ¥
(マドラス心斎橋店; Map p356; ☎06-6213-0858; 2-7-22 Nishi-Shinsaibashi; meals ¥680-1480; ⏲11am-1am; ; Midō-suji or Yotsubashi line to Namba, exit 26d) If you've never tried Japanese-style curry rice, this restaurant on a quiet Ame-Mura side street is a good place to get acquainted with its warm, saucy charms. Choose from tomato-, beef- or chicken-based curries and a variety of toppings (¥50 to ¥330), amid simple but modern decor. You can even get yours with *genmai* (brown rice).

Slices Bar & Cafe CAFE ¥
スライシーズ バーアンドカフェ Map p356; ☎06-6211-2231; www.slicesjapan.com; 2-3-21 Nishi-Shinsaibashi; slices/whole pizza from ¥400/1600, other dishes ¥500-900; ⏲noon-midnight, to 2am Sat; ; Midō-suji line to Namba (exit 24) or Shinsaibashi (exit 7)) If you need a break from Japanese food, step into this casual, foreigner-friendly joint. Pizza lunch sets are especially good value, but there are also calzones, wraps, bagels, desserts, bubble teas and brunch-time pancakes, plus *poutine* (a Montreal speciality of French-fried potatoes topped with gravy and more, courtesy of the Canadian owners) and cocktails.

★ Café Absinthe MEDITERRANEAN ¥¥
(カフェアブサン; Map p356; ☎06-6534-6635; www.absinthe-jp.com; 1-2-27 Kitahorie; mains lunch ¥800-1000, dinner ¥800-1600; ⏲3pm-3am, to 5am Sat & Sun, closed Tue; ; Midō-suji line to Shinsaibashi, exit 7) Friendly and trendy, near the western edge of Ame-Mura, Absinthe serves fantastic cocktails, non-alcoholic drinks and juices, and a rare (for Japan) Mediterranean menu (falafel, hummus and babaganoush, plus pastas and pizzas). It's a tad pricey, but you're paying for quality ingredients, stylish surrounds and laid-back atmosphere; sliding doors create a sidewalk

RESTAURANT HALLS

From upper floors to shopping malls to underground shopping arcades, Osaka positively bursts with restaurant collections, with options for all price ranges. Not all have English menus, but many do have picture menus or food displays and prices in the windows, making it easy to browse.

Grand Front Osaka (グランフロント大阪; Map p354; JR Osaka Station, north exit) At the fancy new shopping mall north of JR Osaka Station, **Umekita Dining** on the 7th through 9th floors of the south building has 36 restaurants, most pretty splashy. For a different experience, **Umekita Cellar** is a food hall with, unusually, both eat-in and take-out options.

JR Osaka Station (JR大阪駅) The 70-plus eateries across multiple buildings here are almost overwhelming. To target your browsing, **Eki Marché** on the southwest side has dozens of small, reasonably priced spots such as **Kani Chahan-no-Mise** (かにチャーハンの店; Map p354; 06-6341-3103; 3-1-1 Umeda, Eki-Marché; mains from ¥680; 10am-10.30pm) for delectable crab fried rice, and a branch of **Kaiten Sushi Ganko** (回転寿司がんこ; Map p354; 06-4799-6811; 3-1-1 Umeda, Eki Marché; sushi plates ¥130-627; 11am-11pm) does *kaiten-sushi* (conveyor-belt sushi).

Gourmet Traveler (グルメトラベラー; Map p354; B2 fl, Herbis Plaza complex; S Yotsubashi line to Nishi-Umeda, JR Osaka Station, south exit) West of JR Osaka Station between the Hilton and the Ritz Carlton hotels, its 16 shops have everything from a Belgian beer restaurant to Indian curry.

Hankyū Sanbangai (阪急三番街; Map p354; www.h-sanbangai.com; Hankyū Umeda Station, B2 fl; Hankyū line to Umeda) Beneath Hankyū Umeda Station is a collection of Japanese and international restaurants, as well as shops selling cakes, pastries and chocolates. You'll know you're in the right place when you see the indoor canal.

Hilton Plaza (ヒルトンプラザ; Map p354; www.hiltonplaza.com; JR line to Osaka) On the B2 floor beneath the Hilton Osaka. Among the restaurants worth trying here is the tempura specialist, **Shinkiraku** (新善楽; Map p354; 06-6345-3461; East B2 fl, Hilton Plaza, 1-8-16 Umeda; lunch/dinner from ¥780/2000; 11am-2.30pm & 5-11pm Mon-Fri, 11am-2.30pm & 4-10pm Sat, Sun & holidays; ; JR line to Osaka).

Namba Parks Mall (Map p356) On the 6th floor alone are 26 restaurants from *kushikatsu* to sushi, Chinese to Italian. At the far end, mostly organic **Sai-ji-ki** (菜蒔季; Map p356; 06-6636-8123; 6th fl, Namba Parks, 2-10-70 Namba-naka; lunch/dinner from ¥1510/1940; 11am-9pm; ; S Midō-suji, Sennichimae, or Yotsubashi line to Namba) is an all-you-can-eat buffet.

Abeno Harukas (あべのハルカス; 1-1-43 Abeno-suji; JR Lines to Tennō-ji, Kintetsu lines to Abenobashi) The main restaurant floors (12 through 14) of Japan's tallest skyscraper have some 44 restaurants among them, with specialities from *fugu* (puffer fish) to pizza. Try for a window seat for sweeping views.

Osaka Maru Building (大阪丸ビル; Map p354; www.marubiru.com/restaurant; B2 fl 1-9-20 Umeda; JR line to Osaka) There is a good variety of restaurants under the distinctive cylindrical Maru Building, including Korean, Indian, *yakitori* and an *omuraisu* (fried rice wrapped in a thin omelette topped with sauce) specialist.

cafe vibe, weather permitting. And, yes, it does serve absinthe.

Nishiya NOODLES ¥¥
(にし家; Map p356; 06-6241-9221; 1-18-18 Higashi Shinsaibashi; mains ¥650-1300, dinner courses ¥3000-5000; 11am-11pm Mon-Sat, to 9.30pm Sun; ; S Midō-suji line to Shinsaibashi, exit 5 or 6) A peaceful retreat from the busy streets, this welcoming Osaka landmark serves udon noodles, hearty *nabe* (cast-iron pot) dishes, and *shabu-shabu* (thin slices of meat and vegetables cooked in a broth and dipped in sauce) for reasonable prices. Look for the traditional three-storey wooden building with sliding-door entrance, just north of the corner.

Le Coccole VEGAN ¥¥
(レ コッコレ; Map p352; 06-6245-5556; www.le-coccole.jp; 3-4-1 Kita-kyuhoji-machi; small plates ¥400-900, mains ¥900-1400; 11.30am-10pm, until 6pm Sun, closed Mon & Tue; ; Midō-suji or Chūō Line to Honmachi, exit 11) At this adorable, all-vegan, mostly organic restaurant, lunch might be Indian curry or brown rice risotto, while dinner gets more Japanese-fusion with dishes like *hijiki* (sea green) samosas, *shiitake* mushroom cutlets, and pasta with dried tofu, *shiitake*, onion, *shiso* leaves and walnut and garlic sauce. From the cafe menu, try smoothies, coffees and tofu cheesecake.

Dōtombori & Around

Lively Dōtombori is crammed with a spin-the-globe assortment of eateries, generally serving heaping portions of tasty food in a casual atmosphere. Because it sees a lot of tourists, most big restaurants here have English menus.

★**Daiki Suisan** SUSHI ¥
(大起水産; Map p356; 06-6214-1055; 1-7-24 Dōtombori; dishes ¥100-500; 11am-11pm;) There's a cheery bustle inside this hard-working *kaiten-sushi* restaurant in a prime Dōtombori location. Over 50 seats zigzag around counters where plates rotate, colour-coded by price and labelled in multiple languages. You can also can get cooked foods including *tori no karaage* (fried chicken) and fried tuna. English-speaking staff help make sense of it all.

Kinryū Rāmen RAMEN ¥
(金龍ラーメン; Map p356; 06-6211-6202; 1-7-26 Dōtombori; regular/chāshū (roast pork) rāmen ¥600/900; 24hr; Midō-suji line to Namba) Beneath the massive green dragon, this indoor-outdoor spot offers house-made noodles and a front-row seat to the Dōtombori scene. Purchase a ticket from a machine, sit at a low table on a tatami platform, top your noodle soup with *kimchi*, garlic or marinated green onion, and slurp away. Don't linger too long, as there always seems to be a queue.

★**Imai Honten** NOODLES ¥¥
(今井本店; Map p356; 06-6211-0319; http://d-imai.com; 1-7-22 Dōtombori; dishes from ¥752; 11am-10pm, closed Wed; ; Midō-suji line to Namba) Step into an oasis of calm amid Dōtombori's chaos to be welcomed by kimono-clad staff at one of the area's oldest and most revered udon specialists. Try *kitsune udon* – noodles topped with soup-soaked slices of fried tofu. Look for the traditional exterior, and the willow tree outside.

★**Chibō** OKONOMIYAKI ¥¥
(千房; Map p356; 06-6212-2211; www.chibo.com; 1-5-5 Dōtombori; mains ¥1004-1652; 11am-1am Mon-Sat, to midnight Sun; ; Midō-suji line to Namba) A popular place to sample Osaka's signature dish. Try the house special *Dōtombori yaki*, a toothsome treat with pork, beef, squid, shrimp and cheese. Another unique speciality: *tonpei-yaki*, an omelette wrapped around fried pork. Some tables look out over the Dōtombori canal.

Zauo SEAFOOD ¥¥
(ざうお難波本店; Map p356; 06-6212-5882; www.zauo.com; Washington Hotel Plaza B1 fl, Nipponbashi 1-1-13; meals ¥680-6000; 5pm-midnight Mon-Fri, 11.30am-midnight Sat & Sun; ; Sakai-suji line to Nipponbashi, exit 6, or Midō-suji line to Namba) In this country where seafood is sometimes eaten so fresh it's still moving, Zauo has tables on long 'fishing boats' over tanks where patrons fish for their own dinner. If you're lucky enough to hook something, there's celebratory drumming and your fish is whisked away to be prepared how you like (priced according to the type of fish).

Alternatively, you can try an eight-piece sushi *omakase nigiri*, or a very tasty *shio-yaki* (salt-grilled) fish set from the menu. There's a ¥300-per-person table charge. Reserve for a 'boat' table.

★**Shoubentango-tei** KAPPŌ-RYŌRI, KAISEKI ¥¥¥
(正弁丹吾亭; Map p356; 06-6211-3208; 1-7-12 Dōtombori; dinner courses from ¥6000, mini kappō-kaiseki from ¥4000; 5pm-10pm; ; Midō-suji line to Namba) On Hōzen-ji Yokochō, the minimalist atmosphere of this graceful shop lets you feast your eyes on *kappō-ryōri*: a multi-course chef-driven extravaganza artfully presented in gorgeous pottery that might come topped with a colourful leaf, or water-misted for just the right sheen. Since peak seasonal ingredients change daily, you may never have the same dish twice here.

Shin-Sekai

Yokozuna KUSHIKATSU ¥
(横綱; Map p352; 06-6630-8440; 3-6-1 Ebisu-higashi; dishes ¥100-550; 10am-11pm; ; Midōsuji line to Dōbutsu-en-mae, exit 5) This

lively local chain sets the standard for *kushikatsu* (¥100 to ¥250), alongside *izakaya* faves like sashimi, sushi and grilled dishes. Yokozuna couldn't be easier to find, behind giant placards painted with sumo wrestlers. If this location is full, two others with the same menu are steps away (2-4-11 Ebisu-higashi and 2-5-9 Ebisu-higashi).

Drinking & Nightlife

Osakans work hard, but when quitting time rolls around, they know how to party. Stroll through Minami on a Friday night and you might think there's one bar for every resident, from *izakaya* to Irish pubs and cocktail bars with stunning views.

There's also a growing craft beer scene – look for the *Osaka Craft Beer Map* for dozens of places to sample it. Also great are summertime rooftop **beer gardens** offering all you can drink and eat in lively, casual surrounds – the one atop Hanshin Department Store (p370) is particularly good.

For club and entertainment events, pick up a copy of the English-language *Kansai Scene* or visit the website (www.kansaiscene.com).

Umeda & Osaka Station Area

Minami might be Osaka's main nightlife district, but there are dozens of bars, clubs and *izakaya* mostly south and east of Osaka Station, and around Hankyū Umeda Station.

Craft Beer Base BAR
(クラフトビアベース; Map p352; 1-2-11 Ōyodo-minami; ⏲11am-11pm, from 3pm Tue; Ⓢ Midōsuji line to Umeda, Ⓡ JR lines to Osaka) In the shadow of the Umeda Sky Building, this bar and bottle shop specialises in local and worldwide craft beers. Order and enjoy around the counter, or climb the narrow stairs to a simple white-walled room. From Osaka or Umeda Stations' north exits, take the underground passage toward Umeda Sky Building, and turn left.

Blarney Stone PUB
(Map p354; www.the-blarney-stone.com; 6th fl, Sonezaki Center Bldg, 2-10-15 Sonezaki; ⏲5pm-1am Mon-Thu, to 5am Fri & Sat, 3.30pm-1am Sun; Ⓡ JR line to Osaka) In Umeda's Ohatsutenjin-dōri arcade, have a Guinness or two and relax in the friendly atmosphere of this Irish-style pub, well liked among local expats and Japanese for after-work drinks and the free live music on weekends. There's a sign at street level.

Captain Kangaroo BAR
(Map p354; 1-5-20 Sonezakishinchi; ⏲6pm-5am Mon-Sat, to midnight Sun; Ⓡ JR line to Osaka) This popular, dimly lit bar in the Kita-Shinchi district is a short walk from JR Osaka Station and draws a good crowd of expats and Japanese. Among other bar-menu standards, they do a good burger with chunky fries, and you can get a meat pie.

G Physique GAY BAR
(Map p354; www.physiqueosaka.com; 8-23 Dōyama-chō, 1st fl Sanyo-Kaikan Bldg; ⏲from 7pm, closing time varies; Ⓢ Midōsuji line to Umeda, Ⓡ JR lines to Osaka) In the warren of tiny bars of the Dōyama-chō, east of Osaka Station, gay men have been coming to this subtly stylish spot since 1993. There's no cover, reasonably priced drinks, and a warm welcome to locals and visitors alike.

Windows on the World BAR
(ウィンドーズオンザワールド; Map p354; 35th fl Hilton Osaka, 1-8-8 Umeda; ⏲5.30pm-12.30am Mon-Thu & Sun, to 1am Fri & Sat; Ⓢ Yotsubashi-suji line to Nishi-Umeda, Ⓡ JR line to Osaka) An unbeatable spot for sophisticated drinks with a view, on the Hilton Osaka's 35th floor. There's a ¥1750 per person table charge (¥1200 for hotel guests) and drinks average ¥2000 each. Popular food menu items include a gourmet plate (¥3300) of smoked salmon, ham, cheese, salami, shrimp and more.

LOCAL KNOWLEDGE

LOOK UP, LOOK DOWN

When wandering the narrow streets of Osaka late at night, convinced that spot you're looking for must have closed or moved, remember that bars and pubs throughout Japan are often tucked away in the upper floors and basements of buildings. Check signs on the sides of buildings showing what's on each floor, and learn how to ask 'Where is...?' in Japanese (*...wa doko des ka?*).

Shinsaibashi, Amerika-Mura & Namba

This is the place for a big night out in Osaka, with numerous bars, clubs and restaurants packed into the streets and alleys of Shinsaibashi, Amerika-Mura and Namba.

★ Onzieme (11) CLUB
(オンジェム; Map p356; www.onzi-eme.com; 11th fl, Midō-suji Bldg, 1-4-5 Nishi-Shinsaibashi; cover charge around ¥2500; Ⓢ Midō-suji line to Shinsaibashi, exit 7) Osaka's largest and liveliest spot for nightlife at its craziest. An assortment of local and internationally acclaimed house, hip-hop and techno DJs showcase their talents nightly, with the posh interior reminiscent of some of the more famous London establishments.

Grand Café CLUB
(グランドカフェ; Map p356; http://grandcafe osaka.com; B1 fl, Spazio Bldg, 2-10-21 Nishi-Shinsaibashi; Ⓢ Midō-suji to Shinsaibashi) This hip underground club in Ame-Mura hosts a variety of electronica-DJ and hip-hop events. There's a comfy seating area and several dance floors. Look for the English sign at street level.

Tavola 36 BAR
(タボラ36; Map p356; 36th fl Swissotel, 5-1-60 Namba, Nankai Osaka; bar table charge per person ¥1300 (free for hotel guests); ⌚ bar 6pm-midnight; Ⓡ Midō-suji line to Namba) With city lights spread beneath you like a twinkling carpet, views are extraordinary from this chichi bar-restaurant. Drinks start at ¥1150, and there are Italian dishes such as the namesake pizza with mascarpone, prawns, mushroom and black truffle (¥2850). Enter the hotel from above Nankai Namba Station.

Rock Rock BAR
(ロックロック; Map p356; www.rockrock.co.jp; 3rd fl, Shinsaibashi Atrium Bldg, 1-8-1 Nishi-Shinsaibashi; ⌚ 6pm-5am, to 1am Sun; Ⓢ Midō-suji line to Shinsaibashi, exit 7) Serving the music-loving community since 1995, Rock Rock has a history of hosting after-parties for international acts and attracting celeb visitors. Regular events with a modest cover charge showcase some of Osaka's finest rock DJs (and famous guests).

Murphy's PUB
(マーフィーズ; Map p356; 6th fl, Reed Plaza Bldg, 1-6-3 Higashi-Shinsaibashi; ⌚ 5pm-1am Sun-Thu, to 4am Fri & Sat; Ⓢ Sakai-suji line to Nagahoribashi) This is one of the oldest Irish-style pubs in Japan, and a good place to rub shoulders with expats and Japanese, enjoy free live music, catch sports matches, and, of course, have a pint. It's on the 6th floor of a futuristic building with what looks like a rocket on the front.

Zerro BAR
(ゼロ; Map p356; 2-3-2 Shinsaibashi-suji; ⌚ 7pm-5am; Ⓢ Midō-suji line to Namba or Shinsaibashi) Zerro has a good range of drinks and food, energetic bilingual bartenders, and a street-level location ideal for a spot of people-watching. Come early for relaxed drinks and conversation; come late on the weekend for DJs, dancing and a lively crowd.

Cinquecento BAR
(チンクエチェント; Map p356; 2-1-10 Higashi-Shinsaibashi; ⌚ 7.30pm-5am Mon-Sat, 8pm-3am Sun; Ⓢ Midō-suji line to Namba or Shinsaibashi) The name is Italian for '500', appropriate since everything at this cosy bar costs ¥500. There's a hearty selection of food and the impressively extensive martini menu. It's not far from the corner of Sakai-suji; look for the number 5 in a red circle.

Shin-Sekai

Nocosare-jima BAR
(のこされ島; Map p352; 2nd fl 1-17-7 Ebisu-higashi; ⌚ 7pm-1am) Pop in for a drink at this cosy, mellow bar with tropical island decor, Southeast Asian munchies and a big window for bang-on views of the Tsūten-kaku tower. It's just inside the Osaka Shin-Sekai arcade, on the right.

☆ Entertainment

For information on upcoming shows, events and concerts, chat with tourist offices or read *Kansai Scene* (www.kansaiscene.com). A number of foreigner-friendly pubs and bars have free live music on weekends, including Murphy's and the Blarney Stone.

★ National Bunraku Theatre THEATRE
(国立文楽劇場; Map p352; ☎ 06-6212-2531; www.ntj.jac.go.jp/english; 1-12-10 Nipponbashi; full performance ¥2400-6000, single act prices vary; ⌚ opening months vary, check website; Ⓢ Sennichimae or Sakai-suji line to Nipponbashi) Japan's best venue for the mesmerising art of *bunraku*, the puppet theatre (p370) closely associated with Osaka. Performances can last all day, with two multiple-act parts up to 4½ hours each (acts are often unrelated). Too long? Non-reserved, same-day single-act tickets are sold on a first-come first-served basis from 9.45am, priced accordingly. Rent the English-language audio guide (full program/single act ¥700/300) for detailed explanations. Shows sell out quickly.

BUNRAKU: OSAKA'S SIGNATURE ART FORM

Bunraku, Japanese traditional **puppet theatre** involving nearly-life-sized puppets manipulated by black-clad, on-stage puppeteers, did not originate in Osaka but was popularised here. *Bunraku*'s most famous playwright, Chikamatsu Monzaemon (1653–1724), wrote plays about Osaka's merchants and the denizens of the pleasure quarters, social classes otherwise generally ignored in the Japanese arts at the time. Not surprisingly, *bunraku* found a wide audience among them, and a theatre was established to stage Chikamatsu's plays in Dōtombori.

Bunraku has been recognised on the Unesco World Intagible Cultural Heritage List, and the National Bunraku Theatre (p369) works to keep the tradition alive, with performances and an exhibition in the lobby about *bunraku*'s history, puppeteers and main characters. Learn more at the Japan Arts Council's website, www2.ntj.jac.go.jp/unesco/bunraku/en/.

Osaka Nōgaku Hall THEATRE
(大阪能楽会館; Map p354; www.pp.iij4u.or.jp/~rohnishi; 2-3-17 Nakasakinishi; most shows ¥5000-6300; JR line to Osaka) A five-minute walk east of Osaka Station, this theatre stages *nō* (stylised dance-drama) shows about twice a month. Look for the relief of a *nō* actor holding a fan on the facade.

Shopping

Osaka has almost as many shops as restaurants: major department stores, international fashion, independent boutiques, electronic goods and secondhand stores. For overseas visitors, major department stores and many other large retailers can waive the sales tax on purchases over ¥10,000. Look for signage in the window or inquire; your passport is required.

For gourmet gifts, sake and confectionary, as well as fresh food, check out department store food halls, where dozens of outlets and counters could keep gourmands busy browsing for hours.

Umeda & Osaka Station Area

Kita is a magnet for department stores clustered around its stations: **Daimaru** (大丸梅田店; Map p354; 06-6343-1231; www.daimaru.co.jp/umedamise; 3-1-1 Umeda; 10am-8pm), **Hankyū** (阪急梅田本店; Map p354; www.hankyu-dept.co.jp/honten; 10am-8pm Sun-Thu, 10am-9pm Fri & Sat), **Hanshin** (阪神梅田; Map p354; www.hanshin-dept.jp/hshonten; 10am-8pm) and the more youth-oriented **Hep Five** (Map p354; www.hepfive.jp; shops 10am-8pm, entertainment 10am-11pm), with the giant Ferris wheel on top. Other big shopping complexes include **Lucua** (ルクア; Map p354; www.lucua.jp; shops 10am-9pm, dining 11am-11pm) in JR Osaka Station, Grand Front Osaka (p366) just north of the station, **Yodobashi Umeda** (Map p354; shops 9am-10pm, restaurants 11am-11pm), with 10 storeys of tech, fashion and dining, and **NU Chayamachi** (NU茶屋町; Map p354; http://nu-chayamachi.com; fashion shops 11am-9pm, Tower Records 11am-11pm, restaurants 11am-midnight) to its north east. Fashion-savvy guys should also check out **Hankyū Men's** (阪急メンズ; Map p354; www.hankyu-dept.co.jp/mens; 11am-9pm Mon-Fri, 10am-9pm Sat, 10am-8pm Sun) in the ship-shaped **Hep Navio** (Map p354) building.

Also in the Osaka Station complex are branches of well-loved Japanese retailers **Tokyū Hands** (東急ハンズ; Map p354; www.tokyu-hands.co.jp; 10th-12th fl, Daimaru, 3-1-1 Umeda; 10am-9pm, to 8.30pm Sun; JR line to Osaka) and **Uniqlo**, and the **Pokemon Centre** (ポケットモンスター; Map p354; 13th fl Daimaru, 3-1-1 Umeda) for branded goods.

Maruzen & Junkudō Umeda BOOKS
(丸善&ジュンク堂書店梅田店; Map p354; www.junkudo.co.jp/MJumeda.html; 7-20 Chayamachi; 10am-10pm; JR line to Osaka) This new behemoth bookshop, the largest in Osaka, is the result of two book specialists joining forces. There's a big range of English-language books on the 6th floor, with travel guides on the 3rd floor. It's in the new Andō Tadao–designed Chaska Chayamachi building.

Kōjitsu Sansō OUTDOOR GEAR
(好日山荘; Map p354; www.kojitusanso.jp; 5th fl, Knowledge Capital, Grand Front Osaka, 3-1 Ōfuka-chō; 10am-9pm; JR line to Osaka) If you need a new backpack or any other kind of outdoor gear, head to this excellent shop in the splashy new Grand Front complex.

Shinsaibashi, Amerika-Mura & Namba Areas

Minami has a huge range of shops. International high-end brands fill Midō-suji, the main boulevard, between Shinsaibashi and Namba subway stations. Head east to the jam-packed Shinsaibashi-suji arcade for popular local and international chains, and Ame-Mura for out-there and vintage clothes, accessories for everything from your person to your car – at outrageously blinged-out **D.A.D** (D.A.D大阪アメリカ村店; Map p356; 2-8-29 Nishi-Shinsaibashi; 11am-9pm; S Midō-suji line to Shinsaibashi, exit 7) – and music. Massive shopping complexes dominate Namba, including **Osaka Takashimaya** (大阪タカシマヤ; Map p356; www.takashimaya.co.jp/osaka/store_information/index.html; 5-1-5 Namba; S Namba) department store and **Namba Parks Mall** (なんばパークス; Map p356; www.nambaparks.com; 2-10-70 Namba-naka; 11am-9pm; S Midō-suji, Sennichimae, Yotsubashi line to Namba).

★Dōguya-suji Arcade MARKET
(道具屋筋; Map p356; www.doguyasuji.or.jp/map_eng.html; S Midō-suji line to Namba) This blocks-long foodie's paradise sells just about anything related to the preparation, consumption and selling of food: all manner of pots, pans, knives, kitchen gadgets, tableware, even shopfront lanterns, bar signs and plastic food models. Start thinking about how to make room in the suitcase for that stuff you never realised you needed.

★Village Vanguard BOOKS, HOMEWARES
(ヴィレッジヴァンガード; Map p356; www.village-v.co.jp; 1-10-28 Nishi-Shinsaibashi; 11am-11pm; S Midō-suji line to Shinsaibashi, exit 7) A great starting point for fun, non-traditional, pop- and street-inspired mementos of your time in Japan. Village Vanguard bills itself as an 'exciting' bookstore, but there's much more to the story: between the cluttered book and magazine racks are offbeat gifts, from animal-shaped coat hooks to design-led T-shirts, mobile-phone cases, kitchen devices, hip-hop hats, shoulder bags, homewares and more.

Tokyū Hands DEPARTMENT STORE
(東急ハンズ; Map p356; www.tokyu-hands.co.jp; 3-4-12 Minamisenba; 10.30am-8.30pm; S Midō-suji line to Shinsaibashi) Nominally a DIY and houseware chain, Tokyū Hands is Japan's favourite place to browse for items you probably didn't need, but will end up loving. It's stacked floor upon floor with everything from obscure tools to design-forward lighting, clocks, curios and craft supplies, just for starters. There's a smaller branch in Umeda.

Bic Camera ELECTRONICS
(ビックカメラ; Map p356; www.biccamera.co.jp/shoplist/nanba.html; 2-10-1 Sennichimae; 10am-9pm; S Midō-suji or Sennichimae line to Namba) This vast store sells everything related to cameras, electronics and computers at competitive prices.

Orientation

Osaka is a gigantic, sprawling city of 223 sq km, but most visitors stay downtown, which is basically divided into two main areas. Kita (Japanese for 'north') contains the business and administrative core of Umeda, and the major transit hub of JR Osaka, Hankyū Umeda and their connected subway stations. Minami ('south') contains the bustling shopping and nightlife zones of Namba, Shinsaibashi, Amerika-Mura and Dōtombori. Namba is the hub of two more major train stations, on the JR and private Nankai lines, and Tennōji to the southeast, is served by JR and Kintetsu line trains. Osaka's extensive subway system connects them all.

DENDEN TOWN & OTAKU ROAD

From the Japanese word for electricity *(denki)*, **Denden Town** – Osaka's version of Tokyo's Akihabara electronics district – is looking a bit tired these days, no doubt due to competition from megastores like Bic Camera and Yodobashi. Still, there's huge variety and some bargains (though make sure your gadget will work in your home country or with your operating system). Most stores are closed on Wednesdays.

One block west is **Otaku Road**, several blocks of shops for manga (Japanese comics), anime (Japanese animation) and their inspired merchandise, plus secondhand video games, and *cosplay* outlets.

Denden Town runs along Sakai-suji, starting southeast of Nankai Namba Station and continuing down to Ebisu-chō Station on the Sakai-suji subway line (exit 1a, 1b or 2).

The de facto dividing line between Kita and Minami is two rivers, Dōjima-gawa and Tosabori-gawa, and the island of Naka-no-shima. Osaka-jō (Osaka Castle) sits about 1km southeast of here. The bayside Tempōzan neighbourhood and Universal Studios are west of the city centre.

Fair warning: Osaka's larger stations can be disorienting, particularly Namba and the Umeda/JR Osaka Station area. Exits are often confusingly labelled, even for Japanese, and English-language directional signage is lacking compared to similar stations in other big Japanese cities.

Adding to the confusion, *shinkansen* (bullet trains) don't stop at any of these hubs, but at Shin-Osaka Station, three subway stops (about five minutes) north of Umeda and JR Osaka Station on the Midō-suji line.

Information

INTERNET ACCESS

Most accommodations have wi-fi or internet access, as do an increasing number of cafes, and Osaka has been expanding free wi-fi in public areas around town (see www.osaka-info.jp/en/wifi).

MONEY

ATMs at Citibank, large post offices, and 7-Eleven stores take international cards. Major banks and post offices have currency exchange services.

Citibank (シティバンク; Map p354; http://citibank.co.jp; 2nd fl, Dai-ichi Semei Bldg, 1-8-17 Umeda; 9am-8pm Mon-Fri, 10am-5pm Sat & Sun, ATM 24hr; JR line to Osaka) Other branches are at Shinsaibashi (Map p356; Midōsuji Diamond Bldg, 2-1-2 Nishi Shinsaibashi; 9am-3pm Mon-Fri, ATM 24hr; S Midō-suji line to Shinsaibashi) and Umeda (Map p354; 7th fl, ABC-MART Umeda Bldg, 1-27 Chayamachi, across from Hankyū Station; 9am-3pm & 5-7pm Mon-Fri, 10am-4pm Sat, ATM 8am-10pm; Hankyū line to Umeda or JR line to Osaka); there's also a 24-hour ATM at Kansai International Airport.

POST

Osaka Central Post Office (大阪中央郵便局; Map p354; 3-2-4 Umeda; postal services 9am-9pm, ATM 7am-11.30pm Mon-Fri, 8am-11.30pm Sat, 9am-9pm Sun; S Midōsuji line to Umeda or Yotsubashi-suji line to Nishi-Umeda, JR line to Osaka)

TOURIST INFORMATION

Tourist offices can help book accommodation if you visit in person. There are offices in the main stations, and information counters at the airports. For the lowdown on upcoming events, pick up a copy of the English-language *Kansai Scene* magazine, available for free at restaurants, nightspots, some hotels and major bookshops.

Osaka Visitors Information Center, Umeda (大阪市ビジターズインフォメーションセンター・梅田; Map p354; 06-6345-2189; www.osaka-info.jp; 1st fl, North Central Gate, JR Osaka Station; 8am-8pm; JR lines to Osaka Station) The main tourist office is inside JR Osaka Station. There is another office on the 1st floor of Nankai Namba Station (大阪市ビジターズインフォメーションセンター・なんば; Map p356; 06-6631-9100; 9am-8pm; S Namba, Nankai line to Namba Station).

TRAVEL AGENCIES

HIS No 1 Travel Osaka (大阪No1トラベル; Map p354; 06-6133-0273; www.no1.his-west.jp; 1st fl, Dai-ichi Semei Bldg, 1-8-17 Umeda; 11am-7pm, to 6.30pm Sun; JR line to Osaka) In Umeda, this helpful travel agency has English speakers and competitive prices.

Getting There & Away

AIR

Two airports serve Osaka: **Kansai International Airport** (KIX; 関西空港; www.kansai-airport.or.jp/en) for all international and some domestic flights; and the domestic **Itami Airport** (ITM; 伊丹空港; http://osaka-airport.co.jp/), also confusingly called Osaka International Airport. KIX is about 50km southwest of the city, on an artificial island in the bay. Itami is located in Osaka itself.

BOAT

China & Korea

Osaka is connected with Shanghai by **Japan China International Ferry Company** (新鑑真, Shin Gan Jin in Japanese, Xin Jian Zhen in Chinese; www.shinganjin.com), departing Osaka on Tuesdays, and Shanghai Ferry Company (p868), departing Osaka on Fridays. One-way 2nd class fares start at ¥20,000 (around 48 hours).

Panstar Ferry Company (p868) connects Osaka and Busan, South Korea (one-way from around ¥13,000, 19 hours), departing Osaka three times a week. There is scant information online in English – ask at the tourist offices for the latest schedules and costs.

Ferries operate from the Osaka Port International Ferry Terminal, reached by the Chuō line or the Nankō Port Town line (aka New Tram) to Cosmo Square Station. It's about a 15-minute walk from the station to the terminal; there are also shuttle buses.

Within Japan

Ferries connect Osaka with several ports on Shikoku, Kyūshū and islands around Okinawa,

GETTING AROUND KANSAI ON THE CHEAP

Three rail passes available only to travellers on temporary visitor visas (you'll have to show your passport) offer inexpensive transit around Kansai.

JR West (www.westjr.co.jp) issues two passes with different coverage areas, durations and price points. The Kansai Area Pass (p876) covers local and express trains (though not *shinkansen*) on JR lines between Himeji and Kyoto, including Kōbe, Osaka and Nara. The Kansai Wide Area Pass (p876) covers all these plus Wakayama Prefecture to the south, Shiga Prefecture to the northeast and Kinosaki to the northwest, and *shinkansen* as far west as Okayama.

Kansai also has an extensive network of non-JR lines, for which the Kansai Thru Pass (p877) offers unlimited travel, as well as on municipal bus and subway lines (though not on JR trains). It also offers discounts at many attractions.

including Beppu (from ¥12,870, 11½ hours) and Kagoshima (from ¥15,650, 15¾ hours). Ferries operate from several piers accessible from the Nankō Port Town line, with additional services from Kōbe. See www.osaka-ferry.net for links to ferry companies and route information in English.

BUS

Long-distance buses operated by **Willer Express** (Map p354; www.willerexpress.com/en) connect Osaka and cities all across Honshū, Shikoku and Kyūshū (to Tokyo one way ¥3600 to ¥9400, eight hours; to Fukuoka one way ¥3900 to ¥7000, 10½ hours); fares vary by schedule and seat type. Willer Express buses depart from next to the Umeda Sky Building (p351). Check with tourist offices for more details and options.

TRAIN

Shin-Osaka Station is on the Tōkaidō-Sanyō *shinkansen* (between Tokyo and Hakata in Fukuoka) and the eastern terminus of the Kyūshū *shinkansen* to Kagoshima. There are direct trains to Tokyo (¥13,620, three hours), Hiroshima (¥9710, 1½ hours), Hakata (¥14,480, three hours), Kagoshima (¥21,380, 4¾ hours) and points in between.

Kyoto

While the *shinkansen* is fastest between Kyoto and Shin-Osaka (from ¥1420, 14 minutes), JR *shinkaisoku* (special rapid train) between Kyoto Station and JR Osaka Station (¥560, 28 minutes) is more convenient to the city centre.

The Hankyū line runs between Hankyū Umeda Station in Osaka and Kawaramachi, Karasuma and Ōmiya stations in Kyoto (*tokkyū* limited express train to Kawaramachi ¥400, 44 minutes). The Keihan line runs between Sanjō, Shijō or Shichijō stations in Kyoto and Yodoyabashi Station in Osaka (*tokkyū* to Sanjō ¥410, 54 minutes), on the Midō-suji subway line.

Kōbe

The *shinkansen* runs between Shin-Kōbe Station and Shin-Osaka Station (from ¥1500, 13 minutes). There is also a JR *shinkaisoku* train between JR Osaka Station and Kōbe's Sannomiya and Kōbe Stations (¥410, 22 minutes).

The Hankyū line is a little cheaper and usually less crowded. It runs from Osaka's Hankyū Umeda Station to Kōbe's Sannomiya Station (*tokkyū*, ¥320, 30 minutes).

Nara

The JR Kansai line links Osaka's Namba and Tennō-ji stations to JR Nara Station via Hōryū-ji (Yamatoji Kaisoku, ¥540, 50 minutes). The Kintetsu Nara line runs from Namba (Kintetsu Namba Station) to Kintetsu Nara Station (¥540, 40 minutes).

Getting Around

TO/FROM THE AIRPORT

Kansai International Airport (KIX)

KIX is well connected to the city with direct train lines and buses.

The all-reserved Nankai Express Rapit runs to/from Nankai Namba Station (¥1430, 35 minutes); Nankai Airport Express trains take about 10 minutes longer and cost ¥920. JR's Haruka limited airport express runs between KIX and Tennō-ji Station (unreserved seat ¥1710, 33 minutes) and Shin-Osaka Station (¥2330, 49 minutes). Regular JR express trains called *kankū kaisoku* also run between KIX, Osaka Station (¥1190, 68 minutes) and Tennō-ji (¥1060, 50 minutes). All these stations connect to the Midō-suji subway line.

Airport limousine buses run to/from Osaka Station/Umeda area, Osaka City Air Terminal (OCAT), Namba, Uehonmachi and the Tempōzan area. The fare is ¥1550 for most routes (¥1050 to OCAT) and it takes an average of 50 minutes, depending on traffic (it can take up to 90 minutes to Umeda). See www.kate.co.jp for timetables.

Trains stop running from the airport at 11.30pm, and the last bus leaves just after midnight. If your flight arrives after this, your other

OSAKA DISCOUNT PASSES

Temporary visitors to Japan can present a passport to purchase the **Osaka Amazing Pass** (大阪周遊パス, www.osaka-info.jp/osp/en, one-/two-day pass ¥2300/3000), which lives up to its name, covering local transit plus admission to 28 of the city's top sights and other discounts. The one-day version is valid on subway and private rail lines (no JR trains), while the two-day pass works on the subway network only. Purchase at city tourist offices in JR Osaka and Nankai Namba Stations, or select hotels.

If you intend to take more than about four transit trips in a day, it's worth investing in the day pass **Enjoy Eco Card** (エンジョイエコカード, per day Monday to Friday/Saturday and Sunday ¥800/600), for unlimited travel on subways, city buses and Nankō Port Town line, plus some admission discounts. At subway ticket machines, push the 'English' button, insert cash, select 'one-day pass' or 'one-day pass weekend'.

option into Osaka is a taxi. It takes about 50 minutes and there are standard fares to Osaka Umeda (¥14,500) and Namba (¥14,000). The late-night fare is an additional ¥2500. It's about ¥18,000 to Shin-Osaka.

Osaka Itami Airport

Frequent limousine buses connect the airport and various parts of Osaka. Buses run to/from Shin-Osaka Station (¥500, 25 minutes), Osaka and Namba stations (¥640, 25 minutes) every 20 minutes from about 8am to 9pm. At Itami, buy your tickets from the machine outside the arrivals hall. See www.okkbus.co.jp for timetables.

BUS

Osaka has an extensive bus system, but the train and subway network is far easier to use.

TRAIN

Osaka has a good subway network and, like Tokyo, a JR loop line (known as the Kanjō-sen) that circles the city area, intersecting with the subways and other train lines. You're not likely to need any other form of transport unless you stay out late and miss the last train.

There are eight subway lines, but the one that short-term visitors will find most useful is the Midō-suji (red) line, running north–south, stopping at Shin-Osaka, Umeda (next to Osaka Station), Shinsaibashi, Namba and Tennō-ji Stations. Most rides cost between ¥200 and ¥300.

Good-value discount passes are available.

KŌBE

078 / POP 1,553,789

Perched on a hillside sloping down to the sea, Kōbe (神戸) is one of Japan's most attractive and cosmopolitan cities. It was a maritime gateway from the earliest days of trade with China and home to one of the first foreign communities after Japan reopened to the world in the mid-19th century.

One of Kōbe's best features is its relatively small size – most sights can be reached on foot from the main train stations, making it a pleasure for casual wandering and stopping in its high quality restaurants and cafes. The most pleasant neighbourhoods to explore are Kitano-chō, Nankinmachi Chinatown and, after dark, the bustling area around Sannomiya Station.

Sights

Kōbe's two main gateways are Sannomiya and Shin-Kōbe stations, with sights, lodging and dining easily accessed on foot, or a short train ride away. Sannomiya marks the city centre, while the *shinkansen* stops at Shin-Kōbe Station, uphill in the northeast corner of town. The two are connected by a quick subway ride or about a 20-minute walk. Pick up a city map at one of the station tourist information offices.

Kōbe City Museum MUSEUM

(神戸市立博物館, Kōbe Shiritsu Hakubutsukan; www.city.kobe.lg.jp/culture/culture/institution/museum/main.html; 24 Kyōmachi; admission ¥200, during special exhibitions up to ¥1000; 10am-5pm, later during special exhibitions, closed Mon; JR, Hankyū or Hanshin lines to Sannomiya Station) Ground yourself in Kōbe's history as a trading port and east–west meeting place, via art and artifacts with decent English signage. Items show foreign influence from clocks and oil lamps to hairstyles. It's pricey during special exhibits, but worth it especially when they include the museum's collection of *namban* (literally 'southern barbarian') art, a school of painting that developed when early Jesuit missionaries taught Western painting techniques to Japanese students.

The Greek revival–style building dates from 1935.

Ikuta Shrine SHINTO SHRINE
(生田神社, Ikuta Jinja; ☎078-321-3851; 1-2-1 Shimo-yamate-dōri; ⏰7am-sunset; 🚉JR, Hankyū or Hanshin lines to Sannomiya Station) FREE Said to have been founded in AD 201, this peaceful, wooded shrine has played a key role in sake brewing history, survived civil wars and WWII, and been a gathering place for residents after natural disasters such as the 1995 earthquake. Its forest and landmark camphor tree are great for a break from the city's bustle.

Nankinmachi (Chinatown) NEIGHBOURHOOD
(南京町; 🚉JR or Hanshin lines to Motomachi Station) This gaudy, bustling, unabashedly touristy collection of Chinese restaurants and trinket and medicinal herb stores should be familiar to anyone who's visited Chinatowns elsewhere. It's fun for a stroll, particularly in the evening when lights illuminate the elaborately painted shop facades. Restaurants tend toward the overpriced (set meals from about ¥850) and may disappoint sophisticated palates, although it's one of the few places in Japan where street snacking is condoned (snacks from about ¥200).

Kōbe Maritime Museum & Kawasaki Good Times World MUSEUM
(神戸海洋博物館 & カワサキワールド Kōbe Kaiyō Hakubutsukan & Kawasaki Wārudo; www.khi.co.jp/kawasakiworld; 2-2 Hatoba-chō, Chūō-ku; admission ¥600; ⏰10am-5pm; Ⓢ Kaigan line to Minato Motomachi Station, 🚉JR Kōbe line to Kōbe or Motomachi) This building is in two parts: an extensive collection of high-quality model ships and displays in the old-school **Maritime Museum**, and the fun, hands-on experience of modern technology in **Kawasaki Good Times World**. You've probably heard of Kawasaki's motorcycles, but this Kōbe-born company has also influenced tech from trains to robotics and aerospace. Clamber aboard a section of the original *shinkansen*, early aeroplanes and some very cool bikes. Yes, it's corporate promo, but it's also pretty impressive.

The museums are in Meriken Park, a seaside location crowned by the 108m-tall, metal lattice **Kōbe Port Tower** (1963).

Kōbe Harbor Land Umie SHOPPING CENTRE
(神戸ハーバーランドumie; www.umie.jp; Ⓢ Kaigan line to Harbor Land, 🚉JR line to Kōbe) Five minutes' walk southeast of Kōbe Station or west of the Maritime Museum, Umie is a busy, multilevel, contemporary megamall with a colourful collection of some 235 big-name retailers and speciality shops, in three separate sections. Even if shopping doesn't appeal, there are awe-inspiring views of the city and some decent dining.

Kitano-chō NEIGHBOURHOOD
(北野町; ijinkan ¥350-750, combination tickets available; ⏰most ijinkan 9am-6pm (to 5pm Oct-Mar); 🚉JR San-yō Shinkansen to Shin-Kōbe or JR, Hankyū or Hanshin lines to Sannomiya) For generations of Japanese tourists, this pleasant, hilly neighbourhood *is* Kōbe, thanks to the dozen or so well-preserved homes of (mostly) Western trading families and diplomats who settled here during the Meiji Period. Its winding streets, nostalgic brick- and weatherboard-built *ijinkan* (literally 'foreigners' houses'), cafes, restaurants and, yes, souvenir shops are great for strolling. All lend a European-American atmosphere, though admittedly it's probably less intriguing for Western visitors than for Japanese.

Kitano Tenman-jinja SHINTO SHRINE
(北野天満神社; ☎078-221-2139; 3-12-1 Kitanocho, Chūō-ku; ⏰7am-5pm; 🚉JR San-yō Shinkansen to Shin-Kōbe or JR, Hankyū or Hanshin lines to Sannomiya Station) FREE This lovely little shrine to academic pursuits holds pride of place in Kitano-chō, up a steep hill and past a touristy stretch of souvenir and snack shops. Even if you aren't studying for an upcoming exam, it's a great place to take a breather and do some lazy people-watching, with views all the way across town to the Inland Sea.

Nunobiki Falls WATERFALL
(布引の滝, Nunobikinotaki; Ⓢ Shin-Kōbe, 🚉Shin-Kōbe) FREE You'd never guess that such a beautiful natural sanctuary could sit so close to the city. This revered waterfall in four sections (the longest is 43m tall) has been the subject of art, poetry and worship for centuries – some of the poems are reproduced on stone tablets at the site. It's accessible by a steep, 400m path, from Shin-Kōbe Station. Take the ground-floor exit, turn left and walk under the station building to the path.

Note: the hike up the stone steps can leave you a sweaty mess, especially in summer – so take it nice and slow and enjoy the river views as you ascend. Alternatively, you can access the falls in about 30 downhill minutes from the lower exit of Nunobiki Herb Gardens (p377) and the midway station of the ropeway (go past the reservoir).

Kōbe

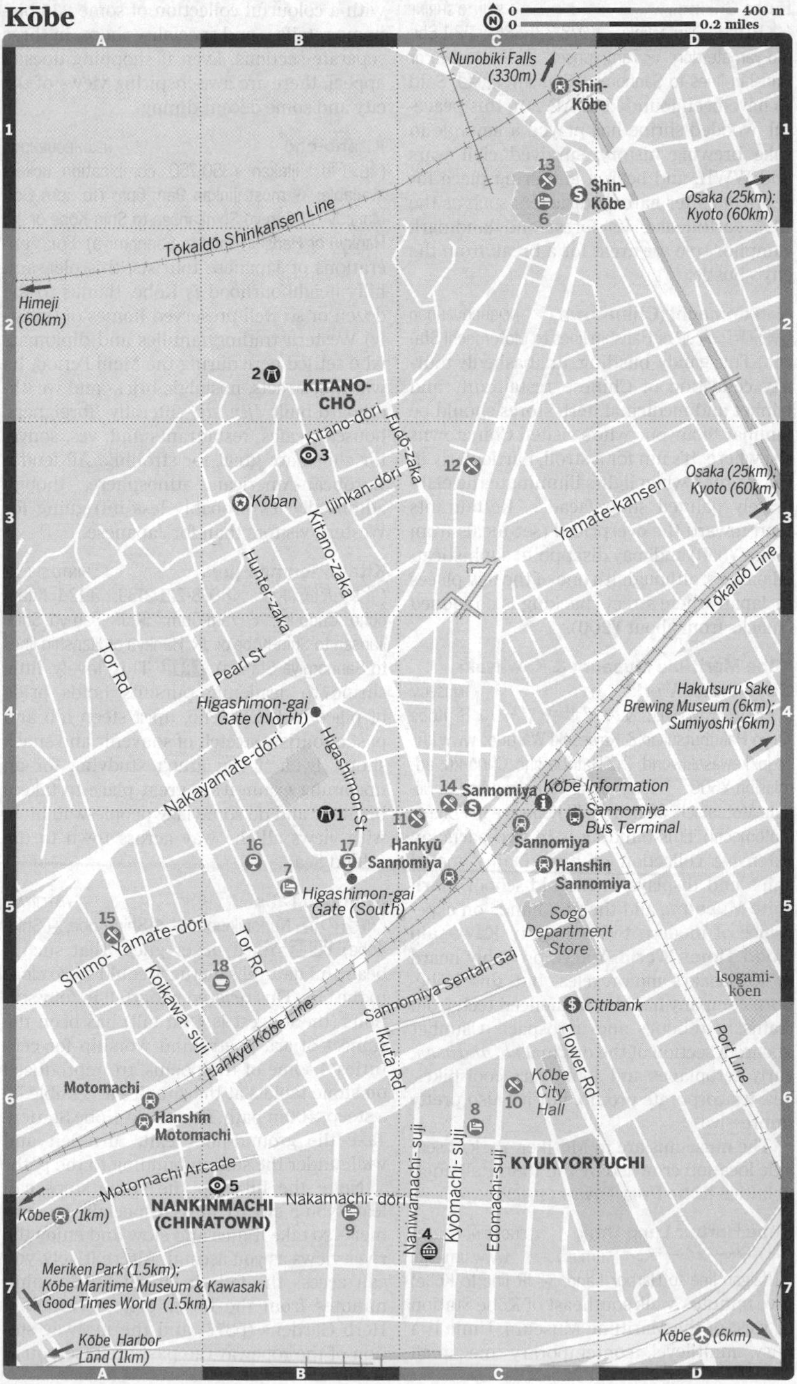
0 400 m
0 0.2 miles
A
B
C
D
1
2
3
4
5
6
7
Nunobiki Falls (330m)
Shin-Kōbe
13
6
Shin-Kōbe
Osaka (25km); Kyoto (60km)
Tōkaidō Shinkansen Line
Himeji (60km)
2
KITANO-CHŌ
Kitano-dōri
Fudō-zaka
3
12
Kōban
Ijinkan-dōri
Kitano-zaka
Hunter-zaka
Yamate-kansen
Osaka (25km); Kyoto (60km)
Tōkaidō Line
Tor Rd
Pearl St
Higashimon-gai Gate (North)
Higashimon St
Nakayamate-dōri
Hakutsuru Sake Brewing Museum (6km); Sumiyoshi (6km)
14
Sannomiya
Kōbe Information
Sannomiya Bus Terminal
1
11
Hankyū Sannomiya
Sannomiya
16
17
7
Hanshin Sannomiya
Higashimon-gai Gate (South)
15
Shimo-Yamate-dōri
Sogō Department Store
Tor Rd
18
Koikawa-suji
Sannomiya Sentah Gai
Isogami-kōen
Citibank
Hankyū Kōbe Line
Ikuta Rd
Flower Rd
Port Line
Motomachi
Hanshin Motomachi
Kōbe City Hall
10
8
Motomachi Arcade
5
KYUKYORYUCHI
Kōbe (1km)
NANKINMACHI (CHINATOWN)
Nakamachi-dōri
9
Naniwamachi-suji
Kyōmachi-suji
Edomachi-suji
4
Meriken Park (1.5km); Kōbe Maritime Museum & Kawasaki Good Times World (1.5km)
Kōbe Harbor Land (1km)
Kōbe (6km)

KANSAI KŌBE

Kōbe

Sights

Sleeping

Eating

Drinking & Nightlife

Kōbe Nunobiki Herb Gardens & Ropeway GARDENS

(神戸布引ハーブ公園・ロープウェイ; Nunobiki Hābu-kōen/Rōpuwei; ropeway one-way/return incl herb gardens ¥900/1400 (¥800 return after 5pm), herb gardens only ¥200; herb gardens 10am-5pm, ropeway 9.30am-4.45pm; herb gardens until 8.30pm, ropeway until 8.15pm 21 Jul–30 Aug and Sat-Sun Sep-Nov; Shin-Kōbe Station) Escape the city on a 400m-high mountain ridge, with sweeping views across town to the bay. Access is via **ropeway** (cable car) departing from near Shin-Kōbe Station. Some twee shops and restaurants near the top station mark the entrance to the **Herb Gardens**, and a paved path leads downhill past themed gardens to the ropeway's mid-station. Exiting the gardens, the trail continues downhill to Nunobiki Falls (p375; about 30 minutes) and Shin-Kōbe Station.

Hakutsuru Sake Brewery Museum MUSEUM

(白鶴造酒資料館; 4-5-5 Sumiyoshi Minami-machi, Higashinada-ku; 9.30am-4.30pm; Hanshin main line to Sumiyoshi) FREE Hakutsuru is the dominant sake brewer in Kōbe's Nada-ku, one of Japan's major sake-brewing centres. The self-guided tour through its historic, wood-built former brewery building (the current, giant concrete factory is behind it) is a fascinating look into traditional sake-making methods. Life-sized models appear on old equipment, and a pamphlet and videos in English help explain. A free sake tasting is available after the tour.

Take the Hanshin line eight stops east from Sannomiya to Sumiyoshi Station (¥190). It's seven minutes if you switch trains at Mikage, 15 minutes if you take the *futsū* (local) train; express trains do not stop. Exit the station, walk south to the elevated highway and cross the pedestrian overpass, make a U-turn at the bottom of the steps, take your first left, then a right; the entrance is on the right. Use the blue-and-white crane logo atop the factory as your guide.

Festivals & Events

Luminarie CULTURAL

Kōbe's biggest annual event is held every evening in early December to celebrate the city's miraculous recovery from a 1995 earthquake that killed over 6000 people (dates change slightly every year; check with information offices). The streets southwest of Kōbe City Hall are decorated with countless illuminated metal archways, which look like the interior of some otherworldly cathedral when viewed from within.

Sleeping

Hotel Trusty BOUTIQUE HOTEL ¥¥

(ホテルトラスティ神戸; 078-330-9111; www.trusty.jp/kobe; 63 Naniwamachi, Chūō-ku; s/d/tw from ¥9800/15,400/18,900; JR, Hankyū or Hanshin lines to Sannomiya) The name screams 'standard-issue business hotel', but this intimate little hotel, south of Sannomiya Station and behind city hall, is actually a super-stylish boutique hotel. Rooms are on the small side, but they are immaculate and have design touches like metal bathroom cups and soap dispensers.

B Kōbe HOTEL ¥¥

(ザ・ビー神戸; 078-333-4880; www.thebhotels.com/the-b-kobe/en; 2-11-5 Shimoyamate St, Chūō-ku; s/d/tw from ¥7200/8800/9800; Seishin-Yamate subway line to Sannomiya, JR, Hankyū or Hanshin lines to Sannomiya) Only steps away from restaurants and nightlife and downhill from Kitano-chō, the B Kōbe is a good, utilitarian choice. Mood-lit hallways lined with earth-tone carpets and wall coverings lead to small-ish rooms (if you're only sleeping here the size shouldn't matter too much). There are laundry machines for guest use and free coffee in the lobby.

★ **Oriental Hotel** HOTEL ¥¥¥

(神戸旧居留地オリエンタルホテル; ☎078-326-1500; www.orientalhotel.jp/en; 25 Kyōmachi, Chūō-ku; d/tw from ¥30,900/34,500; @; 🚉 JR Kōbe line, Hanshin or Hankyū to Sannomiya or Motomachi) One of Japan's most historic hotels (circa 1880), in the old foreigners' settlement, the Oriental was rebuilt after the 1995 earthquake and is now a sleek, elegant tower with a design sense deftly melding old Japan and new. Expect indulgent, English-speaking service and great views of the bay and mountains, from the 17th-storey lobby and restaurant.

ANA Crowne Plaza Hotel Kōbe HOTEL ¥¥¥

(ANAクラウンプラザ神戸; ☎078-291-1121; www.anacrowneplaza-kobe.jp/en; 1-chome, Kitano-chō, Chūō-ku; s/d/tw from ¥9500/15,500/15,500; @ 📶; Ⓢ Seishin-Yamate, 🚉 JR Shinkansen to Shin-Kōbe) Survey the bright lights of Kōbe from this 37-storey tower perched atop the city. Adjacent to JR Shin-Kōbe Station, the Crowne Plaza offers clean, spacious rooms (even if bathroom fixtures feel a bit dated), English-speaking staff, multiple bars and restaurants, and a pool and fitness centre (surcharge ¥1080). More restaurants are downstairs in the **Oriental Avenue shopping centre** (アベニュー).

Eating

Kōbe is famous throughout Japan for beef, Japanese-Western fusion cusine and tasty bakeries. Best restaurant browsing is around Sannomiya Station (with plenty of *izakaya* south of Ikuta Strine) and Chinatown in Nankinmachi.

Mikami SHOKUDŌ ¥

(味加味; ☎078-242-5200; 2-5-9 Kanō-chō; mains ¥480-1500; ⏰11.30am-3pm & 5pm-9.50pm; 📋; 🚉 JR, Hankyū or Hanshin lines to Sannomiya) This cheerfully busy 'food & wine restaurant' offers good-value lunches and dinners, from noodles to Chinese dishes to *teishoku* (set meals) from around ¥650. It's on the block behind Green Hill Hotel; look for the many potted plants and small English sign.

★ **R Valentino** ITALIAN ¥¥

(アール ヴァレンティーノ; ☎078-332-1268; www.r-valentino.com/english; 3rd fl, 4-5-13 Kanō-chō, Chūō-ku; mains ¥950-3200, lunch/dinner set menus from ¥1800/4000; ⏰11.30am-2pm & 5.30-9pm; 🖉📋; 🚉 JR, Hanshin or Hankyū lines to Sannomiya) Run by Italians and popular with Japanese and foreign visitors alike, this easygoing eatery on a Sannomiya side street is casual, comfortable and cosy with stone walls and rustic furniture. Look for dozens of pasta and brick-oven pizza options, plus meat and fish mains. Eager staff help explain the specials and make recommendations.

Wanto Burger BURGERS ¥¥

(ワントバーガー; ☎078-392-5177; www.wantoburger.com; 3-10-6 Shimo-Yamate-dōri; burgers ¥970-4210; ⏰noon-10pm Mon-Sat, noon-5pm Sun; 🚉 JR, Hanshin, Hankyū lines to Sannomiya) Run by a cool young crew, this spot looks like a vintage US diner, with a long counter, groovy tunes and a few tables, but that's where the resemblance ends; it's utterly different in both taste and price because the burgers are made with Kōbe beef (you can also order somewhat less expensive varieties of *wagyū*).

The namesake Wanto Burger comes piled high with a beef patty, sliced steak, garlic chips, bacon, boiled egg slices and steak sauce.

Grill Jūjiya YOSHOKU ¥¥

(グリル十字屋; ☎078-331-5455; 96 Edo-machi; mains ¥750-2300; ⏰11am-8pm Mon-Sat; 🚉 JR, Hanshin, Hankyū lines to Sannomiya) In this city thick with East–West heritage, this old-fashioned charmer specialises in *yōshoku*, Japanese takes on Western cooking: beef stew, grilled chicken, fried seafood, *hayashi* rice (rice with hashed beef, onions and savoury sauce). Wash them down with Japanese craft beers. It's been in business since the 1930s, though the building is newer. Head downstairs, next to the 7-Eleven.

Hirai IZAKAYA ¥¥

(ひら井; ☎078-327-6040; 1-21-8 Kitanagasa-dori, Chūō-ku; dishes ¥390-950; ⏰5pm-1am; 📋; 🚉 JR, Hanshin, Hankyū lines to Sannomiya Station) Northwest of Sannomiya Station is salaryman central, with myriad *izakaya* and bars. Among them, sample Hirai's house speciality, *katsuo wara-yaki* (bonito charred over straw), or house-made *gyōza* (dumplings), alongside *izakaya* standards over beer, sake or highballs. Look for the sake barrels and red lantern outside, two short blocks west of Kitanozaka.

LOCAL KNOWLEDGE

WHERE'S THE BEEF? KŌBE, OF COURSE!

For foodies worldwide, the name Kōbe is synonymous with great beef. The delicate marbling of Kōbe beef lends a supple texture and, many say, sweetness that other varieties of beef lack. It accounts for a mere 0.06% of beef consumption nationwide, which helps explain its sky-high price.

Kōbe beef is just one of many types of *wagyu* (Japanese beef). The name 'Kōbe beef' is a trademark referring to the Tajima breed of Japanese black cows born, raised and slaughtered in Kōbe's home prefecture, Hyōgo. There's a widespread belief that the cows are massaged, fed beer and played soothing music, although the Kōbe Beef Marketing & Distribution Promotion Association (www.kobe-beef.jp) disavows it.

To try it yourself, we like Kōbe Plaisir and Wanto Burger. Tourist information offices and hotels can recommend other spots around town.

Fisherman's Market SEAFOOD ¥¥
(フィシャーマンズマーケット; ☎078-360-3695; www.create-restaurants.co.jp; 2nd fl, Umie Mosaic, 1-6-1 Higashi-kawasaki-chō; lunch/dinner buffet Mon-Fri ¥1799/2399, Sat & Sun ¥1999/2599; ⏲11am-11pm; Ⓢ Kaigan line to Harbor Land) In Kōbe Harbor Land Umie, this giant seafood restaurant features an all-you-can-eat buffet, and, more impressively, million-yen harbour views through tall windows. Seafood preparations span Italian, Chinese, Spanish paella, king crab legs, sushi and more. Even if the eats sometimes feel a bit institutional, it's hard to beat the views and the price.

★ **Kōbe Plaisir** STEAK ¥¥¥
(神戸プレジール; ☎078-571-0141; www.kobe-plaisir.jp/e-index.html; The B Hotel, 2-11-5 Shimo-yamate-dōri; lunch/dinner set menus from ¥3240/6480; ⏲11.30am-3pm, 5pm-10:30pm; Ⓢ Seishin-Yamate line to Sannomiya, Ⓡ JR, Hankyū or Hanshin lines to Sannomiya) You can't get any more locavore; the ingredients come directly from the local branch of the Japan Agricultural Cooperative. You and your party choose your preparation of Kōbe or other steak – *seiro-mushi* (steamed), *teppan-yaki* (grilled on a steel plate) or *shabu-shabu* – and sit back as a multi-course meat-and-veg feast unfolds before you.

Drinking & Nightlife

Kōbe has a large foreign community and a number of bars that attract mixed Japanese and foreign crowds. Come evening, some cafes transform into bars.

Izn't BAR
(イズント; iznt.net; 4th floor, 1-1-8 Shimo-yamate-dōri; ⏲5pm-midnight Sun, 5pm-1am Mon-Thu, 5pm-late Fri & Sat; Ⓡ JR, Hanshin, Hankyū lines to Sannomiya) This lively bar brings Kōbe's Japanese and foreign community together over a rotation of salsa dancing, live bands, acoustic nights and sports broadcasts, plus cocktails, beer, wine and frozen mojitos. There's an international menu of bar snacks, from pizzas and burritos to tandoori wraps and sushi. And, it's mostly non-smoking. Enter off Higashimon Street.

Modernark CAFE
(モダナーク; ☎078-391-3060; 3-11-15 Kitanagasa-dōri, Chūō-ku; ⏲11.30am-10.30pm, to 10pm Sun; Ⓡ JR Kōbe line to Motomachi) An adorably funky, old-school cafe with a wood-accented room, glassed-in verandah and cute gifts for sale. Modernark bills itself as a 'pharm cafe' and emphasises vegetarian and vegan options with its wraps, salads, cakes, coffees and teas (meals from ¥850). Look for the thicket of potted trees out front.

Bar Ashibe BAR
(バーアシベ; ☎078-391-2039; 2-12-21 Shimo-yamate-dori, Chu-o-ku; beer from ¥600, cocktails from ¥800; ⏲6pm-5am; Ⓡ JR, Hanshin, Hankyū lines to Sannomiya) This genteel bar near Ikuta Shrine is a good choice for a mellow drink. Lighting is subdued, staff are discreet and efficient and the vibe invites soulful meditations. The down-tempo R&B soundtrack goes perfectly with the wide selection of spirits.

Information

Citibank (シティバンク; ⏲9am-3pm Mon-Fri, ATM 24hr; Ⓡ JR, Hankyū or Hanshin lines to Sannomiya) South of Sogo Department Store; the ATM accepts international cards.

Kōbe Information (インフォメーション神戸; ☎078-322-0220; ⊙9am-7pm; 🚉JR, Hankyū or Hanshin lines to Sannomiya) The city's main tourist information office is on the ground floor outside JR Sannomiya Station's east gate. There's a smaller information counter on the 2nd floor of Shin-Kōbe Station, outside the main *shinkansen* gate. Both carry reasonably good free maps of the city, pamphlets and the *Kōbe Welcome Coupon* booklet, with discounts to sights.

Getting There & Away

AIR

Skymark Airlines (www.skymark.jp/en) Operates out of Kōbe Airport, with destinations including Tokyo (Haneda; ¥11,800, 70 minutes), Sapporo (Shin-Chitose; ¥13,800, two hours) and Okinawa (Naha; ¥12,800, 2¼ hours).

BOAT

There are regular ferries between Kōbe and Shinmoji (Kitakyūshū, Fukuoka Prefecture) with **Hankyū Ferry** (☎0120-56-3268; www.han9f.co.jp/en, from ¥6890); Niihama (Ehime Prefecture) with **Orange Ferry** (www.orange-ferry.co.jp, from ¥5960); and Ōita (near Beppu on Kyūshū) with **Ferry Sunflower** (www.ferry-sunflower.co.jp, from ¥11,940).

BUS

Overnight buses connect Kōbe's Sannomiya Bus Terminal and Tokyo (Shinjuku highway bus terminal and JR highway bus terminal – JR 高速バスターミナル – at Tokyo Station). The journey costs from ¥6000 and takes around 9½ hours.

TRAIN

Sannomiya Station is the hub for rail travel to/from Osaka on the private Hankyū and Hanshin lines and most JR trains. On the JR Tōkaidō line, *shinkaisoku* (special rapid trains) are the fastest between Sannomiya and Osaka Station (¥410, 22 minutes). Of the private lines, Hankyū is more convenient, connecting Kōbe Sannomiya Station and Hankyū Umeda Station (*tokkyū;* ¥320, 27 minutes), near Osaka Station.

Unless you're on the *shinkansen*, most of the trains to Kyoto require a transfer in Osaka or Umeda.

Shin-Kōbe Station is on the Tōkaidō/San-yō and Kyūshū *shinkansen* lines. Destinations include Fukuoka (Hakata Station; ¥14,160, 2 hours 20 minutes), Tokyo (¥14,160, 3¼ hours), and other major stops including Osaka, Kyoto, Nagoya, Hiroshima and Kagoshima.

Getting Around

TO/FROM THE AIRPORT

Itami Osaka Airport

There are direct limousine buses to/from Osaka's Itami Airport (¥1050, 40 minutes). In Kōbe, the buses stop on the southwestern side of Sannomiya Station.

Kōbe Airport

The Portliner connects Sannomiya (downtown Kōbe) and the airport in 18 minutes and costs ¥330. A taxi costs between ¥2500 and ¥3000 (15 to 20 minutes).

Kansai International Airport (KIX)

The most fun connection between Kōbe and KIX is by Bay Shuttle high-speed boat (¥1850, 31 minutes, approximately hourly), which drops you off by Kōbe's port; take the Portliner the rest of the way. By train, the fastest way is the JR *shinkaisoku* to/from Osaka Station, and the JR *kanku kaisoku* between Osaka Station and the airport (total cost ¥1660, total time 1¾ hours with good connections). There is also a direct limousine bus to/from the airport (¥2000, 1¼ hours), which is more convenient if you have a lot of luggage. The Kōbe airport bus stop is on the southwestern side of Sannomiya Station.

PUBLIC TRANSPORT

Kōbe is small enough to travel around on foot, but JR, Hankyū and Hanshin railway lines run east–west through town. The Seishin-Yamate subway line connects Shin-Kōbe and Sannomiya Stations (¥210, two minutes), or you can walk it in about 20 minutes. Another subway line (the Kaigan line) runs from just south of Sannomiya Station south toward the Harbor Land area. A **city-loop bus service** (per ride/day pass ¥260/660) makes a grand-circle tour of most of the city's sightseeing spots and main stations; look for the retro-style green buses.

HIMEJI

☎079 / POP 543,991

A visit to Himeji (姫路) is a must for any lover of Japanese history, especially castles. The recently renovated Himeji Castle, the finest in all of Japan, towers over this quiet city. Nearby, Kōkō-en is a rambling collection of nine meticulously reconstructed samurai houses and their gardens.

You can visit Himeji, on the *shinkansen* route, as a day trip from Kyoto, Nara, Osaka or Kōbe, or as a stopover en route to Okayama or Hiroshima. The city is flat and easily walkable, or free rental cycles are available from the tourist information office at the station.

Sights

★Himeji-jō CASTLE

(姫路城; Himeji Castle; 68 Honmachi; adult/child ¥1000/300, combination ticket with Kōkō-en ¥1040/360; ⏲9am-5pm Sep-May, to 6pm Jun-Aug) Japan's most magnificent castle, Himeji-jō is one of only a handful of original castles remaining (most are modern concrete reconstructions). Its nickname Shirasagi-jō ('White Egret Castle') comes from its lustrous white plaster exterior and stately form on a hill above the plain. There's a five-storey main keep *(tenshū)* and three smaller keeps, and the entire structure is surrounded by moats and defensive walls punctuated with rectangular, circular and triangular openings for firing guns and shooting arrows.

The main keep's walls also feature *ishiotoshi* – narrow openings that allowed defenders to pour boiling water or oil onto anyone trying to scale the walls after making it past the other defences. On balance, we recommend visitors to pay the admission charge and enter the castle by legitimate means.

Although there have been fortifications in Himeji since 1333, today's castle was built in 1580 by Toyotomi Hideyoshi and enlarged some 30 years later by Ikeda Terumasa. Ikeda was awarded the castle by Tokugawa Ieyasu when the latter's forces defeated the Toyotomi armies. In the following centuries it was home to 48 successive lords.

Now is prime time to visit because much of the castle was closed for a five-year renovation.

It takes around 1½ hours to follow the arrow-marked route around the castle. Last entry is an hour before closing.

★Kōkō-en GARDENS

(好古園; 68 Honmachi; adult/child ¥300/150, combination ticket with Himeji Castle ¥1040/360; ⏲9am-6pm May-Aug, to 5pm Sep-Apr) Across the castle's western moat is this stunning reconstruction of the former samurai quarters. Nine Edo-style homes boast gardens with various combinations of waterfalls, koi ponds, intricately pruned trees, bamboo, flowering shrubs and a wisteria-covered arbor. It feels like a movie set amid the stone and plaster walls lining the paths (in fact, many Japanese historical dramas have been shot here). It is particularly lovely in spring and during the autumn foliage season.

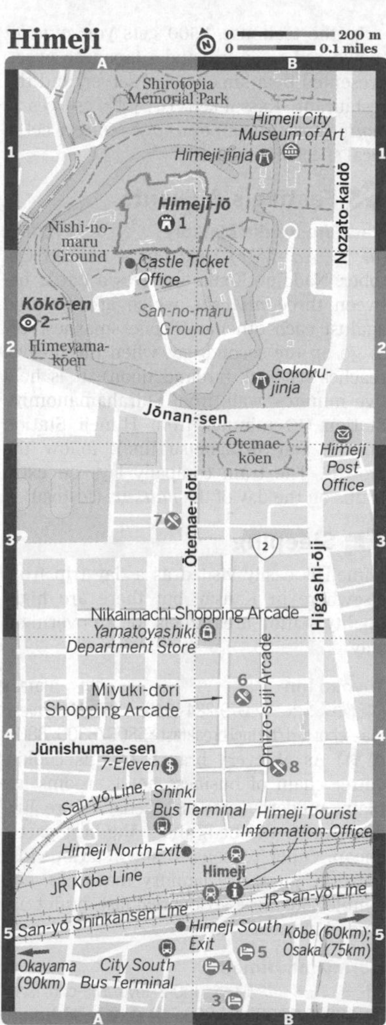

Himeji

Top Sights

1 Himeji-jō A1
2 Kōkō-en A2

Sleeping

3 Dormy Inn Himeji B5
4 Hotel Nikkō Himeji B5
5 Tōyoko Inn B5

Eating

6 Fukutei B4
7 Menme A3
8 Nadagiku Kappa-tei B4

In the teahouse, ¥500 gets you *matcha* (powdered green tea) and a Japanese sweet, presented by a kimono-clad server, and the restaurant Kassui-ken (活水軒) serves a *bentō* (boxed meal) of *anago* (conger eel, a local speciality; ¥2080).

Festivals & Events

Nada-no-Kenka Matsuri FESTIVAL
(灘のけんか祭り) Held on 14 and 15 October, Nada-no-Kenka involves a battle between three *mikoshi*, which are battered against each other until one smashes. Try to go on the second day, when the festival reaches its peak (around noon). It is held five minutes' walk from Shirahamanomiya Station (10 minutes from Himeji Station on the San-yō-Dentetsu line); follow the crowds. The train company lays on extra trains on the day of the *matsuri* (festival).

Sleeping

Himeji is easily visited as a day trip from elsewhere in Kansai, but there are high-quality station-area hotels for an overnight stay.

Tōyoko Inn HOTEL ¥
(東横イン; 079-284-1045; 97 Minamiekimae-chō; s/d/tw incl breakfast ¥5800/8300/8800;) As at every branch of this cookie-cutter chain of business hotels, rooms are plain, modern, spotless, teensy (store luggage under the bed) and – the best part – cheap. Other reasons to stay: station-close location, guest-use laundry machines, and simple Japanese-style breakfast buffet included in rates.

Dormy Inn Himeji HOTEL ¥¥
(ドーミーイン姫路; 160-2 Toyozawa-chō; s/d/tw ¥9200/14,300/16,900;) Although rooms are pretty compact, this new, 12-storey hotel has lots going for it: rooftop *onsen* baths (though only showers in rooms), sauna and laundry machines, crisp, modern-meets-rustic style, Chinese-style PJs instead of the usual *yukata* (bathrobe), all non-smoking rooms and free *rāmen* service nightly. It's a block south of the station.

Hotel Nikkō Himeji HOTEL ¥¥¥
(ホテル日航姫路; 079-222-2231; 100 Minami-ekimae-chō; s ¥13,000, d or tw ¥23,000;) Across from the station's south exit, Himeji's top hotel offers stylish (if somewhat dated) and fairly spacious rooms with Western-style bathtubs, several restaurants (Japanese, Chinese, Western), a relaxation spa, and a bar on the top floor. Significant discounts may be available online.

Eating

Most of the restaurants in Himeji are located in the shopping arcades and underground shopping centre north of the station (on the way to the castle).

Menme NOODLES ¥
(めんめ; 079-225-0118; 68 Honmachi; noodles ¥550-950; 11.30am-6pm, closed Wed;) They make their own noodles at this homey, cheerful little joint a few minutes' walk from the castle. It's not fancy, but it serves an honest, tasty bowl of udon to power you through the day. Look for the white *noren* (doorway curtain) showing noodles being rolled out.

Nadagiku Kappa-tei SHOKUDŌ, IZAKAYA ¥
(灘菊かっぱ亭; 079-221-3573; 58 Higashi Ekimae-chō; dishes ¥210-1000; 11am-9pm Mon-Sat, 11am-8pm Sun) Ceramic sake bottles line the walls of this workmanlike eatery owned by a local sake brewery. Sit on a drum at a woodblock table, and try daily lunch *teishoku* (set meals; ¥620) including the signature *oden* (fish cake and vegie hot-pot) in ginger-soy sauce. It all goes great with the house sake. It's in the arcade, below Octave Cafe.

★ **Fukutei** JAPANESE ¥¥
(福亭; 079-222-8150; 75 Kamei-chō; dishes ¥480-980, lunch set menus ¥1350-2500, dinner ¥3200-4000; 11.30am-2.30pm & 5-10pm Mon-Fri, 11.30am-2.30pm & 5-9pm Sat & Sun;) This approachable, contemporary restaurant is a great choice for a civilised experience. The speciality is the set menus: a little sashimi, some tempura and the usual nibbles on the side. At lunch try the daily special *omakase-zen* (tasting set; ¥1500).

Information

Himeji Tourist Information Office (姫路市観光案内所[姫路観光なびポート]; 079-287-0003; 9am-7pm) Himeji Tourist Information Office is on the ground floor of Himeji Station. Pick up the *Places of Interest Downtown Himeji* map or *Himeji Tourist Guide & Map*.

Getting There & Away

If you've got a Japan Rail Pass or are in a hurry, take the *shinkansen* from Kyoto (from ¥4770, 55 minutes), Hiroshima (¥7790, one hour), Shin-Osaka (¥3240, 35 minutes) and Shin-Kōbe (¥2600, 16 minutes). Otherwise, slower *shinkaisoku* trains on the JR Tōkaidō line run from Kyoto (¥2270, 94 minutes), Osaka (¥1490, one hour) and Kōbe's Sannomiya Station (¥970, 40 minutes).

SHIGA PREFECTURE

Just across the Higashiyama mountains from Kyoto, Shiga Prefecture (滋賀県; Shiga-ken) is dominated by Biwa-ko, Japan's largest lake. Attractions here are easily visited as day trips from Kyoto. The biggest draws are the towns of Nagahama, for its picturesque Kurokabe Square neighbourhood of glass artisans, and Hikone, for its fine original castle. Other worthwhile destinations include the temples Mii-dera and Ishiyama-dera, and the Miho Museum, well worth a trip even if just to see the futuristic building deep in the forest.

Ōtsu 大津

☎077 / POP 342,603

Ōtsu, Shiga-ken's capital, has developed from a 7th-century imperial residence (for five years it was Japan's capital) into a lake port and major post station on the Tōkaidō highway between eastern and western Japan.

The **information office** (☎522-3830; ⏲8.40am-5.25pm) is at JR Ōtsu Station.

Sights

Mii-dera Temple BUDDHIST TEMPLE

(三井寺; 246 Onjōji-chō; admission ¥600; ⏲8am-5pm) Just past its 1200th anniversary (in 2014), these rambling, deeply wooded precincts at the edge of central Ōtsu are the head temple of the Jimon branch of Tendai Buddhism. Four of its buildings are national treasures, others are important cultural properties. The Niō-mon gate here is unusual for its roof, made of layers of tree bark rather than tiles. It looks particularly fine when framed by spring cherry blossoms and autumn colours.

Mii-dera is a short walk northwest of Mii-dera Station on the Keihan Ishiyama-Sakamoto Line (from Kyoto, change trains at Hama-Ōtsu Station).

Festivals & Events

Ōtsu Dai Hanabi Taikai FIREWORKS

Ōtsu's Grand Fireworks Festival starts at dusk on 8 August. Best views are along the waterfront near Keihan Hama-Ōtsu Station. Trains to and from Kyoto are packed for hours before and afterward.

Ōtsu Matsuri CULTURAL

At Tenson-jinja, near JR Ōtsu Station, ornate floats are displayed on the first day and paraded around the town on the second day. Held early to mid-October.

Getting There & Away

From Kyoto, take the JR Tōkaidō line from JR Kyoto Station to JR Ōtsu Station (¥200, 10 minutes), or travel on the Kyoto Tōzai subway line to Hama-Ōtsu Station (¥430, 22 minutes from Sanjō Keihan Station).

Ishiyama-dera

Ishiyama-dera BUDDHIST TEMPLE

(石山寺; 1-1-1 Ishiyama-dera; admission ¥500; ⏲8am-4.30pm) This Shingon-sect temple was founded in the 8th century. Climb the many steps past a garden of massive boulders to the *hondō* (main hall), famed as the place where Lady Murasaki wrote *The Tale of Genji*. Continue exploring on trails winding further uphill through a lovely forest, including the one that leads up to Tsukimitei hall, for great views over Biwa-ko.

The temple is a 10-minute walk from Keihan Ishiyama-dera Station (continue along the road in the direction that the train was travelling). From Kyoto, take the JR Tōkaidō line from JR Kyoto Station to JR Ishiyama Station (*kaisoku* or *futsū* trains only, ¥240, 13 minutes) and switch to the Keihan line for the short journey to Ishiyama-dera Station (¥160). Alternatively, take the subway Tōzai line to Keihan Hama-Ōtsu and transfer to an Ishiyama-dera-bound train (from Sanjo Station: ¥560, 42 minutes including transit time).

Miho Museum

★ **Miho Museum** MUSEUM

(ミホミュージアム; ☎0748-82-3411; www.miho.or.jp; 300, Tashiro Momodani; admission ¥1100; ⏲10am-5pm Jan & Feb, mid-Jun–mid-Jul, mid–end Aug, mid–end Dec, closed some Mon & Tue) Secluded amid hills and valleys near the village of Shigaraki, this knockout museum houses the Koyama family collection of Japanese, Middle Eastern, Chinese and South Asian art, and beautifully displayed special exhibits. The facility is at least as impressive as the collection. The IM Pei–designed main

Shiga Prefecture

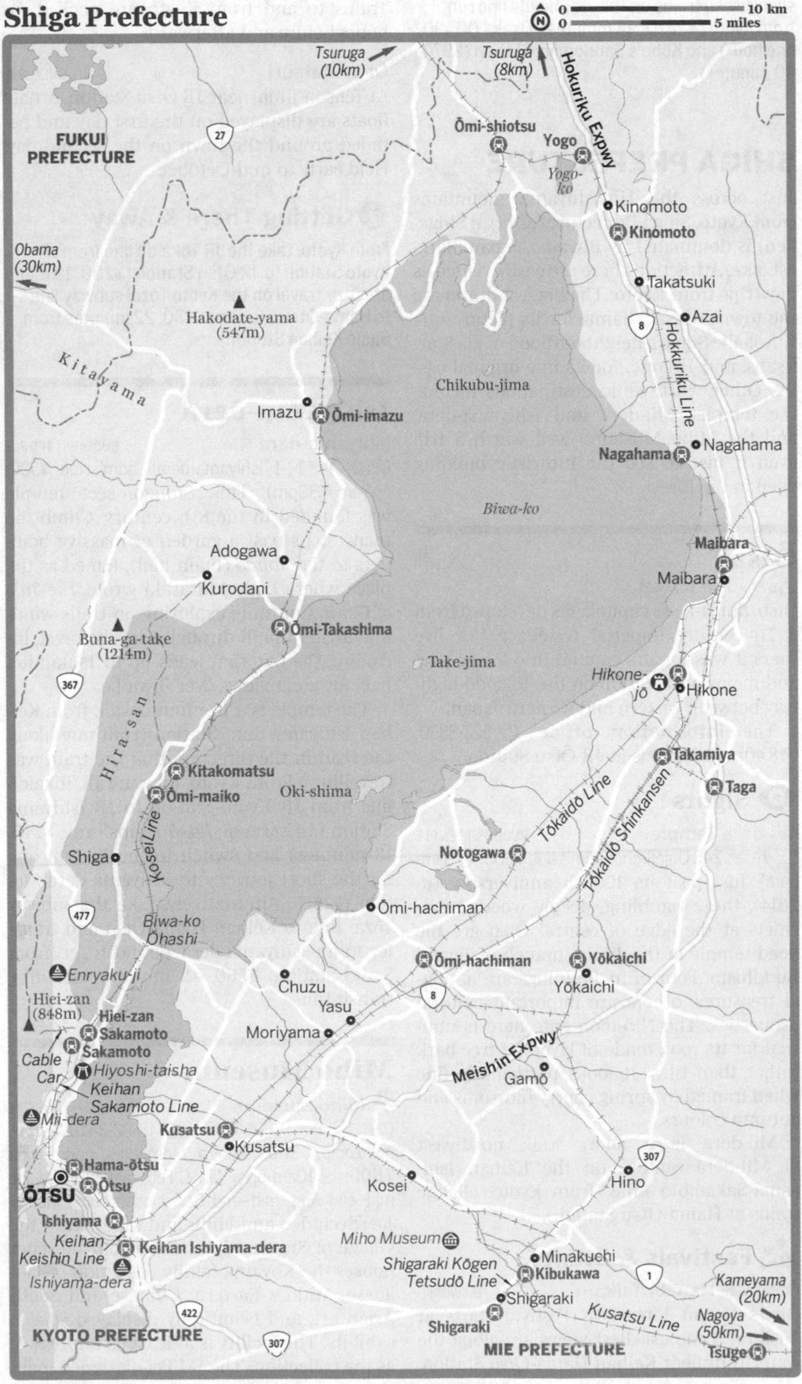

0 10 km
0 5 miles

Tsuruga (10km)
Tsuruga (8km)
Hokuriku Expwy
27
Ōmi-shiotsu
Yogo
Yogo-ko
FUKUI PREFECTURE
Kinomoto
Kinomoto
Takatsuki
Obama (30km)
Hakodate-yama (547m)
8
Azai
Hokkuriku Line
Kitayama
Chikubu-jima
Imazu
Ōmi-imazu
Nagahama
Nagahama
Biwa-ko
Adogawa
Maibara
Kurodani
Maibara
Ōmi-Takashima
Buna-ga-take (1214m)
Take-jima
367
Hikone-jō
Hikone
Hira-san
Takamiya
Kitakomatsu
Ōmi-maiko
Oki-shima
Taga
Tōkaidō Line
Tōkaidō Shinkansen
Kosei Line
Shiga
Notogawa
477
Ōmi-hachiman
Biwa-ko Ōhashi
Enryaku-ji
Ōmi-hachiman
Yōkaichi
Yōkaichi
Chuzu
8
Hiei-zan (848m)
Yasu
Hiei-zan
Moriyama
Sakamoto
Sakamoto
Meishin Expwy
Cable Car
Hiyoshi-taisha
Gamō
Keihan Sakamoto Line
Mii-dera
Kusatsu
Kusatsu
307
Hama-ōtsu
Kosei
Hino
ŌTSU
Ōtsu
Ishiyama
Keihan Keishin Line
Miho Museum
Keihan Ishiyama-dera
Minakuchi
Shigaraki Kōgen Tetsudō Line
Kibukawa
Ishiyama-dera
1
Kameyama (20km)
Shigaraki
Kusatsu Line
422
Nagoya (50km)
KYOTO PREFECTURE
Shigaraki
307
MIE PREFECTURE
Tsuge

KANSAI

building, reached from the ticket centre via a footpath and long pedestrian tunnel opening onto a gorge, feels like a secret hideout in a futuristic farmhouse.

The construction was quite an engineering feat: the top of the mountain was removed, the glass and marble building constructed, and the ground replaced as before around and above it, down to the massive red pine (a video explains it).

Take the JR Tōkaidō line from Kyoto or Osaka to Ishiyama Station, and change to a **Teisan Bus** (Teisan Konan Kōtsu; www.teisan-konan-kotsu.co.jp) bound for the museum (¥820, approximately 50 minutes). Be sure to double-check the website for opening times before setting out, as they can vary.

Hikone 彦根

0749 / POP 112,734

The prefecture's fifth-largest city is of special interest for its lovely castle, which dominates the town. The adjoining garden is also a classic.

Sights

★Hikone Castle CASTLE

(彦根城, Hikone-jō; 1-1 Konki-chō; combined admission with Genkyū-en ¥600; 8.30am-5pm) Completed in 1622, this diminutive castle of the Ii family of *daimyō* (domain lords) is rightly considered a national treasure; much of it remains in its original state. One unusual feature: *teppōzama* and *yazama*, outlets for shooting guns and arrows, designed to be invisible from the outside until being popped out for use. Upper storeys have great views across Biwa-ko. Surrounded by more than 1200 cherry trees, the castle's also very popular for springtime *hanami* (blossom viewing).

The castle is a 10-minute walk up the street from the station (take a left before the shrine, then a quick right, or walk through the shrine grounds).

Genkyū-en GARDENS

(玄宮園; admission incl in Hikone Castle ticket, separate admission ¥200; 8.30am-5pm) This exquisite, Chinese-influenced garden from 1679 is criss-crossed by waterways and wooden bridges. Tree-topped islands, peninsulas and interestingly shaped rocks punctuate its pond. For ¥500 you get a cup of *matcha* and a sweet in the teahouse, to enjoy as you relax and gaze over the scenery. Ask someone at the castle to point you toward the garden.

Yumekyō-bashi Castle Rd NEIGHBOURHOOD

(夢京橋キャッスルロード) About 400m southwest of the castle (accessible via the Omote-mon or Ōte-mon gate of the castle), this street of traditional shops and restaurants is ideal for lunch after exploring the castle. Browse the shops to round out your visit to Hikone.

Eating

Monzen-ya NOODLES ¥

(もんぜんや; 0749-24-2297; 1-6-26 Honmachi; mains ¥700-1500; 11am-6pm, to 3pm Mon, closed Tue) Our favourite spot in Yumekyō-bashi Castle Rd, this little *soba* (buckwheat noodle) place serves specialities such as *nishin-soba* (*soba* with herring; ¥920) and dishes made with local Ōmi beef. From the castle end of the street, it's about 100m on the left – look for the white *noren* curtain with black lettering in the doorway.

Information

Tourist Information Office (0749-22-2954; 9am-5.30pm) The good tourist information office is near the bottom of the steps by Hikone Station's west exit. Pick up the excellent *Street Map & Guide to Hikone* and *A Journey to Hikone*, which has good detail on the castle.

Getting There & Away

Hikone is about an hour from Kyoto on the JR Tōkaidō line (*shinkaisoku*; ¥1110). If you have a Japan Rail Pass or are in a hurry, you can take the *shinkansen* to Maibara (¥3300, 20 minutes from Kyoto) and then backtrack on the JR Tōkaidō line to Hikone (¥190, five minutes).

Nagahama 長浜

0749 / POP 122,783

Easily paired with a trip to Hikone, Nagahama is an appealing little town on the northeast shore of Biwa-ko. The main attraction is the historic preservation district Kurokabe Square.

Sights

★Kurokabe Square NEIGHBOURHOOD

(黒壁スクエア) *Kurokabe* means 'black walls', and you'll find plenty of them in this photogenic historic district (it's not really a square). Many of the old *machiya* (townhouses) and *kura* (storehouses) are now antique shops, galleries or studios showcasing the town's longstanding glass industry.

From Nagahama Station's east exit, follow the street to the left alongside Heiwado supermarket, and take the first left after Shiga Bank; Kurokabe Square begins about 100m further on.

Nagahama Hikiyama Museum MUSEUM
(長浜曳山博物館; ☎0749-65-3300; 14-8 Motohama-chō; admission ¥600; ⌚9am-5pm) From 14 to 16 April, the town's most famous festival, Nagahama Hikiyama Matsuri, takes place; it's scheduled to join the Unesco World Heritage list in 2016. The highlight is costumed five- to 13-year-old children performing kabuki (stylised Japanese theatre) aboard a dozen elaborately ornamented *hikiyama* (festival floats). Floats are about 6m high and weigh about 4.6 tonnes. The rest of the year, check out four of the 13 floats at this museum on the eastern side of Kurokabe Square.

Giant Kaleidoscope LANDMARK
(巨大万華鏡; kyodaimangekyō; ⌚dawn-dusk) FREE One of Kansai's quirkiest attractions is this retro, flower-vase-shaped tower. Stand underneath, hand-crank the wheel and watch what happens above. It's northwest of the Hikiyama Museum; walk to the corner, turn left, and turn right down the alley where you see a sign reading 'Antique Gallery London'. It's surrounded by snack and souvenir stalls.

★Daitsū-ji BUDDHIST TEMPLE
(大通寺; admission ¥500, main hall & grounds free; ⌚9am-4.30pm) Just northeast of Kurokabe Square, this Jōdō-sect temple rivals Kyoto's finest with its collection of dozens of historic *fusuma* (sliding door) and *byōbu* (folding screen) paintings of landscapes and wildlife on gold leaf, including important cultural properties by members of the Kanō school. There's also a stunning inner garden. Even if that's not of interest, peek at the stately main hall and grounds.

Eating

★Yokarō NOODLES ¥
(翼果楼; ☎0749-63-3663; 7-8 Motohama-chō; mains ¥650-900, set meals ¥1340-2040; ⌚11am-5pm) With its tatami room and garden, this intimate, 200-plus-year-old restaurant positively oozes 'old Japan' charm. The signature dish is *yakisaba-sōmen* (grilled mackerel over thin noodles; ¥900) – also available in a set with *yakisaba* (grilled mackerel) sushi (¥1770). Order from the picture menu. It's on the western side of Kurokabe Square, a few doors south of Kurokabe Glass Kan.

Getting There & Away

From Kyoto, most trains to Nagahama (*junkyū* ¥1320, 70 minutes; *shinkansen* ¥3370, 40 minutes, including transfer time) require a transfer in Maibara, a nine-minute ride south of Nagahama. Pick up a map in English at the tourist information office in Nagahama Station.

NARA

☎0742 / POP 364,969

Japan's first permanent capital, Nara (奈良) is one of the country's most rewarding destinations. With eight Unesco World Heritage Sites, it's second only to Kyoto as a repository of Japan's cultural legacy.

The centrepiece is the Daibutsu (Great Buddha), which rivals Mt Fuji and Kyoto's Golden Pavilion (Kinkaku-ji) as Japan's single most impressive sight. The Great Buddha is housed in Tōdai-ji, a soaring temple that presides over Nara-kōen, a park filled with other fascinating sights that lends itself to relaxed strolling amid greenery and tame deer.

Nara is also compact: it's quite possible to pack the highlights into one full day. Many people visit Nara as a side trip from Kyoto, by comfortable express trains in about half an hour, but with an overnight stay (there's high-quality accommodation for all budgets) you might spend one day around the city centre and the other seeing the sights west and southwest of Nara city (areas known as Nishinokyō and Ikaruga, respectively).

History

Nara is at the northern end of the Yamato Plain, where members of the Yamato clan rose to power as the original emperors of Japan. Until the 7th century, however, Japan had no permanent capital, as Shintō taboos concerning death stipulated that the capital be moved with the passing of each emperor. This practice died out under the influence of Buddhism and with the Taika reforms of 646, when the entire country came under imperial control.

At this time it was decreed that a permanent capital be built. Two locations were tried before a permanent capital was finally established at Nara (which was then known as Heijōkyō) in 710. 'Permanent' status, however, lasted a mere 75 years. When a priest named Dōkyō seduced an empress and nearly usurped the throne, it was decided to move the court out of reach of Nara's increasingly powerful clergy. The new capital was established at Kyoto, about 35km north.

Although brief, the Nara Period was extraordinarily vigorous in its absorption of influences from China, laying the foundations of Japanese culture and civilisation. Except for an assault on the area by the Taira clan in the 12th century, Nara was subsequently spared the periodic bouts of destruction wreaked upon Kyoto, and a number of magnificent buildings have survived.

Sights

Nara retains its 8th-century Chinese-style grid pattern of streets. There are two main train stations: JR Nara and Kintetsu Nara. JR Nara Station is a little west of the city centre (but still within walking distance of the sights), while Kintetsu Nara is right in the centre of town. Nara-kōen, which contains most of the important sights, is on the eastern side, against the bare flank of the mountain Wakakusa-yama. It's easy to cover the city centre and the major attractions in nearby Nara-kōen on foot, although buses and taxis do ply the city.

Nara-kōen Area 奈良公園

Many of Nara's most important sites are located around Nara-kōen, a fine park that occupies much of the east side of the city. The park is home to about 1200 deer, which in pre-Buddhist times were considered messengers of the gods and today enjoy the status of National Treasures. They roam the park and surrounding areas in search of handouts from tourists, often descending on petrified children who have the misfortune to be carrying food. You can buy *shika-sembei* (deer biscuits) from vendors for ¥150 to feed to the deer, and *shika-no-fun* (deer poo) chocolates for yourself.

Nara National Museum MUSEUM

(奈良国立博物館; Nara Kokuritsu Hakubutsukan; ☎050-5542-8600; www.narahaku.go.jp; 50 Noboriōji-chō; admission ¥520; ⏲9.30am-5pm, closed Mon) This museum is devoted to Buddhist art and is divided into two sections. Built in 1894, the **Nara Buddhist Sculpture Hall & Ritual Bronzes Gallery** contains a fine collection of *butsu-zō* (statues of Buddhas and Bodhisattvas). Buddhist images here are divided into categories, each with detailed English explanations for an excellent introduction to Mahayana Buddhist iconography. The newer **East and West wings**, a short walk away, contain the permanent collections (sculptures, paintings and calligraphy) and special exhibitions.

A special exhibition featuring the treasures of the Shōsō-in Hall, which holds the treasures of Tōdai-ji, is held from late October to early November (dates vary slightly each year). The exhibits include priceless items from the cultures along the Silk Road. This exhibit is well worth it, but be prepared for crowds. Admission is ¥1000.

Kōfuku-ji BUDDHIST TEMPLE

(興福寺; www.kohfukuji.com) This temple was transferred here from Kyoto in 710. Although the original temple complex had 175 buildings, fires and destruction as a result of power struggles have left only a dozen standing. There are two pagodas – three storeys and five storeys – dating from 1143 and 1426, respectively. The taller of the two is the second-tallest in Japan, outclassed by the one at Kyoto's Tō-ji by a few centimetres.

The Kōfuku-ji National Treasure Hall, in the temple grounds, contains a variety of statues and art objects salvaged from previous structures. A new hall is being built in the centre of the temple grounds, scheduled for completion in 2018.

★**Isui-en & Neiraku Art Museum** GARDENS

(依水園・寧楽美術館; 74 Suimon-chō; admission museum & garden ¥650; ⏲9.30am-4.30pm, closed Tue except for Apr, May, Oct & Nov) This exquisite, contemplative Meiji-era garden features abundant greenery, ponds and walkways with stepping stones designed for you to observe each one as you walk, to appreciate their individual beauty. For ¥850 you can enjoy a cup of tea on tatami mats overlooking the garden. Admission covers the adjoining Neiraku Art Museum, displaying Chinese and Korean ceramics and bronzes in a quiet setting.

Yoshiki-en GARDENS

(吉城園; 68 Noboriōji-chō; free for foreign visitors, ¥250 for Japanese; ⏲9am-5pm, closed Jan & Feb) This garden, located next door to Isui-en (to the right as you enter), is a stunner. Originally a residence of the high priest of Tōdai-ji, the present garden was laid out in 1918 and

Nara

0 800 m
0 0.4 miles

Kyoto (40km)
Sacho-gawa
Saidai-ji (3km); Osaka (30km); Kyoto (40km)
Kintetsu Nara Line
Tōshōdai-ji (3km); Yakushi-ji (4km)
JR Nara
JR Nara Line
Hōryu-ji (12km); Osaka (30km)
Hōryū-ji (14km)
Sakurai (18km); Kashihara-jingū (26km); Yoshino (39km)
Sakurai (18km)
Emperor Kaika's Tomb
Nara Konishi-dōri
Kintetsu Nara
Nobori-Ōji
Kōfuku-ji Hokuen-dō Hall
Kōfuku-ji Nanen-dō Hall
Kōfuku-ji Five-Storey Pagoda
Sanjō-dōri
Sarusawa-ike
Higashi-muki Arcade
Michidono Center-gai Arcade
Shimo-Mikado Arcade
NARAMACHI
Daibutsu-den Hall
Pond
Tōdai-ji
Isui-en & Neiraku Art Museum
Nara-kōen
Tamukeyama-hachimangū
Kasuga Taisha Kamizono
Ni-no-Torii
Mikasa-yama (293m)
1 2 3 4 5 6 7 8 9 10 11 12 13 14 15 16 17 18 19 20 21 22 23 24 25 26 27 28 29 30 31 32 33 34 35 36 37 38 39 40 41

Nara

Top Sights	
1 Daibutsu-den Hall	E1
2 Isui-en & Neiraku Art Museum	E2
3 Tōdai-ji	E1
Sights	
4 Kasuga Taisha	F3
5 Kōfuku-ji	C2
6 Nara National Museum	D2
7 Naramachi Kōshi-no-Ie	C4
8 Naramachi Monogatari-kan	C4
9 Nigatsu-dō & Sangatsu-dō	F1
10 Tōdai-ji Museum	E1
11 Todai-ji Nandai-mon	E2
12 Wakamiya-jinja	G3
13 Yoshiki-en	D2
Sleeping	
14 Guesthouse Nara Backpackers	D1
15 Guesthouse Nara Komachi	A3
16 Guesthouse Sakuraya	C4
17 Hotel Fujita Nara	B2
18 Hotel Nikkō Nara	A3
19 Nara Hotel	D3
20 Nara Ugaya Guesthouse	B3
21 Ryokan Matsumae	C3
22 Super Hotel Lohas JR Nara-eki	A3
23 Wakasa Bettei	D1
Eating	
24 Kameya	C3
25 Kasugano	F2
26 Kura	C3
27 Mellow Café	C2
28 Mizutani-chaya	F2
29 Yumekaze Plaza	E2
Drinking & Nightlife	
30 Drink Drank	C3
31 Nara Izumi Yūsai	C3
32 Sanjō Kitakumae	C2
33 Tachibana	C3
34 Two Mistletoes	C4
Information	
35 Higashi-Muki Post Office	C2
36 JR Nara Station Information Centre	A3
37 Kintetsu Nara Station Information Office	C2
38 Nara City Tourist Information Centre	B3
39 SMBC Bank	C2
Transport	
40 Highway Bus Tickets	C2
41 Local Bus Stop	B2

contains a lovely thatch-roof cottage, a pond and several walking paths. It's particularly lovely in November and early December, when the maples turn a blazing crimson. Look for the small English sign.

★ Tōdai-ji
BUDDHIST TEMPLE

(東大寺) Nara's star attraction is the famous Daibutsu (Great Buddha), housed in the Daibutsu-den Hall of this grand temple. Though Tōdai-ji is often packed with tour groups and school children from across the country, it's big enough to absorb huge crowds and it belongs at the top of any Nara itinerary. Except for the Daibutsu-den Hall, most of Tōdai-ji's grounds can be visited free of charge.

Before entering, check out the **Nandaimon** (東大寺南大門), an enormous gate containing two fierce-looking **Niō guardians**. These recently restored wooden images, carved in the 13th century by the sculptor Unkei, are some of the finest wooden statues in all of Japan, if not the world. They are truly dramatic works of art and seem ready to spring to life at any moment. The gate is about 200m south of the temple enclosure.

★ Daibutsu-den Hall
BUDDHIST TEMPLE

(大仏殿; Hall of the Great Buddha; 406-1 Zōshi-chō; admission ¥500, joint ticket with Tōdai-ji Museum ¥800; ⏲8am-4.30pm Nov-Feb, to 5pm Mar, 7.30am-5.30pm Apr-Sep, to 5pm Oct) Tōdai-ji's Daibutsu-den is the largest wooden building in the world. Incredibly, the present structure, rebuilt in 1709, is a mere two-thirds of the size of the original. The Daibutsu (Great Buddha) inside is one of the largest bronze figures in the world and was originally cast in 746. The present statue, recast in the Edo period, stands just over 16m high and consists of 437 tonnes of bronze and 130kg of gold.

The Daibutsu is an image of Dainichi Nyorai (also known as Vairocana Buddha), the cosmic Buddha believed to give rise to all worlds and their respective Buddhas. Historians believe that Emperor Shōmu ordered the building of the Buddha as a charm against smallpox, which ravaged Japan in preceding years. Over the centuries the statue took quite a beating from earthquakes and fires, losing its head a couple of times (note the slight difference in colour between the head and the body).

Tōdai-ji

The Daibutsu (Great Buddha) at Nara's Tōdai-ji is one of the most arresting sights in Japan. The awe-inspiring physical presence of the vast image is striking. It's one of the largest bronze Buddha images in the world and it's contained in an equally huge building, the Daibutsu-den Hall, which is among the largest wooden buildings on earth.

Tōdai-ji was built by order of Emperor Shōmu during the Nara period (710–784) and the complex was finally completed in 798, after the capital had been moved from Nara to Kyoto. Most historians agree that the temple was built to consolidate the country and serve as its spiritual focus. Legend has it that over two million labourers worked on the temple, but this is probably apocryphal. What's certain is that its construction brought the country to the brink of bankruptcy.

The original Daibutsu was cast in bronze in eight castings over a period of three years. The Daibutsu, or certain parts of it, has been recast several times over the centuries. The original Daibutsu was covered in gold leaf and one can only imagine its impact on Japanese visitors during the eighth century AD.

The temple belongs to the Kegon school of Buddhism, one of the six schools of Buddhism popular in Japan during the Nara period. Kegon Buddhism, which comes from the Chinese Huayan Buddhist sect, is based on the Flower Garland Sutra. This sutra expresses the idea of worlds within worlds, all manifested by the Cosmic Buddha (Vairocana or Dainichi Nyorai). The Great Buddha and the figures that surround him in the Daibutsu-den Hall are the perfect physical symbol of this cosmological map.

FACT FILE

THE DAIBUTSU

» **Height**: 14.98m

» **Weight**: 500 tonnes

» **Nostril width**: 50cm

THE DAIBUTSU-DEN HALL

» **Height**: 48.74m

» **Length**: 57m

» **Number of roof tiles**: 112,589

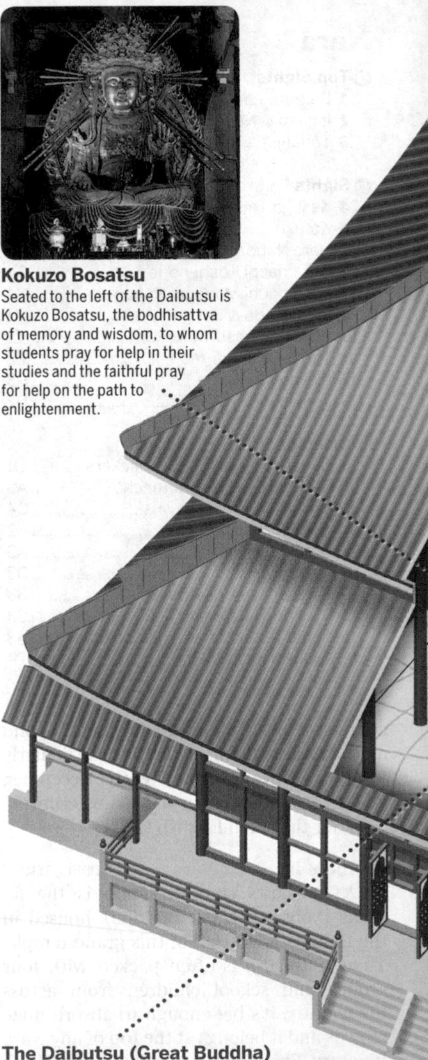

JEFFREY FRIEDL ©

Kokuzo Bosatsu
Seated to the left of the Daibutsu is Kokuzo Bosatsu, the bodhisattva of memory and wisdom, to whom students pray for help in their studies and the faithful pray for help on the path to enlightenment.

The Daibutsu (Great Buddha)
Known in Sanskrit as 'Vairocana' and in Japanese as the 'Daibutsu', this is the Cosmic Buddha that gives rise to all other Buddhas, according to Kegon doctrine. The Buddha's hands send the messages 'fear not' and 'welcome'.

JEFFREY FRIEDL ©

Komokuten
Standing to the left of the Daibutsu is Komokuten (Lord of Limitless Vision), who serves as a guardian of the Buddha. He stands upon a demon (jaki), which symbolises ignorance, and wields a brush and scroll, which symbolises wisdom.
JEFFREY FRIEDL ©
Buddhas Around Dainichi
Sixteen smaller Buddhas are arranged in a halo around the Daibutsu's head, each of which symbolises one of the Daibutsu's different manifestations. They are graduated in size to appear the same size when viewed from the ground.
Tamonten
To the right of the Daibutsu stands Tamonten (Lord Who Hears All), another of the Buddha's guardians. He holds a pagoda, which is said to represent a divine storehouse of wisdom.
JEFFREY FRIEDL ©
Hole in Pillar
Behind the Daibutsu you will find a pillar with a 50cm hole through its base (the size of one of the Daibutsu's nostrils). It's said that if you can crawl through this, you are assured of enlightenment.
JEFFREY FRIEDL ©
Nyoirin Kannon
Seated to the right of the Daibutsu is Nyoirin Kannon, one of the esoteric forms of Kannon Bodhisattva. This is one of the bodhisattva that preside over the six different realms of karmic rebirth.

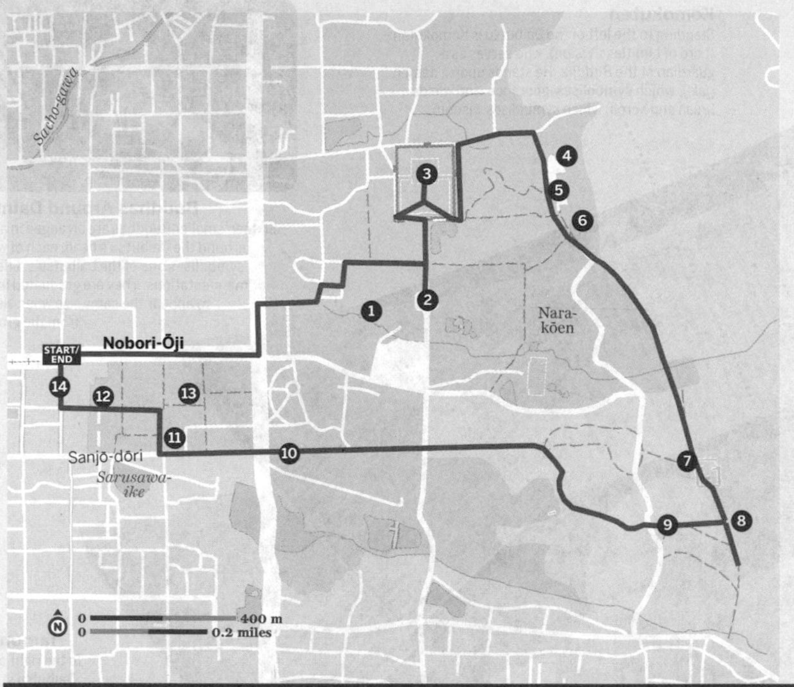

City Walk Nara-kōen

START KINTETSU NARA STATION
END KINTETSU NARA STATION
LENGTH 5KM; HALF A DAY

From Kintetsu Nara Station, walk straight up Nobori-Ōji, passing Kōfuku-ji on your right. Go left and visit **1 Isui-en** (p387), one of Nara's finest gardens. Walk north from the garden entrance, take the next major right after about 100m and walk east to come out in front of Tōdai-ji. Go right to see the massive **2 Nandai-mon** gate. Admire the Niō guardians, then continue to **3 Tōdai-ji** (p389).

Take the southeast exit, then walk left along the temple enclosure. Past the pond, turn right up the hill following the incredibly atmospheric stone-paved path to an open plaza in front of **4 Nigatsu-dō** and **5 Sangatsu-dō halls**. Climb the steps to Nigatsu-dō to enjoy the view of Daibutsuden and the Nara plain.

Return to the plaza and exit south, passing between a log-cabinlike structure and gaudy **6 Tamukeyama-hachimangū**, a shrine overlooking the plaza. Follow the broad path through the woods, descend two staircases and follow the 'Kasuga Shrine' signs to a road leading left left uphill, passing under the slopes of Wakakusa-yama. At Musashino Ryokan (look for the small English sign), walk straight down the steps, cross a bridge, jog left, and at the T-intersection take a left up to **7 Kasuga Taisha**. Walk around the side to find the main entrance.

Leave the shrine via the main entrance and bear left up the path to **8 Wakamiya-jinja**, passing several small shrines on the way. Retrace your steps towards Kasuga Taisha and take a left down the steps which lead back towards the centre of town. You'll pass through **9 Ni-no-Torii**, a large Shintō shrine gate, then continue down the broad wooded arcade to **10 Ichi-no-Torii**, another shrine gate. Cross the street and head to **11 Kōfuku-ji pagoda**. Walk through its grounds, passing between the **12 Nanen-dō** and **13 Hokuen-dō** halls, and take the narrow lane toward Higashi-muki Arcade. A quick right leads you back to **14 Kintetsu Nara Station**.

As you circle the statue towards the back, you'll see a wooden column with a hole through its base. Popular belief maintains that those who can squeeze through the hole, which is exactly the same size as one of the Great Buddha's nostrils, are ensured of enlightenment. There's usually a line of children waiting to give it a try and parents waiting to snap their pictures. A hint for bigger 'kids': try going through with one or both arms above your head – someone on either end to push and pull helps, too.

Nigatsu-dō & Sangatsu-dō BUDDHIST TEMPLE
(二月堂、三月堂; Nigatsu-do free, Sangatsu-do ¥500; ⏲Nigatsu-do 7.30am-6pm Jun-Aug, 8am-5.45pm Apr-May & Sep-Oct, 8am-5.15pm Nov-Mar; Sangatsu-do 8am-4.30pm Nov-Feb, to 5pm Mar & Oct, 7.30am-5.30pm Apr-Sep) These subtemples of Tōdai-ji are uphill from the Daibutsu-den and far less clamorous. Climb a lantern-lined staircase to Nigatsu-dō, a national treasure from 1669 (originally built circa 750). Its verandah with sweeping views across the town (especially at dusk) may remind you of Kiyomizu-dera (p302) in Kyoto. This is where Nara's Omizutori Matsuri (p394) is held.

A short walk south of Nigatsu-dō is Sangatsu-dō, the oldest building in the Tōdai-ji complex and home to a small collection of fine Nara-period statues.

The halls are an easy walk east (uphill) from the Daibutsu-den. Instead of walking straight up the hill, we recommend taking a hard left out of the Daibutsu-den exit, following the enclosure past the pond and turning up the hill. This pathway is one the most scenic walks in all of Nara.

Tōdai-ji Museum MUSEUM
(東大寺ミュージアム; ☎20-5511; Nara-shi, Suimon-chō 100; admission ¥500, joint ticket with Daibutsu-den ¥800; ⏲9.30am-4.30pm) Not far from the Daibutsu-den and Nandai-mon, the stately Tōdai-ji Museum displays several priceless Bodhisattva and other temple treasures, especially appealing to scholars and serious fans of early Nara Buddhism. Plus, the air-conditioning is welcome on hot summer days.

Kasuga Taisha SHINTO SHRINE
(春日大社; 160 Kasugano-chō; ⏲dawn-dusk) FREE This sprawling shrine lies at the foot of a hill in a deeply wooded setting with herds of sacred deer awaiting handouts. Its pathways are lined with hundreds of lanterns, with many hundreds more in the shrine itself. They're illuminated in the twice-yearly Mantōrō (p394) lantern festivals.

Kasuga Taisha was founded in the 8th century by the Fujiwara family and was completely rebuilt every 20 years, according to Shintō tradition, until the end of the 19th century.

There are several subshrines around the main hall. It's worth walking a few minutes south to take a look at the nearby shrine of **Wakamiya-jinja**.

Naramachi 奈良町

South of Sanjō-dōri and Sarusawa-ike pond, Naramachi is a traditional neighbourhood with many well-preserved *machiya* (shophouses) and *kura* (storehouses). It's a mellow place for a stroll away from the busier sights around Nara-kōen. There are several good restaurants, shops, cafes, inns and a creative energy that residents are eager to share with travellers.

Naramachi Kōshi-no-Ie HISTORIC BUILDING
(ならまち格子の家; 44 Gangōji-chō; ⏲9am-5pm, closed Mon) FREE This well-preserved merchant's house is an excellent place to observe architectural details: beamed ceilings, old kitchen, *tansu* stairs and inner garden. Follow signs to 'Naramachi Lattice House'.

Naramachi Monogatari-kan GALLERY
(奈良町物語館; 2-1 Nakanoshinya-chō; ⏲10am-5pm) FREE This interesting little gallery holds some worthwhile art and craft exhibitions, ranging from traditional to modern.

Tours

Information centres (p396) can put you in touch with volunteer guides who speak English and other foreign languages, but you must book at least one day in advance. Try **YMCA Goodwill Guides** (☎45-5920; http://eggnara.tripod.com/home.htm) and **Nara Student Guides** (☎26-4753; www.narastudentguide.org).

Festivals & Events

The dates for some festivals vary, so it's best to check with the Nara or Kyoto tourist information offices.

Yamayaki CULTURAL
(Grass Burning Festival) Held in January on the day before Seijin-no-hi or Coming-of-Age Day, the Grass Burning Festival commemorates a feud many centuries ago between the

monks of Tōdai-ji and Kōfuku-ji: Wakakusa-yama is set alight at 6pm, with an accompanying display of fireworks.

Mantōrō CULTURAL

(3 February on Setsubun from 6pm) Held in early February at Kasuga Taisha at 6pm, the Lantern Festival involves the lighting of 3000 stone and bronze lanterns around Kasuga Taisha – it's impossibly atmospheric. A *bugaku* dance takes place in the Apple Garden on the last day. This festival is also held around 14 August in the O-Bon (Festival of the Dead) holiday period.

Omizutori/Otaimatsu CULTURAL

Every evening from 1 March to 14 March, the monks of Tōdai-ji parade huge flaming torches around the balcony of Nigatsu-dō and rain down embers on the spectators to purify them. On the evening of 12 March, the monks hold a water-drawing ceremony from which the festival takes its name (*mizutori* means 'to take water'). The water-drawing ceremony is performed after midnight.

Takigi Onō DANCE

Open-air performances of *nō* (stylised dance-drama) are held after dark by the light of blazing torches at Kōfuku-ji and Kasuga Taisha, on the third Friday and Saturday of March.

Shika-no-Tsunokiri CULTURAL

Those deer in Nara-kōen are pursued in a type of elegant rodeo into the Roku-en (deer enclosure) close to Kasuga Taisha on the second Saturday, Sunday and the following Monday in October. They are then wrestled to the ground and their antlers sawn off.

Tourist brochures hint that this is to avoid personal harm, though it's not clear whether they are referring to the deer fighting each other or the deer mugging the tourists.

Sleeping

Although Nara can be visited as a day trip from Kyoto or Osaka, spending the night will allow a more relaxing pace. There's fine accommodation for all budgets.

★Guesthouse Nara Backpackers GUESTHOUSE ¥

(ゲストハウス 奈良バックパッカーズ; 0742-22-4557; www.nara-backpackers.com; 31 Yurugichō; dm ¥2400, r without bathroom per person up to ¥3800;) An utterly charming stay in a traditional 1920s building, once a tea master's home. Choose from dorm rooms or three different-sized private tatami-mat rooms, some with garden views. Bathing facilities are shared (bring your own toiletries and towel, or buy or rent them here); shared kitchen for self-caterers. Per-night rates fall the longer you stay.

Children under 10 are not permitted, so as to preserve the home's *shōji* (sliding paper doors) and antique glass windows.

Ryokan Matsumae RYOKAN ¥

(旅館松前; 0742-22-3686; www.matsumae.co.jp/english/index_e.html; 28-1 Higashi-terabayashi-chō; r per person from ¥5400; @) This friendly little ryokan, conveniently located in Naramachi, has Japanese-style rooms with TVs and toilet but no private bath. Some are a little dark, and we could do without the bright green carpeting in hallways, but the overall feeling is warm and relaxing. Bonus: occasional lessons in calligraphy and *kyōgen* (traditional theatrical farce).

Reserve in advance if you'd like Japanese or Western breakfast (from ¥756) or French-Japanese fusion dinner (from ¥4300).

Guesthouse Nara Komachi GUESTHOUSE ¥

(ゲストハウス奈良小町; 0742-87-0556; guesthouse@wave.plala.or.jp; 41-2 Surugamachi; dm from ¥2400, r per person from ¥2995; @) Clean, contemporary, bargain-priced accommodation a few minutes' walk from JR Nara Station. There are both Western-style dorms and tiny private rooms with en suite toilet and shower, separated from the main room by a glass wall (and, fortunately, a privacy curtain). There's a self-catering kitchen and cheap bicycle rentals.

Nara Ugaya Guesthouse GUESTHOUSE ¥

(奈良ウガヤゲストハウス; 0742-95-7739; www.ugaya.net; 4-1 Okukomori-chō; dm from ¥2500, r per person without bathroom from ¥3000; @) This casual backpackers' inn offers a tight warren of bunk-bed dorms and Japanese-style rooms a short walk from Naramachi. Convivial common areas are a good place to meet other travellers, and guests can explore using the inn's excellent city map. Breakfast of *chagayu* (roasted tea rice porridge) costs ¥400 extra.

Ask the owner to give you a demonstration of the *biwa* (traditional Japanese lute).

★Guesthouse Sakuraya GUESTHOUSE ¥¥

(桜舎; www.guesthouse-sakuraya.com; 1 Narukawa-chō; s/d incl breakfast ¥6200/10,400;) This atmospheric stunner in Naramachi, just three quiet guest rooms in a former dyer's workshop, integrates both tradtional and contemporary touches around a lovely courtyard garden and common room and baths. One room has an en suite toilet. The owner offers a 'Discovery of Japanese Culture' course (¥3000). If you're looking for a party, head elsewhere.

Super Hotel Lohas JR Nara-eki BUSINESS HOTEL ¥¥
(スーパーホテルLohas・JR奈良駅; ☎0742-27-9000; www.superhoteljapan.com/en/s-hotels/nara-lohas.html; 1-2 Sanjō-honmachi; s/d/tw incl breakfast ¥7180/12,320/15,220; @📶) Connected to JR Nara Station by an elevated walkway, this hotel has stylish, contemporary design, compact rooms with en suite bathrooms, cheerful, efficient staff (some English-speaking), large communal onsen bath and coin-op laundry. Note: no in-room phones, but there are phones in the lobby.

Hotel Fujita Nara HOTEL ¥¥
(ホテルフジタ奈良; ☎0742-23-8111; http://en.fujita-nara.com; 47-1 Shimosanjō-chō; s/d/tw from ¥8200/11,300/14,000; @📶) In the heart of downtown Nara, about five minutes' walk from either main train station, this efficient hotel offers clean rooms, reasonable prices, some English-speaking staff and Japanese or Western breakfasts (¥1555).

★ **Nara Hotel** HOTEL ¥¥¥
(奈良ホテル; ☎0742-26-3300; www.narahotel.co.jp/en; 1096 Takabatake-chō; s/tw from ¥19,008/34,452; @📶) Founded in 1909, the grande dame of Nara hotels has hosted dignitaries from Edward VIII and Albert Einstein to the Dalai Lama. It retains a Meiji-era style in its traditional exterior, high ceilings, gorgeous woodwork, refined Japanese and Western restaurants, bar and beautifully landscaped grounds. Rooms are spacious and comfortable with big beds, though some have cramped unit bathrooms.

For historic atmosphere, we recommend the Honkan (main building) over the Shinkan (new building).

Hotel Nikkō Nara HOTEL ¥¥¥
(ホテル日航奈良; ☎0742-35-8831; www.nikkonara.jp; 8-1 Sanjō-honmachi; s/d/tw from ¥12,700/22,000/22,000; @📶) The luxe choice in the JR Nara Station area, with plush duvet covers on the beds in the 330 rooms (it's worth paying a bit more for an upgrade from the economy-priced rooms), four restaurants, a lobby lounge, and a soothing common bath in addition to in-room baths.

Wakasa Bettei RYOKAN ¥¥¥
(和鹿彩別邸; ☎0742-23-5858; www.n-wakasa.com/english; 1 Kita-handahigashi-machi; per person with no meals ¥22,727, with 2 meals ¥34,546; 📶) This friendly, contemporary ryokan aims hard to please. The 11 stylish, large Japanese- and Western-style rooms have private facilities including stone or wooden bathtub, and the top-floor common bath has views of Tōdai-ji and Wakakusa-yama. We recommend the newer Bettei over the original (and still friendly) Hotel New Wakasa next door.

Eating

Nara is chock-a-block with good restaurants, mostly near the train stations and in Nara-machi. For restaurant browsing, the covered arcade **Higashi-muki Shōtengai**, between Kintetsu Nara Station and Sanjō-dōri, has about a dozen restaurants: from udon, sushi and Italian to coffee-and-sandwich chains. Look for the local speciality, *kaki-no-ha sushi* (individual pieces of sushi wrapped in persimmon leaf – don't eat the leaf!).

Kameya OKONOMIYAKI ¥
(かめや; ☎0742-22-2434; 9 Tarui-chō; mains ¥680-1140; ⏲11am-10pm; 📖) A giant red lantern marks the entrance to this casual, spirited *okonomiyaki* joint, going strong since the 1960s. There's a seemingly infinite number of combinations for the savoury pancakes; the 'mix okonomiyaki' contains squid, shrimp, pork and scallops. The *yaki-soba* roll has fried noodles inside. No English is spoken, but staff make it work.

Kasugano SHOKUDŌ ¥
(春日野; ☎0742-26-3311; 494 Zōshi-chō; mains ¥600-1000; ⏲8.30am-5pm; 📶📖) Most restaurants between Tōdai-ji and Kasuga Taisha double as souvenir shops, like this one, at the base of Wakakusa-yama and in business since 1927. Dishes span the basic (curry rice, tempura udon, *oyako-don* – chicken and egg over rice) to diverse *gozen* set meals (¥1620). Sit in the woodsy annexe cafe rather than the shop (same menu).

Mellow Café PIZZA, DESSERTS ¥
(メロー　カフェ; ☎0742-27-9099; 1-8 Konishi-chō; mains ¥710-1120, lunch specials ¥1200; ⏲11am-11.30pm; 📶📖) Not far from Kintetsu Nara Station and down a narrow alley (look for the arbour and stone water barrel), this pleasant cafe centres on pasta and

brick-oven pizzas, and desserts such as the *hojicha* parfait (made with roasted-tea ice cream) or the Nara-inspired Bambi roll cake. Drinks include wine, cocktails and coffees.

Mizutani-chaya TEAHOUSE ¥
(水谷茶屋; ☎0742-22-0627; 30 Kasugano-chō; mains ¥590-790; ⏲10am-4pm, closed Wed; 📖) In a small wooded clearing between Nigatsu-dō and Kasuga Taisha, this quaint thatched-roof teahouse is one of Nara's most atmospheric spots. Stop for a cup of *matcha* (powdered green tea; ¥700 including a sweet) or bowl of noodles for a quick pick-me-up.

In warm seasons, sit outside among the greenery and enjoy *kakigōri*, shaved ice with toppings ranging from condensed milk to sweet red beans or fruit-flavoured syrups.

★ **Kura** IZAKAYA ¥¥
(蔵; ☎0742-22-8771; 16 Kōmyōin-chō; dishes ¥100-1000; ⏲5pm-10pm, closed Thu; 📖) This friendly spot in Naramachi, styled like an old storehouse, is just 16 seats around a counter amid dark wood panels and an old beer sign. Indulge in *mini-katsu* (mini pork cutlets), *yakitori* (grilled chicken skewers) and *oden* (fish cake and vegie hot-pot). Order Nara's own Kazenomori sake (¥1200), and everyone will think you're a sake sage.

Yumekaze Plaza RESTAURANT MALL ¥¥
(夢風ひろば; ☎0742-25-0870; www.yume-kaze.com; 16 Kasuganochō; ⏲vary by shop, mostly lunch & dinner) Adjacent to Nara-kōen and across from the Nara National Museum, this convenient collection of a dozen restaurants offers everything from handmade *soba* at **Warabe Yorokobi An** (dishes ¥700-2000) to Italian at **Cafe I-lunga** (dishes ¥1100-1900) and *wagashi* (Japanese sweets) at **Tenpyō-an Cafe**, all in attractively updated old-style buildings.

Drinking & Nightlife

Two Mistletoes CAFE
(トゥーミスルトゥーズ; ☎0742-22-1139; 13 Nakashinyamachi; coffee & tea ¥360-670, lunch set menus ¥1200; ⏲noon-5.30pm Wed-Sun) For a break while in Naramachi, this modernist charmer feels good inside and out with combed plaster walls, lots of wood, garden seating and friendly, modest staff. Teas and vegetarian home-style lunches incorporating medicinal herbs (plus coffees and cakes) may make you feel good inside and out too.

Sanjō Kitakumae BAR
(三条帰宅前; 41-1 Tsunofuri-chō; ⏲3pm-midnight, from 1.30pm Sat & Sun) This tiny, open-sided bar (sealed with clear plastic curtains in inclement weather) is great for people-watching on Sanjō-dōri. *Shōchū* (strong distilled alcohol often made from potatoes) and sake selections vary seasonally (from ¥380 per glass), or choose beer or *umeshu* (plum wine) to wash down small plates including *karaage* (fried chicken pieces) and sausages.

Nara Izumi Yūsai SAKE BAR
(なら泉勇斎; ☎0742-26-6078; 22 Nishi-Terabayashi-chō; ⏲11am-8pm, closed Thu) Drop in on this small standing bar in Naramachi for tastings (¥200 to ¥550) of sake produced in Nara Prefecture (120 varieties from 29 makers, also available for purchase). There is a useful English explanation sheet. Look for the sake barrels and a sign in the window reading 'Nara's Local Sake'.

Drink Drank CAFE
(ドリンクドランク; ☎0742-27-6206; 8 Hashimoto-chō; smoothies ¥700-900; ⏲11am-8pm Thu-Tue) Fruit smoothies are a relatively new thing in Japan; find them at this charming cafe on the east end of Sanjō-dōri. Besides traditional fruits, look for only-in-Japan and seasonal flavours like pumpkin-banana and salty melon. Food offerings include daily lunch specials and light meals (¥520 to ¥570) such as crêpes and panini (grilled sandwiches).

Tachibana CAFE
(たちばな; ☎0742-31-6439; 18-1 Nishiterabayashi-chō; coffee from ¥400; ⏲11am-6pm, closed Wed) This friendly little cafe-gallery in Naramachi is a great place to break for a cup of joe or tea. Then head upstairs to check out the wonderful collection of ceramic or glass art from Kyoto and Nara artists.

Information

The main **JR Nara Station Information Centre** (☎0742-22-9821; www.narashikanko.or.jp/en; ⏲9am-9pm), in the old Nara Station building just outside the east exit of JR Nara Station, is the city's main tourist information centre and English speakers are usually on hand. If arriving at Kintetsu Nara Station, try the helpful **Kintetsu Nara Station Information Office** (☎0742-24-4858; ⏲9am-9pm), near the top of the stairs above exit 3 from the station. Other information offices include the **Nara City Tourist Information Centre** (奈良市観光センター; ☎0742-22-

3900; 23-4 Kami-Sanjō-chō; ⏲9am-9pm). All of the information offices stock useful maps and can assist with same-day hotel reservations.

ℹ Getting There & Away

BUS

There is an overnight bus service between Tokyo's Shinjuku neighborhood and Nara (one way ¥5980 to ¥9500; rates vary by day). In Nara, call **Nara Kōtsū Bus** (☎0742-22-5110; www.narakotsu.co.jp/kousoku in Japanese) or check with the Nara City Tourist Information Centre for details. In Nara, overnight buses leave from stop 4 in front of JR Nara Station east exit and from stop 20 outside Kintetsu Nara Station. In Tokyo, call **Kantō Bus** (☎03-3371-1225; www.kanto-bus.co.jp) or visit the Shinjuku highway bus terminal.

TRAIN

Kyoto

The Kintetsu line is the fastest and most convenient connection between Kyoto (Kintetsu Kyoto Station, in Kyoto Station) and central Nara (Kintetsu Nara Station). Comfortable, all-reserved *tokkyū* trains (¥1130, 35 minutes) run directly; *kyūkō* trains (express; ¥620, 45 minutes) usually require a change at Yamato-Saidai-ji.

For Japan Rail Pass holders, the JR Nara line connects JR Kyoto Station with JR Nara Station (*kaisoku*, rapid; ¥710, 45 minutes) with several departures an hour.

Osaka

The Kintetsu Nara line connects Osaka (Namba Station) with Nara (Kintetsu Nara Station). *Kaisoku* and *futsū* services take about 40 minutes and cost ¥560. All-reserved-seat *tokkyū* trains take five minutes less but cost almost double.

For Japan Rail Pass holders, the JR Kansai line links JR Nara Station with Osaka (Namba and Tennō-ji stations), via *kaisoku* trains; (¥540, 45 minutes and ¥450, 30 minutes respectively).

ℹ Getting Around

TO/FROM THE AIRPORT

Nara Kōtsū operates a **limousine bus service** (www.narakotsu.co.jp/kousoku/limousine/nara_kanku.html) between Nara and Kansai International (KIX; ¥2050, 90 minutes, 6am to 9pm) and Osaka Itami (ITM; ¥1480, 60 minutes, 5am to 5pm) airports, with departures roughly every hour. Buses depart from stop 4 in front of JR Nara Station east exit and stop 20 (Kansai International Airport) and 12 (Itami Airport) outside Kintetsu Nara Station. Purchase tickets at the ticket offices at the respective stations or the airports.

BUS

Although it's a walk of about 15 minutes from JR Nara Station to the temple and shrine districts (about five minutes from Kintetsu Nara), buses are available for ¥210 per ride. Two circular bus routes cover the Nara-kōen area: bus 1 (anticlockwise) and bus 2 (clockwise). For more than two trips, a one-day Free Pass costs ¥500. On Saturday, Sunday and holidays, a tourist-friendly Gurutto Bus covers major sights for ¥100 per ride, several times per hour from about 9am to 5pm.

AROUND NARA

Southern Nara-ken is the birthplace of imperial rule and rich in historical sites easily accessible as day trips from Osaka, Kyoto or Nara; make an early start. Of particular interest are the *kofun* (burial mounds) that mark the graves of Japan's first emperors, concentrated around Asuka. Elsewhere, several isolated temples provide an escape from the crowds. Further afield, the historic refuge, mountaintop town of Yoshino is one of Japan's cherry-blossom meccas.

Easily reached by rail, Yamato-Yagi and Sakurai serve as useful transport hubs for the region. The Kintetsu line is more convenient than JR for most of this region.

Temples Southwest of Nara

While Nara city has some impressive ancient temples and Buddhist statues, three temples southwest of Nara take you to the roots of Japanese Buddhism: Hōryū-ji, Yakushi-ji and Tōshōdai-ji.

Hōryū-ji is one of Japan's most historically important temples. However, its appeal is more academic than aesthetic, and it's a slog through drab suburbs to get there. Thus, for most people we recommend a half-day trip to Yakushi-ji and Tōshōdai-ji, which are easy to reach from Nara and very pleasant for strolling.

If you want to visit all three temples, head to Hōryū-ji first (it's the most distant from the centre of Nara) and then continue by bus 97 or 98 (¥560, 39 minutes) up to Yakushi-ji and Tōshōdai-ji, which are a 10-minute walk apart. Several buses ply the southwest temple route, but bus 97 is most convenient, with English announcements and route maps.

1. Izumo Taisha (p485), Izumo
Huge *shimenawa* (twisted straw ropes) hang at Izumo Taisha, one of the most important shrines in Japan.

2. Ibusuki (p729)
Sand baths – in which people are buried in hot volcanic sand – are popular at this hot-spring resort.

3. Dōtombori (p356), Osaka
With its glittering neon lights and plenty of restaurants and theatres, this is Osaka's liveliest night spot.

2

SYLVAIN GRANDADAM / GETTY IMAGES ©

3

FRANK DEIM / GETTY IMAGES ©

1

TRAVEL PIX / GETTY IMAGES ©

2

4

MASAMI GOTO / SEBUN PHOTO / GETTY IMAGES ©

1. Sapporo Snow Festival (p571)
The elaborate ice sculptures at this annual event have included full-sized stages, Hello Kitty statues and ice slides.

2. Furano (p597)
This attractive town offers skiing in winter and majestic floral displays in warmer months.

3. Itsukushima-jinja, Miyajima (p438)
Appearing to float at high tide, this much-photographed vermilion *torii* (shrine gate) is considered one of the three best views in Japan.

4. Shiretoko National Park (p616)
A visit to this Unesco World Heritage Site includes dramatic views and the chance to soak tired muscles in steaming onsen.

3

Around Nara

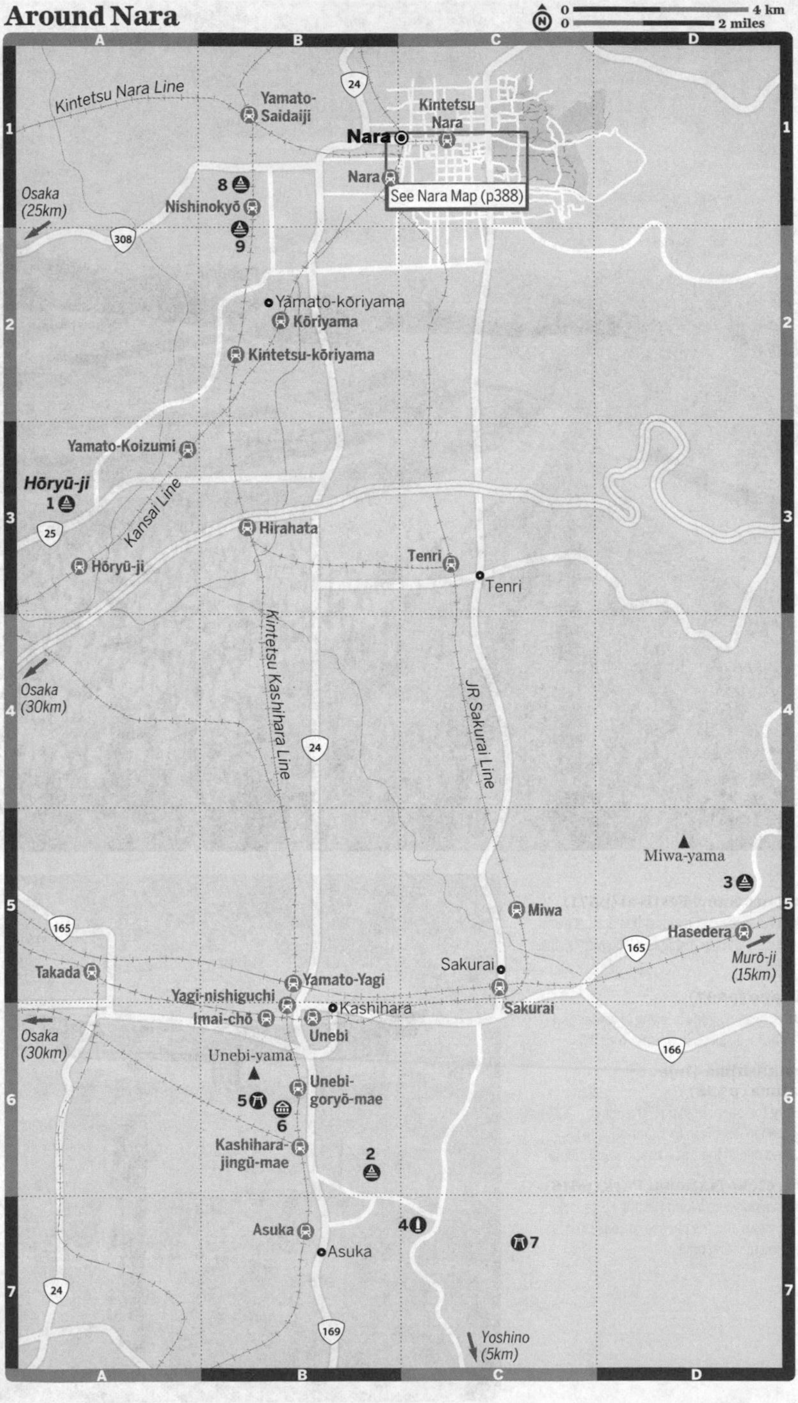

0 — 4 km
0 — 2 miles

Kintetsu Nara Line
Yamato-Saidaiji
Kintetsu Nara
Nara
Nara
See Nara Map (p388)
Osaka (25km)
8
Nishinokyō
9
308
24
Yamato-kōriyama
Kōriyama
Kintetsu-kōriyama
Yamato-Koizumi
Hōryū-ji
1
Kansai Line
25
Hirahata
Hōryū-ji
Tenri
Tenri
Osaka (30km)
Kintetsu Kashihara Line
JR Sakurai Line
24
Miwa-yama
3
Miwa
165
Hasedera
165
Murō-ji (15km)
Takada
Sakurai
Yamato-Yagi
Yagi-nishiguchi
Kashihara
Sakurai
Imai-chō
Unebi
Osaka (30km)
166
Unebi-yama
5
Unebi-goryō-mae
6
Kashihara-jingū-mae
2
Asuka
4
7
Asuka
24
169
Yoshino (5km)

Around Nara

Hōryū-ji 法隆寺

★**Hōryū-ji** BUDDHIST TEMPLE

(法隆寺; Map p402; www.horyuji.or.jp; admission ¥1000; ⊙8am-5pm Feb-Oct, to 4.30pm Nov-Mar) Hōryū-ji was founded in 607 by Prince Shōtoku, considered by many to be the patron saint of Japanese Buddhism. Hōryū-ji is a veritable shrine to Shōtoku and is renowned not only as the oldest temple in Japan, but also as a repository for some of the country's rarest treasures. Several of the temple's wooden buildings have survived earthquakes and fires to become the oldest of their kind in the world.

The temple is divided into two parts, **Sai-in** (West Temple) and **Tō-in** (East Temple); pick up a detailed map and guidebook in English.

The main approach proceeds from the south along a tree-lined avenue and through the Nandai-mon and Chū-mon gates before entering the Sai-in precinct. As you enter, you'll see the **Kondō** (Main Hall) on your right and a pagoda on your left.

The Kondō houses several treasures, including the triad of the Buddha Sakyamuni, with two attendant Bodhisattvas. One of Japan's great Buddhist treasures, it's dimly lit and barely visible – you will need a torch (flashlight) to see it. Likewise, the pagoda contains clay images depicting scenes from the life of Buddha, which are barely visible without a torch.

East of Sai-in are the two concrete buildings of the **Daihōzō-in** (Great Treasure Hall), containing numerous treasures from Hōryū-ji's long history. Continue east through the Tōdai-mon to Tō-in, where the Yumedono (Hall of Dreams) is where Prince Shōtoku is believed to have meditated and received help with problem sutras from a kindly, golden apparition.

Given the cost of admission and the time it takes to get here from central Nara, we recommend that you give careful thought to committing at least half a day to visiting this temple. Take the JR Kansai line from JR Nara Station to Hōryū-ji Station (¥220, 11 minutes). From here, bus 72 shuttles the short distance between the station and the bus stop Hōryū-ji Monmae (¥180, eight minutes). Alternatively, take bus 52 or 97 from either JR Nara Station (stop 10) or Kintetsu Nara Station (stop 8) and get off at the Hōryū-ji-mae stop (¥760, 60 minutes). Walk west about 50m, cross the road and you will see the tree-lined approach to the temple.

Yakushi-ji 薬師寺

Yakushi-ji Temple BUDDHIST TEMPLE

(薬師寺; Map p402; admission ¥500; ⊙8.30am-5pm) This temple houses some of the most beautiful Buddhist statues in all Japan. It was established by Emperor Temmu in 680 as a prayer for the healing of his wife. With the exception of the East Pagoda, which dates to 730 (and is due to be under renovation until 2018), the present buildings either date from the 13th century or are very recent reconstructions.

Entering from the south, turn right before going through the gate with guardian figures and walk to the **Tōin-dō** (East Hall), where a famous, 7th-century Shō-Kannon image shows obvious influences of Indian sculptural styles, making it the progenitor of other Kannon statues throughout Japan.

Then walk west to the **Kondō** (Main Hall). Rebuilt in 1976, it houses several images, including the famous **Yakushi Triad** (the Yakushi Nyorai – healing Buddha – flanked by the Bodhisattvas of the sun and moon), dating from the 8th century. They were originally gold, but a fire in the 16th century turned the images an appealingly mellow black.

Behind (north of) the Kondō is the **Kōdō** (Lecture Hall), which houses yet another fine Buddhist trinity, this time Miroku Buddha with two Bodhisattva attendants. You can exit to the north behind this hall and head to Tōshōdai-ji.

To get to Yakushi-ji, take bus 70 or 72 from JR Nara Station (stop 10) or Kintetsu Nara Station (stop 8) and get off at the Yakushi-ji Parking Lot stop (Yakushijo Chūshajō in

Japanese; ¥250, 15 minutes). Bus 97 from these stations runs to the Yakushi-ji Higashi-guchi stop (¥250, 15 minutes). From here, walk 100m south (in the same direction the bus was travelling) to a Mobil station, cross the road and walk west across a canal. From the main road it's 250m to the temple's south entrance.

You can also take a *futsū* on the Kintetsu Kashihara line (which runs between Kyoto and Kashihara-jingū-mae) and get off at Nishinokyō Station, about 200m north-west of Yakushi-ji (and 600m walk south of Tōshōdai-ji). If you're coming from Nara, change trains at Yamato-Saidaiji (¥260, 25 minutes; *kyūkō* and *tokkyū* do not stop at Nishinokyō). From Kyoto, some trains run direct to Nishinokyō (¥620, 46 minutes); others require a transfer at Yamato-Saidaiji.

Tōshōdai-ji 唐招提寺

Tōshōdai-ji Temple BUDDHIST TEMPLE
(唐招提寺; Map p402; www.toshodaiji.jp; admission ¥600; ⏲8.30am-5pm, last entry by 4.30pm) This temple was established in 759 by the Chinese priest Ganjin (Jian Zhen), who had been recruited by Emperor Shōmu to reform Buddhism in Japan. The temple grounds are pleasantly wooded and mossy, making a good contrast to nearby Yakushi-ji, which is largely devoid of greenery.

The **Kondō** (Golden Hall), roughly in the middle, contains a stunning Senjū (thousand-armed) Kannon image. Behind it, the **Kōdō** (Lecture Hall) contains a beautiful image of Miroku Buddha.

Its buildings, in contrast to the bright colors of Yakushi-ji, have been allowed to age, but you can still see remnants of the colors on the back of the hall.

Tōshōdai-ji is a 500m walk north of Yakushi-ji's northern gate.

Around Yamato-Yagi
大和八木周辺

Easily reached on the Kintetsu line from Osaka, Kyoto or Nara, Yamato-Yagi is the most convenient transport hub for sights in southern Nara-ken. We suggest renting a car here as some of the sights are far flung and hard to reach by public trasportation. From Kyoto take the Kintetsu Nara/Kashihara line direct (*kyūkō*, ¥880, 65 minutes). From Nara take the Kintetsu Nara line to Yamato-Saidaiji and change to the Kintetsu Kashihara line (*kyūkō*, ¥440, 40 minutes with transfer). From Osaka's Tsuruhashi Station, take the Kintetsu Osaka line direct (*kyūkō*, ¥560, 35 minutes). If you've got a Japan Rail Pass, you can reach the Kashihara area from Nara by taking the JR Mahoroba line and getting off at Unebi (¥500, 39 minutes).

Kashihara 橿原

Three stops south of Yamato-Yagi, on the Kintetsu Kashihara line, is Kashihara-jingū-mae Station (¥210 from Yamato-Yagi, five minutes, all trains stop). You can also take the JR Nara/Sakurai line from Nara. There are a couple of interesting sights within easy walking distance of this station.

Kashihara-jingū SHINTO SHRINE
(橿原神宮; Map p402) FREE This shrine, at the foot of Unebi-yama, dates back to 1889, when many of the buildings were moved here from Kyoto Gosho (Kyoto Imperial Palace). The buildings are a good example of classical Shintō architecture, in the same style as those at Ise-jingū (p418). The shrine is dedicated to Japan's mythical first emperor, Jimmu, and a festival is held here each 11 February, the legendary date of Jimmu's enthronement. The vast, parklike grounds are pleasant to stroll around.

The shrine is five minutes' walk from Kashihara-jingū-mae Station; take the central exit and follow the main street toward the mountain.

Nara Prefecture Kashihara Archaeological Museum MUSEUM
(奈良県橿原考古学研究所付属博物館; Nara Ken-ritsu Kashihara Kōkogaku Kenkyūjo Fuzoku Hakubutsukan; Map p402; ☎0744-24-1185; admission Japanese ¥400, non-Japanese free; ⏲9am-5pm, closed Mon) This museum is highly recommended for those with an interest in the history of the Japanese people. The objects on display come from various archaeological sites in the area, including several *kofun*. Although most explanations are in Japanese, there's enough English to give you a general flavour. To get the most out of the museum, bring a Japanese friend to explain things. Foreigners can enter free (bring your passport).

From Kashihara-jingū, walk out of the northern gate of the shrine (to your left when you stand with your back to the main hall), follow the wooded avenue for five minutes, cross the main road, continue for 100m and turn left at the first intersection. It's on the left soon after this turn.

Asuka 飛鳥

0744 / POP 6141

The Yamato Plain in central Nara Prefecture is where the forerunners of Japan's ruling Yamato dynasty cemented their grip on power. In these pre-Buddhist days, deceased emperors were entombed in huge *kofun* (tumuli, or earthen burial mounds). Some of the best examples are around the town of Asuka, about an hour south of Nara. Nowadays, the pitcuresque rolling hills are covered with rice terraces and farmland for crops, including strawberries.

There's a **tourist information office** (0744-54-3624; 8.30am-5pm) outside Asuka Station; it didn't stock any useful maps on our last visit. The best way to explore the area is by bicycle. **Manyō Rent-a-Cycle** (レンタサイクル万葉) rents bikes for ¥300 an hour, or ¥900 a day (¥1000 per day on weekends). Manyō is across the street from the station, and also stocks a useful English map of the area.

Two tombs that are worth seeing are **Takamatsuzuka-kofun** (高松塚古墳; admission ¥250; 9am-5pm) and **Ishibutai-kofun** (石舞台古墳; Map p402; admission ¥250; 8.30am-5pm). Takamatsuzuka-kofun, which looks like a grassy mound, is located in a pleasant wooded park. The interior of the *kofun* is closed to the public, but a hall next door shows painstaking reproductions of the murals inside. Ishibutai-kofun, composed of vast rocks in an open area, is said to have housed the remains of Soga no Umako but is now completely empty.

Also worth visiting is **Asuka-dera** (飛鳥寺; Map p402; admission ¥350; 9am-5.30pm Apr-Sep, to 5pm Oct-Mar), considered the first true Buddhist temple in Japan (founded 596). It houses the **Asuka Daibutsu**, Japan's oldest remaining Buddha image (609). Fifteen tonnes and originally covered in gold, it's said that the statue has never been moved from this spot, meaning that many of the greats of Japanese history have likely stood before it as you can. It's flanked by the Amida Buddha and Prince Shōtoku, the saint credited with bringing Buddhism to Japan.

Asuka can be reached in as little as 12 minutes from Yamato-Yagi (¥230); change at Kashihara-jingū-mae on the Kintetsu Yoshino line.

LOCAL KNOWLEDGE

TAKAMATSUZUKA'S EARLY NOBLES

Murals inside the *kofun* at Takamatsuzuka depict Korean motifs and nobles in Korean court dress, suggesting that the early Yamato nobility may have come from, well, somewhere else. As there is no written documentation as to who was entombed here, one can only wonder.

Around Sakurai

Sakurai (桜井) is a hub of historic temples and shrines and can be reached directly from Nara on the JR Nara/Sakurai line (*futsū*, ¥320, 33 minutes). Connections from Kyoto require a change of trains at Yamato-Yagi to the Kintetsu Osaka line (*tokkyū* and *junkyū*, ¥1840, one hour). Sights within the region are quite spread out, so renting a car is suggested to see them all in one day.

Tanzan-jinja SHINTO SHRINE

(談山神社; Map p402; admission ¥500; 8.30am-4.30pm) Centred around an attractive 13-storey pagoda, this shrine is best viewed against a backdrop of maple trees ablaze with autumn colours (November to early December). It enshrines Nakatomi no Kamatari, patriarch of the Fujiwara clan, which effectively ruled Japan for nearly 500 years. According to legend, Nakatomi met here secretly with Prince Naka no Ōe over games of kickball to discuss the overthrow of the ruling Soga clan, commemorated in scroll paintings and by priests playing kickball on 29 April and 3 November.

The shrine can be reached by Sakurai City Community Bus from stand 1 outside the southern exit of Sakurai Station (¥490, 25 minutes).

Hase-dera BUDDHIST TEMPLE

(長谷寺; Map p402; admission ¥500; 8.30am-5pm Apr-Sep, 9am-4.30pm Oct-Mar) Climb 399 covered steps to the Hondō (main hall) to view a 10m-tall image of Kannon (deity of mercy), Japan's largest wooden sculpture, crafted 1538. There are splendid views from a balcony built on stilts over the mountainside. Expect lots of visitors in spring – for the explosion of blooming peonies and cherry blossoms, which seem to swirl upward in the wind – and autumn, when maples turn vivid red. No wonder it's nicknamed *hana no mitera* (flower-viewing temple).

Hase-dera Station is two stops east of Sakurai on the Kintetsu Osaka line (¥210, six minutes). It's about a 20-minute walk to the temple; walk through the archway, down several flights of steps, turn left, cross the river, then turn right onto the main street toward the temple.

Murō-ji BUDDHIST TEMPLE

(室生寺; admission ¥600; 8.30am-5pm, to 4pm Dec-Feb) Secluded in a thick forest, this temple (founded in the 9th century) is associated with the Shingon sect of Esoteric Buddhism. It's nicknamed 'Women's Kōya-san' because, unusually, it welcomed female students. Top sights include a national treasure – the 9th century, 11-headed Kannon (deity of mercy) with female forms – and, uphill, a five-storey pagoda built in the late 8th century and restored after damage from a 1998 typhoon. Next, continue to Oku-no-in, the innermost sanctum, atop another very steep flight of steps.

Don't feel like climbing? Go about 100m past the pagoda to see a mammoth cedar growing over a huge rock.

From Sakurai, take the Kintetsu Osaka line to Murōguchi-ōno Station (*kyūkō*; ¥350, 16 minutes), then switch to a bus to Murō-ji-mae (¥430, 15 minutes).

Yoshino 吉野

0746 / POP 9053

Yoshino is Japan's top cherry-blossom destination, renowned for the *hito-me-sen-bon* (1000 trees in a glance) viewpoint. For a few weeks in early to mid-April, the blossoms form a floral carpet gradually ascending the mountainsides, and thousands of visitors jam the hilltop village's narrow streets. The rest of the year, Yoshino reverts to a sleepy hamlet with a unique history as a place of refuge. A handful of shrines and temples and some unique foods entertain day trippers and overnight guests.

Sights

Kimpusen-ji TEMPLE

(金峯山寺; admission ¥500; 8.30am-4.30pm, enter by 4pm) A national treasure and Unesco World Heritage Site, this is the head temple of Shugendō, a sect based in Buddhism but borrowing liberally from other traditions. Check out the fearsome **Kongō Rikishi** (guardian figure statues) in the gate and then continue to the **Zaō-dō Hall**, said to be Japan's second-largest wooden building. Early risers can observe morning *otsutome* (worship service), incorporating *taikō* drumming and the sounding of the *horagai* (giant conch shell), reminiscent of storied *yamabushi* (mountain monks).

The temple's trio of central deity statues are a symbol of the city with their fearsome blue faces. They are opened to the public for about one month a year (check at tourist offices for dates and admission fees).

The stone steps to the temple's Niō-mon gate are about 400m uphill from the cable-car station.

Yoshimizu-jinja SHINTO SHRINE

(吉水神社; admission ¥400; 9am-4.30pm) Also on the Unesco World Heritage List, this shrine has provided refuge for important historical figures and now displays scrolls, armour, *nō* (stylised dance-drama) masks and painted *fusuma* (sliding doors) from those times.

Swordsman and general Minamoto Yoshitsune fled here after incurring the wrath of his brother, the first Kamakura shogun. After a dispute for succession in Kyoto, Emperor Go-Daigo set up a rival court in Yoshino and stayed here during palace construction. Toyotomi Hideyoshi hosted a 5000-person *hanami* (blossom-viewing) party in 1594.

From Kimpusen-ji, continue 300m to a side road to the left (the first turn past the post office) leading to this shrine. There are good views back to Kimpusen-ji and the *hito-me-sen-bon* viewpoint.

Nyoirin-ji BUDDHIST TEMPLE

(如意輪時; admission ¥400; 9am-4pm, 7am-5pm Apr) Take the left fork on the road just above Yoshimizu-jinja and the dilapidated Katte-jinja (勝手神社) shrine to reach Nyoirin-ji (about 30 minutes, through the Naka-sen-bon forest of 1000 cherry trees). This temple preserves both the relics of Emperor Go-Daigo's unlucky court and his tomb. In the Hōmotsu-den (Treasure Hall) is a trio of scroll paintings, each with 1000 Buddhas. Legend says that if you look hard enough, you'll find one that looks like yourself.

Sleeping

Ryokan Katō
RYOKAN ¥¥

(旅館歌藤; ☎0746-32-3177; www.kato-yoshino.jp/en; 3056 Yoshinoyama; r per person ¥7560, with breakfast ¥9720, with breakfast & dinner ¥17,280; P) In business for two centuries but marvelously up to date, thanks to warm, young owners, design flair, rough-hewn wooden furniture and a *rotemburo* (outdoor bath) of local stone. We like the modern, log-house-style back building, with a glassed-in rotunda for cherry-tree viewing and gathering around a wood stove. All 14 Japanese-style rooms have shared bath; half have private toilet.

It's about five minutes' walk from the cable car.

Chikurin-in Gumpōen
RYOKAN ¥¥¥

(竹林院群芳園; ☎0746-32-8081; www.chikurin.co.jp/e/home.htm; 2142 Yoshinoyama; r per person with 2 meals ¥13,650-78,000, without bathroom ¥12,600-21,000; @) Generations of emperors have stayed at this temple, which also operates as a ryokan, and it's easy to see why. The main building, with its gorgeous woodwork, dates from the 1790s; rooms are Japan-posh; and baths and the temple garden have sweeping valley views. Some staff speak English. Reservations are essential for cherry-blossom season, and recommended at all other times.

Even if you don't stay over, at least visit the temple's splendid garden (admission ¥300). Single travellers pay a supplement of ¥5250 per night for an overnight stay.

Eating

Many restaurants here are perched on a ridge with inspirational views across the valley. A local speciality is clear, gelatinous sweets made from ground *kuzu* (kudzu or arrowroot) roots.

Tofujaya Hayashi
TOFU ¥

(豆富茶屋林; ☎0746-32-5681; 551 Yoshinoyama; dishes ¥300-800, set menus ¥1000-1300; 9am-5pm, closed Tue;) One of Kansai's most unusual restaurants makes most unexpected creations out of tofu: *hanbāgā* (hamburgers; ¥400); rāmen topped with fried tofu strips, *yuba* (tofu skin) and green onion (¥800); even *dōnatsu* (doughnuts; ¥300). For dessert: soy ice-cream (¥300), of course.

Harukaze
SHOKUDŌ ¥

(はるかぜ; ☎0746-32-3830; mains ¥650-1100, set menus ¥850-1500; 10am-5pm, closed irregularly) With a limited picture menu, this restaurant serves a *kamameshi teishoku* (rice cooked in an iron pot; ¥1500; allow 20 minutes) and other typical lunch favourites. It's about 5m past the information office, on the opposite side – look for the ceramic *tanuki* (Japanese raccoon dog) out front.

Nishizawaya
SHOKUDŌ ¥

(西澤屋; ☎0746-32-8600; mains ¥700-1000; 10am-5pm daily during cherry-blossom and fall-foliage season, irregular closures rest of year;) Run by a bunch of friendly ladies, this homey restaurant serves a *shizuka gozen* set menu, which includes *ayu* (sweetfish) and a small hotpot filled with vegetables and tofu. It's directly across the street from Katte-jinja: look for the plastic food display.

Nakai Shunpūdō
SWEETS ¥

(中井春風堂; ☎0746-32-3043; 545 Yoshinoyama; kuzumanju ¥125; 10am-5pm, closed Wed in summer, Sat & Sun only in winter;) You can watch the chef make *kuzu* (arrowroot gelatin) sweets in the shop window here. Sample it on the spot (as *kuzumanju*, filled with bean paste) or in noodle form dipped in black honey in the spiffy new cafe, fresh with the aroma of newly cut cedar.

Hōkon-an
CAFE ¥

(芳魂庵; ☎0746-32-8207; kuzubana with green tea ¥650; 9am-5pm, closed irregularly;) In business since 1950, this atmospheric little teahouse lets you sip *matcha* with *kuzubana*, made from kudzu and sweet bean paste. Look for the rustic wooden facade and large ceramic urn, just past the post office. Order from the picture menu.

Information

Yoshinoyama Visitor Centre (☎0746-32-8371; 9am-4.30pm Apr, Sat, Sun & holidays May-Nov, closed Dec-Mar) is about 500m up the main street from the top cable-car station, on your right just after Kimpusen-ji (look for the large tan-and-white building). It can help with *minshuku* (guesthouse) bookings if necessary.

Getting There & Away

Visitors to Yoshino first arrive at Yoshino Station, and then make their way up to the village proper by the **Yoshino Ropeway** (吉野大峯ケーブル; one way/return ¥360/610; 9.20am-5.40pm, 7.40am-7.40pm Apr) or on foot. Japan's oldest aerial tram (1929), the ropeway takes about five minutes to climb the 350m (otherwise about a 15-minute walk).

To reach Yoshino Station from Kyoto, take the Kintetsu line to Kashihara-jingū-mae and change trains (*kyūkō* ¥1230, 2¼ hours; *tokkyū* ¥2550, 96 minutes). From Nara, change trains twice at Yamato-Saidaiji and Kashihara-jingū-mae (*kyūkō*, ¥850, about one hour 40 minutes; *tokkyū* ¥1780, about 1¼ hours).

From Osaka, direct trains run on the Kintetsu Minami Osaka–Yoshino line from Abeno-bashi Station (by Tennō-ji Station) to Yoshino (*kyūkō* ¥970, 93 minutes; *tokkyū* ¥1480, 1¼ hours).

The closest JR station to Yoshino is Yoshino-guchi, which has connections with Nara, Osaka and Wakayama. From here, you'll have to take the Kintetsu line (*kyūkō* ¥380, 35 minutes; *tokkyū* ¥890, 26 minutes).

KII PENINSULA

The remote and mountainous Kii Peninsula (紀伊半島; Kii-hantō) is a far cry from central Kansai's bustling urban sprawl. Most of the attractions are in Wakayama Prefecture (Wakayama-ken), including the mountaintop temple complex of Kōya-san, one of Japan's most important Buddhist centres, and the ancient pilgrimage trails and onsen of the Kumano Kodō.

Along the coast are the beachside onsen resort of Shirahama, on the west coast, and the rugged coastline of Shiono-misaki and Kii-Ōshima, at the southern tip.

The JR Kii main line (Kinokuni line) runs around the peninsula's coast, linking Shin-Osaka and Nagoya stations (some to Kyoto Station). Special Kuroshio and Nankii *tokkyū* trains can get you around the peninsula fairly quickly, but once you step off these express trains you're at the mercy of slow local trains and buses.

For most freedom of movement, a rental car is the best way to get around the area. All of Japan's major car rental companies have branches at airports, in big cities and some small towns.

Kōya-san 高野山

☎0736 / POP 3797

Kōya-san is a raised tableland in northern Wakayama-ken covered with thick forests and surrounded by eight peaks. The major attraction here is the Kōya-san monastic complex, which is the headquarters of the Shingon school of Esoteric Buddhism. Though not quite the Shangri-la it's occasionally described as, Kōya-san is one of Japan's most rewarding destinations, not just for the natural setting of the area but also as an opportunity to stay in temples and get a glimpse of long-held traditions of Japanese religious life.

Although it is technically possible to visit Kōya-san as a day trip from Nara, Kyoto or Osaka, we don't recommend it. Instead, take it slow and stay overnight in one of the town's excellent *shukubō* (temple lodgings). Keep in mind that Kōya-san tends to be around 5°C colder than down on the plains, so bring warm clothes if you're visiting in winter, spring or autumn.

Whenever you go, you'll find that getting there is half the fun – near the end of its journey, the train winds through a series of tight valleys with mountains soaring on all sides, and the final vertiginous cable-car leg is not for the faint of heart.

History

The founder of the Shingon sect of Esoteric Buddhism, Kūkai (known after his death as Kōbō Daishi), established a religious community here in 816. Kōbō Daishi travelled as a young priest to China and returned after two years to found the school. He is one of Japan's most famous religious figures and is revered as a Bodhisattva, calligrapher, scholar and inventor of the Japanese *kana* syllabary.

Followers of Shingon believe that Kōbō Daishi is not dead, but rather that he is meditating in his tomb in Kōya-san's Oku-no-in Cemetery, awaiting the arrival of Miroku (Maitreya, the future Buddha). Food is ritually offered in front of the tomb daily to sustain him during this meditation. When Miroku returns, it is thought that only Kōbō Daishi will be able to interpret his heavenly message for humanity. Thus, the vast cemetery here is like an amphitheatre crowded with souls gathered in expectation of this heavenly sermon.

Over the centuries, the temple complex grew in size and attracted many followers of the Jōdo (Pure Land) school of Buddhism. During the 11th century, it became popular with both nobles and commoners to leave hair or ashes from deceased relatives close to Kōbō Daishi's tomb.

Kōya-san is now a thriving centre for Japanese Buddhism, with more than 110 temples. It is the headquarters of the Shingon sect, which numbers 10 million members

Kii Peninsula

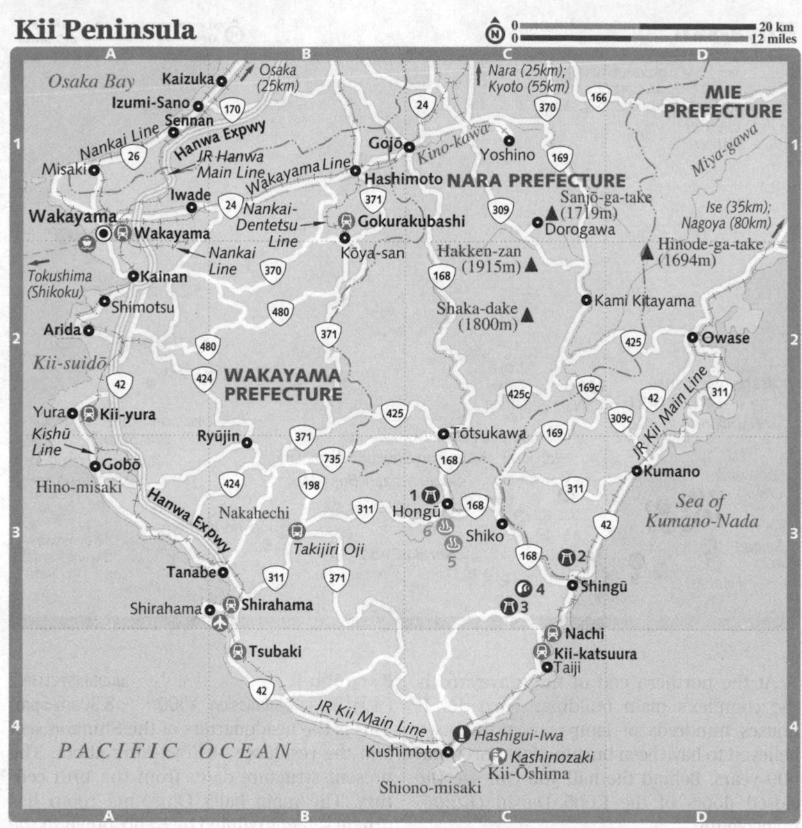

and presides over nearly 4000 temples all over Japan.

Sights

The precincts of Kōya-san are divided into two main areas: the Garan (Sacred Precinct) in the west, where you will find interesting temples and pagodas, and the Oku-no-in, with its vast cemetery, in the east.

A joint ticket (*shodōkyōtsu-naihaiken;* ¥2000) that covers entry to Kongōbu-ji, the Kondō, Dai-tō, Treasure Museum and Tokugawa Mausoleum and more can be purchased at the Kōya-san Shukubō Association (p413) office and the venues themselves.

★Oku-no-in BUDDHIST TEMPLE

(奥の院; Tōrō-dō 6am-5.30pm) FREE One of Japan's most intensely spiritual places, Oku-no-in is a memorial hall to Kōbō Daishi surrounded by a vast, forested Buddhist cemetery. The tall cedars and thousands of peaked stone stupas along the cobblestoned path can be utterly enchanting, especially in swirling mist.

Any Japanese Buddhist who's anybody has had their remains, or at least a lock of hair, interred here to ensure pole position when the Buddha of the Future (Miroku Buddha) comes to earth.

Kii Peninsula

Sights

1	Kumano Hongū Taisha	C3
2	Kumano-Hayatama Taisha	C3
3	Nachi Taisha	C3
4	Nachi-no-taki	C3
	Nachiyama-oku-no-in	(see 4)
	Sanseiganto-ji	(see 3)

Activities, Courses & Tours

5	Kawa-yu Onsen	C3
	Watarase Onsen	(see 5)
6	Yunomine Onsen	C3

Kōya-san

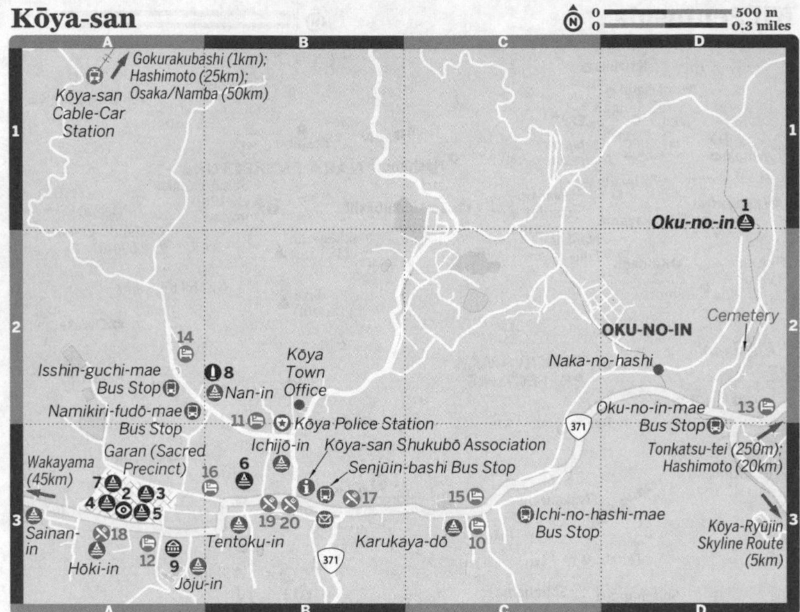

At the northern end of the graveyard is the complex's main building, **Tōrō-dō**. It houses hundreds of lamps, including two believed to have been burning for more than 900 years. Behind the hall you can see the closed doors of the Kōbō Daishi (Kūkai) mausoleum.

Along the way you'll pass the bridge Mimyo-no-hashi. Worshippers ladle water from the river and pour it over the nearby Jizō statues as an offering for the dead. The inscribed wooden plaques in the river are in memory of aborted babies and those who died by drowning.

Between the bridge and the Tōrō-dō is a wooden building the size of a large phone booth, which contains the Miroku-ishi. Pilgrims reach through the holes in the wall to try to lift a large, smooth boulder onto a shelf. The weight of the stone is supposed to change according to your weight of sin. We can only report that the thing was damn heavy!

Oku-no-in is easily reached on foot from the town centre, or you can take the bus east to Ichi-no-hashi-mae bus stop. From here cross the bridge, Ichi-no-hashi, and into the cemetery. Buses return to the centre of town from the Oku-no-mae bus stop (or walk it in about 30 minutes).

Kongōbu-ji BUDDHIST TEMPLE
(金剛峯寺; admission ¥500; ⌚8.30am-5pm)
This is the headquarters of the Shingon sect and the residence of Kōya-san's abbot. The present structure dates from the 19th century. The main hall's Ohiro-ma room has ornate screens painted by Kanō Tanyu in the 16th century.

The rock garden is interesting for the sheer number of rocks used in its composition, giving the effect of a throng of petrified worshippers eagerly listening to a monk's sermon.

Admission includes tea and rice cakes served beside the stone garden.

Garan BUDDHIST TEMPLE
(伽藍; admission per bldg ¥200; ⌚8.30am-5pm)
In this temple complex of several halls and pagodas, the **Dai-tō** (大塔; Great Pagoda) pagoda, rebuilt in 1934 after a fire, is said to be the centre of the lotus-flower mandala formed by the eight mountains around Kōya-san.

The main object of worship is the **Dainichi-nyōrai** (Cosmic Buddha) and his four attendant Buddhas, painted on pillars (originally, it's said, by Kōbō Daishi himself). It's since been repainted and is an awesome sight.

Kōya-san

Top Sights

Sights

Sleeping

Eating

The **Chūmon** (中門) gate was renovated for Kōya-san's 1200th anniversary in 2014. The **Kondō** (金堂; Main Hall; admission ¥200; 8.30pm-5pm) enshrines Yakushi Nyorai, the Buddha of medicine and healing. The current building was rebuilt in 1932. The nearby **Sai-tō** (西塔; Western Pagoda) was most recently rebuilt in 1834 and is more subdued.

Treasure Museum MUSEUM
(霊宝館; Reihōkan; admission ¥600; 8.30am-5.30pm May-Oct, to 5pm Nov-Apr) The Treasure Museum has a compact display of Buddhist works of art, all collected in Kōya-san. There are some very fine statues, painted scrolls and mandalas.

Tokugawa Mausoleum MONUMENT
(徳川家霊台; Tokugawa-ke Reidai; admission ¥200; 8.30am-5pm) Built in 1643, the Tokugawa Mausoleum is actually two adjoining mausoleums in a clearing, of Tokugawa Ieyasu (on the right) and Tokugawa Hidetada (on the left), the first and second Tokugawa shoguns, respectively. They are ornately decorated, as with most structures associated with the Tokugawa regime.

The mausoleum is near the Namikiri-fudō-mae bus stop (波切不動前バス亭).

Tours

Kōyasan Interpreter Guide Club TOUR
(090-1486-2588, 090-3263-5184; www.geocities.jp/koyasan_i_g_c) This club offers four-hour private tours of Kōya-san for ¥5000 per group with a volunteer guide. Professional guides cost from ¥10,000 per four-hour tour. It also offers regularly scheduled tours (Wednesday, April to September) for ¥1000 per person.

The morning tour meets at Ichi-no-hashi at 8.30am, lasts three hours and covers Oku-no-in, Garan and Kongōbu-ji. The afternoon tour meets at Kongōbu-ji at 1pm, takes three hours, and covers Kongōbu-ji, Garan and Oku-no-in.

Festivals & Events

Aoba Matsuri CULTURAL
Held on 15 June to celebrate the birth of Kōbō Daishi. Various traditional ceremonies are performed at the temples around town.

Rōsoku Matsuri CULTURAL
This interesting festival is held on 13 August in remembrance of departed souls. Thousands come to light some 100,000 candles along the approaches to Oku-no-in.

Sleeping

More than 50 temples in Kōya-san offer temple lodgings *(shukubō)*, which serve *shōjin-ryōri* (Buddhist vegetarian cuisine – no meat, fish, onions or garlic) and typically hold morning prayer sessions, which guests are welcome to join or observe.

Most lodgings start at ¥9500 per person and include two meals, with a surcharge for solo guests. Prices can vary widely, both between temples and within them, depending upon the room (most are without en suite bath and toilet), meals and season; generally, the more you pay, the better the room and the meals. Most *shukubō* ask that you check in by 5pm.

Reserve at least seven days in advance through the Kōya-san Shukubō Association (p413); you can fill out a request form online, in English. Most lodgings do not have air-con but do provide fans during warmer months.

★ **Koyasan Guest House Kokuu** GUESTHOUSE ¥
(高野山ゲストハウスKokuu; 0736-26-7216; http://koyasanguesthouse.com; 49-43 Itogun Kōyachō Kōyasan; capsules from ¥3500, s/d/tr

from ¥6000/9000/12,000; @ 📶) This convivial place puts the Kōya-san experience within range of even the most budget-conscious backpackers. It's intimate, clean, woodsy, light and airy, with capsule-style and nice private rooms and shower cabinets down the hall. Knowledgeable, English-speaking staff can help arrange morning prayers and night tours, and prepare inexpensive breakfasts and light meals, such as Indian curry, for dinner. Reserve directly, not through the Shukubō Association.

Rengejō-in SHUKUBO ¥¥
(蓮華定院; ☎0736-56-2233; r per person with meals from ¥9720, single travellers ¥11,880; 📶) This stately temple has superb rooms, a wealth of gardens, fine painted *fusuma* (sliding doors) and interesting art on display. English is spoken and sometimes an explanation of Buddhist practices and meditation is available in the early evening. Wi-fi is in one of the common rooms.

Shōjōshin-in SHUKUBO ¥¥
(清浄心院; ☎0736-56-2006; r per person incl meals from ¥9,720, with private bath from ¥16,200; 📶) Friendly spot with in-room wi-fi and no extra charge for solo travellers. There's an atmospheric old kitchen under a tall wooden ceiling and gold-leaf *fusuma* doors. It's the closest *shukubō* to the entry to Oku-no-in.

Ekō-in SHUKUBO ¥¥
(恵光院; ☎0736-56-2514; ekoin@mbox.co.jp; r per person incl meals from ¥10,800; @ 📶) This lovely hillside temple is run by a friendly bunch of young monks, and rooms look onto beautiful gardens. Ekō-in is known for nighttime tours of Oku-no-in, in English and as one of the two temples in town (the other is Kongōbu-ji) where you can study seated meditation; call ahead. There's no solo traveller surcharge.

Fukuchi-in SHUKUBO ¥¥
(福智院; ☎0736-56-2021; r per person incl meals from ¥12,960, single travellers ¥16,200; @ 📶) This fine temple has outdoor baths with onsen water and a lovely garden designed by the famous designer Shigemori Mirei. Wi-fi is available for limited durations near the temple office. Some staff speak English; sometimes it's busy with Japanese bus tours.

Henjōson-in SHUKUBO ¥¥
(遍照尊院; ☎0736-56-2434; r per person with meals from ¥12,960, with bathroom ¥16,200) Nice rooms and communal baths make this a good choice, with an updated feel.

Sōji-in SHUKUBO ¥¥¥
(総持院; ☎0736-56-2111; r per person with meals from ¥18,360, single travellers ¥29,376) At home with foreign guests, this pleasantly modern temple has a lovely garden, some rooms with ensuite baths and a wheelchair-accessible room with Western-style beds. The top rooms here are among the best in Kōya-san, and the high-quality meals also account for the price differential.

Eating

The culinary speciality of Kōya-san is *shōjin-ryōri,* elaborate and very tasty Buddhist vegan meals served at temple lodgings. If you're not staying over, reserve a *shōjin-ryōri* lunch at a temple; do so ahead of time through the Kōya-san Shukubō Association. Prices are fixed at ¥2700, ¥3800 and ¥5400, depending on the number of courses. Otherwise, most eateries around town close by late afternoon. For snacks and simple meals there's a new **Family Mart** (ファミリーマート; ☎0736-56-2580; 288 Kōyasan) convenience store (big news on the mountain).

★ **Bononsha** VEGETARIAN, CAFE ¥
(梵恩舎; ☎0736-56-5535; 730 Kōyasan; lunch set ¥1200; ⏲9am-5pm, closed Mon, Tue and irregularly; ✎) Run by a delightful French-Japanese couple, this charming cafe with great old wooden beams is a relaxing spot for coffees and cakes such as chocolate cake and tofu cheesecake. Daily lunch set menus are served until they run out (arrive early). It's also a gallery of local pottery.

Tonkatsu-tei SHOKUDŌ ¥
(とんかつ亭; ☎0736-56-1039; 49-48 Kōyasan; mains ¥650-950, set meals from ¥1300; ⏲11am-2pm & 5-10pm, closed Tue; 📋) If after all that Buddhist vegetarian cooking you just need some meat, this mom-and-pop shop on the edge of town serves up an assortment of deep-fried goodness: the namesake *tonkatsu* (pork cutlet), chicken, grilled fish and curry rice. No English spoken, but the sweet older couple who own it make a good go. Look for the yellow roof.

Maruman SHOKUDŌ ¥
(丸万; ☎0736-56-2049; 778 Kōyasan; mains ¥850-1150, set menus ¥850-1880; ⏲9am-5pm, closed irregularly, usually Tue or Wed) This convenient *shokudō* serves standards like *katsu-don*

(fried pork cutlet over rice; ¥820) represented by plastic food models in the window. It's diagonally across from the Shukubō Association office on the main street. **Nankai Shokudō** (南海食堂; ☎0736-56-2128; 777 Kōyasan; mains ¥550-900, teishoku ¥1200-1750) next door is similar.

Information

Kōya-san Shukubō Association (高野山宿坊協会; ☎0736-56-2616; http://eng.shukubo.net; ⌚8.30am-4.30pm Dec-Feb, to 5pm Mar-Jun & Sep-Nov, to 5.45pm Jul & Aug) In the centre of town in front of the Senjūin-bashi bus stop (千手院橋バス停), Kōya-san's well-equipped tourist information centre stocks maps and brochures, and English speakers are usually on hand. It also makes *shukubō* and dining reservations (in advance) and rents an English-language audio guide (¥500) to important sights around town, as well as bikes.

Getting There & Away

Without a rental car, access to Kōya-san is via the Nankai Railway from Osaka. Trains from Namba Station (*kyūkō/tokkyū* ¥1260/2040, one hour and 40 minutes/43 minutes) terminate at Gokurakubashi, at the base of the mountain, where you board a cable car (gondola, five minutes, price included in train tickets) up to Kōya-san itself. From the cable-car station, take a bus into central Kōya-san; walking is prohibited on the connecting road.

Nankai's **Kōya-san World Heritage Ticket** (www.nankaikoya.jp/en/stations/ticket.html; ¥3400) covers return train fare (including one-way *tokkyū* fare from Osaka), buses on Kōya-san and discounted admission to some sites.

From Kyoto, if you've got a Japan Rail Pass, take the JR line to Hashimoto, changing at Nara, Sakurai and Takada en route. At Hashimoto, connect to the Nankai line to Kōya-san (¥830, 50 minutes). Without a Japan Rail Pass, it's easier and quicker to connect to the Nankai line at Namba.

To continue from Kōya-san to Hongū on the Kumano Kodō, return to Hashimoto on the Nankai line and transfer to the JR line to Gōjō (¥210, 15 minutes), then go by bus to Hongū (¥3200, four hours).

Getting Around

Buses run on three routes from the top cable-car station via the town centre to Ichi-no-hashi and Oku-no-in (¥410) via the tourist office at Senjūin-bashi (¥290). The bus office by the top cable-car station sells an all-day bus pass (*ichinichi furee kippu;* ¥830), but once up the hill, the sights are easily walkable in about 30 minutes. Take note of bus schedules before setting out, as buses run infrequently.

Bicycles can be rented (per hour/day ¥400/1200) at the Kōya-san Shukubō Association (p413) office.

Tanabe 田辺

☎0739 / POP 79,631

Tanabe, a small city on the west coast of Wakayama, is the main gateway to the Kumano Kodō. The government of this friendly town has made huge efforts to welcome foreign tourists.

By the train station, the excellent **Tanabe City Kumano Tourism Bureau** (田辺市熊野ツーリズムビューロー; ☎0739-34-5599; www.tb-kumano.jp/en; ⌚9am-6pm) offers useful maps and detailed info on the region as well as a 'gourmet map' of local restaurants with English menus. There are several *izakaya* near the station.

Miyoshiya Ryokan (美吉屋旅館; ☎0739-22-3448; www.miyoshiya-ryokan.com/english.html; 739-7 Minato; r per person from ¥3200; 📶) is a simple travellers' ryokan from the 1940s; the knowledgeable, English-speaking owner makes a stay here worth it. It is located three minutes' walk from the Kii-Tanabe station (turn left at the first traffic signal, follow this road about 300m and it will be on your right).

The JR Kii main line connects Kii-Tanabe with JR Shin-Osaka Station (*tokkyū;* ¥4750, 2¼ hours).

Buses running between Tanabe and Hongū (¥2000, two hours, from stop 2) make a loop of the three surrounding onsen (Watarase, Yunomine and Kawa-yu). These buses also stop at several places that serve as trailheads for the Kumano Kodō.

Shirahama 白浜

☎0739 / POP 23,201

Shirahama, on the southwest coast of the Kii Peninsula, is Kansai's leading beach resort and has all the trappings of a major Japanese tourist attraction – huge resort hotels, aquariums, amusement parks etc. It also has several good onsen, a great white-sand beach and rugged coastal scenery.

Because the Japanese like to do things according to the rules – and the rules say the only time you can swim in the ocean is from late July to the end of August – the place is almost deserted outside the peak season. It's

KUMANO KODŌ: JAPAN'S ANCIENT PILGRIMAGE ROUTE

From earliest times, the Japanese believed the wilds of the Kii Peninsula to be inhabited by *kami*, Shintō deities. When Buddhism swept Japan in the 6th century, these *kami* became *gongen* – manifestations of the Buddha or a Bodhisattva – in a syncretic faith known as *ryōbu*, or 'dual Shintō'.

Japan's early emperors made pilgrimages into the area. The route they followed from Kyoto, via Osaka, Tanabe and over the inner mountains of Wakayama, is known today as the Kumano Kodō: the Kumano Old Road. Over time, the popularity of this pilgrimage spread from nobles to *yamabushi* priests (wandering mountain ascetics) and common folk.

The Kumano faith is based on prehistoric forms of nature worship and over the centuries has mixed with other religions, such as Buddhism. The focal points of worship are the Hongū Taisha, Hayatama Taisha and Nachi Taisha 'grand shrines', which are connected via the Kumano Kodo pilgrimage routes. Interestingly, the Kumano faith is not defined or standardised, and is open to reinterpretation by those who visit; it's a universal sacred site.

In 2004 Unesco declared the Sacred Sites and Pilgrimage Routes in the Kii Mountain Range to be World Heritage Sites. Many sections of the route have been restored and there is good accommodation en route, making it possible to perform your own 'pilgrimage' through the mountains of Wakayama.

The best way to visit Kumano would probably be to follow the general flow of pilgrims from the 9th century – how could over 1000 years of pilgrimage tradition be wrong? Come down the west coast of the Kii Peninsula from Kyoto or Osaka to Tanabe, where there are some great *izakaya* (pub-eateries) and you can get an early start the next morning. Typical routes involve taking a bus from Tanabe, and walking for two days to Hongū, but many variations and longer/shorter trips are possible.

Along the way, most routes converge in Hongū, home of the Hongū Taisha (Grand Shrine) and some excellent onsen, including Yunomine and Kawa-yu, and many visitors spend a few nights here.

The **Tanabe City Kumano Tourism Bureau** (www.tb-kumano.jp/en/index.html), one of the most progressive tourism outfits in all Japan, has detailed information and maps on the routes and an English-language accommodation booking site on its homepage, making trip-planning a snap.

a great place to visit in June or September, and we've swum in the sea here as late as mid-October.

There's a **tourist information office** (☎0739-42-2900; ⏲9.30am-6pm) in the station where you can pick up a map to sights and accommodations. From here, you'll need to take a bus to the main sights (one way/all-day pass ¥340/1100, 15 minutes to the beach).

Sights & Activities

Beaches

Shirara-hama BEACH

(白良浜) Shirara-hama, the town's main beach, is famous for its white sand. If it reminds you of Australia, it's because the town had to import sand from Down Under after the original stuff washed away. This place is packed during July and August, but in the low season it can be quite pleasant. The beach parallels the western side of town.

Coastal Scenery

South of Sakino-yu Onsen are two of Shirahama's natural wonders.

Senjō-jiki (千畳敷; Thousand Tatami Mat Point) is a wildly eroded point with layer after horizontal layer of stratified rock.

Sandan-beki (三段壁; Three-Step Cliff; lift ¥1300; ⏲lift 8am-5pm) is a 50m cliff face which drops away vertiginously into the sea. You can pay to take a lift down to a cave at the base of the cliff, or simply clamber along the rocks to the north of the cliff – it's stunning, particularly when the big rollers are pounding in from the Pacific.

These natural attractions can be reached on foot or bicycle from the main beach in around 30 minutes, or you can take a bus from the station (¥430, 20 minutes to bus stop 'Senjō-guchi').

Onsen

In addition to its great beach, Shirahama has some of Japan's oldest developed onsen. Bring a towel.

Sakino-yu Onsen ONSEN
(崎の湯温泉; 1668 Shirahama-chō Yusaki, Nishi-muro-gun; admission ¥420; ⌚8am-6pm Apr-Jun & Sep, 7am-7pm Jul-Aug, 8am-5pm Oct-Mar, closed Wed year-round) Mentioned in Japan's earliest history book, *Nihon Shōki*, this fantastic bath sits in rocks next to ocean (taller waves might spill into the lower bath). It's 1km south of the main beach along the seafront road, below Hotel Seamore. No soap or shampoo provided, and gents, note that your side of the bath isn't entirely private.

Come early in the day to beat the crowds.

Shirara-yu ONSEN
(白良湯; 3313-1 Shirahama-chō; admission ¥420; ⌚7am-10pm, closed Thu) At the north end of Shirara-hama sits this lovely wooden building with a verandah. Baths are on the second floor for great ocean views. Enter next to Family Mart.

Murono-yu ONSEN
(牟婁の湯; 1665 Shirahama-chō; admission ¥420; ⌚7am-10pm, closed Tue) In front of Shirahama post office, this old-school onsen feels like a simple public bath.

Shirasuna-yu ONSEN
(しらすな湯; 864 Shirahama-chō; admission May-Sep ¥100, Oct-Apr free; ⌚10am-3pm Tue-Sun, to 7pm daily Jul–mid-Sep) This open-air onsen in the middle of Shirara-hama's boardwalk is a footbath most of the year. Between June and 15 September you can wear a swimsuit to soak, then dash into the ocean to cool off.

Sleeping

Minshuku Katsuya MINSHUKU ¥
(民宿かつ屋; ☎0739-42-3814; 3118-5 Shirahama-chō; r per person without meals ¥4000; 📶) This longstanding *minshuku* is the cheapest in town and is very central – only two minutes' walk from the main beach. It's built around a small Japanese garden and has its own natural onsen bath. Downsides: it's showing its age, walls are pretty thin and air-con costs extra.

★ **Hotel Luandon Shirahama** HOTEL ¥¥
(ホテルルアンドン白浜; ☎0739-43-3477; www.luandon.sh.com; 3354-9 Shirahama-chō; r per person from ¥6200) It's an inconvenient 10-minute walk from the beach area, but you're rewarded with en suite bathrooms, crisp, modern room design and bang-on views of Shirahama's inner harbour from the balconies.

Hotel Ginsui HOTEL ¥¥
(ホテル銀翠; ☎0739-42-3316; fax 43-1301; 1356-3 Shirahama-chō; s/d/tw from ¥6480/9720/11,880; 📶) This 48-room hotel is a reasonable choice across the street from the beach (ask for an oceanside room, some with views through the pines to the sunset). Even if we don't love all the design choices (riotous green rope-backed chairs in the lobby?), it's a great deal for the location.

Eating

There are many restaurants in the streets just in from the beach. On the south edge of town, **Fisherman's Wharf** is a new complex for restaurant browsing, including the rooftop beer garden (in warmer months). If you'd like to self-cater, the 24-hour **Gourmet City** supermarket is five minutes' walk from the main beach.

Kiraku SHOKUDŌ ¥
(喜楽; ☎0739-42-3916; 890-48 Shirahama-chō; mains ¥650-800, set menus from ¥1200; ⌚11am-2pm & 4.30-9pm, closed Tue; 📋) This well-kept, cheerful little *shokudō* serves *teishoku* (set meals) like *tonkatsu* (pork cutlet) *tempura* and *katsuo tataki* (lightly roasted bonito). There is a limited picture menu. On Miyuki-dōri, head away from the beach and make the second right, about 150m. It's just in from the corner, close to a coin laundry.

Getting There & Away

Shirahama is on the JR Kii main line. There are *tokkyū* trains from Shin-Osaka Station (¥5080, two hours and 35 minutes). The same line also connects to Kushimoto, Nachi, Shingū and Wakayama city. A cheaper alternative is offered by **Meikō Bus** (www.meikobus.jp; ⌚9am-6pm), which runs buses between JR Osaka Station and Shirahama via Tanabe (one way/return ¥2700/5000, about 3½ to four hours).

Kushimoto, Shiono-misaki & Kii-Ōshima

串本・潮岬・紀伊大島

☎0735

The southern tip of the Kii Peninsula (and southernmost point on Honshu) has some stunning coastal scenery.

The amazing natural rock formation **Hashigui-iwa** is a line of about a dozen spire-like boulders extending into the water like the supports of a bridge. It's popular for a ramble at low tide and for photos at sunrise, and the adjacent visitor centre sells local *ponkan* tangerine-flavoured ice cream.

The main attraction on Kii-Ōshima is the coastal cliffs at the eastern end of the island, around the **Kashino-zaki Lighthouse** (樫野崎灯台; ⌚8.30am-5pm), built circa 1870. In the park around the lighthouse are Turkish-related buildings and monuments, commemorating the sinking of the Turkish ship *Ertugrul* in 1890 and the Japanese who helped rescue the sailors.

Backtracking about 1km, the staid, mostly Japanese-language **Japan–US Memorial Museum** (日米修交記念館; 1033 Kashino, Kushimoto-chō; admission ¥250; ⌚9am-5pm) commemorates the visit of the US ship *Lady Washington* in 1791, a full 62 years before the much more famous landing of Commodore Perry (p805) in Yokohama in 1853.

More interesting, from a lookout just beyond the museum, are the magnificent **Umi-kongō** (海金剛) rock formations along the eastern point of the island, shaped like pyramids and columns jutting out of the ocean.

If you're without your own transport, the best way to explore Kii-Ōshima is by renting a bicycle at **Kushimoto Station** (electric or pedal bicycles ¥1500 per day). Buses from the station are few and far between.

Misaki Lodge Youth Hostel (みさきロッジユースホステル; ☎0735-62-1474; fax 62-0529; 2864-1 Shionomisaki; dm/minshuku without meals per person ¥3780/5500, with 2 meals from ¥6580/8800; 📶) is way better than its name suggests. Honshu's southernmost inn has both hostel and *minshuku*-style accommodation, large Japanese-style ocean-view rooms, some with private toilet (all with shared bath) and a roof deck. Take a Shiono-misaki–bound bus from Kushimoto Station (20 minutes, hourly) and get off at Koroshio-mae.

Kushimoto is 50 minutes from Shirahama by JR *tokkyū* (¥1940) and 3½ hours (¥5940) from Shin-Osaka.

Nachi & Kii-Katsuura
那智・紀伊勝浦

The Nachi and Kii-Katsuura area has several sights grouped around sacred **Nachi-no-taki** (那智の滝), Japan's highest waterfall (133m). The Shintō shrine **Nachi Taisha** (那智大社), near the waterfall, was built in homage to the waterfall's *kami* (spirit god). It's one of the three great shrines of Kii-hantō, and worth the climb up the steep steps for the inspirational views cross the gorges to the waterfall and down to the Pacific.

Next to the shrine is the fine old temple **Sanseiganto-ji** (山青岸渡寺); the gong above the offering box in the main hall is the largest in Japan, a gift from Toyotomi Hideyoshi.

The most atmospheric approach to the falls and the shrine is the fantastic tree-lined arcade of **Daimon-zaka** (大門坂). To get to Daimon-zaka, take a bus from Nachi or Kii-Katsuura Station and get off at the Daimon-zaka stop (ask the bus driver to drop you at Daimon-zaka and he'll point you in the right direction from the stop). The way isn't marked in English, but it's roughly straight uphill just in from the road. From the bus stop to the shrine is roughly 800m, most of it uphill. It's fine in winter, but in summer you'll be a sweaty mess, so consider doing it in reverse (check bus schedules carefully before setting out).

Daimon-zaka takes you up to the steps at the base of the shrine. After visiting the shrine, walk down to the falls. At the base of the falls is **Nachiyama-oku-no-in** (那智山奥の院), where you can pay ¥300 to hike up to a lookout with a better view of the falls.

The **Nachi-no-Hi Matsuri** (Fire Festival) takes place at the falls on 14 July. During this lively event, *mikoshi* are brought down from the mountain and met by groups bearing flaming torches.

Buses to the waterfall and shrine leave from Nachi Station (¥470, 17 minutes) and Kii-Katsuura Station (¥600, 25 minutes). Buses to the Daimon-zaka stop leave from Nachi Station (¥330, 11 minutes) and from Kii-Katsuura Station (¥410, 19 minutes).

ℹ Getting There & Away

Nachi and Kii-Katsuura (two stops apart) can be reached by JR Kii main-line trains from Shin-Osaka Station (*tokkyū*, ¥6160, three hours and 45 minutes) and from Nagoya Station (*tokkyū*, ¥7200, three hours and 40 minutes).

Shingū 新宮

☎0735 / POP 31,398

The small city of Shingū on the east coast of Wakayama is a useful transport hub for access to the Kumano Kodō pilgrimage route and the onsen village of Hongū. There's a helpful **information office** (☎22-2840; ⏲9am-5.30pm) at the station. The end of the pilgrimage route is here, at **Kumano Hayatama Taisha** (熊野速玉大社), which dates from prehistory. The orange pavilions and lanterns stand in sharp contrast to the greenery all around. In town there's a stone staircase, where a 15-minute climb takes you to a larger stone where it is said that the gods originally descended, at Kamikura Shrine.

A two-minute walk north of the station, **Hase Ryokan** (長谷旅館; ☎0735-22-2185; fax 21-6677; 1-7-2 Isada-chō; r per person without meals from ¥4860, with 2 meals from ¥6480, no dinner served on Sun; @📶) is a reasonable choice, though it's ageing and has only Japanese-style toilets (some rooms have private facilities). Call from the station and someone will collect you. Cheap and cheerful **Kishu** (紀州; ☎0735-22-6599; r from ¥3500; 📶) calls itself a 'business hotel' but it's really a small, family run inn with futon bedding on tatami or carpeted floors. Rates rise for rooms with toilet and/or bath.

The JR Kii main line connects Shingū with Nagoya Station (*tokkyū*, ¥6870, three to 3½ hours) and Shin-Osaka Station (*tokkyū*, ¥6690, four hours).

There are buses between Shingū and Hongū, about half of which make a loop of the three surrounding onsen (Watarase, Yunomine and Kawa-yu).

Hongū 本宮

A Unesco World Heritage Site, Hongū is a good starting point for visiting the onsen nearby. The spiffy **Kumano Hongū Heritage Centre** (⏲9am-5pm) has detailed information in English about the sacred Kumano region. Amid rice paddies behind the heritage centre is Japan's largest *torii* (39.9m tall), made out of steel and painted dramatic black. Hongū is also home to **Kumano Hongū Taisha** (熊野本宮大社), one of the three famous shrines of the Kumano Sanzan, near Hongū Taisha-mae bus stop.

Blue Sky Guesthouse (蒼空げすとはうす; ☎42-0800; www.kumano-guesthouse.com/eng.html; 1526 Hongū, Hongū-chō; r per person incl breakfast from ¥6000, single travellers ¥7000; 📶) is an excellent, modern guesthouse with immaculate, comfortable rooms and lots of English-language sightseeing info. Its four Japanese rooms have private facilities. From the Hongū Information Centre, follow the main highway 10 minutes to the south end of town, and look for signs in English.

Hongū is served by infrequent buses from JR Gojō Station in the north (¥3200, four hours), Kintetsu Yamato-Yagi Station in the south (¥3950, five hours and 10 minutes), Kii-Tanabe in the west (¥2000, two hours) and Shingū in the southeast (¥1500, 60 to 80 minutes), which has the most departures of these three. Most Hongū buses also stop at Kawa-yu, Watarase and Yunomine onsen (in that order), but be sure to ask before boarding.

Since bus departures are limited, exploring the area by rental car is a good idea, Tanabe, Shirahama and Wakayama City are good locations.

Yunomine, Watarase & Kawa-yu Onsen

These three onsen are among Kansai's best, each with its own distinct character (worth doing a circuit). There are ryokan and *minshuku* in the area, but if you are on a tight budget it's possible to camp on the riverbanks around Kumano Hongū Taisha.

It's possible to walk among the three onsen. The tunnel at the west end of the village at Kawa-yu connects to Watarase Onsen (the total journey is a little less than 1km). From Watarase Onsen, it's about 3km west along Rte 311 to reach Yunomine.

Yunomine Onsen 湯峰温泉

The authentic, isolated village of Yunomine is nestled around a narrow river in a wooded valley. Most of the town's onsen are inside ryokan or *minshuku*, but charming little **Tsubo-yu Onsen** (つぼ湯温泉; admission ¥770; ⏲6am-10pm, enter by 9.30pm) is open to all. It's right in the middle of town, inside a tiny wooden shack built on an island in the river. Buy a ticket at the *sentō* (public bath) next to **Tōkō-ji** (東光寺), the temple in the middle of town, and it's yours for up to 30 minutes. The *sentō* itself is open the same hours as the onsen and entry is ¥250; of the two baths at the *sentō*, we suggest the *kusuri-yu* (medicine water; ¥380), which is 100% pure hot-spring water. Tsubo-yu Onsen admission also includes the *sentō*.

Sleeping

Yunomine has about a dozen *minshuku* and ryokan. If you're not eating in your inn, there's a public hot spring in town where people boil eggs, corn and more (a nearby shop sells them).

Minshuku Yunotanisō MINSHUKU ¥¥
(民宿湯の谷荘; ☎0735-42-1620; 168-1 Yunomine; r per person with 2 meals ¥8640) At the upper end of the village, this *minshuku* is exactly what a *minshuku* should be: simple, clean and welcoming. The food is good, and rooms have toilet and indoor baths, but be sure to visit the tiny rotemburo: *sweeeeet*!

Ryokan Yoshino-ya RYOKAN ¥¥
(旅館よしのや; ☎0735-42-0101; 359 Yunomine; r per person without meals/with 2 meals from ¥6090/9500, surcharge for solo travellers ¥1080/2160; Wi-fi) Set very close to Tsubo-yu, this is a slightly more upscale place with a lovely *rotemburo* (outdoor bath). It's fairly new, the owners are very friendly, and the location has gorgeous riverside views. Rooms have no private facilities. Wi-fi in the lobby.

Watarase Onsen わたらせ温泉

Built around a bend in the river, **Watarase Onsen** (わたらせ温泉; admission ¥700; ⏲6am-10pm, entry by 9.30pm) is basically one large onsen operation, but what an operation this collection of *rotemburo* is! Baths get progressively cooler as you work your way out from the inside bath.

Kawa-yu Onsen 川湯温泉

Kawa-yu Onsen is a natural wonder where geothermally heated water percolates up through the gravel banks of the river that runs through the middle of the town. You can make your own private bath here by digging out some of the stones and letting the hole fill with hot water; you can then spend the rest of the day jumping back and forth between the bath and the cool waters of the river. Admission is free and the best spots along the river are in front of Fujiya ryokan. We suggest bringing a bathing suit unless you fancy putting on a 'naked *gaijin* (foreigner)' show for the whole town.

In the winter, from December to 28 February, bulldozers are used to turn the river into a giant *rotemburo*. It's known as the **Sennin Buro** (仙人風呂; Thousand-person Bath; ⏲6.30am-10pm) FREE, though whether it holds 1000 people is anyone's guess.

Sleeping

Pension Ashita-no-Mori HOTEL ¥¥
(ペンションあしたの森; ☎0735-42-1525; www.ashitanomori.jp; 1440-2 Kawayu; r per person with meals from ¥10,950; Wi-fi) This Swiss chalet-style building sits across from the riverside hot springs. Shiny wood floors lead to adequate-sized rooms with facilities down the hall. It has its own private onsen bath, and indoor baths are onsen as well. Japanese dinners feature local Kumano beef.

★**Fujiya** RYOKAN ¥¥
(冨士屋; ☎0735-42-0007; www.fuziya.co.jp/english; r per person with meals from ¥16,350, solo surcharge ¥5000-10,000; Wi-fi) This upmarket ryokan features tasteful and spacious rooms, all with river views. There are some Western rooms too, usually an afterthought in most ryokan, but here they're actually beautiful with nature-theme design and private *rotemburo*.

ISE

☎0596 / POP 131,670

The Ise (伊勢) region, on Mie Prefecture's Shima Peninsula, is famous for Ise-jingū, Japan's most sacred Shintō shrine and one of its most impressive. Its only rival is Nikkō's Tōshō-gū, which is as gaudy as Ise-jingū is austere. Ise is easily reached from Nagoya, Kyoto or Osaka and makes a good two-day trip from any of these cities (you can even do it as a day trip from these cities if you take Kintetsu express trains). If you're wondering about how to pronounce Ise, it sounds like 'ee-say'.

Sights

Ise-jingū SHINTO SHRINE
(伊勢神宮, Ise Grand Shrine) Dating back to the 3rd century, Ise-jingū is Japan's most venerated Shintō shrine. It's in two parts: **Gekū** (外宮; Outer Shrine) and the more impressive **Naikū** (内宮; Inner Shrine, (p420), several kilometres away. According to tradition, shrine buildings are rebuilt every 20 years, with exact imitations on adjacent sites according to ancient techniques – no nails, only wooden dowels and interlocking joints. The present buildings were rebuilt in 2013.

Ise-Shima

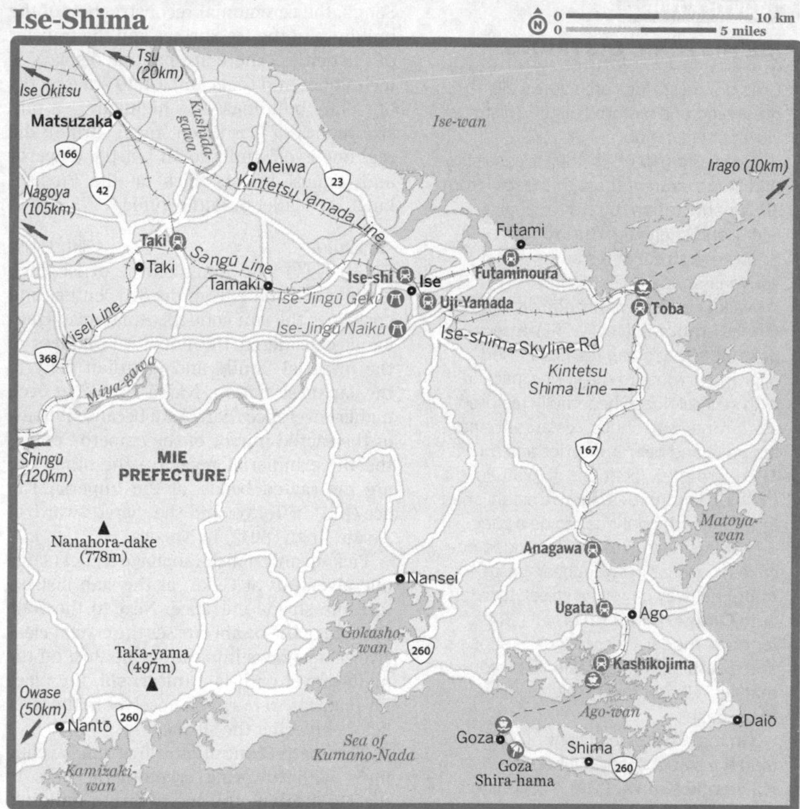

Upon completion of the new buildings, the god of the shrine is ritually transferred to its new home in the Sengū No Gi ceremony, first witnessed by Western eyes in 1953. The wood from the old shrine is then used to reconstruct the *torii* at the shrine's entrance or sent to shrines around Japan for use in rebuilding their structures.

The buildings are stunning examples of pre-Buddhist Japanese architecture, but you may be surprised to discover that the main shrine buildings are almost completely hidden from view behind wooden fences. Only members of the imperial family and certain shrine priests are allowed to enter the inner sanctum. Don't despair, though, as determined neck-craning over fences allows glimpses of the upper parts of buildings (at least if you're tall). You can get a good idea of the shrine's architecture at the new Sengūkan museum or at lesser shrines nearby, which are smaller scale replicas.

Gekū is an easy 10-minute walk from Ise-shi Station; Naikū is accessible by bus from the station or from the stop outside Gekū.

Smoking is prohibited throughout the grounds of both shrines, and photography is forbidden around their main halls. Many Japanese dress fairly neatly to visit the shrines. You might feel distinctly out of place in anything too casual but you don't have to dress formally – you can even wear shorts, but opt on the side of neatness.

Gekū SHINTO SHRINE

(外宮; sunrise-sunset) **FREE** Gekū, the Outer Shrine of Ise-jingū, dates from the 5th century and enshrines the god of food, clothing and housing, Toyouke-no-Ōkami. Daily offerings of rice are made by shrine priests to the deity, who is charged with providing food to Amaterasu-Ōmikami, the goddess enshrined in the Naikū. A stall at the entrance to the shrine provides a leaflet in English with a map.

WORTH A TRIP

ISE HISTORIC DISTRICTS

Outside the shrines are some well-preserved and restored historic districts worth checking out.

Gekū-sandō (外宮参道) is easiest to find; head straight through the *torii* from JR Ise-shi Station toward Ise-jingū's Gekū, and soon you'll be in a retro, Shōwa era street of restaurants and souvenir shops.

Naikū has its own historic district, **Oharai-machi** (おはらい町), a pedestrian street along the Edo Period pilgrimage route to the shrine, packed with several dozen beautifully restored storefronts with shops, restaurants, cafes, sake and beer breweries and more. There are a few locations of Akafuku (赤福), a landmark teahouse established in 1707, which continues to do a gangbuster business in *mochi* (pounded rice cakes) covered in sweet bean paste. About halfway down the street, turn left onto **Okage-yokochō** (おかげ横町), for more modern recreations of shops and a pavilion with occasional performances. Oharai-machi begins just left of Uji-bashi.

On the other side of central Ise, behind the stations, atmospheric **Kawasaki Kaiwai** (河崎界隈) is lined with traditional houses and shops. From the Ise Pearl Pier Hotel, take the side street by Eddy's Supermarket, and turn left about 50m before the canal. The old buildings begin about 200m north.

The main shrine building here is the Goshōden, about 10 minutes' walk from the shrine entrance.

Across the river from the Goshōden are three smaller shrines worth a look (and usually less crowded).

From Ise-shi Station or Uji-Yamada Station it's a 10-minute walk southwest down the main street, Gekū-sandō, to the shrine entrance. It's slightly easier to find if you start from Ise-shi Station (exit the south side).

Sengūkan MUSEUM

(遷宮館; ☎0596-22-6263; 126-1 Toyokawa-chō; admission ¥300; ⏲9am-4.30pm, closed 4th Tue each month) On the Gekū premises, this stunning new museum illustrates Shikinen-Sengū, the ceremonial reconstruction of the buildings of the Ise Shrines and the transfer of the deities. There are pristine displays of techniques and tools and a 1:20 scale model of Gekū's buildings. The highlight is a full-size replica of Goshōden (main shrine); the real one is off limits to all but the emperor and highest priests. Pick up the English-language leaflet or audio guide.

★Naikū SHINTO SHRINE

(内宮) FREE The Inner Shrine of Ise-jingū is thought to date from the 3rd century and enshrines the sun goddess, Amaterasu-Ōmikami, considered the ancestral goddess of the imperial family and guardian deity of the Japanese nation. Naikū is held in even higher reverence than Gekū because it houses the sacred mirror of the emperor, one of the three imperial regalia – the other two are the sacred beads, at the Imperial Palace (p75) in Tokyo, and the sacred sword, at Atsuta-jingū (p212) in Nagoya.

Pick up an English-language leaflet (same one given out at Gekū) at the stall just before the shrine entrance. Next to the stall, the bridge **Uji-bashi** crosses the crystal-clear river Isuzu-gawa into the shrine. Just off the main gravel path is a **mitarashi**, the place for pilgrims to purify themselves in the river before entering the shrine.

The path continues along an avenue lined with towering cryptomeria trees to the **Goshōden**, the main shrine building. As at Gekū, you can only catch a glimpse of the top of the structure from here, past four rows of wooden fences. Closed-circuit TV cameras not so cleverly disguised as trees keep an eye out for potential fence-jumpers!

To get to Naikū, take bus 51 or 55 from bus stop 11 outside Ise-shi Station's south exit (walk south on the main street) or the stop on the main road in front of Gekū (¥410, 15 to 20 minutes). Get off at the Naikū-mae stop. From Naikū, return buses depart from bus stop 2. Alternatively, taxi fare between Ise-shi Station and Naikū costs about ¥2000.

Festivals & Events

As Japan's most sacred shrine, it's not surprising that Ise-jingū's a favourite destination for *hatsu-mōde* (first shrine visit of the new year). Most of the action takes place in the first three days of the year, when millions of worshippers pack the area and accommodation is booked out for months in advance.

The **Kagura-sai**, celebrated in late April and mid-September, is a good chance to see performances of *kagura* (sacred dance), *bugaku* dance, *nō* and Shintō music.

Sleeping

★Ise Guest House Kazami HOSTEL ¥
(風見荘, Kazami-sō; ☎0596-64-8565; www.ise-guesthouse.com; 1-6-36 Fukiage; dm/s/d ¥2600/4000/6000; ⊖@🛜) This hostel may be budget, but it's got a chill, comfy handmade vibe thanks to wood paneling, driftwood 'trees' and whimsical murals. There are rental bikes (¥500 per day), and after sightseeing, relax in the lobby-turned-nighttime bar. Doors are locked at 11.30pm. It's a two-minute walk from JR Ise-shi Station.

Hoshide-kan RYOKAN ¥¥
(星出館; ☎0596-28-2377; www.hoshidekan.jp; 2-15-2 Kawasaki; s/d/tr ¥5350/10,500/15,575, with breakfast ¥6300/12,500/18,750; @🛜) A foreign travellers' favourite, this quaint, 10-room ryokan has heaps of traditional atmosphere, old woodwork and a central garden crisscrossed by a red bridge. No private facilities. From the Ise-shi station area, go straight past Ise City Hotel, and it's on the right at the second light (400m); look for the traditional building with cedars poking in tiny gardens.

Asakichi Ryokan RYOKAN ¥¥
(麻吉旅館; ☎0596-22-4101; fax 22-4102; 109 Nakano-chō; r per person with meals ¥12,920) This atmospheric six-room ryokan, partially dating from the late Edo Period, sits a short ride outside the city centre. There's a nice common bath and four rooms have en suite baths. Take bus 1 or 2 from stop 2 outside Uji-Yamada Station (toward Urata-chō) and get off at Nakano-chō. Taxis from the station cost about ¥1000.

Staff recommend reserving through a travel agent.

Ise Pearl Pier Hotel HOTEL ¥¥
(パールピアホテル; ☎0596-26-1111; www.pearlpier.com; 2-26-22 Miyajiri; s/d/tw ¥8100/16,200/17,280, deluxe s/tw ¥8640/19,400; @🛜) This pleasant, updated business hotel offers coin-op laundry machines, decent restaurants and a small sauna and common bath (¥540 extra). It's worth upgrading to 'deluxe' twin rooms for more space. It's a short walk from Ise-shi Station; request a room facing away from the tracks if you're sensitive to noise.

Eating & Drinking

★Butasute DONBURI ¥¥
(豚捨; ☎0596-23-8802; Okage-yokochō; gyū-don ¥1000; ⏲9am-6pm Apr-Sep, until 5pm Oct-Mar) This atmospheric local institution specialises in *gyū-don* (beef bowls), with the meat thinly sliced, simmered in hearty sauce with onions over rice. It's in the far left corner of Okage-yokochō. There's a new, second location by **Gekū** (⏲11am-9pm Mon-Sat, until 7pm Sun; gyū-don ¥870), next to Magatama-tei.

Sushi-kyū SUSHI ¥¥
(すし久; ☎0596-27-0229; Oharai-machi; teishoku ¥1190-2280; ⏲11am-7pm; 📄) This former ryokan in Oharai-machi oozes Edo Period charm, from its wooden floors to large tatami room. It serves the local speciality, *tekone sushi* – the bonito has been dipped in soy sauce before being placed atop rice in a bowl. The 'ume' set (¥1190) is usually enough for most people. It's on the right, just before the Okage-yokochō entrance.

Daiki SHOKUDŌ ¥¥
(大喜; ☎0596-28-0281; 2-1-48 Iwabuchi; meals from ¥1080; ⏲11am-9pm; 📄) Signage reading 'Japan's most famous restaurant' and 'Royal Family Endorsed' may be an exaggeration, but this is a polished place to sample seafood, including *ise-ebi* (Japanese lobsters, set meals from ¥5400). Simpler meals include sushi and a tempura *teishoku* (¥1620). Look for the wooden building outside and to the right of Uji-Yamada Station.

Magatama-tei BUFFET ¥¥
(勾玉亭; ☎0596-22-7788; 2fl, Hōon-kan (豊恩間), 1-1-31 Iwabuchi; lunch/dinner buffet ¥1620/2376; ⏲11am-2.30pm & 6-9pm) This new buffet restaurant serves some 25 dishes made from local ingredients. The market menu selection changes daily, but look for dishes like Ise *udon* and *tekone sushi*. Expect queues at peak times. Turn left near the Gekū end of Gekū-sandō, and look for the white building with 2nd floor balcony; it's above a local food products shop.

Information

Across the street from Naikū (about 10 minutes' walk from Ise-shi Station), **Ise Tourist Information Centre** (伊勢市観光協会; ☎0596-28-3705; ⏲8.30am-5pm) has the useful *Map of Ise* and can answer your questions and help you find accommodation. There are smaller information offices in both Ise-shi Station and Uji-Yamada Station.

Getting There & Away

There are two stations in Ise: Ise-shi Station and Uji-Yamada Station, only a few hundred metres apart (most trains stop at both). Ise-shi Station is the most useful stop for sights and accommodation.

Ise-shi is connected with Nagoya, Osaka and Kyoto on both the JR and the Kintetsu lines. With a Japan Rail Pass, best connections are via JR Nagoya Station (even if coming from Kyoto/Osaka; take a *shinkansen*) via JR *kaisoku* Mie train to Ise-shi Station (¥2000, 95 minutes).

Without a Japan Rail Pass, the Kintetsu line is most convenient, via comfortable, fast *tokkyū* trains. Kintetsu fares and travel times to/from Ise-shi include Nagoya (*tokkyū*, ¥2770, one hour and 20 minutes), Osaka (Uehonmachi or Namba stations, *tokkyū*, ¥3120, one hour and 46 minutes) and Kyoto (*tokkyū*, ¥3620, two hours).

NORTHERN KANSAI
関西北部

The spectacular coastline of northern Hyōgo and Kyoto Prefectures bursts with sandy beaches, rugged headlands, rocky islets and laid-back atmosphere. JR trains serve some destinations, but to really explore the coastline you'll want wheels: rental car, motorbike, bicycle or thumb.

Without a doubt, the best place to base yourself for exploration is the onsen town of Kinosaki, about 90 minutes from Himeji or two hours from Kyoto by comfortable JR express trains.

Kinosaki 城崎

0796 / POP 4134

In northern Hyōgo Prefecture, Kinosaki is one of Japan's best places to sample the classic onsen experience. A willow-lined canal runs through the town centre, and many of the houses, shops and restaurants retain their traditional charm. Add to this the delights of crab fresh from the Sea of Japan in winter, and you'll understand why this is one of our favourite overnight trips from the cities of Kansai.

Sights & Activities

Kinosaki's biggest attraction is its seven onsen. Overnight guests clip-clop around the canal from bath to bath wearing *yukata* (light cotton kimono) and *geta* (wooden sandals). Most ryokan and hotels in town have their own *uchi-yu* (private baths), but also provide their guests with free tickets to the public baths (*soto-yu*).

Visitors might want to peek at the **Kinosaki Mugiwarazaikudenshokan** (城崎麦わら細工伝承館; 376-1 Yushima; admission ¥300; 9am-5pm, closed Wed), which displays *mugiwarazaiku*, a local craft that employs barley straw cut into tiny pieces and applied to wood to form incredibly beautiful patterns. It's located off the canal, a short walk from Ichi-no-yu onsen.

You can get a map of Kinosaki's onsen from the information office or your lodging.

★Gosho-no-yu ONSEN
(御所の湯; admission ¥800; 7am-11pm, enter by 10.30pm, closed 1st & 3rd Thu) Lovely log construction, a nice two-level *rotemburo* and fine maple colours in autumn. The entry area is decorated like the Kyoto Gosho (Imperial Palace).

Sato-no-yu ONSEN
(さとの湯; admission ¥800; 1-9pm, enter by 8.40pm, closed Mon) Fantastic variety of baths, including Arab-themed saunas, rooftop *rotemburo* and a 'Penguin Sauna' (basically a walk-in freezer – good after a hot bath). Women's and men's baths shift floors daily, so you'll have to go two days in a row to sample all of the offerings.

Kou-no-yu ONSEN
(鴻の湯; admission ¥600; 7am-11pm, enter by 10.30pm, closed Tue) The main feature here is the *teien-buro* (garden bath) that feels like a formal Japanese garden.

Ichi-no-yu ONSEN
(一の湯; admission ¥600; 7am-11pm, enter by 10.30pm, closed Wed) While its main bath is showing its age, the 'cave' bath here is wonderful.

Yanagi-yu ONSEN
(柳湯; admission ¥600; 3-11pm, enter by 10.40pm, closed Thu) Worth a quick soak as you make your way around town. Nice wooden construction.

Mandara-yu ONSEN
(まんだら湯; admission ¥600; 3-11pm, enter by 10.40pm, closed Wed) This is a small wooden *rotemburo*.

Jizo-yu ONSEN
(地蔵湯; admission ¥600; 7am-11pm, enter by 10.40pm, closed Fri) It feels like an old-school *sentō* (public bath) with a spacious main in-

door tub, but no *rotemburo*. Good if others are crowded.

Sleeping

Ryokan Yamamotoya RYOKAN ¥¥
(旅館山本屋; 0796-32-2114; www.kinosaki.com; 835 Yushima, Kinosakichō; r per person incl meals from ¥13,650;) This fine ryokan is comfortable with foreign guests, and has lovely rooms, cosy indoor-outdoor baths and excellent food. It's roughly in the middle of town, near Ichi-no-yu onsen. Rooms have river or mountain views but no private bath (sink and toilet only). Solo travellers are accepted in the spring and autumn only and must pay a single supplement.

Suishōen RYOKAN ¥¥
(水翔苑; 0796-32-4571; www.suisyou.com/en; 1256 Momoshima; r per person without meals ¥6,480-15,876, with meals from ¥18,360;) This excellent, modern, 34-room ryokan boasts a great onsen with indoor and outdoor baths, a sauna and Japanese rooms with en suite bath, around a fabulous garden where *nō* plays are projected on a stage. Western-style rooms are also available. It's a short drive from the town centre, but they'll whisk you to and from the onsen of your choice in their own London taxi. It's a strangely pleasant feeling to ride in the back wearing only a *yukata*!

Mikuniya RYOKAN ¥¥
(三国屋; 0796-32-2414; www.kinosaki3928.com/english/index.htm; 221 Yushima; r per person without/with meals from ¥9,720/16,200;) With 12 rooms in a main building and annexe, this charming ryokan offers clean, freshly redecorated Japanese rooms with toilet and sink, soothing onsen baths and friendly, English-speaking owners. Wi-fi in main building only. It's about 150m on the right, on the street heading into town from the station.

Tsuruya RYOKAN ¥¥
(つるや; 0796-32-2924; www.kinosaki-tsuruya.com/english.html; 606 Yushima; r per person without/with meals from ¥6830/11,550) A few metres before Kou-no-yu onsen (as you approach from the station), this simple ryokan is comfortable with foreign guests. The rooms are plain but sufficient (most don't have private bath or toilet) and the helpful manager speaks some English.

★ **Nishimuraya Honkan** RYOKAN ¥¥¥
(西村屋本館; 0796-32-2211; www.nishimuraya.ne.jp/honkan/english; 469 Yushima; r per person incl 2 meals from ¥30,390, solo travellers from ¥45,510;) Now in its seventh generation, this luxurious hot spring inn is the real deal. Its maze-like layout lends a sense of privacy, the two onsen baths are exquisite, most rooms look out over private gardens, and there's a private gallery of art and historical artifacts. Seasonal *kaiseki* (Japanese haute cuisine) meals are the final touch.

Eating

Crab (*kani*) from the Sea of Japan is a speciality in Kinosaki during the winter months, best enjoyed in *kani-suki* (crab *sukiyaki* in a sake, soy and vinegar broth), cooked at your table with vegetables. Many restaurants in Kinosaki shut down early as most visitors opt for the two-meal option at their accommodation. You should consider doing the same, at least during *kani* season.

Gubigabu PUB ¥¥
(グビガブ; 79 Yushima; mains ¥650-2700; 11am-6pm, closed Wed;) This new craft-beer pub near the town centre serves a diverse menu from pastas, *jidori* (local chicken) and curry rice to beer snacks to accompany the house brews.

Koyume IZAKAYA ¥¥
(こ夢; 0796-32-2695; 691 Yushima; dishes ¥130-1300; 11.30am-2.30pm Nov-Mar, 5.30-11pm year-round) Rub shoulders with locals at this kindly, tiny *izakaya*, over a varied menu including *kani-kamameshi* (crab over steamed rice), *kushikatsu* (fried skewers), *moro-kyu* (cucumber with sweet miso), and plenty of sake. There are a few counter seats and *hori-kotatsu* (well-in-the-floor) seating. Order using pictures on the Japanese menu. It's on the small street behind Jizo-yu and Yanagi-yu.

Daikō Shōten SEAFOOD ¥¥
(大幸商店; 0796-32-3684; 130 Yushima; dishes ¥350-2500; 10am-9pm, to 11pm mid-Apr–Oct;) This seafood shop and *izakaya* serves up freshly caught local seafood fried, grilled, sauteed or raw in a casual atmosphere. The speciality, *kaisen-don* (seafood over rice), is ¥1480 to ¥2500, or you'll never go wrong asking for the master's *osusume* (recommendations). It's diagonally across from Mikuniya; look for the blue awning and fish photos.

Orizuru SUSHI ¥¥

(をり鶴; ☎0796-32-2203; 396 Yushima; meals ¥1250-5700; ⏰11am-2pm & 5-9.30pm, closed Tue; 📋) For decent sushi and crab dishes, try this popular local restaurant on the main street. You can get a *jō-nigiri* (superior sushi set; ¥3700) or try the crab dishes in winter. It's between Ichi-no-yu and Gosho-no-yu, on the opposite side of the street.

Caffe Sorella CAFE

(カフェ ソレッラ; ☎0796-32-2059; 84 Yushima; coffee from ¥340; ⏰9.30am-5.30pm, closed irregularly; 📶) This simple coffee shop, about 75m north of Kinosaki Station on the main street, is a good place for a cuppa, nice brownies and an internet fix (there's free wi-fi if you order a drink). Order from the picture menu.

ℹ Information

Opposite the station is an **accommodation information office** (お宿案内所; ☎0796-32-4141; ⏰9am-6pm), where the staff will gladly help you find a place to stay and make bookings, as well as provide maps of the town. The same office has rental bicycles available for ¥400 for two hours and ¥800 per day (return by 5pm).

ℹ Getting There & Away

Kinosaki is on the JR San-in line and there are a few daily *tokkyū* from Kyoto (¥4320, two hours and 25 minutes), Osaka (¥5080, two hours and 40 minutes) and Himeji (¥3340, one hour and 45 minutes).

Takeno 竹野

Takeno (population about 5000) is a pleasant little fishing village and summer resort with two good sandy beaches: **Takeno-hama** (竹野浜) and **Benten-hama** (弁天浜). For Takeno-hama, go straight out of the station and walk for around 20 minutes. There is an **information office** (☎0796-47-1080; ⏰8.30am-5pm, closed Sun Sep-Jun) on the beachfront in an orange brick building, which can help with accommodation at local inns in the village of charred-wood homes, and suggest sea kayaking, snorkeling and hiking opportunities. Nearby, **Kitamaekan** (北前館; ☎0796-47-2020; onsen adult/child ¥600/350; ⏰10am-9pm) is an onsen complex; baths on the 2nd floor have a great view of the beach and sea.

For Benten-hama, exit Takeno Station, turn left at the first light and walk straight for about 15 minutes (there's a small supermarket en route). Here you'll find **Benten-hama Camping Area** (弁天浜キャンプ場; ☎0796-47-0888; campsites ¥3500, free spaces ¥500 per person, tent charge ¥1000; ⏰daily Jul & Aug, Sat & Sun May, Jun, Sep & Oct), a decent, if crowded, spot to pitch a tent.

Takeno Station is on the JR San-in line, an easy trip from Kinosaki (¥200, nine minutes).

Tango Peninsula 丹後半島

The **Tango-hantō** juts up into the Sea of Japan on the north coast of Kyoto Prefecture. The interior of the peninsula is covered with thick forest, terraced farms, idyllic mountain villages and babbling streams, while the serrated coast alternates between good sandy beaches, gumdrop-shaped islands and rocky points.

The private Kita-kinki Tango Tetsudō rail line runs between Toyooka and Nishi-Maizuru, cutting across the southern base of the peninsula and stopping en route at Amanohashidate. To reach the rest of the peninsula, you'll have to go by road; we suggest renting a car from Kinosaki. Follow the coastal Route 178 around the peninsula for truly spectacular scenery. Along the way, you can stop for a dip at beautiful **Kotobiki-hama Beach** (琴引浜; campsites ¥3000) in the town of Amino. About 16km further is **Ukawa Onsen Yoshino-no-Sato** (宇川温泉 よし野の里; www.ukawaonsen.jp; Kyusō; bathing ¥600, restaurant meals ¥970-1620; ⏰11am-9pm, additional summer hours), a fine hot-spring complex built like a contemporary farmhouse with views down to the sea; its restaurant serves casual meals made from local produce.

About 4km further on, the northernmost point of the Tango Peninsula is **Cape Kyōga-misaki** (経ヶ岬). A car park marks the start of the 0.4km hike to the **Kyōga-misaki Lighthouse** (経ヶ岬灯台) at the end of this cape (though the scenery doesn't really compare with the coast to the west).

On the eastern side of the Tango-hantō, the village of **Ine** (伊根) sits on a perfect little bay where boats moor as if in car ports under special houses called *funaya*, built right over the water. See them up close on a 30-minute boat tour by **Ine-wan Meguri** (伊根湾めぐり; ☎0772-42-0321; ¥680; ⏲9am-4pm Mar-Dec). Buses (¥400, about 55 minutes, hourly) connect Ine with Amanohashidate Station.

Amanohashidate 天橋立

☎0772 / POP 19,808 (MIYAZU CITY)

Amanohashidate (the Bridge to Heaven) is rated as one of Japan's 'three great views'. The 'bridge' is really a long, narrow, tree-covered (8000 pine trees) sand spit, 3.5km in length. There is decent swimming, as well as beach showers, toilet facilities and covered rest areas, the length of the spit. It's a good example of a Japanese tourist circus, but it is pleasant enough.

The town of Amanohashidate consists of two separate parts, one at each end of the spit. At the southern end are a number of hotels, ryokan and restaurants, a popular temple and Amanohashidate Station. There's an **information counter** (☎22-8030; ⏲9am-6pm) at the station. To reach the bridge from the station, take a right out of the station, walk along the main road for 200m to the first light and take a sharp left.

Sleeping & Eating

There's a cluster of restaurants near the southern end of the bridge, most with plastic food models in the windows, serving the local speciality of *asari udon* (clams in noodle soup, around ¥1000) and *shokudō* staples.

Amanohashidate Youth Hostel HOSTEL ¥
(天橋立ユースホステル; ☎0772-27-0121; r per person without/with meals ¥3050/4650; @ Wi-Fi) This fine hostel has good views toward Amanohashidate, friendly owners, well-kept Japanese-style dorm rooms with shared bath, a simple communal kitchen and an excellent hillside location.

Take a bus (¥400, 20 minutes) from Amanohashidate Station and get off at Jinja-mae. At the shrine's main hall, take a right, leave the shrine precinct, turn left up the hill and walk 50m, then take a right and follow the sign for Manai Shrine. Turn at the stone *torii*, walk 200m uphill and it's on the right.

Getting There & Away

Amanohashidate Station is on the Kita-kinki Tango Tetsudō line; best connections to JR stations are Fukuchiyama (*tokkyū*, ¥1520, 35 minutes; *futsū* ¥770, one hour) to the west and Nishi-Maizuru (*futsū*, ¥640, 40 minutes) to the east. There are some direct trains from Kyoto daily via Fukuchiyama (¥3880, two hours), although Japan Rail pass holders will have to fork out ¥1380/1480 for non-reserved/reserved seats for the non-JR part of the route.

Getting Around

You can cross Amanohashidate on foot, by bicycle or on a motorcycle of less than 125cc capacity. Bicycles can be hired at a number of places for ¥400 for two hours or ¥1600 per day.

Maizuru 舞鶴

The ports of Nishi-Maizuru and Higashi-Maizuru are an important transporation hub. Trains from the JR Obama line meet the Kita-kinki Tango Tetsudō railway at Nishi-Maizuru Station; change trains here for Amanohashidate. **Shin-Nihonkai Ferry** (☎06-6345-3881; www.snf.jp) connects Higashi-Maizuru and Otaru in Hokkaidō (2nd class ¥9570, 20 hours). If you have some time to kill, go to **Goro Sky Tower** (五老スカイタワー; 237 Kureya, Ueyasu, Gorogadake Park; admission ¥200; ⏲9am-5pm Dec-Mar, 9am-9pm Apr-Nov), about 6.5km from Nishi-Maizuru Station by car; the inspirational views have been voted among Kansai's best (and you can see them even without paying to enter the tower).

Hiroshima & Western Honshū

Includes ➡

Best Islands

- ➡ Naoshima (p460)
- ➡ Miyajima (p438)
- ➡ Oki Islands (p484)
- ➡ Shiraishi-jima (p464)
- ➡ Ōmi-shima (p447)

Best Historic Sites

- ➡ Itsukushima-jinja (p438)
- ➡ Izumo Taisha (p485)
- ➡ Atomic Bomb Dome (p427)
- ➡ Iwami Ginzan silver mine (p487)
- ➡ Matsue-jō (p481)

Why Go?

Travellers to Western Honshū (本州西部) will find two contrasting coastlines. San-yō (literally 'sunny side of the mountains'), looking out over the Inland Sea, boasts the bigger cities, the narrow-laned portside and hillside towns, ceramic history and the bullet train. This is the coast that holds the region's big name – indelibly scarred, thriving, warm-hearted Hiroshima.

On the other side of the dividing Chūgoku mountain range, San-in (literally 'in the shade of the mountains') gazes out across the expanse of the Sea of Japan. Up here, it's all about an unhurried pace, onsen villages that see few foreigners, historic sites, wind-battered coastlines and great hospitality.

Head inland for hikes along gorges and through caves. Or you can escape the mainland altogether – to the Inland Sea and its galaxy of islands, or to the remote and rugged Oki-shotō in the Sea of Japan.

When to Go

Hiroshima

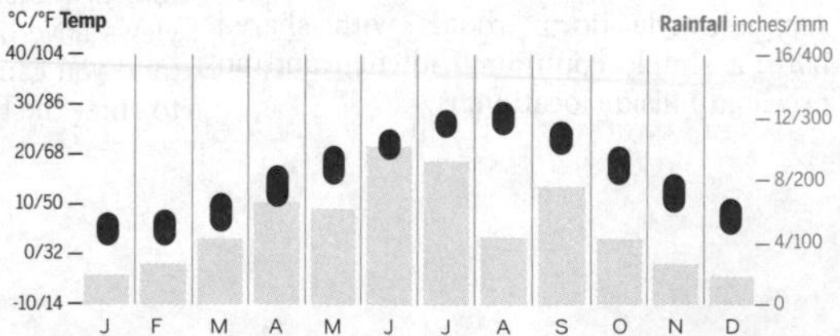

Mar–May & Sep–Nov Mild and photogenic, spring and autumn get most of the attention.

Jul–Sep Beach weather draws crowds to the Inland Sea islands and the Sea of Japan coast.

Aug Hiroshima remembers 6 August with services and a river full of lanterns.

Getting Around

The *shinkansen* (bullet train), linking Osaka and Kyoto with Okayama, Hiroshima and other cities on the way to Shimonoseki, is the fastest way to get around along the Inland Sea coast of Western Honshū. Along the Sea of Japan the *shinkansen* is not an option. Trains operate all the way from Tottori to Hagi, hugging some beautiful rugged coastline on the way, but services are generally infrequent and it's hard to avoid the slow 'local' services. If you're really in a hurry up here (and to get way off the beaten track), it's worth hiring a car. There are few train and bus lines servicing inland destinations – the major rail link between the two coasts runs between Okayama and Yonago.

HIROSHIMA & AROUND

Hiroshima 広島

082 / POP 1,187,000

To most people, Hiroshima means just one thing. The city's name will forever evoke thoughts of 6 August 1945, when Hiroshima became the target of the world's first atomic-bomb attack. Hiroshima's Peace Memorial Park is a constant reminder of that day, and it attracts visitors from all over the world. But leafy Hiroshima, with its wide boulevards and laid-back friendliness, is a far from depressing place. Present-day Hiroshima is home to a thriving and internationally minded community, and it's worth spending a couple of nights here to experience the city at its vibrant best.

Sights

★Atomic Bomb Dome HISTORIC SITE

(原爆ドーム, Genbaku Dome; Genbaku-dōmu-mae) Perhaps the starkest reminder of the destruction visited upon Hiroshima in WWII is the Atomic Bomb Dome. Built by a Czech architect in 1915, it was the Industrial Promotion Hall until the bomb exploded almost directly above it. Everyone inside was killed, but the building was one of very few left standing near the epicentre. A decision was taken after the war to preserve the shell as a memorial.

The building has since become a haunting symbol of the city, and was declared a Unesco World Heritage Site in 1996. Try to wander past in the evening when it's quiet and the propped-up ruins are floodlit.

Peace Memorial Park PARK

(平和記念公園; Heiwa-kinen-kōen; Genbaku-dōmu-mae) Hugged by rivers on both sides, Peace Memorial Park is a large, leafy space criss-crossed by walkways and dotted with memorials. Its central feature is the long tree-lined Pond of Peace leading to the **cenotaph** (原爆死没者慰霊碑). This curved concrete monument holds the names of all the known victims of the bomb. Also at the pond is the **Flame of Peace** (平和の灯), set to burn on until all the world's nuclear weapons are destroyed.

Look through the cenotaph down the pond and you'll see it frames the Flame of Peace and the Atomic Bomb Dome across the river – the park was planned so that these features form a straight line, with the Peace Memorial Museum at its southern end.

Just north of the road through the park is the **Children's Peace Monument**, inspired by Sadako Sasaki, who was two years old at the time of the atomic bomb. When Sadako developed leukaemia at 11 years of age, she decided to fold 1000 paper cranes. In Japan, the crane is the symbol of longevity and happiness, and she believed if she achieved that target she would recover. She died before reaching her goal, but her classmates folded the rest. A monument was built in 1958. Sadako's story inspired a nationwide spate of paper-crane folding that continues to this day. Surrounding the monument are strings of thousands of colourful paper cranes sent here from school children around the country and all over the world.

Nearby is the **Korean Atomic Bomb Victims Memorial** (韓国人原爆犠牲者慰霊碑). Many Koreans were shipped over to work as slave labourers during WWII, and Koreans accounted for more than one in 10 of those killed by the atomic bomb. Just north of this memorial is the **Atomic Bomb Memorial Mound** – the ashes of thousands of unclaimed or unidentified victims are interred in a vault below.

There are other monuments and statues throughout the park, and plenty of benches, including along the riverside looking across to the Atomic Bomb Dome, making this a pleasant area to take a break and reflect.

★Hiroshima Peace Memorial Museum MUSEUM

(広島平和記念資料館; www.pcf.city.hiroshima.jp; 1-2 Nakajima-chō, Naka-ku; admission ¥50; 8.30am-5pm, to 6pm Mar-Nov, to 7pm Aug; Genbaku-dōmu-mae or Chūden-mae) The main

Hiroshima & Western Honshū Highlights

1. Reflecting on a tragic past in cosmopolitan **Hiroshima** (p427).
2. Gaining a new perspective at the art installations and museums of **Naoshima** (p460).
3. Photographing the floating shrine and staying at a ryokan on **Miyajima** (p438).
4. Island-hopping by bicycle via the **Shimanami Kaidō** (p445) to Shikoku.
5. Walking through the shrine gates of **Taikodani-Inari-jinja** (p469) in the mountain town of Tsuwano.

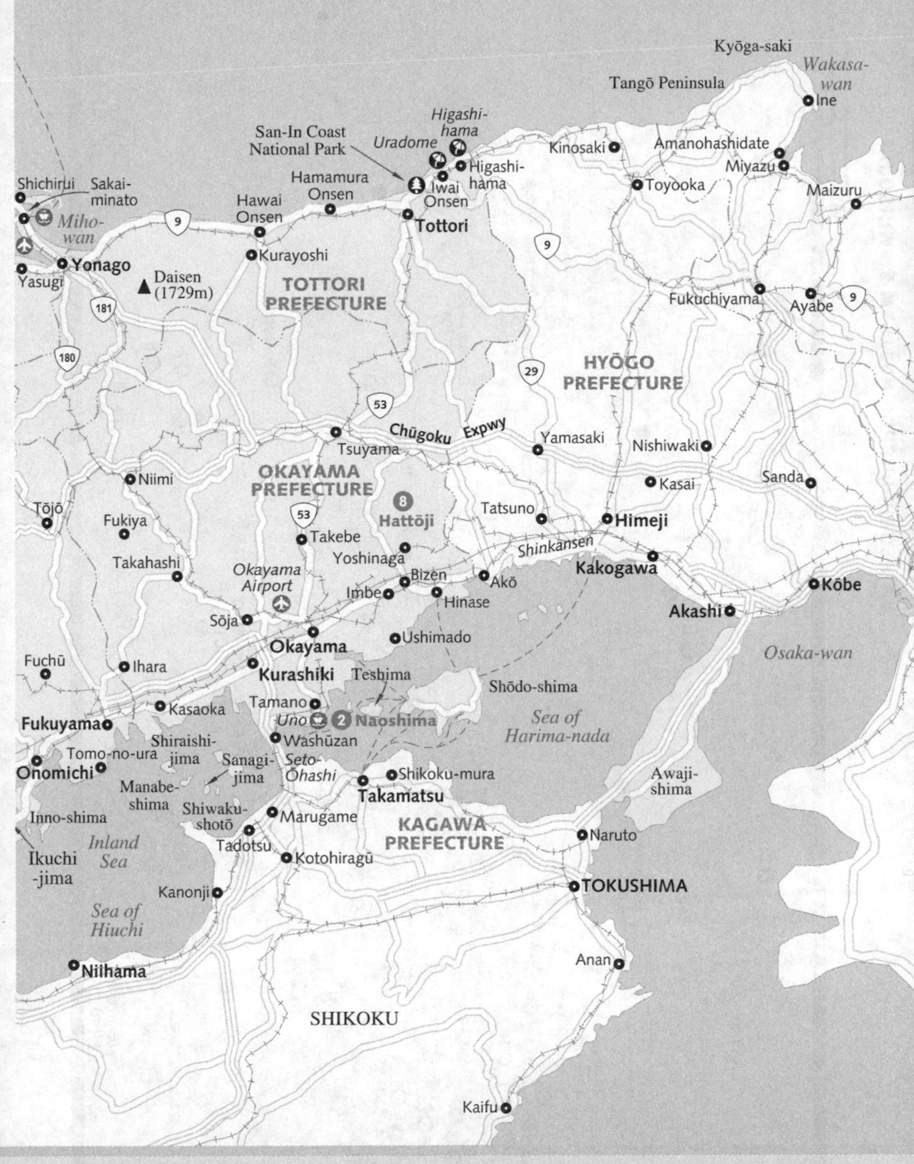

6 Seeing where the gods go on holiday at **Izumo Taisha** (p485).

7 Getting way off the beaten track in the nature- and culture-rich **Oki Islands** (p484).

8 Spending a night in a restored farmhouse in the hills at **Hattōji** (p451).

9 Strolling around the moated castle before a gorgeous sunset in **Matsue** (p480).

10 Exploring the World Heritage **Iwami Ginzan silver mine district** (p487).

Hiroshima

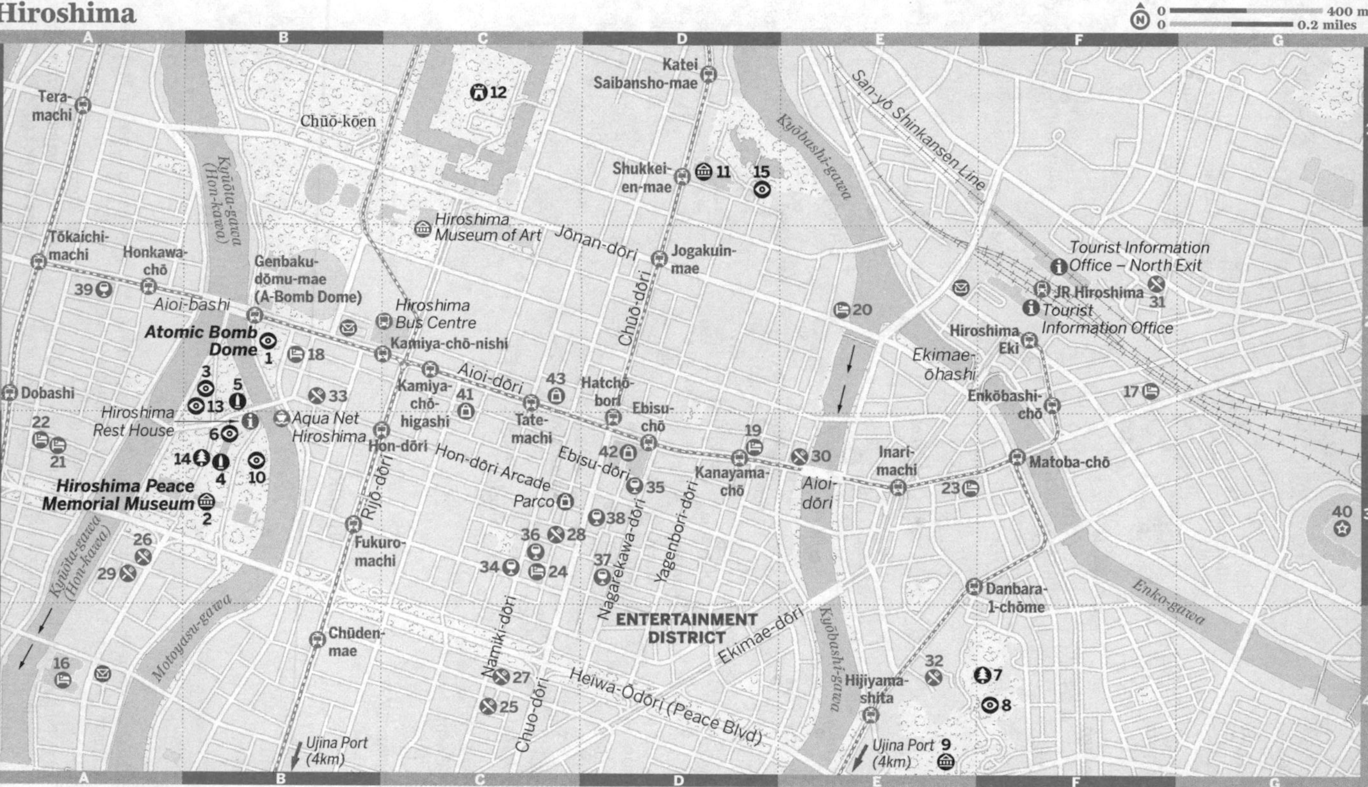

0 400 m
0 0.2 miles
Tera-machi
Chūō-kōen
12
Katei Saibansho-mae
San-yō Shinkansen Line
Kyōbashi-gawa
Kyūōta-gawa (Hon-kawa)
Shukkei-en-mae
11
15
Hiroshima Museum of Art
Jōnan-dōri
Jogakuin-mae
Tourist Information Office – North Exit
Tōkaichi-machi
Honkawa-chō
Genbaku-dōmu-mae (A-Bomb Dome)
39
JR Hiroshima
31
Aioi-bashi
Hiroshima Bus Centre
Chūō-dōri
20
Tourist Information Office
Atomic Bomb Dome
1
18
Kamiya-chō-nishi
Hiroshima Eki
Ekimae-ōhashi
3
5
Aioi-dōri
43
Hatchō-bori
17
Dobashi
33
Kamiya-chō-higashi
41
Ebisu-chō
Enkōbashi-chō
13
Hiroshima Rest House
Aqua Net Hiroshima
Tate-machi
22
6
19
21
Hon-dōri
Hon-dōri Arcade
42
30
Inari-machi
Matoba-chō
14
10
4
Ebisu-dōri
35
Kanayama-chō
Hiroshima Peace Memorial Museum
2
Parco
Aioi-dōri
23
40
26
Rijō-dōri
36
28
38
Yagenbori-dōri
Fukuro-machi
34
24
37
29
Nagarekawa-dōri
Kyūōta-gawa (Hon-kawa)
Danbara-1-chōme
Motoyasu-gawa
Enko-gawa
ENTERTAINMENT DISTRICT
Chūden-mae
Ekimae-dōri
16
Kyōbashi-gawa
32
7
Namiki-dōri
27
Heiwa-Ōdōri (Peace Blvd)
Hijiyama-shita
8
25
Chuo-dōri
Ujina Port (4km)
Ujina Port (4km)
9
A B C D E F G
1 2 3 4

Hiroshima

Top Sights
1 Atomic Bomb Dome B2
2 Hiroshima Peace Memorial Museum ... B3

Sights
3 Atomic Bomb Memorial Mound B2
4 Cenotaph B3
5 Children's Peace Monument B2
6 Flame of Peace B3
7 Hijiyama-kōen F4
8 Hiroshima City Manga Library F4
9 Hiroshima City Museum of Contemporary Art E4
10 Hiroshima National Peace Memorial Hall for the Atomic Bomb Victims B3
11 Hiroshima Prefectural Art Museum D1
12 Hiroshima-jō C1
13 Korean Atomic Bomb Victims Memorial B2
14 Peace Memorial Park B3
15 Shukkei-en D1

Sleeping
16 Aster Plaza International Youth House A4
17 Hana Hostel F2
18 Hiroshima Inn Aioi B2
19 Hotel Active Hiroshima D3
20 Hotel Flex E2
21 Ikawa Ryokan A3
22 J-Hoppers Hiroshima A3
23 K's House Hiroshima E3
24 Sera Bekkan C3

Eating
25 Bakudanya C4
26 Chari A3
27 Hassei C4
28 Okonomi-mura C3
29 Osanpo Masara A3
30 Oyster Conclave Kaki-tei E3
31 Roopali F2
32 Tōshō E4
33 Zucchini B2

Drinking & Nightlife
34 Koba C3
35 Kuro-sawa D3
36 Lotus C3
37 Mac D3
38 Molly Malone's D3
39 Organza A2

Entertainment
40 Mazda Zoom Zoom Stadium G3

Shopping
41 Global Lounge C2
42 Mitsukoshi D3
43 Tokyu Hands C2

building of Hiroshima's premier museum houses a collection of items salvaged from the aftermath of the atomic bomb. The displays are confronting and personal – ragged clothes, a child's melted lunch box, a watch stopped at 8.15am – and there are some grim photographs. While upsetting, it's a must-see in Hiroshima. The east building presents a history of Hiroshima and the development and destructive power of nuclear weapons.

The museum is undergoing major renovations. The east building will be closed until spring 2016, at which point the main building will close until a 2018 grand reopening. During its closure, some items from the main building will be on display in the east building. Check the website for the latest developments.

Hiroshima National Peace Memorial Hall for the Atomic Bomb Victims MEMORIAL
(国立広島原爆死没者追悼平和祈念館; www.hiro-tsuitokinenkan.go.jp; 1-6 Nakajima-chō, Naka-ku; 8.30am-6pm Mar-Nov, to 5pm Dec-Feb, to 7pm Aug; Genbaku-dōmu-mae or Hon-dōri) FREE A softly lit internal walkway leads down into this cool, contemplative space, where the walls show a circular panorama of Hiroshima and the names of its neighbourhoods at the time of the atomic bomb. The fountain at the centre represents the moment the bomb was dropped (8.15am), while the water offers relief to the victims. An adjoining room shows the names and photographs of those who perished. Before leaving, it's well worth taking time to watch the evocative testimonies from survivors.

The memorial hall was built by architect Tange Kenzō, who also designed the Peace Museum, cenotaph and flame.

Shukkei-en GARDENS
(縮景園; 2-11 Kami-nobori-chō, Naka-ku; admission ¥260; 9am-6pm Apr-Sep, to 5pm Oct-Mar; Shukkei-en-mae) Modelled after West Lake in Hangzhou, China, Shukkei-en was built in 1620 for *daimyō* (domain lord) Asano Nagaakira. The garden's name means 'contracted view', and it attempts to re-create grand vistas in miniature. Pathways lead through a series of 'landscapes' and views around an island-dotted pond.

Shukkei-en was destroyed by the bomb, though many of the trees and plants survived to blossom again the following year, and the park and its buildings have long since been restored to their original splendour.

Hiroshima Prefectural Art Museum GALLERY
(広島県立美術館; www.hpam.jp; 2-22 Kami-nobori-chō, Naka-ku; admission ¥510; 9am-5pm Tue-Sun; Shukkei-en-mae) Next to the Shukkei-en garden is the Hiroshima Prefectural Art Museum, featuring Salvador Dalí's *Dream of Venus* and the artwork of Hirayama Ikuo, who was in the city during the atomic bombing. The ground floor has a large light lounge area with floor-to-ceiling windows and garden views.

Hiroshima-jō CASTLE
(広島城, Hiroshima Castle; 21-1 Moto-machi; admission ¥370; 9am-6pm, to 5pm Dec-Feb; Kamiya-chō) Also known as Carp Castle (Rijō; 鯉城), Hiroshima-jō was originally constructed in 1589, but much of it was dismantled following the Meiji Restoration. What remained was totally destroyed by the bomb and rebuilt in 1958. There's a small museum with historical items, but most impressive is the moat, and the surrounding park is a pleasant place for a stroll.

Hijiyama-kōen PARK
(比治山公園; Hijiyama-shita) Hijiyama-kōen is a hilly tree-filled park just outside Hiroshima city centre. It's noted for its cherry blossoms in spring and its autumn foliage, and is a top spot for a stroll. It's also home to the Hiroshima City Museum of Contemporary Art, and the Hiroshima City Manga Library.

Take the number 5 tram (for Hiroshima Port), or walk about 20 minutes south of JR Hiroshima Station. The Hiroshima sightseeing loop bus also stops here.

Hiroshima City Museum of Contemporary Art GALLERY
(広島市現代美術館, MOCA; www.hiroshima-moca.jp; 1-1 Hijiyama-kōen; admission ¥360, more for special exhibitions; 10am-5pm Tue-Sun; Hijiyama-shita) Fans of contemporary art should drop into this modern museum in Hijiyama-kōen, where the exhibits change regularly and may include anything from large-scale installations to video. Outside is a sculpture garden. Check ahead before your visit as there are sometimes special exhibitions.

Hiroshima City Manga Library LIBRARY
(広島市まんが図書館; 082-261-0330; www.library.city.hiroshima.jp/manga; 1-4 Hijiyama-kōen; 10am-5pm Tue-Sun; Hijiyama-shita) An obvious pit stop for manga (Japanese comics) enthusiasts, this library has a small section of foreign-language manga and a collection of vintage and rare manga. Grab the English-language pamphlet and head up to the 2nd floor.

Mazda Museum MUSEUM
(マツダミュージアム; 082-252-5050; www.mazda.com/about/museum; closed Sat, Sun & holidays) FREE Mazda is popular for the chance to see the impressive 7km assembly line. English-language tours (90 minutes) are available at 10am weekdays, but it's best to check the website or at the tourist office for the current times. Reservations are required and can be made online or by phone.

The museum is a short walk from JR Mukainada (向洋) Station, two stops from Hiroshima on the San-yō line

Naka Incineration Plant ARCHITECTURE
(環境局中工場, Kankyō-kyoku Naka Kōjō; 1-5-1 Minami-Yoshijima, Naka-ku; 9am-4pm) FREE Exploring a garbage-processing plant might not sound appealing, but if you're an architecture fan this building is worth a visit. The waterfront building is an imposing sleek-lined glass-and-metal construction designed by Taniguchi Yoshio, architect of the MoMA redesign in New York. Don't miss the tree-lined central atrium, the Ecorium, where you can see the surprisingly clean and quiet internal workings of the plant. Head up to the level 6 viewing gallery for views across the water.

Visitors can walk through the Ecorium and the viewing gallery independent-

HIROSHIMA READING

- *Hiroshima* (1946) by John Hersey – book of the article by Pulitzer Prize–winning writer
- *Hiroshima: Three Witnesses* (1990), edited by Richard H Minear – translation of first-hand accounts of three authors
- *Black Rain* (1965) by Masuji Ibuse – a novel depicting the lives of those who survived
- *Sadako & the Thousand Paper Cranes* (1977) by Eleanor Coerr – aimed at younger readers, based on the true story of Sadako Sasaki

ly. There are information panels dotted around, and the office on level 6 can give you a pamphlet. To get to the plant, take bus 24 for Yoshijima Eigyō-sho and get off at Minami-Yoshijima (¥220, 20 minutes). Walk back to the intersection and turn right. You won't smell garbage in the area, but you may get a waft of *furikake* (seasoning) from a nearby factory.

Festivals & Events

Peace Memorial Ceremony MEMORIAL SERVICE
On 6 August, the anniversary of the atomic bombing, a memorial service is held in Peace Memorial Park and thousands of paper lanterns for the souls of the dead are floated down the Kyūōta-gawa from in front of the Atomic Bomb Dome.

Sleeping

Hiroshima's accommodation is clustered around the station, near Peace Memorial Park, and along the main thoroughfares of Aioi-dōri and Heiwa-Ōdōri, but the city is compact enough so that wherever you base yourself you're never more than a short walk or tram ride away from the main sights.

★Hana Hostel HOSTEL ¥
(広島花宿; 082-263-2980; http://hiroshima.hanahostel.com; 1-15 Kojin-machi; dm/tw from ¥2500/6400;) Hana has a choice of Japanese- or Western-style private rooms, some with private toilet or full (very small) en suite. Cosy lamp lighting and traditional decoration make the tatami rooms the best pick. The only downside for light sleepers is occasional street and train noise. Solo travellers can book a private room at the cost of a twin.

From the station south exit go immediately left along the train tracks, continue past the railway crossing (not over it) and turn right. It's opposite the temple.

★K's House Hiroshima HOSTEL ¥
(ケイズハウス広島; 082-568-7244; www.kshouse.jp/hiroshima-e; 1-8-9 Matoba-chō; dm/s/tw from ¥2600/4800/7400; ; Matoba-chō) K's House has a great location not far from the station. There are small dorms and comfortable tatami rooms with shared shower rooms, or pay a little more for a room with bed and en suite. The kitchen-lounge is modern and a good size, there's a rooftop terrace, and staff are helpful.

The entrance is at the back of the block – turn left off Aioi-dōri to find it.

J-Hoppers Hiroshima HOSTEL ¥
(ジェイホッパーズ広島ゲストハウス; 082-233-1360; http://hiroshima.j-hoppers.com; 5-16 Dobashi-chō; dm/tw from ¥2500/6000; ; Dobashi) This popular old favourite near the Peace Park feels more like someone's house than a standard hostel. The rooms and common areas are small, but it's a cosy place with a friendly crew. There are both dorm beds and private tatami rooms. Singles come at the price of a twin.

Ikawa Ryokan RYOKAN ¥
(いかわ旅館; 082-231-5058; www.ikawaryokan.net; 5-11 Dobashi-chō; s/tw without bathroom ¥4860/8640, with bathroom ¥5940/9720; ; Dobashi) On a quiet side street, this is a large family-run hotel-style ryokan with three connected wings. There are Japanese- and Western-style rooms, all very clean, and many have private bathrooms (though there's also a good common bath). Ikawa often caters to tour and school groups. Wi-fi is in the lobby.

★Hotel Active Hiroshima HOTEL ¥¥
(ホテルアクティブ広島; 082-212-0001; www.hotel-active.com/hiroshima; 15-3 Nobori-chō; s/d incl breakfast from ¥5380/7300; ; Kanayama-chō) With its satiny coverlets and backlit headboards, Hotel Active tries for a little more style than the average business hotel. It's right in the heart of things, and extras like free drink machines, a spa and an included buffet breakfast make this a good-value option.

Some English is spoken; it may be easier to book by phone than via the Japanese-only website.

Aster Plaza International Youth House HOTEL ¥¥
(広島市国際青年会館; 082-247-8700; http://hiyh.pr.arena.ne.jp; 4-17 Kako-machi; s/tw from ¥3720/6420; ; Funairi-machi or Shiyakusho-mae) With good views from the top floors of a huge cultural complex, this city-run hotel represents excellent value for foreign travellers, who get roomy well-equipped modern accommodation at budget prices. Rooms have LAN internet access and there's wi-fi in the lobby. Note that the building is locked at 1am.

Sera Bekkan RYOKAN ¥¥
(世羅別館; 082-248-2251; www.serabekkan.jp; 4-20 Mikawa-chō; r per person with/without meals from ¥11,000/9000; ; Ebisu-chō) Off Namiki-dōri is this traditional ryokan with

good-sized tatami rooms with en suite, large public baths for soaking, a peaceful garden and great hospitality. Look for the dark-red-brick building on a corner across from a small car park.

Hotel Flex HOTEL ¥¥
(ホテルフレックス; 082-223-1000; www.hotel-flex.co.jp; 7-1 Kaminobori-chō; s/d incl breakfast from ¥7150/12,100; @) Curves and concrete are the features at this riverside hotel. Standard rooms are small but there is a more spacious maisonette and high-ceiling room option. All rooms are light, with large windows; naturally, the ones facing the river have the views. There's a bright, breezy cafe downstairs where the included breakfast of a sandwich and drink is served.

★**Hiroshima Inn Aioi** RYOKAN ¥¥¥
(広島の宿相生; 082-247-9331; www.galilei.ne.jp/aioi; 1-3-14 Ōtemachi; r per person with meals from ¥19,900; @; Genbaku-dōmu-mae) At this fine traditional inn, kick back in *a yukata* and enjoy city and park views from your tatami room, or while lazing in the large bath on the 7th floor. The meals are an elaborate traditional spread of dishes, and you can opt for breakfast or dinner only.

Welcoming staff speak just a little English, but do their best to accommodate.

Eating

Hiroshima is famous for oysters and *okonomiyaki* (savoury pancakes; batter and cabbage, with vegetables and seafood or meat cooked on a griddle). The local version, *Hiroshima-yaki,* features individual layers, and noodles as the key ingredient.

★**Hassei** OKONOMIYAKI ¥
(八誠; 4-17 Fujimi-chō; dishes ¥600-1300; 11.30am-2pm & 5-11pm Tue-Sun, dinner only Sun; ; Chūden-mae) The walls of this popular *okonomiyaki* specialist are covered with the signatures and messages of famous and not-so-famous satisfied customers. The tasty, generous servings are indeed satisfying – a half-order is probably more than enough for some at lunchtime.

Hassei is on a side street one block south of Heiwa-Ōdōri.

★**Okonomi-mura** OKONOMIYAKI ¥
(お好み村; www.okonomimura.jp/foreign/english.html; 2nd-4th fl, 5-13 Shintenchi; dishes ¥800-1300; 11am-2am; ; Ebisu-chō) This Hiroshima institution is a touristy but fun place to get acquainted with *okonomiyaki* and chat with the cooks over a hot griddle. Spread over three floors are 26 stalls, each serving up hearty variations of the local speciality. Pick a floor and find an empty stool at whichever counter takes your fancy.

It's in a building off Chūō-dōri, on the opposite side of the square to Parco.

Chari CAFE ¥
(茶里; 2-5 Nakajima-chō; dishes from ¥750; 11am-10pm Mon-Sat; ; Chūden-mae) This low-ceilinged narrow cafe-restaurant near the Peace Memorial Museum is a good place for a coffee or lunch stop after walking around the park. There are a few wooden tables and a solo-diner-friendly long bench. Lunch offerings include a *teishoku* (set meal) of udon, and there are curries and cakes on the menu.

Bakudanya NOODLES ¥
(ばくだん屋; www.bakudanya.net; 6-13 Fujimi-chō; noodles ¥700-1080; 11.30am-midnight; ; Chūden-mae) Try the famous Hiroshima *tsukemen* at this simple street-corner eatery. *Tsukemen* is a *rāmen*-like dish in which noodles and soup come separately. This is the original outlet; the chain has spread across the country. Look for the green awning on the corner.

There are other branches around the city, including on the *shinkansen* side of Hiroshima Station.

Osanpo Masara THAI ¥
(おさんぽまさら; 090-9465-6352; 9-28 Nakajima-chō; curries ¥700-1000; 11am-2.30pm & 6-10pm; ; Chūden-mae) It looks like a shack from the outside – let's call it rustic – and inside there are just a few wooden stools to perch on and a couple of tables. They have a small menu to suit the venue, featuring a very good Thai-style green curry using housemade curry pastes. Follow it up with a soothing coconut ice cream.

★**Tōshō** TOFU ¥¥
(豆匠; 082-506-1028; www.toufu-tosho.jp; 6-24 Hijiyama-chō; sets ¥1800-3000; 11am-3pm & 5-10pm, to 9pm Sun; ; Danbara-1-chōme) In a traditional wooden building overlooking a large garden with a pond and waterfall, Tōshō specialises in homemade tofu, served in a variety of tasty and beautifully presented forms by kimono-clad staff. Even the sweets are tofu based. There is a range of set courses, with some pictures and basic English on the menu.

From the tram stop, continue walking in the direction of the tram and turn left uphill after Hijiyama shrine.

Oyster Conclave Kaki-tei OYSTERS ¥¥
(牡蠣亭; ☎082-221-8990; www.kakitei.jp; 11 Hashimoto-chō; lunch/dinner from ¥1800/3800; ⊙11.30am-2.30pm & 5-10pm, closed Tue & 1st & 3rd Wed of month; ; Kanayama-chō) Come to this intimate riverside bistro for local oysters prepared in a range of mouth-watering ways. Lunch is a set menu of oysters in various guises, served with salad and soup; an à la carte menu is available in the evenings.

Roopali INDIAN ¥¥
(ルーパリ; ☎082-264-1333; http://roopali.jp; 14-32 Wakakusa-chō; lunch sets ¥720-1300, dinner sets from ¥1600; ⊙11am-3pm & 5-10pm;) Choose one of the generous set courses at this large restaurant dishing up filling authentic curries, or put together your own feast – individual dishes start from ¥850. The single naan orders are so big there ought to be a prize for finishing one. There's an English menu and English-speaking staff. It's on the north side of Hiroshima Station.

Zucchini TAPAS ¥¥
(ズッキーニ; ☎082-546-0777; www.in-smart.co.jp/zucchini; 1-5-18 Ōtemachi; dishes ¥400-2800; ⊙11.30am-1am; ; Hon-dōri) Zucchini is a lively Spanish-style tapas restaurant with warm chandelier lighting and the kind of atmosphere that makes you want to sip wine and settle in for a few hours. All the usual ham, cheese and fish goodies are served, plus paellas and steak. It's near the end of Hon-dōri arcade.

Drinking & Nightlife

Hiroshima is a great city for a night out, with bars and pubs to suit whatever mood you're in. The city's main entertainment district is made up of hundreds of bars, restaurants and karaoke joints crowding the lanes between Aioi-dōri and Heiwa-Ōdōri in the city centre. Most places also serve light meals or snacks, and some have live music.

★Koba BAR
(コバ; 3rd fl, Rego Bldg, 1-4 Naka-machi; ⊙6pm-2am Thu-Tue; Ebisu-chō) It's bound to be a good night if you drop into this laid-back place, where the friendly metal-loving musician owner 'Bom-san' can be found serving drinks and cooking up small tasty meals. There is occasional live music. It's up the stairs in a concrete building, just behind Stussy.

OFF THE BEATEN TRACK

SANDAN GORGE

Sandan Gorge (三段峡, Sandan-kyō) is an 11km ravine about 50km northwest of Hiroshima within the Nishi-Chūgoku-Sanchi Quasi-National Park. A trail follows the flow of the Shibaki-gawa through the gorge, providing visitors with access to waterfalls, swimming holes, forests and fresh air. The hike is very popular in autumn, when the leaves change colour. The tourist office in Hiroshima has a hiking map in English, or pick up a copy of Lonely Planet's *Hiking in Japan* for more details.

A dozen buses a day run from the Hiroshima bus centre to Sandan-kyō – it's best to catch the one express service (¥1440, 75 minutes), which leaves Hiroshima in the morning, returning in the afternoon. The bus drops you at the southern end of the gorge.

★Organza BAR, CAFE
(ヲルガン座; ☎082-295-1553; www.organ-za.com; 2nd fl, Morimoto Bldg, Tōkaichi-machi; ⊙5.30pm-2am Tue-Fri, 11.30am-2am Sat, 11.30am-midnight Sun; Honkawa-chō) Bookshelves, old-fashioned furniture, a piano and a stuffed deer head all add to the busy surrounds at this smoky lounge-bar. Organza hosts an eclectic schedule of live events (from acoustic guitar to cabaret), some with a cover charge, and food is also served. Lunch on weekends only.

Molly Malone's PUB
(www.mollymalones.jp; 4th fl, Teigeki Bldg, 1-20 Shintenchi; ⊙5pm-1am Mon-Thu, 5pm-2am Fri, 11.30am-2.30am Sat, 11.30am-midnight Sun; Ebisu-chō) Reliable Irish-style pub with a welcoming Irish expat manager, good beer, good food and occasional live music. It draws a mixed crowd of local expats and Japanese.

Kuro-sawa BAR
(黒澤; 5th fl, Tenmaya Ebisu Bldg, 3-20 Horikawa-chō; ⊙5.30pm-1am, to 2am Sat & Sun; Ebisu-chō) This is a trendy, dimly lit joint, with seating at the sleek bar or at low-to-the-ground tables. There's a good range of sake and cocktails and some tempting dishes to go with your drinks: try the avocado or *ko-iwashi* (sardine) tempura. Be sure to check out the bizarre toilet before you leave.

Kuro-sawa is on the 5th floor of a building in the Ebisu-dōri arcade.

Mac BAR

(マック; 6-18 Nagarekawa-chō; 8pm-late; Ebisu-chō) Long-running Mac draws a mixed crowd: ageing Japanese rockers, expats, travellers and local regulars come here to chat, drink and be merry into the wee hours, while listening to music from the wall of CDs. The owners take requests; choose wisely. Look for the small sign pointing up a stairway at the side of the building.

Lotus BAR

(ロータス; 5th fl, Namiki Curl Bldg, 3-12 Mikawa-chō; 6pm-3am; Ebisu-chō) Take off your shoes and unwind here while reclining among the cushions, or sip cocktails at the bar. It's on a side street just off Namiki-dōri.

Entertainment

Hiroshima is a good place to catch a baseball game and see the beloved local team, the Carp. A love of baseball is not a prerequisite for having a great time – it's fun just watching the rowdy yet organised enthusiasm of the crowd, especially when the despised Yomiuri (Tokyo) Giants come to town. Games are played in the **Mazda Zoom Zoom Stadium** (Hiroshima Municipal Stadium; 2-3-1 Minami-Kaniya), a short walk southeast of the station.

For schedule information in English, see www.japanball.com, or ask at the tourist office.

Shopping

Browse the busy shop-filled Hon-dōri covered arcade for clothes, shoes, accessories and more – there are also conveniently placed cafes for when you need a break. Namiki-dōri is another shopping street, with a range of fashionable boutiques. Hiroshima also has branches of the big-name department stores, such as **Tokyu Hands** (東急ハンズ広島店; http://hiroshima.tokyu-hands.co.jp; 16-10 Hatchō-bori; 10am-8pm, to 8.30pm Fri & Sat; Tate-machi), packed with homewares, must-have gadgets, and gifts; and classy **Mitsukoshi** (広島三越; http://mitsukoshi.mistore.jp/store/hiroshima; 5-1 Ebisu-chō; 10.30am-7.30pm; Ebisu-chō), with its designer labels and great basement-floor food hall.

The edible souvenir of choice from the Hiroshima area is the *momiji-manjū*, a maple-leaf-shaped waffle-like cake filled with a sweet bean paste.

Orientation

Hiroshima's city centre, Peace Memorial Park and most sights are on the south side of the station. The *shinkansen* entrance is on the north side of the station; this is also where the city loop bus pulls in. An underground passageway links the two sides of the station.

Information

INTERNET ACCESS

Hiroshima has a free wi-fi service accessible in a number of spots around the city, including at the Peace Park, along Hon-dōri and Ebisu-dōri, and in some museums. Look for 'Hiroshima Free Wi-fi' to connect. Users need to register when they first connect and usage is limited to 30-minute periods, though you can reconnect as often as you like. There are also computers with internet access at **Global Lounge** (グローバル・ラウンジ; www.hiroshima-no1.com/lounge.html; 2nd fl, Kensei Bldg, 1-5-17 Kamiya-chō; 11.30am-9pm Mon-Thu, to 11pm Fri & Sat; Kamiya-chō-higachi).

MONEY

Higashi Post Office has ATMs that accept international cards and has currency exchange services. ATMs in 7-Elevens also take international cards. The tourist offices have lists of banks and post offices that change money and travellers cheques.

POST

Higashi Post Office (広島東郵便局; 2-62 Matsubara-chō; 9am-7pm Mon-Fri, to 5pm Sat, to 12.30pm Sun) is near the south exit of Hiroshima Station. ATMs are accessible 24 hours except Sunday, when they close at 9pm.

TOURIST INFORMATION

As well as the tourist offices, check out the Hiroshima Navigator website (www.hcvb.city.hiroshima.jp) for tourism and practical information and downloadable audio guides to the sights. *Get Hiroshima* (www.gethiroshima.com), an expat-run website and magazine, has an events calendar, restaurant and bar reviews, and regular feature articles.

Hiroshima Rest House (広島市平和記念公園レストハウス; 082-247-6738; www.mk-kousan.co.jp/rest-house; 1-1 Nakajima-machi; 8.30am-6pm, to 5pm Dec-Feb, to 7pm Aug; Genbaku-dōmu-mae) In Peace Memorial Park next to Motoyasu-bashi bridge, this tourist office has comprehensive information, English-speaking staff and a small shop selling souvenirs.

Tourist Information Office (観光案内所; 082-261-1877; 9am-5.30pm) Tourist office inside the station near the south exit, with English-speaking staff. There is another branch

SAIJŌ, SAKE TOWN

A short train ride east of Hiroshima is the town of Saijō (西条), where seven sake breweries are clustered within easy walking distance of the station. The brewers here know their stuff – Saijō has been producing sake for around 300 years – and most open up their doors to curious and thirsty visitors for free sake tastings.

The **tourist office** (⏲10am-4pm Tue-Sun) on the 2nd floor of the station has a good walking map in English, showing the location of each brewery. Well-known **Kamotsuru** (賀茂鶴; www.kamotsuru.jp) is worth a look as it has a large tasting room screening a video about the district. Nearby is one of Saijō's oldest breweries, **Hakubotan** (白牡丹; www.hakubotan.co.jp), with a lovely broad-beamed display and tasting room with Munakata woodblock prints on the wall. For a bite to eat and a freshly roasted coffee, stop in at **Kugurimon Cafe** (くぐり門; http://kugurimon.com; 17-1 Hon-machi; meals ¥450-850; ⏲10am-5pm, closed 2nd & 4th Tue). They serve up cakes and light meals – try the cheese and sake lees (*sake kasu*) on toast for something different (and surprisingly tasty). When you're done with sake tasting, you can pay your respects to the god of sake at Matsuo-jinja, a short walk to the north of Saijō Station.

If you're in the area in the second weekend of October, don't miss the **Saijō Sake Matsuri** (http://sakematsuri.com), when crowds descend on the town for hours of sampling and events.

Saijō is 35 minutes by train from Hiroshima (¥580).

at the north (shinkansen) exit (☎082-263-6822; ⏲9am-5.30pm).

ℹ Getting There & Away

AIR

Hiroshima Airport (www.hij.airport.jp) is 40km east of the city, with bus connections to/from Hiroshima Station (¥1340, 45 minutes). Buses operate from the airport between 8.30am and 9.40pm; buses run from Hiroshima Station (*shinkansen* exit) between 6am and 7.20pm.

BUS

Long-distance buses connect Hiroshima with all the major cities. Buses depart from the **Hiroshima Bus Centre** (広島バスセンター; www.h-buscenter.com; 🚊Kamiya-chō-nishi), located on the 3rd floor between the Sogo and AQ'A shopping centres.

FERRY

There are connections from Hiroshima port to Matsuyama in Shikoku, with **Setonaikai Kisen Ferry** (瀬戸内海汽船フェリー; ☎082-253-1212; www.setonaikaikisen.co.jp), via standard car ferry (¥3600, two hours and 40 minutes, 10 daily) or high-speed service (¥7100, 1¼ hours, 12 daily). The port (広島港) is the last stop on trams 1, 3 and 5 bound for Ujina (宇品).

There are frequent ferry services to Miyajima (p441).

TRAIN

Hiroshima Station is on the JR San-yō line, which passes westwards to Shimonoseki. It's also a major stop on the Tokyo–Osaka–Hakata *shinkansen* line. Note that if you're travelling from Tokyo or Kyoto, you may need to change trains at Osaka or Okayama en route. Example *shinkansen* fares from Hiroshima:

Hakata ¥8420, 65 minutes
Osaka ¥9710, 1½ hours
Tokyo ¥18,040, four hours

ℹ Getting Around

Most sights in Hiroshima are accessible either on foot or with a short tram (street car) ride. There is also a convenient sightseeing loop bus that links the main attractions.

BICYCLE

Hiroshima is fairly compact and easy for cycling. Many hostels and hotels have bikes for hire from around ¥500 per day.

BUS

The Hiroshima Sightseeing Loop Bus (the *meipurūpu*) has two overlapping routes – orange and green – taking in the main sights and museums of the city, including the Peace Memorial Park and Atomic Bomb Dome. Both routes begin and end on the *shinkansen* entrance (north) side of Hiroshima Station, running from about 9am to 6pm (the green route runs later during summer). Orange route buses run every half-hour; green route buses about every hour.

Passengers can get on and off the bus at any stop. A single ride costs ¥200; an all-day pass is ¥400 (you can buy this from the driver). Those with a JR Pass can ride for free. On the bus there are announcements in English, though the background info on the sights is all in Japanese.

TRAM

Hiroshima's trams (www.hiroden.co.jp) will get you almost anywhere you want to go for a flat fare of ¥160. You pay by dropping the fare into the machine by the driver as you get off the tram. If you have to change trams to get to your destination, you should ask for a *norikae-ken* (transfer ticket).

If you'll be taking at least four tram trips in a day, get a one-day trip card, which gives unlimited travel for ¥600. A one-day card that covers trams plus return ferry to Miyajima is ¥840. The two-day trip card is a good deal at ¥2000, covering tram rides, ferry, and ticket for the ropeway on Miyajima. Buy passes from the tram terminal at the station, from the conductors on board (one-day cards only), or at various hotels and hostels.

Miyajima 宮島

☎0829 / POP 2015

The small island of Miyajima is a Unesco World Heritage Site and one of Japan's most visited tourist spots. Its star attraction is the oft-photographed vermilion *torii* (shrine gate) of Itsukushima-jinja, which seems to float on the waves at high tide – a scene that has traditionally been ranked as one of the three best views in Japan. Besides this feted view, Miyajima has some good hikes on sacred Misen, temples, and cheeky deer that do what they want, when they want, and will eat your map (or JR Pass) right out of your pocket if you're not careful.

Many people visit Miyajima as a day trip, but it's worth staying overnight on the island to enjoy the evening quiet once the crowds have left. Itsukushima-jinja and the *torii* are at their evocative best at sunset, and when lit up after dark.

Turn right as you emerge from the ferry terminal and follow the waterfront for 10 minutes to get to the shrine. The main shopping street, Omotesando, is a block back from the waterfront and packed with souvenir outlets and restaurants. This is also where you will find the world's largest *shakushi* (rice scoop).

Sights

★Itsukushima-jinja SHINTO SHRINE

(厳島神社; 1-1 Miyajima-chō; admission ¥300; ⏲6.30am-6pm Mar–mid-Oct, to 5.30pm mid-Oct–Nov, Jan & Feb, to 5pm Dec) With origins from as far back as the late 6th century, Itsukushima-jinja gives Miyajima its real name.

The shrine's pier-like construction is a result of the island's sacred status: commoners were not allowed to set foot on the island and had to approach by boat through the **torii** (大鳥居; shrine gate) in the bay. Much of the time, though, the shrine and *torii* are surrounded by mud: to get the classic view of the 'floating' *torii*, come at high tide.

The shrine's present form dates from 1168, when it was rebuilt under the patronage of Taira no Kiyomori, head of the doomed Heike clan. On one side of the shrine is a **floating nō stage** (能舞台), built by local lord Asano Tsunanaga in 1680 and still used for *nō* (stylised dance-drama) performances every year from 16 to 18 April.

Senjō-kaku PAVILION

(1-1 Miyajima-chō; admission ¥100; ⏲8.30am-4.30pm) Dominating the hill immediately to the north of Itsukushima-jinja is this huge pavilion built in 1587 by Toyotomi Hideyoshi. The atmospheric hall is constructed with massive pillars and beams, and the ceiling is hung with paintings. It looks out onto a colourful five-storey **pagoda** (五重塔) dating from 1407.

Daigan-ji BUDDHIST TEMPLE

(大願寺; 3 Miyajima-chō; ⏲9am-5pm) Miyajima has several important Buddhist temples, including the 1201 Daigan-ji, just south of Itsukushima-jinja, which dates back to the Heian period and is dedicated to Benzaiten, the Japanese name for Saraswati (the Hindu goddess of good fortune). The seated image of Yakushi Nyorai here is said to have been carved by Kōbō Daishi.

★Daishō-in BUDDHIST TEMPLE

(大聖院; 210 Miyajima-chō; ⏲8am-5pm) Just south of town at the foot of Misen, Daishō-in is a worthwhile stopping point on the way up or down the mountain. This Shingon temple is crowded with interesting things to look at: from Buddhist images and prayer wheels to sharp-beaked *tengu* (bird-like demons) and a cave containing images from each of the 88 Shikoku pilgrimage temples.

Momiji-dani-kōen PARK

(紅葉谷公園; Momiji-dani Park) Momiji means 'maple', and their leaves come alive in autumn here in this pretty park along the river. It's at the foot of Misen, close to the ropeway station.

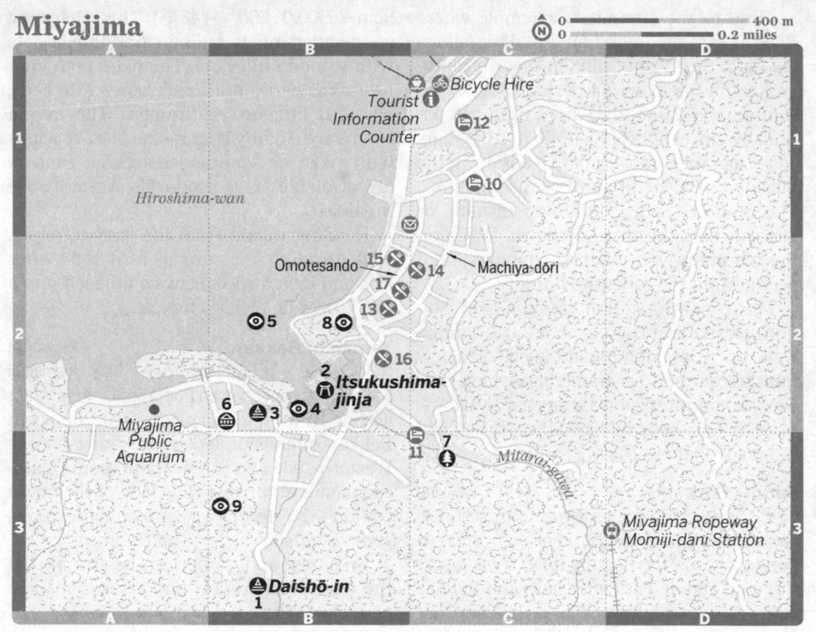

Miyajima

Top Sights

1 Daishō-in ... B3
2 Itsukushima-jinja ... B2

Sights

3 Daigan-ji ... B2
4 Floating Nō Stage ... B2
5 Floating Torii ... B2
6 Miyajima History & Folklore Museum ... B2
7 Momiji-dani-kōen ... C3
8 Senjō-kaku ... B2
9 Tahō-tō ... B3

Sleeping

10 Guest House Kikugawa ... C1
11 Iwasō Ryokan ... C3
12 Yamaichi Bekkan ... C1

Eating

13 Baccano ... B2
14 Kaki-ya ... C2
15 Mame-tanuki ... B2
16 Sarasvati ... B2
17 Yakigaki-no-hayashi ... B2

Tahō-tō PAGODA

(多宝塔) South of Itsukushima-jinja, stone steps (before the History & Folklore Museum) lead up from the road to this picturesque pagoda. There's a pleasant, short path looping around from here and back down to the road.

Miyajima History & Folklore Museum MUSEUM

(歴史民俗資料館; 57 Miyajima-chō; admission ¥300; ⏲8.30am-5pm Tue-Sun) Set in a fine garden, this museum combines a 19th-century merchant house with exhibitions on trade in the Edo period, as well as displays connected with the island.

Activities

★ Misen & Ropeway HIKING

(弥山; http://miyajima-ropeway.info; ropeway one-way/return ¥1000/1800; ⏲ropeway 9am-5pm) Covered with primeval forest, the sacred, peaceful Misen is Miyajima's highest mountain (530m), and its ascent is the island's finest walk. You can avoid most of the uphill climb by taking the two-stage **ropeway**, which leaves you with a 30-minute walk to the top, where there is an excellent observatory.

At the summit observatory, you can kick off your shoes and laze on wooden platforms while enjoying 360-degree views – on clear days you can see across to the mountain ranges of Shikoku.

Close to the summit is a temple where Kōbō Daishi meditated for 100 days following his return from China in the 9th century. Next to the main temple hall close to the summit is a flame that's been burning continually since Kōbō Daishi lit it 1200 years ago. From the temple, a path leads down the hillside to Daishō-in and Itsukushima-jinja. The descent takes a little over an hour, or you can take the ropeway down. While on the mountain you might see monkeys and deer around the ropeway station.

The ropeway station (Momiji-dani Station) to ascend Misen is about a 10-minute walk on from Momiji-dani-kōen, or a few minutes on the free shuttle bus, which runs every 20 minutes from a stop near Iwasō Ryokan. A four-hour hike of Misen is detailed in Lonely Planet's *Hiking in Japan*.

Paddle Park KAYAKING
(☎0829-50-4340; www.paddlepark.com; half-/full-day course ¥6000/10,000) For a different perspective on the floating *torii*, try a kayaking tour. Paddle Park offer half- and full-day courses, or a night-time tour, heading out from the mainland near Maezora Station, which is one stop from Miyajima-guchi. Depending on the conditions on the day, you may even get to kayak through the *torii* itself.

Festivals & Events

★Kangen-sai RELIGIOUS
This Shintō ritual sees decorated wooden boats float by to the sound of traditional drums and flutes. It's held in summer, starting early evening on the 17th of the sixth lunar-calendar month (late July/early August) – check with the tourist office for exact dates for the year you're here.

Hiwatarishiki (Fire Walking Ceremony) RELIGIOUS
The island's monks walk across fire on 3 November. You can join in if you're keen.

Sleeping

Backpackers Miyajima HOSTEL ¥
(バックパッカーズ宮島; ☎0829-56-3650; www.backpackers-miyajima.com; 1-8-11 Miyajima-guchi; dm ¥2300;) This hostel is not actually on Miyajima, but is a good budget base just a short walk from the mainland ferry terminal in Miyajima-guchi. Cash only.

★Guest House Kikugawa RYOKAN ¥¥
(ゲストハウス菊がわ; ☎0829-44-0039; www.kikugawa.ne.jp; 796 Miyajima-chō; s/tw from ¥6500/11,600;) This charming good-value inn is built in traditional style with wooden interiors. There are both tatami rooms with futons and rooms with beds, all with attached bathrooms. The tatami rooms are slightly larger – the most spacious with a cosy mezzanine sleepeng area. Dinners are available, as is a no-frills Western-style breakfast.

Heading inland from the ferry terminal, walk through the tunnel; turn right after this and look for Kikugawa on the left opposite Zonkō-ji (存光寺) temple.

Yamaichi Bekkan RYOKAN ¥¥
(山一別館; ☎0829-44-0700; http://yamaichibekkan.com; r per person from ¥8500;) Just across from the ferry terminal, Yamaichi Bekkan offers simple, clean lodgings in one Western-style and three tatami rooms. Bathrooms are all private. The lady of the house couldn't be more welcoming and speaks some English.

Breakfast and dinner can be arranged at the on-site restaurant and vegetarians can be looked after.

★Iwasō Ryokan RYOKAN ¥¥¥
(岩惣; ☎0829-44-2233; www.iwaso.com; Momiji-dani Miyajima-chō; r per person with 2 meals ¥20,100-42,150;) The Iwasō, open since 1854, offers the grand ryokan experience in exquisite gardens. There are three wings: a stay in a lovely 'Hanare' cottage will set you back the most. Not all rooms have private bathrooms, but you can soak in the onsen in the main building. It's especially stunning in autumn when Momiji-dani (Maple Valley) explodes with colour.

It's about 15 minutes to walk from the ferry port, or a pick-up can be arranged.

Eating & Drinking

There are plenty of places to eat along and around the main shopping strip of Omotesando and near the waterfront. You'll soon realise that oysters are the speciality here, with some restaurants tempting passers-by with oysters grilling in the open. Eel is also popular and can be tried in various meals (on rice, or perhaps in a steamed bun). Lunchtime is often very busy so don't be surprised if you have to wait for a seat. Just one street back from the main strip is the much quieter Machiya-dōri, with a few cafes and eateries. Most restaurants shut down after the crowds go home – the tourist office has a list of those that stay open for dinner.

Sarasvati CAFE ¥
(http://sarasvati.jp; 407 Miyajima-chō; coffees from ¥500, meals ¥990-1500; ⌚8.30am-8pm; 📋) The aroma of roasting coffee beans lures people into this cafe inside a former storehouse building from the early 1900s. Bare wooden floors and tables match a simple menu of traditional coffees (espresso, latte, cappuccino), plus cakes, sandwich and pasta sets.

Baccano ICE CREAM ¥
(バッカーノ; 435 Miyajima-chō; ice cream from ¥450; ⌚10am-6pm; 📋) Baccano gelateria dishes up refreshing swirls of handmade ice cream, from fruity standards to interesting local flavours like roasted green tea and black sesame.

★**Yakigaki-no-hayashi** OYSTERS ¥¥
(焼がきのはやし; ☎0829-44-0335; www.yakigaki-no-hayashi.co.jp; 505-1 Miyajima-chō; dishes ¥900-1600; ⌚10.30am-5pm Thu-Tue; 📋) The oysters in the tank and on the barbecue outside are what everyone is eating here. Try a plate of *nama-gaki* (raw oysters) or *kaki-furai* (crumbed, fried oysters), or go for oysters on udon noodles. It's not all about the slimy shell-dwellers – there are other meals on the menu, such as curry and eel sets.

★**Mame-tanuki** IZAKAYA ¥¥
(まめたぬき; ☎0829-44-2131; 1113 Miyajima-chō; lunch sets ¥1400-2500, dishes ¥500-1500; ⌚11am-3.30pm & 5-11pm; 📋) By day at Mame-tanuki there are lunch sets, such as the tasty *anago meshi* (steamed conger eel with rice) and fried oysters, and at night it is one of the few places open late, serving drinks and *izakaya*-style small dishes. Look for the blue curtain; there's a menu signboard outside. There's no smoking in the evening.

Kaki-ya OYSTERS ¥¥
(牡蠣屋; ☎0829-44-2747; www.kaki-ya.jp; 539 Miyajima-chō; oysters ¥1080-2150; ⌚10am-6pm; 📋) A sophisticated oyster bar on the main street, serving delicious local oysters barbecued in their shells. To try oysters done in a variety of ways, order the '*kakiya* set'. Wash them down with wine from the well-stocked cellar.

Information

Post Office (⌚9am-5pm Mon-Fri, ATM 9am-5.30pm, to 5pm Sat & Sun) Has an international ATM service.

Tourist Information Counter (宮島観光案内所; ☎0829-44-2011; http://visit-miyajima-japan.com; ⌚9am-5pm) Tourist info inside the ferry terminal.

Getting There & Away

Miyajima is accessed by ferry, and is an easy day trip from Hiroshima.

The mainland ferry terminal is a short walk from Miyajima-guchi Station on the JR San-yō line, halfway between Hiroshima (¥410, 26 minutes) and Iwakuni. The ferry terminal can also be reached by tram 2 from Hiroshima (¥260, 70 minutes), which runs from Hiroshima Station, passing the Atomic Bomb Dome on the way. Ferries operated by two companies shuttle regularly across to the island from Miyajima-guchi (¥180, 10 minutes). JR Pass holders can travel on the JR ferry for free.

Setonaikai Kisen (p437) operates high-speed ferries (¥1850, 30 minutes, six to eight daily) direct to Miyajima from Hiroshima's Ujina port. Another option is to take the **Aqua Net ferry** (☎082-240-5955; www.aqua-net-h.co.jp) directly from Peace Memorial Park in central Hiroshima (one way/return ¥2000/3600, 45 minutes, 10 to 15 daily). These boats cruise under the bridges of Kyūōta-gawa before coming out into the bay towards Miyajima. No reservation is required.

Getting Around

Everywhere on Miyajima is within easy walking distance. For **bicycle hire** (per hour ¥100; ⌚9am-5pm), go to the JR office in the ferry terminal. There are also taxis on the island – ask at the tourist office for details.

Iwakuni 岩国

☎0827 / POP 143,800

About an hour away from Hiroshima by train or bus, Iwakuni makes for a worthwhile half-day trip, or a stop-off en-route between Yamaguchi and Hiroshima. The main reason to come here is to see the five-arched bridge Kintai-kyō, and take a walk around the Kikkō-kōen area to which it leads. It's also possible to watch traditional cormorant fishing here during the summer.

Sights

Kintai-kyō BRIDGE
(錦帯橋; admission ¥300, combination incl cable car & castle ¥940; ⌚24hr) Iwakuni's chief claim to fame is the graceful Kintai-kyō, built in 1673 during the rule of feudal lord Kikkawa Hiroyoshi. It has been restored several times since then, but its high arches remain an impressive sight over the wide river, with Iwakuni-jō atop the green hills behind.

In the feudal era only members of the ruling class were allowed to use the bridge, which linked the samurai quarters on the west bank of Nishiki-gawa with the rest of the town. Today, anyone can cross over for a small fee.

Kikkō-kōen PARK

(吉香公園; bridge admission ¥300) What remains of the old samurai quarter in Iwakuni now forms pleasant Kikkō-kōen, accessed via Kintai-kyō bridge. Within the park there are old residences, a pavilion, a couple of museums, ice cream vendors, and spots for picnicking. Worth a look is the **Mekata Family Residence** (旧目加田家住宅; 9.30am-4.30pm Tue-Sun) FREE, the former home of a middle-ranking samurai family from the mid-Edo period.

Reptile enthusiasts and kids might want to pop into the small **White Snake Viewing Facility** (白蛇観覧所; admission ¥100; 9am-5pm), where several of the bizarre albino snakes unique to Iwakuni are on display.

Iwakuni-jō CASTLE

(岩国城; admission ¥260; 9am-4.45pm, closed mid–end Dec, cable car 9am-5pm) The original Iwakuni-jō was built by Hiroie, the first of the Kikkawa lords, between 1603 and 1608. Just seven years later, the Tokugawa shogunate passed a law limiting the number of castles *daimyō* were allowed to build, and the castle at Iwakuni was demolished. It was rebuilt not far from its original setting in 1960. There is nothing much of interest inside, but there are good views from the hilltop setting.

You can get to the castle by cable car (one way/return ¥320/550, every 20 minutes), or you can walk up to the castle among the greenery and birdlife on a pathway that leads up from the west side of the park. The walk takes about 45 minutes.

Eating

There are small eateries in the park and stalls down along the riverside. Local specialities include *iwakuni-zushi,* a sushi made in large square molds, and *renkon* (lotus root) cooked in *korokke* (croquette) form.

Midori-no-sato SUSHI, NOODLES ¥

(緑の里; 1-4-10 Iwakuni; meals ¥600-1080; 10am-6pm;) This restaurant, accessed through a souvenir shop, has a satisfying *iwakuni-zushi* set (¥1080) that comes with a side of *renkon* noodles, plus udon dishes from ¥600. There's no English menu but there are pictures. From the bus centre near Kintai-kyō, walk towards the bridge and take the left opposite the bridge entrance. It's on the right.

Information

Tourist Information (10am-5pm Tue-Sun) Inside JR Iwakuni Station. There is another office at Shin-Iwakuni Station (10.30am-3.30pm Thu-Tue).

Getting There & Away

The bridge and park are a 20-minute bus ride (¥250) from JR Iwakuni Station. There are also buses to the bridge (¥290, 15 minutes) from Shin-Iwakuni. Buses leave regularly. JR Iwakuni Station is on the San-yō line, west of Hiroshima (¥760, 50 minutes). Shin-Iwakuni is on the San-yō *shinkansen* line, connecting to Hiroshima (¥1620, 15 minutes) and Shin-Yamaguchi (¥3390, 30 minutes).

If coming from Hiroshima without a JR Pass, you may find it more convenient to get the Iwakuni bus from Hiroshima bus centre, as it handily drops you at Kintai-kyō (one way/return ¥930/1700, 50 minutes, nine daily).

Tomo-no-ura 鞆の浦

084 / POP 5000

Perfectly situated in the middle of the Inland Sea coast, Tomo-no-ura flourished for centuries as a stopping-off point for boats travelling between western Japan and the capital, until the arrival of steam put an end to the town's glory days. It's now a sleepy port town – at the old harbour, fishing boats quietly bob on the water, and the narrow cobbled streets that surround it retain much of the flavour of the Edo-period heyday. Inland from the harbour there are a dozen or so temples, some tucked within residential streets, and stone steps lead up the hillside to views of the Inland Sea. The small island of Sensui-jima is a short boat ride away.

Film buffs may be interested to know that Tomo-no-ura was the setting for some scenes in *The Wolverine* (2013). It also provided inspiration for renowned Studio Ghibli director Miyazaki Hayao, who spent two months in the town while developing *Gake no ue no Ponyo* (*Ponyo*; 2008). The tourist office has film location maps and information.

The town is good for a few hours of strolling. If you're interested in spending the night, it's worth staying on Sensui-jima. There are a few guesthouses in Tomo-no-ura town, and nearby Fukuyama has a bunch of decent hotels in the station area. The Fukuyama Station tourist office and the Tomo-no-ura tourist office can help with local accommodation bookings.

Sights

Fukuzenji BUDDHIST TEMPLE
(福禅寺; admission ¥200; 8am-5pm) Close to the waterfront, this temple dates back to the 10th century. Adjoining the temple is **Taichōrō** (対潮楼), a reception hall built in the 1690s. This is where you go for a classic view out across the narrow channel to the uninhabited island of Benten-jima and its shrine.

Jōyatō LIGHTHOUSE
(常夜燈) Looking over the harbour area of Tomo-no-ura is this large stone lantern, which used to serve as a lighthouse and has become a symbol of the town.

★Ōta Residence HISTORIC BUILDING
(太田家住宅; admission ¥400; 10am-4.30pm Wed-Mon) On a lane leading back from the harbour area, the former Ōta residence is a fine collection of restored buildings from the mid-18th century. Guided tours (included in admission) take you through the impressive family home and workplace, where *hōmēshu* (sweet medicinal liquor) was once brewed. Some English information is available.

Tomo-no-Ura Museum of History & Folklore MUSEUM
(鞆の浦歴史民俗資料館; www.tomo-rekimin.org; admission ¥150; 9am-5pm Tue-Sun) This museum sits at the top of the hill behind the harbour, with exhibits relating to local industry and craft. On the grounds is the site of the **old castle**, of which nothing remains but a few foundation stones. There are good views across the sea from here.

Iō-ji BUDDHIST TEMPLE
(医王寺) FREE Up a steep hill on the western side of Tomo-no-ura, Iō-ji was reputedly founded by Kōbō Daishi in the 900s. A path leads from the temple to the top of a bluff, from where there are fabulous views.

★Sensui-jima ISLAND
(仙酔島) The island of Sensui-jima is just five minutes across the water from Tomo-no-ura town. There's a walking path that hugs the coast, passing by interesting rock formations and offering views across the water, especially lovely at sunset. After a stroll, drop into **Kokuminshukusha Sensui-jima** (国民宿舎仙酔島; 084-970-5050; www.tomonoura.co.jp/sen; 3373-2 Ushiroji Tomo-chō; r per person with 2 meals from ¥8800;), where nonguests can take a soak in the range of baths for ¥525 (from 10am to 9pm).

The ferry that shuttles passengers across to the island is modelled on the Edo-era steamboat *Iroha Maru*.

There are no English signs on the island, so check with the tourist office in Tomo-no-ura town if you have specific questions on where to go. The ferry runs to the island every 20 minutes from early morning to 9.30pm.

Eating

★Tabuchiya CAFE ¥
(田渕屋; www.tomonoura-tabuchiya.com; 838 Tomo-chō-tomo; set lunch ¥1300; noon-5pm Mon-Sat) At this former merchant building they only serve one meal, but do it very well – *hayashi raisu* (beef in a rich tomato-based sauce on rice). The set lunch comes with a tea or coffee. Walk past the Ōta Residence away from the harbour and look for the small white sign with a green leaf.

Tomo-no-ura @Cafe CAFE ¥
(Jōyatō-mae, Tomo-chō; meals ¥600-1600; 11am-6pm Thu-Tue) This friendly, modern cafe is in a 150-year-old building beside the stone lighthouse on the harbour. There's a small menu consisting of pasta dishes and sandwiches. There's usually some basic English on the chalkboard menu outside.

Information

Tomo-no-ura Tourist Information Centre
(鞆の浦観光情報センター; 084-982-3200; 416-1 Tomo-chō-tomo; 9am-4.30pm) Opposite the Tomo-no-ura bus stop, attached to a souvenir shop. They have English maps and rent out audio guides (¥500).

Getting There & Around

Buses run to Tomo-no-ura every 15 minutes from outside JR Fukuyama Station (¥520, 30 minutes). The tourist office is located at the Tomo-no-ura stop; the bus continues on another 450m or so to the Tomo-kō stop (Tomo Port), which is closest to the central harbour area. JR Fukuyama Station is a main hub and *shinkansen* stop on the San-yō line.

It's easy and most convenient to get around the town on foot. Bikes can be hired (¥300 for two hours) from a booth next to the terminal where the ferries leave for Sensui-jima.

Onomichi 尾道

☎0848 / POP 145,200

Onomichi is a gritty, old-timey seaport town with hills full of temples and literary sites. Film director Ōbayashi Nobuhiko was born in Onomichi, and the town has featured in a number of Japanese movies, notably Ozu's *Tokyo Story*. It's also known for its *rāmen*, and you'll find plenty of places dishing it up. For many travellers, Onomichi is the base from which to cycle the Shimanami Kaidō, the system of road bridges that allows people to island-hop their way across the Inland Sea to Shikoku.

Sights

The modern town stretches east from the station along a thin corridor between the railway tracks and the sea. Most of the places of interest are in the series of steep flagstoned lanes that ladder the hillside behind the tracks. There are also some interesting sights on the islands accessible by ferry or bike from Onomichi; nearby Ikuchi-jima (p447) is a popular half-day trip.

★Temple Walk — BUDDHIST TEMPLES

(古寺めぐり) FREE This trail takes in 25 old temples in the hills behind the town, following narrow lanes and steep stone stairways, where cats laze about here and there in the sunshine. Along the route is a **ropeway** (千光寺山ロープウェイ; one way/return ¥320/500; ⏲every 15min 9am-5.15pm) to an observation tower and a park area (Senkō-ji-kōen), home to **Senkō-ji** (千光寺), the best known and most impressive of Onomichi's temples.

Among the features of Senkō-ji is the *kyō-onrō*, a bell tower whose bell always rings in the new year – its sound is registered as one of the '100 soundscapes of Japan'.

The temple walk starts just east of the station: take the inland road from the station and cross the railway tracks by the statue of local author Hayashi Fumiko. To walk the whole trail takes a couple of hours. You can cut back down into town at various points along the way, or take the ropeway.

Maneki-neko Museum — MUSEUM

(招き猫美術館; Beckoning Cat Museum; http://manekineko-m.jp; admission ¥600; ⏲10am-5pm Thu-Tue) This quirky museum houses hundreds of the ornamental beckoning cats that wave you into shop entrances all over Japan, dating from the Meiji era to modern day. It's not far from the lower ropeway station on Onomichi's temple walk.

Onomichi Literature Museum — MUSEUM

(文学記念室; 13-28 Tsuchidō; admission with Shiga Naoya residence ¥300; ⏲9am-5pm Nov-Mar, to 6pm Apr-Oct, closed Tue Dec-Feb) Close to Hōdo-ji, the fourth temple along Onomichi's temple walk, this museum features displays on the lives and works of Hayashi Fumiko and other writers connected with Onomichi. It's interesting for fans of Japanese literature, and if you can speak or read some Japanese, but there are no English explanations.

Onomichi City Museum of Art — GALLERY

(尾道市立美術館; 17-19 Nishi Tsuchidō-chō; admission varies by exhibition; ⏲9am-5pm Tue-Sun) In Senkō-ji-kōen, downhill from the observation tower, is this museum with changing exhibitions of local and Western art. The building, which has fine views, was remodelled by architect Andō Tadao. There is a bright attached cafe.

Sleeping

★Onomichi Guesthouse Anago no Nedoko — HOSTEL ¥

(あなごのねどこ; ☎0848-38-1005; http://anago.onomichisaisei.com; 2-4-9 Tsuchidō; dm from ¥2800; 🚭@📶) Within a traditional old wooden house restored as part of an NPO project to give life to vacant dwellings, Anago is a budget option with character. As well as the dorms (accessed via narrow stairs), there are private tatami rooms (from ¥3300), a kitchen and a school-room-themed cafe. The entrance is in the *shōtengai* (shopping arcade).

Fuji Hostel — HOSTEL ¥

(フジホステル; ☎0848-36-6215; http://nora-t.p-kit.com; 3-30 Toyohimoto-machi; dm ¥2500; 🚭@📶) Simple, small and cosy, Fuji Hostel has two bedrooms (six bunks in each), one shared bathroom, a kitchen and a living area. The easy-going owner, who lives on site, speaks very little English but manages. The stairs up to the rooms are steep and narrow.

★Hotel Cycle — HOTEL ¥¥¥

(☎0848-21-0550; www.onomichi-u2.com; U2 complex, 5-11 Nishi-gosho-cho; tw from ¥17,000; 🚭@📶) Hotel Cycle is within the large U2 complex right on the waterfront boardwalk, clearly aimed at both the cycling crowd and those with an eye for design. The softly lit rooms (all twins) feature bike storage, and spacious baths, perfect for a soak after a long day of pedalling.

CYCLING THE SHIMANAMI KAIDŌ

The **Setouchi Shimanami Kaidō** (瀬戸内しまなみ海道; Shimanami Sea Route) is a chain of bridges linking Onomichi in Hiroshima Prefecture with Imabari in Ehime Prefecture on Shikoku, via six Inland Sea islands. Besides being remarkable feats of engineering (the monster Kurushima-kaikyō trio at the Imabari end are among the longest suspension bridges in the world), the bridges make it possible to cycle the whole way across. Breezing along 50m or more above the island-dotted sea is an amazing experience, and a highlight of a trip to this part of Japan. Needless to say, it's best enjoyed when the weather is fine.

The Route

The route begins on Mukai-shima (a quick boat ride from Onomichi) and crosses Inno-shima (p447), Ikuchi-jima (p447), Ōmi-shima (p447), Hakata-jima and Ōshima, before the final bridge to reach Imabari. The 'recommended' route is well marked and signed with information boards and maps, but there's nothing stopping you from taking detours along the minor routes around the islands, and plotting your own course from bridge to bridge.

Much of the recommended route is fairly flat, with the odd minor hill, but there are long, thigh-burning inclines leading up to each bridge entrance. The ride takes you through towns and villages, rural areas, past citrus groves and along coastline, but does also hit some less-pretty built-up industrial patches.

Distance & Time

The total recommended route from Onomichi to Imabari is roughly 70km, and could be done in eight or so hours, depending on your fitness and propensity to stop and take pictures. You could take the ferry part of the way, such as to Ikuchi-jima, and bike the rest. Or, a good day trip from Onomichi is to cycle to Ikuchi-jima (about 30km) and return to Onomichi on the ferry in the afternoon.

Some cyclists opt to spend a night on one of the islands on the way across – Ikuchi-jima is a popular stopover point. Or, take it easy and just spend a few hours cycling a section of the route on one of the islands.

Information

The tourist office in Onomichi, and those on each of the islands, can help with all the information you need, including an excellent map in English showing the routes, distances, sights and locations of bike terminals along the way. There's some information in English at www.go-shimanami.jp, from where you can download the English map. You'll also find basic maps, plus bus and ferry schedules, at www.city.onomichi.hiroshima.jp.

If you need to get heavy luggage across, try Kuroneko Yamato (www.kuronekoyamato.co.jp/en), whose *takkyūbin* service will deliver it for you by the next business day (from around ¥1000 depending on size). They pick up from many convenience stores.

Bikes & Costs

Bike hire is ¥500 per day, plus ¥1000 deposit. You don't get the deposit back if you return the bike to a different rental place along the route. There are large bike-hire terminals in Onomichi and in Imabari, and on each island in between. Electric-assist bicycles are also available for ¥800 per day; these have to be returned to the same rental terminal. It's not necessary to reserve a bike, though it's possible to do so and you may want to consider it if you're planning to cycle on a major holiday. Note that reservations can't be made less than a week in advance.

Cyclists also need to pay bridge tolls of between ¥50 and ¥200 per bridge. No one is actually collecting this money; you're trusted to drop the coins into the box at the bridge entrances. During occasional campaigns the tolls are waived and cyclists can cross for free. Check at the tourist offices for the latest.

To take a bike on a ferry costs up to ¥150.

U2 also houses a cafe (where you can 'ride through'), bar, restaurant, bakery and Giant bicycle shop.

Green Hill Hotel Onomichi HOTEL ¥¥¥
(グリーンヒルホテル尾道; ☎0848-24-0100; www.shimanami-gho.co.jp; 9-1 Higashi-gosho-machi; s/tw from ¥7875/15,750;) Directly above the ferry port and a minute's walk from the station, this well-appointed hotel could hardly be better located. Pay a little more for a room on the sea-view side.

Uonobu Ryokan RYOKAN ¥¥¥
(魚信旅館; ☎0848-37-4175; www.uonobu.jp; 2-27-6 Kubo; r per person with meals from ¥16,800) Elegantly old-fashioned Uonobu is a good pick for a ryokan experience, but it's probably best if you can speak a little Japanese. It's renowned for its seafood; nonguests can eat here if they reserve by 5pm the previous day. It's about a 20-minute walk east from the station, just after the city hall (市役所).

Eating

Onomichi Rāmen Ichibankan RĀMEN ¥
(尾道ラーメン壱番館; www.f-ichibankan.com; 2-9-26 Tsuchidō; noodles ¥580-950; ⏲11am-7pm Sat-Thu;) Opposite the Sumiyoshi shrine, a 15-minute walk from the station, this popular noodle shop is a good place to try Onomichi *rāmen,* characterised by thick slabs of juicy pork. Its best seller is the *kaku-ni rāmen* (noodles with eggs and tender cuts of fatty pork).

Yamaneko Cafe CAFE, INTERNATIONAL ¥
(やまねこ; 2-9-33 Tsuchidō; dishes ¥700-1000; ⏲11.30am-10pm, to midnight Fri & Sat, closed Mon;) Retro furnishings, battered-looking walls decorated with local artwork, and a mellow playlist add up to a relaxed spot for a drink or light meal. The menu includes pasta and curry lunch sets, pizza, cakes, coffees and cocktails. Find it on a corner along the waterfront road, a 15-minute walk from the station.

Sumichan OKONOMIYAKI ¥
(すみチャン; 11-17 Higashi-gosho-chō; meals ¥650-1400; ⏲11am-10pm Wed-Mon) Like its neighbour Hiroshima, Onomichi has its own spin on *okonomiyaki* – *Onomichi-yaki* – with the key ingredient being chicken giblets. If you prefer your meals innards-free, there are also Kansai- and Hiroshima-style options on the menu, which has some pictures.

From the station, head west past the shops, then take a left when you reach Yamaguchi Bank.

Neko-no-Te Pan BAKERY ¥
(ネコノテパン; http://pan.catnote.co.jp; 7-7 Higashi-tsuchidō-chō; baked goods ¥120-450; ⏲10am-dusk Thu-Mon) Could this be Japan's smallest bread shop? Pop into 'cat's paw bakery' for a sweet or savoury baked treat and judge for yourself. It's on the steep path that leads to Senkō-ji.

Yasuhiro Sushi SUSHI, SASHIMI ¥¥
(保広寿司; http://yasuhiro.co4.jp; 1-10-12 Tsuchidō; dishes from ¥1600; ⏲11.30am-3pm & 5-9pm Tue-Sun;) Enjoy excellent, fresh local seafood in this traditional black-and-white building on the seafront road, about five minutes' walk from the station and on the left. Try the *sashimi teishoku* (¥1650) at lunchtime. Dinner sets from ¥5400.

Information

Tourist Information Office (☎0848-20-0005; www.ononavi.jp; ⏲9am-6pm) Supplies local maps, has information on the Shimanami Kaidō, and can help with accommodation. It's inside JR Onomichi Station.

Getting There & Away

BICYCLE

Onomichi Port Rent-a-Cycle (☎0848-22-5332; per day ¥500, deposit ¥1000; ⏲7am-6pm) Located in the car park next to the ferry terminal, with multiple bikes. Bikes with gears and electric-assist ones available.

BUS

Regular buses run to Imabari (¥2250), in Shikoku, from Onomichi Station (some originating in Shin-Onomichi Station), all with a transfer at Inno-shima. It takes up to two hours, depending on the connection. Buses also run between Onomichi and Setoda port on Ikuchi-jima (¥1030, 60 minutes, four to seven daily).

FERRY

Ferries travel from Onomichi to Setoda port on Ikuchi-jima (¥820, 40 minutes, nine daily). There are frequent ferries to Mukai-shima (¥110, five minutes). It is up to an additional ¥150 to take a bicycle on the ferries.

TRAIN

Onomichi is on the main JR San-yō line, east of Hiroshima (¥1490, 1½ hours). The Shin-Onomichi *shinkansen* station is 3km north. Regular buses (¥180, 15 minutes) connect the two.

Islands on the Shimanami Kaidō

Six islands are connected by the Shimanami Kaidō bridge system between Onomichi and Imabari. They're accessible by bike or car, and by ferries from Onomichi.

Inno-shima 因島

Famed for its flowers and fruit, Inno-shima is connected by bridge to Mukai-shima, facing Onomichi, and Ikuchi-jima to the west. The Inland Sea was once a haven for pirates, and Inno-shima was the base of one of the three Murakami pirate clans. Today you can get a taste for that time at the modern-replica **pirate castle** (因島水軍城, Suigun-jō; admission ¥310; ⌚9.30am-5pm Fri-Wed), which has some displays of weaponry. It's worth cycling (or driving) up to **Shirataki-yama** (白滝山), a collection of sculptures of the 500 Rakan disciples of the Buddha.

Ikuchi-jima 生口島

Ikuchi-jima is known for its citrus groves and beaches, including Sunset Beach on the west coast.

There's not much doing in the main port town of Setoda, but it does have the remarkable temple complex of **Kōsan-ji** (耕三寺; admission ¥1200; ⌚9am-5pm). Shortly after the death of his beloved mother in 1934, local steel-tube magnate and arms manufacturer Kanemoto Kōzō became a Buddhist priest and sank his fortune into a series of garishly coloured temple buildings. The result is a chaos of over-the-top Buddhist kitsch, consisting of some 2000 exhibits. Don't miss the 1000 Buddhas Cave and its series of graphically illustrated hells.

Just past Kōsan-ji is the **Ikuo Hirayama Museum of Art** (平山郁夫美術館; www.hirayama-museum.or.jp; admission ¥800; ⌚9am-5pm), dedicated to the life and work of the well-travelled, famous Setoda-born artist. The collection here includes several striking works inspired by Ikuo's journeys in India and along the Silk Road.

Ikuchi-jima is a good place to overnight if you're cycling the Shimanami Kaidō. The cheap-and-cheerful **Setoda Private Hostel** (瀬戸田垂水温泉; Setoda Tarumi Onsen; ☎0845-27-3137; www.d1.dion.ne.jp/~sunami/youth; 58-1 Tarumi Setoda-chō; r per person with/without meals ¥4600/3000) is on Sunset Beach and has its own onsen, with accommodation in basic, individual tatami rooms; payment is by cash only. If you're not arriving on two wheels, a pick-up can be arranged from Setoda ferry port. The tourist office in Onomichi can help with reservations.

Ōmi-shima 大三島

The mountainous island of Ōmi-shima is connected by bridge to Ikuchi-jima to the east and Ō-shima to the west. It is home to one of the oldest Shintō shrines in western Japan, **Ōyamazumi-jinja** (大山祇神社; admission Treasure Hall & Kaiji Museum ¥1000; ⌚8.30am-5pm), near Miyaura port. The deity enshrined here is the brother of Amaterasu, the sun goddess. The present structure dates from 1378, but in the courtyard is a 2600-year-old camphor tree, and the treasure hall contains the most important collection of ancient weapons found anywhere in Japan.

It's worth getting off the 'recommended' cycling route to explore Ōmi-shima. With more time on the island, don't miss the **Tokoro Museum** (ところミュージアム大三島; http://museum.city.imabari.ehime.jp/tokoro; admission ¥300; ⌚9am-5pm Tue-Sun), a small but interesting collection of modern sculpture. It's a hilly ride up to the museum, but you're rewarded with fabulous sea views.

OKAYAMA & AROUND

Okayama Prefecture (岡山県; Okayama-ken) is known for its rural character, and the villa at Hattōji offers one of Japan's great countryside getaways. The area is also home to Kurashiki with its well-preserved merchant quarter, and the historic ceramic-making centre of Bizen – all within easy reach of prefectural capital Okayama. The coastline in this area also provides jumping-off points for some of the most popular islands in the Inland Sea, including Naoshima.

Okayama 岡山

☎086 / POP 709,600

The most many travellers see of Okayama is the blur of colour as they fly through on the *shinkansen* to Hiroshima. But it's worth stepping off the train, if only to spend a few hours strolling around Kōraku-en, one of Japan's top-three gardens, which is overlooked

Okayama

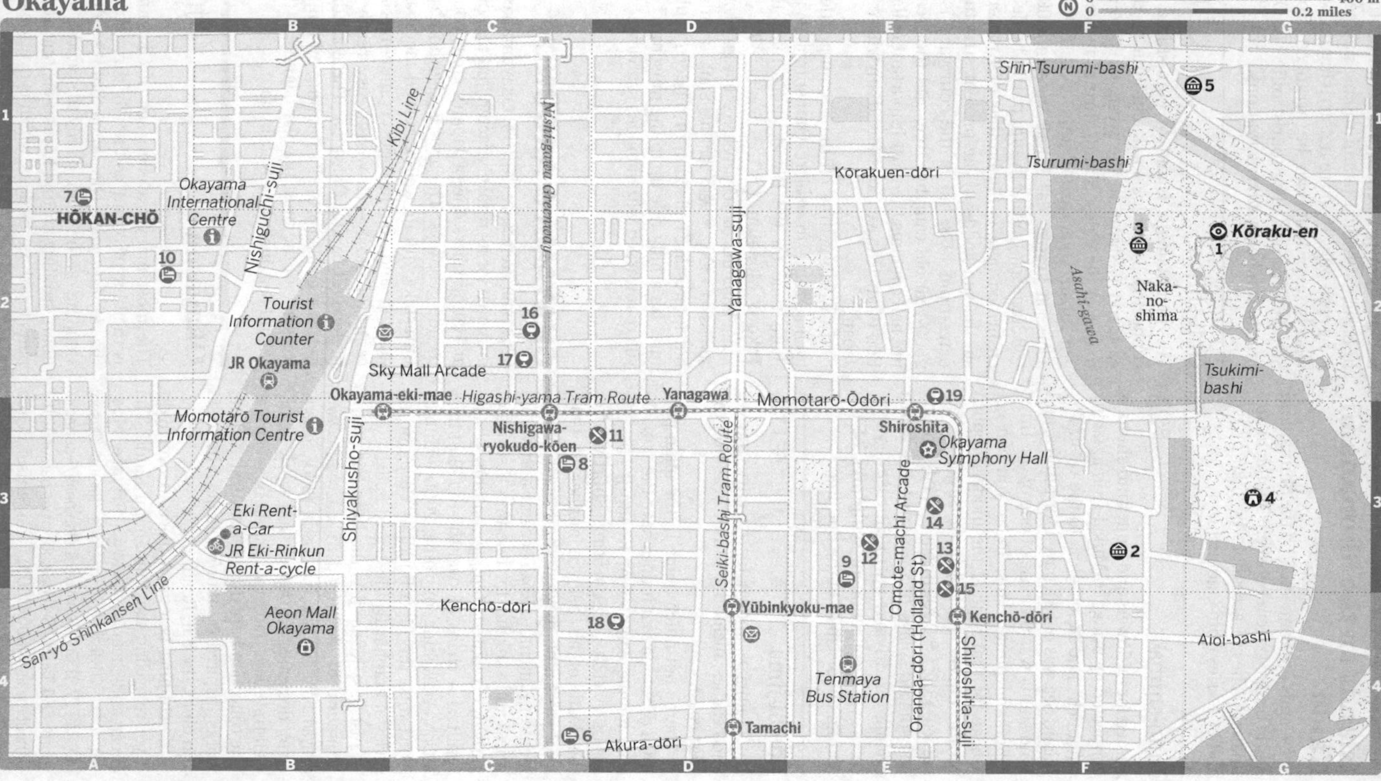
0 400 m
0 0.2 miles
Shin-Tsurumi-bashi
Tsurumi-bashi
Kōrakuen-dōri
Kōraku-en
Naka-no-shima
Asahi-gawa
Tsukimi-bashi
Aioi-bashi
Kibi Line
Nishi-gawa Greenway
Yanagawa-suji
Okayama International Centre
HŌKAN-CHŌ
Nishiguchi-suji
Tourist Information Counter
JR Okayama
Sky Mall Arcade
Okayama-eki-mae
Higashi-yama Tram Route
Yanagawa
Momotarō-Ōdōri
Shiroshita
Okayama Symphony Hall
Momotarō Tourist Information Centre
Nishigawa-ryokudo-kōen
Shiyakusho-suji
Eki Rent-a-Car
JR Eki-Rinkun Rent-a-cycle
San-yō Shinkansen Line
Aeon Mall Okayama
Kenchō-dōri
Seiki-bashi Tram Route
Yūbinkyoku-mae
Omote-machi Arcade
Oranda-dōri (Holland St)
Kenchō-dōri
Shiroshita-suji
Tenmaya Bus Station
Tamachi
Akura-dōri

Okayama

Top Sights
1 Kōraku-en G2

Sights
2 Hayashibara Museum of Art F3
3 Okayama Prefectural Museum F2
4 Okayama-jō G3
5 Yumeji Art Museum G1

Sleeping
6 Central Hotel Okayama C4
7 Kamp Hōkan-chō Backpacker's Inn & Lounge A1
8 Kōraku Hotel C3
9 Okayama View Hotel E3
10 Saiwai-sō A2

Eating
11 Ajitsukasa Nomura D3
12 Okabe E3
13 Padang Padang E3
14 Quiet Village Curry Shop E3
15 Tori-soba Ōta E3

Drinking & Nightlife
16 Aussie Bar C2
17 Izayoi no Tsuki C2
18 Marugo Deli D4
19 Saudade na Yoru E2

by the city's crow-black castle. If you have a few days up your sleeve, make Okayama your base for day trips to other attractions in the region and side trips to islands in the Inland Sea.

The city is proud of its connection to Momotarō, the demon-quelling boy hero of one of Japan's best-known folk tales. You'll spot his face beaming out at you all over town.

Sights

★ Kōraku-en — GARDENS

(後楽園; www.okayama-korakuen.jp; 1-5 Kōraku-en; admission ¥400; 7.30am-6pm Apr-Sep, 8am-5pm Oct-Mar) Kōraku-en draws the crowds with its reputation as one of the three most beautiful gardens in Japan. It has expansive lawns broken up by ponds, teahouses and other Edo-period buildings, including a *nō* theatre stage, and even has a small tea plantation and rice field. In spring the groves of plum and cherry blossoms are stunning, white lotuses unfurl in summer, and in autumn the maple trees are a delight for photographers. There are also seasonal events (fancy some harvest-moon viewing?).

Built on the orders of *daimyō* Ikeda Tsunemasa, the garden was completed in 1700 and, despite suffering major damage during floods in the 1930s and air raids in the 1940s, remains much as it was in feudal times. It was opened to the public in 1884.

From Okayama Station, take the Higashi-yama tram to the Shiroshita stop, from where it's about 10 minutes on foot. Bus 18 from the station will drop you right outside the garden (Kōraku-en-mae stop). Alternatively, walking the entire way will take about 25 minutes.

Okayama-jō — CASTLE

(岡山城; 2-3-1 Marunouchi; admission ¥300, additional charge for special exhibitions; 9am-5pm) Nicknamed U-jō (烏城; Crow Castle) because of its colour, the striking black Okayama Castle has an imposing exterior with gilded fish-gargoyles flipping their tails in the air. You can appreciate its impressive appearance for nix from the grounds or looking from across the river. Inside the *donjon* (main keep), some modern finishes detract from the 16th-century feel, but there are a few interesting museum displays and views from the top floor.

While it was first completed in 1597 under *daimyō* Ukita Hideie, much of the castle was dismantled after the Meiji Restoration and most of what remained burnt down during WWII air raids. It was rebuilt in 1966.

Yumeji Art Museum — GALLERY

(夢二郷土美術館; www.yumeji-art-museum.com; 2-1-32 Hama; admission ¥700; 9am-5pm Tue-Sun) Prominent Taishō-era artist and poet Takehisa Yumeji (1884–1934) is particularly known for his *bijin-ga* (images of beautiful women), and various wistfully posed ladies feature among the paintings, prints and screens on display at this small museum. It's just across the river on the northeast side of Kōraku-en.

Okayama Prefectural Museum — MUSEUM

(岡山県立博物館; www.pref.okayama.jp/kyoiku/kenhaku/hakubu.htm; 1-5 Kōraku-en; admission ¥250; 9am-6pm Tue-Sun) Tools, armoury and Bizen pottery are among the historic artefacts exhibited at this museum. It's located near the entrance to Kōraku-en.

Hayashibara Museum of Art MUSEUM
(林原美術館; www.hayashibara-museumofart.jp; 2-7-15 Marunouchi; admission ¥300; 9am-5pm, closed Mon) This is a small museum with exhibits of scrolls, armour and paintings that were once the property of the Ikeda clan (who ruled Okayama for much of the Edo period). It's near the rear entrance of Okayama-jō. Look for the traditional black-and-white building.

Sleeping

Modern midrange and budget hotels dominate the scene in Okayama. For a more traditional ryokan experience, consider staying in nearby Kurashiki.

Kamp Hōkan-chō Backpacker's Inn & Lounge HOSTEL ¥
(キャンプ; http://kamp.jp; 3-1-35 Hōkan-chō; dm/tw ¥3000/7000;) Dorm rooms are basic (with rather thin walls) but clean at this fresh new hostel option on the west side of Okayama Station. There's plenty of space to relax in the large lounge and bar downstairs, where events and live performances are sometimes held. Find it on a side street just off an old-style sleepy shopping arcade.

★**Kōraku Hotel** HOTEL ¥¥
(後楽ホテル; 086-221-7111; www.hotel.koraku.co.jp; 5-1 Heiwa-chō; s/tw from ¥5900/9200, corner room from ¥13,200; @) Kōraku has classy touches such as local museum pieces displayed on each floor, and pampering extras like complimentary aroma pots for your room. The corner rooms, with large curved windows, are especially spacious. Staff members speak English (and other languages), as does the enthusiastic manager, who you may bump into mingling with guests in the lobby.

There are good discounts for longer stays, and a buffet breakfast for ¥980.

Saiwai-sō HOTEL ¥¥
(ビジネスホテル幸荘; 086-254-0020; http://w150.j.fiw-web.net; 24-8 Ekimoto-chō; s/tw ¥4300/7600;) This 'happy house' declares itself Okayama's first business hotel but it's not typical of that genre, having mostly tatami rooms (go for one of these) in a warren-like building. Some rooms have shared bathrooms. Groups and families are welcomed (up to six people from ¥3800 per person), and what other business hotel has an old-school video-game table in the hotel lounge?

The owners are very welcoming but note that they don't speak English.

Okayama View Hotel HOTEL ¥¥
(岡山ビューホテル; 086-224-2000; www.okaview.jp; 1-11-17 Naka-sange; s/tw from ¥6300/10,500; @) Blonde-wood fittings and beds on the floor in the 'concept' rooms here make this an attractive modern Japanese option. Rooms are small but cosy and the hotel is in a good spot between the station and Kōraku-en.

Central Hotel Okayama HOTEL ¥¥
(セントラルホテル岡山; 086-222-2121; www.c-hotelokayama.co.jp; 1-10-28 Tamachi; s/tw from ¥4800/8000; @) Behind the rather pedestrian name are thoughtfully designed (if small) wood-hued rooms with neatly hidden amenities, friendly service, and a hotel with an interesting history (ask about the room at the top). There is a good restaurant attached, where you can also have breakfast (¥600).

MOMOTARŌ, THE PEACH BOY

Okayama Prefecture and Kagawa Prefecture, on the island of Shikoku, are linked by the legend of Momotarō, the Peach Boy, who emerged from the stone of a peach and, backed up by a monkey, a pheasant and a dog, defeated a three-eyed, three-toed people-eating demon. The island of Megi-jima, off Takamatsu in Shikoku, is said to be the site of the clash with the demon. Momotarō may actually have been a Yamato prince who was deified as Kibitsuhiko. His shrine, Kibitsu-jinja, lies along the route of the Kibiji cycling route.

There are statues of Momotarō at JR Okayama Station, he and his sidekicks feature on manhole covers, and the city's biggest street is named after him. One of the most popular souvenir treats from Okayama is also Momotarō's favoured sweet, *kibi-dango*, a soft *mochi*-like dumpling made with millet flour. And if you can sing the first couple of lines of the well-known old children's tune, Momotarō's Song, you'll impress the locals no end. All together now: *Momotarō-san, Momotarō-san, o-koshi ni tsuketa kibi-dango...*

WORTH A TRIP

HATTŌJI

As you head up through the hills past the farms and thatched-roof houses to Hattōji (八塔寺), the crowds and vending-machine-packed streets of big-city Japan begin to feel delightfully out of reach.

The chief reason to journey out here is to stay at the **Hattōji International Villa** (八塔寺国際交流ヴィラ; 086-256-2535; www.international-villa.or.jp; Kagami Yoshinaga-chō, Bizen-shi; r per person ¥3500, whole house up to 8 people/9-13 people ¥25,000/40,000;), a restored farmhouse that is one of two remaining places established by the prefectural government in the late 1980s as accommodation for foreigners. Spending a night or two here is an excellent way to get a sense of Japan outside the well-touristed urban centres.

The house itself has four large tatami rooms separated by sliding doors, a shared bathroom and kitchen, and bicycles that are free to use. There's an open hearth in the common area, where you can burn charcoal for the full olden-days effect, and near the villa you'll find hiking tracks, shrines and temples (where it's possible to join morning meditation). There are a couple of eateries in the area but hours are irregular – stock up on groceries in Okayama or Yoshinaga before you come to Hattōji. Check availability and reserve online. Payment is cash only.

Buses (¥200, 30 minutes, five to six daily Monday to Saturday) run to Hattōji from Yoshinaga (吉永) on the JR San-yō line, accessible by train (¥580, 40 minutes, roughly every hour) from Okayama. The bus drops you near the villa entrance. See the International Villa Group website for the latest schedule.

While you're near Yoshinaga Station, it's worth visiting the historic Edo-period **Shizutani Gakko** (閑谷学校; Shizutani School; http://shizutani.jp; admission ¥300; 9am-5pm), the first public school in Japan, its wood interiors and Bizen-yaki roof tiles now beautifully preserved. The school is about 3km from the station. There are infrequent buses but it's walkable; ask at the station for directions.

Eating

★Okabe TOFU ¥

(おかべ; 1-10-1 Omote-chō; set meals ¥820-870; 11.30am-2pm Mon-Wed, Fri & Sat) Squeeze in at the counter at this small lunch joint and watch the team of women preparing delicous tofu meals as you wait. It's a simple place and there are only three things on the menu, which has some pictures. Try the *okabe teishoku* for a set of several types of tofu. Okabe is on a corner – look for the illustration of a heavily laden tofu seller in a straw hat.

Ajitsukasa Nomura TONKATSU ¥

(味司野村; 086-222-2234; 1-10 Heiwa-chō; meals ¥700-1200; 11am-9pm;) Step into this quiet bamboo-themed restaurant to try local speciality *demi-katsudon* – deep-fried pork cutlets with a thick, rich demi-glace sauce, served on rice. Place your order by purchasing a ticket from the machine inside the entrance. The machine doesn't have English, but the separate menu does and staff can assist.

Tori-soba Ōta NOODLES ¥

(とりそば太田; www.torisoba.com; 1-7-24 Omote-chō; dishes ¥650-1000; 11am-8pm;) The name of this little countertop restaurant is also its trademark dish: *tori-soba* (steaming bowls of noodles packed with chicken and served in a tasty broth). Other options are variations on the chicken, noodle and spring onion theme and even the small serve is a decent feed. Look for the blue sign with white writing in Japanese.

Quiet Village Curry Shop INDIAN ¥

(クワイエットビレッジカレーショップ; 1-6-43 Omote-chō; dishes ¥780-880; 11.30am-7.30pm Tue-Sun;) This cosy restaurant consists of one long table and counter, where the welcoming owners serve up Bengali-style curries and tasty cups of chai. Some English is spoken and there are vegetarian and vegan options.

Padang Padang ITALIAN, FRENCH ¥¥

(パダンパダン; 086-223-6665; www.padangpadang.jp; 1-7-10 Omote-chō; dishes ¥1000-2400; 6pm-midnight Wed-Mon;) Despite the Asian-sounding name, this mellow, lamp-lit restaurant focuses on French and Italian dishes, deftly whipped up in the small open kitchen. There is occasional live music and it's a good spot for a glass of wine after a day of sightseeing.

DON'T MISS

NAKED FESTIVAL

If you're in the Okayama area on the third Saturday in February, head to Saidai-ji for the **Saidai-ji Eyō**, also known as the Hadaka Matsuri (Naked Festival). It takes place at the Kannon-in temple, where a chaotic crowd of around 10,000 men in loincloths and *tabi* (split-toe socks) fight over two sacred *shingi* (wooden batons) while freezing water is poured over them and crowds around the temple look on. The fun kicks off at 10pm, though there's also a version for elementary-school boys earlier in the evening. Sorry, ladies, only the guys are allowed to strip off and fight for the *shingi*, but anyone can watch. Regular trains run to Saidai-ji from Okayama, about 20 minutes away.

Drinking & Nightlife

Izayoi no Tsuki IZAKAYA
(いざ酔いの月; 1-10-2 Ekimae-chō; ⏲5pm-midnight) A convivial atmosphere, walls decorated with sake labels, and an enormous drink menu – just what you want from a local *izakaya*. There are numerous sakes from Okayama Prefecture and beers from local microbreweries. Try the Doppo pilsner or a Kibi Doteshita Bakushu ale. Izoyoi is just off the Sky Mall arcade. Look for the sign written across a yellow moon.

Saudade na Yoru BAR
(サウダーヂな夜; www.saudade-ent.com/saudade; 2nd fl, Shiroshita Bldg, 10-16 Tenjin-chō; ⏲6pm-3am Mon-Fri, 3pm-3am Sat & Sun) This 2nd-floor lounge bar overlooking the Symphony Hall building makes all the right retro-chic moves, with mismatched furniture, ornate-glass lighting and eclectic background music. It has a good drinks list (most priced around ¥700), coffees and a limited food and snacks menu. A ¥300 cover charge applies after 8pm.

Marugo Deli JUICE BAR
(マルゴ・デリ; 1-1-11 Tamachi; juices ¥420, coffees from ¥315; ⏲11am-11pm Mon-Sat, to 9pm Sun, closed 1st Tue of month) Funky little bar with a good range of fresh juices and coffee and a couple of seats outside. Its sign is a number five in a circle.

Aussie Bar PUB
(オージーバー; 1-10-21 Ekimae-chō; ⏲7pm-late) This casual expat-run watering hole is popular with the city's English-speaking population. Pub grub is also served, such as fish and chips and a range of Aussie-themed burgers (the burger with chilli is named after the notoriously hot outback town Oodnadatta).

Information

Momotarō Tourist Information Centre (ももたろう観光センター; ☎086-222-2912; www.okayama-kanko.net/sightseeing; ⏲9am-8pm) Large office with maps and information on Okayama and the region. The helpful staff speak some English and there's free wi-fi. It's in the basement complex below the station – turn right as you come out of the station's east exit, continue past the police box, and look for the sign and escalators on the left.

Okayama Eki-mae Post Office (岡山駅前郵便局; 1-3-1 Ekimae-chō; ⏲9am-5pm Mon-Fri, ATM 7am-11pm Mon-Fri, 9am-9pm Sat, 9am-7pm Sun) Post office nearest the station, with ATMs accepting international cards.

Tourist Information Counter (観光案内所; ⏲9am-6pm) In the station, by the entrance to the *shinkansen* tracks.

Getting There & Away

BUS

Highway buses connect Okayama with major cities across the region. There are also buses between Okayama and Kansai International Airport (3¼ hours, ¥4650).

Buses to Shin-Okayama port (¥490, 40 minutes, one or two per hour) leave from Okayama Station, stopping at Tenmaya bus station in the city centre on the way.

FERRY

Ferries run to Shōdo-shima (p457) and Naoshima (p463) from Shin-Okayama port and Uno port respectively.

TRAIN

Okayama is on the JR San-yō line and *shinkansen* line, connecting to Osaka (¥5500, 50 minutes) in the east and Hiroshima (¥5500, 35 minutes) to the west. There are also rail links to Takamatsu in Shikoku (¥1510, 55 minutes) and Yonago in Tottori Prefecture on the limited express Yakumo (¥4750, two hours).

Getting Around

Okayama can be seen on foot or with a couple of short tram rides. The Higashi-yama line takes you to the main attractions, going all the way up Momotarō-Ōdōri, then turning right. The Seiki-bashi line turns right earlier, passing the Central Post Office. Travel within the central city area costs ¥100. Okayama is also a good city for cycling.

JR Eki-Rinkun Rent-a-cycle (レンタサイクル駅リンくん; ☎086-223-7081; per day ¥310; ⊙7am-9.50pm) Bike rental on the east side of Okayama Station.

Eki Rent-a-Car (駅レンタカー; ☎086-224-1363; www.ekiren.co.jp; per day from ¥5940; ⊙8am-8pm) Car rental office on the east side of Okayama Station.

Bizen 備前

☎0869 / POP 37,800

The Bizen region has been renowned for its ceramics since the Kamakura period (1185–1333). The pottery produced here tends to be earthy and subdued, and has been prized by dedicated tea-ceremony aficionados for centuries. Travellers with an interest in pottery will find the gritty Bizen town of **Imbe** (伊部) and its kilns a worthwhile side trip from Okayama.

Most places of ceramic interest are within easy walking distance of Imbe Station. The **information counter** (☎0869-64-1001; www.touyuukai.jp; ⊙9am-6pm Wed-Mon), inside the souvenir shop on the left as you exit the platform, has a very good *Inbe Walk* map, in English, showing the locations of kilns, shops and other sites.

On the 2nd floor of the station building is a gallery run by the **Friends of Bizen-yaki Ceramics Society** (岡山県備前焼陶友会; www.touyuukai.jp; ⊙9.30am-5.30pm Wed-Mon) FREE, selling a wide range of ceramics by contemporary potters.

The concrete building to the right as you exit the station is the **Okayama Prefectural Bizen Ceramics Art Museum** (岡山県備前陶芸美術館; admission ¥700; ⊙9.30am-5pm Tue-Sun), with pieces from the Muromachi (1333–1568) and Momoyama (1568–1600) periods, plus work by several modern artists who have been designated 'Living National Treasures'.

Walking up the road leading north from the station, you'll begin to spot the smoking red-brick chimneys and the bamboo groves of the hills behind the town. There are several galleries and shops on this road and more along the road that forms a T-intersection at the end. It's worth stopping in at **Kibido** (黄薇堂; ☎0869-64-4467; www.bizenyakikibido.com; ⊙9am-5pm Mon-Sat, noon-5pm Sun), a kiln and gallery-shop run by the Kimura family, one of the six original families granted official permission in the early 1600s to produce pottery in this region. Here it's possible to take a free tour of the traditional step-style *nobirigama* kiln, and see the current generation of Kimura artists at work. Tours in English are available – they may be able to accommodate if you just drop in, but contact them in advance to avoid disappointment.

It's a short walk up one of the lanes leading uphill from the road to glimpse the large kiln ruins of **Tempogama** (天保窯), c 1832, now fenced off for protection. Continue up from here to the understated and pretty wooden shrine **Imbe-jinja** (忌部神社). Further along is **Amatsu-jinja** (天津神社), decorated with Bizen-yaki figures of the animals of the Chinese zodiac.

Several kilns in the area offer the chance to try your hand at making your own masterpiece. Try **Bishūgama** (備州窯; ☎0869-64-1160; www.gift.or.jp/bisyu; 302-2 Imbe, Bizen-shi; ⊙9am-3pm), where making a piece will cost ¥2700 or ¥3780, depending on the type of firing you choose. The information counter in the station has a list of other kilns and costs.

There is one direct train an hour to Imbe from Okayama (¥580, 40 minutes) on the Akō line (赤穂線), bound for Banshū-Akō (播州赤穂) and Aioi (相生).

Kurashiki 倉敷

☎086 / POP 475,400

Kurashiki's main attraction is its atmospheric Bikan quarter (美観地区), an area of historic buildings along an old willow-edged canal, where a picturesque group of black-and-white warehouses has been converted into museums, and laneways are lined with old wooden houses and shops.

In the feudal era the warehouses here were used to store rice brought by boat from the surrounding countryside. Later, the town became an important textile centre, under the Kurabō Textile Company. Owner Ōhara Magosaburō built up a collection of European art and opened the Ōhara Museum of Art in 1930, which today draws many Japanese tourists.

Kurashiki

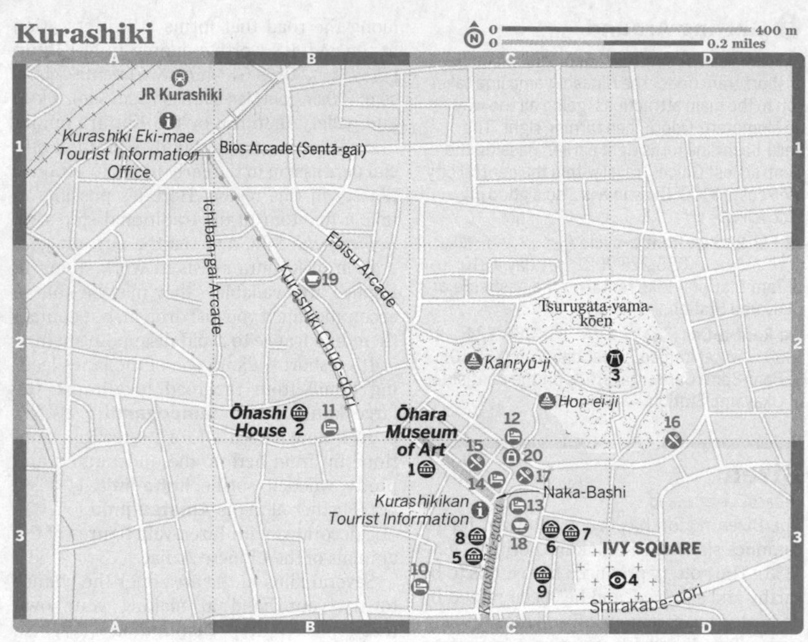

Kurashiki

Top Sights

1	Ōhara Museum of Art	C3
2	Ōhashi House	B2

Sights

3	Achi-jinja	D2
4	Ivy Square	D3
5	Japan Rural Toy Museum	C3
6	Kojima Torajirō Memorial Hall	C3
7	Kurabō Memorial Hall	C3
8	Kurashiki Museum of Folk-craft	C3
9	Momotarō Karakuri Hakubutsukan	C3

Sleeping

10	Cuore Kurashiki	C3
11	Dormy Inn Kurashiki	B2
12	Guesthouse U-Rin-An	C2
13	Ryokan Kurashiki	C3
14	Ryokan Tsurugata	C3

Eating

15	Kamoi	C3
16	KuKu	D2
17	Mamakari-tei	C3

Drinking & Nightlife

18	Kurashiki Coffee-Kan	C3
19	SWLABR	B2

Shopping

20	Tsuneki Tea Shop	C3

Sights

★ Ōhashi House — HISTORIC BUILDING

(大橋家住宅; http://ohashi-ke.com; 3-21-31 Achi; admission ¥500; ⌚9am-5pm Tue-Sun) Between the station and the canal area is the beautifully restored Ōhashi House, built in 1793. The house belonged to one of Kurashiki's richest families and was built at a time when prosperous merchants were beginning to claim privileges that had previously been the preserve of the samurai.

★ Ōhara Museum of Art — GALLERY

(大原美術館; www.ohara.or.jp; 1-1-15 Chūō; admission ¥1300; ⌚9am-5pm, closed Mon except late Jul, Aug & Oct) This is Kurashiki's premier museum, housing the predominantly Western art collection amassed by local textile magnate Ōhara Magosaburō (1880–1943), with the help of artist Kojima Torajirō (1881–1929). The varied assemblage of paintings, prints and sculpture features works by Picasso, Cézanne, El Greco and Matisse, and one of Monet's water-lilies paintings (said to have been bought from the man himself by Torajirō while visiting Monet's home in 1920).

While no rival to the major galleries of Europe, it's an interesting collection and one of the town's biggest attractions for Japanese tourists.

The valid-all-day ticket gets you into the museum's Craft & Asiatic Art Gallery, the contemporary Japanese collection housed in an annexe behind the main building, plus the Kojima Torajirō Memorial Hall (p455).

Japan Rural Toy Museum MUSEUM
(日本郷土玩具館; 1-4-16 Chuō; admission ¥400; ⏲9am-5pm) Four rooms are crammed with displays of wooden toys, masks, dolls and spinning tops (including a world-record breaker), and a colourful array of kites just beckoning to be put on a breeze. You can purchase a new toy of your own in the shop, which also sells crafts and regional artwork.

Ivy Square SQUARE
(アイビースクエア) Present-day Ivy Square was once the site of Ōhara's Kurabō textile factories. The company moved into more modern premises a long time ago, and the red-brick factory buildings (dating from 1889) now house a hotel, restaurants, shops and yet more museums, including the **Kurabō Memorial Hall** (倉紡記念館; www.kurabo.co.jp/kurabo_kinenkan; 7-1 Honmachi; admission ¥350; ⏲9am-5pm), where you can learn all about the history of the Japanese textile industry.

Momotarō Karakuri Hakubutsukan MUSEUM
(桃太郎のからくり博物館; 5-11 Honmachi; adult/child ¥600/400; ⏲10am-5pm) Part gallery and part funhouse, this small museum is devoted to local legend Momotarō (p450), with memorabilia, toys and depictions of the peach boy from over the years. On the ground floor is a collection of amusing displays designed to trick the eye – here you can get a photo of yourself emerging from a peach like Momotarō himself. The 'interactive' displays are dated (think high-school project before computers), but this is part of the charm. Silly fun for a rainy day.

Kojima Torajirō Memorial Hall MUSEUM
(児島虎次郎記念館; www.ivysquare.co.jp/cultural/torajiro.html; 7-2 Honmachi; admission ¥500; ⏲9am-5pm Tue-Sun) Kojima Torajirō was the European-style painter who went above and beyond in helping Ōhara build up his art collection; head to this museum to immerse yourself in his life. Entry is included in the ticket for the Ōhara Art Museum.

Kurashiki Museum of Folk-craft MUSEUM
(倉敷民芸館; http://kurashiki-mingeikan.com; 1-4-11 Chuō; admission ¥700; ⏲9am-5pm Tue-Sun Mar-Nov, to 4.15pm Dec-Feb) Housed in an attractive complex of rice warehouses dating from the late 18th century, with interesting exhibits of ceramics, glassware, textiles and furniture.

Achi-jinja SHINTO SHRINE
(阿智神社; 12-1 Honmachi) A short walk from the canal area are the steep stone steps that lead up to this shrine in **Tsurugatayama-kōen**, a park that overlooks the old area of town. The shrine is home to a wisteria tree throught to be between 300 and 500 years old.

Sleeping

Kurashiki is a good place to spend a night in a ryokan so you can soak up the olde-worlde atmosphere. There are also plenty of Western-style business hotels around the station and along Chuō-dōri.

★ **Cuore Kurashiki** HOSTEL ¥
(クオーレ倉敷; ☎086-486-3443; www.bs-cuore.com; 1-9-4 Chūō; dm/s/tw ¥3500/4500/7500; ⊖📶) Artistic and quirky touches in the rooms and common areas, which were decorated by staff, and a large lounge-cafe-bar area on the ground floor make this a great budget option. The cubby-hole-style dorm beds are a cosy change from a standard bunk, and the 'VIP' private room has a good-sized shower.

Guesthouse U-Rin-An HOSTEL ¥
(☎086-426-1180; www.u-rin.com; 2-15 Honmachi; dm ¥3780; ⊖📶) Friendly U-Rin-An has shared tatami rooms in a traditional old house near the Bikan quarter. There's a kitchen and cafe, and the guesthouse also hosts events. Stay more than one night and the rate is discounted. Cash only.

Dormy Inn Kurashiki HOTEL ¥¥
(ドーミーイン倉敷; ☎086-426-5489; www.hotespa.net/hotels/kurashiki; 3-21-11 Achi; s/tw from ¥6000/8500; ⊖@📶) The pick of the Western-style chains, Dormy Inn is not far from the historic district and has a little something extra to tip the scales in its favour – an onsen on the top floor. There are also complimentary *soba* noodles in the evening.

★Ryokan Kurashiki RYOKAN ¥¥¥
(旅館くらしき; ☎086-422-0730; www.ryokan-kurashiki.jp; 4-1 Honmachi; r per person with 2 meals from ¥29,000; P) By the canal in the heart of the historic district and incorporating several beautifully restored Edo-period buildings, this is probably the best ryokan in town. The spacious suites all have tatami lounge areas with attached twin-bed rooms and bathrooms. Dinner is a multicourse *kaiseki* affair featuring delicacies from the Inland Sea. Some English is spoken.

Ryokan Tsurugata RYOKAN ¥¥¥
(鶴形; ☎086-424-1635; www.turugata.jp; 1-3-15 Chūō; r per person with 2 meals ¥15,220-34,560) This welcoming ryokan in a converted building right in the historic area has tatami rooms overlooking a garden, and meals featuring local seafood. Prices vary according to room size, and most rooms have shared bathrooms. A little English is spoken.

Eating & Drinking

Within the historic area there are numerous eateries and you'll pay a little more for the atmosphere that goes with your food. You'll find cheaper, quick-eats options along Chūō-dōri and in the arcades running from the station.

KuKu INDIAN ¥
(クウクウ; 11-19 Honmachi; meals ¥750-1200; ⏲11.30am-5.30pm Thu-Tue; 🚭 📋) White adobe-style walls and South Asian knick-knacks set the scene at this diminutive cafe-restaurant. There's a menu of simple Indian curries (and a Thai green curry), with set courses at lunch (11.30am to 2pm) including salad, dessert and a tasty cup of chai.

★Mamakari-tei SEAFOOD ¥¥
(ままかり亭; ☎086-427-7112; www.hamayoshi-kurashiki.jp; 3-12 Honmachi; dishes ¥840-3150; ⏲11am-2pm & 5-10pm Tue-Sun; 📋) This traditional eatery, in a 200-year-old warehouse with chunky beams and long wooden tables, is famed for the sardine-like local speciality. The tasty fish is supposed to induce bouts of uncontrollable feasting, so that people are obliged to *kari* (borrow) more *mama* (rice) from their neighbours in order to carry on with their binge.

There are sets at lunch and *kaiseki*-style course options (from ¥4200; reservations recommended) available at dinner, as well as an à la carte menu.

Kamoi SUSHI, SASHIMI ¥¥
(カモ井; ☎086-422-0606; 1-3-17 Chūō; meals ¥1080-2800; ⏲10am-6pm Tue-Sun; 🚭 📋) A large, pleasant canal-side restaurant opposite the Ōhara Museum, serving sashimi set meals, seafood-and-rice dishes, and some desserts. You can get the local sardine-like speciality here in *mamakari-teishoku*. Cash only.

Kurashiki Coffee-Kan CAFE
(倉敷珈琲館; www.kurashiki-coffeekan.com; 4-1 Honmachi; coffees ¥500-850; ⏲10am-5pm) The low-ceilinged, wood-and-brick interior of this caffeine-lovers' paradise is thick with the aroma of freshly roasted beans. The menu features coffee and coffee only, though you can choose hot or cold. It's on the canal next to Ryokan Kurashiki.

SWLABR CAFE, BAR
(2-18-2 Achi; ⏲11.30am-3am) After the Bikan area closes down, relax with the good music and friendly staff at the slightly scruffy SWLABR. By day it serves as a cafe with light meals and cakes; by night it's a bar. It's the green weatherboard house on the corner, a couple of blocks southeast of the station.

Shopping

Kurashiki has numerous shops selling all manner of souvenirs, plus accessories, Bizen ceramics, sweets and more.

★Tsuneki Tea Shop DRINK
(つねき茶舗; http://tsuneki.net; 3-9 Honmachi; ⏲10am-6pm Mon-Sat) Follow the earthy aroma of roasting leaves to this specialist tea shop, where a machine in front churns out fresh *hōjicha* (roasted green tea) to be sold by the bag. You can also buy *mugicha* (barley tea), and tea-brewing instructions in English are available.

Information

Kurashiki Eki-mae Tourist Information Office (倉敷駅前観光案内所; ☎086-424-1220; 2nd fl, Kurashiki City Plaza, 1-7-2 Achi; ⏲9am-7pm, to 6pm Oct-Mar) Just out of the station on the second level and to the right.

Kurashikikan Tourist Information (倉敷館観光案内所; ☎086-422-0542; www.kurashiki-tabi.jp; 1-4-8 Chuō; ⏲9am-6pm) The main tourist centre, in the Bikan quarter.

Getting There & Around

Kurashiki is on the JR San-yō main line just west of Okayama (¥320, 15 minutes). Shin-Kurashiki, on the *shinkansen* line, is two stops from Kurashiki Station (¥200, nine minutes). Kurashiki is easily explored on foot. It's possible to get around by bike, though this may end up being more of a nuisance than convenience, as the lanes are narrow and often crowded.

Shōdo-shima 小豆島

☎0879 / POP 31,200

Famed for its olive groves and as the setting of the classic film *Nijūshi-no-hitomi* (*Twenty-Four Eyes*; it tells the story of a village school teacher and her young charges), Shōdo-shima makes an enjoyable day trip or overnight escape from big-city Japan. It has a smattering of sights but is mainly appealing for its mountainous landscape, scenic coastal roads and Inland Sea vistas.

Tonoshō is the main town and port, and also where you can see the 'world's narrowest navigable strait' (Dobuchi Strait), which runs through the centre of town. The island is popular during summer and when the autumn leaves are at their peak in October and November. Come out of season and you'll find a sleepy isle with very few fellow travellers.

Sights & Activities

Around the Coast

Shōdo-shima Olive Park PARK

(小豆島オリーブ公園; www.olive-pk.jp; 1941-1 Nishimura-misaki; ⏲8.30am-5pm) **FREE** This park is where the island's olive-growing activities are celebrated with several whitewashed buildings, some fake Grecian ruins, a museum and opportunities to buy olive-themed souvenirs. It's worth tolerating the kitsch for the **Sun Olive Onsen** (サン・オリーブ温泉; admission ¥700; ⏲noon-9pm), where you can enjoy fabulous views of the Japanese Aegean from a variety of herbal baths.

★Marukin Soy Sauce Historical Museum MUSEUM

(マルキン醤油記念館; admission ¥210; ⏲9am-4pm) Shōdo-shima was famous for its soy beans long before olives arrived, and several old soy-sauce companies are still in business here. Marukin has a small museum with displays of the sauce-making process, old implements, photos and interesting facts you never knew about the ubiquitous brown stuff. There are good English explanations, and you can try the surprisingly tasty soy-sauce-flavoured ice cream.

It's on the main road between Kusakabe and Sakate.

Twenty-Four Eyes Movie Village MUSEUM

(二十四の瞳映画村; www.24hitomi.or.jp; admission ¥700, combined ticket with the old school ¥790; ⏲9am-5pm) Just north of Sakate is the turn-off to the picturesque fishing village of Tanoura (田ノ浦), site of the village school that featured in the film *Twenty-Four Eyes*. The film was based on a novel by local writer Tsuboi Sakae and was a huge hit in postwar Japan. At this movie village you can see the set used in the 1980s remake of the original 1954 B&W film.

Misaki Branch School HISTORIC BUILDING

(岬の分教場; www.24hitomi.or.jp; admission ¥200, combined ticket with the movie village ¥790; ⏲9am-5pm) Worth visiting in Tanoura is this perfectly preserved 1902 school, setting for the *Twenty-Four Eyes* story and the 1954 film. It's a short walk from the movie village on the road back to Sakate.

Central Mountains

★Kanka Gorge & Ropeway OUTDOORS

(寒霞渓; www.kankakei.co.jp; ropeway one way/return ¥750/1350; ⏲ropeway 8.30am-5pm, to 4.30pm late Dec–late Mar) The cable car (寒霞

SHŌDO-SHIMA FERRIES

ORIGIN	DESTINATION	FARE (¥)	DURATION	FREQUENCY (PER DAY)
Himeji	Fukuda	1520	1hr 40min	7
Shin-Okayama	Tonoshō	1050	70min	13
Takamatsu	Tonoshō (regular)	690	1hr	15
Takamatsu	Tonoshō (high speed)	1170	30min	16
Takamatsu	Ikeda	690	1hr	8
Takamatsu	Kusakabe (regular)	690	1hr	5
Takamatsu	Kusakabe (high speed)	1170	45min	5
Uno	Tonoshō (via Teshima)	1230	1½hr	7

Shōdo-shima

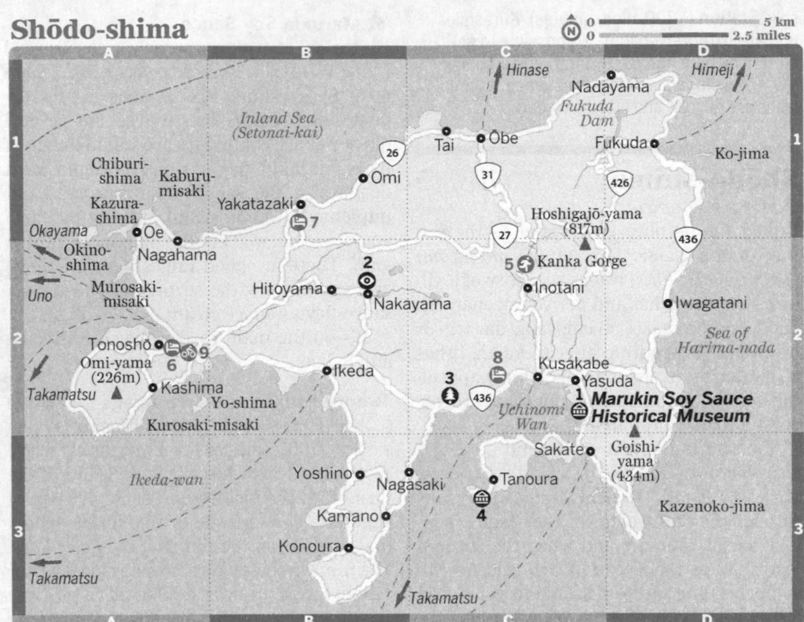

渓ロープウエイ) is the main attraction at Kanka-kei in the central mountains, making a spectacular trip through the gorge, particularly when the foliage is ablaze with autumn colours (drawing scores of leaf-peepers). You can also take in the breathtaking views of the Inland Sea from the area around the upper cable-car station without taking the ride.

An alternative for keen walkers is to climb between the lower and upper cable-car stations via the Omote 12 Views (表12景; 2.3km) and Ura Eight Views (裏8景; 1.8km) tracks. There are other scenic walks from the upper station, including a hike to the eastern peak of Hoshigajō-yama (星ヶ城東峰; 817m).

On weekends, and on weekdays during peak periods, there are four buses a day from Kusakabe port to the lower cable-car station (紅雲亭; Kōuntei), with additional services during the autumn leaf-viewing season. There are no buses during winter.

Nakayama Rice Fields RICE TERRACES

(中山千枚田; Nakayama Senmaida) About 4km inland from the Ikeda ferry terminal are Nakayama's 'thousand rice fields'. The terraces are pretty in any season but are especially picturesque after rice planting in late April or early May, when the water-filled fields become a hillside of mirrors.

Festivals & Events

Nōson Kabuki THEATRE

Shōdo-shima was famous during the Edo period for its tradition of rural kabuki (stylised Japanese theatre), and two 17th-century thatched theatres survive in the mountain villages east of Tonoshō. Performances are held on 3 May at the Rikyū Hachiman Shrine in Hitoyama (肥土山) and on the second Sunday in October at the Kasuga Shrine in Nakayama (中山).

Sleeping & Eating

Minshuku Maruse MINSHUKU ¥

(民宿マルセ; 0879-62-2385; http://new-port.biz/maruse/1.htm; r per person from ¥3700;) This welcoming, neatly kept place next to Tonoshō's post office is a short walk from the ferry terminal. It has Japanese-style rooms with shared bathrooms. Meals are available and feature local seafood.

Shōdo-shima Olive Youth Hostel HOSTEL ¥

(小豆島オリーブユースホステル; 0879-82-6161; www.jyh.gr.jp/shoudo; 1072 Nishimura, Uchinomi-chō; dm ¥2808;) This pleasant hostel near the waterfront has bunk-bed dorms and tatami rooms. Meals and bike rental are available. Buses stop in front of the hostel (at the Shōdoshimi Orību-Yūsu-

Shōdo-shima

Top Sights

1 Marukin Soy Sauce Historical Museum....C2

Sights

Misaki Branch School....(see 4)
2 Nakayama Rice Fields....B2
3 Shōdo-shima Olive Park....C2
4 Twenty-Four Eyes Movie Village....C3

Activities, Courses & Tours

5 Kanka Gorge & Ropeway....C2
Sun Olive Onsen....(see 3)

Sleeping

Business Hotel New Port....(see 6)
6 Minshuku Maruse....A2
7 Resort Hotel Olivean....B1
8 Shōdo-shima Olive Youth Hostel....C2

Eating

Dutch Café Cupid & Cotton....(see 3)

Information

Tourist Information Booth....(see 6)

Transport

Asahiya Rent-a-Cycle....(see 6)
9 Ishii Rent-a-Cycle....A2
Orix Rent-a-Car....(see 6)

mae stop), or it's about a 20-minute walk from Kusakabe port.

Business Hotel New Port HOTEL ¥¥
(ビジネスホテル・ニューポート; 0879-62-6310; www.new-port.biz; s/tw from ¥4180/7780;) Run by the same friendly management as at Minshuku Maruse, this small business hotel is handy if you want a base near the Tonoshō port. They have both Western-style and tatami rooms. Go right when you come out of the ferry terminal – it's on the right about a minute's walk away.

Resort Hotel Olivean RESORT ¥¥¥
(リゾートホテルオリビアン; 0879-65-2311; www.olivean.com; tw with meals from ¥25,000;) This grand complex has it all: tennis courts, open-air onsen, swimming pool, restaurants and sunset views from spacious Western- and Japanese-style accommodation. There are courtesy buses to the resort from Tonoshō.

★**Dutch Café Cupid & Cotton** CAFE ¥
(ダッチカフェキューピッドアンドコトン; 0879-82-4616; lunch set ¥1000; 11am-5pm Fri-Tue;) Inside a knick-knack-filled windmill on a hillside, Dutch Café serves savoury and sweet 'real Dutch' pancakes. Turn right at the top of the Olive Park complex and look for the small sign pointing up a narrow road on the left.

Information

Tonoshō, at the western end of the island, is the biggest town and the usual point of arrival from Takamatsu or Okayama. Check www.town.shodoshima.lg.jp for more information.

Tourist Information Booth (0879-62-5300; 8.30am-5.15pm) Inside the Tonoshō ferry terminal.

Getting There & Away

There are several ferry routes to and from Shōdo-shima's ports.

If you're going to Shōdo-shima from Okayama, pick up a *Kamome bus kippu* (one way ¥1300), a discounted combination ticket covering the bus from Okayama Station to Shin-Okayama port plus the ferry to Shōdo-shima. They're sold at the booth in the bus terminal of Okayama Station, and in the Tonoshō ferry terminal.

Getting Around

The most convenient way to see the island is by car and it's definitely worth hiring one for the day to take in all the scenic routes. Buses do not go everywhere and services are infrequent.

BICYCLE

Cycling can be enjoyable around the coast if you have plenty of time, but you'd want to be very keen to venture inland as there are some serious climbs. Bikes can also be rented at the youth hostel near Kusakabe.

Asahiya Rent-a-Cycle (旭屋レンタサイクル; 0879-62-0162; gearless bikes per hr ¥300; 8.30am-5pm) Inside the Asahiya hotel, opposite the post office in Tonoshō, a short walk from the ferry terminal.

Ishii Rent-a-Cycle (石井レンタサイクル; 0879-62-1866; www7.ocn.ne.jp/~ishii-c/rental.htm; Olive-dōri; gearless bikes per day ¥1000, mountain & electric bikes ¥2000; 8.30am-5pm) It's worth the walk here to get a bicycle with gears. It's about 2km from Tonoshō port. Ask at the ferry terminal for a town map with directions.

BUS

Shōdo-shima Olive Bus (小豆島オリーブバス; 0879-62-0171; www.shodoshima-olive-bus.com) operates services around the island. The most frequent bus, at one or two per hour, runs between Tonoshō and Kusakabe ports, passing Ikeda and Olive Park. Some continue on to Sakate port, passing the Marukin Soy Sauce

Historical Museum; some head north to Fukuda port. There are infrequent services along the north coast, inland to Nakayama, and to Tanoura. A one-/two-day pass is ¥2000/2500, though if you're only taking the bus a couple of times it's cheaper to pay the individual fares as you go.

CAR

There are a handful of car-rental places. Note you can bring a car on some ferries, but it can cost more than hiring one on the island.

Orix Rent-a-Car (オリックスレンタカー小豆島; ☎0879-62-4669; http://car.orix.co.jp; 6hr from ¥4725; ⏲8.30am-6pm) Has a basic touring map in English. Walk about two minutes along the road heading right out of the Tonoshō ferry terminal.

Naoshima 直島

☎087 / POP 3400

As the location of the Benesse Art Site, the island of Naoshima has become one of the region's biggest tourist attractions, offering a unique opportunity to see some of Japan's best contemporary art in gorgeous natural settings.

The Benesse project started in the early '90s, when the Benesse Corporation chose Naoshima as the setting for its growing collection of modern art. Since then, Naoshima has continued to be transformed – once home to a dwindling population subsisting on the proceeds of a small fishing industry and the old-age pension, it now has a number of world-class art galleries and installations, and has attracted creative types from all over the country to set up businesses here. The art movement has not stopped at Naoshima's shores, with museums and art sites popping up on other islands in the Inland Sea.

In addition to the main museums of Naoshima, numerous works of outdoor sculpture are situated around the coast, including Kusama Yayoi's *Yellow Pumpkin*, which has become a symbol of the island.

Sights & Activities

Most sights and activities are clustered around the Honmura (本村), Miyanoura (宮ノ浦) and Benesse Art Site areas.

During holiday seasons the museums can become quite crowded and you may find you have to queue.

★Art House Project ART INSTALLATION
(家プロジェクト; www.benesse-artsite.jp/arthouse; combined ticket ¥1030; ⏲10am-4.30pm Tue-Sun) In Honmura, half a dozen traditional buildings have been turned over to contemporary artists to use as the setting for creative installations. Highlights include Ōtake Shinrō's shacklike **Haisha** (はいしゃ), its Statue of Liberty sculpture rising up through the levels; James Turrell's experiment with light in **Minami-dera** (南寺), where you enter in total darkness…and wait; and Sugimoto Hiroshi's play on the traditional **Go'o Shrine** (護王神社), with a glass staircase, and narrow underground **Stone Chamber**.

The sites are within walking distance of each other. Take the Naoshima bus to the Nōkyō-mae stop to start exploring. Buy a ticket at the tourist counter in the Miyanoura ferry terminal, at Honmura Lounge, or at the tobacco shop near the bus stop.

Benesse House Museum GALLERY
(ベネッセハウス; www.benesse-artsite.jp/benessehouse-museum; admission ¥1030; ⏲8am-9pm) Award-winning architect Andō Tadao designed this stunning museum and hotel on the south coast of the island. Among the works here are pieces by Andy Warhol, David Hockney, Jasper Johns, and Japanese artists such as Ōtake Shinrō.

Chichū Art Museum GALLERY
(地中美術館; www.benesse-artsite.jp/chichu; admission ¥2060; ⏲10am-6pm Tue-Sun, to 5pm Oct-Feb) A short walk from Benesse House is this Andō Tadao creation. A work of art itself, the museum consists of a series of cool concrete-walled spaces sitting snugly underground. Lit by natural light, it provides a remarkable setting for several Monet water-lily paintings, some monumental sculptures by Walter De Maria and installations by James Turrell. Outside is the Chichū garden, created in the spirit of Monet's garden in Giverny.

At peak times a 'timed ticket' system may be in place, designating the time you are able to purchase a ticket and enter.

Lee Ufan Museum GALLERY
(李禹煥美術館; www.benesse-artsite.jp/lee-ufan; admission ¥1030; ⏲10am-6pm Tue-Sun, to 5pm Oct-Feb) Adding to Benesse's suite of museums is yet another design from the irrepressible Andō. It houses works by the renowned Korean-born artist (and philosopher) Lee Ufan, who was a leading figure in the Mono-ha movement of the 1960s and '70s.

Naoshima

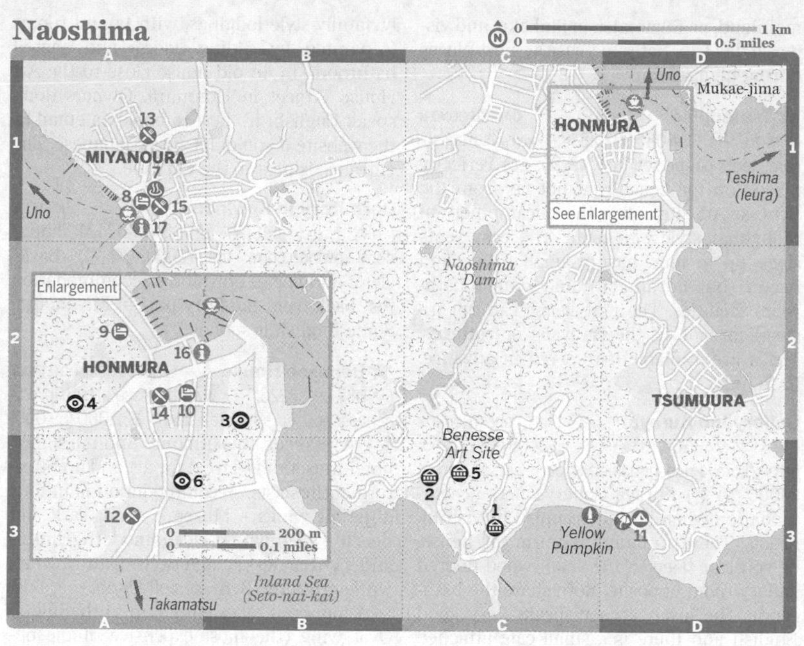

Naoshima

Sights

1 Benesse House Museum C3
2 Chichū Art Museum C3
3 Go'o Shrine B2
4 Haisha A2
5 Lee Ufan Museum C3
6 Minami-dera A3

Activities, Courses & Tours

7 Naoshima Bath – I Heart Yū A1

Sleeping

Benesse House .... (see 1)
8 Dormitory in Kowloon A1
9 Gallery Inn Kuraya A2
10 Minshuku Oyaji-no-Umi A2
11 Tsutsuji-sō D3

Eating

12 Cafe Salon Naka-Oku A3
13 Cin.na.mon A1
14 Genmai-Shinshoku Aisunao A2
Museum Restaurant Issen .... (see 1)
15 Shioya Diner A1

Information

16 Honmura Lounge & Archive A2
17 Marine Station Tourist Information Centre A1

Transport

Cafe Ougiya Rent-a-Cycle .... (see 17)

★ **Naoshima Bath – I Heart Yū** SENTO
(直島銭湯; www.benesse-artsite.jp/en/naoshima sento; admission ¥510; ⏲2-9pm Tue-Fri, 10am-9pm Sat & Sun) For a unique bathing experience, take a soak at this colourful fusion of Japanese bathing tradition and contemporary art, designed by Ōtake Shinrō, where there really is an elephant in the room. It's a couple of minutes' walk inland from Miyanoura port. Look for the building with the palm trees out front.

The name is a play on words – 'Yū' refers to hot water in Japanese.

Sleeping

The accommodation scene is dominated by privately run *minshuku* (guesthouses). Not a lot of English is spoken, but locals are becoming increasingly used to foreign guests. If you prefer hotel-style facilities, Benesse House is your only real option. Alternatively, you can stay in Okayama or Uno port on the mainland, or Takamatsu in Shikoku, and visit it as a day trip. Rates increase at most places during high season.

★Tsutsuji-sō CAMPGROUND ¥
(つつじ荘; ☎087-892-2838; www.tsutsujiso.com; tents per person from ¥3780;) Perfectly placed on the beachfront not far from the Benesse Art Site area is this encampment of Mongolian-style *pao* tents. The cosy tents sleep up to four, have a small fridge and heater (but no air-con), and shared bathroom facilities. The tent-averse can opt instead for one of the caravans or cottages. Meals are available if reserved in advance. Cash only.

Gallery Inn Kuraya GUESTHOUSE ¥
(ギャラリーインくらや; ☎087-892-2253; http://kuraya-naoshima.net; per person from ¥4000;) Kuraya Gallery offers accommodation when it's not occupied by visiting artists. There's a tatami room in the house, or you can sleep in the small wood-floored gallery room opposite. Both share the bathroom. The lovely owner speaks very good English and there is a small cafe attached (irregular hours).

Kuraya is near Honmura port, on the left if you're walking towards the Art House Project's 'Ishibashi'.

Minshuku Oyaji-no-Umi MINSHUKU ¥
(民宿おやじの海; ☎090-5261-7670; http://ameblo.jp/naosima-oyajinoumi; r per person from ¥4200; @) This is a good option for friendly, family-style lodgings, with tatami rooms (separated by sliding doors) and shared bathroom, in an old house close to the Art House Project in Honmura. Owners don't speak English; it's best to book via email or the website if you don't speak Japanese. The entrance is next to the Cat Cafe.

Dormitory in Kowloon HOSTEL ¥
(ドミトリーin九龍; ☎090-7974-2424; http://domi-kowloon.com; dm ¥2900; @) Basic, clean and cheap dormitory accommodation just back from the ferry port in Miyanoura. Some English is spoken.

★Benesse House BOUTIQUE HOTEL ¥¥¥
(☎087-892-3223; www.benesse-artsite.jp/en/benessehouse; tw/ste from ¥32,000/59,000;) A stay at this unique Andō-designed hotel-museum is a treat for art and architecture enthusiasts. Accommodation is in four different wings – Museum, Oval, Park and Beach – each with a clean, modern, clutter- and TV-free design, and decor featuring artworks from the Benesse collection.

A monorail takes guests up to the hilltop Oval wing (the most expensive of the options), where rooms are arranged around a pool of water open to the sky, and there are stunning views from the grassed rooftop. Rooms in Oval are spacious (though the bathrooms are standard issue) and large windows make the most of the views; you may not want to come back down once you're up here. The Beach wing is a newer building by the sea, from where you can see the *Yellow Pumpkin* sculpture. Or stick close to the art with a stay in the Museum lodgings.

Children under seven years old aren't permitted in the Oval and Museum wings. Reserve well in advance.

Eating & Drinking

There are a few cafes in the Art House Project area in Honmura and near the port at Miyanoura. Not many places open in the evenings and hours can be irregular.

★Shioya Diner CAFE ¥
(シオヤダイナー; dishes ¥400-1000; ⊙11am-9pm Tue-Sun;) With rock 'n' roll music, retro furniture and kitsch knick-knacks, Shioya is an odd mix of American diner and grandma's kitchen. The menu features tacos and chilli dogs, and staff sometimes charcoal-grill Cajun chicken on the barbecue out front. It's a great place to relax over a coffee or a meal near Miyanoura port.

DON'T MISS

SETOUCHI ART FESTIVAL

Setouchi Triennale (瀬戸内国際芸術祭; Setouchi International Art Festival; http://setouchi-artfest.jp) This festival of art, music, drama and dance comes around every three years and has a packed calendar of events occurring on multiple Inland Sea islands, many on Naoshima. The 2016 schedule is spread across three seasons: spring (late March to late April), summer (late July to early September) and autumn (early October to early November).

Check the website for the lowdown on events and ferry passes. It's highly recommended you book your accommodation well in advance if you plan to stay on Naoshima during the festival.

★ Cafe Salon Naka-Oku CAFE ¥
(カフェサロン中奥; ☎087-892-3887; www.naka-oku.com; lunch from ¥650, dinner ¥380-750; ⏰11.30am-9pm Wed-Mon; 🗒) Up on a small hill at the rear of a farming plot, Naka-Oku is a good option in the Honmura area, and one of only a couple of places open in the evenings here. It's all wood-beamed warmth and cosiness, with homey specialities like *omuraisu* (omelette filled with rice) at lunchtime, and small dishes with drinks in the evening.

Genmai-Shinshoku Aisunao CAFE ¥
(玄米心食あいすなお; http://aisunao.jp; meals ¥600-900; ⏰11am-5.30pm; 🚭📶✍🗒) 🍃 A tranquil rest stop within the Art House Project area, Aisunao has seating on raised tatami flooring and a decidedly health-conscious menu – try the tasty Aisunao lunch set, with local brown rice, soup and vegies. Desserts (such as soy-milk ice cream), juices and fair-trade coffees are also on offer.

It's around the corner from 'Gokaisho'. Look for the sign with a picture of a bowl of rice.

Cin.na.mon CURRY ¥
(シナモン; www.cin-na-mon.jp; meals ¥650-1000; ⏰11am-3pm & 5-10pm Tue-Sun; 🗒) The laid-back team here serve curries, cakes and smoothies by day, and open up the bar (with some light meals and snacks) at night. It's a short walk from the Miyanoura port.

Museum Restaurant Issen KAISEKI ¥¥¥
(日本料理一扇; ☎087-892-3223; www.benesse-artsite.jp/en/benessehouse/restaurant_cafe.html; breakfasts ¥2100, lunches from ¥2000, dinner courses from ¥6500; ⏰7.30-9.30am, 11.30am-2.30pm & 6-9.45pm; 🚭🗒) The artfully displayed *kaiseki* dinners at this Benesse House basement restaurant are almost too pretty to eat. Courses feature seafood, but there is a veg-dominated option (request a couple of days ahead), and the menu changes with the seasons. Breakfast and lunch are also served. Reservations are recommended.

ℹ Information

The ATMs at the post offices in Miyanoura and Honmura take international cards. Ask at the tourist office for directions.

There are some luggage lockers at Miyanoura port, and luggage can also be left at the Honmura Lounge.

Marine Station Tourist Information Centre (☎087-892-2299; www.naoshima.net; ⏰8.30am-6pm) At the Miyanoura ferry port. Has a comprehensive bilingual map of the island (also downloadable from the website), a walking map and a full list of accommodation options. Note that staff don't make accommodation reservations. Tickets for Art House Project can also be purchased here.

Honmura Lounge & Archive (☎087-840-8273; ⏰10am-4.30pm Tue-Sun) Tourist information in Honmura, with a rest area and left luggage service. Tickets for Art House Project can be purchased.

ℹ Getting There & Away

Naoshima can be visited as a day trip from Okayama or Takamatsu, and it makes a good stopover if you're travelling between Honshū and Shikoku.

From Okayama, take the JR Uno line to Uno (¥580, about an hour); this usually involves a quick change of trains at Chayamachi. Ferries go to Naoshima's main port of Miyanoura from the port near Uno Station (¥290, 15 to 20 minutes, 13 daily). There are also ferries from Uno to the port of Honmura (¥290, 20 minutes, five daily).

Takamatsu is connected to the port of Miyanoura by standard ferry (¥520, 50 minutes, five daily) and high-speed boat (¥1220, 25 minutes, four daily on Fridays, weekends and holidays between March and November; one daily at other times).

Latest ferry timetables can be found on the Benesse Art Site website (www.benesse-artsite.jp) or at the tourist offices in Okayama and Takamatsu.

ℹ Getting Around

Bicycle or the town bus are the best options for getting around Naoshima, though it's possible on foot if you have time – for example, it's just over 2km from Miyanoura port to Honmura and the Art House Project area. There is one **taxi** (☎087-892-3036) on Naoshima, taking up to nine passengers – this has to be reserved before arriving on the island.

BICYCLE

Naoshima is great for cycling and there are a few rental places around Miyanoura ferry port. **Cafe Ougiya Rent-a-Cycle** (☎090-3189-0471; per day ¥300-500; ⏰9am-7pm, to 6pm Dec-Feb) is inside the Marine Station at the port. A few electric bikes (¥1000 per day) and scooters (¥1500 per day) are also available.

BUS

Naoshima 'town bus' minibuses run between Miyanoura, Honmura and Tsutsuji-sō once or twice an hour. It costs ¥100 per ride. From Tsutsuji-sō, there's a free Benesse shuttle, stopping at all the Benesse Art Site museums. In busy seasons buses can fill up quickly, especially towards the end of the day when people are returning to the port to catch ferries. Be sure to check the timetables and allow enough buffer time.

Teshima

If there's not enough to inspire you on Naoshima, get yourself across to Teshima (豊島), a small island between Naoshima and Shōdo-shima with a number of art sites.

A highlight is the **Teshima Art Museum** (豊島美術館; www.benesse-artsite.jp/en/teshima-artmuseum; admission ¥1540; ⊙10am-5pm, 10.30am-4pm Oct-Feb, closed Tue, also closed Wed & Thu Dec-Feb), which is really just an enormous concrete shell, forming a low teardrop-shaped dome on the hillside. Wander through the contemplative space, where cutouts in the shell frame snapshots of blue sky, clouds, or the green of the surrounding hills. Also on the island is the oddly fascinating **Les Archives du Cœur** (心臓音のアーカイブ; www.benesse-artsite.jp/en/boltanski; admission ¥510; ⊙10am-5pm, to 4pm Oct-Feb, closed Tue, also closed Wed & Thu Dec-Feb), a 'heartbeat archive' on a small bay near the Karato port area. There are tens of thousands of registered heartbeats from around the world, and you can listen to them played on a loop in surround sound in the very dark 'heart room' – quite the bizarre experience. For ¥1540 you can record your own and get a keepsake CD.

Be sure to also check out **Teshima Yokoo House** (豊島横尾館; www.benesse-artsite.jp/en/teshima-yokoohouse; admission ¥510; ⊙10am-5pm, to 4pm Oct-Feb, closed Tue Mar-Nov & Tue-Thu Dec-Feb), close to Ieura port. Here an old house has been converted into exhibition spaces, with a colourful take on a traditional Japanese rock garden outside (which locals helped create). Don't miss stepping inside the tower 'waterfall' installation, which is lined with thousands of postcards of waterfalls and seems to go on forever below your feet.

Cycling on the island is highly recommended for getting around. Bikes can be hired at the Ieura port area for ¥500 per day; electric-assist bikes (¥1000 per four hours, ¥100 per additional hour) are also available and a good idea if you're cycling across the island to Karato. There is an infrequent shuttle bus connecting Ieura and Karato (¥200).

Eight ferries a day travel from Uno port on the mainland to Ieura port (¥770, 25 to 40 minutes), with six continuing on to Karato port (¥1030); these ferries also continue to the island of Shōdo-shima. From Takamatsu, three to five ferries go to Ieura daily (¥1330, 35 minutes), some also stopping at Honmura on Naoshima. Two ferries a day go from Naoshima's Miyanoura port to Ieura (¥620, 35 minutes; not every day in low season).

Pick up maps and information (some English spoken) at the tourist office near the Ieura ferry terminal.

Kasaoka Islands 笠岡諸島

Located between Kurashiki and Fukuyama, the port of Kasaoka is the jumping-off point for six small islands only connected to the mainland by boat. In particular, the islands of Shiraishi-jima and Manabe-shima are worth visiting to enjoy the slower pace of life as it used to be lived all over the Inland Sea.

Kasaoka is 40 minutes west of Okayama and 25 minutes west of Kurashiki on the JR San-yō line. From the station, it's a seven-minute stroll down to the port for boats to Shiraishi-jima and on to Manabe-shima.

Shiraishi-jima 白石島

☎0865 / POP 750

Sleepy Shiraishi-jima is popular in the summer for its beaches and there are some good walking paths. Go-everywhere Buddhist saint Kōbō Daishi stopped off here on his way back from China in 806; the temple associated with him, **Kairyū-ji** (開龍寺), incorporates a trail of small shrines leading to a huge boulder on top of the hill.

Visitors can stay at the great-value **International Villa** (☎086-256-2535; www.international-villa.or.jp; r per person ¥3500). The villa is a large house atop a hill, with spacious living areas and kitchen, and an outdoor deck with views of the sea. There are five bedrooms and amenities are shared. It's particularly good for groups or families. The website shows availability, though the Shiraishi Reservations email address is good for seeking more up-to-date general information and for reservations.

There are a handful of eateries on the island, though hours are irregular outside of summer. If you're staying at the Villa, make sure you bring groceries along with you. During summer, resident expat Amy Chavez runs the **Mooo! Bar** (www.mooobar.com) on the beach. It's also possible to rent windsurfing boards and sea kayaks (¥1000 per person per hour).

Eight **Sanyō Kisen** (三洋汽船; ☎0865-62-2866; www.sanyo-kisen.com) ferries run a day to Shiraishi-jima from the port in Kasaoka, about seven minutes from Kasaoka Station. There are four regular services (¥660, 35 minutes) and four high-speed services (¥1130, 22 minutes). The regular services continue on to Manabe-shima. There is also the larger Shiriaishi Ferry (which also takes cars), running four times a day to Shiraishi-jima from Kasaoka (¥530, 45 minutes). Note that this departs from a different dock in Kasaoka, about 20 minutes' walk from the station.

Manabe-shima 真鍋島

☎0865 / POP 300

Manabe-shima is home to more cats than people, and its one small town is an atmospheric maze of old wooden houses, a solitary village shop that has been in business since the Meiji period, and an old-fashioned school. As with everywhere in this part of Japan, Kōbō Daishi got here first – the great man spent time at the **Enpukuji** (円福寺) temple. More recently, the island and all its characters have been wonderfully captured in Florent Chavouet's illustrated book *Manabé Shima*. The locals are sure to show you a copy (and point themselves out in it).

A good reason to venture out here is to stay at the waterfront ryokan **Santora** (島宿三虎; ☎0865-68-3515; www.santora.biz; r per person with 2 meals from ¥10,800;) so you can laze about in its outdoor saltwater bath while watching boats sail by. The rooms are spacious, the shared indoor bathroom has sea views, and the meals feature local seafood and vegies grown by the friendly owners. For something special, go for one of the *hanare* (separate) cabins (from ¥12,900 per person with meals), which have private bathrooms and huge balconies looking out to sea. Note that the owners don't speak English.

There are few places to eat out on the island (most with irregular hours) – the helpful staff at the ferry terminal office can give you some tips.

Eight Sanyo Kisen ferries run a day to Manabe-shima from the port in Kasaoka. There are four regular services (¥1020, one hour and 10 minutes) and four high-speed services (¥1760, 45 minutes), all going via Shiraishi-jima. A water taxi is a convenient alternative option if heading to Santora ryokan, especially for groups, as these can take you from Kasaoka direct to the pier at the ryokan (saving you the walk from the regular ferry dock). Water taxis are ¥10,000 for up to 10 people – Santora can help with details.

YAMAGUCHI & AROUND

Yamaguchi 山口

☎083 / POP 196,600

During the 100 years of civil war that bedevilled Japan until the country was reunited under the Tokugawa in the early 17th century, Yamaguchi prospered as an alternative capital to chaotic Kyoto. In 1550 Jesuit missionary Francis Xavier paused for two months here on his way to the imperial capital, and quickly returned when he was unable even to find the emperor in Kyoto. Yamaguchi today is a surprisingly small prefectural capital with a handful of sights.

Sights & Activities

Yamaguchi City

St Francis Xavier Memorial Church CHURCH
(ザビエル記念聖堂; www.xavier.jp; donation ¥100; visiting hours 9am-5pm Thu-Tue) Yamaguchi was a major centre of Christian missionary activity before the religion was outlawed in 1589. This church resembles a large tent, and sits above the town in Kameyama-kōen. Built in 1952 in honour of St Francis Xavier, it burned down in 1991 and was rebuilt in 1998. The ground-floor **Christian museum** (admission ¥300; 9am-5pm) covers the life of Xavier and early history of Christianity in Japan, mostly in Japanese only. Steps opposite the church lead uphill to views of Yamaguchi.

Yamaguchi Prefectural Art Museum GALLERY
(山口県立美術館; www.yma-web.jp; 3-1 Kameyama-chō; admission ¥300; 9am-5pm Tue-Sun, last admission 4.30pm) This interesting gallery focuses on art of the region, with three rooms showing work from its varied permanent collection, leafy grounds featuring modern sculpture, and regular special exhibitions (admission extra).

Yamaguchi

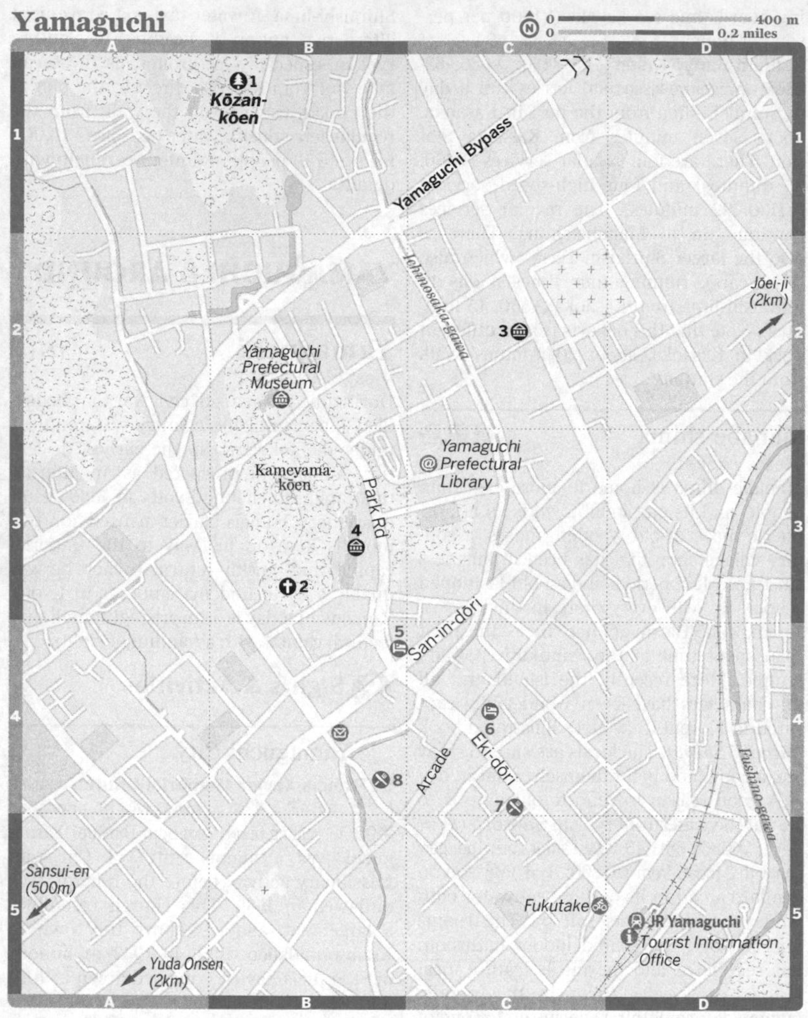

Yamaguchi Furusato Heritage Centre HISTORIC BUILDING
(山口ふるさと伝承総合センター; www.c-able.ne.jp/~denshou; 12 Shimotatekōji; ⏲9am-5pm) FREE The ground floor of the 1886 sake merchant building (the Manabi-kan; まなび館) has a small display of local crafts, including some Ōuchi dolls, and the building itself is interesting. Go upstairs to get a closer look at the large dark-wood beams, and look in the garden for the delightful tea-ceremony room made from old sake-brewing barrels. In the modern learning centre, behind the old building, you can see lacquerware being made.

★Kōzan-kōen PARK
(香山公園) North of the town centre is Kōzan Park, where the five-storey pagoda of **Rurikō-ji** (瑠璃光寺), a National Treasure dating from 1404, is picturesquely situated beside a small lake. A small on-site museum displays miniatures of the 50-plus other five-storey pagodas in Japan. The park is also the site of the **Tōshun-ji** (洞春寺) and the graves of the Mōri lords.

Yamaguchi

Top Sights

1 Kōzan-kōen B1

Sights

Christian Museum .... (see 2)

2 St Francis Xavier Memorial Church B3

3 Yamaguchi Furusato Heritage Centre C2

4 Yamaguchi Prefectural Art Museum ... B3

Sleeping

5 Sunroute Kokusai Hotel B4

6 Taiyō-dō Ryokan C4

Eating

7 Frank C4

8 Sabō Kō B4

Jōei-ji BUDDHIST TEMPLE

(常栄寺; 2001 Miyano-shimo; garden admission ¥300; ⏲garden 8am-5pm, to 4.30pm Oct-Mar) About 4km northeast of JR Yamaguchi Station, temple Jōei-ji is notable for its simple, stone-dotted Zen garden, **Sesshutei**, designed by the painter Sesshū. From the garden, a trail leads uphill through the woods to several more temples. You can reach the temple by bicycle or taxi (about ¥1300) from central Yamaguchi. Or take the train two stops to Miyano and from there it's about a 1km walk.

Yuda Onsen

Just west of Yamaguchi city is the 800-year-old **Yuda Onsen** (湯田温泉). The area is full of hotels and bathing facilities, mostly along a busy main road, which isn't really a place for tottering between baths in your *yukata*. Still, a soak here is a nice way to spend a few hours.

You can take a dip in the indoor and outdoor baths of **Yu-no-Machi Club** (湯の町倶楽部; ☎083-922-0091; 4-6-4 Yudaonsen; admission not incl towel ¥800; ⏲11am-10pm), use the baths at the large **Hotel Kamefuku** (ホテルかめ福; www.kamefuku.com; admission ¥800; ⏲11.30am-10pm) or, for a taste of luxury and a peaceful garden setting, head to **Sansui-en** (山水園; www.yuda-sansuien.com; admission ¥1600; ⏲10am-9pm).

For a full list and map of the baths and hotels, drop in first at the **tourist information office** (☎083-901-0150; 2-1-23 Yuda Onsen; ⏲9am-7pm, foot bath 10am-10pm) on the main road, which also has a free foot bath and towels for sale.

JR and Bōchō Buses run regularly to Yuda Onsen bus stop from Yamaguchi Station (¥220, 15 minutes). They drop you on the main strip, Yuda Onsen-dōri, a short walk from the tourist office (just keep walking in the direction of the bus). Yuda Onsen also has a station, one stop on the local train line from Yamaguchi (¥140), or 20 minutes from Shin-Yamaguchi (¥240). From the station, follow the quiet red road for about 1km to get to the busy main T-intersection and turn right for the tourist office.

Festivals & Events

Gion Matsuri DANCE

On 20, 24 and 27 July, during the Gion Matsuri, the *Sagi-mai* (Egret Dance) is held at Yasaka-jinja.

Tanabata Chōchin Matsuri CULTURAL

From 6 to 7 August, thousands of decorated lanterns illuminate the city.

Sleeping

There's not a great deal of choice in central Yamaguchi, but nearby Yuda Onsen is a good base, especially if you like the idea of an on-site onsen with your accommodation. There are also some good-value Western-style chain hotels clustered around unremarkable Shin-Yamaguchi Station.

Taiyō-dō Ryokan RYOKAN ¥

(太陽堂旅館; ☎083-922-0897; fax 083-922-1152; 2-3 Komeya-chō; r per person from ¥3000; 📶) The Taiyō-dō is a friendly old ryokan in the shopping arcade just off Eki-dōri. The tatami rooms are quite a good size, and there are large communal bathrooms (which you may have private use of, depending on how busy they are). No English is spoken.

Yu Bettō Nohara RYOKAN ¥¥

(湯別当野原; ☎083-922-0018; www.yubettou-nohara.com; 7-8 Yuda Onsen; r per person with 2 meals ¥9000-19,000; 🚭) You'll be welcomed by keen staff at this centrally located ryokan in Yuda Onsen. Most rooms are of the traditional tatami variety; some have both tatami and an area with two single beds. Not all have private bathrooms. Meals are *kaiseki*-style with a seafood focus, and you can stay without meals or with breakfast only.

Sunroute Kokusai Hotel HOTEL ¥¥
(サンルート国際ホテル山口; ☎083-923-3610; www.hsy.co.jp; 1-1 Nakagawara-chō; s/tw from ¥5000/11,775; P ⊖ @ ☜) This modern hotel has stylish, neutral-toned rooms, and is in a good location in the centre of town at the base of tree-lined Park Rd.

★**Matsudaya Hotel** RYOKAN ¥¥¥
(ホテル松田屋; ☎083-922-0125; www.matsudayahotel.co.jp; 3-6-7 Yuda Onsen; r per person with 2 meals from ¥21,600; @ ☜) At this centuries-old, now modernised, ryokan, you can bathe in history – right in the tub where once dipped the plotters of the Meiji Restoration. The ryokan's garden setting and excellent service will likely ease any present-day rebellious thoughts. Matsudaya is on the main drag in Yuda Onsen.

Eating & Drinking

★**Sabō Kō** CAFE ¥
(茶房幸; 1-2-39 Dōjōmonzen; dishes ¥600-900; ⊙11.30am-6pm Wed-Mon; ⊖) A cosy atmosphere prevails in this low-ceilinged little eatery, where customers perch on wooden stools while sipping coffee. The speciality on the Japanese-only menu is the generous, rustic *omuraisu* (omelette filled with fried rice), but there are also curries and *soba*. Look for the small wood-covered place with ceramic pots sticking out of the exterior plasterwork.

Frank CAFE, BAR ¥¥
(フランク; 2nd fl, 2-4-19 Dōjōmonzen; meals ¥880-1280; ⊙11.30am-6pm, to 1am Fri-Sun; ✎) Overlooking the main shopping street, this stylish cafe-restaurant serves Asian-style rice dishes, pastas and curries, and is a relaxing space for a late-night wine or cocktail. Look for 'Frank' painted on the wall at the entrance, just off Eki-dōri.

ℹ Information

Central Post Office (中央郵便局; 1-1-1 Chuo; ⊙9am-7pm, to 5pm Sat, to 12.30pm Sun, ATM 7am-11.30pm Mon-Fri, 9am-9pm Sat, 9am-7pm Sun) Postal and currency exchange services. ATM accepting international cards.

Tourist Information Office (山口観光案内所; ☎083-933-0090; www.yamaguchi-city.jp; ⊙9am-6pm) Inside Yamaguchi Station. There is also an office at Shin-Yamaguchi (☎083-972-6373; 2nd fl, Shin-Yamaguchi Station; ⊙9am-6pm), at the *shinkansen* exit side.

ℹ Getting There & Away

BUS

Chūgoku JR Bus (www.chugoku-jrbus.co.jp) runs nine to 11 buses daily to Hagi (Higashi-Hagi Station; ¥1760, one hour and 10 minutes) from Yamaguchi Station, some originating at Shin-Yamaguchi. **Bōchō Bus** (www.bochobus.co.jp) runs buses to Higashi-Hagi Station (¥2060, 1½ hours, at least hourly) from Shin-Yamaguchi.

TRAIN

Yamaguchi Station is on the JR Yamaguchi line. Shin-Yamaguchi station is 10km southwest in Ogōri on the San-yō *shinkansen* line, which connects to Shimonoseki, Hiroshima, and to Osaka in the east. The Yamaguchi local service connects the Shin-Yamaguchi and Yamaguchi stations (¥240, 25 minutes).

ℹ Getting Around

It's possible to walk to the central sights from Yamaguchi Station, but it's handy to hire a bicycle for the outlying temple areas. Jōei-ji, for example, is about 4km away (closer to Miyano Station). A taxi might be an easier option if you don't want to walk or cycle. For bikes, try **Fukutake** (福武; ☎083-922-0915; Eki-dōri 1-4-6; per day ¥700; ⊙8am-7pm) just across from the station.

Yuda Onsen is served by bus or train from Yamaguchi and Shin-Yamaguchi.

Akiyoshi-dai 秋吉台

Within the **Akiyoshi-dai Quasi-National Park**, the rolling Akiyoshi-dai tablelands are dotted with curious rock spires, beneath which are hundreds of limestone caverns. One of these is **Akiyoshi-dō** (秋芳洞; admission ¥1200; ⊙8.30am-4.30pm), the largest limestone cave in Japan.

It is size that makes the cave impressive. It extends about 10km, at some points 100m wide (though public access is limited to a 1km section), and a river flows through it. The watery reflection of the towering cave walls at times gives the dizzying impression you're walking over a deep ravine. But you can leave the spelunking gear at home – there's a paved route, regular push-button information points that belt out explanations in various languages, and an elevator in the middle that takes you up to a lookout. Despite the development, Akiyoshi-dō is a good side trip from Yamaguchi or Hagi, or a stop en route between the two.

For more on the cave and the surrounding plateau region, a great area for nature walks, go to www.karusuto.com. Information is also available at tourist offices in Yamaguchi and Hagi.

Getting There & Away

Buses go to the cave from major stations in the region. Buses leaving from Yamaguchi Station also stop at Yuda Onsen. JR pass holders coming from Yamaguchi should get the JR bus from Yamaguchi Station.

Higashi-Hagi ¥1810, one hour and 10 minutes, 10.50am and 1.15pm; returning 1pm and 3.40pm

Shimonoseki (via Mine) ¥1800, two hours, eight daily

Shin-Yamaguchi ¥1170, 45 minutes, nine daily

Yamaguchi ¥1210, 55 minutes, 10 daily

Tsuwano 津和野

0856 / POP 8400

A highlight of this region, Tsuwano is a quiet, 700-year-old mountain town with an important shrine, a ruined castle, and an evocative samurai quarter. It also has a wonderful collection of carp swimming in the roadside water channels – in fact, there are far more carp here than people.

Sights & Activities

Tonomachi District

Only the walls and some fine old gates from the former samurai quarter of Tonomachi (殿町) remain, but it's an attractive area for strolling. The water channels that run alongside the picturesque Tonomachi road are home to numerous carp, bred to provide food in case of emergency. As you're walking, look out for *sugidama* (cedar balls) hanging outside a few old sake breweries.

Anno Art Museum GALLERY

(安野光雅美術館; 60-1 Ushiroda; admission ¥800; 9am-5pm, closed 2nd Thu in Mar, Jun, Sep & Dec) Tsuwano-born Anno Mitsumasa is famous for his wonderfully detailed illustrated books, including *Anno's Alphabet* and *Anno's Journey*. You can see his work at this traditional-looking white building near the station, where the large collection is rotated throughout the year.

Around Town

★Taikodani-Inari-jinja SHINTO SHRINE

(太鼓谷稲成神社; 8am-4.30pm) Just above the castle chairlift station, thriving Taikodani-Inari-jinja, built in 1773 by the seventh Lord Kamei Norisada, is one of the five major Inari shrines in Japan. Walk up the hillside to it through a tunnel created by hundreds of *torii,* which are lit up at night, creating a beautiful sight from the town. There are fabulous views of the valley and mountains from the top.

Tsuwano-jō CASTLE

(津和野城; chairlift ¥450; chairlift 9am-5pm, irregular hours winter) The broken walls of Tsuwano-jō brood over the valley. A slightly rickety chairlift takes you slowly up the hillside, and there's a further 15-minute walk through the woods to the castle ruins. There's nothing here except the walls, but there are of course great views.

Morijuku Museum MUSEUM

(杜塾美術館; 542 Morimura; foreigners with ID ¥500; 9am-5pm) This museum is housed in a 150-year-old building that once served as the home of a *shōya* (village headman). Downstairs is a collection of soft-edged scenes painted by local-born artist Nakao Shō, a roomful of bullfight sketches by Goya, and a framed set of beautifully embroidered Taishō-era kimono collars. The caretaker will gladly point out the features of the building, including the pinhole camera hidden away upstairs.

Chapel of St Maria CHAPEL

(マリア聖堂) The tiny Maria-dō dates from 1951. More than 150 'hidden Christians' were imprisoned in a Buddhist temple on this site in the early years of the Meiji Restoration; of these, 36 died before a law allowing freedom of religion was passed in 1873. A procession is held here on 3 May.

South of Town

Nishi Amane Former Residence HISTORIC BUILDING

(西周旧居; 9am-5pm) FREE It's a pleasant walk down the river from Tsuwano town centre to see the peaked-roof former residence of Nishi Amane (1829–97), a philosopher and political scientist prominent in the Meiji government.

Mori Ōgai Former Residence HISTORIC BUILDING

(森鴎外旧宅; www.town.tsuwano.lg.jp/shisetsu/ougai.html; admission ¥100; 9am-5pm, closed Mon Dec-early Mar) Across the river from the Nishi Amane house is the old residence of Mori Ōgai (1862–1922), a highly regarded

Tsuwano

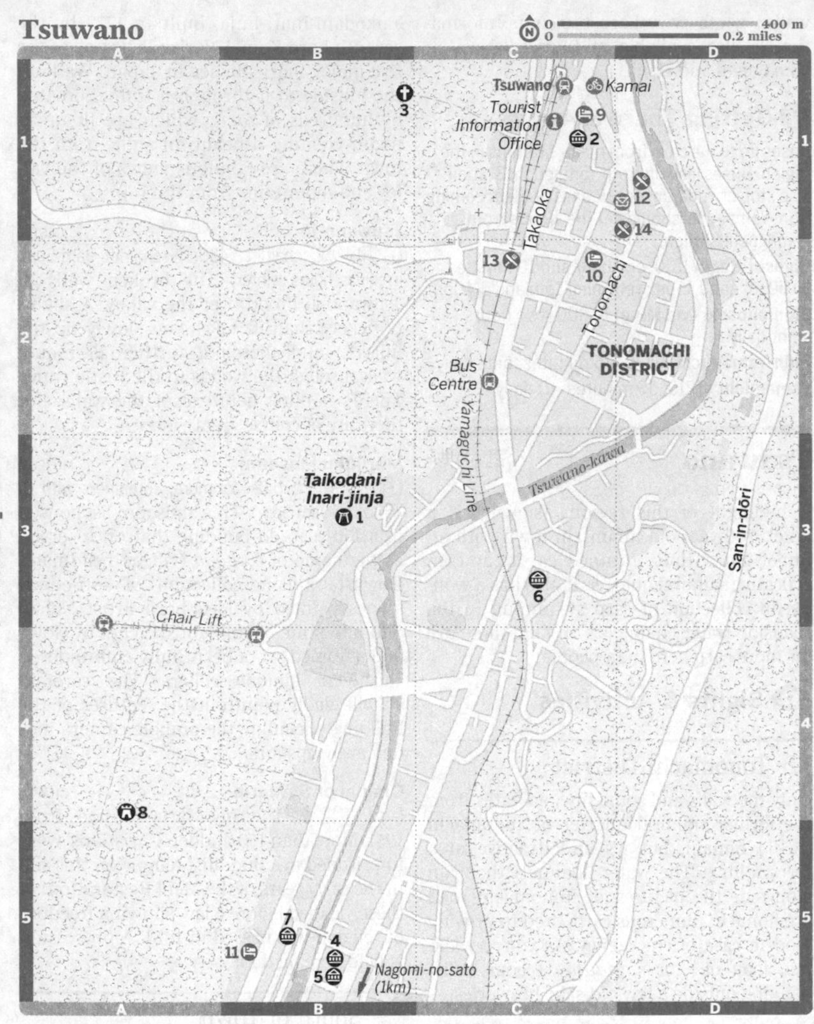

novelist who served as a physician in the Imperial Japanese Army. It's next to the **Mori Ōgai Memorial Museum**.

Nagomi-no-sato ONSEN

(なごみの里; www.nagomi-nosato.com; 256 Washibara; admission ¥600; ⏲10am-9pm Fri-Wed) After a day of sightseeing, take a soak at this onsen complex. It's about 2.5km from the centre of town, or a 15-minute walk from the Mori Ōgai Memorial Museum. Buses do travel here from the station, but there are only three a day (¥200, eight minutes).

Festivals & Events

★Yabusame CULTURAL

At Washibara Hachiman-gū (鷲原八幡宮), south of town about 4km from the station, crowds gather to watch archery contests on horseback on the second Sunday in April.

Sagi-mai Matsuri DANCE

The Heron Dance Festival sees processions of dancers dressed as herons, on 20 and 27 July.

Sleeping

You could see Tsuwano in a day trip from Yamaguchi, but staying the night gives you

Tsuwano

Top Sights
1 Taikodani-Inari-jinja B3

Sights
2 Anno Art Museum C1
3 Chapel of St Maria B1
4 Mori Ōgai Former Residence B5
5 Mori Ōgai Memorial Museum B5
6 Morijuku Museum C3
7 Nishi Amane Former Residence B5
8 Tsuwano-jō A4

Sleeping
9 Hoshi Ryokan C1
10 Noren Yado Meigetsu C2
11 Shokudō Minshuku Satoyama B5

Eating
12 Pino Rosso D1
13 Tsurube C2
14 Yūki D1

the chance to enjoy one of the town's *minshuku* or ryokan, and a walk through the quiet lamp-lit streets in the evening. For information in English online, go to www.gambo-ad.com/english and click on 'Tsuwano' – a few of the local ryokan are listed.

★Hoshi Ryokan MINSHUKU ¥
(星旅館; ☎0856-72-0136; fax 0856-72-0241; 53-6 Ushiroda; r per person with/without meals ¥7000/5000;) You'll get a warm, family welcome at this big, creaky *minshuku* located a minute from the station. The tatami rooms are spacious and there's a shared family-style bathroom.

Shokudō Minshuku Satoyama MINSHUKU ¥
(食堂民宿　さと山; ☎080-1913-9396; www.genki-ya.com/sato; 345 Washibara; s/tw from ¥2500/4500; P@) Satoyama has a spectacular countryside setting. The Japanese-style rooms have mountain views and strong wi-fi, though neglected shared bathrooms. The English-speaking owner cooks decent meals and there is a free-use clothes washer. The mountain-hugging road to Satoyama is flat and easy on a bike; it's walkable but unlit at night. Look for the white house, blue *noren* and red banners.

Noren Yado Meigetsu RYOKAN ¥¥
(のれん宿明月; ☎0856-72-0685; fax 0856-72-0637; 665 Ushiroda-guchi; r per person with 2 meals from ¥10,000) This is a traditional ryokan on a narrow lane in the Tonomachi area. *Fusuma* (sliding screen doors) slide open in the rooms to reveal a garden, and there are soothing, wood-panelled shared bathrooms. Some rooms have private bathrooms. Look for the old-fashioned gate with a red-tiled roof.

Eating & Drinking

There are a few cafes and eateries on the main Tonomachi street, and more along the (less picturesque) street that runs directly south from the station. Not many places open at night, as people tend to eat at their accommodation. If you're looking for something in the evening, try the road that runs south from the station. Restaurants may also close if it's quiet, especially during winter.

★Tsurube NOODLES ¥
(つるべ; 384-1 Ushoroda-guchi; dishes ¥525-900; ⏰11am-4pm Sat-Thu;) The speciality here is fresh wheat noodles handmade on the premises, going into filling dishes like *sansai udon* (noodles with wild vegetables) and *umeboshi udon* (noodles with dried plum). For a little extra, have a side of *omusubi* (rice ball). Tsurube is next to a small graveyard.

Yūki SEAFOOD ¥¥
(遊亀; ☎0856-72-0162; 271-4 Ushiroda; meals ¥1300-3000; ⏰11am-3pm) The *tsuwano teishoku* (a carp-themed sampler of local dishes) is recommended at this elegantly rustic restaurant, which has wooden tables and the sound of running water. There are *koi* (carp) in a pool in the floor here, and more on the menu.

Look for the old-fashioned building with a small pine tree outside. Dinner by appointment only.

Pino Rosso ITALIAN ¥¥
(ピノロッソ; ☎0856-72-2778; www.pinorosso.jp; 284 Ushiroda; lunch/dinner set menus from ¥1200/1500; ⏰10am-9pm Fri-Wed;) The menu at this modern cafe-restaurant includes pasta and pizza, plus there's a range of sweet bready items you can have with your coffee. Reservations are recommended in the evening.

Information

Post office (9am-4pm Mon-Fri, ATM 8.45am-6pm Mon-Fri, 9am-5pm Sat, 9am-1pm Sun) Has an ATM accepting international cards.

Tourist Information Office (津和野町観光協会; 0856-72-1771; www.tsuwano-kanko.net; 9am-5pm) Immediately to the right as you exit the station. Audio sightseeing guides are available for rent (¥300 per day). Free wi-fi, accessible even when closed.

Getting There & Around

Most attractions are within walking or cycling distance of the station. There is a local bus service, but it's not of much use to travellers and runs only a few times a day. Rent bikes at **Kamai** (貸自転車かまい; bike hire per 2/24hr ¥500/800; 8am-sunset), across from the station.

BUS

Long-distance buses go to Higashi-Hagi (¥2190, one hour and 45 minutes, five daily, 8.10am to 5.10pm, JR passes not valid). There are also overnight buses to Kōbe/Osaka and Tokyo.

STEAM TRAIN

The **SL Yamaguchi** (www.c571.jp; adult/child ¥1660/830) steam train trundles through the scenic valleys from Shin-Yamaguchi to Tsuwano between mid-March and late November on weekends and holidays. It's a fun way to travel and is very popular; check the latest schedules and book well ahead at JR and tourist information offices.

TRAIN

Tsuwano is on the JR Yamaguchi line, which runs from Shin-Yamaguchi and Yamaguchi in the south, to Masuda on the Sea of Japan coast (which connects to the San-in line). The *Super Oki* service from Yamaguchi or Shin-Yamaguchi will shave about 25 to 35 minutes off the trip, but costs more than double the standard fare (or free for JR Pass holders).

Masuda ¥580, 40 minutes
Shin-Yamaguchi ¥1140, 100 minutes
Yamaguchi ¥970, 80 minutes

OFF THE BEATEN TRACK

CHŌMON GORGE

If you're travelling between Yamaguchi and Tsuwano, consider a stop at **Chōmon-kyō** (長門峡), a gorge with a walking track, waterfalls, swimming pools and beautiful colours in autumn. The gorge entrance is just near Chōmon-kyō station on the JR Yamaguchi line.

Shimonoseki 下関

083 / POP 280,900

At the extreme western tip of Honshū, Shimonoseki is separated from Kyūshū by a narrow strait, famous for a decisive 12th-century clash between rival samurai clans. The expressway crosses the Kanmon Straits (Kanmon-kaikyō) on the Kanmon-bashi, while another road, the *shinkansen* railway line and the JR railway line all tunnel underneath. You can even walk to Kyūshū through a tunnel under the water. Shimonoseki is also an important connecting point to South Korea. The town is famous for its seafood, particularly *fugu,* the potentially lethal pufferfish.

Sights & Activities

Kyūshū is just across the water and a good side trip from Shimonoseki is a visit to the 'retro' port town of Mojikō.

★Karato Ichiba MARKET
(唐戸市場; www.karatoichiba.com; 5-50 Karato; 5am-1pm Mon-Sat, 9am-3pm Sun) A highlight of a trip to Shimonoseki is an early-morning visit to the Karato fish market. It's a great opportunity to try sashimi for breakfast or lunch, and the fish doesn't get any fresher – a fair bit of it will still be moving. The best days to come are Friday to Sunday, when stallholders set up tables selling *bentō* of sashimi and cooked dishes made from the day's catch. Note that the market is sometimes closed on Wednesdays.

You can take away meals or eat at the counters on the mezzanine level. Buses to Karato (¥220) leave from outside the station and take about seven minutes.

Shimonoseki Kaikyō-kan AQUARIUM
(海響館; www.kaikyokan.com; 6-1 Arukapōto; adult/child ¥2000/900; 9.30am-5.30pm, last entry 5pm) In Karato, Shimonoseki's aquarium has penguins, dolphins and sea-lion shows, plus a blue-whale skeleton and tanks of *fugu.*

Akama-jingū SHINTO SHRINE
(赤間神宮; 4-1 Amidaiji-chō; 24hr) Bright vermilion, Akama-jinjū is a shrine dedicated to the seven-year-old emperor Antoku, who died in 1185 in the battle of Dan-no-ura. On the left is a statue of Mimi-nashi Hōichi (Earless Hōichi), the blind bard whose musical talents get him into trouble with ghosts in a story made famous by Lafcadio Hearn.

The shrine is between Karato and Hino-yama, about a five-minute walk from the Karato market area. From the station, get off the bus at the Akama-jingū-mae bus stop (¥260, 10 minutes).

Hino-yama-kōen PARK

(火の山公園) About 5km northeast of Shimonoseki Station, this park has superb views over the Kanmon Straits from the top of 268m-high Hino-yama. To get to the lookout's **ropeway** (火の山ロープウエイ; one-way/return ¥300/500; ⏲10am-5pm Thu-Mon Mar-Nov), get off the bus at Mimosusōgawa (御裳川; ¥260, 12 minutes). From here it's a steep 10-minute walk to the ropeway entrance. There are buses from Shimonoseki Station that drop you at the ropeway entrance at the Hino-yama ropeway stop (¥290, 15 minutes, hourly).

Dan-no-ura Memorial MEMORIAL

(壇ノ浦銅像) This memorial marks the spot where the decisive clash between the Minamoto and Taira clans took place in 1185. Here, Taira no Tokiko plunged into the sea with the young emperor Antoku in her arms, rather than surrender to the enemy. The statues depict Yoshitsune (the victorious Minamoto general) and Taira no Tomomori, who tied an anchor to his feet and leapt into the sea at Dan-no-ura when it became clear that his side had lost.

It's across the road from the Mimosusōgawa bus stop.

Kanmon Tunnel TUNNEL

(関門トンネル人道; bike admission ¥20; ⏲6am-10pm) FREE This is where you come to get that picture of yourself with one foot in Honshū and the other in Kyūshū. For the 780m submarine walk to Kyūshū, take the bus from the station to the Mimosusōgawa bus stop (¥260, 12 minutes) and take the lifts there to the tunnel.

Kaikyō Yume Tower TOWER

(海峡ゆめタワー; www.yumetower.jp; 3-3-1 Buzenda-chō; observatory adult/child ¥300/150; ⏲9.30am-9.30pm, last entry 9pm) This 153m tower looks like a midget skyscraper topped by a futuristic billiard ball. Head to the observatory for 360-degree views.

Chōfu 長府

Chōfu, east of Shimonoseki Station along the coastal road, is home to the old castle town area. While little remains of the castle itself, there are earth walls and samurai gates, several temples and shrines, and inviting narrow streets, making it an atmospheric spot for a wander.

The **Shimonoseki City Art Museum** (下関市立美術館; ☎083-245-4131; www.city.shimonoseki.yamaguchi.jp/bijutsu; Chōfu-Kuromon Higashi-machi 1-1; admission ¥200, extra during special exhibitions; ⏲9.30am-5pm Tue-Sun, last entry 4.30pm) is on the main road at the edge of the old area. It houses an eclectic collection of local art, which is rotated based on changing themes. There are regular temporary exhibits, sometimes of international artists. Across the road from the museum is pretty **Chōfu-teien** (長府庭園; admission ¥200; ⏲9am-5pm), a garden set around a pond and famous for its flowers in spring and autumn.

A few minutes' walk along the main road from the garden, turn inland to enter the castle-town area. Follow the signs and the small river, Dangu-gawa (壇具川), to walk up to National Treasure **Kōzan-ji** (功山時; ⏲9am-5pm). This is the family burial temple of the local Mōri lords, and has a Zen-style hall dating from 1327, making it the oldest example of Zen Buddhist architecture in Japan. The narrow streets in the area near the temple feature old walls and gates, and close by is the impressive **Chōfu Mōri Residence** (長府毛利邸; admission ¥200; ⏲9am-5pm), a well-preserved 100-year-old home and garden, where you can also have some *matcha* (powdered green tea; ¥400).

There are a few cafes dotted around Chōfu; a good lunch stop is Antiques & Oldies (p475) cafe.

Chōfu is about 20 minutes by bus from Shimonoseki Station. Buses run regularly along the main coastal road, stopping at Karato along the way. For the art museum and garden, get off at Bijutsukan-mae (¥390); for the castle-town area, get off at Jōkamachi-Chōfu (¥410), a couple of stops further along.

Festivals & Events

Sentei Festival CULTURAL

Held at Akama-jingū from 2 to 4 May to remember the Heike women who worked as prostitutes to pay for rites for their fallen relatives. On 3 May women dressed as Heian-era courtesans form a colourful procession at the shrine.

Shimonoseki

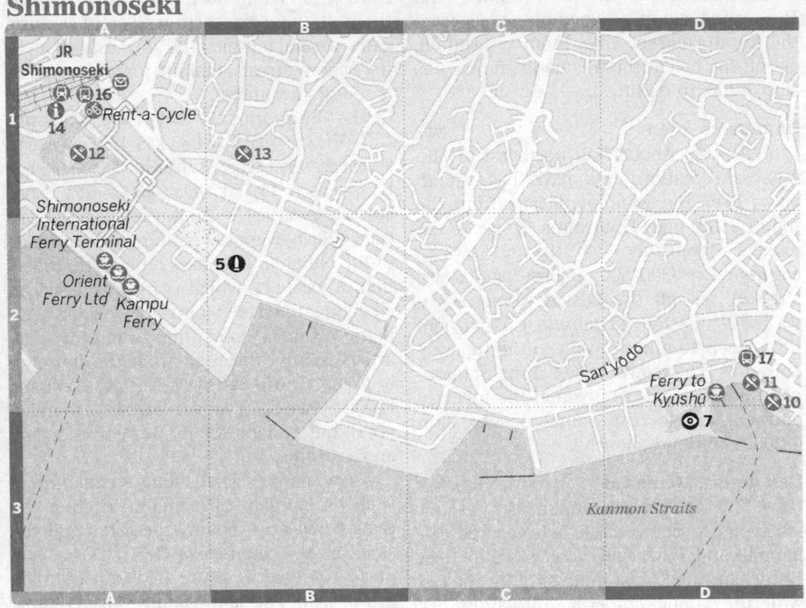

Shimonoseki

Top Sights
1 Karato Ichiba E3

Sights
2 Akama-jingū E2
3 Dan-no-ura Memorial G3
4 Hino-yama-kōen H2
5 Kaikyō Yume Tower B2
6 Kanmon Tunnel G2
7 Shimonoseki Kaikyō-kan D3

Sleeping
8 Hinoyama Youth Hostel H2
9 Kaikyō View Shimonoseki H2

Eating
Kaiten Karato Ichiba Sushi .... (see 1)
10 Kamon Wharf D2
11 Kawaku D2
12 Sea Mall Shimonoseki A1
13 Yabure-Kabure B1

Information
14 Shimonoseki Station Tourist Information Office A1

Transport
15 Akama-jingū-mae Bus Stop E3
16 Bus Terminal A1
17 Karato Bus Stop D2
18 Mimosusōgawa Bus Stop G3
19 Ropeway to Hino-yama Lookout H2

Kanmon Straits Fireworks Festival FIREWORKS
(Hanabi Taikai) A spectacular fireworks display occurring on both sides of the straits at the same time. Held on 13 August.

Sleeping

★ **Hinoyama Youth Hostel** HOSTEL ¥
(火の山ユースホステル; ☎083-222-3753; www.e-yh.net/shimonoseki; 3-47 Mimosusoga-wa-chō; dm ¥3200;) Amazing views of the straits and welcoming service make this one of the best youth hostels in western Honshū. You can take a bus from the station to Hino-yama Observatory (¥290, 15 minutes, hourly), from where it's a short walk. Note that the caretakers sometimes need to pop out – let them know if you're coming to drop off your bags.

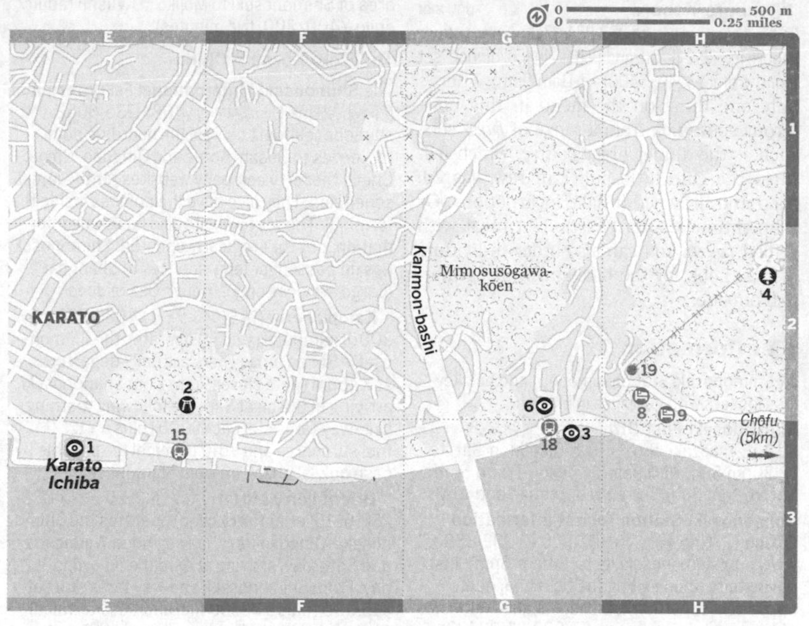

Kaikyō View Shimonoseki HOTEL ¥¥
(海峡ビューしものせき; ☎083-229-0117; www.kv-shimonoseki.com; 3-58 Mimosusogawa-chō; r per person with 2 meals from ¥10,800) Perched up on Hino-yama, Kaikyō View has professional service and the choice of Japanese- or Western-style rooms. Some of the Japanese-style rooms don't have private bathrooms. The hotel has a fabulous onsen with sea views – nonguests can also use it from 11am to 4pm (entry ¥720, last entry 3pm), except Wednesday.

Eating

Close to the fish market is the **Kamon Wharf area**, with eateries and shops specialising in the local goodies. Seekers of only-in-Japan culinary experiences can look out for the *uni*-flavoured ice cream (うにソフトクリーム; sea urchin) and *fugu* burgers (ふぐバーガー). Note that whale meat *(kujira)* is on the menu at many seafood places in Shimonoseki. Check for くじら or クジラ if you'd rather avoid it.

For easy eating near the station, head to the upper floors of the **Sea Mall Shimonoseki** (☎083-232-4705; 4-8 Takezaki-chō; ⊙8am-9pm) shopping complex, where there are restaurants serving local and international food, all with menus and displays in the windows.

Kaiten Karato Ichiba Sushi SUSHI ¥
(海転からと市場寿司; www.kaitenkaratoichibazusi.com; 2nd fl, 5-50 Karato; per plate ¥110-520; ⊙11am-3pm & 5-9pm; 📵) This conveyor-belt sushi restaurant on the 2nd floor, right above the fish market, is a great place to get your hands on the freshest fish without needing to know what they're all called. When the market is closed (on some Wednesdays), the restaurant also closes. Cash only.

Kawaku FUGU ¥
(河久; ☎083-235-4129; 5-1 Karato; dishes ¥200-680, set menus ¥480-980; ⊙10am-6pm; 📵) No puffed-up decor, but you'll catch lots of fresh pufferfish set meals and even a sea breeze at this relaxed corner restaurant on the wharf. English picture menu available. Look for the white *noren* over the entrances.

Antiques & Oldies CAFE ¥
(アンティーク&オールディーズ; ☎083-250-5297; www.aando-since1993.com; 2-3-22 Chōfu-Kawabata; dishes ¥650, sets ¥1200; ⊙11am-6pm, closed Tue & every 2nd & 3rd Mon; 📵) At the back of a charming antique shop in Chōfu's castle-town area is this small cafe, serving up bagel sandwich sets, coffees, juices and cakes. There are just a few tables inside and a shady outdoor terrace. It's near the bend of the river, not far from the entrance to Kōzan-ji. Look for the red signboard.

★**Yabure-Kabure** FUGU ¥¥¥
(やぶれかぶれ; ☎083-234-3711; www.yaburekabure.jp; 2-2-5 Buzenda-chō; lunch/dinner set menu from ¥3240/5400; ⏲11am-9pm) There's only one thing on the menu in this boisterous spot: pick from a range of *fugu* sets, such as the dinner Ebisu course, which features the cute little puffer in raw, seared, fried and drowned-in-sake incarnations. Or a lunchtime *tetsuyaki setto* (set meal with grilled *fugu*). You can also order individual dishes. Look for the blue-and-white pufferfish outside.

ℹ Information

JR Shimonoseki Station is modern and has keyless lockers with guidance in English.

Shimonoseki Post Office (下関郵便局; 2-12-12 Takezaki-chō; ⏲9am-5pm Mon-Sat, to 12.30pm Sun, ATM 9am-6pm Mon-Fri, to 5pm Sat, to 1pm Sun) Currency exchange and ATMs.

Shimonoseki Station Tourist Information Office (下関駅観光案内所; ☎083-232-8383; www.city.shimonoseki.lg.jp; ⏲9am-6pm) Just downstairs upon exiting the ticket barriers, opposite a supermarket. There is another office at the shinkansen station (☎083-256-3422; ⏲9am-6pm).

ℹ Getting There & Around

The main sights outside of the city centre are accessible by regular buses from the train station. To reach the Karato wharf and fish market area, you can also take a pleasant 2km walk east following the water's edge. Shimonoseki is also great for cycling. **Bikes** (per day ¥500; ⏲8am-7pm) can be hired from outside the station from a booth in the car park beside the bus terminal area.

FERRY

Kanmon Kisen (☎083-222-1488; www.kanmon-kisen.co.jp) ferries run about every 20 minutes (6am to 9.29pm) from the Karato wharf area of Shimonoseki to Mojikō in Kyūshū (adult/child ¥400/200, five minutes).

To/From Korea & China

The **Shimonoseki International Ferry Terminal** (下関港国際ターミナル; ☎083-235-6052; shimonoseki-port.com) is the boarding point for ferries to Busan, Korea and Qīngdǎo, China. Check the ferry company websites for the latest schedules. They also have their offices inside the terminal. The port website also has some information, but isn't regularly updated. Shimonoseki has no passenger ferry services to Shanghai (cargo services only), though Osaka does.

Kampu Ferry (関釜フェリー; ☎083-224-3000; kampuferry.co.jp) operates the Shimonoseki–Busan ferry. There are daily departures at 7.45pm (gate closes 7pm) from Shimonoseki, arriving in Busan at 8am the following morning. One-way fares start at ¥9000 (plus a ¥1200 fuel surcharge and ¥610 terminal fee payable by cash only at check-in) from Shimonoseki.

Orient Ferry Ltd (オリエントフェリー; ☎083-232-6615; orientferry.co.jp) operates the Shimonoseki–Qīngdǎo ferry, leaving noon Wednesday and Saturday, arriving at 4pm the following day. From Shimonoseki, one-way fares start at ¥15,000 (plus a ¥2300 fuel and ¥610 terminal fee payable by cash only at check-in). Tickets can't be purchased at the terminal on the day of sailing; make reservations via travel agencies in Japan (such as JTB). See the Orient Ferry website for more details.

TRAIN

JR Shimonoseki is the end of the San-yō line. Shin-Shimonoseki *shinkansen* station is two stops from JR Shimonoseki (¥200, 10 minutes). Shimonoseki also connects to the San-in line, which runs north to Nagato and beyond along the Sea of Japan coast.

> **ℹ DISCOUNT BUS PASS**
>
> If you're taking more than a couple of bus rides in Shimonoseki, pick up a **one-day bus pass** (*ichi-nichi furī jōsha-ken;* ¥700) from the booth at the bus terminal outside the station or at the Karato bus terminal. It's good value (a trip to Chōfu and back alone normally costs more than ¥700) and it saves you the hassle of paying coins each time you get off the bus.

Hagi

☎0838 / POP 53,700

The quiet town of Hagi is known for producing some of the finest ceramics in Japan, and has a well-preserved old samurai quarter. During the feudal period, Hagi was the castle town of the Chōshū domain, which, together with Satsuma (corresponding to modern Kagoshima in southern Kyūshū), was instrumental in defeating the Tokugawa government and ushering in a new age after the Meiji Restoration. Hagi also has a good beach, which is at its best in the summer months.

Western and central Hagi are effectively an island created by the two rivers Hashimoto-gawa and Matsumoto-gawa.

OFF THE BEATEN TRACK

TAWARAYAMA ONSEN

Nestled in the mountains, Tawarayama Onsen (俵山温泉) is a small village that has a reputation as a favoured hidden spa for *tōji* (curative bathing). The story goes that an injured monkey once healed itself in the waters here, but the only monkeys you'll see these days are the ones painted on the street and peering at you from the tasty *manjū* (steamed rice-and-flour bun with filling) sold around town. While Tawarayama draws local tourists, it sees relatively few international travellers.

There is a narrow main strip lined with a mix of old and newer ryokan, none of which have their own bath. Instead, guests go out to bathe in the two public baths: **Machi-no-yu** (町の湯; admission ¥420; ⏲6am-10pm) and the newer **Hakuen-no-yu** (白猿の湯; admission ¥730, early morning & late evening ¥530; ⏲7am-9pm). If you're looking for a place to stay, try popular **Izumiya** (泉屋; ☎0837-29-0231; www.tabi-izumiya.com; r per person with 2 meals from ¥9180), a well-maintained old inn with wooden floors and a garden. The friendly managers can pick up guests at Nagato-Yumoto Station. See www.tawarayamaonsen.com (in Japanese) for more information.

Tawarayama is not especially convenient to anywhere, which for some is part of its appeal. There's a direct bus from Shimonoseki (¥1680, one hour and 50 minutes, eight daily, 7.01am to 5.58pm). Or get to Nagato-Yumoto Station (two stops south of Nagato on the JR Mine line), from where there is one bus an hour (¥530, 25 minutes). If you read Japanese, there is a useful bus journey planner: www.busdayo.jp/sanden.

Eastern Hagi (with the major JR station Higashi-Hagi; get off there for the main sights) lies on the eastern bank of the Matsumoto-gawa.

Sights

The main area of interest is the old samurai residential district of Jōkamachi (城下町), and surrounds, where there are many streets lined with whitewashed walls, enclosing old houses. Nearby is the beach and pretty bay views. There are also a few sights further afield on the edges of town.

★Kikuya Residence HISTORIC BUILDING
(菊屋家住宅; 1-1 Gofuku-machi; admission ¥520; ⏲9.30am-5.30pm) The Kikuya family were merchants rather than samurai. As official merchants to the *daimyō* their wealth and connections allowed them to build a house well above their station. This house dates from 1604 and has a fine gate and attractive gardens, and numerous interesting displays of items used in daily life, including an old public phone box. Don't miss the large old maps of Hagi, which show just how little has changed in the town layout.

Shizuki-kōen PARK
(指月公園) Within this park, there's not much of the old **Hagi-jō** (萩城; ☎0838-25-1826; admission with Asa Mōri House ¥210; ⏲8am-6.30pm Apr-Oct, to 4.30pm Nov-Feb, to 6pm Mar) to see, apart from the typically imposing outer walls and the surrounding carp-filled moat. The castle was built in 1604 and dismantled in 1874 following the Meiji Restoration. But the inner grounds are a pleasant park, with spring cherry blossoms, the **Shizuki-yama-jinja** (志都岐山神社), the **Hanano-e Tea House** (花江茶亭) from the mid-19th century and other buildings. Asa Mōri House is a *nagaya* (Japanese long house). From the castle ruins you can climb the hillside to the 143m peak of Shizuki-yama.

Hagi-jō Kiln CERAMICS
(萩城窯; ☎0838-22-5226; 2-5 Horiuchi; ⏲8am-5pm) *Hagi-yaki* (Hagi ceramic ware) is noted for its fine glazes and delicate pastel colours, and connoisseurs of Japanese ceramics rank it as some of the best. At a number of shops and kilns you can see *hagi-yaki* being made, and browse the finished products, including this one within the walls of the old castle ruins. The tourist office has a complete list of kilns in the area.

Hagi Uragami Museum MUSEUM
(山口県立萩美術館・浦上記念館; ☎0838-24-2400; www.hum.pref.yamaguchi.lg.jp; 586-1 Hiyako; admission ¥300; ⏲9am-5pm Tue-Sun) In this appealing modern building you'll find a superb collection of ceramics and woodblock prints, with fine works by Katsushika Hokusai and Utamaro Kitagawa. There are also regular special exhibitions.

Hagi

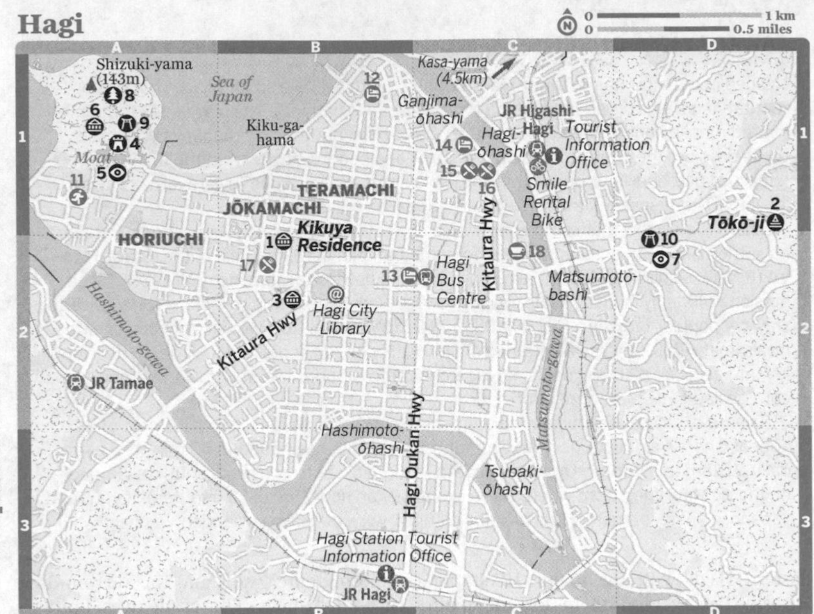

Shōin-jinja SHINTO SHRINE

(松陰神社) This shrine, with a garden and small complex, was founded in 1890 and is dedicated to Meiji Restoration movement leader Yoshida Shōin. His **former house** (8am-5pm) FREE and the school where he agitated against the shogunate in the years leading up to the revolution are also here, as well as a **treasure house** (宝物館; admission ¥500; 9am-5pm). The shrine is located southeast of Higashi-Hagi Station. The circle bus drops you out the front.

Itō Hirobumi House BUILDING

(伊藤博文旧宅; admission ¥100; 9am-5pm) About 200m from Shōin-jinja is the thatched early home of the four-term prime minister, who was a follower of Yoshida Shōin, and who later drafted the Meiji Constitution. It's interesting to see the contrast between this humble place and the impressive mansion he lived in during his years in Tokyo, which is next door, having been moved to Hagi after his death.

★ Tōkō-ji BUDDHIST TEMPLE

(東光寺; www.toukouji.net; 1647 Chintō; admission ¥300; 8.30am-5pm) East of the river, near Shōin-jinja, stands pretty Zen Tōkō-ji, built in 1691 and home to the tombs of five Mōri lords. The stone walkways on the hillside behind the temple are flanked by almost 500 stone lanterns, which were erected by the lords' servants.

Kasa-yama MOUNTAIN

(笠山) About 5km northeast of the town is the 112m dormant volcano Kasa-yama. The top has gorgeous views of the Sea of Japan, and a tiny 30m-deep crater. There is also a walking track around the coast. From late February to late March a beautiful grove of camellias blooms here.

The pond at the mountain's base, **Myōjin-ike** (明神池), is connected to the sea and shelters a variety of saltwater fish. Look and listen for birdlife in the surrounding trees.

About five minutes' walk up the mountain from the pond is **Hagi Glass** (萩ガラス工房; 0838-26-2555; hagi-glass.jp; 9am-6pm, demonstrations 9am-noon & 1-4.30pm) FREE, where quartz basalt from the volcano is used to make extremely tough Hagi glassware. The showroom and shop display beautiful coloured vases, and you can watch the glass-blowing process. Next door is Hagi's own beer and citrus-juice factory, **Yuzuya Honten** (柚子屋本店; e-yuzuya.com; 9am-5pm) FREE. Stop in here to see the very small team at work, taste juice in the attached shop, or have a refreshing *mikan*-flavoured (satsuma) soft cream.

Hagi

Buses go to Kasa-yama from Higashi-Hagi Station once every hour to 1½ hours (¥280, 15 minutes); get off at the Koshi-ga-hama stop, about eight minutes' walk from the base of the mountain and Myōjin-ike.

Activities

Jōzan POTTERY MAKING

(城山; ☎0838-25-1666; 31-15 Horiuchi Nishi-no-hama; lessons ¥1728; ⏰8am-4pm) You can try your hand at making pottery in this large workshop; once fired, items can be shipped anywhere in Japan. Look for the building next to the large kiln.

Sleeping

Hagi doesn't see many foreign tourists and you can't assume all staff at hotels will speak English. The tourist office can help with bookings.

Guesthouse Hagi Akatsukiya HOSTEL ¥

(古民家ゲストハウス萩・暁屋; ☎050-3624-4625; www.guesthouse-hagi-akatsukiya.jimdo.com; 237-1 Hamasakimachi; dm ¥2400-2600;) A polished-up Japanese house with a cute garden and soft bunk beds for a tranquil rest just two minutes from the beach. The well-travelled owner provides good local knowledge, speaks English and rents bikes (¥500, 24 hours). Akatsukiya is beside a shrine – from the northernmost beach, go down the road opposite the blue-tiled toilets and cross the saw mill.

Guesthouse Ruco HOSTEL ¥

(ゲストハウスRuco; ☎0838-21-7435; www.guesthouse-ruco.com; 92 Karahimachi; dm/d with shared bathroom ¥2800/7500;) Ruco is a modern wonderland of handmade furniture and vintage decor. The cafe-bar and even bathroom are stylish and minimalist, making you feel like you're staying in a Muji store. Cramped but clean dorms use clever personal curtains, while Japanese-style doubles are spacious. Helpful staff speak some English. Exit left from Hagi Bus Centre and left again.

Hagi no Yado Tomoe RYOKAN ¥¥¥

(萩の宿常茂恵; ☎0838-22-0150; www.tomoehagi.jp; 608-53 Kōbō-ji Hijiwara; r per person from ¥17,850; @) The finest inn in Hagi, the historic Tomoe has gorgeous Japanese rooms with garden views, beautifully prepared cuisine and luxurious baths. Prices vary according to season, and there are discounted plans on the website (if you don't read Japanese, it may be easier to reserve via email). Cross the bridge from the station and take the road along the river.

Eating & Drinking

★Hotoritei CAFE ¥

(畔亭; www.hotoritei.com; 62 Minami-Katakawa; meals from ¥1000; ⏰11am-5pm, closed Thu & 4-31 Jan) A tranquil rest stop near the Jōkamachi area, Hotoritei is within a large house surrounded by gardens. It mainly serves coffees, teas and cakes – try the fluffy, cream-filled *matcha* (green-tea) roll. There are a few lunch sets; the menu has some pictures. Look for the entrance set back from the road, next to Sam's Irish pub.

Don Don Udonya NOODLES ¥

(どんどん; www.s-dondon.co.jp; 377 San-ku Hijiwara; dishes ¥420-720; ⏰9am-9pm;) A popular spot serving tasty udon and rice dishes. Set meals are *donburi* standards like *oyako-don* (chicken and egg on rice).

There's a cheaper morning selection. It's in a big black-and-white building on the right across the bridge from the station.

Hagi Shinkai SEAFOOD ¥¥
(萩心海; ☎0838-26-1221; 370-71 Hijiwara; set meals ¥3024-6480; ⏰11am-2.30pm & 5-9pm) Seating here is around a large open tank, so you can watch as fish are plucked out by staff while you eat. There are various set-meal options, or ask for the manager-recommended *Shinkai teishoku* (¥1080/1988 at lunch/dinner), which includes sashimi, tempura and *chawanmushi* (steamed savoury egg custard), and isn't on the menu. Look for the white building with the lighthouse.

Cafe Tikal CAFE
(長屋門珈琲・カフェティカル; www.hagi-nagayamoncoffee.jimdo.com; 298-1 Hijiwara; coffee from ¥380; ⏰9.30am-8pm Tue-Sat, to 6pm Sun) Through the old gate of the Kogawa family residence is this small cafe with large windows looking on to a pleasingly unkempt garden. Sit among the games and books at one of the wooden tables and choose from a range of coffees, including a hilly cappuccino. Cakes are also served.

Information

Hagi City Library (萩市立萩図書館; 2nd fl, 552-26 Emukai; ⏰9am-9pm) Free internet access on 2nd floor. You may need to show ID.

Tourist Information Office (萩市観光案内所; ☎0838-25-3145; ⏰9am-5.45pm, to 5pm Dec-Feb) Located inside Higashi-Hagi Station. Staff speak English and provide a good English cycling and walking map. There's another tourist office near Hagi Station.

Getting There & Away

BUS

Long-distance bus connections from Higashi-Hagi Station, via Hagi Bus Centre:

Shin-Yamaguchi ¥2000, 1½ hours, at least hourly

Tsuwano ¥2190, one hour and 45 minutes, five daily

Yamaguchi (JR bus) ¥1760, one hour and 10 minutes, nine to 11 daily

TRAIN

Hagi is on the JR San-in line, which runs along the coast from Tottori and Matsue. Local services between Shimonoseki and Higashi-Hagi (¥1940) take up to three hours, depending on transfers. If you're going to Tsuwano from Higashi-Hagi, go by train up the coast to Masuda (¥970, one hour and 10 minutes), then change to the JR Yamaguchi line (¥580, 40 minutes) or *Super Oki* (¥580, 30 minutes) for Tsuwano. All these journeys are free with a JR Pass. If you have to wait long transferring at sleepy Masuda, try the hidden restaurant street one block north of the station.

POTTED HISTORY

During his Korean peninsula campaigns in 1592 and 1598, Toyotomi Hideyoshi abducted whole families of potters as growing interest in the tea ceremony generated desire for the finest Korean ceramics. The firing techniques brought over all those centuries ago live on in Japanese ceramics today.

Getting Around

It's easy to walk around central Hagi and the Jōkamachi area. Some sights are on the edges of town and Hagi is a good place to explore by bicycle or bus if you're not keen on walking.

BICYCLE

Smile Rental Bike (☎0838-22-2914; hire per 1/24hr ¥200/1000; ⏰8am-5pm) The first of two rental sheds directly left as you exit Higashi-Hagi Station. Smile allows overnight rental, whereas the other doesn't.

BUS

The handy *māru basu* (まぁーるバス; circle bus) takes in all of central Hagi's main attractions. There are east- (東回り) and west-bound (西回り) loops, with two services per hour at each stop. One trip costs ¥100, and one-/two-day passes cost ¥500/700. Both routes stop at Higashi-Hagi Station.

MATSUE & AROUND

Along the San-in coastline on the Sea of Japan is Shimane Prefecture (島根県; Shimane-ken), of which Matsue is the capital. It may be off the beaten track, but there is no shortage of reasons to visit. Cities are few and far between, the pace of life is decidedly slower than on the San-yō coast and the people are particularly friendly towards visitors.

Matsue 松江

☎0852 / POP 193,300

With its fine castle and crowd-pleasing sunsets over Shinji-ko (Lake Shinji), Matsue

DON'T MISS

ADACHI MUSEUM OF ART

East of Matsue, in Yasugi, is this excellent **Adachi Museum of Art** (足立美術館; www.adachi-museum.or.jp; 320 Furukawa-chō, Yasugi-shi; admission ¥2300, foreigners with ID ¥1150; ⌚9am-5.30pm, to 5pm Oct-Mar), founded by local businessman and art collector Adachi Zenkō. The collection includes over 100 paintings by Yokoyama Taikan (1868–1958) and a good selection of works by other major 20th-century Japanese painters. There's also a delightful 'pictures for children' gallery. But for many the real attraction is the stunning gardens, regularly voted among the best in Japan.

Sit and contemplate the perfectly clipped mounds of the Dry Landscape Garden – in the distance, mountains rise up as though part of the garden itself.

From Matsue, take the JR line to Yasugi (安来; ¥410, 22 minutes), where there's a free shuttle bus to the museum (11 daily from 9.05am). The bus also leaves from Yonago Station (12.25pm and 1.15pm, 45 minutes).

is an appealing city with some interesting historical attractions. The city straddles the Ōhashi-gawa, which connects Shinji-ko with Nakanoumi, a saline lake. Most of the main attractions are in a compact area in the north, where you'll find the castle – a rare original. Matsue is also a good base for sojourns to other places of interest in Shimane Prefecture and you could easily spend a few lazy days here.

Sights

★Matsue-jō CASTLE

(松江城, Matsue Castle; www.matsue-tourism.or.jp/m_castle; 1-5 Tonomachi; admission ¥560, foreigners with ID ¥280; ⌚8.30am-6.30pm Apr-Sep, to 5pm Oct-Mar) Dating from 1611, picturesque Matsue-jō has a wooden interior showcasing treasures belonging to the Matsudaira clan. Known as Plover Castle for the graceful shape of its gable ornaments, Matsue-jō is one of only 12 original keeps left in Japan, making it well worth having a look inside. There are dioramas of the city, as well as displays of armoury, including a collection of helmets – the design of each helmet is said to have reflected the personality of its wearer.

From the top of the castle there are great unobstructed views. It's also pleasant to walk around the castle grounds (free entry) and along the surrounding moat, with its charming bridges and pines reaching out across the water. A good way to see the castle area is a trip on a Horikawa Sightseeing Boat (p482).

Matsue History Museum MUSEUM

(松江歴史館; www.matsu-reki.jp; 279 Tonomachi; admission ¥510, foreigners with ID ¥250; ⌚8.30am-6.30pm, to 5pm Oct-Mar, closed 3rd Thu of month) Matsue's excellent modern museum gives a broad-ranging introduction to the history of the region clans, and development of local industry and crafts. Among the displays are old town maps, ceramics, letters and the local speciality Matsue *wagashi* (sweets) – you can taste modern versions in the attached shop. The English audio guide is very good and is free.

Koizumi Yakumo (Lafcadio Hearn) Memorial Museum MUSEUM

(小泉八雲記念館; www.matsue-tourism.or.jp/yakumo; 322 Okudani-chō; admission ¥300, foreigners with ID ¥150; ⌚8.30am-6.30pm Apr-Sep, to 5pm Oct-Mar) This memorial museum has displays on the life and work of former Matsue resident Lafcadio Hearn, as well as some of the writer's personal effects – including his dumb-bells, spectacles and a stack of Japanese newspapers on which he wrote words and phrases to teach English to his son. Hearn enthusiasts should pop round next door to have a look at his **old residence** (小泉八雲旧居; admission ¥300, foreigners with ID ¥150; ⌚8.30am-6.30pm Apr-Sep, to 5pm Oct-Mar).

Buke Yashiki Samurai Residence HISTORIC BUILDING

(武家屋敷; www.matsue-tourism.or.jp/buke; 305 Kitahori-chō; admission ¥300, foreigners with ID ¥150; ⌚8.30am-6.30pm Apr-Sep, to 5pm Oct-Mar) Built for a middle-ranking samurai family during the early 18th century, Buke Yashiki is an immaculately preserved house and garden.

★Shimane Prefectural Art Museum GALLERY

(島根県立博物館; www1.pref.shimane.lg.jp/contents/sam; 1-5 Sodeshi-chō; admission ¥300, foreigners with ID ¥150; ⌚10am-6.30pm Wed-Mon,

Matsue

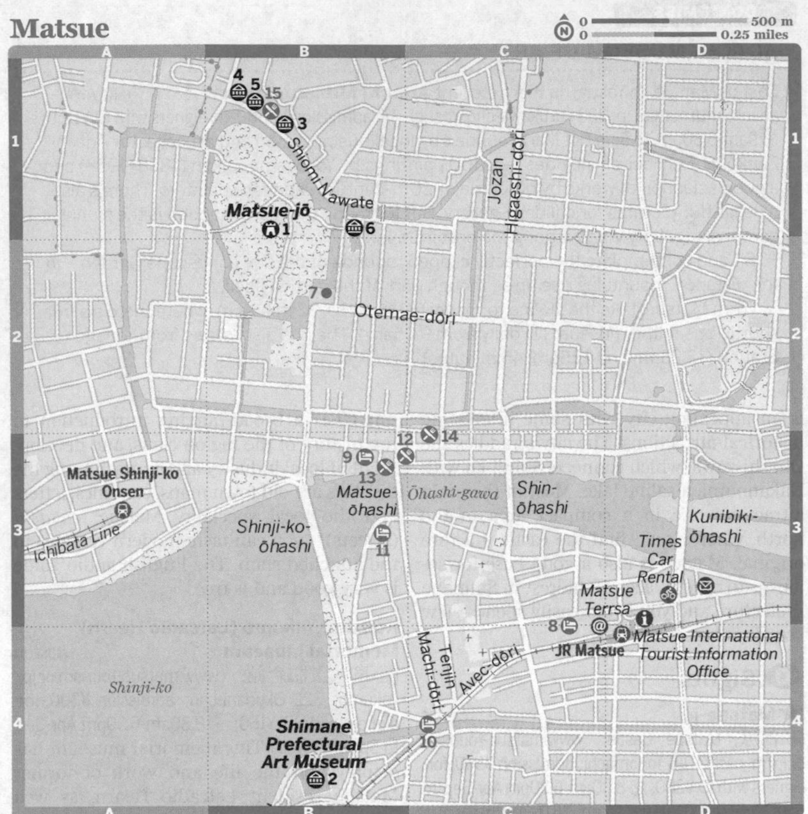

to 30min after sunset Mar-Sep) With its white undulating roof and huge glass windows facing the lake, the museum building itself is an impressive sight. Inside, it displays rotating exhibits from its collection of woodblock prints (there are some Hokusai among them), as well as European paintings and contemporary art. The sunset views from the museum's 2nd-floor platform or outside by the water also draw crowds here. The museum is a 15-minute walk west of the station.

Tours

Horikawa Sightseeing Boat BOAT TOUR
(trips ¥1230, foreigners with ID ¥820; every 15-20min 9am-5pm) The characterful boatmen circumnavigate the castle moat and then zip around the city's canals and beneath a series of bridges. There are a few boarding points; the main one is near the castle entrance.

Festivals

Matsue Suitōro CULTURAL
(松江水燈路; www.suitouro.com; Matsue-jō; 6-9pm) In Matsue's night festival of water and light, hand-painted lanterns create atmospheric paths of light around the moat and up to the castle grounds of Matsue-jō, where there are group drumming battles and outdoor food stalls. Held every Saturday, Sunday and holiday in October.

Sleeping

★ **Terazuya** RYOKAN ¥
(旅館寺津屋; 0852-21-3480; www.mable.ne.jp/~terazuya; 60-3 Tenjin-machi; r per person with/without breakfast ¥5200/4500;) You'll find a warm welcome and simple tatami rooms at this family-run inn, opposite a shrine. The owners speak a little English and can collect you from the station. The bathroom is shared, there's a 10pm cur-

Matsue

Top Sights
1 Matsue-jō ... B1
2 Shimane Prefectural Art Museum ... B4

Sights
3 Buke Yashiki Samurai Residence ... B1
4 Koizumi Yakumo (Lafcadio Hearn) Memorial Museum ... B1
5 Lafcadio Hearn Old Residence ... B1
6 Matsue History Museum ... B1

Activities, Courses & Tours
7 Horikawa Sightseeing Boat ... B2

Sleeping
8 Green Rich Hotel Matsue ... C4
9 Minamikan ... B3
10 Terazuya ... C4
11 Young Inn Matsue ... B3

Eating
12 Kawa-kyō ... B3
13 Naniwa ... B3
14 Tsurumaru ... C3
15 Yakumo-an ... B1

Drinking & Nightlife
Cafe Bar EAD ... (see 13)

few, and coffee and toast is included if you haven't paid for the full breakfast. Cash only.

A canal runs behind the ryokan, as does the JR line – fortunately there's little traffic at night.

Young Inn Matsue GUESTHOUSE ¥
(ヤングイン松江; 0852-25-4500; www.younginn.net; 5 Uo-machi; dm/s/tw ¥2200/2600/5000;) Basic budget accommodation in a good location. The dorms are tatami rooms with futons; quiet private rooms have beds. Shower rooms are shared and there's a lounge-bar. It's not a bad option if you just need a place to sleep.

Green Rich Hotel Matsue HOTEL ¥¥
(グリーンリッチホテル松江駅前; 0852-27-3000; www.gr-matsue.com; 493-1 Asahi-machi; s/tw from ¥5900/10,300;) A modern chain hotel going for a designer look with dark-toned furnishings and back-lit headboards. Most inviting is the large, sunken public bath and sauna. A buffet breakfast is an additional ¥500.

★Minamikan RYOKAN ¥¥¥
(皆美館; 0852-21-5131; www.minami-g.co.jp/minamikan; 14 Suetsugu Hon-machi; r per person with breakfast/2 meals from ¥14,838/22,614) A refined inn on the edge of the lake, Minamikan has a choice of 'modern', 'retro' and 'classic' rooms, all with broad views across the water. The top-end 'modern' has a tatami room with twin beds and private cypress-wood onsen. The cheaper 'classic' has seen the likes of literary great Kawabata Yasunari pass through.

There is also an excellent restaurant. The ryokan entrance is set back from the road.

Eating & Drinking

★Yakumo-an NOODLES ¥
(八雲庵; www.yakumoan.jp; 308 Kita-Horiuchi; dishes ¥700-1150; 10am-3pm;) Next door to the samurai house, this busy *soba* restaurant and its beautiful grounds are an excellent place to sample the local *warigo soba*. Try the tasty *soba kamo nanban* (noodles with slices of duck in broth). Look for a sign on a piece of wood outside.

★Kawa-kyō IZAKAYA ¥
(川京; 0852-22-1312; 65 Suetsugu Hon-machi; dishes ¥800-1575; 6-10.30pm Mon-Sat;) You can count on a friendly welcome at this small *izakaya*, which specialises in the 'seven delicacies' from Shinji-ko and is a good place to try some local sake. The daughter of the owners speaks English. Look for the bamboo-roofed menu display outside. Weekends get busy so book ahead.

Tsurumaru SEAFOOD ¥
(鶴丸; www.tsurumaru2.net; 1-79 Higashi Hon-machi; dishes ¥550-1200; noon-2pm & 5.30-10.30pm Mon-Sat;) The smell of fish grilling over coals permeates this restaurant, which specialises in the cuisine of the Oki Islands. The menu features meals like *eri-yaki konabe* (hot spicy soup cooked over a flame at your table) and sashimi. You'll know it by the *noren* with the crane on it, and the rustic folk-singing that drifts into the street. There's a limited English menu.

Naniwa JAPANESE ¥¥
(なにわ; 0852-21-2835; http://honten.naniwa-i.com; 21 Suetsugu Hon-machi; meals ¥2160-10,800; 11am-9pm) Next to Matsue-ōhashi, this bright, wood-themed restaurant is a tranquil spot for *unameshi* (eel and rice; ¥2700).

LAKE DELICACIES

Matsue's *kyodo ryōri* (regional cuisine) includes the 'seven delicacies' from Shinji-ko.

- *suzuki* – bass, paper-wrapped and steam-baked
- *shirauo* – whitebait, as tempura or sashimi
- *amasagi* – smelt, as sweet tempura or teriyaki
- *shijimi* – freshwater clams, usually in miso soup
- *moroge ebi* – shrimp, steamed
- *koi* – carp, baked in sauce
- *unagi* – freshwater eel, grilled

Or opt for one of the delicately prepared *kaiseki* spreads, such as the Shinji-ko course (¥4320).

Cafe Bar EAD BAR
(カフェバーEAD; 36 Suetsugu Hon-machi; drinks/snacks from ¥540/755; ⏲9pm-1am Thu-Mon) Low lighting, sofas, and a broad terrace with a river view make this relaxed bar-cafe a nice place to end your evening. Snacks include homemade pizzas. It's on the 3rd floor of a building just near the bridge.

ℹ Information

There's free wi-fi in the lobby area (also accessible from outside at all hours) of the large **Matsue Terrsa building** (松江テルサ; ⏲9am-9pm, to 8pm Sat & Sun) near the station.

Matsue Central Post Office (松江中央郵便局; ⏲9am-7pm, to 5pm Sat, to 12.30pm Sun, ATM 7am-11pm Mon-Fri, 9am-9pm Sat, 9am-7pm Sun) Has ATMs accepting international cards.

Matsue International Tourist Information Office (松江国際観光案内所; ☎0852-21-4034; www.kankou-matsue.jp; 665 Asahi-machi; ⏲9am-6pm, to 7pm Jun-Oct) Excellent, friendly assistance in English, French and other languages directly in front of JR Matsue Station. Free wi-fi.

ℹ Getting There & Away

Matsue is on the JR San-in line, which runs along the San-in coast. You can get to Okayama via Yonago on the JR Hakubi line. It's ¥500 to Yonago (30 minutes), then ¥5070 to Okayama by *tokkyū* (2¼ hours). Highway buses operate to Japan's major cities from the terminal in front of the station.

ℹ Getting Around

It's possible to walk around the sights. Matsue is also a good place to explore by bicycle; these can be rented close to Matsue Station at **Times Car Rental** (タイムズカーレンタル; ☎0852-26-8787; 590-4 Asahi-machi; per day ¥300; ⏲8am-6.30pm) and dropped off in six different locations.

There is also a handy city-loop bus: the red streetcar-like Lake Line buses follow a set route around the attractions every 20 minutes. One ride costs ¥200; a day pass is available for ¥500.

Oki Islands 隠岐諸島

POP 21,700

North of Matsue, in the Sea of Japan, are the remote and spectacular Oki-shotō, within the **Oki Islands Geopark**, and with coastal areas that are part of the **Daisen-Oki National Park**. These islands were once used to exile officials (as well as two emperors) who came out on the losing side of political squabbles. Four of the islands are inhabited: the three Dōzen islands – Nishino-shima, Chiburi-jima and Nakano-shima – and the larger Dōgo island. Being cut off from the mainland, there are cultural and religious practices preserved here that aren't observed elsewhere in Japan, the pace of life is decidedly slower, and there's a refreshing lack of development at the tourist spots. Allow at least a couple of days to visit, and keep in mind that ferry services are subject to change, or halt, in bad weather.

The biggest island, **Dōgo** (島後) is notable for its giant, wisened old cedar trees: the 800-year-old Chichi-sugi tree is believed to be the home of a deity; and the Yao-sugi tree at Tamakawasu-no-mikoto-jinja is thought to be 2000 years old, its gnarled sprawling branches propped up with posts. There are nature and coastal walks, and boat tours in the Saigō port area and the northern Shirashima coast. Bull sumo is an attraction throughout the year – not big guy versus bull, but bull versus bull.

West of Dōgo, **Nishino-shima** (西ノ島) boasts the stunning rugged Kuniga coastline, with the sheer 257m Matengai cliff. The coastal hike here is a must-do. The island is also home to interesting shrines, such as Yurahime-jinja, near a small inlet. Legend has it that squid come en masse to this inlet every year in autumn/winter as a way to ask forgiveness from the deity (there are pictures at the shrine to prove it). Nishino-shima is also known for horses, which you'll see roaming the hillsides. You can take diving and kayaking tours, including sunset cave exploration and beginner night dives with **Club Noah Oki** (クラブノア隠岐; ☎08514-6-0825; www.oki.club-noah.net; night dives ¥8400, sunset cave kayaking ¥5500) based at the Beppu port. Instructors knows the essentials in English.

The small **Chiburi-jima** (知夫里島), where the local slogan is *nonbiri Chiburi* (carefree Chiburi), is home to more impressive coastline, featuring the striking Sekiheki, an expanse of rust-coloured cliffs. You can also see stone-wall remains on the island – what is left of a crop-rotation practice that began here in the middle ages. The Akiya coast and Oki-jinja are draws on **Nakano-shima** (中ノ島), also known locally as Ama.

A great choice for accommodation on Chiburi-jima is **Hotel Chibu-no-Sato** (ホテル知夫の里; ☎08514-8-2500; http://tibunosato.com; Chibu 1242-1; r per person with 2 meals from ¥10,800), where the balconied rooms have fabulous sea views and there's an open-air bath (April to October) and free bicycle use for guests. On Nishino-shima, **Oki Seaside Hotel Tsurumaru** (隠岐シーサイドホテル鶴丸; ☎08514-6-1111; http://oki-tsurumaru.jp; r per person with 2 meals from ¥10,800) has a pleasant waterfront location and runs regular cruises. You'll find more accommodation options on Dōgo, particularly in Saigō port. Outside of Saigō is **Hotel Uneri** (ホテル海音里; ☎08512-5-3211; www.oki-island.jp/uneri; cabins ¥13,900-18,500), which has self-catering log cabins. All the islands also have ryokan and *minshuku* (from around ¥5000 up to around ¥8000 with meals); there are campgrounds, but no tents to rent, so BYO.

Each island has a post office with an ATM that accepts international cards, and a tourism office with free wi-fi and at least one native English speaker who can book activities and accommodation and tell you how to get there – essential, as accommodation can be spread out and resemble a regular house. The **Nishino-shima Tourism Office** (☎08514-7-8888; www.nkk-oki.com; ⌚8.30am-5.30pm, to 7pm Jun-Oct) in Beppu port is an excellent source of information and all its Oki Island pamphlets are downloadable from its website. For more on the natural and cultural features of the islands, the **Oki Islands Geopark Promotion Committee** (☎08512-2-9636; www.oki-geopark.jp) produces a very good English guide and map. The tourist office in Matsue is also very helpful.

It's possible to get to some of the main attractions by bike, but to see all of the islands it's best to hire a car or make use of a taxi or eco-tour guide service. There's a local bus on Nishino-shima that goes to the Kuniga coast, though it's infrequent. Ferries go to the Oki Islands from Shichirui (9am) and Sakai-minato (2.25pm, at 2.10pm January to March) ports, northeast of Matsue. They are operated by **Oki Kisen** (☎08512-2-1122; www.oki-kisen.co.jp), calling at the main ports, including Saigō for Dōgo (¥3240, 2½ hours; Rainbow Jet fast ferry from Shichirui ¥6170, 70 minutes). There's also an inter-island ferry service. Buses go to Shichirui from Matsue Station (¥1000, 40 minutes) and Yonago Station (¥870, 40 minutes). Sakai-minato is at the end of the JR Sakai train line, which connects with the JR San-in line at Yonago (¥320, 45 minutes).

Izumo 出雲

☎0853 / POP 143,800

Just west of Matsue, Izumo has one major attraction – the great Izumo Taisha shrine, which ranks with Ise-jingū as one of the most important shrines in Japan. The shrine and surrounding area can be visited as a day trip from Matsue.

Izumo Taisha is 8km northwest of central Izumo. The shrine area is basically one street, lined with eateries and shops, that leads up to the shrine gates. The Ichibata-line Izumo Taisha-mae Station is at the foot of the street.

Sights

★**Izumo Taisha** SHINTO SHRINE

(出雲大社; ⌚6.30am-8pm) FREE Perhaps the oldest Shintō shrine of all, Izumo is second in importance only to Ise-jingū, the home of the sun goddess Amaterasu. The shrine is as old as Japanese recorded history – there are references to Izumo in the *Kojiki,* Japan's oldest book – and its origins stretch back into the age of the gods.

The shrine is dedicated to Ōkuninushi, long revered as a bringer of good fortune, and worshipped as the god of marriage.

Visitors to the shrine summon Ōkuninushi by clapping four times rather than the usual two. According to tradition, the deity ceded control over Izumo to the sun goddess' line – he did this on the condition that a huge temple would be built in his honour, one that would reach as high as the heavens.

MIZUKI SHIGERU'S HORROR MANGA

Eyeballs on taxis, ghostly murals on ferries and ports in the Oki Islands – this is the horror manga of artist Mizuki Shigeru (水木 しげる), Sakai-minato's most famous resident.

His adorably evil *yōkai* (spirit demons) from manga series *GeGeGe No Kitarō* are a take on Japanese folklore, and plaster four train exteriors and interiors from Yonago to Sakai-minato – even announcements are made by one of his characters.

Legions of fans make the trip especially to Mizuki Shigeru Road – outside Sakai-minato Station – to pose with the 134 bronze *yōkai* statues and visit the **Mizuki Shigeru Museum** (水木しげる記念館; ☎0859-42-2171; adult/child ¥700/300, foreigners with ID ¥300; ⏲9.30am-5pm), plus the inevitable souvenir stores. The multimedia museum explains all things ghoulish with free English audio guides, and has rooms that re-create ancient Japan.

Mizuki's undead cast includes: Kitarō, the boy born in a cemetery; his father Medama-oyaji, a reborn eyeball; Neko Musume, the 'Cat Girl' with fangs and a Jekyll and Hyde personality; and Nezumi Otoko, the unwashed 'Rat Man' who uses flatulence as a weapon. Kids love it.

Impressive as the structure is today, it was once even bigger. Records dating from AD 970 describe the shrine as the tallest building in the country; there is evidence that the shrine towered as high as 48m above the ground during the Heian period. It may well have been too high for its own good – the structure collapsed five times between 1061 and 1225, and the roofs today are a more modest 24m.

The current appearance of the main shrine dates from 1744. The main hall underwent one of its periodic rebuildings in 2013, to be done again in another 60 years.

Huge *shimenawa* (twisted straw ropes) hang over the entry to the main buildings. Those who can toss and lodge a coin in them are said to be blessed with good fortune. Visitors are not allowed inside the main shrine precinct, most of which is hidden behind huge wooden fences. Ranged along the sides of the compound are the *jūku-sha*, which are long shelters where Japan's myriad deities stay when they come for their annual conference.

When former-Princess Noriko married the eldest son of the head priest of Izumo Taisha – a 'commoner' – she relinquished her royal status and now lives in a house near the shrine.

Shimane Museum of Ancient Izumo MUSEUM
(島根県立古代出雲歴史博物館; 99-4 Kizuki Higashi Taisha-chō; admission ¥600, foreigners with ID ¥300; ⏲9am-6pm, to 5pm Nov-Feb, closed 3rd Tue of month) Just to the right of the Izumo Taisha shrine's front gate, this museum contains exhibits on local history. These include reconstructions of the shrine in its pomp, and recordings of the annual ceremonies held to welcome the gods to Izumo. There is also a superb collection of bronze from the ancient Yayoi period.

Festivals & Events

Kamiari-sai RELIGIOUS
The 10th month of the lunar calendar is known throughout Japan as Kan-na-zuki (Month without Gods). In Izumo, however, it is known as Kami-ari-zuki (Month with Gods), for this is the month when all the Shintō gods congregate at Izumo Taisha.

The Kamiari-sai is a series of events to mark the arrival of the gods in Izumo. It runs from the 11th to the 17th of the 10th month according to the old calendar; exact dates vary from year to year.

Information

Tourist Information Office (☎0853-30-6015; ⏲9am-5.30pm) Not far from Izumo Taisha-mae Station on the main street.

Getting There & Away

The private, old-fashioned Ichibata line starts from Matsue Shinjiko-onsen Station in Matsue and trundles along the northern side of Shinji-ko to Izumo Taisha-mae Station (¥810, one hour, with a transfer at Kawato; 川跡).

The JR line runs from JR Matsue Station to JR Izumo-shi Station (¥580, 40 minutes), where you can transfer to an Ichibata train to Izumo Taisha-mae (¥490, 20 minutes), or to a bus to the shrine (¥510, 25 minutes).

Long-distance buses run from a few major cities in the region, including Hiroshima, Okayama and Kyoto.

Iwami Ginzan 石見銀山

About 6km inland from Nima Station on the San-in coast west of Izumo is the old Iwami Ginzan silver mine, a Unesco World Heritage Site. In the early 17th century, the mine produced as much as 38 tonnes of silver annually, making it the most important mine in the country at a time when Japan was producing around a third of the world's silver every year. The Tokugawa shogunate had direct control over the 500 or so mines in the area.

The site is spread along a valley, with the small town of Ōmori at its centre. The main streets and the walking path along the river roughly form a long narrow loop, with mine shafts, temples, historic residences and ruins dotted along it and in the wooded hillsides. From one end to the other is about 2km; allow at least four or more hours to do the loop on foot and see the various sites at leisure.

Among the highlights is the **Iwami Ginzan Museum** (石見銀山資料館; 51-1 Omori-chō; admission ¥500; ⌚9am-5pm, to 4pm Dec-Feb), containing various documents, tools and silver-related items. It's inside the Ōmori Daikansho Ato, near the Daikansho Ato bus stop. Nearby is the **Kigami-jinja** (城上神社), with a colourful dragon mural on its ceiling – to hear the dragon 'roar', stand underneath it and clap. Not far from here up the old road is the lovingly restored **Kumagai Residence** (熊谷家住宅; admission ¥500, foreigners with ID ¥300; ⌚9.30am-5pm Tue-Sun), rebuilt in 1801 after an earthquake destroyed most of the town the previous year. The house belonged to a merchant family who made their fortune as officials in the silver trade. Further along is an interesting temple, **Rakan-ji** (羅漢寺; admission incl Gohyakurakan ¥500; ⌚9am-5pm). Opposite is the wonderful **Gohyakurakan** (五百羅漢) where, crowded into two small caves, there are 500 diminutive stone statues of the Buddha's disciples, each showing a different expression – some smiling, some turning their head to chat to their neighbour. The collection was completed in 1766, after 25 years of work. South of Rakan-ji, the **Iwami Ginzan World Heritage Centre** (石見銀山世界遺産センター; 1597-3 Omori-chō; admission ¥300, foreigners with ID ¥200; ⌚8.30am-6pm, to 5.30pm Dec-Feb, closed last Tue of month) has exhibits with explanations in English on the history of the mines and the surrounding area.

Further along the road, don't miss the detour to see the overgrown stone **Shimizudani Refinery Ruins** (清水谷製錬所跡) and, at the far end of the site, the well-lit **Ryūgenji Mabu Shaft** (龍源寺間歩; admission ¥410, foreigners with ID ¥200; ⌚9am-5pm, to 4pm Dec-Mar), which has been widened substantially from its original size. One glance at the original tunnel that stretches beyond the fence at the end of the accessible area should be enough to make most people glad they weren't born as 17th-century miners. Past the Ryūgenji mine shaft, a hiking trail leads 12km to Yunotsu, following the old route along which silver was hauled to port.

There are a few cafes along the old road in town. For a drink and a sweet treat, stop in at **Yamabuki** (やまぶき; ☎0854-89-0676; 28 Omori-chō; donuts ¥100; ⌚10am-5pm Thu-Tue, to 4pm Nov-Mar), where the speciality is sweet-potato doughnuts. It's near Seisui-ji; look for a wooden sign.

Iwami Ginzan could be visited on a (very long) day trip from Matsue. Alternatively, it's good to combine a trip here with a stay in nearby Yunotsu. Another great option for accommodation is near Nima Station, at the **Jōfuku-ji Youth House** (城福寺ユースハウス; ☎0854-88-2233; www14.plala.or.jp/joufukuji; 1114 Nima-machi, Nima-chō; r per person with/without meals ¥4500/3000; @). Accommodation is in comfortable tatami rooms in a Buddhist temple. Meals are available, and the owners can collect you from the station.

There is a booth near the Ōmori Daikansho Ato stop where you can pick up a map and audio guide (¥500), also available at the **tourist information office** (☎0854-89-0333; ⌚9am-5pm, to 4pm Oct-Apr) by the car park close to Rakan-ji. Buses run to the Ōmori Daikansho Ato stop about every half-hour from Ōda-shi Station (¥610, 25 minutes), and from Nima Station (¥390, 15 minutes, four or five per day). There is also a long-distance bus to Hiroshima. Within the mine area, shuttle buses connect Ōmori Daikansho-ato and the World Heritage Centre every 15 minutes (¥200). There are also bikes for rent (¥500 for three hours; ¥700 for an electric-assist bike for two hours).

Yunotsu 温泉津

0855

Three stations south of Nima is the coastal onsen town of Yunotsu, one of the ports from where silver from the Iwami Ginzan mines was shipped to the capital and beyond. Now a protected historic area, it consists of a couple of narrow streets of well-preserved wooden buildings and two atmospheric public baths where you can soak up the mineral-rich waters with the locals.

On the main street of the town, recognisable by the statue outside and the large blue sign, **Motoyu Onsen** (元湯温泉; admission ¥350; 9am-10pm) traces its history back 1300 years, to when an itinerant priest came across a *tanuki* (racoon) nursing its wounded paw in the waters here. No fancy shower heads and racks of shampoo – just grab a wooden bucket and splash yourself down. A short walk away on the other side of the street is the relatively modern **Yakushinoyu Onsen** (薬師湯温泉; admission ¥350; 8am-9pm Mon-Fri, 6am-9pm Sat & Sun), discovered when hot water bubbled up from the ground after an earthquake in 1872.

There are a number of places to stay, including the 100-year-old **Ryokan Masuya** (旅館ますや; 0855-65-2515; www.ryokan-masuya.com; r per person with 2 meals from ¥10,950), down the street towards the sea from the two public baths. A little English is spoken, and accommodation is in tatami rooms (a Western-style room is available, but is not as good). Or try **Yoshidaya** (吉田屋; 0855-65-2014; www.lets.gr.jp/yoshidaya; r per person with/without 2 meals from ¥8700/4700;), a creaky 80-year-old building with spacious tatami rooms. The staff work with the community, including local elderly women farmers who sell *mottainai* vegetables (imperfect-looking vegies that wouldn't normally sell) to use in the meals here. Rooms are available Friday to Sunday only and payment is by cash. Yoshidaya is a few doors down from Motoyu Onsen.

Yunotsu is on the San-in line, down the coast from Matsue (¥1490, 1½ to 2¼ hours), a few stops from Nima and Ōda-shi stations, where there is access to Iwami Ginzan silver mine. When you exit Yunotsu Station, go left, then follow the road around to the right along the waterfront to reach the main street of ryokan. It's a 10- to 15-minute walk.

OFF THE BEATEN TRACK

SANBE-SAN 三瓶山

About 20km inland from Ōda is Sanbe-san, an old volcano with grassy slopes that reaches 1126m. It takes about an hour to climb from **Sanbe Onsen** (三瓶温泉) and five hours to walk around the caldera. You can have a dip in the onsen on your return. Day trippers can try the outdoor baths at **Kokuminshukusha Sanbesō** (国民宿舎さんべ荘; 0854-83-2011; www.sanbesou.jp; Shigaku Sanbe-chō, Ōda-shi; r per person with meals from ¥8740, baths ¥500; 10.30am-9pm), where accommodation is available. The area is a popular ski centre in winter. Buses run between Ōda-shi Station and Sanbe Onsen (¥830, 45 minutes, seven or eight daily).

TOTTORI & AROUND

Although Tottori Prefecture (鳥取県; Tottori-ken) is the least populous of Japan's 47 prefectures, it has a wealth of coastal scenery, sand dunes, onsen and volcanoes. The snag is it takes time and a bit of planning to get to some areas – this is a good place to hire a car. Summer is the best time to visit to get the most out of the beaches.

Tottori 鳥取

0857 / POP 197,300

Tottori is a medium-sized city that attracts crowds of Japanese tourists coming to take pictures of each other next to camels on the famous sand dunes. There's not a lot to keep you here once you've made the obligatory trip to the sand, but it's a decent base for exploring the nearby coastal areas.

Sights & Activities

There are beaches and scenic stretches of coastline within the San-in Coast National Park, a good side trip from Tottori city. The tourist office also has informaton in English about the local beaches.

★**Tottori-sakyū** SAND DUNES

(鳥取砂丘; The Dunes) Used as the location for Teshigahara Hiroshi's classic 1964 film *Woman in the Dunes*, the Tottori sand dunes are on the coast about 5km from the city. There's a viewing point on a hillside overlooking the dunes, along with parking and the usual array of tourist schlock. You can even get a 'Lawrence of Arabia' photo of yourself accompanied by a camel. There are maps at the **Sand Pal Tottori Information Centre** (サンドパルとっとり; 083-17 Yūyama, Fukube-chō; ⌚9am-6pm).

The dunes stretch for over 10km along the coast and, at some points, can be about 2km wide. Buses to the dunes also stop at the **Sakyū-Sentā** (砂丘センター; Dunes Centre), on the hillside, where you can take a **cable car** (one way ¥200; ⌚8.30am-4.30pm) down to the sand.

★Sand Museum MUSEUM
(砂の美術館; www.sand-museum.jp; admission ¥600; ⌚9am-8pm Apr-Jan) You came to see sand? They've got truckloads at this impressive museum of sand sculptures, where sand aficionados from all over the world are invited to created huge, amazingly detailed works based on a particular theme. The exhibition changes each year: check at the tourist office for this year's theme and opening months. The museum is near the sand dunes.

Kannon-in BUDDHIST TEMPLE
(観音院; 162 Ue-machi; admission ¥500; ⌚9am-5pm) The main attraction at this 17th-century temple is its beautiful garden, built around a pond. Gather your thoughts and contemplate the arrangement of stones and trees while sipping a cup of *matcha*, which is included in the admission. The city-loop bus passes near the temple.

Tottori-jō & Jinpū-kaku Villa CASTLE, MUSEUM
(鳥取城跡・仁風閣; 2-121 Higashi-machi; villa admission ¥150; ⌚9am-5pm Tue-Sun) Tottori's castle once overlooked the town, but now only the foundations remain. It's a pleasant walk up the hillside to see them and the views over the city. Below is the elegant Jinpū-kaku Villa, built as accommodation for the Taishō emperor when he visited as Crown Prince in 1907, and now used as a museum.

Hinomaru Onsen SENTO
(日乃丸温泉; 401 Suehiro Onsen-chō; admission ¥400; ⌚6am-midnight, closed 2nd Mon of month except Jan & Aug) There are a number of inner-city onsen within a short walk of the station. If you can brave the scorching hot waters, try soaking with the locals at this public bath in the heart of the entertainment district.

Sleeping

Matsuya-sō GUESTHOUSE ¥¥
(松屋荘; ☎0857-22-4891; 3-814 Yoshikata Onsen; s/tw ¥3780/6480) This *minshuku*-style lodging has no wi-fi or mod cons, but it does have large, clean tatami rooms with washbasins and shared bathrooms. From the station, go straight up the main street and turn right onto Eiraku-dōri (永楽通り). Look for Matsuya-sō on the left after a few blocks; it's about a 15-minute walk from the station. The welcoming owners speak some English.

Green Hotel Morris HOTEL ¥¥
(グリーンホテルモーリス; ☎0857-22-2331; www.hotel-morris.co.jp/tottori; 2-107 Ima-machi; s/tw from ¥5615/11,880;) Stylish, neutral-toned rooms, large spa baths and a sauna make Morris a good-value modern option. It's close to the station, and there's a buffet breakfast for ¥550.

Eating

Tottori-ya YAKITORI ¥
(とっ鳥屋; 585-1 Yamane; skewers from ¥86; ⌚5pm-1am;) This bustling *yakitori* (skewers of grilled chicken) place has a large menu of individual sticks and rice dishes. Get an assortment of six for ¥626 or 12 for ¥1242. As well as chicken there are grilled veg options. It's on Suehiro-dōri, east of the intersection with Eki-mae-dōri. Look for the rope curtain hanging over the door and ask for the English menu.

Jujuan GRILL, SEAFOOD ¥¥
(ジュジュアン; ☎0857-21-1919; 751 Suehiro Onsen-chō; meals ¥2000-10,000; ⌚11am-3pm & 5-11pm) Fresh seafood and local beef *sumibiyaki* (charcoal grilled) are the specialities in this airy restaurant. It does *shabu-shabu*, and set courses, such as the *kaisen gozen* (grilled seafood and vegetables with sides), with a seasonal menu that may include crab and other locally sourced goodies. It's on Suehiro-dōri, east of the intersection with Eki-mae-dōri.

Information

Tourist Information Office (鳥取市観光案内所; ☎0857-22-3318; www.torican.jp; ⌚9.30am-6.30pm) To the right as you exit the station, with English-language pamphlets, maps and English-speaking staff who can book the 1000 Yen Taxi for tourists. Accommodation is only booked at the other tourism office just inside the station entrance.

TOTTORI ONSEN

There are several onsen areas dotted across Tottori Prefecture. With a bit of time, why not put together your own tour of the springs:

Hawai Onsen West of Tottori city and just north of Kurayoshi (倉吉) Station is Tōgō-ike, with Hawai Onsen (はわい温泉) on its western side. Among the many hotels with baths here, you'll find friendly local *sentō* **Hawai Yūtown** (ハワイゆーたうん; www.supersentou.com/4_chugoku/05_hawai.htm; admission ¥350; ⌚9am-9pm Fri-Wed). Pick up a map of the other baths in the area from the information centre. Buses to Hawai Onsen run from Kurayoshi Station. For more on the area, see www.hawai-togo.jp.

Hamamura Onsen Take a dip in the delightful indoor and outdoor baths at Hamamura (浜村), further east along the train line from Kurayoshi. From Hamamura Station, walk straight and take the first major turning on the right. **Hamamura Onsen Kan** (浜村温泉館; www.hal.ne.jp/onsenkan; 780-2 Ketaka-chō; admission ¥430; ⌚10am-10pm, closed 1st Wed of month) is on the left, a seven-minute walk from the station.

Iwai Onsen East of Tottori city is Iwai Onsen (岩井温泉), said to be the oldest onsen in the region and known for its curative waters. This small collection of ryokan is about eight minutes by bus from Iwami Station along Rte 9. Day trippers can relax at modern *sentō* **Iwai Yukamuri Onsen** (岩井ゆかむり温泉; http://yukamuri.net; admission ¥310; ⌚6am-10pm). It's right by the bus stop and has an old-fashioned, white-and-blue exterior.

ℹ Getting There & Away

Tottori is on the coastal JR San-in train line. JR Pass holders going south and west (eg towards Himeji, Okayama, Osaka) must pay a cash fee on board, or when booking, of around ¥1800 for using non-JR tracks; JR-only alternatives add hours. Major destinations:

Matsue ¥2270, two to three hours; express service ¥4620, 1½ hours

Okayama express via Kamigori ¥5010, two hours

Toyooka local service ¥1490, 2½ hours

There are also long-distance buses to major cities in the region.

ℹ Getting Around

BICYCLE

Rent-a-Cycle (per day ¥500; ⌚8am-6.30pm) Outside the station. You can also rent bikes at the Sand Pal Tottori Information Centre (p489) near the dunes.

BUS

The *Kirinjishi* loop bus (¥300/600 per ride/day pass) operates on weekends, holidays and between 20 July and 31 August. It passes the main sights and goes to the dunes. Red- and blue-roofed *Kururi* minibuses (¥100 per ride) ply inner-city loops from the station every 20 minutes, passing by the main city attractions. Regular city buses depart from the station and travel to the dunes area (¥360, 20 minutes). There are maps and timetables available at the information office.

CAR

Cal Rent-a-Car (☎0857-24-0452; www.cal-rent.net; 1-88 Tomiyasu; 24hr from ¥3800; ⌚8am-8pm) Take the main road leading straight out from the south side of the station, then take a left turn at the first major intersection. Cal Rent-a-Car is in a petrol station on the right.

TAXI

1000 Yen Taxi (www.torican.jp; per car for foreigners with ID ¥1000; ⌚8.30am-5.30pm) A great deal for visiting a few sites in a short time. Up to four passengers can hire a taxi for up to three hours, including waiting time at any sites. Passengers are also given a coupon card that can be used with some sites for discounts and free souvenirs (mostly trinkets). Book at the Tourist Information Office.

Daisen 大山

☎0859

Although it's not one of Japan's highest mountains, at 1729m Daisen looks impressive because it rises straight from sea level – its summit is only about 10km from the coast. Daisen is part of the **Daisen-Oki National Park**.

The popular climb up the volcano is a five- to six-hour return trip from **Daisen-ji temple** (大山寺; 9 Daisen; treasure hall ¥300; ⌚9am-4pm, closed Dec-Mar). From the summit, there are fine views over the coast and, in perfect conditions, all the way to the Oki

Islands. Lonely Planet's *Hiking in Japan* has detailed information on the hike.

Even if you're not planning to hike to the summit, there's plenty to keep you occupied. Surrounding Daisen-ji are temples, ruins and forest walking tracks, and you can walk up the stone path to **Ōgamiyama-jinja** (大神山神社), the oldest building in western Tottori-ken. Further along the Daisen Park Way is the **Masumizu Plateau** (Masumizu-kōgen), where a gondola lift takes you up to an observation point and hiking trails. At the edge of the park is the **Shōji Ueda Museum of Photography** (植田正治写真美術館; www.japro.com/ueda; 353-3 Sumura, Hōki-chō; admission ¥800; ⏲9am-5pm, closed Tue & Dec-Feb), showcasing the works of prominent Tottori Prefecture photographer Shōji Ueda (1913–2000), in a large minimalist concrete building with fabulous views across to the mountain.

The mountain catches the northwest monsoon winds in the winter, bringing lots of snow to what is western Japan's top skiing area. **Daisen White Resort** (大山ホワイトリゾート; ☎0859-52-2315; www.daisen-resort.jp) and **Daisen Masumizu-kōgen Ski Resort** (大山ますみず高原スキー場; ☎0859-52-2420; www.masumizu.net/ski) are among the slopes.

The closest station to Daisen is Yonago, about 30 minutes from Matsue and 60 to 90 minutes from Tottori on the San-in line. The Daisen Loop bus (one-/two-day pass ¥1000/2000) runs to Daisen-ji from Yonago Station on weekends and holidays in May and from August to November. It stops at all the main sights around the mountain. Regular buses run to the temple from Yonago (¥820, 50 minutes, five daily) with **Nihon Kōtsū** (www.nihonkotsu.co.jp). At the temple is the large **Daisen-ji Information Centre** (☎0859-52-2502; ⏲8.30am-6pm), with brochures, maps and hiking information. Staff can arrange bookings at the local ryokan. For info online in English, check out http://en.go-to-japan.jp/daisenguide.

San-in Coast National Park 山陰海岸国立公園

The coastline east from the Tottori dunes stretching all the way to the Tango-hantō in Kyoto-fu is known as the San-in Kaigan Kokuritsu-kōen (San-in Coast National Park). There are sandy beaches, rugged headlands and pines jutting into the blue sky. To get the most out of your travels here, having a car is the best option. However, it is possible to get to some sites via train and bus.

Near the edge of Hyōgo Prefecture is **Uradome Kaigan** (浦富海岸), a scenic stretch of islets and craggy cliffs with pines clinging precariously to their sides. Forty-minute cruises with **Uradome Kaigan Cruises** (浦富海岸・島めぐり遊覧船; ☎0857-73-1212; www.yourun1000.com; cruises ¥1300-2100; ⏲every 20min 9.10am-4.10pm Mar-Nov) leave from the fishing port of Ajiro, 35 minutes east of Tottori by bus. From Tottori Station, take a bus bound for Iwami Station (岩美駅) and Iwai Onsen (岩井温泉) and get off at the Tōmeguri Yūransen Noriba-mae stop, which is right outside the cruise ticket office and boarding point. The bus goes via the dunes, so it's possible to visit the dunes and do the cruise as a day trip from Tottori. Note that cruises are sometimes cancelled due to rough conditions; get the tourist office to call and check before you go.

Uradome (浦富) and **Makidani** (牧谷), two popular beaches, are a few kilometres east. The closest station is Iwami on the JR San-in line, where there's a **tourist information office** (☎0857-72-3481; ⏲9am-6pm Tue-Sun). You can take a bus to the beach, rent bicycles and arrange accommodation in the area. **Higashi-hama** (東浜) is a among the best of the swimming beaches along the coast, and is easily accessed by train from Tottori – it's just near Higashi-hama Station (¥410, 30 minutes).

Along this stretch of coast are walking tracks that are part of the **Chūgoku Shizen Hodō** (中国自然歩道; Chūgoku Nature Walking Path), linking to tracks in neighbouring prefectures.

Northern Honshū (Tōhoku)

Includes ➡

Best Onsen

- ➡ Nyūtō Onsen (p528)
- ➡ Aoni Onsen (p539)
- ➡ Sukayu Onsen (p538)
- ➡ Zaō Onsen (p515)
- ➡ Akiu Onsen (p553)

Best Hikes

- ➡ Dewa Sanzan (p517)
- ➡ Hakkōda-san (p538)
- ➡ Iwaki-san (p536)
- ➡ Akita Komaga-take (p527)
- ➡ Oirase Keiryū (p537)

Why Go?

Tōhoku (東北; 'northeast') is Japan's rugged north, a land of hulking volcanic massifs, remote hot springs, ancient folklore and unique customs born of centuries of isolation.

This was a land where, aside from the dramatic and beautiful passage of the seasons, nothing much changed, until the 2011 Great East Japan Earthquake and tsunami changed everything, levelling many coastal communities in Iwate, Miyagi and Fukushima prefectures. Today, new life emerges slowly, with trepidation and courage from the devastation.

The undamaged landscapes of Niigata, Yamagata, Akita and Aomori prefectures are as dramatic and rewarding as ever, home to vibrant festivals and traditions, sensational snow resorts, healing hot springs, mountain hikes along ancient pilgrimage routes, and samurai-era villages.

There's never been a better time to explore Japan's culturally diverse, stunningly beautiful, rugged, great north, and your visit can really make a difference.

When to Go

Aomori

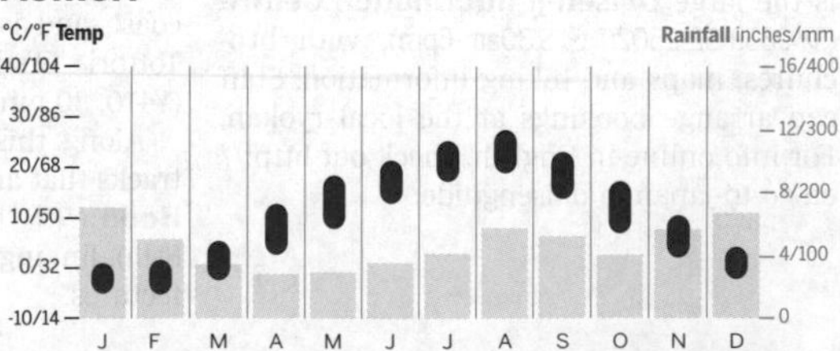

Dec–Feb Skiing galore, winter festivals and *yukimiburo*: onsen snowgazing.

Jun–Aug Mild summers come to life with spirited festivals and magnificent greenery.

Sep–Oct A brief but intense autumn is marked by spectacular displays of foliage.

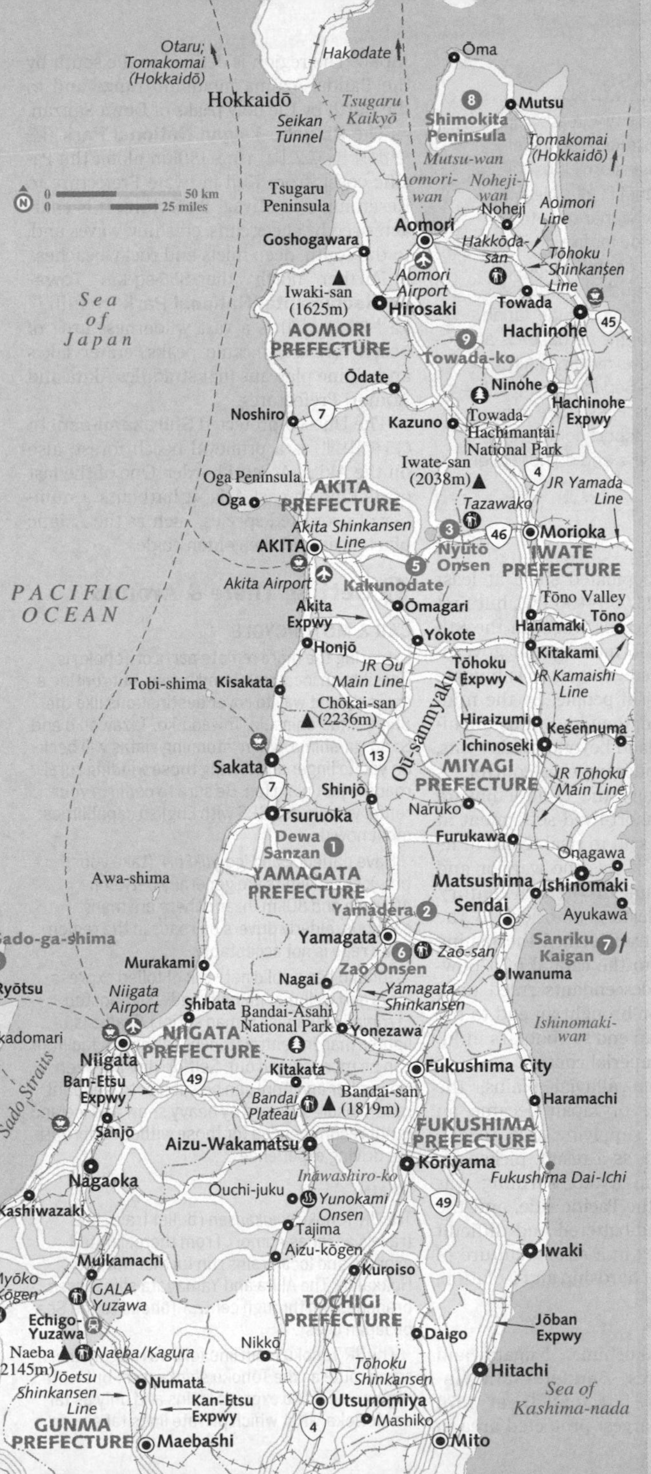

Northern Honshū (Tōhoku) Highlights

1. Following the footsteps of the *yamabushi* (mountain priests) through the sacred peaks of **Dewa Sanzan** (p517).
2. Making pilgrimage to the mountaintop temple of **Yamadera** (p519), as poet Matsuo Bashō once did.
3. Soaking away your worries at **Nyūtō Onsen** (p528), in the mountains above pretty Tazawa-ko.
4. Escaping the mainland crush on scenic **Sado-ga-shima** (p497) island.
5. Venturing back to a time of samurai, on the streets of **Kakunodate** (p525).
6. Dodging the 'ice monsters' at **Zaō Onsen** (p515).
7. Opening your heart along the tsunami-ravaged **Sanriku Kaigan** (p549).
8. Contemplating life at other-worldly Ozore-san on the **Shimokita Peninsula** (p539).
9. Frolicking around the verdant shores of **Towada-ko** (p536).

JR EAST PASS

The **JR East Pass** (www.jreast.co.jp/e/eastpass) offers unlimited rail travel around Tokyo and eastern Honshū (including all of Tōhoku, plus Niigata and Nagano). It's cheaper than the full JR Pass and good for five flexible days in a two-week period. Exchange orders for passes must be purchased from selected agencies outside Japan and surrendered for the actual pass at the JR ticket windows of Narita Airport station or JR Travel Service Centres at major train stations. Passes are only valid for foreign passport holders on a temporary visitor visa and do not cover travel on JR buses.

History

Tōhoku has been populated since at least the Jōmon period (13,000–400 BC), but first entered historical records when, in the 8th century, the newly formed central government in Nara enlisted generals to subjugate the indigenous Emishi people. By the mid-9th century the land, then known as Michinoku (literally 'the land beyond roads') was, if only tenuously, under imperial control.

In the 11th century the Ōshu Fujiwara clan established a short-lived settlement at Hiraizumi that was said to rival Kyoto in its opulence. However, it was the warrior and leader Date Masamune, in the 17th century, who would bring lasting notoriety to the region. Masamune transformed the fishing village of Sendai into the capital of a powerful domain. His descendants ruled until the Meiji Restoration brought an end to the feudal system, and an end to Tōhoku's influence, by restoring imperial control.

Blessed with rich alluvial plains, the coast along the Sea of Japan became an agricultural centre supplying rice to the imperial capital and, as a result, picked up more influence from Kyoto. Farming was less productive on the Pacific side, and the coastline rocky, wind-battered and difficult to navigate, resulting in a strong culture of perseverance born of hardship and isolation.

National Parks

Sprawling over Fukushima, Niigata and Yamagata Prefectures, **Bandai-Asahi National Park** (磐梯朝日国立公園), at 1870 sq km, is the third-largest protected area in Japan. The region is defined to the south by the Bandai-Azuma mountain range and to the north by the holy peaks of Dewa Sanzan.

The **Rikuchū-kaigan National Park** (陸中海岸国立公園) runs 180km along the Pacific coast, from Kuji in Iwate Prefecture to Kesennuma in Miyagi Prefecture. It is characterised by sheer cliffs, crashing waves and, to the south, deep inlets and rocky beaches.

Further north, the 855-sq-km **Towada-Hachimantai National Park** (十和田八幡平国立公園) is a vast wilderness area of beech forests, volcanic peaks, crater lakes and alpine plateaus that straddles Akita and Aomori Prefectures.

The Unesco-protected **Shirakami-sanchi** (白神山地) is a primeval beech forest, also on the Akita–Aomori border. One of the last of its kind in east Asia, it harbours a number of protected species, such as the Asiatic black bear and the golden eagle.

Getting There & Around

CAR & MOTORCYCLE

Exploring the more remote parts of Tōhoku is possible on local trains and buses, but renting a car is a great way to cover destinations like the Shimokita Peninsula, Towada-ko, Tazawa-ko and Sado-ga-shima, where stunning vistas will beckon you to linger and driving those winding rural roads is just plain fun. Be sure to confirm your rental vehicle has GPS with English capabilities: most now do.

Have patience and *'go-yukkuri'* (take your time); speed limits are generally between 40km/h and 80km/h, and there are many cautious, elderly drivers on roads in the region. Road rage is not acceptable.

Tōhoku has a solid network of tolled expressways and well-maintained roads, signposted in *rōmaji* (Japanese roman script). Traffic is lighter than in central Honshū, although facilities can be more spread out. Self-driving between November and April can be subject to frequent road-closures caused by heavy snow and ice and is not recommended for those without appropriate driving experience.

TRAIN

The JR Tōhoku *shinkansen* (bullet train) line travels as far as Aomori. From there, limited express and local trains run further north to Hokkaidō. The Akita and Yamagata *shinkansen* branches run through central Tōhoku to the Sea of Japan coast.

The JR Tōhoku main line follows roughly the same route as the Tōhoku *shinkansen*, but with regular local and express trains and only as far as Morioka, after which private lines take over.

A combination of JR and private lines runs along the east and west coasts.

NIIGATA PREFECTURE

Depending on who you talk to, Niigata-ken (新潟県) isn't technically part of Tōhoku, but its capital city, Niigata, is a transport gateway to the far north. The prefecture receives some of the country's highest snowfalls, burying villages and bewitching powder fiends. Top ski destinations include Myōkō Kōgen, Echigo-Yuzawa Onsen (both now accessible by *shinkansen* from Tokyo) and Naeba, home to the Fuji Rock Festival in the summer. If you just want to *really* get away, pop on over to the delightfully sleepy, sunny, Sado-ga-shima.

Niigata 新潟

025 / POP 811,600

The prefectural capital of Niigata serves as a transit hub and a springboard to nearby Sado-ga-shima. Japan's longest river, the Shinano-gawa, runs through the centre of the city; if you have time to spare, join the locals for a stroll along the riverbank.

Niigata Prefecture

Sights

Saito Family Summer Villa HISTORIC BUILDING
(旧齋藤家別邸, Kyū Saito-ke Bettei; 025-210-8350; www.saitouke.jp; 576 Nishi Ohata-chō; adult/child ¥300/100; 9.30am-5pm Tue-Sun; 3, 13 to Higashi-ōhata Niban-chō) Opened to the public as a museum in June 2012, almost a century after its construction as an indulgent private summer house, this luscious example of turn-of-the-century Japanese architecture and design also features a beautiful garden with huge Edo period pines sheltering over a hundred Japanese maples.

Hakusan-kōen PARK
(白山公園; 025-228-1000; 1-2 Ichiban Horidori-chō; dawn-dusk) Built in 1873 as Japan's first citizen's park, Hakusan-kōen remains a lovely place for a stroll among beautiful, manicured gardens. There's a pond full of koi, a bridge and a shrine.

Nippō Media Ship Sora-no-hiroba OBSERVATION DECK
(新潟日報メディアシップそらの広場; 025-385-7500; 8am-11pm) FREE Come to the 20th floor of this skyscraper for amazing 360-degree views over the Sea of Japan, Niigata city and the distant mountains.

Sleeping

Hotel Nikkō Niigata HOTEL ¥¥
(ホテル日光新潟; 025-240-1888; www.jalhotels.com/domestic/chubu_hokuriku/niigata; 5-1 Bandai-jima; s/d from ¥6750/11,200; P) Niigata's finest hotel is located at the mouth of the Shinano-gawa at the Toki Messe Convention Centre. It's also Niigata's tallest building with views from the Sea of Japan to the distant Alps. Rooms are simply stylish, comfortably appointed and larger than most Japanese hotels. All have fantastic views. Advance purchase discounts are available.

ANA Crowne Plaza Niigata HOTEL ¥¥
(ANAクラウンプラザホテル新潟; 025-245-3333; www.ihg.com; 5-11-20 Bandai; s/tw/d from ¥7225/8925/9775; P) With a 2pm check-in and 11am check-out, you have a little more time to rest in this comfortable, stylish hotel, 10-minutes' walk from the station. Recently refurbished guest rooms come in a variety of shapes and sizes; all have comfortable bedding and good amenities. Enquire about the reasonably priced 50-sq-metre Japanese suites.

Hotel Mets Niigata HOTEL ¥¥¥
(025-246-2100; www.jrhotelgroup.com/eng/index.htm; 1-96-47 Hanazono; s/d from ¥9400/16,000;) New in 2013, this JR Group Hotel has direct access to Niigata station, not to mention compact, well-designed rooms. Rooms on the slick, superior floor are larger (and more expensive).

Eating

Pia Bandai MARKET ¥¥
(ピアBandai; 025-249-2560; 2-10 Bandai-shima, Chūō-ku; meals from ¥1000; 9am-9pm) Conveniently located on the way to Sado Kisen Ferry Terminal, this sprawling complex includes markets and eateries – so you can gawk at the bounty of Niigata's coast and sample it, too. If you're in Niigata with time to eat, a visit here is a must. You'll be spoiled for choice: if you're overwhelmed, the *kaiten-sushi* (conveyor-belt sushi restaurant) **Benkei** (弁慶) ranks highly.

Kanda Grill WESTERN ¥¥
(ぐりるかんだ; 025-246-0820; 1-5-21 Higashi-ōdōri; dishes from ¥700; 11.30am-2pm & 5.30-9pm) Near the station, this *yōshoku* (Western-style) grill house serves up treats for your tastebuds (and enemies of your waistline), such as crumbed *katsu-don* (rice topped with a fried pork cutlet) and *hamburg teishoku* – the cheese hamburg with rice and salad (¥1300) is drippy-licious. There's a photo-menu.

Information

Niigata Central Post Office (新潟中央郵便局; 025-244-3796; 2-6-26 Higashi Ōdori; 9am-7pm)

Niigata University Medical & Dental Hospital (新潟大学医歯学総合病院; 025-227-2460,

NIIGATA SAKE

Niigata Prefecture is one of Japan's top sake-producing regions, known in particular for a crisp, dry style called *tanrei karakuchi*. The long, cold winters produce plenty of fresh mountain snow melt for the valleys below, which translates into delicious rice and then delicious sake. Tipplers should be sure to treat themselves while passing through. In March, a mammoth bacchanal in Niigata city, called **Sake-no-jin** (酒の陣; www.niigata-sake.or.jp/en), highlights more than 90 varieties of sake from around the prefecture.

after hours 025-227-2479; www.nuh.niigata-u.ac.jp/index_e.html; 1-757 Asahimachi-dōri, Ichiban-chō; ⏲ outpatient service 8.30-11.30am Mon-Fri)

Tourist Information Center (新潟駅万代口観光案内センター; ☎ 025-241-7914; www.nvcb.or.jp/en; ⏲ 9am-6pm) Lovely, helpful staff dispense English maps and information to the left of Niigata Station's Bandai exit. The website is good too!

ℹ Getting There & Away

AIR

Niigata Airport (KIJ), 13km north of the city centre, has domestic flights to Sapporo, Nagoya, Osaka, Fukuoka and Okinawa and international flights to Khabarovsk, Vladivostok, Seoul, Shanghai, Harbin and Guam.

Buses to the airport run from stop 5 outside Niigata Station's south exit, roughly every half-hour from 6.30am to 6.40pm (¥400, 25 minutes); a taxi should cost about ¥2500.

BOAT

From the port of Niigata-kō, **Shin-Nihonkai** (新日本海; ☎ 025-273-2171; www.snf.jp) ferries depart at 10.30am daily, except Monday, for Otaru on Hokkaidō (from ¥6480, 18 hours). To get to Niigata-kō, take any bus bound for Rinko-nichōme from stop 6 at the Bandai exit bus pool in front of Niigata Station and get off at Suehiro-bashi (¥200, 25 minutes). A taxi should cost about ¥1500.

Sado Kisen (佐渡汽船; ☎ 025-245-1234; www.sadokisen.co.jp; ⏲ 8am-6pm) runs frequent ferries and hydrofoils to Ryōtsu on Sado-ga-shima. Buses to the ferry terminal (¥200, 15 minutes) leave from stop 5 at the Bandai exit bus pool 45 minutes before sailing. A taxi should cost about ¥1000; alternatively, you can walk there in about 40 minutes.

BUS

Highway buses depart from the **Bandai Bus Center** (万代シテイバスセンター), a big yellow building 1km northwest of the train station, and connect Niigata to major cities throughout Honshū.

CAR & MOTORCYCLE

If you're driving, the **Kan-Etsu Expressway** (関越自動車道) runs between Tokyo and the greater Niigata area. The **Nihonkai-Tōhoku Expressway** (日本海東北自動車道) connects Niigata with Akita.

TRAIN

Shinkansen (bullet trains) on the Jōetsu line run approximately twice an hour between Niigata and Tokyo (¥10,050, 2¼ hours), via Echigo-Yuzawa (¥4860, 45 minutes).

> **ℹ NORTHERN TŌHOKU WELCOME CARD**
>
> The **Northern Tōhoku Welcome Card** (www.northern-tohoku.gr.jp/welcome) offers discounts on admission, lodging and even transport from participating vendors – identified by a red-and-white Welcome Card sticker – in Iwate, Aomori and Akita Prefectures. Print out the card from the website. Note that its use is technically restricted to foreign travellers staying in Japan for less than a year.

There are a few *tokkyū* (limited express trains) each day on the JR Uetsu line between Niigata and Tsuruoka (¥3930, 1¾ hours) and between Niigata and Akita (¥6690, 3¾ hours).

To access the port of Naoetsu-kō, where you can grab a ferry or hydrofoil to the town of Ogi on Sado-ga-shima, there are a few *tokkyū* each day on the JR Shinetsu line between Niigata and Naoetsu (¥4100, 1¾ hours). From Naoetsu Station, it's a 10-minute bus ride (¥200) or about ¥1000 for a taxi to the port.

Sado-ga-shima 佐渡島

☎ 0259 / POP 62,000

Despite being Japan's sixth-largest island, Sado-ga-shima is relatively undeveloped, and is characterised by rugged natural beauty and eccentric reminders of its rich and evocative past. Crowds peak during the third week in August for the Earth Celebration, headlined by the world-famous Kodō Drummers. Outside of the summer holiday season, it's blissfully quiet.

History

Sado has always been something of a far-flung destination, just not always a voluntary one. During the feudal era, the island was a notorious penal colony where out-of-favour intellectuals were forever banished. The illustrious list of former prisoners includes Emperor Juntoku, *nō* (stylised dance-drama) master Ze-Ami, and Nichiren, the founder of one of Japan's most influential Buddhist sects. When gold was discovered near the village of Aikawa in 1601, there was a sudden influx of miners, who were often vagrants press-ganged from the mainland and made to work like slaves.

Sado-ga-shima

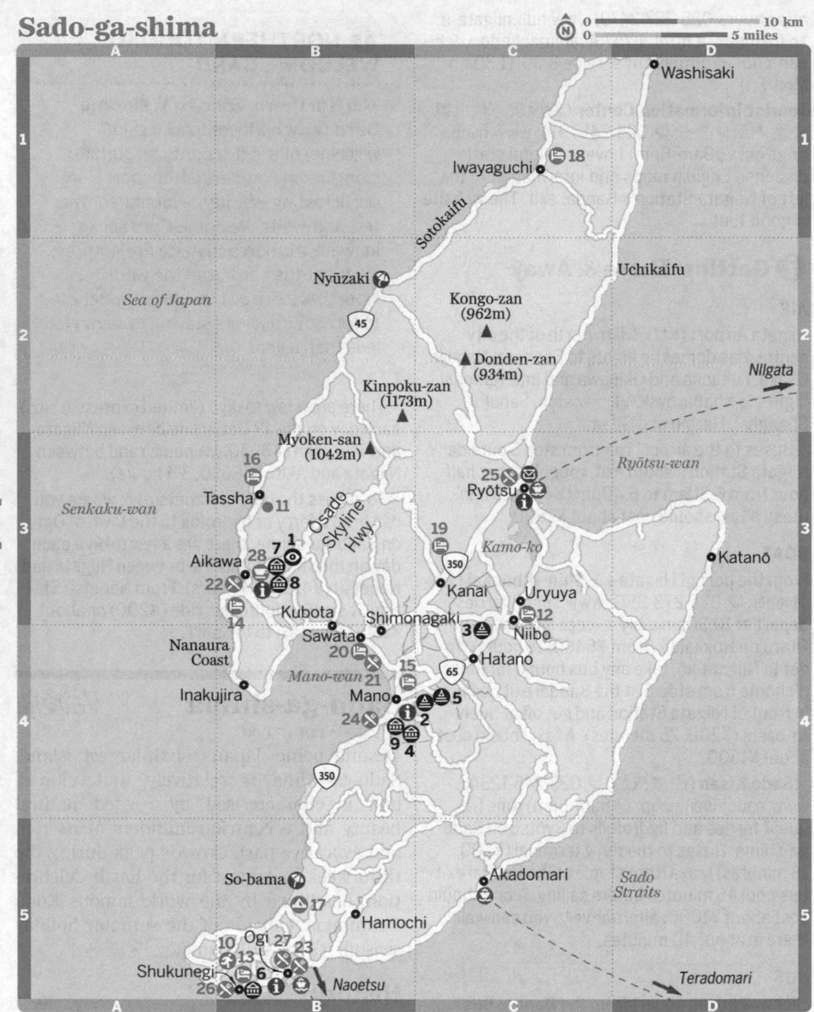

Festivals & Events

Sado is bursting at the seams with culture and known throughout Japan for its many festivals – a testament to the islanders' commitment to a more traditional way of life. *Nō* theatre has a strong following here, with several different groups performing at shrines around the island, often for free. For a full list of all the weird and wonderful events on Sado, including the well-known Earth Celebration (p502), see www.visitsado.com and sado-biyori.com/en.

Getting There & Away

Sado Kisen (佐渡汽船; www.sadokisen.co.jp) runs car ferries and passenger-only hydrofoils between Niigata and Ryōtsu. There are up to six ferries per day (one-way per person/car from ¥2510/17,900, 2½ hours) and 11 jetfoils (one-way ¥6520, one hour) in peak season. Service is greatly reduced outside the summer months. It's generally cheaper to rent a car on the island than take one on the ferry.

From Naoetsu-kō, about 90km southwest of Niigata, there are also up to three daily car-ferry services to Ogi (one-way per person/car from ¥2720/19,500, 2½ hours): particularly useful during Earth Celebration (p502).

Sado-ga-shima

Top Sights	13 Hana-no-ki ... B5
1 Sado Kinzan ... B3	14 Hotel Oosado ... B3
	15 Itōya Ryokan ... B4
Sights	16 Sado Belle Mer Youth Hostel ... B3
2 Kokubun-ji ... C4	17 So-bama Campground ... B5
3 Konpon-ji ... C4	18 Sotokaifu Youth Hostel ... C1
4 Mano Go-ryō ... B4	19 Tōkaen ... C3
5 Myōsen-ji ... C4	20 Urashima ... B4
6 Ogi Folk Museum ... B5	
7 Sado Former Magistrate's Office ... B3	**Eating**
8 Sado Hanga-mura Museum ... B3	21 Aka-chōchin ... B4
9 Sado Museum of History & Tradition ... B4	22 Isonoya ... B3
	23 Shichiemon ... B5
	24 Shima-fūmi ... B4
Activities, Courses & Tours	25 Sushi-no-uohide ... C3
10 Sado Island Taiko Centre ... B5	26 Takobōshi ... B5
11 Senkaku Bay Ageshima Park ... B3	27 Uohara ... B5
Sleeping	**Drinking & Nightlife**
12 Green Village Patio House ... C3	28 Kyōmachi Chaya ... B3

From March to November, there are one to three daily high-speed ferries (one-way, ¥2960, one hour) between Akadomari and Teradomari, 45km south of Niigata.

Getting Around

BICYCLE

Cycling is an enjoyable way to move around the towns, but steep elevations make long-distance cruising a challenge. Tourist information centres in each town rent electric bicycles for a hefty ¥2000 per day (or ¥500 for two hours), while local shops in Ryōtsu and Ogi rent regular bikes for slightly less.

BUS

The island is well served by buses, but services are slow, infrequent and can be confusing.

The Minami line connects Ryōtsu with Mano (¥670, 45 minutes). The Hon line runs from Ryōtsu to Aikawa (¥820, one hour), by way of the large hub of Sawata (¥620, 40 minutes). The Ogi line connects Ogi with Mano (¥820, 55 minutes) and Sawata (¥820, 1¼ hours). Along the northern coast, a few buses run on the Kaifu line each day between Aikawa and Iwayaguchi (¥820, one hour). The Uchikaifu line connects Iwayaguchi and Ryōtsu (¥820, 1½ hours).

The unlimited-ride bus pass (two weekdays/weekend ¥2500/2000) is good value if you plan to cover a lot of ground.

CAR & MOTORCYCLE

Renting a car on the island is the best way to explore: it's much cheaper than bringing a car over on the ferry. Sights and accommodation options are spread out. Expect to pay ¥6000 to ¥10,000 per day, depending on size and availability. **Sado Kisen Car Rental** (☎0259-27-5195) in the ferry terminals is a friendly, helpful operator. Gas stations are few and far between outside the main towns, but you'll often pay a per-kilometre fee for gas and not be required to return the car with a full tank. Unless you plan to circumnavigate the island or stay a long time, you're unlikely to use a full tank.

Ryōtsu & Around 両津

Sado's main hub, Ryōtsu is a low-key port town with little in the way of sights. Head inland and the townscape gives way to rice fields, rustic farmhouses and ancient temples.

Sights

Konpon-ji BUDDHIST TEMPLE

(根本寺; ☎22-3751; 1837 Niibo Ōno; admission ¥300; ⏲9am-4.30pm) This rustic wooden temple, with its thatched roof and pleasant gardens, is where the Buddhist monk Nichiren was first brought when exiled to Sado in 1271. Any bus on the Minami line from Ryōtsu can drop you off at the Konpon-ji-mae bus stop.

Sleeping & Eating

Green Village Patio House HOSTEL ¥

(☎0259-22-2719; www.e-sadonet.tv/~gvyh/eng/index.html; 750-4 Niibo Uryuya; dm/s per person ¥3500/3800, breakfast/dinner ¥700/1000; P ⊜ @ ⓦ) This adorable, spotless, Western-style guesthouse in the heart of

Sado has wonderfully accommodating hosts who speak some English. Accommodation is in six-person dormitories or one of two private rooms with shared facilities. From Ryōtsu, regular buses on the Minami line can drop you off at Niibo Yubinkyoku-mae, 90m past the turn-off for the hostel.

Tōkaen MINSHUKU ¥¥

(桃華園; ☎0259-63-2221; www.on.rim.or.jp/~toukaen; 1636-1 Kanai-Shinbo; r per person from ¥4500, with 2 meals from ¥8800; P 📶) This rambling, isolated *minshuku* (guesthouse) with big, airy rooms is in an attractive, peaceful spot in the middle of the central plains. The kind owners are outdoors-y folk who know every trail on the island. If you don't have a car, take a Hon-line bus from Ryōtsu to Undōkōen-mae and tell the driver you're going to Tōkaen: it's a 3km walk.

Sushi-no-uohide SUSHI ¥¥

(すしの魚秀; ☎0259-27-5610; 136 Ryōtsu-ebisu; meals from ¥1100; ⏱11am-2pm & 4-7pm Thu-Tue) Get a taste of Sado's seas at this counter shop, directly across from the ferry terminal. The *ji-zakana* (local fish) set is a sampling of the day's catch. Look for the characters for sushi (すし) out front.

Information

Tourist Information Center (佐渡観光協会; ☎0259-27-5000; www.visitsado.com/en; 2nd fl, Sado Kisen Ferry Terminal; ⏱8.30am-6pm) There's an excellent selection of English maps and pamphlets here, including walking and cycling guides for all of the island's main areas. The helpful English-speaking staff can help you arrange car rental.

Ryōtsu Post Office (両津郵便局; ☎0259-27-3634; 2-1 Ryōtsu-ebisu; ⏱9am-5pm Mon-Fri) This main post office has an international ATM. Another branch inside the ferry terminal has shorter opening hours.

Mano & Sawata 真野・佐和田

Although Mano was the provincial capital and cultural centre of the island from early times until the 14th century, it has since been dwarfed by the heavily populated administrative capital to the north, Sawata. It's good for Mano, which gets to keep its village feel and its main street lined with wooden buildings and weeping willows.

Sights

A peaceful 7km nature trail east of town winds through paddy fields and past Mano's attractions. The entrance is near the Danpū-jō bus stop, along the Minami bus route between Ryōtsu and Sawata. From the trailhead, it's a short walk to **Myōsen-ji** (妙宣寺; ☎55-2061; ⏱dawn-dusk) FREE, which was founded by one of the Buddhist monk Nichiren's disciples and features a distinctive five-storey pagoda.

From Myōsen-ji, it's a 10-minute walk through farmland and up old wooden steps set into the hillside to **Kokubun-ji** (国分寺; ☎0259-55-2059; 113 Kokubun-ji; ⏱dawn-dusk) FREE, Sado-ga-shima's oldest temple, dating from AD 741. Another 3km takes you past marvellous lookout points to **Mano Go-ryō** (真野御陵), the tomb of Emperor Juntoku. From there, it's a short walk down to **Sado Museum of History & Tradition** (佐渡歴史伝説館, Sado Rekishi Densetsukan; ☎0259-55-2525; www.sado-rekishi.jp; 655 Mano; adult/child ¥800/400; ⏱8am-5.30pm), where tireless animatrons act out scenes from Sado's dramatic past.

Sleeping & Eating

Itōya Ryokan RYOKAN ¥¥

(伊藤屋; ☎0259-55-2019; www.itouyaryokan.com; 278 Mano Shin-machi; r per person ¥5300, with 2 meals ¥7300; P 📶) At the heart of Mano village is the peaceful Itōya Ryokan, just 50m southwest of the Shin-machi traffic signal. This historic house is full of handicrafts from across the island, and evening dishes feature fish and shellfish from the deep sea. Rooms are spotless, the sheets are crisp and there's an inviting *hinoki* (wooden) bath that's perfect for cool evenings.

★ **Urashima** RYOKAN ¥¥¥

(浦島; ☎0259-57-3751; www.urasima.com; 978-3 Kubota; r per person with 2 meals from ¥10,500) This quirky, luxe Sawata ryokan is one for design aficionados: it was once a fishmonger's. Now its friendly, polished staff exemplify the Japanese art of hospitality. Many rooms have balconies facing a pine grove, before the ocean: all are comfortably and smartly furnished with attention to detail. This is a fantastic, modern property in a great spot: the perfect Sado base.

Shima-fūmi CAFE ¥

(シマフウミ; ☎0259-55-4545; www.primosado.jp/shimafumi; 105-4 Daishō; snacks from ¥400; ⏱10am-5pm Fri-Tue) This popular cafe in a delightful spot overlooking Mano bay has coffee and cakes, sandwiches and desserts in a refined-yet-casual setting.

THE GREAT EAST JAPAN EARTHQUAKE

At 2.46pm (JST) on 11 March 2011, a magnitude 9.0 earthquake struck off the eastern coast of Tōhoku.

During the Great East Japan Earthquake (東日本大震災; Higashi-nihon Dai-shinsai), the most powerful to hit Japan since record-keeping began in the early 20th century, and among the five strongest recorded worldwide, the ground shook for a mind-boggling six minutes. It is a testament to Japan's earthquake preparedness that many people received a warning on their mobile phones one minute prior to the event, the same warning stopping high-speed train services automatically: both measures saved countless lives. Due to stringent building codes, few structures collapsed from the shaking.

It was, however, the series of tsunami that followed just 15 minutes later, with wave heights of a staggering 38m in some areas, that caused the devastation. Coastal communities along a continuous 500km stretch of the Sanriku Kaigan (p549) were levelled completely and over 15,000 lives were lost.

Travelling in the Region

Tōhoku is getting back to business. Sendai, the capital of Miyagi Prefecture, whose coastal suburbs suffered greatly, has become a key player in co-ordinating reconstruction efforts. Despite some ongoing repair works to buildings, the vibrant downtown appears undeterred. Matsushima, one of Japan's most beautiful bays, sustained some damage but remains unspoilt. A little further around the coast, Ishinomaki suffered heavy damage, but is once more open for business and tourism. Oku-Matsushima remains in ruins.

In general, the task of 'cleaning-up' the apocalyptic mess that tsunamis make is complete and the long and arduous task of rebuilding and relocation has begun. With it comes a new form of tourism, one which many residents of many towns hope foreign visitors will be a part of. Now that wounds are ever so slowly starting to heal, residents are eager to preserve their history and share the memories of all they have lost, as they work to rebuild new communities and brighter futures for the children of the 'tsunami generation'. It's quite the life-changing experience to rent a car and drive along the coast, visiting the towns that were most affected by the disaster; though keep in mind that sadness still lingers in the hearts of the residents here.

Rail travel remains suspended along sections of six JR lines with buses serving affected destinations: see www.jreast.co.jp/e/eastpass for details. Full restoration of service along the private Sanriku Tetsudō line, serving the coast of Iwate Prefecture, was completed in April 2014.

Aka-chōchin RAMEN ¥
(赤ちょうちん; ☎0259-52-2220; 208-82 Kawarahada-suwa; ramen from ¥500; ⏲11am-1.30pm & 5-11pm) Across the road from the Sawata swimming beach, this family-friendly diner does a mean bowl of *yasai-miso rāmen* (noodles in miso stock with vegetables; ¥850) and the *gyōza* (¥350) are crunchy-licious too! There's a limited picture menu.

ℹ Information

Tourist Information Center (真野観光案内所; ☎0259-55-3589; 488 Mano Shin-machi; ⏲9am-5pm, closed irregularly) Information about hikes and temples in the vicinity and rental cycles is available here, in front of the Mano Shin-machi bus stop.

Ogi & Shukunegi 小木・宿根木

Over Earth Celebration, Ogi heaves with excitement: most performances and workshops are based here. For the rest of the year it's a delightfully sleepy port town – one that celebrated its 400th birthday in 2014! Sleepier still, the must-visit hamlet of Shukunegi, about 3km west of Ogi, is a rare jewel – a tiny, gated, traditional fishing village that feels like a museum, with its weathered wooden merchant houses, narrow alleyways and stone staircases snaking up the hillside.

Sights & Activities

Ogi is famous for its *taraibune,* round boats made from huge barrels designed for collecting shellfish in the many coastal inlets. Today, they're mainly used by women

DON'T MISS

EARTH CELEBRATION

A highlight of any trip to Japan (that coincides with the third week in August), **Earth Celebration** (www.kodo.or.jp/ec/en; mid-Aug) is a one-of-a-kind, three-day, music, arts and environmental love-in, celebrating the diversity of Japanese traditions, the importance of community and the magical power of music. Since 1988, dedicated followers have been returning to Sado to take part in the many activities designed to inform, entertain and bring people together.

The event features a smorgasbord of performances and hands-on workshops, but the main draw are the nightly outdoor performances by the world-renowned Kodō Drummers, based on the island. If you've never experienced *taiko* drumming, you're in for a real treat. Considered one of the most elite drumming groups on the planet, Kodō members are required to adhere to strict physical, mental and spiritual training regimens and spend much of the year on tour.

Rain, hail or shine, themed evening performances proceed to the sheer thrill of adoring fans: it's a pleasure to watch the excitement build up with the heat of the day as crowds gather patiently in groups at **Kisaki Shrine** for the best viewing spots, before ascending the steep path to the beautiful amphitheatre in **Shiroyama Park**. By the time the frenetic drumming commences as the sun starts to set and the temperature cools, the atmosphere is electric. Earth Celebration remains one of those rare and unique opportunities to witness and be part of a historical and cultural lineage, on its home soil.

Earth Celebration's main concerts and workshops take place in and around the village of Ogi, but optional activities and tours are scheduled all over the island. The festival is already well-known worldwide, so accommodation is limited and books up well in advance. Commit to the journey and you will be rewarded.

in traditional fisher-folk costumes to give **rides** (¥500, 10 minutes) to tourists. Tickets are available at the marine terminal, to the west of the ferry pier.

For travellers with their own wheels (two or four will do), the coast west of Ogi is riddled with caves and coves ripe for exploring: follow the road. Further around the point, the rocky coast gives way to sandy beaches, like **So-bama** (素浜), along Mano-wan.

Ogi Folk Museum MUSEUM
(小木民俗博物館; Ogi Minzoku Hakubutsukan; 0259-86-2604; 270-2 Shukunegi; adult/child ¥500/200; 9am-5pm) Come to this former 1920s schoolhouse, saved from demolition to take up a new life as a folk museum, to gawk at all manner of Sado's cultural artefacts (over 30,000 items) and a life-size replica of a 19th-century *sengokubune* freight ship.

Sado Island Taiko Centre DRUMMING
(佐渡太鼓体験交流館, Sado Taiko Taiken Tatakō-kan; 0259-86-2320; www.sadotaiken.jp; 150-3 Ogi-kanetashinden; 9am-5pm Tue-Sun) Come here to have a drumming lesson with members from the elite Kodō drumming group in this beautiful hall perched on a hill overlooking the ocean. Pop in to have a look any time, but lessons must be booked in advance – generally ¥2100 per person, minimum five people.

Sleeping & Eating

So-bama Campground CAMPGROUND ¥
(素浜キャンプ場; 0259-86-3200; sites per person from ¥300, tent rental from ¥1700; May-Oct; P) Right across the road from a tempting stretch of sand and only 6km from Ogi, this attractive campground reaches peak popularity during Earth Celebration, when shuttle buses between it and the festival run several times a day.

★ **Hana-no-ki** RYOKAN ¥¥
(花の木; 0259-86-2331; www.sado-hananoki.com; 78-1 Shukunegi; r per person from ¥6000, with 2 meals from ¥9000; P) To create this enchanting ryokan, the owners painstakingly took apart and reassembled a 150-year-old farmhouse, setting it down among rice paddies along the road to Shukunegi. Accommodation is in Japanese-stye rooms in the main building or detached cottages in the garden. Call ahead for pickup from Ogi.

Shichiemon SOBA ¥
(七右衛門; 0259-86-2046; 643-1 Ogi-machi; noodles from ¥700; 11am-2pm) This long-

established eatery serves slightly flatter-than-usual *teuchi* (handmade) *soba* in all your favourite ways.

Takobōshi SEAFOOD ¥

(たこぼうし; ☎080-1083-4591; Shukunegi; dishes from ¥600; ⊙from 6pm) In little Shukunegi you'll find this spotless, cosy kitchen serving delicious meals made from octopus *(tako)* and sea snails *(sazae)*. The creamy, *yaki sazae karē* (fried sea-snail curry; ¥900) and *tako kara-age* (fried octopus; ¥600), are both something different and delicious.

Uohara SEAFOOD ¥¥

(魚晴; ☎0259-86-2085; 415-1 Ogi-machi; meals from ¥1100; ⊙11am-5pm, closed irregularly) The speciality here is *awabi* (abalone), grilled as a steak (at market rate) or, more affordably, barbecued with a sweet soy-sauce marinade and served over rice. Follow the shop-lined road snaking up the hill behind the tourist information centre for about 250m until you see a white building with red-and-blue writing on the side. There's a picture menu.

Information

Tourist Information Center (小木観光案内所; ☎0259-86-3200; 1935-26 Ogi-machi; ⊙8.30am-5.30pm) English maps and bicycle rentals, a few minutes' walk west of the bus and ferry terminals.

Aikawa 相川

From a tiny hamlet, Aikawa grew into a 50,000-person boom town when gold was discovered nearby in 1601. The conditions for miners were harsh by any standards throughout the Edo period until technological advancements in the Meiji period enabled marginal improvements. Mining operations ceased in 1989. Today, the town is dwindling with each passing generation, but the scars of its mining past remain in the hills, along with the remnants of Kamidera-machi, an area above town once home to scores of temples. Not quite a ghost town yet, Aikawa is a tremendously fascinating place for real history buffs with some Japanese ability. You'll need to dig a little – pun intended.

Sights

★Sado Kinzan HISTORIC SITE

(佐渡金山; ☎0259-74-2389; www.sado-kinzan.com/en; 1305 Shimo-Aikawa; 1/2 courses ¥900/1400; ⊙9am-4:30pm) You'll have to venture up a steep mountain to access this gold mine, which produced large quantities of gold and silver until its demise in 1989. Descend into the chilly depths, where you'll encounter robots that dramatise the tough existence of former miners. A further 300m up the mountain is Dōyū-no-Wareto, the original opencast mine where you can still see the remains of the workings. Public transport is scarce.

Ask for directions to the Kami-AIkawa walk, starting from car park 3: it's a fascinating downhill ramble past hidden temples along a historic street with wonderful vistas.

Sado Hanga-mura Museum MUSEUM

(佐渡版画村美術館; ☎0259-74-3931; 38-2 Aikawa Komeyamachi; adult/child ¥400/200; ⊙9am-5pm Mar-Nov) Lovers of Japanese art will appreciate this rambling gallery where local artists display *hanga* woodblock prints depicting country life in Sado. Workshops (in Japanese) are available.

Sado Former Magistrate's Office MUSEUM

(佐渡奉行所, Sado Bugyō-sho; ☎0259-74-2201; 1-1 Aikawahiroma-machi; admission ¥500; ⊙9am-5pm) Formerly the centre of island government under the Tokugawa shogunate (in the Edo period), these beautifully reconstructed buildings and grounds look the part.

Sleeping

Hotel Oosado HOTEL ¥¥

(ホテル大佐渡; ☎0259-74-3300; www.oosado.com; 288-2 Aikawa-kabuse; r per person with 2 meals from ¥14,000; P ⊖ ᯤ) The best thing about this once-fancy hotel is its clifftop position and *rotemburo,* from where you can watch spectacular sunsets over the Sea of Japan. Accommodation is in either Western-(looking a little grubby) or Japanese-style rooms. All face the ocean. Day bathing (¥700; before 3pm) is a good option.

Eating & Drinking

Isonoya SOBA ¥

(磯の家; ☎0259-74-2213; 16 Aizawa Edozawa-machi; noodles from ¥600; ⊙11am-8pm) This little *soba* shop, a few minutes' walk up the coast from the bus stop, is popular for its *isonoya teishoku* (a crisp assortment of tempura with a side of noodles). Turn right in front of the police station and look for the indigo *noren* curtain where the road bends.

DON'T MISS

TŌHOKU'S FAMOUS FESTIVALS

Tōhoku is known throughout Japan for its traditional festivals, which number among the most elaborate – and raucous – in the country. While every town has its own signature celebration (or two or three), these are the 'big three' not to miss. You'll need to plan ahead though: huge crowds mean the accommodation is booked solidly months in advance.

Sendai Tanabata Matsuri (p553) Thousands of coloured streamers around the downtown area honour a tale of star-crossed lovers.

Aomori Nebuta Matsuri (p531) Local artists outdo themselves in creating elaborate floats, and merrymakers take to the streets in throngs.

Akita Kantō Matsuri (p523) Stunning acrobatics are performed with towering bamboo poles hung with lanterns.

Kyōmachi Chaya CAFE
(京町茶屋; ☎080-1093-6341; 5 Aikawa Yaoya-machi; refreshments from ¥300; ⏲9am-5pm Wed-Mon) Stop in at this wonderfully restored merchant's house for an ice coffee or tea as you walk back down into town. The views and sea breezes from inside, or the small plaza outside, are magnificent.

Information

Tourist Information Center (相川観光案内所; ☎0259-74-2220; 15 Aikawa Haneda-machi; ⏲9am-5pm Apr-Oct) A five-minute walk from the bus stop, behind the police station.

Sotokaifu 外海府

Sado's rugged northern coast is a dramatic landscape of sheer sea cliffs dropping off into deep blue waters. Roads are narrow, windy and subject to frequent roadworks: think harrowing yet exhilarating coastal drives. Buses come here, but you'll really want your own wheels.

Activities

Senkaku Bay Ageshima Park BOAT TOURS
(尖閣湾揚島遊園; ☎0259-75-2311; www.ageshima.eek.jp; 1561 Kitaebisu; boat rides incl park admission ¥1100; ⏲9am-5pm Apr-Nov) Glass-bottomed boat tours of pretty Ageshima Bay depart from this small aquatic-themed amusement park.

Sleeping

Sado Belle Mer Youth Hostel HOSTEL ¥
(佐渡ベルメールユースホステル; ☎0259-75-2011; http://sado.bellemer.jp; 369-4 Himezu; dm with breakfast ¥4320; P⊗) Scenically perched near the shore, about five minutes on foot from the Minami-Himezu bus stop, this longstanding hostel is run by a knowledgable Japanese family, who can give you some good outdoor tips for exploring Sado's wildest stretch of coastline. Rooms are basic dorms, almost all of which have sea views. Meals are available.

Sotokaifu Youth Hostel HOSTEL ¥
(外海府ユースホステル; ☎0259-78-2911; www.sotokaifu.jp; 131 Iwaya-guchi; dm with 2 meals ¥6000; P⊗) Tucked away in a tiny fishing hamlet, this cosy hostel may be just the ticket for solitude-seekers. It's in a traditional Sado house, complete with central hearth, refitted with shared and private rooms. Filling meals include fresh seafood. The hostel is right in front of the Iwayaguchi (岩谷口) bus stop. Think remote.

Echigo-Yuzawa Onsen 越後湯沢温泉

☎025 / POP 8330

If Kawabata Yasunari's famous novel *Yukiguni* (Snow Country), set here, is to be believed, Echigo-Yuzawa was once a hot-spring retreat where geisha competed for guests' affection. Then came skiing and the *shinkansen*. Winter visitors generally head straight to the slopes of GALA Yuzawa and then back home, but there are still plenty of great onsen here, year round.

Sights & Activities

GALA Yuzawa SNOW SPORTS
(ガーラ湯沢; www.galaresort.jp/winter/english; day lift tickets ¥4600; ⏲Dec-Apr) With its own *shinkansen* stop at the base of the mountain, it's possible to wake up in Tokyo, hit the slopes here after breakfast and be back in the big smoke for dinner: the slopes can

get predictably packed. Runs range the full gamut from beginner to intermediate and advanced, with the longest stretching 2.5km. Three quad lifts alongside six triple and double lifts help to thin the crowds. Expect queues at peak times.

English is spoken everywhere, and you'll see plenty of other foreigners. Full equipment rental is available for a somewhat pricey ¥5200 per day. Tokyo travel agents can often arrange cheap packages that include lift and train fare, especially if you're planning to head up on a weekday.

Echigo-Tsumari Art Field ARTS CENTRE
(越後妻有大地の芸術祭の里; www.echigo-tsumari.jp/eng) In 2000 this open-air gallery was conceived as a way to bring people back to this rapidly depopulating, though enchantingly beautiful rural area of green fields and historical wooden farmhouses. Spread out over 770 sq km are scores of installations by Japanese and international artists, set as naturally as possible in the surrounding landscape. Catch a train from Echigo-Yuzawa Onsen to Tōkamachi (¥610, 30 minutes) and download maps online. You'll need a car to make the most of it all.

The area really comes to life during the summer-long Echigo-Tsumari Triennale (next up in 2015).

Yuzawa Town History Museum MUSEUM
(雪国館; Yukiguni-kan; ☎025-784-3965; 354-1 Yuzawa; admission ¥500; ⌚9am-4.30pm Thu-Tue) This wonderful little museum displays memorabilia from the life of Kawabata Yasunari, the first Japanese recipient of the Nobel Prize for Literature, in addition to interesting displays about life in snow country that bring his classic book to life. From the west exit of Echigo-Yuzawa Station, turn right and walk about 500m.

Sleeping & Eating

★Hatago Isen INN ¥¥
(HATAGO井仙; ☎025-784-3361; www.hatago-isen.jp; 2455 Yuzawa; r per person with 1/2 meals from ¥8800/13,075; P) This sumptuous ryokan perfects the aesthetic of an old-time travellers' inn with dim lighting and dark wood, while maintaining modern conveniences. Rooms vary from humble singles to deluxe suites with private *rotemburo*. Meals feature local ingredients and are unusually flexible: you can choose from three different dinner courses and even elect to swap breakfast for lunch and a later checkout.

NASPA New Ōtani HOTEL ¥¥
(NASPAニューオータニ; ☎025-780-6111; www.naspanewotani.com; 2117-9 Yuzawa; r per person with 2 meals & lift pass from ¥18,500; P) This family- and foreigner-friendly resort has its own backyard ski park that is particularly suited to beginners and small children. Rooms are Western-style and reasonably spacious, and there's a whole range of resort facilities, including an onsen. Free shuttles take just five minutes to run between Echigo-Yuzawa Station and the resort.

Kikushin SOBA ¥
(菊新; ☎025-784-2881; 1-1-2 Yuzawa; bowls from ¥900; ⌚11am-2pm & 5.30-9pm Wed-Mon) Just outside the station's East Exit, on the corner, Kikushin serves delicious *soba* (hot or cold) and crunchy *tempura* (including mountain mushrooms; ¥920) – perfect on a cold day.

Getting There & Around

BUS

Echigo-Yuzawa Onsen is connected to Naeba by regular local buses (¥650, 40 minutes). A free shuttle runs between Echigo-Yuzawa Station and GALA Yuzawa.

TRAIN

There are several hourly *shinkansen* on the Jōetsu line from Tokyo to Echigo-Yuzawa (¥6150, 1¼ hours) and, in season, GALA Yuzawa (¥6570, 1½ hours). Trains continue from Echigo-Yuzawa to Niigata (¥4860, 50 minutes).

Naeba 苗場

☎025

Naeba is a little town with a lot going on. Not only does it offer some of the most challenging skiing and snowboarding in the whole of Tōhoku, it's also the setting for Fuji Rock – Japan's biggest outdoor music festival.

Activities

Naeba Ski Resort SNOW SPORTS
(苗場スキー場; ☎025-789-4117; www.princehotels.co.jp/ski/naeba; 202 Mikuni, Yuzawa; day lift ticket/combined Naeba & Kagura ¥5000/5700; ⌚Dec-Apr) The longest of Naeba's 20-plus runs (4km) winds through birch forests and mogul fields prior to dropping a full kilometre. The snow tends to be dry and light, and there are plenty of ungroomed areas where you can carve up some serious powder. English is widespread. Equipment hire starts at ¥5000 per day.

There's also a snow park for kids and freestyle snowboarding course complete with rails, half pipes and kickers. At the bottom of the hill, you'll find the N-Plateau, a massive complex with food court, onsen, convenience store and ski shop.

The awesomely named **Dragondola** (ドラゴンドラ), covering a distance of 5.5km, is reportedly the longest gondola in the world and whisks you away to neighbouring Kagura resort in just 15 minutes.

Kagura Ski Resort SNOW SPORTS
(かぐらスキー場; ☎025-788-9221; www.princehotels.co.jp/ski/kagura; 742 Mitsumata, Yuzawa; day lift ticket ¥5000, combined Naeba & Kagura ¥5700; ⊙Nov-May) Contiguous with Naeba, Kagura is an impressive mountain in its own right with an additional 20-plus runs from beginner to advanced and a lax policy on back-country skiing: experienced alpinists can really have an extreme adventure up here. For those who feel more comfortable sticking to the trails, one of the courses here reaches an impressive 6km.

With the combined pass, you can travel between Naeba and Kagura on the Dragondola at any time. Free shuttle buses depart from the bottom of the Mitsumata area.

Festivals & Events

★ **Fuji Rock Festival** LIVE MUSIC
(www.fujirockfestival.com) Japan's premier event on the world music circuit, Fuji Rock promises three days of musical mayhem in the mountains in late July. Up to a staggering 100,000 people come to see legendary cross-genre big-ticket and upcoming acts. Despite the crowds, the Japanese sense of respect and order prevails and the festival keeps a refreshing emphasis on the music (as it should be) and community.

Sleeping

Prince Hotel Naeba HOTEL ¥¥
(プリンスホテル苗場; ☎025-789-2211; www.princehotels.co.jp/naeba; 202 Mikuni, Yuzawa; r from ¥17,700; P ⊖ @ ⊜ ♿) All of the ski action in Naeba centres on this monolithic resort at the base of the mountain. On offer is a range of Western-style rooms and suites that vary considerably in size, amenities and price – check online for specials – in addition to a slew of bars, cafes, restaurants and health and fitness facilities.

Wadagoya Mountain Hut HUT ¥
(和田小屋; ☎025-789-2211; www.princehotels.com/en/ski/mtnaeba/accommodation; Mt Kagura; dm per person with 2 meals ¥7800; ⊙Dec-May) The Prince Hotel runs this mountain hut on Mt Kagura. Sleeping elbow-to-elbow on futons in a communal room, you'll make friends and cut first tracks in the morning. Arrive in Naeba by 3pm in order to catch the sequence of lifts up to the hut.

BEST SKIING

- Zaō Onsen (p515)
- Naeba (p505)
- Tazawa-ko (p527)
- Myōkō Kōgen
- GALA Yuzawa (p504)

Getting There & Away

Naeba is connected to Echigo-Yuzawa Onsen by regular local buses (¥650, 40 minutes). Free shuttle buses to the Prince Hotel run this route for registered guests.

At the height of the ski season, **Seibu Travel** (☎03-5910-2525; http://bus.seibutravel.co.jp/en) runs a shuttle bus between the Shinagawa Prince Hotel in Tokyo and Naeba (¥3500, four hours).

Myōkō Kōgen 妙高高原

☎0255

This formerly sleepy, up-and-coming snow destination is likely to steal the spotlight once the arrival of the Tōhoku *shinkansen* (scheduled for 2015) brings a surge of new interest to this sprawling collection of powder-rich winter resorts atop the Myōkō mountain range. Proximity to the Sea of Japan means Myōkō gets snow before anywhere else – upwards of 13m per season! At the time of writing, *shinkansen* specifics (short of service commencement date) were under wraps. Tune your eyes to www.myoko.tv/english. One to watch…

Activities

Akakura Onsen Ski Park SNOW SPORTS
(赤倉温泉スキー場; ☎0255-87-2169; www.akakura-ski.com; day lift ticket ¥4200; ⊙Dec-Apr) Akakura Onsen Sukī-Jō is one of the more popular resorts, especially among travellers with small children. All but two of the 20 runs were laid out with the needs of novice skiers in mind, and even the black diamonds are little more than short chutes. But the

high-quality powder and picturesque setting ensure a good time for everyone.

Family restaurants, many drawing inspiration from European chalets, are scattered around the slopes. English signage is generally available.

Dancing Snow SNOW SPORTS
(ダンシングスノー; ☎090-1433-1247; www.dancingsnow.com) For off-piste excitement, check out these local experts for guided tours through the backwoods terrain and snowshoe treks, as well as personalised one-on-one instruction – all in English. Prices depend on the length and type of tour. Check the website for details.

Sleeping

Akakura Onsen, a cosy mountain village with plenty of restaurants, is the perfect base for a long stay.

Hotel Alp INN ¥¥
(ホテルアルプ; ☎0255-87-3388; www.alp-myoko.com/english/index.html; 585-90 Akakura Onsen; r per person with 1/2 meals from ¥11,000/14,000;) The tranquil Hotel Alp lies at the base of the slopes and is extremely conducive to a ski-in, ski-out holiday. There are fewer than 20 rooms on the premises, allowing for a sense of intimacy not found at the resort hotels. Be sure to spend some quality time in the therapeutic sauna and hot-spring bath, perfect for thawing out your joints.

Information

Tourist Information Center (妙高市観光協会; ☎0255-86-3911; www.myoko.tv/english; 291-1 Taguchi; 9am-5pm) Enquire here about multiple mountain and monthly passes especially for overseas travellers, as well as info about accommodation, rentals and ski schools in English. The office is located to the right of Myōkō Kōgen Station, past the bus stop.

Getting There & Away

The Nagano *shinkansen* runs once or twice every hour between Tokyo and Nagano (¥7680, 1¾ hours). Nagano is connected to Myōkō Kōgen by the JR Shinetsu line; hourly *kaisoku* (rapid trains; ¥670, 45 minutes) ply this route. From Myōkō Kōgen Station, shuttle buses and taxis run to Akakura Onsen Sukī-Jō and other ski resorts.

The Joetsu-Myōkō station of the new Hokuriku *shinkansen* line will integrate Wakinoda Station on the Shinetsu Main Line. Services to Myōkō Kōgen (¥500, 30 minutes) are likely to increase in frequency and rapidity once the new line gets up and running. Check www.hyperdia.com for details.

FUKUSHIMA PREFECTURE

Fukushima-ken (福島県), Japan's third-largest prefecture, is Tōhoku's eastern gateway, from where the characteristic mountains of the north begin to rise. Come this far and you've left the Tokyo day trippers behind; the wilds of the beautiful Bandai Plateau attract hikers and skiers seeking deeper exploration. Development is sparse outside a few small cities in this expansive prefecture of diverse terrain. Fukushima's main attraction is the medieval capital of Aizu-Wakamatsu. Sites listed are all well outside the Fukushima Dai-ichi Exclusion Zone (p508).

Aizu-Wakamatsu 会津若松

☎0242 / POP 125,000

Sprawling Aizu-Wakamatsu, a former feudal capital, is a pilgrimage destination for Japanese history buffs. It's looking a little rough around the edges, but plays to its history well. Nanoka-machi-dōri has a number of old-fashioned shops selling local crafts. Aizu is also famous for its sake, and there are a number of breweries around town that do tours and tastings.

History

Aizu-Wakamatsu was once the capital of the Aizu clan, whose reign came to an end in the Bōshin civil war of 1868, when the clan sided with the Tokugawa shogunate against the imperial faction. The fall of Aizu is famous throughout Japan on account of the Byakkotai (White Tigers). This group of teenage samurai committed *seppuku* (ritual suicide by disembowelment) when they saw Tsuruga Castle shrouded in smoke. In reality, it was the surrounding area that was ablaze and it took weeks before defeat was final, but the White Tigers emerged as a powerful symbol of loyalty and fraternity.

Sights

The main sights in Aizu are arrayed around the fringes of downtown. English signage makes it easy to get around on foot: expect a decent amount of walking. Be sure to visit the area around Iimori-yama.

FIGHTING THE FALLOUT: FUKUSHIMA

Like Chernobyl, Fukushima (in English) has become a dirty word, far removed from its ancient origin. The characters *Fuku* (福) and *-shima* (島) mean 'luck, good fortune' and 'island'. It's a cruel irony for the disenfranchised people of this large region, that their name has become synonymous with one of the great man-made misfortunes of our time.

Following the Great East Japan earthquake and tsunami, Fukushima Dai-ichi, a General Electric–designed nuclear power plant, experienced a meltdown in three of its reactors and an explosion in its fourth, severely damaging that building in which highly radioactive spent nuclear fuel is stored. The manual removal and disposal of this precariously located fuel is highly dangerous and will take years to complete. It's an unprecedented and ongoing nuclear disaster (p853).

A 20km exclusion zone remains around the plant, which is on the coast 58km from the capital city of Fukushima and 80km from Sendai. Over 55,000 people were permanently evacuated from their homes. Many still live in crowded, temporary housing. Radioactive contamination exists outside the exclusion zone, but at levels reported to pose no threat to human health. For many travellers to Japan, Fukushima raises the biggest question mark. Risks faced by long-term residents far outweigh those encountered by short-term travellers.

You're well advised to check out **SafeCast** (www.safecast.org) for live radiation maps with data collected by an ever-growing movement of volunteers around Japan. Read up on the event, the nuclear industry and how radiation effects humans, animals and plants: there's a bunch of excellent free content on the website of **Fairewinds Energy Education** (www.fairewinds.org).

Once you've determined your stance, consider a visit to the uncontaminated parts of this ancient prefecture to show the locals they've not been forgotten and that Fukushima is not a dirty word.

Aizu Bukeyashiki HISTORIC BUILDING
(会津武家屋敷; Map p511; ☎0242-28-2525; Innai Higashiyama-machi; adult/child ¥850/450; ⏰9am-4.30pm) This is a superb reconstruction of the *yashiki* (villa) of Saigō Tanomo, the Aizu clan's chief retainer. Wander through the 38 rooms, which include a guest room for the Aizu lord, a tea-ceremony house, quarters for the clan's judge and a rice-cleaning mill, presented here in full, noisy working order.

Tsuruga-jō CASTLE
(鶴ヶ城; Map p511; ☎0242-27-4005; www.tsurugajo.com; 1-1 Ōte-machi; adult/child ¥410/150; ⏰8.30am-4.30pm) The towering 1965 reconstruction of Tsuruga-jō sits in sprawling grounds framed by the original moat and some ruins of the old castle walls. Inside is a museum with historical artefacts from battles and daily life, but the real drawcard is the view from the 5th-floor lookout. Experience a tea ceremony (¥1000) in **Oyakuen**, the 400-year-old teahouse (rescued by a local family when the original castle was destroyed), returned here in 1990.

Iimori-yama HISTORIC SITE
(飯盛山) On the eastern edge of Aizu is Iimori-yama, the mountain where the White Tiger samurai killed themselves. You can take an escalator (¥250) or walk to the top to visit their graves. There are also some creepy old monuments here, gifted by the former fascist regimes of Germany and Italy, in honour of the samurai's loyalty and bravery.

Sazae-dō HISTORIC BUILDING
(さざえ堂; Map p511; ☎0242-22-3163; 1404 Bentenshita; admission ¥400; ⏰9am-5pm) Halfway up Iimori-yama, Sazae-dō is a weird and wonderful hidden gem in a Buddhist temple complex. Built in 1796, the 16.5m high hexagonal wooden structure houses 33 statues of Kannon, the Buddhist goddess of mercy. Once inside you follow a fabulous spiral staircase that, Escher-esque, allows you to journey up and back down again without retracing your steps.

White Tigers Memorial Hall MUSEUM
(白虎隊記念館, Byakkotai Kinenkan; Map p511; ☎0242-24-9170; 33 Bentenshita; adult/child ¥410/200; ⏰8am-5pm Apr-Nov, 9am-4pm Dec-Mar) At the foot of Iimori-yama, the White Tigers Memorial Hall tells the story of the

dramatic suicides and houses the departed samurai's personal possessions.

Festivals & Events

Aizu Aki Matsuri PARADE
(会津秋祭り) This three-day 'Autumn Festival' culminates on 23 September with extravagant processions through the city and an evening lantern parade.

Sleeping

Aizuno Youth Hostel HOSTEL ¥
(会津野ユースホステル; Map p511; ☎0242-55-1020; www.aizuno.com; 88 Kaki-yashiki, Terasaki, Aizu-Takada-chō; dm/s ¥3600/4600; P⊖@) This spick-and-span hostel with Western-style rooms is in a pleasant rural setting outside town, about 20 minutes by foot from Aizu-Takada station along the Tadami line from Aizu-Wakamatsu (¥240, 20 minutes). Pick-up from the station is possible if you call ahead.

Minshuku Takaku MINSHUKU ¥
(民宿多賀来; Map p511; ☎0242-26-6299; www.naf.co.jp/takaku; 104 Innai Higashiyama-machi; r per person ¥4200, with 2 meals ¥6300; P⊖@) This Japanese-style inn offers modest tatami rooms, a pleasant *o-furo* (bath) and an attractive dining area framed by hardwood furnishings. It's located just east of the Aizu Bukeyashiki bus stop; from there, continue along the road, turn left at the post office and it's just behind, on the left.

Aizu Wakamatsu Washington Hotel BUSINESS HOTEL ¥¥
(会津若松ワシントンホテル; Map p511; ☎0242-22-6111; www.aizu-wh.com; 201 Byakko-dōri; s/d from ¥5600/8100; P⊖@) The refurbished rooms in Aizu's fanciest hotel are well priced and the location, three minutes' walk from the station's east exit along Byakkotai-dōri, is just right.

Toyoko Inn Aizu Wakamatsu Ekimae HOTEL ¥¥
(東横イン会津若松駅前; Map p511; ☎0242-32-1045; www.toyoko-inn.com/hotel/00177; 222-1 Byakkomachi; s/d from ¥5300/7300) This generic tourist hotel near the station is meticulously maintained. Rooms on high floors have excellent views and all are compact but comfortable. A light breakfast is included in the rate.

Eating

Aizu is famous for *wappa-meshi,* steamed fish or vegetables over rice, prepared in a round container made from tree bark, which adds a woody fragrance. Alternatively, head over to neighbouring Kitakata for some serious *rāmen* (egg noodles).

Mitsutaya JAPANESE ¥
(満田屋; Map p511; ☎0242-27-1345, 0242-27-1345; 1-1-25 Ōmachi; skewers from ¥120; ⊙10am-5pm Thu-Tue;) A former bean-paste mill dating from 1834, this is an Aizu landmark. The speciality here is *dengaku,* bamboo skewers of tofu, *mochi* (pounded rice cake) or vegetables basted in sweet miso paste and baked over charcoal. Just point at what you want, or go for the *dengaku cōsu* (tasting course; ¥1150 for seven skewers).

★Takino JAPANESE ¥¥
(田季野; Map p511; ☎0242-25-0808; www.takino.jp; 5-31 Sakae-machi; wappa meshi from ¥1480; ⊙11am-9pm;) One of the most famous places to try the sublime *wappa meshi,*

WORTH A TRIP

ŌUCHI-JUKU

A pleasant 45-minute drive from Aizu-Wakamatsu through valleys, farmland and onsen villages, **Ōuchi-juku** (大内宿) is a pretty, photogenic former post town from the Edo period. Most of the buildings lining the compact main street are of the *gasshō zukkuri* style, with steep thatched roofs. Almost all have been converted into restaurants (the local speciality is *takato soba* – noodles eaten using a leek as a spoon!) and tourist shops, selling everything from generic kitsch to local arts and handicrafts. There's also a post office and a worthy museum. A popular sightseeing spot, Ōuchi-juku attracts artists and photographers: for the money shot, climb the stairs leading to the temple at the top end of the street, from where you have a birds-eye view of the pretty village below. If you don't have a rental car, take the private Aizu line train (from Minami Wakamatsu) to Yunokami Onsen (¥730, 30 minutes), from where it's a 15-minute (approximately ¥2000) taxi ride, each way.

Takino offers several versions, including salmon, crab and wild mushroom. There's a picture menu and dining is on tatami mats under polished wooden beams.

Information

Aizu Wakamatsu Post Office (会津若松郵便局; Map p511; ☎0242-22-0840; 1-2-17 Chūō; ⊙9am-7pm) Located on the main street, with an international ATM.

Tourist Information Center (会津若松観光案内所; Map p511; ☎0242-33-0688; www.e.samurai-city.jp; ⊙9am-5.30pm) Inside JR station, staff speak limited English, but have plenty of literature to dispense.

Getting There & Away

BUS

Highway buses connect Aizu-Wakamatsu and Tokyo (¥4800, 4½ hours).

CAR & MOTORCYCLE

The Tōhoku Expressway (東北自動車道) runs between Tokyo and Kōriyama, while the Ban-etsu Expressway (磐越自動車道) connects Kōriyama and Aizu-Wakamatsu.

TRAIN

The JR Tōhoku *shinkansen* runs hourly between Tokyo and Kōriyama (¥7680, 1¼ hours). Kōriyama is connected to Aizu-Wakamatsu by the JR Ban-etsu-saisen line; hourly *kaisoku* (rapid) trains (¥1140, 1¼ hours) ply this scenic route.

There are a couple of daily *kaisoku* on the JR Ban-etsu West line between Aizu-Wakamatsu and Niigata (¥2270, 2¾ hours).

Getting Around

The retro **Classic Town Bus** (まちなか周遊バス; Map p511; single/day pass ¥210/500) departs from outside the train station and does a slow loop of the main sights. Bicycle rental is available at several points around town for ¥500 per day; enquire at the tourist information centre.

Bandai Plateau 磐梯高原

☎0241 / POP 4000

The Bandai Plateau is part of the **Bandai-Asahi National Park** (磐梯朝日国立公園) and its spectacular scenery and vast potential for independent exploration attract hikers, climbers, fishing enthusiasts, skiers and snowboarders. In the centre is **Bandai-san** (磐梯山; 1819m), a once-dormant volcano that erupted suddenly in 1888, spewing forth a tremendous amount of debris that's said to have lowered the mountain's height by 600m. The eruption destroyed dozens of villages and completely rearranged the landscape, resulting in the vast, lake-dotted plateau now known as Bandai-kōgen.

Activities

Goshiki-numa HIKING

(五色沼; Map p511) This popular 3.7km nature trail weaves around a dozen or so pools known as the Five Colours Lakes. Mineral deposits from the 1888 eruption imparted various hues to the waters – cobalt-blue, emerald-green, reddish-brown – which change with the weather. Trailheads begin at Goshiki-numa Iriguchi and Bandai-kōgen bus stops, the main transport hubs beside Hibara-ko, the largest of the Ura-Bandai lakes.

Buses depart from the town of Inawashiro. In April, the Goshiki-numa trail may still be covered in packed snow, and November marks the start of the long Tōhoku winter.

Bandai-san HIKING

(磐梯山; Map p511; ⊙summit accessible May-Oct) Six trails lead to Bandai-san summit and its panorama of mountain ranges and Inawashiro Lake. From Inawashiro Station, catch the bus to Bandai-kōgen to reach the **Ura-Bandai Tozan-guchi** (裏磐梯登山口) trail: it's the easiest to reach by public transport and the most challenging, at seven hours return. After climbing through ski grounds, the path meets the **Happō-dai** (八方台) trail, the shortest, most popular route.

Snow Paradise Inawashiro SNOW SPORTS

(猪苗代スキー場; Map p511; ☎0242-62-5100; 7105 Hayama, Inawashiro-machi; 1-day lift ticket adult/child ¥4600/3800, equipment rental per day ¥4000; ⊙Dec-Mar) Bandai-san's original ski area, Inawashiro has 16 runs – most are beginner and intermediate, which, in conjuction with scant weekday crowds, makes this resort a great choice for novices and families. Veterans may grow bored with the limited options. The slopes are located in the hills above Inawashiro town. Frequent shuttles run between Inawashiro Station and the resort, in season.

Sleeping

Urabandai Youth Hostel HOSTEL ¥

(裏磐梯ユースホステル; Map p511; ☎0241-32-2811; http://homepage3.nifty.com/urabandai/indexe.html; 1093 Kengamine, Hibara, Kita-Shiobara; camping per person ¥1080, dm from ¥3600, dm with 2 meals from ¥5100, cabin from ¥5400;

Bandai Plateau & Around

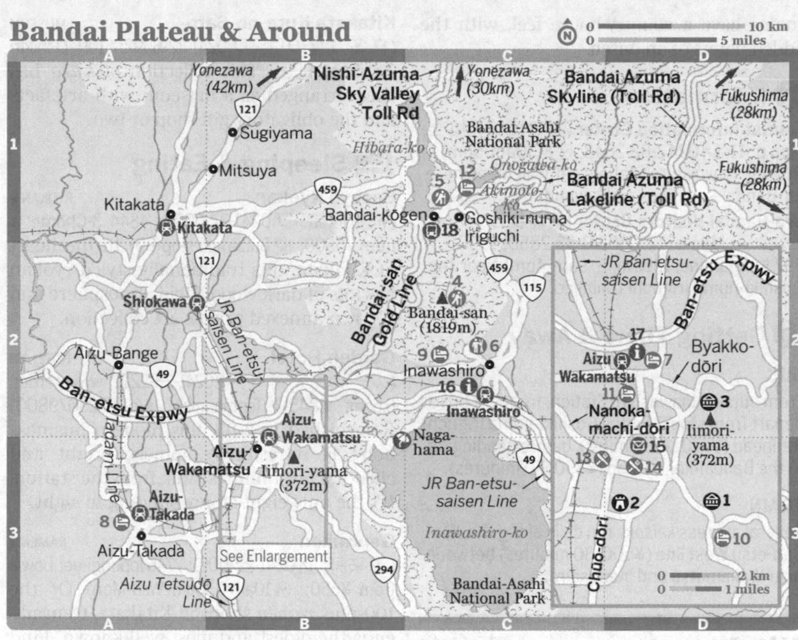

Bandai Plateau & Around

Sights
1 Aizu Bukeyashiki D3
Sazae-dō .... (see 3)
2 Tsuruga-jō D3
3 White Tigers Memorial Hall D2

Activities, Courses & Tours
4 Bandai-san C2
5 Goshiki-numa C1
6 Snow Paradise Inawashiro C2

Sleeping
7 Aizu Wakamatsu Washington Hotel D2
8 Aizuno Youth Hostel A3
9 An English Inn C2
10 Minshuku Takaku D3
11 Toyoko Inn Aizu Wakamatsu Ekimae D2
12 Urabandai Youth Hostel C1

Eating
13 Mitsutaya C3
14 Takino D3

Information
15 Aizu Wakamatsu Post Office D3
16 Tourist Information Center C2
17 Tourist Information Center D2
Ura-Bandai Visitors Center .... (see 5)

Transport
18 Bandai-kōgen Bus Stop C1
Classic Town Bus .... (see 17)
Goshiki-numa Iriguchi Bus Stop .... (see 5)

May-Oct; P @) One of the region's classic mountaineering institutions, this hostel is supremely located by the Goshiki-numa trailhead, a seven-minute walk from the Goshiki-numa Iriguchi bus stop (there are signs). Choose a dorm room for a social atmosphere, camp at the annexed Goshiki Paradise Campground if you want to rough it, or share a romantic cabin in the woods with your better half.

An English Inn PENSION ¥¥
(アン・イングリッシュ・イン; Map p511; 0242-63-0101; http://aei.inawasiro.com; 3449-84 Higashi-Nakamaru, Osada; r per person with 1/2 meals from ¥6500/8900; P) A helpful English-Japanese couple run this pension in Inawashiro, convenient to the slopes. With flowered wallpaper and sloping ceilings reminiscent of attic bedrooms, the Western-style

rooms have a country-house feel, with the added bonus of an onsen.

Information

Tourist Information Center (裏磐梯観光協会; Map p511; ☎0242-62-2048; ⊙8.30am-5pm) Outside Inawashiro Station; get trail maps here for Bandai-san hikes and beyond.

Ura-Bandai Visitors Center (裏磐梯ビジターセンター; Map p511; ☎0241-32-2850; 1093-697 Kengamine, Hibara; ⊙9am-4pm) Near the Goshiki-numa Iriguchi trailhead.

Getting There & Away

BUS

From outside Inawashiro Station, frequent buses depart from stop 3 for the Goshiki-numa Iriguchi trailhead (¥770, 25 minutes), before heading on to the Bandai-kōgen stop (¥890, 30 minutes).

TRAIN

Several express *kaisoku* run daily along the JR Ban-etsu West line (¥500, 30 minutes) between Aizu-Wakamatsu and Inawashiro.

Kitakata 喜多方

☎0241 / POP 49,800

An old Kitakata saying goes: 'A man is not a man unless he has built at least one *kura* (mud-walled storehouse)'. Scattered around this area near Aizu-Wakamatsu, thousands of unique *kura*, constructed between the late 18th and early 20th centuries remain. Kitakata, however, is likely more famous for *rāmen* than its *kura* obsession. Of 120-plus *rāmen* joints in town, the common element is wavy, wide noodles in a hearty pork-and-fish broth made with local spring water, soy sauce and sake. There's no 'best' in town: take your pick based on your preference of hundreds of variations around the typical soy and miso themes.

Sights

Yamatogawa Sake Brewing Museum MUSEUM
(大和川酒蔵北方風土館; ☎0241-22-2233; 4716 Teramachi; ⊙9am-4.30pm) FREE Step inside the Yamatogawa Sake Brewing Museum to peek inside a *kura* that dates from 1790 and, until 20 years ago, functioned as a sake brewery. It's a 15-minute walk north of Kitakata station. East of the museum and across the river, Otazukikura-dōri has a cluster of pretty *kura* that are a drawcard for photographers.

Kitakata Kura-no-Sato MUSEUM
(喜多方倉の里; ☎0241-22-6592; 109 Oshikiri 2-chōme) FREE This collection of *kura* has been arranged as a museum with artefacts and the obligatory gift shop or two.

Sleeping & Eating

Sasaya Ryokan RYOKAN ¥
(笹屋旅館; ☎0241-22-0008; 4844 3-Chōme; r from ¥5500; Burain-go stop B9) In the heart of Kitakata, this traditionally styled ryokan has lots of dark wood, Meiji atmosphere and it's own annexed private art collection.

Garden Hotel HOTEL ¥¥
(ガーデンホテル; ☎0241-23-2221; www.garden6.com; 8845-3 Tenmanmae; s/d ¥5250/9800) Refurbished in 2013, this modern business hotel is refreshingly homely, bright and cheery, a few minutes' walk from the station. It's the only eight-storey building in sight.

Genraiken RAMEN ¥
(源来軒; ☎0241-22-0091; 7745 Ippongi-ue; bowls from ¥650; ⊙10am-7.30pm Wed-Mon) Of the 100-plus *rāmen* shops in Kitakata, Genraiken is the oldest and most well-known. Find it one block north and one block east of the station, with a red facade.

Kōhei RAMEN ¥
(こうへい; ☎0241-22-4328; 6981 Numata; bowls from ¥600; ⊙11am-8pm Thu-Tue) This pure and simple, super-friendly noodle joint has been in the family for decades. Their secret soy-based *shikkoku* (jet black) *rāmen*, for which they're famed, is rich and soupy. The giant handmade *gyōza* alone will fill you up. Look for the red awning: it's on a side street near the NTT tower.

Information

Tourist Information Center (喜多方観光案内所; ☎0241-24-5200; ⊙8.30am-5pm) Inside the station, there are excellent English maps, but no English-speaking staff.

Getting There & Around

Kitakata can be reached from Aizu-Wakamatsu by frequent trains along the JR Ban-etsu West line (¥320, 25 minutes). For drivers, Rte 121 runs between Aizu and Kitakata. Bicycle rentals are available across the street from the station for ¥500 per day.

The town is a little spread out but easily navigable with the English walking map from the tourist information centre. From April to November, catch the hop-on/off *burain-go* tourist bus that loops around the city's sights (and restaurants), also for ¥500 per day.

YAMAGATA PREFECTURE

Visitors to Yamagata-ken (山形県), best known for the three sacred peaks of Dewa Sanzan, revered by *yamabushi* (mountain ascetics) and hikers alike, will be rewarded by the scenic beauty of mountain ranges and coastal vistas, the likes of which once enchanted the legendary travelling poet Matsuo Bashō.

Other highlights include the high-altitude hot springs of Zaō Onsen, with its dramatic caldera lake and challenging ski slopes, and the remarkable clifftop temple, Risshaku-ji, from which the little village of Yamadera got its name. In the warmer months, renting a car is the best way to explore.

Yamagata 山形

023 / POP 254,100

Yamagata is a thriving industrial centre with a sizeable student population, making for a more youthful vibe than in comparable *inaka* (rural) cities. While it's a bit short on sights, Yamagata is an excellent base for day trips to Yamadera and Yonezawa, and also serves as a transit point for Zaō Onsen and Ginzan Onsen.

Sights & Activities

Hirashimizu Pottery District HISTORIC SITE
(平清水焼陶芸地域) In the 19th century there were dozens of fiery kilns lining the Hazukashi-gawa, turning out beautiful bluish-grey mottled pieces known as *nashi-seiji* (pear skin), but now only a few remain. Buses bound for Nishi-Zaō or Geikōdai run hourly or half-hourly from stop 5 outside Yamagata Station to the Hirashimizu stop (¥290, 15 minutes).

Shichiemon-gama POTTERY MAKING
(七右エ門窯; 023-642-7777; 153 Hirashimizu; 8.30am-5.30pm, pottery making 9am-3pm) Try your hand at making your own pottery here in this renowned studio. Lessons (in Japanese) are 90 minutes and priced according to the amount of clay you use (¥2000 per kilogram; shipping fee extra). Finished pieces ship to an address in Japan one month later.

Festivals & Events

Hanagasa Matsuri CULTURAL
(花笠まつり) Large crowds of dancers wear *hanagasa* (flower-laden straw hats) and sing folk songs. Held in early August.

Yamagata International Documentary Film Festival FILM
(www.yidff.jp) This biennial event takes place over one week in October and screens films from all over the world, along with retrospectives, symposiums and a Japanese panorama.

Sleeping & Eating

Guesthouse Mintaro Hut GUESTHOUSE ¥
(ゲストハウスミンタロハット; 090-2797-1687; www.mintarohut.com; 5-13 Ōtemachi; s/d ¥3500/6000; P @) English-speaking Sato-san turned his childhood home into this comfortable guesthouse just off the northeast corner of the central park. The common area is built around a radiant stove, which ensures a warm and familial atmosphere conducive to chatting with fellow travellers, and the kitchen is stocked with supplies for self-caterers.

Richmond Hotel Yamagata-ekimae HOTEL ¥¥
(リッチモンドホテル山形駅前; 023-647-6277; http://yamagata.richmondhotel.jp; 1-3-11 Futaba-chō; s/d from ¥6500/9500; P) A hop, skip and a jump from the station's west exit, Yamagata's new hotel is still in great condition with slightly larger rooms and more comfortable beds than most hotels in this class. Try for a corner room on a high floor for lovely mountain views.

Kitanosuisan IZAKAYA ¥¥
(北野水産; 023-624-0880; 2nd fl, 1-8-8 Kasumicho; table charge ¥500, dishes ¥300-1500; 5pm-midnight) Come here to sample local Yamagata specialities (on the wooden board, with pictures) and sake. Take the first left outside the station's east exit and look for the blue sign across the 2nd floor.

Information

Tourist Information Center (山形市観光案内センター; 023-647-2266; 9am-5.30pm) On the 2nd floor of Yamagata Station, in a small glass booth.

Getting There & Away

The Yamagata *shinkansen* (bullet train) between Tokyo and Yamagata (¥10,450, 2¾ hours) runs hourly, as do *kaisoku* (rapid trains) on the JR

Yamagata Prefecture

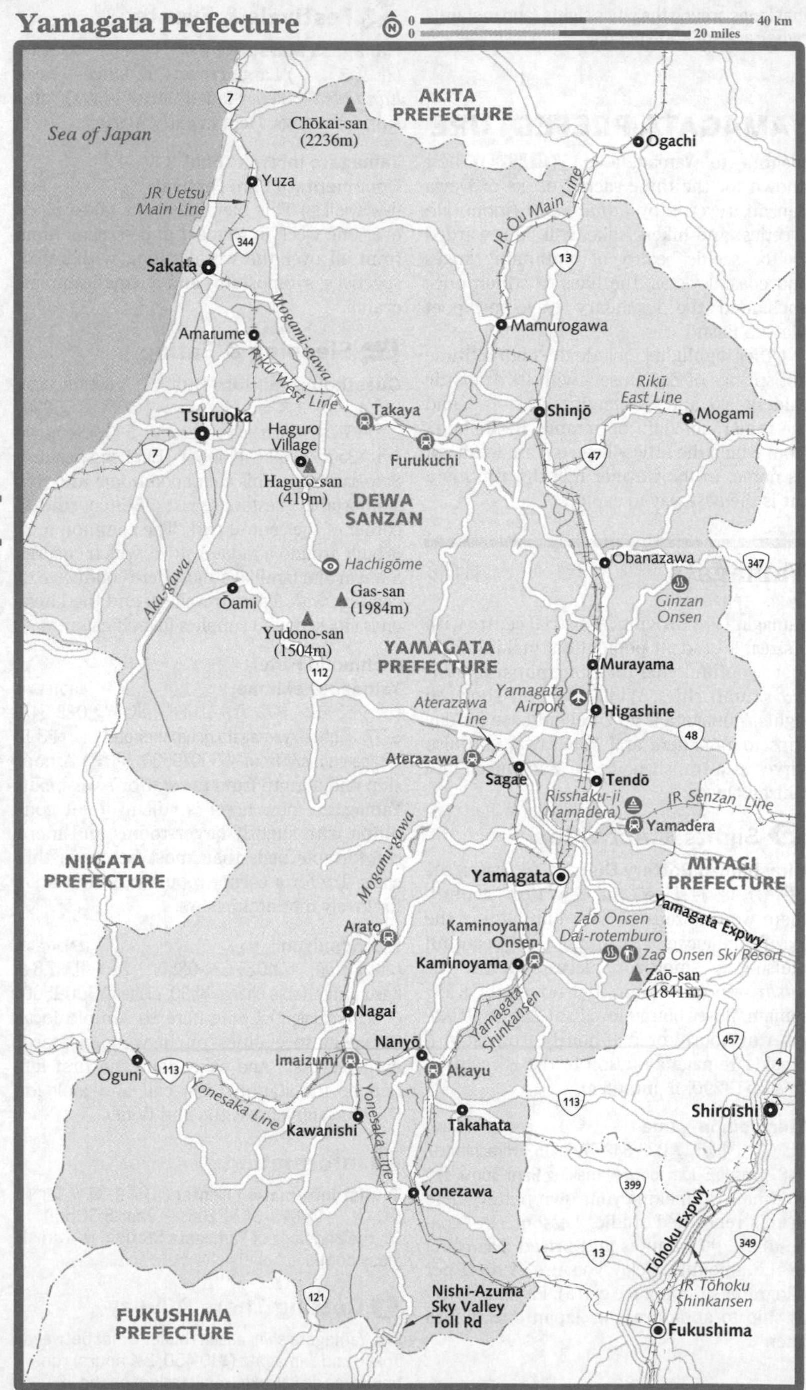

Senzan line between Yamagata and Yamadera (¥240, 15 minutes).

Alternatively, JR highway buses make an overnight trip between Yamagata and Tokyo (¥6400, 6½ hours).

Yonezawa 米沢

0238 / POP 89,390

Famed for its tenderness and flavour, Yonezawa-*gyū* (beef) is said to rival Kobe's own. There are dozens of places in town to tuck in. Of these, 100-year-old **Tokiwa** (登起波; 0238-24-5400; www.yonezawabeef.co.jp/info/eng.html; 7-2-3 Chūō; meals from ¥4200; 11am-9pm, closed Tue) is the best known. Ask the tourist information centre staff in Yonezawa Station for directions – it's a bit out of the way.

Yonezawa is also home to the ruined 17th-century castle of the Uesugi clan. The foundations of the castle now form the boundaries of **Matsugasaki-kōen** (松ヶ崎公園), an attractive park framed by a placid moat filled with lotus flowers. Inside, there's a shrine and a treasury, the **Keishō-den** (稽照殿; 0238-22-3189; 1-4-13 Marunouchi; admission ¥400; 9am-4pm Apr-Nov), which displays armour and works of art belonging to several generations of the Uesugi family.

To really see the feudal era in action, visit on 3 May, when more than a thousand participants in full samurai regalia act out the epic battle of Kawa-naka-jima during the annual **Uesugi Matsuri** (上杉祭り; http://uesugi.yonezawa.info; 3 May).

Yonezawa is a stop on the Yamagata *shinkansen* (bullet train) and regular *futsū* (local) trains plough the JR Ōu main line between Yonezawa and Yamagata (¥840, 45 minutes).

Zaō Onsen 蔵王温泉

023 / POP 14,000

At the summit of a windy mountain road, Zaō Onsen is a magical village with a great name and some big skiing. Even bigger are its *juhyō* (ice monsters); conifers that have been frozen solid by harsh Siberian winds – a phenomenon unique to the area. In warmer months, Zaō promises scenic hiking and the chance to soak in some special *rotemburo,* even if the smell of sulphur is a little on the nose. Year round, morning and evening mists can sweep in unexpectedly, leaving you with that surreal feeling of being above the clouds.

Activities

★Zaō Onsen Ski Resort SNOW SPORTS

(蔵王温泉スキー場; 023-647-2266; www.zao-spa.or.jp; 1-day lift tickets ¥3500-5000; Dec-Apr) Distinguished by its broad and winding runs (some up to 10km long!) and famous **Juhyō Kōgen** (樹氷高原; Ice Monster Plateau) which reaches peak ferocity in frigid February, Zaō has over 40 ropeways and 14 spidery courses with multiple offshoots, including a huge breadth of beginner and intermediate runs. English signage is excellent and full equipment rental is available.

Nightly 'ice-monster' illuminations (January to February) are fun for all (adult/child, ¥2600/1300). Newbies will love that it's possible to ski from the mountain's highest point to the base without accidently turning down a black diamond or getting stuck in a field of moguls, while experienced skiiers will appreciate the sheer scope and variety of terrain.

Zaō Sanroku Ropeway ROPEWAY

(蔵王山麓ロプウェー; 023-694-9518; one-way/return ¥1500/2600; 8.30am-5pm Apr-Nov) This succession of cable cars whisks you over the conifers and up **Zaō-san** (蔵王山) to within spitting distance of **Okama** (御釜), a crater lake of piercing cobalt blue. The walk to the lake passes Buddhist statues and monuments hidden among the greenery, before the terrain breaks up into a sunset-coloured crumble of volcanic rock.

You can extend the hike (and save money) by taking one of the other two shorter ropeways, the Zaō Chūō Ropeway or the Zaō Sky Cable, up or down.

Zaō Onsen Dai-rotemburo ONSEN

(蔵王温泉大露天風呂; 023-694-9417; admission ¥470, lockers ¥100; 6am-7pm May-Oct) Above the village, at the base of the mountain, you'll find this huge open-air hot-spring pool. The sulphur-stained rocks set the stage for the spectacle of dozens of complete strangers bathing naked together in joyful unison. If you arrive for first light in the warmer months, you'll have the place to yourself.

Shinzaemon-no-Yu ONSEN

(新左衛門の湯; 023-693-1212; www.zaospa.co.jp; 905 Kawa-mae; adult/child ¥700/400; 10am-6.30pm Mon-Fri, to 9.30pm Sat & Sun) An upmarket bathing option, this modern hot-spring complex has several spacious pools.

The nicest are outside, set in stone and with wooden canopies.

Sleeping

Accommodation abounds, but reservations are essential if you're visiting during the ski season or on weekends in summer.

Pension Boku-no-Uchi PENSION ¥
(ペンションぼくのうち; ☎023-694-9542; www.bokunouchi.com; 904 Zaō Onsen; r per person from ¥3500, with 2 meals from ¥7800; P 📶) This is a skiers' lodge through and through, from the posters on the wall of the sociable dining room to the prime location right in front of Family Mart and the Chūō Ropeway. Rooms are Japanese-style with communal facilities, including a 24-hour sulphur bath. Don't be put off by the weathered exterior.

Tsuruya Hotel HOTEL ¥¥
(つるやホテル; ☎023-694-9112; www.tsuruyahotel.co.jp; 710 Zaō Onsen; r per person with 2 meals from ¥10,950) Conveniently located opposite the bus terminal, the friendly staff of this small hotel will do their best to ensure you have a wonderful stay. Handsome tatami rooms have beautiful views and a variety of indoor and outdoor baths beckon you to soak your troubles away. A shuttle to the ski-lifts is available.

Zao Spa Hotel Kiraku HOTEL ¥¥
(ホテル喜らく; ☎023-694-2222; www.zao-kiraku.co.jp; 935-25 Zaō Onsen; s/d from ¥9720) Corner rooms on the top floor of this lovingly maintained '80s-style hotel, at the other end of town from the bus terminal, have stunning views of the mountain and valley below. Staff speak little English but are warm and welcoming, as are the *rotemburo*. Rates for solo travellers are a plus.

Yoshida-ya RYOKAN ¥¥
(吉田屋; 13 Zaō Onsen; r per person from ¥4650, breakfast/dinner ¥800/2000; P 📶) Yoshida-ya has a following among foreign travellers for its spacious tatami rooms (communal facilities) and helpful English-speaking staff. It's a modern building, about a 500m uphill walk from both the bus station and the Zaō Sky Cable.

Takamiya RYOKAN ¥¥¥
(高見屋; ☎023-694-9333; www.zao.co.jp/takamiya; 54 Zaō Onsen; r per person with 2 meals from ¥28,080; P 📶) Takamiya is an atmospheric, upmarket ryokan that has been in business for nearly three centuries! There are several beautiful baths here, both indoor and outdoor, made of stone or aromatic cedar. Meals are traditional *kaiseki ryōri* (formal, multiple-course banquet), with top-grade local beef as the headliner. The spacious rooms have tatami sitting areas and fluffy *wa-beddo* (thick futons on platforms).

Eating & Drinking

Matsushima-ya BARBECUE ¥
(松しまや; ☎023-694-9047; 33 Zaō Onsen; meals from ¥900; ⏲11am-8.30pm Thu-Tue; 📋) Lamb barbecued on a hotplate shaped like Ghengis Khan's headgear, *oden* (various goodies stewed in a fish-and-vegetable broth) and *soba* all feature in the varied offerings of this cheery eatery, in a great location in the middle of town.

Robata BARBECUE ¥¥
(ろばた; ☎023-694-9565; 42-7 Kawara; courses from ¥1200; ⏲11am-11pm Fri-Wed; 📋) Mongolian barbecues are popular in Zaō, where the style of cooking is known as *Jingisukan*, with the hotplate oddly resembling Genghis Khan's hat. Grill your own lamb and vegies

MATSUO BASHŌ

Born into a samurai family, Matsuo Bashō (1644–94), regarded as Japan's master of haiku, is credited with elevating this poetic form's status from comic relief to Zen-infused enlightenment. Comparisons have been made between his haiku and Zen *kōan* (short riddles), intended to bring about a sudden flash of insight in the listener. Influenced by the natural philosophy of the Chinese Taoist sage Chuangzi, his work contemplated the rhythms and laws of nature. Later he developed his own poetic principle by drawing on the concept of *wabi-sabi*, a kind of sparse, lonely beauty.

When he reached his 40s, Bashō abandoned his career in favour of travelling throughout Japan, seeking to build friendships and commune with nature as he went. He published evocative accounts of his travels, including *The Records of a Weather-Beaten Skeleton* and *The Records of a Travel-Worn Satchel*, but his collection *The Narrow Road to the Deep North*, detailing his journey throughout Tōhoku in 1689, is the most famous.

OFF THE BEATEN TRACK

GINZAN ONSEN

With its century-old inns forming mirror images on either side of the peaceful Obanazawa, **Ginzan Onsen** (銀山温泉), an out-of-the-way collection of ryokan in the classic Taisho-era style (which adds romantic Western flourishes to traditional architecture), was once the setting for *Oshin*, an enormously popular historical TV drama from the 1980s. Most romantic in the evening or when draped in snow, Ginzan is a pleasant day trip from Yamagata. Several ryokan open their baths for *hi-gaeri* (day) bathing.

Should you decide to stay the night, consider the atmospheric **Notoya Ryokan** (能登屋旅館; ☎0237-28-2327; www.notoyaryokan.com; 446 Ginzan Shin-hata, Obanazawa; r per person with 2 meals from ¥19,500; P). The three-storey structure, complete with balconies, elaborate woodwork and a curious garret tower, dates from 1922, although piecemeal renovations have been completed inside. Make sure you get a room in the main building overlooking the river.

Take the Yamagata *shinkansen* (bullet train) to its terminus in Oishida (¥1420, 30 minutes), then transfer to one of up to five daily buses leaving for Ginzan Onsen (¥710, 40 minutes) from the west exit bus pool.

on the table, but with this much sizzling meat in the room, it's not a place vegetarians will love.

Oto-chaya BAR
(音茶屋; ☎023-694-9081; http://otochaya.com; 935-24 Zaō Onsen; meals from ¥850; ⏲11am-9pm Thu-Tue; 📶) Oto-chaya is a fun and eclectic place at almost all hours: coffee, casseroles, Chinese tea sets, stews, sake and a fully stocked bar! Look for the wooden sign with the teapot, on the main road beyond the Chūō Ropeway.

Information

Tourist Information Center (蔵王温泉観光協会; ☎023-694-9328; www.zao-spa.or.jp; 708-1 Zaō Onsen; ⏲9am-6pm) Just inside the bus terminal. Lots of English-language info is available here.

Getting There & Away

Buses run hourly between the bus terminal in Zaō Onsen and JR Yamagata Station (¥1000, 40 minutes).

At the height of the ski season, private companies run overnight shuttles between Tokyo and Zaō. Prices can be as low as ¥7000 return – enquire at travel agencies in Tokyo for more information.

Dewa Sanzan 出羽三山

☎0235

Dewa Sanzan is the collective title for three sacred peaks – Haguro-san, Gas-san and Yudono-san – which are believed to represent birth, death and rebirth respectively. Together they have been worshipped for centuries by followers of Shugendō, a folk religion that draws from both Buddhism and Shintō. During the annual pilgrimage seasons, you can see white-clad pilgrims equipped with wooden staff, sandals and straw hat, and fleece-clad hikers equipped with poles, waterproof boots and bandana. Of course, it is the *yamabushi*, with their unmistakable conch shells, chequered jackets and voluminous white pantaloons, that keep the ancient traditions alive. Whether stomping along precipitous trails or sitting under icy waterfalls, these devoted mountain men undertake severe ascetic exercises to discipline both body and spirit.

Sights

Tradition dictates that you start at Haguro-san and finish at Yudono-san. You can do the pilgrimage in the opposite direction, though the ascent from Yudono-san to Gas-san is painfully steep. For many, a visit to Haguro-san is rewarding enough.

★**Haguro-san** RELIGIOUS SITE
(羽黒山) The 2446 stone steps through ancient cedars to Haguro-san's summit (419m) have been smoothed by centuries of pilgrims. The climb, taking up to two hours, passes **Gojū-no-tō** (五重塔), a beautiful wooden five-storey pagoda dating from the 14th century. Further along, **Ni-no-saka-chaya** marks the halfway resting place where you'll be greeted by marvellous views and smiling women selling refreshments. At the top, marvel at the **San-shin Gōsaiden**

(三神合祭殿), a vivid red hall that enshrines the deities of all three mountains.

If you're completing the circuit, you must catch the bus from the parking lot beyond the shrine, bound for Hachigōme (八合目; eighth station), where the trail to the top of Gas-san picks up again. The last bus leaves just after 2pm. Most of the old 20km pilgrim trail along the ridgeline to Gas-san became overgrown after a road was built in the 1960s.

Gas-san RELIGIOUS SITE
(月山) Accessible from July to September, Gas-san (1984m) is the highest of these sacred mountains. From **Hachigōme** (八合目; eighth station), the route passes through an alpine plateau to **Kyūgōme** (九合目; ninth station) in 1¾ hours, then grinds uphill for another 1¼ hours. Before entering deeply spiritual **Gassan-jinja** (月山神社; admission ¥500; ⌚5am-5pm Jul–mid-Sep) you must be 'purifed': bow to receive the priest's benediction, then brush yourself head-to-toe with the slip of paper, placing it afterwards in the fountain. Beyond the gate, photography is prohibited.

From here, the pilgrimage route presses on towards the steep descent to Yudono-san. This takes another three hours or so, and you'll have to carefully descend rusty ladders chained to the cliff sides and pick your way down through a slippery stream bed at the end of the trail.

Yudono-san SPIRITUAL
(湯殿山) Accessible from May to October, Yudono-san (1504m) is the spiritual culmination of the Dewa Sanzan trek. Coming from Gas-san, it's a short walk from the stream bed at the end of the descent to **Yudono-san-jinja** (湯殿山神社; admission ¥500; ⌚6am-5pm, closed Nov-Apr). It's forbidden to photograph, and taboo to discuss, this sacred natural shrine, so you'll just have to find out for yourself. It's quite remarkable. Strict rituals prevail: remove your shoes, bow your head before the priest for purification rites then follow the other pilgrims.

To finish the pilgrimage, it's a mere 10-minute hike down the mountain to the trailhead at **Yudono-san Sanrōsho** (湯殿山参籠所), marked by a *torii* (gate) and adjacent to the Sennin-zawa (仙人沢) bus stop.

Ideha Cultural Museum MUSEUM
(いでは文化記念館; Ideha Bunka Kinenkan; ☎0235-62-4727; 7-2 Injū-minami, Haguro-machi; admission ¥400; ⌚9am-4pm, closed Tue Sep-Jun) In Haguro village, this museum has exhibits covering the history of the mountain and *yamabushi* (mountain priest) culture. If you have strong Japanese ability, determination and an interest in *yamabushi* training, enquire here about the residential *Aki-no-mine* (Autumn Peak; men only; in August), *Miko shūgyō* (Shrine maiden; women only; in September) and *Yamabushi Study Experience* (men and women; September) training programs. Fees are upwards of ¥30,000.

Festivals & Events

The peak of Haguro-san is the site of some lively festivals.

Hassaku Matsuri CULTURAL
(八朔祭) *Yamabushi* perform ancient fire rites throughout the night to pray for a bountiful harvest. Held on 31 August.

Shōrei-sai CULTURAL
(松例祭) On New Year's Eve, *yamabushi* perform similar rituals to those of the mountain priests at the Hassaku Matsuri, competing with each other after completing 100-day-long austerities.

Sleeping & Eating

Sleeping options are listed in order from start to finish of the Haguro-san–Yudono-san pilgrimage route; reservations essential.

★ **Saikan** TEMPLE LODGE ¥¥
(斎館; ☎0235-62-2357; 7 Tōge, Haguro-machi; r per person with 2 meals ¥7560; P) Located at the top of Haguro-san, the approach to the basic yet eternally atmospheric Saikan skirts past towering trees, through an imposing gate. The grounds overlook a grand sweep of valleys, while the weathered building is imbued with an air of stoic grandeur. Meals (lunch available) are *shōjin ryōri* (Buddhist cuisine) with foraged mushrooms and mountain vegetables. A very special place.

Midahara Sanrōsho HUT ¥¥
(御田原参籠所; ☎090-2367-9037; r per person with 2 meals ¥7560; ⌚closed Oct-Jun) At the eighth station on Gas-san, this mountain hut is a convenient place to break up the long three-mountain hike. Futons are laid out in one big communal room (*sans* shower), but the meals are filling and the close quarters conducive for swapping stories. Catch the sunrise and you'll be on your way to the peak before the tour buses arrive.

DON'T MISS

YAMADERA

Immortalised by the itinerant haiku master, Matsuo Bashō in *The Narrow Road to the Deep North* (1689), Yamadera (山寺) is home to some very special mountain temple buildings. The town was founded in AD 860 by priests who carried with them the sacred flame from Enryaku-ji near Kyoto, believing that Yamadera's rock faces were the boundaries between this world and the next. Supposedly that flame remains lit to this day.

Risshaku-ji (立石寺; ☎023-695-2843; www.rissyakuji.jp; admission ¥300; ⏲8am-5pm), the Temple of Standing Stones, rests atop a rock-hewn staircase weathered over centuries by unrelenting elements. At the foot of the mountain, guarded by a small lantern, is the sacred flame **Konpon-chūdō** (根本中堂; admission ¥200), said to have been transported from Kyoto many centuries ago. The San-mon (山門) gate marks the start of the 1015 steps pilgrims must climb to reach the temple, past carvings so worn they appear to be part of the landscape and trees so old you feel very small indeed. It's a steep and meditative ascent that makes the views from the top that much more spectacular.

At Nio-mon (仁王門), the second gate through which 'only those with pure souls may enter', the path splits, heading in one direction to the Oku-no-in (奥の院; Inner Sanctuary) and in the other to Godaidō (五大堂), a remarkable 18th-century pavilion perched on the cliff-side with truly arresting views. It's a little obscured: don't miss it!

Although it's possible (though precarious) to visit Yamadera during winter, a visit in the warmer months will be more enjoyable. If you have time, pop in to **Bashō Kinenkan** (山寺芭蕉記念館; ☎023-695-2221; www.yamadera-basho.jp; 4223 Yamadera; admission ¥400; ⏲9am-4.30pm, closed Mon Dec-Feb) to see scrolls and calligraphy related to poet Bashō's famous northern journey.

Hourly *kaisoku* (rapid trains) travel the JR Senzan line between Yamagata and Yamadera (¥240, 15 minutes), onwards to Sendai (¥1140, 1¼ hours).

Yudono-san Sanrōsho LODGE ¥¥
(湯殿山参籠所; ☎0235-54-6131; 7 Rokujuri-yama, Tamugimata; r per person with 2 meals from ¥7560; ⏲Apr-Nov; Ⓟ) This airy mountain lodge at the bottom of Yudono-san has a hot bath and is full of jovial pilgrims celebrating the completion of their multi-day circuit. Hearty meals, beer and sake are available and are usually gratefully received. Lunch sets (from ¥1575), with river fish and mountain vegetables, are served here as well.

Information

If you want to tackle all three mountains – possible from June through September – you need two full days, though three are advised and accommodation should be booked in advance. Stock up on maps at the tourist information office in Tsuruoka.

Getting There & Around

During the summer climbing months, there are up to 10 buses daily (the earliest leaving at 6am) from Tsuruoka to Haguro village (¥820, 35 minutes), most of which then continue to Haguro-sanchō (Haguro summit; ¥1190, 50 minutes). Outside the high season, the schedule is greatly reduced.

From early July to late August, and then on weekends and holidays until late September, there are up to four daily buses from Haguro-sanchō to Gas-san as far as Hachigōme (¥1580, one hour).

Between June and early November, there are up to four daily buses from the Yudono-san Sanrōsho trailhead at Yudono-san to Tsuruoka (¥1880, 1¼ hours), which also pass by Ōami (¥1200, 35 minutes). Transport can grind to a halt once snows begin.

Tsuruoka 鶴岡

☎0235 / POP 136,000

Tsuruoka, in the middle of the Shōnai plain, was established by the Sakai clan, one of feudal Yamagata's most important families. Now, it's the second-largest city in the prefecture and the jumping-off point for the mountains of Dewa Sanzan. Downtown is pretty sleepy; if you need a bite to eat or snacks for the road, try the S-Mall shopping centre, a few minutes on foot from the station.

Sights

Chidō Museum MUSEUM
(致道博物館; ☎0235-22-1199; www.chido.jp; 10-18 Kachū-shinmachi; adult/child ¥700/380;

(⏲9am-4.30pm) Founded in 1950 by the former Lord Shōnai in order to preserve local culture, this museum features Sakai-family artefacts, two Meiji-era buildings, a traditional storehouse and a *kabuto-zukuri* (farmhouse with a thatched roof shaped like a samurai helmet). The museum is on the southwest corner of Tsuruoka-kōen, the site of the former Sakai castle.

Kamo Aquarium AQUARIUM
(加茂水族館; ☎0235-33-3036; www.kamo-kurage.jp; 657-1 Ōkubo, Imaizumi; adult/child ¥1000/500; ⏲9am-5pm) Looking like a streamlined boat pointed towards the ocean, this now high-tech, stylised aquarium was once a rural tourist attraction in decline – until a Nobel Prize–winning scientist, who discovered a fluorescent protein in belt jellyfish, taught the aquarium how to make jellyfish glow. The rest is history. Inside, over 35 species of pulsing, luminous *Aequorea coerulescens* put on a surreal show.

From Tsuruoka station, take the bus bound for Yunohama-onsen and get off at the Kamo Suizokukan stop (30 minutes).

Studio Sedic THEME PARK
(スタジオセディック; ☎0235-62-4299; www.s-sedic.jp; 102 Nakakawadai Haguro-machi, Kawadai; adult/child ¥1300/900; ⏲9am-4pm Apr-Oct) Opened to visitors in 2014, this working movie-set spread out over 4km of countryside on the Shōnai Plain, 20km from Tsuruoka station, has seven distinct areas to explore including convincing reproductions of fishing, farming and mountain villages and an Edo post town. It's a fascinating insight into the Japanese film and TV industry. You'll need a car: there's no public transport.

Festivals & Events

Tenjin Matsuri CULTURAL
(天神祭; ⏲May) On 25 May each year, people stroll around in masks and costumes, serving sake and keeping an eye out for friends and acquaintances. The object is to make it through the festival without anyone recognising you. Manage this feat three years running and local lore claims you'll have good luck for the rest of your life!

Sleeping

Hotel Route Inn Tsuruoka Ekimae HOTEL ¥¥
(ホテルルートイン鶴岡駅前; ☎0235-28-2055; www.route-inn.co.jp; 1-17 Suehiro-machi; s/d ¥6900/10,350) Ask for a high floor at this helpful station-side hotel for great views over Tsuruoka, the Shōnai plain and enveloping mountains. The common areas and compact yet well-appointed rooms are in great shape, staff are friendly and the breakfast buffet great value.

Tokyo Daiichi Hotel Tsuruoka HOTEL ¥¥
(東京第一ホテル鶴岡; ☎0235-24-7611; www.tdh-tsuruoka.co.jp; 2-10 Nishiki-machi; s/d from ¥8800/12,700; P@) Tsuruoka's fanciest digs have comparatively spacious, stylish rooms and a rooftop sauna and *rotemburo*, perfect for a post-hike soak. It's the huge yellow-brick building connected to the S-Mall shopping centre, a few minutes' walk, turning right as you exit the station.

Eating & Drinking

Sapporo Rāmen RAMEN ¥
(サッポロラーメン; ☎0235-23-4300; 15-16 Suehiro-machi; bowls from ¥600; ⏲11.30am-2pm & 5.30-10pm) There's nothing fancy about this little ramen joint run by a delightful husband-and-wife team who've been making buttery noodles here for decades: that's why we love it. Cheep and cheery. Exiting the station, turn left: it's within two blocks, on your left.

High Noon Diner BAR
(ハイヌーン; ☎0235-25-0081; 15-18 Suehiro-machi; ⏲7pm-1am Wed-Mon) Turning left from the station, walk not even two blocks until you see the distinctive neon Pink Flamingo in the window of this cosy retro bar. It has Guinness on tap and is popular with foreign visitors and locals alike.

Information

Tourist Information Center (鶴岡市観光案内所; ☎0235-25-7678; ⏲10am-5pm) To the right as you exit the station, come here for information, bus timetables and English maps for Dewa Sanzan and other attractions.

Getting There & Away

BUS

Buses leave from in front of Tsuruoka Station and from the bus depot at S-Mall for Haguro village (¥840, 35 minutes). There are a few buses each day between Tsuruoka and Yamagata (¥2480, 1¾ hours), though services are often cut back during winter.

TRAIN

A few daily *tokkyū* (limited express trains) run on the JR Uetsu main line between Tsuruoka and

WORTH A TRIP

SECRET SAKATA

Sakata (酒田) flourished in the Edo period when it was a wealthy port cultivated by nobles and merchants. Today, first glances allude to a sad story of a fading rural town with an ageing population. Closer inspection reveals a wealth of cultural and historical attractions waiting to be uncovered. There's a surprising amount of English signage here and plenty to see and do if you have a few hours and sunny weather.

The staff at the **tourist information office** (酒田駅観光案内所; ☎0234-24-2454; www.sakata-kankou.com; ⏲9am-5pm) within Sakata station don't speak much English, but they rent bikes for free and have an excellent English-language walking map. Use it to find the following sights.

Opposite the City Hall, the **Historical Abumiya Residence** (旧鐙屋; ☎0234-22-5001; 14-20 1-chōme; adult/child ¥320/210; ⏲9am-4.30pm) once belonged to a wealthy shipping agent. With a beautiful garden and a fascinating variety of room divisions using *shōji* (sliding screens), it's a wonderful place to contemplate the Japanese aesthetic of bringing the 'outside' in. From here, you can drop down to the **Sakata Kaisen Ichiba** (酒田海鮮市場; ☎0234-23-5522; 5-10 2-chōme; ⏲8am-6pm) market for fresh-off-the-boat seafood and farm-to-table produce. You can eat at a variety of vendors or grab some sushi and picnic goodies and head to picturesque **Hiyoriyama Park** (日和山公園) for an alfresco lunch. On the way, or afterwards, be sure to check out the **Historical Obata ('NK Agent') Building** (旧割烹小幡 (NKエージェント事務所); ☎0234-26-5759; 2-9-37 Hiyoshi-machi; admission ¥100; ⏲9am-5pm), which featured in the 2009 Academy Award–winning Best Foreign Language film, *Okuribito* (おくりびと; Departures). A bunch of other locations around town were used in the film – ask about them here. Alternatively or additionally, the **Sannō Club** (山王クラブ; ☎0234-22-0146; 2-2-25 Hiyoshi-machi; adult/child ¥310/210; ⏲9am-5pm) is a time-warp back to the boom days of the Meiji-era, when this lavish private club would have been a very lively and decadent place indeed. If only those walls could talk...

If you're still hungry and looking for something different, **Pho Son** (フォー ソン; ☎0234-24-7818; 7-7 Niban-chō; noodles from ¥650; ⏲11.30am-2.30pm) in the main shopping district does authentic *pho* noodle bowls and other Vietnamese delights. Yum!

Sakata is an easy day trip from Tsuruoka on the local *fūtsū train* (¥500, 35 minutes) or a pleasant stop en-route to Akita (*tokkyū*, ¥3280, 1½ hours) on the scenic, coast-hugging Uetsu main-line.

Akita (¥3610, 1¾ hours) and between Tsuruoka and Niigata (¥3930, 1¾ hours).

AKITA PREFECTURE

Akita-ken (秋田県) is shaped by the soaring Ōu-sanmyaku and Dewa mountain ranges, which have long kept the region isolated. Even today development is divinely sparse. Akita's peaks shelter remote, rustic hot springs that are among the best in the country: paired with neighbouring Lake Tazawa-ko, Nyūtō Onsen is a unique retreat. Civilisation hums along in Akita's fertile valleys, including the prefectural capital of the same name and the feudal city of Kakunodate, a storehouse of samurai culture. The region also claims the most beautiful women in Japan, the so-called *Akita-bijin*.

Akita 秋田

☎018 / POP 320,150

The northern terminus of the Akita *shinkansen* (bullet train), this sprawling commercial city and prefectural capital is one of the region's principal transport hubs. Like most contemporary cities, it was once a castle town, in this case the seat of power of the Satake clan.

Sights

Akita's few sights are in the city centre near the train station, so you can easily get around on foot.

Senshū-kōen PARK

(千秋公園; ☎018-832-5893) Originally constructed in 1604, Akita's castle was destroyed with other feudal relics during the Meiji Restoration. The moat still guards the

Akita Prefecture

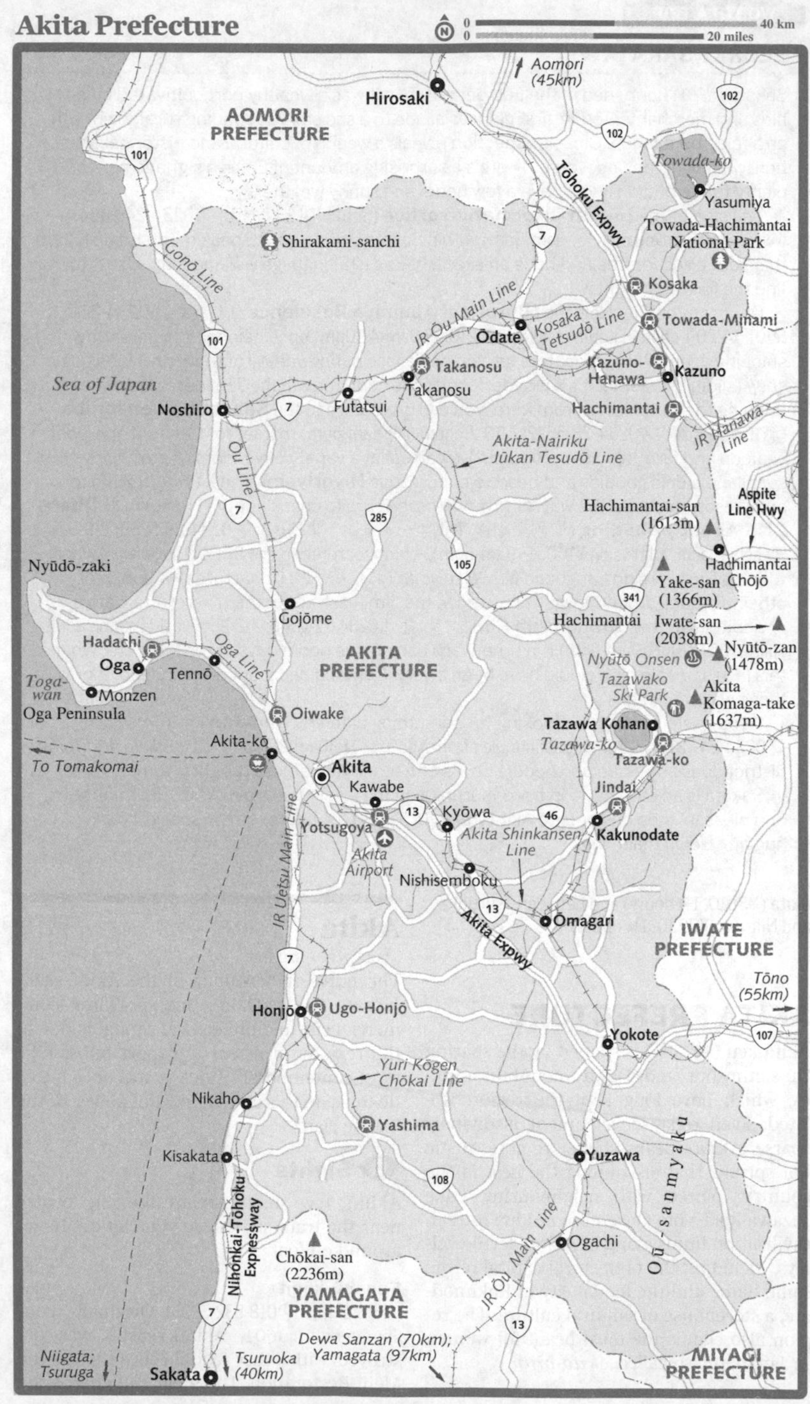

entrance to this leafy park; though hardly sinister, it becomes choked with giant waterlilies in summer. There are also a few pieces of the castle foundation remaining, along with plenty of grassy patches and strolling paths. A reconstruction of a guard tower in the north corner offers views over the city.

Akita Museum of Art MUSEUM
(秋田県立美術館; ☎018-853-8686; http://common3.pref.akita.lg.jp/art-museum; 1-4-2 Naka-dōri; adult/child ¥300/200; ⏲10am-6pm) Akita's most famous painting, Tsuguharu Fūjita's *Events of Akita,* is also reputed to be the world's largest canvas painting, measuring 3.65m by 20.5m and depicting traditional Akita life through the seasons. This work and many others are housed in this shiny new Andō Tadao–designed museum with its wonderful public square. Visitors can rest in the 2nd-floor cafe, from where the reflecting pool seems to run directly into Senshū-kōen's moat.

Akarenga-kan Museum MUSEUM
(赤れんが郷土館, Akarenga Kyōdokan; ☎018-864-6851; www.city.akita.akita.jp/city/ed/ak; 3-3-21 Ō-machi; admission ¥210; ⏲9.30am-4.30pm) Once the opulent headquarters of Akita Bank, this brick structure built in 1912 is now a folk museum. Inside, you'll find fascinating woodblock prints of traditional Akita life by self-taught artist Katsuhira Tokushi.

Festivals & Events

Akita Kantō Matsuri CULTURAL
(秋田竿燈まつり; www.kantou.gr.jp/english/index.htm) At summer's height, Akita celebrates its visually stunning Pole Lantern Festival. As evening falls on the city centre, more than 160 men skilfully balance giant poles, weighing 60kg and hung with illuminated lanterns, on their heads, chins, hips and shoulders, to the beat of *taiko* drumming groups. Held from 3 to 6 August.

Sleeping

Naniwa Hotel MINSHUKU ¥¥
(ホテルなにわ; ☎018-832-4570; www.hotel-naniwa.jp; 6-18-27 Naka-dōri; r per person with 2 meals ¥6800; P⊖@) This small family-run hotel has a variety of tatami rooms (some teeny tiny, others with private sinks and toilets). It also outdoes itself with extras: a beautiful 24-hour *hinoki* (cypress) bath, massage chairs and filling meals that use the owners' home-grown rice. Look for the red building with a wooden entrance.

Toyoko Inn Akita-eki Higashi-guchi HOTEL ¥¥
(東横イン秋田駅東口; ☎018-889-1045; www.toyoko-inn.com/hotel/00087; 4-1 Higashi-dōri; s/d from ¥5600/7600) You can't go past this generic business hotel, adjoining the impressively, recently renovated Akita station, for location and value. It's busy, but staff are friendly and hyper-efficient. Higher floors have nice views.

Richmond Hotel Akita Eki-mae HOTEL ¥¥
(リッチモンドホテル秋田駅前; ☎018-884-0055; www.richmondhotel.jp/en/akita; 2-2-26 Naka-dōri; s/d from ¥6000/8000; ⊖@📶) Remarkably stylish for a business hotel, the Richmond also has a convenient location between the station and the sights. Prices can vary wildly so it's a good idea to book ahead online.

Akita Castle Hotel HOTEL ¥¥
(秋田キャッスルホテル; ☎018-834-1141; www.castle-hotel.co.jp; 1-3-5 Naka-dōri; s/d from ¥7500/11,000; P⊖@📶) It may not look much from the outside, but this is the classiest hotel in town. If you can lock in a discount rate online, it's not a bad deal either. The rooms recently got a stylish makeover; the nicest ones overlook the castle moat.

Eating

Kawabata-dōri, lined with restaurants and bars both classic and seedy, is the city's main nightlife strip. For a picnic lunch, stop by the supermarket in the Naka-Ichi centre.

Kanbun Gonendō UDON ¥
(寛文五年堂; ☎0120-1728-86; www.kanbun5.jp; 1-4-3 Naka-dōri; noodles from ¥900; ⏲11am-10.30pm; 🖉) Sample delicate, fresh *inaniwa udon* (thin wheat noodles) at this popular speciality shop. They're particularly refreshing on a hot day served cold with soy sauce and sesame dipping sauces. Vegetarian dishes are available; ask before ordering. The restaurant is part of the Naka-Ichi shopping centre.

Cafe Pamplemousse CAFE ¥
(パンプルムゥス 秋田; ☎018-801-6677; 3-1-6 Ōmachi; snacks from ¥450; ⏲11am-9pm) Occupying a lovely riverside spot adjacent to a little park, this genial cafe makes cakes and pancakes better than grandma ever did. Well, that's not possible, but you get the drift.

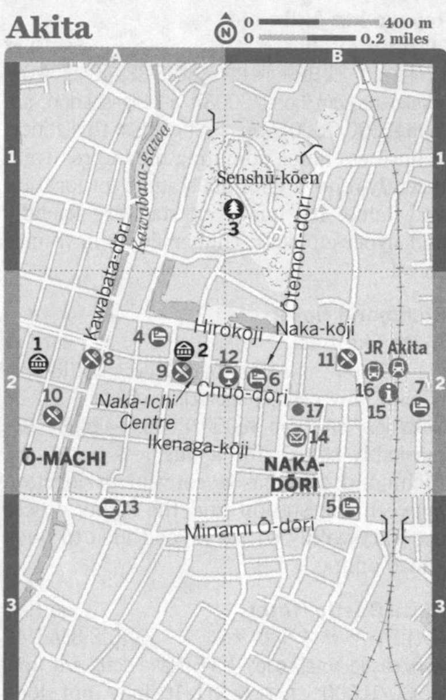

Akita

Sights
1 Akarenga-kan Museum.......................A2
2 Akita Museum of Art A2
3 Senshū-kōen B1

Sleeping
4 Akita Castle Hotel..............................A2
5 Naniwa Hotel......................................B3
6 Richmond Hotel Akita Eki-mae...........B2
7 Toyoko Inn Akita-eki Higashi-guchi...B2

Eating
8 Cafe Pamplemousse...........................A2
9 Kanbun Gonendō................................A2
10 Otafuku...A2
11 Tonkatsu Ichiban-tei B2

Drinking & Nightlife
12 Red House...B2
13 Spica Ryokōsha Cafe & Bar...............A3

Information
14 Akita Eki-mae Post Office..................B2
15 Tourist Information Center................B2

Transport
16 Bus Station..B2
17 Toyota Rent a Car..............................B2

Otafuku JAPANESE ¥¥
(お多福; ☎018-862-0802; 4-2-25 Ōmachi; hotpot dishes from ¥2520; ⊙11.30am-2pm & 5-10.30pm Mon-Fri, 5-10.30pm Sat) This upmarket traditional restaurant does good renditions of classic local dishes such as *kiritanpo-nabe*, a filling hotpot of kneaded and grilled rice (the *kiritanpo*) and vegetables in a chicken and soy-sauce broth. Though pricey, courses (from ¥3675) simplify ordering and include Otafuku's famous pickles.

Tonkatsu Ichiban-tei TONKATSU ¥¥
(とんかつ壱番亭; ☎018-835-6605; 7-1-2 Naka-dōri, 3rd fl, Topico Bldg; sets from ¥930; ⊙8am-10pm) If you're a schnitzel-loving carnivore, you're most likely also a *katsu*-loving carnivore. If so, you should eat here in this spotless establishment when you're in Akita. It's adjacent to the station in the Topico building on the 3rd floor. Set meals start at ¥930 and there's a picture menu.

Drinking & Nightlife

Red House BAR
(レッドハウス; ☎018-836-0588; 1-22 2-chōme; ⊙7pm-1am Mon-Sat) You'll find this supercool sometime live-house bar atop the Ono Flower shop a few blocks' walk from the station. This is where the young, international, open-minded music-lovers hang.

Spica Ryokōsha Cafe & Bar CAFE
(スピカ旅行社カフェ&バー; ☎018-874-8851; 5-4-18 Naka-dōri; ⊙11.30am-11pm Tue-Sat, to 6pm Sun) By day, this colourful cafe serves tasty smoothies and lunch plates. Come night, it morphs into a hip little bar with a nightly happy hour (5pm to 7pm).

Information

Akita Eki-mae Post Office (秋田駅前郵便局; ☎018-832-9899; 4-11-14 Naka-dōri; ⊙9am-6pm)

Akita Red Cross Hospital (秋田赤十字病院; ☎24hr emergency hotline 018-829-5000; www.akita-med.jrc.or.jp; 222-1 Nawashiro-sawa; ⊙outpatient services 8am-11.30am Mon-Fri) Located 5km southeast of the train station, off Rte 41.

Tourist Information Center (秋田市観光案内所; ☎018-832-7941; www.akitacity.info; ⊙9am-7pm) Opposite the *shinkansen* (bullet train) tracks on the 2nd floor of Akita Station.

Getting There & Away

AIR

From Akita Airport, 21km south of the city centre, flights go to/from Tokyo, Osaka, Nagoya, Sapporo and Seoul. Frequent buses leave for the airport from platform 1 in front of Akita Station (¥920, 40 minutes).

BOAT

From the port of Akita-kō, **Shin Nihonkai** (新日本海; ☎018-880-2600; www.snf.jp) has ferries to Tomakomai on Hokkaidō (from ¥4530, 10 hours), departing at 7am on Tuesday, Wednesday, Friday, Saturday and Sunday. A connecting bus leaves at 6.05am from platform 11 outside Akita Station for Akita-kō (¥440, 30 minutes), 8km northwest of the city.

BUS

Highway buses depart from the east exit of the train station, and connect Akita to major cities throughout Honshū.

CAR & MOTORCYCLE

If you're driving, the **Akita Expressway** (秋田自動車道) runs east from Akita until it joins with the Tōhoku Expressway. The **Nihonkai-Tōhoku Expressway** (日本海東北自動車道) runs south along the coast.

Rental cars are scattered around the station, including the reliable **Toyota Rent a Car** (トヨタレンタカー; ☎018-833-0100; 4-6-5 Naka-dōri; ⏲8am-10pm), a few minutes' walk west.

TRAIN

The JR Akita *shinkansen* runs hourly between the northern terminus of Akita and the southern terminus of Tokyo (¥17,460, four hours) via Kakunodate (¥2820, 45 minutes) and Tazawa-ko (¥3160, one hour).

Infrequent local trains also run on the JR Ōu main line between Akita and Kakunodate (¥1320, 1½ hours), with a change at Ōmagari to the JR Tazawako line. There are a few *tokkyū* (limited express trains) each day on the JR Uetsu line, connecting Akita with Niigata (¥6690, 3¾ hours).

Kakunodate 角館

☎0187 / POP 28,300

Established in 1620 by Ashina Yoshikatsu, the lord of the Satake clan, Kakunodate is sometimes referred to as 'Little Kyoto' and presents a thoughtful, immersive experience for anyone interested in catching a glimpse of the samurai era. While the castle that once guarded the feudal town is no more, the *buke yashiki* (samurai district) is splendidly preserved. A veritable living museum of Japanese culture and history, the *buke yashiki* consists of orderly mansions stunningly surrounded by cherry trees and manicured gardens.

Sights

Half-a-dozen villas are open to the public, lining a street shaded by cherry trees a 20-minute walk northwest of the train station. The more elaborate ones are set up like miniature museums; others are simply left as they were and are free for visitors to peek inside.

Aoyagi Samurai Manor Museum MUSEUM
(角館歴史村青柳家; Kakunodate Rekishi-mura Aoyagi-ke; ☎0187-54-3257; www.samuraiworld.com; 3 Omote-machi; adult/child ¥500/300; ⏲9am-4pm) The Aoyagi family compound is impressive in its own right, but inside each well-maintained structure is a fascinating exhibition of family heirlooms. The collection spans generations and includes centuries-old samurai weaponry, folk art and valuable antiques, along with gramophones and classic jazz records.

Bukeyashiki Ishiguro-ke HISTORIC BUILDING
(武家屋敷石黒家; ☎0187-55-1496; 1 Omote-machi; adult/child ¥300/200; ⏲9am-5pm) Built in 1809 as the residence of the Ishiguro family, advisers to the Satake clan, this is one of the oldest buildings in the district. A descendant of the family still lives here, but some rooms are open to the public. In addition to samurai gear, don't miss the weathered maps and the precision scales for doling out rice.

Andō Brewery BREWERY
(安藤醸造; ☎0187-53-2008; 27 Shimo-Shin-machi; ⏲11am-5pm) FREE A centuries-old brewery, Andō makes soy sauce and miso (sorry, tipplers, not that kind of brewery!) in a beautiful, brick storehouse from the late 19th century. You can tour a few rooms and sample some pickles and miso soup (for free!) in the cosy cafe.

Kakunodate Cherry-Bark Craft Center ARTS CENTRE
(角館樺細工伝承館, Kakunodate Kabazaiku Denshōkan; ☎0187-54-1700; 10-1 Omote-machi; adult/child ¥300/150; ⏲9am-4.30pm) Inside are exhibits and demonstrations of *kabazaiku*, the craft of covering household or decorative items in fine strips of cherry bark. This pursuit was first taken up by lower-ranking and masterless samurai in times of hardship.

Festivals & Events

Kakunodate Sakura NATURE

(角館の桜) On the river embankment, a 2km stretch of cherry trees becomes a tunnel of pure pink during the *hanami* (blossom viewing) season, from mid-April to early May. Some of the *shidare-zakura* (drooping cherry) trees in the *buke yashiki* (samurai district) are up to 300 years old.

Kakunodate O-matsuri CULTURAL

(角館のお祭り) As they have done for 350 years, festival participants haul around enormous seven-tonne *yama* (wooden carts) to pray for peaceful times, accompanied by folk music and dancing. From 7 to 9 September.

Sleeping

Akita's countryside has dozens of *nōka minshuku* (farmhouse inns). For a complete list (in Japanese), see www.akita-gt.org/stay.

Room rates rise sharply during cherry blossom and festival seasons.

Iori MINSHUKU ¥

(いおり; ☎0187-55-2262; www.akita-gt.org/stay/minshuku/iori.html; 65 Maeda, Ogata; r per person ¥4500, with 2 meals ¥6000) This working family farm 3km north of Kakunodate Station hosts guests in a delightful, comfortable cabin with whitewashed walls, dark-wood beams, fresh tatami and indigo cushions. Take part in farm life if you choose, or just enjoy a peaceful retreat. Pick-up from Kakunodate Station can be arranged.

Tamachi Bukeyashiki Hotel BOUTIQUE HOTEL ¥¥

(田町武家屋敷ホテル; ☎0187-52-1700; www.bukeyashiki.jp; 23 Tamachi; r per person from ¥8,500, with 2 meals from ¥13,800; P @) This is a modern hotel with traditional styling, but it's fully stocked with modern amenities. Rooms, both Japanese and Western style, are elegant, with dark wooden beams and paper lanterns, but showing a little wear and tear; in comparison, meals are lavish affairs. It's a 10- to 15- minute walk from the station.

Folkloro Kakunodate BUSINESS HOTEL ¥¥

(フォルクローロ角館; ☎0187-53-2070; www.folkloro-kakunodate.com; Nakasuga-zawa 14; s/d/tw from ¥6750/13,500/11,700; P ⊖ @ ☜) This standard but nicely maintained business hotel, part of the JR group, gets points for its convenient location next to the train station and free breakfast spread. Althought it's a bit of a hike from the sights, it's perfect if you're travelling by train: check in, drop your bags and head out on your adventures.

Eating

Chūka-ryōri Yūro CHINESE ¥

(中華料理祐楼; ☎0187-53-3425; 21 Shimonaka-machi; meals from ¥800; ⏲11.30am-2pm & 5-8.30pm Fri-Wed; 📖) This spotless restaurant feels like an art gallery, with beautiful Japanese prints lining the walls. Leave your shoes at the door and venture upstairs where you'll be greeted by the cheery owners and treated to mouthwatering Chinese treats: chilli prawns, dumplings, soups and stir fries. Set menus are available. Look for the red, white and yellow sign on the side of the building.

Kosendō SOBA ¥¥

(古泉洞; ☎0187-53-2902; 9 Higashi-katsuraku-chō; noodles from ¥1050; ⏲10am-4pm; 📖) Kakunodate's most historic lunch spot is this Edo-era wooden schoolhouse, almost 250 years old! The house speciality is *buke-soba* served with *takenoko* (bamboo) and tempura-fried *ōba* (large perilla leaf). It's in the middle of the *buke yashiki* (samurai district); look for the wooden sign above the entrance.

Nishi-no-miyake Restaurant Kita-kura JAPANESE ¥¥

(西宮家レストラン北蔵; ☎0187-52-2438; 11-1 Kami-chō, Tamachi; meals from ¥1100; ⏲11am-5pm; 📖) This sprawling former residence houses a restaurant in a century-old warehouse towards the back of the complex. Here, diners sit under hulking wooden rafters, tucking into classic *yōshoku* (Japanese-style Western food) dishes like *hayashi raisu* (hashed beef on rice) that would have been in vogue when the structure was built. It's halfway between the station and the sightseeing district.

Information

Tourist Information Center (角館町観光協会; ☎0187-54-2700; ⏲9am-5pm) Pick up English maps outside the station in a small building shaped like a *kura* (traditional Japanese storehouse).

Getting There & Around

Several of the *shinkansen* (bullet trains) on the Akita line run hourly between Kakunodate and Tazawa-ko (¥1560, 15 minutes), and between Kakunodate and Akita (¥2940, 45 minutes).

Local trains also run infrequently on the JR Tazawako line between Kakunodate and Tazawa-ko (¥320, 20 minutes), and between Kakunodate and Akita (¥1280, 1½ hours), with a change at Ōmagari to the JR Ōu main line.

Bicycle rentals are available across from the train station for ¥300 per hour.

Tazawa-ko 田沢湖

0187 / POP 12,900

At 423m, idyllic Tazawa-ko is Japan's deepest lake. Its convenient *shinkansen* (bullet train) access makes it a popular summertime escape. The nearby mountains offer excellent views of the lake and four seasons of activity, including skiing. It's highly recommended to pick up a rental car at Tazawa-ko station for a night or two to make the most of the lake and nearby Nyūtō Onsen.

Sights

Tazawa-ko LAKE

(田沢湖) Ringed by mountains, Tazawa-ko's lovely sandy beach, **Shirahama** (白浜), might actually be Japan's best swimming beach outside the remote islands, but only in the warmest months. Rent pleasure-craft at the nearby boathouse from spring to autumn. Romantic sunset strolls are highly recommended any time of year: on the lake's eastern shore, you'll find Tazawa-ko's famed bronze statue of the legendary beauty Tatsuko, sculpted by Funakoshi Yasutake.

A 20km road wraps around the lake, perfect for a slow drive or vigorous cycle – bike rentals are available in the small village of Tazawa Kohan (¥400 per hour). Sightseeing buses depart Tazawa-ko Station and loop around the lake, stopping for 15 minutes to admire the statue of Tatsuko.

Activities

★Akita Komaga-take HIKING

(秋田駒ヶ岳) These mountains straddling the border with Iwate Prefecture are admired for summer wildflowers, autumn foliage and a rare prevalence of both dry and wet plant species. Over two days you can pursue a 17km course that takes in three peaks, overnights in a picturesque mountain hut and ends with a rewarding soak in the reportedly healing waters of Nyūtō Onsen.

Access the trailhead at Komaga-take Hachigōme (eighth station) by taking one of seven daily buses (all departing before 1.30pm) from Tazawa-ko Station (¥1090, one hour). From the eighth station, it's a two-hour hike to the summit of Oname-dake (男女岳; 1637m) before pressing on to the eastern edge of the oval-shaped pond below and claiming your space at the Amida-ike Hinan Goya (阿弥陀池避難小屋) unmanned mountain hut; it's recommended that you leave a small tip (¥1000). You can also double back for 20 minutes or so and scale O-dake (男岳; 1623m).

On the second day, it's a seven-hour descent to Nyūtō Onsen, including first summiting Yoko-dake (横岳; 1583m). The trail down follows the ridgeline most of the way before winding through expansive marshlands rich with birdlife. Emerge at the Nyūtō Onsen bus stop, from where it's a short stroll to a heavenly bath.

Tazawako Ski Park SNOW SPORTS

(田沢湖スキー場; 0187-46-2011; www.tazawako-ski.com; 73-2 Shimo-Takano; 1-day lift ticket adult/child ¥4000/2500, gear rental per day ¥3600; Dec-Apr) Akita's largest winter-sports destination is just over three hours on a *shinkansen* from Tokyo. Of the 13 or so trails, all but the 1.6km Kokutai and Shirakaba runs are on the shorter side, but with an even mix of beginner, intermediate and advanced. The views down the hill to the nearby shores of Tazawa-ko are breathtaking.

There's English signage on the mountains and in the numerous eateries, but a predominantly Japanese clientele. In the winter months, buses leaving Tazawa-ko Station for Nyūtō Onsen stop at Tazawako Sukī-jō (¥550, 30 minutes).

Sleeping

Many elect to bed down in one of neighbouring Nyūtō Onsen's excellent ryokan (p529).

THE LEGEND OF TATSUKO

Legend has it that long ago, a local maiden, Tatsuko, believing that the spring water would make her youthful beauty last forever, drank so much water that she was turned into a dragon and remains in the lake to this day. One version of the mythology adds another dragon, formerly a prince, as her lover. Their passionate nocturnal antics are said to be the reason why Tazawa-ko doesn't freeze in winter!

DELICACIES OF THE DEEP NORTH

Eating in Tōhoku is all about simple seasonal pleasures – the bounty of the land and sea:

- *gyū-tan* (牛タン) Cow's tongue, grilled over charcoal (Sendai).
- *Yonezawa-gyū* (米沢牛) Yonezawa's premium-grade beef.
- *kiritanpo-nabe* (きりたんぽ鍋) Kneaded rice wrapped around bamboo spits, barbecued over a charcoal fire then served in a chicken and soy-sauce hotpot with vegetables (Akita).
- *inaniwa udon* (稲庭うどん) Thinner-than-usual wheat noodles (Akita).
- *wanko-soba* (わんこそば) All-you-can-eat noodles (Morioka).
- *jaja-men* (じゃじゃ麺) Flat wheat noodles topped with sliced cucumber, miso paste and ground meat (Morioka).

Aomori Prefecture's seafood is king:

- *uni* (うに) Sea urchin roe.
- *hotate* (ホタテ) Scallops.
- *maguro* (まぐろ) Tuna; the village of Ōma, at the tip of Honshū, is said to have the finest in the country.

★That Sounds Good PENSION ¥
(ペンションサウンズグッド; ☎0187-43-0127; www.hana.or.jp/~takko; 160-58 Kata-mae; r per person with breakfast from ¥6800; P 📶) The friendly, musical, English-speaking owners of this thoroughly appealing lakefront oasis will pick you up from Tazawa-kohan bus stop, if you don't have a car. The spacious, stylish, comfortable accomodation comprises split-level lofts (shared facilities) and cottages (with bathroom). Activity revolves around an open cafe-bar where meals are served and from where the sounds of weekend jazz billow out over Tazawa-ko.

Drop in, tune out and relax… why not stay a few days?

Tazawa-ko Youth Hostel HOSTEL ¥
(田沢湖ユースホステル; ☎0187-43-1281; www.jyh.or.jp/yhguide/touhoku/tazawako/index.html; 33-8 Kami-Ishigami; dm ¥3890, YHA discount ¥3290, breakfast/dinner ¥650/1050; P 👪) A few minutes' walk from the lake, this rambling hostel is showing its age. Shared *tatami* rooms are clean and overlook the lake. Bathing is a communal affair. Meals are hearty and home-style.

ℹ Information

Tourist Information Center (田沢湖観光情報センター, Folake; ☎0187-43-2111; ⏲8.30am-5.30pm) Inside the train station, with tourist information and free internet available.

ℹ Getting There & Away

BUS

Frequent local buses run between JR Tazawa-ko Station and Tazawa Kohan (¥370, 10 minutes), the tourist hub on the eastern shore of the lake.

Buses also run to Nyūtō Onsen (¥670, 45 minutes). Services terminate after sunset.

CAR & MOTORCYCLE

If you're driving, Rte 46 connects the Akita Expressway (秋田自動車道) with Tazawa-ko.

TRAIN

JR Tazawa-ko Station is located a few kilometres southeast of the lake and serves as the area's main access point.

The Akita *shinkansen* runs several times an hour between Tazawa-ko and Tokyo (¥15,830, three hours) and between Tazawa-ko and Akita (¥3160, 55 minutes) via Kakunodate (¥1560, 15 minutes).

Nyūtō Onsen 乳頭温泉

Visits to this remote *onsen-kyō* (hot-spring village), usually enjoyed in conjunction with contrasting, neighbouring Tazawa-ko, should be considered a must for aspiring onsen-aficionados! The name Nyūtō (meaning 'nipple') comes from the mammary-shaped foothills, from where the spring emerges, although some baths do have milky-white waters. Of the eight establishments here, each has a different character. Most offer *konyoku*: gender-mixed bathing.

Activities

It's possible to enjoy the waters without the expense of overnighting – as a day-bather. Check to see if the excellent-value *hi-gaeri* (day-return) pass, ¥1000, is available from most inns, which open their baths between check-out and check-in: usually between 10am and 3pm. The pass gets you admission to all eight, but it's an on-again, off-again kind of deal. When it's not on offer, you'll need to pay admission (between ¥500 and ¥1000) at each onsen you visit. You'll also need to bring your own towel, or buy one. The caveat is that much of the ambience is lost when you're sharing your stunning mountain *rotemburo* with coach loads of tourists having the same idea.

Sleeping

For the complete list of Nyūtō's inns and some onsen eye-candy, see www.nyuto-onsenkyo.com. If you have the time, you'll appreciate spending a night in these divine surrounds; meals are uniformly special, and there's no other way to enjoy these fine outdoor baths beneath moonlight or in private.

★Tsuru-no-yu Onsen RYOKAN ¥¥
(鶴の湯温泉; 0187-46-2139; www.tsurunoyu.com/english; 50 Kokuyurin, Sendatsui-zawa; r per person with 2 meals ¥8790-16,350, day bathing ¥500; day bathing 10am-3pm Tue-Sun; P) In the business for almost four centuries, Tsuru-no-yu is one of the most aesthetically pleasing *onsen ryokan* we've seen. Accommodation ranges from creaky tatami rooms to compartmentalised suites opening up to the forest. Wherever you sleep, evenings are a nostalgic affair, distinguished by memorable meals and guests in *yukata* socialising by lantern light.

According to lore, the onsen became the official bathhouse of Akita's ruling elite after a hunter once saw a crane *(tsuru)* healing its wounds in the spring. Its milky-white waters are rich in sulphur, sodium, calcium chloride and carbonic acid. The mixed *rotemburo* is positively jubilant, although shyer folk can take refuge in the indoor gender-segregated baths.

Make reservations months in advance. Self-driving is recommended: it's off the beaten track.

Tae-no-yu RYOKAN ¥¥
(妙乃湯; 0187-46-2740; www.taenoyu.com; 2-1 Komagatake; r per person with 2 meals from ¥13,100, day bathing ¥720; day bathing 10am-3pm Wed-Mon; P) What little Tae-no-yu lacks in history, it makes up for in style. Representing exceptional value-for-money, this boutique ryokan aims to please and succeeds. Exquisite locavore meals are based on wild plants foraged on the grounds. Bathing options are comprehensive, including private family onsen, reclining cypress tubs and heavenly *rotemburo*. Single travellers are welcomed.

Kuroyu Onsen RYOKAN ¥¥
(黒湯温泉; 0187-46-2214; www.kuroyu.com; 2-1 Kuroyu-zawa; r per person with 2 meals from ¥12,030, day bathing ¥510; day bathing 9am-4pm May-Nov; P) At the streamside Kuroyu, you'll feel as though you've stepped into a Japanese woodblock print. With a bathing tradition dating back more than 300 years, Kuroyu is famous for its hydrogen-sulphide spring, said to ease an array of ailments; don't miss the waterfall jets. Japanese-style rooms are fairly standard, though the forest setting is the stage for a relaxing retreat.

Getting There & Around

Infrequent buses run from JR Tazawa-ko Station to Nyūtō Onsen (¥820, 50 minutes) and stop at some of the resorts, a few of which are within walking distance from each other. Renting a car from Tazawa-ko will give you the freedom to truly get the most out of a visit to this area.

AOMORI PREFECTURE

Aomori-ken (青森県), at the curious northern tip of Honshū, is split in the middle by Mutsu-wan, the bay cradled in the arm of the axe-shaped Shimokita Peninsula. Having a rental car here will help to open up some of Japan's most remote and exotic areas. From the ethereal and sacred volcanic landscapes around Osore-zan, through to the mysterious highlands of the Hakkōda mountains, down to the verdant shores of Towada-ko and some very special, isolated onsen retreats, Aomori has something for everyone.

Aomori 青森

017 / POP 301,000

Prefectural capital, Aomori is a compact city, a stopover point for travellers en-route to Hokkaidō and a regional transport hub.

Aomori Prefecture

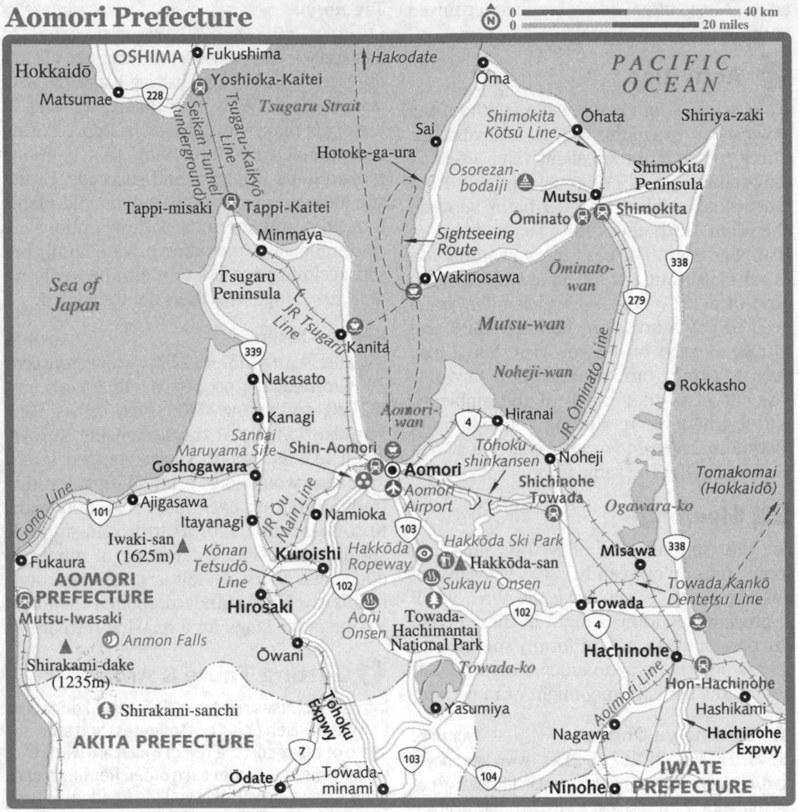

There are a handful of attractions scattered around the city including a pleasant harbourfront area near the station. Aomori's most famous draw is its Nebuta festival, in August.

Most visitors arrive by *shinkansen* into Shin-Aomori Station, one stop away from breezy, waterfront JR Aomori Station on the Ōu line. Shinmachi-dōri, the main drag, rolls east from the station and has a refreshingly sleepy *inaka* (country) vibe. Head down the side streets between the department stores to see farmers hawking their vegies on the sidewalks. Although it's sunny and delightfully cooler than most of Japan in summer, winter here is an icy, frigid state of affairs.

Sights

★ Sannai Maruyama Site ARCHAEOLOGICAL SITE
(三内丸山遺跡; ☎017-766-8282; www.sannaimaruyama.pref.aomori.jp; Sannai Maruyama 305; 9am-5.30pm Jun-Sep, 9am-4.30pm Oct-May) FREE Excavation of this site turned up an astonishing number of intact artefacts from Japan's Jōmon era (10,000–2000 years ago), which are on display at the museum here. The actual archaeological site, along with some reconstructed dwellings, form the grounds out back. Sannai Maruyama is approximately 5km west of Aomori Station. City buses leaving from stop 6 for Menkyō Center stop at Sannai Maruyama Iseki-mae (¥300, 20 minutes).

Aomori Museum of Art MUSEUM
(青森県立美術館; ☎017-783-3000; www.aomori-museum.jp/en/index.html; 185 Chikano, Yasuta; adult/child ¥510/300; 9am-5pm) Artists from Aomori Prefecture feature heavily in the permanent collection here, including pop icon Yoshitomo Nara, master print maker Munakata Shikō, and Tohl Narita, who designed many of the monsters from the iconic *Ultraman* television show. The museum is about 5km west of Aomori Station,

adjacent to the Sannai Maruyama Site; city buses leaving from stop 6 for Menkyō Center stop at Kenritsu-bijyutskan-mae (¥270, 20 minutes).

Nebuta no Ie Wa Rasse MUSEUM
(ねぶたの家ワ・ラッセ; ☎017-752-1311; www.nebuta.or.jp/warasse; 1-1-1 Yasukata; adult/child ¥600/250; ⏰9am-5pm) Even if you missed the festival, you can still gawk at the awesome craftsmanship of the Nebuta floats displayed at this new museum on the waterfront. On weekends there are performances of dancing and drumming as well.

Festivals & Events

Aomori Nebuta Matsuri PARADES
(青森ねぶた祭り; www.nebuta.or.jp/english/index_e) Held from 2 to 7 August, the Nebuta Matsuri has parades of spectacular illuminated floats, accompanied by thousands of rowdy, chanting dancers. The parades start at sunset and last for hours; on the final day, the action starts at about noon. As this is one of Japan's most famous festivals, you'll need to book accommodation way in advance.

Sleeping

Art Hotel Color HOTEL ¥
(アートホテル カラー; ☎017-775-4311; www.arthotelcolor.com; 2-5-6 Shinmachi; s/d from ¥3200/5300) Even by Japanese standards, the unimaginably tiny rooms of this sweet little hotel are strangely comforting: perhaps it's simply the splash of color on the feature wall. Stay here for the excellent rates, including an eclectic and tasty breakfast buffet. Be sure to book on the 'Color Floor' or go for the suite.

Hyper Hotels Passage HOTEL ¥¥
(ハイパーホテルズパサージュ; ☎017-721-5656; 1-8-6 Shinmachi; s/d from ¥5080/7180) One of the closest hotels to JR Aomori Station, this smarter-than-most business hotel even has a chandelier in the lobby. Spotless rooms are bigger than most, the beds are comfortable and the breakfast buffet is decent.

Richmond Hotel Aomori HOTEL ¥¥
(リッチモンドホテル青森; ☎017-732-7655; http://aomori.richmondhotel.jp; 1-6-6 Nagashima; s/d from ¥7000/12,000) Aomori's newest and most imposing chain hotel, about 1km from Aomori Station, offers comfortable, well-appointed rooms that are a cut above the business hotel standard. High floors afford views of the ocean.

Aomori Center Hotel HOTEL ¥¥
(青森センターホテル; ☎017-762-7500; www.aomoricenterhotel.jp; 1-10-9-1 Furukawa; s/d incl breakfast from ¥5100/9100; @) Besides being excellent value, this business hotel is attached to an onsen complex that guests may use for free. Rooms in the brand new *bekkan* (annexe) are the nicest. The hotel (not to be confused with the Aomori Central Hotel) is 500m walk from Aomori Station.

Eating

★**Shinsen Ichiba** MARKET ¥
(新鮮市場; ☎017-721-8000; basement, Auga Bldg, 1-3-7 Shinchō; meals from ¥580; ⏰5am-6.30pm) Aomori is famous for seafood and produce, including scallops, codfish, apples, pickled vegetables and many other foods that are all laid out at this bustling market. There's also a handful of counter restaurants where you can get a fresh *sanshoku-don* (rice topped with scallops, fish roe and sea urchin roe) or a hot bowl of *rāmen* (noodles).

A-Factory FOOD COURT ¥
(エーファクトリー; ☎017-752-1890; 1-4-2 Yanagigawa; meals from ¥700; ⏰11am-8pm;) Part of the city's new waterfront development, A-Factory is a bright, airy food court serving everything from sushi to galettes. Apple cider is brewed on the premises and available by the glass or bottle.

Jūkei CHINESE ¥
(重慶; ☎017-777-4515; 3-7-9 Honchō; dishes from ¥550; ⏰11.30am-9pm) Walking down Shinmachi-dōri from the station, turn left on Zeimusho-dōri (before the Alpha Hotel). Walk towards the water and, on your left, you'll find this refreshingly down-to-earth Chinese diner: *rāmen, gyōza, mābō tōfu, chā-han* (fried rice) with excellent-value set menus (*sābisu teishoku*, ¥750). But the sweet, friendly staff speak no English and the menu's in Japanese. How are your language skills?

Osanai SEAFOOD ¥¥
(食事処おさない; 1-1-17 Shinmachi; dishes from ¥400; ⏰7am-9.30pm Tue-Sun) At the start of Shinmachi-dōri, this popular haunt specialises in *hotate* (scallops) – fried, steamed, in noodles – you name it. Of the more interesting menu items, *marucchi tsumire soba* features dumplings made from apple and scallops on hot *soba* noodles (¥550), and *ringo* (apple) *gyōza* (¥400).

Aomori

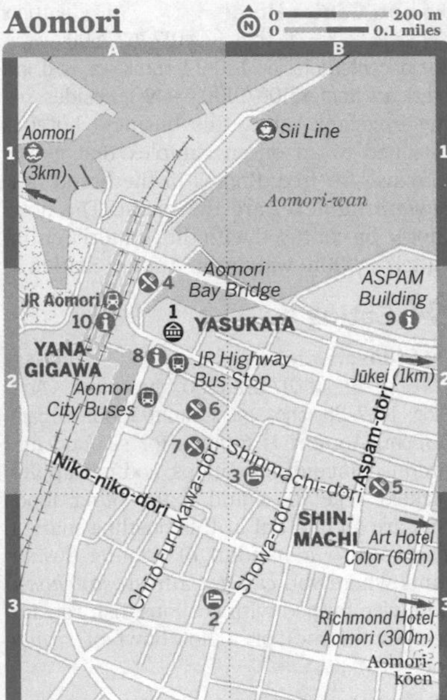

Aomori

Sights

1 Nebuta no Ie Wa Rasse A2

Sleeping

2 Aomori Center Hotel A3
3 Hyper Hotels Passage B2

Eating

4 A-Factory A2
5 Aki B2
6 Osanai A2
7 Shinsen Ichiba A2

Information

8 Aomori Station Tourist Information Center A2
9 ASPAM Building B2
10 Shin-Aomori Station Tourist Information Center A2

Aki STEAK HOUSE ¥¥

(亜希; ☎017-722-3961; 2-1-16 Shinmachi; meals from ¥1100; ⊙11am-9pm Wed-Mon) We love the relaxed, unpretentious atmosphere inside this little steakhouse on the corner: nothing's changed much in 30 years. Steak and *katsu* (crumbed cutlets) in all forms are on the menu. Pork *katsu teishoku* start at ¥1100, depending on your preferred cut of meat.

Information

Aomori City Hospital (青森市民病院; ☎24hr emergency hotline 017-734-2171; 1-14-20 Katsuda; ⊙outpatient services 9am-5pm Mon-Fri) The hospital is 3km southeast of the train station, off Rte 103.

Aomori Station Tourist Information Center (青森市観光交流情報センター; ☎017-723-4670; www.city.aomori.aomori.jp/contents/english; ⊙8.30am-7pm) Everything you need to know about Aomori city and prefecture, in English.

Shin-Aomori Station Tourist Information Center (あおもり観光情報センター; ☎017-752-6311; ⊙8.30am-7pm) On the 2nd floor of the Shinkansen terminus; ask here for info on all things Aomori and for journeys north to Hokkaido.

Getting There & Away

AIR

From Aomori Airport, 11km south of the city centre, there are flights to and from Tokyo, Osaka, Sapporo and Seoul. Airport buses are timed for flights and depart from stop 11 in front of Aomori Station (¥700, 40 minutes).

BOAT

Sii Line (シィライン; ☎017-722-4545; www.sii-line.co.jp) ferries depart twice daily for Wakinosawa (¥2610, one hour) from Aomori-kō Ryokyaku Fune Terminal (青森港旅客船ターミナル).

Tsugaru Kaikyō (津軽海峡; ☎017-766-4733; www.tsugarukaikyo.co.jp) operates eight ferries daily between Aomori and Hakodate (from ¥2220, four hours) year round. Ferries depart from Aomori Ferry Terminal (青森フェリーターミナル) on the western side of the city, a 10-minute taxi ride from Aomori Station (about ¥1600).

BUS

JR highway buses connect Aomori to Sendai (¥5800, five hours) and Tokyo (from ¥8600, 9½ hours).

Buses depart from stop 11 for Hakkōda (¥1090, 50 minutes) and Towada-ko (¥3090, three hours); schedules vary seasonally and run infrequently during winter. Some English schedules are found on www.jrbustohoku.co.jp

CAR & MOTORCYCLE

The **Tōhoku Expressway** (東北自動車道) runs between Tokyo and greater Aomori.

Toyota Rent a Car (トヨタレンタカー; ☎782-0100; http://rent.toyota.co.jp/en/index.html; 104-79 Takama, Ishie; ⊙8am-10pm) can be found outside the west exit of the Shin-Aomori *shinkansen* (bullet train) station and has branches a few blocks from Aomori station.

TRAIN

The Tōhoku *shinkansen* runs roughly every hour from Tokyo Station, by way of Sendai and Morioka, to the terminus at Shin-Aomori Station (¥17,350, 3½ hours).

Futsū (local) trains on the JR Ōu main line connect Aomori with Shin-Aomori (¥190, five minutes) and Hirosaki (¥670, 45 minutes). A few JR Tsugaru *tokkyū* (limited express) trains run daily between Aomori and Akita (¥5080, 2¾ hours) on the same line.

Hourly *tokkyū* trains run on the JR Tsugaru-Kaikyō line between Aomori and Hakodate on Hokkaidō (¥4970, two hours), via the Seikan Tunnel.

One daily *kaisoku* express train on the JR Ōminato line connects Aomori and Shimokita (¥2700, 1½ hours). Otherwise, take a *futsū* train on the private Aoimori Tetsudō line and transfer at Noheji for the JR Ōminato line (¥2180, 1¾ hours).

Getting Around

Shuttle buses (one ride/day pass ¥200/500) circle the city, connecting Shin-Aomori Station, Aomori Station, Aomori Ferry Terminal and most city sights. They may be less direct than regular municipal buses, but are the most economical way to get around the city.

Hirosaki 弘前

0172 / POP 181,000

Established in the feudal era by the Tsugaru clan, the sprawling, historic town of Hirosaki, in the shadow of majestic, Fuji-esque Iwaki-san, remains one of Tōhoku's principal cultural centres, although it faded in prominence after political power shifted to Aomori. The area around Hirosaki station has been lovingly redeveloped, but in other parts of the city, many older structures remain intact but run-down, leaving huge potential for inspiring restorations. Either way, it's a photographer's paradise. Surrounded by farmlands and with some wonderful parks and groves of cherry trees, the area is also Japan's biggest producer of apples.

Sights

★Hirosaki-kōen PARK

(弘前公園) Perfect for picnicking, this enormous public park has been shaped over the centuries by three castle moats, and landscaped with overhanging cherry trees (more than 5000 in total!) that bloom in late April or early May. The remains of **Hirosaki-jō** (弘前城; admission ¥300; 9am-5pm Apr-Nov) lie at the heart of the park; the castle burnt to the ground just 16 years after it was built in 1611.

Chōshō-ji BUDDHIST TEMPLE

(長勝寺; 0172-32-0813; 1-23-8 Nishi-Shigemori; admission ¥300; 9am-4pm) A 10-minute walk southwest of Hirosaki-jō ruins brings you to an atmospheric temple district redolent of feudal times. At the top of the hill, Chōshō-ji comprises the oldest wooden building in Aomori-ken and rows of mausoleums built for the rulers of the Tsugaru clan. Views of Iwaki-san from the imposing stupa to the right of the main temple building are inspiring.

Fujita Memorial Garden GARDEN

(藤田記念庭園; 0172-37-5525; 8-1 Kamishirogane; adult/child ¥310/100; 9am-5pm Tue-Sun Apr-Nov) The former home and garden of the wealthy Fujita family, this beautiful example of a manicured Japanese garden is the second largest in Tōhoku. It features a wonderful teahouse and Western-styled Meiji-era mansion, which now serves as a cafe, replete with grand piano.

Apple Park PARK

(リンゴ公園; 0172-36-7439; www.hi-it.jp/~ringo-kouen; Shimizu Tomita Aza Terasawa 125, Hirosaki City) In season, an excursion to this working orchard, in full view of regal Iwaki-san, is fun for everyone. Pick as many apples as you can carry (2kg for ¥200) – they're goooood! It's possible to ride bikes here, but driving or catching the bus from the station can be a better option: check the homepage for details.

Neputa Mura BUILDING

(ねぷた村; 0172-39-1511; 61 Kamenoko-machi; adult/child ¥550/350; 9am-5pm) Come here to see some of Hirosaki's Neputa floats and try your hand at the giant *taiko* (drums). There are also exhibitions of local crafts. It's a short walk from the Bunka Center stop on the Dote-machi Loop Bus.

Festivals & Events

Hirosaki Castle Snow Lantern Festival LIGHT SHOW

In Hirosaki park, over 200 snow lanterns and 300 miniature igloos light up the winter night. Held in February.

Hirosaki

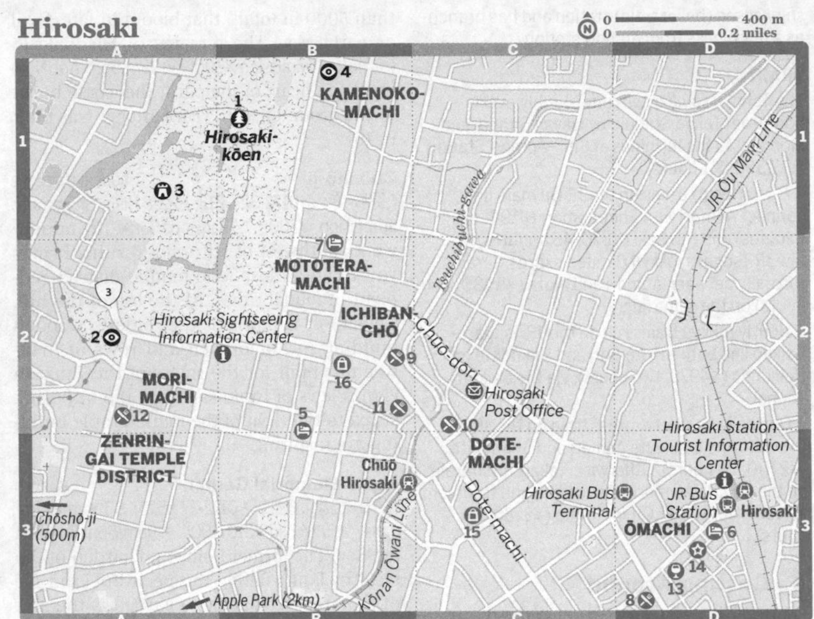

Hirosaki Neputa Matsuri CULTURAL
(弘前ねぷたまつり) Hirosaki's Neputa Matsuri is famous for the illuminated floats parading each evening to the accompaniment of flutes and drums. The festival is considered to signify ceremonial preparation for battle, expressing sentiments of bravery for what lies ahead and heartache for what lies behind. Held from 1 to 7 August.

Oyama-sankei FESTIVAL
In mid-September, area farmers gather for an annual moonlit pilgrimage to the peak of Iwaki-san, where they pray for a bountiful harvest.

Sleeping

★Ishiba Ryokan RYOKAN ¥
(石場旅館; ☎0172-32-9118; www.ishibaryokan.com; 55 Mototera-machi; r per person from ¥4860; P) This labyrinthine, late-19th-century wooden ryokan on a busy street boasts well-maintained tatami rooms (some have private facilities, most overlook a small garden) and a casual, warm vibe. Helpful hosts speak English and some French. Meals and rental bicycles are available. Excellent value for an authentic experience.

Dormy Inn Hirosaki HOTEL ¥¥
(ドーミーイン弘前; ☎0172-37-5489; www.hotespa.net/hotels/hirosaki; 71-1 Honmachi; s/d from ¥6790/10,390) On a hill near Hirosaki Kōen and a bunch of historic sites, this popular hotel has clean, functional rooms, rooftop onsen and *rotemburo* and great views from higher floors. The breakfast buffet is good value. It's a short taxi ride from the station.

Hotel Naqua City Hirosaki HOTEL ¥¥¥
(ホテルナクアシティ弘前; ☎0172-37-0700; www.naquacity-hirosaki.com; 1-1-2 Ōmachi; s/d/tw from ¥6000/7000/10,000; P ⊗ @ ≋ 👪) Rebranded in 2014 (formerly the Best Western), this stylish international-standard hotel is conveniently adjacent Hirosaki Station. Rooms are large by Japanese standards and higher floors afford stunning views of princely Iwaki-san. If you're in the mood for romancin', why not splurge on a stylish, minimalist, freshly refurbished junior suite.

Eating

★Kadare Yokochō FOOD COURT ¥
(かだれ横丁; ☎0172-38-2256; www.kadare.info; 2-1 Hyakkoku-machi; ⊙11am-2am; 🖉) The facade of this nondescript office building (marked by the lanterns out front) deceptively hides a dozen food stalls hawking everything from

Hirosaki

Top Sights
1 Hirosaki-kōen B1

Sights
2 Fujita Memorial Garden A2
3 Hirosaki-jō A1
4 Neputa Mura B1

Sleeping
5 Dormy Inn Hirosaki B2
6 Hotel Naqua City Hirosaki D3
7 Ishiba Ryokan B2

Eating
8 Curry House Hōryū D3
9 Kadare Yokochō B2
10 Kikufuji C2
11 Manchan B2
12 Rairai-ken A2

Drinking & Nightlife
13 Robbin's Nest D3

Entertainment
14 Live House Yamauta D3

Shopping
15 Corrina Corrina C3
16 Tanaka-ya B2

fried noodles to Nepalese curry. It's a lively local hangout. **Hinata-bokko** (日向ぼっこ), with the orange *noren* curtains, is particularly recommended, turning out excellent renditions of *hotate misoyaki* (grilled scallops in miso; ¥600) and *ikamenchi* (fried minced squid; ¥400).

Curry House Hōryū CURRY ¥
(カレーハウス芳柳; ☎0172-33-2189; 2-1-2 Ōmachi; meals ¥600-800; ⏰11am-3pm & 5-8.30pm) Open since 1968 (and they never seem to close), the sweet, creamy curries served up in this humble dining room with only two tables, are moreish. The menu is easy to understand: there are only six choices and a daily special – all curry. We're not sure that the vegie curry doesn't have meat in the stock, but it's delicious. Enquire within.

Rairai-ken CHINESE ¥
(来々軒; ☎0172-32-4828; 16 Ōaza Shigemori-machi; dishes from ¥580; ⏰11am-3pm & 5-9pm Fri-Wed) Despite appearing lonely on its corner near Hirosaki-kōen, this neat little Chinese restaurant is cheery, and cheap! Serving all sorts, from chilli prawns *(ebi-chiri)* to stir-fried vegies *(yasai itame)* and *yaki-soba* (*soba* noodle stir-fry), it's best known for tasty soups, *rāmen* bowls, *gyōza* (and beer).

Manchan CAFE ¥
(万茶ン; ☎0172-35-4663; 36-6 Dote-machi; dessert from ¥600; ⏰11am-6.30pm) Among Hirosaki's numerous coffee shops, this one has the longest history. In business since 1929, it's said to be the oldest in Tōhoku. Once a hangout for the local literati, it's now a lovely spot to sample another Hirosaki speciality: apple pie. Look for the bifurcated cello out front.

Kikufuji JAPANESE ¥¥
(菊富士; ☎0172-36-3300; www.kikufuji.co.jp; 1 Sakamoto-chō; meals from ¥900; ⏰11am-3.30pm & 5-9pm) A variety of set meals and a picture menu make sampling the local cuisine a piece of cake. There's also an extensive list of Aomori sake, which you can try in an *otameshi* (sampler) set of three. Paper lanterns and folk music add atmosphere without being kitschy. Look for the vertical white sign out front.

Drinking & Entertainment

Robbin's Nest PUB
(ロビンズネスト; ☎090-6450-1730; www.robbins-nest.jp; 1-3-16 Ōmachi; ⏰5pm-late) This is an excellent Japanese rendition of a British pub: it's intimate, there's no cover charge (except sometimes when bands are playing), frequent live music, Guinness on tap and a few tables out front (in warmer months) for alfresco drinking.

Live House Yamauta LIVE MUSIC
(ライブハウス山唄; ☎0172-36-1835; www.yamauta.com; 1-2-4 Ōmachi; music ¥800, dinner from ¥3000; ⏰5-11pm, closed alternate Mon) Nightly performances include traditional folk songs and spirited solo improvisation. The dinner course is a good deal, but you can also just sit at the counter with a drink. There's an English sign out front.

Shopping

Tanaka-ya CRAFTS
(田中屋; ☎0172-33-6666; www.tugarunuri.jp; Ichibanchō-kado; ⏰10am-7pm) Tanaka-ya deals in high-grade works by local artisans. The prices aren't cheap, but even if you're not looking to buy, it's worth stopping in for a

peek at the boldly coloured *tsugaru-nuri* (lacquerware of the Tsugaru region), produced in-house.

Corrina Corrina CLOTHING
(コリーナ・コリーナ; ☎0172-32-9878; 133-2 Dote-machi; ⊙11.30am-8pm Fri-Wed) Hippies, hipsters, rockabillies, skaters and wannabees alike will appreciate this eclectic collection of new and used Western clothes, shoes and accessories from around the world at reasonable prices. Seriously cool.

ℹ Information

Hirosaki Post Office (弘前郵便局; 18-1 Kita Kawarake-chō; ⊙post 9am-7pm Mon-Fri, to 3pm Sat, ATM 8am-9pm Mon-Fri, 9am-7pm Sat & Sun) An international ATM is available here.

Hirosaki Sightseeing Information Center (弘前市立観光館; ☎0172-37-5501; www.en-hirosaki.com; 2-1 Shimoshirogane-chō; ⊙9am-6pm) Situated inside the Kankōkan (tourism building), you can rent bikes and grab all manner of English-language materials here. Be sure to check out the plaza and surrounds.

Hirosaki Station Tourist Information Center (弘前市観光案内所; ☎0172-26-3600; ⊙8.45am-6pm) On the ground floor of Hirosaki Station. The best way to see the city is by bicycle – rent them here for an hour or all day for (¥500) and return by 5pm. Very helpful staff.

ℹ Getting There & Around

Tokkyū (limited express) trains on the JR Ōu main line run hourly between Aomori and Hirosaki (¥1180, 35 minutes), and Hirosaki and Akita (¥3930, two hours).

The Tsugaru free pass (adult/child ¥2060/1030) covers area buses and trains, including those that go out to Iwaki-san and Shirakami-sanchi, for two consecutive days. Enquire at the Hirosaki Station Tourist Information Center.

The Dote-machi Loop Bus (¥100 per ride), which circuits the downtown area, leaves from in front of Aomori Station.

Bicycle rental (¥500, 9am to 5pm) is available at either tourist information centre from May through to November.

Towada-ko 十和田湖

☎0176 / POP 6000

Formed by a series of violent volcanic eruptions, Towada-ko, within the Towada-Hachimantai National Park is the largest crater lake in Honshū (52km in circumference), hemmed in by rocky coastlines and dense forests. Just as beautiful, its tributary, the Oirase *keiryū* (mountain stream), winds its way to the Pacific Ocean. Even today, development around the lake remains refreshingly sparse, but for the main tourist hub of Yasumiya. It's easy to feel like you're the only one around.

WORTH A TRIP

IWAKI-SAN & SHIRAKAMI-SANCHI

Looming over Hirosaki, sacred Iwaki-san (Mt Iwaki; 岩木山; 1625m) looks remarkably like Fuji-san from certain angles and at times seems so close you could almost touch it. Should you wish to, daily buses depart the Hirosaki Station bus terminal for **Iwaki-san-jinja** (岩木山神社; ¥720, 40 minutes, April to October), where tradition dictates summit-bound travellers should first make an offering before attempting the ascent. The views from the top are remarkable. A different trail takes you down, past the smaller peak of **Tori-no-umi-san** (鳥ノ海山) to the village of **Dake-onsen** (岳温泉) from where infrequent buses chug back to Hirosaki (¥1050, one hour). The entire 9km hike should take you about seven hours.

If you *were* wondering, Iwaki-san's last recorded eruption was in 1863.

Southwest of Iwaki-san is the isolated **Shirakami-sanchi** (白神山地), a Unesco-protected virgin forest of Japanese beech trees. From the bus stop at Anmon Aqua Village, an hour-long trail leads into the woods to the three **Anmon Falls** (暗門の滝; Anmon-no-taki), the longest of which is 42m. This is part of the park's 'buffer zone', which is open to the public without a permit. Two buses depart Hirosaki Station bus terminal each morning for Anmon Aqua Village (one-way/return ¥1650/2500, 1½ hours, May to October) and two return in the afternoon.

Enquire at the helpful Hirosaki Sightseeing Information Center for maps and timetables if you intend to make either of these trips.

Activities

★Oirase Keiryū HIKING

(奥入瀬渓流) This meandering river is marked by cascading waterfalls, carved-out gorges and gurgling rapids. Casual hikers can follow its path for a 14km stretch connecting Nenokuchi, a small tourist outpost on the eastern shore of the lake, to Yakeyama, from where relatively frequent buses return to either Nenokuchi (¥660, 30 minutes) or the main tourist hub of Yasumiya (¥1100, one hour).

The entire hike should only take you about three hours. Set out in the early morning or late afternoon to avoid slow-moving coach parties.

Towada-ko BOAT TOUR

(十和田; ⌚8am-4pm) To get a sense of the lake's enormous scale, consider a 40-minute scenic cruise from Yasumiya (¥1440, April to November). A ferry also operates between Yasumiya and Nenokuchi (¥1400). You can also rent rowboats and paddleboats next to the dock.

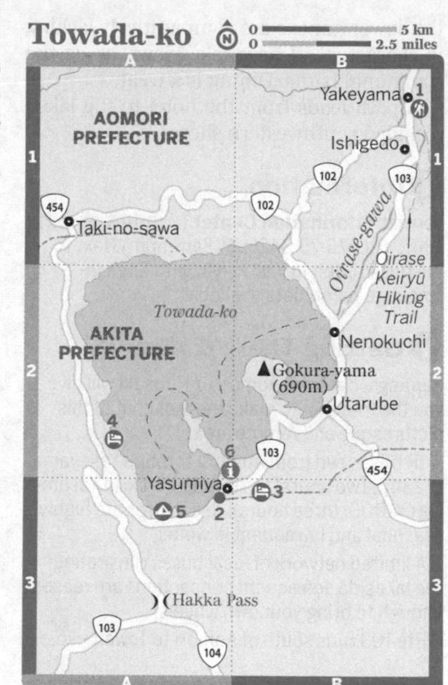

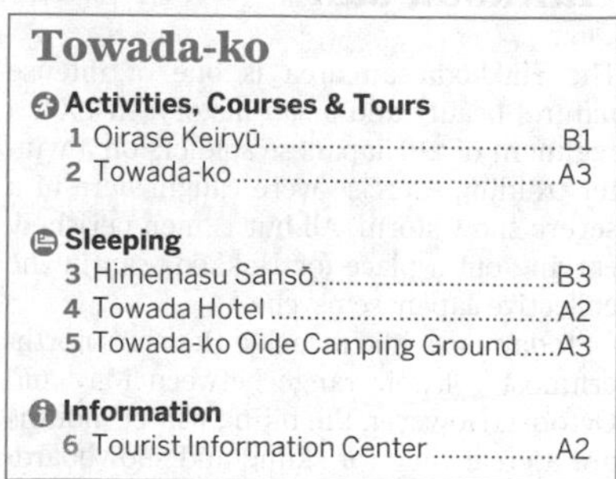

Towada-ko

Activities, Courses & Tours
1 Oirase Keiryū B1
2 Towada-ko A3

Sleeping
3 Himemasu Sansō B3
4 Towada Hotel A2
5 Towada-ko Oide Camping Ground A3

Information
6 Tourist Information Center A2

Sleeping

Hotel rates peak during August (summer holidays) and October, when autumn leaves blaze red.

Towada-ko Oide Camping Ground CAMPGROUND ¥

(十和田湖生出キャンプ場; ☎0176-75-2368; www.bes.or.jp/towada/camp.html; 486 Yasumiya, Towada-kohan; per person ¥300, campsite ¥200, powered sites ¥3000; ⌚25 Apr-5 Nov; Ⓟ) This pretty riverside campground has well-maintained facilities, and rental supplies are available.

Himemasu Sansō MINSHUKU ¥

(ひめます山荘; ☎0176-75-2717; http://himemasusanso.web.fc2.com; 16-15 Yasumiya, Towada-kohan; r per person ¥4400, with 2 meals ¥6500; Ⓟ) A number of the *minshuku* in Yasumiya have seen better days, but not this one. It has eight spotless tatami rooms, an onsen bath and filling spreads of home-cooked food. It's a 15-minute walk from the lake.

★Oirase Keiryū Hotel HOTEL ¥¥

(奥入瀬渓流ホテル; ☎0176-74-2121; www.oirase-keiryuu.jp; 231 Tochikubo, Oirase; r per person with 2 meals from ¥14,500; Ⓟ📶) This stunningly renovated hotel by the trailhead for the Oirase Keiryū hike, has both Japanese- and Western-style rooms and a string of riverside onsen baths. The standout feature is the cavernous dining hall, with picture windows edging the forest and sloping eaves of panelled hardwood. Free transfers from Shin-Aomori station are available: book in advance.

Towada Hotel HOTEL ¥¥

(十和田ホテル; ☎0176-75-1122; www.towada-hotel.com; Namariyama, Towada-ko, Kosaka-machi; r per person with 2 meals from ¥15,500; Ⓟ) The pre-WWII Towada Hotel has a dramatic lobby of hulking timbers, rising to a chandelier-lit cathedral ceiling. The historic main building has elegantly refurbished Japanese-style rooms (with and without baths) whereas the Western-style rooms in the newer annexe are comparatively lacking in character. All have lake views, as do the communal baths. Dining is a treat.

A path leads from the hotel to the lake's secluded southwestern shore.

Information

Tourist Information Center (十和田湖総合案内所; ☎0176-75-2425; ⊙8am-5pm) Next to the bus station in Yasumiya, with English-language pamphlets available.

Getting There & Away

Renting a car from Aomori or Hirosaki will give you the freedom to make the most out of this picturesque and remote area.

JR buses run from Aomori, through Yakeyama (¥2340, two hours) to Towada-ko-eki in Yasumiya (¥1000, three hours); departures are highly seasonal and infrequent in winter.

A limited network of local buses run around the lakeside. Infrequent connections are reason enough to bring your own wheels.

Rte 103 runs south of Aomori to Towada-ko.

Hakkōda-san 八甲田山

☎017

The Hakkōda-san area is one of intense natural beauty and a sad history: in 1902 a regiment of 210 Japanese soldiers on a winter training exercise were caught here in a severe snow storm. All but 11 men perished, carving out a place for Hakkōda-san in the collective Japanese psyche.

Today, most hikers tackle Honshū's northernmost volcanic range between May and October. However, the biting winter months are a great time for skiing and snowboarding. Even if you do catch a chill, take comfort in the fact that Hakkōda-san is home to one of Tōhoku's best onsen, Sukayu.

Sights

Hakkōda Ropeway ROPEWAY

(八甲田山ロープウェー; ☎017-738-0343; www.hakkoda-ropeway.jp; 1-12 Kansuizawa, Arakawa; one-way/return ¥1180/1850; ⊙9am-4.20pm) For anyone who wants a taste of the alpine without having to brave the steep ascent, this scenic ropeway quickly whisks you up to the summit of Tamoyachi-dake (田茂萢岳; 1324m). From there, you can follow an elaborate network of hiking trails, although purists prefer the magnificent one-day loop that starts and finishes just outside the Sukayu Onsen Ryokan.

Activities

★**Hakkōda-san** HIKING

(八甲田山) Hakkōda-san's gruelling but rewarding 12km day-return hike begins near Sukayu Ryokan, in the shadow of **Ōdake** (大岳; 1584m). The ridge trail continues to **Ido-dake** (井戸岳; 1550m) and **Akakura-dake** (赤倉岳; 1548m) before connecting with **Tamoyachi-dake** (田茂萢岳; 1326m) and looping via the ropeway to Sukaya Ryokan.

Things start out relatively flat as you wind through marshlands, but eventually the pitch starts to increase: a good level of fitness and some hiking experience is recommended.

Hakkōda Ski Park SNOW SPORTS

(八甲田スキー場; ☎017-738-0343; www.hakkoda-ropeway.jp; 5-ride pass ¥5050; ⊙9am-4.20pm) Modest Tamoyachi-dake has only two official runs (intermediate) beginning at the top of the Hakkōda Ropeway. The longer of the two, the 5km Forest Course, cuts through the treeline and has a few steep and speedy pitches. The pluses: powder-a-plenty and zero crowding, for serious players. Note that weather conditions can suddenly become severe and getting lost is easy.

Come spring, it's possible to explore a network of unofficial trails that extend to some of the nearby peaks. Even experienced alpinists should only go back-country with a local guide. Equipment rental (¥3500 per day) and a handful of dining options are available in the Ropeway terminals.

Sleeping

Sukayu Camping Ground CAMPGROUND ¥

(酸ヶ湯キャンプ場; ☎017-738-6566; www.sukayu.jp/camp; camping per person ¥500, campsites from ¥500; ⊙late Jun–late Oct; Ⓟ) A good spot to pitch a tent, with clean facilities and rental supplies, located at the end of a small access road immediately south of Sukayu Onsen Ryokan.

★**Sukayu Onsen Ryokan** RYOKAN ¥¥

(酸ヶ湯温泉; ☎017-738-6400; www.sukayu.jp; r per person with 2 meals from ¥11,000, day bathing ¥610; ⊙day bathing 7am-5.30pm; Ⓟ) Straight from an *ukiyo-e* (woodblock print), Sukayu's cavernous, dark-wooded bathhouse is a delight for the senses. The water is hot, acidic and sulphurous (don't get it in your eyes); nothing beats the feel of its penetrating heat. Note that the main bath is *konyoku* (mixed bathing). Rooms in the sprawling

DON'T MISS

AONI ONSEN

You can't get much more rustic, romantic and isolated than **Rampu-no-yado** (ランプの宿; ☎0172-54-8588; www.yo.rim.or.jp/~aoni/index.html; 1-7 Aoni-sawa, Taki-no-ue, Okiura, Kuroishi; r per person with 2 meals from ¥9870, day bathing ¥520; ⏲day bathing 10am-3pm; P) in little Aoni Onsen (青荷温泉). Plopped in a deep valley, surrounded by heavily forested mountains, it's the ultimate escape from civilisation and the present day: oil lamps *(rampu)* are used to light all rooms and corridors. There are no power outlets or wi-fi in the basic tatami rooms. As the sun goes down and the stars come out over the valley, the effect is magical. Have your camera and tripod at the ready.

More magical are the numerous indoor baths and *rotemburo*, spread over several small wooden buildings along both sides of a stream, crossed by a footbridge. With the lack of distractions, you'll have plenty of time to soak and think about what's important.

Dining is a delicious and communal affair, featuring hearty, healthy, mostly vegetarian, locavore cuisine.

Aoni Onsen is located alongside Rte 102 between Hirosaki and Towada-ko. Getting here requires effort or a rental car. Without one, take the private Kōnan Tetsudō line from Hirosaki to Kuroishi (¥440, 30 minutes); connect with a Kōnan bus for Niji-no-ko (¥770, 30 minutes) from where shuttle buses run to Aoni (free, 30 minutes, four daily). From December through March, the narrow lane that winds down to Aoni Onsen is closed to private vehicles; if you're coming by car, park at the Niji-no-ko bus station and catch the free shuttle bus.

Advance reservations are essential.

old-fashioned inn are simple but comfortable, with shared facilities.

Hakkōda-sansō LODGE ¥¥

(八甲田山荘; ☎017-728-1512; www.hakkoda-sanso.com; 1-61 Kansuizawa, Arakawa; r per person ¥5000, with 2 meals ¥9000; P) At the base of the Hakkōda Ropeway, this is the quintessential Japanese skier's lodge. Basic tatami rooms (shared facilities) each have their own TV and overlook the mountain. The dining area, with picture windows facing the peak, also serves lunch.

Hakkōda Hotel HOTEL ¥¥¥

(八甲田ホテル; ☎017-728-2000; www.hakkodahotel.co.jp; 1 Minami-arakawayama, Arakawa; r per person with 2 meals from ¥26,000) The rates for this lovely, woodsy lodge aren't this high for the quality of its amenities, but more for the size of its rooms and its proximity to some of the country's best back-country explorations. This is one for hungry powder-hounds in the winter and hikers in the summer.

Getting There & Away

JR buses leave from stop 11 outside Aomori Station, stopping at Hakkōda Ropeway-eki (¥1100, 50 minutes) and the next stop, Sukayu Onsen (¥1350, one hour). The bus continues to Towada-ko-eki (¥2070, 1½ hours). Bus schedules vary seasonally.

Shimokita Peninsula
下北半島

☎0175 / POP 100,000

Remote, axe-shaped Shimokita-hantō is centred on **Osore-zan** (恐山; 874m), a barren volcano that is regarded as one of the most sacred places in all of Japan. 'Osore', meaning 'fear', is an appropriate name, given that the peak is said to represent Buddhist purgatory. With flocks of jet-black ravens swarming about its sulphur-infused tributaries, it's not too hard to make the metaphysical leap.

There are three main towns on the peninsula: Mutsu (first if arriving by car or train), Wakinosawa (if arriving by ferry) and Ōma, the furthest point north on the Japanese mainland – get here by car or bus. Either way, it's a long, slow ride.

Sights & Activities

★ **Osorezan-bodaiji** BUDDHIST TEMPLE

(恐山菩提寺; ☎0175-22-3825; admission ¥500; ⏲6am-6pm May-Oct) This holy shrine at Osore-zan's summit is a moving, mesmerisingly atmospheric and beautiful place honouring Jizō Bosatsu, protector of children and a much-loved deity in Japanese mythology. It's also said to be located at the entrance to hell: a small brook that flows

ŌMA TUNA

Ōma, at the tip of the Shimokita Peninsula, may look like the end of the earth, but it's the centre of the universe when it comes to tuna. The frigid waters of the Tsugaru Strait, directly off the coast, are said to yield the tastiest *maguro* (bluefin tuna) in Japan. At the height of the season, a prize catch can sell for ¥25,000/kg.

Ōma's fishing co-ops catch fish the old-fashioned way, with hand lines and live bait (and a lot of muscle – these fish are enormous). It's a way of life that sets them squarely against large-scale commercial interests and in favour of greater regulation to protect the bluefin population.

Tuna is caught fresh between late August and January, although most shops close up by mid-November when the cold winds turn fierce.

into the beautiful crater lake, Usori, is said to represent the legendary Sanzu river, which souls must cross on their way to the afterlife. Fittingly, people visit mourning lost children or seeking to commune with the dead.

Several stone statues of Jizō overlook hills of craggy, sulphur-strewn rocks and hissing vapour. Visitors are encouraged to help lost souls with their underworld penance by adding stones to the cairns. You can even bathe on hell's doorstep at the free onsen off to the side as you approach the main hall. Allow an hour or two to wander the landscape in deep contemplation.

Hotoke-ga-ura BOAT TOUR
(仏ヶ浦) The western edge of the peninsula is a spectacular stretch of coastline dotted with 100m-high wind-carved cliffs, which are said to resemble images of Buddha. Boats depart for sightseeing round-trips from Wakinosawa to Hotoke-ga-ura between April and October at 10.45am and 2.55pm (¥3900, two hours). Services are often suspended in poor weather.

Festivals & Events

Osore-zan Taisai SPIRITUAL
(恐山大祭) These two annual festivals attract huge crowds of people, who come to consult *itako* (mediums) in order to contact deceased family members. Held from 20 to 24 July and 9 to 11 October.

Sleeping & Eating

★ Wakinosawa Youth Hostel HOSTEL ¥
(脇野沢ユースホステル; ☎0175-44-2341; www.wakinosawa.com; 41 Senokawame, Wakinosawa; dm ¥3900, breakfast/dinner ¥630/1050; P⊖📶) This standout hostel is perched on a hillside at Wakinosawa village, about 15 minutes west of the ferry pier – call ahead for a pick-up if you don't have a car. Western and Japanese dorms are available, adorned with rich hardwoods and country furnishings. While it helps to speak a bit of Japanese, the genial owners are extremely accommodating and will help you spot the local snow monkeys.

Plaza Hotel Mutsu HOTEL ¥¥
(プラザホテルむつ; ☎0175-23-7111; www.ph-m.jp; 2-46 Shimokita-chō, Mutsu; s/tw from ¥5700/9000; ⊖@📶) A bit dated, but comfortable enough, this hotel is a two-minute walk from Shimokita Station. Look for the brick-coloured (but not brick) building.

Sun Hotel Ōma HOTEL ¥¥
(サンホテル大間; ☎0175-37-2001; 2 Okoppe shita-michi, Ōma; s/d from ¥5500/7800) If you make it this far north and haven't got the energy to drive or bus all the way back down, this simple business hotel does the trick. It ain't the Ritz, but it won't break the bank either.

Kaikyōsō SUSHI ¥¥
(海峡荘; ☎0175-37-3691; 17-734 Ōma-taira, Ōma; meals from ¥1100; ⏲11am-3pm late Apr–early Nov) Here in Ōma, tuna is served literally sea-to-table, and you can see the locals barbecuing fish heads on the street. Kaikyōsō, in the bright green building, does a *maguro-don* (tuna sashimi over rice) with thick melt-in-your-mouth cuts of *akami* (lean red meat), *chū-toro* (medium-grade fatty tuna) and ohhhhhhh, *ō-toro* (top-grade fatty tuna). If you've come this far, go for the good stuff…

Getting There & Away

BOAT

Sii Line (p532) operates two daily ferries between Wakinosawa and Aomori (¥2610, one hour).

Tsugaru Kaikyō (p532) runs two to three ferries daily from Ōma to Hakodate on Hokkaidō (from ¥1810, 1¾ hours).

BUS

From May to October, there are up to five buses departing from Shimokita Station for Osore-zan (¥750, 45 minutes). Year-round, buses connect Shimokita and Ōma (¥1990, two hours). There are a few buses each day to Wakinosawa from Ōminato Station (¥1800, 70 minutes).

TRAIN

One daily *kaisoku* express train on the JR Ōminato line connects Aomori, Shimokita and Ōminato (¥2700, 1½ hours).

Otherwise, take a *futsū* train on the private Aoimori Tetsudō line from Aomori and transfer at Noheji for the JR Ōminato line (¥2180, 1¾ hours).

IWATE PREFECTURE

Japan's second-largest prefecture, Iwate-ken (岩手県) is a quiet place, largely characterised by sleepy valleys, a rugged coastline and some pretty serious mountain ranges. Although the region once played host to warring states and feudal rule, there are few remnants of this turbulent past, aside from the magnificent temples at Hiraizumi. Indeed, Iwate feels more provincial – in the best of ways – and stopping in places like the Tōno valley, which influenced a rich collection of folk tales, can feel almost like turning back time.

Morioka 盛岡

019 / POP 298,400

Morioka is a pretty, former castle-town framed by three flowing rivers and a brooding volcano, Iwate-san. Once the seat of the Nanbu domain, it is now the prefectural capital and a regional transport hub. Though the castle itself is long gone, the park in its place and surrounding area make for a pleasant stroll. Morioka is also famous for its cast-iron artisan work and an obsession with noodles. Must. Eat. Here.

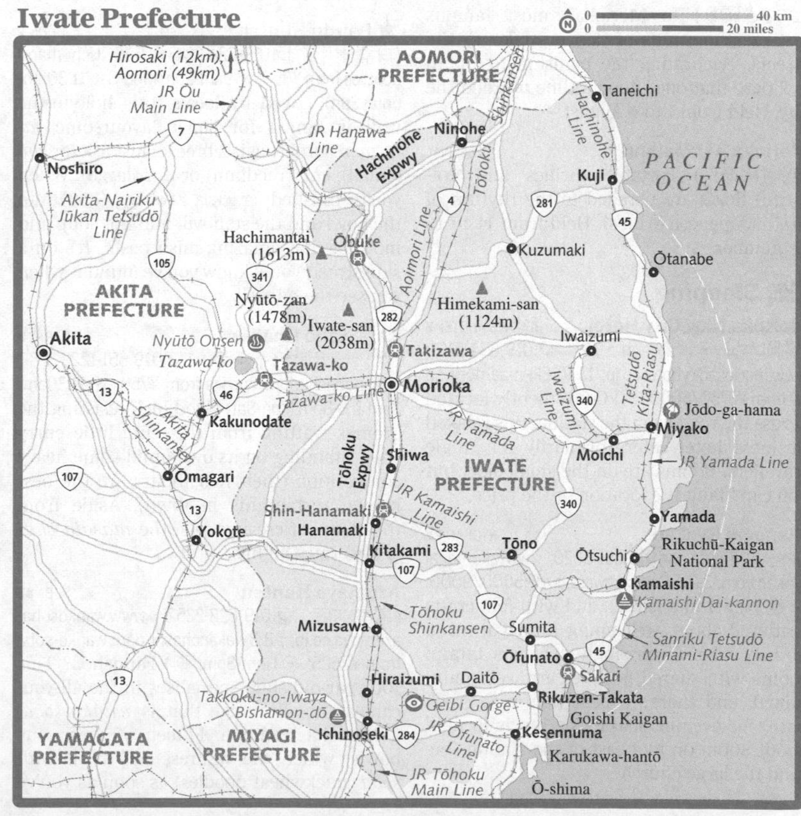

Sights

Iwate-kōen PARK
(岩手公園) If you head east on foot from the station along Kaiun-bashi for about 20 minutes, you'll eventually come to this landscaped park, where Morioka-jō once stood. All that remains of the castle, completed in 1633 and destroyed in 1874, are its moss-covered stone foundation walls. Still, you can get a sense of its scale.

Rock-Splitting Cherry Tree LANDMARK
(石割桜, Ishiwari-zakura) A few blocks north of Iwate-kōen, in front of the Morioka District Court, is this much-loved local attraction: a 300-year-old cherry tree, which sprouted from the crack in a huge granite boulder. Some claim that it has pushed its way through over time, and while that's clearly an impossible feat, it's nevertheless a sight to behold.

Festivals & Events

Sansa Odori DANCE
(さんさ踊り) In Morioka's most famous festival, thousands of dancers take to the streets, celebrating the banishment of an evil ogre that once upon a time plagued the city. Held from 1 to 4 August.

Morioka Aki Matsuri FESTIVAL
(盛岡秋祭り) Portable shrines and colourful floats are paraded to the rhythm of *taiko* (Japanese drums). Held from 14 to 16 September.

Sleeping

Morioka New City Hotel BUSINESS HOTEL ¥
(盛岡ニューシティホテル; ☎019-654-5161; www.moriokacityhotel.co.jp; 13-10 Eki-mae-dōri; s/tw from ¥3750/6000; 📶) Conveniently located across the road from the station, this relaxed business hotel caters primarily for single travellers. Rooms are on the small side, but you can't fault the location or the price.

Kumagai Ryokan RYOKAN ¥¥
(熊ヶ井旅館; ☎019-651-3020; www.kumagairyokan.com; 3-2-5 Ōsawakawara; s/d ¥5000/9000; 🚭@📶) Set in a garden and with folk crafts scattered about, welcoming Kumagai has a homely vibe. Surprisingly spacious tatami rooms with shared facilities are well maintained, and there's a neat *iwa-buro* (rock bath) for evening soaks. The inn is located about 800m on foot east of the station (behind the large church).

Daiwa Roynet Morioka HOTEL ¥¥
(ダイワロイネットホテル盛岡; ☎019-604-2155; www.daiwaroynet.jp/morioka; 1-8-10 Ō-dori; s/d from ¥7300/9800; 📶) Pleasant, modern rooms with a splash of colour and a good location, about 1km east of the station towards Iwate-kōen, make this a good choice if you're planning to explore.

Eating & Drinking

Short of changing trains, dining may be the standalone reason to make a stop here. Noodle fans should note that Morioka has some delicious and unusual varieties. Try *wanko-soba* (わんこそば), buckwheat noodles served by the mouthful in tiny wooden bowls: it's like a competition between you and the waitress, who tries to top up your bowl faster than you can say you're full.

Prefer to savour at your own pace? Go for *jaja-men* (じゃじゃめん), udon-like noodles heaped with cucumber, miso paste and ground meat – mix all this up and add vinegar, spicy oil and garlic to taste.

★**Pairon Honten** UDON ¥
(白龍本店; ☎019-624-2247; 5-15 Uchi-maru; noodles from ¥350; ⏰9am-9pm Mon-Sat, 11.30am-6pm Sun) Loved by locals, this hole-in-the wall is famed for super-flavoursome *jaja-men*. Ordering is a breeze: just ask for *shō* (small), *chū* (medium) or *dai* (large). When you're finished, crack a raw egg (¥50) into the bowl and the staff will add hot soup and more of that amazing miso paste. It's on a side-street; you'll know you've found it when you see the queue.

Karē Kōbō Chalten CURRY ¥
(カレー工房チャルテン; ☎019-651-1223; 1-8-1 Nakanohashi-dōri; curries from ¥750; ⏰11.30am-3pm & 6-8pm Mon-Sat) Good luck resisting the aromas wafting from this cute little curry shop, standing on its own amid some heavy competition (their neighbours are the best known restaurants in town). Aside from the range of creamy eats, the *masala chai* (¥400) rates highly.

Azumaya Honten SOBA ¥¥
(東屋本店; ☎019-622-2252; www.wankosoba-azumaya.co.jp; 1-8-3 Nakanohashi-dōri; wanko-soba from ¥2625; ⏰11am-8pm; 📋) Famished? This 100-year-old shop specialises in the all-you-can-eat noodle binge that is *wanko-soba*, a Morioka tradition. Fifteen of these tiny bowls, which the waitress will refill with *soba* (buckwheat noodles) as soon as you've

Morioka

Morioka

Sights
1 Iwate-kōen C2
2 Rock-Splitting Cherry Tree C1

Sleeping
3 Daiwa Roynet Morioka C1
4 Kumagai Ryokan B2
5 Morioka New City Hotel A1

Eating
6 Karē Kōbō Chalten D2
7 Azumaya Honten D2
8 Nepina's Kitchen Nirvana B1
9 Pairon Honten D2

Drinking & Nightlife
10 Fukakusa D2

Shopping
11 Kamasada Honten D2

put the last one down, is equivalent to one ordinary bowl – but the average customer will put away 50 (and 100 or 200 is not unheard of).

Nepina's Kitchen Nirvana INDIAN ¥¥
(ニルヴァーナ盛岡市大通本店; 019-626-5777; www.nirvanafoods.org/english; 2-7-22 Ō-dōri, 2F Ohara Bldg; dishes from ¥750; 11am-3pm & 5-11pm;) Not far from the station, there's an extensive menu of Nepalese and Indian delights from the tandoor in this cheery, popular diner – good for when you can't stomach another bowl of noodles! Dinner sets (from ¥1590) and all-you-can-drink specials (gosh!) are great value.

Fukakusa CAFE, BAR
(ふかくさ; 019-622-2353; 1-2 Konya-chō; coffee ¥350, beer ¥450; 11.30am-3pm & 5-11pm Mon-Sat, noon-5pm Sun) This little hideaway on the banks of the Nakatsu-gawa is the perfect place to stop for a pick-me-up or to unwind after a long afternoon. Look for the ivy out front.

Shopping

Gozaku, the area just east of the Nakatsu-gawa, is the old merchants' district, now home to craft studios and cafes.

Kamasada Honten HOMEWARES
(釜定本店; 019-622-3911; 2-5 Konya-chō; 9am-5.30pm Mon-Sat) Morioka is known for its *nanbu tekki* (cast ironware), notably tea kettles. There are some beautiful examples at this venerable old shop, along with more affordable items, like wind chimes and incense holders.

Information

Iwate Medical University Hospital (岩手医科大学附属病院; 24hr emergency hotline 019-651-5111; www.iwate-med.ac.jp/hospital; 19-1 Uchi-maru; outpatient services 8.30am-11am, 1-4pm Mon-Fri)

Morioka Central Post Office (盛岡中央郵便局; 019-624-5353; 1-13-45 Chūō-dōri; 9am-7pm Mon-Fri) An international ATM is available here.

Northern Tōhoku Tourism Center (北東北観光センター; 019-625-2090; 9am-5pm) Located on the 2nd floor of Morioka Station, with English speakers and help available to book accommodation.

Tourist Information Center (盛岡観光コンベンション協会; ☎019-604-3305; www.hello-morioka.jp; 2nd fl, Odette Plaza, 1-1-10 Nakanohashi-dōri; ⊙9am-6pm, closed 2nd Tue each month) The friendly staff near the Nakanohashi district speak some English and are happy to welcome you to Morioka.

Getting There & Away

BUS

Regional buses depart from outside the east exit of the train station, and connect Morioka with Sendai (¥2890, 2½ hours) and Hirosaki (¥2980, 2¼ hours). Night buses depart for Tokyo (¥7870, 7½ hours) from the east exit.

CAR & MOTORCYCLE

If you're driving, the Tōhoku Expressway (東北自動車道) runs between Tokyo and the greater Morioka area.

TRAIN

There are hourly *shinkansen* (bullet trains) on the JR Tōhoku line between Tokyo and Morioka (¥14,740, 2½ hours), and Morioka and Shin-Aomori (¥6130, 1¼ hours).

Frequent trains run on the JR Akita *shinkansen* line between Morioka and Akita (¥4620, 1½ hours) via Tazawa-ko (¥2030, 30 minutes) and Kakunodate (¥2840, 50 minutes). The local Tazawa-ko line covers the same route in about twice the time for around half the price; you may need to transfer at Ōmagari.

Getting Around

The charmingly named Dendenmushi ('electric transmission bug') tourist trolley makes a convenient loop around town, departing in a clockwise direction from stop 15 in front of Morioka Station (anticlockwise from stop 16) between 9am and 7pm. One ride costs ¥250, a day pass is ¥600.

Bicycles can be rented from **Sasaki Jitensha Shōkai** (佐々木自転車商会; ☎019-624-2692; 10-2 Morioka Eki-mae-dōri; per hour/day ¥200/1000; ⊙8.30am-6pm), near Morioka Station.

Hiraizumi 平泉

☎0191 / POP 8000

Hiraizumi's grandeur once rivalled that of Kyoto. From 1089 to 1189, three generations of the Ōshu Fujiwara clan used their gold-mining wealth to create a living paradise devoted to the principles of Buddhism. However, feudal strife brought these ambitions to an abrupt, tragic end. Today only a few sights bear testament to Hiraizumi's former glory, yet this pleasantly rural town remains one of Tōhoku's premier cultural attractions. Hiraizumi's sights were added to the Unesco World Heritage list in 2011.

History

Hiraizumi's fate is indelibly linked to that of Japan's favourite tragic hero, Minamoto-no-Yoshitsune. A great warrior, Yoshitsune earned the jealous contempt of his elder half-brother – Japan's first shogun, Minamoto-no-Yoritomo – and fled east, eventually taking refuge at Hiraizumi in 1187. This gave Yoritomo the perfect excuse to attack, resulting in both the defeat of the Ōshu Fujiwara and the death of Yoshitsune. Yoritomo was said to be so impressed with the temples of Hiraizumi that he allowed them to remain, and it was the Kamakura shogunate (military government) that later sponsored the construction of the first wooden hall to protect the Konjiki-dō mausoleum.

Sights & Activities

★Chūson-ji BUDDHIST TEMPLE
(中尊寺; ☎0191-46-2211; www.chusonji.or.jp/en; adult/child ¥800/300; ⊙9am-5pm) Established in AD 850 by the priest Ennin, the complex was expanded by the Ōshu Fujiwara family in the 12th century. A total of 300 buildings with 40 temples was constructed. Ironically, the family's grand scheme to build a Buddhist utopia was destroyed when a massive fire ravaged nearly everything in 1337. Only two of the original constructions, the **Konjiki-dō** (金色堂, Golden Hall; ⊙8am-4.30pm Apr-Oct, 8.30am-4pm Nov-Mar) and **Kyōzō** (経蔵; Sutra Repository), remain alongside more recent reconstructions. The sprawling site is reached via a steep cedar-lined avenue.

Mōtsū-ji GARDENS
(毛越寺; ☎0191-46-2331; admission ¥500; ⊙9am-5pm) Established by the priest Ennin in AD 850 at the same time as Chūson-ji, Mōtsū-ji was once Tōhoku's largest and grandest temple complex. The buildings are all long gone, but the enigmatic 12th-century 'Pure Land' gardens, designed with the Buddhist notion of creating an earthly paradise, remain.

Takkoku-no-Iwaya Bishamon-dō BUDDHIST TEMPLE
(達谷窟毘沙門堂; ☎0191-46-4931; admission ¥300; ⊙8am-5pm, varies seasonally) Located 6km outside town, this temple built into a

Hiraizumi

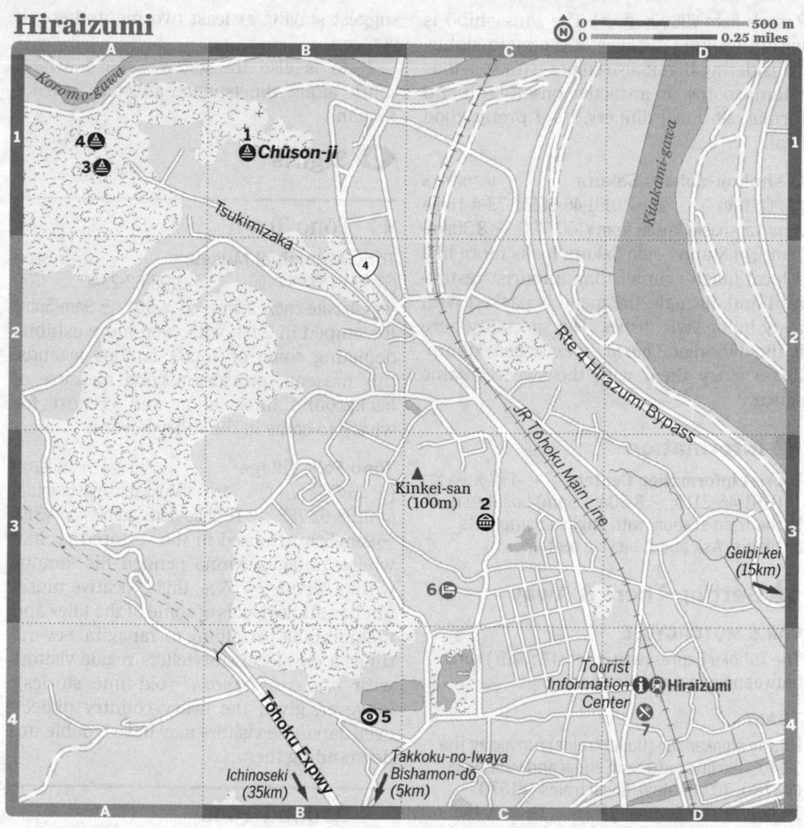

Hiraizumi

Top Sights

1 Chūson-ji B1

Sights

2 Hiraizumi Cultural Heritage Center C3
3 Konjiki-dō A1
4 Kyōzō A1
5 Mōtsū-ji B4

Sleeping

6 Hotel Musashibō C3

Eating

7 O-shokuji-dokoro Sakura D4

cave is dedicated to Bishamon, the Buddhist guardian of warriors. It was built by the general Sakanoue-no-Tamuramaro in AD 801 after his victory against a local warlord. You can cycle here from Mōtsū-ji along a paved path in about 30 minutes.

Hiraizumi Cultural Heritage Center MUSEUM
(平泉文化遺産センター; 44 Hanadate; ⏲9am-5pm) FREE This new museum charts Hiraizumi's rise and fall, and there are English explanations throughout.

Geibi Gorge BOAT TOUR
(厳美渓; 90 min cruise ¥1600; ⏲8.30am-4pm) Singing boatmen on flat-bottomed wooden boats steer passengers down the Satetsu River, which cuts through a ravine flanked by towering limestone walls. Geibi-kei is 15km east of Hiraizumi; take the hourly bus from stop 7 outside Ichinoseki Station (¥640, 40 minutes) or the *kaisoku* (rapid train) from Ichinoseki to Geibi-kei Station on the JR Ōfunato line (¥500, 30 minutes).

Sleeping & Eating

Hotel Musashibō HOTEL ¥¥
(ホテル武蔵坊; ☎0191-46-2241; www.musasibou.co.jp; 15 Hiraizumi-ōsawa; r per person with

2 meals from ¥9800; P @) The Musashibō is within walking distance of the main sights. Considering that it also comes with spacious tatami rooms, an attractive onsen bath and formal, sit-down dinners, it's a pretty good deal.

O-shokuji-dokoro Sakura JAPANESE ¥
(お食事処さくら; ☎0191-46-5651; 73-4 Hiraizumi-ya; snacks/meals from ¥100/700; ⊙8.30am-7pm;) Station-side Sakura looks more like a local lunch counter than a tourist restaurant and, fittingly, the menu is packed with tasty home-style dishes. The speciality here is the handmade *hatto gozen* (wheat dumplings) – try them with the sweet sesame sauce.

Information

Tourist Information Center (平泉町観光協会; ☎0191-46-2110; ⊙8.30am-5pm) Located next to the train station, with English pamphlets available. Ask about bicycle rental.

Getting There & Away

CAR & MOTORCYCLE

The Tōhoku Expressway (東北自動車道) runs between Sendai and Hiraizumi.

TRAIN

Hourly *shinkansen* (bullet trains) run along the JR Tōhoku line between Sendai and Ichinoseki (¥3780, 30 minutes). Local trains (¥1670, 1¼ hours), running every hour or two, ply the same route on the JR Tōhoku main line and also connect Ichinoseki and Hiraizumi (¥210, 10 minutes).

Ichinoseki is connected to Morioka by the JR Tōhoku *shinkansen* (¥3780, 40 minutes) and the JR Tōhoku main-line *futsū* (¥1670, 1½ hours).

Tōno 遠野

☎0198 / POP 29,300

Surrounded by verdant rice fields and dramatic mountains, Tōno speaks to a time when people lived intimately, off their land. Superstitious residents, in turn, developed a healthy mix of fear and admiration for the natural world, which led to the creation of a whole assortment of *yōkai* (ghosts, demons, monsters and spirits) and made Tōno the heartland for some of Japan's most cherished folklore.

Here, a bike ride through the woods can transport you to a mythical 'Lost Japan', where the wild things roamed free. We'd suggest staying at least two nights here, if you can.

Tōno is also the gateway for journeys south along the tsunami-affected Sanriku Kaigan.

Sights

Tōno Town

Tōno Municipal Museum MUSEUM
(遠野市立博物館; ☎0198-62-2340; 3-9 Higashidate-chō; admission ¥310; ⊙9am-5pm) Revamped in 2014, with even more exhibits depicting some of Tōno's famous legends, this museum provides a good measure of background information and context for what's to come in the valley beyond.

Tōno Folk Village MUSEUM
(とおの昔話村, Tōno Mukashibanashi-mura; ☎0198-62-7887; 2-11 Chūō-dōri; admission ¥310; ⊙9am-5pm) Housed in the restored ryokan where Yanagita Kunio penned his famous work *Legends of Tōno,* this evocative museum has audiovisuals of some of the tales and memorabilia pertaining to Yanagita. Several times a day, local storytellers regale visitors with *mukashi-banashi* (old-time stories); however, given the heavy country dialect, even Japanese visitors may have trouble understanding them.

Around Tōno

The best way to see the countryside is by bicycle, made all the easier by a fantastic riverside trail. The Tōno Valley opens up into some beautiful terrain, particularly to the east. Most of the sights below are dotted throughout the valley. Finding them is half the fun. Rent a bicycle, grab a walking map from the tourist information centre (p548) and don't be (too) afraid to explore. The mythical world is well signposted in English, but don't let that stop you setting off down unmarked roads – you never know what you might find.

About 2.5km southwest of Tōno Station is **Unedori-sama** (卯子酉様; ☎0198-62-2111; Shimokumi-chō), the matchmaking shrine. According to legend, if you tie a strip of red cloth around one of the pines, using only your left hand, you'll meet your soul mate. In the hills above, the **Gohyaku Rakan** (五百羅漢) are eerie, moss-covered rock carvings of 500 disciples of Buddha that were fashioned by a priest to console the spirits of

Tōno Valley

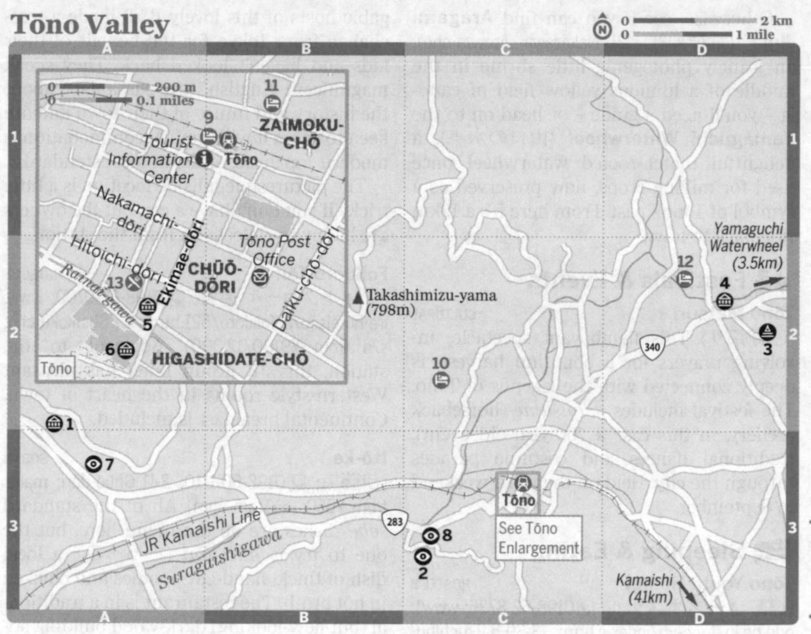

Tōno Valley

Sights

1 Chiba Family Magariya........................A2
2 Gohyaku Rakan........................C3
3 Jōken-ji........................D2
4 Tōno Denshōen........................D2
5 Tōno Folk Village........................A2
6 Tōno Municipal Museum........................A2
7 Tsuzuki-ishi........................A3
8 Unedori-sama........................C3

Sleeping

9 Folkloro Tōno........................B1
10 Kuranoya........................C2
11 Minshuku Tōno........................B1
12 Tōno Youth Hostel........................D2

Eating

13 Itō-ke........................A2

those who died in a 1754 famine. It's a truly unique site – approach respectfully.

If you continue west along Rte 283 towards Morioka for about 8km, you'll eventually come to **Tsuzuki-ishi** (続石). A curious rock that rests amid aromatic cedars: either a natural formation or a *dolmen* (primitive tomb). A short, steep hike rewards you with views across the valley, but take heed as hungry ogres (and bears) are reported to lurk in these parts. One kilometre past Tsuzuki-ishi is the **Chiba Family Magariya** (南部曲り家千葉家; 0198-62-9529; adult/child ¥310/100; 9am-4pm), a grand 200-year-old farmhouse in the traditional L-shaped Tōno style.

About 5km east of the town centre is **Denshōen** (遠野伝承園; 0198-62-8655; www.densyoen.jp; 6-5-1 Tsuchibuchi, Tsuchibuchi-chō; admission ¥310; 9am-4pm), another traditional farmhouse containing a small cultural museum. The highlights here are the thousand Oshira-sama deities fashioned from mulberry wood. A few hundred metres southeast is **Jōken-ji** (常堅寺; 0198-62-1333; 7-50 Tsuchibuchi, Tsuchibuchi-chō), a peaceful temple dedicated to the deity image of Obinzuru-sama. Behind the temple is the **Kappa-buchi pool**, where Tōno's famous water sprites lurk. It is said that if pregnant women worship at the shrine on the riverbank, they'll produce plenty of milk, but only if they first produce a breast-shaped offering. The tiny altar is filled with small red or white cloth bags, most replete with nipple.

Otherwise, see if you can find **Aragami Jinja** (荒神神社; 21 Nakazawa, Aozasa-chō), an isanely photogenic little shrine in the middle of a lumious yellow field of canola – you'll need a guide – or head on to the **Yamaguchi Waterwheel** (山口の水車), a delightful thatch-roofed waterwheel once used for milling crops, now preserved as a symbol of Tōno's past. From here it's a 12km ride back to town.

Festivals & Events

Tōno Matsuri CULTURAL

(遠野祭り) This flamboyant spectacle, involving prayers for a bountiful harvest, is deeply connected with the legends of Tōno. The festival includes *yabusame* (horseback archery, in this case a 700-year-old event), traditional dances and costume parades through the city. Held on the third weekend in September.

Sleeping & Eating

Tōno Youth Hostel HOSTEL ¥

(遠野ユースホステル; ☎0198-62-8736; www1.odn.ne.jp/tono-yh/index-e.htm; 13-39-5 Tsuchibuchi, Tsuchibuchi-chō; dm from ¥3400, breakfast/dinner ¥600/1200; P ⊖ @) Fronted by rice fields, this remote farmhouse hostel pays homage to Tōno of yesteryear. The amicable manager, who speaks a decent smattering of English, is well versed in local lore and captivates imaginations with nightly reports on rumoured sightings. Accommodation is in simple dorms that share open-air baths, while meals feature seasonal produce and are served communally. Bicycle rental is available.

From Tōno Station, take a bus bound for Saka-no-shita to the Nitagai stop (¥290, 12 minutes). From there, it's a 10-minute walk, with the hostel clearly signposted along the way (look for the small wooden signs at knee-level).

Minshuku Tōno MINSHUKU ¥¥

(民宿とおの; ☎0198-62-4395; www.minshuku-tono.com; 2-17 Zaimoku-chō; r per person with 2 meals from ¥9450; P) This dignified *minshuku*, behind the station, has large, airy tatami rooms and delicious home-style cooking, including home-brewed *doburoku* (unfiltered sake).

Kuranoya MINSHUKU ¥¥

(くら乃屋; ☎0198-60-1360; www.kuranoya-tono.com; 45-136 Sanchiwari, Kōkōji, Matsuzaki-chō; r per person from ¥6500) The friendly, knowledgable hosts of this lovely B&B made a tree-change from Tokyo for the benefit of their kids and haven't looked back. They speak magnificent English, are passionate about the history and future of their town and are keen to share it with you. Accommodation is modern Japanese, of the highest standards.

The picturesque hillside location is a little tricky if you don't have a car, but the owners are happy to collect you from the station.

Folkloro Tōno HOTEL ¥¥

(フォルクローロ遠野; ☎0198-62-0700; www.jre-hotels.jp/e/folkloro/521.html; 5-7 Shinkoku-chō; s/d from ¥9100/12,300) Adjacent to the station, this JR group hotel has pleasant Western-style rooms in the heart of town. Continental breakfast is included.

Itō-ke SOBA ¥

(伊藤家; ☎0198-60-1110; 2-11 Chūō-dōri; mains from ¥650; ⊙11am-5pm) All of the standard *soba* dishes are on the menu here, but the one to try is *hittsumi* (ひっつみ), a local dish of thick, hand-cut noodles and chicken in hot broth. The restaurant is in a traditional (but new-looking) dark-wood building adjacent to the Tōno Folk Village; look for the wooden sign over the sliding doors.

Information

Tōno Post Office (遠野郵便局; ☎0198-62-2830; 6-10 Chūō-dōri; ⊙9am-5pm Mon-Fri) An international ATM is available here.

Tourist Information Center (遠野市観光協会; ☎0198-62-1333; www.tonojikan.jp; ⊙9am-5pm) Across from the train station, friendly, helpful staff await your arrival with bicycle rentals (¥1000 per day), English maps and free internet. Ask if the hop-on, hop-off town bus (¥3000 per day) is operating when you're in town.

Getting There & Away

Trains run hourly on the JR Tōhoku line between Hiraizumi and Hanamaki (¥840, 45 minutes). The JR Kamaishi line connects Hanamaki to Tōno (¥840, one hour), while the JR Tōhoku line connects Hanamaki to Morioka (¥670, 45 minutes).

If you're coming from Sendai, take the Tōhoku *shinkansen* (bullet train) to Shin-Hanamaki (¥5910, one hour) and transfer to the JR Kamaishi line for Tōno (¥760, 45 minutes). The *shinkansen* also connects Shin-Hanamaki to Morioka (¥1530, 15 minutes).

From 2014, a very special SL *Ginga* series steam locomotive re-entered service along the route from Hanamaki to Kamaishi via Tōno, inspired by the novel *Night on the Galactic Railroad*. Departure times vary and are limited. Train buffs and travelling families should check www.jr-morioka.com/sl/index for details, although the site is in Japanese.

The Sennin-Tōge expressway links up with Rte 283 between Tōno and Kamaishi, for journeys around the Sanriku Kaigain.

SANRIKU KAIGAN

Extending from Aomori prefecture in the north, through Iwate and Miyagi prefectures to the south, the vast Sanriku Kaigan (三陸海岸, Sanriku Coast) is a rugged and beautiful stretch of ria coastline marked by steep rocky cliffs. A 'ria' is characterised by having a broad estuary that funnels into a long narrow inlet. It is on the low-lying land around the rias of the Sanriku Kaigan that communities developed. Ironically, these topographical peculiarities that sustain life here also amplify tsunami. And so, the Sanriku coast bore the brunt of destruction and the greatest loss of life when the Great East Japan Earthquake and subsequent tsunami struck in March 2011.

This is not the first time towns of the Sanriku Kaigan have been hit by tsunami, nor will it be the last. In 1933, the Sanriku Earthquake, measuring 8.4 on the Richter scale, generated tsunami waves of up to 28m. Countless lives and buildings were

TAKUYA'S STORY

'As usual, I left for work in a rush without saying a word to my parents. On that day, I was working in Miyako-city, about 60km north of my hometown, Ōtsuchi.

It began like every other boring work day. And then it happened. The ground started shaking. It shook so hard that you couldn't stand and *kept on shaking*. When it finally stopped, I feared a tsunami and drove up the hill, even before I heard the warnings. I phoned my parents but there was no signal. After many hours, I reached my uncle's house. Listening to the radio, I realised returning to Ōtsuchi was impossible, so I spent the long night awake there, my mind racing, unable to focus on any one thought: fear of losing my family, denial and hope for my family's survival.

The road to Ōtsuchi remained impassable. Four days later, I heard rumours that people were fleeing Ōtsuchi using an old mountain path. I left in search of my family. After hours of walking through the forest, imagining that somehow Ōtsuchi had been spared, I arrived in the town. In an instant, my hope was shattered and the worst was before my eyes. There was nothing, absolutely nothing left but endless piles of rubble.

The rest is a blur. I remember passing where my house used to be but wasn't anymore. I made it to an elementary school nearby.

I found my mother. Alive. She screamed when she saw me. I felt my knees weaken with relief and then her words stiffened my body: "I can't find your father."

Exactly one month later, I found my father. Finally. After I'd opened hundreds of other body bags searching for him. A part of me said, "Finally". Then my heart went numb. Frozen, after holding on to that hope that he might be alive, for so long.

That was three years ago now. I lost hope, but now I live with hope in the same town that stole my hope.

In these three years, I met my partner, Mio, who came to Ōtsuchi on a rescue team, and married her. Life plays a game on you like that. If there was no tsunami, I wouldn't have gone through that devastation, but I would never have met my wife.

Ōtsuchi lost 10% of its population. Everyone here lost someone they love. Some people lost everyone.

If I could give you one gift from this disaster, it would be to make each day count. Love the ones you love. We're sad because the ones we love are gone. We're sad because we can't talk to them anymore. We'll never be sure if they knew how much we loved them.

So, if you hear our story, and it inspires you to tell your loved ones how much you love them, every day – to say "Good morning", "Goodbye" and "Goodnight", it will be a requiem for the ones we have lost, so our journeys will not have been in vain.'

If you're lucky, you might run into Takuya and Mio at the Ōtsuchi Yume-no-hiroba (p551).

ROAD TO RECOVERY

Almost all of the low-lying areas of towns and villages along this vast stretch of coastline were levelled in the 2011 tsunami. It's a humbling experience to see what remains first hand and to try to imagine what was here before. Optimistic estimates figure recovery and reconstruction will take at least 10 to 15 years.

If you're interested in seeing where things are at, we recommend self-driving. The following listings are best supplemented by your own research, and cover a broad area. The inland towns of Tōno, to the north, and Ichinoseki, to the south, make good bases for exploring the coast.

Below is a summary of what you might expect in each town:

Kamaishi Western areas survived unscathed, low-lying areas flattened and 1250 lives were lost. Outwardly, Kamaishi appears to be getting on with business.

Ōtsuchi Levelled. Roughly 10% of the town's 16,000 people were lost. Rebuilding continues slowly.

Ōfunato Waves 24m in height travelled 3km inland, destroying much of the town. Residents heeded warnings and loss of life was comparatively small.

Rikuzen-takata Around 5000 buildings swept away and 2000 lives lost. Rebuilding continues fervently. A vast network of conveyor belts ferries soil from neighbouring mountains into the town, where it's used to raise the ground level. The sheer scale of devastation is easily appreciated here.

Kesennuma Almost 2000 lives lost in this busy port city, one of the largest towns in the region. Coastal areas remain levelled but life goes on in the hilly suburbs. 'Recovery Markets' in temporary buildings have sprung up across the city; why not spend some tourist yen?

Minami-Sanriku Of the town's 80 evacuation sites, 31 were inundated and 95% of the town was destroyed. Thousands of people reached higher ground and survived. Visually, the scope of devastation is easy to comprehend here.

lost. Monuments and memorials were erected, but with 'progress' and the passing of time, people forgot. The recurring message in each of the towns decimated by this disaster is that although people knew tsunami would come, many didn't consider it a serious threat.

Survivors are determined that now, people won't forget, nor be forgotten.

Visitors now have the opportunity to witness and be part of the rebirth of these towns and villages, their people eager to protect and share their history and culture with the world. There's a real sense of resilience and the appreciation of life here, which can touch the heart of anyone who visits.

Sights

The area offers some touching memorials, sights on higher ground that survived the disaster, and the opportunity for inspired communication.

★RIAS Ark Art Gallery MUSEUM

(リアスアーク美術館; 0226-24-1611; www.riasark.com; 138-5 Akaiwamakisawa, Kesennuma; admission ¥300; 9.30am-4.30pm Wed-Sun) High in the hills above Kesennuma, this local art museum houses the largest collection of photographs and artefacts relating to the 2011 Great East Japan Earthquake and tsunami in existence. A comprehensive booklet containing an English translation of each exhibit is available. The sheer volume and nature of the collection might be a little overwhelming.

Kamaishi Dai-kannon BUDDHIST MONUMENT

(釜石大観音; 0193-24-2125; www.kamaishi-daikannon.com; 3-9-1 Ōdaira; adult/child ¥500/300) In the hills above Kamaishi, this enormous (48.5m tall) statue of the Goddess of Mercy has witnessed much tragedy below, but remains a source of hope for thousands of pilgrims each year. You can climb the inside of the structure for eye-opening views.

Goishi Kaigan COASTLINE

(碁石海岸) This 6km scenic stretch of rocky coastline and picturesque beaches around Ōfunato is part of the Sanriku Recovery National Park. Around 4km of walking trails hug the clifftops.

Rikuzen-takata Ippon-matsu MEMORIAL

(陸前高田一本松; www.city.rikuzentakata.iwate.jp/kategorie/fukkou/ipponmatu/ipponmatu.html) Thousands of pine trees lined the coastline around Rikuzen-takata. Remarkably, all but one were destroyed in the 2011 tsunami. That tree survived for over a year, until salination from the inundation caused its demise. A replica was constructed in its place and serves as a touching memorial, symbolising hope.

Ue-no-yama Ryokuchi PARK

(上の山緑地) This little park in Minami-Sanriku was one of the elevated evacuation zones. From here you can see the sheer scale of the devastation and reconstruction. Say a prayer or ring the bell at the nearby shrine.

Minami-Sanriku Crisis Management Centre MEMORIAL

(南三陸防災対策庁舎) The steel shell is all that remains of this three-storey building, standing alone in what was once Minami-Sanriku. It's been preserved by the locals as a touching memorial to the lives that were lost here.

Tours

★Yume-no-hiroba WALKING TOUR

(夢の広場; ☎0193-55-5120; www.oraga-otsuchi.jp; 23-37-3 Ōtsuchi; tours per person from ¥1000; ⊙by appointment) In Ōtsuchi, the resilient, forward-thinking and compassionate folk at this local organisation run individual and group tours around Ōtsuchi, sharing personal, first-hand accounts of the disaster and educating visitors on disaster management and humanitarian concerns. Prepare to have your heart melt a little. Okay, a lot. Very highly recommended.

Sleeping

Consider basing yourself in Tōno or Ichinoseki for trips along the coast. The limited accommodation here is routinely filled with construction workers.

Hotel Route Inn Kamaishi HOTEL ¥¥

(ホテルルートイン釜石; ☎0193-22-0301; www.route-inn.co.jp; 2-5-17 Ōhara, Kamaishi; s/d from ¥7300/12,000; P 📶) New in 2014, this business hotel has compact, state-of-the-art rooms and on-site onsen baths.

Chisun Inn Ichinoseki IC HOTEL ¥¥

(チサンイン岩手一関インター; ☎0191-25-6911; www.solarehotels.com/en/hotel/tohoku/chisuninn-iwate-ichinoseki; 188-2 Aza Tsukimachi, Akoogi, Ichinoseki; s/d from ¥4950/6600) By the Ichinoseki interchange, this hotel has bright, airy rooms with comfortable beds, a pleasant outlook and complimentary breakfast. Best for self-drivers. There are a bunch of restaurants and facilities nearby.

Information

Kamaishi Tourist Information Society (釜石観光物産協会; ☎0193-22-5835; 22-1 Suzuko-chō, Kamaishi; ⊙9am-5pm) By Kamaishi station, friendly staff are able to assist with information and maps on the surrounding areas.

Getting There & Away

Depending on how much you wish to explore, car rental (from Morioka, Sendai, or Ichinoseki) is highly recommended. Roads in, out and around the area are in excellent shape, with many new roads and highways under construction. The prevalence of heavy, slow-moving trucks can be hazardous. Have patience.

Rail services on the JR Kamaishi line are fully operational, but buses have replaced trains on large sections of the JR Ōfunato, Kesennuma and Yamada lines.

The private Sanriku Tetsudō's coastal Kita-Riasu (between Miyako and Kuji) and Minami-Riasu (between Sakari and Kamaishi), which were heavily damaged by the tsunami, returned to full service in April 2014. The Kita-Riasu line connects with the JR Hachinohe line in Kuji, for journeys north as far as Hachinohe, in Aomori prefecture, from where it's possible (though time consuming) to continue on to Aomori city, or north to the Shimokita peninsula, on the private Aoimori line. As schedules in the area are subject to change, refer to www.hyperdia.com for detailed information on connections, travel times and prices.

MIYAGI PREFECTURE

Miyagi-ken (宮城県) is something of a transition zone between the rural hinterlands of the far north and the massive urban development that typifies much of central Honshū. Its capital, Sendai, has excellent tourist infrastructure, unique culinary offerings and plenty of cultural attractions to boot.

Of course, if you want to escape the urban trappings and get back to the nature that most likely brought you up this way, then don't miss the healing waters of Akiu Onsen and Matsushima, a worthy contender for the title of Japan's most beautiful bay.

Miyagi Prefecture

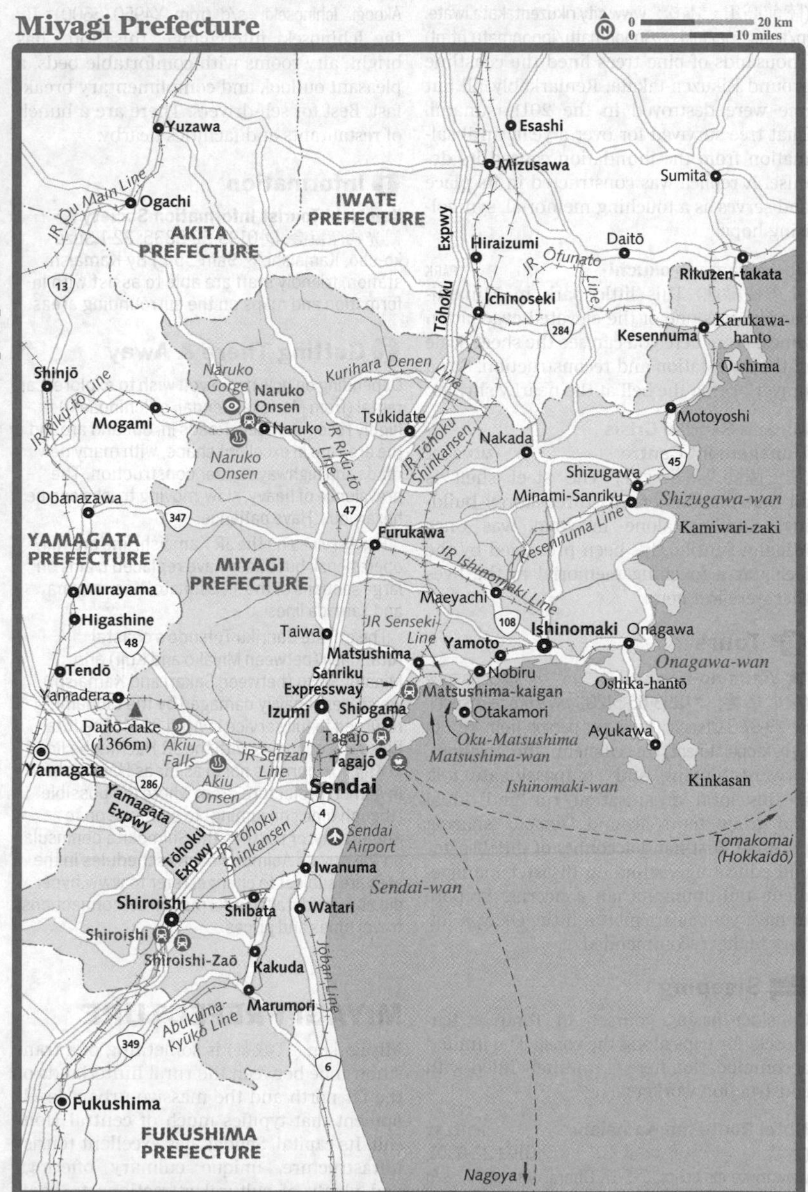

Sendai 仙台

022 / POP 1,060,000

For Tōhoku's largest city, Sendai is fairly compact, with well-ordered, tree-lined streets that front a ruined castle. Japanese are quick to associate the city with its

WORTH A TRIP

AKIU ONSEN

Wonderful Akiu Onsen (秋保温泉) was the Date clan's favourite therapeutic retreat, with a natural saltwater spring that's said to be a curative for back pain and arthritis. There are dozens of inns here that offer up their baths to day trippers.

You can also stretch your legs along the rim of **Rairai Gorge** (磊々峡; Rairai-kyō), a 20m-deep gorge that runs through the village. Pick up maps and a list of bathhouses at the **Tourist Information Center** (秋保温泉観光案内所; ☎022-398-2323; www.akiuonsenkumiai.com/en; Akiu Sato Center; ⏲9am-6pm). In the hills west of town is **Akiu Falls** (秋保大滝; Akiu Ōtaki), a 6m-wide, 55m-high waterfall designated as one of Japan's three most famous waterfalls. View the falls from a scenic outlook or hike down 20 minutes to the bottom.

Buses leave hourly for Akiu Onsen from stop 8 at Sendai Station's west bus pool (¥800, 50 minutes). On weekends there are two buses daily that continue to Akiu Ōtaki (¥1100, 1½ hours). Otherwise, catch one of the few buses for the falls from the Akiu Sato Center (¥670, 20 minutes).

samurai benefactor, Date Masamune, and its spectacular Tanabata Matsuri, one of Japan's most famous festivals.

Sendai's downtown lies far enough inland to have been spared by the 2011 tsunami, though its coastal suburbs weren't so lucky.

It's business as usual in this vibrant city. With the best nightlife in the north and excellent transport connections, Sendai is worth a stopover on its own strengths or en route somewhere else.

History

Sendai, 'city of a thousand generations', was established by Date Masamune in 1600. A ruthless, ambitious *daimyō* (domain lord), Masamune turned Sendai into a feudal capital that controlled trade routes, salt supplies and grain milling throughout much of Tōhoku. The Date family ruled the Sendai-han until the Meiji Restoration brought an end to the feudal era in 1868.

Sights

Most sights can be reached by the Loople tourist bus.

★Zuihō-den Mausoleum HISTORIC BUILDING
(瑞鳳殿; ☎022-262-6250; www.zuihoden.com; 23-2 Otamaya-shita, Aoba-ku; adult/child ¥550/200; ⏲9am-4pm; 🚌Loople stop 4) The mausoleum of Date Masamune sits majestically atop the summit of a tree-covered hill by the Hirose-gawa. Built in 1637 but destroyed by Allied bombing during WWII, the current building, completed in 1979, is an exact replica of the original, faithful to the ornate and sumptuous Momoyama style.

Sendai Castle Ruins CASTLE
(仙台城跡; ☎022-261-1111; www.sendaijyo.com; 1 Kawauchi, Aoba-ku; 🚌Loople stop 6, regular bus stop 'Sendai Jō Ato Minami') Built on Aoba-yama in 1602 by Date Masamune and destroyed during Allied bombing, Sendai-jō still looms large over the city. Giant moss-covered walls, as imposing as they are impressive, are still intact and the grounds offer sweeping views over the city.

Sendai City Museum MUSEUM
(仙台市博物館; ☎022-225-3074; 26 Kawauchi, Aoba-ku; adult/child ¥400/200; ⏲9am-4.45pm Tue-Sun; 🚌Loople stop 5) The city museum offers a comprehensive account of samurai Masamune's epic life, as well as more than 13,000 artefacts on loan from the Date family with plenty of explanations in English.

Sendai Mediatheque LIBRARY
(仙台メディアテーク; ☎022-713-3171; www.smt.city.sendai.jp; 2-1 Kasuga-machi, Aoba-ku; ⏲9am-10pm, gallery hours vary) FREE Housed in an award-winning structure designed by Japanese architect Itō Toyō, this cultural hub includes a library, art galleries and event space. Check the website to see if anything is going on when you're in town. Highly recommended.

Festivals & Events

Donto-sai CULTURAL
(どんと祭) On 14 January, men brave subzero weather to don loincloths and pray for good fortune for the new year.

Sendai Tanabata Matsuri CULTURAL
(仙台七夕まつり; Star Festival; www.sendaitanabata.com) Sendai's biggest event, held

Central Sendai

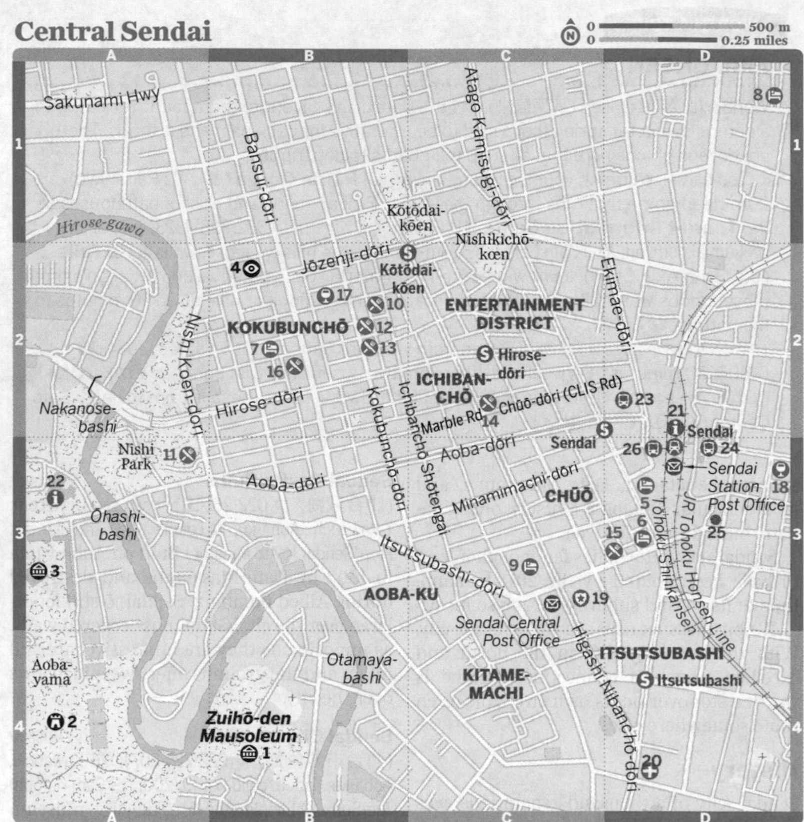

from 6 to 8 August, celebrates a Chinese legend about the stars Vega and Altair. Vega was the king's daughter who fell in love with and married Altair, a common herder. The king disapproved, so he formed the Milky Way between them. Once a year magpies are supposed to spread their wings across the universe so that the lovers can meet – traditionally on 7 July (on the old lunar calendar).

Jōzenji Street Jazz Festival LIVE MUSIC
(定禅寺ストリートジャズフェスティバル; www.j-streetjazz.com; ⌚2nd weekend in Sep) Hundreds of buskers from across Japan perform in Sendai's streets and arcades. Book your accommodation way, way in advance.

Sendai Pageant of Starlight LIGHT SHOW
(SENDAI光のページェント; www.sendaihikape.jp; ⌚mid–late Dec) About 600,000 festive lights illuminate Aoba-dōri and Jōzenji-dōri.

Sleeping

★Dōchū-an Youth Hostel HOSTEL ¥
(道中庵ユースホステル; ☎022-247-0511; www.jyh.or.jp/yhguide/touhoku/dochuan; 31 Kita-yashiki, Ōnoda, Taihaku-ku; dm ¥3750, YHA discount ¥3150; P ⊖ @) This evocative former farmhouse has cosy Japanese-style rooms, genial managers, bike rental, free internet and a fantastic old cedar bath. Located south of the city centre, the closest station is Taishidō (¥180, eight minutes from Sendai Station) on the JR Tōhoku line, from where it's a six-minute walk; ask for a map at the station or print one from the website.

Minshuku Keyaki MINSHUKU ¥
(民宿欅; ☎022-796-4946; 13-4 Tachimachi, Aoba-ku; dm ¥2800) In the heart of Kokubunchō, this smart guesthouse has cheap-as-chips dorms and friendly staff.

Central Sendai

Top Sights
1 Zuihō-den Mausoleum B4

Sights
2 Sendai Castle Ruins A4
3 Sendai City Museum A3
4 Sendai Mediatheque B2

Sleeping
5 Hotel Metropolitan Sendai D3
6 Hotel Washington D3
7 Minshuku Keyaki B2
8 Sendai Chitose Youth Hostel D1
9 Westin C3

Eating
10 Aji Tasuke B2
11 Gengo Chaya A3
12 Hosoya B2
13 Jiraiya B2
14 Manhattan Bakery C2
15 Ohisamaya D3
16 Santarō B2

Drinking & Nightlife
17 Gallo B2
18 The Ha'penny Bridge D3

Entertainment
Club Shaft .... (see 12)

Information
19 Sendai Central Police Station C3
20 Sendai City Hospital D4
21 Sendai City Information Center D2
22 Sendai International Centre A3

Transport
23 Bus Stop 34 .... D2
24 JR Tōhoku Bus Center D3
Loople .... (see 26)
25 Toyota Rent a Car D3
26 West Bus Terminal D3

Sendai Chitose Youth Hostel HOSTEL ¥
(仙台千登勢ユースホステル; ☎022-222-6329; www.ryokanchitoseya.co.jp; 6-3-8 Odawara, Aoba-ku; dm ¥3800;) Within walking distance of the centre, this hostel has snug Japanese-style rooms in a residential area north of the train station. From the east exit, walk through the bus pool and take a left on the main road, walking for 15 minutes until you see a drugstore, then take a left, followed by the second right onto a narrow street.

Hotel Washington HOTEL ¥¥
(仙台ワシントンホテル; ☎022-745-2222; http://sendai.washington-hotels.jp; 4-10-8 Chūō; s/d from ¥9100/12,600) Sendai's newest offering, by the station, has stylish, state-of-the-art rooms that are well priced for their high standard. The location can't be beat.

Westin HOTEL ¥¥¥
(ウェスティンホテル仙台; ☎022-722-1234; www.westin.com; 1-9-1 Ichiban-chō, Aoba-ku; r from ¥13,500) The luxury Westin has some of Sendai's largest and best-appointed rooms with unrivalled views across the city. If you're looking to live it up a little, search no further. This is a true, international-standard five-star hotel with all the trimmings.

Hotel Metropolitan Sendai HOTEL ¥¥¥
(ホテルメトロポリタン仙台; ☎022-268-2525; www.sendai.metropolitan.jp; 1-1-1 Chūō, Aoba-ku; s/d ¥13,500/23,200;) For comfort and convenience, you can't beat the Metropolitan, which is part of the Sendai Station complex. Rooms here are smart, well appointed and comfortably plush.

Eating

Gyūtan (charcoal-grilled cow's tongue) is a much-loved local delicacy.

Manhattan Bakery BAKERY ¥
(マンハッタンベーカリー; ☎022-208-5566; 1-7-18 Chūō, Aoba-ku; sandwiches from ¥380; 7am-8pm) This spotless hole-in-the-wall with just a few tables, off the CLIS Rd shopping street (before Marble Rd) makes delicious sandwiches to order from a variety of fresh toppings. Better still, they do an amazing eggs Benedict.

Hosoya BURGERS ¥
(ほそや; ☎022-462-4139; 2-10-7 Kokubunchō, Aoba-ku; burgers from ¥450; noon-10pm, to 8pm Sun;) This vintage burger counter has grilled more than a million patties since opening in 1950, and still serves up old-school soda-fountain treats like ice-cream floats. There are also a few options for vegetarians, like egg and cheese sandwiches. Look for the English sign out front.

Gengo Chaya TEAHOUSE ¥
(源吾茶屋; ☎022-222-2830; 1-1 Sakuragaoka-kōen, Aoba-ku; snacks from ¥350; 11am-6pm;) In business for 130 years, this teahouse is known for its *zunda-mochi,*

CAUTION: MISCHIEVOUS RIVER IMPS AHEAD

At the beginning of the 20th century, writer and scholar Yanagita Kunio (1875–1962) published *Tōno Monogatari* (遠野物語; Legends of Tōno), a collection of local folk tales based on interviews with Sasaki Kyōseki, an educated man from a peasant family who had committed to memory more than 100 *densetsu* (local legends). The book captured the nation's imagination, bringing into focus the oral traditions of a region that had previously been ignored. Read the English translation before you visit, if you can.

A weird and wonderful cast of characters and situations draws heavily on the concept of animism, whereby an individual spirit is attributed to everything that exists, including animals and objects. Of particular importance to Tōno is the story of Oshira-sama. It begins with a farm girl who develops a deep affection for her horse; eventually the two marry, against her father's will. One night, the father finds her sleeping in the stables and, outraged, slaughters the animal. Distraught, the daughter clings to the horse's head and together they are spirited up to the heavens, becoming the deity, Oshira-sama.

There are also shape-shifting foxes and *oni* (ogres) who live in the hills and eat lost humans. But best known are the *kappa* (yes, from Super Mario Bros. fame): impish water sprites with thick shells, scaly skin and pointed beaks, responsible for all sorts of mischief and grief. Tōno's many *kappa* reputedly have a nasty habit of pulling people's intestines out through their bum to feed on their *shirikodama*, a mythical ball that humans would call a soul and *kappa* would call delicious.

Points to note: *kappa* love cucumbers, so keep some handy – your generosity might earn you a temporary reprieve. (Astute connoisseurs of sushi will note that a *kappa-maki* is none other than a cucumber hand roll.) If you meet a *kappa* in the woods, remember to bow, as it will return the gesture, spilling out the water stored in its head and becoming temporarily powerless. *Kappa* will always repay a favour and are highly knowledgable in medicine, agriculture and games of skill.

Throughout all of the *Tōno Monogatari* stories there is a common theme: the struggle to overcome the everyday problems of rural life.

pounded rice cakes topped with a jam made from fresh soybeans – a Sendai speciality. You can get meals here, too, but the *mochi* alone is incredibly filling. The teahouse is on the eastern edge of Sakuragaoka Park, with white *noren* (sunshade) curtains out front.

★ Aji Tasuke JAPANESE ¥¥

(味太助; ☎022-225-4641; www.aji-tasuke.co.jp; 4-4-13 Ichiban-chō, Aoba-ku; mains from ¥1470; ⏰11.30am-10pm Wed-Mon; 📋) At this landmark restaurant it's not what you order, but how much. Everyone is here to sample the famous *gyūtan* – charcoal-grilled cow's tongue, served with a side of pickled cabbage and tail soup. Perch at the counter to watch – and smell – the grilling in action. It's next to a small *torii* (shrine gate), and usually has a queue.

Jiraiya IZAKAYA ¥¥

(地雷也; ☎022-261-2164; www.jiraiya.com/pc; basement, 2-1-15 Kokubunchō, Aoba-ku; dishes from ¥1100; 📋) Local seafood and sake are the drawcards here. Seating is elbow-to-elbow at the counter, but the atmosphere is warm and jovial. If you can splurge, try the charcoal-grilled *kinki* (also called *kichiji*, or rockfish), the house speciality. Jiraiya's entrance is on a side street, marked by a giant red lantern. Reservations are recommended on weekends, especially for groups.

Ohisamaya VEGETARIAN ¥¥

(おひさまや; ☎022-224-8540; 4-8-17 Chūō, Aoba-ku; meals from ¥1260; ⏰11.30am-2.30pm Mon-Sat) Vegetarians will rejoice at this vendor of macrobiotic magic offering an ever-changing menu of vegetarian pastas, rice dishes and salads.

Santarō JAPANESE ¥¥¥

(三太郎; ☎022-224-1671; www.santarou.jp; 1-20 Tachimachi, Aoba-ku; dishes from ¥1200, sets from ¥1700, kaiseki courses per person ¥8000-16,000; ⏰11.30am-2pm & 5-10pm) Spectacular evening *kaiseki* courses and crunch-for-lunch tempura are served in this evocative traditional building in the heart of Kokubun-chō. Best for dining with two or more.

Drinking & Entertainment

The Kokubunchō area is Tōhoku's largest entertainment district. It's noisy, slightly chaotic and bright, with everything from hole-in-the-wall bars and British-styled pubs to raging dancing clubs and seedy strip shows. Note that there are a fair number of hostess and host clubs here, as well as seemingly ordinary bars, that levy steep cover charges; it's a good idea to check before ordering.

The Ha'penny Bridge PUB

(ザ ハーフペニー ブリッジ; ☎022-256-6881; www.h2.dion.ne.jp/~hapenny/; 4-5-1 Tsutsujigaoka Miyagino-ku; ⊙6pm-1am) Behind the station, this cosy pub has free wi-fi, a variety of import beers on tap, and a real Mother England kinda vibe.

Gallo BAR

(ガッロ; ☎022-765-7493; 2-12-23 Kokubunchō, Aoba-ku; cover charge ¥500; ⊙7pm-2am, closed irregularly) Bucking the trend for flash and brashness in Kokubunchō, this tiny basement bar has a mellow vibe and retro-pop soundtrack. The menu features fruit-infused spirits from around Japan. Our pick is the lemon-and-ginger-spiked *umeshū* (plum wine; ¥650). Look for the hand-painted English sign.

Club Shaft CLUB

(クラブシャフト; ☎022-722-5651; 4th fl, Yoshiokaya Dai 3 Bldg, 2-10-11 Kokubunchō, Aoba-ku; ⊙8pm-late Mon-Thu, from 10pm Fri & Sat) This perennial venue spins a shuffled playlist of hip-hop, house and J-pop. You'll have a great time here, and most likely regret it once the hangover kicks in.

Information

EMERGENCY

Sendai Central Police Station (仙台中央警察署; ☎022-222-7171; 1-3-19 Itsutsubashi, Aoba-ku)

MEDICAL SERVICES

Sendai City Hospital (仙台市立病院; ☎022-266-7111, 24 hr emergency hotline 022-216-9960; http://hospital.city.sendai.jp; 3-1 Shimizu-kōji, Wakabayashi-ku; ⊙outpatient service 8.30am-11.30am Mon-Fri)

MONEY & POST

Sendai Central Post Office (仙台中央郵便局; ☎022-267-8035; 1-7 Kitame-machi, Aoba-ku; ⊙9am-9pm) There's an international ATM here.

TOURIST INFORMATION

Sendai City Information Center (仙台市観光案内所; ☎022-222-4069; www.sentabi.jp; 2nd fl, JR Sendai Station; ⊙8.30am-7pm) Pick up English maps and brochures here.

Sendai International Centre (仙台国際センター; ☎022-265-2471; www.sira.or.jp/icenter/english/index.html; Aoba-yama, Aoba-ku; ⊙9am-8pm) English-speaking staff, plus an international newspaper library and bulletin board.

Getting There & Away

AIR

From Sendai airport, 18km south of the city centre, flights head for Tokyo, Osaka, Nagoya, Hiroshima, Sapporo and many other destinations.

The Sendai Kūkō Access line leaves for the airport from Sendai Station roughly every 20 minutes (¥630, 25 minutes).

BOAT

From the port of Sendai-kō, **Taiheyo Ferry** (☎022-263-9877; www.taiheiyo-ferry.co.jp/english/index.html) has one daily ferry to Tomakomai on Hokkaidō (from ¥7200, 15 hours), and three to four ferries per week to Nagoya (from ¥6700, 22 hours).

Buses leave from stop 34 at Sendai Station for Sendai-kō (¥510, 40 minutes), but only until 6pm.

BUS

Highway buses depart from outside the east exit of the train station, and connect Sendai to major cities throughout Honshū. Purchase tickets at the **JR Tōhoku Bus Center** (☎022-256-6646; www.jrbustohoku.co.jp; ⊙6.50am-7.30pm), next to bus stop 42.

CAR & MOTORCYCLE

The Tōhoku Expressway (東北自動車道) runs between Tokyo and the greater Sendai area.

Toyota Rent a Car (☎022-293-0100; https://rent.toyota.co.jp; 1-5-3 Tsutsujigaoka, Miyagino-ku; ⊙8am-8pm) has an office a few blocks east of the station.

SENDAI MARUGOTO PASS

The **Sendai Marugoto Pass** (仙台まるごとパス; adult/child ¥2600/1300) covers unlimited travel for two days on the Loople tourist bus, Sendai subway and area trains and buses going as far as Matsushima-kaigan, Akiu Onsen and Yamadera (in Yamagata Prefecture). Pick one up at JR Sendai Station.

TRAIN

The JR Tōhoku *shinkansen* (bullet train) runs hourly between Tokyo and Sendai (¥11,200, two hours), and between Sendai and Morioka (¥6670, 45 minutes).

There are several daily *kaisoku* (rapid trains) on the JR Senzan line between Sendai and Yamagata (¥1140, 1¼ hours) via Yamadera (¥820, one hour). Local trains on the JR Senseki line connect Sendai and Matsushima-kaigan (¥420, 35 minutes); be sure to get one going all the way to Takagi-machi, or you'll have to transfer at Higashi-Shiogama.

Getting Around

The Loople (one ride/day pass ¥250/600) tourist trolley leaves from the west bus pool's stop 15-3 every 30 minutes from 9am to 4pm, making a useful loop around the city in a clockwise direction.

Sendai's single subway line runs from Izumi-chūō in the north to Tomizawa in the south, but doesn't cover any tourist attractions; single tickets cost from ¥200 to ¥350.

Matsushima 松島

022 / POP 15,800

Matsushima's glorious bay, studded with some 260 pine-covered islands, is one of Japan's Nihon Sankei (Three Great Sights). Over the centuries, the trees have been slowly twisted by the winds, while their rocky bases have been eroded by the lapping waves. The result is a spectacular monument to nature's dramatic powers. Local residents credit the islands, which served as a natural breakwater, with sparing Matsushima from the devastation experienced elsewhere along the coast in the 2011 tsunami.

Matsushima is the most popular tourist destination on the northeast coast and can get very crowded, especially on summer weekends. Still, its charms are undeniable.

Sights

Matsushima-kaigan, where the sights are, is essentially a small village, easily navigated on foot.

Zuigan-ji BUDDHIST TEMPLE

(瑞巌寺; admission ¥700; 8am-5pm Apr-Sep, closes earlier Oct-Mar) Tōhoku's finest Zen temple, Zuigan-ji was established in AD 828. The present buildings were constructed in 1606 by Date Masamune to serve as a family temple. Zuigan-ji is undergoing a major restoration that will take until 2019 to complete. As a result, some buildings are closed and others are sheathed in tarps, though it's possible to enter them. Still open is the excellent Seiryūden (temple museum), which has a number of well-preserved relics from the Date family, including national treasures.

The temple is 500m north of Matsushima-kaigan station. Follow the signs.

Kanran-tei PAVILION

(観瀾亭; admission ¥200; 8.30am-5pm Apr-Oct, to 4.30pm Nov-Mar) This pavilion was presented to the Date family by the *daimyō* (domain lord) Toyotomi Hideyoshi in the late 16th century. It served as a genteel venue for tea ceremonies and moon-viewing parties – the name means 'a place to view ripples on the water'. Today it's a peaceful spot for sipping a bowl of whisked *matcha* (powdered green tea).

Kanran-tei is at the northern end of the park opposite Matsushima-kaigan station.

Godai-dō BUDDHIST TEMPLE

(五大堂) Date Masamune constructed this small wooden temple in 1604. Although it stands on an island in the bay, connected to the mainland by a short bridge, it was miraculously untouched by the 2011 tsunami. The temple doors open to the public only once every 33 years (next in 2039). Come instead for the sea views and to see the 12 animals of the Chinese zodiac carved on the eaves.

Godai-dō is located in the park across from Matsushima-kaigan station, about 600m walk, past the boat wharves.

Fuku-ura-jima ISLAND

(福浦島; admission ¥200; 8am-5pm Mar-Oct, to 4.30pm Nov-Feb) You can't miss the 252m-long red wooden bridge connecting Fuku-ura-jima to the mainland. The shady trails here, which wind along the coast through native pines and a botanic garden, make for a pleasant hour-long stroll.

Activities

Matsushima-wan CRUISE

(松島湾; www.matsushima.or.jp; adult/child ¥1500/750; 9am-3pm) To get a sense of the scale of the bay and its dense cluster of pine-topped islands, which sit like so many bonsai floating in a giant's backyard pond, cruise boats depart hourly from the central ferry pier, completing a 50-minute loop. Be-

OFF THE BEATEN TRACK

NARUKO ONSEN 鳴子温泉

Naruko Onsen is famous for having nine distinct springs, whose waters have a different composition of minerals and thus different healing qualities, and for its *kokeshi* (traditional wooden dolls). Take advantage of the Yu-meguri Ticket (¥1300), which you can buy at the **Tourist Information Center** (鳴子観光・旅館案内センター; ☎0229-83-3441; www.naruko.gr.jp; ⏲8.30am-6pm), to visit the baths at several different inns.

Be sure to take a soak in **Taki-no-yu** (滝の湯; admission ¥150; ⏲7.30am-10pm), a fabulously atmospheric wooden bathhouse that's hardly changed in 150 years. It's known for its therapeutic relief of high blood pressure and hardened arteries.

Northwest of town, 100m-deep **Naruko Gorge** (鳴子峡, Naruko-kyō) is particularly spectacular in autumn when maples ignite, but makes for a scenic visit year round.

If you like the pace of this fading rural enclave, consider spending a night at charming **Yusaya Ryokan** (ゆさや旅館; ☎0229-83-2565; www.yusaya.co.jp; 84 Yumoto; r per person with 2 meals from ¥14,800; P @), with its impressive *rotemburo* (outdoor bath) and elegant banquets of river fish and mountain vegetables.

There is an hourly service on the JR Tōhoku *shinkansen* between Sendai and Furukawa (¥3220, 15 minutes). Hourly trains run on the JR Rikū-tō line between Furukawa and Naruko Onsen (¥670, 45 minutes).

tween April and October, you can opt for a longer course (¥2700, 1¾ hours) that goes all the way to Oku-Matsushima.

Festivals & Events

Zuigan-ji Tōdō RELIGIOUS
(瑞巌寺灯道) The approach to Zuigan-ji is lit with candlesticks to honour the ancient shrine. From 6 to 8 August.

Matsushima Ryūtōe Umi-no-bon CULTURAL
(松島流灯会海の盆; http://uminobon.jp) In mid-August, the souls of the departed are honoured with the O-Bon (Festival of the Dead) ritual, when lighted lanterns are floated out to sea.

Sleeping & Eating

Bistro Abalon PENSION ¥¥
(びすとろアバロン; ☎022-354-5777; www.bistroabalon.com/06/index.html; 26-21 Sanjugari; s/d from ¥6500/12,000; P ⊖ ≋) This pension looks like a little chateau perched on a hill. Inside, however, are dark-wood beams, rattan furniture and bamboo shades. The nicer rooms have balconies and sea views. Meals are a feast of locally sourced seafood, beef and produce. It's a seven-minute walk up the hill behind Matsushima-kaigan Station.

Hotel Ubudo HOTEL ¥¥¥
(ホテル海風土; ☎022-355-0022; www.ubudo.jp; 5-3 Higashi-hama; r per person with 2 meals from ¥19,000; P @ ≋) Fancy catching the sunrise over the bay from your window, or perhaps from the bath? This onsen-hotel gets top billing for its fabulous *rotemburo* (outdoor bath) overlooking the bay; the priciest rooms have private balcony baths! Meals are lavish *kaiseki* showcasing the rich variety of local seafood. The hotel is past the Fukuura-jima bridge, within walking distance of the main sights.

Santori Chaya JAPANESE ¥
(さんとり茶屋; 24-4-1 Senzui; meals from ¥980; ⏲11.30am-3pm & 5-10pm Thu-Tue) Perennial local favourites from land and sea such as *kaisen-don* (mixed sashimi on rice) and *gyūtan* (chargrilled cow's tongue) feature here, along with seasonal specialities like Matsushima's famous oysters. Seating is on floor cushions on the 2nd floor; try to get a table by the window. It's in a beige building with an indigo banner and has a picture menu.

Information

Tourist Information Center (松島観光協会; ☎022-354-2263; www.matsushima-kanko.com; Matsushima-kaigan Station; ⏲9.30am-4.30pm Mon-Fri, 8.30am-5pm Sat & Sun) At the station; come here for English brochures, accommodation bookings and the latest info on Oku-Matsushima.

Getting There & Away

CAR & MOTORCYCLE

By road, Matsushima can be reached from Sendai via the Sanriku Expressway (三陸自動車道).

OKU-MATSUSHIMA

On the eastern curve of the bay, remote Oku-Matsushima (奥松島) was devastated by the tsunami and remains in ruins. It's still possible to visit **Ōtakamori** (大高森), a hill in the middle of Miyato Island that offers stunning views of the bay. The 20-minute trek up and down is highly recommended, but only if you have a rental car to get there, as public transport has all but disintegrated. If you have time, take a drive out here to get a sense of the devastation, but be respectful of what has been lost.

TRAIN

There are frequent trains on the JR Senseki line that connect Sendai and Matsushima-kaigan (¥410, 35 minutes).

Sights are at Matsushima-kaigan Station, not Matsushima Station – an easy mistake. Just to confuse, Matsushima is on the Jōban line from (Sendai, platform 3), Matsushima-kaigan is on the Senseki line (Sendai, platform 10 – *jūban*, in Japanese).

Due to tsunami damage, the rail service is disrupted between Takagi-machi (one stop after Matsushima-kaigan) and Rikuzen-Ono. A bus runs along this route instead, leaving from Matsushima-kaigan Station and travelling to Yamoto (one stop after Rikuzen-Ono). It stops near all the train stations along the way, including Nobiru (¥250, 20 minutes), the closest stop for Oku-Matsushima. Buy a regular JR ticket at the train station to use on the bus. Pick up the Senseki line for Ishinomaki in Yamoto.

Ishinomaki 石巻

☎0225 / POP 152,000

Heavily damaged by the 2011 tsunami, Ishinomaki's singular tourist attraction, the **Ishinomaki Mangattan Museum** (石ノ森萬画館; ☎0225-96-5055; www.man-bow.com/manga; 2-7 Nakase; adult/child ¥800/200; ⊙9am-5pm), which recently reopened after extensive reconstruction, matters big to manga fans. Looking like an otherworldly spaceship, this museum is packed with tributes to influential *manga-ka* (cartoonist) and local hero Shōtarō Ishinomori, most famous for creating the *Cyborg 009* and *Kamen Rider* series. The museum is a 20-minute walk from the station: along the way you'll spot a few statues of Ishinomori's characters, a teaser for what's to come.

In the hills above Ishinomaki, 56m above sea level, the beautiful **Hiyori-yama Kōen** (日和山公園) stands on the site of the former Ishinomaki castle. Offering sweeping views over the city, it's a wonderful spot to relax. On a more sombre note, it's also the best vantage point to comprehend the scale of the 2011 tsunami's destruction.

Most travellers just come for the afternoon, but if you'd like to spend more time getting to know the city, now in the process of rebuilding, you can bed down for the night at the guesthouse run by Ishinomaki 2.0, a collective of creative types from Sendai and Tokyo, NPO workers and local merchants, working to 'upgrade' the city post-tsunami. Find out more from http://ishinomaki2.com/v2/english.

ℹ Getting There & Away

The damaged JR Senseki line, connecting Sendai and Ishinomaki, has not yet been repaired. Coming from Matsushima-kaigan, take a bus to Yamoto and reconnect with the Senseki line for Ishinomaki (¥480, 1½ hours). Direct highway buses leave for Ishinomaki roughly twice an hour from stop 33 in front of Sendai Station (¥800, 1½ hours). Get the latest info from the **Tourist Information Center** (石巻観光案内所; ☎93-6448; www.i-kanko.com; ⊙9am-5.30pm) at the station.

Sapporo & Hokkaidō

Includes ➡

Best Hikes

- ➡ Rishiri-zan (p608)
- ➡ Asahi-dake (p600)
- ➡ Yōtei-zan (p592)
- ➡ Shiretoko Traverse (p617)
- ➡ Poroshiri-dake (p597)

Best Brewery Pubs

- ➡ Sapporo Beer Garden & Museum (p576)
- ➡ Abashiri Bīru-kan (p614)
- ➡ Taisetsu Ji-bīru-kan (p596)
- ➡ Hakodate Beer (p581)
- ➡ Otaru Sōko No 1 (p585)

Why Go?

Hokkaidō (北海道) defies the image of Japan as a crowded nation. It's a different world up here, or at least it feels like it, with 20% of Japan's land area but only 5% of its population. Japanese identify this northern land with its wildlife and mountains, greenery and agriculture, snowy winters, temperate summers and arrow-straight roads disappearing into the horizon.

But there's more to it than the scenery. The Ainu, Hokkaidō's indigenous people, are making a determined return after a century of forced assimilation. Sapporo is a bustling modern city that can meet all your urban needs before you head out to explore. And the island is winning a reputation as a haven for thrill-seeking travellers wanting to ski and hike in its mountains, explore its magnificent national parks, relax in its hidden onsen (hot springs), and experience its offerings at their own pace. Enjoy it at your leisure.

When to Go

Sapporo

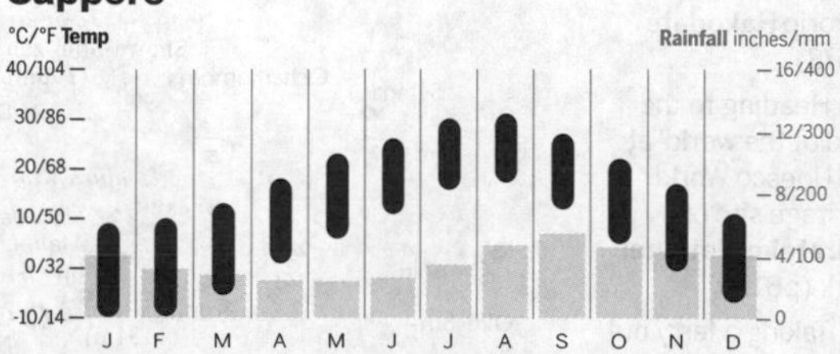

Jun–Aug Hiking season reaches its peak during the holidays of July and August.

Sep & Oct A brief but intense autumn is marked by changing leaves.

Dec–Mar Sub-zero chill and Siberian snowfalls herald the ski season.

Sapporo & Hokkaidō Highlights

1. Drinking beer straight from the source in **Sapporo** (p576).
2. Staring down a Hello Kitty snow-woman at the **Sapporo Snow Festival** (p571).
3. Carving up the slopes at **Niseko** (p586) or **Furano** (p597).
4. Charting a path through the wilderness in **Daisetsuzan National Park** (p601).
5. Saying goodbye to stress as you steam at **Noboribetsu Onsen** (p592).
6. Discovering enormous, ancient *marimo* (balls of algae) in **Akan National Park** (p620).
7. Dining on fresh *uni* (sea-urchin roe) and *ikura* (salmon eggs) in **Otaru** (p583).
8. Strolling through 19th-century streetscapes in historic **Hakodate** (p578).
9. Heading to the 'end of the world' at the Unesco World Heritage site of **Shiretoko National Park** (p616).
10. Taking a ferry out to the remote islands of **Rishiri-Rebun-Sarobetsu National Park** (p608) to climb Rishiri-zan.

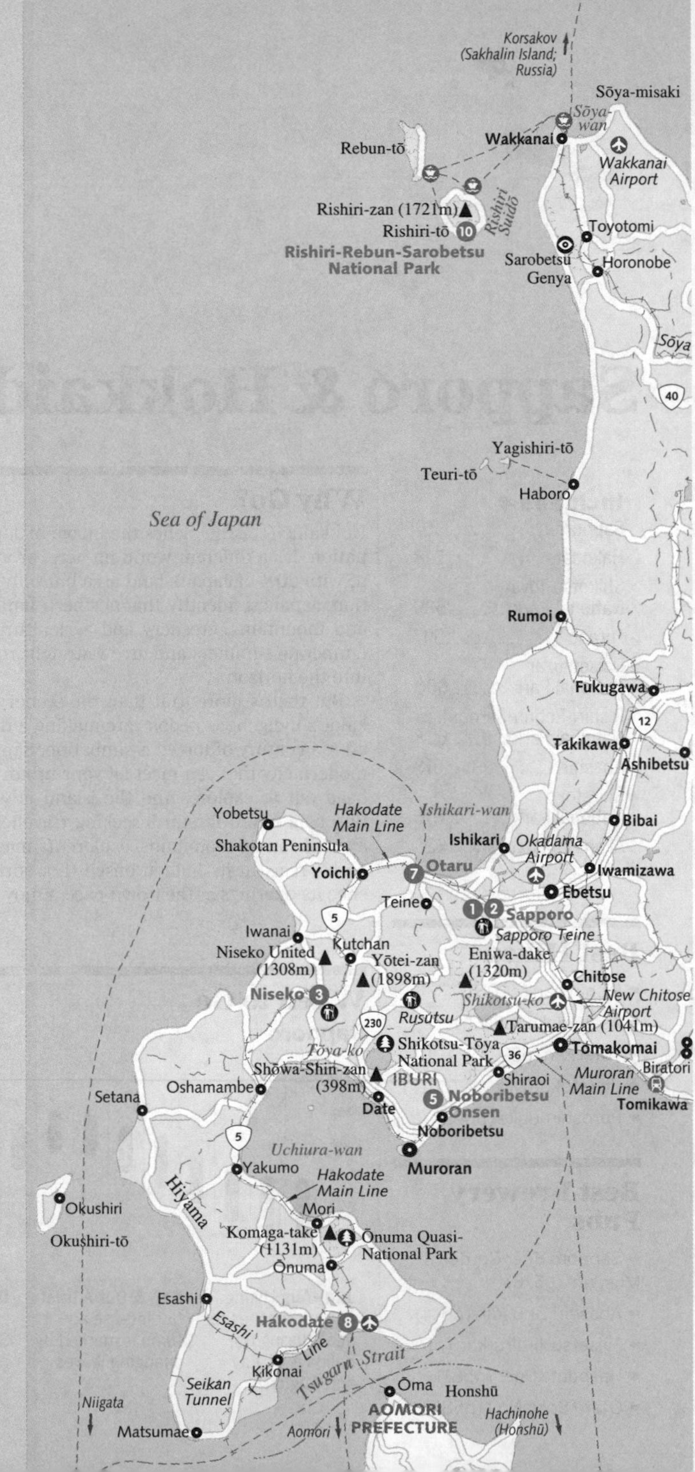

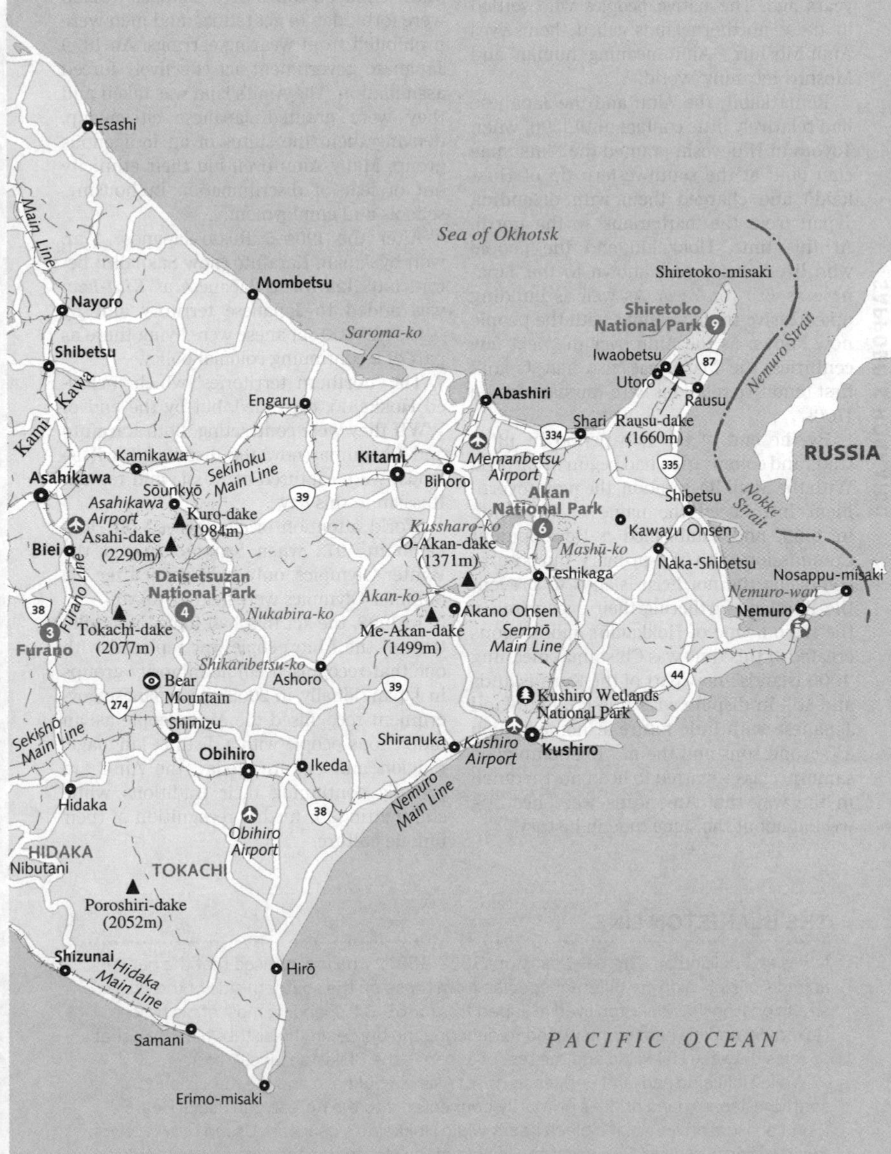

Sea of Okhotsk
Esashi
Main Line
Nayoro
Shibetsu
Kami Kawa
Mombetsu
Saroma-ko
Engaru
Abashiri
Shiretoko-misaki
Shiretoko National Park
Iwaobetsu
Utoro
Rausu
Nemuro Strait
Shari
Rausu-dake (1660m)
RUSSIA
Kamikawa
Asahikawa
Sekihoku Main Line
Kitami
Bihoro
Memanbetsu Airport
Sōunkyō
Asahikawa Airport
Kuro-dake (1984m)
Asahi-dake (2290m)
Biei
Furano Line
Daisetsuzan National Park
Akan National Park
Kussharo-ko
O-Akan-dake (1371m)
Kawayu Onsen
Shibetsu
Nokke Strait
Mashū-ko
Naka-Shibetsu
Teshikaga
Nosappu-misaki
Nemuro-wan
Nemuro
Akan-ko
Akano Onsen
Nukabira-ko
Tokachi-dake (2077m)
Furano
Me-Akan-dake (1499m)
Senmō Main Line
Shikaribetsu-ko
Ashoro
Bear Mountain
Kushiro Wetlands National Park
Sekishō Main Line
Shimizu
Shiranuka
Kushiro Airport
Kushiro
Obihiro
Ikeda
Nemuro Main Line
Hidaka
Obihiro Airport
HIDAKA
Nibutani
TOKACHI
Poroshiri-dake (2052m)
Shizunai
Hidaka Main Line
Hirō
Samani
PACIFIC OCEAN
Erimo-misaki
0 100 km
0 60 miles

History

Hokkaidō was connected to north Asia via Sakhalin and the Kuril islands during the glacial age and it is thought that humans moved into the region around 20,000 years ago. The native peoples who settled in these northern lands called themselves Ainu Moshiri – Ainu meaning 'human' and Moshiri meaning 'world'.

Remarkably, the Ainu and the Japanese had relatively little contact until 1590, when Toyotomi Hideyoshi granted the Matsumae clan land at the southwestern tip of Hokkaidō and charged them with defending Japan from the 'barbarians' to the north. At this time, Hokkaidō and the people who lived there were known to the Japanese as *Ezo* (or *Yezo*). As well as building up exclusive trade relations with the people now known as the Ainu over the next few centuries, the Matsumae also had Japan's first tentative relations with Russians in the 1700s.

By the end of the Edo period in 1868, trade and colonisation had begun in earnest. With the Meiji Restoration, the new government introduced the name of Hokkaidō in 1869, and established a Development Commission with the primary purpose of colonising the northern islands to prevent the Russians furthering their expansion in the region. One of Hokkaidō's subdivisions created at this time was Chishima (meaning '1000 islands'; now part of the Kuril islands and still in dispute with Russia). Mainland Japanese with little future at home – such as second sons and the newly unemployed samurai class – started to head north, much in the way that Americans were heading west at about the same time in history.

By the start of the 20th century, the mainland Japanese population on the island topped one million, and by the time the Meiji period ended, the Ainu had become de-facto second-class citizens in their own land. Many Ainu customs were banned, women were forbidden to get tattoos, and men were prohibited from wearing earrings. An 1899 Japanese government act effectively forced assimilation. The Ainu's land was taken and they were granted Japanese citizenship, denying them the status of an indigenous group. Many Ainu even hid their ethnicity out of fear of discrimination in housing, schools and employment.

After the 1904–5 Russo-Japanese War, won by Japan, Karafuto (now Sakhalin; before 1905 known to Japanese as *Kita-Ezo*) was added to Japanese territory and by 1940, 400,000 Japanese were living there as part of a continuing colonial policy.

The 'northern territories', which included Hokkaidō, expanded, but by the end of WWII they were contracting. Both Karafuto and Chishima (now the disputed Kuril islands) were captured by Russia and remain Russian to this day.

World attention briefly focused on Hokkaidō in 1972 when Sapporo hosted the Winter Olympics, only eight years after the Summer Olympics were held in Tokyo.

In 1998, the act that had forced assimilation on the Ainu people was replaced with one that recognised ethnic minority groups in Japan. Finally, in 2008, the Japanese government recognised the Ainu people as 'an indigenous people with a distinct language, religion and culture'. Today, the Ainu are proudly continuing their traditions while still fighting for further recognition of their unique culture.

THE BLAKISTON LINE

It was an Englishman, Thomas Blakiston (1832–1891), who first noticed that the native animals of Hokkaidō are different species from those on the southern side of the Tsugaru straits on Honshū. Blakiston lived in Japan from 1861–84, spending most of his time in Hakodate, and his name is now used to describe the border in the distribution of animal species between Hokkaidō and the rest of Japan – 'the Blakiston Line'.

While Hokkaidō had land bridges to north Asia via Sakhalin and the Kuril islands, southern Japan's land bridges primarily connected it to the Korean peninsula. Bears found on Honshu are Asiatic black bears while Hokkaidō's bears are Ussuri brown bears, found in northern Asia. On the southern side of the straits, Japanese macaque monkeys are found on Honshū as far north as Aomori, but not in Hokkaidō. Among other species north of the Blakiston line are Siberian chipmunks, Hokkaidō red squirrels, the *ezo-jika* (Hokkaidō deer), *kita-kitsune* (northern fox), northern pika and Blakiston's Fish Owl.

Geography & Climate

Shaped a bit like the squashed head of a squid, Hokkaidō is a very big island and is far and away Japan's largest prefecture. In terms of area, it is almost exactly the same size as Ireland. However, many will find it surprising to hear that in terms of latitude, Hokkaidō is closer to the equator than Ireland.

Surprisingly, Sapporo, at about 43°N, is about the same latitude as Marseille in the south of France and southern Oregon in the USA. Hokkaidō's winter weather, however, is affected by its proximity to Siberia and cold northwesterly winds, which causes frigid weather and significant snowfall, especially on the Sea of Japan side of the island – the kind of powdery snow that excites winter sports enthusiasts. On the Sea of Okhotsk side of Hokkaidō, winter brings drift ice from the north, which clogs up the sea.

Hokkaidō supposedly misses out on *tsuyu*, the rainy season in June and July that covers the rest of Japan in rain, humidity and stickiness – but in these days of climate change, there are claims that Hokkaidō is getting hotter and more humid. Summer is generally warm and pleasant, cooler in the mornings and evenings. *Taifu* (typhoons) seldom make it as far north as Hokkaidō, usually petering out after pounding southern Japan, and/or heading out to sea.

Autumn brings gorgeous fall colours and Hokkaidō is renowned throughout Japan for its beauty in this season, particularly mid-September to mid-October.

Hokkaidō is often divided into four subprefectures: Dō-nan (道南; southern), Dō-ō (道央; central), Dō-hoku (道北; northern) and Dō-tō (道東; eastern).

National Parks

Hokkaidō boasts some of Japan's oldest and most beautiful national parks.

Daisetsuzan National Park (p600), in the centre of the island, is a stunning expanse of mountain ranges, volcanoes, onsen, lakes and hiking tracks. It is Japan's largest national park, covering 2309 sq km.

As far north as you can get in Japan, Rishiri-Rebun-Sarobetsu National Park (p608) offers superb hiking and views of seaside cliffs, a mammoth Fuji-like volcano and, in season, flowers galore.

Shiretoko National Park (p616), in eastern Hokkaidō, is as remote as it gets: a peninsula so impressive, with mountain wilds and rugged coastline, that it is a Unesco World Heritage–listed site.

Still in the east, Akan National Park (p620) has onsen, caldera lakes, volcanoes, *marimo* (famous green algae balls) and plenty of hiking.

Kushiro Wetlands National Park (p626), Japan's largest remaining marshland, plays host to the *tanchō-zuru*, the Japanese crane, known as the symbol of longevity... and Japan Airlines.

South of Sapporo, Shikotsu-Tōya National Park (p589) has caldera lakes, hot springs villages and active volcanoes, and has even hosted a G8 summit.

Getting There & Away

AIR

With the advent of budget airlines in Japan, travelling by air has become the fastest, most convenient and, if you book early enough, cheapest way to get to Hokkaidō.

Sapporo's New Chitose Airport (p576), 40km southeast of Hokkaidō's main city, is the region's hub. Flights arrive in Chitose from all over Japan and an increasing number of direct international flights wing in from around Asia and the Pacific, including Taiwan, Hong Kong, China, Korea, Thailand, Guam, Hawaii and even Sakhalin.

For cheap airfares, check budget airlines such as Vanilla Air, Peach, Air Do, Jetstar and Skymark Airlines – all offer flights to Hokkaidō.

BOAT

Domestic ferries from Honshū are a low-cost, fun way to get to Hokkaidō. Even the cheapest of tickets on a long-distance ferry buys you tatami space.

Hokkaidō's main ferry ports are Tomakomai, Hakodate and Otaru.

Keep the following options in mind:

MOL Ferry (www.sunflower.co.jp) Down the Pacific side between Tomakomai and Ōarai (Ibaraki-ken).

Seikan Ferry (www.seikan-ferry.co.jp) Between Hakodate and Aomori.

Shin-Nihonkai Ferry (www.snf.jp) These guys operate down the Japan Sea side of Honshū. Ferries run between Tomakomai, Akita, Niigata and Tsuruga (Fukui-ken); and between Otaru, Niigata and Maizuru (Kyoto-fu).

Silver Ferry (www.silverferry.jp) Between Tomakomai and Hachinohe (Aomori-ken).

Taiheiyō Ferry (www.taiheiyo-ferry.co.jp) Down the Pacific coast of Honshū, between Tomakomai, Sendai and Nagoya.

Tsugaru Kaikyō Ferry (www.tsugarukaikyo.co.jp) Operates between Hakodate and Aomori.

and Hakodate and Ōma at the northernmost tip of Honshū.

An intriguing international ferry route from Hokkaidō operates from Wakkanai to Sakhalin (p607).

TRAIN

If you have a JR Pass, getting to Hokkaidō is relatively simple. Take a Tohoku *shinkansen* (bullet train) from Tokyo to Aomori, then change to a limited express to Hakodate – this train heads through the Seikan Tunnel to Hokkaidō. The *shinkansen* is expected to have a service to Hakodate by 2016, possibly earlier, and there are plans for a service all the way to Sapporo in 2025.

Getting Around

AIR

While it's possible to travel around Hokkaidō by air, it's definitely not the cheapest way to do things and the number of flights are limited.

ANA (www.ana.co.jp) Offers a number of options, especially seasonal ones such as those that run from Sapporo's New Chitose Airport to Rishiri-tō from 1 June to 30 September.

Hokkaidō Air System (HAC; www.hac-air.co.jp) Operates a number of routes in Hokkaidō, mainly from Sapporo's secondary airport, Okadama. Also flies direct to Rishiri-tō.

BICYCLE

Hokkaidō is a great place to tour by bike. Cyclists are a common sight all over the island, especially during summer. For those looking to hit the road under their own steam, the Cycle Tourism Hokkaido Promotion Network has produced a very useful booklet called Hokkaido Cycle Tourism which can be downloaded online at www.hkd.mlit.go.jp/kanribu/chosei/hct_e.pdf.

Rider houses or cycling terminals are cheap, common and great places to meet other cyclists, as well as bikers.

ROAD TRIP

Hokkaidō's highlights are its national parks, magnificent mountains, hidden hot springs, remote gorges and capes – and public transport struggles to get you to where you want to be. Trains and buses provide limited access and you won't get the chance to explore.

If you really want to see what Hokkaidō has to offer, we heartily recommend that you get your own wheels and take a road trip. The advent of multilingual car-navigation systems for Japan has made driving in Hokkaidō relatively simple for foreign visitors – the bigger rental-car companies have them. Some rental cars even come with pocket wi-fi!

BUS

Within cities, buses are convenient and usually cheap. Ask about a *norihōdai* (all-day) pass if you're going to use them a lot – there's often a substantial discount.

Between cities, there are a number of bus routes. Here are a few:

Chūō Bus (www.chuo-bus.co.jp) Operates between Sapporo and Hakodate, Asahikawa, Obihiro, Kitami, Abashiri, Shiretoko and Kushiro, among others. These guys go everywhere.

Dōhoku Bus (www.dohokubus.com) Between Asahikawa and Obihiro, Kushiro and Sapporo.

Dōnan Bus (www.donanbus.co.jp) Operates mainly between Sapporo and points south, including Hakodate, New Chitose Airport, Tomakomai, Niseko, Rusutsu, Jōzankei, Tōya-ko Onsen and Noboribetsu Onsen.

Sōya Bus (www.soyabus.co.jp) Between Sapporo and Wakkanai.

CAR & MOTORCYCLE

Car-rental rates vary, but if you walk in off the street expect to pay between ¥7000 and ¥10,000 per day, plus the cost of fuel. The best Hokkaidō rental-car deals are booked online and in English before you go.

JR Hokkaido Rent a Car (www.jrh-rentacar.com)

Nippon Rent-a-Car Hokkaido (www.nrh.co.jp/foreign)

Nissan Rent a Car (http://nissan-rentacar.com/english/)

Toyota Rent-a-Car (www.toyotarentacar.net/english)

If you are flying into New Chitose Airport, there are shuttles that takes you directly to the airport car depots, where friendly English-speaking staff will get you on your way.

Roads & Driving

- Hokkaidō's roads are very well maintained.
- There is an expanding pay-your-way expressway system (高速道路; *kōsoku-dōro*), which is relatively expensive and you won't need to use unless you're in a hurry. A reduced-price Hokkaidō Expressway Pass is available for foreign visitors and can be purchased through rental-car companies.
- Major roads are dotted with *Michi-no-eki* (道の駅; road stations), which usually have toilets, refreshments for sale, and often house a small tourist information office.
- Rules are not made to be broken in Japan. Do your best not to exceed what may seem like

exasperatingly slow speed limits (even when the road is a straight as an billiard cue!) and don't park illegally.

➡ Before you go, check out Visit Hokkaidō's (https://en.visit-hokkaido.jp/) downloadable 'Must-have Handbook for Driving in Hokkaidō'.

TRAIN

Trains run frequently on the trunk lines, but there are few lines and reaching remote locations involves infrequent connections. Hokkaidō is a big island with a low population density, so coverage isn't particularly good, especially when compared with the rest of Japan.

In addition to the country-wide JR Rail Pass, there is also a Hokkaidō Rail Pass costing ¥15,000 for three days, ¥19,500 for five days and ¥22,000 for seven days. Check out your options at www2.jrhokkaido.co.jp/global/.

SAPPORO

POP 1.90 MILLION / ☎011

Japan's fifth-largest city, and the prefectural capital of Hokkaidō, Sapporo (札幌) is a surprisingly dynamic and cosmopolitan urban centre that pulses with energy. Designed by European and American architects in the late 19th century, Sapporo is shaped by its wide grid of tree-lined streets and ample public parks, which contribute to the city's surprising level of liveability. After a day of exploring the city you can get your energy back over a hot meal, a great proposition given Sapporo's wholly deserved gastronomic reputation.

As the island's main access point and transport hub, Sapporo serves as an excellent base for striking out into the wilds. But don't check out too quickly: Sapporo is a major tourist destination in itself, especially for those partial to the delicious liquid gold that is Sapporo beer. If you're planning long periods of time hiking in isolation, you might want to first indulge in a bit of the raucous nightlife of the Susukino district. And, of course, if the calendar month happens to read February, don't miss out on the Sapporo Snow Festival (Yuki Matsuri), a winter carnival highlighted by frozen sculptures of everything from brown bears and *tanuki* (racoon dogs) to Godzilla and Doraemon.

History

Sapporo is one of Japan's newest cities, and lacks the temples and castles found in its more southerly neighbours. However, it has a long history of occupation by the Ainu, who first named the area Sari-poro-betsu or 'a river which runs along a plain filled with reeds'.

The present-day metropolis was once nothing but a quiet hunting and fishing town in the Ishikari Plain of Hokkaidō. While the Ainu were left alone until 1821, everything changed when the Tokugawa shogunate (military government) created an official trading post that would eventually become Sapporo. The city was declared the capital of Hokkaidō in 1868, and its growth was carefully planned.

In the 20th century Sapporo emerged as a major producer of agricultural products. Sapporo Beer, the country's first brewery, was founded in 1876 and quickly became synonymous with the city itself. In 1972, Sapporo hosted the Winter Olympics, while the city's annual Sapporo Snow Festival, begun in 1950, attracts more than two million visitors.

In recent years, Sapporo has experienced something of a cultural and spiritual renaissance, especially as more and more youths are choosing to flee their lives in the Tokyo and Osaka areas in search of a new start.

Sights

Sapporo is a very walkable city for much of the year. The gridded streets (a rarity in Japan) make for very simple navigation, and most of the major sights are clustered together in the city centre.

We're not going to lie to you though – Sapporo can be bitterly cold in winter, especially when the Arctic winds are blowing and the snow is piling up. Dress appropriately – and maybe get a beer or two into your system – if you're planning to walk in winter.

Of course, if your body starts to go numb, you can always take advantage of the city's super-efficient subway, tram and bus lines. There is also what seems to be a whole other city underground, with walkways and shopping malls linking JR Sapporo Station with Ōdōri Kōen and Susukino.

High season runs from April to October; most attractions have reduced hours the rest of the year.

★Ōdōri Kōen PARK

(大通公園; www.sapporo-park.or.jp/odori/; Ⓢ Ōdōri) Ōdōri Kōen is the long, block-wide park that splits Sapporo into its north-south grid. Fully 13 blocks (1.5km) long, with the TV Tower at its eastern end, the park plays host to the city's major events and festivals.

Sapporo

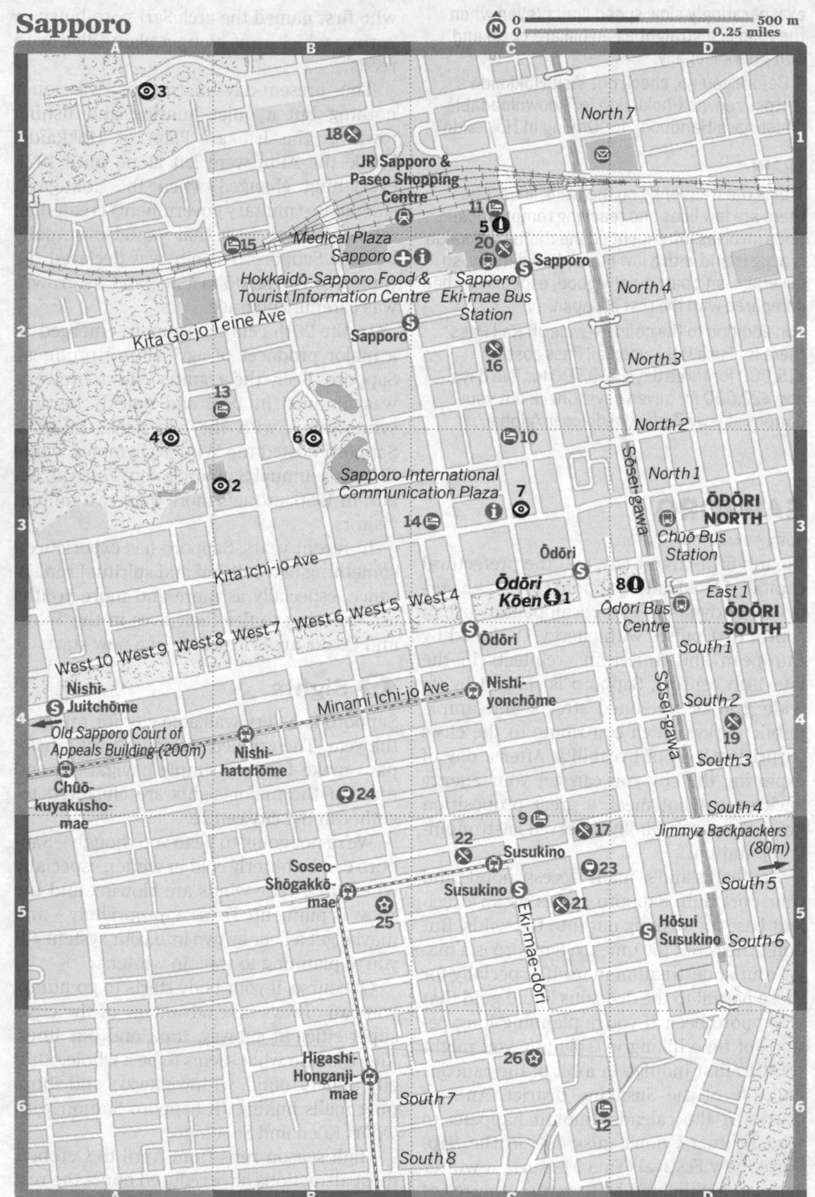

Beautifully manicured flower gardens match the green lawns, overhanging trees and the plentiful artwork, fountains, statues and benches to relax on. A haven in the heart of the city, the park is a 10-minute walk south from JR Sapporo Station along Eki-mae-dōri.

Sapporo TV Tower TOWER
(さっぽろテレビ塔, Sapporo Terebi-tō; www.tv-tower.co.jp; Ōdōri-nishi 1-chōme; admission

Sapporo

Top Sights
1 Ōdōri Kōen C3

Sights
2 Hokkaidō Ainu Center B3
3 Hokkaidō University A1
4 Hokkaidō University Botanical Garden A3
5 JR Tower C1
6 Old Hokkaidō Government Office Building B3
7 Sapporo Clock Tower C3
8 Sapporo TV Tower D3

Sleeping
9 Capsule Inn Sapporo C5
10 Cross Hotel Sapporo C3
11 JR Tower Hotel Nikko Sapporo C1
12 Marks Inn Sapporo C6
13 Nakamuraya Ryokan B2
14 Sapporo Grand Hotel C3
15 Sapporo House Youth Hostel B2

Eating
16 Kani-honke C2
17 Kani-honke (Susukino) C5
18 Kushidori B1
19 Ni-jō Ichiba D4
20 Rāmen Kyōwakoku C2
21 Rāmen Yokochō C5
22 Yosora-no-Jingisukan C5

Drinking & Nightlife
23 500 Bar C5
24 TK6 .... B4

Entertainment
25 alife B5
26 Booty C6

¥700; 9am-10pm; S Ōdōri) There's no way you'll miss this 147m-high Eiffel Tower–shaped affair at the eastern end of Ōdōri Kōen, which stands alongside Tokyo Tower in the category of misplaced monuments. Still, the views from the observation deck at 90m are very impressive, especially when the sun drops below the horizon and Sapporo lights up for the night.

Old Sapporo Court of Appeals Building MUSEUM
(札幌市資料館, Shiryokan; 011-251-0731; www.s-shiryokan.jp/; W13 Ōdori; 9am-7pm Tue-Sun; S Nishi-juitchōme) FREE At the western end of Ōdōri Kōen stands this impressive brick building that was built in 1926 as the Sapporo High Court. While the grounds and gardens seem like an extension of the park, the building houses a popular free museum on Sapporo's history.

JR Tower TOWER
(ＪＲタワー; 011-209-5100; www.jr-tower.com; N5W2 Chūō-ku; admission ¥700; 10am-11pm) The 38-floor JR Tower (173m) offers the best views of Sapporo. It's easy, all indoors, and there are shopping, eating and drinking options galore in the huge complex that surrounds JR Sapporo Station.

Sapporo Clock Tower LANDMARK
(札幌市時計台; Sapporo Tokei-dai; http://sapporoshi-tokeidai.jp; N1W2 Chūō-ku; admission ¥200; 8.45am-5pm; S Ōdōri) No Japanese tourist can leave Sapporo without snapping a photo of the city's signature landmark, the clock tower. Built in 1878, the clock has not missed tolling the hour for more than 130 years. That's impressive, but these days Sapporo's encroaching urban metropolis somewhat dwarfs the small building. The clock tower is just two minutes on foot from Ōdōri station, or a 10-minute walk from JR Sapporo Station.

Old Hokkaidō Government Office Building BUILDING
(北海道庁旧本庁舎; 011-204-5019; N3W6 Chūō-ku; 8.45am-6pm; S Sapporo) FREE Known by all as Akarenga (red bricks), this magnificent neo-baroque building was constructed of bricks in 1888 and is surrounded by lovely lawns and gardens. There are various historical exhibits and art on show. While Akarenga closes at 6pm, the gardens are open until 9pm and are a popular place for a stroll.

Sapporo Winter Sports Museum MUSEUM
(札幌ウィンタースポーツミュージアム; 011-641-8585; www.sapporowintersportsmuseum.com; 1274 Miyano-mori Chūō-ku; admission ¥600; 8.30am-6pm) Housed in the ski-jump stadium built for the Sapporo Olympics west of the central city, this highly amusing museum includes a computerised ski-jump simulator that allows you to try your skills without breaking every bone in your body. And if you do land a few virtual jumps, a chairlift ride to the launch point of the actual ski jump used in the 1972 games should serve as a quick reality check.

To reach the museum, take the Tōzai subway line to Maruyama Kōen (円山公園), then take exit 2 for the Maruyama bus terminal. Next, take bus 14 to Ōkurayama-kyōgi-jō-iriguchi (大倉山競技場入り口; ¥200, 15 minutes); from here, it's a 10-minute walk uphill to the stadium.

Moiwa-yama Ropeway CABLE CAR
(藻岩ロープウェイ; ☎011-561-8177; www.sapporo-dc.co.jp/eng; one way/return ¥900/1700; ⏲10.30am-10pm; 🚊Rōpuwei-iriguchi) Panoramic views of Sapporo can be had from this scenic ropeway and cable-car system, which runs up to the top of Moiwa-san (531m) to the southwest of the central city. You are on the gondola (ropeway) for five minutes, then on the cable car for two more to reach the top, from where there are magnificent views. You can easily access the ropeway by taking the tram to the Rōpuwei-iriguchi stop, and then hopping on the free shuttle bus.

Hokkaidō University UNIVERSITY
(北海道大学, Hokkaidō Daigaku; www.hokudai.ac.jp/en/index.html; ⏲dawn-dusk; 🚆JR Sapporo) Established in 1876, this university is a scenic spot, with a number of unique buildings. The Furukawa Memorial Hall and the Seikatei are noteworthy, and several campus museums are open to the public. The bust of William S Clark, the founding vice-president of the university, is a well-known landmark. Upon his departure in 1877, Professor Clark famously told his students: 'Boys, be ambitious!'

Hokkaidō University Botanical Garden GARDENS
(北大植物園, Hokudai Shokubutsuen; ☎011-221-0066; www.hokudai.ac.jp/fsc/bg; N3W8; admission ¥400; ⏲9am-4pm Tue-Sun) 🍃 One of Sapporo's must-see sights, this beautiful outdoor garden is the botanical showpiece of Hokkaidō University. Here you'll find more than 4000 plant varietals, all attractively set on a meandering 14-hectare plot just 10 minutes on foot southwest of JR Sapporo station. Of particular note is the small section dedicated to Ainu wild foods and medicinal plants.

Hokkaidō Ainu Center CULTURAL CENTRE
(北海道アイヌ協会, Hokkaidō Ainu Kyōkai; ☎011-221-0462; www.ainu-assn.or.jp/english/eabout01.html; 7th fl, Kaderu 2.7 Bldg, N2W7 Chūō-ku; ⏲9am-5pm Mon-Sat; Ⓢ JR Sapporo) FREE Across the street from Hokkaidō University Botanical Garden, this cultural centre offers an interesting display room of robes, tools and historical information on the Ainu.

Hokkaidō Jingu SHINTO SHRINE
(北海道神宮; www.hokkaidojingu.or.jp/eng/index.html; Ⓢ Maruyama-kōen) FREE To the west of the city, this shrine is nestled in a forest so dense it's easy to forget that Sapporo is just beyond the grounds. Dating back to 1869, this is one of the oldest shrines in Hokkaidō and is known for its spectacular cherry and plum blossoms in spring. A few blocks west of Maruyama-kōen subway station (円山公園).

Hokkaidō Museum of Modern Art MUSEUM
(北海道立近代美術館, Hokkaidō Ritsukindai-bijutsukan; www.aurora-net.or.jp/art/dokinbi; N1W17 Chūō-ku; admission ¥500; ⏲9.30am-5pm Tue-Sun; Ⓢ Nishi-juhatchōme) A comprehensive collection of modern works primarily by Japanese artists. The museum is a few blocks north of Nishi-juhatchōme Station (exit 4) on the Tōzai line.

Moerenuma-kōen SCULPTURE PARK
(モエレ沼公園; www.sapporo-park.or.jp/moere/english; 1-1 Moerenuma-kōen; ⏲7am-10pm) FREE Completed in 2005, this former waste-treatment plant to the northeast of the central city is now an impressive reclaimed green belt full of modern sculptures, originally designed by the legendary Noguchi Isamu before his death in 1988. Taking pride of place is the *Glass Pyramid*. To reach the park, take bus 69 or 79 from the Kanjo-dōri Higashi subway stop.

Activities

Sapporo Teine SKIING, SNOWBOARDING
(サッポロテイネ; ☎011-223-5830; www.sapporo-teine.com/snow; day passes ¥4800; ⏲9am-4pm) You can't beat Teine for convenience, as the slopes, which hosted skiing events for the 1972 Winter Olympics, lie quite literally on the edge of Sapporo. Teine has two zones: the lower, more beginner- and family-oriented Olympia Zone, including the Pandaruman Kids' Park; and the higher, more challenging Highland Zone. There are 15 runs and nine lifts. Full equipment rental for skiers/snowboarders is available for ¥4950 per day. English signage is limited and there are few foreigners compared to Niseko.

Just 15 minutes from Sapporo by local train, Teine can get very crowded, particularly on weekends and school holidays. Frequent trains on the JR Hakodate line run between Sapporo and Teine (¥260). From JR Teine Station, shuttle buses conveniently whisk you back and forth to the slopes.

A good option is the Bus Pack, which gets you a return bus trip from Sapporo central city hotels and a seven-hour lift ticket for ¥4800/2800 per adult/child. This deal requires pre-booking by a week, but is perfect if you are heading to Sapporo with your family. Check the website for a list of hotels and timetables.

Sapporo Dome STADIUM
(札幌ドーム; ☎011-850-1020; www.sapporo-dome.co.jp; Ⓢ Fukuzumi) Built for the 2002 FIFA World Cup, the Sapporo Dome was tested early, hosting the hotly contested England vs Argentina match. You can take tours of the Dome on the hour from 10am to 4pm for ¥1000, but book ahead. The Dome is a 10-minute walk from Fukuzumi Station (福住) on the Tōho subway line (地下鉄東豊線).

This intriguing stadium, with a fixed roof, is interesting in that it switches surfaces depending on the sport being played. Sapporo is home to baseball's Hokkaidō Nippon Ham Fighters (www.fighters.co.jp), who play on an artificial surface. The local soccer team is Consadole Sapporo (www.consadole-sapporo.jp) – for their matches a natural grass pitch is slid into the stadium. The Fighters have extremely boisterous crowds and a trip to the Sapporo Dome is a great way to see parochial Japan in action. Check out the website for schedules.

NAC Sapporo ROCK CLIMBING
(ＮＡＣ札幌; ☎011-812-7979; www.nac-web.com/sapporo; Īas Sapporo A Town 1 Fl, イーアス札幌Ａタウン１Ｆ; day pass ¥1950; ⏲10am-10pm; Ⓢ Higashi-Sapporo) Sapporo's version of the Niseko Adventure Centre (NAC) features Japan's largest indoor climbing wall, covering a whopping 1200 sq m inside a shopping centre. You can take '1st step' lessons or aim higher once experienced. Īas Sapporo A Town is a three-minute walk from Higashi-Sapporo (東札幌) Station on the Tōzai subway line (東西線).

Tours

Hokkaidō Chūō Bus Tours BUS TOUR
(北海道中央バス; ☎011-231-0500; http://teikan.chuo-bus.co.jp/en) As well as half- and full-day tours of Sapporo's attractions, Chūō Bus runs day tours to Furano, Biei, Asahidake Onsen, Asahiyama Zoo, Sōunkyō Onsen, Shikotsu-ko and Tōya-ko, Niseko, Jōzankei and Otaru to name just a few.

There are flower tours, onsen tours, market tours… Take a look at the English website and take your pick.

Festivals & Events

Sapporo hosts a lot of festivals and there is always something going on throughout the year.

★**Sapporo Snow Festival** CULTURAL
(さっぽろ雪まつり, Sapporo Yuki Matsuri; www.snowfes.com/english) Drawing more than two million visitors, the annual Sapporo Yuki Matsuri takes place in early February, and is arguably one of Japan's top festivals. From humble beginnings in 1950, when local high-school students built six snow statues in Ōdōri Kōen, these days the festival hosts an international snow sculpture contest attracting teams from around the world.

There's everything from entire frozen stages for visiting musical acts to ice slides and ice mazes for the kiddies and – of course – a cutesy-cool Hello Kitty statue or two. You can view these icy behemoths in Ōdōri Kōen as well as in other locations around the city. The festival also highlights the best in regional food and drink from across the island, and you can expect all kinds of wild and drunken revelry, particularly once the sun sets (at these latitudes, it's quite early!). Finding reasonably priced accommodation can be extremely difficult, so book as far in advance as possible.

Sapporo Beer Festival BEER
(札幌ビールまつり) The summer beer festival is held in Ōdōri Kōen from mid-July to mid-August. The big names plus microbrewers set up outdoor beer gardens, offering a variety of beers and other beverages, as well as food and snacks. A whole month of beer drinking in the sun!

Sapporo Autumn Fest FOOD
(さっぽろオータムフェスト; www.sapporo-autumnfest.jp/english) A new kid in terms of Sapporo festivals, Autumn Fest has been going since 2008 and is extremely popular. Held in the second half of September, it is based on that great Japanese enthusiasm for consuming exquisite food and drink. Stalls are set up with vendors from all over Hokkaidō selling every kind of consumable product imaginable. A must for foodies.

Sleeping

Sapporo offers a diverse range of accommodation ranging from budget crash pads to lavish escapes. Advance reservations are necessary during the Sapporo Snow Festival, and on weekends during peak winter snowfall and the summer holiday periods.

For those on a budget, book online and early for some amazing deals. Hotel prices in Sapporo change by the night – the best deals are in the Sunday to Thursday slot.

★Ino's Place HOSTEL ¥

(イノーズプレイス; ☎011-832-1828; http://inos-place.com/e/; dm/s/d from ¥2900/4300/7600; @📶; Ⓢ Shiroishi) Ino's Place is a popular backpackers' spot with all the fixings – friendly, bilingual staff are on hand to make your stay warm and welcome, while clean rooms, private lockers, free internet, free coffee and tea, no curfew, a Japanese bath, laundry facilities, a kitchen and a communal lounge space sweeten the deal.

To reach Ino's, take the Tōzai subway line to the Shiroishi stop (白石; don't go to JR Shiroishi Station); take exit 1 and walk straight for a few minutes along the main street in the direction of the Eneos petrol station. Turn right at the fourth traffic light and you'll see a detached two-storey white building – you've arrived! The English website tells you all you need to know.

Jimmyz Backpackers HOSTEL ¥

(☎011-206-8632; www.jimmyzbp.com/english; S5E3 Chūō-ku; dm per person ¥2950; 📶; Ⓢ Hōsui Susukino) With only 10 beds in total – six in a mixed dorm and four in a female dorm – Jimmyz isn't huge. In a normal Japanese house converted into a small, homely backpackers, it's convenient though, located only a few blocks east of Susukino.

It's simple, but everything you could want is here, from free tea and coffee to free internet. There's a good English website.

Sapporo International Youth Hostel HOSTEL ¥

(札幌国際ユースホステル; ☎011-825-3120; www.youthhostel.or.jp/kokusai; 6-5-35 Toyohira-ku; dm/r per person from ¥3200/3800; @📶; Ⓢ Gakuen-mae) Housed in a surprisingly modern and stylish building, this well-conceived youth hostel has perfected the basics by offering simple rooms to budget travellers. Both Western- and Japanese-style private rooms are available, as well as 'dorm rooms' featuring four full-sized beds.

The closest subway stop is Gakuen-mae (学園前; exit 2) on the Tōhō line; the hostel is just two minutes from the station behind the Sapporo International Student Centre.

Capsule Inn Sapporo CAPSULE HOTEL ¥

(カプセル・イン札幌; ☎011-251-5571; www.capsuleinn-s.com/english; S3W3 Chūō-ku; r per person ¥2800; @📶; Ⓢ Susukino) If you're a man of simple needs who doesn't get scared easily by small spaces, this XY-chromosome-only capsule hotel offers your standard berth plus a sauna, large bathroom, coin laundry and even a 'book corner' with reclining chairs. A stone's throw from the main Susukino crossing right in the heart of the action. Check-in from 1pm; check-out by 10am.

There's a full explanation in English on their website on how to make the most out of a capsule hotel.

★Nakamuraya Ryokan RYOKAN ¥¥

(中村屋旅館; ☎011-241-2111; www.nakamura-ya.com/english.html; N3W7-1 Chūō-ku; r per person high season from ¥7875, low season ¥7350; @📶; Ⓢ JR Sapporo) Located on a side street near the entrance to the Hokkaidō University Botanical Garden, this charming Japanese-style inn is a wonderful introduction to the pleasures of the island. A variety of different plans are available, featuring tatami rooms of varying shapes and sizes, as well as lavish feasts incorporating the unique flavours of Hokkaidō. There is internet and wi-fi in the lobby.

All guests can also relax in the onsite bath, and the owner-managers are well equipped to deal with the needs of foreign travellers. It's a 10-minute walk from JR Sapporo Station.

Sapporo House Youth Hostel HOSTEL ¥¥

(札幌ハウスユースホステル; ☎011-726-4235; http://yh-sapporo.jp/english/index.html; N6W6-3-1 Kita-ku; dm/tw from ¥3460/8000; @📶; Ⓢ JR Sapporo) Only five minutes on foot west of JR Sapporo Station, just north of the train tracks, the Sapporo House Youth Hostel is in an excellent location. Though it looks like an office building and is slightly sterile, it's a good option for those wanting a cheap place to lay their head.

Marks Inn Sapporo HOTEL ¥¥

(マークスイン札幌; ☎011-512-5001; www.marks-inn.com; S8W3 Chūō-ku; s/d from ¥4500/6000; @📶; Ⓢ Nakajima-kōen) For private accommodation, you really can't get cheaper or more convenient than this business hotel on the edge of the Susukino entertainment district, right across from the canal. Rooms are a bit cramped, but it's easy to find after a night out, the beds are soft, and breakfast is free.

Cross Hotel Sapporo HOTEL ¥¥
(クロスホテル札幌; ☎011-272-0010; www.crosshotel.com/eng_sapporo; N3W2 Chūō-ku; s/d from ¥6000/9600; @📶; Ⓢ JR Sapporo) This shimmering tower is located about five minutes south of the JR Sapporo Station on foot. The interior is a veritable designer's showcase, with chic rooms categorised according to three thematic styles: urban, natural and hip. There's also a steel-and-glass-enclosed onsen that allows you to stare out at the city while you soak in a steaming tub.

Sapporo Grand Hotel HOTEL ¥¥¥
(札幌グランドホテル; ☎011-261-3311; www.grand1934.com/english/index.html; N1W4 Chūō-ku; r from ¥19,000; @📶; Ⓢ JR Sapporo) Established in 1934 as the first European-style hotel in Sapporo, this grand old dame now occupies three adjacent buildings that lie at the southeast corner of the former Hokkaidō government building. Fairly subdued rooms vary considerably in price and style, though all guests are seemingly treated to VIP service from arrival to checkout.

JR Tower Hotel Nikko Sapporo HOTEL ¥¥¥
(ＪＲタワーホテル日航札幌; ☎011-251-2222; www.jrhotelgroup.com/eng/hotel/eng101.htm; N5W2 Chūō-ku; s/d/tw from ¥24,000/33,000/38,000; @📶; Ⓢ JR Sapporo) You can't beat the location of this lofty hotel, virtually on top of JR Sapporo Station. Taking advantage of such great heights, the Hotel Nikko Sapporo offers plush rooms priced by floor, a spa with a view, and both Western and Japanese restaurants perched on the 35th floor. The views from the top are some of the best in Sapporo.

Eating

In addition to its namesake beer, Sapporo is famous for its miso-based *rāmen* (egg noodles), which makes use of Hokkaidō's delicious butter and fresh corn. The city also serves up some truly incredible seafood, winter-warming stews and *jingisukan*, an easy-to-love dish of roasted lamb that pays tribute to everybody's favourite Mongol warlord, Genghis Khan.

★ **Rāmen Yokochō** RAMEN ¥
(元祖さっぽろラーメン横丁; Rāmen Alley; www.ganso-yokocho.com; ⏲11am-3am; Ⓢ Susukino) This famous alleyway in the Susukino entertainment district is crammed with *rāmen* shops. Anyone with a yen for *rāmen* shouldn't miss it, but it can be tricky to find. From the main Susukino crossroads, walk south to the first crossroad. Turn left (east); Rāmen Yokochō is halfway down on the right, running parallel to Eki-mae-dōri.

If you can't find it just ask – it's one place people will know. Hours vary for different shops, though prices are consistently reasonable, with a bowl of noodles setting you back around ¥1000. This is the original Rāmen Yokochō, and they are keen to distance themselves from all imposters.

Rāmen Kyōwakoku RAMEN ¥
(らーめん共和国, Rāmen Republic; www.sapporo-esta.jp/ramen; 10th fl, ESTA Bldg, JR Sapporo Station; bowl of rāmen ¥700-1000; ⏲11am-10pm; Ⓢ JR Sapporo) If Rāmen Yokochō is the original Rāmen Alley with history and atmosphere on its side, then these guys are the shameless copycats. The thing is, Japan is renowned for copying things and improving them. Rāmen Kyōwakoku is a 'clean', touristy version of the original, but it is also very good.

It's all here in eight different shops – Sapporo *miso-rāmen*, Asahikawa *shōyu-rāmen* and Hakodate *shio-rāmen*. A Hokkaidō rāmen odyssey! No early morning noodles here after a hard night's drinking though – it all closes down with the department stores.

Ni-jō Ichiba MARKET ¥
(二条市場; S3E1&2 Chūō-ku; ⏲7am-6pm; Ⓢ Ōdōri) While Ni-jō Ichiba is starting to look a tad tired, there is still plenty to poke your nose into. Buy a bowl of rice and select your own sashimi toppings, gawk at the fresh delicacies such as sea urchin and crab, or chow down on Hokkaidō's version of 'Mother and Child' *(oyakodon)*, rice topped with salmon and roe.

Get there early for the freshest selections and the most variety; individual restaurants have their own hours. The market is just over the Sōsei-gawa at the eastern end of the Tanuki-kōji shopping arcade.

Yosora-no-Jingisukan JINGISUKAN ¥¥
(夜空のジンギスカン; ☎011-219-1529; www.yozojin.com; S4W4 Chūō-ku, 9th & 10th fl; plates

A FOOD LOVER'S GUIDE TO HOKKAIDŌ

From a gourmet's perspective, it is something of a tragedy that little tangible evidence remains of Hokkaidō's indigenous cuisine. In 1878, a Yorkshire woman by the name of Isabella Bird dined with Ainu, and wrote the following lip-smacking account: 'Soon, the evening meal was prepared by the chief's principal wife, who tipped into a soot pot swinging over the flames a mixture of wild roots, beans, seaweed, shredded fish, dried venison, millet paste, water and fish oil, and left the lot to stew for three hours.'

Of course, the frontier spirit is still alive and well on the island, and Hokkaidō does remain a foodie's paradise. One Ainu dish that has survived the passage of time is *ruibe* (ルイベ), which is simply a salmon that has been left out in the Hokkaidō midwinter freeze, sliced up sashimi style, and then served with soy sauce and water peppers.

The Ainu tradition of hotpots is also being fostered by modern Japanese, and you'll find winter-warming *nabemono* (鍋物) all across the island. A particularly delicious variant of this dish is *ishikari-nabe* (石狩鍋), a rich stew of cubed salmon, miso, mirin, potatoes, cabbage, tofu, leek, kelp, wild mushrooms and sea salt. Sapporo-ites are also fond of their original *sūpu-karē* (スープカレー), which is quite literally a soupy variant of Japanese curry.

In addition to salmon, another cold-water speciality is *kani-ryōri* (かに料理; crab cuisine). The long-legged crabs of Wakkanai and Kushiro fetch the highest prices, though anything from Hokkaidō's icy waters will be packed with flavour.

Dairy cows flourish in the island's wide open expanses, which is reason enough to add a bit of lactose to your diet. Hokkaidō milk is used in everything from ice cream and cappuccinos to creamy soups and sauces, while Hokkaidō butter is best served atop a bowl of *rāmen* (ラーメン).

There are variants of everybody's favourite soup-noodle dish across the island, though the most famous is the miso-based Sapporo *rāmen*. If you want to be a purist, wash down your bowl with a pint of the legendary lager that is Sapporo *bīru* (札幌ビール).

And finally, no culinary account of Hokkaidō is complete without mention of Sapporo's beloved *jingisukan* (ジンギスカン), which was perhaps best summed up by British writer Alan Booth in his book *The Roads to Sata* (1985): 'I ordered the largest mug of draught beer on the menu and a dish of mutton and cabbage, which the Japanese find so outlandish that they have dubbed it *jingisukan* (Genghis Khan) after the grandfather of the greatest barbarian they ever jabbed at. The beer, as always, was about one-third froth, but a single portion of Ghenghis was so huge that it took an hour to eat – compensation for the loss of fluid ounces…'

from ¥850; 5pm-1am; Susukino) There is *jingisukan* everywhere you look in Sapporo, though at this speciality place, located on the 9th and 10th floors of the My Plaza building, you can grill up lamb from around the world while checking out the city views. The handy picture menu makes ordering a breeze.

Highly recommended is the two-hour, ¥3100 per head, eat-all-you-can, drink-all-you-can plan on the 9th floor. The My Plaza building is at the opposite end of the same block as McDonald's at Susukino Crossing.

Sushi-no-uo-masa SUSHI ¥¥

(鮨の魚政; 011-644-9914; www.asaichi-maruka.jp; Chūō Oroshi-uri-ichiba Maruka Centre 1F, N12W21, 中央卸売市場マルカセンター１Ｆ; 5am-11am; JR Sōen) This is something special: sushi for breakfast out at the fish markets. It's going to take an effort to get here, but the sushi is the best and you can wander around the Sapporo fish markets before and after eating. It's out at N12W21, a 10-minute walk from JR Sōen Station (桑園) or a 10-minute drive from Sapporo station.

Sushi-no-uo-masa is smack in the middle of the stalls on the ground floor of the Maruka Centre. If you're asking locals for directions, ask for the Chūō Oroshi-uri-ichiba.

Kushidori YAKITORI ¥¥

(串鳥; 011-758-2989; http://kushidori.com; N7W4-8-3 Kita-ku; skewers from ¥150; 11am-12.30am; JR Sapporo) A famous Sapporo chain serving a variety of *yakitori* (skewers of grilled chicken) and grilled vegetables,

Kushidori has a simpe picture menu. Point at what you want, and the chef will grill it for you – choose from either *tare* (sauce) or *shio* (salt).

There are locations all around the city, including this one just a few blocks north of JR Sapporo Station. There are also two at Susukino crossing. Look for the red sign with 串鳥 on it.

★Kani-honke SEAFOOD ¥¥¥

(札幌かに本家; ☎011-222-0018; www.kani-honke.jp/e; N3W2 Chūō-ku; set courses from ¥4400; ⏱11.30am-10pm; 📄; 🚉JR Sapporo) These are THE crab guys! The frigid seas surrounding Hokkaidō are bountiful and yield some of the tastiest crustaceans on the planet. Kani-honke is legendary for its crab offerings – try the recommended Kani-isuki menu for ¥4400 per person. Crab and vegetables are cooked in a pot, consumed, then rice and egg are added to the remaining soup.

There are two Kani-honke restaurants in Sapporo. One is near JR Sapporo station and the other one block east of Susukino crossing. For both, look for the sign with the huge crab and the enormous かに本家 sign on top of the building.

Drinking & Nightlife

Sapporo-ites are famous for their love of the drink, and if you want to drop delicious Sapporo lager straight from the source, don't miss Sapporo Beer Garden (p576). While there are literally hundreds of bars and clubs scattered throughout the city, all of the action and nightlife revolves around Susukino, the largest entertainment district north of Tokyo. All bars in this area are within easy stumbling distance of the Susukino subway station.

★TK6 BAR

(☎011-272-6665; http://tk6.jp; S2W6 Chūō-ku; ⏱4pm-late; 📶; Ⓢ Susukino) Sapporo's top sports bar, TK6 keeps everybody bubbling with happy hour from 4pm to 7pm daily, free wireless for all patrons and international sports events on the big screen. Get some tips on what to do in town from the locals, both Japanese and foreign. The bar food is as good as the beer.

500 Bar BAR

(ファイブハンドレッドバー; S4W2 Chūō-ku, 1st fl, Hoshi Bldg; ⏱6pm-5am Mon-Sat, to 3am Sun & holidays; Ⓢ Susukino) This place, with reasonable and easy to add up prices, is usually packed with a mix of foreign and local clientele, even on weekdays. Every drink on the menu here is ¥500, hence the name (pronounced 'gohyakubaa'). This is one of the franchise's several locations in Sapporo, one block east of Susukino crossing.

Booty CLUB

(ブーティー; www.booty-disco.com; S7W4 Chūō-ku; ⏱8pm-close Fri & Sat; Ⓢ Susukino) Booty has built up a deserved reputation as a top party place in Sapporo. Only open on Fridays and Saturdays, it offers Western-style fast food alongside urban beats. The rotating schedule – which you can check out online – incorporates the best in hip-hop, R&B and reggae, and attracts a young, clubby crowd. No entry charge.

alife CLUB

(エーライフ; www.alife.jp/pc; S4W6 Chūō-ku, B1F Taiki Bldg; ⏱8pm-close; Ⓢ Susukino) This well-heeled club, which has just charged past its 10th anniversary, brings a bit of the Tokyo high life to the far north. Although the thermometer might be dropping outside, it's always hot and heavy in this cavernous joint, so dress to impress!

Orientation

Sapporo, laid out in a Western-style grid pattern, has to be one of the easiest cities in the world to navigate.

Blocks are labelled East or West and North or South in relation to a central point near the TV Tower in the city centre. The grass-covered park Ōdōri Kōen divides the city into its north–south halves. The address is either north or south of Ōdōri Kōen. The east–west divider is officially the canal-like Sōsei-gawa (創成川). Addresses are either west or east of the river. Most of the central city and its points of interest are west.

Sitting almost perfectly on the intersecting points is Sapporo Terebi-tō, just to the west of the river. As the TV Tower can be easily seen, everyone gets their bearings from it.

It's all very simple. For example, the famous landmark Tokei-dai (Clock Tower) is in the block of North 1, West 2 (Kita Ichi-jo, Nishi Ni-chōme) – N1W2.

JR Sapporo Station is at N5W2. South of Ōdōri is the downtown shopping district with shops and arcades. Susukino, the club and entertainment district, is located mainly between the South 2 and South 6 blocks.

DON'T MISS

SAPPORO BEER

Let's face it: 'Sapporo' means beer. After visiting Germany (and being favourably impressed), Kihachirō Ōkura returned and selected Sapporo as the lucky place to start what would become Japan's first beer brewery, founded in 1876.

Sapporo Beer Garden & Museum (サッポロビール園; www.sapporoholdings.jp/english/guide/sapporo/; N7E9 Higashi-ku; ⊙beer garden 11.30am-10pm, museum 10.30am-6pm) Part museum, part beer garden, this legendary Sapporo attraction is in the original Sapporo Beer brewery, almost due east of JR Sapporo Station. There are free one-hour tours of the museum (recorded English commentary provided) followed by tastings (¥200 per beer). The adjoining beer garden has four restaurants spanning a variety of cuisines.

Purists should note that pints of Sapporo were meant to be enjoyed with the local grilled-lamb speciality, *jingisukan* (Genghis Khan). There is also a great gift shop selling beer memorabilia.

Take the Tōhō subway to the Higashi-Kuyakusho-mae stop (exit 4) and walk for 10 minutes, or hop on the 'Sapporo Walk' (Kan 88) bus at the south side of JR Sapporo Station and get off at the Sapporo Beer Factory stop.

Hokkaidō Brewery (サッポロビール北海道工場; ☎011-748-1876; www.sapporoholdings.jp/english/guide/hokkaido/; Toiso 542-1, Eniwa-shi; ⊙tours 10am-4pm Tue-Sun) A must for die-hard beer fans, Hokkaidō Brewery, the current brewing and bottling facility, is housed in a mammoth production plant that looks like something out of a James Bond film. Technicians in white lab coats peer into test tubes; immaculate stainless-steel tanks are covered with computerised gauges and dials; and video cameras monitor the bottles as they whiz by.

English is minimal on the 40-minute self-guided tour, but you'll be rewarded with a refreshing 20 minutes to tipple at the end.

Admission is free, but you need to make reservations by 5pm the day before.

Hokkaidō Brewery is a 40-minute train ride from Sapporo; take the JR Chitose line towards the airport and get off at the Sapporo Beer Teien Station. By bus, take the Sapporo to Chitose bus and get off at the Sapporo Beer Hokkaido Brewery stop.

ℹ Information

MEDICAL SERVICES

For good advice on health in Hokkaidō, visit www.healthhokkaido.com.

Medical Plaza Sapporo (メディカルプラザ札幌; ☎011-209-5450; www.medical-plaza.jp; N5W2 Chūō-ku; Ⓢ JR Sapporo) Conveniently located on the 7th and 8th floors of the JR Tower in JR Sapporo Station.

Sapporo City General Hospital (市立札幌病院; ☎011-726-2211; www.city.sapporo.jp/hospital; N11W13 1-1 Chūō-ku; ⊙24hr) Offers 24-hour emergency care.

POST

Sapporo Central Post Office (札幌中央郵便局, Sapporo Chūō Yūbinkyoku; ☎011-748-2451; N6E1-2-1 Higashi-ku; ⊙9am-8pm Mon-Fri, 9am-7pm Sat, 9am-5pm Sun; Ⓢ JR Sapporo) Located just east of Sapporo JR Station. Take the north exit and turn right. The ATMs stay open longer than the window.

TOURIST INFORMATION

Hokkaidō-Sapporo Food & Tourist Information Centre (北海道さっぽろ「食と観光」情報館; ☎011-213-5088; www.welcome.city.sapporo.jp/english; JR Sapporo Station; ⊙8.30am-8pm; Ⓢ JR Sapporo) Located on the ground floor of Sapporo Stellar Pl, inside JR Sapporo Station, this is the island's mother lode of tourist information. Stock up on maps, timetables, brochures and pamphlets, and be sure to make use of the friendly and helpful bilingual staff. JR also has English-speaking staff in here to answer your train questions.

Sapporo International Communication Plaza (札幌国際プラザ; ☎011-211-3678; www.plaza-sapporo.or.jp/en; N1W3 Chūō-ku, 3rd fl, MN Bldg; ⊙9am-5.30pm Mon-Sat; Ⓢ Ōdori) Directly opposite the Sapporo Clock Tower, this place is set up to cater for the needs of foreign residents and visitors. There is an extensive list of English resources, free internet access and helpful, friendly staff.

ℹ Getting There & Away

AIR

New Chitose Airport (CTS; www.new-chitose-airport.jp/en/) Sapporo's main airport is about 40km southeast of the city. Domestic destinations include Tokyo, Osaka, Nagoya, Hiroshima and many others.

Okadama Airport (丘珠空港; Okadama Kūkō) Small airport about 10km north of Sapporo with limited service to cities in Hokkaidō.

BUS

Highway buses connect Sapporo with the rest of Hokkaidō, are generally cheaper than trains and are even time-competitive on some routes.

- **Sapporo Eki-mae Bus Station** (札幌駅前バスターミナル) is the main terminal, just southeast of JR Sapporo Station, beneath Esta.
- **Chūō Bus Station** (中央バスターミナル; Ōdōri E1), the bus terminal for Hokkaidō Chūō Bus company, is located just northeast of Sapporo TV Tower.
- **Ōdōri Bus Centre** (大通バスターミナル; S1E1) was formerly a main terminus but usage is now declining. It's just southeast of Sapporo TV Tower.

At all three departure points you will find ticket booths from where you can purchase tickets to major cities throughout Hokkaidō.

Some sample destinations, which have frequent daily departures from Sapporo Eki-mae:

Asahikawa ¥2000, two hours
Furano ¥2100, three hours
Niseko ¥2300, three hours
Noboribetsu Onsen ¥2100, two hours
Tōya-ko Onsen ¥2700, 2¾ hours
Wakkanai ¥6000, six hours

From Chūō bus station there are a few departures a day to Abashiri (¥6210, 6¼ hours) and Obihiro (¥3670, 4¼ hours).

Buses to Hakodate depart from both the Chūō and Ōdōri bus stations (¥4680, 5¼ hours).

CAR & MOTORCYCLE

The best place in Hokkaidō to pick up a rental car is at the New Chitose Airport. There are a dozen companies located in the arrivals area on the 1st floor. Most companies also have outlets in Sapporo.

TRAIN

Getting to Sapporo by train is relatively easy. If you're coming from Honshū, the easiest way is to get to Aomori, the northern terminal for the Tohoku *shinkansen*. Once there, transfer to the JR Tsugaru Kaikyō line – trains run through the Seikan Tunnel between Aomori and Hakodate (¥5340, two hours), and then change to the JR Hakodate line between Hakodate and Sapporo (¥8590, 3½ hours).

The *shinkansen* is expected to have a service to Hakodate by 2016, possibly earlier, and has plans for a service all the way to Sapporo in 2025.

Getting Around

TO/FROM THE AIRPORT

New Chitose Airport is accessible from Sapporo by *kaisoku* (rapid) train (¥1340, 35 minutes) or bus (¥1000, 1¼ hours). There are also convenient bus services connecting the airport to various Hokkaidō destinations including Niseko.

For Okadama airport, shuttle buses depart from Sakaemachi subway station, the northernmost stop on the Tōhō subway line, every 20 minutes (¥210, five minutes).

BUS & TRAM

JR Sapporo Station is the main terminus for local buses.

Year-round between 7am and 11pm, the 'Sapporo Walk' tourist bus (Kan 88) loops through major sights and attractions including the Sapporo Beer Garden, Ōdōri Park and the Clock Tower; a one-day pass costs ¥750, single trips are ¥210.

There is a single tram line in Sapporo that heads west from Ōdōri, turns south, then loops back to Susukino. The fare is a flat ¥170.

SUBWAY

Sapporo's three subway lines are extremely efficient. Fares start at ¥200 and one-day passes cost ¥800 (weekend-only passes are ¥500 per day).

TAXI

Taxis are a quick and comfortable way to move around the city, but you'll pay substantially for the convenience factor. Flagfall is ¥650, which gives you 1.6km; it's then an additional ¥260 per kilometre.

PUBLIC TRANSPORT PASSES

Common Use One-Day Card Includes the use of subways, trams and city buses for ¥1000 per day.

Kitaca JR Hokkaidō's rechargeable pay-in-advance IC card that can be used on JR trains in the greater Sapporo region including Shin-Chitose Airport and Otaru, as well as on subways, trams and buses.

Sapica A rechargeable pay-in-advance IC card that covers Sapporo's subways, city buses and trams.

With You Card Pay-in-advance non-rechargeable card (various denominations available from ¥500 to ¥10,000) that can be used on subways, trams and city buses.

SOUTHERN HOKKAIDŌ

Southern Hokkaidō (道南; Dō-nan) is often bypassed entirely by Sapporo-bound travellers. That's a shame as Hakodate, a prominent Meiji-era port, is one of the most atmospheric cities in Hokkaidō and is certainly worth a visit. Dō-nan is also home to a couple of small but historically significant towns, which bear striking architectural reminders of the Edo period.

Hakodate 函館

POP 280,000 / ☎0138

Built on a narrow strip of land between Hakodate Harbour to the west and the Tsugaru Strait to the east, Hakodate is the southern gateway to the island of Hokkaidō. Under the Kanagawa Treaty of 1854, the city was one of the first ports to open up to international trade, and as such hosted a small foreign community. Much of that influence can still be seen in the Motomachi district, a steep hillside that is sprinkled with wooden buildings and brick churches. You can also get a sense of the town's history by riding nostalgic trams through the orderly streets.

The latest big news for Hakodate is that the *shinkansen* (bullet train) is almost here. Operations to Hakodate from Honshū through the Seikan Tunnel should be up and running by 2016.

Sights

Hakodate-yama & Ropeway MOUNTAIN

(函館山; ☎0138-23-3105; www.334.co.jp/eng; one way/return ¥660/1200; ⏲10am-10pm) Mention you've been to Hakodate and every Japanese person you know will ask if you saw the night view from atop Hakodate-yama – it's that famous! Take the ropeway (gondola) to the top for amazing views over the city. Take tram 2 or 5 to the Jūjigai stop, and walk uphill to the ropeway station.

Alternatively, a summit-bound bus (¥360, 30 minutes) leaves directly from JR Hakodate Station, and stops at several viewing places as it winds to the top. You can also drive up or take the hiking track (from May to late October).

★**Hakodate Morning Market** MARKET

(函館朝市, Hakodate Asa-ichi; www.hakodate-asaichi.com; ⏲5am-noon) FREE Located just to the south of JR Hakodate Station, this market is a great place for hungry seafood lovers. Like tightly packed ammo, freshly caught squid glisten in ice-stuffed styrofoam. Most of the live commerce is over by 8am, but you can still pick up snacks and souvenirs later in the morning.

Red-brick Warehouse District HISTORIC BUILDINGS

(赤レンガ倉庫) Hakodate's red-brick warehouses were built around 1907 and now house food markets, cafes, shops and galleries. This extremely popular part of town sits on the waterfront between JR Hakodate Station and Motomachi. If your feet get a tad tired, give them a rest in the *ashi-yu* (foot bath) out the back of La Vista Hakodate Bay Hotel.

Hakodate Museum of Northern Peoples MUSEUM

(函館市北方民族資料館; Hakodate-shi Hoppō-minzoku Shiryōkan; ☎0138-22-4128; www.zaidan-hakodate.com/hoppominzoku/#sisetu; 21-7 Suehiro-chō; admission ¥300; ⏲9am-7pm; 🚋5, stop Suehirō-chō) The Hakodate City Museum of Northern Peoples is a recommended place to learn about the Ainu and their culture. The exhibits are immaculate and English signage has been added to some.

Motomachi District

On Mt Hakodate's lower slopes, Motomachi is home to many historic buildings such as foreign churches, consulates and residences from the 19th century. Scattered around the hillside among more modern neighbourhoods, they command stunning panoramic views of the bay.

Take tram 5 from JR Hakodate Station and get off at the Suehirō-chō stops, then walk uphill.

Old Public Hall of Hakodate Ward MUSEUM

(旧函館区公会堂, Kyū-Hakodate Kukōkaidō; www.zaidan-hakodate.com/koukaido; 11-13 Motomachi; admission ¥300; ⏲9am-7pm; 🚋5, stop Suehirō-chō) The old Public Hall of Hakodate Ward, built in 1910, is an ornate mansion awash in pale blues and yellows that reigns regally over the district. Inside are items of historical interest relating to the city, although its main appeal is the wonderful colonial-style architecture.

Old English Consulate MUSEUM

(旧イギリス領事館, Kyū-Igirisu Ryōjikan; www.hakodate-kankou.com/british/en/; 33-14 Motomachi; admission ¥300; ⏲9am-7pm; 🚋5, stop Suehirō-chō) From 1913 to 1934, this

Central Hakodate

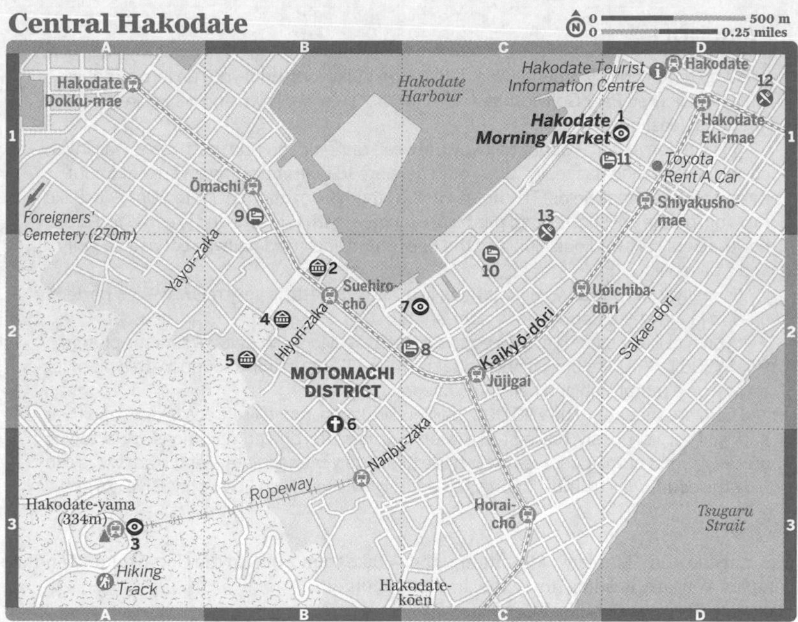

Central Hakodate

Top Sights
1 Hakodate Morning Market ... D1

Sights
2 Hakodate Museum of Northern Peoples ... B2
3 Hakodate-yama & Ropeway ... A3
4 Old English Consulate ... B2
5 Old Public Hall of Hakodate Ward ... B2
6 Orthodox Church ... B2
7 Red-brick Warehouse District ... C2

Sleeping
8 B&B Pension Hakodate-mura ... C2
9 Hakodate Perry House ... B1
10 La Vista Hakodate Bay Hotel ... C2
11 Tōyoko Inn Hakodate Eki-mae Asaichi ... D1

Eating
12 Daimon Yokochō ... D1
13 Hakodate Beer ... C1

whitewashed mansion served as the British consulate. Today it's primarily used as a tea salon for sightseers in need of some afternoon respite.

Orthodox Church CHURCH
(函館ハリストス正教会, Hakodate Harisutosu Seikyōkai; http://orthodox-hakodate.jp; 3-13 Motomachi; donation ¥200; ⏲10am-5pm Mon-Fri, 10am-4pm Sat, 1-4pm Sun; 🚋5, stop Suehirō-chō) Dating from 1916, this beautiful old Russian Orthodox church is adorned with distinctive copper domes and spires.

Foreigners' Cemetery CEMETERY
(外国人墓地, Gaikokujin Bochi; 23 Funamichō; ⏲dawn-dusk; 🚋5, stop Hakodate Dokku-mae) The Foreigners' Cemetery, an interesting slice of local history, contains the graves of sailors, clergy and others who died far away from their homelands. Many of the graves are marked with English, Russian or French inscriptions. The first to be buried here were two sailors from the American Navy's 1854 visit.

Greater Hakodate

★Yunokawa Onsen Monkeys ONSEN
(湯の川温泉猿; ☎0138-57-7833; www.hako-eco.com/english_leaflet.pdf; 3-1-15 Yunokawa-cho; admission ¥300; ⏲9.30am-6pm Apr-Oct, 9.30am-4.30pm Nov-Mar) While the onsen monkeys

PARK GOLF

If you do much driving around Hokkaidō it won't take long until you run into a meticulously manicured Park Golf course (パークゴルフ) – every town and village in Hokkaidō has got at least one.

This version of golf – about halfway between real golf and putt-putt golf – was invented in Hokkaidō and has really taken off. There are 18 holes covering an area of about three or four football fields. The holes vary in length from about 40m to 80m – just like real golf, par 3s are shorter and par 5s are longer – with bunkers and greens. You are, however, only allowed one club and the ball is hard and sized halfway between a golf ball and a baseball.

It's really fun, you can wear what you like, and etiquette is very relaxed – it's perfectly okay to laugh at your opponent's poor shots!

If you feel like a bit of fun, stop your car and take a look. Most local courses charge from ¥300 to ¥500 to play; it should take around 1½ hours for a round. With a bit of luck there'll be a rental club and ball you can use.

There are thought to be 700,000 'parkers' in Japan, mostly retirees. Many take their park golf very seriously, having town-wide tournaments and competitions. Most towns are very proud of their courses, which are absolutely immaculate – and whoever is running the course will be most impressed if foreign visitors turn up to play. Give it a go!

are outside on Monkey Mountain, the complex you are heading to is the indoor Hakodate Tropical Botanical Garden at Yunokawa Onsen. While the garden is nice, the undoubted stars of the show, especially in winter, are the Japanese macaque monkeys who soak in their own private onsen, often surrounded by snow.

If they're feeling enthused, you might get to see them jumping off their high wires into the onsen. If watching the monkeys gets you excited about getting into hot water too, don't forget that Yunokawa Onsen is a hot springs area and the nearby hotels will be happy to relieve you of your yen so you can have a bath, too. To get here, take Hakodate Bus from outside Hakodate Station for 20 minutes to the Nettai Shokubutsuen-mae stop.

Goryō-kaku Fort Park FORT

(五稜郭公園) FREE Japan's first Western-style fort was built in 1864 in the shape of a five-pointed star (*goryō-kaku* means 'five-sided fort'), and was designed to trap attackers in deadly crossfire. Nothing remains of the actual fort structure, but the landscaped grounds and moat are picturesque, and 1600 cherry trees make this a great spot in spring.

The 98m **Goryō-kaku Tower** (☎0138-51-4785; www.goryokaku-tower.co.jp; admission ¥840; ⊙8am-7pm) was opened in 2006 so that the five-pointed star can be viewed from above. Take tram 2 or 5 to the Goryōkaku-kōen-mae stop.

Festivals & Events

Hakodate has plenty going on throughout the year. For the full scoop, see www.hakodate.travel/en/event/.

Hakodate Goryō-kaku Matsuri CULTURAL

(函館五稜郭祭り) Held on the third weekend in May, this festival features a parade of townsfolk dressed in the uniforms of the soldiers who took part in the Meiji Restoration battle of 1868.

Hakodate Port Festival CULTURAL

(函館港祭り, Hakodate Minato Matsuri) During the Hakodate Port Festival in early August, groups of seafood-fortified locals (reportedly 10,000 of them) move like waves doing an energetic squid dance.

Sleeping

Hakodate Perry House GUESTHOUSE ¥

(函館ぺりーハウス; ☎0138-83-1457; www.hakodate-perryhouse.com; 3-2 Ōmachi; r per person ¥2000-3500; Ōmachi) Opened exactly 160 years after Perry's American Navy ships visited Hakodate, this simple guesthouse is named after the great naval captain. Rooms are smallish and the bathroom and toilet facilities are shared, but the price is right and the location is convenient near the Ōmachi tram stop.

B&B Pension Hakodate-mura PENSION ¥¥
(B＆Bペンションはこだて村; ☎0138-22-8105; www.bb-hakodatemura.com; 16-12 Suehiro-chō; s/d from ¥5940/9500; @☎; Jūjigai) In a great location near the corner of the harbour, everything is close here. Expect a friendly welcome and English speakers at this B&B with restaurant and lounge on the ground floor, and rooms upstairs. There are plenty of room options – check out the website. Breakfast available for ¥840.

Tōyoko Inn Hakodate Eki-mae Asaichi HOTEL ¥¥
(東横イン函館駅前朝市; ☎0138-23-1045; www.toyoko-inn.com/e_hotel/00063/index.html; 22-7 Ōtemachi; s/d from ¥4000/6000; @☎; JR Hakodate) Hakodate's version of the Tōyoko Inn is an affordable choice for budget-conscious travellers in need of private space. Includes breakfast, supper, internet and a host of other services. It's located just steps away from the morning market, and only three minutes on foot from JR Hakodate Station.

La Vista Hakodate Bay Hotel HOTEL ¥¥¥
(ラビスタ函館ベイ; ☎0138-23-6111; www.hotespa.net/hotels/lahakodate; 12-6 Toyokawa-chō; r from ¥13,000; @☎; Uōichiba-dori) This excellent upmarket hotel benefits from its waterfront district location. Rooms are smallish but attention to detail is excellent. There is a rooftop onsen and spa complex, complete with soaking tubs overlooking the mountains and the bay.

Eating & Drinking

Daimon Yokochō FOOD STALLS ¥
(大門横丁; ☎0138-24-0033; 7-5 Matsukaze-chō; JR Hakodate) Head east from JR Hakodate Station for five minutes to find this collection of food stalls with all sorts of cuisine on offer. Hakodate is known for its *shio-rāmen* with a clear, salty soup. There are plenty of opportunities to try it here.

★ **Hakodate Beer** PUB FOOD ¥¥
(はこだてビール; ☎0138-23-8000; www.hakodate-factory.com/beer; 5-22 Ōtemachi; dishes from ¥650; 11am-10pm; ; Uōichiba-dori) Scan the English menu at Hakodate Beer and choose from a variety of microbrews – from cold ales and golden wheat beers to dark stouts – to complement homemade pizzas and items from the grill including freshly caught squid and locally made sausages. Beer enthusiasts will love this place.

Information

Hakodate Tourist Information Centre (函館市観光案内所; ☎0138-23-5440; www.hakodate.travel/en; 9am-7pm Apr-Oct, 9am-5pm Nov-Mar; JR Hakodate) Inside JR Hakodate Station, this information centre has plenty of English brochures and maps. The Travel Hakodate website is extremely well done.

Getting There & Away

AIR

From Hakodate Airport, just a few kilometres east of the city centre, there are international flights to Seoul and Taipei, and domestic flights to various destinations including Sapporo, Tokyo and Kansai.

Frequent buses run direct between Hakodate Airport and JR Hakodate Station (¥300, 20 minutes), or you can simply take a taxi (¥2000).

BOAT

Tsugaru Kaikyō Ferry (津軽海峡フェリー; www.tsugarukaikyo.co.jp/global/english/) operates ferries (departing year-round) between Aomori and Hakodate (from ¥2700, 3¾ hours), and between Hakodate and Ōma (¥2200, 1¾ hours) on the Shimokita Peninsula. The ferry terminal, where you also buy your tickets, is on the northeast corner of Hakodate Harbour.

Regular shuttle buses (¥310, 15 minutes) and taxis (¥1500) run between the ferry terminal and JR Hakodate Station.

BUS

There are daily buses between JR Hakodate Station and Sapporo's Chūō bus station and Ōdōri bus centre (¥4680, 5¼ hours).

CAR & MOTORCYCLE

If you've just arrived in Hokkaidō, Hakodate is a good place to pick up a rental car and start your road-tripping adventure across the island.

Toyota Rent A Car (トヨタレンタカー函館駅前; ☎0138-26-0100; rent.toyota.co.jp/en; 19-2 Ōtemachi; 8am-8pm) has a branch office a few blocks southwest of JR Hakodate Station.

Nippon Rent a Car (www.nrh.co.jp) is right outside the station.

TRAIN

The JR Tsugaru Kaikyō line runs between Hakodate and Aomori (¥5340, two hours) via the Seikan Tunnel. The JR Hakodate line runs between Hakodate and Sapporo (¥8590, 3½ hours).

A combination of *tokkyū* (limited express) and *kaisoku* (rapid) trains run on the JR Hakodate line between Hakodate and Niseko via Oshamambe (¥5410, 3½ hours).

The *shinkansen* will soon be bulleting to Hakodate.

OFF THE BEATEN TRACK

AN ONSEN IN THE SEA

If you have your own wheels and are up for an adventure, head out on Route 278 to the Kameda peninsula east of Hakodate. When the road heads inland, follow it up and over to the far coast, then turn right on Route 231 and drive southeast to the end of the road.

Mizunashi Kaihin Onsen (水無海浜温泉) is one of those hidden jewels – an onsen in the sea! You'll need to turn up at the right time as the two main rockpools are covered by the sea when the tide is in, but if you time it right, you're in for a special treat.

There are changing facilities and while some bathers go naked, others wear bathing suits. It's up to you. To get your timing right for the onsen, ask about tides at the Hakodate Tourist Information Centre before you leave Hakodate. You'll want to be there an hour or two either side of low tide.

Getting Around

Single-trip fares on trams and buses generally cost between ¥210 and ¥250, depending on how long you ride.

One-day (¥1000) passes offer unlimited rides on both trams and buses (¥600 for tram alone), and are available at the tourist information centre or from the drivers.

West of Hakodate

To the west of Hakodate are a couple of interesting towns that can be visited as a day trip, especially if you have your own wheels.

Matsumae 松前

Prior to the start of the Meiji era, this town was the stronghold of the Matsumae clan and the centre of Japanese political power in Hokkaidō. As a result, Matsumae is home to the only castle on the island – the northernmost castle in Japan.

Sights

Matsumae-jō CASTLE

(松前城; www.e-matsumae.com; admission ¥360; 9am-5pm Apr–Dec) Matsumae-jō, originally built in 1606, has undergone plenty of changes and currently houses feudal relics and a small collection of Ainu items. Around 10,000 cherry trees blossom in the park around the castle for about a month from late April to mid-May.

Getting There & Away

Frequent *tokkyū* on the JR Esashi line run between Hakodate and Kikonai (¥2070, 35 minutes). Regular buses run between JR Kikonai Station and Matsumae (¥1370, 1½ hours).

Esashi 江差

If Matsumae was Hokkaidō's Edo-period political centre, then Esashi was its economic lifeblood. It is even said that at its height, Esashi was more prosperous than Edo. Prior to the depletion of fishing stocks in the early 20th century, a number of *nishingoten* (herring barons' homes) dominated the shoreline.

Sights

Nakamura-ke NOTABLE BUILDING

(中村家住宅; www.hokkaido-esashi.jp/modules/english/content0005.html; admission ¥300; 9am-5pm Tue-Sun Apr-Oct) This historic, well-preserved residence typifies Esashi's prosperous past with a gabled roof made of cypress and a foundation of stones shipped from the Hokuriku region. More than a residence, it was also office and storehouse for the merchant who built it.

Getting There & Away

Frequent *tokkyū* on the JR Esashi line run between Hakodate and Kikonai (¥1620, 35 minutes). Kikonai is connected to Esashi by the JR Esahi line – a few daily *kaisoku* ply this route (¥900, one hour).

Ōnuma Regional Park 大沼国定公園

Only about 25km north of Hakodate, Ōnuma Kōen is the coastal city's version of a mountain and lake playground. Sitting beneath the impressive Komagatake (駒ケ岳) volcano (1131m) are three lakes – Ōnuma (大沼), Konuma (小沼) and Junsainuma (じゅんさい沼) – easily accessed by train or car.

International visitors have been enjoying Ōnuma since the early Meiji era when Hakodate was one of the few Japanese ports open for foreign trade. Members of the Italian and German royal families turned up in the late 1800s, but things really took off when Emperor Meiji came for a look in 1881, attracting national attention.

These days visitors show up to cruise on the lakes, cycle around them and explore Ōnuma's many small islands on bridged footpaths. The park is perfect for a family day out. There are eating options around the station.

Sights & Activities

Rental bicycles (¥500 per hour, ¥1020 per day) are available outside JR Ōnuma Kōen Station and cycling the 14km around Ōnuma is a good option. Rental Segway are also available. A series of linked walking paths around Ōnuma's small islands starts not far from the train station.

While it is possible to hike up Komagatake on the Akaigawa Tozan-dō (赤井川登山道), the high peaks are off limits due to ongoing volcanic activity.

★Ōnuma Beer BREWERY
(大沼ビール; ☎0138-67-16110; www.onumabeer.co.jp; ⏲9am-4pm) For those who get a bit hot and thirsty, a five-minute walk from JR Ōnuma Kōen Station will bring you to Ōnuma Beer, a top spot to relax and try the highly recommended local brews.

Ōnuma Cruises CRUISES
(大沼遊船; ☎0138-67-2229; www.onuma-park.com; cruise ¥1100) Ōnuma Cruises runs popular 30-minute cruises out on the lake and also rents out rowing dinghies, swan-shaped pedal boats and fishing boats.

Sleeping

B&B Chairo-tori B&B ¥
(B&B茶色い鳥; ☎0138-67-2231; http://birdinn.web.fc2.com; per person with/without breakfast ¥4500/3800) In the yellow building right next to JR Ōnuma Kōen Station is B&B Chairo-tori, a good place to stay. The owner speaks English and greets international visitors enthusiastically. The rooms here are Japanese-style with shared facilities.

Information

Ōnuma Tourist Information Centre (大沼観光案内所; ☎0138-67-2170; www.onuma-guide.com; ⏲8.30am-6pm) Next to the station, this impressive information centre has helpful staff and good English information.

Getting There & Away

JR Ōnuma Kōen Station is on the JR Hakodate line. Trains head south to Hakodate (¥1880, 20 minutes) and north to Sapporo (¥8500, 2½ hours). If you've got your own wheels, Route 5 runs right through the park.

CENTRAL HOKKAIDŌ

Central Hokkaidō (道央; Dō-ō) is where Hokkaidō garners its deserved reputation for stunning national parks, world-class ski slopes and rustic hot-spring villages. The scenic port town of Otaru is worth a visit, but the focus in winter is on Niseko, where legendary powder attracts skiers and snowboarders from across the globe. Shikotsu-Tōya National Park offers up caldera lakes, a towering Fuji-san look-alike and steaming onsen towns.

Otaru 小樽

POP 131,000 / ☎0134

One of Hokkaidō's most popular tourist destinations for Japanese visitors, Otaru is a romantic port town steeped in a rich history that dates back to its glory days as a major herring centre. Otaru was the terminal station for Hokkaidō's first railroad, and today nostalgic warehouses and buildings still line the picturesque canal district. There are great options for foodies, and if you're into music boxes or any kind of glass object imaginable, you'll go gaga in Otaru.

JR Otaru Station is up the hill and inland from the canal and port. Head out the main doors and straight down Chūō-dōri for 10 minutes to get to the canal.

Sights

★Otaru Canal CANAL
(小樽運河) Go for a stroll beneath the old Victorian-style gas lamps lining this historic canal and admire the charismatic warehouses dating from the late 19th and early 20th centuries.

Nihon Yūsen Building HISTORIC BUILDING
(旧日本郵船株式会社小樽支店; admission ¥300; ⏲9.30am-5pm Tue-Sun) Lying behind the park at the northern end of the canal is the old Nihon Yūsen Company Building. Before the collapse of the herring industry, many of Hokkaidō's shipping orders were processed here. The interior of the building

Otaru

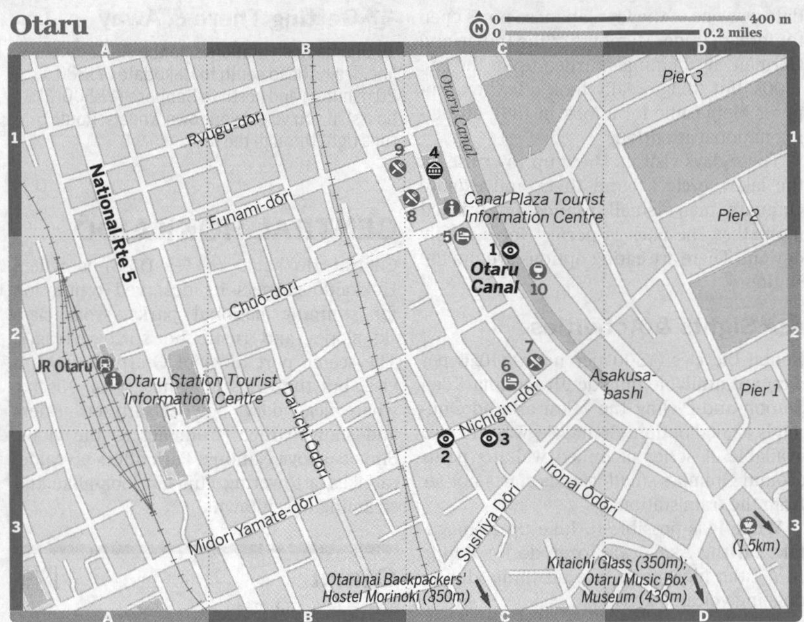

Otaru

Top Sights
1 Otaru Canal C2

Sights
2 Nichigin-dōri C3
3 Old Bank of Japan Building C3
4 Otaru Museum C1

Sleeping
5 Hotel Nord Otaru C2
6 Hotel Vibrant Otaru C2

Eating
7 Kita-no-aisukurīmu Yasan C2
8 Otaru Sushi-kō C1
9 Uminekoya B1

Drinking & Nightlife
10 Otaru Sōko No 1 .... C2

has been restored to its former grandeur and provides a revealing look at the opulence of the era.

Otaru Museum MUSEUM
(小樽市総合博物館; ☎0134-22-1258; admission ¥300; ⏲9.30am-5pm Tue-Sun) This small but engaging half of Otaru Museum, known as the Ungakan (運河館), is housed in a restored warehouse dating from 1893 near the canal. It has displays on Hokkaidō's natural history, some Ainu relics, and various special exhibitions on herring, ceramics and literature.

Nichigin-dōri STREET
(日銀道り) Once known as the 'Wall Street of the North', Nichigin-dōri is lined with elegant buildings that speak to Otaru's past life as a prominent financial centre.

Old Bank of Japan Building NOTABLE BUILDING
(日本銀行旧小樽支店金融資料館; Nichigin-dōri; ⏲9.30am-5pm Tue-Sun) FREE Don't miss the old Bank of Japan (日本銀行), a classic brick building that was designed by the same architect responsible for Tokyo Station. The exterior is marked by owl keystones, which pay homage to the Ainu guardian deity, while an impressive 100m-high ceiling highlights the interior.

Otaru Music Box Museum MUSEUM
(小樽オルゴール堂; ☎0134-21-3101; www.otaru-orgel.co.jp; ⏲9am-6pm) FREE At the Marchen Crossroads (メルヘン交差点), a 15-minute walk east of the canal, the main music box museum is mind-boggling. So is the fact that they've got another five buildings about town! There are over 25,000 music boxes and if you're really keen, you can make your own.

Sleeping

Otarunai Backpackers' Hostel Morinoki HOSTEL ¥
(おたるないバックパッカーズホステル杜の樹; ☎0134-23-2175; www.infotaru.net; 4-15 Aioi-chō; dm ¥3000; @📶) This great little backpacker spot is worlds apart from your usual Japan YH offerings. Accommodation is in fairly simple male and female dormitories, though guests are treated to kitchen, laundry and internet facilities, as well as bilingual staff, communal lounges, and a laid-back, congenial vibe. The hostel is about a 15-minute walk from JR Otaru Station.

★ **Hotel Vibrant Otaru** HOTEL ¥¥
(ホテルヴィブラントオタル; ☎0134-31-3939; www.vibrant-otaru.jp/en_index.html; Nichigin-dōri; s/d from ¥5500/8500, vault r from ¥10,500; @📶) A stylish renovation of a historic Otaru bank resulted in this justifiably 'vibrant hotel', which is located across the road from the main post office. The lobby and cafe are very attractive with period furniture, including wrought-iron tables. For a memorable night's stay, shell out a bit of extra cash and bed down in the old bank vault!

Hotel Nord Otaru HOTEL ¥¥
(ホテルノルド小樽; ☎0134-24-0500; www.hotelnord.co.jp/en/index.php; 1-4-16 Ironai; s/d from ¥7350/12,600; @📶) This European-style hotel fronts the warehouses along Otaru Canal. Rooms are priced according to size and view – the larger, canal-facing rooms are by far the most atmospheric.

Eating & Drinking

★ **Kita-no-aisukurīmu Yasan** ICE CREAM ¥
(北のアイスクリーム屋さん; ☎0134-23-8983; 1-2-18 Ironai; ice cream from ¥350; ⏲9.30am-5pm; 📖) Housed in a converted warehouse that was built in 1892, just back from the canal (look for the ice-cream banner), this legendary Otaru ice-cream parlour scoops up some seriously stomach-turning flavours. If you're up to the challenge, you can sample *nattō* (fermented soy beans), tofu, crab, sea urchin, beer and even a jet-black scoop of squid ink.

Uminekoya SEAFOOD ¥¥
(海猫屋; ☎0134-32-2914; 2-2-14 Ironai; dishes from ¥750; ⏲lunch & dinner; 📖) Housed in a crumbling brick warehouse laced with ivy, this famous bar-restaurant has been the setting for several novels of Japanese literary fame. The English menu helps with the ordering, though it's best to ask the waiter for their *osusume* (recommendation), as the catch of the day and some local sake is generally what you're after here.

Otaru Sushi-kō SUSHI ¥¥
(小樽すし耕; ☎0134-21-5678; sushi set from ¥1470; ⏲noon-8.30pm; 📖) For Japanese travellers, eating in Otaru is *all* about sushi – local specialities include *sake* (salmon), *ikura* (salmon roe), *uni* and *kani*. This tiny grey-brick warehouse is a tad hard to find but worth the effort. It's just back from the Canal Plaza Tourist Information Centre.

Otaru Sōko No 1 PUB
(小樽倉庫 No.1; http://otarubeer.com/jp; dishes from ¥800; ⏲11am-10pm) Housed in a converted warehouse on the harbour side of the canal, Sōku No 1 offers a nice selection of microbrewed drafts, plus German culinary fare to complement its Bavarian decor. Look for the 'Otaru Beer' sign.

Shopping

Kitaichi Glass GLASS
(北一硝子; ☎0134-33-1933; www.kitaichiglass.co.jp; ⏲8.45am-6pm) A 15-minute walk east of the canal area, the Kitaichi Glass area virtually fills a street with 16 shops, galleries, cafes and museums with everything imaginable made of glass.

Information

Canal Plaza Tourist Information Centre (運河プラザ観光案内所; ☎0134-33-2555; ⏲9am-6pm) A 10-minute walk straight down Chūō-dōri from JR Otaru Station will bring you to the canal. On the corner at the bottom, the information centre is housed in Otaru's oldest warehouse. All sorts of information is available here.

Otaru Station Tourist Information Centre (小樽駅観光案内所; ☎0134-29-1333; ⏲9am-6pm) If arriving by train, drop in here to pick up good maps and information in English.

Getting There & Away

BOAT

Shin-Nihonkai Ferries (新日本海フェリー; ☎0134-22-6191; www.snf.jp) runs between Otaru and Tsuruga (Fukui-ken) and Maizuru (Kyoto-fu). Check the website for the latest details. These ferries, which operate on the Japan Sea side of Japan, are good options for getting between Hokkaidō and Kansai.

To get to the ferry terminal, take the bus from stop 4 in front of JR Otaru Station (¥210, 30 minutes).

TRAIN

There are hourly *kaisoku* on the JR Hakodate line between Otaru and Sapporo (¥640, 45 minutes). Trains also continue on the same line to Niseko (¥1450, two hours).

Niseko ニセコ

POP 4650 / ☎0136

Hokkaidō is dotted with world-class ski resorts, but the reigning prince of powder is unquestionably Niseko. There are four interconnected resorts with more than 800 skiable hectares along the eastern side of the mountain, Niseko Annupuri. Soft and light powdery snow and an annual average snowfall of more than 15m make Niseko extremely popular with international skiers. Many own second homes here – resulting in a diverse dining and nightlife scene that is atypical of far-flung rural Japan.

But Niseko is not just about winter. Growing efforts to turn the area into a year-round resort are reaping rewards and visitors are also turning up for the hiking, biking, rafting, canoeing, fishing and other outdoor opportunities. Think of Niseko as Japan's version of Whistler or Queenstown.

The first thing you'll be struck by in Niseko is the perfect conical volcano Yōtei-zan (羊蹄山; 1898m), which looms ominously across the valley and provides a dramatic backdrop unlike any other.

Sights

Milk Kōbō (Milk Factory) GALLERY

(ミルク工房; ☎0136-44-3734; www.milk-kobo.com; ⌚9.30am-6pm) On the road up to Niseko Village, this complex of milk-related shops and galleries is a popular spot. What they're selling is made onsite – there's the Cake Corner, Ice-cream Corner, Yoghurt factory, Coffee Shop (using local milk of course!) and they've expanded into vegetables, souvenirs and the Prativo Restaurant (p588). All under the gaze of Yōtei-zan.

Activities

★**Niseko United** SKIING, SNOWBOARDING

(ニセコユナイテッド; www.niseko.ne.jp/en; 8hr/1-day pass ¥5600/6400; ⌚8.30am-8.30pm Nov-Apr) Niseko United is the umbrella name for four resorts, namely Niseko Annupuri, Niseko Village, Grand Hirafu and Hanazono. What makes Niseko United stand out from the competition is that you can ski or snowboard on all four slopes by purchasing a single all-mountain pass.

This electronic tag gives you access to 18 lifts and gondolas, 60 runs, as well as free rides on the inter-mountain shuttle bus. If you're planning on skiing for several days, a week or even the season, you can also buy discounted multiday passes.

Rental equipment is of very high quality, and can be picked up virtually everywhere at affordable prices. Rental shops typically have a few foreign staff on hand to help English-speaking customers. A high percentage of visitors to Niseko are from abroad, with plenty of Australians and growing numbers from Europe and North America. English is everywhere you look and listen.

At the base, most of the après-ski action is in Hirafu; though luxury-seekers harbour in the Hilton at Niseko Village, and locals tend to stick to Annupuri.

Communal bathing in an onsen after a day on the slopes is a chance to jump into Japanese culture. Most hotels either have an onsen on the premises, or can point you in the direction of the nearest bathhouse.

Niseko Adventure Centre (NAC) OUTDOORS

(ニセコアドベンチャーセンター; ☎0136-23-2093; www.nac-web.com) These guys are the innovators in Japan, following examples set in other mountain resorts throughout the world. In winter they offer everything from ski and snowboard lessons to snowshoe and backcountry tours. In summer they offer rafting, hiking, sea kayaking and canyoning tours...plus more!

Based in a massive purpose-built building in Hirafu, there's an 11m indoor climbing wall and Jojo's Café & Restaurant on the top floor. Definitely check it all out online before you go.

Niseko Circuit Hike HIKING

(ニセコサーキットハイキング) Summer is the best time of year to tackle some of the area's challenging wilderness hikes. The 16km Niseko Circuit that starts around the back of Niseko Annupuri at Goshiki Onsen is a good one. Fully described in Lonely Planet's *Hiking in Japan*, it takes six to seven hours, and the trailhead is accessible by local bus lines.

From Goshiki Onsen (五色温泉), it climbs Nitonupuri (ニトヌプリ; 1080m), Chisenupuri (チセヌプリ; 1134m), then rounds the ponds Chō-numa (長沼) and Ō-numa (大沼) and finishes back at Goshiki Onsen.

Onsen

Niseko has a brochure with 25 onsen options in the area, be they for use in winter or summer. Prices are generally around ¥500 to ¥700 per person.

Winter visitors may like to opt for luxury at the Hilton Niseko Village (¥1000) or at the Niseko Grand Hotel (¥700), while those with their own wheels in summer will love Niimi Onsen (¥500) and Goshiki Onsen (¥600), both away in the mountains to the west of Niseko Annupuri and its ski fields.

Sleeping

Niseko proper is spread out along the base of the four slopes. The closer you get to the slopes themselves, the more options you'll have. Hirafu and Annupuri host the vast majority of accommodation, while Niseko Village is centred on the upmarket Hilton. Most places will provide pick-up and drop-off for the slopes in winter, or you can take buses and shuttles to move about. It's strongly recommended that you book well in advance in winter.

Youth Hostel Karimpani Niseko HOSTEL ¥
(ユースホステルカリンパニ・ニセコ藤山; ☎0136-44-1171; www.karimpani-niseko.com/english; 336 Aza Niseko; dm from ¥3650, breakfast/dinner ¥600/1200; P @ ♿) In an 80-year-old converted schoolhouse, Max and Yūko's place is super-friendly and clean. Old classrooms now house dorms and concerts are held regularly in the gymnasium. The meals are first-class. The family lived in New Zealand for five years and they speak excellent English. They'll do transfers for free – a five-minute drive to the Annupuri slopes.

Eki-no-yado Hirafu MINSHUKU ¥
(駅の宿ひらふ; ☎0136-22-1956; http://hirafu-eki.com; dm per person with/without 2 meals ¥5700/3500; @) An excellent budget choice with character in an operating JR train station. Yes, that means trains rolling through every hour or so. Shared rooms are upstairs in the station building, the compact dining room is downstairs and the bath is made from a big hollowed-out log.

If you leave the door open you can lie back and watch the trains pass by 5m away. They do ski field transfers for ¥200. And, of course, you can come by train!

> **SEIKAN TUNNEL**
>
> A marvel of Japanese engineering, the Seikan railway tunnel travels beneath the Tsugaru Strait, connecting the islands of Honshū and Hokkaidō. With a total length of 53.85km, including a 240m-deep and 23.3km-long undersea portion, the Seikan Tunnel (青函トンネル) is the deepest and longest undersea tunnel in the world. It will soon have the *shinkansen* winging its way through it.

Niseko Annupuri Youth Hostel HOSTEL ¥
(ニセコアンヌプリユースホステル; ☎0136-58-2084; www.annupuri-yh.com; 470-4 Niseko; dm with/without 2 meals from ¥5190/3460; P 📶) This friendly mountain lodge constructed entirely from hardwood sits conveniently within a five-minute walk of the Annupuri ski grounds. Guests congregate in front of the fire, swapping ski tips and tucking into delicious meals.

Hotel Niseko Alpen HOTEL ¥¥
(ホテルニセコアルペン; ☎0136-22-1105; www.grand-hirafu.jp/hotel_niseko-alpen/en; r from ¥12,000; P @ 📶 🏊 ♿) Right next to the Welcome Centre and the lifts in Hirafu, this spacious place has it all. Plush Western-style rooms, an indoor pool, onsen and buffet meals make staying here a real pleasure – and you're not far from the restaurants and bars of Hirafu. A very good option.

Hilton Niseko RESORT ¥¥¥
(ニセコヒルトンヴィレジ; ☎0136-44-1111; www.placeshilton.com/niseko-village; r from ¥20,000; P @ 📶 ♿) The Hilton enjoys the best location of all – it is quite literally attached to the Niseko Gondola. Spacious Western-style rooms are complemented by a whole slew of amenities spread out across a self-contained village. Check the website before arriving as special deals are usually available, which combine discounted room rates with breakfast and dinner buffets.

Eating & Drinking

Many of the lodges and ryokan offer great meals, and the slopes have plenty of snacks, pizza, *rāmen* and other goodies. After hours things are tricky because lodging is spread out and buses are inconvenient, but there are plenty of watering holes in Hirafu.

WORTH A TRIP

RUSUTSU

Compared to neighbouring Niseko, Rusutsu (ルスツ; population 2000) is much less developed, and pales in size and scope. On the flip side, however, the slopes aren't nearly as crowded, and the lack of foreigners results in a decidedly more traditional ambience.

There is some serious powder waiting for you at the **Rusutsu Resort** (ルスツリゾート; ☎0136-46-3111; http://en.rusutsu.co.jp; lift tickets day/night ¥5500/2300, r from ¥9500; ⏰day 9am-5pm, night 4-9pm Nov-Apr), which boasts well-groomed trails and fantastic tree runs. The resort caters equally to skiers and snowboarders, has trails of all difficulty levels, 18 lifts, more than three dozen runs, a half-pipe and numerous off-piste options.

The resort website is easy to follow in English and gives you all the options. The lodge offers Western-style rooms, while larger suites overlook the slopes in the modern tower. Book in advance as discounted packages including room, lift ticket and meal plan are often available.

If you're staying in Niseko, Rusutsu is only a 20- to 30-minute drive away. Various operators offer Rusutsu day trips if you don't have your own wheels.

During the ski season, several companies run highway buses from Sapporo and New Chitose Airport to Niseko via Rusutsu (¥1990, two hours). If you're driving, note that Rte 230 runs between Sapporo and Tōya-ko via Rusutsu.

★**Graubunden** CAFE ¥
(グラウビュンデン; ☎0136-23-3371; www.graubunden.jp; ⏰8am-7pm Fri-Wed) Seriously good sandwiches, cakes, cookies and drinks in Hirafu East Village. A local favourite that has been open for decades, Graubunden is the perfect spot to chill out with good service, good food and a relaxed atmosphere.

Jojo's Café & Restaurant CAFE ¥
(ジョジョズカフェ; ☎0136-23-2220; www.nac-web.com/niseko/cafe.html; mains from ¥750; ⏰11am-9pm; 📋) Excellent casual dining to be had at the Niseko Adventure Centre (NAC). We're talking burgers, salads, pasta and tacos, and stupendous views of Yōtei-zan from out on the terrace on a good day.

Green Farm Café CAFE ¥
(☎0136-23-3354; http://nisekogreenfarm.com; mains from ¥800; ⏰8am-5pm summer, 8am-10pm winter) In the heart of Hirafu, Green Farm Café offers up a tasty range of dishes using organic produce from its nearby Niseko Green Farm. Pastas, burgers, coffees and even organic wine will fill the spot at this popular cafe.

Restaurant Prativo INTERNATIONAL ¥¥
(レストランプラテイーヴォ; ☎0136-55-8852; www.milk-kobo.com/prativo/e; buffet ¥1550; ⏰11am-3pm) Part of the extremely popular Milk Kōbō complex (p586) on the road to Niseko Village, Prativo offers a salad buffet with meat, fish or pasta main dishes at lunchtime. Locals believe it's the best.

ℹ Information

Spread around the eastern base of the mountain are several towns and villages that compose Niseko 'resort'.

Most of the restaurants and bars are clustered together in Hirafu (ひらふ), while Annupuri (アンヌプリ), Niseko Village (ニセコビレッジ) and Hanazono (花園) are much quieter and less developed.

Further east are Kutchan (倶知安) and Niseko (ニセコ) proper, which are more permanent population centres that remain decidedly Japanese.

Information Centre Plat (☎0136-22-3344; www.town.kutchan.hokkaido.jp; ⏰10am-7pm) If you head straight down the street outside JR Kutchan Station, on the left hand side after 200m you'll find the very helpful Information Centre Plat, which stocks English-language brochures and maps.

Hirafu Welcome Centre (ひらふウエルカムセンター; ☎0136-22-0109; www.grand-hirafu.jp/winter/en/index.html; ⏰8.30am-9pm) To meet the winter crush, the Hirafu Welcome Centre – where direct buses to/from New Chitose Airport originate and terminate – also provides English-language information.

Niseko Tourist Information (ニセコ観光案内所; ☎0136-44-2468; www.nisekotourism.com; ⏰9am-6pm) Has offices at JR Niseko Station and at the View Plaza Michi-no-Eki on Rte 66 heading into town. They have pamphlets, maps and bus timetables and will help with bookings.

Getting There & Away

BUS

During the ski season, **Chūō Bus** (☎011-231-0500; www.chuo-bus.co.jp) runs from JR Sapporo Station and New Chitose Airport to Niseko. The trip takes around three hours depending on road conditions, costs ¥2300 (return ¥3850) and drops off at the Welcome Centre in Hirafu, the Hilton and Annupuri. Reservations are necessary, and it's recommended that you book well ahead of your departure date.

CAR & MOTORCYCLE

Scenic Route 5 winds from Sapporo to Otaru around the coast, and then cuts inland through the mountains down to Niseko. Having a car will make it easier to move between the various ski slopes, though drive with extreme caution. In the summer (low season), public transport services drop off, which provides more incentive to pick up a car in Sapporo or at New Chitose Airport.

TRAIN

While there is a JR Hirafu Station, it is far from the town itself, and is not well serviced by local buses. From JR Niseko and JR Kutchan Stations, you will need to switch to local buses to access the villages at the base of the ski slopes. Trains run on the JR Hakodate line between Sapporo and Niseko (¥2470, two hours) via Kutchan (¥2150, 1¾ hours).

Getting Around

There are twice-hourly local buses linking JR Kutchan and JR Niseko Stations to Hirafu, Niseko Village, Annupuri and Hanazono. Pick up a schedule from the tourist information centres so that you don't miss your connection. Also, if you've purchased an all-mountain pass, you can ride the hourly shuttle bus between the villages.

Shikotsu-Tōya National Park 支笏洞爺国立公園

To the south and southwest of Sapporo, Shikotsu-Tōya National Park (993 sq km) is very spread out and largely mountainous wilderness. It is marked by picturesque caldera lakes, two of Hokkaidō's top hot-spring towns, and Yōtei-zan, also known as Ezo-Fuji (the Fuji-san lookalike of Hokkaidō.).

Shikotsu-ko 支笏湖

Directly south of Sapporo and surrounded by soaring volcanoes, Shikotsu-ko is the second-deepest lake in Japan. While it is 250m above sea level, its deepest spot is 363m, 113m below sea level. Not easy to reach without your own wheels, it's a superb spot for independent exploration and excellent for campers.

Shikotsu-ko Onsen (支笏湖温泉), on the eastern side of the lake, is the only town. This compact little resort village has some nice short walks, including a nature trail for birdwatchers. Sightseeing boats head out onto the lake and there are rental bicycles, boats and canoes.

Activities

Tarumae-zan HIKING

(樽前山) On the southern side of the lake is Tarumae-zan (1041m), an active volcano that is the area's most popular hike. The crater itself is usually closed, but you can reach and go around the rim from the **seventh station** (650m; only accessible by private car). Allow 1½ hours for the return hike to the rim.

From the same trailhead you can also climb **Fuppushi-dake** (風不死岳; 1102m) in five to six hours return, which offers excellent views of the lake and park. Locals suggest a bear bell is essential for this hike.

Eniwa-dake HIKING

(恵庭岳) On the northwestern side of the lake, Eniwa-dake (1320m) is a pointed mountain with a crater on its eastern side. Allow five to six hours for the rewarding return hike. Downhill ski racing for the 1970 Winter Olympics was held on a course on its southwestern side.

Sleeping

Shikotsu-ko is great for campers. There is a lakeside camping area at Okotan to the southwest of Eniwa-dake just off Route 78. Other camping areas are at **Morappu** in the east and **Bifue** in the west, both off Route 276.

★**Log Bear** MINSHUKU ¥

(ログベアー; ☎0123-25-2738; http://logbear.moto-nari.com/shikotsu/Welcome.html; per person ¥5000; 📶) A top spot to stay, Log Bear is right in the middle of Shikotsu-ko Onsen, and is run by a real character called Robin. Log Bear is also a coffee shop and restaurant. You're likely to be sent to the youth hostel for your onsen, but it's a very fun place.

Information

Shikotsu-ko Visitor Centre (支笏湖ビジターセンター; ☎0123-25-2404; www15.ocn.ne.jp/~sikotuvc/; Shikotsu-ko Onsen; ⏲9am-5.30pm Apr-Nov, 9am-4.30pm Dec-Mar) The

Shikotsu-Tōya National Park

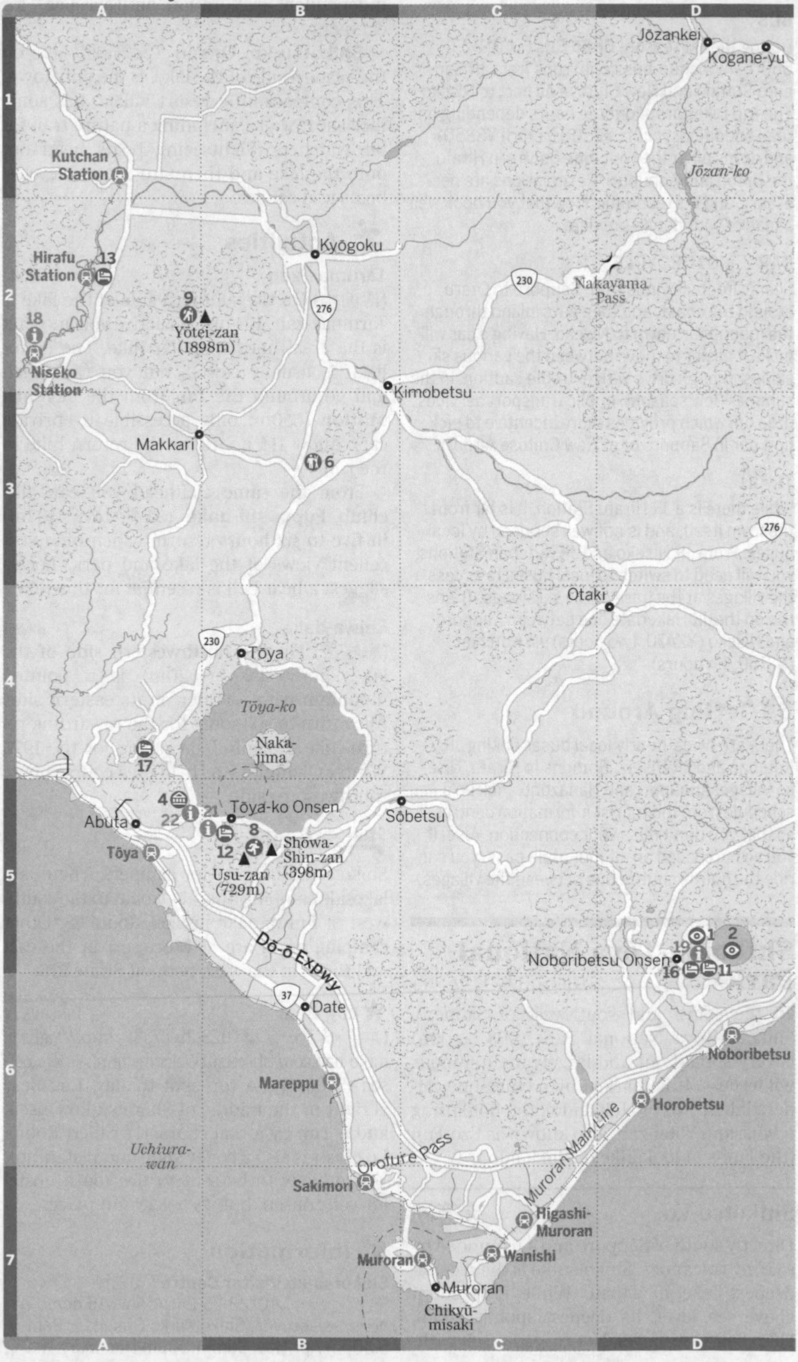

Kutchan Station
Hirafu Station
13
18
Niseko Station
9
Yōtei-zan (1898m)
Kyōgoku
276
230
Jōzankei
Kogane-yu
Jōzan-ko
Nakayama Pass
Kimobetsu
Makkari
6
276
Otaki
230
Tōya
Tōya-ko
Naka-jima
17
4
22
21
Abuta
Tōya
Tōya-ko Onsen
8
12
Usu-zan (729m)
Shōwa-Shin-zan (398m)
Sōbetsu
Dō-ō Expwy
37
Date
Mareppu
Uchiura-wan
Orofure Pass
Sakimori
Muroran Main Line
Horobetsu
Noboribetsu
Noboribetsu Onsen
19
1
2
16
11
Higashi-Muroran
Wanishi
Muroran
Muroran
Chikyū-misaki

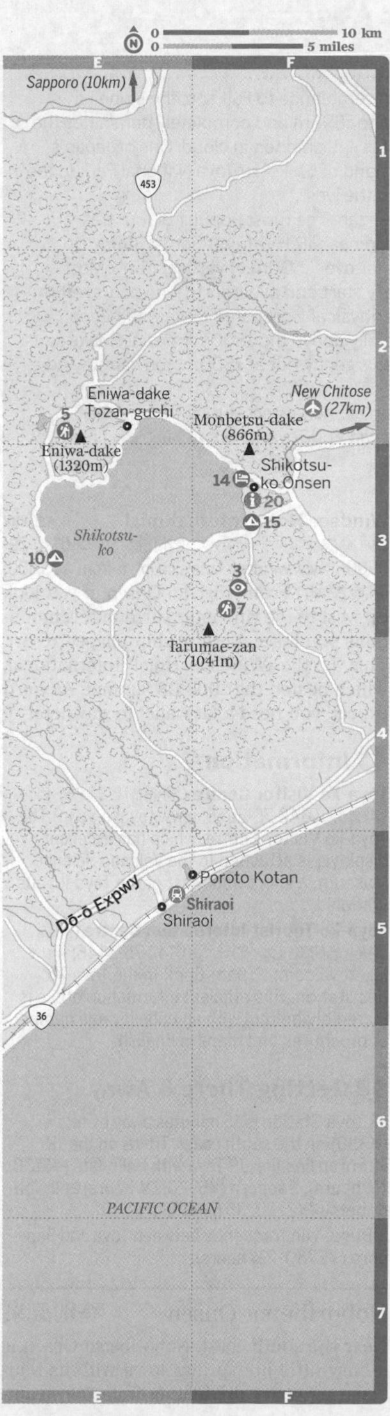

Shikotsu-Tōya National Park

Sights

1	Jigoku-dani	D5
2	Kuttara-ko	D5
3	Seventh Station	F3
4	Volcano Science Museum	A5

Activities, Courses & Tours

5	Eniwa-dake	E2
6	Rusutsu Resort	B3
7	Tarumae-zan	F3
8	Usu-zan Ropeway	B5
9	Yōtei-zan	A2

Sleeping

10	Bifue	E3
11	Dai-ichi Takimoto-kan	D5
12	Daiwa Ryokan	B5
13	Eki-no-yado Hirafu	A2
14	Log Bear	F3
15	Morappu	F3
16	Shōkōin	D5
17	Windsor Hotel International	A4

Information

18	Niseko Tourist Information	A2
19	Noboribetsu Park Service Centre	D5
20	Shikotsu-ko Visitor Centre	F3
21	Tōya-ko Tourist Information Centre	B5
22	Tōya-ko Visitor Centre	A5

Shikotsu-ko Visitor Centre has good displays, English brochures and maps, and helpful staff. They also rent out bicycles for ¥300 per day.

Tōya-ko 洞爺湖

At the southwestern side of Shikotsu-Tōya National Park, Tōya-ko is an almost classically round caldera lake with a large island (Naka-jima) sitting in the middle.

On the southern side of the lake are two active volcanoes, Shōwa-Shin-zan (昭和新山; 398m) and Usu-zan (有珠山; 729m). The former, which popped up out of a wheat field in 1944 and was given the name meaning 'the new mountain of the Shōwa period', regularly belches sulphurous fumes, while the latter has quieted somewhat since erupting in 2000 and covering the region in ash. That eruption made television news worldwide – as did the G8 Summit that was held at Tōya-ko in 2008.

Tōya-ko Onsen (洞爺湖温泉) is a sizeable town with an attractive waterfront that is keen to attract visitors. It has 12 free hand- and foot-baths throughout town (think of it

WORTH A TRIP

CLIMBING YŌTEI-ZAN

Also known as Ezo-Fuji because of its striking resemblance to Fuji-san, the stunning volcanic cone of **Yōtei-zan** (羊蹄山) towers up to 1898m and completely dominates the surrounding landscape. The only way to miss it is if it's hidden in cloud. One of Japan's 100 Famous Mountains, it sits in its own little island of Shikotsu-Tōya National Park to the north of Tōya-ko. Niseko is barely 10km away to the west.

Be prepared for a big climb if you tackle Yōtei-zan. The most popular of four trailheads is Yōtei-zan Tozan-guchi, south of Kutchan near JR Hirafu Station at 350m. Do your maths and you'll calculate that you are in for over 1500m of vertical climb. Most people climb and descend in a day – get an early start and allow six to nine hours return, depending on how fit you are. Be mentally and physically prepared – the weather can change quickly on this exposed volcano, especially above the 1600m tree line. Make sure you have enough food and drink. There is an emergency hut at 1800m. You can stay here but you'll have to bring everything with you.

The upper reaches of Yōtei-zan are covered in alpine flowers during the summer. From the peak, the Sea of Japan, the Pacific Ocean and Tōya-ko are all visible – unless, of course, you are inside a cloud!

as an onsen treasure-hunt!), a fireworks display on the lake every night from April until October at 8.45pm, and paddle-steamers running lake cruises. The 50km circumference of the lake features 58 statues in an outdoor art gallery that can be rounded by car or bicycle.

Sights & Activities

Usu-zan Ropeway ROPEWAY
(有珠山ロープウェイ; www.wakasaresort.com; return ¥1500; 8.30am-5pm) The Usu-zan Ropeway runs up from between Usu-zan and Shōwa-Shin-zan to a couple of viewing platforms and some stunning views of the lake and the steaming crater.

Volcano Science Museum MUSEUM
(火山科学館; 0142-75-2555; www.toyako-vc.jp; admission ¥600; 9am-5pm) This impressive museum is a must for anyone interested in the spectacular landforms of the national park. You can even 'experience' an eruption in the Volcanic Eruption Theatre. A short walk west from the Tōya-ko bus station.

Sleeping

Daiwa Ryokan RYOKAN ¥
(大和旅館; 0142-75-2415; http://daiwa-ryokan.jp; r per person 1/2/4 people ¥4350/3825/3300; P @) Two blocks east of the Tōya-ko bus station, Daiwa Ryokan is a simple Japanese-style ryokan that ticks all the boxes and offers a warm welcome. Nonguests can use the onsen here for ¥400.

Windsor Hotel International HOTEL ¥¥¥
(ザ・ウィンザーホテル洞爺; 0120-29-0500; www.windsor-hotels.co.jp; r from ¥33,600; P @) From Tōya-ko Onsen, if you look up west to the rim of the surrounding mountains you'll see a cruise ship–shaped resort. This is the Windsor Hotel International, which hosted the 2008 G8 Summit. As you'd expect, you need a fat wallet to stay here!

Information

Tōya-ko Visitor Centre (洞爺湖ビジターセンター; 0142-75-2555; www.toyako-vc.jp) The Tōya-ko Visitor Centre, which has excellent displays, is attached to the Volcano Science Museum, a short walk west of the Tōya-ko bus station.

Tōya-ko Tourist Information Centre (洞爺湖観光情報センター; 0142-75-2446; www.laketoya.com; 9am-6pm) In the Tōya-ko bus station, this efficient information office is incredibly helpful with an unbelievable number of brochures and maps in English.

Getting There & Away

JR Tōya Station is 15 minutes away by bus (¥330) on the south coast. Trains on the JR Muroran line link JR Tōya with Hakodate (¥5130, 1¾ hours), Sapporo (¥5920, 1¾ hours) and Noboribetsu (¥2720, 35 minutes).

Buses run frequently between Tōya and Sapporo (¥2780, 2¾ hours).

Noboribetsu Onsen 登別温泉

Near the south coast, Noboribetsu Onsen is a busy little hot springs town with its rejuvenating water originating from the steaming and hissing Jigoku-dani just above the village.

Noboribetsu is very serious about its baths, which received great fame when the town was designated as a health resort for injured soldiers following the 1904–5 Russo-Japanese War. You can have a bath at just about all of the hotels without staying, with prices ranging from ¥400 all the way up to ¥2000.

While you're wandering around the village, keep an eye open for an interesting selection of 'demon statues' which supposedly bring success in business, study and love.

Sights

Jigoku-dani HOT SPRINGS

(地獄谷; Hell Valley) A short walk uphill reveals what may await us in the afterlife: sulphurous gases, hissing vents and seemingly blood-stained rocks. A number of short tracks run up through Jigoku-dani. Those keen on a walk can carry on over to Oyunuma, a hot steamy lake about a 30-minute walk from town.

Kuttara-ko LAKE

(倶多楽湖) If you have your own wheels, head up through town past Jigoku-dani and keep going on Route 350 as it becomes a narrow mountain road. Eventually, after about 8km, you'll reach Kuttara-ko, a circular volcanic caldera lake which is remarkable for two things – there's not a single river flowing into or out of it, and it has been left almost completely untouched by human hands. Lap up the natural environment before carrying on back down to the real world.

Sleeping

★Shōkōin MINSHUKU ¥

(聖光院; ☎0143-84-2359; http://jodo.jp/01-063/; dm per person ¥3400; 📶) Those on a budget will love staying at the Shōkōin temple. Not many temples look like a three-storey green office building, but this one does! The entrance is on the ground floor, the temple rooms are on floor two, and the priest's wife runs a *minshuku* on floor three.

You'll have to head out for meals, but the tatami rooms are clean, the onsen is open 24 hours and there is wireless internet. The temple is also known locally as Kannon-ji (観音寺).

Dai-ichi Takimoto-kan HOTEL ¥¥

(第一滝本館; ☎0143-84-3322; www.takimotokan.co.jp/english; r per person with 2 meals from ¥10,950; @📶👪) The Dai-ichi Takimoto-kan is a superb place to stay with an English website explaining all the options. A long history is complemented by 'hot spring heaven'. Nonguests can use the bath from 9am to 6pm for ¥2000.

Information

Noboribetsu Park Service Centre (登別パークサービスセンター; ☎0143-84-3311; www.noboribetsu-spa.jp; ⏲8.30am-5pm) At the entrance to Jigoku-dani is this information centre, which does a good job of introducing you to this volcanic wonderland. You can pick up English brochures and maps here, and it is the starting spot for a number of good nature trails.

Getting There & Away

JR Noboribetsu Station is 15 minutes away by bus (¥330), down on the coast. Trains run on the JR Muroran line to Hakodate (¥6890, 2½ hours), Sapporo (¥4480, 1¼ hours), and JR Tōya Station (¥2720, 35 minutes).

Buses run frequently between Noboribetsu and Sapporo (¥2100, two hours).

Jōzankei 定山渓

At the northernmost extent of Shikotsu-Tōya National Park and less than an hour's drive to Sapporo on Route 230, Jōzankei is the closest major onsen town to Hokkaidō's main city and an easy escape for those after some R&R. History tells us that the hot springs were first discovered in 1866 by a wandering ascetic monk, Miizumi Jōzan.

Stretching along a gorge of the Toyohira-gawa, Jōzankei is particularly well known for its stunning autumn colours, which can easily be viewed from the bath. Most hotels and ryokan offer use of their onsen for nonguests for ¥500 to ¥1500. If soaking just your feet will do, head to the free stone *ashi-yu* next to Iwato Kannon-dō.

Sights

Ainu Culture Promotion Centre CULTURAL CENTRE

(札幌ピリカコタン, Sapporo Pirka Kotan; ☎011-596-5961; www.city.sapporo.jp/shimin/pirka-kotan/en; Kogane-yu; exhibition room admission ¥200; ⏲9am-5pm Tue-Sun) Sapporo city's excellent Ainu Culture Promotion Centre is in Kogane-yu, 3km east of Jōzankei. The whole place is very well done and visitors can touch and hold exhibits in the exhibition hall.

AINU RENAISSANCE

Although Ainu culture was once declared 'dead' by the Japanese government, the past few decades have seen people of Ainu descent assert their ethnicity both politically and culturally. If you're interested in learning more about the Ainu, visit the website of the **Ainu Culture Centre** (アイヌ文化交流センター; Ainu Bunka Kōryū Centā; ☎03-3245-9831; www.frpac.or.jp/english/index.html) in Tokyo as well as the following Hokkaidō hotspots.

Shiraoi

Between Tomakomai and Noboribetsu on the south coast in central Hokkaidō, Shiraoi's **Poroto Kotan** (ポロトコタン) is a lakeside village of reconstructed traditional Ainu buildings, anchored by the **Ainu Museum** (アイヌ民族博物館; ☎0144-82-3914; www.ainu-museum.or.jp/en/; admission ¥750; ⏲8.45am-5pm). Museum exhibits are labelled in both Japanese and English, and in the village you might catch demonstrations of Ainu crafts and cultural performances. Shiraoi is on the JR Muroran line.

Nibutani

In the northern outskirts of Biratori village on Route 237, north of Tomikawa on the south coast of central Hokkaidō, **Nibutani Ainu Culture Museum** (二風谷アイヌ文化博物館; www.town.biratori.hokkaido.jp/biratori/nibutani; admission ¥400; ⏲9am-5pm mid-Apr–mid-Nov, 9am-5pm Tue-Sun mid-Nov–mid-Apr, closed mid-Dec–mid-Jan) has very good collections and attractive displays, although most information is in Japanese only. On the eastern side of Nibutani's main street, the **Kayano Shigeru Ainu Memorial Museum** (萱野茂二風谷アイヌ資料館; admission ¥400; ⏲9am-5pm Apr-Nov, by appointment Dec-Mar) houses the private collection of Kayano Shigeru, the first person of Ainu descent to be elected to the Japanese Diet. You'll need your own wheels to get to Nibutani.

Akan National Park

Make sure to visit the Ainu Village (p623) in Akanko Onsen. There are Ainu handicraft shops, restaurants and cultural performances in the theatre Ikor (p623). Further east in the park, on the shores of Kussharo-ko, are the Museum of Ainu Folklore (p621) and Marukibune (p625).

Kogane-yu & Sapporo

Forty minutes by car, southwest of Sapporo on Route 230, is the Ainu Culture Promotion Centre (p593) at Sapporo Pirka Kotan, a new centre with displays and an excellent exhibition room. In Sapporo itself, head to the **Ainu Association of Hokkaidō** (北海道アイヌ協会; ☎011-221-0462; www.ainu-assn.or.jp).

Iwato Kannon-dō BUDDHIST TEMPLE
(岩戸観音堂; ☎011-598-2012; ⏲7am-8pm) This small temple fronts a 120m-long cave that has 33 statues of Kannon, the Buddhist deity of compassion, and is dedicated to road workers who lost their lives constructing roads in the area. At the time of research, the cave was closed due to rockfalls. Check out the lovely old Jōzankei photographs on display.

Sleeping

Jōzankei View Hotel HOTEL ¥¥
(定山渓ビューホテル; ☎011-598-3339; http://karakami-kankou.jp/en/jv; r from ¥8000; P@👪) A good spot to stay, especially if you're with children. This monster complex (647 rooms) may look as if it has seen better days, but it more than meets most needs and there are some good deals to be had, especially if booking online. There are underground and rooftop onsen, a family-fun 'Water Kingdom', restaurants and loads of parking.

Information

Jōzankei Tourism Office (☎011-598-2012; http://jozankei.jp; ⏲9am-5pm) Right on Route 230, the main road through the valley, this exceptionally helpful office has English brochures and maps, an English-speaker, and features a small museum with photos of Jōzankei in the booming years of days gone by. Worth a visit.

Getting There & Away

Buses run regularly between Sapporo and Jōzankei (¥750, 1¼ hours).

Tomakomai 苫小牧

Just as New Chitose Airport acts as the airport hub for Sapporo and Hokkaidō, the industrial port town of Tomakomai, only 20km south of Chitose, is the main port of entry for long-distance ferries. Most visitors are there because they're getting on or off a ferry.

Sleeping

There really is no reason to stay in Tomakomai unless your ferry arrives or departs at a very nasty hour.

Toyoko Inn Tomakomai Eki-mae HOTEL ¥¥
(東横イン苫小牧駅前; 0144-32-1046; www.toyoko-inn.com/e_hotel/00108/index.html; s/d from ¥4980/6480; P@) Right next to the station, Toyoko Inn Tomakomai Eki-mae is part of the Japan-wide chain of Toyoko Inns. While there might not be a lot of character on hand, there is free internet, breakfast and supper – plus you are guaranteed spotless rooms.

Getting There & Away

Hokkaidō Chūō Bus (www.chuo-bus.co.jp) runs highway buses between Tomakomai Ferry Terminal and Sapporo Eki-mae Bus Station (¥1310; 1¾ hours). **Dōnan Bus** (www.donanbus.co.jp) runs between the ferry terminal and JR Tomakomai Station (¥240; 15 minutes).

JR Tomakomai Station is on the JR Muroran Line, 45 minutes from Sapporo (¥3020).

FERRY

There are quite a few options for arriving in and departing from Hokkaidō by ferry via Tomakomai:

Taiheiyō Ferry (www.taiheiyo-ferry.co.jp) Down the Pacific coast of Honshū, between Tomakomai, Sendai and Nagoya.

Shin-Nihonkai Ferry (www.snf.jp) These guys operate down the Japan Sea side of Honshū. Options are between Tomakomai, Akita, Niigata and Tsuruga (Fukui-ken).

Silver Ferry (www.silverferry.jp) Between Tomakomai and Hachinohe (Aomori-ken).

MOL Ferry (www.sunflower.co.jp) Down the Pacific side between Tomakomai and Ōarai (Ibaraki-ken).

NORTHERN HOKKAIDŌ

Northern Hokkaidō (道北; Dō-hoku) is where the majestic grandeur of the natural world takes over. Southeast of Asahikawa, the second-largest city on the island, Daisetsuzan National Park is a raw virgin landscape of enormous proportions. Way up north, west of Wakkanai and in the shadow of Siberia, Rishiri-Rebun-Sarobetsu National Park is a dramatic island-scape famous for its wildflowers. And, in case you still need a few reminders of human settlement, Furano is one of Hokkaidō's most famous ski resorts, and home to one of the world's only belly-button appreciation festivals!

Asahikawa 旭川

POP 350,000 / 0166

Asahikawa carries the dual honour of having the most days with snowfall in all of Japan, as well as the record for the coldest temperature (-40°C). It is mainly used by travellers as a transit point for Wakkanai to the north, Daisetsuzan National Park to the southeast, and Biei and Furano to the south, but is also a pleasant city in which to spend a day or two.

Sights

Asahiyama Zoo ZOO
(旭山動物園; 0166-36-1104; www5.city.asahikawa.hokkaido.jp/asahiyamazoo; admission ¥820; 9.30am-5.15pm May-Oct, 10.30am-3.30pm Nov-Apr) Known Japan-wide, the country's northernmost zoo attracts visitors with its stars from cold climates: polar bears and penguins. It's well done and extremely popular. Buses 41, 42 or 47 run between bus stop 5 in front of the station and the entrance to the zoo (¥400, 40 minutes).

Otokoyama Sake Brewery Museum BREWERY
(男山酒造り資料館; 0166-47-7080; www.otokoyama.com/english/index.html; 2-7 Nagayama; 9am-5pm) FREE If you want to try the local tipple, take the 30-minute tour of this legendary brewery, which appears in old *ukiyo-e* (woodblock prints) and historic literature. These guys export all over the world. Take bus 67, 68, 70, 71, or 669 from bus stop 18 in front of JR Asahikawa Station, and get off at Nagayama 2-jō 7-chōme (¥200, 20 minutes).

Kawamura Kaneto Ainu Memorial Hall MUSEUM
(川村カ子トアイヌ記念館; ☎0166-51-2461; http://ainu-museum.sakura.ne.jp; 11 Kitamonchō; admission ¥500; ⊙9am-5pm) Kaneto Kawamura, an Ainu chief, became a master surveyor and helped to lay the tracks for several of Hokkaidō's railways. In 1916, after eye problems forced him to retire, he used his accumulated wealth to create the first Ainu museum. Take bus 24 from stop 14 in front of JR Asahikawa Station to the Ainu Kinenkan-mae stop (¥170, 15 minutes).

Festivals & Events

Get the full scoop on Asahikawa's year-round events at www.asahikawa-daisetsu.jp/e/event/index.html.

Winter Festival FESTIVAL
(冬祭り; Fuyu Matsuri; www.city.asahikawa.hokkaido.jp/files/kankou/awf) Held every February and into its sixth decade, this is one of Japan's top winter festivals. The International Ice Sculpture Competition is a highlight, along with local food and fun seasonal events.

Kotan Matsuri CULTURAL
(コタン祭り; www.asahikawa-daisetsu.jp/e/event/event_kotanmatsuri.html) Held on the autumn equinox in September on the banks of the Chubestu-gawa, south of the city. There are traditional Ainu dances, music and prayer ceremonies offered to the deities of fire, the river, *kotan* (the village) and the mountains.

Sleeping

Guest House Asahikawa GUESTHOUSE ¥
(ゲストハウス旭川; ☎0166-73-8269; www.guesthouseasahikawa.jp; Rokujō-dōri 7-chōme 31-10; dm ¥3000; @) On the 2nd floor of what used to be an office building, this guesthouse has been crafted with loving care. It's a bit squashy, but the owners are enthusiastic, there's free coffee and internet, a kitchen, games and a book exchange. It's about a 10-minute walk from JR Asahikawa Station.

Tōyoko Inn Asahikawa Ekimae HOTEL ¥¥
(東横イン旭川駅前; ☎0166-27-1045; www.toyoko-inn.com/e_hotel/00069/index.html; 9-164-1 Ichijō-dōri; s/d incl breakfast from ¥5980/7480; P@) This popular chain's clean and convenient Asahikawa hotel is a short walk from JR Asahikawa station. There is free breakfast and wireless internet.

Loisir Hotel Asahikawa HOTEL ¥¥¥
(ロワジールホテル旭川; ☎0166-25-8811; www.solarehotels.com/en/hotel/hokkaido/loisir-asahikawa; s/d from ¥8000/10,000; P@) An easy-to-spot white tower block, the Loisir is Asahikawa's top hotel. First-class amenities include a large gym and spa as well as four fine restaurants, one of which is a 15th-floor bistro with a view. Book early online for good deals.

Eating & Drinking

Asahikawa is famous for its *shōyu* (soy sauce) *rāmen*, and there are *rāmen* shops on virtually every street in the city.

Furarīto Alley (ふらりーと小路; www.furari-to.com) is a rambling collection of 18 restaurants running the length of an alley between Yonjō-dōri and Gojō-dōri about a 10-minute walk north of JR Asahikawa Station. Very popular with locals, it's the place to go. Wander along (loosely translated, *furarīto* means wander) and see what looks good. Virtually everything is on offer.

★ **Taisetsu Ji-bīru-kan** BREWERY
(大雪地ビール館; ☎0166-25-0400; www.ji-beer.com; 1604-1 Miyashita-dōri 11-chōme; ⊙11.30am-10pm) To try the local award-winning brew, walk east of JR Asahikawa Station for five minutes to Taisetsu Ji-bīru-kan. Taisetsu Beer is good! You can drink it, buy it, try beer jelly and, of course, sit down and consume it with a plate of *jingisukan* or a bowl of *rāmen*. Highly recommended.

Information

Asahikawa's new JR Station is a stunner, and a haven from the cold in the depths of winter. A large pedestrian avenue extends north of it for eight blocks, and most of the hotels and restaurants are within easy walking distance of the station.

Asahikawa International Centre (旭川国際交流センター; ☎0166-25-7491; http://asahikawaic.jp/en; Feeeal Asahikawa 7F, Ichijō-dōri 8-chōme; ⊙10am-7.30pm) A useful spot a few minutes north of JR Asahikawa Station on the 7th floor of the Feeeal Building. Information on Asahikawa and Hokkaidō as a whole, as well as free internet use. Take some time out and relax here.

Tourist Information Counter (旭川観光案内所; ☎0166-26-6665; www.asahikawa-daisetsu.jp/e/index.html; ⊙8.30am-7pm Jun-Sep, 9am-7pm Oct-May) Inside JR Asahikawa Station on

OFF THE BEATEN TRACK

CLIMBING POROSHIRI-DAKE

Take a look at any map of Hokkaidō and you'll see that there is a large gap with virtually nothing marked between Central Hokkaidō and the Tokachi region of Eastern Hokkaidō.

Actually, this gap is filled with the 130km-long **Hidaka mountain range**, surely the least-penetrated region and most-remote area in Japan. From the township of Hidaka almost all the way to the tip of Erimo-misaki there is nothing but forested tectonically-uplifted mountains. Road penetration and signs of human habitation are minimal.

Highest of the Hidaka peaks is **Poroshiri-dake** (幌尻岳; 2052m), one of Japan's Hyakumeizan, the 100 Famous Mountains. For those trying to conquer the 100, Poroshiri is legendary as the hardest to get to and the one where you're bound to get your feet wet – there are 23 crossings of the Nukabira-gawa! There is a hut, however, after those 23 crossings, offering the chance to dry out.

Allow two days for the 40km loop hike that starts at Torisui Dam (取水ダム), climbs Poroshiri-dake and **Tottabetsu-dake** (1959m; トッタベツ岳) and ends back at the dam. You can stay at the Poroshiri-sansō hut or camp beside it for one or two nights.

Get a copy of Lonely Planet's *Hiking in Japan*, the right map – Shōbunsha's Yama-to-kōgen Chizu 3 (昭文社山と高原地図 3 大雪山) – and get a Japanese-reader to check out www5.ocn.ne.jp/~biratori for the latest in information for getting to the trailhead. Access is from the township of Furenai (振内) on Route 237 to the west of the mountains.

This is a great hike, but do not attempt it after heavy rains or if they are forecast, as the river will be uncrossable.

the ground floor, everyone is very helpful and friendly; there are English-speakers, English maps and brochures.

Getting There & Around

AIR

Asahikawa Airport is 10km southeast of the city. There are domestic flights to Tokyo, Nagoya, Osaka and elsewhere, as well as international flights to various Asian destinations. Buses between the airport and JR Asahikawa Station (¥600, 30 minutes) are timed to connect with arrivals and departures.

BUS

There are frequent daily departures from bus stops in front of JR Asahikawa Station to Sapporo (¥2000, two hours), Wakkanai (¥4700, 4¾ hours), Furano (¥860, 1½ hours) and Biei (¥520, 50 minutes).

CAR & MOTORCYCLE

If you want to pick up a car before heading either north, south or east, **Toyota Rent-a-Car** (トヨタレンタカー; ☎0166-23-0100; www.toyotarentacar.net/english; 9-396-2 Miyashita-dōri; ⏲8am-8pm Apr-Oct, to 7pm Nov-Mar) has a branch office at Asahikawa Airport and one right outside JR Asahikawa Station. **Nippon Rent A Car** also has locations at the airport and station (www.nrh.co.jp).

TRAIN

Super Kamui *tokkyū* run twice an hour between Asahikawa and Sapporo (¥5010, 1½ hours). There are just a couple of *tokkyū* on the JR Sōya line each day between Asahikawa and Wakkanai (¥8500, 3¾ hours), and on the JR Sekihoku line between Asahikawa and Abashiri (¥8170, four hours). Finally, there are regular *kaisoku* on the JR Furano line between Asahikawa and Furano (¥1070, 1¼ hours) via Biei (¥540, 30 minutes).

Furano 富良野

POP 26,000 / ☎0167

Furano is a delight in all seasons. One of Japan's most inland towns, it receives extreme amounts of powdery snow, and is ranked one of the country's top skiing and snowboarding destinations. Somewhat surprisingly, a continental climate descends on the area outside the winter months, fostering a burgeoning wine industry, producing award-winning cheeses and enabling sprawling fields of lavender to spring to life.

The centre of town and the train station are in the valley, while the ski district is a couple of kilometres west at the base of the mountains.

Sights

The real appeal of Furano is simply exploring and getting lost in the rural landscape surrounding the town, but there are also a number of attractions worth checking out. Having the luxury of your own wheels will greatly enhance your visit.

DON'T MISS

BIEI

More or less halfway between Asahikawa and Furano, with the dramatic mountains of Daisetsuzan National Park in the background, Biei (美瑛; population 11,000) is an artist's and nature-lover's mecca. With the freedom of a rental car, you can cruise for hours along blissful country roads lined with fields of sunflowers, lavender and white birch. The so-called Patchwork Road to the west of town will get you lost for sure.

Route 237 runs between Asahikawa, Biei and Furano, but the real appeal of Biei is simply exploring the detours, getting lost and stopping to enjoy the rural flavour – so get off the main road. If you don't have a car, there are *kaisoku* (rapid trains) on the JR Furano line between Biei and Asahikawa (32 minutes) and Biei and Furano (36 minutes).

Whether you arrive by train or car, a visit to Biei's lovely old stone station should be on your agenda. It has been voted one of Japan's 100 top train stations!

Biei Potato-no-Oka (美瑛ポテトの丘; Map p602; ☎0166-92-3255; www.potatovillage.com/eng/top.html; dm/r per person from ¥4960/6100, 4-person cottages ¥22,000, 3-/5-person log houses ¥13,650/21,000; P @) An endearing place perched at the top of a field of potatoes. A variety of accommodation options are available in dormitories, rooms with private bathrooms, and adorable cottages and log houses. Guests congregate at night for hearty dinners (extra cost) featuring local produce, most notably potatoes! They'll pick you up at Biei station if you book ahead.

Biei Tourist Information Office (美瑛観光案内所; Map p602; ☎0166-92-4378; www.biei-hokkaido.jp; 8.30am-7pm May-Oct, 8.30am-5pm Nov-Apr) With enthusiastic English-speaking staff, this office has English maps and brochures, and even map codes for Biei highlights for your car navigation system. Rental bicycles are available for ¥200 per hour.

★**Ningle Terrace** ARTS CENTRE
(ニングルテラス; Map p602; ☎0167-22-1111; www.princehotels.co.jp/newfurano; noon-8.45pm Sep-Jun, 10am-8.45pm Jul-Aug) FREE Anyone into arts, crafts and shopping should not miss visiting Ningle Terrace at the New Furano Prince Hotel. With 15 log cabins all specialising in different crafts connected by boardwalks in the forest, there is everything from wooden toys to glass-blowing to candles to paper products. The mini-woodwind instruments shop is captivating. Everything is made onsite.

Farm Tomita FARM
(ファーム富田; Map p602; ☎0167-39-3939; www.farm-tomita.co.jp/en; 9am-4.30pm Oct-late Apr, 8.30am-6pm late Apr-Sep) FREE You really have to see Farm Tomita to believe it: try to imagine huge fields of brightly coloured flowers blooming like a rainbow. The Japanese tend to go wildest over the lavender, but the seasonal fields produce just as many squeals of delight.

The cafe and gift shop sell lavender-infused products including soft-serve ice-creams, puddings, jellies, pastries and soft drinks.

This place is so popular that from June to September, JR actually opens up a temporary train station known as Lavender Batake (ラベンダー畑; Lavender Farm) to accommodate the influx of visitors. Otherwise, the closest station is JR Naka-Furano.

Furano Winery WINERY
(ふらのワイン工場; Map p602; ☎0167-22-3242; www.furanowine.jp; 9am-4.30pm Sep-May, 9am-6pm Jun-Aug) FREE About 4km northwest of JR Furano station and overlooking the valley, it's almost obligatory to visit this winery, check out the wine-making process and indulge in a complimentary tipple.

Furano Cheese Factory CHEESE FACTORY
(富良野チーズ工房, Furano Chīzu Kobō; Map p602; ☎0167-23-1156; www.furano-cheese.jp; 9am-5pm Apr-Oct, to 4pm Nov-Mar) FREE Foodies should head to the cheese factory, about 2km south of JR Furano station. Try the wine-infused cheddar, as well as other Furano milk products such as ice cream. There's a pizza restaurant and the opportunity to try your hand at making things such as cheese and ice cream, but you need to book ahead. Check out the website.

Activities

Furano Ski Area SKIING, SNOWBOARDING
(富良野スキー場; www.snowfurano.com; lift tickets full day/night only ¥4900/1600, children 12 & under free; day 8.30am-5pm, night 5-8pm)

Situated between two Prince hotels, this world-class winter-sports resort has hosted numerous FIS World Ski and Snowboarding events, yet remains relatively undiscovered by foreign visitors as compared to Niseko.

Open from late November until the start of May, the slopes are predominantly beginner and intermediate, but there is a handful of steep advanced runs.

Eleven lifts, including the fastest gondola in Japan, help to keep the crowds in check. The two Prince hotels provide a wonderful après-ski atmosphere of fine dining, lively drinking and curative onsen soaking.

If you've got kids in tow, a major bonus here is that children aged 12 and under get a free lift pass. Full equipment rental is available for ¥4500 per day. English signage is adequate. Check the website for the latest.

Furano Ropeway ROPEWAY
(富良野ロープウェー; ☎0167-22-1111; www.princehotels.com/en/newfurano/furano-ropeway; one way/return ¥1200/1900) With its base at the New Prince Hotel, the Furano Ropeway (a 100-person gondola) zips visitors up to 900m for magnificent views over the Furano valley. The main lift in winter for skiers and boarders, it is also open and running from June to October. A number of hiking options are available from the top, including walking back down.

Festivals & Events

Heso Matsuri FESTIVAL
(www.furano.ne.jp/hesomatsuri/en) Humorously known as Heso-no-machi (Belly-Button Town), Furano is in the centre of Hokkaidō. This geographical distinction has given rise to the town's famous navel festival on 28 and 29 July. If you're in town, take the opportunity to strip off, have a humorous face painted on your midriff and join the Bellybutton Dance plus other inventive events.

Furano Wine Festival WINE
This harvest festival on the third Sunday in September offers all kinds of drink and food tastings along with other events. In an effort towards sustainability, organisers ask revellers to bring their own chopsticks!

Sleeping

Alpine Backpackers HOSTEL ¥
(アルパインバックパッカーズ; Map p602; ☎0167-22-1311; www.alpn.co.jp/english/index.html; dm per person ¥2500, tw/q ¥5000/10,000; P@W) Conveniently located just a few minutes' walk from the lifts, this is a great spot for skiers and active types. Backpackers are well catered for with cooking and laundry facilities, and a boiling onsen. There are also all sorts of activities from rafting to fishing to hot-air ballooning on offer. Check out the website.

Furano Youth Hostel HOSTEL ¥
(富良野ユースホステル; Map p602; ☎0167-44-4441; www4.ocn.ne.jp/~furanoyh/english.htm; 3-20 Okamati Naka-Furano-Cho; dm incl breakfast & dinner ¥3450; P@) Five minutes' walk west of JR Naka-Furano Station (not JR Furano Station), the Furano Youth Hostel occupies a big farmhouse overlooking the countryside. Breakfast and dinner are on the house (except Sunday night – the chef takes a break). Meals are simple, tasty and feature local produce. Private rooms may be available for an extra ¥2100 per room.

★**New Furano Prince Hotel** HOTEL ¥¥¥
(新富良野プリンスホテル; Map p602; ☎0167-22-1111; www.princehotels.com/en/newfurano; s/d with breakfast & lift tickets from ¥15,000/18,000; P@W) The New Prince hotel is a snazzy place with a variety of restaurants, bars and lounge areas. The rooms are plush, the service is impeccable, and the convenience factor of being virtually at the bottom of the Ropeway helps to maximise your slope time. Note that the cheapest prices are available if you book online well in advance.

Furano Natulux Hotel BOUTIQUE HOTEL ¥¥¥
(富良野ナチュラクスホテル; ☎0167-22-1777; www.natulux.com/en/index.html; s/d from ¥15,850/21,000; P@W) Located directly across from JR Furano Station, this boutique hotel has style. Rooms are on the small side, but there is a spa with bath and sauna. The cafe is a great place to indulge in a wine and cheese fondue set – both locally sourced, of course!

Eating

★**Chīzu Rāmen-no-mise Karin** RAMEN ¥
(チーズラーメンの店かりん; ☎0167-22-1692; 9-12 Moto-machi; dishes from ¥1000; ⏰11am-8pm; 📋) Furano is famous for its cheese and one way the locals eat it is shredded over a bowl of rāmen. This excessively high-calorie indulgence can be found in a nondescript brown-and-white building (look for the red curtain) a few minutes' walk southwest of JR Furano Station. There

is an English menu and the elderly owners will be ecstatic to greet you.

Kunen-kōbō Yamadori CURRY ¥

(くんえん工房 YAMADORI; ☎0167-39-1810; 4-14 Asahi-machi; dishes from ¥1000; ⊙lunch Fri-Wed;) Furano is famous for its omelette curries known as *omu-karē* (オムかれー) and Yamadori tops off that dish with a slice of bacon for ¥1000. You'll find this neat little treat in a cutesy-cool pink farmhouse with white trim a couple of minutes' walk from JR Furano Station.

Information

Tourist Information Office (富良野観光案内所; Map p602; ☎0167-23-3388; www.furanotourism.com; ⊙9am-6pm) Stock up on English maps and pamphlets, get some last-minute help booking accommodation, rent bicycles and even check your internet for free at JR Furano Station. There is also an office below the Kitanomine Gondola Station in the ski district. The website is very good.

Getting There & Away

BUS

Frequent buses run between Furano and Sapporo (¥2260, 2½ hours), as well as between Furano and Asahikawa (¥880, 1½ hours).

CAR & MOTORCYCLE

Route 237 runs between Asahikawa, Biei and Furano. It is 59km to Asahikawa by road, and 142km to Sapporo. Be extremely careful in the winter months as roads in this area can be icy and treacherous.

TRAIN

There are frequent *kaisoku* on the JR Furano line between Furano and Asahikawa (¥1070, 1¼ hours). For Sapporo (¥4140, 2½ hours), take a *futsū* on the JR Nemuro line to Takikawa, and then change to the hourly Super Kamui *tokkyū*.

Daisetsuzan National Park 大雪山国立公園

Known as 'Nutakukamushupe' in Ainu, Daisetsuzan or 'Big Snow Mountain' is Japan's largest national park, designated in 1934 and covering more than 2300 sq km. A vast wilderness area of soaring mountains, active volcanoes, remote onsen, clear lakes and dense forests, Daisetsuzan is something special in Japan.

Virtually untouched by human hands, the park has minimal tourism, with most visitors basing themselves in the hot-spring villages on the periphery.

The three main access points into the park are **Asahidake Onsen** in the northwest, **Sōunkyō Onsen** in the northeast and **Tokachi-dake Onsen** in the southwest.

Another special spot on the eastern side of the park is **Daisetsu Kōgen Onsen**.

Asahidake Onsen 旭岳温泉

☎0166

This hot-springs village, at 1100m above sea level, has a few inns at the base of Asahi-dake, Hokkaidō's tallest peak. There are plenty of hiking options and healing onsen for afterwards.

Most of the onsen, even those at the higher-end hotels, are open for day use to the general public. Prices range from ¥500 up to ¥1500.

Be prepared. There are no ATMs, shops or restaurants at Asahidake Onsen, so you'll need to have cash, and food sorted out if you are going camping or contemplating taking on the Grand Traverse. If you are staying, order meals at your accommodation house when you book.

Activities

Asahidake Ropeway ROPEWAY

(旭岳 ロープウェイ; Map p602; ☎0166-68-9111; http://wakasaresort.com/eng; one way/return 1 Jun-20 Oct ¥1650/2900, 21 Oct-31 May ¥1100/1800; ⊙6am-5.30pm Jul–mid-Oct, 9am-4pm mid-Oct–Jun) This ropeway runs from Asahidake Onsen (1100m) up to Sugatami (姿見) at 1600m, making **Asahi-dake** (旭岳; 2290m) a very feasible day hike. There are all sorts of hiking options and on a good day, the views are magnificent.

Asahidake Skiing SKIING

(Map p602; http://wakasaresort.com/eng; day pass ¥4000; ⊙1 Dec-6 May) This is an extreme skiing experience on a smoking volcano – it is definitely not for beginners. The only lift is the Asahidake Ropeway, but it is possible to hike up higher. There is plenty in the way of dry powder and scenic views, but it is recommended to ski with an experienced mountain guide.

For up-to-date information, check out www.snowjapan.com.

HIKING IN DAISETSUZAN NATIONAL PARK

There are many options for hiking in the national park ranging from half-day trips to the Daisetsuzan Grand Traverse, a hardcore five- to seven-day, 55km hike the length of the park.

Get a copy of Shōbunsha's Yama-to-Kōgen Chizu Map 3: Daisetsuzan (昭文社山と高原地図３大雪山), be prepared, and check the weather forecast. Visitor centre staff will be more than happy to update you on conditions.

From Asahidake Onsen

From the top of the ropeway at 1600m...

- There is a very nice, short loop walk around Sugatami-daira (姿見平) that will take less than an hour.
- Alternatively, climb the well-trodden track to Asahi-dake (2290m), Hokkaidō's highest point and one of Japan's Hyakumeizan (100 Famous Mountains), for amazing views and an excellent day trip of four to five hours hiking (return).
- If you are really keen and organised, get an early start and hike from Asahi-dake all the way over to Kuro-dake (黒岳; 1984m), then take the chairlift and ropeway down to Sōunkyō Onsen. You'll need to check ropeway start and finish times and allow six to eight hours for the hike between the ropeway stations. This is an excellent hike!

From Sōunkyō Onsen

From the top of the ropeway and chairlift at 1520m...

- Kuro-dake is only an hour or so climb away on a rocky trail renowned for its alpine flowers. Allow a couple of hours' walking for the return trip.
- From Kuro-dake you can carry on over to Asahi-dake and take the ropeway down to Asahidake Onsen. Allow six to eight hours for this mission, a reversal of the Asahi-dake to Kuro-dake hike.
- Another good day hike from Sōunkyō Onsen involves taking the bus to Ginsen-dai (銀泉台; 1400m; check bus times at the visitor centre) and climbing Aka-dake (赤岳; 2078m). This is a lovely track. Allow four to five hours and make sure you're back in time for the return bus.

From Tokachi-dake Onsen

As well as being the end point for the Grand Traverse, a couple of excellent full-day hikes can be tackled from here. Tokachi-dake Onsen is at 1270m.

- A return trip up Tokachi-dake (十勝岳; 2077m), one of Japan's Hyakumeizan, will take six to eight hours return and reveal some marvellous volcanic landscapes.
- Alternatively, head south and climb Furano-dake (富良野岳; 1912m) for great views out over Furano and the valley. A return trip up here will take four to six hours.

Daisetsuzan Grand Traverse

You will need to be seriously prepared for this extremely rewarding five- to seven-day hike the length of the park. This is anything but a walk in the park!

The season for this hike runs from early July to October. A tent and camping gear may be preferable to the extremely bare-bones huts. You'll need to carry in your own food and cooking supplies. This is also bear country, so be smart and tie a bell to your rucksack (see p616).

You could start at either Asahidake Onsen or Sōunkyō Onsen and you'll finish at Tokachi-dake Onsen. Pick up a copy of Lonely Planet's *Hiking in Japan*, do your homework before you go, and make the most of this adventure.

Sleeping

Daisetsuzan Shirakaba-sō INN ¥

(大雪山白樺荘; Map p602; ☎0166-97-2246; http://park19.wakwak.com/~shirakaba/english.html; incl 2 meals, dm from ¥6890, r per person ¥7940; P @) A cross between a youth hostel and a ryokan, this mountain lodge near the ropeway's lower terminal offers comfortable

Daisetsuzan National Park

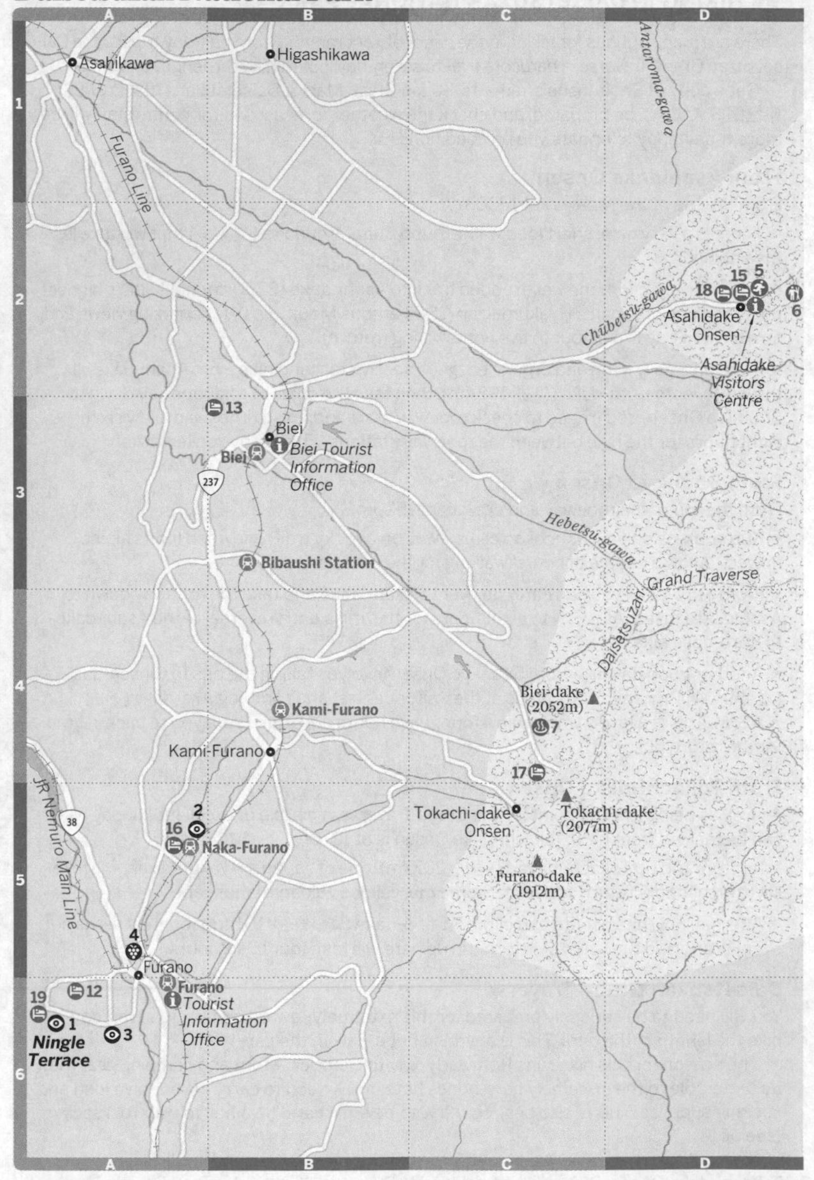

Japanese- and Western-style rooms and hot-spring baths. There is a large kitchen available if you're self-catering, but it's worth going for the meal plan. Lots of options, so check out the website. Nonguests can use the onsen for ¥500.

★Lodge Nutapukaushipe LODGE ¥¥
(ロッジ・ヌタプカウシペ; Map p602; 0166-97-2150; r per person with 2 meals from ¥8000; P) This log cabin–style place is an absolute joy, run by a real character who has handcrafted most of the furniture and

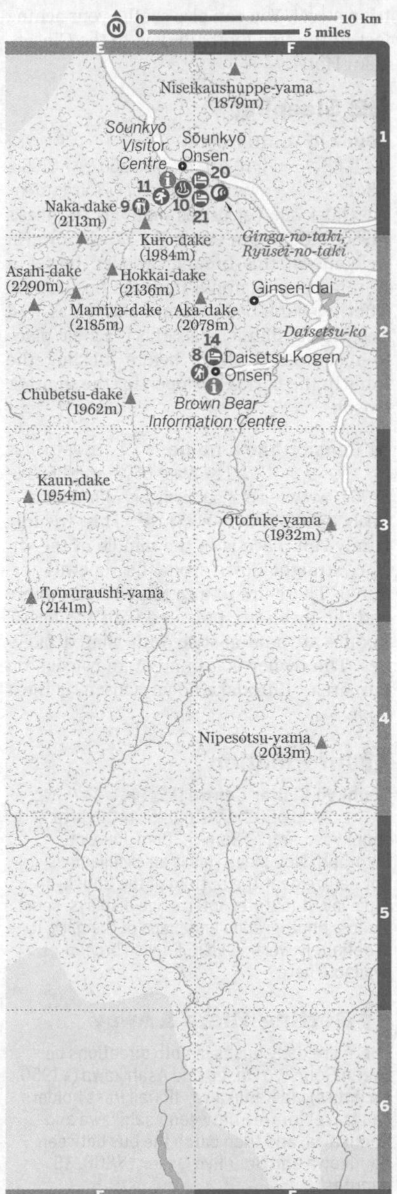

fittings from local timber. The onsen is superb, as are the meals. You'll have to make a bit of an effort though as there isn't a website. Pick up the phone and speak slowly. You won't be disappointed.

Daisetsuzan National Park

Top Sights
1 Ningle Terrace....A6

Sights
2 Farm Tomita....A5
3 Furano Cheese Factory....A6
4 Furano Winery....A5

Activities, Courses & Tours
5 Asahidake Ropeway....D2
6 Asahidake Skiing....D2
7 Fukiage Roten-no-yu....C4
8 Kōgen-numa Meguri Hike....F2
9 Kurodake Skiing....E1
10 Kurodake-no-yu....E1
11 Sōunkyō Ropeway....E1

Sleeping
12 Alpine Backpackers....A6
13 Biei Potato-no-Oka....B3
14 Daisetsu Kōgen Sansō....F2
15 Daisetsuzan Shirakaba-sō....D2
16 Furano Youth Hostel....A5
17 Kamihoro-sō....C4
18 Lodge Nutapukaushipe....D2
19 New Furano Prince Hotel....A6
20 Pension Yama-no-ue....F1
21 Sōunkyō Youth Hostel....F1

Information

Asahidake Visitors Centre (旭岳ビジターセンター; Map p602; 0166-97-2153; www.town.higashikawa.hokkaido.jp/vc; 9am-5pm Jun-Oct, 9am-4pm Nov-May) Has excellent maps that the staff will mark with daily track conditions. If you're heading out on a long hike, inform them of your intentions.

Getting There & Away

There are three buses in both directions daily between bus stop 4 in front of JR Asahikawa Station and Asahidake Onsen (¥1320, 1½ hours). The first bus leaves Asahikawa at 9.25am, returning from Asahidake Onsen at 11am.

Sōunkyō Onsen 層雲峡温泉

01658

The national park's main gateway on its northeastern side is Sōunkyō Onsen. Sōunkyō is a good base for forays into the park's interior, and there are some impressive natural attractions in the area that are worth seeking out.

The town has ATM facilities, restaurants and a couple of convenience stores, though if you are heading out into the backcountry, you'd be better to organise supplies before coming. There is no petrol station.

Sights

Sōunkyō (層雲峡; Layer Cloud Gorge) is a string of gorges 15km long formed by the Ishikari River, the very same Ishikari River that empties out into the Sea of Japan just north of Sapporo.

Popular with visitors are the waterfalls **Ryūsei-no-taki** (流星の滝; Shooting Stars Falls) and **Ginga-no-taki** (銀河の滝; Milky Way Falls). Also noteworthy are **Ōbako** (大箱; Big Box) and **Kobako** (小箱; Little Box), two unique sections of perpendicular rock formations, though getting to see them is difficult.

Activities

A number of shops along the main street rent out mountain bikes (¥2000 per day).

Sōunkyō Ropeway ROPEWAY
(大雪山層雲峡・黒岳ロープウェイ; Map p602; www.rinyu.co.jp/kurodake; 8am-7pm Jul-Aug, closed intermittently in winter) This combination ropeway-chairlift provides fast and easy access to Kuro-dake. From Sōunkyō Onsen at 670m, the ropeway will fly you up to 1300m for ¥1100/1950 (one way/return). From there, the chairlift can take you up to 1520m for ¥400/600 (one way/return). The peak of Kuro-dake is at 1984m. Hiking up here is a favourite with alpine plant and flower enthusiasts.

Kurodake Skiing SKIING
(Map p602; www.rinyu.co.jp/kurodake; pass ¥3700) Not a standard ski field, Kuro-dake is becoming popular with hardcore enthusiasts who like vertical and challenging terrain. With a season from early November to early May, and heaps of snow, this is not a place for beginners. The only problem is that the ropeway and chairlift close for maintenance for parts of January and February – time your visit well.

For up-to-date information, check out www.snowjapan.com.

Kurodake-no-yu ONSEN
(黒岳の湯; Map p602; 01658-5-3333; www.sounkyo.com/kurodakenoyu.html; admission ¥600; 10am-9pm) After a hard day of play, Kurodake-no-yu offers handsome hot-spring baths including a 3rd-floor *rotemburo* (outdoor bath) – it's on the town's main pedestrian street. You can also soothe your aching feet in the free footbath next to the Ginsenkaku Hotel.

Sleeping

Sōunkyō Youth Hostel HOSTEL ¥
(層雲峡ユースホステル; Map p602; 01658-5-3418; www.youthhostel.or.jp/sounkyo/en/index.html; dm per person with/without 2 meals ¥4950/3200; Jun-Oct; P @) Expect a warm welcome at this humble wooden hostel, a 10-minute walk uphill from the bus station. Offering bunk-bed accommodation, as well as basic but filling meals, this is a great place to meet other hikers before tackling the trails in the park. Only open for the summer season.

★ **Pension Yama-no-ue** PENSION ¥¥
(ペンション山の上; Map p602; 01658-5-3206; www.p-yamanoue.com; r with/without 2 meals ¥8800/5800; P @) This friendly family-run place is in the middle of the village, straight down from the ropeway terminal. There are nature photos everywhere and the meals are prepared with great care. Rooms are tatami-style with shared facilities. The owner is a mine of knowledge on the area. Kurodake-no-yu Onsen is next door.

Information

Sōunkyō Visitor Centre (層雲峡ビジターセンター; Map p602; 01658-9-4400; http://sounkyovc.net; 8am-5.30pm Jun-Oct, 9am-5pm Nov-May) This is an excellent visitor centre near the bottom of the Sōunkyō ropeway. It features interactive displays, short videos, photographs and maps of the park. It is definitely worth a visit. English brochures available here.

Getting There & Away

There are daily buses in both directions between Sōunkyō Onsen and Asahikawa (¥1950, 1¾ hours) via Kamikawa. JR Rail Pass holders can travel for free between Asahikawa and Kamikawa, and then catch the bus between Kamikawa and Sōunkyō Onsen (¥800, 35 minutes).

There are also a couple of buses a day to Kushiro (¥4790, 5¼ hours) via Akanko Onsen (¥3260, 3½ hours) in Akan National Park; and buses to Obihiro (¥2200, 80 minutes).

If you're driving, Route 39 connects Sōunkyō Onsen to Asahikawa in the west and Abashiri in the east.

DON'T MISS

FUKIAGE ROTEN-NO-YU

If you like sitting naked in small pools of hot steaming water surrounded by pristine forest, then head to **Fukiage Roten-no-yu** (吹上露天の湯; Map p602). This semi-secret spot is about 5km from Tokachi-dake Onsen – head down Route 291, then right on Route 966 – easy to get to if you have a good map and your own wheels.

There's a big sign on the downhill side of the road, a parking area and a 200m track down through the forest. There's nothing there except two hot pools. The one higher up is hotter than the other.

It's not for the shy: strip off and hop in! There's no charge...and this place is *konyoku*, meaning men and women bathe together. You might like to take a small 'modesty towel' if you've got one.

Daisetsu Kōgen Onsen 大雪高原温泉

On the eastern side of the park about 20km south of Sōunkyō Onsen, this is about as remote as it gets! Ten kilometres up an unsealed road in the middle of nowhere you'll find a couple of buildings in the heart of the national park. Make the effort – this is a highly recommended mountain adventure.

There are no shops, ATMs or petrol stations here.

Activities

Kōgen-numa Meguri Hike HIKING
(高原沼めぐり登山コース; Map p602; ⊙22 Jun-10 Oct) This four-hour hiking course around the Kōgen-numa (small lakes) is your best chance to see a brown bear in the wild. It's strictly regulated. Hikers must listen to a lecture at the Brown Bear Information Centre and are only allowed to head out on the hike between 7am and 1pm. Hikers must be off the track by 3pm.

Staff are out on the track each day, radioing in bear whereabouts and keeping an eye on both the hikers and the bears. This is a wonderful day hike beneath the high peaks. Soak in Kōgen Onsen after your walk.

Sleeping

Daisetsu Kōgen Sansō LODGE ¥¥
(大雪高原山荘; Map p602; ☎01658-5-3818; www.daisetsu-kogen.com; per person with meals from ¥10,950; ⊙10 Jun-10 Oct) Only open 123 days each year, this haven at the end of the road is well worth a visit. Rooms are simple with shared facilities, but the food is good, the onsen is hot and the air is fresh.

Make the most of your foray into the mountains – this is like staying at a mountain hut without having to walk five hours to get there. There are two buses per day from Sōunkyō Onsen for overnight guests, but having your own wheels is the best option. If you're not staying, you can use the onsen for ¥700.

Information

Brown Bear Information Centre (ヒグマ情報センター; Map p602; ⊙22 Jun-10 Oct) This small building has all sorts of 'bear info' and it is mandatory for hikers to listen to a 'bear lecture' here before heading out on the Kōgen-numa Meguri hike. Pay attention! Staff are out daily on the hike, radioing in bear locations to keep hikers safe.

Getting There & Away

Daisetsu Kōgen Onsen is at the end of a 10km unsealed road off Route 273 to the east of the park. The turnoff is signposted about 15km southeast from Sōunkyō Onsen. A car navigational system is useful to help you get here.

Alternatively, make a booking for the night at Daisetsu Kōgen Sansō and use their twice-daily bus for guests from Sōunkyō Onsen.

Tokachi-dake Onsen 十勝岳温泉

The main gateway to the national park in the southwest is Tokachi-dake Onsen, northeast of Furano.

This remote hot-spring village is not only the end point for the Grand Traverse hike, but is also a great spot for starting day hikes into the park. It is much less crowded than Asahidake and Sōunkyō Onsen. There are no shops, ATMs or petrol stations, so come prepared.

Sleeping

Kamihoro-sō LODGE ¥¥
(カミホロ荘; Map p602; ☎0167-45-2970; http://tokachidake.com/kamihoro; per person incl 2 meals

from ¥6500; P @) A decent place where you can unwind after hiking, with pleasant Japanese-style rooms and hot-spring baths fronting the distant mountains. Nonguests can use the bath for ¥600.

Getting There & Away

Kami-Furano train station is 15 minutes north of Furano on the JR Furano line. Kami-Furano Station is connected to Tokachi-dake Onsen by three buses (¥500, 40 minutes) each day.

Wakkanai 稚内

POP 40,000 / ☎0162

Wakkanai, Japan's most northern city, changes wildly with the seasons. From November to March, it's something akin to a remote Siberian outpost, home to hearty fishermen, kelp farmers and a harp-seal colony. Outside the winter months, it's a pleasantly mild port city that serves as a departure point for ferries to Rishiri-tō and Rebun-tō, two dramatic wildflower-dotted islands that rank among Hokkaidō's highlights, and – assuming you have your visa in order – a trip across the border to the Russian island of Sakhalin. And yes, those translations on the street signs about town are in Russian.

While it may seem to beat the northerly end of the world, Wakkanai is actually 45°N in latitude, about the same as Portland, Oregon, and Milan, Italy.

Sights

If you think that the huge breakwater protecting Wakkanai harbour from pounding waves from the north looks a bit odd, take a closer look. It was first built in 1936 to look like a straightened version of the Colosseum in Rome. Around 427m long, it has 70 columns that are 13.6m high. It's a popular spot for a stroll.

★Fukukō-ichiba MARKET
(副港市場; Map p610; ☎0162-29-0829; www.wakkanai-fukukou.com) About a 10-minute walk south of JR Wakkanai Station, this complex houses everything from a food market to souvenir shops to restaurants to the **Minato-no-yu Onsen** (港の湯温泉; ☎0162-22-1100; admission ¥700; ⏲10am-10pm). It's a bit like a living museum as fascinating historical corners show photos and videos of the history of Wakkanai and Karafuto (Sakhalin – when it was part of Japan before 1945).

Wakkanai Centennial Memorial Tower TOWER
(稚内開基百年記念塔; Map p610; ☎0162-24-4019; admission ¥400; ⏲closed Nov-Apr) Atop a grassy hill a few blocks (but a big climb) from JR Wakkanai Station is the town's centennial memorial tower, the Shikai Hyakunen Kinen-tō. On a clear day you can see Russia and get great views of Japan's northernmost points. If you turn up around dusk, you'll likely run into a surprisingly bold band of *ezo-jika* (Hokkaidō deer).

Noshappu-misaki CAPE
(ノシャプ岬; Map p610) On a good day this cape, the second most-northern point in mainland Japan, is a nice place for a picnic. It's a pleasant walk (45 minutes) or bike ride (20 minutes) north of town. Along the way, look out for the kelp-drying yards along the shoreline. If the weather is good, look out to the west for Rishiri-tō.

Sōya-misaki CAPE
(宗谷岬) At 30km east of Wakkanai, Sōya-misaki is mainland Japan's northernmost point. Birdwatchers will love the seagulls and terns, while people-watchers will enjoy the stream of tour buses and groups being photographed before the 'northernmost point' monument. This is where length-of-Japan walkers or cyclists either start or finish, so if there's a person getting their photo taken in front of the monument, go up and shake their hand. Buses depart regularly from JR Wakkanai Station (¥2430, 50 minutes).

Sarobetsu Genya MARSHLANDS
(サロベツ原野; Map p610) While technically part of Rishiri-Rebun-Sarobetsu National Park, these marshlands are best accessed from Wakkanai. Approximately 35km south of town, Sarobetsu Genya is full of colour every year, best in June and July, with dramatic wildflower blooms. Frequent *futsū* (local trains) on the JR Sōya line run between Wakkanai and Toyotomi (¥900, 45 minutes). Toyotomi is connected to the park entrance by regular local buses (¥430, 15 minutes).

Activities

There is some wonderful wildlife-watching in Bakkai (抜海), where harp seals arrive each year in November and stay until May. A basic viewing hut provides shelter, a toilet and some information about the seals. Frequent *futsū* run on the JR Sōya line between Wakkanai and Bakkai (¥260, 15 minutes).

Dress warmly. It's a 30-minute walk from the station to the port where the seals are. Your own wheels would be useful.

Festivals & Events

Japan Cup Dogsled Race SPORTS
(Zenkoku Inu-zori Wakkanai Taikai; www.city.wakkanai.hokkaido.jp) In February Wakkanai hosts the biggest dogsled race in Japan at Wakkanai Airport Park. The track winds through some truly inhospitable frozen terrain, though everyone warms up back in the city where festivities carry on well into the night.

Sleeping

Wakkanai Moshiripa Youth Hostel HOSTEL ¥
(稚内モシリパユースホステル; Map p610; 0162-24-0180; www.moshiripa.net; 2-9-5 Chūō; dm/r from ¥3960/4800; @) Conveniently located a few blocks north of JR Wakkanai Station, this dark-blue, three-storey building offers functional, unfussy dormitories and private rooms. But the management is warm and friendly, even when the temperatures outside are cold and unforgiving.

★**Tenpoku no Yu** HOTEL ¥¥
(天北の湯 (ドーミーイン稚内); Map p610; 0162-24-5489; www.japanican.com/en/hotel/detail/1101015; 2-7-13 Chūō; s/d from ¥6000/8000; @) Formerly known as Dormy Inn Wakkanai and only four minutes' walk from JR Wakkanai Station, this hotel is a good choice. There's an onsen on the top floor, coin laundry facilities, free internet and early breakfast for those wanting to catch the first ferry out to the islands. Standard spotless and functional rooms. Book early online for great rates.

ANA Crowne Plaza Wakkanai HOTEL ¥¥
(ANAクラウンプラザホテル稚内; Map p610; 0162-23-8111; www.ana-hotel-wakkanai.co.jp; s/d incl breakfast from ¥14,000/16,500; P @) Tall, sleek and stylish, if a little weather-worn, this place seems a bit out of place in downtown Wakkanai – walk to the waterfront and you can't miss it. Book early online and you'll be surprised how reasonable prices can be.

Eating

★**Pechika** RUSSIAN ¥
(ペチカ; 0162-23-7070; www.w-kenki.com/pechka; Fukukō-ichiba; set menu from ¥1000; 5-11pm) This Russian restaurant in the Fukakō-ichiba complex is a joy, proudly displaying friendship on a local level between Wakkanai and its neighbour. There's Russian beer, Russian music and the place is packed with locals. The Saharin Course (サハリンコース; Sakhalin Course, ¥1500) is a popular choice.

Take-chan SEAFOOD ¥
(竹ちゃん; 0162-22-7130; http://take-chan.co.jp; 2-8-7 Chūō; dishes from ¥500; 11am-11pm;) If you make it past the huge tank of live crabs just inside the front door you're in for a treat at this legendary Wakkanai restaurant. There's an English menu and if you're into seafood, you can't go wrong. Try the *tako-shabu* (¥1575), an octopus variant of traditional *shabu-shabu*. A five-minute walk from JR Wakkanai Station.

Information

Tourist Information Counter (0162-22-2384; www.welcome.wakkanai.hokkaido.jp/en; 10am-6pm) You can pick up maps and get your bearings at the tourist information counter located inside JR's Wakkanai Station.

FERRY TO RUSSIA

From June to September an unusual excursion from Wakkanai is a ferry trip to the city of Korsakov on Sakhalin Island in Russia. Most Japanese tourists, many of whom are actually travelling to see where they were born or to visit *ohaka* (family gravesites), make this journey with a tour group, but with a little planning it's fairly easy to go on your own.

Russia has recently changed to an online visa service for visitors. Check online for the latest. There are rumours that the Wakkanai–Korsakov trip will become visa-free for stays of less than 72 hours.

From Wakkanai Harbour, Heartland Ferry (p608) operates five to nine monthly ferries (June to September) in both directions between Wakkanai and Korsakov (5½ hours). A 2nd-class one-way/return ticket costs ¥25,000/40,000. If you are not returning to Japan, you may be asked to show an onward ticket at customs in Russia.

Getting There & Around

JR's Wakkanai Station is right next to the bus terminal and both are just 10 minutes on foot from the ferry port.

AIR

From Wakkanai Airport, about 10km east of the city centre, there are year-round daily flights to Sapporo and Tokyo, plus seasonal flights to Nagoya and Osaka. Regular buses run between JR Wakkanai Station and the airport (¥600, 35 minutes).

BUS

There are a couple of daily buses in either direction between JR Wakkanai Station and Sapporo (¥6000, six hours), as well as Asahikawa (¥4700, 4¾ hours).

BOAT

Heartland Ferry (ハートランドフェリー; ☎011-233-8010; www.heartlandferry.jp/english/index.html) has sailings to Rishiri-tō and Rebun-tō as well as Russia.

CAR & MOTORCYCLE

Long and lonely Route 40 runs between Asahikawa and Wakkanai. If you're heading out to Rishiri-tō or Rebun-tō, parking is available at the ferry terminal for ¥1000 per night.

TRAIN

Wakkanai is at the end of the line. There are just a couple of *tokkyū* each day on the JR Sōya line between Asahikawa and Wakkanai (¥8500, four hours).

Rishiri-Rebun-Sarobetsu National Park
利尻礼文サロベツ国立公園

For a remote island adventure, take a trip out to Rishiri-tō and Rebun-tō, which lie off the coast of Wakkanai to the west. While the islands are virtually abandoned in the winter months, from May to August they burst to life with wildflower blooms, drawing visitors by the boatload. This is also the best time to summit Rishiri-zan (1721m), a near-perfect cone rising like a miniature Mt Fuji from the surrounding sea. The national park also includes the flower-filled marshlands of Sarobetsu Genya (p606), best accessed from Wakkanai.

Rishiri-tō 利尻島

POP 5100 / ☎0163

Author and alpinist Fukada Kyūya did Rishiri-tō a huge favour in 1962, ensuring its prosperity when he named it as one of his Nihon Hyakumeizan, Japan's '100 Famous Mountains'. These days, every Japanese hiker has it on his bucket list, ensuring a steady supply of visitors throughout the northern summer. While hikers head to Rishiri-tō, flower enthusiasts flock to Rebun-tō.

Activities

Rishiri-zan HIKING

(利尻山; Map p610) Also known as Rishiri-Fuji for its resemblance to Fuji-san, Rishiri-zan is a big climb. The main trailhead is about 4km from the ferry port at Oshidomari (鴛泊) at 220m above sea level. The peak is at 1721m, meaning you've got 1500 vertical metres to climb.

While this can be an incredibly rewarding hike with amazing views, do not underestimate the fitness required to make such a climb or the changeable nature of the weather on this exposed stand-alone volcano. June through September is the best time to attempt it.

Limited bus service runs to the start of the track; otherwise you must walk, hitch, taxi or ask staff at your lodging if they can drop you off. The return hike to the top will take eight to 10 hours. At 1230m, just past the eighth station, Rishiri-dake yamagoya (利尻岳山小屋) is an unstaffed mountain hut perched on the edge of a precipice that provides the bare minimum of a roof over your head (no water). It is possible to spend the night here.

There are actually two peaks, Kita-mine (北峰) and Minami-mine (南峰), the latter just 2m higher. You may only be allowed to climb to Kita-mine for safety reasons.

For the descent, it's also possible to head down the trail to Kutsugata (沓形) on the island's west coast. The track, which passes Rōsoku-dake (ローソク岩; Candle Rock) near the top, runs into road at 430m and you'll have to find a way to get down to Kutsugata from there, probably using your feet. Buses run regularly on the 18km road between Kutsugata and Oshidomari. Alternatively, stay the night in Kutsugata.

Get a copy of Shobunsha's excellent map, Yama-to-kōgen Chizu 1 Rishiri; Rausu (昭文社 山と高原地図 1 利尻；羅臼).

Rishiri-Fuji Onsen ONSEN

(利尻富士温泉; Map p610; ☎0163-82-2388; admission ¥600; ⏰11am-9pm Jun-Aug, noon-9pm Sep-May) Could there be a better place to go to recover from climbing Rishiri-zan?

We don't think so. The onsen is on the road from Oshidomari to the trailhead. Pick it out on your way to the climb in the morning so you know where to go on the way back.

Sleeping

Hokuroku Campground CAMPGROUND ¥
(利尻北麓野営場; Map p610; ☎0163-82-2394; campsites per person ¥300, cabins ¥3000; ⊙15 May-15 Oct; P) Located at the start of the Rishiri-zan track, this camping ground is a good spot to stay if you want to get an early start to the hike. It's a 10-minute drive or 60-minute walk from the ferry terminal. There are four other campgrounds on the island. Check at the tourist information booth when you get off the ferry.

Rishiri Green Hill Inn HOSTEL ¥
(利尻ぐりーんひるinn; Map p610; ☎0163-82-2507; http://rishiri-greenhill.net; dm from ¥3800; P ⊖ @ ≋ ✈) A former youth hostel, this is a sociable backpacker spot with dormitories. There's kitchen usage, free internet, coin laundry and a convivial atmosphere. Call ahead for a ride from the ferry. The friendly owners will drop guests up at the start of the Rishiri-zan track. It's a bit out of the way, but a good budget option.

★ **Maruzen Pension Rera Mosir** PENSION ¥¥
(マルゼンペンションレラモシリ; Map p610; ☎0163-82-2295; www.maruzen.com/tic/oyado; per person with/without 2 meals from ¥9500/6300; P @ ≋) Open year-round, this place is set up to cater for all needs. With a lovely design, stylish rooms and restaurant, outdoor baths and terrace, this is *the* place to stay. They do free port pick-ups, can arrange rental cars and will drop off at the Rishiri-zan trailhead.

Owner Toshiya is a surfing and mountain guide.

Eating

There are not a lot of restaurants on the island, so eating where you stay is a good option.

★ **Sunset Dream Cafe** CAFE ¥
(サンセットドリームカフェ; Map p610; ☎0163-82-2033; www.hi-ho.ne.jp/m-1949; ⊙10am-5pm May-Sep) This place, perched above the port, may be your salvation in horrible weather when hiking is out of the question. There are tasty coffees, teas and snacks, soothing jazz, plus the wonderful photos of Matsui Hisayuki on display in the attached gallery. A perfect port in a storm!

Tsuki Café CAFE ¥
(月カフェ; Map p610; ☎0163-82-2305; http://tsukirishiri.wix.com/tsuki; ⊙10am-2am Thu-Tue) Upstairs in Oshidomari's new ferry terminal, Tsuki is a sparkling cafe enthusiastically serving visitors and those waiting for ferries with tasty coffees, cookies and full meals. Their Rishiri-*rāmen* (¥1200) is excellent. After the last ferry has gone, Tsuki transforms into an *izakaya* (pub-eatery) and is open until the wee hours.

Information

Oshidomari Tourist Information Office (Map p610; ☎0163-82 2201; www.rishiritou.com; ⊙8am-5.30pm 15 Apr-15 Oct) On the ground floor of the new ferry terminal, this information office provides English maps and details about transport, sights and hiking. Staff can also help you book accommodation and/or ferry services.

SKIING & SURFING AT RISHIRI

Yes, you read that right. There is skiing and surfing to be had on Rishiri, but neither is for beginners. Toshiya Watanabe at **Rishiri Nature Guide Service** (利尻自然ガイドサービス; ☎0163-82-2295; www.maruzen.com/tic/guide) is at the forefront of adventure tourism in these remote islands and has some intriguing options for adrenalin-seekers.

Toshiya swears his surfing tours (available from May to October), run in conjunction with his Maruzen Pension Rera Mosir, are spectacular and he should know – he used to run a surf shop in a more tropical realm. Also on offer are sea-kayaking tours (May through October), hiking tours, salmon-fishing tours (September and October) and winter ski tours and snowshoe tours.

Toshiya's ski guiding is true backcountry stuff (think no lifts) with plenty of hiking up, followed by steep descents on a Fuji-type volcano that doesn't see many skiers or boarders.

We re-emphasise: these tours are for the adventurous. If you're keen, contact Toshiya through his website; it would be helpful to have a Japanese-speaker on hand.

Rishiri-Rebun-Sarobetsu National Park

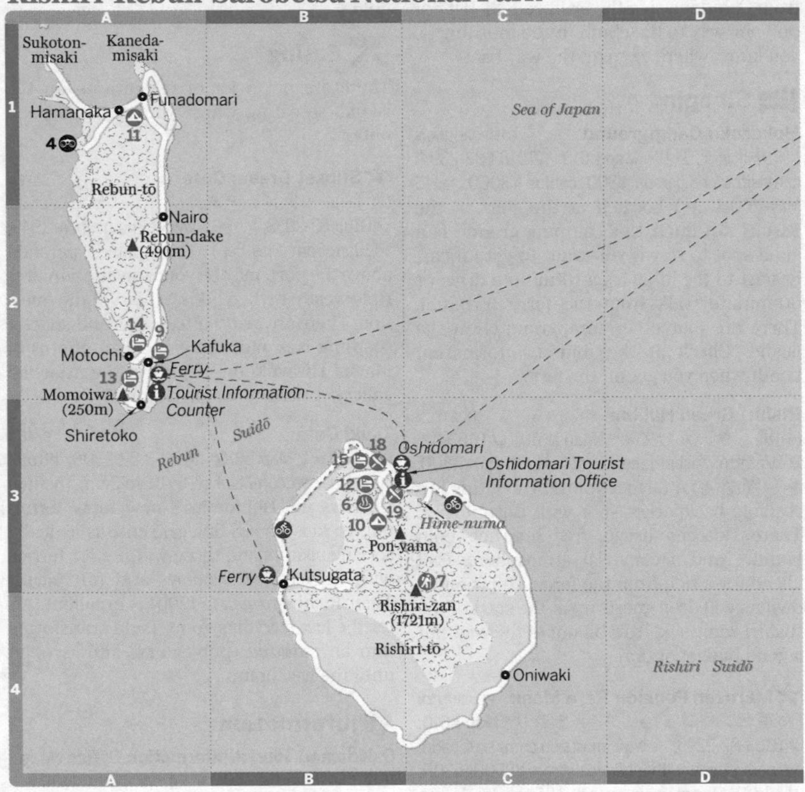

Rishiri-Rebun-Sarobetsu National Park

Top Sights
1 Fukukō-ichiba ... F1

Sights
2 Noshappu-misaki ... E1
3 Sarobetsu Genya ... F4
4 Sukai-misaki ... A1
5 Wakkanai Centennial Memorial Tower ... E1

Activities, Courses & Tours
6 Rishiri-Fuji Onsen ... B3
7 Rishiri-zan ... C3

Sleeping
8 ANA Crowne Plaza Wakkanai ... F1
9 Hana Rebun ... A2
10 Hokuroku Campground ... B3
11 Kushu-kohan Campground ... A1
12 Maruzen Pension Rera Mosir ... B3
13 Momoiwa-sō Youth Hostel ... A2
14 Pension Uni ... A2
15 Rishiri Green Hill Inn ... B3
16 Tenpoku no Yu ... E1
17 Wakkanai Moshiripa Youth Hostel ... E1

Eating
18 Sunset Dream Cafe ... B3
19 Tsuki Café ... B3

Getting There & Around

AIR

From Rishiri-tō Airport, just a few kilometres west of Oshidomari, there are year-round flights to Sapporo, with more operating in the summer tourist season. Check out **ANA** (www.ana.co.jp) and **Hokkaidō Air System** (HAC; www.hac-air.co.jp).

Local buses run infrequently by the airport; a taxi into town costs around ¥1200.

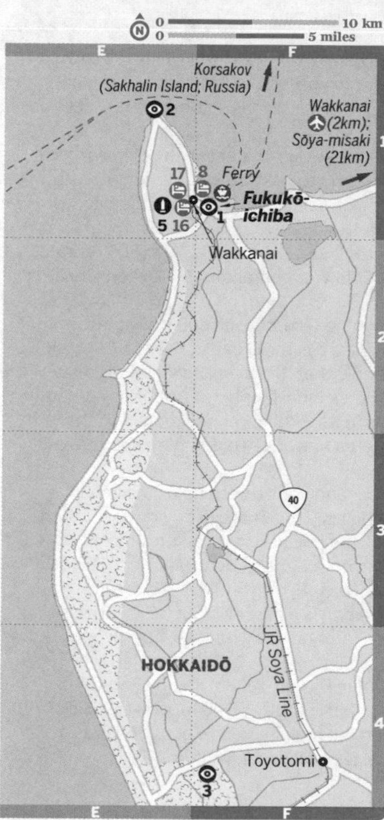

BICYCLE

Cycling is a great way to see the island – rent a bike from the shops near the Oshidomari ferry terminal.

A leisurely circuit of the island (56km) takes anywhere from five to seven hours. There is also a 25km cycling path that runs through woods and coastal plains from Oshidomari to past Kutsugata.

BOAT

Rishiri's brand new ferry terminal at **Oshidomari** (Map p610) is up and running.

Heartland Ferry (ハートランドフェリー; ☎011-233-8010; www.heartlandferry.jp) operates two to four daily ferries (year-round) between Wakkanai and Oshidomari (from ¥2340, 1¾ hours). Slightly less frequent ferries run in both directions from Oshidomari and Kutsugata Harbours to Kafuka (¥960, 45 minutes) on Rebun-tō.

All ferry tickets are available for purchase at the various ports.

BUS

Regular local buses run in both directions around the island's perimeter, completing a circuit in about two hours (¥2200). The trip from Oshidomari to Kutsugata (¥730) takes 30 to 50 minutes, depending on whether the bus stops at the airport. Pick up a bus schedule at the tourist information booth in the ferry terminal.

CAR & MOTORCYCLE

Rental cars are available down by the port.

Rebun-tō 礼文島

POP 2800 / ☎0163

While Rishiri-tō is a volcanic cone towering out of the sea, Rebun-tō is completely different, shaped like a long dried squid with a high point of just 490m. In the summertime, fields of wildflower explode into colour attracting visitors. The terrain is varied, and a number of tracks are maintained around the island.

Activities

Most people come to Rebun-tō to hike, whether it's an eight- to 10-hour trek traversing the length of the island or a shorter two- to four-hour option.

For starters, it's a good idea to take a bus to the northern tip of the island, **Sukoton-misaki** (スコトン岬). Keep your eyes open for harp seals, which can be seen year-round here, in **Funadomari Bay** (船泊湾) and at **Kaneda-misaki** (金田岬).

From Sukoton-misaki, you can hike your way back south to **Sukai-misaki** (澄海岬; Map p610) in 2½ hours. From here, either turn east and inland for 45 minutes to reach the bus stop at **Hamanaka** (浜中), or alternatively, you can continue south and hike the entire length of the island.

Another popular hike is from **Nairo** (内路), halfway down the east coast, to the top of **Rebun-dake** (礼文岳; 490m). It's a pleasant four-hour return journey, and the view from the summit helps to give perspective on the shape of Rebun.

Near the port in **Kafuka** (香深) there is a wildflower trail leading across a backbone of highlands to **Momoiwa** (桃岩; Peach Rock). The track then winds down through more flowers to the lighthouse at **Shiretoko** (知床). Take the bus back to Kafuka.

Usuyuki-no-yu Onsen ONSEN
(うすゆきの湯; ☎0163-86-2345; admission ¥600; ⏲noon-10pm) This impressive onsen is right on the waterfront in Kafuka, a couple

DRIVING THE OKHOTSK LINE

If the name Okhotsk doesn't sound very Japanese to you, you're dead right. The Japanese never had a name for the sea that borders the eastern coast of Hokkaidō, so they've adopted (and adapted!) the Russian name.

Take a look at a map and you'll see that the Okhotsk Sea falls between Sakhalin (formerly known as Karafuto and part of Japan from 1905 to 1945), a long stretch of eastern Siberia, the Kamchatka Peninsula, the Kuril Islands (including the Northern Territories still in dispute between Japan and Russia) and Hokkaidō.

The name Okhotsk may even make you shiver – it just sounds cold. With 80% covered in ice floes in winter and the scene of countless Cold War operations, the Okhotsk Sea just doesn't seem to be the most inviting place.

Strange then, considering the history and ongoing territorial disputes, that the Japanese have called that region of Hokkaidō that faces the Okhotsk Sea the Okhotsk Region (オホーツク地方; Ohōtsuku-chihō). Not only that, the long and lonely road that runs the length of the coast is known as the Okhotsk Line, Monbetsu Airport is named Monbetsu Okhotsk Airport and the region revels in its Okhotsk connection. If you've spent a bit of time in Japan, you'll find that this area has a very different feel to the rest of the country.

If you're driving around Hokkaidō in a rental car and you've been up to Wakkanai and Rishiri-Rebun-Sarobetsu National Park, we heartily recommend driving back south by the Okhotsk Line. After rounding Sōya-misaki, the northernmost point in mainland Japan, and turning south, you'll be stunned at the nothingness. No towns, no traffic lights, few cars and only wind-battered coastline. For Tokyo drivers this is a dream come true and will shatter any thoughts you had that Japan is a densely populated, crowded country. The closer to Abashiri you get, the more farming you'll run into, but savour the remoteness.

If you want to break up the drive, stay the night in Esashi, 100km south of Sōya-misaki, at the **Hotel New Kohrin** (ホテルニュー幸林; ☎0163-62-4040; www.esashi.biz/new-kohrin; per person from ¥3000; P @). Right on the main road, this place features a big onsen in which to sit and contemplate your remote Hokkaidō adventure.

of minutes' walk from the ferry terminal. A great place for a soak after a day spent hiking.

Sleeping

Kushu-kohan Campground CAMPGROUND ¥
(久種湖畔キャンプ場; Map p610; ☎0163-87-3110; campsites per person/tent ¥600/500, 4-person cabins ¥2000; ⏲May-Oct) This campground offers attractive lakeside camping and woodsy cabins beside Lake Kushu at the northern end of the island. You'll need to take the bus to get there (¥1030, 45 minutes). There is another tents-only campground at Midori-ga-oka Kōen, near Kafukai, 5km north of Kafuka.

Momoiwa-sō Youth Hostel HOSTEL ¥
(桃岩荘ユースホステル; Map p610; ☎0163-86-1421; www.youthhostel.or.jp/n_momoiwaso.htm; dm ¥3600, breakfast/dinner ¥600/1000; ⏲Jun-Sep; @) This eclectic youth hostel (located in an old herring house) has a devoted cult following. Beds are a combination of Japanese-style dorms (on tatami mats) and bunks. Staff can pick you up when the ferry docks: look for the flags. Keep in mind that this is a hardcore youth hostel.

Pension Uni PENSION ¥¥
(ペンションうーにー; Map p610; ☎0163-86-1541; www.p-uni.burari.biz; r per person with/without 2 meals from ¥8860/5860; P @) Up the hill from the port, this bright blue pension offers both a cheery reception and cheery rooms. Everything is immaculate here. Make the most of the offer of a ride from/to the ferry terminal.

Hana Rebun HOTEL ¥¥¥
(花れぶん; Map p610; ☎0163-86-1177; www.hanarebun.com; r with 2 meals from ¥15,000; @) This upmarket spot in the middle of Kafuka packs in the crowds during the busy summer months. There is an excellent *rotemburo* here that overlooks Rishiri-zan, and sumptuous banquet dinners that are attended to by a professional staff.

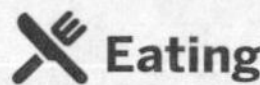

Eating

★Robata Chidori SEAFOOD ¥

(炉ばたちどり; ☎0163-86-2130; ⊙11am-10pm) Chidori is a lovely little intimate spot along the waterfront in Kafuka, about five minutes' walk from the ferry terminal. This is real *robata-yaki*, with a small grill in each table that you cook your food on. The speciality of the house is *Hokke Chanchan-yaki* (¥1400). *Hokke* is similar to a mackerel, and you grill it yourself over charcoal.

Information

Tourist Information Counter (Map p610; ☎0163-86-2655; www.rebun-island.jp; ⊙8am-5pm mid-Apr–Oct) In the new ferry terminal, helpful English-speaking staff can assist with transport, sights, hiking and accommodation. Open until the last ferry departs.

Getting There & Around

BICYCLE

Rental bicycles can be found outside the Kafuka ferry terminal.

BOAT

From Wakkanai Harbour, Heartland Ferry (p611) operates two to five daily ferries (year-round) between Wakkanai and Kafuka (from ¥2570, two hours). Less-frequent ferries run in both directions from Kafuka to Oshidomari and Kutsugata Harbours (¥960, 45 minutes) on Rishiri-tō. All ferry tickets are available for purchase at the various ports.

BUS

Buses run along the island's main road from Kafuka in the south to Sukoton-misaki in the north (¥1250, 70 minutes). There are also bus routes from Kafuka to Shiretoko (¥300, 15 minutes) and Motochi (¥450, 20 minutes). Pick up a timetable at the tourist information counter in the Kafuka ferry terminal on arrival.

CAR & MOTORCYCLE

Scooters and cars are readily available outside the Kafuka ferry terminal. Having your own wheels gives you the opportunity to explore Rebun to the max.

EASTERN HOKKAIDŌ

Eastern Hokkaidō (道東; Dō-tō) is a harsh yet hauntingly beautiful landscape that has been shaped by volcanoes and vast temperature extremes. In the winter months, dramatic ice floes off the coast of Abashiri in the Okhotsk Sea can be seen from the decks of ice-breakers. Both Akan and Shiretoko National Park, the latter a World Heritage-listed site, are best explored during the mild summers when there are great hiking opportunities. Kushiro Wetlands National Park offers the chance to see the red-crested white crane, the symbol of longevity in Japan.

Abashiri 網走

POP 40,000 / ☎0152

To the Japanese, Abashiri is as synonymous with the word 'prison' as Alcatraz is to Americans. Winters here are as harsh as they come, and the mere mention of the prison (still in operation) sends chills through the spines of even the most hardened individuals. Abashiri is also famous for its frozen seas, which can be explored on ice-breakers, and its coral-grass blooms, which burst into life every September. Throughout the warmer months, Abashiri serves as a jumping-off point for both Akan National Park and Shiretoko National Park.

Sights

From June to October, a tourist-loop bus connects the bus and train stations to the three museums, all of which are a few kilometres southwest of town.

Abashiri Prison Museum MUSEUM

(網走監獄博物館; ☎0152-45-2411; www.kangoku.jp/world/index.htm; admission ¥1080; ⊙8am-6pm Apr-Oct, 9am-5pm Nov-Mar) Housed in the remains of the original Meiji-era structure, the dark and foreboding Kangoku Hakubutsukan details the reasons this historic prison was so feared.

Okhotsk Drift Ice Museum MUSEUM

(オホーツク流氷館; ☎0152-43-5951; www.ryuhyokan.com; admission ¥520; ⊙8am-6pm Apr-Oct, 9am-4.30pm Nov-Mar) The Ryūhyōkan sits atop a hill with great viewing platforms, interesting displays and the tiny *kurione* (sea angel), a funky relative of the sea slug that has become the de-facto Abashiri mascot.

Hokkaidō Museum of Northern Peoples MUSEUM

(北海道立北方民族博物館; ☎0152-45-3888; www.hoppohm.org/english; admission ¥550; ⊙9.30am-4.30pm Tue-Sun) The Hoppōminzoku Hakubutsukan, southwest of town,

DON'T MISS

A BEER WITH THE INNOVATORS

While in Abashiri, all beer-lovers should take the opportunity to visit the innovators at **Abashiri Bīru-kan** (網走ビール館; www.takahasi.co.jp/beer/yakiniku/index.html; Minami-ni-jō-nishi, Yon-chōme; meat plates from ¥780, beers from ¥500; ⏲lunch & dinner) – the guys who brought you Bilk. This amazing concoction, made up of 70% beer and 30% Hokkaidō milk, may not have survived its first season in the bottles (for lack of sales), but these guys keep trying.

On offer now is the most mind-bogglingly colourful range of beers on the planet: the Ryūhyō (drift ice) Draft, representing winter, is a startlingly bright blue; the Hamanasu Draft, developed for summer in the colour of the *hamanasu* flower, is cherry red; the Jaga (potato) Draft is somewhat surprisingly shocking pink; and the Shiretoko Draft nicely represents the colours of the national park by being alarmingly green. The latest offering is Kangoku-no-kuro (Extreme Black), also known as Abashiri Prison Stout.

All beers are up for tasting with brilliant yaki-niku (grilled meat) meals. Think of it as a Japanese version of beers around the BBQ, even if the beers are the colours of the rainbow!

The Abashiri Bīru-kan brewery restaurant is on the main drag about a 10-minute walk east of Abashiri Station. You may also find the brews for sale in bottles in supermarkets and convenience stores in the region.

is dedicated to northern cultures. A state-of-the-art place, it has numerous exhibits on Ainu, Native American, Aleutian and other indigenous cultures.

Activities

★Aurora CRUISE
(MSおーろら; ☎0152-43-6000; http://ms-aurora.com/abashiri/en; cruises ¥3300; ⏲9am-6pm) From roughly late January to late March, the ice-breaker *Aurora* departs four to six times a day from Abashiri port for one-hour cruises into the frozen Sea of Okhotsk. Dress warmly.

Abashiri Nature Cruise CRUISE
(網走ネイチャークルーズ; ☎0152-44-5849; cruises ¥8000; ⏲Apr-Oct) Once the ice disappears from the Sea of Okhotsk (usually by April), popular three-hour nature cruises depart twice daily and head out looking for whales, dolphins and seabirds.

Sango Sōgunraku NATURE WALK
(サンゴ草群落) Known as salt pickle or glasswort in other parts of the world, coral glass, the otherwise humble marsh plant, gets its moment of fame in September when it turns bright red. There are a few boardwalk viewing spots about 10km west of town at Lake Notoro (能取湖).

Ryūhyō Norokko-gō SCENIC RIDE
(流氷ノロッコ号) Running roughly from late January to late March, this sightseeing train putters along twice a day from Abashiri to Shiretoko-shari Station (¥810, one hour) through a field of utterly white snow. Stare out at this frozen landscape while eating dried *surume* (squid) and nursing a can of Sapporo lager.

Cycling Road CYCLING
A cycling road runs for 25km west from Abashiri to Lake Saroma (サロマ湖), taking in the coral-grass-viewing areas and featuring beautiful views of lakes, forests and pumpkin fields.

Festivals & Events

Okhotsk Drift Ice Festival FESTIVAL
(オホーツク流氷まつり; ⏲mid-Feb) What an opportunity to celebrate the cold! Ice sculptures and statues, illuminated at night, plus lots of warm sake to keep your blood flowing.

Orochon-no-hi Festival CULTURAL FESTIVAL
(オロチョンの火祭り) Held on the last Saturday in July, this fire festival prays for a good harvest and consoles the spirits of those who have passed.

Sleeping

Minshuku Lamp MINSHUKU ¥
(民宿ランプ; ☎0152-43-3928; http://travel.rakuten.com/hotel/info/13793; r per person ¥2800; Ⓟ@) A 10-minute walk from JR Abashiri Station, Minshuku Lamp is the best budget option in town, with simple Japanese-style rooms with shared facilities. There's a coin

laundry and rental bicycles on site. Book ahead or ask the tourist information office to call for you.

Toyoko Inn Okhotsk Abashiri Eki-mae HOTEL ¥¥
(東横インオホーツク網走駅前; ☎0152-45-1043; www.toyoko-inn.com/e_hotel/00003/index.html; s/d from ¥4800/6300; P@) Directly opposite JR Abashiri Station, Abashiri's Toyoko Inn may be a simple business hotel, but it is clean, convenient and keen to attract business. Internet, buffet breakfasts and curry-rice dinners are free for guests.

Hotel Route Inn Abashiri Eki-mae HOTEL ¥¥
(ホテルルートイン網走駅前; ☎0152-44-5511; www.route-inn.co.jp/search/hotel/index_hotel_id_502; s/d ¥6050/10,450; @) Conveniently located across from JR Abashiri Station, this instalment of the Route Inn chain offers the usual, however, a nice perk is the large winter-warming onsen.

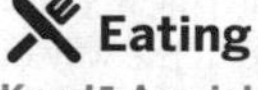

Eating

Kandō Asa-ichi MARKET ¥
(感動朝市; ☎0152-43-7670; ⌚6.30-9.30am Mon-Fri, to 10.30am Sat & Sun Jul-Sep) Head to the morning market for a seafood breakfast. Local farmers and fishermen turn up to sell their wares; there are plenty of hearty *ohayō gozaimasu*'s (greetings) and tasty eating options.

Information

Tourist Information Office (☎0152-44-5849; http://abashiri.jp/tabinavi/en/index.html; ⌚9am-5pm) The tourist information office inside Abashiri Station has English-language maps and a wide offering of pamphlets on eastern Hokkaidō.

There's another office at the *michi-no-eki* (road station) on Route 23 at the port. Both can help with accommodation bookings.

Getting There & Away

AIR

From Memanbetsu Airport, about 15km south of the city centre, there are domestic flights to various destinations including Sapporo, Tokyo and Osaka. Airport buses (¥900, 30 minutes) are approximately timed to flights and run from the bus station via Abashiri Station to the airport.

BICYCLE

Rental bicycles are readily available next to the station.

BUS

There are highway buses each day in both directions between the bus terminal in Abashiri (1km east of the train station) and the Chūō bus station in Sapporo (¥6210, 6¼ hours). Between June and mid-October there are buses from Memanbetsu Airport via Abashiri bus terminal and Shari to Utoro in Shiretoko National Park (¥3200, 2½ hours).

CAR & MOTORCYCLE

Hiring a car is the best option for those who want to get to the more remote sections of Shiretoko and Akan National Parks. Various car-rental agencies, including **JR Hokkaido Rent-a-Lease** (ジェイアール北海道レンタリース; www.jrh-rentacar.jp; ⌚8am-6pm Jan-Apr & Nov-Dec, to 8pm May-Oct), are located in front of JR Abashiri Station.

TRAIN

The JR Sekihoku line runs between Abashiri and Asahikawa (¥8170, four hours). One way to Akan National Park is to catch the train to Bihoro (¥540, 30 minutes), then catch an onward bus into the park.

The JR Senmō main line runs between Abashiri and Kushiro (¥3670, 3½ hours). On the way it passes through Shiretoko-Shari (¥840, 50 minutes), the closest station to Shiretoko National Park, and through Kawayu Onsen (¥1640, two hours) in Akan National Park.

Shari 斜里

POP 13,000 / ☎0152

The town of Shari sits on the coast about 40km east of Abashiri and acts as a gateway to Shiretoko National Park. JR Shiretoko-Shari is the closest train station to the World Heritage–listed site, but you're still about an hour by bus or car from the entrance to the national park.

Sights

Koshimizu Gensei-kaen PARK
(小清水原生花園; ⌚closed Nov-Apr) FREE A spectacular 20km stretch of wildflowers along the coast between Abashiri and Shari, this is like a wide open park. Visit in early summer and catch it at its peak, with over 40 species of flowers simultaneously blooming.

Gensei-kaen has its own tiny JR station with an information centre plus short walks through the flora and dunes out to the sea. There are also rental bicycles.

Activities

Shari-dake HIKING

(斜里岳) Shari township has a magnificent mountain that it can call its own directly to the south. Shari-dake (1547m) is a spectacular volcanic cone that casts a big shadow and is one of Japan's 100 Famous Mountains.

It is a great hike; either use your own wheels to get to the trailhead at the Kiyodake-sō (清岳荘) hut at 680m, or hop off the train at JR Kiyosato (清里町) Station and take a taxi to the trailhead (¥4000, 30 minutes).

Allow seven to eight hours for the return hike which involves plenty of stream crossings plus spots with ropes and chains to help you. The views from the top are superb. If you get stuck, you can stay at the Kiyodake-sō for ¥1540 but there are no meals. Go between June and October, take supplies and use a bear bell.

Sleeping

Minshuku Yumoto-kan MINSHUKU ¥

(民宿湯元館; ☎0152-23-3486; www.yumotokan.info; r per person from ¥3300; P @) This pleasant place is a 20-minute walk from JR Shiretoko-Shari Station. There are lots of options and meals are available onsite. Nonguests can use the onsen here for ¥400 between 7am and 8pm.

Hotel Grantia HOTEL ¥¥

(ホテルグランティア斜里; ☎0152-22-1700; www.hotel-grantia.co.jp/shiretoko; s/d from ¥6850/10,050; P @) For those who decide to stay in Shari, right outside the station and dwarfing everything else around is Hotel Grantia with attractive and comfortable rooms, free internet and an onsen.

Information

Tourist Information Counter (☎0152-23-2424; ⏲8.30am-5.30pm Apr-Oct) There is a useful tourist information counter inside JR Shiretoko-Shari Station with maps, bus timetables and brochures.

Getting There & Away

Trains run on the JR Senmō main line between Shiretoko-Shari and Abashiri (¥840, 50 minutes), and between Shiretoko-Shari and Kushiro (¥2810, 2½ hours). Between Shari and Kushiro is Kawayu Onsen (¥930, 45 minutes) in Akan National Park.

There are between five and nine buses daily between Shari and Utoro (¥1500, 50 minutes) in Shiretoko National Park.

Shiretoko National Park
知床国立公園

Shiretoko-hantō, the peninsula that makes up Shiretoko National Park, was known in Ainu as 'the end of the world'. This magnificent stretch of land has little in the way of vehicle access; unless you are a keen hiker, you will be limited to viewing the park from a cruise boat or seeing minimal parts of it from a bus. The rewards of a visit, however, are obvious. Shiretoko, a Unesco World Heritage Site, is Japan's last true wilderness.

The park has two access points, at Utoro (ウトロ) on the northwestern side of the peninsula, and at Rausu (羅臼) on its southeastern side. If you're using public transport, chances are you'll be bussing from Shari to Utoro.

WARNING: BEAR ACTIVITY

The Shiretoko peninsula is home to around 600 *higuma* (brown bears), the highest density in Hokkaidō. *Higuma* are a whole different story to the smaller black bears on Honshū – they're much bigger and much more aggressive.

Take all precautions, especially in the early morning and at dusk, and avoid hoofing it alone. Make a lot of noise; like Japanese hikers, tie a *kuma-yoke* (bear bell) to your rucksack. Remember, the bears want to avoid you just about as much as you want to avoid them and if they hear you coming, they'll take evasive action.

If you're camping, use the steel food bins or tie up your food and do not bury your rubbish.

Note that bear activity picks up noticeably during early autumn when the creatures are actively foraging for food ahead of their winter hibernation. Be especially cautious at this time.

WORTH A TRIP

GETTING INTO HOT WATER

The Shiretoko peninsula offers some great opportunities to get into hot water. These onsen are sought out by onsen connoisseurs – free pools of hot water that you can just strip off and hop into. Some are in the forest, some by the sea, but none of them are for the timid. They are free because, in most cases, there is nothing there...just hot water. You'll need your own wheels to reach most of them.

Iwaobetsu Onsen (岩尾別温泉) At the end of the Iwaobetsu road. While there is also an onsen in the Iwaobetsu Onsen Hotel Chinohate, head down the trail at the back end of the car park to find three hidden hot pools in the forest. The third, and smallest, is 100m after the first two.

Kamuiwakka-yu-no-taki (カムイワッカ湯の滝) This is a popular warm waterfall that is at the end of the road on the northwestern side of the peninsula. Most bathers wear bathing suits here. Unfortunately, the hot water further upstream has been made off-limits for safety reasons by the bureaucrats.

Kuma-no-yu (熊の湯) A few kilometres up and inland from Rausu, this pair of steaming pools on the far side of the steaming river is superb. Park by the road and cross the bridge. Some locals come every day. The onsen is segregated by sex and has changing facilities.

Seseki Onsen (セセキ温泉) A man-made rockpool by the sea, the heat of the water in here is determined by whether the tide is in or not. Soak it in while staring out to sea. Made famous by a popular television drama.

Aidomari Onsen (相泊温泉) This little boiler, almost at the end of the road on the eastern side of the peninsula, has two little pools, side-by-side, segregated by sex and a makeshift shed during the busy summer season. It's freely accessible the rest of the year. Gaze out towards the sea because it backs onto the road and a fair bit of concrete.

Sights

Shiretoko Pass Lookout LOOKOUT

(知床峠展望台) If hiking isn't your thing, you can obtain dramatic views by driving Route 334 between Utoro and Rausu and stopping at the Shiretoko Pass Lookout (740m), which sits just to the southwest of Rausu-dake (1660m). Route 334 winds through magnificent forest; keep your eyes open for deer.

Activities

★Shiretoko Traverse HIKING

The classic traverse is a two-day hike that stretches for 25km from Iwaobetsu Onsen (岩尾別温泉) to Kamuiwakka-yu-no-taki (カムイワッカ湯の滝). You'll need to be properly equipped to tackle this route. You'll climb Rausu-dake (羅臼岳; 1660m), traverse along the tops to **Iō-zan** (硫黄山; 1563m), then descend to Kamuiwakka--yu-no-taki, a 'waterfall onsen'.

There are four camping areas along the top that have steel food bins (think bears!). Don't underestimate the difficulty of the terrain. The last bit of this track has recently been reopened. Whatever you do, make sure you drop in at the Shiretoko Nature Centre for the latest on conditions and advise them of your intentions.

Rausu-dake HIKING

(羅臼岳) One of Japan's 100 Famous Mountains, Rausu-dake (1660m) makes a great day hike, best tackled from Iwaobetsu Onsen (岩尾別温泉; 340m). Allow six to eight hours for the return trip. From the top there are stunning views of Kunashiri-tō, one of the Kuril islands still in dispute with Russia.

These days there are no buses up to Iwaobetsu Onsen so you'll either need your own wheels, or you'll have to hitch or walk the last 4km up to the trailhead from the Iwaobetsu bus stop. The good news is that the Iwaobetsu Onsen *rotemburo* are waiting for you when you come down.

Shiretoko-go-ko Nature Trail WALKING

(知床五湖; www.goko.go.jp/english; ⏲7.30am-6pm late Apr-late Nov) This little group of five lakes *(go-ko)* is well worth a visit, but unfortunately it's trapped in a bureaucratic quagmire. Eighteen kilometres north of Utoro, a short walk of 800m on an elevated

Shiretoko National Park

boardwalk (40 minutes return) from the entrance to the rather unromantically named Lake 1 (*Ichi-ko*) is free and requires no applications.

If you want to go on to Lakes 2 to 5, however, you need to submit applications, pay the right fee and attend a lecture first. See the website for the exact requirements.

Nature Cruises

A number of companies operate nature cruises along the northwestern side of the peninsula from Utoro. Cruises on offer range from 90-minute return trips as far as Kamuiwakka-yu-no-taki (around ¥3000 per person) to 3½-hour trips all the way out to the cape and back (around ¥7000 per person). **Aurora Cruises** (おーろら; ☎0152-24-2147; http://ms-aurora.com/shiretoko/en) offers both options, as well as drift-ice trips aboard ice-breakers from Abashiri in winter. **Godzilla-Iwa Cruises** (ゴジラ岩観光; ☎0152-24-3060; http://kamuiwakka.jp) offers similar trips, with smaller, faster and more flexible boats. They also run winter cruises from Utoro among the ice from January to April.

Shiretoko National Park

Sights

1	Shiretoko Pass Lookout	B4

Activities, Courses & Tours

2	Aidomari Onsen	D3
3	Iwaobetsu Onsen	B4
4	Kamuiwakka-yu-no-taki	B3
5	Kuma-no-yu	B5
6	Rausu-dake	B4
7	Seseki Onsen	D3
8	Shiretoko Traverse	B4
9	Shiretoko-go-ko Nature Trail	A3

Sleeping

10	Marumi	B5
11	Oyado Kiraku	A4
12	Rausu Dai-Ichi Hotel	B5
13	Shiretoko Iwaobetsu Youth Hostel	A4

Nature cruises also operate out of Rausu on the southeastern side of the peninsula. **Marumi Cruises** (まるみ観光船; ☎0153-88-1313; http://shiretoko-rausu.com) has daily 9am departures in both summer and winter to see local wildlife such as whales, dolphins, seals, seabirds and eagles.

Sleeping

Oyado Kiraku MINSHUKU ¥

(お宿来羅玖; ☎0152-24-2550; http://travel.rakuten.com/hotel/info/130733; r per person with/without 2 meals ¥7500/4000; @) A short walk from the *michi-no-eki* (road station) in Utoro, Kiraku is a bargain with tatami rooms, shared facilities, tasty meals and a convenient location. The staff at the information counter at the *michi-no-eki* will call for you, but it pays to book ahead in summer.

Shiretoko Iwaobetsu Youth Hostel HOSTEL ¥

(知床岩尾別ユースホステル; ☎0152-24-2311; www.youthhostel.or.jp/English/e_iwaobetsu.htm; dm from ¥3900, breakfast/dinner from ¥700/1260; Mar-Nov; P @) At the Iwaobetsu bus stop, 5km north of Utoro, this is a popular base for hikers. The hostel also provides numerous chances to spot wildlife, as bears, deer and foxes live in the surrounding woods. A sea-kayak tour is run by the hostel on demand. The road up to Iwaobetsu Onsen and the trailheads starts here.

★ Marumi RYOKAN ¥¥

(羅臼の宿まるみ; ☎0153-88-1313; www.shiretoko-rausu.com; r per person with/without 2 meals from ¥8750/5660; P @) Eight kilometres southwest of Rausu on Route 335, Marumi has more of everything than you need. There is an onsen, sauna, restaurant, internet and simple but clean tatami rooms overlooking the sea. This friendly place also runs daily nature cruises out of Rausu year-round.

Rausu Dai-Ichi Hotel HOTEL ¥¥

(羅臼第一ホテル; ☎0153-87-2259; http://rausu-daiichi-hotel.jp; per room from ¥12,000; P) This upmarket place is a couple of kilometres inland from Rausu township in the valley on Route 334. There is a large onsen with *rotemburo,* restaurant and parking onsite. Rooms are Japanese-style with private facilities. A great spot from which to explore the national park with your own wheels.

Information

There are information centres left, right and centre, as well as simple information desks at the *michi-no-eki*, the big roadside drive-ins in both Utoro and Rausu.

Rausu Visitor Centre (羅臼ビジターセンター; ☎0153-87-2828; http://rausu-vc.jp; 9am-5pm Tue-Sun) On the Rausu side of the peninsula on Route 334, this place has displays, maps and information, much of it in English. Worth a visit. Take a look out the back and spot some deer.

Rusa Field House (ルサフィールドハウス; ☎0152-24-4354; http://shiretoko-whc.jp/rfh; 9am-5pm Wed-Mon May-Oct, 10am-4pm Wed-Mon Feb-Apr) This excellent log-house facility at the park entrance on Route 87, 13km northeast of Rausu, has informative displays and staff. Every year in summer around 100 to 200 hardy souls walk from Aidomari to Shiretoko-misaki (Cape Shiretoko) – this 50km round-trip hike is not recommended except for the highly intrepid and well prepared. You must check in and out here. Likewise for adventurous sea-kayakers heading out to the cape.

Shiretoko Nature Centre (知床ネイチャーセンター; ☎0152-24-2114; http://center.shiretoko.or.jp/en; 8am-5.40pm mid-Apr–mid-Oct, 9am-4pm mid-Oct–mid-Apr) Run by the Shiretoko Nature Foundation, this is effectively the national park visitor centre. Be sure to register here before heading off into the wilds. Tell staff what you are up to and they will bring you up-to-date with the latest weather, track and bear conditions. You can pick up maps and English brochures here.

Getting There & Around

BUS

There are buses daily between Shari and Utoro (¥1500, 50 minutes); from Utoro, buses continue on as far as Shiretoko-go-ko (¥690, 25 minutes).

A shuttle bus operates from the Shiretoko Nature Centre to Kamuiwakka-yu-no-taki (¥1300) from 1 August to 25 August and 15 September to 24 September. The road from Shiretoko-go-ko to Kamuiwakka-yu-no-taki is closed to private traffic during these periods. Outside of these dates, you can drive to the end of the road.

There are buses daily between Utoro and Rausu (¥1310, 55 minutes) via the dramatic Shiretoko Pass. Daily buses also run between Rausu and Kushiro (¥4740, 3½ hours).

CAR & MOTORCYCLE

Having your own wheels will greatly enhance your visit.

Akan National Park
阿寒国立公園

One of Japan's first groups of national parks, Akan National Park was designated in 1934 and covers 905 sq km of volcanic peaks, large caldera lakes, thick forests and rejuvenating onsen. A marvellous place to explore!

If you are using trains, the eastern part of the park will be easiest to get to. The JR Senmō line runs between Abashiri and Kushiro and has useful stops in the park at JR Kawayu Onsen Station and at JR Mashū Station in the town of Teshikaga, a little further south. You'll need to hit the road, either by bus or car, to get to Akanko Onsen and western parts of the park. A rental car will be very useful here.

Kawayu Onsen 川湯温泉

☎015

Kawayu is a quiet onsen town with a dozen or so hot-spring hotels, but it's in the surrounding area that Akan National Park really comes to life.

Kawayu Onsen township is a five-minute bus ride from JR Kawayu Onsen Station.

Sights & Activities

★Mashū-ko LAKE

(摩周湖) Considered by many to be Japan's most beautiful lake, Mashū-ko once held the world record for water clarity. The island in the middle was known by the Ainu as the Isle of the Gods. A road runs along the western rim of this impressive caldera lake. You can't get down to lake level, but there are two official viewing points called Viewpoint 1 and Viewpoint 3. There's no parking fee at Viewpoint 3.

★Mashū-dake Trail HIKING

(摩周岳) The trailhead for this excellent hike is at Mashū-ko Viewpoint 1 (400m) at the southern end of the lake. You can take a bus, drive or hitch (see p873) to this point.

The walk to the top of Mashū-dake (857m) takes you around the lake to its eastern side and back (four to six hours return), and you will be rewarded with amazing volcanic views for much of the hike.

Kawayu Eco-Museum Centre MUSEUM

(川湯エコミュージアムセンター; ☎015-483-4100; www6.marimo.or.jp/k_emc; ⏲8am-5pm May-Oct, 9am-4pm Nov-Apr) FREE This museum and visitors centre in Kawayu Onsen has impressive displays, handy hiking maps and helpful staff. Check out how the volcanic landscape was formed. A number of short nature trails start here.

Iō-zan VOLCANO

(硫黄山) This steaming, hissing mountain (512m), a couple of kilometres south of Kawayu Onsen, comes complete with sunshine-yellow sulphur and onsen-steamed eggs. Chances are you'll hear the sellers calling *Tamago! Tamago! Tamago!* (Eggs!) even before you reach the car park.

Tsutsuji-ga-hara Nature Trail WALKING

(つつじヶ原ネイチャートレイル) This nature trail connects the Kawayu Eco-Museum Centre and Iō-zan with a very pleasant 2.5km walkway. While climbing Iō-zan is prohibited for safety reasons, the nature trail allows you to get up close to the volcanic activity and smell the sulphur!

Kussharo-ko LAKE

(屈斜路湖) The park's biggest lake is famous for its swimming, boating and volcanically warmed sands, and its own version of the Loch Ness monster, Kusshi. Roads run around its southern and eastern shores, which are fun for exploring.

Wakoto Peninsula Nature Trail WALKING

(和琴半島ネイチャートレイル) FREE At the southern end of Kussharo-ko, the Wakoto peninsula was created by a volcanic eruption much later than that which formed the lake. A circular 'island' is connected to the

WORTH A TRIP

ROTEMBURO RELAXING

If you just can't get enough of open-air onsen, try these beauties. All are free, but bear in mind there are few or no facilities.

Kawayu Onsen Ashi-no-yu (川湯温泉足の湯) This one is just for the feet. Smack in the middle of Kawayu Onsen, this 'footbath' has seating and is covered by a roof for shelter when it's raining. Right beside the steaming stream running through the township.

Suna-yu (砂湯) On the eastern side of Kussharo-ko. You've got to dig your own hole, literally! Hot water comes up through sand at the side of the lake. Bury your feet in it or dig a hole and wallow. There's no privacy here though.

Ike-no-yu (池の湯) You'll need a car navigational system or a good map to find this huge rockpool of hot water on the eastern side of Kussharo-ko. It's worth the effort though.

Kotan-yu (コタン湯) On the southern shores of Kussharo-ko, in the Ainu *kotan* (village), this *rotemburo* offers great views out to the lake. It's one pool with a big rock in the middle splitting it into male and female sides.

Wakoto-yu (和琴湯) At the base of the Wakoto Peninsula at the south of Kussharo-ko, this big rockpool is easy to find at the start of the Wakoto Peninsula Nature Trail. Changing rooms here.

mainland by a narrow neck of land and has a lovely 2.5km nature trail around it.

The walk will take about an hour. Relax in the free onsen at the trailhead after your walk. There is also a campground here next to the car park on the 'mainland'.

Museum of Ainu Folklore MUSEUM
(コタンアイヌ民族資料館; ☎015-484-2128; admission ¥420; ⏲9am-5pm late-Apr–Oct) In the village of Kussharo Kotan on the southern shores of Kussharo-k, this museum displays traditional Ainu tools and crafts.

Taihō Sumo Museum MUSEUM
(大鵬相撲記念館; ☎015-483-2924; www12.plala.or.jp/k-hirao/kankou/38_09.html; admission ¥400; ⏲9am-9pm Jun-Sep, 9am-5pm Oct-May) Sumo fans will enjoy this museum in Kawayu Onsen township dedicated to legendary hometown hero, Taihō (大鵬; 1940–2013). He was born on Karafuto (Sakhalin) to a Ukrainian father and Japanese mother, brought up in Kawayu Onsen, and went on to become one of the greatest *yokozuna* (grand champions) of all time. Taihō retired in 1971.

Sleeping

Onsen Minshuku Mako MINSHUKU ¥
(温泉民宿摩湖; ☎015-482-5124; www.onsenmako.com; r per person with/without 2 meals ¥5000/3500; P@) A 20-minute walk from JR Mashū station, this family-run place has simple tatami rooms, an onsen, a convivial atmosphere and serves meals. A good option, especially if you have your own wheels.

Mashū-ko Youth Hostel HOSTEL ¥
(摩周湖ユースホステル; ☎015-482-3098; www.masyuko.co.jp; dm from ¥3300, breakfast/dinner ¥760/1260; P@) A 10-minute drive from Teshikaga on the road to Mashū-ko, this youth hostel offers dorms and Western-style rooms with shared facilities. There is a restaurant onsite and if you don't have a car, the English-speaking staff will pick you up at JR Mashū Station with an advance reservation.

Wakoto Peninsula Lakeside Campground CAMPGROUND ¥
(和琴半島湖畔キャンプ場; ☎015-484-2350; campsites ¥500, cabins ¥4500; ⏲mid-May–Oct; P) There's a number of camping areas in the vicinity. This one is at the Wakoto Peninsula on the southern shores of Kussharo-ko.

Kussharo-Genya Youth Guesthouse HOSTEL ¥
(屈斜路原野ユースゲストハウス; ☎015-484-2609; www.gogogenya.com/intro/e-intro.htm; dm/r per person from ¥4300/5200, breakfast/dinner ¥600/1300; P@ᯤ) On a backroad off Route 243 on the southern shores of Kussharo-ko, this wonderfully designed youth hostel is an architectural treat, with vaulted ceilings, lofty skylights and polished wooden floors. If you don't have a car, the

Akan National Park

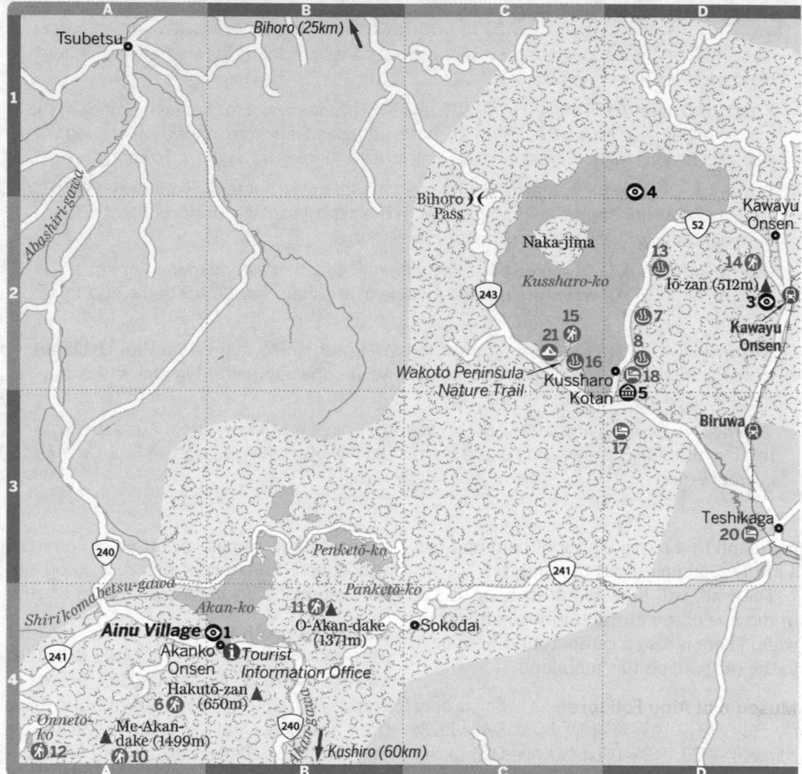

English-speaking staff will pick you up from JR Mashū Station provided you make an advance reservation.

Kinkiyu Hotel ONSEN HOTEL ¥¥
(欣喜湯; ☎015-483-2211; www.kinkiyu.com; r per person with/without meals ¥9000/6000) This big hotel in central Kawayu Onsen may have seen better days, but it is a great deal for its well-kept, spotless tatami rooms, its meticulous Japanese meals and its cavernous onsen.

ℹ Information

JR Mashū Station Tourist Information
(☎015-482-2642; www.masyuko.or.jp; ⏲9am-5pm May-Oct, 10am-4pm Nov-Apr) In JR Mashū Station, this helpful counter has English maps and brochures and can help with accommodation bookings. Two stations south of Kawayu Onsen.

ℹ Getting There & Around

BUS

In the high season, daily buses run by **Akan Bus** (阿寒バス; ☎0154-37-8651; www.akanbus.co.jp; 4-day pass ¥4000; ⏲mid-Jul–Oct) connect Abashiri and Kushiro, travelling through the park via Kawayu Onsen, Mashū-ko, JR Mashū Station and Akanko Onsen. There are various multi-day pass options.

CAR & MOTORCYCLE

Your own wheels will allow you to fully explore the park. Between Mashū Station and Akanko Onsen on Route 241 is a particularly scenic stretch with an outstanding lookout at Sokodai that overlooks Penketō-ko and Panketō-ko.

TRAIN

Trains run north on the JR Senmō main line between Kawayu Onsen and Shiretoko-shari (¥930, 45 minutes), and south between Kawayu Onsen and Kushiro (¥1840, 1¾ hours) via Mashū (¥360, 15 minutes).

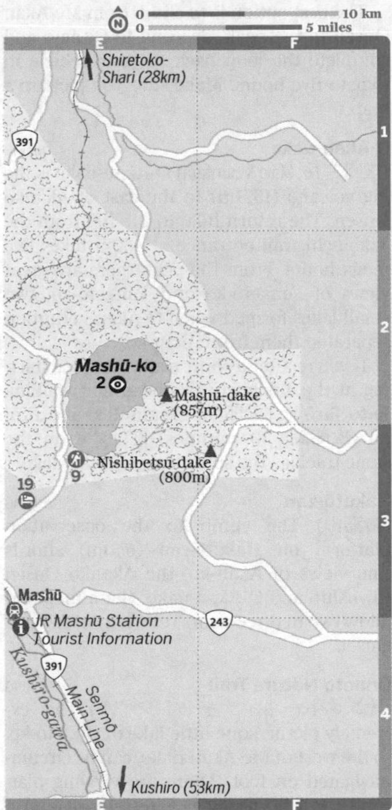

JR Kawayu Onsen Station is a five-minute bus ride from the town centre (¥300); buses are timed to meet most of the trains.

Akanko Onsen 阿寒湖温泉

☎0154

The resort town of Akanko Onsen, in the western part of the Akan National Park, is on the southern shores of Akan-ko. It has one of the largest Ainu *kotan* in Hokkaidō, and is a recommended destination for anyone interested in this ancient culture.

Here you can also catch a glimpse of *marimo,* the most famous algae ever to bob to the surface of the water (see p624). The lake is also known as one of Japan's top fly-fishing spots, so don't be surprised if you see fishermen out in their waders during your early morning stroll.

Akan National Park

Top Sights
1 Ainu Village B4
2 Mashū-ko E2

Sights
3 Iō-zan D2
4 Kussharo-ko D1
5 Museum of Ainu Folklore D3

Activities, Courses & Tours
6 Hakutō-zan A4
7 Ike-no-yu D2
8 Kotan-yu D2
9 Mashū-dake Trail E3
10 Me-Akan-dake A4
11 O-Akan-dake B4
12 Onneto Nature Trail A4
13 Suna-yu D2
14 Tsutsuji-ga-hara Nature Trail D2
15 Wakoto Peninsula Nature Trail C2
16 Wakoto-yu C2

Sleeping
17 Kussharo-Genya Youth Guesthouse D3
18 Marukibune D2
19 Mashū-ko Youth Hostel E3
20 Onsen Minshuku Mako D3
21 Wakoto Peninsula Lakeside Campground C2

Sights

★ Ainu Village VILLAGE

(アイヌコタン, Ainu Kotan) While it's definitely tourist-oriented, the *kotan* on the western edge of Akanko Onsen is inhabited by one of the largest remaining Ainu communities in Hokkaidō. There are Ainu shops selling woodcrafts, leatherwork and other handmade items, and restaurants offering traditional Ainu food.

Ikor THEATRE

(イコロ; www.akanainu.jp/) An impressive theatre complex in the Ainu *kotan,* Ikor (meaning 'treasure') gives local Ainu the chance to share their culture. There are daily Ainu dance performances (¥1000) and puppet plays. You can also try making and playing *mukkuri* (similar to a mouth harp), wood carving and embroidery. Book at least a day in advance for the three craft experiences. Check out the website for more.

Ainu Folklore Museum MUSEUM

(アイヌ生活記念館, Ainu Seikatsu Kinenkan; www.akanainu.jp/; admission ¥300; ⏲10am-9pm) At the top of the hill in the Ainu *kotan,* this small museum complex celebrates Ainu lifestyles of yesteryear. There are a number of Ainu buildings you can poke your nose into to get a feel for the old ways.

Akan Kohan Eco-Museum Centre MUSEUM

(阿寒湖畔エコミュージアムセンター; http://business4.plala.or.jp/akan-eco; ⌚9am-5pm Wed-Mon) FREE At the eastern edge of town, this place has well-maintained exhibits with lots of photographs, and a number of *marimo* in aquarium tanks. It also has hiking maps and displays about the local flora and fauna.

The *bokke* (bubbling clay pools) walk starts from the museum. It makes a shaded, breezy loop out to Akan-ko and back through the forest to some volcanic mudpools.

Activities

As an onsen town, a number of hotels offer use of their baths to nonguests. This can cost anywhere from ¥500 to ¥1500. There are a number of *ashi-yu* (foot baths) and *te-yu* (hand baths) about town. Feel free to soak your hands or feet.

★**Me-Akan-dake** HIKING

(雌阿寒岳, Female Mountain) The highest mountain in the park, Me-Akan-dake (1499m) is an active volcano that is one of Japan's 100 Famous Mountains. From Akanko Onsen (430m) the climb takes five to seven hours return, but if you've got your own wheels, head to the trailhead at Me-Akan Onsen (720m) from where the return climb takes three to four hours.

The best option is to climb from Me-Akan Onsen to the peak, descend to Onneto and complete the loop back to your vehicle in four to five hours. Make sure you pick up a map.

O-Akan-dake HIKING

(雄阿寒岳, Male Mountain) O-Akan-dake is the big volcano (1371m) to the east of Akanko Onsen. The return hike to the top from the Takiguchi trail entrance at 450m takes five to six hours. From the peak there are great views of Penketō-ko and Panketō-ko, two small lakes formed when O-Akan's eruption separated them from Akan-ko.

If you're after a short walk, consider starting at the Takiguchi trailhead and walking in to Tarō-ko (太郎湖; 15 minutes) and Jirō-ko (次郎湖; 30 minutes). They're on the same track as the summit of O-Akan-dake.

Hakutō-zan HIKING

(白湯山) The climb to the observation platform on Hakutō-zan (650m) affords fine views of Akan-ko, the Akanko Onsen township and O-Akan-dake. Get a map and allow two to three hours return from Akanko Onsen.

Onneto Nature Trail WALKING

(オンネトーネイチャートレイル) This extremely picturesque little lake of Onneto-ko, to the west of Me-Akan-dake, can be circumnavigated on foot. There are viewing platforms, toilets, parking, a restaurant and a number of short nature trails. Allow an hour to circle the lake and less than that for the return trip to Yu-no-taki (湯の滝) waterfall.

MARIMO VIEWING

Akan-ko is legendary throughout Japan for its *marimo (まりも; Cladophora aegagropila),* spheres of green algae that are both biologically intriguing – it takes as long as 200 years for them to grow to the size of a baseball – and very, very *kawaii* (cute). This is what most Japanese visitors to Akanko Onsen are here to see. The *marimo* became endangered after being designated a national treasure: suddenly, everyone in Japan needed to have one.

The Ainu came to the rescue by starting the **Marimo Matsuri** (まりも祭り), held in mid-October, which returns *marimo* to Akan-ko.

While there are *marimo* on display at the Akan Kohan Eco-Museum Centre, the proper way to see it is to head out on the lake.

Akan-ko Sightseeing Cruise (☎0154-67-2511; www.akankisen.com; trips ¥1850) The best way to get up close and personal with *marimo* is to take a sightseeing cruise, which makes an 85-minute loop around the lake. Included in the trip is a brief 15-minute stop at a small observation centre where you can hopefully spot a few balls of algae photosynthesising on the surface of the water.

DON'T MISS

AN AINU EXPERIENCE

Marukibune (丸木舟; ☎015-484-2644; www.sh.rim.or.jp/~moshiri; per person with/without meals from ¥8500/6500; P) Atuy's place in the Ainu *kotan* at the southern end of Kussharo-ko is a special spot, especially if you stay out here. There's a restaurant downstairs offering up tasty Ainu dishes, and a great range of rooms with a stunning onsen with a view upstairs. Atuy is a real Ainu character, with impromptu Ainu music sessions a common occurrence.

Positioned between the Museum of Ainu folklore and the outdoor *rotemburo* by the lake, Marukibune also offers Ainu culture tours and fishing tours over the summer. Top dishes in the restaurant include the sashimi of *parimono* (a local river fish; ¥1000) and the white *rāmen* (¥1000). If you get the opportunity to stay in Atuy's lovingly developed 'Ainu-*shitsu*' (per person with meals ¥30,000), take it! If you can't afford to stay in this special room (it's like an art museum), ask for a look.

There is a campsite at the southern end of the lake.

Sleeping

★Minshuku Kiri MINSHUKU ¥
(民宿桐; ☎0154-67-2755; www10.plala.or.jp/kiriminsyuku; r per person with/without breakfast ¥4500/4000; 📶) Expect tiny rooms and shared facilities at this great-value *minshuku* above a souvenir shop a couple of minutes' walk from the Ainu *kotan*. The rooms may be small but you'll enjoy your stay. There is a wooden onsen, excellent meals and a friendly welcome here.

Akanko Onsen Campground CAMPGROUND ¥
(阿寒湖温泉キャンプ場; ☎0154-67-3263; 5-1 Akan Onsen; campsites per person ¥630; ⊙Jun-Sep; P) About a five-minute walk west of Akanko Onsen centre, across Route 241 from the Ainu theatre this campground has shady pitches and an *ashi-yu* (foot bath) for relaxing tired feet.

Gozensui Hotel HOTEL ¥¥
(ホテル御前水; ☎0154-67-2031; www.akanko.co.jp/gozensui-top.html; 4-5-1 Akan Onsen; r per person from ¥7500; P@📶) One of the big hotels along the waterfront, Gozensui is good value and right in the middle of town. Both tatami and Western-style rooms are on offer, along with an attractive onsen complex.

Akan Yuku-no-sato Tsuruga RYOKAN ¥¥¥
(あかん遊久の里鶴雅, Lake Akan Tsuruga Resort Spa; ☎0154-67-4000; www.tsuruga.com/en; 4-6-10 Akan Onsen; r per person with 2 meals from ¥14,500; P@📶🏊) The top spot in town, expect to be greeted by a virtual sculpture and art gallery in the lobby. The meals are like edible art, the rooms offer exquisite views and the two floors of onsen have it all, from ceramic tubs to open-air rock-garden baths.

Eating

★Poronno AINU CUISINE ¥
(ポロンノ; ☎0154-67-2159; www.poronno.com; ⊙10am-9.30pm May-Oct, 12pm-8.30pm Nov-Apr) If you're interested in Ainu culture, head to this tiny place in the Ainu *kotan*. Lovingly run, Poronno will have you admiring both Ainu handicraft and culinary skills. Try the *yukku-don* (venison on rice; ¥1000).

Onsen Kōbō Akan CAFE ¥
(温泉工房あかん; ☎0154-67-2847; ⊙8am-5pm) Seldom do you get the opportunity to soak your feet in an indoor *ashi-yu* (foot bath) while consuming delicious coffees, cakes and pastas. This place, two streets back from Akanko Onsen's sightseeing boat docks, offers just that. Strip off your shoes and socks and soak away! The *zari-bonara* (freshwater crayfish pasta) for ¥900 is superb.

Information

Tourist Information Office (☎0154-67-3200; www.lake-akan.com/en/index.html; ⊙9am-6pm) This big new building in the middle of town has parking and can help with your needs in Akanko Onsen. There are English brochures and maps, along with helpful staff.

Getting There & Away

There are daily buses in both directions between Asahikawa and Akanko Onsen (¥5210, 4½ hours) via Sōunkyō Onsen (¥3260, 3½ hours) in Daisetsuzan National Park. There are also buses between Akanko Onsen and Kushiro (¥1500, two hours).

If you're driving, Akanko Onsen is on Route 240, which (of course!) has been renamed Marimo Highway (まりも国道).

Kushiro Wetlands National Park 釧路湿原国立公園

Kushiro Shitsugen National Park, at 269 sq km, is Japan's largest expanse of undeveloped wetland. Sitting directly north of the coastal city of Kushiro, it was designated a national park in 1987 to combat urban sprawl and protect the wetland habitat of numerous species of wildlife, chiefly the *tanchō-zuru* (red-crested white crane), the traditional symbol of both longevity and Japan.

In the early 20th century, Japanese cranes were thought to be extinct due to overhunting and habitat destruction. In 1926, however, a group of about 20 birds was discovered in the marshes around Kushiro, and with concentrated conservation efforts they now number more than 1200 birds. The cranes can be seen year-round, but the best time is during winter when they gather at feeding spots. Popular with Japanese photographers, the cranes often dance exotically in pairs.

While it is difficult to get out into the middle of the park, the JR Senmō line that links Kushiro with Kawayu Onsen, Shiretoko-Shari and Abashiri, runs up its eastern fringes. Route 53 runs up the park's western fringes. If you have your own wheels, you can explore the park at length, including various viewpoints.

Train-users can ride from Kushiro to JR Kushiro Shitsugen Station (¥350, 20 minutes), then walk uphill for 15 minutes to the **Hosooka Marsh Viewpoint** (細岡展望台) from where you can easily appreciate the grand scale of this wetland preserve.

Sights

Japanese Crane Reserve WILDLIFE RESERVE
(釧路市丹頂鶴自然公園; 0154-56-2219; http://kushiro-tancho.jp; admission ¥470; 9am-6pm Apr-Sep, 9am-4pm Oct-Mar) Head to this bird park near Kushiro airport for year-round close-up views of red-crested white cranes. While there are fences, cranes and other birds can fly both in and out. Run by Kushiro Zoo, this place has been instrumental in increasing the numbers of these magnificent birds. There's a bus from Kushiro Airport and JR Kushiro station.

Akan International Crane Centre 'GRUS' WILDLIFE RESERVE
(阿寒国際ツルセンター "グルス"; 0154-66-4011; www.tecs.jp/photobook/tancho/; admission ¥460; 9am-5pm) On the western side of the park, this place has an excellent English website and is accessible from the Kushiro–Akanko bus (¥1410, one hour) that travels along Route 240. Attached is the Crane Observation Centre, a winter feeding ground that is your best chance to see cranes outside of a bird park. The Observation Centre is open from 8.30am to 4.30pm November to March.

Sleeping

★ **Kushiro Shitsugen Tōro Youth Hostel** HOSTEL ¥
(釧路湿原とうろユースホステル; 0154-87-2510; www.tohro.net; dm from ¥3456, breakfast/dinner ¥650/1080; P @) A few minutes' walk from JR Tōro (塘路) Station is this extremely friendly and efficient place with bunk-style rooms and a great viewing deck from where you can survey the national park. From May to November the hostel runs canoe tours and offers a guiding service, while from December to March they offer tours to see the cranes.

These eco-minded people even produce their own solar power.

Kushiro 釧路

POP 181,000 / 0154

The most populous city in eastern Hokkaidō, Kushiro is an industrial port that came to prominence as its harbour is relatively free of ice in winter. It is an important transport hub for visitors heading to or from the region's spectacular national parks as flights arrive here from all over Japan and JR train lines meet here.

Trains on the JR Senmō line run north to JR Kushiro Shitsugen, for Kushiro Wetlands National Park. These same trains continue on to JR Mashū and JR Kawayu Onsen stations for Akan National Park, and then on to JR Shiretoko-Shari, the station closest to Utoro (the northern gateway for Shiretoko National Park).

Buses run from here to Rausu, the southern gateway for Shiretoko National Park, and also to Akanko Onsen in Akan National Park.

Get into Kushiro early enough in the day to make onward connections. If you do

NORTHERN TERRITORIES DISPUTE

If you want to see Russia, head to Nemuro (根室; population 3000), at the end of the JR Nemuro line and hop on a bus to Nosappu-misaki (納沙布岬; one way/return ¥1040/1900, 50 minutes), the easternmost point of mainland Japan. This is as close to Russia as you can get!

Barely 10km away are the Habomai islets, uninhabited apart from a Russian border guard outpost. These islets are part of the disputed Chishima Retto (千島列島; Kuril Islands).

The Kurils are a volcanic archipelago that stretches for 1300km northeast to Kamchatka, Russia, and separates the Sea of Okhotsk from the Pacific Ocean.

There have been tit-for-tat squabbles over who owned what between Japan and Russia since the early 1800s, but it got really messy at the end of WWII. Japan agreed to the terms of surrender in the Potsdam Declaration and the war finished on 15 August 1945, however, Russia was not party to that agreement and had only just declared war on Japan on 9 August. Russian military forces started their invasion of the Kuril islands on 18 August, three days after Japan had surrendered.

The ongoing dispute has blighted the Japan–Russia relationship ever since, to the point that they have yet to sign a peace treaty since the end of WWII.

Although sparsely populated, the Kurils have valuable mineral deposits, possibly oil and gas reserves, and are surrounded by rich fishing grounds. In 2010, Russian President Dmitry Medvedev landed on the Kurils and promised its residents development assistance. Medvedev later stated that the islands were an 'inseparable' part of the country and a strategic Russian region.

The Northern Territories continue to be a hot topic in Hokkaidō and if you are driving around, particularly in eastern Hokkaidō, you may be surprised at roadside signs calling for the islands to be returned to Japan. Don't hold your breath!

decide to spend the night here, there are a number of business hotels near the train station.

Sights

Washō Market MARKET
(和商市場, Washō Ichiba; www.washoichiba.com; 8am-6pm Mon-Sat) A couple of minutes' walk from the south side of JR Kushiro Station, Washō Ichiba features every kind of seafood imaginable. It's as much a sightseeing spot as a place to eat. Try the local speciality known as *Katte-don* (勝手丼), where you buy a bowl of sushi rice then add your choice of delectable seafood options on top.

Sleeping

Toyoko Inn Kushiro Jūji-gai HOTEL ¥¥
(東横イン釧路十字街; 0154-23-1045; www.toyoko-inn.com/e_hotel/00084/index.html; s/d ¥4980/6980; P@) There's not tons of character here, but you can't go wrong with a Toyoko Inn. Kushiro's version is a five-minute walk south of JR Kushiro Station along Kita-ōdori (北大通り) and offers spotless efficiency along with free breakfast, supper and internet.

Getting There & Away

AIR

Kushiro's airport is located about 10km west of the city. From here, there are flights to various domestic destinations including Tokyo, Osaka, Nagoya and others. Buses between the airport and JR Kushiro Station (¥910, 45 minutes) are timed to connect with arrivals and departures.

BUS

Buses run daily between Asahikawa, Sōunkyō Onsen and Kushiro (¥5450, 6½ hours) via Akanko Onsen (¥1530, 2¼ hours). There are also daily buses between Rausu and Kushiro (¥4740, 3½ hours).

TRAIN

Kushiro is on the JR Nemuro line, which runs all the way from Sapporo (¥8920, four hours) to Kushiro, and on to Nemuro (¥2420, 2¼ hours).

Heading north from Kushiro, the JR Senmō main line runs between Kushiro and Abashiri (¥3570, 3½ hours) via Shiretoko-shari (¥2730, 2½ hours), Kawayu Onsen (¥1790, 1½ hours) and Kushiro Shitsugen (¥350, 20 minutes).

DON'T MISS

BEAR MOUNTAIN

Hokkaidō is bear country and, let's face it, these aren't the small black bears that inhabit Honshū. These are *higuma* (Ussuri brown bear), thought to be the ancestor of the North American grizzly bear. And they are every hiker's nightmare.

If you are going to do any hiking in Hokkaidō, make sure you have a *kuma-yoke* (bear repeller) in the form of a small bell tied to your backpack. The theory goes that a bear wants to meet you face to face about as much as you want to meet him face to face and if he hears you coming, he'll avoid you at all costs. This is a good theory…

So while hikers want to avoid meeting a bear in the wild, there is a certain fascination with these massive, potentially ferocious creatures. Everyone wants to see one up close, but in most cases, without putting their life on the line. It's similar to that 'shark in the water' phenomena.

Bear Mountain (ベアマウンテン; ☎0156-64-7007; www.sahoro.co.jp/language/english/green/bear/bear.html; admission per person with/without bus option ¥3000/2000; ⏲9am-4pm late Apr-Oct) is a 15-hectare enclosure at the Sahoro Resort in northern Tokachi that meets bear-watching requirements perfectly. Thirteen male *higuma* roam the forested enclosure, which has very clever viewing facilities.

For ¥2000 you can stroll along a 370m boardwalk 5m above ground level and look down on the bears. The more expensive entrance price includes a ride in a heavily fortified bus that looks like it's going into a war zone. In either case, you're virtually guaranteed a close-up of a massive (300kg to 400kg!) *higuma*.

There's an observation point at ground level where you are only separated from the bears by a very thick window. It is a sobering experience…and an absolute must. Bear Mountain is closed during the winter as all the bears are hibernating.

You'll need your own wheels to get to Bear Mountain. It's part of the Sahoro Resort (サホロリゾート) complex on Route 38, 54km northeast of Obihiro and 66km southeast of Furano.

Tokachi 十勝

The name Tokachi is as synonymous with wine in Japan as Beaujolais is in Europe. Tokachi was a historic but short-lived province that was established in the late 19th century. Today, the region is part of the Dō-tō (道東) subprefecture, is largely agricultural and has few major tourist draws, though it does boast some lovely wine-scented countryside.

Obihiro 帯広

POP 170,000 / ☎0155

A former Ainu stronghold, the modern city of Obihiro was founded in 1883 by the Banseisha, a group of colonial settlers from Shizuoka Prefecture in Central Honshū. Squeezed in between the Hidaka and Daisetsuzan mountain ranges, Obihiro is a friendly, laid-back city without much to offer tourists.

Sleeping

Toipirka Kitaobihiro Youth Hostel HOSTEL ¥
(トイピルカ北帯広ユースホステル; ☎0155-30-4165; http://homepage1.nifty.com/TOIPIRKA/english/main_eng.htm; dm from ¥3450, breakfast/dinner ¥750/1300; Ⓟ@📶) A great place to break for the night is this attractive log house with extremely friendly owners. It's near Tokachigawa Onsen, a cluster of resort-style onsens and hotels along the Tokachi-gawa. If you phone ahead, the staff can pick you up from JR Obihiro Station. It's about a 15-minute drive east of the city.

Toyoko Inn Tokachi Obihiro Ekimae HOTEL ¥¥
(東横イン十勝帯広駅前; ☎0155-27-1045; www.toyoko-inn.com/e_hotel/00067; s/d from ¥5300/6300; Ⓟ@📶) It's standard stuff but it's very reasonable and you know what you're getting at the local version of this super-efficient Japan-wide chain. Near JR Obihiro Station, it offers free parking, internet and breakfast.

Getting There & Away

AIR

Obihiro's airport is 25km south of the city. There are flights to Tokyo, Osaka, Nagoya and other domestic destinations. Buses between the airport and JR Obihiro Station (¥1000, 40 minutes) are timed to connect with arrivals and departures.

BUS

Buses run between Obihiro and the Chūō bus station in Sapporo (¥3670, 4¼ hours). Regular buses also run between Obihiro and Sōunkyō Onsen (¥2200, 80 minutes).

TRAIN

The JR Nemuro line runs between Obihiro and Sapporo (¥7220, 2½ hours), and between Obihiro and Kushiro (¥4810, 1½ hours).

Ikeda 池田

POP 8100 / ☎015

Located amid the grape fields of the eastern Tokachi plain, Ikeda is a small farming town that became famous in the 1960s when the municipal government started experimenting with winemaking. While conservative oenophiles might not consider Japanese wines in the same league as Old World classics and other New World upstarts, pull out a bottle of Ikeda and decide for yourself. Judging by the giant corkscrew sculpture and the wine-glass fountain at the station, the folks here hope you will.

Getting around the various sights is much easier if you have your own wheels. Pick up a map and cruise.

Sights & Activities

★Ikeda Wine Castle WINERY

(ワイン城 Wain-jō; ☎015-572-2467; www.tokachi-wine.com; factory tours 9am-5pm) FREE Some perfectly quaffable wines are made at the Ikeda Wine Castle, set on a hillside overlooking the town, only 10 minutes' walk south of the station. There are tours and tastings, along with a souvenir shop and an excellent restaurant.

Happiness Dairy FARM

(ハッピネスデーリィ; ☎015-572-2001; http://happiness-dairy.com; 9.30am-5.30pm Mon-Fri, 9.30am-6pm Sat, Sun & holidays) FREE This family-friendly place, only a two-minute drive northeast of the Wine Castle, produces cheese to complement the region's wine. Taste the cheese then wander over to the dairy and try the excellent ice creams, or just relax and take in the rural ambiance.

Moon Face Gallery & Cafe GALLERY

(画廊喫茶ムーンフェイス; ☎015-572-2198; 10am-6pm Wed-Mon) FREE This burgeoning artists' community in Ikeda produces some lovely craft goods. The Moon Face Gallery & Cafe displays works by locals while serving up tasty cappuccinos and espressos.

Spinner's Farm Tanaka FARM

(スピナーズファーム ・タナカ; ☎015-572-2848; www12.plala.or.jp/spinner; 10am-6pm Apr-Oct, 10am-5.30pm Nov-Mar) FREE This place specialises in wool, offering an opportunity to feed the sheep outside, then spin their wool inside. There are classes, but you'll need to book ahead for these. They have all sorts of woollen articles to meet your Hokkaidō souvenir requirements.

Sleeping

Ikeda Kita-no-Kotan Youth Hostel HOSTEL ¥

(池田北のコタンユースホステル; ☎015-572-3666; www11.plala.or.jp/kitanokotan; dm with 2 meals from ¥5600; P@☎) Friendly management and delicious dinners, including a complimentary glass of local wine, make Ikeda Kita-no-Kotan Youth Hostel a real treat. The hostel is within easy walking distance of the Toshibetsu Station, one stop west of Ikeda (¥210, five minutes).

Oyado Tatsumi RYOKAN ¥

(お宿たつみ; ☎015-572-2615; www.kankou-ikeda.com/?shops=stay; r per person from ¥4000; P) With lovely tatami-mat rooms and a superb stone bath, Tatsumi is a good option within a one-minute walk of Ikeda Station. Breakfast is also available for ¥1000.

Eating

Restaurant Yonekura RESTAURANT

(レストランよねくら; ☎015-572-2032; 9am-8pm Fri-Wed) Just across from Ikeda Station, Yonekura is a popular eating spot serving up a local speciality, *buta-don* (¥900) – thick, juicy pork on a bed of rice with a tasty sauce. They've also come up with another local favourite – banana-*manjū*, a sweet banana-flavoured dessert. Don't get there too late in the day or they'll have sold out.

Getting There & Away

Trains run on the JR Nemuro line between Obihiro and Ikeda (¥450, 30 minutes) and Kushiro and Ikeda (¥4480, 70 minutes).

Shikoku

Includes ➡

Best Outdoor Adventures

- ➡ Rafting Yoshino-gawa (p643)
- ➡ Hiking Ishizuchi-san (p665)
- ➡ Hiking Tsurugi-san (p644)
- ➡ Surfing the Tokushima coastline (p647)
- ➡ Canyoning in Nametoko Valley (p656)

Best Temples

- ➡ Zentsū-ji (p666)
- ➡ Konpira-san (p667)
- ➡ Ishite-ji (p659)
- ➡ Kongōfuku-ji (p654)
- ➡ Yashima-ji (p672)

Why Go?

The birthplace of revered Buddhist ascetic Kōbō Daishi (774–835), Shikoku (四国) is synonymous with natural beauty and the pursuit of spiritual perfection. It's home to the 88 Temple route, Japan's most famous pilgrimage, even if some *henro* (pilgrims) today bus it rather than hoof it.

But Shikoku is not just for the seeker of enlightenment – the island's stunning Iya Valley, rugged Pacific coastline, gorgeous free-flowing rivers and mountain ranges all beckon to be explored with hiking boot, kayak, surfboard and your own earthly vessel. Your physical incarnation will feast upon the historic castles and gardens, excellent regional cuisine and modern pleasures of Kōchi, Matsuyama and Takamatsu.

Easy to access from Honshū via two bridge systems – glorious feats of engineering – Shikoku offers an adventurous retreat from the outside world. Just like Kōbō Daishi would have wanted.

When to Go

Takamatsu

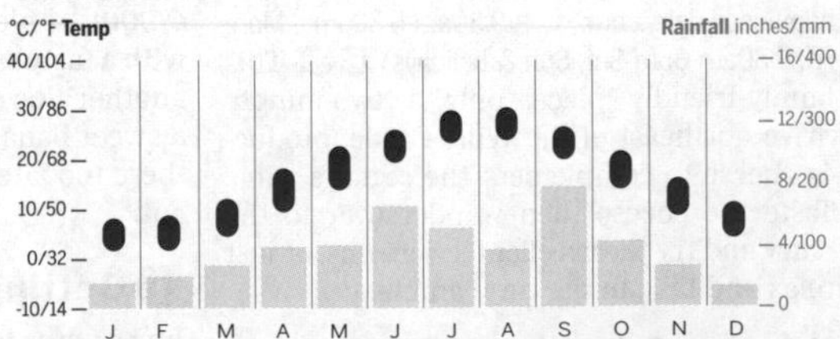

Apr Enlightenment may know no weather, but any pilgrimage is best taken in spring.

Jul–Sep Rivers are running, surf is rolling and the sun is, well, shining.

Aug Join every man, woman and child for Awa-odori Matsuri, Japan's wildest dance party.

Getting There & Around

Most visitors to Shikoku over the past 1200 years have followed a clockwise route starting near Tokushima. Most now usually arrive on the island by train from Okayama or by highway bus from Osaka, Kyoto and Tokyo. The Iya Valley and the two southern capes are probably best explored by car, as many towns there have tricky bus and train connections.

AIR

All Nippon Airways (www.ana.co.jp) and **Japan Airlines** (www.jal.co.jp) services connect Matsuyama, Kōchi, Takamatsu and Tokushima in Shikoku with Tokyo, Osaka and other major centres.

BOAT

Nankai Ferry (南海フェリー; 088-636-0750; www.nankai-ferry.co.jp in Japanese) runs daily connections between Tokushima and Wakayama (two hours, six daily).

Ocean Tōkyū Ferry (オーシャン東九フェリー; 088-662-0489; www.otf.jp in Japanese; 9am-5pm) departs once daily to/from Tokyo/Tokushima (18 hours).

Setonaikai Kisen Ferry (瀬戸内海汽船; Matsuyama booking office 089-953-1003; www.setonaikaikisen.co.jp; 7am-9pm) has regular hydrofoil connections between Matsuyama and Hiroshima (1¼ hours, 12 daily).

Jumbo Ferry (087-811-6688; www.ferry.co.jp) runs between Takamatsu and Kōbe (three hours and 40 minutes, five daily).

BUS

Three bridge systems link Shikoku with Honshū. In the east, the Akashi Kaikyō-ōhashi connects Tokushima with Kōbe in Hyōgo-ken via Awaji-shima (Awaji Island). The Shimanami Kaidō is an island-hopping series of nine bridges (with bike paths!) leading from Imabari in Ehime-ken to Onomichi near Hiroshima.

TRAIN

The Seto-ōhashi (Seto Bridge) runs from Okayama to Sakaide, west of Takamatsu. This is the only one of the bridges to carry trains. JR and private Kotoden trains run to all regions, except the tips of the two southern capes.

INTERNATIONAL DRIVING PERMIT

If you plan on renting a car to explore Shikoku's more out-of-the-way destinations – such as the Iya Valley and the southern surf beaches – be sure to procure an International Driving Permit before leaving your home country.

TOKUSHIMA PREFECTURE

The traditional starting point for generations of pilgrims, Tokushima Prefecture (徳島県) is home to the first 23 of Shikoku's 88 Temples. Notable attractions in this region include the lively Awa-odori Matsuri, which takes place in Tokushima in August; the mighty whirlpools of the Naruto Channel between Tokushima and Awaji-shima; the dramatic scenery of the Iya Valley; and the surf beaches of the southern coast.

Tokushima 徳島

088 / POP 257,718

With Mt Bizan looming in the west, and the Shinmachi-gawa cutting a gentle swath through the middle, Tokushima is its eponymous prefecture's pleasant capital. With a number of nearby temples, the city makes a solid starting point for pilgrims.

Every August, the Awa-odori Matsuri, a traditional dance festival, attracts thousands of Japanese from across the country. Book accommodation well ahead and expect to pay a premium if visiting during this time.

Sights & Activities

★Bizan MOUNTAIN

(眉山) At the foot of Bizan, the 280m-high summit at the southwestern end of Shinmachibashi-dōri, **Awa Odori Kaikan** (阿波おどり会館; 088-611-1611; www.awaodori-kaikan.jp; 2-20 Shinmachibashi; admission ¥300; 9am-5pm, closed 2nd & 4th Wed) features extensive exhibits relating to the Awa-odori Matsuri and dance. The dance is performed at 2pm, 3pm and 4pm daily (and at 11am as well on weekends), with a nightly performance at 8pm (afternoon/evening ¥600/800). From the 5th floor, the **Bizan Ropeway** (088-652-3617; one way/return ¥610/1020; 9am-5:30pm Nov-Mar, to 9pm Apr-Oct & during special events) whizzes you to the top of Bizan for fine city views. A combined ticket for the museum, cable car and dance show is ¥1620.

Tokushima Modern Art Museum MUSEUM

(徳島県立近代美術館; 088-668-1088; www.art.tokushima-ec.ed.jp; Bunka-no-mori-kōen, Hachiman-chō; admission ¥200; additional ¥600 for special exhibitions; 9.30am-5pm Tue-Sun) With a permanent collection that includes modern masters both Japanese and Western,

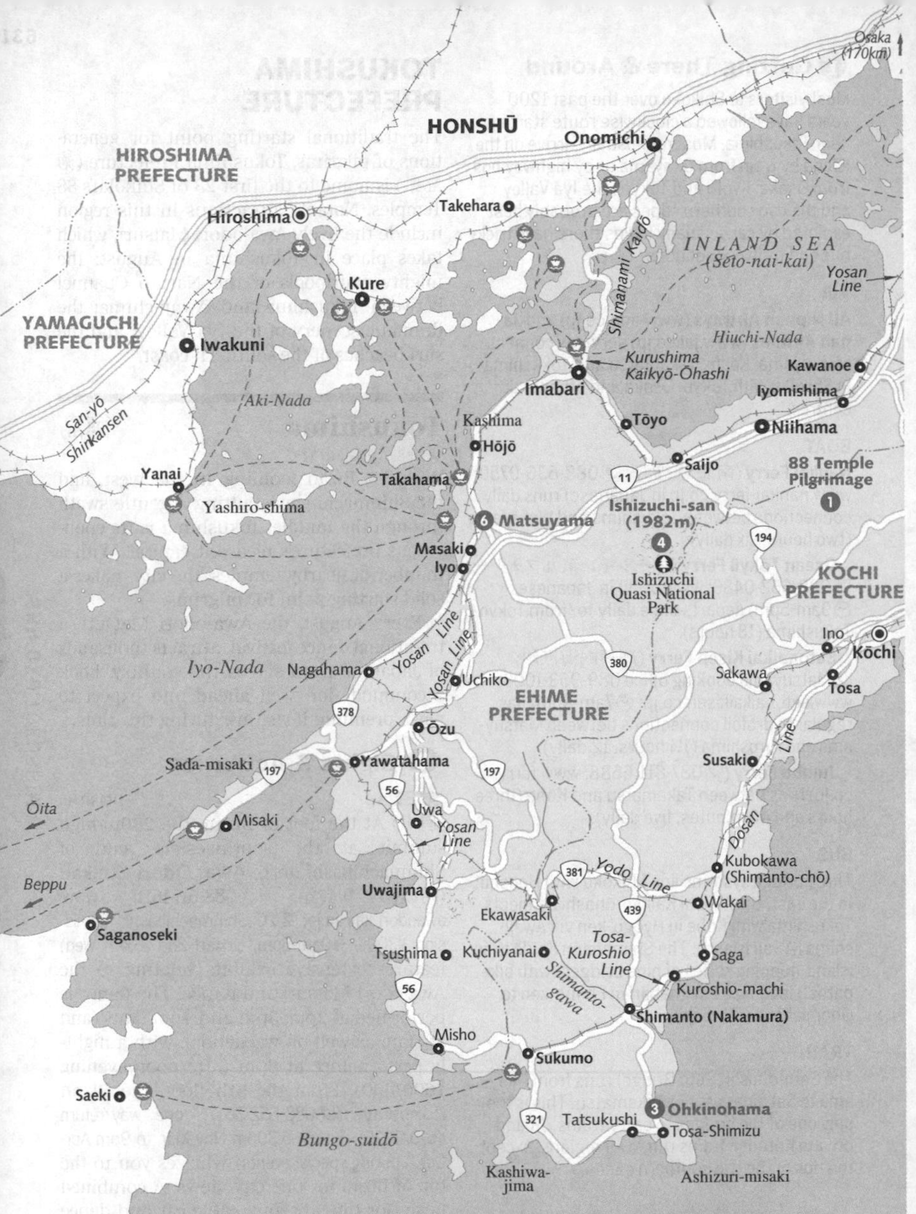

Shikoku Highlights

1. Walking the time-worn route of the **88 Temple pilgrimage** (p641).
2. Finding seclusion, if not enlightenment, like Kōbō Daishi did at **Muroto-misaki** (p648).
3. Surfing beautiful swells or snorkelling pristine streams at **Ohkinohama** (p653).
4. Hiking up sacred **Ishizuchi-san** (p665), one of Japan's most gripping ascents.
5. Picking your way across swaying vine bridges and rafting the white-water of Yoshino-gawa in the gorgeous

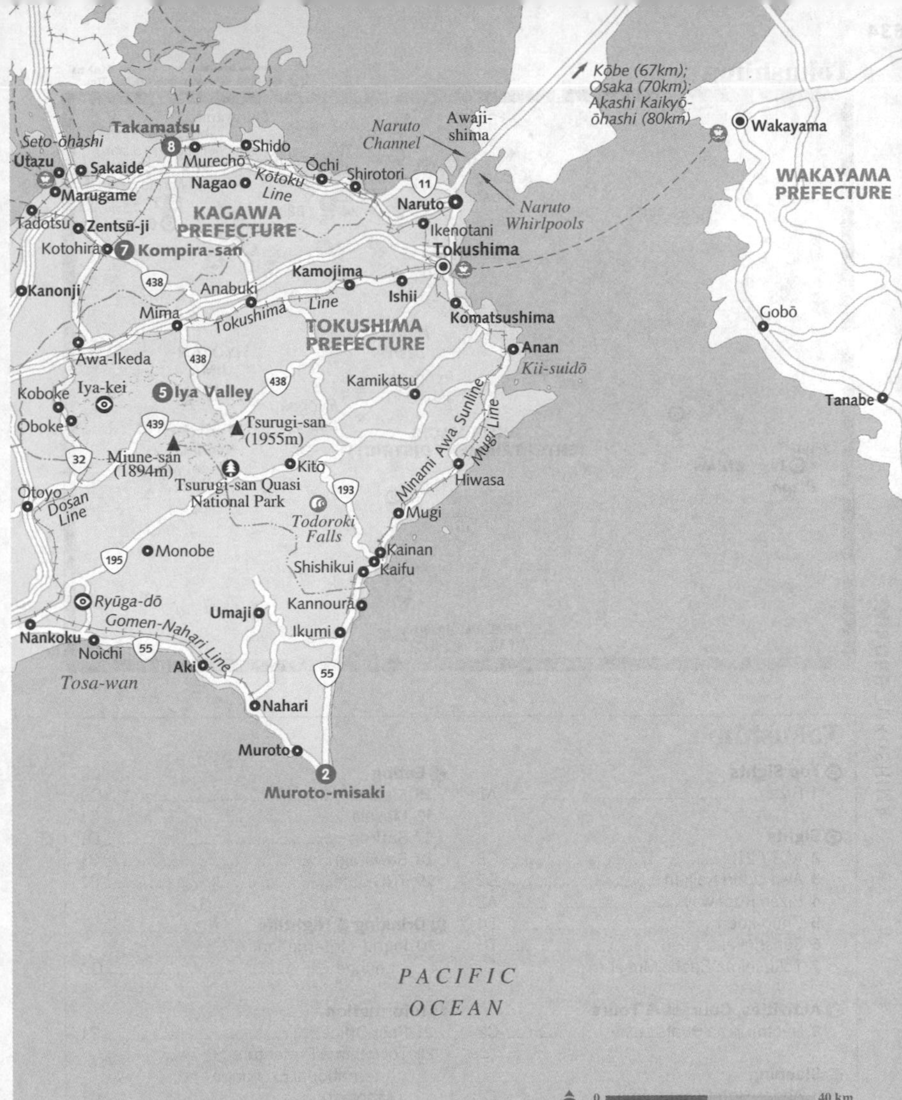

isolation of the **Iya Valley** (p643).

❻ Soaking in the venerable waters of historic **Dōgo Onsen** (p662) in the castle-town metropolis of Matsuyama.

❼ Trekking up 1368 stone steps to pay homage to the god of seafarers at **Konpira-san** (p667).

❽ Walking off Japan's most famous *udon* with a stroll through Takamatsu's exquisite Edo-period garden, **Ritsurin-kōen** (p669).

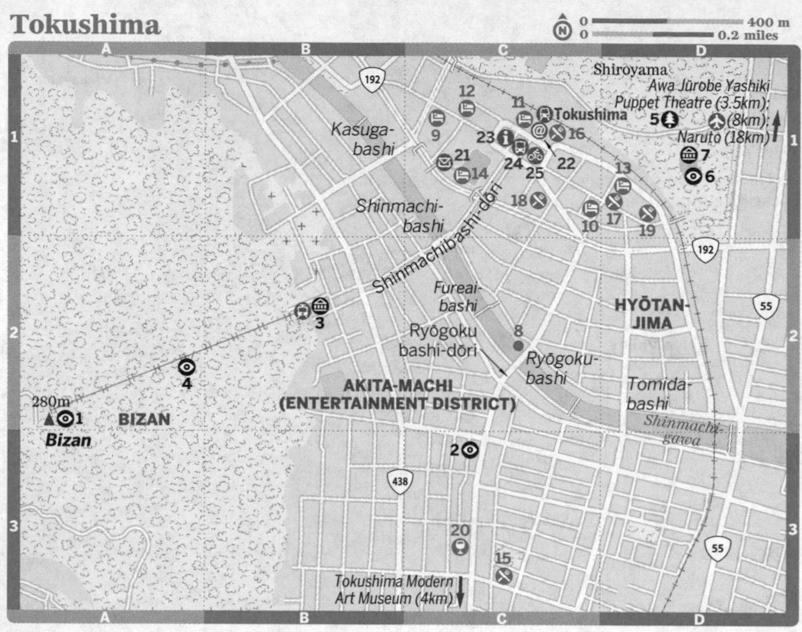

Tokushima

Top Sights
1 Bizan A2

Sights
2 ACTY 21 .... C3
3 Awa Odori Kaikan B2
4 Bizan Ropeway A2
5 Chūō-kōen D1
6 Senshūkaku-teien D1
7 Tokushima Castle Museum D1

Activities, Courses & Tours
8 Hyōtan-jima Boats C2

Sleeping
9 Agnes Hotel Tokushima C1
10 Hotel Astoria C1
11 Hotel Clement Tokushima C1
12 Hotel Four Season Tokushima C1
13 Sakura-sō D1
14 Tokushima Tōkyū Inn C1

Eating
15 Kisuke C3
16 Masala C1
17 Saffron D1
18 Sawaragi C1
19 YRG Café D1

Drinking & Nightlife
20 Ingrid's International Lounge C3

Information
21 Post Office C1
22 Tokushima Prefecture International Exchange Association C1
23 Tourist Information Office C1

Transport
24 Bus Terminal C1
25 Rental Bicycles C1

this surprisingly sophisticated prefectural museum houses two- and three-dimensional art by Picasso and Klee as well as Kaburagi and Seishi. It is particularly interesting to compare the more familiar European works to their Japanese counterparts, especially the pieces reflecting Japan's postwar identity; the fusion of traditional and Western-influenced styles embodies the zeitgeist of the period.

To get to the museum, catch a bus (¥210, 20 minutes) from stop No 3 on the middle island at the Tokushima bus terminal. Bunka-no-mori-kōen is a great option for rainy days, as the complex houses several museums and the prefectural library. The **Tokushima Prefectural Museum** (徳島県立博物館; ☎088-668-3636; www.museum.tokushima-ec.ed.jp; Bunka-no-mori-kōen; adult/child ¥200/¥50; ⏰9:30am-5pm Tue-Sun), full of huge dinosaur skeletons and engaging natural-history exhibits, will keep kids entertained for hours.

Awa Jūrobe Yashiki Puppet Theatre THEATRE
(阿波十郎兵衛屋敷; ☎088-665-2202; http://joruri.info/jurobe; 184 Miyajima Motoura, Kawauchi-chō; museum admission ¥410; ⏰9.30am-5pm, to 6pm Jul & Aug) For hundreds of years, puppet theatre thrived in the farming communities around Tokushima. Performances can still be seen here, in the former residence of Bandō Jūrobe, a samurai who allowed himself to be executed for a crime he didn't commit in order to preserve the good name of his master. The tale inspired the drama *Keisei Awa no Naruto,* first performed in 1768. Sections from the play are performed at 11am daily, and at 11am and 2pm on weekends.

To get to the museum, take a bus for Tomiyoshi Danchi (富吉団地) from bus stop No 7 at Tokushima bus terminal and get off at the Jūrobe Yashiki-mae stop (¥270, 25 minutes). More puppets can be seen at the nearby **Awa Deko Ningyō Kaikan** (阿波木偶人形会館; Awa Puppet Hall; ☎088-665-5600; 1-226 Miyajima Motoura, Kawauchi-chō; admission ¥400; ⏰9am-5pm, closed 1st & 3rd Wed of the month).

Chūō-kōen PARK
(中央公園) Northeast of the train station is Tokushima's central park, Chūō-kōen, where you'll find the scant ruins of Tokushima-jō (Tokushima Castle) and the beautiful **Senshūkaku-teien** (千秋閣庭園; admission ¥50, incl in museum ticket), an intimate 16th-century garden featuring rock bridges and secluded ponds. You can get a glimpse into the castle's former grandeur at **Tokushima Castle Museum** (徳島城博物館; ☎088-656-2525; www.city.tokushima.tokushima.jp/johaku/index.shtml; 1-8 Jōnai; admission ¥300; ⏰9:30am-5pm Tue-Sun), whose structure is based on the original castle's architecture and location. The museum contains a model of the castle town at its peak as well as artefacts from this period.

Built in 1585 for Hachisuka Iemasa after he was granted the fiefdom of Awa by Toyotomi Hideyoshi, most of the castle was destroyed in 1875 following the Meiji Restoration. On display in the museum are the *daimyō*'s (domain lord's) boat, suits of armour, and letters to the local lord from Hideyoshi and the first Tokugawa shogun, Ieyasu. Though displays are all in Japanese, an excellent English pamphlet is available.

Tours

Boats (ひょうたん島周遊船; ☎090-3783-2084) cruise around the 'gourd-shaped' Hyōtan-jima (Hyōtan Island) in central Tokushima. The tours cost ¥100 and leave from Ryōgoku-bashi (両国橋; Ryōgoku Bridge) on the Shinmachi-gawa every 20 minutes from 1pm to 3.40pm Monday to Friday from mid-March to mid-October, and daily from 20 July to 31 August. In July and August there are additional departures every 40 minutes from 5pm to 7.40pm.

Festivals & Events

Every August Tokushima is the location for one of the biggest parties in Japan, when the fabulous **Awa-odori Matsuri** (Awa-odori Festival) takes place to mark the O-bon holidays.

Sleeping

Sakura-sō MINSHUKU ¥
(さくら荘; ☎088-652-9575; 1-25 Terashima-honchō-higashi; per person without bathroom ¥3300; 📶) The delightful older lady in charge readily welcomes lost foreigners to her charming *minshuku* (Japanese guesthouse), which has 12 large, good-value tatami rooms. It's a few blocks east of the train station, just before the NHK TV studio. Look for the sign in Japanese.

Agnes Hotel Tokushima BOUTIQUE HOTEL ¥¥
(アグネスホテル徳島; ☎088-626-2222; www.agneshotel.jp; 1-28 Terashima-honchō-nishi; s/d with breakfast from ¥6500/13,000; P 🚭 @ 📶) Hip little Agnes lies 200m west of the station and offers a more sophisticated aesthetic than the usual business hotel. The rooms have stylish interiors, and the foyer pastry cafe is a destination in its own right. There's internet access in the lobby, and LAN access in all rooms.

Hotel Four Season Tokushima BOUTIQUE HOTEL ¥¥
(☎088-622-2203; www.fshotel.jp; 1-54-1 Terashima-honchō-nishi; s/tw with breakfast from ¥5900/11,800; 🚭 @ 📶) It's not *quite* the famous chain, but the 23 rooms are quite decent nonetheless – if a bit dowdier than those of its sister hotel, the Agnes, just down the road.

Hotel Astoria HOTEL ¥¥
(ホテルアストリア; ☎088-653-6151; 2-26-1 Ichiban-cho; s/tw ¥5400/8640; P⊜@ᯤ) An informal vibe pervades this neat family hotel tucked off the main drag. The narrow rooms are well appointed, with spacious bathrooms and firm beds. There is LAN internet access in rooms, and a popular cafe-restaurant in the lobby. It's across the road and down a block from the giant Tōyoko Inn signage.

Tokushima Tōkyū Inn HOTEL ¥¥
(徳島東急イン; ☎088-626-0109; www.tokyu hotels.co.jp; 1-24 Motomachi; s/d from ¥7800/12,960; P⊜@ᯤ) A step up in comfort and class from more cramped business hotels, the Tōkyū Inn offers clean, relatively spacious rooms and is conveniently located across the plaza from the JR Tokushima Station. Find the hotel entrance on the river side of the Sogō department store building. Book online for more competitive rates.

Hotel Clement Tokushima HOTEL ¥¥¥
(ホテルクレメント徳島; ☎088-656-3111; www.hotelclement.co.jp; 1-61 Terashima-honchō-nishi; s/d from ¥10,690/14,260; P⊜@) Directly on top of the station building, luxurious Hotel Clement boasts 18 floors and 250 comfortable, spacious Western-style rooms. Although it's more expensive than other business hotels, the extra yen gets you a slew of amenities including a spa and a range of restaurants and bars.

Eating & Drinking

Tokushima's main entertainment district is in Akita-machi across the river, along the streets around the landmark ACTY 21 building.

AWA-ODORI MATSURI

The Awa-odori is the largest and most famous *bon* (Japanese Buddhist custom that honours one's ancestors) dance in Japan. Every night from 12 to 15 August, men, women and children don *yukata* (light cotton kimono) and straw hats and take to the streets to dance to the samba-like rhythm of the theme song 'Awa Yoshikono', accompanied by the sounds of *shamisen* (three-stringed guitars), *taiko* (drums) and *fue* (flutes). More than a million people descend on Tokushima for the festival every year, and accommodation is at a premium.

YRG Café CAFE ¥
(☎088-656-7899; 1-33-4 Terashima Honchō Higashi; meals ¥700-1500; ⏲11.30am-3pm & 8-10pm Fri-Wed; 📋) This adorable coffee shop down by the train tracks is run by super-talented, English-speaking Takao. 'Yellow, Red, Green' can hospitalise (repair) your ailing laptop but is better known for serving up whopping cups of chai and nutritious, comforting meals that change weekly.

Saffron CAFE ¥
(☎088-656-0235; 2-10-2 Ichiban-cho; meals ¥800-1000; ⏲10am-4pm) The huge Japanese *omuraisu* (omelette filled with spiced rice and covered in sweet, brown sauce) at this very cosy lunch spot make delicious hangover food. Linger for a scoop of homemade ice cream and hang out with the friendly owner. Look for the English sign propped outside.

Masala INDIAN ¥
(マサラ; ☎088-654-7122; Terashima-honchō-nishi; dishes ¥480-680; ⏲11am-9.30pm; 📋) Sometimes all you need is a good, authentic curry. The Indian staff serve veggie curries and a range of enormous, piping hot naan. This branch of the small Shikoku-based chain is on the 5th floor of the Clement Plaza.

Sawaragi JAPANESE ¥¥
(さわらぎ; ☎088-625-2431; 5-3 Ichiban-chō; lunch ¥980; ⏲11.30am-1.30pm & 5.30-10pm) Its beige facade looks unremarkable, and its atmosphere unassuming, but the traditional Japanese dishes served at this family-run restaurant are beautifully prepared. Choose from three dinner courses (¥1620 to ¥5500, according to how hungry you are), which feature a variety of seasonal dishes.

Kisuke IZAKAYA ¥¥
(喜助; ☎088-652-1832; 1-20 Chūō-dōri; dishes ¥500-800; ⏲6pm-midnight Mon-Sat) Named after an anime character who always arrives in the nick of time, Kisuke has built a reputation for imaginative seafood dishes. Get a recommendation for the freshest specials by asking, *'Osusume wa arimasu ka?'* To find it, take Ryōgoku-bashi south through Akita-machi. Turn left just before the big Kyoei supermarket, and look for Kisuke's striking, modern exterior on the next corner.

Ingrid's International Lounge KARAOKE BAR
(☎088-626-0067; ingridsinternational.wordpress.com; 2-7-1 Sakaemachi; ⏲6pm-late) Filipina Ingrid is Tokushima's go-to girl for expat

BEST SCENIC DRIVE: SHIMANTO-GAWA

Little traffic and stunning scenery make Shikoku one of the best driving destinations in Japan. There's also a lack of regular public transport services in some areas, namely around the two southern capes and the Iya Valley, so your international licence can at last come in handy. Our favourite drive is along the banks of the Shimanto-gawa on Rte 381. Here you vie with the odd truck for single-lane access to some of the narrowest, bendiest, prettiest roads in the country, boxed in by rocky cliffs on one side and the shimmering Shimanto-gawa on the other. It feels like you're in a rally driving video game where the animated cars just know how to avoid you.

gossip and all-night karaoke. The lounge is hard to find, tucked among the hostess clubs in the southwest of Akita-machi, but there's nothing duplicitous about this Tokushima travellers' institution. Beware: Ingrid never forgets a face!

Information

ATMs at the post office accept international cards.

Tokushima Prefecture International Exchange Association (徳島県国際交流協会; TOPIA; 088-656-3303; www.topia.ne.jp; 6th fl, Clement Plaza, 1-61 Terashima Honchō-nishi; 10am-6pm) English-speaking staff, with internet access available (¥50 for 10 minutes).

Tourist Information Office (徳島総合観光案内所; 088-622-8556; 9am-8pm) In a booth on the plaza outside the station.

Getting There & Around

TO/FROM THE AIRPORT

Tokushima's **airport** (徳島阿波おどり空港; 088-699-2831; www.tokushima-airport.co.jp/en) is reached by bus (¥440, 30 minutes, buses timed to coincide with flights) from bus stop No 1 in front of the station.

BUS

Highway buses connect Tokushima with Tokyo (¥10,180, nine hours) and Nagoya (¥6790, 5 hours); there are also buses to Takamatsu (¥1650, 1½ hours), Hiroshima (¥6150, 3¾ hours, two daily) and Kansai airport (¥4100, 2¾ hours).

BIKE

Rental Bicycles (貸し自転車; 088-652-6661; per half/full day ¥270/450, deposit ¥3000; 9am-8pm) Available from the underground bike park to the left as you leave the station.

TRAIN

Tokushima is just over an hour by train from Takamatsu (¥2640 by *tokkyū* – limited express). For the Iya Valley and Kōchi, change trains at Awa-Ikeda (阿波池田, ¥2820, 1½ hours).

Around Tokushima

Naruto Whirlpools 鳴門の渦潮

At the change of tides, seawater whisks through the narrow channel between Shikoku and Awaji-shima at such speed that ferocious whirlpools are created. The Naruto-no-Uzushio are active twice a day. Check www.uzusio.com for a timetable or visit the tourist office.

For an up-close and personal view of the whirlpools, you can venture out into the Naruto Channel on one of the **tourist boats** that depart from the waterfront in Naruto. **Naruto Kankō Kisen** (鳴門観光汽船; 088-687-0101; per person ¥1530-2530; every 20 mins 9am-4.20pm) is one of several companies making regular trips out from the port, next to the Naruto Kankō-kō (鳴門観光港) bus stop. For a bird's-eye view, you can walk out along **Uzu-no-michi** (渦の道; 088-683-6262; www.uzunomichi.jp; admission ¥510; 9am-6pm, to 5pm Oct-Feb), a 500m-long walkway underneath the Naruto-ōhashi, which puts you directly above the action.

To get to the whirlpools, take a bus bound for Naruto-kōen (鳴門公園) from bus stop 1 in front of Tokushima Station (¥710, 1½ hours, hourly from 9am).

If you want to stare into the abyss a bit longer, **Ryokan Kōen Mizuno** (旅館公園水野; 088-772-0013; s/d from ¥5500/11,000) has beautiful, Japanese-style rooms with sea views and efficient, foreigner-friendly service.

The First Five Temples: Ryōzen-ji to Jizō-ji

Naruto is the starting point for Shikoku's 88 Temple pilgrimage. The first five temples are all within easy walking distance of each other, making it possible to get a taste of the *henro* (pilgrim) trail on a day trip from Tokushima.

88 Temples of Shikoku

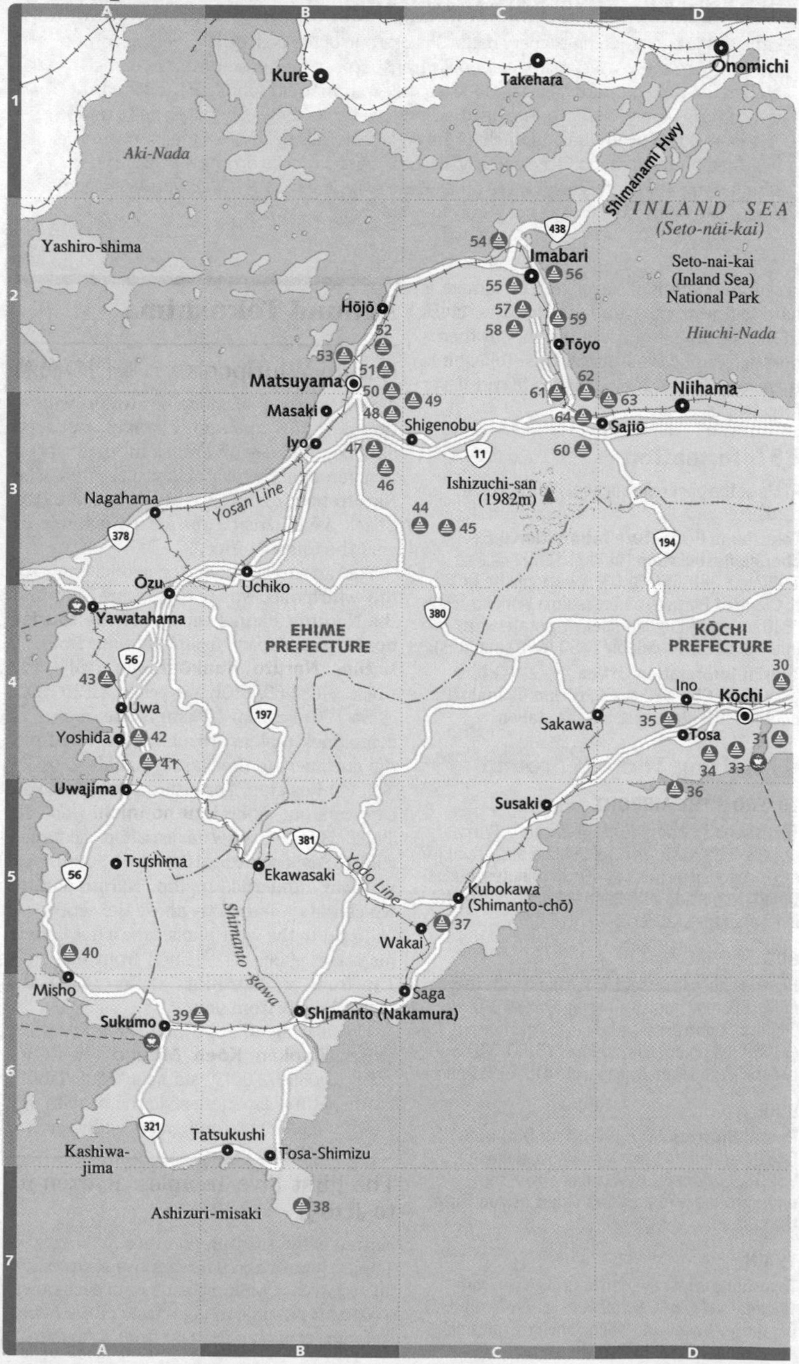

SHIKOKU

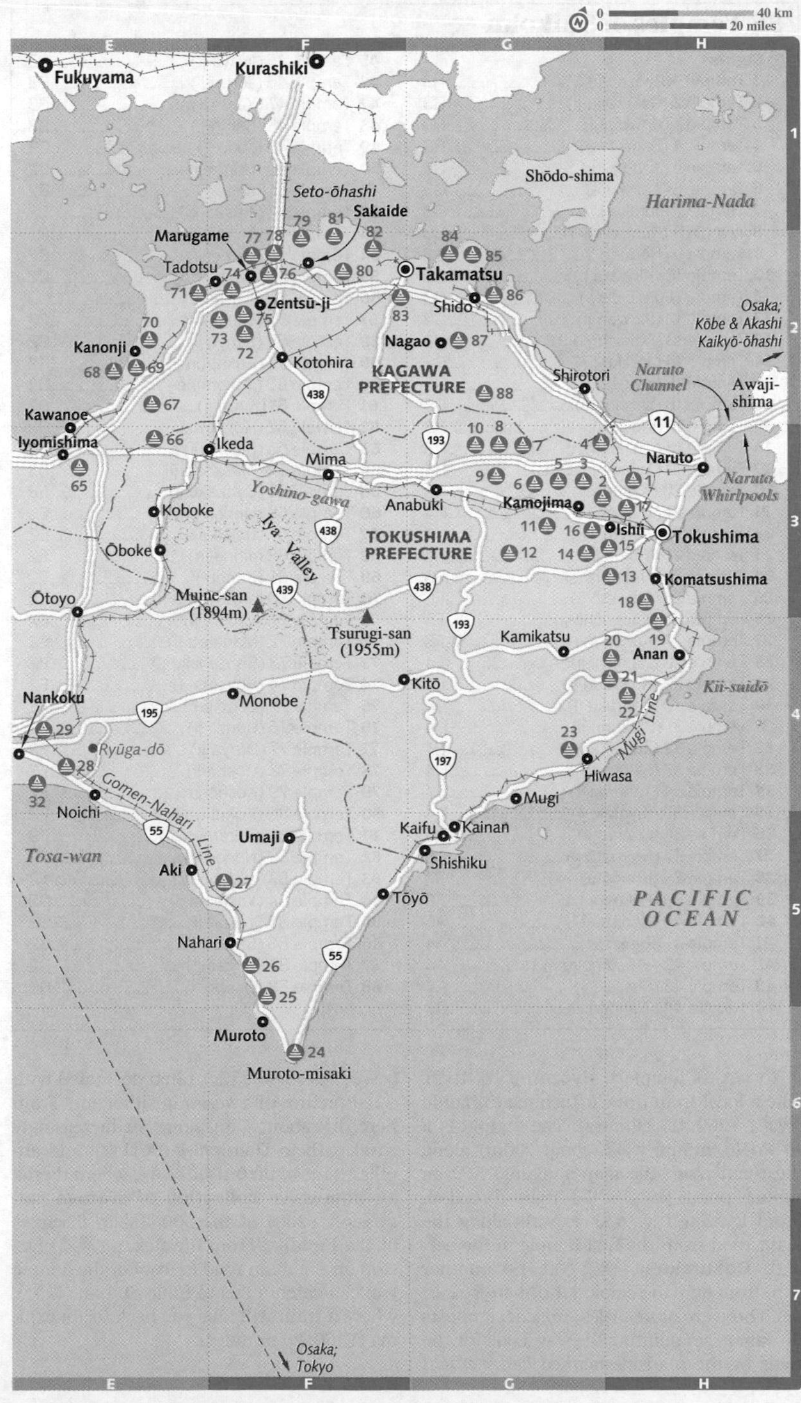

Fukuyama
Kurashiki
Seto-ōhashi
Shōdo-shima
Harima-Nada
Sakaide
Marugame
Tadotsu
Takamatsu
Zentsū-ji
Shido
Osaka; Kōbe & Akashi Kaikyō-ōhashi
Nagao
Kanonji
Kotohira
KAGAWA PREFECTURE
Shirotori
Naruto Channel
Awaji-shima
Kawanoe
Iyomishima
Ikeda
Mima
Naruto
Naruto Whirlpools
Yoshino-gawa
Anabuki
Kamojima
Koboke
Iya Valley
TOKUSHIMA PREFECTURE
Ishii
Tokushima
Ōboke
Komatsushima
Ōtoyo
Muine-san (1894m)
Tsurugi-san (1955m)
Kamikatsu
Anan
Kitō
Kii-suidō
Nankoku
Monobe
Ryūga-dō
Mugi Line
Hiwasa
Gomen-Nahari Line
Noichi
Mugi
Kaifu
Kainan
Umaji
Shishiku
Tosa-wan
Aki
Tōyō
PACIFIC OCEAN
Nahari
Muroto
Muroto-misaki
Osaka; Tokyo
SHIKOKU
0 40 km
0 20 miles

88 Temples of Shikoku

Sights

1 Temple 1 (Ryōzen-ji) H3
2 Temple 2 (Gokuraku-ji) G3
3 Temple 3 (Konsen-ji) G3
4 Temple 4 (Dainichi-ji) G3
5 Temple 5 (Jizō-ji) G3
6 Temple 6 (Anraku-ji) G3
7 Temple 7 (Juraku-ji) G3
8 Temple 8 (Kumadani-ji) G3
9 Temple 9 (Hōrin-ji) G3
10 Temple 10 (Kirihata-ji) G3
11 Temple 11 (Fujii-dera) G3
12 Temple 12 (Shōzan-ji) G3
13 Temple 13 (Dainichi-ji) H3
14 Temple 14 (Jōraku-ji) G3
15 Temple 15 (Kokubun-ji) H3
16 Temple 16 (Kannon-ji) G3
17 Temple 17 (Ido-ji) H3
18 Temple 18 (Onzan-ji) H3
19 Temple 19 (Tatsue-ji) H4
20 Temple 20 (Kakurin-ji) H4
21 Temple 21 (Tairyō-ji) H4
22 Temple 22 (Byōdō-ji) H4
23 Temple 23 (Yakuō-ji) G4
24 Temple 24 (Hotsumisaki-ji) F6
25 Temple 25 (Shinshō-ji) F5
26 Temple 26 (Kongōchō-ji) F5
27 Temple 27 (Kōnomine-ji) F5
28 Temple 28 (Dainichi-ji) E4
29 Temple 29 (Kokubun-ji) E4
30 Temple 30 (Zenraku-ji) D4
31 Temple 31 (Chikurin-ji) D4
32 Temple 32 (Zenjibu-ji) E4
33 Temple 33 (Sekkei-ji) D4
34 Temple 34 (Tanema-ji) D4
35 Temple 35 (Kiyotaki-ji) D4
36 Temple 36 (Shōryū-ji) D5
37 Temple 37 (Iwamoto-ji) C5
38 Temple 38 (Kongōfuku-ji) B7
39 Temple 39 (Enkō-ji) A6
40 Temple 40 (Kanjizai-ji) A5
41 Temple 41 (Ryūkō-ji) A4
42 Temple 42 (Butsumoku-ji) A4
43 Temple 43 (Meiseki-ji) A4
44 Temple 44 (Taihō-ji) C3
45 Temple 45 (Iwaya-ji) C3
46 Temple 46 (Jōruri-ji) B3
47 Temple 47 (Yasaka-ji) B3
48 Temple 48 (Sairin-ji) B3
49 Temple 49 (Jōdo-ji) C3
50 Temple 50 (Hanta-ji) B2
51 Temple 51 (Ishite-ji) B2
52 Temple 52 (Taisan-ji) B2
53 Temple 53 (Enmyō-ji) B2
54 Temple 54 (Enmei-ji) C2
55 Temple 55 (Nankō-bō) C2
56 Temple 56 (Taisan-ji) C2
57 Temple 57 (Eifuku-ji) C2
58 Temple 58 (Senyū-ji) C2
59 Temple 59 (Kokubun-ji) C2
60 Temple 60 (Yokomine-ji) C3
61 Temple 61 (Kōon-ji) C2
62 Temple 62 (Hōju-ji) C2
63 Temple 63 (Kisshō-ji) D3
64 Temple 64 (Maegami-ji) C3
65 Temple 65 (Sankaku-ji) E3
66 Temple 66 (Unpen-ji) E3
67 Temple 67 (Daikō-ji) E2
68 Temple 68 (Jinne-in) E2
69 Temple 69 (Kanon-ji) E2
70 Temple 70 (Motoyama-ji) E2
71 Temple 71 (Iyadani-ji) E2
72 Temple 72 (Mandara-ji) F2
73 Temple 73 (Shusshaka-ji) F2
74 Temple 74 (Kōyama-ji) F2
75 Temple 75 (Zentsū-ji) F2
76 Temple 76 (Konzō-ji) F2
77 Temple 77 (Dōryū-ji) F2
78 Temple 78 (Gōshō-ji) F2
79 Temple 79 (Kōshō-in) F2
80 Temple 80 (Kokubun-ji) F2
81 Temple 81 (Shiramine-ji) F2
82 Temple 82 (Negoro-ji) F2
83 Temple 83 (Ichinomiya-ji) F2
84 Temple 84 (Yashima-ji) G2
85 Temple 85 (Yakuri-ji) G2
86 Temple 86 (Shido-ji) G2
87 Temple 87 (Nagao-ji) G2
88 Temple 88 (Ōkubo-ji) G2

To get to Temple 1, **Ryōzen-ji** (霊山寺), take a local train from Tokushima to Bandō (板東; ¥260, 25 minutes). The temple is a 10- to 15-minute walk (about 700m) along the main road; the map at Bandō Station should point you in the right direction. From Ryōzen-ji it's a short walk along the main road from the first temple to the second, **Gokuraku-ji** (極楽寺), and another 2km from here to Temple 3, **Konsen-ji** (金泉寺). There are more-or-less regular signposts (in Japanese) pointing the way. Look for the signs by the roadside marked *henro-michi* (へんろ道 or 遍路道), often decorated with a red picture of a *henro* in silhouette. From here, it's about 5km along an increasingly rural path to **Dainichi-ji** (大日寺), and another 2km to **Jizō-ji** (地蔵寺), where there's an impressive **collection of statues** (admission ¥200) of the 500 Rakan disciples of the Buddha. From the Rakan (羅漢) bus stop on the main road in front of the temple you can catch a bus to Itano Station (板野), where a train will take you back to Tokushima (¥360, 25 minutes).

WALKING PILGRIMS

The *henro* (pilgrim on the 88 Temple walk) is one of the most distinctive sights of any trip to Shikoku. They're everywhere you go, striding along busy city highways, cresting hills in remote mountain valleys – solitary figures in white, trudging purposefully through heat haze and monsoonal downpour alike on their way from temple to temple. Who are these people, and what drives them to make a journey of more than 1400km on foot?

Although the backgrounds and motives of the *henro* may differ widely, they all follow in the legendary footsteps of Kōbō Daishi, the monk who established Shingon Buddhism in Japan and made significant contributions to Japanese culture. Whether or not it is true that Kōbō Daishi actually founded or visited all 88 sacred sites, the idea behind making the 88-temple circuit is to do so accompanied by the spirit of Kōbō Daishi himself – hence the inscription on so many pilgrims' backpacks and other paraphernalia: 同行二人 (*dōgyō ninin*), meaning 'two people on the same journey'.

Regardless of each *henro's* motivations, the pattern and routine of life on the road is very similar for everyone who undertakes the trail. The dress is uniform, too: *hakue* (white garments) to signify sincerity of purpose and purity of mind; the *sugegasa* (straw hat) that has protected pilgrims against sun and rain since time immemorial; and the *kongōzue* (colourful staff). The routine at each temple is mostly the same, too: a bang on the bell and a chant of the Heart Sutra at the Daishi-dō (one of the two main buildings in each temple compound), before filing off to the *nōkyōchō* (desk), where the pilgrims' book is inscribed with beautiful characters detailing the name of the temple and the date of the pilgrimage.

If you're eager to become an *aruki henro* (walking pilgrim) yourself, you'll need to budget around 60 days (allowing for an average distance of 25km a day) to complete the circuit. To plan your pilgrimage, the website www.shikokuhenrotrail.com and the guidebook *Shikoku Japan 88 Route Guide* (Buyodo Publishing) are both excellent English-language resources; the book can also be purchased at Temple 1, Ryōzen-ji.

Travellers who don't have the time or inclination for the whole thing can get a taste of what it's all about by following one of the *henro*-for-a-day minicircuits. Aside from Naruto (p637), cities with concentrations of temples within easy reach of each other include Matsuyama (p659; Temples 46 through 53), and Zentsū-ji (p666) in Kagawa Prefecture.

Iya Valley 祖谷渓

The spectacular Iya Valley is a special place, its staggeringly steep gorges and thick mountain forests luring travellers to seek respite from the hectic 'mainland' lifestyle. Winding your way around narrow cliff-hanging roads as the icy blue water of the Yoshino-gawa shoots along the ancient valley floors is a blissful travel experience. The active soul can pick up some of the country's finest hiking trails around Tsurugi-san or try world-class white-water rafting in the Ōboke and Koboke Gorges.

For the more sedentary, three top-notch onsen (hot springs) are well within reach, while evening entertainment is nothing more strenuous than sampling the local Iya *soba* (buckwheat noodles) and reliving your day's visual feast.

The earliest records of the valley describe a group of shamans fleeing from persecution in Nara in the 9th century. At the end of the 12th century, Iya famously became the last refuge for members of the vanquished Heike clan following their defeat at the hands of the Minamoto in the Gempei Wars. Their descendants are believed to live in the mountain villages to this day.

Ōboke & Koboke 大歩危・小歩危

Ōboke and Koboke are two scenic gorges on the Yoshino-gawa, which fluctuates from languid green waters to Class IV rapids. Driving through these rural river valleys provides the first verdant glimpse into the magic of Iya.

To orient yourself in this maze of valleys, stop by **Lapis Ōboke** (ラピス大歩危; ☎0883-84-1489; 1553-1 Kamimyo; admission ¥500; ⏲9am-6pm Apr-Nov, to 5pm Dec-Mar) for basic tourist information. Its primary role is as a geology and local *yōkai* (ghost) museum – skip the rocks, but get acquainted

Iya Valley

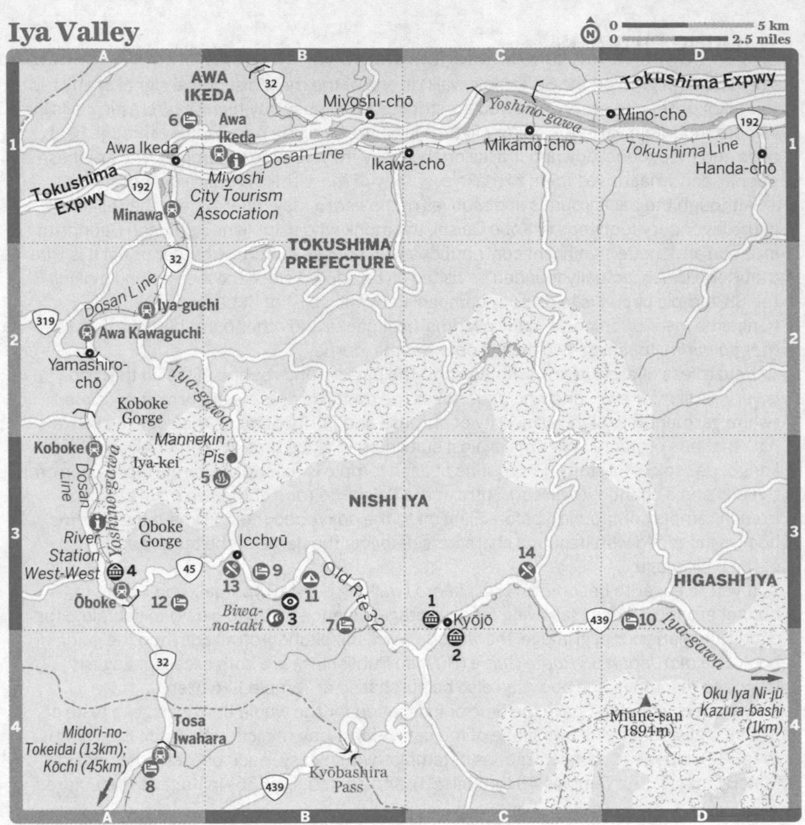

Iya Valley

Sights

1 Buke Yashiki	C3
2 Higashi Iya History & Folk Museum	C4
3 Kazura-bashi	B3
4 Lapis Ōboke	A3

Activities, Courses & Tours

Happy Raft	(see 8)
5 Iya Onsen	B3

Sleeping

6 Awa Ikeda Youth Hostel	A1
7 Chiiori	B3
8 Happy Guest House	A4
9 Hotel Kazura-bashi	B3
10 Iyashi no Onsen-kyō	D3
11 Kazura-bashi Camping Village	B3
12 Ku-Nel-Asob	A3

Eating

13 Iya Bijin	B3
Momiji-tei	(see 4)
14 Soba Dōjō	C3

with the folkloric apparitions, colourfully represented in a hall of delightful horrors (explained with some English signage).

Stop by the tourist complex **River Station West-West** (☎0887-84-1117; www.west-west.com) for river gear at the Mont Bell shop, road snacks and pit stops at the *konbini* (convenience store), and excellent *soba* at the restaurant **Momiji-tei** (もみじ亭; ☎0883-84-1117; meals ¥900-2000; ⏲10am-5.30pm Thu-Tue) – try the *tempura soba* set (¥1450), either hot or cold.

Activities

Happy Raft RAFTING
(ハッピーラフト; ☎0887-75-0500; www.happyraft.com; 221-1 Ikadagi) South of Ikeda on Rte 32 between Koboke and Ōboke, around 20 companies run white-water rafting and kayaking trips from mid-March to mid-October. Happy Raft, steps from JR Tosa Iwahara Station, operates sensational rafting trips and canyoning adventures (¥9000) with English-speaking guides (half-day ¥5500 to ¥7500, full day ¥10,000 to ¥15,500).

Iya Onsen ONSEN
(祖谷温泉; ☎0883-75-2311; www.iyaonsen.co.jp; 367-2 Matsuo Matsumoto; onsen ¥1500; ⊙7am-6pm for day-use guests) On Old Rte 32, this onsen is a great place to warm up after a chilling plunge through white water. A cable car descends a steep cliff-face to some sulphurous, open-air baths on the riverside. The hotel is a fantastic place to slow down, enjoy spectacular views of the forested gorge and, of course, soak in the onsen.

Accommodation includes beautifully prepared meals incorporating valley-sourced venison, vegetables and fish; rates begin at ¥16,350 per person.

Sleeping

Happy Guest House GUESTHOUSE ¥
(☎0887-75-0500; dm per person ¥3000; P) Run by the local outfit Happy Raft, this trio of small guesthouses can each accommodate up to 10, and all come with a kitchen. The original guesthouse is a self-contained and fully restored farmhouse, with a tatami room overlooking the Yoshino Valley.

Ku-Nel-Asob GUESTHOUSE ¥
(空音遊; ☎090-9778-7133; www.k-n-a.com; 442 Enoki; r per person with dinner/breakfast & dinner ¥7000/8100; P 📶) Five simple, attractive tatami rooms are available in this near-century-old house, perched on a beautiful bluff overlooking the river. Meals here are vegan and served family-style. Since the house doesn't have a bath, the friendly English-speaking owners provide transfers and entry to a local onsen for ¥500. Reservations must be made at least three days in advance.

The owners also offer free pick-ups/drop-offs at JR Ōboke Station, 3km away.

Midori no Tokeidai GUESTHOUSE ¥
(みどりの時計台; ☎0887-72-0202; http://midorinotokeidai.com; 665 Kawaguchi; per person ¥3500; P) This delightfully decorated former school building houses many 'in-the-know' Japanese and foreign guests.

Awa Ikeda Youth Hostel HOSTEL ¥
(阿波池田ユースホステル; ☎0883-72-5277; 3798 Sako, Nishiyama; dm ¥3600, breakfast/dinner ¥530/1050; P) 🍃 This isolated hostel with huge communal tatami rooms and a do-it-yourself vibe sits alongside the serene Mitsugon-ji mountain temple. Make sure you book ahead if you need to be picked up at JR Awa-Ikeda Station, 5km away, and if you require meals. It's quite difficult to find, so we've included its GPS coordinates: 133°48'3"E, 34°2'26"N.

Nishi Iya 西祖谷

The extravagant greenery and river-smoothed stones along the Iya-gawa form a verdant backdrop to the Nishi Iya's famous vine bridge. Rte 32 follows the river valley to connect with Higashi Iya to the east.

Sights

Kazura-bashi BRIDGE
(かずら橋; admission ¥500; ⊙8am-5pm) This remarkable vine bridge is one of only three left in the valley (the other two are further east in Higashi Iya). Stepping onto the creaking vine bridge, with the river sparkling between the gaps, is worth the slightly depressing approach via the monstrous car park. Check out the nearby Biwa-no-taki, an impressive, 50m-high waterfall.

Sleeping & Eating

Kazura-bashi Camping Village CAMPGROUND ¥
(かずら橋キャンプ村; ☎090-1571-5258; campsite ¥510, plus per person ¥200, 4-5-person bungalow ¥5350; ⊙Apr-Nov) This rustic but well-maintained campground lies 500m upriver from the vine bridge. Showers are free, and rental equipment – from tents to kitchenware – is available at reasonable rates. If you don't speak Japanese, have a Japanese speaker call ahead to reserve, as walk-ins are problematic for the friendly but non-English speaking caretaker. Check in between 9am and 5pm.

★**Hotel Kazura-bashi** RYOKAN ¥¥¥
(ホテルかずら橋; ☎0883-87-2171; www.kazurabashi.co.jp; 33-1 Zentoku; r per person with 2 meals from ¥15,900; P 🚭 📶) At the base of a steep hillside about 1km north of the bridge, this lovely hotel offers spacious, comfortable Japanese-style rooms with mountain views.

Beautifully prepared traditional meals are served in the tatami dining room by the unobtrusively attentive staff. A funky cable car ferries guests up to the hotel's highlight: a gorgeous, open-air onsen on the hill.

Nonguests are welcome to use the onsen (¥1200) between 10am to 4pm.

Iya Bijin SOBA ¥
(祖谷美人; ☎0883-87-2009; www.iyabijin.jp; 9-3 Zentoku; meals ¥700-3700; ⏲8am-5pm; 📵) For a taste of local Iya *soba,* try Iya Bijin, in an attractive black-and-white building with lanterns hanging out the front. Try a simple plate of *zaru soba* (cold noodles with dipping sauce), or a lunch set that includes local dishes such as *dekomawashi* (grilled skewers of taro, tofu and *konnyaku* – devil's tongue), boar and wild vegetables.

Higashi Iya 東祖谷

About 30km east of Nishi Iya, Rte 439 winds deeply into the green gulches of Higashi Iya (also known as Oku Iya).

Sights & Activities

Oku Iya Ni-jū Kazura-bashi BRIDGE
(奥祖谷二重かずら橋; admission ¥500; ⏲7am-5pm) The spectacular Oku Iya Ni-jū Kazura-bashi are two secluded vine bridges hanging side by side high over the river. A self-propelled, three-seated wooden cable-cart is another fun way to cross the river; there's a small public camping area on the other side.

Higashi Iya History & Folk Museum MUSEUM
(東祖谷歴史民俗資料館; ☎0883-88-2286; 14-3 Kyōjo; admission ¥410; ⏲8.30am-5pm) This folk museum is in a large red building in Kyōjō, displaying historic artefacts and everyday tools, as well as items relating to the Heike legend.

Buke Yashiki HISTORIC BUILDING
(武家屋敷喜多家; ☎0883-88-2040; admission ¥300; ⏲9am-5pm, closed Tue & Dec-Mar) Several kilometres up a narrow, winding road near Kyōjō, Buke Yashiki is a thatched-roof samurai-house museum commanding spectacular views of the valley. Beside the house is a Shintō shrine that is home to a massive cedar tree dating back more than 800 years.

Sleeping & Eating

Iyashi no Onsen-kyō HOTEL ¥¥¥
(いやしの温泉郷; ☎0883-88-2975; http://iyashino-onsenkyo.com; 28 Sugeoi, Higashi Iya; r per person with meals from ¥14,000; ⏲onsen 10am-9pm) Off the main road between Kyōjō and the Higashi Iya vine bridges is this lovely and unpretentious hotel and hot-springs complex, with Japanese- and Western-style rooms, an onsen and a restaurant. A smattering of Japanese-language skills would be helpful here; at the very least, ask a Japanese speaker to book ahead for you.

Soba Dōjō SOBA ¥
(そば道場; ☎0883-88-2577; zaru soba ¥800; ⏲11am-5pm Fri-Wed) At Soba Dōjō on Rte 439, you can sample a bowl of *zaru soba* and even make your own (¥2500; reservations required). The restaurant has a reddish roof, and a yellow curtain hanging over the door.

Tsurugi-san 剣山

At 1955m, Tsurugi-san is the second-highest mountain in Shikoku and provides excellent and challenging hiking opportunities, as well as some fairly basic snowboarding from December to February. A **chairlift** (one way/return ¥1000/1800; ⏲9am-5pm, last return 4.45pm) goes most of the way up, after which it is a leisurely 30-minute walk to the summit. If you decide to climb all the way, you'll

VINE BRIDGES

The wisteria vine bridges of the Iya Valley are glorious remnants of a remote and timeless Japan. Crossing the bridges has for centuries been notoriously difficult, which well suited the bandits and humbled warriors who took refuge in the secluded gorges. The bridges are feats of ancient engineering, undertaken roughly 1000 years ago, and were formed by tying together the wild vines that hung on either side of the 45m-wide valley. Only in recent years have the bridges been reinforced with side rails, planks and wire. But it's not only the acrophobic among us who will get the wobbles.

Only three *kazura-bashi* survive, one heavily touristed bridge at Nishi Iya and another pair of 'husband and wife' bridges at Higashi Iya, which is a further 30km east – the secluded, deep gorge setting is worth the extra effort.

CHIIORI – A RURAL RETREAT

High on a mountainside in the remote Iya Valley, looking out over forested hillsides and plunging gorges, is one of Japan's most unusual places to stay.

Chiiori (www.chiiori.org; s/d high season from ¥21,000/22,000; lower rates for larger groups) – 'The Cottage of the Flute' – is a once-abandoned 18th-century thatched-roof farmhouse that has been painstakingly restored towards its original brilliance. Unlike many such examples of cultural heritage in Japan, where concrete and plastic have wrecked the architectural aesthetic, here glistening red-pine floorboards surround open-floor hearths under soaring rafters. Set amid steep hillsides dotted by thatched houses and forests strewn with narrow mountain paths, Iya was for centuries an example of an untouched coexistence of humans and nature, albeit one that offered residents little hope of wealth and comfort.

In recent decades, however, the locals' traditional lifestyle and the balance with the environment have been rapidly upset; employment moved from agriculture to government-subsidised and frequently pointless construction, the effects of which – eg paved riverbeds – can be seen from almost any roadside. Part of the project's mission has been working with residents to promote sustainable, community-based tourism and realise the financial potential of traditional life, which until recently many locals saw as backward and valueless. It is a work in progress – many thatched roofs in the area are still hidden by corrugated tin sheets – but by adding to the growing number of tourists visiting the area, largely because of the work of those involved in Chiiori, staying here helps to encourage those conservation efforts.

The house was bought as a ruin by the author and aesthete Alex Kerr in the early 1970s, and he went on to romanticise the Iya Valley in his award-winning book *Lost Japan*. Chiiori remains a beautiful and authentic destination for sensitive travellers, with its *shōji* (movable screens), antique furnishings and *irori* (traditional hearths) – all complemented by a gleaming, fully-equipped modern kitchen and gorgeous bathroom, complete with *hinoki* (Japanese cypress) tub. Since the establishment of the nonprofit Chiiori Trust in 2005, the local government has approached the Trust to help restore several smaller traditional houses in the area. These houses have been renovated to a similarly high standard and aesthetic as Chiiori and are also available as accommodation. All are outfitted with modern kitchens and bathrooms, and even washing machines. Follow the Higashi-Iya Ochiai link on the Chiiori Trust website for information and rates on these smaller houses.

To stay in these extraordinary environs, you must reserve in advance through **Chiiori Trust** (☎0883-88-5290; www.chiiori.org; 209 Tsurui, Higashi-Iya; ⏱9am-6pm); payments must be made in cash. Because of the remote locations of Chiiori and the other houses, the Chiiori Trust strongly recommends that guests bring private vehicles.

pass the Tsurugi-jinja (Tsurugi Shrine) en route, which is close to a natural spring of drinkable water.

Just below the peak, **Tsurugi-san Chōjō Hutte** (剣山頂上ヒュッテ; ☎088-622-0633; http://tsurugisan-hutte.com; Tsurugi-san; r with/without meals ¥8000/4800) offers basic lodgings in this mountaintop sea of clouds. For more detailed information on ascending Tsurugi-san and Miune-san, check out Lonely Planet's *Hiking in Japan*.

ℹ Information

The **Miyoshi City Tourism Association** (三好市観光協会; ☎0883-76-0877; info@miyoshicity-kankokyokai.or.jp; 1810-18 Sarada, Ikeda-chō; ⏱9am-6pm) is an excellent place to get your bearings. Located right outside the JR Awa-Ikeda Station, it offers a plethora of English-language maps, pamphlets and public transport schedules for the Iya Valley, and there's usually an English speaker on duty.

ℹ Getting There & Around

Access to the area is via Ōboke Station, reached by limited-express train from Takamatsu (¥2990) or Tokushima (¥3280) with a change at Awa-Ikeda, or from Kōchi (¥2460). From Honshū, Nanpū limited-express trains depart hourly from Okayama (¥4020, 1¾ hours); Okayama is on the Sanyō Shinkansen line.

WORTH A TRIP

ALL DOLLED UP

If you're travelling along Rte 439, it's not a matter of 'blink and you'll miss it,' but blink, and blink again, because you may have a hard time believing your eyes when you hit **Nagoro** (Nagoro Scarecrow Village; 名頃かかしの里; 12km west of Oku Iya Ni-jū Kazura-bashi). Those 'people' – waiting at the bus stop, gossiping on a porch, toiling in the fields – are not people at all, but life-sized scarecrow-type dolls made by resident Ayano Tsukimi as a way of memorialising former inhabitants of her hometown. The figures are surprisingly lifelike from afar and strikingly expressive up close, their postures and faces each uniquely individual. Equal parts eerie and sweet, the dolls create a surreal tableau amid the quiet river valley.

For a look into the village, check out the beautiful short film *Valley of Dolls* (http://vimeo.com/92453765), created by a German filmmaker who visited with Ayano-san.

Getting around the valley itself involves some planning, because Iya's sights are widespread, and public transport is sporadic at the best of times. Four buses per day travel between Ōboke and Iya (¥660, 40 minutes). **Ōboke Taxi** (☎0883-84-1225) is one of several companies filling the gaps in the bus schedule.

The best way to explore the region is with your own wheels; you will thank the Daishi for the freedom and flexibility a car offers here. Rental cars are available in Shikoku's larger cities.

SOUTHERN TOKUSHIMA PREFECTURE 徳島県南部

The slow-paced highway running south from Tokushima-shi (Tokushima City) passes through prosperous little agricultural towns fronted by lazy surf beaches and marine industry machinery, and is flanked by hidden temples and spectacular rocky bluffs.

The JR Mugi line runs down the coast as far as Kaifu, just short of the border. From Kaifu, the private Asa Kaigan railway runs two stops further to Kannoura, just across the border. From here, you can continue by bus to the cape at Muroto-misaki and on to Kōchi city. Coming the other way, trains run from Kōchi as far as Nahari – but you'll have to rely on buses to get you around the cape.

Hiwasa 日和佐

☎0884

The major attraction in the small coastal town of Hiwasa is **Yakuō-ji** (薬王寺), Temple 23, and the last temple in Tokushima Prefecture. Yakuō-ji dates back to the year 726, and is famous as a *yakuyoke no tera* (a temple with special powers to ward off ill fortune during unlucky years). The unluckiest age for men is 42; for women, 33 is the one to watch out for. Kōbō Daishi is said to have visited in 815, the year of his own 42nd birthday. The long set of stone steps leading up to the main temple building comes in two stages: 33 steps for the women, followed by another 42 for the men. The tradition is for pilgrims to put a coin on each step – when it's busy, you may find the steps practically overflowing with ¥1 coins. Make your way to the pagoda at the top, and fork over ¥100 to view the basement gallery – to see the (figuratively) dark artwork of this underworld, you'll need to creep along the wall of a (literally) pitch-dark hall.

Road-weary pilgrims will find refreshment at the rest stop in the middle of town, which, in addition to the usual food stalls, immaculate restrooms and small market, also has a free *ashi-yu* (foot bath).

About 1.5km from the centre of town is the beach of **Ōhama** (大浜), a long stretch of sand where sea turtles come to lay their eggs from May to August each year.

South to Muroto-misaki

A short train ride south from Hiwasa is the sleepy fishing town of **Mugi** (牟岐), where the winding streets of the old fishing port make an interesting stopover. A 45-minute (3km) walk along the coast past the fishing port is **Mollusc Mugi Shell Museum** (貝の資料館モラスコむぎ; ☎0884-72-2520; 198-1 Shimohamabe; admission ¥400; ⏲9am-4.30pm Tue-Sun), a mollusc-shaped structure on an idyllic beach – inside, there's an impressive collection of shells, as well as live tropical specimens including moray eels and nautilus. There is an old Hachiman shrine in the centre of the town, and boats run out to the island of Teba-jima (出羽島).

Blue Marine (ブルーマリン; ☎0884-76-3100, 0884-76-1401; www.kaiyo-kankou.jp/index.php/marine-home; 28-45 Takegashima; cruises ¥1800, guided kayaking trips ¥2500-3000; ⏱8am-5pm Wed-Mon) operates glass-bottomed boat tours around Takegashima island near Shishikui, as well as guided sea-kayaking tours.

Sleeping & Eating

There are plenty of attractive places to stay along the coast at Kannoura, Shishikui and Ikumi.

Minshuku Ikumi MINSHUKU ¥
(民宿いくみ; ☎0887-24-3838; www.ikumiten.com; 7-1 Ikumi; r per person with breakfast ¥4400; P 📶) This cosy, family-run *minshuku* sits right alongside the highway in Ikumi. It's a popular surfer's choice, thanks to the well-presented rooms and the helpful, knowledgable owner, Ten.

South Shore INN ¥
(サウスショア; ☎0887-29-3211; www.southshore-ikumi.com; 12-10 Ikumi; r per person with/without meals ¥7250/3800; P 📶 🏊) A sunny, simple inn with shared bathrooms, South Shore sits about a block from the beach in Ikumi and has a relaxed Hawaiian-esque vibe. The cute attached cafe and tiny pool area are convivial spots to hang out après-surf.

★ **Pension Shishikui** PENSION ¥¥
(ペンションししくい; ☎0884-76-2130; www.p-shishikui.com; 84-18 Akazome; per person with meals from ¥9250; P @ 👪) Perfect for families or romantic getaways, charming Pension Shishikui occupies a snug cove with a private crescent of beach (protected by a seawall). All rooms, whether in the main house or free-standing log cabins, have ocean views and private bathrooms. The English-speaking owner rents surfboards, kayaks and bikes, and the property includes a tennis court and two communal baths.

Consult the map on the website for its location, on the first road just south of Shishikui Bridge.

Ikumi White Beach Hotel HOTEL ¥¥
(生見ホワイトビーチホテル; ☎0887-29-3018; www.wbhotel.net; 575-11 Ikumi; s/d with breakfast ¥5200/8400; P) This clean, laid-back Ikumi beachfront hotel has Japanese- and Western-style rooms with big beach views. It also runs an inexpensive restaurant called **Olu-Olu** (オルオル; meals ¥800-1000; ⏱7am-2pm & 5-8pm), featuring a picture menu and shelves of Japanese surf mags.

Hotel Riviera HOTEL ¥¥¥
(ホテルリビエラ; ☎0884-76-3300; www.hotel-riviera.co.jp; 226-1 Aza Matsubara; per person with meals from ¥13,000; P 📶) In Shishikui, this large hotel features upmarket Western- and Japanese-style rooms. Nonguests can use the sea-view onsen (¥600; from 6.30am to 9am and 11am to 10pm).

Aunt Dinah CURRY ¥
(☎0887-29-2080; 24-107 Kawauchi, Tōyō-chō; meals ¥800-1500; ⏱10am-9pm Wed-Mon) Japanese country music and a range of curries are available at this old-timey spot near the main crossroad in Kannoura. House specialities include a filling Thai coconut curry for ¥1390.

SURFING TOKUSHIMA

Southern Tokushima is a surfer's paradise, with world-class river mouths, consistent barrels and relatively few surfers in the water. Despite the prevalence of concrete on the shoreline, this region has mostly gorgeous white-sand beaches and relaxed, friendly locals.

Surfboards are available for hire (around ¥3000 for 24 hours) at numerous places in the one-street beach-bum town of **Ikumi** (生見), where you'll find most of the best places to stay. If you're just here to surf for the day, parking will run you ¥1000. For money, there is a post office with an international ATM in Kaifu, and another in Kannoura.

Getting There & Away

Trains run as far south as Kannoura. There are also buses from Mugi to Kannoura (¥780, 45 minutes, 14 per day), stopping at Kaifu and Shishikui on the way. Seven buses a day run from Kannoura to Muroto-misaki, via Ikumi (¥1520, 40 minutes). Buses run as far as Aki (安芸; ¥2880, 2½ hours), where you can transfer to a train to Kōchi. On the last 40km to the cape, the road hugs the coast, hemmed in by mountains and sea.

KŌCHI PREFECTURE

The largest of Shikoku's four prefectures, Kōchi Prefecture spans the entire Pacific coastline between the two capes of Muroto-misaki and Ashizuri-misaki. Cut off from the rest of Japan by the mountains and sea, the province once known as Tosa was traditionally regarded as one of the wildest and most remote places in the country.

Although the trip through Tosa makes up more than a third of the pilgrimage, only 16 of the 88 Temples are located in the province. In fact, it's 84km from the last temple in Tokushima Prefecture at Hiwasa before you get to the first temple in Kōchi Prefecture at Muroto-misaki. The longest distance between temples is also in Kōchi: a crippling 87km from Temple 37 (岩本寺; Iwamoto-ji) in Kubokawa to Temple 38 (金剛福寺; Kongōfuku-ji) at Ashizuri-misaki.

Kōchi Prefecture is a good place for outdoor types. Whale-watching, rafting, hiking and camping are all options here. Kōchi Prefecture brims with scenic spots, especially along the Shimanto-gawa, one of the last undammed rivers in Japan.

Tokushima to Kōchi

Continuing further south, you'll pass more pretty fishing villages tucked away along a painfully slow-paced oceanside highway. It's a beautiful, desolate coastal drive, and all the more remarkable for its proximity to the bright lights of Kōchi.

Muroto-misaki 室戸岬

☎0887

Kōbō Daishi found enlightenment on this gorgeous, wild cape (Muroto-misaki; 室戸岬), and it's easy to ponder why as you reach the 'doorway to the land of the dead'. Visitors can explore Kōbō Daishi's rather murky bathing hole among the rock pools, and the Shinmeikutsu (神明窟), the cave where he once meditated.

A huge white statue of the saint stares out to sea just north of the cape. A kilometre or so around the bend, a winding road leads up to Temple 24, **Hotsumisaki-ji** (最御崎寺, also known as Higashi-dera), which was founded by Kōbō Daishi in the early 9th century. It's at the top of a steep hill directly above the point. Next to the temple, accommodation is available at the peaceful **shukubō** (☎0887-23-0024; Hotsumisaki-ji; r per person with/without meals ¥6500/4200), a modern building with spotless tatami rooms.

For something completely different, **Hoshino Resort Utoco Auberge & Spa** (星野リゾートウトコオーベルジュ＆スパ; ☎0887-22-1811, 050-3786-0022; www.utocods.co.jp; 6969-1 Muroto-misaki-chō; r per person with meals from ¥23,000; P ♨) is a remarkable concept hotel founded by the late cosmetics giant Uemura Shū. Pumping water from 1000m below the surface, the spa and resort aim to harness the restorative powers of mineral-rich, deep-sea water. The design is elegant and minimalist, each room a spacious retreat with sea-view bathtubs and beds precisely placed so that the occupant's gaze rests parallel to the horizon. A whole menu of massage and saltwater spa therapy is available, with day courses that include lunch and two deep-sea water treatments for ¥12,400. Utoco is on the shoreline, 100m before Daishi's statue and adjacent to another day spa with attached restaurant.

Several buses a day run west from the cape to Nahari or Aki (安芸; ¥1720, 1½ hours), where you can change to the JR line for a train to Kōchi (one hour). Trains between Aki and Kōchi take anywhere between 45 minutes and 1½ hours, depending on connections at Gomen (tickets cost between ¥1170 and ¥1490). There are also buses up the east coast to Kannoura and Mugi in Tokushima Prefecture.

Ryūga-dō 龍河洞

☎0887

Accessible by bus from Tosa-Yamada Station on the Dosan line is the limestone cave **Ryūga-dō** (龍河洞; ☎0887-53-2144; www.ryugadou.or.jp; 1424 Sakagawa, Tosa-Yamada; admission ¥1100; ⏲8:30am-5pm, to 4.30pm Dec-Feb). The cave has some interesting stalactites and stalagmites, and traces of prehistoric habitation. The route gets quite steep in places. Visitors on a standard ticket will see about 1km of the 4km cave. Advance reservations and an additional ¥1000 are required for the *bōken kōsu* (adventure course; 冒険コース), where you get to don helmet and overalls and follow a guide for a 90-minute exploration of the inner reaches of the cave.

There are five buses a day to Ryūga-dō from Tosa-Yamada Station (¥440, 20 minutes). Tosa-Yamada Station is 30 minutes from Kōchi by local train (¥360), or 15 minutes by *tokkyū* (limited-express train; ¥680).

Kōchi 高知

☎088 / POP 338,909

Kōchi is a smart, compact city with a deserved reputation for enjoying a good time. The castle here is largely undamaged, and remains a fine example of Japanese architecture. Excellent access to Ashizuri-misaki, Iya Valley and southern Tokushima, and easy day trips to caves, beaches and mountains make Kōchi a perfect base for travels around the island. Also claimed by Kōchi is a samurai of great national significance – during the Meiji Restoration, Sakamoto Ryōma was instrumental in bringing down the feudal government.

Sights & Activities

★Kōchi-jō CASTLE

(高知城; 1-2-1 Marunouchi; admission ¥400; 9am-5pm) Kōchi-jō is one of just a dozen castles in Japan to have survived with its original *tenshu-kaku* (keep) intact. The castle was originally built during the first decade of the 17th century by Yamanouchi Katsutoyo, who was appointed *daimyō* by Tokugawa Ieyasu after he fought on the victorious Tokugawa side in the Battle of Sekigahara in 1600. A major fire destroyed much of the original structure in 1727, and the castle was largely rebuilt between 1748 and 1753.

The castle was the product of an age of peace – it never came under attack, and for the remainder of the Tokugawa period it was more like a stately home than a military fortress.

Godaisan PARK

(五台山) Several kilometres east of the town centre is the mountain of Godaisan, where there are excellent views over the city from a **lookout point** (展望台). A short walk away at the top of the hill is **Chikurin-ji** (竹林寺), Temple 31. Descending the steps by the temple's Treasure House brings you to the entrance gates of the **Kōchi Prefectural Makino Botanical Garden** (高知県立牧野植物園; 088-882-2601; www.makino.or.jp; 4200-6 Godaisan; admission ¥720; 9am-5pm), a beautiful network of gardens and parkland featuring more than 3000 different plant species.

The main hall of Chikurin-ji was built by the second Tosa *daimyō,* Yamanouchi Tadayoshi, in 1644. The extensive grounds also feature a five-storey pagoda and thousands of statues of the Bodhisattva Jizō, guardian deity of children and travellers. The temple's **Treasure House** (宝物館; admission ¥400; 9am-5pm) hosts an impressive collection of Buddhist sculpture from the Heian and Kamakura periods; the same ticket gets you into the lovely late-Kamakura-period garden opposite.

The My-Yū bus (p652) stops at Godaisan, and you can also purchase a Godaisan one-day pass (¥300 for foreigners showing a passport upon purchase).

Katsura-hama BEACH

(桂浜) Katsura-hama is a popular beach 13km south of central Kōchi at the point where Kōchi's harbour empties out into the bay. Unfortunately, strong currents prohibit swimming, but it's a lovely spot to stroll, with a small shrine perched on an oceanside promontory. Just before the beach itself is **Sakamoto Ryōma Memorial Museum** (坂本龍馬記念館; 088-841-0001; www.ryoma-kinenkan.jp; 830 Urado-shiroyama; admission ¥500; 9am-5pm), with exhibits dedicated to the life of a local hero who was instrumental in bringing about the Meiji Restoration in the 1860s.

Born in Kōchi in 1835, Ryōma brought about the alliance between the Satsuma (modern Kagoshima) and Chōshū (Yamaguchi) domains that eventually brought down the Tokugawa shogunate. He was killed in Kyoto in 1867, aged 32.

Public buses run to Katsura-hama from Kōchi Station (¥690, 35 minutes, six daily) and Harimaya-bashi (¥620, 25 minutes, frequent). The My-Yū bus runs as far as Katsura-hama before heading back to Kōchi.

Sunday Market MARKET

(日曜市; 5am-6pm Sun Apr-Sep, 6am-5pm Sun Oct-Mar) Our favourite street market in Shikoku is 300 years old, and takes place every Sunday along the main road leading to the castle. Colourful stalls sell fresh produce, tonics and tinctures, knives, flowers, garden stones and wooden antiques.

Ino Japanese Paper Museum MUSEUM

(いの町紙の博物館; 088-893-0886; 110-1 Saiwai-chō, Ino-chō; admission ¥500; 9am-5pm Tue-Sun) Make your own Japanese paper for ¥300 at this museum, about 10km west of Kōchi. From the Harimaya-bashi tram stop, take a tram to the last stop in Ino. From there, walk westward until the next main intersection, turn right and find the museum 100m ahead.

Festivals

Kōchi's lively **Yosakoi Matsuri** (よさこい祭り; Yosakoi Festival) on 10 and 11 August perfectly complements Tokushima's Awa-odori Matsuri (12 to 15 August). There's a night-before event on 9 August and a

Kōchi

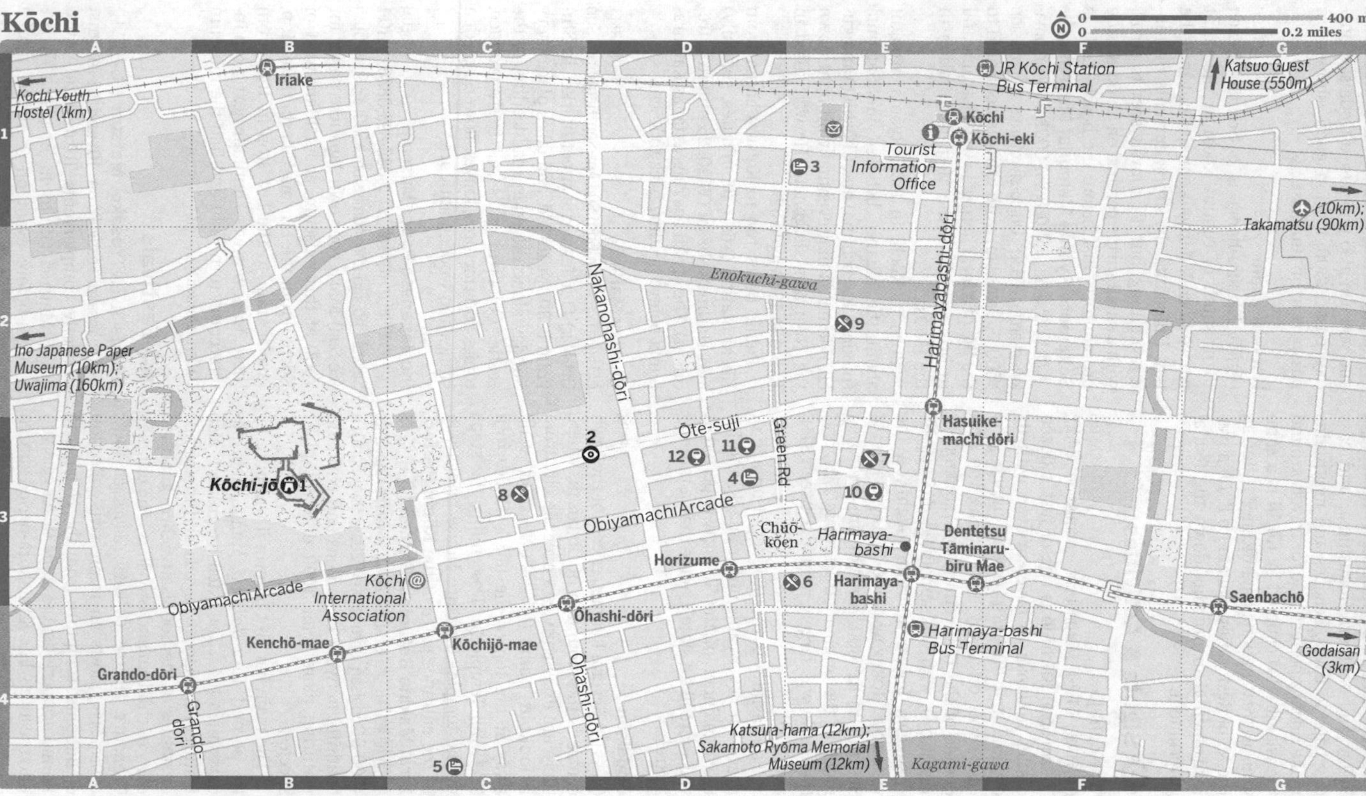
0 400 m
0 0.2 miles
Kochi Youth Hostel (1km)
Iriake
JR Kōchi Station Bus Terminal
Katsuo Guest House (550m)
Kōchi
Kōchi-eki
Tourist Information Office
3
(10km); Takamatsu (90km)
Enokuchi-gawa
Harimayabashi-dōri
9
Ino Japanese Paper Museum (10km); Uwajima (160km)
Nakanohashi-dōri
Hasuike-machi dōri
Ōte-suji
2
11
12
Green Rd
7
4
10
Kōchi-jō 1
8
Obiyamachi Arcade
Chūō-kōen
Harimaya-bashi
Dentetsu Tāminaru-biru Mae
Horizume
6
Harimaya-bashi
Kōchi @ International Association
Obiyamachi Arcade
Saenbachō
Ōhashi-dōri
Harimaya-bashi Bus Terminal
Kenchō-mae
Kōchijō-mae
Godaisan (3km)
Grando-dōri
Grando-dōri
Ōhashi-dōri
Katsura-hama (12km); Sakamoto Ryōma Memorial Museum (12km)
5
Kagami-gawa

Kōchi

Top Sights

Sights

Sleeping

Eating

Drinking & Nightlife

night-after effort on 12 August, but 10 and 11 August are the big days.

Sleeping

★Kochi Youth Hostel HOSTEL ¥

(高知ユースホステル; ☎088-823-0858; www.kyh-sakenokuni.com; 4-5 Fukuigashi-machi; dm/s ¥2500/3000; P⊖@🛜) Sitting along a canal near Engyōjiguchi (円行寺口) Station, this immaculate wood-panelled hostel has simple, comfortable rooms and a welcoming, homely vibe. Spring for the ¥400 breakfast, as they are excellent value. The friendly, English-speaking host Kondo Tomio is a former sake company rep and offers sake sampling courses for ¥500. Find detailed directions on the website.

Katsuo Guest House GUESTHOUSE ¥¥

(かつおゲストハウス; ☎070-5352-1167; 4-7-28 Hijima-chō; dm/s/d ¥2500/3500/7000; P⊖🛜) Good things come in small packages, as is the case with Katsuo Guest House. In a residential Kōchi neighbourhood, this intimate spot (there's one dorm room and one private) is a haven for those yearning for impromptu jams on the house guitar or djembe, a DIY meal in the communal kitchen and artistic nods to local landmarks adorning the shared bathroom.

Petit Hotel BUSINESS HOTEL ¥¥

(プチホテル高知; ☎088-826-8156; www.phk.jp; 1-8-13 Kitahon-machi; s/d from ¥6000/8000; P⊖@🛜) This excellent business hotel near Kōchi Station is an astute alternative to the larger chains. Service is efficient and friendly, and the rooms are reasonably spacious, particularly the sparkling clean bathrooms.

Richmond Hotel HOTEL ¥¥

(リッチモンドホテル高知; ☎088-820-1122; www.richmondhotel.jp/en/kochi; 9-4 Obiyamachi; s/d from ¥7600/12,200; P⊖@🛜) Kōchi's most swish business hotel has the spotless, modern rooms and professional service expected of accommodation of this class, plus it's located just off the main shopping arcade in the heart of the city. Parking (¥700 per day) is a short distance off-site, but the hotel's convenient placement puts you in the middle of dining, nightlife and city walkability.

Sansuien HOTEL ¥¥

(三翠園; ☎088-822-0131; www.sansuien.co.jp; 1-3-35 Takajō-machi; r per person with breakfast from ¥6500; P⊖@) Three blocks south of the castle along Kenchō-mae Dōri is this classy multistorey hotel with luxurious onsen baths and a garden incorporating a series of buildings that once formed part of the *daimyō's* residence. The Japanese tatami rooms far outweigh their Western counterparts for both size and comfort. Nonguests can use the baths from 10am to 4pm (¥900).

Eating

Kōchi's main entertainment district is in the area around the Obiyamachi Arcade and the Harimaya-bashi junction where the tramlines meet. Local specialities include *katsuo tataki* (lightly seared bonito fish). After a night of drinking, head to Green Rd, a small street lined till late with open-air noodle stalls.

★Hirome Ichiba JAPANESE ¥

(ひろめ市場; ☎088-822-5287; 2-3-1 Obiyamachi; dishes ¥300-900; ⏲8am-11pm, from 7am Sun; 📄) Some hundred or so mini-restaurants specialising in everything from *gomoku rāmen* (seafood noodles) to *tako-yaki* (octopus balls) surround communal tables; this is the hub of Kōchi's cheap eats scene. On weekends, it positively heaves with young people drinking hard and happy. It's at the end of the main arcade, just before the castle.

Habotan IZAKAYA ¥

(葉牡丹; ☎088-823-8686; 2-21 Sakai-machi; dishes ¥150-1100; ⊙11am-11pm) Red lanterns mark out this locals' *izakaya* (pub-eatery) that opens at the shockingly early hour of 11am. The food is under glass on the counter, so you can point at what you'd like to order. *Sashimi moriawase* (a selection of sashimi) is ¥1050. Local booze includes Tosa-tsuru sake and Dabada Hiburi, a *shōchū* (distilled grain liquor) made from chestnuts.

Hakobe OKONOMIYAKI ¥

(はこべ; ☎088-823-0084; 1-2-5 Obiyamachi; dishes ¥650-1000; ⊙11am-midnight) This is one of the few remaining cook-it-yourself *okonomiyaki* joints in Kōchi serving cheap and cheerful Japanese pancakes (¥650), with good English spoken by the waiters. The 'mix' of *ika* (squid) and *ebi* (shrimp) and *tori* (chicken) is heavenly. Other alternatives include *buta* (pork) and *yasai* (vegetables). It's slap bang in the heart of the arcade.

Uofuku IZAKAYA ¥¥

(魚福; ☎088-824-1129; 2-13 Nijūdai-chō; dishes ¥600-1500; ⊙5.30-11pm Mon-Sat) Uofuku is a fabulous curb-side *izakaya* on a quiet backstreet behind the arcade. Fish is the order of the day, handpicked from the tank by the door. The menu is a mess of kanji; try the *katsuo tataki* (around ¥1200) or ask for an *osusume* (recommendation). This is a good place for adventurous eaters.

If you're feeling brave, try the *shutō* – the pickled and fermented innards of the bonito fish (¥450), which locals regard as a delicacy.

Drinking & Nightlife

Amontillado PUB

(アモンティラード; ☎088-875-0899; 1-1-17 Obiyamachi; ⊙5pm-1am) When you're *izakaya*'d out and crave fish-and-chips with a pint of Guinness (¥900), pop into this Irish pub off Obiyamachi Arcade.

Boston Cafe Bar BAR

(ボストンカフェ; ☎088-875-7730; 1-7-9 Ōte-suji; ⊙5.30pm-2am, later on Sat & Sun) Across the alley from the backside of the Richmond Hotel, this is a friendly, American-themed neighbourhood bar.

Love Jamaican CLUB

(☎088-872-0447; 3rd fl, 1-5-5 Obiyamachi; ⊙7pm-3am) This fully legit reggae and hip-hop club is a hive of after-hours mayhem thanks to the excellent sound system, generous drink deals and manicured young crowd.

Information

A left-luggage office is in the station, and international ATMs are available at the post office down the street from the station.

Kōchi International Association (高知県国際交流協会; ☎088-875-0022; www.kochi-kia.or.jp; 2nd fl, 4-1-37 Honmachi; ⊙8.30am-5.15pm Mon-Sat, closed Sat in Aug) Offers free internet access, a library and English newspapers.

Tourist Information Office (高知観光案内所; ☎088-826-3337; Kita Honmachi; ⊙9am-5pm, accommodation info 8.30am-7.30pm) The helpful tourist information pavilion in front of JR Kōchi Station provides English-language maps and Kōchi mini-guidebooks.

Getting There & Around

TO/FROM THE AIRPORT

Kōchi's Ryōma airport, about 10km east of the city, is accessible by bus (¥720, 40 minutes) from the station. There are daily flights to/from Tokyo, Osaka and Fukuoka.

BUS

The **My-Yū bus** (MY遊バス; 1-day/2-day pass ¥1000/1600) runs to Godaisan and Katsurahama from Kōchi Station; show a foreign passport upon purchase and you'll get it at half price.

TRAIN

Kōchi is on the JR Dosan line, and is connected to Takamatsu (*tokkyū* ¥4580, two hours and 10 minutes) via Awa-Ikeda (*tokkyū* ¥2820, 70 minutes). Trains also run west to Kubokawa (*tokkyū* ¥2640, one hour), where you can change for Shimanto-shi (formerly known as Nakamura; *tokkyū* ¥4140).

TRAM

Kōchi's colourful tram service (¥200 per trip) has been running since 1904. There are two lines: the north–south line from the station intersects with the east–west tram route at the Harimaya-bashi (はりまや橋) junction. Pay when you get off, and ask for a *norikae-ken* (transfer ticket) if you have to change lines.

Kōchi to Ashizuri-misaki

The quiet stretch of coast between Kōchi and Ashizuri-misaki passes towns of traditionally tiled rooftops adorned with solar panels, and busy working harbours. Though Tosa-wan (Tosa Bay) was once a major whaling centre, nowadays whale-watching is the going attraction. Other diversions of the region include sea-kayaking along the Shimanto-gawa (one of the last free-flowing

WORTH A TRIP

OHKINOHAMA

About 40 minutes south of Shimanto City, on the bus to Ashizuri-misaki, is **Ohkinohama** (大岐の浜), Shikoku's most magnificent sandy white beach. The only souls to frequent this unspoilt 2km stretch are the pick of the region's surfers, some egg-laying turtles and the odd, grinning clam diver. Facing east means you can watch the sun and moon rise from your beach towel, and warm currents ensure swimming is possible year-round. If you're just sunning and surfing for the day, stop for an udon lunch at **Hōbai** (朋輩; ☎0880-83-6700; udon ¥400-700; ⊙11.30am-4pm Mon-Fri, 11am-sellout Sat & Sun), a little roadside shop whose exterior has been pieced together out of driftwood.

Most travellers do shoot through en route to the cape, but a stay at the serene, eco-rustic **Kaiyu Inn** (海癒; ☎0880-82-8500; www.kaiyu-inn.jp; 2777-12 Ohki; s ¥7000-23,000, each additional person ¥2500; P ⊖ ☎ ♿) is itself worth the visit to Shikoku. The accomplished owner, Mitsu, studied agriculture in the USA before serving a hotel apprenticeship in Bali. Here he has redesigned a white concrete 1960s conference centre into a sublime yet affordable contemporary retreat. Each self-contained studio apartment has been designed by a different emerging Japanese architect and, coupled with Mitsu's keen aesthetical eye and extensive designer furniture collection, has created spaces worthy of magazine covers, each with Pacific Ocean views. The communal dinners (not included in room rates) are inventive, super-fresh and organic, and feature famed local clams, the catch of the day, and loads of fruits and vegetables. Dinners must be reserved in advance.

While the Kaiyu concept is about slowing down and savouring the area's rivers and ocean (long-term is the norm here), visitors are also welcome for one-night stays and day visits to the boiler-fired **onsen** (guests/nonguests ¥700/950; ⊙1-7pm Wed-Mon) – advance reservations required. This eco-friendly spa is itself a day-trip destination, with tranquil views of Ohkinohama from the stylish baths, featuring imported heat-conducive stone and adjustable temperature gauges. Never has the word 'wellness' felt so apt.

rivers in Japan), surfing, beach-combing, exploring the rugged scenery and Temple 38 on the pilgrimage route.

The train line from Kōchi parts at Wakai. The JR Yodo line heads northwest through the mountains to Uwajima in Ehime-ken, while the private Tosa-Kuroshio line heads around to Shimanto City (formerly known as Nakamura) and ends at Sukumo. There is also a bus service to Ashizuri-misaki from Nakamura Station (¥1930, one hour and 45 minutes, nine daily).

Activities

Ōgata Whale Watching WHALE-WATCHING
(大方ホエールウォッチング; ☎0880-43-1058; http://nitarikujira.com; adult/child ¥5000/1000; ⊙8.30am-5pm) In the town of Kuroshio-machi, not far from Shimanto City, Ōgata Whale Watching runs three four-hour trips daily between late April and October, leaving at 8am, 10am and noon. Tosa Irino and Tosa Kamikawaguchi are the closest stations to Kuroshio-machi on the Tosa-Kuroshio railway line.

Sleeping

Kawarakko CAMPGROUND ¥
(かわらっこ; ☎0880-31-8400; www.kawarakko.com; campsite from ¥3300) A neatly maintained riverside campground run by an adventure company. Canoes, mountain bikes and even tents are available to hire should you fancy a spontaneous night under the stars.

Shimanto City 四万十市

☎0880 / POP 35,655

Shimanto, formerly called **Nakamura** (中村), is a good place to organise trips on the beautiful **Shimanto-gawa** (四万十川). Staff at the **tourist information office** (四万十市観光協会; ☎0880-35-4171; www.shimanto-kankou.com; 383-15 Uyama; ⊙8:30am-5.30pm), located at the crossroads of Routes 56 and 439, can provide information on kayaking and canoe trips, and camping and outdoor activities. A number of companies offer **river cruises** on traditional fishing boats called Yakata-bune (¥2000 for 50 minutes) and kayak rental (half-day/full day from ¥3500/5000); the tourist information office has a full list. Bike rental is available here too (per five hours/full day ¥600/1000), allowing you to scoot out to the river under your own steam.

Conveniently located in front of the station but otherwise unremarkable, the **Nakamura Dai-ichi Hotel** (中村第一ホテル; ☎0880-34-7211; 5-15 Ekimae-chō; s/d ¥5300/9800) works in a pinch. A post office with international ATM is a short walk away.

Ashizuri-misaki 足摺岬

☎0880

Like Muroto-misaki, Ashizuri-misaki (Ashizuri Cape; 足摺岬) is a rugged, picturesque promontory that's famous for its otherworldly appearance and violent weather.

On a bluff at Ashizuri-misaki there's an imposing statue of locally born hero John Manjirō. Born in 1836 as Nakahama Manjirō, the young fisherman was swept onto the desolate shores of Tori-shima, 600km from Tokyo Bay, in 1841. Five months later, he and his shipmates were rescued by a US whaler passing by, and granted safe passage to Hawaii. After moving to Massachusetts and learning English, 'John' finally returned to Japan and later played a leading role in diplomatic negotiations with the USA and other countries at the end of the Tokugawa period.

Ashizuri-misaki is also home to Temple 38, **Kongōfuku-ji** (金剛福寺), whose setting has breathtaking views of the promontory and the Pacific Ocean. A short walk back towards civilisation is **Ashizuri Youth Hostel** (足摺ユースホステル; ☎0880-88-0324; dm ¥3500), run by a cute older couple who provide large, well-cared-for tatami rooms. With advance notice meals are available. More upmarket is **Ashizuri Kokusai Hotel** (足摺国際ホテル; ☎0880-88-0201; www.ashizuri.co.jp; r per person with meals from ¥14,040), which has onsen baths overlooking the sea. It's located along the main road into town.

EHIME PREFECTURE

Occupying the western region of Shikoku, Ehime Prefecture (愛媛県) has the largest number of pilgrimage temples – 27 of them, to be precise. Like Tosa, the southern part of the prefecture has always been considered wild and remote; by the time pilgrims arrive in Shikoku's largest city, Matsuyama, they know that the hard work has been done. There are large clusters of temples around Matsuyama and the Shimanami Kaidō bridge system, which links Shikoku with Honshū and makes for a spectacular bike ride.

Prefectural highlights are the immaculately preserved feudal castle and historic Dōgo Onsen in Matsuyama, and the sacred peak of Ishizuchi-san (1982m), the tallest mountain in western Japan.

Uwajima 宇和島

☎0895 / POP 83,070

An unhurried castle town, Uwajima draws a steady trickle of titillated travellers to its academically inclined sex museum and attached Shintō fertility shrine. Though most travellers bypass Uwajima en route to Matsuyama, the town makes a pleasant stop and retains some noteworthy traditions, such as pearl farming, terraced agriculture and bloodless bullfighting.

Sights & Activities

Taga-jinja & Sex Museum SHINTO SHRINE

(多賀神社 & 凸凹神堂; ☎0895-22-3444; www3.ocn.ne.jp/~dekoboko; admission ¥800; ⏲8am-5pm) Once upon a time, many Shintō shrines had a connection to fertility rites. Of those that remain, Taga-jinja is one of the best known. The grounds of the shrine are strewn with tree-trunk phalluses and numerous statues and stone carvings. Inside, the museum is packed with anthropological erotica from all corners of the procreating world – you can pay for the privilege of photographing it with a scant ¥20,000.

Uwajima-jō CASTLE

(宇和島城; 1 Marunouchi; admission ¥200; ⏲9am-4pm) Dating from 1601, Uwajima-jō is a small three-storey castle on an 80m-high hill in the centre of town. The present structure was rebuilt in 1666 by the *daimyō* Date Munetoshi. The *donjon* (main keep) is one of only 12 originals left in Japan; there is nothing much to see inside. The surrounding park, **Shiroyama-kōen** (城山公園), is open from sunrise to sunset, and is a pleasant place for a stroll.

Date Museum MUSEUM

(伊達博物館; 9-14 Goten-machi; admission ¥500; ⏲9am-5pm Tue-Sun) The well-presented exhibits at the excellent Date Museum are dedicated to the Date family, who ruled Uwajima from the castle for 250 years dur-

Uwajima

Uwajima

Sights

1 Date Museum ... A4
2 Municipal Bullfighting Ring ... D1
3 Shiroyama-kōen ... B3
4 Taga-jinja & Sex Museum ... A1
5 Uwajima-jō ... B3

Sleeping

6 Kiya Ryokan ... C4
7 Uwajima Oriental Hotel ... B1

Eating

8 Boulangerie Riz ... B2
9 Cafe Penguin Hotel ... C3
10 Hozumi-tei ... B2
11 Wabisuke ... B2

ing the Tokugawa period. The explanations are mostly in Japanese, but a lot of the stuff on display – swords, armour, palanquins and lacquerware – is pretty self-explanatory.

Temples 41-42 BUDDHIST TEMPLE

A great way to get a taste of the 88 Temple pilgrimage without having to slog it out along busy main roads is to follow this mini-circuit that starts and ends in Uwajima. This walk between Temple 42, Butsumoku-ji (仏木寺) and Temple 41 Ryūkō-ji (龍光寺), covers a little over 5km.

Take a bus from Uwajima Station direct to Temple 42, Butsumoku-ji. After admiring the thatched bell-house and the statues of the seven gods of good fortune, follow the clearly marked *henro* trail back through picturesque farming villages and rice paddies to Temple 41, Ryūkō-ji. Here, a steep stone staircase leads up to a pleasant temple and shrine overlooking the fields. From outside Ryūkō-ji there are signs to Muden Station (務田駅), a 15-minute (800m) walk away. From here, you can catch a train or bus back to Uwajima.

Municipal Bullfighting Ring BULLFIGHTING RING
(宇和島市営闘牛場; admission ¥3000) *Tōgyū* (闘牛) is probably best described as a type of bovine sumo. In these bloodless 'wrestling' matches, victory is achieved when one animal forces the other to its knees, or when one turns tail and flees from the ring. Fights are held on 2 January, the first Sunday of April, 24 July, 14 August and the fourth Sunday of October. Directions to the bullfighting ring are available at the tourist information office.

★**Forest Canyon** ADVENTURE SPORTS
(フォレストキャニオン; ☎0895-42-0063, 0895-49-6663; http://nametoko.net; Meguro, Matsuno-chō; canyoning full day/half day ¥10,500/8500) If temple-viewing and hiking aren't meeting your adrenaline requirements, try canyoning in the beautiful Nametoko Valley (an easy day trip from Uwajima). Forest Canyon is dedicated to safety, with experienced guides, so guests can freely leap into deep pools, climb up some waterfalls, abseil down others and swoosh down natural slides (including one that's 40m long!) created by the river.

All equipment – including wetsuit, helmet and life jacket – is included in the rate.

Sleeping & Eating

Mori-no-Yado Uwajima Youth Hostel HOSTEL ¥
(森の宿うわじまユースホステル; ☎0895-22-7177; www2.odn.ne.jp/~cfm91130/eigo.htm; 166-11 Daichojioku Hinoe; dm/s/tw ¥2500/3600/7200; P ⊖ @) This friendly, low-key hostel is hidden away in the forest 2.5km uphill from the station. The place is spotless, the bike rentals are free and the setting is serene. Look for the directions to Uwatsuhiko-jinja (English sign) and the small blue-and-yellow 'YH' signs leading to a small path up to the hostel. Call ahead for reservations, as the hostel occasionally closes. Prices given here are the foreign traveller special rates.

Uwajima Oriental Hotel BUSINESS HOTEL ¥¥
(宇和島オリエンタルホテル; ☎0895-23-2828; www.oriental-web.co.jp/uwajima; 16-10 Tsurushima-chō; s/d ¥5800/10,500; P @) North of the station, this friendly business hotel has clean, typically small rooms with unobstructed views of the city from the upper floors. Perks include a pillow menu, a *konbini* (convenience store) on the 1st floor, free parking and bike rentals.

★**Kiya Ryokan** RYOKAN ¥¥¥
(木屋旅館; ☎0895-22-0101; http://kiyaryokan.com; 2-8-2 Honmachiōte; ryokan rental per night ¥21,600, plus ¥5400 per person, incl breakfast) A rare opportunity to rent an entire house where literary greats have stayed, Kiya Ryokan offers a compelling reason for an Uwajima stop. Though not a traditional ryokan experience – no in-house staff nor elaborate *kaiseki* (Japanese haute cuisine) dinners – it is uniquely modern and appealing. Best enjoyed and most economical for groups (the house sleeps up to eight).

A glass floor between the entry and a second-storey room creates an unexpected, harmonious view of the house's architectural lines. Coloured LED lights and remote-controlled screens allow guests to create their own ambience. The house surrounds an inner courtyard garden, and bathing facilities are a beautifully integrated combination of modern and traditional. Even if you don't stay, it's worth a stop to browse its tiny, well-curated boutique and get the lowdown on current happenings around town.

Boulangerie Riz BAKERY ¥
(ブランジュリーリズ; ☎0895-22-8800; 1-4-22 Ebisu-machi; pastries ¥50-250; ⏲9am-4pm Fri-Wed) Heavenly, light pastries and breads made with rice flour (50% – not gluten-free) are the house speciality at this bakery along the Kisaiya Road (きさいやロード) shopping arcade. Enjoy a simple breakfast at the counter while watching the bakers expertly turning out handmade treats, such as croissants flecked with local citrus, and rolled *matcha* (powdered green tea) cake.

Cafe Penguin Hotel ASIAN ¥
(カフェぺんぎんほてる; ☎0895-23-3007; 2-2-1 Chūō-chō; lunch set ¥900; ⏲11am-5pm) Penguin…no, hotel…no, cafe…yes! This cosy lunch spot offers lovingly prepared meals of pan-Asian cuisine, from bulgogi to Thai curry, served in a salubriously airy and peaceful environment. There's an outdoor terrace, a room outfitted with kids' toys and books, and yet another room with a more grownup but equally relaxed feel.

Wabisuke SEAFOOD ¥¥
(和日輔; ☎0895-24-0028; 1-2-6 Ebisu-machi; dishes ¥1000-1500; ⏲11am-10pm Thu-Tue) This restaurant, washed by the gentle sounds of running water, is an elegant spot to try the local *tai* (sea bream) specialities, available here as a *tai-meshi gozen* (sea bream set

course; ¥1880). There is a picture menu, and the young staff speak some English.

Hozumi-tei IZAKAYA ¥¥
(ほづみ亭; ☎0895-25-6590; 2-3-8 Shinmachi; dishes ¥750-1500; ⏲11am-1.30pm & 5-10.30pm, closed some Sun) This formal *izakaya* has been serving up local food for over 70 years. If you request '*Kyōdo ryōri*' (郷土料理) – meaning 'local cuisine' – the friendly owner should unlock his secrets. There's usually an English-speaker on hand to interpret the menu, but we highly recommend the *tai-meishi* course (¥2100), as this allows you to sample several interesting local dishes.

ℹ Information

There are international ATMs at the post office across from the station.

Tourist Information Office (宇和島市観光協会; ☎0895-22-3934; ⏲9am-6pm) At Kisaiya Hiroba at the port; find a more conveniently located information booth (☎0895-23-5530; ⏲9am-6pm) at the JR station.

ℹ Getting There & Around

Uwajima is on the JR Yosan line, and can be reached from Matsuyama (*tokkyū* ¥2990, 1½ hours) via Uchiko (*tokkyū* ¥2270, one hour). You can hire bicycles (per hour ¥100; h9:30am-5pm) at the station, in the corner office on the left after you exit the building.

Uwajima to Matsuyama

Several worthwhile stops along the western coast include the unhurried and unpretentiously bewitching Ōzu, with its recently reconstructed castle, and Uchiko, a town that grew rich on wax in the 19th century and is home to an elegant historic district. From Uwajima, the JR Yodo line runs to Kubokawa and Kōchi; the JR Yosan line heads north to Matsuyama.

Yawatahama 八幡浜

☎0894 / POP 37,380

Throughout the centuries, pilgrims from Kyūshū traditionally arrived in Yawatahama by ferry, and then started and ended their pilgrimage at nearby Temple 43 – **Meiseki-ji** (明石寺).

Take the **Uwajima Unyu Ferry** (宇和島運輸フェリー; ☎0894-23-2536; www.uwajimaunyu.co.jp) from Yawatahama to Beppu (¥3100, three hours, six daily) and Usuki (¥2310, 2½ hours, six or seven daily) on Kyūshū. Yawatahama port is a five-minute bus ride (¥150) or taxi ride (around ¥630); because buses are so infrequent, the 20-minute (1.5km) walk from Yawatahama Station is often faster than waiting for a bus. To walk there, turn left out of the station and head straight until you hit the sea.

If you need to stay overnight, **Super Hotel Yawatahama** (スーパーホテル八幡浜; ☎0894-20-9000; www.superhotel.co.jp; 1460-123 Chiyoda-machi; s/d incl breakfast ¥6150/8200; P⊝☎), just off the main north–south thoroughfare, is the best choice.

Ōzu 大洲

☎0893 / POP 46,911

On the Yosan line northeast of Yawatahama is Ōzu, where traditional **ukai** (鵜飼; cormorant river fishing) takes place on the Hiji-kawa from 1 June to 20 September. **Sightseeing boats** (☎0893-57-6655; per person noon/night tour ¥4000/6000; ⏲noon or 6pm) follow the fishing boats down the river as the cormorants catch fish. Reservations are required.

Sights

Ōzu-jō CASTLE
(大洲城; ☎0893-24-1146; 903 Ōzu; admission ¥500, joint ticket with Garyū-sansō ¥800; ⏲9am-5pm) One of Japan's most authentically reconstructed castles, Ōzu-jō and its outlying buildings are original survivors from the Edo period. The castle is an impressive sight above the river, but exploring its interior is particularly fascinating – cross-sections of its roof construction, displays of armour and a scale model of the castle's bones are displayed in pristine condition.

Garyū-sansō GARDENS
(臥龍山荘; ☎0893-24-3759; 411-2 Ōzu; admission ¥500, joint ticket with Ōzu-jō ¥800; ⏲9am-5pm) Across town from Ōzu-jō, Garyū-sansō is an elegant Meiji-period teahouse and garden in an idyllic spot overlooking the river. On Sundays from April to October, you can partake in the tea ceremony (¥400; from 10am to 4pm).

Sleeping

Ōzu Kyōdokan Youth Hostel HOSTEL ¥
(大洲郷土館ユースホステル; ☎0893-24-2258; http://homepage3.nifty.com/ozuyh; Sannomaru; dm per person ¥3200) A delightful place to stay at the foot of Ōzu-jō, with a modernist garden below it. The tatami rooms are fit for

an army, and the hostel doubles as a museum, featuring interesting curios and antique ceramics from the town's boom years as a Tokugawa-period castle town.

Uchiko 内子

0893 / POP 18,045

Uchiko is undergoing a mini-renaissance, with a growing number of domestic travellers taking interest in this attractive town with its prosperous past. During the late Edo and early Meiji periods Uchiko boomed as a major producer of wax, resulting in a number of exquisite houses that still stand today along a street called Yōkaichi.

Sights

You can buy a combined ticket (¥900) for admission to Uchiko-za, the Museum of Commerce & Domestic Life and the Japanese Wax Museum, available for purchase at any of the three sights. It's also possible to line up an English-speaking volunteer guide if you book ahead at www.we-love-uchiko.jp.

Uchiko-za THEATRE

(内子座; 0893-44-2840; 1515 Uchiko; admission ¥400; 9am-4.30pm) About halfway between the station and Yōkaichi is Uchiko-za, a magnificent traditional kabuki theatre. Originally constructed in 1916, the theatre was completely restored in 1985, complete with a revolving stage. Performances are still held at the theatre about 40 times per year; call ahead for a schedule.

Museum of Commerce & Domestic Life MUSEUM

(商いと暮らし博物館; 0893-44-5220; 1938 Uchiko; admission ¥200; 9am-4.30pm) A few minutes' walk north along the main road from Uchiko-za is the Museum of Commerce & Domestic Life, which exhibits historical materials and wax figures portraying a typical merchant's home of the early 20th century. If you understand Japanese, the recorded voicing of various characters in the house is entertainingly campy; otherwise, get the lowdown from the English flyer.

Yōkaichi Historic District HISTORIC SITE

(八日市) Uchiko's picturesque main street has a number of interesting buildings, many now serving as museums, souvenir stalls, craft shops and charming teahouses. The old buildings typically have cream-coloured plaster walls and 'wings' under the eaves that serve to prevent fire spreading from house to house.

On the left as you walk up the street, look for **Ōmori Wa-rōsoku** (大森和ろうそく; 9am-5pm, closed Mon & Fri), Uchiko's last remaining candle manufacturer. The candles are still made by hand here according to traditional methods, and you can watch the candle-makers at work.

As the road makes a slight bend, several well-preserved Edo-era buildings come into view, including Ōmura-tei and Hon-Haga-tei, the latter of which is a fine example of a rich merchant's home. The Hon-Haga family established the production of fine wax in Uchiko, winning awards at World Expositions in Chicago (1893) and Paris (1900).

Further on, the exquisite Kamihaga-tei is a wax merchant's house within a large complex of buildings related to the wax-making process. The adjacent **Japanese Wax Museum** (木蝋資料館; admission ¥500; 9am-4.30pm) has excellent English explanations on the wax-making process and the town's prosperous past.

Finally, at the end of the historic district, you'll see signs pointing to **Kōshō-ji** (高昌寺; 9am-4.30am), the shrine up the hill. It's just a few minutes' walk up to the large reclining Buddha in front of the shrine.

Sleeping & Eating

Matsunoya Ryokan RYOKAN ¥¥

(松乃屋旅館; 0893-44-5000; www.dokidoki.ne.jp/home2/matunoya; 1913 Uchiko; per person with meals ¥10,500; P @) Still the best place to stay in town, this smart, central ryokan has neatly kept tatami rooms, a lovely communal bath and beautiful meals. The management is not the warmest you'll encounter in Shikoku, but staff are welcoming to foreign guests. The attached Poco a Poco restaurant serves delicious pasta. Set meals (including *crème brûlée!*) start at ¥1000.

Auberge Uchiko INN ¥¥¥

(オーベルジュ内子; 0893-44-6565; www.orienthotel.jp/uchiko; 485-2 Ikazaki Otsu; per person with meals ¥26,120-32,600) Worth a splurge if you've got your own wheels and can speak Japanese. Five freestanding modern cubes in the hills above Uchiko have glass walls affording views of the surrounding woods and town below. 'Nouvelle Uchiko' cuisine is the order of the day, and there's an onsen that nonguests can use for ¥1000.

Uchiko Fresh Park Karari MARKET ¥
(内子フレッシュパークからり; ☎0893-43-1122; 2452 Uchiko; ⏲9am-5pm) Above the Oda River, this farmers market offers fresh, locally grown produce, prepared *bentō* (boxed meals), regional specialities and a **restaurant** (レストランからり; Karari set ¥1200; ⏲11am-7.30pm) serving good *teishoku* (set) meals. Try the Karari set and from the picture menu choose a main, served with bread or rice.

Mother Restaurant CAFE ¥
(洋食マザー; ☎0893-44-5717; Uchiko; lunch ¥800-1000; ⏲11.30am-2.30pm & 5.30-9pm Tue-Sun) Near the turn-off to Yōkaichi is this friendly Japanese diner that prepares a tasty two-choice lunch menu and good, strong coffee.

Information

Uchiko Visitor Centre (内子町ビジターセンター; ☎0893-44-3790; www.we-love-uchiko.jp; 2020 Uchiko; ⏲9am-5.30pm Apr-Sep, to 4.30pm Oct-Mar) Offers maps, brochures, and local information, and can also arrange English-speaking volunteer guides, with advance booking.

Getting There & Around

Uchiko is 25 minutes from Matsuyama by *tokkyū* (¥1280, hourly) and by *futsū* (local train; ¥760, one hour). Yōkaichi is 1km north of Uchiko Station, and is well signposted in English.

Matsuyama 松山

☎089 / POP 513,000

Located in a lush river basin, Shikoku's largest city is handsome and refined, with a hint of 'mainland' hustle. Matsuyama is famed across Japan for Dōgo Onsen Honkan, a luxurious 19th-century public bathhouse built over ancient hot springs. The finest castle on the island towers above the stylish trams criss-crossing the city streets and the harbour glistening in the distance. Matsuyama is also home to seven of the 88 Temples, including Ishite-ji, one of the most famous stops on the pilgrimage.

Sights

★**Matsuyama-jō** CASTLE
(松山城; ☎089-921-4873; admission ¥510; ⏲9am-5pm, to 5.30pm Aug, to 4.30pm Dec & Jan) Perched on top of Mt Katsuyama in the centre of town, the castle dominates the city, as it has for centuries. Matsuyama-jō is one of Japan's finest surviving castles, and one of the very few with anything interesting to peruse inside: the castle has a treasure trove of artefacts with excellent English-language displays. A ropeway (one way/return ¥270/510) is on hand to whisk you up the hill, though there is a pleasant pathway if you prefer to walk.

It's worth walking down via the back slopes of the castle and stopping off at **Ninomaru Shiseki Tei-en** (二之丸史跡庭園; admission ¥100; ⏲9am-5pm, to 5.30pm Aug, to 4.30pm Dec & Jan) in the outer citadel of the fort, consisting of old gardens and modern water features.

Ishite-ji BUDDHIST TEMPLE
(石手寺) East of Dōgo Onsen is Ishite-ji, 51st of the 88 Temples, and one of the largest and most impressive in the circuit. *Ishite* means 'stone hand' and comes from a legend associated with Kōbō Daishi. A statue of Kōbō Daishi overlooks the temple from the hillside.

Shiki Memorial Museum MUSEUM
(松山市立子規記念博物館; ☎089-931-5566; http://sikihaku.lesp.co.jp; 1-30 Dōgo-kōen; admission ¥400; ⏲9am-6pm May-Oct, to 5pm Nov-Apr) This memorial museum celebrates the life and work of Matsuyama-born poet Masaoka Shiki (1867--1902), as well as the history of Matsuyama. Shiki initiated the reform of haiku and tanka (two forms of traditional poetry), and influenced a generation of poets after him. The museum has some English-language signage but also offers English-speaking volunteer guides with advance reservations.

Dōgo-kōen PARK
(道後公園; www.dogokouen.jp; Dōgo-kōen) A small park containing the site of Yuzuki-jō, the former residence of the Kōno clan that ruled Iyo province in feudal times. Articles unearthed during recent excavations are on display in **Yuzuki-jō Museum** (湯築城資料館; ☎089-941-1480; Dōgo-kōen; ⏲9am-5pm Tue-Sun) FREE, near the west entrance of the park.

Isaniwa-jinja SHINTO SHRINE
(伊佐爾波神社; 173 Sakuradani-chō) Designated a National Treasure, this shrine was modelled on Kyoto's Iwashimizu-Hachimangū and was built in 1667. It's located a short walk east of Dōgo Onsen.

Matsuyama

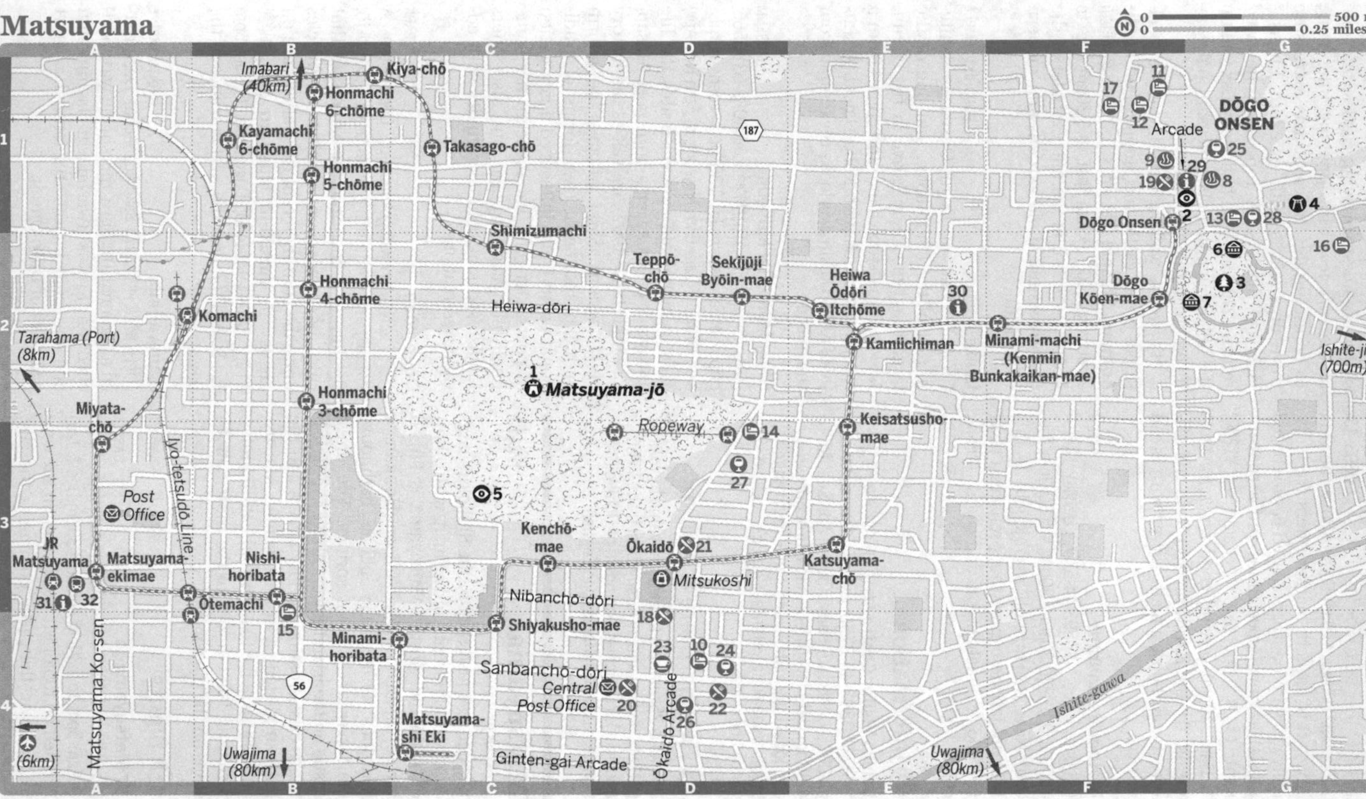
500 m
0.25 miles
Imabari (40km)
Kiya-chō
Honmachi 6-chōme
Kayamachi 6-chōme
Takasago-chō
Honmachi 5-chōme
187
Shimizumachi
Honmachi 4-chōme
Komachi
Heiwa-dōri
Tarahama (Port) (8km)
Teppō-chō
Sekijūji Byōin-mae
Heiwa Ōdōri Itchōme
Kamiichiman
Minami-machi (Kenmin Bunkakaikan-mae)
Dōgo Kōen-mae
Dōgo Onsen
DŌGO ONSEN
Arcade
Ishite-ji (700m)
Matsuyama-jō
Honmachi 3-chōme
Miyata-chō
Ropeway
Keisatsusho-mae
Post Office
Iyo-tetsudō Line
JR Matsuyama
Matsuyama-ekimae
Nishi-horibata
Ōtemachi
Kenchō-mae
Ōkaidō
Mitsukoshi
Katsuyama-chō
Nibanchō-dōri
Shiyakusho-mae
Minami-horibata
Sanbanchō-dōri
Central Post Office
Ōkaidō Arcade
56
Matsuyama Ko-sen
Matsuyama-shi Eki
Uwajima (80km)
Ginten-gai Arcade
Ishite-gawa
Uwajima (80km)
(6km)

Matsuyama

Top Sights
1 Matsuyama-jō C2

Sights
2 Botchan Karakuri Clock G1
3 Dōgo-kōen G2
4 Isaniwa-jinja G1
5 Ninomaru Shiseki Tei-en C3
6 Shiki Memorial Museum G2
7 Yuzuki-jō Museum G2

Activities, Courses & Tours
8 Dōgo Onsen Honkan G1
9 Tsubaki-no-yu F1

Sleeping
10 Check Inn Matsuyama D4
11 Dōgo Kan F1
12 Dōgo Yaya F1
13 Funaya G1
14 Guest House Matsuyama D3
15 Hotel JAL City B4
16 Matsuyama Youth Hostel G2
17 Sen Guesthouse F1

Eating
18 Café Bleu D4
19 Dōgo-no-machiya F1
20 Goshiki Sōmen D4
21 Takizawa D3
22 Tengu no Kakurega D4

Drinking & Nightlife
23 Cafe BC D4
24 Chocobar D4
25 Dōgo Bakushukan G1
26 Sala Sol D4
27 Underground Cafe D3
28 Wani to Sai G1

Information
29 Dōgo Onsen Tourist Information Office G1
30 Ehime Prefectural International Centre E2
31 Tourist Information Office A3

Transport
32 Bus Stop A3
JR Matsuyama Rental Bicycles .... (see 31)

Sleeping

Guest House Matsuyama GUESTHOUSE ¥
(ゲストハウス松山; 089-934-5296; www.sophia-club.net/guesthouse; 8-3-3 Ōkaidō-chō; dm/s/tw/apt ¥2000/2500/4000/8000;) Community-minded Tamanoi-san welcomes foreign guests to her guesthouse and cafe, components of her nonprofit endeavour to foster cultural exchange. Formerly an international-student liaison, she creates customised language and cultural classes (think aikidō, tea ceremony, *taiko* drumming) for her guests at very reasonable rates. Accommodation is no-frills, although some options include kitchens, and is best for unfussy travellers. Email ahead for reservations.

Matsuyama Youth Hostel HOSTEL ¥
(松山ユースホステル; 089-933-6366; www.matsuyama-yh.com/english; 22-3 Dōgo-himezuka; dm ¥2800, r per person ¥3600;) The health-conscious, communal atmosphere at this hilltop hostel makes it a great base for multiple visits to Dōgo Onsen, since it's a 10-minute walk up the hill east of the complex. Breakfast and dinner are also available for an additional fee. It's a good idea to reserve in advance here.

★ **Sen Guesthouse** GUESTHOUSE ¥¥
(泉ゲストハウス; 089-961-1513; www.senguesthouse-matsuyama.com; 4-14 Dōgo-takōchō; dm/s/d ¥2700/4500/7000;) This welcoming guesthouse is *the* place in Shikoku to get the lowdown on all things pilgrimage. Run by a super-friendly young American/Japanese couple, Sen has spacious tatami rooms with shared facilities, a roomy and well-equipped kitchen, a small bar and a tidy, homey communal area. The rooftop is a great place to catch the sunset over Matsuyama.

The guesthouse is a five-minute walk from Dōgo Onsen, and the owners rent out bicycles and happily share local info on Matsuyama and beyond, as well as advice on undertaking a pilgrimage.

★ **Dōgo Yaya** HOTEL ¥¥
(道後やや; 089-907-1181; www.yayahotel.jp; 6-1 Dōgo-takōchō; s/d from ¥7800/10,800;) Easy on the eyes and the budget, Dōgo Yaya is aesthetically pleasing as well as a smashing deal. The 68 rooms of various layouts are models of clean, contemporary style infused with traditional Japanese elements: raised tatami platforms for the cushy Western beds, sliding *shōji*-type doors and wood-slat embellishments. No onsen, but guests

AN INSIDER'S GUIDE TO DŌGO ONSEN

According to legend, Dōgo Onsen (道後温泉) was discovered during the age of the gods when a white heron was found healing itself in the spring. Since then, Dōgo has featured prominently in a number of literary classics, and won itself a reputation for the curative powers of its waters. The mono-alkaline spring contains sulphur, and is believed to be particularly effective at treating rheumatism, neuralgia and hysteria.

Dōgo Onsen Honkan (5-6 Dōgo-yunomachi; ⏲6am-10pm, to 11pm for kami-no-yu), the main building, was constructed in 1894, and designated an important cultural site in 1994. The three-storey, castle-style building incorporates traditional design elements, and is crowned by a statue of a white heron to commemorate its legendary origins. Although countless famous people have passed through its doors, Dōgo Onsen Honkan is perhaps best known for its inclusion in the famous 1906 novel *Botchan* by Natsume Sōseki, the greatest literary figure of Japan's modern age, who based his novel on his time as a school teacher in Matsuyama in the early 20th century.

Even if you're well versed in onsen culture, Dōgo can be a bit confusing as there are two separate baths (and four pricing options) from which to choose. The larger and more popular of the two baths is *kami-no-yu* (神の湯; water of the gods), separated by gender and adorned with heron mosaics. A basic bath is ¥410, while a bath followed by tea and *senbei* (rice crackers) in the 2nd-floor tatami room is ¥840 and includes a rental *yukata* (light cotton kimono). A rental towel and soap will set you back a further ¥50. The smaller, more private of the two baths is the *tama-no-yu* (魂の湯; water of the spirit), which is also separated by gender and adorned with simple tiles. A bath followed by tea and *botchan dango* (sweet, skewered rice dumplings) in the 2nd-floor tatami room costs ¥1250, while the top price of ¥1550 allows you to enjoy your snack in a private 3rd-floor tatami room.

There are English-language pamphlets to clarify the correct sequence of steps, but you might want to review this rundown before heading to Dōgo Onsen. After paying your money outside, you should enter the building and leave your shoes in a locker. If you've paid ¥410, go to the *kami-no-yu* changing room (signposted in English), where you can use the free lockers for your clothing. If you've paid ¥840 or ¥1250, first go upstairs to receive your *yukata*, and then return to either the *kami-no-yu* or *tama-no-yu* (also signposted in English) changing room. After your bath, you should don your *yukata* and retire to the 2nd-floor tatami room to sip your tea and gaze down on the bath-hoppers clip-clopping by in *geta* (traditional wooden sandals). If you've paid top whack, head directly to the 3rd floor, where you will be escorted to your private tatami room. Here, you can change into your *yukata* before heading to the *tama-no-yu* changing room, and also return after your bath to sip tea in complete privacy.

Regardless of which option you choose, you are allowed to explore the building after taking your bath. On the 2nd floor, there is a small **exhibition room** displaying artefacts relating to the bathhouse, including traditional wooden admission tickets. If you've taken one of the pricier upstairs options, you can also take a guided tour (in Japanese) of the private **imperial baths**, last used by the royal family in 1950. On the 3rd floor, the corner tatami room (the favourite of Natsume Sōseki) has a small **display** (in Japanese) on the writer's life.

Dōgo can get quite crowded, especially on weekends and holidays, although at dinner time it's usually empty as most Japanese tourists will be dining at their inns. If you want to escape the crowds, one minute on foot from the Honkan (through the shopping arcade) is **Tsubaki-no-yu** (椿の湯; admission ¥360; ⏲6.30am-11pm), Dōgo Onsen's hot-spring annexe, frequented primarily by locals. If you don't want a full bath, there are also nine free **ashi-yu** (足湯; foot baths) scattered around Dōgo Onsen where you can take off your shoes and socks and warm your feet. The most famous one is located just opposite the station at the start of the arcade. Here, you can also check out **Botchan Karakuri Clock** (坊ちゃんからくり時計), which was erected as part of Dōgo Onsen Honkan's centennial in 1994. It features figures based on the main characters from *Botchan*, who emerge to take a turn on the hour from 8am to 10pm. The spectacle is utterly delightful.

receive discounted entry to nearby Dōgo Onsen.

Check Inn Matsuyama HOTEL ¥¥
(チェックイン松山; ☎089-998-7000; www.checkin.co.jp/matsuyama; 2-7-3 Sanban-chō; s/tw from ¥5120/7920; P ⊜ @ ☎) This business hotel is excellent value for money, with well-equipped modern rooms with free wi-fi, a *konbini* in the lobby and an onsen on the roof (the women's onsen is on the 2nd floor). A short walk from the Ōkaidō arcade (大街道), the hotel is super convenient to the city's nightlife and restaurants.

Dōgo Kan HOTEL ¥¥¥
(道後舘; ☎089-941-7777; www.dogokan.co.jp; 7-26 Dōgo-takōchō; per person with meals Mon-Fri from ¥24,100, Sat & Sun from ¥28,000; P ☎) The Kurokawa Kishō–designed Dōgo-kan lies on a slope behind the Tsubaki-no-yu public baths. Indoor ponds and supremely gracious staff complement the grand tatami rooms and an elaborate series of communal baths. The Western rooms are appreciably cheaper but lack any real 'Dōgo-ness' which is presumably the attraction to this atmospheric spot.

Funaya RYOKAN ¥¥¥
(ふなや; ☎089-947-0278, toll-free 0120-190-278; www.dogo-funaya.co.jp; 1-33 Dōgo-yunomachi; r per person with meals from ¥22,050) Natsume Sōseki took refuge here from his writer's block and aching limbs, and so should you if you can afford it. The beauty lies inside, from the central garden and private onsen to the exquisite surrounding tatami rooms fit for Japanese royalty. It's a short walk from the Dōgo Onsen tram station along the road that leads up to Isaniwa-jinja.

Hotel JAL City HOTEL ¥¥¥
(☎089-913-2580; www.jalhotels.com/matsuyama; 1-10-10 Otemachi; s/tw from ¥9050/19,060; P @ ☎) The No 5 tram runs right past the door of the best business hotel in Matsuyama, which is a short walk from the castle. Hotel JAL City is a tasteful offering with attentive service and exemplary dining. The rooms are a bit bland, but very spacious and comfortable.

Eating

The area around the Ginten-gai and Ōkaidō shopping arcades in central Matsuyama is full of places to eat and drink.

Dōgo-no-machiya CAFE ¥
(道後の町屋; ☎089-986-8886; www.dogonomachiya.com; 14-26 Dōgo-yunomachi; meals ¥650-1000; ⊙9am-10pm Wed-Mon, closed every 3rd Wed; ⊜ ▤) With a traditional shopfront along the Dōgo arcade, this former teahouse now serves as a bakery-cafe offering burgers, sandwiches and soul-satisfying coffee and tea drinks. Its shotgun-style layout leads through beautifully preserved dark-wood rooms to a Japanese garden and tatami room out back.

Café Bleu CAFE ¥
(☎089-907-0402; 4th fl, 2-2-8 Ōkaidō; meals ¥600-900; ⊙11.30am-midnight) This lovely little music cafe serves tasty, simple sustenance to a bookish clientele. There's a picture menu and daily specials. The decor includes photos of Andy Warhol and Mick Jagger spying on you in the bathroom, vintage typewriters and shelves of superb art books. Beer (including Guinness on draught) and generous cocktails also available.

Tengu no Kakurega IZAKAYA ¥
(てんぐの隠れ家; ☎089-931-1009; 2-5-17 Sanban-chō; dishes ¥400-1200; ⊙noon-midnight, to 1am Fri & Sat) A chic *izakaya* serving *yakitori* and other dishes in a pleasant setting; try the *omakase* (chef's choice) set of grilled, skewered carnivorous delights (¥1260). Paper screens give onto a little garden at the back. Look for the *tengu* (long-nosed goblin) hung above the doorway, on the right-hand side of the second block heading east from the Ōkaidō arcade.

Goshiki Sōmen NOODLES ¥¥
(五色そうめん; ☎089-933-3838; 3-5-4 Sanban-chō; meals ¥780-2000; ⊙11am-10.30pm, sometimes closed 3-5pm; ▤) Next to the central post office is this elegant Matsuyama institution, which specialises in *goshiki sōmen* (thin noodles in five different colours). You'll recognise it by the piles of colourful noodles in the window waiting to be taken home as souvenirs. Set meals are around ¥1500; there is a picture menu with English descriptions of the most popular dishes.

Takizawa JAPANESE ¥¥
(たきざわ; ☎089-931-9377; 3-4-4 Ōkaidō; meals ¥850-2500; ⊙11.30am-2pm & 5-10pm Tue-Sat, closed every 1st & 3rd Sun) Near the castle ropeway, this warmly austere restaurant serves simple, beautifully balanced Matsuyama-style cuisine at reasonable prices. Rice lunch sets (¥850) change daily but are invariably

A CYCLING PILGRIMAGE

For *henro* (pilgrims) who wish to start or finish their pilgrimage on two wheels, a fantastic way to travel between Shikoku and Hiroshima Prefecture is via the Shimanami Kaidō (p445), a bicycle route that crosses a series of bridges across six Inland Sea islands. **Sunrise Itoyama** (サンライズ糸山; ☎0898-41-3196; www.sunrise-itoyama.jp; 2-8-1 Sunaba-chō; bicycle rental per day ¥500; ⊙8am-8pm Apr-Sep, to 5pm Oct-Mar) in Imabari is the most convenient starting point on the Shikoku side. It's also a good idea to send heavy luggage ahead with a courier service like Yamato; many guesthouses and convenience stores can help you with the paperwork.

skillfully prepared with subtle flavours and nods to local specialities. Try the *tai kamameshi* (kettle-steamed rice with snapper, ¥1000).

Drinking & Nightlife

The bulk of drinking establishments are concentrated in Ichiban-chō and Niban-chō amid the network of neon-lit streets either side of the Ōkaidō arcade.

Sala Sol BAR
(☎090-7571-4386; 3rd fl, Ciel Bldg, 2-3-5 Sanbanchō; drinks from ¥600; ⊙8.30pm-3am Tue-Sun) The town's most popular bar with foreigners is surprisingly cool, with excellent music and generous drink specials. It's also one of the few places in town where people dance…all night long. You'll have to look closely for the little sandwich board pointing out the stairwell.

Dōgo Bakushukan BREWERY
(道後麦酒館; ☎089-945-6866; 20-13 Dōgo-yunomachi; ⊙11am-10pm) Right by Dōgo Onsen Honkan, this brewery is a good spot for a locally made beer and a bite to eat after a relaxing soak. The names of the brews are allusions to novelist Natsume Sōseki and his famous novel, *Botchan*. There's also a decent range of food available from a picture menu (such as *iwashi no karaage* – fried sardines).

Wani to Sai BAR
(ワニとサイ; ☎080-3319-2765; 1-39 Dōgo-yunomachi; drinks from ¥600; ⊙7pm-late) Easily the funkiest little spot in Matsuyama, Wani to Sai is a 'circus bar' run by a fascinating native son who set off to Florence to study fresco painting and wound up creating marionettes and busking around Europe for eight years instead. Wanting to hang with an artsy crowd? You've come to the right place.

Underground Cafe BAR
(☎089-998-7710; 3-6-6 Ōkaidō; ⊙6pm-4am) A local and expat secret bar hang-out that feels more Honshū than Shikoku and serves Japanese-style Mexican food on the side. It's off the street leading to the ropeway; look for the Union Jack flag, so coolly out of context.

Chocobar BAR
(☎089-933-2039; 2-2-6 Sanbanchō; drinks from ¥700; ⊙5pm-late) This tiny shot bar located on a busy road has a regular hip-hop soundtrack and colourful decor. It's one of the few places in Matsuyama where passers-by can watch you get drunk.

Cafe BC CAFE
(☎089-945-9295; 2-2-20 Ōkaidō; ⊙9am-10pm Mon-Wed, Fri & Sat, 9am-7pm Thu & Sun) The best coffee in Matsuyama. The lady of the house also makes killer sandwiches, perfect for a light lunch; sandwich lunch sets cost ¥650 to ¥750.

Information

ATMs accepting international cards can be found at the central post office and at the post office that's a couple of minutes' walk north of JR Matsuyama Station.

Ehime Prefectural International Centre (愛媛県国際交流協会; EPIC; ☎089-917-5678; www.epic.or.jp; 1-1 Dōgo Ichiman; ⊙8.30am-5pm Mon-Sat) Provides advice, internet access and bike rental. EPIC is near the Minami-machi (南町; aka Kenmin Bunkakaikan-mae) tram stop. Look for the red question mark.

Tourist Information Office (☎089-931-3914; ⊙8.30am-8.30pm) The main office is located inside JR Matsuyama Station, while a branch office (☎089-943-8342; ⊙8am-8pm) is opposite the tram terminus for Dōgo Onsen.

Getting There & Away

BOAT

The superjet hydrofoil, run by the Setonaikai Kisen (p631) ferry, has regular hydrofoil connections between Matsuyama and Hiroshima (¥7100, 1¼ hours, 13 daily). The Hiroshima–Matsuyama ferry (¥3600, 2½ hours, 10 daily) is also a popular way of getting to/from Shikoku.

BUS

There are JR Highway buses that run to/from Osaka (¥6900, 5½ hours, five daily) and Tokyo (¥12,200, 12 hours, one daily). Note that fares to Tokyo vary considerably depending on the date. There are frequent buses to major cities in Shikoku.

TRAIN

The JR Yosan line connects Matsuyama with Takamatsu (*tokkyū* ¥5670, 2½ hours), and there are also services across the Seto-ōhashi to Okayama (*tokkyū* ¥6310, 2¾ hours) on Honshū.

Getting Around

TO/FROM THE AIRPORT

Matsuyama's airport, 6km west of the city, is easily reached by bus (¥310, 15 minutes, half-hourly) from the front of the JR Matsuyama Station.

BICYCLE

JR Matsuyama Rental Bicycles (per day ¥300; ⏲9am-6pm Mon-Sat) Available at the large bicycle park to the right as you exit JR Matsuyama Station.

TRAM

Tickets cost a flat ¥160 for each trip (pay when you get off). A day pass costs ¥400. Lines 1 and 2 are loop lines, running clockwise and anti-clockwise around Katsuyama (the castle mountain). Line 3 runs from Matsuyama-shi station to Dōgo Onsen, line 5 goes from JR Matsuyama Station to Dōgo Onsen, and line 6 from Kiya-chō (木屋町) to Dōgo Onsen. You can also ride the vintage Botchan Ressha (坊ちゃん列車), small trains that were imported from Germany in 1887. Named for Natsume Sōseki's famous novel, they ran up and down Matsuyama's streets for 67 years, and they're back in occasional use. Combo tickets for the Botchan Ressha plus a one-day tram pass cost ¥500.

Ishizuchi-san 石鎚山

☎0897

At 1982m, Ishizuchi-san is the highest peak in western Japan, and was traditionally considered to be a holy mountain. Ishizuchi attracts pilgrims and climbers alike, particularly during the July and August climbing season. During the winter (late December to late March) skiing is possible.

To get to the Nishi-no-kawa cable-car station (on the northern side of the mountain), take the direct bus (¥990, 55 minutes, four daily) from Iyo-Saijo Station. The **cable car** (石鎚登山ロープウェイ; ☎0897-59-0331; www.ishizuchi.com; one way/return ¥1030/1950; ⏲8am-6pm Jul & Aug, hrs vary Sep-Jun) carries hikers to an elevation of 1300m; from here, plan on about a five-hour round-trip hike to the summit.

You can climb up one way and down the other or make a complete circuit from Nishi-no-kawa to the summit, down to Tsuchi-goya and then back to Nishi-no-kawa. Allow all day and an early start for the circuit. For detailed information on hiking Ishizuchi-san, see Lonely Planet's *Hiking in Japan*.

Accommodation is available at **Ishizuchi Fureai-no-Sato** (石鎚ふれあいの里; ☎0897-59-0203; 1-25-1 Nakaoka, Saijo-shi; per person r ¥1170, cabins from ¥2920), where the cabins are cosy and the complex includes a small onsite restaurant, *ofuro* (public bath) and outdoor cooking area. Reserve accommodation and meals in advance, as it's a destination for school groups.

KAGAWA PREFECTURE

Formerly known as Sanuki, Kagawa Prefecture (香川県) is the smallest of Shikoku's four regions, and the smallest of the country's 47 prefectures. Its attractions include the celebrated shrine of Konpira-san in Kotohira, and the lively port city of Takamatsu with its world-renowned Japanese garden.

The region's hospitable weather and welcoming people have always been a comfort to pilgrims as they come to the end of their journey. Today, it's a main point of arrival, since the only rail link with Honshū is via the Seto-ōhashi bridge to Okayama. More interestingly, it's a gateway and short ferry ride to the remarkable Inland Sea islands and their growing art scene.

Matsuyama to Takamatsu

The JR Yosan line runs around the coast between Takamatsu and Matsuyama. At Tadotsu, the JR Dosan line splits off and runs south to Zentsū-ji and Kotohira, through the Iya Valley and eventually to Kōchi.

Kanonji 観音寺

☎0875 / POP 63,128

Coming east from Ehime-ken, the first town of consequence in Kagawa Prefecture is Kanonji, notable as the only spot on the

OFF THE BEATEN TRACK

CO-MACHI-NO-IE

For a taste of immersion in a small-town historic district, where nothing caters to tourists, book a night or two in the town of Utazu. Along the old *henro* (pilgrim) trail, the local government recently teamed up with the Chiiori Trust to preserve and utilise two historic houses, known as **Co-machi-no-ie** (古街の家; ☎0877-85-6941; http://co-machi-no-ie.jp; s/d/tr from ¥14,000/16,000/21,000). One house has traditional bones and tatami rooms that feature original ornamental woodwork. The neighbouring Shōwa-period house is a complete contrast, with a blocky, minimalist exterior – its interior is a beautiful fusion of Japanese and Western, with unusually high ceilings, original Japanese details and contemporary furnishings.

The Comachi houses are best for self-caterers looking to connect with the community, and who welcome the micro-adventures of interacting with the local shopowners, poking around Gōshō-ji (郷照寺; Temple 78) and checking out the landscape paintings housed in the waterfront **Higashiyama Kaii Setouchi Art Museum** (東山魁夷せとうち美術館; ☎0877-44-1333; www.pref.kagawa.jp/higashiyama/english/museum; 224-13 Aza Minami-dōri, Shamijima, Sakaide; admission ¥300; ⏲9am-5pm Tue-Sun). Utazu is a good base for self-driving visitors, with easy access to Marugame, Zentsū-ji and Konpira-san. Email for reservations.

pilgrimage trail to have two of the 88 Temples on the same grounds: Temple 68, **Jinne-in** (神恵院), and Temple 69, **Kanon-ji** (観音寺). It's also known for the odd **Zenigata** (銭形), a 350m-circumference coin-shaped sculpture in the sand dating from 1633. The coin and its inscription are formed by huge trenches dug in the sand, and are said to have been dug overnight by the local population as a welcome present to their feudal lord. For the best views of the sculpture, you'll need to climb the hill in Kotohiki-kōen, 1.9km northwest of Kanonji Station (not far from the two temples). A small **tourist information office** (☎0875-25-3839), over the bridge from the station, has maps. Kanonji is considerably closer to Takamatsu (*tokkyū* ¥2270, 45 minutes) than Matsuyama (*tokkyū* ¥4260, 1¾ hours).

Marugame 丸亀

☎0877 / POP 113,414

An interesting detour from the 88 Temple circuit is in Marugame, home to **Marugame-jō** (丸亀城; 1 Marugame; admission ¥200; ⏲9am-4.30pm). The castle dates from 1597, and is one of only 12 castles in Japan to have its original wooden *donjon* intact.

Marugame also has two interesting little museums – right outside the station is **Marugame Genichiro-Inokuma Museum of Contemporary Art** (MIMOCA; 丸亀市猪熊弦一郎現代美術館; ☎0877-24-7755; www.mimoca.org; 80-1 Hamamachi; admission ¥300; ⏲10am-6pm), showcasing two- and three-dimensional work of its eponymous artist, as well as rotating exhibitions. From here, a 15-minute walk towards the harbour brings you to the **Uchiwa-no-Minato Museum** (うちわの港ミュージアム; ☎0877-24-7055; 307-15 Minato-machi; ⏲9.30am-5pm Tue-Sun) FREE, which has displays and demonstrations on how *uchiwa* (round paper fans) are made. Around 90% of Japan's *uchiwa* are still made in Marugame.

Across from the station, **bike hire** (☎0877-25-1127; per day ¥200, deposit ¥300; ⏲7am-5pm) is available from the bicycle park. By bike, it is less than an hour from Marugame to Zentsū-ji. Marugame is easily covered as a day trip from Takamatsu (*tokkyū* ¥1070, 20 minutes).

Zentsū-ji 善通寺

☎0877 / POP 33,183

If you only have time for one temple, then make it **Zentsū-ji** (善通寺) FREE, number 75 of the 88 Temples and the place where Kōbō Daishi was born. It is also the largest temple – most of the other 88 could fit comfortably into the car park here. The temple boasts a truly magnificent five-storey pagoda and giant camphor trees that are said to date back as far as Daishi's childhood. Visitors can venture into the basement of the **Mie-dō** (御影堂; admission ¥500; ⏲8am-5pm) and traverse a 100m-long passageway (戒壇めぐり) in pitch darkness: by moving carefully along with your hand pressed to the wall (painted with mandalas, angels and lotus flowers), you are said to be safely following Buddha's way. If you're on a bike, there are several other pilgrimage temples within easy reach of this one, including Temple 73, **Shusshaka-ji** (出釈迦寺) FREE.

The temple is about 1km from the JR Zentsū-ji Station, straight ahead as you exit. On the right you'll find a number of well-priced, casual restaurants. Zentsū-ji is a quieter alternative to Kotohira, if you're also planning to visit Konpira-san. On a main road that's part of the *henro* trail, the hostel **Kaze-no-Kuguru** (風のくぐる; ☎0877-63-6110; www.kuguru.net; dm ¥2900, s/d from ¥3700/6400) is an excellent choice: friendly, immaculate and flooded with natural light. It's a 15-minute walk from the station; find a map on the website.

Kotohira 琴平

☎0877 / POP 9967

The small mountain village of Kotohira is home to one of Shikoku's most famous tourist attractions, Konpira-san, a Shintō shrine dedicated to the god of seafarers. The 1368 steep stone steps are a rite of passage for many Japanese, with plenty of interesting en-route distractions.

Sights

★Konpira-san SHINTO SHRINE

(金刀比羅宮; 892-1 Kotohira-chō; Hōmotsu-kan admission ¥800, Shoin admission ¥800; Hōmotsu-kan & Shoin 8.30am-4.30pm) Konpira-san or, more formally, Kotohira-gū, was originally a Buddhist and Shintō temple dedicated to the guardian of mariners. It became exclusively a Shintō shrine after the Meiji Restoration.

A lot of fuss is made about how strenuous the climb (1368 steps) to the top is, but if you've made it this far in Japan, you've probably completed a few long ascents to shrines already.

The first notable landmark on the long climb is **Ō-mon** (大門), a stone gateway that leads to **Hōmotsu-kan** (宝物館; Treasure House), where the collection of treasures is pretty underwhelming for such a major shrine. Nearby you will find five traditional-sweets vendors at tables shaded by large white parasols. A symbol of ancient times, the vendors (the Gonin Byakushō – Five Farmers) are descendants of the original families that were permitted to trade within the grounds of the shrine. Further uphill is **Shoin** (書院; Reception Hall), a designated National Treasure that dates from 1659 and has some interesting screen paintings and a small garden.

Continuing the ascent, you eventually reach large **Asahi-no-Yashiro** (旭社; Shrine of the Rising Sun). Built in 1837, this large hall is dedicated to the sun goddess Amaterasu, and is noted for its ornate wood-carving. From here, the short final ascent, which is the most beautiful leg of the walk, brings you to **Gohonsha** (御本社; Gohon Hall) and **Ema-dō** (絵馬堂; Ema Pavilion). The latter is filled with maritime offerings ranging from pictures of ships and models to modern ship engines. From this level, there are spectacular views that extend right down to the coast and over the Inland Sea.

Incurable climbers can continue for another 500 or so steps up to Oku-sha (Inner Shrine), which features stone carvings of *tengu* (bird-like demons) on the cliff.

★Kanamaru-za THEATRE

(金丸座; ☎0877-73-3846; admission ¥500; 9am-5pm) Japan's oldest kabuki playhouse, though it had a lengthy stint as a cinema before falling out of use. The restorations are superb; wander backstage and see the revolving-stage mechanism, basement trapdoors and a tunnel out to the front of the theatre. The playhouse is 200m east of the main approach to Konpira-san. There's a good English leaflet available, and English-speaking volunteer guides are sometimes on hand.

Kinryō-no-Sato MUSEUM

(金陵の郷; ☎0877-73-4133; 623 Kotohira-chō; 9am-4pm Mon-Fri, 9am-6pm Sat & Sun) FREE This sake museum, located along the main approach to the shrine, is in the old premises of a brewery that has owned the building since 1789. There's an English leaflet explaining the sake-making process, but sadly, the sake-tasting component is no longer offered.

Sleeping & Eating

Kotobuki Ryokan RYOKAN ¥¥

(ことぶき旅館; ☎0877-73-3872; 245-5 Kotohira-chō; per person with breakfast from ¥6480; P @) This welcoming ryokan with comfortable tatami rooms and warm hospitality is conveniently situated by the riverside. Umbrellas, internet access and spotless shared bathrooms are all available. Turn left for the arcade and some small restaurants; turn right for the shrine.

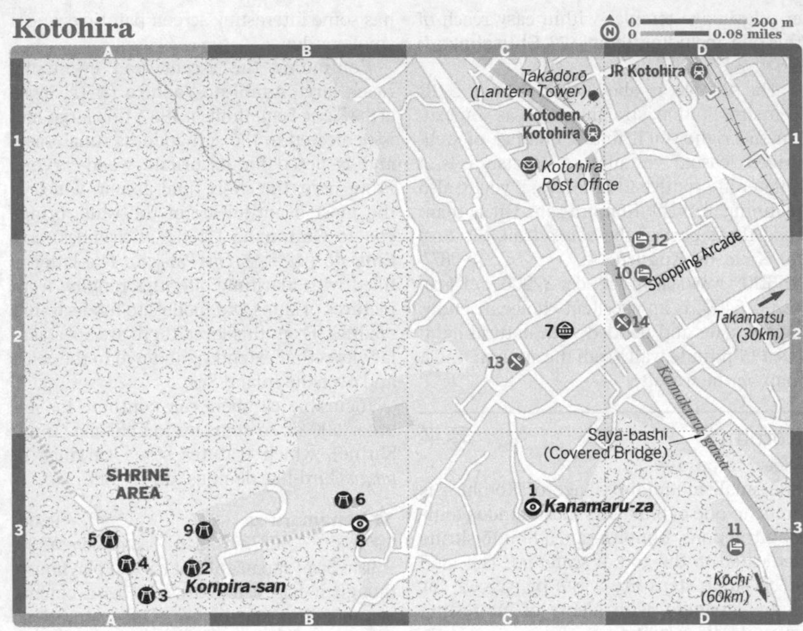

Kotohira

Top Sights

1	Kanamaru-za	C3
2	Konpira-san	A3

Sights

3	Asahi-no-Yashiro	A3
4	Ema-dō	A3
5	Gohonsha	A3
6	Hōmotsu-kan	B3
7	Kinryō-no-Sato	C2
8	Ō-mon	B3
9	Shoin	A3

Sleeping

10	Kotobuki Ryokan	D2
11	Kotohira Kadan	D3
12	Kotohira Riverside Hotel	D2

Eating

13	Konpira Udon	C2
14	New Green	D2

Kotohira Riverside Hotel HOTEL ¥¥
(琴平リバーサイドホテル; ☎0877-75-1800; 246-1 Kotohira-chō; s/d with breakfast ¥7560/12,960;) This well-run business hotel has comfortable Western-style rooms. There's an in-house bath, but guests also receive discounted rates at its sister property's onsen nearby.

Kotohira Kadan RYOKAN ¥¥
(琴平花壇; ☎0877-75-3232; www.kotohira-kadan.jp; 1241-5 Kotohira-chō; r/villa per person from ¥11,880/23,760;) A luxurious refuge after a climb up Konpira-san, this elegant ryokan is about three minutes' walk from the centre of Kotohira. Most of the rooms are Japanese style, with three standalone villas as well, all within a garden setting. Soak weary muscles in the house onsen or in your own tub (some of the tubs are open-air).

Beautifully presented meals feature local seafood and regional specialities, and though the staff don't speak much English, they are extremely warm and accommodating.

Konpira Udon UDON ¥
(こんぴらうどん; ☎0877-73-5785; meals ¥500-1200; 8am-5pm) Just short of the first set of steps leading up Konpira-san, this is one of dozens of *Sanuki udon* joints in Kotohira. You can't miss it, as the front window shows off the busy udon-makers rolling out dough and slicing noodles by hand. Try the *kake udon* (¥500), hot or cold noodles in broth.

New Green CAFE ¥

(ニューグリーン; ☎0877-73-3451; 722-1 Kotohira-chō; meals ¥850-1600; ⏲8.30am-8.30pm; 🄔) A cute neighbourhood spot where the local ladies cackle over coffee, New Green is also one of the few restaurants in town open for dinner. If the salads, *kaki-furai* (breaded, fried oysters) and *omuraisu* (omelette filled with fried rice) leave you wanting, there's cake as well.

Information

There are coin lockers and tourist brochures at the JR station. The ATMs at the post office accept international cards.

Getting There & Away

You can travel to Kotohira on the JR Dosan line from Kōchi (*tokkyū* ¥3930, 1½ hours) and Ōboke (¥2270; 45 minutes). For Takamatsu and other places on the north coast, change trains at Tadotsu. The private Kotoden line also has regular direct trains from Takamatsu (¥620, one hour).

Takamatsu 高松

☎087 / POP 429,352

The buoyant port city of Takamatsu hums a vibrant, many-part harmony – venerable castle grounds that host contemporary crafts fairs, the small-town-big-city energy of a prefectural capital, regional culinary specialities like *Sanuki udon* and the heritage of traditional gems like Ritsurin-kōen. It's urban Japan at its most pleasant and pretension-free.

On a practical and pleasurable level, Takamatsu also serves as a jumping-off point for day trippers to intriguing destinations like the snowballing art scene on the islands of the Inland Sea.

Sights

★Ritsurin-kōen PARK

(栗林公園; ☎087-833-7411; http://ritsuringarden.jp; 1-20-16 Ritsurin-chō; admission ¥410; ⏲sunrise-sunset) One of the most beautiful gardens in the country, Ritsurin-kōen dates from the mid-1600s and took more than a century to complete. Designed as a walking garden for the *daimyō*'s enjoyment, the park winds around a series of ponds, tearooms, bridges and islands. To the west, Shiun-zan (Mt Shiun) forms an impressive backdrop to the garden. The classic view of Engetsu-kyō bridge with the mountain in the background is one of the finest in Japan.

Enclosed by the garden are a number of interesting sights, including **Sanuki Folkcraft Museum** (讃岐民芸館; ⏲8.45am-4.30pm) FREE, which displays local crafts dating back to the Tokugawa dynasty. There are a number of teahouses in the park, including 17th-century **Kikugetsu-tei** (掬月亭; matcha ¥710; ⏲9am-4pm), where you can sip *matcha* with a traditional sweet and enjoy various garden tableaux from the tatami rooms. Or try the lovely thatched-roof **Higurashi-tei**, which dates from 1898.

The easiest way to reach Ritsurin-kōen is by taking the frequent direct bus (¥230, 15 minutes) from JR Takamatsu Station.

Takamatsu-jō CASTLE

(高松城; 2-1 Tamamo-chō; admission ¥200; ⏲western gate sunrise-sunset, eastern gate 7am-6pm Apr-Sep, 8.30am-5pm Oct-Mar) The site of Takamatsu's castle now forms delightful Tamamo-kōen, a park where the walls and seawater moat survive, along with several of the original turrets. Each spring a swimming race is held in the moat to honour an age-old chivalrous tradition. The original castle was built in 1588 for Itoma Chikamasa, and was the home of the region's military rulers until the Meiji Restoration, which happened nearly 300 years later. Reconstruction of the main keep is slated for completion in 2015; watch this space.

Takamatsu City Museum of Art MUSEUM

(高松市美術館; ☎087-823-1711; 10-4 Konyamachi; admission ¥200; ⏲9.30am-7pm Tue-Sat, to 5pm Sun) This impressive inner-city gallery is testament to Takamatsu's quality art scene. The light and spacious refitting of a former Bank of Japan building is a stroke of curatorial genius, well served by interesting exhibitions on rotation from across Japan and the world.

Sleeping

There's one great budget spot in Takamatsu, but midrange hotels here represent great value if you can spend up a little.

Chottoco-ma GUESTHOUSE ¥

(ちょっとこま; chottoco-ma.com; 3-7-5 Ōgi-machi; dm/d ¥2500/6000; 📶) Spotless, bright and intimate, the charming Chottoco-ma is run by a friendly young couple, the English-speaking Yutaka and Emi. This tiny guesthouse (reservations essential) has only two dorm rooms and one private room, all sharing bathroom facilities. Located about

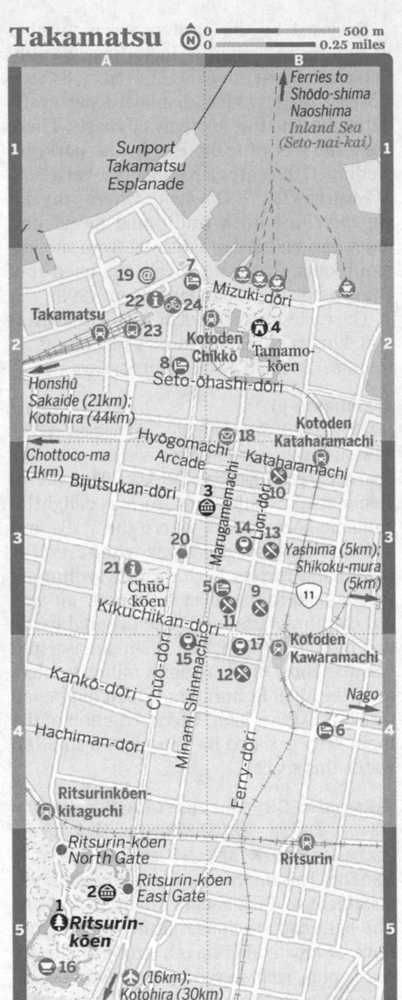

Takamatsu

Top Sights
1 Ritsurin-kōen.....A5

Sights
2 Sanuki Folkcraft Museum.....A5
3 Takamatsu City Museum of Art.....B3
4 Takamatsu-jō.....B2

Sleeping
5 Dormy Inn Takamatsu.....B3
6 Hotel No 1 Takamatsu.....B4
7 JR Hotel Clement Takamatsu.....A2
8 Takamatsu Terminal Hotel.....A2

Eating
9 Bijin-tei.....B3
10 Kawafuku.....B3
11 Ofukuro.....B3
12 Tokiwa Saryō.....B4
13 Tsurumaru.....B3

Drinking & Nightlife
14 Anbar.....B3
15 Grandfather's.....A4
16 Kikugetsu-tei.....A5
17 King's Yawd.....B4

Information
18 Central Post Office.....B2
19 e-TOPIA.....A2
20 JTB.....A3
21 Kagawa International Exchange.....A3
22 Tourist Information Office.....A2

Transport
23 Bus Terminal.....A2
24 Takamatsu-shi Rental Cycles.....A2

a kilometre from central Takamatsu, it's in an interesting harbourside neighbourhood with nearby onsen and good local seafood restaurants. Find transport details and a map on their website.

★ Dormy Inn Takamatsu HOTEL ¥¥
(ドーミーイン高松; ☎087-832-5489; www.hotespa.net/hotels/business; 1-10-10 Kawaramachi; s/d from ¥7000/9000; ⊜@📶) The Dormy is a little different from the usual big hotel fare, with its keen eye for design and a location at the heart of the entertainment district. The rooms are sleek and spacious, while service is top notch for the price. The onsen and *rotemburo* (outdoor bath) on the top floor are welcome additions, as is the wi-fi throughout.

Hotel No 1 Takamatsu BUSINESS HOTEL ¥¥
(ホテルNo.1高松; ☎087-812-2222; www.hotelno1.jp/takamatsu; 2-4-1 Kankō-dōri; s/tw ¥5290/8100; P⊜@) Three blocks east and three blocks south of Kotoden Kawaramachi Station, this is a sparkling business hotel with standard rooms and a rooftop men-only *rotemburo* with sweeping views of the city (the women's baths are on the 2nd floor). There is internet access in the lobby, and there are LAN connections in all rooms.

Takamatsu Terminal Hotel HOTEL ¥¥
(高松ターミナルホテル; ☎087-22-3731; www.webterminal.jp; 10-17 Nishinomaru-chō; s/d from ¥5400/8640; P@📶) It could use a minor

makeover, but this homey little hotel has more personality than the neighbouring business hotels. It's conveniently located about a minute's walk from the station. Solo travellers should opt for bigger singles, with semi-double beds.

JR Hotel Clement Takamatsu HOTEL ¥¥¥
(JRホテルクレメント高松; ☎087-811-1111; www.jrclement.co.jp; 1-1 Hamano-chō; s/d from ¥12,830/21,390; P ⊖ @ ⓦ) This eye-catching ultramodern hotel is one of the first buildings you see as you exit JR Takamatsu Station. The rooms are spacious, and there's a good selection of bars and restaurants with sweeping views of the Inland Sea.

Eating

Restaurants and bars are clustered in the covered arcades and entertainment district to the west side of the tracks between Kotoden Kataharamachi and Kawaramachi stations. People in Takamatsu are serious about their udon, and no trip here would be complete without at least one bowl of the famous speciality, *Sanuki udon*. Look for the words *te-uchi udon* (手打ちうどん), meaning 'handmade noodles'.

Kawafuku UDON ¥
(川福; ☎087-822-1956; 2-1 Daiku-machi; udon lunch set ¥600; ⊙11am-midnight) One of Takamatsu's best-known udon shops, Kawafuku serves its silky *Sanuki udon* in a variety of ways. Choose from the plastic food models outside. Look for the red-and-white striped lanterns in front, along Lion-dōri.

Tsurumaru UDON ¥
(鶴丸; ☎087-821-3780; 9-34 Furubaba-chō; curry udon ¥700; ⊙8pm-4am Mon-Sat) Sit at the counter and watch the noodles being pounded by hand in this popular spot, which is busy with the bar-hopping crowd until late into the night. The delicious *karē udon* (curry udon) is the most popular choice here. Look for the curtain over the door with a picture of a crane on it.

Ofukuro IZAKAYA ¥
(おふくろ; ☎087-862-0822; 1-11-12 Kawara-machi; dishes ¥500-1500; ⊙5-10pm Mon-Sat; ⓔ) This fabulous *washofu* (local eating house) in the heart of the entertainment district offers a well-priced and hearty dining experience. A number of delicious, pre-prepared vegetarian and fish dishes sit on the counter, served with complimentary salad and miso soup. Find it east of Minami Shinmachi.

Bijin-tei IZAKAYA ¥¥
(美人亭; ☎087-861-0275; 2-2-10 Kawara-machi; dishes ¥700-1500; ⊙5-10pm Mon-Sat) Smiling *mama-san* sees all at this discreet seafood *izakaya*. Point to the menu items already plated – the pickled *tako* (octopus) is a mouthful – or ask for an *osusume* (recommendation). It's on the ground floor of a building containing several snack bars and karaoke joints. Look for the sign with the shop's name on it in kanji.

Tokiwa Saryō SEAFOOD ¥¥
(ときわ茶寮; ☎087-861-5577; 1-8-2 Tokiwa-chō; dishes ¥1200-3600; ⊙11am-3.30pm & 5-11.30pm) An old Japanese inn with a pond and excellent sashimi and tempura sets; there's an easy-to-understand picture menu. It's off the Tokiwa arcade from Ferry Dōri, take the second left; it's the building on the right with the big white lantern.

Drinking & Nightlife

★ **King's Yawd** BAR
(☎087-837-2660; 1-2-2 Tokishin-machi; ⊙6pm-2am Tue-Sat) The chilled-out, dreadlocked Sato-san holds court over a diverse crew that hangs out at this Jamaican bar. She slings authentic Jamaican food (think jerk chicken and ackee), while her staff pour generous cocktails, all to a background of reggae and red, gold and green decor. Justifiably popular with both locals and expats.

Grandfather's BAR
(グランドファーザーズ; ☎087-837-5177; B1 fl, 1-6-4 Tamachi-chō; ⊙7pm-late) The scene here is so smooth you'll fall off your seat as the bookish owner spins vintage '60s and '70s funk and soul records from his enormous collection. Meanwhile, otherworldly waitresses hover through smoke to present your free-poured, icy cool beverages.

Anbar BAR
(アンバー; 1st fl, Dai-ichi Bldg, 8-15 Furubaba-chō; ⊙8pm-late Fri-Wed) The company of surreal feline imagery is an interesting companion to a fine whisky. There's an English sign outside, and plenty of hip weirdos inside.

Information

There's a left-luggage office at JR Takamatsu Station, and international ATMs at the central post office (located near the northern exit of Marugamemachi Arcade).

e-TOPIA (e-とぴあ; 4th fl, Takamatsu Symbol Tower; ⊙10am-8pm Tue-Sun) Free internet access in a large, sunny facility; in the Sunport complex between the JR Station and the port.

JTB (☎087-851-2117; 7-6 Kajiyamachi; ⏲10am-6pm Mon-Sat) For reliable help with travel arrangements.

Kagawa International Exchange (アイパル香川国際交流会館; I-PAL Kagawa; ☎087-837-5908; www.i-pal.or.jp; 1-11-63 Banchō; ⏲9am-6pm) In the northwest corner of Chūō-kōen, this international exchange association has a small library, satellite TV and internet access.

Tourist Information Office (高松市観光案内所; ☎087-851-2009; ⏲9am-6pm) In the plaza outside the station.

Getting There & Around

BICYCLE

Takamatsu is flat, and excellent for biking. The city offers a great deal on its 'blue bicycles' (¥100 per 24 hours; photo ID is required), which can be picked up at **Takamatsu-shi Rental Cycles** (高松駅前広場地下レンタサイクルポート; ☎087-821-0400; ⏲7am-10pm) in the underground bicycle park outside JR Takamatsu Station.

BOAT

Jumbo Ferry (ジャンボフェリー; ☎087-811-6688; www.ferry.co.jp) Runs between Takamatsu and Kōbe (¥1940, four hours). Free buses shuttle passengers from the port to JR Takamatsu Station.

BUS

There are bus services to/from Tokyo (¥10,300, 9½ hours, three daily), Nagoya (¥7000, 5½ hours, two daily), Kyoto (¥4950, three hours and 40 minutes, six daily) and most other major cities.

TRAIN

Takamatsu is the only city in Shikoku with regular rail links to Honshū. There are frequent trains to Okayama (¥1510, 55 minutes, every half-hour), where you can connect to *shinkansen* (bullet train) services that will whiz you to any of the major cities in just a few hours.

From Takamatsu, *tokkyū* trains on the JR Kōtoku line run southeast to Tokushima (¥2640, one hour and seven minutes, hourly); the JR Yosan line runs west to Matsuyama (¥5670, 2½ hours, hourly); and the JR Dosan line runs to Kōchi (¥4910, 2½ hours, hourly). The private Kotoden line also runs direct to Kotohira (¥620, one hour, frequent).

Around Takamatsu

Takamatsu is a great base for exploring the olive groves of Shōdo-shima (p457) and the art scene of Naoshima (p460) and islands of the Inland Sea, all less than an hour by boat.

Yashima 屋島

About 5km east of Takamatsu is the 292m-high tabletop plateau of Yashima, where you'll find **Yashima-ji** (屋島寺), number 84 of the 88 Temples. This was the site of a decisive battle between the Genji and Heike clans in the late 12th century, and the temple's **Treasure House** (admission ¥500; ⏲9am-5pm) exhibits artefacts relating to the battle. Just behind the Treasure House is the **Pond of Blood,** where victorious Genji warriors washed the blood from their swords.

At the bottom of Yashima, about 500m north of the station, is **Shikoku-mura** (四国村; ☎087-843-3111; www.shikokumura.or.jp; 91 Yashima-nakamachi; admission ¥800; ⏲8.30am-6pm Apr-Oct, 8.30am-5.30pm Nov-Mar), an excellent village museum that houses old buildings transported from all over Shikoku and neighbouring islands. The village's fine kabuki stage came from Shōdo-shima, which is famous for its traditional farmers' kabuki performances. There is also an excellent restaurant serving, you guessed it, *Sanuki udon* (from ¥450) in an old farmhouse building as you leave the village.

Yashima is six stops from Kawaramachi on the private Kotoden line (¥240). Shuttle buses run from the station to the top of the mountain (¥100) every half an hour from 9.30am to 4.30pm, but it's a very pleasant hour-long hike up the forested back side of the plateau to the temple.

Isamu Noguchi Garden Museum イサム・ノグチ庭園美術館

It's worth considering an excursion to the town of Murechō, east of Takamatsu, to witness the fascinating legacy of noted sculptor Isamu Noguchi (1904–88). Born in Los Angeles to a Japanese poet and an American writer, Noguchi set up a studio and residence here in 1970. Today the **complex** (イサムノグチ庭園美術館; ☎087-870-1500; www.isamunoguchi.or.jp; 3-5-19 Mure-chō; tours ¥2160; ⏲tours 10am, 1pm & 3pm Tue, Thu & Sat by appointment) is filled with hundreds of Noguchi's works, and holds its own as an impressive art installation. Inspiring sculptures are on display in the beautifully restored Japanese buildings and in the surrounding landscape.

Visitors should fax or email ahead for reservations, preferably two weeks or more in advance (see the website for reservations and access details).

Kyūshū

Includes ➡

Best Onsen

- ➡ Ibusuki Sunamushi Kaikan Saraku (p729)
- ➡ Takegawara Onsen (p741)
- ➡ Shitan-yu (p746)
- ➡ Kirishima-Yaku National Park (p727)
- ➡ Takeo Onsen (p691)

Best Places to Eat

- ➡ Zauo (p683)
- ➡ Tōsenkyō Sōmen Nagashi (p731)
- ➡ Kawashima Tōfu (p689)
- ➡ Shippoku Hamakatsu (p702)
- ➡ Takamori Dengaku-no-Sato (p717)

Why Go?

Japan's southern- and westernmost main island is arguably its warmest, friendliest and most beautiful, with active volcanic peaks, rocky, lush and near-tropical coastlines, and great onsen virtually everywhere. Much Japanese history was made in Kyūshū (九州). Jōmon ruins, Shintō's sun goddess, wealthy trading ports, cloistered foreigners, samurai rebels and one of the earth's greatest wartime tragedies all loom large.

Today, burgeoning Fukuoka is a multicultural metropolis. In sweet, picturesque Nagasaki, tragedy contrasts with a colourful trading history, Kumamoto's castle is one of Japan's finest, and the volcanic Aso caldera is the world's largest. Saga Prefecture boasts *three* legendary pottery centres. Steam pours from the earth in Beppu, Miyazaki's Nichinan coast boasts vistas, monkeys, and Japan's best surfing, while Kagoshima, heart of the Meiji Restoration, smoulders – literally – with active volcanoes. Peppered throughout are relaxing hot-spring towns, trekking trails and family-friendly fun.

When to Go

Fukuoka

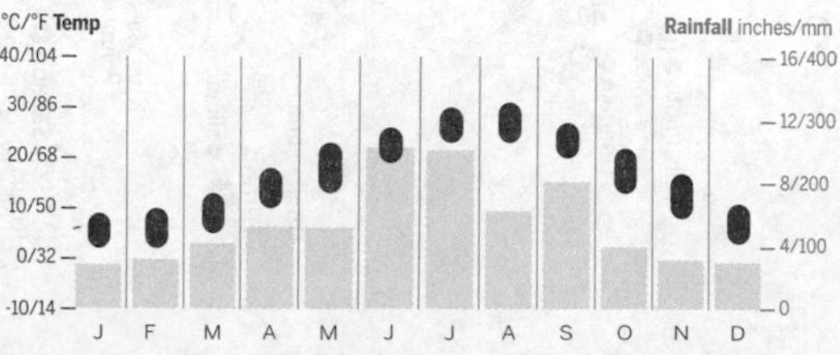

Apr–May Temperate weather and blooming azaleas on the volcanic slopes.

Jul–Aug Beat the night-time heat at delicious *yatai* (food stalls) in Fukuoka.

Oct–Nov Pleasant temperatures bring energetic festivals, such as Nagasaki's Kunchi Matsuri.

Kyūshū Highlights

1 Joining the night owls for beer and *yakitori* skewers at a *yatai* food stall in **Fukuoka** (p682).

2 Being moved – and charmed – by the unique history of **Hirado** (p704).

3 Getting buried in warm volcanic sand in **Ibusuki** (p729).

4 Seeing where the last samurai made their last stand at **Kumamoto Castle** (p712).

5 Touring the eerie, deserted 'ghost island' of **Hashima** (aka *Gunkanjima*, p700).

6 Marvelling at Japan's unique ceramics traditions in **Arita** (p690), **Imari** (p690) and **Karatsu** (p688).

7 Rowing amid waterfalls and hungry

ducks in **Takachiho Gorge** (p738).

8 Recharging in a riverside *rotemburo* (outdoor bath) in tranquil **Kurokawa Onsen** (p717).

9 Surfing some breaks along the **Nichinan coast** (p737).

10 Sipping sweet-potato *shōchū* in **Kagoshima** (p718) as the Sakurajima volcano burps and billows ash across the bay.

History

Excavations dating to around 10,000 BC indicate that southern Kyūshū was the likely entry point of the Jōmon culture, which gradually crept north.

Japan's trade with China and Korea began in Kyūshū, and the arrival of Portuguese ships in 1543 initiated Japan's at-times thorny relationship with the West and brought on the beginning of its 'Christian Century' (1549–1650). With Christianity, the Portuguese also brought gunpowder weaponry, heralding the ultimate decline of the samurai tradition.

In 1868 rebels from Kyūshū were instrumental in carrying through the Meiji Restoration, which ended the military shogunate's policy of isolation, marking the birth of modern Japan. During the ensuing Meiji era (1868–1912), rapid industrialisation caused profound social, political and environmental change.

Sadly, this historically rich region is best known for one event – the 9 August 1945 atomic bombing of Nagasaki.

Getting There & Away

AIR

Fukuoka Airport is Japan's fourth busiest, servicing destinations in Asia and Japan. In addition to domestic connections, Ōita (closest airport to Beppu), Kagoshima, Kumamoto, Miyazaki and Nagasaki airports all have flights to Seoul, and Kagoshima and Nagasaki airports serve Shanghai, Taipei and Hong Kong. Miyazaki serves Taipei, but not always daily, and Kitakyūshū serves Busan. Many airlines offer space-available 'Visit Japan' discount fares for foreign visitors, connecting many Kyūshū airports to Tokyo and Naha (Okinawa).

BOAT

There are sea connections to Kyūshū from Osaka and Okinawa. High-speed ferries shuttle between Fukuoka and Busan, in South Korea.

CHEAP TRANSPORT

There are discounted all-you-can-ride passes on JR Kyūshū and Kyūshū buses, from ¥8000/10,000 for three days in northern Kyūshū /all of Kyūshū, or a four-day all-Kyūshū Pass for ¥14,000. For further information visit www.sunqpass.jp/english/pass/index.html.

TRAIN

The opening of the Kyūshū *shinkansen* (bullet train) in March 2011 brought high-speed rail travel directly from Shin-Osaka to Kagoshima, via Hakata Station (Fukuoka) and Kumamoto, making this fascinating area more accessible than ever before.

Getting Around

BUS

Kyūshū's extensive highway bus system is often the most efficient and cheapest way around the island. See www.atbus-de.com for routes and reservations.

CAR

Outside the cities, car rental is the best way to reach many of the best-preserved and least-known landscapes, particularly in rural southern and northeastern Kyūshū and around Aso-san. Car-rental agencies are conveniently located all over Kyūshū.

TRAIN

Kyūshū *shinkansen* lines run north–south through western Kyūshū between Hakata and Kagoshima, and other major Kyūshū cities are connected by *tokkyū* (limited express) train services.

There's even an ultra-luxury **Seven Stars Sleeper train** (http://www.cruisetrain-seven-stars.jp/en/index.html; 2 days/1 night, s/d from ¥750,000/960,000). A four-day/three-night trip is also available.

FUKUOKA PREFECTURE

Fukuoka

092 / POP 1,474,400

Fukuoka (福岡) is Kyūshū's largest city (and Japan's sixth largest) and still growing. It's made up of two former towns, the Fukuoka castle town on the west bank of the Naka-gawa and Hakata on the east. The two towns merged in 1889 as Fukuoka, though the name Hakata is still widely in use (for instance, it's Fukuoka Airport but Hakata Station).

Hakata traces its trading history back some 2000 years, which continues today with visitors from Seoul and Shanghai. Among Japanese, the city is famed for its 'Hakata *bijin*' (beautiful women), SoftBank Hawks baseball team and hearty Hakata rāmen (egg noodles).

OFF THE BEATEN TRACK

HIKING HOTSPOTS

Hikers will discover that Kyūshū boasts some of Japan's most awe-inspiring treks. Nearly every prefecture has great getaways. Below are some top spots, several of which follow still-active volcanoes, making for jaw-droppingly awesome vistas...and sometimes requiring special precautions, too. Also look for the *Kyūshū Olle* brochure, available in many tourist booths, for trekking routes through towns and trails.

- Kirishima-Yaku National Park (p727), Kagoshima
- Unzen (p706), Nagasaki
- Hirado (p704), Nagasaki
- Kaimon-dake (p730), Kagoshima
- Aso-san (p715), Kumamoto
- Kujyū-san (p748), Ōita

Fukuoka's warmth and friendliness make it a great gateway to Kyūshū, and warm weather and contemporary attractions – art, architecture, shopping and cuisine – make it a good base for regional excursions.

Sights & Activities

Hakata Area

★Fukuoka Asian Art Museum MUSEUM
(福岡アジア美術館; ☎092-263-1100; http://faam.city.fukuoka.lg.jp; 7th & 8th fl, Riverain Centre Bldg, 3-1 Shimo-Kawabata-machi; adult/child/student ¥200/free/¥150; ⏰10am-8pm Thu-Tue; 🚇Nakasu-Kawabata) On the upper floors of the large Hakata Riverain Centre (博多リバレイン), this large museum houses the world-renowned **Asia Gallery** and additional galleries for special exhibits (admission fee varies) and artists in residence. Changing exhibits cover contemporary works from 23 countries, from East Asia to Pakistan.

★Hakata Machiya Furusato-kan MUSEUM
(博多町家ふるさと館; ☎092-281-7761; www.hakatamachiya.com; 6-10 Reisen-machi; admission ¥200; ⏰10am-6pm; 🚇Gion) Spread over three *machiya* (traditional townhouses), this folk museum recreates a Hakata *nagare* (neighbourhood unit) from the late Meiji era. The replica buildings house historical photos and displays of traditional Hakata culture, festivals, crafts and performing arts, as well as recordings of impenetrable Hakata-ben (dialect). Artisans are frequently on hand offering demonstrations.

Canal City SHOPPING CENTRE
(キャナルシティ; www.canalcity.co.jp; 1-2 Sumiyoshi; ⏰shops 10am-9pm, restaurants 11am-11pm) Canal City shopping centre is Fukuoka's biggest mall, boasting an eponymous artificial canal with illuminated fountain symphony, hotels, a multiplex cinema, playhouse and about 250 boutiques, bars and bistros. It was designed by Jon Jerde, who later created Tokyo's Roppongi Hills.

Tenjin Area

Fukuoka-jō & Ōhori-kōen HISTORIC SITE
(福岡城・大濠公園; 🚇Ōhori-kōen) Only the walls of Fukuoka-jō (Fukuoka Castle) remain, but the castle's hilltop site (Maizuru-kōen) provides good views of the city and great views of aircraft landing at nearby Hakata airport.

Ōhori-kōen, an expansive park and pond (once part of the castle's moat system) is just adjacent to the castle grounds, and has the traditionally styled **Nihon-teien** (日本庭園; Japanese Garden; ☎092-741-8377; 1-7 Ōhori-kōen; adult/child ¥240/¥120; ⏰9am-5pm Sep-May, to 6pm Jun-Aug Tue-Sun; 🚇Ōhori-kōen). It's a more recent construction (1984) around a pond with stone gardens and a teahouse.

Nearby, **Fukuoka Art Museum** (福岡市美術館; ☎092-714-6051; www.fukuoka-art-museum.jp/english; 1-6 Ōhori-kōen; admission ¥200; ⏰9.30am-5pm Tue-Sun Sep-May, to 7pm Tue-Sat, to 5pm Sun Jul & Aug; 🚇Ōhori-kōen) has ancient pottery and Buddhist guardians on one floor; works by Basquiat, Brancusi, Rothko and Warhol upstairs; and galleries pairing Western artists with Japanese contemporaries. Most exhibits change every few months.

Tenjin Chūō-kōen PARK
(天神中央公園; 🚇Nakasu-Kawabata or Tenjin) Some attractive historic Western architecture populates this park by City Hall, most

Central Fukuoka

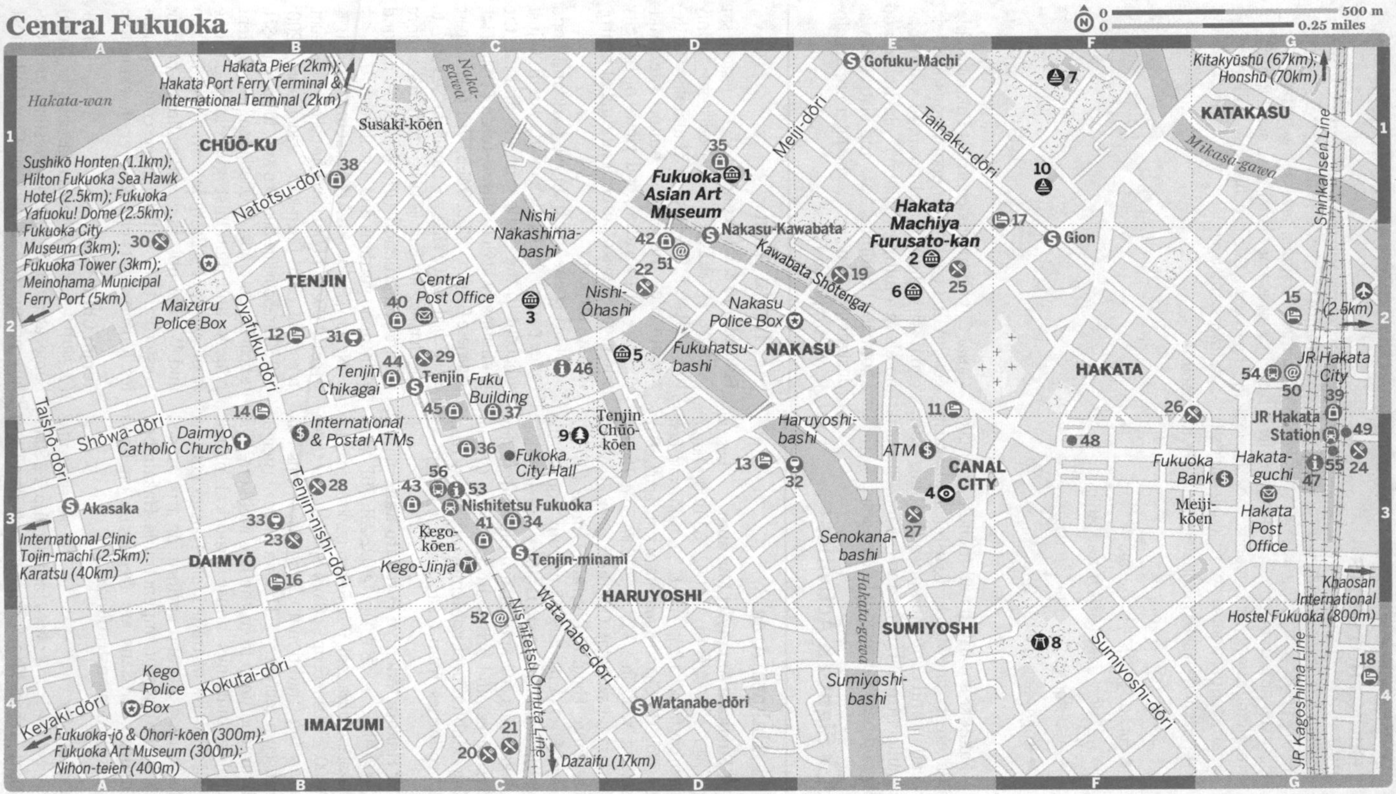

0 500 m
0 0.25 miles

Hakata-wan
Hakata Pier (2km); Hakata Port Ferry Terminal & International Terminal (2km)
Naka-gawa
Susaki-kōen
Gofuku-Machi
7
Kitakyūshū (67km); Honshū (70km)
KATAKASU
Mikasa-gawa
Shinkansen Line
CHŪŌ-KU
Sushikō Honten (1.1km); Hilton Fukuoka Sea Hawk Hotel (2.5km); Fukuoka Yafuoku! Dome (2.5km); Fukuoka City Museum (3km); Fukuoka Tower (3km); Meinohama Municipal Ferry Port (5km)
30
38
Natotsu-dōri
35
Fukuoka Asian Art Museum 1
Meiji-dōri
Taihaku-dōri
10
Nishi Nakashima-bashi
42
51
Nakasu-Kawabata
Kawabata Shōtengai
Hakata Machiya Furusato-kan 2
17
Gion
TENJIN
Central Post Office
40
3
22
Nishi-Ōhashi
19
6
25
Maizuru Police Box
Oyafuku-dōri
12
31
Nakasu Police Box
15
(2.5km)
44
29
Tenjin Chikagai
Tenjin
Fuku Building
37
46
5
Fukuhatsu-bashi
NAKASU
HAKATA
54
50
JR Hakata City
39
14
45
Tenjin Chūō-kōen
9
Haruyoshi-bashi
11
26
JR Hakata Station
49
Taishō-dōri
Shōwa-dōri
Daimyo Catholic Church
International & Postal ATMs
36
Fukoka City Hall
ATM
48
13
32
CANAL CITY
4
Fukuoka Bank
Hakata-guchi
55
24
47
28
56
43
53
Nishitetsu Fukuoka
Akasaka
33
23
Kego-kōen
41
34
27
Meiji-kōen
Hakata Post Office
International Clinic Tojin-machi (2.5km); Karatsu (40km)
DAIMYŌ
Kego-Jinja
Tenjin-minami
Senokana-bashi
16
Tenjin-nishi-dōri
HARUYOSHI
Watanabe-dōri
Hakata-gawa
Khaosan International Hostel Fukuoka (800m)
52
Nishitetsu Ōmuta Line
SUMIYOSHI
8
Sumiyoshi-dōri
18
Kego Police Box
Kokutai-dōri
Sumiyoshi-bashi
Watanabe-dōri
JR Kagoshima Line
Keyaki-dōri
Fukuoka-jō & Ōhori-kōen (300m); Fukuoka Art Museum (300m); Nihon-teien (400m)
IMAIZUMI
21
20
Dazaifu (17km)

Central Fukuoka

Top Sights
1 Fukuoka Asian Art Museum D1
2 Hakata Machiya Furusato-kan E2

Sights
3 Akarenga Bunka-kan C2
4 Canal City E3
5 Former Prefectural Hall & Official Guest House D2
6 Hakata Local History Museum E2
Rakusuien .... (see 8)
7 Shōfuku-ji F1
8 Sumiyoshi-jinja F4
9 Tenjin Chūō-kōen C3
10 Tōchō-ji F1

Sleeping
11 Dormy Inn Premium E2
12 Hotel Etwas Tenjin B2
13 Il Palazzo D3
14 La Soeur Fukuoka Hotel Monterey B2
15 Nishitetsu Inn Hakata G2
16 Plaza Hotel Premier B3
17 Ryokan Kashima Honkan F1
18 With the Style G4

Eating
19 Curry Honpo E2
20 Fish Man C4
21 Henry & Cowell C4
22 Ichiran D2
23 Ippudō B3
24 Ippudō G3
25 Murata E2
No No Budo .... (see 36)
26 Rāmen Jinanbō F2
27 Rāmen Stadium E3
28 Tenjin Nobunaga B3
29 Yatai Food Stalls C2
30 Zauo A2

Drinking & Nightlife
31 International Bar B2
32 Mitsubachi D3
33 Morris B3

Shopping
34 Daimaru C3
35 Hakata-ori no Sennen Kōbō D1
36 IMS building C3
37 Junkudō Fukuoka C2
38 Mandarake B1
39 Maruzen G2
40 mina tenjin C2
41 Mitsukoshi C3
42 Shōgetsudō D2
43 Solaria Plaza C3
44 Tenjin Chikagai B2
45 Tenjin Core C2

Information
46 ACROS Fukuoka C2
47 Hakata Station General Information Center G3
48 HIS Travel F3
49 JR Kyūshū Travel Agency G3
50 Media Café Popeye – Hakata-ekimae G2
51 Media Café Popeye – Nakasu D2
52 Media Café Popeye – Tenjin C4
53 Nishitetsu Tenjin Bus Center Tourist Information C3
Rainbow Plaza .... (see 36)

Transport
54 Fukuoka Kōtsū Centre G2
55 JR Hakata Station G3
56 Nishitetsu Tenjin Bus Terminal C3

notably the French Renaissance-styled **Former Prefectural Hall & Official Guest House** (旧福岡県公会堂貴賓館; 6-29 Nishi-nakasu; admission ¥240; ⌚9am-5pm Tue-Sun), dating from 1910 and including a cafe. A couple of blocks north, the copper-turreted **Akarenga Bunka-kan** (福岡市赤煉瓦文化館; Red Brick Cultural Centre; ⌚9am-9pm Tue-Sun) FREE was built in 1909 by the same architect who designed Tokyo Station, and now hosts simple historical exhibits.

Coastal Fukuoka

Fukuoka's northwest coast is a modern mix of corporate headquarters, hotels, large shopping and entertainment venues and apartment blocks, easiest reached by bus from Tenjin or Hakata.

Several pretty islands are a quick ferry ride's reach from the mainland and offer a nice day trip diversion for those with extra time.

Fukuoka Tower OBSERVATORY
(福岡タワー; www.fukuokatower.co.jp; 2-3-26 Momochi-hama; adult/child/student & senior ¥800/200/500; ⌚9.30am-10pm Apr-Sep, to 9pm Oct-Mar) Standing above the Momochi district is the 234m-tall Fukuoka Tower, a symbol of the city and mostly hollow (its main purpose is as a broadcast tower). There's an observation deck at 123m and a cafe for soaking up the views, especially at dusk. Ask

SHRINES & TEMPLES

The intimate **Kushida-jinja**, municipal Shintō shrine of Hakata, traces its history to AD 757 and sponsors the Hakata Gion Yamakasa Matsuri, in which storeys-high floats make their way through the streets. A one-room **local history museum** (博多歴史館; 1-41 Kami-kawabata; museum admission ¥300; ⊙10am-5pm Tue-Sun; Ⓜ Gion or Nakasu-Kawabata) covers the festival, plus swords, ancient pottery and more.

Other temples/shrines worth visiting:

Sumiyoshi-jinja (住吉神社; 2-10-7 Sumiyoshi) Sumiyoshi-jinja is said to be the original *taisha* (grand shrine) of Shintō's Sumiyoshi sect. On its north side is **Rakusuien** (楽水園; http://rakusuien.net; admission/tea ¥100/300; ⊙9am-5pm Wed-Mon), a pretty garden and teahouse built by a Meiji-era merchant, which offers an outdoor tea ceremony.

Tōchō-ji (東長寺; 2-4 Gokushō-machi; Ⓜ Gion) Tōchō-ji has Japan's largest wooden Buddha (10.8m high, 30 tonnes, created in 1992) and some impressively carved Kannon (goddess of mercy) statues. The temple is said to date from AD 806 and to have been founded by Kūkai, founder of the Shingon school of Buddhism.

Shōfuku-ji (聖福寺; 6-1 Gokushō-machi; Ⓜ Gion) Shōfuku-ji is a Zen temple founded in 1195 by Eisai, who introduced Zen and tea to Japan; the nation's first tea plants are said to have been planted here. Note: its buildings are closed to the public, but tree-lined stone paths make a nice ramble.

for the foreigner discount. While you're in the area, drop into Robosquare nearby.

Fukuoka City Museum MUSEUM
(福岡市博物館; http://museum.city.fukuoka.jp; 3-1-1 Momochi-hama; admission ¥200; ⊙9.30am-5.30pm Tue-Sun Sep-Jun, to 7.30pm Tue-Sat, to 5.30pm Sun Jul & Aug) This smart museum displays artefacts from local history and culture, and the pride of the collection is an ancient 2.3 sq cm, 108g golden seal with an inscription proving Japan's historic ties to China.

Fukuoka Yafuoku! Dome STADIUM
(福岡ヤフオク！ドーム; www.softbankhawks.co.jp/stadium) This monolithic, retractable-roof stadium is the home field of Fukuoka's much-loved SoftBank Hawks baseball team. Tours (in Japanese) are offered and there's a museum of the life of Oh Sadaharu, the world's all-time home-run king (best for die-hard fans).

Nokonoshima ISLAND
(能古島) A quick ferry ride from Fukuoka, pretty **Nokonoshima** (能古島) mixes natural and man-made parks. The latter, called **Island Park** (アイランドパーク; www.nokonoshima.com; adult/child ¥1000/500), gets the most visitors, with a swimming beach, fields of seasonal wildflowers, huts selling crafts, and sweeping ocean views.

Bicycle rental (per hour/day ¥300/1000) and English maps are available at Noko Market (のこの市), by the ferry dock. Buses 300 and 301 depart frequently from Nishitetsu Tenjin bus terminal (¥360, 20 minutes) for Meinohama Municipal Ferry Port (not to be confused with Meinohama on the subway line).

Shikanoshima ISLAND
(志賀島) Delightfully rural, this island has fresh seafood restaurants that line the harbourside streets. Ferries depart hourly (¥670, 33 minutes) from Bayside Place, along with seasonal sightseeing cruises around Hakata Bay. Shikanoshima also has a fishing shrine (志賀海神社), decorated with deer antlers, and a popular beach about 5km east of the shrine.

Festivals & Events

Hakozaki-gū Tamaseseri CULTURAL
On 3 January, two groups of young men clad in loincloths raucously chase a wooden ball in the name of good fortune at Hakozaki-gū shrine.

Hakata Dontaku Minato Matsuri CULTURAL
Tracing its roots to the port festival, on 3 and 4 May, Fukuoka's Meiji-dōri vibrates to the percussive shock of *shamoji* (wooden serving spoons) being banged together like castanets, with *shamisen* (three-stringed banjo) accompaniment.

Hakata Gion Yamakasa Matsuri CULTURAL

The city's main festival is held from 1 to 15 July, climaxing at 4.59am on the 15th, when seven groups of men converge at Kushida-jinja to race along a 5km-long course carrying huge portable shrines called *yamakasa*. According to legend, the festival originated after a 13th-century Buddhist priest was carried aloft, sprinkling holy water over victims of a plague.

Kyūshū Bashō Sumo Tournament SUMO

Held over two weeks at the Fukuoka Kokusai Centre during mid-November. Spectators start lining up at dawn for limited same-day tickets (*tōjitsu-ken;* ¥3400 to ¥15,000).

Sleeping

Fukuoka is a destination for both business and pleasure, with plenty of quality accommodation at all budgets. Stay near JR Hakata Station for convenience if railing around, although Tenjin is a better bet if you plan to spend a few days shopping and playing.

Hakata Area

★Ryokan Kashima Honkan RYOKAN ¥

(和風旅館 鹿島本館; ☎092-291-0746; fax 092-271-7995; 3-11 Reisen-machi; s/d Sun-Thu ¥4000/7000, Fri & Sat ¥6300/10,000; @📶; 🚇Gion) This charmingly creaky, unpretentious Taishō-era ryokan is a historic landmark, pleasantly faded and focused around a small garden with a stone lantern. Oozing atmosphere, it's a great place to sample traditional Japan. The friendly owners communicate well in English. No private baths, but Japanese/Western breakfasts are available for ¥800/700.

Khaosan International Hostel Fukuoka HOSTEL ¥

(☎092-404-6035; www.khaosan-fukuoka.com; 11-34 Hiemachi; dm/s/tw from ¥2400/3500/5200; 🚭@📶; 🚇Hakata) This 19-room hostel offers bare-bones accommodation and a communal TV and DVDs, plus a roof deck for meeting other travellers. From Hakata Station, head down Chikushi-dōri and turn left at Hotto Motto *bentō* shop.

Nishitetsu Inn Hakata HOTEL ¥¥

(西鉄イン博多; ☎092-413-5454; www.n-inn.jp; 1-17-6 Hakata-ekimae; s/d/tw from ¥8300/10,300/15,400; 🚭@📶; 🚇Hakata) Across from the station, this shiny, spotless 503-room hotel has decent-sized rooms but really scores points for its common baths and sauna (in addition to en suite facilities). Visit them in a spiffy waffle-pattern *yukata* (light cotton kimono).

Dormy Inn Premium BUSINESS HOTEL ¥¥

(ドーミーインプレミアム; ☎092-272-5489; www.hotespa.net; 9-1 Gionmachi; s/d Sun-Thu from ¥9290/13,490, d Fri & Sat from ¥25,600; P🚭@📶) Rates are not the cheapest in town and rooms are pretty cramped, but that doesn't tell the whole story. The Dormy Inn has a natural onsen (hot spring) in addition to in-room showers, and rates include nightly bowls of rāmen. Plus, the location next to Canal City is hard to beat. Rates rise substantially on weekends, and note: no children are allowed.

Its 122 rooms (all nonsmoking) are done up in warm earth tones and bold Hakata-ori weaving patterns, and sliding doors keep corridor noise at bay. Look for discounts on the website.

★With the Style HOTEL ¥¥¥

(ウィズザスタイル福岡; ☎092-433-3900; www.withthestyle.com; 1-9-18 Hakataeki-minami; r from ¥45,200; 🚭@; 🚇Hakata) We don't know what the name means, but 'style' is indeed the byword at this sleek designer hotel. You could easily imagine yourself poolside in Hollywood around the fountain courtyard. Each of the 16 rooms exude rock star cool, all include breakfast, minibar and welcome drinks, and guests can reserve complimentary private use of the rooftop spa or penthouse bar. With a steakhouse on-site, it's an inner-city retreat to savour.

Tenjin Area

Hotel Etwas Tenjin HOTEL ¥¥

(ホテルエトワス天神; ☎092-737-3233; www.hoteletwas.co.jp; 3-5-18 Tenjin; s/d ¥6000/8000; 🚭@📶; 🚇Tenjin) Recently refurbished and good value. Its 84 rooms are tiny, but clean and good value for the location: with lively Oyafuko-dōri around the corner, it's hard to complain. Free breakfast and lobby wi-fi sweeten the deal. There are even automatic check-in machines, a glimpse of the future!

Plaza Hotel Premier HOTEL ¥¥

(プラザホテルプルミエ; ☎092-734-7600; www.plaza-hotel.net; 1-14-13 Daimyō; s/d/tw from ¥8100/13,500/15,550; P🚭@📶; 🚇Tenjin or Akasaka) Location, location and location is the main reason to stay here in trendy Daimyō, yet business-hotel-size rooms rival far pricier hotels. The night vibe on the street outside is ubercool and its ground floor trattoria, AW Kitchen, looks like it belongs on a fashionable Tokyo side street. Check online for discount coupons.

La Soeur Fukuoka Hotel Monterey HOTEL ¥¥¥
(ホテルモントレ ラ・スール福岡; ☎092-726-7111; www.hotelmonterey.co.jp/en; 2-8-27 Daimyō; s/d from ¥16,200/25,500; P ⊖ @ ; Tenjin) A popular wedding spot, this 182-room property has a prime location and well-appointed rooms with contemporary French touches and parquet floors. Check the website for bargains.

Il Palazzo HOTEL ¥¥¥
(☎092-716-3333; www.ilpalazzo.jp; 3-13-1 Haruyoshi; s/d/tw from ¥17,000/26,000/29,000; ⊖ @; Nakasu-Kawabata) Don't be put off by the windowless, colonnaded facade of burnt orange and obsidian by Uchida Shigeru, whose work also includes boutiques for fashion designer Yohji Yamamoto. The lobby is as glossy as black lipstick, the 62 rooms are slick and soothing, staff couldn't be sweeter, and you're just steps from Nakasu-gawa and Tenjin hot spots (yet hidden on a quiet street).

Coastal Fukuoka Area

Hilton Fukuoka Sea Hawk HOTEL ¥¥¥
(ヒルトン福岡シーホーク; ☎092-844-8111; www.hilton.com; 2-2-3 Jigyohama; s/d from ¥15,444/21,740; P ⊖ @) If you want to make an impression, you can hardly do better anywhere in Japan. The lobby restaurant of this César Pelli–designed hotel soars like its namesake bird, and at 1052 rooms, it's Asia's largest Hilton.

Eating

To most Japanese, Hakata means *tonkotsu rāmen* – noodles in a distinctive broth made from pork bones. Other specialities include *yakitori* (grilled chicken on skewers), *yakiniku* (Korean-style grilled beef) and fresh seafood.

The Fukuoka way to eat is at *yatai* (屋台), mobile hawker-style food carts with simple counters and seats; Fukuoka claims about 150 *yatai,* more than in the rest of Japan combined! Let the aromas and chatty conversation lead you to the best cooking and the best companions. For a more local experience, try the **yatai** (dusk; Tenjin) around Tenjin or Nagahama. Get there early as most seats are soon taken. (Note that if you talk too much without ordering enough you'll be asked to move on.)

For other restaurant browsing, greater Tenjin is a good bet, or try the restaurants on the 9th and 10th floors of JR Hakata City (the Hakata Station building). Or grab some takeaway from the *depachika* (food hall) in the basement of Hankyu or Amu, nearby.

Curry Honpo CURRY ¥
(伽哩本舗; ☎092-262-0010; www.curry-honpo.com; 6-135 Kami-kawabata; curry from ¥700; 11am-9.30pm; ; Nakasu-Kawabata) Try the Kawabata Shōtengai location of the famous shop for some *yaki-curry* (broiled curry rice with cheese), which the English menu disturbingly refers to as 'combustion curry'. The standard is pork combustion curry (¥700). It's the wood-panelled and faux-brick storefront in the arcade.

Murata NOODLES ¥
(信州そばむらた; ☎092-291-0894; 2-9-1 Reisen-machi; soba from ¥700; 11.30am-9pm, closed 2nd Sun of month; ; Gion) Down the street from the Hakata Machiya Furusato-kan, this lovely eatery makes homemade *soba* (buckwheat noodles) from the Shinshū area of central Japan (around Nagano), prepared in a variety of ways including *kakesoba* (in hot broth, ¥700), *zaru-soba* (cold with dipping sauce, ¥850) and *oroshi-soba* (cold, topped with grated *daikon,* ¥1000).

★ **Fish Man** IZAKAYA ¥¥
(Sakana Otoko; 魚男フィッシュマン; ☎092-717-3571; 1-4-23 Imaizumi; teishoku ¥680-1500; 11.30am-3pm & 5.30pm-1am; Tenjin-minami) Fish Man's post-industrial vibe has lacquered plywood and big windows, which show off the unconventional presentations of seafood fresh from the Nagahama market across town: *kaidan-zushi* (sushi served on a wooden spiral staircase, ¥1500), *tsubotai no misoyaki* (miso-grilled snapper, ¥880) or a *maguro* hamburger served on a steel plate (¥980).

There's no English menu here, but the English-speaking staff can help explain. Look for the banner outside reading 'No Fish, No Life'.

Afterwards, stop for dessert at Fish Man's adorable affiliated cake shop **Henry & Cowell** (☎092-741-7888; 1-3-11 Imaizumi; 11am-9pm), just down the street. It also has a small selection of takeaway foods.

HAKATA'S RĀMEN KINGS

Fukuokans and non-Fukuokans alike salivate at the mention of Hakata rāmen. The distinctive local version of these ubiquitous noodles is called *tonkotsu rāmen*, served in a hearty broth made from pork bones.

And if for some reason Hakata-style rāmen doesn't satisfy you, in Canal City there's **Rāmen Stadium** (ラーメンスタジアム; ☎092-282-2525; 5th fl, Canal City; rāmen from ¥550; ⊙11am-11pm), an entire floor of eight rāmen vendors imported from the length and breadth of Japan.

Ichiran (一蘭; ☎092-262-0433; www.ichiran.co.jp/english/; 5-3-2 Nakasu; rāmen from ¥790; ⊙24hr; 📋; 🚇Tenjin) Ichiran has been serving noodles for 39 years. Customers eat at individual cubicles, and fill out forms requesting precisely how they want their noodles prepared. Flavour strength, fat content, noodle tenderness, quantity of special sauce and garlic content can all be regulated. An English-language request form is also available.

Their corporate office/main location in Nakasu has two stories: the upper floor has the signature individual booths the chain is known for, the ground floor is more traditional, with sit-down tables and a bar. Look for the bright green and red awning.

Ippudō (一風堂; ☎092-781-0303; 1-12-61 Daimyō; rāmen ¥700-800; ⊙11am-2am Sun-Thu, 10.30am-4am Fri & Sat; 📋; 🚇Tenjin) Has workmanlike and always bustling branches in Tenjin, serving the best-selling Akamaru Modern (with black sesame oil and a fragrant *umami-dama*, or flavour ball), Shiromaru Classic (with thin noodles) and Karaka (spicy rāmen). There's also a **second branch** (☎092-413-5088; 10th fl, JR Hakata City, 1-1 Hakata-eki-chūō-gai; rāmen ¥700-800; ⊙11am-midnight; 🚇Hakata) in the JR Hakata City shopping centre.

Rāmen Jinanbō (ラーメン二男坊; ☎092-473-5558; 2-16-4 Hakata Eki-mae; rāmen ¥700-1100; ⊙11am-midnight Mon-Sat, 11am-9pm Sun; 🚇Hakata) Cozy rāmen/pub that's just a few minutes from Hakata's Higashi-guchi. No frills, just thick, Fukuoka-style broth, noodles and draughts, with most of the seating at the bar. Also has a branch in Rāmen Stadium.

★Zauo — SEAFOOD ¥¥

(ざうお; ☎092-716-9989; www.zauo.com; 1-4-15 Nagahama; catch your own fish from ¥3660; ⊙5pm-11.30pm Mon-Fri, 11.30am-11pm Sat & Sun; 👪; 🚇Akasaka) Staff equip you with fishing rods, bait and nets to fish your own *tai* (sea bream), *hirame* (flounder) and more from giant tanks surrounding tables on boat-shaped platforms. When you make a catch, they'll bang drums before taking the fish away to prepare to your taste: sashimi, grilled, fried etc. Kitschy, but fun. There are other *izakaya*-style dishes if fish isn't your thing.

Sushikō Honten — SUSHI ¥¥

(すし幸本店; ☎092-761-1659; 2-11-18 Minatomachi; meals from ¥1050; ⊙11am-10pm; 🚇Ōhori-kōen) Sushi here can be two completely different experiences: elegant and dignified on the 2nd floor, or served together with other dishes in a rollicking upstairs beer garden that's open year-round for dinner only and covered in inclement weather (all you can eat and drink for women/men from ¥2500/3150).

Tenjin Nobunaga — YAKITORI ¥¥

(天神信長; ☎092-721-6940; 2-6-21 Tenjin; skewers ¥105-263; ⊙5pm-1am Mon-Sun; 🚇Tenjin) Nobunaga is raucous and rowdy, and that's just the chefs. There's no English menu but it's easy to choose from the skewers behind the counter. Another house speciality is *potato-mochiage* (¥420), a fried dumpling of mashed potato, cheese and *mochi* (pounded rice). Look for the red lanterns just to the right of Big Echo karaoke hall.

No No Budo — BUFFET ¥¥

(野の葡萄; ☎092-714-1441; IMS Bldg, 1-7-11 Tenjin; lunch/dinner ¥1680/2200; ⊙11am-4pm & 5-11pm Mon-Sun; 🚇Tenjin) The IMS building (天神イムズ) has prime skyline views from its 12th- and 13th-floor restaurants, including No No Budo. The busy self-serve gourmet buffet has good-for-you Japanese and Western fish and meat dishes, noodles, salads, soups and nice pastries. An extra ¥1300 buys all-you-can-drink beer, wine and cocktails.

🍷 Drinking & Nightlife

The weekend starts on Thursday in multicultural, party-friendly Fukuoka. Tenjin and

Daimyō's streets are safe, easy to explore and great for people-watching. The main drag, Oyafuko-dōri, roughly translates to 'street of unruly children' because of the cram schools that once lined it. In a way, the cap still fits. Nakasu Island, while one of Japan's busiest entertainment districts, is often sleazy.

International Bar BAR
(インターナショナルバー; 4th fl, Urashima Bldg, 3-1-13 Tenjin; 7pm-late; Tenjin) There's free karaoke on Tuesdays at this tiny bar. Like the name implies, it's one of the original places in Fukuoka for locals and *gaijin* (foreigners) to connect, in a time warp of red-velvet seating and hip-hop beats.

Mitsubachi BAR
(ミツバチ; 092-739-3800; 5th Hotel East, 3-4-65 Haruyoshi; 6pm-5am Mon-Sat , 6pm-1am Sun & holidays; Nakasu-Kawabata) Enjoy views of Hakata and Canal City across the Naka-gawa through giant windows in this pretty dining bar. With lots of glass and mirrors, it's a flashy spot to make a first impression.

Nishijin Saisei Sakaba BAR
(西新再生酒場; 050-5572-3966; 4-9-13 Nishijin; yakitori from ¥110, beers ¥600; 5pm-3am Mon-Sun; ; Nishijin) This may be Japan's only *izakaya* (pub-eatery) with private, no-smoking rooms – come here to drink, laugh, sing karaoke, enjoy great pub-style food, and (for once) you don't have to be coughing through the clouds.

Morris PUB
(モーリス; 092-771-4774; 7th fl, Stage 1 Nishidōri Bldg, 2-1-4 Daimyō; from 5pm; ; Tenjin) One of the better pub chains in Japan, this chain attracts a nice mix of Japanese and *gaijin*. Begin your evening with happy-hour cocktails (¥250; 5pm to 7pm) on the awesome patio perched high above trendy Daimyō. There's a good beer selection and tasty pub food.

Shopping

Big department stores dominate the skyline of Tenjin and around Hakata Station. Fukuoka's department stores occupy a three-block gauntlet of Watanabe-dōri in Tenjin. **Tenjin Core** (天神コア; 092-721-8436), **Mitsukoshi** (三越; 092-724-3111), **Daimaru** (大丸; 092-712-8181), **Solaria Plaza** (ソラリアプラザ; 092-733-7777), the **IMS Building** (天神イムズ; 092-733-2001; Tenjin 1-7-11) and **Mina Tenjin** (ミーナ天神; 092-713-3711) are all favourites, as is the subterranean **Tenjin Chikagai** (天神地下街; 092-711-1903;).

For contemporary fashion, low-rise boutiques in the Daimyō district show off local designers, and lining the avenue Keyaki-dōri are intimate shops for antiques, design items and foreign crafts.

Shōgetsudō ARTS & CRAFTS
(松月堂; 092-291-4141; 5-1-22 Nakasu; 9am-7pm; Nakasu-Kawabata) White-faced clay Hakata *ningyō* (dolls) depicting women, children, samurai and geisha are a popular Fukuoka craft. This place sells them and offers painting workshops (¥1575 to ¥3150).

Hakata-ori no Sennen Kōbō KIMONO
(博多織の千年工房; 092-283-8111; B1 fl, Hakata Riverain, 3-1 Shimo-Kawabata-machi; 10.30am-7.30pm; Nakasu-Kawabata) Hakata is also renowned for its weaving tradition, called Hakata-ori, and this elegant shop offers obis, kimonos and accessories from business-card holders to handbags in the distinctive style. None of it is cheap (silk obi start at around ¥10,000), but it's meant to last generations. Hakata-ori is also available at Tenjin's department stores.

Mandarake MANGA
(まんだらけ; 092-716-7774; 2-9-5 Daimyō; noon-8pm; Tenjin) The Fukuoka branch of Mandarake is Kyūshū's largest manga store, with several storeys of games, comic books and DVDs.

Junkudō Fukuoka BOOKS
(ジュンク堂書店; 1st-4th fl, Media Mall; 10am-8.30pm; Tenjin) This bookshop sells foreign paperbacks.

Maruzen BOOKS
(丸善; 8th fl, Hakata Station Bldg, Hakata-eki; 10am-9pm; Hakata) Maruzen has a huge selection of Japanese- and English-language books, magazines and DVDs.

Orientation

For visitors, Fukuoka can be divided into three main districts. Hakata, the old *shitamachi* (downtown), is now dominated by Fukuoka's *shinkansen* stop, the busy JR Hakata Station. Three subway stops away and across the river Naka-gawa is Fukuoka's beating heart, the Tenjin district, bursting with department stores, boutiques, eateries and nightlife. Above ground, Tenjin centres around Watanabe-dōri, paralleled underground by Tenjin Chikagai, a long shopping arcade with mood lighting and cast-ironwork ceilings that make it a cool refuge from the

WORTH A TRIP

MOJIKŌ & YAHATA

Kitakyūshū is at the island's far north. Its two enclaves can be a good day trip.

Mojikō (門司港) has been a port since 1889, and its harbourside 'Retro Town' is a trove of Meiji- and Taishō-period architecture, handsome brick buildings that once housed shipping companies and customs houses, and a drawbridge for pedestrians. Check www.en.mojiko.info before you go for sightseeing tips. You can walk under the Kanmon Strait via the tunnel to Shimonoseki on Honshū. A row of shops along the waterfront serves Mojikō's signature dish, *yaki-curry* (curry rice broiled with melted cheese on top).

Yahata (八幡) is a one-time industrial town that has cleaned up its act with inspirational results. **Kitakyūshū Kankyō Museum** (北九州市環境ミュージアム; Kitakyūshū Environment Museum; www.eco-museum.com; 2-2-6 Higashida Yahata; 9am-5pm Tue-Sun) FREE has 'radioramas' (with sound available in English) that tell of the environmental degradation of Kyūshū in the early industrial period (including the notorious Minamata disease that struck near Kumamoto in the 1950s, a poisoning caused by mercury released into Minamata Bay by a chemical factory which polluted, knowingly, for more than three decades, according to a 1968 government ruling). Interactive exhibits illustrate the effects of pollution. Steps away, the futuristic **Kitakyūshū Innovation Gallery & Studio** (北九州イノベーションギャラリー; www.kigs.jp; 2-2-11 Higashida Yahata; 9am-7pm Tue-Fri, to 5pm Sat & Sun) offers changing special exhibits (varies, often ¥500) and an excellent chronology of technological innovation. Across the road is a towering **steel foundry** from 1901, now cleaned up and a great place for a *bentō* (boxed meal) picnic.

From Hakata, transfer at Kokura (*shinkansen* ¥3390, 16 minutes; *tokkyū* limited express ¥1320, 40 minutes). From Kokura local trains cost ¥280 to either Mojikō (13 minutes) or Space World Station (for Yahata, 10 minutes).

summer heat. West of Tenjin is trendy Daimyō, Fukuoka's homage to Tokyo's Harajuku, minus the crowds, heading towards Fukuoka's former castle grounds.

The coastal neighbourhoods, best reached by bus or taxi, have many attractive sights, restaurants and hotels.

Information

INTERNET ACCESS

Fukuoka is refreshingly wired, with free public wi-fi available at city hall, major train and subway stations, the airport, tourist information centres and in the Tenjin Chikagai (underground arcade). **Media Cafe Popeye** (www.media-cafe.net) has branches at **Hakata-ekimae** (メディアカフェポパイ博多駅前; 8th fl, Fukuoka Kōtsū Centre Bldg; 24hr; Hakata), **Nakasu** (メディアカフェポパイ中州店; 8th fl, Spoon Bldg, 5-1-7 Nakasu; 24hr; Nakasu-Kawabata) and **Tenjin** (メディアカフェポパイ天神店; 2nd fl, Nishitetsu Imaizumi Bldg, 1-12-23 Imaizumi; 24hr; Tenjin-minami). Each has a free soft-drink bar, massage chairs and couples' booths. Offers ¥420 for the first 60 minutes, then ¥80 per subsequent 10 minutes.

MEDICAL SERVICES

International Clinic Tojin-machi (092-717-1000; http://internationalclinic.org; 1-4-6 Jigyo; 9am-1pm & 2:20-6pm Mon, Tue, Thu & Fri, 9am-1pm Sat; Tōjin-machi, Exit 1) Multilingual clinic for general medical services and emergencies. It's two blocks from the station.

MONEY

In addition to the post office and Seven Bank ATMs, banks and ATMs offer currency exchange at Fukuoka Airport, there's a 24-hour Citibank ATM (シティバンク ATM) in Tenjin, and most banks around JR Hakata Station and Tenjin handle foreign-exchange services.

POST

The **central post office** (福岡中央郵便局; 9am-7pm Mon-Sat, to 12.30pm Sun & holidays, ATM 12.05am–11.55pm Mon-Sat, to 9pm Sun & holidays) is one block northeast of Tenjin subway station, and **Hakata post office** (博多郵便局) is just outside JR Hakata Station's Hakata-guchi.

TOURIST INFORMATION

Fukuoka City Tourist Information Counters (福岡市観光案内所) at Fukuoka Airport, **Hakata Station General Information Center** (福岡市観光案内所JR博多駅支店; 092-431-3003; 8am-9pm) and **Nishitetsu Bus Center** (福岡市観光案内所天神支店; 092-751-6904; 10am-6.30pm) in Tenjin dispense maps, coupons and the helpful *City Visitor's Guide*, and can help with lodging, transport and car-rental information. Information centres at

WORTH A TRIP

TACHIARAI

From 1919 to 1945, the isolated farm village of Tachiarai (大刀洗) hosted a training school for Japanese fighter pilots, including some on kamikaze suicide missions. Expanded in 2009, **Tachiarai Heiwa Kinenkan** (大刀洗平和記念館; Tachiarai Peace Memorial Museum; ☎0946-23-1227; http://tachiarai-heiwa.jp; admission ¥500; ⊙9am-5pm) shows the rigorous training these men endured. English signage is basic, but the artefacts are evocative (uniforms, medals, gold-plated sake cups etc). The centrepiece is a jet fighter shot down during the war and recovered from Hakata Bay in 1996. The museum also memorialises kamikaze pilots and townspeople who died during a USAF B-29 bombing on 27 March 1945.

The museum is across from Tachiarai Station. From Fukuoka, take the Nishitetsu line to Nishitetsu Ogōri (¥500, 30 minutes); from Dazaifu (¥330) it takes 25 minutes plus transfer time at Nishitetsu Futsukaichi. Then walk to Ogōri Station on the Amagi Railway for the trip to Tachiarai (¥280, 15 minutes). JR passengers can transfer to the Amagi Railway at Kiyama (¥330, 20 minutes).

ACROS Fukuoka (アクロス福岡; ☎092-725-9100; www.acros.or.jp/r_facilities/information.html; Cultural Information Centre, 2nd fl, ACROS Bldg, 1-1-1 Tenjin; ⊙10am-6pm, closed 29 Dec-3 Jan; Ⓡ Nakasu-Kawabata or Tenjin) and **Rainbow Plaza** (レインボープラザ; ☎092-733-2220; www.rainbowfia.or.jp; 8F, IMS Bldg, 1-7-11 Tenjin; ⊙10am-8pm, closed 3rd Tue most months) are targeted mostly at foreign residents.

Fukuoka Now (www.fukuoka-now.com) is an indispensable monthly English-language street mag with detailed city maps.

Yokanavi.com (www.yokanavi.com/eg) is a comprehensive Fukuoka/Hakata tourist information site.

TRAVEL AGENCIES

HIS Travel (☎092-735-5545; www.his-j.com; 4th fl, Yodobashi Hakata Bldg., 6-12 Chūō-gai; ⊙10am-8.30pm; Ⓡ Hakata) Discount international and domestic arrangements can be made at the Hakata branch of this international chain.

JR Kyūshū Travel Agency (☎092-431-6215; 1-1 Chuo-gai; ⊙10am-8pm Mon-Sat, to 6pm Sun; Ⓡ Hakata) Provides bookings and advice for travel within Kyūshū and Japan. Located within JR Hakata Station.

Getting There & Away

AIR

Fukuoka Airport (☎ domestic terminal 092-621-6059, international terminal 092-621-0303; ⊙ domestic 6.20am-10.20pm, international 7am-9.30pm; Ⓡ Fukuoka Airport) is an international hub serving carriers from east and Southeast Asia, as well as many domestic routes including Tokyo (from Haneda/Narita airports), Osaka and Okinawa (Naha).

Cut-rate carrier **Skymark** (☎ in Tokyo 0570-051-330; www.skymark.co.jp/en) flies to Haneda Airport.

BOAT

Ferries from Hakata connect to Okinawa and other islands off Kyūshū. **Beetle** (☎ in Japan 092-281-2315, in Korea 051-469-0778; www.jrbeetle.co.jp) high-speed hydrofoils connect Fukuoka with Busan in Korea (one way/round trip ¥13,000/26,000, three hours, at least three daily). The **Camellia line** (☎ in Japan 092-262-2323, in Korea 051-466-7799; www.camellia-line.co.jp) has a regular ferry service from Fukuoka to Busan (one way/return ¥9000/17,100, six hours, daily at 12.30pm). Both ships dock at Chūō Futō (Hakata Port Ferry Terminal) via bus 88 from JR Hakata Station (¥230), or bus 80 from Tenjin (Solaria Stage-mae; ¥190).

BUS

Long-distance buses (☎ ask operator for English interpreter 0570-00-1010) depart from the **Fukuoka Kōtsū Centre** (福岡交通センター) next to JR Hakata Station (Hakata-gate) and also from the **Nishitetsu Tenjin Bus Terminal** (西鉄天神バスセンター). Destinations include Tokyo (economy/business ¥8300/12,000, 14½ hours), Osaka (from ¥8800, 9½ hours), Nagoya (¥7500, 11 hours) and many towns in Kyūshū; ask about discounted round-trip fares.

TRAIN

JR Hakata Station (JR博多駅; ☎ English information 471-8111, JR English info line 03-3423-0111) is a hub in northern Kyūshū. *Shinkansen* services operate to/from Tokyo (¥22,750, five hours), Osaka (¥15,110, 2½ hours), Hiroshima (¥8940, 62 minutes), Kumamoto (¥4930, 38 minutes) and Kagoshima-Chūō (¥10,250, 77 minutes).

Within Kyūshū, non-*shinkansen* trains run on the JR Nippō line through Beppu to Miyazaki; the Sasebo line runs from Saga to Sasebo; and the Nagasaki line runs to Nagasaki. You can also travel by subway and JR train to Karatsu and continue to Nagasaki by train.

Getting Around

TO/FROM THE AIRPORT

The subway takes just five minutes to reach JR Hakata Station (¥260) and 11 minutes to Tenjin (¥260). Shuttle buses connect domestic and international terminals.

Taxis cost around ¥1600 to Tenjin/Hakata.

BUS

City bus services operate from the Fukuoka Kōtsū Centre adjacent to JR Hakata Station and from the Nishitetsu Tenjin Bus Terminal (西鉄天神バスセンター). Many stop in front of the station (Hakata-guchi). Specially marked buses have a flat ¥100 rate for city-centre rides, or one-day passes cost ¥600/1000 for one/two adults.

TRAIN

Fukuoka has three **subway lines** (http://subway.city.fukuoka.lg.jp; ⌚5.30am-12.25am) of which visitors will find the Kūkō (Airport) line most useful, running from Fukuoka Airport to Meinohama Station via Hakata, Nakasu-Kawabata and Tenjin stations. Fares start at ¥200 (¥100 if going just one stop); a one-day pass costs adult/child ¥600/300.

Dazaifu 太宰府

☎092 / POP 71,245

Dazaifu, former government centre of Kyūshū, has a beautiful cluster of temples, a famous shrine and a striking national museum, making for a popular day trip from Fukuoka.

Sights

★Kyūshū National Museum MUSEUM

(九州国立博物館; www.kyuhaku.com; 4-7-2 Ishizaka; adult/student ¥430/130; ⌚9.30am-5pm Tue-Sun) Built into the tranquil hills of Dazaifu and reached through more escalators than the average airport, this striking structure (built in 2005) resembles a massive space station for the arts. One of the best (if not *the* best) and biggest collections of art in Kyūshū, this is a must-see for art aficionados.

Highlights include a fascinating exhibit of the relationship between Japanese arts and culture and those of the rest of Asia, varying special exhibits, pottery and a wonderful 'please touch' section for the youngest visitors.

★Tenman-gū SHINTO SHRINE

(太宰府天満宮; www.dazaifutenmangu.or.jp; 4-7-1 Saifu; ⌚sunrise-sunset) Poet-scholar Sugawara-no-Michizane was a distinguished Kyoto figure until his exile to distant Dazaifu, where he died two years later. He became deified as Tenman Tenjin, god of culture and scholars. Among the countless visitors to the grand, sprawling Tenman-gū, his shrine and burial place are students hoping to pass college entrance exams. The *hondō* (main hall) was rebuilt in 1591.

Behind the shrine is the **Kankō Historical Museum** (菅公歴史館; ☎092-922-8225; admission ¥200; ⌚9am-4.30pm Thu-Mon), with dioramas showing Tenjin's life (an English leaflet provides explanations). Across the grounds, the **Daizifu Tenman-gū Museum** (太宰府天満宮宝物殿; admission ¥400; ⌚9am-4pm Tue-Sun) has artefacts from his life including some excellent swords. This is a near-mandatory stop on the bus tour route, so expect to see swarms of people even on weekdays.

Kōmyōzen-ji BUDDHIST TEMPLE

(光明禅寺; ☎092-922-4053; admission ¥200; ⌚8am-4.30pm) Secreted away on the southern edge of Dazaifu, this small temple has an exquisite jewel of a Zen garden. It's a peaceful contrast to the crowds at the nearby shrine.

Kaidan-in MONASTERY

(戒壇院) Across town, nestled among rice paddies and reachable by bus (¥100), Kaidan-in dates from 761 and was one of the most important Buddhist ordination monasteries in Japan.

Kanzeon-ji BUDDHIST TEMPLE

(観世音寺) Adjacent to the monastery, this temple dates from 746 but only the great bell (said to be Japan's oldest) remains from the original construction. Its **treasure hall** (宝蔵; ☎092-922-1811; admission ¥500; ⌚9am-4.30pm) has an impressive collection of statuary, most of it wood, dating from the 10th to 12th centuries. Many of the items show Indian or Tibetan influence.

Dazaifu Exhibition Hall MUSEUM

(大宰府展示館; ☎092-922-7811; ⌚9am-4.30pm Tue-Sun) FREE Dazaifu Exhibition Hall displays finds from local archaeological excavations. Nearby are the **Tofurō ruins** (都府楼) of ancient government buildings.

Enoki Shrine (榎社) is where Sugawara-no-Michizane died. His body was transported to Tenman-gū on the ox cart that appears in so many local depictions.

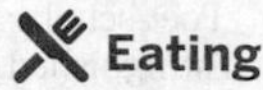

Eating

Kasanoya CAFE ¥

(かさの家; ☎092-222-1010; www.kasanoya.com; 2-7-24 Zaifu; 5 bean cakes ¥600, meals from ¥750; ⏲9am-6pm; 🚉Nishi-tetsu Dazaifu) The best reason to come here is to grab some of the best *umegaemochi* (a sweet-bean-paste-filled cake with toasted *mochi* rice on the outside) this street has to offer, assuming you're willing to wait in line. You can eat here too – either set menus or items à la carte. From the station, it's on your right as you head towards the temple, just after you pass the second *torii* (entrance) gate.

Shopping

The main street between the station and the temple has over 40 stores all selling the local *meibutsu* (delicacy) – in this case, it's *umegaemochi*. There's a plum branch insignia, which represents the plum branch that Tenjin was given to 'cheer him up' in exile.

Information

The **tourist information office** (太宰府市観光案内所; ☎092-925-1880; ⏲9am-5pm) at Nishitetsu Dazaifu Station has helpful staff and an English-language map.

Getting There & Around

The private Nishitetsu train line connects Nishitetsu Fukuoka (in Tenjin) with Dazaifu (¥400, 30 minutes). Change trains at Nishitetsu Futsukaichi Station. A new bus to Dazaifu leaves from JR Hakata Station (¥600, 40 minutes) and the airport (¥500, 30 minutes). Bicycles can be rented for ¥500 per day at Nishitetsu Dazaifu Station. Electric bikes cost ¥800 per day.

SAGA PREFECTURE

Occupying Kyūshū's northwestern corner, scenic Saga Prefecture (佐賀県; Saga-ken) is chiefly known for three towns: Karatsu, Imari and Arita. The towns were central to Japan's historic pottery trade.

Karatsu 唐津

☎0955 / POP 129,000

Karatsu is at the base of the scenic Higashi-Matsuura Peninsula, an ideal location for its historic pottery trade. Korean influences elevated the town's craft from useful ceramics to art.

In Karatsu pottery fanatics will be in their element viewing earth-toned vases and tea bowls that sell for more than a luxury car. For everyone else, there's a hilltop castle, historic buildings, a simple Shōwa-era town centre and a pretty seaside cycling trail. Outside of town, the coastline, pounded into shape by the roiling Sea of Genkai, makes for dramatic vistas and nice day hikes.

The Nakamachi shopping area, five minutes away, offers nice restaurants and souvenirs all within an easy stroll.

Sights & Activities

It's about 25 minutes' walk from JR Karatsu Station to the sea, and around town are ceramic shops, and kilns and studios where you can see local potters at work.

A **walking and cycling path** cuts through the pine trees planted behind the 5km-long Niji-no Matsubara Beach.

Nakazato Tarōemon MUSEUM

(中里太郎右衛門; 3-6-29 Chōda; ⏲9am-5.30pm) FREE This kiln-gallery is dedicated to the life and work of the potter (1923–2009) responsible for the revival of Karatsu ware. His work is in the inner gallery.

Karatsu Ware Federation Exhibition Hall GALLERY

(唐津焼総合展示場; 2nd fl, Arpino Bldg; ⏲9am-6pm) FREE Adjacent to Karatsu Station, this exhibition hall displays and sells (from ¥500) local potters' works.

Kyū-Takatori-tei HISTORIC BUILDING

(旧高取邸; 5-40 Kita-jōnai; adult/child ¥510/260; ⏲9.30am-5pm Tue-Sun) Kyū-Takatori-tei is a fabulously restored late-Meiji Period villa of a local trader, built in a mix of Japanese and Western styles, with lantern-filled gardens, a Buddhist altar room, a wealth of paintings on cedar boards and an indoor *nō* (dance-drama) stage. An English audioguide rents for ¥300.

Karatsu-jō CASTLE

(唐津城; 8-1 Higashi-jōnai; adult/child ¥410/200; ⏲9am-5pm) This 1608 castle (rebuilt 1966) is picturesquely perched on a hill overlooking the sea, and houses antique ceramics, samurai armour and archaeological displays. It's a formidable sight even from the outside. To avoid the climb through the park, Maizuru-kōen, take the outdoor elevator (¥100/50 per adult/child per ride).

WORTH A TRIP

YOBUKO

A colourful **morning market** (朝市; ⏲7.30am-noon) for squid, fish and produce animates the quaint, dwindling fishing port of Yobuko (呼子) each day, drawing visitors from all over the region. At the far end of the market is the **Nakao Mansion** (中尾家屋敷; ☎095-582-0309; adult/child ¥200/100; ⏲9am-5pm Thu-Tue), the painstakingly refurbished home and processing house of a whaling family, opened in 2011. It's filled with historical exhibits explained in English and excellent architectural details; whales were hunted in nearby waters until 1877.

Buses connect from Karatsu's Ōteguchi Bus Centre (Shōwa bus; ¥750, 30 minutes).

An overnight stay at one of the ryokan across the road from the waterfront (from around ¥15,000 including meals) will allow you to watch the flickering lights of fishing boats heading out to sea.

Hikiyama Festival Float Exhibition Hall MUSEUM

(曳山展示場; 6-33 Nishi-jōnai; admission ¥300; ⏲9am-5pm) Contains the 14 amazing floats used in the annual Karatsu Kunchi Matsuri. Floats include the Aka-jishi (Red Lion, constructed 1819), samurai helmets, and the auspicious phoenix and sea bream. There's good signage in English and a video shows festival scenes. It's near scenic **Karatsu-jinja** (唐津神社; 3-13 Minami-jōnai), the shrine that sponsors the festival.

Festivals & Events

Doyō-yoichi FOOD

Held in the town centre over four consecutive Saturdays from late July into early August.

Karatsu Kunchi Matsuri CULTURAL

From 2 to 4 November, Karatsu comes to life in this spectacular festival, dating from 1592 and designated a festival of national cultural importance. The highlight is a parade of massive, exquisitely decorated *hikiyama* (floats).

Sleeping & Eating

Karatsu Dai-Ichi Hotel HOTEL ¥¥

(☎0955-74-1000; www.kugimoto.co.jp/dai-ichi.info.htm; 488-1 Nishi-Teramachi; s/d/tw from ¥5700/9900/10,800; P⊖@) Seven minutes on foot from Karatsu Station, this hotel doesn't win style points, but has clean rooms and friendly, accommodating staff. Some singles are nonsmoking. Rates include a simple breakfast buffet.

★**Yōyōkaku** RYOKAN ¥¥¥

(洋々閣; ☎0955-72-7181; www.yoyokaku.com; 2-4-40 Higashi-Karatsu; r per person incl 2 meals from ¥18,360; P@🛜) In a word: gorgeous. Here are some more words: rambling, minimalist, woodwork, pine garden and Karatsu-yaki pottery for your in-room seafood meals. A real getaway, yet under 10 minutes' walk from the castle. Can't stay here? Visit the on-site gallery of Nakazato family pottery.

Karatsu Bāgā BURGERS ¥

(からつバーガー; www.karatsu-burger.com; burgers ¥340-460; ⏲9am-8pm) In the middle of nowhere (in a carpark) in Niji no Matsubara is a brown and white Toyota serving burgers so famous people line up to buy them, and have for decades. The 'Special' is the most popular: a steaming cheeseburger topped with a fried egg and ham slice. There's also a **branch** (からつバーガー; ☎080-9101-6912; 1513-18 Nakamachi; ⏲10am-8pm; 🅡Karatsu) in Nakamachi, near Karatsu station.

★**Kawashima Tōfu** TOFU ¥¥

(川島豆腐店; ☎0955-72-2423; www.zarudoufu.co.jp; Kyōmachi 1775; set meals lunch ¥1620-2675, dinner ¥5000-10,000; ⏲8am-10pm, meal seatings 8am, 10am, noon, 5.30pm) On the shopping street near the station, this renowned tofu shop has been in business since the Edo period and serves set meals starring tofu plus other seasonal specialities (reservations required) around the 10-seat counter in a jewel box of a back room. Soft, warm, fresh – this is tofu as good as it gets. There's also frozen tofu 'soft cream' for ¥300.

Information

At JR Karatsu Station, the **tourist information office** (☎0955-72-4963; ⏲9am-6pm) has a selection of English-language tourist maps and brochures, and some enthusiastic English-speaking staff who can book accommodation.

Getting There & Around

From Fukuoka, take the Kūkō (Airport) subway line from Hakata or Tenjin to the end of the line at Meinohama. Many trains continue directly (or you may need to switch) to the JR Chikuhi line to reach Karatsu (¥1140, 70 minutes). From Karatsu to Nagasaki (¥4020, three hours) take the JR Karatsu line to Saga, and the Kamome *tokkyū* on the JR Nagasaki line from there.

From Karatsu's **Ōteguchi Bus Centre** (☎0955-73-7511), highway buses depart for Fukuoka (¥1030, 70 minutes) and Yobuko (¥750).

At the **Arpino** (☎0955-75-5155) building, next to the station, are a few loaner bicycles for day trips (free, 9am to 6pm); the station no longer rents bicycles.

Imari 伊万里

☎0955 / POP 57,700

You can tell you're getting close to Imari by the blue and white tiles that start appearing everywhere: street signs, bridge totems, even crushed gravel has shards of Imari's signature blue and white. The town proper lies near the border of Nagasaki Prefecture. Tourist brochures are available at **Imari City Information** (伊万里市観光協会; ☎0955-23-3479; ⏲9am-6pm) at Imari Station on the regional Matsūra Railway, across the street from JR Imari Station.

The pottery kilns are concentrated on photogenic **Ōkawachiyama** (大川内山), a 15-minute bus ride from the station. Around 30 workshops and public galleries make for a lovely ramble uphill alongside streams, cafes and a bridge covered with local shards. Arrive by noon to allow for exploring and shopping. About six buses per day (¥150) make the trip. Alternatively, the taxi fare is approximately ¥1800 each way.

Back in the town centre, near the river Imari-gawa, **Imari City Ceramic Merchant's Museum** (伊万里市陶器商家資料館; ☎0955-22-7934; ⏲10am-5pm Tue-Sun) FREE houses some priceless pieces of Ko-imari (as old Imari ware is known) from the 18th and 19th centuries, inside the handsomely preserved home of a merchant family; there's an excellent English leaflet. There's also a gallery on the 2nd floor of the Matsūra station.

A few hundred metres from the station area, family-run **Kippō** (天ぷらの吉峰; ☎0955-23-3563; 196 Tatemachi; lunch set menus from ¥1,260; ⏲11am-9pm Thu-Tue) serves up super-fresh tempura, some on Imari-ware dishes. No English is spoken, so just say '*setto o kudasai*' (set menu, please).

Imari is connected to Karatsu (¥650, 48 minutes) by the JR Chikuhi line, and also to Arita by the private Matsūra-tetsudō line (¥420, 24 minutes).

Arita 有田

☎0955 / POP 21,500

Kaolin clay was discovered here in 1615 by Ri Sampei, a naturalised Korean potter, enabling the manufacture of fine porcelain in Japan for the first time. By the mid-17th century, the porcelain was being exported to Europe.

KYŪSHŪ POTTERY TOWNS

In mountainous Kyūshū, many villages had difficulty growing rice and looked towards other industries to survive. Access to good clay, forests and streams made pottery-making a natural choice, and a number of superb styles can be found here.

Karatsu, Arita and Imari are the major pottery towns of Saga-ken. From the early 17th century, pottery was produced in this area by captive Korean potters, experts who were zealously guarded so that neither artist nor the secrets of their craft could escape. When trade routes opened up to the West, potters in Japan began imitating the highly decorative, Chinese-style ware popular in Europe. Pottery styles are often called by the suffix *-yaki* (pottery) added to the town name.

Arita Highly decorated porcelain, often with squares of blue, red, green or gold.

Imari Fine porcelain, originally blue and white, bursting into vibrant colours in the mid-Edo period.

Karatsu Marked by subtle earthy tones, prized for its use in the tea ceremony.

In southern Kyūshū, Kagoshima Prefecture is known for Satsuma-yaki (Satsuma is the feudal name for that region). Styles vary from crackled glazes to porcelains painted with gleaming gold, and rougher, more ponderous 'black Satsuma' ware.

The staff at the tiny **tourist information desk** (☎0955-42-4052; www.arita.or.jp/index_e.html; ⊙9am-5pm) inside Arita Station can assist with maps in English, timetables and accommodation, predominantly small private *minshuku* (guesthouses). Be sure to grab a *hama* (ceramic disk used in firing) as a free souvenir.

Between the station and Kyūshū Ceramic Museum is the **Yakimono Sanpo-michi** (Pottery Promenade) of around 16 galleries. The tourist office has a map that's in Japanese but is easy enough to follow. Arita's streets fill with vendors for the **annual pottery market**, held from 29 April to 5 May.

Out of the town centre, two of Arita-yaki's prime practitioners have been at it for 14 generations. The **Imaemon Gallery** (今右衛門ギャラリー; ☎0955-42-5550; admission ¥300; ⊙9.30am-4.30pm Tue-Sun) and **Kakiemon Kiln** (柿右衛門窯; ☎0955-43-2267; admission free; ⊙9am-5pm) FREE both have museums in addition to sales shops. **Genemon Kiln** (源石衛門窯; ☎0955-42-4164; http://genemon.co.jp; ⊙workshop 8am-5pm, gallery 8am-5.30pm Mon-Sun) FREE makes and sells more contemporary styles. These can be reached by a short taxi ride (about ¥1000), or infrequent community bus from the station.

Taxi or Arita bus (¥200, five to seven buses daily) can also take you out to the **clay mines** (磁石場; *jisekiba*). From here you can walk back to the station in about an hour, via a route lined with numerous old houses with leftover pottery used in the bricks, as well as many galleries.

A short train ride east of Arita, **Takeo Onsen** is a modern hot-springs town with about a dozen onsen hotels. The original **Takeo Onsen** (武雄温泉; admission ¥400; ⊙6.30am-midnight) has a 1300-year history and is said to have refreshed the armies of Toyotomi Hideyoshi. Its impressive lacquered Chinese-style entrance gate was built without nails, and the oldest existing bathing building (Moto-yu) is a wooden hall from 1870. It's a 15-minute walk west of the station's north exit. The complex even has *roten* (outdoor) baths and *kashikiri* (private reservable baths for families or couples) baths, making it a good spot for people uncomfortable bathing nude among others.

You can also stay among hot spring baths at the 14-room **Takeo Onsen Youth Hostel** (武雄温泉ユースホステル; ☎0954-22-2490; fax 0954-20-1208; 16060-1 Nagashima; dm with breakfast member/nonmember ¥3400/4000), with a green and orange paint job so bright it's likely visible from space. The friendly owners can pick you up if you ring ahead saying you'll be later than the 4pm check-in. A few loaner bikes are available. Rates include a simple breakfast of *onigiri* (rice balls) and coffee, but no dinner is served, so if you're not dining in a local restaurant, the shuttle can stop at local shops for provisions.

DON'T MISS

KYŪSHŪ CERAMIC MUSEUM

The best ceramics museum in the region, about five minutes on foot from Arita Station, is the large, hilltop **Kyūshū Ceramic Museum** (九州陶磁文化館; admission free, charge for special exhibits; ⊙9am-5pm, closed Mon) FREE. The Shibata Collection comprehensively showcases the development and styles of Kyūshū's many ceramic arts, with excellent English signage.

The private Matsūra-tetsudō line connects Arita with Imari (¥420, 24 minutes). JR *tokkyū* trains between Hakata (¥3060, 80 minutes) and Sasebo (¥460, 31 minutes) stop at Arita and Takeo Onsen. Takeo Onsen is also connected to Arita by local trains (¥280, 20 minutes). Infrequent community buses (¥150) cover most sights, but you'll save time by taking taxis (about ¥1000 to most sights). Arita Station rents out bicycles (¥300 per day).

NAGASAKI PREFECTURE

History

Nagasaki Prefecture's multilayered role in Japanese history started when an off-course Chinese ship landed in Kagoshima Prefecture in 1543, carrying guns and Portuguese adventurers. Catholic missionaries arrived soon thereafter, ushering in Japan's 'Christian Century' (1549–1650), centred in Nagasaki, Hirado and other local communities.

By 1570 Nagasaki was a wealthy, fashionable port, as Portuguese traders shuttled between Japan, China and Korea and missionaries converted Japanese. In 1580 the *daimyō* (domain lord) briefly ceded Nagasaki to the Society of Jesuits.

The shogun then reclaimed Nagasaki, expelled the Jesuits and, in 1597, crucified 26 European and Japanese Christians.

Christianity was officially banned altogether in 1613, yet some 'hidden Christians' continued to practise.

After a peasant uprising at Shimabara in 1637–38, the shogunate forbade all foreigners from Japan and Japanese from travelling overseas, beginning a period called *sakoku* (national seclusion), which lasted over two centuries. The single exception was Dejima, a man-made island in Nagasaki harbour where Dutch traders lived under close scrutiny.

When Japan reopened its doors to the West in the 1850s, Nagasaki was uniquely positioned to become a major economic force, particularly in shipbuilding, the industry that ultimately led to its tragic bombing on 9 August 1945.

Nagasaki 長崎

☎095 / POP 440,000

It's both unfortunate – and important – that the name Nagasaki is synonymous with the dropping of the atomic bomb. Unquestionably, this history overshadows everything else, yet today Nagasaki is a vibrant, charming and totally unique gem that begs to be explored far beyond the bomb museums, monuments and memorials. Not that the WWII history can be overlooked or denied: it's as much a part of the city's fabric as the hilly landscape and cobblestones. A visit to the scenes of atomic devastation is a must, but you'll find that this welcoming, peaceful city boasts a colourful trading history, alluring churches, shrines, temples and an East-meets-West culinary scene, prettily set around a gracious harbour. A few days will let you scratch the surface, so plan for a week or more if you have the extra time.

Sights

Urakami (Northern Nagasaki)

Urakami, the hypocentre of the atomic explosion, is today a prosperous, peaceful suburb. While nuclear ruin seems comfortably far away seven decades later, many sights here keep the memory alive.

★Nagasaki Atomic Bomb Museum MUSEUM

(長崎原爆資料館; www.city.nagasaki.lg.jp/peace/english/abm; 7-8 Hirano-machi; admission ¥200, audio guide ¥150; ⌚8.30am-6.30pm May-Aug, to 5.30pm Sep-Apr; 🚊Matsuyama-machi) An essential Nagasaki experience, this sombre place recounts the city's destruction and loss of life through photos and artefacts, including mangled rocks, trees, furniture, pottery and clothing, a clock stopped at 11.02 (the hour of the bombing), first-hand accounts from survivors and stories of heroic relief efforts. Exhibits also include the postbombing struggle for nuclear disarmament, and conclude with a chilling illustration of which nations bear nuclear arms.

★Nagasaki National Peace Memorial Hall for the Atomic Bomb Victims MEMORIAL

(国立長崎原爆死没者追悼平和祈念館; www.peace-nagasaki.go.jp; 7-8 Hirano-machi; ⌚8.30am-6.30pm May-Aug, to 5.30pm Sep-Apr; 🚊Matsuyama-machi) FREE Adjacent to the Atomic Bomb Museum and completed in 2003, this minimalist memorial by Kuryū Akira is a profoundly moving place. It is best approached by quietly reading the carved inscriptions and walking around the sculpted water basin. In the hall below, 12 glass pillars, containing shelves of books of the names of the deceased, reach skyward.

★Peace Park PARK

(平和公園; Heiwa-kōen; 🚊Ōhashi) FREE North of the hypocentre, the Peace Park is presided over by the 10-tonne bronze **Nagasaki Peace Statue** (平和祈念像), designed in 1955 by Kitamura Seibo. It also includes the dove-shaped Fountain of Peace (1969) and the Peace Symbol Zone, a sculpture garden with contributions on the theme of peace from around the world. On 9 August, a rowdy antinuclear protest is held within earshot of the more respectful official memorial ceremony for those lost to the bomb.

Atomic Bomb Hypocentre Park PARK

(長崎爆心地公園; 🚊Matsuyama-machi) FREE The park has a smooth, black stone column marking the point above which the bomb exploded. Nearby are bomb-blasted relics, including a section of the wall of the Urakami Cathedral.

Urakami Cathedral CHURCH

(浦上天主堂; 1-79 Motō-machi; ⌚9am-5pm Tue-Sun; 🚊Ōhashi) FREE Once the largest church in Asia (1914), the cathedral took three decades to complete and three seconds to flatten. This smaller replacement cathedral was completed in 1959 on the ruins of the original. Walk around the side of the hill to see a belfry lying in state where the original building fell after the blast.

Nagai Takashi Memorial Museum MUSEUM
(永井隆記念館; 22-6 Ueno-machi; admission ¥100; ⏲9am-5pm; 🚋Ōhashi) This small but quietly moving museum celebrates the courage and faith of one man in the face of overwhelming adversity. Already suffering from leukaemia, Dr Nagai survived the atomic explosion but lost his wife to it. He immediately devoted himself to the treatment of bomb victims until his death in 1951. In his final days, he continued to write prolifically and secure donations for survivors and orphans, earning the nickname 'Saint of Nagasaki'. Ask to watch the video in English.

Next door is **Nyokodō** (如己堂), the simple hut from which Dr Nagai worked – its name comes from the biblical commandment 'love thy neighbour as thyself'.

Shiroyama Elementary School HISTORIC BUILDING
(城山小学校; ☎095-861-0057; 23-1 Shiroyama-chō; ⏲8.30am-4.30pm Mon-Fri; 🚋Matsuyama-machi) FREE This was the closest school to the nuclear blast, up a hill a mere 500m away, where 1400 children were vaporised. It's hard not to be moved by the very ordinariness that exists here today. Except for one building that still stands as it did following the bombing (to the right at the top of the stairs), this functioning school looks much like any other, albeit with the addition of sculptures, monuments and memorials commemorating the loss of life.

The last of these is laden with strands of 1000 origami cranes, the traditional children's prayer for peace.

One-Pillar Torii MONUMENT
(一本柱鳥居; 🚋Daigakubyōin-mae or Urakami-eki-mae) FREE The blast knocked down half of the stone entrance arch to the Sanno-jinja shrine, 800m southeast of the hypocentre, but the other pillar remains, a quiet testimony to the power of strength and resilience.

Central Nagasaki

★Dejima HISTORIC SITE
(出島; 🚋Dejima) In 1641, the Tokugawa shogunate banished all foreigners from Japan, with one exception: Dejima, a fan-shaped, artificial island 560m in circumference (15,000 sq m) in Nagasaki harbour. From then until the 1850s, this tiny Dutch trading post was the sole sanctioned foreign presence in Japan. Today the city has filled in around the island and you might miss it. Don't. Seventeen buildings, walls and structures (plus a miniature Dejima) have been painstakingly reconstructed into the **Dejima Museum** (出島資料館; nagasakidejima.jp/en; 6-1 Dejima-machi; admission ¥510; ⏲8am-6pm, to 7pm mid-July to mid-Oct; 🚋Dejima).

THE ATOMIC EXPLOSION

When USAF B-29 bomber *Bock's Car* set off from the Marianas on 9 August 1945 to drop a second atomic bomb on Japan, the target was Kokura on Kyūshū's northeastern coast. Due to poor visibility, the crew diverted to the secondary target, Nagasaki.

The B-29 arrived over Nagasaki at 10.58am amid heavy cloud. When a momentary gap appeared and the Mitsubishi Arms Factory was sighted, the 4.57-tonne 'Fat Man' bomb, with an explosive power equivalent to 21.3 kilotonnes of TNT (almost twice that of Hiroshima's 'Little Boy'), was released over Nagasaki.

The bomb missed the arms factory, its intended target, and exploded at 11.02am, at an altitude of 500m almost directly above the largest Catholic church in Asia (Urakami Cathedral). In an instant, it annihilated the suburb of Urakami and 74,000 of Nagasaki's 240,000 people. Ground temperatures at the hypocentre were estimated at between 3000°C and 4000°C, and as high as 600°C 1.5km away. Everything within a 1km radius of the explosion was destroyed, and searing winds up to 170km/h (typhoons generally top out at 150km/h) swept down the valley of the Urakami-gawa towards the city centre. With able-bodied men at work or at war, most victims were women, children and senior citizens, as well as 13,000 conscripted Korean labourers and 200 Allied POWs. Another 75,000 people were horribly injured (and it is estimated that as many people died due to the after-effects). After the resulting fires burned out, a third of the city was gone.

Yet the damage might have been even worse had the targeted arms factory been hit. Unlike in the flatlands of Hiroshima or the Nagasaki port itself, the hills around the river valley protected outlying suburbs from greater damage.

Nagasaki

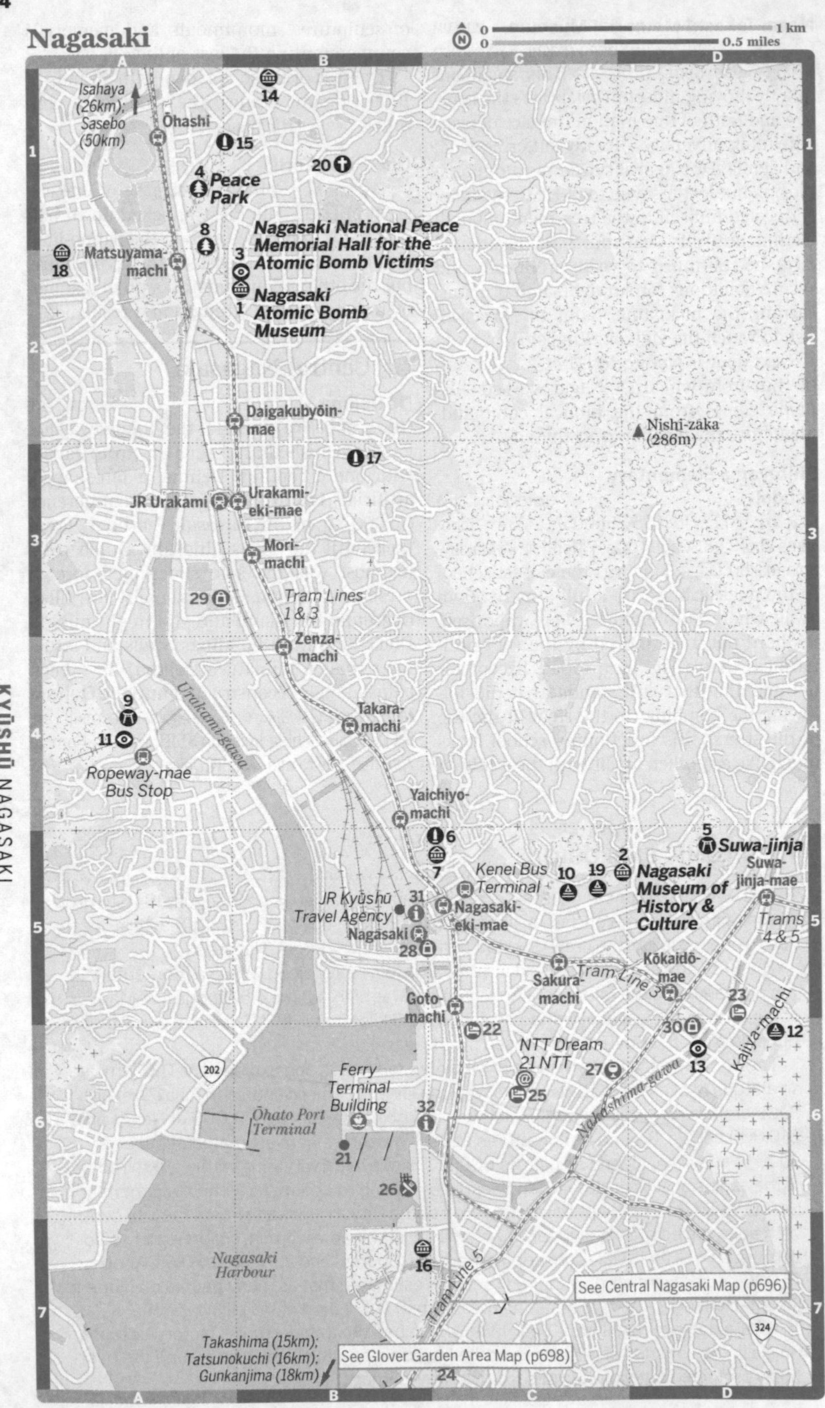

0 1 km
0 0.5 miles
Isahaya (26km); Sasebo (50km)
Ōhashi
14
15
20
4 Peace Park
8
Nagasaki National Peace Memorial Hall for the Atomic Bomb Victims
3
18
Matsuyama-machi
1
Nagasaki Atomic Bomb Museum
Daigakubyōin-mae
Nishi-zaka (286m)
17
JR Urakami
Urakami-eki-mae
Mori-machi
29
Tram Lines 1 & 3
Zenza-machi
Urakami-gawa
9
11
Takara-machi
Ropeway-mae Bus Stop
Yaichiyo-machi
6
7
5 Suwa-jinja
Kenei Bus Terminal
10
19
2 Nagasaki Museum of History & Culture
Suwa-jinja-mae
JR Kyūshū Travel Agency
31
Nagasaki-eki-mae
Nagasaki
28
Trams 4 & 5
Sakura-machi
Kōkaidō-mae
Tram Line 3
Goto-machi
22
23
30
12
Kajiya-machi
NTT Dream 21 NTT
13
27
Nakashima-gawa
202
Ferry Terminal Building
25
Ōhato Port Terminal
32
21
26
Nagasaki Harbour
16
Tram Line 5
See Central Nagasaki Map (p696)
324
Takashima (15km); Tatsunokuchi (16km); Gunkanjima (18km)
See Glover Garden Area Map (p698)
24

Nagasaki

Top Sights

1 Nagasaki Atomic Bomb Museum......... B2
2 Nagasaki Museum of History & Culture......... C5
3 Nagasaki National Peace Memorial Hall for the Atomic Bomb Victims......... B2
4 Peace Park......... A1
5 Suwa-jinja......... D5

Sights

6 26 Martyrs Memorial......... C5
7 26 Martyrs Museum......... C5
8 Atomic Bomb Hypocentre Park......... A1
9 Fuchi-jinja......... A4
10 Fukusai-ji Kannon......... C5
11 Inasa-yama Cable Car......... A4
12 Kōfuku-ji......... D6
13 Megane-bashi......... D6
14 Nagai Takashi Memorial Museum......... B1
15 Nagasaki Peace Statue......... B1
16 Nagasaki Prefectural Art Museum......... B7
17 One-Pillar Torii......... B3
18 Shiroyama Elementary School......... A2
19 Shōfuku-ji......... C5
20 Urakami Cathedral......... B1

Activities, Courses & Tours

21 Nagasaki Harbour Cruises......... B6

Sleeping

22 Chisun Grand Nagasaki......... C6
23 Hostel Akari......... D5
24 Hotel Monterey Nagasaki......... C7
25 Sakamoto-ya......... C6

Eating

AlettA......... (see 29)
26 Dejima Wharf......... B6

Drinking & Nightlife

27 Inokuchiya......... C6

Shopping

28 Amu Plaza......... B5
29 Mirai Nagasaki Cocowalk......... A3
30 Shōkandō......... D6

Information

31 Nagasaki City Tourist Information Centre......... B5
32 Nagasaki Prefectural Tourism Association & Visitors Bureau......... B6

Restored and reopened in 2006 and constantly being upgraded, the buildings here are as instructive inside as they are good-looking outside, with exhibits covering the spread of trade, Western learning and culture, archaeological digs, and rooms combining Japanese tatami (woven floor matting) with Western wallpaper. There's excellent English signage. Allow at least two hours. There's even a a kimono rental shop (¥1000 per hour) for those who want to feel even more in character.

★ Nagasaki Museum of History & Culture — MUSEUM

(長崎歴史文化博物館; www.nmhc.jp; 1-1-1 Tateyama; admission ¥600; 8.30am-7pm, closed 3rd Tue of month; Sakura-machi) This large museum with attractive displays opened in 2005 to focus on Nagasaki's proud history of international exchange. The main gallery is a fabulous reconstruction of a section of the Edo-period Nagasaki Magistrate's Office, which controlled trade and diplomacy. Detailed English-language explanations were in the works at the time of research.

★ Suwa-jinja — SHINTO SHRINE

(諏訪神社; 18-15 Kaminishiyama-machi; 24hr; Suwa-jinja-mae) Situated on a forested hilltop and reached via multiple staircases, this enormous shrine was established in 1625. Around the grounds are statues of *komainu* (protective dogs), including the *kappa-komainu* (water-sprite dogs), which you pray to by dribbling water onto the plates on their heads. The *gankake komainu* (turntable dog) was often called on by prostitutes, who prayed that storms would arrive, forcing the sailors to stay at the port another day.

Between 7 and 9 October each year, the shrine comes to life with the dragon dance of Kunchi Matsuri (p700), Nagasaki's most important annual festival.

Nagasaki Station Area — NEIGHBOURHOOD

The Nagasaki Station area includes a number of key sights that are within easy reach of the train station. It's a busy nexus of shops, skyscrapers, streets and alleyways not far from the harbor. Of most interest are the 26 Martyrs Memorial, with info and relics from a crackdown on Christianity; Shōfuku-ji, with its lovely gardens; and Fukusai-ji Kannon, a turtle, a goddess and a pendulum.

The **26 Martyrs Memorial** (日本二十六聖人殉教地) features reliefs commemorating the six Spanish and 20 Japanese crucified in 1597, when authorities cracked down on practising Christians. The youngest killed were boys aged 12 and 13. Behind the memorial is a simple Christianity-related

Central Nagasaki

Central Nagasaki

Top Sights

1 Dejima ... A2

Sights

2 Dejima Museum ... B2
3 Shinchi Chinatown ... B3
4 Sōfuku-ji ... G3

Sleeping

5 Hotel Dormy Inn Nagasaki ... C3
6 Richmond Hotel Nagasaki Shianbashi ... E3

Eating

7 Hōuntei ... E3
8 Kairaku-en ... C3
9 Organic Restaurant Tia ... C2
10 Ryōtei Kagetsu ... E4
11 Shippoku Hamakatsu ... F2
12 Tsuru-chan ... E2
13 Yosso ... D1

Drinking & Nightlife

14 Panic Paradise ... D1

Shopping

15 Fukusaya ... E3

museum (二十六聖人記念館; 095-822-6000; www.26martyrs.com; 7-8 Nishisaka-machi; admission ¥500; 9am-5pm).

The gardens of the temple **Shōfuku-ji** (聖福寺; 3-77 Tamazono-machi; 24hr; Sakura-machi) contain an arched stone gate dating from 1657. It's worth the significant uphill climb to reach the palm-filled inner court and main building, dating from 1715. Also note the interesting *onigawara* (ogre-covered wall) and sacred kiln used for the ceremonial burning of disused Buddhist scriptures.

Fukusai-ji Kannon (福済寺·長崎観音; Nagasaki Universal Kannon Temple; 2-56 Chikugo-machi; admission ¥200; 8am-4pm; Sakura-machi) is in the form of a huge astral turtle carrying an 18m-high figure of the goddess Kannon. Inside, a Foucault pendulum, demonstrating the rotation of the earth, hangs from the top.

Nagasaki Prefectural Art Museum MUSEUM
(長崎県美術館; 095-833-2110; www.nagasaki-museum.jp/english; 2-1 Dejima-machi; admission ¥400; 10am-8pm, closed 2nd & 4th Mon each month; Shimin-Byōin-mae) Designed by Kuma Kengo (the architect behind Tokyo's Nezu Museum), this museum straddles a canal in an environmentally friendly building (note the roof garden). The permanent collection covers both Nagasaki-related art and Spanish art, and special exhibits are eclectic, from Chinese to Chagall. There's a lovely cafe in the bridge over the canal.

Sōfuku-ji BUDDHIST TEMPLE
(崇福寺; 7-5 Kajiya-machi; admission ¥300; 8am-5pm; Shōkakuji-shita) In Teramachi, this Ōbaku temple (Ōbaku is the third-largest Zen sect after Rinzai and Sōtō) was built in 1629 by Chinese monk Chaonian. Its red entrance gate (*Daiippo-mon)* exemplifies Ming dynasty architecture. Inside the temple you can admire a huge cauldron that was used to prepare food for famine victims in 1681, and a statue of Maso, goddess of the sea, worshipped by early Chinese seafarers. There's also a *matcha* tea service (¥700) served with sweets.

Kōfuku-ji BUDDHIST TEMPLE
(興福寺; 4-32 Tera-machi; admission ¥300; 8am-5pm; Kōkaidō-mae) This temple in Teramachi dates from the 1620s and is noted for the Ming architecture of the main hall. Like Sōfuku-ji, it is an Ōbaku Zen temple – and the oldest in Japan.

Nakashima-gawa Bridges BRIDGE
(中島川; Kōkaidō-mae or Nigiwai-bashi) FREE Parallel to Teramachi, the Nakashima-gawa is crossed by a picturesque collection of 17th-century stone bridges. At one time, each bridge was the distinct entranceway to a separate temple. Best known is the double-arched **Megane-bashi** (めがね橋; Spectacles Bridge), originally built in 1634 and so called because the reflection of the arches in the water looks like a pair of Meiji-era spectacles. Six of the 10 bridges, including Megane-bashi, were washed away by flooding in 1982 and restored using the recovered stones.

Shinchi Chinatown NEIGHBOURHOOD
(新地中華街; Tsuki-machi) During Japan's long period of seclusion, Chinese traders were theoretically just as restricted as the Dutch, but in practice they were relatively free. Only a couple of buildings remain from the old area, but Nagasaki still has an energetic Chinese community, evident in the city's culture, architecture, festivals and cuisine. Visitors come from far and wide to eat here and shop for Chinese crafts and trinkets.

Glover Garden Area

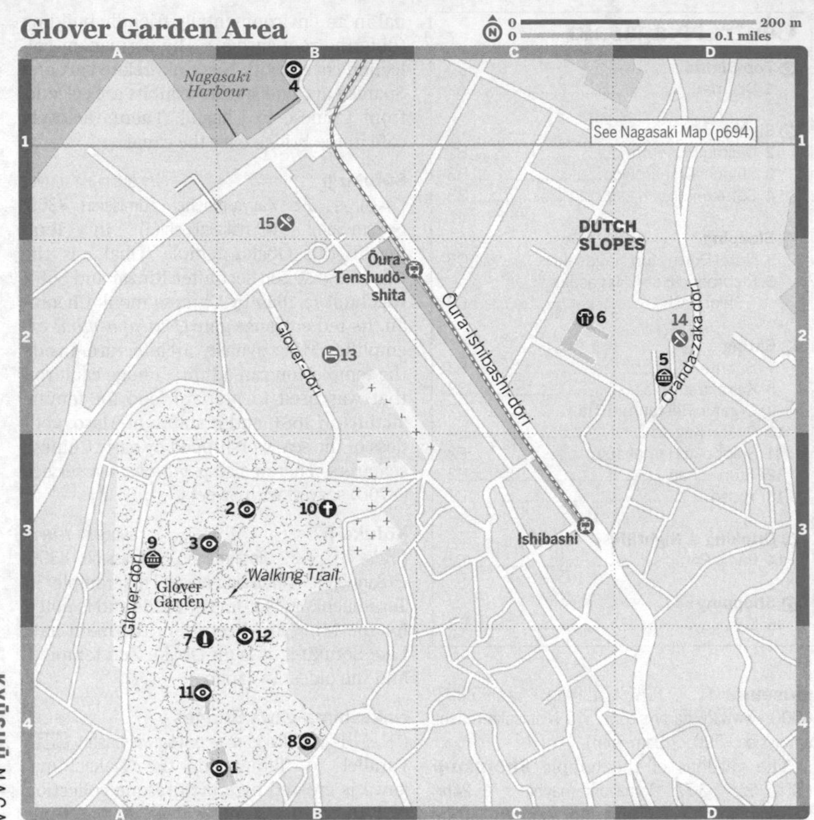

Inasa-yama LANDMARK

(稲佐山) West of the harbour, a **cable car** (長崎ロープウェイ; www.nagasaki-ropeway.jp; return ¥1230; 9am-10pm; 🚊) ascends every 20 minutes to the top of 333m-high Inasa-yama, offering superb views over Nagasaki, particularly at night. From 7am to 10pm there's a free shuttle from five Nagasaki hotels (reserve at front desk) and JR Nagasaki Station going towards Shimo-Ōhashi; get off at the **Ropeway-mae bus stop** (ロープウェイ前) and walk up the steps through the grounds of **Fuchi-jinja** (淵神社).

Elsewhere on the mountainside is **Onsen Fukunoyu** (温泉ふくの湯; 095-833-1126; 451-23 Iwami-machi; admission ¥800; 9.30am-1am Sun-Thu, 9.30am-2am Fri-Sat). In addition to wet baths, try the gabanyoku stone baths (additional ¥700), with temperatures from a balmy 38°C to the are-you-nuts? 70°C. There's a free shuttle from JR Nagasaki and Urakami Stations (20 minutes, twice per hour).

Southern Nagasaki

Glover Garden GARDENS

(グラバー園; 095-822-8223; www.glover-garden.jp; 8-1 Minami-yamate-machi; adult/student ¥610/300; 8am-9.30pm 29 Apr–mid-Jul, to 6pm mid-Jul–28 Apr; 🚊 Ōura Tenshudō-shita) Some former homes of the city's Meiji-period European residents have been reassembled in this hillside garden. Glover Garden is named after Thomas Glover (1838–1911), the Scottish merchant who built Japan's first railway, helped establish the shipbuilding industry and whose arms-importing operations influenced the course of the Meiji Restoration. It's a lovely spot to stroll around.

The best way to explore the garden is to take the moving walkways to the top of the hill then walk back down. The **Mitsubishi No 2 Dock building** (旧三菱第２ドックハウス; adult/student ¥610/300; 8am-9.30pm 29 Apr–mid-Jul, to 6pm mid-Jul–28 Apr) is high-

Glover Garden Area

Sights

1 Alt House ... B4
2 Glover Garden ... B3
3 Glover House ... A3
4 Gunkanjima Concierge ... B1
5 Ko-shashin-shiryōkan ... D2
6 Kōshi-byō & Historical Museum of China ... C2
7 Madame Butterfly Statue ... A4
Maizō-shiryōkan ... (see 5)
8 Mitsubishi No 2 Dock building ... B4
9 Nagasaki Traditional Performing Arts Museum ... A3
10 Ōura Catholic Church ... B3
11 Ringer House ... A4
12 Walker House ... B4

Sleeping

13 ANA Crowne Plaza Nagasaki Gloverhill ... B2

Eating

14 Higashi-yamate Chikyū-kan ... D2
15 Shikairō ... B1

est, with panoramic views of the city and harbour from the 2nd floor. Next highest is **Walker House** (旧ウォーカー住宅), filled with artefacts donated by the families, followed by **Ringer House** (旧リンガー住宅), **Alt House** (旧オルト住宅) and finally **Glover House** (旧グラバー住宅; adult/student ¥610/300; ⏲8am-9.30pm 29 Apr–mid-Jul, to 6pm mid-Jul–28 Apr). Halfway down is the **Madame Butterfly Statue** of Japanese opera singer Miura Tamaki, inspiration for the famous opera by Puccini – the story took place here in Nagasaki. Exit the garden through the **Nagasaki Traditional Performing Arts Museum** (長崎伝統芸能館; adult/student ¥610/300; ⏲8am-9.30pm 29 Apr–mid-Jul, to 6pm mid-Jul–28 Apr), which has a display of dragons and floats used in Nagasaki's colourful Kunchi Matsuri.

Ōura Catholic Church CHURCH
(大浦天主堂; ☎095-823-2628; 5-3 Yamatemachi; admission ¥300; ⏲8am-6pm; Ōura Tenshudō-shita) This hilltop church, Japan's oldest (1865), is dedicated to the 26 Christians who were crucified in Nagasaki in 1597. It's more like a museum than a place of worship, with an ornate Gothic altar and bishop's chair, and an oil painting of the 26 martyrs. To pray for free, use the regular church across the street.

Dutch Slopes HISTORIC SITE
(オランダ坂; Oranda-zaka; Ishibashi) The gently inclined flagstone streets known as the Dutch Slopes were once lined with wooden **Dutch houses**. Several buildings here have been beautifully restored and offer glimpses of Japan's early interest in the West. The quiet **Ko-shashin-shiryōkan** (古写真資料館; Museum of Old Photographs; 6-25 Higashi-yamatemachi; ⏲9am-5pm Tue-Sun) and **Maizō-shiryōkan** (埋蔵資料館; Museum of Unearthed Artefacts; 6-25 Higashi-yamatemachi; ⏲9am-5pm Tue-Sun) showcase the area's history (note that most signage is in Japanese). Admission to both museums is ¥100.

Kōshi-byō & Historical Museum of China CONFUCIAN SHRINE
(孔子廟・中国歴代博物館; ☎095-824-4022; 10-36 Ōuramachi; shrine & museum admission ¥600; ⏲8.30am-5.30pm; Ishibashi) The jauntily painted Kōshi-byō shrine claims to be the only Confucian shrine built by and for Chinese outside China, and the statues of sages in its courtyard certainly make you feel like you've journeyed across the sea. The original 1893 building was destroyed by fire following the A-bomb explosion.

Behind it, a glossy museum of Chinese art spans jade artefacts and Neolithic archaeological finds to terracotta warriors and Qing-dynasty porcelain. There's also a large gift shop with Chinese trinkets, from classy to kitschy.

Tours

One-hour **Nagasaki Harbour Cruises** (長崎港めぐりクルーズ; ☎095-822-5002; Nagasaki Harbour Terminal Bldg; adult/child ¥2000/1000, sunset cruise ¥2500/1250) are a great way to glimpse picturesque Nagasaki. Check at the ferry terminal for up-to-date schedules.

Festivals & Events

Peiron Dragon Boat Races CULTURAL
Colourful boat races were introduced by the Chinese in the mid-1600s, and held to appease the god of the sea. They still take place in Nagasaki Harbour in late July.

Shōrō-nagashi CULTURAL
On 15 August lantern-lit boats are floated on the harbour to honour ancestors. The boats

WORTH A TRIP

GHOST ISLAND HASHIMA

Hashima, aka *Gunkanjima* (battleship island), is an eerie, abandoned cluster of buildings rising out of the bay that from afar resembles a battleship. Once the world's most densely populated area, Hashima became a ghost island as soon as the coal mines that had operated since the 1890s were closed. Since 1974 it has been left to the elements. Once considered as a refuse dump, thanks to the tireless work of some concerned Nagasaki citizens the island was protected and is now in the process of being designated of world cultural interest by UNESCO. It looks like it comes straight out of an apocalyptic manga, so much so that it was the backdrop for the villian's lair in the 2012 James Bond film *Skyfall*.

Much of the island is unsafe and several structures have collapsed or been damaged due to recent hurricanes; however, guided tours operate several times a day, allowing visitors to ramble on safe walkways among the long-disused skyscrapers, concrete remnants of conveyor belts and impressive fortified walls. Some of the architecture (such as the iconic 'X' stairways, alas, not visible on the tour) is considered remarkable for its time, as engineers tackled the challenges of designing for such cramped living. While most of the spoken guiding is in Japanese, English info is available.

Three-hour cruises are by reservation (conditions permitting) and run daily from April to October, with fewer departures November to March. Contact **Gunkanjima Concierge** (軍艦島コンシェルジュ; ☎095-895-9300; http://www.gunkanjima-concierge.com/en/index.html; Tokiwa town 1-60 Tokiwa terminal building 102; adult ¥3900) for reservations.

are of various sizes and handcrafted from a variety of materials (bamboo, wood, rice stems etc). Eventually they are carried out to sea and destroyed by the waves. The best viewpoint for the procession is at the Ōhato ferry terminal.

Kunchi Matsuri CULTURAL

Held from 7 to 9 October, this energetic festival features Chinese dragons dancing all around the city but especially at Suwa-jinja. The festival is marked by elaborate costumes, fireworks, cymbals and giant dragon puppets.

Sleeping

For ease of transport and access to restaurants and nightlife, we recommend staying near JR Nagasaki Station or Shianbashi.

Hostel Akari HOSTEL ¥

(ホステルあかり; ☎095-801-7900; www.nagasaki-hostel.com; 2-2 Kajiya-machi; dm/s from ¥2600/3300, d & tw from ¥6600; ⊙reception 8am-8pm; ⊖@☜; 🚋Kōkaidō-mae) This commendably friendly 28-bed hostel sets the standard, with bright, clean Japanese-style rooms with Western-style bedding and bathrooms, uber-helpful staff, an open kitchen and a dedicated crew of local volunteers who lead free walking tours around the city. It's by the lovely Nakashima-gawa. Towel rental is ¥100.

Hotel Dormy Inn Nagasaki BUSINESS HOTEL ¥¥

(ドーミーイン長崎; ☎095-820-5489; www.hotespa.net/hotels/nagasaki; 7-24 Dōza-machi; s/d/tw from ¥6290/8290/13,900; ⊖@; 🚋Tsuki-machi) Adjacent to Chinatown, this hotel would be worth it just for the location. The rooms are crisp and neat as a pin, with quality mattresses. There are large, gender-separated common baths and saunas in addition to in-room facilities. The breakfast buffet (¥1100) includes *sara-udon*, and there's free *soba* served from 9.30pm to 11pm. Prices vary widely based on season and online discounts.

ANA Crowne Plaza Nagasaki Gloverhill HOTEL ¥¥

(ANAクラウンプラザ長崎グラバーヒル; ☎095-818-6601; www.anacrowneplaza-nagasaki.jp; 1-18 Minami-yamate-machi; s/d/tw from ¥8700/13,400/16,440; P⊖@☜; 🚋Ōura-Tenshudō-shita) Near Glover Garden, Ōura Catholic Church and the Dutch Slopes, this hotel has three types of room: Standards that are relatively plain, then Superior and Deluxe, which are both quite stylish thanks to recent renovation. About the only downside: no view to speak of.

Chisun Grand Nagasaki BUSINESS HOTEL ¥¥

(チサングランド長崎; ☎095-826-1211; www.solarehotels.com/english; 5-35 Goto-machi; s/d/tw ¥12,000/16,000/18,000; ⊖@☜; 🚋Goto-machi)

On the main drag, look for this hotel with 153 sleek rooms that come with dark wood panelling, separate shower, tub and vanity. Staff are used to foreign guests and there's a coin laundry. Look for discounted rates on the website.

★ Sakamoto-ya RYOKAN ¥¥¥
(料亭旅館坂本屋; ☎095-826-8211; www.sakamotoya.co.jp; 2-13 Kanaya-machi; r per person incl 2 meals from ¥15,575; P @; Goto-machi) This magnificent old-school ryokan has been in business since 1894. Look for art-filled rooms, hallways lined with Arita-yaki pottery, postage-stamp-sized gardens off 1st-floor rooms, *kaiseki* meals (Japanese haute cuisine) and only 11 rooms for personal service, each with a *hinoki-buro* (cypress wood bath). From Goto-machi tram stop, walk past Chisun Grand Hotel and turn left. It's diagonally across from the TV broadcast tower.

Richmond Hotel Nagasaki Shianbashi HOTEL ¥¥¥
(リッチモンドホテル長崎思案橋; ☎095-832-2525; nagasaki.richmondhotel.jp; 6-38 Motoshikkui-machi; s/d/tw from ¥11,000/16,000/19,000; @; Shianbashi) You can't be closer to the heart of Shianbashi than this travellers' favourite. Deluxe rooms are large by Japanese standards. There's cheerful, English-speaking staff and a terrific breakfast buffet (¥1000) including Nagasaki specialities.

Hotel Monterey Nagasaki HOTEL ¥¥¥
(ホテルモントレ長崎; ☎095-827-7111; www.hotelmonterey.co.jp/nagasaki; 1-22 Ōura-machi; s/tw from ¥12,600/23,600; @; Ōura-Tenshudōshita) At this Portuguese-themed hotel, near the Dutch Slopes and Glover Garden, rooms are spacious and light filled, beds are comfy, and staff are courteous and used to the vagaries of foreign guests. Look for online discounts.

Eating

Nagasaki is a culinary crossroads reflecting its rich international history. *Champon* is a local take on rāmen featuring squid, octopus, pork and vegetables in a milky, salt-based broth. *Sara-udon* nests the same toppings in a sauce over crispy fried noodles. Chinese and Portuguese influences converge in *shippoku ryōri*, Nagasaki-style *kaiseki*. *Kakuni-manju* is Chinese, pork belly in a sweet sauce, often found at street stalls. And *chirin-chirin* (ding ding) flavoured shaved ice is sold from tiny carts around town in warmer months.

The Mirai Nagasaki Cocowalk (p702) shopping mall features some 20 restaurants on its 4th and 5th floors. **AlettA** (アレッタ; ☎095-801-5245; lunch/dinner ¥1650/2070; 11am-3.30pm & 5-11pm; Mori-machi) is an airy buffet restaurant on the 4th floor, with a different national theme each month.

Other good places for restaurant browsing include the restaurant floors of the shopping mall Amu Plaza (p702), and **Dejima Wharf** (出島ワーフ; Dejima), a picturesque, harbourside collection of open-air restaurants (seafood to Italian) at a variety of price points, plus bars and galleries, just west of Dejima.

★ Organic Restaurant Tia JAPANESE ¥
(ティア; ☎095-828-2984; www.tia-nagasaki.com; 6-24 Ginza-chō; breakfast buffet ¥1150, meals from ¥700; 7-10am, 11:30am-3pm & 6-9pm; Kankō-dōri) Mouth-watering homestyle Japanese cooking made with local, organic products. What's not to love? The breakfast buffet is fantastic. Below the Victoria Inn.

Hōuntei IZAKAYA ¥
(宝雲亭; ☎095-821-9333; 1-8 Motoshikkui-machi; dishes ¥360-520; 5-11pm; Shianbashi) Patrons have been ordering the *hito-kuchi gyōza* (one-bite *gyōza;* ¥380 for 10) at this rustic hole-in-the-wall since the 1970s. Also try *butaniratoji* (pork and shallots cooked omelette style; ¥540). There's a picture menu. Look for the lantern and brown *noren* (door curtain) across from With Nagasaki.

Shikairō CHINESE ¥
(四海楼; ☎095-822-1296; 4-5 Matsugae-machi; champon or sara-udon ¥997; 11.30am-3pm & 5-9pm; ; Oura-Tenshudō-shita) This huge, freestanding Chinese restaurant (look for the giant red pillars) near Glover Garden is credited as the creator of *champon* and has been in operation since 1899. There are dead-on harbour views and a small *champon* museum.

Tsuru-chan CAFE ¥
(ツル茶ん; ☎095-824-2679; 2-47 Aburaya-machi; Toruko rice ¥980-1180; 9am-10pm; Shianbashi) Despite the name Toruko (Turkish) rice, there's nothing much Turkish about this hearty Nagasaki signature dish: pork cutlets in hearty, curry-flavoured gravy over pasta and rice (¥1080). This retro *kissaten* (coffee shop) claims to have invented it. Creative

WORLD FOODS WEEKLY

In the Dutch Slopes, the 'World Foods Restaurant' inside **Higashi-yamate Chikyū-kan** (東山手「地球館」; ☎095-822-7966; www.h3.dion.ne.jp/~chikyu; 6-25 Higashiyamate-machi; ⏰cafe 10am-5pm Thu-Tue, restaurant noon-3pm Sat & Sun; 🚋Ishibashi) operates most weekends; each week a different chef comes to prepare inexpensive meals from their home country – some 70 nations and counting. This little gem is what cultural exchange – and Nagasaki – is all about.

preparations include chicken, beef and even cream sauce. For dessert, try the 'Nagasaki Milkshake', so thick it must be eaten, not drunk.

★Shippoku Hamakatsu KAISEKI ¥¥
(卓袱浜勝; ☎095-826-8321; www.sippoku.jp; 6-50 Kajiya-machi; lunch/dinner from ¥1500/2940; ⏰11.30am-10pm; 📖; 🚋Shianbashi) Come here if you would like to experience *shippoku ryōri* and still afford your airfare home. Course menus are filling and varied (the Otakusa Shippoku is served on a dramatic round tray). In addition, there is a choice of either Japanese- or Western-style seating.

Yosso JAPANESE ¥¥
(吉宗; ☎095-821-0001; www.yossou.co.jp; 8-9 Hama-machi; set meals from ¥1350; ⏰11am-8pm; 🚋Shianbashi) People have been coming to eat *chawanmushi* (Japanese egg custard) since 1866. Look for the traditional shopfront festooned with red lanterns. The Yosso *teishoku* (¥2376) adds fish, *soboro* (sweetened, ground chicken over rice), *kakuni* (stewed pork belly), dessert and more. There's no English menu, but a display case makes ordering easy.

Kairaku-en CHINESE ¥¥
(会楽園; ☎095-822-4261; www.kairakuen.tv; 10-16 Shinchi-chō; dishes ¥800-1600; ⏰11am-4pm & 5-9.30pm; 📖; 🚋Tsuki-machi) At this Shinchi Chinatown standby, the cheerful staff dressed in black with white aprons has been serving southern Chinese cuisine since the Shōwa Era. The ¥800 lunch set meals (noodle dishes, sweet and sour pork etc) are a good deal, or for a splurge, try Peking duck (¥5000).

Ryōtei Kagetsu KAISEKI ¥¥¥
(史跡料亭花月; ☎095-822-0191; www.ryoutei-kagetsu.co.jp; 2-1 Maruyama-machi; set meals lunch/dinner from ¥10,080/13,860; ⏰noon-3pm & 6-10pm, closed most Tue; 🚋Shianbashi) A sky-high *shippoku* restaurant dating to 1642, when it was a high-class brothel. If you have Japanese skills or a chaperone, dining companions and a love of food, you might not flinch at the price.

Drinking & Nightlife

Nagasaki doesn't bustle after dark, but little nightspots punctuate the narrow lanes around Hamano-machi and Shianbashi.

Panic Paradise BAR
(パニックパラダイス; ☎095-824-6167; basement, 5-33 Yorozuya-machi; drinks from ¥700; ⏰9pm-late; 🚋Kankō-dōri) Cool but friendly, this dark basement bar is a bit of a local icon, cluttered with rock memorabilia. There's a huge collection of tunes, cosy booths with dim lamps and the staff has pride in the environment.

Inokuchiya WINE BAR
(猪ノ口屋; ☎095-821-0454; 4-11 Sakae-machi; ⏰5.30-11pm Mon-Sat; 🚋Nigiwaibashi) Away from Shianbashi but worth the trip, this cool spot has a wine store fronting a warren of rooms for sampling wines, *shōchū* (alcoholic beverage made from potatoes or grains) and Nagasaki sake, alongside delectable small plates of pâté, carpaccio and salads. Not much English on the menu, but you can usually make yourself understood.

Shopping

Local crafts and products are sold around and opposite JR Nagasaki Station, as well as in shops along busy Hamano-machi shopping arcade near Shianbashi tram stop. Ignore tortoiseshell crafts (べっ甲) sold around town: these may actually land you in jail if they're endangered species.

For mall shopping, **Amu Plaza** (アミュプラザ長崎) at the station is nice and easy, and you can't miss **Mirai Nagasaki Cocowalk** (みらい長崎ココウォーク; ☎095-848-5509; www.cocowalk.jp; 1-55 Morimachi; ⏰10am-9pm; 🚋Mori-machi, 🚉JR Urakami), a massive shopping, dining and cinema complex with a Ferris wheel on the roof (¥500).

The yellow, brick-shaped castella cake remains a must-have Nagasaki sweet. Two of the finer shops are **Fukusaya** (福砂屋; www.castella.co.jp; 3-1 Funadaiku-machi; ⏰8.30am-8pm;

Shianbashi), making the cakes since 1624; and **Shōkandō** (匠寛堂; 095-826-1123; www.shokando.jp; 7-24 Sakana-no-machi; 9am-7pm; Kōkaidō-mae), across from Megane-bashi, supplier to the Japanese imperial family.

Orientation

Nagasaki's sights are scattered over a broad area, but once you're in a district it's easy to walk from one location to the next. The atomic bomb hypocentre is in the suburb of Urakami, about 2.5km north of JR Nagasaki Station. Central and southern Nagasaki are where you'll find sights related to its history of trade and foreign influence. Main enclaves are around JR Nagasaki Station and about 2km south: Shinchi Chinatown, the Dutch Slopes and Glover Garden. Near Shinchi Chinatown, Shianbashi is the main nightlife and shopping district.

Parts of Nagasaki are quite hilly, so bring good walking shoes. Because of the hills, people rarely bike, and even driving can be challenging.

Information

INTERNET ACCESS

Nagasaki offers free wi-fi in many public places including JR Nagasaki Station, Dejima Wharf and Shinchi Chinatown. Visit www.ninjin-area.net/sites/map to find locations, and look for ninjin.net in your browser to sign on (there's an option in English).

Cybac Café (サイバックカフェ; 095-818-8050; 3rd & 4th fl, Hashimoto Bldg, 2-46 Aburaya-chō; registration fee ¥320, 1st 30/subsequent 15min ¥320/110; Shianbashi) This enormous internet cafe has showers, darts, drinks and more.

MONEY

In addition to postal and 7-Eleven ATMs, several branches of **18 Bank** (十八銀行) handle foreign-currency exchange.

TOURIST INFORMATION

In addition to tourist brochures available at locations following, look for the free English-language magazine *Nagazasshi*, published by local expats, containing events, sightseeing tips and features. A new multilingual **call centre** (095-825-5175) caters to English-speaking visitors.

Nagasaki City Tourist Information Centre (長崎市総合観光案内所; 095-823-3631; www.at-nagasaki.jp/foreign/english; 1st fl, JR Nagasaki Station; 8am-8pm) Can assist with finding accommodation and has brochures and maps in English.

Nagasaki Prefectural Tourism Association & Visitors Bureau (095-828-9407; visit-nagasaki.com; 8th fl, 14-10 Motofuna-machi; 9am-5.30pm, closed 27 Dec-3 Jan; Ōhato) Its website has detailed info on tourism and activities.

TRAVEL AGENCIES

JR Kyūshū Travel Agency (095-822-4813; JR Nagasaki Station; 10.30am-7pm Mon-Fri, 10am-6pm Sat & Sun) Handles domestic travel and hotel arrangements.

Getting There & Away

AIR

There are flights between Nagasaki and Tokyo (Haneda; JAL & ANA/Solaseed Air), Osaka (Itami), Okinawa and Nagoya; Seoul and Shanghai too.

BOAT

Ferries sail from a few places around Nagasaki, including Ōhato terminal, south of JR Nagasaki Station. The Shanghai–Nagasaki connection was still suspended at the time of research.

BUS

From the Kenei bus station opposite JR Nagasaki Station, buses depart for Unzen (¥1800, 1¾ hours), Sasebo (¥1500, 1½ hours), Fukuoka (¥2570, 2¼ hours), Kumamoto (¥3700, 3¼ hours) and Beppu (¥4630, 3½ hours). Night buses for Osaka (¥10,900, 10 hours) leave from both the **Kenei bus terminal** (県営バスターミナル) and the **Shinchi bus terminal** (新地バスターミナル).

TRAIN

JR lines from Nagasaki head for Sasebo (¥1650, 1¾ hours), Hirado (¥2870, 3¼ hours) or Fukuoka (Hakata Station; *tokkyū* ¥4500, two hours). Most other destinations require a change of train. Nagasaki is not currently served by *shinkansen*.

Getting Around

TO/FROM THE AIRPORT

Nagasaki's **airport** (0957-52-5555; http://www.nabic.co.jp/; 593 Mishima-machi, Ōmura-shi) is located about 40km from the city. Airport

DON'T MISS

HIDDEN MAJESTY

Nagasaki is just as interesting underwater as it is above ground: a plethora of soft and hard corals are easily viewable from several points along some of Japan's northernmost reefs. Snorkel from nearby Takashima or beach dive from Tatsunokuchi, about 30 minutes' drive from Nagasaki centre.

buses (¥800, 35 minutes) operate from stand 4 of the Kenei bus terminal opposite JR Nagasaki Station and outside the Shinchi bus terminal. A taxi to the airport costs about ¥10,000.

BICYCLE

Bicycles can be rented from JR Nagasaki Station at the **Eki Rent-a-Car** (☎095-826-0480; per 2hr/day ¥500/1500, 20% discount for JR Pass holders). They are electric powered; however, due to the hilly nature of the terrain, bikes are not the ideal way to get around.

BUS

Buses cover a wider area than trams do, but they're less user-friendly for non-Japanese speakers.

TRAM

The best way of getting around Nagasaki is by tram. There are four colour-coded routes numbered 1, 3, 4 and 5 (route 2 is for special events) and stops are signposted in English. It costs ¥120 to travel anywhere in town, but you can transfer for free at the Tsuki-machi (築町) stop only (ask for a *noritsugi*, or transfer pass), unless you have a ¥500 all-day pass for unlimited travel, available from tourist information centres and many hotels. Most trams stop running around 11.30pm.

Hirado 平戸

☎0950 / POP 36,000

The tragic irony of sweet, off-the-beaten-path Hirado is that it was once *the* spot where foreigners visited Japan before *sakoku* (isolationism) and Dejima island. As trains, then airplanes surpassed ships as the main entry to Japan, Hirado has been all but forgotten, especially since the town lies off a private, non-JR rail line. This secluded yet lovely little island has many reminders of early Western involvement, particularly of *kakure-Kirishitan* (hidden Christians) who populated this region. It's also a popular beach getaway and has a lovely old-style shopping street, great seafood, a castle and wonderful museums.

Sights & Activities

★Ji-in to Kyōkai no Mieru Michi STREET
寺院と教会の見える道; Street for Viewing Temples & a Church) Rising up a steep hill from town is this street, one of the most photogenic vantage points in all of Kyūshū. The Buddhist temples and large Christian church are testimony to the island's history.

★Oranda Shōkan HISTORIC BUILDING
(オランダ商館; ☎0950-26-0636; 2477 Okubo; admission ¥300; ⊙8.30am-5pm, closed 3rd Tue, Wed & Thu of Jun) Across from the waterfront, this was the **trading house of the Dutch East India Company**. Shogunal authorities took the Gregorian date on the front of the building (1639) as proof of forbidden Christianity, ordered it destroyed and used it to justify confining Dutch traders to Dejima (p693). It has been rebuilt according to the original plans and now houses displays of textiles, pewter ware, gin and pottery traded.

Hirado-jō CASTLE
(平戸城; ☎0950-22-2201; 1458 Iwanoue-machi; admission ¥510; ⊙8.30am-5.30pm) Hirado-jō presides over the town, with an enormous number of rebuilt structures. Inside you'll see traditional armour and clothing, and photos and models of old Hirado.

Matsūra Historical Museum MUSEUM
(松浦史料博物館; ☎0950-22-2236; www.matsura.or.jp; 12 Kagamigawa-chō; admission ¥500; ⊙8.30am-5.30pm) Across the bay, the museum is housed in the stunning residence of the Matsūra clan, who ruled the island from the 11th to the 19th centuries. You'll find armour that you can don to pose for photos, *byōbu* (folding screen) paintings, and the thatched-roof **Kanun-tei**, a *chanoyu* (tea ceremony) house for the unusual Chinshin-ryū warrior-style tea ceremony (¥500) that is still practised on the island.

If you can get here on a Friday, be sure to participate in the tea ceremony offered between 9.30am and 5pm. Clothed in a traditional kimono, you'll partake in a tea service very similar to those served when this custom was first brought to Japan from China centuries ago. Along with the tea, old-style Hirado sweets are also served.

Hirado Christian Museum MUSEUM
(平戸切支丹資料館; ☎0950-28-0176; admission ¥200; ⊙9am-5.30pm Thu-Tue) Across the middle of the island, this small museum displays items including a Maria-Kannon statue that the hidden Christians used in place of the Virgin Mary.

Kawachi Pass HIKING
(川内峠) FREE West of central Hirado, this series of grassy hilltops offers views of both sides of the island – east towards the Japanese mainland and west towards the East China Sea – and above the tiny islands that populate the waters.

Cape Shijiki BEACH
From Hirado, it's about a 40km (one-hour) drive to the island's southern tip at Cape Shijiki, from where there are views of the Gotō-rettō archipelago. En route, **Hotel Ranpū** (ホテル蘭風; ☎0950-23-2111; per day ¥1000) rents out fishing equipment.

Long **Neshiko Beach** on Hirado's lovely west coast is popular for swimming.

Festivals & Events

Hirado's famous **Jangara Matsuri** folk festival, held on 18 August, is particularly colourful, reminiscent of Okinawa or Korea. Arrive in Hirado by late morning for the afternoon events. From 24 to 27 October, the **Okunchi Matsuri** has dragon and lion dancing at Kameoka-jinja.

Sleeping & Eating

While there are sleeping and eating options throughout Hirado, two of the best choices are on the mainland side.

Grass House Youth Hostel HOSTEL ¥
(平戸ユースホステル・グラスハウス; ☎0950-57-1443; www.grass-house.com; 1111-3 Ōkubo, Tabira-chō; dm ¥3606, d per person incl 2 meals ¥6954; P@) In Hirado-guchi, the closest mainland town, is this unexpectedly awesome hostel with koi pond, hilltop water views, two lovely *rotemburo* (outdoor baths) and a sprawling grassy campground. There are also private rooms and a restaurant. A taxi from Tabira-Hirado-guchi Station costs about ¥600.

Samson Hotel RESORT ¥¥
(サムソンホテル; ☎0950-57-1110; www.samson-hotel.jp; 210-6 Nodamen, Tabira-chō; capsule ¥3240, r per person incl 2 meals from ¥9720; P⊖@) This 10-storey, hot-spring hotel on the mainland reopened in 2012 after an expansion and renovation. Public baths are like lookouts over the water, and pricey giant suites contain multiple rooms, some with balconies. By contrast, capsule hotel beds are as simple as you can get (meals not included), and there's a summertime beer garden. Rates listed are for the old building.

Shunsenkan SEAFOOD ¥
(旬鮮館; ☎0950-22-4857; 655-13 Miyanomachi; Kaisen-don ¥700; ⏲11am-3pm Wed-Mon) Across from the tourist information office and operated by local fishing families, this cooperative is basically a market with picnic tables, where staff will prepare meals. Look for the red building and ask for *sashimi moriawase* (assorted sashimi, ¥400), *kaisen-don* (seafood over rice) or just point.

Ichiyama STEAK ¥¥
(市山; ☎0950-22-2439; 529 Tsukiji-machi; set meals from ¥3800; ⏲11.30am-2pm & 5-9.30pm Wed-Mon) Hirado beef compares well in taste with other *wagyu* varieties. Try it at this spacious and comfy spot for *yakiniku* (Korean-style grilled beef). Multicourse set menus are a good deal.

Orientation

The island's main town, Hirado, is small enough to navigate on foot, but you'll need your own transport for points elsewhere. The brand new **tourist information centre** (☎0950-22-2015; 776-6 Sakigata; ⏲8.30am-6pm) is near the ferry terminal and has lots of English-language materials, free computers/wi-fi and helpful staff who can assist with booking accommodation.

Getting There & Around

Hirado is closer to Saga-ken than to Nagasaki city, joined to Kyūshū by a mini Golden Gate–lookalike bridge from Hirado-guchi. The closest train station, Tabira-Hirado-guchi on the private Matsūra-tetsudō line (to Imari ¥1120, 67 minutes; Sasebo ¥1220, 80 minutes), is Japan's westernmost; and local buses cross the bridge to the island (¥260, 10 minutes). From Nagasaki, journey to Sasebo by JR/express bus (¥1600/1450, both 1½ hours) and continue to Hirado by bus (¥1300, 1¼ hours).

Rental bikes are available at the tourist information centre for ¥500 per four hours. Rental cars starting at ¥6000 per day are well worth it if you plan to see the furthest sights or beaches.

SHIMABARA PENINSULA

The hilly Shimabara Peninsula (島原半島) along the calm Ariake Sea is a popular route between Nagasaki and Kumamoto, via ferry from Shimabara.

The 1637–38 Shimabara Uprising led to the suppression of Christianity in Japan and the country's subsequent two centuries of seclusion from the West. Peasant rebels made their final stand against overwhelming odds (37,000 versus 120,000 people) and held out for 80 days before being slaughtered.

More history was made on 3 June 1991, when the 1359m peak of **Unzen-dake** erupted after lying dormant for 199 years, taking the lives of 43 journalists and scientists. Over

12,000 people were evacuated from nearby villages before the lava flow reached the outskirts of Shimabara.

Unzen 雲仙

☎0957

Unzen-Amakusa National Park, said to be Japan's first, is another gem that's off the beaten path but spectacularly worth going to. It boasts dozens of onsen and woodsy trekking through volcanic landscapes. Unzen village (population 1089) is easily explored in an afternoon, and once the day trippers clear out it's a peaceful night's stay in some great hot-spring accommodation.

Sights & Activities

Hot Springs

A path just outside the village winds through the bubbling *jigoku* (meaning 'hells'; boiling mineral hot springs). Unlike the touristy *jigoku* of Beppu, these natural wonders are broken up only by stands selling *onsen tamago* (onsen-steamed hard-cooked eggs). A few centuries ago, these *jigoku* lived up to their name, when some 30 Christian martyrs were plunged alive into Oito Jigoku.

Onsen

Check at Unzen Tourist Association for which lodgings accept visitors during your stay. The following public facilities are open regularly, and several of the hotels offer *higaeri* (day use) entry:

Kojigoku ONSEN
(小地獄温泉館; ☎0957-73-3273; 500-1 Unzen; admission ¥400; ⏲9am-9pm) A super-rustic wooden public bath, a few minutes' drive or about 15 minutes on foot from the village centre.

Shin-yu ONSEN
(新湯共同浴場; ☎0957-73-3233; 320 Unzen; admission ¥100; ⏲9am-11pm Thu-Tue) Simple *sentō* (public bath) style with lots of local colour.

Yunosato ONSEN
(湯の里温泉; ☎0957-73-2576; 303 Unzen; admission ¥200; ⏲9am-11pm, closed 10th & 20th each month) *Sentō* style, known for its distinctive round stone bathtubs.

Hiking

From the town, popular walks to Kinugasa, Takaiwa-san and Yadake are all situated within the national park. The **Mt Unzen Visitors Centre** (雲仙お山の情報館; ☎0957-73-3636; ⏲9am-7pm Fri-Wed 20 Jul–Aug, to 5pm 1 Sep–19 Jul) has displays on volcanoes, flora and fauna, and information in English.

Nearby, via Nita Pass, is **Fugen-dake** (1359m), part of the Unzen-dake range. Its hiking trail has incredible views of the lava flow from the summit. A shared **Heisei Taxi** (☎0957-73-2010; each way per person ¥430) ride takes you to the Nita-tōge parking area, starting point for the Fugen-dake walk. A **cable car** (Ropeway; ☎0957-73-3572; each-way ticket ¥610; ⏲8.55am-5.23pm) gets you close to a shrine and the summit of **Myōken-dake** (1333m), from where the hike via **Kunimi-wakare** takes just under two hours return. Walk 3.5km back from the shrine to Nita via the village and valley of Azami-dani.

For a longer excursion (three hours), detour to **Kunimi-dake** (1347m) for a good glimpse of Japan's newest mountain, the smoking lava dome of **Heisei Shinzan** (1483m), created in November 1990 when Fugen-dake blew its stack.

Sleeping & Eating

Unzen has numerous hotels, *minshuku* and ryokan, with nightly rates from around ¥9500 including dinner and breakfast.

Shirakumo-no-Ike Camping Ground CAMPGROUND ¥
(白雲の池キャンプ場; ☎0957-73-2543; www.dango.ne.jp/unzenvc/camp.html; campsites from ¥400; ⏲25 Apr-5 May & 19 Jul-30 Aug) This picturesque summertime campsite next to Shirakumo Pond is about a 600m walk downhill from the post office, then a few hundred metres from the road. Tent hire is available (¥3000) or you may pitch your own tent (one/two people ¥600/2000).

★**Fukudaya** HOTEL ¥¥
(福田屋; ☎0957-73-2151; www.fukudaya.co.jp; Unzen Kokuritsu Koen; r from ¥9900) Fukudaya is a stylish, hip, funky onsen hotel that mixes Western and Japanese decor. The rooms with private outdoor baths are gorgeous, with milky water and decks that overlook a small creek running below. A cafe/lounge in the lobby serves steaks sizzling on heated lava stones. The bar has an expansive LP record collection of classic to eclectic. There's even a disco ball.

Unzen Sky Hotel HOTEL ¥¥
(雲仙スカイホテル; ☎0957-73-3345; www.unzen-skyhotel.com; r per person with/without 2 meals from ¥11,150/6630; P 🛜) The lobby is a

bit kitschy, but the well-maintained rooms (mostly Japanese-style) are a great deal. The *rotemburo* is in an attractive garden, and the boat-shaped indoor bath is the largest in Unzen. Families will appreciate the baby seats for the bath. Day-use bathing is also fine. There's even a table tennis table! Unlike many hotels, this one can prepare vegetarian meals on request.

Unzen Kankō Hotel HOTEL ¥¥
(雲仙観光ホテル; 0957-73-3263; www.unzenkankohotel.com; s from ¥12,030, d & tw from ¥19,740; P) Designers of this 1936 luxury hotel clearly had a Swiss chalet in mind. A destination in itself, with lots of history on the walls, it has a charming library, woody billiard room, decadent onsen baths (day use with lunch ¥1080) and large, ornate but not overdone rooms with clawfoot tubs. The cafe has tasty food, and dinners here start at ¥9800.

Kyūshū Hotel HOTEL ¥¥¥
(九州ホテル; 0957-73-3234; www.kyushuhtl.co.jp/language/en; r per person with 2 meals from ¥17,430; P) Unzen's *jigoku* make a dramatic backdrop for this five-storey, mid-century property updated with a stylish lobby, a variety of tempting room types (Japanese and Western, some with open-air baths and balconies), lovely indoor–outdoor common baths, fusion meals and lots of photos on the walls. If you'll be hiking you can reserve a box lunch to eat on the trail.

Information

For town maps and accommodation bookings, consult **Unzen Tourist Association** (雲仙観光協会; 0957-73-3434; 320 Unzen; 9am-5pm).

Getting There & Away

Three buses run daily between Nagasaki and Unzen (¥1800, one hour and 40 minutes). Unzen is also a stop on the more frequent bus route from Shimabara (¥730, 45 minutes) to Isahaya (¥1300, one hour and 20 minutes), with train connections to Nagasaki (¥460, 34 minutes).

Shimabara 島原

0957 / POP 48,815

This relaxed castle town (and ferry gateway to Kumamoto) flows with springs so clear that koi-filled waterways line the street. The springs first appeared following the 1792 eruption of nearby Mt Unzen, and the town still vividly recalls the deadly 1991 eruption, commemorated with a harrowing museum. Other attractions to note include the reconstructed Shimabara castle, a samurai street and a reclining Buddha. Because of the delicious water, foods like *dango*, (soft rice-flour balls), shaved ice and *sōmen* (vermicelli) noodles are popular.

LOCAL KNOWLEDGE

THE TEAHOUSES OF SHIMABARA

With all the clear water flowing through the town, Shimabara is known for its teahouses. For a quick break, the city-owned former villa **Shimeisō** (四明荘; 0957-63-1121; 2-125 Shinmachi; 9am-5pm) FREE sits on stilts over a spring-fed pond and serves tea for free (you can see the sand literally bubbling). Off Shimabara's central arcade, the delightful, Meiji-era **Shimabara Mizuyashiki** (しまばら水屋敷; 0957-62-8555; www.mizuyashiki.com; 513 Yorozumachi; tea & sweets ¥315-683; 11am-5pm) features a lovely garden, spring-fed pond and obsessive collection of *maneki-neko* (lucky cat) figurines from all over Japan, some for sale. The enthusiastic owner has created a detailed walking map of sights and restaurants in town.

Sights

★**Shimabara-jō** CASTLE
(島原城; 0957-62-4766; 9am-5.30pm) Hilltop Shimabara Castle was ruled mostly by the Matsudaira Clan from the 1660s, played a part in the Shimabara Rebellion and was rebuilt in 1964. Amid lotus ponds, tangled gardens, almost 4km of mossy walls, picturesque pines and staff dressed in period costumes, the grounds house four **museums** (combined admission adult/child ¥540/260). The main castle displays arms, armour and items of the Christian uprising with English explanations. **Seibō Kinenkan** (西望記念館) is dedicated to the work of native son Kitamura Seibō, sculptor of the Nagasaki Peace Statue.

★**Samurai Houses** BUILDINGS
(武家屋敷) FREE In the Teppō-machi area, northwest of the castle, are *buke yashiki* (samurai houses) set along a pretty, 450m-long gravel road with a stream down the middle. Most of the houses are currently inhabited, but several are open to the public.

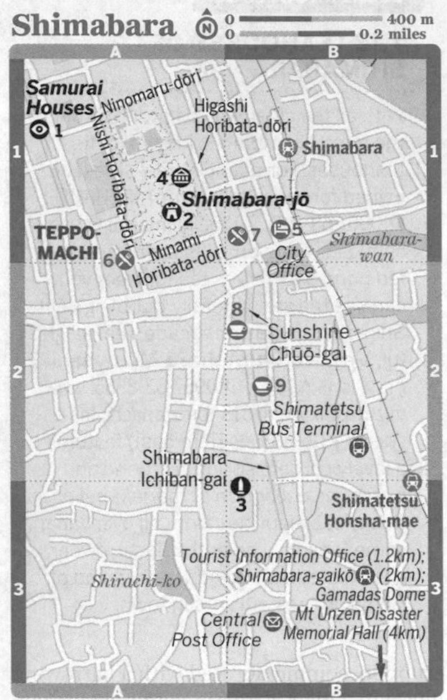

Shimabara

Top Sights

1 Samurai Houses ... A1
2 Shimabara-jō ... A1

Sights

3 Nehan-zō ... B3
4 Seibō Kinenkan ... A1

Sleeping

5 Hotel & Spa Hanamizuki ... B1

Eating

6 Himematsu-ya ... A1
7 Inohara ... B1

Drinking & Nightlife

8 Shimabara Mizuyashiki ... B2
9 Shimeisō ... B2

Nehan-zō STATUE

(ねはん像) FREE In the cemetery of Kōtō-ji Buddhist temple (江東寺) is this tranquil Nirvana statue, dating from 1957. At 8.6m, it's the longest reclining Buddha in Japan.

Gamadas Dome Mt Unzen Disaster Memorial Hall MUSEUM

(がまだすドーム雲仙岳災害記念館; ☎0957-65-5555; www.udmh.or.jp; 1-1 Heisei-machi; admission ¥1000; ⊙9am-6pm) About 4km south of the town centre, this excellent high-tech museum about the 1991 eruption and vulcanology in general is plonked eerily at the base of the lava flow. Get the free English audioguide, and visit the disturbingly lifelike simulation theatre.

Festivals & Events

The town's **water festival** is held in early August.

Sleeping & Eating

★ **Hotel Nampuro** HOTEL ¥¥

(ホテル南風楼; ☎0957-62-5111; www.nampuro.com; 7331-1 Bentenmachi; s from ¥9000, d with/without 2 meals ¥17,600/11,600; P ⊖ @ ☎ ≋ ♿) Whether you're coming from Kumamoto or Unzen, stop at Hotel Nampuro if you're ready for a splurge. Or a splash, if you're into onsen bathing: their multiple *rotemburo* offer stunning ocean views. The hotel is large yet staff take time to make you feel at home, and there's even a large family-friendly play area for young kids, inflatable toys and a cage with *kabuto* beetles.

A new hotel, the Nampuro is trying to (really!) have something for everyone: they've got a free beverage and ice-cream bar, table tennis tables, lawn games, even their own cotton candy machine.

Hotel & Spa Hanamizuki BUSINESS HOTEL ¥¥

(花みずき; ☎0957-62-1000; 548 Nakamachi; s/tw ¥5300/9500; P ⊖ @) Near Shimabara Station, this kindly 42-room tower has communal baths with wooden tubs (in addition to in-room baths), sauna and Japanese-style breakfast (¥800). Parking is ¥500 extra.

★ **Inohara** CAFÉ ¥

(猪原金物店; ☎0957-62-3117; www.inohara.jp; 912 Ueno-chō; shave ice ¥400, curry ¥450-650; ⊙11am-6pm, closed 1st & 3rd Wed each month) This blade and sharpening store is filled with incredible knives, hatchets, swords, and even ninja *shuriken* (throwing stars), but it is also a lovely cafe, offering good Japanese curry, *sōmen*, *dango* and shave ice. All made with fresh Shimabara water and using hand-sharpened blades.

Himematsu-ya JAPANESE ¥

(姫松屋; ☎0957-63-7272; 1-1208 Jōnai; dishes ¥550-800, set meals ¥750-2100; ⊙10am-8pm, closed 2nd Tue each month; 📖) This venerable restaurant across from the castle serves Shimabara's best-known dish, *guzōni* (¥980), a clear broth with *mochi* (pounded rice dumplings), seafood and vegetables. There's more standard Japanese fare too, and Unzen-raised *wagyu* beef goes for ¥1600.

Information

The main **Tourist Information Office** (島原温泉観光協会; ☎0957-62-3986; 7-5 Shimokawashiri-machi; ⌚8.30am-5.30pm) is located inside the ferry-terminal bus station (note: *not* in the train station!).

Getting There & Around

JR trains from Nagasaki to Isahaya (*futsū/tokkyū* ¥460/1070, 34/17 minutes) connect with hourly private Shimabara-tetsudō line trains to Shimabara/Shimabara-gaikō Stations (¥1430/1510, 1½/1¾ hours) respectively by the castle/port.

Ferries to Kumamoto Port depart frequently from Shimabara Port (7am to 7pm), both fast **Ocean Arrow ferries** (オーシャンアロー; ☎0957-63-8008; www.kumamotoferry.co.jp; adult/child ¥1000/500, 30 minutes; ⌚7am-5.30pm) and car ferries (adult/child ¥680/340, one hour). From Kumamoto Port, buses take you to the city (¥480, 30 minutes).

Local buses shuttle between Shimabara Station and the port (¥170) or train station (¥150). Bikes can also be rented at Shimabara-gaikō Station (per hour regular/electric ¥150/300).

KUMAMOTO PREFECTURE

Kumamoto-ken (熊本県) is the crossroads of Kyūshū. Chief draws are the city of Kumamoto, whose castle played a key role in Japanese history, and Mt Aso (Aso-san), the gigantic and very active volcanic crater at the island's centre. It's also got its own rampantly popular icon, Kumamon, soon to take its place along side Kitty-chan and Pikachu in the *kawaii* (cute) culture hall of fame.

Kumamoto 熊本

☎096 / POP 734,300

Kumamoto is deeply proud of its greatest landmark, Kumamoto-jō, the castle around which the city radiates. There's a tempting collection of restaurants, bars and shopping around the busy arcades east of the castle. Kumamoto is also the gateway to the Aso-san region, which is fortunate indeed since in summer Kumamoto is one of the warmest cities in Japan.

Sights

Former Hosokawa Gyōbutei BUILDING

(旧細川刑部邸; 3-1 Furukyō-machi; admission with/without castle ¥640/300; ⌚8.30am-5.30pm Mar-Nov, to 4.30pm Dec-Feb) North of the castle, down paths of immaculately raked gravel, is the large villa and garden built for the Hosokawa clan. Inside are displays of furniture and art pieces.

Kumamoto Prefectural Traditional Crafts Centre GALLERY

(熊本県伝統工芸館; 3-35 Chibajō-machi; admission ¥210; ⌚9am-5pm, closed Mon & 28 Dec-4 Jan) Near the prefectural art museum annexe, this large facility displays local Higo inlay, Yamaga lanterns, porcelain and woodcarvings, many for sale in the excellent museum shop (free entry). **Sakuranobaba Johsaien** (桜の馬場城彩苑) and the **Kumamoto Prefectural Products Centre** (熊本県物産館; NTT Bldg, 3-1 Sakura-machi) also sell craft items (plus food and *shōchū* liquor).

Honmyō-ji BUDDHIST TEMPLE

(本妙寺) On the grounds of this sprawling hillside temple complex northwest of the castle, 176 steps lined with hundreds of lanterns lead to the mausoleum of Katō Kiyomasa (加藤清正公の墓; 1562–1611), *daimyō* and architect of Kumamoto castle. The mausoleum was designed at the same height as the castle's *tenshūkaku* (central tower). A **treasure house** (宝物館; 4-13-20 Hanazono; admission ¥300; ⌚9am-4.30pm Sat & Sun) exhibits Kiyomasa's crown and other personal items.

Shimada Museum of Art MUSEUM

(島田美術館; 4-5-28 Shimazaki; admission ¥700; ⌚10am-5pm Wed-Mon) Through the winding backstreets south of Honmyō-ji (about 20 minutes on foot), this quiet museum displays the calligraphy and scrolls of Miyamoto Musashi (1584–1645), samurai, artist and strategist. Current artists' work is on display in adjoining galleries. There's also a cafe at the museum if you're feeling peckish.

Lafcadio Hearn's House HISTORIC BUILDING

(小泉八雲熊本旧居; ☎0963-54-7842; 2-6 Ansei-machi; admission ¥200; ⌚9.30am-4.30pm, closed Mon & 29 Dec–3 Jan) Irish-Greek immigrant Lafcadio Hearn (aka Koizumi Yakumo; 1850–1904) became one of the foremost interpreters of Japanese culture to the outside world. He lived in town from 1891 to 1894, in this house dating from 1877.

Central Kumamoto

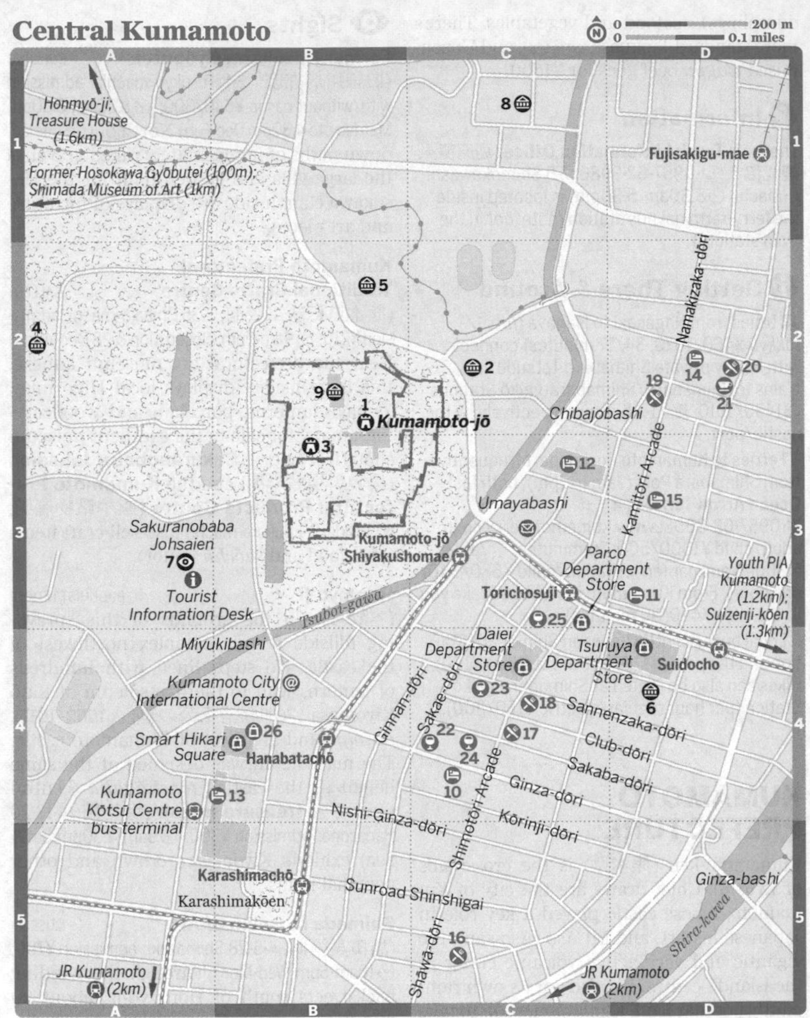

Sōseki Memorial Hall HISTORIC BUILDING
(夏目漱石内坪井旧居; 4-22 Tsuboi-machi; admission ¥200; ⏲9.30am-4.30pm Tue-Sun) Meiji-era novelist Natsume Sōseki (1867–1916) is honoured at the pretty 1870s home where he lived during his four years teaching English in Kumamoto. The home has some fine architectural details, and in the garden you can stroll in the master's footsteps. It's about a 100m walk west of the river, Tsuboi-gawa.

Suizenji-kōen GARDENS
(水前寺公園; Suizenji Park; www.suizenji.or.jp; 8-1 Suizenji-kōen; admission ¥400; Kokindenju-no-ma Teahouse tea & Hosokawa sweets ¥550-650; ⏲9am-5pm) Southeast of the city centre, this photogenic lakeside garden represents the 53 stations of the Tōkaidō (the old road that linked Tokyo and Kyoto). The miniature Mt Fuji is instantly recognisable, though much of the rest of the analogy is often lost in translation.

Festivals & Events

Takigi Nō CULTURAL
Traditional performances at Suizenji-kōen take place by torchlight on the first Saturday in August from 6pm.

Central Kumamoto

Hi-no-kuni Festival CULTURAL
Kumamoto lights up with fireworks and dancing for the Land of Fire Festival in mid-August.

Autumn Festival CULTURAL
From mid-October to early November, Kumamoto-jō stages its grand cultural festival, which includes *taiko* drumming.

Sleeping

Youth PIA Kumamoto HOSTEL ¥
(ユースピア熊本[熊本県青年会館]; ☎096-381-6221; www.ks-kaikan.com; 3-17-15 Suizenji; dm HI member/nonmember ¥3240/3600; P ⊖ @) Away from the town centre, about seven minutes' walk from JR Suizen-ji Station, this institutional-style hostel has dorms and private rooms (Japanese and Western style) and a 10pm curfew. A simple restaurant serves *shokudō* (inexpensive) standards.

Extol Inn Kumamoto BUSINESS HOTEL ¥¥
(エクストールイン熊本銀座通; ☎096-351-2111; www.extol-inn.jp; 1-9-8 Shimotōri; s/tw incl breakfast ¥5700/8500; ⊖ @ ≋) A clean, very reasonably priced option dead in the heart of Ginza street, steps away from where the nightlife happens and just a 10-minute walk to Kumamoto castle. Assuming one doesn't mind a business hotel, this is a perfect option for a cheap, clean night's stay.

Maruko Hotel RYOKAN ¥¥
(丸小ホテル; ☎096-353-1241; www.maruko-hotel.jp; 11-10 Kamitōri-machi; per person with/without 2 meals from ¥12,960/6480; P @ ≋) Features old-school Japanese-style rooms, a top-storey *o-furo* (common bath), a tiny ceramic *rotemburo* and some English-speaking staff. It's just outside the covered arcade. Parking costs ¥1000.

JR Kyūshū Hotel Kumamoto BUSINESS HOTEL ¥¥
(JR九州ホテル熊本; ☎096-354-8000; www.jrhotelgroup.com/eng/hotel/eng150.htm; 3-15-15 Kasuga; s/tw from ¥8700/10,800; P ⊖ @) The best place to stay among the hotels around JR Kumamoto Station, this 150-room tower has a comfortably contemporary design, some English-speaking staff and larger-than-usual rooms for a business hotel. Thick-paned glass minimises train noise, but request a room away from the tracks if sensitive. Discounts and promotions may drop the price at times.

Kumamoto Kōtsū Centre Hotel BUSINESS HOTEL ¥¥
(熊本交通センターホテル; ☎096-326-8828; www.kyusanko.co.jp/hotel; 3-10 Sakuramachi; s/tw from ¥5850/9750; P ⊖ @ ≋) In a prime location above the main bus terminal, this hotel has a mid-century Japanese look and pleasant staff. Look for discounted rates online or by phone. Just ¥900 gets you a large breakfast buffet. There are bargain 'windowless singles' for ¥4350. Wi-fi is only in the lobby.

Wasuki HOTEL ¥¥
(和数奇; ☎096-352-5101; www.wasuki.jp; 7-35 Kamitōri-machi; s/d/tw from ¥8800/13,200/17,600; P @ ≋) Done in the style of

DON'T MISS

KUMAMOTO-JŌ

Dominating the skyline, Kumamoto's robust **castle** (熊本城; ☎096-322-5900; admission ¥500; ⊙8.30am-6pm Mar-Nov, to 5pm Dec-Feb) is one of Japan's best, built in 1601–07 by *daimyō* Katō Kiyomasa, whose likeness is inescapable around the castle (look for the distinctive tall pointed hat). From 1632 it was the seat of the powerful Hosokawa clan.

Though a reconstruction, Kumamoto-jō is best known as the scene of the story of the last samurai. During the 1877 Satsuma Rebellion, rebels against the new imperial order held out for a 50-day siege here before the castle was burned, leaving the Meiji government to rule unfettered.

The castle's massive curved stone walls, 5.3km in circumference, are crammed with 13 photogenic buildings, turrets, keeps and the soaring black **Tenshūkaku** (main building, 29.5m tall), today a historical museum with 6th-storey lookouts. Next door, the 2008 reconstruction of the **Honmaru Palace** (Honmaru Goten) fairly gleams with fresh wood and gold leaf paintings, particularly in the **Sho-kun-no-ma** receiving room. Free castle info is offered in English; call to check availability.

Within the castle walls, the **Kumamoto Prefectural Museum of Art** (熊本県立美術館; 2 Ninomaru; admission ¥270; ⊙9.30am-5.15pm, closed Mon & 25 Dec-4 Jan) has ancient Buddhist sculptures and modern paintings. Across the castle park, the museum's postmodern **Chibajo Annexe** (2-18 Chibajō-machi; ⊙9.30am-6.30pm, closed Mon & 25 Dec-4 Jan) FREE, built in 1992 by the Spanish architects Elias Torres and José Antonio Martínez-Lapeña, is an architectural landmark.

Kumamoto Castle, with a charcoal exterior, white plaster, dark beams and brooding *tansu*-style (wooden) furniture in the generously sized rooms, most combining tatami, hardwood floors and Western-style bedding. It's well located for eating and nightlife, and there are common baths on the top floor (plus in-room facilities). Staff are friendly, but there's little English signage to aid in getting around.

★Kumamoto Hotel Castle HOTEL ¥¥¥
(熊本ホテルキャッスル; ☎096-326-3311; www.hotel-castle.co.jp; 4-2 Jōtō-machi; s/d/tw from ¥10,098/17,820/19,008, Japanese-style r ¥35,640; P⊖☜) Overlooking the castle, this posh, upmarket hotel has professional, friendly service (staff wear Hawaiian shirts in Kumamoto's hot summers), a beamed ceiling inspired by its namesake, and rooms with slick renovations in muted browns and whites. Request a castle-view room.

Hotel Nikko Kumamoto HOTEL ¥¥¥
(ホテル日航熊本; ☎096-211-1111; www.nikko-kumamoto.co.jp; 2-1 Kamitōri-chō; s/d/tw from ¥17,820/47,520/32,076; P⊖@☜) The classic Japanese hotel experience, Kumamoto's premier hotel offers staff in crisp uniforms, fine-grained woods, soothing marble and spacious rooms with big bathrooms and views to the castle or Aso-san.

Eating

The Kamitōri and Shimotōri arcades and vicinity are happy grazing grounds for Japanese and foreign cuisines, from gourmet extravaganzas to fast food. Kumamoto is famous for *karashi-renkon* (fried lotus root with mustard) and *Higo-gyū* (Higo beef) and the Chinese-inspired *taipien*, bean vermicelli soup with seafood and vegetables. However, the most popular dish seems to be *basashi* (raw horsemeat). Other menus include whale meat (*kujira;* 鯨), which we hope you'll avoid.

To sample many foods in one place, visit Sakuranobaba Johsaien (p709), a tourist complex near the castle, with lots of stalls and restaurants serving local specialities.

Ramen Komurasaki RAMEN ¥
(熊本ラーメンこむらさき; ☎096-325-8972; 8-16 Kamitōri; rāmen ¥570-1030; ⊙11am-10pm Tue-Sun; ⓔ) This rāmen joint is next to Yoshinoya at the north end of the Kamitōri Arcade. The signature 'king rāmen' (¥620) is garlicky, cloudy Kumamoto-style *tonkotsu* (pork) broth with bamboo shoots, julienned mushrooms and *chashū* (roast pork) so lean you'd think it had been working out.

Chocolat CAFE ¥
(ショコラ; ☎096-355-3157; www.chocolat-kumamoto.com; 2-5-10 Shimotōri; crêpes ¥650-1000; ⊙noon-11pm Tue-Sun) A couple of blocks south

of the Shimotōri Arcade, amid sidestreets reminiscent of Tokyo's trendy Omote-Sando, this charming shop has mottled walls like a Parisian boudoir and specialises in sweet and savoury crêpes like ham, cheese and vegetables. Galettes are crêpes made with *soba* (buckwheat) flour.

★Kome no Kura IZAKAYA ¥¥

(米の蔵; ☎096-212-5551; 2nd fl, 1-6-27 Shimotōri; dishes ¥250-950; ⏲5.30pm-midnight; 📋) This black-walled, quietly chic *izakaya*, with cosy private booths and *hori-kotatsu* (well in the floor for your feet) seating, has a whole menu of Kumamoto specialities along with standard fare. *Tsukune* (ground chicken) is served pressed around a bamboo skewer. Look for 'dynamic kitchen' on its sign.

If you're having trouble finding it, look for Docomo: it's next door.

★Yokobachi IZAKAYA ¥¥

(☎096-351-4581; 11-40 Kaminoura; small plates ¥480-1200; ⏲5pm-midnight; 📋) Yokobachi's leafy courtyard and open kitchen are distinctive. Standout small plates include spicy *tebasaki* (chicken wings), an inventive Caesar salad with sweet potato and lotus root chips, delicately fried *mābō-nasu* (eggplant in spicy meat sauce) and, if you dare, *basashi* (¥880). There are 13 *shōchū* liquors to choose from.

Kōran-tei CHINESE ¥¥

(紅蘭亭; ☎096-352-7177; 5-26 Ansei-machi; meals from ¥850; ⏲11am-9.30pm Mon-Sat, 11am-9pm Sun; 🚭@📋📋👪) On the second storey above a Swiss pastry shop on the Shimotōri Arcade, this glossy restaurant has an endless menu. Enjoy the action on the arcade as you tuck into *taipien* (¥750; 'bean noodle with vegetable' on the English menu), daily lunch specials (¥850) or a six-course feast for a mere ¥1650.

Drinking & Nightlife

The laneways off Shimotōri Arcade and the hip Namikizaka-dōri area at the north end of Kamitōri Arcade are lively after dark.

★Andcoffeeroasters CAFE

(アンドコーヒーロースターズ; ☎096-273-6178; andcoffeeroasters.com; 11-22 Kamitōri-chō; ⏲8am-8pm) Delightful boutique coffee shop with freshly roasted beans and a 'tart of the day', such as persimmon or Earl Grey. Coffee nerds will feel right at home with the rich lattes, creamy cappuccinos and other speciality espresso drinks. It's outside the north end of the arcade.

Sanctuary CLUB

(サンクチュアリー; ☎096-325-5853; 4-16 Tetori Honmachi; ⏲8pm-late) The city's biggest night club has bars, food, darts, billiards, karaoke, dancing, lounges and DJs spinning alt-rock to hip hop, for an international crowd. If there's a cover charge (up to ¥500), it often includes a drink ticket. Fridays and Saturdays are busiest.

Jeff's World Bar BAR

(ジェフズワールドバー; 2nd fl, 1-4-3 Shimotōri; ⏲8pm-2am) *Gaijin* (expats) and local Japanese frequent this 2nd-floor pub. There's dancing some weekends, and it's a bit of a meat market for those on the prowl. Look for the basketball-sized, blue, world sign across from the red and white '7 Bldg' or you might walk right by.

Good Time Charlie BAR

(5th fl, 1-7-24 Shimotōri; ⏲8pm-2am Thu-Tue) Charlie Nagatani earned the rank of Kentucky Colonel for his contributions to the world of country music (he runs the Country Gold Festival near Aso-san), and this bar is his home base. Look for live music, a tiny dance floor and thousands of pictures on the walls.

Rock Bar Days BAR

(☎096-323-7110; 3rd fl SMILE Bldg, 1-7-7 Shimotōri; ⏲8pm-5am) It's Kumamoto's grunge underground, three storeys up. Request a tune and they will dutifully find it in the vast library of over 6000 primarily foreign CDs that adorn the walls. Dance if you have the space, or make friends at the bar (drinks are around ¥600) or in comfy chairs.

Information

Visit www.kumamoto-icb.or.jp for city information. **Higo Bank** (肥後銀行) handles currency exchange, and there are conveniently located postal ATMs.

Kumamoto City International Centre (熊本市国際交流会館; ☎096-359-2020; 4-18 Hanabata-chō; ⏲9am-8pm Mon-Sat, to 7pm Sun & holidays) Has free wi-fi on the 1st and 2nd floors, plus BBC News and English-language magazines.

Tourist Information Desks (熊本駅総合観光案内所) Branches at JR Kumamoto Station (熊本駅総合観光案内所; ☎096-352-3743; ⏲8.30am-8pm) and Sakuranobaba Johsaien

(桜の馬場城彩苑総合観光案内所; ☎096-322-5060; ⌚8.30am-5.30pm, to 6.30pm Mar-Nov). Both locations have English-speaking assistants and accommodation listings.

ℹ Getting There & Away

JR Kumamoto Station is an inconvenient few kilometres southwest of the centre (though an easy tram ride). It's a stop on the Kyūshū *shinkansen* with destinations including Kagoshima-Chūō (¥6740, 43 minutes), Fukuoka (Hakata Station; ¥4930, 33 minutes), Hiroshima (¥13,340, 1¾ hours) and Shin-Osaka (¥18,340, 3¼ hours), as well as Beppu (¥4930, three hours) via the JR Hōhi line. Flights connect Aso-Kumamoto Airport with Tokyo and Osaka.

Highway buses depart from the Kumamoto Kōtsū Centre (熊本交通センター) bus terminal. Routes include Fukuoka (¥2060, two hours), Kagoshima (¥3700, 3½ hours), Nagasaki (¥3700, 3¼ hours) and Miyazaki (¥4630, three hours).

ℹ Getting Around

TO/FROM THE AIRPORT

Buses to and from the airport (¥730, 50 minutes) stop at Kumamoto Kōtsū Centre and JR Kumamoto Station.

BUS

City buses are generally hard to manage without Japanese skills, with one exception: the Castle Loop Bus (per ride/day pass ¥150/400) connecting the bus centre with most sights in the castle area at least every half-hour, between 9am and 5pm daily.

CAR & MOTORCYCLE

Renting a car is recommended for trips to Aso and beyond (from about ¥5250 per 12 hours). Rental services line the street across from JR Kumamoto Station.

TRAM

Kumamoto's tram service (Shiden) reaches the major sights for ¥150 per ride. One-/two-day passes (¥500/800) can be bought onboard, offer discounted admission to sights and can be used on city buses.

Aso-san Area 阿蘇山

☎0967 / POP 30,000

Halfway between Kumamoto and Beppu lies the Aso-san volcanic caldera. It's among the world's largest (128km in circumference), so big that it's hard at first to understand its scale, and strikingly beautiful. Formed through a series of eruptions over the past 300,000 years, the current outer crater is about 90,000 years old and now accommodates towns, villages and train lines.

Aso-san is still active, and the summit is frequently off-limits due to toxic gas emissions or wind conditions. Check with the tourist information centre or www.aso.ne.jp/~volcano/eng/ for updates in English.

Sights

★Aso-gogaku MOUNTAINS

(阿蘇五岳) The **Five Mountains of Aso** are the smaller mountains within the outer rim: Eboshi-dake (1337m), Kijima-dake (1321m), Naka-dake (1506m), Neko-dake (1408m), furthest east, and the highest, Taka-dake (1592m).

Naka-dake is the active volcano: *very* active in recent years, with fatal eruptions occurring in 1958 and 1979, and other significant eruptions in 1989, 1990 and 1993.

If Naka-dake is behaving, a cable car whisks you up to the crater's edge in just four minutes; from there, it's a 30-minute walk.

It'll cost ¥600 in tolls and parking if driving yourself. The **cable car** (Ropeway; one way/round trip ¥750/1200; ⌚8.30am-6pm mid-Mar–Oct, 8.30am-5pm Nov, 9am-5pm Dec–mid-Mar) is 3km from the Aso Volcano Museum. Don't miss the 100m-deep crater – with pale green waters bubbling and steaming below, it varies in width from 400m to 1100m, and there's a walk around the southern edge of the crater rim. Arrive early in the morning to glimpse a sea of clouds hovering inside the crater, with Kujū-san (1787m) on the horizon.

Aso Volcano Museum MUSEUM

(阿蘇火山博物館; ☎0967-34-2111; www.asomuse.jp; 1930-1 Akamizu; admission ¥840, parking ¥410; ⌚9am-5pm) This unique museum has a real-time video feed from inside the active crater, informative English-language brochures and audioguides (free), and a video presentation of Aso friends showing off.

Opposite the museum, you can go hiking on **Kusasenri** (草千里), a grassy meadow with two 'lakes' in the flattened crater of an ancient volcano. It's postcard-perfect on a clear day. Just off the road from the museum to Aso town is the perfectly shaped cone of **Kome-zuka** (954m), another extinct volcano.

Aso-jinja SHINTO SHRINE

(阿蘇神社) FREE Dedicated to the 12 gods of the mountain, this shrine is about a 1.3km walk north of JR Miyaji Station, and is one of only three shrines in Japan with its original gate. The drinking water here is so delicious that visitors fill canteens to take home.

Activities

From the top of the cable-car run you can **walk** around the crater rim to the peak of Naka-dake and on to Taka-dake. Ask at tourist information offices about trail conditions before setting out for **Sensui Gorge** (Sensui-kyō), which blooms with azaleas in mid-May; or between Taka-dake and Neko-dake and on to Miyaji, the next train station east of Aso.

Shorter walks include the easy ascent of Kijima-dake from the Aso Volcano Museum, about 25 minutes to the top. You can then return to the museum or take the branch trail to the Naka-dake ropeway in about 30 minutes. The walk around Kusasenri takes about one hour, and can be combined with a climb to the top of Eboshi-dake (about 80 minutes).

Yume-no-yu Onsen ONSEN
(阿蘇坊中温泉夢の湯; 1538-3 Kurokawa; admission ¥400; ⏲11am-10pm, closed 1st & 3rd Mon of the month) After a long hike, this welcoming onsen, just in front of JR Aso Station, has wonderful indoor and outdoor pools, a large sauna and private 'family' bath (¥1000 per hour).

Festivals & Events

Hi-furi Matsuri CULTURAL
A spectacular fire festival, Hi-furi Matsuri is held at Aso-jinja in mid-March.

Sleeping & Eating

Most accommodation is in Aso or Takamori. Away from the towns, restaurants and lodgings are scattered and hard to reach by public transport. Stocking up on snacks is suggested, and there's a cluster of eateries on Hwy 57 near JR Aso Station. Two hostels, **Asobigokoro** (阿蘇び心; ☎0967-34-0315; www.aso.ne.jp/asobi-gokoro/; 211 Kurokawa; dm ¥2000, r per person ¥2800; @📶; 🚉Aso) and **Aso Base Backpackers** (阿蘇ベースバックパッカーズ; ☎0967-34-0408; www.aso-backpackers.com; 1498 Kurokawa; dm/s/tw/d without bathroom ¥2800/5500/6000/6600; ⏲closed mid-Jan–mid-Feb; P@📶) offer the lowest-cost accommodation, the latter just steps from the train station.

Aso Town

Shukubō Aso RYOKAN ¥¥
(宿坊あそ; ☎0967-34-0194; fax 0967-34-1342; 1076 Kurokawa; r per person with/without 2 meals from ¥12,000/5000; P📶) In a reconstructed 300-year-old samurai house, this lovely, rustic ryokan has modern touches and a tree-lined setting less than 500m from Aso Station. Its 12 rooms have private toilet and shared bath, and a dinner of local meats and fish is served around an *irori* (hearth). It's near Saiganden-ji temple, which dates from AD 726. (It's *not* non-smoking though.)

Sanzoku-Tabiji JAPANESE ¥
(山賊旅路; ☎0967-34-2011; 2127-1 Kurokawa; meals ¥650-1500; ⏲11am-6pm Thu-Tue; ✎📋👪) Cute shop known for *dangojiru* (miso soup with thick-cut noodles) and *takana ryōri* (dishes using mustard greens), beneath a ceiling strung with traditional ceramic bells. It's on Hwy 57, opposite the Villa Park Hotel, 10 minutes' walk west from JR Aso Station.

Takamori

Murataya Ryokan Youth Hostel HOSTEL ¥
(ユースホステル村田家旅館; ☎0967-62-0066; www13.ocn.ne.jp/~okuaso; 1672 Takamori; per person dm HI member/nonmember ¥3132/3780, ryokan with 2 meals ¥8208; P) This 1930s building in central Takamori feels like a private home. Its seven rooms are identical and have shared facilities, but at the ryokan rate you'll have a better grade of services (like laying out of futons) and meals. It's about 800m from the station (if needed, they can offer pick up). At the youth hostel rate, dinner/breakfast cost ¥1080/650 extra. The bath is still heated with logs, like old times.

Bluegrass INN ¥
(ブルーグラス; ☎0967-62-3366; www.aso-bluegrass.com; 2814 Takamori; r per person ¥3240; P) This cowboy ranch house and inn has attractive clean tatami rooms, and a 'stay & ride' package for horse fans. The restaurant serves burgers, steaks and local cuisine (lunch and dinner from ¥1100, closed first and third Wednesday of the month) from a picture menu. It's on Hwy 325, about a 20-minute hike from the station. Look for the US flag marking the driveway.

Kyūkamura Minami-Aso HOTEL ¥¥
(休暇村南阿蘇; ☎0967-62-2111; www.qkamura.or.jp/aso; 3219 Takamori; s/d with 2 meals from

Aso-san

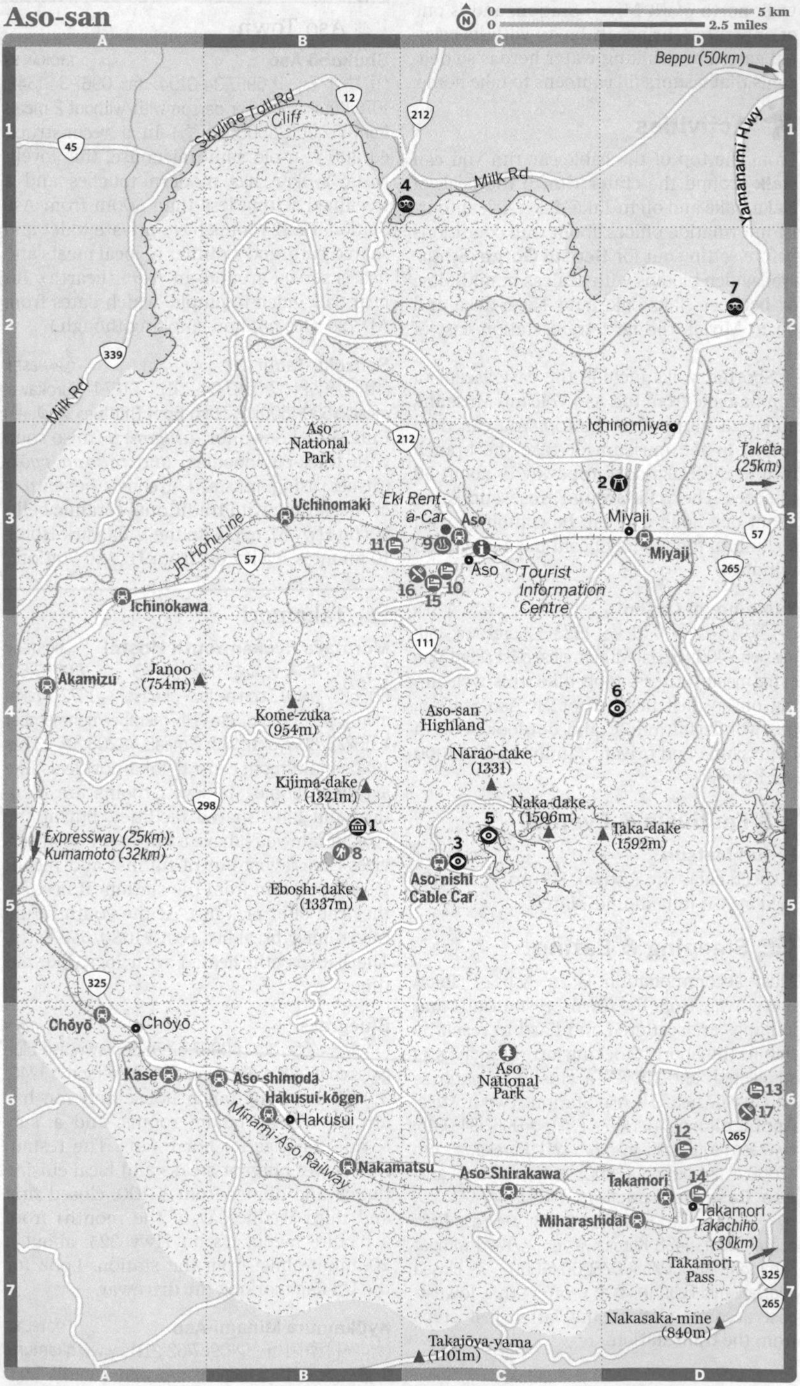
0 5 km
0 2.5 miles
A
B
C
D
1
2
3
4
5
6
7
Beppu (50km)
Skyline Toll Rd
Cliff
12
212
45
Yamanami Hwy
Milk Rd
4
7
339
Milk Rd
Aso National Park
212
Ichinomiya
Taketa (25km)
2
Uchinomaki
Eki Rent-a-Car
Aso
Miyaji
Miyaji
57
JR Hōhi Line
11
9
Aso
Tourist Information Centre
57
265
16
10
15
Ichinokawa
111
Akamizu
Janoo (754m)
Kome-zuka (954m)
6
Aso-san Highland
Narao-dake (1331)
Kijima-dake (1321m)
298
Naka-dake (1506m)
1
5
Taka-dake (1592m)
Expressway (25km); Kumamoto (32km)
3
8
Aso-nishi Cable Car
Eboshi-dake (1337m)
325
Chōyō
Chōyō
Aso National Park
Kase
Aso-shimoda
Hakusui-kōgen
Hakusui
13
17
Minami-Aso Railway
12
265
Nakamatsu
Aso-Shirakawa
Takamori
14
Takamori
Miharashidai
Takachiho (30km)
Takamori Pass
325
265
Nakasaka-mine (840m)
Takajōya-yama (1101m)
KYŪSHŪ

Aso-san

Sights

1 Aso Volcano Museum B5
2 Aso-jinja D3
3 Cable Car C5
4 Daikanbō Lookout C1
5 Naka-dake Crater C5
6 Sensui Gorge D4
7 Shiroyama Tembōdai Lookout D2

Activities, Courses & Tours

8 Kusasenri B5
9 Yume-no-yu Onsen C3

Sleeping

10 Aso Base Backpackers C3
11 Asobigokoro B3
12 Bluegrass D6
13 Kyūkamura Minami-Aso D6
14 Murataya Ryokan Youth Hostel D6
15 Shukubō Aso C3

Eating

16 Sanzoku-Tabiji C3
17 Takamori Dengaku-no-Sato D6

¥11,800/21,700;) This vacation village is beautifully maintained, with magnificent peak views. Rates vary, but all include access to onsen and *rotemburo*. A kid-friendly play area is a plus for families. Rates rise in high season: July and August.

★ **Takamori Dengaku-no-Sato** GRILL ¥¥
(高森田楽の里; 0967-62-1899; 2685-2 Ōaza-Takamori; set meals ¥1680-2500; 10am-7.30pm;) A fantastic thatch-roofed ex-farmhouse, where around your own *irori* embedded in the floor the staff use oven mitts to grill skewers of vegetables, meat, fish and tofu, some covered in the namesake *dengaku* (sweet miso) paste. It's a few minutes by car or taxi (about ¥600) from Takamori Station.

Orientation

Best explored by car, the region offers fabulous drives, diverse scenery and peaceful retreats. Routes 57, 265 and 325 encircle the outer caldera, and the JR Hōhi line runs across the northern section from Kumamoto. If you're driving, **Daikanbō Lookout** (大観峰) is one of the best places to take it all in, but it's often crowded with tour buses. **Shiroyama Tembōdai** (Yamanami Hwy) is a nice alternative. Aso is the main town, but Takamori, to the south, is more intimate and charming.

Information

Next to JR Aso Station, the helpful **Tourist Information Centre** (道の駅阿蘇施設案内所; 0967-35-5088; 1440-1 Kurokawa; 9am-6pm) offers free road and hiking maps and local information in English, and coin lockers. A postal ATM is 100m south, across Hwy 57.

Getting There & Around

Aso is on the JR Hōhi line between Kumamoto (*tokkyū/futsū*; ¥2240/1110, 70/86 minutes) and Ōita (¥3570, 1½ hours). Some buses from Beppu (¥2950, three hours) continue to the Aso-nishi cable-car station (an extra ¥540).

For Takamori, transfer from the JR Hōhi line at Tateno (¥370, 30 minutes) to the scenic Minami-Aso private line, which terminates at Takamori (¥480, 30 minutes). Buses from Takamori continue southeast to Takachiho (¥1280, 80 minutes, two daily).

Buses operate approximately hourly from JR Aso Station via the volcano museum to Aso-nishi cable-car station (¥650, 40 minutes), stopping at Kusasenri (¥570).

Rent electric bikes at JR Aso Station (¥400 for two hours), or cars at **Eki Rent-a-Car** (駅レンタカー; 0967-34-1120; www.ekiren.co.jp; per half day/day from ¥4720/5790; 9am-6pm), adjacent to the train station (reserve in advance).

Kurokawa Onsen 黒川温泉

0967 / POP 302

Nestled on either sides of a steep gorge about one hour northeast of Aso Town, tranquil Kurokawa Onsen is one of Japan's prettiest hot-spring villages and has won top onsen honours several years in a row. Safely secluded from the rest of the world, it's the perfect spot to experience what an onsen ryokan getaway is all about.

For day trippers, a *nyūtō tegata* (onsen passport; ¥1300) allows access to three baths from Kurokawa's 24 ryokan (open 8.30am to 9pm). Buy one at the tourist information desk (p718) and ask which locations are open during your visit. Favourites include Yamamizuki, Kurokawa-sō and Shimmei-kan, with cave baths and riverside *rotemburo* (Kurokawa is especially famous for its *rotemburo*). Many places offer *konyoku* (mixed bathing).

Sleeping

Kurokawa's onsen ryokan aren't cheap, but this isn't an experience you'll have every day. English is spoken to varying degrees, and some ryokan can arrange pick-up from Kurokawa Onsen bus stop.

Chaya-no-Hara Campground CAMPGROUND ¥
(茶屋の原キャンプ所; ☎0967-44-0220; 6323 Manganji; campsite per person from ¥600, plus ¥600 per tent & ¥600 per car) About 5km before Kurokawa Onsen is this place, which is essentially a sloping lush green field with inspirational views.

Aso Kujū-Kōgen Youth Hostel HOSTEL ¥
(阿蘇くじゅう高原ユースホステル; ☎0967-44-0157; www.asokujuuyh.sakura.ne.jp; 6332 Oguni-machi Senohara; dm HI member/non-member from ¥2000/2600) About 6km from Kurokawa Onsen, this friendly hostel has English information about hiking Kujū-san and other high peaks in the area, which can be viewed from the property; there's also a couple of log cabins. Breakfast (¥500) and dinner (¥1000) are available.

Sanga Ryokan RYOKAN ¥¥¥
(山河旅館; ☎0967-44-0906; www.sanga-ryokan.com; r per person with 2 meals from ¥16,350; P) Deep in the gorge, about 1.5km from the town centre, this romantic ryokan has 16 deluxe rooms, all but one of which have private onsen attached. Exquisite *kaiseki* meals, attention to detail and heartfelt service make this a place to experience the Japanese art of hospitality.

Okyakuya Ryokan RYOKAN ¥¥¥
(御客屋旅館; ☎0967-44-0454; www.okyakuya.jp; r per person with 2 meals from ¥15,270; P) At Kurokawa Onsen's oldest ryokan (in its seventh generation of the same family) all 10 rooms have river views, plus sink and toilet, and share common onsen baths; the riverside *rotemburo* is worth it by itself.

Information

Tourist Information Desk (Ryokan Association; 旅館組合; ☎0967-44-0076; www.kurokawaonsen.or.jp/english; Kurokawa-sakura-dōri; ⌚9am-6pm) Sells the *nyūtō tegata* (onsen passport; ¥1300) and dispenses friendly, helpful information.

Getting There & Away

Experiencing this area is most enjoyable by car, but several daily buses connect Kurokawa Onsen with Kumamoto/Aso (¥2000/960, 2½ hours/one hour), and a couple continue on to Beppu (¥2900, 2½ hours) via Yufuin (¥2300). Check timetables if you intend to make this a day trip.

KAGOSHIMA PREFECTURE

Kagoshima-ken (鹿児島県) is mainland Japan's southernmost prefecture and some say the nation's most friendly, beautiful and relaxed. Kagoshima city lies in the shadow of the highly active Sakurajima volcano, with the fertile coastal plains of the Satsuma Peninsula to the south. To the north is the striking Kirishima-Yaku National Park, with its own string of active volcanoes.

Kagoshima 鹿児島

☎099 / POP 609,250

Sunny Kagoshima has a personality to match its climate, voted Japan's friendliest city nationwide. Its backdrop/deity is Sakurajima, a very active volcano *just* across the bay. Locals raise their umbrellas against the mountain's recurrent eruptions, when fine ash coats the landscape like snow and obscures the sun like fog – mystical and captivating. The entire prefecture even has a special 'Ash Forecast' as part of the weather report. Once ash starts falling you'll understand why: it stings, coats your teeth with grit, dirties futons and laundry, and makes anyone who has just washed their car burst into tears.

History

Once called Satsuma, it was ruled by the Shimazu clan for a remarkable 700 years. The location helped it grow wealthy through trade, particularly with China. Contact was also made with Korea, whose pottery methods were influential in the creation of Satsuma-yaki.

When Japan opened to the world in the mid-19th century, Satsuma's government competed with the shogunate, engaging in war with Britain and hosting a Satsuma pavilion – independent from the Japanese pavilion – at the 1867 Paris Expo. Satsuma's best known samurai, the complicated and (literally) towering figure of Saigō Takamori, played a key role in the Meiji Restoration. There's a **statue of Saigō Takamori** in central Kagoshima.

Sights

★Museum of the Meiji Restoration MUSEUM

(維新ふるさと館; 23-1 Kaijiya-chō; admission ¥300; ⌚9am-5pm; 🚉JR Kagoshima-Chūō) The museum offers insights into the unique social system of education, samurai loyalty and sword techniques that made Satsuma one of Japan's leading provinces, with a great audioguide in English. There are hourly audiovisual presentations about the groundbreaking visits of Satsuma students to the West and the Satsuma Rebellion told by animatronic Meiji-era reformers, including Saigō Takamori and Sakamoto Ryōma.

Sengan-en (Iso-teien) GARDENS

(仙巌園[磯庭園]; ☎099-247-1551; 9700-1 Yoshinochō; admission with/without guided villa tour & tea ceremony ¥1500/1000; ⌚8.30am-5.30pm) In 1658, the 19th Shimazu lord laid out this hilly, rambling bayside property of groves, gardens, hillside trails and one of Japan's most impressive pieces of 'borrowed scenery': the fuming peak of Sakurajima. It was a place of pleasure and a strategically important lookout for ships entering Kinkō-wan.

Allow at least 30 minutes for a leisurely stroll, 20 minutes more to tour the 25-room **Goten**, a former villa of the Shimazu clan (traditional tea and sweets provided).

Shops around the garden sell *jambo-mochi* (pounded rice cakes on a stick) and Kiriko cut glass.

The adjacent **Shōko Shūseikan** (尚古集成館; admission free with garden ticket; ⌚8.30am-5.15pm) museum once housed Japan's first factory (1850s). Exhibits relate to the Shimazu family and Japanese industrial history, with over 10,000 items and precious heirlooms, including scrolls, military goods, Satsuma-yaki pottery, and Japan's earliest cannons, steam engines and cut glass.

The garden is about 2km north of the city centre. Nearby is **Iso-hama**, the city's popular, kid-friendly swimming beach.

Reimeikan MUSEUM

(黎明館; Kagoshima Prefectural Museum of Culture; 7-2 Shiroyama-chō; admission ¥310; ⌚9am-6pm, closed Mon & 25th of each month; 🚊Shiyakushō-mae) The Reimeikan has extensive displays on Satsuma history and ancient swordmaking. It's inside the site of Kagoshima's castle, Tsurumaru-jō (1602); the walls and moat are all that remain, and bullet holes in the stones are still visible. It's behind Kagoshima's city hall and government buildings.

WORTH A TRIP

UENOHARA JŌMON-NO-MORI

Archaeology enthusiasts will want to detour to this **museum** (上野原縄文の森; ☎0995-48-5701; 1-1 Uenohara Jōmon-no-mori, Kokubu; admission ¥310; ⌚9am-5pm Tue-Sun), on the site where the oldest authenticated Jōmon-era pottery shards were discovered during excavations for nearby office parks. Based on these findings, anthropologists began to conclude that the first humans may have come to Japan from the south rather than the north, via canoes or rafts along the Ryūkyū island chain. Look also for a re-created village of Jōmon-era dwellings, demonstrations, tools and artefacts. The museum can be reached by train from Kagoshima to Kokubu, from where it's about 8km (20 minutes) by taxi or private car.

Kagoshima City Museum of Art MUSEUM

(鹿児島市立美術館; 4-36 Shiroyama-chō; admission ¥300; ⌚9.30am-6pm Tue-Sun; 🚊Asahi-dōri) The Kagoshima City Museum of Art has a small, permanent collection of works by modern-day Kagoshima painters, as well as some 16th-century porcelains and woodblock prints, and a wonderful collection of Sakurajima paintings.

★Kagoshima City Aquarium AQUARIUM

(かごしま水族館; 3-1 Honkō Shinmachi; adult/child ¥1500/750; ⌚9.30am-6pm; 🚊Asahi-dōri) Beautiful seascapes brim with marine life by the harbour, plus there are dolphin and seal shows and great English signage. Perhaps the coolest exhibit is the giant tank where whale sharks, tuna and other deep-water fish circle around (and above!) you.

Onsen ONSEN

Kagoshima boasts some 50 bathhouses, most meant for locals and recalling the humble, everyday *sentō* of old. They include **Nishida Onsen** (西田温泉; 1-2-17 Takashi; admission ¥360; ⌚5.30am-10.30pm, closed 2nd Mon each month), about five minutes' walk from JR Kagoshima-Chūō Station; and **Kagomma Onsen** (かごっま温泉; 3-28 Yasui-chō; admission ¥360; ⌚10am-1am, closed 15th of each month) near city hall. A great onsen brochure is available in most tourist info desks and many hotel lobbies.

Central Kagoshima

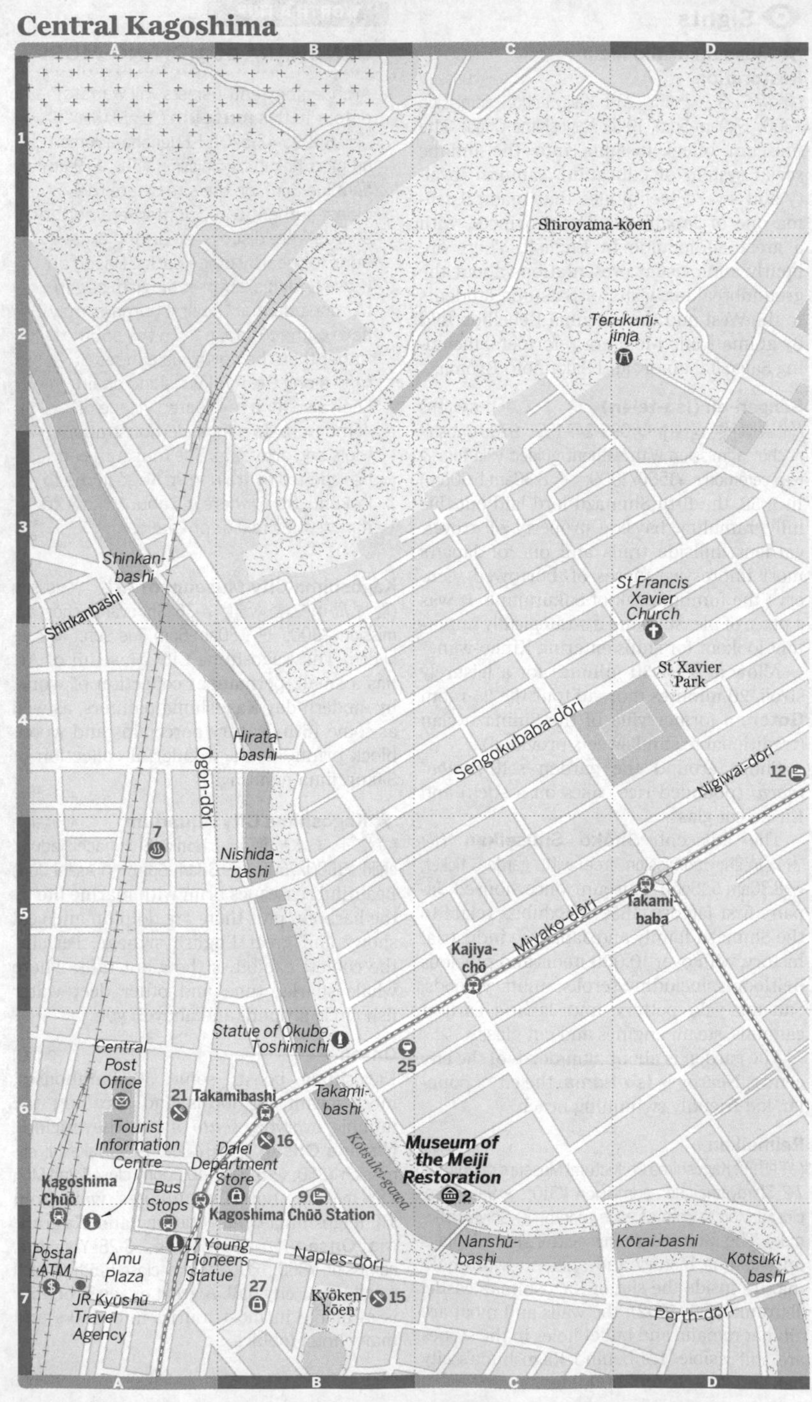

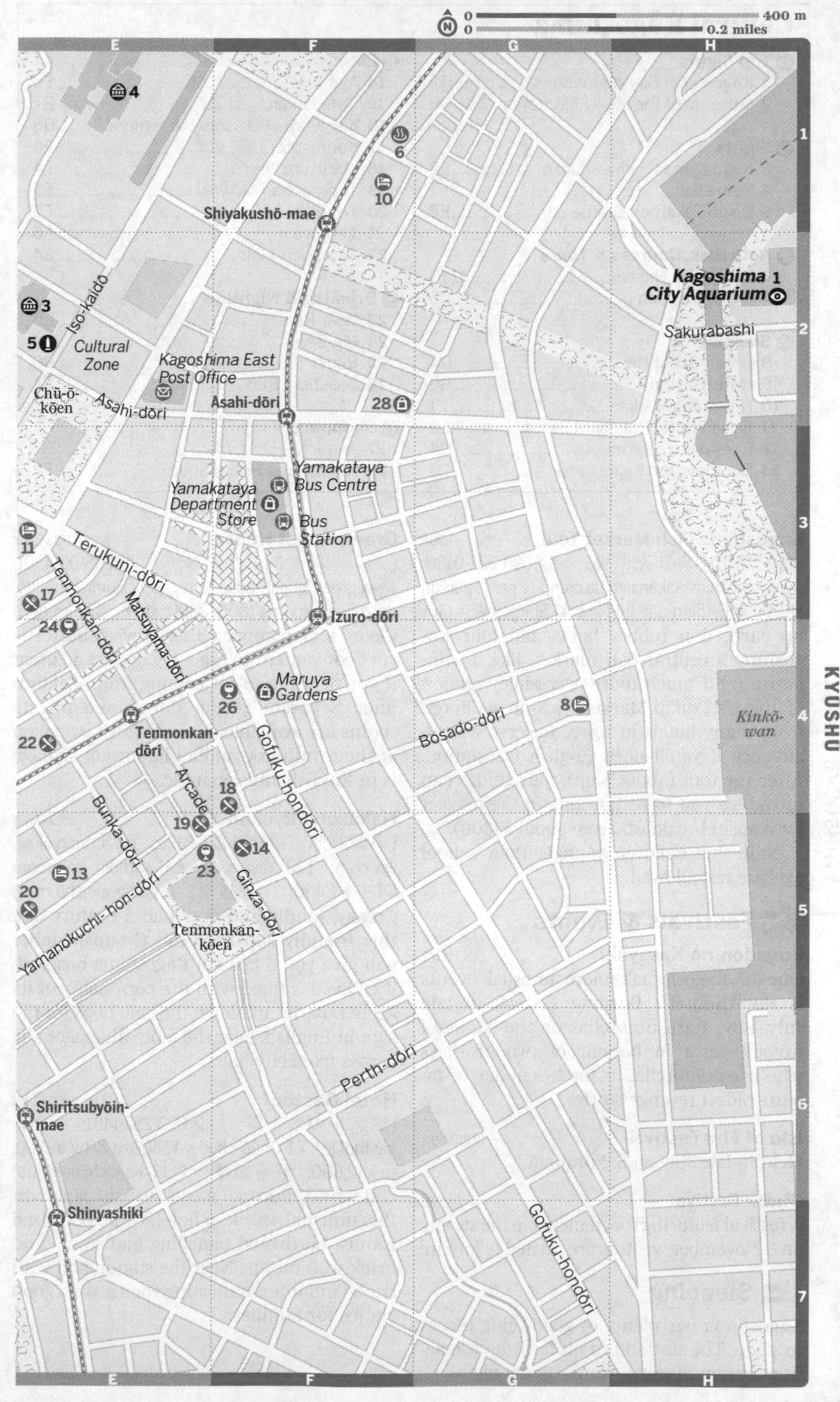

0 400 m
0 0.2 miles
E
F
G
H
1
2
3
4
5
6
7
4
6
10
Shiyakushō-mae
Iso-kaidō
3
5
Cultural Zone
Kagoshima East Post Office
Kagoshima City Aquarium 1
Sakurabashi
Chū-ō-kōen
Asahi-dōri
Asahi-dōri
28
Yamakataya Bus Centre
Yamakataya Department Store
Bus Station
11
Terukuni-dōri
Tenmonkan-dōri
Matsuyama-dōri
17
24
Izuro-dōri
Maruya Gardens
26
8
Kinkō-wan
22
Tenmonkan-dōri
Gofuku-hondōri
Bosado-dōri
Arcade
18
19
14
23
Bunka-dōri
13
20
Ginza-dōri
Yamanokuchi-hon-dōri
Tenmonkan-kōen
Perth-dōri
Shiritsubyōin-mae
Shinyashiki
Gofuku-hondōri
KYŪSHŪ

Central Kagoshima

Top Sights
1 Kagoshima City Aquarium H2
2 Museum of the Meiji Restoration C6

Sights
3 Kagoshima City Museum of Art E2
4 Reimeikan E1
5 Saigō Takamori Statue E2

Activities, Courses & Tours
6 Kagomma Onsen F1
7 Nishida Onsen A5

Sleeping
8 Green Guest House G4
9 Hotel Gasthof B6
10 Nakazono Ryokan F1
11 Onsen Hotel Nakahara Bessō E3
12 Remm Kagoshima D4
13 Sun Days Inn Kagoshima E5

Eating
14 Ajimori F5
15 Cafe Lakan B7
16 Kagomma Furusato Yatai-mura B6
17 Kumasotei E3
18 Marutora Ikka F4
19 Tenmonkan Mujyaki E5
20 Tontoro E5
21 Tontoro A6
22 Yamauchi Nōjō E4

Drinking & Nightlife
23 Beer Reise E5
24 Big Ben E4
25 Recife B6
26 Salisbury Pub F4

Shopping
27 Asa-ichi B7
28 Kagoshima Brand Shop F2

Kagoshima Fish Market Tour TOUR
(鹿児島市中央卸売市場; ☎099-222-0180; www.kagoshimasakanaichiba.com; per person ¥800; ⏲6.45am Sat Jul-Nov; Shinyashiki) Get up early, don rubber boots and tour Kagoshima's central fish market, like a miniature (and much more accessible) version of Tokyo's Tsukiji Market. Pick-up is offered from many hotels in town. Reserve well in advance if you'll need English translation. After the tour (about 8am), tour guides can introduce you to restaurants in the market for a sushi breakfast (from about ¥1000).

Note that children younger than 'school age' are not allowed.

Festivals & Events

Sogadon-no-Kasayaki CULTURAL
One of Kagoshima's more unusual events is the Umbrella Burning Festival in late July. Boys burn umbrellas on the banks of Kōtsuki-gawa in honour of two brothers who used umbrellas as torches in one of Japan's oldest revenge stories.

Isle of Fire Festival CULTURAL
Held in late July on Sakurajima.

Ohara Festival DANCE
A festival featuring folk dancing in the streets on 3 November; visitors are invited to join in.

Sleeping

Kagoshima has plenty of good-value places to sleep. The station is a bit far from the action, so aim to stay towards Tenmonkan.

Green Guest House HOSTEL ¥
(グリーンゲストハウス; ☎0998-02-4301; www.green-guesthouse.com; 5-7 Sumiyoshi-chō; dm/private room ¥1800/2800; @ ; Izuro-dōri) Clean and compact, this newish hostel is very convienent to the ferry docks and great if you're going to (or coming from) Sakurajima. Separate gender dorms and private rooms are available. Some English is spoken at the front desk, and all important signage is in English and Japanese.

Nakazono Ryokan RYOKAN ¥
(中薗旅館; ☎099-226-5125; nakazonoryokan.wix.com; 1-18 Yasui-chō; s/d without bathroom ¥4200/8400; @ ; Shiyakushō-mae) Creaky, kindly and over half a century old, this friendly Japanese Inn Group member will give you a taste of Kagoshima hospitality. Plus, it's filled with the personality of its keeper. Baths are down the hall. Look for the sign in English, near the footpath diagonally across from city hall.

Hotel Gasthof HOTEL ¥¥
(ホテルガストフ; ☎099-252-1401; www.gasthof.jp; 7-1 Chūō-chō; s ¥5500, d & tw ¥8900, tr ¥12,600; P @ ; JR Kagoshima-Chūō) Old-world Europe meets urban Japan at this unusual 48-room hotel, with good-sized rooms, hardwood panelling and stone- and brick-wall motifs. Near the station and with triple and interconnecting rooms, it's a good choice for families.

Sun Days Inn Kagoshima BUSINESS HOTEL ¥¥
(サンデイズイン鹿児島; ☎099-227-5151; www.sundaysinn.com; 9-8 Yamanokuchi-chō; s/tw ¥6300/8300; P ⊖ @ ᯤ; Tenmonkan-dōri) Good value at the heart of Tenmonkan. Rooms are compact, but the beds, showers and warm decor make up for it, and the hotspots are steps away. Rates are cheaper booked online (in Japanese). The breakfast buffet (some 30 choices including local specialities) is a bargain at ¥500.

★ **Onsen Hotel Nakahara Bessō** HOTEL ¥¥¥
(温泉ホテル中原別荘; ☎099-225-2800; www.nakahara-bessou.co.jp; 15-19 Terukuni-chō; r per person with/without 2 meals from ¥12,960/8640; P ⊖ @ ᯤ; Tenmonkan-dōri) Just outside Tenmonkan and across from a park, this family-owned inn traces its history to 1904. Ignore its boxy exterior; inside are a modern *rotemburo*, spacious Japanese-style rooms with private bath, traditional artwork and a good *Satsuma-ryōri* (regional cuisine) restaurant. Non-smokers will appreciate the strict policy, and wi-fi is available as well.

Remm Kagoshima HOTEL ¥¥¥
(レム鹿児島; ☎099-224-0606; kagoshima-remm.hh-hotels.jp; 1-32 Higashi-sengoku-chō; s/d/tw from ¥10800/15,120/19,980; ⊖ @ ≋; Tenmonkan-dōri) At this hotel in Tenmonkan rooms are business-hotel-sized but futuristic in style and amenities: custom-designed beds, fluffy white duvets, massage chairs, rain showers and glass windows in the bathrooms for natural light (and, thoughtfully, curtains). The public spaces' ageless design incorporates ancient stones and hardwoods, and it's worth springing for the extensive breakfast buffet (guest/non-guest ¥1000/1100) in the restaurant.

Eating

Kagoshima's regional cuisine, *Satsuma-ryōri*, is prized for dishes like *kurobuta shabu-shabu* (black pork hotpot), *tonkotsu* (pork ribs) seasoned with miso and brown sugar, *jidori* (local chicken), *katsuo* (bonito, locally called *buen*), and *Satsuma-age* (deep-fried fish cake). Other produce includes *Satsuma-imo* (purple sweet potatoes) and *Satsuma-mikan* (oranges).

The JR Kagoshima-Chūō Station area, the backstreets of Tenmonkan and the Dolphin Port shopping centre near the ferry terminals all abound with restaurants. Local friends will think you're really in the know if you venture into the narrow lanes of the Meizanbori neighbourhood southeast of City Hall, crammed with tiny yet often chic purveyors of everything from *yakitori* and curry rice to French and Spanish cuisine.

★ **Yamauchi Nōjō** IZAKAYA ¥
(山内農場; ☎099-223-7488; 2nd fl, 1-26 Higashi-sengoku-chō; dishes ¥390-1250; ⏲4pm-midnight Sun, to 2am Mon-Thu, to 3am Fri & Sat; Tenmonkan-dōri) *Kuro Satsuma-dori* (black Satsuma chicken) is the name of the bird served here, and also what it looks like after being grilled *sumibi-yaki*-style over open charcoal. Other local dishes: marinated *katsuo* (bonito) sashimi (¥770), *kurobuta* (black pork) salad (¥680) and *tsukune* (chicken meatballs, ¥490) with cheese or raw egg. Decor is modern-meets-rustic. Enter around the corner from Remm Kagoshima Hotel.

★ **Cafe Lakan** FUSION ¥
(カフェラカン; ☎0992-10-5572; 3-1 Uenosono-chō; set meals from ¥900; ⏲11am-5pm Mon & Tue, 11am-10pm Thu-Sun; ⊖; JR Kagoshima-Chūō) Lovely little fusion cafe with delicious daily specials that mix Japanese, Italian and other Western cuisine. Decor is dark wood with a bar. It's the kind of place where you'll see groups of office ladies out for lunch, salarymen there for a glass of wine after work, or someone in the back with a book. Entirely non-smoking, too, so you can taste the food.

Kagomma Furusato Yatai-mura JAPANESE ¥
(かごっまふるさと屋台村; ☎099-255-1588; 6-4 Chūō-chō; prices vary; ⏲lunch & dinner, individual stall hours vary; JR Kagoshima-Chūō) *Yatai-mura* means 'food stall village', and some two dozen stalls near Kagoshima-Chūō Station offer a taste of Kagoshima of old. Follow your nose to your favourite stalls for *sumibi-yaki* (coal-fired chicken), sashimi, teppanyaki beef and fish dishes. Booth No 7 serves delicious onsen-water-boiled Kagoshima *kurobuta* (wild boar), *shabu-shabu* style. Yum!

Tenmonkan Mujyaki SWEETS ¥
(天文館むじゃき; ☎099-222-6904; 5-8 Sennichi-chō; large/small shirokuma ¥683/483; ⏲11am-10pm, from 10am Jul, Aug, Sat & Sun year-round; Tenmonkan-dōri) Quench your thirst during Kagoshima's steamy summers with highly refreshing *kakigori* (shaved ice with condensed milk, fruits and beans). Go for the *shirokuma*, with toppings arranged to look like its namesake polar bear. Look for the polar bear outside.

Tontoro RAMEN ¥
(豚とろ; rāmen dishes from ¥650;) Tontoro's two locations are local institutions for rāmen in thick *tonkotsu* pork broth, finished with scallions and a hint of garlic. The branch at **Yamanokuchi** (099-222-5857; 9-41 Yamanokuchi; 11am-3.30am; Tenmonkan-dōri), in the corner house with the red trim, is rather workaday; while the one near JR Kagoshima-Chūō Station, on **Chūō-machi** (099-258-9900; 3-3 Chūō-machi; 11am-midnight; JR Kagoshima-Chūō), is more polished.

THE WONDERS OF SAKURAJIMA

Kagoshima's iconic symbol Sakurajima has been spewing an almost continuous stream of smoke and ash since 1955, and it's not uncommon to have over 1000 mostly small 'burps' per year. In 1914 over three billion tonnes of lava swallowed numerous island villages – over 1000 homes – and joined Sakurajima to the mainland to the southeast.

Despite its volatility, Sakurajima is currently friendly enough to get fairly close. Among the volcano's three peaks, only Minami-dake (South Peak; 1040m) is active. Climbing the mountain is prohibited, but there are several lookout points.

On the mainland, Kagoshima residents speak proudly of Sakurajima. It is said to have *nanairo* (seven colours) visible from across Kinkō-wan, as the light shifts throughout the day on the surface of the mountain.

The volcanic island is best enjoyed by car; the drive around takes an hour, more depending on stops. A drive along the tranquil north coast and then inland will lead you to **Yunohira Lookout** (湯之平展望所), for views of the mountain and back across the bay to central Kagoshima. On the east coast, the top of a once-3m-high **torii** (黒神埋没鳥居; gate to a Shinto shrine) emerges from the volcanic ash at Kurokami, the rest buried in the 1914 eruption.

Before you head off, stop first at the **Sakurajima visitors centre** (099-293-2443; http://www.sakurajima.gr.jp/svc/english; 9am-5pm), nearish the ferry terminal, with exhibits about the volcano including a model showing its growth, with helpful English-speaking staff. There's an *ashi-yu* (footbath) close to the visitors centre. Continuing along the south coast, Arimura Lava Observatory is one of the best places to observe the smoky Minami-dake and the lava flow.

Karasujima Observation Point (烏島展望台) overlooks where the 1914 lava flow engulfed a small island that had once been 500m offshore.

About 650m from the ferry terminal, the large, ageing **Sakurajima Youth Hostel** (桜島ユースホステル; 099-293-2150; www.e-yh.net/kagoshima; 189 Yokoyama-chō; dm without meals ¥2650;) has dorm and Japanese bunk-bed rooms, plus onsen baths with brown waters. Curfew is 10pm, but since there's zero nightlife here it's not a problem.

Adjacent to the ferry terminal, the light-filled **Rainbow Sakurajima Hotel** (レインボー桜島; 099-293-2323; www.rainbow-sakurajima.com; 188-1 Yokoyama-chō; per person d & tw with 2 meals from ¥9700;) faces the puffing volcano in one direction and central Kagoshima across the bay in the other. Most rooms are Japanese style. There's an onsen open to the public (¥300) from 10am to 10pm, and a bayside beer garden over summer weekends.

Sakurajima Island View Buses (one way ¥120-440, day pass ¥500, 8 per day; 9am-4.30pm) loop around Sakurajima. Alternatively, try **Sakurajima Rentacar** (099-293-2162; 2hr/day from ¥4800/6500), which also rents out bikes (¥300 per hour), though biking is not recommended since, if the volcano erupts during your ride, you may find yourself unprotected from breathing the ash.

Frequent passenger and car ferries shuttle around the clock between Kagoshima and Sakurajima (¥160, 15 minutes). Reach the ferry terminal, near the aquarium, via City View Bus or other buses headed for Suizokukan-mae, or by tram to Suizokukan-guchi. The **Yorimichi Cruise** (よりみちクルーズ船; 099-223-7271; adult/child ¥500/250; 11.05am) takes one of six circuitous sightseeing routes from Kagoshima Port to Sakurajima Port in about 50 minutes. Purchase a regular ferry ticket back from Sakurajima to Kagoshima.

Marutora Ikka IZAKAYA ¥
(〇虎一家; ☎099-219-3948; 2nd fl, 14-17 Sennichi-chō; dishes from ¥400; ⏲6pm-3am Tue-Sun; 📖; 🚊Tenmonkan-dōri) This happy spot is festooned with an eclectic collection of Shōwa-period (1926–89) pop-culture memorabilia, where young Japanese come to hang out over a few rounds of beer and comfort food like bite-sized black pork *hitokuchi-gyōza* (10 pieces for ¥450!). Look for the dark wooden street frontage and staircase leading upstairs, down the block from 7-Eleven.

★**Kumasotei** JAPANESE ¥¥
(熊襲亭; ☎099-222-6356; 6-10 Higashi-Sengoku-chō; set meals lunch/dinner from ¥1500/3000; ⏲11am-2.30pm & 5-10pm; 📶📖; 🚊Tenmonkan-dōri) This atmospheric multistorey restaurant near central Tenmonkan covers all your *Satsuma-ryōri* needs: *Satsuma-age, tonkotsu, kurobuta shabu-shabu*, and lots of fresh fish and seafood.

Ajimori JAPANESE ¥¥
(あぢもり; ☎099-224-7634; 13-21 Sennichi-chō; shabu-shabu courses from ¥4320; ⏲11.30am-2pm & 5.30-8.45pm Wed-Mon; 📖; 🚊Tenmonkan-dōri) This classy multistorey shop claims to have invented *kurobuta shabu-shabu*. Set meals come with handmade udon noodles and side dishes depending on the price. There are also *tonkatsu* (deep-fried pork cutlet) meals (from ¥650 at lunchtime, except Sunday). It's just north of the arch with giant eyeglasses on it.

Drinking & Nightlife

Tenmonkan is where most of the action happens – shot bars, clubs and karaoke boxes. Most dance clubs don't get going until around 11pm and many bars charge admission (average ¥500 to ¥1000). Many also charge a 'table fee' or 'service' for the snacks or bar nuts they'll serve, whether you eat them or not.

Recife BAR
(レシフェ; ☎099-213-9787; 1-3 Kajiya-chō; ⏲noon-11pm, to midnight Fri & Sat, closed Tue; 🚊JR Kagoshima-Chūō) This arty, mellow three-floor shop-bar-restaurant also has DJ decks and hosts occasional parties. It's popular with locals and expat groovers, and has Latin-American eats before turning into a bar for the wee hours. Though an old standard in the Kagoshima scene, it's in a new location, along Miyako-dōri between Kajiya-chō and Takamibashi tram stops.

SHŌCHŪ

Reviled for ages, Kagoshima's Prefectural drink has of late become one of its many prides. *Shōchū*, a strong distilled liquor (sometimes nicknamed Japanese vodka), is now drunk in high-end bars all across Japan. Kagoshima-ken claims the highest consumption in Japan, which may well explain why everyone's so friendly! Each prefecture is known for its own particular variety. In Kumamoto, *shōchū* is usually made from rice; in Ōita, it's barley, and here it's *imo-jōchū* from sweet potatoes. Drink it straight, with soda or over ice, but the most traditional way is *oyu-wari*, with water heated in a stone pot over glowing coals. Drink until you yourself begin to glow.

Big Ben PUB
(☎099-226-4470; basement, 8-23 Higashi-Sengoku-chō; ⏲5pm-2am, to 4am Fri & Sat; 🚊Tenmonkan-dōri) This basement meeting spot has dozens of beers from around the world, footy and memorabilia from around the world, and patrons from – wait for it – around the world. Meals include *kurobuta* burgers and steamed mussels, alongside fish and chips.

Beer Reise BAR
(ビアライゼ; ☎099-227-0088; Hirata Bldg, 9-10 Sennichi-chō; ⏲5pm-3am; 🚊Tenmonkan-dōri) In a new location, this cheery narrow bar has Guinness and Hoegaarden, a variety of German and Belgian beers, and ¥100-off happy hour from 5pm to 7pm. Enter from the side door to the left of the tobacco shop.

Salisbury Pub BAR
(ソールズベリーパブ; ☎099-223-2386; 2nd fl, 1-5 Gofuku-chō; ⏲6pm-2am Wed-Mon; 🚊Tenmonkan-dōri) This classy, quiet bar appeals to a 30-something crowd and stocks a good selection of foreign beers and wines and a few single malts. Food is available, but the menu is in Japanese.

Shopping

Regional specialities include Satsuma Kiriko cut glass, Tsumugi silk, bamboo and wood products, and Satsuma-yaki pottery (most typically in austere black and white). Some are for sale at Sengan-en and the **Kagoshima Brand Shop** (鹿児島ブランドショップ; 1st fl, Sangyo Kaikan Bldg, 9-1 Meizan-chō;

9am-6pm; Asahi-dōri) near Tenmonkan. Pick up the free English-language *A Guide to Kagoshima Products*.

Fun shopping experiences include the **Asa-ichi** (朝市; Morning Market; 4.30am-1pm Mon-Sat) just south of JR Kagoshima-Chūō Station.

Orientation

Kagoshima spreads north–south beside the bay and has two JR stations, the main one being Kagoshima-Chūō to the south. The centre of the action is about 1km northeast where the Tenmonkan-dōri shopping arcade crosses the tramlines.

Information

Tourist information is available on the prefectural site, www.kagoshima-kankou.com/for. The city website (www.city.kagoshima.lg.jp) has detailed info on transit, sights and living in town. For sightseeing info and arts and entertainment listings, see www.kic-update.com.

The **central post office** (鹿児島中央郵便局; ATM 7am-11pm Mon-Fri, 9am-9pm Sat, 9am-7pm Sun & holidays) near JR Kagoshima-Chūō Station has an ATM.

JR Kyūshū Travel Agency (JR九州旅行鹿児島支店; 099-253-2201; 2nd fl, JR Kagoshima-Chūō Station; 10am-7pm Mon-Fri, 10am-6pm Sat & Sun) Can assist with domestic travel bookings.

Tourist Information Centre (鹿児島中央駅総合観光案内所; 099-253-2500; inside JR Kagoshima-Chūō Station; 8am-8pm) Has plenty of information in English and the handy *Kagoshima* visitor's guide. Near the Museum of the Meiji Restoration, the **Tourism Exchange Centre** (観光交流センター; 099-298-5111; 1-1 Uenosono-chō; 9am-7pm) has pamphlets and can make hotel reservations.

Getting There & Away

AIR

Kagoshima Airport has connections to Shanghai, Hong Kong, Taipei and Seoul, and convenient domestic flights, including to Tokyo, Osaka and Okinawa (Naha).

BOAT

Ferries depart from Minami-futō pier to Yakushima (jetfoil ¥9100, one hour and 50 minutes; regular ferry ¥4900, four hours). From Kagoshima Shin-kō (Kagoshima New Port), **Marix Line** (099-225-1551) has ferries to Okinawa (Naha) via the Amami archipelago (¥15,870, 25 hours).

BUS

Long-distance buses depart from the Express bus centre located opposite the east exit of Kagoshima-Chūō Station and from streetside stops nearby and near Yamakataya department store in Tenmonkan.

Routes include Miyazaki (¥2780, 2¾ hours), Fukuoka (¥5450, 3¾ hours), Ōita (¥5660, 5½ hours), Nagasaki (¥6690, 5½ hours) and overnight to Osaka (¥12,400, 12 hours).

TRAIN

JR Kagoshima-Chūō Station is the terminus of the Kyūshū *shinkansen*, with stops including Kumamoto (¥6740, 45 minutes), Hakata (¥10,450, 1¾ hours), Hiroshima (¥17,880, 2¼ hours) and Shin-Osaka (¥22,100, 3¾ hours). Also stopping at Kagoshima Station, the JR Nippō line goes to Miyazaki (*tokkyū;* ¥4220, two hours) and Beppu (¥10,110, five hours).

Getting Around

TO/FROM THE AIRPORT

Express buses depart every five to 20 minutes to and from JR Kagoshima-Chūō Station/Tenmonkan (¥1250, one hour/55 minutes).

BICYCLE

Bikes can be rented (two hours/day ¥500/1500, 40% discount for JR pass holders) at JR Kagoshima-Chūō Station.

BUS

Hop-on, hop-off City View Buses (¥190, every 30 minutes, 9am to 6.30pm) loop around the major sights in two routes. A one-day pass (¥600) is also valid on trams and city bus lines and offers discounted admission to many attractions. Otherwise, local buses tend to be inconvenient, particularly if you don't speak Japanese (you're better off with trams).

CAR & MOTORCYCLE

Many outlets around JR Kagoshima-Chūō Station rent cars for trips around the region.

TRAM

If you're doing only a limited amount of sightseeing, trams are the easiest way around town. Route 1 starts from Kagoshima Station and goes through the centre into the suburbs. Route

CUTE TRANSIT CARDS

Visitors with passports can take advantage of the Cute transit card (one/two days ¥1200/1800) covering city buses (including the City View and Sakurajima Island View buses), trams, Sakurajima ferries and the Yorimichi Cruise. Cardholders can also get discounted admission to many attractions. Pick it up at tourist information offices.

2 diverges at Takami-baba (高見馬場) to JR Kagoshima-Chūō Station and terminates at Korimoto. Either pay the flat fare (¥170) or buy a one-day travel pass (¥600) from the tourist information centre or onboard.

Kirishima-Yaku National Park 霧島屋久国立公園

This mountainous park straddling northern Kagoshima-ken and western Miyazaki-ken has excellent hikes of many lengths, although ash eruptions, toxic gases and other volcanic activity sometimes changes accessibility. The area is known for its wild azaleas, hot springs and the 75m waterfall, **Senriga-taki**. It is also famous in Japanese mythology as being the place where the gods first descended to earth and began the imperial dynasty, unbroken to this day.

Hikers should monitor the weather closely before setting out. Thunderstorms and fog are common during the rainy season (mid-May to June) and winters can be bitter; otherwise, the vistas are superb.

Sights

Kirishima-jingū SHINTO SHRINE

(霧島神宮; 2608-5 Kirishima-Taguchi; 24hr) Picturesque, tangerine Kirishima-jingū has a good vantage point. Though the original dates from the 6th century, the present shrine was built in 1715. It is dedicated to Ninigi-no-mikoto, who, according to *Kojiki* (a book compiled in 712), led the gods from the heavens to the Takachiho-no-mine summit. The shrine is accessible by bus (¥240, 15 minutes) from JR Kirishima-jingū Station.

There's a small village with inns and restaurants at the foot of the shrine.

Activities

This area has numerous **onsen**, both 'wild' ones (just hot spots in rivers) to expansive onsen hotels. You will see steam rising up from numerous places as you travel around. All of the hotels in this area have baths, and a number of them offer them to day-only visitors. Some have mixed-gender bathing pools as well as segregated male and female baths.

The **Ebino-kōgen circuit** is a relaxed 4km stroll around a series of volcanic lakes – **Rokkannon Mi-ike** is a stunning, intensely cyan lake. Across the road from the lake, **Fudō-ike**, at the base of Karakuni-dake, is a steaming *jigoku*. The stiffer climb to the 1700m summit of **Karakuni-dake** skirts the edge of the volcano's deep crater before arriving at the high point on the eastern side. The panoramic view southwards is outstanding, taking in the perfectly circular caldera lake of Ōnami-ike, **Shinmoe-dake** (the one that erupted in January 2011; parts remain inaccessible) and the perfect cone of **Takachiho-no-mine**. On a clear day, you can see Kagoshima and the smoking molar of Sakurajima. Friendly wild deer roam freely through the town of **Ebino-kōgen** and are happy to be photographed. Several of the rivers here have pools hot enough for bathing, and you'll find the routes leading up here thick with *higaeri* (day use) onsen lodges.

Two buses per day connect the Kirishima-jingū area with Ebino-kōgen, but this area is vastly more accessible by car.

Sleeping & Eating

Lodgings are clustered near Kirishima-jingū or in Ebino-kōgen village, with good accommodation options but few eateries. Most village shops close by 5pm.

Kirishima Jingū-mae Youth Hostel HOSTEL ¥

(霧島神宮前ユースホステル; 0995-57-1188; 2459-83 Kirishima-Taguchi; dm HI member/nonmember ¥3390/3990, minshuku rates per person incl 2 meals ¥7710; P @) A few minutes from Kirishima-jingū, this neat, comfy youth hostel has Japanese rooms and mountain views from its onsen baths. Breakfast/dinner costs ¥540/1080. It also operates as a more expensive *minshuku*, with better meals and amenities.

Minshuku Kirishima-ji MINSHUKU ¥

(民宿きりしま路; 0995-57-0272; 2459 Kirishima-Taguchi; r per person with/without 2 meals ¥7560/4500; P) This spartan but friendly six-room inn, just across the gorge from the shrine, has forest views and shared onsen baths. Day visitors can stop here for a lunch of house-made *soba* dishes (¥480 to ¥880) including a house-special *champon*. Day use of the bath is possible as well for ¥300.

Ebino-Kōgen Campground & Lodge CAMPGROUND ¥

(えびの高原キャンプ村; 0984-33-0800; 1470 Ōaza Suenaga; campsites/tent rental/lodge cabins per person from ¥830/1440/1640; mid-winter closing dates vary; P) A pretty stream runs through the middle of this delightful campground with onsen baths (open 5pm to 8pm), 500m from the Eco-Museum Centre. Rates rise in July and August.

★Ebino-Kōgen Sō HOTEL ¥¥¥
(えびの高原荘; ☎0984-33-0161; www.ebinokogenso.com; 1489 Ōaza Suenaga; r per person incl 2 meals with/without bathroom from ¥11,200/10,200; P⊜) This friendly onsen hotel boasts some excellent facilities including mountain-view rooms and coin laundry. The lovely *rotemburo* is open to the public from 11.30am to 8pm (¥520), and there's a mixed-gender bath deep in the forest. The location, near Ebino-Kōgen village, is superb and the restaurant makes tasty meals. Rates may be lower depending on the meal calibre, so ask when you reserve.

There's a shuttle bus to JR Kirishima-Jingū and JR Kobayashi Stations; ring ahead to get one.

Information

Nature centres at each end of the volcano walk have bilingual maps and hiking information, and exhibits on local wildlife.

Ebino-kōgen Eco Museum Centre (えびのエコミュージアムセンター; ☎0984-33-3002; ⏲9am-5pm) This lodge-like tourist centre has information, maps, some dioramas of the area and helpful staff.

Kirishima City Tourist Information (霧島市観光案内所; ☎0995-57-1588; 2459-6 Taguchi; ⏲9am-5pm) Right near the giant *torii* gate at the entrance to Kirishima-jingū. There's an *ashi-yu* (foot onsen) a few steps from the entrance.

Takachiho-gawara Visitors Centre (高千穂河原ビジターセンター; ☎0995-57-2505; ⏲9am-5pm) A small visitors centre at the base of Takachiho with hiking info, maps and safety suggestions.

ERUPTION OF SHINMOE-DAKE

On 26 January 2011, the massive eruption of Shinmoe-dake, in the centre of the mountainous park, shut down roads and air travel and blanketed much of the region in a thick layer of ash. It also left impassable a popular 15km hiking route along the summit of the park's other volcanic peaks: Karakuni-dake (1700m) via Shishiko-dake, Naka-dake and Takachiho-gawara to the summit of Takachiho-no-mine (1574m). Check with local authorities in case of a change in conditions.

Getting There & Away

The main train junctions are JR Kobayashi Station, northeast of Ebino Plateau, and Kirishima-jingū Station to the south.

Satsuma Peninsula
薩摩半島

The peninsula south of Kagoshima city has fine rural scenery, samurai houses, a haunting kamikaze museum and spectacular sand baths. While buses operate to Chiran and trains to Ibusuki, renting a car from Kagoshima will save time and hassles. You'll also find wonderful views along Ibusuki Skyline Rd of Kinkō-wan and the main islands' southernmost mountains. Time permitting, zip all the way to the tip for great glimpses of Kaimon-dake, this area's 'Mt Fuji'.

Chiran 知覧

☎0993 / POP 40,391 (MINAMI-KYŪSHŪ CITY)

A river runs through Chiran, 34km south of Kagoshima, parallel to a collection of restored samurai houses. On the town's edge is a fascinating memorial to WWII's kamikaze pilots.

Seven of the mid-Edo period residences along Chiran's 700m street of **samurai houses** (武家屋敷; 6198 Chiran-chō; combined admission to all houses ¥500; ⏲9am-5pm) have gardens open to the public, in which water is usually symbolised by sand, *shirasu* (volcanic ash) or gravel. Allow up to one leisurely hour to view them all. Ask for info at the **Chiran Samurai Residence & Garden Preservation Association** (知覧武家屋敷庭園保存会; ☎0993-58-7878; www.chiranbukeyashiki.jp; 13731-1 Chiran-chō; ⏲9am-5pm).

Just off the samurai street, **Taki-An** (高城庵; ☎0993-83-3186; 6329 Chiran-chō; soba ¥650, set meals from ¥2100; ⏲10.30am-3pm) is a lovely restaurant in another traditional house where you can sit on tatami and admire the garden over a bowl of hot *soba* (¥650) or Satsuma specialities such as *tonkotsu teishoku* (pork set meal, ¥1620) and Chiran's famous green tea. Picture menu available.

Chiran Eikoku-kan (知覧英国館; Tea World; ☎0993-83-3963; 13746-4 Chiran-chō; tea from ¥530; ⏲10am-6pm Wed-Mon) is across the main road from the samurai houses and marked by a post box and a slightly dented double-decker British-style bus. It offers tea, a cup of which entitles you to take the tour of the tiny one-room collection of newspaper accounts, photos and memorabilia of the **Anglo-Satsuma Museum**. It commemorates the 1862 war between Britain and Satsuma, which started when British visitors refused to bow to a samurai of the Shimazu clan. Eikoku-kan's Yumefuki loose tea, made with Chiran leaves, has won Britain's Great Taste Award for several years running.

Around 2km west of town, Chiran's air base was the point of departure for 1036 WWII kamikaze pilots *(tokkō)*, the largest percentage in the Japanese military. On its former site, the large, thought-provoking **Kamikaze Peace Museum** (知覧特攻平和会館; ☎0993-83-2525; www.chiran-tokkou.jp; 17881 Chiran-chō; admission ¥500; ⏲9am-5pm) presents aircraft, mementos and photographs of the fresh-faced young men selected for the Special Attack Corps. It's worth paying for the English-language audioguide (¥100), which tells individual pilots' harrowing stories.

Kagoshima Kōtsū (鹿児島交通) buses to Chiran (samurai houses/Peace Museum; ¥890/930, 80/85 minutes, hourly) run from the Yamakataya bus centre (山形屋バスセンター) in Tenmonkan and JR Kagoshima-Chūō Station. From Chiran, buses run five times daily to Ibusuki (¥940, 69 minutes).

Ibusuki 指宿

☎0993 / POP 44,200

In southeastern Satsuma Peninsula, around 50km from Kagoshima, the hot-spring resort of Ibusuki is quiet, particularly in the low season, and more especially after dark. Ibusuki Station is located about 1km from the beachfront and most accommodation, but the few eateries are near the station.

Sights & Activities

Ibusuki's biggest attraction is sand baths, in which onsen steam rises through sand, reputedly with blood-cleansing properties.

Chiringashima ISLAND

(知林ヶ島) Lovely Chiringashima is connected to the mainland by a thin land bridge that appears only at low tide, when hikers, beachcombers and tide-pool explorers can walk the coral- and shell-strewn connector and visit a small shrine on the island itself. Hours vary with the tides, which you may have to race if you walk too slowly. A taxi from Ibusuki Station takes 10 minutes; the over-sand hike, one-way, takes about half an hour, more if you stop along the way.

CAPE SATA

Collectors of 'mosts' will want to journey around Kinkō-wan to Cape Sata (佐多岬, Sata-misaki), the most southern point in the Japanese main islands, at the tip of the Ōsumi Peninsula and site of Japan's oldest lighthouse. **Sata Day Go Boats** (さたでい号; ☎0994-27-3355; http://www.town.minamiosumi.lg.jp/minami04/minami10.asp; Sata-Misaki; 30min tours adult/child ¥2000/1000) offer day cruises to see coral, sea turtles, *fugu* (pufferfish), dolphins and sharks. Boats run only when weather permits, so call first. Cape Sata is best reached by car.

Ibusuki Sunamushi Kaikan Saraku SAND BATH

(いぶすき砂むし会館 砂楽; ☎0993-23-3900; 5-25-18 Yunohama; admission sand bath & onsen ¥920, onsen only ¥610; ⏲8.30am-9pm, closed noon-1pm Mon-Fri) Pay at the entrance, change into the provided *yukata* and wander down to the beach where, under a canopy of bamboo slat blinds, women with shovels bury you in hot volcanic sand. Reactions range from panic to euphoria. It's said that 10 minutes will get rid of impurities, but many stay longer. When you're through, head back up to soak in the onsen.

Yaji-ga-yu SENTO

(弥次ヶ湯; 1068 Jūcchō; admission ¥300; ⏲7am-9pm, closed 2nd & 4th Thu each month) There's loads of atmosphere in this historic wooden *sentō* (1892) away from the town centre, so old it has no showers; you wash by dipping buckets in the tub. A crib in the ladies' bath makes bathing easier for families with toddlers.

Yoshi-no-yu SENTO

(吉乃湯; 4-2-41 Yunohama; admission ¥300; ⏲2-9.30pm Fri-Wed) Up-to-date *sentō* with a pretty *rotemburo* in a garden.

Sleeping & Eating

Tamaya Youth Hostel HOSTEL ¥

(圭屋ユースホステル; ☎0993-22-3553; 5-27-8 Yunohama; dm with no meals/breakfast/2 meals ¥2800/3280/4250; P ⊝ @ ☜) This 25-bed, three-storey hostel is rather plain, but it's located diagonally across from the sand baths and has kayaks for rent in summer. There's both Japanese- and Western-style bedding.

DON'T MISS

SATSUMA DENSHŌKAN

The **Satsuma Denshōkan** (薩摩伝承館; www.satsuma-denshokan.com; 12131-4 Higashikata; admission ¥1500; ⌚8.30am-7pm) museum is striking, offering a history of Satsuma plus displays of Chinese ceramics and gleaming Satsuma-yaki in a temple-style building that seems to float on its own lake. There are English-language audioguides. It's about 3.5km (taxi ¥1000, 10 minutes) from Ibusuki Station, at the Hakusuikan onsen hotel.

Minshuku Takayoshi MINSHUKU ¥
(民宿たかよし; ☎0993-22-5982; 5-1-1 Yunohama; r without/with 2 meals ¥3880/6630; P 📶) No frills, clean *minshuku* just seven minutes' walk from the sand baths. Homegrown vegies/produce is used in the meals.

Tsukimi-sō RYOKAN ¥¥
(月見荘; ☎0993-22-4221; www.tsukimi.jp; 5-24-8 Yunohama; r per person with 2 meals from ¥13,110; P 📶) Rooms at this spotless seven-room ryokan across from the sand baths have private facilities, in addition to pretty indoor and outdoor baths and meals featuring *Satsuma-ryōri* such as *tonkotsu* and sashimi. There's not much English spoken, but amenable staff make it work. Wi-fi is in the lobby only (along with a giant Totoro doll and other curios).

Ryokan Ginshō RYOKAN ¥¥¥
(旅館吟松; ☎0993-22-3231; www.ginsyou.co.jp; 5-26-27 Yunohama; r per person with 2 meals from ¥16,200; P @ 📶) The exquisite 2nd- and 9th-floor *rotemburo* of this upmarket beachfront ryokan have broad views and a lovely relaxation garden. Ocean-facing rooms start from ¥17,280 and rooms with baths on the balcony are available. There's an onsen vent right in your dinner table, as genteel servers cook *Satsuma-age* before your eyes. Day use of the bath (¥1000) is from 6pm to 9pm.

Hakusuikan HOTEL ¥¥¥
(白水館; ☎0993-22-3131; www.hakusuikan.co.jp/en; 12126-12 Higashi-kata; r per person with 2 meals from ¥18,510; P @ 📶 🏊) Visiting dignitaries might stay in one of the stratospheric-priced rooms in the sumptuous, 40-room Rikyū wing, but we of more modest means can splurge on the less expensive of its 164 rooms. The opulent onsen/*rotemburo*/sand baths are worth the stay by themselves. The Fenice restaurant in the Denshōkan building is as tasty as it is attractive.

Ibusuki Iwasaki Hotel HOTEL ¥¥¥
(指宿いわさきホテル; ☎0993-22-2131; http://ibusuki.iwasakihotels.com/en; 3775 Jūni-chō; tw from ¥16,632; P 🚭 📶 🏊 👪) Straight out of 1980s Hawaii, this kid-friendly pink tower has a putting green, onsen, pools and acres of lush, palm-filled gardens. All rooms face the ocean and have balconies, and there are sports equipment rentals including bikes and tennis courts. Sand baths cost ¥1080. Look for evening Hawaiian dance shows in summer.

Aoba IZAKAYA ¥
(青葉; ☎0993-22-3356; 1-2-121 Minato; dishes from ¥320; ⌚11am-3pm & 5.30-10pm Wed-Mon) Behind the yellow-green *noren* (door curtain) a minute's walk left of the station, this cheery shop serves satisfying *kurobuta rōsukatsu* (black pork cutlet) *teishoku* (¥1420) or, if you dare, *Satsuma jidori sashimi* (raw sliced chicken, ¥1000). Picture menu available.

Information

Ibusuki City Tourist Information Centre
(指宿市観光協会; ☎0993-22-3252; 2-5-33 Minato; ⌚9am-5pm) A 15-minute walk from the station, this tourist information centre is large and has a variety of brochures, maps and information. Staff are helpful and friendly, though English may be hit or miss. The station information desk (指宿観光案内所; ☎0993-22-4114; ⌚9am-6pm) has wi-fi, basic maps and can assist with directions and accommodation.

Getting There & Around

Ibusuki Station is about 1½ hours from Kagoshima by bus (¥950) or 51 minutes by train from Kagoshima-chūō (*tokkyū* ¥2130). Train geeks and sightseers will love the special wood-panelled Ibutama *tokkyū* with specially angled seats for breathtaking bay views. Rent bikes (¥500 for two hours) from the station. Car-rental offices are steps away.

Around Satsuma Peninsula

Ikeda-kō is a volcanic caldera lake west of Ibusuki, inhabited by giant eels kept in tanks by the parking lot. South of the lake is **Cape Nagasaki-bana**, from where you can see offshore islands on a clear day.

In a gorge near Ikeda-kō, **Tōsenkyō Sōmen Nagashi** (唐船峡そうめん流し; ☎0993-32-2143; 5967 Jūchō; sōmen ¥570; ⊙10am-5pm, later in summer) is a pilgrimage for many Japanese (an estimated 200,000 annual visitors!) as the 1967 birthplace of *nagashi-sōmen* (flowing noodles). *Sōmen* (vermicelli) spin around tyre-shaped table-top tanks of swiftly flowing 13°C water; catch the noodles with your chopsticks and dip in sauce to eat. It's lots of fun and ultra-refreshing on hot days. *Teishoku* (from ¥1340) come with *onigiri* (rice balls), miso soup and grilled *masu* (trout), which swim (along with sturgeon) in pools around the restaurant.

The beautifully symmetrical 924m cone of **Kaimon-dake**, nicknamed 'Satsuma Fuji', dominates the southern skyline and can be climbed in two hours. An early start may reward you with views of Sakurajima, Cape Sata, and Yakushima and Tanegashima islands.

At the southwestern end of the peninsula, about one hour from Ibusuki, is **Makurazaki**, a port famous for *katsuo* (bonito). By the port, the workmanlike **Makurazaki O-Sakana Centre** (枕崎お魚センター; ☎0993-73-2311; http://makurazaki-osakana.com/; 33-1 Matsunō-chō; ⊙9am-5pm) has 20 or so vendors (you can watch real *katsuo-bushi* – bonito flakes – being made), souvenir shops and a simple restaurant. Fish fans should head to humble **Daitoku** (だいとく; ☎0993-72-0357; 17 Origuchi-chō; funajin meshi ¥880; ⊙11am-3.30pm & 5.30-8.30pm, closed irregularly) on the main drag, for award-winning *katsuo funado meshi* (called *funajin meshi* here) – a *donburi* (dish served over rice) with fresh bonito, bonito flakes, green onion, *nori* strips and rice crisps in *katsuo* broth. Makurazaki is the terminus of the train line from Kagoshima.

Seahorse House AQUARIUM

(タツノオトシゴハウス; ☎0993-38-1883; www.seahorseways.com; 5202-2 Beppu, Ei-chō; ⊙10am-4.30pm Wed-Mon) FREE This seahorse hatchery is totally unique, offering close-up looks at thousands of hatchling seahorses, plus information, videos, souvenirs and a small cafe. One of the exhibits is the only two-headed seahorse ever seen (preserved, as it did not live long). Plans for expansion may mean more to see/do in the future. There are also great walking trails, some tide pools, beaches perfect for shell collecting, and stunning views of Kaimon-dake on a clear day.

Best visited as a stop on your way to Makurazaki or as a day-trip out of Ibusuki.

MIYAZAKI PREFECTURE

Miyazaki-ken (宮崎県) is best known for its surfing breaks along the palmy, balmy coastline from the city of Miyazaki southwards. Coastal drives here may remind you of California or the Italian Riviera. At the prefecture's northern reaches (easier accessed from Kumamoto) is lovely Takachiho, mythical home of the sun goddess Amaterasu. (Note that it's not *Mt Takachiho,* in nearby Kagoshima – the two are often confused.)

Although there are train and bus services, the most rewarding way to explore this diverse prefecture is by car.

Miyazaki 宮崎

☎0985 / POP 405,900

The prefectural capital makes a convenient base for forays around the region, with a friendly, low-key vibe and fun, unique restaurants and night spots in the Nishitachi nightlife district, about 700m from the station.

Sights

Miyazaki-jingū SHINTO SHRINE

(宮崎神宮; 2-4-1 Jingū) This shrine honours the Emperor Jimmu, the semi-mythical first emperor of Japan and founder of the Yamato court. Spectacular centuries-old wisteria vines cover the thickly forested grounds, and bloom in April. It's a 500m walk from Miyazaki-jingū Station, one stop (¥160, three minutes) north of Miyazaki Station.

Just north of the shrine, **Miyazaki Prefectural Museum of Nature & History** (宮崎県総合博物館; 2-4-4 Jingū; ⊙9am-5pm Wed-Mon) FREE exhibits items on local history, archaeology, festival artefacts and folkcrafts. Behind the museum, **Minka-en** (民家園) FREE features four traditional-style Miyazaki farmhouses and other outbuildings.

Heiwadai-kōen PARK

(平和台公園; Peace Park) The park's centrepiece is the 37m-high **Peace Tower** monument constructed in 1940, a time when peace in Japan was about to disappear. Its timeless design may remind you of ancient

Miyazaki

Miyazaki

Sights
1 Miyazaki Science Centre ... D1

Sleeping
2 Youth Hostel Sunflower Miyazaki ... B3
3 Hotel Route Inn ... A1
4 Miyazaki Kankō Hotel ... B4
5 Richmond Hotel Miyazaki Ekimae ... D1

Eating
6 Bon Belta Department Store ... A1
7 Bosco ... A1
8 Izakaya Seoul ... A1
9 Maruman Honten ... A1
10 Miyachiku ... B4
11 Ogura Honten ... B1
12 Ogura Segashira Branch ... C3
13 Okashi no Hidaka ... A2
14 Togakushi ... A1
15 Togakushi ... A3
16 Yamakataya Department Store ... A1

Drinking & Nightlife
17 Igokochiya Anbai ... A2
18 Lifetime ... C1
19 One Coin Bar ... A2
20 Suntory Shot Bar 4665 ... A2
21 The Bar ... B1

Shopping
22 Miyazaki Prefectural Products Promotion Exhibition Hall ... B3

Inca or Khmer monuments, and it's made of stones from all over the world. The **Haniwa Garden** is dotted with reproductions of clay *haniwa* (earthenware figures found in Kōfun-period tombs) excavated from the Saitobaru burial mounds, set among mossy hillocks.

Heiwadai-kōen is about 1km north of Miyazaki-jingū. Buses from Miyazaki Station stop along Tachibana-dōri (¥290, 20 minutes, at least two per hour).

Miyazaki Science Centre MUSEUM
(宮崎科学技術館; 0985-23-2700; 1-1-2 Miyazaki-eki Higashi; admission with/without sky show ¥750/540; 9am-4.30pm Tue-Sun) Steps away from Miyazaki Station, this interactive science museum boasts one of the world's largest planetariums; some exhibits include English translations.

Festivals & Events

Yabusame CULTURAL
Witness samurai-style horseback archery at Miyazaki-jingū on 2 and 3 April.

Erekocha Matsuri CULTURAL
Miyazaki's newest festival with dancers and *taiko* drummers filling Tachibana-dōri in mid-July.

Fireworks FIREWORKS
One of Kyūshū's largest fireworks shows lights up the summer sky over the Ōyodo-gawa in early August.

Miyazaki-jingū Grand Festival CULTURAL
In late October, this festival brings in the autumn with horses and *mikoshi* (portable shrines) being carried through the streets.

Sleeping

Youth Hostel Sunflower Miyazaki HOSTEL ¥
(ユースホステルサンフラワー宮崎; 0985-24-5785; 1-3-10 Asahi; dm HI member/non-member ¥3240/3888;) Near the prefectural office, this institutional-style, 20-bed hostel has both Japanese and Western-style rooms and doubles as a community centre during the day. There's a giant kitchen, loaner bikes (free for guests), coin laundry, a restaurant and a nominal 10pm curfew.

Hotel Route Inn BUSINESS HOTEL ¥¥
(ホテルルートイン宮崎; 0985-61-1488; www.route-inn.co.jp; 4-1-27 Tachibana-dōri-nishi; s/d/tw with breakfast ¥6800/11,300/11,800;) Across from the Nishitachi district, this 200-plus-room hotel is excellent value, with a great breakfast buffet, spacious, decently appointed rooms, free coffee in the granite lobby and common baths (in addition to private bathrooms).

Richmond Hotel Miyazaki Ekimae BUSINESS HOTEL ¥¥
(リッチモンドホテル宮崎駅前; 0985-60-0055; www.richmondhotel.jp; 2-2-3 Miyazaki-eki-higashi; s/d/tw with breakfast members from ¥6500/8600/11,800, non-members ¥12,000/15,000/22,000;) Behind Miyazaki Station, this light-filled business hotel has clean, modern furnishings, larger-than-average rooms and a breakfast buffet including local specialities. The membership is well worth asking for, as it reduces the cost of a stay substantially.

Miyazaki Kankō Hotel HOTEL ¥¥¥
(宮崎観光ホテル; 0985-27-1212; www.miyakan-h.com; 1-1-1 Matsuyama; s/tw from ¥8790/17,580, about ¥3000 per person more in new wing;) This towering hotel has two buildings; the west and recently remodeled east wings. All rooms are relatively spacious. There's an on-site onsen with *rotemburo*, plus a baby grand piano in the lobby. While being next to the river means some nice strolls in the evening, it's quite far from the station and nightlife district, so plan on using a taxi to get to and back.

Eating

Miyazaki is famous for *chikin nanban* (sweet fried chicken with tartar sauce), *hiya-jiru* (cold summer soup made from baked tofu, fish, miso paste and cucumbers, served over rice), *jidori* (local chicken) and *kama-age udon* (wheat noodles boiled in a cauldron). Miyazaki *gyū* (beef) has won national competitions. Snack foods include *nikumaki onigiri* (rice balls wrapped in marinated pork) and *chiizu manjū* (cream-cheese-filled dumplings). Local produce includes mango and *yuzu* (citron), sometimes mixed with pepper for spicy *yuzu-kōshō* paste.

The Nishitachi neighbourhood is great for restaurant browsing, although don't expect many English menus. For takeaway food, try the basement marketplaces at **Bon Belta** (ボンベルタ橘; 10am-8pm or later) and **Yamakataya** (山形屋; 10am-8pm or later) department stores, or pick up a *shiitake ekiben* (mushroom boxed lunch) at Miyazaki Station.

★ **Ogura Honten** JAPANESE ¥
(おぐら本店; 0985-22-2296; 3-4-24 Tachibana-higashi; chikin nanban ¥980; 11am-3pm & 5-10pm Wed-Mon) *Chikin nanban* was invented here over half a century ago, and crowds

still flock to Ogura's red-and-white awning in the alley just behind Yamakataya department store. For shorter queues, try the larger, kitsch-filled crosstown **branch** (おぐら瀬頭店; ☎0985-23-5301; 2-2-23 Segashira; ⊙11am-10pm; 👪).

★Togakushi NOODLES ¥

(戸隠; ☎0985-24-6864; 7-10 Chūō-dōri; noodles ¥600-900; ⊙6pm-2am) Workmanlike Togakushi has no English menu, but come anyway, for the delicate, thin *kama-age-udon* (¥600) for dipping in tangy sauce of *negi* (green onion), *tempura-ko* (tempura crispies) and refreshing *yuzu* (Japanese citron); pour the water from the noodles into the sauce to make soup. It's what locals crave after a bender. Look for the giant red lantern. During the day, there's another **branch** (戸隠|市役所前支店; 1-3-3 Tachibana-nishi-dōri; ⊙11am-5pm Mon-Sat) near city hall.

Okashi no Hidaka SWEETS ¥

(お菓子の日高; ☎0985-25-5300; 2-7-25 Tachibana-dōri-nishi; sweets from ¥105; ⊙9.30am-9.30pm) Peruse, if you will, the refrigerator case of luscious-looking Japanese and Western pastries, but order the giant *nanjakō-daifuku* (dumpling of sweet bean paste, strawberry, chestnut and cheese in a wrapper of airy *mochi;* ¥336). Cheese *manju* (dumplings; ¥157) are another signature taste of Miyazaki.

Izakaya Seoul KOREAN ¥¥

(韓国居酒屋ソウル; ☎0985-29-8883; 1st fl, 7-26 Chūōmachi; most mains ¥1000-1200; ⊙6pm-2am; 📋) This Korean restaurant does a brisk business in barbecue made with Miyazaki *gyū, bibimba* (rice hotpot) and *pajeon* (savoury pancakes).

Maruman Honten YAKITORI ¥¥

(丸万本店; ☎0985-22-6068; 3-6-7 Tachibana-dōri-nishi; grilled chicken ¥1100; ⊙5.30pm-1.30am Thu-Sat, Mon, Tue, to midnight Sun) This homely shop serves *jidori,* full of flavour but tougher and cooked rarer than you may be used to. The standard is *momoyaki* (grilled chicken leg), but *tataki* (seared; ¥600) and *sashimi* (what you think it is; ¥650) are also popular, and meals come with a light and delicious chicken broth. For more thorough cooking, say '*yoku yaite kudasai*'. Basic English spoken. Look for the red marble facade.

Bosco ITALIAN ¥¥

(ぼすこ; ☎0985-23-5462; 1st fl, 7-22 Chūōmachi; mains ¥950-1260; ⊙6pm-midnight, closed alternate Sun; 📋) This nice trattoria has an open kitchen, two large tables and a long counter badly in need of some 'no smoking' signs, as even a few people lighting up in such a tiny space make it hard to taste the (otherwise excellent) meals. The shrimp and avocado spaghetti in cream sauce is the signature dish, but anything is sure to satisfy those Italian cravings.

★Miyachiku STEAK ¥¥¥

(みやちく; ☎0985-62-1129; 2nd fl, Miyazaki Kankō Hotel, 1-1-1 Matsuyama; lunch/dinner set menu from ¥2300/¥5150; ⊙11am-3pm & 5-10pm) If you're going to splurge on Miyazaki *gyū,* make it at this gracious *yakiniku* (Korean-style barbecue) and steak house with river views. Lunch set menus are a nice deal with appetiser, salad, beef, vegetables, dessert and coffee.

🍷 Drinking & Nightlife

Miyazaki also plays to the wee hours, especially in the summer, with hundreds of tiny bars. Most of the action is in Nishitachi.

The Bar BAR

(ザ・バー; www.thebarmiyazaki.com; 3rd fl, Paul Smith Bldg, 3-7-15 Tachibana-dōri-higashi; ⊙8pm-3am) This hub of the expat community and its local friends draws a cheery mixed crowd who are proud of the city and keen to welcome visitors over a few cold beers. There's even a full-sized billiard table.

One Coin Bar BAR

(ワンコインバー; 8-21 Chūō-dōri; ⊙6pm-3am Wed-Mon) All drinks are ¥500 (one coin!) at this smart, eight-stool hole-in-the-wall with a regular clientele who return for the conversation. The well-mannered 'master' speaks English and dispenses pizzas and spaghetti from the world's tiniest kitchen.

Lifetime BAR

(ライフタイム; 2nd fl, 2-3-8 Hiroshima; admission Fri ¥500; ⊙11.45am-2pm & 5pm-12.30am Mon-Sat) Modern jazz is alive and well in Miyazaki with near-nightly jams at this upstairs bistro-bar. Drinks start at ¥600, with coffee, snacks and steaks on the menu.

Suntory Shot Bar 4665 BAR

(サントリーショットバー4665; 1-12 Chūō-dōri; ⊙7pm-2am Tue-Sat, to midnight Sun) Drink a highball at nightfall at this subdued art deco-styled spot with many malt whiskies and hand-carved ice for cocktails. The owner speaks some English.

Igokochiya Anbai BAR
(いごこち屋　あんばい; 1st fl, 7-30 Chūō-dōri; ⏲6pm-1am Mon-Sat) Tucked away on Chūō-dōri, Anbai is a sophisticated *izakaya* with more than 350 varieties of *shōchū*, Guinness on tap, well-chosen local dishes and cool jazz background music. It's across the street from the Onishi Clinic.

Shopping

Miyazaki Prefectural Products Promotion Exhibition Hall ARTS & CRAFTS
(みやざき物産館; 1-6 Miyata-chō; ⏲9.30am-7pm Mon-Fri, 9.30am-6.30pm Sat & Sun) This place sells local wood crafts, clay *haniwa,* lots of snacks and a wall of *shōchū* liquors.

Information

Located inside JR Miyazaki Station, the helpful **tourist information centre** (宮崎市観光案内所; ☎0985-22-6469; ⏲9am-6pm) has maps of the city and its surroundings. There are international ATMs both at the station and at the **central post office** (⏲ATM 7am-11pm Mon-Fri, 9am-9pm Sat, 9am-5pm Sun & holidays), five minutes' walk west along Takachiho-dōri. Opposite the post office, the **Miyazaki Prefectural International Plaza** (宮崎県国際交流協会; ☎0985-32-8457; 8th fl, Carino Bldg; ⏲10am-7pm Tue-Sat) has satellite TV as well as various foreign-language newspapers and magazines.

Near the station's west exit is the internet cafe **E-Planet** (☎0985-60-7306; 2-12-20 Hiroshima; membership ¥100, first 30 min ¥250, then 15 min ¥100; ⏲24hr).

Getting There & Away

AIR

Miyazaki is connected by air with Tokyo (ANA & JAL/Solaseed), Osaka, Okinawa and Fukuoka (IBEX), plus a few flights weekly to Seoul and Taipei on Asiana Airlines.

BOAT

Miyazaki Car Ferry (宮崎カーフェリー; ☎0985-29-5566; www.miyazakicarferry.com; from 2nd-class ¥11,200) links Miyazaki with Kōbe; it's a 13-hour trip.

BUS

Routes include Kagoshima (¥2780, 2¾ hours), Kumamoto (¥4630, 3¼ hours), Nagasaki (¥6690, 5½ hours) and Fukuoka (¥4630, four hours). Phone the **Miyazaki Eki Bus Centre** (宮崎駅バスセンター; ☎0985-23-0106).

TRAIN

The JR Nippō line runs down to Kagoshima (*tokkyū,* ¥4220, two hours) and up to Beppu (*tokkyū,* ¥5990, 3¼ hours).

VISIT MIYAZAKI BUS CARD

For budget travellers not in a hurry, this bus pass (¥1000 per day) is a fabulous deal, covering city and regional buses including to Aoshima and Nichinan Coast. Buy it at tourist counters and some hotels. There's also a 'One Coin' ¥500 pass on weekends.

Getting Around

Miyazaki's airport is connected to the city centre by bus (¥440, 30 minutes) or train (¥350, 10 minutes) from JR Miyazaki Station. Most city bus services use the Miyazaki Eki Bus Centre opposite the station.

Car rental is the most convenient way to explore the coastal region outside the city. There are many agencies outside the station's west exit (12 hours from about ¥5500).

Aoshima 青島

☎0985

Aoshima is a tiny palm-covered island (1.5km in circumference), and also the name of the adjacent mainland town, one of Japan's more relaxed, alternative communities. Surfers and sunbathers come for its lovely beaches, which are strewn with sand-dollars after rough storms. A great alternative to staying in central Miyazaki.

Sights & Activities

The first thing you'll notice as you cross the water to the island of Aoshima is the unique geological feature surrounding it. Called the **devil's washboard** (*oni no sentaku-ita,* 鬼の洗濯板), it looks just like a washboard of centuries ago. On the island, the photogenic Shintō shrine **Aoshima-jinja** (青島神社) is reputedly good for matchmaking, and the **Legend of Hyūga Hall** (日向神話館; ⏲8am-5pm, to 6pm Jul & Aug) tells the story of Amaterasu, Emperor Jimmu and the founding of Japan in wax-museum-style dioramas with English explanations. An estimated 200 species of plants and animals can be found in its small circumference.

On the landside, the **Prefectural Subtropical Plant Garden** (青島亜熱帯植物園; admission free, greenhouse ¥200; ⏲9am-5pm) boasts 64 different species of fruit trees.

West of town, an 8km-long, well-maintained **hiking path** winds through **Kaeda Gorge** (加江田渓谷) following the Kaeda-gawa, a refreshingly clear stream filled with boulders and excellent swimming holes. Lush foliage includes banana palms and mountain cedars. Your own transport is helpful to get here; turn off Rte 220 onto prefectural road 339.

Festivals & Events

On the second Monday in January, loincloth-clad locals dive ceremoniously into the ocean at Aoshima-jinja. At the end of July there's more splashing as *mikoshi* are carried through the shallows to the shrine.

Sleeping & Eating

Miyazaki Cocona Shirahama Drive-in Campsite CAMPGROUND ¥
(宮崎白浜オートキャンプ場ココナ; 0985-65-2020; tent hire ¥1620, camp sites from ¥3020, cabins for up to 4 people ¥10260;) Opposite Shirahama beach, this modern complex has plenty of room and some nice rustic cabins set back from the main area.

★**ANA Holiday Inn Resort Miyazaki** HOTEL ¥¥
(ANA ホリデイインリゾート宮崎; 0985-65-1555; www.anahirmiyazaki.com; 1-16-1 Aoshima; s/tw from ¥7000/11,000; P@) This shiny white, semi-cylindrical, beachfront tower with glass elevators has ocean-view rooms and onsen baths (day use ¥1000). In the off-season rooms are surprisingly reasonable given the quality of the stay; however, in peak season it can be ¥5000 or more higher than what's listed here. There's a large fountain and pool, some kiddie attractions and the beach couldn't be closer.

Nearly all the 200+ rooms have ocean views but a few do not. Those may be cheaper; it's worth asking if you're trying to save yen.

★**Minshuku Misakisō** GUESTHOUSE ¥¥
(民宿みさき荘; 0985-65-0038; www.misakisou.com; 1 chōme 5-4; s/d ¥4500/8000; P) Gracious and friendly, the Misakisō is a one-stop-shop: it's a place to stay, a bar (guests only), cafe and surf rental (boards from ¥2500; cafe and rental closed Wednesday). Rooms are mainly Japanese-style, but there's one Western option, and all are clean and very convenient for anyone planning to surf or sunbathe: just cross the street and you're at the beach. No English is spoken, but foreigners are welcomed just the same.

Route Inn Grantia Aoshima Taiyōkaku HOTEL ¥¥
(ルートイングランティアあおしま太陽閣; 0985-65-1531; www.route-inn.co.jp/english; 1-16-2 Aoshima-nishi; s/d/tw from ¥6100/11,600/12,650; P@) On the hillside midway between Aoshima and Kodomo-no-kuni stations, this hot-spring property offers excellent value. Day use of onsen, *rotemburo* and *ganbanyoku* (stone bath) costs from ¥600 (¥770 on weekends).

Minato Aoshima SEAFOOD ¥¥
(港あおしま; 0985-65-1044; 3-5-1 Aoshima; set menus ¥1000-1500; 11am-2pm Tue-Sun) Owned and run by the local fisherman's collective, this take-your-shoes-off spot offers some of the finest and freshest seafood that Aoshima has to offer. Most meals are sets, including several side dishes and miso soup.

Getting There & Around

Aoshima is on the JR Nichinan line from Miyazaki (¥360, 30 minutes). Buses from Miyazaki Station stop at Aoshima (¥700, 40 minutes, hourly) en route to Udo-jingū. It's about 800m to the island from the station.

Udo-jingū 鵜戸神宮

Reached via a coastal path, this brightly painted **Shintō shrine** (0987-29-1001; 3232 Ōaza Miyaura) occupies an open cavern overlooking unusual rock formations in the cove below. It's protocol to buy five *undama* (luck stones, ¥100), make a wish and try to hit the shallow depression on top of the turtle-shaped rock. Men use their left hand, women their right when making the throw. Wishes are usually related to marriage, childbirth and lactation, because the boulders in front of the cavern are said to represent Emperor Jimmu's grandmother's breasts (No, really!).

Hourly buses from Aoshima (¥1020, 40 minutes) and Miyazaki (¥1470, 1½ hours) stop on the highway. From the bus stop, it's about a 700m walk to the shrine past interesting rock formations and picturesque fishing boats.

Obi 飫肥

In this quaint town nicknamed 'Little Kyoto', the wealthy Ito clan ruled from Obi castle for 14 generations beginning in 1587, somehow surviving the 'one kingdom, one castle' ruling in 1615. There's **tourist info** (飫肥城観光案内; ☎0987-25-3308; ⏲9.30am-4.30pm) right at the castle.

Only the walls of the original **Obi-jō** (飫肥城; ☎0987-25-4411; admission ¥610; ⏲9am-4.30pm) are intact, but the grounds have six important buildings, including the impressive, painstakingly reconstructed **Ōte-mon gate** and **Matsuo-no-maru**, the lord's private residence. The **museum** has a collection relating to the Itō clan's long rule over Obi. **Yoshokan**, formerly the residence of the clan's chief retainer, stands just outside the castle entrance and has a large garden with Mt Atago (Atago-san) as 'borrowed scenery'.

Once you've seen these sights, rent bikes (¥500 per day) at the castle carpark to explore the rest of the town, with its photogenic streetscapes, shrines and historic shopping street; your admission ticket has a simple map.

By the castle, **Obiten** (おび天; ☎0987-25-5717; 9-1-8 Obi; mains ¥850-1150; ⏲9am-4pm) serves a local version of *Satsuma-age* (fried cakes of fish paste and vegetables, here called *tempura*). The signature Obiten with udon is ¥850.

The JR Nichinan line connects Obi with Miyazaki (*kaisoku*, ¥940, 65 minutes) via Aoshima. From Obi Station, it's a 10-minute walk to the castle. Buses from Miyazaki (¥2080, 2¼ hours, last return bus 4pm) stop below the castle entrance.

Nichinan-kaigan & Toi-misaki 日南海岸・都井岬

The palm-lined stretch of coastal road from Aoshima to Toi-misaki (Cape Toi) via the town of Nichinan is a rewarding drive, with seaside cliffs and views of the islands reminiscent of gumdrops and camels.

Just off the coast from **Ishinami-kaigan**, the tiny island of **Kō-jima** is home to a group of monkeys that apparently rinse their food in the ocean before eating, but they're a fickle bunch, and hard to spot. Boats shuttle visitors back and forth for ¥3000 per person return.

From here heading south, it's about another 7km to **Toi-misaki**, famed for wild horses and a dramatic fire festival on the last weekend in September. Lest you think this is galloping stampedes of never-seen-a-human-before stallions, it's not: these 'wild' horses are sedate and well-fed, much like one would see in a dude ranch in the American west or Australian outback. If you want wild – wild monkeys that is – then detour up into the mountain roads here and drive slowly: several bands of monkeys inhabit the slopes and it's often possible to see them. Earthworms the size of garter snakes are another curious denizen. En route is **Koigaura-hama** (Koigaura Beach) where the *surf-zoku* (surf tribe) hang out.

Lodging along the way is few and far between. **Kushima Spa** (串間温泉いこいの里; ☎0987-75-2000; www.kushima-spa.com; 987 Honjyō; d incl 2 meals without/with bath ¥16,240/20,160; ⏲closed 3rd Wed each month), 25 minutes from Toi-misaki, is sort of like a *Michi no Eki* (highway rest area) on steroids, offering reasonable rooms, great onsen (including a nice *rotemburo*), tourist info, a cafe, and souvenirs and snacks. It's a good midpoint between Miyazaki and Kagoshima, if you're doing the coastal route. It's almost worth the detour just to feed the enormous carp that surround the property's many pools.

Saitobaru 西都原

☎0983

North of Miyazaki, the **Saitobaru Burial Mounds Park** looks like a golf course at first glance, but the hillocks dotting the several square kilometres of fields and forests are actually more than 300 *kofun* (tumuli, or burial mounds). These mostly keyhole-shaped mounds, dating from AD 300 to 600, served much the same function as Egyptian pyramids for early Japanese nobility. Bike rental is free.

The large **Saitobaru Archaeological Museum** (西都原考古博物館; ☎0983-41-0041; ⏲10am-6pm Tue-Sun) FREE displays excavated items like Jōmon pottery, ancient swords, armour and *haniwa*. Rent the English audioguide (¥400); signage is in Japanese. A hall nearby is built around an excavation site.

Buses run twice a day to Saitobaru from Miyakō City bus terminal (¥1140, 70 minutes), but you'll need your own transport if you want to explore the tomb-strewn countryside. Saitobaru is not on the Visit Miyazaki Bus Card.

In the nearby town of Saito, drummers wear odd pole-like headgear for the unique **Usudaiko dance festival** in early September. A harvest festival lasts from 12 to 16 December, highlighted by **Shiromi Kagura** performances on the 14th and 15th.

Takachiho 高千穂

☎0982 / POP 14,000

In far northern Miyazaki-ken, this pretty mountain town is a remote but rewarding destination, and the site where legend says Japan's sun goddess brought light back to the world. As if that weren't reason enough to visit, there's a deep and dramatic gorge through the town centre.

Sights

★Ama-no-Iwato-jinja SHINTO SHRINE

(天岩戸神社; 1073-1 Iwato; ⏲24hr, office 8.30am-5pm) One of Shintō's loveliest shrines honours the cave where Amaterasu hid. The cave itself is off-limits, but Nishi Hongū (the shrine's main building) sits right across the river Iwato-gawa. If you're with a Japanese speaker, ask a staff member to show you the viewpoint behind the *honden* (main hall). Buses leave approximately hourly (¥300, 20 minutes) from Takachihō's Miyakō bus centre.

A seven-minute walk beside a picturesque stream takes you to **Ama-no-Yasukawara**, a deep cave where tradition says that thousands of other deities discussed how to lure Amaterasu from the cave. Modern-day visitors have left innumerable stacks of stones in tribute, imparting a sort of Indy Jones feeling.

Takachiho Gorge GORGE

(高千穂峡; Takachiho-kyō) Takachiho's magnificent gorge, with its waterfall, overhanging rocks and sheer walls, was formed over 120,000 years ago by a double volcanic eruption. There's a 1km-long nature trail above the gorge. Or view it up close from a **rowboat** (☎0982-73-1213; per 30 min ¥2000, up to 3 adults per boat; ⏲8.30am-5pm), though during high season it can be as busy as rush hour. In season, rowers will be mobbed by throngs of hungry ducks, but so far no deaths have been reported…

SUN GODDESS DISAPPEARS! WORLD GOES DARK!

According to Shintō legend, the sun goddess Amaterasu, angered by the misbehaviour of her brother, exiled herself into a cave sealed by a boulder, plunging the world into darkness. Alarmed, other gods gathered at another nearby cave to discuss how to get her to re-emerge. Eventually the goddess Ame-no-Uzume performed a bawdy dance which aroused Amaterasu's curiosity, and she emerged from the cave and light was restored to earth. *Iwato kagura* dances performed in Takachiho today re-enact this story.

Takachiho-jinja SHINTO SHRINE

(高千穂神社) Takachiho-jinja, about 10 minutes' walk from the bus centre, is dramatically set in a grove of cryptomeria pines, including one that's over 800 years old. Some of the buildings here look like they could almost be the same age.

Festivals & Events

Takachiho's artistic claim to fame is **kagura** (sacred dance). In May, September and November (the dates change annually), performances are held at Ama-no-Iwato-jinja from 10am to 10pm, while hour-long performances of **yokagura** (night-time kagura; tickets ¥700; ⏲8pm) take place nightly at Takachiho-jinja. Arrive up to an hour early for front row seating.

There are also all-night performances *(satokagura)* in farmhouses on 19 nights from November to February. In all, 33 dances are performed from 6pm until 9am the next morning. If you brave the cold until morning, you'll be caught up in a wave of excitement. Contact the tourist information office for details.

Sleeping & Eating

Takachiho has about 30 hotels, ryokan, *minshuku* and pensions, which all typically book out during the autumn foliage season.

Takachiho Youth Hostel HOSTEL ¥

(高千穂ユースホステル; ☎0982-72-3021; 5899-2 Mitai; dm HI member/nonmember ¥2800/3400; P ⊖ @) This large hostel is far from the sights but clean, efficient and deep in the woods. Rooms are Japanese-style, with breakfast/dinner (¥500/900) available, as are laundry machines and pick-up from the bus centre.

Chiho-no-ie NOODLES ¥

(千穂の家; ☎0982-72-2115; 62-2 Owazamukoyama; sōmen ¥500, set meals from ¥1100; ⏲9am-5pm) At the base of the gorge (though, sadly, with no water views), this simple building serves *nagashi-sōmen* (¥500) – have fun catching tasty noodles with your

Takachiho

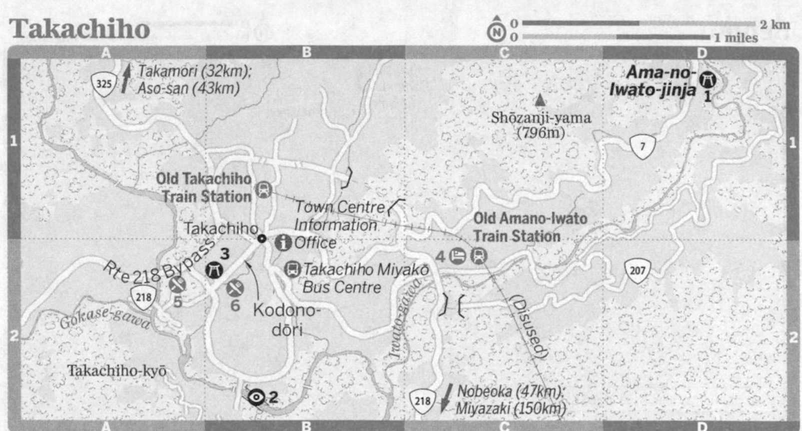

Takachiho

Top Sights

Sights

Sleeping

Eating

chopsticks as they float by in halved bamboo shafts. Another building near the carpark has the popular set meals.

Gamadase Ichiba MARKET ¥¥
(がまだせ市場; ☎Nagomi 0982-73-1109; 1099-1 Mitai; Nagomi lunch set menus ¥1400-2500, dinner set menus ¥1750-6000; ⊙markets & Nagomi 11am-2.30pm & 5-9pm, closed 2nd Wed each month) Operated by the local agricultural collaborative, this facility has markets for local produce and the Nagomi (和) restaurant for local beef set menus. Be sure to say 'hi' to the full-size replicas of beloved now-departed bovines that stand outside.

Information

Town Centre Information Office (街中案内所; ☎0982-72-4680; 1296-5 Mitai; ⊙8.30am-5.30pm) This info office has helpful staff and a variety of maps, brochures, info, postcards, and souvenirs.

Getting There & Around

Takachiho is most easily reached by car from the Aso-san area in Kumamoto Prefecture. Two buses daily serve Takachiho's **Miyakō Bus Centre** (高千穂宮交バスセンター; ☎0982-72-4133) from Kumamoto (¥2300, 2¾ hours) via Takamori (¥1280, 1¼ hours). From the bus centre it's walkable to the gorge and Takachiho-jinja, but you'll need transport to reach other sights. The town centre information office has wi-fi and rents out electric bicycles for ¥300 per hour or ¥1500 per day.

ŌITA PREFECTURE

Beppu 別府

☎0977 / POP 121,870

You don't have to look far in Beppu, in Ōita Prefecture (大分県), to see the reason for its popularity: steam rising from vents in the earth means onsen bathing opportunities galore. Beppu is at turns quaint, touristy, modern, traditional, solid and rickety, but the charm of this hilly, hospitable city grows on visitors as sure as the waters are warm. Winter visitors get the seasonal treat of seeing the entire town filled with warm, escaping steam.

Sights & Activities

Hot Springs

Beppu has two types of hot springs, collectively pumping out more than 100 million litres of hot water every day. *Jigoku* (hells) are for looking at; *onsen* are for bathing.

Beppu

0 — 1 km
0 — 0.5 miles

A B C D
1 2 3 4 5 6 7

Kunisaki Peninsula (20km)
Kamegawa
6
2 3
See Kannawa Hells Area Map (p745)
KANNAWA HELLS AREA
11
500
645
Beppu Daigaku
7
Yamanami Hwy
Matsuyama; Osaka
Haruki-gawa
Beppu Traditional Bamboo Crafts Centre 1
Beppu-wan
HORITA
Sakai-gawa
5
8
Yufuin (24km)
52
Fujimi-dori
9
Beppu-Koen
Beppu
4
See Central Beppu Map (p742)
Rakutenchi Amusement Park
10
Asami-gawa
10
Ōita (14km)
Usuki (20km)

Beppu

Top Sights

1 Beppu Traditional Bamboo Crafts Centre B5

Sights

2 Chi-no-ike Jigoku B1
3 Tatsumaki Jigoku B1

Activities, Courses & Tours

4 Ichinoide Kaikan B7
5 Kitahama Termas Onsen D6
6 Shibaseki Onsen A1
7 Shōnin-ga-hama Sand Bath D3

Sleeping

8 Suginoi Hotel A6

Eating

9 Shinanoya C6
10 Tomonaga Panya D7

Hells HOT SPRINGS

(each hell/combination ticket ¥400/2110; 8am-5pm) Beppu's most hyped attraction is the **jigoku meguri** (hell circuit), where waters bubble forth from underground with unusual results. Unlike Unzen, where the geothermal wonders are unadorned, the circuit's eight stops have become mini amusement parks, each with a theme and some loaded with tourist kitsch; consider yourself warned.

The hells are in two groups, six at **Kannawa**, over 4km northwest of Beppu Station, and two about 2.5km further north. In the Kannawa group are steaming blue **Umi Jigoku** (海地獄; Sea Hell), **Oniishibōzu Jigoku** (Demon Monk Hell), where bubbling mud looks like a monk's shaved head, **Shira-ike Jigoku** (白池地獄; White Pond Hell) and **Kamado Jigoku** (かまど地獄; Oven Hell), named because it was once used for cooking. At **Oni-yama Jigoku** (鬼山地獄; Devil's Mountain Hell) and **Yama Jigoku** (山地獄; Mountain Hell), a variety of animals are kept in enclosures that look uncomfortably small. Take a bus from Beppu Station to Umi-Jigoku-mae (¥330).

The smaller group of hells has **Chi-no-ike Jigoku** (血の池地獄; Blood Pool Hell; Map p740), with its photogenic red water, and **Tatsumaki Jigoku** (龍巻地獄; Tornado Hell; Map p740), where a geyser shoots off about every 35 minutes.

Onsen

Beppu has eight onsen districts, **Beppu Hattō** (www.city.beppu.oita.jp/01onsen/english/index.html). Onsen aficionados spend their time in Beppu moving from one bath to another and consider at least three baths a day *de rigueur;* bathing costs from ¥100 to ¥1000. Bring your own soap, washcloth and towel, as some places don't rent them.

In central Beppu, the *very* hot **Takegawara Onsen** (竹瓦温泉; Map p742; 16-23 Moto-machi; admission ¥100, sand bath ¥1030; 6.30am-10.30pm, sand bath 8am-9.30pm, sand bath closed 3rd Wed each month) occupies a fabulous wooden building dating back to the Meiji era (present building from 1938). Bathing is simple; scoop out water with a bucket, wash yourself, then soak. There's also a sand bath where a *yukata* is provided so you can lie in a shallow trench and get buried up to your neck in hot sand; arrive earlier for warmest sand. The simple half-timber building and *hinoki* (cypress) bath of **Ekimae Kōtō Onsen** (駅前高等温泉; Map p742; 13-14 Ekimae-machi; admission ¥200; 6am-midnight) is just a couple of minutes' walk from the station.

Downhill from Kannawabus stop is **Kannawa Mushi-yu** (鉄輪蒸し湯; 1-gumi Kannawa-kami; ¥510; 6.30am-8pm) where, wrapped in a *yukata,* you steam at 65°C (ow!) on top of Japanese rush leaves. Eight to 10 minutes here is said to have the detoxifying power of up to 30 minutes in a sauna. Nearby **Hyōtan Onsen** (ひょうたん温泉; 159-2 Kannawa; admission before/after 6pm ¥700/550, yukata ¥200; 9am-1am) has multiple pools, *rotemburo,* sand baths and private baths.

Shibaseki Onsen (柴石温泉; Map p740; 4-kumi Noda; admission ¥210; 7am-8pm, closed 2nd Wed of each month) is en route to the smaller pair of hells. You can rent a private *kazoku-buro* (family bath) for ¥1620 per hour.

Nearby, popular **Onsen Hoyōland** (温泉保養ランド; 5-1 Myōban; admission ¥1100; 9am-8pm) has giant mud baths, plus open-air and mixed-gender bathing.

Between JR Beppu Station and the Kamegawa onsen area, **Shōnin-ga-hama sand bath** (上人ヶ浜; Map p740; admission ¥1030; 8.30am-6pm Apr-Oct, 9am-5pm Nov-Mar) has a great beach location and some English-speaking staff.

For a seaside onsen experience, head to **Kitahama Termas Onsen** (北浜温泉テルマス; Map p740; admission ¥510; 10am-10pm Fri-Wed). You'll need a bathing suit, as the outside *rotemburo* mixes it up.

Central Beppu

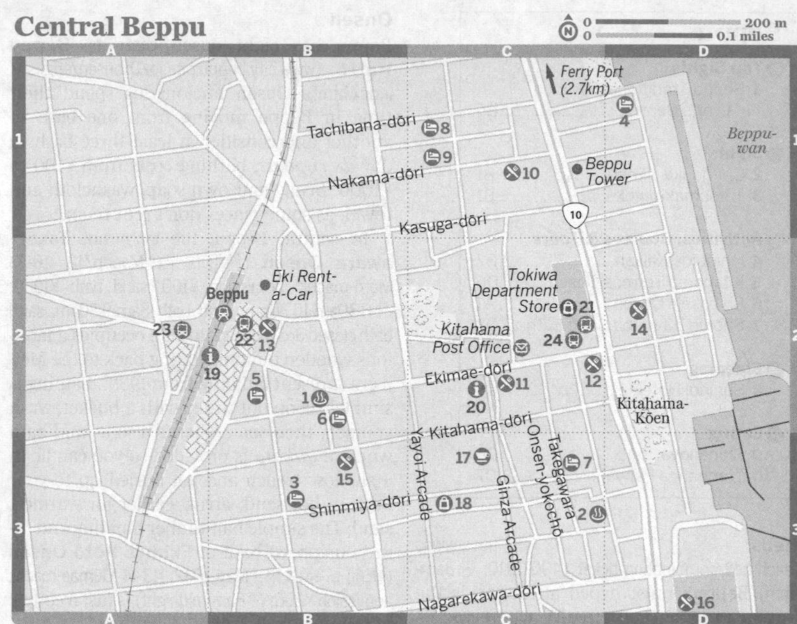

Central Beppu

Activities, Courses & Tours
1 Ekimae Kōtō Onsen B2
2 Takegawara Onsen C3

Sleeping
3 Beppu Guest House B3
4 Beppu Hotel Umine D1
5 Hotel Seawave Beppu B2
6 Kokage International Minshuku B2
7 Nogami Honkan Ryokan C3
8 Spa Hostel Khaosan Beppu C1
9 Yamada Bessou C1

Eating
10 Fugu Matsu C1
11 Gyōza Kogetsu C2
12 Jin Robata & Beer Pub C2
13 Toyotsune B2
14 Toyotsune D2
15 Ureshi-ya B3
16 You Me Town D3

Drinking & Nightlife
17 Kissa Natsume C3

Shopping
18 Yamashō C3

Information
19 Foreign Tourist Information Office B2
20 Foreign Tourist Information Office C2

Transport
21 Airport Bus Stop C2
22 Beppu Station Bus Stop (East side) B2
23 Beppu Station Bus Stop (West side) A2
24 Bus Stop for Kannawa Onsen C2

The owner of **Ichinoide Kaikan** (いちのいで会館; Map p740; 14-2 Uehara-machi; ⌚11am-5pm) loves onsen so much that he built three pool-sized *rotemburo* in his backyard. There are fabulous views over Beppu to the sea. The general deal is that you order a delicious *teishoku* (¥1470), prepared while you bathe. Ask for directions at the tourist information offices.

Museums

★ Beppu Traditional Bamboo Crafts Centre MUSEUM
(別府市竹細工伝統産業会館; Map p740; ☎0977-23-1072; 8-3 Higashi-sōen; admission ¥300; ⌚8.30am-5pm Tue-Sun) The hands-on crafts centre displays refined works from Edo-period masters as well as current examples of uses for this versatile material, which

grows copiously in this region. If you'd like to try your hand at crafting bamboo, request a reservation at least one week ahead (¥400/1000, depending on the complexity of the item). From Beppu Station, take bus 22 or 25 to Takezaiku-densankan-mae or bus 1 to Minami-baru (about 200m away).

Festivals & Events

Onsen Festival CULTURAL

Held during the first weekend in April.

Tanabata Matsuri CULTURAL

In adjacent Ōita city, held over three days from the first Friday in August.

Sleeping

Beppu Guest House HOSTEL ¥

(別府ゲストハウス; Map p742; ☎0977-76-7811; www.beppu.cloudline.com; 1-12 Ekimae-chō; dm/s ¥1500/2500; P ⊖ @ ☎) The big kitchen and living rooms are great places to hang out with fellow travellers at this arty, funky and welcoming hostel. Other positives: free loaner bikes, laundry machines and English-speaking staff with local knowledge. There's no bath on-site, but a ¥100 public bath is nearby.

Spa Hostel Khaosan Beppu HOSTEL ¥

(スパホステルカオサン別府はまゆう; Map p742; ☎0977-23-3939; www.khaosan-beppu.com; 3-3-10 Kitahama; dm/s ¥2000/3000; P ⊖ @ ☎) About eight years old, this place is excellent value with clean, renovated rooms (mix of Japanese and Western styles) and hot-spring baths. Look for the Thai *tuk-tuk* out front. Prices can be even cheaper during slow season.

★**Yamada Bessou** RYOKAN ¥¥

(山田別荘; Map p742; ☎0977-24-2121; http://yamadabessou.jp; 3-2-18 Kitahama; r per person with 2 meals from ¥6500; P ⊖ @ ☎ 👪) You could be stepping back in time at this sprawling family-run 1930s inn with wonderfully well-preserved rooms and fabulous art deco features and furnishings. The onsen and private *rotemburo* are so lovely you'll hardly mind that only a couple of its eight rooms have full bath and toilet.

Kokage International Minshuku MINSHUKU ¥¥

(国際民宿こかげ; Map p742; ☎0977-23-1753; ww6.tiki.ne.jp/~kokage; 8-9 Ekimae-chō; s/d ¥4350/7650; P @ ☎) Off an alley near Ekimae-dōri, this cosy nine-room inn is old and friendly, chock-full of atmospheric woodwork, antiques and trinkets. There's a lovely stone onsen, and toast and coffee for breakfast. Rooms over the entrance are quietest.

Nogami Honkan Ryokan RYOKAN ¥¥

(野上本館; Map p742; ☎0977-22-1334; www.yukemuri.net; 1-12-1 Kitahama; r per person with/without breakfast from ¥6000/3000; P @ ☎) In a classic, boxy 1950s building near Takegawara Onsen, most of the 25 rooms here don't have private bathrooms. Three small baths can be reserved for private use, and owner Ken is a knowledgable and gracious host. Rates vary with the season.

Hotel Seawave Beppu BUSINESS HOTEL ¥¥

(ホテルシーウェーブ別府; Map p742; ☎0977-27-1311; www.beppuonsen.com; 12-8 Ekimae-chō; s/tw/ste from ¥6000/8600/18,000; P ⊖ @ ☎) For late arrivals or early getaways, this hotel with small rooms is right across from the station. There are in-room baths and a recently opened in-house onsen.

★**Beppu Hotel Umine** HOTEL ¥¥¥

(別府ホテルうみね; Map p742; ☎0977-26-0002; www.umine.jp; 3-8-3 Kitahama; r per person with breakfast from ¥15,120; P ⊖ @) In-room onsen baths with water views, gorgeous common baths, savvy contemporary design, excellent restaurants and oodles of personal service make this Beppu's top stay. Rates are expensive but include drinks and snacks in the library lounge.

Suginoi Hotel HOTEL ¥¥¥

(杉乃井ホテル; Map p740; ☎0977-24-1141; www.suginoi-hotel.com/english; 1 Kankaiji; r per person with 2 meals from ¥10,000; P ⊖ @) On a hillside above town, Suginoi offers the tiered rooftop Tanayu *rotemburo*, the Aqua Garden onsen swimming pool (combined day-use ¥1300, bathing suit required) and high standards indoors. Japanese-style rooms are more alluring than Western ones, but the 15 Ceada Floor rooms are slick and special. Note that rates vary widely with the season.

Eating & Drinking

Beppu is renowned for *toriten* (chicken tempura), freshwater fish, *Bungō-gyū* (local beef), *fugu* (pufferfish), wild mountain vegetables and *dangojiru*. On the 1st floor of the **You Me Town shopping mall** (ゆめタウン別府; Map p742), English-friendly restaurants include conveyor-belt sushi, noodles and a buffet.

DON'T MISS

JIGOKU MUSHI KŌBŌ

Ingenious! Amid the hells of Kannawa, you can cook your own meal in onsen steam in this **workshop** (地獄蒸し工房; Hell Steaming Workshop; ☎0977-66-3775; 5-kumi Furomoto; egg ¥150, dishes from ¥600-1300, steamers ¥510 per 30min, seafood set ¥2500; ⏰9am-9pm, closed 3rd Wed of month). Purchase ingredients on the spot (or bring your own), and steam them in *kama* (vats) roiling from the onsen below. It shares a building with the Foreign Tourist Information Office, so there's usually an English speaker on hand to help until 5pm. It can be crowded at peak times such as weekend lunch.

★ Toyotsune JAPANESE ¥
(Map p742; ☎0977-22-3274; 2-13-11 Kitahama; ⏰11am-2.30pm & 5-9pm Thu-Tue) Toyotsune nails the Beppu specialities: *toriten*, *Bungō-gyū* and lots of fresh fish, plus tempura. This main branch is on the corner behind Jolly Pasta; a **second branch** (とよ常; Map p742; ☎0977-22-2083; 3-7 Ekimae-honmachi; mains ¥630-1580; ⏰11am-2.30pm & 5-9pm Fri-Wed; 📖) is across from Beppu Station.

★ Gyōza Kogetsu GYŌZA ¥
(餃子湖月; Map p742; ☎0977-21-8062; 3-7 Ekimae-honmachi; gyōza ¥650; ⏰2-9.30pm Wed-Mon) This seven-seat counter shop with a manic local following has only two things on the menu, both ¥600 – generous plates of *gyōza* fried to a delicate crunch, and bottles of beer. It's in the tiny alley behind the covered arcade; look for the display case filled with cat figurines.

Tomonaga Panya BAKERY ¥
(友永パン屋; Map p740; ☎0977-23-0969; Chiyo-machi 2-29; pastries from ¥100; ⏰8.30am-5.30pm Mon-Sat) This charming, historic bakery has been in business since 1916, and people still queue for its ever-changing selection of oven-fresh breads and pastries. The *wanchan* (doggie) bun (¥110) is filled with custard cream and uses raisins for the eyes and nose. Note: the shop closes when sold out.

Ureshi-ya SHOKUDO ¥
(うれしや; Map p742; ☎0977-22-0767; 7-12 Ekimae-honmachi; dishes ¥220-950; ⏰5pm-2am Tue-Sun) You'll get your money's worth at this friendly and busy *shokudō* with *donburi*, sashimi, *oden* (hotpot), noodle dishes and more, displayed for you to choose. Can be *packed* at times.

Shinanoya CAFE, NOODLES ¥
(信濃屋; Map p740; ☎0977-25-8728; 6-32 Nishi-noguchi; mains ¥600-1300; ⏰9am-9pm, to 6pm Tue & Wed) A few minutes from the station's west exit and dating back to 1926, this kindly *kissaten* also serves a renowned *dangojiru* loaded with vegies and best enjoyed while viewing the piney garden, or sitting around a giant common table in plush, green-velvet armchairs. It's the traditional building just before Family Mart.

Jin Robata & Beer Pub IZAKAYA ¥
(ろばた仁; Map p742; ☎0977-21-1768; 1-15-7 Kitahama; dishes ¥350-1140; ⏰5pm-midnight) A neon fish sign directs you to this welcoming international pub. To go with your booze, pick from the rows of fresh fish on display (get it sashimi or cooked) or sample *toriten*, local beef and more. Or try the ever-popular fried chicken if you're hankering for a taste of home.

Kissa Natsume CAFE ¥
(喫茶なつめ; Map p742; 1-4-23 Kitahama; ⏰10am-8.30pm Thu-Tue) This retro snack and dessert spot in the covered arcade is best known for its own *onsen kōhī* (¥530), coffee made with hot-spring water. Look for the wooden barrel above the door.

Fugu Matsu FUGU ¥¥¥
(ふぐ松; Map p742; ☎0977-21-1717; www.fugumatsu.jp; 3-6-14 Kitahama; fugu set meals from ¥8640; ⏰11am-9pm; 📖) This friendly shop has been serving simple *fugu* since 1958. Sit on *hori-kotatsu* seating and chow on sashimi, *karaage* (fried fugu) and *hiresake* (sake boiled with a grilled *fugu* fin). Reservations are required.

Shopping

For over a century, the must-have souvenir for Japanese holidaymakers in Beppu was everyday-use bamboo products (such as baskets); nowadays the trend is towards art pieces. Find them at shops like **Yamashō** (山正; Map p742; 4-9 Kusunoki-machi; ⏰10am-6pm) in the central shopping arcades, although be forewarned that many pieces are

Kannawa Hells Area

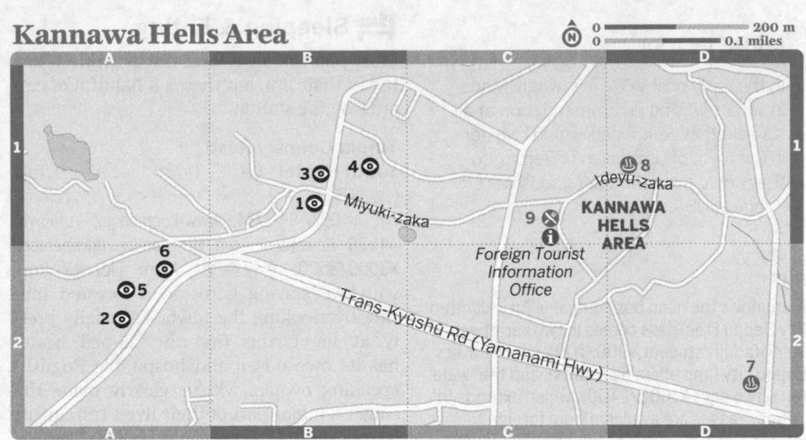

Kannawa Hells Area

Sights

1 Kamado Jigoku B1
2 Oniishibōzu Jigoku A2
3 Oni-yama Jigoku B1
4 Shira-ike Jigoku B1
5 Umi Jigoku A2
6 Yama Jigoku A2

Activities, Courses & Tours

7 Hyōtan Onsen D2
8 Kannawa Mushi-yu D1

Eating

9 Jigoku Mushi Kōbō C1

Chinese imports. Ask *'Nihon-sei des ka?'* (Is this made in Japan?) to check.

Information

International ATMs can be found at Beppu Station, **Kitahama post office** (別府北浜郵便局; Map p742; ⌚ATM 9am-5.30pm Mon-Fri, 9am-5pm Sat & Sun) and the nearby Cosmopia shopping centre. Ōita Bank (大分銀行) handles foreign-exchange services.

Foreign Tourist Information Offices (別府外国人観光客案内所; www.beppuftio.blogspot.com) Branches at Beppu International Plaza (Map p742; ☎0977-21-6220; 12-13 Ekimae-machi; ⌚9am-5pm), Beppu Station (Map p742; ☎0977-23-1119; cnr Ekimae-dōri & Ginza Arcade; ⌚10am-5pm) and Kannawa (☎0977-66-3855; 5-kumi Furomoto; ⌚9am-5pm). Well equipped with helpful bilingual volunteers and an arsenal of local information and advice.

Getting There & Away

AIR

Flights go to **Ōita Airport** (☎0978-67-1174; http://www.oita-airport.jp) from Tokyo Haneda (ANA, JAL, Solaseed Air) and Osaka. Flights also operate to Seoul.

BOAT

The **Ferry Sunflower Kansai Kisen** (☎0977-22-1311) makes an overnight run between Beppu and Osaka and Kōbe (¥11,940, 11 hours), stopping at Matsuyama (4½ hours). The evening boat departs at 6.45pm to western Honshū and passes through the Inland Sea, arriving at 6.35am the next morning. For the port, take bus 20 or 26 from Beppu Station's west exit.

BUS

There's a Kyūshū Odan (Trans-Kyūshū) bus to Aso Station (¥2980, 3¼ hours) and Kumamoto (¥3960, five hours). Buses from Fukuoka Airport run every hour to Kitahama Station (¥3190, two hours).

TRAIN

The Kyūshū *shinkansen* from Hakata (Fukuoka) connects with the JR Nippō line at Kokura (*shinkansen* and *tokkyū*, ¥5580, 90 minutes) to Beppu. The JR Nippō line continues to Miyazaki via Ōita (*tokkyū*, ¥5330, 3¼ hours). Kagoshima-Chūō is close to a six-hour ride (¥10,110).

Getting Around

TO/FROM THE AIRPORT

Beppu Airport buses to Ōita Airport stop outside Tokiwa department store (¥1450, 45 minutes) and Beppu Station.

MADE IN USA

In the early post-WWII era, when 'Made in Japan' was no recommendation at all, it's said that companies would register in the town of Usa, north of Beppu, so they could proclaim their goods were 'Made in USA'.

BUS

Kamenoi is the main bus company. An unlimited 'My Beppu Free' pass comes in two varieties: 'mini' (adult/student ¥900/700), which covers Beppu city (and offers discounts); and the 'wide' (one/two days ¥1600/2400), which extends to Yufuin. Passes are available from foreign tourist information offices and some lodgings. From JR Beppu Station, buses 2, 5, 7, 41 and 43 go to Kannawa (15 to 25 minutes), and buses 16 and 26 serve Chi-no-ike and Tatsumaki *jigokus*.

Yufuin 由布院

☎0977 / POP 35,800

About 25km inland from Beppu, delightful Yufuin sits in a ring of mountains, with the twin peaks of Yufu-dake especially notable. The town lives for tourism and is a good place to see contemporary Japanese crafts; ceramics, clothing, woodworking and even interesting foods abound in its narrow lanes. However, Yufuin gets crowded on holidays and weekends. If staying overnight, arrive before dusk, when the day trippers leave and wealthier Japanese retreat to the sanctuary of their ryokan.

As in Beppu, making a pilgrimage from one onsen to another is a popular activity. Most historic is **Shitan-yu** (下ん湯; admission ¥200, deposit money in slot outside; ⏲9am-9pm), a one-room thatched bathhouse with mixed bathing only, on the northern shore of **Kinrin-ko** (Lake of Golden Fish Scales, named by a Meiji-era philosopher). Most local baths *are* separated by gender, such as nearby **Nurukawa Onsen** (ぬるかわ温泉; ☎0977-84-2869; 1490-1 Kawakami Takemoto; admission ¥430; ⏲8am-8.30pm), a cluster of small bathing rooms with lots of character and mountain views.

Double-peaked **Yufu-dake** (1584m) volcano overlooks Yufuin and takes about 90 minutes to climb. Some buses from Yufuin stop at the base of Yufu-dake at Yufu-tozanguchi (由布登山口; ¥360, 16 minutes, hourly).

Sleeping & Eating

Most patrons have their meals while relaxing in their inn, but there's a handful of eateries by the station.

Yufuin Country Road Youth Hostel HOSTEL ¥

(湯布院カントリーロードユースホステル; ☎0977-84-3734; www4.ocn.ne.jp/~yufuinyh; 441-29 Kawakami; dm HI member/nonmember ¥3000/3500; P ⊖ @ ☰) John Denver fans will love staying here, on a forested hillside overlooking the town. Especially pretty at night, this first-rate 25-bed hostel has its own onsen and hospitable English-speaking owners who've clearly made the singer a major part of their lives. Infrequent buses (¥200, Monday to Friday only) service the area, or you can arrange for pick up, but call ahead first.

Two meals are available for an extra ¥1750.

★**Makiba-no-ie** RYOKAN ¥¥

(牧場の家; ☎0977-84-2138; 2870-1 Kawakami; r per person with 2 meals from ¥13,110; P) There's atmosphere aplenty in these thatched-roof huts with sink and toilet surrounding a beautiful *rotemburo*. The antique-filled garden restaurant offers *jidori* (local chicken) and *Bungō-gyū teishoku* meals from ¥1600. Visitors can use the *rotemburo* for ¥600.

Yufu-no-Oyado Hotaru RYOKAN ¥¥

(由布のお宿ほたる; ☎0977-84-5151; www.yufuin-hotaru.com; 1791-1 Kawakita; r per person from ¥13,000; ⏲reception 7am-9pm; P) Lovely, family-run traditional ryokan nestled in cypress and bamboo. A variety of onsen baths make this a lovely spot for dippers, and one of the owners speaks excellent English.

Kamenoi Bessō RYOKAN ¥¥¥

(亀の井別荘; ☎0977-84-3166; www.kamenoi-bessou.jp; 2633-1 Kawakami; r per person with 2 meals from ¥35,790; P @) For the no-holds-barred Yufuin splurge, look no further. From Kinrin-ko, enter the *kayabuki* (thatched roof) gate down gravel paths to this campus of craftsman-style wooden buildings encircling stone baths with peaked wooden roofs. Meals are sure to contain local specialities, and staff seem never to have heard of the concept 'no'. Choose from Japanese, Western and combination Japanese-Western-style guest rooms.

Hidamari JAPANESE ¥
(陽だまり; ☎0977-84-2270; 2914 Kawakami; mains ¥756-1620; ⏰lunch 11am-3pm, shop 8.30am-5.30pm) Operated by local farming families, this informal restaurant and produce market nails the local standards like *toriten, dangojiru* and local beef in *teishoku* (set meals); order from the picture menu. The rest of the day you can buy *bentōs,* local yoghurt and ice cream. It's about 150m from the station, at the intersection with the large stone *torii*.

Izumi Soba NOODLES ¥¥
(泉そば; ☎0977-85-2283; 1599-1 Kawakami; soba from ¥1296; ⏰11am-5pm) There are less expensive *soba* shops in town, but at this classy place with a view of Kinrin-ko you can watch the noodles being made in the window before you sit down. The standard is *seirō-soba* (on a bamboo mat); *oroshi-soba* comes topped with grated daikon.

ℹ Information

Tourist Information Office (由布院温泉観光案内所; ☎0977-84-2446; ⏰9am-6pm) The tourist Information office inside the train station has some information in English, including a detailed walking map showing galleries, museums and onsen. Bicycles are available for rent from 9am to 5pm.

ℹ Getting There & Away

Trains connect Beppu with Yufuin (*futsū/tokkyū* ¥1110/1930, 1¼ hours/one hour) via Ōita.

Buses connect JR Beppu Station with Yufuin throughout the day (¥900, 50 minutes). Express buses serve Fukuoka (¥2800, 2¼ hours), Aso (¥2370, 2½ hours) and Kumamoto (¥3550, 4½ hours).

Electric bikes can be rented at the JR station (two hours with/without JR pass ¥400/500).

Usuki 臼杵

☎0972 / POP 41,500

Just outside Usuki are the thousand-year-old **Usuki Stone Buddhas** (臼杵石仏; Fukata; admission ¥540; ⏰6am-6pm, to 7pm Apr-Sep). Four clusters comprising 60-plus images (59 are designated national treasures) lie in a series of niches in a ravine. Some are complete statues, whereas others have only the heads remaining. It's truly a spiritual place if it's uncrowded.

Usuki has several temples and well-preserved traditional houses and a pretty downtown of historic wood and stucco homes and shops. On the last Saturday in August, the town hosts a **fire festival**, and other festivities are held throughout the year; ask for details at the **tourist information office** (臼杵市観光情報協会; ☎0972-63-2366; Usuki Station; ⏰9am-3pm) adjacent to Usuki Station. Find local history exhibits at the community centre **Sala de Usuki** (サーラデ臼杵; ☎0972-64-7271; ⏰9am-7pm).

About a dozen local restaurants boast some of the best *fugu* in Japan; expect to pay from about ¥5000/8000 for a lunch/dinner set, including sake.

Usuki is 40km southeast of Beppu. Take the JR Nippō line to Usuki Station (*tokkyū/futsū* ¥2070/940, 45/60 minutes), usually involving a change in Ōita. From here infrequent buses take 20 minutes to the Buddha images, or it's about ¥2020 by taxi or 30 minutes via bike. You can rent normal bikes (free!) or electric bikes (¥300 per hour) at the station.

Kunisaki Peninsula
国東半島

It would be easy to overlook this remote corner of Kyūshū north of Beppu, underserved as it is by public transport, but you'd be missing some of the most undisturbed *pawā spotto* (power spots, Japanese slang for spiritual places) in the nation. The town of Bungo-takada is nicknamed 'Buddha's Village' and the region is noted for its early Buddhist influence, including some rock-carved images linked to the more famous ones at Usuki. Your own car is useful for getting around the region efficiently.

The national treasure, 11th-century **Fuki-ji** (富貴寺; admission ¥200; ⏰8.30am-4.30pm) in Bungo-takada, is the oldest wooden structure in Kyūshū and one of the oldest wooden temples in Japan. Its overgrown grounds and moss-covered stupas complement the structure beautifully. Ōita Kōtsū buses from Usa Station go to Bungo-takada (¥810, 20 minutes); from there, it's a 10-minute taxi ride (around ¥1000).

In the centre of the peninsula, near the summit of Futago-san (721m), is **Futago-ji** (両子寺; 1548 Futago, Akimachi; admission ¥200; ⏰8am-5pm), founded in 718 and dedicated to Fudō-Myō-o, the fire-enshrouded, sword-wielding deity. It's a lovely climb, especially in spring or autumn and there are plenty of subtemples to explore around its forested gorges.

OFF THE BEATEN TRACK

KUJYŪ-SAN 九重山

Tucked in Ōita's southwest corner lies its biggest mountain range, collectively known as Kujyū-san, a favourite for hikers and mountaineering clubs. Accessed by car either from Ōita or from Kumamoto (via Aso National Park) it offers more than 20 peaks, including the island's highest, Naka-dake (1791m). Because of this, the range is known as the 'rooftop of Kyūshū'. One of the most popular climbs is from Makinotoi-tōge, which is an easy day hike thanks to access via a circuitous yet lovely road that goes most of the way. It's more peopled than other peak ascents. From there the avid can hike all the way to Naka-dake if they want to. The Aso Kujū-Kōgen Youth Hostel (p718) in Kurokawa Onsen is a good base camp for excursions.

Nearby **Taizō-ji** (胎蔵時; admission ¥200; ⌚8.30am-5pm) is known for its famously uneven stone stairs. Local legend says that they are so random and haphazard that the Oni (devils) must have created them in a single night.

Around 2km south of **Maki Ōdō Hall**, and deep in a forest along a mossy riverbed, are two Heian-period Buddha images carved into a cliff, a 6m figure of the Dainichi Buddha and an 8m figure of Fudō-Myō-o. Known as **Kumano Magaibutsu** (熊野磨崖仏; admission ¥200; ⌚8.30am-5pm), these are the largest Buddhist images of this type in Japan. If you thought the few hundred steps to the carvings were tough, wait until the next few hundred to the shrine at the top.

The sprawling, wooded and water-crossed **Usa-jingū** (宇佐神社; 2859 Ōaza), the original of which dates back some 1200 years, is the chief shrine among some 40,000 in Japan dedicated to the warrior-god Hachiman. It's a 4km bus or taxi ride from Usa Station (get off at Usa-Hachiman-mae), on the JR Nippō line from Beppu. Parking costs ¥400.

Timed right, this might be the most spectacular view you see your entire trip: the glowing setting sun sinking into the ocean or behind mud flats that seem to go right out to the horizon. **Soba Cafe Yuuhi** (ソバカフェゆうひ; ☎0978-25-8533; www.facebook.com/sobacafeyuuhi; 5125 Usuno; soba dishes ¥800-1000; ⌚11am-6pm Wed-Mon), a humble *soba* shop in a roadside turnout, sells handmade *soba* and rents SUP boards (¥2000 per hour) for use at high tide. On clear evenings you can even see the green flash, a rare phenomenon that causes a greenish color in the sun's final ray. Seeing it is thought to bring good luck.

Okinawa & the Southwest Islands

Includes ➡

Best Beaches

- ➡ Ida-no-hama, Iriomote-jima (p786)
- ➡ Sunset Beach, Ishigaki-jima (p782)
- ➡ Sunayama Beach, Miyako-jima (p777)
- ➡ Nishibama Beach, Aka-jima (p774)
- ➡ Furuzamami Beach, Zamami-jima (p774)

Best Diving Destinations

- ➡ Yonaguni-jima (p789)
- ➡ Kerama Islands (p774)
- ➡ Ishigaki-jima (p780)
- ➡ Iriomote-jima (p786)

Why Go?

Japan's Southwest Islands (南西諸島; Nansei-shotō) are a Japan you may not know exists: a chain of semitropical, coral-fringed islands evocative of Hawaii or Southeast Asia. They're a nature lover's paradise: in the northern Kagoshima Prefecture lush primeval forests hide among the craggy peaks of Yakushima, and the starfish-shaped Amami-Ōshima has fine beaches on its convoluted coastline. Heading south, Okinawa-hontō (沖縄本島) is the bustling main island of Okinawa Prefecture and jumping-off point for the nearby Keramas, tiny gems with white-sand beaches and crystal-clear waters. Miyako-jima boasts killer beaches and laid-back, retro appeal. And furthest south, the Yaeyama Islands boast Japan's best coral reefs, subtropical jungles and mangrove swamps.

But spectacular nature is only part of it – the Southwest Islands exude a peculiarly 'un-Japanese' culture. Indeed, they made up a separate country for most of their history, and the Ryūkyū cultural heart still beats strongly here.

When to Go

Naha

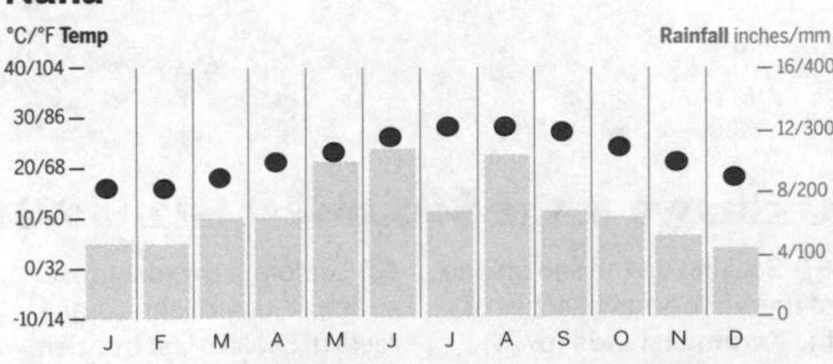

May & Jun Travel may coincide with the rainy season; while it's not too intense, sunshine may be scarce.

Jul–Sep This is the best time to enjoy the beaches, but expect some big crowds.

Oct–Mar The water is cooler but swimmable, and you'll have entire beaches to yourself.

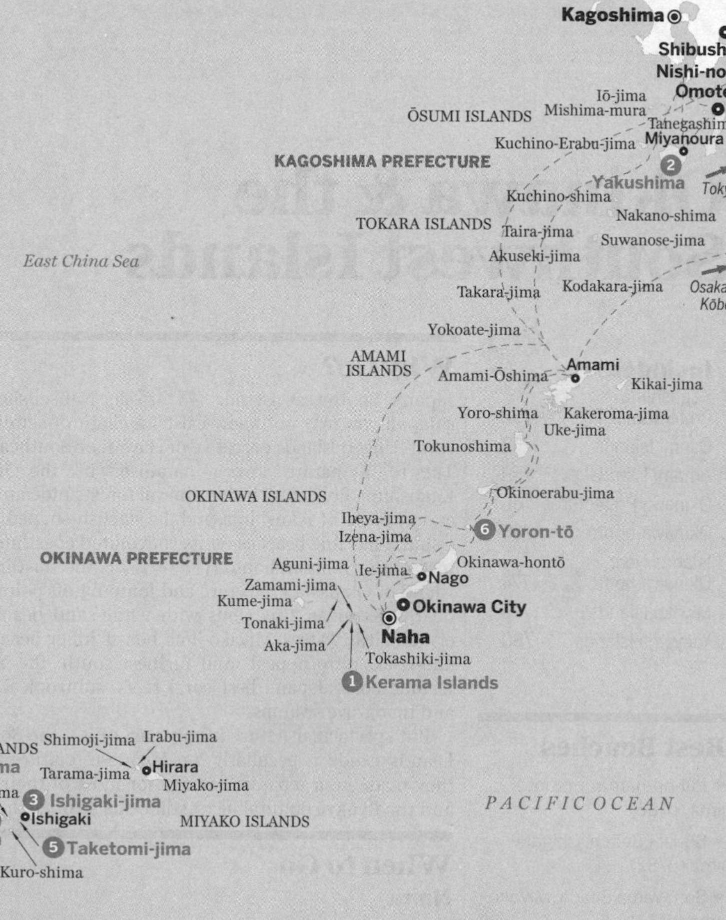

Okinawa & the Southwest Islands Highlights

1. Soaking up the sun on one of the white-sand beaches of the **Kerama Islands** (p774).
2. Hiking into the mountainous heart of **Yakushima** (p752) to commune with ancient *yakusugi* trees.
3. Diving with playful mantas off **Ishigaki-jima** (p780).
4. Exploring the mangrove swamps, jungles and coral reefs of Japan's last frontier, **Iriomote-jima** (p786).
5. Taking a ferry to a simpler time on the 'living museum' island of **Taketomi-jima** (p788).
6. Chilling out on peaceful **Yoron-tō** (p764), with its blissful scenery of beaches and sugarcane.
7. Searching the horizon for Taiwan from **Yonaguni-jima** (p789), Japan's westernmost island, and diving its mysterious underwater rock formations.

History

For centuries ruled by *aji* (local chieftains), in 1429 Okinawa and the Southwest Islands were united by Sho Hashi of the Chūzan kingdom, which led to the establishment of the Ryūkyū dynasty. During this period Sho Hashi increased contact with China, which contributed to the flourishing of Okinawan music, dance, literature and ceramics. In this 'Golden Era', weapons were prohibited, and the islands were rewarded with peace and tranquillity.

But the Ryūkyū kingdom was not prepared for war when the Shimazu clan of Satsuma (modern-day Kagoshima) invaded in 1609. The Shimazu conquered the kingdom easily and established severe controls over its trade. The islands were controlled with an iron fist, and taxed and exploited greedily for the next 250 years.

With the restoration of the Meiji emperor, the Ryūkyūs were annexed to Japan as Okinawa Prefecture in 1879. However, life hardly changed for the islanders as they were treated as foreign subjects by the Japanese government. Furthermore, the Meiji government stamped out local culture by outlawing the teaching of Ryūkyū history in schools, and establishing Japanese as the official language.

In the closing days of WWII, the Japanese military made a decision to use the islands of Okinawa as a shield against Allied forces. Sacrificing it cost the islanders dearly: more than 100,000 Okinawan civilians lost their lives in the Battle of Okinawa.

Following the war, the occupation of the Japanese mainland ended in 1952, but Okinawa remained under US control until 1972. Its return, however, was contingent upon Japan agreeing to allow the Americans to maintain bases on the islands and some 30,000 American military personnel remain.

Climate

The Southwest Islands have a subtropical climate. With the exception of the peaks of Yakushima, which can be snowcapped between December and February, there's no real winter. You can comfortably travel the Southwest Islands any time of year, but swimming might be uncomfortable between late October and early May, unless you're the hardy sort.

The average daily temperature on Okinawa-hontō in December is 20°C, while in July it is 30°C. The islands of Kagoshima Prefecture average a few degrees cooler, while those of the Yaeyama Islands and Miyako Islands are a few degrees warmer. The islands are most crowded during June, July and August and during the Golden Week holiday in early May. Outside of these times, the islands are often blissfully quiet.

The main thing to keep in mind when planning a trip to the Southwest Islands is the possibility of typhoons, which can strike any time between June and October. If you go then, build flexibility into your schedule, as typhoons often cause transport delays. Ideally, purchase tickets that allow changes without incurring a fee. The website of the **Japan Meteorological Agency** (www.jma.go.jp/en/typh) has the latest details on typhoons approaching Japan.

Language

Although the Ryūkyū islands used to have their own distinctive language, this has by and large disappeared. Standard Japanese is spoken by almost every resident of the islands. That said, travellers who speak some standard Japanese might find the local dialects and accent a little hard to catch.

Getting There & Away

There are flights between major cities in mainland Japan and Amami-Ōshima, Okinawa-hontō (Naha), Miyako-jima and Ishigaki-jima. Kagoshima has flights to/from all these islands and many of the smaller islands as well. Other islands such as Yonaguni-jima and Kume-jima can be reached from Naha or Ishigaki.

There are ferries between Tokyo, Osaka/Kōbe and Kagoshima to the Amami Islands and Okinawa-hontō, as well as plentiful ferries between Kagoshima and Yakushima and Tanegashima. Once you arrive in a port such as Amami (previously called Naze) on Amami-Ōshima or Naha on Okinawa-hontō, there are local ferry services to nearby islands. However, you cannot reach the Miyako Islands or Yaeyama Islands by ferry from mainland Japan or Okinawa-hontō; it's necessary to fly to these destinations.

If you are arriving in Japan by air, it is worth noting that Japan Airlines and All Nippon Airways both offer 'visit Japan'–type airfares for domestic flights within Japan – as long as they are bought outside Japan in conjunction with a ticket to Japan. Such tickets, if used to Okinawa, are an incredible saving from standard domestic airfares bought within the country.

ALL-YOU-CAN-SAIL TICKET

A Line Ferry (☎in Kagoshima 099-226-4141, in Tokyo 03-5643-6170; www.aline-ferry.com) sails from Kagoshima to Naha and offers a little-known but great deal in its *norihōdai kippu* (2nd-class sleeping rooms; ¥14,600), which lets you get on and off its south- or north-bound ferries freely within seven days; ferries stop at Amami-Ōshima, Tokunoshima, Okinoerabu-jima, Yoron-tō, and Motobu on Okinawa-hontō. On each leg of the trip, you must inform staff that you're hopping on and off, and you can travel in one direction only, but the savings on individual 2nd-class trips is more than ¥6000.

Getting Around

Aside from ferries, there are also excellent air networks throughout the islands. While most islands have public bus systems, there are usually not more than a few buses per day on each route. We recommend bringing an International Driving Permit and renting a car or scooter, particularly on Yakushima, Ishigaki, Iriomote and Okinawa-hontō.

KAGOSHIMA PREFECTURE

The northern end of the Southwest Islands is part of Kagoshima Prefecture (鹿児島県; Kagoshima-ken), and contains three island groups (island groups are called 'shotō' or 'rettō' in Japanese). All are accessible by ferry or plane.

Northernmost are the Ōsumi Islands, which are home to the island of Yakushima, one of the most popular destinations in the Southwest Islands. Next are the Tokara Islands, consisting of 12 rarely visited volcanic islets; these are the most remote destinations in the region. Southernmost are the Amami Islands, which are home to the population centre of Amami-Ōshima as well as several more picturesque islands. Located 380km south of Kyūshū, this group has a pronounced tropical feel.

Ōsumi Islands 大隅諸島

The Ōsumi Islands comprise the two main islands of Yakushima and Tanegashima and the seldom-visited triumvirate of islands known as Mishima-mura. The all-star attraction in the group is Yakushima, a virtual paradise for nature lovers that attracts large numbers of both domestic and international travellers. Tanegashima, which is famous as the home of Japan's space program, sees few foreign travellers, though it is a popular surfing destination for Japanese. The most commonly visited island in the Mishima-mura group is tiny Iō-jima, a rarely visited gem of a volcanic island with excellent onsen (hot springs).

Yakushima 屋久島

☎0997 / POP 13,054

Designated a Unesco World Heritage Site in 1993, Yakushima is one of the most rewarding islands in the Southwest Islands. The craggy mountain peaks of the island's interior are home to the world-famous *yakusugi* (屋久杉; *Cryptomeria japonica*), ancient cedar trees that are said to have been the inspiration for some of the scenes in Miyazaki Hayao's animation classic *Princess Mononoke*.

Hiking among the high peaks and mossy forests is the main activity on Yakushima, but the island is also home to some excellent coastal onsen and a few sandy beaches.

Keep in mind that Yakushima is a place of extremes: the mountains wring every last drop of moisture from the passing clouds and the interior of the island is one of the wettest places in Japan. In the winter the peaks may be covered in snow, while the coast is still relatively balmy. Whatever you do, come prepared and don't set off on a hike without a good map and the proper gear. An International Driving Permit will also vastly increase your enjoyment here, as buses are few and far between.

Sights

Yakushima's main port is Miyanoura (宮之浦), on the island's northeast coast. This is the most convenient place to be based, as most buses originate from here. From Miyanoura, a road runs around the perimeter of the island, passing through the secondary port of Anbō (安房) on the east coast, and then through the hot-springs town of Onoaida (尾の間) in the south. Heading north from Miyanoura, the road takes you to the town of Nagata (永田), which has a brilliant stretch of white-sand beach.

★Yakusugi Museum MUSEUM
(屋久杉自然館; ☎0997-46-3113; 2739-343 Anbō; admission ¥600; ⏲9am-5pm, closed 1st Tue of the month) In a forested spot with sea views, the Yakusugi Museum has informative, beautifully designed exhibits about *yakusugi* and the history of the islanders' relationship to these magnificent trees. The museum offers an excellent audioguide in English. It's conveniently located on the road leading up to Yakusugi Land.

Nagata Inaka-hama BEACH
(永田いなか浜) On the island's northwest coast in the village of Nagata is a beautiful beach for sunsets, and it's where sea turtles lay their eggs from May to July. It's beside the Inaka-hama bus stop, served by Nagata-bound buses from Miyanoura.

Umigame-kan MUSEUM
(うみがめ館; ☎0997-49-6550; 489-8 Nagata; admission ¥200; ⏲9am-5pm Wed-Mon) This nonprofit organisation has displays and information about turtles, mostly in Japanese. During nesting (June and July) and hatching (August) seasons, they arrange night tours on the beach. In order to protect the nesting turtles, eggs and hatchlings, it is imperative that visitors go with a sanctioned tour.

Issō-kaisuiyokujō BEACH
(一湊海水浴場) A fine beach, located on the north coast of the island, about midway between Miyanoura and Nagata. It's a short walk from the Yahazu bus stop (served by any Nagata-bound bus from Miyanoura).

Ōko-no-taki WATERFALL
(大川の滝) On the west coast is Yakushima's highest waterfall, at 88m. It's a five-minute walk from Ōko-no-taki bus stop, which is the last stop for some of the buses running south and west from Miyanoura and Anbō (note that only two buses a day run all the way out here).

Yakushima Environmental & Cultural Village Center MUSEUM
(屋久島環境文化村センター; ☎0997-42-2900; admission & film ¥520; ⏲9am-5pm, closed 3rd Tue) In Miyanoura at the corner of the ferry-terminal road. It has exhibits about the island's natural environment and history, with limited English signs. It screens a 25-minute film (sparsely subtitled in English) at 20 minutes past the hour.

Activities

Hiking

Hiking is the best way to experience Yakushima's beauty. If you're planning anything more than a short stroll around Yakusugi Land, pick up a copy of the Japanese-language *Yama-to-Kougen-no-Chizu-Yakushima* (山と高原の地図屋久島; ¥1080), available at major bookshops in Japan.

Even though trails can be very crowded during holidays, be sure to alert someone at your accommodation of your intended route and fill in a *tōzan todokede* (route plan) at the trailhead.

The most popular hike is to **Jōmon-sugi** (縄文杉), a monster of a *yakusugi* estimated to be between 3000 and 7000 years old. Most hikers reach the tree via the 19.5km, eight-to-10-hour round-trip from the **Arakawa-tozanguchi** (荒川登山口) trailhead (604m). From March through November, in order to limit traffic congestion, all hikers must transfer to an Arakawa Mountain Bus (¥1740 round-trip; five departures and nine returns daily) at the Yakusugi Museum carpark. You must buy a ticket at least a day in advance; also note that this fare is not covered by the one- or two-day bus passes. Two daily buses run to and from Miyanoura (¥930, one hour 20 minutes, March to November).

A shorter and arguably more beautiful hike is the round trip from the **Shiratani-unsuikyō-tozanguchi** (白谷雲水峡登山口) trailhead (622m), served by up to 10 daily buses to and from Miyanoura (¥530, 40 minutes, March to November). Budget three or four hours for this hike, and bring ¥300 for admission.

The granddaddy of hikes here is the day-long outing to the 1935m summit of **Miyanoura-dake**, the highest point in

> **YAKUMONKEY**
>
> The yakumonkey.com website is a super-handy planning resource for visitors to Yakushima. If you're going to do some serious hiking on the island, it's worth purchasing the excellent *Yakumonkey Guide to Yakushima* before you arrive, as it's near impossible to find on the ground. Full of useful information on Yakushima, it includes detailed descriptions of hikes and trails. It's available in both print and ebook formats.

Yakushima

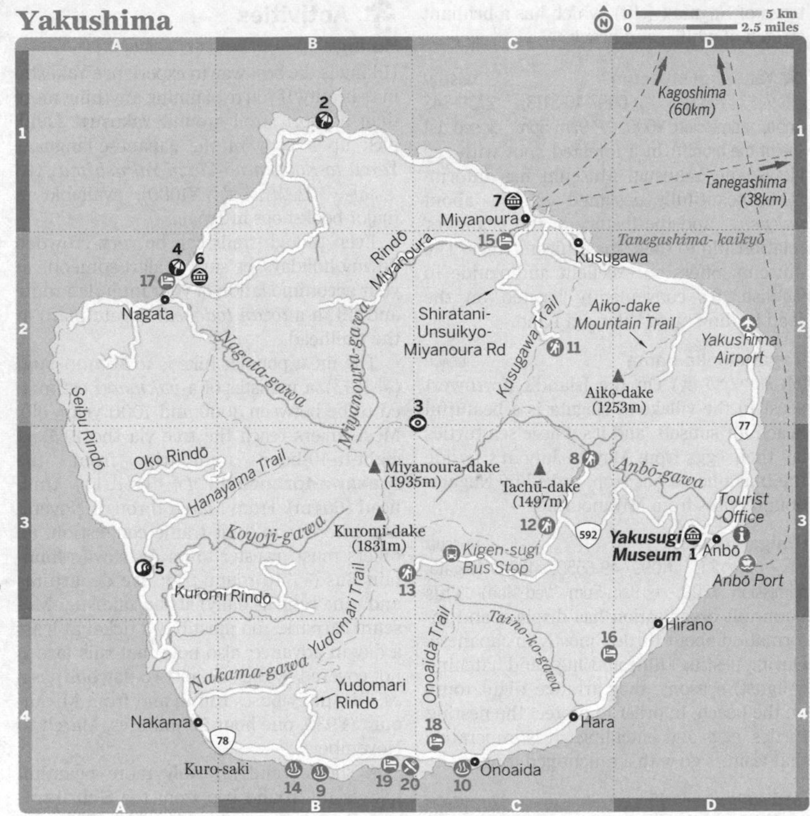

southern Japan. Fit climbers should allow about seven hours return from **Yodogawa-tozanguchi** (淀川登山口) trailhead (1370m). Yodogawa-tozanguchi is about 1.5km (about 30 minutes) beyond the **Kigen-sugi bus stop**, served by two buses a day to/from Anbō (¥910, one hour). The buses do not give you sufficient time to complete the round-trip in a day – an early-morning taxi from Miyanoura (around ¥11,000) gives you time to make the second bus back to Anbō.

Finally, it's possible to make a traverse of Miyanoura-dake with a stop at Jōmon-sugi en route. Do not attempt this in a day; you'll have to spend the night in one of the *yama-goya* (mountain huts) above Jōmon-sugi. Typical routes are between Yodogawa and Arakawa or Yodogawa and Shiratani-unsuikyō. A full traverse of the island is described in Lonely Planet's *Hiking in Japan*.

If you're feeling a little less adventurous, a visit to **Yakusugi Land** (ヤクスギランド; admission ¥300; ⏲9am-5pm) is a great way to see some *yakusugi* without a long trek into the forest. It offers shorter hiking courses over wooden boardwalks, and longer hikes deep into the ancient cedar forest. There are four buses a day to and from Anbō (¥720, 40 minutes).

Onsen

Yakushima has several onsen (hot springs), from beautifully desolate seaside pools to upmarket hotel facilities. The seaside onsen listed here are *konyoku* onsen (mixed-sex baths) where swimsuits are not allowed; women traditionally wrap themselves in a thin towel for modesty.

Hiraiuchi Kaichū Onsen ONSEN
(平内海中温泉; admission ¥100; ⏲24hr) Onsen lovers will be in heaven here. The outdoor baths are in the rocks by the sea and can only

Yakushima

be entered at or close to low tide. You can walk to the baths from the Kaichū Onsen bus stop, but the next stop, Nishikaikon, is actually closer. From Nishikaikon, walk downhill towards the sea for about 200m and take a right at the bottom of the hill.

Yudomari Onsen ONSEN
(湯泊温泉; admission ¥100; 24hr) This blissfully serene onsen can be entered at any tide. Get off at the Yudomari bus stop and take the road opposite the post office in the direction of the sea. Once you enter the village, the way is marked. It's a 300m walk and you pass a great banyan tree en route.

Onoaida Onsen ONSEN
(尾之間温泉; 136-2 Onoaida; admission ¥200; 7am-9.30pm May-Oct, to 9pm Nov-Apr, from noon Mon) In the village of Onoaida is a rustic indoor bathhouse that is divided by gender. Expect to rub shoulders with the village elders here. The water is naturally, divinely hot. It's about 350m uphill from the Onoaida Onsen bus stop.

Sleeping

The most convenient place to be based is Miyanoura. You'll also find lodgings in larger villages and several bare-bones *yama-goya* in the mountains. In July and August and the spring Golden Week holiday, it's best to try to reserve ahead since places fill up early.

★ **Sankara Hotel & Spa** HOTEL ¥¥¥
(0997-47-3488, toll-free 0800-800-6007; www.sankarahotel-spa.com; 553 Haginoue, Mugio; r per person with breakfast from ¥35,000; P @) Overlooking Yakushima's southeast coast, this stunning collection of luxury villas blends ocean views with Balinese design elements. Sustainable practices at Sankara include all water used on the property sourced from mountain runoff, and the restaurant utilising as much local and organic produce as possible, much of which is grown expressly for the hotel. Guests 15 years and older only.

The main restaurant's French fusion cuisine is created by Chef Takei Chiharu, who trained at several three-Michelin-star establishments in France. Staff can pick you up, but if you have transport, look for the green signs in English along the road between Hirano and Hara.

MIYANOURA

Miyanoura Portside Youth Hostel HOSTEL ¥
(宮之浦ポートサイドユースホステル; 0997-49-1316; www.yakushima-yh.net; 278-2 Miyanoura; dm/d ¥3800/4400; P @) This simple and clean youth hostel doesn't offer meals, but there are several good restaurants close by. It's a 10-minute walk from Miyanoura port – turn left off of the main port road and veer left after passing the portside park; it's about 100m further.

Lodge Yaedake-sansō LODGE ¥¥
(ロッジ八重岳山荘; 0997-42-1551; www17.ocn.ne.jp/~yakusima/lodge/index.html; Miyanoura; r per person with meals ¥8100; P) This secluded accommodation features Japanese- and Western-style rooms in rustic riverside cabins connected by wooden walkways. Soak up the beauty of your surroundings in the communal baths; children will enjoy splashing in the river. Meals served in the tatami dining room are balanced and exquisite. The lodge is located inland on the Miyanoura-gawa; staff can pick you up in Miyanoura.

If it's full, the lodge also runs the **Minshuku Yaedake Honkan** (民宿八重岳本館; ☎0997-42-2552; 208 Miyanoura; r per person incl meals ¥6800; P) in town.

ONOAIDA

★Yakushima Youth Hostel HOSTEL ¥
(屋久島ユースホステル; ☎0997-47-3751; www.yakushima-yh.net; 258-24 Hirauchi; dm/s ¥3540/5640; P@🛜) This well-run youth hostel is about 3km west of Onoaida, nestled into the forest. Accommodation is in either Japanese- or Western-style dorms, and the shared kitchen and bathroom facilities are spotless. Get off any southbound buses from Miyanoura at the Hirauchi-iriguchi bus stop and take the road towards the sea for about 200m.

Yakushima Iwasaki Hotel HOTEL ¥¥¥
(屋久島いわさきホテル; ☎0997-47-3888; http://yakushima.iwasakihotels.com; 1306 Onoaida; d from ¥26,140; P@🛜🏊) This luxury hotel commands an impressive view from its hilltop location above Onoaida. Spacious Western-style rooms have either ocean or mountain views. The hotel has its own onsen and meals are available in two restaurants. Southbound buses from Miyanoura stop right in front.

NAGATA

★Sōyōtei RYOKAN ¥¥
(送陽邸; ☎0997-45-2819; www.soyotei.com; r per person incl meals ¥13,650; P) On the northwest coast near Nagata Inaka-hama, this gorgeous, family-run guesthouse has a collection of semidetached units that boast private verandahs and ocean views. The traditional structures feature rooftops unique to Yakushima, with stones anchoring the roof tiles – you'll recognise the place immediately. There are several baths for private use, including an outdoor bath overlooking the crashing waves.

Lovely seafood-focused meals are served in a communal, open-air dining room that looks out over Inaka-hama and the sea.

Eating

There are a few restaurants in each of the island's villages, with the best selection in Miyanoura. If you're staying anywhere but Miyanoura, ask for the set two-meal plan at your lodgings. If you're going hiking, you can ask your lodging to prepare a *bentō* (boxed meal) the night before you set out.

If you need to stock up on supplies for camping or hiking, you'll find **Yakuden** (ヤクデン; ⏲9am-10pm) supermarket on the main street in Miyanoura, just north of the entrance to the pier area.

Naa Yuu Cafe CAFE ¥
(なーゆーカフェ; ☎0997-49-3195; 349-109 Hirauchi; lunch sets ¥850-1250; ⏲11.30am-8pm Tue-Sun, closed 2nd & 4th Tue; 📋) Down a dirt road and facing a field of wild reeds, this cute cafe feels vaguely Hawaiian. The menu, however, leans more toward Thailand. Lunch sets range from red curry to Kagoshima black pork–sausage pizza. Look for a green sign in English, about 3km west of Onoaida.

Restaurant Yakushima JAPANESE ¥
(レストラン屋久島; ☎0997-42-0091; 2nd fl, Yakushima Kankō Centre; meals ¥1000; ⏲9am-4pm; @) This simple restaurant serves a ¥520 morning set breakfast with eggs, toast and coffee and a tasty *tobi uo sashimi teishoku* (flying fish sashimi set meal; ¥980) for lunch.

SEA TURTLES

Loggerhead sea turtles and green sea turtles come ashore on the beaches of Yakushima to lay their eggs. Unfortunately, human activity can significantly interfere with the egg-laying process. Thus we recommend that you keep the following rules in mind when visiting the beaches of Yakushima (particularly those on the northwest coast):

- Never approach a sea turtle that has come ashore.
- Do not start fires on the beach as the light will confuse the chicks (who use moonlight to orient themselves). Likewise, do not shine torches (flashlights) or car headlights at or near the beach.
- Do not walk on the beach at night.
- Be extremely careful when you walk on the beach, as you might inadvertently step on a newly hatched turtle.
- If you want to observe the turtles, enquire at Umigame-kan (p753).

Look for the green, two-storey building on the main road, near the road to the pier.

Shiosai SEAFOOD ¥¥
(潮騒; ☎0997-42-2721; 305-3 Miyanoura; dishes ¥1200; ⏲11.30am-2pm & 5.30-9.30pm Fri-Wed) Find a full range of Japanese standards such as *sashimi teishoku* (sashimi set; ¥1700) or *ebi-furai teishoku* (fried shrimp set; ¥1400). Look for the blue and whitish building with automatic glass doors along the main road through Miyanoura.

Information

The best place to get money on Yakushima is at one of the island's post offices, the most convenient of which is in Miyanoura.

Tourist Information Centre (☎0997-42-1019; ⏲8.30am-5pm) Miyanoura's ferry terminal has a useful information centre in the round white building as you emerge from the ferry offices. It can help you find lodgings and answer all questions about the island.

Tourist Office (☎0997-46-2333; ⏲9am-5.30pm) In Anbō there's a smaller tourist office in the first alley off the main road just north of the river.

Getting There & Away

AIR

Japan Air Commuter (JAC) has flights between Kagoshima and Yakushima. Yakushima's **airport** (屋久島空港; ☎0997-42-1200) is on the northeastern coast between Miyanoura and Anbō. Hourly buses stop at the airport, though you can usually phone your accommodation for a pick-up or take a taxi.

BOAT

Hydrofoil services operate between Kagoshima and Yakushima, some of which stop at Tanegashima en route. **Tane Yaku Jetfoil** (☎in Kagoshima 099-226-0128, in Miyanoura 0997-42-2003) runs four Toppy and Rocket hydrofoils per day between Kagoshima (leaving from the high-speed ferry terminal just to the south of Minamifutō pier) and Miyanoura (¥9100, one hour 45 minutes for direct sailings, two hours 40 minutes with a stop in Tanegashima). There are also two hydrofoils per day between Kagoshima and Anbō Port (2½ hours) on Yakushima.

The normal ferry *Yakushima 2* sails from Kagoshima's Minamifutō pier for Yakushima's Miyanoura port (one way/return ¥4800/8300). It leaves at 8.30am and takes four hours.

The *Hibiscus* also sails between Kagoshima and Yakushima, leaving at 6pm, stopping overnight in Tanegashima, and arriving at Miyanoura at 7am the following day (one way/return ¥3600/7200). Reservations aren't usually necessary for this ferry; it normally leaves from Kagoshima's Taniyama pier.

> **STAY DRY!**
>
> Yakushima is one of the wettest places on earth; it rains *a lot* in the island's interior. Be sure to prepare adequately for hiking in rainforests in which you may find yourself slogging through torrential rain for a whole day. Mountain huts *(yama-goya)* have no staff, food or sleeping bags, so bring what you need.
>
> **Nakagawa Sports** (ナカガワスポーツ; ☎0997-42-0341; http://yakushima-sp.com; 421-6 Miyanoura; rainwear rentals ¥1200-2400; ⏲9am-7pm, closed every other Wed) in Miyanoura rents everything from rainwear and waterproof hiking boots (also in large sizes) to tents and baby carriers.

Getting Around

Local buses travel the coastal road part way around Yakushima roughly every hour or two, though only a few head up into the interior. Buses are expensive and you'll save a lot of money by purchasing a *Furii Jōsha Kippu*, which is good for unlimited travel on Yakushima Kotsu buses. One-/two-day passes cost ¥2000/3000 and are available at the Tane Yaku Jetfoil office in Miyanoura.

Hitching is also possible, but the best way to get around the island is to rent a car. **Toyota Rent-a-Car** (☎0997-42-2000; https://rent.toyota.co.jp; up to 12hr from ¥5250; ⏲8am-8pm) is located near the terminal in Miyanoura.

Tanegashima 種子島

☎0997 / POP 30,298

A long, narrow island about 20km northeast of Yakushima, Tanegashima is a laid-back destination popular with Japanese surfers and beach lovers. Home to Japan's Space Centre, Tanegashima was where firearms were first introduced to Japan by shipwrecked Portuguese in 1543. Good ferry connections make this island easy to pair with a trip to Yakushima. Unfortunately, the relative lack of buses makes it difficult to enjoy this island without a rental car or scooter, or, at least, a good touring bicycle.

The island's main port of **Nishi-no-Omote** (西の表) is located on the northwest coast of the island, while the airport is about halfway down the island near the west coast.

WORTH A TRIP

GET AWAY FROM IT ALL

Depending on when you go, the more remote Southwest Islands can be havens of tranquillity with few other travellers. But if you really want to escape, it's just a question of hopping on the right ferry. In Kagoshima Prefecture, **Iō-jima** (硫黄島) is a tiny bamboo-covered island with a smouldering volcano and two brilliant seaside onsen. **Mishima Sonei Ferry** (☎099-222-3141) sails there from Kagoshima. The city is also home to **Ferry Toshima** (☎099-222-2101) which plies the **Tokara-rettō** (トカラ列島), a chain of seven inhabited and five uninhabited islands between Yakushima and Amami-Ōshima that offer plenty of hiking, fishing and onsen. Even for the Japanese, they seem like the end of the world.

The best beaches and most of the surfing breaks are on the east coast of the island, which is also home to an onsen.

Sights & Activities

Space Science & Technology Museum MUSEUM
(宇宙科学技術館; ☎0997-26-9244; Kukinaga, Minamitane-chō; ⏰9.30am-5.30pm Tue-Sun, closed on launch days) FREE Tanegashima's Space Centre, on the spectacular southeastern coast of the island, is a large parklike complex with rocket-launch facilities. Its Space Science & Technology Museum details the history of Japan's space program, with some English labels. There are models of Japan's rockets and some of the satellites it has launched.

Buses running from Nishi-no-Omote all the way to Tanegashima Space Center take two hours.

Tanegashima Development Centre – Gun Museum MUSEUM
(種子島開発総総合センター・鉄砲館; ☎0997-23-3215; 7585 Nishi-no-Omote; admission ¥420, combo ticket ¥550; ⏰8.30am-5pm, closed 25th of each month) Though one focus is on the history of guns in Tanegashima, with an excellent collection of antique firearms, this is actually a cultural and natural-history museum as well. If you make as straight a beeline as possible up the hill from the port, you'll find it at a crossroads; the building looks like the stern of an old galleon. The combined ticket includes admission to an interesting **samurai house** (月窓亭; ☎0997-22-2101; http://gessoutei.blogspot.com/p/english.html; 7528 Nishi-no-Omote; admission ¥200; ⏰9am-5pm, closed 25th of each month) about 50m away.

Takezaki-kaigan BEACH
(竹崎海岸) Nearby to the Space Centre, this coastline is home to a beautiful stretch of white sand popular with surfers. The best spot to enjoy it is the beach in front of the Iwasaki Hotel (closest bus stop: Iwasaki Hotel), which has some impressive rock formations.

Nagahama-kaigan BEACH
(長浜海岸) The west coast of Tanegashima is also home to a 12km stretch of beach that is equally popular with surfers and egg-laying sea turtles.

Nakatane-chō Onsen Center ONSEN
(中種子町温泉保養センター; ☎0997-27-9211; 5542 Sakai, Nakatane; per person ¥300; ⏰11am-8pm Fri-Wed) Hot springs at Kuma-no-kaigan; the closest bus stop is Kuma-no-kaisuiyokujō.

Sleeping

Most travellers base themselves in the port town of Nishi-no-Omote. Listings in this section begin in Nishi-no-Omote and end on Tanegashima's east coast

Nagareboshi MINSHUKU ¥
(流れ星; ☎0997-23-0034; www.t-shootingstar.com; 7603-10 Nishi-no-Omote; r with shared bathroom from ¥3500; P @ 📶) Run by a friendly, English-speaking woman, charming Nagareboshi has spotless, spacious rooms and a very laid-back vibe. From the pier road in Nishi-no-Omote, walk to the stoplight and jog around the right side of the post office, then walk uphill, bearing right at the top of the steps. Look for the sign upslope, and veer right towards the temple.

Miharu-sō RYOKAN ¥
(美春荘; ☎0997-22-1393; 7486-6 Nishi-no-Omote; r per person with breakfast ¥5400; P ⊖ 📶) Tidy Japanese-style rooms in this family-run ryokan in Nishi-no-Omote are cosy and full of natural light. If you speak Japanese, you can hit up the owner for local info on surf spots. If not, he's likely to point you in the right direction anyhow.

Mauna Village BUNGALOWS ¥¥
(マウナヴィレッジ; ☎0997-25-0811; www.mauna-village.com; 9668-40 Genna; r per person ¥4500-7300; P 📶) On the east coast, this collection of seven cute, red-roofed cottages is popular with surfers and families. Some units have sea views and all have toilets, but bathing facilities are shared. Guests can use the small communal kitchen.

East Coast BUNGALOWS ¥¥
(イーストコースト; ☎0997-25-0763; www.eastcoast.jp; Kanehama-kaigan; s/d/tr from ¥2700/5400/8100; large cabin ¥13,000; P) With only two cosy, fully-equipped bungalows near the local break, this place is (as you might guess) on the east coast of Tanegashima. Reservations are essential. The owner is an English-speaking Japanese surfer who also runs a great on-site cafe (open from 11am to 5pm).

Eating

Surf Bar Dolphin BAR ¥
(☎0997-23-0747; www.dolphintrip.net; 21 Higashi-chō; burger sets ¥1100-2000; ⏲11.30am-2.30pm & 7pm-2am; 📄) During the day, this chilled-out surf bar in Nishi-no-Omote is famous for its Tanegashima burger (with egg, bacon, lettuce, tomato, cheddar), flying-fish burger and fries; by night, it spins funky grooves and friendly conversation. It's a short walk south from the post office, with bright red signage in English.

Koryōri Shirō IZAKAYA ¥¥
(小料理しろう; ☎0997-23-2117; 24-6 Higashi-chō; dishes from ¥500; ⏲5-11pm) Head to this friendly little *izakaya* (pub-eatery) in Nishi-no-Omote to sample tasty dishes such as the *sashimi teishoku* (sashimi set; ¥1200). There are plants out the front and blue-and-white *noren* (doorway curtains). It's along the main road east of the post office.

Information

There is a helpful **information office** (種子島観光案内所; ☎0997-23-0111; ⏲9am-5pm) at the pier in Nishi-no-Omote, inside the Cosmo ferry office/waiting room. The road from the Nishi-no-Omote pier dead-ends at the post office, which houses an international ATM.

Getting There & Away

Tanegashima has five flights to and from Kagoshima (30 minutes) on Japan Air Commuter (JAC).

Tane Yaku Jetfoil (p757) has four daily high-speed ferries (¥7700, 1½ hours) between Kagoshima and Yakushima, some of which stop at Tanegashima. Finally, **Kashō Kaiun** (☎099-261-7000) operates one normal ferry a day between Kagoshima and Tanegashima (¥3500, three hours and 40 minutes).

Amami Islands 奄美諸島

The islands of the Amami group are the southernmost in Kagoshima Prefecture. Amami-Ōshima, the largest and most popular island, lies at the northern end of the group. It serves as the main transport hub and boasts excellent beaches, as well as dense jungle. The other islands in the chain are dominated by sugarcane fields but also have some good beaches. Heading south, Tokunoshima is famous for its 'bovine sumo', Okinoerabu-jima has intriguing caves and tiny Yoron-tō is fringed with intriguing beaches.

Amami-Ōshima 奄美大島

☎0997 / POP 62,532

Amami-Ōshima is Japan's third-largest offshore island after Okinawa-hontō and Sado-ga-shima. With a mild subtropical climate year-round, the island is home to some unusual flora and fauna, including tree ferns and mangrove forests. The coastline of the island is incredibly convoluted – a succession of bays, points and inlets, punctuated by the occasional white-sand beach – making the island an interesting alternative to islands further south.

The main city and port, Amami (also called Naze; 名瀬), is on the north coast. The island's tiny airport is 55 minutes away by bus (¥1100, almost hourly, buses are timed to meet flights) on the northeast end of the island. The best beaches are also at the northeast end.

Sights & Activities

Amami-Ōshima is great to explore by touring bike or rental car. The coastal route to **Uken** (宇検) on the west coast has some lovely stretches. Another option is Rte 58 south to **Koniya** (古仁屋), from where you can continue southeast to the **Honohoshi-kaigan** (ホノホシ海岸), a rocky beach with incredible coastal formations, or catch a ferry to **Kakeroma-jima** (加計呂麻島), a small island with a few shallow beaches.

Amami-Ōshima

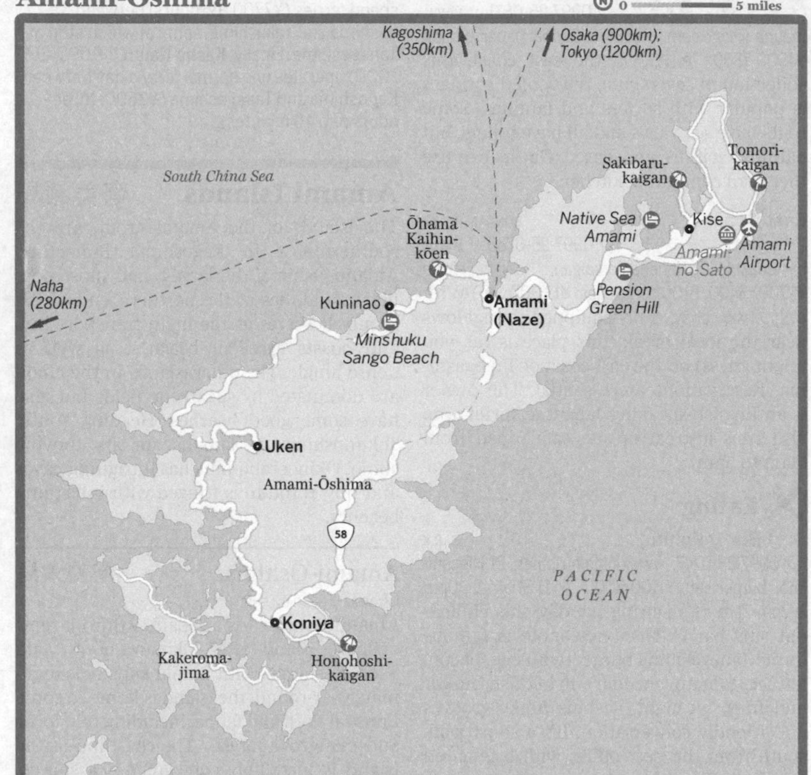

Ōhama-kaihin-kōen BEACH
(大浜海浜公園) The closest beach to Amami, it's popular for swimming, snorkelling and sea kayaking in summer. It can get crowded and is not as nice as beaches further afield, but it's convenient. Take an Ōhama-bound bus from Amami and get off at the Ōhama stop (¥400).

Sakibaru-kaigan BEACH
(崎原海岸) This stunner of a beach lies about 4.5km down a point of land just north of Kise (about 20km northeast of Amami). Take a Sani-bound bus from Amami and get off at Kiseura (¥950), and then walk. If you're driving, it's marked in English off the main road (be prepared for *narrow* roads).

Tomori-kaigan BEACH
(土盛海岸) It's easy to get to this beach, which also offers brilliant white sand and some great snorkelling with a channel leading outside the reef. It's about 3km north of the airport. Take a Sani-bound bus from Amami and get off at Tomori (¥1210).

Amami-no-Sato MUSEUM
(奄美の郷; 0997-55-2333; www.amamipark.com; 1834 Setta, Kasari-chō; admission ¥620; 9am-6pm, to 7pm Jul & Aug, closed 1st & 3rd Wed) Though most displays are in Japanese, there's enough multimedia to make this Amami cultural and natural-history museum interesting even if finer details are lost. Short documentary films illustrating island traditions, musical exhibits and dioramas of local homes all bring Amami traditions to life. This cultural centre, as well as an art museum showcasing the work of Tanaka Isson, are part of Amami Park, five minutes by bus from the airport.

Sleeping

Minshuku Sango Beach MINSHUKU ¥¥
(民宿さんごビーチ; ☎0997-57-2580; sango beach0315@gmail.com; 68 Kuninao; r per person incl 2 meals from ¥6800; P @) Overlooking a lovely sandy beach, this laid-back *minshuku* (Japanese guesthouse) offers peace in abundance. Guests sleep in six semidetached units and meals are taken overlooking the sea. Call ahead for a pick-up from the ferry port or from Amami. From the airport, take a bus heading to Amami (¥800), and get off at the West Court–mae stop.

Pension Green Hill GUESTHOUSE ¥¥
(ペンショングリーンヒル; ☎0997-62-5180; www.greenhill-amami.com; 1728-2 Akaogi, Tatsugō-chō; s/d with 2 meals ¥9180/17,280; P @) A favourite among Japanese surfers, convivial Green Hill has ocean views (including the local surf spot, Tebiro Point), and Japanese- and Western-style rooms, some with lofts. It's about 30 minutes from the airport and a few minutes' walk to the beach. Have a Japanese speaker call ahead to request a pick up for you; very little English is spoken here.

Amami Sun Plaza Hotel BUSINESS HOTEL ¥¥
(奄美サンプラザホテル; ☎0997-53-5151; www.amami-sunplaza.co.jp; 2-1 Minato-machi; s/tw from ¥6500/9500; P @) This squeaky-clean, comfortable, accommodating business hotel is right in downtown Amami, with nearby access to local restaurants. It's a five-minute taxi ride to the port, making it very convenient if you're leaving town on an early ferry.

Native Sea Amami HOTEL ¥¥¥
(ネイティブシー奄美; ☎0997-62-2385; www.native-sea.com; 835 Ashitoku, Tatsugō-chō; per person incl 2 meals from ¥16,200; P @) About 28km east of Amami (or 3km from the Akaogi bus stop), this dive centre–resort has comfortable wood-floored, Western-style accommodation in a room block perched on a promontory over a lovely bay. There is a nice shallow beach below the resort and the dining room and guest rooms have gorgeous, sweeping views.

Eating

Okonomiyaki Mangetsu OKONOMIYAKI ¥
(お好み焼き満月; ☎0997-53-2052; 2-2 Irifune-chō; dishes ¥1000; ⏲noon-2am) Locals pile in for the excellent *okonomiyaki* (batter and cabbage cakes cooked on a griddle) at this excellent Amami eatery. For carnivores, we recommend the *kurobuta* mix (pork-shrimp-squid mix; ¥1260), and for vegies, the *isobecchi* (*mochi* rice and *nori;* ¥750). There's a picture menu.

Hokorashi-ya IZAKAYA ¥¥
(誇羅司屋; ☎0997-52-1158; 13-6 Irifune-chō; meals ¥3000; ⏲5.30pm-midnight) An atmospheric *izakaya* in downtown Amami, Hokorasha-ya dishes up toothsome Amami specialities such as *aosa-no-tempura* (fish-and-shellfish cakes fried in a freshwater seaweed batter; ¥600) and a regional *chāhan* (fried rice flecked with bonito and egg; ¥800), as well as beautifully plated sushi and sashimi specials. There's a picture menu.

Information

Tourist Information Counter (☎0997-63-2295; ⏲8am-5.30pm) In the airport arrivals hall; can help with maps and bus schedules.

Getting There & Around

Amami-Ōshima has flights to/from Tokyo, Osaka and Kagoshima with Japan Airlines (JAL) or JAC.

Ryukyu Air Commuter (RAC) operates a daily flight between Naha and Amami-Ōshima. There are also flights between Amami-Ōshima and the other islands in the Amami group.

Amami-Ōshima has a good bus system, but you will definitely appreciate a rental car if you have an International Driving Permit. **Times Car Rental** (タイムズレンタカー; ☎0997-63-0240; 467 Kasari-chō; ⏲8am-7pm) has subcompacts from ¥5500, with a branch in Amami and another across from the airport.

A Line Ferry (☎in Kagoshima 099-226-4141; www.aline-ferry.com) Operates four or five ferries a month running to/from Tokyo (¥23,110, 37 hours) and Osaka/Kobe (¥17,580, 29 hours), as well as daily ferries to and from Kagoshima (¥10,310, 11 hours). Most of these ferries continue on to Naha (¥10,050, 13 hours), so you can travel in the reverse direction from Naha to Amami-Ōshima as well.

Marix Line (マリックスライン; ☎0997-53-3112, in Kagoshima 099-225-1551; www.marix-line.co.jp) Having joined forces commercially, Marix and A Line still run their own ferries along the same routes for the same rates, but on alternating days. If you find that one does not offer a route on the day you wish to travel, simply book with the other company.

Tokunoshima 徳之島

☎0997 / POP 24,282

Tokunoshima, the second-largest island of the Amami Islands, has some interesting coastal rock formations and a few good beaches. The island is famous for **tōgyū** (闘牛大会, bovine sumo), which has been practised on the island for more than 500 years. Attractions include decent diving and snorkelling and views that occasionally call to mind parts of Hawaii.

On the island's east coast is the main port of **Kametoku-kō** (亀徳港) and the main town of **Kametsu** (亀津). Tokunoshima's airport is on its west coast, not far from the secondary port of **Hetono** (平土野).

Sights & Activities

If the spectacle of bulls locking horns interests you, there are 13 official *tōgyū* (bovine sumo) venues on the island that stage tournaments. In *tōgyū*, the animals are goaded on by human handlers, and the bloodless match ends when one bull retreats; it's more like eight-legged sumo than anything resembling European bullfighting. The three biggest tournaments are held in January, May and October – call the tourist office to confirm details.

Several good beaches are dotted around the coast, including the excellent **Aze Prince Beach** (畦プリンスビーチ), which is near the Aze/Fruits Garden bus stop on the northeast coast.

About 9km north of the airport at the northwestern tip of the island, **Mushiroze** (ムシロ瀬) is an interesting collection of wave-smoothed rocks that makes a great picnic spot. On a point on the southwest coast of the island, the **Innojō-futa** (犬の門蓋) is a collection of bizarrely eroded upthrust coral that includes a formation that resembles a giant pair of spectacles. Blink and you'll miss the sign on the main road about 10km south of the airport. From the turnoff into the maze of sugarcane fields, it's a bit poorly signed in kanji.

Sleeping

Aze Campground CAMPGROUND
(畦キャンプ場; P) FREE This fine little campground at Aze Prince Beach has showers, nice grassy campsites and a trail down to its own private beach.

★**Pension Shichifukujin** MINSHUKU ¥
(ペンション七福人; ☎0997-82-1126; 1637-3 Kametoku; s/d ¥3000/4000; P) Run by the effusive Shikasa-san, this hillside *minshuku* has spacious, comfortable Japanese- and Western-style rooms in the main building and an additional block. There's a cheery kitchen area, and discounts are available for long-term stays. Add ¥1590 per person to include two meals in the deal. The family also runs a cheap **minshuku** (コーポ七福人; ☎0997-82-2618; 7446-2 Kametsu; r per person ¥3000; P @) in town.

Kanami-sō MINSHUKU ¥¥
(金見荘; ☎0997-84-9027; www.kanamiso.com; r per person with/without meals ¥9980/4730; P @) In the village of Kanami at the very northeast tip of the island, this friendly divers' lodge has a great location overlooking a good snorkelling beach. Some of the upstairs rooms have sweeping views; cheaper rooms with shared bath are also available. The place specialises in *ise ebi ryōri* (Japanese lobster cuisine).

Information

A small **tourist information office** (徳之島観光協会; ☎0997-82-0575; ⏲9am-5.30pm Mon-Sat) at the ferry building has a detailed Japanese pamphlet and a simple English one about the island. It can help with accommodation, but you're best off booking ahead.

Getting There & Around

Tokunoshima has flights to/from Kagoshima (JAL) and Amami-Ōshima (JAC).

Tokunoshima is served by Marix (p761) and A Line (p761) ferries, which run between Kagoshima (some originating in Honshū) and Naha, and Amami Kaiun ferries, which run between Kagoshima and Okinoerabu-jima.

There are bus stations at both ports, and a decent bus system to all parts of the island, but you'll definitely appreciate the convenience of a car, scooter or touring bicycle. **Toyota Renta Car** (トヨタレンタカー; ☎0997-82-0900; ⏲9am-6pm) is right outside Kametoku Port pier. There are also car-rental places near the airport.

Okinoerabu-jima 沖永良部島

☎0997 / POP 13,240

About 33km southwest of Tokunoshima, Okinoerabu is a sugarcane-covered island with some excellent beaches, interesting coastal formations and a brilliant limestone cave.

Wadomari (和泊), the island's main town, is decidedly retro. The airport is at the eastern tip of the island, with **Wadomari Port** (和泊港) in Wadomari, 6km away on the east coast.

A FOOD LOVER'S GUIDE TO OKINAWA

Reflecting the islands' geographic and historical isolation, Okinawa's food shares little in common with that of mainland Japan. The cuisine originated in the splendour of the Ryūkyū court and from the humble lives of the impoverished islanders. Healthy eating is considered to be extremely important; indeed, islanders have long held that medicine and food are essentially the same. Today, the island's staple foods are pork, which is acidic and rich in protein, and *konbu* (a type of seaweed), which is alkaline and calorie-free.

Every part of the pig is eaten. *Mimigā* (ミミガー) is thinly sliced pig's ears marinated in vinegar, perfect with a cold glass of local Orion beer (オリオンビール). *Rafutē* (ラフテー) is pork stewed with ginger, brown sugar, rice wine and soy sauce until it falls apart. If you're looking for a bit of stamina, you should try some *ikasumi-jiru* (イカスミ汁), which is stewed pork in black squid ink.

While stewing is common, Okinawans prefer stir-frying, and refer to the technique as *champurū* (チャンプルー). Perhaps the best known stir-fry is *gōyā champurū* (ゴーヤーチャンプルー), a mix of pork, bitter melon and the island's uniquely sturdy tofu, *shima-dōfu* (島豆腐). Occasionally, you'll come across an unusual tofu variant known as *tōfuyō* (豆腐痒), which is sorely fermented, violently spicy and fluorescent pink – taste it with caution!

The ubiquitous *okinawa-soba* (沖縄そば) is udon (thick white noodles) served in a pork broth. The most common variants are *sōki-soba* (ソーキそば), topped with pork spare ribs; and *Yaeyama-soba* (八重山そば), which contains thin white noodles and is flecked with bits of tender pork.

Finally, there's nothing quite like Blue Seal (ブルーシール) brand ice cream, an American favourite introduced here after WWII. It's best savoured at a shop rather than in pre-packed containers.

Sights & Activities

There are excellent beaches all around the island. You'll also find Japan's biggest banyan tree and several 'secret' little beaches off the coastal road between Fūcha and the airport.

The island's coast has many impressive geographical landforms. **Tamina-misaki** (田皆崎), at the northwest tip of the island, has ancient coral that has been upthrust to form a 40m cliff. At the island's northeast tip, **Fūcha** (フーチャ) is a blowhole in the limestone rock, which shoots water 10m into the air on windy days.

Okidomari Kaihin-kōen BEACH
(沖泊海浜公園) Backed by green cliffs, the white sand and offshore coral formations make this beach a worthwhile stop; it's at the northwest end of the island.

Shōryū-dō CAVE
(昇竜洞; ☎0997-93-4536; 1520 Yoshino; admission ¥1000; ⏲9am-5pm) On the southwest slopes of Ōyama (the mountain at the west end of the island), you will find this brilliant limestone cave with 600m of walkways and illumination. It's a few kilometres inland from the southwest coastal road.

Sleeping & Eating

Okidomari Campground CAMPGROUND
(沖泊キャンプ場; P) FREE This excellent beachfront campground at Okidomari Kaihin-kōen has showers and large grassy areas with trees for shade.

Business Hotel Ugurahama HOTEL ¥¥
(ビジネスホテルうぐら浜; ☎0997-92-2268; www.erabu.net/ugurahama; 6-1 Wadomari; r per person with/without meals from ¥6500/4800; P @) This friendly hotel has simple Japanese- and Western-style rooms. From the port, take a left on the main road and follow it over the bridge and through the town; look for the white building with blue trim on your right.

Mōri Mōri IZAKAYA ¥¥
(もおりもおり; ☎0997-92-0538; 582 Wadomari; meals from ¥1500; ⏲5pm-midnight, closed some Sun) This superfriendly *izakaya* in Wadomari offers small dishes such as *gōyā champurū* (bitter melon stir-fry; ¥500). See if you can break the local beer-chugging record, which stands at under three seconds. It's a little hard to spot: from the Menshiori Shopping St (when coming from port), take

LIVING LANGUAGES

If you spend a little time in Okinawa, you might hear bits of the Okinawan language: *'mensōre'* (welcome) instead of the standard Japanese *'yōkoso'* – or *'nifei dēbiru'* instead of *'arigatō'*. What you may not realise is that besides Okinawan, there exists a colourful diversity of distinct dialects throughout the island chain – all considered Ryukyuan languages. Sadly, many of these dialects are dying out with older generations.

According to Unesco, of the existing 7000 or so languages spoken in the world, around 2500 are considered endangered. When Kiku Hidenori (owner of Yoron Minzoku-mura on Yoron-tō) heard this statistic several years ago, he was dismayed to find the Amami, Okinawa and Yoron dialects were included among these endangered tongues. As someone who actively preserves traditional Yoron culture and grew up speaking Yoron-hōgen (Yoron dialect), he decided that he needed to help save his island's language from extinction.

Kiku explains, 'People of my generation – I'm 50 years old – can still speak Yoron-hōgen. Nowadays, there's a television in every house, broadcasting in standard Japanese. Children don't grow up in the same homes as their grandparents, so they just don't hear Yoron-hōgen. We are beginning to lose the dialect.'

For his part, Kiku has begun teaching Yoron-hōgen in the local elementary schools, and bringing junior high school students to Yoron Minzoku-mura to give older kids a sense of pride in their unique heritage and dialect. His independent work has attracted the attention of Japanese professors of language. 'Obviously, one must try one's very best individually, but I think that networking is crucial,' he says. Kiku is actively liaising with other dialect preservationists elsewhere in Japan to find the best strategies and methods for keeping these tongues alive. With any luck, such grassroots efforts by him and others can bring these island dialects back from the brink.

the first right, then the first left, and look for the dark-wood shopfront.

Sō IZAKAYA ¥¥
(草; ☎0997-92-1202; 512-7 Tedechina; meals from ¥1800; ⏰5pm-midnight) Head towards the port from town, and on the main road after the bridge, you'll spy an ersatz waterwheel in front of a corner restaurant. Step inside and you'll find a friendly, cosy *izakaya* serving interesting local specialities like *yagi-jiru* (goat soup, ¥800) and *yachimochi* (rice cake made with black sugar, ¥650), as well as more typical *izakaya* items.

Information

There is a small **tourist information booth** (☎0997-92-2901; ⏰8.30am-5pm) at Wadomari port on the 2nd floor of the terminal building, which has maps of the island (the office is next to the ferry ticket window).

Getting There & Around

Okinoerabu has flights to and from Kagoshima and Yoron-tō on JAC.

Okinoerabu-jima is served by Marix (p761) and A Line Ferry (p761), which run between Kagoshima (some originating in Honshū) and Naha, and Amami Kaiun ferries, which run between Kagoshima and Okinoerabu-jima.

The island has a decent bus system, but you'll definitely welcome the convenience of a car, scooter or touring bicycle. You'll find **Toyota Renta Car** (トヨタレンタカー; ☎0997-92-2100; ⏰9am-6pm) right outside the airport.

Yoron-tō 与論島

☎0997 / POP 5258

Fringed with white, star-sand-speckled beaches and extensive coral reefs, Yoron-tō is one of the most appealing islands in the Southwest Islands chain. A mere 5km across, it is the southernmost island in Kagoshima Prefecture. On a good day, Okinawa-hontō's northernmost point of Hedo-misaki is visible 23km to the southwest.

The harbour is next to the airport on the western tip of the island, while the main town of **Chabana** (茶花) is 1km to the east.

Sights & Activities

On the eastern side of the island, Yoron-tō's best beach is the popular **Oganeku-kaigan** (大金久海岸). About 500m offshore from Oganeku-kaigan is **Yurigahama** (百合ヶ浜), a stunning stretch of white sand that disappears completely at high tide. Boats (¥2000 return) putter back and forth, ferrying visitors out to it. Other good beaches include **Maehama-kaigan** (前浜海岸), on the southeast coast, and **Terasaki-kaigan** (寺崎海岸), on the northeast coast.

★Yoron Minzoku-mura MUSEUM
(与論民族村; 693 Higashi; admission ¥400; ⏲9am-6pm) At the island's southeastern tip, the excellent Yoron Minzoku-mura is a collection of traditional thatch-roof island dwellings and storehouses that contain exhibits on the island's culture and history. If at all possible, bring along a Japanese speaker, as the owner is an incredible source of information on the island's heritage and dialect.

Southern Cross Center MUSEUM
(サザンクロスセンター; ☎0997-97-3396; 3313 Ricchō; admission ¥400; ⏲9am-6pm) A short walk from the Ishini (石仁) bus stop, 3km south of Chabana, is a lookout that serves as a museum of Yoron-tō and Amami history and culture. Offering good views south to Okinawa, it celebrates the fact that Yoron-tō is the northernmost island in Japan from where the Southern Cross can be seen.

Sleeping

Shiomi-sō MINSHUKU ¥¥
(汐見荘; ☎0997-97-2167, 0997-97-3582; 2229-3 Chabana; r per person without bathroom incl meals ¥5940; Ⓟ@) This friendly and casual *minshuku* is popular with young people. Some Western-style rooms are available, though most are Japanese-style; all share bathrooms. Starting from Chabana harbour, take the main road north (uphill) out of town and look for the cute little white house on the left after the turn. Staff will pick you up if you phone ahead.

★Pricia Resort HOTEL ¥¥¥
(プリシアリゾート; ☎0997-97-5060; www.pricia.co.jp; 358-1 Ricchō; r per person incl breakfast from ¥10,810; Ⓟ@) These relaxing whitewashed cottages by the airport evoke Yoron-tō's sister island Mykonos in Greece. The best cottages are the beachfront 'B type' units. Breezy Western-style rooms and jacuzzi baths are popular with Japanese divers and holidaying US servicemembers from Okinawa. The hotel offers an entire menu of activities, including windsurfing, snorkelling and banana-boat rides.

Eating & Drinking

There's a large supermarket and two mini-markets in the centre of Chabana.

Umi Café CAFE ¥
(海カフェ; ☎0997-97-4621; 2309 Chabana; meals from ¥800; ⏲11am-6pm, from 1pm Sat;) This delightful terraced gallery-cafe with ocean views is something you'd expect to find perched on a Greek cliff; it's no surprise to find chicken gyros (¥700) on the menu. Go to the village office at the top of the main drag, turn left and then right at the end of the street. Look for small signs pointing uphill.

The owner also runs a small hostel (dorm beds ¥1500).

Bar Natural Reef BAR
(ナチュラルリーフ; 16-1 Chabana; snacks from ¥600; ⏲9pm-1am) This tiki bar on Chabana's main drag is the best watering hole on the island, with plenty of *yū sen,* a local *shōchū* (strong distilled alcohol) made from sugarcane, to keep everyone happy. Owner Kowaguchi-san has lots of tips about the best spots on Yoron-tō.

Information

Beside the city office in Chabana is the friendly **tourist information office** (ヨロン島観光協会; ☎0997-97-5151; 32-1 Chabana; ⏲8.30am-5.30pm), which provides an English-language map of the island and can make accommodation bookings. There is an international ATM at the post office in Chabana.

Getting There & Around

Yoron-tō has direct flights to/from Kagoshima (JAC) and Naha (RAC).

Yoron-tō is served by Marix (p761) and A Line Ferry (p761), which run between Kagoshima (some originating in Honshū) and Naha, and Amami Kaiun ferries, which run between Kagoshima and Okinoerabu-jima.

Yoron-tō has a bus system, but you'll definitely appreciate the convenience of a car, scooter or touring bicycle. **Yoron Rentacar** (ヨロンレンタカー; ☎0997-97-3633; 48-7 Chabana; ⏲8am-6pm), located in Chabana, will meet car- or scooter-rental clients at the airport, and may offer you an energy drink when sending you on your way. If you don't opt for the convenient airport pick-up, find Yoron Rentacar on the road just east of the post office, off Chabana's main drag.

OKINAWA PREFECTURE

Japan's southernmost prefecture, Okinawa Prefecture (沖縄県; Okinawa-ken) makes up the southern half of the Southwest Islands. The prefecture stretches from the southern islands in Kagoshima Prefecture to within 110km of Taiwan. Three island groups make up the prefecture. From north to south, they are the Okinawa Islands, Miyako Islands and Yaeyama Islands.

The northernmost island group is the Okinawa Islands, which contains Okinawa-hontō (meaning 'Okinawa Main Island' in Japanese), home to the prefectural capital, Naha. This is the prefecture's transport hub, easily accessed by flights and ferries to/from the mainland. Plentiful ferries run between Naha and the Kerama Islands, which lie about 30km west of Okinawa-hontō.

Located 300km southwest of Okinawa-hontō, the Miyako Islands are home to the popular beach destination of Miyako-jima. There is no ferry access to this group; you must arrive via flights from the mainland, Naha or Ishigaki.

The Yaeyama Islands, a further 100km southwest, include the coral-fringed island of Ishigaki and the nearby jungle-clad Iriomote-jima. Like the Miyako Islands, you have to fly in.

Okinawa-hontō 沖縄本島

098 / POP 1.32 MILLION

Okinawa-hontō is the largest island in the Southwest Islands, and the historical seat of power of the Ryūkyū dynasty. Although its cultural differences with mainland Japan were once evident in its architecture, almost all traces were completely obliterated in WWII. Fortunately, Allied bombing wasn't powerful enough to completely stamp out other remnants of Okinawan culture, and today the island is home to a unique culinary, artistic and musical tradition.

The island is also home to some excellent beaches, delicious food and friendly people, many of whom speak a little more English than their mainland counterparts. Of course, with US Air Force jets flying overhead from time to time, it's hard to forget the reality of the continuing American military presence on the island and the history behind that presence.

Prefectural capital Naha is a transport hub for the other islands. War memorials are clustered in the south of the island, while there are some good beaches and other attractions on the Motobu peninsula. The north is relatively undeveloped.

It's worth noting that Okinawa-hontō has been somewhat overdeveloped for domestic tourism. If you seek Southeast Asian–style beaches and fewer big resorts, the majority of your time is best spent on Okinawa Prefecture's smaller islands.

Naha 那覇

POP 321,077

Flattened during WWII, the prefectural capital of Naha is now a thriving urban centre. The city sports a convenient elevated monorail and a rapidly expanding skyline of modern high-rise apartments, as well as the inevitable traffic jams.

The city plays host to an interesting mix of young Japanese holidaymakers, American GIs looking for off-base fun and a growing number of foreign tourists. The action centres on Kokusai-dōri (International Blvd), a colourful and energetic 2km main drag of hotels, restaurants, bars, clubs and just about every conceivable type of souvenir shop. And overlooking it all from a safe distance to the east is Shuri-jō, a wonderfully restored castle that was once the home of Ryūkyū royalty.

Sights & Activities

Naha is fairly easy to navigate, especially since the main sights and attractions are located in the city centre. The main drag is Kokusai-dōri, while the Tsuboya pottery area is to the southeast via a series of covered arcades. The Shuri district is located about 3km to the east of the city centre.

The city's main artery, **Kokusai-dōri** (国際通り), is a riot of neon, noise, souvenir shops, bustling restaurants and Japanese young things out strutting their stuff. It's a festival of tat and tackiness, but it's a good time if you're in the mood for it.

Many people prefer the atmosphere of the three shopping arcades that run south off Kokusai-dōri: **Ichibahon-dōri** (市場本道り), **Mutsumibashi-dōri** (むつみ橋通り) and **Heiwa-dōri** (平和通り).

★Tsuboya Pottery Street NEIGHBOURHOOD
(壷屋やちむん道り; Tsuboya Yachimun-dōri)
One of the best parts of Naha is this neighbourhood, a centre of ceramic production from 1682, when Ryūkyū kilns were consolidated here by royal decree. Most shops

Okinawa-hontō

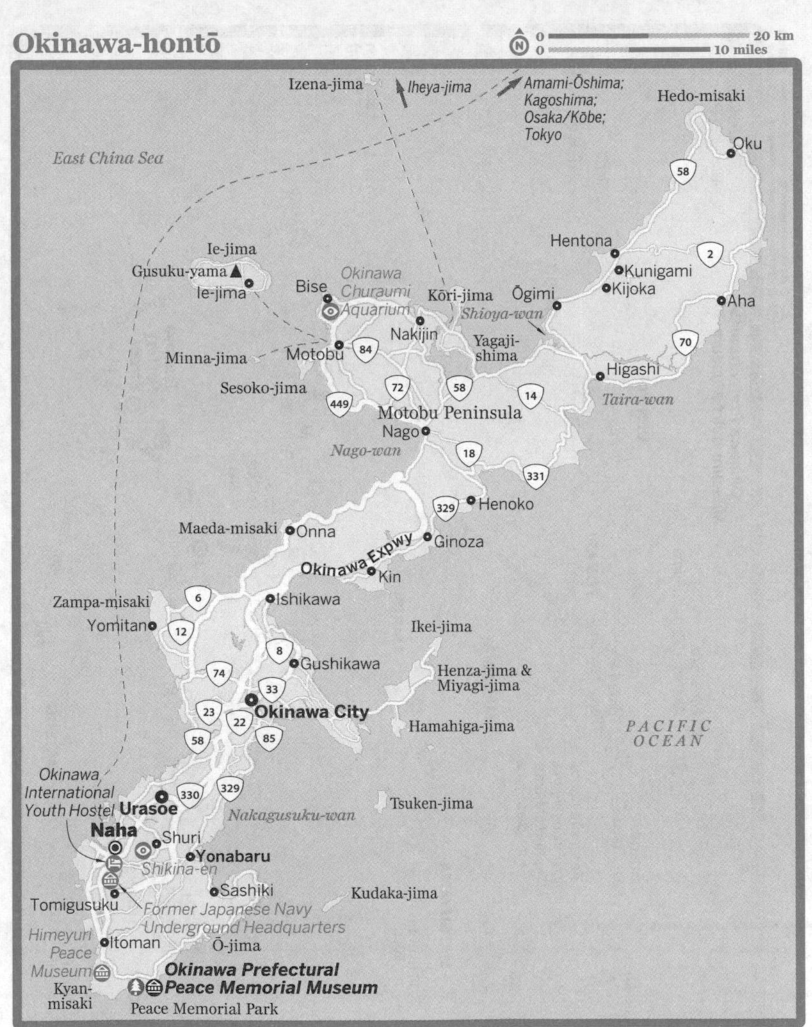

along this atmospheric street sell all the popular Okinawan ceramics, including *shiisā* (lion-dog roof guardians) and containers for serving *awamori,* the local firewater. The lanes off the main street here contain some classic crumbling old Okinawan houses. To get here from Kokusai-dōri, walk south through the entirety of Heiwa-dōri arcade (about 350m).

★Okinawa Prefectural Museum & Art Museum MUSEUM
(沖縄県立博物館・美術館; ☎098-941-8200; www.museums.pref.okinawa.jp; Omoromachi 3-1-1; admission prefectural/art museum ¥410/310; ⌚9am-6pm Tue-Thu & Sun, to 8pm Fri & Sat) Opened in 2007, this museum of Okinawa's history, culture and natural history is easily one of the best museums in Japan. The displays are well laid out, attractively presented and easy to understand, with excellent bilingual interpretive signage. The art museum section holds interesting special exhibits (admission prices vary) with an emphasis on local artists. It's about 15 minutes' walk northwest of the Omoromachi monorail station.

Naha

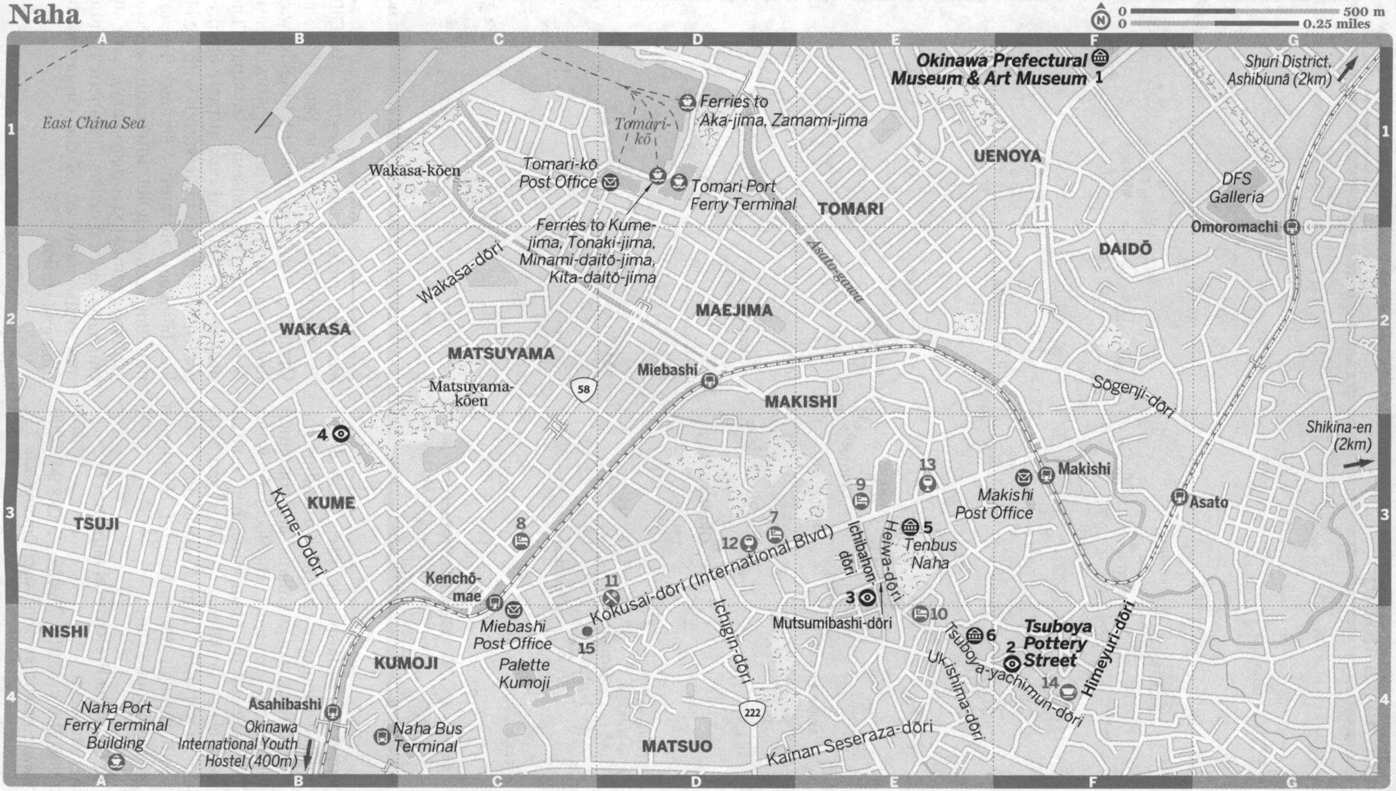

0 500 m
0 0.25 miles

Okinawa Prefectural Museum & Art Museum 1
Shuri District, Ashibiunā (2km)
East China Sea
Ferries to Aka-jima, Zamami-jima
Tomari-kō
UENOYA
Wakasa-kōen
Tomari-kō Post Office
Tomari Port Ferry Terminal
TOMARI
DFS Galleria
Omoromachi
Ferries to Kume-jima, Tonaki-jima, Minami-daitō-jima, Kita-daitō-jima
Asato-gawa
DAIDŌ
Wakasa-dōri
MAEJIMA
WAKASA
MATSUYAMA
Miebashi
58
Matsuyama-kōen
MAKISHI
Sōgenji-dōri
4
Shikina-en (2km)
13
9
Makishi
Asato
Makishi Post Office
KUME
TSUJI
8
7
5
Tenbus Naha
12
Ichibahon-dōri
Heiwa-dōri
Kume-Ōdōri
Kokusai-dōri (International Blvd)
Kenchō-mae
11
3
10
Himeyuri-dōri
NISHI
Miebashi Post Office
Ichigin-dōri
Mutsumibashi-dōri
6
Tsuboya Pottery Street 2
15
KUMOJI
Palette Kumoji
Tsuboya-yachimun-dōri
Uk-ishima-dōri
14
Naha Port Ferry Terminal Building
Asahibashi
Okinawa International Youth Hostel (400m)
Naha Bus Terminal
222
MATSUO
Kainan Seseraza-dōri

Naha

Top Sights
1 Okinawa Prefectural Museum & Art Museum F1
2 Tsuboya Pottery Street F4

Sights
3 Daichi Makishi Kōsetsu Ichiba E3
4 Fukushū-en B3
5 Naha City Traditional Arts & Crafts Center E3
6 Tsuboya Pottery Museum E4

Sleeping
7 Hotel JAL City Naha D3
8 Hotel Sun Palace Kyūyōkan C3
9 Lohas Villa E3
10 Stella Resort E4

Eating
11 Yūnangi D3

Drinking & Nightlife
12 Helios Pub D3
13 Rehab E3
14 Uchinā Chaya Buku Buku F4

Information
Manga Kissa Gera Gera .... (see 13)
15 Okinawa Tourist C4
Tourist Information Office .... (see 5)

Tsuboya Pottery Museum MUSEUM
(壺屋焼物博物館; ☎098-862-3761; www.edu.city.naha.okinawa.jp/tsuboya; 1-9-32 Tsuboya; admission ¥315; ⊙10am-6pm Tue-Sun) The excellent Tsuboya Pottery Museum houses some fine examples of traditional Okinawan pottery. Here you can also inspect potters' wheels and *arayachi* (unglazed) and *jōyachi* (glazed) pieces. There's even a cross-section of a *nobori-gama* (kiln built on a slope) set in its original location, where crushed pieces of pottery that date back to the 17th century lay suspended in earth.

Daichi Makishi Kōsetsu Ichiba MARKET
(第一牧志公設市場; 2-10-1 Matsuo; ⊙10am-8pm) Our favourite stop in the arcade area is the covered food market just off Ichibahon-dōri, about 200m south of Kokusai-dōri. The colourful variety of fish and produce on offer here is amazing, and don't miss the wonderful local restaurants upstairs.

Fukushū-en GARDENS
(福州園; ☎098-869-5384; 2-29 Kume; ⊙9am-6pm Thu-Tue) FREE Garden fans should take a stroll through Chinese-style Fukushū-en. All materials were brought from Fuzhou, Naha's sister city in China, including the pagoda that sits atop a small waterfall.

Shikina-en GARDENS
(識名園; ☎098-855-5936; 421-7 Aza Māji; admission ¥400; ⊙9am-6pm Thu-Tue) Around 4km east of the city centre is a Chinese-style garden containing stone bridges, a viewing pavilion and a villa that belonged to the Ryūkyū royal family. Despite its flawless appearance, everything here was painstakingly rebuilt after WWII. To reach the garden, take bus 2, 3 or 5 to the Shikinaen-mae stop (¥220, 20 minutes).

Naha City Traditional Arts & Crafts Center ART GALLERY
(那覇市伝統工芸館; ☎098-868-7866; 2nd fl, 3-2-10 Makishi; admission ¥300; ⊙9am-6pm) Right on Kokusai-dōri, this gallery houses a notable collection of traditional Okinawan crafts by masters of the media. You can also try your hand at Ryukyuan glass-blowing, weaving, *bingata* (painting on fabric) and pottery-making in the workshops (¥1500 to ¥3000), and make your own souvenir from Okinawa.

SHURI DISTRICT 首里

The original capital of Okinawa, Shuri's temples, shrines, tombs and castle were all destroyed in WWII, but the castle and surrounding structures were rebuilt in 1992.

Shuri-jō CASTLE
(首里城; ☎098-886-2020; http://oki-park.jp/shurijo/; 1-2 Kinjō-chō; admission ¥820, discounted to ¥660 with 1-day monorail pass; ⊙8.30am-7pm Apr-Jun, Oct & Nov, to 8pm Jul-Sep, to 6pm Dec-Mar, closed Wed & Thu in Jul) This reconstructed castle was originally built in the 14th century and served as the administrative centre and royal residence of the Ryūkyū kingdom until the 19th century. Enter through the Kankai-mon (歓会門) and go up to the Hōshin-mon (奉神門), which forms the entryway to the inner sanctum of the castle. Visitors can enter the impressive **Seiden** (正殿), which has exhibits on the castle and the Okinawan royals.

There is also a small collection of displays in the nearby **Hokuden** (北殿).

To reach the complex, which sits atop a hill overlooking Naha's urban sprawl, take the Yui-rail monorail to Shuri Station. Exit to the west, go down the steps, walk straight, cross one big street, then a smaller one and go right on the opposite side, then walk about 350m and look for the signs on the left.

Iri-no-Azana VIEWPOINT
(西のアザナ) While you're at the castle, visit the Iri-no-Azana, a viewpoint about 200m west of the Seiden that affords great views over Naha and as far as the Kerama Islands.

Festivals & Events

Dragon-Boat Races CULTURAL
Held in early May, particularly in Itoman and Naha. These races *(hari)* are thought to bring luck and prosperity to fishermen.

Ryūkyū-no-Saiten CULTURAL
Brings together more than a dozen festivals and special events celebrating Okinawan culture for three days at the end of October.

Naha Ōzunahiki SPORTS
Takes place in Naha on Sunday around the national Sports Day Holiday in October, and features large teams that compete in the world's biggest tug of war, using a gigantic 1m-thick rope weighing over 40 tonnes.

Sleeping

Naha is the most convenient (and fun) base for exploring Okinawa-hontō.

Stella Resort GUESTHOUSE ¥
(ステラリゾート; ☎098-863-1330; www.stella-cg.com; 3-6-41 Makishi; dm ¥1400, s/d ¥3000/4200; P @ wi-fi) Between Heiwa-dōri arcade and the Tsuboya pottery area, this tropical-themed guesthouse has private loft rooms, pool table, an aquarium room for zoning out and some English-speaking staff. Look for the turquoise building at the end of the covered section of Heiwa-dōri and climb the stairs to the lobby. The guesthouse also runs **Lohas Villa** (ロハスヴィラ; ☎098-867-7757; www.lohas-cg.com; 3rd fl, Breath Bldg, 2-1-6 Makishi; dm/s/d ¥1600/3600/5200; @ wi-fi), just off Kokusai-dōri.

Okinawa International Youth Hostel HOSTEL ¥
(沖縄国際ユースホステル; ☎098-857-0073; www.oiyh.org; 51 Ōnoyama; dm ¥4410, r per person with/without bathroom ¥5670/5145; P non-smoking @) This excellent youth hostel is located in Ōnoyama-kōen, a five-minute walk from the Tsubogawa Station; find detailed directions on the website. Prices are cheaper for Hostelling International members. Take note that unmarried couples are not welcome to share rooms.

★ **Hotel Sun Palace Kyūyōkan** HOTEL ¥¥
(ホテルサンパレス球陽館; ☎098-863-4181; www.palace-okinawa.com/sunpalace; 2-5-1 Kumoji; s/d incl breakfast from ¥6500/9800; P non-smoking @) About three minutes' walk from Kokusai-dōri, the Sun Palace is a step up in warmth and quality from a standard business hotel. Staff are friendly, the fairly spacious rooms include small potted plants and a welcoming Okinawan feel, and there's even a rooftop terrace, a refreshing bit of outdoor space laced with greenery.

Hotel JAL City Naha HOTEL ¥¥¥
(ホテルJALシティ那覇; ☎098-866-2580; http://naha.jalcity.co.jp; 1-3-70 Makishi; s/d from ¥13,000/16,000; P non-smoking @ wi-fi) In the middle of the action on Kokusai-dōri, JAL City has 304 swish, modern rooms, in which even the single beds are wide enough to serve as cosy doubles. Though staff here speak limited English, the service is excellent.

Eating & Drinking

In Naha, a great place to sample Okinawan cuisine is at one of the 2nd-floor eateries at Daichi Makishi Kōsetsu Ichiba (p769); roam around for a look at what others are eating and grab a seat.

★ **Ashibiunā** OKINAWAN ¥
(あしびうなぁ; ☎098-884-0035; 2-13 Shurijō; lunch sets ¥800-1250; ⏲11.30am-3.30pm & 5.30pm-midnight; English menu) Perfect for lunch after touring Shuri-jō, Ashibiunā has a traditional ambience and picturesque garden. Set meals feature local specialities such as *gōyā champurū*, *okinawa-soba* (thick white noodles in a pork broth) and *ikasumi yakisoba* (stir-fried squid-ink noodles). On the road leading away from Shuri-jō, Ashibiunā is on the right, just before the intersection to the main road.

Yūnangi OKINAWAN ¥¥
(ゆうなんぎい; ☎098-867-3765; 3-3-3 Kumoji; dishes ¥1200; ⏲noon-3pm & 5.30-10.30pm Mon-Sat; English menu) You'll be lucky to get a seat here, but if you do, you'll be treated to some of the best Okinawan food around, served in traditional but bustling surroundings. Try the *okinawa-soba* set (¥1400), or choose among

THREE-STRING HARMONY

Stroll through any Okinawa town and before long you'll likely hear the tinkly sound of the *sanshin*, a banjolike precursor to the ubiquitous *shamisen* that is played on Japan's main islands. Typically constructed of a wooden frame covered with python skin, the *sanshin* has a long lacquered neck, a bamboo bridge and three strings that are struck with a plectrum, often carved from the horn of a water buffalo.

Introduced from China in the 16th century, the *sanshin* was used for court music during the Ryūkyū kingdom and later prized by commoners for its soothing sound; in the devastation after WWII, *sanshin* made of tin cans and nylon string cheered the exhausted survivors. Today, you can hear folksongs featuring *sanshin* all over Japan. Musicians such as Takashi Hirayasu and Yoriko Ganeko have helped popularise the sound in and out of Japan so you can even find *sanshin* groups overseas.

the appealing options in the picture menu. On a sidestreet off Kokusai-dōri, look for the wooden sign with white lettering above the doorway.

★Uchinā Chaya Buku Buku TEAHOUSE
(うちなー茶屋ぶくぶく; ☎098-861-2952; 1-28-3 Tsuboya; tea ¥800; ⏰10am-6pm) This incredibly atmospheric teahouse near the east end of the Tsuboya pottery area is worth a special trip. It takes its name from the traditional frothy Okinawan tea served here: *buku buku cha* (¥800), jasmine tea topped with toasty rice foam and crushed peanuts. It's up a small lane just north of Tsuboya-yachimun-dōri and overlooks an historic 160-year-old house. Children aged seven and older are welcome.

Rehab BAR
(☎098-988-1198; www.rehabokinawabar.com; 3rd fl, 2-4-14 Makishi; ⏰7pm-late) This 3rd-floor international bar on Kokusai-dōri attracts a friendly, mixed crowd and has cosy nook seating, imported beer, and two-for-one drinks on Tuesdays. The cool bartenders here speak English.

Helios Pub PUB
(ヘリオスパブ; ☎098-863-7227; 1-2-25 Makishi; ⏰11.30am-11pm Sun-Thu, 11.30am-midnight Fri & Sat) Craft beer lovers who tire of Orion can perk up bored palates with a sample flight of four house brews (¥900) and pints for ¥525. Edibles cover the pub-menu gamut, all very reasonably priced.

ℹ Information

Post offices are scattered around town, including the **Miebashi post office** (美栄橋郵便局; 1-1-1 Kumoji; ⏰ATM 7am-11pm Mon-Fri, 9am-9pm Sat, 9am-7pm Sun), on the ground floor of the Palette Kumoji building, the **Tomari-kō post office** (泊ふ頭郵便局; 3-25-5 Maejima; ⏰ATM 9am-7pm Mon-Fri, 9am-5pm Sat & Sun), in the Tomari port building, and the **Makishi post office** (牧志郵便局; 3-13-19 Makishi; ⏰ATM 9am-11pm Mon-Fri, 9am-7pm Sat & Sun), around the corner from Makishi Station. All of these post offices have international ATMs.

Manga Kissa Gera Gera (まんが喫茶ゲラゲラ; ☎098-863-5864; 2nd fl, 2-4-14 Makishi; per hr ¥480; ⏰24hr) A convenient net cafe on Kokusai-dōri. It's just a little east of the Family Mart convenience store.

Okinawa Tourist (沖縄ツーリスト; OTS; ☎098-862-1111; 1-2-3 Matsuo; ⏰9.30am-6.30pm Mon-Fri, to 5pm Sat) On Kokusai-dōri, a competent travel agency with English speakers who can help with all manner of ferry and flight bookings.

Tourist Information Counter (☎098-857-6884; 1F Arrivals Terminal, Naha International Airport; ⏰9am-9pm) At this helpful prefectural counter, we suggest picking up a copy of the *Naha Guide Map* before heading into town, and an *Okinawa Guide Map* if you plan to explore outside Naha.

Tourist Information Office (那覇市観光案内所; ☎098-868-4887; 3-2-10 Makishi; ⏰9am-8pm) The city office has internet access and luggage storage for a small fee, and free maps and information. It's in the Tenbus Building, which also houses the Naha Traditional Arts & Crafts Center.

ℹ Getting There & Away

AIR

Naha International Airport (OKA) has connections with Seoul, Taipei, Hong Kong and Shanghai. Connections with mainland Japan include Fukuoka, Osaka, Nagoya and Tokyo; significant discounts (*tabiwari* on All Nippon Airways and *sakitoku* on JAL) can sometimes be had if you purchase tickets a month in advance. Note that this is only a partial list; most large Japanese cities have flights.

Naha also has air connections with Kume-jima, Aka-jima, Miyako-jima, Ishigaki-jima and Yoron-tō, among other Southwest Islands.

BOAT

Naha has regular ferry connections with ports in Honshū (Tokyo and Osaka/Kōbe) and Kyūshū (Kagoshima).

Marix (☎0997-53-3112, in Kagoshima 099-225-1551; www.marix-line.co.jp) and **A Line** (☎ in Naha 098-861-1886, in Tokyo 03-5643-6170; www.aline-ferry.com) operate four to six ferries a month running to/from Tokyo (¥27,230, 47 hours) and Osaka/Kōbe (¥21,790, 42 hours), as well as daily ferries to/from Kagoshima (¥15,870, 25 hours). Note that if you ask for a *norihōdai kippu* you can sail from Kagoshima to Naha and get on and off the ferries freely within seven days.

There are three ports in Naha, and this can be confusing: Amami Islands ferries operate from Naha Port (Naha-kō); Tokyo/Osaka/Kōbe/Kagoshima ferries operate from Naha Shin Port (Naha Shin-kō); and Kume-jima and Kerama Islands ferries operate from Tomari Port (Tomari-kō).

Note that there is no ferry service to the Miyako Islands or Yaeyama Islands from Naha.

ℹ Getting Around

The Yui-rail monorail runs from Naha International Airport in the south to Shuri in the north. Prices range from ¥200 to ¥290; day passes cost ¥700. Kenchō-mae Station is at the western end of Kokusai-dōri, while Makishi Station is at its eastern end.

Naha Port is a 10-minute walk southwest from Asahibashi Station, while Tomari Port is a similar distance north from Miebashi Station. Bus 101 from Naha bus terminal (那覇バスターミナル) heads further north to Naha Shin Port (20 minutes, hourly).

When riding on local town buses, simply dump ¥200 into the slot next to the driver as you enter. For longer trips, take a ticket showing your starting point as you board and pay the appropriate fare as you disembark. Buses run from Naha to destinations all over the island.

A rental car makes everything easier when exploring Okinawa-hontō. The rental-car counter in the arrivals hall of Naha International Airport offers information on the dozen or so rental companies in Naha, allowing you to comparison shop.

Southern Okinawa-hontō 沖縄本島の南部

During the closing days of the Battle of Okinawa, the southern part of Okinawa-

AMERICAN BASES IN OKINAWA

The US officially returned Okinawa to Japanese administration in 1972, but it negotiated a Status of Forces Agreement that guaranteed the Americans the right to use large tracts of Okinawan land for military bases, most of which are on Okinawa-hontō. These bases are home to approximately 19,000 American servicemembers.

Although the bases have supported Okinawa's economic growth in the past, they now contribute to about 5% the Okinawa economy. The bases are a sore spot for islanders due in part to occasional crimes committed by American servicemen. Antibase feelings peaked in 1996, after three American servicemen abducted and raped a 12-year-old Okinawan girl. Similar incidents in recent years have perpetuated animosity, including several in 2012 alone.

Plans to relocate the base from Futenma to the less-densely populated Henoko district were officially approved by both the US and Japan in 1996 but have continually met with vocal opposition from Okinawa residents, the majority of whom would like to see the US military presence take leave of the island entirely.

In April 2010, 90,000 protesters gathered to call for an end to the bases, the biggest such demonstrations in 15 years. That year, then Prime Minister Hatoyama Yukio fell on his sword after breaking a promise to move Futenma air base off the island; he finally admitted it would stay.

Though the US formally agreed in early 2012 to move 9000 Marines (amounting to around half of the Marines on Okinawa) to bases on Guam, Hawaii and elsewhere in the Pacific, this plan will not begin manifesting until the mid-2020s.

At the time of research, an opponent of the relocation plan, Onaga Takeshi, had just been elected governor of Okinawa. Whether he has the power to block the establishment of the Henoko base remains to be seen.

hontō served as one of the last holdouts of the Japanese military and an evacuation point for wounded Japanese soldiers. A visit to the area, a day or half-day trip from Naha, is highly recommended for those with an interest in wartime history.

Okinawa's most important war memorials are clustered in the **Peace Memorial Park** (平和祈念公園; ⌚dawn-dusk), located in the city of Itoman on the southern coast of the island. The centrepiece of the park is the **Okinawa Prefectural Peace Memorial Museum** (沖縄県平和祈念資料館; ☎098-997-3844; www.peace-museum.pref.okinawa.jp; 614-1 Aza Mabuni, Itoman; admission ¥300; ⌚9am-5pm), which focuses on the suffering of the Okinawan people during the invasion of the island and under the subsequent American occupation. While some material may stir debate, the museum's mission is to serve as a reminder of the horrors of war so that such suffering is not repeated. A free English-language audioguide is available, providing great detail of the 2nd-floor exhibit. Outside the museum is the **Cornerstone of Peace** (⌚dawn-dusk), inscribed with the names of everyone who died in the Battle of Okinawa.

To reach the park, take bus 89 from Naha bus terminal to the Itoman bus terminal (¥560, one hour, every 20 minutes), then transfer to bus 82, and get off at Heiwa Kinendō Iriguchi (¥460, 30 minutes, hourly).

An interesting, if haunting, stop en route to the Peace Park is the **Himeyuri Peace Museum** (ひめゆり平和祈念資料館; ☎098-997-2100; www.himeyuri.or.jp; 671-1 Ihara, Itoman; admission ¥310; ⌚9am-5pm), located above a cave that served as an emergency field hospital during the closing days of the Battle of Okinawa. Here, 240 female high-school students were pressed into service as nurses for Japanese military wounded. As American forces closed in, the students were summarily dismissed and the majority died. This is another monument whose mission is to promote peace, driven by survivors and alumnae of the school. Excellent, comprehensive interpretive signage is provided in English. Bus 82 stops outside.

Directly south of Naha in Kaigungo-kōen is the **Former Japanese Navy Underground Headquarters** (旧海軍司令部壕; Kyūkaigun Shireibu-gō; ☎098-850-4055; 236 Tomishiro, Tomigusuku; admission ¥440; ⌚8:30am-5pm), where 4000 men committed suicide or were killed as the battle for Okinawa drew to its bloody conclusion. Only 250m of the tunnels are open, but you can wander through the maze of corridors, see the commander's final words on the wall of his room, and inspect the holes and scars in other walls from the grenade blasts that killed many of the men. To reach the site, take bus 55, 88 or 98 from Naha bus terminal to the Uebaru Danchi-mae stop (¥220, 20 minutes, several hourly). From there it's a five-minute walk – follow the English signs (the entrance is near the top of the hill).

Motobu Peninsula 本部半島

Jutting out to the northwest of Nago, the hilly peninsula of Motobu (Motobu-hantō) is home to some scenic vistas, islets and decent beaches, as well as an incredibly popular aquarium. Motobu peninsula is served by frequent loop lines from Nago – buses 66 and 65 respectively run anticlockwise and clockwise around the peninsula.

A couple of kilometres north of Motobu town is the **Ocean Expo Park** (海洋博公園), the centrepiece of which is the wonderful **Okinawa Churaumi Aquarium** (沖縄美ら海水族館; ☎098-048-3748; http://oki-churaumi.jp; 424 Ishikawa, Motobu-chō; adult/child ¥1850/610; ⌚8.30am-6.30pm Oct-Feb, to 8pm Mar-Sep). The aquarium is built around the world's largest aquarium tank, which houses a fantastic variety of marine life, including whale sharks. Unfortunately, this place is on the checklist of every single tourist to the island, and it can be packed. From Nago, buses 65, 66 and 70 run directly to the park (¥860, 50 minutes).

About 1km north of the aquarium is the quaintly preserved village of **Bise** (備瀬), a leafy community of traditional Okinawan houses along a beach. An atmospheric lane lined with old garcinia trees (フクギ並木) is perfect for strolling, and a few shops sell seashell crafts. Near the lane's southern end, **Cahaya Bulan** (チャハヤブラン; ☎098-051-7272; 429-1 Bise; ajian-soba ¥800; ⌚noon-sunset Thu-Tue, Fri-Tue in winter;) is a relaxing cafe with noodle dishes such as *ajian-soba* (Asian-style *soba*) and a patio with views of Ie-jima.

If you're after natural attractions and have your own wheels, we recommend a drive out to **Kōri-jima** (古宇利島) via **Yagaji-jima** (屋我地島). The bridge between the two islands is surrounded by picturesque turquoise water, and there's a decent beach on either side of the road as you reach Kōri-jima. The bridge to Yagaji-jima starts just north of the Motobu peninsula off Rte 58.

Northern Okinawa-hontō 沖縄本島の北部

The northern part of Okinawa-hontō is largely undeveloped and comparatively wild and rugged. Since there is limited public transport in the north, you will probably need a rental car. Rte 58 hugs the west coast all the way up to **Hedo-misaki** (辺戸岬; Hedo Cape), which marks the northern end of Okinawa. The point is an incredibly scenic spot backed by hills, with rocks rising from the dense greenery. On a good day, Yoron-tō, the southernmost island in the Amami Islands, is easily seen only 23km to the northeast.

Islands Near Okinawa-hontō

Most travellers don't come this far just to souvenir-shop for clay *shiisā* in Naha. Even if your time on Okinawa-hontō is limited, it's a short ferry ride from Naha to some of the most attractive islands in the entire Southwest Island chain – the clear azure waters and white-sand beaches of the Kerama Islands are only 30km offshore, and about 60km beyond the Keramas lies the rarely visited Kume-jima.

To fall even further off the map, venture out to the other nearby islands: Ie-jima, Iheya-jima, Izena-jima, Aguni-jima, Kitadaitō-jima and Tonaki-jima. Naha's Tourist Information Office (p771) can help with the preliminaries.

Kerama Islands 慶良間諸島

The islands of the Kerama group are a world away from the buzz of Okinawa-hontō, though even these isles can get crowded during the summer holiday season. Each of the three main islands – Zamami-jima, Aka-jima and Tokashiki-jima – can be visited easily as a day trip from Naha. But to really savour their slow-paced pleasures, stay a few days in one of the islands' *minshuku*.

AKA-JIMA 阿嘉島

☎098 / POP 279

A mere 2km in diameter, tiny Aka-jima makes up for in beauty what it lacks in size. With some of the best beaches in the Keramas and an extremely peaceful atmosphere, it's easy to get stuck here for several days. There's also some great snorkelling and diving nearby.

If you keep your eyes open around dusk you might spot a **Kerama deer** (慶良間シカ), descendants of deer that were brought by the Satsuma from Kagoshima when they conquered the Ryūkyūs in 1609. The deer are smaller and darker than their mainland cousins, and have been designated a National Treasure.

There are great beaches on every side of the island, but for sheer postcard-perfect beauty, it's hard to beat the 1km stretch of white sand on the northeast coast known as **Nishibama Beach** (西浜ビーチ). It can be crowded in summer; if you want privacy, there are quieter beaches on the other sides of the island.

Dive shop-hotel **Marine House Seasir** (マリンハウスシーサー; ☎0120-10-2743, in English 090-8668-6544; www.seasir.com; s/d with 3 meals from ¥9000/16,000; P 📶) at the west end of the main village has good, clean Western- and Japanese-style rooms. Most of the guests are divers.

Kawai Diving (☎098-987-2219; http://oki-zamami.jp/~kawai/; 153 Aka; s/d incl meals from ¥7780/15,550; P @ 📶), located along Maehama Beach on the south coast, has simple rooms and a family atmosphere. English-speaking staff are happy to tell guests about the island and take them diving (one/two dives ¥6480/10,840, including equipment rental).

Zamami Sonei Ferry (☎098-868-4567) has two fast ferries a day (¥3140, one hour 10 minutes) and one regular ferry (¥2120, 1½ hours) to/from Naha's Tomari Port. A motorboat also makes four trips a day between Aka-jima and Zamami-jima (¥300, 15 minutes).

Due to its small size, the best way to get around the island is on foot.

ZAMAMI-JIMA 座間味島

☎098 / POP 586

A stone's throw from Aka-jima, Zamami-jima is *slightly* more developed, with its own lovely beaches. It's got some brilliant offshore islands and great diving and snorkelling in the surrounding waters. Pick up a map and excellent English-language information at the port's **Zamami Village Tourist Information Center** (☎098-987-2277; ⏲9am-5pm).

Furuzamami Beach (古座間味ビーチ), approximately 1km southeast from the port

DOGGED DEVOTION

Just outside Aka-jima port stands a statue of a dog named Shiro.

Shiro's family lived on Zamami-jima before moving to Aka-jima. After his family relocated to Aka-jima, they discovered, after repeated disappearances, that Shiro had been swimming the 3km across sometimes rough seas to visit his canine companion Marilyn on Zamami-jima, after which he'd make the return trip to his family.

Shiro's devotion became famous among the islanders, who would spot him paddling between the two islands. As the story goes, Shiro and Marilyn had three litters of puppies together, and after Shiro died, the people on Aka-jima collected the funds to build a monument to his memory.

On the western side of Zamami-jima you'll find a matching monument of Marilyn sitting, looking out across the water, waiting for her love.

(over the hill), is a stunning 700m stretch of white sand that is fronted by clear, shallow water and a bit of coral. The beach is well developed for day trippers, with toilets, showers and food stalls. You can also rent snorkelling gear here (¥1000).

If you fancy a little solitude, you'll find picturesque empty beaches in several of the coves on the other sides of the island. The best beaches, however, are on **Gahi-jima** (嘉比島) and **Agenashiku-jima** (安慶名敷島), which are located about a kilometre south of the port. Ringed by delightful white-sand beaches, they are perfect for a half-day *Robinson Crusoe* experience. One boat operator who can take you to these islands and arrange snorkelling trips is **Zamami Tour Operation** (098-987-3586). The tourist information office can also help arrange boat tours (¥1500 per person round-trip).

Whale-watching is possible between the months of December and April. For more information, either enquire at the tourist information office or call the **Zamami-mura Whale-Watching Association** (座間味村ホエールウォッチング協会; 098-896-4141; www.vill.zamami.okinawa.jp/whale; adult/child ¥5400/2700), which has one to two tours daily (two hours).

Stay overnight at **Joy Joy** (ジョイジョイ; 098-987-2445, 0120-10-2445; http://keramajoyjoy.com/index.html; 434-2 Zamami; r per person without bathroom incl breakfast from ¥5400;), a pension in the northwest corner of the village with Western- and Japanese-style rooms that surround a small garden. It also runs a dive shop, with beach and sea dive tours (in Japanese only) from ¥4860.

A new option for accommodation is the convivial **Zamamia International Guesthouse** (098-987-3626; www.zamamia-guesthouse.com; dm/s/d ¥2000/5000/6000;), run by a super-friendly Canadian expat who often organises barbecue dinners for guests. Dorm beds here are spacious and outfitted with privacy curtains; bathrooms are shared.

Zamami Sonei (098-868-4567) has two or three fast ferries a day (¥3140, 50 minutes) and one regular ferry (¥2120, two hours) to/from Naha's Tomari Port. The ferries usually stop at Aka-jima en route from Naha to Zamami.

A motorboat also makes four trips a day between Aka-jima and Zamami-jima (¥300, 15 minutes).

Rental cars, scooters and bicycles are available near the pier.

TOKASHIKI-JIMA 渡嘉敷島

098 / POP 730

Tokashiki-jima, the largest island of the Kerama Islands, is a long, skinny, north–south island that has some great beaches. It's very popular with young Japanese holidaymakers, but is slightly less appealing than Aka-jima and Zamami-jima. Ferries arrive at the port of Tokashiki (渡嘉敷) on the east coast.

The island's most attractive beaches are **Tokashiku Beach** (トカシクビーチ) and **Aharen Beach** (阿波連ビーチ), both of which are located on the west coast. Both beaches are well developed for tourism, and have toilets, showers, food stalls and shops where you can rent snorkelling gear (¥1000).

If you plan to spend the night, Aharen is the place to be. **Southern Cross** (サザンクロス; 098-987-2258, 090-1941-1232; 170 Aharen; r per person with/without meals from ¥8500/6500; P), a family-run inn with simple Western- and Japanese-style rooms, is practically on the beach. Rates are a little cheaper if you opt for shared bathrooms. A little further back in the village you'll find

Kerama-sō (けらま荘; ☎098-987-2125; 93 Aharen; r per person with/without breakfast from ¥4725/3675), which is a larger, more organised *minshuku* with basic Japanese-style rooms and reasonable rates. Staff will pick you up at the pier if you can get someone to make a reservation in advance in Japanese.

Marine Liner Tokashiki (マリンライナーとかしき; ☎098-987-3122) operates two or three fast ferries a day (¥2430, 40 minutes), while **Ferry Tokashiki** (フェリーとかしき; ☎098-868-7541) runs one regular ferry (¥1620, one hour 10 minutes) from Naha's Tomari Port.

Buses run from Tokashiki Port to the beaches on the west coast. Bicycles, cars and scooters are available in Tokashiki Port; **Kariyushi Rentasābisu** (かりゆしレンタサービス; ☎098-987-3311; http://kariyushi-kerama.com; 1779-10; ⌚9.30am-6.30pm) is one rental spot just outside the port area.

Kume-jima 久米島

☎098 / POP 8296

The furthest flung of the outer islands, Kume-jima is a quiet island that sees fewer visitors than the Keramas. It's mostly flat and covered with sugarcane, with a few good beaches and the mother of all sandbars off its east coast.

The airport is at the western extreme of the island, with the main port of Kanegusuku (兼城) just a few kilometres south. There is a **tourist information office** (☎098-985-7115) at the airport that opens to meet incoming flights in summer.

The most popular beach on the island is **Eef Beach** (イーフビーチ), on the east coast. *Iifu (Eef)* means 'white' in the local Kume dialect, and not surprisingly, the beach is known for its powdery white sand. The attractive **Shinri-hama** (シンリ浜), a beach on the west coast near the airport, is known for its sunsets over the East China Sea.

Kume-jima's most famous attraction is **Hate-no-hama** (はての浜), a 7km sandbar that extends from the eastern point of the island, pointing back towards Okinawa-hontō. If you arrive by air, you can't miss this coral-fringed strip of white framed by the turquoise waters of the sea. The best way to get there is on an excursion with **Hatenohama Kankō Service** (はての浜観光サービス; ☎090-8292-8854; ⌚9am-5pm), which runs a three-hour tour to the sandbar for ¥4500. If you book in advance, staff members can pick you up from your accommodation.

On tiny **Ōjima** (奥武島), which is connected to Kume-jima's east coast by a causeway, you'll find the intriguing **Tatami-ishi** (畳石), a natural formation of flat pentagonal rocks that covers the seashore.

Eef Beach is the place to stay, and there are plenty of choices along the 1.5km waterfront. Splurge a little and stay on the beach at the slightly retro **Kumejima Eef Beach Hotel** (久米島イーフビーチホテル; ☎098-985-7111; www.courthotels.co.jp/kumejima; 548 Janadō; s/d with breakfast from ¥7150/18,900; P @).

JTA and RAC operate six flights a day between Naha and Kume-jima. **Kume Shōsen** (久米商船; ☎098-868-2686) runs one or two daily ferries from Naha's Tomari Port to/from Kume-jima (¥3390, three hours).

Kume-jima has an efficient bus system, and there are several rental-car companies at the port and airport.

Miyako Islands 宮古諸島

Located just north of the Tropic of Cancer, the Miyako Islands have some of the finest beaches in the Southwest Islands, and there is good diving and snorkelling in the waters offshore. This island group contains the main island of Miyako-jima, and the nearby islands of Ikema-jima, Irabu-jima, Shimoji-jima and Kurima-jima, as well as a scattering of tiny islets.

Miyako-jima 宮古島

☎0980 / POP 55,006

The main island in the Miyako group, Miyako-jima is a mostly flat expanse of sugarcane edged with excellent beaches, with long fingers of land pointing out into the sea. Lying just offshore are four smaller islands, three of which are connected to the main island by bridges.

You can happily spend your days here hopping from one great beach to the next, with a spot of snorkelling at each one if you're so inclined. If you tire of that, a seaside drive to the various capes and wetlands is a great way to spend a few hours.

Sights & Activities

On the southeast corner of Miyako-jima are several attractions including **Boraga Beach** (保良泉ビーチ), which is a popular spot for snorkelling and kayaking (with a hair-raisingly steep access road). Around the cape

Miyako Islands

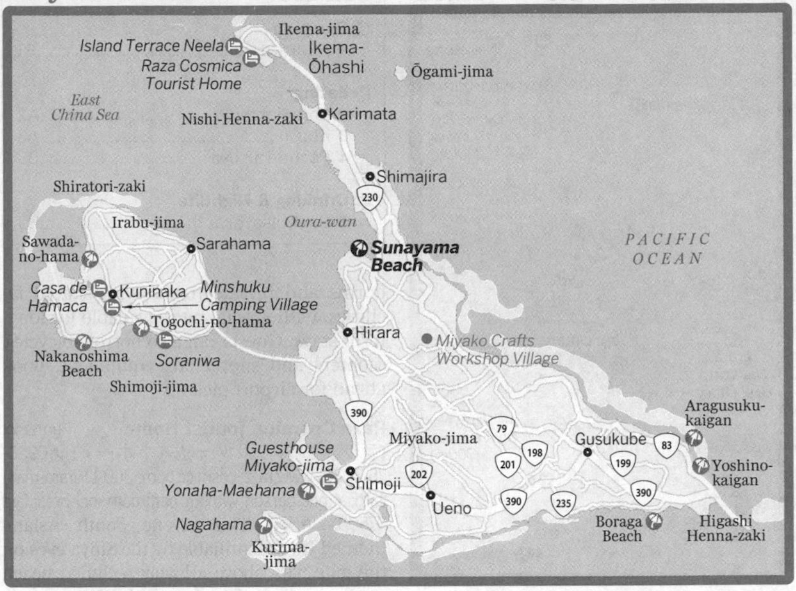

to the north, you'll find **Yoshino-kaigan** (吉野海岸; Yoshino Coast) and **Aragusuku-kaigan** (新城海岸; Aragusuku Coast), two relatively shallow beaches with a lot of offshore coral (much of it dead).

If you've got a car, we recommend a drive out to the end of **Higashi Henna-zaki** (東平安名崎), a narrow finger of land that extends 2km into the Pacific Ocean. There are picnic tables, walking trails and a lighthouse at the point to explore.

Another good drive is across **Ikema-Ōhashi** (池間大橋) to **Ikema-jima** (池間島). The shallow turquoise water on either side of this 1.4km bridge is insanely beautiful on a sunny day (just try to keep your eyes on the road). You'll find several **private pocket beaches** around the coast of Ikema-jima.

★ Sunayama Beach BEACH

(砂山ビーチ) Just 4km north of Hirara you will find this excellent little beach, which lies at the bottom of a large sand dune (hence the name 'Sand Mountain Beach'). A cool stone arch at one side of the beach provides a bit of shade.

Yonaha-Maehama BEACH

(与那覇前浜ビーチ) On the southwest coast, beautiful Yonaha-Maehama is a 6km stretch of white sand that attracts a lot of families and young folks due to its shallow waters. It's a lovely beach, but it can get crowded and the presence of the occasional jet-ski is a drawback. It's just before the Kurima-Ōhashi bridge, on the north side.

Nagahama BEACH

(長浜) If you've had a look at the crowds at Yoneha-Maehama and decided that you want something quieter, head across the Kurima-Ōhashi and drive to the northwest coast of **Kurima-jima** (来間島), where you will find the brilliant (and usually uncrowded) Nagahama.

Miyako Crafts Workshop Village COURSE

(宮古島市体験工芸村; ☎0980-73-4111, 090-7165-9862; www.miyakotaiken.com; 1166-286 Higashi-nakasone, Hirara; workshops from ¥1500; ⌚10am-6pm) At this crafts village adjoining the Miyako Botanical Garden, you can learn about Miyako-jima's traditional handicrafts with some hands-on creativity. Courses, most of which are suitable for kids, include making *shiisā* from clay, cooking Miyako specialities, and traditional weaving (*Miyako-jōfu*). Though some workshops accommodate walk-ins, it's best to make reservations beforehand.

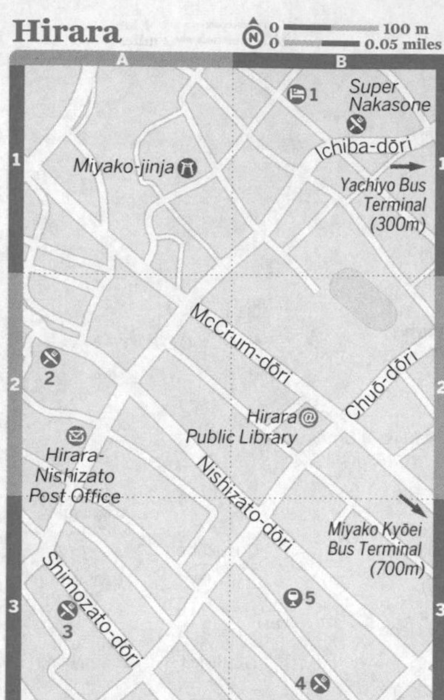

Hirara

Sleeping
1 Hiraraya B1

Eating
2 Koja Honten A2
3 Kuusu A3
4 Pōcha Tatsuya B3

Drinking & Nightlife
5 Bar Pulse B3

Sleeping

Most of the accommodation is located in the town of Hirara, but you'll also find places to stay closer to the beaches. There are free campgrounds at many beaches, including Yonaha-Maehama, Boraga and Aragusuku.

Hiraraya GUESTHOUSE ¥
(ひららや; ☎0980-75-3221; www.miyako-net.ne.jp/~hiraraya; 282 Higashi-nakasone; dm night/week ¥2000/12,000, r per person night/week ¥3000/18,000; P 📶) Located in central Hirara around the corner from Nakasone Super (look for the doorway curtain that says 'Hiraraya'), the genial, English-speaking Hiro presides over this laid-back spot where young neighbours and friends cruise in to hang out. Accommodation is available in a dorm with huge beds, or a Japanese-style private room; there are special rates available for longer-term stays.

Guesthouse Miyako-jima GUESTHOUSE ¥
(ゲストハウス宮古島; ☎0980-76-2330, 090-1583-6520; www2.miyako-ma.jp/yonaha/test-top.html; 233 Yoneha; dm/s/d ¥1800/3500/6000; P 📶) This bright and cheery guesthouse run by a kite-boarding enthusiast has a scenic location near Yoneha-Maehama beach. Accommodation is in cosy Western-style dorms and private rooms with shared facilities, with special rates available for long-term stays. Guests can also borrow bicycles, scooters and snorkelling equipment. Book ahead for airport pick-up.

Raza Cosmica Tourist Home HOTEL ¥¥
(ラザ・コスミカツーリストホーム; ☎0980-75-2020; www.raza-cosmica.com; 309-1 Hirara-maezato; r per person without bathroom incl breakfast ¥7500; P 📶) This serene South Asian-themed inn, identifiable by the Shiva eyes on the gate, sits above a lovely secluded beach on Ikema-jima. Wood-floored, Western-style rooms offer peace and quiet – especially as children under 12 are not permitted. Spotless bathroom facilities are shared. Because of its somewhat isolated location, it's best to rent a car. Reservations must be made in advance via email.

Island Terrace Neela BOUTIQUE HOTEL ¥¥¥
(アイランドテラス・ニーラ; ☎0980-74-4678; www.neela.jp; 317-1 Hirara-maezato; s/d incl breakfast from ¥38,500/70,000; P 📶 🏊) Overlooking a serene white-sand beach on Ikema-jima, this intimate high-end resort looks like a whitewashed Mediterranean resort airlifted to Japan. The private villas would make a decadent honeymoon destination. Rates are moderately less expensive during slower seasons.

Eating & Drinking

There are eateries scattered here and there across the island, but you'll find the best selection in the town of Hirara.

Koja Honten SOBA ¥
(古謝本店; ☎0980-72-2139; 165 Nishizato; dishes ¥550-950; ⏰10am-8pm) One block northwest of the intersection between Ichiba-dōri and Nishizato-dōri, this nondescript noodle house is something of a local legend. For more than 50 years, Koja has been serv-

ing up steaming bowls of *sōki-soba* (noodles with pork; ¥700). Look for the white tiles around the entryway; the owner speaks a bit of English.

Kuusu SOUTHEAST ASIAN ¥
(☎0980-75-5963; 553-3 Shimozato; dishes ¥500-800; ⏲6pm-2am Fri-Wed; 📖) Fresh spring rolls, green curry, *gōyā champurū* and nasi goreng all feature on the menu here, and a young crowd keeps it lively if you're just here for a Singha beer or a sip of *awamori*.

★ **Pōcha Tatsuya** IZAKAYA ¥¥
(ぽうちゃたつや; ☎0980-73-3931; 275 Nishizato; meals ¥3000-4000; ⏲6.30-11pm Wed-Mon) This hospitable *izakaya* is a warm, efficient bastion of Miyako-jima quality, serving fresh, thoughtfully prepared local fare such as *kobushime-yawaraka-ni* (steamed cuttlefish; ¥730) and *sūchiki* (vinegared pork with bitter melon; ¥630). Its justified popularity necessitates making reservations. Some Japanese skills are helpful here, as the specials change often, but requesting *omakase* (chef's choice) will result in a succession of regional delights.

Bar Pulse BAR
(バーパルス; ☎0980-73-6441; 299-7 Nishizato; drinks ¥700; ⏲8pm-4am) Run by the English-speaking P-Boo, who spins tunes from his extensive and eclectic collection, this bar is a welcome aural refuge from Okinawa's ubiquitous soft-samba covers of Beatles ditties. The interior is pretty bare bones, but there's no cover and the company is interesting. Look for the pink neon sign outside.

ℹ Information

Hirara Public Library (平良市立図書館; cnr McCrum-dōri & Chūō-dōri, Hirara; ⏲10am-7pm Tue-Fri, 10am-6pm Sat, 10am-5pm Sun) Free internet access on the 2nd floor.

Hirara-Nishizato Post Office (平良西里郵便局; Ichiba-dōri; ⏲9am-5pm Mon-Fri, ATM 9am-7pm) This centrally located post office has an international ATM.

Tourist Information Desk (☎0980-72-0899; ⏲9am-6pm) In the arrivals hall of the airport, you can pick up a copy of the *Miyako Island Guide Map*. Travellers who can read Japanese should also pick up a copy of the detailed *Guide Map Miyako*.

ℹ Getting There & Away

Miyako-jima has direct flights to/from Tokyo's Haneda Airport (JTA), Naha (JTA/RAC/ANA) and Ishigaki (RAC/ANA).

ℹ Getting Around

Miyako-jima has a limited bus network that operates from two bus stands in Hirara. Buses run between the airport and Hirara (¥210, 10 minutes). Buses also depart from Yachiyo bus terminal for Ikema-jima (¥500, 35 minutes), and from the Miyako Kyōei bus terminal, 700m east of town, to Yoshino-kaigan/Boraga Beach (¥500, 50 minutes). Yet another line runs between Hirara and Yoneha-Maehama/Kurima-jima (¥390, 30 minutes).

IN DEEP WATER

Stunning both above and below the water's surface, the Southwest Islands set the scene for some excellent diving with an impressive variety of species such as whale sharks, manta rays, sea snakes, turtles and corals. Keeping it even more interesting are underwater wrecks, cavern systems and some mysterious ruins (…or very unusual rock formations).

Costs for diving in the Southwest Islands are higher than you might pay in Southeast Asia, but standards of equipment and guiding are fairly high. If you are not in possession of a valid diving certification, many operators offer introductory diving programs for novices. To rent equipment, you should know your weight in kilograms, your height in metres and your shoe size in centimetres.

Here are some English-speaking operators who welcome foreigners:

Umicoza (海講座; ☎0980-88-2434; www.umicoza.com/english; 1287-97 Kabira, Ishigaki-jima; 1/2 dives ¥9450/12,600, equipment rental ¥5250; ⏲8am-6pm)

Piranha Divers (☎080-4277-1155, 098-967-8487; www.piranha-divers.jp; 2288-75 Aza-Nakama, Okinawa-hontō; full-day dives from ¥13,000, equipment rental ¥4000)

Penguin Divers (ペンギンダイバーズ; ☎0980-79-5433; www.diving-penguin.com/english.htm; 1st fl, 27 Shimozato, Hirara, Miyako-jima; 2 boat dives ¥13,000)

Sou Wes (Yonaguni-jima; see p790)

The island's flat terrain is perfectly suited to biking; rent bicycles at the guesthouse Hiraraya (p778) in Hirara. If you want to move faster, there are rental-car counters at the airport and offices in Hirara.

Irabu-jima & Shimoji-jima 伊良部島・下地島

With the completion of the Irabu Bridge (伊良部大橋) in early 2015, the bucolic, rural character of Irabu-jima and Shimoji-jima may undergo some transformation with the new ease of access. Not much goes on here, aside from sugarcane cultivation and the 'touch-and-go' (landing and immediate take-off) exercises by ANA pilots. These islands are blessed with uncrowded beaches and a snail-paced vibe – well worth a day trip from Miyako-jima.

The best swimming beach is **Toguchi-no-hama** (渡口の浜) on Irabu-jima's west coast. Easily the best snorkelling beach is **Nakanoshima Beach** (中の島ビーチ), protected by a high-walled bay on the west coast of Shimoji-jima. Look for the sign reading 'Nakano Island the Beach'.

An intriguing site for a stroll or dive is **Tōri-ike** (通り池), two seawater 'ponds' on the west coast of Shimoji-jima that are actually sink-holes in the coral that formed the island.

If you seek an out of the ordinary experience, opt for an overnight on Irabu-jima at the quirkily delightful **Casa de Hamaca** (カサ・デ・アマカ; ☎080-3277-8941; 621-3 Kuninaka; s/d without bathroom ¥3000/5400; ⏰closed Jan-Mar; P 📶). Run by Japanese runner and world traveller Sekiyama Tadashi, this is likely the only accommodation in Japan outfitted solely with hammocks *and* a Spanish-speaking proprietor. Another inexpensive option is **Minshuku Camping Village** (民宿キャンプ村; ☎0980-78-3100; http://m-souken.on.omisenomikata.jp; 645-1 Kuninaka; s/d ¥3000/4000, campsites ¥500) just over the bridge in Shimoji-jima.

For a more secluded and romantic experience, head to **Soraniwa** (そらにわ; ☎0980-74-5528; www.soraniwa.org; 721-1 Irabu-azairabu; s/tw from ¥10,500/13,650, apt from ¥25,000, lunch ¥900-1200; ⏰cafe 11.30am-10pm; P @) on Irabu-jima's south coast. This small, stylish cafe-hotel is run by a young couple transplanted from the 'mainland'. The restaurant uses local, organic ingredients, while the intimate, modern hotel features sumptuous beds, shelves made from repurposed wood and a rooftop Jacuzzi looking onto the sea.

Yaeyama Islands 八重山諸島

At the far southwestern end of the Southwest Islands are the gorgeous Yaeyama Islands, which include the main islands of Ishigaki-jima and Iriomote-jima as well as a spread of 17 isles. Located near the Tropic of Cancer, they are renowned for their lovely beaches, superb diving and lush landscapes.

The Yaeyama Islands are arguably the top destination in the Southwest Islands. They offer Japan's best snorkelling and diving, and some of the country's last intact subtropical jungles and mangrove swamps (both on Iriomote-jima). Perhaps the best feature of the Yaeyamas is their variety and the ease with which you can explore them: plentiful ferry services run between Ishigaki City and nearby islands such as Iriomote-jima and Taketomi-jima, and you can easily explore three or four islands in one trip.

Ishigaki-jima 石垣島

☎0980 / POP 48,910

Blessed with excellent beaches and brilliant dive sites, Ishigaki-jima also possesses an attractive, rugged geography that invites long drives and day hikes. Located 100km southwest of Miyako-jima, Ishigaki is the most populated and developed island in the Yaeyama group. Some places around the island may seem reminiscent of Hawaii, but Ishigaki is tropical Japan through and through.

Sights & Activities

Ishigaki City (石垣市) occupies the south-western corner of the island. You'll find most of the action in the two shopping arcades, which run parallel to the main street, Shiyakusho-dōri. The city is easily walkable, and can be explored in an hour or two.

A series of roads branch out from Ishigaki City and head along the coastline and into the interior. There are several settlements near the coast, though most of the interior is mountains and farmland.

Some of the best beaches on the island are found on the west coast. It's also worth spending a half-day exploring some of the city's sights to get a feel for its culture.

The sea around Ishigaki-jima is famous among the Japanese diving community for its large schools of manta rays, particularly from June to October. The most popular

Ishigaki City

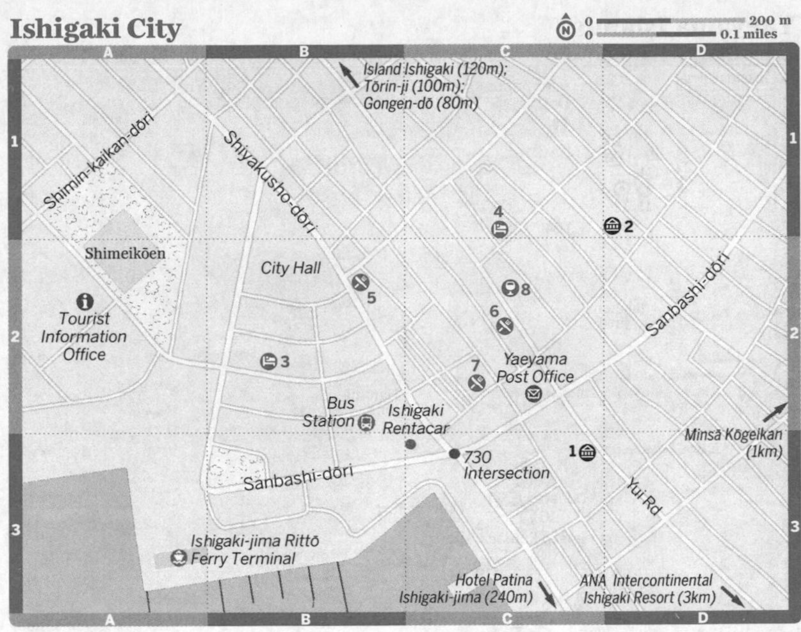

Ishigaki City

Sights

1 Ishigaki City Yaeyama Museum C3
2 Miyara Dōnchi D1

Sleeping

3 Pension Yaima-biyōri B2
4 Rakutenya... C1

Eating

5 Eifuku Shokudō B2
6 Ishigaki-jima Kids.................................C2
7 Paikaji C2

Drinking & Nightlife

8 Mori-no-Kokage C2

spot is **Manta Scramble**, off the coast of Kabira Ishizaki. Although you'll likely be sharing with a fair number of dive boats, you're almost guaranteed to see a manta (or four). There are a number of dive shops on Ishigaki-jima.

Ishigaki City Yaeyama Museum MUSEUM
(石垣市立八重山博物館; ☎0980-82-4712; 4-1 Tonoshiro; admission ¥200; ⏰9am-5pm Tue-Sun) This modest museum has exhibits on the culture and history of the island, which are quite well presented with English explanations. Notable among the more typical cultural artefacts: a few informational pages about some of Japan's oldest human remains (estimated, using carbon dating, to be 24,000 years old), discovered on Ishigaki in 2011 during construction of the new airport.

Miyara Dōnchi HISTORIC BUILDING
(宮良殿内; 178 Ōkawa; admission ¥200; ⏰9am-5pm) The unique home of a Ryūkyū kingdom official dating from 1819; walk north along Sanbashi-dōri until you see signs in English. The house is still an actual residence, so you can only peer into the open rooms from the outside and enjoy the small garden.

Tōrin-ji BUDDHIST TEMPLE
(桃林寺; 285 Ishigaki; ⏰9am-7pm) Founded in 1614, the Zen temple of Tōrin-ji, near the intersection of Shimin-kaikan-dōri and Rte 79, is home to the 18th-century guardian statues of Deva kings. Adjacent to the temple is **Gongen-dō** (権現堂; ⏰9am-7pm), a small shrine rebuilt after being destroyed by a tsunami in 1771.

Yonehara Beach BEACH
(米原海岸) On the north coast of Ishigaki along Rte 79, Yonehara Beach is a nice sand beach with a good bit of reef offshore. You can rent snorkel gear (¥1000) at any of the

Yaeyama Islands

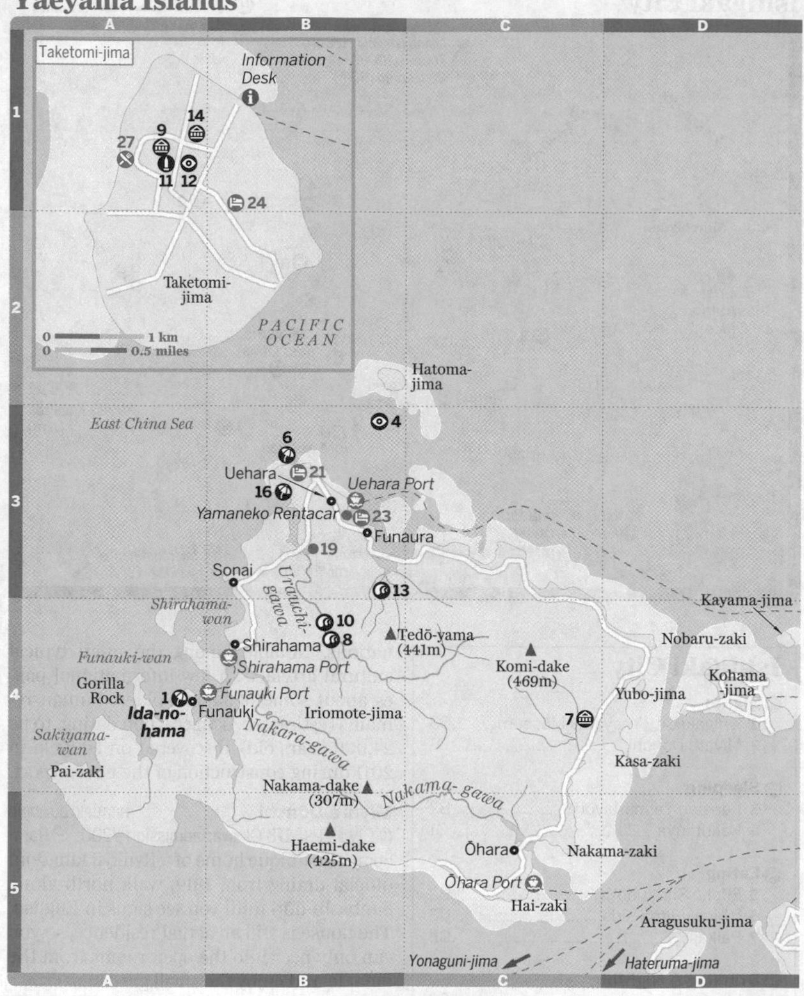

shops along the main road, where you'll also find plentiful cafes.

★Kabira-wan BEACH

(川平湾) Kabira-wan is a sheltered bay with white-sand shores and a couple of interesting clumplike islands offshore. This is more of a wading beach than a swimming beach and it's usually busy with glass-bottomed boat traffic, which detracts somewhat from its beauty.

★Sunset Beach BEACH

(サンセットビーチ) At the north end of the island, on the west coast, you will find a long strip of sand with a bit of offshore reef. As the name implies, this is a good spot to watch the sun set into the East China Sea.

Sleeping

★Iriwa GUESTHOUSE ¥

(イリワ; ☎0980-88-2563; http://iriwa.org; 599 Kabira; dm ¥2500, s/d from ¥4500/7600; P @) Just above Kabira-wan on the north coast, Iriwa is a comfortable guesthouse with dorm beds, two large private rooms and a small self-contained cottage, all warmly decorated with a Hawaiian aesthetic. It's run by a super-chill, friendly young Korean/

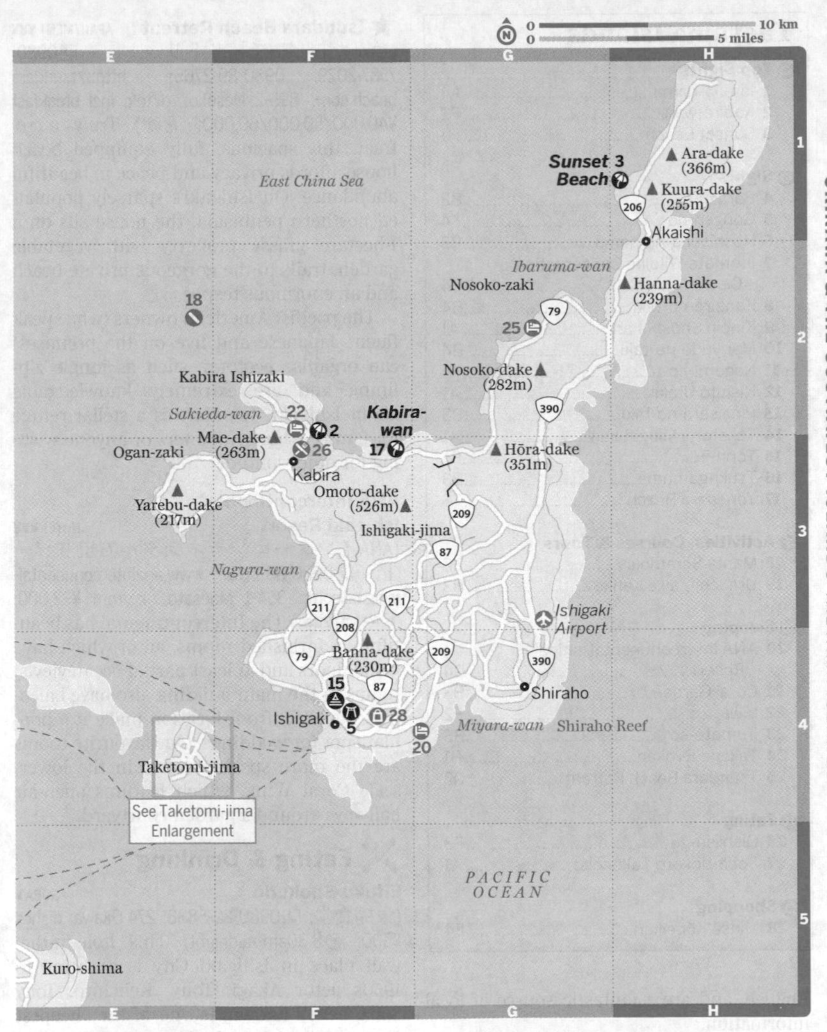

Japanese couple who like to share meals and snorkelling expeditions with guests.

The main house has a communal lounge room and spacious, sunny kitchen – the roof, the highest point in Kabira village, offers excellent views of the sea during the day and stars at night.

Pension Yaima-biyōri GUESTHOUSE ¥
(ペンションやいま日和; ☎0980-88-5578; http://yaimabiyori.com; 10-7 Miaski-chō; s/d without bathroom ¥3200/5600, with bathroom ¥3600/6600; P @) Centrally located in Ishigaki City two blocks north of the ferry and bus station, this welcoming pension offers appealing, spacious Western- and Japanese-style rooms with shared facilities or private bathrooms.

Rakutenya GUESTHOUSE ¥
(楽天屋; ☎0980-83-8713; www3.big.or.jp/~erm8p3gi; 291 Ōkawa; r per person without bathroom ¥3500; P @) This quaint guesthouse is two blocks north of the covered markets in Ishigaki City, and has attractive Western- and Japanese-style rooms in a couple of rickety, old wooden houses. The managers are a friendly Japanese couple who speak some

Yaeyama Islands

Top Sights

1 Ida-no-hama ... A4
2 Kabira-wan ... F2
3 Sunset Beach ... H1

Sights

4 Barasu-tō ... B3
5 Gongen-dō ... F4
6 Hoshisuna-no-hama ... B3
7 Iriomote Wildlife Conservation Center ... C4
8 Kanpire-no-taki ... B4
9 Kihōin Shūshūkan ... A1
10 Mariyudō-no-taki ... B4
11 Nagomi-no-tō ... A1
12 Nishitō Utaki ... A1
13 Pinaisāra-no-taki ... B3
14 Taketomi Mingei-kan ... A1
15 Tōrin-ji ... F4
16 Tsuki-ga-hama ... B3
17 Yonehara Beach ... F3

Activities, Courses & Tours

18 Manta Scramble ... E2
19 Urauchi-gawa Kankō ... B3

Sleeping

20 ANA Intercontinental Ishigaki Resort ... G4
21 Coral Garden ... B3
22 Iriwa ... F2
23 Irumote-sō ... B3
24 Takana Ryokan ... B1
25 Tsundara Beach Retreat ... G2

Eating

26 Oishiisā-gu ... F3
27 Soba-dokoro Takenoko ... A1

Shopping

28 Minsā Kōgeikan ... F4

English, and are a fantastic source of local information.

Hotel Patina Ishigaki-jima HOTEL ¥¥
(ホテルパティーナ石垣島; ☎0980-87-7400; www.patina.in; 1-8-5 Yashima-chō; s/tw incl breakfast from ¥7300/10,500; P ⊜ @ ☜) Just a few minutes' walk from the port and central Ishigaki City, Hotel Patina is a small, friendly hotel that's far enough from downtown to be quiet at night. A French bakery across the way supplies snacks or a post-breakfast breakfast, while the relaxed hotel offers bike and scooter rentals as well as free laundry (dryers are coin operated).

★Tsundara Beach Retreat APARTMENT ¥¥¥
(つんだらビーチ・リトリート; ☎0980-7587-2029, 0980-89-2765; http://tsundarabeach.com; 895-2 Nosoko; d/tr/q incl breakfast ¥40,000/50,000/60,000; P @) Truly a retreat, this spacious, fully equipped beach house affords privacy and peace in beautiful abundance. On Ishigaki's sparsely populated northern peninsula, the house sits on a 1-hectare grassy property with vegetable garden, trails to the gorgeous private beach and an enormous teepee.

The pacifist American owners (who speak fluent Japanese and live on the premises) can organise ecotours such as jungle ziplining and are extremely knowledgable about Ishigaki. Tsundara is a stellar refuge for families, honeymooners or anyone wishing for quiet solitude.

ANA Intercontinental Ishigaki Resort HOTEL ¥¥¥
(ANAインターコンチネンタル石垣リゾート; ☎0980-88-7111; www.anaintercontinental-ishigaki.com; 354-1 Maesato; r from ¥22,000; P ⊜ @ ☜ ≋) The Intercontinental has beautifully refurbished rooms, all of which have wood floors and at least partial ocean views; rooms in the main building also have balconies. Its beachfront location make it a popular spot for weddings. Our favourite rooms are the more spacious ones in the lower-scale Coral Wing, which features open-air hallways around a garden courtyard.

Eating & Drinking

Eifuku Shokudō SOBA ¥
(栄福食堂; ☎0980-82-5838; 274 Ōkawa; dishes ¥500; ⊙8.30am-midnight) This hole-in-the-wall place in Ishigaki City is a shrine to 1950s actor Akagi 'Tony' Keiichirō. Tony Soba, as it's known, is one of the cheapest places on the island for *Yaeyama-soba* (thin noodles in broth; ¥300), though we recommend the stinky (but tasty) *yagi-soba* (goat *soba;* ¥500). Look for the blue building with Tony's visage illustrating the wall.

Oishiisā-gu NOODLES ¥
(おいシーサー遇; ☎0980-88-2233; 906-1 Kabira; meals ¥600-1000; ⊙11am-6pm, to 7pm in summer; 📋) This sunlit *soba* place in Kabira serves local dishes like chilled *yomogi-soba* (mugwort *soba*) served in a conch shell, or *tebichi soba,* Okinawan *soba* topped with stewed pork trotters. Even better, you can follow your lunch with some homemade

gelato, in novel flavours like Ishigaki beer, *gōyā* or black sesame and soybean.

Ishigaki-jima Kids SOBA ¥
(石垣島キッズ; ☎0980-83-8671; 203-1 Ōkawa; meals ¥850; ⏲noon-2pm & 6-9pm Thu-Tue) In one of the covered arcades, Ishigaki-jima Kids serves good Ishigaki-style cafe fare – *sōki-soba,* taco rice and the like – all detailed in a picture menu. There's usually a great lunch set of taco rice or *Yaeyama soba* with a glass of beer for ¥1250.

★ **Paikaji** IZAKAYA ¥¥
(南風; ☎0980-82-6027; 219 Ōkawa; dishes ¥700; ⏲5pm-midnight) No relation to Naha's Paikaji chain, this Ishigaki City favourite serves all the Okinawan and Yaeyama standards. Both the atmosphere and kitchen get top marks. Try the *ikasumi chahan* (squid ink fried rice; ¥700), the *gōyā champurū* (¥750) or the *sashimi moriawase* (sashimi assortment; ¥750 to ¥1800 depending on size). Look for the traditional front, coral around the entryway and a red-and-white sign.

Mori-no-Kokage IZAKAYA
(森のこかげ; ☎0980-83-7933; 199 Ōkawa; dishes ¥800; ⏲5pm-midnight Fri-Wed) This little Ishigaki City *izakaya* has warmth and natural ambience. Local treats are sliced steak of Ishigaki beef (¥1280) and the microbrew *ishigaki-jima-zake* (¥500). Look for the plants and tree trunks outside.

Shopping

A good place to shop for *o-miyage* (souvenirs) is the main shopping arcade, which also has a public market. Shopkeepers start slashing prices in the hour or so before closing up shop in the early evening.

Minsā Kōgeikan ARTS
(みんさー工芸館; ☎0980-82-3473; 909 Tonoshiro; ⏲9am-6pm) Minsā Kōgeikan is a weaving workshop and showroom with exhibits on Yaeyama Islands textiles. You can also try your hand at weaving a coaster (¥1500); you'll need to reserve ahead by phone. The building is located between the city centre and the airport, and can be reached via the airport bus (there's a Minsā Kōgeikan stop).

Information

Information Counter (☎0980-87-0468; Airport; ⏲7.30am-9pm) Small but helpful.

Island Ishigaki (アイランド ishigaki; ☎0980-82-7848; www.island-ishigaki.jp; 3 Arakawa; internet 1hr ¥400; ⏲24hr) A clean, well-lit place to surf the web or spend the night if you're in a bind, this *manga kissa* (comic-book coffee shop) is a short walk from the Ishigaki City centre.

Tourist Information Office (石垣市観光協会; ☎0980-82-2809; 1st fl, Ishigaki-shi Shōkō Kaikan; ⏲8.30am-5.30pm Mon-Fri) Sometimes has friendly English-speaking staff and always has an English-language Yaeyama Islands brochure. Japanese readers should pick up the *Ishigaki Town Guide* and the *Yaeyama Navi*.

Yaeyama Post Office (八重山郵便局; Sanbashi-dōri; ⏲lobby 9am-7pm Mon-Fri, to 3pm Sat, ATM 8am-9pm) Has international ATMs.

Getting There & Away

AIR

Ishigaki-jima has direct flights to/from Tokyo's Haneda Airport (JTA/ANA), Osaka's Kansai International Airport (JTA/ANA), Naha (JTA/ANA), Miyako-jima (RAC/ANA) and Yonaguni-jima (RAC).

BOAT

Ishigaki-jima Rittō Ferry Terminal (石垣港離島ターミナル) serves islands including Iriomote-jima, Kohama-jima, Taketomi-jima and Hateruma-jima. Departures are frequent enough that you can usually just turn up in the morning and hop on the next ferry departing for your intended destination (except during the summer high season). The three main ferry operators are **Yaeyama Kankō Ferry** (八重山観光フェリー; ☎0980-82-5010; www.yaeyama.co.jp), **Ishigaki Dream Kankō** (石垣島ドリーム観光; ☎0980-84-3178; www.ishigaki-dream.co.jp) and **Anei Kankō** (安栄観光; ☎0980-83-0055; www.aneikankou.co.jp). To get to the ferry terminal, head southwest along the waterfront from the 730 Intersection.

Getting Around

The bus station is across the road from the ferry terminal in Ishigaki City. Several buses an hour go to the airport (¥540, 45 minutes). A few daily buses go to Kabira-wan (¥680, 50 minutes), Yonehara Beach (¥820, one hour) and Shiraho (¥500, 30 minutes). One-day (¥1000) and five-day bus passes (¥2000) are available for purchase directly from the driver.

Rental cars, scooters and bicycles are available at shops throughout the city centre. If you're comfortable on a scooter, it's a scenic four- to five-hour cruise around the island; plan for longer if you want to spend some time relaxing on the island's beaches. **Ishigaki Rentacar** (石垣島レンタカー; ☎0980-82-8840; 25 Ōkawa; ⏲8am-7pm) is located in the city centre and has reasonable rates.

Iriomote-jima 西表島

☎0980 / POP 2272

Although it's only 20km west of Ishigaki-jima, Iriomote-jima could easily qualify as Japan's last frontier. Dense jungles and mangrove swamp blanket more than 90% of the island, and it's fringed by some of the most beautiful coral reefs in all Japan. If you're super lucky, you may even spot one of the island's rare *yamaneko*, a nocturnal and rarely seen wildcat (they are most often seen crossing the road at night, so drive carefully after dark).

Several rivers penetrate far into the lush interior of the island and these can be explored by riverboat or kayak. Add to the mix sun-drenched beaches and spectacular diving and snorkelling, and it's easy to see why Iriomote-jima is one of the best destinations in Japan for nature lovers.

Sights & Activities

The majority of the island's beaches are shallow due to the extensive coral reef that surrounds the island.

★Ida-no-hama BEACH
(イダの浜) From **Shirahama** (白浜), at the western end of the north coast road, there are four daily boats to the isolated settlement of **Funauki** (船浮; ¥500). Once there, it's a mere 10-minute walk on to the absolutely gorgeous Ida-no-hama.

Hoshisuna-no-hama BEACH
(星砂の浜; Star Sand Beach) If you're looking to do a bit of snorkelling, head to this beach on the northwestern tip of the island. The beach is named after its star sand, which actually consists of the dried skeletons of marine protozoa. If you are a competent swimmer and the sea is calm, make your way with mask and snorkel to the outside of the reef – the coral and tropical fish here are spectacular.

Tsuki-ga-hama BEACH
(月ヶ浜; Moon Beach) The best swimming beach on the island is Tsuki-ga-hama, a crescent-shaped yellow-sand beach at the mouth of the Urauchi-gawa on the north coast.

Iriomote Wildlife Conservation Center MUSEUM
(西表野生生物保護センター; ☎0980-85-5581; Komi Taketomi; ⏲10am-4pm Tue-Sun, closed noon-1pm) FREE If you are at all intrigued by the *yamaneko*, it's worth stopping by this natural-history centre. Though exhibits are all in Japanese, of interest is a short documentary film about the *yamaneko* and its declining population on an island with hazards like human refuse and fast cars. A basic pamphlet in English is available for ¥100.

Hiking

Iriomote has some great hikes, but do not head off into the jungle interior without notifying police: the trails in the interior are hard to follow – many people have become lost and required rescue. We strongly suggest that you stick to well-marked tracks like the one listed here, or arrange for a guide through your accommodation (from ¥20,000).

At the back of a mangrove-lined bay called Funaura-wan, a few kilometres east of Uehara, you can make out a lovely waterfall plunging 55m down the cliffs. This is **Pinaisāra-no-taki** (ピナイサーラの滝), Okinawa's highest waterfall at 55m. When the tide is right, you can paddle a kayak across the shallow lagoon and then follow the Hinai-gawa (on the left) to the base of the falls. The short Māre-gawa (on the right) meets a trail where it narrows. This climbs to the top of the falls, from where there are superb views down to the coast. From the river, walk inland until you come to a pumping station, then turn around and take the right fork in the path. The walk takes less than two hours, and the river is great for a cooling dip.

Unfortunately, it is difficult to find a tour company that will rent you a kayak without requiring you to join a guided tour (half-/full days cost about ¥6000/10,000). Other day hikes you can do independently include the ones along the Urauchi-gawa.

Diving

Much of the brilliant coral fringing Iriomote's shores is accessible to proficient snorkellers. Most of the offshore dive sites around Iriomote are served by dive operators based on Ishigaki.

One spot worth noting is the unusual **Barasu-tō** (バラス島), between Iriomote-jima and Hatoma-jima, which is a small island formed entirely of bits of broken coral. In addition to the island itself, the reefs nearby are in quite good condition and make for good boat-based snorkelling on a calm day.

Tours

Iriomote's number-one attraction is a boat trip up the **Urauchi-gawa** (浦内川), a winding brown river reminiscent of a tiny stretch of the Amazon. From the mouth of the river, **Urauchi-gawa Kankō** (浦内川観光; ☎0980-85-6154; www.urauchigawa.com) runs boat tours 8km up the river (round-trip ¥1800, 30 minutes each way, multiple departures daily between 9.30am and 3.30pm). At the 8km point, the boat docks and you can walk a further 2km to the scenic waterfalls of **Mariyudō-no-taki** (マリユドウの滝), from where another 200m brings you to the **Kanpire-no-taki** (カンピレーの滝). The walk from the dock to Kanpire-no-taki and back takes around two hours. You can also opt to just take the boat trip to the dock and back. The pier (浦内川遊覧船乗場) is about 6km west of Uehara.

Sleeping

Iriomote-jima's accommodation is spread out around the island. Most places will send a car to pick you up from the ferry terminal if you let them know what time you will be arriving.

Kanpira-sō MINSHUKU ¥
(カンピラ荘; ☎0980-85-6508; www.kanpira.com; 545 Uehara; r per person with/without meals from ¥5000/3000, with meals & private bathroom ¥6000; P) Two minutes' walk from the ferry landing in Uehara, hospitable Kanpira has basic Japanese-style rooms and an informative manager who produces extraordinarily good, bilingual maps of the island. From the ferry, walk to the main road; you'll soon see it on the right.

Irumote-sō HOSTEL ¥
(いるもて荘; ☎0980-85-6255; 870-95 Uehara; dm with/without dinner from ¥5300/4000, r per person with/without dinner ¥6050/4750; P @ 📶) Between Uehara Port (上原港) and Funaura Port (船浦港), this hillside hostel has comfortable dorms and simple Japanese-style private rooms. Meals are served in the large communal dining room. We recommend calling for a pick-up before you arrive as it's hard to find.

Coral Garden PENSION ¥¥
(コーラルガーデン; ☎0980-85-6027; www.e-iriomote.com; 289-17 Uehara; s/d incl breakfast from ¥5800/11,600, plus ¥1000 for single night stay; ⏲closed Dec-Feb; P @ 📶 🏊) A five-minute drive from Uehara, this beachfront pension has simple Japanese- and Western-style rooms overlooking Hoshisuna-no-hama. There's a small pool, and a path leading down to the beach, which is a great spot for snorkelling. Call ahead for pick-up from the port.

Eating

With few restaurants on the island, most travellers prefer to take meals at their accommodation (or self-cater). But for a meal out, we recommend the following:

Laugh La Garden OKINAWAN ¥
(ラフラガーデン; ☎0980-85-7088; 2nd fl, 550-1 Uehara; dishes ¥900; ⏲11.30am-2.30pm & 6.30pm-last order, Fri-Wed) Near the road from Uehara Port and beside the petrol station, this relaxed cafe-restaurant has sets such as *ishigakibuta-no-misokatsu teishoku* (miso-seasoned Ishigaki pork cutlets; ¥950) and Iriomote delicacies such as *inoshishi-sashimi* (wild boar sashimi; ¥600).

Densā Shokudō JAPANESE ¥
(デンサー食堂; ☎0980-85-6453; 558 Uehara; meals ¥850; ⏲11.30am-6pm Thu-Mon, to 4pm Tue) This cosy daytime eatery serves up Okinawan favourites, like the *gōyā champurū teishoku* (¥850) and *Yaeyama soba* (¥500), in a homey dining room with an outdoor terrace. Browse a selection of manga (comics) while you wait. It's directly across the road once you head out of the Uehara port.

Getting There & Around

Iriomote-jima has a 58km-long perimeter road that runs about halfway around the coast. No roads run into the unspoiled interior.

Yaeyama Kankō Ferry (八重山観光フェリー; ☎0980-82-5010; www.yaeyama.co.jp), **Ishigaki Dream Kankō** (石垣島ドリーム観光; ☎0980-84-3178; www.ishigaki-dream.co.jp) and **Anei Kankō** (安栄観光; ☎0980-83-0055; www.aneikankou.co.jp) operate ferries between Ishigaki City (on Ishigaki-jima) and Iriomote-jima. Ferries from Ishigaki sail to/from two main ports on Iriomote: Uehara Port (上原港; ¥2360, one hour, up to 20 daily), convenient for most destinations, and Ōhara Port (大原港; ¥1800, 40 minutes, up to 27 daily). Strong north winds will require Uehara-bound ferries to travel the safer route to Ōhara; in these cases, buses at the port will shuttle passengers to Uehara for free.

Six or nine buses daily run between Ōhara Port and Shirahama (¥1240, 1½ hours); raise your hand to get on anywhere. There's a 'free pass' for buses (one-/three-day passes ¥1030/1540) that also gives you 10% off attractions such as the Urauchi-gawa cruise.

If you have an International Driving Permit, try **Yamaneko Rentacar** (やまねこレンタカー; ☎0980-85-6111; 584-1 Uehara; ⏰8am-6pm). Most of the island accommodation also rent bicycles to guests.

Taketomi-jima 竹富島

☎0980 / POP 352

A mere 15-minute boat ride from Ishigaki-jima, the tiny islet of Taketomi-jima is a living museum of Ryūkyū culture. Centred on a flower-bedecked village of traditional houses complete with red *kawara* (tiled) roofs, coral walls and *shiisā* statues, Taketomi is a breath of fresh air if you're suffering from an overdose of modern Japan.

In order to preserve the island's historical ambience, residents have joined together to ban some signs of modernism. The island is criss-crossed by crushed-coral roads and free of chain convenience stores.

While Taketomi is besieged by Japanese day trippers in the busy summer months, the island remains blissfully quiet at night. This is true even in summer, as the island offers little in the way of after-dark entertainment. If you have the chance, it's worth spending a night here as Taketomi truly weaves its spell after the sun dips below the horizon.

Sights & Activities

There are a number of modest sights in Taketomi village, though it's best for simply wandering around and soaking up the atmosphere. Taketomi-jima also has some decent beaches. **Kondoi Beach** (コンドイビーチ) on the west coast offers the best swimming on the island. Just south is **Kaiji-hama** (カイジ浜), which is the main *hoshi-suna* (star sand) hunting ground.

Nagomi-no-tō MONUMENT
(なごみの塔; ⏰24hr) FREE Roughly in the centre of the village, the modest lookout tower of Nagomi-no-tō has good views over the red-tiled roofs of the pancake-flat island.

Nishitō Utaki SHRINE
(西塘御獄) Near Nagomi-no-tō is a shrine that's dedicated to a 16th-century ruler of the Yaeyama Islands who was born on Taketomi-jima.

Kihōin Shūshūkan MUSEUM
(喜宝院蒐集館; ☎0980-85-2202; admission ¥300; ⏰9am-5pm) At the west of the village, this private museum houses a diverse collection of folk artefacts.

Taketomi Mingei-kan GALLERY
(竹富民芸館; ☎0980-85-2302; 381-4 Taketomi; ⏰9am-5pm) FREE Where the island's woven *minsā* belts and other textiles are produced.

Sleeping & Eating

Many of the traditional houses around the island are Japanese-style ryokan serving traditional Okinawan cuisine. Note that Taketomi fills up quickly in the summer, so be sure to book ahead.

Takana Ryokan HOSTEL ¥
(高那旅館; ☎0980-85-2151; www.kit.hi-ho.ne.jp/hayasaka-my; 499 Taketomi; dm with/without meals ¥5000/3500, r per person with meals from ¥8800) Opposite the tiny post office, Takana consists of a basic youth hostel and an attached upmarket ryokan. Basic Western-style dorms in the youth hostel are a great option if you're on a budget, although the Japanese-style tatami rooms in the ryokan are a bit more comfortable.

Soba-dokoro Takenoko NOODLES ¥
(そば処竹の子; ☎0980-85-2251; 101-1 Taketomi; dishes ¥800; ⏰10.30am-4pm & 6.30pm-midnight) This tiny restaurant on the northwest side of the village (look for the blue banner and the umbrellas) serves up *sōki-soba* (¥800) and *Yaeyama soba* (*soba* topped with tiny pieces of tender pork, bean sprouts and scallions; ¥600) in amazing broth.

Information

Ferries arrive at the small port on the northeast corner of the island, while Taketomi village is located in the centre of the island. There's a small **information desk** (☎0980-84-5633; ⏰7.30am-6pm) in the port building, and an international ATM in the post office in Taketomi village.

Getting There & Around

Yaeyama Kankō Ferry (八重山観光フェリー; ☎0980-82-5010), **Ishigaki Dream Kankō** (石垣島ドリーム観光; ☎0980-84-3178) and **Anei Kankō** (安栄観光; ☎0980-83-0055) operate ferries between Ishigaki City (on Ishigaki-jima) and Taketomi-jima (¥690, 10 minutes, up to 45 daily).

Rental bicycles are great for exploring the crushed-coral roads. Since the island is only 3km long and 2km wide, it is easily explored on foot or by bicycle. An assortment of bike-rental outfits meet arriving ferries at the port and run free shuttles between their shops and the port. The going rate for bike rentals is ¥300 per hour or ¥1500 for the day. Another way to see the island is by taking a tour in a water buffalo cart.

Two operators in the village offer 30-minute rides (hosted in Japanese) for ¥1200 per person.

Hateruma-jima 波照間島

☎0980 / POP 543

Forty-five kilometres south of Iriomote-jima is the tiny islet of Hateruma-jima, Japan's southernmost inhabited island. Just 15km around, Hateruma-jima has a couple of beauteous beaches and a seriously laid-back vibe.

Ferries arrive at the small port on the northwest corner of the island, while Hateruma village is in the centre.

Just to the west of the port is **Nishihama** (ニシ浜), a perfect beach of snow-white sand with some good coral offshore. Here you will find free public showers, toilets and a campground. At the opposite southeast corner of the island, directly south of the airport, is the impressive **Takanasaki** (高那崎), a 1km-long cliff of Ryūkyū limestone that is pounded by the Pacific Ocean. At the western end of the cliffs is a small monument marking **Japan's southernmost point** (日本最南端の碑), which is an extremely popular photo spot for Japanese visitors.

There are several *minshuku* on the island, including **Pension Sainantan** (ペンション最南端; ☎0980-85-8686; www5.ocn.ne.jp/~besuma/; 886-1 Hateruma; r per person incl meals from ¥8800; P @), which offers Japanese-style rooms with small terraces downstairs and Western-style rooms with balconies upstairs. There's also a rooftop terrace with spectacular views of the beach and sea, and it's all three minutes' walk from Nishihama.

Another great choice is **House Minami** (ハウス美波; ☎0980-85-8050, 090-8437-3132; http://homepage2.nifty.com/minami85; 3138 Hateruma; r per person ¥3000-4500; P), east of the town centre. Arranged around a cosy courtyard, these fully equipped, detached quarters sit in a village close to sugarcane fields. Though the proprietors don't speak English, they are very foreigner-friendly.

Anei Kankō (安栄観光; ☎0980-83-0055) has three ferries a day to Hateruma-jima from Ishigaki (¥3090; one hour). There is no public transport on the island, but rental bicycles and scooters are available for hire.

Yonaguni-jima 与那国島

☎0980 / POP 1745

About 125km west of Ishigaki and 110km east of Taiwan is the islet of Yonaguni-jima, Japan's westernmost inhabited island. Renowned for its strong sake, small horses and marlin fishing, the island is also home to the jumbo-sized Yonaguni atlas moth, the largest moth in the world.

However, most visitors come to see what lies beneath the waves. In 1985, a diver discovered what appeared to be human-made 'ruins' off the south coast of the island. In addition, the waters off the west coast are frequented by large schools of hammerhead sharks. This makes the island perhaps the most famous single diving destination in Japan.

Sights

Just as Hateruma-jima has a monument to mark Japan's southernmost point, Yonaguni-jima has a rock to mark the country's **westernmost point** (日本最西端の碑) at **Irizaki** (西崎). If the weather is perfect, the mountains of Taiwan are visible far over the sea (this happens only about twice a year – don't be disappointed if you can't see them).

Yonaguni has an extremely rugged landscape, and the coastline is marked with great rock formations, much like those on the east coast of Taiwan. The most famous of these are **Tachigami-iwa** (立神岩), literally 'Standing-God Rock' (although another name might come to mind); the dramatic **Gunkan-iwa** (軍艦岩; Battleship Rock); and **Sanninu-dai** (サンニヌ台), all of which are off the southeast coast. At the eastern tip of the island, Yonaguni horses graze in the pastures leading out to the lighthouse at **Agarizaki** (東崎).

Higawa-hama BEACH

(比川浜) On the south coast of the island is the pleasant little village of Higawa, which has a wide, sandy crescent of beach. The water here is clear and shallow, making it a great spot for swimming and snorkelling.

Kokusen Awamori BREWERY

(国泉泡盛; ☎0980-87-2315; ⊙8am-5pm) If you want to sample Hanazake, the island's infamous local brew, head to Kokusen Awamori, which is located in Sonai and offers free tastings and sales on-site.

Activities

Local divers have long known about the thrills that await at **Irizaki Point** (西崎ポイント); in winter, the waters are frequented by large schools of hammerhead sharks.

Kaitei Iseki DIVING
(海底遺跡; Underwater Ruins) The Kaitei Iseki were discovered by chance in 1985 by marine explorer Aratake Kihachirō. Some claim that these ruins, which look like giant blocks or steps of a sunken pyramid, are the remains of a Pacific Atlantis, although there are equally compelling arguments that they are just the random result of geological processes.

One Yonaguni dive shop with English-speaking guides is **Sou Wes** (☎0980-87-2311; www.yonaguni.jp; 59-6 Yonaguni; 1/2 dives ¥8000/12,000, equipment rental ¥5000; ⏰8am-6pm), who also offers glass-bottomed boat tours over the ruins for nondivers. When visibility is poor due to choppy water, passengers can watch a DVD about the ruins on board. **Mosura no Tamago** (もすらのたまご; ☎0980-87-2112; 4022-380 Yonaguni; per person ¥3700) also offers glass-bottomed boat tours.

Marlin Fishing FISHING
In addition to diving, the seas off Yonaguni are also renowned for marlin, and the All-Japan Billfish Tournament is held here each year in June or July. If you're interested in trolling, boats in Kubura can be chartered from ¥55,000 a day – call the **Yonaguni Fishing Co-operative** (☎in Japanese 0980-87-2803) for information.

Sleeping & Eating

It's wise to book accommodation ahead of your visit; Yonaguni is quite a distance to travel without a reservation.

There's a decent campground on the south coast near the village of Higawa, next to a nice beach called Kataburu-hama. Self-caterers will find two simple supermarkets in the centre of Sonai.

Fujimi Ryokan RYOKAN ¥
(ふじみ旅館; ☎0980-87-2143; 71-1 Yonaguni; r per person incl 2 meals from ¥6000; P) This basic ryokan is a good choice if you're looking for more traditional accommodation. Coming from the airport, take the main road through Sonai and turn left at the traffic light, then make another left at the second alley thereafter. You'll see the sign on the right. Staff can pick you up at the airport or ferry port with prior arrangement.

Minshuku Yoshimaru-sō MINSHUKU ¥¥
(民宿よしまる荘; ☎0980-87-2658; www.yonaguniyds.com; 3984-3 Yonaguni; dm/r per person incl breakfast ¥6000/7050; P 📶) Up the hill from the port in Kubura, Yoshimaru-sō is ideal for divers, as the friendly owners also operate the on-site and long-standing Yonaguni Diving Service. Simple Japanese- and Western-style rooms have nice views of the nearby port and spacious communal bathing facilities. The real appeal of this *minshuku* is the owners' local diving expertise (two-dive boat trips cost ¥12,500). Book ahead to get picked up at the airport or ferry terminal.

Dōurai IZAKAYA ¥¥
(どぅーらい; ☎0980-87-2909; 62 Yonaguni; dishes ¥800; ⏰6pm-midnight Mon-Sat) In the centre of Sonai is this delightful little Okinawan *izakaya* that serves local specialities such as *Ishigakigyū-sutēki* (Ishigaki-style steak; ¥1300) and *rafutē* (gingered, stewed pork; ¥700). It's about 100m southeast of the post office in Sonai. It's next door to a barber shop with a striped pole in front.

Information

The ferry port of Kubura (久部良) is at the island's western extreme. The main settlement is around the secondary port of Sonai (祖納) on the north coast. In between, on the northwest coast, you'll find the airport.

There is an **information counter** (☎0980-87-2402; ⏰8.30am-noon, call after) in the airport, which can help you find accommodation. You can also pick up the Japanese-language *Yonaguni-jima* map, and an English-language version that includes set locations of the erstwhile TV drama *Dr Koto's Clinic*, which was set on Yonaguni.

Each post office in Kubura and Sonai has an international ATM.

Getting There & Around

RAC has flights between Yonaguni and Naha. RAC also operates flights between Yonaguni and Ishigaki-jima.

Fukuyama Kaiun (福山海運; ☎0980-82-4962) operates two ferries a week between Ishigaki-jima and Kubura Port on Yonaguni (¥3550, 4½ hours) – these are not for the faint of stomach.

There are public buses here, but they make only four trips around the island per day, so the best transport is rental car or scooter. **Yonehama Rentacar** (米浜レンタカー; ☎0980-87-2148; ⏰8am-6pm) offers very reasonable rates and has a counter inside the airport terminal.

Understand Japan

Japan Today

'Morning in Japan' might seem hyperbolic, but the country is clawing its way out of three decades of economic stagnation and rebuilding from the disastrous earthquake and tsunami of 2011, and there is a sense of optimism in the air. Indeed, standing on a street corner in Tokyo these days, you might just feel a frisson of that old 1980s 'bubble economy' magic, when it seemed Japan could do no wrong.

Best Books

A Different Kind of Luxury (Andy Couturier; 2010) Several Japanese who've decided to chase 'a different kind of luxury' – time and freedom.

Kitchen (Yoshimoto Banana; 1988) Contemporary Japan through the lives of two young women.

The Wages of Guilt: Memories of War in Germany and Japan (Ian Buruma; 1994) A comparison of postwar Japan and Germany.

The Wind-Up Bird Chronicle (Murakami Haruki; 1994) A series of quests starting with a search for a missing cat in postwar Tokyo.

The Roads to Sata: A 2000-Mile Walk Through Japan (Alan Booth; 1985) A beautiful account of a walking journey through Japan.

Dogs and Demons: Tales from the Dark Side of Japan (Alex Kerr; 2002) The hard truth about modern Japan. Read it on the way home.

Best Films

Lost in Translation (2003) Directed by Sofia Coppola, it's one of the few foreign films about Japan that captures some of its reality without cliches.

Miyazaki Anime Director Miyazaki Hayao's animated films are classics. Start with *My Neighbor Totoro* or *Castle in the Sky*.

A Change of Course

Japan was hammered by the global financial crisis of 2008. The country faced previously unthinkable unemployment numbers and the old certainties of lifetime employment and age-based promotions started to look like mere pipe dreams. And to make matters worse, nations like China and South Korea were taking huge bites out of market sectors that Japan used to dominate. In the general election of 2012, the people of Japan made their dissatisfaction with this state of affairs plain by choosing the Liberal Democratic Party (LDP) over the previously ruling Democratic Party of Japan. Headed by Abe Shinzō, the LDP wasted no time in bringing in changes.

Under the banner of 'Abenomics', the LDP pushed through a raft of policies that were decidedly radical in famously conservative Japan: inflationary monetary schemes, quantitative easing, and various forms of direct fiscal stimulus. One of the main aims of Abenomics was to weaken the yen, thereby making Japanese products cheaper overseas and (hopefully) increasing demand for Japanese exports. The early results were encouraging. Japan enjoyed a 1.5% GDP growth in 2013 and the yen started to slide against other world currencies. The people of Japan re-elected Abe and the LDP by a landslide in 2014.

The World Returns to Japan

In recent times, the yen has been trading against the US dollar at levels not seen since the late 1990s. For foreign travellers to the country, this means one thing: Japan seems positively cheap (well, at least outside of Tokyo). Sure, there's been a little inflation, but Japan is now arguably one of the cheapest countries in the developed world.

Foreign travellers who had avoided the country in the aftermath of the 2011 earthquake and tsunami are now returning in record numbers. In October 2014, 1,272,000 foreign travellers visited Japan – a record for a single month. The largest growth has been in visitors from other Asian nations like China, Taiwan, Thailand and Korea.

Healing Rifts

This surge of visitors from Asian countries couldn't have come at a better time for Japan. Despite the progressive economic policies of the LDP, the party is undeniably nationalist. And the statements and views of influential LDP politicians have inflamed passions in Asian countries that suffered Japanese aggression during WWII. Tensions between Japan and China focused on the ownership of a small group of islands known in Japan as the Senkaku Islands and in China as the Diaoyu Islands. Located about 400km west of the Okinawan city of Naha, the rocky islands are of almost no worth in terms of resources, but priceless in terms of national pride, at least for right-wingers in both countries.

For a while, it looked as if tensions might actually escalate into a military conflict, but cooler heads have so far prevailed. In December 2014, after much backstage maneuvering, Abe met President Xi Jinping of China and actually shook hands (no small gesture considering the histories involved). The two essentially agreed to disagree, acknowledging that the countries held different positions on the ownership of the islands.

Looking Forward to the Olympics

For Japan, the best news of all in recent times was the September 2013 decision by the International Olympic Committee to award the 2020 Summer Olympics to Tokyo. The decision was a huge boon to the country and it's added a new urgency to a spate of infrastructure projects, including extended *shinkansen* (bullet train) lines, expanded international airports, and a drive to further develop facilities and services for tourists.

POPULATION: **127.3 MILLION**

GDP: **US$4.73 TRILLION**

INFLATION: **2.4%**

UNEMPLOYMENT: **3.5%**

if Japan were 100 people

64 would be 15-64 years old
23 would be over 65 years old
13 would be 0-14 years old

belief systems
(% of population)

Shintoism Buddhism

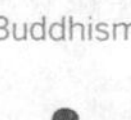

2 Christianity
8 Other

Note: total exceeds 100% as many people follow both Shinto and Buddhist belief systems.

population per sq km

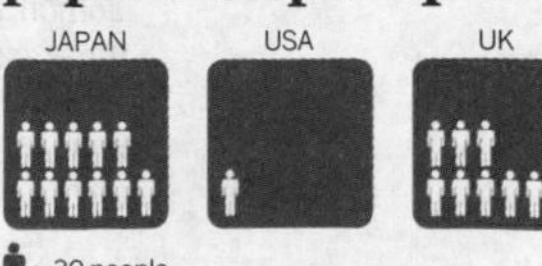

≈ 30 people

History

The history of Japan is greatly characterised by the distance of its islands from the mainland. Although over the centuries there has been contact between Japan and other parts of Asia, its separation from the mainland has been pivotal in Japan evolving into the unique country you find today. Japan's history may be broadly divided into five main periods: prehistory (ending in about 400 BC); pre-classical (to AD 710); classical (to 1185); medieval (to 1600); and pre-modern to modern (from 1600).

Jōmon pottery vessels dating back some 15,000 years are the oldest-known ceramic pots in the world.

Ancient Japan: From Hunter-Gatherers to Divine Rule

Once upon a time, the male and female deities Izanagi and Izanami came down to a watery world from Takamagahara (The Plains of High Heaven), to create land. Droplets from Izanagi's 'spear' solidified into the land now known as Japan, and Izanami and Izanagi then populated it with gods. One of these was Japan's supreme deity, the Sun Goddess Amaterasu (Light of Heaven), whose great-great-grandson Jimmu became the first emperor of Japan, reputedly in 660 BC.

This is the seminal creation myth of Japan but, more certainly, humans were present in Japan at least 200,000 years ago (though the earliest human remains go back only 30,000 years or so). Until the end of the last ice age about 15,000 years ago, a number of land bridges linked Japan to the continent – Siberia to the north, Korea to the west and probably present-day Taiwan to the south – so access was not difficult.

The first recognisable culture to emerge was the neolithic Jōmon (named after a 'rope-mark' pottery style), from about 13,000 BC. The Jōmon were mostly hunter-gatherers and preferred coastal regions, though agriculture, developing from about 4000 BC, brought more stable settlement and larger tribal communities. Northern Japan's indigenous Ainu people are of Jōmon descent.

From about 400 BC there were waves of immigrants, later known as Yayoi (from the earliest site of their reddish wheel-thrown pottery). They first arrived in the southwest, probably from the Korean Peninsula,

TIMELINE

c 13,000 BC

First evidence of the hunter-gatherer Jōmon, ancestors of the present-day Ainu of northern Japan and producers of the world's earliest pottery vessels.

c 400 BC

Yayoi people appear in southwest Japan (probably via Korea), practising wet rice cultivation and using metal tools. They also promote inter-regional trade and a sense of territoriality.

3rd century AD

Queen Himiko reigns over Yamatai (Yamato) and is recognised by Chinese visitors as 'over-queen' of Japan's more than 100 kingdoms.

and brought iron and bronze technology, and highly productive wet rice farming techniques.

The Jōmon were gradually forced north, although modern Japanese have significant amounts of Jōmon DNA, indicating some intermingling of the races. The Yayoi had spread to the middle of Honshū by the 1st century AD, but northern Honshū could still be considered Jōmon territory until at least the 8th century.

The Yayoi's new technologies brought increased and more diverse production, and greater intertribal trade. At the same time, rivalry increased between regional tribal groups, often over resources, and there was greater social stratification.

Yamato Clan

Agriculture-based settlement led to territories and boundaries being established. According to Chinese sources, by the end of the 1st century AD there were more than a hundred kingdoms in Japan, and by the middle of the 3rd century these were largely ruled by an 'over-queen' named Himiko, whose own territory was known as Yamatai (later Yamato). Its location is disputed, with some scholars favouring northwest Kyūshū, but most favouring the Nara region. The Chinese treated Himiko as sovereign of all Japan (with the name Yamato eventually applied to Japan as a whole) and, through tributes, she acknowledged her allegiance to the Chinese emperor.

After her death in 248 Himiko is said to have been buried – along with 100 sacrificed slaves – in a massive barrow-like tomb known as a *kofun*, indicative of the importance of status. Other dignitaries chose burial in similar tombs, and so from this point on, till the establishment of Nara as a capital in 710, Japan is usually referred to as being in the Kofun or Yamato period.

The period saw the confirmation of the Yamato as the dominant – indeed imperial – clan in Japan. They appear to have consolidated their power by negotiation and alliance with (or incorporation of) powerful potential foes. This was a practice Japan was to continue through the ages whenever it could, though it was less accommodating in the case of perceived weaker foes.

The first verifiable emperor was Suijin (died c 318). He was likely a member of the Yamato clan, though some scholars think he led a group of 'horse-riders' believed to have entered Japan from the Korean Peninsula around the start of the 4th century. The period also saw the adoption of writing, based on Chinese but first introduced by scholars from the Korean kingdom of Paekche in the mid-5th century. Scholars from Paekche also introduced Buddhism a century later.

Top Historic Sites

- *Ishibutai-kofun, Asuka*
- *Tōdai-ji, Nara*
- *Tō-ji, Kyoto*
- *Daibutsu, Kamakura*
- *Imperial Palace, Tokyo*
- *Dejima, Nagasaki*

mid-5th century

Scholars from the Korean kingdom of Paekche introduce writing. Using Chinese characters to express spoken Japanese produces a highly complex writing system.

mid-6th century

Scholars from Paekche introduce Buddhism. Its texts can be read by a now-literate elite, who use it to unify and control the nation.

710

Japan's first capital is established at Nara, based on Chinese models. Japan is arguably a nation-state by this stage.

712 & 720

The compilation of two major historical works, *Kojiki* (712) and *Nihon Shoki* (720), allow the imperial family to trace its 'divine' origins and, in this way, legitimise its right to rule.

The Yamato rulers promoted Buddhism as a way to unify and control the land. Though Buddhism originated in India, the Japanese regarded it as a Chinese religion, and it was one of the 'things Chinese' they adopted to achieve recognition as a civilised country – especially by China. By copying China, Japan hoped it too could become powerful.

In 604 the regent Prince Shōtoku (573–620) enacted a constitution with a very Chinese flavour. Its 17 articles promoted harmony and hard work. In 645 major Chinese-style reforms followed, such as centralised government, nationalisation and allocation of land, and codes of law. Starting under Emperor Temmu (r 673–86), the imperial family had historical works compiled, such as the *Kojiki* (Record of Old Things; 712) and *Nihon Shoki* (Record of Japan; 720), to legitimise their power by claiming divine descent. It had the desired effect, and despite a number of perilous moments Japan continues to have the world's longest unbroken monarchy.

Not all things Chinese were emulated. Confucianism, for example, condoned removing an unvirtuous ruler who had lost the 'mandate of heaven', but this idea was not promoted in Japan. Nor was the Chinese practice of achievement of high rank through examination, for the Japanese ruling class preferred birth over merit.

By the early 8th century, Japan, with its estimated five million people, had all the characteristics of a nation-state (with the exclusion of northern Japan). It was effectively unified, with a centralised government, systematic administration, legitimised power, social stratification, a written constitution and legal code, and external recognition.

The Age of Courtiers

In 710 a capital was established at Nara (Heijō-kyō). The influence of Buddhism is still seen today in the Tōdai-ji, which houses a huge bronze Buddha and is the world's largest wooden building (and one of the oldest).

Emperor Kammu (r 781–806) decided to relocate the capital in 784. His decision may have been prompted by a series of disasters following the move to Nara, including a massive smallpox epidemic that killed up to one-third of the population in 735–37. In 794 the capital was transferred to nearby Kyoto (Heian-kyō), which remained Japan's capital for more than a thousand years, though it was not necessarily the centre of actual power.

In Kyoto, over the next few centuries, courtly life reached a pinnacle of refined artistic pursuits and etiquette, captured famously in the novel *The Tale of Genji,* written by the court-lady Murasaki Shikibu in about 1004. It showed courtiers indulging in diversions such as guessing flowers by their scent, building extravagant follies and sparing no expense for the latest luxury. On the positive side, it was a world that encouraged aesthetic sensibilities, such as of *mono no aware* (the bitter-sweetness of things) and *okashisa* (pleasantly surprising incongruity), which have en

TALE OF GENJI

The Tale of Genji, written by the courtesan Murasaki Shikibu in about 1004, is widely believed to be the world's first novel.

740

Construction begins on the vast Tōdai-ji temple complex in Nara. It is thought the complex was built to provide a focus for the nation and to ward off smallpox.

700s

The classical age of Japanese religious sculpture, in which some of Japan's greatest works of Buddhist art are produced (some still visible in and around Nara).

794

In response to a series of misfortunes, including a smallpox epidemic, Japan's formal capital is relocated from Nara to Heian (present-day Kyoto), where it remains for more than a thousand years.

804

After travelling to China to study Buddhism, Kūkai (also known as Kōbō Daishi) founds Shingon (Esoteric) Buddhism in Japan and establishes the famous Kōya-san religious centre.

HISTORICAL PERIODS

PERIOD	DATE	KEY EVENTS
Jōmon	c 13,000 BC–c 400 BC	Neolithic peoples migrate from mainland Asia to Japan
Yayoi	c 400 BC–c AD 250	Technologically advanced Yayoi immigrants arrive in Japan by boat from the Korean peninsula
Kofun/Yamato	250–710	The forerunners of the Yamato Dynasty consolidate their power over central Japan
Nara	710–94	The first permanent capital of Japan is established in the city of Nara
Heian	794–1185	The capital of Japan is moved to Kyoto and a period of peace and cultural refinement ensues
Kamakura	1185–1333	The country is torn by civil war and is ruled by warlords (shogun) based in the eastern city of Kamakura
Muromachi	1333–1568	The Kamakura shogun lose their grip on power and a new shogun is installed in Kyoto
Azuchi-Momoyama	1568–1600	A period of intense civil war comes to a close when Toyotomi Hideyoshi unites the country, establishing the Tokugawa shogunate
Edo/Tokugawa	1600–1868	The Tokugawa shogunate closes the country and ushers in a period of significant peace and prosperity
Meiji	1868–1912	The arrival of Westerners destabilises Japan, leading to the fall of the Tokugawa shogunate and the 'restoration' of the emperor
Taishō	1912–26	Japan modernises at a furious pace and sides with the Entente power in WWI
Shōwa	1926–89	Japan expands its empire throughout East Asia in the 1930s, and enters into full-scale war with the Allied Powers in WWII
Heisei	1989–present	After a miraculous post-war recovery, Japan's 'Bubble Economy' bursts in 1990, followed by decades of economic stagnation

dured to the present day. But it was also a world increasingly estranged from the real one and it lacked muscle. The court's effeteness was made worse by the weakness of the emperors, manipulated over centuries by the politically powerful Fujiwara family.

While the nobles immersed themselves in courtly pleasures and intrigues, out in the provinces powerful military forces were developing.

9th–12th centuries

The court becomes culturally sophisticated, but is increasingly effete and removed from the real world. Actual power is held by provincial military clans.

1156

The major provincial families Taira and Minamoto are employed by rival court factions and engage in bitter warfare, with the Taira prevailing under its warrior-leader Kiyomori.

1185

Minamoto Yoritomo topples the Taira and, as the most powerful man in the land, brings a level of unity. A suspicious man, he kills many of his own relatives.

1192

Yoritomo takes the title shogun (generalissimo) from a largely puppet emperor and establishes the *bakufu* (shogunate) in his home territory at Kamakura, heralding the start of feudalism in Japan.

They were typically led by minor nobles, often sent on behalf of court-based major nobles to carry out 'tedious' local duties. Some were distant imperial family members, barred from succession claims – a practice known as 'dynastic shedding' – and hostile to the court. Their retainers included skilled warriors known as samurai (literally 'retainer').

The two main 'shed' families, the Minamoto (also known as Genji) and Taira (Heike), were enemies. In 1156 they were employed to help rival claimants to the Fujiwara family leadership, but these figures soon faded into the background when a feud developed between the Minamoto and the Taira.

The Taira prevailed, under their leader Kiyomori (1118–81), who based himself in the capital and, over the next 20 years, fell prey to many of the vices that lurked there. In 1180 he enthroned his two-year-old grandson, Antoku. When a rival claimant requested the help of the Minamoto family, who had regrouped, their leader, Yoritomo (1147–99), was more than ready to agree. Both Kiyomori and the claimant died shortly afterwards, but Yoritomo and his younger half-brother Yoshitsune (1159–89), continued the campaign against the Taira – interrupted by a pestilence during the early 1180s. By 1185 Kyoto had fallen and the Taira had been pursued to the western tip of Honshū. A naval battle ensued, won by the Minamoto. In a well-known tragic tale, Kiyomori's widow leapt into the sea with her grandson Antoku (now aged seven), rather than have him surrender. Minamoto Yoritomo, now the most powerful man in Japan, was to usher in a martial age.

The Age of Warriors

Yoritomo did not seek to become emperor, but wanted the new emperor to give him legitimacy by conferring the title of shogun (generalissimo), which was granted in 1192. He left many existing offices and institutions in place and set up his base in his home territory of Kamakura rather than Kyoto. While in theory he represented the military arm of the emperor's government, in practice he was in charge of government. His 'shogunate' was known in Japanese as the *bakufu,* meaning the tent headquarters of a field general, though it lasted almost 700 years as an institution.

In 1191 the Zen monk Eisai is said to have brought tea leaves from China, starting Japan's tradition of tea drinking.

The system of government became feudal, centred on a loyalty-based lord-vassal system. It was more personal and 'familial' than medieval European feudalism, particularly in the extended *oya-ko* relationship ('parent-child', in practice 'father-son'), which became another enduring feature of Japan.

But 'families' were not always happy, and the more ruthless power-seekers did not hesitate to kill family members they saw as threats. Yoritomo, apparently suspicious by nature, killed off so many of his own

1199
After Yoritomo's suspicious death, his formidable wife, Masako (the 'nun shogun') becomes the most powerful figure in Japan, establishing her family, the Hōjō, as shoguns.

1200–50
Hōnen and Shinran promote the 'Pure Land' schools of Buddhism, which remain the country's most popular Buddhist sects.

1223
The monk Dōgen studies Chang Buddhism in China and later returns to found the influential Sōtō school of Zen Buddhism.

13th century
Zen Buddhism becomes established in Japan, especially among warriors, and also influences Japanese aesthetics. 'Mass-appeal' forms of Buddhism are also established.

SAMURAI

The prime duty of a samurai – a member of the warrior class from about the 12th century onwards – was to give faithful service to his lord. In fact, the term 'samurai' is derived from a word meaning 'to serve'. Ideally, 'service' meant being prepared to give up one's life for one's lord, though, at least initially, it was typically only hereditary retainers who felt such commitment. At the other end of the ranks, samurai were professional mercenaries who were unreliable and often defected.

The renowned samurai code, *bushidō* (the way of the warrior), developed over centuries but was not formally codified until the 17th century, by which time there were no real battles to fight. The code was greatly idealised, with its intention appearing to have been to show samurai as moral exemplars, to counter criticism that they were parasitic.

Core samurai ideals included *gaman* (endurance), *isshin* (wholehearted commitment) and *makoto* (sincerity). Samurai were supposed to be men of Zen-like austerity who endured hardship without complaint. Even though samurai were often highly educated and sometimes paralleled European knights, their chivalry was not so dominant.

Samurai who became lordless were known as *rōnin* (wanderers or masterless samurai); they acted more like brigands and were a serious social problem.

Samurai who fell from grace were generally required to commit seppuku (ritual suicide by disembowelment) to show the purity of the soul, which was believed to reside in the stomach.

The samurai's best-known weapon was the *katana* sword, though in earlier days the bow also featured. Arguably the world's finest swordsmen, samurai were formidable opponents in single combat. During modernisation in the late 19th century, the government – itself comprising samurai – realised that a conscript army was more efficient as a unified fighting force and disestablished the samurai class. However, samurai ideals such as endurance and fighting to the death were revived through propaganda prior to the Pacific War, and underlay the determination of many Japanese soldiers.

family members that there were difficulties with the shogunal succession when he died in 1199 (after falling from his horse in suspicious circumstances). His half-brother Yoshitsune, whom he had killed, earned an enduring place in Japanese literature and legend as the archetypical tragic hero.

Yoritomo's widow Masako (1157–1225) was a formidable figure, controlling the shogunate for much of her remaining life. Having taken religious vows on her husband's death, she became known as the 'nun shogun'. She was instrumental in ensuring that her own family, the Hōjō, replaced the Minamoto as shoguns. The Hōjō shogunate continued to use Kamakura as the shogunal base, and lasted till the 1330s.

1274 & 1281

Under Kublai Khan, the Mongols twice attempt to invade Japan, but fail due to poor planning, spirited Japanese resistance and, especially, the destruction of their fleets by typhoons.

1333

General Ashikaga Takauji, initially allied with Emperor Go-Daigo, topples the unpopular Hōjō shōgunate. Takauji requests the title of shogun, but Go-Daigo declines and a rift develops.

1338–92

Takauji installs a puppet emperor who names him shogun, establishing the Ashikaga shogunate at Muromachi. Two rival emperors exist till Go-Daigo's line is betrayed by Takauji's grandson Yoshimitsu in 1392.

1400s–1500s

Japan is in almost constant internal warfare, including the particularly fierce Ōnin War of 1467–77. The era, especially from the late 15th to late 16th centuries, is known as the Sengoku (Warring States) period.

Mongol Threats

It was during the Hōjō shogunate that the Mongols twice tried to invade, in 1274 and 1281. Under Kublai Khan (r 1260–94), the Mongol empire was close to its peak and after conquering Korea in 1259 he sent requests to Japan to submit to him, but these were ignored.

Kublai Khan's expected first attack came in November 1274, allegedly with about 900 vessels carrying 40,000 men, though these figures may be exaggerated. They landed near Hakata in northwest Kyūshū and, despite spirited Japanese resistance, made progress inland. However, for unclear reasons, they retreated to their ships and shortly afterwards a violent storm blew up, damaging about a third of the fleet. The remainder returned to Korea.

A more determined attempt was made by China seven years later. Kublai had a fleet of 4400 warships built to carry a force of 140,000 men – again, these are questionable figures. In August 1281 they landed once more in northwest Kyūshū and again met spirited resistance and had to retire to their vessels. Once more, the weather intervened – this time a typhoon – and half their vessels were destroyed. The survivors went back to China, and there was no further Mongol attempt to invade Japan.

The typhoon of 1281 prompted the idea of divine intervention to save Japan, with the coining of the term kamikaze (literally 'divine wind'). Later this term was used about the Pacific War suicide pilots who, said to be infused with divine spirit, gave their lives to protect Japan from invasion. It also led the Japanese to feel that their land was indeed the Land of the Gods.

KAMIKAZE

The kamikaze ('divine wind') of 1281 is said to have drowned 70,000 Mongol troops. If true, it would be the world's worst maritime disaster.

Demise of the Hōjō Shogunate

Despite its successful defence of Japan, the Hōjō shogunate suffered. Its inability to make promised payments to those involved in repelling the Mongols caused considerable dissatisfaction, while the payments it did make severely depleted its finances.

It was also during the Hōjō shogunate that Zen Buddhism was brought from China. The austerity and self-discipline of Buddhism appealed greatly to the warrior class, and it was also a factor in the appeal of aesthetic values such as *sabi* (elegant simplicity). More popular forms of Buddhism were the Jōdo (Pure Land) and Jōdo Shin (True Pure Land) sects.

Dissatisfaction towards the shogunate came to a head under the unusually assertive emperor Go-Daigo (1288–1339). After escaping from exile imposed by the Hōjō, he started to muster anti-shogunal support in western Honshū. In 1333 the shogunate dispatched troops to counter this threat, under one of its most promising generals, the young Ashikaga Takauji (1305–58). However, recognising the dissatisfaction towards the Hōjō and that together he and Go-Daigo would have considerable

1543

Portuguese, the first Westerners, arrive by chance in Japan, bringing firearms and Christianity. Firearms prove popular among warlords, while Christianity has a mixed reception.

1568

The warlord Oda Nobunaga seizes Kyoto and becomes the supreme power, though he does not take the title of shogun. He is noted for his massive ego and brutality.

1582

Nobunaga is betrayed and forced to commit suicide. Power transfers to one of his loyal generals, Toyotomi Hideyoshi, who becomes increasingly paranoid and anti-Christian. Hideyoshi takes the title of regent.

late 1500s

Sen-no-Rikyū lays down the form of the tea ceremony, the ritualised drinking of tea originally practised by nobility and later spreading to wealthy commoners.

military strength, Takauji threw in his lot with the emperor and attacked the shogunal offices in Kyoto. Others also soon rebelled against the shogunate itself in Kamakura.

This was the end for the Hōjō shogunate, but not for the institution. Takauji wanted the title of shogun, but his ally Go-Daigo feared that conferring it would weaken his own imperial power. A rift developed, and Go-Daigo sent forces to attack Takauji. But Takauji emerged victorious and turned on Kyoto, forcing Go-Daigo to flee into the hills of Yoshino about 100km south of the city, where he set up a court in exile. In Kyoto, Takauji installed a puppet emperor from a rival line, who returned the favour by declaring him shogun in 1338. The two courts co-existed until 1392 when the 'southern court' (at Yoshino) was betrayed by Ashikaga Yoshimitsu (1358–1408), Takauji's grandson and third Ashikaga shogun.

Warring States

Takauji set up his shogunal base in Kyoto, at Muromachi. With a few exceptions such as Takauji and his grandson Yoshimitsu (who had Kyoto's famous Kinkaku-ji built and once declared himself 'King of Japan'), the Ashikaga shoguns were relatively weak. Without strong, centralised government and control, the country slipped into civil war as regional warlords – who came to be known as *daimyō* (domain lords) – engaged in seemingly interminable feuds and power struggles. Starting with the Ōnin War of 1467–77 and for the next hundred years, the country was almost constantly in civil war. This time was known as the Sengoku (Warring States) era.

Ironically, perhaps, during the Muromachi period a new flourishing of the arts took place, such as in the refined *nō* drama, ikebana (flower arranging) and *chanoyu* (tea ceremony). Key aesthetics were *sabi* (weathered and altered with age), *yūgen* (elegant and tranquil otherworldliness, as seen in *nō*), *wabi* (subdued taste) and *kare* (severe and unadorned).

The first Europeans arrived in 1543; three Portuguese traders blown ashore the island of Tanegashima, south of Kyūshū. Soon other Europeans arrived, bringing with them Christianity and firearms. They found a land torn apart by warfare and ripe for conversion to Christianity – at least in the eyes of missionaries such as Francis Xavier, who arrived in 1549. But the Japanese warlords were more interested in the worldly matter of guns.

Historical Reads

- *The Coming of the Barbarians* (Pat Barr; 1967)
- *Samurai William* (Giles Milton; 2003)
- *Inventing Japan* (Ian Buruma; 2004)
- *Embracing Defeat* (John Dower; 2000)

Reunification

Nobunaga Seizes Power

One of the most successful of the warlords using firearms was Oda Nobunaga (1534–82), from what is now Aichi Prefecture. Starting from a relatively minor power base, his skilled and ruthless generalship produced a series of victories over rivals. In 1568 he seized Kyoto and installed one

1592 & 1597–98 Hideyoshi twice tries to conquer Korea as part of a plan to control Asia, the second attempt ending after his death in 1598. The invasions seriously damage relations between Japan and Korea.

1600 The warlord Tokugawa Ieyasu breaks an earlier promise to the dying Hideyoshi to protect his young son and heir Hideyori, and seizes power at the Battle of Sekigahara.

1603 Ieyasu becomes shogun, with policies aimed at retaining power by maintaining the status quo and minimising threats.

1638 Westerners have been expelled, except for a small Protestant Dutch population on a tiny island off Nagasaki. Shogunal forces massacre Japanese Christians in the Christian-led Shimabara Rebellion.

of the Ashikaga clan (Yoshiaki) as shogun, then drove him out in 1573 and made his own base at Azuchi. Although he did not take the title of shogun, Nobunaga was the supreme power in the land.

Noted for his brutality, Nobunaga was not a man to cross. He hated Buddhist priests, and tolerated Christianity as a counterbalance to them. His massive ego led him to erect a temple where he could be worshipped and to declare his birthday a national holiday. His stated aim was 'Tenka Fubu' ('A Unified Realm under Military Rule') and he went some way to achieving this by redistributing territories among the *daimyō*, having land surveyed and standardising weights and measures.

HIDDEN CHRISTIANS

Japan's so-called 'Christian Century' began in 1549 with the arrival of Portuguese missionaries on the island of Kyūshū. Within decades, hundreds of thousands of Japanese, from peasants to *daimyō*, were converted.

The rapid rise of Christian belief, as well as its association with trade, Western weaponry and control of Japanese territory, came to be viewed as a threat by the *bakufu* under Toyotomi Hideyoshi. In 1597 Hideyoshi ordered the crucifixion of 26 Japanese and Spanish Franciscans in Nagasaki. Despite his death in 1598, an era of suppression of Christians had begun and, with the expulsion of missionaries ordered in 1614 by Tokugawa Hidetada, thousands of Christians were persecuted over the following six decades. Many thousands of Christian peasants resisted in the 1637–38 Shimabara Rebellion, after which Christianity was outlawed completely.

Other persecution took the form of *fumi-e,* in which suspected Christians were forced to walk on images of Jesus. The Gregorian date on the Dutch trading house on the island of Hirado was taken as proof of the Dutch traders' Christianity and used to justify their exile to Nagasaki's Dejima, ushering in more than two centuries of *sakoku* (closure to the outside world).

Japanese Christians reacted by going undercover as *kakure Kirishitan* (hidden Christians). Without priests, they worshipped in services held in secret rooms inside private homes. On the surface, worship resembled other Japanese religions, including using *kamidana* (Shintō altars) and *butsudan* (Buddhist ancestor-worship chests) in homes, and ceremonial rice and sake. But *kakure Kirishitan* also kept hanging scrolls of Jesus, Mary and saints, as well as statues like the Maria-Kannon, depicting Mary in the form of the Buddhist deity of mercy holding an infant symbolising Jesus. The sounds of worship, too, mimicked Buddhist incantations. Scholars estimate there were about 150,000 hidden Christians.

It was not until 1865 – 12 years after the arrival of the American expedition led by Commodore Matthew Perry, who eventually forced Japan to re-open to the West – that Japan had its first large-scale church again, Oura Cathedral in Nagasaki. The Meiji government officially declared freedom of religion in 1871. Today, there are estimated to be between one and two million Japanese Christians (about 1% of the population).

1689–91

Matsuo Bashō, the greatest name in haiku poetry, completes a journey around Japan that inspires his most famous collection of poems, *The Narrow Road to the Deep North*.

1600s–1800s

The Tokugawa shogunate is based at Edo (later renamed Tokyo). Life is tightly controlled, and the nation is shut off from most of the world. Nonetheless 'Edo merchant culture' emerges.

1701–03

The mass suicide of the 'Forty-Seven Rōnin', after avenging their lord's death, is seen by many as a model for samurai ethics.

mid- to late 1700s

Itō Jakuchū creates a flamboyant and seminaturalistic style of painting with hints of Western influence, but retaining a Japanese heart.

The Ambitions of Hideyoshi

In 1582 Nobunaga was betrayed by one of his generals and forced to commit suicide. However, the work of unification was continued by another of his generals, Toyotomi Hideyoshi (1536–98), a foot soldier who had risen through the ranks to become Nobunaga's favourite. He, too, was an extraordinary figure. Small and with simian features, he was nicknamed 'Saru-chan' ('Little Monkey') by Nobunaga, but his huge will for power belied his physical size. He disposed of potential rivals among Nobunaga's sons, took the title of regent, continued Nobunaga's policy of territorial redistribution and insisted that *daimyō* should surrender their families to him as hostages to be kept in Kyoto – his base being at Momoyama. He also banned weapons for all classes except samurai.

In his later years, Hideyoshi became increasingly paranoid, cruel and megalomaniacal. He would saw in half messengers who gave him bad news, and had young members of his own family executed for suspected plotting. He also issued the first expulsion order of Christians (1587), whom he suspected were an advance guard for an invasion. In 1597 he crucified 26 Christians, nine of them Europeans. His grand scheme for power included a pan-Asian conquest, and as a first step he attempted an invasion of Korea in 1592, which failed amid much bloodshed. He tried again in 1597, but the campaign was abandoned when Hideyoshi died of illness in 1598.

The Japanese religion of Shintō is one of the few religions in the world with a female solar deity.

Shogun Ieyasu

On his deathbed, Hideyoshi entrusted one of his ablest generals, Tokugawa Ieyasu (1542–1616), with safeguarding the country and the succession of his young son Hideyori (1593–1615). Ieyasu betrayed that trust. In 1600, in the Battle of Sekigahara, he defeated those trying to protect Hideyori and effectively became the overlord of Japan. In 1603 his power was legitimised when the emperor gave him the title of shogun, and his Kantō base, the once tiny fishing village of Edo – later renamed Tokyo – became the real centre of power and government in Japan.

Through these three men – Nobunaga, Hideyoshi and Ieyasu – by fair means, or more commonly, foul, the country was reunified within three decades.

A Time of Stability

Having secured power for the Tokugawa, Ieyasu and his successors were determined to retain it. Their basic strategy was to enforce the status quo and minimise any potential for challenge.

Their policies included tight control over military families, including requiring authorisation for castle-building and marriages. They continued to redistribute (or confiscate) territory and, importantly, required

1808

The British ship HMS *Phaeton* captures several Dutch personnel at the island of Dejima and demands supplies. The British leave with the supplies before Japanese reinforcements arrive.

1800–50

Ukiyo-e, highly stylised woodblock prints depicting entertainment districts and landscapes, become popular. The movement is led by Utagawa Hiroshige and Katsushika Hokusai.

c 1830

Hokusai carves his famous woodblock print, *The Wave*, depicting Fuji-san and a huge crashing wave.

early to mid-19th century

The nation's isolation is threatened by increasing numbers of foreign whalers and other vessels entering Japanese waters. Treatment of those attempting to land is harsh

daimyō and their retainers to spend every second year at Edo, where their families were kept permanently as hostages.

The shogunate also directly controlled ports, mines, major towns and other strategic areas. Movement was severely restricted by deliberately destroying many bridges, setting up checkpoints and requiring written authority for travel. Wheel transport was banned, potentially ocean-going vessels were strictly monitored, and overseas travel for Japanese was banned as well as the return of those already overseas.

Social movement was also banned, with society divided into four main classes: in descending order *shi* (samurai), *nō* (farmers), *kō* (artisans) and *shō* (merchants). Detailed codes of conduct, including clothing, food, housing and even the siting of the toilet, applied to each of these classes.

Though not greatly popular, Christianity threatened the shogunate's authority, and missionaries were expelled in 1614. Following the Christian-led Shimabara Rebellion, Christianity was banned, several hundred thousand Japanese Christians were forced into hiding, and all Westerners except the Protestant Dutch were expelled by 1638.

David Mitchell's *Thousand Autumns of Jacob de Zoet: A Novel* tells the story of the Dutch living on the island of Dejima during the period of *sakoku*.

The shogunate found Protestantism less threatening than Catholicism (knowing that the Vatican could muster one of the biggest military forces in the world) and would have let the British stay on if the Dutch had not convinced it that Britain was a Catholic country. Nevertheless, the Dutch were just a few dozen men confined to a tiny trading base on the artificial island of Dejima, near Nagasaki.

Retreat From the World

Japan entered an era of *sakoku* (closure to the outside world) that was to last for more than two centuries. Within the isolated and severely prescribed world of Tokugawa Japan, breaching even a trivial law could mean execution. Even 'rude behaviour', defined as 'acting in an unexpected manner', was a capital offence. Punishments could be cruel, such as crucifixion, and meted out collectively or by proxy, with, for example, a village headman punished for a villager's misdemeanour. Secret police reported on misdeeds.

As a result, people learned the importance of obedience to authority, collective responsibility and 'doing the right thing'. These are values still prominent in present-day Japan.

Merchants Rise as Samurai Decline

For all the constraints, the Tokugawa period had a considerable dynamism, especially among the merchants, who as the lowest class were often ignored by the authorities and had relative freedom. They prospered greatly from the services and goods required for *daimyō* processions to

1853–54	1854–67	1867–68	1870s–early 1890s
US Commodore Matthew Perry uses 'gunboat diplomacy' to force Japan to open up for trade and re-provisioning. In response, many Japanese criticise the ineffective shogunate.	Opposition to the shogunate grows, led by samurai from the Satsuma and Chōshū domains. Initially hostile to foreigners, they soon realise Japan's defensive limitations.	The Meiji Restoration disestablishes the shogunate and restores imperial authority, but 15-year-old emperor Mutsuhito is a puppet, and oligarchs rule. Japan's capital is moved to Edo, renamed Tokyo.	The oligarchs bring in policies of modernisation and Westernisation, such as creating a conscript army (1873), disestablishing the samurai (1876) and adopting a constitution (1889).

and from Edo, which were so costly that *daimyō* had to convert much of their domain's produce into cash. This boosted the economy in general.

A largely pleasure-oriented merchant culture thrived and produced the popular kabuki drama, with its colour and stage effects. Other entertainments included bunraku (classic puppet theatre), haiku, popular novels and *ukiyo-e* (woodblock prints), often of female geisha, who came to the fore during this time.

Samurai had no major military engagements. Being well-educated, most ended up fighting paper wars as administrators and managers. Ironically, it was during this period of relative inactivity that the renowned samurai code of *bushidō* was formalised. Though largely idealism, occasionally the code was put into practice, such as the loyalty shown in 1701–03 by the 'Forty-Seven Rōnin', masterless samurai who waited two years to avenge the unfair enforced seppuku (ritual suicide by disembowelment) of their lord, killing the man responsible and then committing seppuku themselves.

The disorienting collapse of the regimented Tokugawa world produced a form of mass hysteria called *Ee Ja Nai Ka* (Who Cares?), with traumatised people dancing naked and giving away possessions.

A Time for Learning

Confucianism was officially encouraged, with the apparent aim of reinforcing the idea of hierarchy and status quo, but it also encouraged learning and literacy. By the end of the period, up to a third of the 30 million Japanese were literate – far ahead of Western populations of the time. However, a strong trend of nationalism, centred on Shintō and the ancient texts, also occurred. Its focus on the emperor's primacy was unhelpful to the shogunate. Certainly, by the early to mid-19th century, there was considerable dissatisfaction with the shogunate, fanned also by corruption and incompetence among officials.

It is questionable how much longer the Tokugawa shogunate and its secluded world might have continued, but as it happened, external forces were to hasten its demise.

Modernisation

A number of Western vessels had appeared in Japanese waters since the start of the 19th century. Any Westerners who landed, even through shipwreck, were almost always expelled or even executed. This was not acceptable to Western powers. America in particular was keen to expand its interests across the Pacific, with its numerous whaling vessels in the northwest needing regular provisioning.

In 1853 and again the following year, US Commodore Matthew Perry steamed into Edo-wan with a show of gunships and demanded Japan open up to trade and provisioning. The shogunate was no match for Perry's firepower and had to agree to his demands. Soon an American consul arrived, and other Western powers followed suit. Japan was obliged to give 'most favoured nation' rights to all the powers, and lost control over its own tariffs.

1894–95

Japan starts a war with China, at this stage a weak nation. Defeating China in the Sino-Japanese War (1895), Japan gains Taiwan and its territorial expansion begins.

1902

Japan signs the Anglo-Japanese Alliance, the first-ever equal alliance between a Western and non-Western nation. Effectively, this means Japan has become a major power.

1904–05

Japan wins the Russo-Japanese War. Antipathy towards Russia had developed after the Sino-Japanese War, when Russia pressured Japan to renounce Chinese territory that it then occupied.

1910

Free of any Russian threat, Japan formally annexes Korea, in which it had been increasingly interested since the 1870s. The international community makes no real protest.

Meiji Restoration

Anti-shogunal samurai, particularly in the outer domains of Satsuma (southern Kyūshū) and Chōshū (western Honshū), capitalised on the humiliation of the shogunate, the nation's supposed military protector. A movement arose to 'revere the emperor and expel the barbarians' *(sonnō jōi)*.

Unsuccessfully skirmishing with the Western powers, the reformers realised that while expelling the barbarians was not feasible, restoring the emperor was. Their coup, known as the Meiji (Enlightened Rule) Restoration, in late 1867 to early 1868, 'restored' the new teenage emperor Mutsuhito (1852–1912; later known as Meiji), following the convenient death of his father Kōmei (1831–67).

THE REAL LAST SAMURAI

Saigō Takamori (1828–77) was a giant for his day, at about 180cm (6ft) tall, with a broad build, square head and large eyes. His importance in Japanese history is equally large.

Born to a samurai family in Kagoshima, Kyūshū (then called Satsuma Province, in the southwestern corner of the main islands), Saigō was an ardent supporter of the emperor Meiji and field commander of the imperial army against the forces of the Tokugawa shogunate. A rebellion of Tokugawa loyalists quashed at Ueno in Tokyo in 1868 cemented the Meiji Restoration.

But things did not turn out as Saigō had hoped. The samurai system was abolished once Meiji ascended the throne, and by 1872 this system of professional warriors had given way to a Western model of military conscription. Saigō, by then part of the Meiji government, recommended invading Korea, and after this idea was rejected in 1873 he resigned and returned to Satsuma.

By 1874 the new army had put down small riots by former samurai that broke out around the country. Other former samurai rallied around Saigō and urged him to lead a rebellion against the imperial forces. The resulting 1877 siege of Kumamoto Castle lasted 54 days, with a reported force of 40,000 samurai and armed peasants arrayed against the imperial army. When the castle was incinerated and defeat became inevitable, it is said that Saigō retreated to Kagoshima and committed seppuku.

The Satsuma Rebellion, as it came to be called, soon gained legend status among common Japanese. Capitalising on this fame, the Meiji government posthumously pardoned Saigō and granted him full honours, and today he remains an exemplar of the samurai spirit. Statues of his image can be found most prominently in Kagoshima and, walking his faithful dog, in Tokyo's Ueno-kōen. His most famous maxim, *keiten aijin*, translates to 'Revere heaven, love humankind'.

Fans of the 2003 movie *The Last Samurai* may recognise elements of this story in Katsumoto, the character played by Watanabe Ken. However, there is no evidence that any Western soldier, such as the one played by Tom Cruise, had any role in these events in Saigō's life.

1912

Emperor Meiji (Mutsuhito) dies, after seeing Japan rise from a remote pre-industrial nation to a world power in half a century. His mentally disabled son, Yoshihito, succeeds him.

1914–15

Japan uses the involvement of Western countries in WWI in Europe to occupy German territory in the Pacific in 1914 (as Britain's ally), and in 1915 to present China with 'Twenty-One Demands'.

1920s

Japan becomes increasingly disillusioned with the West, feeling unfairly treated by decisions such as the Washington Conference naval ratios (1921–22) and the USA's immigration policies in 1924.

1923

The Great Kantō Earthquake strikes Japan near Tokyo, killing an estimated 100,000 to 140,000 people. Much of the destruction is caused by fires sweeping through Tokyo and Yokohama after the quake.

After some initial resistance, the last shogun, Yoshinobu (1837–1913), retired to Shizuoka to live out his remaining years peacefully. The shogunal base at Edo became the new imperial base and was renamed Tokyo (Eastern Capital).

Mutsuhito did as he was told by those who had restored him, though they would claim that everything was done on his behalf and with his sanction. His restorers, driven by both personal ambition and genuine concern for the nation, were mostly leading Satsuma or Chōshū samurai aged in their early 30s, the most prominent of them Itō Hirobumi (1841–1909), who later became prime minister on no fewer than four occasions. Fortunately for Japan, they proved a very capable oligarchy.

Japan was also fortunate that the Western powers were distracted by richer and easier pickings in China and elsewhere, and did not seriously seek to occupy or colonise Japan. Nevertheless, the fear of colonisation made the reformers act with great urgency. Far from being colonised, they wanted to be colonisers and make Japan a major power.

The salaries of foreign specialists invited to Japan during the Meiji period are believed to have amounted to 5% of all government expenditure during the period.

Westernisation

Under the banner of *fukoku kyōhei* (rich country, strong army), the young men who now controlled Japan decided on Westernisation as the best strategy. Another slogan, '*oitsuke, oikose*' (catch up, overtake), suggests they even wanted to outdo their models. Missions were sent overseas to observe Western institutions and practices, and specialists were brought to Japan to advise in areas from banking to transport to mining.

In the following decades Japan Westernised quite substantially, not just in material ways such as telegraphs, railways and clothing, but also by establishing a modern banking system and economy, a legal code, a constitution and legislative assembly, elections and political parties, and a conscript army.

Where necessary, existing institutions and practices were disestablished. *Daimyō* were 'persuaded' to give their domain land to the government in return for governorships or other compensation, enabling a prefectural system to be set up. The four-tier class system was scrapped, and people were freed to choose their occupation and place of residence. Even the samurai class was phased out by 1876 to pave the way for a more efficient conscript army.

New Ideologies

The ban on Christianity was lifted, though few took advantage of it. Nevertheless, numerous Western ideologies entered the country, one of the most popular being 'self-help' philosophy, which provided a guiding principle for a population newly liberated from a world in which everything had been prescribed for them. The government quickly realised that

The rickshaw was not developed until 1869, after the Tokugawa ban on wheeled transport was lifted.

1931

Increasingly defiant of the West, Japan invades Manchuria and then dramatically withdraws from the League of Nations in response to criticism. Japan's behaviour becomes more aggressive.

1937

During an attempted occupation of China, Japan commits an atrocity at Nanjing, torturing and killing many thousands of people, mostly innocent civilians.

1941

Japan enters WWII by striking Pearl Harbor without warning on 7 December, destroying much of the USA's Pacific fleet and drawing America into the war.

1942

After early military successes, Japan's expansion is thwarted at the Battle of Midway in June, with significant losses. From this time, Japan is largely ir retrea nationalism could usefully harness these new energies. People were encouraged to make a success of themselves and become strong, and in so doing show the world what a successful and powerful nation Japan was.

Leaning Towards Democracy

The government took responsibility for establishing major industries and then selling them off at bargain rates to chosen 'government-friendly' industrial entrepreneurs – a factor in the formation of huge industrial conglomerates known as *zaibatsu*. While the government's actions were not really democratic, this was typical of the day. Another example is the 'transcendental cabinet' that was responsible only to the emperor, who followed his advisers, who were members of the same cabinet! Meiji Japan was outwardly democratic, but internally retained many authoritarian features.

The 'state-guided' economy was helped by a workforce that was well educated, obedient and numerous, and traditions of sophisticated commercial practices such as futures markets. In the early years, Japan's main industry was textiles and its main export silk, but later in the Meiji period it moved into manufacturing and heavy industry, becoming a major world shipbuilder. Improvement in agricultural technology freed up farming labour to move into these manufacturing sectors.

The World Stage

A key element of Japan's aim to become a world power with overseas territory was the military. Following Prussian (army) and British (navy) models, Japan built up a formidable military force. Using the same 'gunboat diplomacy' on Korea that Perry had used on the Japanese, in 1876 Japan was able to force on Korea an unequal treaty of its own, and increasingly meddled in Korean politics. In 1894, using Chinese 'interference' in Korea as a justification, Japan manufactured a war with China, a weak nation at this stage despite its massive size, and easily emerged victorious. As a result, it gained Taiwan and the Liaotung Peninsula. Russia pressured Japan into renouncing the peninsula and then promptly occupied it, leading to the Russo-Japanese War of 1904–05, won by Japan. An important benefit was Western recognition of its interests in Korea, which it annexed in 1910.

The Coming of the Barbarians, by Pat Barr, is perhaps the most interesting account of the mid-19th-century opening of Japan.

By the time of Mutsuhito's death in 1912, Japan was recognised as a world power. In addition to its military victories and territorial acquisitions, in 1902 it had signed the Anglo-Japanese Alliance, the first-ever equal alliance between a Western and non-Western nation. The unequal treaties had also been rectified. Western-style structures were in place. The economy was world ranking. The Meiji period had been a truly extraordinary half-century of modernisation. But where to next?

1945
Following intensive firebombing of Tokyo in March, Hiroshima and Nagasaki become victims of an atomic bombing on 6 and 9 August, leading Japan's leader, Hirohito, to surrender on 15 August.

1945–52
Japan undergoes USA-led occupation and a rapid economic recovery follows. Hirohito is spared from prosecution as a war criminal, angering many American allies.

1954
Godzilla makes his first appearance in an animated movie of the same name, directed by Honda Ishirō, with the premise that Godzilla was a monster created by the atomic bombings of WWII.

1964
Tokyo hosts the Summer Olympics, an event that for many Japanese marked Japan's full re-entry into the international community and the completion of its recovery from WWII.

Growing Dissatisfaction with the West

Mutsuhito was succeeded by his son Yoshihito (Taishō), whose mental deterioration led to his own son Hirohito (1901–89) becoming regent in 1921.

The Taishō period (Great Righteousness; 1912–26) saw continued democratisation, the extension of the right to vote and a stress on diplomacy. Until WWI Japan benefitted economically from the reduced presence of the Western powers, and politically from its alliance with Britain, and was able to occupy German possessions in East Asia and the Pacific. However, Japan also used the reduced Western presence in 1915 to aggressively try to gain control of China, issuing its notorious 'Twenty-One Demands', which were eventually modified.

Japan was arguably the first Asian nation to defeat a Western nation in a military conflict (the Russo-Japanese War of 1904–05).

There was a growing sense of dissatisfaction in Japan towards the West, and a sense of unfair treatment. The Washington Conference of 1921–22 set naval ratios of three capital ships for Japan to five American and five British, which upset the Japanese, despite being well ahead of France's 1.75. Around the same time, a racial-equality clause Japan proposed to the newly formed League of Nations was rejected. And in 1924 America introduced race-based immigration policies that effectively targeted Japanese.

This dissatisfaction intensified in the Shōwa period (Illustrious Peace), which started in 1926 with the death of Yoshihito and the formal accession of Hirohito. Not a strong emperor, he was unable to curb the rising power of the military, which pointed to a growing gap between urban and rural living standards and accused politicians and big businessmen of corruption. The situation was not helped by repercussions from the Great Depression in the late 1920s. The cause of these troubles, in Japanese eyes, was the West, with its excessive individualism and liberalism. According to the militarists, Japan needed to look after its own interests, which meant a resource-rich, Japan-controlled Greater East Asian Co-Prosperity Sphere that even included Australia and New Zealand.

Japan invaded Manchuria in 1931 and set up a puppet government. When the League of Nations objected, Japan promptly left the league. It soon turned its attention to China, and in 1937 launched a brutal invasion that saw atrocities such as the infamous Nanjing Massacre of December. Casualty figures for Chinese civilians at Nanjing vary from 40,000 to over 300,000. Many of the tortures, rapes and murders were filmed and are undeniable, but even today, Japanese attempts to downplay this and other massacres in Asia remain a stumbling block in Japan's relations with many Asian nations.

WWII

Japan did not reject all Western nations, for it admired the new regimes in Germany and Italy and in 1940 entered into a pact with them. This

1972

The USA returns administrative control of Okinawa to Japan, but keeps many bases in place, which is a continuing source of tension.

1990

The so-called 'Bubble Economy', based on overinflated land and stock prices, finally bursts in Japan. By the end of the year, the stock market has lost 48% of its value.

2005

Japan's population declines for the first year since WWII, and is a continuing trend.

2010

China surpasses Japan as the world's second-largest economy after the USA.

gave it confidence to expand further in Southeast Asia, principally seeking oil. However, the alliance didn't lead to much cooperation, and since Hitler was openly talking of the Japanese as *untermenschen* (lesser beings) and the 'Yellow Peril', Japan was never sure of Germany's commitment. The USA was increasingly concerned at Japan's aggression, and applied sanctions. Diplomacy failed and war seemed inevitable.

The Yamato dynasty is the longest unbroken monarchy in the world, and Hirohito's reign from 1926 to 1989 the longest of any Japanese monarch.

Japanese forces struck at Pearl Harbor on 7 December 1941, damaging much of the USA's Pacific fleet and apparently catching the USA by surprise (though some scholars believe Roosevelt and others deliberately allowed the attack, to overcome isolationist sentiment and to bring the USA into the war against Germany). Whatever the reality, the USA certainly underestimated Japan's commitment, which led to widespread occupation of Pacific islands and parts of Asia. Most scholars agree that Japan never expected to beat the USA, but hoped to bring it to the negotiating table and emerge better off.

The tide started to turn against Japan from the Battle of Midway in June 1942, when much of its carrier fleet was destroyed. Japan had over-extended itself, and over the next three years was subjected to an island-hopping counter-attack. By mid-1945 Japan, ignoring the Potsdam Declaration calling for unconditional surrender, was preparing for a final Allied assault on its homeland. On 6 August the world's first atomic bomb was dropped on Hiroshima, killing 90,000 civilians. Russia, which Japan had hoped might mediate, declared war on 8 August. And on 9 August another atomic bomb was dropped, this time on Nagasaki, resulting in another 50,000 deaths. The emperor formally surrendered on 15 August.

The Modern Period

Japan's recovery from the war is now the stuff of legend. The American occupation officially ended in 1952, with the USA engaged in yet another war, this time on the Korean Peninsula. Many historians, both Japanese and American, say Japan's role as a forward base reignited the Japanese economy. Whatever the case, its growth from the 1950s on can only be termed miraculous. It wasn't until 1990, with the bursting of the 'Bubble Economy', that it finally came down to earth.

Until Japan was occupied by the USA and other Allies following WWII, the nation had never been conquered or occupied by a foreign power.

The following decades were marked by protracted economic stagnation that was only worsened by the 2008 Global Financial Crisis. As if that wasn't bad enough, only three years later, Japan was devastated by the Great East Japan Earthquake and Tsunami of 2011, in which more than 15,000 people perished. At this point, one might have expected Japan to throw in the towel, but the country has a history of bouncing back from adversity. By 2013 the country was once again experiencing economic growth, and is now gearing up for the 2020 Tokyo Summer Olympics with a mood of optimism and healthy determination.

2011

On 11 March, the Great East Japan Earthquake strikes off the coast of northeast Japan (Tōhoku), generating a tsunami that kills many thousands and setting off a crisis at a nuclear powerplant in Fukushima Prefecture.

2012

The Ōi nuclear reactor in Fukui-ken is restarted, but, in response to public protest, it is closed again the following year.

2013

The Japanese government approves the Special Secrecy Law, raising fears of censorship and threats to freedom of speech.

2013

The International Olympic Committee awards Tokyo the right to host the 2020 Summer Olympics.

The People of Japan

The uniqueness and peculiarity of the Japanese is a favourite topic of both Western observers and the Japanese themselves. It's worth starting any discussion about the people of Japan by noting that there is no such thing as 'the Japanese'. Rather, there are 127 million individuals in Japan, each with their own unique character, interests and habits. Despite popular stereotypes to the contrary, Japanese people are as varied as any others on earth.

Defying Stereotypes

While stereotypes of the Japanese are usually exaggerated and often inaccurate, it's true that the Japanese do collectively show certain cultural characteristics that reflect their unique history and interaction with their environment. First, Japan is an island nation. Second, until WWII, Japan was never conquered by an outside power, nor was it heavily influenced by Christian missionaries. Third, until the beginning of last century, the majority of Japanese lived in close-knit rural farming communities. Fourth, most of Japan is covered in steep mountains, so the few flat areas of the country are quite crowded – people literally live on top of each other. Finally, for almost all of its history, Japan has been a strictly hierarchical place, with something approximating a caste system during the Edo period.

It is thought that the modern Japanese population emerged from the mixing of early Jōmon people, who walked to Japan via land bridges formed during an ice age, and later Yayoi people, who arrived from the Korean Peninsula in boats.

All of this has produced a people who highly value group identity and social harmony – in a tightly packed city or small farming village, there simply isn't room for colourful individualism. One of the ways harmony is preserved is by forming consensus and concealing personal opinions and true feelings. Thus, the free-flowing exchange of ideas, debates and even heated arguments that one expects in the West are far less common in Japan. This reticence to share innermost thoughts may contribute to the Western image of the Japanese as somewhat mysterious.

Of course, there is a lot more to the typical Japanese character than just a tendency to prize social harmony. Any visitor to the country will soon discover a people who are remarkably conscientious, meticulous, industrious, honest and technically skilled. A touching shyness and sometimes almost painful self-consciousness are also undoubted features of many Japanese. These characteristics result in a society that is a joy for the traveller to experience.

And let us say that any visit to Japan is a good opportunity to explode the myths about Japan and the Japanese. While you may imagine a nation of suit-clad conformists or enigmatic automatons, a few rounds in a local *izakaya* (pub-eatery) will quickly put all of these notions to rest.

Lifestyle

The way most Japanese live today differs greatly from the way they lived before WWII. As the birth rate has dropped and labour demands have drawn more workers to cities, the population has become increasingly urban. At the same time, Japan continues to soak up influences from abroad and the traditional lifestyle of the country is quickly disappearing

THE LANGUAGE FACTOR

Why is it that the Japanese are often perceived as aloof or even bizarre? These stereotypes are largely rooted in language: few Japanese are able to speak English as well as, say, your average Singaporean or Hong Kong Chinese, not to mention most Europeans. This difficulty with English is largely rooted in the country's English-education system, and is compounded by cultural factors, including a natural shyness and a perfectionist streak, and the nature of the Japanese language itself, which contains fewer sounds than many other major languages (making pronunciation of other languages difficult). Thus, what appears to the casual observer to be a maddening inscrutability is more likely just an inability to communicate effectively. Outsiders who become fluent in Japanese discover a people whose thoughts and feelings are surprisingly – almost boringly – similar to those of folks in other developed nations.

in the face of a dizzying onslaught of Western material and pop culture. These days, the average young Tokyoite has a lot more in common with her peers in Melbourne or London than she does with her grandmother back in her *furusato* (home town).

In the City

The overwhelming majority of Japanese live in the bustling urban environments of major cities. These urbanites live famously hectic lives dominated by often gruelling work schedules and punctuated by lengthy commutes from more affordable outlying neighbourhoods and suburbs to city centres.

Until fairly recently, the nexus of all this activity was the Japanese corporation, which provided lifetime employment to the legions of blue-suited white-collar workers, almost all of them men, who lived, worked, drank, ate and slept in the service of the companies for which they toiled. These days, as the Japanese economy makes the transition from a manufacturing economy to a service economy, the old certainties are vanishing. On the way out are Japan's famous 'cradle to grave' employment and age-based promotion system. Now, a recent college graduate is just as likely to become a *furitaa* (part-time worker) as he is to become a salaryman. Needless to say, all this has wide-ranging consequences for Japanese society.

Most Japanese babies are born with a Mongolian spot *(mōkohan)* on their lower backs. This harmless birthmark is composed of melanin-containing cells and usually fades by the age of five. It's common in several Asian populations and in Native Americans.

Most families once comprised a father who was a salaryman, a mother who was a housewife, kids who studied dutifully in order to earn a place at one of Japan's elite universities, and an elderly in-law who had moved in. Although the days of this traditional model may not be completely over, it has been changing fast in recent years. As in Western countries, *tomobataraki* (both spouses working) is now increasingly common.

The kids in the family probably still study like mad. If they are not yet in high school, they will be working towards gaining admission to a select high school by attending an evening cram school, known as a *juku*. If they are already in high school, they will be attending a *juku* in the hopes of passing university admission exams.

As for the mother- or father-in-law, who in the past would have expected to be taken care of by the eldest son in the family, they may have found that beliefs about filial loyalty have changed substantially since the 1980s, particularly in urban centres. Now, more and more Japanese families are sending elderly parents and in-laws to live out their dotage in *rōjin hōmu* (literally 'old folk's homes').

In the Country

Only one in 10 Japanese live in the small farming and fishing villages that dot the mountains and cling to the rugged coasts. Mass postwar emigration from these rural enclaves has doubtless changed the weave of Japanese social fabric and the texture of its landscape, as the young continue their steady flight to the city, leaving untended rice fields to slide down the hills from neglect.

Today only 15% of farming households continue to make ends meet solely through agriculture, with most rural workers holding down two or three jobs. Though this lifestyle manages to make the incomes of some country dwellers higher than those of their urban counterparts, it also speaks clearly of the crisis that many rural communities are facing in their struggle to maintain the traditional way of life.

The salvation of traditional village life may well rely on the success of the 'I-turn' (moving from urban areas to rural villages) and 'U-turn' (moving from country to city, and back again) movements. Although not yet wildly successful, these movements have managed to attract young people who work at home, company workers who are willing to put in a number of hours on the train commuting to the nearest city, and retirees looking to spend their golden years among the thatched roofs and rice fields that symbolise a not-so-distant past.

Religion

Shintō and Buddhism are the main religions in Japan. Most Japanese practice some rites from both religions (though these are sometimes practiced without any particular religious fervour) and are likely to pay an annual visit to a shrine and a temple, particularly during important holidays like O-bon and New Year's.

Shintō, or 'the way of the gods' is the indigenous religion of Japan. Shintoists believe that *kami* (gods) are present in the natural world, or, at the very least, animate the natural world. Consisting of thousands of deities, the Shintō pantheon includes both local spirits and global gods and goddesses. Therefore, a devout Shintoist might worship the spirit of

VISITING A SHINTŌ SHRINE

Entering a Japanese shrine can be a bewildering experience for travellers. In order to make the most of the experience, follow these guidelines and do as the Japanese do.

➡ Just past the *torii* (shrine gate), you'll find a *chōzuya* (trough of water) with long-handled ladles (*hishaku*) perched on a rack above. This is for purifying yourself before entering the sacred precincts of the shrine. Some Japanese forgo this ritual and head directly for the main hall. If you choose to purify yourself, take a ladle, fill it with fresh water from the spigot, pour some over one hand, transfer the spoon and pour water over the other hand. Then pour a little water into a cupped hand and rinse your mouth, spitting the water onto the ground beside the trough, not into the trough.

➡ Next, head to the *haiden* (hall of worship), which sits in front of the *honden* (main hall) enshrining the *kami* (god of the shrine). Here you'll find a thick rope hanging from a gong, with an offerings box in front. Toss a coin into the box and ring the gong by pulling on the rope (to summon the deity). Then pray, clap your hands twice, bow and then back away from the shrine. Some Japanese believe that a ¥5 coin is the best for an offering at a temple or shrine and that the luck engendered by the offering of a ¥10 coin will come further in the future (since 10 can be pronounced *tō* in Japanese, which can also mean 'far').

➡ If photography is forbidden at a shrine, it will be posted as such. Otherwise, it is permitted and you should simply use your discretion when taking photos.

a nearby waterfall or that of a uniquely shaped rock, while simultaneously revering the most celebrated Shintō deity Amaterasu, the goddess of the sun. The majority of Japanese would say that their religion is Shintō, but what they would mean by this would vary widely from person to person.

Buddhism arrived from India via China and Korea sometime in the 6th century and has for the most part coexisted peacefully with Shintō. About 85 million people in Japan currently practice some form of Buddhism, though most combine their practice with the exercise of periodic Shintō rites. Japanese Buddhism is mostly Mahayana Buddhism, which is notable for its belief in bodhisattva, beings who put off entry into nirvana in order to save all beings stuck in the corrupt world of time.

Japanese Buddhists often call on the assistance of these bodhisattva, usually by chanting mantras or otherwise invoking their names rather than meditating. Zen Buddhism, however, although being a Mayahana sect, places great emphasis on meditation.

Population

Japan has a population of approximately 127 million people and, with 91% of it concentrated in urban centres, population density is extremely high. Areas such as the Tokyo–Kawasaki–Yokohama conurbation are so densely populated that they have almost ceased to be separate cities, running into each other and forming a vast coalescence that, if considered as a whole, would constitute the world's largest city.

One notable feature of Japan's population is its relative ethnic and cultural homogeneity. This is particularly striking for visitors from the USA, Australia and other multicultural nations. The main reason for this ethnic uniformity lies in Japan's strict immigration laws, which have ensured that only a small number of foreigners settle in the country.

The largest non-Japanese group in the country is made up of 650,000 *zai-nichi kankoku-jin* (resident Koreans). For most outsiders, Koreans are an invisible minority. Indeed, even the Japanese themselves have no way of knowing that someone is of Korean descent if they adopt a Jap-

MINORITY CULTURES

The Ainu, of whom there are roughly 24,000 living in Japan, are the indigenous people of Hokkaidō and, some would argue, the only people who can claim to be natives of Japan. Due to ongoing intermarriage and assimilation, almost all Ainu consider themselves bi-ethnic. Today, fewer than 200 people in Japan can claim both parents with exclusively Ainu descent.

The *burakumin* are a largely invisible (to outsiders, at least) group of Japanese whose ancestors performed work that brought them into contact with the contamination of death – butchering, leatherworking and disposing of corpses. The *burakumin* were the outcasts in the social hierarchy (some would say caste system) that existed during the Edo period. While the *burakumin* are racially the same as other Japanese, they have traditionally been treated like an inferior people by much of Japanese society. Estimates put the number of hereditary *burakumin* in present-day Japan at anywhere between 890,000 and three million.

While discrimination against *burakumin* is now technically against the law, there continues to be significant discrimination against them in such important aspects of Japanese social life as work and marriage. It is common knowledge, though rarely alluded to, that information about any given individual's possible *burakumin* origin is available to anyone (generally employers and prospective fathers-in-law) who is prepared to make certain discreet investigations. Many Japanese consider this a very culturally sensitive issue and may prefer to avoid discussion of this topic with foreigners.

anese name. Nevertheless, Japanese-born Koreans, who in some cases speak no language other than Japanese, were only recently released from the obligation to carry ID cards with their fingerprints at all times. Some still face discrimination in the workplace and other aspects of their daily lives. Aside from Koreans, most foreigners in Japan are temporary workers from China, Southeast Asia, South America and Western countries.

Indigenous groups such as the Ainu have been reduced to very small numbers, due to intermarriage with non-Ainu and government attempts to hasten their assimilation into general Japanese society. At present, Ainu are concentrated mostly in Hokkaidō, the northernmost of Japan's main islands.

The most notable feature of Japan's population is the fact that it is shrinking. Japan's astonishingly low birth rate of 1.4 births per woman is among the lowest in the developed world and Japan is rapidly becoming a nation of elderly citizens. The population began declining in 2005, and is predicted to reach 100 million in 2050 and 67 million in 2100. Needless to say, such demographic change will have a major influence on the economy in coming decades.

Women in Japan

Traditional Japanese society restricted the woman's role to the home where, as housekeeper, she wielded considerable power, overseeing all financial matters, monitoring the children's education and, in some ways, acting as the head of the household. Even in the early Meiji period (1868–1912), this ideal was rarely matched by reality: labour shortfalls often resulted in women taking on factory work and, even before that, women often worked side by side with men in the fields.

Most Japanese identify themselves as both Shintō and Buddhist, but many young Japanese get married in Christian ceremonies performed by foreign 'priests' (many of whom are not real Christian priests).

As might be expected, the contemporary situation is complex. There are, of course, women who stick to established roles. They tend to opt for shorter college courses, often at women's colleges, and see education as an asset in the marriage market. Once married, they leave the role of breadwinner to the husband. Part of the reason for this is the prevalence of gender discrimination in Japanese companies. Societal expectations, however, also play a role: Japanese women are often forced to choose between having a career and having a family. Not only do most companies refuse to hire women for career-track positions, many Japanese men are simply not interested in having a career woman as a spouse. This makes it very intimidating for a Japanese woman to step out of her traditional gender role and follow a career path.

Increasingly, however, Japanese women are choosing to forgo or delay marriage in favour of pursuing their own career ambitions. However, changing aspirations do not necessarily translate into changing realities, and Japanese women are still significantly underepresented in upper management and political positions. There is a disproportionately high number of females employed as so-called OLs (office ladies). OLs do a lot of the grunt work in many Japanese companies, with tasks often extending beyond secretarial work to include a lot of the day-to-day running of company affairs. In some conservative companies their duties also include making and serving tea to their male colleagues and visitors to the company.

Those women who do choose full-time work suffer from one of the worst gender wage gaps in the developed world: Japanese women earn only 68% of what Japanese men earn, compared to 77% in the USA, 81% in the UK and 82% in Australia (according to figures released by the respective governments). In politics, the situation is even worse: Japanese women hold only 11.7% of seats in the Diet, the nation's governing body.

Japanese Cuisine

Those familiar with Japanese cuisine *(nihon ryōri)* know that eating is half the fun of travelling in Japan. Even if you've already tried some of Japan's better-known dishes, you're likely to be surprised by how delicious the original is when served on its home turf. More importantly, the adventurous eater will be delighted to find that Japanese food is far more than just sushi, tempura or sukiyaki. Indeed, it is possible to spend a month in Japan and sample a different speciality restaurant every day.

Eating in a Japanese Restaurant

What's What in Japanese Restaurants: A Guide to Ordering, Eating and Enjoying (Robb Satterwhite; 2011) is a brilliant guide to Japanese restaurants. With thorough explanations of the various types of dishes and sample menus, this is a must for those who really want to explore and enjoy what's on offer.

When you enter a restaurant in Japan, you'll be greeted with a hearty *irasshaimase* (Welcome!). In all but the most casual places, the waiter will next ask you *nan-mei sama* (How many people?). Answer with your fingers, which is what the Japanese do. You will then be led to a table, a place at the counter or a tatami room.

At this point you will be given an *o-shibori* (hot towel), a cup of tea and a menu. The *o-shibori* is for wiping your hands and face. When you're done with it, just roll it up and leave it next to your place. Now comes the hard part: ordering. If you don't read Japanese, and don't have a phrasebook or other language reference to point to, there are two phrases that may help: *o-susume wa nan des ka* (What do you recommend?) and *o-makase shimas* (Please decide for me).

When you've finished eating, you can signal for the bill by crossing one index finger over the other to form the sign of an X. This is the standard sign for 'Bill, please'. You can also say *o-kanjō kudasai*. Remember, there is no tipping in Japan and tea is free of charge. Usually you will be given a bill to take to the cashier at the front of the restaurant. Only the bigger and more international places take credit cards, so cash is always the safer option.

Eating Etiquette

When it comes to eating in Japan, there are quite a number of implicit rules, but they're fairly easy to remember. If you're worried about putting your foot in it, relax – the Japanese don't expect you to know what to do and they are unlikely to be offended as long as you follow the standard rules of politeness from your own country. Here are a few major points to keep in mind:

Chopsticks in rice Do not stick your *hashi* (chopsticks) upright in a bowl of rice. This is how rice is offered to the dead in Buddhist rituals. Similarly, do not pass food from your chopsticks to the chopsticks of someone else. This is another funeral ritual.

Polite expressions When eating with other people, especially when you're a guest, it is polite to say *itadakimasu* (literally 'I will receive') before digging in. This is as close as the Japanese come to saying grace. Similarly, at the end of the meal, you should thank your host by saying *gochisō-sama deshita,* which means 'It was a real feast'.

Kampai It is bad form to fill your own glass. You should fill the glass of the person next to you and wait for them to reciprocate. Raise your glass a little off the table while it is being filled. Once everyone's glass has been filled, the usual starting signal is a chorus of *kampai*, which means 'Cheers!'.

Slurp When you eat noodles in Japan, it's perfectly OK, even expected, to slurp them. In fact, one of the best ways to find *rāmen* (egg noodle) restaurants in Japan is to listen for the loud slurping sound that comes out of them!

Restaurant Types & Sample Menus

With the exception of *shokudō* (all-round restaurants) and *izakaya* (pub-eateries), most Japanese restaurants concentrate on a particular speciality cuisine. In this chapter we discuss the main types of restaurants you are likely to encounter and provide sample menus for each type. If you familiarise yourself with the main types of restaurants and what they serve, you'll be able to get the most out of Japan's incredible culinary scene.

Of course, you may baulk at charging into a restaurant where both the language and the menu are likely to be incomprehensible. Those timid of heart should take solace in the fact that the Japanese will go to extraordinary lengths to understand what you want and will help you order.

Shokudō

A *shokudō* is the most common type of restaurant in Japan, and is usually found near train stations, tourist spots and just about any other place where people congregate. Easily distinguished by the presence of plastic food displays in the window, these inexpensive places usually serve a variety of *washoku* (Japanese dishes) and *yōshoku* (Western dishes).

At lunch, and sometimes dinner, the easiest meal to order at a *shokudō* is a *teishoku* (set-course meal), which is sometimes also called *ranchi setto* (lunch set) or *kōsu* (course). This generally includes a main dish of meat or fish, a bowl of rice, *miso-shiru* (bean-paste soup), shredded cabbage and some *tsukemono* (Japanese pickles). In addition, most *shokudō* serve a fairly standard selection of *donburi-mono* (rice dishes) and *menrui* (noodle dishes). When you order noodles, you can choose between

JAPANESE CHAIN RESTAURANTS

Japan is awash with foreign chain restaurants. In cities like Tokyo and Kyoto, you can't walk more than a few blocks without running into a branch of 'Sutaba' (Starbucks) and 'Makudo' (McDonald's). Fortunately, for those who want to 'go local', there are some great homegrown chains that are at least as good. Here are some of our favourites; most have either picture menus, English menus, or both.

Curry House CoCo Ichibanya Better known as 'Coco Ichi', this is the place to try *wa-kare* (Japanese-style curry and rice).

Doutor This humble coffee and sandwich chain can be a lifesaver when you just fancy something familiar like a Western-style sandwich and a hot cup of coffee. The sandwiches are often much better than those found at regular Japanese bakeries and convenience stores.

Ootoya For healthy sets of filling Japanese standards like noodles, rice and fish, along with plenty of vegies, served in clean well-lit surroundings, this chain of modern *shokudō* is a great choice.

MOS Burger This Japanese burger chain has a loyal following of foreign customers who go for the juicy handmade burgers and delights like *ebi* (shrimp) rice burgers and *wagyū* (Japanese beef) burgers.

Yoshinoya *Gyūdon* (sukiyaki-style beef served over a bowl of rice) is the speciality here and it's filling and super cheap. Go in the morning for a healthy salmon and rice set meal *(sake teishoku)*.

soba and udon, both of which are served with a variety of toppings. If you're at a loss as to what to order, simply say *kyō-no-ranchi* (today's lunch) and they'll do the rest. Expect to spend from ¥600 to ¥1000 for a meal at a *shokudō*.

katsu-don	かつ丼	rice topped with a fried pork cutlet
oyako-don	親子丼	rice topped with egg and chicken
ten-don	天丼	rice topped with tempura prawns and vegetables

ŌTA KAZUHIKO ON JAPAN'S IZAKAYA

Ōta Kazuhiko is considered by many to be Japan's leading authority on *izakaya,* Japan's beloved pub-eateries. Ōta-san travels the length of Japan seeking out the best traditional *izakaya*. He has published his findings in more than a dozen books, including *Ōta Kazuhiko no Izakaya Mishuran,* the 'Mishuran' in the title being a play on the famed Michelin restaurant guide series.

What is the definition of an izakaya? Simply put, an *izakaya* is a place where you can enjoy sake. More broadly, an *izakaya* is a place where you can enjoy sake and food. In addition, they are places that you can easily enter alone.

What is the history of the izakaya? Prior to the Meiji period, *saka-ya* (sake shops) would serve alcohol to customers who dropped by for a drink. The customers would stand around and drink their sake out of *masu* (square wooden boxes used to measure sake). Thus, these places were *tachi-nomiya* (stand-and-drink places). Later, some *saka-ya* turned the sake barrels into seats for their customers, so they could relax and enjoy their drink. Thus, they became *izakaya* (the *i* means 'to be', which, added to *saka-ya,* forms *izakaya,* meaning a *saka-ya* where you can stay and drink). Later on, some places started to serve snacks to go with the sake, and this evolved into proper food to go with the sake.

What role did izakaya play in Japanese society? *Izakaya* played an important role in Japanese society. Traditionally, after men finished work at a company, they would go together to an *izakaya*. The older members of the group or the boss would often pay for the younger workers. While they drank, they could talk freely about work and also about things outside work, like their personal lives and their past. The older guys would teach the young ones how to drink, how to order, and also about the ways of the world. Thus, the *izakaya* served as a place of human and social education, not just a drinking place.

What should you order in an izakaya? First of all, don't rush. Just have a look around. Maybe start with some *ginjō-shu* (a high-grade sake). Have the first one cold. Then, consider having some hot sake. As for food, seafood is the way to go: sashimi, stewed fish, grilled fish or shellfish. You can also try some chicken dishes. Have a look at what the other customers are eating or check out the specials board. If you can't speak or read Japanese, you can point at things or bring along a Japanese friend to help you order.

Where can you find good izakaya? Well, there are lots of chain *izakaya* near the train stations in most cities, but the best place to look for really good ones is in the old *hankagai* (entertainment district), which is usually not where the train station is. The best places have been run for generations by the same family, and the customers have also been coming for generations. So, the master might have watched his customers grow up. These are the places that take pride in their work and are the most reliable.

What is the best thing about izakaya? *Izakaya* are places where people show their true selves, their true hearts. The sake allows people to drop their pretensions and let their hair down. *Izakaya* are places where people show their individuality. They bind people together, whether strangers or friends. I think all countries have a place like this, but in Japan, if you want to see the way people really are, the *izakaya* is the place to go.

Izakaya

An *izakaya* is the Japanese equivalent of a pub-eatery. It's a good place to visit when you want a casual meal, a wide selection of food, a hearty atmosphere and, of course, plenty of beer and sake. When you enter an *izakaya,* you are given the choice of sitting around the counter, at a table or on a tatami floor. You usually order a bit at a time, choosing from a selection of typical Japanese foods, such as *yakitori,* sashimi and grilled fish, as well as Japanese interpretations of Western foods like French fries and beef stew.

Izakaya can be identified by their rustic facades and the red lanterns outside their doors bearing the kanji for *izakaya* (居酒屋). Many also stack crates of beer and sake bottles outside. Since *izakaya* food is casual fare to go with drinking, it is usually fairly inexpensive. Depending on how much you drink, you can expect to get away with spending ¥2500 to ¥5000 per person.

agedashi-dōfu	揚げだし豆腐	deep-fried tofu in a *dashi* (stock) broth
hiyayakko	冷奴	a cold block of tofu with soy sauce and spring onions
jaga-batā	ジャガバター	baked potatoes with butter
niku-jaga	肉ジャガ	beef and potato stew
sashimi mori-awase	刺身盛り合わせ	a selection of sliced sashimi
shio-yaki-zakana	塩焼魚	a whole fish grilled with salt
yaki-onigiri	焼きおにぎり	a triangle of grilled rice with *yakitori* sauce

FUGU

Since 2000 there have been 23 cases of poisoning caused by improperly prepared *fugu* (globefish or pufferfish). Government sources, however, attribute these deaths to home, rather than restaurant, meals.

Yakitori

Yakitori (skewers of charcoal-grilled chicken and vegetables) is a popular after-work meal. *Yakitori* is not so much a full meal as an accompaniment for beer and sake. At a *yakitori-ya* (*yakitori* restaurant) you sit around a counter with the other patrons and watch the chef grill your selections over charcoal. The best way to eat here is to order several varieties, then order seconds of the ones you really like. Ordering in these places can be a little confusing since one serving often means two or three skewers (be careful – the price listed on the menu is usually that of a single skewer).

In summer, the beverage of choice at a *yakitori* restaurant is beer or cold sake, while in winter it's hot sake. A few drinks and enough skewers to fill you up should cost ¥3000 to ¥4000 per person. *Yakitori* restaurants are usually small places, often located near train stations, and are best identified by a red lantern outside and the smell of grilled chicken.

hasami/negima	はさみ/ねぎま	pieces of white meat alternating with leek
kawa	皮	chicken skin
piiman	ピーマン	small green capsicums (peppers)
rebā	レバー	chicken livers
sasami	ささみ	skinless chicken-breast pieces
shiitake	しいたけ	Japanese mushrooms
tama-negi	玉ねぎ	round white onions
tebasaki	手羽先	chicken wings
tsukune	つくね	chicken meatballs
yaki-onigiri	焼きおにぎり	a triangle of grilled rice with *yakitori* sauce

TASTY TRAVEL

There's one word every food lover should learn before coming to Japan: *meibutsu*. It means 'speciality', as in regional speciality, and Japan has loads of them. In fact, it never hurts to simply ask for the *meibutsu* when you order at a restaurant or *izakaya*. More often than not, you'll be served something memorable. Here are some of Japan's more famous local specialities, listed by region.

Hiroshima *kaki* (oysters); *Hiroshima-yaki* (Hiroshima-style *okonomiyaki;* batter and cabbage cakes cooked on a griddle)

Hokkaidō *kani-ryōri* (crab cuisine); salmon

Kyoto *kaiseki* (Japanese haute cuisine); *wagashi* (Japanese traditional sweets); *yuba* (the skim off the top of tofu, or soy-milk skin); *Kyō-yasai* (Kyoto-style vegetables)

Kyūshū *tonkotsu-rāmen* (pork-broth *rāmen*); *Satsuma-imo* (sweet potatoes)

Northern Honshū *wanko-soba* (eat-till-you-burst *soba*); *jappa-jiru* (cod soup with Japanese radish and miso)

Okinawa *gōya champurū* (bitter melon stir-fry); *sōki-soba* (*rāmen* with spare ribs); *mimiga* (pickled pigs' ears)

Osaka *tako-yaki* (grilled octopus dumplings); *okonomiyaki*

Shikoku *sansai* (wild mountain vegetables); *sanuki-udon* (a type of wheat noodles); *katsuo tataki* (lightly seared bonito)

Shimonoseki *fugu* (poisonous blowfish or pufferfish)

Tokyo sushi

Sushi & Sashimi

Like *yakitori,* sushi is considered an accompaniment for beer and sake. Nonetheless, both Japanese and foreigners often make a meal of it, and it's one of the healthiest options around. All proper sushi restaurants serve their fish over rice, in which case it's called sushi; without rice, it's called sashimi or *tsukuri* (or, politely, *o-tsukuri*).

There are two main types of sushi: *nigiri-zushi* (served on a small bed of rice; the most common variety) and *maki-zushi* (served in a seaweed roll).

Sushi is not difficult to order. If you sit at the counter of a sushi restaurant you will be able to simply point at what you want, as most of the selections are visible in a refrigerated glass case between you and the sushi chef. You can also order à la carte from the menu. When ordering, you usually order *ichi-nin mae* (one portion), which normally means two pieces of sushi. Be careful, since the price on the menu will be that of only one piece.

If ordering à la carte is too daunting, you can take care of your whole order with just one or two words by ordering *mori-awase,* an assortment plate of *nigiri-zushi*. These usually come in three grades: *futsū nigiri* (regular *nigiri*), *jō nigiri* (special *nigiri*) and *toku-jō nigiri* (extra-special *nigiri*). The difference is in the type of fish used. Most *mori-awase* contain six or seven pieces of sushi.

Be warned that meals in a good sushi restaurant can cost upwards of ¥10,000, while an average establishment can run from ¥3000 to ¥5000 per person. One way to sample the joy of sushi on the cheap is to try an automatic sushi place, usually called *kaiten-zushi,* where the sushi is served on a conveyor belt that runs along a counter. Here you simply reach up and grab whatever looks good to you (which certainly takes the pain out of ordering). You are charged by the number of plates of sushi that you have eaten. Plates are colour-coded by their price and the cost is written either somewhere on the plate itself or on a sign on the wall. You can usually fill yourself up in one of these places for ¥1000 to ¥2000 per person.

The Tsukiji Fish Market in Tokyo is the world's largest. It handles around 2000 tonnes of marine products a day (more than 450 kinds of fish!).

Before eating the sushi, dip it very lightly in *shōyu* (soy sauce), which you pour from a small decanter into a low dish specially provided for the purpose. If you're not good at using *hashi* (chopsticks), don't worry – sushi is one of the few foods in Japan that is perfectly acceptable to eat with your hands. Slices of *gari* (pickled ginger) are served to refresh the palate. The beverage of choice with sushi is beer or sake (hot in winter, cold in summer), with a green tea at the end of the meal.

Note that most of the items on this sample sushi menu can be ordered as sashimi. Just add the words *no o-tsukuri* to get the sashimi version. So, for example, if you wanted some tuna sashimi, you would order *maguro no o-tsukuri*. Note that you'll often be served a different soy sauce to accompany your sashimi; if you like wasabi with your sashimi, you can add some directly to the soy sauce and stir.

The book *Ivan Ramen* (2013) by Ivan Orkin tells the unlikely tale of an American chef's successful *rāmen* restaurant in Tokyo.

ama-ebi	甘海老	sweet shrimp
awabi	あわび	abalone
ebi	海老	prawn or shrimp
hamachi	はまち	yellowtail
ika	いか	squid
ikura	イクラ	salmon roe
kai-bashira	貝柱	scallop
kani	かに	crab
katsuo	かつお	bonito
maguro	まぐろ	tuna
tai	鯛	sea bream
tamago	たまご	sweetened egg
toro	とろ	the choice cut of fatty tuna belly
unagi	うなぎ	eel with a sweet sauce
uni	うに	sea-urchin roe

Sukiyaki & Shabu-shabu

Restaurants usually specialise in both of these dishes. Popular in the West, sukiyaki is a favourite of most foreign visitors to Japan. Sukiyaki consists of thin slices of beef cooked in a broth of *shōyu*, sugar and sake, and accompanied by a variety of vegetables and tofu. After cooking, all the ingredients are dipped in raw egg before being eaten. When made with high-quality beef, such as Kōbe beef, it is a sublime experience.

Shabu-shabu consists of thin slices of beef and vegetables cooked by swirling the ingredients in a light broth, then dipping them in a variety of special sesame-seed and citrus-based sauces. Both of these dishes are prepared in a pot over a fire at your private table. Don't fret about preparation – the waiter will usually help you get started, and keep a close watch as you proceed. The key is to go slow, add the ingredients a little at a time and savour the flavours.

Sukiyaki and *shabu-shabu* restaurants usually have traditional Japanese decor and sometimes a picture of a cow to help you identify them. Ordering is not hard. Simply say 'sukiyaki' or *shabu-shabu* and indicate how many people are dining. Expect to pay from ¥3000 to ¥10,000 per person.

Tempura

Tempura consists of portions of fish, prawns and vegetables cooked in a light batter. When you sit down at a tempura restaurant, you will be given a small bowl of *ten-tsuyu* (a light brown sauce) and a plate of grated *daikon* (Japanese radish) to mix into the sauce. Dip each piece of tempura into this sauce before eating it. Tempura is best when it's hot, so don't wait too long – use the sauce to cool each piece and dig in.

While it's possible to order à la carte, most diners choose to order *teishoku,* which includes rice, *miso-shiru* and *tsukemono.* Some tempura restaurants offer courses that include different numbers of tempura pieces.

Expect to pay between ¥2000 and ¥10,000 for a full tempura meal. Finding these restaurants is tricky as they have no distinctive facade or decor. If you look through the window, you'll see customers around the counter watching the chefs as they work over large woks filled with oil.

kaki age	かき揚げ	tempura with shredded vegetables or fish
shōjin age	精進揚げ	vegetarian tempura
tempura moriawase	天ぷら盛り合わせ	a selection of tempura

Rāmen

More than five billion servings of instant *rāmen* are consumed each year in Japan. The leading purveyors of this snack are convenience stores, which also offer hot water to prepare them in.

The Japanese imported this dish from China and put their own spin on it to make what is one of the world's most delicious fast foods. *Rāmen* dishes are big bowls of noodles in a meat broth, served with a variety of toppings, such as sliced pork, bean sprouts and leeks.

In some restaurants, particularly in Kansai, you may be asked if you'd prefer *kotteri* (thick and fatty) or *assari* (thin and light) soup. Other than this, ordering is simple: just sidle up to the counter and say *rāmen,* or ask for any of the other choices usually on offer. Expect to pay between ¥500 and ¥900 for a bowl. Since *rāmen* is derived from Chinese cuisine, some *rāmen* restaurants also serve *chāhan* or *yaki-meshi* (both dishes are fried rice), *gyōza* (dumplings) and *karaage* (deep-fried chicken pieces).

Rāmen restaurants are easily distinguished by their long counters lined with customers hunched over steaming bowls. You can sometimes *hear* a *rāmen* shop as you wander by – it's considered polite to slurp the noodles and aficionados claim that slurping brings out the full flavour of the broth.

chāshū-men	チャーシュー麺	*rāmen* topped with slices of roasted pork
miso-rāmen	みそラーメン	*rāmen* with miso-flavoured broth
rāmen	ラーメン	soup and noodles with a sprinkling of meat and vegetables
wantan-men	ワンタン麺	*rāmen* with meat dumplings

Soba & Udon

Soba (thin brown buckwheat noodles) and udon (thick white wheat noodles) are Japan's answer to Chinese-style *rāmen.* Most Japanese noodle shops serve both *soba* and udon in a variety of ways.

Noodles are usually served in a bowl containing a light, bonito-flavoured broth, but you can also order them served cold and piled onto a bamboo screen along with a cold broth to dip the noodles in (this is called *zaru soba*). If you order *zaru soba,* you will also receive a small plate of wasabi and sliced spring onions – you put these into the cup of broth and then eat the noodles by dipping them into this mixture. When you have finished your noodles, the waiter will give you some hot broth to mix with the leftover sauce, which you drink as if it is a kind of tea. As with *rāmen,* you should feel free to slurp as loudly as you please.

Soba and udon places are usually quite cheap (about ¥800 a dish), but some fancy places can be significantly more expensive (the decor is a good indication of the price).

kake soba/udon	かけそば/うどん	*soba*/udon noodles in broth
kitsune soba/udon	きつねそば/うどん	*soba*/udon noodles with fried tofu
tempura soba/udon	天ぷらそば/うどん	*soba*/udon noodles with tempura prawns
tsukimi soba/udon	月見そば/うどん	*soba*/udon noodles with raw egg

Unagi

Unagi (eel) is an expensive and popular delicacy in Japan. Even if you can't stand the creature when it's served in your home country – or if you've never tried it – you owe it to yourself to try *unagi* at least once while you're visiting Japan. *Unagi* is cooked over hot coals and brushed with a rich sauce of *shōyu* and sake. Full *unagi* dinners can be expensive, but many *unagi* restaurants also offer *unagi bentō* (boxed meals) and lunch sets for around ¥1500. Most *unagi* restaurants display plastic models of their set meals in their front windows, and may have barrels of live eels to entice passers-by.

kabayaki	蒲焼き	skewers of grilled eel without rice
una-don	うな丼	grilled eel over a bowl of rice
unagi teishoku	うなぎ定食	full-set *unagi* meal with rice, grilled eel, eel-liver soup and pickles
unajū	うな重	grilled eel over a flat tray of rice

KŌBE BEEF

All meals involving Kōbe beef should come with the following label: warning, consuming this beef will ruin your enjoyment of any other type of beef. We're not kidding. It's that good.

The first thing you should know about Kōbe beef is how to pronounce it: 'ko-bay' (rhymes with 'no way'). In Japanese, Kōbe beef is known as *Kōbe-gyū*. Second, Kōbe beef is actually just one regional variety of *wagyū* (literally 'Japanese beef'). *Wagyū* can be any of several breeds of cattle bred for the extreme fatty marbling of their meat (the most common breed is Japanese black). Kōbe beef is simply *wagyū* raised in Hyogō-ken, the prefecture in which the city of Kōbe is located.

There are many urban legends about Kōbe beef – circulated, we suppose, by the farmers who raise them or simply by imaginative individuals who ascribe to cows the lives they'd like to lead. It is commonly believed that Kōbe-beef cattle spend their days drinking beer and receiving regular massages. However, in all our days in Japan, we have never seen a single tipsy cow or met a cow masseur. More likely, the marbling pattern of the beef is the result of selective breeding and the cow's diet of alfalfa, corn, barley and wheat straw.

The best way to enjoy Kōbe beef, or any other type of *wagyū*, is when it is cooked on a *teppan* at a *wagyū* specialist, known as *teppan-yaki-ya*. Due to the intense richness (and price) of a good *wagyū* steak, it is usually consumed in relatively small portions – say, smaller than the size of your hand. The meat is usually seared quickly, then cooked to medium rare – cooking a piece of good *wagyū* to well done is something akin to making a tuna-fish sandwich from the best cut of *toro* sashimi.

Although Kōbe beef and *wagyū* are now all the rage in Western cities, like most Japanese food, the real thing consumed in Japan is far superior to what is available overseas. And – surprise, surprise – it can be cheaper to eat it in Japan than elsewhere. You can g a fine *wagyū* steak course at lunch for around ¥5000, and at dinner for around double that. Of course, the best place for Kōbe beef is – you got it – Kōbe.

Tonkatsu

Tonkatsu is a deep-fried breaded pork cutlet that is served with a special sauce, usually as part of a set meal *(tonkatsu teishoku)*. *Tonkatsu* is served both at speciality restaurants and at *shokudō*. Naturally, the best *tonkatsu* is to be found at the speciality places, where a full set will cost ¥1500 to ¥2500. When ordering *tonkatsu*, you are able to choose between *rōsu* (a fatter cut of pork) and *hire* (a leaner cut).

hire katsu	ヒレかつ	*tonkatsu* fillet
tonkatsu teishoku	とんかつ定食	a set meal of *tonkatsu*, rice, *miso-shiru* and shredded cabbage

Okonomiyaki

Sometimes described as Japanese pizza or pancake, the resemblance is in form only. Actually, *okonomiyaki* are various forms of batter and cabbage cakes cooked on a griddle.

At an *okonomiyaki* restaurant you sit around a *teppan* (iron hotplate), armed with a spatula and chopsticks to cook your choice of meat, seafood and vegetables in a cabbage and vegetable batter.

Some restaurants will do most of the cooking and bring the nearly finished product over to your hotplate for you to season with *katsuo-bushi* (bonito flakes), *shōyu*, *ao-nori* (an ingredient similar to parsley), Japanese Worcestershire-style sauce and mayonnaise. Cheaper places, however, will simply hand you a bowl filled with the ingredients and expect you to cook it for yourself. If this happens, don't panic. First, mix the batter and filling thoroughly, then place it on the hotplate, flattening it into a pancake shape. After five minutes or so, use the spatula to flip it and cook for another five minutes. Then dig in.

Most *okonomiyaki* places also serve *yaki-soba* (fried noodles with meat and vegetables) and *yasai-itame* (stir-fried vegetables). All of this is washed down with mugs of draught beer.

One final word: don't worry too much about the preparation of the food – as a foreigner you will be expected to be awkward, and the waiter will keep a sharp eye on you to make sure no real disasters occur.

FOODIE FILM

The film *Tampopo* (Itami Jūzō; 1987) is essential preparation for a visit to Japan – especially if you intend to visit a *rāmen* shop while you're there! It's about two fellows who set out to help a *rāmen* shop owner improve her restaurant, with several food-related subplots woven in for good measure.

gyū okonomiyaki	牛お好み焼き	beef *okonomiyaki*
ika okonomiyaki	いかお好み焼き	squid *okonomiyaki*
mikkusu	ミックスお好み焼き	*okonomiyaki* with a mix of fillings, including seafood, meat and vegetables
modan-yaki	モダン焼き	*okonomiyaki* with *yaki-soba* and a fried egg
negi okonomiyaki	ネギお好み焼き	thin *okonomiyaki* with spring onions

Kaiseki

Kaiseki is the pinnacle of Japanese cuisine, where the ingredients, preparation, setting and presentation come together to create a dining experience quite unlike any other. Born as an adjunct to the tea ceremony,

COOKING COURSES

- Buddha Bellies (p111), Tokyo
- A Taste of Culture (p111), Tokyo
- Uzuki (p320), Kyoto
- Haru Cooking Class (p321), Kyoto

kaiseki is a largely vegetarian affair; though fish is often served, meat never appears on the *kaiseki* menu. One usually eats *kaiseki* in the private room of a *ryōtei* (an especially elegant style of traditional restaurant), often overlooking a private, tranquil garden. The meal is served in several small courses, giving the diner an opportunity to admire the plates and bowls, which are carefully chosen to complement the food and season. Rice is eaten last (usually with an assortment of pickles) and the drink of choice is sake or beer.

All this comes at a steep price – a good *kaiseki* dinner costs upwards of ¥10,000 per person. A cheaper way to sample the delights of *kaiseki* is to visit a *kaiseki* restaurant for lunch. Most places offer a boxed lunch containing a sampling of their dinner fare for around ¥2500.

You can enter *kaiseki* places at lunchtime without a reservation, but you should ask your hotel or ryokan to call ahead to make arrangements for dinner.

bentō	弁当	boxed meal, usually of rice, with a main dish and pickles or salad
kaiseki	懐石	traditional, Kyoto-style haute cuisine
matsu	松	extra-special course
take	竹	special course
ume	梅	regular course

The average Japanese person consumes 58kg of rice per year. The vast majority of this is made up of *shiro-gohan* (a white, steamed rice), but some health-food enthusiasts prefer *genmai* (brown rice).

Sweets

Although most restaurants don't serve dessert (plates of sliced fruit are sometimes served at the end of a meal), there is no lack of sweets in Japan. Most Japanese sweets (known generically as *wagashi*) are sold in speciality stores for you to eat at home. Many of the more delicate-looking ones are made to balance the strong, bitter taste of the special *matcha* (powdered green tea) served during the tea ceremony.

Some Westerners find Japanese sweets a little challenging, due to the liberal use of a sweet, red *azuki*-bean paste called *anko*. This unusual filling turns up in even the most innocuous-looking pastries. The next main ingredient is often pounded sticky rice *(mochi)*, which has a a sticky, soft and chewy consistency.

With such a wide variety of sweets, it's impossible to list all the names. However, you'll probably find many variations on the *anko*-covered-by-*mochi* theme.

Okashi-ya (sweet shops) are easy to spot: they usually have open fronts with their wares laid out in wooden trays to entice passers-by. Buying sweets is simple – just point at what you want and indicate with your fingers how many you'd like.

anko	あんこ	sweet paste or jam made from *azuki* beans
kashiwa-mochi	柏餅	pounded glutinous rice with a sweet filling, wrapped in an aromatic oak leaf
mochi	餅	pounded rice cakes made of glutinous rice
wagashi	和菓子	Japanese-style sweets
yōkan	ようかん	sweet red-bean jelly

The highly prized Japanese *matsutake* mushroom can sell for up to US$2000 per kilogram. They are usually enjoyed in the autumn, sometimes in the form of a tea, at other times grilled or with rice.

Vegetarians & Vegans

Travellers who eat fish should have almost no trouble dining in Japan: almost all *shokudō, izakaya* and other common restaurants offer a set meal with fish as the main dish. Vegans and vegetarians who don't eat fish will have to get their protein from tofu and other bean products.

Note that most *miso-shiru* is made with *dashi* broth that contains fish, so if you want to avoid fish, you'll also have to avoid miso soup.

Most big cities in Japan have vegetarian or organic restaurants, which naturally serve a variety of choices that appeal to vegetarians and vegans. In the countryside, you'll have to do your best to find suitable items on the menu, or try to convey your dietary preferences to the restaurant staff. Note that many temples in Japan serve *shōjin-ryōri* (Buddhist vegetarian cuisine), which is made without meat, fish or dairy products. A good place to try this is Kōya-san in Kansai.

Drinks

Drinking plays a big role in Japanese society, and there are few social occasions where beer or sake is not served. Alcohol (in this case, sake) also plays a ceremonial role in various Shintō festivals and rites, including the marriage ceremony. As a visitor to Japan, you'll probably find yourself in lots of situations where you are invited to drink, and tipping back a few beers or glasses of sake is a great way to get to know the locals. However, if you don't drink alcohol, it's no big deal. Simply order *oolong cha* (oolong tea) in place of beer or sake. While some folks might put pressure on you to drink alcohol, you can diffuse this pressure by saying *sake o nomimasen* (I don't drink alcohol).

What you pay for your drink depends on where you drink and, in the case of hostess bars, with whom you drink. Hostess bars are the most expensive places to drink (up to ¥10,000 per drink), followed by upmarket traditional Japanese bars, hotel bars, beer halls and casual pubs. If you are not sure about a place, ask about prices and cover charges before sitting down. As a rule, if you are served a small snack (called *o-tsumami,* or 'charm') with your first round, you'll be paying a cover charge (usually a few hundred yen, but sometimes much more).

The most important Shintō deity is Inari, traditionally the god of the rice harvest. Reflecting the changing nature of the Japanese economy, Inari is now the god of all sorts of commerce.

Izakaya and *yakitori-ya* are cheap places for beer, sake and food in a casual atmosphere resembling that of a pub. All Japanese cities, whether large or small, will have a few informal bars with reasonable prices. These are popular with young Japanese and resident *gaijin* (foreigners), who usually refer to them as *gaijin* bars. In summer, many department stores and hotels in big cities open up beer gardens on the roof. Many of these places offer all-you-can-eat/drink specials for around ¥3000 per person.

Most of the non-alcoholic drinks you're used to at home will be available in Japan, with a few colourfully named additions like Pocari Sweat and Calpis Water. One convenient aspect of Japan is the presence of drink-vending machines on virtually every street corner and, at ¥120, refreshment is rarely more than a few steps away.

Sake

Despite being overtaken in recent years by beer and *shōchū* (distilled grain liquor), most Japanese still consider sake to be the national drink. The Japanese name reflects this: it's commonly known as *nihonshu* (the drink of Japan). Sake has played an important part in Japanese culture for as long as there has been a Japanese culture. It plays an important part in a variety of Shintō rituals, including wedding ceremonies, and many Shintō shrines display huge barrels of sake in front of their halls (before you get any ideas, be aware that most of them are empty).

Although consumption has been on the wane in recent years, it is generally agreed that the quality of sake available is better than ever. Many of the best sakes have a complexity of flavours and aromas comparable to the fine wines and beers of Europe.

Not surprisingly, sake makes the perfect accompaniment to traditional Japanese food, and sake pubs *(izakaya)* generally also serve excellent seasonal fish and other foods to go with the booze. Sake can be drunk *reishu* (chilled), *jō-on* (at room temperature), *nuru-kan* (warmed) or *atsu-kan* (piping hot), according to the season and personal preference. The top-drawer stuff is normally served well chilled. Sake is traditionally presented in a ceramic jug known as a *tokkuri*, and poured into tiny cups known as *o-choko* or *sakazuki*. A traditional measure of sake is one *gō* (一合), which is a little over 180mL or 6oz. In speciality bars, you will have the option of ordering by the glass, which will often be filled to overflowing and brought to you in a wooden container to catch the overflow. If you have company, the tradition is to pour your neighbour's drink and then wait for them to reciprocate. When they pour your drink, it's polite to lift your glass; women should place one hand underneath their glass when someone is pouring their drink.

Sake is always brewed during the winter, in the cold months that follow the rice harvest in September. The main ingredients of sake are rice and yeast, together with a mould known as *kōji* that helps convert the starch in the rice into fermentable sugars. Sake is categorised by law into two main classes: *futsū-shu* (ordinary sake); and *tokutei-meishōshu* (premium sake), which is further classified by the extent to which the rice is refined before fermentation. This is generally shown on the label as the *seimai buai*, which expresses how much of the rice is polished away before being fermented. As a general rule, the lower this number, the better (or at least, the more expensive) the sake will be. Sake made from rice kernels with 40% to 50% of their original volume polished away is known as *ginjō*. Sake made from rice kernels with 50% or more of their original volume polished away is known as *dai-ginjō*. It is believed that sake made from the inner portion of the rice kernel is the smoothest and most delicious of all. Sake made only with rice and *kōji* (without the use of added alcohol) is known as *junmai-shu* (pure rice sake).

The Insider's Guide to Sake (Philip Harper; 1998) offers a fine introduction to sake, including information on how to choose a good sake and the history of the drink.

ama-kuchi	甘口	sweet flavour
ama-zake	甘酒	sweet sake served at winter festivals
dai-ginjō	大吟醸	sake made from rice kernels with 50% or more of their original volume polished away
futsū-shu	普通酒	ordinary sake
genshu	原酒	undiluted sake, often with alcohol content close to 20%
ginjō	吟醸	sake made from rice kernels with 40% to 50% of their original volume polished away
jizake	地酒	'local sake', often from small, traditional breweries
junmai-shu	純米酒	'pure rice sake', made from only rice, *kōji* and water
kara-kuchi	辛口	dry, sharp flavour
kōji	麹	the mould that helps to convert the starch in the rice into fermentable sugars
kura/sakagura	蔵/酒蔵	sake brewery
nama-zake	生酒	fresh, unpasteurised sake
nigori-zake	濁り酒	milky-white 'cloudy sake', often rather sweet
nihonshu	日本酒	Japanese word for 'sake'
o-choko	お猪口	small cups traditionally used for sake
seimai buai	精米歩合	the percentage of the original size to which the grain is reduced by polishing before the brewing process starts
tokkuri	徳利	traditional ceramic serving vessel
tokutei-meishōshu	特定名称酒	premium sake

SIPPING A LOCAL SAKE

Sake is brewed in every prefecture in Japan – with the single exception of Kagoshima in southern Kyūshū, the traditional stronghold of the distilled drink known as *shōchū* – and there are more than 1500 breweries in operation today. Niigata and other parts of Northern Honshū are particularly famous for the quality of their sake, with Hiroshima and Nada-ku (in Kōbe) also major centres of the brewing industry. Almost everywhere you go in Japan you will have an opportunity to drink sake brewed just a few kilometres from where you are staying. A foreign visitor who shows an interest in the *jizake* (local brew) is likely to be treated to enthusiastic recommendations and the kind of hospitality that has been known to lead to sore heads the next morning.

Beer

Introduced at the end of the 1800s, *biiru* (beer) is now the favourite tipple of the Japanese. The quality is generally excellent and the most popular type is light lager, although some breweries have been recently experimenting with darker brews. The major breweries are Kirin, Asahi, Sapporo and Suntory. There are also a growing number of microbreweries, and craft beer has seen a boom in popularity in recent years. Beer is dispensed everywhere, from vending machines to beer halls, and even in some temple lodgings. A standard can of beer from a vending machine is about ¥250, although some of the gigantic cans cost more than ¥1000. At bars, a beer starts at ¥500 and the price climbs upwards, depending on the establishment. *Nama biiru* (draught beer) is widely available, as are imported beers.

A few years ago, the Japanese Ministry of Agriculture established a team to assess the quality of Japanese restaurants abroad. The so-called 'Sushi Police' are intended to put a stop to third-rate restaurants serving poor imitations of real Japanese food. Does this spell the end of the California roll?

biiru	ビール	beer
biniru	瓶ビール	bottled beer
nama biiru	生ビール	draught beer

Shōchū

For those looking for a quick and cheap escape route from the sorrows of the world, *shōchū* is the answer. It's a distilled spirit made from a variety of raw materials, including potato (in which case it's called *imo-jōchū*) and barley *(mugi-jōchū)*. It's quite strong, with an alcohol content of about 30%. In recent years it has been resurrected from its previous lowly status (it was used as a disinfectant in the Edo period) to become a trendy drink. You can drink it *oyu-wari* (with hot water) or *chūhai* (in a highball with soda and lemon). A 720mL bottle sells for about ¥600, which makes it a relatively cheap option compared with other spirits.

chūhai	チューハイ	*shōchū* with soda and lemon
oyu-wari	お湯割り	*shōchū* with hot water
shōchū	焼酎	distilled grain liquor

Coffee & Tea

Kōhii (coffee) served in a *kissaten* (coffee shop) tends to be expensive in Japan, costing between ¥350 and ¥500 a cup, with some places charging up to ¥1000. For a caffeine fix, a cheap alternative is one of the coffee-restaurant chains like Doutor or Pronto, or doughnut shops such as Mr Donut (which offers free coffee refills). An even cheaper alternative than these is a can of coffee, hot or cold, purchased from a vending machine. Although unpleasantly sweet, at ¥120 the price is hard to beat.

When ordering coffee at a coffee shop in Japan, you will be asked whether you would like it *hotto* (hot) or *aisu* (cold). Black tea also comes hot or cold, and is served with *miruku* (milk) or *remon* (lemon). A good way to start a day of sightseeing in Japan is with a *mōningu setto* (morning set) of tea or coffee, toast and eggs, which generally costs around ¥400.

American kōhii	アメリカンコーヒー	weak coffee
burendo kōhii	ブレンドコーヒー	blended coffee, fairly strong
kafe ore	カフェオレ	*café au lait*, hot or cold
kōcha	紅茶	black English tea
kōhii	コーヒー	regular coffee
orenji jūsu	オレンジジュース	orange juice

Japanese Tea

Unlike black tea, most Japanese tea is green and contains a lot of vitamin C and caffeine. The powdered form used in the tea ceremony is called *matcha* and is drunk after being whipped into a frothy consistency. The more common form, a leafy green tea, is simply called *o-cha*, and is drunk after being steeped in a pot. In addition to green tea, you'll probably drink a lot of a brownish tea called *bancha*, which restaurants serve for free. In summer, a cold beverage called *mugicha* (roasted barley tea) is served in private homes.

The superb Tokyo Food Page (www.bento.com) offers explanations of Japanese dishes, great places to eat in Tokyo and much, much more.

bancha	番茶	ordinary-grade green tea, with a brownish colour
matcha	抹茶	powdered green tea used in the tea ceremony
mugicha	麦茶	roasted barley tea
o-cha	お茶	leafy green tea
sencha	煎茶	medium-grade green tea

Arts

Japan is graced with a sublime artistic tradition that transcends gallery walls, the pages of books and the kabuki stage to seep into everyday life. The country has a long history of receiving cultural imports from continental Asia and later the West, as well as a tendency to refine techniques and materials to an extreme degree. The result is a creative heritage that is as varied, deep and rich as any on the planet.

Traditional Visual Art

Ceramics

Jōmon pottery, with its distinctive cordlike decorative patterns, dates back up to 15,000 years, making it the oldest indigenous artform. When the Jōmon people were displaced by the Yayoi people, starting around 400 BC, a more refined style of pottery developed, with clear continental Asian influences and techniques. Continental techniques and even artisans continued to dominate Japanese ceramic arts for the next millennium or more; around the 5th century AD Sue ware was introduced from Korea, and around the 7th century Tang Chinese pottery became influential.

In the medieval period Japan's great ceramic centre was Seto in Central Honshū. Here, starting in the 12th century, Japanese potters took Chinese forms and adapted them to Japanese tastes and needs to produce a truly distinctive pottery style known as Seto ware. One Japanese term for pottery and porcelain, *setomono* (literally 'things from Seto'), clearly derives from this still-thriving ceramics centre.

Today, there are more than 100 pottery centres in Japan, with scores of artisans producing everything from exclusive tea utensils to souvenir folklore creatures. Department stores regularly organise exhibitions of ceramics and offer the chance to see some of this fine work up close.

Pottery Towns

Arita *Old Imari, Kakiemon and Nabeshima styles.*

Bizen *Simple, earthy style.*

Hagi *Tea-ceremony pottery.*

Kanazawa *Overglazed porcelain.*

Mashiko *Beautiful, functional pottery.*

Shikki (Lacquerware)

The Japanese have been using lacquer to protect and enhance the beauty of wood since the Jōmon period (13,000–400 BC). In the Meiji era (1868–1912), lacquerware became very popular abroad and it remains one of Japan's best-known products. Known in Japan as *shikki* or *nurimono,* lacquerware is made using the sap from the lacquer tree *(urushi),* a close relative of poison oak. Raw lacquer is actually toxic and causes severe skin irritation in those who have not developed immunity. Once hardened, however, it becomes inert and extraordinarily durable.

The most common colour of lacquer is amber or brown, but additives are used to produce black, violet, blue, yellow and even white lacquer. In better pieces, multiple layers of lacquer are painstakingly applied and left to dry, and finally polished to a luxurious shine.

Famous laquerware-producing areas include Wajima in Ishikawa Prefecture, where it takes over 100 steps to create pieces that are are known for their sturdy elegance, and Okinawa, where the style known as Ryūkyū-*shikki* incorporates designs of flowers and dragons more common to Chinese art.

Painting

From the Heian period (794–1185) up until the beginning of the Edo period (1600–1867), Japanese painting borrowed from Chinese and Western techniques and media, ultimately transforming them for its own aesthetic ends. By the Edo period, which was marked by the enthusiastic patronage of a wide range of painting styles, Japanese art had come completely into its own. The Kanō school, initiated more than a century before the beginning of the Edo era, continued to be in demand for its depiction of subjects connected with Confucianism, mythical Chinese creatures and scenes from nature. The Tosa school, which followed the *yamato-e* style of painting (often used on scrolls during the Heian period), was also kept busy with commissions from the nobility, who were eager to see scenes re-created from the classics of Japanese literature.

The Rimpa school (from 1600) not only absorbed the styles of painting that had preceded it, but progressed beyond well-worn conventions to produce a strikingly decorative and delicately shaded form of painting. The works of art produced by a trio of outstanding artists from this school – Tawaraya Sōtatsu, Hon'ami Kōetsu and Ogata Kōrin – rank among the finest of this period.

The screen paintings of Hasegawa Tohaku, created almost 400 years ago, are said to be the first examples of Impressionist art.

Calligraphy

Shodō (the way of writing) is one of Japan's most valued arts, cultivated by nobles, priests and samurai alike, and is still studied by Japanese schoolchildren today as *shūji*. Like the characters of the Japanese script, the art of *shodō* was imported from China. In the Heian period, a fluid, cursive, distinctly Japanese style of *shodō* called *wayō* evolved, though the Chinese style remained popular in Japan among Zen priests and the literati for some time.

In both Chinese and Japanese *shodō* there are three important types. Most common is *kaisho* (block-style script). Due to its clarity, this style is favoured in the media and in applications where readability is key. *Gyōsho* (running hand) is semi-cursive and is often used in informal correspondence. *Sōsho* (grass hand) is a truly cursive style. *Sōsho* abbreviates and links the characters together to create a flowing, graceful effect.

One of the most famous *ukiyo-e* is *The Great Wave* by Hokusai (1760–1849), one of his series *Thirty-Six Views of Mt Fuji*. Visit the Hokusai Museum in Obuse where the artist spent his final years.

Ukiyo-e (Woodblock Prints)

The term *ukiyo-e* means 'pictures of the floating world' and derives from a Buddhist metaphor for the transient world of fleeting pleasures. The subjects chosen by artists for these woodblock prints included characters and scenes from the tawdry, vivacious 'floating world' of the entertainment quarters in Edo (latter-day Tokyo), Kyoto and Osaka, as well as postcard-style views of landscapes such as Mt Fuji.

The floating world, centred on pleasure districts such as Edo's Yoshiwara, was a topsy-turvy kingdom, an inversion of the usual social hierarchies that were held in place by the power of the Tokugawa shogunate. Here, money meant more than rank, while actors and artists were the arbiters of style, and prostitutes elevated their art to such a level that their accomplishments matched those of the women of noble families.

The vivid colours, novel composition and flowing lines of *ukiyo-e* caused great excitement in the West, sparking a vogue that one French art critic dubbed *japonisme*. *Ukiyo-e* became a key influence on Impressionists (such as Toulouse-Lautrec, Manet and Degas) and post-Impressionists. Among the Japanese, the prints were hardly given more than passing consideration – millions were produced annually in Edo. They were often thrown away or used as wrapping paper for pottery. For many years, the Japanese continued to be perplexed by the keen interest foreigners took in this art form, which they considered of ephemeral value.

Hiroshige, noted for many collec tions of *ukiyo-* prints includi *One Hundr Famous Vie Edo*, was a fighter by though retired t a Budd

Ikebana

The Japanese art of flower arranging known as *ikebana* is thought to date back to the 6th century when Buddhism entered the country, bringing with it the tradition of leaving flowers as offerings for the spirits of

Arts Festivals

Echigo-Tsunari Art Triennale (www.echigo-tsumari.jp)

Festival/Tokyo (www.festival-tokyo.jp)

Fukuoka Asian Art Triennale (www.fukuokatriennale.ajibi.jp)

Sapporo International Arts Festival (www.sapporo-internationalart festival.jp)

Setouchi Triennale (www.setouchi-art fest.jp)

Yokohama Triennale (www.yokohama triennale.jp)

the dead. However, given the older Shintō religion's deification of nature, it's possible that the roots of the art go back even further. Either way, by the 16th century *ikebana* had reached its artistic zenith with its incorporation into the rituals and tradition of the tea ceremony.

Although there are several distinct styles of *ikebana,* they all tend to lean heavily on minimalism; a display may typically have just one or two blooms deliberately arranged among a similarly sparse number of sticks and leaves. The main contemporary schools of *ikebana* are the Kyoto-based **Ikenobo** (www.ikenobo.jp), and the Tokyo-based **Ohara** (www.ikebanahq.org/ohara.php) and **Sōgestsu** (www.sogetsu.or.jp).

Contemporary Visual Art

In the years that followed WWII, Japanese artists struggled with issues of identity. They explored whether Western artistic media and methods could convey the space, light, substance and shadows of the Japanese spirit, or whether this essence could only truly be expressed through traditional Japanese artistic genres.

Today's artists and movements have no such anxiety about co-opting, or being co-opted by, Western philosophies and aesthetics. Instead there is an insouciant celebration of the smooth, cool surface of the future articulated by fantastic colours and shapes. This exuberant aesthetic is exemplified by Takashi Murakami, whose work derives much of its energy from *otaku,* the geek culture that worships characters that figure prominently in manga, Japan's ubiquitous comic books. Murakami's spirited, prankish images and installations have become emblematic of the Japanese aesthetic known as *poku* (a concept that combines pop art with an *otaku* sensibility), and his *Super Flat Manifesto,* which declares that 'the world of the future might be like Japan is today – super flat', can be seen as a primer for contemporary Japanese pop aesthetics.

Beyond the pop scene, artists continue to create works whose textures and topics relay a world that is broader than the frames of a comic book. Three notable artists to look for are Sakai Yoshie, whose ethereal oil paintings, replete with pastel skies and deep waters, leave the viewer unsure whether they are floating or sinking; Ambe Noriko, whose sculptural works with paper can resemble sand dunes shifting in the Sahara,

WABI-SABI

No, it isn't the spicy green stuff you eat with your sushi. Rather, *wabi-sabi* is one of the fundamental visual principles governing traditional Japanese ideals of beauty. The idea of *wabi-sabi* is an aesthetic that embraces the notion of ephemerality and imperfection as it relates to all facets of Japanese culture.

The term *wabi-sabi* comes from the Japanese *wabi* and (you guessed it) *sabi* – both with quite convoluted definitions. *Wabi* roughly means 'rustic' and connotes the loneliness of the wilderness, while *sabi* can be interpreted as 'weathered', 'waning' or 'altered with age'. Together the two words signify an object's natural imperfections that arise during its inception and the acknowledgement that the object will evolve as it confronts mortality.

This penchant for impermanence and incompleteness transcends Japanese visual ulture, from the fragrant cherry blossoms that bloom in spring to the slightly asymmet- *Hagi-yaki* pottery, but is perhaps most palpable in landscape design and traditional hitecture. Japanese teahouses reflect *wabi-sabi* motifs with their natural construction erials, handmade ceramics and manicured gardens.

hough the origins of *wabi-sabi* can be traced back to ancient Buddhism, these tic ideals are still present in modern Japan and can even be found throughout the ative cityscapes we see today.

or your high-school biology textbook; and the indomitable Tenmyouya Hisashi, whose work chronicles the themes of contemporary Japanese life, echoing the flat surfaces and deep impressions of woodblock prints, while singing a song of the street.

Contemporary art is booming in Japan off the back of art tourism to places such as Naoshima, home to the various art museums and installations sponsored by publishing company Bennesse. Asahi Breweries also sponsor the **Asahi Arts Festival** (www.asahi-artfes.net), which in 2014 included 60 programs across the country as well as in South Korea.

Traditional Performing Arts

Nō

Sometimes transliterated as noh, this is the oldest of Japan's traditional performing arts, with its roots in Shintō rites. The hypnotic masked dance-dramas of *nō* reflect the minimalist aesthetics of Zen. The movement is glorious, the chorus and music sonorous, the expression subtle. A sparsely furnished cedar stage directs full attention to the performers, who include a chorus, drummers and a flautist.

There are two principal characters: the *shite,* who is sometimes a living person but more often a ghost whose soul cannot rest or a demon; and the *waki,* who leads the main character towards the play's climactic moment. The haunting masks of *nō* theatre always depict female or nonhuman characters; adult male characters are played without masks. Each *nō* school has its own repertoire, and the art form continues to evolve and develop.

Providing light relief to the sometimes heavy going drama of *nō* are the comic vignettes known as *kyōgen*, some of which reference the main play, others which stand alone. Colloquial language is used, so they are easier to understand for a contemporary audience than the esoteric *nō*.

Kabuki

The first performances of kabuki, staged early in the 17th century by an all-female troupe, were highly erotic and attracted enthusiastic support from the merchant class. In true bureaucratic fashion, Tokugawa officials feared for the people's morality and banned women from the stage in 1629. Since that time, kabuki has been performed exclusively by men, giving rise to the institution of *onnagata,* or *ōyama* – male actors who specialise in female roles.

Over the course of several centuries, kabuki has developed a repertoire that draws on popular themes, such as famous historical accounts and stories of love-suicide, while also borrowing copiously from *nō, kyōgen* (comic drama) and bunraku (classical puppet theatre). Most kabuki plays border on melodrama, although they vary in mood.

Formalised beauty and stylisation are the central aesthetic principles of kabuki. The acting is a combination of dancing and speaking in conventionalised intonation patterns, and each actor prepares for a role by studying and emulating the style perfected by his predecessors. Kabuki actors are born into the art form, and training begins in childhood. Today, they enjoy great social prestige and their activities on and off the stage attract as much interest as those of popular film and TV stars.

Shochiku runs Japan's premier kabuki theatres in Tokyo (Kabuki-za and Shimbashi Embujō), Kyoto (Minama-za) and Osaka (Shokichu-za). For more information and to book tickets, see www.kabuki-bito.jp.

Bunraku

Japan's traditional puppet theatre developed at the same time as kabuki, when the *shamisen* (a three-stringed instrument resembling a lute or banjo), imported from Okinawa, was combined with traditional puppetry techniques and *jōruri* (narrative chanting). Bunraku, as it came to be known in the 19th century, addresses many of the same themes as kabuki; in fact, many famous plays in the kabuki repertoire were originally written for puppet theatre. Bunraku involves large puppets – nearly two-thirds life-sized – manipulated by up to three black-robed puppeteers. The puppeteers do not speak; a seated narrator tells the story and provides character voices. The best places to see bunraku are at Osaka's National Bunraku Theatre and Tokyo's National Theatre.

Rakugo

A traditional Japanese style of comic monologue, *rakugo* (literally 'dropped word') dates back to the Edo period. The performer, usually in kimono, sits on a square cushion on a stage. Props are limited to a fan and hand towel. The monologue begins with a *makura* (prologue), which is followed by the story itself and, finally, the *ochi* (punch line or 'drop', which is another pronunciation of the Chinese character for *raku* in *rakugo*). Many of the monologues in the traditional *rakugo* repertoire date back to the Edo and Meiji periods and, while well known, reflect a social milieu unknown to modern listeners. Current practitioners write new monologues addressing issues relevant to contemporary life.

Tokyo Art Beat (www.tokyoartbeat.com) is a bilingual art and design guide, with a regularly updated list of events focusing on the capital.

Contemporary Theatre & Dance

Contemporary theatre and dance are alive and well in Japan, though most major troupes are based in Tokyo. The 1960s *shōgekijō* (small theatre) movement has given Japan many of its leading playwrights, directors and actors, including such now-international luminaries as Ninagawa Yukio and Noda Hideki. *Shōgekijō* arose as a reaction to the realism and structure of *shingeki* (a 1920s movement that borrowed heavily from Western dramatic forms), and featured surrealistic plays that explored the relationship between human beings and the world. Like their counterparts in the West, these productions took place in any space available – in small theatres, tents, basements, open spaces and street corners.

Blending elements of Japanese pop culture, folklore and acrobatic dance are Tokyo Dolores (www.facebook.com/TokyoDolores/info), an all-female performance-art group.

More recent *shōgekijō* productions have dealt with realistic and contemporary themes, such as modern Japanese history, war, environmental degradation and social oppression. Changing cultural perceptions have propelled the movement in new directions, notably towards socially and politically critical dramas. Names to watch out for include Okada Toshiki, the artistic director of **chelftisch** (www.chelfitsch.net), and Miura Daisuke, leader of envelope-pushing theatre company Potsudo-ru; both are past winners of the Kishida Drama Award, Japan's top playwriting prize, named after the early 20th-century dramatist who is regarded as the father of modern Japanese theatre.

Butō

In many ways, *butō* is Japan's most accessible – there are no words except for the occasional grunt – and exciting performing art. It is also its newest dance form, dating from only 1959, when Hijikata Tatsumi (1928–86) gave the first *butō* performance. *Butō* was born out of a rejection of the excessive formalisation that characterises traditional forms of Japanese dance. It also stems from the desire to return to the ancient roots of the Japanese soul, and is therefore also a rejection of the Western influences that flooded Japan in the postwar years.

Displays of *butō* are best likened to performance-art happenings rather than traditional dance performances. During a *butō* performance, one or more dancers use their naked or seminaked bodies to express the most elemental and intense human emotions. Nothing is sacred in *butō*, and performances often deal with topics such as sexuality and death. For this reason, critics often describe *butō* as scandalous, and *butō* dancers delight in pushing the boundaries of what can be considered tasteful in artistic performance.

Butō tends to be more underground than the more established forms of Japanese dance and, consequently, it is harder to catch a performance. Top Tokyo-based troupes include **Sankai Juku** (www.sankaijuku.com) and **Dairakudakan Kochūten** (www.dairakudakan.com).

Arts Online

KIE (http://int.kateigaho.com) International edition of the glossy arts and culture magazine Kateigaho.

Performing Arts Network (www.performingarts.) Covers a broad ıge of performing arts.

Literature

Japan lays claim to the world's first novel with Murasaki Shikibu's *Genji Monogatari* (The Tale of Genji). This detailed, lengthy tome documents the intrigues and romances of early Japanese court life and, although it is perhaps Japan's most important work of literature, its extreme length probably limits its appeal to all but the most ardent Japanophile or literature buff.

Some of the earliest examples of Japanese literature were penned by women who, with no access to education in Chinese, used the simplified phonetic script *hiragana*. Their male counterparts at the time were busy copying and perfecting the imported Chinese characters known as *kanji*.

Most of Japan's important modern literature has been penned by authors who live in and write about cities. Though these works are sometimes celebratory, many lament the loss of a traditional rural lifestyle that has given way to the pressures of a modern, industrialised society. *Kokoro,* the modern classic by Sōseki Natsume, outlines these rural-urban tensions, as does *Snow Country,* by Nobel laureate Kawabata Yasunari. These works touch upon the tensions between Japan's nostalgia for the past and its rush towards the future, between its rural heartland and its burgeoning metropolises.

The works of Mishima Yukio are considered unrepresentative of Japanese culture by many Japanese themselves, but his compelling novels, which include *Confessions of a Mask*, *Forbidden Colours* and *After the Banquet* still make for very interesting and insightful reading.

Ōe Kenzaburo, Japan's second Nobel laureate, has produced some of Japan's most disturbing, energetic and enigmatic literature. *A Personal Matter* is the work for which he is most widely known. In this troubling novel, which echoes Ōe's frustrations at having a son with autism, a 27-year-old cram-school teacher's wife gives birth to a brain-damaged child. His life claustrophobic and his marriage failing, he dreams of escaping to Africa while planning the murder of his son.

Contemporary Writers

Murakami Ryū's *Almost Transparent Blue* is strictly sex and drugs, and his ode to the narcissistic early 1990s, *Coin Locker Babies,* recounts the toxic lives of two boys who have been left to die in coin lockers by their mothers. Like Murakami Ryū, Yoshimoto Banana is known for her ability to convey the prevailing Zeitgeist in easily, um, digestible form. In her novel *Kitchen* she relentlessly chronicles Tokyo's fast-food menus and '80s pop culture, though underlying the superficial digressions are hints of a darker and deeper world of death, loss and loneliness. For light relief, try Kawakami Hiromi's quirky romance *Strange Weather in Tokyo*.

Academic Kathryn Hemmann's Contemporary Japanese Literature (www.japaneselit.net) has reviews not only of Japanese novels but also non-fiction and manga, too.

Most frequently talked about as the next Japanese Nobel laureate is Murakami Haruki. The one-time jazz-club owner hit a home run with his 1979 debut novel *Hear the Wind Sing,* which was inspired by watching a baseball game. Other major novels have followed including ill-fated romance *Norwegian Wood,* set in the late '60s against the backdrop of student protests and adapted into a movie in 2010; the metaphysical mysteries *A Wild Sheep Case* and *The Wind-Up Bird Chronicles*; and his mega three-part opus *1Q84*. Murakami has also penned an excellent short memoir about his marathon running (and his creative writing process) *What I Talk About When I Talk About Running*.

Music

Japan has a huge, shape-shifting music scene supported by a local market of audiophiles willing to try almost anything. Jazz has a very dedicated following, as does rock, house and electronica. Among homegrown sounds are *min'yo* (folk music), including the instrumental *shamisen*-style Tsugaru and the traditional drumming popularised by the likes of Kodō based on Sado-ga-shima; and *enka*, a unique and melodramatic synthesis of Japanese and Western styles that is epitomised by the powerful, sobbing vocal technique of Hibari Misora.

WHO'S WHO OF J-POP

Japanese pop music, commonly shortened to J-pop, is a major driver of the country's fashion industry. If you can't tell Morning Musume (eight-girl idol group, big in the early 2000s) from Arashi (five-member one-time boy band), then read on for a brief who's who of current J-pop royalty.

AKB48 Consisting of 60-plus fresh-faced young girls from all over Japan, including one who is entirely computer generated, AKB48 has taken the manufactured idol group to its limit. Divided into three teams, the AKB48 girls have their own TV show, and their own concert hall, coffee shop and theatre in Akihabara. Fans, mostly grown men, line up daily to see these young idols on stage.

Hamasaki Ayumi Noted for her chameleon style and high-concept videos, the empress of J-pop, known as Ayu to her adoring fans, is one of the brightest stars in the Avex universe: Avex is one of Japan's biggest recording labels. She has shifted more than 50 million albums since her debut in 1998.

B'z Matsumoto Tak and Inaba Koshi have been rocking the Japanese charts since 1988. Pronouced 'beez', the duo is one the nation's biggest-selling J-pop acts.

Kyary Pamyu Pamyu This pop princess (whose real name is Takemura Kiriko) has been a runaway success since her musical debut in 2011 with PonPonPon. She's been compared to Lady Gaga for her outrageous fashions and self-promotion, which includes being the Harajuku ambassador of *kawaii* (cuteness).

Mr Children Nicknamed Misu-Chiru, this four-member band formed in 1988 and have gone on to sell in excess of 50 million albums. Lead singer Sakurai Kazutoshi composes most of their songs.

More mainstream are the *aidoru,* idol singers whose popularity is generated largely through media appearances and is centred on a cute, girl-next-door image. These days, J-pop (Japan pop) is dominated by female vocalists who borrow heavily from American pop stars.

Cinema

Japan has a vibrant film industry and proud, critically acclaimed cinematic traditions. Renewed international attention since the mid-1990s has reinforced interest in domestic films, which account for an estimated 40% of box-office receipts, nearly double the level in most European countries. Of course, this includes not only artistically important works, but also films in the samurai, science-fiction, horror and 'monster stomps Tokyo' genres, for which Japan is also known.

From the 1920s, Japanese directors starting producing films in two distinct genres: *jidaigeki* (period films) and *gendaigeki* (films dealing with modern themes). The more realistic storylines of the new films soon reflected back on the traditional films with the introduction of *shin jidaigeki* (new period films).

The golden age of Japanese cinema kicked off with Kurosawa Akira's *Rashōmon,* winner of the Golden Lion at the 1951 Venice International Film Festival and the Oscar for best foreign film. The increasing realism and high artistic standards of the period are evident in such landmark films as *Tōkyō Monogatari* (Tokyo Story; 1953) by the legendary Ōzu Yasujirō; Mizoguchi Kenji's classics *Saikaku Ichidai Onna* (The Life of Oharu; 1952) and *Ugetsu Monogatari* (Tales of Ugetsu; 1953); and Kurosawa's 1954 masterpiece *Shichinin no Samurai* (Seven Samurai). Despite falling attendances at cinemas in the 1960s, '70s and '80s, the industry remained a major artistic force. These decades gave the world such landmark works as Ichikawa Kon's *Chushingura* (47 Samurai; 1962) and Kurosawa's *Yōjimbo* (1961), *Kagemusha* (1980), which shared the Palme d'Or at Cannes, and *Ran* (1985).

Imamura Shōhei's heart-rending *Narayama Bushiko* (The Ballad of Narayama) won the Palme d'Or at Cannes in 1983. Itami Jūzō became perhaps the most widely known Japanese director outside Japan after

Kurosawa, with such biting satires as *Osōshiki* (The Funeral; 1987), *Tampopo* (Dandelion; 1987) and *Marusa no Onna* (A Taxing Woman; 1987). Ōshima Nagisa, best known for controversial films such as *Ai no Corrida* (In the Realm of the Senses; 1976), scored a critical and popular success with *Senjo no Merry Christmas* (Merry Christmas, Mr Lawrence) in 1983.

In 1997, Japanese directors received top honours at two of the world's most prestigious film festivals: *Unagi* (Eel), Imamura Shōhei's black-humoured look at human nature's dark side, won the Palme d'Or at Cannes, making him the only Japanese director to win this award twice; and Kitano 'Beat' Takeshi took the Golden Lion in Venice for *Hana-bi*, a tale of life and death, and the violence and honour that links them. In 2009, Takita Yojiro's film *Okuribito* (Departures) won the Oscar for best foreign film.

In recent years Koreeda Hirokazu has had critical hits both in Japan and internationally with his low-key and charming domestic dramas *Kiseki* (I Wish; 2011) and *Soshite Chichi ni Naru* (Like Father Like Son; 2013), which won the Jury Prize at Cannes in 2013.

The plots of most modern Japanese horror films can be traced back to the popular *kaidan* (traditional horror or ghost stories) of the Edo and Meiji periods.

Anime

The term anime covers the very broad range of animations made in Japan – everything from the highly polished hand-drawn output of Studio Ghibli (which are branded by the studio as 'animated films' to make them distinct from much of the rest of the industry) to the cookie-cutter series churned out each season for Japanese TV.

Anime targets all age and social groups and encompasses all genres, from science fiction and action adventure to romance and historical drama. The medium includes deep explorations of philosophical questions and social issues, humorous entertainment aimed at kids and bizarre fantasies. Some works can offer breathtakingly realistic visuals, exquisite attention to detail, complex and expressive characters, and elaborate plots. Leading directors and voice actors are accorded fame and respect, while characters become popular idols.

Among the best-known anime is *Akira* (1988), Ōtomo Katsuhiro's psychedelic fantasy set in a future Tokyo inhabited by speed-popping biker gangs and psychic children. *Ghost in the Shell* (1995) is an Ōishii Mamoru film with a sci-fi plot worthy of Philip K Dick involving cyborgs, hackers and the mother of all computer networks. The works of Kon Satoshi (1963–2010), including the Hitchcockian *Perfect Blue* (1997), the charming *Tokyo Godfathers* (2003) and the sci-fi thriller *Paprika* (2006), are also classics of the medium.

Recent movies of note include those directed by Hosada Mamoru including *Summer Wars* (2009) and *Ōkami Kodomo no Ame to Yuki* (Wolf Children; 2012), and the Nishikubo Mizuho-directed *Joban'ni no Shima* (Giovanni's Island; 2014), set on the northern island of Shikotan during and immediately after WWII.

Author, poet, playwright, actor and film director Mishima Yukio (1925–1970) courted controversy throughout his life and is perhaps best known for his ritual suicide by seppuku in 1970 after leading a failed coup.

Studio Ghibli

In 2014, Studio Ghibli, Japan's most critically successful producer of animated movies, announced it would be halting production to regroup in the light of the retirement of one of its creative lights, Miyazaki Hayao, and the advanced age of another, Takahata Isao, Miyazaki's mentor from their time working together in the 1960s for animation studio Tōei, and the director of anime classics including *Grave of the Fireflies* (1988) and *Only Yesterday* (1991).

Of the two it is Miyazaki who has done the most to put Japanese animation in the international spotlight by winning an Oscar for *Spirited Away* (2001) and an Academy Honorary Award in 2014.

Beloved TV anime *Astro Boy* and *Kimba the White Lion* are based on hit manga by Tezuka Osamu (1928–1989), an artist frequently referred to as *manga no kamisama* – the 'god c manga'.

MANGA

Walk into any convenience store in Japan and you can pick up several phone-directory-sized weekly manga anthologies. Inside you'll find about 25 comic narratives spanning everything from gangster sagas and teen romance to bicycle racing and *shōgi* (Japanese chess), often with generous helpings of sex and violence. The more successful series are collected in volumes *(tankōbon)*, which occupy major sections of bookshops.

No surprise then that manga accounts for about a third of all sales of Japan's US$30 billion book and magazine publishing industry. Manga's roots can be traced back centuries to ancient scroll paintings that told a story; words were first married with this graphic art in *kibyōshi* woodblock print publications of the Edo period. Today's major publishers, including Kodansha and Kadokawa are based in Tokyo and this is where many *mangaka* (manga artists) get their start in the industry. Recently, faced with declining print magazine sales, publishers have expanded into the booming market for *keitai* manga – comics read on smart phones.

An excellent introduction to the art of manga is the Kyoto International Manga Museum. **Comiket** (www.comiket.co.jp; short for 'Comic Market') is a massive twice-yearly convention in Tokyo for fan-produced amateur manga known as *dōjinshi*. To the untrained eye, *dōjinshi* looks like 'official' manga, but most are parodies (sometimes of a sexual nature) of famous manga titles.

Miyazaki was born in 1941 in wartime Tokyo and his father was the director of a firm that manufactured parts for the famous Japanese Zero fighter plane. This early exposure to artificial flight had a deep impression on Miyazaki, and one of the hallmarks of his films is skies filled with whimsical flying machines; his swan song *The Wind Rises* (2013) is a fictionalised bio-pic about Zero-designer Hirokoshi Jirō. The studio's name Ghibli (pronounced zhibli) comes from an Italian scouting plane used in WWII.

In high school, Miyazaki saw Japan's first feature-length anime, *Hakujaden* (known overseas as *Panda and the Magic Serpent*; 1958) and resolved to become an animator himself. After graduating from university in 1963, he joined Tōei and worked on some of the studio's most famous releases, including *Little Norse Prince* (1968), where he first teamed up with Takahata. His debut as a movie director was in 1979 on *Lupin III: Castle of Cagliostro*.

In 1984, Miyazaki directed an anime version of his manga *Nausicaa of the Valley of the Winds*. The movie provides a brilliant taste of many of the themes that run through Miyazaki's subsequent work, including environmental concerns and the central role of strong female characters. The film's critical and commercial success established Miyazaki as a major force in the world of Japanese anime and led to the creation of the animation studio, Studio Ghibli, through which he has produced all his later works.

In 1988 Studio Ghibli released *My Neighbor Totoro*. Much simpler and less dense than many Miyazaki films, *Totoro* is the tale of two young girls who move with their family to the Japanese countryside while their mother recuperates from an illness. There they befriend Totoro, a magical creature who lives in the base of a giant camphor tree. For anyone wishing to make an acquaintance with the world of Miyazaki, this is the perfect introduction.

Even though Miyazaki has made it clear he doesn't intend to direct any more movies, his colleague Takahata hopes he will change his mind. And who can blame him: Takahata's *The Tale of Princess Kaguya* was released in 2013. Although it was his first feature in 14 years, 79-year-old Takahata refuses to say it will be his last.

STUDIO GHIBLI

All Studio Ghibli fans will want to make a pilgrimage to the delightful Ghibli Museum in the Tokyo suburb of Mitaka.

Architecture

Long before the Japanese borrowed and bested Western design motifs, the island nation honed its architectural craft during two centuries of self-inflicted isolation under the Tokugawa shogunate. A preference for understated buildings in harmony with nature developed as the prime aesthetic, and is still evident today, be it in Japan's carved wooden temples and shrines, or the concrete, metal and glass structures that grace its cities.

Shrines, Temples & Castles

Japan's shrines and temples are undoubtedly the best examples of the nation's early architectural abilities. Important religious complexes were usually quite large and featured a great hall surrounded by smaller structures such as pagodas – the ancient version of the skyscraper – and buildings that served as quarters for devotees. Shrines can always be recognised by the *torii* – the simple gateways typically made of wood (although you also come across them in stone and concrete), while Buddhist temples often reference their Chinese roots in their hip-roof construction and more florid ornamentation.

Equally impressive are the country's collection of feudal castles, although most of the bastions we see today are largely concrete replicas of the original wooden structures destroyed by war, fire or decay. Initially, the feudal castles were simple mountain forts that relied more on natural terrain than structural innovation for defence. Castle construction boomed during the 16th and 17th centuries, each one more impressive than the next; most were later razed by Edo and Meiji governments.

Four of Japan's castles have structures that are classed as national treasures: Himeji-jō (p381), Matsumoto-jō (p257), Hikone-jō (p385) and Inuyama-jō (p220). Jcastle (www.jcastle.info) is an online guide to 293 castles around Japan.

Traditional Homes

Principally simple and refined, the typical house was constructed using post-and-beam timber, with sliding panels of wood or rice paper making up the exterior walls and tatami mats on the floors. *Shōji* (movable

TOP FIVE WOODEN WONDERS

Hōryū-ji (p403)This temple complex in the ancient capital of Nara is commonly believed to feature the two oldest wooden structures in the world: the pagoda (rising just over 32m) and the Kondō (golden or main hall).

Tōdai-ji (p389) Although the current Daibutsu-den Hall of this Buddhist temple in Nara is only two-thirds of its original 8th-century size, it can still boast to being the largest wooden building on earth.

Chion-in (p303) Characterised by graceful buildings and expansive courtyards, this stunning temple complex in Kyoto features a two-storey wooden San-mon, or temple gate – the largest of its kind in all of Japan.

Kiyomizu-dera (p302) The pièce de résistance of this beloved Kyoto temple is the main hall with its signature verandah sitting atop a scaffolding-like structure.

Byōdō-in (p316) Another Kyoto temple, its Amida-dō (Phoenix Hall; also known as Hōō-dō) is featured on the ¥10 coin.

screens) would divide the interior rooms. In more densely populated areas, traditional housing took the form of *machiya* (traditional Japanese townhouses), usually built by merchants. Although most of the neat, narrow rows of these structures have been replaced with flashier modern dwellings, one can still stumble across *machiya* in Kyoto. The reasoning behind the gossamer construction of domestic dwellings was twofold: light materials were favourable during hot summer months and heavier building products were inadvisable due to the frequency of earthquakes.

The most distinctive type of Japanese farmhouse was the thatch-roofed *gasshō-zukuri,* so named for the shape of the rafters, which resemble a pair of palms pressed together in prayer. While these farmhouses appear cosy and romantic, they were often home for up to 40 people and the occasional farm animal. The dark floorboards, soot-covered ceilings and lack of windows starkly contrasted with the breezy merchant houses in more populated areas.

Early Modern Architecture

The Meiji Restoration (1868) re-opened Japan's doors to international architectural influences. Josiah Conder, a British architect, was invited to Tokyo to design many structures that embodied the pillars of Western architecture. Conder erected numerous buildings in Gothic, Renaissance, Moorish and Tudor styles, energising Tokyo's heterogeneous cityscape. Conder was trying to develop an adaptation of Western architecture that could be understood as uniquely Japanese, but the adaptation of so many Western styles exhibited the difficulty of choosing and propagating a Japanese architecture. The Meiji administration was not pleased. They sought a ubiquitous Western aesthetic rather than a garish mishmash of colonial styles. Offended that Conder tried to impose a synthetic 'Japanisation' of the Western style, the Meiji administration rescinded his contract.

This resistance to Western architecture continued until after WWI, when foreign architects such as Frank Lloyd Wright came to build the Imperial Hotel in Tokyo. Wright was careful to pay homage to local sensibilities when designing the Imperial's many elegant bridges and unique guest rooms (though he famously used modern, cubic forms to ornament

TRADITIONAL JAPANESE GARDENS

Touring some of Japan's best gardens is likely to be a revelation, as the Japanese have elevated the art of gardening from mere hobby to the realm of fine art. The major types of gardens you'll encounter during your horticultural explorations:

Funa asobi Meaning 'pleasure boat' and popular in the Heian period, such gardens feature a large pond for boating and were often built around noble mansions. The garden that surrounds Byōdō-in (p316) in Uji is a vestige of this style.

Shūyū These 'stroll' gardens are intended to be viewed from a winding path, allowing the design to unfold and reveal itself in stages and from different vantages. Popular during the Heian, Kamakura and Muromachi periods, a celebrated example is the garden at Ginkaku-ji (p308) in Kyoto.

Kanshō Zen rock gardens (also known as *kare-sansui* gardens) are an example of this type of 'contemplative' garden intended to be viewed from one vantage point and designed to aid meditation. Kyoto's Ryōan-ji (p310) is perhaps the most famous example.

aiyū The 'varied pleasures' garden features many small gardens with one or more teauses surrounding a central pond. Like the stroll garden, it is meant to be explored on and provides the visitor with a variety of changing scenes, many with literary allus. The imperial villa of Katsura Rikyū (p316) in Kyoto is the classic example.

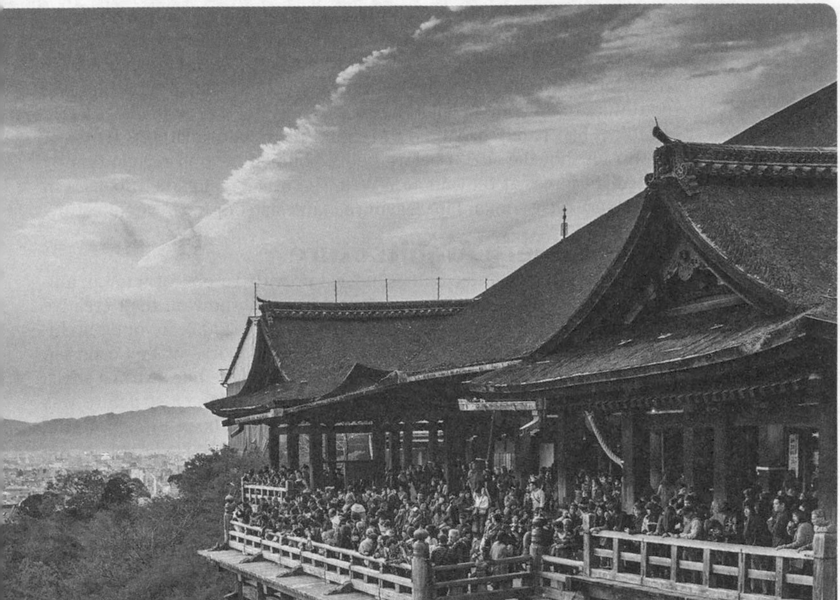

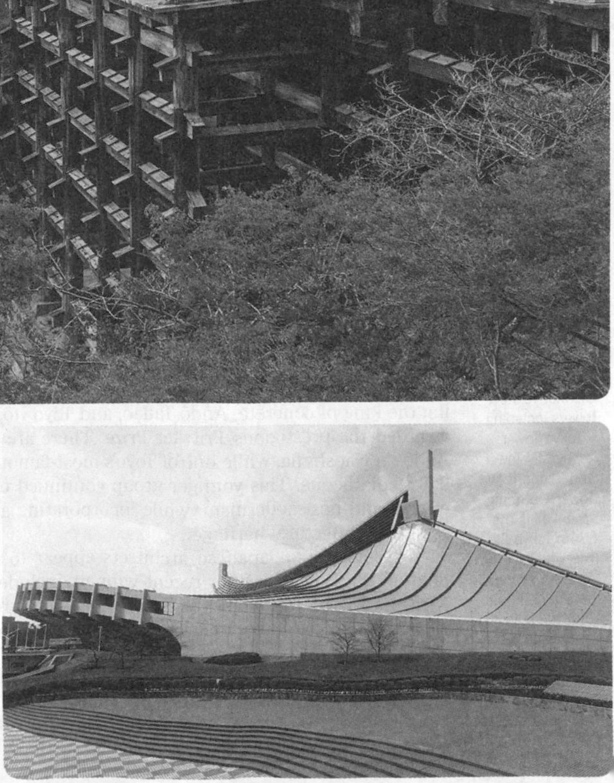

Top Kiyomizu-dera (p302)
Bottom Yoyogi National Gymnasium, designed by Tange Kenzō for the 1964 Summer Olympic Games in Tokyo

DAN HERRICK / GETTY IMAGES ©

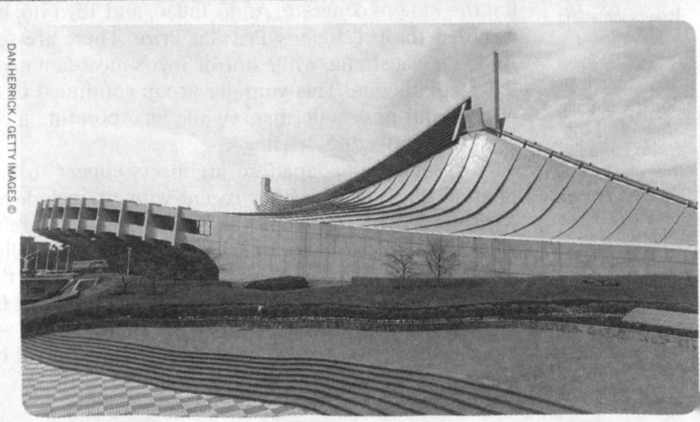

the interiors of the hotel). The building was demolished in 1967 to make way for the current Imperial Hotel, which shows little of Wright's touch. Part of the hotel survives in Meiji Mura (p221), an architectural park near Inuyama, while Wright's charming wooden train station building continues to function in Nikkō.

Tokyo had barely had time to rebuild in the aftermath of the Great Kantō Earthquake (1923) before being bombed beyond recognition by the Allied forces at the end of WWII. The other major metropolises in Japan suffered a similar fate, leaving a blank slate for future architecture.

Late Modern Architecture

Many foreign talents have also made their mark in the freewheeling, anything-goes world of Tokyo architecture including Phillipe Starck (Super Dry Hall), Rafael Viñoly (Tokyo International Forum), Sir Norman Foster (Century Tower) and Herzog & de Meuron (Prada Building).

Tokyo's Summer Olympic Games in 1964 provided a platform for an ambitious new generation of Japanese architects to show off their creative chops. Leading the way was Tange Kenzō (1913–2005), a young architect whose ideas were highly influenced by the works of Le Corbusier. His designs for the two large Olympic stadiums were like swirling shells plucked from the depths of an alien ocean. The larger structure was shaped as though the hull of a majestic boat had been flipped upside down. The gracious gestures of the design masked the sheer volume required to house thousands of spectators. Indeed, the entire world was captivated by these inspired compositions. Tange went on to have a very successful career, and would later design the Tokyo Metropolitan Government Offices (1991).

Also in the 1960s, architects such as Shinohara Kazuo, Kurokawa Kisho, Maki Fumihiko and Kikutake Kiyonori began a movement known as Metabolism, which promoted flexible spaces and functions instead of fixed forms in building. Shinohara came to design in a style he called Modern Next, incorporating both modern and postmodern ideas combined with Japanese influences. This style can be seen in his Centennial Hall at Tokyo Institute of Technology: an elegant and uplifting synthesis of clashing forms clad in shiny metal.

Kurokawa's architecture blends Buddhist building traditions with modern influences; while Maki, the master of minimalism, pursued design in a modernist style while still emphasising the elements of nature – like the roof of his Tokyo Metropolitan Gymnasium (near Sendagaya Station), which takes on the form of a sleek metal insect. Another Maki design, the Spiral Building, built in Aoyama in 1985, is a favourite with Tokyo residents, and its interior is also a treat.

Contemporary Architecture

The telecommunications age has bequeathed Japan with many distinctive steel towers including Tokyo Tower, Nagoya TV Tower and Sapporo TV Tower. Outdoing them all is the 634m Tokyo Sky Tree, officially the tallest tower in the world, though not the tallest structure.

Skip ahead a decade and Japan's second generation of architects began gaining recognition within the international architecture scene, including the king of concrete, Andō Tadao, and Toyo Itō, both of whom were awarded the prestigious Pritzker Prize. There are several buildings by Andō on Naoshima, while one of Toyo's most-famous designs is the Sendai Mediatheque. This younger group continued to explore both modernism and postmodernism, while incorporating a renewed interest in Japan's architectural heritage.

In recent years, Japanese architects appear to have had a strangle hold on the Pritzker. Other recent winners include Sejima Kazuyo and Nishizawa Ryue who helm the SANAA firm and are noted for their unwavering dedication to creating luminous form-follows-function spaces. They have dozens of impressive projects under their belt, including the 21st Century Museum of Contemporary Art in Kanazawa, and the other-worldly Teshima Art Museum. In 2014 they were joined by Ban Shigeru who is best known for recycling cardboard tubes and shipping containers into sustainable, low-cost constructions.

Traditional Japanese Accommodation

Let's face it: a hotel is a hotel wherever you go. And while some of Japan's hotels are very nice indeed, you're probably searching for something unique to the culture. If this is what you're after, you'll be pleased to learn that Japan is one of the last places in Asia where you can find truly authentic traditional accommodation: ryokan, *minshuku* and *shukubō*.

Ryokan

Simply put, ryokan are traditional Japanese inns. They are where Japanese travellers stayed before they had heard the word *hoteru* (hotel). These Japanese-style accommodations boast tatami-mat rooms and futons instead of beds, and most serve Japanese-style breakfast and dinner as well. This simple explanation, however, doesn't do justice to ryokan.

It is said that there are more than 80,000 ryokan in Japan, but that number decreases each year as modern Japanese find hotels to be more convenient.

A high-end ryokan is the last word in relaxation. The buildings themselves set the tone: they employ traditional Japanese architecture in which the whole structure is organic, made entirely of natural materials such as wood, earth, paper, grass, bamboo and stone. Indeed, a good ryokan is an extension of the natural world. And nature comes into the ryokan in the form of the Japanese garden, which you can often see from the privacy of your room or even your own bathtub.

But more than the building, the service is what sets ryokan apart from even the best hotels. At a good ryokan, you will be assigned a personal maid who sees to your every need. These ladies seem to have a sixth sense: as soon as you finish one course of your dinner, you hear a knock on the door and she brings the next course. Then, when you stroll down the hall to take a bath, she dashes into your room and lays out your futon.

Many ryokan in Japan pride themselves on serving *kaiseki ryōri* (Japanese haute cuisine), which rivals that served in the best restaurants. Staying at one of these so-called *ryōri ryokan* (cuisine ryokan) is like staying at a first-class 'residential restaurant', where you sleep in your own private dining room.

Another wonderful variety is the onsen ryokan: a ryokan with its own private hot-spring bath. These places were like luxury spas long before anyone had heard the word 'spa'. Some of the top places have rooms with private en suite onsen baths, usually built overlooking gardens. When you stay at an onsen ryokan, your day involves a gruelling cycle of bathe-nap-eat-repeat. A night at a good onsen ryokan is the perfect way to get over your jet lag when you arrive in the country or a special treat to round out your journey in Japan.

Of course, it would be irresponsible to suggest that all ryokan fit this description. A lot of places that call themselves ryokan are really just hotels with Japanese-style rooms. Some places may not even serve dinner. That isn't to say they aren't comfortable: simple ryokan are often very friendly and relaxing and they may cost less than hotels in some places.

But if you can do it, we strongly recommend staying in a high-end ryokan for at least one night of your trip.

Note that ryokan may not have en suite bathtubs or showers, and at some simple places even the toilet facilities are shared. If this is an issue, be sure to enquire when you make a reservation.

Staying in a Ryokan

Due to language difficulties and unfamiliarity, staying in a ryokan is not as straightforward as staying in a Western-style hotel. However, it's not exactly rocket science and, with a little education, it can be a breeze, even if you don't speak a word of Japanese. Note that much of what is noted here will also apply to staying at a *minshuku*.

Best Ryokan in Japan

- Tawaraya (p323), Kyoto
- Hiiragiya Ryokan (p323), Kyoto
- Kayōtei (p250), Yamanaka Onsen
- Nishimuraya Honkan (p423), Kinosaki

Here's the basic drill. When you arrive, leave your shoes in the *genkan* (entry area or foyer) and step up into the reception area. Here, you'll be asked to sign in. Next, you'll be shown around the place and then to your room, where you will be served a cup of tea. You'll find that there is no bedding to be seen in your room – your futon is in the closet and will be laid out later. You can leave your luggage anywhere except the *tokonoma* (sacred alcove) that will usually contain some flowers or a hanging scroll. If it's early enough, you can then go out to do some sightseeing.

When you return, you'll change into your *yukata* (lightweight Japanese robe) and will be served dinner in your room or in a dining room. After dinner, it's time for a bath. If it's a big place, you can generally bathe anytime in the evening until around 11pm. If it's a small place, you'll be given a time slot. While you're in the bath, some mysterious elves will go into your room and lay out your futon so that it's waiting for you when you return all toasty from the bath.

In the morning, you'll be served a Japanese-style breakfast (some places these days serve a simple Western-style breakfast for those who can't stomach rice and fish in the morning). You pay on check-out, which is usually around 11am.

Minshuku

A *minshuku* is usually a family-run private lodging, rather like a B&B in Europe or the USA. In some very simple *minshuku* you're really just staying with a Japanese family that has turned a few of the rooms in their house into guestrooms. Other places are purpose-built to serve as accommodation. In either case, the rooms will be Japanese style, with tatami mats and futons. Bathroom facilities are usually shared and meals are usually eaten in a common dining room. Unlike at a ryokan, in a *minshuku* you are usually expected to lay out and put away your own bedding.

Staying at a *minshuku* can be like staying with your extended family over the holidays. If you've got a few boisterous relatives in the room next door, you'll probably hear what they're saying. Still, most guests are pretty good at observing quiet hours (midnight to 8am).

The average price per person per night, including two meals, is around ¥5500. *Minshuku* are a little hard to find on your own if you don't speak and read Japanese. And, needless to say, owners are less likely to speak English than at hotels or popular ryokan. The best way to find a *minshuku* is to ask at a local tourist information office, where they will usually call ahead and make all arrangements for you.

Shukubō

A *shukubō* is lodging offered at Buddhist temples, traditionally for pilgrims or official visitors to the temple, but these days just as often for casual travellers.

Shukubō vary tremendously in style and amenities: some are downright luxurious and rival the best ryokan in Japan, while others are merely spartan rooms that resemble those found at a cheap hostel or guesthouse. Most are somewhere in between. Rooms are almost always

JAPANESE ACCOMMODATION MADE EASY

A number of foreign travellers have turned up unannounced in a ryokan or *minshuku* and been given a distinctly cold reception, then concluded that they have been the victim of discrimination. More than likely, they simply broke one of the main rules of Japanese accommodation: don't surprise them. With this in mind, here are a few tips to help you find a bed each night in Japan. Note that the following also goes for hotels, although these are generally a little more flexible than traditional accommodation.

Reservations Make reservations whenever possible, even if it's just a quick call a few hours before arriving.

Email or fax The Japanese are much more comfortable with written than spoken English. If you email or fax a room request with all your details, you will find a warm welcome. You can always follow it up with a phone call, once you're all on the same page.

The baton pass Get your present accommodation to call ahead and reserve your next night's lodging. This will put everyone at ease – if you're acceptable at one place, you'll be just fine at another.

Tourist information offices Even in the smallest hamlet or island in Japan, you'll find tourist information offices, usually right outside train stations or ferry terminals. These exist just to help travellers find accommodation (OK, they also give brilliant directions). They will recommend a place and call to see if a room is available, then they will tell you exactly how to get there. This is another form of introduction.

Lastly, there will be times when you just have to slide that door open and hope for the best. Even the surprise-averse Japanese have to resort to this desperate expediency from time to time. The secret here is to try to minimise the shock. Smile like you're there to sell them insurance, muster your best *konbanwa* (good evening) and try to convince them that you actually prefer futons to beds, green tea to coffee, chopsticks to forks, and baths to showers.

traditionally Japanese, meaning tatami mats on the floor and a futon for sleeping. Occasionally, sexes will be segregated, but most places allow couples to stay together. Sometimes you are simply allocated a room in the temple precincts and left to your own devices. At other places, you may also be allowed (or even required) to participate in prayers, services or meditation. If you're lucky, you might find an English-speaking monk on hand who will be willing to give you a tour of the temple and explain the treasures and history of the place.

When reserving a night in a *shukubō*, be sure to ask about food. Many places serve simple meals, while others serve nothing at all, leaving guests to bring their own food or eat at local restaurants.

Without question, the most popular spot to try a *shukubō* in Japan is at the mountain monastery complex of Kōya-san (p408) in Wakayama-ken (Kansai), about two hours by train south of Osaka. A popular Shingon (Esoteric) Buddhist pilgrimage spot, almost all temples here offer *shukubō* and some of them are truly spectacular, with rooms boasting magnificent garden views, fine decorations, private baths and superb prayer halls. Most are slightly less grand, of course, but they're usually a step up from the spartan (albeit cheaper) places found at many other pilgrimage centres. The speciality of Kōya-san is *shōjin-ryōri* (Buddhist vegetarian cuisine) and some temples here offer truly memorable fare. Thus, for anyone wishing to give *shukubō* a try, Kōya-san is highly recommended.

You can find *shukubō* all across Japan, including at temples in Kyoto and Nara. Many options can be found by searching online or by asking at the local tourist information offices.

Sport

The Japanese love sports and are enthusiastic fans of traditional sumo wrestling and martial arts, as well as imported games such as baseball and soccer. Basketball, figure skating and golf are also highly popular and have created stars such as golfer Ishikawa Ryō and skater Hanyū Yuzuru. In 2019 the country will host the Rugby World Cup, which will be but a prelude to the hoopla surrounding the 2020 Summer Olympics in Tokyo.

Sumo

The national sport is a ritualistic form of wrestling that developed out of ancient Shintō rites for a good harvest. Two overweight, amply muscled men, clothed only in *mawashi* (loin cloths) with their hair slicked back into a topknot, battle it out in a packed earth *dōyo* (ring) over which hangs a roof that resembles that of a shrine. Before bouts, which typically last only seconds, the *rikishi* (wrestlers) rinse their mouths with water and toss salt into the ring – both purification rituals. They also perform the *shiko* movement, where they squat, clap their hands and alternately raise each leg as high as it can go before stamping it down – all shows of strength and agility.

Grand Tournaments (*bashō*) are held over a 15-day period, six times a year (January, May and September in Tokyo, March in Osaka, July in Nagoya and November in Fukuoka) and they are well worth a visit. It's the pageantry as much as the actual wrestling of a *bashō* that is so memorable, including spectacles such as the ceremonial entrance of *maku-uchi* (top division) wrestlers in their decorative *keshō-mawashi* aprons and the bow-twirling moves of the *yokozuna*, sumo's supreme champions.

Sumo Online

Nihon Sumo Kyokai (www.sumo.or.jp) Online ticket sales.

Sumo Fan Magazine (www.sumofanmag.com) Multilingual online fanzine.

Sumotalk (www.sumotalk.com) The skinny on all things sumo.

Baseball

The Japanese call it *yakyū* and it's been played here since 1873, when it was introduced by Horace Wilson, an American teacher in Tokyo. The US connection is still alive and well, with top Japanese players snapped up to play in the States, and American baseball stars on their way down tending to flow in the opposite direction.

Games are played between April and October across the country in two pro leagues (Central and Pacific; www.npb.or.jp), each with six teams sponsored by big businesses. The victors in each league then duke it out in the end-of-season seven match Japan Series. The most successful team by a wide margin is Tokyo-based Yomiuri Giants, who have 35 Central League and 22 Japan Series titles to their name.

Soccer

The beautiful game also has a 150-year-old pedigree in Japan, but it was only with the creation of the professional J-League (www.j-league.or.jp) in 1993 that it began to gain wider spectator popularity. In 2002 Japan co-hosted a very successful World Cup with Korea.

As of 2014 there were 18 clubs in the premier J1 division and 20 in the J2 division; all compete in the Yamazaki Nabisco Cup, with games held between March and October.

SUMO MOVES

Size is important in sumo, but woe betide any *rikishi* who relies solely on bulk as, more often than not, it's *kimari-te* (wrestling techniques) that win the day. There are 82 official *kimari-te* a *rikishi* may legitimately employ, including:

Abisetaoshi Using body weight to push an opponent backwards to the ground.

Oshidashi Pushing underneath an opponents arms or in the chest to force him out of the ring.

Oshitaoshi Pushing an opponent to the ground either inside or outside the ring.

Shitatenage Tackling an opponent by grabbing inside his arms.

Tsukiotoshi Grabbing an opponent underneath the arm or on his side and forcing him down at an angle.

Uwatenage Grabbing an opponent's *mawashi* (loin cloth) from outside the opponent's arms and throwing him to the ground.

Uwatedashinage As above but also dragging an opponent.

Yorikiri Lifting an opponent out of the ring by his *mawashi*.

Moves that will get a wrestler disqualified include punching with a closed fist, boxing ears, choking, grabbing an opponent in the crotch area, and pulling his hair.

Martial Arts

Although they have roots in the combat techniques honed over centuries by samurai and other warriors, the martial arts that are most closely associated with Japan today developed in the modern era. These *gendai budō* aim for self-improvement and self-protection rather than aggression.

Judo

An Olympic sport since 1964, judo (literally meaning 'the gentle way') is a wrestling-style of martial art that developed at the end of the 19th century from the more harmful jujitsu fighting school. The controlling body is the Tokyo-based **All-Japan Judo Federation** (www.judo.or.jp), which offers classes and has a hostel at which recommended students can stay. Also check their website for details of judo contests held throughout the year.

Karate

Meaning 'empty hand', karate came to mainland Japan from Okinawa and is a fusion of an Okinawan martial art known as *ke* and Chinese martial arts. Today there are various styles of karate, with the **Japan Karate Association** (www.jka.or.jp) representing the most popular Shokotan tradition. The association's *dōjō* (practice hall) in Tokyo welcomes visitors who wish to join a training session.

Kendō

An evolution of *kenjutsu* (the art of sword-fighting), practitioners of kendō use blunt bamboo swords (*shinai*) and light body armour (*bōgu*). The sport is governed by the **All-Japan Kendō Federation** (www.kendo-fik.org) based at Tokyo's Nippon Buddōkan, where many of the championship matches are held.

Aikidō

Developed in the early 20th century, this form of self defence combines elements of judo, karate and kendō so that the practitioner uses, rather than opposes, an adversary's attack through techniques such as throws and controls. Tokyo's Hombu-dōjō is the headquarters of the **International Aikidō Federation** (www.aikikai.or.jp) and you can sign up for classes there.

There are over 2300 18-hole golf courses in Japan and you can find details about them all, plus golf driving ranges, at Golf in Japan (www.golf-in-japan.com).

Living Art of the Geisha

No other aspect of Japanese culture is as widely misunderstood as the geisha. First – and let's get this out of the way – geisha are not prostitutes. Nor is their virginity sold off to the highest bidder. Nor do they have to sleep with regular patrons. Simply put, geisha are highly skilled entertainers who are paid to facilitate and liven up social occasions in Japan.

Memoirs of a Geisha (1997) by Arthur Golden is an entertaining fictional account of the life of a Kyoto geisha.

Origins

The origins of geisha are subject to some debate, but most historians believe that the institution of the geisha started in the Edo period (1600–1868). At this time, there were various types of prostitutes who served men in the pleasure quarters of the large cities. Some of these ladies became very accomplished in various arts and it is said that some pleasure houses even employed male performers to entertain customers. Some believe that these male entertainers were the first to be dubbed 'geisha', which means 'artistic person'.

Eventually, there arose a class of young ladies who specialised exclusively in entertainment and who did not engage in sexual relations with clients. These were the first true female geisha, and over the years they became prized for their accomplishments in a wide variety of Japanese arts.

Geisha Central

Without a doubt, Kyoto is the capital of the geisha world. Confusingly, in Kyoto they are not called 'geisha'; rather, they are called *maiko* or *geiko*. A *maiko* is a girl between the ages of 15 and 20, who is in the process of training to become a fully fledged *geiko* (the Kyoto word for 'geisha'). During this five-year period, she lives in an *okiya* (geisha house) and studies traditional Japanese arts, including dance, singing, tea ceremony and *shamisen* (a three-stringed instrument). During this time, she will also start to entertain clients, usually in the company of a *geiko*, who acts like an older sister.

Due to the extensive training she receives, a *maiko* or *geiko* is like a living museum of Japanese traditional culture. In addition to her skills, the kimono she wears and the ornaments in her hair and on her obi (kimono sash) represent the highest achievements in Japanese arts. It's therefore hardly surprising that both Japanese and foreigners consider a meeting with a geisha to be a magical occurrence.

While young girls may have been sold into this world in times gone by, these days girls make the choice themselves, often after coming to Kyoto to see one of the city's famous geisha dances. The proprietor of the *okiya* will meet the girl and her parents to determine if the girl is serious and if her parents are willing to grant her permission to enter the world of the geisha (the *okiya* makes a considerable investment in terms of training and kimonos, so they are loathe to take girls who may quit).

GEISHA MANNERS

There's no doubt that catching a glimpse of a geisha is a once-in-a-lifetime Japanese experience. Unfortunately, the sport of 'geisha-spotting' has really gotten out of hand in Kyoto's Gion district (the city's main geisha district). It's to such a pitch that *The Telegraph* reported in 2014 that some of Kyoto's geisha are now being trained in self-defence by the city's police department. In order to make life easier for everyone involved, it's probably best to keep the following in mind if you join the ranks of geisha-spotters in Gion:

➡ The geisha you see in Gion are usually on the way to or from an appointment and cannot stop for photos or conversation.

➡ You shouldn't touch or grab a geisha, or physically block their progress.

➡ If you really want to get close to a geisha, private tour agencies and high-end ryokan or hotels can arrange geisha entertainment.

➡ Finally, if you are intent on getting a few photos of geisha, you will find plenty of 'tourist geisha' in the streets of Higashiyama during the daytime. These are tourists who have paid to be made up as geisha. They look pretty much like the real thing and they are usually more than happy to pose for pictures.

Once a *maiko* completes her training and becomes a *geiko,* she is able to move out of the *okiya* and live on her own. At this point she is free to have a boyfriend, but if she gets married she has to leave the world of the geisha. It's very easy to spot the difference between a *maiko* and a *geiko: maiko* wear their own hair in an elaborate hairstyle with many bright hair ornaments called *kanzashi,* while *geiko* wear wigs with minimal ornamentation (usually just a wooden comb in the wig). Also, *maiko* wear elaborate long-sleeve kimonos, while *geiko* wear simpler kimonos with shorter sleeves.

Geisha Entertainment

Maiko and *geiko* entertain their clients in exclusive restaurants, banquet halls, 'teahouses' (more like exclusive traditional bars) and other venues. An evening of *maiko/geiko* entertainment usually starts with a *kaiseki* (Japanese haute cuisine) meal. While their customers eat, the *maiko/geiko* enter the room and introduce themselves in Kyoto dialect.

They proceed to pour drinks and make witty banter with the guests. Sometimes they even play drinking games, and we can tell you from experience that it's hard to beat geisha at their own games! If it's a large party with a *jikata* (*shamisen* player), the girls may dance after dinner.

As you might guess, this sort of entertainment does not come cheap: a dinner with one *maiko* and one *geiko* and a *jikata* might cost about US$900, but it's definitely worth it for a once-in-a-lifetime experience. Let's face it: 'I had dinner with a geisha' is a pretty good entry in any 'been there, done that' contest.

It's impossible to arrange private geisha entertainment without an introduction from an established patron. However, these days geisha entertainment can be arranged through top-end hotels, ryokan and some private tour operators in Kyoto.

Knowledgeable sources estimate that there are about 65 *maiko* and just over 185 *geiko* in Kyoto (the latter figure includes *jikata*). Geisha can also be found in other parts of the country, most notably Tokyo. However, it is thought that there are less than 1000 geisha or *geiko* and *maiko* remaining in all of Japan.

The best way to see geisha – a whole lot of geisha – is to attend one of Kyoto's spring or autumn geisha dances.

Environment

Stretching from the tropics to the Sea of Okhotsk, the Japanese archipelago is a fantastically varied place. Few countries enjoy such a variety of climates and ecosystems, with everything from coral-reefed islands to snowcapped mountains. Unfortunately, this wonderful landscape is also one of the world's most crowded, and almost every inch of the Japanese mainland bears the imprint of human activity.

The Land

In 2005 the Japanese Ministry of the Environment launched the 'Cool Biz' campaign to cut CO_2 emissions. The program encouraged 'casual Fridays' in offices and raising thermostats in summer (to use less air-con). After a year it was estimated that annual CO_2 emissions were reduced by over 1 million tonnes.

Japan's four main islands, Honshū (slightly larger than Britain), Hokkaidō, Kyūshū and Shikoku are home to the bulk of the nation's population. A further 6848 smaller islands make up the archipelago, which stretches from the Ryūkyū Islands (of which Okinawa is the largest) at around 25°N to the northern end of Hokkaidō at 45°N. Cities at comparable latitudes are Miami (south) and Montreal (north). Japan's total land area is 377,435 sq km, of which mountains comprise around 80%. Before the last Ice Age, Japan was connected by a land bridge to the East Asian continent.

Situated along the 'Ring of Fire', Japan occupies one of earth's most seismically active regions. In March 2011 the 9.0-magnitude Great East Japan Earthquake, one of the strongest in history, caused a tsunami that devastated coastal areas of northeast Honshū. Officially, 15,884 people lost their lives. Many of the thousands of tremors that strike Japan each year aren't even felt, but should you find yourself in a coastal area during a significant earthquake, waste no time: avoid driving and immediately head for higher ground or above the 3rd storey of a reinforced concrete building.

Japan has many volcanoes, including majestic Mt Fuji. In February 2009 Mt Asama in Nagano sent smoke 2km into the air and scattered ash over Tokyo. In 2014 an unexpected eruption of Ontake-san, also in Nagano, killed 56 hikers, though volcanic fatalities are generally uncommon. Kyūshū's volcanoes are the most active: spectacular Sakura-jima in Kagoshima frequently puts on a show.

Although Japan's environment has been manipulated by human activity over centuries, pockets of startling beauty remain, some surprisingly close to heavily populated areas. Fortunately, conservation and environmental consciousness is on the rise.

Human Impact

Visitors to Japan are often shocked at the state of the Japanese landscape. It seems that no matter where you look, the hills, rivers, fields and coastline bear the unmistakable stamp of human activity. Population density, outdated land-management policies and politics-for-profits have all contributed to this disfigurement of Japan's environment. Generally, it is only in the higher peaks or on the most remote coasts that one finds nature unbridled.

Almost 70% of Japan's available land mass is forested. Of this, almost 40% has been planted with uniform rows of *sugi* conifers (Cryptomeria japonica). Such forests account for 33% of Japan's total lumber output, and not even national forests are exempt from tree farming. The result: large chunks of Japan's many mountains look like a patchwork quilt of monotonous *sugi* and swathes of clear-cut hillside. These monoculture forests and clear-cutting techniques reduce topsoil stability, causing frequent landslides. To combat this, ugly concrete retaining walls are erected over huge stretches of hillside.

Worse still, it's estimated that only three of Japan's almost 30,000 rivers are un-dammed, with concrete channels and embankments built around even the most inaccessible mountain streams.

Rural areas yield enormous power in Japanese politics, as representation is determined more by area than by population. In order to ensure the support of their constituencies, rural politicians have little choice but to lobby for government spending on public-work projects, as employment prospects are limited in these depopulating areas. Despite the negative effects on the environment Japanese politicians seem unable to break this habit.

The upshot of all this is a landscape that looks, in many places, like a giant construction site. Fortunately, a new ecofriendly generation of young Japanese seem to care more about the environment. Hybrid and electric cars are now commonplace, and Japan's first offshore solar power plant (generating enough electricity to power 22,000 homes) commenced operation in 2013. Groups such as **Japan for Sustainability** (japanfs.org), **Green Action** (www.greenaction-japan.org) and **Greenpeace Japan** (www.greenpeace.org/japan) each lobby for environmental concerns such as de-nuclearisation, the research and development of renewable energy technologies and reducing carbon emissions.

Wildlife

The latitudinal spread of Japan's islands makes for a wide diversity of flora and fauna. The Nansei and Ogasawara archipelagos in the far south are subtropical, and flora and fauna in this region are related to those found on the Malay peninsula. Mainland Japan (Honshū, Kyūshū and Shikoku) shows more similarities with Korea and China, while Hokkaidō shares some features with Russia's nearby Sakhalin Island.

Animals

Japan's land bridge to the Asian continent allowed the migration of animals from Korea and China. There are also species that are unique to Japan, such as the Japanese giant salamander and the Japanese macaque. In addition, Nansei-shotō, which has been separated from the mainland for longer than the rest of Japan, has a few examples of fauna that are classified by experts as 'living fossils', such as the Iriomote cat.

Japan's largest carnivorous mammals are its bears. Two species are found in Japan – the *higuma* (brown bear) of Hokkaidō, and the *tsukinowaguma* (Asiatic brown bear) of Honshū, Shikoku and Kyūshū.

HONSHŪ BLOSSOM & FOLIAGE SEASONS

Early February–mid-March

Whether white or pink, plum blossoms signal winter is loosening its grip.

March & April

Camellias grace gardens and temples, overlapping with the plums and cherries.

Mid-March–mid-April

Sakura season. Wherever you are, in a really good cherry-blossom year it can seem like Mother Nature has decided to put on her best party dress and go mad; crowds gather everywhere for *hanami* (cherry-blossom viewing).

April & May

Hikers delight in the many varieties of wild azaleas that festoon the highlands.

Late April-May

In Japanese, a word exists to describe the luminous green that typifies the trees of Japan for the first few weeks after budding: *shinryoku*. Photographers use the word 'oversaturation'.

May

Divine purple blossoms of draping wisteria decorate temple gardens and mountainsides

Late Octobe[illegible] early Decemb[illegible]

The brilliant spectacle o[illegible] (autumn foliage se[illegible] sees *momiji* (maples[illegible] and other broadlea[illegible] cycle through yello[illegible] orange and [illegible]

SUSTAINABLE TRAVEL IN JAPAN

As a traveller, you can minimise your impact on the Japanese environment in several simple ways.

Refuse packaging The Japanese art of over-packaging is out of date. At the cash register, you can say: '*Fukuro wa irimasen*' (I don't need a bag).

Carry your own chopsticks Grab a pair of '*hashi*' (washable chopsticks with a carrying case) from a convenience store.

Less tuna, please Try to avoid species of endangered fish, such as *maguro* (tuna) – including *toro* (fatty tuna belly). We know, this one hurts!

Use public transport Japan's public transport system is among the best in the world – use it.

Hop on a bike Rent bikes (often for free) to explore the countryside or join the legions of Japanese who commute on their *mama-charis* (shopping bikes).

The International Union for Conservation of Nature and Natural Resources (IUCN) 'Red List' currently tallies 92 endangered fauna species in Japan, of which 24 are 'critically endangered'. The widely consumed Japanese eel is among them, along with the Iriomote cat, Tsushima cat, Blakiston's fish eagle and Japanese river otter. A further 111 species are listed as 'vulnerable', including the Asiatic black bear, and a variety of sharks and whales.

Plants

The flora of Japan today is not what the Japanese saw hundreds of years ago. This is not just because a lot of Japan's natural landscape has succumbed to modern urban culture, but also because much of Japan's flora is imported. It is thought that 200 to 500 plant species have been introduced to Japan since the Meiji period, mainly from Europe, but also from North America.

A large portion of Japan was once heavily forested. The cool to temperate zones of Central and Northern Honshū and southern Hokkaidō were home to broad-leaf mixed deciduous forests. These days, however, you are much more likely to see monotonous stands of *sugi*.

Fortunately, the sheer inaccessibility of much of Japan's mountainous topography has preserved some areas of great natural beauty – in particular the alpine regions of Central Honshū, the lovely national parks of Hokkaidō and the semitropical island of Iriomote.

According to a 2008 report in the *Proceedings of the Japan Academy*, there are 1690 endangered and threatened species of vascular plants in Japan. For more information, visit the website of the Biodiversity Center of Japan at www.biodic.go.jp.

WOODEN CHOPSTICKS

Twenty-five ...llion pairs of ...ibashi (dis-...ble wooden ...ticks) are ...n Japan ...lly – ... to the ...eded ...000

National Parks

Japan has 31 *kokuritsu kōen* (national parks) and 56 *kokutei kōen* (quasi-national parks), ranging from the far south (Iriomote National Park) to the northern tip of Hokkaidō (Rishiri-Rebun-Sarobetsu National Park). Although national and quasi-national parks account for less than 1% of Japan's total land area, the World Bank lists 16.5% of Japan's total land mass as 'Terrestrial Protected Areas'.

Few of the parks have facilities that you might expect in national parks (ranger stations, campgrounds, educational facilities etc). More importantly, national park status doesn't necessarily mean that the area in question is free from residential, commercial or even urban development.

For descriptions of Japan's parks, see www.env.go.jp/en/np.

Environmental Issues

Japan has spent a lot of time in the spotlight recently due to environmental issues. The 2009 film, *The Cove* focusing on the annual slaughter of dolphins in the town of Taiji (southern Kansai) won the Academy Award for best documentary feature, although few Japanese have seen it: only six cinemas nationwide showed it. The Taiji fishermen claim that they were lied to and misrepresented by the filmmakers.

THE FUKUSHIMA NUCLEAR INCIDENT

The tsunami caused by the Great East Japan Earthquake (p501) devastated coastal areas of northeast Honshū, home to several nuclear power plants. Most avoided calamity, however, to the south of the most tsunami-devastated areas, the seaside, six-reactor Fukushima Dai-ichi plant (alarmingly just 240km northeast of Tokyo) suffered unimaginable damage.

At the time of the quake, three reactors were offline for maintenance. The remaining three were automatically shut down. A series of hydrogen explosions caused further structural damage, which remains a significant complication. The seawalls built to protect the plant from tsunami inundation failed dismally, and the facility was flooded, damaging buildings and knocking out generators, resulting in a catastrophic loss of essential cooling capacity, causing a total core meltdown in three reactors. No evidence is publicly available to confirm the actual location of these melted cores. Some experts have speculated that the cores may have breached their containment vessels into the ground beneath: an unprecedented situation.

While it is thought that much of the deadly radioactive material remains contained on-site, a significant amount of radiation was dispersed in a plume to the northwest. Radioactive water continues to leak or be released into the Pacific Ocean. Hundreds of makeshift tanks have been filled with contaminated water used to cool spent fuel. TEPCO (www.tepco.co.jp/en), the plant's highly criticised operator, remains PR-positive but tight-lipped. The pro-nuclear Liberal Democratic Party government's 2013 'State Secrecy Act' ensures this remains the status quo.

Short of a handful of international experts who were permitted on-site following the disaster, the outside world has little knowledge of how decommissioning is proceeding and what risks remain. A frightening amount of highly combustible radioactive material remains in damaged buildings susceptible to further strong earthquakes in coming years. Should that material catch fire or explode, the effects are unthinkable. Some estimates put the task of decommissioning at half a century.

An exclusion zone with a radius of 20km exists around the plant. The safety of food throughout Japan remains a lingering concern and it is difficult to get a clear overall picture of the risks. The general consensus is that radiation measurements in food remain at acceptable levels. The onus remains with local municipalities and farmers to conduct voluntary checks. As always, it's best to do your own research. Start with the impartial sites: www.safecast.org and www.fairewinds.org.

Following the disaster, all of Japan's 48 reactors (which generated about 30% of the nation's power) were shut down, with the last one going offline in May 2012. In July 2012, a plant in the town of Ōi (in Fukui Prefecture) became Japan's only operational reactor, until September 2013, when it was shut down in response to public protest. In November 2014, two reactors in Kagoshima prefecture were approved to be restarted. It's a near certainty that the re-election of Shinzo Abe's LDP in the December 2014 election will see more reactors coming online soon.

While research indicates that radiation outside Fukushima Dai-ichi's exclusion zone appears to pose no health risks to visitors to Japan, it seems clear that until the plant is fully decommissioned, its precarious location, volume of highly explosive nuclear fuel and the scale of damage it received likely make it the greatest single threat to the safety of not only the people of Japan but the global environment as a whole.

Under the 1997 Kyoto Protocol, Japan pledged to cut CO_2 emissions by 6% from 1990 levels, but emissions to 2013 rose by 14% (to their second-highest level) in the wake of the suspension of nuclear power generation.

Japan remains under international criticism for continuing to hunt whales, despite a 1982 International Whaling Commission moratorium on commercial whaling. Japan claims that it is whaling for research purposes, but critics point out that killing more than 900 minke, 50 fin and 50 humpback whales per season is impossible to justify in the name of research, and question why whale meat is widely sold for human consumption. In January 2010 the issue came to a head when the anti-whaling organisation Sea Shepherd's vessel *Ady Gil* was rammed and sunk by Japanese whalers, who then turned their water cannons on the stricken crew. People within Japan and overseas were further enraged when it was revealed in December 2011 that US$29 million of funds earmarked for tsunami recovery efforts had gone to shore up the whaling industry. Whaling and dolphin hunting has become so politicised in Japan that meaningful dialogue seems impossible. The domestic media refuses to say anything critical about the practices and most politicians interpret any such criticism as 'Japan bashing'.

In 2014 the International Court of Justice ruled that Japan's whaling program was not scientific and ordered Japan to cease whaling, although there appears no official national plans to do so. The issue will likely continue to make global headlines.

Japan's over-fishing of tuna, a species which many biologists say could be driven extinct if commercial fishing is not banned, also receives global criticism. In 2010 Japan's opposition to the Convention on International Trade in Endangered Species (CITES) proposed ban on commercial tuna fishing was instrumental in the bill's defeat.

In 2009 environmentalists were briefly cheered by the results of the general election in which the Democratic Party of Japan (DJP) took power from the Liberal Democratic Party of Japan (LDP). The DJP had promised to end the sort of unrestrained public-works projects that have left Japan littered with what many consider needless dams, bridges, concrete retaining walls and other eyesores. Soon after taking power, the DJP announced plans to cancel 48 large public-works projects. Unfortunately, they ran headlong into the power of the bureaucrats who are intimately tied to such projects, as well as the local communities that have become dependent on the so-called 'construction state'. The LDP were re-elected in 2012 and again in December 2014.

Survival Guide

Directory A–Z

Accommodation

Japan offers a wide range of accommodation, from cheap guesthouses to first-class hotels. In addition to the Western-style hotels, you'll also find distinctive Japanese-style places such as ryokan and *minshuku*. For more on traditional Japanese accommodation, see p843.

Reservations

- It can be hard to find accommodation during high-season holiday periods (cherry-blossom season, autumn-foliage season, Golden Week holiday and the Obon holiday period). If you plan to be in Japan during these periods, you should make reservations as far in advance as possible.
- Tourist information offices at main train stations can usually help with reservations, and are often open until about 6.30pm or later. Even if you are travelling by car, the train station is a good first stop in town for information, reservations and cheap car parking.
- Making phone reservations in English is usually possible at larger hotels and foreigner-friendly ryokan. Providing you speak clearly and simply, there will usually be someone around who can get the gist of what you want.
- **Japanese Inn Group** (06-6225-3611; www.japaneseinngroup.com) is a collection of foreigner-friendly ryokan and guesthouses. You can book member inns via its website or phone/fax. Pick up a copy of its excellent guide to member inns at major tourist information centres in Japan.

Camping

Camping is possible at official campgrounds across Japan, some of which are only open during the summer high season of July and August. Camping is also possible year-round (when conditions permit) at campgrounds in the mountains or around certain mountain huts. 'Guerrilla' or unofficial camping is also possible in many parts of rural Japan, but we recommend asking a local person about acceptable areas before setting up your tent.

Cycling Terminals

Cycling terminals *(saikuringu tāminaru)* provide low-priced accommodation of the bunk-bed or tatami-mat variety and are usually found in scenic areas suited to cycling.

Cycling-terminal prices compare favourably with those of a youth hostel: around ¥3000 per person per night, or ¥5000 including two meals.

Hostels & Guesthouses

Japan has an extensive network of youth hostels, often located in areas of interest to travellers. The network is administered by **Japan Youth Hostels, Inc** (JYH; 03-3288-1417; www.jyh.or.jp/english/index.html; 2-21-4 Yanagibashi Taito-ku Tokyo 111-0052). You can stay at youth hostels in Japan without

SLEEPING PRICE RANGES

The following price ranges refer to a double room for hotels, and per person without meals for ryokan. Unless otherwise stated, the national 8% consumption tax is included in the price, but note that some hotels quote exclusive of taxes.

less than ¥6000 (less than ¥8000 in Tokyo)

¥6000–15,000 (¥8000–25,000 in Tokyo)

more than ¥15,000 (more than ¥25,000 in Tokyo)

being a member of either the JYH or the International Youth Hostel Federation (IYHA). Hostellers are expected to check in between 3pm and 8pm to 9pm. There is usually a curfew of 10pm or 11pm. Checkout is usually before 10am and dormitories are closed between 10am and 3pm. Bath time is usually between 5pm and 9pm, dinner is between 6pm and 7.30pm, and breakfast is between 7am and 8am.

If you'd like to join JYH, a one-year membership costs ¥2800. For more details, a downloadable English-language map of member hostels, and a useful guide, visit the JYH website.

In addition to the JYH hostels, you'll find various independent hostels and guesthouses in cities and towns frequented by travellers. These places are usually much more relaxed than official youth hostels and they usually lack curfews. Prices are similar to those charged by official hostels, sometimes even a bit cheaper. Among the more popular are the K's House and J-Hoppers groups.

Finally, the Toho network (www.toho.net) is a diverse collection of places that has banded loosely together to offer a more flexible alternative to youth hostels. Most of the network's 90 members are in Hokkaidō, although there are a few scattered around Honshū and other islands further south. Prices average ¥4000 per person for dormitory-style accommodation, or ¥5000 with two meals. Private rooms are sometimes available for about ¥1000 extra.

COSTS

Typical hostel charges:

One-night stay (dorm) ¥3000

One-night stay (private room) ¥4000

Breakfast ¥500

Dinner ¥900

Sheet rental ¥100

Towel rental ¥100

BOOK YOUR STAY ONLINE

For more accommodation reviews by Lonely Planet authors, check out http://lonelyplanet.com/hotels/. You'll find independent reviews, as well as recommendations on the best places to stay. Best of all, you can book online.

Hotels

You'll find a range of Western-style hotels in most Japanese cities and resort areas. So-called business hotels are efficient, utilitarian hotels that are geared to Japan's business travellers; while the rooms tend to be small, they are usually perfectly adequate for a night's stay. Luxury hotels are what you'd find anywhere else in the world.

CAPSULE HOTELS

One of Japan's most famous forms of accommodation is the *capseru hoteru*. As the name implies, the 'rooms' in a capsule hotel consist of banks of neat white capsules stacked in rows two or three high. The capsules are about the size of a spacious coffin. Inside is a bed, a TV, a reading light, a radio and an alarm clock. Personal belongings are kept in a locker room. Most capsule hotels have the added attraction of a sauna and a large communal bath.

Capsule hotels are common in major cities and often cater to workers who have partied too hard to make it home or have missed the last train. The majority of capsule hotels only accept male guests, but some also accept women. Given the fact that many of the guests at capsule hotels are inebriated salarymen, it's not entirely surprising that these aren't the most salubrious places to spend the night. The exceptions to this are the new breed of foreigner-friendly capsule hotels that have recently opened in places like Tokyo and Kyoto, which are very nice (if small!) places to stay.

LOVE HOTELS

As the name implies, love hotels are used by Japanese couples for discreet trysts. You can use them for this purpose as well, but they're also acceptable for overnight accommodation.

To find a love hotel on the street, just look for flamboyant facades and signs clearly stating the rates. Love hotels are designed for maximum privacy: entrances and exits are kept separate; keys are provided through a small opening without contact between desk clerk and guest; and photos of the rooms are displayed to make the choice easy for the customer.

Most love hotels are comfortable with foreign guests, but travellers have reported being turned away at some places. Same-sex couples may have more trouble than heterosexual couples.

COSTS

In addition to the 8% consumption tax that is levied on all accommodation in Japan, you may have to pay an additional 10% or more as a service charge at luxury hotels. Sample hotel charges:

Business hotel single ¥8000

Business hotel double ¥12,000

Luxury hotel single ¥17,000

Luxury hotel double ¥23,000

Capsule hotel ¥3800

'Love hotel' double (overnight) ¥6500

Kokumin-shukusha

Kokumin-shukusha (people' lodges) are government-supported institutions offe ing affordable accommod tion in scenic areas. Priva Japanese-style rooms ar the norm, though some

ADDRESSES IN JAPAN

In Japan, finding a place from its address can be difficult, even for locals. The problem is twofold: first, the address is usually given by an area rather than a street; and second, the numbers are not necessarily consecutive, as prior to the mid-1950s numbers were assigned by date of construction.

To find an address, the usual process is to ask directions. Have your address handy. The numerous local police boxes are there largely for this purpose. Businesses often include a small map in their advertisements or on their business cards to show their location.

Most taxis and many rental cars now have satellite navigation systems, which make finding places a breeze, as long as you can program the address or phone number into the system. You'll have to be able to read Japanese to input the address, but phone numbers should be fine.

places offer Western-style rooms. Prices average ¥5500 to ¥6500 per person per night, including two meals.

Mountain Huts

Mountain huts *(yama-goya)* are common in many of Japan's hiking and mountain-climbing areas. While you'll occasionally find free emergency shelters, most huts are privately run and charge for accommodation. These places offer bed and board (two meals) at around ¥5000 to ¥8000 per person; if you prepare your own meal, that figure drops to ¥3000 to ¥5000 per person. It's best to call ahead to reserve a spot (contact numbers are available in Japanese hiking guides and maps, and in Lonely Planet's *Hiking in Japan*), but you won't usually be turned away if you show up without a reservation.

Rider Houses

Catering mainly to touring motorcyclists, rider houses *(raidā hausu)* provide extremely basic shared accommodation from around ¥1500 per person per night. You should bring your own sleeping bag or ask to rent bedding from the owner. For bathing facilities, you will be directed to the local *sentō* (public bath).

Rider houses are most common in Hokkaidō, but you'll also find them in places such as Kyūshū and Okinawa. If you can read some Japanese, spiral-bound *Touring Mapple* maps, published by Shobunsha and available in Japan, mark almost all of the rider houses in a specific region, as well as cheap places to eat along the way. Readers of Japanese will also find the **Rider House Database** (www.tabizanmai.net/rider/index_new.html) useful.

Customs Regulations

Customs allowances:

Alcohol Up to three 760mL bottles.

Gifts/souvenirs Up to ¥200,000 in total value.

Perfume Up to 2oz.

Tobacco products Up to 100 cigars or 400 cigarettes or 500g.

You must be over the age of 20 to qualify for these allowances. Customs officers will confiscate pornographic materials in which pubic hair is visible.

There are no limits on the importation of foreign or Japanese currency. The export of foreign currency is also unlimited, but there is a ¥5 million export limit for Japanese currency.

Visit **Japan Customs** (www.customs.go.jp) for more information on Japan's customs regulations.

Discount Cards

➡ Japan is an excellent place for senior travellers, with discounts available on entry fees to many temples, museums and cinemas. To qualify for widely available senior discounts, you have to be aged over 60 or 65, depending upon the place or company. In almost all cases a passport will be sufficient proof of age.

➡ Japanese domestic airlines (JAS, JAL and ANA) offer senior discounts of about 25% on some flights. See their websites for details.

Electricity

Tokyo and eastern Japan are on 50Hz, and western Japan, including Nagoya, Kyoto and Osaka, is on 60Hz.

Embassies & Consulates

Australian Embassy (Map p72; ☎03-5232-4111; www.australia.or.jp/en; 2-1-14 Mita, Minato-ku, Tokyo)

Australian Consulate (☎06-6941-9271; www.australia.or.jp/en/consular/osaka; 16th fl, Twin 21 MID Tower, 2-1-61 Shiromi, Chūō-ku, Osaka)

Canadian Embassy (☎03-5412-6200; www.canadainternational.gc.ca/japan-japon; 7-3-38 Akasaka, Minato-ku, Tokyo)

Canadian Consulate (☎052-972-0450; www.canadainternational.gc.ca/japan-japon; Nakatō Marunouchi Bldg, 6F, 3-17-6 Marunouchi, Naka-ku, Nagoya)

French Embassy (☎03-5798-6000; www.ambafrance-jp.org; 4-11-44 Minami Azabu, Minato-ku, Tokyo)

German Embassy (☎03-5791-7700; www.japan.diplo.de; 4-5-10 Minami Azabu, Minato-ku, Tokyo)

German Consulate (☎06-6440-5070; www.japan.diplo.de; 35th fl, Umeda Sky Bldg Tower East, 1-1-88-3501 Ōyodonaka, Kita-ku, Osaka)

Irish Embassy (☎03-3263-0695; www.irishembassy.jp; Ireland House, 2-10-7 Kōji-machi, Chiyoda-ku, Tokyo)

Netherlands Embassy (☎03-5776-5400; http://japan.nlembassy.org; 3-6-3 Shibakōen, Minato-ku, Tokyo)

Netherlands Consulate (☎06-6944-7272; http://japan.nlembassy.org; 33rd fl, Twin 21 MID Tower, 2-1-61 Shiromi, Chūō-ku, Osaka)

New Zealand Embassy (☎03-3467-2271; www.nzembassy.com/japan; 20-40 Kamiyama-chō, Shibuya-ku, Tokyo)

Russian Embassy (Map p82; ☎03-3583-4445; www.rusconsul.jp; 2-1-1, Azabudai, Minato-ku, Tokyo)

South Korean Embassy (☎03-3455-2601; http://jpn-tokyo.mofa.go.kr/worldlanguage/asia/jpn-tokyo/main; 1-7-32 Minami Azabu, Minato-ku, Tokyo)

South Korean Consulate (☎092-771-0461; http://jpn-fukuoka.mofa.go.kr/worldlanguage/asia/jpn-fukuoka/main/index.jsp; 1-1-3 Jigyōhama, Chūō-ku, Fukuoka)

UK Embassy (☎03-5211-1100; www.gov.uk/government/world/organisations/british-embassy-tokyo; 1 Ichiban-chō, Chiyoda-ku, Tokyo)

UK Consulate (☎06-6120-5600; www.gov.uk/government/world/organisations/british-embassy-tokyo/office/british-consulate-general-osaka.ja; 19th fl, Epson Osaka Bldg, 3-5-1 Bakurōmachi, Chūō-ku, Osaka)

USA Embassy (米国大使館; Map p82; ☎03-3224-5000; http://japan.usembassy.gov; 1-10-5 Akasaka, Minato-ku, Tokyo; Ⓢ Ginza line to Tameike-sannō, exits 9, 12 & 13)

USA Consulate (☎06-6315-5900; http://osaka.usconsulate.gov; 2-11-5 Nishitenma, Kita-ku, Osaka)

Food

For information on eating in Japan see Eat & Drink Like a Local (p54) and Japanese Cuisine (p816).

EATING PRICE RANGES

The following price ranges refer to a standard main meal.

¥ less than ¥1000 (less than ¥2000 in Tokyo)

¥¥ ¥1000–4000 (¥2000–5000 in Tokyo)

¥¥¥ more than ¥4000 (more than ¥5000 in Tokyo)

Gay & Lesbian Travellers

With the possible exception of Thailand, Japan is Asia's most enlightened nation with regard to the sexual preferences of foreigners. Shinjuku-nichōme in Tokyo is an established scene where English is spoken and meeting men is fairly straightforward.

In rural areas, there may be one drinking establishment where gay men meet. It would, however, often be difficult to locate such places without a local friend to guide the way.

The lesbian scene is growing but is still elusive for most non-Japanese-speaking foreigners. Outside Tokyo you may find it difficult to break into the local scene unless you spend considerable time in a place or have local contacts who can show you around.

Staying in hotels is simple as most have twin rooms, but love hotels are less accessible; if you know someone Japanese and can overcome the language barrier, a stay in a love hotel may be possible, although some are not particularly foreigner friendly.

Utopia (www.utopia-asia.com) is the site most commonly frequented by English-speaking gays and lesbians.

There are no legal restraints to same-sex sexual activities of either gender. Public displays of affection are not really common, whether the couple be same-sex or heterosexual, but they are not usually a problem in cities. In the countryside, they may raise some eyebrows, but that's probably al

Health

Japan is an advanced co try with high standards hygiene and few ende diseases. There are n cial immunisations r visit and, other thar prescription medic from home, no special preparations to make. Hospitals and clinics can be found all over the archipelago, and only the smallest outer islands lack medical facilities. That said, there are some things to keep in mind.

Medical Care in Japan

While the Japanese medical system is extensive and comprehensive, the level of care can be uneven. Here are some things to note if you need to seek medical attention:

➡ It is better to seek care at university hospitals or other large hospitals, rather than clinics.

➡ Japanese doctors and hospitals are sometimes reluctant to treat foreigners. It helps to carry proof of insurance and be willing to show it. If a doctor or hospital seems reticent about giving care, you should insist on it (even though Japan has no Hippocratic oath, doctors can be told that they have to treat patients in need of care).

➡ Most hospitals and clinics have regular hours (usually in the mornings) when they will see patients.

➡ Hotels and ryokan that cater to foreigners will usually know the best hospitals in a particular area and will also know hospitals with English-speaking doctors.

➡ Most doctors speak some English. However, it helps to bring along a Japanese speaker if possible to help you explain your condition and to navigate the hospital.

[illegible]surance

[illegible]vel-insurance policy to [illegible] theft, loss and medical [illegible]ms is essential. Some [illegible] will specifically ex[illegible]ngerous activities', [illegible] include scuba [illegible]torcycling and even [illegible]you plan to engage in such activities, you'll want a policy that covers them.

You may prefer a policy that pays doctors or hospitals directly rather than having you pay on the spot and claim later. If you have to claim later, make sure you keep all documentation. Some policies ask you to call (reverse charge) a centre in your home country where an immediate assessment of your problem is made. Check that the policy covers ambulances or an emergency flight home.

Be sure to bring your insurance card or other certificate of insurance to Japan; Japanese hospitals have been known to refuse treatment to foreign patients with no proof of medical insurance.

Worldwide travel insurance is available at www.lonelyplanet.com/travel-insurance. You can buy, extend and claim online anytime – even if you're already on the road.

Internet Access

➡ You'll find internet cafes (with rates running from ¥200 to ¥700 per hour) and other access points in most major Japanese cities. As a rule, internet connections are fast and reliable.

➡ In accommodation reviews, an internet symbol indicates that the accommodation option has at least one computer with internet for guest use and/or LAN cable internet access in guest rooms. We also note where wi-fi is available.

➡ Most hotels and hostels offer free wi-fi for their guests, but some still charge for it and some places have no in-room wi-fi at all (this is particularly true of small older hotels in smaller cities and towns).

➡ Note that some hotels have in-room LAN cable internet access instead of wi-fi. The hotels usually provide LAN cables, but you may want to bring your own to avoid having to ask for one everywhere you stay. These LAN connections usually work fine, but you may occasionally find it difficult to log on due to software or hardware compatibility issues or configuration problems – the front-desk staff *may* be able to help.

Wi-fi

Wi-fi is everywhere in some form, but is often only available to subscribers of various Japanese services, many of which are not easy for travellers to join (especially those who don't speak and read Japanese). There are a number of ways to get online, though, and Japan has been trying to improve the options for travellers.

Freespot Map (www.freespot.com/users/map_e.html) Has a list of internet hot spots. It's not exhaustive and the maps are in Japanese, but it's still quite useful.

Starbucks All Starbucks stores in Japan offer free wi-fi to customers. You must register online to use the service (go to http://starbucks.wi2.co.jp).

Iijmio Japan Travel SIM cards You can buy Iijmio Japan Travel SIM cards (https://t.iijmio.jp/en) from major electronics shops in Japan. Your device must be unlocked and you must be able to input the APN settings to use these. The cards are good for three months and offer 2GB of data. The company is tied in with Brastel and you can also make (but not receive) voice calls with these. Unlike some other SIM cards, no telephone call is required to activate these cards, making them a great choice for travellers.

B-Mobile SIM cards You can buy B-Mobile Visitor SIM cards from major electronics shops in Japan. You can also order them online (www.bmobile.ne.jp/english) and have them delivered to your first night's lodgings or even to the post office at your arrival airport. These data-only cards will usually allow internet use for a specific length of time (a month is common). Note that the amount of data you can download is limited and your device must be unlocked and you must be able to input the APN settings. A call is required to activate these cards (usually, but not always, someone at the shop can make the call).

Japan Connected Download this app (www.ntt-bp.net/jcfw) and register ahead of time for free wi-fi service, courtesy of the national telecom provider NTT. Connect at a variety of spots in Tokyo (including 7-11 convenience stores and Narita/Haneda airports) and a few other places across the country (primarily in Hiroshima, Fukuoka, Osaka and Kanazawa); visit their Coverage Areas page for details.

Boingo Subscribers to Boingo's global plan (www.boingo.com) can use BB Mobilepoint wi-fi at McDonald's restaurants, some convenience stores and some restaurants.

Portable internet connections You can rent data cards, USB dongles or pocket wi-fi devices from various phone-rental companies. The most user-friendly option with English service is provided by **Rentafone Japan** (☎from overseas 81-75-212-0842, toll free within Japan 0120-746-487; www.rentafonejapan.com), which offers two types of pocket wi-fi from ¥3900 per week with unlimited use.

Free city wi-fi Several cities in Japan, including Kyoto, Osaka and Hiroshima have launched free wi-fi services in train stations, tourist areas, and sometimes other areas. Check with local tourist offices or online for details.

Legal Matters

Japanese police have extraordinary powers. They can detain a suspect for up to three days without charging them; after this time a prosecutor can decide to extend this period for another 20 days. Police can also choose whether to allow a suspect to phone their embassy or lawyer, though if you find yourself in police custody you should insist that you will not cooperate in any way until allowed to make such a call. Your embassy is the first place you should call if given the chance.

Police will speak almost no English; insist that a *tsūyakusha* (interpreter) be summoned. Police are legally bound to provide one before proceeding with any questioning. Even if you do speak Japanese, it's best to deny it and stay with your native language.

If you have a problem, call the **Japan Helpline** (☎0570-000-911; www.jhelp.com/en/jhlp.html; ⏲24hr), a nationwide emergency number that operates 24 hours a day, seven days a week.

Maps

If you'd like to buy a map of Japan before arriving, both Nelles and Periplus produce reasonable ones. If you want something more detailed, wait until you get to Tokyo or Kyoto, where you'll find lots of detailed maps in both English and Japanese.

➡ The JNTO's free *Tourist Map of Japan*, available at JNTO-operated tourist information centres inside the country and JNTO offices abroad, is a reasonable English-language map that is suitable for general route planning.

➡ The *Japan Road Atlas* (Shobunsha) is a good choice for those planning to drive around the country; unfortunately, it's out of print (you might be able to find a copy online, but it won't be cheap). Those looking for something less bulky should pick up a copy of the *Bilingual Atlas of Japan* (Kodansha). Of course, if you can read a little Japanese, you'll do much better with one of the excellent *Super Mapple* road atlases published by Shobunsha.

Money

The currency in Japan is the yen (¥). The Japanese pronounce yen as 'en', with no 'y' sound. The kanji for yen is 円.

Yen denominations:

¥1 coin; lightweight, silver colour

¥5 coin; bronze colour, hole in the middle, value in Chinese character only

¥10 coin; copper colour

¥50 coin; silver colour, hole in the middle

¥100 coin; silver colour

¥500 coin; large, silver colour

¥1000 banknote

¥2000 banknote (rare)

¥5000 banknote

¥10,000 banknote

ATMs

Automated teller machines are almost as common as vending machines in Japan.

WARNING: JAPAN IS A CASH SOCIETY

Be warned that cold hard yen is the way to pay in Japan. While credit cards are becoming more common, cash is still much more widely used, and travellers cheques are rarely accepted. Never assume that you can pay for things with a credit card; always carry sufficient cash. The only places where you can count on paying by credit card are department stores, large hotels and at major JR ticket offices.

For those without credit cards, it would be a good idea to bring some travellers cheques as a back-up. As in most other countries, the US dollar is still the currency of choice in terms of exchanging cash and cashing travellers cheques.

Unfortunately, most of these do not accept foreign-issued cards. Even if they display Visa and MasterCard logos, most accept only Japan-issued versions of these cards.

Fortunately, Japanese postal ATMs accept cards that belong to the following international networks: Visa, Plus, MasterCard, Maestro, Cirrus, American Express, Diners Club, Discover and China Unionpay cards. You'll find postal ATMs in almost all post offices, and you'll find post offices in even the smallest Japanese villages.

Note that postal ATMs work only with bank or cash cards – you cannot use credit cards, even with a pin number. That is to say, you cannot use postal ATMs to perform a cash advance.

Most postal ATMs are open 9am to 5pm Monday to Friday, 9am to noon on Saturday, and are closed on Sunday and holidays. Some postal ATMs in very large central post offices are open longer hours; the central post offices in major cities are open *almost* 24 hours a day. Postal ATMs are relatively easy to use and have an English Guide button.

In addition, 7-Eleven convenience stores across Japan have linked their ATMs to international cash networks, and these often seem to accept cards that for one reason or other will not work with postal ATMs. These *are* open 24 hours. So, if you can't find an open post office or your card won't work with postal ATMs, don't give up: ask around for a 7-Eleven (pronounced like 'sebun erebun' in Japanese).

International cards also work in the ATMs at **Citibank Japan** (www.citibank.co.jp/en/banking/branch_atm). If you find that your card doesn't work in a postal or 7-Eleven ATM, this is a good last-ditch bet.

Credit Cards

Cash and carry is still very much the rule in Japan. If you do decide to bring a credit card, you'll find Visa the most useful, followed by MasterCard, Amex and Diners Club. Note also that Visa cards can be used for cash advances at Sumitomo Mitsui banks in Japan, but you might have to go to a specific branch to do this.

International Transfers

To make an international transfer you'll have to find a Japanese bank associated with the bank transferring the money. Start by asking at the central branch of any major Japanese bank. If it doesn't have a relationship with your bank, it can usually refer you to a bank that does. Once you find a related bank, you'll have to give your home bank the exact details of where to send the money: the bank, branch and location, and the bank's SWIFT code. A credit-card cash advance is a worthwhile alternative.

Moneychangers

You can change cash or travellers cheques at most banks, major post offices, discount ticket shops, some travel agencies, some large hotels and most big department stores. Note that discount-ticket shops (known as *kakuyasu kippu uriba* in Japanese) often have the best rates. These can be found around major train stations. However, only US dollars and euros fetch decent exchange rates.

CURRENCY WARNING

Exchange rates for the US dollar and euro are reasonable in Japan. All other currencies, including the Australian dollar and the currencies of nearby countries, fetch very poor exchange rates. If you want to bring cash to Japan, we suggest US dollars or euros. Or, if you must change other currencies into yen, we suggest doing so in your home country.

Tipping

There is little tipping in Japan. If you want to show your gratitude to someone, give them a gift rather than a tip. If you do choose to give someone a cash gift (your maid at a ryokan, for instance), place the money in an envelope first.

Opening Hours

Business hours in Japan are fairly standard. Almost all museums, many other sights and many businesses close over the New Year period (30 or 31 December to 3 or 4 January). Also, most museums in Japan are closed on Monday. Note that when a place is normally closed on a Monday, it will usually open on any national holiday Monday (in which case it will most likely be closed on the following Tuesday). Typical business hours:

Banks 9am to 3pm weekdays.

Bars 6pm to midnight or later, closed one day a week.

Department stores 10am to 7pm, closed one or two days a month. Often open for all or part of the New Year's holidays.

Museums 9am or 10am to 5pm, Tuesday to Sunday.

Offices 9am to 5pm or 6pm Monday to Friday.

Post offices Local 9am to 5pm Monday to Friday; Central 9am to 7pm Monday to Friday and 9am to 3pm Saturday (larger city post offices may have an after-hours window open 24/7).

Restaurants 11am to 2pm and 6pm to 11pm, closed one day a week.

Smaller shops 9am to 5pm, may be closed Sunday.

Post

➡ The Japanese postal system is extremely reliable, efficient and, for regular postcards and airmail letters, not markedly more expensive than in other developed countries.

➡ The airmail rate for postcards is ¥70 to any overseas destination; aerograms cost ¥90. Letters weighing less than 25g are ¥90 to other countries within Asia, ¥110 to North America, Europe or Oceania (including Australia and New Zealand), and ¥130 to Africa and South America.

➡ You will be charged extra if your writing runs over onto the address side (the right side) of a postcard.

➡ The symbol for post offices is a red T with a bar across the top on a white background (〒).

➡ Mail can be sent to, from or within Japan when addressed in English (Roman script).

GOVERNMENT TRAVEL ADVICE

The following government websites offer travel advisories and information on current hot spots.

Australian Department of Foreign Affairs (www.smarttraveller.gov.au)

British Foreign Office (www.gov.uk/foreign-travel-advice)

US State Department (http://travel.state.gov/content/passports/english/country.html)

Public Holidays

Japan has 16 national holidays. When a public holiday falls on a Sunday, the following Monday is taken as a holiday. If that Monday is already a holiday, the following day becomes a holiday as well. And if two weekdays (say, Tuesday and Thursday) are holidays, the day in between also becomes a holiday.

Ganjitsu (New Year's Day) 1 January

Seijin-no-hi (Coming-of-Age Day) Second Monday in January

Kenkoku Kinem-bi (National Foundation Day) 11 February

Shumbun-no-hi (spring equinox) 20 or 21 March

Shōwa-no-hi (Shōwa Emperor's Day) 29 April

Kempō Kinem-bi (Constitution Day) 3 May

Midori-no-hi (Green Day) 4 May

Kodomo-no-hi (Children's Day) 5 May

Umi-no-hi (Marine Day) Third Monday in July

Yama-no-hi (Mountain Day) 11 August (starting 2016)

Keirō-no-hi (Respect-for-the-Aged Day) Third Monday in September

Shūbun-no-hi (autumn equinox) 22 or 23 September

Taiiku-no-hi (Health-Sports Day) Second Monday in October

Bunka-no-hi (Culture Day) 3 November

Kinrō Kansha-no-hi (Labour Thanksgiving Day) 23 November

Tennō Tanjōbi (Emperor's Birthday) 23 December

You will find transport crowded and accommodation bookings hard to come by during the following high-season travel periods:

Shōgatsu (New Year) 31 December to 3 January

Golden Week 29 April to 5 May

O-Bon mid-August

Safe Travel

Japan has its share of natural disasters, including earthquakes, tsunami, volcanic eruptions, typhoons and landslides. Fortunately, there are robust public warning systems and evacuation procedures in place, should one of these things occur. Your lodgings will be a good source of information in the event of an emergency.

The Great East Japan Earthquake of March 2011 and the resulting tsunami caused a huge amount of destruction in northeast Japan. While most of the tsunami damage has been cleaned up and the local infrastructure largely restored, an exclusion zone with a radius of 20km is in effect around the Fukushima Dai-Ichi nuclear power plant, which was damaged by the tsunami. The plant is in Fukushima Prefecture in northeast Honshū.

Telephone

Japanese telephone numbers consist of an area code plus the number. You do not dial the area code when making a call in that area. When dialling Japan from abroad, dial the country code ☎81, followed by the area code (drop the '0') and the number. The most common toll-free prefixes are ☎0120, 0070, 0077, 0088 and 0800. Directory-assistance numbers:

Local directory assistance ☎104 (¥60 to ¥150 per call)

Local directory assistance in English ☎0120-36-4463 (9am to 5pm Monday to Friday)

International directory assistance ☎0057

Local Calls

The Japanese public-telephone system is reliable and efficient. Unfortunately the number of pay phones decreasing fast as more a more Japanese buy mob phones. Local calls from phones cost ¥10 per minute; unused ¥10 coins are returned after the call is completed but no change is given on ¥100 coins.

In general it's much easier to buy a telephone card *(terefon kādo)* when you arrive rather than worry about always having coins on hand. Phone cards are sold in ¥500 and ¥1000 denominations (the latter earns you an extra ¥50 in calls) and can be used in most green or grey pay phones. Cards are available from vending machines (some of which can be found in public phone booths) and convenience stores. They come in myriad designs and are also a collectable item.

Mobile Phones

Japan's mobile-phone networks use 3G (third generation) mobile-phone technology on a variety of frequencies. Thus, non-3G mobile phones cannot be used in Japan and most foreign mobile phones will not work in Japan. Furthermore, SIM cards are not commonly available in Japan. For most people who want to use a mobile phone while in Japan, the only solution is to rent one.

Several telecommunications companies in Japan specialise in short-term mobile-phone rentals, including **Rentafone Japan** (☎from overseas 81-75-212-0842, toll free within Japan 0120-746-487; www.rentafonejapan.com), which offers rentals starting at ¥3900 per week (domestic rates from ¥35 per minute and overseas calls from ¥45 per minute).

Prepaid International Phone Cards

Because of the lack of pay phones from which you can make international phone calls in Japan, the easiest way to make a call is to buy a prepaid international phone card. Most convenience stores carry at least one of the following types of phone cards: KDDI Superworld Card; NTT Communications World Card; or SoftBank Telecom Comica Card. These cards can be used with any regular pay phone in Japan.

Useful International Numbers

For international operator-assisted calls dial ☎0051 (KDDI; operators speak English).

There's very little difference in the rates of direct-dial international numbers. Dial one of the numbers, then the international country code, the local code and the number.

- KDDI ☎001-010
- NTT ☎0033-010
- SoftBank Telecom ☎0041-010

Time

All of Japan is in the same time zone: nine hours ahead of Greenwich Mean Time (GMT). Sydney and Wellington are ahead of Japan (by one and three hours respectively), and most of the world's other big cities are behind: (New York by 14 hours, Los Angeles by 17 and London by nine). Japan does not have daylight-savings (summer) time.

Toilets

- You will come across both Western-style toilets and Asian squat toilets in Japan. When you have to squat, the correct position is facing the hood, away from the door.
- Public toilets are free. The *katakana* for 'toilet' is トイレ, and the kanji is お手洗い. You'll often also see the kanji signs for female (女) and male (男).
- Toilet paper isn't always provided, so carry tissues with you. You may also be given small packets of tissues on the street – a common form of advertising.
- In many bathrooms, separate toilet slippers are provided – usually located just inside the toilet door. These are for use in the toilet only, so remember to change out of them when you leave.
- It's quite common to see men urinating in public – the unspoken rule is that it's acceptable at night time if you happen to be drunk.

Tourist Information

You will find tourist information offices (*kankō*

PRACTICALITIES

Newspapers & Magazines There are three main English-language daily newspapers in Japan: the *Japan Times*, *Daily Yomiuri* and *Asahi Shimbun/International Herald Tribune*. In the bigger cities, these are available at bookstores, convenience stores, train-station kiosks and some hotels. In the countryside, you may not be able to find them anywhere. Foreign magazines are available in major bookshops in the bigger cities.

Radio Recent years have seen an increase in the number of stations aimed specifically at Japan's foreign population. InterFM (76.1FM; www.interfm.co.jp) is a favourite of Tokyo's expat community, and the Kansai equivalent is FM Cocolo (76.5FM; www.cocolo.jp).

TV & DVDs Japan uses the NTSC system.

Weights & Measures Japan uses the international metric system.

annai-sho; 観光案内所) in most cities and towns and even in some small villages. They are almost always located inside or in front of the main train station. Staff members may speak some English, but don't count on it. English-language materials are usually available. Naturally, places that get a lot of foreign visitors are more likely to have English-speaking staff and English-language materials. Nonetheless, with a little patience and a smile you will usually be able to get the information you need from even the smallest local tourist information office.

The **Japan National Tourism Organization** (www.jnto.go.jp) is Japan's main English-language information service for foreign travellers. JNTO produces a great deal of useful literature, which is available from its overseas offices as well as its Tourist Information Center in Tokyo. Most of its publications are available in English and, in some cases, other European and Asian languages. The organisation's website is a very useful tool when planning your journey to Japan.

JNTO has overseas offices in Australia, Canada, France, Germany, the UK and the USA (see the JNTO website for locations and contact details).

Travellers with Disabilities

Japan gets mixed marks in terms of ease of travel for those with disabilities. On the plus side, many new buildings have access ramps, traffic lights have speakers playing melodies when it is safe to cross, train platforms have raised dots and lines to provide guidance for the visually impaired, and some ticket machines in Tokyo have Braille. Some attractions also offer free entry for disabled persons and one companion. On the negative side, many of Japan's cities are still rather difficult for disabled persons to negotiate, often due to the relative lack of normal sidewalks on narrow streets.

Train cars on most lines have areas set aside for people in wheelchairs. Those with other physical disabilities can use the seats near the train exits, called *yūsen-zaseki*. You will also find these seats near the front of buses; usually they're a different colour from the regular seats.

The **Accessible Japan** (www.tesco-premium.co.jp/aj/index.htm) website is not updated regularly, but details the accessibility of hundreds of sites in Tokyo, including hotels, sights and department stores, as well as offering general information about getting around Japan. For good bilingual information on accommodation, activities, sights, shops etc, click the 'Accessible Tokyo' link on the **Japanese Red Cross Language Service Volunteers** (www.tok-lanserv.jp/eng) website.

Visas

Generally, visitors who are not planning to engage in income-producing activities while in Japan are exempt from obtaining visas and will be issued a 90-day *tanki-taizai* (temporary-visitor) visa on arrival. Nationals of Australia, Canada, France, Ireland, Italy, the Netherlands, New Zealand, Spain, the UK and the USA are eligible for this visa.

Stays of up to six months are permitted for citizens of Austria, Germany, Ireland, Mexico, Switzerland and the UK. Citizens of these countries will almost always be given a 90-day temporary-visitor visa upon arrival, which can usually be extended for another 90 days at immigration bureaux inside Japan.

Japanese law requires that visitors entering on a temporary-visitor visa possess an ongoing air or sea ticket or evidence thereof. In practice, few travellers are asked to produce such documents, but it pays to be on the safe side.

For additional information on visas and regulations, contact your nearest Japanese embassy or consulate, or visit the website of the **Ministry of Foreign Affairs of Japan** (www.mofa.go.jp). Here you can find out about the different types of visas available, read about working-holiday visas and find details on the Japan Exchange & Teaching (JET) program, which sponsors native English speakers to teach in the Japanese public school system.

On entering Japan, all short-term foreign visitors are photographed and fingerprinted.

Resident Card

Anyone who will stay in Japan longer than 90 days, which usually means those entering on various mid- to long-term visas rather than tourist visas, will be issued with a 'resident card' (在留カード). These cards replace the old *gaikokujin torokusho* cards (commonly known as '*gaijin* cards'). If you're entering Japan on a visa that allows you to stay for longer than 90 days, you'll be issued one of these at the airport.

You must carry your card at all times as the police can stop you and ask to see it. If you don't have it, you may be taken back to the police station and will have to wait there until someone fetches the card for you.

Visa Extensions

With the exception of those nationals whose countries have reciprocal visa exemptions and can stay for six months, the limit for most nationalities is 90 days. To extend a temporary-visitor visa beyond the standard 90 days, apply at the nearest immigration office. **The Japanese Immigration Bureau** (www.immi-moj.go.jp/english/soshiki/index.html)

website lists the offices in Japan. You must provide two copies of an Application for Extension of Stay (available at the immigration office), a letter stating the reasons for the extension, supporting documentation and your passport. There is a processing fee of ¥4000.

Work Visas

Unless you are on a cultural visa and have been granted permission to work, or hold a working-holiday visa, you are not permitted to work without a proper work visa. If you have the proper paperwork and an employer willing to sponsor you, the process is straightforward, although it can be time consuming.

Once you find an employer willing to sponsor you, it is necessary to obtain a Certificate of Eligibility from the nearest immigration office. The same office can then issue you your work visa, which is valid for one or three years. The whole procedure usually takes two to three months.

Working-Holiday Visas

Citizens of Australia, Canada, Denmark, France, Germany, Hong Kong, Ireland, New Zealand, the Republic of Korea and the UK who are aged between 18 and 25 (the limit can be pushed up to 30 in some cases) can apply for a working-holiday visa. The program is also open to residents of Hong Kong and Taiwan.

This visa allows a six-month stay and two six-month extensions. It is designed to enable young people to travel during their visit; although employment is supposed to be part-time or temporary, in practice many people work full time.

A working-holiday visa is much easier to obtain than a work visa and is popular with Japanese employers. Single applicants must have the equivalent of US$2000 of funds, a married couple must have US$3000, and all applicants must have an onward ticket from Japan. For details, enquire at your closest Japanese embassy or consulate.

Volunteering

Japan doesn't have as many volunteer opportunities as some other Asian countries. However, there are positions out there for those who look. One of the most popular options is provided by **Worldwide Opportunities on Organic Farms Japan** (www.wwoofjapan.com). This organisation places volunteers on organic farms and provides participants with a good look at Japanese rural life and the running of an organic farm. It's also a great chance to improve your Japanese-language skills.

Alternatively, you can look for volunteer opportunities once you arrive. There are occasional ads for volunteer positions in the various English-language journals in Japan. Word of mouth is also a good way to search. Hikers, for example, are sometimes offered short-term positions in Japan's mountain huts.

Women Travellers

Japan is a relatively safe country for women travellers, though perhaps not quite as safe as some might think. Crimes against women are generally believed to be widely under-reported, especially by Japanese women. Foreign women are occasionally subjected to some forms of verbal harassment or prying questions. Physical attacks are very rare, but have occurred.

The best advice is to avoid being lulled into a false sense of security by Japan's image as one of the world's safest countries and to take the normal precautions you would in your home country. If a neighbourhood or establishment looks unsafe, then treat it that way. As long as you use your common sense, you will most likely find that Japan is a pleasant and rewarding place to travel as a woman.

Several train companies have recently introduced women-only cars to protect female passengers from *chikan* (men who grope women and girls on packed trains). These cars are usually available during rush-hour periods on weekdays on busy urban lines. There are signs (usually in pink) on the platform indicating where you can board these cars, and the cars themselves are usually labelled in both Japanese and English (again, often in pink).

If you have a problem and you find the local police unhelpful, you can call the **Japan Helpline** (☎0570-000-911; www.jhelp.com/en/jhlp.html; ⏲24hr), a nationwide emergency number that operates 24 hours a day, seven days a week.

Finally, an excellent resource for any woman setting up in Japan is Caroline Pover's *Being A Broad in Japan*.

Work

Japan is an interesting place to live and work for a year or two and you'll find expats in all the major cities doing just that. Teaching English is still the most common job for Westerners, but bartending, hostessing, modelling and various writing-editorial jobs are also possible. It is illegal for non-Japanese to work in Japan without a proper visa.

The key to success is doing your homework and presenting yourself properly. You will definitely need a sharp outfit for interviews, a stack of *meishi* (business cards) and the right attitude. If you don't have a university degree, you won't be eligible for most jobs that qualify you for a work visa. Any qualification, such as an English-teaching certificate, will be a huge boost.

Outside of the entertainment, construction and English-teaching industries, you can't expect a good job unless you speak fluent Japanese.

Transport

GETTING THERE & AWAY

While most travellers fly to Japan via Tokyo, there are several other ways of getting into and out of the country. For a start, there are many other airports, which can make better entry points than Tokyo's somewhat inconvenient Narita International Airport. It's also possible to arrive by sea from South Korea, China and Russia.

Flights, tours and rail tickets can be booked online at lonelyplanet.com/bookings.

Entering the Country

For most travellers, entering Japan is simple and straightforward. Visas (p865) are given on arrival for many nationalities. Foreigners are now fingerprinted and photographed on arrival.

Air

There are flights to Japan from all over the world, usually to Tokyo, but also to a number of other airports. Although Tokyo may seem the obvious arrival and departure point, for many visitors this may not be the case. For example, if you plan to explore western Japan or the Kansai region, it might be more convenient to fly into Kansai International Airport near Osaka.

Airports & Airlines

There are international airports situated on the main island of Honshū (Nagoya, Niigata, Osaka/Kansai, Haneda and Tokyo Narita), as well as on Kyūshū (Fukuoka, Kagoshima, Kumamoto and Nagasaki), Okinawa (Naha) and Hokkaidō (Sapporo).

Two major international carriers with extensive domestic networks in Japan are **Japan Airlines** (☎03-5460-0522, 0570-025-121; www.jal.co.jp/en) and **All Nippon Airways** (☎0570-029-709, in Osaka 06-7637-6679, in Tokyo 03-6741-1120; www.ana.co.jp).

Tokyo The majority of international flights to/from Tokyo use Narita International Airport (www.narita-airport.jp), about an hour from Tokyo by express train, but some international flights now go via Tokyo International Airport (www.tokyo-airport-bldg.co.jp), better known as Haneda Airport, about 30 minutes from Tokyo by monorail.

Osaka Most of Osaka's international flights go via Kansai International Airport (www.kansai-airport.or.jp), which serves the key Kansai cities of Kyoto, Osaka, Nara and Kōbe.

Nagoya Central Japan International Airport (www.centrair.jp) has international connections with several countries.

Fukuoka At the northern end of Kyūshū, Fukuoka is the main arrival point for western Japan. Fukuoka International Airport

CLIMATE CHANGE & TRAVEL

Every form of transport that relies on carbon-based fuel generates CO_2, the main cause of human-induced climate change. Modern travel is dependent on aeroplanes, which might use less fuel per kilometre per person than most cars but travel much greater distances. The altitude at which aircraft emit gases (including CO_2) and particles also contributes to their climate change impact. Many websites offer 'carbon calculators' that allow people to estimate the carbon emissions generated by their journey and, fc those who wish to do so, to offset the impact of the greenhouse gases emitted with c tributions to portfolios of climate-friendly initiatives throughout the world. Lonely P offsets the carbon footprint of all staff and author travel.

(www.fuk-ab.co.jp), conveniently located near the city, has connections with several countries, mostly in Asia.

Kagoshima On Kyūshū, Kagoshima Airport (www.koj-ab.co.jp) has flights to/from Hong Kong, Shanghai, Seoul and Taipei.

Naha Located on Okinawa-hontō (the main island of Okinawa), Naha Airport (www.naha-airport.co.jp) has flights to/from Beijing, Hong Kong, Pusan, Seoul, Shanghai, Taichung and Taipei.

Niigata Central Honshū's Niigata Airport (www.niigata-airport.gr.jp) has flights to/from Guam, Harbin, Khabarovsk, Seoul, Shanghai, Taipei and Vladivostok.

Kumamoto Kyūshū's Kumamoto Airport (www.kmj-ab.co.jp) has flights to/from Seoul and Kaohsiung.

Nagasaki Flights to/from Shanghai and Seoul are through Nagasaki Airport (www.nabic.co.jp).

Sapporo On Hokkaidō, New Chitose Airport (www.new-chitose-airport.jp) has connections with several countries, mostly in Asia.

Sea

China

Japan China International Ferry Company (☎in China 021-63257642, in Japan 06-6536-6541; www.shinganjin.com) Shanghai–Osaka/Kōbe, 2nd class ¥20,000, 48 hours, departs Osaka on Tuesday.

Orient Ferry Ltd (☎in China 0532-8387-1160, in Japan 083-232-6615; www.orientferry.co.jp) Qingdao–Shimonoseki, ¥15,000, 28 hours, departs Shimonoseki on Wednesday and Saturday.

Shanghai Ferry Company (上海フェリー; www.shanghai-ferry.co.jp) Shanghai–Osaka/Kōbe, 2nd class ¥20,000, 48 hours, departs Osaka on Friday.

Russia

Heartland Ferry (☎in Japan 011-233-8010, in Russia 7-4242-72-6889; www.heartlandferry.jp) Korsakov (Sakhalin Island, Russia)–Wakkanai (Hokkaidō), ¥25,000/40,000 one way/return, 7½ hours, June to September.

South Korea

South Korea is the closest country to Japan and there are several ferry connections between them.

Panstar Ferry Line (www.panstar.jp) Busan–Osaka/Kōbe, 2nd class ¥13,000, 19 hours, departs Osaka three times a week.

Beetle (☎in Japan 092-281-2315, in Korea 051-441-8200; www.jrbeetle.co.jp/internet/english/index.html) Busan–Fukuoka, ¥13,000, three hours, at least three daily.

Camellia Line (☎in Japan 092-262-2323, in Korea 051-466-7799; www.camellia-line.co.jp) Busan–Fukuoka, from ¥9000, six hours from Fukuoka to Busan, six to 10 hours from Busan to Fukuoka, daily.

Kampu Ferry (☎in Japan 083-224-3000, in Korea 82-2-730-2137, in Korea 463-3165(-8); www.kampuferry.co.jp) Busan–Shimonoseki, from ¥9000 (plus ¥1200 fuel surcharge and ¥610 terminal fee), 12 hours, daily.

GETTING AROUND

Japan has one of the best public-transport systems in the world, which makes getting around the country an absolute breeze.

Air

Air services in Japan are extensive, reliable and safe. In many cases, flying is much faster than even *shinkansen* (bullet trains) and not that much more expensive. Flying is also an efficient way to travel from the main islands to the many small islands, particularly the Southwest Islands (the southern islands of Kagoshima and Okinawa Prefectures).

In most of Japan's major cities there are travel agencies where English is spoken. For an idea of the latest prices in Tokyo check the travel ads in the various local English-language publications, and in Kansai, check *Kansai Scene*.

Airlines in Japan

Japan Airlines (☎03-5460-0522, 0570-025-121; www.jal.co.jp/en) A major international carrier with an extensive domestic network.

All Nippon Airways (☎0570-029-709, in Osaka 06-7637-6679, in Tokyo 03-6741-1120; www.ana.co.jp) A major Japanese domestic and international carrier.

BAGGAGE FORWARDING

If you have too much luggage to carry comfortably or just can't be bothered, you can do what many Japanese travellers do: send it to your next stop by *takkyūbin* (express-shipping companies). Prices are surprisingly reasonable and overnight service is the norm. Perhaps the most convenient service is Yamato Takkyūbin, which operates from most convenience stores. Simply pack our luggage and take it to the nearest convenience ore; staff will help with the paperwork and arrange for k-up. Note that you'll need the full address of your destination in Japanese, along with the phone ber of the place. Alternatively, ask the owner of your modation to come and pick it up (this is usually e, but might cost extra).

Japan Trans Ocean Air (☎03-5460-0522, 0570-025-071; www.jal.co.jp/jta) A smaller domestic carrier that mostly services routes in the Southwest Islands. Website in Japanese only.

Shinchūō Kōkū (New Central Air Service; ☎0422-31-4191; www.central-air.co.jp) Has light-plane flights between Chōfu Airport, outside Tokyo, and the islands of the Izu Archipelago. Website in Japanese only.

SAT Airlines (UTS; エアーサービス株式会社; ☎011-222-1433; www.uts-air.com) Has flights between Sakhalin (Russia) and Hokkaidō. Website in Japanese only.

Discount Tickets & Air Passes

➡ For domestic flights, return fares are usually around 10% cheaper than buying two one-way tickets. You can also get advance-purchase reductions: both All Nippon Airways (ANA) and Japan Airlines (JAL) offer discounts of up to 50% if you purchase your ticket a month or more in advance, with smaller discounts for purchases made one to three weeks in advance.

➡ Seniors over 65 also qualify for discounts on most Japanese airlines, but these are sometimes only available if you fly on weekdays.

➡ ANA also offers the Star Alliance Japan Airpass for foreign travellers on ANA or Star Alliance network airlines. Provided you reside outside Japan, purchase your tickets outside Japan, and carry a valid international ticket on any airline, you can fly up to five times within 60 days on any ANA domestic route for only ¥10,000 per flight (a huge saving on some routes). Visit www.ana.co.jp/wws/th/e/wws_common/fare/special/airpass.html for more information.

BUDGET AIRLINES IN JAPAN

Japan has opened up its skies to low-cost carriers and the result is a proliferation of budget airlines flying to various parts of the archipelago. This has brought previous expensive and distant destinations like Hokkaidō and Okinawa within the reach of even budget travellers. Keep in mind that budget airlines often come and go, so we cannot guarantee that all of these will be flying when you're in country, but we definitely recommend checking their fares online when making travel plans – you might save a bundle.

Jetstar (www.jetstar.com)

Peach (www.flypeach.com)

Skymark Airlines (www.skymark.co.jp)

Bicycle

Japan is a good country for bicycle touring, and several thousand cyclists, both Japanese and foreign, traverse the country every year. Favourite bike-touring areas include Kyūshū, Shikoku, the Japan Alps (if you like steep hills!), the Noto Peninsula and Hokkaidō.

There's no point in fighting your way out of big cities by bicycle. Put your bike on the train or bus and get out to the country before you start pedalling. To take a bicycle on a train you may need to use a bicycle-carrying bag, available from good bicycle shops.

A useful series of maps is *Touring Mapple* (Shōbunsha), which is aimed at motorcyclists, but is also very useful for cyclists.

For more info on cycling in Japan, check out the excellent website of **KANcycling** (www.kancycling.com).

Hire

You will find bicycle-rental shops outside the train or bus stations in most of Japan's popular tourist areas, as well as near the ferry piers on many of the country's smaller islands. Typical charges are around ¥200/1000 per hour/day. Kyoto, for example, is ideally suited to bicycle exploration and there are plenty of cheap hire shops to choose from.

Note that the bicycles for rent are not usually performance vehicles. More commonly they're what the Japanese call *mama chari* (literally 'mama's bicycles'): one- or three-speed shopping bikes that are murder on hills of any size. They're also usually too small for anyone more than 180cm in height.

Many youth hostels also have bicycles to rent.

Purchase

In Japan, prices for used bicycles range from a few thousand yen for an old shopping bike to several tens of thousands of yen for good mountain and road bikes. New bikes range from about ¥10,000 for a shopping bike to ¥100,000 for a flash mountain or road bike.

Touring bikes are available in Japan, but prices tend to be significantly higher than you'd pay back home. If you're tall, you may not find any suitably sized bikes in stock. One solution for tall riders, or anyone who wants to save money, is to buy a used bike – in Tokyo, check the English-language publications; in Kyoto, visit the Kyoto International Co[illegible]munity House and check t[illegible] message board.

Boat

Japan is an island nation and there are many ferry services between islands and between ports on the same island. Ferries can be an excellent way of getting from one place to another and for seeing parts of Japan you might otherwise miss. Taking a ferry between Osaka (Honshū) and Beppu (Kyūshū), for example, is a good way of getting to Kyūshū and – if you choose the right departure time – seeing some of the Inland Sea on the way.

On overnight ferries, 2nd-class travel means sleeping in tatami-mat rooms where you simply unroll your futon on the floor and hope that your fellow passengers aren't too intent on knocking back the booze all night. In this basic class, fares are usually lower than equivalent land travel, but there are also more-expensive private cabins. Bicycles can be brought along and most ferries also carry motorcycles and cars.

Information on ferry routes, schedules and fares is found in the *JR Jikokuhyō* and on information sheets from the **Japan National Tourism Organization** (JNTO; www.jnto.go.jp).

FERRY FARES & DURATIONS

ROUTE	FARE (¥)	DURATION (HR)
Hokkaidō–Honshū		
Otaru–Maizuru	9570–16,350	21½
Otaru–Niigata	6480–12,860	19½
Tomakomai–Hachinohe	5000–7500	7-9
Tomakomai–Ōarai	8740–18,000	19
From Tokyo		
Shinmoji (Kitakyūshū)	16,120–18,220	35
Tokushima (Shikoku)	10,640–12,740	18-19½
From Osaka/Kōbe		
Beppu (Kyūshū)	11,320–14,820	12
Miyazaki (Kyūshū)	11,920–15,220	14
Naha (Okinawa)	21,790–27,960	38
hibushi (Kyūshū)	13,790–17,500	15
inmoji (Kitakyūshū)	6880–10,180	12½
shū–Okinawa		
shima–Naha	15,870–22,040	25

Bus

Japan has a comprehensive network of long-distance buses. These 'highway buses' are nowhere near as fast as the *shinkansen*, but the fares are comparable with those of normal *futsū* (local) trains. For example, the trip between Tokyo and Kyoto takes just over 2½ hours by *shinkansen* and about eight hours by bus. Of course, there are many places in Japan where trains do not run and bus travel is the only public-transport option.

Bookings can be made through any travel agency in Japan or at the *midori-no-madoguchi* (green counters – look for the counter with the green band across the glass) in large Japan Rail (JR) stations. The Japan Rail Pass is valid on some highway buses, but in most cases the *shinkansen* would be far preferable (it's much faster and more comfortable).

Night Services

Night buses are a good option for those on a tight budget without a Japan Rail Pass. They are relatively cheap, spacious (allowing room to stretch out and get some sleep) and they also save on a night's accommodation. They typically leave at around 10pm or 11pm and arrive the following day at around 6am or 7am.

Car & Motorcycle

Driving in Japan is quite feasible, even for just the mildly adventurous. The major roads are signposted in English; road rules are generally adhered to and driving is safer than in a lot of other Asian countries; and petrol, while expensive, is not prohibitively so. Indeed, in some areas of the country it can prove much more convenient than other forms of travel and, between a group of people, it can also prove quite economical.

In some parts of Japan (most notably Hokkaidō, the Noto Peninsula, some parts of Kyūshū and the Southwest Islands), driving is really the only efficient way to get around unless you have a good touring bicycle or fancy long waits for buses each time you need to make a move.

Crash helmets are compulsory for motorcyclists in Japan.

Automobile Associations

If you're a member of an automobile association in your home country, you're eligible for reciprocal rights with the **Japan Automobile Federation** (JAF; ☎0570-00-2811, 03-6833-9000; www.jaf.or.jp; 2-2-17 Shiba, Minato-ku, Tokyo 105-0014). Its office is near Onarimon Station on the Tōei Mita line.

BARGAIN BUSES

Japan Railways (JR) operates the largest network of highway buses in Japan, and we quote its prices for most long-distance bus routes. However, several budget bus companies have recently sprung up in Japan and these are gaining popularity with backpackers. One such company is **Willer Express** (from outside Japan 050-5805-0383; http://willerexpress.com), which offers fares significantly cheaper than those of JR. It also offers three-/four-/five-day bus passes that are great value. Booking is possible in English online. Check the website for the latest details and pick-up/drop-off points.

Another good deal is offered by a group of bus companies on Kyūshū, which have banded together to offer the **SUNQ Pass** (www.sunqpass.jp; 3-/4-day ¥10,000/14,000, 3-day northern Kyūshū only ¥8000), which offers unlimited travel. Kyūshū buses reach many places trains don't.

Driving Licences

Travellers from most nations are able to drive (both cars and motorcycles) in Japan with an International Driving Permit backed up by their own regular licence. The International Driving Permit is issued by your national automobile association. Make sure it is endorsed for cars and motorcycles if you're licensed for both.

Travellers from Switzerland, France and Germany (and others whose countries are not signatories to the Geneva Convention of 1949 concerning international driving licences) are not allowed to drive in Japan on a regular International Driving Permit. Rather, travellers from these countries must have their own licence backed by an authorised translation of the same licence. These translations can be made by their embassy or consulate in Japan or by the JAF. If you are unsure which category your country falls into, contact the nearest JNTO office for more information.

Foreign licences and International Driving Permits are only valid in Japan for six months. If you are staying longer, you will have to get a Japanese licence from the local department of motor vehicles.

Expressways

The expressway system is fast, efficient and growing all the time. Tolls cost about ¥24.6 per kilometre. Tokyo to Kyoto, for example, will cost ¥10,050 in tolls.

There are good rest stops and service centres at regular intervals. A prepaid highway card, available from tollbooths or at the service areas, saves you having to carry so much cash and gives you a 4% to 8% discount in the larger card denominations. You can also pay tolls with most major credit cards. Exits are usually fairly well signposted in English, but make sure you know the name of your exit as it may not necessarily be the same as the city you're heading towards.

Fuel

You'll find *gasoreen sutando* (petrol stations) in almost every town and in service stations along the expressways. The cost of petrol per litre ranged from ¥135 to ¥144 for regular and ¥146 to ¥155 for high octane at the time of writing.

Hire

➡ You'll usually find car-rental agencies clustered around train stations and ferry piers. Typical rates for a small car are ¥5000 to ¥7000 per day, with reductions for rentals of more than one day. On top of the rental charge, there's about a ¥1000-per-day insurance cost.

➡ Communication can sometimes be a major problem when hiring a car. Some of the offices will have a rent-a-car phrasebook, with questions you might need to ask in English.

BUS FARES & DURATIONS

Some typical long-distance one-way fares and travel times out of Tokyo include the following (note that the cheapest fares on each route are shown).

DESTINATION	FARE (¥)	DURATION (HR)
Aomori	7500	9½
Hakata	8300	14½
Hiroshima	11,900	11½
Kōbe	5000	10
Kyoto	5000	8
Nagano	3200	4
Nagoya	5250	5½
Nara	5000	8½
Osaka	5000	8½

Otherwise, just speak as slowly as possible and hope for the best. A good way to open the conversation is to say '*kokusai menkyō wo motteimasu*' (I have an international licence).

➡ **Toyota Rent-a-Car** (☎in Japan 0800-7000-111, outside Japan 81-3-5954-8020; http://rent.toyota.co.jp) has the largest rental network and has a very informative website that allows reservations from overseas.

➡ Hiring a motorcycle for long-distance touring is not as easy as hiring a car, although small scooters are available in many places for local sightseeing.

➡ Small motorcycles (those below 125cc) are banned from expressways and are generally not suitable for long-distance touring, but people have ridden from one end of Japan to the other on little 50cc scooters (taking the back roads, of course). An advantage of these bikes is that you can ride them with just a regular driving licence, so you won't need to get a motorcycle licence.

Parking

In most big cities, free curbside parking spots are almost nonexistent, while in rural areas you'll be able to park your car just about anywhere you want. In the cities you'll find that you usually have to pay ¥200 per hour for metered street parking, or anywhere from ¥300 to ¥600 per hour for a spot in a multistorey car park. You'll find car parks around most department stores and near some train stations. Fortunately, most hotels have free parking for guests, as do some restaurants and almost all department stores.

Road Rules

Driving is on the left. There are no unusual rules or interpretations of them and most signposts follow international conventions. JAF has a *Rules of the Road* book available in English and five other languages for ¥1000.

Maps & Navigation

➡ If you can find a used copy of the *Road Atlas Japan* (Shōbunsha), grab it. It's all in English (romaji) with enough names in kanji to make navigation possible even off the major roads. Unfortunately, it's out of print and hard to find these days. If you're really intent on making your way through the back blocks, a Japanese map will prove useful even if your knowledge of kanji is nil. The best Japanese road atlases by far are the *Super Mapple* series (Shōbunsha), which are available in bookshops and some convenience stores.

➡ There is a reasonable amount of signposting in romaji, so getting around isn't all that difficult, especially in developed areas. If you are attempting tricky navigation, use your maps imaginatively – watch out for the railway lines, the rivers, the landmarks. They're all useful ways of orienting yourself when you can't read the signs. A compass will also come in handy when navigating.

➡ These days, many rental cars come equipped with satellite navigation systems, making navigation a snap, provided you can figure out how to work the system; ask the person at the rental agency to explain it and

DRIVING IN JAPAN

Unless you plan on driving in central Tokyo or Osaka or forget that the Japanese drive on the left, you should have no major problems driving in Japan. In fact, driving here is remarkably sane compared to many countries (perhaps because it's so difficult to pass the test). Still, there are a few peculiarities that are worth keeping in mind.

Turn signals Some Japanese drivers have the annoying habit of turning on their turn signals only after they stop at a light or enter an intersection. This seems to defeat the purpose of a signal (ie to tell people *in advance* what you plan to do). This doesn't cause too many problems, but be ready for it.

Petrol stations While self-serve petrol stations are becoming popular, full-service stations are still the rule. And in Japan, when they say 'full service', they really mean it. They'll empty your ashtray, take any garbage you have, wipe your windshield and then wave you back into traffic. And if you're wondering how to say 'fill 'er up' in Japanese, it's '*mantan*' (full tank). And you might be asked how you intend to pay; the two possible answers are '*genkin*' (cash) or '*kaado*' (credit card).

Chains If you drive in mountain areas in winter, you might be required to put chains on your car. If you rent a car in these areas, it will probably come equipped. Petrol stations in mountain areas will usually put the chains on for a charge (¥1000 to ¥2000). There may be police stops in these areas to make sure that cars have chains.

be sure to take notes or, if you're just going from point A to point B, have them set it for you. With most of these systems, you can input the phone number of your destination, which is easy, or its address, which is just about impossible if you don't read Japanese. Even without programming in your destination, with the device on the default '*genzai-chi*' (present location) setting, you will find it very useful.

Hitching

Hitching is never entirely safe, and we don't recommend it. Travellers who decide to hitch should understand that they are taking a small but potentially serious risk. In particular, Japan is a dangerous place for solitary female hitchhikers; there have been cases of solitary female hitchers being attacked, molested and raped. People who do choose to hitch will be safer if they travel in pairs and let someone know where they are planning to go.

Provided you understand the risks and take appropriate precautions, Japan is known as a good country for hitchhiking. Many hitchhikers have tales of extraordinary kindness from motorists who have picked them up.

The rules for hitchhiking are similar to those anywhere else in the world. Dress neatly and look for a good place to hitch – expressway on-ramps and expressway service areas are probably your best bets.

Truck drivers are particularly good for long-distance travel as they often head out on the expressways at night. If a driver is exiting before your intended destination, try to get dropped off at one of the expressway service areas. The *Service Area Parking Area* (SAPA) guide maps are excellent for hitchhikers. They're available free from expressway service areas and show full details of each interchange (IC) and rest stop. These are important orientation points if you have a limited knowledge of Japanese.

Local Transport

All the major cities offer a wide variety of public transport. In many cities you can get day passes for unlimited travel on bus, tram or subway systems. Such passes are usually called an *ichi-nichi-jōsha-ken*. If you're staying for an extended period in one city, commuter passes are available for regular travel.

Bus

Almost every Japanese city has an extensive bus service, but it's usually the most difficult public-transport system for foreign travellers to use. Destinations and stops are often written only in Japanese.

Fares are usually paid when you get off. In Tokyo and some other cities, there's a flat fare regardless of distance. In the other cities, you take a ticket (known as a *seiri-ken*) as you board that indicates the zone number at your starting point. When you get off, an electric sign at the front of the bus indicates the fare charged at that point for each starting zone number. You simply pay the driver the fare that matches your zone number (you put both the *seiri-ken* and the fare into the fare box). There is often a change machine near the front of the bus that can exchange ¥100 and ¥500 coins and ¥1000 notes.

Taxi

Taxis are convenient and can be found even in very small cities and on tiny islands; the train station is the best place to look. Fares are fairly uniform throughout the country. Flagfall (posted on the taxi windows) is ¥600 to ¥710 for the first 2km, after which it's around ¥100 for each 350m (approximately). There's also a time charge if the speed drops below 10km/h. A red light in the lower right corner of the windshield indicates if a taxi is available (it says 'vacant' in Japanese) – this can be difficult to spot during the day. At night, taxis usually have the light on their roof on when they're vacant and off when they're occupied, but there are regional variations.

Don't open the door to get into a taxi; the driver does that with a remote release. The driver will also shut the door when you leave the taxi.

Communication can be a problem with taxi drivers, but perhaps not as much as you fear. If you can't tell the driver where you want to go, it's useful to have the name written down in Japanese. At hotel front desks there will usually be business cards complete with name and location, which can be used for just this purpose.

Tipping is not necessary. A 20% surcharge is added after 11pm or for taxis summoned by radio. There may also be an added charge if you arrange the taxi by phone or reserve the taxi. Finally, taxis can usually take up to four adult passengers (one person can sit in the front). Drivers are sometimes willing to bend the rules for small children.

Train & Subway

Several cities, especially Osaka and Tokyo, have mass-transit rail systems comprising a loop line around the city centre and radial lines into the central stations and the subway system. Subway systems operate in Fukuoka, Kōbe, Kyoto, Nagoya, Osaka, Sapporo, Tokyo and Yokohama. They are usually the fastest and most convenient way to get around the city.

For subways and local trains, you'll most likely have to buy your ticket from a machine. They're pretty easy to understand even if you can't read kanji as there is a diagram explaining the routes; from this you can find out what your fare should be. If you can't work the fare out, a solution is to buy a ticket for the lowest fare. When you finish your trip, go to the fare-adjustment machine *(seisan-ki)* or the staffed counter before you reach the exit gate and pay the difference. JR train stations and most subway stations have posted above the platform not only their names in kanji and romaji but also the names of the preceding and following stations.

Tram

Many cities have tram lines, in particular, Nagasaki, Kumamoto and Kagoshima on Kyūshū; Hiroshima on Honshū, Kōchi and Matsuyama on Shikoku; and Hakodate on Hokkaidō. These are excellent ways of getting around as they combine many of the advantages of bus travel (good views of the passing parade) with those of subways (it's easy to work out where you're going). Fares work on similar systems to bus travel and there are also unlimited-travel day tickets.

Train

Japanese rail services are among the best in the world: they are fast, frequent, clean and comfortable. The 'national' railway is Japan Railways, commonly known as 'JR', which is actually a number of separate private rail systems providing one linked service.

The JR system covers the country from one end to the other and also provides local services around major cities such as Tokyo and Osaka. JR also operates buses and ferries, and convenient ticketing can combine more than one form of transport.

In addition to JR services, there is a huge network of private railways. Each large city usually has at least one private train line that services that city and the surrounding area, or connects that city to nearby cities. These are often a bit cheaper than equivalent JR services.

Types of Trains

The slowest trains stopping at all stations are called *futsū* or *kaku-eki-teisha*. A step up from this is the *kyūkō* (ordinary express), which stops at only a limited number of stations. A variation on the *kyūkō* trains is the *kaisoku* (rapid) service (usually operating on JR lines). The fastest regular (non-*shinkansen*) trains are the *tokkyū* (limited-express) services, which are sometimes known as *shin-kaisoku* (again, usually operating on JR lines).

SHINKANSEN

The fastest and best-known services are JR's *shinkansen*, Japan's famed 'bullet trains'. *Shinkansen* lines operate on separate tracks from regular trains, and, in some places, the *shinkansen* station is a fair distance from the main JR station (as is the case in Osaka).

On most *shinkansen* routes, there are two or three types of service: faster express services stopping at a limited number of stations, and slower local services stopping at more stations. There is no difference in fare, except for the Green Car (1st-class) carriages, which cost slightly more.

Most *shinkansen* cars are nonsmoking, but there are also a limited number of smoking cars on each train. There are reserved and unreserved cars on all trains. If you're travelling outside peak travel periods, you can usually just show up and expect to get a seat in an unreserved car. If you're travelling during a peak period, it is a good idea to stop at a JR station to make a reservation a few days prior to your departure.

Classes

Most long-distance JR trains, including *shinkansen*, have regular and Green Car carriages. The seating is slightly more spacious in Green Car

TRAIN RESERVATIONS FROM ABROAD

➡ Keep in mind that you do not usually have to make reservations in advance for train travel in Japan. Do consider reserving in advance, though, for Golden Week, O-bon (mid-August) and New Year travel.

➡ It is not possible to make reservations for JR trains online in English. However, most travel agents who handle the Japan Rail Pass can also make train reservations and sell you tickets in advance (for a fairly hefty surcharge).

➡ Note that if you have a Japan Rail Pass, you will not be able to reserve travel through a travel agent outside Japan, as you must activate the pass in Japan and show the pass when you make reservations.

➡ It is always possible to walk into a JR office once in Japan and book all your train travel (you can reserve travel up to a month in advance). Because it is difficult and expensive to reserve train travel from abroad, many people reserve all their train travel for their trip soon after arriving in Japan at the nearest JR office.

carriages (think of a typical business-class seat on an aircraft). The Green Car carriages also tend to be quieter and less crowded. However, all Green Car seats are reserved, so if you've got a Green Japan Rail Pass, you'll have to reserve every trip in advance (with a regular pass you just go through the turnstiles and get on the next available train).

Costs

JR fares are calculated on the basis of *futsū-unchin* (basic fare), *tokkyū-ryōkin* (an express surcharge levied only on express services) and *shinkansen-ryōkin* (a special charge for *shinkansen* services). Note that if you buy a return ticket for a trip that is more than 600km each way, you qualify for a 10% discount on the return leg.

The following are some typical basic/*shinkansen* fares from Tokyo or Ueno (prices given for *shinkansen* are the total price of the ticket):

Hakata ¥13,820/21,810

Hiroshima ¥11,660/18,040

Kyoto ¥8210/13,080

Morioka ¥8420/14,940

Nagoya ¥6260/10,360

Niigata ¥5620/10,050

Okayama ¥10,480/16,300

Shin-Osaka ¥8750/13,620

Shin-Shimonoseki ¥13,500/22,350

SURCHARGES

Fares for reserved seats are slightly higher during peak travel seasons (21 March to 5 April, 28 April to 6 May, 21 July to 31 August and 25 December to 10 January). The surcharge is usually ¥200 during these periods.

Further surcharges apply for overnight sleepers, and these vary with the berth type. Japan Rail Pass users must still pay the sleeper surcharge.

TRAIN TERMINOLOGY

PRONUNCIATION	SCRIPT	ENGLISH
futsū	普通	local
green-sha	グリーン車	1st-class car
jiyū-seki	自由席	unreserved seat
kaisoku	快速	JR rapid or express
kaku-eki-teisha	各駅停車	local
katamichi	片道	one way
kin'en-sha	禁煙車	nonsmoking car
kitsuen-sha	喫煙車	smoking car
kyūkō	急行	ordinary express
ōfuku	往復	round trip
shin-kaisoku	新快速	JR special rapid train
shinkansen	新幹線	bullet train
shitei-seki	指定席	reserved seat
tokkyū	特急	limited express
wan-man-kā	ワンマンカー	only one driver/attendant on board

Passes & Discount Tickets

Train travel in Japan can be costly, especially if one rides the *shinkansen* and buys tickets individually. Fortunately, there are some really great rail passes on offer. These can save you a lot of money and anyone considering even a modest exploration of Japan should consider one of these passes. The Japan Rail Pass is the main pass that will be of most use to typical travellers to Japan. However, there are several other passes that might be cheaper and more suitable if you intend to explore only one specific region.

JAPAN RAIL PASS

The **Japan Rail Pass** (www.japanrailpass.net) is a must for anyone planning to do extensive train travel within Japan. Not only will it save you a lot of money, it will save you from having to fish for change each time you board a train.

➡ The Japan Rail Pass *must* be purchased outside Japan. It is available to foreign tourists and Japanese overseas residents (but not foreign residents of Japan).

➡ The pass cannot be used for the super express Nozomi *shinkansen* service but is OK for everything else (including other *shinkansen* services).

➡ Children between the ages of six and 11 qualify for child passes, while those aged under six ride for free.

➡ Regular passes cost ¥29,110/14,550 per adult/child for seven days, ¥46,390/23,190 for 14 days and ¥59,350/29,670 for 21 days.

➡ Green passes cost ¥38,880/19,440 per adult/child for seven days, ¥62,950/31,470 for 14 days and ¥81,870/40,930 for 21 days.

Since a one-way reserved-seat Tokyo–Kyoto *shinkansen* ticket costs ¥13,080, you only have to make one round-trip between Tokyo and Kyoto on the *shinkansen* to make a seven-day pass come close to paying off (add a round-trip between Narita and Tokyo and you're already saving money). Note that the pass is valid only

NEW RAIL PASSES

Note that the situation regarding rail passes in Japan is currently changing and new passes are being introduced at a furious pace. We strongly recommend that you check the latest offerings on the sites of **JR East** (www.jreast.co.jp), **JR West** (www.westjr.co.jp) and **JR Kyūshū** (www.jrkyushu.co.jp).

on JR services; you will still have to pay for private-train services.

In order to get a pass, you must first purchase an 'exchange order' outside Japan at a JAL or ANA office or a major travel agency. Once you arrive in Japan, you must bring this order to a JR Travel Service Centre (in most major JR stations and at Narita and Kansai International Airports). When you validate your pass, you'll have to show your passport in addition to the exchange order.

When you validate the pass, you select the date on which you want the pass to become valid. You can choose to make it valid immediately or on a later date. So, if you just plan to spend a few days in Kyoto or Tokyo before setting out to explore the country by rail, set the validity date to the day you start your exploration outside the city. This can save you a lot of money (because the pass really pays for itself when taking long *shinkansen* trips – rather than a few local JR trips around a city like Tokyo or Kyoto.

For more information on the pass and overseas purchase locations, visit the Japan Rail Pass website.

JR EAST RAIL PASSES

JR East (www.jreast.co.jp) operates rail lines in the north and eastern areas of Honshū, including the Tokyo area. They offer two passes that cover all or part of their service area. For JR east, anyone over 12 is considered an adult, anyone between the ages of six and 11 is considered a child, and anyone below the age of six travels for free.

JR East Pass The **JR East Pass** (www.jreast.co.jp/e/eastpass) is a great deal for those who only want to travel in eastern Japan. The passes are good on all JR lines in eastern Japan (including Tōhoku, Yamagata, Akita, Jōetsu and Nagano *shinkansen,* but not including the Tōkaidō *shinkansen*). This includes the area around Tokyo and everything north of Tokyo to the tip of Honshū, but doesn't include Hokkaidō. The passes are good for travel on any five days of a 14-day period that starts with purchase or activation of the pass in Japan. The travel dates do not have to be declared in advance. The passes cost ¥22,000/11,000 per adult/child. The passes are only good for travel in ordinary cars (ie there are no Green Car passes). Unlike the Japan Rail Pass, the pass can be purchased inside Japan (by those holding tourist visas), as well as outside Japan. The passes can also be purchased online.

JR East Kantō Area Pass The **JR East Kantō Area Pass** (www.jreast.co.jp/e/kantoareapass) is a good option for those who want to explore only Tokyo and the surrounding area. It covers travel on all JR lines, including *shinkansen* in the Tokyo and surrounding area (see the website for the exact lines covered). It will get you as far as places such as Nikkō, Karuizawa and the Izu Peninsula. The passes cost ¥8300/4200 per adult/child. The passes are only good for travel in ordinary cars (ie there are no Green Car passes).

JR WEST RAIL PASSES

JR West (www.westjr.co.jp) offers rail passes valid in the western parts of Honshū (Kansai, the Okayama area, the Hiroshima area and the Yamaguchi area). For these passes, 'child' means anyone between six and 11 (children aged under six travel free). Unlike the Japan Rail Pass, the pass can be purchased inside Japan at major stations in the areas covered by the respective passes (by those holding tourist visas), as well as outside Japan (at the same places where you can purchase Japan Rail Passes). The passes can also be purchased online. See the website for further details.

Kansai Area Pass A great deal for those who only want to explore the Kansai area, the Kansai Area Pass covers unlimited travel on JR lines between most major Kansai cities, such as Himeji, Kōbe, Osaka, Kyoto and Nara. It also covers JR trains to/from Kansai International Airport, but does not cover any *shinkansen* lines. The pass also entitles holders to reserved seats at no extra charge (you'll have to reserve each trip before boarding the train). Passes are only good on consecutive days. Passes cost a couple of hundred yen more if purchased within Japan.

DURATION	REGULAR (ADULT/CHILD)
1 day	¥2200/1100
2 days	¥4300/2150
3 days	¥5300/2650
4 days	¥6300/3150

Kansai Wide Area Pass This is similar to the Kansai Area Pass, but it also allows travel on the Sanyō *shinkansen* between Osaka and Okayama as well as trains going as far as Kinosaki in the north and Shingū in the south, including a variety of *tokkyū* (limited express trains). The pass is valid for four days and costs ¥8500/4250 per adult/child when purchased outside Japan or online; ¥9000/4500 if purchased inside Japan.

West Hokuriku Area Pass This is a rather specialised pass that covers travel on all JR local and limited express trains in the Hokuriku Area of Central Honshū. This area includes the prefectures of Ishikawa, Kanazawa and Toyama. The pass is valid for four days and costs ¥4500/2250 per adult/child.

Kansai-Hiroshima Area Pass This pass covers covers most JR trains, including express trains in Kansai, as well as the Sanyō *shinkansen* between Osaka and Hiroshima, plus other JR trains in the Hiroshima area. The pass is valid for five days and costs ¥13,000/6500 per adult/child when purchased outside Japan or online; ¥14,000/7000 per adult/child when purchased inside Japan.

Hiroshima-Yamaguchi Area Pass This pass covers most JR trains, including express trains in Kansai, as well as the Sanyō *shinkansen* between Mihara and Hakata, and other JR trains in the Hiroshima area and Yamaguchi area of far Western Honshū. The pass is valid for five days and costs ¥11,000/5500 per adult/child when purchased outside Japan or online; ¥12,000/6000 per adult/child when purchased inside Japan.

Sanyo-San'in Area Pass This pass covers most JR trains, including express trains in central Kansai, and the Okayama, Hiroshima and far Western Honshū areas, as well as the Sanyō *shinkansen* between Osaka and Hakata. The pass is valid for five days and costs ¥19,000/9500 per adult/child when purchased outside Japan or online; ¥20,000/10,000 per adult/child when purchased inside Japan.

JR KYŪSHŪ RAIL PASSES

JR Kyūshū (www.jrkyushu.co.jp) offers two passes: one that covers all JR lines in the northern part of Kyūshū and another that is good for all JR lines in Kyūshū (see the website for areas covered).

For these passes, 'child' means anyone between six and 11 (those below six travel free). These passes can be purchased both inside Japan (at travel agencies in major train stations in Kyūshū) and outside Japan at the same locations as the Japan Rail Pass. It can only be used by those on a temporary visitor visa. If you purchase an exchange order overseas, you can pick up your pass at major train stations in Kyūshū.

Three-day all-area passes per adult/child cost ¥14,400/7200; five days costs ¥17,490/8745. For Northern Kyūshū it's ¥7200/3600 for three days and ¥9260/4630 for five.

SEISHUN JŪHACHI KIPPU

If you don't have a Japan Rail Pass, one of the best deals going is a five-day **Seishun Jūhachi Kippu** (www.jreast.co.jp/e/pass/seishun18.html), literally a 'Youth 18 Ticket'. Despite its name, it can be used by anyone of any age. Basically, for ¥11,850 you get five one-day tickets valid for travel anywhere in Japan on JR lines. The only catches are that you can't travel on *tokkyū* or *shinkansen* trains and each ticket must be used within 24 hours. However, even if you only have to make a return trip, say, between Tokyo and Kyoto, you'll be saving a lot of money. Seishun Jūhachi Kippu can be purchased at most JR stations in Japan. Sale and validity periods are outlined in the following table:

SEASON	SALES PERIOD	VALIDITY PERIOD
Spring	20 Feb–31 Mar	1 Mar–10 Apr
Summer	1 Jul–31 Aug	20 Jul–10 Sep
Winter	1 Dec–10 Jan	10 Dec–20 Jan

Note that these periods are subject to change. For more information, ask at any JR ticket window. If you don't want to buy the whole book of five tickets, you can sometimes purchase separate tickets at the discount-ticket shops around train stations.

KANSAI THRU PASS

This pass is a real bonus to travellers who plan to do a fair bit of exploration in the Kansai area. It enables you to ride on city subways, private railways and city buses in Kyoto, Nara, Osaka, Kōbe and Wakayama. It also entitles you to discounts at many attractions in the Kansai area. A two-day pass costs ¥4000 and a three-day pass costs ¥5200. It is available at the Kansai airport travel counter on the 1st floor of the International Arrivals Hall and at the main bus information centre in front of Kyoto Station. For more information, visit www.surutto.com.

STORED VALUE (IC) CARDS

There are several useful stored value cards (known as 'IC Cards' in Japan) that may be of use to some travellers. These can usually be used on all JR trains in a particular area as well as in many local shops (especially convenience stores). The two most likely to be of interest to travellers are the **Suica Card** (www.jreast.co.jp/e/pass/suica), which works in the JR East region (eastern Honshū, including Tokyo and around) and the **Icoca Card** (www.jr-odekake.net/icoca; in Japanese), which works in the Kansai region. These can be purchased at the JR ticket offices of major train stations in the respective areas. Note that these cards can also be used outside of their main areas of coverage, but cannot be used for continuous travel between areas – so forget about using them, for instance, to take the *shinkansen* from Tokyo to Kyoto.

DISCOUNT-TICKET SHOPS

Discount-ticket shops are known as *kakuyasu-kippu-uriba* (格安切符売り場) or *kinken shoppu* (金券ショップ) in Japanese. These shops deal in discounted tickets for trains, buses, domestic flights, ferries, and a host of other things such as cut-rate stamps and phone cards. You can typically save between 5% and 10% on *shinkansen* tickets. Discount-ticket agencies are found around train stations in medium and large cities – ask at your lodgings for the nearest one.

Schedules & Information

The most-complete timetables can be found in the *JR Jikokuhyō* (Book of Timetables), which is available at all Japanese bookshops, but is written in Japanese. JNTO, however, produces a handy English-language *Railway Timetable* booklet that explains a great deal about the services in Japan and gives timetables for the *shinkansen* services, JR *tokkyū* and major private lines. If your visit to Japan is a short one and you will not be straying far from the major tourist destinations, this booklet may well be all you need.

Major train stations all have information counters, and you can usually get your point across in simplified English.

If you need to know anything about JR, such as schedules, fares, fastest routes, lost baggage, discounts on rail travel, hotels and car hire, call the **JR East Infoline** (☎from inside Japan 050-2016-1603, from overseas 81-50-2016-1603; www.jreast.co.jp/e/customer_support/infoline.html; ⏰10am-6pm). Information is available in English, Korean and Chinese. It operates from 10am to 6pm daily except during the New Year's period. The website **Hyperdia** (www.hyperdia.com) is also a useful online source for schedules and is probably the most user-friendly English-language site.

Tickets & Reservations

Tickets for most journeys can be bought from train-station vending machines, ticket counters and reservation offices. For reservations of complicated tickets, larger JR train stations have *midori-no-madoguchi*, which function as JR's inhouse travel agency. Major private travel agencies in Japan also sell reserved-seat tickets.

On *futsū* services, there are no reserved seats. On the faster *tokkyū* and *shinkansen* services you can choose to travel reserved or unreserved. However, if you travel unreserved, there's always the risk of not getting a seat and having to stand, possibly for the entire trip. This is a particular danger at weekends, peak travel seasons and on holidays. Reserved-seat tickets can be bought any time from a month in advance to the day of departure.

Information and tickets can be obtained from travel agencies, of which there are a great number in Japan. Nearly every train station of any size will have at least one travel agency in the station building to handle all sorts of bookings in addition to train services. Japan Travel Bureau (JTB) is the big daddy of Japanese travel agencies. However, for most train tickets and long-distance bus reservations, you don't need to go through a travel agency – just go to the ticket counters or *midori-no-madoguchi* of any major train station.

Language

IJapanese is spoken by more than 125 million people. While it bears some resemblance to Altaic languages such as Mongolian and Turkish and has grammatical similarities to Korean, its origins are unclear. Chinese is responsible for the existence of many Sino-Japanese words in Japanese, and for the originally Chinese kanji characters which the Japanese use in combination with the home-grown hiragana and katakana scripts.

Japanese pronunciation is easy to master for English speakers, as most of its sounds are also found in English – if you read our coloured pronunciation guides as if they were English, you'll be understood. Note though that in Japanese, it's important to make the distinction between short and long vowels, as vowel length can change the meaning of a word. The long vowels, shown in our pronunciation guides with a horizontal line on top of them (ā, ē, ī, ō, ū), should be held twice as long as the short ones. It's also important to make the distinction between single and double consonants, as this can produce a difference in meaning. Pronounce the double consonants with a slight pause between them, eg sak·ka (writer).

Note also that the vowel sound ai is pronounced as in 'aisle', air as in 'pair' and ow as in 'how'. As for the consonants, ts is pronounced as in 'hats', f sounds almost like 'fw' (with rounded lips), and r is halfway between 'r' and 'l'. All syllables in a word are pronounced fairly evenly in Japanese.

WANT MORE?

For in-depth language information and handy phrases, check out Lonely Planet's *Japanese Phrasebook*. You'll find it at **shop.lonelyplanet.com**, or you can buy Lonely Planet's iPhone phrasebooks at the Apple App Store.

BASICS

Japanese uses an array of registers of speech to reflect social and contextual hierarchy, but these can be simplified to the form most appropriate for the situation, which is what we've done in this language guide too.

Hello.	こんにちは。	kon·ni·chi·wa
Goodbye.	さようなら。	sa·yō·na·ra
Yes.	はい。	hai
No.	いいえ。	ī·e
Please. (when asking)	ください。	ku·da·sai
Please. (when offering)	どうぞ。	dō·zo
Thank you.	ありがとう。	a·ri·ga·tō
Excuse me. (to get attention)	すみません。	su·mi·ma·sen
Sorry.	ごめんなさい。	go·men·na·sai

You're welcome.
どういたしまして。 dō i·ta·shi·mash·te

How are you?
お元気ですか? o·gen·ki des ka

Fine. And you?
はい、元気です。 hai, gen·ki des
あなたは? a·na·ta wa

What's your name?
お名前は何ですか? o·na·ma·e wa nan des ka

My name is ...
私の名前は wa·ta·shi no na·ma·e wa
…です。 ... des

Do you speak English?
英語が話せますか? ē·go ga ha·na·se·mas ka

I don't understand.
わかりません。 wa·ka·ri·ma·sen

Does anyone speak English?
どなたか英語を do·na·ta ka ē·go o
話せますか? ha·na·se·mas ka

ACCOMMODATION

Where's a ...?	…が ありますか?	... ga a·ri·mas ka
campsite	キャンプ場	kyam·pu·jō
guesthouse	民宿	min·shu·ku
hotel	ホテル	ho·te·ru
inn	旅館	ryo·kan
youth hostel	ユース ホステル	yū·su· ho·su·te·ru

Do you have a ... room?	…ルームは ありますか?	...rū·mu wa a·ri·mas ka
single	シングル	shin·gu·ru
double	ダブル	da·bu·ru

How much is it per ...?	…いくら ですか?	... i·ku·ra des ka
night	1泊	ip·pa·ku
person	1人	hi·to·ri

air-con	エアコン	air·kon
bathroom	風呂場	fu·ro·ba
window	窓	ma·do

DIRECTIONS

Where's the ...?
…はどこですか? ... wa do·ko des ka

Can you show me (on the map)?
(地図で)教えて くれませんか? (chi·zu de) o·shi·e·te ku·re·ma·sen ka

What's the address?
住所は何ですか? jū·sho wa nan des ka

Could you please write it down?
書いてくれませんか? kai·te ku·re·ma·sen ka

behind ...	…の後ろ	... no u·shi·ro
in front of ...	…の前	... no ma·e
near ...	…の近く	... no chi·ka·ku
next to ...	…のとなり	... no to·na·ri
opposite ...	…の 向かい側	... no mu·kai·ga·wa
straight ahead	この先	ko·no sa·ki

Turn ...	…まがって ください。	... ma·gat·te ku·da·sai
at the corner	その角を	so·no ka·do o
at the traffic lights	その信号を	so·no shin·gō o
left	左へ	hi·da·ri e
right	右へ	mi·gi e

SIGNS

入口	**Entrance**
出口	**Exit**
営業中/開館	**Open**
閉店/閉館	**Closed**
インフォメーション	**Information**
危険	**Danger**
トイレ	**Toilets**
男	**Men**
女	**Women**

EATING & DRINKING

I'd like to reserve a table for (two people).
(2人)の予約を お願いします。 (fu·ta·ri) no yo·ya·ku o o·ne·gai shi·mas

What would you recommend?
なにが おすすめですか? na·ni ga o·su·su·me des ka

What's in that dish?
あの料理に何 が入っていますか? a·no ryō·ri ni na·ni ga hait·te i·mas ka

Do you have any vegetarian dishes?
ベジタリアン料理 がありますか? be·ji·ta·ri·an ryō·ri ga a·ri·mas ka

I'm a vegetarian.
私は ベジタリアンです。 wa·ta·shi wa be·ji·ta·ri·an des

I'm a vegan.
私は厳格な 菜食主義者 です。 wa·ta·shi wa gen·ka·ku na sai·sho·ku·shu·gi·sha des

I don't eat ...	…は 食べません。	... wa ta·be·ma·sen
dairy products	乳製品	nyū·sē·hin
(red) meat	(赤身の) 肉	(a·ka·mi no) ni·ku
meat or dairy products	肉や 乳製品は	ni·ku ya nyū·sē·hin
pork	豚肉	bu·ta·ni·ku
seafood	シーフード 海産物	shī·fū·do/ kai·sam·bu·tsu

Is it cooked with pork lard or chicken stock?
これはラードか鶏の だしを使って いますか? ko·re wa rā·do ka to·ri no da·shi o tsu·kat·te i·mas ka

I'm allergic to (peanuts).
私は (ピーナッツ)に アレルギーが あります。 wa·ta·shi wa (pī·nat·tsu) ni a·re·ru·gī ga a·ri·mas

That was delicious!
おいしかった。 oy·shi·kat·ta

Cheers!
乾杯! kam·pai

Please bring the bill.
お勘定をください。 o·kan·jō o ku·da·sai

Key Words

appetisers	前菜	zen·sai
bottle	ビン	bin
bowl	ボール	bō·ru
breakfast	朝食	chō·sho·ku
cold	冷たい	tsu·me·ta·i
dinner	夕食	yū·sho·ku
fork	フォーク	fō·ku
glass	グラス	gu·ra·su
grocery	食料品	sho·ku·ryō·hin
hot (warm)	熱い	a·tsu·i
knife	ナイフ	nai·fu
lunch	昼食	chū·sho·ku
market	市場	i·chi·ba
menu	メニュー	me·nyū
plate	皿	sa·ra
spicy	スパイシー	spai·shī
spoon	スプーン	spūn
vegetarian	ベジタリアン	be·ji·ta·ri·an
with	いっしょに	is·sho ni
without	なしで	na·shi de

Meat & Fish

beef	牛肉	gyū·ni·ku
chicken	鶏肉	to·ri·ni·ku
duck	アヒル	a·hi·ru
eel	うなぎ	u·na·gi
fish	魚	sa·ka·na
lamb	子羊	ko·hi·tsu·ji
lobster	ロブスター	ro·bus·tā
meat	肉	ni·ku
pork	豚肉	bu·ta·ni·ku
prawn	エビ	e·bi
salmon	サケ	sa·ke
seafood	シーフード/海産物	shī·fū·do/kai·sam·bu·tsu
shrimp	小エビ	ko·e·bi
tuna	マグロ	ma·gu·ro
turkey	七面鳥	shi·chi·men·chō
veal	子牛	ko·u·shi

KEY PATTERNS

To get by in Japanese, mix and match these simple patterns with words of your choice:

When's (the next bus)?
(次のバスは)何時ですか? (tsu·gi no bas wa) nan·ji des ka

Where's (the station)?
(駅は)どこですか? (e·ki wa) do·ko des ka

Do you have (a map)?
(地図)がありますか? (chi·zu) ga a·ri·mas ka

Is there (a toilet)?
(トイレ)がありますか? (toy·re) ga a·ri·mas ka

I'd like (the menu).
(メニュー)をお願いします。 (me·nyū) o o·ne·gai shi·mas

Can I (sit here)?
(ここに座って)もいいですか? (ko·ko ni su·wat·te) mo ī des ka

I need (a can opener).
(缶切り)が必要です。 (kan·ki·ri) ga hi·tsu·yō des

Do I need (a visa)?
(ビザ)が必要ですか? (bi·za) ga hi·tsu·yō des ka

I have (a reservation).
(予約)があります。 (yo·ya·ku) ga a·ri·mas

I'm (a teacher).
私は(教師)です。 wa·ta·shi wa (kyō·shi) des

Fruit & Vegetables

apple	りんご	rin·go
banana	バナナ	ba·na·na
beans	豆	ma·me
capsicum	ピーマン	pī·man
carrot	ニンジン	nin·jin
cherry	さくらんぼ	sa·ku·ram·bo
cucumber	キュウリ	kyū·ri
fruit	果物	ku·da·mo·no
grapes	ブドウ	bu·dō
lettuce	レタス	re·tas
nut	ナッツ	nat·tsu
orange	オレンジ	o·ren·ji
peach	桃	mo·mo
peas	豆	ma·me
pineapple	パイナップル	pai·nap·pu·ru
potato	ジャガイモ	ja·ga·i·mo

QUESTION WORDS

How?	どのように?	do·no yō ni
What?	なに?	na·ni
When?	いつ?	i·tsu
Where?	どこ?	do·ko
Which?	どちら?	do·chi·ra
Who?	だれ?	da·re
Why?	なぜ?	na·ze

pumpkin	カボチャ	ka·bo·cha
spinach	ホウレンソウ	hō·ren·sō
strawberry	イチゴ	i·chi·go
tomato	トマト	to·ma·to
vegetables	野菜	ya·sai
watermelon	スイカ	su·i·ka

Other

bread	パン	pan
butter	バター	ba·tā
cheese	チーズ	chī·zu
chilli	唐辛子	tō·ga·ra·shi
egg	卵	ta·ma·go
honey	蜂蜜	ha·chi·mi·tsu
horseradish	わさび	wa·sa·bi
jam	ジャム	ja·mu
noodles	麺	men
pepper	コショウ	ko·shō
rice (cooked)	ごはん	go·han
salt	塩	shi·o
seaweed	のり	no·ri
soy sauce	しょう油	shō·yu
sugar	砂糖	sa·tō

Drinks

beer	ビール	bī·ru
coffee	コーヒー	kō·hī
(orange) juice	(オレンジ) ジュース	(o·ren·ji·) jū·su
lemonade	レモネード	re·mo·nē·do
milk	ミルク	mi·ru·ku
mineral water	ミネラル ウォーター	mi·ne·ra·ru· wō·tā
red wine	赤ワイン	a·ka wain
sake	酒	sa·ke
tea	紅茶	kō·cha
water	水	mi·zu
white wine	白ワイン	shi·ro wain
yogurt	ヨーグルト	yō·gu·ru·to

EMERGENCIES

Help!	
たすけて!	tas·ke·te
Go away!	
離れろ!	ha·na·re·ro
I'm lost.	
迷いました。	ma·yoy·mash·ta
Call the police.	
警察を呼んで。	kē·sa·tsu o yon·de
Call a doctor.	
医者を呼んで。	i·sha o yon·de
Where are the toilets?	
トイレはどこですか?	toy·re wa do·ko des ka
I'm ill.	
私は病気です。	wa·ta·shi wa byō·ki des
It hurts here.	
ここが痛いです。	ko·ko ga i·tai des
I'm allergic to ...	
私は… アレルギーです。	wa·ta·shi wa ... a·re·ru·gī des

SHOPPING & SERVICES

I'd like to buy ...	
…をください。	... o ku·da·sai
I'm just looking.	
見ているだけです。	mi·te i·ru da·ke des
Can I look at it?	
それを見ても いいですか?	so·re o mi·te mo ī des ka
How much is it?	
いくらですか?	i·ku·ra des ka
That's too expensive.	
高すぎます。	ta·ka·su·gi·mas
Can you give me a discount?	
ディスカウント できますか?	dis·kown·to de·ki·mas ka
There's a mistake in the bill.	
請求書に間違いが あります。	sē·kyū·sho ni ma·chi·gai ga a·ri·mas

ATM	ATM	ē·tī·e·mu
credit card	クレジット カード	ku·re·jit·to· kā·do
post office	郵便局	yū·bin·kyo·ku
public phone	公衆電話	kō·shū·den·wa
tourist office	観光案内所	kan·kō·an·nai·jo

TIME & DATES

What time is it?
何時ですか?　nan·ji des ka

It's (10) o'clock.
(10)時です。　(jū)·ji des

Half past (10).
(10)時半です。　(jū)·ji han des

am	午前	go·zen
pm	午後	go·go

Monday	月曜日	ge·tsu·yō·bi
Tuesday	火曜日	ka·yō·bi
Wednesday	水曜日	su·i·yō·bi
Thursday	木曜日	mo·ku·yō·bi
Friday	金曜日	kin·yō·bi
Saturday	土曜日	do·yō·bi
Sunday	日曜日	ni·chi·yō·bi

January	1月	i·chi·ga·tsu
February	2月	ni·ga·tsu
March	3月	san·ga·tsu
April	4月	shi·ga·tsu
May	5月	go·ga·tsu
June	6月	ro·ku·ga·tsu
July	7月	shi·chi·ga·tsu
August	8月	ha·chi·ga·tsu
September	9月	ku·ga·tsu
October	10月	jū·ga·tsu
November	11月	jū·i·chi·ga·tsu
December	12月	jū·ni·ga·tsu

TRANSPORT

boat	船	fu·ne
bus	バス	bas
metro	地下鉄	chi·ka·te·tsu
plane	飛行機	hi·kō·ki
train	電車	den·sha
tram	市電	shi·den

What time does it leave?
これは何時に出ますか?　ko·re wa nan·ji ni de·mas ka

Does it stop at (...)?
(…)に停まりますか?　(...) ni to·ma·ri·mas ka

Please tell me when we get to (...).
(…)に着いたら教えてください。　(...) ni tsu·i·ta·ra o·shi·e·te ku·da·sai

A one-way/return ticket (to ...).
(…行きの)片道/往復切符。　(...·yu·ki no) ka·ta·mi·chi/ō·fu·ku kip·pu

bus stop	バス停	bas·tē
first	始発の	shi·ha·tsu no
last	最終の	sai·shū no
ticket window	窓口	ma·do·gu·chi
timetable	時刻表	ji·ko·ku·hyō
train station	駅	e·ki

I'd like to hire a ...　…を借りたいのですが。　o ka·ri·tai no des ga

4WD	四駆	yon·ku
bicycle	自転車	ji·ten·sha
car	自動車	ji·dō·sha
motorbike	オートバイ	ō·to·bai

Is this the road to ...?
この道は…まで行きますか?　ko·no mi·chi wa ... ma·de i·ki·mas ka

(How long) Can I park here?
(どのくらい)ここに駐車できますか?　(do·no·ku·rai) ko·ko ni chū·sha de·ki·mas ka

NUMBERS

1	一	i·chi
2	二	ni
3	三	san
4	四	shi/yon
5	五	go
6	六	ro·ku
7	七	shi·chi/na·na
8	八	ha·chi
9	九	ku/kyū
10	十	jū
20	二十	ni·jū
30	三十	san·jū
40	四十	yon·jū
50	五十	go·jū
60	六十	ro·ku·jū
70	七十	na·na·jū
80	八十	ha·chi·jū
90	九十	kyū·jū
100	百	hya·ku
1000	千	sen

GLOSSARY

For lists of culinary terms, see p787; for useful words when visiting an onsen, see the box, p817; and for train terminology, see p847.

Ainu – indigenous people of Hokkaidō and parts of Northern Honshū
Amaterasu – sun goddess and link to the imperial throne
ANA – All Nippon Airways
annai-sho – information office
asa-ichi – morning market

bama – beach; see also *hama*
bashō – *sumō* tournament
bonsai – the art of growing miniature trees by careful pruning of branches and roots
bugaku – dance piece played by court orchestra in ancient Japan
buke yashiki – *samurai* residence
bunraku – classical puppet theatre which uses huge puppets to portray dramas similar to *kabuki*
Burakumin – traditionally outcasts associated with lowly occupations such as leatherwork; literally 'village people'
bushidō – a set of values followed by the *samurai;* literally 'the way of the warrior'
butsudan – Buddhist altar in Japanese homes

chō – city area (in large cities) between a *ku* and a *chōme* in size; also a street
chōchin – paper lantern
chōme – city area of a few blocks

Daibutsu – Great Buddha
daimyō – regional lord under the *shōgun*
daira – plain; see also *taira*
dake – peak; see also *take*
dani – valley; see also *tani*
danjiri – festival float
dera – temple; see also *tera*
dō – temple or hall of a temple

eki – train station

fu – prefecture; see also *ken*
fusuma – sliding screen door
futsū – local train; literally 'ordinary'

gaijin – foreigner; literally 'outside people'
gasoreen sutando – petrol station
gasshō-zukuri – an architectural style (usually thatch-roofed); literally 'hands in prayer'
gawa – river; see also *kawa*
geiko – the Kyoto word for *geisha*
geisha – woman versed in arts and drama who entertains guests; *not* a prostitute
gekijō – theatre
genkan – foyer area where shoes are removed or replaced when entering or leaving a building
geta – traditional wooden sandals
gū – shrine
gun – county

habu – a venomous snake found in Okinawa
haiku – 17-syllable poem
hama – beach; see also *bama*
hanami – blossom viewing (usually cherry blossoms)
haniwa – earthenware figure found in tombs of the Kōfun period
hantō – peninsula
hara – uncultivated field or plain
hari – dragon-boat race
hatsu-mōde – first shrine visit of the new year
henro – pilgrim on the Shikoku 88 Temple Circuit
Hikari – the second-fastest type of *shinkansen*
hiragana – phonetic syllabary used to write Japanese words
hondō – main route or main hall
honsen – main rail line

ichi-nichi-jōsha-ken – day pass for unlimited travel on bus, tram or subway systems
ikebana – art of flower arrangement
irezumi – a tattoo or the art of tattooing
irori – hearth or fireplace
izakaya – pub-style eatery

JAF – Japan Automobile Federation
JAL – Japan Airlines
ji – temple
jigoku – boiling mineral hot spring, which is definitely not for bathing in; literally 'hells'
jikokuhyō – timetable or book of timetables
jima – island; see also *shima*
jingū – shrine
jinja – shrine
jizō – small stone statue of the Buddhist protector of travellers and children
JNTO – Japan National Tourism Organization
jō – castle
JR – Japan Railways
JTB – Japan Travel Bureau
juku – after-school 'cram' school
JYHA – Japan Youth Hostel Association

kabuki – a form of Japanese theatre based on popular legends, characterised by elaborate costumes, stylised acting and the use of male actors for all roles
kaikan – hall or building
kaikyō – channel/strait
kaisoku – rapid train
kaisū-ken – a book of transport tickets
kami – Shintō gods; spirits of natural phenomena
kamikaze – typhoon that sunk Kublai Khan's 13th-century invasion fleet and the name adopted by suicide pilots in the waning days of WWII; literally 'divine wind'
kana – the two phonetic syllabaries, *hiragana* and *katakana*
kanji – Chinese ideographic script used for writing Japanese; literally 'Chinese script'
Kannon – Bodhisattva of Compassion (commonly referred to as the Buddhist Goddess of Mercy)

karaoke – bar where you sing along with taped music; literally 'empty orchestra'

katakana – phonetic syllabary used to write foreign words

katamichi – one-way transport ticket

katana – Japanese sword

kawa – river; see also *gawa*

ken – prefecture; see also *fu*

kendo – oldest martial art; literally 'the way of the sword'

ki – life force, will

kimono – brightly coloured, robe-like traditional outer garment

kin'en-sha – nonsmoking train carriage

kippu – ticket

kissaten – coffee shop

ko – lake

kō – port

kōban – police box

kōen – park

kōgen – high plain (in the mountains); plateau

kokumin-shukusha – people's lodge; an inexpensive form of accommodation

kokuritsu kōen – national park

kotatsu – heated table with a quilt or cover over it to keep the legs and lower body warm

koto – 13-stringed instrument derived from a Chinese zither that is played flat on the floor

ku – ward

kūkō – airport

kura – earth-walled storehouse

kyō – gorge

kyūkō – ordinary express train (faster than a *futsū,* only stopping at certain stations)

machi – city area (in large cities) between a *ku* and *chōme* in size; also street

machiya – traditional Japanese townhouse or merchant house

maiko – apprentice *geisha*

mama-san – woman who manages a bar or club

maneki-neko – beckoning or welcoming cat figure frequently seen in restaurants and bars; it's supposed to attract customers and trade

manga – Japanese comics

matsuri – festival

meishi – business card

midori-no-madoguchi – ticket counter in large Japan Rail stations, where you can make more complicated bookings (look for the green band across the glass)

mikoshi – portable shrine carried during festivals

minato – harbour

minshuku – the Japanese equivalent of a B&B; family-run budget accommodation

misaki – cape; see also *saki*

mon – gate

mura – village

N'EX – Narita Express

NHK – Nihon Hōsō Kyōkai (Japan Broadcasting Corporation)

Nihon – Japanese word for 'Japan'; literally 'source of the sun'; also *Nippon*

ningyō – Japanese doll

Nippon – see *Nihon*

nō – classical Japanese drama performed on a bare stage

noren – cloth hung as a sunshade, typically carrying the name of the shop or premises; indicates that a restaurant is open for business

norikae-ken – transfer ticket (trams and buses)

NTT – Nippon Telegraph & Telephone Corporation

o- – prefix used to show respect to anything it is applied to

ōfuku – return ticket

o-furo – traditional Japanese bath

OL – 'office lady'; female clerical worker; pronounced 'ō-eru'

onnagata – male actor playing a woman's role (usually in *kabuki*)

onsen – hot spring; mineral-spa area, usually with accommodation

oshibori – hot towel provided in restaurants

pachinko – popular vertical pinball game, played in *pachinko* parlours

rakugo – Japanese raconteur, stand-up comic

rettō – island group; see also *shotō*

Rinzai – school of Zen Buddhism which places an emphasis on *kōan* (riddles)

romaji – Japanese roman script

rōnin – student who must resit university entrance exam; literally 'masterless *samurai*', sometimes referred to as 'wanderer'

ropeway – Japanese word for a cable car, tramway or funicular railway

rotemburo – open-air or outdoor bath

ryokan – traditional Japanese inn

saki – cape; see also *misaki*

sakoku – Japan's period of national seclusion prior to the Meiji Restoration

sakura – cherry blossom

salaryman – male white-collar worker, usually in a large firm

sama – even more respectful suffix than *san;* used in instances such as *o-kyaku-sama* – the 'honoured guest'

samurai – warrior class

san – mountain; also suffix which shows respect to the person it is applied to

san-sō – mountain hut or cottage

sentō – public bath

seppuku – ritual suicide by disembowelment

shamisen – a three-stringed traditional Japanese instrument that resembles a banjo or lute

shi – city (used to distinguish cities from prefectures of the same name, eg Kyoto-shi)

shikki – lacquerware

shima – island; see also *jima*

shinkaisoku – express train or special rapid train (usually on JR lines)

shinkansen – super-express train, known in the West as 'bullet train'

Shintō – the indigenous religion of Japan; literally 'the way of the gods'

shirabyōshi – traditional dancer

shitamachi – traditionally the low-lying, less affluent parts of Tokyo

shodō – Japanese calligraphy; literally the 'way of writing'

shōgekijō – small theatre

shōgi – a version of chess in which each player has 20 pieces and the object is to capture the opponent's king

shōgun – former military ruler of Japan

shōgunate – military government

shōji – sliding rice-paper screen

shōjin ryōri – Buddhist vegetarian meal (served at temple lodgings etc)

shokudō – all-round restaurant

shotō – archipelago or island group; see also *rettō*

Shugendō – offbeat Buddhist school, which incorporates ancient shamanistic rites, *Shintō* beliefs and ascetic Buddhist traditions

shūji – a lesser form of *shodō;* literally 'the practice of letters'

shukubō – temple lodging

soapland – Japanese euphemism for a bathhouse offering sexual services, eg massage parlour

Sōtō – a school of Zen Buddhism which places emphasis on *zazen*

sumi-e – black-ink brush painting

sumō – Japanese wrestling

tabi – split-toed Japanese socks used when wearing *geta*

taiko – drum

taira – plain; see also *daira*

taisha – great shrine

take – peak; see also *dake*

taki – waterfall

tani – valley; see also *dani*

tanuki – racoon or dog-like folklore character frequently represented in ceramic figures

tatami – tightly woven floor matting on which shoes are never worn; traditionally, room size is defined by the number of tatami mats

teien – garden

tera – temple; see also *dera*

to – metropolis, eg Tokyo-to

tō – island

tokkyū – limited express train; faster than a *kyūkō*

tokonoma – sacred alcove in a house in which flowers may be displayed or a scroll hung

torii – entrance gate to a Shintō shrine

tōsu – lavatory

uchiwa – paper fan

ukiyo-e – woodblock print; literally 'pictures of the floating world'

wa – harmony, team spirit; also the old *kanji* used to denote Japan, and still used in Chinese and Japanese as a prefix to indicate things of Japanese origin, eg *wafuku* (Japanese-style clothing)

wabi – enjoyment of peace and tranquillity

wan – bay

washi – Japanese handmade paper

yabusame – samurai-style horseback archery

yakimono – pottery or ceramic ware

yakuza – Japanese mafia

yama – mountain; see also *zan*

yamabushi – mountain priest (Shugendō Buddhism practitioner)

yama-goya – mountain hut

yamato – a term of much debated origins that refers to the Japanese world

yamato-e – traditional Japanese painting

yatai – festival float; hawker stall

yukata – light cotton summer *kimono,* worn for lounging or casual use; standard issue when staying at a *ryokan*

zaibatsu – industrial conglomerate; the term arose pre-WWII but the Japanese economy is still dominated by huge firms such as Mitsui, Marubeni and Mitsubishi, which are involved in many different industries

zaki – cape

zan – mountain; see also *yama*

zazen – seated meditation emphasised in the Sōtō school of Zen Buddhism

Zen – an offshoot of Buddhism, introduced to Japan in the 12th century from China, that emphasises a direct, intuitive approach to enlightenment rather than rational analysis

Behind the Scenes

SEND US YOUR FEEDBACK

We love to hear from travellers – your comments keep us on our toes and help make our books better. Our well-travelled team reads every word on what you loved or loathed about this book. Although we cannot reply individually to your submissions, we always guarantee that your feedback goes straight to the appropriate authors, in time for the next edition. Each person who sends us information is thanked in the next edition – the most useful submissions are rewarded with a selection of digital PDF chapters.

Visit **lonelyplanet.com/contact** to submit your updates and suggestions or to ask for help. Our award-winning website also features inspirational travel stories, news and discussions.

Note: We may edit, reproduce and incorporate your comments in Lonely Planet products such as guidebooks, websites and digital products, so let us know if you don't want your comments reproduced or your name acknowledged. For a copy of our privacy policy visit lonelyplanet.com/privacy.

OUR READERS

Many thanks to the travellers who used the last edition and wrote to us with helpful hints, useful advice and interesting anecdotes:

Akira Ueda, Alexander Ritter, Alison Gray, Ana Ruiz, Aurélien Ta, Brian Knox, Chenchen Wu, David McSherry, Dennis Hansen, Gilyong Ryu, Gordan Barrett, Greg Hewson, Gustav Lönn, Gwen Hasenauer, Haris Lazanitis, Jasmin Morley, Joosje Peters, Jordan Owens, Jos Vandendriessche, Joseph Sorensen, Lanie McCarry, Larry Cannon, Lisa Scheinin, Lu Yao, Marcelo Bustani, Marianna Gentilin, Marijke Claes, Marlon Goos, Martin Hensch, Michael Heilbronn, Michael Singer, Mio Ebisu, Claudine Mouilleau, Pagasa Serrano, Paul Das, Phil McGowan, Sandra Zemp, Sara Bandali Wren & Andrew Wren, Senan Fox, Sint Suthirachartkul, Steve Hoy, Tessa Leigh, Tim Laslavic, Toru Kato, Veronica Teo, Yumi Kan

AUTHOR THANKS

Chris Rowthorn

I would like to thank my family for their patience and support during the writing of this guide. I would also like to thank Kitayama Jun, SK, KT, HK and IK for their assistance. Thanks are also due to the people of Kyoto, who help me every day in countless ways. Finally, I would like to thank all readers of Lonely Planet for their feedback and input. And if any readers see me in Kyoto, please don't hesitate to stop me and let me know what you think!

Ray Bartlett

Thanks first to the amazing people of Japan: for opening your doors and hearts to me as I crisscrossed your lovely land. Thanks to Snoopy for 'Hayakaken!' and airport fun. Kaori, for some great yatai. Sena, for vital moral support. Thanks, Yuki, for the tips and discoveries. Many thanks to the 'pink, fluffy unicorn' for some great 'stuffsies' and help and laughs. And thanks to my family, the whole reason I'm an expert in this area in the first place.

Andrew Bender

Special thanks to Yohko Scott, Nishimura Tetsuya, Daniel Lee, Eddie Bessler, Sanj Powell, Adam Benz, Jorge Girón, Urakami Masahiro, Hashimoto Akira, Yanai Maki, Fujita Shūji, Amy Jo Shapiro, Louise Dendy, Uoi Shingō, Brad Towle, Shimamoto Kumiko, Sakamoto Yūsuke, Colin Fukai, Akagi Hideyuki, Doi Kōsuke, Kuzumoto Masanori, Yoshida Haruyuki, Tani Tomoe, Nishimura Jun, Nishikubo Tomomi and Tsukada Keiji.

Laura Crawford

Much appreciation goes to fellow travellers who shared their experiences, insights and recommendations; and to the many locals who provided friendly conversation, directions and tea. Big thanks also to the dedicated and knowledgeable team of fellow writers, and to the hardworking inhouse gang. Finally, thank you to Mitsue Nagase and Yoshino Kawaura;

steadfast friend Naoko Akamatsu; and partner in life and other things, Amrit Parmar.

Craig McLachlan

A hearty thanks to all those who helped me out on the road, but most of all to my living kanji dictionary and exceptionally beautiful wife, Yuriko, who let me know when I'd reached my daily quota of local Hokkaido brews!

Rebecca Milner

A big thanks to my mom for her company and to my husband for his tireless patience. To Emi and Steph for their willingness to visit 'just one more bar' and to Jon and Kanna for their cooking. Mike and Ivan: thank you for your 'local knowledge'. Will, Tabata-san, Sayuri, Miyawaki-san, Tristan, Toshiko and Kenichi: I'm grateful for your help and recommendations. And finally to Simon and Laura – thank you for all your help, guidance and patience.

Simon Richmond

Dōmo arigatō gozaimasu to Kylie Clark and colleagues at JNTO London; Tabata Naoko and colleagues at TCVB; Asono Akiko and colleagues at YCVB; Osawa Kei at Intermediateque; Tokyo friends Toshiko, Kenichi, Giles and William; Masami Takahashi in Hakone; Angela and Yasu in Kisami; Brent Potter for expert advice on Fuji and for getting me safely up to the summit and back; Tokyo co-author Rebecca and Laura and Diana for keeping it all running smoothly at LPHQ.

Phillip Tang

Thanks to the generous Japanese people who make me love Japan. Thank you Nicola Jones and the patient women in the tourism offices. Big thanks to Laura Crawford, the eds and Japan team. *Dōmo arigatō* Nic Williamson and Ayako Noguchi for the sushi and whiskey times in Tokyo. A huge thanks to Daniel Belfield for leaping head first into internet cafes, Masuda supermarkets, coastal backroads, electric cycling, and morning-after trains with my stuff. Hagi Hagi. Thank you Vek Lewis, Ernesto Alanis Cataño and Lisa N'paisan for love and family.

Benedict Walker

My eternal gratitude for you, Mum (Trish Walker): your unfaltering and unconditional love and support has given me more second chances and golden opportunities than I probably deserve. I hope I make you proud. Thanks as always to my Japanese family, Kaori, Takashi and Wako Shimizu: I love you dearly. To my Japanese friends and colleagues who helped me on the road (you know who you are), I look forward to our next meeting. Finally, I dedicate this work and the love and enthusiasm with which it was written, to the people of Tohoku who lost so much, with the hope that it will bring even a tiny flicker of light back into your communities, and to my new pals Takuya and Mio for touching my heart in a way that nobody ever has.

Wendy Yanagihara

Grateful thanks to Mitsu and Tae, Junta and friends, Toru, Tamanoi-san, Kiku-san, Hiro, Matthew and Nori. Thanks also to Laura, Chris and all my fellow authors for pulling together another wonderful book. *Muchas gracias y amor a mi hermanito* Jason for traveling with me in Yakushima and Tanegashima, my Susono family for keeping me rooted, and my Carp family for fostering my freedom.

ACKNOWLEDGEMENTS

Climate map data adapted from Peel MC, Finlayson BL & McMahon TA (2007) 'Updated World Map of the Köppen-Geiger Climate Classification', Hydrology and Earth System Sciences, 11, 163344.

Tokyo Subway Route Map, Bureau of Transportation, Tokyo Metropolitan Government, Tokyo Metro Co Ltd © 2014.6.

Illustrations pp100-1 and pp390-1 by Michael Weldon.

Cover photograph: Geisha, Kyoto, William Chu/Getty.

THIS BOOK

This 14th edition of Lonely Planet's *Japan* guidebook was researched and written by Chris Rowthorn, Ray Bartlett, Andrew Bender, Laura Crawford, Craig McLachlan, Rebecca Milner, Simon Richmond, Phillip Tang, Benedict Walker and Wendy Yanagihara. This guidebook was produced by the following:

Destination Editor Laura Crawford

Product Editor Luna Soo

Senior Cartographer Diana Von Holdt

Book Designer Virginia Moreno

Assisting Editors Michelle Bennett, Kate Chapman, Nigel Chin, Melanie Dankel, Victoria Harrison, Kate James, Rosie Nicholson, Lauren O'Connell, Sally Schafer, Saralinda Turner

Assisting Cartographers Corey Hutchison, Alison Lyall

Cover Researcher Naomi Parker

Thanks to Naoko Akamatsu, Sasha Baskett, Ryan Evans, James Hardy, Elizabeth Jones, Kate Morgan, Martine Power, Kirsten Rawlings, Wibowo Rusli, Dianne Schallmeiner, Lauren Wellicome

Index

Map Pages **000**
Photo Pages **000**

B

Map Pages **000**
Photo Pages **000**

Map Pages **000**
Photo Pages **000**

N

Map Pages **000**
Photo Pages **000**

Map Pages **000**
Photo Pages **000**

Map Legend

Sights

- Beach
- Bird Sanctuary
- Buddhist
- Castle/Palace
- Christian
- Confucian
- Hindu
- Islamic
- Jain
- Jewish
- Monument
- Museum/Gallery/Historic Building
- Ruin
- Shinto
- Sikh
- Taoist
- Winery/Vineyard
- Zoo/Wildlife Sanctuary
- Other Sight

Activities, Courses & Tours

- Bodysurfing
- Diving
- Canoeing/Kayaking
- Course/Tour
- Sento Hot Baths/Onsen
- Skiing
- Snorkelling
- Surfing
- Swimming/Pool
- Walking
- Windsurfing
- Other Activity

Sleeping

- Sleeping
- Camping

Eating

- Eating

Drinking & Nightlife

- Drinking & Nightlife
- Cafe

Entertainment

- Entertainment

Shopping

- Shopping

Information

- Bank
- Embassy/Consulate
- Hospital/Medical
- Internet
- Police
- Post Office
- Telephone
- Toilet
- Tourist Information
- Other Information

Geographic

- Beach
- Hut/Shelter
- Lighthouse
- Lookout
- Mountain/Volcano
- Oasis
- Park
- Pass
- Picnic Area
- Waterfall

Population

- Capital (National)
- Capital (State/Province)
- City/Large Town
- Town/Village

Transport

- Airport
- Border crossing
- Bus
- Cable car/Funicular
- Cycling
- Ferry
- Metro/MRT/MTR station
- Monorail
- Parking
- Petrol station
- Skytrain/Subway station
- Taxi
- Train station/Railway
- Tram
- Underground station
- Other Transport

Note: Not all symbols displayed above appear on the maps in this book

Routes

- Tollway
- Freeway
- Primary
- Secondary
- Tertiary
- Lane
- Unsealed road
- Road under construction
- Plaza/Mall
- Steps
- Tunnel
- Pedestrian overpass
- Walking Tour
- Walking Tour detour
- Path/Walking Trail

Boundaries

- International
- State/Province
- Disputed
- Regional/Suburb
- Marine Park
- Cliff
- Wall

Hydrography

- River, Creek
- Intermittent River
- Canal
- Water
- Dry/Salt/Intermittent Lake
- Reef

Areas

- Airport/Runway
- Beach/Desert
- Cemetery (Christian)
- Cemetery (Other)
- Glacier
- Mudflat
- Park/Forest
- Sight (Building)
- Sportsground
- Swamp/Mangrove

Craig McLachlan

Sapporo & Hokkaidō Craig has walked the length of Japan (3200km in 99 days!), climbed Japan's 100 Famous Mountains, hiked the 88 Sacred Temples of Shikoku and scaled all of Japan's 3000m peaks. Books on his exploits have been published in English and Japanese and he has co-authored multiple editions of Lonely Planet's *Hiking in Japan* and *Japan* guidebooks. A 'freelance anything', Craig has an MBA and is also a pilot, karate instructor, tour leader, hiking guide, Japanese interpreter and budding novelist. See www.craigmclachlan.com.

Read more about Craig at:
http://auth.lonelyplanet.com/profiles/craigmclachlan

Rebecca Milner

Tokyo Rebecca came to Tokyo for 'just one year' in 2002 and still hasn't been able to tear herself away. She's lived west of Shinjuku and east of the Sumida and now shares an apartment in Shibuya (the quiet part) with her husband and cat. Her writing has appeared in the *Guardian*, *Japan Times*, *CNN Travel* and *BBC Travel* and Lonely Planet guides to Japan.

Simon Richmond

Mt Fuji & Around Tokyo Travel writer, photographer and videographer Simon Richmond won travel guidebook of the year for his first co-authored guidebook on Japan published in 1999. He's also written guides to Tokyo (where he lived and worked for several years as a journalist and editor in the early 1990s) and books on anime and manga. He's been an author with Lonely Planet since 1999, working on many titles for the company and features for its website. Read more about his travels at www.simonrichmond.com and on Twitter and Instagram @simonrichmond.

Phillip Tang

Yamaguchi & Around, Matsue & Around, Tottori & Around Phillip has been visiting Japan since 2004 and doesn't think it strange to pop in mainly for the matcha, pockets of serenity and ¥100 stores. He grew up in Australia, then London and Mexico, and now finds being internationally homeless useful for writing Lonely Planet guides to Mexico, China and Korea. Check out his website philliptang.co.uk and the photos he Instagrammed for this trip @mrtangtangtang.

Benedict Walker

The Japan Alps & Central Honshū, Northern Honshū (Tōhoku) Currently hanging by the beach near his mum, in hometown Newcastle, Ben's plan of 'livin' the dream', spending his days between his three great loves, Australia, North America and Japan, seems to be coming to fruition: it's not greedy – it's just sharing the love! This is the third time he's written for Lonely Planet's *Japan* guidebook, which he first received as a 12th birthday gift. Passionate about (almost) all things Japanese, Ben speaks the lingo pretty well: he's convinced he was a monk in a past life. Ben has also co-written Lonely Planet's *Canada*, *Florida* and *Australia* guidebooks, written and directed a play, toured Australia managing travel for rockstars and is an avid photographer toying with his original craft of film-making. He's an advocate of following your dreams – they can come true. For updates, see www.wordsandjourneys.com.

Wendy Yanagihara

Shikoku, Okinawa & the Southwest Islands As the daughter of an Issei (first-generation Japanese-American) in California, Wendy grew up summering in Japan with her mother. But it wasn't until two years ago that she had the pleasure of exploring the 88-temple pilgrimage, the diversity of Ryukyuan dialects and an affinity for *jiimami-dōfu*. Previously, she has worked on several editions of the *Japan* and *Tokyo* guidebooks, among the 20+ guidebooks on which she has worked for Lonely Planet.

OUR STORY

A beat-up old car, a few dollars in the pocket and a sense of adventure. In 1972 that's all Tony and Maureen Wheeler needed for the trip of a lifetime – across Europe and Asia overland to Australia. It took several months, and at the end – broke but inspired – they sat at their kitchen table writing and stapling together their first travel guide, *Across Asia on the Cheap*. Within a week they'd sold 1500 copies. Lonely Planet was born.

Today, Lonely Planet has offices in Franklin, London, Melbourne, Oakland, Beijing and Delhi, with more than 600 staff and writers. We share Tony's belief that 'a great guidebook should do three things: inform, educate and amuse'.

OUR WRITERS

Chris Rowthorn

Coordinating Author, Kyoto Chris has been based in Kyoto since 1992. He became a regional correspondent for the *Japan Times* in 1995 and joined Lonely Planet in 1996. He's worked on Lonely Planet's *Japan*, *Kyoto*, *Hiking in Japan* and *Tokyo* guidebooks. He speaks and reads Japanese fluently and has appeared on local TV to introduce secret temples in Kyoto. Chris's wife is from Kyoto's Arashiyama district and his two children are proudly multicultural. Chris runs Chris Rowthorn Tours (www.chrisrowthorn.com), which offers private tours and consulting about Kyoto and the rest of Japan. He also curates www.insidekyoto.com, his personal blog about the city of Kyoto.

Ray Bartlett

Kyūshū Ray arrived in Kagoshima in 1993 and in many ways never left: it's now a second home. While hailing from Japan's 'most southern mainland prefecture' he's proudly crisscrossed Kyūshū so many times he's lost count. His hobbies include onsen baths, surfing and hiking, all of which he enjoyed while researching this edition of *Japan*. For more info or to contact Ray, visit www.Kaisora.com or check out his onsen suggestions at www.OnsenJapan.net. He divides his time between Japan, Mexico and the USA.

Read more about Ray at:
http://auth.lonelyplanet.com/profiles/kaisora

Andrew Bender

Kansai France was closed, so after college Andrew left his native New England for a job in Japan. It was a life-changing experience, as visits to Japan often are. He's since mastered chopsticks, the language, karaoke and shoe etiquette. Now based in Los Angeles, he writes about Japan for the *Los Angeles Times*, inflight magazines and about a dozen Lonely Planet titles, as well as the Seat 1A travel blog for Forbes. He also does cross-cultural consulting for Japanese businesses and escorts visitors around Japan. His website is www.wheres-andy-now.com.

Laura Crawford

Hiroshima & Around, Okayama & Around Laura first discovered Japan as an undergraduate studying Japanese in Kansai. She later travelled up and down the country, set up home in Osaka for two years, wrote a thesis on Japanese English, and eventually landed a job as an editor at Lonely Planet's Melbourne branch. She now works as a Destination Editor in London, but was kindly let out of the office to go on the road again in Japan. She tweets @crawfplanet.

Read more about Laura at:
http://auth.lonelyplanet.com/profiles/crawfplanet

OVER PAGE MORE WRITERS

Published by Lonely Planet Publications Pty Ltd
ABN 36 005 607 983
14th edition – Sep 2015
ISBN 978 1 74321 674 3

10 9 8 7 6 5 4 3 2 1
Printed in China